Dictionary of
American Family
Names

Dictionary of American Family Names

PATRICK HANKS

Editor

VOLUME TWO

G–N

OXFORD

UNIVERSITY PRESS

2003

Oxford University Press

Oxford   New York
Auckland   Bangkok   Buenos Aires   Cape Town   Chennai
Dar es Salaam   Delhi   Hong Kong   Istanbul   Karachi   Kolkata
Kuala Lumpur   Madrid   Melbourne   Mexico City   Mumbai
Nairobi   São Paulo   Shanghai   Taipei   Tokyo   Toronto

Published by Oxford University Press, Inc.
198 Madison Avenue, New York, New York, 10016
http://www.oup-usa.org

Oxford is a registered trademark of Oxford University Press

Library of Congress Cataloging-in-Publication Data

Dictionary of American family names / Patrick Hanks, editor.
   p. cm.
Includes bibliographical references.
   ISBN 0-19-508137-4 (set : acid-free paper) — ISBN 0-19-516557-8 (v. 1
: acid free paper) — ISBN 0-19-516558-6 (v. 2 : acid free paper) —
ISBN 0-19-516559-4 (v. 3 : acid free paper)
   1. Names, Personal—United States—Dictionaries.   I. Hanks, Patrick.
   CS2485.D53 2003
   929.4′0973—dc21

                                                          2003003844

Printing number: 9 8 7 6 5 4 3 2 1

Printed in the United States of America
on acid-free paper

EDITORIAL STAFF

Editor in Chief
Patrick Hanks

Managing Editor
Kate Hardcastle

Eastern European Editor
Gábor Bátonyi

Editorial Assistants
Claire Bland, Louise Jones

Project Administrator (1991–2000)
Valerie Fairhurst

Name Frequencies and Data Management
D. Kenneth Tucker

Computational Text Validation Routines
D. Kenneth Tucker, Ian Batten

OXFORD UNIVERSITY PRESS

Publisher
Karen Day

Director of Editorial Development
Timothy J. DeWerff

Director of Editorial, Design, and Production
John Sollami

Managing Editor, Dictionaries Program
Constance Baboukis

Copy Editors, Proofreaders
Linda Costa, Melissa A. Dobson, Louise B. Ketz, Christine A. Lindberg,
Jane McGary, Joseph Patwell, Abigail Powers, Ryan Sullivan, Meera Vaidyanathan
Publication Services, Inc.: Jerome Colburn, Jyothirmai Gubili, Elisa B. Laird,
Peter A. Nelson, Jenny Putnam, Rob Siedenburg, Scott Stocking,
Rebecca E. Taylor, Joyce Wiehagen

Cover Design
Joan Greenfield

Information Systems, Type Composition
Stephen Perkins, dataformat.com, LLC

CONTRIBUTORS AND CONSULTANTS

For Names from the British Isles

English	David Mills, Patrick Hanks, Kate Hardcastle
Welsh	Hywel Wyn Owen
Scottish	William Nicolaisen, Patrick Hanks
Irish	Kay Muhr
Scottish Gaelic	Kay Muhr

For Names from Western Europe

French	Susan Whitebook
German	Edda Gentry, Jürgen Eichhoff
Dutch	Charles Gehring

For Scandinavian and Finnish Names

Norwegian and Danish	Olav Veka
Swedish	Lena Peterson
Finnish	Hannele Jönsson-Korhola, Kate Moore

For Names from Southern Europe

Spanish and other Iberian Languages	Dieter Kremer Roser Saurí Colomer
Italian	Enzo Caffarelli
Greek	Nick Nicholas, Johanna Kolleca

For Jewish Names

Jewish	Alexander Beider

For Slavic and East European Names

Polish	Aleksandra Cieślikowa
Czech	Dobrana Moldanová
Slovak	Peter Ďurčo
Russian and Ukrainian	Alexander Beider
Armenian	Bert Vaux
Slovenian	Simon Lenarčič
Croatian	Dunja Brozović
Serbian	Svetozar Stijović, Tvrtko Prćić
Hungarian	Gábor Bátonyi
Latvian and Lithuanian	Laimute Balode

For Names from the Middle East and Indian Subcontinent

Indian	Rocky Miranda
Muslim names	Salahuddin Ahmed
Arabic names	Paul Roochnik

For Names from East Asia

Chinese	Mark Lewellen
Japanese	Fred Brady
Korean	Gary Mackelprang

Genealogical Notes
Project team; Additional notes: Marion Harris, M. Tracey Ober

KEY TO THE DICTIONARY

*Consult the General Introduction and the essay
by D. Kenneth Tucker for further explanation.*

Main entry (one of the more than 70,000 surnames listed in DAFN)

Frequency of this surname in the sample of 88.7 million listings in the DAFN database

Explanation and etymology —

Register (3259) English: perhaps from Middle English, Old French *registre* 'register', 'book for recording enactments', hence perhaps a metonymic occupational name for a scribe or clerk.

Surname type (e.g., occupational, habitational, patronymic, nickname)

Language or culture of origin —

Regner (420) German: **1.** (Bavarian): habitational name for someone from Regen (a place on the Regen river, for which it is named). **2.** from a Germanic personal name composed of the elements *ragin* 'counsel' + *hari, heri* 'army'.

Region where this surname probably originated

Etymon (a word or element from which the surname is derived; in italics)

Gloss on the etymon (in single quotation marks)

GIVEN NAMES German 4%. *Alois* (2), *Kurt* (2), *Erwin, Franz, Otto.*

Regnier (926) French (**Régnier**): from the personal name *Régnier*, of Germanic origin (see RAYNER 1).

Cross-reference to a related main entry (in capital and small capital letters)

FOREBEARS A Regnier from La Rochelle, France, is documented in Pointe-aux-Trembles, Quebec, in 1708, with the secondary surname BRION or Brillon.

Forebear note for an early bearer of this surname in North America

GIVEN NAMES French 6%. *Lucien* (2), *Micheline* (2), *Pierre* (2), *Andre, Celestine, Felicie, Guilene, Marcel, Marcelle, Patrice, Romain.*

Selection of diagnostic given names from U.S. telephone directories

Rego (1493) **1.** Portuguese and Galician: habitational name from any of the numerous places in Portugal and Galicia called Rego, named with *rego* 'ditch', 'channel', 'furrow'. **2.** Dutch: from a Germanic personal name with the first element *ragin* 'counsel' + *guda* 'god', or *gōda* 'good', or *gauta* 'Goth'. **3.** Dutch: variant of REGA 2. **4.** Hungarian (**Regő**): occupational name for a musician or poet, from *rege* 'song', 'tale'.

Number of occurrences of this diagnostic given name with this particular surname in the DAFN database

Multiple origins

Alternate form in the language of origin (usually with diacritics)

GIVEN NAMES Spanish 15%; Portuguese 9%. *Manuel* (32), *Jose* (25), *Armando* (5), *Eduardo* (5), *Carlos* (4), *Fernando* (4), *Francisco* (4), *Ramon* (4), *Humberto* (3), *Juan* (3), *Luis* (3), *Mario* (3); *Joao* (5), *Duarte* (2), *Adauto, Albano, Goncalo, Guilherme, Serafim.*

Statistical confidence measure that this surname is in fact Spanish, based on analysis of the associated given names

Diagnostic given names grouped by language or cultural group (separated by semicolons)

Dictionary of American Family Names

G

Gaa (96) German: Bavarian dialect variant of GAU.
GIVEN NAMES French 5%; German 4%. *Lucienne; Manfred.*

Gaal (327) **1.** Hungarian: variant of **Gál** (see GAL). **2.** Dutch: habitational name from a place so named in the province of North Brabant.
GIVEN NAMES Hungarian 15%. *Geza* (4), *Imre* (2), *Laszlo* (2), *Mihaly* (2), *Sandor* (2), *Zoltan* (2), *Arpad, Attila, Ferenc, Gyula, Jozsef, Miklos.*

Gaar (173) **1.** Dutch (**van de Gaar**): habitational name for someone from De Gader, an area of Hasselt in northeastern Belgium. **2.** Dutch: variant of **van de Geer**, a topographic name for someone living by a piece of land that tapered to a point. **3.** German: in Austria a nickname for a person who was ready and willing (to do a task), from Middle High German *gar* 'ready', 'prepared'.

Gaarder (167) Norwegian: habitational name from any of numerous farmsteads in southeastern Norway named *Gårder* (plural of *gård* 'farm' from Old Norse *garðr*).
GIVEN NAME Scandinavian 6%. *Erik.*

Gaba (166) **1.** Hungarian: from a pet form of the personal name *Gábor* or *Gábriel* (see GABRIEL). **2.** Czech and Slovak (**Gába**): from a pet form of the personal name GABRIEL. **3.** Polish: nickname for a bully, from *gabać* 'to provoke or molest'. **4.** Indian (Panjab): Hindu (Arora, Khatri) and Sikh name, meaning 'calf' in Panjabi (from Sanskrit *garbha* 'embryo').
GIVEN NAMES Indian 8%. *Ashok, Deepak, Mahender, Nandlal, Prakash; Marthe.*

Gabaldon (563) Spanish (**Gabaldón**): habitational name from Gabaldón in the province of Cuenca.
GIVEN NAMES Spanish 24%. *Manuel* (10), *Jose* (5), *Carlos* (3), *Roberto* (3), *Alfredo* (2), *Epitacio* (2), *Fernando* (2), *Francisco* (2), *Lupe* (2), *Miguel* (2), *Nestor* (2), *Ramon* (2).

Gabay (261) Jewish (Sephardic and eastern Ashkenazic): status name from Hebrew *gabay* 'warden', denoting a trustee or warden of a Jewish public institution, especially a synagogue, or a manager of the affairs of a Hasidic rabbi.
GIVEN NAMES Jewish 21%. *Haim* (3), *Meyer* (2), *Amnon, Amram, Arie, Avram, Efrat, Eyal, Iren, Itzhak, Izak, Meir.*

Gabbard (1945) Americanized spelling of German GEBHARDT.

Gabbay (122) **1.** Jewish (Sephardic and eastern Ashkenazic): variant of GABAY. **2.** Iranian: unexplained.
GIVEN NAMES Muslim 25%; Jewish 15%. *Amir* (2), *Ebrahim* (2), *Goli, Hamid, Kamal, Nematollah, Rouhollah, Saleh, Soltan; Meir* (2), *Ofer* (2), *Aviva, Moshe, Shimon.*

Gabbert (1061) German: **1.** from a personal name, a variant of GEBHARDT. **2.** habitational name from a place so named in Pomerania. **3.** perhaps a nickname for a clown or buffoon (see GABE 1).

Gabe (252) **1.** French: nickname from Old French *gabe* 'joke' (of Old Norse origin). **2.** German: from a short form of Germanic personal name formed with *geba* 'gift'. Compare GEBHARDT.

Gabehart (246) Altered spelling of German GEBHARDT.

Gabel (2640) **1.** German and Jewish (Ashkenazic): metonymic occupational name for a maker and seller of forks, from Middle High German *gabel(e)*, German *Gabel* 'fork'. The reference is to any of the various pieces of agricultural equipment denoted by this word, for example hay forks, shearlegs, etc. Table forks were not used in Germany for eating before the 16th century. **2.** German: topographic name for someone who lived near a fork in a road or river, or owned a forked piece of land, from the German word in this transferred sense. **3.** German: habitational name from any of the places called Gabel in Germany, in Schleswig, Thuringia, Silesia, and in particular one in Bohemia, which derive their name from Slavic *jablo* 'apple tree'. **4.** German: from a short form of GABRIEL. **5.** Americanized spelling of German *Gäbel* (see GAEBEL) or *Göbel* (see GOEBEL). **6.** Jewish (Ashkenazic): adoption of 1–3 above.

Gabelman (123) German (**Gabelmann**) and Jewish (Ashkenazic): variant of GABEL.

Gaber (454) **1.** Muslim (Egyptian Arabic): variant of JABER. **2.** Jewish (eastern Ashkenazic): variant of HABER. **3.** German: from a short form of the personal name GABRIEL. **4.** Slovenian: from a short form of the personal name *Gabrijel* (see GABRIEL). **5.** Slovenian: topographic name from *gaber* 'hornbeam', denoting someone who lived by a place where hornbeams grew. It may also be a shortened

American form of the surnames **Gaberšek** or **Gaberščfek**, which have the same origin.
GIVEN NAMES Muslim 8%; German 4%. *Mohamed* (3), *Ahmed* (2), *Hossam* (2), *Osama* (2), *Abdelaziz, Abdo, Ahmad, Ali, Anwar, Elsayed, Farag, Hesham; Kurt, Otto, Volker.*

Gabert (257) German (also **Gäbert**): variant of GEBHARDT.

Gabhart (159) Altered spelling of German GEBHARDT.
GIVEN NAME German 4%. *Kurt.*

Gable (3535) **1.** Northern English: of uncertain origin, perhaps a habitational name from a minor place named with Old Norse *gafl* 'gable', which was applied to a triangular-shaped hill. The mountain called Great Gable in Cumbria is named in this way. **2.** Americanized spelling of German and Jewish GABEL. **3.** Possibly an altered spelling of German **Göbel** (see GOEBEL).

Gabler (790) **1.** German and Swiss German (also **Gäbler**), Jewish (Ashkenazic): occupational name for a maker of forks, from an agent derivative of Middle High German *gabel(e)*, German *Gabel* 'fork'. **2.** habitational name for someone from a place called *Gabel* in German, *Jablone* in Czech (see GABEL 3). **3.** English: occupational name for a tax collector or usurer, Old French *gabelier, gableor*, a derivative of *gable* 'tax', 'revenue', of Germanic origin.
GIVEN NAMES German 5%. *Klaus* (3), *Erwin* (2), *Gerd* (2), *Fritz, Irmgard, Jurgen, Otto, Theodor, Willi.*

Gabor (681) Hungarian (**Gábor**) and Jewish (from Hungary): from the personal name *Gábor*, Hungarian form of GABRIEL.

Gaboriault (191) French: variant of GABOURY.
GIVEN NAMES French 16%. *Alcide* (2), *Armand* (2), *Adrien, Amedee, Arsene, Gaston, Laurent, Marcel, Renald.*

Gaboury (364) French: nickname for a joker, from a diminutive of Norman French dialect *gab* 'joke' (see GABE).
GIVEN NAMES French 10%. *Fernand* (2), *Gabrielle, Gaston, Germain, Jacques, Jean-Louis, Marcel, Normand.*

Gabrick (107) Probably an Americanized spelling of a Polish or other Slavic name based on the personal name GABRIEL, or from a derivative of *gaber* 'hornbeam'.
GIVEN NAME French 6%. *Lucien* (2).

Gabriel (6688) English, Scottish, French, German, Spanish, Portuguese, and Jewish:

from the Hebrew personal name *Gavriel* 'God has given me strength'. This was borne by an archangel in the Bible (Daniel 8:16 and 9:21), who in the New Testament announced the impending birth of Jesus to the Virgin Mary (Luke 1:26–38). It has been a comparatively popular personal name in all parts of Europe, among both Christians and Jews, during the Middle Ages and since. Compare MICHAEL and RAPHAEL. It was the name of a famous patriarch and archbishop of Serbia (died 1659). In Russia it was the official Christian name of St. Vsevolod (died 1138). In the U.S. this name has absorbed cognate names from other European languages, for example the Greek patronymics **Gabrielis, Gabrielatos, Gabrielidis, Gabrielakos, Gabrieloglou.**

Gabriele (740) Italian: from the personal name *Gabriele*, Italian form of GABRIEL.
GIVEN NAMES Italian 18%. *Luigi* (3), *Pasquale* (3), *Salvatore* (3), *Antonio* (2), *Domenic* (2), *Gino* (2), *Giuseppe* (2), *Guido* (2), *Mauro* (2), *Nino* (2), *Santo* (2), *Amedeo.*

Gabrielle (125) Variant spelling of Italian GABRIELE.
GIVEN NAMES Italian 9%. *Antonio, Cosmo, Gennaro, Sal.*

Gabrielli (300) Italian: patronymic from the personal name *Gabriello*, a variant of GABRIELE.
GIVEN NAMES Italian 14%; Spanish 9%. *Erminio* (3), *Amedeo, Angelo, Domenico, Enrico, Flavio, Gasper, Gino, Luciano, Luigi, Romolo, Silvio; Mario* (4), *Armando* (2), *Julio* (2), *Americo, Fabio, Jacinto, Luisa, Maria Delcarmen, Mariano, Orlando.*

Gabrielse (118) Dutch: variant of GABRIELSEN.

Gabrielsen (246) Dutch and Scandinavian: patronymic from the personal name *Gabriel.* See GABRIEL.
GIVEN NAMES Scandinavian 14%; German 6%. *Alf, Thorvald; Gerhard, Hans.*

Gabrielson (976) Patronymic from GABRIEL; probably a respelling of Swedish **Gabrielsson** or Danish and Norwegian GABRIELSEN.
GIVEN NAMES Scandinavian 7%. *Erik* (6), *Nels, Nils, Sven, Tor.*

Gabris (119) **1.** Czech (**Gábriš**), Slovak (**Gabriš, Gábriš**) and Polish: see GABRYS. **2.** Hungarian (**Gábris**): from a pet form of the personal name *Gábor* (see GABOR). **3.** Latvian: derivative of the personal name *Gabrieliu* (see GABRIEL). **4.** Greek: from a pet form of the personal name GABRIEL.

Gabrys (134) **1.** Polish (**Gabryś**) and Czech (**Gabryš**): from a derivative of the personal name GABRIEL. **2.** Lithuanian: derivative of the personal name *Gabrieliu* (see GABRIEL).
GIVEN NAMES Polish 7%. *Grazyna, Jozef, Miroslaw, Zdzislawa, Zofia.*

Gaby (241) Southern French: from a pet form of the personal name GABRIEL.

Gac (108) Polish: from a pet form of various personal names such as GABRIEL, *Gaudentius*, or *Gaweł* (see GALL).
GIVEN NAMES Polish 7%. *Dariusz, Kazimierz.*

Gaccione (158) Italian: of uncertain derivation: **1.** possibly a variant of **Caccione**, from an augmentative of CACCIA. **2.** alternatively, from a doubly suffixed (with *-acci* and *-one*) reduced derivative of a personal name ending in *-go*, as for example *Alberigo* (see ALBERICO), ARRIGO, or *Federigo* (see FRIGO).
GIVEN NAMES Italian 29%. *Angelo* (5), *Salvatore* (3), *Carmine* (2), *Pasquale* (2), *Antonio, Ciro, Guiseppe, Santina, Vincenzo.*

Gacek (323) Polish: **1.** nickname from *gacek* 'bat' (the animal). **2.** from a pet form of GAC.
GIVEN NAMES Polish 12%. *Andrzej* (2), *Jozef* (2), *Piotr* (2), *Aniela, Danuta, Henryk, Jerzy, Lech, Lucyna, Ryszard, Tadeusz, Wladyslaw.*

Gach (270) **1.** German: from Middle High German *gāch* 'fast', 'rash'; probably a nickname for an impetuous man. **2.** Polish: from a pet form of various personal names such as GABRIEL, *Gaudentius*, or *Gaweł* (see GALL).

Gacke (117) German: unexplained; perhaps a variant of **Gack**, a nickname from Middle High German *geck* 'childish', 'foolish' (compare GACKLE). Most occurrences are in IA and MN.

Gackle (116) German (**Gäckle**): from a diminutive of *geck* 'childish', 'foolish'. This name is one of the German family names that were established in Russia in the 19th century.

Gad (159) **1.** English: variant spelling of GADD. **2.** Danish: from a medieval nickname *Gad* meaning 'sting', 'point', or from the Biblical male personal name *Gad.* **3.** Muslim: from a personal name based on Arabic *jād* 'serious', 'earnest'.
GIVEN NAMES Muslim 32%. *Ahmed* (3), *Mostafa* (2), *Said* (2), *Sarwat* (2), *Amera, Ashraf, Ehab, Emad, Fadel, Hassan, Khadiga, Mohamed.*

Gadberry (588) Variant of English GADBURY.

Gadbois (571) French: variant spelling of **Gadebois** (Artois), itself a variant of **Gâtebois**, a topographic name composed of the elements *gâté* 'spoilt', 'laid waste' + *bois* 'wood'. In New England, this has been rendered as WOOD in English.
GIVEN NAMES French 8%. *Michel* (4), *Armand* (2), *Henri* (2), *Benoit, Marcel, Marcelle, Martial, Oliva, Ovila, Pierre, Raoul, Yvan.*

Gadbury (125) English: habitational name from Cadborough, alias Gateborough, in Rye, Sussex, probably so named from Old English *gāt* 'goat' + *beorg* 'hill'.

Gadd (994) English: from northern Middle English *gad* 'goad', 'spike', 'sting' (Old Norse *gaddr*), hence a metonymic occupational name for a cattle driver or, more likely, a nickname for a persistent and irritating person. The Old Norse word is attested as a byname (see GADSBY).

Gaddie (478) Scottish: variant of GEDDIE.

Gaddis (3006) Scottish and northern Irish: variant of GEDDES.

Gaddy (2498) Northern Irish: variant of GEDDIE.

Gade (492) **1.** Danish and Swedish: topographic name for someone who lived by a main street, from *gade* 'street', 'thoroughfare'. **2.** German: from a personal name, a short form of the various compound names (for example GOTTLIEB) formed with Middle Low German *gōd* 'good' or *god*, *got* 'god', or from Old Saxon *gigado*, Middle High German *gate* 'companion', a byname for a compatible man. **3.** (**Gäde**): see GAEDE. **4.** Indian (Maharashtra); pronounced as two syllables: Hindu (Maratha) name, probably from Marathi *gaa* 'cart'.
GIVEN NAMES Indian 6%; Scandinavian 5%; German 4%. *Arun* (2), *Anuradha, Prasad, Radhika, Rajendra, Ravindra, Satya, Sreedhar, Sreenivasa, Surendra, Usha; Bernt, Bjorn, Gudrun, Niels, Thor; Armin* (2), *Hans, Klaus, Lorenz.*

Gaden (110) **1.** North German: patronymic from a short form of a compound name formed with *gōd* 'good' or *god*, *got* 'god'. **2.** English (Severn Valley): unexplained.
GIVEN NAME German 5%. *Hans.*

Gadient (118) Swiss German: unexplained. Most occurrences are in IA and MO.

Gadomski (334) Polish: habitational name for someone from a place called Gadomiec in Ostrołęka voivodeship.
GIVEN NAMES Polish 7%. *Bronislaw, Casimir, Feliks, Tadeusz, Tomasz, Wieslaw.*

Gadoury (161) French: from a diminutive of **Gadaud**, a personal name of Germanic origin, composed of the elements *wadi* 'pledge', 'security' + *waldan* 'to govern'. This was borne by a 9th-century bishop of Marseilles.
GIVEN NAMES French 14%. *Marcel* (2), *Armand, Henri, Julien, Marie-Laure.*

Gadow (161) Eastern German: habitational name from places so named in Mecklenburg and Brandenburg.
GIVEN NAMES German 5%. *Bernd, Wolfgang.*

Gadsby (231) English: habitational name from Gaddesby in Leicestershire, recorded in Domesday Book as *Gadesbi* and so named from the Old Norse personal name *Gaddr* (or from Old Norse *gaddr* 'spur (of land)') + *býr* 'settlement'.

Gadsden (578) English: habitational name from Gaddesden in Hertfordshire, recorded in Domesday Book as *Gatesdene*, from an Old English personal name *Gǣte(n)* + Old English *denu* 'valley'.

Gadson (899) English: variant of GADS-DEN, assimilated by folk etymology to the common patronymic ending -son.

Gadway (176) Probably an Americanized form of the French name **Gadoin**, from a personal name of Germanic origin, composed of the elements wadi 'pledge', 'security' + wini 'friend'. Alternatively, it may be an Americanized form of **Gadaud** (see GADOURY) or some other name with the same first element.

Gadzinski (156) Polish (**Gadziński**): most probably a habitational name from a lost or unidentified place.
GIVEN NAME Polish 5%. Dariusz.

Gaebel (163) German (**Gäbel**): **1.** from the personal name Gabelo, a derivative of Gabo, of unexplained origin. **2.** habitational name from a house distinguished by the sign of a fork (see GABEL). **3.** South German: from Middle High German gebel 'skull', 'head', presumably a nickname for someone with a peculiarity of the skull.
GIVEN NAMES German 10%. Kurt (2), Dieter, Ewald, Klaus.

Gaebler (124) German (**Gäbler**): from an agent derivative of GABEL; generally an occupational name for a fork maker, but possibly also a topographic name for someone who lived at a fork in the road.
GIVEN NAMES German 4%. Johann, Kurt.

Gaede (481) German (**Gäde**): from the personal name Gaddo, Gedde, a variant of GADE 2.

Gaer (119) Jewish (eastern Ashkenazic): variant of GEIER.
GIVEN NAME Jewish 4%. Meyer.

Gaertner (788) German (**Gärtner**): see GARTNER.
GIVEN NAMES German 8%. Otto (3), Franz (2), Helmut (2), Kurt (2), Dieter, Erna, Ernst, Gerhard, Hans, Irmgard, Karl Heinz, Ulrich.

Gaeta (952) **1.** Italian: habitational name from Gaeta, a place in Latina province. **2.** Italian: probably a habitational name from Gaeta in Italy (see 1 above and GAYTAN). **3.** Catalan (**Gaetà**): probably a variant spelling of the Catalan family name **Gaietà**.
GIVEN NAMES Spanish 18%; Italian 12%. Juan (6), Jose (4), Jesus (3), Luis (3), Manuel (3), Mario (3), Ramon (3), Alberto (2), Guadalupe (2), Humberto (2), Maria Elena (2), Miguel (2); Salvatore (4), Antonio (3), Pasquale (3), Carmine (2), Dante (2), Domenic (2), Filomena (2), Rocco (2), Sabato (2), Vito (2), Angelo, Cosmo.

Gaetani (162) Italian: patronymic from GAETANO.
GIVEN NAMES Italian 15%; French 6%. Donato (3), Angelo, Dino, Salvatore, Silvio; Alphonse, Armand, Camille.

Gaetano (483) Italian: from the personal name Gaietano, medieval Latin Caietanus, originally a Latin ethnic name denoting

someone from Caieta in Latium. According to legend the place was named after the elderly nurse of Aeneas, who died there after fleeing with him from the ruins of Troy. The name persisted among early Christians and was popular in the Middle Ages. The religious reformer St. Gaetano (1480–1547) was born in Vicenza, a member of a Venetian noble family. He is not to be confused with his contemporary Cardinal Gaetano, an active opponent of Martin Luther.
GIVEN NAMES Italian 12%. Salvatore (3), Angelo (2), Dino, Francesco, Giovanni, Mauro, Nunzio, Pasquale, Primo, Rocco, Sal, Silvio.

Gaeth (158) North German (**Gäth**): from Middle Low German gade 'fitting', 'suitable', 'stately', probably a nickname for a compatible person.

Gaetz (205) German (**Gätz**): a variant of GADE.

Gaff (345) **1.** English: metonymic occupational name for someone who made or used iron hooks or crooks, Old French, Middle English gaffe. **2.** German: from a derivative of the stem geb- (see GAFFKE).

Gaffaney (105) Variant of Irish GAFFNEY.

Gaffey (454) Irish: reduced Anglicized form of Gaelic **Mac Eachaidh** 'son of the horseman' or **Mac Gáibhthigh** 'son of the fierce one' (see McGAFFEY).
GIVEN NAMES Irish 5%. Brendan (2), John Patrick.

Gaffin (224) Irish: reduced form of McGAF-FIN, an Anglicization of Gaelic **Mac Eacháin** (see McGAHAN).

Gaffke (149) German: from a short form of Germanic personal name formed with geba 'gift' (as in GEBHARDT) + the diminutive suffix -ke.

Gaffner (104) Swiss German: topographic name, found mainly in Wallis canton (Valais) for someone who lived in an Alpine hut or shelter, from Romansch Gafene 'large basket'.

Gaffney (4960) **1.** Irish: reduced Anglicized form of Gaelic **Ó Gamhna** 'descendant of Gamhain', a byname meaning 'calf'. On occasion the English surname CAULFIELD was adopted as equivalent. **2.** Possibly an altered spelling of Swiss German **Gaf(f)ner**, a topographic name for a cottage dweller, from dialect Gafene 'large basket', 'Alpine (dairy) hut'.
GIVEN NAMES Irish 6%. Brendan (2), Declan, Kieran, Niall, Ronan.

Gafford (941) **1.** English: probably a variant of GIFFORD. **2.** Probably a respelling of German **Gaffert**, a habitational name from Gaffert near Köslin, Brandenburg, or from a personal name formed with Middle High German gate 'fellow', 'companion'.

Gafner (117) Swiss German: variant of GAFFNER.

Gagan (180) Irish: variant of GAHAN or GEOGHEGAN.

Gagas (100) Lithuanian: nickname or occupational name from gagas 'gander'. Compare GANDER.

Gage (6070) **1.** English: from Middle English, Old French ga(u)ge 'measure', probably applied as a metonymic occupational name for an assayer, an official who was in charge of checking weights and measures. **2.** English and French: from Middle English, Old French gage 'pledge', 'surety' (against which money was lent), and therefore a metonymic occupational name for a moneylender or usurer.

Gagel (182) German: habitational name from a place so named near Magdeburg.

Gagen (277) **1.** Irish: variant of GAHAN or GEOGHEGAN. **2.** German: topographic name from the Tyrolean term Gagen 'Alpine dairy hut'.

Gager (487) **1.** English: occupational name for an assayer, from an agent derivative of Middle English, Old French ga(u)ge 'measure' (see GAGE). **2.** German: probably a topographic name from Tyrolean Gagen 'alpine dairy hut'.

Gagliano (1275) Italian: habitational name from any of various places so named, derived from the Latin personal name Gallius, for example Gagliano Castelferrato.
GIVEN NAMES Italian 18%; Spanish 11%; French 4%. Salvatore (11), Sal (6), Angelo (5), Carlo (3), Guido (3), Rosario (3), Carmelo (2), Domenico (2), Luigi (2), Mario (2), Achille, Antonino, Antonio, Biagio, Carmine; Salvador (3), Diego (2), Alfonso, Alfredo, Ana, Edgardo, Liborio, Rico; Andre, Camille, Thierry.

Gagliardi (1801) Italian: patronymic from GAGLIARDO.
GIVEN NAMES Italian 13%. Rocco (6), Angelo (4), Carmelo (4), Pasquale (4), Enrico (3), Antonio (2), Carmine (2), Domenic (2), Ezio (2), Gennaro (2), Giuseppe (2), Salvatore (2).

Gagliardo (478) Southern Italian: from a nickname or medieval personal name Gagliardo, a loanword from Occitan galhard or French gaillard 'strong', 'robust'.
GIVEN NAMES Italian 20%. Salvatore (5), Carlo (4), Antonino (2), Francesco (2), Sal (2), Angelo, Carmine, Cesare, Domenico, Gioacchino, Giuseppe, Ignazio.

Gaglio (278) Southern Italian: nickname for someone with grizzled hair or beard, from Sicilian gagghiu 'spotted', 'dappled'.
GIVEN NAMES Italian 28%. Salvatore (10), Vito (4), Antonio (3), Pietro (3), Filippo (2), Caesar, Carmelo, Cesare, Domenico, Giovanni, Nichola, Nunzio.

Gaglione (302) Italian: **1.** from an augmentative of GAGLIO. **2.** from Neapolitan guaglione 'youth', 'lad'.
GIVEN NAMES Italian 27%. Salvatore (4), Elia (3), Carmine (3), Gennaro (2), Aniello, Assunta, Carmine, Giovanni, Luciano,

Luigi, Marco, Mariano, Mario, Pellegrino, Valerio.

Gagnard (120) French: from a pejorative derivative of *gagner* 'to make money', applied as a nickname in the sense 'pillager' and by extension for a cruel or unscrupulous man.

Gagne (3885) French: occupational name for a farmer or peasant, from Old French *ga(i)gnier* 'to cultivate or work (the land)'. Numerous variants and Americanized forms are found (see GAGNER, GONYEA).
GIVEN NAMES French 17%. *Armand* (17), *Lucien* (17), *Marcel* (14), *Andre* (10), *Fernand* (10), *Normand* (9), *Donat* (6), *Jacques* (6), *Rosaire* (6), *Adrien* (5), *Cecile* (5), *Emile* (5).

Gagner (563) French: from *gagneur* 'cultivator', an agent derivative of Old French *ga(i)gnier* 'to cultivate' (see GAGNE).
GIVEN NAMES French 7%. *Armand* (3), *Andre* (2), *Cecile, Clovis, Gaston, Gilles, Hilaire, Laurent.*

Gagnier (405) French: variant of GAGNER.
GIVEN NAMES French 7%. *Andre, Camille, Christophe, Dominique, Pierre.*

Gagnon (8559) French: **1.** nickname for an aggressive or belligerent man, from Old French *gagnon* ' mastiff', 'guard dog'. **2.** possibly from Occitan *ganhon* 'young pig', applied as an offensive nickname. See also GONYEAU.
GIVEN NAMES French 14%. *Armand* (38), *Andre* (27), *Marcel* (27), *Normand* (20), *Emile* (14), *Jacques* (14), *Pierre* (14), *Gilles* (11), *Cecile* (10), *Fernand* (9), *Georges* (9), *Laurent* (9).

Gago (129) Spanish and Portuguese: nickname for a man afflicted with a stammer, from Spanish, Portuguese *gago* 'stammering', 'stuttering' (of imitative origin).
GIVEN NAMES Spanish 33%; German 5%. *Jose* (3), *Manuel* (3), *Andres* (2), *Francisco* (2), *Albino, Alfredo, Amparo, Angel, Arcenio, Emilio, Esteban, Fernando; Otto* (3).

Gagon (109) Variant of Irish GEOGHEGAN.

Gahagan (682) Irish: variant of GAVIGAN.

Gahan (467) Irish: **1.** reduced form of MCGAHAN, an Anglicized form of Gaelic *Mac Eacháin*, 'son of *Eachán*'. **2.** in Leinster, a reduced Anglicized form of Gaelic Ó Gaoithin 'descendant of *Gaoithín*', a personal name from a diminutive of *gaoth*, an adjective meaning 'wise' (probably the sense here) or a noun meaning 'wind'; hence in Connacht the name is sometimes 'translated' as WYNNE or WYNDHAM. Occasionally it may be an Anglicized form of **Mac Gaoithín** 'son of *Gaoithín*', although this is more commonly found as MCGEEHAN, an Ulster name.
GIVEN NAME Irish 4%. *Brendan.*

Gahm (227) German: habitational name for someone from Gahme near Pössneck in Thuringia.

Gahn (217) German: from a short form of the personal name *Johannes* (see JOHN).

Gahr (238) **1.** North German (**Gähr**): from a short form of a Germanic personal name formed with the element *gār, gēr* 'spear'. **2.** South German: see GAAR.

Gaia (134) **1.** Italian: from the personal name *Gaia*, feminine form of *Gaio* (from Latin *Caius, Gaius*). **2.** Portuguese: habitational name from Gaia in northern Portugal.
GIVEN NAMES Italian 7%. *Camillo* (2), *Angelo, Sylvio.*

Gaida (191) **1.** Lithuanian: nickname from *gaidys* 'rooster'. **2.** Latvian: from a personal name, *Gaida*, based on the verb *gaidīt* 'to wait'. **3.** Polish and Lithuanian: variant spelling of GAJDA. **4.** Respelling of French **Gaide**, from *Gaido*, a personal name of Germanic origin, possibly related to *gār, gēr* 'lance', 'spear'.

Gaier (242) **1.** South German and Austrian form of GEYER. **2.** German: occupational name for a forest warden, from a derivative of Slavic *gaj* 'grove'.
GIVEN NAMES German 4%. *Elfriede, Nicolaus.*

Gaige (168) Variant spelling of English GAGE.

Gail (407) **1.** English: variant spelling of GALE. **2.** French: nickname from Old French *gail* 'cheerful', 'jolly'. **3.** German: variant of GEIL.

Gailes (116) English: variant spelling of GALES.
GIVEN NAME French 4%. *Marcell.*

Gailey (1107) **1.** English: habitational name from a place in Staffordshire named Gailey, from Old English *gagel* 'bog-myrtle' + *lēah* 'woodland clearing'. **2.** In some instances, an altered spelling of South German **Gailer** (variant of GEILER) or of Swiss **Gälli** (see GALL).

Gaillard (767) English (of Norman origin) and French: **1.** nickname from French *gaillard* 'strong', 'robust', possibly from Gaulish *galia* 'strength' + the suffix *-ard*. **2.** from Old French *gaile* 'cheerful' (of Germanic origin; compare GALE 1) + the pejorative suffix *-ard*.
FOREBEARS Gaillard was brought to America by the Huguenots, and is sometimes Americanized as GAYLORD.
GIVEN NAMES French 7%. *Philippe* (2), *Pierre* (2), *Andre, Andree, Ketly, Marcel, Mirlande, Monique.*

Gain (371) English: variant of GAINES.

Gainer (1592) Irish: variant spelling of GAYNOR.

Gaines (12628) **1.** English (of Norman origin): nickname for a crafty or ingenious person, from a reduced form of Old French *engaine* 'ingenuity', 'trickery' (Latin *ingenium* 'native wit'). The word was also used in a concrete sense of a stratagem or device, particularly a trap. **2.** This surname has

also assimilated reduced variants of Welsh GURGANUS.

Gainey (2369) Irish (mainly Connacht): reduced Anglicized form of Gaelic Ó Geigheannaigh 'descendant of *Géibheannach*' or **Mac Géibheannaigh** 'son of *Géibheannach*', a byname meaning 'fettered'.

Gainor (236) Irish: variant spelling of GAYNOR.

Gainous (284) Reduced form of Welsh GURGANUS.

Gains (171) English: variant of GAIN.

Gair (215) Scottish: habitational name from places so named in Dumfries and Galloway, Strathclyde, and the Border regions.

Gaiser (685) German: occupational name for a goatherd or a nickname for a capricious person, from an agent derivative of Middle High German *geiz* 'goat'.
GIVEN NAMES German 5%. *Hans* (2), *Dieter, Gerhard, Gottlob, Helmuth, Kurt, Manfred, Otto.*

Gaisford (140) English: habitational name from a lost or unidentified place.

Gaitan (731) Hispanic: variant of Italian GAETANO.
GIVEN NAMES Spanish 44%. *Jose* (19), *Carlos* (12), *Jesus* (9), *Juan* (9), *Francisco* (8), *Manuel* (7), *Raul* (6), *Luis* (5), *Roberto* (5), *Alfonso* (4), *Ernestina* (4), *Fernando* (4).

Gaiter (148) English and Scottish: variant of GAITHER.
GIVEN NAMES French 8%; German 4%. *Andre* (2), *Leonce; Franz.*

Gaither (3319) English: occupational name from Middle English *gaytere* 'goatherd', an agent derivative of Middle English *gayte* 'goat' (a northern spelling of Old English *gāt*, or from the related Old Norse word *geit*).

Gaito (160) Italian (Naples): unexplained. It may be a habitational name from a place so named, from Arabic *gaydah* 'wood'.

Gaj (117) Polish and Slovak: **1.** from a short form of the personal name *Gajus*. **2.** topographic name from *gaj* 'grove'.
GIVEN NAMES Polish 12%; German 4%. *Bogdan, Casimir, Elzbieta, Ewa, Tadeusz.*

Gajda (298) Polish, Slovak, and Hungarian: from Slavic *gajda* 'bagpipe', in particular the kind of folk instrument found in the Carpathians. The word is ultimately of Turkish origin. The surname probably arose as a metonymic occupational name for a piper, but perhaps in some cases as a nickname, as the Polish word also has the figurative meanings 'fat legs' or 'awkward person'.
GIVEN NAMES Polish 16%. *Jacek* (2), *Wojciech* (2), *Andrzej, Casimir, Gerzy, Grazyna, Janusz, Jerzy, Marzena, Stanislaw, Tadeusz.*

Gajdos (122) **1.** Hungarian: nickname for a ribald person, from *gajdolni* 'to sing in a raucous or drunken way' (from Slavic

gajda 'bagpipe'). In some cases it may be an occupational name for a player of pipes or bagpipes. **2.** Polish and Slovak (**Gajdoš**): from a derivative of GAJDA.
GIVEN NAMES Hungarian 6%. *Bela, Imre, Zoltan.*

Gajeski (127) Polish: variant of GAJEWSKI.
GIVEN NAME German 5%. *Kurt* (2).

Gajewski (1013) Polish: habitational name for someone from any of the various places named Gaj (from *gaj* 'grove'), Gajew, or Gajewo.
GIVEN NAMES Polish 9%. *Zbigniew* (3), *Casimir* (2), *Jerzy* (2), *Mieczyslaw* (2), *Pawel* (2), *Tomasz* (2), *Wieslaw* (2), *Zygmunt* (2), *Boguslaw, Ewa, Henryk, Janusz.*

Gal (277) **1.** Polish, Slovak (**Gál**), and Slovenian: from a personal name, Latin *Gallus* (see GALL), which was widespread in Europe in the Middle Ages. There are many pet forms and other derivatives of this personal name; the American surname could also be a shortening of any of them. See also GALL. **2.** Hungarian (**Gál**): from the ecclesiastical name *Gál*, a short form of *Gál(l)os*, from Latin *Gallus* (see GALL). **3.** French: from the personal name *Gallus* (see 1), the name of a 6th-century bishop of Clermont. **4.** French: habitational name for someone from either of two places named Saint Gal, in Lozère and Puy-de-Dôme, or from Saint Jal in Corrèze. **5.** French: nickname from southern French *gal* 'rooster' (Old French *jal*, Latin *gallus*). As a French name, it appears to have been brought to the U.S. by Swiss bearers. **6.** Jewish (Israeli): ornamental name from Hebrew *gal* 'wave'.
GIVEN NAMES Jewish 14%; Hungarian 9%; Polish 6%. *Aharon* (2), *Eti* (2), *Ofer* (2), *Aviva, Dorit, Dov, Gadi, Iddo, Ido, Moshe, Noam, Ronen; Imre* (3), *Sandor* (3), *Janos* (2), *Laszlo* (2), *Bela, Ildiko; Andrej, Dariusz, Feliks, Kazimierz, Stanislaw, Wlodzimierz.*

Gala (270) **1.** Indian (Gujarat): Jain name of unknown meaning. **2.** Polish and Hungarian: from a derivative of the personal name GAL.
GIVEN NAMES Indian 29%. *Bharat* (2), *Jayant* (2), *Kanti* (2), *Umesh* (2), *Ashok, Chetan, Daksha, Dilip, Hardev, Hema, Hemant, Himanshu.*

Galambos (225) Hungarian: metonymic occupational name for a keeper of doves, from *galamb* 'dove', 'pigeon'.
GIVEN NAMES Hungarian 4%. *Bela, Laszlo, Nandor.*

Galan (873) Spanish (**Galán**): nickname from *galán* 'beau', 'suitor', a loanword from French *galant*.
GIVEN NAMES Spanish 39%. *Jose* (19), *Carlos* (10), *Luis* (10), *Manuel* (10), *Juan* (8), *Francisco* (6), *Pedro* (6), *Rafael* (6), *Alfonso* (5), *Jesus* (5), *Jorge* (5), *Raul* (5).

Galang (312) Filipino: unexplained. Possibly an altered form of Spanish GALAN.

GIVEN NAMES Spanish 43%. *Jaime* (4), *Jose* (4), *Manuel* (3), *Renato* (3), *Alfredo* (2), *Angel* (2), *Conrado* (2), *Domingo* (2), *Ernesto* (2), *Jesus* (2), *Miguel* (2), *Ramon* (2); *Antonio* (4), *Clemente.*

Galanis (227) Greek: nickname for someone with pale blue eyes, from the adjective *galanos* 'azure', 'milky blue'.
GIVEN NAMES Greek 17%. *Constantine* (2), *Constantinos* (2), *Andreas, Aristotelis, Christos, Demetrios, Evangelos, Georgios, Kostantinos, Manos, Nickolaos, Panagiota.*

Galano (144) **1.** Spanish: nickname for an elegant man, from an adjectival derivative of *galán* 'beau', 'dandy' (see GALAN). **2.** Italian (Calabria): nickname, of Greek origin, for someone with blue eyes. Compare Greek GALANIS.
GIVEN NAMES Spanish 22%; Italian 15%. *Jose* (2), *Luis* (2), *Rogelio* (2); *Adriano, Alberto, Ana, Angel, Armando, Augusto, Blanca, Caridad, Erasmo; Crescenzo* (2), *Antonio, Carmela, Carmine, Dante, Egidio, Luigi.*

Galanos (114) Greek: variant of GALANIS.
GIVEN NAMES Greek 6%. *Demosthenes, Diogenes, Labros.*

Galant (173) French: nickname for a cheerful or high-spirited person, from *galant*, the present participle of Old French *galer* 'to be in good humor', 'enjoy oneself', a word of Germanic origin (see GALE 1 and GAILLARD). The meanings 'gallant' and 'attentive to women' are later developments, which may lie behind some examples of the surname.
GIVEN NAMES Jewish 4%. *Shraga, Sol.*

Galante (1333) Italian and Portuguese: nickname for a chivalrous person, from *galante* 'courteous', 'gallant' (from French *galant*), also applied as a medieval personal name.
GIVEN NAMES Italian 16%. *Salvatore* (9), *Angelo* (8), *Antonio* (6), *Dante* (3), *Lorenzo* (3), *Pietro* (3), *Rocco* (3), *Vito* (3), *Gasper* (2), *Gino* (2), *Giuseppe* (2), *Marino* (2).

Galanti (242) Italian: variant of GALANTE.
Galantis is also found as a Greek family name.
GIVEN NAMES Italian 11%. *Salvatore* (2), *Angelo, Carmela, Ceasar, Dino, Gianna, Nazzareno, Sal, Stefano.*

Galardi (148) Basque: topographic name for someone who lived in an area of abundant firewood, from Basque *galar* 'kindling', 'dead wood' + *-di*, a suffix denoting abundance.

Galarneau (335) French: from a diminutive of Old French *galerne* 'northwest wind'.
FOREBEARS Bearers of this name from La Rochelle, France, had reached Canada by 1665.
GIVEN NAMES French 8%. *Pierre* (3), *Lucien* (2), *Alcide, Ludger, Rosaire.*

Galarza (866) Basque: topographic name, cognate with GALARDI, from *galar* 'kindling', 'dead wood' + the collective suffix *-tza.*

GIVEN NAMES Spanish 50%. *Luis* (15), *Jose* (14), *Juan* (12), *Carlos* (10), *Jesus* (8), *Miguel* (8), *Raul* (8), *Jorge* (7), *Julio* (7), *Guillermo* (5), *Ignacio* (5), *Javier* (5).

Galas (259) **1.** Polish: from a derivative of the personal name GAL. **2.** Hungarian: from the personal name *Gálos* (see GAL). **3.** Dutch: variant of GALLAS. **4.** Spanish: variant of GALAZ.
GIVEN NAMES Polish 9%. *Beata, Bronislaus, Edyta, Elzbieta, Janina, Piotr, Wladyslawa, Wojciech.*

Galaska (114) Polish (**Gałazka**): nickname for a small or insignificant person from *gałązka* 'twig', 'branch'.

Galassi (238) Italian: patronymic from GALASSO.
GIVEN NAMES Italian 16%; French 4%. *Reno* (2), *Arduino, Carlo, Domenica, Gilda, Gino, Giulio, Leno, Marino, Naldo, Natale, Nino; Armand, Normandie.*

Galasso (792) Italian (mainly Venice): from an Italianized form of the personal name *Galahad*, name of a character in Arthurian legend.
GIVEN NAMES Italian 15%. *Salvatore* (6), *Angelo* (3), *Dino* (2), *Donato* (2), *Gino* (2), *Luigi* (2), *Sal* (2), *Ugo* (2), *Vincenzo* (2), *Alessandra, Antonio, Carmine.*

Galat (132) Polish: possibly a derivative of the Silesian dialect word *galoty* 'trousers', thus a nickname for someone who used to wear elegant trousers.

Galatas (142) Greek: occupational name for a seller of milk, an agent noun from *gala* 'milk'.
GIVEN NAMES French 6%. *Albertine, Andre.*

Galati (684) Italian: from the medieval Greek personal name *Galatēs*, originally meaning 'person from Galatia or Gaul'. Galatia was an ancient territory of central Asia Minor, so called from its inhabitants, Celtic speakers who invaded from the west in the 3rd century BC. Gaul (Latin *Gallia*) consisted originally of the Celtic-speaking territories of what is now France; the Latin term was extended to include northern Italy after the Celtic invasions of the 4th and 3rd centuries BC.
GIVEN NAMES Italian 25%. *Salvatore* (8), *Rocco* (6), *Carmine* (5), *Vito* (5), *Giuseppe* (3), *Saverio* (3), *Carmelo* (2), *Giovanni* (2), *Leonardo* (2), *Mauro* (2), *Vincenzo* (2), *Angelo.*

Galaviz (501) Hispanic (Mexico): unexplained.
GIVEN NAMES Spanish 52%. *Jose* (13), *Juan* (8), *Manuel* (8), *Raul* (7), *Luis* (6), *Pedro* (5), *Ramon* (5), *Jesus* (4), *Ruben* (4), *Armando* (3), *Eduardo* (3), *Juana* (3).

Galayda (121) Origin unidentified.

Galaz (163) Spanish (**Gálaz**) and Portuguese: possibly from a personal name of literary origin. Compare GALASSO.
GIVEN NAMES Spanish 45%. *Ruben* (4), *Jesus* (3), *Luis* (3), *Alfredo* (2), *Armando* (2),

Fernando (2), *Jose* (2), *Lupe* (2), *Manuel* (2), *Adolfo*, *Alonzo*, *Ana*.

Galban (143) Spanish (**Galbán**): variant of **Galván** (see GALVAN).

GIVEN NAMES Spanish 47%. *Jose* (6), *Manuel* (5), *Leandro* (3), *Eduardo* (2), *Jorge* (2), *Juan* (2), *Ofelia* (2), *Ana*, *Angel*, *Armando*, *Arnulfo*, *Beatriz*.

Galbo (207) Italian: from Latin *galbus* 'yellowish', hence probably a nickname for someone with fair hair or a light-colored beard.

GIVEN NAMES Italian 19%. *Sal* (3), *Salvatore* (2), *Antonino*, *Concetta*, *Enzo*, *Filippo*, *Giuliano*, *Guiseppe*, *Marco*, *Pietro*, *Santo*.

Galbraith (3646) Scottish: ethnic name for someone descended from a tribe of Britons living in Scotland, from Gaelic *gall* 'stranger' (see GALL) + *Breathnach* 'Briton' (i.e. 'British foreigner'). These were either survivors of the British peoples who lived in Scotland before the Gaelic invasions from Ireland in the 5th century (in particular the Welsh-speaking Strathclyde Britons, who survived as a distinctive ethnic group until about the 14th century), or others who had perhaps migrated northwestwards at the time of the Anglo-Saxon invasions.

FOREBEARS This name is first recorded as a surname in the area of Lennox, a rich agricultural region north of Glasgow under the Campsie Fells, in the 12th century. In early medieval times, the region to which Lennox belongs was an independent Welsh-speaking kingdom, with its capital at Dumbarton. It was not integrated into the rest of Scotland until 1124. The first recorded chief of the Galbraiths was Gilchrist 'the Briton', living in 1193.

Galbreath (1865) Scottish: variant spelling of GALBRAITH.

Galbreth (111) Scottish: variant spelling of GALBRAITH.

Galczynski (63) Polish (**Gałczyński**): habitational name for someone from Gałczyn in Ciechanów or Konin voivodeships, places so named from **Gałka** (see GALKA).

GIVEN NAMES Polish 11%. *Ignacy*, *Wojciech*.

Galdamez (287) Spanish (**Galdámez**): Castilianized form of Basque **Galdames**, a habitational name from Galdames in Biscay, Basque Country.

GIVEN NAMES Spanish 56%. *Carlos* (8), *Jose* (8), *Roberto* (5), *Juan* (4), *Luis* (4), *Manuel* (4), *Alfredo* (3), *Jorge* (3), *Pedro* (3), *Rafael* (3), *Ricardo* (3), *Alfonso* (2); *Antonio* (4), *Marco* (3), *Amelio*, *Francesca*.

Galdi (143) **1.** Italian: unexplained. **2.** Hungarian (**Gáldi**): habitational name for someone from a place called Gáld in Fejér county.

GIVEN NAMES Italian 12%. *Santo* (2), *Antonio*, *Giuseppe*.

Gale (6094) **1.** English: nickname for a cheerful or boisterous person, from Middle English *ga(i)le* 'jovial', 'rowdy', from Old English *gāl* 'light', 'pleasant', 'merry', which was reinforced in Middle English by Old French *gail*. Compare GAIL 2. **2.** English: from a Germanic personal name introduced into England from France by the Normans in the form *Gal(on)*. Two originally distinct names have fallen together in this form: one was a short form of compound names with the first element *gail* 'cheerful', 'joyous'. Compare GAILLARD, the other was a byname from the element *walh* 'stranger', 'foreigner'. **3.** English: metonymic occupational name for a jailer, topographic name for someone who lived near the local jail, or nickname for a jailbird, from Old Northern French *gaiole* 'jail' (Late Latin *caveola*, a diminutive of classical Latin *cavea* 'cage'). **4.** Portuguese: from *galé* 'galleon', 'war ship', presumably a metonymic occupational name for a shipwright or a mariner. **5.** Slovenian: from a pet form of the personal name GAL (Latin *Gallus*), formed with the suffix *-e*, usually denoting a young person.

Galea (328) Italian and Spanish: from *galea* 'galleon', '(war)ship', presumably a metonymic occupational name for a shipwright or a sailor.

GIVEN NAMES Italian 11%; Spanish 8%; French 4%. *Carmel* (2), *Agostino*, *Carlo*, *Carmelo*, *Guiseppe*, *Sal*, *Salvatore*, *Santo*, *Vincenzo*; *Jesus*, *Jose*, *Nadina*, *Roberto*; *Monique* (2), *Armand*.

Galeana (105) Hispanic (Mexico): unexplained.

GIVEN NAMES Spanish 67%. *Francisco* (4), *Juan* (3), *Carlos* (2), *Javier* (2), *Jose* (2), *Luis* (2), *Pedro* (2), *Ramon* (2), *Adan*, *Amada*, *Amador*, *Andres*.

Galeano (307) Spanish: probably a variant of GALIANO.

GIVEN NAMES Spanish 47%. *Jose* (13), *Carlos* (5), *Julio* (5), *Jorge* (4), *Luis* (4), *Blanca* (3), *Rafael* (3), *Alejandro* (2), *Alvaro* (2), *Ana* (2), *Arturo* (2), *Esperanza* (2); *Antonio* (4), *Marco* (2), *Angelo*, *Emidio*, *Lia*, *Nicola*, *Salvatore*.

Galeas (105) Spanish (common in Honduras): unexplained.

GIVEN NAMES Spanish 56%. *Jose* (10), *Carlos* (2), *Carlos Alberto* (2), *Pablo* (2), *Santos* (2), *Absalon*, *Alvaro*, *Armando*, *Armondo*, *Blanca*, *Carlos Ernesto*, *Edgardo*.

Galeazzi (106) Italian: from the personal name *Galeazzo*, of uncertain origin.

GIVEN NAMES Italian 14%. *Dino* (2), *Albo*, *Angelo*, *Dante*, *Massimo*, *Remo*, *Sante*.

Galecki (137) Polish (**Gałecki**): habitational name from any of various places named Gałki, probably from *gałka* 'knob'. These are found in the voivodeships of Radom, Siedlce, and Sieradz; also (during the Middle Ages) in the southern borderland of Poland, now part of Ukraine.

GIVEN NAMES Polish 12%. *Andrzej*, *Gerzy*, *Jerzy*, *Jozef*, *Krystyna*, *Leszek*, *Urszula*.

Galella (104) Italian: variant of **Gallello**, which is probably from a pet form of the personal name *Gallo* (see GALLI).

GIVEN NAMES Italian 16%. *Luigi* (2), *Carmela*, *Donatella*, *Valentino*.

Galen (281) **1.** Reduced form of the Dutch surname **van Galen**, a habitational name, probably from Gaal in the province of North Brabant, or perhaps from the German town of Gahlen in North Rhine-Westphalia. **2.** English: variant of GALYON.

Galentine (177) See GILLENTINE.

Galer (285) **1.** English: variant of GALE 3. **2.** Possibly a respelling of German **Gähler**, a variant of GEHLER.

Gales (989) **1.** English: from Middle English *Gallis*, variant of WALLIS. **2.** Possibly an Americanized form of German **Gölz** (see GOELZ).

Galewski (113) Polish: habitational name for someone from Galew, Galewice, or Galów in the voivodeships of Kalisz, Kielce, or Konin. See also GALL 2.

Galey (519) **1.** English: variant spelling of GALLEY. **2.** Ukrainian: nickname meaning 'hasten', 'hurry', from Proto-Slavic *galiti* 'to shout'.

Galford (234) **1.** English: habitational name from a place in Devon so named, from Old English *gafol* 'tax', 'toll' + *ford* 'ford'. The surname is now not found in England. **2.** Possibly an Americanized spelling of German **Galfert**, from a Germanic personal name based on Old High German *galan* 'to sing', or of **Gelfort**, **Gelfert**, or **Gelfart(h)**, from a Germanic personal name composed with Middle High German *gelfen* 'to cry', 'to boast' or *gelf* 'scorn'.

Galgano (341) Italian: from *Galgano*, a development of the medieval personal name *Galvano*, an equivalent of Celtic *Gawain* (Old French *Gauvain*), which was widely popularized through the Arthurian romances (see GAVIN).

GIVEN NAMES Italian 6%. *Rocco* (3), *Angelo*.

Galiano (315) **1.** Spanish and Italian: from the Late Latin personal name *Gallianus*, a derivative of *Gallius*, from *Gallus* (see GALL 2). **2.** Italian: habitational name from a place called Galiano.

GIVEN NAMES Spanish 16%; Italian 11%. *Jose* (4), *Luis* (3), *Blanca* (2), *Jaime* (2), *Jorge* (2), *Juan* (2), *Julio* (2), *Pedro* (2); *Dino* (2), *Eduardo* (2), *Rolando* (2), *Adolfo*, *Aida*, *Angelo*, *Fausto*, *Gennaro*, *Luciano*, *Nunzio*, *Rocco*.

Galica (145) Polish: from a pet form of the personal name GAL.

GIVEN NAMES Polish 4%. *Mieczyslaw*, *Stanislaw*.

Galicia (500) Spanish: ethnic name for someone from the former kingdom of Galicia, now an autonomous region of northwestern Spain.

GIVEN NAMES Spanish 53%. *Jose* (8), *Carlos* (7), *Juan* (7), *Manuel* (5), *Juana* (4), *Mario*

(4), *Miguel* (4), *Pedro* (4), *Rodolfo* (4), *Alicia* (3), *Arturo* (3), *Fidel* (3); *Antonio* (2), *Carmelo, Cirino, Enrico, Fausto, Federico, Severiano.*

Galicki (71) Polish and Jewish (eastern Ashkenazic): habitational name for someone from a lost place called Galice.
GIVEN NAMES Polish 11%; Jewish 5%; German 5%. *Krzysztof* (2); *Gershon; Aloysius.*

Galik (246) Polish and Hungarian (**Gálik**): from a pet form of a personal name: Polish *Gal*, Hungarian *Gál* (see GAL).

Galin (171) **1.** Jewish (eastern Ashkenazic): habitational name for someone from the village of Galino in Lithuania. **2.** Polish: from a pet form of the personal name GAL.
GIVEN NAMES Jewish 7%. *Nir, Shoshi, Tsilya.*

Galindez (120) Spanish (**Galíndez**): patronymic from the personal name GALINDO.
GIVEN NAMES Spanish 47%. *Orlando* (3), *Aracelis* (2), *Carlos* (2), *Jose Luis* (2), *Margarita* (2), *Miguel* (2), *Telmo* (2), *Alfredo, Angel, Arcadio, Efrain, Efren.*

Galindo (3286) Spanish: from the medieval personal name *Galindo*, of predominantly Aragonese origin and distribution, but of unknown etymology.
GIVEN NAMES Spanish 48%. *Jose* (59), *Juan* (47), *Manuel* (37), *Jesus* (29), *Pedro* (28), *Carlos* (27), *Jaime* (22), *Luis* (20), *Mario* (19), *Francisco* (17), *Jorge* (17), *Ramon* (16).

Galinis (101) Lithuanian: topographic name for someone living at the end of a village, from *galas* 'end'.
GIVEN NAMES Lithuanian 5%. *Algimantas, Vytautas.*

Galinski (179) **1.** Polish (**Galiński**): habitational name from Galiny Duże in Skierniewice voivodeship. **2.** Jewish (eastern Ashkenazic): habitational name for someone from Galińce in northeastern Poland, Galinka in Ukraine, or Galiniai in Lithuania.
GIVEN NAMES Polish 6%. *Basia, Jozef, Zygmunt.*

Galinsky (181) Jewish (Ashkenazic): variant spelling of GALINSKI.
GIVEN NAMES Jewish 8%; Russian 7%; German 4%. *Eyal* (2), *Eliezer, Irina, Meyer, Sima; Elizaveta, Galina, Igor, Mikhail, Raisa, Semyon, Vitaly; Klaus, Ulrich.*

Galioto (233) **1.** Italian: occupational name from *galeotto* 'sailor on a galleon'. **2.** Portuguese: variant of **Galiote**, from *galiote* 'pirate', 'corsair'.
GIVEN NAMES Italian 17%. *Mario* (2), *Mariano* (2), *Rosario* (2), *Agostino, Angelo, Benedetto, Carlo, Guiseppe, Sal, Salvatore, Vincenza.*

Galipeau (344) **1.** French: from Old French *galipe* 'galley,' an occupational nickname for a seaman. **2.** Possibly a respelling of French **Galipot**, from *garipot* 'pine tar', used to seal joints in ships; thus also an occupational name for a seaman.

GIVEN NAMES French 15%. *Armand* (2), *Michel* (2), *Normand* (2), *Andre, Aurel, Henri, Jacques, Lorette, Ludger, Marcel, Monique, Pierre.*

Galka (285) Polish (**Gałka**): nickname from Polish *gałka* 'knob', 'lump', probably denoting someone who was disfigured by a prominent carbuncle. This name is also established in German-speaking lands.
GIVEN NAMES Polish 7%. *Andrzej, Eugeniusz, Franciszek, Ignacy, Irek, Krzysztof.*

Galkin (131) **1.** Jewish (from Belarus): habitational name for someone from the village of Galki in eastern Belarus. **2.** Russian: patronymic from *Galka*, a nickname meaning 'jackdaw', used to denote a thievish or talkative person.
GIVEN NAMES Russian 11%; Jewish 5%. *Nikolay* (2), *Leonid, Lev, Mikhail, Nikolai, Yevgeny; Hyman, Isaak.*

Galkowski (92) Polish (**Gałkowski**): habitational name for someone from Gałkowo in Suwałki voivodeship or Gałków in Piotrków voivodeship, both places named from *gałka* 'knob', 'lump'.

Gall (3390) **1.** Scottish, Irish, and English: nickname, of Celtic origin, meaning 'foreigner' or 'stranger'. In the Scottish Highlands the Gaelic term *gall* was applied to people from the English-speaking lowlands and to Scandinavians; in Ireland the same term was applied to settlers who arrived from Wales and England in the wake of the Anglo-Norman invasion of the 12th century. The surname is also found at an early date in Lincolnshire, where it apparently has a Breton origin, having been introduced by Breton followers of the Norman Conquerors. **2.** French, German, Polish, Slovak, Czech, Danish, etc.: from a personal name (*Gallus* in Latin) which was widespread in Europe during the Middle Ages, due to the cult of a 7th-century Irish monk and missionary, St. *Gall*. He established a Christian settlement to the south of Lake Constance, which became the monastery later known as St. Gallen. His name was taken into Czech as *Havel* and into Polish as *Gaweł*, the extra syllable being introduced by analogy with Latin *Paulus*, which yielded Czech *Pavel* and Polish *Paweł*. **3.** Hungarian (**Gáll**): variant of **Gál** (see GAL).

Galla (358) **1.** Polish, Czech, and Slovak (Moravian): from the personal name *Gallus*, from Latin *Gallus* or *Gaulus* (see GALL 2). **2.** Hungarian: from a pet form of *Gál* (see GAL). **3.** Italian: possibly a nickname from a derivative of *gallo* 'rooster'; alternatively it could be from medieval Latin *gadda* 'oak', or perhaps a variant of CALLA. **4.** Muslim: variant of KALLA.
GIVEN NAMES Italian 5%; Muslim 5%. *Guillermo; Amal, Farid, Fereshteh.*

Gallacher (285) Scottish spelling of GALLAGHER.

Gallager (173) Irish: variant of GALLAGHER.

Gallagher (27736) Irish: reduced Anglicized form of Gaelic **Ó Gallchobhair** 'descendant of *Gallchobhar*', a personal name from the elements *gall* 'strange', 'foreign' + *cabhair* 'help', 'support'.
GIVEN NAMES Irish 5%. *Brendan* (22), *Siobhan* (6), *Declan* (5), *Brigid* (3), *Eamon* (3), *Padraic* (3), *Clancy* (2), *Conal* (2), *Dermot* (2), *Donal* (2), *Donovan* (2), *Dymphna* (2).

Gallahan (267) Irish: probably a variant of GALLIGAN.

Gallaher (1578) Irish: variant of GALLAGHER.

Gallahue (135) Irish: variant of GALLAGHER.
GIVEN NAME Irish 9%. *Kieran* (2).

Gallamore (177) English: probably a variant of CULLIMORE.

Galland (369) French: variant of GALANT.

Gallant (3737) **1.** English: nickname for a cheerful or high-spirited person, from Old French, Middle English *galant* 'bold', 'dashing', 'lively'. The meanings 'gallant' and 'attentive to women' are further developments, which may lie behind some examples of the surname. **2.** French: variant spelling of GALANT, cognate with 1.
GIVEN NAMES French 6%. *Adrien* (5), *Gilles* (4), *Yvon* (4), *Alphonse* (2), *Andre* (2), *Camille* (2), *Emile* (2), *Lucien* (2), *Normand* (2), *Pierre* (2), *Adelard, Alban.*

Gallardo (2623) Spanish: from a Germanic personal name composed of the elements *gail* 'cheerful', 'joyous' + *hard* 'hardy', 'brave', 'strong'.
GIVEN NAMES Spanish 46%. *Jose* (62), *Juan* (36), *Manuel* (26), *Carlos* (22), *Luis* (21), *Francisco* (19), *Jesus* (19), *Ramon* (17), *Jorge* (16), *Rafael* (16), *Enrique* (13), *Mario* (13).

Gallas (351) **1.** Dutch: from a pet form of the Germanic personal name GERLACH. **2.** Dutch: possibly also a nickname from *galasse* 'cobblestone' or 'gall stone'. **3.** Polish: variant of GALAS. **4.** Eastern German: variant of GALL 2, with the Slavic suffix -*as*.

Gallaspy (100) Variant spelling of Scottish or Irish GILLESPIE.

Gallatin (455) Swiss French (from Savoy): of Rhaeto-Romansch or Ladin origin, but unexplained. The name is also recorded in the Italian form **Gallatini**.

Gallaugher (128) Irish: see GALLAGHER. This spelling is found chiefly in northern Ireland and England.

Gallaway (909) Respelling of the Scottish regional name GALLOWAY.

Galle (738) French: **1.** (**Gallé**) nickname for a cheerful lively person, from a diminutive of Old French *gail* 'pleasant', 'merry'. **2.** Breton: variant of GALL 1. **3.** German: variant of GALL, or nickname for an evil person, from Middle High German *galle* 'bile', 'bitterness', 'falsehood'. **4.** Danish and Swedish: perhaps from an old byname *Galle*, believed to derive from Old Danish and Old Swedish *galle* 'fault', 'defect'. **5.** Slovenian: Germanized spelling of GALE 5.

GIVEN NAMES French 4%. *Andre* (2), *Amie*, *Colette*, *Yves*.

Gallego (736) Spanish: ethnic name for someone from Galicia, Spanish *gallego*.

GIVEN NAMES Spanish 41%. *Jose* (16), *Juan* (12), *Carlos* (8), *Luis* (8), *Jesus* (6), *Julio* (5), *Enrique* (4), *Guillermo* (4), *Jorge* (4), *Luz* (4), *Manuel* (4), *Alvaro* (3).

Gallegos (8231) Spanish: habitational name from any of the numerous places named Gallegos, originally denoting a place settled by 'people from Galicia'.

GIVEN NAMES Spanish 35%. *Jose* (138), *Juan* (89), *Manuel* (76), *Carlos* (46), *Ruben* (38), *Francisco* (32), *Jorge* (32), *Luis* (32), *Jesus* (29), *Ramon* (26), *Mario* (24), *Fernando* (23).

Galleher (130) Irish: variant of GAL-LAGHER.

Gallemore (160) English: probably a variant of CULLIMORE.

Gallen (326) Northern Irish: reduced Anglicized form of Gaelic **Ó Galláin** 'descendant of *Gallán*', a personal name from a diminutive of *gall* 'rooster'.

GIVEN NAME Irish 4%. *Michael Patrick*.

Gallenstein (122) German: unexplained; perhaps a habitational or topographic name from a minor or lost place so named, either from the family name **Galle**, which derived from the personal name *Gallus* (Latin for 'rooster') or from *galle* 'wet, damaged spot (in a field)' + STEIN.

Gallentine (321) German: see GILLENTINE.

Galler (353) **1.** German: patronymic from a personal name (Latin *Gallus*) which was widespread in Europe in the Middle Ages (see GALL 2). **2.** German: nickname for someone in the service of the monastery of St Gallen, or a habitational name for someone from the city in Switzerland so named. **3.** English: variant of GALLIER. **4.** Hungarian (**Gallér**): from *gallér* 'collar', hence a metonymic occupational name for a taylor, in particular a maker of military garments. **5.** Jewish (Ashkenazic): from German *Galle* 'bile', 'gall', with the agent suffix *-er*. This surname seems to have been one of the group of names selected at random from vocabulary words by government officials.

GIVEN NAMES German 6%; Jewish 5%. *Dieter* (2), *Fritz*, *Otto*, *Reinhold*; *Hyman* (2), *Emanuel*, *Meyer*, *Myer*, *Naum*.

Gallerani (172) Italian: from the medieval personal name *Gallerano*, from *Galerant*, the eponymous hero of a French romance.

GIVEN NAMES French 5%; Italian 4%. *Emile*; *Franca*, *Petrina*, *Ugo*.

Gallery (278) Irish: reduced Anglicized form of Gaelic **Mac Giolla Riabhaigh** 'son of the brindled lad' (see McELRATH).

Galles (339) **1.** Germanized spelling of the French name **Gallois** (meaning 'Gallic'), which was taken to Germany by Huguenot refugees who settled east of the Rhine. **2.** In some cases possibly Catalan **Gallès**, an ethnic name from *gallès* 'Gallic', from Late Latin *gallense*.

Gallet (146) French: from a diminutive of GALLE.

FOREBEARS A family named Galais-Lafleur, from Brittany, was established in Quebec city by 1689.

GIVEN NAMES French 19%. *Jacques* (4), *Alain*, *Gilberte*, *Michel*, *Pierre*, *Vernice*, *Yves*.

Galletta (345) Italian: **1.** from a diminutive or pet form of GALLO. **2.** in some cases, possibly from *galletta* '(ship's) biscuit', 'hard tack'.

GIVEN NAMES Italian 15%. *Salvatore* (3), *Nunzio* (2), *Filippo*, *Rocco*, *Santo*.

Galletti (214) Italian: patronymic from a patronymic or diminutive of GALLO.

GIVEN NAMES Italian 18%. *Primo* (2), *Sebastiano* (2), *Aldo*, *Alfredo*, *Gino*, *Giovanna*, *Guido*, *Julio*, *Odilia*, *Premo*, *Reno*, *Silvia*.

Galley (613) **1.** English: metonymic occupational name for a seaman, from Middle English *galy(e)* 'ship', 'barge' (Old French *galie*, of uncertain origin). **2.** English: nickname for someone who had been on a pilgrimage to the Holy Land, from a reduced form of the place name *Galilee*. **3.** Scottish: variant of GALL 1, from the derivative *gallda* or the collective form *gallaich*. **4.** German: presumably a derivative of GALL. **5.** Northern French: variant of GALLET. This name is also found in French Switzerland and may have been brought to the U.S. from there.

Galli (1230) **1.** Italian: patronymic from GALLO. **2.** Swiss German: variant of GALLE 3. **3.** Hungarian: variant of *Gáli*, pet form of the ecclesiastical name *Gallus* (see GAL).

GIVEN NAMES Italian 11%. *Angelo* (9), *Guido* (4), *Carlo* (2), *Cesare* (2), *Dino* (2), *Domenic* (2), *Enzo* (2), *Gino* (2), *Primo* (2), *Rino* (2), *Savino* (2), *Stefano* (2).

Gallia (129) Italian: habitational name from a minor place so named.

Gallian (123) Variant of Italian GALLIANO or French GALLIEN.

Galliano (221) Italian: from a medieval personal name from Latin *Gallianus*, from an adjective meaning 'Gaulish'.

GIVEN NAMES French 5%; Italian 4%. *Alain*, *Monique*; *Dante*, *Enrico*, *Geno*.

Gallicchio (154) Italian: habitational name from Gallicchio, a place in Potenza province.

GIVEN NAMES Italian 19%. *Rocco* (2), *Antonio*, *Emilio*, *Luigi*, *Mario*, *Pasquale*, *Salvatore*, *Valentino*, *Vito*.

Gallick (194) Americanized spelling of **Gallic**, a Breton name for a French immigrant to Brittany.

Gallien (467) French: from a medieval name from Latin *Gallianus*, from *gallianus* 'of Gaul', 'Gallic'.

Gallier (229) French and English: nickname for a jovial man, from an agent derivative of Old French *galer* 'to make merry'. Compare English WALLER 4.

Galligan (1326) Southern Irish: reduced Anglicized form of Gaelic **Ó Gealagáin** 'descendant of *Gealagán*', a personal name from a double diminutive of *geal* 'bright', 'white'.

GIVEN NAMES Irish 6%. *Brendan* (3), *Aileen*, *Liam*.

Galligher (150) Irish: variant spelling of GALLAGHER.

Galliher (482) Irish: variant spelling of GALLAGHER.

Gallihugh (126) Origin uncertain; perhaps a variant of Irish GALLAGHER.

Gallik (164) Probably a reduced form of Swiss German **Galliker**, of uncertain origin, or a variant spelling of German GOLICK.

Gallimore (1282) English: probably a variant of CULLIMORE.

Gallin (114) **1.** English: perhaps a variant spelling of GALLON. **2.** Jewish (Ashkenazic): variant of GALIN.

GIVEN NAMES Jewish 6%. *Hyman*, *Meyer*.

Gallina (545) Italian: from *gallina* 'hen', 'chicken'; possibly a nickname for someone thought to resemble a hen, or perhaps a metonymic occupational name for someone who kept poultry.

GIVEN NAMES Italian 15%. *Angelo* (6), *Sal* (3), *Antonio* (2), *Filippo* (2), *Giovanni* (2), *Giuseppe* (2), *Salvatore* (2), *Antonino*, *Cataldo*, *Dino*, *Domenico*, *Gaspare*.

Gallinger (240) German: habitational name for someone from Galling in Bavaria or from Gallingen in East Prussia.

Gallino (110) Italian: **1.** from a diminutive of GALLO. **2.** habitational name from a place so named.

Gallion (1059) French: from a diminutive of Old French *galier* 'man with a cheerful disposition'.

Gallipeau (112) French: from Old French *galippe*, which in the 15th century was the name of a type of galley, hence a metonymic occupational name for someone who made or manned such a vessel.

GIVEN NAME French 6%. *Gregoire*.

Gallis (120) Probably a variant spelling of GALLES or KALLIS.

Gallison (102) English: unexplained.

Gallivan (674) Irish: reduced Anglicized form of Gaelic **Ó Gealbháin** (see GALVIN).

This form is associated particularly with County Kerry.

GIVEN NAME Irish 6%. *Brendan*.

Gallman (717) Swiss German (**Gallmann**): variant of GALL 2, reinforced by the addition of Middle High German *man* 'man'.

Gallmeyer (122) German: distinguishing name for a farmer in the service of a feudal lord named *Gall(es)*, from the medieval personal name **Gallus** (Latin 'rooster').

GIVEN NAME German 6%. *Kurt*.

Gallo (6977) **1.** Italian and Spanish: nickname from *gallo* 'rooster' (Latin *gallus*), given originally to a person with some of the attributes associated with a rooster, as for example a powerful voice or sexual prowess. **2.** Italian: from the medieval personal name *Gallo* (see GALL 2). **3.** Italian and Greek (**Gallos**): ethnic name for someone from France or Gaul (Latin *Gallus*). **4.** Italian: habitational name from any of numerous places named with this word, especially in southern Italy, as for example Gallo Matese in Caserta province.

GIVEN NAMES Italian 22%; Spanish 12%. *Angelo* (31), *Salvatore* (26), *Mario* (16), *Rocco* (12), *Antonio* (11), *Pasquale* (11), *Carmine* (10), *Luigi* (6), *Vito* (8), *Armando* (7), *Alfonso* (6), *Cono* (6), *Sal* (6), *Carlo* (5), *Domenic* (5); *Jose* (15), *Carlos* (11), *Pedro* (11), *Jorge* (10), *Luis* (10), *Julio* (9), *Raul* (6), *Fernando* (5), *Juan* (5).

Gallogly (284) Irish: reduced Anglicized form of Gaelic **Mac an Ghalloglaigh**, from *galloglach* 'gallogass'. Galloglasses were a class of warriors retained by Irish chieftains. This was formerly a Donegal surname, but is now found mainly in central Ireland.

Gallon (309) English (chiefly Northumberland) and French: perhaps a variant of GALE 2.

Gallop (631) English: nickname for a rash or impetuous person or a metonymic occupational name for a messenger, from modern English *gallop* (Old French *galop*, probably of imitative origin).

Gallow (296) Americanized spelling of GALLO.

GIVEN NAMES French 4%. *Alcide*, *Landry*, *Orelia*, *Vernice*.

Galloway (11743) Scottish: regional name from Galloway in southwestern Scotland, named as 'place of the foreign Gaels', from Gaelic *gall* 'foreigner' + *Gaidheal* 'Gael'. From the 8th century or before it was a province of Anglian Northumbria. In the 9th century it was settled by mixed Gaelic-Norse inhabitants from the Hebrides and Isle of Man.

Gallucci (873) Italian: patronymic from a diminutive of GALLO.

GIVEN NAMES Italian 9%. *Antonio* (3), *Angelo* (2), *Salvatore* (2), *Vito* (2), *Aldo*, *Amedeo*, *Carmela*, *Eliseo*, *Emidio*, *Fiore*, *Pasco*, *Pasquale*.

Galluccio (161) Italian: from a diminutive or pet form of GALLO.

GIVEN NAMES Italian 20%. *Mario* (2), *Adolfo*, *Angelo*, *Antonio*, *Armano*, *Assunta*, *Carmine*, *Luca*, *Vito*.

Gallup (1674) English: variant spelling of GALLOP.

Gallups (143) Apparently a variant of GALLOP.

Gallus (221) Swiss German and Czech: variant of GALL 2.

Galluzzo (352) Italian: from a variant of GALLUCCIO.

GIVEN NAMES Italian 24%. *Salvatore* (5), *Angelo* (4), *Carmelo* (3), *Sal* (3), *Carlo* (2), *Marino* (2), *Natale* (2), *Rocco* (2), *Antonio*, *Carmela*, *Cosimo*, *Ermanno*.

Gally (102) Swiss variant of German GALLE.

Galm (123) German: probably a nickname related to Middle High German *galm* 'noise', or a habitational name from Galm near Magdeburg.

GIVEN NAME German 5%. *Willi*.

Galo (193) Catalan (**Galó**): from *galó* 'braid'.

GIVEN NAMES Spanish 35%. *Jose* (6), *Alejandro* (2), *Ana* (2), *Cruz* (2), *Ezequiel* (2), *Gustavo* (2), *Jorge* (2), *Manuel* (2), *Adelino*, *Alfredo*, *Alvaro*, *Americo*.

Galovich (118) Croatian: unexplained.

Galow (100) Eastern German: habitational name from Galow in Silesia, Poland.

GIVEN NAMES German 8%. *Horst* (2), *Wolfgang*.

Galper (110) Jewish (eastern Ashkenazic): Russianized form of HALPERN.

GIVEN NAMES Russian 17%; Jewish 13%. *Yevgeniya* (2), *Yevgeny* (2), *Arkadiy*, *Igor*, *Leonid*, *Valeriy*, *Yelena*; *Ilya* (2), *Ari*, *Aron*, *Sol*, *Sura*.

Galperin (220) Jewish (eastern Ashkenazic): Russianized form of HALPERN.

GIVEN NAMES Russian 24%; Jewish 19%. *Boris* (4), *Mikhail* (4), *Vladimir* (4), *Sergey* (3), *Anatoly* (2), *Leonid* (2), *Lev* (2), *Semyon* (2), *Aleksandr*, *Arkadiy*, *Arkady*, *Grigory*; *Inna* (2), *Semen* (2), *Emanuel*, *Igal*, *Irina*, *Isadore*, *Jascha*, *Levi*, *Menashe*, *Shlomit*, *Shlomo*, *Volf*.

Galpin (366) English: occupational name for a messenger or scullion (in a monastery), from Old French *galopin* 'page', 'turnspit', from *galoper* 'to gallop'.

Galster (260) German and Swiss German: nickname for a trickster, from Middle High German *galster* 'deceit', also, in Swabia, 'magpie', and in this sense it may have been a nickname for a pilferer or petty thief.

Galt (507) **1.** English: variant spelling of GAULT. **2.** Scottish: variant of GALL 1.

Galton (109) English: habitational name from a place in Dorset named Galton.

Galus (186) Polish variant of GALLUS. Also a variant of Hungarian *Gálos*, a derivative of GALLUS.

GIVEN NAMES Polish 7%. *Andrzej*, *Boguslaw*, *Boleslaw*, *Piotr*, *Wojciech*.

Galusha (647) Origin unidentified.

Galuska (183) **1.** Czech (Moravian; **Galuška**) and Slovak: variant of Czech **Haluška** 'pasta' (see HALUSKA), probably a nickname for someone with a mole or other facial blemish. **2.** Polish: variant of GALUSZKA.

Galuszka (108) Polish (also **Gałuszka**): **1.** derivative of GAL. **2.** nickname from the Polish dialect word *gałuska* 'little ball', 'little knob', probably denoting someone with a prominent mole or carbuncle.

GIVEN NAMES Polish 8%. *Andrzej*, *Stanislaw*, *Wlodzimierz*.

Galvan (4494) Spanish (**Galván**): from a medieval personal name. This is in origin the Latin name *Galbanus* (a derivative of the Roman family name *Galba*, of uncertain origin). However, it was used in a number of medieval romances as an equivalent of the Celtic name *Gawain* (see GAVIN), and it is probably this association that was mainly responsible for its popularity in the Middle Ages.

GIVEN NAMES Spanish 49%. *Jose* (129), *Juan* (72), *Manuel* (47), *Jesus* (38), *Carlos* (34), *Luis* (30), *Guadalupe* (29), *Raul* (26), *Francisco* (24), *Miguel* (24), *Ruben* (23), *Pedro* (22).

Galvao (109) Portuguese form of GALVAN.

GIVEN NAMES Spanish 39%; Portuguese 19%; Italian 9%. *Manuel* (7), *Jose* (4), *Luiz* (4), *Celso* (2), *Mario* (2), *Telmo* (2), *Alirio*, *Carlos*, *Fernando*, *Hilario*, *Isaura*, *Jacinto*; *Joao*, *Terezinha*; *Antonio* (4), *Flavio*, *Marcello*, *Umberto*.

Galvez (1700) Spanish (**Gálvez**): patronymic from the medieval personal name *Galve* (Arabic *Ghālib* 'triumphant'), which was borne by various Moorish chieftains in Spanish history and legend, notably the father-in-law of Al-Mansūr, the 10th-century vizier of Córdoba.

FOREBEARS General Bernardo de Gálvez was Spanish governor of LA in 1777, and fought against the British in the American Revolution. The city of Galveston, TX, is named for him.

GIVEN NAMES Spanish 50%. *Jose* (48), *Jorge* (29), *Carlos* (26), *Juan* (21), *Luis* (15), *Miguel* (15), *Jesus* (10), *Manuel* (10), *Rafael* (9), *Roberto* (9), *Mario* (8), *Ramon* (8).

Galvin (4494) **1.** Irish: reduced Anglicized form of Gaelic **Ó Gealbháin** 'descendant of *Gealbhán*', a personal name from *geal* 'bright' + *bán* 'white'. **2.** French: nickname for a cheerful drunkard, from Old French *galer* 'to enjoy oneself', also used in a transitive sense with the meaning 'waste', 'consume' + *vin* 'wine' (Latin *vinum*). **3.** French: from a variant of the personal name *Gauvain* (see GAVIN).

GIVEN NAMES Irish 5%. *Brendan* (4), *Eamon* (2), *Colm, Connor, Conor, Fergus, Fidelma, Padraig*.

Galvis (146) Catalan (also **Galbis**): probably a Catalan equivalent of Spanish **Gálvez** (see GALVEZ).

GIVEN NAMES Spanish 47%. *Carlos* (5), *Luis* (5), *Jaime* (3), *Juan* (3), *Alvaro* (2), *Claudio* (2), *Jorge* (2), *Jose* (2), *Sergio* (2), *Agustin, Amparo, Ana*.

Galway (174) Irish: probably a variant of Scottish GALLOWAY, rather than a habitational name from the place of this name in southern Connacht. During the Middle Ages Galways were wealthy merchants on the south coast of Ireland, but now the name is largely confined to Ulster.

Galyan (105) Origin unidentified. Compare GALYEAN, GALYEN, GALYON.

Galyean (516) Origin unidentified. Compare GALYAN, GALYEN, GALYON.

Galyen (201) Origin unidentified. Compare GALYAN, GALYEAN, GALYON.

Galyon (544) Origin unidentified. Compare GALYAN, GALYEAN, GALYEN.

Gama (340) Portuguese: probably from *gama* 'fallow deer doe', feminine form of *gamo*, possibly as a topographic or habitational name.

GIVEN NAMES Spanish 44%; Portuguese 10%. *Jose* (9), *Armando* (5), *Carlos* (5), *Jesus* (5), *Manuel* (3), *Ramon* (3), *Silvestre* (3), *Alejandro* (2), *Emilio* (2), *Javier* (2), *Julio* (2), *Lupe* (2); *Joao* (3), *Paulo*; *Antonio* (2), *Alfonse, Dioscoro, Gennaro, Lorenzo, Luciano, Marco*.

Gamache (1635) French: habitational name from places in Eure and Somme called Gamaches, first recorded in the 8th century as *Gannapio* and *Gammapium* respectively. The place names are of uncertain origin; one suggestion is that they may have been named with the Celtic elements *cam* 'bent', 'winding' + *apia* 'water'.

FOREBEARS A family of this name was established in Château Richer, Quebec, by 1676.

GIVEN NAMES French 11%. *Armand* (7), *Normand* (7), *Adrien* (4), *Lucien* (3), *Marcel* (3), *Aime* (2), *Andre* (2), *Camille* (2), *Fernand* (2), *Pierre* (2), *Raoul* (2), *Aldege*.

Gamage (257) English (of Norman origin): habitational name from any of various places in France called Gamaches (see GAMACHE).

Gamarra (138) Basque: habitational name from any of several towns called Gamarra, in Araba, Basque Country.

GIVEN NAMES Spanish 55%. *Luis* (7), *Carlos* (5), *Jorge* (4), *Miguel* (4), *Roberto* (4), *Eduardo* (3), *Jose* (3), *Julio* (3), *Fernando* (2), *Raul* (2), *Adalid, Agustin*.

Gamba (289) Italian: nickname for a person with some peculiarity of the legs or gait, from *gamba* 'leg', Late Latin *gamba*, from Greek *kampē* 'bend', 'joint', 'knee'.

GIVEN NAMES Italian 13%; Spanish 9%. *Angelo* (3), *Salvatore* (3), *Antonio* (2), *Amelio, Arcangelo, Carlo, Carmela, Duilio, Margherita, Serafino, Spartaco*; *Jose* (3), *Emilio* (2), *Teresita* (2), *Alfonso, Angelina, Camilo, Eduardo, Ernesto, Gilberto, Gonzalo, Guillermo, Jorge*.

Gambale (210) Italian: from *gambale* 'leg armor', 'greave', 'leggings' (from *gamba* 'leg'); a metonymic occupational name for a maker of greaves or leggings, or possibly a nickname for an habitual wearer of leggings or for someone who wore leggings of a distinctive kind.

GIVEN NAMES Italian 17%. *Angelo* (4), *Nicola* (2), *Antonio, Carlo, Enrico, Ugo*.

Gambardella (455) Southern Italian: from a pet form of the unexplained personal name *Gambardo*.

GIVEN NAMES Italian 15%; French 4%. *Carmine* (2), *Ciro* (2), *Pasquale* (2), *Aldo, Antonio, Attilio, Carmel, Dante, Fabrizio, Giuseppe, Matteo, Sal*; *Alphonse* (5), *Patrice*.

Gambaro (100) Italian: habitational name from a place in Piacenza called Gambara, from a personal name of Germanic origin.

GIVEN NAMES Italian 16%; French 6%. *Cesare, Marco, Oreste, Paolo, Salvatore*; *Laurent, Marcelle*.

Gambee (104) English: variant spelling of GAMBY.

Gambel (140) **1.** German: from a variant of the Germanic personal name *Gambert*, or some other personal name formed with Old High German *gam(an)* 'joy', 'play'. **2.** English: variant spelling of GAMBLE.

GIVEN NAME French 5%. *Patrice*.

Gambell (132) English: variant spelling of GAMBLE.

Gamber (601) German: occupational or nickname for an entertainer or a buffoon, from Middle High German *gampen* 'to hop or jump'.

Gambetta (116) Italian and Swiss Italian (Ticino): nickname for a person with some peculiarity of the legs or gait, from a diminutive of *gamba* 'leg' (see GAMBA). This name is also well established in Argentina and Uruguay.

GIVEN NAMES Spanish 13%; Italian 10%; French 6%. *Miguel* (4), *Luis* (2), *Consuelo, Raul, Ruben*; *Carlo* (2), *Mario, Primo, Ricardo*; *Emile* (2).

Gambill (1522) Americanized spelling of German **Gamperl** or **Gampl**, or Swiss **Gämperle**, variants of GAMPER (see GAMBEL).

Gambini (115) Italian: variant (plural) of GAMBINO.

GIVEN NAMES Italian 8%. *Aldo, Antonio, Chiara, Domenic, Tommaso*.

Gambino (1465) Italian: from a diminutive of *gamba* 'leg', probably applied as a nickname for someone with short legs. The surname, probably of Italian origin, is also found in Spain and Portugal.

GIVEN NAMES Italian 21%. *Salvatore* (31), *Angelo* (11), *Vincenzo* (4), *Vito* (4), *Giovanni* (3), *Rocco* (3), *Sal* (3), *Calogero* (2), *Carlo* (2), *Carmine* (2), *Francesco* (2), *Gaetano* (2).

Gamble (10294) **1.** English: from the Old Norse byname *Gamall* meaning 'old', which was occasionally used in North England during the Middle Ages as a personal name. **2.** Altered spelling of German GAMBEL.

Gambles (78) English: patronymic from GAMBLE.

Gamblin (761) Americanized form of German **Gmelin** (see GIMLIN).

Gamboa (1829) Basque: topographic name composed of the elements *gain* 'peak', 'summit' + *boa* 'rounded'.

GIVEN NAMES Spanish 45%. *Jose* (47), *Juan* (20), *Manuel* (20), *Luis* (18), *Carlos* (17), *Francisco* (16), *Jesus* (12), *Mario* (11), *Miguel* (11), *Pedro* (10), *Armando* (9), *Jaime* (9); *Antonio* (13), *Marco* (5), *Angelo* (3), *Constantino* (3), *Eliseo* (3), *Lorenzo* (3), *Dante* (2), *Adalgisa, Bartolo, Carmelo, Clemente, Dario*.

Gambone (236) Italian: from an augmentative of GAMBA.

GIVEN NAMES Italian 17%. *Salvatore* (5), *Caesar, Ciro, Domenic, Domenico, Erminio, Nunzie, Pasquale, Reno, Rocco, Sal, Santi*.

Gambrel (533) English: variant spelling of GAMBRELL.

Gambrell (1611) **1.** English: unexplained; probably of French origin (see 2). **2.** Respelling of French **Gambrelle**, a reduced form of **Gambarelle**, a nickname denoting someone with long legs, from a derivative of *gambe*, Norman and Picard form of *jambe* 'leg'.

Gambrill (195) English (Kent): variant spelling of GAMBRELL.

Gamby (123) English (Bedfordshire): unexplained.

Game (186) **1.** English: from Middle English *game, gamen* 'amusement', 'pastime' (Old English *gamen*), hence a nickname for a merry or sporty person. **2.** German (**Gä(h)me**): from a Germanic personal name formed with Old High German *gaman* 'fun', 'game'.

Gamel (494) Southern French: from Old French *gamel* 'oatmeal', which was used for cleaning and degreasing woolen cloth; the surname may therefore have arisen as a metonymic occupational name for a textile worker or perhaps for a miller or baker.

Gamelin (183) **1.** French: from pet form of any of the compound personal names formed with *gamal*, related to Old Norse *gamall*, Old German *gamel* 'old', 'aged'.

2. Possibly a respelling of German **Gammelin**, a habitational name from a place in Mecklenburg called Gammelin. FOREBEARS A family of this name from Blois was in Trois Rivières, Quebec, by 1661.
GIVEN NAMES French 13%. *Aime* (2), *Alberic*, *Alphonse, Cecile, Emile, Leopaul.*

Gamer (177) Jewish (eastern Ashkenazic): from the Russian pronunciation of HAMER.
GIVEN NAMES Jewish 4%. *Semen, Yaakov.*

Gamero (109) Spanish: unexplained. This name is particularly common in Mexico, also well established in Peru.
GIVEN NAMES Spanish 60%. *Jose* (5), *Carlos* (3), *Ramon* (3), *Miguel* (2), *Orlando* (2), *Virgilio* (2), *Alberto, Amado, Ana, Angel, Arnulfo, Bartolome.*

Games (305) **1.** Spanish: variant of **Gámez** (see GAMEZ). **2.** English: variant of GAME.

Gamet (178) French: from a pet form of *Gamo*, a short form of a Germanic personal name formed with *gam-*, a short form of Old High German *gaman* 'joy' or *gamal* 'old', 'aged'.

Gamez (1900) Spanish (**Gámez**): patronymic from *Gamo*, a personal name of unexplained origin.
GIVEN NAMES Spanish 51%. *Jose* (48), *Juan* (27), *Carlos* (23), *Manuel* (21), *Jesus* (16), *Francisco* (15), *Luis* (15), *Mario* (14), *Alfredo* (12), *Pedro* (12), *Raul* (11), *Alberto* (10).

Gamino (291) Spanish: from a pet form of the personal name *Gamo* (see GAMEZ).
GIVEN NAMES Spanish 52%. *Jose* (10), *Adolfo* (4), *Sergio* (4), *Jesus* (3), *Juan* (3), *Juanita* (3), *Margarita* (3), *Salvador* (3), *Bernardo* (2), *Carlos* (2), *Cesar* (2), *Guadalupe* (2); *Dino* (2), *Angelo, Ciro, Dario, Eliseo, Marco Antonio, Salustia.*

Gamlin (120) **1.** English: from a pet form of *Gamel*, from the Old Norse personal name *Gamall* (see GAMBLE). **2.** Americanized form of French GAMELIN.

Gamm (261) German: habitational name for someone from Gamme, near Hamburg, or from a Germanic personal name based on Old High German *gaman* 'joy', 'fun', 'game'. Compare GAMMEL.

Gamma (132) Swiss Italian: unexplained. This name is also found in Germany and in Brazil.
GIVEN NAMES Italian 6%; German 5%. *Enrico, Marco; Hans* (2), *Lorenz.*

Gammage (439) English: variant spelling of GAMAGE.

Gammel (342) **1.** German: nickname for a jovial man, from Middle High German *gamd* 'gaiety', 'merriment', or from a Germanic personal name based on Old High German element with the same meaning (see GAMM). **2.** French: variant spelling of GAMEL.

Gammell (362) **1.** English: variant of GAMBLE. **2.** Respelling of German GAMMEL.

Gammill (814) English: variant of GAMBLE.

Gammon (2426) English: **1.** variant of GAME. **2.** from Anglo-Norman French *gambon* 'ham', a diminutive of *gambe*, Norman-Picard form of Old French *jambe* 'leg' (Late Latin *gamba*), hence probably a nickname for someone with some peculiarity of the legs or gait.

Gammons (661) English: variant of GAMMON.

Gamon (138) Spanish (**Gamón**): probably a topographic name from *gamón* 'asphodel'.
GIVEN NAMES Spanish 28%. *Jose* (4), *Alfredo* (2), *Jesus* (2), *Luis* (2), *Alejandro, Angel, Arsenio, Ernesto, Esperanza, Gregoria, Javier, Jose Angel.*

Gamroth (137) Eastern German: of Slavic origin but unexplained etymology. There is a habitational name **Gamrodt** in Silesia, Poland, also recorded as **Gamerad** and **Gamerote**, which is the name of a vessel for drinking and a metonymic occupational name there for a maker of such vessels.

Gan (529) **1.** Chinese 甘: although the character for Gan is the same as that in the name of the western province Gansu, the two sources of the surname are not related to that of the province. One source of the surname is Gan Pan, a senior minister to the Shang dynasty king Wu Ding (1324–1266 BC). The other source is a town named Gan in Shaanxi province that was granted to a descendant of Wu Wang (who established the Zhou dynasty in 1122 BC). The grantee's descendants adopted the place name as their surname. **2.** Hispanic (Filipino): unexplained.
GIVEN NAMES Chinese 11%. *Li* (4), *Hong* (2), *Hua* (2), *Jee* (2), *Jian* (2), *Cheong, Chin, Chuan, Eng, Hui Ming, Jianmin, Jing.*

Ganas (181) Greek: **1.** occupational name for a coppersmith, from *gana* 'coating', 'verdigris'. **2.** possibly also a variant of GANIS.
GIVEN NAMES Greek 6%. *Constantine, Demos, Konstantinos, Stavros, Taso.*

Ganaway (214) Variant spelling of English GANNAWAY.

Gancarz (208) Polish: variant of **Garncarz**, occupational name from *gancarz* 'potter'.
GIVEN NAMES Polish 12%. *Elzbieta* (2), *Andrzej, Janina, Kazimierz, Stanislaw, Thadeus, Wlodzimierz, Zbigniew.*

Ganci (232) Italian: Sicilian variant of GANGI.
GIVEN NAMES Italian 22%. *Salvatore* (9), *Sal* (2), *Antonio, Camillo, Ciro, Domenica, Giuseppi, Paolo, Rosolino, Sebastiano.*

Gandara (469) Portuguese and Galician: habitational name from any of numerous places in northern Portugal and Galicia so named from *gandara* 'barren land'.
GIVEN NAMES Spanish 47%. *Jose* (17), *Arturo* (6), *Manuel* (6), *Luis* (5), *Pedro* (5), *Carlos*

(4), *Gerardo* (4), *Rafael* (4), *Alejandro* (3), *Ana* (3), *Angel* (3), *Arnulfo* (3).

Gandee (490) Variant spelling of English GANDY.

Gander (547) **1.** English: from Middle English *gander*, Old English *gand(r)a* 'gander', 'male goose', hence a metonymic occupational name for a keeper of geese, or a nickname for someone supposedly resembling a gander in some way. **2.** English: variant of GANTER. **3.** North German: perhaps a habitational name from Gandern in Brandenburg. **4.** North German: nickname for a vain or self-important man from *ganter* 'male goose', 'gander'. **5.** South German and Swiss German: habitational name from a place named with Middle High German *gant* 'scree' (Swiss *gand*), or topographic name for someone living by an area of scree.

Gandhi (929) Indian (Gujarat, Bombay city, Rajasthan, Panjab): Hindu (Bania, Vania, Arora, Jat), Jain, Parsi, and Sikh occupational name meaning 'perfume seller' in modern Indic languages, from Sanskrit *gāndhika*, from *gandha* 'perfume'. In Gujarati the word also means 'grocer' or 'pharmacist'. This name occurs chiefly in Gujarat among Vanias and Parsis. It is also found among the Oswal Banias of Rajasthan and among the Aroras and the Jats of the Panjab.
GIVEN NAMES Indian 90%. *Rajesh* (16), *Ashok* (14), *Ramesh* (14), *Pravin* (12), *Bharat* (11), *Dilip* (11), *Sanjay* (11), *Dinesh* (10), *Suresh* (10), *Anil* (9), *Mukesh* (8), *Rajendra* (8).

Gandia (108) Catalan: habitational name from Gandia, in Valencia.
GIVEN NAMES Spanish 39%. *Alfredo* (3), *Edmundo* (3), *Jose* (3), *Carlos* (2), *Eduardo* (2), *Salvador* (2), *Altagracia, Bienvenido, Bonifacio, Delfin, Digna, Erlinda.*

Gandolfi (189) Italian: patronymic or plural form of GANDOLFO.
GIVEN NAMES Italian 11%. *Giovanni* (2), *Attillo, Ettore, Geno, Gino, Larraine, Valentino.*

Gandolfo (494) Italian: from *Gandolfo*, a Germanic personal name composed of the elements *gand* 'spell' + *wulf* 'wolf'.
GIVEN NAMES Italian 22%; Spanish 6%. *Angelo* (4), *Salvatore* (4), *Carmelo* (2), *Carmine* (2), *Vito* (2), *Antonino, Antonio, Bartolo, Carlo, Carmela, Dante, Eduardo, Ricardo, Rosario; Antonieta, Baldo, Carlos, Diego, Elena, Jorge, Mario, Raymondo.*

Gandrud (100) Norwegian: unexplained.

Gandy (3338) English (of Norman origin): of uncertain origin. The most plausible suggestion is that it is a nickname for someone who was in the habit of wearing gloves, from Old French *ganté*, a derivative of *gant* 'glove' (see GANT) or an occupational name for a glove-maker, Old French *gantier*. However, a certain Hugh de Gandy was High Sheriff of Devon in 1167; it is possible that his surname is a habitational name from some unidentified place in France or even from Ghent in Flanders (see GAUNT 1).

Gane (137) English: variant spelling of GAIN.

Ganem (240) Arabic or Turkish: variant of GHANEM.
GIVEN NAMES Spanish 6%; French 4%. *Jorge* (2), *Jose* (2), *Beatriz, Eduardo, Juan, Maria Rosa, Marina, Roberto; Jacques, Joffre.*

Ganesan (118) Indian (Kerala, Tamil Nadu): Hindu name from Sanskrit *gaṇeṣa* 'lord of the army' (see GANESH) + the Tamil-Malayalam third-person masculine singular suffix -*n*. This is found only as a given name in India, but has come to be used as a family name in the U.S.
GIVEN NAMES Indian 96%. *Kumar* (3), *Ram* (3), *Ganesh* (2), *Guru* (2), *Krishna* (2), *Ramesh* (2), *Ravi* (2), *Sridhar* (2), *Sriram* (2), *Subramanian* (2), *Suresh* (2), *Anand.*

Ganesh (131) Indian (southern states): Hindu name from Sanskrit *gaṇeṣa* 'lord of the army' (from *gaṇa* 'army' + *īśa*), an epithet of the elephant-headed god who is the son of Shiva. Among Tamil and Malayalam speakers who have migrated from their home states it is a variant of GANESAN. It is found only as a male given name in India, but used as a family name in the U.S. among South Indians.
GIVEN NAMES Indian 80%. *Krishna* (2), *Muthu* (2), *Ramesh* (2), *Ravi* (2), *Anil, Arumugam, Deodath, Dinesh, Gopala, Jaishankar, Jyoti.*

Ganey (566) Variant spelling of Irish GAINEY.

Gang (471) **1.** German: (**Gäng**) variant of GENG. **2.** German: variant of GANGE 2. **3.** Korean: variant of KANG. **4.** Chinese 耿: variant of GENG 2.

Gange (236) **1.** English (of Norman origin): of uncertain derivation. It may be a habitational name, perhaps from a place called Ganges in southern France. This is recorded in the 12th century as *Agange* and *Aganthicum*, perhaps from a derivative of Latin *acanthus* 'bear's-foot'. On the other hand, it may be from the Old Norse personal name *Gangi*, a cognate of Old English *Gegn*. **2.** German (**Gänge**): from Middle High German *genge* 'common', 'circulating (among the people)', 'sprightly', hence an occupational name for a hawker or peddler; perhaps also a nickname for an energetic person (see GENGE 2). **3.** German (**Gange** or **Gänge**): from a short form of the personal names *Wolfgang* or *Gangulf*, both formed with Old High German *gang*- 'gait', 'walk' (+ *wolf* 'wolf').
GIVEN NAMES Italian 5%. *Angelo, Carmino, Salvatore, Vito.*

Gangel (107) German (**Gängel**): variant of GANGL.
GIVEN NAME Jewish 4%. *Miriam.*

Gangemi (343) Italian: variant of CANGEMI.
GIVEN NAMES Italian 14%. *Carmine* (2), *Rocco* (2), *Saverio* (2), *Guiseppe, Nazareno, Nazzareno, Nicola, Sal, Santo.*

Ganger (356) **1.** English: from an agent derivative of Old English *gangan* 'to walk', hence possibly a nickname for someone with a peculiar gait; by the period of surname formation, however, the word had acquired the sense 'go-between' and it is likely that this meaning lies behind the surname in some instances. **2.** German (usually **Gänger**): variant of GENGLER.

Gangestad (100) Scandinavian: unexplained.

Gangi (490) Southern Italian (Sicily): habitational name from Gangi in Palermo.
GIVEN NAMES Italian 9%; French 4%. *Angelo* (3), *Salvatore* (3), *Carmelo* (2), *Antonio, Clemente, Domenic, Gaeton, Lia; Camille, Serge.*

Gangl (311) South German and Austrian: from the short form of the personal name *Gangolf* or its reversal *Wolfgang*, from Old High German *gang*- 'gait', 'walk' + *wolf* 'wolf'.

Gangle (108) Variant of German GANGL.

Gangloff (353) German: from the Germanic personal name *Gangulf*, composed of the elements *gang* 'walk' + *wolf, wulf* 'wolf'.
GIVEN NAMES French 4%. *Andree, Collette, Serge.*

Ganguly (105) Indian (Bengal): Hindu (Brahman) name, whose Sanskrit form, **Gangopadhyaya**, means 'teacher from the village of Ganga'. Sanskrit *upādhyāya* means 'teacher'. Compare CHATTERJEE, BANERJEE, MUKHERJEE.
GIVEN NAMES Indian 89%. *Arun* (2), *Chandra* (2), *Gopa* (2), *Amitava, Devi, Dipak, Dipankar, Gautam, Indrani, Indranil, Jyoti, Kalyan.*

Gangwer (164) German: see GONGAWARE.

Ganim (180) Arabic and Turkish: variant of GHANEM.
GIVEN NAMES Muslim 6%. *Abrahim* (2), *Ibrahim* (2), *Afaf, Hassan, Mazin, Mohamad, Nasser, Shukri.*

Ganis (111) **1.** Greek and Turkish: nickname for a rich man, from Turkish *gani* 'rich', of Arabic origin. **2.** English: unexplained.

Ganje (135) South German: unexplained; perhaps a respelling of **Gänge**, a nickname from Middle High German *genge* 'fit', or a pet form of **Johann**, a variant of the personal name JOHANNES.

Ganje (135) South German: unexplained; perhaps a respelling of **Gänge**, a nickname from Middle High German *genge* 'fit'.

Ganley (775) Irish: reduced Anglicized form of Gaelic **Mag Sheanlaoich**, from *sean* 'old' + *laoch* 'hero', 'warrior'.
GIVEN NAMES Irish 5%. *Brendan, Marypat.*

Gann (4513) **1.** Irish: reduced form of McGANN. **2.** German: from the personal name *Gano*, or, in Austria, a short form of *Candidus*, a personal name from Latin *candidus* 'bright', 'white', 'clear', 'beautiful' (see KANN). **3.** German: topographic name for someone who lived near an expanse of scree, Middle High German *gant*.

Gannaway (637) English: habitational name from *Janaways*, the Middle English name for someone from the seaport of Genoa in Italy. This was taken as a plural, but is in fact an English spelling of the Old French adjectival form, *Genoveis*, Italian *Genovese* 'Genoese' (see GENOVESE).

Gannett (272) English: nickname probably for a voracious or raucous person, from Middle English *ganet* 'solan goose', 'gannet', from Old English *ganot*.

Gannon (5713) Irish: reduced Anglicized form of Gaelic **Mag Fhionnáin**, a patronymic from the personal name *Fionnán*. This name, from a diminutive of *fionn* 'white', 'fair', was borne by several early Irish saints.
GIVEN NAMES Irish 4%. *Brendan* (3), *Brigid, Donal, Liam, Niall, Padraic, Ronan.*

Gano (682) French: variant of **Ganeau**, **Ganot**, or **Guéneau**, all derived from a personal name based on the Germanic element *wān* 'hope'. This name came to America with the Huguenots.

Ganoe (390) French: see GANO.

Ganong (171) Origin unidentified.

Gans (1001) German and Dutch: **1.** from Dutch and German *gans* 'goose', hence a nickname for a foolish person or a metonymic occupational name for someone who bred or tended geese, or a habitational name for someone who lived at a house distinguished by the sign of a goose. **2.** nickname for a healthy or strong person, from Middle Low German *gans* 'whole', 'complete', 'healthy'.

Ganschow (123) German: habitational name for someone from a place so named in Mecklenburg.
GIVEN NAMES German 5%. *Erwin* (2), *Otto.*

Gansemer (106) German: variant of GENSEMER, which is probably a variant of **Genzmer**, or a reduced form of **Gansheimer** (see GENSHEIMER). Most occurrences are in IA and NE.

Gansen (175) Dutch: from Middle Dutch *gans*; a metonymic occupational name for someone who kept or sold geese; alternatively, it may have been a nickname for someone thought to resemble the bird, or, in some cases, a habitational name for someone who lived at a house distinguished by a sign depicting geese.

Ganser (477) German: occupational name for a breeder or keeper of geese, from an agent derivative of Middle High German *gans* 'goose'.

Ganske (292) German: probably from a short form of a Germanic personal name formed with *gans*, a cognate of German *ganz* 'whole' (as in *Gansmar*), or possibly related to *gand* 'magic'. In northern Germany, it could be a variant of **Gänsicke**, a diminutive of GANS 1.

Ganson (191) Scottish and English: probably, as Black suggests, a patronymic from the personal name GAVIN.

Ganster (152) German: **1.** nickname for a vivacious or fiery man, from Middle High German *ganster* 'spark'. **2.** nickname or occupational name from South German *ganster* 'gander'. Compare GANTER.

Gansz (106) German: variant of GANS.

Gant (3932) **1.** French and English: metonymic occupational name for a maker or seller of gloves, from Old French *gant* 'glove' (of Germanic origin). **2.** German: of uncertain origin. In the south, it may be a topographic name from Middle High German *gant* 'scree', or a habitational name from a place named with this word. Compare GANDER. It could also be a metonymic occupational name for an auctioneer from Middle High German *gant* 'auction' (see GANTER 1), for which a glove (*gantus*, French *gant*) was set up as a sign (see 1). A third possibility is that it is a variant of GANS, from Low German *gante* 'goose'.

Gantenbein (191) Swiss and South German: derogatory nickname meaning 'goose leg', presumably from Romansh *ganta* 'wild goose' + Middle High German *bein* 'bone', 'leg'.
GIVEN NAMES German 4%. *Florian, Heinrich, Kurt.*

Ganter (399) **1.** South German: occupational name for an official in charge of the legal auction of property confiscated in default of a fine; such a sale was known in Middle High German as a *gant* (from Italian *incanto*, a derivative of Late Latin *inquantare* 'to auction', from the phrase *In quantum?* 'To how much (is the price raised)?'). **2.** German: metonymic occupational name for a cooper, from Middle High German *ganter, kanter* 'barrel rack'. **3.** German: variant of GANDER 3. **4.** English: occupational name for a glover, from Old French *gantier*, an agent derivative of *gant* 'glove' (see GANT).
GIVEN NAMES German 5%. *Kurt* (2), *Otto* (2), *Franz, Frieda.*

Gantert (123) German and Swiss German: **1.** in the north from a Germanic personal name *Ganthas*, of uncertain origin, or a nickname from Middle Low German *ganter* 'gander'. **2.** in the south probably an occupational name for an auctioneer, from Middle High German *gant* 'court-ordered auctioneer', or a topographic name from Middle High German (originally Romansch) *gant* 'scree', in all cases with excrescent *-t*.
GIVEN NAME French 4%. *Armand.*

Ganther (146) German: variant of GANTER.
GIVEN NAME French 5%. *Andre.*

Gantner (346) South German and Swiss German: variant of GANTER 1 and 2.
GIVEN NAMES German 5%. *Egon, Erhard, Erwin, Florian, Franz, Manfred.*

Gantt (2817) Origin uncertain: probably a variant of French, English, or German GANT.

Gantz (1126) German and Jewish (Ashkenazic): variant spelling of GANZ.

Gantzer (162) German: variant of GANZER.

Ganus (224) Reduced form of GURGANUS.

Ganz (1158) **1.** German and Swiss German: variant of GANS 'goose'. **2.** German: from a short form of the Germanic personal name *Ganso*, a cognate of modern German *ganz* 'whole', 'all'. **3.** German: possibly also from an altered form, under Russian influence, of the personal name *Hans*, a short form of *Johannes* (see JOHN). **4.** Jewish (Ashkenazic): ornamental name from German *ganz* 'whole'.
GIVEN NAMES Jewish 5%; German 4%. *Sol* (4), *Miriam* (2), *Zvi* (2), *Avner, Baruch, Ber, Hersch, Hershel, Hyman, Isak, Mandel, Mayer; Hans* (4), *Armin, Erwin, Hans Peter, Ulrich.*

Ganzel (153) German: from a diminutive of GANZ.
GIVEN NAMES German 5%. *Elke, Fritz, Hans Peter.*

Ganzer (296) German: **1.** South German: variant of GANSER. **2.** Slavic habitational name from a place so named in the district of Ruppin.

Gao (937) Chinese 高: from the name of the area of Gao in the state of Qi during the Western Zhou dynasty (1122–771 BC). A son of the royal family of Qi was granted the area of Gao, and subsequently his descendants adopted Gao as their surname.
GIVEN NAMES Chinese 69%. *Feng* (17), *Yan* (11), *Hong* (10), *Ming* (10), *Xiang* (9), *Wei* (8), *Chao* (7), *Yang* (7), *Hua* (6), *Yi* (6), *Jian* (5), *Ping* (5), *Min* (4), *Tian* (3), *Chang* (2), *Shen.*

Gaona (707) Spanish: of uncertain origin; a connection with the place name Gauna (in Araba, Basque Country) is doubtful because of the consistent spelling of the surname with *-o-*.
GIVEN NAMES Spanish 51%. *Jose* (16), *Manuel* (10), *Juan* (8), *Jesus* (7), *Raul* (7), *Rodolfo* (7), *Armando* (5), *Mario* (5), *Miguel* (5), *Pedro* (5), *Roberto* (5), *Ruben* (5); *Antonio* (7), *Marco* (3), *Angelo, Bartolo, Ciro, Geronimo, Heriberto, Rino, Romeo.*

Gapen (108) Respelling of French **Gapin**, from a diminutive of *gap*, a variant of *gab* 'joke', 'mockery', presumably applied as a nickname for a joker.
GIVEN NAME French 6%. *Patrice.*

Gapinski (390) Polish (**Gapiński**): habitational name for someone from a place called Gapinin, in Piotrków voivodeship.
GIVEN NAMES Polish 4%. *Andrzej, Zbigniew.*

Gapp (199) **1.** English: from Middle English *gappe*, Old Norse *gap* 'chasm', 'breach', hence a topographic name for someone who lived near a gap in a wall, hedge, or (in Norfolk and Suffolk) cliffs. **2.** German: from the personal name *Gabo*, a short form of *Gebolf* (see GEBHARDT).

Gappa (281) Possibly of Slavic origin: unexplained.

Gara (201) **1.** Hungarian: variant of GARAY. This is one of the few Hungarian habitational names without the regular *-i* suffix. **2.** Irish: reduced form of O'GARA. **3.** Indian (Gujarat and Bombay city): Parsi name of unknown meaning.
GIVEN NAMES German 5%; Indian 4%. *Otto* (2); *Radha, Ravi, Siva.*

Garabedian (720) Armenian: patronymic from the western Armenian personal name *Garabed* 'leader'. Compare KARAPETIAN.
GIVEN NAMES Armenian 25%; French 5%. *Garabed* (8), *Haig* (8), *Aram* (5), *Krikor* (5), *Garo* (4), *Armen* (3), *Bedros* (3), *Hrair* (2), *Kerop* (2), *Meline* (2), *Mihran* (2), *Minas* (2); *Armand* (2), *Aide, Andre, Edouard, Michel, Monique, Pierre.*

Garafalo (140) Italian: variant of GAROFALO.
GIVEN NAMES Italian 18%. *Angelo* (3), *Salvatore* (2), *Antonio, Sal.*

Garafola (226) Italian: variant of GAROFALO.
GIVEN NAMES Italian 12%. *Angelo* (2), *Salvatore* (2), *Domenic, Sal.*

Garand (258) French: variant of GARANT.
GIVEN NAMES French 17%. *Andre* (2), *Armand* (2), *Pierre* (2), *Adelard, Antoine, Benoit, Gilles, Jacques, Jean-Marie, Jeremie, Lucien, Raoul.*

Garant (267) French: from *garant* 'guarantor'.
FOREBEARS A family of this name from Rouen was established in Sainte Famille, Île d'Orléans, by 1669.
GIVEN NAMES French 15%. *Normand* (4), *Andre* (2), *Herve* (2), *Germain, Monique, Philias, Pierre, Yvan.*

Garard (136) English: from a variant of the personal name *Gerard* (see GARRETT 1).

Garate (122) Basque: habitational name from a town called Garate in Basque Country, or topographic name, possibly from a derivative of Basque *gara* 'height', 'peak'.
GIVEN NAMES Spanish 51%. *Carlos* (6), *Jose* (4), *Juan* (3), *Luis* (3), *Manuel* (2), *Agustin, Alfredo, Alicia, Amparo, Angel, Arsenio, Cesar.*

Garavaglia (252) Italian: of uncertain derivation. Possibly a habitational name; compare the place names Garavagna (Cuneo) and Garavoglie (Vercelli).

Garay (1300) **1.** Basque: Castilianized form of **Garai**, a habitational name from Garai, in Biscay, Basque Country, or from one of the five other, smaller places of the same name, also in Biscay, all named from

Basque *garai* 'high', a derivative of *gara* 'height', 'peak'. **2.** Hungarian: habitational name for someone from a place called Gara.

GIVEN NAMES Spanish 46%. *Jose* (34), *Carlos* (20), *Juan* (18), *Luis* (14), *Javier* (9), *Manuel* (9), *Jesus* (8), *Francisco* (7), *Julio* (7), *Raul* (7), *Ana* (6), *Cesar* (6).

Garb (177) **1.** German: occupational name for a tanner, from the dialect word *garb*, Middle High German *garwe*. See also GERBER. **2.** German: from a short form of a personal name formed with Old High German *gēr* 'spear', 'lance'. Compare GERHARDT. **3.** Jewish (eastern Ashkenazic): descriptive nickname from Polish *garb* 'hump'.

GIVEN NAMES Jewish 5%. *Yaakov, Zelik.*

Garbacz (207) Polish: nickname from the dialect word *garbacz* 'hunchback', from *garb* 'hump'.

GIVEN NAMES Polish 11%. *Stanislaw* (2), *Andrzej, Elzbieta, Henryk, Janusz, Slawomir, Wieslawa.*

Garbarini (187) Italian: patronymic from GARBARINO.

Garbarino (576) Italian: probably a habitational name from Garbarino, a locality of Rovegno in Genoa province or Garbarini in Tribogna, Genoa. The forms **Garberino**, **Garberini** occur in southern Italy and Caracausi links these with Sicilian *galberi* 'golden oriole', the species of bird.

GIVEN NAMES Italian 7%. *Angelo* (3), *Enrico, Marco.*

Garbe (545) **1.** English and French: from Middle English, Old French *garbe* 'wheatsheaf', applied as a metonymic occupational name for a reaper or harvester, or for someone who collected wheatsheaves owed in rent. **2.** German: variant of GARB.

GIVEN NAMES German 8%. *Kurt* (4), *Gerhard* (2), *Gunther* (2), *Armin, Erwin, Gunter, Hans, Manfred, Reinhold, Wolfgang.*

Garber (5335) **1.** English: occupational name for a reaper or harvester, or for someone who collected wheatsheaves owed in rent, from an agent derivative of Middle English *garbe* 'wheatsheaf' (see GARBE). **2.** North German: from a personal name composed of *geri, gari* 'spear' + *berht* 'bright', 'famous'. **3.** North German form of GERBER. **4.** Jewish (Ashkenazic): variant of GERBER, from Yiddish *garber*.

Garbers (201) **1.** North German: variant of GARBER 2. **2.** Danish: patronymic from the German family name GERBER or a variant of **Garbarsch** (from *Garbe* 'sheaf', 'bundle').

Garbett (284) English (chiefly West Midlands): from *Gerberht*, a Norman personal name composed of the Germanic elements *gār, gēr*, 'spear', 'lance' + *berht* 'bright', 'famous' (see GEBERT 1). There has been some confusion with GARBUTT.

Garbin (160) French: probably from a diminutive of *garbe*, Picard form of *gerbe* 'ear (of grain)', 'head of grass'.

GIVEN NAMES Italian 7%. *Angelo* (2), *Corrado, Marino, Primo.*

Garbisch (152) German: probably an altered form of *Gaubisch*, a variant, under Slavic influence, of the personal name *Jacobus* (see JACOB).

Garbo (173) Italian: **1.** apparently a nickname from Italian *garbo* 'polite', 'kind'; 'kindness', 'graciousness'; or alternatively from the same word in Venetian dialect meaning 'curt', 'abrupt'. **2.** Sicilian variant of GALBO.

FOREBEARS The medieval Florentine doctors Dino and Tommaso Garbo took their surname from the via del Garbo in Florence.

GIVEN NAMES Italian 8%. *Carmelo, Ennio, Nunzio, Palma, Salvatore.*

Garbrecht (103) German: variant of **Gerbert** (see GERBRACHT).

GIVEN NAMES German 12%. *Gottlieb, Jurgen, Kurt, Otto.*

Garbus (110) Jewish (from Belarus): nickname from Belorussian *garbuz* 'pumpkin', used figuratively to denote a decrepit old man.

GIVEN NAMES Jewish 8%. *Sol* (2), *Isadore.*

Garbutt (414) English (of Norman origin): **1.** from *Geribodo*, a Germanic personal name composed of the elements *gār, gēr*, 'spear', 'lance' + *bodo* originally 'lord', 'master', but early reinterpreted as 'messenger'. The name was borne notably by a 7th-century saint, bishop of Bayeux; as a result of his cult the name was popular among the Normans and introduced by them into England. **2.** from *Geribald*, a Germanic personal name composed of the elements *geri, gari* 'spear' + *bald* 'bold', 'brave'. This name owed its popularity largely to a 9th-century saint, bishop of Châlons-sur-Seine.

Garceau (631) French: nickname from a derivative of *gars* 'boy'. The surname is particularly associated with Acadia, and hence also with the Cajuns of LA.

GIVEN NAMES French 7%. *Armand* (2), *Normand* (2), *Ovila* (2), *Adrien, Celina, Emile, Gaston, Germaine, Jean-Paul, Lucien, Marcel, Stephane.*

Garcelon (117) French (Channel Islands): unexplained.

Garces (749) Spanish, Catalan (**Garcés**), and Portuguese (**Garcês**): variant of the patronymic **Garciez**, from the personal name *García* (see GARCIA).

GIVEN NAMES Spanish 52%; Portuguese 10%. *Jorge* (16), *Carlos* (13), *Juan* (12), *Jose* (8), *Manuel* (8), *Cesar* (7), *Rafael* (7), *Luis* (6), *Fernando* (5), *Gustavo* (5), *Javier* (5), *Mario* (5); *Albeiro, Paulo.*

Garcia (105882) Spanish (**García**) and Portuguese: from a medieval personal name of uncertain origin. It is normally found in medieval records in the Latin form *Garsea*, and may well be of pre-Roman origin, perhaps akin to Basque *(h)artz* 'bear'.

GIVEN NAMES Spanish 47%; Portuguese 9%. *Jesus* (915), *Carlos* (845), *Luis* (760), *Francisco* (637), *Pedro* (585), *Miguel* (518), *Jorge* (499), *Mario* (468), *Raul* (458), *Roberto* (455), *Ramon* (450), *Rafael* (432); *Wenceslao* (8), *Joao* (7), *Paulo* (7), *Catarina* (6), *Albeiro* (3), *Ligia* (3), *Zaragoza* (3), *Godofredo* (2), *Lidio* (2), *Wenseslao* (2), *Adao, Afonso.*

Garczynski (177) Polish (**Garczyński**): habitational name for someone from a place called Garczyn, in Gdańsk and Siedlce voivodeships.

GIVEN NAME Polish 5%. *Casimir* (3).

Gard (1797) **1.** French: metonymic occupational name for a gardener, from the objective case (*gard*) of Old French *gardin* 'garden'. **2.** English: variant spelling of GUARD. **3.** Norwegian: habitational name from a farmstead so named, from Old Norse *garðr* 'farm'. **4.** Swedish (**Gård**): topographic or ornamental name from *gård* 'farm'.

Garde (245) **1.** Basque: habitational name from a place so named in Navarre, Basque Country, from Basque *garde* 'place where wild oats grow'. **2.** French: from Old French *garde* 'watch', 'protection'; an occupational name for someone who kept watch or guard, or a topographic name for someone who lived near a vantage point or watchtower. **3.** Swedish (**Gård**): variant of **Gård** (see GARD). **4.** Indian (Maharashtra); pronounced as *gur-day*: Hindu (Brahman) name, found among the Konkanasth Brahmins, probably from Marathi *gǝra* 'belch'.

GIVEN NAMES Indian 5%. *Vasant* (2), *Ajay, Anand, Tanuja.*

Gardea (348) Basque: variant of GARDE.

GIVEN NAMES Spanish 43%. *Jose* (7), *Manuel* (6), *Raul* (5), *Jesus* (4), *Juanita* (3), *Leticia* (3), *Ramon* (3), *Ricardo* (3), *Sergio* (3), *Alejandro* (2), *Armando* (2), *Corina* (2).

Gardell (114) Altered spelling of French **Gardel** or **Gardelle**, both derivatives of GARDE.

Gardella (753) Italian: probably a pet form of *Garda*, feminine form of *Gardo*, a short form of various personal names such as *Edgardo, Ildegardo, Mingardo.*

GIVEN NAMES French 4%. *Amie, Emile.*

Garden (642) **1.** English: metonymic occupational name for a gardener, from Old Anglo-Norman French *gardin* 'garden'. Compare GARDENER. **2.** Americanized form of French DESJARDINS.

Gardener (371) **1.** English: from Anglo-Norman French *gardinier* 'gardener'. In medieval times this normally denoted a cultivator of edible produce in an orchard or kitchen garden, rather than one who tended ornamental lawns and flower beds. **2.** Americanized form of French DESJARDINS or German *Gärtner* (see GARTNER).

Gardenhire (398) Americanized form of German **Gertenhäuer**, an occupational name for someone who cut canes or made rods, from Middle High German *gerte* 'cane', 'rod' + *hou(w)er* 'cutter'.

Gardin (215) French, northern Italian (Venice), and Spanish: metonymic occupational name for a gardener, from Old French *gardin* 'garden', or an Italian or Spanish cognate.
GIVEN NAMES Spanish 5%; Italian 4%. *Jose* (3), *Homero* (2), *Ramonda*, *Ruben*; *Mario*, *Orlando*.

Gardiner (4344) English: variant spelling of GARDENER.
FOREBEARS Lion Gardiner came from England in 1635 to Saybrook, CT, the settlement of Earl of Warwick patentees at the mouth of the Connecticut River, and built a fort there. Born in 1636, his son, David, was the first white child born in the settlement. Lion later bought the Isle of Wight, now Gardiners Island, from the Indians, and moved his family there until 1653, when he bought land in what is now Easthampton, Long Island, NY.

Gardinier (277) French: occupational name for a gardener, from an agent derivative of Old French *gardin* 'garden'.

Gardipee (128) Altered form of French **Gariépy**, a surname from Gascony, known in Canada since 1756. The etymology is unknown.

Gardner (50507) **1.** English: reduced form of GARDENER. **2.** Probably a translated form of German *Gärtner* (see GARTNER).

Gardocki (137) Polish: habitational name for someone from a place called Gardoty, in Łomża voivodeship.
GIVEN NAMES Polish 10%. *Andrzej*, *Bogdan*, *Wojciech*.

Gardon (102) **1.** French: from a derivative of GARDE. **2.** German: unexplained. Compare GERDON. **3.** Probably an altered form of English and Scottish GARDEN or Scottish GORDON. **4.** Spanish: unexplained.
GIVEN NAMES Spanish 9%. *Rodolfo* (3), *Julio*, *Vicente*.

Garduno (466) Galician (**Garduño**): habitational name from a place named Garduña, in Lugo, Galicia, or from the Garduña mountain range in Portugal, named with *garduña* 'pine marten'.
GIVEN NAMES Spanish 41%. *Jose* (10), *Juan* (8), *Francisco* (6), *Alejandro* (4), *Roberto* (4), *Raul* (3), *Ricardo* (3), *Sergio* (3), *Adriana* (2), *Alberto* (2), *Alicia* (2), *Armando* (2).

Gardy (119) French: southern variant of GARDIN.

Gareau (237) French: nickname from the dialect word *gar(r)el*, *gar(r)eau* 'limping', 'bow legged'.
FOREBEARS A bearer of this name from Saintonge was in Boucherville, Quebec, by 1670.

GIVEN NAMES French 11%. *Andre*, *Armand*, *Emile*, *Gaston*, *Germain*, *Laurent*, *Monique*, *Raoul*.

Garee (118) Origin unidentified. Perhaps an altered spelling of GAREY.

Gareis (131) German: **1.** from a reduced form of the Latin personal name *Gregorius* (see GREGORY). **2.** metonymic occupational name for a blacksmith, from a compound of Middle High German *gar(e)* 'ready' + *īsen* 'iron'. **3.** from *Gero*, a short form of a Germanic personal name composed with *ger* 'spear'.
GIVEN NAMES German 5%. *Gerhard*, *Hans*, *Helmut*.

Garelick (228) Jewish (from Belarus): variant of GORELIK.
GIVEN NAME Jewish 5%. *Sol*.

Garen (135) German: probably a variant of **Geeren** (see GEER).

Gares (146) Of uncertain origin: possibly an altered form of German **Görres**, GAREIS or **Gareus**, all reduced forms of the Latin personal name *Gregorius* (see GREGORY).

Garey (1087) **1.** English: variant of GEARY 2. **2.** Scottish: reduced and altered form of McGARRY.

Garfield (1672) **1.** English: probably a habitational name from a lost or unidentified place, generally from a field name denoting a triangular area, Old English *gāra* (see GORE) at the corner of an open field after rectangular furlongs had been laid out. **2.** Jewish: Americanized form of one or more like-sounding Jewish surnames.
FOREBEARS U.S. President James Abram Garfield (1831–81) was preceded by at least six Garfields born in America, his immigrant ancestor having come to Massachusetts Bay with John Winthrop in 1630.

Garfinkel (800) Jewish (Ashkenazic): ornamental name or nickname, from Yiddish *gorfinkl* 'carbuncle', German *Karfunkel*. This term denoted both a red precious or semi-precious stone, especially a garnet or ruby cut into a rounded shape (in which case it is an ornamental name), and a large inflamed growth on the skin like a large boil (in which case it is a descriptive nickname).
GIVEN NAMES Jewish 7%. *Sol* (4), *Chaim* (3), *Dov* (2), *Yair* (2), *Abbe*, *Avrohom*, *Chana*, *Ilan*, *Pesach*, *Pincus*.

Garfinkle (322) Jewish (American): variant of GARFINKEL.
GIVEN NAMES Jewish 4%. *Chaim*, *Jakob*.

Garfunkel (138) Jewish (Ashkenazic): variant of GARFINKEL.
GIVEN NAMES Jewish 6%. *Moshe*, *Talya*.

Garg (396) Indian (northern states): Hindu (Bania) and Jain name, which goes back to the name of an ancient Hindu sage. The Agarwal Banias and the Oswal Banias both have clans called Garg.
GIVEN NAMES Indian 94%. *Amit* (7), *Anil* (7), *Ashok* (7), *Sanjay* (7), *Narendra* (6), *Rajiv*

(6), *Arun* (5), *Atul* (5), *Om* (5), *Rakesh* (5), *Vijay* (5), *Ajay* (4).

Gargan (279) Irish: reduced Anglicized form of Gaelic **Ó Geargáin** 'descendant of *Geargán*' or **Mac Geargáin** 'son of *Geargán*', a personal name from a diminutive of *garg* 'fierce'.

Gargano (851) Italian: apparently a regional name from Gargano, an extensive area of Apulia, but more likely from a typically Sicilian variant of the personal name *Galgano*, itself a variant of *Galvano*, Italian equivalent of *Gawain* (see GALVIN).
GIVEN NAMES Italian 17%. *Angelo* (9), *Antonio* (4), *Rocco* (3), *Aldo* (2), *Carmine* (2), *Domenic* (2), *Gaetano* (2), *Salvatore* (2), *Aniello*, *Annamaria*, *Biagio*, *Carlo*.

Gargaro (114) Southern Italian: from the Greek stem *gargar-*, denoting either a 'babbling' or 'clear' stream of water, or 'gargling'. Only the latter sense is attested as a vocabulary word in Southern Italian Greek.
GIVEN NAMES Italian 14%. *Angelo* (2), *Antonio*, *Luigi*, *Salvatore*.

Gargas (110) Altered form of **Garrigus**, an Americanized form of the French Huguenot name GARRIGUES.

Garger (173) German: **1.** habitational name for someone from Garge near Lüneburg, a place name that is probably of Slavic origin. **2.** variant of **Karger** (see KARG).
GIVEN NAMES German 4%. *Alois*, *Hans*, *Ignatz*.

Garges (177) Altered form of **Garrigus**, an Americanized form of the French Huguenot name GARRIGUES.

Gargis (176) Altered form of **Garrigus**, an Americanized form of the French Huguenot name GARRIGUES.

Gargiulo (738) Southern Italian: probably from a diminutive of Sicilian *gargia* 'jaw', 'mandible' or Calabrian *gargia* 'open mouth', presumably applied as a nickname.
GIVEN NAMES Italian 21%. *Salvatore* (8), *Enrico* (2), *Mario* (2), *Aldo*, *Angelo*, *Antonio*, *Armando*, *Carlo*, *Ciro*, *Claudio*, *Elio*, *Emilio*, *Gaetano*, *Gennaro*, *Luca*, *Mariano*, *Valerio*.

Garguilo (253) Variant of Italian GARGIULO.
GIVEN NAMES Italian 12%. *Salvatore* (3), *Federico* (2), *Amerigo*, *Angelo*, *Guido*, *Sal*, *Vito*.

Gargus (278) Altered form of **Garrigus**, an Americanized form of the French Huguenot name GARRIGUES.

Garhart (102) Altered form of German GERHARDT.

Garibaldi (567) Italian (Liguria): patronymic from the medieval personal name *Garibaldo*, from a Germanic personal name composed of the elements *gār*, *gēr* 'spear', 'lance' + *bald* 'bold', 'brave'.
GIVEN NAMES Spanish 14%; Italian 7%. *Juan* (3), *Concepcion* (2), *Cruz* (2), *Graciela* (2), *Guadalupe* (2), *Julio* (2), *Manuel* (2), *Raul* (2), *Adan*, *Alejandro*, *Alicia*, *Andres*;

Caesar (2), *Enrico* (2), *Gino* (2), *Angelo,*
Cesario, Dario, Filiberto, Fiore, Gaetano,
Giovanni, Giuseppe, Renzo.

Garibay (997) Basque: Castilianized form
of Basque **Garibai**, a habitational name
from a place called Garibai in Gipuzkoa,
Basque Country, or from a field name composed of the elements *garo* 'bracken',
'fern' or *gara* 'height' + *(i)bai* 'stream'.
GIVEN NAMES Spanish 52%. *Jose* (28), *Juan*
(16), *Manuel* (14), *Javier* (11), *Jesus* (10),
Jorge (10), *Carlos* (8), *Luis* (8), *Miguel* (8),
Pedro (8), *Rafael* (8), *Salvador* (8).

Garica (153) possibly variant of Basque
Gerrika (alongside **Garrica** and **Gerica**), a
habitational name from Gerrika, a town in
Biscay, Basque Country.
GIVEN NAMES Spanish 44%. *Carlos* (3), *Jose*
(3), *Mario* (2), *Pedro* (2), *Rodolfo* (2),
Rufino (2), *Alfonso, Armando, Arturo,*
Demetrio, Esteban, Gelacio; Antonio (2),
Heriberto, Savino.

Gariepy (438) French (**Gariépy**): unexplained.
FOREBEARS The name is found in Canada
from 1657 on, coming from Gascony in
France, although the earliest bearer was
also known as PICARD.
GIVEN NAMES French 11%. *Michel* (2), *Serge*
(2), *Gaston, Germain, Germaine, Gilles,*
Lucien, Marcel, Normand, Yvan, Yves.

Garin (243) **1.** Southern French: from the
Germanic personal name *G(u)arinus*, from
wari(n)- 'protection', 'shelter'. This name
is also found in Switzerland and may have
been brought to the U.S. from there.
2. Russian: patronymic from a short form
of the personal name *Gerasim.*
GIVEN NAMES Spanish 7%. *Benedicto* (2),
Beatriz, Consuelo, Dinora, Eduardo, Ines,
Manuel, Marta, Noemi, Rodolfo, Rogelio,
Simona.

Garing (141) German: possibly an altered
spelling of German **Gähring**, a variant of
GEHRING.

Garinger (193) German: probably altered
spelling of Gähringer, see GARING, or
possibly an altered spelling of German
GEHRINGER.

Garino (107) **1.** Probably a variant of
Italian GUARINO. **2.** Respelling of French
Garinot, Garinaud, from a pet form of
GARIN.
GIVEN NAMES Italian 11%; French 7%. *Aldo,*
Dino, Enzo, Guido, Romolo; Marie-
Claude, Raoul, Veronique.

Garis (304) **1.** German: variant of GEHRIS.
2. French: variant of GARRIS. **3.** Greek (of
Albanian origin): of uncertain origin; possibly a topographic name from Albanian
garre 'ditch'.

Garity (189) Irish: reduced form of
MCGARITY. Compare GARRITY.

Garl (143) **1.** German: probably a northern
variant of GERL, a topographic name from
a field named with *girlet* 'alder stand or
copse'. **2.** English: variant of **Garle**, a

nickname from Middle English *girle, garle*
'child'.

Garland (9095) English: **1.** metonymic occupational name for a maker of garlands or
chaplets, perhaps also a habitational name
from a house sign. The word is first attested
in the 14th century, from Old French, and
appears to be of Germanic origin. **2.** habitational name from a minor place, such as
Garland in Chulmleigh, Devon, named
from Old English *gāra* 'triangular piece of
land' (see GORE) + *land* 'cultivated land',
'estate'.

Garley (121) English (Northamptonshire):
unexplained; probably a habitational name
from a lost or unidentified place.
GIVEN NAMES Spanish 5%. *Eloy* (2), *Osvaldo,*
Tomas.

Garlick (855) **1.** Jewish (American): Americanized form of GORELIK. **2.** English
(chiefly Lancashire): from Middle English
garlek 'garlic', hence a metonymic occupational name for a grower or seller of garlic
or perhaps a nickname for someone who
ate a lot of garlic. An alternative derivation
of the English name is from an unrecorded
survival into Middle English of the Old
English personal name *Gārlāc*, which is
composed of the elements *gār* 'spear' + *lāc*
'sport', 'play'. **3.** German: altered form of
Garlich (see GERLICH).

Garlin (148) German: habitational name
from a place so named in Mecklenburg.

Garling (377) North German form of
GERLING.

Garlinger (125) Altered spelling of German
Gerlinger, a topographic name from the
collective noun *girlet* 'stand of alder trees'
(see GERL).

Garlinghouse (194) Americanized form of
German **Gerlinghaus**, a habitational name
from a place named Gerlinghausen in the
Sieg district in northwestern Germany.

Garlington (572) English: habitational
name from a lost or unidentified place, possibly in Lancashire, where the surname is
most frequent.

Garlitz (314) **1.** German: habitational name
from any of two places so named in
Mecklenburg and near Berlin. **2.** Possibly
an altered spelling of the German surname
Görlitz, a habitational name from any of
several places named Garlitz.

Garlock (999) **1.** Jewish (American):
Americanized form of GORELIK. **2.** Americanized spelling of German GERLACH or
the North German form **Garlach**.

Garlough (109) Americanized spelling of
Jewish GORELIK or German GERLACH or
the North German form **Garlach**.

Garlow (376) Origin unidentified.

Garman (2863) **1.** Irish: variant of GOR-
MAN 1. **2.** English: variant of GORMAN 2.
3. German: variant of GERMAN.

Garmany (225) Altered spelling of the
French habitational name **Garmigny**, from
Germigny in Seine-et-Marne, named from

the Romano-Gallic estate name *Germinia-
cum*. This name is found chiefly in AL and
GA.

Garmon (1706) **1.** Irish: variant of GOR-
MAN 1. **2.** English: variant of GORMAN 2.
3. Altered spelling of German GEHRMANN.

Garms (251) North German: reduced form
of *Garmens*, a patronymic from GERMAN.

Garn (420) German: **1.** metonymic occupational name for a producer of or dealer in
yarn, Middle High German *garn*. **2.** (in
eastern Germany) from Slavic *gorn-*
'mountain dweller'.

Garnand (134) Origin unidentified.

Garneau (577) French: from a pet form of
the Germanic personal name *Warinwald*,
composed of the elements *war(in)* 'guard'
+ *waldan* 'to govern'.
FOREBEARS A bearer of this name from
Poitou was in Quebec city by 1663.
GIVEN NAMES French 13%. *Andre* (3), *Emile*
(3), *Lucien* (3), *Marcel* (3), *Armand* (2),
Pierre (2), *Aldea, Alphonse, Benoit,*
Fernand, Gilles, Jean-Luc.

Garner (24679) **1.** English: from Anglo-
Norman French *gerner* 'granary' (Old
French *grenier*, from Late Latin *granarium*, a derivative of *granum* 'grain'). It may
have been a topographic name for someone
who lived near a barn or granary, or a metonymic occupational name for someone in
charge of the stores kept in a granary.
2. English: variant of WARNER 1, from a
central Old French form. **3.** English: reduced form of GARDENER. **4.** South German: from an agent derivative of Middle
High German *garn* 'thread'; by extension,
an occupational name for a fisherman.
5. Altered spelling of GERNER.

Garnes (516) Norwegian and English: variant spelling of GARNESS.

Garness (125) **1.** Norwegian: habitational
name from any of several farmsteads
named Gardnes, probably from Old Norse
garðr 'fence' + *nes* 'headland'. **2.** English
(Worcester): variant spelling of **Garniss**,
of uncertain origin, perhaps a derivative of
Old French *gernon* 'moustache'.
GIVEN NAME Scandinavian 9%. *Ordell.*

Garnett (3177) English: **1.** from Old
French *Guarinot, Warinot*, a pet form of the
personal name *Guarin, Warin*, from Germanic *wari(n)-* 'protection', 'shelter'.
2. possibly a metonymic occupational
name for a maker or fitter of garnets, a type
of hinge, Middle English *garnette*, or for a
jeweler, from Middle English *garnette,*
gernet 'garnet'. **3.** from a diminutive of
GARNER 1.

Garney (161) **1.** English: unexplained; perhaps a variant of **Garneys**, itself a variant
of **Garniss** (see GARNESS 2). **2.** Name of
unknown etymology found among people
of Indian origin in Guyana and Trinidad.
GIVEN NAMES Indian 4%. *Narine, Seeram,*
Sunita.

Garnica (413) Basque: variant of **Gernika**, a habitational name from Guernica in Biscay, Basque Country.
GIVEN NAMES Spanish 49%. *Jose* (10), *Juan* (6), *Mario* (6), *Jesus* (4), *Angel* (3), *Gonzalo* (3), *Guadalupe* (3), *Jorge* (3), *Jose Luis* (3), *Manuel* (3), *Pablo* (3), *Pedro* (3); *Antonio* (3), *Marco* (2), *Caesar*, *Cecilio*, *Eliseo*, *Lorenzo*.

Garnick (135) Eastern German: variant of **Gornich** or **Gornig**, from Slavic *gora* 'mountain'; a topographic name for a mountain dweller or a metonymic occupational name for a miner.

Garnier (326) **1.** French: from a Germanic personal name, *Warinhari*, composed of the elements *war(in)* 'guard' + *hari*, *heri* 'army'. **2.** English: variant of GARNER 1.
FOREBEARS This name was also brought to America by the Huguenots. A priest called Garnier from Paris was in Quebec by 1636, and working in St. Jean en Huronie; he was killed in 1649, and canonized on June 29, 1930. There was a family from Maine in Quebec by 1663 and one from Normandy in Château Richer by 1671.
GIVEN NAMES French 17%. *Francois* (3), *Jacques* (3), *Achille* (2), *Jean-Pierre* (2), *Philippe* (2), *Andre*, *Antoine*, *Laurent*, *Marcel*, *Michel*, *Olivier*, *Patrice*.

Garno (136) Americanized spelling of French GARNEAU.

Garnsey (273) English: **1.** Norman habitational name for someone from Germisay in Haut-Marne, France. **2.** habitational name from Guernsey in the Channel Islands.

Garnto (179) Of English origin: see GORNTO. The name in this spelling is found mainly in GA.

Garofalo (1779) Southern Italian: from *garofalo* 'carnation', from Greek *karyophyllon*, standard modern Italian *garofano*. Southern Italian Greek has the more conservative *karofaddho*; the standard modern Greek form is *garifalo*. This is presumably a nickname for one who habitually sported a carnation, a topographic name for someone who lived where carnations grew, or a metonymic occupational name for a grower or seller of these flowers. De Felice notes that the Calabrese and Sicilian dialect forms, *garofalu* and *garofolo*, denote other species of plant, as well as a whirlwind or vortex, senses which could also have contributed to the surname.
GIVEN NAMES Italian 22%. *Angelo* (15), *Salvatore* (15), *Mario* (8), *Sal* (8), *Carmine* (6), *Gasper* (5), *Alfonso* (3), *Giovanni* (3), *Santo* (3), *Antonino* (2), *Antonio* (2), *Camillo* (2), *Domenic* (2), *Fausto* (2), *Fernando* (2), *Roberto* (2), *Rosario* (2).

Garofano (220) Italian: from *garofano* 'carnation', 'gilliflower' (see GAROFALO).
GIVEN NAMES Italian 11%. *Antonio* (2), *Angelo*, *Ciro*, *Luigi*, *Rocco*, *Salvatore*, *Saverio*, *Umberto*.

Garofolo (205) Southern Italian: variant of GAROFALO.
GIVEN NAMES Italian 10%. *Angelo*, *Carmelo*, *Carmine*, *Silvio*, *Vito*.

Garon (525) French: **1.** from a personal name of Germanic origin, *Garo*, meaning 'ready'. **2.** habitational name from places so named in Loire and Rhône, from Gaulish *gar*, a variant of *car* 'rock', 'stone'.
GIVEN NAMES French 6%. *Adrien* (2), *Andre*, *Antoine*, *Jacques*, *Jean Luc*, *Laurien*, *Lucien*, *Marcel*.

Garone (271) **1.** Italian: unexplained. **2.** French: perhaps an altered spelling of the habitational name **Garonne**, from the places so named in Gironde and Basses Pyrénées.
GIVEN NAMES Italian 7%. *Angelo*, *Concetta*, *Nicola*.

Garoutte (449) Southern French: nickname or occupational name from Occitan *garouto*, denoting a type of pea.

Garr (939) **1.** Irish or Scottish: reduced form of MCGARR. **2.** Altered form of German **Gorr**, from a short form of the personal name *Gregor*, Latin *Gregorius* (see GREGORY). **3.** Possibly an altered spelling of German **Garre**, a nickname for someone with a croaky voice, from a derivative of Middle High German, Middle Low German *garren* 'to whistle', 'to groan'. **4.** Alternatively, a metonymic occupational name for a cartwright, from Middle High German *garre*, *karre* 'cart'.

Garrabrant (266) Probably an altered spelling of North German **Garbrand** or **Gerbrant**, from a Germanic personal name, composed of the elements *gār*, *gēr* 'spear', 'lance' + *brand* 'fire', 'flame'.

Garrahan (161) Irish: reduced Anglicized form of Gaelic **Mag Aracháin**.
GIVEN NAME Irish 6%. *Patrick Michael*.

Garramone (208) Italian: according to Caracausi, from a metathesized variant of *camarruni* 'spurge' (sp. *Euphorbia*), but perhaps also a metathesized form of **Cammaro**, an occupational name, found exclusively in Sicily, from Arabic *ḥammār* 'muleteer' or *khammār* 'wine merchant'.
GIVEN NAMES Italian 18%. *Rocco* (11), *Antonio*, *Pasco*, *Sal*, *Salvatore*.

Garrand (158) Altered spelling of French GARANT or GARAND.

Garrant (128) French and English: unexplained.
GIVEN NAMES French 5%. *Camille*, *Emile*.

Garrard (1224) **1.** English: variant of GARRETT 1. **2.** French: variant of **Gérard** (see GERARD).

Garratt (270) English: variant spelling of GARRETT.

Garraway (172) English: **1.** from the Old English personal name *Gārwīg* 'spear war' **2.** habitational name for someone from Garway in Herefordshire. The place name, recorded in 1189 as *Langarewi*, is probably

from Welsh *llan* 'church' + the personal name *Guoruoe*.

Garrell (161) **1.** Respelling of French **Garrel**, possibly from a derivative of Old French *garre* 'colorful', 'two-tone'. **2.** Possibly a respelling of German **Garrel**, a habitational name from a place so named near Oldenburg.

Garrels (216) Dutch and North German: patronymic from the personal name *Gerold*, composed of the Germanic elements *gār*, *gēr* 'spear', 'lance' + *wald* 'rule'.

Garrelts (245) Dutch and North German: variant of GARRELS.

Garren (1280) **1.** English: probably a variant of GARRANT. **2.** Respelling of German GAREN.

Garret (147) **1.** French: humorous nickname for a man with shapely legs, from *jarrett* 'hock'. **2.** French: variant spelling of **Garet**, which has various explanations: from Old French *garet* 'shelter', a derivative of *garer* 'to protect', hence a metonymic occupational name for a herdsman or a topographic name for someone who lived by a covered shelter for animals, or a habitational name for someone from a place named with this word, for example in Allier and Puy-de-Dôme; or alternatively from a pet form of any of the various Germanic personal names beginning with the element *geri*, *gari* 'spear' or *ward* 'guard', 'protect'. **3.** English: variant spelling of GARRETT.
GIVEN NAMES French 5%. *Napoleon*, *Olivier*.

Garretson (1454) English: patronymic from GARRETT.

Garrett (36302) English: from either of two Germanic personal names introduced to Britain by the Normans: *Gerard*, composed of the elements *gar*, *ger* 'spear', 'lance' + *hard* 'hardy', 'brave', 'strong'; and *Gerald*, composed of the elements *gār*, *gēr* 'spear', 'lance' + *wald* 'rule'.

Garrette (135) Variant spelling of French GARRET.

Garrettson (114) Evidently a patronymic form of GARRETT.

Garrick (954) **1.** Americanized spelling of the French topographic name *Garrigue* (see GARRIGUES). **2.** Scottish: variant of **Garioch**, a habitational name from the district in Aberdeenshire so named. **3.** English: habitational name from Garwick in Lincolnshire, named from an Old English personal name *Gǣra* + Old English *wīc* '(dairy) farm'.
FOREBEARS The name is closely associated with the Huguenots. The English actor-manager David Garrick (1717–79) was the grandson of David de la Garrique, who fled Bordeaux in 1685, changing his family name to Garric on arrival in England. Other Garricks (Garicks) were in SC in the 1820s.

Garrido (896) Spanish and Portuguese: nickname from Spanish, Portuguese *garrido* 'elegant', 'handsome', 'comely'.
GIVEN NAMES Spanish 45%; Portuguese 12%. *Jose* (35), *Carlos* (14), *Manuel* (10), *Juan* (8), *Ernesto* (7), *Luis* (7), *Miguel* (7), *Pedro* (7), *Angel* (6), *Enrique* (6), *Jorge* (6), *Julio* (6); *Aderito, Joao; Antonio* (13), *Dante* (3), *Leonardo* (3), *Lorenzo* (3), *Luciano* (2), *Marco* (2), *Angelo, Elio, Filiberto, Gabino, Gabriele, Primo.*

Garriga (237) Catalan and southern French (Occitan): topographic name, from *garriga* 'barren land, where only holm oaks grow'.
GIVEN NAMES Spanish 36%. *Jose* (5), *Juan* (4), *Enrique* (3), *Francisco* (3), *Alicia* (2), *Alvaro* (2), *Juana* (2), *Luis* (2), *Ramon* (2), *Agustin, Alejandra, Alejandro.*

Garrigan (555) Irish: reduced Anglicized form of Gaelic **Mac Geargáin** or sometimes **Ó Geargáin**, from a diminutive of *garg* 'fierce'.
GIVEN NAMES Irish 4%. *Delma, Liam.*

Garrigues (151) Southern French: from Old Provençal *garrique* 'grove of holm oaks or kermes oaks'; a topographic name for someone who lived by such a grove, or a habitational name from any of various places named with this word, such as Les Garrigues in Tarn-et-Garonne and Vaucluse. After the revocation of the edict of Nantes (1685), a French family from Languedoc with this name migrated to Prussia, and thence to England, where it is found in the form GARRICK, and America, where the surname is found in a profusion of forms. In Berlin it also appears in the form **Jar(r)iges**.
GIVEN NAMES French 4%. *Caspar, Jacques, Leonie.*

Garrigus (253) Altered spelling of French GARRIGUES, which originated in Germany.

Garringer (476) German: probably an altered spelling of GERINGER or GEHRINGER.

Garriott (480) French Canadian variant of the southern French habitational name **Gariot**, from a derivative of *garer* 'to shelter or protect'.

Garris (2298) **1.** French: habitational name from a place so named in Saint-Palay canton in Pyrénées Atlantiques. **2.** German: variant of GEHRIS.

Garrish (136) English: variant of GERRISH.

Garrison (18603) English: patronymic from GARRETT.

Garriss (113) **1.** German: variant of **Gorris**, **Görres** or GAREIS, reduced forms of the Latin personal name *Gregorius* (see GREGORY). **2.** It could also be a variant of the French Huguenot name GARRIGUES.

Garritano (177) Italian: possibly a habitational name from an adjectival form of the place name Garro, a small district in Cosenza province.
GIVEN NAMES Italian 16%. *Antonio* (2), *Carmine* (2), *Dante, Dominico, Ezio, Luigi, Romeo.*

Garritson (107) English: patronymic from GARRETT.

Garrity (2768) Irish: reduced form of **McGarity**, an Anglicized form of Gaelic **Mag Oireachtaigh** 'son of *Oireachtach*'.
GIVEN NAMES Irish 5%. *Brigid, Colum, John Patrick, Liam, Murphy.*

Garro (285) **1.** Catalan (**Garró**): from *garró* 'calf', presumably applied as a nickname. **2.** Portuguese: nickname from *garro* 'leper'.
GIVEN NAMES Spanish 15%; Italian 13%. *Carlos* (3), *Amparo* (2), *Gerardo* (2), *Luis* (2), *Mario* (2), *Alejandro, Alvaro, Atilio, Guillermo, Javier, Juan, Julio; Guido* (2), *Salvatore* (2), *Angelo, Carmine, Cesario, Domenic, Eligio, Nunzio, Rocco, Sal, Santo, Sebastiano.*

Garrod (248) English: variant of GARRETT 2.

Garron (216) French: variant of GARON 1.

Garrott (242) Variant spelling of the French surname **Garrot**, from an Old French and Occitan word meaning 'withers (of a horse)', 'trajectory of an arrow' or in Old French 'stick'. The French surname is also established in Spain and Portugal.

Garrow (879) **1.** Scottish: descriptive nickname from Gaelic *garbh* 'brawny', 'rough'. **2.** English: variant of GARRAWAY. **3.** Americanized spelling of French GAREAU.

Garry (1215) Irish: reduced Anglicized form of McGARRY or O'GARA.
GIVEN NAMES Irish 4%. *Brendan* (2), *Mahon.*

Garsee (100) Origin unidentified.

Garside (474) English (Lancashire and Yorkshire): habitational name from Gartside or Garside in Oldham, Lancashire, apparently so named from northern Middle English *garth* 'enclosure' (Old Norse *garðr*) + *side* 'hill slope' (Old English *sīde*).

Garske (409) Eastern German: of Slavic origin, perhaps a habitational name from Görzke near Jerichow or a respelling of GARTZKA.

Garski (117) German (of Slavic origin): variant of GARSKE.

Garson (490) French and Scottish (Orkney): occupational name for a young servant, from the oblique case of Old French *gars* 'boy', 'lad'.

Garst (695) German (of Slavic origin): unexplained.

Garstka (152) Polish: from *garstka* 'handful', 'bunch', possibly applied as a nickname for a small person.
GIVEN NAMES Polish 8%. *Czeslawa, Dariusz, Wlodzimierz, Zigmund.*

Garten (658) **1.** German: metonymic occupational name for a gardener or overseer of a garder or enclosure. Originally the term denoted the keeper of an enclosure for deer, later of a vineyard or smallholding, from Middle High German *garte* 'garden', 'enclosure'. Compare *Hofgarten* 'courtyard',

Weingarten 'vineyard'. Alternatively, it may be a short form of any of the various compound names formed with this element, e.g. Swiss *Gart(en)mann*, *Gartenhauser*. **2.** Jewish (Ashkenazic): ornamental name from German *Garten* 'garden'.

Gartenberg (152) Jewish (Ashkenazic): ornamental name composed of German *Garten* 'garden' + *Berg* 'mountain', 'hill'.
GIVEN NAMES Jewish 7%; German 4%. *Golda, Meyer, Moshe; Erwin, Wolf.*

Garth (812) **1.** Northern English: topographic name for someone who lived near an enclosure, normally a paddock or orchard, from northern Middle English *garth* 'enclosed area', 'yard' (from Old Norse *garðr* 'enclosure'). **2.** German (also **Gärth**): topographic name from Old Saxon *gard* 'enclosure', 'farm(yard)', originally denoting a settlement protected by a fence.

Garthe (106) **1.** German: habitational name from a place so named near Cloppenburg. **2.** German: variant of GARTH. **3.** Eastern German: variant of Slavic **Jarota**, from a short form of personal name *Jaroslaw*.
GIVEN NAMES Scandinavian 7%. *Erik, Lars, Norvald.*

Garthwaite (280) English: habitational name from a lost place in northern England; the second element of the place name is probably Old Norse *þveit* 'clearing'.

Gartin (401) English: variant spelling of GARTON.

Gartland (741) **1.** English: unexplained. **2.** This name is also found in Ireland as **(Mac) Gartlan(d)**, which MacLysaght describes as a Gaelicized form of GARLAND.

Gartley (204) **1.** Scottish: habitational name from the former barony of Garntuly (now Gartly), in Aberdeenshire. **2.** Perhaps also an altered spelling of German **Gartler**, a variant of GARTNER or *Gärtler* (see GERTLER).

Gartman (790) South German and Swiss German (**Gartmann**): **1.** occupational name for a gardener (see GARTNER); in some cases it may refer to the owner of a small (enclosed or fenced) farm or a worker at a deer preserve (see GARTH). **2.** habitational name from Garte near Osnabrück.

Gartner (2159) German (also **Gärtner**), Slovenian, Jewish (Ashkenazic): occupational name for a gardener or vintner, from an agent derivative of Middle High German *garte* 'enclosure', 'garden'.
GIVEN NAMES German 5%. *Hans* (6), *Kurt* (4), *Gerda* (3), *Johann* (2), *Lorenz* (2), *Otto* (2), *Wolfgang* (2), *Bernd, Dieter, Frieda, Fritz, Gerhard.*

Garton (1312) English: habitational name from Garton in East Yorkshire or from various minor places so named, from Old English *gāra* 'triangular plot of land' + *tūn* 'farmstead'.

Gartrell (564) English (Cornwall): unexplained. This name is found mainly in GA.

Gartside (150) English: variant of GARSIDE.

Gartz (106) Eastern German (under Slavic influence): habitational name from any of several places so named.

Gartzke (164) Eastern German (of Slavic origin): unexplained.
GIVEN NAMES German 6%. *Arno, Detlef, Rainer.*

Garufi (112) Italian: variant of **Garufo**, which is from Arabic, from, amongst other possibilities, *qarūf* 'hard', 'cruel', *'arūf* 'constant', 'persevering', or *'arūf(ah)* 'one who knows'.
GIVEN NAMES Italian 20%. *Santo* (3), *Carmelo* (2), *Domenica, Francesca, Mario, Remo, Sal, Salvatore, Tino.*

Garven (141) **1.** German: from a variant of the personal name *Gerwin* (see GERWIN). **2.** Perhaps a variant spelling of GARVIN.

Garver (1859) German: variant of GARBER 3, itself a variant of GERBER.

Garverick (171) Probably an Americanized spelling of German **Gerberich**, a variant of *Gerbert* (see GERBRACHT).

Garvey (4646) Irish: reduced Anglicized form of Gaelic **Ó Gairbhshíth** 'descendant of *Gairbhshíth*', a personal name from *garbh* 'rough', 'cruel' + *síth* 'peace'. See also McGARVEY.
GIVEN NAMES Irish 5%. *Brendan* (6), *Kieran* (2), *Colm, John Patrick, Kilian, Seamus, Sean Patrick.*

Garvie (167) Scottish spelling of Irish GARVEY.

Garvin (4645) Irish: reduced Anglicized form of Gaelic **Ó Gairbhín** 'descendant of *Gairbhín*', a personal name derived from a diminutive of *garbh* 'rough', 'cruel'.

Garvis (119) English: variant of JARVIS.

Garwood (1436) English: habitational name from a lost or unidentified minor place, possibly in East Anglia, where the name is most common, and probably so called from Old English *gāra* 'gore', 'triangular piece of land' + *wudu* 'wood'.

Gary (6265) **1.** English: variant of GEARY 2. **2.** Irish: reduced form of McGARY. **3.** Respelling of Swiss German **Gehri** or **Gehry**, variants of GEHR.

Garza (18643) Spanish: from *garza* 'heron', probably applied as a nickname for someone with long legs.
GIVEN NAMES Spanish 48%. *Jose* (369), *Juan* (287), *Jesus* (195), *Manuel* (143), *Raul* (143), *Carlos* (132), *Ruben* (118), *Guadalupe* (107), *Mario* (99), *Armando* (94), *Roberto* (91), *Luis* (90).

Garzia (100) Italianized form of Spanish GARCIA.
GIVEN NAMES Spanish 12%; Italian 9%. *Mario* (2), *Alfredo, Ernestina, Fernando, Juan, Pedro, Ricardo; Angelo, Antonio, Ciro, Corrado.*

Garzon (417) Spanish (**Garzón**): **1.** from *garzón* 'boy', 'lad' (from French *garçon*); probably a nickname with derogatory overtones. **2.** from an augmentative of *garza* 'heron'. **3.** habitational name from any of three places in Andalusia named Garzón. The surname is found among Sephardic Jews in Morocco.
GIVEN NAMES Spanish 50%. *Jose* (11), *Jorge* (5), *Luis* (5), *Juan* (4), *Miguel* (4), *Pablo* (4), *Roberto* (4), *Arturo* (3), *Carlos* (3), *Fernando* (3), *Francisco* (3), *Hernando* (3); *Marco* (3), *Antonio* (2), *Caesar, Fausto, Flavio, Marcello, Valentino.*

Garzone (120) Italian: **1.** occupational name for a young servant, from *garzone* 'boy', 'lad', 'servant', possibly a loanword from French *garçon*. **2.** alternatively, it has been suggested that it could be from a derivative of *garzo* 'head of a species of thistle used for teasing cloth', presumably applied as a topographic or metonymic occupational name, or *garza* 'heron', or Calabrian and Sicilian *garzu* 'sweetheart', 'lover'.
GIVEN NAMES Italian 15%. *Angelo, Luigi, Palma, Tullio, Vincenzo.*

Gasaway (779) Possibly an Americanized spelling of German **Gösswein**, from the Germanic personal name *Goswin*, composed of the elements *gos* or possibly *Gauta* 'Goth' + *wine* 'friend'.

Gasbarro (244) Italian: variant of GASPARRO.
GIVEN NAMES Italian 16%; French 4%. *Pasco* (4), *Angelo* (3), *Guido* (2), *Antonio, Emidio, Gino; Armand* (2), *Pascal* (2), *Achille.*

Gasca (332) Aragonese and also Catalan: ethnic name from the feminine form of *Gasc* 'Basque'.
GIVEN NAMES Spanish 46%. *Jose* (8), *Francisco* (5), *Manuel* (5), *Guadalupe* (4), *Ricardo* (4), *Eduardo* (3), *Luis* (3), *Miguel* (3), *Alberto* (2), *Alvaro* (2), *Arturo* (2), *Enrique* (2).

Gasch (158) **1.** German: probably from a reduced form of a personal name, which may be *Gottfried* or *Gottschalk* in eastern Germany, or from the Polish personal name *Gaweł* (from Latin *Gallus*), or, in southern Germany, from Latin *Castulus* meaning 'the pure one'. **2.** Catalan: variant of the ethnic name **Gasc**, from *gasc* 'Basque'. This surname is also established in southern France.

Gaschler (134) German: probably a variant of Alemannic *Kastler*, from a short form of a personal name from Old High German *gast* 'guest', 'foreign warrior', or alternatively a variant of GASCH.

Gascho (135) Origin unidentified; probably Hungarian.

Gascoigne (225) English: from Old French *Gascogne* 'Gascony', hence a regional name. The name of the region derives from that of the Basques, who are found close by and formerly extended into this region as well; they are first named in Roman sources as *Vascōnes*, but the original meaning of the name, derived from a root *eusk-* in the non-Indo-European language that they still speak today, is completely obscure. By the Middle Ages the Basques had been displaced from most of Gascony by speakers of Gascon (a dialect of Occitan, related to French), who were proverbial for their boastfulness. In the 11th century Gascony united with Aquitaine and was thus held by England between 1154 and 1453. See GASCON.

Gascon (381) French, Spanish (**Gascón**), and English: regional name for someone from the province of Gascony, Old French *Gascogne* (see GASCOIGNE).
GIVEN NAMES Spanish 18%; French 8%. *Jose* (4), *Manuel* (3), *Jaime* (2), *Mario* (2), *Miguel* (2), *Rafael* (2), *Ruben* (2), *Amado, Ana, Ana Maria, Angel, Caridad; Andre* (2), *Irby* (2), *Chantal, Jean-Guy, Jean-Philippe, Monique, Serge, Simonne.*

Gascoyne (101) English: variant spelling of GASCOIGNE.

Gase (185) German (also **Gäse**): unexplained; perhaps a nickname from Polish *geś* 'goose' or a cognate word in a related Slavic language.

Gash (613) **1.** Scottish and English: from a central French form of the Norman personal name *Wazo*, apparently derived from a compound Germanic name formed with *wad* 'to go' as the first element. **2.** Americanized spelling of German GASCH.

Gasior (370) Polish (**Gąsior**): from Polish *gąsior* 'gander', hence a nickname for a man thought to resemble a gander in some way, or metonymic occupational name for a keeper of geese.
GIVEN NAMES Polish 13%. *Izabela* (3), *Wojciech* (3), *Jozef* (2), *Andrzej, Bronislaw, Casimir, Dorota, Grazyna, Jerzy, Jozefa, Mieczyslaw, Pawel.*

Gasiorowski (216) Polish (**Gąsiorowski**): habitational name for someone from a place called Gąsiorowo, for example in Kalisz or Poznań voivodeships.
GIVEN NAMES Polish 7%. *Czeslaw, Krzysztof, Piotr, Zygmunt.*

Gaska (194) **1.** Polish (**Gąska**): nickname for a naive person, from *gąska* 'little goose'. **2.** Hungarian: from a pet form of the personal name *Gáspár*, Hungarian form of KASPAR.
GIVEN NAMES Polish 11%. *Beata, Cecylia, Czeslaw, Jaroslaw, Jozefa, Leszek, Stanislawa, Tadeusz, Tomasz, Zofia.*

Gaskamp (130) German: topographic name, possibly from Westphalian *Gast* 'barley' (standard German *Gerste*) + *kamp* 'field', 'domain'.
GIVEN NAMES German 4%. *Erwin* (2), *Otto.*

Gaskell (529) English: variant spelling of GASKILL.

Gaskey (244) Perhaps an altered spelling of French **Gasquet**, **Gasqué**, from diminutives of *Gasc* 'Gascon' (see GASQUE).
GIVEN NAMES French 4%. *Honore, Marcel.*

Gaskill (2251) English (Lancashire): habitational name from Gatesgill in Cumbria, so named from Old Norse *geit* 'goat' + *skáli* 'shelter'.

Gaskin (2099) English: variant of GASCON.

Gaskins (3120) English: variant of GASCON.

Gasko (104) Jewish (eastern Ashkenazic): Russianized form of the Yiddish personal name *Haske*, a pet form of *Haskl* (see EZEKIEL).
GIVEN NAMES Jewish 6%; German 4%. *Miriam* (2), *Yigal*; *Kurt.*

Gasner (224) German: variant spelling of GASSNER.

Gaspar (1413) **1.** French, Spanish, Catalan, Portuguese, and Hungarian (**Gáspár**): from the personal name, which was common in central Europe up to the 18th century (see CASPER). **2.** Slovenian (mainly Prekmurje in easternmost Slovenia; **Gašpar**): from a dialect form of the personal name **Gašper** (see CASPER).
GIVEN NAMES Spanish 21%; Portuguese 7%. *Jose* (24), *Manuel* (16), *Francisco* (7), *Carlos* (5), *Jesus* (5), *Alfredo* (4), *Juan* (4), *Julio* (4), *Mario* (4), *Miguel* (4), *Rafael* (4), *Ana* (3); *Joao* (5), *Agostinho, Catarina, Vasco.*

Gaspard (1494) French: variant of GASPAR.
GIVEN NAMES French 7%. *Camile* (2), *Gabrielle* (2), *Minos* (2), *Pierre* (2), *Andre, Berthony, Carmelle, Cecile, Emile, Eusebe, Gervais, Ghislaine.*

Gaspari (264) Italian: patronymic from the personal name *Gaspare* (see CASPER). This name is also found in Slovenia, where it is either an importation from Italy or an Italianized form of the Slovenian patronymic **Gašparič**.
GIVEN NAMES Italian 20%. *Angelo* (3), *Rocco* (2), *Sante* (2), *Stefano* (2), *Aldo, Antonio, Cesare, Domenic, Donato, Emidio, Flavio, Gaetano.*

Gasparian (110) Armenian: patronymic from the western Armenian personal name *Gaspar* (see KASPAR).
GIVEN NAMES Armenian 51%; Russian 4%. *Armen* (7), *Gevork* (2), *Oganes* (2), *Akop, Ashot, Azniv, Grigor, Gurgen, Haig, Hasmik, Hrach, Hrair*; *Svetlana, Vladimir.*

Gasparini (235) Italian: from a pet form of the personal name *Gaspare* (see CASPER).
GIVEN NAMES Italian 29%. *Angelo* (3), *Gino* (2), *Lino* (2), *Aldo, Benigno, Dario, Geno, Giordano, Giorgio, Giuliano, Graziano, Leonardo, Mario, Massimo, Mauro, Ofelia.*

Gasparovic (112) Croatian and Serbian (**Gašparović**): patronymic from the personal name *Gašpar* (see CASPER).

Gasparro (166) Italian: from a variant of the personal name *Gaspare*, Italian equivalent of CASPER. The form **Gasparos** is also found as a Greek family name.
GIVEN NAMES Italian 25%. *Vito* (4), *Angelo* (2), *Antonio, Costantino, Donato, Giuseppe, Leonardo, Mauro, Michelangelo, Nichola, Nicola.*

Gasper (1715) **1.** German: variant of **Kaspar** (see CASPER). **2.** Slovenian (**Gašper**): from the personal name *Gašper* (see CASPER). It may also be a reduced form of the Slovenian patronymics **Gašperšič** or **Gašperčič**.

Gasperini (184) Italian: variant of GASPARINI.
GIVEN NAMES Italian 14%. *Graziano* (2), *Guido* (2), *Franco, Lorenzo, Marcello, Marco, Orlando, Piero, Renato, Silvio, Tulio.*

Gasperson (151) Americanized form of a Danish, Swedish, or other patronymic from the personal name CASPER. Compare CASPERSON.

Gasque (339) French (Huguenot): regional name denoting someone from Gascony in southwestern France (see GASCON).

Gass (2617) **1.** South German, Swiss, and Jewish (Ashkenazic): topographic name for someone who lived in a street in a city, town, or village, Middle High German *gazze*, German *Gasse*, Yiddish *gas* 'street', 'side street'. **2.** English: variant of GASH. **3.** Altered spelling of German GAST, found in the areas of Swiss settlement.

Gassaway (570) See GASAWAY.

Gassel (138) German and Jewish (Ashkenazic): diminutive of GASS.

Gassen (265) German: habitational name from any of several places so named in Bavaria, Hessen, Rhineland, Brandenburg.
GIVEN NAME French 4%. *Marcel* (2).

Gasser (1172) German and Swiss German (also **Gässer**) and Jewish (Ashkenazic): topographic name for someone who lived in a side street or alley, from a derivative of Middle High German *gazze*, German *Gasse*, Yiddish *gas*.

Gassert (233) South German: variant of GASSER.

Gassett (406) Respelling of Swiss French **Gasset** or French **Gassette**, topographic name for someone who lived in a muddy location, from a variant of *gache* 'pool', 'puddle'.

Gassler (108) German (**Gässler**): topographic name for someone who lived in a side street, from a noun derivative of *gazze* (see GASS).
GIVEN NAME German 4%. *Gottfried.*

Gassman (727) Jewish (Ashkenazic): see GASS.

Gassmann (206) Jewish (Ashkenazic): see GASS.
GIVEN NAMES German 4%. *Almut, Erwin.*

Gassner (450) **1.** German, Swiss, and Jewish (Ashkenazic): topographic name for someone who lived in a side street or alley (see GASSER). **2.** Swiss German: variant of the occupational name GEISNER 'goatherd'.
GIVEN NAMES German 6%. *Erwin, Ewald, Hans, Heinz, Kurt, Rainer, Rudi, Wilhelm.*

Gasson (116) English and French: perhaps a variant of GARSON.

Gast (1874) **1.** German and Jewish (Ashkenazic): nickname for a stranger or newcomer to a community, Middle High German *gast* 'foreigner', 'guest', 'stranger', German *Gast*. **2.** German and Swiss German: from a short form of a personal name *Gastolf*, or Alemannic from the personal name ARBOGAST. **3.** French: topographic name for someone who lived on a patch of waste land, Old French *gast*.
GIVEN NAMES German 4%. *Otto* (3), *Fritz* (2), *Dieter, Elfriede, Gerhardt, Hertha, Kurt, Lorenz, Lothar.*

Gastelum (424) probably a variant of Basque **Gaztelu**, a habitational name from any of the towns called Gaztelu in Araba, Biscay, Gipuzkoa and Navarre, in Basque Country. This variant is mainly found in Mexico.
GIVEN NAMES Spanish 53%. *Jose* (8), *Jesus* (6), *Miguel* (5), *Juan* (3), *Manuel* (3), *Rodolfo* (3), *Sergio* (3), *Adelaida* (2), *Alberto* (2), *Carlos* (2), *Jaime* (2), *Leopoldo* (2).

Gaster (287) German: from a variant of a personal name formed with GAST.

Gastineau (449) French: topographic name from Old French *gaste* 'uncultivated or ravaged land.'
FOREBEARS The name is mentioned in Trois Rivières, Quebec, in 1650, and a bearer of the name was married there in 1663.

Gaston (5566) French: from the Old French oblique case of a Germanic personal name, originally probably a byname from *gasti* 'stranger', 'guest', 'host'. Compare GUEST. The surname is also found in England and Ireland, where it is probably a Huguenot importation.

Gatch (263) Probably an Americanized spelling of German **Götsch** (see GOETSCH) or **Gattsche**, a variant of GADE.

Gatchel (156) Irish: variant spelling of GATCHELL.

Gatchell (501) **1.** Irish: unexplained. MacLysaght comments that this was the name of a prominent Quaker family from Waterford. **2.** Americanized form of Swiss **Götschel**, from a pet form of **Götsch** (see GOETSCH).

Gateley (259) **1.** English: habitational name from a place in Norfolk, so named from Old English *gāt* 'goat' + *lēah* 'woodland clearing'. **2.** Possibly a variant spelling of the Irish surname GATELY or English GATLEY.

Gately (1099) **1.** Irish: reduced Anglicized form of Gaelic **Ó Gatlaoich**, 'descendant of *Gotlaoch*', a byname composed of the elements *got* 'stammering' + *laoch* 'warrior', 'hero'. **2.** Variant spelling of the English surnames GATELEY or GATLEY.

Gatens (119) Irish: probably a variant of **Gaitens**, **Gattins**, Donegal variants of MCGETTIGAN.

GIVEN NAMES Irish 5%. *Brigid, Colum.*

Gater (160) English: variant spelling of GAITER.

Gates (18742) **1.** English: topographic name for someone who lived by the gates of a medieval walled town. The Middle English singular *gate* is from the Old English plural, *gatu*, of *geat* 'gate' (see YATES). Since medieval gates were normally arranged in pairs, fastened in the center, the Old English plural came to function as a singular, and a new Middle English plural ending in -s was formed. In some cases the name may refer specifically to the Sussex place Eastergate (i.e. 'eastern gate'), known also as *Gates* in the 13th and 14th centuries, when surnames were being acquired. **2.** Americanized spelling of German **Götz** (see GOETZ). **3.** Translated form of French **Barrière** (see BARRIERE).

FOREBEARS In New England, Gates was the preferred English version of the name of an extensive French family, called Barrière dit Langevin. Horatio Gates, a British military officer born in Maldon, England, in about 1728, fought on the colonial side in the American Revolution, settled in VA after the war, and died in NY.

Gatewood (2396) English: habitational name of uncertain origin. There are places called Gate Wood End, South Yorkshire, Gatewood Hill, Hampshire, and Gatewood House Farm, Leicestershire. The first is named from an Old Norse *geyt* 'rushing stream or spring'; the second is from Old English *gāt* 'goat'; the etymology of the Leicestershire place name is not known.

FOREBEARS The Gatewood family has been established in Essex Co., VA, and Spotsylvania since the 17th century.

Gath (228) **1.** Scottish: reduced form of MCGATH. **2.** English: variant of GARTH. **3.** North German (**Gäth**): variant of **Gäde** (see GAEDE). **4.** North German: topographic name from Middle Low German *gate* 'street', 'alley'.

GIVEN NAME German 4%. *Otto* (2).

Gathers (445) Possibly an altered form of North German **Gather**, a habitational name for someone from either of two places called Gath (near Krefeld and in Schleswig).

Gathings (284) German (**Gäthings**): patronymic from **Gäth,**, a variant of **Gäde** (see GAEDE).

Gathman (179) German (**Gathmann**): topographic name for someone who lived in a street or alley, from Middle Low German *gate* 'street', 'alley' + *man* 'man'.

Gathright (483) English: origin uncertain; probably a variant of CARTWRIGHT.

Gatica (200) Basque: Castilianized form of Basque **Gatika**, a habitational name from a place called Gatika in Biscay, Basque Country.

GIVEN NAMES Spanish 43%. *Jose* (7), *Jorge* (5), *Manuel* (4), *Pedro* (4), *Juan* (3), *Francisco* (2), *Guillermo* (2), *Mario* (2), *Rolando* (2), *Sergio* (2), *Alberto*, *Alejandro*; *Antonio*.

Gatley (169) **1.** English: variant of GATLIFF. **2.** Variant spelling of English GATELEY or Irish GATELY.

Gatliff (201) English: habitational name for someone from Gatley in Greater Manchester (formerly in Cheshire), recorded in 1290 as *Gateclyve*, from Old English *gāt* 'goat' + *clif* 'cliff', 'bank'.

Gatlin (3223) **1.** English: of uncertain origin; probably a variant of CATLIN or **Gadling**, a nickname from Old English *gædeling* 'kinsman', 'companion', but also 'low fellow'. **2.** Possibly an altered spelling of German **Göttling**, from a Germanic personal name formed with *god* 'god' or *gōd* 'good' + -*ling* suffix of affiliation, or, like **Gättling** (of which this may also be an altered form), a nickname from Middle High German *getlinc* 'companion', 'kinsman'. Compare 1.

Gatling (687) **1.** English: variant of GATLIN. **2.** Possibly a respelling of German **Gättling** (see GATLIN 2).

Gato (115) Spanish (Valladolid): unexplained.

GIVEN NAMES Spanish 39%. *Jose* (3), *Rodolfo* (2), *Ana, Andres, Aurelio, Benito, Claudio, Elba, Eulogio, Felicidad, Francisco, Gilberto.*

Gatrell (232) English: of uncertain origin; it may be, as Reaney suggests, a voiced variant of the habitational name CATTERALL.

Gatson (504) Origin uncertain. Perhaps a metathesized form of GASTON.

Gatt (168) **1.** Scottish: of uncertain derivation. Black believes it may be local to Dunfermline, where it was first recorded in 1579. **2.** South German: from a short form of a Germanic personal name formed with the same root as Middle High German *gate* 'companion', 'compatible person'.

Gatta (252) Italian: apparently a nickname from Old Italian *gatta* 'cat'. Compare GATTO, which derives from the later, masculinized form of the same word.

GIVEN NAMES Italian 17%. *Pasquale* (3), *Antonio* (2), *Ciriaco* (2), *Pasco* (2), *Attilio, Caesar, Enrico, Lorenzo, Oreste, Rocco, Vincenzo, Vittorio.*

Gatten (269) Variant spelling of English GATTON.

Gatti (1019) Italian: patronymic or plural form of GATTO.

GIVEN NAMES Italian 11%. *Angelo* (6), *Rocco* (3), *Salvatore* (3), *Aldo* (2), *Carlo* (2), *Dante* (2), *Dario* (2), *Franco* (2), *Lucio* (2), *Nino* (2), *Pompeo* (2), *Ricco* (2).

Gattis (876) English: occupational name for a watchman, from Middle English, Old French *gaite* 'watchman'.

Gatto (1507) Italian: nickname for someone thought to resemble a cat in any of many possible physical or abstract ways, from Italian *gatto* '(tom) cat', Late Latin *cattus*. Compare English CATT.

GIVEN NAMES Italian 22%. *Angelo* (11), *Mario* (10), *Salvatore* (8), *Carmine* (2), *Dino* (2), *Domenic* (2), *Giuseppe* (2), *Liborio* (2), *Luciano* (2), *Vincenzo* (2), *Vito* (2), *Americo, Basilio, Antonio, Carlo, Claudio, Domingo, Elena, Francisco, Gabriela, Noemi.*

Gatton (666) English: habitational name for someone from a place in Surrey so named, from Old English *gāt* 'goat' + *tūn* 'enclosure'.

Gattone (133) Italian: augmentative of GATTO.

GIVEN NAMES Italian 14%. *Antonio, Domenic, Gino, Rocco, Vito.*

Gatts (127) Possibly an Americanized spelling of German **Götz** (see GOETZ).

Gattuso (397) Italian (Liguria and Lombardy): from a derivative of GATTO.

GIVEN NAMES Italian 19%. *Sal* (5), *Salvatore* (5), *Angelo* (2), *Carmelo* (2), *Domenic* (2), *Rocco* (2), *Antonio, Carmine, Francesco, Giovanni, Luigi.*

Gatwood (127) English: probably a variant of **Gatward**, an occupational name for a gate keeper or goatherd, from Old English *geat* 'gate' or *gāt* 'goat' + *weard* 'ward', 'keeper'.

Gatz (566) **1.** German: from *Gato*, a short form of an old personal name formed with the same root as Middle High German *gate* 'companion'. **2.** German (in eastern Germany): possibly from the Slavic personal name *Gaczko*. **3.** German: habitational name from a place so named in Pomerania. **4.** Americanized spelling of Ukrainian and Polish GAC.

Gatza (130) German (of Polish origin): from Polish *Gaca*, a pet form of GAC.

Gatzemeyer (101) German: variant of KATZENMEYER.

Gatzke (411) Eastern German: pet form from GATZ 2.

GIVEN NAMES German 5%. *Otto* (5), *Ewald.*

Gau (501) **1.** German: habitational name from any of various places named with Middle High German *gau, göu* 'area of fertile agricultural land'. **2.** Chinese 高: variant of GAO.

Gaub (165) German: from a Swabian form of the personal name *Gabo*, meaning 'gift'. Compare GEBHARDT.

Gaubatz (149) Eastern German: nickname for a braggart or boaster, Sorbian *gubatz.*

GIVEN NAMES German 8%. *Dieter, Fritz, Heinz, Klaus.*

Gaubert (241) French (Normandy and Picardy): from a Germanic name of uncertain origin. The first element is probably

the tribal name *Gaut* (apparently the same as Old English *Gēatas*, the Scandinavian people to which Beowulf belonged, and also akin to the name of the *Goths*); the second is *berht* 'bright', 'famous'.
GIVEN NAMES French 12%. *Thierry* (2), *Arnaud, Aurore, Clothilde, Irby, Jacques, Monique, Raoul, Reynald.*

Gauch (148) South German and Swiss German: nickname for a fool, from Middle High German *gouch* 'cuckoo', 'madman'.

Gaucher (235) **1.** New England variant of the French surname GAUTIER. **2.** Variant of German GAUCH.
GIVEN NAMES French 11%. *Emile* (2), *Armand, Francoise, Jacques, Laurette, Lucien, Philippe.*

Gauci (107) Italian: unexplained.
GIVEN NAMES Italian 15%. *Silvio* (2), *Carmel, Carmelo, Reno, Salvatore.*

Gauck (106) German: **1.** perhaps, as Bahlow suggests, from the Frisian personal names *Jeuck* or *Geuken*. **2.** in the south a nickname for a silly person, a fool, from Middle High German *gouch*.

Gaudet (1911) French: from the Germanic personal name *Waldo* (from *waldan* 'to govern').
GIVEN NAMES French 7%. *Armand* (6), *Pierre* (4), *Andre* (3), *Marcel* (3), *Emile* (2), *Normand* (2), *Adelard, Alphonse, Andrus, Camille, Chantel, Fernand.*

Gaudette (1351) Altered (North American) spelling variant of GAUDET.
GIVEN NAMES French 7%. *Armand* (3), *Normand* (3), *Eulice* (2), *Aime, Alphonse, Andre, Dominique, Donat, Emile, Eugenie, Fernand, Henri.*

Gaudin (446) French: from the Germanic personal name *Waldo* (from *waldan* 'to govern') or a derivative of *gaut-* 'Goth'.
FOREBEARS A Huguenot family called **Gaudin**, from La Rochelle, was in Quebec city in 1655. Another, from Burgundy, was in Montreal in 1654; and one from Normandy had arrived in Quebec city by 1656.
GIVEN NAMES French 13%. *Pierre* (5), *Andre* (2), *Alphonse, Colette, Emile, Georges, Henri, Irby, Leonce, Michel, Monique.*

Gaudino (217) Italian: possibly from a diminutive of GAUDIO.
GIVEN NAMES Italian 22%. *Antonio* (3), *Salvatore* (3), *Angelo* (2), *Luigi* (2), *Sal* (2), *Baldassare, Cosmo, Dino, Francesco, Gaspare, Nunzio.*

Gaudio (637) Italian: nickname for a cheerful person, from *gaudio* 'joy', 'happiness', also sometimes applied with the implied meaning '(son whose birth has brought) joy'.
GIVEN NAMES Italian 19%. *Francesco* (5), *Pasquale* (4), *Angelo* (3), *Sal* (3), *Salvatore* (3), *Dante* (2), *Giuseppe* (2), *Santo* (2), *Agostino, Alessandro, Carmel, Concetta.*

Gaudioso (210) Italian: nickname from *gaudioso* 'joyful'.

GIVEN NAMES Italian 23%. *Ercole* (4), *Carmelo* (3), *Matteo* (3), *Angelo, Domenic, Domenico, Franco, Pasquale, Vito.*

Gaudreau (806) French: from a pet form of *Waldhari*, a personal name of Germanic origin formed with *wald* 'rule', 'power' + *hari, heri* 'army'.
FOREBEARS Bearers of the name who are of Acadian origin are descended from a François Gauterot, who arrived in 1636, from a village near Loudun, in the Loire region of France. A Gaudreau or Gotreau removed from Port-Royal, Acadia, to Quebec city in 1665; and another, from the Isle de Ré, to Île d'Orléans by 1671.
GIVEN NAMES French 15%. *Gilles* (3), *Marcel* (3), *Armand* (2), *Fernand* (2), *Michel* (2), *Adrien, Andre, Celine, Donat, Euclide, Gaetane, Germaine.*

Gaudreault (157) French: variant of GAUDREAU.
GIVEN NAMES French 25%. *Armand* (4), *Aime, Alain, Benoit, Fernand, Jean-Guy, Jean-Marie, Laurent, Marcel, Pascal, Pierre, Rodrigue.*

Gauer (401) German: **1.** from a derivative of Middle High German *gou* 'country', a topographic name for someone from the country, or (in the Rhine area) an occupational name for a squire, farmer, or local craftsman. **2.** habitational name, probably for someone from Gauern near Gera in Thuringia or possibly from Gauernitz on the Saale river.
GIVEN NAMES German 6%. *Otto* (3), *Klaus* (2), *Hermann, Manfred.*

Gauerke (144) German: from a pet form of a Germanized form of the Slavic personal name *Gabor, Gawor*.

Gauger (973) German: from Middle High German *gougern* 'to wander around or stagger', presumably a nickname for someone with a peculiar gait.

Gaugh (160) **1.** Irish: reduced form of McGAUGH. **2.** Perhaps also an Americanized spelling of German GACH or GAUCH.

Gaughan (1347) Irish: reduced Anglicized form of Gaelic **Ó Gaoithin** (see GAHAN).
GIVEN NAMES Irish 6%. *Eamon* (2), *Brendan.*

Gaughran (155) Irish: reduced Anglicized form of Gaelic **Mag Eachráin**, a patronymic from the personal name *Eachrán*, of uncertain origin, perhaps containing the element *each-* 'horse'. Compare GAHAN 1.

Gaugler (446) South German and Swiss German: occupational name for a jester or entertainer, Middle High German *goukelære, gougelære*.

Gaukel (106) South German: occupational name, and occasionally a nickname, for a traveling entertainer, from Middle High German *gaukeln* 'to perform magic', 'do tricks'.
GIVEN NAME German 4%. *Kurt.*

Gauker (102) German: variant of GAUKEL.

Gaul (1673) **1.** Scottish and Irish: variant of GALL 1. **2.** German: nickname for a un-

mannered person, from Middle Low German *gūl* 'horse', 'workhorse', 'stallion'.

Gauld (135) English: variant of GAULT.

Gaulden (309) See GAULDIN.

Gauldin (442) Origin uncertain: perhaps a variant of English GOLDEN.

Gaulding (193) Perhaps an altered spelling of the English surname GOULDING.

Gauley (116) Reduced form of Irish McGAULEY.

Gaulin (428) French: reduced form of the Germanic personal name *Gaudelin*.
FOREBEARS A bearer of this name from Perche is recorded in Quebec city in 1567.
GIVEN NAMES French 13%. *Pierre* (2), *Rodolphe* (2), *Adelard, Alcide, Aldege, Andre, Camille, Emile, Francois, Jean Pierre, Lucien, Rosaire.*

Gaulke (462) Eastern German: variant of GOHLKE.
GIVEN NAMES German 4%. *Kurt* (2), *Erwin, Otto.*

Gault (2483) **1.** English: nickname from the wild boar, Middle English *galte, gaute, gault* (Old Norse *gǫltr*). Wild boars were common in the British Isles from the earliest times, and became extinct only with the clearing of the large tracts of forest which formerly covered the country; hunting them was a favorite pastime in the Middle Ages. **2.** French: from Germanic *walþu-* 'wood', 'forest'; a topographic name for someone who lived in or near a wood, or a habitational name for someone from any of the places named with this word, for example Le Gault in Loir-et-Cher, Marne, and Eure-et-Loir.

Gaultney (227) English: habitational name from Gaultney in Rushton, Northamptonshire, probably so named from Old Norse *gǫltr* 'boar' + Old Danish *klint* 'steep cliff or bank' with the later addition of Middle English *heye* 'enclosure'. The surname is not found in the U.K. In the U.S., it is concentrated in GA. Compare GAUTNEY.

Gaumer (469) German: occupational name for an official moral censor, a supervisor, or overseer, Middle High German *goumer*.

Gaumond (223) French: of uncertain origin; probably from a Germanic personal name, *Walmund*, composed of the elements *wala* 'death in battle' + *mund* 'protection'. The second element was assimilated by folk etymology to *mont* 'hill'.
FOREBEARS A bearer of the name from the Paris region is recorded in Quebec city in 1671.
GIVEN NAMES French 11%. *Herve* (2), *Armand, Girard, Pierre.*

Gauna (336) Basque: habitational name from Gauna, a place in Araba province, Basque Country.
GIVEN NAMES Spanish 36%. *Jose* (5), *Jesus* (4), *Juan* (4), *Amada* (3), *Manuel* (3), *Ramon* (3), *Benito* (2), *Ercilia* (2), *Fernando* (2), *Guadalupe* (2), *Ricardo* (2),

Abelino; Eliseo (3), *Antonio* (2), *Lorenzo* (2), *Leonardo, Lucio, Sal.*

Gaunce (192) **1.** Scottish and Irish: Anglicized form of Gaelic **Mac Aonghuis** (see MCCANCE). **2.** Perhaps also an Americanized spelling of German GANZ.
GIVEN NAME Irish 5%. *Brennan* (2).

Gaunt (918) English: **1.** habitational name from Ghent in Flanders, from which many wool workers and other skilled craftsmen migrated to England in the early Middle Ages. The surname is found most commonly in West Yorkshire, around Leeds. The Flemish place name is first recorded in Latin documents as *Gandi* and *Gandavum*; it is apparently of Celtic origin, but of uncertain meaning. **2.** from a nickname from Middle English *gaunt* 'thin', 'wasted', 'haggard' (of uncertain, possibly Scandinavian, origin). **3.** variant of GANT.

Gauntlett (136) English: unexplained; perhaps a diminutive of GAUNT.

Gauntt (495) Apparently an altered spelling of GAUNT.

Gaus (534) German: **1.** from Middle Low German *gōs, gūs* 'goose' (or Bavarian and Alemannic *gaus*), a nickname for a foolish person or metonymic occupational name for a breeder of geese. **2.** from a short form of an old personal name formed with Old High German *gawi* 'fertile region', 'district'.
GIVEN NAMES German 4%. *Otto* (4), *Franz, Hans, Kurt.*

Gause (1428) Eastern German: **1.** of Old Prussian origin; unexplained. **2.** from Czech-Sorbian *hus* 'goose', probably applied as a metonymic occupational name for a goose farmer. **3.** possibly also a habitational name for someone from Gaussig near Bautzen.

Gausman (227) German (**Gausmann**): variant of **Gossmann** (see GOSSMAN).

Gauss (448) German: variant of GAUS.
GIVEN NAMES German 4%. *Eldred, Erwin, Kurt, Siegfried.*

Gaustad (252) Norwegian: habitational name from any of several farmsteads so named. The first element is from either of two personal names (*Gaute* or Old Norse *Guðrekr*, a compound of *guð* 'god' + *rekr* 'powerful'), or possibly a river name. The second element is Old Norse *staðr* 'farmstead'.

Gaut (452) English and French: variant of GAULT.

Gauthier (6407) French: from a Germanic personal name composed of the elements *wald* 'rule' + *hari, heri* 'army' (see WALTER). This name is also found in Switzerland and may have been brought to the U.S. from there.
GIVEN NAMES French 11%. *Armand* (15), *Pierre* (15), *Andre* (14), *Marcel* (10), *Gaston* (8), *Jacques* (8), *Michel* (8), *Francois* (7), *Emile* (6), *Fernand* (6), *Monique* (6), *Normand* (6).

Gauthreaux (351) Variant spelling (found in LA) of the French surname GAUDREAU.

Gautier (711) French: variant of GAUTHIER. In this spelling, the name has been established in both Italy (Turin) and Germany (Brunswick) since about 1700.
GIVEN NAMES French 6%; Spanish 4%. *Andre* (2), *Camille* (2), *Antoine, Francois, Marcel, Pascale, Philippe, Remy, Thierry; Jose* (5), *Jorge* (2), *Miguel* (2), *Adelina, Altagracia, Ana, Andres, Arnaldo, Artemio, Augusto, Carlos, Edilberto.*

Gautney (216) English: variant of GAULTNEY. The surname is not found in the U.K.; in the U.S., it is found chiefly in AL.

Gautreau (528) French: variant of GAUDREAU.
GIVEN NAMES French 6%. *Amedee* (2), *Ancil, Armand, Camille, Lucien, Marcel, Normand, Remi.*

Gautreaux (942) French: variant of GAUDREAU.
GIVEN NAMES French 7%. *Alcide* (2), *Antoine* (2), *Eulice* (2), *Leonce* (2), *Pierre* (2), *Andree, Camile, Camille, Francois, Gabrielle, Gillis, Laure.*

Gauvin (862) French: from the Old French personal name *Gauvin* (see GAVIN).
FOREBEARS A bearer of the name from La Rochelle is recorded in Quebec city in 1665.
GIVEN NAMES French 18%. *Emile* (3), *Jacques* (3), *Normand* (3), *Pierre* (3), *Armand* (2), *Gisele* (2), *Laurent* (2), *Lucien* (2), *Raynald* (2), *Yves* (2), *Adrien, Aime.*

Gauvreau (141) French: of uncertain origin; possibly from a pet form of the Old French personal name *Gauvin* (see GAVIN).
FOREBEARS A bearer of the name from Poitou is recorded in Quebec city in 1668.
GIVEN NAMES French 12%. *Emile* (2), *Andre, Gaston, Jacques.*

Gavaghan (125) Irish (Connacht): probably a reduced Anglicized form of Gaelic **Ó Gáibhtheacháin** 'descendant of *Gáibhtheachán*', a personal name derived from a derivative of the adjective *gáibhtheach* 'fierce', 'eager'.
GIVEN NAME Irish 9%. *Declan.*

Gavan (142) Irish: variant spelling of GAVIN.

Gavel (219) French (southwestern): metonymic occupational name for a harvester, from *javelle*, a term for a sheaf of grain which was loosely bound and left on the ground to ripen.

Gavenda (103) Czech (East Moravian): nickname for a chatterbox, from dialect *gavenda* 'talkative'.
GIVEN NAMES Czech and Slovak 4%. *Antonin, Blanka.*

Gaver (365) Possibly an altered spelling of German *Köber* (see KOBER) or *Göber* (see GOBER).

Gavett (107) **1.** English: variant of GAVITT. **2.** Alternatively, perhaps, French: variant of GAVETTE.

Gavette (138) French Canadian spelling of French **Gavet**, which is probably a habitational name from Gavet in Isère or alternatively a topographic name from Gascon *gavet* 'fast-flowing stream'.

Gavigan (441) Irish: **1.** probably a reduced Anglicized form of Gaelic **Ó Gáibhtheacháin** (see GAVAGHAN). **2.** (Ulster) reduced Anglicized form of Gaelic **Mag Eachagáin** 'son of *Eachagán*', a diminutive of the personal name *Eachaidh*, from *each* 'horse'. Compare GAHAN 1.

Gavin (4712) **1.** Irish: reduced Anglicized form of Gaelic **Ó Gábháin** or **Ó Gáibhín**, both of which Woulfe derives from diminutives of *gábhadh* 'want' or 'danger' (the second being the more likely meaning here). **2.** Scottish: reduced form of MCGAVIN, which is believed to be an Anglicized form of Gaelic **Mac Gobhann** 'son of the smith'. **3.** Scottish and northern English: from a personal name popular in the Middle Ages in the Middle English form *Gawayne* as well as the Old French *Gauvin*. The name was introduced from French versions of the Arthurian romances, where this name was borne by one of the knights of the Round Table, the brother of Galahad and Mordred and a nephew of Arthur. It is probably from an Old Welsh personal name composed of the elements *gwalch* 'hawk' + *gwyn* 'white', influenced in part by Breton forms. **4.** French and Swiss French: possibly a nickname for someone with a goiter or prominent Adam's apple, from a word meaning 'throat', 'crop'. **5.** In some cases possibly Castilianized form of Aragonese **Gabín**, a habitational name from Gabín, a place in Uesca province, Aragon.

Gavino (119) Italian and Spanish: from the personal name *Gavino*, equivalent of Celtic *Gawain* (Old French *Gauvain*), which was widely popularized through the Arthurian romances (see GAVIN).
GIVEN NAMES Spanish 39%; Italian 12%. *Jose* (3), *Conchita* (2), *Guadalupe* (2), *Luis* (2), *Alejandro, Bienvenido, Carlos; Antonio* (2), *Augusto, Candido, Carlo, Celestino, Elva, Eusebio, Fructuoso, Romeo.*

Gavinski (107) Polish (**Gawiński**): habitational name from from Gawin in Włocławek province.

Gaviria (187) Basque: Castilianized form of **Gabiria**, a habitational name from Gabiria in Gipuzkoa, Basque Country, so named from Basque *gabi* 'smith's hammer' + *-iri* 'near'.
GIVEN NAMES Spanish 53%. *Luis* (9), *Eduardo* (3), *Jose* (3), *Juan* (3), *Miguel* (3), *Andres* (2), *Carlos* (2), *Fernando* (2), *Francisco* (2), *Jairo* (2), *Jesus* (2), *Liliana* (2).

Gavitt (288) English: of uncertain origin. Perhaps an altered spelling of **Gabbett**, which is from a pet form of the personal name GABRIEL.

Gavlick (136) Variant spelling of German and possibly Polish **Gawlik**, a short form of the Polish personal name *Gaweł* (see GAWEL).

Gaw (634) **1.** Scottish and Irish: reduced form of MCGAW, which is an Anglicized form of Gaelic **Mag Ádhaimh** 'son of Adam'. **2.** German: variant (old) spelling of GAU.

Gawel (330) **1.** Polish (**Gaweł**): from a personal name (Latin *Gallus*) which was widespread in Europe during the Middle Ages (see GALL 2). **2.** German: from a pet form of a Germanic personal name formed with *gawi* 'country', 'fertile region'. Compare GAU.
GIVEN NAMES Polish 8%. *Janusz* (2), *Franciszek, Halina, Jolanta, Lucyna, Ludwik, Tadeusz, Wladyslaw, Zbigniew.*

Gawlak (129) Polish: from a patronymic form of the personal name *Gaweł* (see GALL 2).
GIVEN NAMES Polish 7%. *Andrzej, Janina, Tadeusz.*

Gawley (115) **1.** Irish and Scottish: reduced form of **McGauley**, a variant of MCCAULEY. **2.** probably an Americanized form of German **Golle**, a variant of GOHL 1.
GIVEN NAME German 4%. *Kurt.*

Gawlik (498) Polish: from a pet form of the personal name *Gaweł*, Latin *Gallus* (see GALL 2).
GIVEN NAMES Polish 5%. *Andrzej, Feliks, Janina, Pawel, Rafal, Tadeusz, Zygmunt.*

Gawne (207) English: variant of GAVIN.

Gawron (365) **1.** Polish: nickname from *gawron* 'rook'. **2.** German: habitational name of Slavic origin from a place so named near Breslau.
GIVEN NAMES Polish 13%. *Aleksander, Casimir, Franciszek, Grazyna, Jacek, Lech, Ludwik, Marcin, Miroslaw, Piotr, Stanislaw, Stanistaw.*

Gawronski (392) Polish (**Gawroński**): habitational name for someone from Gawrony, so named from Polish *gawron* 'rook'.
GIVEN NAMES Polish 8%. *Casimir* (2), *Zygmunt* (2), *Andrzej, Beata, Jacek, Jerzy, Leszek, Stanislaus, Zigmund.*

Gawrych (112) Polish: from a derivative of the personal name *Gawrzyjał*, a vernacular form of GABRIEL.
GIVEN NAMES Polish 9%. *Andrzej, Danuta, Jozef.*

Gawrys (151) Polish: from a derivative of the personal name *Gawrzyjał*, a vernacular form of GABRIEL.
GIVEN NAMES Polish 8%. *Agnieszka, Eugeniusz, Jozef, Mariusz, Wladyslaw.*

Gawthrop (192) English (Yorkshire): habitational name from any of several places in West Yorkshire called Gawthrop or Gaw-thorpe, all of which are named from Old Norse *gaukr* 'cuckoo' + *þorp* 'enclosure' (see THORPE).

Gaxiola (234) Mainly found in Mexico: unexplained.
GIVEN NAMES Spanish 45%. *Alvaro* (3), *Carlos* (3), *Gerardo* (3), *Ana* (2), *Armida* (2), *Efrain* (2), *Fernando* (2), *Jose* (2), *Luz* (2), *Manuel* (2), *Rafael* (2), *Sergio* (2); *Antonio, Cecilio, Fausto, Federico.*

Gay (11046) **1.** English and French: nickname for a lighthearted or cheerful person, from Middle English, Old French *gai*. In Middle English the term could also mean 'wanton', 'lascivious' and this sense may lie behind the surname in some instances. **2.** English (of Norman origin): habitational name from places in Normandy called Gaye, from an early proprietor bearing a Germanic personal name cognate with WADE. **3.** probably from the Catalan personal name *Gai* (Latin *Gaius*), or in some cases a nickname from Catalan *gay* 'cheerful'. **4.** Variant of German GAU. **5.** North German: from a Frisian personal name *Gay*.
FOREBEARS A Congregational clergyman and one of the forerunners of the Unitarian movement in New England, Ebenezer Gay (1696–1787) was born in Dedham, MA, which had been founded by his grandfather, John Gay, who came to America from Wiltshire, England, about 1630 and settled in Watertown, MA. Ebenezer's great-grandson Howard was editor of the *American Anti-Slavery Standard.*

Gayda (152) Polish: variant of GAJDA; also a German spelling of the same name.

Gayden (304) English: variant spelling of **Gaydon**, a habitational name from a place in Warwickshire, so named from an Old English personal name *Gǣga* + *dūn* 'hill'. Reaney suggests that the surname may also have derived from a personal name (recorded as *Gaidun*).

Gaydos (981) Americanized spelling of Hungarian GAJDOS.

Gaydosh (207) Americanized spelling of Hungarian GAJDOS.

Gaye (215) English: variant spelling of GAY.
GIVEN NAMES African 9%. *Amadou* (2), *Cheikh* (2), *Awa, Penda.*

Gayer (498) German: variant spelling of GAIER 1.

Gayhart (338) Variant of GAYHEART.

Gayheart (404) Of uncertain origin; possibly an Americanized (translated) form of French JOLICOEUR or an Americanized spelling of German GERHARDT.

Gayle (1703) English: variant spelling of GALE.

Gayler (284) **1.** Americanized spelling of GAILLARD. Compare GAYLORD. **2.** German: variant of **Geiler**, from a noun derivative of GEIL.

Gayles (246) **1.** English (northeast): probably a variant of GALE. **2.** Possibly also an Americanized spelling of German **Gölz** (see GOELZ).

Gaylor (1213) Americanized spelling of GAILLARD, associated in particular with the Huguenots.

Gaylord (2041) Americanized spelling of GAILLARD, associated in particular with the Huguenots.

Gayman (318) **1.** English: occupational name meaning 'servant of GAY'. **2.** French: from a Germanic personal name *Gaidman* or *Gaidmar*, of which the first element is *gaida* 'point (of a lance)'. **3.** German (**Gaymann**): variant of GAU 1, reinforced by the addition of *man* 'man'. **4.** Americanized spelling of German **Gehmann** (see GEHMAN).

Gaymon (202) **1.** French: from pet form of *Gaimo*, a short form of a Germanic personal name formed with *gaid* 'point (of a spear)' + a second element beginning with *m-* (for examples, see GAYMAN). **2.** Probably an Americanized spelling of German **Gehmann** (see GEHMAN). This name is concentrated in SC.

Gaynes (137) English: variant spelling of GAINES.

Gaynor (2222) **1.** Irish: reduced Anglicized form of Gaelic **Mag Fhionnbhairr** 'son of *Fionnbharr*', a personal name composed of *fionn* 'fair', 'white' + *barr* 'top', 'head'. **2.** Welsh and English: from the female personal name *Gaenor* (a form of Welsh *Gwenhwyfar*, a compound of *gwen* 'fair', 'white' + (g)*wyf* 'smooth', 'yielding' + *fawr* 'large'. This was the name of King Arthur's queen *Guinevere*).

Gaytan (897) Spanish (**Gaytán**): probably variant of Spanish GAITAN.
GIVEN NAMES Spanish 56%. *Jose* (23), *Juan* (18), *Jesus* (17), *Manuel* (13), *Francisco* (10), *Ricardo* (9), *Raul* (8), *Carlos* (7), *Felipe* (7), *Roberto* (7), *Sergio* (7), *Arturo* (6).

Gayton (616) **1.** English: habitational name from any of several places in Merseyside, Norfolk, Northamptonshire, and Staffordshire called Gayton, or from Gayton le Marsh or Gayton le Wold in Lincolnshire. The Northamptonshire and Staffordshire place names are from an Old English personal name *Gǣga* + *tūn* 'farmstead'; the others are from Old Norse *geit* 'goat' + *tún* 'farmstead'. **2.** French: diminutive of **Gayte**, a southern variant of *guette* 'watch', and hence an occupational name for a watchman.
GIVEN NAMES Spanish 5%. *Rafael* (3), *Cesar* (2), *Alfredo, Ana, Apolonio, Ezequiel, Fernando, Francisco, Gregorio, Gustabo, Jesus, Jose.*

Gaza (115) Origin unidentified.
GIVEN NAMES Spanish 5%. *Ruben* (2), *Luisito, Rey, Vicenta.*

Gazaway (529) See GASAWAY. This name is common in GA.

Gazda (452) **1.** Polish, Slovak, and Czech (Moravian): occupational name from the vocabulary word *gazda* 'highland farmer', 'uplander'. **2.** Hungarian: status name from the vocabulary word *gazda* 'farmer', in particular a relatively well-off small-holder. The word is of Slavic origin, as in 1 above, but the meaning in Hungarian is different.
GIVEN NAMES Polish 4%. *Andrzej, Irena, Malgorzata, Wojciech, Zbigniew.*

Gazdik (174) Polish (**Gaździk**): from a pet form of GAZDA 'uplander'.

Gazzara (137) Italian (mainly Sicily): possibly from a nickname based on Arabic *ghazārah* 'commotion', 'turmoil'.
GIVEN NAMES Italian 15%. *Carmela, Gaetano, Guido, Sebastiano.*

Gazzo (122) Italian: of uncertain etymology. It is probably from medieval Greek *Gatsos*, a pet form of *Georgatsos*, a derivative of *Geōrgios* (see GEORGE). However, Caracausi proposes that it is a nickname from Sicilian *gazzu* 'blue-eyed' (also 'short-sighted'), or from Old Italian *gazzo* 'deep blue' (like the feathers of a magpie, Italian *gazza*). It could also be a habitational name from Gazzo in Padova province, Gazzo Veronese in Verona province, or from a reduced form of *Agazzo*, from Late Latin *Agathius*, either a masculine form of *Agata* or from the analogous Germanic personal name *Agathio*.
GIVEN NAMES Italian 15%. *Angelo* (4), *Almando, Attilio, Julio, Salvatore.*

Gazzola (200) Italian: **1.** nickname for someone considered to resemble a magpie in some way: possibly a person known for chattering or pilfering, from a diminutive of *gazza* 'magpie'. **2.** habitational name from Gazzola, a place in Piacenza province.
GIVEN NAMES Italian 26%. *Angelo* (3), *Orlando* (2), *Cesare, Emilio, Ernesto, Fermino, Giorgio, Guillermo, Philomena, Reno.*

Gbur (155) Southern German and Austrian: status or occupational name for a farmer, a variant of GEBAUER.
GIVEN NAMES Slavic 4%. *Halina, Jozefa.*

Ge (189) **1.** Chinese 葛: in ancient China there existed a clan called Ge, whose descendants came to use Ge as their surname. Another source of the name is from an area named Ge during the Xia dynasty (2205–1766 BC) in present-day Henan province. The descendants of the rulers of Ge eventually adopted the place name as their surname. **2.** Chinese 戈: from the ancient state of Ge that was granted to a descendant of the model emperor Yu (2205–2198 BC). Later descendants adopted the place name as their surname. **3.** French (**Gé**): variant of **Gée**.

GIVEN NAMES Chinese 61%. *Jian* (4), *Ping* (3), *Haiping* (2), *Huilan* (2), *Ling* (2), *Ming* (2), *Pei* (2), *Qiong* (2), *Song* (2), *Wen* (2), *Xun* (2), *Yan* (2).

Geagan (125) Irish: variant of GEOGHEGAN.

Gean (293) **1.** Most probably a reduced Anglicized form of Irish **Ó Géibhinn**, itself a reduced form of **Ó Géibheannaigh**, from *géibheannach* 'fettered'. **2.** Alternatively, it could be an Americanized spelling of German **Gien**, which is from a short form of HEINRICH.

Gear (726) **1.** English: nickname from Middle English *gere* 'fit of passion' (see GEARY 3). **2.** German: possibly an altered spelling of GIER.

Gearhart (2906) Americanized spelling of German **Gierhard**, a variant of GERHARDT.

Gearheart (347) Americanized spelling of German **Gierhard**. Compare GEARHART.

Gearin (284) Origin uncertain. Perhaps a variant of GEARING.

Gearing (413) **1.** English: patronymic from a Germanic personal name beginning with the element *gēr, gār* 'spear' (see GEARY 2). **2.** Probably an Americanized spelling of German GEHRING.

Gears (108) English: variant of GEAR.

Gearty (113) Irish: reduced form of GERAGHTY.
GIVEN NAME Irish 6%. *Brendan.*

Geary (4733) **1.** Irish: reduced Anglicized form of Gaelic **Ó Gadhra** 'descendant of Gadhra' (see O'GARA). See also McGEARY. **2.** English: from a personal name derived from Germanic *gēr, gār* 'spear', a short form of any of various compound names with this as a first element (see, for example GARRETT). **3.** English: nickname for a wayward or capricious person, from Middle English *ge(a)ry* 'fickle', 'changeable', 'passionate' (a derivative of *gere* 'fit of passion', apparently a Scandinavian borrowing). **4.** Possibly an altered spelling of German GEHRING or GEHRIG.
FOREBEARS Most present-day Irish bearers of the name Geary and its variants and derivatives are descended from a single 10th-century ancestor, a nephew of Eadhra, who founded the family O'HARA in Connacht. The family is now spread more widely.

Geathers (147) Probably a variant of German GATHERS or English GAITHER.

Gebauer (507) German, Austrian: status name for a landowner, from Middle High German *gebūre* 'neighboring farmer'.
GIVEN NAMES German 9%. *Gerhard* (3), *Jutta* (2), *Bodo, Dieter, Gerda, Horst, Johann, Kurt, Lothar, Manfred, Otto.*

Gebben (109) Dutch and German: probably a patronymic of the Frisian short form **Gebbe** of the personal name **Gebbert**, a variant of GEBHARDT.

Gebbia (227) Southern Italian: topographic name from Sicilian *gebbia* 'irrigation cistern', from Arabic *ğabiyah*, or a habitation-

al name from any of various places named with this word.
GIVEN NAMES Italian 12%; French 4%. *Salvatore* (4), *Carmela; Armand, Monique.*

Gebbie (164) Scottish: from a pet form of the Norman personal name *Giselbert* (see GILBERT).

Gebel (276) German: variant of **Gäbel** (see GAEBEL).
GIVEN NAMES German 6%. *Ewald, Franz, Kurt, Markus, Mathias.*

Gebers (115) German: patronymic from a variant of GEBHARDT.
GIVEN NAMES German 4%. *Erwin, Wilhelm.*

Gebert (665) German: variant of GEBHARDT.
GIVEN NAMES German 5%. *Kurt* (3), *Annelies, Franz, Fritz, Horst, Ulrich, Wolfgang.*

Gebhard (790) German: variant of GEBHARDT.
GIVEN NAMES German 5%. *Fritz* (2), *Hans* (2), *Arno, Dieter, Heinrich, Ilse, Kurt, Manfred.*

Gebhardt (2156) German: from a Germanic personal name composed of the elements *geb* 'gift' + *hard* 'hardy', 'brave', 'strong'. A saint of this name was bishop of Constance around the end of the 10th century, and his popularity may have had an influence on the continued use of the personal name into the Middle Ages.
GIVEN NAMES German 5%. *Otto* (7), *Hans* (3), *Klaus* (2), *Arno, Bernd, Dieter, Elke, Ernst, Erwin, Georg, Gottlieb, Hildegarde.*

Gebhart (1349) German: variant spelling of GEBHARDT.

Gebler (146) German: variant of GABLER.
GIVEN NAMES French 5%; German 4%. *Armand; Kurt.*

Gebo (386) Respelling of French **Gibault**, from a Germanic personal name composed of the elements *geb-* 'gift' + *wald* 'rule'.
FOREBEARS A family of this name from Poitou was in Quebec city by 1662.

Geck (230) **1.** North German: nickname from Middle Low German *geck* 'fool'. **2.** German: from a short form of JACOB.

Geckle (122) German: from a pet form of GECK 2.

Geckler (114) German: nickname from an agent derivative of Middle High German *gecke* 'fool'.
GIVEN NAMES German 11%. *Dieter, Ernst, Kurt, Otto.*

Geddes (1485) Scottish and northern Irish: there is a place of this name in Nairn, but the name is more likely to be a patronymic from GEDDIE.

Geddie (315) Scottish and northern Irish: of uncertain origin. It may be a much altered form of McADAM. Compare KEDDIE. If this is correct, the initial *G-* represents a trace of Gaelic *mac* 'son (of)', while *Eddie* is variant of *Addie*, a pet form of ADAM. It could alternatively be a nickname meaning 'greedy', from a diminutive of the Scottish dialect word *gedd* 'pike', also attested in metaphorical application to a person who was a voracious eater.

Geddings (429) Welsh: variant of GITTINGS.

Geddis (362) Northern Irish: variant spelling of GEDDES.

Gedeon (422) French (**Gédéon**) and Hungarian: from the French, Hungarian, or some other form of the personal name GIDEON.

GIVEN NAMES French 12%. *Gedeon* (2), *Henri* (2), *Andre, Andree, Antoine, Cecile, Francois, Jean-Robert, Marcel, Marie Carmel, Odette, Rodrigue.*

Gedman (102) **1.** English: unexplained. **2.** Swedish: unexplained.

Gedney (314) English: habitational name from a place in Lincolnshire, probably so named from an Old English personal name *Gǣda* or *Gydda* (genitive *-n*) + *ēg* 'island'.

GIVEN NAME French 4%. *Laurette.*

Gee (7397) **1.** Irish and Scottish: reduced form of MCGEE, Anglicized form of Gaelic **Mac Aodha** 'son of *Aodh*' (see MCCOY). **2.** English: this is a common name in northern England, of uncertain origin. The existence of a patronymic form **Geeson** points to a personal name, but this has not been satisfactorily identified. It may in fact be the Irish or Scottish name in an English context. **3.** French (**Gée**): habitational name from any of several places called Gé or Gée, for example in Maine-et-Loire, derived from the Gallo-Roman domain name *Gaiacum.*

Geelan (131) Irish (County Galway): reduced Anglicized form of Gaelic **Ó Gialláin**, which MacLysaght suggests may be derived from a diminutive of *giall* 'hostage'.

GIVEN NAMES Irish 6%. *Brendan, Niall.*

Geels (110) **1.** Dutch: perhaps a patronymic from the Germanic personal name *Gailo*; otherwise, a variant of GILLIS. **2.** English and Scottish: possibly, as Black proposes, a variant of GILES.

Geen (126) **1.** Cornish: unexplained. **2.** Dutch and North German: from a short form of a derivative of the Germanic personal name *Gerard.*

Geenen (133) Dutch and Belgian: reduced form of **Van Geenen**, which is probably a habitational name from Gene near Vreren, in Limburg, Belgium.

Geer (3268) **1.** English: variant of GEARY 3. **2.** North German: from a personal name derived from *gēr, gār* 'spear' (see GEARY 2). **3.** Dutch: reduced form of **van den Geer**, a topographic name from *geer* 'headland'.

Geerdes (257) North German: variant of GERDES.

Geers (441) Dutch: patronymic from a short form of any of various personal names formed with the Germanic element *gār, gēr* 'spear', 'lance', for example GERHARDT.

Geerts (205) Dutch: variant of GEERS.

GIVEN NAME German 4%. *Dieter.*

Geery (116) Irish: variant spelling of GEARY.

Geesaman (228) Americanized spelling of North German **Gesemann**, a variant of GIESE.

Geese (101) German: variant spelling of GIESE.

Geesey (361) Americanized spelling of German GEESE or GIESE.

Geeslin (309) Probably an altered spelling of German **Giessling** (a variant of GIESEL), or of KIESLING.

Geeter (107) Origin unidentified.

Geeting (165) Probably respelling of German **Gütig**, from a short form of a name formed with Slavic *god* 'beauty', or of German **Gütting**, from a Germanic personal name formed with Old High German *got* 'god' or *guot* 'good'.

Geffen (196) **1.** Jewish (Israeli): ornamental name from Hebrew *gefen* 'vine', a Hebraicization usually of the various Ashkenazic surnames from German WEIN. **2.** North German: from a Germanic personal name formed with *geba* 'gift', for example GEBHARDT.

GIVEN NAMES Jewish 10%. *Haim, Moshe, Zev.*

Geffert (241) North German: from a Low German form of GEBHARDT.

Geffner (160) **1.** German: perhaps from a short form of GEBHARDT, or a habitational name for someone from Geffern on the Rhine near Baden-Baden. **2.** Jewish (Ashkenazic): unexplained.

GIVEN NAMES Jewish 13%. *Avi* (3), *Sol* (2), *Hyman.*

Geffre (237) Variant of French of GEOFFROY (see JEFFREY).

Gefroh (125) German: unexplained. This is one of the German names that became established in Odessa, Ukraine, in the 19th century.

Gegenheimer (167) German: topographic name for someone whose home is across the way, from *gegen* 'against', 'across' + *heim* 'home' + *-er* suffix denoting an inhabitant.

Gegg (185) South German: variant of GECK.

Gegner (104) German: topographic name for someone who lived 'across the way', but also a nickname for a hostile person, from Middle Low German *gegenēre* 'enemy'.

Gehl (554) German: **1.** from the short form of an old personal name formed with Middle High German *geil* 'voluptuous', 'mischievous', 'rich'. **2.** from an Old Frisian personal name formed with a cognate of Old High German *modal* 'ancestral estate', 'home country'. **3.** nickname for someone with blond hair or a pale complexion, from Middle Low German,

Middle High German *gel* 'yellow', 'blond'. **4.** in eastern Germany, from a much altered short form of the personal name DANIEL.

Gehlbach (163) German: habitational name from an unidentified place, named with a compound of *Gehl* 'wet lowland' + *Bach* 'stream'.

Gehle (212) German: variant of GEHL.

GIVEN NAMES German 5%. *Erhard, Helmut, Otto.*

Gehlen (113) German and French (Alsace): in the northwest from a topographic name denoting wet, low-lying ground.

GIVEN NAMES French 7%. *Elzear, Pierre.*

Gehler (118) German: reduced form of **Gelhaar**, a nickname for someone with fair hair, from Middle High German *gel* 'yellow' + *har* 'hair'.

GIVEN NAME German 7%. *Niklaus.*

Gehlert (116) German: variant of GEHLER.

GIVEN NAMES German 6%. *Ernst, Klaus.*

Gehlhausen (209) German: probably a habitational name, from a place or farm named with *Gehl* 'wet lowland' + *-hausen* 'at the houses'.

GIVEN NAMES German 4%. *Kurt, Otto.*

Gehling (255) German: habitational name from a place near Hagen, Westphalia.

Gehm (311) German: **1.** perhaps a habitational name for someone from Gehmen in Saxony or from any of several places named Gemen. **2.** from a short form of a personal name formed with Old High German *gam(an)* 'joy', 'play', 'fun'. **3.** from a short form of the medieval personal name *Gemianus.*

GIVEN NAMES German 5%. *Ewald* (2), *Hans, Helmut, Otto.*

Gehman (865) Swiss German (**Gehmann**): probably a variant of GEHM 2.

FOREBEARS Two brothers called Geeman landed in Philadelphia in 1732.

Geho (166) Origin uncertain; probably an American form of French GUILLOT.

Gehr (414) German: from a short form of the various personal names formed with *gār, gēr* 'spear', 'lance' (see, for example, GERHARDT, GERHOLD), or from a field name, from the same word used to denote a wedge-shaped plot.

Gehres (218) German: variant of GEHRING. Compare GEHRIS.

GIVEN NAMES German 4%. *Rainer* (2), *Erwin.*

Gehret (277) German and Swiss German: from a reduced form of the personal name *Gerhard* (see GERHARDT) or possibly *Gerold* (see GERHOLD).

Gehrig (456) German and Swiss German: variant of GEHRING.

GIVEN NAMES German 6%. *Otto* (2), *Bernhard, Franz, Gerhard, Hanspeter, Klaus, Lothar, Manfred.*

Gehring (2068) German and Swiss German: from a medieval personal name, a short form of *Gerhard* or a similar name, formed with the first element *gēr, gār* 'spear' + the patronymic suffix *-ing*.

Gehringer (560) German: **1.** patronymic from the personal name *Gerung, Gering*, variants of GEHRING. **2.** habitational name from any of various places named Gehring, in particular in Bavaria, or from a place in Rhineland named Gering.

Gehris (208) German: Eastphalian variant of GEHRING.

Gehrke (1810) North German: from a pet form of GEHR.
GIVEN NAMES German 4%. *Gerhard* (3), *Hans* (3), *Otto* (3), *Erwin* (2), *Inge* (2), *Fritz, Guenter, Gunter, Helmuth, Johannes, Kurt, Leonhard.*

Gehrman (254) Americanized spelling of GEHRMANN.

Gehrmann (171) North German: variant of GEHR.
GIVEN NAMES German 8%; Scandinavian 4%. *Alfons, Bernhard, Franz, Hans.*

Gehrs (123) North German: patronymic from GEHR.

Gehrt (244) German: reduced form of GERHARDT.

Geib (1112) German: from an old word for 'dirt', 'grime', presumably applied as a derogatory nickname.

Geibel (383) German: from a personal name or topographic name formed with Old High German *gāwi* 'fertile region', 'countryside' (as opposed to a town).
GIVEN NAMES German 4%. *Fritz, Kurt.*

Geidel (177) South German: **1.** nickname from Middle High German *giudel* 'braggart' or 'squanderer'. **2.** variant of KEIDEL.
GIVEN NAME German 5%. *Gerhard* (2).

Geier (1724) **1.** German: see GEYER. **2.** Jewish (Ashkenazic): occupational name from Yiddish *geyer* 'peddler' (a derivative of *geyn* 'to go') or in some cases perhaps an unflattering name from German *Geier* 'vulture', as in 1, bestowed by non-Jewish government officials in central Europe at the time when surnames became compulsory.
GIVEN NAMES German 4%. *Horst* (4), *Otto* (3), *Hans* (2), *Kurt* (2), *Florian, Franz, Frieda, Helmut, Markus, Siegfried, Winfried.*

Geiger (8738) South German and Jewish (Ashkenazic): occupational name for a violin player or maker, Middle High German *gīger* (an agent derivative of *gīge* 'violin'), German *Geiger*.

Geigle (199) South German (Swabian): metonymic occupational name for a violinist, from Middle High German *gīge* 'violin' + the South German diminutive suffix *-ele*.
GIVEN NAMES German 5%. *Armin, Erwin, Otto.*

Geiken (153) North German: probably a patronymic from the Frisian personal name *Geick, Geike*.
GIVEN NAMES German 5%. *Frieda, Gerhard, Matthias.*

Geil (456) German: nickname from Middle High German *geil* 'mischievous', 'boisterous', 'happy'.

Geiler (176) South German: **1.** nickname for a boisterous or mischievous man, from a noun derivative of GEIL. **2.** from Middle High German *gīlære, gīler* 'beggar', 'vagrant'.

Geiling (127) German: from Middle Low German *geilink* 'thrush', hence possibly a nickname for someone with a fine singing voice or for someone who kept or caught songbirds.
GIVEN NAMES German 7%. *Fritz, Hermann.*

Geiman (304) German (**Geimann**): topographic name for someone who lived in open countryside, as opposed to a city dweller, from Middle High German *gouw, göu* 'fertile country', 'open country'.

Geimer (245) German: possibly from a personal name formed with *Gini-* (as in *Gimmo*) + *her(i)* 'army' or alternatively a dialect variant of GAUMER.

Geis (1440) German: **1.** from the personal name *Giso*, a short form of any of the various personal names with the initial element *Gis-* such as *Giselbrecht, Giselher*. **2.** probably a respelling of GEISS, GIES, GIESE.

Geise (679) German: variant of GEIS 1.

Geisel (533) German: from a short form of a personal name formed with *Gisel-* (see GIESEL).

Geiselman (221) German: from an extended form of GEISEL.

Geisen (267) German: patronymic from *Giso* (see GEIS).
GIVEN NAMES German 4%. *Kurt* (2), *Karlheinz.*

Geiser (1504) German and Swiss German: occupational name for a goatherd, from a derivative of Middle High German *geiz* 'goat'.

Geisert (218) **1.** German and Swiss German: variant of GEISER. **2.** German: from a reduced form of the personal name **Geishard**, from Old High German *gīsil* 'scion' + *hard* 'hardy', 'bold', 'brave'.
GIVEN NAMES German 6%. *Eldor, Kurt, Otto, Reinhard.*

Geisinger (426) German and Swiss German: habitational name for someone from Geisingen in southwestern Germany or Geising, south of Dresden.
GIVEN NAME German 4%. *Kurt* (3).

Geisler (2496) **1.** German (Bavaria and Austria) from the personal name *Giselher* (see GIESELER). **2.** altered spelling of Swiss **Geissler**, an occupational name for a goatherd, from an agent derivative of from Middle High German *geiz* 'goat'.

Geiss (525) German: **1.** variant of GEIS. **2.** (southern) metonymic occupational name for a goatherd, from Middle High German *geiz* 'goat'.

GIVEN NAMES German 5%. *Christoph, Gunther, Hans, Heinz, Juergen, Kurt, Otto, Reinhold.*

Geisser (119) German: variant spelling of GEISER.

Geissinger (218) German: variant spelling of GEISINGER.

Geissler (871) German: variant spelling of GEISLER.
GIVEN NAMES German 7%. *Otto* (4), *Christoph, Dieter, Ernst, Franz, Heinz, Helmut, Kurt, Markus, Rudi, Ulrich.*

Geist (2326) **1.** German: metonymic occupational name for a goatherd or nickname for a stubborn person, from Middle High German *geiz* 'goat'. **2.** German: habitational name for someone who lived in a house marked with the sign of the Holy Spirit (normally depicted as a dove), from Middle High German *geist* 'spirit'. Both *Geist* and *Heilgeist* occur as house signs in Frankfurt am Main in the mid–14th century. **3.** North German: topographic name for someone who lived in an area of barren sandy soil, Middle Low German *gēst*.

Geister (201) German (Silesia): occupational name for a goatherd, from an agent derivative of GEIST 1.

Geisz (125) German: unexplained.
GIVEN NAMES German 11%. *Franz, Gerhard, Johann, Nikolaus, Otto.*

Geiszler (173) Apparently a variant spelling of German GEISLER.
GIVEN NAMES German 4%. *Alois* (3), *Gottlieb.*

Geitner (175) German: **1.** nickname from an agent derivative of Middle High German *giuden* 'to boast or show off'. **2.** habitational name for someone from Geithain (earlier *Geiden, Geidten*) in Saxony.
GIVEN NAME French 4%. *Jacques.*

Geitz (149) German: unexplained.
GIVEN NAME German 4%. *Lorenz.*

Gekas (109) Greek: ethnic name for someone from northern Albania, from Albanian *Gegë* 'Geg'.
GIVEN NAMES Greek 14%. *Constantine* (3), *Ilias, Kostas, Speros, Xenofon.*

Gelardi (205) Italian: variant of GILARDI.
GIVEN NAMES Italian 18%. *Stefano* (2), *Angelo, Carlo, Carmela, Carmelina, Carmelo, Domenica, Francesca, Gasper, Giacomo, Nino, Pasquale.*

Gelatt (106) Origin unidentified.

Gelb (780) Jewish (Ashkenazic): nickname for a man with red hair (see GELL).
GIVEN NAMES Jewish 7%. *Avner* (2), *Emanuel* (2), *Chana, Lipot, Mandel, Miriam, Pinchas, Sol, Surie, Yanky, Yehoshua, Yehuda.*

Gelbard (107) Jewish (Ashkenazic): nickname from German *gelb* 'yellow' + *Bart* 'beard'.
GIVEN NAMES Jewish 6%. *Ephraim, Hyman.*

Gelber (562) Jewish (Ashkenazic): inflected form of GELB.
GIVEN NAMES Jewish 7%. *Sol* (3), *Herschel* (2), *Gershon, Hyman, Itshak.*

Gelder (217) **1.** English (Yorkshire): occupational name for a person responsible for looking after oxen and castrated horses, from Middle English *geld* 'sterile', 'barren (animal)' (Old Norse *geldr*) + *herde* 'herdsman', Old English *hierde* (see HEARD). **2.** Dutch: habitational name from the Dutch province of Gelderland or from Geldern in northwestern Germany (see GELLER 1).

Gelfand (746) Jewish (from Belarus and Ukraine): ornamental name from Yiddish *helfand* 'elephant' (see OLIPHANT); the change from *h* to *g* is due to the influence of Russian, which has no *h*.
GIVEN NAMES Jewish 14%; Russian 10%. *Yakov* (6), *Hyman* (3), *Marat* (2), *Meyer* (2), *Mikhael* (2), *Sol* (2), *Avrohom, Chana, Chaya, Emanuel, Fira, Genya; Leonid* (6), *Vladimir* (5), *Boris* (4), *Mikhail* (4), *Galina* (3), *Yefim* (3), *Gennadiy* (2), *Yelizaveta* (2), *Anatoliy, Anatoly, Fanya, Grigoriy.*

Gelfman (107) Jewish (eastern Ashkenazic): variant of HELFMAN under Russian influence. Russian has no *h* and alters *h* to *g* in borrowed words.
GIVEN NAMES Jewish 16%; Russian 4%. *Hyman* (3), *Avrom, Meyer, Rakhil, Rina; Leonid, Yury.*

Gelfond (126) Jewish (from Belarus and Ukraine): variant of GELFAND.
GIVEN NAMES Jewish 10%; Russian 6%; Scandinavian 4%; Scottish 4%. *Noam* (2), *Anchel, Semen; Arkadi, Boris, Lev; Alf.*

Gelhar (140) German: nickname for a fair-haired person, from Middle High German *gël* 'yellow' + *hār* 'hair'.

Gelhaus (137) German: probably a habitational name from a farm or house named with *gel* 'swamp', 'mire', a frequent component of field and place names in northwestern Germany.
GIVEN NAME German 4%. *Jochen.*

Gelin (161) **1.** French: possibly a back formation from Old French *geline* 'hen'. **2.** Jewish (from Belarus and Ukraine): variant of GELLES.
GIVEN NAMES French 21%; German 7%; Jewish 5%. *Gabrielle, Jacques, Jean Robert, Pierre, Rodolphe, Sauveur, Serge, Stephane, Yves, Yvon; Fritz, Hans, Hermann; Moisey, Naum.*

Gelinas (1036) French (**Gélinas**): possibly from an augmentative of Old French *gelin* or *geline* 'hen'. It is often found in Canada with LACOURSE as a secondary surname.
FOREBEARS A bearer of the name from Saintonge was in Quebec city by 1666.
GIVEN NAMES French 15%. *Andre* (6), *Marcel* (5), *Armand* (3), *Emile* (3), *Jean-Guy* (3), *Alain* (2), *Fernand* (2), *Jacques* (2), *Michel* (2), *Pierre* (2), *Rosaire* (2), *Aime.*

Gelineau (268) Western French: from a diminutive of GELIN.
GIVEN NAMES French 11%. *Armand* (2), *Marcel* (2), *Germaine, Ghislaine, Jean-Paul, Leodore, Lucien, Napoleon.*

Gell (257) **1.** Jewish (eastern Ashkenazic): nickname for a man with red hair, from Yiddish *gel* 'red-headed', Middle High German *gel* 'yellow', German *gelb* (see GELLER). **2.** German: unexplained. **3.** English: from a short form of the personal name JULIAN. **4.** Variant of French GILLE.

Gellatly (183) English: variant of GOLIGHTLY.

Geller (3053) **1.** North German: habitational name from the North German town of Geldern or from the Dutch province of Gelderland, earlier *Geler* and *Gelre*. Both places get their names from what may be an ancient element descriptive of marshland. **2.** German: occupational name for a town crier, Middle High German *gellære* (from *gellen* 'to shout or yell'). **3.** Jewish (Ashkenazic): nickname for a man with red hair, from the strong form of Yiddish *gel* 'red-headed' (Middle High German *gel* 'yellow'). There has been considerable confusion with German *gelb* 'yellow', since the meaning change from 'yellow' to 'red' took place only in Yiddish and only with reference to people's complexion or hair coloring. **4.** Jewish (eastern Ashkenazic): variant of HELLER 3, originating under Russian influence, since Russian has no *h* and alters *h* in borrowed words to *g*. **5.** German: variant of GEHLER. **6.** Hungarian: variant of **Gellért** (see GELLERT).
GIVEN NAMES Jewish 7%. *Hyman* (3), *Miriam* (3), *Moishe* (3), *Moysey* (3), *Sholom* (3), *Ari* (2), *Avrum* (2), *Chaim* (2), *Eliyahu* (2), *Esfir* (2), *Ilya* (2), *Rina* (2).

Gellerman (202) Jewish (eastern Ashkenazic): variant of GELLER 3 or 4.
GIVEN NAMES Jewish 5%. *Aron, Hersh.*

Gellert (330) **1.** German: variant of GELLER 2. **2.** German: from the Germanic personal name *Gelhard*, a cognate of the verb *gelten* 'to sacrifice', 'to recompense'. **3.** Hungarian (**Gellért**): from a personal name composed of the Germanic elements *gār, gēr* 'spear', 'lance' + *hard* 'hardy', 'brave', 'strong'.
GIVEN NAMES German 6%. *Dieter, Heinz, Klaus, Reinhard.*

Gelles (247) German and Jewish (eastern Ashkenazic): metronymic from the female personal name *Gele.*
GIVEN NAMES German 5%. *Heinz* (2), *Erna, Kurt.*

Gelling (104) English: unexplained; most probably a derivative of an unidentified Old English personal name.

Gellings (111) English: variant of GELLING.

Gellis (181) Jewish (eastern Ashkenazic): variant of GELLES.

Gellman (459) **1.** Jewish (Ashkenazic): variant of GELLER 3. **2.** German (**Gellmann**): perhaps a habitational name for someone from any of various places named Gellen in Oldenburg, Brandenburg, and East Prussia.

GIVEN NAMES Jewish 6%. *Emanuel* (2), *Mort* (2), *Ari, Hyman, Sima, Sol, Toba.*

Gellner (229) German: occupational name for someone who worked with gold, a refiner, jeweler, or gilder, from an agent derivative of Middle High German *golt* 'gold'.
GIVEN NAMES German 9%. *Kurt* (3), *Otto* (2), *Bernhard, Uwe.*

Gelman (951) Jewish (Ashkenazic): variant of GELLER 3.
GIVEN NAMES Jewish 14%; Russian 9%. *Ilya* (3), *Meyer* (3), *Genya* (2), *Hyman* (2), *Rina* (2), *Sol* (2), *Yakov* (2), *Aba, Arieh, Aron, Avram, Chaim; Boris* (4), *Mikhail* (4), *Yefim* (4), *Igor* (3), *Iosif* (3), *Lev* (3), *Aleksandr* (2), *Inessa* (2), *Anatoly, Arkagy, Efim, Etel.*

Gelnett (111) German: unexplained. Possibly an alteration of **Gennet**, a German adaptation of French GENET, according to Gottschald, or of German GERNERT.

Gelo (143) Italian: **1.** possibly from a short form of the personal name ANGELO. **2.** from *gelo* 'frost', possibly applied to someone with a frosty temperament or as a topographic name for someone who lived in a place prone to frost. **3.** Croatian: unexplained.
GIVEN NAMES Italian 12%; South Slavic 4%. *Salvatore* (3), *Calogero, Settimio, Vincenzo; Anto, Ruza.*

Gelpi (182) Catalan (**Gelpí**): unexplained.
GIVEN NAMES Spanish 14%; French 10%. *Juan* (3), *Jose* (2), *Rafael* (2), *Raul* (2), *Aurea, Candelaria, Isidoro, Mercedes, Orlando, Ricardo; Marcel* (2), *Pierre* (2), *Andre, Andree.*

Gelsinger (185) German: of uncertain origin. Probably a topographic or habitational name composed with *Gelsing-*, the root of the place name Gelsenkirchen.

Gelsomino (124) Italian: from the personal name *Gelsomino* (from *gelsomino* 'jasmine'), or in some cases possibly a topographic name with the same meaning.
GIVEN NAMES Italian 24%. *Rocco* (2), *Angelo, Carmine, Guido, Nino, Nunzio, Salvatore, Vincenzo, Vito.*

Gelston (153) English: habitational name from a place so named in Lincolnshire. The place name, recorded in the Domesday book as *Cheuelestune*, is probably from an Old Norse personal name *Gjǫfull* + Old English *tūn* 'farmstead', 'village'.

Geltz (188) German: from Middle High German *gelze* 'castrated hog', presumably a metonymic occupational name or perhaps an unflattering nickname.

Gelvin (172) Probably a variant of Irish GALVIN.

Gelwicks (121) Origin unidentified.

Gemar (128) German: from Middle High German *gemare* 'someone who provides a horse to make up a team', 'supportive neighbor', 'companion' (a derivative of *marh* 'horse'), hence a nickname for a farmer with only one horse or for a good neighbor.

Gembala (120) German: probably an Americanized form of South German (Austrian) **Gambele** or any of its variants (see GAMBEL, GAMBILL, GAMBLE).

Gemberling (244) Variant spelling of South German **Gamperling**, a variant of **Gamper** (see GAMBER).

Gemeinhardt (104) South German: apparently a topographic name for someone living in or near a municipal forest, from Middle High German *gemein* 'common' + *hard(t)* 'wood', 'forest'. In northern Germany, however, the name is a fake formation of a personal name from *Gemein(d)er*, *Gemeinert* 'co-owner', 'companion' + the name component *hard*, as in *Gebhard*, *Hartwig* (Old High German *hart* 'strong'). One reason for this development is probably the semantic change of *gemein* from 'common' to 'bad', 'mean'.
GIVEN NAME German 9%. *Otto* (3).

Gemelli (113) Italian: from a plural or patronymic form of the personal name *Gemello*, from Latin *Gemellus* 'twin'.
GIVEN NAMES Italian 10%. *Giampiero*, *Iolanda*, *Massimo*.

Gemignani (152) Italian (Tuscany): from the personal name *Gemignano*, a vernacular form of the Late Latin name *Geminianus*, a derivative of *geminus* 'twin'.
GIVEN NAMES Italian 18%. *Carlo* (2), *Gino* (2), *Edo*, *Ezio*, *Guido*, *Lido*, *Otello*, *Piero*, *Rino*.

Gemma (307) Italian (Tuscany and throughout the south): from the popular medieval female personal name *Gemma* (from *gemma* 'gem', 'precious stone').
GIVEN NAMES Italian 10%; French 4%. *Angelo* (2), *Gino* (2), *Nunzio* (2), *Marco*, *Rocco*, *Santina*; *Armand* (2), *Alphonse*.

Gemme (204) **1.** French: metonymic occupational name for a jeweller, from *gemme* 'gem', 'precious stone'. **2.** German: perhaps a metonymic name derived from a stem *Gam-*, as in the 16th century female personal name *Gemeke*.
GIVEN NAMES French 14%. *Adelard*, *Alexina*, *Benoit*, *Gaston*, *Jean Jacques*, *Laurent*, *Pierre*.

Gemmel (130) **1.** Scottish: variant of GAMBLE. **2.** German: nickname for a cheerful person from Middle Low German *gemelik* 'happy', 'funny', 'boisterous'. Compare GAMMEL.

Gemmell (593) **1.** Scottish: variant of GAMBLE. **2.** Altered spelling of German GEMMEL.

Gemmer (175) German: from a personal name *Gamer*, from Old High German *gamel* 'joy', 'play'. Compare GAMMEL.
GIVEN NAME German 5%. *Otto*.

Gemmill (537) Scottish: variant of GAMBLE.

Genao (180) Hispanic (Dominican Republic): unexplained.

GIVEN NAMES Spanish 53%. *Jose* (6), *Rafael* (4), *Ana* (3), *Cristina* (2), *Esteban* (2), *Francisca* (2), *Francisco* (2), *Juan* (2), *Julio* (2), *Luz* (2), *Maximo* (2), *Miguel* (2).

Genaro (113) Variant spelling of Italian GENNARO.
GIVEN NAMES Spanish 13%; Italian 7%. *Diaz* (2), *Gilberto* (2), *Alicia*, *Jose*; *Antonio* (2).

Genaw (116) **1.** Probably an Americanized spelling of German GNAU. **2.** Possibly an altered spelling of French JUNEAU.

Gencarelli (169) Italian: patronymic or plural form of *Gencarello*, which is probably a nickname from *gencarello*, a derivative of southern Italian *genco* 'bullock'.
GIVEN NAMES Italian 38%. *Angelo* (6), *Elio* (3), *Luigi* (2), *Orlando* (2), *Ernesto*, *Federico*, *Gennaro*, *Gino*, *Giorgio*, *Giovanni*, *Guiseppe*, *Mario*, *Natale*, *Pasquale*, *Salvatore*.

Genco (409) Italian: nickname for a strong man, from southern Italian *genco* 'bullock' (from Latin *iuvencus*).
GIVEN NAMES Italian 14%. *Salvatore* (4), *Angelo*, *Antonio*, *Carmel*, *Concetta*, *Cosimo*, *Giuseppe*, *Luigi*, *Pasquale*, *Sal*, *Santina*, *Santo*.

Gendel (116) Jewish (eastern Ashkenazic): variant of HENDEL, under Russian influence, since Russian has no *h* and alters *h* in borrowed words to *g*.
GIVEN NAMES Jewish 10%; Russian 9%. *Chaim*, *Polina*, *Zinaida*; *Anatoly*, *Leonid*, *Mikhail*, *Vladimir*, *Yevgeniy*.

Gendelman (164) Jewish (eastern Ashkenazic): variant of HANDLER, originating under Russian influence, since Russian has no *h* and alters *h* in borrowed words to *g*.
GIVEN NAMES Jewish 22%; Russian 22%. *Fira* (2), *Asher*, *Boruch*, *Genya*, *Golda*, *Ilya*, *Rina*, *Semen*, *Shmul*, *Sima*, *Yakov*, *Yankel*; *Mikhail* (4), *Boris* (3), *Lev* (3), *Vladimir* (3), *Leonid* (2), *Oleg* (2), *Aleksandr*, *Dmitry*, *Genady*, *Igor*, *Lyubov*, *Raisa*.

Gendler (184) Jewish (Ashkenazic): variant of HANDLER, originating under Russian influence, since Russian has no *h* and alters *h* in borrowed words to *g*.
GIVEN NAMES Russian 13%; Jewish 8%. *Boris* (2), *Efim* (2), *Sofiya* (2), *Vladimir* (2), *Fanya*, *Grigoriy*, *Igor*, *Iosif*, *Lev*, *Nadezhda*, *Sofya*; *Hymie*, *Isaak*, *Naum*, *Rochel*.

Gendreau (769) French: variant of GENDRON.
GIVEN NAMES French 12%. *Armand* (8), *Normand* (3), *Alcide* (2), *Fernand* (2), *Gisele* (2), *Lucien* (2), *Marcel* (2), *Ovide* (2), *Andre*, *Camille*, *Florent*, *Herve*.

Gendron (1935) French: **1.** from a diminutive of Old French *gendre* 'son-in-law' (Latin *gener*). **2.** habitational name from Gendron in Namur province, Belgium.
FOREBEARS A bearer of the name Gendreau, from Saintonge, was in Château Richer, Quebec, by 1663, while someone called

Gendron, also from Saintonge, was in Quebec city from 1656; another, from Brittany, was in Montreal by 1664; and a third, again from Saintonge, was in Quebec city by 1710.
GIVEN NAMES French 12%. *Armand* (8), *Pierre* (5), *Gilles* (4), *Henri* (4), *Normand* (4), *Antoine* (3), *Lucien* (3), *Marcel* (3), *Andre* (2), *Francois* (2), *Urgel* (2), *Aime*.

Gene (101) French: from a reduced form of the personal name *Eugène* (see EUGENE).
GIVEN NAME French 4%. *Francois*.

General (186) Origin uncertain. Possibly an altered form of French **Généreux** (see GENEREUX).

Genereux (350) French (**Généreux**): nickname from *généreux* 'generous', 'giving'.
GIVEN NAMES French 7%. *Armand*, *Donat*, *Emile*, *Ovila*, *Serge*, *Simonne*.

Genest (451) **1.** French: topographic name for someone who lived by a patch of broom, Old French *genest(e)* (from Late Latin *(planta) genesta*). **2.** German: cognate of 1, from Latin.
FOREBEARS A bearer of the name Genest, of unknown origin, was in Île d'Orléans by 1670.

Geoffrey **Plantagenet** was so called from wearing in his cap a sprig of the broom plant. He was the father of Henry II (1133–89), the first Plantagenet King of England. His descendants ruled England until ousted by the House of Tudor at the end of the Wars of the Roses.
GIVEN NAMES French 17%. *Emile* (3), *Fernand* (3), *Florent* (3), *Laurent* (3), *Pierre* (3), *Armand* (2), *Laurette* (2), *Normand* (2), *Adelard*, *Benoit*, *Gaetan*, *Gilles*.

Genet (273) French: **1.** variant of GENEST 1. **2.** from a reduced pet form of the personal name *Eugène* (see EUGENE).
GIVEN NAMES French 7%. *Odile* (2), *Adrien*, *Christophe*.

Genett (111) Probably a respelling of French GENET.

Genetti (126) Italian: patronymic or plural form of *Genetto*, a reduced pet form of the personal name *Eugenio*, from Latin *Eugenius* (see EUGENE).
GIVEN NAME German 4%. *Otto*.

Geng (228) **1.** South German: nickname for a lively, alert person, from Middle High German *genge* 'sprightly'. **2.** Chinese 耿: this surname was adopted during the Shang dynasty (1766–1122 BC) by inhabitants of an area called Geng. According to one source, Geng was a state; after it was conquered, some of the inhabitants adopted the name of the state as their surname. According to another source, Geng was the name of the city that was made capital of the region.
GIVEN NAMES Chinese 18%. *Jing* (3), *Lei* (2), *Xin* (2), *Yan* (2), *Dong Hong*, *Fu*, *Jia*, *Li*, *Lifeng*, *Liping*, *Mei*, *Ming Hui*.

Genge (130) German: variant of German GENG.
GIVEN NAMES German 5%. *Kurt*, *Ulrich*.

Gengenbach (128) German: habitational name from Gengenbach in Baden-Württemberg.
GIVEN NAMES German 10%. *Kurt* (2), *Egon, Erwin*.

Gengler (696) South German: occupational name for a traveling merchant or buyer of coins, Middle High German *gengeler*.

Gengo (127) Italian: possibly from the Germanic personal name *Gengwald*, composed of the elements *gang* 'walk', 'path' + *wald* 'rule'.
GIVEN NAMES Italian 16%. *Angelo* (2), *Orlando* (2).

Genin (130) Jewish (eastern Ashkenazic): metronymic from the Yiddish female given name *Henye*, a pet form of HANNA. The initial *G* is due to Russian influence, since Russian has no *H* and alters *H* in borrowed words to *G*.
GIVEN NAMES Russian 8%; Jewish 7%. *Anatoly, Demitry, Oleg, Vladimir, Yevgeniy, Zinoviy; Esfir, Izya*.

Genis (202) Catalan (**Genís**): from the personal name *Genís*, a variant of **Ginés** (see GINES).
GIVEN NAMES Russian 9%; Spanish 5%. *Galya* (2), *Aleksandr, Boris, Igor, Lyubov, Mikail, Oleg, Semyon, Sofya, Vladimir; Javier* (2), *Jose* (2), *Alicia, Amado, Damacia, Edmundo, Ignacio, Miguel*.

Genn (124) **1.** English (Cornish): from a short form of the female personal name *Jennifer*, from Welsh *Gwenhwyfar* (see GAYNOR). Until the 19th century *Jennifer* was a characteristically Cornish name. **2.** German: of uncertain origin; possibly from a Celtic root or from a short form of *Heinrich* (see HENRY) or *Johannes* (see JOHN).

Genna (281) Southern Italian: topographic name from Arabic *jannah* 'garden'.
GIVEN NAMES Italian 22%. *Vito* (5), *Salvatore* (4), *Antonino, Antonio, Camillo, Gino, Giovanni, Girolamo, Giuseppe, Ignazio, Rocco*.

Gennarelli (129) Italian: from a pet form of the personal name GENNARO.
GIVEN NAMES Italian 24%. *Gino* (2), *Carlo, Carmine, Dante, Franco, Lia, Macario, Marco, Mario, Valentino*.

Gennari (158) Italian: patronymic or plural form of the personal name GENNARO.
GIVEN NAMES Italian 26%; French 4%. *Angelo* (3), *Aldo* (2), *Luigi* (2), *Remo* (2), *Romolo* (2), *Antonio, Cesare, Dante, Elio, Francesco, Gino, Guido; Alain, Pascal*.

Gennaro (510) Italian: from the personal name *Gennaro* 'January'. The name is associated with the cult of *Januarius*, a 3rd-century bishop of Benevento, who became the patron saint of Naples.
GIVEN NAMES Italian 16%. *Vito* (7), *Antonio* (2), *Rocco* (2), *Salvatore* (2), *Carmelo, Concetta, Franco, Gasper, Giuseppe, Guido, Luigi, Nicola*.

Gennett (158) Variant of French GENET.

Gennette (117) Variant of French GENET.

Gennusa (125) Italian: of uncertain etymology.
GIVEN NAMES Italian 14%. *Salvatore* (3), *Gaetano, Gino*.

Gennuso (114) Italian: variant of GENNUSA.
GIVEN NAMES Italian 10%. *Gaetano, Orazio, Sal, Santo*.

Geno (341) New England variant of French Canadian JUNEAU or **Jouineau**, from French JUNOD or JUNOT. Alternatively, it may derive from a popular form of the personal name *Jovin*, (Latin *Iovinus*, a derivative of *Iovis*).

Genova (680) Italian: habitational name from Genoa (Italian *Genova*) in Liguria, which during the Middle Ages was one of the great seaports of the Mediterranean and a flourishing mercantile and financial center. The origin of the name of the city is uncertain. It has been associated with Latin *janua* 'door', but is more probably of pre-Roman origin. The surname in its various forms is distributed throughout southern Italy, *Genova* and *Genovese* being particularly common in Calabria and Sicily.
GIVEN NAMES Italian 16%. *Angelo* (7), *Aldo* (4), *Antonio* (3), *Pasquale* (3), *Carmelo* (2), *Salvatore* (2), *Vito* (2), *Attilio, Carmela, Carmine, Domenic, Domenica*.

Genovese (1787) Southern Italian: habitational name for someone from Genoa in Liguria (see GENOVA), from the adjectival form of the place name. In medieval times the Genoese were regarded as clever individuals, and it is possible that the surname is sometimes a nickname with this sense.
GIVEN NAMES Italian 14%. *Angelo* (11), *Salvatore* (8), *Rocco* (4), *Aldo* (2), *Dante* (2), *Domenic* (2), *Domenica* (2), *Enrico* (2), *Filippa* (2), *Nicolo* (2), *Vito* (2), *Antonino*.

Genovesi (200) Italian: patronymic or plural form of GENOVESE.
GIVEN NAMES Italian 24%. *Mario* (3), *Angelo* (2), *Dario* (2), *Santo* (2), *Alfonse, Amleto, Biagio, Carlo, Enrico, Geno, Gino, Giuseppe, Luciano, Sergio*.

Genrich (284) Russian (of German origin) and Jewish (eastern Ashkenazic): from a Russianized form of the German personal name *Heinrich* (see HENRY).

Gens (205) **1.** German: variant of JENS. **2.** Jewish (eastern Ashkenazic) and Polish (**Gęś**): ornamental name from Polish *gęś* 'goose'.

Gensch (150) Eastern German: from the personal name *Gensch*, a short form of the Sorbian form of JOHN.
GIVEN NAMES German 5%. *Fritz, Gerlinda*.

Gensel (210) German (also **Gänsel**): nickname from a diminutive of GANS 'goose'.

Gensemer (148) **1.** German: of uncertain origin. Possibly a variant spelling of **Genzmer**, a variant of GANZ, or a dialect variant of GENSHEIMER. **2.** Possibly an al-

tered form of German **Gensemeyer**, an occupational name for someone who raised and sold geese, from Middle High German *gans* 'goose' + *meier* '(tenant) farmer'.

Genser (145) **1.** German and Jewish (Ashkenazic): occupational name for someone who kept, tended, or sold geese, from Middle High German *gans* 'goose'. **2.** habitational name for someone from a place called Gensen, near Waldsee.
GIVEN NAMES Jewish 4%; German 4%. *Moshe; Mathias, Matthias*.

Gensheimer (142) German: habitational name for someone from Gansheim near Donauwörth, Bavaria.
GIVEN NAMES German 8%. *Alois, Fritz, Klaus, Kurt*.

Genske (165) Probably an altered spelling of German **Genzke**, a derivative of GANS or GANZ.

Gensler (637) **1.** South German and Swiss German: variant of GANSER. **2.** Jewish (Ashkenazic): occupational name for a breeder of geese, from an agent derivative of German *Gans* 'goose'.
GIVEN NAMES German 4%. *Otto* (2), *Erwin, Kurt, Siegfried, Taube, Wilhelm*.

Genson (226) French spelling of JANSON.
GIVEN NAME French 4%. *Franck*.

Gent (717) **1.** English and French: nickname, possibly sometimes applied ironically, from Middle English *gente*, Old French *gent(il)* 'well born', 'noble', 'courteous'. Compare GENTLE. **2.** German and English: habitational name for someone from Ghent in Flanders, French name *Gand*.

Genter (328) South German: variant of GANTER 1.

Gentes (166) **1.** Possibly a variant of French GENT. **2.** Dutch and German: patronymic from a short form of a Germanic personal name formed with *gand* 'spell', such as *Gandolfus*.
GIVEN NAMES French 11%. *Andre, Armand, Henri, Lucien, Marcel, Normand*.

Genthe (121) German: variant spelling of GENTE or a habitational name from Gentha in Saxony Anhalt, east of Wittenberg.

Genther (172) German: **1.** variant of GENT. **2.** from a personal name formed with an element related to Old Norse *gandr* 'enchantment', 'magic', 'werewolf'. **3.** variant of GENTER.
GIVEN NAMES German 5%. *Fritz, Otto*.

Genthner (240) South German: occupational name for a cooper, a South German variant of GANTER 2.

Gentilcore (134) Italian: nickname for a good-hearted person, from *gentil* 'courteous', 'kind' + *core* 'heart', an old or dialect form of *cuore* (Latin *cor*).
GIVEN NAMES Italian 19%. *Angelo* (2), *Achille, Luciano, Rocco*.

Gentile (5473) **1.** Italian: from the personal name *Gentile*, a continuation of Late Latin *Gentilis* meaning 'of the same stock (Latin *gens*)' and then 'non-Christian', 'pagan'; as a medieval name it was an omen name with the sense 'noble', 'courteous', also 'delicate', 'charming', 'graceful' (Italian *gentile*). In some cases the surname may have arisen from a nickname, sometimes possibly ironical, from the same word. **2.** English: variant of GENTLE.

GIVEN NAMES Italian 16%. *Angelo* (24), *Salvatore* (21), *Carmine* (12), *Vito* (12), *Domenic* (11), *Rocco* (11), *Giuseppe* (10), *Gino* (9), *Antonio* (7), *Pasquale* (7), *Gennaro* (6), *Sal* (6).

Gentili (111) Italian: patronymic from GENTILE.

GIVEN NAMES Italian 15%. *Amilcare, Enrico, Leno, Primo, Romolo, Sylvio, Vincenzo.*

Gentilini (130) Italian: from a diminutive of GENTILE.

GIVEN NAMES Italian 9%. *Aldo* (2), *Gino* (2), *Bruna, Dante.*

Gentis (118) North German and Dutch: variant of GENTES.

GIVEN NAME French 4%. *Thierry.*

Gentle (753) English: nickname, sometimes ironic, from Middle English, Old French *gentil* 'well born', 'noble', 'courteous' (Latin *gentilis*, from *gens* 'family', 'tribe', itself from the root *gen-* 'to be born').

Gentleman (139) **1.** English: status name for a man of good birth (see GENTLE). **2.** Translation of any of the various equivalents of 1 in other languages, for example Italian GENTILUOMO or French GENTILHOMME.

GIVEN NAME French 4%. *Jean-Paul.*

Gentles (180) English: variant of GENTLE.

Gentner (533) South German: variant of GANTER 1.

Gentry (15386) English: nickname, sometimes perhaps ironic, from Middle English, Old French *genterie* 'nobility of birth or character'. Compare GENTLE.

Gentsch (133) Eastern German (of Slavic origin): from a Sorbian-Saxon short form of the personal name *Johannes* (see JOHN).

GIVEN NAMES German 4%. *Hans, Kurt.*

Gentz (550) German: from a short form of the personal name *Gen(dr)ich*, Slavic form of HEINRICH.

GIVEN NAMES German 4%. *Heinz* (2), *Bernhard, Hertha, Kurt.*

Gentzel (140) Eastern German: from a pet form of JANTZ.

Gentzler (288) South German: variant of GANSER.

Genua (102) Italian: habitational name from the city of Genoa (Italian *Genova*), from the Latin form *Genua*.

GIVEN NAMES Italian 23%. *Vito* (4), *Ciriaco, Dante, Gennaro, Giulio, Nicolo.*

Genung (289) Origin unidentified. Compare GANONG.

Genz (376) German: variant spelling of GENTZ.

GIVEN NAMES German 5%. *Kurt* (3), *Armin, Erwin.*

Genzel (103) Eastern German: from a pet form of JANTZ.

Genzer (140) **1.** German: occupational name of Slavic origin, from Sorbian *gjancar* 'potter'. **2.** Jewish (eastern Ashkenazic): occupational name from Yiddish *gendzer* 'goose dealer'.

GIVEN NAMES Russian 5%; Jewish 5%. *Gennady, Maks; Hyman, Irina, Semen.*

Geoffrey (151) English: variant spelling of JEFFREY.

GIVEN NAMES French 13%. *Colette* (2), *Marcel* (2), *Alain, Andre.*

Geoffrion (236) French: from a pet form of GEOFFROY.

GIVEN NAMES French 12%. *Lucien* (2), *Andre, Camille, Damien, Emile, Francoise, Pierre.*

Geoffroy (347) French: from a variant spelling of the personal name *Geofroi* (see JEFFREY).

GIVEN NAMES French 13%. *Armand* (3), *Pierre* (2), *Camille, Christophe, Emile, Jean-Marie, Laurent, Normand, Sylvian, Telesphore.*

Geoghagan (112) Irish: variant of GEOGHEGAN.

Geoghan (144) Irish: reduced form of GEOGHEGAN.

GIVEN NAME Irish 6%. *Caitlin.*

Geoghegan (700) Irish: reduced Anglicized form of Gaelic **Mag Eochagáin**, a patronymic from the personal name *Eochagán*, a diminutive of *Eochaidh*, *Eochaidhe* 'horseman'. Compare CAUGHEY.

GIVEN NAMES Irish 7%. *Dermot, Eamon, Eamonn, Kieran, Seamus, Siobhan.*

Georg (241) German: from a German vernacular form of the Greek personal name *Geōrgios* (see GEORGE).

GIVEN NAMES German 5%. *Erwin, Gerd, Kurt, Manfred.*

Georgas (112) Greek: from a reduced form of patronymic surnames such as **Georgiadis**, from the Greek personal name *Geōrgios* (see GEORGE).

GIVEN NAMES Greek 15%. *Costas* (2), *Antonios, Constantine, Eleni, Loukas, Stavros.*

George (40227) English, Welsh, French, South Indian, etc.: from the personal name *George*, Greek *Geōrgios*, from an adjectival form, *geōrgios* 'rustic', of *geōrgos* 'farmer'. This became established as a personal name in classical times through its association with the fashion for pastoral poetry. Its popularity in western Europe increased at the time of the Crusades, which brought greater contact with the Orthodox Church, in which several saints and martyrs of this name are venerated, in particular a saint believed to have been martyred at Nicomedia in AD 303, who, however, is at best a shadowy figure historically. Nevertheless, by the end of the Middle Ages St. George had become associated with an unhistorical legend of dragon-slaying exploits, which caught the pop-

ular imagination throughout Europe, and he came to be considered the patron saint of England among other places. As an American family name, this has absorbed cognates from other European languages, including German **Georg** and Greek patronymics such as **Georgiou**, **Georgiadis**, **Georgopoulos**, and the status name **Papageorgiou** 'priest George'. In English-speaking countries, this surname is also found as an Anglicized form of Greek surnames such as **Hatzigeorgiou** 'George the Pilgrim' and patronymics such as **Giorgopoulos** 'son of George'. It is used as a given name among Christians in India, and in the U.S. has come to be used as a surname among families from southern India.

Georgeff (93) Americanized spelling of the Bulgarian and Macedonian surname **Georgiev**, a patronymic from the personal name *Georgi*, from Greek *Geōrgios* (see GEORGE).

GIVEN NAMES South Slavic 4%. *Goran, Vassil.*

Georgen (104) German: habitational name from a place called St. Georgen or a patronymic from the personal name *Georg* (see GEORGE).

Georger (100) **1.** German (also **Geörger**): patronymic from the personal name *Georg* (see GEORGE), or possibly a habitational name for someone from a place named with this personal name (see, e.g. GEORGEN), or a nickname for someone with service obligations to a monastery or church dedicated to St. George. **2.** French: from a pet form of GEORGE.

GIVEN NAME French 4%. *Girard.*

Georges (1155) French: variant of GEORGE. This name is also common in Germany, taken there by the Huguenots.

GIVEN NAMES French 11%. *Pierre* (4), *Raymonde* (3), *Marcel* (2), *Maryse* (2), *Philippe* (2), *Regine* (2), *Serge* (2), *Yves* (2), *Alain, Andre, Constant, Emile.*

Georgescu (101) Romanian: patronymic from the personal name *Georgiu* (see GEORGE).

GIVEN NAMES Romanian 53%; Russian 4%. *Florin* (4), *Constantin* (3), *Ionel* (3), *Anca* (2), *Corneliu* (2), *Doru* (2), *Grigore* (2), *Laurentiu* (2), *Mihai* (2), *Mircea* (2), *Radu* (2), *Vasile* (2); *Andrei.*

Georgeson (422) English (chiefly Northumberland): patronymic from the personal name *George* (see GEORGE).

Georgetti (104) Variant spelling of Italian **Giorgetti**, from a pet form of the personal name GIORGIO (see GEORGE).

GIVEN NAMES Italian 20%. *Angelo* (4), *Amleto, Pasquale.*

Georgi (296) German: patronymic from the Latin form of the personal name *Georg* (see GEORGE).

GIVEN NAMES German 12%. *Otto* (5), *Erwin, Fritz, Guenther, Gunter, Heinz, Ingeborg, Manfred, Reinhold.*

Georgia (458) Americanized form of any of several derivatives in various European languages of the Greek personal name *Geōrgios* (see GEORGE), for example Greek GEORGIADIS. It is unlikely to be connected with the female personal name *Georgia*, still less with the state or country called *Georgia*.

GIVEN NAMES German 4%. *Erwin, Frieda, Herta.*

Georgiades (158) Greek: variant spelling of GEORGIADIS.

GIVEN NAMES Greek 22%. *Nicos* (2), *Andreas, Constantine, Costas, Ioannis, Kyriakos, Nikos, Panagiotis, Panayiotis, Savvas, Spiro, Takis.*

Georgiadis (162) Greek: patronymic from the personal name *Geōrgios* (see GEORGE). The *-ides* patronymic suffix is classical, and was revived by Greeks from Asia Minor in particular.

GIVEN NAMES Greek 31%. *Vasilios* (3), *Christos, Demetrios, Despina, Dimitrios, Georgios, Iraklis, Konstantinos, Kostas, Marios, Panagiotis, Sotirios.*

Georgian (105) Armenian: **1.** probably an Americanized form of **Gurjian**, patronymic from an ethnic name for someone from Georgia, a state in the Caucasus mountains to the north of Armenia. **2.** perhaps also an Americanized form of **Geworgian**, a patronymic from the western Armenian personal name *Geworg* (see KEVORKIAN).

GIVEN NAMES Armenian 7%. *Hovsep, Ohannes, Razmik, Takouhi.*

Georgiou (292) Greek: patronymic from the genitive case of the personal name *Geōrgios* (see GEORGE). Patronymics formed with the genitive case are typical in particular of Cyprus.

GIVEN NAMES Greek 30%. *Andreas* (8), *Christos* (2), *Demetrios* (2), *Ioannis* (2), *Loucas* (2), *Markos* (2), *Yannis* (2), *Anastasios, Aristos, Constantine, Costas, Dimitrios.*

Georgopoulos (162) Greek: patronymic from the personal name *Geōrgios* (see GEORGE) + the patronymic ending *-poulos*. This ending occurs chiefly in the Peloponnese. It is derived from Latin *pullus* 'nestling', 'chick'.

GIVEN NAMES Greek 27%. *Andreas* (2), *Christos* (2), *Dimitrios* (2), *Dionisios* (2), *Angelos, Apostolos, Athas, Demetre, Demetrios, Ilias, Joannis, Odysseus.*

Gepford (130) Americanized spelling of German **Gepfert**, one of the many variants of GOTTFRIED, or from a personal name formed with the stem *Geb-* as in GEBHARDT.

Gephart (944) Variant spelling of German GEBHARDT.

Gepner (115) German: of uncertain origin. Possibly an unrounded variant of **Göpner**,

which is perhaps a habitational name derived from any of several places named Goben in Bavaria.

Geppert (299) German: variant of *Göpfert*, itself a variant of GOTTFRIED.

GIVEN NAME German 4%. *Otto.*

Gera (185) **1.** Indian (Panjab): Hindu (Arora) and Sikh name meaning 'dove', based on the name of a Jat clan. **2.** Hungarian: from a pet form of the personal names *Germán* (see GERMAN 2), or *Gergely*, Latin *Gregorius* (see GREGORY). **3.** German: habitational name from a place in Thuringia so named.

GIVEN NAMES Indian 29%. *Anil* (3), *Krishan* (2), *Sunil* (2), *Ved* (2), *Amita, Arun, Kamlesh, Mohan, Nihal, Prabha, Renuka, Sanjay.*

Gerace (843) Italian: variant of GERACI.

GIVEN NAMES Italian 12%. *Salvatore* (4), *Angelo* (3), *Ciro* (2), *Domenic* (2), *Rocco* (2), *Sal* (2), *Amerigo, Bonaventura, Carlo, Cosmo, Dino, Gaetano.*

Geraci (1343) Italian (Calabria and Sicily): habitational name for someone from Gerace or Gerace Marina in Calabria, or from Geraci Siculo in Sicily. The places are named with medieval Greek *geraki* 'hawk', classical Greek *hierax*. **Gerakis** 'hawk' has been known as a surname and nickname in Greece since Byzantine times.

GIVEN NAMES Italian 16%. *Salvatore* (17), *Angelo* (7), *Santo* (5), *Sal* (3), *Domenic* (2), *Gaetano* (2), *Gino* (2), *Pietro* (2), *Vito* (2), *Benedetto, Biagio, Carmela.*

Gerads (185) German: from a dissimilated form of *Gerard*, a variant of GERHARDT.

Geraghty (1346) Irish: reduced Anglicized form of Gaelic **Mag Oireachtaigh** 'son of *Oireachtach*', a byname meaning 'member of the assembly' or 'frequenting assemblies'.

GIVEN NAMES Irish 8%. *Brendan* (3), *Seamus* (3), *Ciaran, James Patrick, Siobhan.*

Gerald (1555) English and French (**Gérald**): from the personal name *Gerald, Gérald*, composed of the Germanic elements *gēri, gāri* 'spear' + *wald* 'rule'; it was introduced to Britain from France by the Normans.

Geralds (226) Variant of or patronymic from English GERALD.

Gerard (3487) English (chiefly Lancashire) and French (**Gérard**): from the personal name *Gerard, Gérard*, introduced to Britain from France by the Normans; it is composed of the Germanic elements *gār, gēr* 'spear', 'lance' + *hard* 'hardy', 'brave', 'strong'.

GIVEN NAMES French 4%. *Andre* (4), *Camille* (3), *Jean-Pierre* (3), *Murielle* (3), *Emile* (2), *Pascal* (2), *Pierre* (2), *Agathe, Alain, Aldes, Antoine, Armand.*

Gerardi (934) Italian: patronymic from the Germanic personal name *Gerardo* (see GERARD).

GIVEN NAMES Italian 11%. *Vito* (7), *Enzo* (2), *Gaspare* (2), *Luigi* (2), *Rocco* (2), *Antonio, Canio, Carmine, Filippo, Francesco, Giovanni, Libero.*

Gerardo (326) Spanish and Italian: from the personal name *Gerardo* (see GERARD).

GIVEN NAMES Spanish 36%. *Jose* (4), *Francisco* (3), *Alberto* (2), *Alfredo* (2), *Aurelio* (2), *Carlos* (2), *Jesus* (2), *Juan* (2), *Norberto* (2), *Ramon* (2), *Tomas* (2), *Ana; Antonio, Carmine, Dino, Enrico, Marco, Marco Antonio.*

Gerardot (124) Variant of French GIRARDOT.

Gerardy (115) Origin unidentified. Many early occurrences in KS.

Geraty (108) Irish: variant spelling of GERAGHTY.

Gerbasi (143) Italian: variant of GERVASI.

GIVEN NAMES Italian 12%. *Antonio* (2), *Francesco, Gino, Paolo, Salvatore.*

Gerber (7101) German, Swiss, and Jewish (Ashkenazic): occupational name for a tanner, Middle High German *gerwer* (from Old High German *(ledar) garawo* 'leather preparer'), German *Gerber*.

Gerberding (183) German: Westphalian patronymic from the personal name *Gerbert*, composed of the elements *gēr, gār* 'spear' + *berht* 'bright', 'famous'.

Gerberich (117) German: from the personal name *Gerberich*, composed of the Germanic elements *gār, gēr* 'spear' + *berht* 'bright', 'famous'.

Gerbig (187) German: from the personal name *Gerwig*, composed of the elements *gēr, gār* 'spear' + *wīg* 'battle'.

GIVEN NAMES German 5%. *Horst, Kurt, Otto.*

Gerbino (219) Italian: of uncertain derivation; Caracausi proposes various possibilities: **1.** from the personal name *Gerbino*, possibly from Tuscan *gerbo* 'grimace'. **2.** from a pet form from a short form of a personal name such as *Gerberto*. **3.** from Sicilian *girbinu* meaning 'light blue' (with reference to eyes) or 'blond' (with reference to hair color). **4.** topographic name from Italian *gérbo* 'uncultivated land', whence *terra gerbina* 'land on which only grasses grow'. **5.** habitational name for someone from the Tunisian island of Gerba.

Gerbitz (137) **1.** German: habitational name from a place called Gerbitz, in Anhalt (near Nienburg an der Saale). **2.** Germanized form of Slovenian **Gerbec**, **Grbec** or **Gerbic**, nicknames for a hunchback, from *grba* 'hunch'.

GIVEN NAME German 4%. *Kurt.*

Gerbracht (150) German: variant of **Gerbert**, from a personal name composed Old High German *gēr* 'spear' + *berht* 'bright', 'famous'.

GIVEN NAME German 4%. *Hermann.*

Gerde (104) German: probably a variant of GERDES, or a habitational name from a place near Hannover named Gerden.

Gerdeman (208) German (**Gerdemann**): habitational name for someone from a place near Hannover named Gerden.
GIVEN NAME German 5%. *Otto* (3).

Gerdes (2441) North German: patronymic from the personal name *Gerd*, reduced form of GERHARDT.
GIVEN NAMES German 5%. *Otto* (5), *Gerhard* (3), *Armin* (2), *Erwin* (2), *Gerd* (2), *Hartmut* (2), *Kurt* (2), *Ralf* (2), *Wolfgang* (2), *Beate*, *Bernhard*, *Fritz*.

Gerding (588) North German: patronymic from the personal name *Gerd*, reduced form of GERHARDT.

Gerdon (106) **1**. Scottish: altered spelling of GORDON. **2**. German: unexplained. Compare GARDON. **3**. French: perhaps a variant of GARDON

Gerdts (246) North German: patronymic from the personal name *Gerdt*, reduced form of GERHARDT.
GIVEN NAMES German 6%. *Detlef*, *Klaus*, *Reiner*, *Uwe*.

Gere (386) **1**. Americanized form of German GEHR. **2**. English: perhaps a variant of GEARY 3. **3**. Hungarian: from a reduced form of the personal name *Gergely*, Latin *Gregorius* (see GREGORY).

Gereau (137) French (**Géreau**): from a vernacular form of the personal names *Gérald* (see GERALD) or *Gérou* (see GEROU).

Gerecke (154) North German: from a pet form of a personal name formed with *gēr*, *gār* 'spear' as the first element.
GIVEN NAMES German 8%. *Dieter*, *Heinz*, *Lorenz*, *Manfred*.

Geremia (312) Italian form of JEREMIAH.
GIVEN NAMES Italian 10%. *Dino* (2), *Franco* (2), *Angelo*, *Antonietta*, *Carmine*, *Domenic*, *Enrico*, *Lorenzo*, *Pasquale*, *Salvatore*.

Geren (587) Respelling of German **Gehren**, a variant of GEHR 1.

Gerena (266) Spanish: habitational name from Gerena, a place in Seville province.
GIVEN NAMES Spanish 44%. *Jose* (5), *Juan* (5), *Luis* (5), *Luz* (4), *Miguel* (3), *Digna* (2), *Felicita* (2), *Francisco* (2), *Jaime* (2), *Margarita* (2), *Nilda* (2), *Adelaida*; *Antonio* (3), *Angelo*, *Caesar*, *Carmela*, *Dante*, *Eliseo*, *Leonardo*.

Gerety (289) Irish: variant of GERAGHTY.
GIVEN NAMES Irish 7%. *Brigid* (2), *Keelin*, *Liam*.

Gerfen (135) German: of uncertain origin; probably from a short form (*Gerbo*) of a personal name composed with Old High German *gēr* 'spear'.

Gerg (102) German: from a dialect form of the personal name GEORG.
GIVEN NAME German 4%. *Othmar*.

Gergel (140) **1**. South German and Austrian: from a pet form of the personal name *Georg* (see GEORGE). **2**. Hungarian: variant of GERGELY.

Gergely (275) Hungarian: from the personal name *Gergely*, Hungarian form GREGORY.
GIVEN NAMES Hungarian 6%. *Arpad* (2), *Bela* (2), *Attila*, *Dezso*, *Laszio*, *Mihaly*.

Gergen (416) German: from a variant of the personal name *Georg* (see GEORGE).

Gerger (146) South German: **1**. patronymic from GEORGE 2. **2**. habitational name for someone from any of several places named St. Georgen, in Austria and southern Germany.
GIVEN NAMES German 10%. *Erwin*, *Klaus*, *Manfred*, *Volker*.

Gerges (122) Arabic: variant of GIRGIS.
GIVEN NAMES Arabic 56%. *Amir* (2), *Ashraf* (2), *Maher* (2), *Nabil* (2), *Safwat* (2), *Afaf*, *Amira*, *Anwar*, *Badie*, *Bahaa*, *Bassam*, *Bassem*.

Gerhard (1115) German: variant of GERHARDT.
GIVEN NAMES German 5%. *Kurt* (5), *Hans* (2), *Rudi* (2), *Albrecht*, *Armin*, *Erwin*, *Fritz*, *Lothar*, *Otto*, *Reinhold*.

Gerhardstein (100) German: perhaps an altered form of **Gerhardshain**, a habitational name from a place so named in the Rhineland Palatinate, altered as if the second element were *Stein* 'stone'.
GIVEN NAME French 5%. *Alphonse* (2).

Gerhardt (2055) German: from a Germanic personal name composed of the elements *gēr*, *gār* 'spear' + *hard* 'hardy', 'brave', 'strong'.
GIVEN NAMES German 4%. *Kurt* (5), *Armin* (2), *Wilhelm* (2), *Bernhard*, *Dieter*, *Eldred*, *Erwin*, *Gerda*, *Gerhardt*, *Heinrich*, *Heinz*, *Horst*.

Gerhart (1705) German: variant of GERHARDT.

Gerhartz (113) German: patronymic from the personal name GERHARDT.

Gerhold (290) German: from a personal name composed of Old High German *gēr*, *gār* 'spear' + *wald* 'rule'.
GIVEN NAMES German 4%. *Eldred*, *Gitta*, *Kurt*.

Gerich (128) **1**. German: variant of **Gerrick**. **2**. Slovenian (**Gerič**): metronymic from the female personal name *Gera*, short form of *Gertruda*, Slovenian form of German *Gertrud* (see TRUDE).
GIVEN NAMES German 9%; Slavic 8%. *Horst*, *Mathias*; *Andrei*, *Milan*, *Natalya*.

Gericke (239) North German: from a pet form of a personal name beginning with the element *gēr*, *gār* 'spear', for example *Gerhard* (see GERHARDT).
GIVEN NAMES German 6%. *Bernhard*, *Helmut*, *Otto*.

Gerig (418) German: variant of GEHRIG.

Gerik (119) Americanized form of German GEHRIG.

Gering (509) North German: variant of GEHRING.
GIVEN NAMES German 4%. *Armin*, *Georg*, *Johannes*, *Kurt*, *Reinhold*.

Geringer (399) German: patronymic from GERING.

Gerity (131) Irish: variant of GERAGHTY.

Gerk (155) **1**. Variant of German **Gerke** (see GERKEN). **2**. Possibly also Slovenian: ethnic name for a Greek, from Slovenian *Gerk*, an old spelling of *Grk* 'Greek'.

Gerke (966) German: variant of GERKEN.
GIVEN NAMES German 4%. *Kurt* (2), *Bernhard*, *Dieter*, *Frieda*, *Fritz*, *Heinrich*, *Markus*, *Reinhardt*.

Gerken (1446) North German: patronymic from a short form of a personal name beginning with *gēr*, *gār* 'spear', as in *Gerhard* (see GERHARDT).
GIVEN NAMES German 4%. *Kurt* (5), *Eldor* (3), *Erwin*, *Ewald*, *Otto*, *Siegmar*, *Wilhelm*.

Gerkin (308) Variant of German GERKEN.

Gerl (131) **1**. German: from a regional field name *girlet* denoting a stand or copse of alders. **2**. Perhaps an altered spelling of German **Gerle**, from a short form of GERLACH.
GIVEN NAME German 4%. *Franz*.

Gerlach (2998) **1**. German and Dutch: from the personal name *Gerlach*, composed of the elements *gēr*, *gār* 'spear' + *lach*, a cognate of Old High German *leich* 'sport', 'play'. **2**. Jewish (Ashkenazic): ornamental adoption of the German name.
GIVEN NAMES German 5%. *Kurt* (7), *Dieter* (4), *Juergen* (4), *Otto* (4), *Erwin* (2), *Hans* (2), *Horst* (2), *Klaus* (2), *Alois*, *Eberhard*, *Franz*, *Frederich*.

Gerland (116) Variant of English GARLAND.

Gerleman (168) German (**Gerlemann**): from **Gerle** (see GERL 2) + *man* 'man'.

Gerlich (226) **1**. German and Jewish (eastern Ashkenazic): variant of GERLACH. **2**. Jewish (eastern Ashkenazic): variant, under Russian influence, of **Herlich**, itself a variant of EHRLICH.

Gerling (592) German: patronymic from a short form of a Germanic personal name beginning with the element *gār*, *gēr* 'spear', 'lance'.

Gerlitz (116) Jewish (Ashkenazic) and German: habitational name for someone from Görlitz in Saxony.
GIVEN NAMES Jewish 9%; German 6%. *Chaim* (3), *Emanuel*, *Zeev*; *Kurt*.

Gerlock (142) Americanized spelling of German GERLACH.

Gerloff (274) German: from a personal name *Gerulf*, composed of Old High German *gēr* 'spear' + *-loff*, *wolf* 'wolf'.
GIVEN NAME German 4%. *Erhard*.

Gerlt (123) German: from a short form of the personal name *Gerald* (from *Gerwald*, Old High German *gēr* 'spear' + *walt* 'rule').

Germain (2143) **1**. French: from the Old French personal name *Germain*. This was popular in France, where it had been borne by a 5th-century saint, bishop of Auxerre. It

derives from Latin *Germanus* 'brother', 'cousin' (originally an adjective meaning 'of the same stock', from Latin *germen* 'bud', 'shoot'). In the Romance languages, especially Italian, the popularity of the equivalent personal name has been enhanced by association with the meaning 'brother (in God)', and in Spanish the cognate surname is derived from the vocabulary word meaning 'brother' rather than from a personal name. The feminine form, *Germaine*, which occurs as a place name in Aisne, Marne, and Haute-Marne, is associated with a late 16th-century saint from Provençal, the daughter of a poor farmer, who was canonized in 1867. **2.** English: variant of GERMAN.
GIVEN NAMES French 10%. *Pierre* (6), *Armand* (2), *Jacques* (2), *Raoul* (2), *Wesner* (2), *Andre*, *Andree*, *Camil*, *Camille*, *Christophe*, *Dieudonne*, *Easton*.

Germaine (465) French: variant of GERMAIN 1.
GIVEN NAMES French 4%. *Michel* (2), *Emile*, *Henri*.

German (4277) **1.** English: ethnic name from Old French *germain* 'German' (Latin *Germanus*). This sometimes denoted an actual immigrant from Germany, but was also used to refer to a person who had trade or other connections with German-speaking lands. The Latin word *Germanus* is of obscure and disputed origin; the most plausible of the etymologies that have been proposed is that the people were originally known as the 'spear-men', with Germanic *gēr*, *gār* 'spear' as the first element. **2.** English (of Norman origin): from the Old French personal name *Germain* (see GERMAIN). **3.** Americanized spelling of Spanish **Germán** or Hungarian **Germán**, cognates of 2. **4.** German: from the saint's name *German(us)*. See also GERMANN. **5.** Jewish (eastern Ashkenazic): Russianized variant of HERMANN. **6.** Greek: reduced form of **Germanos**, a Greek personal name, bestowed in honor of saints of the Eastern Church distinct from St. Germain: in particular, St. Germanos in the 8th century, liturgical poet and patriarch of Constantinople. The Greek surname can also denote someone associated with Germany or someone with blond hair.

Germani (225) Italian: patronymic or plural form of the personal name GERMANO.
GIVEN NAMES Italian 19%. *Gasper* (3), *Salvatore* (3), *Angelo*, *Giuseppe*, *Orazio*, *Rasario*, *Rosaria*, *Sal*, *Vita*, *Vito*.

Germann (1021) **1.** English, German, and Swiss German: variant of GERMAN. **2.** German: variant of GEHRMANN.

Germano (956) Italian: from the personal name *Germano* (see GERMAN 2).
GIVEN NAMES Italian 13%. *Rocco* (4), *Antonio* (3), *Domenico* (3), *Nino* (3), *Sal* (3), *Salvatore* (3), *Angelo* (2), *Carmello* (2), *Franco* (2), *Geno* (2), *Guido* (2), *Carmelo*.

Germany (982) English (eastern counties): apparently a variant of GERMAN.

Germer (311) **1.** German and French: from the Germanic personal name *Germar*, composed of the elements *gār*, *gēr* 'spear', 'lance' + *mār*, *mēri* 'famous'. **2.** German: of Slavic origin, variant of the personal name *Jaromir*, from a cognate of Czech *jary* 'lively', 'vehement'.

Germond (239) French and Swiss French: from the Germanic personal name *Germund*, composed of the elements *gār*, *gēr* 'spear', 'lance' + *mund* 'protection'.

Germundson (107) Swedish (**Germundsson**): patronymic from the personal name *Germund* (see GERMOND).

Gernand (136) German: from a Germanic personal name formed with *gār*, *gēr* 'spear', 'lance'.
GIVEN NAME German 4%. *Erwin*.

Gerndt (101) German: from a reduced form of the Germanic personal name *Gernot*, composed of the elements *ger*, *gar* 'spear' + *not* 'battle', 'skirmish'.

Gerner (659) **1.** English and German: variant of GARNER 1. **2.** German: habitational name for someone from any of the five places in Bavaria called Gern.

Gernert (254) **1.** German: from a reduced form of the Germanic personal name *Gernhard* (see GERNHARDT). **2.** English and German: variant of GERNER.

Gernhardt (113) German: from the Germanic personal name *Gernhard*, which is either a variant of GERHARDT, or may be formed with a first element that is related to Middle High German *gern* 'to desire'.

Gernon (112) English: nickname for a man with a moustache, from Old French *gernon*, *grenon* 'moustache'.

Gero (504) **1.** Americanized spelling of French **Gérald** (see GERALD) or **Gérou** (see GEROU). **2.** Hungarian (also **Geró** or **Gerő**): from the personal name *Gerő*, pet form of *Gergely*, Hungarian form of GREGORY. **3.** German: from a short form of a Germanic personal name formed with *gār*, *gēr* 'spear', 'lance'. **4.** Reduced form of any of various Greek distinguishing nicknames beginning with *gero-* 'old', e.g. *Gerovassilis* 'old Basil', *Gerocostas* 'the elder Constantine', etc.
GIVEN NAMES French 4%. *Amie*, *Andre*, *Camille*, *Gisele*, *Marcelle*.

Gerold (296) **1.** English: variant of GARRETT 1. **2.** German: from the Germanic personal name *Gerwald*, composed of the elements *gār*, *gēr* 'spear', 'lance' + *wald-* 'rule'.
GIVEN NAMES French 4%. *Christien*, *Pierre*.

Gerome (124) French (**Gérome**, **Gérôme**): variant spelling of **Gérôme** (see JEROME).
GIVEN NAMES French 9%; Italian 5%. *Delouis*, *Jacques*, *Marielle*, *Rodrigue*; *Silvio* (2), *Romeo*.

Geron (166) French: from the personal name *Gero*, *Gerone*, a short form of a Ger-

manic personal name formed with *gār*, *gēr* 'spear', 'lance', as for example *Gérard* (see GERARD).

Gerondale (115) Perhaps an Americanized form of Scandinavian GRONDAHL. This is a common name in WI.

Geronimo (300) Spanish (**Gerónimo**) and Italian: from the personal name *Geronimo*, from Greek *Hierōnymos* (see HIERONYMUS).
GIVEN NAMES Spanish 39%; Italian 8%. *Alfredo* (3), *Carlito* (3), *Jose* (3), *Roberto* (3), *Rolando* (3), *Angel* (2), *Gerardo* (2), *Javier* (2), *Jesus* (2), *Leopoldo* (2), *Luz* (2), *Tomas* (2); *Antonio* (2), *Romeo* (2), *Vito* (2), *Fausto*, *Gilda*, *Jovencio*, *Leonardo*.

Gerou (130) **1.** French: from a reduced form of the Germanic personal name *Gerwulf*, composed of the elements *gēr*, *gār* 'spear' + *wulf* 'wolf'. **2.** Greek: patronymic from the genitive case of Greek *geros* 'old', 'elder' (see GERO 4).

Gerould (122) French (**Gérould**): variant of **Géraud** (see GERALD).

Geroux (180) French (**Géroux**): variant of GEROU.

Gerow (726) **1.** Americanized spelling of French GEROU or GIRAUD. **2.** Possibly an Americanized spelling of the German habitational name **Gerau**, from a place so named in Hesse.

Gerrald (167) Altered spelling of GERALD.

Gerrard (732) English: variant of GARRETT 1.

Gerren (107) Perhaps an altered form of English **Gerrans**, a habitational name from Gironde (Gascony) or a patronymic from an Old French personal name, *Gerin*, of Germanic origin.

Gerrick (132) **1.** Possibly an altered spelling of the English surname GARRICK. **2.** Possibly an altered spelling of German **Gerrich**, from a Germanic personal name formed with *gār*, *gēr* 'spear', 'lance'. In some instances it could be a habitational name from Gerrick in northern Germany.
GIVEN NAME German 4%. *Kurt*.

Gerrie (116) Scottish: probably a variant of Irish GEARY.

Gerring (126) Origin unidentified. Perhaps an altered form of German GEHRING.

Gerringer (272) Altered spelling of German GERINGER.

Gerrior (166) Anglicized form of French GUERRIER. This name is concentrated in MA.

Gerrish (761) **1.** English: nickname for an unpredictable, wayward person, from Middle English *gerysshe* 'wild', 'changeable'. Compare GEARY. **2.** Possibly an altered spelling of German **Gerisch**, a variant of GIERSCH.

Gerrits (364) Dutch: patronymic from a Germanic personal name composed of the elements *gār*, *gēr* 'spear', 'lance' + *hard* 'hardy', 'brave', 'strong'; a variant of GERHARDT.

FOREBEARS The name **Gerritse** is recorded in Beverwijck in New Netherland (Albany, NY) in the mid 17th century.

Gerritsen (253) Dutch: variant of GERRITS.
GIVEN NAMES Dutch 8%. *Gerrit* (3), *Jeroen* (2), *Berend, Derk, Hendrik, Henk*.

Gerrity (657) Irish: variant of GERAGHTY.

Gerry (1132) **1.** English: variant of GEARY. **2.** Possibly an altered spelling of German **Gehri**, a variant of GEHR 1.

Gersbach (118) Swiss German: habitational name from a place so named northeast of Lörrach in Baden.
GIVEN NAMES German 9%. *Gunter* (2), *Erhard*.

Gersch (256) **1.** German: variant of GIERSCH. **2.** Jewish (eastern Ashkenazic): variant of HIRSCH 2 and 3, under Russian influence.
GIVEN NAMES German 8%. *Wolfgang* (3), *Gotthard, Kurt, Willi*.

Gersh (295) **1.** Jewish (Ashkenazic): variant of HIRSCH 2 and 3. **2.** Americanized spelling of German GERSCH.
GIVEN NAMES Jewish 5%. *Berko, Dorit, Sol, Yitzchak*.

Gershen (102) Jewish (Eastern Ashkenazic): variant of GERSHON.

Gershenson (131) Jewish (from Ukraine and Bessarabia): Russianized form of **Hershenson**, a patronymic from the Yiddish personal name *Hersh* (see HIRSCH).
GIVEN NAMES Jewish 14%. *Moshe* (2), *Hillel, Hyman, Meir*.

Gershman (436) Jewish (from Ukraine and Belarus): variant of HIRSCH, under Russian influence (see GOREN).
GIVEN NAMES Jewish 13%; Russian 8%. *Hyman* (2), *Ari, Aron, Faina, Isadore, Khaim, Khana, Leyb, Mort, Semen, Yakov; Mikhail* (4), *Leonid* (3), *Oleg* (3), *Boris* (2), *Fima* (2), *Aleksandr, Anatoly, Galina, Genady, Grigory, Leya, Vladimir*.

Gershon (457) Jewish: from the Hebrew personal name *Gershon, Gershom*, of uncertain origin. It may mean 'exile', but is usually interpreted as 'sojourner', from Hebrew *ger sham* meaning 'a stranger there'.
GIVEN NAMES Jewish 8%. *Ari* (2), *Chaim, Isak, Moshe, Nissim, Semen, Sol, Varda, Zev*.

Gershowitz (99) Jewish (eastern Ashkenazic): variant, under Russian influence (Russian having no *h*), of **Herschowitz**, a patronymic from *Hersh*, a dialect variant of HIRSCH 2.
GIVEN NAMES Jewish 8%. *Hyman, Tova*.

Gerson (1265) German form or Jewish variant of GERSHON.
GIVEN NAMES Jewish 6%. *Isak* (3), *Sol* (3), *Elihu* (2), *Esti, Golde, Hershel, Hyman, Maier, Meyer, Mort, Reuven, Shoshana*.

Gerst (723) German: metonymic occupational name for a grower of or dealer in barley, or possibly more generally for a farmer, from Middle High German *gerste* 'barley'.

Gerstein (602) **1.** German: of uncertain origin; probably a variant of **Kerstein**, itself a variant of KIRST. **2.** Jewish (eastern Ashkenazic): of uncertain origin; perhaps an ornamental name composed of German *Gerst* 'barley' + *Stein* 'stone'.
GIVEN NAMES Jewish 5%. *Mayer* (2), *Meyer* (2), *Sol* (2), *Emanuel, Hyman, Zev*.

Gerstel (215) German: diminutive of GERST.

Gersten (406) **1.** German: habitational name from a place near Lingen in East Friesland named Gersten. **2.** German: variant of GERST. **3.** Jewish (Ashkenazic): ornamental name or metonymic occupational name from German *Gersten* 'barley' (see 2).
GIVEN NAMES Jewish 6%. *Hyman* (2), *Baruch, Leib, Mendel, Miriam, Pnina, Shimon*.

Gerstenberger (307) German: habitational name for someone from a place called Gerstenberg in Thuringia.
GIVEN NAMES German 12%. *Kurt* (3), *Erwin* (2), *Helmut* (2), *Otto* (2), *Egon, Ernst, Gerhard, Gunther, Rudi*.

Gerstenfeld (104) Jewish (Ashkenazic): ornamental name compound composed of German *Gerst(en)* 'barley' + *Feld* 'field'.
GIVEN NAMES French 8%; Jewish 6%; German 5%. *Jacques* (2), *Cecile; Sol, Zahava; Erwin, Walburga*.

Gerstenkorn (108) Jewish (Ashkenazic): ornamental name compound composed of German *Gerst(en)* 'barley' + *Korn* 'grain'.

Gerster (151) South German and Swiss German: occupational name for a farmer, or specifically a grower of or dealer in barley, from an agent derivative of Middle High German *gerste* 'barley'. See also GERST.
GIVEN NAMES French 5%; German 4%. *Pierre, Stephane; Ingo*.

Gerstle (192) South German: from a field name, presumably denoting one in which barley was grown, or a metonymic occupational nickname for a farmer (see GERST).
GIVEN NAMES German 7%. *Heinz, Helmut, Kurt*.

Gerstman (174) German (**Gerstmann**) and Jewish (Ashkenazic): occupational name for a dealer in barley or a farmer who grew barley (see GERSTER).
GIVEN NAMES Jewish 7%. *Bluma, Hyman, Sol*.

Gerstner (861) South German and Swiss German: variant of GERSTER.

Gerszewski (165) Polish: from a derivative of the personal name *G(i)ersz*, a pet form of GERHARDT.

Gerten (120) **1.** German: patronymic from the personal name *Gert(h)*, a short form of GERHARDT. **2.** Possibly a respelling of English GIRTON.

Gerth (824) German and Swiss German: **1.** from a reduced form of GERHARDT. **2.** habitational name for someone from Gerthe near Bochum.
GIVEN NAMES German 4%. *Horst* (2), *Kurt* (2), *Erwin, Gerhard*.

Gertler (226) German and Jewish (Ashkenazic): variant of *Gürtler* (see GURTLER) or, in some instances, of *Gärtner* (see GARTNER).
GIVEN NAME Jewish 5%. *Ari* (2).

Gertner (274) German and Jewish (Ashkenazic): variant spelling of **Gärtner** 'gardener' (see GARTNER).
GIVEN NAMES Jewish 11%. *Alter* (2), *Ilya* (2), *Chaim, Izidor, Mendel, Meyer, Shimon, Shmuel, Zalman*.

Gertsch (240) Swiss German: from a short form of any of the Germanic personal names formed with *gēr, gār* 'spear', 'lance'.
GIVEN NAMES German 5%. *Markus, Ulrich*.

Gertz (783) **1.** North German: patronymic from a Germanic personal name composed of *gār, gēr* 'spear', 'lance' + *hard* 'hardy', 'brave', 'strong'. **2.** Jewish (eastern Ashkenazic): variant, under Russian influence (see GOREN), of HERZ.

Gervais (1952) French: from the Norman personal name *Gervase*, of disputed etymology. The name was borne by a certain St. Gervasius, around whom a cult grew up following the discovery of his remains in Milan in 386.
FOREBEARS A family Gervais from Bordeaux was in Quebec city by 1665; another bearer of the name, from La Rochelle, went to Quebec city in 1669; one from Normandy was in Île d'Orléans by 1672; one from Paris had removed to Montreal by 1676; and one from Brittany had settled in Quebec city by 1697.
GIVEN NAMES French 13%. *Marcel* (11), *Normand* (8), *Armand* (4), *Aime* (3), *Andre* (3), *Emile* (3), *Pierre* (3), *Raoul* (3), *Alain* (2), *Alcide* (2), *Camille* (2), *Cecile* (2).

Gervase (175) **1.** Americanized form of Italian GERVASIO. **2.** English: variant of JARVIS.
GIVEN NAMES Italian 9%. *Angelo, Rocco, Salvatore*.

Gervasi (464) Italian: patronymic or plural form of GERVASIO.
GIVEN NAMES Italian 21%. *Angelo* (6), *Vito* (3), *Gaetano* (2), *Gino* (2), *Antonino, Biagio, Canio, Concetto, Cosimo, Domenica, Giacinto, Giovan*.

Gervasio (240) Italian: from the personal name *Gervasio* (see GERVAIS, JARVIS).
GIVEN NAMES Italian 16%; Spanish 8%; French 4%. *Emilio* (2), *Aldo, Angelo, Antonio, Dino, Egidio, Eluterio, Francesca, Gregorio, Raffaele, Ugo; Fidel, Jose, Manuel, Maurilio, Romana; Camille* (2), *Noele*.

Gervin (129) **1.** German: habitational name from Gervin near Kolberg, southeast of Berlin. **2.** French: perhaps an altered form of **Gerboin**, from a pet form of the Germanic personal name *Gerbert* (see GERBRACHT).

Gerwe (111) German: occupational name for a tanner, from Middle High German *gerwe*, a variant of GEBER.

Gerwig (346) German: from the Germanic personal name *Gerwig*, composed of the elements *gēr* 'spear' + *wīg* 'battle', 'fight'. GIVEN NAMES French 4%. *Andre, Henri*.

Gerwin (189) German: from a Germanic personal name composed of the elements *gēr, gār* 'spear' + *wine* 'friend'.

Gerwitz (144) Jewish (from Ukraine): of uncertain origin; perhaps a variant of HOROWITZ or alternatively an altered form of GEWIRTZ.

Gery (226) **1.** Southern French (**Géry**): variant of GILLE. **2.** French (**Géry**): from the Germanic personal name *Gaugeric*, which was borne by a 6th-century bishop of Cambrai. **3.** Possibly a respelling of Swiss German **Gehry**, a variant of GEHR.

Gesch (118) North German: from *Gesch*, a metronymic from a pet form of *Gertrud*, the first syllable deriving from Old High German *ger, gar* 'spear'. GIVEN NAMES German 6%. *Fritz, Wolfgang*.

Geschke (199) **1.** North German: from the personal name *Gesche*, a pet form of any of several personal names beginning with *G-*. **2.** Polish: variant of JESCHKE. GIVEN NAMES German 5%. *Dietrich, Juergen, Ralf*.

Geschwind (131) German: nickname for a speedy individual, from Middle High German *geswinde* (modern German *geschwind*) 'fast', 'impetuous'.

Gesell (442) German: from Middle High German *geselle* 'companion' (Old High German *gisell(i)o*, a derivative of *sal* 'hall', originally referring to someone who shared living accommodation). In the medieval trade guilds, this word acquired the specialized sense of 'journeyman', i.e. one who had completed his apprenticeship and was working in the workshop of a master craftsman; the surname may well be derived from this specialized sense, rather than merely from a nickname meaning 'companion' or 'friend'. GIVEN NAMES German 4%. *Dieter, Gerhard, Hans, Inge*.

Geske (564) German: **1.** variant of GESCHKE. **2.** habitational name for someone from Geseke near Lippstadt, Westphalia.

Gesler (143) Probably an altered spelling of German GESSLER.

Gesner (232) Variant spelling of German GESSNER.

Gess (298) German: probably from a variant (possibly Slavic) of the Germanic personal name *Gero*, a short form of the various personal names formed with *gār, gēr* 'spear', 'lance'.

Gessel (200) South German: probably a variant spelling of **Gessele** or **Gessl**, diminutives of *Gasse* 'alley', 'side street', a topographic name for someone who lived in a side street or alley.

Gesser (108) South German: variant of GASSER. GIVEN NAME German 5%. *Ilse*.

Gessert (187) German: probably a variant of **Gassert**, which is a variant of GASSER.

Gessler (368) South German: variant spelling of **Gässler** (see GASSLER). GIVEN NAMES German 6%. *Kurt* (2), *Otto* (2), *Alois, Johannes, Klaus*.

Gessner (1135) **1.** German: variant of GASSER. **2.** Swiss German: occupational name for a goat herd, from Middle High German *geiz* 'goat' + *-(n)er* agent suffix. GIVEN NAMES German 4%. *Kurt* (5), *Gerhard* (2), *Otto* (2), *Egon, Matthias, Reinhold, Udo*.

Gest (311) North German: **1.** topographic name for someone who lived in one of the areas of geest (sandy soil) in northwestern Germany. **2.** habitational name from any of several places so named in the Lower Rhine region.

Gesualdi (188) Italian: patronymic or plural form of GESUALDO. GIVEN NAMES Italian 28%. *Vito* (4), *Rocco* (3), *Angelo* (2), *Arcangelo, Carmine, Gerardo, Giovanni, Luigi, Salvatore, Santo*.

Gesualdo (114) Italian: apparently from the medieval personal name *Gesualdo*, composed of the Germanic elements *gīsil* 'pledge', 'hostage', 'noble offspring' (see GIESEL) + *wald* 'rule', or perhaps a hybrid construction of which the first element is Italian *Gesù* 'Jesus'. However, it is possible that the family name is rather habitational in origin, from Gesualdo in Avellino province. GIVEN NAMES Italian 16%. *Americo, Antonio, Domenic, Fausto, Giacomo, Gustavo, Rocco, Sal*.

Getchell (1015) **1.** Altered spelling of Irish GATCHELL. **2.** Altered spelling of South German **Götschel**, **Goetschel**, from a short form of GOTTFRIED or GOTTSCHALK.

Geter (645) **1.** German: occupational name presumably for a field or garden worker, from Middle High German *jeten* 'to weed'. **2.** In some cases it may be an altered spelling of French **Jetté** (see JETTE).

Gethers (248) Origin unidentified. Perhaps a variant of German GATHERS or English GAITHER.

Gethin (18) Welsh: Anglicized form of *cethin*, a nickname meaning 'dark', 'swarthy' or 'ugly'.

Getman (662) Jewish (from Belarus and Ukraine): nickname from Russian *getman* 'Cossack chief', Polish *hetman*. See HETMAN.

Getsinger (200) Altered spelling of German **Getzinger**, a habitational name from

Götzingen in Baden, formerly called *Gezinchheim*.

Getson (125) English: voiced variant of **Jetson**, a patronymic from the personal name *Jutt*, a pet form of JORDAN. Compare JUDSON.

Gettel (255) German: Americanized spelling of **Göttel** (see GOETTEL).

Gettelfinger (113) French (Alsatian): habitational name from Gettelfingen, a place name of German origin.

Getter (395) Probably an altered spelling of German **Götter**, a derivative from a short form of a personal name composed with Old High German *got* 'god' or Old Saxon *gōd* 'good', as in GOTTFRIED.

Gettig (154) **1.** German: from a short form of a personal name derived from Middle High German *gate* 'companion'. See GETTEL 1. **2.** Altered spelling of German **Göttig**, a variant of GETTER 1.

Getting (155) **1.** German: variant of GETTIG or **Götting** (see GOETTING). **2.** From an Anglicized form of the Welsh personal name *Gutyn* (see GITTINGS).

Gettinger (316) **1.** German: variant of GETTIG 1. **2.** Americanized spelling of German **Göttinger**, a habitational name for someone from Götting in Bavaria or from any of the places called Göttingen in Lower Saxony, Westphalia, Hesse, and Württemberg. **3.** Jewish (eastern Ashkenazic): variant of OETTINGER, with an inorganic initial *H* transformed into *G* under Russian influence. GIVEN NAMES Jewish 4%. *Emanuel* (2), *Miriam* (2), *Yisrael* (2), *Isadore, Yerachmiel*.

Gettings (435) Welsh: variant of GITTINGS.

Gettis (172) Variant of northern Irish GETTY.

Gettle (332) Respelling of German GETTEL.

Gettler (226) German: **1.** probably a spelling variant of **Gättler**, from Middle High German *gate* 'companion', see GETTIG 1. **2.** altered spelling of Swiss **Göttler**, from a short form of the personal names GOTTFRIED or *Gotthard*.

Gettman (311) German (**Gettmann**): variant of German and Swiss **Göttmann** or **Goettmann**, a variant of **Gottmann** (see GOTTMAN).

Getto (134) Italian: possibly from a pet form of a personal name ending in *-gio*, as for example *Ambrogetto* from *Ambrogio*.

Getts (256) Altered spelling of Jewish GETZ or German **Götz** (see GOETZ).

Getty (1124) Northern Irish (Derry): reduced Anglicized form of Gaelic **Mag Eitigh** 'son of *Eiteach*', a personal name from *eiteach* 'winged'.

Gettys (595) Variant of northern Irish GETTY.

Getz (3141) German and Jewish (Ashkenazic): variant of **Götz** (see GOETZ).

Geurin (290) Origin unidentified: perhaps a variant of French and Irish GUERIN. This name is clustered in AR and KY.

Geurink (127) Dutch (**Geurinck**): reduced form of **Goederick**, from a Germanic personal name composed of the elements *god* 'god' + *rīc* 'power(ful)' or alternatively a patronymic from a derivative of the personal name *Gregorius* (see GREGORY) or of a Germanic personal name such as *Goder(t)* (see GOTHARD) or *Go(de)rik*.

Geurts (368) Dutch: patronymic from the Germanic personal names *Godevaard* (see GODFREY) or *Godert* (see GOTHARD).
GIVEN NAMES French 4%. *Florent* (2), *Jacques*.

Gevedon (137) Perhaps an altered spelling of French **Gévaudan**, a regional name denoting someone from a former area of France corresponding to the modern department of Lozère and part of Haute–Loire.

Geving (213) Norwegian: unexplained.

Gewirtz (248) Jewish (eastern Ashkenazic): metonymic occupational name for a spicer, from Yiddish *gevirts* 'spice' (Middle High German, Old High German *(ge)würz* 'herb', 'plant', 'root').
GIVEN NAMES Jewish 18%. *Yosef* (3), *Gershon* (2), *Yonah* (2), *Hinda*, *Mordechai*, *Shimon*, *Shmuel*, *Varda*, *Zipporah*.

Geyer (3276) German: nickname for a greedy or rapacious person, from Middle High and Middle Low German *gīr(e)* 'large bird of prey', 'vulture'. Some early examples may be a habitational name from houses bearing the sign of a bird of prey or from a place named Geyer near Zwickau, in Saxony, which is probably ultimately from the same word.
GIVEN NAMES German 4%. *Hans* (7), *Franz* (3), *Kurt* (3), *Otto* (3), *Frieda* (2), *Horst* (2), *Arno*, *Bernhardt*, *Ernst*, *Erwin*, *Gerhard*, *Hannelore*.

Geyman (140) Russianized form of German GEHMAN.
GIVEN NAMES Russian 12%. *Aleksandr* (2), *Grigory* (2), *Anatoly*, *Fanya*, *Michail*, *Serafima*.

Gfeller (226) South German: topographic name for someone who lived by a gorge, Middle High German *gevelle*, or a habitational name for someone from any of various places in Bavaria and Austria named from this word.

Ghaffari (154) Muslim: from the Arabic family name **Ghaffārī**, denoting someone descended from an ancestor bearing the name *Ghaffār*, from Arabic *ghaffār* 'merciful'. *Al-Ghaffār* 'the Merciful' is an attribute of Allah.
GIVEN NAMES Muslim 71%. *Ali* (4), *Mehrdad* (3), *Mohammad* (3), *Mohsen* (3), *Ramin* (3), *Abbas* (2), *Ahmad* (2), *Fereydoon* (2), *Mahmoud* (2), *Mohamad* (2), *Nader* (2), *Saeed* (2).

Ghan (136) Reduced form of Irish MCGHAN, a variant of MCGANN.

Ghanem (125) Muslim (Arabic and Turkish): from a personal name based on Arabic *ghanem* 'successful', 'prosperous'.
GIVEN NAMES Muslim 60%. *Nabil* (4), *Ahmed* (3), *Khalil* (3), *Mohamed* (3), *Bassam* (2), *Abdullah*, *Ali*, *Assaf*, *Ayman*, *Bahjat*, *Fady*, *Ghanem*.

Ghani (166) Muslim: from a personal name based on Arabic *ghanī* 'rich'.
GIVEN NAMES Muslim 85%. *Abdul* (7), *Usman* (6), *Mohammed* (4), *Javed* (3), *Abdool* (2), *Abu* (2), *Ali* (2), *Ashraf* (2), *Jalil* (2), *Jamal* (2), *Mohammad* (2), *Rashid* (2).

Ghannam (108) Arabic: occupational name from *ghannām* 'shepherd'.
GIVEN NAMES Arabic 67%. *Mahmoud* (4), *Ahmad* (3), *Khalil* (3), *Aziz* (2), *Ghanem* (2), *Jalil* (2), *Sabri* (2), *Suha* (2), *Ameen*, *Anwar*, *Farha*, *Farida*.

Ghant (101) English and Scottish: variant of GHENT, a habitational name for someone from Ghent in Flanders.

Gharibian (101) Armenian: patronymic from Turkish dialect *gharib* 'stranger', 'wanderer', 'impoverished person'.
GIVEN NAMES Armenian 65%; Scandinavian 4%. *Razmik* (4), *Vigen* (3), *Kevork* (2), *Anahid*, *Antranik*, *Ara*, *Armen*, *Arsen*, *Artush*, *Dikran*, *Galoust*, *Garegin*.

Ghattas (137) Muslim: unexplained.
GIVEN NAMES Muslim 49%; French 5%. *Amin* (2), *Asad* (2), *Habeeb* (2), *Naguib* (2), *Roshdy* (2), *Samir* (2), *Samy* (2), *Adib*, *Aiman*, *Amgad*, *Assad*, *Bahgat*; *Emile* (2), *Pascal*, *Pierre*.

Ghazal (102) Muslim: from a personal name based on Arabic *ghazāl* 'gazelle'. Abū Ḥāmid al-Ghazāli (died 1111) was a famous Muslim sage.
GIVEN NAMES Muslim 49%; French 10%. *Fadi* (3), *Ahmed* (2), *Ismat* (2), *Nabil* (2), *Samira* (2), *Ahmad*, *Antoun*, *Esam*, *Eyad*, *Faris*, *Ibtissam*, *Maher*; *Alain*, *Antoine*, *Lucien*, *Michel*, *Pierre*.

Ghazarian (168) Armenian: patronymic from the personal name *Ghazar*, variant of *Łazar* (see LAZAR).
GIVEN NAMES Armenian 69%. *Ghazar* (4), *Ara* (3), *Anahid* (2), *Armen* (2), *Avedis* (2), *Garo* (2), *Nerses* (2), *Norair* (2), *Rouben* (2), *Shahen* (2), *Vahan* (2), *Vahe* (2).

Ghazi (106) Muslim: from a personal name based on Arabic *ghāzī* 'conqueror', 'fighter for the faith'. This was a title borne by the Mughal emperor Aurangzeb (1658–1707).
GIVEN NAMES Muslim 67%; French 4%. *Abdol* (2), *Ali* (2), *Bassam* (2), *Hassan* (2), *Nasser* (2), *Saeed* (2), *Sultan* (2), *Abbas*, *Abdo*, *Ahmad*, *Ebrahim*, *Faisal*; *Antoine*, *Jean-Yves*.

Ghee (347) Irish and Scottish: variant of GEE.

Gheen (369) Probably an Americanized form of Irish GEOGHEGAN.
FOREBEARS Thomas and Joseph Gheen are recorded in 1768 in the tax records of West Bradford Township, Chester County, PA.

Ghent (437) English: habitational name for someone from Ghent in Flanders. Compare GENT.

Gherardi (190) Italian: patronymic or plural form of *Gherardo*, one of the many Italian equivalents of GERARD.
GIVEN NAMES Italian 15%. *Silvio* (2), *Alessandro*, *Angelo*, *Antonio*, *Donato*, *Egidio*, *Ennio*, *Enzo*, *Gildo*, *Lucio*, *Luigi*, *Primo*.

Ghere (120) Variant of GERE.
GIVEN NAME German 5%. *Otto* (2).

Ghezzi (169) Italian: patronymic or plural form of a nickname from Old Italian *ghezzo* 'dark', with reference to hair-, beard-, or skin-color. The term originally related to horses, and in some cases the name may have alluded to the owner of an animal of this color. *Ghezzo* is also recorded as a personal name, of Germanic origin.
GIVEN NAMES Italian 14%. *Giovanni* (2), *Reno* (2), *Angelo*, *Bartolomeo*, *Guilio*, *Leno*, *Lido*, *Nino*, *Severino*, *Tiziano*.

Ghilardi (136) Italian (Lombardy): patronymic or plural form of the Germanic personal name *Ghilardo*, one of the many Italian equivalents of GERARD.
GIVEN NAMES Italian 16%. *Mario* (3), *Franco* (2), *Renato* (2), *Enrico*, *Geno*, *Lino*, *Lorenzo*, *Silvano*.

Ghilarducci (104) Italian: patronymic or plural form of *Ghilarduccio*, a pet form of *Ghilardo* (see GHILARDI).
GIVEN NAMES Italian 11%. *Amato*, *Angelo*, *Dino*.

Ghio (170) Northern Italian: variant of GUIDO.
GIVEN NAMES French 5%. *Serge* (2), *Anatole*.

Gholson (845) Variant of English GOLD-STONE 2 and 3.

Gholston (554) Variant of English GOLD-STONE 2 and 3.

Ghormley (289) Variant of Irish GORMLEY.

Ghose (100) Indian: variant of GHOSH.
GIVEN NAMES Indian 73%. *Amitava* (2), *Anjan* (2), *Sudipta* (2), *Anupam*, *Arup*, *Bharati*, *Biswa*, *Chandra*, *Dipankar*, *Gautam*, *Manash*, *Nimai*.

Ghosh (602) Indian (Bengal) and Bangladeshi: Hindu (Kayasth) occupational name, from Sanskrit *ghoṣa* 'cowherd'.
GIVEN NAMES Indian 85%. *Amit* (6), *Arun* (5), *Ashok* (5), *Kalyan* (5), *Swapan* (5), *Amitava* (4), *Shyamal* (4), *Ananta* (3), *Ashim* (3), *Asish* (3), *Atish* (3), *Bijoy* (3).

Ghrist (186) French and English: perhaps a variant of CHRIST.
GIVEN NAMES French 4%. *Mechelle*, *Michel*.

Giacalone (582) Southern Italian: from Sicilian *ggiaccluni* 'small field rat', 'shrew'.

GIVEN NAMES Italian 20%. *Vito* (8), *Giuseppe* (4), *Sal* (3), *Gaspare* (2), *Mario* (2), *Nicolo* (2), *Nino* (2), *Pietro* (2), *Salvatore* (2), *Angelo, Antonino, Gabriele, Rosario.*

Giaccone (130) Italian: augmentative form of **Giacco**, from a reduced form of the personal name GIACOMO (see JAMES).
GIVEN NAMES Italian 22%. *Mario* (2), *Sal* (2), *Salvatore* (2), *Antonio.*

Giachetti (132) Italian: patronymic from a pet form of the personal name *Giacomo* (see JAMES, JACOB).
GIVEN NAMES Italian 18%. *Angelo* (2), *Salvatore* (2), *Gaetano, Pierluigi, Romano.*

Giacinto (102) Italian: from the personal name *Giacinto*, Greek *Hyakinthos*, a name borne by various saints, including one venerated especially in the Eastern Church. Compare Spanish JACINTO.
GIVEN NAMES Italian 19%. *Sal* (2), *Benito, Ernesto, Rocco, Silvio.*

Giacobbe (355) Italian: from the personal name *Giacobbe*, one of the Italian forms of JACOB.
GIVEN NAMES Italian 14%. *Nicola* (2), *Rocco* (2), *Salvatore* (2), *Alessandro, Angelo, Antonino, Antonio, Dino, Francesco, Nino.*

Giacomelli (154) Italian: patronymic or plural form of *Giacomello*, a pet form of the personal name *Giacomo* (see JAMES).
GIVEN NAMES Italian 18%. *Geno* (2), *Angelo, Carlo, Giancarlo, Lia, Marcellino, Nino, Olindo, Rino, Umberto.*

Giacometti (110) Italian: from a pet form of the personal name GIACOMO (see JAMES).
GIVEN NAMES Italian 21%. *Guido* (3), *Alfeo, Alfredo, Alredo, Augusto, Luigi, Marco, Marino, Mario, Primo, Tiziana.*

Giacomini (329) Italian: patronymic from a pet form of the personal name GIACOMO.
GIVEN NAMES Italian 8%. *Reno* (2), *Angelo, Dino, Enrico, Geno, Guerino, Matteo, Nino, Paolo, Romano, Salvatore.*

Giacomo (181) Italian: from the personal name *Giacomo*, from Latin *Jacobus* via Late Latin *Jac(o)mus* (see JAMES).
GIVEN NAMES Italian 6%. *Domenico, Gino, Salvatore.*

Giacona (105) Italian: variant of GIACONE.
GIVEN NAMES Italian 33%. *Corrado* (3), *Salvatore* (3), *Amedeo, Benedetto, Domenic, Gasper, Giorgio, Giovanni, Giuseppe.*

Giacone (158) Italian: from an augmentative of *Giaco*, a short form of the personal name GIACOMO.
GIVEN NAMES Italian 15%. *Carlo* (4), *Salvatore* (3), *Luigi.*

Giaimo (372) from an Italianized spelling of the Spanish personal name JAIME, equivalent to Italian *Giacomo* (see JAMES).
GIVEN NAMES Italian 21%. *Angelo* (8), *Salvatore* (6), *Mario* (5), *Rosario* (3), *Sal* (2), *Basilio, Carmel, Francesca, Giovanni, Ignazio, Matteo, Natale, Santo, Vita.*

Gialanella (141) Italian: unexplained.
GIVEN NAMES Italian 21%. *Americo, Angelo, Antonio, Gaetano, Giovanni, Mario, Ovidio, Raffaele.*

Giallombardo (129) Italian: from a compound of the personal name GIANNI + *Lombardo* (see LOMBARDI).
GIVEN NAMES Italian 22%. *Salvatore* (4), *Angelo* (2), *Luciano* (2).

Giambalvo (291) Italian: from the personal name *Giambalvo*, composed of the personal names GIANNI + *Balvo*, a southern variant of BALBO.
GIVEN NAMES Italian 14%. *Santo* (4), *Angelo* (2), *Biagio, Gaspare, Guiseppe, Pietro, Saverio, Vita, Vito.*

Giambattista (115) Italian: from the compound personal name *Giambattista*, composed of GIANNI + BATTISTA. Compare French JEAN-BAPTISTE.
GIVEN NAMES Italian 10%. *Crescenzo, Dominico, Lucio.*

Giambra (193) Italian: topographic name from *ciambra* 'vault', 'chamber'; in Calabria, the same word denoted a guard's post raised above the ground.
GIVEN NAMES Italian 14%. *Angelo* (3), *Santo* (3), *Biagio.*

Giambrone (495) Italian: probably from an augmentative of GIAMBRA, or alternatively directly from French *chambron*, an augmentative of *chambre* 'room'.
GIVEN NAMES Italian 18%. *Angelo* (5), *Salvatore* (5), *Vito* (2), *Aldo, Antonio, Benedetto, Carmine, Gino, Graziella, Maurizio, Nicolo, Rocco.*

Giambruno (114) Italian: from the compound personal name *Giambruno*, composed of GIANNI + BRUNO.
GIVEN NAMES Italian 7%. *Salvatore, Vito.*

Giammanco (122) Italian: either from the compound personal name *Giammanco*, composed of GIANNI + *manco* 'left-handed' (see MANCO), or in some cases an assimilated form of **Giambanco**, which is a compound of GIANNI + *Banco*.
GIVEN NAMES Italian 32%. *Angelo* (6), *Ciro* (2), *Giuseppe* (2), *Salvatore* (2), *Piero, Pietro, Rosolino, Salvator.*

Giammarco (223) Italian: from a compound personal name composed of GIANNI + MARCO.
GIVEN NAMES Italian 30%. *Mario* (3), *Pasquale* (3), *Alfonso, Americo, Antonio, Armando, Attilio, Carlo, Cesare, Dante, Emilio, Ettore, Filippo, Guerino, Luigi, Massimo, Nino, Orlando, Ovidio, Panfilo, Renato, Rico.*

Giammarino (189) Italian: from a compound of the personal names GIANNI + MARINO.
GIVEN NAMES Italian 29%. *Angelo* (3), *Adriano* (2), *Antonio* (2), *Donato* (2), *Pasquale* (2), *Salvatore* (2), *Carmine, Claudio, Concetta, Domenic, Gaetano, Gennaro, Giuseppe, Vito.*

Giammona (156) Italian: from the female personal name *Giambona*, a compound of *Gianna* (feminine form of GIANNI) + BONA.
GIVEN NAMES Italian 23%. *Ciro* (5), *Carmine, Giovanna, Guiseppe, Rosario, Salvatore, Vincenzo, Vito.*

Giampa (173) Italian (**Giampà**): from a short form of various compound names such as *Giampaglia*, GIAMPAOLO, GIAMPAPA, etc.
GIVEN NAMES Italian 16%. *Alfredo, Domenic, Emilio, Luciano, Marco, Natale.*

Giampaolo (155) Italian: from a compound personal name composed of the personal names GIANNI + PAOLO.
GIVEN NAMES Italian 24%. *Mario* (4), *Rocco* (3), *Angelo, Antonio, Artenio, Casimiro, Constantino, Dante, Enrico, Giuseppe, Marco, Paolo, Pasquale, Umberto, Vito.*

Giampapa (111) Italian: from a compound of the personal name GIANNI + PAPA.
GIVEN NAMES Italian 39%. *Santo* (7), *Salvatore* (3), *Francesco* (2), *Cirino, Gianni, Gioacchino, Giuseppe.*

Giampietro (328) Italian: from a compound personal name composed of the personal names GIANNI + PIETRO.

Gianakos (113) Greek: patronymic from *Giannis*, vernacular form of the personal name *Iōannēs* 'John' (see JOHN). The *-akos* patronymic suffix is associated with the Mani peninsula in the southwestern Peloponnese.
GIVEN NAMES Greek 8%. *Constantinos, Evangelos, Spiro.*

Giancola (514) Italian: from a compound personal name composed of the elements *Gian* (a short form of GIANNI) + *Cola* (a short form of *Nicola*; see NICHOLAS).
GIVEN NAMES Italian 12%. *Angelo* (4), *Dante* (3), *Alessandro, Antonio, Carmine, Cosimo, Domenico, Donato, Guiseppe, Marcello, Nicola, Nino.*

Gianelli (124) Italian: **1.** variant of GIANNELLI. **2.** possibly from a pet form of the rare personal name *Giano*, from Latin *Janus*.
GIVEN NAMES Italian 8%. *Antonio, Giuseppe, Nino, Vito.*

Gianfrancesco (154) Italian: from a compound personal name composed of GIANNI + FRANCESCO.
GIVEN NAMES Italian 28%. *Luigi* (4), *Antonio* (2), *Domenic* (2), *Domenico, Filomena, Franco, Gianni, Gino, Liberato, Salvatore, Ugo.*

Giang (404) Vietnamese: unexplained.
GIVEN NAMES Vietnamese 51%; Chinese 20%. *Ha* (11), *Hoa* (7), *Dung* (6), *Hung* (6), *Minh* (6), *Vinh* (6), *Linh* (4), *Muoi* (4), *Son* (4), *Anh* (3), *Cuong* (3), *Doan* (3); *Hong* (7), *Chi* (5), *Hon* (2), *Chu, Chun, Dong, Ho, Sang, Song, Tong.*

Giangiulio (105) Italian: from a compound personal name composed of GIANNI + *Giulio*, Italian form of JULIUS.

GIVEN NAMES Italian 14%. *Nicola* (2), *Arduino, Elio, Luciano.*

Giangrande (202) Italian: nickname meaning 'big John', from a compound of the personal name *Gian*, a reduced form of GIOVANNI, + *grande* 'big'.
GIVEN NAMES Italian 13%. *Salvatore* (2), *Alberto, Alfonso, Camillo, Emilio, Ercole, Gaetana, Gino, Mario.*

Giangrasso (109) Italian: nickname meaning 'fat John', from a compound of the personal name *Gian*, a reduced form of GIOVANNI, + *grasso* 'fat'.
GIVEN NAMES Italian 28%. *Angelo, Annamaria, Carlo, Filippo, Gaetano, Giacomo, Nicolo, Sal, Salvatore.*

Giangreco (146) Italian: nickname meaning 'John the Greek', from a compound of *Gian*, a reduced form of the personal name GIOVANNI, + GRECO.
GIVEN NAMES Italian 16%. *Carmine* (2), *Corrado, Gaetano, Gino, Giuseppe, Leonardo, Salvatore.*

Giangregorio (151) Italian: from a compound personal name composed of the elements GIANNI + GREGORIO.
GIVEN NAMES Italian 25%. *Angelo* (8), *Antonio* (3), *Carmine, Ciriaco, Domenico, Duilio, Lorenzo, Silvio.*

Gianino (207) Italian: **1.** dialect variant of GIANNINO. **2.** possibly from a pet form of the personal name *Giano*, from Latin *Janus*.
GIVEN NAMES Italian 16%. *Salvatore* (6), *Carmelo* (2), *Angelo, Luciano, Orazio, Sal.*

Giannantonio (141) Italian: from a compound personal name composed of the elements GIANNI + ANTONIO.
GIVEN NAMES Italian 20%. *Aldo, Gildo, Gino, Guido, Lelio, Nicola, Rocco.*

Giannattasio (188) Italian: from a compound personal name composed of the elements GIANNI + a reduced form of ATTANASIO.
GIVEN NAMES Italian 18%. *Agostino, Americo, Angelo, Gerardo, Mario, Onofrio, Orlando, Rocco.*

Giannelli (283) Italian: from a pet form of the personal name GIANNI.
GIVEN NAMES Italian 19%. *Saverio* (2), *Aldo, Antonio, Carmela, Carmine, Domenic, Erminio, Ettore, Fiore, Giovanni, Guido, Oronzo.*

Giannetta (110) Italian: from a feminine form of the personal name GIANNETTO. The feminine form is probably due to the influence of the Italian word *famiglia* 'family'.
GIVEN NAMES Italian 20%. *Salvatore* (3), *Amelio* (2), *Amedio, Angelo, Eliseo, Rocco.*

Giannetti (396) Italian: patronymic or plural form of the personal name GIANNETTO.
GIVEN NAMES Italian 17%. *Gino* (3), *Silvio* (3), *Enrico* (2), *Rocco* (2), *Antonio, Bartolomeo, Carmino, Cosimo, Dante, Dario, Domenica, Donato.*

Giannetto (165) Italian: from a pet form of the personal name GIANNI.
GIVEN NAMES Italian 25%. *Carlo* (3), *Santo* (3), *Angelo* (2), *Antonio* (2), *Cosimo, Gaetano, Giovanni, Salvatore.*

Gianni (328) Italian: from the personal name *Gianni*, a reduced form of *Giovanni*, Italian equivalent of JOHN.
GIVEN NAMES Italian 14%. *Rocco* (5), *Angelo* (3), *Gaetano* (2), *Croce, Fiorella, Giovanni, Pierina, Reno, Saverio.*

Giannini (1333) Italian: patronymic or plural form of the personal name GIANNINO.
GIVEN NAMES Italian 13%. *Angelo* (6), *Dino* (5), *Luigi* (4), *Aldo* (3), *Pasquale* (3), *Salvatore* (3), *Umberto* (3), *Vito* (3), *Emidio* (2), *Guido* (2), *Marino* (2), *Alessandro.*

Giannino (154) Italian: from a pet form of the personal name GIANNI.
GIVEN NAMES Italian 13%. *Salvatore* (2), *Angelo, Ennio, Giuseppe, Sal.*

Giannola (122) Italian: from a pet form of the personal name GIANNI.
GIVEN NAMES Italian 30%. *Vito* (3), *Antonino* (2), *Salvatore* (2), *Carmela, Dino, Gino, Giuseppe, Pietro, Stefano.*

Giannone (600) Italian: from an augmentative of the personal name GIANNI, a nickname meaning 'Big John'.
GIVEN NAMES Italian 22%. *Angelo* (6), *Sal* (5), *Mario* (4), *Salvatore* (4), *Carmelo* (2), *Enrico* (2), *Onofrio* (2), *Rinaldo* (2), *Rocco* (2), *Aldo, Alfonse, Alfonso, Antonio, Carlo, Marta, Rosario.*

Giannoni (119) Italian: patronymic from the personal name GIANNONE.
GIVEN NAMES Italian 13%; Spanish 9%. *Angelo, Battista, Corrado, Gino, Renzo; Mario* (5), *Alberto, Benito, Domingo, Gerardo, Lino, Sergio.*

Giannopoulos (120) Greek: patronymic (pronounced 'Yannopoulos') from *Giannis*, vernacular form of *Iōannēs* 'John' (see JOHN) + the patronymic ending -*poulos*. This ending occurs chiefly in the Peloponnese; it is derived from Latin *pullus* 'nestling', 'chick'.
GIVEN NAMES Greek 24%; Italian 7%. *Nikolaos* (2), *Vasilios* (2), *Anastasios, Angeliki, Athanasios, Despina, Ilias, Kyriakos, Nicolaos, Spiro, Stelios; Angelo* (5).

Giannotti (425) Italian: patronymic or plural form of *Giannotto*, a pet form of the personal name GIANNI.
GIVEN NAMES Italian 14%. *Giovanni* (3), *Aldo* (2), *Attilio* (2), *Franco* (2), *Salvatore* (2), *Angelo, Gennaro, Gino, Guido, Leno, Lorenzo, Marino.*

Giannuzzi (125) Italian: from the personal name *Giannuzzo*, a pet form of the personal name GIANNI.
GIVEN NAMES Italian 27%. *Vito* (4), *Angelo* (2), *Aldo, Alessio, Antonio, Francesco, Gino, Giovanni, Onofrio, Santo.*

Gianopoulos (105) Greek: variant spelling of GIANNOPOULOS.
GIVEN NAMES Greek 6%. *Spero, Stylianos.*

Gianotti (154) Italian: variant of GIANNOTTI.
GIVEN NAMES Italian 9%. *Marco, Paolo.*

Giaquinto (483) Italian: from a variant of the personal name GIACINTO.
GIVEN NAMES Italian 13%. *Angelo* (3), *Carmine* (2), *Antonio, Biagio, Corrado, Domenic, Giovanni, Guido, Pasquale, Salvatore, Sebastiano, Silvio.*

Giard (315) French: possibly a reduced form of **Girard**, the French form of GARRETT.
FOREBEARS A family named Giard from Poitiers was in Montreal by 1665.
GIVEN NAMES French 11%. *Emile* (2), *Normand* (2), *Armand, Herve, Jacques, Joffre, Laurette, Maryse, Pierre, Yvan.*

Giardina (1110) Italian: **1.** from a feminine form of GIARDINO. **2.** from the medieval female personal name *Iardina, Giardina*.
GIVEN NAMES Italian 21%. *Salvatore* (21), *Angelo* (8), *Giuseppe* (7), *Vito* (5), *Sal* (3), *Santo* (3), *Antonio* (2), *Bartolomeo* (2), *Biagio* (2), *Domenico* (2), *Gaetano* (2), *Saverio* (2).

Giardini (207) Italian: patronymic or plural form of GIARDINO.
GIVEN NAMES Italian 18%. *Angelo* (3), *Dino* (2), *Giacomo* (2), *Nino* (2), *Carmine, Dante, Donato, Guido, Luigi, Remo.*

Giardino (384) Italian (mainly south): from *giardino* 'garden', hence a metonymic occupational name for a gardener (see GARDNER), a topographic name for someone who lived by a garden, or a habitational name from any of various places named Giardino, for example in Bologna, or from Giardina Gallotti, or Giardinello in Palermo.
GIVEN NAMES Italian 16%. *Angelo* (7), *Salvatore* (3), *Cosmo, Nicola, Rocco, Romeo, Sal, Vito.*

Giarraputo (121) Italian: origin uncertain; possibly from Sicilian *ggiarraùtu* or *ggiaragutu* 'wild rose'
GIVEN NAMES Italian 11%. *Salvatore* (2), *Pietrina.*

Giarratana (101) Southern Italian (Sicily): habitational name from a place so named in Ragusa.
GIVEN NAMES Italian 19%. *Rosario* (2), *Angelo, Sal, Salvatore, Silvio.*

Giarratano (287) Southern Italian (Sicily): **1.** habitational name for someone from Giarre in Catania province, Sicily, from an adjectival form of the place name. **2.** in some instances possibly a nickname for a charlatan or quack, Sicilian *giarratanu, iarratanu.*
GIVEN NAMES Italian 19%. *Angelo* (5), *Salvatore* (4), *Carmela* (2), *Gaspare* (2), *Nino* (2), *Carmelo, Gasper, Pasquale, Sarino.*

Giarrusso (338) Italian: from a compound personal name composed of a reduced form of the personal name GIOVANNI + the personal name *Russo* or the adjective *russo* 'red' (see ROSSO).
GIVEN NAMES Italian 16%. *Angelo* (2), *Antonio* (2), *Carlo* (2), *Vito* (2), *Alessandro*, *Carmelo*, *Carmine*, *Dante*, *Domenic*, *Enrico*, *Franco*, *Leonardo*.

Giasson (118) Respelling of French **Chiasson**.
GIVEN NAMES French 14%. *Andre*, *Jacques*, *Jean Claude*, *Jinette*, *Marcel*, *Michel*.

Giauque (153) Swiss French: variant spelling of JACQUES.

Giba (107) Polish: nickname from *gibać* 'to bow' or 'to wobble'.
GIVEN NAMES Polish 6%; Russian 4%. *Krystyna*, *Piotr*, *Urszula*; *Dmytro*.

Gibas (173) Polish: 1. from a derivative of *gibać* 'to bow' or 'to wobble'. Compare GIBA. 2. nickname from the dialect word *gibas* 'tall, slim man'.
GIVEN NAME Polish 4%. *Franciszek*.

Gibb (1485) English: from the common medieval personal name *Gib*, a short form of GILBERT. This surname is also frequent in Scotland and South Wales.

Gibbar (103) English: variant of GIBBARD.

Gibbard (167) English: from a Germanic personal name composed of the elements *geba* 'gift' + *hard* 'hardy', 'brave', 'strong' (see GEBHARDT).

Gibbens (714) 1. English: patronymic from GIBBON 1. 2. German: patronymic from a short form of a Germanic personal name formed with *geba* 'gift'.

Gibbins (442) English: patronymic from GIBBON 1.

Gibble (329) 1. English: probably a variant of KIBBLE. 2. Americanized spelling of German **Gibel** or **Gibbel** (see GIEBEL).

Gibbon (510) English: from the medieval personal name *Gibbon*, a pet form of GIBB.

Gibboney (299) Irish: variant of GIBNEY.

Gibbons (11057) English: patronymic from GIBBON.

Gibbs (21183) English: patronymic from GIBB.

Gibby (529) Welsh: probably a derivative of GIBBS or GIBBON, although in some cases it may represent the Welsh personal name *Cybi*.

Gibeau (246) French: variant of GIBEAULT.
GIVEN NAMES French 7%. *Andre*, *Henri*, *Normand*.

Gibeault (188) French: 1. from a derivative of *gib-* 'back', as for instance in *gibbeux* 'hunchbacked'. 2. from a pet form of a Germanic personal name composed with the element *geb* 'gift'.
GIVEN NAMES French 9%. *Laurent*, *Marcel*, *Michel*.

Gibeaut (113) Apparently a respelling of French GIBEAULT.

Gibel (100) French: from a pet form of a compound personal name formed with *Gib* (from Old High German *geba* 'gift') as the first element.

Giberson (649) English: probably a variant spelling of **Gibbeson**, a patronymic from GIBB.

Gibert (212) French and German: variant of GILBERT.

Gibilisco (136) Italian: topographic name for a mountain dweller, from Arabic *jabal* 'mountain' + the Italian suffix *-esco* denoting belonging or association.
GIVEN NAMES Italian 19%. *Salvatore* (3), *Santo* (3), *Angelo*, *Carlo*, *Raffaele*.

Gibler (339) German: variant of GIEBLER.

Giblin (1177) 1. Scottish and Irish: from a pet form of GIBB. 2. French: reduced form of **Gibelin**, from a pet form of a Germanic personal name formed with *gi-*.
GIVEN NAMES Irish 5%. *Brendan* (3), *Cormac*, *Murphy*.

Gibney (904) Irish (Midlands and Ulster): reduced Anglicized form of Gaelic Ó **Gibne** 'descendant of *Gibne*', a byname meaning 'hound'. See also McGIBNEY.
GIVEN NAMES Irish 4%. *Brendan*, *Conn*.

Giboney (211) Northern Irish: variant of GIBNEY.

Gibson (61941) Scottish and English: patronymic from GIBB.

Gick (263) South German: presumably from a cognate of Old Norse *gyggr* 'giant(ess)', and hence a nickname for an exceptionally tall or strange man.

Gidcumb (173) Probably of English origin. It appears to be a habitational name formed with Old English *cumb* 'combe', 'valley'; however, no likely source has been identified, and the surname is not found in England. In the U.S., there are clusters of this name in IL and KY.

Gidden (111) English: variant of GIDDINGS.

Giddens (2261) English: variant of GIDDINGS.

Giddings (1758) English: habitational name from a group of villages near Huntingdon, called Great, Little, and Steeple Gidding, named from Old English *Gyddingas* 'people of *Gydda*', a personal name of uncertain origin.

Gideon (1355) Jewish: from the Biblical name meaning 'one who cuts down' in Hebrew. It was borne by an Israelite leader appointed to deliver his people from the Midianites (Judges 6:14).

Gidley (492) English: habitational name for someone from Gidleigh in Devon, so named from an Old English personal name *Gydda* + *lēah* 'woodland clearing'.

Gidney (219) English: variant of GEDNEY.

Giebel (388) German: from Middle High German *gebel*, *gibel*, meaning 'gable' but also 'head', 'skull', hence probably a name for someone living at a house with promi-

nent gables or a nickname for someone with a large or otherwise remarkable head. The personal name *Giebold* or *Geb(w)alt*, from the stem *geb-* 'gift', may have been the origin in some instances.

Giebler (211) German: 1. from an agent derivative of Middle High German *gebel*, *gibel* 'gable'; 'head', 'skull' (see GIEBEL). 2. from a short form of a Germanic personal name formed with *geba* 'gift'.
GIVEN NAMES German 5%. *Erwin* (2), *Alois*, *Udo*.

Gieck (142) German: probably a variant spelling of **Giek**, from Middle High German *giege* 'fool', 'bewitched person', or a variant of GICK, which appears to be related in meaning.
GIVEN NAME French 4%. *Camille*.

Giedd (139) German: probably a variant of **Gött** (see GOTT). This name is one of the German names that were established in Ukraine during the 19th century.

Giefer (227) German: from a Low German form of the personal name GEBHARDT.

Gieger (220) German: variant spelling of GEIGER.

Giegerich (173) German: derivative of GICK.

Giel (204) German: 1. from a medieval personal name of which the original form was Latin *Aegidius*, from Greek *aigidion* 'kid', 'young goat'. Compare English GILES. 2. in some instances, an altered spelling of GEIL.

Gielow (290) Eastern German (under Slavic influence): habitational name from Gielow, near Malchin, in Mecklenburg.

Gienger (238) German: habitational name for someone from either of two places in Württemberg: Giengen (near Heidenheim) or Gingen (near Geislingen).
GIVEN NAMES German 8%. *Gottlieb*, *Ludwing*, *Otto*, *Reinhard*, *Ulrich*.

Gier (653) 1. German: nickname from Middle High German *gir* 'greedy', 'rapacious'. 2. North German: Low German form of GEYER.

Gierach (142) German: probably a variant of the Germanic personal name *Gero*, formed with *gār*, *gēr* 'spear', 'lance', under Slavic influence.
GIVEN NAMES German 11%. *Eldred*, *Fritz*, *Gerhard*, *Helmuth*, *Kurt*.

Giere (191) German: topographic name from a Rhineland field name, probably denoting a wedge-shaped field (see GEHR 2).

Gierhart (209) North German: variant of GERHARDT.

Giering (116) German: variant of GEHRING.

Gieringer (145) German: variant of GIERING 2.
GIVEN NAMES German 5%. *Kurt*, *Otto*.

Gierke (338) German: from a pet form, under Slavic influence, of the personal name GERHARDT.

Gierman (141) Variant of North German **Giermann**, from a short form of a personal name beginning with the element *Ger-*, for example GERHARDT.

Giersch (174) German: from the female personal name *Gerusch* or *Gerisch*, pet forms of *Gertrud* (see TRUDE), with the Slavic suffix *-usch* or *-isch*.

Giertz (127) German (Lower Rhine): patronymic, ultimately from the personal name GERHARDT.

Gies (742) **1.** North German: variant of GIESE. **2.** Altered spelling of South German **Giess**, a variant of **Güss** (see GUESS).

Giesbrecht (288) German: from a personal name composed of Old High German *gīsil* 'hostage', 'pledge', 'noble offspring' (see GIESEL) + *berht* 'bright', 'famous', a cognate of *Giselbert*.
GIVEN NAMES German 4%. *Erna, Franz, Reinold, Wilhelm.*

Giese (3026) German and Danish: from a short form of the personal name *Giselbert* (see GIESBRECHT), or any other Germanic name with *gīsil* as the first element.
GIVEN NAMES German 5%. *Otto* (9), *Klaus* (4), *Erwin* (3), *Heiner* (3), *Heinz* (2), *Uwe* (2), *Aloysius, Armin, Dieter, Erhard, Ewald, Frieda.*

Giesecke (199) German: variant of GIESEKE.
GIVEN NAMES German 16%; Scandinavian 4%. *Hans* (4), *Helmut* (2), *Benno, Ernst, Gunter, Klaus, Kurt, Otto, Rainer; Karsten.*

Gieseke (444) North German: from the personal name *Giesecke*, a pet form of *Giselbert* (see GIESBRECHT).

Gieseking (142) North German: patronymic from the personal name GIESEKE.

Giesel (129) German: from the personal name *Giesel*, a short form of any of several Germanic personal names with the first element *gīsil* 'pledge', 'hostage', 'noble offspring'. In ancient and medieval Germanic society, the younger children of kings and princes were sometimes sent to be brought up at the court of a neighboring ruler, as a pledge of peace between the two nations or clans. Thus, the male personal name *Gisil* and its feminine equivalent *Gisela* mean both 'pledge' and 'noble offspring'.

Gieseler (137) German: from a variant of the Germanic personal name *Giselher*, from *gīsil* 'offspring', 'pledge', 'noble offspring' (see GIESEL) + *heri* 'army'.
GIVEN NAME German 4%. *Manfred.*

Gieselman (221) North German (**Gieselmann**): variant of **Geiselmann** (see GEISEL).

Giesen (457) North German: **1.** patronymic from GIESE. **2.** habitational name from Giessen in Hesse, which derives its name from a castle *ze den Giezzen* 'on the streams'.

Gieser (241) German: occupational name for a foundryman, from an agent derivative of Middle High German *giezen* 'to pour or cast'.

Giesey (177) Probably an Americanized spelling of German GIESE or of Swiss German GIESEL.

Giesing (119) Dutch, North German, and Danish: patronymic from GIES(E), a short form of the personal name *Giselbert* (see GIESBRECHT).

Gieske (192) Reduced form of the German surname GIESECKE.
GIVEN NAMES German 5%. *Guenther, Juergen.*

Giesler (871) German: **1.** reduced form of German GIESELER. **2.** it may also be a topographic name derived from South German *giessel* 'waterfall', 'whirlpool'. **3.** In the U.S., it is also an altered spelling of GEISLER.
GIVEN NAMES German 5%. *Hans* (3), *Kurt* (3), *Otto* (2), *Theodor* (2), *Frieda.*

Giesy (125) Probably an Americanized spelling of German GIESE or of Swiss German GIESEL. Compare GIESEY.

Gietzen (258) German: probably a topographic name for someone living by a stream or flood plain, from Middle High German *gieze* 'torrent', 'flood'. Compare GIESEN.

Giffen (447) Irish and English: variant spelling of GIFFIN.

Giffin (1557) **1.** Irish: reduced form of McGIFFIN, an Anglicized form of Gaelic *Mag Dhuibhfhinn* 'son of *Duibhfhionn*'. **2.** English: from a pet form of the Norman personal name *Geffrei* (see JEFFREY).

Gifford (7509) English: **1.** habitational name for someone from Giffords Hall in Suffolk. It was originally named in Old English as *Gyddingford* 'ford associated with Gydda'. Compare GIDDENS. **2.** possibly in some cases a variant spelling of **Giffard**, which may derive from an Old German personal name, *Gifard*, or from a Middle English nickname from Old French *giffard* 'chubby-cheeked', 'bloated' (a pejorative of *giffel* 'jaw', 'cheek', of Germanic origin).

Gift (580) **1.** English: possibly from the vocabulary word *gift* used as a personal name, in the sense 'gift of God', with reference to a child. Compare THEODORE. However, the name is most common in Cornwall and may be of Cornish origin. **2.** German: unexplained. Apparently an unflattering nickname meaning 'poison'.

Gigante (351) Italian: from *gigante* 'large', hence a nickname for a big person, in a physical or abstract sense, or possibly an ironical nickname applied to someone who was short in stature.
GIVEN NAMES Italian 24%. *Salvatore* (6), *Cosmo* (3), *Sal* (3), *Antonio* (2), *Armando, Arturo, Corrado, Demetrio, Dino, Domenic, Domenico, Giovanni, Michelangelo, Mario, Nicola, Sergio, Vito.*

Giganti (136) Italian: patronymic or plural form of GIGANTE.
GIVEN NAMES Italian 10%. *Geno, Nino, Salvatore.*

Giger (400) Swiss or Americanized spelling of German GEIGER.
GIVEN NAMES German 5%; French 4%. *Hannes, Hanspeter, Theodor, Urs; Romain* (2), *Jean Guy.*

Giggey (143) Americanized spelling of Swiss German **Gigy** or **Gygi**, which is most probably an unflattering nickname from Middle High German *giege* 'fool'.

Gigler (113) South German: variant of GEIGER or, more likely, a nickname for a silly person or fool, from Middle High German *gi(e)gel* 'beguiler', 'fool'.
GIVEN NAME German 4%. *Manfred.*

Giglia (196) Italian: from the personal name *Giglia*, feminine form of GIGLIO.
GIVEN NAMES Italian 25%. *Angelo* (4), *Alfonso* (3), *Salvatore* (2), *Alfonse, Carmelo, Ignazio, Nicolo, Pietro, Sal, Salvator, Santina, Santo, Vita.*

Giglio (1636) Italian: from the personal name *Giglio*, from *giglio* 'lily' (Latin *lilium*), a plant considered to symbolize the qualities of candor and purity.
GIVEN NAMES Italian 16%. *Salvatore* (17), *Angelo* (8), *Sal* (5), *Carmine* (4), *Antonio* (3), *Giacomo* (3), *Caesar* (2), *Carmelo* (2), *Dante* (2), *Francesca* (2), *Francesco* (2), *Gioacchino* (2).

Gigliotti (1015) Italian: patronymic or plural form of *Gigliotto*, a pet form of the personal name GIGLIO.
GIVEN NAMES Italian 16%. *Angelo* (12), *Carmine* (5), *Francesco* (3), *Luigi* (3), *Antonio* (2), *Cosimo* (2), *Ferdinando* (2), *Natale* (2), *Agostino, Aldo, Carmelo, Corrado.*

Gignac (334) French: habitational name for someone from any of various places so called in Bouches-du-Rhône, Hérault, Lot, and Vaucluse.
GIVEN NAMES French 12%. *Gilles* (2), *Cecile, Fernand, Jean-Guy, Jean-Pierre, Lucienne, Marcel, Marcelle, Yvan.*

Giguere (1073) French (**Giguère**): unexplained.
FOREBEARS Bearers of the name Giguère, from Perche, were in Quebec city by 1652.
GIVEN NAMES French 18%. *Andre* (4), *Cecile* (4), *Fernand* (3), *Gaston* (3), *Lucien* (3), *Alcide* (2), *Armand* (2), *Emile* (2), *Henri* (2), *Herve* (2), *Laurent* (2), *Normand* (2).

Gikas (156) Greek: from *Gjika*, an Albanian short form of the personal name NIKITAS.
FOREBEARS Gikas or Ghica is the name of a famous Albanian-Greek family which played a significant role in the history of Moldavia and Wallachia. Helena Ghica (1829–88) wrote under the pen name *Dora d'Istria*.
GIVEN NAMES Greek 21%. *Evangelos* (2), *Xenophon* (2), *Angeliki, Athanasios,*

Joannis, Lazaros, Sotirios, Sotiris, Spyros, Stamatis, Theodoros, Xenofon.

Gil (2696) **1.** Spanish, Catalan, Portuguese, Dutch, and German: from the personal name *Gil*, from French *Gille(s)*, from Latin *Aegidius* (see GILES). **2.** German: from Slavic *gil* 'bullfinch', probably a nickname for a simpleton.

GIVEN NAMES Spanish 45%; Portuguese 11%. *Jose* (76), *Luis* (34), *Manuel* (34), *Carlos* (33), *Juan* (30), *Francisco* (21), *Jesus* (18), *Jorge* (15), *Pedro* (14), *Mario* (13), *Miguel* (13), *Ana* (11); *Joao* (2), *Ligia*.

Gilardi (276) Italian: patronymic or plural form of *Gilardo*, a Germanic personal name composed of the elements *gār*, *gēr* 'spear', 'lance' + *hard* 'hardy', 'brave', 'strong'. See also GERARD.

GIVEN NAMES Italian 9%. *Salvatore* (2), *Carlo, Gasper, Nicola*.

Gilb (173) German: from a short form of the personal name GILBERT.

Gilberg (313) **1.** Jewish (Ashkenazic): unexplained. **2.** Danish: habitational name from any of several places named Gjelbjerg. **3.** German: from a Germanic personal name based on a cognate of modern *gelten* originally 'to sacrifice', then 'to recompense', 'to retaliate'.

GIVEN NAMES Scandinavian 5%; Jewish 4%. *Nels* (2), *Anders, Gudrun*; *Dalit* (2), *Meyer, Miriam, Sol*.

Gilbert (41247) **1.** English (of Norman origin), French, and North German: from *Giselbert*, a Norman personal name composed of the Germanic elements *gīsil* 'pledge', 'hostage', 'noble youth' (see GIESEL) + *berht* 'bright', 'famous'. This personal name enjoyed considerable popularity in England during the Middle Ages, partly as a result of the fame of St. Gilbert of Sempringham (1085–1189), the founder of the only native English monastic order. **2.** Jewish (Ashkenazic): Americanized form of one or more like-sounding Jewish surnames.

FOREBEARS The Devon family of Gilbert can be traced to Geoffrey Gilbert (died 1349), who represented Totnes in Parliament in 1326. His descendants included Sir Humphrey Gilbert (died 1583), who discovered Newfoundland. A French family called Gilbert, from Poitou, was in Neuville, Quebec by 1683; another bearer of the name, from La Rochelle, had migrated to Trois Rivières, Quebec, by 1685.

Gilberti (197) Italian: patronymic or plural form of the personal name GILBERTO.

GIVEN NAMES Italian 14%. *Giovanna* (2), *Carmel, Carmela, Carmine, Nunzio, Salvator, Vito*.

Gilberto (123) Italian: from a reduced form of the personal name GILIBERTO.

GIVEN NAMES Italian 16%; Spanish 8%. *Pasquale* (2), *Domenic, Gino, Massimo, Pietro, Sebastiano, Segundo*; *Ana, Fernando, Gonzalez, Jose, Maldonado*.

Gilbertsen (115) Norwegian: patronymic from the personal name GILBERT.

Gilbertson (3852) **1.** English: patronymic from the personal name GILBERT. **2.** Americanized form of Norwegian GILBERTSEN or a cognate in Danish or Swedish.

Gilbo (198) Americanized spelling of the French surname **Gilbaut**, from a Germanic personal name composed of the elements *gī(si)l* 'hostage', 'pledge', 'noble youth' + *bald, bold* 'bold', 'brave'.

Gilboy (218) Irish: **1.** reduced Anglicized form of Gaelic **Ó Giolla Bhuidhe** 'descendant of the yellow-haired (*buidhe*) servant'. This is a Connacht surname, sometimes replaced with Scottish OGILVIE. **2.** adoption of the English habitational name **Gilby**, from a place in Lincolnshire, so named from the Old Norse personal name *Gilli*, which is abstracted from the various Irish personal names containing Gaelic *giolla* 'servant' + Old Norse *býr* 'farm', 'settlement'.

GIVEN NAME Irish 5%. *Brendan*.

Gilbreath (1925) Variant of Scottish GALBRAITH.

Gilbreth (348) Variant of Scottish GALBRAITH.

Gilbride (413) Irish and Scottish: Americanized form of Gaelic **Mac Giolla Brighde** (Irish) or **Mac Gille Brighde** (Scottish) 'son of the servant of (Saint) Brigit', more often Americanized as MCBRIDE. The name *Brighid* (modern *Brigit*) almost certainly means 'exalted'. Brighid was probably originally a pagan fire goddess, many of whose attributes became attached to the historical figure of St. Brigit of Kildare (452–523), founder of the first Irish convent.

GIVEN NAME Irish 5%. *Brendan*.

Gilcher (111) German: variant of GILGER.
GIVEN NAMES German 6%. *Heinz, Otto*.

Gilchrest (250) Variant spelling of Scottish GILCHRIST.

Gilchrist (4287) Scottish: from the Gaelic personal name *Gille Crìosd* 'servant of Christ'.

Gilcrease (380) Probably an altered form of Scottish GILCHRIST.

Gilcrest (167) Variant of Scottish GILCHRIST.

Gilday (331) Scottish and English: perhaps a variant of Irish GILDEA.

Gilde (106) Dutch and North German: habitational name from a place so named near Gifhorn in Lower Saxony.

GIVEN NAMES German 6%. *Hans* (2), *Hans-Georg*.

Gildea (827) Irish: reduced Anglicized form of Gaelic **Mac Giolla Dhé** 'son of the servant of God', from *Dia* 'God'. The name originated with a monastic family in Donegal in the 11th century.

GIVEN NAMES Irish 5%. *Eilis, Fergal, Sinead*.

Gildehaus (154) German: topographic name for someone who lived by a guild house, Middle Low German *gildehuse*, or a habitational name from a place near Bentheim in Lower Saxony, named with this word. This name found predominantly in MO.

GIVEN NAMES German 5%. *Armin, Kurt*.

Gildemeister (124) North German: occupational name for the head of a craft guild, Middle Low German *gildemēster* 'guild master'.

GIVEN NAMES German 11%. *Bernhard, Fritz, Kurt, Otto, Willi*.

Gilden (348) Dutch: patronymic from GILLEN.

Gilder (619) English: variant of GOLD 1.

Gildersleeve (670) English: nickname for a flamboyant dresser, from Middle English *gyldenesleve* 'golden sleeve'.

Gildner (287) **1.** Jewish (eastern Ashkenazic): ornamental name or metonymic occupational name for a worker in gold, from Yiddish *gildner* 'golden'. **2.** German: variant of **Güldner** (see GULDNER).

GIVEN NAMES German 5%. *Claus, Eldred, Manfred*.

Gildon (151) English: from Old English *gylden* 'golden', perhaps applied for someone with golden hair.

Gildow (110) Origin unidentified. This name is found mainly in OH.

Gile (998) French: variant of GILES 1.

Giles (13195) **1.** English and French: from a medieval personal name of which the original form was Latin *Aegidius* (from Greek *aigidion* 'kid', 'young goat'). This was the name of a 7th-century Provençal hermit, whose cult popularized the name in a variety of more or less mutilated forms: *Gidi* and *Gidy* in southern France, *Gil(l)i* in the area of the Alpes-Maritimes, and *Gil(l)e* elsewhere. This last form was taken over to England by the Normans, but by the 12th century it was being confused with the Germanic names *Gisel*, a short form of GILBERT, and *Gilo*, which is from *Gail* (as in GAILLARD). **2.** Irish: adopted as an Anglicized equivalent of Gaelic **Ó Glaisne**, a County Louth name, based on *glas* 'green', 'blue', 'gray'.

Gilfillan (513) Scottish: reduced Anglicized form of Gaelic **Mac Gille Faoláin** 'son of the servant of (Saint) Faolán' (see WHELAN).

Gilford (388) English: variant spelling of GUILFORD.

Gilgen (110) German and Swiss German: from the inflected form of a house name 'at the lily', based on Middle High German *lilge, gilge* 'lily', or a habitational name for someone from a place called, St Ägidi (earlier, Aegilius) near Passau, for instance.

GIVEN NAME German 4%. *Heinz*.

Gilgenbach (112) German: habitational name from a place so named.

Gilger (212) German: patronymic from a medieval personal name, a derivative of *Aegilius*, a later form of *Aegidius* (see GILES 1).

Gilham (420) English: variant of WILLIAM, influenced by the French form, *Guillaume*.

Gilhooley (134) Irish: variant spelling of GILHOOLY.
GIVEN NAME Irish 5%. *Seamus*.

Gilhooly (212) Irish: reduced Anglicized form of Gaelic **Mac Giolla Ghuala** 'son of the gluttonous lad', from *gola* 'gullet', 'gut'.
GIVEN NAME Irish 9%. *John Patrick*.

Giliberti (108) Italian: patronymic or plural form of the Germanic personal name GILIBERTO.
GIVEN NAMES Italian 38%. *Salvatore* (2), *Arcangelo, Claudio, Cosimo, Eduardo, Ezio, Gerardo, Lorenzo, Mario, Marisa, Octavio, Vito* .

Giliberto (100) Italian: from a Germanic personal name (see GILBERT).
GIVEN NAMES Italian 35%. *Sal* (3), *Salvatore* (2), *Constantino, Costantino, Emilio, Rosario, Santo, Sebastiano, Vittorio*.

Gililand (154) Northern Irish: variant of GILLILAND.

Gilinsky (104) **1.** Jewish (from Lithuania): habitational name from the village of Gili in Lithuania. **2.** Polish (**Giliński**): habitational name for someone from Gilino in Płock voivodeship, Poland.
GIVEN NAMES French 5%; Polish 4%; Jewish 4%. *Armand* (2); *Karol; Itai, Yetta*.

Gilio (112) Italian: **1.** from the personal name *Giglio*, a derivative of the Latin personal name *Aegidius* (see GILES). **2.** in some instances, possibly a variant of GIGLIO.
GIVEN NAMES Italian 10%. *Angelo, Giuseppe*.

Gilkerson (551) English: variant spelling of Scottish GILKISON.

Gilkes (232) English (Oxfordshire, Warwickshire): patronymic from a pet form of the personal name GILL.

Gilkeson (202) Scottish: variant spelling of GILKISON.

Gilkey (1222) Northern Irish: unexplained. It may be a pet form of the Scottish personal name GILCHRIST.

Gilkison (348) Scottish: patronymic from a pet form of GILCHRIST.

Gill (23601) **1.** English: from a short form of the personal names GILES, JULIAN, or WILLIAM. In theory the name would have a soft initial when derived from the first two of these, and a hard one when from *William* or from the other possibilities discussed in 2–4 below. However, there has been much confusion over the centuries. **2.** Northern English: topographic name for someone who lived by a ravine or deep glen, Middle English *gil(l)*, Old Norse *gil* 'ravine'. **3.** Scottish and Irish: reduced Anglicized form of Gaelic **Mac Gille** (Scottish), **Mac Giolla** (Irish), patronymics from an occu-

pational name for a servant or a short form of the various personal names formed by attaching this element to the name of a saint. See MCGILL. The Old Norse personal name *Gilli* is probably of this origin, and may lie behind some examples of the name in northern England. **4.** Scottish and Irish: reduced Anglicized form of Gaelic **Mac An Ghoill** (see GALL 1). **5.** Norwegian: habitational name from any of three farmsteads in western Norway named Gil, from Old Norse *gil* 'ravine'. **6.** Dutch: cognate of GILES. **7.** Jewish (Israeli): ornamental name from Hebrew *gil* 'joy'. **8.** German: from a vernacular short form of the medieval personal name *Aegidius* (see GILGER). **9.** Indian (Panjab): Sikh name, probably from Panjabi *gil* 'moisture', also meaning 'prosperity'. There is a Jat tribe that bears this name; the Ramgarhia Sikhs also have a clan called Gill.
GIVEN NAMES Indian 4%. *Avtar* (8), *Amritpal* (4), *Darshan* (4), *Hardip* (4), *Nirmal* (4), *Sohan* (4), *Ajit* (3), *Balwinder* (3), *Charan* (3), *Jasvir* (3), *Kewal* (3), *Navdeep* (3).

Gillam (1227) English: variant of WILLIAM, from a central French form in which *W* is replaced by *G*.

Gillan (614) Irish: **1.** reduced Anglicized form of Gaelic **Ó Giolláin**, from a diminutive of *giolla* 'lad'. **2.** reduced form of GILLILAND.

Gilland (720) **1.** Scottish and northern Irish: reduced form of GILLILAND. **2.** In Scotland possibly a habitational name from Gullane near Edinburgh, locally pronounced *Gillan*.

Gillard (1096) **1.** English: from a pejorative derivative of the personal name GILES. **2.** English and French: from an assimilated form of the personal name *Gislehard*, a compound of Old High German *gīsel* 'hostage', 'pledge', 'noble youth' (see GIESEL) + *hard* 'hardy'. This name is also found in Switzerland, whence it may have been brought to the U.S.

Gillaspie (599) Variant spelling of Scottish or Irish GILLESPIE.

Gillaspy (340) Variant spelling of Scottish or Irish GILLESPIE. The spelling *Gillaspy* is found mainly in and around Manchester, England.

Gille (401) **1.** French: variant of GILES. **2.** German: variant of GILL. **3.** German: from a short form of a Germanic personal name ultimately related to a verb meaning 'to sacrifice, repay, or reward'.
GIVEN NAMES French 4%. *Gisele, Pierre*.

Gillean (214) Variant spelling of Irish or English GILLIAN.

Gilleland (878) Northern Irish: variant of GILLILAND.

Gillem (177) English and Scottish: from the personal name *Gillem*, a variant of *Guillaume*, French form of WILLIAM.

Gillen (3133) **1.** Irish: variant spelling of GILLAN or reduced form of MCGILLEN.

2. Dutch: patronymic from *Gil*, a personal name that is a much reduced and altered vernacular form of Latin *Aegidius* (see GILES). **3.** German: variant of GILBERT. See also GILLE 2.

Gillentine (276) Americanized spelling of German **Gellentin**, **Gellenthin**, a habitational name from a place named Gellenthin in Pomerania.

Gillenwater (1091) Altered spelling of the English surname **Gillingwater**, which Reaney suggests is probably a topographic name from Old English *gylden* 'yellow' + *wæter* 'water', 'stream'.

Gilleo (113) Origin unidentified.

Giller (430) **1.** English: variant of GUILER. **2.** German: variant of GILLE 2. **3.** German: habitational name for someone from Gill near Neuss, in the Rhineland. **4.** Jewish (eastern Ashkenazic): from the Yiddish male personal name *Hiller*, a variant of *Hillel*. The initial *G* is due to Russian influence, since Russian has no *h* and alters *h* to *g* in borrowed words.
GIVEN NAMES Jewish 5%; Russian 4%. *Avraham, Hymen, Irina, Meyer, Pinchas; Leonid* (3), *Asya, Boris, Ivetta, Lev, Matvey, Polya, Svetlana, Yury*.

Gilleran (169) Irish: reduced Anglicized form of Gaelic **Mac Giollaráin** or **Ó Giollaráin**, according to Woulfe, formerly **Mac Giolla Éanáin** 'son of the servant of (Saint) *Eanán*'.

Gilles (1363) **1.** French: variant spelling of GILES. **2.** German: from the personal name *Gilius*, from *Aegilius*, a Late Latin variant of *Aegidius* (see GILES 1).
GIVEN NAMES French 5%. *Jacques* (2), *Pierre* (2), *Amie, Arsene, Berthony, Ghislaine, Gilles, Jean Marie, Jean-Baptiste, Maryse, Maxime, Odette*.

Gillespie (15841) Scottish and Irish: reduced Anglicized form of Gaelic **Mac Gille Easbuig** (Scottish), **Mac Giolla Easpaig** (Irish), patronymics from a byname meaning 'servant of the bishop'.

Gillet (222) **1.** English: variant spelling of GILLETT. **2.** French: from a pet form of the personal name GILES 1.
GIVEN NAMES French 13%. *Andre* (2), *Mireille* (2), *Emile, Henri, Jean-Jacques, Jean-Louis, Marcel*.

Gillett (1926) English: **1.** from a pet form of the personal names GILES, JULIAN, or WILLIAM (see GILL 1). **2.** topographic name for someone living at the top of a glen or ravine, from northern Middle English *gil(l)* 'glen' + *heved* 'head'.

Gillette (4778) **1.** English: from a feminine form of GILLETT 1. **2.** French: variant spelling of GILLET.

Gilley (3611) Perhaps an altered spelling of Scottish GILLIE, or an Americanized spelling of French **Gillet**.

Gillham (705) English: variant of WILLIAM, from a central French form in which *W* is replaced by *G*. The spelling of this name has been further influenced by English habitational names ending in *ham*.

Gilliam (9265) English: variant of WILLIAM, from a central French form in which *W* is replaced by *G*.

Gillian (442) **1.** English: variant of JULIAN. **2.** Irish (Tyrone and Derry): reduced Anglicized form of Gaelic **Mac Gileáin** 'son of *Gileán*', a variant of the personal name *Gealán*, from a diminutive of *geal* 'bright', 'white'.

Gilliand (238) **1.** Irish: variant of GILLIAN. **2.** Swiss French: unexplained.

Gilliard (869) **1.** English and northern Irish (county Down): probably a variant of GILLARD. **2.** French and Swiss French: from a derivative of **Gillier**, from the Germanic personal name *Giselher*, composed of *gīsil* 'hostage', 'pledge', 'noble offspring' (see GIESEL) + *heri* 'army'.

Gilliatt (180) English: variant of GILLETT 1.

Gillick (308) English: variant of GULICK.

Gillie (398) Scottish: variant of GILLIS.

Gillies (1118) Scottish: variant of GILLIS or McGILLIS.

GIVEN NAMES Scottish 4%. *Dugald* (2), *Alastair, Iain*.

Gillig (253) German: **1.** from the personal name *Gilius*, a German form of GILES. **2.** from a Germanic personal name, see GILLE 2.

Gilligan (2320) Irish (Ulster): reduced Anglicized form of Gaelic **Mac Giolla-gáin**, a double diminutive of *giolla* 'lad'.

GIVEN NAMES Irish 5%. *Brendan* (3), *Grainne, Michael Sean*.

Gillihan (462) Variant of Irish GILLIGAN.

Gillikin (483) Variant of Irish GILLIGAN.

Gillilan (339) Irish: variant of GILLILAND.

Gilliland (5125) Scottish and northern Irish: reduced Anglicized form of Gaelic **Mac Gille Fhaoláin** (Scottish) or **Mac Giolla Fhaoláin** (Irish) 'son of the servant of St *Faolán*'. Compare McCLELLAN. Woulfe thinks that the Irish version died out and all modern forms were taken to Ulster from Scotland.

Gillim (104) English: variant of GILLIAM.

Gillin (500) Irish: variant of GILLAN.

Gilling (100) English: **1.** from a variant of the personal name JULIAN. **2.** habitational name from either of two places in North Yorkshire, Gilling East and Gilling West, named in Old English as '(settlement of) the people (Old English *ingas*) of a man called Gȳthia or Gētla'.

Gillingham (772) English: habitational name from places in Dorset, Norfolk, and Kent, named Gillingham, 'homestead (Old English *hām*) of the people of *Gylla*', an unattested Old English personal name.

Gillings (156) English: patronymic or metronymic from the personal name JULIAN.

Gillins (155) English: variant of GILLINGS.

Gilliom (100) English: variant of GILLIAM, which is itself a variant of WILLIAM.

Gillion (136) English: from a variant of the personal name JULIAN.

Gillis (7045) **1.** Scottish: reduced form of Gaelic **Mac Gille Iosa** 'son of the servant of Jesus'. Compare McLEISH. The usual spelling in Scotland is GILLIES. **2.** Dutch form of GILES.

Gillison (214) Scottish: patronymic from GILLIS 1.

Gillispie (1648) Variant spelling of Scottish or Irish GILLESPIE.

Gilliss (102) Variant spelling of Scottish GILLIS.

Gillitzer (116) German: unexplained.

Gillman (1675) **1.** English: from a personal name, Old French *Guillemin*, Anglo-Norman French *Williman*, pet forms of *Guillaume, Willelm* (see WILLIAM). **2.** German (**Gillmann**): variant of GILLE 2.

Gillmer (101) Variant spelling of Scottish GILMER, itself a variant of GILMORE.

Gillmor (141) Variant spelling of Scottish GILMER, itself a variant of GILMORE.

Gillmore (687) Scottish and Irish: variant spelling of GILMORE.

Gillock (238) Perhaps a variant of GULICK.

Gillogly (262) Scottish: variant of Irish GALLOGLY.

Gillon (401) French: from a pet form of the personal name GILES 1.

Gillooly (304) Irish: variant spelling of GILHOOLEY, now found chiefly in England and Scotland.

GIVEN NAME Irish 5%. *Sean Michael*.

Gillott (220) English: variant of GILLETT 1.

Gillotti (179) Italian: **1.** from a derivative of the personal names GILIO or GIGLIO, or directly from French *Gillot*, a pet form of GILLE. **2.** possibly a habitational name from Gillotti, a district of Colosimi Cosenza in Calabria.

GIVEN NAME Italian 6%. *Angelo*.

Gillow (119) English: habitational name from a place in Herefordshire, named from Welsh *cil* 'retreat' + *llwch* 'pool'.

Gills (519) **1.** English: variant of GILL. **2.** Scottish and English: habitational name from Gills in the parish of Canisbay, Caithness.

Gillson (180) English: variant spelling of GILSON.

Gillum (1639) English: variant of WILLIAM, from a central French form in which *W* is replaced by *G*.

Gillund (133) Scottish and northern Irish: reduced form of GILLILAND.

Gilly (254) **1.** French: variant of GILES 1. **2.** German: variant of GILL.

Gillyard (145) See GILYARD.

Gilman (5361) **1.** English: variant spelling of GILLMAN. **2.** Altered spelling of German **Gillmann** (see GILLMAN).

Gilmartin (1213) Irish: reduced Anglicized form of Gaelic **Mac Giolla Mhartain**, a patronymic from the personal name *Giolla Mhartain* 'servant of (Saint) Martin' (see MARTIN).

GIVEN NAMES Irish 5%. *Aidan, Brendan, Declan, Dermot, Niall*.

Gilmer (2410) **1.** Scottish and Irish: variant of GILMORE. (In Ireland, it is most likely an Americanized form of the Sligo name *Mac Giolla Mhir*.) **2.** German: from the short form of a Germanic personal name composed with *gīsil* 'pledge', 'hostage', 'noble youth' (see GIESEL).

Gilmore (16106) **1.** Scottish and Irish (Ulster): reduced Anglicized form of Gaelic **Mac Gille Mhoire** (Scots), **Mac Giolla Mhuire** (Irish), patronymics from personal names meaning 'servant of (the Virgin) Mary'. **2.** Irish: in Armagh, reduced Anglicized form of Gaelic **Mac Giolla Mhura** 'servant of St. Mura (of Fahan, Donegal)' or, in Sligo, of **Mac Giolla Mhir** 'son of the spirited lad'.

Gilmour (1214) Scottish and Irish: variant spelling of GILMORE.

Gilner (137) English: unexplained.

Gilpatric (116) Variant spelling of Irish GILPATRICK.

Gilpatrick (482) Irish: reduced Anglicized form of Gaelic **Mac Giolla Phádraig** 'son of the servant of (Saint) Patrick' (see KILPATRICK).

Gilpin (2307) **1.** English: in the northeast, from the Gilpin river in Cumbria; in southern counties, probably a variant of GALPIN. **2.** Irish (Connacht): reduced Anglicized form of Gaelic **Mac Giolla Fionn** 'son of the fair-haired lad'. In Ulster, the name may be of northern English origin (see 1 above).

Gilreath (1371) Scottish: of uncertain origin.

Gilroy (1551) Irish: reduced Anglicized form of Gaelic **Mac Giolla Ruaidh** 'son of the red-haired lad', from *ruadh* 'red'. Compare McELROY.

GIVEN NAMES Irish 4%. *Brendan, Brennan, Kieran*.

Gilsdorf (381) German: possibly a habitational name from Gelsdorf near Remagen, Rhineland.

Gilsenan (121) Irish: reduced form of **MacGils(h)enan**, an Anglicized form of Gaelic **Mac Giolla Seanáin** 'son of the servant or devotee of St. Senan'.

GIVEN NAMES Irish 8%. *Brendan, Colm*.

Gilson (2895) **1.** English: patronymic from GILES. **2.** French: reduced form of **Gilesson**, a derivative of GILES 1.

Gilster (162) German: probably a nickname, either from an agent derivative of Middle High German *gelstern* 'to yell or shout' or from Low German *gilsterig* 'lascivious'.

Gilstrap (1759) English: probably a habitational name from a lost or unidentified place with a name such as *Gil(l)sthorp(e)*, the first element being on Old English or Old Norse personal name, the second being Old Norse *þorp* 'hamlet', 'settlement', or possibly an Anglicized form of a Danish habitational name from Gelstrup or Gølstrup in Jutland. The surname is found in SC, GA, and TX.

Giltner (458) South German: occupational name for a maker or seller of wooden buckets, from an agent derivative of Middle Low German *gilte* 'wooden bucket'.

Giltz (104) German and Luxembourgeois: from a short form of the personal name *Ägilius* (variant of *Ägidius*) (see GILES).

Gilvin (137) Perhaps a variant spelling of the Irish surnames GILPIN, **Gilvane** (see KILBANE), or GALVIN.

Gilyard (364) English: possibly a variant of GILLARD. Compare GILLIARD.

Gima (136) Japanese: found mostly in the Ryūkyū Islands, there are several different characters used in various combinations to write this name, the most common ones meaning 'ceremony' and 'space'.
GIVEN NAMES Japanese 23%. *Yasuo* (2), *Hideko, Hitoshi, Kazuhiko, Masa, Masahiro, Michiko, Sakae, Shingo, Tatsuya, Tsuyoshi, Yasuko.*

Gimbel (637) **1.** Jewish (western Ashkenazic): variant of GIMPEL. **2.** German: nickname for a simpleton, from Middle High German *gümpel* 'bullfinch'. **3.** German: nickname (probably obscene), from Middle High German *gimpel* 'springer', 'jumper', also 'penis'. **4.** German: from a Germanic personal name formed with *gund* 'fight', 'battle' (see GOMBERT).

Gimbert (102) French and English: from *Gimberht*, a personal name of Germanic origin, of which the second element is *berht* 'bright', 'shining'.
GIVEN NAMES French 8%. *Alain, Dominique.*

Gimble (104) Respelling of German GIMBEL.

Gimenez (347) Spanish (**Giménez**): variant of **Jiménez** (see JIMENEZ).
GIVEN NAMES Spanish 39%. *Carlos* (11), *Jose* (7), *Eduardo* (5), *Angel* (4), *Juan* (3), *Manuel* (3), *Alejandro* (2), *Alfredo* (2), *Gerardo* (2), *Luis* (2), *Lupe* (2), *Alberto*; *Antonio* (4), *Federico* (2), *Sal* (2).

Gimlin (173) Americanized form of German **Gmelin**, a nickname for an unhurried person, from Middle High German *gmēle*, based on the adjective *gemach* 'comfortable', 'calm'.

Gimpel (266) **1.** German: from a pet form of the personal name *Gumprecht* (see GOMBERT). **2.** Jewish (Ashkenazic): from the Yiddish personal name *Gimpl*, a derivative of German *Gumprecht*.

Gimple (106) German and Jewish (Ashkenazic): variant of GIMPEL.

Gin (395) **1.** English: variant of GINN. **2.** Perhaps a respelling of French JEAN. **3.** East Asian: unexplained.
GIVEN NAMES Southeast Asian 11%. *Yuen* (3), *Yee* (2), *Ying Chun* (2), *Bik, Bock, Cheuk, Chow, Chun, Fong, Gan, Hong, Kan.*

Ginder (723) German: variant of **Günther** (see GUENTHER).

Gindi (197) Jewish: unexplained.
GIVEN NAMES Jewish 12%. *Isadore* (2), *Hyman, Nissim.*

Gindlesperger (238) Possibly a German topographic name for someone who lived on a mountain near Gindels, Bavaria.

Gindt (104) German and Alsatian: from the Germanic personal name *Gundo*, from *gund* 'war', 'battle'.

Gines (409) Catalan (**Ginés**): from a medieval personal name, Latin *Genesius*, from Greek *gennēsios* 'well-born', 'legitimate'.
GIVEN NAMES Spanish 18%. *Jose* (3), *Ruben* (3), *Elba* (2), *Juan* (2), *Luis* (2), *Miguel* (2), *Abundio, Amado, Americo, Andres, Aracelia, Artemio.*

Ging (237) **1.** German and Swiss German: unexplained. **2.** Irish: reduced form of **McGing**, a variant of MCGINN, from a dialect pronunciation of Gaelic *-inn* as *-ing*.

Gingell (204) **1.** English (common in Bristol): variant of GINGOLD, of which the origin is unexplained. **2.** Respelling of German **Gingel**, a common Bavarian surname, derived from a short form of the Germanic personal name *Gangulf*, composed of the elements *gangan* 'to walk or go' + *(w)ulf* 'wolf'.

Ginger (433) **1.** German: habitational name for someone from Gingen or Giengen in Württemberg. **2.** English: from Middle English *gingivere, gyngure, gingere* 'ginger', hence a metonymic occupational name for a dealer in spices, or possibly a nickname for someone with reddish hair or a fiery temperament.

Gingerich (1440) Americanized form of Swiss German **Güngerich** (see GINGRICH).

Gingery (306) Americanized form of Swiss German **Güngerich** (see GINGRICH).

Gingles (163) Northern Irish: probably from the hybrid name **Mac Inglis** (Gaelic and English), meaning 'son of the English speaker', from Scottish INGLIS.

Gingold (261) Jewish (eastern Ashkenazic): ornamental name from Yiddish *gingold* 'fine gold'.
GIVEN NAMES Jewish 7%. *Miriam* (3), *Sol* (3).

Gingras (1090) French Canadian variant of French **Gingreau**, unexplained.
FOREBEARS A family of this name from Poitou was in Sillery, Quebec, by 1665.
GIVEN NAMES French 15%. *Laurent* (5), *Andre* (4), *Armand* (4), *Emile* (4), *Aime* (2), *Alcide* (2), *Antoine* (2), *Gaetan* (2), *Lucien* (2), *Marcel* (2), *Normand* (2), *Amie.*

Gingrich (1440) Americanized spelling of German **Güngerich**, from a Germanic personal name formed with *gund* 'battle' + *rīc* 'power(ful)'.

Ginkel (104) German: perhaps a variant of KUNKEL.
GIVEN NAMES German 6%. *Ernst, Kurt.*

Ginley (211) Irish: reduced form of MCGINLEY, an Anglicized form of Gaelic *Mag Fhionnghaile* 'son of *Fionnghal*'.

Ginn (2999) **1.** Irish: reduced form of MCGINN, an Anglicized form of Gaelic **Mag Finn** 'son of *Fionn*'. **2.** English: from Middle English *gin* 'trick', 'contrivance', 'snare', a reduced form of Middle English *engin* (see INGHAM 2), hence a metonymic occupational name for a trapper or a nickname for a cunning person.

Ginnetti (141) Italian: probably from a derivative of the personal name *Gino*, with a doubling of the *n* due to the influence of *Gi(ov)anni*.
GIVEN NAMES Italian 8%. *Dante, Orlando* (2), *Mario, Rocco.*

Ginocchio (186) Italian: **1.** from *ginocchio* 'knee', hence probably a nickname for someone with distinctive knees. **2.** from a pet form of the personal name *Gino*.

Ginsberg (2390) Jewish (Ashkenazic): ornamental variant of GINSBURG.
GIVEN NAMES Jewish 8%. *Meyer* (7), *Aron* (6), *Isadore* (4), *Sol* (4), *Binyomin* (3), *Chaim* (2), *Emanuel* (2), *Hyman* (2), *Sholom* (2), *Zvi* (2), *Ari, Aryeh.*

Ginsburg (1659) Jewish (Ashkenazic): habitational name for someone from Günzburg in Swabia, which derives its name from the river Günz (in early Latin records *Guntia*, probably of Celtic origin) + Old High German *burg* 'fortress', 'walled town'.
GIVEN NAMES Jewish 6%. *Moshe* (3), *Gershon* (2), *Aron, Beril, Chaim, Chana, Dov, Eliezer, Herzl, Hyman, Ilysa, Margalit.*

Ginter (1480) **1.** German and Polish: variant of **Günther** (see GUENTHER). **2.** Respelling of GINTHER.

Ginther (1116) South German: variant of **Günther** (see GUENTHER).

Ginty (258) Irish: reduced form of MCGINTY, an Anglicized form of Gaelic **Mag Fhionnachtaigh**.
GIVEN NAMES Irish 4%. *Conal, Patrick Sean.*

Gintz (153) German: from a short form of a Germanic personal name formed with *gund* 'battle', as for example GUENTHER.

Ginyard (170) Possibly of English origin: unexplained.

Ginzburg (201) Jewish (Ashkenazic): variant of GINSBERG.
GIVEN NAMES Russian 33%; Jewish 28%. *Lev* (7), *Mikhail* (4), *Anatoly* (3), *Arkadiy* (3), *Boris* (3), *Leonid* (3), *Aleksandr* (2), *Efim* (2), *Sofiya* (2), *Yevgeny* (2), *Arkady, Fanya*; *Naum* (3), *Uri* (3), *Aron* (2), *Yakov* (2), *Yankel* (2), *Ari, Basya, Chaim, Filipp, Gershon, Ilya, Inna.*

Gioe (118) Italian (**Gioè**): perhaps a reduced form of **Gioeli**, from the personal name *Gioele*.
GIVEN NAMES Italian 16%. *Salvatore* (2), *Agostino, Carlo, Gasper, Matteo.*

Gioffre (189) Italian (**Gioffré**): from the personal name *Gioffré*, a borrowing from French (see GEOFFROY).

GIVEN NAMES Italian 31%. *Rocco* (3), *Carmelo* (2), *Alfredo, Antonino, Carmela, Gaetano, Giacomo, Giovanna, Giuseppe, Rino, Salvatore.*

Gioia (906) Italian: **1.** from the personal name *Gioia*, derived from *gioa* 'jewel', 'precious object'. This is normally a feminine name, but there are occasional records of its use as a masculine personal name in the Middle Ages. It may also have been a nickname for someone who frequently used the expression *mia gioia* 'my joy'. In the form **Tzogias** this is also found as a Greek family name. **2.** habitational name from any of various places in southern Italy named with this word, including Gioia del Colle (Bari), Gioia Sannitica (Caserta), and Gioia Tauro (Calabria).

GIVEN NAMES Italian 17%. *Angelo* (7), *Salvatore* (6), *Vito* (4), *Antonio* (3), *Elio* (2), *Giovanni* (2), *Giuseppe* (2), *Luigi* (2), *Rocco* (2), *Alessandra, Annunziata, Benedetto.*

Gion (108) French: from an old form of the personal name *Gidon*, a pet named derived from a short form of a compound Germanic personal name formed with *gid* 'song'.

GIVEN NAMES French 5%. *Alphonse, Philippe.*

Gionet (237) French: possibly from a pet form of the personal name *Gion*, an old form of *Gidon*, of Germanic origin.

GIVEN NAMES French 10%. *Euclide* (2), *Lucien* (2), *Armand, Marcel, Urbain.*

Gionfriddo (198) Italian: probably a variant of **Giuffrido**, from the personal name *Goffredo* (Italian equivalent of JEFFREY).

GIVEN NAMES Italian 18%. *Santo* (3), *Sal* (2), *Angelo, Biagio, Concetto, Gino, Nicola, Sebastiano.*

Gionta (121) Italian: variant of GIUNTA.

GIVEN NAMES Italian 26%. *Salvatore* (3), *Umberto* (3), *Camillo, Dante, Guido, Luigi, Pietro, Quinto, Romeo, Sal.*

Giordani (164) Italian: patronymic or plural form of GIORDANO. **Giordanis** also occurs as a Greek family name.

GIVEN NAMES Italian 9%; French 5%; Spanish 5%. *Angelo, Ettore, Francesco, Gennaro, Gino, Luciano, Marcello; Gardy, Michel; Enrique* (2), *Armondo, Valdir.*

Giordano (5950) Italian: from the personal name *Giordano*, Italian equivalent of JORDAN.

GIVEN NAMES Italian 17%. *Angelo* (36), *Salvatore* (28), *Rocco* (20), *Antonio* (16), *Pasquale* (14), *Carmine* (11), *Vito* (10), *Domenic* (8), *Gaetano* (8), *Giuseppe* (8), *Sal* (7), *Santo* (5).

Giorgi (501) Italian: patronymic or plural form of the personal name GIORGIO. In the form **Tzortzis** this also occurs as a Greek family name.

GIVEN NAMES Italian 18%. *Angelo* (3), *Amedeo* (2), *Antonio* (2), *Aldo, Amedio, Attilio, Carlo, Carmello, Dante, Dino, Elio.*

Giorgianni (173) Italian (Sicily): from a compound of the personal names GIORGIO + GIANNI.

GIVEN NAMES Italian 26%. *Salvatore* (3), *Nicola* (2), *Sal* (2), *Domenic, Gaetano, Nino, Nunzio, Reno, Rocci, Santo, Valentino.*

Giorgio (529) Italian: from the personal name *Giorgio*, Italian equivalent of GEORGE.

GIVEN NAMES Italian 14%. *Vito* (6), *Salvatore* (4), *Angelo* (2), *Amedeo, Antonio, Cataldo, Franco, Giuseppe, Marco, Nicola, Rocchina.*

Giorlando (105) Italian: variant of **Gerlando**, from a personal name of Germanic origin.

GIVEN NAMES Italian 18%; French 4%. *Carlo* (2), *Salvatore* (2), *Angelo, Franco, Nicola, Sal; Gaspard.*

Giorno (139) Italian: from a reduced form of BONGIORNO.

GIVEN NAMES Italian 26%. *Antonio* (2), *Luigi* (2), *Amedeo, Angelo, Bernardino, Domenic, Fabio, Gildo, Mario Natale, Ottavio, Paolo.*

Giovacchini (100) Italian: from the personal name *Giovacchino*, Italian form of the biblical name JOACHIM.

GIVEN NAMES Italian 16%. *Aquilino, Dante, Dario, Gino, Guido, Lido, Lino, Marino, Mario, Rocco, Saverio.*

Giovanelli (170) Italian: variant spelling of GIOVANNELLI.

GIVEN NAMES Italian 17%. *Angelo* (2), *Pasquale* (2), *Attilio, Cesare, Domenic, Gaetano, Silvio.*

Giovanetti (195) Italian: from a pet form of GIOVANNI.

GIVEN NAMES Italian 10%. *Aldo, Battista, Carlo, Domenic, Donato, Lia, Luigi.*

Giovanini (118) Italian: from a pet form of the personal name GIOVANNI.

GIVEN NAMES Italian 6%. *Domenic, Primo.*

Giovannelli (109) Italian: from a pet form of the personal name GIOVANNI.

GIVEN NAMES Italian 13%. *Vito* (2), *Amerigo, Rocco.*

Giovannetti (256) Italian: from a pet form of the personal name GIOVANNI.

GIVEN NAMES Italian 13%. *Angelo* (2), *Dante* (2), *Giancarlo* (2), *Amedeo, Carlo, Federico, Geno, Leno, Mafalda, Reno.*

Giovanni (250) Italian: from the personal name *Giovanni*, Italian equivalent of JOHN. In spite of the long-standing popularity of the personal name in Italy, the surname is rare; the present-day frequency is less than 20.

GIVEN NAMES French 4%; Italian 4%. *Armand* (2); *Antonietta, Marino, Nunzio, Romeo.*

Giovanniello (214) Italian: from the personal name *Giovanniello*, a pet form

Giovanni (Italian equivalent of JOHN) formed with the Neapolitan and southern suffix *-iello*.

GIVEN NAMES Italian 31%. *Rocco* (6), *Angelo* (2), *Antonio* (2), *Giuseppe* (2), *Vito* (2), *Carmine, Corrado, Ermanno, Filomena, Leonardo, Nicolo, Nunzio.*

Giovannini (272) Italian: patronymic from a pet form of the personal name GIOVANNI.

GIVEN NAMES Italian 28%. *Mario* (4), *Alberto* (3), *Carlo* (3), *Marco* (2), *Marina* (2), *Renzo* (2), *Aldo, Alfio, Angelo, Battista, Elvio, Enrico, Ettore, Geno.*

Giovannoni (186) Italian: patronymic from an augmentative form of GIOVANNI.

GIVEN NAMES Italian 9%. *Amerigo, Carlo, Dino, Geno, Gino, Luigi.*

Giovannucci (100) Italian: from a pet form of GIOVANNI.

GIVEN NAMES Italian 26%. *Mario* (2), *Angelo, Domenic, Erminio, Lino, Luciano, Rocco, Verino.*

Giove (116) Italian: **1.** from *Giòve* ('Jupiter'), the name of the chief Roman deity, perhaps a nickname for someone who habitually swore *per Giove* 'by Jove'. **2.** from Sicilian *ggiòve, iòvi* 'Thursday', applied as a personal name for someone born or baptized on that day of the week. **3.** habitational name from Giove in Terni province, Umbria. **4.** possibly from a variant of the personal name *Giobbe* (see JOB).

GIVEN NAMES Italian 12%. *Salvatore* (2), *Angelo, Raffaele, Rocco.*

Giovenco (146) Italian: from *giovenco* 'young ox', 'bullock', possibly applied as a nickname reflecting someone's physical or behavioral characteristics.

GIVEN NAMES Italian 20%. *Marcello* (2), *Salvatore* (2), *Antonio, Carmelo, Fortunata, Gino, Grazia, Guiseppe, Pietro.*

Giovinazzo (209) Italian: habitational name from Giovinazzo in Bari province, Apulia.

GIVEN NAMES Italian 21%. *Rocco* (4), *Angelo* (3), *Vito* (2), *Antonio, Domenica, Raffaele, Santo.*

Giovino (131) Southern Italian: variant of either *Iovíno* (see IOVINO 2) or of *Giovene*, *Giovine* (see IOVINE).

GIVEN NAMES Italian 14%. *Angelo* (3), *Carlo, Carmine, Marco, Salvatore.*

Gipe (629) Probably a respelling of German **Geib**, a surname of uncertain origin from the Palatinate; according to Bahlow it is a topographic name from a term denoting dirt or decay.

Gipp (206) **1.** English: variant of GIBB. **2.** German: from a short form of a Germanic personal name formed with the stem *geb* 'gift', as in *Gebhard* (see GEBHARDT).

Gipple (190) **1.** Americanized spelling of German **Gibel** or **Gibbel** (see GIEBEL). **2.** German: from a diminutive of Middle High German *gippe* 'jacket' (modern Bavarian *Joppe*), hence a metonymic occupational name for a tailor or a nickname for someone who habitually sported a colorful or unusual jacket.

Gips (105) Jewish (eastern Ashkenazic): origin uncertain; perhaps a variant of HIPSHER, with initial *G* replacing *H* due to Russian influence and final *s* replacing *sh* due to the confusion between these two sounds in the Yiddish dialect spoken in Lithuania and Belarus.
GIVEN NAMES Jewish 8%. *Mordechai, Yaffa, Yitzchok.*

Gipson (5293) English: patronymic from GIBB.

Giraldi (117) Italian: patronymic or plural form of the personal name GIRALDO.
GIVEN NAMES Italian 12%. *Orlando* (2), *Carlo, Elida, Rudolfo, Sergio.*

Giraldo (590) Spanish, Portuguese, and Italian: from the Germanic personal name *Giraldo*, equivalent to GERALD.
GIVEN NAMES Spanish 54%; Portuguese 13%. *Luis* (16), *Carlos* (15), *Jose* (15), *Jorge* (8), *Blanca* (6), *Fernando* (6), *Gustavo* (6), *Hernan* (6), *Juan* (6), *Luz* (6), *Alberto* (5), *Diego* (5); *Albeiro* (2), *Ligia.*

Girard (4980) French: variant of **Gérard** (see GERARD).
FOREBEARS A family named Girard from Normandy was in Quebec city by 1660; another, from Le Mans, was in Quebec in 1663; and a third, from Poitou, was in Quebec city by 1666.
GIVEN NAMES French 10%. *Armand* (12), *Andre* (10), *Luc* (9), *Marcel* (8), *Fernand* (7), *Lucien* (7), *Dominique* (6), *Laurent* (6), *Alphonse* (5), *Emile* (5), *Adrien* (4), *Jacques* (4).

Girardeau (127) French: from a pet form of **Gérard** (see GERARD).

Girardi (679) Italian: patronymic or plural form of *Girardo*, one of the many Italian forms of the personal name GERARD.
GIVEN NAMES Italian 21%; Spanish 5%. *Angelo* (4), *Antonio* (2), *Arturo, Attilio, Biagio, Carmin, Carmine, Cosimo, Domenico, Donato, Erminio, Ezio, Fabio, Filomena, Gerardo, Germano; Juan Pablo* (2), *Jaime, Javier, Julio, Luisa.*

Girardin (371) French: from a pet form of **Gérard** (see GERARD).
GIVEN NAMES French 8%. *Marcel* (2), *Normand* (2), *Armand, Emile, Gaston.*

Girardot (220) French: from a pet form of **Gérard** (see GERARD).
FOREBEARS A family of this name from La Rochelle was in Montreal by 1687.

Giraud (337) French: from a vernacular form of **Gérald** (see GERALD).
FOREBEARS One immigrant of this name was established in Montreal by 1681; others, from Brittany, were in Beauport, Quebec, by 1700.
GIVEN NAMES French 10%. *Pierre* (2), *Alain, Emile, Franck, Herve, Laurent, Marie-Noelle, Sylvain.*

Girdler (290) **1.** English: occupational name for a girdle maker, from an agent derivative of Middle English *gurdel* 'girdle' (Old English *gyrdel*). **2.** Probably also an Americanized spelling of North German **Gördeler**, a variant of **Gürtler** (see GURTLER).

Girdley (138) **1.** English (Yorkshire and Lincolnshire): unexplained; possibly a habitational name from a lost or unidentified place. **2.** Probably an Americanized spelling of German **Gördeler** (see GURTLER 2).

Girdner (286) Americanized spelling of any of the names discussed at GURTNER.

Gire (144) Americanized spelling of German GAIER or GEYER.

Girgenti (183) Southern Italian: habitational name for someone from Agrigento in Sicily, which was called Girgenti until 1927.
GIVEN NAMES Italian 25%. *Sal* (4), *Alfio* (3), *Salvatore* (3), *Gaetano* (2), *Santo* (2), *Angelo, Gaeton, Giuseppe.*

Girgis (262) Arabic form of the Greek personal name *Geōrgios* (see GEORGE).
GIVEN NAMES Arabic 70%. *Nabil* (5), *Sami* (4), *Adly* (3), *Amal* (3), *Girgis* (3), *Medhat* (3), *Melad* (3), *Monir* (3), *Nader* (3), *Wagdy* (3), *Fayez* (2), *Fikry* (2).

Girling (134) **1.** English (East Anglia): much reduced and altered form of the medieval French nickname *coeur de lion* 'lion heart'. Compare CODLING. **2.** Probably a variant of German **Gierling**, itself a variant of GERLING.

Girman (116) **1.** English: variant spelling of GERMAN. **2.** German: see GIERMAN.

Giro (106) **1.** Catalan (**Giró**): probably a habitational name for someone from Girona, Catalonia, from a derivative of the place name. **2.** in some cases perhaps Aragonese (**Giró**): habitational name from Giró in Uesca province. **3.** Italian: unexplained, possibly from a pet form of an unidentified personal name.
GIVEN NAMES Spanish 26%. *Jorge* (2), *Jose* (2), *Miguel* (2), *Rafael* (2), *Alicia, Andres, Angel, Eduardo, Fernando, Ladislao, Luis, Raul; Aldo* (2), *Nino.*

Girod (384) French: variant spelling of GIRAUD.
GIVEN NAMES French 6%. *Marcel* (2), *Alain, Chantal, Jacques, Olivier, Romain.*

Giroir (354) French: variant spelling of GIROUARD.
GIVEN NAMES French 4%. *Albertine, Monique.*

Girolami (145) Italian: patronymic or plural form of the personal name GIROLAMO. This name is also found in Corsica.
GIVEN NAMES Italian 28%. *Guido* (4), *Claudio* (2), *Adelio, Aldo, Antonio, Attilio, Domenic, Francesca, Remo, Romeo, Silvio.*

Girolamo (210) Italian: from a popular variant of the personal name *Geronimo*, from Greek *Hierōnymos* (see HIERONYMUS).
GIVEN NAMES Italian 12%. *Rocco* (2), *Carlo, Gino, Michelina, Nicola, Pasquale.*

Giron (1337) **1.** French: variant of **Géron** (see GERON). **2.** Spanish (**Girón**): from a medieval nickname *Girón*, from Galician *girón* (*xirón*) 'hem', 'remnant'.
GIVEN NAMES Spanish 44%. *Jose* (32), *Carlos* (25), *Juan* (22), *Luis* (12), *Julio* (10), *Francisco* (8), *Jesus* (8), *Manuel* (8), *Ana* (7), *Jorge* (7), *Miguel* (7), *Mario* (6).

Gironda (140) **1.** Italian: of uncertain origin; possibly from a variant of Italian *ghironda* 'barrel-organ'. **2.** Southern French (Occitan) and Catalan: habitational name from Gironda, at the confluence of the Garona (Gironda) and the Dordonha, rivers in Occitania, or a regional name from the department of the same name. **3.** Galician: habitational name from Gironda in Galicia (Ourense).
GIVEN NAMES Italian 14%. *Vito* (3), *Antonio, Onofrio, Pasquale, Raffaele.*

Girone (124) Italian: from a Germanic personal name *Gero, Geronis* (see GERON), also occurring in the form *Gerone.*
GIVEN NAMES Italian 24% *Angelo, Carmela, Emilio, Gennaro, Marta, Rodolfo, Vito.*

Girouard (1278) French: from *Gérouard*; according to Morlet, from the Germanic personal name *Geroward, Giroward*, composed of the elements *gār, gēr* 'spear', 'lance' + *ward* 'guardian'. Dauzat, on the other hand, describes it as a derivative of *Geroul*, a compound of *gār, gēr* + *wolf, wulf* 'wolf'.
GIVEN NAMES French 11%. *Armand* (7), *Andre* (4), *Lucien* (4), *Emile* (3), *Fernand* (2), *Jacques* (2), *Marcel* (2), *Maxime* (2), *Adelard, Adrien, Camille, Chanel.*

Giroux (1954) French: variant of **Géroux** (see GEROU).
FOREBEARS A family named Giroux from Perche was established in Quebec city by 1654.
GIVEN NAMES French 11%. *Armand* (5), *Lucien* (5), *Marcel* (4), *Pierre* (4), *Andre* (3), *Rosaire* (3), *Gabrielle* (2), *Gaston* (2), *Gilles* (2), *Laurent* (2), *Luc* (2), *Monique* (2).

Girt (149) **1.** Northern Irish: reduced form of MCGIRT. **2.** Probably also an Americanized variant of **Gert(h)**, from a short form of GERHARDT.

Girten (237) **1.** German: probably a variant of GERTEN. **2.** Possibly a respelling of English GIRTON.

Girtman (197) South German and Swiss German: probably an occupational name for a maker of belts and straps or for a groom (in charge of harnesses and saddles), from Middle High German *gürten* 'to gird'.

Girton (656) English: habitational name from places in Cambridgeshire and Nottinghamshire called Girton, from Old English *grēot* 'grit', 'gravel' + *tūn* 'enclosure', 'settlement'.

Girty (117) Possibly a variant spelling of Irish **Gerty**, a reduced form of GERAGHTY.

Girtz (103) German: variant spelling of GERTZ.

Girvan (209) Scottish and northern Irish: habitational name from Girvan, a place in Ayrshire.

Girvin (407) Scottish and northern Irish: variant spelling of GIRVAN.

Gisclair (227) Perhaps a variant of the French family name **Gisclard**, which Dauzat derives from the female personal name *Gisele* (from the Germanic personal name *Gisela*) + *hard* 'hardy', 'brave', 'strong'.
GIVEN NAMES French 6%; Irish 4%. *Antoine, Clovis, Gaston, Jean Marie*; *Murphy, Patrick James*.

Gise (100) English: variant spelling of GUISE.

Gisel (125) Swiss German and German: variant spelling of GIESEL or GEISEL.

Gish (1545) German (**Gisch**): from a short form of the Germanic personal name *Gisulf*, from *gīsil* 'pledge', 'hostage', 'noble youth' (see GIESEL) + *wolf*, *wulf* 'wolf'.
FOREBEARS Matthias Gisch from Assweiler in the Palatinate arrived in Philadelphia in 1733 with a group of Mennonites. From him are descended all American Gish families.

Gisi (193) Swiss German: from a pet form of the personal name GIESEL.

Gislason (134) Icelandic: patronymic from the personal name *Gisli* (see GIESEL).

Gisler (322) **1.** Swiss German: variant of GIESELER. **2.** Altered spelling of German GEISLER.
GIVEN NAMES German 8%. *Otto* (3), *Erwin* (2), *Hans* (2), *Armin, Hedwig, Matthias*.

Gismondi (153) Italian: patronymic or plural form of *Gismondo*, a reduced form of the personal name *Sigismondo*, of Germanic origin (see SIEGMUND).
GIVEN NAMES Italian 18%. *Gaetano* (2), *Cataldo, Domenico, Franco, Giuseppe, Nicola, Pasquale*.

Gissel (117) North German and Danish: from a Germanic personal name based on *gīsil* 'pledge', 'hostage', 'noble youth' (see GIESEL).

Gissendanner (132) Altered spelling of **Giezendanner**, a Swiss German topographic name, probably from South German *giesse* 'waterfall', 'torrent' + *tanner* 'dweller near a pine forest'.

Gist (1934) English (Devon and Cornwall): probably a variant spelling of GUEST.

Gitchel (128) German: unexplained.

Gitchell (149) Americanized spelling of German GITCHEL.

Gitelman (131) Jewish (eastern Ashkenazic): variant of GITTELMAN.
GIVEN NAMES Jewish 26%; Russian 22%. *Ephraim* (2), *Esfir, Gersh, Haya, Naum, Osher, Shmil, Srul, Yitzhak, Zvi; Leonid* (4), *Yefim* (4), *Boris* (3), *Igor* (2), *Lev* (2),

Anatoly, Dmitry, Maks, Mikhail, Valeriy, Yevgeniy, Zhanna.

Githens (313) Variant of Welsh GITTINGS.

Gitlin (479) Jewish (from Belarus): metronymic from a pet form of the female personal name GUTE.
GIVEN NAMES Jewish 8%. *Sol* (3), *Blyuma, Izrail, Miriam, Moisey*.

Gitlitz (124) Jewish (from Belarus): metronymic from the Yiddish female personal name *Gitle*, a pet form of GUTE.
GIVEN NAME Jewish 4%. *Meyer*.

Gitt (114) **1.** German: perhaps a shortened form of a family name formed with *Gitt-* as the first element, such as GITTINGER. **2.** English: unexplained.

Gittelman (154) Jewish (eastern Ashkenazic): metronymic from a pet form of the female personal name GUTE.
GIVEN NAME Jewish 5%. *Arye*.

Gittens (591) Variant of Welsh GITTINGS.

Gitter (320) **1.** German: from Middle High German *gitter* 'railing', 'bar', hence a topographic name for someone who lived by a gate or barrier, or a metonymic occupational name for a janitor. **2.** German: habitational name from a place called Gitter near Brunswick; the place name is ancient name of uncertain origin, probably Celtic. **3.** Jewish (from Poland and Ukraine): nickname or ornamental name from Yiddish dialect *giter* 'good', equivalent of GOOD.
GIVEN NAMES German 7%. *Kurt* (3), *Wolf* (2), *Aloys, Benno, Frieda, Hermann*.

Gittinger (131) German: probably from a Germanic personal name composed with a cognate of Old Saxon *gidd* 'poem', 'song', or alternatively a variant spelling of **Güttinger**, a habitational name from either of two places named Güttingen: near Konstanz, Württemberg, or Thurgau in Switzerland.
GIVEN NAMES German 5%. *Kurt, Theodor, Ute*.

Gittings (439) Welsh: **1.** from the Welsh personal name *Gutyn, Guto*, a pet form of *Gruffydd* (see GRIFFITH), with the redundant addition of English patronymic -*s*. **2.** possibly also a patronymic from a byname from Welsh *cethin* 'dusky', 'swarthy'.

Gittins (337) Welsh: variant of GITTINGS.

Gittleman (310) Jewish (American): Americanized spelling of GITTELMAN.
GIVEN NAMES Jewish 8%. *Hyman* (3), *Sol* (3), *Mayer, Shira*.

Gittler (114) Jewish (Ashkenazic): metronymic from the female personal name *Gitl*, a pet form of GUTE.

Gittleson (113) Jewish: Americanized variant of **Gittelson**, metronymic from the Yiddish female personal name *Gitl*, a pet form of GUTE, + German *Sohn* 'son'.
GIVEN NAME Jewish 6%. *Isadore* (2).

Gitto (167) Italian: from a short form of a personal name ending with -*gitto*, such as *Ambrogitto*, a pet form of *Ambrogio*.

GIVEN NAMES Italian 18%. *Salvatore* (3), *Concetta, Fortunato, Nunzie, Rocco, Rudolfo, Sal, Saverio*.

Giudice (394) Italian: occupational name for an officer of justice, *giudice* (Latin *iudex*, from *ius* 'law' + *dicere* 'to say'). In some cases it may have been applied as a nickname for a solemn and authoritative person thought to behave like a judge.
GIVEN NAMES Italian 21%. *Salvatore* (6), *Sal* (5), *Angelo* (4), *Gaetano* (2), *Baldassare, Carmine, Cosimo, Emanuele, Ennio, Gino, Giuseppe*.

Giudici (156) Italian: patronymic or plural form of GIUDICE.
GIVEN NAMES Italian 17%. *Angelo* (4), *Giuliano, Livio, Luigi, Paolo, Reno, Salvatore, Tullio*.

Giuffre (448) Southern Italian (**Giuffré**): from the personal name *Giuffré* (see GIOFFRE).
GIVEN NAMES Italian 22%. *Angelo* (6), *Salvatore* (3), *Augustino, Bartolo, Biagio, Carlo, Carmelo, Carmine, Cosimo, Franco, Gino, Giuseppe, Julio, Mario*.

Giuffrida (298) Italian (mainly Sicily): from the personal name *Giuffrido*, a variant of GIOFFRE.
GIVEN NAMES Italian 23%. *Angelo* (3), *Giulio* (3), *Rosario* (3), *Sal* (2), *Salvatore* (2), *Alfio, Alfredo, Biagio, Carmela, Carmelo, Carmine, Cirino, Concetta, Concetto*.

Giuliani (732) Italian: patronymic or plural form of GIULIANO.
GIVEN NAMES Italian 17%. *Domenic* (4), *Antonio* (3), *Geno* (3), *Angelo* (2), *Dante* (2), *Giulio* (2), *Guido* (2), *Tullio* (2), *Alessandro, Antonietta, Dino, Elio*.

Giuliano (1056) Italian: **1.** from the personal name *Giuliano*, Italian equivalent of JULIAN. **2.** in some cases, a habitational name from for example Giuliano di Roma or Giuliàno Teatino.
GIVEN NAMES Italian 19%. *Salvatore* (6), *Vito* (6), *Antonio* (4), *Sal* (4), *Carlo* (3), *Pasquale* (3), *Angelo* (2), *Concetto* (2), *Domenic* (2), *Domenico* (2), *Filippo* (2), *Gaetano* (2).

Giunta (913) Italian: from a short form of the personal name *Bonag(g)iunta*, literally 'good addition', a name commonly given in the late Middle Ages to a long-awaited or much-desired son. Found throughout Italy, the name is common only in the south, specifically in Calabria and Sicily.
GIVEN NAMES Italian 17%. *Salvatore* (8), *Santo* (5), *Angelo* (4), *Sal* (4), *Carmelo* (2), *Ciro* (2), *Edvige* (2), *Marco* (2), *Rocco* (2), *Aldo, Antonio, Carmela*.

Giuntoli (105) Italian: from a derivative of GIUNTA.
GIVEN NAMES Italian 23%. *Vito* (2), *Alessandro, Domenic, Enzo, Gino, Marino, Palmiro, Plinio, Remo, Reno, Silvano*.

Giusti (692) Italian: patronymic or plural form of the personal name GIUSTO.

GIVEN NAMES Italian 17%. *Angelo* (6), *Gino* (4), *Aldo* (3), *Silvio* (3), *Camillo* (2), *Costantino* (2), *Dante* (2), *Donato* (2), *Elio* (2), *Franco* (2), *Luigi* (2), *Paolo* (2).

Giustino (138) Italian: from the personal name *Giustino*, from Latin *Iustinus*, a derivative of *Iustus* (see GIUSTO).

GIVEN NAMES Italian 27%. *Rocco* (5), *Angelo* (2), *Vito* (2), *Cosmo, Marino, Oronzo, Vincenzo*.

Giusto (305) Italian: from the personal name *Giusto*, derived from the Latin name *Iustus* meaning 'honorable', 'upright'.

GIVEN NAMES Italian 12%. *Domenic* (2), *Salvatore* (2), *Angelo, Gaetano, Giuseppe, Oreste, Pasquale, Sal.*

Givan (418) Scottish and northern Irish: variant spelling of GIVEN.

Givans (132) English and northern Irish: variant spelling of *Givens*, itself a variant of GIVEN.

Given (1514) Irish: reduced Anglicized form of Gaelic **Mag Dhuibhín** or **Mag Dhuibhfhinn** (see McGIFFIN).

Givens (7040) Northern Irish: variant of GIVEN, with English patronymic *-s*.

Givhan (148) Perhaps a variant of GIVEN. This name is concentrated in AL.

Givlden (101) Probably a respelling of French **Givaudan**, a regional name from Gévaudan, an ancient region of France corresponding to present-day Lozère and part of Haute-Loire.

Givins (96) Northern Irish: variant spelling of GIVENS.

Givler (214) German: dialect variant of GIBLER.

Givner (104) Origin unidentified.

Giza (349) **1.** Polish: nickname from *giża* 'hind leg of an ox or swine', possibly applied as a metonymic occupational name for a butcher. **2.** Albanian (**Gjizë**): occupational name for a maker or seller of cheese, from *gjizë* 'skim-milk cheese'. In the form **Gizas** this is also found as a Greek and Aromanian family name.

GIVEN NAMES Polish 9%. *Halina* (2), *Zbigniew* (2), *Zygmund* (2), *Bogdan, Jerzy, Ludwik, Zdzislaw, Zigmund.*

Gizinski (101) Polish (**Giziński**, also **Gizyński**): habitational name from Giżyn in Ciechanów voivodeship.

GIVEN NAME Polish 4%. *Casimir.*

Gizzi (449) Italian: probably a patronymic from *Gizio*, a reduced form of the personal name *Egizio*, from an ethnic name relating to Egypt.

GIVEN NAMES Italian 20%. *Angelo* (4), *Carmine* (4), *Amedeo* (2), *Antonio* (2), *Carlo* (2), *Dino* (2), *Elio* (2), *Gino* (2), *Giovanni* (2), *Marino* (2), *Costantino, Domenic.*

Gjerde (296) Norwegian: habitational name from any of numerous farmsteads so named, from Old Norse *gerði* 'enclosed land' (i.e. pasture).

GIVEN NAMES Scandinavian 13%. *Per* (2), *Anders, Aslaug, Gunner, Lars, Obert.*

Glaab (176) German: from Polish *głab* 'cabbage stalk', probably a nickname for a cabbage grower or for a simpleton.

Glab (169) Polish (**Głąb**): nickname from *głąb* 'fool' (literally, 'cabbage-stalk').

GIVEN NAMES Polish 16%. *Alicja, Beata, Czeslaw, Dariusz, Grzegorz, Janusz, Krystyna, Krzysztof, Stanislaw, Urzula, Zofia.*

Glace (197) Welsh: Anglicized form of **Glas**, a nickname meaning 'gray', 'green', 'silver-haired'.

Glacken (224) Irish: variant spelling of GLACKIN.

Glackin (251) Scottish and northern Irish: reduced Anglicized form of Gaelic **Ó Glacáin**, based on a diminutive of *glac* 'grasp'.

GIVEN NAMES Irish 5%. *Aidan, Brigid.*

Glad (435) **1.** English: from a short form of the various Old English personal names with a first element *glæd* 'shining', 'joyful'. Compare GLADWIN. **2.** English and Scandinavian: nickname for a cheerful person, from Middle English, Scandinavian *glad* 'merry', 'jolly'.

GIVEN NAMES Scandinavian 5%. *Gudrun, Sten.*

Gladbach (104) German: habitational name from any of various (mainly Rhineland) places named Gladbach, Gladbeck, Gladebeck.

Gladd (169) English (possibly also Scandinavian): variant spelling of GLAD.

Gladden (2194) English: patronymic from GLAD 1.

Gladding (433) English: variant of GLADDEN.

Glade (451) **1.** Northern Irish: reduced form of McGLADE. **2.** English: topographic name for someone who lived in a glade, Middle English *glade*. **3.** English: from an Old English personal name *Glæd*. **4.** German (also **Gläde**): nickname for a handsome man, from Middle Low German *glad(de)* 'smooth', 'shining'.

Gladen (132) English: variant of GLADDEN.

Gladfelter (509) Variant spelling of Swiss German **Glattfelder**, a habitational name for someone from a place north of Zurich named Glattfelden, from Old High German *glat* 'plane', 'shiny' + *feld* 'open country'.

Gladhill (240) English: variant of GLEDHILL.

Gladieux (200) French (southwest): according to Morlet, an altered form of **Cladel**, a southern derivative of *cleda* 'hurdle', hence a metonymic occupational name for a hurdle maker.

Gladin (114) French (southwest): according to Morlet, an altered form of **Cladel**, a southern derivative of *cleda* 'hurdle', hence a metonymic occupational name for a hurdle maker.

Gladis (150) German: of Slavic origin (see GLADISH), or a dialect variant of *Claudius*, the name of a 7th-century archbishop of Besançon.

Gladish (293) **1.** English: habitational name from Glydwish in Burwash, Sussex, which is named from Old English *glida* 'kite' + Old English *wisc* 'marshy meadow'. **2.** Altered spelling of German **Gladisch**, from the personal name *Gladu*, Slavic form of *Claudius*, or a nickname for a proper looking person, from Slavic *gladki* 'smooth'.

Gladkowski (102) Polish (**Gładkowski**): habitational name for someone from Gładków in Warszawa voivodeship.

GIVEN NAMES Polish 6%. *Tadeusz, Wlodzimierz.*

Gladman (204) English: variant of GLAD 2.

Gladney (1125) English: unexplained.

Gladson (377) English: unexplained. In form, this appears to be a patronymic from GLAD, but there is no evidence that this was ever a personal name. It may be an English variant of Scottish GLADSTONE. The surname appears to have died out in Britain.

Gladstein (191) Jewish (eastern Ashkenazic): variant of **Glatshteyn** (see GLADSTONE).

GIVEN NAMES Jewish 9%. *Hyman, Itzhak.*

Gladstone (1239) **1.** Scottish: habitational name from a place near Biggar in Lanarkshire, apparently named from Old English *gleoda* 'kite' + *stān* 'stone'. **2.** Jewish (American): Americanized form of **Glatshteyn**, an ornamental surname composed of Yiddish *glat* 'flat' + *shteyn* 'stone'.

Gladu (258) French Canadian: variant of GLADIEUX.

GIVEN NAMES French 6%. *Armand, Mireille, Pierre.*

Gladue (154) French Canadian: variant of GLADIEUX.

GIVEN NAMES French 7%. *Alphonse* (2), *Andre.*

Gladwell (354) English: apparently a habitational name, from an unidentified place, perhaps in East Anglia, where the surname is most common today.

Gladwin (232) English: from the late Old English personal name *Glædwine*, composed of the elements *glæd* 'shining', 'joyful' + *wine* 'friend'.

Gladys (124) Americanized spelling of Polish **Gładysz** (see GLADYSZ).

GIVEN NAMES Polish 4%. *Andrzej, Danuta.*

Gladysz (128) Polish (**Gładysz**): nickname for a dandy, Polish *gładysz*, from *gładki* 'smooth'.

GIVEN NAMES Polish 10%. *Janusz* (2), *Witold, Zygmunt.*

Glaeser (524) German (also **Gläser**): **1.** variant of GLASER. **2.** variant of *Kleser*, a short form of the personal name *Nikolaus* (see NICHOLAS) in Siegerland district.

GIVEN NAMES German 7%. *Heinz* (3), *Hans* (2), *Bernd*, *Guenther*, *Kurt*, *Manfred*, *Matthias*, *Rudi*, *Wilhelm*.

Glagola (109) Origin unidentified.

Glahn (244) German: **1.** nickname for a lethargic person, from Middle High German *glan* 'sluggish'. **2.** habitational name from a place so named near Hannover.

GIVEN NAMES German 4%. *Konrad* (2), *Kurt*.

Glance (172) Americanized spelling of German GLAN(T)Z.

Glancey (142) Irish: variant spelling of GLANCY.

GIVEN NAME Irish 5%. *Pegeen*.

Glancy (747) Irish: reduced Anglicized form of Gaelic **Mag Fhlannchaidh** 'son of *Flannchadh*' (see CLANCY).

Glander (489) German: **1.** nickname from Middle High German *glander* 'shine', 'radiance'. **2.** habitational name for someone from Glann, near Salzburg, named from *Glander*, a South German term for an enclosure or fence constructed of palings.

GIVEN NAMES German 4%. *Herwig* (2), *Erhard*, *Erwin*, *Otto*.

Glandon (350) Perhaps an altered spelling of the English habitational name **Clandon** (see CLANTON).

Glandorf (102) German: habitational name from a place so called near Osnabrück.

Glandt (109) German: nickname from Middle High Geman *glander* 'gleam', 'sparkle', 'shine', for someone with such a temperament.

GIVEN NAMES German 7%. *Darrold*, *Otto*.

Glanton (339) Probably an altered spelling of the English habitational name CLANTON.

Glantz (706) **1.** German: nickname from Middle High German *glanz* 'shine', 'radiance'. **2.** Jewish (Ashkenazic): ornamental name from German *Glanz* 'shine', 'radiance', Yiddish *glants*.

GIVEN NAMES Jewish 4%. *Emanuel* (3), *Miriam* (2), *Hyman*, *Ronit*, *Zalman*.

Glanville (462) English (chiefly Devon): **1.** (of Norman origin) habitational name from a place in Calvados, France, named from a Germanic personal name of uncertain form and meaning + Old French *ville* 'settlement'. **2.** habitational name from Glanvill Farm in Devon, Clanville in Somerset and Hampshire, or Clanfield in Hampshire, or from some other place likewise named with Old English *clǣne* 'clean' (i.e. free of brambles and undergrowth) + *feld* 'pasture', 'open country' (see FIELD).

Glanz (488) South German and Jewish: variant spelling of GLANTZ.

Glanzer (349) South German (also **Glänzer**) and Jewish (Ashkenazic): from a derivative of GLAN(T)Z.

Glanzman (138) Swiss German (**Glanzmann**) and Jewish (Ashkenazic): elaborated form of GLAN(T)Z.

GIVEN NAMES Jewish 5%. *Ilan*, *Sol*.

Glaros (122) Greek: from medieval Greek *glaros* 'seagull', classical Greek *laros*, a nickname for a person thought to resemble a seagull, for example in having a voracious appetite.

GIVEN NAMES Greek 5%. *Constantinos*, *Vassilios*.

Glas (257) **1.** Jewish (Ashkenazic): variant spelling of GLASS. **2.** German: variant of GLASS 1 or 3. **3.** German: from a short form of the medieval personal name *Gelasius*, the name of a pope (492–96). **4.** Welsh: nickname meaning 'gray', 'green', 'silver-haired'.

GIVEN NAMES German 5%. *Fritz*, *Georg*, *Gerhard*, *Johann*.

Glasby (171) Scottish and Irish: reduced form of GILLESPIE.

Glasco (709) English and Welsh: variant of GLASCOCK.

Glascock (812) English and Welsh: variant spelling of GLASSCOCK.

Glascoe (205) Northern Irish form of GLASSCOCK.

Glaser (4640) **1.** German and Swiss German (also **Gläser**): occupational name for a glass blower or glazier, from an agent derivative of Middle High German *glas* 'glass'. This name is widespread throughout central Europe. **2.** Jewish (Ashkenazic): occupational name for a glass blower or glazier, from the German word *Glaser*.

Glasford (119) Scottish: variant of GLASSFORD.

Glasgow (3356) **1.** Scottish: local name from the city on the Clyde (first recorded in 1116 as *Glasgu*), or from either of two minor places with the same name in Aberdeenshire. The etymology of the place name is disputed; it is probably from Welsh *glas* 'gray', 'green', 'blue' + *cau* 'hollows'. **2.** Scottish and Irish: altered form of **Closkey**, reduced and Anglicized form of Gaelic **Mac Bhloscaidhe** 'son of *Bloscadh*' (see MCCLOSKEY). **3.** Irish: variant of the English family name GLASS-COCK, which was once common in County Kildare.

Glasheen (179) Irish (Munster): Anglicized form of Gaelic **Ó Glaisín**, based on a diminutive of *glas* 'green', 'blue', 'gray'. Compare GLEASON.

Glasier (133) Probably a variant spelling of English GLAZIER or an Americanized form of the German cognate GLASER.

Glasner (202) German and Jewish (Ashkenazic): variant of GLASER.

Glasow (112) Northern German: habitational name from any of several place so named in Mecklenberg-Pomerania or one in Brandenburg.

Glaspell (115) English: unexplained; this is a Hampshire surname, also written **Glass-pel(l)**, **Glas(s)pool(e)**, and **Glasspole**. Possibly, it may be a habitational name from Glaspwll in Powys, Wales.

Glasper (428) English (County Durham, Cleveland): unexplained.

Glaspey (141) Irish or Scottish: reduced form of GILLESPIE.

Glaspie (442) Scottish: reduced form of GILLESPIE.

Glaspy (123) Irish or Scottish: reduced form of GILLESPIE.

Glass (15454) **1.** English and German: metonymic occupational name for a glazier or glass blower, from Old English *glæs* 'glass' (akin to GLAD, referring originally to the bright shine of the material), Middle High German *glas*. **2.** Irish and Scottish: Anglicized form of the epithet *glas* 'gray', 'green', 'blue' or any of various Gaelic surnames derived from it. **3.** German: altered form of the personal name *Klass*, a reduced form of *Nikolaus* (see NICHOLAS). **4.** Jewish (Ashkenazic): ornamental name from German *Glass* 'glass', or a metonymic occupational name for a glazier or glass blower.

Glassberg (233) Jewish (Ashkenazic): ornamental name composed of German *Glas* 'glass' + *Berg* 'mountain', 'hill'.

GIVEN NAMES Jewish 6%. *Gerson*, *Meyer*, *Sol*.

Glassburn (376) Possibly an Americanized form of German **Glas(s)brenner**, an occupational name for a glass maker, from German *Glas* 'glass' + *Brenner* 'burner'.

Glassco (218) English (found mainly in Wales): variant of GLASSCOCK 2.

Glasscock (1548) **1.** English: habitational name from Glascote near Tamworth in Staffordshire, named from Old English *glæs* 'glass' + *cot* 'hut', 'shelter'; it was probably once a site inhabited by a glass blower. **2.** Welsh: habitational name from Glascoed in Monmouthshire (Gwent), named from Welsh *glas* 'gray', 'green' + *coed* 'wood'. This name is also found in Ireland and may also have been brought to the U.S. from there.

Glassel (104) German: diminutive of GLASS.

GIVEN NAMES German 10%. *Ernst* (3), *Ilse*.

Glasser (1844) German and Jewish (Ashkenazic): variant spelling of GLASER.

Glassey (165) Swiss French: unexplained.

Glassford (328) Scottish: habitational name for someone from Glassford in Lanarkshire.

Glassman (1892) German (**Glassmann**) and Jewish (Ashkenazic): occupational name for a glazier (see GLASS 1).

GIVEN NAMES Jewish 4%. *Sol* (5), *Ephraim* (2), *Hyman* (2), *Miriam* (2), *Erez*, *Isadore*, *Meyer*, *Myer*, *Rina*, *Shmuel*, *Yetta*, *Zvi*.

Glassmeyer (149) German: identifying name for a tenant farmer called Nikolaus, from *Glass*, a reduced and altered form of the personal name *Nikolaus*, + Middle High German *meier* 'tenant farmer'.

Glassner (223) German: variant spelling of GLASNER.

Glasson (356) **1.** English (of Cornish origin): metonymic occupational name for a glazier or glass blower. **2.** Scottish: reduced form of MCGLASSON. **3.** French and Swiss French: from a diminutive of *glace* 'ice', hence a nickname for a cold person.

Glastetter (179) Altered spelling of German **Glasstetter**, probably a habitational name from an unidentified place where glass was made.

Glatfelter (258) Altered spelling of Swiss German **Glattfelder** (see GLADFELTER).

Glatt (529) Jewish (Ashkenazic) and South German: nickname from Yiddish and Middle High German *glat* (modern German *glatt*) 'smooth', 'sleek'.

GIVEN NAMES Jewish 4%. *Avi* (3), *Avram, Sol.*

Glatter (135) South German: **1.** habitational name for someone from either of two places called Glatt, in Switzerland and Württemberg, so named from *glatt* 'flat', 'level'. **2.** nickname for a sleek man, from a noun derivative of Middle High German *glat* 'smooth', 'sleek'. Compare GLATT.

Glatz (520) German and Jewish (Ashkenazic): **1.** nickname for a bald man, from Middle High German *gla(t)z* 'bald head', 'bald' (a derivative of Middle High German, Old High German *glat* 'smooth', 'shiny', an equivalent of GLAD), German *Glatze* 'baldness'. In some cases the German surname may be topographic for someone living on a bare, treeless hill. **2.** habitational name from Glatz, the German name of Kłodzko in Lower Silesia.

Glatzer (181) German and Jewish (Ashkenazic): from a noun derivative of GLATZ, denoting either a bald man or an inhabitant of Glatz.

GIVEN NAMES Jewish 18%. *Yehuda* (4), *Avraham, Boruch, Chaim, Gershon, Levi, Noam, Sender, Shlomo, Yael.*

Glaub (189) German: from Slavic *glava* 'head', a nickname for someone with a large or otherwise remarkable head.

GIVEN NAMES German 4%. *Mathias* (2), *Klaus.*

Glauber (187) **1.** Jewish (Ashkenazic): nickname or ornamental name meaning 'believer', from German *glauben* 'to believe' + the noun suffix *-er*. **2.** German: from a personal name based on Old High German *glou* 'intelligent', 'perspicacious', or a nickname with the same meaning, from a noun derivative of Middle High German *glau, glou.*

GIVEN NAMES Jewish 9%; German 6%. *Baruch, Boruch, Pinchos, Pinchus, Yonah, Zalmen; Kurt, Wilhelm, Wolf.*

Glaude (240) French: variant of CLAUDE.

GIVEN NAMES French 13%. *Adelard* (2), *Alcide, Armand, Germain, Gilles, Lucien, Marcel, Normand.*

Glauner (109) German: descriptive nickname from a Swabian word denoting a cross-eyed person.

Glaus (207) Swiss German: from the dialect personal name *Glaus*, a reduced form of *Nikolaus* (see NICHOLAS).

Glauser (288) Swiss German: patronymic from GLAUS.

GIVEN NAME German 4%. *Hans* (2).

Glavan (194) Slovenian, Croatian, Serbian, Romanian, and Greek (**Glavanis**): nickname for a big-headed person, from a derivative of South Slavic *glava* 'head'.

GIVEN NAMES South Slavic 9%; Romanian 4%. *Branko, Davor, Ivica, Petar, Slavica; Constantin, Dorel, Mihai, Serban; Carmella, Manuel, Miguel, Pedro, Rafael.*

Glave (119) **1.** Irish: reduced form of **MacGlave**, an Anglicized form of Gaelic **Mag Laithimh** (see GLAVIN 2). **2.** English: variant of GLEAVE. **3.** German: habitational name from a place so named in Mecklenberg-West Pomerania.

GIVEN NAMES German 5%; Irish 4%. *Andreas, Hermann, Lorenz; Conan, Donovan.*

Glaves (120) English (Yorkshire): variant of GLEAVE.

Glaviano (114) Italian: according to Caracausi this name occurs repeatedly in the parish registers of Piana degli Albanesi; it is probably derived from the Albanian habitational name **Glava**.

GIVEN NAMES Italian 24%. *Marco* (2), *Angelo, Carmelo, Sal, Salvatore.*

Glavin (513) Irish: **1.** reduced Anglicized form of Gaelic **Ó Gláimhin**, from a diminutive of *glámh* 'satirist'. **2.** reduced Anglicized form of Gaelic **Mag Láimhín**, formerly **Mag Fhlaithimhín**, from *flaitheamh* 'ruler'. Mag Láimhín has sometimes been 'translated' *Hand*, from the similarity of the reduced form to *lámh* 'hand'.

GIVEN NAMES Irish 4%. *Niall, Dermot.*

Glawe (316) German: **1.** habitational name from Glave in Mecklenburg. **2.** nickname for someone with a large or otherwise remarkable head, from Slavic *glava* 'head'. **3.** (**Gläwe**): either a variant of 1 or more probably from the personal name KLAUS.

Glawson (117) Probably an Americanized spelling of North German **Klausen** or **Klassen**, patronymics from the personal name KLAUS.

Glaza (236) Polish (**Głaza**): from a derivative of *głaz* 'big stone', possibly a nickname for a hard-hearted person.

Glaze (2366) English (chiefly West Midlands): variant of GLASS 1.

Glazebrook (337) English: habitational name from a place in Cheshire, named from the Glaze Brook, the stream on which it stands (a British name, from Welsh *glas* 'gray', 'green', 'blue') + Old English *brōc* 'stream'. The surname is also common in Devon, where it probably derives from a place by a stream similarly named, a small tributary of the Avon.

Glazener (180) Probably an Americanized form of German **Glasner** or **Gläsner**, variants of GLASER.

Glazer (1865) **1.** Americanized spelling of German and Ashkenazic Jewish GLASER or **Gläser** (see GLASER). **2.** Slovenian spelling of German GLASER. It is found mainly in the foothills of Pohorje mountain in eastern Slovenia, where many glassworks were in operation until the end of the 19th century.

GIVEN NAMES Jewish 7%. *Isadore* (5), *Dov* (3), *Hyman* (3), *Sol* (3), *Hillel* (2), *Ari, Avram, Bentzion, Doron, Elik, Eytan, Limor.*

Glazewski (107) Polish (**Głażewski**): habitational name for someone from Głażewo in Ostrołęka voivodeship.

GIVEN NAMES Polish 8%. *Stanisław, Tadeusz.*

Glazier (1415) English: variant of GLASS 1.

Glazner (165) Americanized spelling of German GLASNER. This name is concentrated in TX and AL.

Gleason (10160) Irish (Munster): reduced Anglicized form of Gaelic **Ó Glasáin**, from a diminutive of *glas* 'green', 'blue', 'gray'.

Gleaton (644) Possibly a variant of CLEATON. This name is common in SC and GA.

Gleave (241) English: from Middle English *gle(y)ve* 'sword' (Old French *gleive, glaive*, Latin *gladius*), hence a metonymic occupational name for a maker or seller of swords or a nickname for an accomplished swordsman.

GIVEN NAMES German 4%. *Erwin, Kurt, Otto.*

Gleaves (366) English (chiefly Lancashire): variant of GLEAVE.

Gleba (150) Ukrainian and Polish: **1.** from the eastern Slavic personal name *Gleb*. Gleb, murdered son of Prince Vladimir of Kiev (10th century), is revered as a saint along with his brother Boris. **2.** possibly also from *gleba* 'soil'.

Gleckler (178) Americanized spelling of German **Glöckler**, a variant of GLOECKNER.

Gledhill (577) English: habitational name from Gledhill, a place in West Yorkshire, named from Old English *gleoda* 'kite' + *hyll* 'hill'.

Gleed (144) Southern English: nickname from Middle English *glede* 'kite' (Old English *glida, gleoda*), probably applied with reference to the bird's rapacious qualities.

Gleeson (1146) Irish: variant spelling of GLEASON.

GIVEN NAMES Irish 6%. *Donal* (2), *Siobhan* (2), *Brendan, Conor.*

Gleghorn (271) English (Newcastle and Durham): probably a variant spelling of the Scottish surname CLEGHORN.

Gleich (331) German: from Middle High German *gelīche* 'equal', 'even', 'appropriate', an element in numerous habitational names from which the surname may have

arisen, for example Gleichen bei Kassel and Gleichen bei Brettach in Württemberg.
GIVEN NAMES German 4%. *Kurt* (2), *Heinz*.

Gleicher (160) **1.** German: occupational name for an iron worker who flattened out the metal into sheets, from an agent derivative of Middle High German *gelīchen* 'to smooth or even out'. **2.** Jewish (Ashkenazic): from the inflected form of German *gleich* 'same', one of names from vocabulary words that were selected at random by government officials when surnames were made compulsory.
GIVEN NAME Jewish 5%. *Iren*.

Gleim (303) German: from Middle High German *glīme, gleime* 'glow worm', attested as the name of various knights during the Middle Ages; the surname may also have arisen as a habitational name from Gleima, a place in Thuringia.
GIVEN NAMES German 4%. *Erwin, Heinrich, Kurt, Manfred*.

Gleisner (176) Variant spelling of German GLEISSNER.

Gleissner (114) German: derogatory nickname for a hypocrite, Middle High German *glīsenære*.
GIVEN NAMES German 5%. *Alois, Jurgen, Konrad*.

Glen (849) **1.** Scottish: topographic name for someone who lived in a valley, Gaelic *gleann*, or a habitational name from a place named with this word, such as Glen near Peebles. **2.** English: habitational name from a place in Leicestershire, so named from an Old English word *glean* 'glen', 'valley' (from Celtic *glinn*). **3.** Jewish (Ashkenazic): presumably an Americanized form of one or more like-sounding Jewish names.
FOREBEARS A Scottish family of this name settled among the Dutch at Beverwijck in New Netherland in the 17th century and later became prominent in Schenectady.

Glende (134) German: variant of GLANZ.

Glendening (309) Scottish: variant spelling of GLENDENNING.

Glendenning (509) Scottish: habitational name from a place in the parish of Westerkirk, Dumfries, recorded in 1384 as *Glendonwyne*. It is probably named from Welsh *glyn* 'valley' + *din* 'fort' + *gwyn* 'fair', 'white'.

Glendinning (228) Scottish: variant of GLENDENNING.

Glendon (124) **1.** English: habitational name from a place so named in Devon or from Glendon Hall in Northamptonshire. The first is named from Cornish *glynne* 'valley' + Old English *dūn* 'hill', while the Northamptonshire place name is from Old English *clǣne* 'clean' (i.e. clear of weeds) + *dūn*. **2.** Irish: reduced and altered form of **MacAlinden**, an Anglicized form of Gaelic **Mac Giolla Fhionntáin** 'son of a devotee of (Saint) *Fintan*'. Compare LINDY.

Glenn (16611) Scottish and Irish (Donegal): see GLENNY.

Glenna (103) Irish: variant of GLENNY.

Glenney (144) Irish: variant spelling of GLENNY.

Glennie (207) Scottish spelling of GLENNY. In the U.K. this spelling is concentrated in Aberdeenshire.

Glennon (1402) Irish (Leinster): reduced Anglicized form of Gaelic **Mag Leannáin** 'son of *Leannán*', a byname from *leann* 'cloak'.
GIVEN NAMES Irish 4%. *Aileen, Brendan, Liam*.

Glenny (162) Irish and Scottish: topographic name for someone who lived in a valley, Gaelic *an Ghleanna* 'of the glen'.
GIVEN NAMES French 4%; Irish 4%. *Emile, Jobe; Brendan, Dympna, Seamus*.

Glenz (128) German: variant of GLANTZ.

Glerum (137) Altered spelling of Norwegian **Glærum**, a habitational name from any of several farmsteads in northwestern Norway named Glærem, from Old Norse *gljúfr* 'ravine' + *heim* 'farm'.

Gless (121) German: **1.** habitational name for someone from Glessen near Cologne or from Glesse on the river of that name near Hameln. **2.** perhaps a reduced form of Swiss **Glesser** or **Glessmann**, variants of GLASER.
GIVEN NAMES German 4%. *Gerd, Wolfgang*.

Glessner (691) German: variant of GLASER.

Glew (199) English (Yorkshire): nickname for a cautious, prudent, or wise man, from Middle English *glew* 'wise', 'prudent' (Old English *glēaw*).

Glick (3905) Jewish (Ashkenazic): variant of **Glück** (see GLUCK).
GIVEN NAMES Jewish 4%. *Hyman* (8), *Myer* (4), *Sol* (4), *Chaim* (2), *Dov* (2), *Emanuel* (2), *Miriam* (2), *Zvi* (2), *Aaron David, Akiva, Anat, Ari*.

Glickman (1444) Jewish (Ashkenazic): elaborated form of **Glück** (see GLUCK).
GIVEN NAMES Jewish 7%. *Miriam* (5), *Sol* (5), *Emanuel* (2), *Hyman* (2), *Arye, Avraham, Hagit, Haim, Hyam, Hymen, Hymie, Meyer*.

Glicksman (179) Jewish (Ashkenazic): elaborated form of **Glück** (see GLUCK).
GIVEN NAMES Jewish 10%. *Morry* (2), *Aron, Hyman, Sol*.

Glickstein (217) Jewish (Ashkenazic): ornamental name composed of modern German *Glück* 'luck' (Yiddish *glik*) + *Stein* 'stone'.
GIVEN NAMES Jewish 7%. *Hyman, Sol*.

Glidden (1907) English (Devon): apparently a habitational name possibly from Glidden in Hampshire, which is named from Old English *gleoda* 'kite' + *dūn* 'hill'. Compare GLEDHILL. However, the concentration of the surname in Devon suggests that it may also have arisen from another place, now lost.

Glidewell (1261) English (Buckinghamshire): possibly a habitational name from a lost or unidentified place. Compare GLADWELL.

Glime (148) Origin uncertain. Probably a respelling of German GLEIM.

Glines (600) Welsh: possibly an altered form of GLYNN, with English patronymic -*s*.

Gliniecki (125) Polish: habitational name for someone from Gliniec in Radom voivodeship, or perhaps from a place called Glinice.
GIVEN NAMES Polish 4%. *Bronislaw, Zbigniew*.

Glinka (161) **1.** Polish and Belorussian: derivative of *glina* 'clay'. **2.** Polish: habitational name for someone from a place called Glinki. One in Poland is in Warszawa voivodeship. This is also established as a family name in German-speaking lands.
GIVEN NAMES Polish 7%; German 5%. *Casimir, Jerzy, Mariusz, Tomasz; Erwin, Gunter*.

Glinski (486) Polish (**Gliński**): habitational name for someone from a place named Glina, from *glina* 'clay'.
GIVEN NAMES Polish 6%. *Andrzej, Bogdan, Dariusz, Elzbieta, Jacek, Janusz, Stanislaw, Wieslaw, Zbigniew, Zofia*.

Glinsky (121) Jewish (eastern Ashkenazic): habitational name from any of numerous villages in Ukraine and Belarus named with Eastern Slavic *glina* 'clay'.
GIVEN NAMES Jewish 4%. *Aron, Ilya*.

Glisan (134) Possibly an altered spelling of Irish GLEASON. This name is concentrated in IL and PA.

Glissman (104) German (**Glissmann**): **1.** nickname for someone with something shining about him or his appearance, from Middle High German *gliz* 'sheen', 'sparkle'. **2.** habitational name for someone from either of two places called Glissen in Lower Saxony, west of the Weser.

Glisson (1486) Perhaps a variant of Irish GLEASON.

Glista (120) Polish: nickname for someone who used to intrude himself everywhere, from *glista* 'worm', 'earthworm'.
GIVEN NAME Polish 4%. *Wladyslaw*.

Glock (478) German: from Middle High German (Old High German *glocka*, apparently ultimately from a Celtic source), hence a topographic name for someone who lived by the bell tower of a church, a habitational name from a house distinguished by the sign of a bell, or a metonymic occupational name for a sexton (who among other duties was responsible for ringing the church bell) or a town crier (who used a handbell to draw attention).

Glockner (227) German (also **Glöckner**): topographic, habitational, or occupational name, from an agent derivative of Middle High German *glocke, glogge* 'bell' (see GLOCK). In some parts of Germany,

Glockner is the usual term for a sexton. Compare KIRCHNER, MESNER, and OPPERMANN.

GIVEN NAMES German 4%. *Hans, Rudie.*

Glod (182) **1.** Polish (**Głód**): from *głód* 'hunger', possibly applied as a nickname for someone who was very thin or, ironically, for someone who was excessively fat. **2.** German: probably from a Germanic personal name composed with Old High German *(h)lūt* 'clear', 'famous'.

GIVEN NAMES Polish 8%. *Grazyna, Jaroslaw, Mieczyslaw, Tadeusz, Tomasz.*

Glodek (116) Polish (**Głodek**): diminutive of **Głód** (see GLOD).

GIVEN NAMES Polish 9%. *Jadwiga, Miroslawa, Zosia.*

Gloden (116) **1.** German (**Glöden**): variant of GLOD. **2.** North German: probably a metonymic occupational name for a blacksmith, from Middle Low German *glode* 'iron', 'tongs'.

Glodowski (347) Polish (**Głodowski**): habitational name for someone from any of various places named Głodowo.

Gloe (145) North German: of uncertain origin; possibly a variant of **Kloë** or **Gloël**, variants of *Nicolaus* (see NICHOLAS).

GIVEN NAMES German 5%. *Aloys, Fritz.*

Gloeckner (152) German (**Glöckner**): occupational name for a bell-ringer or sexton, Middle High German *glockenære*. See also GLOCKNER.

GIVEN NAMES German 6%. *Erwin, Konrad, Manfred.*

Gloede (153) North German (**Glöde**): **1.** habitational name from Glöthe near Calbe on the Saale river. **2.** metonymic occupational name for a blacksmith, from Middle Low German *glode, glude* 'iron', 'tongs'.

Glogowski (263) Polish (**Głogowski**) and Jewish (from Poland): habitational name from any of various places named with Polish *głóg* 'hawthorn'. One such place is Głogów in western Poland, the German name of which is Glogau.

GIVEN NAMES Polish 9%; German 4%. *Beata, Bogdan, Casimir, Irena, Jozef, Stanislaw, Tadeusz, Witold; Siegmund.*

Glomb (176) Polish: variant of **Głąb** (see GLAB). This name is also established in German-speaking lands.

Glomski (173) Americanized spelling of Polish *Głąbski* or *Głębski*, habitational names for someone from an unidentified place named with *głąb* 'cabbage stalk' or *głębia* 'depth', 'bottom'.

Gloor (295) Swiss German: from a derivative of the Latin personal name *Hilarius* (see HILLARY).

Glor (147) Swiss German: variant of GLOOR.

Glore (471) **1.** German: from *Glöre*, a derivative of the Latin personal name *Hilarius* (see HILLARY). **2.** Possibly a respelling of Swiss GLOOR.

Gloria (610) **1.** Spanish, Italian, Portuguese (**Glória**), and French (Brittany and Provence): **2.** metronymic from the female personal name *Gloria*. **3.** according to Morlet, an occupational nickname for a singer, from 'Gloria in excelsis Deo', part of the mass.

FOREBEARS A family named Gloria from Rouen was in Quebec city by 1652; another, also called Desrochers, from Angoulême, was in Repentigny, Quebec, by 1694.

GIVEN NAMES Spanish 38%; Portuguese 7%. *Jose* (14), *Carlos* (5), *Juan* (5), *Luis* (4), *Francisco* (3), *Guadalupe* (3), *Jesus* (3), *Manuel* (3), *Raul* (3), *Rodolfo* (3), *Alberto* (2), *Carolina* (2); *Joaquim; Antonio* (4), *Ireneo* (2), *Lorenzo* (2), *Marco, Marco Antonio, Reynato, Romeo.*

Glorioso (544) Italian: nickname from *glorioso* 'glorious', 'arrogant', 'vainglorious'.

GIVEN NAMES Italian 16%. *Salvatore* (9), *Angelo* (7), *Mauro* (2), *Sal* (2), *Santo* (2), *Giuseppe, Ireneo, Vincenza.*

Glos (126) **1.** German: variant of KLAUS, a reduced form of the personal name *Nikolaus*, German form of NICHOLAS. **2.** Polish: from *głos* 'voice', presumably applied as a nickname for someone with a loud, mellifluous, or otherwise remarkable voice.

Glose (123) Probably an Americanized form of German GLOS.

Gloss (378) **1.** German: variant of KLAUS, a reduced form of the personal name *Nikolaus*, German form of NICHOLAS. **2.** English: nickname for a flatterer, from Old French *glose* 'flattery'.

GIVEN NAMES German 5%. *Erwin* (2), *Bernd, Guenther, Otto.*

Glosser (395) German (also **Glösser**): variant of GLASER.

Glossner (105) German: from a medieval short form of a Germanic personal name formed with *(h)lūt* 'clear' (modern German *laut*) as a first element, as in LUDWIG.

GIVEN NAMES German 4%. *Merwin, Wolfgang.*

Glosson (396) Probably an Americanized spelling of German **Klausen** (see GLAWSON).

GIVEN NAMES French 4%. *Antoine, Monique.*

Gloster (247) English: habitational name from the city of Gloucester. The place originally bore the British name *Glēvum* (apparently from a cognate of Welsh *gloyw* 'bright'), to which was added the Old English element *ceaster* 'Roman fort or walled city' (Latin *castra* 'legionary camp').

Glotfelty (323) Americanized spelling of Swiss German **Glattfelder** (see GLADFELTER).

Glotzbach (213) German: of uncertain origin; possibly from a creek so named or a variant of **Glutzbach**, from Old High German *(h)lūt* 'clear' + *bach* 'stream'.

Glotzer (121) **1.** Jewish (eastern Ashkenazic): nickname from Yiddish *glotser* 'gaper'. **2.** German: probably a nickname from Middle High German *glotzen* 'to stare'. **3.** German: possibly a variant of GLATZER.

GIVEN NAMES Jewish 5%. *Hirsch, Sol.*

Glover (19862) English: occupational name for a maker or seller of gloves, Middle English *glovere*, an agent noun from Old English *glōf* 'glove'.

Glovier (112) English: variant of GLOVER.

Glow (130) **1.** Irish: reduced form of **McGlow**, itself an altered form of MCCLOY. **2.** Americanized form of Polish GLOWA or German GLOE, or perhaps a translation of German GLANTZ.

Glowa (103) Polish (**Głowa**): nickname from Polish *głowa* 'head'.

GIVEN NAMES Polish 6%. *Jozef* (2), *Wasyl.*

Glowacki (952) Polish (**Głowacki**): habitational name for someone from Głowaczówice, Głowaczewo, or Głowaczowa, place names (from *głowa* 'head').

GIVEN NAMES Polish 8%. *Piotr* (3), *Tadeusz* (3), *Boguslaw* (2), *Jerzy* (2), *Aloisius, Augustyn, Bogdan, Darek, Grzegorz, Halina, Janusz, Jozef.*

Glowinski (106) Polish (**Głowiński**): habitational name for someone from Głowino in Toruń voivodeship or Głowno in Łódź voivodeship, both named with *głowa* 'head'.

Gloyd (297) Variant of Welsh LLOYD.

Gluck (1548) **1.** German (also **Glück**): from Middle High German *g(e)lücke* 'luck' (of uncertain origin, not attested before the late 12th century), hence a nickname for an individual considered fortunate, perhaps someone who had had a narrow escape. **2.** Jewish (Ashkenazic): ornamental name from German *Glück* 'luck' (Yiddish *glik*), or one expressing hope for good luck in the future.

GIVEN NAMES Jewish 9%. *Miriam* (7), *Emanuel* (5), *Aron* (4), *Chaim* (3), *Mendel* (3), *Ari* (2), *Arie* (2), *Avrohom* (2), *Hyman* (2), *Mayer* (2), *Mordechai* (2), *Rozalia* (2).

Gluckman (294) **1.** Jewish (Ashkenazic): elaborated form of **Glück** (see GLUCK). **2.** German (**Glückmann**): nickname for a fortunate or lucky man (see GLUCK).

Glucksman (182) Jewish (Ashkenazic): variant of GLUCKMAN.

GIVEN NAMES Jewish 10%; German 4%. *Moshe* (3), *Aharon, Dov; Hellmut, Willi.*

Glueck (400) German and Jewish (Ashkenazic) (**Glück**): see GLUCK.

GIVEN NAMES French 4%; German 4%. *Ghislaine; Eberhard, Klaus, Siegbert.*

Glueckert (120) German (**Glückert**): nickname for a lucky or optimistic person, a derivative of *Glück* (see GLUCK).

Glunt (410) Possibly a variant of German **Glund**, a nickname for a noisy person, from Middle High German *klunderen* 'to crash about'.

Glunz (141) German: from Middle High German *glunse* 'spark', hence a nickname

for someone with a lively intelligence or possibly an explosive temperament.
GIVEN NAME German 5%. *Markus*.

Gluth (227) German: from a short form of a Germanic personal name formed with Old High German *(h)lūt* 'clear', also 'famous'.

Glymph (197) Origin unidentified. This name is concentrated in SC.

Glynn (3784) **1.** Welsh and Cornish: topographic name for someone who lived in a valley, Welsh *glyn*, Cornish *glin*, or a habitational name from a place named with this word. Morgan proposes Glynllifon in Caernarfon as a probably source of the Welsh surname. **2.** Irish: reduced form of Gaelic **Mag Fhloinn** (see MCGLYNN).
GIVEN NAMES Irish 5%. *Brendan* (2), *Malachy* (2), *Dermot, Eamon, Liam, Niall, Ronan, Sean Patrick, Siobhan*.

Gmeiner (124) South German and Austrian: from a nickname from Middle High German *gemein(d)er* 'co-owner', 'partner in a debt', 'companion'.

Gmerek (107) Polish: nickname for an untidy person, from a derivative of Polish dialect *gmerać* 'to rummage about'.

Gmitter (102) German: perhaps a locative name with a shortened intensifying prefix *ge-* + *mitte* 'middle' for someone who lived or had property in the center of a village or other area, such as a field. Compare GMEINER.

Gnadt (136) **1.** South German: topographic name for someone living on an incline, from Old High German *gināda* 'incline', 'slope'. **2.** Northern and central German: from Middle High German *genāde* 'inclination to help', 'grace', 'favor', probably a nickname for someone who enjoyed the favor of his feudal lord.

Gnagey (135) **1.** Altered spelling of Swiss German **Gnaegi, Gnägi**, of uncertain origin. It may be from Middle High German *nâhe* 'near', 'close', hence a nickname for a neighbor. **2.** In some cases possibly an altered spelling of Hungarian GNAGY.

Gnagy (129) **1.** Hungarian: from the common Hungarian family name NAGY, with the addition of the letter *g-* representing the first character of someone's initials, their place of origin, or a nickname. This method of altering the most frequent surnames such as *Kis* 'small' (see KISS), NAGY 'big', *Kovács* 'smith' (see KOVACS), or SZABO 'tailor' is a peculiar feature of Hungarian naming. **2.** Possibly an altered spelling of Swiss German **Gnägi** (see GNAGEY 1).

Gnall (108) South German and Swiss German: unexplained.

Gnann (146) South German and Swiss German: **1.** from Middle High German *genanne, gename* 'relative' 'kinsman', 'namesake', denoting a relative, e.g. father or grandfather, with the same personal name. **2.** status name for a councilor, from Middle High German *genant* 'nominated'.
GIVEN NAME German 4%. *Otto*.

Gnau (189) German: nickname for an economical person, from Middle High German *genou* 'thrifty', 'careful'.

Gneiting (113) German: possibly a nickname for a person with a hostile, resentful disposition, from Middle High German *nīt* 'eagerness', 'envy', 'hatred'.

Gniadek (133) Polish: nickname for someone with chestnut hair, from *gniadek* 'reddish brown', from *gniady* 'brown'.
GIVEN NAMES Polish 6%. *Jerzy, Jozef, Krzysztof*.

Go (631) **1.** Filipino: unexplained. **2.** Indonesian: unexplained. **3.** Japanese (**Gō**): variously written; the most common form simply means 'village'. The surname is found in eastern Japan and on Amami in the Ryūkyū Islands. **4.** Chinese 吴: variant of WU 1. **5.** Chinese 伍: variant of WU 4.
GIVEN NAMES Spanish 20%. *Ramon* (4), *Rolando* (4), *Jose* (3), *Bienvenido* (2), *Corazon* (2), *Cristina* (2), *Elena* (2), *Eleuterio* (2), *Estrellita* (2), *Jaime* (2), *Simplicio* (2), *Adolfo*.

Goacher (129) English: variant of GOUCHER.
GIVEN NAMES Scandinavian 5%. *Anders, Erik*.

Goad (3372) Probably an Americanized spelling of German **Gohde** or **Godde**, variants of GOTT 1.

Goan (155) Northern Irish form of GOWAN.

Goans (184) Possibly altered spelling of German GANS or GANZ.

Goar (307) Scottish: unexplained. Black associates this name with Orkney, citing the example of Andrew Gor, tacksman of Pretty, 1490. The few bearers of this surname found in the U.K. today are found mainly in Scotland.

Goard (188) English: possibly a variant spelling of GOURD.

Goates (260) **1.** English: unexplained; probably a variant of **Goate** which may derive either from Middle English *gat* (Old English *gāt*), hence a metonymic occupational name for someone who kept goats or a nickname for someone thought to resemble a goat in some way, or a topographic name for someone who lived by a watercourse or sluice, Middle English *gote*. Possibly in some instances the name may be an altered form of COATES. **2.** Possibly an Americanized spelling of German **Götz** (see GOETZ).

Goatley (193) English: habitational name from Goatley in Northiam, Sussex, so named from Old English *gāt* 'goat' + *lēah* 'woodland clearing'.

Gobbell (116) Variant spelling of GOEBEL.

Gobbi (145) Italian (chiefly Lombardy and Venetia): patronymic or plural form of *Gobbo*, a nickname for a hunchback.
GIVEN NAMES Italian 13%. *Dante, Elio, Evo, Francesca, Graziano, Nunzio, Remo, Umberto*.

Gobble (705) **1.** English: possibly a variant of GOBLE or GOBEL. **2.** Perhaps an Americanized spelling of French GOBEIL. It is a common name in NC, VA, and TN.

Gobeil (142) French: unexplained. Compare GOBEILLE.
FOREBEARS A bearer of the name Gobeil from Nior is documented in Beaupré, Quebec, in 1666.
GIVEN NAMES French 22%. *Huguette* (2), *Normand* (2), *Emile, Jean-Guy, Lucien, Marcelle, Michel, Yves*.

Gobeille (136) French: unexplained. Compare GOBEIL.
GIVEN NAME French 10%. *Emile*.

Gobel (541) **1.** German (usually **Göbel**): see GOEBEL. **2.** French and English: metonymic occupational name for a maker or seller of goblets and tankards, from Old French *gobel* 'drinking vessel', 'cup' (apparently from Celtic *gob* 'mouth'). **3.** English: in some cases possibly a variant of GODBOLD. Compare GOBLE.

Gobeli (132) Swiss German: variant of **Göbel** (see GOEBEL).

Goben (349) German: habitational name from Gobbin on Rügen Island (Pomerania) or from any of several places named Goben in Bavaria.

Gober (1530) German: variant of GABRIEL or GOBERT.

Gobert (411) German and English: from a medieval personal name, *Godebert*, composed of the Germanic elements *gōd* 'good' or *god, got* 'god' + *berht* 'bright', 'famous'. The name was popularized in England by the Normans, and probably absorbed an Old English form *Godbeorht*. An Exeter moneyer named *Godbryt* is recorded in the reign of King Canute (1016–35).
GIVEN NAMES French 4%. *Andre, Antoine, Marie-France, Monique*.

Gobin (393) **1.** French: from a pet form of GOBERT. **2.** Guyanese and Trinidadian name found among people of Indian origin: from the Hindu personal name *Govind*, from Sanskrit *govinda* 'lord of herdsmen', an epithet of the god Krishna.
FOREBEARS A family called Gobin from Tours was in Quebec city by 1681.
GIVEN NAMES Indian 5%; French 4%. *Bhola, Boodram, Mohan, Narine, Parmanand, Pooran, Shiva; Andre, Marcelle, Pierre*.

Goble (3144) **1.** English: variant of GODBOLD. **2.** Americanized spelling of German **Göbel** (see GOEBEL).

Goblirsch (194) German (of Slavic origin): a variant of **Koblischke**, a nickname for someone with a sweet tooth, from Czech *koblížka* 'sweet tooth'.
GIVEN NAMES German 5%. *Kurt* (2), *Aloysius, Wenzel*.

Gobrecht (124) German: variant of GOBERT.

Goch (117) **1.** North German: habitational name from any of the various minor places which get their names from an ancient

Germanic element *goch*, *gog* 'marsh', 'bog', 'fen'. **2.** Polish: from a pet form of various personal names, such as *Goczałek*, *Gościsław*, or *Gotart*.

GIVEN NAMES Polish 6%. *Pawel, Zuzanna, Zygmunt.*

Gochanour (128) Respelling of German **Gauchenauer** (see GOCHENOUR).

Gochenaur (115) Respelling of German **Gauchenauer** (see GOCHENOUR).

Gochenour (530) Americanized spelling of Swiss German **Gauchenauer**, a habitational name from a place named Gauchenau, named with Alemannic *gauch(e)* 'cuckoo', 'fool' + *au* 'water meadow' (Middle High German *ouwe*).

FOREBEARS Jacob Goughnour emigrated from Switzerland in 1770, settling near Hagerstown, MD.

Gochnauer (159) Of Swiss German origin: see GOCHENOUR.

Gochnour (160) Of Swiss German origin: see GOCHENOUR.

Gocke (157) German (**Göcke**): see GOECKE.

Gockel (212) **1.** North German: habitational name for someone from a place in Westphalia called Gockeln. According to Bahlow, the place name is derived from *gok*, an obsolete word for a bog. **2.** South German: from Middle High German *gogel* 'cheerful', 'lively', either a nickname for someone with a cheerful disposition or an occupational name for an entertainer (modern German *Gaukler*). **3.** South German: nickname from a regional term *gockel* 'rooster'.

Gockley (192) Americanized spelling of German **Gockler** or Swiss **Göckler**, probably a nickname or an occupational name for a clown or entertainer, from an agent derivative of Middle High German *gogelen* 'to clown'. Compare GOCKEL 2.

Goda (253) **1.** Hungarian: from the old Hungarian secular personal name *Goda*, probably from a short form of *Godimir*, *Godislav*, or some other Slavic name. **2.** Japanese: (**Gōda**): 'connected rice paddies'. The name is not common in Japan; this pronunciation is found mostly on the island of Shikoku. In western Japan it is pronounced *Aita*. **3.** Indian (Gujarat): Jain name of unknown meaning, based on the name of a Jain community.

GIVEN NAMES Japanese 12%; Indian 4%. *Junko* (2), *Shohei* (2), *Hideki, Kazuhiro, Kunihiro, Masao, Masayoshi, Nobuko, Takehiko, Tomio, Toshihiko, Yasumasa; Jignesh, Jitendra, Jyotsna, Kishor, Viral, Vish.*

Godar (171) Variant spelling of French GODDARD.

FOREBEARS A family called Godaire, dit L'Angevin, was present in Montreal by 1715.

Godard (408) English and French: variant spelling of GODDARD.

FOREBEARS A family Godard, also called Lapointe, from Senlis (Oise) was in Beaupré, Quebec, by 1687.

GIVEN NAMES French 15%. *Pierre* (2), *Reynald* (2), *Alcide, Armand, Aurel, Celine, Cyprien, Dominique, Emile, Etienne, Euclide, Gilles.*

Godat (104) Swiss French: unexplained.

GIVEN NAMES French 9%. *Andre, Dominique.*

Godbee (413) English: variant spelling of GODBY.

Godbey (849) English: variant spelling of GODBY.

Godbold (612) English (of Norman origin): from the personal name *Godebald*, composed of the Germanic elements *gōd* 'good' or *god, got* 'god' + *bald, bold* 'bold', 'brave'.

Godbolt (317) English: variant of GOD-BOLD.

Godbout (654) French: from the Norman personal name *Godebald*, composed of the Germanic elements *god* 'good' or *god, got* 'god' + *bald, bold* 'bold', 'brave'.

FOREBEARS There have been people called Godbout in Canada since 1662.

GIVEN NAMES French 19%. *Marcel* (4), *Alain* (3), *Pierre* (3), *Alphonse* (2), *Andre* (2), *Gilles* (2), *Jacques* (2), *Achille, Aime, Armand, Aubert, Emilienne.*

Godby (626) English: habitational name for someone from either of two places in Leicestershire, Goadby or Goadby Marwood, named from the Old Norse personal name *Gauti* + *býr* 'farmstead', 'settlement'.

Goddard (6022) **1.** English (of Norman origin) and French: from *Godhard*, a personal name composed of the Germanic elements *gōd* 'good' or *god, got* 'god' + *hard* 'hardy', 'brave', 'strong'. The name was popular in Europe during the Middle Ages as a result of the fame of St. Gotthard, an 11th-century bishop of Hildesheim who founded a hospice on the pass from Switzerland to Italy that bears his name. This surname and the variant *Godard* are also borne by Ashkenazic Jews, presumably as an Americanized form of one or more like-sounding Jewish surnames. **2.** Possibly also an Americanized spelling of German **Gotthard** (see GOTHARD).

Godden (326) **1.** English: variant of GODIN. **2.** North German (**Gödden**): from a Low German form of GOTHARD 2.

Goddin (113) Variant spelling of English GODIN.

Godding (156) German: from a pet form of any of numerous Germanic personal name formed with the elements *god, got* 'god' or *gōd* 'good'.

Goddu (114) French: perhaps a variant of **Godu**, from a derivative of Old French *gode* in the sense 'debauched'.

FOREBEARS A family Godu, also called Sancoucy, from Poitiers, was in Varennes, Quebec, by 1698.

Godeaux (135) French: **1.** from a pet form of a Germanic compound personal name formed with *god, got* 'god' or *gōd* 'good' (see for example GODDARD). **2.** from a Germanic personal name composed of the elements *god + wald* 'rule', 'power'. **3.** from a diminutive of *gode* a French dialect term meaning 'simple', 'silly'.

GIVEN NAMES French 12%. *Curley* (2), *Antoine, Nolton, Orise.*

Godec (104) Slovenian or Croatian: unexplained.

Godek (331) Polish: **1.** from a pet form of the personal name *Godzisław*, composed of Slavic *godzic* 'to reconcile' + *slav* 'glory'. **2.** (**Gǫdek**) see GONDEK.

GIVEN NAMES Polish 4%. *Aleksander, Casimir, Danuta, Stanislaus.*

Godel (117) **1.** English: from an Old German personal name, *Godilo, Godila*. **2.** German (**Gödel**): from a pet form of a compound personal name beginning with the element *gōd* 'good' or *god, got* 'god'. **3.** Variant of **Godl** or **Gödl**, South German variants of **Gote**, from Middle High German *got(t)e, gö(t)te* 'godfather'. **4.** Jewish (Ashkenazic): from the Yiddish male personal name *Godl*, a pet form of *God*, a variant of biblical *Gad*.

Godette (213) Respelling of southern French **Gaudet**, from a nickname from the root *gaud-* 'happy', 'lively' (Latin *gaudere* 'to rejoice').

FOREBEARS Claude Godet, Lord of Maretz, was in Quebec at various times between 1609 and 1623.

Godfrey (10192) **1.** English: from the Norman personal name *Godefrei, Godefroi(s)*, composed of the Germanic elements *god, got* 'god' + *frid(u), fred* 'peace'. See also JEFFREY. **2.** Americanized form of Irish **Mac Gothraidh** or **Ó Gothraidh**, patronymics from the Irish equivalent of Godfrey (see 1 above), borrowed from the Vikings. **3.** Americanized form of the French surname **Godefroi**, of the same origin as 1.

FOREBEARS An Irish family of the name Godfrey originated in Romney, Kent. The first of them to settle in Ireland was Colonel John Godfrey, who was rewarded with lands in Kerry for his services in the 1641 rebellion. Godefroy, Lord of Normanville, from Normandy, was married in Trois Rivières, Quebec, in 1636. He was captured by the Iroquois in 1652. His brother, Lord of Linctot, from Rouen, was also married in 1636 in Trois Rivières, and lived from 1629 to 1632 among the Hurons. Another Godefroy, from Paris, was a trader and interpreter from 1623.

Godin (1404) French, English, and Dutch: from the Germanic personal name *Godin-*, a pet form of any of various compound names beginning with *god, got* 'god'. Compare GODBOLD, GODDARD, and GOD-FREY.

FOREBEARS A family called Goddin or Gaudin, descended from Huguenots of La Rochelle, France, was established in Canada by 1655. Another family of this name, also known as Châtillon, from Burgundy, was in Montreal by 1654. A third, from Rouen, Normandy, was in Quebec city by 1656.
GIVEN NAMES French 11%. *Normand* (8), *Marcel* (4), *Armand* (3), *Donat* (3), *Gilles* (3), *Pierre* (3), *Andre* (2), *Lucien* (2), *Michel* (2), *Alphy*, *Amiee*, *Cecile*.

Godina (270) **1.** Catalan: from the female personal name *Godina*, possibly of Germanic origin. **2.** Catalan: variant of **Codina**, a topographic name from *codina* 'stony field'. **3.** Slovenian: nickname from the adjective *goden* 'ripe', 'mature', formed with the augmentative suffix *-ina*.
GIVEN NAMES Spanish 47%. *Jose* (10), *Manuel* (7), *Felipe* (3), *Fernando* (3), *Juan* (3), *Carlos* (2), *Emilio* (2), *Fidel* (2), *Jesus* (2), *Manuela* (2), *Marcos* (2), *Olegario* (2).

Godines (140) Spanish and Portuguese: variant spelling of **Godínez** (see GODINEZ).
GIVEN NAMES Spanish 54%; Portuguese 14%. *Jesus* (3), *Jose* (3), *Juan* (3), *Luis* (3), *Arturo* (2), *Manuel* (2), *Ricardo* (2), *Roberto* (2), *Abelardo*, *Agustin*, *Alda*, *Alfredo*; *Figueroa*.

Godinez (1357) Spanish (**Godínez**): patronymic from the personal name GODINO.
GIVEN NAMES Spanish 53%. *Jose* (51), *Jesus* (16), *Juan* (16), *Salvador* (16), *Luis* (14), *Carlos* (13), *Jorge* (13), *Pedro* (13), *Manuel* (12), *Miguel* (11), *Armando* (9), *Francisco* (8).

Goding (376) **1.** English: variant of GOODING. **2.** German (**Göding**): variant of GODDING.

Godinho (140) Portuguese form of GODINO.
GIVEN NAMES Spanish 21%; Portuguese 14%. *Manuel* (6), *Carlos* (3), *Jose* (3), *Arnaldo* (2), *Anselmo*, *Cristina*, *Helio*, *Mario*, *Palmira*, *Pedro*; *Altair*, *Henrique*, *Paulo*.

Godino (176) **1.** Spanish: from the medieval personal name *Godino*, of Visigothic origin, from *Gaut* 'Goth' or *guþ* 'god'. Compare GODIN. **2.** Italian: pronounced *Godìno*, this is probably from a personal name of Germanic origin formed with the element *god*, *got* 'god' (compare GODIN). The name pronounced *Gòdino*, on the other hand, is of Greek origin, but unexplained etymology.
GIVEN NAMES Italian 21%; Spanish 6%. *Angelo* (5), *Antonio*, *Benito*, *Francisco*, *Gregorio*, *Luigi*, *Mario*, *Octavio*, *Riccardo*, *Rino*; *Ignacio*, *Manuel*, *Marcelina*, *Marcelino*, *Romaldo*.

Godkin (187) English: from a pet form of the Old English personal name *Goda*, which was in part a byname and in part a short form of various compound names with the first element *gōd*.

GIVEN NAMES Russian 6%. *Vladimir* (2), *Grigoriy*, *Mikhail*, *Yefim*, *Yevgeniy*.

Godleski (172) Altered spelling GODLEWSKI.

Godlewski (659) Polish and Jewish (from Poland): habitational name for someone from Godlewo in Łomża voivodeship.
GIVEN NAMES Polish 12%. *Stanislaw* (4), *Andrzej* (2), *Slawomir* (2), *Bogdan*, *Boleslaw*, *Casimir*, *Danuta*, *Grzegorz*, *Juliusz*, *Kazimierz*, *Krzysztof*, *Ludwik*.

Godley (711) English: habitational name from Godley in Cheshire or Goodleigh in Devon, both named from the Old English byname *Gōda* meaning 'good' + Old English *lēah* 'woodland clearing'.

Godlove (175) Translation of German and Jewish GOTTLIEB.

Godman (225) English: variant of GOODMAN.

Godown (171) Origin unidentified. Perhaps an Americanized spelling of German **Godau**, which may be a habitational name from Göda (formerly *Godaw*), a place in Saxony.

Godoy (946) Galician: habitational name from Godoy, a place in Galicia. The origin of the place name is uncertain, but a connection has been suggested with the Gothic elements *gu{dh}s* 'god' + *wīhs* 'saint'.
GIVEN NAMES Spanish 50%. *Jose* (31), *Carlos* (10), *Gustavo* (9), *Luis* (9), *Mario* (9), *Alicia* (7), *Jaime* (7), *Jorge* (7), *Pedro* (7), *Ricardo* (7), *Cesar* (6), *Juan* (6); *Antonio* (4), *Franco* (2), *Gilda* (2), *Leonardo* (2), *Marco* (2), *Sal* (2), *Amadeo*, *Fausto*, *Federico*, *Flavio*, *Gabriella*, *Lorenzo*.

Godsey (1912) Americanized form of German GOETZE.

Godshalk (148) Americanized spelling of German GOTTSCHALK.

Godshall (567) Americanized spelling of **Gottschall**, a variant of GOTTSCHALK.

Godsil (160) English: habitational name for someone from Gadshill in Kent, either of two places called Godshill in Hampshire and the Isle of Wight, or Godsell Farm in Wiltshire, which were all originally named *Godeshyll* 'God's hill'.

Godwin (8332) English: variant of GOODWIN.

Goe (274) Korean: variant of KO.

Goeb (102) German (**Göb**): variant of **Gob**, from a short form of the Germanic personal name *Godebald*.
GIVEN NAMES German 5%. *Helmut*, *Walburga*.

Goebel (3669) German (**Göbel**): from the personal name *Göbel*, a pet form of the Old High German name *Godebert*, composed of the elements *gōd* 'good' or *god* 'god' + *berht* 'bright', 'famous'.
GIVEN NAMES German 4%. *Kurt* (11), *Franz* (3), *Horst* (3), *Otto* (3), *Gerd* (2), *Hans* (2), *Helmut* (2), *Aloysius*, *Bernd*, *Christoph*, *Dieter*, *Dietmar*.

Goecke (249) North German (**Göcke**): Low German form of GOEDEKE.

Goeckel (161) South German: variant of GOCKEL 2.
GIVEN NAMES German 11%. *Hans* (2), *Fritz*, *Hanspeter*, *Heinz*.

Goeckner (130) German (**Göckner**): probably a variant of **Göckler** (see GOCKLEY) or of **Göcke** (see GOCKE).
GIVEN NAMES German 6%. *Fritz*, *Hans*, *Kurt*.

Goedde (308) North German: from the personal name *Gödde*, a short form of *Goeddert* (see GOTHARD).
GIVEN NAMES German 5%. *Eckhard* (2), *Alois*, *Gerhard*.

Goede (329) **1.** North German: from the personal name *Göde*, a popular short form of any of the Germanic names formed with *god*, *got* 'god' or *gōd* 'good' (e.g. GOTTFRIED). **2.** German (**Goede**): habitational name from a place near Bautzen in Saxony called Göda. **3.** Dutch: nickname for a good and kindly man, from *goed* 'good'.
GIVEN NAMES German 5%. *Heinz* (2), *Hans*, *Helmuth*.

Goedecke (218) North German: from a pet form of *Godefried*, Low German form of GOTTFRIED.
GIVEN NAMES German 9%. *Kurt* (2), *Elfriede*, *Erwin*, *Heinrich*, *Klaus*, *Manfred*, *Otto*.

Goedeke (129) North German (**Gödeke**): variant of GOEDECKE.

Goeden (278) **1.** Dutch: variant of GOEDE 2 or GODIN. **2.** German: variant of GOEDE 1.

Goedert (262) Dutch and North German: from the Germanic personal name *Godehart* composed of the elements *gōd* 'good' or *god*, *got* 'god' + *hard* 'hardy', 'brave', 'strong'.
GIVEN NAMES French 4%. *Michel*, *Olivier*.

Goedken (199) German: reduced form of **Goedeken**, a patronymic from GOEDECKE.

Goeglein (132) German: from a pet form of GOGEL.

Goehl (138) Eastern German (**Göhl**): variant of GOHL.

Goehner (173) Swiss and German (**Göhner**): probably an occupational name for a tub maker, from Middle High German *gon* 'vat', 'tub', 'container for liquids'.
GIVEN NAME German 4%. *Otto*.

Goehring (1243) German (**Göhring**): see GEHRING.
GIVEN NAMES German 4%. *Erwin* (2), *Otto* (2), *Alois*, *Ewald*, *Frieda*, *Heinz*, *Kurt*, *Lorenz*, *Lutz*, *Marliese*, *Milbert*, *Reinhold*.

Goeke (406) German (**Göke**): from a reduced form of **Gödeke** (see GOEDECKE).

Goeken (205) North German: variant of **Gödeke** (see GOEDECKE).

Goel (384) Indian (northern states): Hindu (Bania) and Jain name of unknown origin, based on the name of a clan in the Agarwal Bania community.

GIVEN NAMES Indian 91%. *Anil* (6), *Arun* (6), *Deepak* (6), *Sanjay* (6), *Vijay* (6), *Vinod* (6), *Mohan* (5), *Sudhir* (5), *Ajay* (4), *Arvind* (4), *Ashok* (4), *Manish* (4).

Goeller (434) South German (**Göller**): variant of GELLER 2.
GIVEN NAMES German 4%. *Kurt* (2), *Horst*, *Klaus*, *Leonhard*, *Otto*.

Goellner (175) German (**Göllner**): occupational name for someone who worked with gold (a refiner, jeweler, or gilder), from an agent derivative of Old High German *gold* 'gold'.
GIVEN NAME German 6%. *Dietmar*.

Goelz (431) German: **1.** dialect variant of GELTZ. **2.** (**Gölz**): habitational name from Göls in Holstein or from either of two places, Göl(t)zscha or Göltzschen, in Saxony. **3.** nickname for a bald man from Slavic *gol-* 'naked', 'bald'.

Goelzer (103) German (**Gölzer**): **1.** dialect variant of GELTZ. **2.** habitational name from Göl(t)zscha or Göltzschen in Saxony.

Goeman (238) **1.** Dutch: from a short form of the medieval personal name *Go(e)dman*, composed of the Germanic elements *gōd* 'good' or *god*, *got* 'god' + *man* 'man'. **2.** Dutch: occupational name for an arbitrator in a civil dispute, i.e. a trusted or respected person, from *goedeman*, literally 'good man'. **3.** In some cases perhaps an altered spelling of German **Gö(h)mann** (see GOHMAN).

Goen (387) Dutch and North German (also **Göen**): from a pet form of a Germanic personal name beginning with the element *gond* 'battle'.

Goenner (119) North German (**Gönner**): from the personal name *Gönner*, a variant of GUNTER, composed of the elements *gund* 'battle' + *hari*, *heri* 'army'. Compare GONNERMAN.

Goens (309) **1.** Dutch: patronymic from GOEN. **2.** German (**Göens**): Frisian patronymic from the personal name *Göde* (see GOEDE, cognate with 1).

Goepfert (292) Swiss German: from a variant of GOTTFRIED.
GIVEN NAMES German 8%. *Franz* (2), *Gerhard* (2), *Hans*, *Helmuth*, *Otto*.

Goerdt (134) German (**Gördt**): variant and reduced form of the Germanic personal name GERHARDT.

Goeres (108) North German (**Göres**): from a reduced form of the Latin personal name *Gregorius* (see GREGORY, and compare GORR).
GIVEN NAMES German 7%. *Erwin*, *Markus*.

Goergen (341) North German (**Görgen**): patronymic from a Low German form of the personal name *Georg* (see GEORGE).

Goering (907) Eastern German (**Göring**): **1.** variant of GEHRING. **2.** topographic name from Slavic *gora* 'mountain', 'hill'.

Goeringer (147) German: variant of GOERING.

GIVEN NAMES German 12%. *Otto* (3), *Erwin*, *Ewald*, *Kurt*.

Goerke (330) Eastern German (under Slavic influence): **1.** from a pet form of the personal name *Georg* (see GEORGE). **2.** possibly a habitational name from any of several places in Pomerania so called, from Slavic *gora* 'mountain', 'hill'.
GIVEN NAMES German 11%. *Reinhardt* (2), *Benno*, *Bernhard*, *Dieter*, *Fritz*, *Gerhard*, *Guenter*, *Hans*, *Heinz*, *Kurt*, *Siegfried*, *Ulrich*.

Goerlich (146) East German (**Görlich**): variant of GERLACH.
GIVEN NAMES German 12%. *Gerhard*, *Klaus*, *Kurt*, *Reimund*, *Wolfgang*.

Goerlitz (161) Eastern German (**Görlitz**): habitational name for someone from a Silesian city so named, now forming part of the border between Germany and southern Poland.
GIVEN NAMES German 5%; Scandinavian 4%. *Erhard*, *Erwin*, *Gerda*.

Goerner (186) German (**Görner**): **1.** habitational name from Görna in Saxony or Görne in Brandenburg. **2.** variant of GERNER.
GIVEN NAMES German 7%. *Helmut*, *Horst*, *Johannes*.

Goers (354) North German (**Görs**): patronymic from *Goer*, a Low German form of the Latin personal name *Gregorius* (see GREGORY).
GIVEN NAMES German 4%. *Armin*, *Klaus*, *Otto*.

Goertz (635) German (**Görtz**): probably of Slavic origin, a habitational name from any of various places in eastern and northern Germany named Görtz or Görz.
GIVEN NAMES German 5%. *Alois* (2), *Christoph*, *Erwin*, *Guenter*, *Juergen*, *Kurt*, *Otto*.

Goertzen (394) German: probably a variant of *Göretz*, a reduced form of *Gerhards* (see GERHARDT), or a variant of GOERTZ.
GIVEN NAMES German 4%. *Kurt*, *Waltraut*.

Goes (236) **1.** Dutch and North German: from Middle Dutch *goes* 'goose', hence probably a metonymic occupational name for someone who kept geese, or a nickname for a silly person. **2.** Portuguese: unexplained.
GIVEN NAMES Portuguese 6%; Spanish 6%. *Joaquim*, *Paulo*; *Manuel* (3), *Alvaro*, *Carlos*, *Julio*, *Luiz*, *Marcelo*, *Mario*, *Orlando*, *Raul*, *Virgilio*.

Goeser (205) North German (**Göser**): occupational name for a breeder or keeper of geese, from an agent derivative of Low German *gōs* 'goose'. Compare GANSER.
GIVEN NAMES German 6%. *Kurt* (3), *Gitta*, *Monika*.

Goessling (130) German: probably a variant of **Gösling**, from the personal name *Gozzelin*, or from a pet form of *Gozzo*, a short form of *Gozzelin*. Alternatively, it may be from a short form of the personal

names *Goswin*, *Gossold*, or *Gotfrid* (see GOTTFRIED), which belong to the southwestern part of the country.
GIVEN NAME German 5%. *Erwin*.

Goethals (187) Dutch: from *goed ale* 'good ale', hence a metonymic occupational name for a brewer. The *h*, according to Debrabandere, results from a folk interpretation of the second element as *hals* 'throat', 'neck'.
GIVEN NAMES French 6%. *Colette*, *Gaston*, *Ignace*.

Goethe (287) German (also **Göthe**): from a short form of the personal name *Godo*, formed with the Germanic element *god*, *got* 'god', or from Middle High German *göte* 'godfather'.

Goetsch (902) German and Swiss German (**Götsch**): from a pet form of GOTTFRIED or GOTTSCHALK.

Goetschius (135) German humanistic name: a Latinate spelling of GOETSCH.

Goett (103) German: variant spelling of **Gött**, a variant of GOTT 2.

Goette (177) **1.** South German (**Götte**): from Middle High German *götte*, *gotte* 'godfather'. **2.** North German: variant of GOEDDE.
GIVEN NAME German 5%. *Erna*.

Goettel (240) South German (**Göttel**): from a pet form of GOTTFRIED, or any of the other personal names formed with *Got(t)-*.
GIVEN NAMES German 10%. *Klaus* (2), *Otto* (2), *Gerhard*, *Heinrich*, *Othmar*, *Wolfgang*.

Goetter (122) German (**Götter**): from the personal name *Godechar*, formed with the Germanic elements *god*, *got* 'god' or *gōd* 'good'.
GIVEN NAME German 6%. *Erwin* (2).

Goetting (200) German (**Götting**): **1.** habitational name from any of several places in Westphalia named Göttingen, or from Götting in Bavaria. **2.** patronymic from the personal name *Goette*, *Gotte* (see GOTT 1).
GIVEN NAMES German 5%. *Helmut*, *Kurt*.

Goettl (318) South German (**Göttl**): variant spelling of GOETTEL.

Goettsch (347) German (**Göttsch**): variant spelling of GOETSCH.
GIVEN NAMES German 4%. *Hans* (2), *Manfred*.

Goettsche (115) German: variant of **Götsche**, itself a variant of *Götsch* (see GOTSCH).
GIVEN NAMES German 9%. *Erwin*, *Reinhard*, *Uwe*, *Wilhelm*.

Goetz (5749) South German (**Götz**): from a short form of any of the various compound names with the first element *gōd* 'good' or *god*, *got* 'god'.

Goetze (375) German (**Götze**): variant of GOETZ.
GIVEN NAMES German 8%; Scandinavian 4%. *Dieter* (3), *Fritz*, *Hans*, *Hartmann*, *Helmut*, *Klaus*, *Rainer*, *Wilhelm*; *Erik* (3).

Goetzinger (388) German: habitational name for someone from any of three places called Götzing in Bavaria, from Götzingen in Baden, or from Gotzing in Bavaria.

Goetzke (182) Eastern German (**Götzke**): from GOETZ + the Slavic suffix *-k*.

Goetzman (161) South German (**Götzmann**): **1.** variant of **Götz** (see GOETZ). **2.** from late Middle High German *gotesman* 'man of God', hence a nickname for a particularly pious person, or perhaps for someone who worked in a church.

Goewey (209) **1.** Dutch: Americanized spelling of **Goewie**, for which Debrabandere offers various explanations, including the following: **2.** variant of **Degouy**, a habitational name for someone from any of several minor places in northern France named Gouy. **3.** from the personal name *Gauvain*, French form of a Celtic name found in English as *Gawain*. **4.** from a Germanic personal name, a compound of *god, got* 'god' + *hari, heri* 'army'. FOREBEARS The Goewey family were established in Beverwijck in New Netherland (Albany, NY) in the 17th century. For example, the Dutch Reformed Church registers show that Sara Goewey married Gerritt Sybrantse Van Schayk on January 4, 1684/85.

Goff (11811) **1.** Welsh: nickname for a redhaired person (see GOUGH). **2.** English (of Cornish and Breton origin): occupational name from Cornish and Breton *goff* 'smith' (cognate with Gaelic *gobha*). The surname is common in East Anglia, where it is of Breton origin, introduced by followers of William the Conqueror. **3.** Irish: reduced form of MCGOFF. FOREBEARS Edward Goffe was a farmer in Cambridge MA whose house was acquired by Harvard College some time before 1654 and used as a dormitory, known as Goffe's College.

Goffe (162) English: variant spelling of GOFF.

Goffin (172) **1.** English (East Anglia): either a diminutive of GOFF or from a pet form of the personal name GODFREY. **2.** French: nickname from a diminutive of Old French *goffe* 'heavy', 'coarse'.

Goffinet (259) French: diminutive of GOFFIN 2.

Goffman (102) Jewish (Eastern Ashkenazic): variant, under Russian influence, of HOFFMAN. Russian has no *h* and alters *h* to *g* in borrowed words and names.

GIVEN NAMES Jewish 7%; German 4%. *Hirsch; Erwin.*

Goffney (123) Irish: variant of GAFFNEY.

Goffredo (149) Italian: from the personal name *Goffredo*, Italian equivalent of GODFREY.

GIVEN NAMES Italian 22%. *Alfonso, Angelo, Carmine, Carolina, Marina, Mario, Nicola, Savino, Vito.*

Gofman (138) Jewish (eastern Ashkenazic): variant of HOFFMAN under Russian influ-

ence, since Russian has no *h* and alters *h* in borrowed words to *g*.

GIVEN NAMES Russian 44%; Jewish 27%. *Aleksandr* (3), *Boris* (3), *Semyon* (3), *Vladimir* (3), *Fruma* (2), *Genrikh* (2), *Igor* (2), *Leonid* (2), *Zoya* (2), *Anatoly, Arkadiy, Evgeni; Ilya* (2), *Izya* (2), *Yakov* (2), *Chaim, Fira, Gersh, Inna, Irina, Isak, Izrail, Khana, Marat.*

Goforth (3067) Probably an Americanized spelling of German **Goffarth**, a Lower Rhine variant of *Godefried* (see GOTTFRIED), or an Americanized spelling of the Dutch cognate **Goeffoet**.

Goga (146) Greek (**Gogas**) and Albanian: nickname from Albanian *kokë* 'head'.

Gogan (253) **1.** Irish: reduced Anglicized form of Gaelic **Mac Cogadháin** 'son of *Cogadhán*' (see COOGAN). **2.** Hungarian (**Gogán**): from an old secular personal name *Gogán* (also found as *Gogány* and *Gógány*).

GIVEN NAME Irish 5%. *Liam.*

Gogel (307) German: nickname from Middle High German *gogel* 'lively', 'boisterous'.

GIVEN NAMES German 4%. *Alois, Gerhard, Rainer.*

Gogerty (112) Irish: reduced form of **Mac Gogarty**, an Anglicized form of Gaelic **Mag Fhógartaigh**. Compare FOGARTY.

Goggans (532) Apparently a variant of GOGGIN. It is a common name in AL and TX.

Goggin (1094) Irish: variant of COOGAN.

GIVEN NAMES Irish 4%. *Brendan, Caitlin.*

Goggins (897) Irish: variant of COOGAN, with English patronymic *-s*.

Goglia (193) Italian: habitational name from Goglia in Novara province.

GIVEN NAMES Italian 14%. *Salvatore* (2), *Dino, Gennaro, Natale, Pasquale, Rocco, Silvio, Sylvio.*

Gogol (130) **1.** Polish, Ukrainian, and Jewish (from Ukraine): from Ukrainian *gogol* 'wild duck', 'mallard', a nickname denoting a wildfowler or acquired on account of some other association with the bird. The Jewish name may be ornamental. **2.** Jewish (from Poland): habitational name from Gogole, a village in northeastern Poland.

GIVEN NAMES Polish 13%. *Danuta* (2), *Janusz* (2), *Andrzej, Darek, Jozef, Stanislawa.*

Gogola (124) **1.** Polish: nickname from either *gogołka* 'unripe fruit' or *gogol* 'wild duck', 'mallard'. See GOGOL. **2.** Greek (**Gogolas**): unflattering nickname for a stupid person, from Albanian *kungull* 'squash', 'pumpkin'.

GIVEN NAMES Polish 10%. *Danuta, Henryk, Jozef, Michalina, Mieczyslaw, Zbigniew.*

Gogolin (116) German: probably a topographic name from Polish (dialect) *gogoła, gógoła* 'wild apple tree'.

GIVEN NAMES German 17%. *Kurt* (4), *Otto*(2), *Heinz, Uwe.*

Goguen (614) Variant spelling of French **Goguin**, a nickname for a prankster or joker, from Old French *gogue* 'joke'.

GIVEN NAMES French 9%. *Alcide* (3), *Donat* (2), *Aurele, Camille, Cecile, Emile, Evariste, Gisele, Normand, Ovila, Placide.*

Goh (275) **1.** Chinese 吴: variant of WU 1. **2.** Chinese 伍: variant of WU 4.

GIVEN NAMES Chinese 21%. *Swee* (3), *Chae* (2), *Ching* (2), *Boon, Chan, Cheng, Gim, Guan, Han, Jin, Jin Hui, Kau.*

Gohde (122) North German: from a short form of any of the personal names composed with the Germanic element *gōd* 'good' or *god, got* 'god', such as *Godefrid*.

Goheen (688) Origin unidentified.

Gohl (443) **1.** Eastern German (of Slavic origin): nickname from *goły* 'bald', 'naked', or topographic name from *gola* 'bare heathland', 'place without trees', or a habitational name from a place named with this word. **2.** Swiss German: probably a nickname for a loud person, from Middle High German *goln* 'to howl'.

Gohlke (326) Eastern German (of Slavic origin): from a derivative of GOHL.

Gohman (196) Altered spelling of German **Gö(h)mann**, a nickname for a farmer or country dweller, from Middle High German *göu, geu* 'region', 'country' + *man* 'man' (see GAU 1), or, in the north, possibly a topographic name from the field name *An der Gö* 'at the water meadow'.

Gohn (389) German: from a reduced form of the personal name *Johann* (see JOHN).

Gohr (243) German: **1.** from Middle Low German *gor* 'quagmire', 'bog', an element in various habitational names from which the surname may have arisen, including Gohr near Neuss; alternatively, it may simply be a topographic name for someone living near a bog. **2.** in eastern Germany, possibly from Polish *gora* 'mountain' or *gor* 'fire', 'burning' (denoting cleared forest), elements contained in various fieldnames and place names.

Gohring (110) German (**Göhring**): variant of GOERING. This is one of the German names that became established in Ukraine in the 19th century.

Goicoechea (119) Basque: topographic name from Basque *goi* 'higher', 'upper' + *eche* 'house'.

GIVEN NAMES Spanish 30%. *Aurelio* (2), *Jose* (2), *Benito, Carlos, Elia, Eugenio, Isidro, Jesus, Jose Luis, Josefina, Juan, Julio.*

Goike (129) **1.** German (of Slavic origin): from a diminutive of Sorbian *haj* 'grove', either a topographic name for someone who lived by a copse or a metonymic occupational name for a forest warden. **2.** Germanized spelling of Polish **Gajek**, of the same meaning as 1, from a diminutive of *gaj* 'grove'.

Goin (970) French: variant of **Gouin**, itself a variant of GODIN.

Goines (759) Probably an altered form of Irish GOING.

Going (548) **1.** Irish: reduced Anglicized form of Gaelic *Mac an Ghabhann* or *Mac Gabhann* 'son of (the) smith' (see McGOWAN) or, in some cases, an Anglicized spelling of the French family name GOUIN, which has been established in Tipperary since the end of the 17th century. **2.** German (**Göing**): variant of **Göding** (see GODING).

Goings (1085) **1.** Irish: variant of GOING. **2.** Possibly an altered form of German **Göing** (see GOING).

Goins (6594) **1.** Irish: variant of GOING. **2.** Possibly an altered form of German **Göing** (see GOING).

Gokey (605) Much altered Americanized form of French GAUTHIER.

Gokhale (105) Indian (Maharashtra); pronounced *gokh-lay*: Hindu (Brahman) name found among Konkanasth Brahmans, probably from Marathi *gokhla* 'round window', literally 'cow eye', from Sanskrit *gavākṣa* (from *go* 'cow' + *akṣa* 'eye'), + the suffix *-la*.
GIVEN NAMES Indian 91%. *Ajit* (3), *Anjali* (3), *Anil* (2), *Madhu* (2), *Parag* (2), *Sanjay* (2), *Sudhir* (2), *Vinayak* (2), *Abhay, Alaka, Amita, Anuradha*.

Gola (242) **1.** Italian: topographic name from *gola* 'mountain hollow', 'cavity'. **2.** Italian: variant of COLA. **3.** Polish: nickname from *goły* 'naked', 'bare', 'bald'. **4.** Polish: topographic name *gola* 'heath', 'moor', 'place without trees'. **5.** Indian (Himachal Pradesh, U. P.): Hindu (Prajapati) name of unknown meaning.
GIVEN NAMES Indian 4%. *Amod, Anil, Bharat, Madhu.*

Golab (150) Polish (**Gołąb**): nickname for a mild-mannered or peace-loving man, from Polish *gołąb* 'dove'.
GIVEN NAMES Polish 14%. *Casimir, Danuta, Janina, Jerzy, Pawel, Rafal, Tomasz, Zbigniew.*

Golan (333) Jewish (Israeli): ornamental name from the Golan Heights in Israel.
GIVEN NAMES Jewish 26%. *Elchanan* (4), *Zeev* (4), *Aviva* (3), *Avi* (2), *Moshe* (2), *Nachum* (2), *Anat, Ari, Arie, Arieh, Aryeh, Asaf.*

Golas (296) Polish: nickname from *golas* 'naked man'.
GIVEN NAME Polish 4%. *Danuta.*

Golaszewski (168) Polish: habitational name for someone from a place called Gołaszew or Gołaszewo.
GIVEN NAMES Polish 18%. *Dariusz* (2), *Krzysztof* (2), *Zigmund* (2), *Jadwiga, Radoslaw, Tadeusz, Wieslaw, Zygmunt.*

Golay (312) **1.** French and Swiss French: unexplained. **2.** Probably a variant of Irish GOOLEY.

Golba (133) Polish: **1.** possibly a nickname for a man with knobbly knees, from the dialect word *golba* 'protruding knee'. **2.** alternatively, perhaps, from a pet form of the Germanic personal name *Golbert*.
GIVEN NAMES Polish 7%. *Zygmunt* (2), *Jozef.*

Golberg (185) **1.** German: from the name of a wood near Aken in Anhalt, but the surname is also taken to be a variant of GOLDBERG. **2.** Jewish (Ashkenazic): variant of GOLDBERG.
GIVEN NAMES Scandinavian 6%; Jewish 6%. *Bjorn, Nels; Aron, Frima, Polina, Yakov.*

Gold (9282) **1.** Jewish (Ashkenazic): ornamental name from modern German *Gold*, Yiddish *gold* 'gold'. In North America it is often a reduced form of one of the many compound ornamental names of which *Gold* is the first element. **2.** English and German: from Old English, Old High German *gold* 'gold', applied as a metonymic occupational name for someone who worked in gold, i.e. a refiner, jeweler, or gilder, or as a nickname for someone who either had many gold possessions or bright yellow hair. **3.** English: from an Old English personal name *Golda* (or the feminine *Golde*), which persisted into the Middle Ages as a personal name. The name was in part a byname from *gold* 'gold', and in part a short form of the various compound names with this first element.
GIVEN NAMES Jewish 5%. *Sol* (13), *Emanuel* (8), *Miriam* (7), *Meyer* (6), *Mayer* (5), *Hyman* (4), *Ari* (3), *Avram* (3), *Mendel* (3), *Moshe* (3), *Shraga* (3), *Aviva* (2).

Golda (198) **1.** Jewish (Ashkenazic): from a female personal name meaning 'gold' (see GOLDE). **2.** Polish (**Gołda**): nickname from the dialect word *gołdać* 'to swill'. **3.** German: variant of GOLD 2 as a nickname.
GIVEN NAMES Polish 5%; German 4%. *Stanislaw, Zbigniew; Helmut, Reinhard.*

Goldade (252) Origin unidentified. Probably German, perhaps with a Slavic ending. This surname is found predominantly in ND.

Goldammer (226) German: metonymic occupational name for a bird catcher or dealer, from German *Goldammer* 'yellow hammer'.
GIVEN NAMES German 5%. *Matthias, Otto, Rainer.*

Goldbach (380) **1.** Jewish (Ashkenazic): ornamental name composed of German *Gold* 'gold' + *Bach* 'stream'. **2.** German and Jewish (Ashkenazic): habitational name from any of 22 places named Goldbach.
GIVEN NAMES German 5%. *Fritz* (2), *Klaus* (2), *Elfriede, Otto.*

Goldbaum (184) Jewish (Ashkenazic): ornamental name, a compound of German *Gold* 'gold' + *Baum* 'tree'.
GIVEN NAMES Jewish 17%. *Isadore* (4), *Dov* (3), *Chaim, Meyer, Yisroel, Zev.*

Goldbeck (225) German and Jewish (Ashkenazic): habitational name from any of ten places named Goldbeck, from Middle Low German *gold* 'gold' + *bek* 'stream', 'creek'. In some cases, the Jewish name may be ornamental.

Goldberg (16563) **1.** German: habitational name from any of numerous places named Goldberg. **2.** Jewish (Ashkenazic): ornamental name, a compound of German *Gold* 'gold' + *Berg* 'mountain', 'hill', or occasionally a habitational name of the same origin as 1.
GIVEN NAMES Jewish 7%. *Sol* (31), *Hyman* (28), *Isadore* (19), *Miriam* (19), *Meyer* (14), *Emanuel* (13), *Myer* (8), *Ilya* (6), *Mort* (6), *Hymen* (5), *Ari* (4), *Aron* (4).

Goldberger (779) Jewish (Ashkenazic): ornamental name meaning 'person from golden hill' (see GOLDBERG).
GIVEN NAMES Jewish 21%. *Moshe* (6), *Chaim* (5), *Mayer* (5), *Mendel* (4), *Zvi* (4), *Aron* (3), *Arieh* (2), *Arye* (2), *Elye* (2), *Emanuel* (2), *Mordechai* (2), *Pincus* (2).

Goldblatt (864) Jewish (Ashkenazic): ornamental name, composed of German *Gold* 'gold' + *Blatt* 'leaf'.
GIVEN NAMES Jewish 6%. *Emanuel* (2), *Meyer* (2), *Aron, Chaim, Hyman, Isadore, Shimon, Yehuda.*

Goldblum (159) Jewish (Ashkenazic): ornamental name, a compound of German *Gold* 'gold' + *Blume* 'flower'.
GIVEN NAMES Jewish 10%. *Moshe* (2), *Irit, Miriam, Yetta.*

Golde (218) **1.** Jewish (Ashkenazic): from the Yiddish female personal name *Golde* meaning 'gold'. **2.** German: from a short form of any of several Germanic personal names composed with *gold, guld* 'gold', 'bright'.
GIVEN NAMES German 5%; Jewish 4%. *Hellmut* (2), *Erwin; Hirsch.*

Golden (17758) **1.** English: nickname for someone with golden hair, from Middle English *gelden, golden* (from Old English *gylden*). **2.** Irish: reduced Anglicized form of Gaelic **Mag Ualghairg** (see McGOLDRICK).

Goldenberg (1745) Jewish (Ashkenazic): ornamental name, a compound of German *golden* 'golden' + *Berg* 'mountain', 'hill'.
GIVEN NAMES Jewish 10%; Russian 5%. *Yakov* (4), *Sol* (3), *Chaim* (2), *Emanuel* (2), *Mazal* (2), *Moishe* (2), *Aron, Avi, Berish, Boruch, Chaya, Elchonon; Boris* (8), *Igor* (6), *Leonid* (5), *Mikhail* (3), *Oleg* (3), *Vladimir* (3), *Arkady* (2), *Dmitry* (2), *Iosif* (2), *Lev* (2), *Sofya* (2), *Aleksandr.*

Goldenstein (228) Jewish (Ashkenazic): ornamental name, a compound of German *golden* 'golden' + *Stein* 'stone'.
GIVEN NAMES French 7%; German 4%. *Jean-Claude* (2), *Pascale, Pierre; Kurt.*

Golder (653) **1.** English: from the Old English personal name *Goldhere*, composed of the elements *gold* 'gold' + *here* 'army'.

2. English: habitational name from a place in Oxfordshire, so named from Old English *golde* 'marigold' (a derivative of *gold*) + *ōra* 'slope'. **3.** German (also **Gölder**): variant of GOLDNER. **4.** Jewish: variant of GOLD.
GIVEN NAMES Jewish 4%. *Myer* (2), *Genya*, *Hershel*, *Meyer*.

Goldey (181) English: from an Old English female name, *Goldgifu*, which is not independently attested but is found as an element of place names.
GIVEN NAMES French 6%. *Camille*, *Fanchon*.

Goldfarb (2134) Jewish (Ashkenazic): ornamental name composed of German *Gold* 'gold' + *Farbe* 'color'.
GIVEN NAMES Jewish 7%. *Hyman* (8), *Emanuel* (4), *Aron* (2), *Aviva* (2), *Isadore* (2), *Ari*, *Avi*, *Ber*, *Meyer*, *Miriam*, *Moishe*, *Moshe*.

Goldfeder (149) Jewish (Ashkenazic): ornamental name composed of German *Gold* 'gold' + *Feder* 'feather'.
GIVEN NAMES Jewish 8%. *Avrom*, *Sholom*, *Sol*, *Yehudah*, *Yoel*.

Goldfein (113) Jewish (Ashkenazic): ornamental name from German *goldfein* 'fine as gold'.
GIVEN NAMES Jewish 9%. *Miriam*, *Mort*, *Yisroel*.

Goldfield (178) Jewish: Americanized form of the Ashkenazic ornamental name **Goldfeld** 'gold field'.
GIVEN NAMES Jewish 11%. *Herschel* (2), *Inna*.

Goldfine (254) Jewish: Americanized spelling of Ashkenazic GOLDFEIN 'fine as gold'.
GIVEN NAMES Jewish 11%; German 4%. *Sol* (2), *Hyman*, *Isadore*, *Meyer*; *Erwin* (2), *Frieda*.

Goldfinger (248) Jewish (Ashkenazic): ornamental name composed of German *Gold* 'gold' + *Finger* 'finger'.
GIVEN NAMES Jewish 9%. *Chaim*, *Chaya*, *Moshe*, *Sol*.

Goldhammer (215) **1.** Jewish (Ashkenazic): ornamental name composed of German *Gold* 'gold' + *Hammer* 'hammer'. **2.** German: variant of GOLDAMMER.

Goldie (507) **1.** Scottish: from a diminutive of GOLD. **2.** Scottish: nickname for a wall-eyed person with an unnatural pigmentation of one eye, from Middle English *gold* 'gold' + *ie* 'eye'. **3.** English: variant spelling of GOLDY.

Goldin (925) Jewish (from Belarus): metronymic from the Yiddish female personal name GOLDE.
GIVEN NAMES Russian 8%; Jewish 8%. *Lev* (5), *Yefim* (5), *Leonid* (3), *Yelena* (3), *Arkadiy* (2), *Grigory* (2), *Mikhail* (2), *Vladimir* (2), *Alexey*, *Boris*, *Daniil*, *Fima*; *Sol* (4), *Avraham* (2), *Hyman* (2), *Isaak* (2), *Asher*, *Berka*, *Ehud*, *Eliyahu*, *Khana*, *Shmuel*, *Yakov*, *Yuly*.

Golding (1859) **1.** English: from the late Old English personal name *Golding*, in form a patronymic from *Golda* (see GOLD 4). **2.** German: patronymic from a short form of a Germanic personal name formed with *gold*, *guld* 'gold', 'bright'. **3.** Jewish (from Latvia and Lithuania): habitational name from *Golding*, the German and Yiddish name of the city of Kuldīga in Latvia.

Goldinger (156) German and Jewish (Ashkenazic): variant of GOLDING.

Goldizen (132) Americanized form of German **Goldeisen**, a metonymic occupational name for a gold panner or goldsmith, from Middle High German *gold* 'gold' + *īsen* 'iron'.

Goldman (12475) **1.** German (**Goldmann**) and Jewish (Ashkenazic): variant of GOLD. **2.** Jewish (Ashkenazic): metronymic from the Yiddish female personal name GOLDE.
GIVEN NAMES Jewish 6%. *Hyman* (22), *Sol* (16), *Meyer* (14), *Miriam* (11), *Emanuel* (10), *Isadore* (6), *Yakov* (6), *Aron* (5), *Meir* (5), *Dov* (4), *Shlomo* (4), *Mort* (3).

Goldmann (237) **1.** German: variant of GOLD. **2.** Jewish (Ashkenazic): variant spelling of GOLDMAN.
GIVEN NAMES German 8%. *Erna*, *Ernst*, *Florian*, *Klaus*, *Kurt*, *Wolfgang*.

Goldner (776) **1.** German (also **Göldner**): occupational name for someone who worked with gold, from an agent derivative of Old High German *gold* (see GOLD). **2.** Jewish (Ashkenazic): variant of GOLD.

Goldrich (147) **1.** English and German: from an Old English and Germanic personal name composed of the elements *gold* 'gold' + *rīc* 'ruler'. **2.** Jewish (Ashkenazic): Americanized spelling of the Ashkenazic ornamental name **Goldreich**, composed of the German elements *Gold* 'gold' + *reich* 'rich'.
GIVEN NAME Jewish 5%. *Avi* (2).

Goldrick (231) **1.** Irish: reduced form of McGOLDRICK. **2.** German: Americanized spelling of GOLDRICH.

Goldring (351) **1.** English, German, and Jewish (Ashkenazic): from the Middle English, German, or Yiddish elements *gold* + *ring*. As an English or German surname it is most probably a nickname for someone who wore a gold ring. As a Jewish surname it is generally an ornamental name. **2.** Scottish: habitational name from Goldring in the bailiary of Kylestewart.
FOREBEARS The name is found in England as early as 1230, when Thomas Goldring is recorded as holding property in Essex and Hertfordshire. The name was quite common in London, Sussex, and Hampshire from early times, and descendants of these bearers are now also well established in Canada. The first known bearer in Scotland is Thomas of Goldringe, who held land in Prestwick in 1511.

GIVEN NAMES Jewish 7%. *Shmuel* (2), *Benzion*, *Emanuel*, *Isadore*, *Shlomo*, *Tzvi*, *Yaacov*.

Goldsberry (1036) Variant of English GOLDSBOROUGH.

Goldsborough (446) English: habitational name for someone from either of two places in North Yorkshire called Goldsborough. One, near Knaresborough is named from the Old English (or Old German) personal name *Godel* + Old English *burh* 'fortified place'. The other, near Whitby, is named from the Old English personal name *Golda* + *burh*.

Goldsby (508) English: habitational name from a place in Lincolnshire named Goulceby, from the Old Norse personal name *Kolkr* + Old Norse *bý* 'farm', 'settlement'.

Goldschmidt (759) German and Jewish (Ashkenazic): occupational name for a worker in gold, Middle High German *goltsmit*, German *Goldschmied*.
GIVEN NAMES German 10%; Jewish 4%. *Kurt* (7), *Hans* (4), *Egon* (2), *Erwin* (2), *Gunter* (2), *Ilse* (2), *Bernhard*, *Ernst*, *Fritz*, *Heinrich*, *Hermann*, *Klaus*; *Isadore* (2), *Azriel*, *Ehud*, *Ephraim*, *Ilan*, *Miriam*, *Nili*.

Goldsmith (6864) English: occupational name for a worker in gold, a compound of Old English *gold* 'gold' + *smið* 'smith'. In North America it is very often an English translation of German or Jewish GOLDSCHMIDT.

Goldson (201) English: variant of GOLDSTONE 2 and 3.

Goldstein (16343) **1.** Jewish (Ashkenazic): ornamental name composed of German *Gold* 'gold' + *Stein* 'stone'. **2.** German: from a medieval personal name, nickname, or occupational name from Middle High German, Middle Low German *golste(i)n* 'gold stone', 'precious stone', (probably chrysolite or topaz, which was used as a testing stone by alchemists).
GIVEN NAMES Jewish 7%. *Sol* (29), *Hyman* (28), *Miriam* (20), *Meyer* (17), *Isadore* (12), *Emanuel* (8), *Myer* (6), *Ari* (5), *Aron* (4), *Avram* (4), *Dov* (4), *Mort* (4).

Goldston (735) English: variant of GOLDSTONE 2 and 3.

Goldstone (490) **1.** Jewish: Americanization of Ashkenazic GOLDSTEIN. **2.** English: from the Old English personal name *Goldstān*, composed of the elements *gold* 'gold' + *stān* 'stone'. **3.** English: habitational name for someone from a place in Shropshire named Goldstone, from the genitive case of the Old English personal name *Golda* (see GOLD 4) + Old English *stān* 'stone'; or from one in Kent, recorded in the early 13th century as *Goldstanestun* 'settlement (Old English *tūn*) of *Goldstān*'.

GIVEN NAMES Jewish 5%. *Emanuel, Malki, Menachem, Miriam, Moshe, Yaakov, Yitzchok.*

Goldsworthy (476) English: variant spelling of **Galsworthy**, a habitational name from a place in Devon named Galsworthy, possibly from Old English *gagel* 'gale', 'bog myrtle' + *ora* 'hill slope'.

Goldthwaite (266) English: habitational name, perhaps from Guilthwaite in South Yorkshire, which is named from Old Norse *gil* 'ravine' + Old Norse *þveit* 'clearing'. However, the modern surname is associated with Essex, suggesting some other source, now lost.

Goldwasser (298) **1.** German: topographic name for someone who lived by a stream where gold was found, from Middle High German *golt* 'gold' + *wazzer* 'water', or possibly an occupational nickname for a gold panner. **2.** Jewish (Ashkenazic): ornamental name composed of German *Gold* 'gold' + *Wasser* 'water'.

GIVEN NAMES Jewish 6%. *Eliezer* (2), *Hyman, Isadore, Meir, Sol.*

Goldwater (228) Americanized form of German and Jewish GOLDWASSER.

Goldwire (148) Jewish (American): perhaps an English translation of **Golddraht** (from German) or **Goldendrut** (from Yiddish dialect), both meaning 'golden wire'.

Goldwyn (102) **1.** English: from the Old English personal name *Goldwine*, composed of the elements *gold* 'gold' + *wīn* 'friend'. **2.** Jewish: Americanization of a like-sounding Ashkenazic surname.

GIVEN NAMES Jewish 6%. *Irit, Miriam, Sol.*

Goldy (316) Variant spelling of English GOLDEY or Scottish and English GOLDIE.

Gole (107) **1.** Indian (Maharashtra); pronounced as two syllables: Hindu (Brahman) name found among Konkanasth Brahmans, probably from Sanskrit *gola* 'globe'. **2.** Slovenian: nickname or topographic name from the adjective *gol* 'hairless', 'naked', or 'bare', 'treeless'. Compare GOLIA, GOLEC. **3.** Slovenian: derivative of the medieval male personal name *Gal*, Latin *Gallus*. Compare GALE 5.

GIVEN NAMES Indian 11%. *Abhijeet, Dileep, Dilip, Neelima, Suvarna.*

Golebiewski (146) Polish (**Gołębiewski**): habitational name for someone from Gołębie, Gołębiewo, or any of various places called Gołębiów, all named with *gołąb* 'dove'.

FOREBEARS The names Gołębiewski and Gołębiowski, borne by Polish noble families, date back to the 14th century.

GIVEN NAMES Polish 12%. *Ignatius, Leslaw, Miroslaw, Tadeusz, Zdzislaw.*

Golec (252) **1.** Polish: nickname from Polish *golec* (a noun derivative of the adjective *goły* 'naked') in various possible senses. The basic meaning is 'naked man' or 'hairless man'. It could therefore be a nickname for someone penniless, totally destitute, a naked wretch, which is one of the meanings of the vocabulary word. Equally, it could be a nickname for a bald or clean-shaven man. **2.** Slovenian: nickname from the adjective *gol* 'hairless' (probably in the old sense 'beardless youngster').

GIVEN NAMES Polish 8%. *Stanislaw* (2), *Teofil, Tomasz, Zdzislaw.*

Goleman (170) Americanized spelling of German **Gollmann**: **1.** habitational name for someone from any of several places called Golm in eastern Germany. **2.** status name for someone in feudal bondage to a lord or to the Church, from Middle High German *goll* 'feudal bondage' (from Latin *collata* 'bondage', 'obligation') + *man* 'man'.

Golembeski (232) Variant of Polish GOLE-BIEWSKI.

Golembiewski (427) Variant of Polish GOLEBIEWSKI.

Golemon (127) Variant of German **Gollmann** (see GOLEMAN).

Golen (192) Origin unidentified.

Goley (266) **1.** English: variant of GULLEY. **2.** Possibly a variant of Irish GOOLEY.

Golia (163) **1.** Italian: from the Biblical personal name *Golia* 'Goliath', a nickname for a very large man. **2.** Altered spelling of Slovenian **Golja**, topographic name derived from *gol* 'treeless' or *goljava* 'barren land'.

GIVEN NAMES Italian 17%. *Aldo, Annamaria, Gino, Nunzio, Oreste, Pasquale.*

Golias (157) **1.** Hungarian (**Góliás**) and Slovak (**Goliáš**): from the Biblical personal name *Golias* 'Goliath', a nickname for a very large man. **2.** Greek: variant of COLLIAS 1.

Golick (149) **1.** Jewish (from Ukraine): nickname from Russian *golik* 'beggar', 'ragamuffin'. **2.** Altered spelling of German **Gölich**, a nickname from Sorbian *golik* 'the bald one'.

GIVEN NAME French 5%. *Roch.*

Golightly (724) **1.** English: nickname, perhaps for a messenger, from Middle English *gō(n)* 'to go' (Old English *gān*) + *lihtly* 'lightly', 'swiftly' (Old English *lēoht(līc)*). **2.** Scottish: altered form of a surname of uncertain origin, possibly an unidentified habitational name. The earliest known bearer is William Galithli, who witnessed a charter at the beginning of the 13th century. Henry Gellatly, an illegitimate son of William the Lion, of whom little or nothing is known, was the grandfather of Patric Galythly, one of the pretenders to the crown of Scotland in 1291. **3.** Irish: adopted as an English equivalent of Gaelic **Mac an Ghallóglaigh** 'son of the galloglass', Irish *gallóglach*. A galloglass was a mercenary retainer or auxiliary soldier (a compound of *gall* 'foreigner' (see GALL 1) + *óglach* 'youth', 'warrior'). The name is also found pseudo-translated as ENGLISH.

Golik (129) Polish: nickname from *goły* 'naked'. Compare GOLEC.

GIVEN NAMES Polish 13%; German 5%. *Wojciech* (2), *Boleslaw, Eugeniusz, Jerzy, Wladyslawa; Florian, Monika, Viktor.*

Golin (154) **1.** Jewish (eastern Ashkenazic): habitational name for someone from the village of Golna in Belarus. **2.** Jewish: American shortened form of any Jewish (eastern Ashkenazic) name starting with *Golin*, for example GOLINSKI.

GIVEN NAMES Jewish 7%. *Marat, Miriam, Musya, Shoshana.*

Golini (106) Italian: patronymic or plural form of GOLINO.

GIVEN NAMES Italian 8%. *Alfio, Michelina, Umberto.*

Golino (133) Italian: from a short form of the personal name *Ugolino*, which may be a pet form of *Ugo* (Italian equivalent of HUGH) or alternatively from a Germanic compound personal name.

GIVEN NAMES Italian 38%. *Carlo* (3), *Sal* (3), *Antonio* (2), *Alessandro, Angelo, Antonino, Assunta, Fabrizio, Giuseppe, Mafalda, Reynaldo, Rinaldo, Rosario, Santo.*

Golinski (183) Polish (**Goliński**): habitational name for someone from a place called Golina or Gola, for example in Kalisz voivodeship, named with *goły* 'naked'.

GIVEN NAMES Polish 9%; German 5%. *Karol, Leszek, Miroslaw, Thadeus, Zbigniew; Aloysius, Horst.*

Golis (108) Origin unidentified.

Goll (674) **1.** English: nickname for a silly person, from Middle English *golle* 'unfledged bird'. There is evidence of a female personal name *Golla* and it is possible that this also may have given rise to the surname. **2.** German and Swiss German: unflattering nickname from dialect *goll* 'bullfinch', in the sense 'simpleton'; or perhaps a variant of **Gollmann** (see GOLEMAN 2).

Golla (332) **1.** Eastern German: nickname from a Slavic word meaning 'bald'. Compare Polish *goły*. **2.** Eastern German: habitational name from any of the places called Gollau, in Lower Saxony, East Prussia, and Bavaria. **3.** Indian (Andhra Pradesh): Hindu name meaning 'herdsman' in Telugu.

GIVEN NAMES German 5%; Indian 5%. *Dieter* (2), *Alois, Erwin, Gunter; Vinay* (2), *Krishna, Padma, Prasad, Satyanarayana.*

Golladay (395) Probably an Americanization of French **Galaudet**. It is recorded as a Huguenot name.

Gollaher (125) Variant of Irish GALLAGHER.

Gollehon (113) Probably an altered form of Irish CALLAGHAN.

Goller (480) German: **1.** from Middle High German *goller, koller* 'neck cover', 'sleeveless vest', hence a metonymic occupational name for a maker of such garments. **2.** habitational name for someone from Gollern or Gollau, both in Lower Saxony.

GIVEN NAMES German 5%. *Erwin, Ingo, Siegfried, Wolfgang.*

Golliday (207) Probably an Americanization of French **Galaudet**. See GOLLADAY.

Golliher (246) Irish: variant of GALLAGHER.

Gollin (121) German: habitational name for someone from a place so named near Templin in Brandenburg.

GIVEN NAMES German 9%. *Ernst, Gerhard, Manfred, Wilhelm.*

Gollinger (116) German (Austrian): habitational name for someone from a place near Salzburg called Golling.

Gollnick (225) Eastern German: from Slavic *gola* 'heath', hence an indirect occupational name for a heath or moor ranger.

GIVEN NAMES German 7%. *Horst* (2), *Kurt* (2).

Gollon (106) Scottish: variant spelling of **Gollan**, a habitational name from Gollan in Kinross-shire.

Gollub (104) German: variant spelling of GOLUB.

GIVEN NAMES German 5%. *Frieda, Wilhelm.*

Golly (177) **1.** English (Cornwall): variant of GULLEY. **2.** German: variant of GOHL, or in the south of GOLL.

GIVEN NAMES German 5%. *Berthold, Gerd.*

Golob (315) Slovenian: from Slovenian *golob* 'dove', hence a nickname for a mild-mannered or peace-loving person or possibly a metonymic occupational name for a dove handler or breeder. This is also found as a German and Jewish name.

GIVEN NAMES Jewish 5%. *Meyer* (2), *Shmuel* (2), *Aryeh.*

Golod (105) Jewish (from Belarus): nickname from Russian *golod* 'hunger'.

GIVEN NAMES Russian 27%; Jewish 23%. *Vladimir* (4), *Boris* (3), *Galina* (2), *Mikhail* (2), *Yefim* (2), *Anatoly, Lev, Liliya, Oleg, Raisa, Yelizaveta, Yevgeny; Ilya* (3), *Isaak* (2), *Aron, Inna, Khanan, Semen, Slava, Yakov.*

Golomb (293) **1.** Polish: variant of **Gołąb** (see GOLAB). **2.** Jewish (eastern Ashkenazic): ornamental name from Polish *gołąb* 'dove' (Latin *columba*).

Golombek (116) **1.** Polish: nickname for a peace-loving man (see GOLAB). **2.** Jewish (eastern Ashkenazic): ornamental name from Polish *gołąbek* 'little dove', 'little pigeon' (see GOLOMB).

GIVEN NAMES Jewish 8%. *Eyal, Meyer, Zvi.*

Golon (120) Polish: nickname from *golony* 'shaven'.

Golonka (212) Polish: nickname from either *golonka* 'hand of pork' or *golony* 'clean-shaven'.

GIVEN NAMES Polish 11%. *Zbigniew* (3), *Janina* (2), *Casimir, Ewa, Maciej.*

Golphin (132) French and English: unexplained.

GIVEN NAMES French 8%. *Camille, Germaine.*

Golson (737) English: variant of GOLD-STONE 2 and 3.

Golston (318) English: variant of GOLD-STONE 2 and 3.

Goltry (106) English: variant of **Galtry**, a Yorkshire surname of unexplained derivation.

Goltz (595) **1.** Jewish (eastern Ashkenazic): ornamental name or occupational name for a woodcutter or someone who sold wood, from German *Holz* 'wood', altered under Russian influence, since Russian has no *h* and alters *h* in borrowed words to *g*. **2.** Eastern German (under Slavic influence): habitational name for someone from Golz or Golssen in eastern Germany, place names that may derive from Slavic *gola* 'heath'.

GIVEN NAMES German 5%. *Kurt* (3), *Otto* (2), *Dieter, Erwin, Gottlieb, Helmut.*

Golub (1022) **1.** Jewish (eastern Ashkenazic), Ukrainian, and Belorussian: variant of HOLUB. **2.** German: from Sorbian *golub* 'dove', a metonymic occupational name for someone who bred or looked after doves, which were reared for food in the Middle Ages. See also HOLUB.

GIVEN NAMES Jewish 7%; Russian 4%. *Ilya* (4), *Aharon, Avrum, Hyman, Hymen, Inna, Irina, Isadore, Marat, Mariya, Miriam, Moisey; Boris* (3), *Arkadiy* (2), *Vladimir* (2), *Aleksandr, Arkadi, Dmitry, Gennady, Grigory, Iosif, Leonid, Mikhail, Nataly.*

Golubski (158) Polish (**Gołubski**): habitational name for someone from Golub-Dobrzyń in Toruń voivodeship or Golubie in Suwałki voivodeship.

Golz (313) **1.** German and Jewish (eastern Ashkenazic): variant spelling of GOLTZ. **2.** Possibly an altered spelling of German GOELZ.

GIVEN NAMES German 7%. *Kurt* (2), *Bernhard, Erwin, Friedhelm, Hans, Otto.*

Goman (150) **1.** Jewish (from Belarus): of uncertain origin. Perhaps a nickname for a wicked person, from Hebrew *Haman*, pronounced *homen* by Ashkenazic Jews, the *H* then being altered to *G* under Russian influence. Haman is a personage in the biblical book of Esther. **2.** German: variant of **Gömann** (see GOHMAN).

GIVEN NAMES Russian 8%; Jewish 6%. *Boris, Galina, Grigory, Lev, Natalya, Oleg, Semyon; Isaak, Yakov.*

Gombar (155) Slovak: occupational name for a craftsman who made buttons, from *gomba* 'big button'.

GIVEN NAMES Russian 4%. *Aleksandr, Grigory, Yelena.*

Gomberg (317) German and Jewish (Ashkenazic): unexplained.

GIVEN NAMES Jewish 9%; Russian 7%. *Miriam* (2), *Ilya, Inna, Mandel, Sol; Aleksandr, Arkadiy, Boris, Galina, Grigory, Iosif, Mordko, Vitaly, Vladimir, Yevgeniy, Yevgeniya, Yulia.*

Gombert (174) French and German: from *Gundbert*, a Germanic personal name composed of the elements *gund* 'battle' + *berht* 'bright', 'famous'. The name was relatively popular in both France and Germany during the Middle Ages, and was also adopted by Ashkenazic Jews. See also GIMPEL.

Gombos (241) Hungarian: occupational name for a wool comber, from Hungarian *gomb* 'comb'.

GIVEN NAMES Hungarian 8%. *Ferenc* (2), *Bela, Erzsebet, Gabor, Geza, Miklos, Sandor.*

Gomer (445) English: from Middle English *Godmer*, a blend of two names, Old English *Godmær* and Old Northern French *Godmar*, both composed of the Germanic elements *gōd* 'good' or *god* 'god' + *mēri, māri* 'famous'.

Gomes (4812) Portuguese: from the medieval personal name *Gomes*, probably Visigothic in origin, from *guma* 'man'. This name is also common on the west coast of India, where it was taken by Portuguese colonists.

GIVEN NAMES Spanish 18%; Portuguese 11%. *Manuel* (102), *Jose* (83), *Carlos* (24), *Fernando* (23), *Luis* (18), *Francisco* (15), *Jorge* (11), *Mario* (10), *Domingos* (8), *Jaime* (8), *Julio* (8), *Luiz* (8); *Joao* (20), *Joaquim* (9), *Paulo* (8), *Catarina* (3), *Henrique* (3), *Agostinho* (2), *Amadeu* (2), *Ademir, Aderito, Aloisio, Conceicao, Ilidio.*

Gomez (31277) Spanish (**Gómez**): from a medieval personal name, probably of Visigothic origin, from *guma* 'man'. Compare GOMES.

GIVEN NAMES Spanish 48%. *Jose* (870), *Juan* (390), *Manuel* (308), *Carlos* (260), *Luis* (259), *Jesus* (225), *Francisco* (219), *Miguel* (186), *Pedro* (167), *Jorge* (165), *Ramon* (160), *Rafael* (151).

Gomillion (264) **1.** Americanized form of German **Gmelin** (see GIMLIN). **2.** Of French origin: variant of GREMILLION.

Gomm (150) English: variant of GUMM.

Gomoll (161) Eastern German: nickname from Slavic *gomóly* 'hornless', 'bare'.

GIVEN NAMES German 9%. *Otto* (2), *Erwin, Heinz, Wolfgang.*

Gompers (101) Dutch and North German: patronymic from the personal name *Gundbert* (see GOMBERT).

Gompf (111) South German: perhaps a variant of GUMP.

Goncalves (1198) Portuguese (**Gonçalves**): patronymic from a personal name of Visigothic origin, *Gonçalo*, formed with *gunþ* 'battle'.

GIVEN NAMES Spanish 38%; Portuguese 26%. *Jose* (82), *Manuel* (44), *Carlos* (28), *Fernando* (13), *Luis* (11), *Domingos* (10), *Jorge* (9), *Ana* (7), *Jaime* (7), *Francisco* (6), *Alfredo* (5), *Armando* (5); *Joao* (25), *Joaquim* (14), *Paulo* (7), *Sebastiao* (3), *Albano, Catarina, Duarte, Henrique,*

Marcio, Martinho, Serafim, Terezinha; *Antonio* (52), *Antonino, Filomena, Licinio, Luciano, Marco*.

Gonce (254) **1.** Greek (**Gontsis**): ornamental name from Turkish *gonce* 'bud'. **2.** It may also be French, from a reduced form of a Germanic personal name formed with *gund* 'battle'.

Gonda (385) Hungarian: from a pet form of the personal name *Konrád* (see KONRAD).

Gondek (448) Polish: variant of **Gǫdek**, a nickname from Old Polish *gǫdzić* 'to play on an instrument'.

GIVEN NAMES Polish 7%. *Zofia* (2), *Dariusz, Ewa, Leszek, Maciej, Tadeusz, Wieslaw, Wieslawa, Wojciech*.

Gonder (426) Possibly a respelling of German GANDER.

Gonet (166) Polish (of French origin): from a pet form of the personal name *Hugo*, French form of HUGH.

GIVEN NAMES Polish 7%; German 4%. *Slawomir* (2), *Beata, Jolanta, Karol*; *Rainer* (2).

Gong (965) **1.** Chinese 龔: the origin of this surname dates back to the time of the legendary emperor Huang Di (2697–2595 BC). An adviser held the surname Gonggong, comprised of two different characters that are pronounced *Gong* in modern Chinese. The first of these characters served as the basis for two later surnames: some descendants combined the symbol for 'water' with that for Gong, creating the surname *Hong* (see HONG 1); others added the character for 'dragon', creating the surname *Gong*. **2.** Chinese 宮: from a character meaning 'palace', part of the title of an official in charge of guarding the palace. During the Spring and Autumn period (722–481 BC), descendants of such an official adopted Gong as their surname. **3.** Chinese 巩: from the name of the state of Gong-Bo, located in Henan province during the Zhou dynasty (1122–221 BC). **4.** Chinese 公: of uncertain origin; this character came into use as a surname during the Spring and Autumn period (722–481 BC) in the state of Lu in present-day Shandong province. **5.** Chinese 弓: from a character meaning 'bow'. This name originated with Hui, a grandson of the legendary emperor Huang Di (2697–2595 BC). Hui invented bows and arrows, an accomplishment that inspired two surnames: **Gong**, the character for 'bow', and **Zhang** (see ZHANG), which is composed of the characters for 'bow' + 'long'.

GIVEN NAMES Chinese 30%. *Jin* (5), *Min* (4), *Yan* (4), *Ying* (4), *Bin* (3), *Sing* (3), *Wai* (3), *Wing* (3), *Chang* (2), *Chung* (2), *Gang* (2), *Jiansheng* (2), *Kwong* (2), *Lai* (2), *Li* (2), *In Sook, Sung Do, Tian, Yiming, Yiu, Youn*.

Gongaware (205) German: probably an Americanized form of the common Bavarian name **Ganghofer**, a habitational name for someone from any of the places named Gangkofen in northern Bavaria.

FOREBEARS John Jacob Gangewere (born 1705 in Bavaria, Germany) and his brother Michael emigrated to Westmoreland County, PA, in 1725.

Gongola (107) Origin unidentified.

Gongora (326) Spanish (**Góngora**) from Basque: habitational name from Basque Gongora, a place in the Aranguren valley in Navarre, Basque Country.

GIVEN NAMES Spanish 45%; Portuguese 10%. *Jose* (9), *Carlos* (4), *Manuel* (4), *Luis* (3), *Alberto* (2), *Ernesto* (2), *Esperanza* (2), *Estanislao* (2), *Guadalupe* (2), *Gustavo* (2), *Jesus* (2), *Jorge* (2); *Paulo; Leonardo* (2), *Antonio, Marco, Marco Antonio*.

Gongwer (103) Of German origin: variant of GONGAWARE.

Gonia (166) **1.** Americanized form of French **Gagné** (see GAGNE). **2.** Polish: nickname from a derivative of *gonić* 'to chase'.

Gonnella (351) Italian: from Old Italian *gonnella* 'tunic', 'cloak', 'mantel', hence probably a metonymic occupational name for a maker of such garments.

GIVEN NAMES Italian 18%. *Angelo* (2), *Rocco* (2), *Carmine, Concetta, Dante, Dino, Domenico, Ennio, Gino, Massimo, Pasquale, Severino*.

Gonnering (142) North German (**Gönnering**), Dutch, and Luxembourgeois: patronymic from the personal name *Gönner* (see GOENNER).

Gonnerman (181) German: reduced form of **Gundermann**, from the personal name *Gundram*, composed of the elements *gund* 'battle' + *ram* 'raven'.

Gonsales (95) Spanish and Portuguese: variant of **González** (see GONZALEZ).

GIVEN NAMES Spanish 36%. *Jose* (5), *Francisco* (2), *Ruben* (2), *Arcadio, Artemio, Erasmo, Ernesto, Eusebio, Juan, Lupe, Manuel, Miguel*; *Angelo, Quirino*.

Gonsalez (248) Spanish (**Gonsález**) and Portuguese: variant of **González** (see GONZALEZ).

GIVEN NAMES Spanish 58%. *Jose* (11), *Carlos* (4), *Ruben* (4), *Ignacio* (3), *Manuel* (3), *Alfredo* (2), *Elena* (2), *Felipe* (2), *Guadalupe* (2), *Gustavo* (2), *Jesus* (2), *Jorge* (2).

Gonsalves (2277) Variant spelling of Portuguese **Gonçalves** (see GONCALVES). This name is also found in western India, where it was taken by Portuguese colonists.

GIVEN NAMES Spanish 10%; Portuguese 5%. *Manuel* (54), *Jose* (11), *Fernando* (4), *Americo* (3), *Joaquin* (3), *Jorge* (3), *Luis* (3), *Miguel* (3), *Bernardo* (2), *Jose Carlos* (2), *Juvenal* (2), *Pedro* (2); *Joao* (2), *Joaquim*.

Gonser (375) German: Swabian variant of GANSER.

Gonsior (126) Germanized or Americanized form of Polish **Gąsior** (see GASIOR).

GIVEN NAMES Polish 5%. *Bogdan, Henryk*.

Gonsoulin (242) French: of uncertain origin. **1.** It may be an altered form of **Goncelin, Gonssolin**, from a pet form of a Germanic compound personal name formed with *gund* 'battle'. **2.** Alternatively, perhaps, an altered form of **Consolin**, in southeastern France an occupational name for a magistrate.

GIVEN NAMES French 4%. *Michel, Ulysse*.

Gonter (119) **1.** German: from a variant of the German personal name *Günter* (see GUNTER). **2.** Jewish (eastern Ashkenazic): occupational name, a Yiddishized form of Ukrainian *gontar* 'shingle maker'.

GIVEN NAMES German 5%; Jewish 5%. *Bernhardt, Frieda*; *Avrohom* (2).

Gonterman (195) Variant of German **Gundermann** (see GUNDERMAN).

Gonthier (175) French and Swiss French: from the Old French personal name *Gontier*, composed of the Germanic elements *gund* 'battle' + *hari, heri* 'army'. Compare GUNTER.

FOREBEARS A family called Gonthier from Paris was in Quebec city by 1676.

GIVEN NAMES French 18%. *Henri* (2), *Alexandre, Andre, Chantale, Denys, Gilles, Monique, Normand, Piere, Renald*.

Gonya (181) Americanized spelling of French GAGNE, found predominantly in New England.

GIVEN NAMES French 4%. *Mechelle, Patrice*.

Gonyea (696) Americanized spelling of French GAGNE, found predominantly in New England.

Gonyeau (109) Respelling of French GAGNON, found predominantly in New England, possibly also of **Gagneau**, from a diminutive of GAGNE.

Gonyer (226) Americanized spelling of French GAGNE, found predominantly in New England.

Gonyo (166) Americanized spelling of French GAGNE, found predominantly in New England.

Gonzaga (252) Spanish: habitational name from a place so named in Mantua, Italy; this was the home of the ruling family of Mantua for almost four centuries, whose most famous son was St. Louis Gonzaga.

GIVEN NAMES Spanish 37%. *Ana* (2), *Eduardo* (2), *Guillermo* (2), *Juanito* (2), *Luz* (2), *Manuel* (2), *Ricardo* (2), *Rufina* (2), *Teodosio* (2), *Alicia, Andres, Aniceto*; *Caesar* (4), *Fausto* (2), *Clemente, Leonardo*.

Gonzales (33171) Variant of Spanish **González** (see GONZALEZ).

GIVEN NAMES Spanish 34%. *Jose* (517), *Manuel* (342), *Juan* (311), *Carlos* (192), *Jesus* (159), *Luis* (147), *Ramon* (123), *Ruben* (116), *Pedro* (109), *Raul* (97), *Guadalupe* (91), *Lupe* (91).

Gonzalez (65991) Spanish (**González**): patronymic from the personal name GONZALO, a personal name of Visigothic origin, based on the Germanic element *gunþ* 'battle'. Compare Portuguese **Gonçalves** (see GONCALVES).

GIVEN NAMES Spanish 53%. *Juan* (1045), *Carlos* (712), *Luis* (702), *Manuel* (695), *Jesus* (614), *Jorge* (463), *Pedro* (463), *Francisco* (454), *Miguel* (411), *Ramon* (372), *Raul* (372), *Mario* (362).

Gonzalo (122) Spanish: from the personal name *Gonzalo*, of Visigothic origin, formed with *gunþ* 'battle'.

GIVEN NAMES Spanish 51%. *Miguel* (2), *Pedro* (2), *Albino, Amador, Angelina, Arana, Arnaldo, Blanco, Carlos, Casimiro, Castro, Diego*; *Antonio, Flavio, Lido, Marino*.

Goo (357) Korean: variant of KU.

Gooch (4074) **1.** English (mainly East Anglia): variant of GOFF. **2.** Possibly an Americanized spelling of German GUTSCH.
FOREBEARS Several bearers of the name Gooch came from England to VA in the 17th century, with family tradition placing them in a town called Goochland. The best known of these early immigrants was VA colonial governor Sir William Gooch (1681–1751).

Good (13148) **1.** English: nickname from Middle English *gode* 'good' (Old English *gōd*). **2.** English: from a medieval personal name, a survival of the Old English personal name *Gōda*, which was in part a byname and in part a short form of various compound names with the first element *gōd*. **3.** Americanized form of like-sounding names in other languages, for example German GUT or GUTH.

Goodacre (131) **1.** English: probably a habitational name from Goodacre in Devon. **2.** Possibly an Americanized form of German **Gutacker**, a topographic name for someone who owned or farmed a 'good field', or a habitational name from a place so named near Datteln.

Goodale (1306) English: variant of GOODALL 2.

Goodall (1861) English (chiefly Yorkshire and Nottinghamshire): **1.** habitational name from Gowdall in East Yorkshire, named from Old English *golde* 'marigold' + Old English *halh* 'nook', 'recess'. **2.** from Middle English *gode* 'good' + *ale* 'ale', 'malt liquor', hence a metonymic occupational name for a brewer or an innkeeper.

Goodart (102) **1.** Variant of English GODDARD. **2.** Perhaps also an Americanized form of German GOTHARD.

Goodbar (169) Possibly an altered spelling of the English family name **Godber**, from the medieval personal name *Godebert* (see GOBERT), or of **Goodbeer**, **Godbear**, when not a variant of *Godber*, an occupational nickname for a brewer or a nickname for a toper. Alternatively, it may be an Americanized form of the German cognate **Gutbier** ('good beer').
GIVEN NAME German 4%. *Fritz* (2).

Goodbody (110) English (Norfolk): from Middle English *gode* 'good' + *body* 'person', 'creature', apparently a nickname for a good person. Reaney, however, notes that the expression was used as a polite term of address, and the surname may therefore have arisen as a nickname for someone who habitually used this expression.

Goodbread (136) English translation of German **Gutbrod**, an occupational nickname for a baker, from Middle High German *guot* 'good' + *brōt* 'bread'.

Goodchild (393) **1.** English (mainly southern): from a Middle English personal name, a survival of Old English *Gōdcild*, composed of the elements *gōd* 'good' + the late Old English name-forming element *cild* (see CHILD). This name may also have been used in the Middle English period as a nickname for a good person. **2.** English: nickname from *godchild*, i.e. someone who was the godchild of an important member of the community. Compare **Godson**, which was similarly confused with GOODSON. **3.** English translation of German **Gutkind** (see GUTKIN).

Goode (7271) English: variant spelling of GOOD.

Goodell (1978) Variant spelling of English GOODALL.

Goodemote (113) Perhaps an Americanized spelling of German GUTERMUTH.

Gooden (2734) English: possibly a nickname from Middle English *gode* 'good' + *hine* 'servant'. Compare GOODHUE.

Goodenough (680) English: **1.** nickname from Middle English *gode* 'good' + *enoh* 'enough' (Old English *genōh*). Reaney suggests that it was bestowed on one who was easily satisfied; it may also have been used with reference to one whose achievements were average, 'good enough' though not outstanding. **2.** possibly a nickname meaning 'good lad' or 'good servant', from Middle English *gode knave*, from Old English *gōd* 'good' + *cnafa* 'boy', 'servant'.

Goodenow (276) English: variant spelling of GOODENOUGH.

Gooder (132) English: from a Middle English personal name *Godere*, Old English *Gōdhere*, composed of the elements *gōd* 'good' + *here* 'army'.

Goodermote (107) See GOODEMOTE.

Goodfellow (1101) English: nickname for a congenial companion, from Middle English *gode* 'good' + *felawe* 'fellow'.

Goodfriend (343) **1.** English: nickname for a reliable friend or neighbor, from Middle English *gode* 'good' + *frend* 'friend'. **2.** English translation of German **Gutfreund** cognate of 1, from Middle High German *guot* 'good' + *vriunt* 'friend'.

Goodgame (181) English: nickname for a merry or sporty person, from Middle English *gode* 'good' + *game, gamen* 'sport', 'pastime'.

Goodger (140) English: variant of GOODYEAR.

Goodgion (133) English (Yorkshire): variant of GUDGEON.

Goodhart (543) **1.** English: nickname for a kindly person, from Middle English *gode* 'good' + *herte* 'heart'. **2.** Probably also an Americanized form of German GOTHARD or Swiss **Gutherz**, a nickname for a charitable person, from Middle High German *guot* 'good' + *herze* 'heart'.

Goodheart (263) **1.** English: variant spelling of GOODHART. **2.** Americanized form of German and Swiss German **Gutherz** (see GOODHART 2). **3.** Probably also an Americanized spelling of German GOTHARD.

Goodhue (594) English **1.** nickname for a trusted servant, from Middle English *gode* 'good' + *hewe* 'servant' (a derivative of Old English *hīwan* 'retinue', 'household'). **2.** from an Old Norse personal name composed of the elements *guð* 'battle' + *hugi* 'mind', 'spirit'.

Goodie (129) English: apparently a variant spelling of GOODY.

Goodier (189) English: variant of GOODYEAR.

Goodin (2349) English: perhaps a variant of GOODING or an Americanized spelling of French GODIN.

Goodine (280) Perhaps an Americanized spelling of GODIN.
GIVEN NAMES French 4%. *Andre, Celine*.

Gooding (2341) English: patronymic from GOOD.

Goodison (126) English: metronymic from GOODY.

Goodkin (135) English: variant of GODKIN.

Goodkind (101) **1.** English: unexplained; possibly an altered form of **Goodkin**, from a pet form of the Old English personal names *Goda* or *Gode*. **2.** Possibly an Anglicized form of German and Jewish GUTKIN.

Goodlet (144) Scottish: variant spelling of GOODLETT.

Goodlett (632) Scottish (common in Orkney and Shetland): nickname for a trusted servant, from Middle English *gode* 'good' + *ladde* 'lad', 'servant' (see LADD and compare GOODHUE 1, GOODENOUGH 2).

Goodley (147) **1.** English: variant of GODLEY. **2.** Probably also an Americanized spelling of South German and Swiss German **Gütle** (or the variants **Güttly** and **Gütler**), a status name for a smallholder (see GOODLIN).

Goodlin (184) See GOODLING.

Goodling (415) Perhaps an Americanized spelling of German **Gütlein**, a status name for a smallholder, from Middle High German *guot* 'landholding', 'small farm' + the diminutive suffix *-lein -li*, *-lin*. Alternatively, **Güthlein** and **Güthling** may be from a nickname for a good and kindly person, from Middle High German *güetlich*, later changed as though derived from a personal name composed with Germanic *god*, *got* 'god' or *gōd* 'good'.

Goodloe (777) English (Lancashire): unexplained. There are many bearers of this name in AL.

Goodlow (260) English: variant of GOODLOE.

GIVEN NAME French 4%. *Andre* (2).

Goodman (28049) **1.** English: status name from Middle English *gode* 'good' + *man* 'man', in part from use as a term for the master of a household. In Scotland the term denoted a landowner who held his land not directly from the crown but from a feudal vassal of the king. **2.** English: from the Middle English personal name *Godeman*, Old English *Gōdmann*, composed of the elements *gōd* 'good' or *god* 'god' + *mann* 'man'. **3.** English: from the Old English personal name *Gūðmund*, composed of the elements *gūð* 'battle' + *mund* 'protection', or the Old Norse cognate *Guðmundr*. **4.** Americanized form of Jewish GUTMAN or German GUTMANN.

FOREBEARS This name was brought independently to New England by many bearers from the 17th century onward. Richard Goodman was one of the founders of Hartford, CT, (coming from Cambridge, MA, with Thomas Hooker) in 1635.

Goodmanson (142) Americanized form of Icelandic **Guðmansson**, patronymic from the Norse personal name *Guðmundr* (see GOODMAN).

Goodner (710) English: variant of GOODENOUGH.

Goodness (180) **1.** English: nickname from Old English *gōdnes* 'goodness'. **2.** English translation of the French Canadian surname LABONTE.

Goodnight (1259) Americanized form of German GUTKNECHT.

Goodno (144) Altered spelling of English GOODENOUGH.

Goodnough (355) English: reduced form of GOODENOUGH.

Goodnow (466) English: variant of GOODENOUGH.

Goodpaster (609) Of Swiss German origin: variant of GOODPASTURE.

Goodpasture (360) Probably a mistranslation of Swiss German VOLLENWEIDER, a topographic name actually meaning 'foal pasture', but wrongly interpreted as 'full pasture'.

Goodreau (380) Americanized spelling of French GAUDREAU.

Goodrich (7539) **1.** English: from the Middle English personal name *Goderiche*, Old English *Gōdrīc*, composed of the elements *gōd* 'good' + *rīc* 'power'. **2.** Americanized spelling of German **Güttrich**, cognate with 1.

FOREBEARS William Goodrich emigrated

from England to Wethersfield, CT, in about 1643.

Goodrick (233) **1.** English: variant of GOODRICH. **2.** Americanized spelling of German **Güttrich** (see GOODRICH).

Goodridge (771) **1.** English: variant of GOODRICH. **2.** Americanized spelling of German **Güttrich** (see GOODRICH).

Goodroad (108) Probably an altered form of French GAUDREAU.

Goodroe (219) Americanized spelling of French GAUDREAU.

Goodrow (503) Americanized spelling of French GAUDREAU.

Goodrum (902) English (mainly Norfolk): from an Old Norse personal name which Reaney identifies as *Guðormr*, a compound of *guð* 'god' + *ormr* 'snake', 'serpent', but which could be *Guðþormr*, a compound of *guð* 'god' + *þormr* 'to respect or honor', 'to spare'.

Goods (181) Probably a variant of English GOOD.

GIVEN NAME French 4%. *Camille*.

Goodsell (814) **1.** English: nickname from Middle English *gode* 'good' + *saule*, *soule* 'soul'. **2.** Probably also an Americanized form of German **Gutseel** or **Gutsell**; like 1, these are a nickname for a kindly person (literally 'good soul'). Alternatively, it could be a reduced Americanized form of south German **Gutgsell**, a nickname or journeyman's name, from *gut* 'good' + *Gesell(e)* 'fellow', 'journeyman'.

Goodson (5385) **1.** English (chiefly East Anglia and East Midlands): nickname for a dutiful son, from Middle English *gode* 'good' + *sone* 'son'. **2.** English: from a Middle English survival of the Old English personal name *Gōdsunu*, composed of the elements *gōd* 'good' + *sunu* 'son'. **3.** Possibly an Americanized form of German **Gutersohn**, a nickname or pet name meaning 'good son' for one of out of many sons.

Goodspeed (843) English: from the expression 'God speed (you)'; a wish for success for one setting out on an enterprise, presumably applied as a nickname for someone who habitually used this expression.

Goodstein (503) Part-translation of the Jewish ornamental name **Gutstein**, from German *gut* 'good' + *Stein* 'stone'.

GIVEN NAMES Jewish 5%. *Ahuva*, *Kieve*, *Miriam*, *Sol*.

Goodwater (115) Probably a translation of German **Gutwasser**, a habitational name from any of numerous places in Bohemia and Moravia named for their supply of good water.

Goodwill (497) English (Yorkshire): nickname for a friendly or amiable person, from Middle English *gode* 'good' + *will* 'desire'. The compound is attested in the sense 'favorable disposition' since before the Norman Conquest.

Goodwin (25763) English: from the Middle English personal name *Godewyn*, Old English *Gōdwine*, composed of the elements *gōd* 'good' + *wine* 'friend'.

FOREBEARS This name was brought independently to New England by many bearers from the 17th century onward. William Goodwin was one of the founders of Hartford, CT, (coming from Cambridge, MA, with Thomas Hooker) in 1635.

Goodwine (251) Americanized form of German **Gut(t)wein**, literally 'good wine', but probably derived from the personal name *Guotwin* from Old High German *guot* 'good' + *win(e)* 'friend'.

Goodwyn (537) English: variant spelling of GOODWIN.

Goody (262) English: **1.** from Middle English *god dai* 'good day', possibly applied as a nickname for someone who frequently used this greeting. **2.** from a Middle English female personal name *Godeve*, Old English *Gōdgifu*, composed of the elements *gōd* 'good' or *god* 'god' + *gifu* 'gift'. This name has perhaps absorbed a less common name with the second element *gūð* 'battle'. **3.** nickname for a widow or an independent woman, from Middle English *goodwife* 'mistress of a house', from Old English *gōd* 'good' + *wīf* 'woman'. Compare GOODMAN 1.

Goodyear (1248) **1.** English: probably a nickname from Middle English *gode* 'good' (Old English *gōd*) + *year*, *yere* 'year', bestowed on someone who frequently used the expression, perhaps in the sense '(as I hope to have a) good year' or as a New Year salutation. Alternatively, it may have been from an Americanized form of French GAUTHIER. **2.** English translation of German **Gutjahr**, originally a nickname for someone born on New year's Day.

FOREBEARS The inventor of vulcanized rubber, Charles Goodyear (1800–60) was of the fourth generation descended from Stephen Goodyear (1598–1658), who succeeded Gov. Theophilus Eaton as leader of the company of London merchants that founded the New Haven colony in CT in 1638.

Googe (237) English: variant of GOOCH, itself a variant of GOFF.

Googins (178) Perhaps a variant of Irish COGAN. Compare GOGGINS.

Gookin (295) Irish: reduced Anglicized form of Gaelic **Mac Guagáin** (see McGUIGAN).

FOREBEARS Born in 1612 in England or Ireland of an Irish father, the soldier and magistrate Daniel Gookin spent time in VA on his father's plantation as a teenager. In 1644 he moved to MA to escape the persecutions of Governor Berkeley. He was a stalwart defender of the rights of the Indians and wrote two books on the subject, *Historical Collections of the Indians in New England*, written in 1674 and *The*

Doings and Sufferings of the Christian Indians, completed in 1677. Gookin also wrote a *History of New England*, the manuscript of which was unfortunately destroyed without being published. He died in 1687.

Goold (436) English: variant of GOULD.

Gooley (315) **1.** Americanized spelling of French GOULET. **2.** Irish: reduced Anglicized form of Gaelic **Ó Gabhlaigh**, from *gabhlach* 'forked'.

Goolsby (2555) English: probably a reduced form of **Gooldsbury**, a variant of GOLDSBOROUGH.

Goon (272) Perhaps a reduced form of Irish **McGoohan**, an Anglicized form of Gaelic **Mac Cuacháin** or **Mag Cuacháin**, a patronymic from a byname from *cuach* 'cuckoo'.

Goonan (174) Irish: reduced Anglicized form of Gaelic **Ó Gamhnáin**, from a diminutive of *gamhra* 'calf'. Compare GAFFNEY.

Goos (272) **1.** North German: metonymic occupational name for a breeder or keeper of geese, from Middle Low German *gōs* 'goose'. **2.** South German: from a short form of a Germanic personal name based on *Gote* 'Goth' or *got* 'god'.
GIVEN NAMES German 4%. *Claus, Ernst, Gunther.*

Goosby (238) See GOOLSBY.
GIVEN NAME French 4%. *Monique.*

Goosen (168) Variant spelling of Dutch and North German GOOSSEN.

Goosman (124) **1.** North German (**Goosmann**): occupational name for a breeder or keeper of geese (see GOOS). **2.** German (**Goosmann**): variant of **Gossmann** (see GOSSMAN).

Goossen (316) Dutch and North German: patronymic from the Germanic personal name *Gozzo*, a short form of the various compound names with *gōd* 'good' or *god, got* 'god'.

Goossens (202) Dutch and North German: variant of GOOSSEN.
GIVEN NAMES French 9%; German 5%. *Emile, Jacques, Laurent, Monique; Alfons, Fritz.*

Goostree (187) English (Lancashire): habitational name from a place in Cheshire called Goostrey.

Gootee (419) Americanized spelling of French GAUTHIER.

Gopal (167) Indian (southern states): Hindu name, from Sanskrit *gopāla* 'cowherd' (from *go* 'cow' + *pāla* 'protector'), an epithet of the god Krishna. It is only a male given name in India, but has come to be used as a surname among South Indians in the U.S.
GIVEN NAMES Indian 89%. *Raj (5), Ram (5), Madan (3), Ganesh (2), Haresh (2), Indira (2), Kishore (2), Nanda (2), Rajeev (2), Ravi (2), Siva (2), Ajay.*

Goplen (111) Norwegian and Danish: unexplained.

Gora (285) Polish (**Góra**) and Jewish (from Poland): from Polish *góra* (Slavic *gora*) 'mountain', 'hill', hence a topographic name for someone who lived on a hillside or in a mountainous district, or perhaps a nickname for a large person.
GIVEN NAMES Polish 10%. *Irena, Ireneusz, Jolanta, Krystyna, Lech, Leszek, Mieczyslaw, Miroslawa, Wlodzimierz, Zigmont, Zofia.*

Goracke (184) German (of Slavic origin): topographic name from a diminutive of Old Slavic, Sorbian *gora* 'mountain'.

Gorak (106) Polish (**Górak**): patronymic from **Góra** (see GORA).
GIVEN NAMES Polish 7%. *Jozef, Tadeusz.*

Goral (339) Polish (**Góral**): topographic name denoting someone from the mountains of southern Poland, from *góral*, a derivative of *góra* 'mountain' (see GORALSKI).
GIVEN NAMES Polish 4%. *Dorota, Mieczyslaw, Slawek, Wladyslaw, Wojciech.*

Goralski (273) Polish (**Góralski**): habitational name for someone from a place named Górale, in Piotrków, Sieradz, and Toruń voivodeships, named with *góral* 'mountainous'.

Goranson (450) Respelling of Swedish **Göransson**, a patronymic from the personal name *Göran*, Swedish form of GEORGE.
GIVEN NAMES Scandinavian 5%. *Nels, Sven.*

Gorbet (123) English: variant of GARBUTT.

Gorbett (134) English: variant of GARBUTT.

Gorby (666) English: possibly a variant of CORBY.

Gorczyca (323) Polish: metonymic occupational name for a mustard grower, from *gorczyca* 'white mustard'.
GIVEN NAMES Polish 10%. *Casimir (2), Krzysztof (2), Danuta, Elizbieta, Fryderyk, Jozef, Kazimierz, Ryszard, Teofil.*

Gorczynski (141) Polish (**Gorczyński, Górczyński**): habitational name for someone from Gorczyn in Sieradz voivodeship or Górczyn in Poznań voivodeship.
GIVEN NAMES Polish 12%. *Andrzej, Boleslaw, Jerzy, Ryszard, Tadeusz.*

Gord (100) English: unexplained; perhaps a variant of GOURD.

Gordan (430) **1.** Variant of German JORDAN. **2.** English: perhaps an altered spelling of GORDON.

Gordanier (112) Possible respelling of French GARDINIER.

Gorden (982) Altered spelling of GORDON.

Gorder (453) German (**Görder**): variant of **Gärtner** (see GARTNER).

Gordillo (326) Spanish: from a pet form of the nickname **Gordo**, from Spanish *gordo* 'fat' (Late Latin *gurdus*, of uncertain origin).

GIVEN NAMES Spanish 50%. *Jose (8), Carlos (6), Luis (6), Juan (5), Manuel (5), Pedro (5), Jorge (4), Sergio (4), Alfredo (2), Ana (2), Arturo (2), Emilio (2).*

Gordin (194) Jewish (from Russia): variant of GORDON 4 and 5.
GIVEN NAMES Jewish 18%; Russian 7%. *Eyal (2), Moisey (2), Yakov (2), Zalman (2), Erez, Faina, Haya, Inna, Mendel; Leonid (4), Aleksandr, Boris, Feiga, Genady.*

Gordinier (152) French: variant of GARDINIER.

Gordley (151) Probably an Americanized spelling of German **Gördeler**, a variant of **Gürtler** (see GURTLER).

Gordner (216) **1.** Variant of Swiss and German **Gortner** (see GORTNEY). **2.** Perhaps also a variant of English GARDNER.
GIVEN NAME German 4%. *Fritz (2).*

Gordon (57047) **1.** Scottish: habitational name from a place in Berwickshire (Borders), named with Welsh *gor* 'spacious' + *din* 'fort'. **2.** English (of Norman origin) and French: habitational name from Gourdon in Saône-et-Loire, so called from the Gallo-Roman personal name *Gordus* + the locative suffix *-o, -ōnis*. **3.** Irish: adopted as an English equivalent of Gaelic **Mag Mhuirneacháin**, a patronymic from the personal name *Muirneachán*, a diminutive of *muirneach* 'beloved'. **4.** Jewish (from Lithuania): probably a habitational name from the Belorussian city of Grodno. It goes back at least to 1657. Various suggestions, more or less fanciful, have been put forward as to its origin. There is a family tradition among some bearers that they are descended from a son of a Duke of Gordon, who converted to Judaism in the 18th century, but the Jewish surname was in existence long before the 18th century; others claim descent from earlier Scottish converts, but this is implausible. **5.** Spanish and Galician **Gordón**, and Basque: habitational name from a place called Gordon (Basque) or Gordón (Spanish, Galician), of which there are examples in Salamanca, Galicia, and Basque Country. **6.** Spanish: possibly in some instances from an augmentative of the nickname *Gordo* (see GORDILLO).

Gordy (1438) Americanized form of French **Gourdeau**, a topographic name from Old French *gort* 'stretch of water rich in fish'.
FOREBEARS A family called Gourdeau, from Poitou, was in Quebec city by 1652.

Gore (8696) **1.** English: habitational name from any of various places, for example in Kent and Wiltshire, named Gore, from Old English *gāra* 'triangular piece of land' (a derivative of *gār* 'spear', with reference to the triangular shape of a spearhead). **2.** French: nickname for a gluttonous and idle individual, from Old French *gore* 'sow' (of allegedly imitative origin, reflecting the grunting of the animal).

Gorecki (821) Polish (**Górecki**) and Jewish (from Poland): habitational name from any of the numerous places in Poland named Górka or Górki, from Polish *góra* 'mountain', 'hill'.
GIVEN NAMES Polish 8%. *Casimir* (3), *Jerzy* (3), *Tadeusz* (3), *Krzysztof* (2), *Lech* (2), *Piotr* (2), *Andrzej*, *Ignatius*, *Jacek*, *Jaroslaw*, *Kazimierz*, *Maciej*.

Goree (751) **1.** Americanized form of a French name, probably **Gorré**, from Old French *goré* 'deceived', 'betrayed'. **2.** variant spelling of Scottish and Irish GOREY.

Goreham (125) English: variant of GORHAM.

Gorelick (358) Jewish (from Belarus): Americanized spelling of GORELIK.
GIVEN NAMES Jewish 15%. *Chaim* (3), *Isadore* (2), *Meyer* (2), *Aba*, *Avrohom*, *Chana*, *Chiam*, *Isser*, *Mayer*, *Moshe*, *Shmuel*, *Sol*.

Gorelik (337) Jewish (from Belarus): nickname for someone who had had a house fire, from Belorussian *gorelyj* 'burnt' + the noun suffix *-ik*.
GIVEN NAMES Russian 36%; Jewish 30%. *Boris* (17), *Leonid* (8), *Mikhail* (8), *Vladimir* (6), *Arkady* (5), *Oleg* (5), *Semyon* (5), *Igor* (4), *Grigoriy* (3), *Yefim* (3), *Yelena* (3), *Aleksey* (2); *Yakov* (7), *Zinaida* (5), *Aron* (3), *Elihu* (2), *Inna* (2), *Isaak* (2), *Sima* (2), *Zalman* (2), *Esfir*, *Faina*, *Gersh*, *Irina*.

Goren (522) Jewish (Ashkenazic): altered form of HORN 5, under Russian influence; since Russian has no *h* and alters *h* in borrowed words to *g*. In Israel the name has been reinterpreted by folk etymology as being from Hebrew *goren* 'threshing floor', which is in fact etymologically and semantically unrelated.
GIVEN NAMES Jewish 15%. *Hershel* (3), *Emanuel* (2), *Erez* (2), *Yehuda* (2), *Ayal*, *Danit*, *Doron*, *Dov*, *Elad*, *Elihu*, *Eran*, *Haim*.

Gorenflo (179) German: Huguenot name, originally from Friedrichstal (founded by Huguenots), now Stutensee, near Karlsruhe.
GIVEN NAME German 4%. *Ewald* (2).

Gorenstein (137) Jewish (eastern Ashkenazic): altered form of HORNSTEIN under Russian influence, since Russian has no *h* and alters *h* in borrowed words to *g*.
GIVEN NAMES Jewish 14%. *Aryeh* (2), *Hyman*, *Ilya*, *Meyer*, *Moisey*.

Gores (297) North German (**Göres**): patronymic from the personal name *Gör(e)*, a Low German form of Latin *Gregorius* (see GREGORY).

Gorey (338) Scottish and Irish: reduced Americanized form of **Mac Gafraidh** or **Mac Gofraidh** 'son of *Gafradh*' (see MCCAFFREY).

Gorga (124) **1.** Southern Italian and Catalan: topographic name from Sicilian *gorga*, Catalan *gorg(a)* 'place where water collects', 'mill pond', 'gorge'. **2.** Catalan: habitational name from Gorga in Alacant.
GIVEN NAMES Italian 20%. *Angelo* (2), *Adamo*, *Alfonso*, *Carmine*, *Domenic*, *Donato*, *Eduardo*, *Giacinto*, *Julio*, *Umberto*.

Gorgas (173) Catalan: variant spelling of **Gorgues**, a topographic name from the plural of *gorga* 'gorge' (see GORGA).
GIVEN NAME French 4%. *Carolle* (2).

Gorges (311) **1.** English and French: topographic name for someone who lived by or in a deep valley, from Middle English, Old French *gorge* 'gorge', 'ravine' (from Old French *gorge* 'throat'). There are various places in England and France named with this word, and the surname may be a habitational name from any of these. **2.** German: unexplained.
FOREBEARS A family by the name of Gorges originated in the village of Gorges near Périers in Normandy, France, where Ralph de Gorges was living in the late 11th century. A branch of the family was established in England when Thomas de Gorges lost his lands to the King of France. He became warden of Henry III's manor of Powerstock, Devon. Sir Ferdinando Gorges, an English proprietor, was granted the province of Maine in 1639, and his brother, Thomas Gorges, was governor of Maine in the 1640s.
GIVEN NAMES German 5%. *Claus*, *Erwin*, *Heinz*, *Otto*, *Wilhelm*.

Gorgone (205) Italian: apparently a humanistic nickname from Greek *Gorgōn* 'gorgon'. In classical mythology the Gorgons were three sisters who had the power to turn to stone anyone who looked at them.
GIVEN NAMES Italian 13%. *Salvatore* (5), *Angelo*, *Carmelo*, *Gaetano*, *Sal*.

Gorham (3004) English (Kent): apparently a habitational name from a lost or unidentified place, possibly so named from Old English *gāra* 'triangular piece of land' + *hām* 'homestead'.
FOREBEARS Born in England, John Gorham emigrated to MA and in 1643 married Desire Howland, daughter of John Howland, who came to America on the *Mayflower*. His descendant Nathaniel (1738–96) was born in Charlestown, MA, and was one of the signers of the Declaration of Independence.

Gori (238) Northern Italian: patronymic or plural form of the common medieval personal name *Goro*, a reduced form of *Gregorio* (see GREGORY).
GIVEN NAMES Italian 18%. *Gino* (3), *Italo* (2), *Lido* (2), *Marco* (2), *Aldo*, *Angelo*, *Dino*, *Domenic*, *Fabiano*, *Livio*, *Luca*, *Secondo*.

Gorin (454) **1.** Jewish (eastern Ashkenazic): variant of GOREN. **2.** English: variant of GORING 1. **3.** French: diminutive of GORE.
GIVEN NAMES Jewish 9%; Russian 4%. *Meyer* (3), *Yakov* (2), *Hersh*, *Miriam*, *Moises*, *Shlomo*, *Sol*, *Tuvia*, *Zeev*; *Iosif* (2), *Anatoly*, *Boris*, *Fanya*, *Grigori*, *Grigoriy*, *Igor*, *Mikhall*, *Svetlana*.

Goring (227) **1.** English: habitational name from places in Oxfordshire and West Sussex named Goring, from Old English *Gāringas* 'people of Gāra', a short form of the various compound names with the first element *gār* 'spear'. **2.** German (**Göring**): see GOERING.

Goris (306) Galician: probably a habitational name from Gorís in Pontevedra province, Galicia.
GIVEN NAMES Spanish 16%. *Jose* (5), *Juan* (3), *Julio* (3), *Alicia* (2), *Manuel* (2), *Maribel* (2), *Rafael* (2), *Agusto*, *Ana*, *Bernardina*, *Edmundo*, *Eladio*.

Gorka (370) Polish (**Górka**): habitational name from a place called Górka or Górki (see GORECKI).
GIVEN NAMES Polish 9%. *Danuta* (2), *Stanislaw* (2), *Andrzej*, *Jacek*, *Jerzy*, *Jozef*, *Kazimierz*, *Krystyna*, *Pawel*, *Zygmund*.

Gorley (242) **1.** Northern English variant of Scottish GOURLEY. **2.** Possibly also an Americanized spelling of French **Gourlé** (see GURLEY).

Gorman (12427) **1.** Irish: reduced Anglicized form of Gaelic **Mac Gormáin** and **Ó Gormáin** 'son (or descendant) of *Gormán*', a personal name from a diminutive of *gorm* 'dark blue', 'noble'. Compare O'GORMAN. **2.** English: from the Middle English personal name *Gormund*, Old English *Gārmund*, composed of the elements *gār* 'spear' + *mund* 'protection'. **3.** English: topographic name for someone who lived by or on a triangular patch of land (see GORE). **4.** German (**Görmann**): variant of GEHRMANN. **5.** German (**Görmann**): of Slavic origin, occupational name for a miner, from Slavic *góra* 'mountain'.

Gormley (2086) Irish: reduced Anglicized form of Gaelic **Ó Gormghaile** 'descendant of *Gormghal*', a personal name from *gorm* 'noble', 'dark blue' + *gal* 'valor'.
GIVEN NAMES Irish 4%. *Brendan* (2), *Aileen*, *Brigid*, *Declan*, *Eamonn*, *Nuala*.

Gormly (174) Irish: variant spelling of GORMLEY.

Gornall (157) English (Lancashire): apparently a habitational name from a place so called, perhaps Gornalwood near Birmingham, which is probably named from Old English *cweorn* 'mill' + *halh* 'recess', 'hollow'.

Gorney (614) **1.** English: variant of GURNEY. **2.** Altered spelling of Polish GORNY. **3.** Possibly an altered spelling of German **Gornig**, **Görnig**, occupational names for a miner, from Polish *góra* 'mountain'.

Gorniak (150) Polish (**Górniak**): **1.** patronymic from **Górny** (see GORNY). **2.** habitational name for someone from a place called Górna or Górne.

GIVEN NAMES Polish 6%. *Andrzej, Dorota, Wojciech.*

Gornick (302) Americanized spelling of Slovenian or Polish GORNIK.

Gornik (166) **1.** Polish: occupational name from *górnik* 'miner'. **2.** Polish: topographic name, an agent derivative of *górny* 'upper part of a settlement' (see GORNY). **3.** Slovenian: from *gora* 'mountain', 'hill', in any of several senses. It may be a topographic name for someone who lived on a hill; a habitational name from any of several places named with *gora* or the adjective *gornji* 'upper'; or a feudal status name for the steward of a vineyard, from *gora* in the sense 'hill planted with vines'.
GIVEN NAMES Polish 4%. *Andrzej, Wieslaw.*

Gornto (155) Altered form of an unidentified English surname; said to be an altered form of BRINTON.
FOREBEARS Edward Brinton, alias Gornto, is listed as one of the original settlers (a mason) in Jamestown VA in 1607.

Gorny (299) Polish (**Górny**): **1.** habitational name for someone from a place called Górne. **2.** from the adjective *górny* 'upper', 'superior', applied either as a topographic name for someone who lived in the upper part of a settlement, etc., or as a nickname for someone considered to have superior abilities.
GIVEN NAMES Polish 7%. *Andrzej, Krzysztof, Miroslaw, Ryszard, Wieslaw.*

Gorospe (175) Basque: topographic or habitational name, possibly composed of Basque *gorosti* 'holly' or *gurutz* (*goroz*) 'cross' + *-be* 'below'.
GIVEN NAMES Spanish 31%. *Jose* (3), *Cesar* (2), *Honorio* (2), *Manuel* (2), *Renato* (2), *Adolfo, Angelita, Benedicto, Cornelio, Fernando, Gerardo, Herminio.*

Gorr (381) German: **1.** from a reduced form of the Latin personal name *Gregorius* (see GREGORY). **2.** nickname from Middle High German *gorre* 'bad horse'.

Gorrell (1276) English: **1.** nickname from Middle English *gorrell* 'fat man' (from Old French *gorel* 'pig'). **2.** from the Old English personal name *Gārwulf*, composed of the elements *gār* 'spear' + *wulf* 'wolf'. **3.** habitational name from any of various places named with Old English *gor* 'dirt', 'mud' + *wella* 'spring', 'stream', such as Gorwell in Essex and Dorset, or Gorrell in Devon.

Gorrie (159) Scottish and Irish: reduced form of McGORRY.
GIVEN NAMES Irish 4%. *Brennan, Sheelagh.*

Gorringe (111) English: variant of GORING.

Gorry (132) Irish and Scottish: reduced form of McGORRY.

Gorse (119) **1.** English (mainly Lancashire): topographic name from Old English *gors(t)* 'gorse', or a habitational name from some minor place named with this word. **2.** Slovenian (**Gorše**): shortened form of the personal name *Gregor*, Latin *Grego-*

rius. **3.** Slovenian (**Gorše**): topographic name from a derivative of *gora* 'mountain', 'hill planted with vines', 'wood in a hill country' (see GORNIK).

Gorski (2762) Polish (**Górski**) and Jewish (eastern Ashkenazic): habitational name for someone from any of numerous places called Góra, Górka, or Górki, from *góra* 'mountain', 'hill'.
GIVEN NAMES Polish 6%. *Jerzy* (3), *Jozef* (3), *Andrzej* (2), *Casimir* (2), *Piotr* (2), *Ryszard* (2), *Stanislaw* (2), *Tadeusz* (2), *Witold* (2), *Zbigniew* (2), *Agnieszka.*

Gorsky (295) Jewish (eastern Ashkenazic): variant spelling of GORSKI.

Gorsline (276) Perhaps an altered spelling of French GOSSELIN.

Gorsuch (1024) English: habitational name from the hamlet of Gorsuch, Lancashire, earlier *Gosefordsich*, from Old English *Gōsford* 'goose ford' + *sīc* 'small stream'.
FOREBEARS This name is first recorded as that of a manor near Ormskirk held by Walter de Gosefordsich in the late 13th century.

Gort (282) **1.** French: from Old French *gort* (Gaulish *gorto*), denoting a particular kind of trap placed on a river bed to catch fish; the surname may have arisen as a topographic name or as a habitational name from any of numerous settlements named Le Gort in, for example, Charente, Eure-et-Loir, Loir-et-Cher. **2.** Variant of French GARD.
GIVEN NAMES Spanish 7%. *Wilfredo* (3), *Lazaro* (2), *Aida, Alfredo, Eduardo, Efren, Esteban, Jesus, Jose, Mario, Vicente, Wifredo.*

Gorter (220) Dutch: occupational name for a grower of barley, and possibly by extension a brewer, Middle Dutch *gruter, gurter.*
GIVEN NAMES Dutch 5%; German 4%. *Geert, Gerrit, Jacobus; Hans, Klaus, Wilhelmina.*

Gortney (169) Possibly an altered spelling of German **Gort(h)ner**, a metonymic occupational name for a miller, from an agent derivative of Low German *gorte* 'groats'.

Gorton (1602) English: habitational name from a place in Lancashire, so named from Old English *gor* 'dirt', 'mud' + *tūn* 'enclosure', 'settlement'.
FOREBEARS Introduced in America by a family from Gorton, Lancashire, England (three miles from Manchester), the name Gorton was also adopted by a religious group known as the Gortonites. They were followers of Samuel Gorton (*c.* 1592–1677), whose unorthodox religious beliefs, which included denying the doctrine of the Trinity, caused him to seek religious toleration by emigrating to Boston in 1637 with his family. In conflict with authorities in Massachusetts Bay, Plymouth, and Newport, he eventually settled in Shawomet, RI, and renamed it Warwick. He died there in 1677, leaving three sons and at least six daughters.

Gorum (186) Probably an altered spelling of English GORHAM. It is found chiefly in AL and LA.

Gory (134) **1.** Irish or Scottish: reduced form of McGORRY. **2.** Altered spelling of Swiss **Göhry**, a variant of GEHRING or of **Gori**, from a pet form of the personal name *Georg* (see GEORGE).

Goryl (106) Polish: nickname from *goryl* 'gorilla'.
GIVEN NAMES Polish 5%. *Janina, Zofia.*

Gorzynski (118) Polish (**Gorzyński**, **Górzyński**): habitational name for someone from any of various places called Gorzyń, Górzyń, or Górzno, all named with *góra* 'mountain', 'hill'.
GIVEN NAMES Polish 7%. *Dariusz, Wlodzimierz.*

Gosa (320) Origin unidentified.

Gosch (479) **1.** North German: from a reduced form of the personal name **Godschalk**, Low German form of GOTTSCHALK. **2.** German: nickname from Sorbian *goch* 'chap', 'fellow'.
GIVEN NAMES German 5%. *Hans* (3), *Claus, Erwin, Guenther, Heinz, Helmut, Kurt.*

Goscinski (119) Polish (**Gościński**, **Goszczyński**): habitational name for someone from Goszczyn, Goszczyna, Goszczynno, or Goszczyno, all places named with a personal name, *Goszcza*, ultimately from *gość* 'guest'.
FOREBEARS The surname Gościński or Goszczński, borne by a Polish noble family, can be traced back to the 14th century.

Gosda (101) East German: habitational name from a place so named near Cottbus in the Lausitz district.
GIVEN NAME German 4%. *Dieter.*

Gosdin (210) Possibly a variant spelling of the English habitational name **Gosden**, from a lost place in Slaugham, Sussex, so named from Old English *gōs* 'goose' + *denn* 'woodland pasture'.

Gose (624) German: **1.** topographic name for someone living by the Gose river near Goslar in the Harz Mountains. **2.** from a Germanic personal name, from *god, got* 'god' or *gōd* 'good'.

Gosha (185) Possibly an Americanized spelling of German **Gosche, Gösche**, from a short form of a Germanic personal name formed with *god, got* 'god' or *gōd* 'good'.
GIVEN NAMES French 6%. *Angelle, Mechelle, Monique.*

Goshen (133) **1.** Jewish (Israeli): unexplained. **2.** Americanized spelling of the North German family name **Göschen**, a patronymic from a short form of the personal name GOTTSCHALK.
GIVEN NAMES Jewish 6%. *Dov, Drora, Shmuel.*

Goshert (160) Possibly an altered spelling of German **Gosshart**, from the Germanic personal name *Gozzo* (see GOSSE) + *hart* 'hard', 'brave', 'strong'.

Goshorn (570) Probably a variant of South German **Ganshorn**, presumably a topographic name, in which the suffix -*horn* denotes a promontory or horn of land; Low German *gōs* 'goose' corresponds with standard *Gans*.

Goslee (273) English: unexplained.

Goslin (627) **1.** English: variant of JOSLIN. **2.** French: variant of GOSSELIN. **3.** South German (**Göslin**): from a pet form of any of several personal names formed with *Gos-*, for example *Gossbert*.

Gosline (177) Variant spelling of GOSLIN, found chiefly in MD.

Gosling (298) **1.** English: variant of JOSLIN. **2.** English: nickname from Middle English *gosling* 'young goose' (from Old English *gōs* + the Germanic suffix -*ling*, partly in imitation of Old Norse *gæslingr* from *gás*). **3.** German: from a short form of a Germanic personal name formed with *god, got* 'god' or *gōd* 'good'.

Gosman (167) **1.** Jewish (eastern Ashkenazic): nickname from Yiddish *goz* 'hare' + *man* 'man'. **2.** Variant spelling of German **Gossmann** (see GOSSMAN).

Gosnell (2565) Irish: from an Irish adaptation (**Góiséir**) of English HOSIER, the name of a family in Munster in the late 16th century.

Gosney (729) **1.** English (Yorkshire): possibly a habitational name from Goosnargh in Lancashire, so named from the Old Irish personal name *Gussān* + Old Norse *erg* 'hill pasture'. **2.** Probably an Americanized form of German **Gossner** or **Gössner**, variants of GASSNER.

Goss (9449) **1.** English (chiefly West Country): variant of GOSSE. **2.** German: from the Germanic personal name *Gozzo*, a short form of the various compound names with the first element *gōd* 'good' or *god, got* 'god'.

Gossage (566) English: variant of GORSUCH.

Gossard (668) **1.** French: from the Germanic personal name *Gozhard*, composed of an unexplained firt element *goz-* + *hard* 'hardy', 'brave', 'strong'. **2.** English (Midlands): occupational name for a keeper of geese, Middle English *goseherde*, from Old English *gōs* 'goose' + *hierde* 'herdsman', 'keeper'.

Gosse (401) English (of Norman origin), French, and North German: from the Old French personal name *Gosse*, representing the Germanic personal name *Gozzo*, a short form of the various compound names beginning *gōd* 'good' or *god, got* 'god'.

Gosselin (2567) French: from a pet form of the Old French personal name GOSSE.
FOREBEARS A man from Normandy, France, called Gosselin or Guiselin was married in Quebec city in 1653.
GIVEN NAMES French 15%. *Gaston* (8), *Armand* (7), *Lucien* (6), *Benoit* (5), *Marcel* (5), *Normand* (5), *Andre* (4), *Laurent* (4), *Adrien* (3), *Aime* (3), *Alphonse* (3), *Germain* (3).

Gossen (319) Dutch: variant of GOOSSEN.

Gosser (505) German: variant of GASSER.

Gossett (3981) English and French: from a pet form of GOSSE.
FOREBEARS A bearer of the name Gossett from Normandy, France, was established in Quebec city by 1677.

Gossman (715) German (**Gossmann**, **Gössmann**) and French: from a Germanic personal name composed of the elements *goz* 'Goth' + *man* 'man'.

Gossom (103) Probably a variant of English GOSSON.

Gosson (111) English: possibly a variant of **Godson** (see GOODSON) or a patronymic from the personal name *Gotte* (see GOTT).

Gostomski (196) Polish: habitational name for someone from Gostomie in Gdańsk voivodeship or Gostomin in Ciechanów voivodeship.

Goswami (148) Indian (northern states): Hindu (Brahman) name, from Sanskrit *gosvāmī* 'lord', 'religious mendicant', from Sanskrit *go*, a word with many meanings, including 'earth' and 'cow', + *svāmī* 'lord' (see SWAMY).
GIVEN NAMES Indian 86%. *Sanjay* (3), *Ashok* (2), *Gautam* (2), *Mangal* (2), *Ram* (2), *Ajit*, *Amit*, *Anand*, *Animesh*, *Anuj*, *Ashish*, *Ashoke*.

Goswick (366) English: habitational name from Goswick in Northumberland, so named from Old English *gōs* 'goose' + *wīc* 'outlying farm'.

Gosz (116) Hungarian: unexplained.

Gotay (138) Catalan: most probably variant of **Godall** (alongside **Goday** and **Gotall**), from Catalan *godall* 'calf', presumably applied as a nickname.
GIVEN NAMES Spanish 37%. *Luis* (3), *Pedro* (3), *Alberto* (2), *Ana* (2), *Jose* (2), *Angel*, *Berenice*, *Domingo*, *Elba*, *Esmeralda*, *Esperanza*, *Eugenio*.

Gotch (247) **1.** Welsh: variant of GOOCH. **2.** Americanized spelling of German **Götsch** (see GOTSCH).

Gotcher (418) Origin uncertain: perhaps a variant spelling of English GOUCHER, or alternatively an Anglicized spelling of French GAUTHIER.

Gotelli (127) Italian (Liguria): probably from a pet form of the Germanic personal name *Gotto*, or from a diminutive of the ethnic name *Goto* 'Goth'.

Goth (270) **1.** North German and Danish: tribal name from medieval German *Gote* 'Goth'. **2.** German (**Göth**): variant of GOTT 1.

Gotham (320) English: habitational name from Gotham in Nottinghamshire, so named from Old English *gāt* 'goat' + *hām* 'homestead' or *hamm* 'water meadow'.

Gothard (717) **1.** English: occupational name for a keeper of goats, Middle English *gotherde*, from Old English *gāt* 'goat' + *hierde* 'herdsman', 'keeper'. **2.** German: from a personal name composed of the elements *gōd* 'good' or *god, got* 'god' + *hard* 'hardy', 'brave', 'strong'.

Gotlieb (145) Variant spelling of German and Jewish GOTTLIEB.
GIVEN NAMES Jewish 16%. *Yosef* (2), *Avner*, *Cheskel*, *Hyman*, *Itzhak*, *Miriam*, *Pincus*, *Rochel*.

Goto (514) Japanese (**Gotō**): 'later wisteria', indicating descendants of the FUJIWARA clan through various branches. This name occurs chiefly along the southeastern seaboard of Japan and in the Ryūkyū Islands.
GIVEN NAMES Japanese 64%. *Makoto* (4), *Takashi* (4), *Takeshi* (4), *Akira* (3), *Hideo* (3), *Hiroshi* (3), *Masayuki* (3), *Toshiyuki* (3), *Yumi* (3), *Atsushi* (2), *Hiroko* (2), *Kaoru* (2).

Gotsch (230) German (**Götsch**): from a short form of the personal name GOTTFRIED or GOTTSCHALK.
GIVEN NAMES German 7%. *Hans* (3), *Helmut* (2), *Erwin*, *Otto*.

Gotschall (288) Variant spelling of German GOTTSCHALK.

Gotshall (188) Americanized spelling of German GOTTSCHALK.

Gott (1808) **1.** German: from short form of the various Germanic compound personal names with the first element *gōd* 'good' or *god, got* 'god'. **2.** South German and Swiss German: from Middle High German *got(t)e* 'godfather'. **3.** English (of Norman origin): from a personal name having the same etymology as 1 above.

Gotta (151) Italian: variant of GOTTO.

Gotter (105) German (**Götter**): from the Germanic personal name *Godehar*, formed with *gōd* 'good' or *got* 'god' + *hari* 'army'.

Gottesman (695) Jewish (Ashkenazic): ornamental name, literally meaning 'God's man', from modern German or Yiddish.
GIVEN NAMES Jewish 14%; German 4%. *Moshe* (4), *Menachem* (3), *Shlomo* (3), *Elihu* (2), *Amrom*, *Bernat*, *Chaim*, *Dov*, *Dovid*, *Emanuel*, *Hershel*, *Hyam*; *Erwin* (2), *Armin*, *Frieda*, *Otto*.

Gottfried (1000) **1.** German: from a Germanic personal name composed of the elements *god, got* 'god' + *frid(u)* 'peace'. **2.** Jewish (Ashkenazic): ornamental name composed of German *Gott* 'God' + *Friede* 'peace', or ornamental adoption of the German personal name as a surname.
GIVEN NAMES German 4%. *Kurt* (4), *Alois*.

Gotthardt (189) German: variant of GOTHARD.

Gotthelf (120) **1.** German: from the personal name *Gotthelf* (literally 'God's help'), which was first recorded at the beginning of the 18th century; it was formed in imitation of older German male names but stressing a Christian (Protestant) attitude and became popular through the

Pietist movement in Germany. In some cases at least, it was a late adoption as a surname; for instance, the Swiss minister and writer Albert Bitzius (1797–1854) dubbed himself Jeremias Gotthelf. **2.** Jewish (Ashkenazic): ornamental name with the same meaning as 1, from German *Gott* 'God' + *Helfe* 'help'.
GIVEN NAME Jewish 7%. *Meyer* (3).

Gotti (106) **1.** Italian: patronymic or plural form of GOTTO. **2.** Swiss German: variant of GOTT 1.
GIVEN NAMES French 4%; Italian 4%. *Andre*; *Angelo, Vito.*

Gottier (112) Variant of French GAUTHIER.

Gottlieb (3625) **1.** German and Jewish (Ashkenazic): from the personal name *Gottlieb.* As a German personal name this is for the most part a translation of Greek *Theophilos* ('one who loves God') that became very popular in the 17th and 18th centuries with the rise of the Pietist movement. Among German Jews, it existed, independently from German Christians, since the Middle Ages. **2.** German: from the personal name *Goteleib,* based on Old High German *god, got* 'god' + *leiba* 'offspring', 'son'.
GIVEN NAMES Jewish 7%. *Meyer* (7), *Sol* (6), *Emanuel* (5), *Cheskel* (3), *Heshy* (3), *Isadore* (3), *Miriam* (3), *Moshe* (3), *Chaim* (2), *Feivel* (2), *Hyman* (2), *Isser* (2).

Gottlob (113) German: from a personal name composed of the elements *god, got* 'god' + *lob* 'praise'. This was one of the German personal names that became popular in the 17th and 18th centuries with the rise of the Pietist movement.

Gottman (193) **1.** Jewish (Ashkenazic): variant of GOTTESMAN. **2.** German (**Gottmann**): from a short form of any of the Germanic personal names formed with *gōd* 'good' or *got, god* 'god' (for example GOTTFRIED, GOTTHARDT, GOTTSCHALK) + *man* 'man'.

Gotto (215) Italian: from a short form of a personal name ending with *-gotto,* as for example *Rigotto, Ugotto.*

Gotts (189) **1.** English: patronymic from the personal name GOTT 1. **2.** Possibly an Americanized spelling of German **Götz** (see GOETZ).

Gottsch (164) German (**Göttsch**): variant spelling of **Götsch** (see GOTSCH).

Gottschalk (1864) German and Jewish (western Ashkenazic): from a medieval personal name composed of Middle High German *got* 'God' (Old High German *got*) + *scalh* 'servant', 'serf' (Old High German *scalc*).
GIVEN NAMES German 6%. *Kurt* (12), *Hans* (3), *Armin* (2), *Horst* (2), *Otto* (2), *Arno, Franz, Fritz, Gunther, Heinz, Ingo, Klaus.*

Gottschall (408) German: variant of GOTTSCHALK.

Gottschling (98) Eastern German: probably from a variant of the Slavic personal name *Godslaw.*
GIVEN NAMES German 11%. *Helmut, Manfred, Ulrich.*

Gottshall (352) Americanized spelling of German GOTTSCHALK.

Gottstein (115) German and Swiss German: unexplained.
GIVEN NAME German 4%. *Fritz.*

Gottula (113) German: unexplained. In the 19th century, this name is recorded as common in Elpersheim, Württemberg.

Gottwald (287) Eastern German: from a medieval personal name composed of the elements *got* 'God' or *gōd* 'good' + *walt(an)* 'rule'.
GIVEN NAMES German 7%. *Hans* (3), *Armin, Fritz, Johannes, Kurt.*

Gotwalt (134) Americanized spelling of GOTTWALD.

Gotz (182) South German (also **Götz**): from a short form of the personal name GOTT-FRIED.
GIVEN NAMES German 5%. *Manfred, Otto, Viktor.*

Goubeaux (168) French: variant of GOBEL.

Goucher (511) **1.** English: nickname from Middle English *gode* 'good' + *chere* 'face' (Old French *chier*). **2.** Anglicized spelling of French GAUTHIER.

Goude (172) **1.** English: variant of GOOD. **2.** Dutch: metonymic occupational name for a goldsmith, from *goud* 'gold'.

Goudeau (540) French: **1.** from a personal name, a short form of the various Germanic compound names with the first element *gōd* 'good' or *god, got* 'god'. **2.** from a diminutive of Old French *gode,* in various dialects a term for a simpleton. This name is found chiefly in LA.
GIVEN NAMES French 4%. *Alphonse, Firmin, Marcel.*

Goudelock (129) **1.** Variant spelling of **Goudielock,** a Scottish surname of uncertain origin, presumably a nickname for someone with curly yellow hair. **2.** Jewish: Americanization of some Ashkenazic surname of similar sound or meaning.
GIVEN NAMES Jewish 5%. *Mendel, Miriam.*

Goudey (116) Scottish: variant of GOLDIE.

Goudie (310) Scottish: variant of GOLDIE.

Goudreau (502) Altered spelling of French GAUDREAU.
GIVEN NAMES French 11%. *Michel* (2), *Adrien, Andre, Aurore, Cecile, Chanel, Donat, Fernand, Germaine, Gilles, Jacques, Lucien.*

Goudy (801) Scottish: variant of GOLDIE.

Gouge (1005) English: variant of GOOCH, itself a variant of GOFF.

Gougeon (180) French: **1.** metonymic occupational name for maker or pegs or stakes, from *goujon* 'peg', 'stake'. **2.** nickname from the gudgeon, Old French *gougon* (Latin *gobio,* genitive *gobionis*).

The fish is considered easy to catch, and so the nickname may have denoted a greedy or gullible person.
FOREBEARS A bearer of the name Gougeon, from Poitou, was in Quebec city by 1686.
GIVEN NAMES French 7%. *Andre, Franck, Jacques.*

Gouger (205) Altered spelling of German GAUGER.

Gough (3302) **1.** Welsh: nickname for a red-haired person, from Welsh *coch* 'red'. **2.** Irish: reduced form of MCGOUGH.

Goughnour (172) Americanized form of German **Gauchenauer** (see GOCHENOUR).

Gouin (494) **1.** French: variant of GODIN. **2.** Breton: nickname for a person with fair hair or a light complexion, from *gwen* 'light', 'white', 'fair'. See also GWYNN.
FOREBEARS A bearer of the name Gouin, from Poitou, was in Trois Rivières, Quebec, by 1663.
GIVEN NAMES French 15%. *Normand* (4), *Andre* (2), *Emile* (2), *Francois* (2), *Michel* (2), *Zoel* (2), *Armand, Donat, Edline, Fernand, Gilles, Jean Charles.*

Gouker (312) **1.** Variant spelling of German GAUGER. **2.** Americanized spelling of French GAUTHIER.

Goulart (685) French: nickname for a glutton, from Old French *goule* 'throat' (Latin *gula*) + the pejorative suffix *-art.* This name is also established in Brazil.
GIVEN NAMES Spanish 16%. *Manuel* (28), *Jose* (12), *Carlos* (5), *Belmiro* (2), *Jorge* (2), *Aida, Alfredo, Alvarino, Alvaro, Ana, Cesar, Eduardo.*

Goularte (125) Altered spelling of French GOULART.

Goulas (103) Greek: nickname from the vocabulary word *goula* 'turnip', or else from Latin *gula* 'gullet'.
GIVEN NAMES Greek 9%. *Evagelos, Evangelos, Panagiotis, Pantelis.*

Gould (16172) English: variant of GOLD.

Goulden (272) English: variant of GOLDEN.

Goulder (138) English: variant of GOLDER.

Gouldin (103) English: variant of GOLDEN.

Goulding (819) English: from the late Old English personal name *Golding.*

Goulet (2258) French: nickname for a greedy or voracious man, from Old French *goulet* 'gullet', a diminutive of *goule* 'throat' (Latin *gula*). It may also be in part a topographic name for someone who lived by a narrow pass or defile.
FOREBEARS A family of this name, from Chartres, was in Quebec city in 1646 and in Château Richer in later years.
GIVEN NAMES French 14%. *Normand* (10), *Andre* (8), *Marcel* (6), *Lucien* (5), *Armand* (4), *Adrien* (3), *Benoit* (3), *Fernand* (3), *Jacques* (3), *Michel* (3), *Aime* (2), *Camille* (2).

Goulette (483) French Canadian spelling of GOULET.
GIVEN NAMES French 4%. *Arnaud, Calice, Emile, Marcel.*

Gounaris (104) Greek: occupational name for a furrier, from a derivative of *gouna* 'fur'.

GIVEN NAMES Greek 17%. *Anastasios, Andreas, Antonios, Constantinos, Dimitrios, Isidoros, Kostas, Spiros.*

Goupil (182) French: nickname for someone with red hair or for a cunning person, from Old French *goupil* 'fox', Late Latin *vulpiculus*, a diminutive of classical Latin *vulpes*, a distant cognate of WOLF. This was replaced as a vocabulary word during the Middle Ages by *renard*, originally a personal name. Compare REYNARD, the name borne by the fox in the popular beast tales.

FOREBEARS René Goupil, born in Angers, France, on May 13, 1608, arrived as a Jesuit priest in Canada in 1640, and was killed by the Iroquois in what is now NY in 1642. He was canonized on June 29, 1930. Another bearer of this name, from Normandy, was married in Quebec city in 1650.

GIVEN NAMES French 19%. *Normand* (4), *Andre, Dominique, Fernand, Julien, Leonce, Marcel.*

Gour (100) Indian (northern states): Hindu (Rajput) name, based on the name of a Rajput clan.

GIVEN NAME Indian 6%. *Mayank.*

Gourd (156) **1.** English: perhaps an occupational name for a maker of bottles or cups, from Old French *gourde* 'water vessel', 'flask', but possibly of the same derivation as 2. **2.** French: from Old French *gourd* 'heavy', 'dull', 'sluggish', hence a nickname for a slow lumbering person.

GIVEN NAMES French 7%. *Henri* (2), *Andre.*

Gourdin (133) French: nickname from Old French *gourdin* 'madman', 'fool'.

GIVEN NAMES French 7%; Jewish 4%. *Julien, Patrice; Aron, Miriam.*

Gourdine (180) French: from Old French *gourdine* 'woman of loose morals'.

Gourlay (259) Scottish: variant of GOURLEY.

Gourley (2369) Scottish: of uncertain origin; possibly a Norman habitational name from an unidentified place in Normandy or England.

Gourneau (104) French: perhaps a variant of **Gournay** (see GURNEY).

Gouse (141) Americanized spelling of German GAUS.

Gouthro (111) Americanized form of an uncertain original, perhaps Scottish GUTHRIE. This name is strongly associated with Nova Scotia.

Gouveia (733) Portuguese: habitational name from any of various places so called, in particular one in the province of Beira Baixa. The place name is first recorded in the Latin forms *Gaudela* and *Goudela*; it is of obscure origin.

GIVEN NAMES Spanish 14%; Portuguese 8%. *Manuel* (17), *Jose* (10), *Carlos* (4), *Alvaro*

(2), *Fernando* (2), *Luis* (2), *Marcos* (2), *Mario* (2), *Renato* (2), *Roberto* (2), *Altino, Americo; Paulo* (2), *Albano, Joao.*

Govan (619) Scottish: **1.** habitational name from Govan near Glasgow, first recorded c.1134 as *Guven*, possibly meaning 'place of the smith', although more recently a Cumbric word *gir* 'hill' has been suggested. **2.** from a reduced Anglicized form of Gaelic **Mac a'Ghobhainn** 'son of the smith', from *gobha* 'smith'.

FOREBEARS Christian, widow of Simon de Govane, held lands in Govan in 1293.

Gove (1124) Scottish (Inverness): variant of GOFF.

Govea (397) Variant of Portuguese GOUVEIA.

GIVEN NAMES Spanish 47%. *Jose* (11), *Juan* (6), *Carlos* (4), *Luis* (4), *Manuel* (4), *Adolfo* (3), *Benito* (3), *Francisco* (3), *Gerardo* (3), *Guadalupe* (3), *Jesus* (3), *Jorge* (3); *Antonio* (9), *Eliseo, Heriberto, Leonardo, Lucio, Marco.*

Goveia (99) Variant of Portuguese GOUVEIA.

Gover (787) English: most probably, as Reaney proposes, a variant of **Gofair**, a nickname from Middle English *go(n)* 'to go' (Old English *gān*) + *fair* 'lovely', 'quiet(ly)' (see FAIR).

Govern (130) Irish or Scottish: reduced form of McGOVERN.

Governale (262) Italian: possibly from Old Italian *governale* 'rudder', 'helm', probably applied as a metonymic occupational name for a helmsman or for a guide.

GIVEN NAMES Italian 12%. *Angelo* (2), *Carlo, Carmela, Franco, Saverio, Vincenzo.*

Governor (110) American English: occupational name for a member of the household of a governor.

Govero (113) Origin unidentified. This name is strongly associated with MO.

Govert (136) German: from a Germanic personal name, a variant of GOTTFRIED.

Govier (142) English (Devon): unexplained. It may be a variant of GOVER, but early examples with a definite article, e.g. Richard le Gofiar (Somerset 1327), point to an origin as an occupational name or perhaps a nickname, from an unknown element.

Govoni (341) Italian: **1.** habitational name from Govone, a place in Cuneo province, Piedmont. **2.** in northern Italy, from a short form of IACOVONE.

GIVEN NAMES Italian 5%. *Caesar* (2), *Aldo, Angelo, Antonio, Deno, Dino, Gildo, Guido, Licinio, Quinto.*

Gow (751) Scottish: occupational name from Gaelic *gobha* 'smith'.

Gowan (1207) **1.** Irish (Cavan): reduced Anglicized form of Gaelic **Ó Gobhann** 'descendant of the smith'. **2.** Scottish and Irish: shortened form of McGOWAN or from the genitive (*gobhainn*) of *gobhan* 'smith'. In Ireland (in the south, especial-

ly), these names were also translated as SMITH.

Gowans (337) Scottish: variant of McGOWAN 'son of the smith', in which the Gaelic patronymic prefix *Mac* has been replaced by the English patronymic suffix *-s*.

Goward (111) English (East Anglia): **1.** derivative of GOFF. **2.** variant of COWARD.

Gowder (117) Perhaps an Americanized spelling of German **Gauder**, a nickname for a braggart or wastrel, from an agent derivative of Middle High German *giuden* 'to brag or squander'.

Gowdy (775) **1.** Northern Irish: variant of GOLDIE. **2.** Possibly an Americanized spelling of **Gaude**, an eastern German name under Slavic influence, or of German **Gaudig**, a nickname for a waster, from Middle High German *giudec* 'wasteful'.

Gowell (214) English: presumably a nickname for an habitual user of the expression 'Go well' (Old English *gān* 'go' + *wel* 'well'), or possibly a nickname for a messenger.

Gowen (1313) **1.** Scottish or Irish: reduced and altered spelling of McGOWAN. **2.** English (East Anglia): variant of GOWING.

Gowens (344) Scottish: variant spelling of GOWANS.

Gower (2587) **1.** English (of Norman origin): regional name for someone from the district north of Paris known in Old French as *Gohiere*. **2.** English (of Norman origin): habitational name from any of the various places in northern France called Gouy (from the Gallo-Roman personal name *Gaudius* + the locative suffix *-acum*), with the addition of the Anglo-Norman French suffix *-er*. **3.** English: from a Norman personal name, *Go(h)ier*, cognate with the Old English name mentioned at GOODER. **4.** Welsh: from the peninsula in southern Wales, of which the Welsh name is *Gŵyr*. **5.** Probably an Americanized spelling of German GAUER.

Gowers (118) Irish: variant of GOWER.

GIVEN NAME Irish 4%. *Liam.*

Gowin (599) **1.** English: variant of GOWING. **2.** variant of Scottish or Irish GOWAN.

Gowing (297) **1.** English: from a Middle English personal name, *Gowin*, from Old French *Gouin*, a variant of GODIN. **2.** Irish: variant of GOWAN.

Gowins (172) **1.** Variant of English GOWING. **2.** Variant of Scottish GOWANS.

Gowland (130) English: habitational name from Gowlands in Moor Monkton, West Yorkshire.

Goy (145) **1.** French: from the Old French word *goi* (Latin *gubia*) denoting a type of bill hook or knife used by vine-growers or coopers, hence possibly a metonymic occupational name for a maker or user of such implements. **2.** English (of Norman origin): habitational name from any of various places in France named Gouy, for example in Aisne or Pas-de-Calais. **3.** Galician: probably a habitational name from Goy in Lugo province, Galicia. **4.** German: north-western variant of GAU.

GIVEN NAMES French 5%. *Andre, Jacques.*

Goya (177) **1.** Japanese: found mostly in the Ryūkyū Islands, this name is usually written with characters meaning 'barbarian room' or 'give room'. **2.** Basque: variant of **Goia**, a topographic name from Basque *goi* 'upper part' + the definite article *-a*. **3.** Galician: habitational name from Goya in Lugo province, Galicia.

GIVEN NAMES Japanese 25%; Spanish 5%. *Hideo* (2), *Chiyo, Fumio, Kameko, Kazuo, Keiji, Kimie, Masafumi, Masanari, Nobuhiko, Ryuji, Sadao; Adolfo* (2), *Alberto, Augusto, Carlos, Ernesto, Francisco, Jorge, Juan, Miguel, Nestor, Ramon.*

Goyal (281) Indian: variant of GOEL.

GIVEN NAMES Indian 94%. *Ashok* (6), *Ajay* (5), *Amit* (5), *Madan* (5), *Prem* (5), *Anil* (4), *Meera* (4), *Raj* (4), *Ramesh* (4), *Subhash* (4), *Vinod* (4), *Dinesh* (3).

Goyen (123) English (Cornwall): unexplained. Compare GOYNE.

Goyer (346) **1.** French: occupational name for a maker of bill hooks or vine knives, from an agent derivative of *goy* (GOY). **2.** Dutch: habitational name for someone from Het Gooi area of the Netherlands. This is a common name in the Albany area, as many settlers came from that area. **3.** Possibly an Americanized spelling of German **Geuer**, a variant of GAUER.

GIVEN NAMES French 8%. *Andre* (2), *Francois, Gilles, Jacques, Jean Claude, Luc, Mireille, Pierrette, Thierry.*

Goyette (1247) Variant of French **Guyet** (see GUYETTE).

GIVEN NAMES French 12%. *Normand* (6), *Armand* (5), *Marcel* (5), *Aime* (3), *Emile* (3), *Philippe* (3), *Martial* (2), *Monique* (2), *Raoul* (2), *Alain, Alcide, Alexandre.*

Goyne (250) **1.** English (Cornwall): unexplained. **2.** Irish: perhaps a variant of COYNE. **3.** Possibly also a variant spelling of French GOUIN.

Goynes (174) English: unexplained. Compare GOYNE, GOINES.

Goza (649) Origin unidentified.

Grab (395) **1.** Polish: topographic name from Polish *grab* 'hornbeam'. **2.** German: topographic name, from Middle High German *grabe(n)* 'ditch', '(track alongside a) moat'. This name is also found in the German-speaking part of Switzerland.

GIVEN NAMES German 4%. *Otto* (2), *Markus.*

Grabarek (101) Polish: occupational name from a diminutive of *grabarz* 'grave digger'.

GIVEN NAMES Polish 11%. *Casimir, Jadwiga, Jaroslaw, Stanislaus.*

Grabau (303) Eastern German: habitational name from any of several places in northern

and eastern Germany named with Sorbian *grab* 'hornbeam'. Compare GRABOW.

GIVEN NAMES German 4%. *Gerhardt, Hans, Otto.*

Grabb (103) Altered form of North German KRABBE.

Grabbe (182) North German variant of KRABBE.

Grabe (231) German: topographic name for someone who lived by a dike or ditch (see GRAB), or habitational name from either of two places in Thuringia named with this word: Grabe and Graba.

GIVEN NAMES German 5%. *Arno, Ernst, Klaus, Ulrich.*

Grabel (195) **1.** South German: variant of GRABLE. **2.** Possibly also an Americanized spelling of Swiss German **Krähbühl** (see GRAYBILL).

Graben (145) German: variant of GRAB 2.

Grabenstein (140) German: **1.** topographic name from Middle High German *grabe(n)* 'ditch', '(track alongside a) moat' + *stein* 'rock'. **2.** habitational name from Grafenstein near Wohlau, Silesia.

GIVEN NAMES German 5%. *Albrecht, Erwin, Kurt.*

Graber (3384) **1.** German: from an agent derivative of Middle High German *graben* 'to dig or excavate', hence an occupational name for a digger of graves or ditches, or an engraver of seals. This name is also found in the German-speaking part of Switzerland. **2.** Jewish (Ashkenazic): occupational name for a grave-digger, either from German *Gräber* or from a Yiddishized form of Polish *grabarz*.

Grabert (247) German: **1.** (also **Gräbert**): variant of GRABER. **2.** nickname for someone with gray hair, from Middle High German *grā(w)*, Middle Low German *grāw*.

Grabiec (133) Polish: occupational name from an agent derivative of *grabić* 'to rake up', also 'to plunder'.

GIVEN NAMES Polish 15%. *Zbigniew* (3), *Stanislaw* (2), *Henryk, Jacek.*

Grabill (470) Americanized spelling of Swiss German **Kräh(en)bühl** (see GRAYBILL).

Grabinski (250) Polish (**Grabiński**): habitational name for someone from any of the numerous places throughout Poland called Grabin, Grabina, or Grabiny, all named with *grab* 'hornbeam'.

GIVEN NAMES Polish 10%. *Janusz* (3), *Boleslaw, Eugeniusz, Ewa, Jadwiga, Lech, Wojciech.*

Grable (1136) South German (**Gräble**): occupational name for a grave or ditch digger, from an agent noun from Middle High German *graben* 'ditch'; in some cases the name may be topographic, denoting someone who lived by a ditch.

Grabner (266) **1.** German: topographic name from Middle High German *graben* 'ditch', 'moat' or a habitational name from a place named with this word, the *-er* suffix

denoting an inhabitant. **2.** German (**Gräbner**): variant of GRABER. **3.** Slovenian (eastern Slovenia): topographic name from a derivative of *graben* 'small ravine', a German borrowing that replaced the Slovenian word *grapa* with the same meaning.

GIVEN NAMES German 8%. *Helmut* (2), *Kurt* (2), *Math, Viktor.*

Graboski (185) Variant of Polish and German GRABOWSKI.

Grabow (671) Eastern German: topographic name for someone living by a hornbeam, Slavic *grab*, or habitational name from a place named with this word.

Grabowski (3302) Polish, Jewish (eastern Ashkenazic), and eastern German: habitational name from any of various places named with Slavic *grab* 'hornbeam' (the wood which was used for making yokes), for example Grabów, Grabowa, Grabowo.

GIVEN NAMES Polish 6%. *Zbigniew* (6), *Stanislaw* (4), *Tadeusz* (4), *Andrzej* (3), *Casimir* (3), *Grzegorz* (3), *Jerzy* (3), *Leszek* (3), *Jacek* (2), *Janusz* (2), *Walenty* (2), *Alicja.*

Grabski (220) Polish: habitational name from any of various places called Grab, Graby, or Grabia, from *grab* 'hornbeam'.

GIVEN NAMES Polish 9%. *Casimir, Kazimierz, Krystyna, Tomasz, Zbigniew.*

Graca (146) Portuguese (**Graça**): from a short form of the religious epithet *da Graça* meaning 'of mercy', from *graça* 'grace', 'mercy'.

GIVEN NAMES Portuguese 14%; Spanish 14%; Dutch 4%; Italian 4%. *Joao* (3); *Adriano* (2), *Ana* (2), *Carlos* (2), *Jose* (2), *Manuel* (2), *Mario* (2), *Amancio, Julio, Pedro, Teo; Helder* (2); *Antonio* (5).

Grace (9496) English: **1.** nickname from Middle English, Old French *grace* 'charm', 'pleasantness' (Latin *gratia*). **2.** from the female personal name *Grace*, which was popular in the Middle Ages. This seems in the first instance to have been from a Germanic element *grīs* 'gray' (see GRICE 1), but was soon associated by folk etymology with the Latin word meaning 'charm'.

Graceffa (145) Southern Italian: unexplained.

GIVEN NAMES Italian 25%. *Alfio* (3), *Sal* (3), *Carlo* (2), *Salvatore* (2), *Angelo, Carmelo, Francesco, Gerlando, Pietro, Salavatore, Stefano.*

Gracey (764) English: variant of GRACE.

Graci (202) Southern Italian: unexplained.

GIVEN NAMES Italian 35%. *Angelo* (15), *Salvatore* (7), *Sal* (3), *Carmel* (2), *Gino* (2), *Carmela, Carmelo, Carmine, Giovanna, Giuseppe, Stefano.*

Gracia (1059) Spanish and Catalan (**Gràcia**): from a short form of the religious epithet *da Gracia* meaning 'of mercy', from *gracia* 'grace', 'mercy'.

GIVEN NAMES Spanish 41%. *Jose* (29), *Carlos* (9), *Juan* (9), *Manuel* (9), *Francisco* (8),

Jesus (8), *Luis* (8), *Guadalupe* (6), *Mario* (6), *Pedro* (6), *Javier* (5), *Jorge* (5).

Graciano (193) Spanish and Portuguese: from the personal name *Graciano*, from the Roman name *Gratianus*.

GIVEN NAMES Spanish 53%. *Jose* (5), *Juan* (4), *Alfredo* (3), *Carlos* (3), *Francisco* (3), *Manuel* (3), *Ruben* (3), *Jesus* (2), *Julio* (2), *Margarita* (2), *Miguel* (2), *Ramon* (2).

Gracie (326) **1.** Scottish: variant of GRASS 3. **2.** English: variant of GRACE.

Gracy (226) Respelling of GRACIE.

Gracyalny (104) Polish (**Gracjalny**): nickname from the adjective *gracjalny* 'gracious', 'full of grace'.

Graczyk (603) Polish: from *graczyk* 'player', diminutive of *gracz*, an agent noun from *grać* 'to play', in various senses: to play cards or to play a musical instrument, hence a nickname for a gambler or musician.

GIVEN NAMES Polish 6%. *Zigmund* (2), *Andrzej*, *Casimir*, *Grazyna*, *Grzegorz*, *Jacek*, *Jadwiga*, *Miroslawa*, *Ryszard*, *Zbigniew*, *Zofia*.

Grad (391) **1.** Slovenian: topographic name from *grad* 'castle'. **2.** Possibly also a Slovenian and Polish nickname from the obsolete noun *grad* 'hail' (in the sense 'precipitation'). **3.** German: borrowing of 1 or alternatively a nickname either from Middle High German *grātac* 'greedy' or, in the south, from Middle High German *gerāde* 'swift', 'skillful'. **4.** Jewish (Ashkenazic): ornamental name from German *gerade* 'upright'.

GIVEN NAMES Jewish 4%. *Emanuel*, *Miriam*, *Shraga*, *Yonatan*.

Graddick (111) **1.** English: unexplained; perhaps a variant of **Craddick**, itself a variant of CRADDOCK. **2.** German: possibly an Americanized form of **Gredig**, a habitational name from a place named Greding in Bavaria, or a nickname for a greedy person, related to Old High German *grātag* 'greedy'.

GIVEN NAME French 4%. *Arianne*.

Graddy (509) Irish (Munster): reduced Anglicized form of Gaelic **Ó Greada**, possibly from *greid* 'champion' (genitive *greada*).

Grade (212) German and Jewish (Ashkenazic): variant of GRAD.

GIVEN NAMES German 5%. *Hans*, *Kurt*, *Lothar*, *Reinhold*.

Gradel (147) German: **1.** (also **Grädel**): variant of GRAD. **2.** (Bavaria and Austria): topographic name for someone living on a ridge or terrace, from Middle High German *grāt* 'step', 'ridge'.

Graden (265) Scottish: habitational name from the lands of Graden in Berwickshire.

Grader (100) **1.** South German: topographic name for someone who lived on or by terraced land, from a noun derivative of Middle High German *grāt* 'step' (Latin

gradus) (see GRADERT). **2.** Dutch: unexplained.

Gradert (101) South German and Danish: possibly a topographic name for someone who lived on terraced land, from *grad* 'terrace', or a nickname for a skillful person, from Middle High German *gerāt* 'swift', 'dexterous', 'efficient' + the strong adjective ending *-er* + inorganic *-t*.

Gradin (106) **1.** Swedish: unexplained. **2.** German: unexplained. **3.** English: unexplained.

Gradney (169) Origin unidentified.

GIVEN NAMES French 8%. *Curley*, *Easton*, *Prosper*.

Grado (242) **1.** Asturian-Leonese and Aragonese: Castilianized form of **Grau**, a habitational name from Grau (Asturies) or Lo Grau (Uesca, Aragon). **2.** Italian: possibly from a variant of the omen name *Grado* or from a short form of a compound name formed with this element, or alternatively a habitational name from a place called Grado. See DE GRADO.

GIVEN NAMES Spanish 36%; Italian 6%. *Jose* (6), *Ramon* (4), *Miguel* (3), *Jesus* (2), *Juan* (2), *Juana* (2), *Mario* (2), *Marta* (2), *Alfonso*, *Alonzo*, *Amador*, *Ana Maria*; *Angelo*, *Eligio*, *Fausto*, *Federico*, *Lorenzo*, *Marco*, *Salvatore*.

Gradowski (107) Polish: habitational name for someone from a place called Gradowo in Włocławek voivodeship.

Gradwell (123) **1.** English (mainly Lancashire): **2.** Probably an Americanized form of German GRATHWOHL.

Gradwohl (135) German: variant of GRATHWOHL.

GIVEN NAMES French 4%. *Armand*, *Lucien*.

Grady (9312) Irish: **1.** (Munster and Connacht) reduced Anglicized form of Gaelic **Ó Gráda** 'descendant of *Gráda*', a byname meaning 'noble' (see O'GRADY). **2.** reduced Anglicized form of Gaelic **Mag Bhrádaigh** (see McGRADY).

Graeber (609) German (**Gräber**): see GRABER 1.

GIVEN NAMES German 5%. *Kurt* (2), *Fritz*, *Helmut*, *Hermann*, *Ralf*, *Ulrich*, *Winfried*.

Graebner (172) German (**Gräbner**): variant of GRABNER.

GIVEN NAMES German 4%. *Erwin*, *Kurt*.

Graef (663) Dutch and North German: status name for the chairman of a town council. Compare GRAF.

GIVEN NAMES German 10%. *Egon* (2), *Lothar* (2), *Otto* (2), *Armin*, *Claus*, *Erwin*, *Franz*, *Friedrich*, *Hans*, *Helmut*, *Hermann*, *Jochen*.

Graefe (202) German (Rhine-Westphalia): variant of GRAF 1.

GIVEN NAMES German 8%. *Armin*, *Arno*, *Goetz*, *Horst*, *Johannes*.

Graeff (493) Variant spelling of Dutch and North German GRAEF.

Graeser (142) German (**Gräser**): variant of the topographic name GRAS, the *-er* suffix denoting an inhabitant.

Graesser (131) Swiss German: variant of GRASSER 2.

Graessle (170) **1.** Americanized spelling of German **Gräss(e)l**, a diminutive of GRASS 1. **2.** South German (**Grässle**): nickname for a greedy person, from Old High German *grātag* 'greedy'.

GIVEN NAMES German 4%. *Horst*, *Otto*.

Graeter (128) German: occupational name for a worker or overseer in a granary or warehouse, from an agent derivative of Middle High German *grede* 'warehouse', 'municipal granary'.

GIVEN NAMES German 6%. *Beate*, *Erwin*, *Helmut*.

Graetz (200) German (**Grätz**): see GRATZ.

GIVEN NAME German 4%. *Helmut*.

Graeve (147) Dutch (**de Graeve**) and North German: variant of GRAEF.

Graf (5840) **1.** German: status name from Middle High German *grāve*, *grābe*, which was used as a title denoting various more or less aristocratic dignitaries and officials. In later times it became established as a title of nobility equivalent to the Romance count. The vocabulary word also denoted a variety of different minor local functionaries in different parts of Germany. In the Grand Duchy of Hesse, for example, it was used for the holder of the comparatively humble office of village headman. Compare MAYER, SCHULTZ, and VOGT. The surname could have originated from any of these senses or be an occupational name for a servant or retainer of a count, or a nickname for someone who gave himself airs and graces. **2.** Variant spelling of Dutch GRAEF. **3.** Jewish (Ashkenazic): ornamental name selected, like HERZOG and other words denoting titles, because of their aristocratic connotations.

GIVEN NAMES German 5%. *Hans* (10), *Kurt* (9), *Otto* (7), *Erwin* (5), *Ernst* (4), *Fritz* (4), *Gerhard* (4), *Hermann* (4), *Horst* (4), *Manfred* (3), *Udo* (3), *Alois* (2).

Grafe (287) German: Rhineland variant of GRAF.

GIVEN NAMES German 5%. *Fritz* (2), *Ralf*.

Graff (5325) **1.** German (also **Gräff**), Dutch, and Jewish (Ashkenazic): variant of GRAF. **2.** English: metonymic occupational name for a clerk or scribe, from Anglo-Norman French *grafe* 'quill', 'pen' (a derivative of *grafer* 'to write', Late Latin *grafare*, from Greek *graphein*).

Graffam (251) English: habitational name from Graffham in Sussex or Grafham in Cambridgeshire, so named from Old English *grāf* 'grove' + *hām* 'homestead', 'manor' or *hamm* 'enclosure hemmed in by water'.

Graffeo (355) Southern Italian: variant spelling of **Grafeo**, an occupational name, from Greek *grapheus* 'scribe'.

GIVEN NAMES Italian 16%. *Salvatore* (7), *Angelo* (3), *Carlo, Ignazio, Luciano, Salvato, Veto, Vita.*

Graffis (122) Latinized form of German GRAF or Dutch GRAEF.

Graffius (194) Latinized form of German GRAF or Dutch GRAEF.

Graft (341) Dutch: **1.** habitational name from either of two places so named, in North Holland and Zeeland. **2.** variant of **Gracht**, a topographic name for someone who lived by a canal in a city, Dutch *gracht.*

Grafton (1282) English: habitational name from any of the numerous places so named from Old English *grāf* 'grove' + *tūn* 'enclosure', 'settlement'.

Grage (228) North German form of GRAU 1.
GIVEN NAMES German 4%. *Hans* (2), *Kurt, Theodor.*

Gragert (159) North German: nickname for someone with gray hair from a derivative of Middle Low German *grāge* 'gray'. The term later came to denote a 'gray monk' or an old horse, and it is possible that the nickname arose from either of these meanings.

Gragg (1967) **1.** English: possibly a variant of CRAGG. **2.** Probably a respelling of German **Grag**, a nickname for a person with gray hair, from Middle Low German *grāge* 'gray'. This name is found predominantly in NC.

Graham (69312) Scottish and English: habitational name from Grantham in Lincolnshire, recorded in Domesday Book as *Graham* (as well as *Grantham, Grandham,* and *Granham*). See also GRANTHAM.
FOREBEARS The surname Graham is now most common in Scotland and northern Ireland. It was taken to Scotland at the beginning of the 12th century by the Norman baron William de Graham, holder of the manor in Lincolnshire, from whom many if not all modern bearers are probably descended.

Grahame (113) Scottish and English: variant spelling of GRAHAM.

Grahek (257) Slovenian: from a diminutive of *grah* 'pea', hence a nickname for a small man or an occupational name for a grower of peas.

Grahl (297) German: habitational name for someone from Graal in Mecklenburg.
GIVEN NAMES German 5%. *Friedrich* (2), *Kurt.*

Grahm (107) English and Scottish: reduced form of GRAHAM.

Grahn (584) **1.** Eastern German (under Slavic influence): perhaps a habitational name from such places as Granow, Grana, and Gran. **2.** North German (**Grä(h)n**): a North German variant of **Grün** (see GRUEN). **3.** Swedish: ornamental spelling of *gran* 'spruce'. This may be an ornamental name, a topographic name, or possibly a habitational name from a place called Gran.
GIVEN NAMES Scandinavian 6%. *Gunhild, Lars.*

Grahovac (105) Serbian and Croatian: habitational name for someone from any of numerous places named Grahovo, named with *grah* 'beans'.
GIVEN NAMES South Slavic 12%. *Milan* (2), *Jure, Milos, Zlatko.*

Graichen (144) German: habitational name for someone from Graicha in Thuringia.
GIVEN NAMES German 7%. *Claus, Gunther.*

Grainger (1565) English: variant spelling of GRANGER.

Grajales (140) Spanish (common in Mexico): unexplained.
GIVEN NAMES Spanish 48%. *Jose* (3), *Marcos* (3), *Carlos* (2), *Francisco* (2), *Juan* (2), *Loida* (2), *Manuel* (2), *Tomas* (2), *Adiela, Alba, Ana, Andres.*

Grajeda (414) Spanish: from *grajo* 'rook', hence a topograpic name for someone who lived by a rookery or in a place frequented by rooks.
GIVEN NAMES Spanish 48%. *Jose* (14), *Carlos* (7), *Juan* (7), *Manuel* (6), *Roberto* (6), *Javier* (5), *Arturo* (4), *Mario* (4), *Miguel* (4), *Pedro* (4), *Raul* (4), *Alfredo* (3).

Grajek (115) Polish (also found as a German surname in the Ruhr): unexplained.

Grajewski (117) Polish: habitational name for someone from a place called Grajewo, in Łomża voivodeship.
GIVEN NAMES Polish 11%. *Franciszek, Jerzy, Mariusz, Wojciech, Zdzislaw.*

Grala (105) Polish (also **Grała**): occupational nickname for a musician, from *grać* 'to play a musical instrument'.
GIVEN NAMES Polish 7%. *Bronislaw, Jolanta.*

Graley (203) **1.** English: variant of GREELEY. **2.** Possibly an Americanized form of German GREULICH.

Grall (298) German: nickname for an irascible person, from Middle High German *gral* 'angry', 'furious'.

Gralla (108) Jewish (from Poland): occupational name from Polish *grala* 'musician'.
GIVEN NAMES Jewish 10%; German 4%. *Isser, Izaak, Meyer, Simcha; Heinz.*

Gram (532) **1.** Danish: habitational name from any of several farmsteads named Gram, from *grāt* 'gray' + Old Danish *hēm* 'farmstead'. **2.** South German: nickname for an irascible man, from Middle High German *gram* 'angry'.
GIVEN NAMES Scandinavian 5%. *Anders, Erik, Hilmar, Holger, Maren.*

Gramajo (137) Spanish (common in Guatemala and Argentina): unexplained.
GIVEN NAMES Spanish 49%. *Armando* (2), *Jesus* (2), *Jose* (2), *Juan* (2), *Luis* (2), *Aida, Alfredo, Amado, Andres, Artemio, Camilo, Carlos.*

Gramann (117) German: nickname for an irascible man, from Middle High German *gram* 'angry' + *man* 'man', or for a gray-haired person, from Middle Low German *grā.*
GIVEN NAME German 4%. *Wolfgang.*

Grambo (131) Norwegian: habitational name from a farmstead so named in Trysil, of unknown etymology.

Gramer (232) German: **1.** (also **Grämer**): variant of KRAMER. **2.** variant of GRABNER. **3.** from a personal name from Germanic *hramn, hrafn, hraban* 'raven'.
GIVEN NAMES German 5%. *Gerhard, Ingeborg, Kurt.*

Grames (193) Possibly an altered spelling of German **Gramm(e)s**, from a short form of the personal name *Hieronymus.*

Gramke (107) German: habitational name from Gramke in Lower Saxony or Grambke near Bremen.

Gramley (146) Americanized form of German **Grämmle**, a Swabian variant of GRAMLICH.

Gramlich (625) German (also **Grämlich**): nickname for an irascible person, from Middle High German *gramelich, gremlich* 'angry'.

Gramling (760) Altered spelling of German GRAMLICH.

Gramm (402) **1.** German: habitational name from a place so called in Schleswig. **2.** South German: variant of GRAM.

Grammatico (140) Italian and Greek (**Grammatikos**): from Greek *grammatikos* 'scholar', 'clerk', 'record keeper', hence an occupational name or, in Italian, sometimes a nickname applied to a studious person.
GIVEN NAMES Italian 16%. *Cosimo, Domenic, Fedele, Natale, Salvatore, Santino, Vincenzo.*

Grammer (1267) **1.** English: occupational name for a scholar or astrologer, from Old French *gramaire* 'grammarian', 'scholar', also 'astrologer'. **2.** German: variant of GRAMER.

Grams (1325) **1.** Probably an Americanized form of a Polish or eastern German (Sorbian) nickname meaning 'one who limps'. Compare Polish GRAMZA. **2.** German: from a reduced form of the personal name *Hieronymus.*

Gramse (108) Eastern German: of Slavic origin; see GRAMS.

Gramza (200) Polish: nickname for shambling person, from the dialect word *gramza* 'shambling'.
GIVEN NAMES Polish 4%. *Ludwik, Zygmund.*

Gran (626) **1.** Swedish: ornamental surname from *gran* 'Norway spruce', adopted in the 19th century. This belongs to the large class of ornamental surnames taken from natural features of the landscape. **2.** German: habitational name from Gran in Hungary. **3.** German (**Grän**): variant of GREIN.
GIVEN NAMES Scandinavian 5%. *Erik* (3), *Nils* (2), *Helmer, Lennart, Thor.*

Grana (351) **1.** Galician (**Graña**): habitational name from any of the numerous places in Galicia named Graña. **2.** Italian: habitational name from Grana in Asti province.

GIVEN NAMES Spanish 19%; Italian 8%. *Juan* (5), *Adolfo* (4), *Jose* (4), *Faustino* (2), *Generosa* (2), *Gilberto* (2), *Luis* (2), *Alejandro, Andres, Bernardo, Blanca, Concepcion; Antonio* (2), *Ciro* (2), *Romeo* (2), *Domenic, Leonardo, Neno, Nicolo, Salvatore.*

Granada (123) Spanish: habitational name from the city of Granada in southern Spain.
GIVEN NAMES Spanish 26%. *Rodrigo* (2), *Alvaro, Argentina, Carlos, Carmelita, Eduardo, Elvira, Erlinda, Luis, Mario, Marta, Miguel.*

Granade (198) Altered form of Spanish GRANADA.
FOREBEARS This spelling and the variant **Grenade** are borne by descendants of a Spanish Moorish family who established themselves in Brussels in the 16th century. Some members of the family moved to the Palatinate, and emigrated from there to NC.

Granado (655) Spanish and Portuguese: **1.** nickname from Spanish *granado* 'mature', 'experienced', 'distinguished'. **2.** topographic name or metonymic occupational name for a grower or seller of pomegranates, from *granado* 'pomegranate tree', Latin *(pomum) granatum* (see GARNETT 1).
GIVEN NAMES Spanish 44%. *Jose* (13), *Manuel* (12), *Juan* (6), *Domingo* (5), *Francisco* (5), *Arturo* (4), *Guadalupe* (4), *Jesus* (4), *Pedro* (4), *Ruben* (4), *Concepcion* (3), *Ignacio* (3).

Granados (1706) Spanish: topographic name from the plural of *granado* 'pomegranate tree' (see GRANADO 2).
GIVEN NAMES Spanish 53%. *Jose* (60), *Juan* (31), *Manuel* (30), *Carlos* (20), *Ramon* (17), *Luis* (15), *Pedro* (15), *Jorge* (13), *Mario* (13), *Jesus* (12), *Francisco* (11), *Miguel* (9).

Granahan (228) Irish: reduced form of McGRANAHAN, an Anglicized form of Irish Gaelic *Mac Reannacháin* 'son of *Reannachán*'.
GIVEN NAME Irish 7%. *Brendan.*

Granat (318) **1.** Swedish: soldier's name from *granat* 'grenade', 'shell'. **2.** Polish and Jewish (eastern Ashkenazic): from *granat* meaning 'pomegranate' in Polish and 'garnet' in Yiddish; a nickname in Poish and an ornamental name in Yiddish. **3.** Southern French: from Old French *granat*, originally 'pomegranate', later 'garnet' and hence a metonymic occupational name for a jeweler or dealer in semiprecious stones. **4.** French: from the past participle of *granar* 'to provide with seeds'; an indirect occupational name for a prosperous farmer.
GIVEN NAMES Polish 5%; Jewish 4%. *Zbigniew* (2), *Aniela, Zigmund; Meyer.*

Granata (699) Italian: **1.** from *granata* 'pomegranate', hence a metonymic occupational name for a grower or seller of the fruit, or a nickname for someone with red hair or a red complexion. **2.** habitational name from a locality so named in Santa Maria del Cedro, in Cosenza province. **3.** habitational name from the Spanish city of Granada, *Granata* in Italian.
GIVEN NAMES Italian 15%. *Angelo* (5), *Domenic* (4), *Sal* (3), *Attilio* (2), *Dino* (2), *Giuseppe* (2), *Antonio, Biagio, Carlo, Carmelo, Delio, Enrico.*

Granath (157) Swedish: variant spelling of GRANAT.
GIVEN NAMES Scandinavian 9%; German 5%. *Lars* (2), *Erik; Fritz, Kurt.*

Granato (511) Italian: metonymic occupational name for a jeweler or lapidary, from *granato* 'garnet'.
GIVEN NAMES Italian 11%. *Salvatore* (4), *Rocco* (3), *Sal* (3), *Carmine* (2), *Pasquale* (2), *Girolamo, Guido, Ippolito, Santo.*

Granberg (408) **1.** Swedish: ornamental name composed of the elements *gran* 'spruce' + *berg* 'mountain', 'hill'. **2.** Norwegian: habitational name from any of several farmsteads so named, from *gran* 'spruce' + *berg* 'hill'.
GIVEN NAMES Scandinavian 11%; German 4%. *Lars* (2), *Elof, Erik, Mauritz, Nils, Pontus; Kurt* (3).

Granberry (552) Probably an Americanized spelling of GRANBERG.

Granby (104) English: habitational name from a place in Nottinghamshire named Granby, from the Old Norse personal name *Grani* + *bý* 'farmstead'.

Grand (702) **1.** French and English (East Anglia): variant of GRANT. **2.** German: topographic name for someone who lived in a gravelly area, from Middle Low German *grand* 'coarse gravel'. **3.** German: nickname from a southern word of uncertain origin meaning 'frustration', 'anger', 'ire'. **4.** Danish: nickname from *grand* 'pure'.

Granda (435) Asturian-Leonese and Galician: habitational name from any of various places in Asturies and Galicia named with *granda* 'rocky plain', 'scrub-covered upland with poor soil' (from pre-Roman *gándara*).
GIVEN NAMES Spanish 39%. *Jose* (17), *Manuel* (7), *Julio* (6), *Angel* (5), *Luis* (4), *Orlando* (4), *Ramon* (4), *Francisco* (3), *Miguel* (3), *Benigno* (2), *Blanca* (2), *Carlos* (2).

Grandberry (337) Probably an Americanized form of Norwegian and Swedish GRANBERG.

Grandbois (149) French: topographic name from *grand* 'large' + *bois* ' wood', 'copse'.
GIVEN NAMES French 19%. *Andre* (2), *Marcell* (2), *Yvon* (2), *Amedee, Laurent, Lucien.*

Grandchamp (163) French: topographic name from *grand* 'large' + *champ* 'field'.
GIVEN NAMES French 8%. *Celina, Jean-Luc, Luc.*

Grande (1877) **1.** Italian, Spanish, and Portuguese: nickname for someone of large stature, in either a literal or figurative sense, from *grande* 'tall', 'large'. **2.** German: habitational name from Grande in Holstein or Grand in Bavaria. **3.** Norwegian: habitational name from any of several farmsteads so named, from Old Norse *grandi* 'sandbank'.
GIVEN NAMES Italian 22%; Spanish 8%. *Angelo* (11), *Salvatore* (9), *Rocco* (8), *Domenic* (6), *Mario* (6), *Antonio* (5), *Santo* (4), *Orlando* (3), *Americo* (2), *Carmine* (2), *Gennaro* (2), *Luigi* (2), *Pasquale* (2), *Saverio* (2), *Alberico; Jose* (10), *Carlos* (7), *Alicia* (4), *Ricardo* (4), *Jorge* (3), *Juan* (3), *Raul* (3), *Angel* (2), *Atilio* (2).

Granderson (271) Variant of English or Scottish GRANDISON.

Grandfield (219) Americanized form of the French topographic names GRANDCHAMP or GRANDPRE.

Grandi (155) Italian: patronymic or plural form of GRANDE.
GIVEN NAMES Italian 15%. *Elio* (3), *Dante* (2), *Dino, Geno, Pietro.*

Grandin (164) **1.** French: from a diminutive of GRAND. See also GRANT. **2.** Italian: from a derivative of GRANDE. **3.** English: possibly a variant of **Crandon** or **Craden** (see GRANDON).

Grandinetti (307) Italian: plural of **Grandinetto**, a patronymic from a diminutive of GRANDE.
GIVEN NAMES Italian 9%. *Angelo* (2), *Aldo, Antonio, Carmin, Domenic, Guido, Martino.*

Grandison (332) English and Scottish: said to be a habitational name from Granson on Lake Neuchâtel. The first known bearer of the surname is Rigaldus de Grancione (*fl.* 1040). The name was taken to Britain by Otes de Grandison (died 1328) and his brother. They were among a group of Savoyards who settled in England when Henry III married a granddaughter of the Count of Savoy.

Grandjean (148) French: from French *grand* 'tall', 'large' + *Jean* (French equivalent of JOHN), hence a nickname ('Big John'), or a distinguishing name for the older of two bearers of the same personal name. As a nickname it may have been applied in a literal or ironical sense, or as a means of distinguishing between members of the same family with a common personal name. This is a common name in Switzerland, and in some instances may have been brought to the U.S. from there.

Grandmaison (214) French: compound name composed of the elements *grand* 'large' + *maison* 'house', used to denote someone who lived or possibly worked in a large house.
GIVEN NAMES French 15%. *Renaud* (2), *Cecile, Fernand, Gaston, Lucien, Normand, Rosaire, Thaddee.*

Grandon (270) English: probably a variant of **Crandon**, a habitational name from Crandon in Somerset or Crandean in Falmer, Sussex. Compare GRANDIN.

Grandpre (156) French (**Grandpré**): topographic name for someone who lived near a large meadow, from French *grand* 'large' + *pré* 'meadow', 'field'.
GIVEN NAMES French 9%. *Emile, Pierre, Raoul.*

Grandstaff (728) Americanized form of German **Grenzhof** or **Granzow** (see GRINDSTAFF).

Grandt (195) German: topographic name for someone who lived in a gravelly area, from Middle Low German *grand* 'coarse gravel'.
GIVEN NAMES German 6%. *Erwin, Fritz, Horst, Otto.*

Grandy (946) English: unexplained; possibly a variant of GRUNDY or GRANBY.

Granelli (90) Italian: variant of **Granello** (see GRANILLO).
GIVEN NAMES Italian 24%. *Mario* (2), *Sergio* (2), *Attillo, Ettore, Gino.*

Graner (318) **1.** French: southern variant of GRANIER. **2.** German: variant of GRAN, + the *-er* suffix denoting an inhabitant. **3.** German: Swabian occupational name for a peddler. **4.** German (**Gräner**): variant of GREINER.

Granese (152) Italian: most probably from a reduced form of *Agranese*, a habitational name for an inhabitant of Agrano, a former municipality in present-day Verbania province, from an adjectival form of the place name. However, the surname occurs predominantly in Campania and it may be that an alternative source should be sought.
GIVEN NAMES Italian 10%. *Lucio, Rocco, Salvatore.*

Graney (615) **1.** Irish: reduced Anglicized form of Gaelic **Mag Raighne** 'son of *Raighne*', a pet form of *Raghnall*. MacLysaght describes this as a north Ulster name which is sometimes changed to Grant. **2.** Possibly a respelling of Swiss German **Gräni**, of unexplained origin.

Granfield (176) Americanized form of the French topographic names GRANDCHAMP or **Grandpré** (see GRANDPRE). Compare GRANDFIELD.

Grange (543) English and French: topographic name for someone who lived by a granary, from Middle English, Old French *grange* (Latin *granica* 'granary', 'barn', from *granum* 'grain'). In some cases, the surname has arisen from places named with this word, for example in Dorset and West Yorkshire in England, and in Ardèche and Jura in France. The Marquis de Lafayette owned a property named *Lagrange*, and there used to be a place in VT so named in his honor.

Granger (6067) English and French: occupational name for a farm bailiff, responsible for overseeing the collection of rent in kind into the barns and storehouses of the lord of the manor. This official had the Anglo-Norman French title *grainger*, Old French *grangier*, from Late Latin *granicarius*, a derivative of *granica* 'granary' (see GRANGE).

Granholm (184) Swedish: ornamental name composed of the elements *gran* 'spruce' + *holm* 'island'.
GIVEN NAMES Scandinavian 13%. *Alf* (3), *Erik, Lars, Lasse, Nels.*

Granier (299) French: occupational name for a grain merchant (from Latin *granarius*), or a topographic name for someone who lived by a granary (from Latin *granarium*) or a metonymic occupational name for someone who supervised or owned one.
GIVEN NAMES French 6%. *Andre, Emile, Marcel, Nemour, Pierre, Thierry.*

Granieri (164) Italian: metonymic occupational name for a grain merchant, from *graniere* 'barn', a borrowing of French *grénier*; otherwise from a metathesized form of French GARNIER.
GIVEN NAMES Italian 14%. *Vito* (3), *Emanuele, Salvatore.*

Granillo (393) Italian: nickname for someone with pockmarks or similar blemishes, from *granello* 'speck', a diminutive of *grano* 'grain' (Latin *granum*).
GIVEN NAMES Spanish 41%. *Jose* (10), *Manuel* (8), *Francisco* (5), *Ramon* (4), *Raul* (4), *Alfonso* (3), *Carlos* (3), *Jaime* (3), *Jesus* (3), *Miguel* (3), *Alberto* (2), *Blanca* (2).

Graning (114) Swedish: ornamental name composed of *gran* 'spruce' + the common surname suffix *-ing* (see ARNING).

Granite (117) Origin unidentified. Possibly of Russian Jewish origin.

Granito (172) Italian: **1.** topographic name from Sicilian *granitu* 'area of grain cultivation' (Latin *granetum*). **2.** otherwise a nickname from Italian *granito* 'granite', denoting a particularly strong or rugged individual.
GIVEN NAMES Italian 10%. *Dante, Gennaro.*

Granlund (339) Swedish and Norwegian: ornamental name composed of the elements *gran* 'spruce' + *lund* 'grove'.

Grannan (288) Irish: reduced form of **MacGrannan**, an Anglicized form of Gaelic **Mag Raghnainn**, a form of **Mac Raghnaill**, cognate with REYNOLDS.

Granneman (120) Variant of German GRANNEMANN.
GIVEN NAME German 5%. *Hans* (5).

Grannemann (110) German: perhaps a variant of **Grandemann**, itself a variant of GRANDE.

Grannis (386) Probably an altered form of English **Crannis**, a habitational name from Cranes in Nevendon, Essex.

Grano (284) Italian and Spanish: from *grano* 'grain' (Latin *granum*), probably applied as a metonymic occupational name for a farmer or grain merchant.

GIVEN NAMES Italian 17%; Spanish 8%. *Angelo* (3), *Domenic* (2), *Sal* (2), *Alessandro, Armando, Carmela, Carmin, Cecilio, Cosmo, Dante, Dario, Enzo, Eugenio, Lucrezia; Alicia, Ana, Julio, Lourdes, Maria Guadalupe, Manuel, Osvaldo, Raul.*

Granoff (220) Jewish (eastern Ashkenazic): alternative spelling of **Granov**, a habitational name from Granov in Ukraine. In the U.S. this is also found as a reduced form of **Granovsky**, the local form of this surname in Ukraine.
GIVEN NAMES Jewish 6%. *Hyman, Isadore.*

Granquist (292) Swedish: ornamental name composed of the elements *gran* 'spruce' + *quist*, an old or ornamental spelling of *kvist* 'twig'.
GIVEN NAMES Scandinavian 6%. *Erik, Nels, Nils.*

Gransee (100) German: habitational name from a place so called near Neuruppin in Brandenburg.

Granstrom (144) Swedish (**Granström**): ornamental name composed of the elements *gran* 'spruce' + *ström* 'river'.

Grant (43607) **1.** English and (especially) Scottish (of Norman origin), and French: nickname from Anglo-Norman French *graund, graunt* 'tall', 'large' (Old French *grand, grant*, from Latin *grandis*), given either to a person of remarkable size, or else in a relative way to distinguish two bearers of the same personal name, often representatives of different generations within the same family. **2.** English and Scottish: from a medieval personal name, probably a survival into Middle English of the Old English byname *Granta* (see GRANTHAM). **3.** Probably a respelling of German GRANDT or GRAND.
FOREBEARS The U.S. president General Ulysses S. Grant (1822–85), born in OH, was the descendant of a Puritan called Matthew Grant, who landed in Massachusetts with his wife, Priscilla, in 1630. This family of Grants continued in New England until Captain Noah Grant, having served throughout the Revolution, emigrated to PA in 1790 and later to OH.

Grantham (4026) English: habitational name from Grantham in Lincolnshire, of uncertain origin. The final element is Old English *hām* 'homestead'; the first may be Old English *grand* 'gravel' or perhaps a personal name *Granta*, which probably originated as a byname meaning 'snarler'. See also GRAHAM.

Grantland (127) English: habitational name from Grantland in Poughill, Devon, possibly so named from an Old English personal name *Granta* + Old English *land* 'cultivated land', 'estate'.

Grantz (306) Eastern German: habitational name from any of various places in northeastern Germany named with Slavic *gran(t)z* 'frontier', 'border'.

Granucci (107) Italian (Lucca): perhaps a nickname for someone with pockmarks or similar blemishes. Compare GRANILLO.

Granum (185) Norwegian: habitational name from any of several farmsteads in southeastern Norway, so named from Old Norse *Granheimr*, a compound of *grǫn* 'spruce' + *heimr* 'farmstead'.
GIVEN NAMES Scandinavian 5%. *Hilma, Iver.*

Granville (586) English (of Norman origin): habitational name from any of various places in northern France called Grainville, from the Germanic personal name *Guarin* (see WARING) + Old French *ville* 'settlement'.

Granzow (296) German: habitational name from any of several places in northeastern Germany named Granzow, from Slavic *gran(t)z* 'frontier', 'border'.
GIVEN NAMES German 6%. *Helmut, Klaus, Kurt.*

Grap (128) North German: variant of GRAPE.

Grape (149) North German: metonymic occupational name for a maker of metal or earthenware vessels, from Middle Low German *grope* 'pot'.

Graper (238) North German (**Gräper**): occupational name for a maker of metal or earthenware vessels, from an agent derivative of Middle Low German *grope* 'pot'. Compare GRAPE.

Grapes (271) English (East Anglia): perhaps a habitational name from a house bearing the sign of a bunch of grapes. The vocabulary word is attested from the 13th century (at first in the compound *wingrape*), and comes from Old French *grape*, which is probably related to a Germanic element meaning 'hook'.

Gras (223) **1.** French: nickname for a stout person, from Old French *cras* 'fat' (from Latin *crassus*). **2.** Catalan: nickname for a stout person, from Latin *crassus* 'fat'. **3.** German: variant of GRASS 2.
GIVEN NAMES French 7%; Spanish 6%; German 4%. *Clemence, Francoise, Michel, Philippe; Francisco* (3), *Baudilio, Guadalupe, Jesus, Jose Pedro, Juan, Juana; Dieter* (2).

Graser (409) South German: from Middle High German *gras* 'grass' + the agent suffix *-er*, a topographic name for someone who owned or lived on a patch of meadowland or an occupational name for a reaper who cut grass with a sickle for fresh fodder.
GIVEN NAMES German 7%. *Kurt* (2), *Franz, Gerhardt, Hilde, Horst, Theodor, Wilhelm.*

Grasley (129) **1.** Americanized spelling of South German **Gräsle** or Swiss German **Gräsli**, diminutives of *Gras* (see GRASS). **2.** Perhaps an Americanized spelling of **Grässle** or **Grässling**, from a Germanic personal name reflected by Old High German *grātag* 'greedy'.

Grasmick (289) **1.** Altered form of Russian **Gerasimek**: from a diminutive of the personal name *Gerasim* (Greek *Gerasimos*, a derivative of *geras* 'old age', or of the homonymous *geras* 'honor'), which was borne by a 5th-century saint, venerated in the Eastern Church, who was chiefly famous for the devotion he is said to have inspired in a lion from whose paw he extracted a thorn. **2.** German: of disputed etymology; possibly of the same origin as 1 or from the bird name *Grasmücke* 'warbler'.
GIVEN NAMES German 5%. *Kurt* (2), *Gottlieb, Reinhold.*

Grass (1609) **1.** English and German: topographic name for someone who owned or lived by a meadow, or a metonymic occupational name for someone who made or sold hay, from Middle English *gras*, Middle High German *gras* 'grass', 'pasture', 'grazing'. **2.** English: nickname for a stout man, from Anglo-Norman French *gras* 'fat', from Latin *crassus* (which was itself used as a Roman family name), with the initial changed under the influence of *grossus* (see GROSS). **3.** Scottish: occupational name, reduced from Gaelic *greusaiche* 'shoemaker'. A certain John Grasse alias *Cordonar* (Middle English *cordewaner* 'shoemaker') is recorded in Scotland in 1539. **4.** South German: nickname for an irascible man, from Middle High German *graz* 'intense', 'angry'.

Grasse (278) **1.** German: variant of GRASS 4. **2.** French: habitational name from the city of Grasse, in Alpes-Maritimes, which was a Huguenot center, sacked by François I in 1536. **3.** Perhaps a reduced form of French **Degrâce** (see DE GRACE).
GIVEN NAMES German 6%. *Kurt* (2), *Erwin, Helmut, Merwin, Uwe.*

Grassel (269) South German (**Grässel**): **1.** from a diminutive of GRASS 1. **2.** nickname for a greedy person, from Old High German *grātag* 'greedy'.

Grasser (415) **1.** South German: nickname for an irascible person, from an inflected form of Middle High German *graz* 'intense', 'angry'. **2.** South German (**Grässer**): from Middle High German *gras* 'grass' + the agent suffix *-er* (see GRASER). **3.** Swiss German: nickname for a complainer, from Middle High German *graz* 'passionate', 'furious'.

Grassi (967) Italian: patronymic or plural form of the nickname GRASSO.
GIVEN NAMES Italian 15%. *Angelo* (6), *Carlo* (4), *Guido* (4), *Rocco* (4), *Ciro* (3), *Dante* (3), *Dino* (3), *Geno* (3), *Antonio* (2), *Biagio* (2), *Marco* (2), *Salvatore* (2).

Grassia (134) Italian: from a metathesized form of the personal name *Garsia*, from Spanish *García* (see GARCIA).
GIVEN NAMES Italian 22%. *Angelo* (3), *Amedeo* (2), *Maurizio, Pasquale, Rocco, Salvatore.*

Grassie (140) Scottish: variant of GRASS 3.

Grassl (189) German: variant of GRASSEL.
GIVEN NAME German 5%. *Hans* (2).

Grassman (304) **1.** German (**Grassmann**): elaborated form of of GRASS 1 and 4. **2.** English: occupational name for a seller of grease, from Old French *graisse, greisse, gresse* 'grease'. **3.** English: occupational name from Middle English *grasman, gresman* 'cottager', from Middle English *gras, gres* 'grass', 'pasture' + *man*.

Grassmyer (101) German (**Grassmeyer**): distinguishing name for a tenant farmer who lived who lived by a meadow, from Middle High German *gras* 'grass', 'pasture' + MEYER.

Grasso (2855) Italian: nickname for a stout man, from *grasso* 'fat' (Latin *crassus*).
GIVEN NAMES Italian 16%. *Salvatore* (27), *Angelo* (24), *Sal* (8), *Domenic* (6), *Vito* (5), *Carmine* (4), *Rocco* (4), *Carmelo* (3), *Luigi* (3), *Pasquale* (3), *Santo* (3), *Alfio* (2).

Grasty (361) English: unexplained.

Grate (460) French (**Graté**): from the past participle of *gratter* 'to till or scratch (the soil)', possibly applied as a nickname for a dilettante.

Grater (262) **1.** English: from Old French *grateor, gratour, gratier* 'one who grates', hence possibly an occupational name for a furbisher. **2.** German (**Gräter**): see GRAETER.
GIVEN NAME German 4%. *Otto* (3).

Grathwohl (196) South German: from a contraction of the phrase *es gerate wohl!* ('may it turn out well'), an expression which originated among the medieval craft guilds and subsequently came to denote a journeyman.
GIVEN NAMES German 7%. *Kurt* (2), *Erwin, Fritz, Otto.*

Grattan (463) English: variant spelling of GRATTON.
GIVEN NAME Irish 4%. *Brendan.*

Gratton (802) English: habitational name from any of various places so named. Gratton in Derbyshire is from Old English *grēat* 'great' + *tūn* 'enclosure', 'settlement'. Gratton in High Bray, Devon, is probably 'great hill', from Old English *grēat* + *dūn*. A number of minor places in Devon are named from the dialect word *gratton, gratten* 'stubble-field'.
GIVEN NAMES French 8%. *Andre* (2), *Fernand* (2), *Adelard, Armand, Aurore, Emile, Gaston, Gilles, Julien, Monique, Normand, Remi.*

Gratz (848) South German (also **Grätz**): **1.** habitational name from several places so named in Austria, Bohemia, and Moravia. **2.** from a short form of a Germanic personal name reflected by Old High German *grātag* 'greedy'. **3.** from a short form of the personal name PANKRATZ.

Gratzer (169) German: **1.** habitational name for someone from a place called Gratz or Grätz (see GRATZ). **2.** German: (**Grätzer**): variant of KRETZER 2.
GIVEN NAMES Hungarian 4%. *Antal, Laszlo, Miklos.*

Grau (1533) **1.** German and Jewish (Ashkenazic): nickname for someone with gray hair or a gray beard, from German *grau* 'gray'. **2.** Southern French: topographic name for someone who lived near a canal giving access to the sea, Occitan *grau* (Latin *gradus* 'step'). **3.** French: from Old French *grau* denoting a type of agricultural fork with curved tines (apparently of Germanic origin), hence a metonymic occupational name for a maker, seller, or user of such implements. **4.** Catalan: topographic name from *grau* (Latin *gradum*). **5.** Catalan: from a reduced form of the common medieval personal name *Guerau* (see GERALD).
GIVEN NAMES German 5%. *Kurt* (3), *Otto* (3), *Fritz* (2), *Heinz* (2), *Horst* (2), *Dieter, Frieda, Gerhard, Herta, Joerg, Johann, Manfred.*

Graubard (111) Jewish (Ashkenazic): nickname for someone with a gray beard, from German *grau* 'gray' + *Bart* 'beard'.
GIVEN NAME Jewish 5%. *Meyer.*

Grauberger (191) **1.** German: habitational name for someone from a place called Grauberg 'gray mountain'. **2.** Jewish (Ashkenazic): ornamental name from German *grau* 'gray' + *Berg* 'mountain', 'hill' + the agent suffix *-er*.

Graue (244) German: **1.** habitational name from a place so named near Hannover. **2.** variant of GRAU.

Grauel (199) German: **1.** habitational name from any of three places so named in northern Germany. **2.** variant of GREUEL.

Grauer (584) German and Jewish (Ashkenazic): nickname for someone with gray hair or a gray beard, from an inflected form of German *grau* 'gray'.

Graul (428) German: variant of GREUEL.

Graulich (137) German: variant of GREULICH.
GIVEN NAMES German 8%. *Erhardt, Kurt.*

Grauman (198) Jewish variant spelling or respelling of German GRAUMANN.

Graumann (207) German and Jewish (Ashkenazic): nickname for someone with gray hair or a gray beard (see GRAU).
GIVEN NAMES German 12%. *Berthold* (2), *Heinz* (2), *Erwin, Ewald, Kurt, Ralf, Reiner.*

Graunke (175) German: of uncertain origin. Perhaps from *grau* 'gray' (see GRAU) + Slavic suffix, or from a place name (see GRAUE).
GIVEN NAME German 4%. *Kurt.*

Graupman (116) German (**Graupmann**): occupational name for someone who produced or dealt in grits and legumes, from early Modern German *graupe* 'pot barley' (from Bohemian *krupa*) + *man* 'man' (compare GRAUPNER).

Graupner (109) German: **1.** occupational name for a producer of or dealer in pot barley, from the Bohemian loan word *krupa* 'pot barley' + the German agent suffix *-ner*. **2.** habitational name for someone from Graupen (Krupka in Czech) in Bohemia.
GIVEN NAMES German 7%. *Kurt, Volker.*

Gravatt (529) English: topographic name for someone living near a small grove or copse, from Old English *gráfet, grǽfet* 'little grove' (from Old English *gráf(e), grǽfe* 'grove', 'copse' + the diminutive suffix *-et*).

Grave (196) **1.** English: occupational name from Middle English *greyve* 'steward', from Old Norse *greifi* or Low German *grēve* (see GRAF). **2.** English: topographic name, a variant of GROVE. **3.** French: topographic name for someone who lived on a patch of gravelly soil, from Old French *grave* 'gravel' (of Celtic origin). **4.** North German: either from the northern form of GRAF, but more commonly a topographic name from Middle Low German *grave* 'ditch', 'moat', 'channel', or a habitational name from any of several places in northern Germany named with this word.
GIVEN NAMES Spanish 5%. *Manuel* (2), *Alejandro, Domingo, Florentino, Jose, Juan, Octavio, Rafael.*

Gravel (831) **1.** French: diminutive of GRAVE 3. **2.** North German: nickname for someone with gray hair or a gray beard, from Low German *grāw*.
GIVEN NAMES French 18%. *Marcel* (4), *Normand* (4), *Gaston* (3), *Jean Guy* (3), *Lucien* (3), *Pierre* (3), *Serge* (3), *Donat* (2), *Felicien* (2), *Fernand* (2), *Gilles* (2), *Michel* (2).

Graveline (336) French: diminutive of GRAVE 3.
GIVEN NAMES French 4%. *Adrien, Alcide, Raynald.*

Gravell (172) Respelling of French GRAVELLE.
GIVEN NAME French 4%. *Jean-Paul.*

Gravelle (823) French: from a diminutive of GRAVE.

Gravely (986) **1.** English: habitational name from Gravely in Cambridgeshire or Graveley in Hertfordshire. The first is possibly from Old English *grǽf* 'pit', 'trench' + *lēah* 'woodland clearing'. The second is from Old English *grǽfe, gráf(a)* 'grove', 'copse' + *lēah*. **2.** Possibly an altered spelling of Swiss **Gräffi**, a variant of GRAF.

Graven (437) North German: **1.** topographic name for someone living near a ditch or moat, from Middle Low German *grave* 'ditch', 'moat', 'channel'. Compare GRABE. **2.** possibly a reduced form of any of various compound habitational names such as **Gravenhorst** or **Gravenstein**. **3.** Norwegian: habitational name from any of several farmsteads so named, from Old Norse *grof* 'hollow', 'depression'.

Graver (817) **1.** English: occupational name for an engraver, from Old English *grafere, grǽfere* 'engraver', 'sculptor' (Old French *graveur*). It is possible that the name was also an occupational name for a miner, from Old English *grafan* 'to dig'. **2.** German (also **Gräver**): variant of GRABER.

Graves (29311) **1.** English: patronymic from GRAVE 1. **2.** French: topographic name from the plural of Old French *grave* 'gravel' (see GRAVE).

Gravett (342) **1.** English: topographic name for someone who lived by a copse or small grove, Middle English *gravette, grevette* (from a diminutive of Old English *gráf* 'grove'). **2.** Altered spelling of French **Gravet**, cognate with 1.

Gravette (197) English: variant spelling of GRAVETT.

Gravina (202) Italian: habitational name from any of various places named Gravina, especially one in Puglia, near Bari.
GIVEN NAMES Italian 20%. *Vito* (2), *Alfredo, Mario, Orlando, Rocco, Santo, Vincenza, Vincenzo.*

Gravino (188) Italian: from a masculinized form of GRAVINA.
GIVEN NAMES Italian 13%. *Dante* (2), *Angelo, Biagio, Gaetano, Guido, Lia, Marco, Rocco.*

Gravitt (998) English: variant spelling of GRAVETT.

Gravitte (108) Respelling of English GRAVETTE.

Gravlee (105) Probably an Americanized form of English GRAVELY.

Gravley (575) **1.** English: variant spelling of GRAVELY. **2.** Possibly also a variant spelling of Swiss German *Gräfli* (see GRAVELY).

Gravlin (210) English (Norfolk and Suffolk): unexplained.

Gravois (242) French: topographic name for someone who lived in an area of coarse gravel, from Old French *grave* (of Celtic origin).
GIVEN NAMES French 7%. *Antoine, Francois, Gaston, Laurent.*

Graw (213) North German: variant of GRAU.

Grawe (246) North German: variant of GRAUE.

Gray (84423) **1.** English: nickname for someone with gray hair or a gray beard, from Old English *grǽg* 'gray'. In Scotland and Ireland it has been used as a translation of various Gaelic surnames derived from *riabhach* 'brindled', 'gray' (see REAVEY). In North America this name has assimilated names with similar meaning from other European languages. **2.** English and Scottish (of Norman origin): habitational name from Graye in Calvados, France, named from the Gallo-Roman personal name *Gratus*, meaning 'welcome', 'pleasing' + the locative suffix *-acum*. **3.** French and Swiss French: habitational name from Gray in Haute-Saône and Le Gray in Seine-Maritime, both in France, or from Gray-la-ville in Switzerland, or a regional name from the Swiss canton of Graubünden.

FOREBEARS A leading English family called Grey, holders of the earldom of Stamford, can be traced to Henry de Grey, who was granted lands at Thurrock, Essex, by Richard I (1189–99). They once held great power, and Henry Grey, Duke of Suffolk (1517–54), married a granddaughter of Henry VII. Because of this he felt entitled to claim the throne for his daughter, Lady Jane Grey (1537–54), after the death of Henry VIII. For this, and for his part in Wyatt's rebellion, both he and his daughter were beheaded. Another family of the same name originated in Northumbria, where they held land at Wark-on-Tweed in 1398. Members include the Earls Grey, of whom the best known is probably Charles, 2nd Earl Grey (1764–1845), the prime minister under whom the 1832 Reform Bill was passed.

Graybeal (860) See GRAYBILL.

Graybill (1550) Americanized spelling of the Swiss German habitational name **Kräh(en)bühl**, literally 'crow hill' (see KRAHENBUHL).

Graydon (415) English: unexplained.

Grayer (330) **1.** English: unexplained. **2.** Possibly an Americanized form of German GRAUER. **3.** Alternatively, perhaps a respelling of French **Gruyer**, an occupational name from Old French *gruier* 'forester'.

Grays (376) English: probably a patronymic from GRAY, or possibly a variant spelling of GRACE.

Grayson (5172) English: patronymic from GRAVE 1.

Graziadei (118) Italian: from the baptismal name *Graziadei*, a translation of the Latin phrase *gratia Dei* 'grace of God', bestowed also in the sense 'gift of God'.
GIVEN NAMES Italian 23%. *Rocco* (3), *Carlo* (2), *Salvatore* (2), *Carmela*.

Graziani (451) Italian and Jewish (from Italy): patronymic or plural form of the personal name GRAZIANO.
GIVEN NAMES Italian 12%. *Angelo* (2), *Carlo* (2), *Dante* (2), *Amerigo*, *Antonio*, *Enrico*, *Francesco*, *Franco*, *Gino*, *Giovanni*, *Graziano*, *Luigi*.

Graziano (2592) Italian: from the personal name *Graziano*, Latin *Gratianus*, a derivative of *gratus* 'welcome', 'pleasing'.
GIVEN NAMES Italian 16%. *Sal* (19), *Salvatore* (13), *Vito* (12), *Angelo* (8), *Rocco* (5), *Antonio* (4), *Augustino* (3), *Domenic* (3), *Enrico* (3), *Gino* (3), *Aldo* (2), *Carmela* (2).

Grazier (294) English: occupational name for someone who reared or grazed cattle, from a noun derivative of Old English *grasian* 'to graze'.

Grazioli (101) Italian: from a derivative of the personal name *Grazio*, masculine form of *Grazia* (see DE GRAZIA).
GIVEN NAMES Italian 14%. *Enrico*, *Primo*, *Stefano*.

Graziosi (144) Italian: patronymic or plural form of GRAZIOSO.
GIVEN NAMES Italian 34%. *Angelo* (5), *Paolo* (2), *Alberto* (2), *Americo* (2), *Antonio*, *Armando* (2), *Caesar*, *Eduardo*, *Filippo*, *Gino*, *Guiseppe*, *Luigi*, *Mario*, *Nicola*, *Orlando*, *Pasquale*, *Piero*, *Rocco*.

Grazioso (108) Italian: from the personal name *Grazioso* (Italian *grazioso* 'full of grace'), a continuation of the Latin personal name *Gratiosus*.
GIVEN NAME Italian 6%. *Carmelo*.

Grealish (166) Irish: reduced Anglicized form of **Mag Riallghuis**, variant of **Mac Niallghuis** (see MCNELIS).

Greaney (555) Irish (Kerry and Galway): **1.** reduced Anglicized form of Gaelic **Ó Gráinne** 'descendant of *Gráinne*', a female personal name. **2.** possibly a reduced Anglicized form of **Mag Raighne** (see MCRANEY).
GIVEN NAMES Irish 7%. *Aidan*, *Conor*, *Maeve*, *Siobhan*.

Greany (125) Irish: reduced Anglicized form of Gaelic **Ó Gráinne** 'son of *Gráinne*', a female personal name.

Grear (366) Scottish: variant spelling of *Grier*, itself a variant of GREGOR.

Greaser (237) Americanized spelling of the Swiss and South German topographic name **Griesser** (see GRIESER).

Greason (194) Possibly a variant spelling of French **Grison**, a nickname for a man with gray hair, from *gris* 'gray'. This name also occurs in Germany, mainly in Baden, near the French border, and may have been taken from there to the U.S. It is found chiefly in MO and GA.

Great (151) **1.** Americanized form of Dutch DE GROOT or German GROSS. **2.** English: variant of **Greet**, a nickname from Old English *grēat* 'big', 'stout', a habitational name from Greet in Gloucestershire or Greete in Shropshire, both named from an Old English *grēote* 'gravelly place', or a topographic name with the same meaning.
GIVEN NAME Dutch 4%. *Arco*.

Greathouse (2388) North German and Dutch: Americanized form of **Grothaus**, habitational name from any of various farms so called, literally 'big house', in particular one in Westphalia.

Greatorex (147) English (Derbyshire): habitational name from a place in Derbyshire called Greterakes.

Greaux (104) French (**Gréaux**): metathesized form of **Géraud** (see GERALD).
GIVEN NAMES French 14%. *Andre* (2), *Jean-Pierre*.

Greaver (138) English (also **Griever**): unexplained; perhaps a variant of GRAVER.

Greaves (1674) English: topographic name from Old English *grǣfe* 'brushwood', 'thicket', or a habitational name from any of the places named with this word, for ex-

ample in Cumbria, Lancashire, and Staffordshire.

Greb (517) Polish: variant of GRAB.

Grebe (572) German (Hesse): variant of GRAF.
GIVEN NAMES German 5%. *Kurt* (3), *Erwin*, *Fritz*, *Hans*, *Willi*.

Greber (158) **1.** Jewish (Ashkenazic): variant of GRABER. **2.** German and Swiss German: variant of **Gräber** (see GRABER).

Grebner (190) German: variant of **Gräbner** (see GRABNER).

Grecco (392) Variant spelling of GRECO.
GIVEN NAMES Italian 12%. *Rocco* (2), *Aldo*, *Angelo*, *Carmine*, *Gaetano*, *Gasper*, *Giovanni*, *Orest*, *Sal*.

Grech (405) **1.** Maltese: unexplained. **2.** Polish or eastern German (Sorbian): from *Grech*, a vernacular pet form (in Silesia and elsewhere) of the Latin personal name *Gregorius* (see GREGORY).
GIVEN NAMES Italian 7%; Spanish 6%. *Angelo* (4), *Mario* (3), *Carmel*, *Dante*, *Nazareno*;; *Armondo* (2), *Joaquin* (2), *Jaime*, *Marta*, *Ruben*, *Xavier*.

Greco (6180) Italian: ethnic name for a Greek, from Italian *Greco* (Latin *Graecus*). In some cases it may have been applied as a nickname for a crafty or guileful person, for these were qualities traditionally attributed to the Greeks.
GIVEN NAMES Italian 15%. *Salvatore* (41), *Angelo* (37), *Vito* (19), *Sal* (12), *Antonio* (8), *Gaetano* (7), *Pasquale* (7), *Rocco* (7), *Vincenzo* (6), *Domenic* (5), *Francesco* (5), *Carlo* (4).

Greear (459) Probably a variant spelling of Scottish GRIER.

Greek (465) Of uncertain origin. **1.** English (Devon): possibly a variant of CREEK. **2.** Possibly an Americanized spelling of German KRIEG or Dutch *Kriek* (see CREEK). **3.** ethnic name for a Greek, a translation of Italian GRECO or of a word with the same meaning in some other language.

Greeley (1780) English (of Norman origin): nickname for someone with a pock-marked face, from Old Northern French *greslé* 'pitted', 'scarred' (from *gresle* 'hailstone', of Germanic origin).

Greely (365) English: variant spelling of GREELEY.

Green (131873) **1.** English: one of the most common and widespread of English surnames, either a nickname for someone who was fond of dressing in this color (Old English *grēne*) or who had played the part of the 'Green Man' in the May Day celebrations, or a topographic name for someone who lived near a village green, Middle English *grene* (a transferred use of the color term). In North America this name has no doubt assimilated cognates from other European languages, notably German *Grün* (see GRUEN). **2.** Jewish (American): Americanized form of German **Grün** or

Yiddish **Grin**, Ashkenazic ornamental names meaning 'green' or a short form of any of the numerous compounds with this element. **3.** Irish: translation of various Gaelic surnames derived from *glas* 'gray', 'green', 'blue'. See also FAHEY. **4.** North German: short form of a habitational name from a place name with *Gren-* as the first element (for example **Greune**, **Greubole**).

Greenamyer (100) Americanized form of German **Grünemeier** or **Grön(e)meier** (see GRONEMEYER), a compound name from Middle High German *grüene* 'green', 'fresh' or Middle Low German *gröne* + Middle High German *meier* '(tenant) farmer', probably, in the early period of surname formation, denoting a farmer whose land was in a woodland clearing. In later formations, the first element, taken from a place name or topographic feature, may have been added to distinguish the bearer from other bearers of the common surname **Meyer**.

Greenan (362) **1.** Irish (mainly Cavan and Sligo): reduced Anglicized form of Gaelic **Ó Grianáin** 'descendant of *Grianán*', probably from a diminutive of *grian* 'sun', *grianach* 'sunny', 'cheerful'. **2.** Scottish: habitational name from either of two places so named in Strathclyde region, probably named with the same word.

Greenawald (131) Americanized form of German **Grünewald** (see GRUNWALD).

Greenawalt (1148) Americanized form of German **Grünewald** (see GRUNWALD).

Greenaway (347) **1.** English: variant of GREENWAY. **2.** Americanized form of Dutch GROENEWEG.

Greenbaum (1489) **1.** Partly Americanized form of the Ashkenazic Jewish ornamental name **Grünbaum**, a compound of German *grün* 'green' + *Baum* 'tree'. **2.** Partly Americanized form of German **Grünbaum**, from Middle High German *grüene* 'green' + *boum* 'tree', probably a habitational name from a house distinguished by the sign of a tree in leaf.
GIVEN NAMES Jewish 7%. *Hyman* (3), *Sol* (3), *Meyer* (2), *Shlomo* (2), *Shraga* (2), *Ari*, *Arie*, *Aron*, *Avi*, *Emanuel*, *Herschel*, *Hershel*.

Greenberg (11353) Partly Americanized form of German and Ashkenazic Jewish **Grünberg** (see GRUNBERG).
GIVEN NAMES Jewish 6%. *Sol* (21), *Meyer* (19), *Hyman* (10), *Miriam* (9), *Emanuel* (6), *Ari* (5), *Chaim* (4), *Isadore* (4), *Arie* (3), *Avrohom* (3), *Avrom* (3), *Moshe* (3).

Greenberger (340) Partly Americanized form of German and Ashkenazic Jewish **Grünberger**. As a Jewish surname it is ornamental, while the German name is habitational, from *Grünberg* (see GRUNBERG)+ the habitational suffix *-er*.
GIVEN NAMES Jewish 8%. *Isidor* (2), *Binyomin*, *Mendel*, *Meyer*, *Sol*, *Zeev*.

Greenblatt (1055) Partly Americanized form of the Ashkenazic Jewish ornamental name **Grünblatt**, a compound of German *grün* 'green' + *Blatt* 'leaf'.
GIVEN NAMES Jewish 8%. *Gershon* (3), *Emanuel* (2), *Hyman* (2), *Menachem* (2), *Zev* (2), *Aviva*, *Chaja*, *Chana*, *Isadore*, *Meyer*, *Miriam*, *Myer*.

Greenburg (486) Americanized form of the Ashkenazic Jewish ornamental name **Grünburg**, a compound of German *grün* 'green' + *Burg* 'castle'.
GIVEN NAMES Jewish 4%. *Gerson* (2), *Ari*, *Aron*, *Avraham*, *Boruch*, *Moshe*.

Greene (44408) **1.** Irish: translation of Gaelic **Ó hUainín** 'descendant of *Uainín*' (see HONAN 2). **2.** variant spelling of GREEN as an English name or as an Americanized form of name of similar meaning in some other European language.

Greenebaum (132) Partly Americanized form of Ashkenazic Jewish **Grünbaum** (see GREENBAUM).

Greener (633) **1.** English: habitational name from Greenhaugh in Northumberland, named from Old English *grēne* 'green' + *halh* 'nook', 'recess'. Compare GREENHALGH. **2.** Americanized spelling of Ashkenazic Jewish **Griner** (see GREEN). **3.** Americanized spelling of German **Grüner** (see GRUENER).

Greeney (121) English: probably a variant of GREENHALGH.

Greenfeld (264) Partly Americanized form of the Ashkenazic Jewish ornamental name GRUN(E)FELD or **Grinfeld**, a compound of Yiddish *grin* + German *Feld* 'field', or of German **Grünfeld** (see GRUNFELD).
GIVEN NAMES Jewish 18%; German 4%. *Chaim* (4), *Avrohom* (2), *Mayer* (2), *Mozes* (2), *Ben Zion*, *Bluma*, *Chaya*, *Meyer*, *Moishe*, *Naftali*, *Naftaly*, *Shimshon*; *Armin*, *Dieter*.

Greenfield (5251) **1.** English: habitational name from any of numerous minor places named Greenfield, from Old English *grēne* 'green' + *feld* 'pasture', 'open country' (see FIELD). **2.** English: variant of GRANVILLE. **3.** English translation of German and Ashkenazic Jewish **Grünfeld** (see GRUNFELD).

Greenhagen (132) Americanized form of German **Grönhagen**, probably a topographic name in northwestern German, from Low German *grön* 'green' (standard *grün*) + *Hagen* 'hedge', 'enclosure'.

Greenhalgh (1022) English (Lancashire): habitational name from either of two places in Lancashire called Greenhalgh, from Old English *grēne* 'green' + *holh* 'hollow'. Compare GREENER.

Greenhaw (538) **1.** Probably a respelling of English GREENHOW or GREENHALGH. **2.** Possibly a respelling of German **Grünhag(e)**, a variant of **Grünhagen** (see GRUENHAGEN).

Greenhill (713) **1.** English: habitational name from any of the various minor places in England named Greenhill, usually from Old English *grēne* 'green' + *hyll* 'hill'. However, Greenhill in Worcestershire is probably named from Old English *grīma* 'specter', 'goblin' + *hyll* 'hill'. **2.** English translation of Ashkenazic Jewish **Grünberg**.

Greenhoe (143) Probably a respelling of English GREENHOW.

Greenhouse (399) **1.** English: topographic name for someone who lived in a house by a village green, from Middle English *grene* 'green' + *hous* 'house'. (The term was not used to denote a glasshouse for the cultivation of 'greens' or sensitive plants until the late 17th century.) **2.** Jewish (American): English translation of Ashkenazic **Grünhaus**, an oramental name composed of German *grün* 'green' + *Haus* 'house'.

Greenhow (132) English: habitational name from either of two places called Greenhow, in North and West Yorkshire, or from Gerna in the parish of Downham, Lancashire, all of which are named with Old English *grēne* 'green' + *hōh* 'mound' (or the cognate Old Norse *haugr*).

Greenhut (195) Americanized form of the Ashkenazic Jewish surname **Gru(e)nhut**, a habitational name for someone who lived at a house distinguished by the sign of a green hat, from German *grün* 'green' + *Hut* 'hat'.
GIVEN NAMES German 5%; Jewish 4%. *Kurt*; *Baruch*, *Mendel*, *Sol*.

Greenia (143) Americanized form of French GRENIER.

Greenidge (364) English: habitational name for someone from Greenhedge Farm in Aslockton, Nottinghamshire, so named from Old English *grēne* 'green' + *hecg* 'hedge'.

Greenier (127) Americanized spelling of French GRENIER.

Greening (889) **1.** English: derivative of GREEN. **2.** Americanized spelling of German **Grüning**, a variant of GROENING.

Greenland (490) **1.** English: topographic name for someone who lived near a patch of land left open as communal pasturage, from Middle English *grene* 'green' + *land* 'land'. **2.** Translated form of German **Grönland**, a topographic name with the same meaning as 1, from Low German *grön* 'green' + *Land* 'land'.

Greenlaw (862) Scottish: habitational name from lands so named in Berwickshire.

Greenleaf (1597) **1.** English: from Old English *grēne* 'green' + *lēaf* 'leaf', presumably applied as a nickname, the significance of which is now lost. **2.** Jewish (American): English translation of the Ashkenazic ornamental surname **Grünblatt**, a compound of German *grün* + *Blatt* 'leaf'.

Greenlee (3212) English: habitational name from any of various minor places, for example in Staffordshire, so named from Old English *grēne* 'green' + *lēah* 'woodland clearing'.

Greenlees (127) Scottish: habitational name from (East or West) Greenlees in Lanarkshire, named from Older Scots *grēne* 'green' + *ley(s)* 'piece of open country', later 'meadow'.

Greenley (337) English: variant spelling of GREENLEE.

Greenlief (131) Probably a respelling of English or Jewish GREENLEAF.

Greenlund (109) Partly Americanized form of Swedish **Grönlund** (see GRONLUND).

Greenly (304) English: variant spelling of GREENLEE.

Greenman (1054) **1.** English: nickname or topographic name from Middle English *grene* + *man* 'man' (see GREEN). **2.** Probably a translation of German **Grunemann** or **Grünemann**, possibly a topographic name with the same sense as *Grönland* (see GREENLAND), or a habitational name for someone from any of numerous places named Grüna, Grünau, or Grüne.

Greeno (590) Respelling of French GRIGNON.

Greenough (743) **1.** English (Lancashire): variant of GREENHOW. **2.** Americanized spelling of French GRIGNON.

Greenshields (104) Scottish: habitational name from Greenshields in the parish of Liberton, Lanarkshire.

Greenslade (234) English: topographic name for someone who lived near a fertile valley, from Middle English *grene* 'green' + *slade* 'valley', 'dell'.

Greenspan (1395) Americanized form of the Ashkenazic Jewish ornamental surname **Grünspan**, from German *Grünspan* 'verdigris' (Middle High German *gruenspān*, which is a calque of medieval Latin *viride hispanicum* 'Spanish green').
GIVEN NAMES Jewish 6%. *Avrohom* (2), *Emanuel* (2), *Mayer* (2), *Aryeh*, *Hymie*, *Isadore*, *Mendy*, *Meyer*, *Miriam*, *Nachum*, *Shlomo*, *Sholom*.

Greenspon (161) Jewish: see GREENSPAN.
GIVEN NAME Jewish 4%. *Morty*.

Greenstein (1554) Partly Americanized form of the Ashkenazic Jewish ornamental surname **Gru(e)nstein**, from German *grün* 'green' (Yiddish *grin*) + *Stein* 'stone'.
GIVEN NAMES Jewish 6%. *Shosh* (2), *Avraham*, *Batsheva*, *Dafna*, *Myer*, *Ronen*, *Shalom*, *Sol*, *Zeev*.

Greenstone (138) English translation of Ashkenazic Jewish **Gru(e)nstein** (see GREENSTEIN).

Greenstreet (316) English (Kent): topographic name from Middle English *grene* 'green' + *strete* 'road', 'way'.

Greenup (363) English: topographic name for someone who lived in a fertile valley, from Middle English *grene* 'green' + *hope* 'valley'. Compare GREENSLADE.

Greenwade (129) **1.** Americanized form of German **Grün(e)wald** (see GRUN-

WALD). **2.** Perhaps also an altered spelling of English **Greenwood**, a topographic name from Middle English *grene* 'green' + *wode* 'wood'.

Greenwald (3115) Partly Americanized form of German and Jewish **Grün(e)wald** (see GRUNWALD).
GIVEN NAMES Jewish 4%. *Hyman* (3), *Shlomo* (3), *Emanuel* (2), *Miriam* (2), *Peretz* (2), *Aron*, *Avraham*, *Bernat*, *Dov*, *Dovid*, *Faigie*, *Meyer*.

Greenwaldt (152) Variant of German and Jewish **Grün(e)wald** (see GRUNWALD).

Greenwalt (897) Partly Americanized form of German and Jewish **Grün(e)wald** (see GRUNWALD).

Greenway (2001) **1.** English: topographic name for someone who lived by a grassy path, from Middle English *grene* 'green' + *weye* 'path' (see WAY). **2.** Welsh: Anglicized form of the Welsh personal name *Goronwy*, of unexplained origin. **3.** Translation of Dutch GROENEWEG or German **Grüneweg**, **Gröneweg**, topographic names with the same meaning as 1.

Greenwell (2421) English (Northumberland): topographic name for someone who lived by a stream among lush pastures, from Middle English *grene* 'green' + *welle* 'spring', 'stream', or habitational name from a minor place so named.
FOREBEARS The main English family of this name came originally from Greenwell, Wolsingham, County Durham, where they are recorded as owning land as early as 1183.

Greenwood (9211) **1.** English: topographic name for someone who lived in a dense forest, from Middle English *grene* 'green' + *wode* 'wood', or a habitational name from a minor place so named, as for example Greenwood in Heathfield, East Sussex. **2.** English translation of Ashkenazic Jewish **Grünholz**, an ornamental compound of German *grün* 'green' + *Holz* 'wood', and probably of German *Grünwald* (see GRUENWALD). **3.** English translation of French BOISVERT.

Greer (19626) Chiefly northern Irish: variant of GRIER.

Greeson (1274) Scottish: patronymic from GRIEVE.

Greever (230) **1.** Variant spelling of Dutch and North German GREVER. **2.** Possibly also a variant spelling of English GREAVER.

Grefe (261) North German: variant of GRAF.
GIVEN NAMES German 6%. *Erhardt*, *Gerhard*, *Gerhart*, *Kurt*.

Grefenstette (16) North German: habitational name from Greven near Münster in North Rhine-Westphalia, with the addition of *stette*, variant of STADT 'city'.

Greff (207) French (Alsace and Lorraine): variant of German GRAFF.

Greg (125) English: variant spelling of GREGG.

Grega (367) Polish and eastern German: variant of GREGER.

Greger (493) Polish and eastern German: from a vernacular form of the Latin personal name *Gregorius* (see GREGORY).

Gregersen (384) North German, Danish, and Norwegian: patronymic from the personal name *Greger* (see GREGORY).
GIVEN NAMES Scandinavian 8%; German 5%. *Erik* (2), *Nels* (2), *Nils* (2), *Aksel*, *Bjorn*, *Dagny*, *Juel*; *Hans* (3), *Detlef*, *Erna*, *Hermann*, *Jurgen*.

Gregerson (693) Americanized spelling of GREGERSEN.
GIVEN NAMES Scandinavian 6%. *Juel*, *Lars*, *Viggo*.

Gregg (9717) English: from a short form of GREGORY.

Greggs (370) English: patronymic from GREGG.

Grego (382) Spanish and Portuguese: ethnic name from *grego* 'Greek'.

Gregoire (1996) French (**Grégoire**): from the personal name *Grégoire*, French form of GREGORY.
GIVEN NAMES French 15%. *Emile* (9), *Armand* (7), *Marcel* (5), *Normand* (5), *Alphonse* (3), *Cecile* (3), *Fernand* (3), *Gilles* (3), *Jacques* (3), *Alain* (2), *Alphee* (2), *Georges* (2).

Gregor (1622) **1.** Scottish: reduced form of McGregor. **2.** German: from the personal name *Gregor*, a vernacular form of Latin *Gregorius* (see GREGORY). This surname has also been adopted by Ashkenazic Jews. It is also found as a family name in Slovenian and other Slavic languages. In some cases it may be a reduced form of the Slovenian patronymic **Gregorčič**.

Gregorek (108) Polish: from a diminutive of the personal name **Gregor**, variant of *Grzegorz*, vernacular form of Latin *Gregorius* (see GREGORY).
GIVEN NAMES Polish 20%. *Jerzy* (2), *Jozef*, *Krzysztof*, *Lucjan*, *Lucyna*, *Miroslaw*, *Tadeusz*, *Zygmunt*.

Gregori (214) **1.** Italian: patronymic or plural form of GREGORIO. **2.** Catalan: from the personal name *Gregori* (see GREGORY).
GIVEN NAMES Italian 16%; Spanish 8%. *Agostino*, *Alessandro*, *Antonio*, *Bartolo*, *Caterina*, *Cesare*, *Duilio*, *Emanuele*, *Emidio*, *Giorgio*, *Giovanni*, *Ivano*; *Henrique* (4), *Lino* (2), *Wilfredo* (2), *Alicia*, *Augusto*, *Ernesto*, *Luisa*, *Mario*, *Maurilio*, *Reinaldo*.

Gregorian (121) Armenian: variant of GRIGORIAN.
GIVEN NAMES Armenian 26%. *Armen* (3), *Zareh* (2), *Andranik*, *Arsen*, *Avanes*, *Avo*, *Garen*, *Hrach*, *Karineh*, *Massis*, *Roobik*, *Vartan*; *Philomena* (4), *Antonio*.

Gregorich (463) Slovenian (**Gregorič**) and Croatian (**Gregorić**): patronymic from the personal name *Gregor* (Slovenian) or *Gregorije* (Croatian) (see GREGORY), vernacular forms of Latin *Gregorius* (see GREGORY).

Gregorie (137) French (**Grégorie**): from the female personal name *Grégorie*, feminine form of *Grégoire* (see GREGORY).

GIVEN NAME French 4%. *Yvon.*

Gregorio (796) Italian, Spanish, and Portuguese (**Gregório**): from the personal name *Gregorio* (see GREGORY).

GIVEN NAMES Spanish 18%; Italian 10%; Portuguese 6%. *Manuel* (7), *Mario* (5), *Fernando* (4), *Jose* (4), *Ramon* (4), *Juan* (3), *Roberto* (3), *Ana* (2), *Cesar* (2), *Francisco* (2), *Adolfo*, *Alberto*; *Angelo* (6), *Antonio* (4), *Salvatore* (3), *Carmine* (2), *Gennaro* (2), *Federico*, *Franco*, *Heriberto*, *Italo*, *Marco*, *Nicola*; *Henrique*, *Joaquim*, *Paulo.*

Gregorius (141) German, Dutch, etc.: humanistic name from the Latin form of **Gregor** (see GREGORY).

GIVEN NAMES German 4%. *Hans, Wolfgang.*

Gregory (31453) English: from a personal name that was popular throughout Christendom in the Middle Ages. The Greek original, *Grēgorios*, is a derivative of *grēgorein* 'to be awake', 'to be watchful'. However, the Latin form, *Gregorius*, came to be associated by folk etymology with *grex, gregis*, 'flock', 'herd', under the influence of the Christian image of the good shepherd. The Greek name was borne in the early Christian centuries by two fathers of the Orthodox Church, St. Gregory Nazianzene (*c.* 325–390) and St. Gregory of Nyssa (*c.* 331–395), and later by sixteen popes, starting with Gregory the Great (*c.* 540–604). It was also the name of 3rd- and 4th-century apostles of Armenia. In North America the English form of the name has absorbed many cognates from other European languages. (For forms, see Hanks and Hodges 1988).

Gregson (863) English: patronymic from *Greg*, a short form of the personal name GREGORY.

Gregston (170) Perhaps an altered form of GREGSON.

Gregus (146) Eastern German: unexplained. Perhaps from a short form of GREGORY.

GIVEN NAMES German 6%. *Helmut, Jurgen, Kurt.*

Greider (311) Variant of Dutch (**de**) **Gruyter** (see GRYDER).

Greif (675) **1.** German: habitational name from a house distinguished by the sign of a gryphon, Middle High German *grīf(e)* (Old High German *grīf(o)*, from Late Latin *gryphus*, Greek *gryps*, of Assyrian origin). **2.** German: nickname for a grasping man, the gryphon in folk etymology having come to be associated with Middle High German *grīfen* 'to grasp or snatch'. **3.** English: variant of GRIEF.

GIVEN NAMES Jewish 4%. *Arnon* (2), *Emanuel* (2), *Aron, Avner, Hyman, Igal, Meyer.*

Greiff (166) German: variant spelling of GREIF 1.

GIVEN NAMES German 5%. *Gerhard, Hans.*

Greig (1066) Scottish: from a short form of the personal name GREGORY.

Greil (122) German: variant of GREUEL.

GIVEN NAMES German 4%. *Gerhardt, Kurt.*

Greim (170) **1.** South German: from a short form of a compound personal name beginning with the element *grīm* 'mask', 'helmet'. **2.** Scottish: variant of GRAHAM.

Greiman (152) **1.** Respelling of German GREIMANN. **2.** Jewish (Ashkenazic): of uncertain origin; perhaps a variant of GRAUMAN.

Greimann (105) German: from GREIM or GREIN, with the addition of Middle High German *man* 'man'.

Grein (348) German: **1.** nickname for an argumentative person, from Middle High German *grīn* 'loud cry', 'loud'. **2.** habitational name from places so named in Bavaria and Austria.

GIVEN NAMES German 6%. *Eldor* (2), *Hans* (2), *Jochen, Klaus.*

Greiner (3463) South German: **1.** nickname for a cantankerous or quarrelsome person, from Middle High German *grīner* 'squabbler', 'quarreler', an agent derivative of *grīn* 'loud cry', 'shout'. **2.** habitational name for someone from a place called Grein (see GREIN 2).

Greinke (164) German: of uncertain origin. Perhaps a nickname for a small person, from Middle Low German *gren* 'grain' + the North German diminutive suffix *-k-*.

GIVEN NAME German 4%. *Klaus.*

Greis (204) **1.** German: descriptive nickname for a gray-haired man, from Middle High German *grīs* 'gray'. **2.** Respelling of German GRIES.

GIVEN NAMES German 6%. *Kurt* (2), *Gunther, Helmut.*

Greisen (146) Danish: patronymic from the personal name *Greis*, a reduced form of *Gregers*, Danish form of GREGORY.

GIVEN NAMES German 4%. *Hans, Theodor.*

Greiser (124) German: descriptive nickname for a gray-haired man, from Middle High German *grīs* 'gray' (see GREIS).

Greiss (120) **1.** German: variant of GREIS. **2.** Muslim: unexplained.

GIVEN NAMES Muslim 7%. *Hani* (2), *Kamal, Raouf, Rashad.*

Greitzer (118) Jewish (Ashkenazic): **1.** ornamental name from Yiddish *graytser* 'kreuzer', the old Austro-Hungarian unit of currency. **2.** metonymic occupational name from Yiddish *graytser* 'corkscrew'.

GIVEN NAME Jewish 4%. *Sol.*

Greive (127) Scottish and northern English: variant spelling of GRIEVE.

Greiwe (176) German: possibly a nickname from Middle High German *greibe* 'sharp', 'tangy', 'dour'. Compare GREY.

Grell (600) German: **1.** nickname for an irritable, irascible person, from Middle High German, Middle Low German *grellen* 'to be angry'. **2.** habitational name from a place named Grelle.

GIVEN NAMES German 4%. *Hans* (4), *Kurt* (2), *Claus, Dietrich, Franz, Guenter.*

Grella (387) Italian: probably from a reduced form of *Agrella*, feminine form of *Agrello*, a derivative of *Agro*, from *agro* 'rough', 'hard'.

GIVEN NAMES Italian 17%. *Angelo* (5), *Carmine* (3), *Nunzio* (3), *Giuseppe* (2), *Pasquale* (2), *Antonio, Carmino, Emanuele, Gino, Giovanni, Lorenzo, Nunzi.*

Grelle (196) German: variant of GRELL.

Gremillion (949) Possibly a variant spelling of the French surname **Gremillon**, a habitational name from either of two places: Gremillon in Vienne or Le Grémillon.

FOREBEARS The name is specifically associated with LA; its bearers are descended from one Louis Gremillion dit Sans Quartier, who came from Courcival, near Le Mans, in the French province of Maine, shortly before 1747.

GIVEN NAMES French 6%. *Marcel* (2), *Monique* (2), *Pierre* (2), *Andre, Camille, Emile, Gaston, Landry, Normand, Octave, Ovide.*

Gremminger (143) Swiss German: of uncertain origin; possibly from a Germanic personal name based on *grim* 'mask', 'helmet', or, more likely, a nickname for an irascible person, from Middle High German *gram* 'angry'.

Grems (111) German: derogatory nickname from a derivative of Middle High German *gremzen* 'to be moody or objectionable'.

Gren (163) Swedish: ornamental surname from Swedish *gren* 'branch' (Old Norse *grein*). In some cases the name may have been chosen with some reference to the notion of the 'branches' making up a family 'tree', but it also falls into the category of words denoting natural features, which were drawn on heavily when Swedish surnames came to be formed wholesale in the 19th century.

GIVEN NAMES Scandinavian 8%. *Gunner, Lars.*

Grenda (166) Polish: variant of **Grzęda**, a nickname from *grzęda* 'perch', 'roost', 'patch'.

GIVEN NAMES Polish 6%. *Casimir, Rafal, Zygmond.*

Grendahl (129) **1.** Swedish: ornamental name from *gren* 'branch' + *dahl* 'valley'. **2.** Norwegian: habitational name from a farm in Trøndelag, named with *gren* (of uncertain origin) + *dal* 'valley'.

GIVEN NAMES Scandinavian 4%. *Erik, Thor.*

Grenell (145) Perhaps a variant of GREENHILL.

Grenfell (358) English: variant of GREEN-FIELD 2.

Grenier (2653) French: variant of GRANIER.
GIVEN NAMES French 15%. *Gilles* (8), *Lucien* (8), *Normand* (7), *Andre* (6), *Armand* (6), *Marcel* (6), *Emile* (5), *Camille* (4), *Alcide* (3), *Henri* (3), *Herve* (3), *Laurent* (3).

Greninger (248) Swiss German: of uncertain origin; perhaps from a personal name as assumed by A. Socin from the family name of Henricus *Greninc*, recorded in a Freiburg document of *c*.1200.

Grenke (144) German: variant of *Grönke* (see GROENKE), or of GREINKE.
GIVEN NAMES German 5%. *Alois, Otto*.

Grennan (378) **1.** English: variant of GERNON. **2.** Irish: reduced Anglicized form of Gaelic **Ó Grianáin** (see GREENAN).
GIVEN NAMES Irish 6%. *Brendan, Eamon, Kieran*.

Grennell (117) English: variant of GREEN-HILL 1.

Grenon (321) French (Normandy): nickname for someone who wore a moustache (at a time when men were generally clean shaven), from Old French *gernon, grenon* 'moustache'.
GIVEN NAMES French 14%. *Henri* (2), *Jean-Francois* (2), *Anatole, Andre, Collette, Gisele, Jean-Louis, Luc, Lucien, Normand, Rejeanne, Rosaire*.

Grenz (403) German: **1.** nickname for someone with a deformity or peculiarity of the mouth or nose, from Middle High German *grans* 'beak', 'snout'. **2.** from a topographic name for someone who lived near a border, from Polish *granica*, which became German *Grenze* 'border' after the 16th century.
GIVEN NAMES German 7%. *Klaus* (2), *Otto* (2), *Reinhard* (2), *Erna, Frieda, Manfred, Milbert*.

Gresens (144) **1.** Dutch and German: patronymic from a vernacular form of Latin *Gratianus*, a derivative of *Gratius*, itself a derivative of *gratus* 'pleasing', 'lovely'. St. Gratian (died *c*. 337) was a disciple of St. Denis of Paris; he became the first bishop of Tours. **2.** German: variant spelling of **Gresenz**, from the medieval personal name *Crescentius* (Latin *crescens* 'growing').
GIVEN NAMES German 5%. *Erwin* (2), *Kurt*.

Greseth (116) Norwegian: habitational name from either of two farms, in Møre and Trøndelag, named with Old Norse *grjót* 'stone' + *setr* 'farmstead', 'dwelling'.

Gresh (474) Americanized spelling of German **Gresch**, from a short form of GREGOR.

Gresham (3771) English: habitational name from a place in Norfolk, so named from Old English *græs, gærs* 'grass(land)', 'pasturage' + *hām* 'homestead' or *hamm* 'enclosure hemmed in by water'.

Gresko (321) Variant of Ukrainian HRESKO.

Gresock (101) Americanized form of Slovak **Krišák**.

Gress (1437) German and Danish: **1.** from a short form of a Germanic nickname that may be derived from Old High German *grātag* 'greedy'. **2.** from Middle Low German *grese* 'horror', 'fear', a nickname for someone who was feared in the community. **3.** habitational name from Gress, a place in Mecklenburg.

Gressel (147) South German: **1.** diminutive of GRESS 1. **2.** nickname for a big person, from a variant of *grössl*, a diminutive of *gross* 'big'. **3.** variant of **Grässel** (see GRASSEL). **4.** variant of the personal name *Erasmus*, Latinized form of Greek *Erasmos*, a derivative of *erān* 'to love'. St. Erasmus (died 303) was a bishop of Formiae in Campania, martyred under Diocletian; he is numbered among the Fourteen Holy Helpers and is a patron of sailors.

Gresser (225) German: variant of GRASER.

Gressett (375) Respelling of French **Gresset**, from a derivative of *graisse* 'fat'.

Gressler (113) German: variant of **Grässler**, itself a variant of GRASER.
GIVEN NAME German 4%. *Volker*.

Gressley (168) Altered spelling of the German Swiss family name **Gressly**, a variant of GRESSEL.

Gressman (155) German (**Gressmann**): habitational name for someone from Gress in Mecklenburg.
GIVEN NAME German 4%. *Reinhold*.

Greth (183) German: from a short form of a personal name formed with Old High German *grātag* 'greedy'.

Grether (276) **1.** Swiss German: variant of GRAETER. **2.** South German: from the female personal name *Grete*.
GIVEN NAMES German 6%. *Hans* (3), *Heinz* (2), *Dieter, Traute*.

Gretz (308) **1.** German: from a short form of a Germanic personal name cognate with Old High German *grātag* 'greedy'. **2.** Jewish (Ashkenazic): habitational name from Grätz, the German name of the Polish town Grodzisk, near Poznań.

Gretzinger (199) German and Jewish (western Ashkenazic): habitational name for someone from any of three places named Grötzingen (Old High German *Grezzingun*) in Baden-Württemberg.
GIVEN NAMES German 6%. *Kurt* (2), *Otto*.

Greubel (163) German: of uncertain origin; possibly a variant of GREUEL 2 or alternatively a habitational name from a Grevel near Dortmund or Grübel in Bavaria.

Greuel (244) German: **1.** habitational name from any of several places in the Rhineland named Greuel. **2.** nickname from Middle High German *griuwel* 'horror'.

Greulich (364) German: nickname from Middle High German *griuwelich* 'horrifying'.
GIVEN NAMES German 8%. *Gunther* (2), *Bernd, Dieter, Friedhelm, Friedrich, Hedwig, Irmgard, Kurt*.

Greunke (135) North German: Lower Rhine variant of **Gröhnke** (see GROEN).
GIVEN NAMES German 5%. *Armin, Kurt*.

Greve (1126) **1.** North German and Scandinavian: status name from Middle Low German and Danish *greve*, equivalent to German GRAF. **2.** English: variant of GREAVES.
GIVEN NAMES German 5%. *Gerhard* (2), *Otto* (2), *Reinhold* (2), *Bernhardt, Claus, Erna, Erwin, Ewald, Fritz, Kurt*.

Greven (108) **1.** Dutch: from a derivative of *grave* 'official', 'governor', 'count' (see GRAEF). **2.** German: variant of GREVE. **3.** German: habitational name from either of two places so named, one near Münster, the other in Mecklenburg.
GIVEN NAMES German 14%; Dutch 6%. *Otto* (2), *Erwin, Meinrad, Wolfgang*; *Dirk* (2), *Gerrit*.

Grever (170) Dutch and North German: occupational name for a digger (of graves or ditches), Middle Dutch *graver*, Middle Low German *grever(e)*.

Greving (117) North German and Dutch: patronymic derivative of Low German *greve* 'count', 'official' (see GREVE), or the Dutch cognate *grave*.

Grew (236) **1.** English: nickname for a tall, scrawny person, from Middle English, Old French *grue* 'crane' (Late Latin *grua*, for classical Latin *grus*). **2.** Irish: reduced form of MULGREW.

Grewal (411) Indian (Panjab): Sikh name based on the name of a Jat tribe, of unexplained origin.
GIVEN NAMES Indian 86%. *Balwinder* (5), *Hardev* (2), *Jagdish* (2), *Kiran* (2), *Lakhbir* (2), *Mohan* (2), *Raj* (2), *Rajpal* (2), *Sandip* (2), *Sanjay* (2), *Sukhpal* (2), *Ajit*.

Grewe (642) **1.** English and Irish: variant of GREW. **2.** German: variant of GREVE.
GIVEN NAMES German 6%. *Alois* (2), *Hans* (2), *Johannes* (2), *Arno, Erna, Gunther, Lorenz, Manfred, Oskar, Otto*.

Grewell (203) **1.** English: metonymic occupational name for a miller or baker, from Old French *gruel* 'fine flour', 'meal'. **2.** Perhaps also an Americanized spelling of German GREUEL.

Grey (3561) **1.** English: variant spelling of GRAY 1. **2.** German: dialect variant of GRAU.

Grgurich (140) Croatian and Serbian (**Grgurić**): patronymic from the personal name *Grgur*, a vernacular form of Latin *Gregorius* (see GREGORY).

Gribben (381) Irish: reduced Anglicized form of Gaelic **Mac (Mag) Roibín**, a patronymic from the Norman personal name *Robin*, a pet form of ROBERT.
GIVEN NAMES Irish 4%. *Liam, Dympna, Seamus*.

Gribbin (411) Irish: variant spelling of GRIBBEN.

Gribbins (210) Irish: variant of GRIBBEN.

Gribble (1504) **1.** English: from a Norman personal name *Grimbald*, composed of the

Germanic elements *grīm* 'mask', 'helmet' + *bald*, *bold* 'bold', 'brave'. **2.** Respelling of German **Gribbel**, from a pet form of a personal name formed with GREIF.

Gribbon (139) Irish: variant spelling of GRIBBEN.

Gricar (43) Slovenian (**Gričar**): topographic name for someone who lived by a low hill, from Slovenian *grič* 'low hill'.

Grice (2923) English: **1.** nickname for a gray-haired man, from Middle English *grice*, *gris* 'gray' (Old French *gris*, apparently of Germanic origin, and probably a distant cognate of GRAY 1). **2.** from Middle English *grice*, *grise* 'pig' (Old Norse *gríss*, probably akin to 1), hence a metonymic occupational name for a swineherd or a nickname. **3.** Possibly an Americanized spelling of German GREIS.

Grider (2378) Variant of Dutch (**de**) **Gruyter** (see GRYDER).

Gridley (793) English: nickname for someone with a pock-marked face (see GREELEY).

FOREBEARS Richard Gridley arrived in Boston about 1630. His fourth-generation descendant Richard (1710/11–96) was born in Boston and became a military engineer and iron smelter.

Grieb (495) Possibly a variant spelling of the Swiss German family name **Griebe**, an occupational name for a butcher or fat dealer, from Middle High German *griebe*, *griube* 'rendered bacon pieces', 'crackling'.
GIVEN NAMES German 5%. *Erhard*, *Ernst*, *Erwin*, *Ewald*, *Gerhard*.

Griebel (577) **1.** South German: variant of **Grübel** (see GRABLE). **2.** South German: topographic name for someone living in a hollow, from a diminutive of Middle High German *gruobe* 'hollow'. **3.** Westphalian nickname for a clever person, from Middle Low German *grievel* 'badger'.

Grieco (1305) Italian: variant of GRECO.
GIVEN NAMES Italian 14%. *Angelo* (9), *Vito* (6), *Carmine* (5), *Donato* (5), *Antonio* (4), *Pasquale* (3), *Salvatore* (3), *Ciriaco* (2), *Rocco* (2), *Alessandra*, *Amedeo*, *Carmel*.

Grieder (200) Swiss German: variant of KREIDER.

Grief (156) **1.** English (Norfolk): from an Old Norse personal name *Greifi*, a byname from Old Norse *greifi*, Old Danish or Old Swedish *grefe* 'count', 'earl'. **2.** French: nickname from Old French *grief* 'sad'. **3.** German: variant spelling of GREIF 1.
GIVEN NAME French 5%. *Lucien*.

Grieff (111) English (Norfolk): variant spelling of GRIEF.

Grieger (398) German: from the personal name *Grieger*, one of the German forms of Latin *Gregorius* (see GREGORY).

Griego (1758) Spanish: ethnic name from *griego* 'Greek' (Latin *graecus*).
GIVEN NAMES Spanish 21%. *Manuel* (16), *Carlos* (9), *Orlando* (9), *Juan* (8), *Jose* (7),

Alfonso (6), *Ruben* (6), *Leandro* (4), *Mario* (4), *Armando* (3), *Benito* (3), *Celestino* (3).

Grieme (125) German: from a short form of a compound personal name beginning with the Germanic element *grīm* 'mask', 'helmet'. Compare GREIM.

Griep (365) North German variant of GREIF 1.

Griepentrog (189) North German: from a sentence meaning 'reach in(to) the vat'; a late medieval nickname for a journeyman baker or perhaps for a greedy person.

Grier (3807) Scottish: from the personal name *Grier*, a common medieval Scottish vernacular form of GREGORY.

Grierson (401) Scottish: patronymic from GRIER.
FOREBEARS A Scottish family by the name of Grierson claim descent from Gilbert, son of Malcolm MacGregor (died 1374), 11th Lord of MacGregor. Gilbert was known as both MacGregor and Gregorson. In 1400 he was granted lands by the Earl of March in the name Grierson. The numerous northern Irish bearers of the name Greer claim descent from this same Gilbert.

Gries (728) **1.** South German: topographic name for someone who lived in a sandy place, from Middle High German *griez* 'sand'. **2.** Perhaps a reduced form of German GRIESE.

Griesbach (455) German: topographic name for someone living near a stream with a sandy bottom, from Middle High German *griez* 'sand' + *bach* 'brook', 'stream'.

Griesbaum (122) German: variant of KIRSCHBAUM 1.

Griese (456) North German: nickname for a gray-haired man, from Middle Low German *grīs* 'gray'.

Griesel (153) South German (Bavaria) and Swiss German: from a diminutive of Middle High German *griez* 'coarsely ground grain'; perhaps an occupational nickname for a miller, farmer, or farm worker, or alternatively a topographic name for someone who lived on sandy soil, from the same word in this sense.
GIVEN NAMES German 6%. *Gerhard*, *Otto*.

Griesemer (361) German: **1.** reduced form of **Griesemeier**, a distinguishing name for a tenant farmer whose farm was on sandy soil, from Middle High German *griez* 'sand', 'sandy bank (of a river)' + *meier* 'tenant farmer' (see MEYER). **2.** perhaps also a dialect reduction of **Griesheimer**, a habitational name for someone from any of several places in southern Germany named Griesheim.
GIVEN NAMES German 5%. *Manfred* (3), *Kurt*.

Grieser (520) South German: topographic name for someone living on a sandy site, from Middle High German *griez* 'sand' + *-er* suffix denoting an inhabitant.
GIVEN NAMES German 4%. *Fritz* (3), *Dieter*, *Gerhard*.

Grieshaber (333) South German: from Middle High German *griez* 'coarse milled grain' + *haber* 'he who has', hence an occupational nickname for a farmer.
GIVEN NAMES German 9%. *Otto* (3), *Erwin*, *Georg*, *Gerd*, *Gunther*, *Nikolaus*, *Wolfgang*.

Grieshop (170) German: topographic name for someone living on a sandy site, from Middle High German *griez* 'sand' + Middle Low German *hōp* 'heap', 'pile'. (Phonologically mixed forms occur in certain dialect areas, e.g. in the Rhineland and in later settlement areas east of the Elbe, due to the geographically uneven consonant changes of the second or Old High German sound shift.)
GIVEN NAME French 4%. *Patrice*.

Griesinger (190) German: habitational name for someone from a place named Griesingen in Bavaria.
GIVEN NAMES German 4%. *Dieter*, *Wolfgang*.

Griesmer (152) German: variant of GRIESEMER.

Griess (485) German: variant of GRIES.
GIVEN NAMES German 4%. *Ewald* (2), *Kurt* (2), *Egon*, *Heinz*, *Otto*.

Griesser (157) South German: variant spelling of GRIESER.
GIVEN NAMES German 9%. *Horst* (2), *Kaspar*, *Kurt*, *Wolfgang*.

Griest (329) **1.** English: unexplained; perhaps a variant of GRIST. **2.** German: unexplained.

Grieve (861) Scottish and northern English: occupational name for a steward or estate manager, Middle English *greve*, Old English *græfa*. Compare REEVE and SHERIFF. This word was originally distinct from GRAVE 1, but some confusion has occurred as a result of the close similarity in both form and meaning.

Grieves (329) Scottish: patronymic from GRIEVE.

Griff (215) **1.** English: topographic name for someone living near a pit or hollow, from Old Norse *gryfja* 'pit', 'hollow', or a habitational name from Griff in Warwickshire, Griffe in Derbyshire, or Griff Farm in Rievaulx, North Yorkshire, all probably named with this word. **2.** Welsh: short form of GRIFFITH. **3.** Possibly also a reduced form of Irish McGRIFF. **4.** German: variant of GREIF 1.

Griffee (229) Irish: reduced Anglicized form of Gaelic Ó Gríobhtha (see GRIFFIN).

Griffel (127) **1.** Dutch, German, and Jewish (Ashkenazic): metonymic occupational name from Middle Dutch and Middle Low German *griffel* 'slate pencil', modern German *Griffel*. **2.** Dutch: topographic name from Dutch *griffe* 'swamp ditch'. **3.** German: variant of **Gribbel** (see GRIBBLE 2).
GIVEN NAMES Jewish 8%; German 4%. *Giora* (2), *Baruch*, *Moshe*, *Tali*; *Hertha*.

Griffen (853) English: variant spelling of GRIFFIN.

Griffes (120) French: from the plural of *griffe* 'claw' (Old French *grif*), presumably a nickname for someone with clawlike hands or grasping habits.

Griffeth (636) Altered spelling of GRIFFITH.

Griffey (1007) Irish: reduced Anglicized form of Gaelic **Ó Gríobhtha** (see GRIFFIN).

Griffie (300) Irish: variant spelling of GRIFFEY.

Griffin (64218) **1.** Welsh: from a medieval Latinized form, *Griffinus*, of the Welsh personal name *Gruffudd* (see GRIFFITH). **2.** English: nickname for a fierce or dangerous person, from Middle English *griffin* 'gryphon' (from Latin *gryphus*, Greek *gryps*, of Assyrian origin). **3.** Irish: Anglicized (part translated) form of Gaelic **Ó Gríobhtha** 'descendant of *Gríobhtha*', a personal name from *gríobh* 'gryphon'.

Griffing (524) Variant spelling of GRIFFIN.

Griffis (2847) Reduced form of Welsh GRIFFITHS.

Griffith (28835) Welsh: from the Old Welsh personal name *Gruffudd*, Old Welsh *Grip(p)iud*, composed of the elements *grip*, of uncertain significance, + *iud* 'chief', 'lord'.

Griffiths (5409) Welsh: patronymic from GRIFFITH.

Griffitt (136) Altered spelling of GRIFFITH.

Griffitts (395) Altered spelling of GRIFFITHS.

Griffo (305) **1.** Italian: from *grifo* 'gryphon' (Latin *gryphus*, Greek *gryps*, of Assyrian origin), hence a nickname for someone thought to resemble the mythical beast **2.** Italian **Griffò**: probably from *Grifo*, *Crifo*, derived from Greek *kryphos* 'secret', 'hidden', 'enigmatic'. **3.** Perhaps a respelling of French **Griffaud**, which Morlet speculates may be from one of the Germanic compound personal names beginning with the element *grif*, a derivative of Old High German *grifan* 'to grasp or seize'.

GIVEN NAMES Italian 12%. *Salvatore* (4), *Filippo, Paolo, Rocco, Vito*.

Griffon (121) French: from a diminutive of Old French *griffe* 'claw', hence a nickname for a grasping or vicious person, or perhaps for someone with a deformed or otherwise remarkable hand.

GIVEN NAMES French 7%. *Dominique, Heloise, Irby.*

Griffy (202) Irish: reduced Anglicized form of Gaelic **Ó Gríobhtha** (see GRIFFIN).

Grifka (123) German (of Slavic origin): probably a variant of **Grifke**, like **Gniffke** from (Polish) *gniew* 'anger', hence a nickname for an irascible person.

Grigas (220) Lithuanian: unexplained.

Grigg (1838) English: from a short form of the personal name GREGORY.

Griggers (131) Patronymic from a vernacular form of the Latin personal name *Gregorius* (see GREGORY).

Griggs (8353) English: patronymic from the personal name GRIGG.

Grignon (247) French: nickname equivalent to *grignard* 'angry', 'contemptuous', from Old French *grignier* 'to grit the teeth or curl the lips', gestures of fierce contempt. The verb is of Germanic origin and was originally probably an imitative formation suggestive of grunting through clenched teeth.

GIVEN NAMES French 7%. *Pierre* (2), *Henri, Laurent, Marcel.*

Grigorian (246) Armenian: patronymic from the Armenian personal name *Grigor* (see GREGORY).

GIVEN NAMES Armenian 49%; Russian 5%. *Grigor* (4), *Ashot* (3), *Varouj* (3), *Andranik* (2), *Ara* (2), *Araksi* (2), *Ararat* (2), *Armen* (2), *Arshaluys* (2), *Gevork* (2), *Hakop* (2), *Rouben* (2); *Vladimir* (2), *Barkev, Guennadi, Leonid, Sergei.*

Grigoryan (156) Armenian: variant spelling of GRIGORIAN.

GIVEN NAMES Armenian 35%; Russian 29%; Jewish 7%. *Grigor* (3), *Gayane* (2), *Grach* (2), *Vardan* (2), *Anahid, Aram, Armenak, Armine, Arsham, Arusyak, Edik, Garen*; *Vladimir* (3), *Yuriy* (3), *Aleksandr* (2), *Grigoriy* (2), *Oleg* (2), *Sergey* (2), *Galina, Kima, Mayya, Mikhail, Natalya, Ninel*; *Irina.*

Grigsby (3802) English (Kent): habitational name from a lost or unidentified place.

Grigson (133) English: patronymic from the personal name GRIGG.

Grijalva (882) Spanish: habitational name from any of various places named Grijalba, in particular the one in Burgos province. The place name is from *iglesia* 'church' + Old Spanish *alva* 'white'.

GIVEN NAMES Spanish 37%. *Manuel* (13), *Jose* (12), *Ruben* (11), *Francisco* (10), *Carlos* (8), *Raul* (7), *Jesus* (6), *Jorge* (6), *Armando* (5), *Galo* (4), *Juan* (4), *Luis* (4).

Grill (1399) **1.** English: nickname for a fierce or cruel man, from Middle English *grill(e)* 'angry', 'vicious' (from Old English *gryllan* 'to rage', 'to gnash the teeth'; compare 4). **2.** German: nickname for a cheerful person, from Middle High German *grille* 'cricket' (Old High German *grillo*, from Late Latin *grillus*, Greek *gryllos*). The insect is widely supposed to be of a cheerful disposition, no doubt because of its habit of infesting hearths and warm places. The vocabulary word is confined largely to southern Germany and Austria, and it is in this region that the surname is most frequent. **3.** German: habitational name from any of eight places in Upper Bavaria and Austria, perhaps so named from Middle High German *grille* 'cricket'. **4.** North German: nickname for an angry man from Middle Low German *grellen* 'to be furious', 'to shriek'. Compare 1.

GIVEN NAMES German 5%. *Erwin* (4), *Franz* (2), *Otto* (2), *Alois, Bernhard, Ernst,* *Gerhard, Hermann, Klaus, Konrad, Manfred, Monika.*

Grilley (132) Possibly an altered form of Irish CRILLY.

Grilli (372) Italian: **1.** patronymic or plural form of the nickname GRILLO. **2.** possibly a reduced form of the compound name **Mazzagrilli**, meaning 'kill the crickets', i.e. an ironic nickname for a idler.

GIVEN NAMES Italian 19%. *Guido* (3), *Salvatore* (3), *Donato* (2), *Enzo* (2), *Vito* (2), *Aldo, Angelo, Dino, Enrico, Ettore, Francesco, Geno.*

Grilliot (181) French: variant of GRILLOT.

Grillo (2110) **1.** Italian: nickname for a cheerful person, from *grillo* 'cricket' (Late Latin *grillus*). **2.** Respelling of French GRILLOT.

GIVEN NAMES Italian 23%. *Salvatore* (12), *Rocco* (8), *Angelo* (7), *Vito* (7), *Mario* (6), *Sal* (6), *Carmela* (4), *Orlando* (4), *Aldo* (3), *Alfredo* (3), *Carlo* (3), *Domenic* (3), *Evelio* (3), *Rosario* (3), *Pasquale* (3), *Antonio* (2), *Carmine* (2), *Raul* (2), *Roberto* (2), *Sergio* (2).

Grillot (180) French: nickname for a cheerful person, from a variant of *grillon* 'cricket'.

GIVEN NAMES French 7%. *Emile* (2), *Francois.*

Grills (338) English: patronymic from GRILL 1.

Grim (2834) **1.** Dutch: nickname for a dour and forbidding person, from Middle Dutch *grim, grem* 'stern', 'severe'. **2.** English: nickname with the same meaning as 1, from Old English *grim* 'fierce', 'grim'. **3.** Respelling of German GRIMM.

Grima (137) Italian and Maltese: according to Caracausi, from the Germanic female personal name *Grima* (from *grīm* 'mask', 'helmet').

GIVEN NAMES Italian 18%. *Angelo* (2), *Mario* (2), *Carmel, Carmine, Sante.*

Grimaldi (1520) Italian: patronymic or plural form of the personal name GRIMALDO. This name is also found in Greece, Corsica, and elsewhere.

FOREBEARS This is the name of the ruling family of the principality of Monaco. They came to Monaco from Genoa in the 13th century.

GIVEN NAMES Italian 21%; Spanish 5%. *Mario* (8), *Angelo* (6), *Antonio* (3), *Giuseppe* (3), *Sal* (3), *Santo* (3), *Aniello* (2), *Ascanio* (2), *Carmela* (2), *Franco* (2), *Giovanni* (2), *Marco* (2), *Marino* (2), *Massimo* (2); *Manuel* (3), *Jose* (2), *Luis* (2), *Carlos.*

Grimaldo (384) Spanish and Italian: from a Germanic personal name composed of the elements *grīm* 'mask', 'helmet' + *wald* 'rule'. This name is common in Mexico and Peru.

GIVEN NAMES Spanish 54%. *Jose* (19), *Juan* (12), *Jesus* (9), *Manuel* (7), *Luis* (5), *Francisco* (4), *Pedro* (4), *Gerardo* (3),

Jorge (3), *Pablo* (3), *Roberto* (3), *Rogelio* (3).

Grimard (171) French: from *Grimhard*, a Germanic personal name composed of the elements *grīm* 'mask', 'helmet' + *hard* 'strong'.
GIVEN NAMES French 18%. *Jacques* (2), *Marcel* (2), *Alphonse, Fernand, Gisele, Jean-Paul, Normand, Yvan, Yves.*

Grimaud (129) French: from a Germanic personal name composed of the elements *grim* 'mask' + *waldan* 'to govern'.
GIVEN NAMES French 6%. *Armand* (2), *Michel.*

Grimball (132) Probably a variant spelling of GRIMBLE.

Grimble (109) English: variant of GRIBBLE.
GIVEN NAME Irish 5%. *Murphy.*

Grime (256) English: from the Old Norse personal name *Grímr*, which remained popular as a personal name in the form *Grim* in Anglo-Scandinavian areas well into the 12th century. It was a byname of Woden with the meaning 'masked person' or 'shape-changer', and may have been bestowed on male children in an attempt to secure the protection of the god. The Continental Germanic cognate *grīm* was also used as a first element in compound names. Compare GRIMAUD and GRIBBLE, with the original sense 'mask', 'helmet'. Some examples of the surname may derive from short forms of such names.

Grimes (17241) English: patronymic from GRIME.

Grimley (346) **1.** English: habitational name from a place in Worcestershire, probably so named from Old English *grīma* 'specter', 'goblin' + Old English *lēah* 'woodland clearing'. **2.** Irish: variant of GORMLEY.
GIVEN NAMES Irish 4%. *Connor, Liam.*

Grimm (8731) German and Swiss German: **1.** nickname for a dour and forbidding individual, from Old High German *grim* 'stern', 'severe'. **2.** from a Germanic personal name from *grīma* 'mask', 'helmet'.

Grimme (285) German and Swiss German: variant of GRIMM.

Grimmer (763) **1.** English: from a Norman personal name *Grimier*, composed of the Germanic elements *grīm* 'mask', 'helmet' + *hari, heri* 'army'. **2.** German: variant of GRIMM 2. **3.** German: variant of KRIMMER.
GIVEN NAMES German 4%. *Manfred* (2), *Wolfgang* (2), *Fritz, Hanni, Kurt, Otto.*

Grimmett (1204) English: from a pet form of a short form of any of the Germanic personal names beginning with *grīm* 'mask', 'helmet' (see GRIME).

Grimshaw (818) English: habitational name from either of two places in Lancashire, named Grimshaw, from the Old Norse personal name *Grímr* (see GRIME) or Old English *grīma* 'specter', 'goblin' + Old English *sceaga* 'copse'.

Grimsley (1987) English: habitational name from a lost or unidentified place, possibly in the Midlands, where the name is now concentrated.

Grimsrud (172) Norwegian: habitational name from any of several farmsteads in southeastern Norway, so named from Old Norse *Grímr*, a personal name meaning 'man with a mask or helmet' + *ruð* 'cleared field'.
GIVEN NAMES Scandinavian 11%; German 6%. *Lars* (2), *Anders, Erik, Jorgen, Knut; Kurt* (2), *Otto.*

Grimstad (167) Norwegian: habitational name from any of about fifteen farmsteads so named from the Old Norse personal name *Grímr* (see GRIMSRUD) + *staðr* 'farmstead'.
GIVEN NAMES Scandinavian 16%. *Gudrun, Oystein, Steinar.*

Grimstead (130) English: **1.** habitational name from Grimstead in Wiltshire, probably so named from Old English *grēne* 'green' + *hām-stede* 'homestead'. **2.** variant of GRINSTEAD.
GIVEN NAME German 5%. *Otto* (2).

Grimwood (193) English: from the Germanic personal name *Grimward*, composed of *grīm* 'mask', 'helmet' + *ward* 'guard'.

Grinage (170) Perhaps in part an altered spelling of GREENIDGE.
GIVEN NAME French 4%. *Osborn.*

Grinberg (447) **1.** Jewish (eastern Ashkenazic): variant of **Grünberg** (see GRUNBERG). **2.** Swedish: ornamental name composed of an unexplained first element + *berg* 'hill', 'mountain'.
GIVEN NAMES Jewish 30%; Russian 30%. *Yakov* (7), *Irina* (4), *Isaak* (4), *Ilya* (2), *Meyer* (2), *Moises* (2), *Semen* (2), *Avram, Borukh, Chaim, Chiam, Fayvel; Boris* (13), *Aleksandr* (10), *Mikhail* (8), *Vladimir* (7), *Grigoriy* (5), *Igor* (5), *Leonid* (5), *Lev* (4), *Yefim* (4), *Arkady* (3), *Oleg* (3), *Anatoly* (2).

Grinde (305) Norwegian: habitational name from any of several farmsteads in western Norway, so named from Old Norse *grind* 'gate'.
GIVEN NAMES Scandinavian 4%. *Erik, Obert.*

Grindel (118) **1.** German: topographic name for someone who lived by a swamp or moor. **2.** English: variant of GRINDLE.

Grindell (124) **1.** English: variant of GRINDLE. **2.** Probably also a respelling of German **Grindel** (see GRINDLE 2).

Grinder (403) English: occupational name for a grinder of grain, i.e. a miller, Middle English, Old English *grindere*, an agent noun from Old English *grindan* 'to grind'. Less often it may have referred to someone who ground blades to keep their sharpness or who ground pigments, spices, and medicinal herbs to powder.

Grindle (1179) **1.** English: topographic name from Middle English *grene* 'green' + *dale* 'dale', 'valley' or *hille, hull* 'hill'; al-

ternatively, the surname may have arisen from either of two habitational names meaning 'green valley': Greendale in Devon or Grindale in East Yorkshire, or from Grindal ('green hill') in Shropshire. **2.** South German: from Middle High German *grindel* 'latch', 'beam', 'pole', probably a metonymic occupational name for a doorman. **3.** Respelling of North German GRINDEL.

Grindley (148) **1.** English: habitational name from any of various minor places, for example in Staffordshire, so named from Old English *grēne* 'green' + *lēah* 'woodland clearing'. **2.** Altered spelling of German **Grindler**, a variant of **Grindel** (see GRINDLE).

Grindrod (154) English: habitational name from a minor place in the parish of Rochdale, Lancashire, so named from Old English *grēne* 'green' + *rod* 'clearing' (see RHODES).
▪ FOREBEARS This name is first recorded in Rochdale in 1541 in the spelling *Greneroade*.

Grindstaff (1341) Americanized form of German **Grenzhof**, a habitational name from a place so named near Heidelberg, or of **Granzow** (see GRANZOW).

Grine (152) **1.** English: probably a variant of **Grein, Grain**, a topographic name for someone who lived by an inlet or at the fork of a river, Middle English *greine, grayne*. **2.** Altered spelling of German GREIN. **3.** Possibly an Americanized form of Norwegian **Grini**, a common habitational name from any of numerous farmsteads in southeastern Norway named Grini, from Old Norse *grǫnvin*, a compound of *grǫn* 'spruce' + *vin* 'meadow'.
GIVEN NAMES Spanish 4%. *Carlos* (2), *Alfonso, Juanita, Luis, Manuel, Polito.*

Griner (1533) **1.** Americanized spelling of German GREINER. **2.** Jewish (eastern Ashkenazic): from an inflected form of Yiddish *grin* 'green' (see GREEN).

Gring (149) German: nickname for a slight or unimportant person, from Middle High German *gering* 'small', 'slight'.

Grinnan (158) Possibly an Americanized spelling of French GRIGNON.

Grinnell (1345) English: variant of GREENHILL 1.

Grinstead (947) English: **1.** habitational name from East or West Grinstead in Sussex, or from Greensted or Greenstead in Essex, all named from Old English *grēne* 'green' + *stede* 'place'. **2.** variant of GRIMSTEAD.

Grinter (144) English: of uncertain origin. It is probably an occupational name for an official in charge of a granary, Anglo-Norman French *grenetier*, but it could also be a variant of GRINDER.
▪ FOREBEARS The name Grinter is fairly common in Dorset, England, from the 16th to

the 18th centuries. It is recorded as Grenter in 1570 in that county.

Gripp (302) **1.** English: topographic name for someone who lived in a deep valley, from Middle English *grype* 'kettle', 'caldron' (Old English *gripu*). **2.** German: variant of GREIF 1.

Grippe (153) Apparently of Italian origin; perhaps a respelling of GRIPPI.
GIVEN NAME Italian 7%. *Rocco* (3).

Grippi (164) Italian: patronymic or plural form of GRIPPO.
GIVEN NAMES Italian 21%. *Mario* (3), *Salvatore* (3), *Sal* (2), *Casimiro*, *Domenica*, *Giuseppi*, *Santa*.

Grippo (393) Italian: **1.** from a Germanic personal name *Grippo*, from *grīm* 'mask', 'helmet'. **2.** from the Calabrian dialect word *grippa* 'wrinkle', probably a nickname for someone with a wrinkled complexion.
GIVEN NAMES Italian 16%. *Carmine* (3), *Angelo* (2), *Lorenzo* (2), *Aniello*, *Enrico*, *Gaetano*, *Giacomo*, *Gino*, *Pasquale*, *Piero*, *Ral*, *Rocco*.

Grisanti (250) Italian (Sicily): from the personal name *Grisanto*, *Crisanto*, Greek *Khrysanthēs*, from the vocabulary word *khrysanthon* 'chrysanthemum' (literally 'flower of gold').
GIVEN NAMES Italian 19%; Spanish 5%. *Carlo* (4), *Dino* (2), *Mario* (2), *Aldo*, *Angelo*, *Cosimo*, *Giuseppe*, *Rinaldo*, *Salvatore*, *Vito*; *Alejandro*, *Ana Maria*, *Carlos*, *Elena*, *Jorge*.

Grisby (249) English: unexplained; possibly a habitational name from a lost or unidentified place.

Griscom (213) English: probably a habitational name from a lost or unidentified place called **Griscombe**.

Grise (395) **1.** English: variant of GRICE. **2.** French (**Grisé**): variant spelling of **Griset**, a nickname for someone with gray hair, a gray complexion, or perhaps one who habitually wore gray, from Old French *gris* 'gray'.
GIVEN NAMES French 4%. *Elphege*, *Lucien*, *Normand*.

Grisez (126) French: variant spelling of **Griset** 'gray' (see GRISE).
GIVEN NAME French 4%. *Germain*.

Grishaber (127) Americanized spelling of German GRIESHABER.

Grisham (2613) **1.** English: variant of GRESHAM. **2.** Possibly an altered spelling of German **Griesheim**, a habitational name for someone from any of several places so named in southern Germany.

Grismer (170) Americanized spelling of German GRIESEMER.

Grismore (165) Americanized spelling of German GRIESEMER.

Grissett (543) Anglicized or Germanized spelling of French **Griset** 'gray' (see GRISE). The name was probably taken to Germany by Huguenot refugees in the late

17th century, and thence to North America (NC).

Grissinger (225) Variant spelling of German GRIESINGER.

Grisso (219) Probably an Americanized spelling of French **Grisseau** or German **Gressow**.

Grissom (3969) English: diminutive of GRICE 1.

Grisson (133) English: variant of GRISSOM.

Grist (491) English: of uncertain origin. It may be an occupational nickname for a miller, from the Middle English abstract noun *grist* 'grinding', Old English *grist*, a derivative of *grindan* (see GRINDER). The word was not used in the concrete sense of grain to be ground until the 15th century.

Griswell (169) English: of uncertain origin. Perhaps an altered form of GRISWOLD or CRESWELL. In the U.S. it is found chiefly in GA.

Griswold (4406) English: habitational name from Griswolds Farm in Snitterfield, Warwickshire, which is probably named with Old English *grēosn* 'gravel' + *weald* 'woodland'.
FOREBEARS Edward Griswold (1607–91) and his family were Puritans who came to the American colonies from Wootton Wawen, Warwickshire, England, on the *Mary and John*, arriving on 30 May 1630. They settled first in Dorcester MA, and in 1639 moved to Windsor VT. Matthew Griswold emigrated to New England in 1639, settling first in Windsor, CT, and later in Lyme, CT.

Gritter (145) Altered spelling of German **Grütter**. **1.** In German-speaking Switzerland this is a topographic name for someone living or farming on newly cleared land, from Middle High German *geriute* + *-er*, suffix denoting an inhabitant. Compare KREIDER. **2.** In northern Germany, an occupational name for a miller, Middle Low German *grütter*.
GIVEN NAME Dutch 4%. *Gerrit* (3).

Grittner (103) German: **1.** (Silesia): occupational name for a grist miller, from Middle Low German *grutte* 'grits', 'coarsely ground flour'. **2.** metronymic from the female personal name *Grite*, *Grete*.
GIVEN NAME German 4%. *Kurt*.

Gritton (377) English: habitational name from any of various places named Gretton. One in Northamptonshire is named from Old English *grēot* 'gravel' + *tūn* 'enclosure', 'settlement'. Gretton in Shropshire is named from Old English *grēoten* 'gravelly' + *tūn*, while Gretton, Gloucestershire, is 'farmstead (*tūn*) near Greet (Old English *grēote* 'gravelly place')'.

Gritz (305) Altered spelling of German **Grütz**, a metonymic occupational name for a miller, from Middle High German *griuze*, *grütz e* 'grits', or possibly a reduced form of derivatives such as *Grützmacher* (see GRUETZMACHER).

Gritzmacher (147) Altered spelling of South German **Grützmacher** (see GRUETZMACHER).
GIVEN NAMES German 4%. *Bernd*, *Erwin*.

Grivas (135) Greek: nickname for a man with graying hair, or who owned a gray horse, from Bulgarian *grivŭ* 'gray speckled with blue', possibly via Aromanian *griv* 'gray', or from the derivative Greek word *grivas* 'gray horse'.
GIVEN NAMES Greek 12%. *Spiro* (2), *Angelos*, *Apostolos*, *Demetre*, *Demetrios*, *Efstathios*.

Grizzaffi (103) Southern Italian: nickname from medieval Greek *khrysaphi* 'gold' (classical Greek *khrysos*, Southern Italian Greek *grisafi*).
GIVEN NAME Italian 7%. *Biaggio*.

Grizzard (753) Variant spelling of French **Grizard**, a pejorative derivative of *gris* 'gray' (see GRIZZLE).

Grizzell (396) Americanized form of French and Swiss French **Grisel** or **Grizel**, derivatives of **Gris**, from Old French *gris* 'gray', hence a nickname for a man with gray hair, a gray complexion, or who habitually wore gray.

Grizzle (1417) Americanized form of French and Swiss French **Grisel** or **Grizel**, derivatives of **Gris**, from Old French *gris* 'gray', hence a nickname for a man with gray hair, a gray complexion, or who habitually wore gray.

Groah (110) Variant of German GROH.

Groark (132) Irish: reduced Anglicized form of Gaelic **Mag Ruaire**, a patronymic from a personal name derived from Norse *Hrothrekr* (see RODERICK). Compare O'ROURKE.

Groat (744) **1.** Scottish: probably a nickname imported from Low German or Dutch *groot* 'big', 'large'. **2.** Americanized spelling of the cognates GROTH, GROOT, or GROTT.

Grob (688) **1.** German (Switzerland): nickname for a strong, heavy man, or for a lout, from Middle High German *g(e)rop* 'coarse'. **2.** Jewish (Ashkenazic): from Yiddish *grob*, cognate with 1, which also means 'fat' and may have been applied in this sense.
GIVEN NAMES German 4%. *Elfriede*, *Erwin*, *Franz*, *Hans*, *Heinz*, *Markus*.

Grobe (558) German: **1.** variant of GROB. **2.** (**Gröbe**): variant of **Gröber** (see GROBER 1).

Grober (204) **1.** German (**Gröber**): habitational name for someone from any of various places, for example near Potsdam and Jena, named Gröber, or from either of the places near Bitterfeld or Meissen called Gröbern. **2.** German (**Gröber**): variant of GRABER 1. **3.** North German: variant of GROVER.

Grobman (164) Jewish (Ashkenazic): nickname meaning 'coarse man' or 'heavy man'.

GIVEN NAMES Jewish 9%; Russian 7%. *Aron, Moisey, Ranan; Mikhail* (3), *Anzhelika, Iosif, Leonid, Lev.*

Groce (1826) **1.** English: variant spelling of GROSS. **2.** Respelling of German GROSS.

Groch (132) Polish and eastern German: **1.** occupational name or nickname for someone who grew peas, from Polish, Sorbian *groch* 'pea'. **2.** from a pet form of a personal name such as *Grodzisław*.
GIVEN NAMES Polish 5%. *Andrzej, Czeslaw.*

Grocholski (81) Polish: habitational name for someone from any of the places called Grocholice, in Piotrków, Sieradz, or Tarnobrzeg voivodeships, all named with Polish *groch* 'pea'.
GIVEN NAMES Polish 11%; French 9%. *Wlodzimierz* (2), *Jerzy, Jozef; Francois* (2), *Patrice.*

Grochowski (618) Polish: habitational name from any of various places called Grochów, Grochy, or Grochowce, from *groch* 'pea'.
GIVEN NAMES Polish 10%. *Henryk* (2), *Aleksander, Casimir, Cecylia, Elzbieta, Feliks, Halina, Jadwiga, Janusz, Jaroslaw, Jerzy, Jozef.*

Grocki (127) Polish: variant of Polish **Grodzki** (see GRODSKY).

Grode (239) North German: topographic name from Low German *groden* 'grassland', 'drained plot of land'.

Groden (186) German: habitational name from a place named Groden, near Hadeln in northern Germany.

Grodi (123) Origin uncertain; apparently of French or Swiss origin, but unexplained.

Grodin (179) Probably Scottish, but unexplained.

Grodsky (145) **1.** Altered spelling of Polish **Grodzki**, a habitational name from Grodziec or Grodzie, places named with *gród* 'castle', 'fortification' (cognate with Russian *grad*). **2.** Jewish (eastern Ashkenazic): habitational name (see 1).
GIVEN NAME Jewish 8%. *Emanuel.*

Grody (142) **1.** Irish: reduced form of **MacGrody**, an Anglicized form of Gaelic **Mag Rodaigh** 'son of *Rodach*', a personal name from *rod* 'strong'. **2.** Polish: habitational name from any of various places called Grody, named with *grody* 'castles'.

Grodzicki (121) Polish: habitational name from any of various places called Grodziec, Grodzisk, Grodzisko, or Grodziszcze. All are named with *gród* 'castle', 'fortification'.
GIVEN NAMES Polish 9%. *Janusz, Karol, Krzysztof, Ryszard.*

Groeber (136) German (**Gröber**): see GROBER.
GIVEN NAME German 6%. *Eugen.*

Groebner (201) German (**Gröbner**): variant of GRABNER.

Groeger (156) German (**Gröger**): variant of GREGER.

GIVEN NAMES German 17%. *Klaus* (3), *Gunter, Hans, Karlheinz, Kurt, Reinhard, Siegfried, Wilfried.*

Groen (640) **1.** Dutch: nickname for someone who habitually dressed in green, from Middle Dutch *groene* 'green'. **2.** North German (**Grön**): variant of **Grün** (see GRUEN).
GIVEN NAMES Dutch 4%. *Gerrit* (2), *Klaas* (2), *Cornelis, Henk, Jaap, Marinus.*

Groendyke (108) Dutch (**Groendijk**): habitational name from a locality named as 'the green dike'.

Groene (238) Variant of Dutch and North German GROEN.

Groeneveld (278) Dutch: habitational name from any of various minor places named Groeneveld, from Middle Dutch *groene* 'green' + *veld* 'pasture'.
GIVEN NAMES German 6%; Dutch 4%. *Benno* (2), *Kurt* (2), *Johannes, Otto; Hendrik* (2), *Bram, Gerrit, Wim.*

Groeneweg (138) Dutch and North German: topographic name for someone who lived by a grassy path, from Middle Dutch *groene* 'green' + *weg* 'path'.

Groenewold (167) Dutch: habitational name from any of various places (for example, in North Brabant, Gelderland, and South Holland) named Groenewoud, from Middle Dutch *groene* 'green' + *woudt* 'wood', 'forest'
GIVEN NAMES German 4%. *Hans, Kurt.*

Groening (132) North German: from Middle Low German *grönink* 'yellowhammer' (a species of bunting), a metonymic occupational name for a bird catcher, or perhaps a nickname.
GIVEN NAMES German 8%. *Juergen, Kurt, Manfred.*

Groenke (130) North German (**Grönke**): from a diminutive of **Groen** (see GRUEN).
GIVEN NAMES German 8%. *Fritz, Hans, Klaus, Kurt.*

Groesbeck (478) Dutch: habitational name from Groesbeek, south of Nijmegen.
FOREBEARS The name is recorded in Beverwijck in New Netherland (Albany, NY) in the mid 17th century.

Groeschel (155) German (**Gröschel**): from a diminutive of GROSCH.
GIVEN NAME German 4%. *Gerhard.*

Groesser (108) German: variant of GROSSER 2, comparative form of Middle High German *grōz* 'big', 'tall', 'important'.
GIVEN NAMES German 6%. *Fritz, Nikolaus.*

Groetsch (152) German (**Grötsch**, of Slavic origin): from Sorbian *grod* 'castle', 'fortified town' (Old Slavic *gradu*).
GIVEN NAMES German 9%. *Ewald* (2), *Kurt* (2), *Siegmar* (2).

Groezinger (109) South German (**Grözinger**): variant of **Grötzinger** (see GRETZINGER).
GIVEN NAMES German 8%. *Armin, Friedrich, Reinhard.*

Grof (101) **1.** Hungarian: status name from *gróf* 'count'. Compare German GRAF. This name is also found in Slovenia. As a surname it is probably an ironic nickname. **2.** German: variant of GROB. **3.** Possibly an Americanized spelling of the Norwegian habitational name **Grov**, from any of several farmsteads so named, from Old Norse *grof* 'pit', 'hollow'.
GIVEN NAMES Hungarian 5%. *Geza, Zoltan.*

Groff (3859) **1.** Dutch: from the personal name *Grof*, a reduced form of *Gerolf*. **2.** Hungarian: variant of GROF.

Groft (339) English: of uncertain origin; perhaps an altered form of CROFT.

Grogan (4423) Irish: **1.** reduced Anglicized form of Gaelic **Ó Grúgáin** 'descendant of *Grúgán*', a personal name from a diminutive of *grúg* 'anger', 'fierceness'. **2.** reduced Anglicized form of Gaelic **Ó Gruagáin** 'descendant of *Gruagán*', a personal name from a diminutive of *gruag* 'hair'. The patronymic form **Mac Gruagáin** (Anglicized **McGrogan**) is much rarer.

Grogg (624) German and Swiss German: from a short form of a Germanic personal name derived from Gothic *hrukjan* 'to crow' or related to Middle High German *rōhen* 'to roar', 'cry (in battle)', probably originally a byname for a warrior (as the name may also be cognate with Gothic *hrotheigs* 'victorious').

Groh (1656) German: nickname for a grizzled or gray-haired man, from Middle High German *grā* 'gray'.

Grohe (100) German: variant of GROH.
GIVEN NAME German 5%. *Heinrich.*

Grohman (269) Respelling of German GROHMANN.

Grohmann (104) German: nickname for a grizzled or gray-haired man (see GROH).
GIVEN NAMES German 12%; Scandinavian 7%; Dutch 4%. *Erwin* (2), *Eckhart, Hans, Klaus, Udo; Erik* (2), *Knud; Gert.*

Grohowski (120) Polish: variant spelling of GROCHOWSKI.
GIVEN NAME Polish 4%. *Kazimir.*

Grohs (354) **1.** German: variant spelling of GROSS. **2.** Altered form of German GROH.
GIVEN NAMES German 8%. *Detlef, Florian, Gerhard, Hans, Heinz, Helmut, Kurt, Lothar, Otto.*

Groleau (409) French: possibly a nickname for someone who habitually bawled or squawked, from *gouleau*, a diminutive of *grole* 'crow', 'raven' (ultimately from Latin *graculus*).
GIVEN NAMES French 9%. *Lucien* (2), *Normand* (2), *Alphee, Armand, Colette, Emile, Herve, Marcel, Marthe, Pierre.*

Groll (544) **1.** North German: habitational name from Groll in Westphalia or Grollo in Drente, (from Dutch *Gronlo* 'fen'). **2.** German: perhaps a nickname for an angry person from Middle High German *groll* 'anger', 'wrath'. **3.** North German: nick-

name from Middle Low German *krul* 'shock of hair'.
GIVEN NAMES German 4%. *Dieter (3), Eckhard, Franz, Klaus.*

Groller (114) South German (**Gröller**): variant of **Greller**, a nickname for a loud, man, from an agent derivative of Middle High German *grellen* 'to shout angrily'.

Grom (183) Polish and Slovenian: nickname for a noisy or obstreperous person, from *grom* 'thunder', 'crashing', 'loud noise'. This name is also found in German-speaking countries.

Gromacki (112) Polish: variant of **Gromadzki**, a habitational name for someone from Gromadzice in Kielce voivodeship.

Groman (315) German (**Gromann**): variant of GROHMANN.

Gromek (142) Polish: from a diminutive of GROM.
GIVEN NAMES Polish 12%. *Urszula (2), Bogdan, Krystyna, Miroslaw, Stanislaw.*

Gromer (180) German: **1.** from a reduced form of the personal name *Gerom*, Latin *Hieronymus* (see JEROME). **2.** variant of KRAMER. **3.** (also **Grömer**): from a short form of a Germanic personal name, reflected by Old High German *hruom* 'fame'.

Gromley (112) Irish: possibly a metathesized form of GORMLEY.

Grona (103) Perhaps a respelling of German GRONE, or a habitational name from any of several places named Gronau.
GIVEN NAMES German 7%. *Fritz, Hans, Otto.*

Gronau (247) German: habitational name from any of eleven places in northern Germany so named, from Middle Low German *grōne* 'green' + *ōwe* 'water meadow' or 'river island'.
GIVEN NAMES German 10%. *Kurt (4), Hans (2), Eldred, Erwin, Heinz, Lothar.*

Gronbach (103) German: probably a habitational name from a place so named, the first syllable of which may derive from a North German word for 'green' or for 'crane' (the bird) + *bach* 'stream'.
GIVEN NAME German 4%. *Helmut.*

Gronberg (219) Swedish (**Grönberg**): ornamental name composed of the elements *grön* 'green' + *berg* 'mountain', 'hill'.
GIVEN NAMES Scandinavian 6%. *Anders, Erik.*

Grondahl (206) **1.** Swedish (**Gröndahl**): ornamental name composed of the elements *grön* 'green' + *dahl*, an ornamental (old) spelling of *dal* 'valley'. **2.** Norwegian and Danish: habitational name from the common place name Grøndal, a compound of *grønn* 'green' + *dal* 'valley'.
GIVEN NAMES Scandinavian 6%. *Helmer, Viljo.*

Grondin (691) French: nickname for a gloomy curmudgeon, from *gronder* 'to mutter or grumble' (Latin *grundire*).
GIVEN NAMES French 19%. *Marcel (5), Andre (2), Armand (2), Gaston (2), Lucien (2),*

Normand (2), Pierre (2), Alcide, Cecile, Donat, Emile, Francois.

Grone (152) **1.** German: habitational name from Grone near Göttingen or other places so named in Lower Saxony. **2.** North German: variant of **Grün** (see GRUEN). **3.** North German: unflattering nickname for a lecher, from Middle Low German *grone* 'lascivious'.

Gronek (104) Polish: occupational name for someone who sold or cultivated grapes, from *grono* 'grape'.
GIVEN NAMES Polish 7%. *Casimir, Franciszek, Jerzy.*

Groneman (114) North German: unflattering nickname meaning 'lascivious man' (see GRONE 3).

Gronemeyer (148) German (Westphalia): variant spelling of **Gronmeier** (see GREENAMYER).

Groner (560) German: **1.** habitational name for someone from Grone (see GRONE 1). **2.** unflattering name for a lecher (see GRONE 3).
GIVEN NAMES Jewish 6%. *Shimon (3), Yossef (2), Zev (2), Hinda, Leib, Mordechai, Schneur, Zalman.*

Gronert (102) German: variant of GRONER.
GIVEN NAMES German 8%. *Armin, Bernd.*

Gronewold (306) North German (also **Grönewold**): topographic name for someone who lived by a verdant forest, from Middle Low German *grōne* 'green' + *wald* 'woods', or a habitational name from a place named with this word, for example Grönwohld near Trittau.

Groninger (211) German (also **Gröninger**): habitational name for someone from Groningen (Netherlands) or from Gröningen near Halberstadt (Thuringia), or perhaps a nickname for an immature person, from Middle Low German *gröninc*, literally 'greenling'.

Gronlund (270) **1.** Swedish (**Grönlund**): ornamental name composed of the elements *grön* 'green' + *lund* 'grove'. **2.** Norwegian and Danish (**Grønlund**): ornamental name, or a habitational name from any of numerous places so named; the name is a compound of *grønn* 'green' + *lund* 'grove'.
GIVEN NAMES Scandinavian 9%. *Bent, Erik, Lars, Matts.*

Gronowski (182) Polish: habitational name for someone from a place called Gronów, of which there are numerous examples throughout Poland, or Gronówek.
GIVEN NAMES German 6%. *Hans (2), Alfons, Kurt.*

Gronquist (130) Swedish (**Grönquist**): ornamental name composed of the elements *grön* 'green' + *quist*, an old or ornamental spelling of *kvist* 'twig', 'branch'.
GIVEN NAME Scandinavian 4%. *Nels.*

Gronseth (187) Norwegian: habitational name from any of numerous farmsteads,

notably in central Norway, named Gronseth, from *grøn* 'green' + *set* 'farmland'.

Gronski (209) Polish (**Groński**): habitational name from Grońsko in Poznań voivodeship.

Groom (1930) English (common in East Anglia): occupational name for a servant or a shepherd, from Middle English *grōm(e)* 'boy', 'servant' (of uncertain origin), which in some places was specialized to mean 'shepherd'.

Groome (415) English: variant spelling of GROOM.

Groomer (116) Possibly an Americanized spelling of German **Grummer**, probably from a personal name formed with Old High German *gruoni* 'green' + *māri* 'famous'.

Groomes (329) **1.** English: variant of GROOM. **2.** Possibly an Americanized spelling of German **Grummes**, from a short or pet form of the personal name *Hieronymus* (see JEROME).

Grooms (3395) English: variant of GROOM.

Groos (147) North German: variant of GROSS 1.

Groot (265) Dutch: nickname for a big man, from Middle Dutch *grōt* 'great', 'large'.
GIVEN NAMES Dutch 9%. *Hendrik (4), Pieter (3), Willem.*

Grooters (179) Probably an altered spelling of Dutch **Grootaers**, a nickname for someone with a big behind, from Middle Dutch *grōt* 'large', 'tall' + *aers, e(e)rs* 'buttocks'.

Groothuis (160) Dutch: topographic name for someone who lived in or by a large house, from Middle Dutch *grōt* 'large', 'great' + *hous* 'house'.

Groover (1296) Americanized form of German GRUBER.

Gropp (321) German: **1.** from a Germanic personal name formed with a cognate of Gothic *hrōtheigs* 'victorious'. **2.** variant of GROB. **3.** from *Gropp* 'grouper' (the fish); possibly a metonymic occupational name for a fisherman, or a nickname for someone with a large head and wide mouth like a grouper.
GIVEN NAMES German 7%. *Claus (2), Dieter, Egon, Erwin, Manfred, Wolfgang.*

Groppe (122) German: **1.** from a short form (*Robbo*) of a Germanic personal name formed with *(h)rod* 'fame', 'victory' as the first element, for example ROBERT. **2.** nickname for someone who somehow resembled a fish called (in the south) *Groppe*, known for its big head and mouth.
GIVEN NAME German 4%. *Erwin.*

Gropper (238) **1.** German: occupational name for someone who fished for grouper, from GROPP + -*er* suffix denoting human agency. **2.** North German (**Gröpper**): Westphalian occupational name for a maker of metal or earthenware vessels, from Middle Low German *grope* 'pot' + agent suffix -*er*.
GIVEN NAME Jewish 4%. *Morry (2).*

Gros (992) **1.** French: nickname for a large man, from Old French *gros* 'big', 'fat', Late Latin *grossus*, of Germanic origin. See also LEGROS. **2.** Jewish (Ashkenazic) and English: variant spelling of GROSS. **3.** Slovenian spelling of German GROSS.

GIVEN NAMES French 8%. *Emile* (3), *Camile* (2), *Irby* (2), *Albon*, *Alcide*, *Arsene*, *Chantelle*, *Clovis*, *Elphege*, *Etienne*, *Francois*, *Gabrielle*.

Grosch (427) German: from Middle High German, Middle Low German *grosch* 'groschen', a gold or silver coin, a metonymic occupational name for a moneyer, or possibly a nickname for an avaricious person.

GIVEN NAMES German 4%. *Kurt* (3), *Erwin*, *Heinz*.

Grose (1937) **1.** Cornish: topographic name for someone who lived near a stone cross set up by the roadside or in a marketplace, Cornish *crous* (Latin *crux*, *crucis*). Compare CROSS. **2.** English: nickname for a large or fat man, from Old French *gros*, 'big', 'fat' (see GROS).

Groseclose (523) Americanized spelling of German **Grossklos** (*Gross Klaus* 'big Klaus'), probably a distinguishing nickname for the larger (or older) of two bearers of the personal name KLAUS in the same family.

Grosenick (100) Variant of German **Grossnick**, literally 'big Nick', probably used to distinguish the elder or larger of two people called NIKOLAUS.

GIVEN NAMES German 9%. *Armin*, *Ernst*, *Otto*.

Grosh (238) Americanized spelling of any of various names of central and eastern European origin, all of them originating with reference to a coin, hence a metonymic occupational name for a moneyer or a nickname for a wealthy or money-conscious individual. Possible source names include German GROSCH; Polish GROSZ; Ukrainian **Groshok**, from *groshi*, denoting coins or money in general; and Russian **Groshev**, from *grosh*, a coin worth half a kopek. The relevant vocabulary word in all of these languages is derived from medieval Latin *(denarius) grossus*, literally 'thick coin'.

Groshans (111) German: literally 'big Hans', a distinguishing name for the older or larger of two bearers of the same personal name, *Hans*, a reduced form of JOHANNES, German equivalent of JOHN.

Groshek (186) Americanized spelling of Polish GROSZEK, also found as a Jewish name.

GIVEN NAMES German 4%. *Florian*, *Gerhart*.

Groshong (304) Americanized spelling of French GROSJEAN.

Grosjean (281) French and Swiss French: compound name from *gros* 'big', 'large' + the personal name *Jean* (French form of JOHN); it may have been applied as a nick-

name to distinguish between two bearers of the same personal name, denoting either the older or the larger, or simply to denote an exceptionally large (or small) man. *Grosjean* is also used in French as a nickname for a stupid fellow.

GIVEN NAME French 5%. *Philippe*.

Groskopf (163) German and Jewish (Ashkenazic): variant spelling of GROSSKOPF.

Groskreutz (155) German: habitational name from a place named Gross-Kreuz in Brandenburg.

Grosman (139) **1.** Jewish (Ashkenazic): elaborated form of GROSS. **2.** Slovenian or other respelling of German GROSSMANN.

GIVEN NAMES Jewish 17%; Russian 12%. *Dov* (3), *Yosef* (2), *Gerson*, *Miriam*, *Rotem*, *Zeev*; *Leonid* (3), *Aleksandr*, *Galina*, *Grigoriy*, *Klavdiya*, *Matvey*, *Velya*.

Gross (30150) **1.** German and Jewish (Ashkenazic): nickname for a big man, from Middle High German *grōz* 'large', 'thick', 'corpulent', German *gross*. The Jewish name has been Hebraicized as **Gadol**, from Hebrew *gadol* 'large'. This name is widespread throughout central and eastern Europe, not only in German-speaking countries. **2.** English: nickname for a big man, from Middle English, Old French *gros* (Late Latin *grossus*, of Germanic origin, thus etymologically the same word as in 1 above). The English vocabulary word did not develop the sense 'excessively fat' until the 16th century.

Grossbard (103) Jewish: nickname for someone with a large beard, from German *gross* 'big' + *Bard* 'beard'.

GIVEN NAMES Jewish 13%. *Hyman* (2), *Aharon*, *Aron*, *Moshe*.

Grossberg (354) **1.** Jewish (Ashkenazic): ornamental name composed of German *gross* 'large' + *Berg* 'mountain', 'hill'. **2.** German: habitational name from either of two places so named.

GIVEN NAMES Jewish 5%. *Chaim* (2), *Aron*, *Hyman*, *Miriam*.

Grosse (932) German: variant of GROSS.

GIVEN NAMES German 6%. *Kurt* (4), *Bernd*, *Eberhard*, *Erwin*, *Gerhard*, *Gerhardt*, *Hans*, *Hermann*, *Ingo*, *Otto*, *Reinhold*, *Uwe*.

Grossen (169) Dutch and Swiss German: from a pet form of a Germanic compound name beginning with the element *grōz* 'large'.

GIVEN NAME Scandinavian 4%. *Thor* (2).

Grossenbacher (212) Swiss German: habitational name from a place called Grossenbach.

GIVEN NAMES French 5%; German 5%. *Armand*, *Emile*, *Gabrielle*, *Pierre*; *Franz*, *Frieda*, *Klaus*.

Grosser (602) German: **1.** nickname for a big man, from an inflected form of GROSS. **2.** (also **Grösser**) distinguishing epithet for the larger or older of two bearers of the

same personal name, from the comparative form of the adjective *gross* 'big', 'large'.

GIVEN NAMES German 5%. *Kurt* (3), *Alois*, *Bernhard*, *Christoph*, *Ernst*, *Gunther*, *Siegfried*, *Wolf*.

Grosshans (200) German: compound name from Middle High German *grōz* 'large' + *Hans*, a pet form of the personal name *Johann(e)s* (see JOHN), hence a nickname used to denote a large man called Hans or to distinguish between two bearers of this personal name.

GIVEN NAMES German 8%. *Erwin* (2), *Kurt* (2), *Guenther*, *Winfried*.

Grossheim (102) German: **1.** possibly a habitational name from a place of this name. **2.** variant of the nickname or distinguishing name *Grosshain* 'big Henry' (see HEINRICH), which 17th-century records show was altered to the form of a place name.

GIVEN NAME German 5%. *Kurt*.

Grossi (911) Italian: patronymic or plural form of the nickname GROSSO.

GIVEN NAMES Italian 16%; French 4%. *Angelo* (4), *Rocco* (3), *Antonio* (2), *Carlo* (2), *Carmine* (2), *Dino* (2), *Domenic* (2), *Egidio* (2), *Elio* (2), *Ezio* (2), *Gino* (2), *Marco* (2); *Alphonse* (2), *Remy* (2), *Achille*, *Camille*, *Guille*, *Jacques*, *Jean-Jacques*, *Michel*, *Raoul*, *Serge*.

Grossinger (118) Jewish: unexplained.

GIVEN NAMES Jewish 7%. *Hershy*, *Shloime*.

Grosskopf (406) German and Jewish (Ashkenazic): nickname from a compound of Middle High German *grōz* 'large', German *gross* + Middle High German *kopf*, German *Kopf* 'head'.

GIVEN NAMES German 5%. *Otto* (2), *Hilde*, *Kurt*, *Oskar*, *Reinholdt*.

Grosskreutz (123) German: habitational name from a place named Gross Kreutz in Brandenburg, or a similarly named place elsewhere.

GIVEN NAME German 4%. *Otto*.

Grossman (9033) Jewish (Ashkenazic): descriptive nickname for a large man (see GROSSMANN).

GIVEN NAMES Jewish 5%. *Sol* (11), *Emanuel* (4), *Hyman* (4), *Isadore* (4), *Mort* (4), *Ari* (3), *Avi* (3), *Miriam* (3), *Myer* (3), *Yosef* (3), *Ilya* (2), *Isidor* (2).

Grossmann (547) German and Jewish (Ashkenazic): descriptive nickname for a large man, from *gross* 'large' (see GROSS) + *Mann* 'man'.

GIVEN NAMES German 10%. *Dieter* (2), *Erwin* (2), *Hans* (2), *Kurt* (2), *Otto* (2), *Franz*, *Goetz*, *Gottlieb*, *Gunter*, *Heinz*, *Helmut*, *Horst*.

Grossnickle (434) Americanized spelling of German **Grossnickel**, a compound of *gross* 'large' + *Nickel*, a pet form of the personal name *Nikolaus* (German form of NICHOLAS). It may have been applied as a nickname to denote a large or corpulent man or to distinguish between two bearers of the same name.

Grosso (1542) Italian: nickname for a large or corpulent man, from Italian *grosso* 'big', 'large' (Late Latin *grossus*).
GIVEN NAMES Italian 11%. *Rocco* (7), *Angelo* (4), *Salvatore* (3), *Vito* (3), *Antonio* (2), *Dante* (2), *Domenic* (2), *Pasquale* (2), *Santo* (2), *Amato*, *Battista*, *Carlo*.

Grosvenor (510) English (of Norman origin): status name for a person who was in charge of the arrangements for hunting on a lord's estate, from Anglo-Norman French *gros* 'great', 'chief' (see GROSS) + *vene-o(u)r* 'hunter' (Latin *venator*, from *venari* 'to hunt').
FOREBEARS This is the name of one of the wealthiest families in Britain, which holds the title Duke of Westminster. They have been long established in Cheshire, with strong links with the city of Chester. One of the earliest recorded bearers of the name was Robert le Grosvenor of Budworth, who was granted lands by the Earl of Chester in 1160. The family's fortunes were founded by Thomas Grosvenor (born 1656), who in 1677 married an heiress, Mary Davies, whose inheritance included Ebury Farm, Middlesex. This now forms an area of central London that includes Grosvenor Square and Belgrave Square.

Grosz (730) **1.** Polish and Jewish (eastern Ashkenazic): nickname from Polish *grosz*, a coin of small value (see GROSH). **2.** Hungarian, Jewish (from Hungary), and Polish spelling of the German name GROSS, a nickname meaning 'large'.

Groszek (78) Polish and Jewish (from Poland): from *groszek*, a diminutive of *grosz*, a copper coin, hence a metonymic occupational name for a moneyer or a nickname for a wealthy or money-conscious individual.
GIVEN NAMES Polish 9%. *Boleslaw*, *Urszula*.

Grote (1734) North German: variant of GROTH.

Grotenhuis (139) Dutch: variant of GROOTHUIS.
GIVEN NAMES Dutch 4%. *Dirk*, *Marinus*.

Groth (2788) North German, Dutch, and Danish: nickname for a large man, from Low German *grot(h)*. Compare GROSS.
GIVEN NAMES German 4%. *Erwin* (5), *Hans* (4), *Otto* (3), *Siegfried* (2), *Volker* (2), *Bernhard*, *Claus*, *Ernst*, *Ewald*, *Gerhard*, *Heinrich*, *Heinz*.

Grothaus (257) North German: topographic name for someone who lived in or by a large house or farmstead, from Low German *grot(h)* 'large', 'great' + central or standard German *Haus* 'house'.

Grothe (765) North German and Dutch: variant of GROTH.
GIVEN NAMES German 5%. *Hans* (2), *Egon*, *Elke*, *Ernst*, *Fritz*, *Gerhard*, *Guenter*, *Kurt*, *Uwe*, *Wolfram*.

Grotheer (137) North German: derogatory nickname for a braggart, from Middle Low German *grōt* 'big', 'great' + *hēre* 'gentleman', 'lord', 'master'.
GIVEN NAMES German 18%. *Kurt* (4), *Dieter* (2), *Claus*, *Helmut*, *Ingeborg*.

Groton (109) Possibly English, a habitational name from any of various places in Suffolk, probably named in Old English as 'sandy or gravelly stream'.

Grott (127) North German: variant of GROTH.

Grotte (138) North German: variant of GROTH.

Grotts (106) Americanized spelling of German GROTZ.

Grotz (205) South German: **1.** topographic name for someone living by a pine forest, from *Grotz* 'pine tree top'. **2.** nickname from Alemannic and Swabian *grotz* 'little man', 'shrimp', originally 'butt end' (e.g. of an apple).
GIVEN NAME German 4%. *Kurt* (2).

Groulx (293) French Canadian spelling of **Groult**, **Grould**, possibly reduced forms of *Gréoul*, a personal name of Germanic origin, composed of the elements *gred* 'hunger' + *wolf*, *wulf* 'wolf'.
GIVEN NAMES French 9%. *Armand* (2), *Adrien*, *Andre*, *Donat*, *Francois*, *Gabrielle*, *Herve*.

Ground (185) **1.** English: unexplained. Compare GROUNDS. **2.** Perhaps an Americanized form of German GRUND.

Grounds (675) English: unexplained. There are four farms so named in Warwickshire, one in Oxfordshire, and one in Worcestershire, and the surname is most probably derived from one of these.

Group (253) Probably an Americanized spelling of German **Grupp**, a variant of GROPP 1, or KRUPP 2. This name is concentrated in PA.

Grout (795) English: metonymic occupational name for a dealer in coarse meal, Old English *grūt*, Old Norse *grautr* 'porridge'.

Groux (108) French: habitational name from any of various places called Le Groux (Charente) or Les Groux (Oise, Yvelines).
GIVEN NAME French 6%. *Jean-Michel*.

Grove (8781) **1.** English: topographic name for someone who lived by a grove or thicket, Middle English *grove*, Old English *grāf*. **2.** English (Huguenot): Americanized spelling of the French surname **Le Grou(x)** or **Le Greux** (see GROULX). **3.** North German form of GROB. **4.** North German: habitational name from any of several places named Grove or Groven in Schleswig-Holstein, which derive their name from Middle Low Germany *grōve* 'ditch', 'channel'. In some cases the name is a Dutch or Low German form of GRUBE. **5.** Altered form of German GRAF.
FOREBEARS The surnames Grove and Groves are common mainly in the West Midlands. A Huguenot family who acquired the name Grove are descended from

a certain Isaac Le Greux or Grou(x) or his brother. They fled from Tours in France in the late 17th century and settled in Spitalfields, London. Their children were known as Grou(x) or Grove; their grandchildren also used the form Grew; but their great-grandchildren, born at the end of the 18th century, were universally Grove.

Groven (121) Norwegian: habitational name from any of several farmsteads, so named from Old Norse *gróf* 'pit', 'hollow' (originally 'stream' by which a hollow is eroded).
GIVEN NAME Scandinavian 5%. *Erik*.

Grover (6203) **1.** North German: occupational name for a ditch or grave digger, from Middle Low German *grove* 'hollow', 'grave'. **2.** Americanized form of German and Swiss GRUBER. **3.** Southern English: topographic name for someone who lived by a grove, a variant of GROVE 1 + the suffix *-er* denoting an inhabitant. **4.** Indian (Panjab): Hindu and Sikh name of unknown origin.
GIVEN NAMES Indian 4%. *Rakesh* (4), *Raj* (3), *Rajiv* (3), *Sanjay* (3), *Subhash* (3), *Vijay* (3), *Amrit* (2), *Atul* (2), *Harish* (2), *Naveen* (2), *Rashmi* (2), *Sunil* (2).

Groves (8950) English: variant of GROVE 1.

Grow (1953) North German: **1.** variant of GROH, **2.** variant of GROWE.

Growden (121) English: voiced variant of the habitational name CROWDEN. This form appears to have arisen from the place in Devon, 44 of the 49 bearers listed in the 1881 British census having been born in Cornwall or Devon.

Growe (136) North German: **1.** variant of GROH. **2.** variant of GRUBE.

Growney (197) Irish: reduced Anglicized form of Gaelic **Ó Gramhna**, which McLysaght describes as a corrupt form of **Mac Carrghamhna** 'son of *Corrghamhain*' (see McCARRON).

Gruba (176) Polish: from *gruby* 'big', 'coarse', 'thick', hence a nickname referring either to an individual's physical appearance or to his coarse behavior.

Grubaugh (463) Probably an Americanized form of German **Grunbach**, a habitational name for someone from a place so named near Stuttgart.

Grubb (5549) **1.** English: derogatory nickname for a small person, from Middle English *grub* 'insect larva'. **2.** This is a PA name probably representing German GRUBE.

Grubbe (119) **1.** German: from a Germanic personal name formed with an element reflected in Gothic *hrotheigs* 'victorious' (which in Old High German merges with *rōt* 'red'). **2.** English: variant spelling of GRUBB.

Grubbs (5658) English: variant of or patronymic form of GRUBB.

Grube (1704) German: **1.** topographic name for someone who lived in a depression or hollow, from Middle High German

gruobe 'pit', 'hollow'. See also GRUBER.
2. from a personal name *Grubo*, which merged completely with 1.

FOREBEARS The earliest known American bearer of the surname Grube was the Moravian missionary Bernhard Adam Grube, who was born in 1715 in Thüringen, at Walschleben near Erfurt, Germany. He was sent to PA in the spring of 1748, where he was a teacher. Subsequently, he volunteered for work among the Indians. He lived out his years in Bethlehem, PA.

GIVEN NAMES German 4%. *Kurt* (3), *Ernst* (2), *Klaus* (2), *Wolfgang* (2), *Grete*, *Wilhelm*.

Gruben (161) German: of uncertain origin. Possibly: **1.** a nickname of Slavic origin, from Polish *gruby* 'big', 'coarse' or a cognate in some other Slavic language. **2.** a reduced form of **Grubenheimer**, a name attached to the Waldenses in the 14th century in Germany because they met in isolated places, or a reduced form of Swiss *Grubenmann*, a variant of GRUBE.

GIVEN NAMES Dutch 4%; German 4%. *Kornelis*, *Onno*; *Hans*, *Kurt*.

Gruber (5997) **1.** German (**Grüber**) and Jewish (Ashkenazic): topographic name for someone who lived in a depression or hollow, from (respectively) Middle High German *gruobe*, German *Grube* 'pit', 'hollow' + the suffix *-er* denoting an inhabitant. As a Jewish name it can also be one of names randomly distributed by government officials. **2.** Jewish (eastern Ashkenazic): nickname from an inflected form of Yiddish dialect *grub* 'rude, impolite'.

GIVEN NAMES German 4%. *Kurt* (7), *Otto* (5), *Franz* (4), *Manfred* (3), *Alois* (2), *Aloysius* (2), *Armin* (2), *Hans* (2), *Heinz* (2), *Helmut* (2), *Markus* (2), *Wolfgang* (2).

Grubert (108) German: variant of GRUBER.

GIVEN NAMES German 8%. *Bodo*, *Heinz*.

Grubich (122) Eastern German (of Slavic origin) or Polish: nickname from Polish *gruby* 'big', 'coarse' or from a Sorbian cognate.

Grubman (133) **1.** German (**Grubmann**) and Jewish (Ashkenazic): topographic name for a man who lived in a hollow (see GRUBER). **2.** Jewish (eastern Ashkenazic): variant of GRUBER 2.

GIVEN NAMES Jewish 7%. *Isadore*, *Naum*.

Gruca (125) Polish: from *gruca* 'grain of cereal', probably a nickname for an insignificant person or a metonymic occupational name for a grower of or dealer in grain.

GIVEN NAMES Polish 13%; German 4%. *Jerzy* (2), *Krystyna*, *Miroslaw*, *Tomasz*, *Witold*; *Konrad*, *Wolf*.

Gruden (117) Slovenian (western and central Slovenia): nickname from *gruda* 'clod', 'soil'. It may also be connected with *gruden* 'December', which is derived from the same word. Compare Polish GRUDZIEN.

Grudzien (176) Polish (**Grudzień**): literally, 'December', hence a surname bestowed on someone with some particular association with the month, such as being due to pay rent then or having been baptized then.

GIVEN NAMES Polish 11%. *Arkadiusz*, *Dariusz*, *Halina*, *Krystyna*, *Zbigniew*, *Zofia*.

Grudzinski (280) Polish (**Grudziński**): habitational name from any of various places called Grudna or Grudno, named with the Polish word *gruda* 'clod of earth' (from which the name of the month *Grudzień* 'December' is derived). See also GRODSKY.

GIVEN NAMES Polish 6%. *Andrzej*, *Tadeusz*, *Wojciech*, *Zygmunt*.

Grue (117) French: possibly a nickname for a tall thin man, from *grue* 'crane'.

Gruel (206) **1.** German: from a Germanic personal name formed with an element reflected in Gothic *hrōtheigs* 'victorious'. **2.** French and English: metonymic occupational name for a miller or baker, from Old French *gruel* 'fine flour', 'meal'. **3.** Perhaps also an altered form of French **Groult** or **Grould** (see GROULX).

Gruen (649) **1.** German (**Grün**): from Middle High German *grüene* 'green', 'fresh', 'raw', hence a nickname for someone who habitually dressed in green, a topographic name for someone who lived in a green and leafy place, or a habitational name for someone from a place named with this word, such as Gruna, Grunau in Silesia. **2.** Jewish (Ashkenazic): ornamental name from German *grün* 'green'.

GIVEN NAMES German 6%; Jewish 4%. *Kurt* (4), *Dieter*, *Dietrich*, *Georg*, *Hans*, *Heinz*, *Hermann*, *Hertha*; *Ehud* (2), *Eliezer*, *Isadore*, *Isidor*, *Meyer*, *Rivka*, *Shimon*, *Shlomo*, *Shoshana*.

Gruenberg (371) Jewish (Ashkenazic) and German: variant spelling of **Grünberg** (see GRUNBERG).

GIVEN NAMES German 7%. *Hans* (2), *Helmuth* (2), *Juergen*, *Kurt*.

Grueneberg (113) German: variant of **Grünberg** (see GRUNBERG).

GIVEN NAMES German 5%. *Fritz*, *Hermann*.

Gruener (185) German and Jewish (Ashkenazic): from an inflected form of GRUEN.

GIVEN NAMES German 8%. *Manfred* (2), *Erna*, *Hannelore*, *Kurt*.

Gruenewald (286) Jewish (Ashkenazic) and German: variant spelling of **Grün(e)wald** (see GRUNWALD).

GIVEN NAMES German 9%. *Kurt* (2), *Arno*, *Guenter*, *Hannelore*, *Manfred*.

Gruenhagen (222) Jewish (Ashkenazic) and German (**Grünhagen**): habitational name from any of several places named Grünhagen, in northern and eastern Germany.

GIVEN NAMES German 4%. *Eldor*, *Otto*.

Gruenke (145) German: variant of GROENKE.

GIVEN NAMES German 7%. *Lothar*, *Mathias*.

Gruenwald (446) Jewish (Ashkenazic) and German: alternative spelling of **Grünwald** (see GRUNWALD).

GIVEN NAMES German 4%. *Bernd*, *Fritz*, *Heinz*, *Oskar*.

Grueser (106) German: probably an occupational name for a grain merchant, from an agent noun based on Middle High German *grūz* 'grain' (of sand or cereal). Alternatively, it may be a topographic name for someone living on sandy soil, from a derivative of the same word in the sense 'sand'.

Grueter (107) German (**Grüter**): **1.** Swiss German: Alemannic variant of **Greuter**, a topographic name from Middle High German *geriute* 'land cleared for cultivation'. **2.** North German: according to Bahlow, an occupational name for a brewer who used rosemary instead of hops, from an agent derivative of Middle Low German *grut* 'rosemary'.

Gruetzmacher (282) German (also **Grützmacher**): occupational name for a producer (miller) of grits or groats, from a standardized form of Middle Low German *grüt(te)maker*.

GIVEN NAMES German 7%. *Eldor*, *Ewald*, *Friedrich*, *Fritz*, *Gerhardt*.

Grugan (112) Irish: variant of GROGAN.

Gruhlke (157) Eastern German: variant of GRULKE.

Gruhn (369) North German: variant spelling of GRUEN.

GIVEN NAMES German 6%. *Otto* (2), *Hans*, *Heinz*, *Ralf*, *Rudi*.

Gruis (157) Northwestern German: from Dutch *gruis* 'dust', 'powder', 'dregs', hence a nickname for a farmer living on fine or sandy soil.

Grulke (225) German: perhaps a reduced form of **Grugelke**, a nickname for a fearsome person, from Middle Low German *grüwel* 'horror' or Low German *grügel* 'capercaillie', 'grouse' + the diminutive suffix *-ke*.

GIVEN NAMES German 4%. *Otto*, *Reinhard*.

Grullon (336) Spanish (**Grullón**): possibly from a derivative of *grulla* 'crane', presumably applied as a nickname for tall thin person; in Mexico, however, *grulla* denotes a crafty person.

GIVEN NAMES Spanish 56%. *Jose* (15), *Juan* (12), *Ana* (9), *Rafael* (7), *Carlos* (3), *Luis* (3), *Miguel* (3), *Altagracia* (2), *Arturo* (2), *Bernarda* (2), *Emilio* (2), *Francisco* (2); *Antonio* (3), *Carmelo* (2), *Filomena* (2), *Cecilio*, *Dario*, *Mirella*.

Grum (119) **1.** Probably respelling of German **Grumm**, a habitational name from Grumme, near Bocholt, apparently so named from Low German *grum* 'dirt', 'mud', or a topographic name for someone from a muddy place. **2.** Alternatively, it may be a respelling of German KRUMM. **3.** Slovenian: unexplained.

GIVEN NAME German 4%. *Ignatz*.

Gruman (155) Jewish (eastern Ashkenazic): variant of GRAUMANN.

GIVEN NAMES Jewish 8%. *Zev* (2), *Herschel*, *Yakov*.

Grumbach (126) Swiss German and French (Alsatian): habitational name from any of 14 places so named.

GIVEN NAMES German 6%; French 5%. *Kurt* (2), *Dieter*; *Andre*, *Pierre*.

Grumbine (178) Americanized spelling of German **Krumbein**, a nickname for someone with a deformed limb, from Middle High German *krump* 'crooked' + *bein* 'bone', 'leg'.

Grumbles (215) **1.** Apparently a variant of the English family name **Grumble**, itself a variant of GRIBBLE. **2.** Alternatively, perhaps, an Americanized form of German **Krumholz** (see CRUMBLISS). This surname is found mainly in TX.

Grumbling (113) Origin unidentified. It is probably an Americanized form of an unidentified German original.

Grumet (172) **1.** French: metonymic occupational name for a fuller, from Old Picard *grumet* 'oats', which were used in the fulling process. **2.** German and Jewish (Ashkenazic): respectively from Middle High German *gruonmāt*, modern German *Grummet* 'aftermath', 'second cut (of grass for hay)'. As a German name it is an occupational nickname for a mower; as a Jewish name it is of ornamental origin.

GIVEN NAMES Jewish 10%. *Meyer* (2), *Eliezer*, *Rivky*, *Zvi*.

Grummer (107) English: unexplained; perhaps an altered form of GRAMMER.

Grun (144) German and Jewish (Ashkenazic): variant of **Grün** (see GRUEN).

GIVEN NAMES Jewish 11%; German 9%; Polish 4%. *Herschel* (2), *Izhak* (2), *Moise*, *Rebekkah*, *Schmuel*, *Shoshana*; *Otto* (2), *Ulrika*, *Willibald*; *Maciek* (2), *Jozef*.

Grunberg (209) **1.** Jewish (Ashkenazic): ornamental name from German *grün* 'green' + *Berg* 'mountain', 'hill'. **2.** German (**Grünberg**): habitational name from any of numerous places named Grünberg.

GIVEN NAMES Jewish 6%; German 6%. *Pnina* (2), *Anat*, *Avraham*, *Emanuel*, *Shoshana*; *Angelika*, *Wolf*, *Wolfgang*.

Grund (615) German: topographic name for someone who lived at the bottom of a deep valley, from Middle High German *grunt* 'deep valley', 'valley bottom'.

Grunden (318) German: possibly a variant of GRUND.

Grunder (303) Swiss German (also **Gründer**): variant of the topographic name GRUND, the *-er* suffix denoting an inhabitant.

GIVEN NAMES German 4%. *Armin*, *Hermann*, *Walther*.

Grundman (379) Variant of German GRUNDMANN.

Grundmann (130) South German: topographic name for someone who lived at the bottom of a deep valley (see GRUND, MANN).

GIVEN NAMES German 14%; Scandinavian 5%. *Hans* (2), *Manfred* (2), *Frieda*, *Heinz*, *Volker*.

Grundmeier (118) German: distinguishing name for a tenant farmer whose farm lay at the bottom of a deep valley stream (see GRUND, MEYER).

Grundstrom (148) Swedish (**Grundström**): ornamental name composed of the elements *grund* 'ground' + *ström* 'current', 'stream'.

Grundy (1212) English (chiefly Lancashire): probably a Middle English metathesized form of the Old French personal name *Gondri*, *Gundric* (see GUNDRY).

Gruner (575) **1.** Swiss German and Jewish (Ashkenazic): habitational name denoting someone from a place named Grunau or Gruna. **2.** German and Ashkenazic Jewish (**Grüner**): see GRUENER.

GIVEN NAMES German 9%. *Kurt* (3), *Otto* (3), *Oskar* (2), *Wenzel* (2), *Dieter*, *Engel*, *Erwin*, *Helmut*, *Horst*, *Johann*, *Ute*, *Wolfgang*.

Grunert (232) German: **1.** variant of GRUNER. **2.** (**Grünert**): variant of **Grüner** (see GRUENER).

GIVEN NAMES German 13%. *Kurt* (3), *Arno* (2), *Heinrich*, *Jurgen*, *Konrad*, *Nikolaus*, *Otto*, *Sieg*.

Grunewald (780) Jewish (Ashkenazic) and German: variant of **Grünwald** (see GRUNWALD).

Grunfeld (140) **1.** Jewish (Ashkenazic): ornamental name composed of German *grün* 'green' + *Feld* 'field'. **2.** German (**Grünfeld**): habitational name from any of several places in northern and central Germany named Grünfeld, named with elements meaning 'green open country'.

GIVEN NAMES Jewish 22%; German 8%; Hungarian 5%. *Baruch* (4), *Chaim* (2), *Shulem* (2), *Aron*, *Avraham*, *Benzion*, *Bernath*, *Ishai*, *Isidor*, *Leser*, *Mordechai*, *Pinchas*; *Armin* (2), *Ernst* (2); *Tibor* (3), *Geza*, *Kalman*.

Grunke (120) German (**Grünke**): possibly a standardized form of Low German GROENKE or GREUNKE.

Grunow (284) German: habitational name from any of several places (mainly in Brandenburg) called Grunow or Grunau.

GIVEN NAMES German 10%. *Otto* (5), *Kurt* (2), *Dieter*, *Horst*.

Grunst (115) German: unexplained.

GIVEN NAMES German 4%. *Hans*, *Hertha*.

Grunwald (894) **1.** German and Swiss German (**Grünwald**): habitational name from any of various places named Grün(e)wald, from Middle High German *grüene* 'green' + *walt* 'wood', 'forest'. **2.** Jewish (Ashke-

nazic): ornamental surname, with the same meaning as 1.

GIVEN NAMES German 9%; Jewish 8%. *Otto* (5), *Hans* (3), *Kurt* (3), *Erwin* (2), *Heinz* (2), *Reinhard* (2), *Armin*, *Dieter*, *Ernst*, *Ewald*, *Fritz*, *Gerhard*; *Chaim* (4), *Amrom* (2), *Amron* (2), *Aron* (2), *Arie*, *Cheskel*, *Eitan*, *Elchonon*, *Hersch*, *Mayer*, *Mendel*, *Miriam*.

Grupe (313) North German: topographic name for someone living near a water channel, from Middle Low German *grüppe* 'ditch', 'channel'.

GIVEN NAMES German 4%. *Fritz*, *Manfred*.

Grupp (304) **1.** German: variant of GROPP 1. **2.** North German: variant of GRUPE.

GIVEN NAMES German 10%. *Otto* (3), *Gunther* (2), *Fritz*, *Hans*, *Helmut*, *Matthias*.

Gruse (131) Probably a variant of German GRUSS.

GIVEN NAME German 4%. *Klaus*.

Grush (195) Americanized form of German GROSCH.

Gruskin (135) Jewish (from Belarus): habitational name from the village of Grushki in Belarus.

GIVEN NAMES Jewish 9%. *Mayer*, *Meyer*, *Moshe*.

Gruss (355) German: **1.** from Middle High German *grūz* 'grain', 'groats', 'dregs'; possibly a derogatory occupational nickname for a grain merchant, or a topographic name for someone living on sandy soil. **2.** (also **Grüss**): from a Germanic personal name formed with an element reflected in Gothic *hrōtheigs* 'victorious'. **3.** perhaps of Slavic origin: from a pet form of a vernacular form of the Latin personal name *Gregorius* (see GREGORY).

GIVEN NAMES German 4%. *Otto* (2), *Ilse*.

Grussing (178) German (**Grüssing**): patronymic from **Grüss** (see GRUSS 2).

Gruszczynski (87) Polish (**Gruszczyński**): habitational name for someone from Gruszczyno in Siedlce voivodeship, any of several places called Gruszczyn, in the voivodeships of Kielce, Poznań, and Radom, or Gruszczyce in Sieradz voivodeship. All these places are named with *gruszka* 'pear'.

GIVEN NAMES Polish 15%. *Jaroslaw*, *Jolanta*, *Krzysztof*, *Zbigniew*, *Zygmunt*.

Gruszecki (82) Polish: habitational name from Gruszka in the voivodeship of Zamość or from Gruszki in the voivodeship of Suwałki. Both places are named with Polish *gruszka* 'pear'.

GIVEN NAMES Polish 9%; Czech and Slovak 4%; German 4%. *Marcin*, *Wojciech*; *Wilhelm*.

Gruszka (229) Polish (common in Silesia) and Jewish (from Poland): from *gruszka* 'pear', hence a metonymic occupational name for someone who grew or sold pears, or a nickname for someone thought to resemble the fruit. As a Jewish surname it is mainly ornamental.

GIVEN NAMES Polish 24%. *Andrzej* (2), *Casimir* (2), *Jerzy* (2), *Tadeusz* (2), *Danute, Dorota, Elzbieta, Grazyna, Jozef, Kazimierz, Lucyna.*

Gruttadauria (106) Italian: altered form of **Guttadaurio**, recorded in the 12th century as *Gutta da Auro* 'drop of gold'.

GIVEN NAMES Italian 23%. *Salvatore* (3), *Vito* (2), *Armando, Carmella, Ettore, Filippa.*

Grutzmacher (105) German (**Grütz-macher**): see GRUETZMACHER.

Gruver (1148) Possibly an altered spelling of German GRUBER, reflecting the Pennsylvania German pronunciation.

Gruwell (286) **1.** Altered spelling of **Grüwel(l)**, an Alemannic form of GREUEL. **2.** Possibly an altered spelling of Dutch **Grouwels** or **Grauwels**, a nickname from Middle Dutch *gruwel* 'fright', 'terror'.

Gryder (442) Altered spelling of Dutch **(de) Gruyter**, an occupational name for a brewer or grower or supplier of bog myrtle, apparently an ingredient of beer, later replaced by hops.

Grygiel (196) Polish: from a pet form of the personal name *Grzegorz*, from Latin *Gregorius* (see GREGORY).

GIVEN NAMES Polish 5%. *Bogdan, Czeslaw, Krzysztof, Zofia.*

Grymes (134) English: variant spelling of GRIMES.

Grzegorczyk (113) Polish: from a pet form of the personal name *Grzegorz*, vernacular form of Latin *Gregorius* (see GREGORY).

GIVEN NAMES Polish 13%; German 4%. *Andrzej, Czeslaw, Danuta, Marzena, Piotr, Zofia; Erwin.*

Grzegorzewski (66) Polish: habitational name for someone from Grzegorzowice or Grzegorzewice, both named with the personal name *Grzegorz*, Latin *Gregorius* (see GREGORY).

GIVEN NAMES Polish 9%. *Ireneusz, Jerzy.*

Grzelak (237) Polish: patronymic from *Grzela*, a dialect pet form of *Grzegorz*, vernacular form of Latin *Gregorius* (see GREGORY).

GIVEN NAMES Polish 10%. *Dariusz, Jacek, Krystyna, Stanislaw, Wladyslaw, Wlodzimierz, Wojciech, Zbigniew.*

Grzesiak (159) Polish: patronymic from a short form of *Grzegorz*, vernacular form of Latin *Gregorius* (see GREGORY).

GIVEN NAMES Polish 5%. *Zbigniew, Zygmunt.*

Grzesik (133) Polish: from a pet form of *Grzegorz*, vernacular form of Latin *Gregorius* (see GREGORY).

GIVEN NAMES Polish 11%. *Casimir, Grzegorz, Krystyna, Mieczyslaw.*

Grzeskowiak (178) Polish (**Grześkowiak**): patronymic from the personal name *Grzesiek*, a pet form of *Grzegorz*, vernacular form of Latin *Gregorius* (see GREGORY).

GIVEN NAMES Polish 6%. *Casimir, Krzysztof, Zdzislaw, Zophia.*

Grzyb (296) Polish: from *grzyb* 'mushroom', applied as a nickname for a dull old man, or a metonymic occupational name for someone who collected and sold edible fungi.

GIVEN NAMES Polish 12%. *Danuta* (2), *Eugeniusz, Grazyna, Henryka, Janina, Janusz, Mariusz, Miroslaw, Tadeusz, Wojciech, Zbigniew.*

Grzybowski (588) Polish: habitational name for someone from any of various places called Grzybowa, Grzybowo, or Grzybów, all named with *grzyb* 'mushroom'.

GIVEN NAMES Polish 8%. *Tadeusz* (2), *Tomasz* (2), *Wieslaw* (2), *Andrzej, Bartosz, Boguslaw, Mikolaj, Piotr, Rafal, Ryszard, Zigmond, Zofia.*

Grzywa (81) Polish: nickname from *grzywa* 'mane', 'shock of hair'.

GIVEN NAMES Polish 6%; German 4%. *Jerzy; Florian.*

Grzywacz (199) Polish and Jewish (from Poland): nickname from *grzywacz* 'ring-necked dove' or from *grzywa* 'mane', with reference to a man with long hair. As a Jewish name it is mainly ornamental.

GIVEN NAMES Polish 9%. *Zbigniew* (2), *Boguslawa, Boleslaw, Jerzy, Piotr, Weislaw, Zofia.*

Grzywinski (102) Polish: habitational name for someone from a place called Grzywnie in Toruń voivodeship, named with *grzywna*, an old monetary unit.

GIVEN NAME Polish 5%. *Wladyslaw.*

Gschwend (103) South German: habitational name from any of various places in Bavaria, Baden-Württemberg, Lower Austria, and elsewhere called Gschwand, Gschwend(t), or Geschwend (meaning 'cleared land').

GIVEN NAMES German 12%. *Kurt* (3), *Otto.*

Gschwind (191) Swiss German and South German: nickname for an impetuous man, from Middle High German *geswinde* 'quick', 'impetuous'.

GIVEN NAMES German 6%; French 5%. *Wilhelm; Philippe* (2), *Germain.*

Gsell (298) Swiss German and German: variant of GESELL.

Gu (676) **1.** Chinese 顾: from the place name Gu. Records of the this surname go back to the Xia dynasty (2205–1766 BC), when there existed a state called Gu. Much later, during the Spring and Autumn period (722–481 BC), there existed another state of Gu. Eventually, some descendants of the ruling class of both these areas adopted the place name as their surname. **2.** Chinese 谷: from a word meaning 'valley'. During the Zhou dynasty (1122–221 BC) there existed in the state of Qin a certain Viscount Fei Zi, a descendant of the legendary emperor Zhuan Xu of the 26th century BC. Viscount Fei Zi was granted the area Qin

Valley, and his descendants later adopted the word *gu* 'valley', as their surname. **3.** Chinese 古: from the name of the grandfather of the virtuous duke Wen Wang (1231–1135 BC), known as Gu Gong Tan Fu. The character for Gu, which also means 'ancient', was adopted by some of his descendants as a surname.

GIVEN NAMES Chinese 69%. *Hong* (7), *Wei* (7), *Qing* (5), *Ning* (4), *Ping* (4), *Shudong* (4), *Xin* (4), *Chen* (3), *Hua* (3), *Jin* (3), *Ming* (3), *Xiang* (3), *Chong* (2), *Min* (2), *Neng* (2), *Wee, You.*

Guadagni (104) Italian: patronymic or plural form of GUADAGNO.

GIVEN NAMES Italian 18%. *Antonio, Dante, Dino, Guilio, Maurizio, Neri, Pasquale, Rocco.*

Guadagnino (146) Italian: from a pet form of the personal name GUADAGNO.

GIVEN NAMES Italian 19%. *Carmelo* (2), *Eduardo* (2), *Aldino, Angelo, Antonino, Antonio, Carmine, Domenico, Leonardo, Sal, Salvatore, Santo.*

Guadagno (436) Italian: from the medieval personal name *Guadagno* or a shortening of the compound form *Buonguadagno* (*buon* 'good' + *guadagno* 'advantage', 'gain'); both forms were popularly used to denote a long-awaited and much-wanted child.

GIVEN NAMES Italian 17%. *Angelo* (5), *Carmine* (4), *Carlo* (2), *Guido* (2), *Luigi* (2), *Aldo, Carmelo, Luciano, Palma, Pasquale, Romeo, Sal.*

Guadagnoli (108) Italian: from patronymic or plural form of **Guadagnolo**, a pet form of the personal name GUADAGNO.

GIVEN NAMES Italian 28%. *Alfredo, Angelo, Antonio, Costantino, Domenic, Donato, Emilio, Gabriele, Germano, Gino, Leonida, Pasco.*

Guadalupe (357) Spanish: from the female personal name *Guadalupe*, a Marian name derived from the place so named in Cáceres province. The place name is named as 'the valley of the wolves', from Arabic *wādī* 'valley', 'riverbed' + Latin *lupi* 'wolves'. Guadalupe is the site of a Hieronymite convent founded in the 14th century, which possesses a famous image of the Virgin Mary. In some cases, the surname may have arisen as a habitational name from the same place

GIVEN NAMES Spanish 46%. *Jose* (16), *Luis* (5), *Luz* (5), *Carlos* (4), *Fernando* (3), *Francisco* (3), *Manuel* (3), *Aida* (2), *Ana* (2), *Andres* (2), *Angel* (2), *Cruz* (2).

Guadarrama (272) Spanish: from the name of the mountain range between Segovia and Madrid, or rather from a valley that gave its name to the whole mountain range, from Arabic *wādī al-ramah*. The first element is *wādī* 'valley', 'riverbed'; the second is unexplained.

GIVEN NAMES Spanish 59%. *Jose* (12), *Carlos* (5), *Francisco* (4), *Alfredo* (3), *Cesar* (3),

Fernando (3), *Jesus* (3), *Juan* (3), *Arturo* (2), *Cesareo* (2), *Eduardo* (2), *Gregorio* (2).

Guagenti (114) Italian: Caracausi derives this from a metathesized form of an unattested personal name *Gaujenti*, from Latin *gaudiens, gaudientis* 'one who rejoices'.
GIVEN NAMES Italian 22%. *Angelo* (2), *Sal* (2), *Antonio, Carmine, Salvator, Salvatore.*

Guagliardo (225) Italian: variant spelling of GAGLIARDO.
GIVEN NAMES Italian 15%. *Salvatore* (5), *Carlo, Carmela, Dante, Fedele, Ignazio, Leonardo, Sal.*

Guajardo (1605) Spanish: unexplained. Perhaps a habitational name from a place so named in Estremadura. This name is common in Argentina, Chile, and Mexico.
GIVEN NAMES Spanish 48%. *Jose* (39), *Juan* (37), *Jesus* (18), *Ruben* (17), *Arturo* (13), *Luis* (13), *Manuel* (13), *Ricardo* (13), *Carlos* (9), *Javier* (9), *Pedro* (9), *Jaime* (7).

Gualdoni (140) Italian: **1.** from an augmentative of the personal name *Gualdo*, from an old German personal name, *Waldo*, a pet form of a Germanic personal name formed with *wald* 'power'. **2.** otherwise, from an augmentative of Old Italian *gualdo* 'woods'.
GIVEN NAMES Italian 7%. *Attilio, Caesar, Cesare.*

Gualtieri (424) Italian: from a Germanic personal name, *Gualtieri*, composed of *wald* 'rule' + *hari, heri* 'army'. Compare GAUTHIER, WALTER.
GIVEN NAMES Italian 26%. *Mario* (5), *Rocco* (4), *Antonio* (3), *Deno* (2), *Rosario* (2), *Agostino, Angelo, Carmine, Claudio, Dino, Domenic, Domenico, Egidio, Fernando, Francesco, Gregorio, Jose, Orlando, Ricardo, Roberto, Ubaldo.*

Guan (616) **1.** Chinese 关: from a character meaning 'mountain pass' or 'guarded passage'. This formed part of the title of an official in charge of guarding strategic passes. Descendants of one such official are known to have adopted the character as their surname. Another source is Guan Longfeng, a senior official during the Xia dynasty (2205–1766 BC). **2.** Chinese 管: from the name of the short-lived state of Guan created when the Zhou dynasty was established in 1122 BC. The third son of Wen Wang, Guan Shu, was granted this state. He soon betrayed his family's trust, however, by allying himself, along with two of his brothers, with the descendants of the Shang dynasty that the Zhou had just displaced. This rebellion was put down and Guan Shu was killed. His clan dispersed, but some descendants later adopted the name Guan as their surname. The character for this name also means 'tube' or 'pipe' and 'manage'.
GIVEN NAMES Chinese 67%. *Wei* (6), *Jian* (5), *Ming* (4), *Hui* (3), *Li* (3), *Wen* (3), *Ying* (3),

Chi (2), *Heng* (2), *Hua* (2), *Hui Zhen* (2), *Jianmin* (2), *Yiping* (2), *Yong Chan, You.*

Guarascio (120) Italian: unexplained.
GIVEN NAMES Italian 17%. *Luigi, Natale, Salvatore, Saverio.*

Guard (592) English: occupational name for a watchman, from Old French *garde* 'watch', 'protection', a word of Germanic origin. Compare WARD 1.

Guardado (715) Portuguese and Spanish: from an adjectival derivative of *guardar* 'to guard'.
GIVEN NAMES Spanish 57%. *Jose* (34), *Carlos* (9), *Juan* (9), *Luis* (9), *Jesus* (8), *Julio* (8), *Pedro* (7), *Alfredo* (6), *Miguel* (6), *Ana* (5), *Jorge* (5), *Rafael* (5).

Guardia (155) Catalan (**Guàrdia**), Spanish, and Italian: from Catalan *guàrdia*, Spanish and Italian *guardia* 'guard', 'watch', a topographic name for someone who lived by a watch place, an occupational name for a member of the town guard, or a habitational name from any of the numerous places named (La) Guardia.
GIVEN NAMES Spanish 26%; Italian 19%. *Jose* (3), *Enrique* (2), *Alejandro, Alicia, Angel; Ricardo* (5), *Marco* (3), *Vito* (2), *Armando, Arturo, Celestino, Eduardo, Elvira, Ettore, Vincenzo.*

Guardino (363) Italian: from a pet form of the personal name *Guardo*, from the old German personal name *Wardo*.
GIVEN NAMES Italian 13%; Spanish 4%. *Sal* (5), *Carmela* (2), *Leonardo* (2), *Salvatore* (2), *Antonio, Calogero, Lorenzo, Saverio, Stefano; Agustin, Diego, Mireya.*

Guardiola (343) Catalan: habitational name from any of the numerous places named Guardiola, from *guardiola*, a diminutive of *guàrdia* 'guard'.
GIVEN NAMES Spanish 53%. *Juan* (11), *Jose* (7), *Luis* (7), *Jesus* (5), *Raul* (5), *Ricardo* (4), *Armando* (3), *Eduardo* (3), *Ignacio* (3), *Manuel* (3), *Alberto* (2), *Alejandro* (2).

Guarente (121) Italian (Campania): possibly from Old Tuscan *guarente* 'guarantor'.
GIVEN NAMES Italian 8%. *Carlo, Nerina, Saverio.*

Guariglia (208) Italian: according to Caracausi, a habitational name from a minor place in Sicily.
GIVEN NAMES French 5%. *Pierre* (2), *Armand.*

Guarin (132) Spanish (**Guarín**): Castilianized form of Catalan **Guarí** (see GUARINO).
GIVEN NAMES Spanish 43%. *Luis* (3), *Avelino* (2), *Carlos* (2), *Jose* (2), *Urbano* (2), *Ana Cecilia, Aracely, Armando, Camilo, Diego, Dioselina, Eduvina.*

Guarini (175) Italian: patronymic or plural form of GUARINO.
GIVEN NAMES Italian 10%. *Pasquale* (2), *Antonio, Rocco, Salvatore.*

Guarino (2473) Italian: from the personal name *Guarino*, derived from the Germanic element *war(n)* 'guard', 'protect'.
GIVEN NAMES Italian 15%. *Angelo* (23), *Rocco* (14), *Salvatore* (13), *Vito* (9),

Antonio (5), *Pasquale* (4), *Sal* (4), *Aldo* (3), *Carmela* (3), *Francesco* (3), *Vincenzo* (3), *Carmine* (2).

Guarisco (235) Southern Italian: possibly from a personal name formed with the suffix *-isco*, from Germanic *-isk*, denoting belonging.
GIVEN NAMES Italian 10%. *Sal* (2), *Antonino, Cesare, Enza, Neno, Ottavio.*

Guarnera (114) Italian: variant (feminine in form) of GUARNERI.
GIVEN NAMES Italian 10%. *Cosimo* (2), *Giuseppe, Salvatore.*

Guarneri (237) Southern Italian: patronymic or plural form of *Guarnero*, a Germanic personal name composed of the elements *war(in)* 'guard' + *hari, heri* 'army'.
GIVEN NAMES Italian 27%. *Sal* (5), *Salvatore* (5), *Carmine* (2), *Pasquale* (2), *Vito* (2), *Angelo, Camillo, Carlo, Carmela, Carmelo, Elia, Julio, Mario, Rosario.*

Guarnieri (507) Southern Italian: variant of GUARNERI.
GIVEN NAMES Italian 18%. *Salvatore* (5), *Aldo* (3), *Angelo* (3), *Carmine* (3), *Sal* (3), *Attilio* (2), *Concetta, Enrico, Gesualdo, Gino, Guido, Nunzio.*

Guastella (294) Southern Italian: according to Caracausi, from Sicilian *guastedda* 'focaccia' (flat loaf) (from Old French *gastel*, or rather Norman French *guastel, wastel*), presumably a metonymic occupational name for a baker or perhaps a nickname for a thin person. Alternatively, it may be derived from some minor place name.
GIVEN NAMES Italian 21%. *Salvatore* (5), *Sal* (3), *Ciro* (2), *Gasper* (2), *Calogero, Carmella, Carmelo, Carmine, Francesco, Giovanni, Julio, Mario, Nicolo, Vitina.*

Guay (1289) French: **1.** variant spelling of GAY. **2.** nickname from Old French *guai* 'unfortunate', 'ill-starred'.
GIVEN NAMES French 18%. *Normand* (8), *Andre* (6), *Armand* (6), *Lucien* (6), *Fernand* (5), *Marcel* (4), *Adrien* (3), *Pierre* (3), *Raoul* (2), *Camille* (2), *Emile* (2), *Jean Pierre* (2).

Guba (189) **1.** Hungarian: metonymic occupational name from *guba* 'overcoat'. **2.** Belorussian and Ukrainian: descriptive nickname from *guba, huba* 'lip'.

Gubala (103) Polish: nickname from a derivative of Old Polish *gubać* 'to crouch'.
GIVEN NAMES Polish 12%. *Andrzej* (2), *Stanislaw, Zbigniew, Zofia.*

Gubbels (198) German: probably a variant spelling of Rhenish **Göbbels**, a pet form of the Germanic personal name *Godebert*, from *gōd* 'good' or *god, got* 'god' + *berht* 'shining', or a patronymic from the Frisian personal name *Gubbe*.

Gubbins (226) English: patronymic from a variant of the personal name *Gibbon*, a pet form of GIBB.
GIVEN NAME Irish 6%. *Liam* (2).

Guber (102) Jewish (eastern Ashkenazic): variant of HUBER under Russian influence, since Russian has no *h* and alters *h* to *g* in borrowed words and names.

GIVEN NAMES Jewish 11%; Russian 4%. *Zev* (2), *Sol*; *Dmitri, Yelena.*

Guberman (203) Jewish (from Ukraine): variant of HUBERMAN, under Russian influence (see GOREN).

GIVEN NAMES Jewish 9%; Russian 4%. *Emanuel, Frima, Limor, Shlomo, Sol*; *Boris* (2), *Efim, Sergey, Vladimir.*

Gubler (336) Swiss German: topographic name from the South German dialect term *gubel* 'mountain crest', 'rocky outcrop' + the *-er* suffix denoting an inhabitant.

Gubrud (112) Norwegian: from *Gubberud*, name of seven places in eastern Norway, named with *Gubbi*, a pet form of the Old Norse male name *Guðbrandr*, + *rud* 'clearing'.

Gubser (170) Swiss German: of uncertain origin. It may be a nickname from the South German dialect word *gubitz* 'plover', or, more likely, a status name for a cottager from Old High German *chupisi* 'peasant's cottage'.

GIVEN NAMES French 6%; German 4%. *Veronique*; *Bernhard, Erwin.*

Gucciardo (163) Italian (Sicily): from the personal name *Gucciardo*, a revival of French *Guichard*, of Germanic origin, probably composed of the elements *wīg* 'battle' or *wisa* 'experience' + *hard* 'strong', 'brave', 'hardy'.

GIVEN NAMES Italian 15%. *Carmine* (4), *Biagio, Pasquale, Sal.*

Guccio (7) Italian: from the late medieval personal name *Guccio*, a reduced pet form of any of various names ending in *-go*, for example *Arrigo* (see HENRY) or *Ugo* (see HUGH).

Guccione (245) Italian (Sicily): from an augmentative form of the personal name GUCCIO.

GIVEN NAMES Italian 24%. *Salvatore* (4), *Sal* (2), *Antonio, Attilio, Biagio, Enrico, Gaetano, Giovanna, Matteo.*

Guck (210) South German: **1.** from the Bavarian word for a toad, applied either as a nickname or a topographic name. **2.** nickname from Middle High German *guck* 'cuckoo'.

Guckenberger (102) German: habitational name for someone from any of numerous places, especially in Bavaria and southern Germany, called Guggenberg.

Guckert (170) South German: variant of GUCK 2.

GIVEN NAMES German 5%. *Horst* (2), *Ralf.*

Gucwa (141) Polish: Polonized pet form of the German personal name *Gozwin*, a derivative of an ancient Germanic personal name meaning 'friend of the Goths'.

GIVEN NAMES Polish 6%. *Mieczyslaw, Piotr.*

Gudaitis (133) Lithuanian: ethnic name from *gudas* 'Belorussian'.

Gudde (104) German: **1.** variant of GUDE 1. **2.** (also Frisian): from a short form of a

Germanic personal name composed with *got* 'god' or *gōd* 'good'.

Gude (441) **1.** North German: complimentary nickname from *gude* 'the good one'. **2.** German: nickname from Sorbian *khudy* 'poor'.

Gudeman (150) North German: complimentary nickname from *guder man* 'good man'.

Gudenkauf (189) Dutch: nickname, literally meaning 'good bargain', but perhaps an altered form of the North German family name **Godekopp**, a nickname meaning 'good head', Low German *kopp* 'head' having been confused with Dutch *koop* 'buy', 'bargain'.

Guderian (186) North German: nickname from a reduced form of *guter Johann* 'good John'.

GIVEN NAME German 4%. *Guenther.*

Gudgel (246) Possibly an Americanized spelling of German GOTTSCHALL. Compare GUTSHALL.

Gudgeon (153) English: from Middle English *gojon, gogen*, Old French *gougon* 'gudgeon' (the fish) (Latin *gobio*, genitive *gobionis*), applied as a nickname or perhaps as a metonymic occupational name for a seller of these fish. The gudgeon is considered easy to catch, so the nickname may have denoted a gullible person.

Gudger (269) **1.** English: variant form of GOODYEAR. **2.** German: altered form of the South German and Swiss family name *Gutjahr*, nickname from a New Year's greeting, 'Good year'.

Gudino (333) Spanish: **1.** habitational name from a place called Gudino, of which there are two examples in Salamanca province. **2.** variant of GODINO.

GIVEN NAMES Spanish 60%. *Jose* (13), *Juan* (6), *Francisco* (5), *Salvador* (5), *Jesus* (4), *Jorge* (4), *Jose Luis* (4), *Rafael* (4), *Ramon* (4), *Alfonso* (3), *Arturo* (3), *Gonzalo* (3).

Gudmundson (321) Swedish (**Gudmundsson**), Danish and Norwegian (**Gudmundsen**): patronymic from the Scandinavian personal name *Gudmund*, from Old Norse *Guðmundr*, composed of the elements *guð* 'god' + *mundr* 'protection'.

GIVEN NAMES Scandinavian 5%. *Erik.*

Gue (330) French (**Gué**): topographic name for someone who lived near a ford, from Old French *wad* 'ford', 'crossing place'.

GIVEN NAMES French 5%. *Andre, Giraud.*

Guebert (127) German or French (**Guébert**): variant of GUILBERT.

GIVEN NAMES German 4%. *Erwin, Lorenz.*

Guedes (117) Portuguese: unexplained.

GIVEN NAMES Spanish 33%; Portuguese 26%; Italian 8%; French 4%. *Jose* (5), *Luiz* (4), *Carlos* (3), *Sergio* (3), *Alfredo* (2), *Orlando* (2), *Adriano, Ana, Carolina, Ernesto, Fernando, Geraldo; Joao* (3), *Joaquim* (3), *Afonso* (3), *Agostinho, Anabela; Agostino, Antonio, Lia, Riccardo; Alphonse, Jean-Pierre.*

Guedry (194) French: see GUIDRY.

Guel (166) Castilianized variant (**Güel**) of Catalan **Güell** (see GUELL).

GIVEN NAMES Spanish 48%. *Jose* (7), *Raul* (4), *Jorge* (3), *Pablo* (3), *Alejandrino* (2), *Isidro* (2), *Juan* (2), *Mario* (2), *Ramiro* (2), *Adolfo, Alberto, Alejandro.*

Guelker (134) North German (**Gülker**): habitational name derived from *Gülke*, the old Rhenish name of the city now called Jülich; in the 4th century it was named in Latin as *Juliacum* 'settlement of Julius', and in 1094 it is documented as *Guliche*.

Guell (136) **1.** German (**Güll**): from the personal name *Aegilius*. **2.** South German and Swiss German: topographic name from Middle High German *gülle* '(swampy) puddle'. **3.** Catalan (**Güell**): habitational name from any of the places named Güell, in particular in Girona and Lleida provinces, Catalonia, named with Latin *vadellum* 'little ford'.

Guenette (200) Altered spelling of French **Guenet**, a pet form of **Guène**, from a Germanic personal name, a short form of a compound name formed with *wān* 'hope'.

GIVEN NAMES French 16%. *Andre, Antoine, Cecile, Gaston, Gilles, Jean-Claude, Lucienne, Marcel, Pierre, Rudolphe.*

Guenin (140) French (**Guénin**): from a derivative of **Guène**, from the Germanic personal name *Wano*, a pet form of a compound name formed with *wan* meaning 'hope', 'expectation'.

GIVEN NAMES French 5%. *Pierre, Remy.*

Guenther (4081) German (**Günther**): from a Germanic personal name composed of *gund* 'battle' + *hari, heri* 'army'.

GIVEN NAMES German 6%. *Kurt* (12), *Hans* (6), *Otto* (5), *Fritz* (3), *Gerhard* (3), *Lutz* (3), *Christoph* (2), *Helmut* (2), *Klaus* (2), *Manfred* (2), *Oskar* (2), *Ulrich* (2).

Guenthner (337) German (**Günthner**): habitational name from Gunthen in West Prussia or Gunthenen in East Prussia.

Guentner (101) Variant of German **Günther** (see GUENTHER).

Guenzel (110) German: from a pet form of the personal name *Günther* (see GUENTHER).

GIVEN NAMES German 8%. *Hans, Otto, Rudi.*

Guerard (210) French (**Guérard**): from a Germanic personal name composed of *war(in)* 'guard' + *hard* 'hardy', 'strong'.

GIVEN NAMES French 14%. *Laurent* (2), *Pierre* (2), *Alcide, Antoine, Benoit, Jacques, Jean-Paul, Lucien, Marcel.*

Guercio (465) Italian: nickname for a person with a squint, from *guercio* 'cross-eyed'.

GIVEN NAMES Italian 11%. *Salvatore* (2), *Santo* (2), *Antonio, Carlo, Concetta, Geno, Girolamo, Giuseppe, Sal, Savino, Stefano.*

Guereca (102) of Basque origin: unexplained.

GIVEN NAMES Spanish 54%. *Jose* (5), *Juan* (3), *Guadalupe* (2), *Manuel* (2), *Sergio* (2),

Alberto, Alejandro, Alicia, Angel, Bernardo, Candelaria, Carlos.

Guerette (230) See GUERRETTE.
GIVEN NAMES French 15%. *Normand* (4), *Aurel, Aurele, Emile, Herve, Laurent.*

Guerin (2291) French (**Guérin**): from the Germanic personal name *Warin*, a short form of various compound names beginning with *war(in)* 'guard'. This is found as a Huguenot name, established in Ireland (County Limerick).
GIVEN NAMES French 6%. *Armand* (5), *Emile* (4), *Marcel* (4), *Normand* (4), *Andre* (2), *Dominique* (2), *Aime, Alain, Arsene, Benoit, Francois, Gilles.*

Guerino (154) Italian: variant of GUARINO.
GIVEN NAMES Italian 12%. *Sirio* (2), *Aldo, Mario, Premo.*

Guernsey (979) English: apparently a habitational name from the island of Guernsey in the Channel Islands. It is now a rare surname in Britain.

Guerra (8679) **1.** Spanish, Portuguese, and Italian: nickname for a belligerent person or for a soldier, from *guerra* 'war'. In some cases the Italian name may represent a short form of various compound personal names containing this element, for example **Vinciguèrra**. The Iberian name may in some cases reflect a misinterpretation of the Basque base *ezquerra, esquerra*, from *esker* 'left-handed'. **2.** Basque: Castilianized form of Basque **Gerra**, a topographic name for someone who lived in a break or depression in a range of hills, from Basque *gerri* 'waist'.
GIVEN NAMES Spanish 43%; Portuguese 9%. *Jose* (207), *Juan* (125), *Manuel* (83), *Carlos* (71), *Jesus* (63), *Luis* (62), *Raul* (51), *Mario* (48), *Armando* (45), *Francisco* (45), *Jorge* (44), *Roberto* (43); *Henrique, Joao, Paulo, Sil; Antonio* (41), *Marco* (11), *Dario* (9), *Lorenzo* (9), *Leonardo* (7), *Romeo* (7), *Aldo* (6), *Ciro* (6), *Luciano* (6), *Vito* (6), *Angelo* (5), *Sal* (5).

Guerrant (250) French: nickname for a belligerent person or alternatively for a valiant soldier, from *guerrer* 'to fight'.

Guerreiro (127) Portuguese and Galician: nickname for a belligerent person or alternatively for a valiant soldier, from *guerreiro* 'warrior'.
GIVEN NAMES Spanish 33%; Portuguese 20%. *Jose* (10), *Manuel* (3), *Ricardo* (2), *Sergio* (2), *Carlos, Dulce, Edmundo, Elvira, Enrique, Francisco, Humberto, Josefina; Paulo* (2), *Joao, Joaquim; Antonio* (4), *Angelo, Silvio.*

Guerrera (580) Italian: from a feminine form of GUERRERO.
GIVEN NAMES Italian 34%. *Angelo* (10), *Salvatore* (9), *Antonio* (8), *Mario* (8), *Nicola* (5), *Domenic* (3), *Donato* (3), *Pasquale* (3), *Rocco* (3), *Sal* (3), *Enrico* (2), *Fortunato* (2), *Vittorio* (2), *Alberto, Alessandro, Emilio, Eufemia, Imelda, Juan, Mauricio, Rodolfo, Rosario.*

Guerrero (10757) Spanish, Portuguese, and Italian: nickname for an aggressive person or for a soldier, from an agent derivative of *guerra* 'war'. Compare GUERRA.
GIVEN NAMES Spanish 49%; Portuguese 10%. *Jose* (279), *Juan* (172), *Jesus* (98), *Luis* (93), *Manuel* (89), *Carlos* (86), *Francisco* (76), *Raul* (72), *Miguel* (67), *Jorge* (63), *Pedro* (60), *Roberto* (60); *Wenceslao* (6), *Ligia* (5), *Anatolio, Calixtro, Lidio, Omero, Paulo.*

Guerrette (352) Apparently of French origin: perhaps related to *guerre* 'war'.
GIVEN NAMES French 13%. *Antoine* (2), *Armand* (2), *Germaine* (2), *Adrien, Alphee, Camil, Camille, Josephe, Lucien, Ludger, Marcel, Rosaire.*

Guerrier (317) French: nickname for an aggressive person or occupational name for a soldier, from Old French *guerrier* 'warrior'.
GIVEN NAMES French 40%; German 5%. *Yves* (4), *Rodrigue* (2), *Cecile, Ermite, Franck, Georges, Gilberte, Gisele, Hugues, Jean Luc, Jean-Jacques, Laurent; Fritz* (2), *Walther.*

Guerrieri (550) Italian: patronymic or plural form of GUERRIERO.
GIVEN NAMES Italian 21%. *Salvatore* (5), *Angelo* (3), *Mario* (3), *Claudio* (2), *Gasper* (2), *Alfredo, Americo, Antonio, Aurelio, Bernardino, Biagio, Carmine, Chiara, Corrado, Domenico, Emidio, Enrico, Ernesto, Francesco, Melio, Orlando, Renato.*

Guerriero (771) Italian: nickname for a belligerent person or an occupational name for a soldier, from an agent noun from *guerra* 'war'.
GIVEN NAMES Italian 19%. *Angelo* (7), *Carmine* (7), *Sal* (5), *Antonio* (4), *Salvatore* (4), *Carlo* (2), *Domenic* (2), *Nunzio* (2), *Pasquale* (2), *Aniello, Carmela.*

Guerrini (192) Italian: patronymic or plural form of the medieval personal name *Guerrino*, derived from *guerra* 'war', which was popularized by Andrea da Barberino's *Guerrin Meschino*.
GIVEN NAMES Italian 19%. *Alfonso, Arnaldo, Dante, Guido, Leandro, Luca, Mario, Mauro, Oreste, Osvaldo, Remo, Tommaso, Tosca.*

Guerro (113) Spanish: unexplained, but probably a derivative of *guerra* 'war' (compare GUERRA).
GIVEN NAMES Spanish 34%; Italian 7%. *Amparo* (2), *Armando* (2), *Jose* (2), *Manuel* (2), *Patricio* (2), *Alicia, Angel, Baldomero, Carlos, Dominga, Francisco, Gustavo; Carmine.*

Guerry (325) French and Swiss French: nickname for an aggressive person or occupational name for a soldier. Compare GUERRIER.

Guertin (1285) French: of uncertain derivation; possibly a short form of the various Germanic compound personal names

formed with *wert*, reflected by Old High German *werd* 'noble', 'honorable'.
GIVEN NAMES French 10%. *Armand* (8), *Emile* (3), *Andre* (2), *Antoine* (2), *Lucien* (2), *Marcel* (2), *Normand* (2), *Pierre* (2), *Zoel* (2), *Adrien, Amie, Celestin.*

Guertler (111) German: variant spelling of **Gürtler** (see GURTLER).
GIVEN NAMES German 16%. *Hans* (2), *Klaus* (2), *Elke, Horst, Siegfried.*

Guess (2585) **1.** English: probably a variant of GUEST. **2.** South German (**Güss**): topographic name for someone who lived near a torrent or on a flood plain, from Middle High German *güsse* 'flood', 'flooding'. **3.** German: variant of GEIS.

Guessford (146) Possibly an altered form of English **Gosford**, a habitational name from places so named in Oxfordshire, Somerset, Suffolk, and Warwickshire, or from Gosforth in Cumbria. All are named from Old English *gōs* 'goose' (genitive plural *gósa* 'of the geese') + *ford* 'ford'.

Guest (3450) English: nickname for a stranger or newcomer to a community, from Middle English *g(h)est* 'guest', 'visitor' (from Old Norse *gestr*, absorbing the cognate Old English *giest*).

Guetschow (146) German (**Gütschow**): habitational name from Gützkow near Anklam in northeastern Germany.

Guetter (101) Jewish (Ashkenazic): variant of GUTTER.
GIVEN NAMES French 4%. *Alexandre, Alphonse.*

Guettler (218) South German (**Güttler**): status name for the holder of a small farm, from Middle High German *güetelin* 'small holding', ultimately from *guot* 'property'.
GIVEN NAMES German 4%. *Arno, Franz.*

Guevara (3453) Basque: Castilianized form of Basque **Gebara**, a habitational name from a place in the Basque province of Araba. The origin and meaning of the place name are uncertain; it is recorded in the form *Gebala* by the geographer Ptolemy in the 2nd century AD. This is a rare name in Spain.
GIVEN NAMES Spanish 51%. *Jose* (134), *Carlos* (53), *Juan* (51), *Luis* (40), *Jesus* (30), *Francisco* (29), *Jorge* (21), *Ana* (18), *Miguel* (17), *Julio* (16), *Manuel* (16), *Roberto* (16).

Guevarra (216) Variant spelling of GUEVARA.
GIVEN NAMES Spanish 52%. *Jose* (3), *Andres* (2), *Artemio* (2), *Carlos* (2), *Edgardo* (2), *Jesus* (2), *Manuel* (2), *Adelaida, Adoracion, Aida, Altagracia, Aristedes.*

Guevin (110) French (**Guévin**): unexplained.

Gueye (121) West African: unexplained.
GIVEN NAMES African 45%; Muslim 26%; French 6%. *Cheikh* (6), *Mamadou* (6), *Fatou* (2), *Ousmane* (2), *Aliou, Amadou, Aminata, Boubacar, Djibril, Modou, Momar, Serigne; Ibrahima* (4), *Moussa* (2),

Moustapha (2), *Abdoul, Abdoulaye, Aly, Daouda, Elhadji, Fadel, Ismaila, Karim, Khadim; Alain, Patrice.*

Guffey (2461) Irish and Scottish: reduced form of MCGUFFEY.

Guffin (183) Irish: reduced form of MCGUFFIN (see MCGIFFIN).

Guffy (236) Irish and Scottish: variant spelling of GUFFEY.

Gugel (301) German: from Middle High German *gugel* 'cowl', 'hood (of a coat or jacket)' (Latin *cuculla*), a metonymic occupational name for a maker of hoods or alternatively a nickname for someone who habitually wore one. In some cases the surname may have arisen from topographic names containing this element.
GIVEN NAMES Russian 6%; German 5%. *Aleksandr* (3), *Lev, Oxana, Saveliy, Vladimir, Yury; Arno, Gerhard, Hannelore.*

Guggenheim (292) Jewish (western Ashkenazic): habitational name from Gugenheim in Alsace or, less likely, Jugenheim (earlier *Guggenheim*) near Bensheim (Hesse). In both cases the second element is from Old High German *heim* 'homestead', while the first is of obscure and disputed etymology.
GIVEN NAMES German 5%. *Hans* (2), *Ernst, Erwin, Manfred.*

Guggino (104) Southern Italian: variant of GUGINO.
GIVEN NAMES Italian 20%. *Domenic, Gasper, Ignacio, Mario, Salvadore.*

Guggisberg (173) Swiss German and South German: habitational name from a place named with *gugge* 'cuckoo' or 'toad' + *berg* 'mountain', 'hill'. According to some, *gug* may be an old word meaning 'swamp' and South German *guggi* 'toad' a derivative of it.
GIVEN NAME French 4%. *Michel.*

Gugino (273) Southern Italian: apparently from *cugino* 'cousin', reflecting the voiced pronunciation of *c*, typical of Sicily.
GIVEN NAMES Italian 9%. *Salvatore* (2), *Carmelo, Cosmo.*

Guglielmetti (161) Italian: patronymic or plural form of *Guglielmetto*, a pet form of the personal name GUGLIELMO.
GIVEN NAMES Italian 24%. *Aldo* (3), *Antonio, Domenico, Fausto, Mario, Matteo, Rocco, Vincenzo, Vita.*

Guglielmi (304) Italian: patronymic or plural form of GUGLIELMO.
GIVEN NAMES Italian 31%. *Cosmo* (4), *Mario* (3), *Egidio* (2), *Gino* (2), *Alessandra, Alfredo, Amadeo, Amedeo, Antonio, Carlo, Carmine, Dante, Domenic, Domenico, Elena, Manuela, Marina, Roberto, Sergio.*

Guglielmino (122) Italian: from a pet form of the personal name GUGLIELMO.
GIVEN NAMES Italian 11%. *Sal* (2), *Salvatore* (2), *Franco, Giovanni, Marco.*

Guglielmo (742) Italian: from the personal name *Guglielmo*, Italian equivalent of WILLIAM.

GIVEN NAMES Italian 22%. *Angelo* (9), *Antonio* (5), *Rocco* (5), *Salvatore* (5), *Nicola* (4), *Aniello* (3), *Giuseppe* (3), *Luigi* (3), *Pasquale* (3), *Fedele* (2), *Amedeo, Antonino.*

Gugliotta (280) Italian: **1.** from a pet form of the personal name *Guglia*. **2.** from a pet form of **Aguglia**, a topographic name for someone living by an obelisk or obelisk-shaped mountain peak, from medieval Latin *aguglia* 'obelisk'.
GIVEN NAMES Italian 15%. *Carmelo* (2), *Salvatore* (2), *Aldo, Angelo, Antonino, Antonio, Gaetano, Giuseppe, Natale, Nicola, Vito.*

Gugliotti (195) Italian: variant, plural or patronymic in form, of GUGLIOTTA.
GIVEN NAMES Italian 34%. *Carmine* (5), *Rocco* (5), *Angelo* (2), *Antonio* (2), *Orazio* (2), *Domenic, Donato, Elio, Enrico, Fiore, Nicola, Nunzio.*

Gugliuzza (210) Italian: from a derivative of the personal name *Guglia* (see GUGLIOTTA).
GIVEN NAMES Italian 19%. *Salvatore* (2), *Carmelo, Domenico, Nicola, Santo, Veto.*

Guha (108) Indian (Bengal) and Bangladeshi: Hindu (Kayasth) name from Sanskrit *guhā* 'cave', or 'heart', 'mind'.
GIVEN NAMES Indian 90%. *Ratan* (3), *Amitava* (2), *Asim* (2), *Manju* (2), *Prabir* (2), *Ranjan* (2), *Sanjiv* (2), *Aloke, Amala, Amit, Anima, Arun.*

Guhl (323) **1.** Eastern German: either from a Slavic personal name, or perhaps a habitational name from places in eastern Germany called Guhle(n), Guhlau, or Guhlow. **2.** South German (Swiss): of uncertain origin; perhaps a nickname from late Middle High German *gūl* 'bad horse', also 'monster'.
GIVEN NAMES German 5%. *Otto* (2), *Franz, Ruediger, Wolfgang.*

Guibord (123) Probably an altered spelling of French **Guibaud**, from a Germanic personal name composed of the elements *wīg* 'battle', 'fight' + *bald, bold* 'bold', 'brave'.

Guice (944) Americanized spelling of German GEIS.

Guichard (187) French: from a Germanic personal name composed of the elements *wīg* 'battle', 'combat' + *hard* 'hardy', 'strong'.
GIVEN NAMES French 8%; Spanish 8%. *Andre, Betrand, Gilles, Michel, Thierry; Alvaro, Julio* (2), *Ramon* (2), *Alicia, Ana Maria, Elena, Juan, Maria Luisa, Osvaldo.*

Guida (958) Italian: **1.** patronymic or plural form of GUIDO. **2.** from a short form of a personal name formed with *guida* 'guide', for example the Tuscan names **Bonaguida** 'good guide' and **Cacciaguida** 'hunting guide'. **3.** (**Guidà**) occupational name for a goatherd, from Greek *aigidion* 'kid'. Compare the modern Greek surname **Gidás**.

GIVEN NAMES Italian 19%. *Angelo* (6), *Antonio* (4), *Salvatore* (4), *Humberto* (3), *Mario* (3), *Gaetano* (2), *Luciano* (2), *Vito* (2), *Alfonso, Angelina, Arcangelo, Armando, Carmelo, Ciro, Domenica, Domenico, Eugenio, Geraldo, Orlando.*

Guider (304) **1.** Irish (Tipperary and mid-Ulster): unexplained. It may be a reduced Anglicized form of Gaelic **Mac Giodaire**, from *giodar* 'haste'. **2.** Probably an Americanized spelling of South German **Geider**, a nickname for a braggart, Middle High German *giuder*. Compare GEITNER.

Guidera (202) Of uncertain origin. The name is found (though rarely) in Italy, where, according to Caracausi, it is of Albanian origin, being recorded in documents relating to the Albanian-speaking community of Sicily.

Guidetti (122) Italian: from a pet form of the personal name GUIDO.
GIVEN NAMES French 6%; Italian 6%. *Pierre* (2); *Giampiero, Giovanni.*

Guidi (460) Italian: patronymic or plural form of the personal name GUIDO.
GIVEN NAMES Italian 28%. *Enzo* (5), *Paolo* (4), *Armando* (3), *Aldo* (2), *Antonio* (2), *Carlo* (2), *Gino* (2), *Guido* (2), *Mario* (2), *Maurizio* (2), *Silvio* (2), *Agostino, Angelo, Giuliano, Lilio, Orlando, Remigio, Sergio.*

Guidice (291) Metathesized spelling of Italian GIUDICE.
GIVEN NAMES Italian 12%. *Carmine* (2), *Carmela, Dino, Domenic, Orazio, Vincenzo, Vito.*

Guido (1727) Italian: from the personal name *Guido*, Italian equivalent of GUY.
GIVEN NAMES Italian 23%; Spanish 12%. *Salvatore* (10), *Angelo* (7), *Carmine* (4), *Armando* (3), *Gino* (3), *Mariano* (3), *Rocco* (3), *Gaetano* (2), *Pasquale* (2), *Santo* (2), *Umberto* (2), *Vito* (2); *Jose* (5), *Guadalupe* (2), *Juan* (2), *Luis* (2), *Manuel* (2), *Pura* (2), *Alejandro, Alfonso.*

Guidone (170) Italian: from an augmentative of the personal name GUIDO.
GIVEN NAMES Italian 13%. *Corrado* (2), *Giovanni* (2), *Franco, Marco, Rocco.*

Guidotti (315) Italian: from a pet form of the personal name GUIDO.
GIVEN NAMES Italian 5%. *Guido* (3), *Aldo, Alessandro, Angelo, Antonio, Edo, Geno.*

Guidroz (562) Swiss French (Vaud): unexplained.
GIVEN NAMES French 6%. *Antoine, Camille, Emile, Pierre, Sylvian, Yves.*

Guidry (6818) **1.** French: from a personal name based on the Germanic root *waido* 'hunt'. The name is particularly associated with Cajuns in LA, who seem all to be descended from Claude Guédry dit Grivois, who arrived in Acadia before 1671. **2.** Variant of **Guitry**, which is based on a personal name composed of the Germanic elements *wid(u), wit-* 'wood' + *rīc* 'power(ful)'.

GIVEN NAMES French 6%. *Camille* (6), *Curley* (6), *Alphonse* (5), *Cecile* (5), *Emile* (5), *Alcide* (4), *Ulysse* (4), *Amie* (3), *Angelle* (3), *Antoine* (3), *Gillis* (3), *Jacques* (3).

Guier (169) **1.** Probably an Americanized spelling of German GEIER. **2.** Possibly an altered spelling of French **Guyet**, from a pet form of GUY.

Guiffre (176) Southern French: from a Germanic personal name composed of the elements *wīg* 'battle', 'combat' + *frid(u)* 'peace'.
GIVEN NAME Italian 5%. *Salvatore.*

Guignard (119) French: nickname from Old French *guingnart* 'someone who winks'.
GIVEN NAMES French 17%. *Alain* (2), *Dominique, Francois, Luc, Yvon.*

Guiher (111) Probably a respelling of French **Guihard**, from a Germanic personal name composed of the elements *wit* 'wood' + *hard* 'strong', 'hardy'.

Guilbault (370) North American spelling of French **Guilbaut**, from a Germanic personal name composed of the elements *wil* 'will', 'desire' + *bald, bold* 'bold', 'brave'.
GIVEN NAMES French 11%. *Andre* (3), *Emile, Gaston, Jean Guy, Jean-Paul, Lucien, Marcel, Normand.*

Guilbeau (648) French: see GUILBAULT.
GIVEN NAMES French 9%. *Andre* (2), *Emile* (2), *Lucien* (2), *Octave* (2), *Cyprien, Fabien, Julien, Laurent, Marcelle, Monique, Onezime, Pierre.*

Guilbeault (174) French: see GUILBAULT.
GIVEN NAMES French 17%. *Adelard* (2), *Adrien, Armand, Donat, Emile, Laurent, Lucien, Normand.*

Guilbeaux (226) French: see GUILBAULT.
GIVEN NAMES French 10%. *Alphe, Camille, Cecile, Easton, Minus, Nolton, Renald, Yoland.*

Guilbert (279) French: from a Germanic personal name composed of the elements *wil(j)-* 'will' + *berht* 'bright', 'famous'.
GIVEN NAMES French 11%. *Normand* (2), *Andre, Camille, Emile, Gaston, Gisele, Lucien, Pierre, Raoul.*

Guild (1199) **1.** Scottish: apparently a nickname for someone who played a prominent part in a medieval guild. It may, however, be a Scottish variant of GOLD. **2.** Welsh: Anglicized form of the Welsh surname **Gwyllt**, a nickname meaning 'wild'.

Guile (295) **1.** Most probably a variant of GILL, in any of the senses pronounced with a hard *g*. **2.** It could also be Scottish, English, or French, an uncomplimentary nickname from Old French *guile*, Middle English *gile* 'deceit' or 'treachery'. **3.** Possibly also an Americanized spelling of German GEIL.

Guiler (137) **1.** English: nickname for a wiley or deceitful person, from Old French *guileor* 'deceiver', 'traitor'. **2.** Americanized spelling of German GEILER.

Guiles (419) Of uncertain origin; it could be a variant of French GUILL or of English GUILE or GILES.

Guilfoil (196) Irish: variant spelling of GUILFOYLE.

Guilford (933) English: habitational name from Guildford in Surrey, which is probably named with Old English *gylde* 'golden' (perhaps used here to denote a sandy hill) + *ford* 'ford'.

Guilfoyle (695) Irish: reduced Anglicized form of Gaelic **Mac Giolla Phóil**, a patronymic from the personal name *Giolla Phóil* 'servant of (Saint) Paul'.

Guiliani (123) Metathesized spelling of Italian GIULIANI.
GIVEN NAMES Italian 5%. *Aldo, Angelo.*

Guiliano (355) Metathesized spelling of Italian GIULIANO.
GIVEN NAMES Italian 19%. *Angelo* (5), *Salvatore* (5), *Carmine* (4), *Antonio* (2), *Matteo* (2), *Dino, Fiore, Pasquale, Reno, Sal.*

Guill (632) **1.** French: from the personal name *Guille*, a short form of GUILLAUME (see WILLIAM). **2.** Perhaps a reduced form of the Irish family name **McGuill**, an Anglicized form of Gaelic **Mac Cuill** 'son of Coll'.

Guillaume (563) French: from the personal name *Guillaume*, French form of WILLIAM.
GIVEN NAMES French 19%. *Pierre* (5), *Jacques* (2), *Jean-Pierre* (2), *Marcel* (2), *Patrice* (2), *Yvon* (2), *Anite, Antoine, Edrice, Francois, Gesner, Ghislaine.*

Guillemette (387) French: in most cases probably from *Guillemette*, a female personal name derived from GUILLAUME, or in some cases a respelling of **Guillemet**, from a masculine pet form of the same name.
GIVEN NAMES French 22%. *Andre* (3), *Normand* (3), *Armand* (2), *Gilles* (2), *Jean-Paul* (2), *Leonie* (2), *Alcide, Anatole, Cecile, Emile, Fernand, Fernande.*

Guillen (2369) Spanish (**Guillén**): from the personal name *Guillén*, Spanish equivalent of WILLIAM.
GIVEN NAMES Spanish 51%. *Jose* (81), *Juan* (38), *Francisco* (31), *Manuel* (28), *Carlos* (27), *Luis* (25), *Pedro* (21), *Miguel* (18), *Jesus* (15), *Rafael* (15), *Ruben* (15), *Enrique* (14).

Guillermo (381) Spanish: from the personal name *Guillermo*, Spanish equivalent of WILLIAM.
GIVEN NAMES Spanish 52%. *Juan* (4), *Jose* (3), *Julio* (3), *Luis* (3), *Amador* (2), *Carlos* (2), *Claudio* (2), *Emeterio* (2), *Eugenio* (2), *Lopez* (2), *Luz* (2), *Margarita* (2).

Guillet (211) French: from a pet form of the personal name **Guille**, a short form of *Guillaume* (see WILLIAM).
GIVEN NAMES French 13%. *Andre* (2), *Jean Marc, Philippe, Pierre, Romain, Yvan.*

Guillette (228) Characteristic French Canadian spelling of GUILLET.

GIVEN NAMES French 13%. *Marcel* (2), *Andre, Armand, Emile, Lucien, Manon, Telesphore, Virginie.*

Guilliams (596) Welsh: patronymic from GWILLIAM, with English patronymic *-s.*

Guillory (4235) French: from a Germanic name composed of the elements *wil* 'will', 'desire' + *rīc* 'power(ful)'.
FOREBEARS Simon Guillory emigrated from Chartre-sur-Cher to Canada in 1646; his grandson Joseph-Grégoire moved to Opelousas, LA, in 1764.
GIVEN NAMES French 5%. *Andre* (4), *Antoine* (4), *Alcide* (2), *Elcie* (2), *Ferrel* (2), *Leonce* (2), *Nolton* (2), *Odile* (2), *Yves* (2), *Aldes, Alexandre.*

Guillot (1628) French: from a pet form of the personal name **Guille**, itself a short form of GUILLAUME.
GIVEN NAMES French 6%. *Emile* (3), *Francois* (2), *Landry* (2), *Serge* (2), *Amelie, Andree, Angelle, Antoine, Eugenie, Jacques, Jean Louis, Joffre.*

Guillotte (314) French Canadian spelling of GUILLOT, reflecting the Canadian pronunciation.
GIVEN NAMES French 9%. *Alcide, Andre, Emile, Normand, Oneil, Theophile, Ulysse, Vernice.*

Guilmette (554) French: variant **Guillemet**, from a pet form of *Guillaume* (see WILLIAM).
GIVEN NAMES French 8%. *Armand* (4), *Edmour* (2), *Andre, Antoine, Cecile, Emile.*

Guimaraes (182) Portuguese (**Guimarães**): habitational name from any of various places called Guimarães, especially the provincial capital of Minho; its name is derived from a Germanic personal name.
GIVEN NAMES Spanish 39%; Portuguese 24%; Italian 7%. *Jose* (6), *Carlos* (4), *Eduardo* (4), *Fernando* (3), *Luiz* (3), *Roberto* (3), *Jorge* (2), *Marcos* (2), *Mario* (2), *Viriato* (2), *Abilio, Albino; Joaquim* (2), *Paulo* (2), *Amadeu, Anabela, Joao, Marcio, Vasco; Antonio* (8), *Luciano, Plinio.*

Guimond (735) French: from a Germanic personal name composed of the elements *wīg* 'battle', 'combat' + *mund* 'protection'.
GIVEN NAMES French 9%. *Armand* (3), *Andre* (2), *Normand* (2), *Valmore* (2), *Auguste, Camil, Cecile, Emile, Ghislain, Gilles, Lucien, Pierre.*

Guimont (188) French: variant of GUIMOND.
GIVEN NAMES French 10%. *Andre, Armand, Germain, Ludger, Rejean.*

Guin (923) **1.** French: from a Germanic personal name or short form of various compound names formed with *wini* 'friend'. **2.** Perhaps a reduced form of McQUINN. This name is clustered in NC, AL, and LA.

Guinan (586) Irish: reduced Anglicized form of two distinct Gaelic names, which have now become confused: **Ó Cuinneáin** 'descendant of *Cuinneán*', a personal name from a diminutive of *conn* 'chief', and **Ó Cuineáin** 'descendant of *Cuineán*', a personal name from a diminutive of *cana* 'whelp'.

GIVEN NAMES Irish 5%. *Kieran, Kiernan, Spud.*

Guinane (108) Irish: variant of GUINAN.

Guinard (114) French: from a Germanic personal name composed of the elements *wini* 'friend' + *hard* 'hardy', 'strong'.

GIVEN NAME French 4%. *Laurent.*

Guindon (275) French: possibly from a derivative of Old French *guinde* 'winch'.

GIVEN NAMES French 10%. *Gaston* (2), *Michel* (2), *Andre, Germain, Jean Marie, Marcel, Yannick.*

Guinee (128) Irish: variant spelling of GUINEY.

Guiney (403) Irish (Connacht): reduced Anglicized form of Gaelic **Mac Géibheannaigh**, 'son of *Géibheannach*', from *géibheannach* 'fettered'. See also KEAVENY.

GIVEN NAME Irish 6%. *Siobhan.*

Guinn (4546) Irish: reduced and altered form of McQUINN.

Guinta (270) Probably a metathesized spelling of Italian GIUNTA.

GIVEN NAMES Italian 15%. *Angelo* (2), *Marco* (2), *Salvatore* (2), *Salvo* (2), *Santo* (2), *Carmine, Rocco, Sal.*

Guinther (276) Americanized spelling of German GUENTHER.

Guinto (185) Probably a metathesized spelling of Italian **Giunto**, a variant of GIUNTA.

GIVEN NAMES Spanish 34%; Italian 6%. *Pedro* (3), *Virgilio* (3), *Arsenio* (2), *Vicente* (2), *Adriana, Alberto, Alfredo, Anabel, Angelita, Artemio, Augustina, Benedicto; Carlo, Enrico.*

Guinyard (149) North American spelling of French GUIGNARD.

Guion (400) French: from the Germanic personal name *Wido* (see GUY).

GIVEN NAMES French 4%. *Camille, Colette, Michel.*

Guire (181) **1.** Reduced form of Irish and Scottish McGUIRE. **2.** Americanized spelling of German GEIER.

Guirguis (203) Arabic: variant of GIRGIS.

GIVEN NAMES Arabic 66%. *Maged* (5), *Samir* (5), *Maher* (4), *Mounir* (3), *Nabil* (3), *Raouf* (3), *Amir* (2), *Habib* (2), *Hany* (2), *Moneer* (2), *Nader* (2), *Sherif* (2).

Guise (505) **1.** English and French: regional name for someone from the district of France of this name, which is of unexplained origin. **2.** French: from a short form of a Germanic personal name formed with *wid* 'leader'.

Guisinger (276) Americanized spelling of German GEISINGER.

GIVEN NAME French 4%. *Laure* (3).

Guist (108) Of uncertain origin. Possibly a metathesized spelling of Italian **Giust**, a variant of GIUSTI.

Guisti (127) Metathesized spelling of Italian GIUSTI.

GIVEN NAMES Italian 5%; German 4%. *Rinaldo, Vincenzo; Kurt* (2).

Guitar (119) Southern French: from the Germanic personal name *Withard*, composed of the elements *wid(u), wit* 'wood', 'forest' + *hard* 'hardy', 'brave', 'strong'.

Guitard (91) Southern French: from the Germanic personal name *Withard*, composed of the elements *wid(u), wit* 'wood', 'forest' + *hard* 'hardy', 'brave', 'strong'.

GIVEN NAMES French 12%; German 4%. *Jean-Pierre, Laurent, Leandre, Patrice; Waltraud.*

Guite (123) French: from the Germanic personal name *Wido*, from *wid* 'wood'.

GIVEN NAMES French 14%. *Marcel* (2), *Gilles, Maurille, Michel, Renaud.*

Guiterrez (425) Spanish (**Guitérrez**): respelling of Spanish **Gutiérrez** (see GUTIERREZ).

GIVEN NAMES Spanish 51%. *Jose* (10), *Juan* (7), *Luis* (6), *Arturo* (5), *Francisco* (5), *Alfredo* (4), *Jesus* (4), *Rafael* (4), *Raul* (4), *Carlos* (3), *Guadalupe* (3), *Jose Luis* (3).

Guitierrez (110) Spanish (**Guitiérrez**): respelling of Spanish *Gutiérrez* (see GUTIERREZ).

GIVEN NAMES Spanish 60%. *Jose* (3), *Juan* (3), *Enrique* (2), *Jaime* (2), *Manuel* (2), *Miguel* (2), *Ofelia* (2), *Ricardo* (2), *Salvador* (2), *Andres, Argentina, Armando.*

Guiton (128) French: variant spelling of GUYTON.

GIVEN NAMES French 6%. *Jacques, Landry, Michel.*

Guitron (146) Spanish (**Guitrón**): unexplained; possibly a variant of Spanish *guitarrón*, an augmentative of *guitarra* in the colloquial sense 'rogue'.

GIVEN NAMES Spanish 43%. *Guillermo* (4), *Francisco* (3), *Miguel* (3), *Alfredo* (2), *Jose* (2), *Jose Angel* (2), *Juan* (2), *Maria Del* (2), *Roberto* (2), *Alfonso, Armida, Blanca.*

Guity (107) Hispanic: unexplained.

GIVEN NAMES Spanish 51%. *Justo* (3), *Encarnacion* (2), *Juan Ramon* (2), *Pablo* (2), *Ana, Ana Julia, Arcadio, Bernardo, Catalina, Dinora, Dominga, Esteban.*

Guizar (206) reduced form of the family name of Basque origin **Jaureguizar**, a topographic name from Basque *jauregui* 'palace', 'principal home' + *zar* 'old'.

GIVEN NAMES Spanish 52%. *Jose* (5), *Mario* (4), *Miguel* (3), *Ramon* (3), *Angel* (2), *Braulio* (2), *Francisco* (2), *Jesus* (2), *Jose Luis* (2), *Luis* (2), *Manuel* (2), *Margarita* (2); *Antonio, Caesar, Dario, Eliseo, Lorenzo, Marco, Marco Antonio.*

Gula (532) Polish: **1.** descriptive nickname for someone with a prominent bump or wart, Polish *gula*. **2.** nickname for a reveler, from a derivative of the dialect verb

gulać 'to make merry'. **3.** Hungarian: variant of *Gulya*, metonymic occupational name for a herdsman, from *gulya* 'cattle'.

Gulan (127) Polish: from a derivative of GULA.

GIVEN NAMES Polish 5%. *Jerzy, Tomasz.*

Gularte (104) Portuguese (Azores): unexplained.

GIVEN NAMES Spanish 9%. *Alvaro, Beatriz, Edmundo, Leticia, Manuel, Rey.*

Gulas (186) Polish: from a derivative of GULA or **Goły** (see GOLEC).

Gulati (268) Indian (Panjab): Hindu (Arora) and Sikh name of unknown meaning, based on the name of a clan in the Arora community.

GIVEN NAMES Indian 91%. *Anil* (8), *Manish* (4), *Prem* (4), *Ravi* (4), *Amar* (3), *Raj* (3), *Rajeev* (3), *Rajesh* (3), *Rakesh* (3), *Sunil* (3), *Suresh* (3), *Chander* (2).

Gulbrandsen (219) Scandinavian: patronymic from the Old Norse personal name *Guðbrandr*, a compound of *guð* 'god' + *brandr* 'sword'.

GIVEN NAMES Scandinavian 23%. *Erik* (4), *Bjorn* (2).

Gulbrandson (180) Scandinavian: variant of GULBRANDSEN.

GIVEN NAMES German 4%. *Hans, Kurt.*

Gulbransen (152) Danish: variant of GULBRANDSEN.

Gulbranson (403) Scandinavian: variant of GULBRANDSEN.

GIVEN NAMES Scandinavian 4%. *Erik, Iver, Nels.*

Gulczynski (102) Polish (**Gulczyński**): habitational name from a place called Gulcz in Piła voivodeship, named with *golec* 'naked' (see GOLEC).

GIVEN NAMES Polish 7%; German 4%. *Karol; Erwin.*

Guldan (141) Origin uncertain. Possibly a respelling of GULDEN.

Gulden (465) **1.** German (also **Gülden**): from the name of the coin (English *guilder*), from Middle High German *guldīn* 'golden'; it was probably applied as a nickname, or a status name with reference to a medieval tax obligation. **2.** German: nickname or topographic name for someone living near a cesspool, a euphemistic application of Middle Low German *gülden*, *gulden*, Middle High German *guldin* 'gold', 'golden'. **3.** Jewish (Ashkenazic): ornamental name from German *Gulden*, Yiddish *guldn*, or Polish *gulden* 'guilder' (see 1 above).

Guldin (189) **1.** Jewish (eastern Ashkenazic): variant of GULDEN. **2.** Swiss German: probably a derivative of GOLD.

FOREBEARS A Swiss Anabaptist family by the name of Guldin is recorded in the 16th century.

Guldner (116) German (also **Güldner**): occupational name for someone who worked in gold (for example a goldsmith, gilder, or jeweler), from Middle Low German,

Middle High German *gulden*, *gülden* 'to gild'.

GIVEN NAMES German 5%. *Guenter, Kurt.*

Guler (123) Muslim: unexplained.

GIVEN NAMES Muslim 15%. *Ali* (2), *Ahmet, Cemal, Evren, Fatih, Fevzi, Ismail, Yakup, Zakir.*

Gulick (1527) **1.** English: from the Middle English personal name *Gullake, Gudloc* (Old English *Gūðlāc*, composed of the elements *gūð* 'battle' + *lāc* 'sport', 'play', reinforced by the Old Norse cognate *Guðleikr*). **2.** See GULLICK.

Gulino (517) Italian: variant of GOLINO.

GIVEN NAMES Italian 29%. *Angelo* (5), *Salvatore* (5), *Sal* (4), *Mario* (3), *Rosario* (3), *Alberto* (2), *Carmelo* (2), *Dante* (2), *Ignazio* (2), *Aldo, Antonino, Antonio, Ateo, Benito, Biagio, Calogero.*

Gull (338) **1.** English: nickname from Middle English *gulle* 'gull' or *gul(le)* (Old Norse *gulr*) 'yellow', 'pale' (of hair or complexion). **2.** Swiss German: nickname for an irascible or unreliable person, from an Alemannic form of Latin *gallus* 'rooster'. See also GUELL.

Gulla (372) Italian: from a feminine form of GULLO.

GIVEN NAMES Italian 14%. *Mario* (2), *Salvatore* (2), *Antonio, Carmine, Egidio, Giuseppe, Giusto, Guido, Orlando, Rocco, Sal, Vito.*

Gullage (110) Variant of GULLEDGE.

Gullatt (215) Probably an altered spelling of GULLETT.

Gulledge (1439) **1.** Probably an Americanized spelling of German **Gullich** or **Guhlich** (see GULLICK). **2.** Possibly English, a variant of COLLEDGE or COOLIDGE.

Gullekson (103) Variant spelling of Swedish GULLICKSON.

Gullett (1386) English: unexplained.

Gullette (344) Origin uncertain. Possibly an altered spelling of GULLETT or perhaps a variant of a pet form of French GUILLAUME (see WILLIAM). Compare, for example, GUILLEMETTE.

Gulley (2977) **1.** English: descriptive nickname for a giant or a large man, from Middle English *golias* 'giant', from the Hebrew personal name *Golyat* Goliath. In the Bible Goliath was the champion of the Philistines, who stood 'six cubits and a span'; he was defeated in single combat by the shepherd boy David (I Samuel 17), who killed him with a stone from his sling. There is unlikely to be any connection with the English vocabulary word *gully* (from Old French *goulet* 'neck of a bottle'), which is not attested in this sense before the 17th century. **2.** Perhaps an altered spelling of French **Goulley**, a variant of GOULET.

Gulli (185) Italian: patronymic or plural form of GULLO.

GIVEN NAMES Italian 21%. *Francesco* (2), *Aurelio, Carmelo, Franco, Giuseppe,* *Mario, Nicolo, Pietro, Rocco, Salvatore, Vincenzo, Vito.*

Gullick (291) **1.** English: variant spelling of GULICK. **2.** Dutch (**van Gullick**): habitational name for someone from Jülich (Dutch *Gulik*) in North Rhine-Westphalia. **3.** Altered spelling of German **Gullich** or **Güllich**, nickname for a bald or clean-shaven man, from Slavic (Sorbian) *holy* 'naked', 'beardless'. Compare GULLEDGE.

Gullickson (1072) Swedish: patronymic from the personal name *Gullik*, from Old Norse *Guðleikr*, a compound of *guð* 'god' + *leikr* 'fight', 'struggle'.

Gulliford (223) English: variant of GULLIVER, altered by association with place names ending in *-ford*.

Gulliksen (112) Danish: see GULLICKSON.

GIVEN NAMES Scandinavian 15%. *Jorgen* (3), *Erik, Fredrik.*

Gullikson (160) Swedish: variant of GULLICKSON.

Gulling (129) English: nickname from a noun derivative of Middle English *gull*, Old Norse *gulr* 'pale'.

Gullion (566) Reduced form of Irish **Magullion** or **Mac Gullian**, Anglicized forms of Gaelic *Mac Gilleáin*, a diminutive of *gile* 'brightness', *geal* 'bright', or *giolla* 'lad'.

Gulliver (354) English: nickname for a greedy person, from Old French *goulafre* 'glutton'.

Gullo (779) Southern Italian: nickname from Southern Italian Greek *kouddho, skouddho*, from classical Greek dialect *kolos* 'hornless', a term used metaphorically to denote someone childless. The form **Gulló**, with the stress on the final syllable, may derive from Greek *kyllos* 'bandy-legged' or modern Greek *koullos* 'mutilated'.

GIVEN NAMES Italian 12%. *Salvatore* (6), *Sal* (5), *Angelo* (2), *Carmine* (2), *Santo* (2), *Valentino* (2), *Aldo, Biaggio, Carmelo, Egidio, Filippo, Filomena.*

Gullotti (100) Italian: from a diminutive of GULLO.

GIVEN NAMES Italian 13%. *Angelo* (2), *Dante.*

Gully (574) English: variant spelling of GULLEY.

Gulotta (401) Italian: from the female personal name, a pet form of *Gulla*.

GIVEN NAMES Italian 15%. *Gasper* (4), *Vito* (3), *Carlo* (2), *Angelo, Carmelo, Domenica, Geno, Ignazio, Marco, Nino, Pietro, Rino.*

Gulsby (111) Probably a reduced form of English: **Gooldsbury**, a variant of GOLDSBOROUGH.

Gulseth (128) Norwegian: habitational name from a farm in Telemark, named with the Old Norse personal name *Guli* + *set* 'farmstead', 'dwelling'.

Gulsvig (106) Norwegian: habitational name from a farm named with the Old Norse personal name *Guli* + *vig*, an older (Danish) spelling of *vik* 'bay'.

Gulyas (186) Hungarian (**Gulyás**): occupational name for a herdsman, from *gulya* 'cattle'.

GIVEN NAMES Hungarian 17%. *Laszlo* (5), *Imre* (3), *Akos, Attila, Gabor, Miklos.*

Gum (984) North German: **1.** from a by-name from Old Saxon *gumo* 'man'. **2.** variant spelling of GUMM.

Gumaer (161) Probably Dutch or Frisian: from a personal name from Germanic *Gundemar*, from *gund* 'battle' + *mār, mēri* 'famous'. This name is concentrated in NY.

Guman (104) Swiss German (**Gumann**): unexplained.

Gumbel (138) English and German (also **Gümbel**): from the Germanic personal name *Gumbald*, composed of the elements *gund* 'battle' + *bald* 'bold', 'brave'; it was taken to Britain from France by the Normans.

Gumbert (270) North German: variant of GOMBERT.

Gumble (111) Americanized spelling of German GUMBEL.

Gumbs (393) English: variant of **Gumb**, itself a variant of GUMM.

GIVEN NAMES French 5%. *Gabrielle, Germain, Julien, Vernice.*

Gumina (221) Southern Italian: from *gomena* 'cable', 'hawser', hence probably a metonymic occupational name for a cable maker.

GIVEN NAMES Italian 13%. *Sal* (3), *Pietro* (2), *Salvatore* (2), *Angelo, Antonio, Francesca, Santo.*

Gumm (997) **1.** English: from a nickname or byname from Middle English *gome*, Old English *guma* 'man'. **2.** German: probably a variant of **Gumme**, from a Frisian personal name or a short form of a Germanic personal name such as *Gundemar* (*gund* 'battle' + *mār, mēri* 'famous').

Gummer (137) **1.** English: variant of GOMER. **2.** German: variant of GUMM 2.

Gummere (158) English: variant of GOMER.

Gummo (152) Cornish: unexplained.

Gummow (102) Variant of Cornish GUMMO.

Gump (856) Swiss German and South German: **1.** occupational name or nickname from Middle High German *gumpen*, *gumpeln* 'to clown'. **2.** from a short form of a Germanic personal name formed with *gund* 'battle', 'war'. Compare GOMBERT.

Gumpert (226) German: variant of GOMBERT.

GIVEN NAMES German 7%; French 4%. *Gunther, Hans, Lothar, Ralf; Armand, Patrice.*

Gums (145) German: from the Slavic place name *Gümse* (earlier *Gumisa*), name of a place in Lusatia.

Gumz (230) German: variant of GUMS.

GIVEN NAMES German 4%. *Eldred* (2), *Klaus.*

Gunawan (111) Southeast Asian: unexplained.

GIVEN NAMES Southeast Asian 5%. *Indra, Rusi.*

Gunby (263) English: habitational name from Gunby in East Yorkshire, which is named from the Old Norse female personal name *Gunnhildr* + Old Norse *bý̆r* 'farmstead', 'settlement', or from Gunby St. Nicholas or Gunby St. Peter in Lincolnshire, named from the Old Norse male personal name *Gunni* + *bý̆r* 'farmstead', 'settlement'.

Gund (138) German (also **Günd**): from a short form of any of various Germanic personal names formed with *gund* 'battle' as the first element.

GIVEN NAME German 5%. *Heinz* (2).

Gundel (174) South German (also **Gündel**): from a short form of any of various Germanic personal names beginning with *gund* 'battle'.

GIVEN NAME German 4%. *Hans.*

Gunder (339) German: variant of **Günther** (see GUNTER).

Gunderman (532) German (**Gundermann**): **1.** from the Germanic personal name *Gundram*, composed of the elements *gund* 'battle' + *hramn, hrafn, hraban* 'raven'. **2.** elaborated form of GUNDER.

Gundersen (977) Danish and Norwegian: patronymic from an Old Norse personal name, *Gunnarr*, a compound of *gunn* 'battle' + *arr* 'warrior'.

GIVEN NAMES Scandinavian 17%; German 4%. *Erik* (7), *Alf* (2), *Knut* (2), *Anders, Astrid, Bjorn, Fredrik, Gudrun, Helmer, Hilmar, Hilmer, Johan; Hans* (5), *Kurt* (4), *Bernhard, Elke.*

Gunderson (5566) Americanized spelling of GUNDERSEN.

Gundlach (830) German: from a Germanic personal name, a compound of *gund* 'battle' + *lach* 'jousting', 'jumping in battle'.

GIVEN NAMES German 6%. *Heinz* (5), *Erna* (2), *Kurt* (2), *Eldor, Otto, Rudiger.*

Gundling (111) German: enlarged form of a short form (*Gundo*) of a Germanic personal name composed with *gund* 'battle', as in GUENTHER.

Gundrum (530) German: from the Germanic personal name *Gundram* composed of the elements *gund* 'battle' + *hramn, hrafn, hraban* 'raven'.

Gundry (223) English (of Norman origin): from *Gondri, Gundric*, an Old French personal name introduced to Britain by the Normans, composed of the Germanic elements *gund* 'battle' + *rīc* 'power(ful)'.

Gundy (470) English: from the Norman personal name *Gundi*, of Germanic origin, a pet form of any of various names beginning with *gund* 'battle'. See for example GUNDRY.

Gunia (167) Polish: nickname for someone from the Carpathian Mountains, from *gunia*, a term denoting the overcoat forming part of the national costume of dwellers in the Carpathians.

GIVEN NAMES Polish 6%; German 5%. *Bogdan, Czeslaw, Ryszard; Kurt* (2).

Gunion (114) Scottish: reduced form of **Mac Gille Gunnin** 'son of the devotee or servant of *Finnén* (St. Finnbarr)'.

Gunkel (469) German: variant of KUNKEL 1.

Gunlock (121) Possibly an Americanized spelling of German GUNDLACH.

Gunn (8178) **1.** Scottish: name of a clan associated with Caithness, derived from the Old Norse personal name *Gunnr* (or the feminine form *Gunne*), a short form of any of various compound names with the first element *gunn* 'battle'. **2.** Scottish: sometimes an Anglicized form of Gaelic **Mac Gille Dhuinn** 'son of the servant of the brown one' (see DUNN). (According to Woulfe a name of the same form also existed in Sligo, Ireland.) **3.** English: metonymic occupational name for someone who operated a siege engine or cannon, perhaps also a nickname for a forceful person, from Middle English *gunne, gonne* 'ballista', 'cannon', 'gun'. The term originated as a humorous application of the Scandinavian female personal name *Gunne* or *Gunnhildr*.

Gunnarson (231) Swedish (**Gunnarsson**): patronymic from the personal name *Gunnar*, from Old Norse *Gunnarr*, a compound of Old Norse *gunn* 'battle' + *arr* 'warrior'.

GIVEN NAMES Scandinavian 11%. *Agust, Lennart, Nils, Sven, Thor.*

Gunnell (778) **1.** English: from the Middle English female personal name *Gunnilla, Gunnild*, Old Norse *Gunnhildr*, composed of the elements *gunn* 'battle' + *hild* 'strife'. This was a popular name in those parts of England that were under Scandinavian influence in the Middle Ages. **2.** Irish: reduced Americanized form of *Mag Congail*, a Donegal name more often Americanized as MCGONIGLE. **3.** Respelling of German **Günnel**, from a short form of the Germanic personal names *Gundram* or GUNDLACH.

Gunnells (457) **1.** Irish: variant of GUNNELL 2, with English patronymic *-s*. **2.** Metronymic from English GUNNELL 1.

Gunnels (830) See GUNNELLS.

Gunner (258) **1.** English: from the Old Norse female personal name *Gunvǫr*, composed of the elements *gunn* 'battle' + *vǫr*, the feminine form of *varr* 'defender', or possibly from the Old Norse male personal name *Gunnarr*. **2.** English: occupational name for an operator of heavy artillery (see GUNN). **3.** Americanized spelling of German **Gönner**, a habitational name for someone from any of numerous places named Gönne.

Gunnerson (269) Americanized spelling of any of numerous Scandinavian family names that are patronymics from the personal name *Gunnar*, such as Swedish *Gunnarsson* (see GUNNARSON), or Danish and Norwegian GUNDERSEN.

Gunnett (134) Northern English: from the Middle English female personal name

Gunnot, a pet form of the Old Norse female name *Gunne* (see GUNN 1).

Gunnin (144) English (Herefordshire): possibly an altered form of Irish GUNNING.

Gunning (1297) Irish: reduced Anglicized form of Gaelic **Ó Conaing** 'descendant of *Conaing*', a personal name, a borrowing of Anglo-Saxon *cyning* 'king'.

Gunnink (117) Possibly a respelling of Irish GUNNING.

Gunnison (138) Northern English: metronymic from the female personal name *Gunne* (see GUNN).

Gunnoe (346) Americanized form of a French Huguenot name of unexplained origin.

GIVEN NAMES French 4%. *Andre, Mechelle, Pierre.*

Gunsallus (149) Variant of GUNSALUS.

Gunsalus (111) perhaps an American form of Spanish **González** (see GONZALEZ), or **Gonzalos** (alongside the variants **Gonsalos, Gonzalus, Gonsalus, Gunsallus**).

Gunsch (140) German (**Günsch**): from a short form of the personal name *Günther* (see GUNTER).

GIVEN NAME French 4%. *Henri.*

Gunselman (115) Americanized spelling of German **Günzelmann**, from a pet form of the personal name *Gunther* + Middle High German *man* 'man'.

Gunsolus (105) Variant of GUNSALLUS.

Gunson (103) English: reduced form of GUNNISON.

Gunst (164) **1.** German: from a much altered short form of the personal name CONSTANT or CONSTANTINE. **2.** Danish and Swedish: unexplained.

GIVEN NAMES German 7%. *Helmut* (2), *Otto, Ulrike.*

Gunter (8347) German (also **Gunther, Günt(h)er**) and English: from the Germanic personal name *Gunter* (Old French *Gontier*), composed of the elements *gund* 'battle' + *hari, heri* 'army'.

Gunther (3338) German and English: variant of GUNTER.

GIVEN NAMES German 4%. *Kurt* (7), *Gerhard* (4), *Fritz* (2), *Otto* (2), *Rudi* (2), *Alphons, Arno, Bernd, Dieter, Ehrhardt, Erwin, Gunther.*

Gunton (98) English: habitational name from either of two places in East Anglia, one in Norfolk and the other in Suffolk, both named with the Old Norse personal name *Gunni* (see GUNN 1) + Old English *tūn* 'enclosure', 'settlement'.

Guntrum (115) Variant of German **Guntram**, from the Germanic personal name *Gundram*, composed of *gund* 'battle' + *ram* 'raven'.

Gunville (143) Origin uncertain. In some cases it may be an altered spelling of French **Quinville**; however, the name is rare in the eastern states, which argues against French.

Gunzenhauser (123) German and Jewish (western Ashkenazic): habitational name for someone from either of two places named Gunzenhausen, one in Württemberg and the other in Bavaria.
GIVEN NAMES German 5%; Jewish 4%. *Kurt*; *Sol*.

Guo (1069) **1.** Chinese 郭: from an area in Shanxi province named Guo (written with a different character, pronounced the same). A younger brother of the famed virtuous duke Wen Wang (12th century BC) was enfeoffed this area and given the name Guo Shu. The Chinese character for the area was pronounced in the same way as a different character, the source of the present-day surname **Guo**, and people began to refer to Guo Shu with this homophonic character. **2.** Chinese 国: from a character that also means 'kingdom' or 'state'. Descendants of the founder of the state of Qi during the Warring States period (403–221BC) adopted this character as their surname. **3.** Chinese 过: from the name of a state of Guo that existed during the Xia dynasty (2205–1766 BC). Following defeat of this state, residents of the area adopted its name as their surname.
GIVEN NAMES Chinese 70%. *Ying* (11), *Wei* (10), *Hong* (9), *Jian* (8), *Ping* (7), *Yan* (7), *Jin* (6), *Li* (6), *Xin* (6), *Min* (5), *Yi* (6), *Hua* (5), *Wen* (5), *Xuan* (3), *Quan* (2), *Que* (2), *Anh, Bang, Chang, Dai, Du, Lan, Long, Tuan, Yiping*.

Guppy (133) English: habitational name from a place in Wootton Fitzpaine, Dorset, *Gupehegh* in Middle English. This is named with the Old English personal name *Guppa* (a short form of *Gūðbeorht* 'battle bright') + *(ge)hæg* 'enclosure'. The tropical fish denoted by this word was named in the 19th century in honor of R.J.L. Guppy, a clergyman in Trinidad who first presented specimens to the British Museum.
FOREBEARS The earliest known bearer of the name is Nicholas de Gupehegh (Somerset, 1253/4). Most if not all present-day bearers of the name are thought to descend from a certain William Guppy of Chardstock, Devon, who in 1497 was fined forty shillings for his alleged part in the rebellion of Perkin Warbeck.
GIVEN NAME French 4%. *Monique* (2).

Gupta (2743) Indian (northern states): Hindu (Bania) and Jain name, from Sanskrit *gupta* 'secret', 'protected'. This is a well-known name of ancient India; the two greatest empires of ancient northern India were both founded by persons named Chandragupta (see also CHANDRA). The founder of the Maurya empire in the 4th century BC was Chandragupta Maurya. In the 4th century AD, the Gupta empire was founded by another Chandragupta, and a long line of Gupta kings ruled India for about 200 years.
GIVEN NAMES Indian 93%. *Sanjay* (45), *Rakesh* (40), *Ajay* (34), *Vijay* (33), *Ashok*

(30), *Anil* (29), *Sunil* (28), *Suresh* (26), *Ramesh* (25), *Raj* (24), *Sandeep* (20), *Satish* (20).

Guptill (572) English: unexplained. It is said to be a variant of **Gubtail**, which is likewise unexplained. This name is found predominantly in ME.

Gupton (913) English: apparently a habitational name from a lost or unidentified place. Only two bearers of the surname, both female, were recorded in the 1881 British Census, and it now appears to be extinct in the British Isles. In the U.S. it is concentrated in NC, where it is common, and also in TN.

Gura (388) **1.** Polish and Jewish (from Poland): variant of GORA. **2.** Ukrainian and Belorussian: from a pet form of *Gury*, a variant of *Hury* (see GEORGE). **3.** Albanian: from *gur(i)* 'stone', either a topographic name or a nickname for a tough character, or from a place called Gura, named with this word.

Gural (225) Polish: variant of GORAL.

Guralnick (128) Jewish (from Ukraine): occupational name from Ukrainian *guralnyk*, Yiddish *guralnik* 'distiller'.
GIVEN NAMES Jewish 6%. *Hyman, Sol*.

Gurecki (112) Polish: variant of GORECKI.

Gurevich (427) Jewish (from Belarus and Lithuania): variant of HOROWITZ.
GIVEN NAMES Russian 34%; Jewish 27%. *Boris* (19), *Vladimir* (13), *Leonid* (9), *Mikhail* (9), *Lev* (8), *Dmitry* (5), *Igor* (5), *Anatoly* (4), *Arkadiy* (4), *Yefim* (4), *Arkady* (3), *Aleksandr* (2); *Isaak* (7), *Naum* (5), *Yakov* (5), *Ilya* (4), *Isak* (3), *Hyman* (2), *Inna* (2), *Irina* (2), *Semen* (2), *Sima* (2), *Zalman* (2), *Zinaida* (2).

Gurewitz (110) Jewish (from Belarus and Lithuania): variant of HOROWITZ.

Gurganious (148) Variant of Welsh GURGANUS.

Gurganus (768) Of Welsh origin: from an Anglicized form of the personal name *Gwrgenau*, composed of the elements *gwr* 'man', 'warrior' + *cenau* 'whelp', 'young dog', a term used in Welsh heroic poetry for a soldier ferocious in attack.
FOREBEARS The name is recorded as early as 1617 in Jamestown VA, when Edward Gurgany from England patented a land grant at Curles Neck VA.

Gurian (163) **1.** German: unexplained. **2.** possibly an altered form of Armenian **Gurjian**, patronymic from an ethnic name for someone from Georgia, to the north of Armenia in the Caucasus mountains.
GIVEN NAME German 4%. *Erwin*.

Gurin (153) **1.** Jewish (from Belarus): habitational name for someone from the village of Gury in Belarus. **2.** Russian: patronymic from the personal name *Gury* (variant of *Yuri*) or *Georgi*, derivatives of Greek *Geōrgios* (see GEORGE).
GIVEN NAMES Jewish 7%; Russian 5%. *Sol*; *Vladimir* (2), *Boris, Sergey, Yelena*.

Gurka (248) **1.** Ukrainian: from a pet form of *Gury*, a variant of *Hury* (see GEORGE). **2.** Polish: variant of GORKA.
GIVEN NAMES Polish 4%. *Jozef* (3), *Urszula*.

Gurkin (195) Russian: patronymic from a pet form of *Gury*, a variant of *Yuri* or *Georgi* (see GEORGE).

Gurley (2973) **1.** English (Warwickshire): apparently a variant of GOURLEY or GORLEY. **2.** Possibly an Americanized spelling of French **Gourlé**, from Old French *gourle* 'money belt'. Its application as a surname is not clear; it may have been a metonymic occupational name for a maker of such receptacles, or perhaps a nickname for someone who was tight with his money. **3.** Alternatively, it may be an Americanized form of German GERLING or GERLICH.

Gurman (151) **1.** Dutch: from the personal name *Goeder* (from a Germanic personal name composed of the elements *gōd* 'good') + *man* 'man'. **2.** Jewish (eastern Ashkenazic): etymology unexplained.
GIVEN NAMES Jewish 16%. *Efrat, Haim, Isadore, Kalmen, Menachem, Miriam, Sol*.

Gurnee (194) Variant spelling of English GURNEY.

Gurnett (108) English: from Middle English *gurnard, gurnade* 'gurnard', 'gurnet', a marine fish with a large spiny head, mailed cheeks, and three pectoral rays (genus *Trigla*), possibly named from French *grognard* 'grumbler', on account of the grunting noise it makes.

Gurney (1854) English (of Norman origin): habitational name from any of various places in France named Gournay, notably Gournay-en-Brai in Seine-Maritime.

Gurnsey (143) English: apparently an altered spelling of GUERNSEY.

Gurr (417) German: derisive nickname for a useless person or a wicked woman, from Middle High German *gurre* 'bad mare'

Gurrieri (140) Italian: variant of GUERRIERI.
GIVEN NAMES Italian 24%. *Angelo* (6), *Salvatore* (3), *Gianni, Giovanni, Nicola, Nunzio, Sebastiano*.

Gurrola (532) Basque: reduced form of Basque **Egurrola**, a topographic name from Basque *egur* 'firewood', 'kindling' + the locative suffix *-ola*.
GIVEN NAMES Spanish 49%. *Jesus* (10), *Jose* (10), *Manuel* (6), *Raul* (6), *Rafael* (5), *Alfredo* (4), *Felipe* (4), *Guadalupe* (4), *Juan* (4), *Mario* (4), *Ricardo* (4), *Carlos* (3).

Gurry (165) Irish: variant of GORRY.

Gurske (107) Eastern German and Jewish (eastern Ashkenazic): variant of Slavic GORSKI.

Gurski (281) Polish (**Górski**) and Jewish (eastern Ashkenazic): variant of GORSKI.

Gursky (376) Polish (**Górski**) and Jewish (eastern Ashkenazic): variant of GORSKI.

Gurtler (154) **1.** English: variant of GIRDLER. **2.** German (**Gürtler**): occupational name for a maker of straps and belts, from Middle High German *gurtel* 'belt' (specifically a leather belt with brass fittings, from which a purse would be hung).

Gurtner (188) **1.** Swiss German (**Gurtner**) and South German (**Gürtner**): variant of **Gürtler** (see GURTLER). **2.** German: habitational name for someone from Gurten in Bavaria.

Gurule (929) Spanish: unexplained.
GIVEN NAMES Spanish 16%. *Manuel* (10), *Ramon* (6), *Jose* (5), *Epifanio* (3), *Juan* (3), *Marcos* (3), *Orlando* (3), *Ruben* (3), *Adolfo, Alfonso, Alfredo, Augustina.*

Gurwell (105) German (of Slavic origin): unexplained.

Gurwitz (149) Jewish (from Ukraine): variant of HOROWITZ.
GIVEN NAMES Jewish 11%. *Hersch, Moshe, Yitzchak, Zeev.*

Gusa (107) Origin unidentified.

Guse (642) **1.** Eastern German: patronymic from a reduced form of the personal name AUGUST. **2.** German (also **Güse**): habitational name from Güsen, near Genthin.
GIVEN NAMES German 5%. *Frieda* (2), *Erwin, Ewald, Gebhard, Hans, Inge, Kurt, Rainer, Reinhardt, Reinhold.*

Guseman (180) See GUSMAN.

Gush (119) English (Devon): Reaney derived this from an Old Swedish personal name *Gus(s)e*, but the present-day concentration of the surname in Devon suggests that another source may be involved.

Gushee (100) Probably a variant of GUSHUE.

Gushue (145) Probably an altered form of English GOUCHER or French GAUTHIER.
FOREBEARS This name is found from the early 1600s in Newfoundland.

Guske (138) Altered spelling of German GUSTKE.
GIVEN NAMES German 4%. *Ewald, Horst.*

Gusky (138) Polish (**Guski**): habitational name from a place called Gusin in Konin or Siedlce voivodeships.

Gusler (274) German: probably a habitational name, a variant of **Gosler**, from Goslar in the Harz Mountains, or Gosel.

Gusman (422) **1.** Spanish (**Gusmán**): variant of Spanish **Guzmán** (see GUZMAN). **2.** Jewish (eastern Ashkenazic): occupational name for a metalworker, from Yiddish *gus* 'casting' + *man* 'man'. **3.** Perhaps an altered spelling of German **Güssmann** (see GUSSMAN).
GIVEN NAMES Spanish 23%. *Jose* (4), *Carlos* (3), *Juan* (3), *Blanca* (2), *Jorge* (2), *Manuel* (2), *Salvador* (2), *Santiago* (2), *Adolfo, Alejandro, Alfonso, Alvino.*

Guss (697) German: **1.** nickname for an impetuous or effusive person, from Middle High German *gus* 'outpouring', 'effusion'. **2.** variant spelling of **Güss** (see GUESS).

Gussler (114) German (**Güssler**): variant of **Giessler** (see GIESSLER), a topographic name.

Gussman (157) **1.** German (**Güssmann**): from the personal name *Goswin*, composed of the elements *gōss* 'Gaut' (name of a tribe) + *wine* 'friend'. **2.** Altered spelling of Spanish **Guzmán** (see GUZMAN).

Gust (1366) **1.** German: from a short form of the personal name *Jodocus*, which is either a Latinized form of a Breton name, *Iodoc*, borne by a 7th-century Breton saint (compare JOST and JOYCE) or from a reduced form of the personal name AUGUSTUS. **2.** Eastern German: probably from Slavic *gost* 'stranger', 'guest', hence a nickname like GAST.
GIVEN NAMES German 4%. *Otto* (4), *Dieter, Eldor, Ewald, Florian, Frieda, Fritz, Helmut, Hermann, Johann.*

Gustafson (12090) Americanized spelling of Swedish **Gustafsson**, **Gustavsson**, or Danish and Norwegian **Gustavsen**, **Gustafsen**, patronymics from the Old Swedish personal name *Götstaf*, of uncertain origin.
GIVEN NAMES Scandinavian 5%. *Erik* (23), *Nels* (8), *Lennart* (4), *Swen* (4), *Lars* (3), *Nils* (3), *Sven* (3), *Anders* (2), *Britt* (2), *Ejnar* (2), *Helmer* (2), *Hjalmer* (2).

Gustafsson (130) Swedish: variant of GUSTAFSON.
GIVEN NAMES Scandinavian 49%; German 6%. *Lars* (3), *Per* (3), *Erik* (2), *Mats* (2), *Anders, Bjorn, Lennart, Niklas, Nils, Ragner, Sig; Hans, Ulrika.*

Gustason (119) Scandinavian: variant of GUSTAFSON.

Gustave (117) French: from the personal name *Gustave*, of Scandinavian origin (see GUSTAFSON).
GIVEN NAMES French 15%. *Dieudonne, Fernand, Luckner, Pierre.*

Gustaveson (152) Variant of Scandinavian GUSTAFSON.

Gustavsen (118) Danish: see GUSTAFSON.

Gustavson (773) Scandinavian: variant of GUSTAFSON.
GIVEN NAMES Scandinavian 13%. *Nils* (4), *Sten* (3), *Bernt* (2), *Erik* (2), *Sven* (2), *Aksel, Evald, Gunner, Lars, Owe, Ragner.*

Guster (111) German: variant of KUSTER.

Gustin (1943) **1.** German and French: reduced form of AUGUSTIN. **2.** Slovenian (**Guštin**): reduced form of the personal name *Avguštin* (see AUGUSTIN).

Gustine (119) French: variant of GUSTIN or metronymic from a reduced form of the female personal name *Augustine*.

Gustke (141) Eastern German: variant of GUST 2, or perhaps a pet form of GUST 1.

Gustus (147) German: from a reduced form of the personal name *Augustus* or a variant of the medieval personal name *Justus* (from Latin *iustus* 'just').
GIVEN NAME French 4%. *Andre.*

Gut (164) German, Jewish (Ashkenazic), and Polish: variant of German GUTH.
GIVEN NAMES Polish 10%; German 6%; Jewish 5%. *Franciszek, Irena, Jozef, Krystian, Krystyna, Ludwik, Wojciech; Erwin, Hans, Hertha, Urs; Moshe, Shai.*

Gute (139) Jewish (Ashkenazic): from the Yiddish female personal name *Gute* 'good'.

Gutekunst (291) German: nickname for a skilled artist or workman, from Middle High German *guot* 'good' + *kunst* 'skill', 'art'.
GIVEN NAMES German 4%. *Eugen, Ilse.*

Guterman (159) Jewish (Ashkenazic): nickname or ornamental name from Yiddish *guterman*, literally 'good man'. Compare GUTMAN.
GIVEN NAMES Jewish 13%; Russian 7%. *Polina* (2), *Hyman; Iosif* (2), *Fanya, Mikhail, Mikhall, Yevgeny.*

Gutermuth (164) German: probably a nickname from Middle High German *guot* 'good' + *muot* 'spirit'. In the Middle Ages, journeymen of different trades were frequently referred to by a specific, more or less appropriate and often humorous nickname. Compare FREIMUTH.

Gutgsell (103) South German: nickname meaning 'good companion', from Middle High German *guot* 'good' + *geselle* 'friend', 'companion', 'journeyman'.
GIVEN NAMES German 7%. *Alois, Bernd, Otto.*

Guth (1446) German and Jewish (Ashkenazic): from modern German and Yiddish *gut*, Middle High German *guot* 'good' or 'capable'. This may be a nickname, but in the Middle Ages the term also denoted a freeman or a vassal of noble birth, and the surname may be a status name from this sense. As a Jewish surname it is often ornamental. Compare GUTMAN.
GIVEN NAMES German 4%. *Hans* (3), *Kurt* (3), *Fritz* (2), *Gerhard* (2), *Erwin, Heinz, Otto, Reinhold, Siegfried, Wilhelm.*

Gutheil (124) German: from the expression *gutes Heil* 'good blessing or success', probably a nickname for someone who was well received by the community or who habitually used the expression.
GIVEN NAMES German 5%. *Helmut, Horst.*

Gutherie (126) Variant of Scottish GUTHRIE.

Guthery (290) Variant of Scottish GUTHRIE.

Guthier (108) German: Huguenot name.

Guthman (129) German (**Guthmann**): status name from Middle High German *guot man*, literally 'capable man'. In the Middle Ages this term denoted a highly placed vassal who was a freeman or a man of noble birth. Compare GUTH.
GIVEN NAME French 4%. *Raoul.*

Guthmiller (372) Americanized form of German **Guthmüller**, a nickname from Middle High German *guot* 'good' (see GUTH) + *müler* 'miller'.
GIVEN NAMES German 4%. *Reinhold* (2), *Milbert, Otto.*

Guthridge (289) **1.** Possibly an altered spelling of German **Güttrich** (see GUTTERY). **2.** English: perhaps a variant of GUTTRIDGE.

Guthrie (12077) **1.** Scottish: habitational name from a place near Forfar, named in Gaelic with *gaothair* 'windy place' (a derivative of *gaoth* 'wind') + the locative suffix *-ach*. **2.** Possibly an Anglicized form of Scottish Gaelic **Mag Uchtre** 'son of *Uchtre*', a personal name of uncertain origin, perhaps akin to *uchtlach* 'child'. **3.** Irish: adopted as an English equivalent of Gaelic **Ó Fhlaithimh** 'descendant of *Flaitheamh*', a byname meaning 'prince'. This is the result of an erroneous association of the Gaelic name in the form **Ó Fhlaithimh** (*Fh* being silent), with the Gaelic word *laithigh* 'mud', and of mud with gutters, and an equally erroneous association of the Scottish surname *Guthrie* with the word 'gutter'. Compare LAFFEY. FOREBEARS Samuel Guthrie (1782–1848), who invented a replacement for the flintlock musket, also discovered chloroform in 1831. His ancestor John Guthrie came to North America from Edinburgh, Scotland, and died in Litchfield Co., CT, in 1730.

Gutierez (130) Spanish (**Gutiérez**): variant spelling of **Gutiérrez** (see GUTIERREZ).
GIVEN NAMES Spanish 48%. *Jesus* (3), *Jose* (3), *Ignacio* (2), *Manuel* (2), *Adalberto*, *Ana Maria*, *Angel*, *Carlota*, *Emilio*, *Exiquio*, *Felipe*, *Fermin*.

Gutierres (143) Spanish: variant spelling of **Gutiérrez** (see GUTIERREZ).
GIVEN NAMES Spanish 47%. *Jose* (4), *Ramon* (4), *Jesus* (2), *Juan* (2), *Manuel* (2), *Alberto*, *Alfonzo*, *Alvaro*, *Ana*, *Andres*, *Antelmo*, *Catalina*.

Gutierrez (24787) Spanish (**Gutiérrez**): patronymic from the medieval personal name *Gutierre*, from a Visigothic personal name of uncertain form and meaning, perhaps a compound of the elements *gunþi* 'battle' + *hairus* 'sword'.
GIVEN NAMES Spanish 48%. *Jose* (732), *Juan* (354), *Luis* (241), *Jesus* (233), *Manuel* (228), *Carlos* (215), *Francisco* (167), *Jorge* (156), *Pedro* (144), *Raul* (134), *Miguel* (132), *Roberto* (126).

Guttierrez (98) Spanish: variant spelling of **Gutiérrez** (see GUTIERREZ).
GIVEN NAMES Spanish 38%. *Jesus* (2), *Jose* (2), *Pablo* (2), *Raul* (2), *Reina* (2), *Adolfo*, *Beatriz*, *Carlos*, *Diego*, *Evangelina*, *Felicita*, *Humberto*; *Antonio*, *Heriberto*, *Luciano*.

Gutkin (151) **1.** Jewish (eastern Ashkenazic): metronymic from a pet form of the female personal name GUTE. **2.** German: from *Gutkind*, a pet name meaning 'good child'.
GIVEN NAMES Russian 19%; Jewish 9%. *Leonid* (2), *Vladimir* (2), *Anatoliy*, *Arkadiy*, *Boris*, *Dmitriy*, *Esya*, *Galina*, *Gennady*, *Grigori*, *Lev*, *Mikhail*; *Ari*, *Izak*.

Gutknecht (469) Swiss German and German: status name for a page of noble birth (Middle High German *guot kneht*). The name has been Americanized as

Goodknecht, **Goodknight**, **Goodnight**, and **Goodnite**.
GIVEN NAMES German 5%. *Kurt* (2), *Erwin*, *Ewald*, *Frieda*, *Hannelore*, *Otto*.

Gutkowski (237) Polish: habitational name for someone from any of many places named Gutków, Gutkowo, or Gutkowice.
GIVEN NAMES Polish 5%; German 4%. *Jerzy*, *Stanislaw*; *Florian* (2), *Monika* (2).

Gutman (1221) **1.** Jewish (Ashkenazic): ornamental name or nickname from German, Yiddish *gut* 'good' + *man(n)* 'man'; it was also used as a male personal name, from which the surname may be derived in some cases. **2.** Americanized spelling of German **Gut(h)mann** (see GUTHMANN).
GIVEN NAMES Jewish 12%; Russian 7%. *Yechiel* (4), *Irina* (3), *Aron* (2), *Avrohom* (2), *Faigy* (2), *Faina* (2), *Ilya* (2), *Yakov* (2), *Arie*, *Aryeh*, *Avi*, *Avrum*; *Boris* (10), *Lev* (5), *Igor* (4), *Leonid* (4), *Dmitry* (3), *Aleksandr* (2), *Vlad* (2), *Zhanna* (2), *Anatoliy*, *Anisim*, *Arkady*, *Dusya*.

Gutmann (464) **1.** Swiss German: literally 'good man', a term for the master of a household. **2.** Jewish (Ashkenazic): variant of GUTMAN.
GIVEN NAMES German 12%. *Kurt* (4), *Hans* (3), *Alois* (2), *Willi* (2), *Aloysius*, *Fritz*, *Guenter*, *Heinz*, *Helmut*, *Hermann*, *Katharina*, *Manfred*.

Gutowski (960) Polish: habitational name for someone from any of many places in central and northern Poland called Gutowo or Gutów.
GIVEN NAMES Polish 6%. *Bogdan* (2), *Mieczyslaw* (2), *Witold* (2), *Andrzej*, *Boleslaw*, *Iwona*, *Jerzy*, *Karol*, *Lucja*, *Miroslawa*, *Piotr*, *Tomasz*.

Gutridge (232) English: **1.** variant of GOODRICH. **2.** from the Middle English personal name *Cuterich*, Old English *Cūðrīc*, composed of the elements *cūð* 'famous', 'well known' + *rīc* 'power'.

Gutsch (128) **1.** German: nickname from Slavic *god* 'beauty'. **2.** Probably a respelling of GOTSCH.

Gutschow (120) German (**Gütschow**): habitational name from Gützkow near Anklam.

Gutshall (664) Altered spelling of the German surname *Gottschall*, a variant of GOTTSCHALK.

Gutstein (102) **1.** Jewish (Ashkenazic): ornamental compound of *gut* 'good' +*Stein* 'stone'. Most occurrences are in NY. **2.** East German: probably from a topographic or habitational name.

Gutt (220) **1.** German: from an Old Prussian name. **2.** Jewish (Ashkenazic): variant of GUTH.
GIVEN NAMES German 10%. *Bernd* (2), *Dieter*, *Folker*, *Gerda*, *Gottfried*, *Gunther*, *Lorenz*.

Guttenberg (177) **1.** German and Jewish (Ashkenazic): habitational name from any of various places, for example in Bavaria,

called Guttenberg, from the weak dative case (originally used after a preposition and article) of Old High German *guot* 'good' + *berg* 'mountain', 'hill'. The shortening of the vowel in the first syllable is a feature found in various dialects of German. **2.** Jewish (Ashkenazic): ornamental name composed of German *gut* 'good' + *Berg* 'mountain', 'hill'.
GIVEN NAMES Jewish 5%; German 4%. *Aryeh* (2), *Sol*; *Kurt*.

Gutter (190) Jewish (Ashkenazic): nickname from German *Guter* 'good (man)'.
GIVEN NAMES Jewish 11%. *Benzion* (2), *Zvi* (2), *Chaim*, *Hymie*, *Zalmen*.

Gutterman (369) Jewish (Ashkenazic): variant of GUTMAN.
GIVEN NAMES Jewish 8%. *Arie* (2), *Yaakov* (2), *Dafna*, *Dvora*, *Hyman*, *Miriam*, *Tzvi*.

Guttery (128) **1.** Irish: perhaps a variant of Scottish GUTHRIE. **2.** Possibly an altered spelling of the German occupational name **Gutterer**, denoting a maker of balloon-shaped glass bottles, or of German **Güttrich**, from a Germanic personal name formed with *god*, *got* 'god' or *gōd* 'good' + *rih* 'powerful'.
GIVEN NAME Scottish 4%. *McQueen*.

Guttierrez (98) Spanish: variant spelling of GUTIERREZ.
GIVEN NAMES Spanish 38%. *Jesus* (2), *Jose* (2), *Pablo* (2), *Raul* (2), *Reina* (2), *Adolfo*, *Beatriz*, *Carlos*, *Diego*, *Evangelina*, *Felicita*, *Humberto*; *Antonio*, *Heriberto*, *Luciano*.

Guttilla (101) Southern Italian: of uncertain derivation; possibly from a pet form of the Germanic personal name *Gotto*, or alternatively a variant of **Cutilla**, a topographic name, or possibly a nickname, from a diminutive of **Cuti**, from Sicilian *cuti* 'pebble'.
GIVEN NAMES Italian 25%. *Salvatore* (3), *Sal* (2), *Vito* (2), *Antonio*, *Francesca*, *Gasper*.

Gutting (225) **1.** German (also **Gütting**): of uncertain origin. Probably from a Germanic personal name formed with *gōd* 'good' or *god*, *got* 'god'. **2.** Perhaps an altered spelling of English CUTTING.

Guttman (784) **1.** Jewish: variant spelling of GUTMAN(N). **2.** Americanized spelling of German GUT(T)MANN.
GIVEN NAMES Jewish 10%; Hungarian 4%. *Mayer* (4), *Moshe* (3), *Emanuel* (2), *Gershon* (2), *Mendel* (2), *Sol* (2), *Ari*, *Elimelech*, *Hyman*, *Isidor*, *Miriam*, *Nachman*; *Jeno* (5), *Zoltan* (4), *Lajos* (2), *Sandor* (2), *Andras*.

Guttmann (205) German and Jewish (Ashkenazic): variant spelling of GUTMANN.
GIVEN NAMES German 8%; Jewish 4%. *Inge* (2), *Otto* (2), *Bernhard*, *Gerhard*; *Bernat*.

Guttormson (135) Scandinavian: patronymic from the personal name *Guttorm*.

Guttridge (112) English: **1.** from the Middle English personal name *Goderiche* (from Old English *Gōdrīc*, composed of the elements *gōd* 'good' + *rīc* 'power'). **2.** from the Middle English personal name *Cuterich* (from Old English *Cūðrīc*, composed of the elements *cūð* 'famous' + *rīc* 'power').

Gutwein (228) German (**Guttwein**): from the Germanic personal name *Gutwin*, a compound of Old High German *guot* 'good' + *win* 'friend'. The notion that the name means 'good wine' is a product of folk etymology.
GIVEN NAMES German 7%; Jewish 7%. *Fritz, Hans, Kurt, Manfred; Isadore* (2), *Miriam* (2), *Baruch, Hersch, Hersh, Jakob, Yehuda.*

Gutz (150) Eastern German: variant of **Götz** (see GOETZ).

Gutzler (108) German: perhaps a variant of **Gutzer**, a Swabian nickname for a curious person, from (dialect) *gutzen* 'to look', 'peek'.

Gutzman (237) German (**Gutzmann**): variant of **Götzmann** (see GOETZMAN).
GIVEN NAMES German 4%. *Kurt* (2), *Reinhold.*

Gutzmer (214) Eastern German: from a Slavic personal name *Gotzmer*, from *Gostimir*, a compound of *gosti* 'guest' + *mir* 'peace'.
GIVEN NAMES German 4%. *Armin, Florian, Otto.*

Gutzwiller (228) Swiss German: probably a habitational name from a deserted settlement in Sundgau region (Alsace) called Guzwiler.

Guy (9095) **1.** English (of Norman origin) and French: from a French form of the Germanic personal name *Wido*, which is of uncertain origin. This name was popular among the Normans in the forms *Wi, Why* as well as in the rest of France in the form *Guy*. **2.** English: occupational name for a guide, Old French *gui* (a derivative of *gui(d)er* 'to guide', of Germanic origin).

Guye (109) English: variant spelling of GUY.

Guyer (2008) **1.** English: occupational name from Old French *guyour* 'guide' (see GUY 2). **2.** Americanized spelling of German GEYER. **3.** Swiss German: from a contraction of the expression *gut Jahr* ('good year') which as a greeting in rural Switzerland meant 'I wish you a good harvest this year'.

Guyett (196) Variant of French **Guyet** (see GUYETTE).

Guyette (970) Respelling of French **Guyet**, from a pet form of the personal name GUY. Compare GUYOT.

Guymon (441) Probably a North American spelling of French GUIMOND, GUIMONT.

Guynes (388) Origin uncertain; perhaps a variant of Irish **Guinness**, a reduced form of McGINNIS. This name is found predominantly in TX.

Guynn (675) Origin uncertain; perhaps a variant of French GUYON or of Welsh GWYNN.

Guyon (244) English and French: variant of GUY, from the subject case of the name in Old French.
GIVEN NAMES French 6%. *Gaston, Jean-Francois, Virginie.*

Guyot (298) French: from a pet form of the personal name GUY.
GIVEN NAMES French 6%. *Celine, Jean-Luc, Patrice, Stephane.*

Guyse (113) English and French: variant spelling of GUISE.

Guyton (2169) **1.** English (Norfolk): possibly a variant of the habitational name GAYTON. **2.** French: from a derivative of the personal name GUY.

Guza (172) Polish: nickname for someone with a prominent carbuncle, from *guz* 'knob', 'lump'.

Guzek (219) Polish: nickname from a diminutive of *guz* 'knob', 'lump'.
GIVEN NAMES Polish 5%. *Grzegorz, Karol, Stanislaw, Teofil.*

Guzik (538) Polish: nickname for a small person, from *guzik* 'button'.
GIVEN NAMES Polish 9%. *Lucyna* (2), *Piotr* (2), *Tadeusz* (2), *Andrzej, Beata, Boguslaw, Bronislaw, Casimir, Ferdynand, Grazyna, Grzegorz, Stanislaw.*

Guzinski (84) Polish (**Guziński**): habitational name, possibly for someone from a place called Guzy, in Białystok or Suwałki voivodeships.
GIVEN NAME Polish 4%. *Wojciech.*

Guzman (11712) **1.** Spanish (**Guzmán**): of uncertain and disputed etymology, probably from a Germanic personal name. **2.** Jewish (eastern Ashkenazic): variant of GUSMAN.
GIVEN NAMES Spanish 52%. *Jose* (372), *Juan* (172), *Luis* (123), *Carlos* (121), *Manuel* (97), *Jesus* (88), *Francisco* (87), *Miguel* (84), *Pedro* (73), *Rafael* (62), *Ramon* (60), *Raul* (60).

Guzowski (141) Polish: habitational name from a place called Guzów, of which there is one in Radom voivodeship and another in Skierniewice.
GIVEN NAMES Polish 5%. *Danuta, Ryszard.*

Guzy (201) Polish (Silesia): **1.** variant of GUZA. **2.** nickname for a thin person, from dialect *guzy* 'scanty', 'narrow'.

Guzzardo (200) Northern Italian: variant of GUCCIARDO, with the transition of *-cc-* to *-zz-* typical of northeastern dialects.
GIVEN NAMES Italian 7%. *Angelo, Salvatore.*

Guzzetta (194) Italian: feminine variant of **Guzzetto**, a pet form of GUZZO. The feminine form is no doubt due to the influence of the Italian word *famiglia* 'family'.
GIVEN NAMES Italian 7%. *Angelo, Sal.*

Guzzi (330) Italian: patronymic or plural form of GUZZO.
GIVEN NAMES Italian 10%. *Angelo* (4), *Carmela, Dante, Sal, Santo.*

Guzzo (503) Italian: **1.** from a late medieval personal name *Guzzo*, a reduced pet form of various personal names, for exam-

ple *Arriguzzo*, from *Arrigo* (see HENRY), and *Uguzzo*, from *Ugo* (see HUGH). **2.** in the south, from the Sicilian and Calabrian dialect word *guzzu* '(aggressive) small dog', 'puppy', applied as a nickname.
GIVEN NAMES Italian 14%. *Rocco* (3), *Angelo* (2), *Salvatore* (2), *Agostino, Carmelina, Domenic, Gildo, Giorgio, Nunzio, Santo, Saverio.*

Gwaltney (1004) Anglicized form of the Welsh family name **Gwalchmai**, which is from the Welsh personal name *Gwalchmai* 'hawk of the plain'.

Gwartney (202) Variant of Welsh GWALTNEY.

Gwiazdowski (86) Polish: habitational name from a place called Gwiazdowo, in the voivodeship of Poznań.
GIVEN NAME Polish 6%. *Casimir.*

Gwilliam (149) Welsh: from the personal name *Gwilym*, Welsh form of WILLIAM. The initial *G-* was acquired by analogy with names such as GWYN, of which the lenited form is WYN.

Gwin (1586) Variant spelling of Welsh GWYNN.

Gwinn (1532) Variant spelling of Welsh GWYNN.

Gwinner (152) South German: nickname from Middle High German *gewinnen* 'to achieve fortune and wealth through hard work'.

Gwizdala (22) Polish (**Gwizdała**): nickname for someone noted for his cheerful whistling, from a derivative of *gwizdać* 'to whistle'.
GIVEN NAMES Polish 20%. *Kazimierz, Waclaw.*

Gwozdz (190) Polish (**Gwóźdź**): from *gwóźdź* 'nail', applied either as a metonymic occupational name for a nailmaker or as a nickname for a tall, thin person.
GIVEN NAMES Polish 12%. *Feliks* (2), *Jerzy* (2), *Henryk, Jarek, Ludwika, Wojciech, Zbigniew.*

Gwyn (747) Welsh: variant spelling of GWYNN.

Gwynn (1065) Welsh: from *gwyn* 'light', 'white', 'fair'. This word was widely used as a personal name in the Middle Ages. It may also be a nickname for a person with fair hair or a noticeably pale complexion. See also WINN.

Gwynne (218) Welsh: variant spelling of GWYNN.

Gyger (95) Variant spelling in Slavic regions and in Switzerland of German GEIGER.
GIVEN NAME German 4%. *Willi.*

Gyles (128) English: variant spelling of GILES.

Gyure (75) Hungarian (**Gyüre**): from a pet form of the personal name *György*, Hungarian form of GEORGE.

H

Ha (2232) **1.** Vietnamese (**Hà**): unexplained. **2.** Korean: there are two Ha clans, each with a unique Chinese character. The founding ancestor of the larger Ha clan was named Ha Kong-jin and settled in the Chinju area around AD 1010. Most of the modern descendants of Ha Kong-jin live in the Kyŏngsang and Chŏlla provinces. The founding ancestor of the smaller of the two clans was named Ha Hŭm, and he settled in the Taegu area after emigrating from Song China some time in the early part of the twelfth century. Most of the modern descendants of Ha Hŭm still live in the Taegu area. **3.** Chinese 夏: variant of XIA. **4.** English: unexplained.

GIVEN NAMES Vietnamese 40%; Chinese/Korean 32%. *Quang* (17), *Vinh* (16), *Thanh* (15), *Cuong* (13), *Hai* (13), *Binh* (11), *Anh* (10), *Minh* (10), *Tu* (10), *Tuan* (10), *Tam* (6), *Tinh* (5), *Tuong* (5); *Young* (10), *Jung* (6), *Kwang* (5), *Kyung* (5), *Sung* (5), *Chae* (4), *Han* (4), *Soo* (4), *Jeong* (2), *Jung Hoon* (2), *Moon Soo* (2); *Hung* (20), *Dung* (9), *Hong* (9), *Dong* (8), *Sang* (8), *Chi* (8), *Chung* (4), *Chang* (3), *Chong* (2).

Haab (201) German and Swiss German: from a short form of a Germanic personal name composed of the elements *had(u)* 'battle', 'strife' + *berht* 'bright', 'famous'.

GIVEN NAMES German 7%; French 4%. *Guenter* (2), *Erwin, Kurt; Gaston* (2), *Jean-Marc.*

Haack (1617) **1.** North German: occupational name from Middle Low German *hoke, hoker* 'huckster', 'hawker', 'peddler' or possibly from Middle Low German *hake* 'young fellow'. **2.** North German and Dutch: from Middle Low German *hāke*, Dutch *haak* 'hook' (e.g. a fish-hook), perhaps a nickname for someone with some deformity such as a hunch back or a metonymic occupational name for someone who made or used hooks.

GIVEN NAMES German 4%. *Erwin* (5), *Otto* (4), *Ernst, Ewald, Fritz, Gerda, Gottlieb, Helmut, Kurt, Ralf, Reinhart.*

Haacke (218) North German: variant of HAACK.

GIVEN NAMES German 4%. *Erwin, Gottfried, Hans.*

Haaf (201) **1.** North German: variant of HAFF. **2.** South German: metonymic occupational name for a potter, from Middle High German *hafen* 'pot'. **3.** Swedish: topographic name, an altered spelling of *hav* 'sea', 'ocean', or an adoption of the North German name (see 1 above).

Haag (3997) **1.** German and Dutch: topographic name from Middle High German *hac* 'enclosure', 'hedge', Middle Dutch *haghe*, or a habitational name from any of the many places named with this word. **2.** Shortened form of Dutch **Van den Haag**, a habitational name from The Hague. **3.** South German and Swiss German: from the Germanic personal name *Hago*, a short form of any of the various compound names beginning with *hagan* 'enclosure', 'protected place', 'scrub'. **4.** Swedish: probably an ornamental adoption of the German name.

Haage (140) **1.** German and Dutch: variant of HAAG 'hedge', 'enclosure'. **2.** South German: nickname from Old High German *hago* 'bull'.

GIVEN NAMES German 10%. *Claus* (2), *Hans* (2), *Kurt* (2).

Haagen (128) **1.** Danish and Norwegian: from the Old Norse personal name *Hákon*, probably a compound of *hár* 'high' or a word meaning 'horse' + *kyn* 'family' or *konr* 'son', 'descendant'. **2.** German: variant of HAAG or HAAGE. **3.** Dutch (**van Haagen**) and North German: habitational name from any of various places named Hagen, for example in North Rhine-Westphalia and the Palatinate.

Haagensen (113) Danish and Norwegian: patronymic from the personal name HAAGEN.

GIVEN NAMES Scandinavian 14%. *Erik* (2), *Paal, Viktor.*

Haagenson (228) Americanized spelling of Danish and Norwegian HAAGENSEN or the Swedish cognate **Håkensson**.

GIVEN NAMES Scandinavian 6%. *Erik* (2), *Helmer, Nels.*

Haak (907) **1.** North German and Dutch: variant of HAACK. **2.** Swedish: unexplained.

GIVEN NAMES German 4%. *Claus, Helmut, Hubertus, Klaus, Kurt, Otto, Wilhelm.*

Haake (636) **1.** German: variant of HAACK. **2.** Swedish: possibly from the soldier's name *Hake*, which may be a metonymic occupational name from *hakebössa* 'arquebus' (a type of 16th-century firearm that was supported on a tripod or a forked rest).

GIVEN NAMES German 5%. *Eldor* (3), *Alois, Erwin, Hermann, Klaus, Konrad, Kurt, Otto.*

Haakenson (315) Altered spelling of Norwegian **Haakensen**, **Håkensen** (see HAAGENSEN).

GIVEN NAMES Scandinavian 7%. *Helmer* (2), *Selmer* (2), *Idar.*

Haaland (449) Norwegian: habitational name from any of numerous farmsteads named Haaland or Håland, in Agder and southwestern Norway, notably in the county of Rogaland. The farm name is from Old Norse *Hávaland*, from Old Norse *hár* 'high' + *land* 'farm'.

GIVEN NAMES Scandinavian 16%; German 5%. *Erik* (2), *Aksel, Carsten, Hjalmer, Juel, Lars, Maren, Per, Thora, Vidar; Hans, Hilde, Kurt, Otto, Waltraud.*

Haan (703) **1.** Dutch: from *haan* 'rooster', a nickname for someone thought to resemble a cockerel or a habitational name from a house distinguished by the sign of a rooster. **2.** Belgian and Dutch (**van Haan**): habitational name from any of several places named Haan, in particular in Brabant and West Flanders. **3.** German: variant of HAHN.

Haapala (226) Finnish: from *haapa* 'aspen' + the local suffix *-la*. Originally it was a habitational name for someone living or working at a farmstead so named, but in other cases the surname was an ornamental adoption during the name conversion movement in the 19th and early 20th centuries. It occurs chiefly in western Finland.

GIVEN NAMES Finnish 10%. *Eino* (2), *Urho* (2), *Ensio, Hannele, Irja, Kauko, Niilo, Onni, Waino.*

Haar (819) **1.** German and Jewish (Ashkenazic): nickname for someone with a copious or otherwise noticeable head of hair, from Middle High German *hār* 'hair', German *Haar* 'hair'. **2.** German: metonymic occupational name for someone who worked with raw flax (Middle High German *har*) in the production of linen. **3.** North German and Dutch: topographic name for someone who lived by a swamp, from Middle Low German *hōr*, *hār* 'dirt', 'mud'. **4.** Probably a shortened form of Dutch **van Haar**, a habitational name for someone from Ter Haar in Groningen or any of three places named De Haar (in Drente, Overijssel, and Gelderland).

Haarmann (128) North German: topographic name for someone who lived by a swamp, a variant of HAAR 3, with the addition of *man* 'man'.

GIVEN NAMES German 6%. *Aloysius, Kurt.*

Haarstad (118) Norwegian: habitational name from a place called Haarstad.
GIVEN NAMES Scandinavian 11%. *Knut, Oivind*; *Otto* (2), *Hans*.

Haas (15135) Dutch, German, and Jewish (Ashkenazic): from Middle Dutch, Middle High German *hase*, German *Hase* 'hare', hence a nickname for a swift runner or a timorous or confused person, but in some cases perhaps a habitational name from a house distinguished by the sign of a hare. As a Jewish name it can also be an ornamental name or one of names selected at random from vocabulary words by government officials when surnames became compulsory.

Haasch (140) Dutch: nickname meaning 'hare-like', from an adjectival derivative of HAAS.

Haase (3748) German, Dutch, and Jewish (Ashkenazic): variant of HAAS.
GIVEN NAMES German 5%. *Kurt* (11), *Gerhard* (5), *Otto* (4), *Klaus* (3), *Dieter* (2), *Guenter* (2), *Heinz* (2), *Manfred* (2), *Arno, Benno, Bernd, Claus.*

Haasl (112) South German: nickname from a diminutive of HAAS 'hare'.

Haass (183) Variant of North German and Dutch HAAS.
GIVEN NAMES German 6%. *Erwin* (3), *Otto.*

Haataja (150) Finnish: possibly from the dialect word *haataa* 'to toil'. This is an old Finnish family name, which occurs throughout the northern part of the country and in the Savo region in central eastern Finland.
GIVEN NAME Scandinavian 5%. *Nels.*

Haba (119) **1.** Czech: from a shortened form of any of various Old Czech traditional personal names formed with *habat* 'to take', or from a pet form of HAVEL. **2.** Polish: perhaps a variant of **Chaba**, from a dialect word meaning 'rib' or 'dry branch'. **3.** Jewish (from Poland): metonymic occupational name from Polish *chaba*, a kind of coarse white woolen cloth.
GIVEN NAMES Polish 6%; Jewish 4%. *Janina, Janusz*; *Shlomo.*

Habben (219) Frisian: patronymic from a Germanic personal name composed of the elements *had(u)* 'battle', 'strife' + *berht* 'bright', 'famous'.

Habeck (505) North German: variant of HABIG, from Middle Low German *havec* 'hawk'.
GIVEN NAMES German 5%. *Kurt* (2), *Alfons, Heino, Helmut, Klaus, Uwe.*

Habecker (265) North German: (**Häbecker**) occupational name for a hawker (see HAWKER), from an agent derivative of Middle Low German *havec* 'hawk', *heveker.*

Habeeb (247) Muslim: variant of HABIB.
GIVEN NAMES Muslim 6%. *Mohamed* (2), *Awni, Ghani, Ibrahim, Jamil, Marwan, Mohamad, Musa, Nadirah, Safia, Taha, Tanios.*

Habegger (337) South German and Swiss German: variant of HABECKER.

Habel (682) **1.** German: from a pet form of the Germanic personal name *Habo*, a short form of various compound names formed with *had(u)* 'battle', 'strife'. **2.** Dutch: topographic name from *abeel*, denoting a type of poplar tree. **3.** Dutch: from the personal name *Abel* (see ABEL). **4.** Czech and German: Germanized variant of Czech HAVEL, from the saint's name *Gallus* 'Gall'.
GIVEN NAMES German 5%. *Kurt* (2), *Theodor* (2), *Berthold, Eberhard, Heinz, Mathias, Ulrike.*

Habenicht (215) German: nickname for a poor man, a compound of Middle High German *habe(n)* 'have' + *niht* 'nothing'.
GIVEN NAMES German 4%. *Fritz, Kurt.*

Haber (2596) **1.** German and Jewish (Ashkenazic): metonymic occupational name for a grower of or dealer in oats, from Middle High German *haber(e)* 'oats', modern German *Hafer*. As a Jewish surname, it is in many cases ornamental. **2.** Jewish (Ashkenazic): habitational name from a place called Haber in Bohemia.
GIVEN NAMES Jewish 5%. *Sol* (3), *Aron* (2), *Eitan* (2), *Emanuel* (2), *Hyman* (2), *Moshe* (2), *Aviva, Chanie, Dafna, Isadore, Kalmen, Meyer.*

Haberberger (135) German: habitational name for someone from a place called Haberberg.

Haberer (365) German and Jewish (Ashkenazic): occupational name for a grower or seller of oats, from an agent derivative of Middle High German *haber(e)* 'oats'. As a Jewish name it is often an ornamental adoption.

Haberkorn (461) **1.** German: metonymic occupational name for a dealer in oats, from Middle High German *haber(e)* 'oats' + *korn* 'grain'. **2.** Jewish (Ashkenazic): adoption of 1, probably as an ornamental-occupational name for a grain merchant.

Haberl (158) German: diminutive of HABER.
GIVEN NAMES German 11%. *Erwin, Hans, Helmuth, Helmut, Klaus, Manfred.*

Haberland (220) German: topographic name from Middle High German *haber(e)* 'oats' + *land* 'land', or a habitational name from any of various places so called.
GIVEN NAMES German 11%. *Kurt* (3), *Bernhard, Dieter, Erwin, Fritz, Hans, Heinz, Helmut.*

Haberle (265) South German and Swiss German (also **Häberle**): diminutive of HABER.

Haberman (1704) German or Jewish: variant of HABERMANN.

Habermann (280) German and Jewish (Ashkenazic): occupational name for a grower or seller of oats, composed of the elements HABER + the agent suffix *-mann*.
GIVEN NAMES German 9%. *Kurt* (2),

Brunhilde, Erwin, Hans, Helmut, Helmuth, Hermann, Ralf.

Habermehl (235) German: metonymic occupational name for a producer or seller of oatmeal, from Middle High German *haber(e)* 'oats' + *mël* 'flour'.
GIVEN NAMES German 4%. *Hans, Heinz, Rainer.*

Habersham (135) English (Yorkshire): metonymic occupational name for a maker of habergeons, Middle English, Old French *haubergeon*. The habergeon was a sleeveless jacket of mail or scale armor, which was also worn for penance.
FOREBEARS Born in Beverley, Yorkshire, England, James Habersham emigrated to the infant colony of Georgia in 1738 with his friend George Whitefield. Together they established what is believed to be America's first orphanage. Habersham was married in Bethesda, GA, in 1740 and had three surviving sons, all of whom were educated at Princeton and became ardent patriots.

Haberstroh (294) German: from Middle High German *haber(e)* 'oats' + *strō* 'straw', hence probably a metonymic occupational name for a grower of oats.

Habetz (102) German: unexplained. Possibly an altered spelling of **Habets**, from a Germanic personal name, variant of *Hadebert* (see HAAB).
GIVEN NAMES German 9%. *Alois, Gerhard, Wenzel.*

Habib (933) Muslim and Jewish (Sephardic): from an Arabic personal name based on *habīb* 'beloved', 'friend', used by both Muslims and Jews. **Habibullah** 'beloved of Allah' is an epithet of Mohammad.
GIVEN NAMES Muslim 51%. *Ahsan* (9), *Mohammad* (9), *Mohammed* (9), *Mohamed* (7), *Abdul* (5), *Amir* (4), *Habib* (4), *Muhammad* (4), *Nabil* (4), *Nagi* (4), *Jamal* (3), *Kamil* (3).

Habibi (122) Muslim: from an adjectival derivative of HABIB.
GIVEN NAMES Muslim 71%. *Ali* (4), *Hamid* (4), *Mohammad* (3), *Habib* (2), *Hassan* (2), *Majid* (2), *Amir, Arshad, Asif, Behzad, Bijan, Esfandiar.*

Habich (133) **1.** South German (also **Häbich**): variant of HABIG. **2.** Slovenian (central Slovenia; **Habič**): patronymic from a derivative of the medieval personal name *Habjan*, a variant of the personal name *Fabjan* (see FABIAN).

Habicht (168) German: variant of HABIG.
GIVEN NAMES German 10%. *Ernst* (2), *Helmut* (2), *Bernd.*

Habig (340) German: from Middle High German *habech* 'hawk', hence a nickname for someone who was thought to resemble the bird or a metonymic occupational name for someone who trained hawks for hunting (see HAWK).

Habiger (189) German: occupational name

for someone who trained hawks for hunting, from Middle High German *habich* 'hawk' + the agent suffix *-er*.
GIVEN NAME German 4%. *Kurt*.

Hable (299) German: variant of HABEL, or in some cases an Americanized spelling of this name.

Haby (192) Swiss German: unexplained.

Hach (235) German: **1.** nickname or occupational name from Middle High German *hache* 'young man', 'guy', 'boy', 'servant'. **2.** possibly a North German topographic name, from Low German *hach* 'dirty water'. **3.** (Eastern German) from a Slavic-influenced pet form of the personal name HANS.
GIVEN NAMES German 6%. *Dieter* (2), *Gerhard* (2), *Katharina*.

Hache (110) **1.** French and English: from Old French *hache* 'axe', 'battleaxe', hence a metonymic occupational name for someone who made or used axes or battleaxes. **2.** German: variant of HACH 1.
GIVEN NAMES French 16%; German 6%; Spanish 5%; Italian 4%. *Alphonse, Amedee, Euclide, Josee, Laurent, Lucien, Yvon; Gerhard* (2), *Friedrich Wilhelm, Hans Diedrich; Altagracia, Jorge, Mario, Pedro; Marco* (2), *Lorenzo*.

Hachey (375) Altered spelling of French **Hachet** or **Hachée**, occupational names for an axeman or woodman or a maker of woodmen's implements, from derivatives of Old French *hache* 'axe', 'battleaxe' (see HACHE).
GIVEN NAMES French 6%. *Cecile, Celina, Emile, Fernande, Napoleon, Placide, Romain*.

Hachmeister (130) North German: variant of HAGEMEISTER.

Hachtel (152) German: habitational name from a place called Hachtel, near Bad Mergentheim in Baden-Württemberg.

Hack (2257) **1.** North German: occupational name for a peddler (see HAACK 1). **2.** North German: topographic name for someone who lived by a hedge (see HECK 2). **3.** North German: perhaps also a topographic name from *hach, hack* 'dirty, boggy water'. **4.** Frisian, Dutch, and North German: from a Frisian personal name, *Hake*. **5.** Jewish (Ashkenazic): metonymic occupational name from Yiddish *hak* 'axe'. **6.** English: variant of HAKE 1.
FOREBEARS George Hack (c. 1623–c. 1665) was born in Cologne, Germany, of a Schleswig-Holstein family, and emigrated to New Amsterdam where he practiced medicine and entered the VA tobacco trade. Colony records show that he and his wife, Anna, were formally made naturalized citizens of VA in 1658. He had two daughters, neither of whom married, and two sons: George Nicholas Hack, the founder of the Norfolk branch of the family; and Peter, for many years a member of the VA House of Burgesses, the founder of the Maryland

branch. Hack's descendants eventually changed the spelling of the name to Heck.

Hackathorn (220) Americanized form of German HAGEDORN.

Hackbart (187) German: variant of HACKBARTH.

Hackbarth (1054) German: from the Germanic personal name *Hagabert*, composed of *hag* 'hedge', 'enclosure' + *berht* 'bright', 'famous'.
GIVEN NAMES German 4%. *Kurt* (4), *Otto* (4), *Horst* (2), *Erwin, Siegfried*.

Hacke (131) **1.** German: from the Germanic personal name *Hago*, a short form of various Germanic personal names formed with *hag* 'hedge', 'enclosure'. **2.** Jewish (Ashkenazic): metonymic occupational name from German *Hacke* 'axe'.
GIVEN NAME German 4%. *Kurt*.

Hackel (370) German (also **Häckel**): from a diminutive of *Hack* 'cutter', i.e. either 'butcher' or 'woodcutter' (see HACKER).
GIVEN NAMES German 5%. *Kurt* (3), *Otto* (3).

Hackenberg (464) German: habitational name from any of several places called Hackenberg.

Hackenburg (107) Either a respelling of German HACKENBERG or of **Hachenburg**, a habitational name from a place in Rhineland-Palatinate called Hachenburg.
GIVEN NAME German 6%. *Fritz* (2).

Hacker (4868) **1.** German (also **Häcker**), Dutch, and Jewish (Ashkenazic): occupational name for a butcher, possibly also for a woodcutter, from an agent derivative of Middle High German *hacken*, Dutch *hakken* 'to hack', 'to chop'. The Jewish surname may be from Yiddish *heker* 'butcher', *holtsheker* 'woodcutter' (German *Holzhacker*), or *valdheker* 'lumberjack', or from German *Hacker* 'woodchopper'. **2.** English (chiefly Somerset): from an agent derivative of Middle English *hacken* 'to hack', hence an occupational name for a woodcutter or, perhaps, a maker of *hacks* (*hakkes*), a word used in Middle English to denote a variety of agricultural tools such as mattocks and hoes.

Hackert (170) German and Dutch: variant of HACKER.

Hackett (7436) **1.** Scottish: variant of **Halkett**, which is probably a habitational name from the lands of Halkhead in Renfrewshire, named with Middle English *hauk, halk* 'hawk' + *wude* 'wood'. **2.** English (mainly central England): from a pet form of the medieval personal name *Hack, Hake* (see HAKE). **3.** English: from Middle English *haket*, a kind of fish, hence perhaps a nickname for someone supposed to resemble such a fish, or a metonymic occupational name for a fisherman or fish seller. **4.** Irish: when it is not the English name, this may also be an Anglicized form of Gaelic *Mac Eachaidh* (see CAUGHEY, MCGAFFEY).
FOREBEARS This name was established in

Ireland by William de Haket, who accompanied King John and was granted estates in Tipperary in the early 13th century. The form *de Haket* suggests this is the Scottish habitational name. The spelling Hackett was first used by his descendants in the 16th century.

Hacking (260) English (Lancashire): habitational name from Hacking in Lancashire, the name of which is of uncertain origin. Early forms appear with the definite article, and the name may represent an Old English term for a fish weir, a derivative of *hæcc* 'hatch', 'low gate', or *haca* 'hook'.

Hackl (268) German (Bavarian): variant of HACKEL.
GIVEN NAMES German 8%. *Franz* (2), *Alphons, Guenter, Heinz, Matthias*.

Hackleman (237) Americanized spelling of **Häckelmann**, a South German variant of HACKEL, with the addition of Middle High German *man*.

Hackler (1153) German (**Häckler**): **1.** South German: occupational name for someone who used a small hoe in the field or a vineyard, see HECKLER. **2.** an occupational name for a haberdasher, dry goods dealer.

Hackley (656) **1.** English: probably a habitational name either from a lost or unidentified place, or a variant of HAGLEY. **2.** Possibly a variant of German HACKLER.

Hackman (1603) **1.** English: occupational name for a servant (Middle English *man*) of a man named *Hake* (see HAKE). **2.** Respelling of German HACKMANN, or a Jewish spelling variant of this name. **3.** Respelling of German **Hachmann**, topographic name for someone living near a hedge or enclosure, from Middle Low German *hach* 'hedge', 'enclosure', 'fenced pasture or woodland', or habitational name from a place called Hachum (dialect *Hachen*) in Lower Saxony.

Hackmann (268) **1.** German and Jewish (Ashkenazic): occupational name for a butcher or a woodcutter (see HACKER 1). **2.** North German: variant of HAACK 'peddler', 'hawker'.
GIVEN NAMES German 6%. *Ernst* (2), *Kurt* (2), *Arno, Heinz*.

Hackney (3318) English and Scottish: **1.** habitational name from Hackney in Greater London, named from an Old English personal name *Haca* (genitive *Hacan*) + *ēg* 'island', 'dry ground in marshland'. **2.** from Middle English *hakenei* (Old French *haquenée*), an ambling horse, especially one considered suitable for women to ride; perhaps therefore a metonymic occupational name for a stablehand. This surname has also been found in Scotland since medieval times.

Hackworth (1399) English: habitational name, probably from Hackworthy in Devon, which is named from an Old

English personal name *Haca* + Old English *worð* or *worðig* 'enclosure'.

Hada (201) Japanese: variously written, usually with characters used phonetically. It is an alternative pronunciation of the ancient name HATA and is listed with it in the Shinsen shōjiroku. *Hada*, and another variant pronunciation **Haneda**, both written with characters meaning 'wings' and 'rice paddy', are found predominantly in eastern Japan.
GIVEN NAMES Japanese 25%. *Akiko, Isamu, Kaz, Kazumi, Kyoko, Masaye, Masayo, Mitsugi, Mitsuji, Mitsuo, Morio, Noboru.*

Hadad (187) Arabic and Jewish (Sephardic): variant of HADDAD 'blacksmith', a common form of this name among Sephardic Moroccan Jews.
GIVEN NAMES Jewish 9%; Muslim 7%; Spanish 5%. *Sima* (2), *Eliezer, Haim, Igal, Moshe, Nuriel, Sol, Yochanan*; *Abdalla, Atta, Ibrahim, Jalal, Jamal, Najib, Nawal, Raouf, Salem, Soliman*; *Patricio* (2), *Alejandro, Eduardo, Jose, Manuel, Marivel, Miguel.*

Hadaway (691) English: variant of HATHAWAY.

Hadcock (113) English: variant of ADCOCK.

Hadd (113) English: unexplained.

Haddad (3054) Arabic and Jewish (Sephardic): occupational name for a blacksmith, Arabic *ḥaddād.*
GIVEN NAMES Muslim 24%; French 5%. *Samir* (11), *Khalil* (9), *Nabil* (9), *Sami* (9), *Nadim* (8), *Fouad* (7), *Ghassan* (7), *Ibrahim* (7), *Kamel* (7), *Salim* (7), *Jamal* (6), *Bassam* (5); *Emile* (9), *Michel* (9), *Antoine* (8), *Andre* (3), *Camille* (2), *Georges* (2), *Pierre* (2), *Aime, Christophe, Jacques, Leonie, Philippe.*

Haddan (110) Scottish: variant spelling of HADDEN.

Haddaway (203) English: variant of HATHAWAY.

Hadden (2345) **1.** Scottish: variant of HOWDEN 1. **2.** English: variant of HADDON. **3.** Irish (Ulster and County Louth): though mainly Scottish, this surname is sometimes used as an Anglicized form of Gaelic Ó hÉidín 'descendant of *Éidín* (see HAYDEN). **4.** North German (Frisian): from the personal name *Hadder*, a derivative of any of the Germanic compound names formed with *had* 'battle', 'strife' as the first element.

Hadder (137) **1.** Frisian: from the personal name *Hadder*, derived from a Germanic name composed of the elements *hadu* 'strife' + *ward* 'guard', 'protector'. **2.** English: unexplained.

Haddix (989) English: patronymic form of HADDOCK 1.

Haddock (2827) English: of three possible origins: **1.** from a medieval survival with added initial *H-* of the Old English personal name *Ædduc*, a diminutive of *Æddi*, itself a short form of various compound names with the first element *ēad* 'prosperity', 'fortune'. **2.** habitational name from Haydock near Liverpool, which is probably named from Welsh *heiddog* 'characterized by barley'. **3.** from Middle English *hadduc* 'haddock', hence a metonymic occupational name for a fisherman or fish seller, or a nickname for someone supposedly resembling the fish.

Haddon (694) English: habitational name from any of the various places, in Derbyshire, Northamptonshire, and Devon, named with Old English *hǣð* 'heathland', 'heather' + *dūn* 'hill', or from Haddon in Cambridgeshire, which is probably named from the Old English personal name *Headda* + *dūn.*

Haddow (201) Scottish: habitational name from Haddo in Aberdeenshire, named with Older Scots *half* + *davach, dauch*, from Gaelic *dabhach*, a land measure equivalent to four plowgates.
GIVEN NAME Scottish 7%. *Alastair* (3).

Haddox (804) English: patronymic form of HADDOCK.

Hade (212) Irish: possibly an Anglicized form of Gaelic Ó hAidíthe, later Ó hÉididh 'descendant of *Éideadh*', from *éideadh* 'clothes', 'armor', which was first Anglicized as **Haidy**.

Hadel (150) German: variant of *Hatto*, a short form of any of the Germanic personal names formed with *hadu* 'strife' as their first element.

Haden (1191) **1.** English (West Midlands) and Irish: variant spelling of HAYDEN. **2.** German: perhaps an altered spelling of HADDEN or HEIDEN.

Hader (219) **1.** German and Jewish (Ashkenazic): nickname for a quarrelsome person, from Middle High German *hader* 'discord', 'argument', 'quarrel', German *Hader.* **2.** German and Jewish (Ashkenazic): from Middle High German *hader* 'tattered clothes', 'rags', German *Hader*, hence a nickname for a scruffy person or a metonymic occupational name for a trader in rags. **3.** German (**Häder**): variant of HEIDER.

Hadfield (886) English: habitational name from a place in Derbyshire, named from Old English *hǣð* 'heathland', 'heather' + *feld* 'pasture', 'open country'.

Hadi (120) Muslim: from a personal name based on Arabic *hādi* 'leader', 'guide'. *Al-Ḥādi* 'the Guide' is one of the names of Allah. It is also a title of 'Ali ibn Muhammad Naqi, tenth imam of the Shiites (died 868).
GIVEN NAMES Muslim 71%. *Abdul* (6), *Ali* (4), *Mohammed* (4), *Abbas* (2), *Amirali* (2), *Jamal* (2), *Laith* (2), *Mohamed* (2), *Mohammad* (2), *Omar* (2), *Abdallah, Abdulhadi.*

Hadland (111) English (Oxfordshire): unexplained.

Hadler (333) German: habitational name for someone from Hadeln, a marshy region west of the Elbe estuary, originally named as *Hadulo(un)*, from *hadu* 'marsh' + *lo* 'woods'.
GIVEN NAME French 4%. *Jacques* (4).

Hadley (7453) English (chiefly West Midlands): habitational name from either of two places named Hadley, in Worcestershire and Shropshire, or from either of two places named Hadleigh, in Essex and Suffolk. The first is named from the Old English personal name *Hadda* + *lēah* 'wood', '(woodland) clearing'; the other three are from Old English *hǣð* 'heathland', 'heather' + *lēah.*

Hadlock (684) English: unexplained. Probably a habitational name from an unidentified place, possibly Hadleigh in Suffolk. The name has died out in England.
FOREBEARS Nathanael Hadlock is recorded in Charlestown, MA, in 1638, having emigrated from Great Bromley in Essex, England. The family subsequently moved to Roxbury, MA.

Hadnot (255) Variant of English HODNETT.

Hadorn (104) Variant spelling of German HAGEDORN.

Hadsall (179) English: unexplained. It is most probably a habitational name from an unidentified place in the West Midlands, possibly Hadzor Hall in Worcestershire.

Hadsell (412) English: see HADSALL.

Hadwin (143) English: from an Old English personal name composed of the elements *hadu* 'strife' + *win(e)* 'friend'.

Hady (117) English: unexplained.

Haeberle (206) German (**Häberle**): see HABERLE.

Haecker (241) German (**Häcker**): see HACKER.
GIVEN NAMES German 5%. *Arno, Claus, Fritz.*

Haefele (260) South German (**Häfele**): metonymic occupational name for a potter, from a diminutive of Middle High German *hafen* 'pot'. Compare HAFNER.
GIVEN NAME German 4%. *Ilse.*

Haeffner (177) German: variant of HAEFNER.

Haefner (733) German (**Häfner**): variant of HAFNER. This is the normal term for a potter in southwestern Germany, and the surname is largely confined to this area of the country.

Haeg (149) German and Dutch: variant of HAAG.

Haegele (336) German (**Hägele**): see HAGELE.
GIVEN NAMES German 5%. *Ingeborg, Klaus, Kurt, Siegfried.*

Haeger (262) German (**Häger**): see HAGER.
GIVEN NAMES German 5%. *Hans, Kurt, Wilhelm, Willi.*

Haehn (139) German: variant of HAHN.

Haehnel (100) German: from a pet form of HAHN 1 and 2.
GIVEN NAMES German 10%. *Erwin, Ingo, Kurt.*

Haemmerle (115) South German (**Hämmerle**): from a diminutive or pet form of HAMMER 1.

GIVEN NAMES German 10%. *Florian, Fritz, Manfred.*

Haen (340) Probably a shortened form of Dutch **de Haen**, a variant of DE HAAN.

Haenel (177) German (**Hänel**): from a pet form of the personal name *Johann(es)* (see JOHN).

GIVEN NAMES German 8%. *Horst* (2), *Manfred.*

Haener (110) **1.** Swiss German: variant of HAINER. **2.** German: altered spelling of **Hähner** or **Hänner**, pet forms of the personal name *Hainer* or *Heinrich* respectively.

Haer (120) German: **1.** topographic name for someone who lived by a swamp, a variant of HAAR 3. **2.** altered spelling of **Hähr** (common in Württemberg), from Middle High German *heher* 'jay' (the bird). **3.** Alternatively, it may be a topographic name from Middle Low German *hare* 'hill'.

GIVEN NAMES German 4%. *Georg, Otto.*

Haering (183) Dutch and North German (**Häring**): variant spelling of HARING or HERRING.

GIVEN NAME German 5%. *Otto.*

Haerr (111) German: variant of HAER.

Haertel (182) German (**Härtel**) and Dutch: from a pet form of various compound personal names formed with the Germanic element *hard* 'hardy', 'brave', 'strong'.

GIVEN NAME German 4%. *Fritz.*

Haertling (113) German: probably a variant of HARTLING.

Haese (271) German and Dutch: variant of HAAS.

Haessig (110) German (**Hässig**): **1.** from an adjectival form of the regional name *Hesse*, denoting someone from that territory (see HESS). **2.** from a short form of a Germanic personal name, possibly one formed with *hadu* 'strife' or from a pet form of HERMANN or HEINRICH. **3.** unflattering nickname from Middle High German *hazzec, hezzec* 'hostile', 'malevolent'.

GIVEN NAMES German 4%. *Hans* (2), *Reiner.*

Haessler (108) German (**Hässler**): habitational name for someone from any of various places called Hassel or Haslach, the name of which is based on *haslo* 'swampy woodland'.

GIVEN NAMES German 8%. *Reiner, Reinhard.*

Haessly (169) Altered spelling of Swiss German **Hässli**, diminutive of HAAS.

Haeussler (143) South German (**Häussler**): variant of **Häusler** (see HAUSLER).

GIVEN NAMES German 10%. *Armin, Erwin, Juergen, Karl Heinz.*

Hafeez (101) Muslim: from a personal name based on Arabic *ḥāfiz* 'protector'. This is also an honorific title given to someone who has memorized the whole of the

Qur'an. *Al-Ḥāfiz* 'the Protector' is an attribute of Allah.

GIVEN NAMES Muslim 88%. *Abdul* (13), *Mohammad* (8), *Mohammed* (6), *Syed* (5), *Tahir* (4), *Alia* (3), *Muhammad* (3), *Abdool* (2), *Khalid* (2), *Mohamed* (2), *Shahid* (2), *Tariq* (2).

Hafele (163) South German (**Häfele**): see HAEFELE.

Hafeman (180) Americanized spelling of North German HAFEMANN.

Hafemann (113) North German: status name for a steward on an estate. Compare South German HOFFMANN.

GIVEN NAMES German 7%. *Erna, Lorenz.*

Hafemeister (101) North German: occupational name for a steward on an estate or the supervisor of a court. Compare HOFFMEISTER.

Hafen (320) South German: metonymic occupational name for a potter, from Middle High German *hafen* 'pot'.

Hafer (1474) German and Jewish (Ashkenazic): metonymic occupational name for a grower of or dealer in oats, from German *Hafer* 'oats'. Compare HABER. As a Jewish surname, it is in many cases ornamental.

Haferkamp (123) German and Dutch: variant spelling of HAVERKAMP.

GIVEN NAMES German 7%. *Hans, Hermann, Johann, Rudi.*

Hafey (165) Irish: variant spelling of HAFFEY, a variant of HAUGHEY.

Haff (454) North German: **1.** dialect variant of HOFF 'farm'. **2.** from Middle Low German *haf* 'sea', 'lagoon', most likely denoting someone living by one of the lagoons on the Baltic coast, German *Haff*.

Haffer (92) German: from the Middle High German personal name *Haffer*, reduced form of *Hadufrid*, composed of the Germanic elements *hadu* 'battle' and *fridu* 'peace'.

Haffey (403) Irish: variant of HAUGHEY.

Haffner (1334) German: variant spelling of HAFNER.

Hafford (385) Irish (especially County Westmeath): variant of HARFORD.

Hafler (153) South German (**Häfler**): occupational name for a potter. Compare HAFNER.

Hafley (368) Americanized form of South German HAEFELE.

Hafner (2185) South German and Austrian: occupational name for a potter, Middle High German *hafner*, an agent derivative of Middle High German *hafen* 'pot', 'dish'. This is the normal term for the occupation in southeastern Germany and Austria, and the German surname is found mainly in this area, also in Slovenia.

Haft (417) **1.** German and Jewish (Ashkenazic): metonymic occupational name for a maker and seller of various sorts of clamps and fastenings, from Middle High German

haft 'clasp'. **2.** Jewish (eastern Ashkenazic): metonymic occupational name for an embroiderer, from Yiddish *haft* 'embroidery'.

Haga (1061) **1.** Norwegian: habitational name from any of numerous farmsteads in southern Norway, so named from Old Norse *haga*, dative case of *hagi* 'enclosure'. This surname is also established in Sweden. **2.** Japanese: written with characters meaning 'fragrant' and 'congratulations', the name is found mostly in northeastern Japan and is probably taken from a place in Shimotsuke (now Tochigi prefecture) by that name.

GIVEN NAMES Japanese 6%. *Masao* (2), *Naoko* (2), *Hirokazu, Katsuhiko, Kenji, Koji, Madoka, Masayuki, Ryo, Satoshi, Shigeru, Takehiko.*

Hagadone (110) Americanized form of German HAGEDORN.

Hagadorn (346) Variant spelling of German HAGEDORN.

Hagaman (584) Variant of German HAGEMANN or Dutch HEGEMAN.

Hagan (7690) Irish: **1.** reduced Anglicized form of Gaelic **Ó hÁgáin** 'descendant of *Ógán*', a personal name from a diminutive of *óg* 'young'. **2.** reduced Anglicized form of Gaelic **Ó hAodhagáin** 'descendant of *Aodhagán*', a personal name formed from a double diminutive of *Aodh* meaning 'fire'.

Hagans (851) Northern Irish: variant of HAGAN, with the addition of English patronymic -*s*.

Hagar (1100) Variant of HAGER.

Hagarty (236) Irish: variant spelling of HAGGERTY.

GIVEN NAME Irish 8%. *Brendan.*

Hagberg (759) Swedish: probably an ornamental name from *hage* 'enclosure' + *berg* 'mountain', 'hill'.

GIVEN NAMES Scandinavian 6%. *Nils* (5), *Erik* (2), *Arnt, Helmer, Lennart.*

Hage (959) **1.** German: topographic name from Middle High German *hac* 'enclosure', 'hedge'. **2.** Dutch: variant of HAAG. **3.** Norwegian: habitational name from any of several farmsteads so named, from the Old Norse indefinite singular form *hagi* 'enclosure' (see HAGA). This surname is also established in Sweden.

Hagedorn (1748) **1.** German: topographic name from Middle High German *hagedorn* 'hawthorn', from *hac* 'hedge' + *dorn* 'thorn'. Compare HAWTHORNE. This surname is also well established in Denmark. **2.** Dutch: habitational name from the common place name Hagedoorn, of the same etymology as 1.

Hagee (199) Probably an altered form of German HAGE, spelled thus to preserve the second syllable as pronounced in German; but see also HAGY.

Hagel (746) **1.** German (also **Hägel**): variant of HEGEL. **2.** Dutch: nickname from *hagel* 'hail'. **3.** variant of HAGELE 3.

GIVEN NAMES German 4%. *Hans* (2), *Klaus* (2), *Brendt, Dieter, Erwin, Florian, Kurt, Lieschen, Otto, Wolfgang.*

Hagele (130) German (**Hägele**): **1.** from a pet form of the personal name *Hagin* (see HAGEN). **2.** topographic name from Middle High German *hagen* 'hedge', 'enclosure'. **3.** nickname or metonymic occupational nickname from a Swabian dialect word denoting a breeding bull.

GIVEN NAMES German 11%. *Otto* (2), *Armin, Erwin, Gerd.*

Hagelin (162) **1.** Swiss German (**Hägelin**): variant of HAGELE. **2.** Dutch: from a derivative of the Germanic personal name HAGEN. **3.** Swedish: ornamental name from *hage* (see HAGA) + the common surname suffix *-lin.*

GIVEN NAMES Scandinavian 5%. *Anders, Lars.*

Hagelstein (128) German: nickname for a hot-headed, irascible man, from Middle High German *Hagelstein* 'hailstone'.

GIVEN NAMES German 4%; Scandinavian 4%. *Hans* (2); *Holger.*

Hageman (2146) **1.** Dutch: topographic name for someone who lived by an enclosure, from Middle Dutch *haghe* 'hedge', 'enclosure' + *man* 'man'. **2.** Respelling of German HAGEMANN. **3.** Swedish: either of German origin (see HAGEMANN), or an ornamental or topographic name from Swedish *hage* 'enclosed pasture' + *man* 'man'.

Hagemann (860) **1.** German: topographic name for someone who lived by a hedge or enclosure, from Middle High German *hac* 'enclosure', 'hedge', Middle Low German *hage* + *mann* 'man'. **2.** Danish: either of German origin (see 1) or an occupational name for a gardener, Danish *haghman.*

GIVEN NAMES German 6%. *Kurt* (3), *Fritz* (2), *Egon, Hans, Helmut, Horst, Ilse, Juergen, Otto, Rudi, Wilhelm, Willi.*

Hagemeier (263) German: variant spelling of HAGEMEYER.

GIVEN NAMES German 5%. *Wilhelm* (2), *Fritz, Guenter.*

Hagemeister (186) North German: from Middle Low German *hege* 'hedge', 'enclosure' + *meister, mēster* 'supervisor', an occupational name for a person in charge of cultivating and settling new areas, who often became the civil administrator of the settlement.

GIVEN NAMES German 4%. *Hans* (2), *Erwin.*

Hagemeyer (297) German: distinguishing name for the tenant farmer (see MEYER) of a farm by an enclosure, from Middle Low German *hac* 'hedge', 'enclosure', dative *hage.*

Hagen (9950) **1.** North German and Dutch: topographic name from Middle Low German *hage(n)*, Middle Dutch *haghe* 'enclosure', 'hedge'. **2.** German, Dutch, and Danish: from a Germanic personal name, a short form of the various compound names formed with *hag* 'enclosure', 'protected place' as the first element. **3.** German: nickname from Middle High German *hagen* 'breeding bull'. **4.** Jewish (Ashkenazic): of uncertain origin; perhaps the same as 1. **5.** English: from an Old Scandinavian or continental Germanic personal name *Hǫgni* 'protector', 'patron' (Old Norse), *Haghni* (Old Danish), *Hagano* (Old Germanic). **6.** Norwegian: habitational name from any of numerous farmsteads so named, from the definite singular form of *hage*, from Old Norse *hagi* 'enclosure'. **7.** Swedish: ornamental or topographic name from the definite singular form of *hage* 'enclosed pasture'.

Hagenbuch (366) German: habitational name from any of various places so named, including Hagenbach near Neckarsulm, which was formerly called Hagenbuch.

Hagenow (170) Eastern German: habitational name from places in Pomerania and Mecklenburg called Hagenow.

GIVEN NAMES German 5%. *Arno, Otto.*

Hagens (356) North German and Dutch: patronymic form of HAGEN 2.

Hager (8091) **1.** Dutch and North German: from a Germanic personal name composed of *hag* 'hedge', 'enclosure' + *hari, heri* 'army'. **2.** from a Germanic personal name, *Hadugar*, composed of the elements *hadu-* 'combat', 'strife' + *gari*, from *garwa* 'ready', 'eager'. **3.** German (also **Häger**): topographic name for someone who lived by a hedged or fenced enclosure, Middle High German *hac.* **4.** German and Jewish (Ashkenazic): nickname for a thin man, from Middle High German, German *hager* 'thin', 'gaunt'. **5.** English: occupational name for a woodcutter, from an agent derivative of Middle English *haggen* 'to cut or chop'.

Hagerman (1900) North German (**Hägermann**): Westphalian variant of HAGER.

Hagert (133) German: variant of HAGER 3, 4.

Hagerty (2265) Irish: variant spelling of HAGGERTY.

GIVEN NAMES Irish 4%. *Brigid* (3), *Brendan, Roisin.*

Hagewood (250) **1.** Americanized form of Dutch **Hagewoud**, a topographic or habitational name composed of the elements *hage* 'hedge' + *woud* 'wood'. **2.** Variant of northern English HAGWOOD 1.

Hagey (300) Americanized form of German HAGE, reflecting its pronunciation as two syllables in German, or an altered spelling of Swiss German **Hägi** or its variant **Hegi**, see HAGY.

Hagg (353) **1.** Swedish (**Hägg**): ornamental name from *hägg* 'bird cherry' (*Prunus padus*). This is one of the surnames drawn from the vocabulary of nature and adopted more or less arbitrarily in the 19th century. **2.** English: from Old Norse *Hagi*, which

has been identified as a byname from *hagr* 'deft', 'dextrous', although it could equally well be a habitational name meaning 'the enclosure', see HAGEN. **3.** South German: variant of HAACK.

GIVEN NAME Scandinavian 6%. *Iver.*

Haggan (114) Irish: variant of HAGAN 1.

Haggar (197) English: variant of HAGGARD.

Haggard (3062) **1.** English: nickname from Middle English, Old French *hagard* 'wild', 'untamed'. This word was adopted into Middle English as a technical term in falconry to denote a hawk that had been captured and trained when already fully grown, rather than being reared in captivity; the surname may have developed as a metonymic occupational name for a falconer. **2.** Americanized form of Danish *Ågård* (see AGARD).

Haggart (319) **1.** Scottish: according to Black, an altered form of McTAGGART. However, it seems more likely to be an altered form of HAGGARD. **2.** Dutch: topographic name denoting someone who lived by an enclosure or hedge, from an agent noun based on Middle Dutch *haghe.*

Haggarty (153) Scottish spelling of Irish HAGGERTY.

Hagge (340) **1.** South German: variant of HAACK. **2.** Frisian: from an unexplained personal name. **3.** Swedish (**Hägge**): variant of **Hägg** (see HAGG).

Hagger (126) English: **1.** variant of HAGGARD. **2.** variant of HAGER.

Haggerty (4295) Irish (Ulster): Anglicized form of Gaelic **Ó hÉigceartaigh** 'descendant of *Éigceartach*', a byname meaning 'unjust'.

GIVEN NAMES Irish 6%. *Brendan* (4), *Connor, Delma, Dermod, Ethna, James Patrick, Liam, Michael Sean.*

Haggett (319) English: variant of HACKETT 2.

Haggins (277) Variant of Irish HIGGINS.

Hagglund (240) Swedish (**Hägglund**): ornamental name composed of the elements *hägg* 'bird cherry' + *lund* 'grove'.

GIVEN NAMES Scandinavian 15%; German 4%. *Erik* (2), *Alf, Lars, Niels; Kurt.*

Haggstrom (140) Swedish (**Häggström**): ornamental name composed of the elements *hägg* 'bird cherry' + *ström* 'river'.

GIVEN NAMES Scandinavian 12%; German 5%. *Lars* (2), *Erik, Olle; Kurt.*

Hagie (142) Scottish: variant of HEGGIE.

Hagin (356) **1.** Irish: variant spelling of HAGAN. **2.** Possibly a respelling of HAGEN.

Hagins (511) Origin uncertain. Perhaps an altered form of Irish HIGGINS.

Hagiwara (101) Japanese: 'bush clover plain', also pronounced *Hagihara*; both versions are found mostly in the Tōkyō area, and *Hagihara* is also found in the island of Okinawa.

GIVEN NAMES Japanese 80%. *Takeshi* (3), *Eiji* (2), *Tatsuo* (2), *Toshio* (2), *Toshiyuki* (2), *Yoshi* (2), *Chiaki, Haruo, Hideko, Hiroko, Hiroshi, Isamu.*

Hagle (305) German (**Hägle**): diminutive of HAGE.

Hagler (2009) German (also **Hägler**): topographic name for someone who lived by a hedge or enclosure, Middle High German *hac*, + the suffix *-er* denoting an inhabitant (compare DOERFLER), or a habitational name from a place named with this word.

Hagley (156) English: habitational name from either of two places, in Worcestershire and Somerset, named Hagley, from Old English *hagga* 'haw', 'berry' + *lēah* 'wood', 'glade'.

GIVEN NAME German 5%. *Kurt* (2).

Haglund (1080) Swedish: ornamental name composed of the elements *hag(e)* 'enclosure' + *lund* 'grove'. In America, there has probably been some confusion with HAGGLUND.

GIVEN NAMES Scandinavian 5%. *Erik* (2), *Alf, Bjorn, Knute, Nels, Per.*

Hagman (672) **1.** Swedish: ornamental or topographic name for someone who lived by an enclosure, from *hag(e)* 'enclosure' + *man* 'man'. **2.** Altered spelling of German HAGEMANN.

GIVEN NAMES Scandinavian 5%; German 4%. *Erland, Lennart, Per, Swen; Kurt* (2), *Hans.*

Hagmann (248) German: variant of HAGEMANN.

GIVEN NAMES French 6%; German 4%. *Patrice* (3); *Hans, Siegfried.*

Hagner (359) German (also **Hägner**): habitational name from any of numerous places named Hagen, for example in Westphalia.

Hagood (1379) Variant of English HAPGOOD. This is a common name in AL and TX.

Hagopian (753) Armenian: patronymic from the personal name *Hagop*, classical Armenian *Yako(v)b* (see JACOB).

GIVEN NAMES Armenian 28%. *Hagop* (17), *Haig* (6), *Sarkis* (6), *Aram* (5), *Nubar* (4), *Armen* (3), *Raffi* (3), *Vartkes* (3), *Zaven* (3), *Dikran* (2), *Noubar* (2), *Vahan* (2).

Hagos (132) Ethiopian: unexplained.

GIVEN NAMES Ethiopian 72%; Muslim 8%. *Alem* (3), *Almaz, Berhane* (3), *Berhe, Beyene* (2), *Afework, Asefaw, Azeb, Fikre, Fitsum, Genet, Getachew, Haddis, Kifle, Yonatan; Abdul, Jamal, Jemal, Mana, Said, Saleh.*

Hagstrom (1007) Swedish (**Hagström**): ornamental name formed with *hag(e)* 'enclosure' + *ström* 'river'. See also HAGGSTROM.

GIVEN NAMES Scandinavian 9%. *Erik* (4), *Lars, Anders, Mats, Nels, Nils.*

Hague (1978) **1.** English (mainly South Yorkshire): variant spelling of HAIGH or HAIG. **2.** Irish (County Cavan): variant spelling of HAIG.

Haguewood (112) Americanized form of Dutch **Hagewoud** (see HAGEWOOD).

Hagwood (318) **1.** English: possibly a variant of **Hackwood**, a habitational name from a minor place so named. One example, in Northamptonshire, is named from Middle English *hacked* 'cut' + *wode* 'wood'; another, in Basingstoke, Hampshire is named from Old English *haca* 'hook', 'bend' + *wudu* 'wood'. In the U.S. this name is frequent in NC. **2.** See HAGEWOOD 1.

Hagy (996) Probably an altered spelling of Swiss German **Hägi, Haegi, Hägy**, or **Hegi**, topographic names or, in the case of **Hegi**, also a habitational name derived from Middle High German *hac* 'briar hedge' or 'enclosure (for habitation)'. Compare HAGEY and HEAGY.

Hahl (138) German: habitational name from Hahl in Westphalia, Hahlen near Minden, or from a place on the Hahle river, all named with *hal* 'marsh', 'mire'.

Hahm (202) **1.** German: metonymic occupational name for a sealer of weights and measures, from Middle High German *hāme* '(standard) measure'. **2.** Korean: variant of HAM.

GIVEN NAMES Korean 21%. *Sung* (2), *Yong* (2), *Byung, Chang, Dong, Hyun, Jae, Jee, Jong, Jong Hun, Jong Hyun, Moon Hee, Jung Suk, Sang, Seok, Seung, Soon, Sungtae, Taeyong.*

Hahn (16939) **1.** German: from Middle High German *hane* 'rooster', hence a nickname for a conceited or sexually active man. In some instances it may have been a habitational name from a house bearing the sign of a rooster. **2.** German: patronymic from a reduced form of the personal name *Johannes* (see JOHN). This surname is also found in Denmark and Sweden. **3.** Jewish (Ashkenazic): ornamental name from German *Hahn* 'rooster', one of the many Ashkenazic surnames based on vocabulary words denoting birds or animals.

Hahne (417) German (also **Hähne**): from a short form of the personal name *Johannes* (see JOHN).

GIVEN NAMES German 6%. *Lutz* (3), *Friedrich, Jutta, Wolfgang.*

Hahner (127) **1.** South German: occupational name for a poultry farmer, from an agent derivative of Middle High German *hane* 'rooster'. **2.** German: habitational name for someone from any of several places called Hahn or Hag. **3.** German (**Hähner**): see HAENER.

Hahs (229) German: variant spelling of HASS.

Hai (132) **1.** Muslim: from a personal name based on Arabic *hayy* 'alive'. Al-Hayy, 'the Living', is one of the attributes of Allah. **2.** Chinese 海: from the name of Hai Qun, a senior minister from the state of Wei during the Spring and Autumn period (722–481 BC). The character for this name also means

'ocean'. **3.** Vietnamese: unexplained. **4.** Jewish (Israeli): ornamental name from Hebrew *chai* 'alive', 'vivid'.

GIVEN NAMES Muslim 32%; Vietnamese 15%; Jewish 5%. *Abdul* (8), *Syed* (2), *Arifa, Atta, Faiz, Hamid, Iftekhar, Iskandar, Mohamed, Mohammad, Mohannad; Mui* (2), *Pham* (2), *Tran* (2), *Vo* (2), *Bui, Cao, Chau, Dinh, Duong, Nguyen, Sau, Vo Van; Ilan, Ronen, Shlomo; Chan, Chiming, Lung, Wai Fun, Yin.*

Haid (322) South German: variant of HEID.

Haidar (115) Muslim: from a personal name based on Arabic *haidar* 'lion'. This was an epithet of ʿAlī ibn Abi Talib, fourth of the 'rightly guided' khalifs (ruled 656–61), the first imam of the Shiite Muslims.

GIVEN NAMES Muslim 67%. *Ali* (8), *Hassan* (3), *Mohammad* (3), *Ahmad* (2), *Hani* (2), *Khalil* (2), *Mohamad* (2), *Nabil* (2), *Adiba, Ahmed, Akram, Amir.*

Haider (793) **1.** Muslim: variant spelling of HAIDAR. **2.** South German: habitational name for someone from a place called Haid, or a topographic name for someone who lived on a heath (see HEID).

GIVEN NAMES Muslim 34%. *Syed* (31), *Ghulam* (8), *Ali* (5), *Mohammad* (5), *Mohammed* (4), *Sayed* (4), *Ahmad* (3), *Muhammad* (3), *Nadeem* (3), *Sajjad* (3), *Salman* (3), *Abbas* (2).

Haidet (141) Origin unidentified, probably French. This name is concentrated in OH.

Haidle (115) **1.** South German: variant of HEIDEL. In this spelling, the name is associated with a family of 19th-century German settlers in Russia. **2.** English (Gloucestershire): unexplained.

Haifley (102) Americanized spelling of South German HAEFELE or **Höfle**, see HOEFLE.

Haig (581) **1.** Scottish (of Norman origin): habitational name from any of various places in northern France named with Old Norse *hagi* 'enclosure', a word with cognates in most Germanic languages. Compare HAY. **2.** English: variant spelling of HAIGH. **3.** Irish (County Cavan): reduced Anglicized form of Gaelic **Mac Thaidhg** (see MCCAIG).

FOREBEARS The Scottish Borders family of Haig were Normans from La Hague in Manche, Normandy. Their first ancestor in Scotland was Petrus del Hage, whose name appears on documents of the 1160s. The direct line died out in 1867 and the ancestral manor of Bemersyde passed into other hands, but in 1921 it was purchased by the nation and presented to Field Marshal Sir Douglas Haig (1861–1928), who had been created 1st Earl Haig in 1919.

Haigh (1165) English (chiefly Yorkshire): topographic name for someone who lived by a hedged or fenced enclosure (Old English *haga*), or a habitational name from a place named with this word (or its Old

Norse cognate *hagi*), especially three places called Haigh, two in West Yorkshire and the other near Manchester.

Haight (2676) English: topographic name for someone who lived at the top of a hill (see HIGHT).

Haigler (832) Americanized spelling of German **Hägler** (see HAGLER).

Haigwood (126) Americanized form of Dutch **Hagewoud** (see HAGEWOOD).

Haik (216) **1.** Jewish (Ashkenazic): unexplained. **2.** Arabic (**Hā'ik**): occupational name for a weaver.
GIVEN NAMES Jewish 4%. *Meyer, Yossi.*

Hail (594) **1.** English: nickname from Old Norse *heill* 'healthy', 'sound', 'whole'. **2.** South German: variant of HEIL.

Haile (1500) **1.** Scottish and northern English: variant spelling of HALE 1. **2.** English: variant spelling of HAIL.
GIVEN NAMES Ethiopian 15%. *Lemlem* (4), *Senait* (4), *Bereket* (3), *Seifu* (3), *Abrehet* (2), *Amanuel* (2), *Berhane* (2), *Dawit* (2), *Dehab* (2), *Fekade* (2), *Fekadu* (2), *Hagos* (2).

Hailes (144) **1.** Scottish: habitational name from Hailes in Lothian, originally in East Lothian, named from the Middle English genitive or plural form of *hall* 'hall'. **2.** English: habitational name from Hailes in Gloucestershire, which is named from an old British river name meaning 'polluted'. Compare Welsh *halog* 'dirty'. **3.** English: variant spelling of HALES.

Hailey (2408) English: habitational name from places in Oxfordshire and Hertfordshire named Hailey, from Old English *hēg* 'hay' + *lēeah* 'wood', '(woodland) clearing'.

Hails (173) English and Scottish: variant spelling of HAILES.

Hailstone (106) English: habitational name from Hailstone Hill in Wiltshire or Hailstone Farm in Gloucestershire.

Hailu (151) Ethiopian: unexplained.
GIVEN NAMES Ethiopian 67%; African 6%. *Girma* (3), *Abiy* (2), *Alem* (2), *Aynalem* (2), *Tewodros* (2), *Wondwossen* (2), *Abate*, *Abeba*, *Abraha*, *Alemu*, *Amha*, *Araya*; *Almaz.*

Haim (135) **1.** Jewish: variant of HEIM. **2.** French: topographic name from Old French *haim* 'homestead', 'hamlet', 'settlement' (cognate with Old English *ham*).
GIVEN NAMES Jewish 10%; French 6%. *Dror, Haim, Mazal, Mendel, Shimon, Yitzhak; Alain, Jacques, Marcel.*

Haimes (176) **1.** English: patronymic from the Norman personal name *Hamo* (see HAMMOND). **2.** Jewish: Americanized form of some like-sounding Jewish name.
GIVEN NAMES Jewish 5%. *Miriam, Yacov, Yosef.*

Haimowitz (123) Jewish (eastern Ashkenazic): patronymic from the Yiddish personal name *Khayim* (from Hebrew *chayim* 'life').

GIVEN NAMES Jewish 9%; German 4%. *Azriel, Hyman; Frieda.*

Hain (1087) **1.** English: habitational name from any of various places named with Middle English *heghen*, a weak plural of *hegh*, from Old English *(ge)hæg* 'enclosure'. See also HAYNES. **2.** English: from the Middle English personal name *Hain*, *Heyne*. This is derived from the Germanic personal name *Hagano*, originally a byname meaning 'hawthorn'. It is found in England before the Conquest, but was popularized by the Normans. In the Danelaw, it may be derived from Old Norse *Hagni*, *Hǫgni* (see HAGAN), a Scandinavianized version of the same name. **3.** English: nickname for a wretched individual, from Middle English *hain(e)*, *heyne* 'wretch', 'niggard'. **4.** German: topographic name for someone who lived by a patch of enclosed pastureland, Middle High German *hage(n)* (see HAGEN 1), *hain*, or a habitational name from a place named Hain, from this word. **5.** German: from the Germanic personal name *Hagin*, originally a byname from the same element as in 2 above. **6.** Jewish (eastern Ashkenazic): metronymic from the Yiddish personal name *Khaye* 'life' + the Slavic possessive suffix *-in*.

Haine (128) English and German: variant spelling of HAIN.
GIVEN NAME French 6%. *Michel.*

Hainer (221) South German: from the Germanic personal name *Haginher*, composed of the elements *hag* 'hedge', 'enclosure' + *hari*, *heri* 'army'.

Haines (11562) English and Irish: variant spelling of HAYNES.

Hainey (230) **1.** Irish: variant of HEANEY. **2.** Americanized form of German or Dutch HEINE.

Hainley (203) Americanized spelling of German HEINLE.

Hainline (458) Americanized spelling of German HEINLEIN.

Hains (401) English: variant spelling of HAYNES.
FOREBEARS Two brothers of this name were captured in New England by the French; one was married at Ange-Gardien, Quebec, in 1710.
GIVEN NAMES French 4%. *Andre* (2), *Monique, Nolton.*

Hainsworth (273) English (common in West Yorkshire): **1.** habitational name from Hainworth in West Yorkshire, named from the Old English personal name *Hagena* + Old English *worð* 'enclosure'. **2.** habitational name from Ainsworth in Lancashire, from the Old English personal name *Ægen* + *worð* 'enclosure'. Names such as *de Haynesworth* and *de Heynesworth* occur in the surrounding area in the 14th century.

Hair (2822) **1.** Scottish spelling of Irish HARE. **2.** English: nickname for someone

with some peculiarity of the hair, from Middle English *here* 'hair'.

Haire (2029) Northern Irish: variant spelling of HARE.

Hairell (100) Variant spelling of English or Irish HARRELL.

Hairfield (241) English: probably a variant of **Harefield**, a habitational name from a place so named, for example the one Greater London or Harefield in Selling, Kent, which are both apparently named from Old English *here* 'army' + *feld* 'open country'.

Hairgrove (154) Probably an altered form of the English habitational name HARGROVE.

Hairr (188) **1.** Variant spelling of Irish or English HARE or of English HAIR. **2.** Perhaps an Americanized spelling of German HERR.

Hairrell (113) Variant spelling of English or Irish HARRELL.

Hairston (3694) Scottish: habitational name from a place named Harestone or Harestane. The surname has died out in Scotland.

Haisch (117) South German: from a short form of a Germanic personal name beginning with *heid* 'heath'.
GIVEN NAMES German 8%. *Klaus, Manfred.*

Haisler (94) German: variant spelling of HEISLER.

Haisley (192) English and northern Irish: variant spelling of HAZLEY.

Haislip (645) Probably a variant of Scottish HYSLOP.

Haist (243) **1.** Probably a variant of German HEIST. **2.** English (Yorkshire): possibly a reduced form of HAYHURST. See also HAST.
GIVEN NAMES German 4%. *Erwin, Gernot.*

Haisten (178) **1.** English (Cumbria): possibly a habitational name from a place named Hayston, examples of which are found in Strathclyde, Tayside, and Dyfed, or from Haystoun near Peebles in the Scottish Borders. **2.** Dutch: variant spelling of HASTEN.

Hait (169) **1.** Jewish: variant spelling of CHAIT. **2.** French: nickname from Old French *haid* 'joy', 'gladness'.
GIVEN NAMES Jewish 9%. *Hyman* (3), *Gershon, Miriam, Sol.*

Haith (346) English (Lincolnshire): variant spelling of HEATH.

Haithcock (413) Variant spelling of English HEATHCOCK.

Haitz (112) German: variant of HEITZ.

Haizlip (153) American variant spelling of Scottish HYSLOP.

Hajdu (175) Hungarian (**Hajdú**): from *hajtó* 'drover'. Drovers traveled armed, and sometimes ended up as highwaymen, mercenaries, or retainers in the service of local landowners. *Hajdú* acquired all these

meanings, but the surname is chiefly associated with the settlement of some 10,000 mercenaries in eastern Hungary by Prince István Bocskay as a reward for their support. Their towns, dating from 1605, still retain *Hajdú-* as a first element. The name is also borne by Hungarian Jews, generally as an ornamental adoption of the Hungarian name.
GIVEN NAMES Hungarian 13%. *Istvan* (3), *Aladar, Bela, Erzsebet, Karoly, Katalin, Laszlo, Sandor.*

Hajduk (369) Polish: occupational name for a drover, from a term borrowed from Hungarian (see HAJDU), which was also used to denote a Hungarian foot soldier in the Polish army in the 16th century.
GIVEN NAMES Polish 8%. *Casimir* (2), *Bogdan, Czeslaw, Krzysztof, Malgorzata, Mariusz, Michalina, Miroslaw, Zbigniew.*

Hajec (110) Czech (**Hájec**): variant of HAJEK.

Hajek (897) Czech (**Hájek**): **1.** occupational name for a woodman or topographic name for someone who lived by a thicket or grove, from Czech *hájek* 'thicket', from *háj* 'grove', or directly from *háj* 'grove', the diminutive suffix *-ek* being added in forming the surname. **2.** occupational name for a keeper of animals (a herd), especially one who looked after horses (an ostler), from *hájit* 'to protect', 'to defend'.
GIVEN NAMES German 4%. *Otto* (5), *Hans* (3), *Elke, Klaus, Monika.*

Hajjar (406) Arabic: occupational name from *hajjar* 'stonemason'.
GIVEN NAMES Arabic 20%; French 6%. *Abdulla* (2), *Fadi* (2), *Fareed* (2), *Fawaz* (2), *Naji* (2), *Sami* (2), *Waleed* (2), *Ahmad, Amer, Atallah, Aysha, Aziz; Fabien* (2), *Antoine, Emile, Germaine, Jean-Jacques, Michel, Serge.*

Hajny (134) Czech (**Hajný**): occupational name for a woodman or a gamekeeper, a derivative of *háj* 'grove'.
GIVEN NAME German 5%. *Otto* (2).

Hajovsky (116) Czech (**Hájovský**): habitational name for someone from any of various places named with *hájek* 'thicket'.

Hak (116) **1.** Dutch: variant spelling of HAACK. **2.** Swedish: unexplained. **3.** Southeast Asian: unexplained.
GIVEN NAMES Southeast Asian 11%. *Seng* (2), *Chea, Heng, Hok, Meng, Song.*

Hakala (596) Finnish: topographic or ornamental name from *haka* 'pasture', 'paddock' + the local suffix *-la. Haka* is a common element of Finnish place names. It was widely adopted as an ornamental surname during the name conversion movement in the 19th and early 20th centuries, especially in western Finland.
GIVEN NAMES Finnish 6%. *Reino* (3), *Toivo* (3), *Eino, Esa, Esko, Jukka, Oiva, Onni, Pentti, Sirpa, Wilho.*

Hakanson (303) Swedish (**Håkansson,**

Håkanson): patronymic from the personal name *Håkan* (see HAAGENSEN).
GIVEN NAMES Scandinavian 10%. *Lennart* (2), *Thor* (2), *Alf, Erik, Nils, Sten.*

Hake (1329) **1.** English: from the Old Norse byname *Haki* (cognate with HOOK), given originally to someone with a hunched figure or a hooked nose. **2.** North German: variant of HAACK. **3.** Dutch and North German: from the Germanic personal name *Hac(c)o*, a short form of a compound name beginning with the element *hag* 'hedge', 'enclosure'. **4.** Jewish (Ashkenazic): variant spelling of HACKE.

Hakeem (104) Muslim: see HAKIM.
GIVEN NAMES Muslim 40%. *Abdul, Ahmed, Atiya, Ayesha, Azim, Aziz, Bassam, Dirar, Ehab, Habibah, Hasan, Kareem.*

Haken (112) South German: variant of HAACK 1.
GIVEN NAMES German 18%. *Ernst, Franz, Gerhard, Wolfgang.*

Haker (130) **1.** North German: occupational name from Middle Low German *hoker* 'peddler', 'hawker'. **2.** Jewish (Ashkenazic): variant spelling of HACKER.

Hakes (939) English: patronymic from HAKE 1.

Hakey (114) English: unexplained.

Hakim (722) Muslim: from a personal name based on Arabic *hakīm* 'learned', 'wise'. *Al-Hakīm* 'the All-Wise' is an attribute of Allah. It may also be a status name from the Arabic noun *hākim* 'governor', 'judge', 'scholar' or Persian *haekim* 'wise man', 'philosopher', or 'physician'. In the Indian subcontinent it generally denotes a physician, in particular one specializing in traditional herbal remedies. *Al-Hākim* 'the Judge' is also an attribute of Allah.
GIVEN NAMES Muslim 42%; French 4%. *Abdul* (8), *Ali* (4), *Karim* (4), *Mohamad* (4), *Ashfaq* (3), *Khalil* (3), *Mohammed Abdul* (3), *Adnan* (2), *Akber* (2), *Bilal* (2), *Faiz* (2), *Hussein* (2); *Jacques* (3), *Camille* (2), *Alain, Andre, Eugenie, Henri.*

Hakimi (205) Arabic and Iranian: from an adjectival derivative of HAKIM.
GIVEN NAMES Muslim 64%. *Bijan* (3), *Changiz* (3), *Mansour* (3), *Mansoor* (2), *Mehdi* (2), *Mitra* (2), *Moussa* (2), *Abdul Rahman, Afsaneh, Ahmad, Alireza, Aslam.*

Hakimian (162) Armenian and Iranian: patronymic from an occupational name for a physician, Turkish *hakim*, or judge, Turkish *hâkim*, both of Arabic origin (see HAKIM). In the Ottoman Empire many Armenians were physicians.
GIVEN NAMES Muslim 53%; Armenian 6%. *Afshin* (2), *Bijan* (2), *Ebrahim* (2), *Roozbeh* (2), *Abdol, Abrahim, Afsaneh, Ali, Amir, Davoud, Ezatollah, Farrokh; Hagop, Kevork, Krikor, Maral, Vahan, Varoujan.*

Hakola (126) Finnish: habitational name from a farmstead so called, probably named with western Finnish dialect *hako* 'spruce branch' + the local ending *-la.*

However, in some cases, the element *Hako* may be from a Germanic personal name.

Halabi (102) Arabic: habitational name from Arabic *Halabī*, adjectival derivative of *Halab* 'Aleppo', a city in Syria.
GIVEN NAMES Arabic 65%; French 4%. *Samir* (4), *Ali* (3), *Walid* (3), *Abdullah* (2), *Khaled* (2), *Marwan* (2), *Mohamad* (2), *Moussa* (2), *Nadim* (2), *Oussama* (2), *Abdallah, Abed; Emile, Michel.*

Halaby (125) Muslim: see HALABI.
GIVEN NAMES Muslim 33%. *Fouad* (2), *Hussam* (2), *Jamil* (2), *Shukri* (2), *Ahmed, Assad, Fadi, Issam, Jalal, Kasim, Nabil, Naim.*

Halama (190) Polish and Czech: unflattering nickname meaning 'big, lumbering fellow', 'lout'.

Halas (350) **1.** Czech and Polish (**Hałas**): nickname for a noisy person, from Czech *halas* 'uproar', Polish *hałas* 'noise'. **2.** Respelling, especially in eastern Slovenia, of Hungarian **Halász** 'fisherman' (see HALASZ).

Halasz (264) Hungarian (**Halász**): occupational name for a fisherman, from *hal* 'fish' + the occupational suffix *-ász.*
GIVEN NAMES Hungarian 14%. *Sandor* (4), *Laszlo* (3), *Imre* (2), *Istvan, Jozsef, Karoly, Laszio, Tibor, Zoltan.*

Halbach (434) **1.** German: topographic name from *hal* 'marsh', 'mire' + *bach* 'stream'. **2.** Dutch and German: habitational name from any of three places called Halbach, near Remscheid, North Rhine-Westphalia.
GIVEN NAMES German 5%. *Klaus* (2), *Alois, Hans, Kurt, Otto.*

Halberg (415) **1.** German: habitational name from two places called Halberg, one near Braunschweig, the other in Swabia. **2.** Swedish: variant of HALLBERG. **3.** Jewish (Ashkenazic): unexplained.

Halberstadt (285) German: habitational name from any of various places so named, notably the city near Magdeburg and Halberstadt near Königstein in Saxony.
GIVEN NAMES German 6%. *Kurt* (2), *Ernst, Hans, Manfred, Ullman.*

Halberstam (154) Jewish (eastern Ashkenazic): ornamental form of a habitational name from the town of Halberstadt in Saxony. The last syllable was replaced with German *Stamm* 'trunk'.
GIVEN NAMES Jewish 53%. *Chaim* (14), *Baruch* (6), *Benzion* (6), *Sinai* (6), *Naftali* (3), *Aron* (2), *Shlomo* (2), *Yitzchok* (2), *Alter, Arie, Boruch, Chana.*

Halbert (1724) **1.** Scottish: of uncertain origin. One suggestion is that it is an occupational name for a soldier who used a halberd (see 2); another is that it may be from a Scandinavian personal name. **2.** French: metonymic occupational name for a maker of halberds and similar weapons, from Old French *hallebarte* 'halberd' (ultimately from Middle High German *helmbarde*, from *helm* 'handle' + *barde* 'hatchet').

Halbig (171) German: from the medieval personal name *Heilwig*, *Helwig* (see HELWIG).

GIVEN NAMES German 9%. *Wolfgang* (2), *Alois*, *Bernhard*.

Halbleib (171) German: metonymic occupational name for a baker, meaning 'half-loaf', from a tax levy of this amount.

Halbrook (614) English: variant of HOLBROOK.

Halbrooks (200) English: variant of HOLBROOK.

Halbur (262) German: a variant or altered spelling of **Halbauer** or HALLBAUER, a status name for a farmer who owed half of the proceeds of his land in rent, from *halb* 'half' + *Bauer* 'farmer'. See HALLBAUER. This surname occurs chiefly in IA.

Halcomb (1222) English: variant of HOLCOMB, probably specifically from Halcombe in Wiltshire.

Hald (154) South German and Danish: topographic name for someone living near or on a slope, from Middle High German *halde*, Danish *hall* 'slope', or a habitational name from any of several places in Denmark named from this word.

GIVEN NAMES Scandinavian 9%. *Bent*, *Borge*, *Torleif*.

Haldane (162) **1.** Scottish and English: from an old personal name, Old Norse *Halfdanr*, Old Danish *Halfdan*, Anglo-Scandinavian *Healfdene*, meaning 'half-Dane'. **2.** Scottish: variant of HOWDEN.

Haldeman (1252) Southern German (**Haldemann**): topographic name for someone who lived on a mountainside or slope, from Middle High German *halde* 'slope' + *man(n)* 'man'.

Halden (110) English and Scottish: variant of HALDANE.

Halder (236) **1.** German: topographic name for someone who lived on a mountainside or slope, from an agent derivative of Middle High German *halde* 'slope'. **2.** Indian (Bengal) and Bangladeshi: Hindu (usually, Brahman) name, also written **Haldar**. It is probably derived from Sanskrit *haladhara* 'one who holds a plow', an epithet of Balarama, the brother of the god Krishna. Balarama is said to have used a weapon shaped like a plowshare.

GIVEN NAMES Indian 8%; German 4%. *Amit*, *Anup*, *Narayan*, *Purna*, *Ratan*, *Tapan*; *Kurt* (2).

Halderman (419) German (**Haldermann**): **1.** variant of HALDEMAN. **2.** variant of **Haltermann** (see HALTERMAN).

Haldiman (130) Swiss German (**Haldimann**): variant of HALDEMAN.

Haldorson (100) Scandinavian: patronymic from the personal name *Haldor*.

GIVEN NAMES Scandinavian 14%. *Helmer*, *Obert*.

Hale (30486) **1.** English (also well established in South Wales): topographic name for someone who lived in a nook or hollow, from Old English and Middle English *hale*, dative of *h(e)alh* 'nook', 'hollow'. In northern England the word often has a specialized meaning, denoting a piece of flat alluvial land by the side of a river, typically one deposited in a bend. In southeastern England it often referred to a patch of dry land in a fen. In some cases the surname may be a habitational name from any of several places in England named with this fossilized inflected form, which would originally have been preceded by a preposition, e.g. *in the hale* or *at the hale*. **2.** English: from a Middle English personal name derived from either of two Old English bynames, *Hæle* 'hero' or *Hægel*, which is probably akin to Germanic *Hagano* 'hawthorn' (see HAIN 2). **3.** Irish: reduced Anglicized form of Gaelic **Mac Céile** (see MCHALE). **4.** Jewish (Ashkenazic): variant spelling of HALLE.

FOREBEARS Robert Hale, who settled in Cambridge, MA, in 1632, was an ancestor of the revolutionary war patriot and spy Nathan Hale (1755–76) of CT. The common English surname was brought independently in the 17th century to VA and MD.

Halek (104) Czech (**Hálek**): from the personal name *Hálek*, pet form of HAVEL.

Halen (112) Dutch: patronymic from a short form of a Germanic personal name formed with the element *had(u)* 'battle', 'strife'.

Haler (124) **1.** English: possibly an occupational name for a porter or carrier, from an agent derivative of Middle English *hailen* 'to haul', 'to drag', from Old French *haler* 'to pull'. **2.** Slovenian: variant spelling of German HALLER.

Hales (2991) **1.** English (widespread, especially in the southeast): from the genitive singular or nominative plural form of Old English *halh* 'nook', 'recess' (see HALE). **2.** Irish: when not of English origin, this may be a variant of HEALY or MCHALE.

Haley (13929) English (chiefly West Yorkshire): habitational name from any of several places named with Old English *hēg* 'hay' + *lēah* 'wood', 'clearing'.

Halfacre (360) English: habitational name from Halfacre in Northill, Cornwall, or a topographic name for someone who lived on a holding of a half acre of land.

Halferty (226) Irish: Anglicized form of Gaelic **Ó hAilbheartaigh** 'descendant of *Ailbeartach*', a personal name or byname probably derived from *ilbeartach* 'accomplished'.

Halfhill (306) Americanized form of German HALBERG, wrongly assumed to be from German *halb* 'half' + *Berg* 'hill'.

Halfman (153) Respelling of German HALFMANN.

Halfmann (401) North German: status

name denoting the tenant of a farm who paid half of its produce in rent.

GIVEN NAMES German 6%. *Dieter* (2), *Kurt* (2), *Erwin*, *Hans*, *Hartmut*, *Otto*.

Halfon (126) Jewish (Sephardic): occupational name for a moneychanger, from Hebrew.

GIVEN NAMES Jewish 14%; Spanish 6%; French 5%. *Sol* (3), *Uri* (3), *Moshe* (2), *Haim*, *Isak*, *Miriam*, *Zohar*; *Roberto* (2), *Eduardo*, *Juanita*, *Ramon*; *Jacques* (2).

Halford (1291) English (chiefly Midlands): habitational name from any of various places called Halford. Most, for example those in Warwickshire and Shropshire, are named from Old English *halh* 'nook', 'recess' + *ford* 'ford'.

Halfpenny (108) English: nickname probably for a tenant whose feudal obligations included a regular payment in cash or kind (for example bread or salt) of a halfpenny.

Halgren (174) Swedish: variant spelling of HALLGREN.

GIVEN NAMES Scandinavian 6%. *Nels*, *Sven*, *Thor*.

Haliburton (268) Scottish: see HALLIBURTON. This is a common name in TX.

Halicki (116) Polish: habitational name from a place called Halicz, now in Ukraine.

GIVEN NAMES Polish 22%. *Zygmunt* (2), *Dariusz*, *Halina*, *Henryk*, *Jadwiga*, *Janucz*, *Janusz*, *Jaroslaw*, *Katarzyna*, *Wlodzimierz*, *Zdzislaw*.

Halik (162) Czech (**Halík**): from a personal name, a pet form of HAVEL.

Halim (222) Muslim: from a personal name based on Arabic *halīm* 'patient', 'tolerant'. *Al-Halīm* 'the Forgiving' is an attribute of Allah.

GIVEN NAMES Muslim 53%. *Abdul* (14), *Abbas* (2), *Amin* (2), *Mohammad* (2), *Omar* (2), *Samir* (2), *Afifa*, *Ahmed*, *Arif*, *Ashraf*, *Aslam*, *Chaudhary*.

Haling (137) German **1.** (**Häling**): nickname for a secretive person, from Middle High German *hælinc* 'secret'. **2.** a short form of the personal name *Alexander*.

Halk (115) Hungarian: nickname from *halk* 'quiet'.

Halker (142) English and Scottish: unexplained; possibly a variant spelling of HAWKER.

Halkias (129) Greek: occupational name for a coppersmith, classical Greek *khalkeus*.

GIVEN NAMES Greek 16%. *Constantine* (2), *Antonios*, *Demetrios*, *Dimos*, *Ioannis*, *Pericles*, *Vassilios*.

Halko (280) Finnish: from *halko* 'split log', probably acquired as a nickname by a proficient log splitter.

Hall (166370) English, Scottish, Irish, German, and Scandinavian: from Middle English *hall* (Old English *heall*), Middle High German *halle*, Old Norse *hǫll* all meaning 'hall' (a spacious residence), hence a topographic name for someone who lived in or near a hall or an occupational name for a servant employed at a hall. In some cases it may be a habitational name from places named with this word, which in some parts of Germany and Austria in the Middle Ages also denoted a salt mine. The English name has been established in Ireland since the Middle Ages, and, according to MacLysaght, has become numerous in Ulster since the 17th century. FOREBEARS Hall is one of the commonest and most widely distributed of English surnames, bearing witness to the importance of the hall as a feature of the medieval village. John Hall, an Englishman born in Kent in 1584 who emigrated to New England in 1632, founded a notable American family, whose members have included Lyman Hall (1724–90), politician and one of the signers of the Declaration of Independence; Asaph Hall (1829–1907), astronomer, who discovered the two satellites of Mars; and Stanley Hall (1844–1924), pioneer in psychophysics. Another John Hall emigrated to America in about 1652, settling in MA. His descendants include Charles M. Hall (1863–1914), who invented a process for the mass production of aluminum. A certain David Hall, born in Edinburgh around 1714, became a partner of Benjamin Franklin's in the printing business.

Halla (231) **1.** Finnish: topographic name from *halla* 'frost', by extension 'fallow field'. This name is found mainly in northern Finland (Ostrobothnia and Kainuu). It is also found as an ornamental name, adopted by Finns with Swedish names during the name conversion movement in the 19th and early 20th centuries. **2.** Finnish: from an old personal name of Germanic origin. **3.** Variant of German HALLE (see HALL), found in France, Austria, Bohemia, and elsewhere.

Hallada (146) Perhaps an altered spelling of Scottish and English HALLIDAY.

Halladay (613) Scottish and English: variant of HOLLIDAY.

Hallahan (514) Irish: Anglicized form of Gaelic *Ó hÁilleacháin* 'descendant of *Áilleachán*', a personal name from a diminutive of *áille* 'beauty'. This Cork surname is sometimes confused with HALLIGAN, an Ulster surname.

Hallal (112) Muslim: from the Arabic epithet *hallal* 'solver', 'resolver'.
GIVEN NAMES Muslim 11%. *Nadim* (3), *Abeer, Ezzat, Issam, Samir, Tarek.*

Hallam (1108) English (chiefly southern Yorkshire and East Midlands): regional name from the district in southern Yorkshire around Sheffield and Ecclesfield called Hallam, or a habitational name from a place of this name in Derbyshire. The Derbyshire name is from Old English *halum*, dative plural of *halh* 'nook', 'recess' (see HALE 1). The Yorkshire district, sometimes called *Hallamshire*, is possibly

of the same derivation or alternatively from *hallum*, dative plural of Old English *hall* 'stone', 'rock', Old Norse *hallr*.

Hallas (385) **1.** Greek: probably from Turkish *halâs* 'exemption', a status name for someone who was exempt from payment of rent or taxes. **2.** English (Yorkshire): variant of HOLLOWS. **3.** Possibly an altered spelling of Czech **Halas**, a nickname for a noisy person, from *halas* 'uproar', from *halasit* 'to be noisy'.
GIVEN NAMES Greek 4%. *Spiro* (3), *Basilios, Constantine, Spyros.*

Hallauer (162) South German: habitational name for someone from Hallau near Schaffhausen.

Hallaway (110) English: variant of **Alaway**, from the Old English personal name *Æðelwīg*, composed of the elements *æðel* 'noble' + *wīg* 'war'.

Hallbauer (100) German: occupational name from Middle High German *halp* 'half' + *būre* 'farmer', denoting a farmer who farmed only half of a holding or who paid half the produce of his land in rent.
GIVEN NAMES German 9%. *Gerhard, Klaus, Otto.*

Hallberg (1081) **1.** Swedish: ornamental or topographic name composed of the elements *häll* 'stone', 'rock' or *hall* 'hall' + *berg* 'hill'. **2.** North German: variant of HALBERG.
GIVEN NAMES Scandinavian 6%. *Erik* (4), *Lars* (2), *Johan, Per, Sven, Swen.*

Halldorson (112) Norwegian: patronymic from the personal name *Halldor*.

Halle (660) **1.** German: variant of HALL. **2.** French (also **Hallé**): topographic name from Old French *halle*, 'covered market', from *halla* 'covered room'. **3.** Dutch and Belgian (**van Halle**): habitational name from places in Belgium named Halle (Brabant, Antwerp), Hal in North Brabant, or Hall and Halle in Gelderland. **4.** Jewish (Ashkenazic): habitational name from the city of Halle, in Saxony, Germany.
GIVEN NAMES French 8%. *Rejean* (3), *Marcel* (2), *Andre, Arianne, Armand, Camille, Fernand, Gaspard, Laurent.*

Halleck (297) German: of uncertain origin; a topographic name from the Brunswick area (Lower Saxony) along with other *Hall*-compound names or possibly a habitational name from a place named with Middle High German *ecke* 'corner'.

Hallee (144) Respelling of French **Hallé** (see HALLE).
GIVEN NAMES French 15%. *Alain* (2), *Armand, Fernand, Henri, Napoleon, Renald, Urbain.*

Hallen (306) **1.** Swedish (**Hallén**): variant of HALL, with the addition of the adjectival suffix *-én*. **2.** Possibly a shortened form of Dutch **van der Hallen**, a topographic or habitational name from Middle Dutch *halle* 'hall' (see HALL).

GIVEN NAMES Scandinavian 7%. *Erik* (2), *Thor.*

Hallenbeck (808) Dutch and North German: probably a habitational name from *Halenbeck* in Mecklenburg, or a similarly named place elsewhere.
FOREBEARS This name is recorded in Beverwijck in New Netherland (Albany, NY) in the mid 17th century.

Haller (4071) **1.** German and English: topographic name for someone who lived or worked at a hall. from HALL + the suffix *-er* denoting an inhabitant. **2.** Swiss German: topographic name, a variant of HALTER 1. **3.** German: variant of HELLER 1.
GIVEN NAMES German 4%. *Kurt* (9), *Hans* (7), *Otto* (4), *Franz* (2), *Gunther* (2), *Juergen* (2), *Ulrich* (2), *Bernhard, Erwin, Guenther, Heinrich, Heinz.*

Halleran (196) Irish: variant of HALLORAN.

Hallet (176) English: variant spelling of HALLETT.
GIVEN NAME French 4%. *Jean-Pierre* (2).

Hallett (2148) English (mainly Somerset and Devon): from the Norman personal name *Hallet* or *Aylett*, pet forms of *Aylard* (see ALLARD).

Halley (1738) **1.** Scottish: habitational name from a place the location of which is disputed. Black gives two Scottish options, the first with no explanation, the second being Halley in Deerness, Orkney. Modern Scottish bearers may well get it from the Irish names (see 3 and 4 below). **2.** English: in part possibly a habitational name from Hawley in Hampshire, named from Old English *heall* 'hall', 'large house' + *lēah* 'woodland clearing'. **3.** Irish (Counties Waterford and Tipperary): shortened Anglicized form of Gaelic *Ó hAilche* 'descendant of *Ailche*', possibly from the byname *Ailchú* meaning 'gentle hound'. In some cases **Halley** has been used to replace MULHALL. **4.** Irish (County Clare): shortened Anglicized form of Gaelic *Ó hÁille* 'descendant of *Áille*', apparently from *áille* 'beauty', but possibly a variant of *Ó hÁinle* (see HANLEY).

Hallford (581) English: variant spelling of HALFORD.

Hallgren (496) Swedish: **1.** ornamental name formed with *hall* 'stone', 'rock', 'hall' + *gren* 'branch'. **2.** (**Hällgren**): ornamental compound name composed of the elements *häll* 'rock' + *gren* 'branch'.
GIVEN NAMES Scandinavian 8%; German 4%. *Sven* (2), *Nels, Odvar, Swen; Otto* (2), *Hans, Kurt.*

Halliburton (932) Scottish: habitational name from Haliburton in Berwickshire.

Halliday (1861) Scottish and northern English: variant of HOLLADAY. Halliday is also found in Ireland, where it is of English origin. Black notes that Scottish bearers of the name took it to France, where they became Viscounts of Pontaudemer.

Halligan (1286) Irish: shortened Anglicized form of Gaelic **Ó hÁil(l)eagáin** 'descendant of *Áil(l)eagán*', a double diminutive of *áille* 'beauty'. There has been confusion between this Ulster surname and HALLAHAN.

GIVEN NAMES Irish 7%. *Brendan, Clancy, Liam, John Patrick.*

Hallin (313) **1.** Swedish: ornamental name composed of the elements *hall* (see HALL) + the suffix *-in*, derived from Latin *-in(i)us* 'descendant of'. **2.** Irish: shortened Anglicized form of Gaelic **Ó hAilín** 'descendant of *Ailín*', a personal name of uncertain origin, perhaps a diminutive from *ail* 'noble', 'rock'.

GIVEN NAMES Scandinavian 5%. *Bjorn, Kjersten, Nels.*

Hallinan (568) Irish: shortened Anglicized form of Gaelic **Ó hÁilgheanáin** 'descendant of *Áilgheanán*', a pet form of a personal name composed of old Celtic elements meaning 'mild, noble person'.

GIVEN NAMES Irish 7%. *Conn, Conor.*

Halling (446) **1.** English (Gloucestershire): habitational name from Hawling in Gloucestershire or possibly from Halling in Kent. Halling was named in Old English as 'family or followers of a man called *Heall*'; Hawling may have the same etymology or it may have meant 'people from Hallow' (a place in Worcestershire named in Old English with *halh* + *haga* 'enclosure'), or 'people at the nook of land', Old English *halh* (see HALE 1). **2.** German: variant of **Häling** (see HALING).

Hallisey (355) Irish (mainly Counties Cork and Kerry): shortened Anglicized form of Gaelic **Ó hÁilgheasa** 'descendant of *Áilgheas*', a personal name from *áilgheas* 'eagerness'.

GIVEN NAME Irish 6%. *Brendan* (2).

Halliwell (359) Northern English (Lancashire): habitational name from a place near Manchester called Halliwell, from Old English *hālig* 'holy' + *well(a)* 'well', 'spring', or from any of the numerous other places named with these elements (see HOLLOWELL).

Halliwill (103) Northern English: variant of HALLIWELL.

GIVEN NAME French 5%. *Camille.*

Hallman (3612) **1.** English: occupational name for a servant at a hall (see HALL). **2.** English: topographic name for someone who lived in a hollow or nook, Middle English *hale*, Old English *halh*. **3.** Swedish: compound of *hall* 'hall' + *man* 'man'. **4.** Respelling of German **Hallmann**, a variant of HELLMANN.

Hallmark (1727) English: from Middle English *halfmark* 'half a mark', probably a nickname or status name for someone who paid this sum in rent.

Hallock (1957) English: unexplained.

Halloran (2341) Irish: shortened Anglicized form of Gaelic **Ó hAllmhuráin** 'descendant of *Allmhurán*', a personal name from a diminutive of *allmhurach* 'foreigner' (from *all* 'beyond' + *muir* 'sea').

GIVEN NAMES Irish 5%. *Brendan, Liam.*

Halloway (197) English: variant of ALLOWAY.

Hallowell (979) Northern English and Scottish: variant of HALLIWELL.

Hallows (122) English: topographic name from Middle English *hal(l)owes* 'nooks', 'hollows', from Old English *halh* (see HALE 1). In some cases the name may be genitive, rather than plural, in form, with the sense 'relative or servant of the dweller in the nook'.

Hallquist (302) Swedish: ornamental name composed of the elements *hall* 'stone', 'rock', 'hall' + *quist*, an old or ornamental spelling of *kvist* 'twig'.

GIVEN NAMES Scandinavian 4%. *Nils* (2), *Erik, Hjalmer, Knute.*

Halls (435) English: variant of HALL.

Hallsted (103) English: variant spelling of HALSTEAD.

Hallstrom (576) Swedish: **1.** (**Hallström**): ornamental name composed of the elements *hall* 'stone', 'rock', 'hall' + *ström* 'river'. **2.** (**Hällström**): ornamental name composed of the elements *häll* 'rock' + *ström* 'river'.

GIVEN NAMES Scandinavian 7%. *Erik, Nels, Nils, Thor.*

Hallum (644) **1.** English and Scottish: variant spelling of HALLAM. **2.** Norwegian: habitational name from any of three farmsteads so named in southeastern Norway, from either the dative plural of Old Norse *holl* 'slope' or Old Norse *Hallheimr*, a compound of *hallr* 'slope' + *heimr* 'farmstead'.

Hallums (170) English: probably a habitational name from Hallams Farm in Wonersh, Surrey, Middle English *Hullehammes* 'hill enclosures', 'enclosures (by the) hill', or alternatively a variant of HALLUM, with the addition of a genitive *-s* indicating 'servant of', 'widow of', etc.

Hally (205) Variant spelling of HALLEY.

Halm (531) South German: metonymic occupational name for a peasant farmer, from Middle High German *halm* 'stalk', 'blade of grass', indicating someone who grew cereal crops.

Halman (108) English: variant spelling of HALLMAN.

Halonen (141) Finnish: **1.** in eastern Finland, from the Karelian personal name *Hali*, earlier *Fali* (a derivative of the Russian Orthodox name *Falalei*, from Greek *Thalelaios*) + the common surname ending *-nen*. **2.** in western Finland, it is probably from a Germanic personal name containing the element *Hal-*.

GIVEN NAMES Finnish 8%. *Pekka* (2), *Helvi, Jussi, Toivo.*

Halpain (132) Scandinavian: unexplained.

GIVEN NAME Scandinavian 4%. *Erik* (2).

Halper (580) Jewish (Ashkenazic): variant of HALPERN.

GIVEN NAMES Jewish 4%. *Emanuel* (2), *Ari, Isador, Miriam, Mort.*

Halperin (903) Jewish (Ashkenazic): variant of HALPERN.

GIVEN NAMES Jewish 7%. *Meyer* (5), *Aron* (3), *Avi, Avinoam, Hyman, Itzhak, Limor, Miriam, Mordechi, Shimon, Sol, Zvi.*

Halpern (2336) Jewish (Ashkenazic): habitational name from the city of Heilbronn in Württemberg, which had a large and influential Jewish population in medieval times. See also HEILBRUNN.

GIVEN NAMES Jewish 7%. *Sol* (7), *Hyman* (4), *Meyer* (4), *Miriam* (4), *Emanuel* (3), *Isadore* (3), *Peleg* (2), *Arie, Arieh, Aron, Benzion, Chaim.*

Halpert (366) Jewish: variant of HALPERN.

GIVEN NAMES Jewish 12%; German 4%. *Mendel* (2), *Moshe* (2), *Alter, Berish, Emanuel, Hershel, Menachem, Mordche, Pinkas, Shlomo, Sol, Yehuda*; *Eugen, Ignatz, Otto.*

Halphen (103) French and Jewish (Ashkenazic): **1.** perhaps, as Morlet suggests, a derivative of Hebrew *chalfi* (Aramaic *halphai*) meaning 'God has replaced (a dead child)', or from Hebrew *chalfon* 'money changer'. **2.** Alternatively, it could be a habitational name for someone from Heilbronn (see HALPERN).

GIVEN NAMES French 7%; Spanish 6%. *Leonce, Philippe*; *Osvaldo* (3), *Fabio* (2), *Demetrio.*

Halpin (2367) Irish: shortened Anglicized form of Gaelic **Ó hAilpín** 'descendant of *Alpín*', an ancient personal name, which MacLysaght and Woulfe link etymologically with *alp* 'lump'.

GIVEN NAMES Irish 5%. *Brendan* (4), *Dermot* (2), *Eamon* (2), *Declan, Kieran, Murphy, Senan.*

Halprin (185) Jewish (Ashkenazic): variant of HALPERN.

GIVEN NAMES Jewish 6%. *Meyer* (2), *Emanuel, Sol.*

Halsall (103) English (Lancashire): habitational name from a place in Lancashire named Halsall, from an Old English personal name *Hæle* + *halh* 'nook of land'.

Halse (133) **1.** English: from Middle English *hals* 'neck' (Old English *h(e)als*). This was a nickname for a man with a long neck or for a conspicuous sufferer from goiter (a common affliction in medieval times). **2.** English (Devon): topographic name denoting someone living on a neck of land (from Middle English *atte halse* 'at the neck'), or a habitational name from either of two places in Devon and Somerset named Halse, from this word. To a lesser extent Halse in Northamptonshire, named from Old English *hals* + *hōh* 'ridge', may also have contributed to the surname. **3.** Norwegian: habitational name from any of three farmsteads in the county of Møre og Romsdal. The farmsteads are so named from the Old Norse dative singular of *hals* 'neck', referring to a neck of land, or a ridge between two valleys.

Halsell (341) English: variant spelling of HALSALL.

Halsema (146) Frisian: unexplained.

Halseth (248) Norwegian: habitational name from any of several farmsteads, notably in the Trøndelag region, named Halseth, from a combination of either Old Norse *hallr* 'slope' or the personal name *Halli* + *set* 'farm'.

Halsey (2882) English: habitational name of uncertain origin. The surname is common in London, and may be derived from Alsa (formerly *Assey*) in Stanstead Mountfitchet, Essex (recorded as *Alsiesheye* in 1268). Another possible source is Halsway in Somerset, named from Old English *hals* 'neck' + *weg* 'way', 'road'.

Halstead (3363) English: **1.** habitational name from any of the various places bearing this name, for example in Essex (*Haltesteda* in Domesday Book), Kent, and Leicestershire, all of which are probably named from Old English *h(e)ald* 'refuge', 'shelter' + *stede* 'site', or possibly Hawstead in Suffolk, which has the same origin. However, the name is now most frequent in Lancashire and Yorkshire, where it is from High Halstead in Burnley, named as the 'site of a hall', from Old English *h(e)all* 'hall' + *stede* 'place'. **2.** occupational name for someone employed at 'the hall buildings', Middle English *hallested*, an ostler or cowhand, for instance.

Halsted (519) English: variant spelling of HALSTEAD.

Halstrom (118) Respelling of Swedish **Hallström** or **Hällström** (see HALL-STROM).
GIVEN NAMES Scandinavian 4%. *Erik, Lars.*

Halt (175) **1.** German: topographic name for someone who lived by pastureland, Middle High German *halte* 'pasture' or 'stopping place'. **2.** English and North German: nickname from Middle English, Middle Low German *halte* 'lame' (Old English *h(e)alt*) 'lame'.

Halteman (238) Altered spelling of German **Haldemann** (see HALDEMAN) or **Halter-mann** (see HALTERMAN).

Halter (1700) **1.** German: topographic name for someone who lived by a meadow or pastureland, from Middle High German *halte* 'pasture' + the suffix *-er* denoting an inhabitant. **2.** South German and Jewish (Ashkenazic): from Middle High German *haltære* 'keeper', 'shepherd', German *Halter*. **3.** English: occupational name for a maker of halters for horses and cattle, Middle English *haltrere* (from Old English *hælftre* 'halter'). **4.** Dutch: metonymic occupational name for a halter-maker, from Middle Dutch *halfter, haelter, halter* 'halter'.

Halterman (1235) North German (**Haltermann**): habitational name for someone from places in Westphalia and Hannover called Haltern.

Haltiwanger (209) Southern German: topographic name from Middle High German *halti, halde* 'slope' + *wange* 'grassy mountain slope' + the suffix *-er* denoting an inhabitant. This name occurs chiefly in SC.

Haltom (666) Possibly an altered spelling of English or Irish HALTON.

Halton (380) **1.** English (mainly Lancashire): habitational name from any of several places named Halton, usually from Old English *h(e)alh* 'nook', 'hollow' + *tūn* 'enclosure', 'settlement'. Halton in Cheshire, however, is possibly named from an Old English *hāthel* 'heathery place' + *tūn*, and Halton in Northumberland from an Old English *hāw* 'look out' + *hyll* 'hill' + *tūn*. **2.** Irish: altered form of **O'Haltahan**, an Anglicized form of Gaelic **Ó hUltacháin** 'descendant of *Ultachán*', a diminutive of *Ultach* 'Ulsterman'. This is a rare Fermanagh surname, which is sometimes Anglicized as NOLAN.
FOREBEARS Most English bearers of this name trace their descent from William de Halton, who was living at Halton, Lancashire, in 1346.

Haluska (294) Czech and Slovak (**Haluška**): from Czech and Slovak *halušky* 'pasta pieces'. The application as a surname is unclear; it may in fact have been a nickname for someone with a prominent mole.

Halverson (4896) Americanized spelling of Norwegian or Danish HALVORSEN.

Halverstadt (126) Variant of German HALBERSTADT.

Halvorsen (1435) Danish and Norwegian form of HALVORSON.
GIVEN NAMES Scandinavian 10%. *Erik* (10), *Age* (2), *Lars* (2), *Alf, Bjorn, Egil, Iver, Knut, Maren, Per, Vidar.*

Halvorson (2845) Scandinavian (mostly Norwegian): patronymic from the personal name *Halvor*, Old Norse *Hallvarðr*, composed of the elements *hallr* 'rock' + *varðr* 'guardian', 'defender'.
GIVEN NAMES Scandinavian 4%. *Erik* (7), *Arndt* (2), *Selmer* (2), *Thor* (2), *Helmer, Hilma, Knute, Obert.*

Ham (5753) **1.** English (mainly southwestern England): variant spelling of HAMM. **2.** French: habitational name from any of the various places in northern France (Ardennes, Pas-de-Calais, Somme, Moselle) named with the Germanic word *ham* 'meadow in the bend of a river', 'water meadow', 'flood plain'. **3.** Dutch: variant of HAMME. **4.** Korean: there is only one Chinese character for the Ham surname. Some sources report that there are sixty different Ham clans, but only the *Kangnŭng* Ham clan can be documented. Although some records have been lost and a few gen-

erations are unaccounted for, it is known that the founding ancestor of the Ham clan is Ham Kyu, a Koryŏ general who fought against the Mongol invaders in the thirteenth century. His ancestor, Ham Hyŏk, was a Tang Chinese general who stayed in Korea after Tang China helped Shilla unify the peninsula during the seventh century. Another of Ham Hyŏk's ancestors, Ham Shin, accompanied Kim Chu-wŏn, the founding ancestor of the Kangnŭng Kim family, to the Kangnŭng area, and hence the Ham clan became the Kangnŭng Ham clan. The first prominent ancestor from Kangnŭng whose genealogy can be verified is Ham Kyu, the Koryŏ general. Accordingly, he is regarded as the Kangnŭng Ham clan's founding ancestor.
GIVEN NAMES Korean 4%. *Young* (5), *Ok* (3), *Nam* (3), *Chul, Eun Hee, Eun Young, Hae Jung, Il Hwa.*

Hamacher (307) German (Lower Rhine): occupational name for a harness and collar maker for draught animals, Middle Low German *hamaker* (from Middle Low German *hame* 'collar'). Compare Dutch HAMMAKER.

Hamad (250) Muslim: from an Arabic personal name, *Ḥammād* 'much praising', an intensive form of HAMID.
GIVEN NAMES Muslim 61%. *Mohamed* (4), *Abdel* (3), *Salam* (3), *Ahmad* (2), *Ali* (2), *Ashraf* (2), *Hassan* (2), *Hussein* (2), *Karim* (2), *Khaled* (2), *Maher* (2), *Mahmoud* (2).

Hamada (543) Japanese: 'seashore rice paddy'; found in the island of Shikoku and in the Ryūkyū Islands. Several unrelated families bearing this name descend from the FUJIWARA, TAIRA, Kikuchi, Arakida, and other clans.
GIVEN NAMES Japanese 46%. *Hiroshi* (3), *Isao* (3), *Kenji* (3), *Koichi* (3), *Koji* (3), *Masaru* (3), *Sadao* (3), *Haruo* (2), *Hiroyuki* (2), *Iwao* (2), *Junichi* (2), *Katsuyuki* (2).

Hamady (108) Muslim: from an adjectival derivative of HAMAD.
GIVEN NAMES Muslim 13%. *Akram, Fakhri, Ghassan, Jamal, Jamil, Kahlil, Nasri, Salim.*

Hamaker (586) Dutch: variant of HAMMAKER.

Hamalainen (128) Finnish (**Hämäläinen**): regional name for someone from Häme province, in central Finland. This is a well-established Finnish family name dating back to the 16th century.
GIVEN NAMES Finnish 30%; Scandinavian 6%. *Reino* (5), *Pekka* (2), *Aimo, Arvi, Jukka, Jussi, Olavi, Pirjo, Raija, Timo, Wiljo.*

Hamamoto (199) Japanese: '(one who lives) near the seashore'; mostly found in western Japan and the Ryūkyū Islands.
GIVEN NAMES Japanese 38%. *Akira, Giichi, Goichi, Kazuo, Kazuto, Kiyomi, Kiyoshi, Masahiko, Masao, Masaru, Masato, Mitsuo.*

Haman (819) Respelling of German HAMANN.

Hamann (2388) German (also found in Denmark): from a much reduced form of the personal name *Johannes* (see JOHN) + *Mann* 'man', i.e. 'John's man (servant)'.
GIVEN NAMES German 4%. *Heinz* (2), *Horst* (2), *Armin, Erhard, Ernst, Erwin, Fritz, Hans, Helmut, Ilse, Inge, Juergen.*

Hamar (216) Norwegian: habitational name from several farmsteads named Hamar, from Old Norse *hamarr* 'hammer', denoting a hammer-shaped cliff or crag.

Hamasaki (130) Japanese: 'seashore cape'; found mainly in western Japan and the Ryū kyū Islands.
GIVEN NAMES Japanese 39%. *Iwao* (2), *Shigemi* (2), *Yuzuru* (2), *Akira, Haru, Hidekazu, Kimiko, Kiyoshi, Miwa, Ryo, Shinji, Tomo.*

Hambel (118) German: possibly a variant of HAMPEL.

Hambelton (141) English: variant spelling of HAMBLETON.

Hamberg (332) **1.** German, Danish, and Jewish (Ashkenazic): habitational name from any of several places named Hamberg. **2.** Jewish (Ashkenazic): variant of HAMBURG.
GIVEN NAMES French 4%; Scandinavian 4%. *Marcelle* (3), *Jeanmarie; Bjorn, Erik, Johan, Nels.*

Hamberger (245) **1.** German and Jewish (Ashkenazic): habitational name for someone from any of various places named HAMBERG. **2.** Jewish (Ashkenazic): variant of HAMBURGER.

Hamblen (821) English: variant spelling of HAMBLIN.

Hamblet (204) English: variant spelling of HAMLETT.

Hambleton (690) English: habitational name from any of several places named Hambleton, Hambleden, or Hambledon, in particular Hambleton in Lancashire, which is named from Old English *hamel* 'crooked (hill)' + *tūn* 'enclosure', 'settlement'.

Hamblett (168) English: variant spelling of HAMLETT.

Hambley (209) English: variant spelling of HAMBLY.

Hamblin (2789) **1.** English: variant of HAMLIN. **2.** Variant of French **Hamelin**.

Hambly (294) English: **1.** from the Norman personal name *Hameley*, a double diminutive of *Hamo* (see HAMMOND). **2.** habitational name from Hamly Bridge in Chiddingly, Sussex, named from an Old English personal name *Eamba* + Old English *lēah* 'wood', '(woodland) clearing'.

Hambrecht (129) German: from the Germanic personal name *Haginberht*, a compound of *hagin* 'enclosed area' + *berht* 'bright', 'famous'.
GIVEN NAMES German 7%. *Helmut, Uwe.*

Hambric (122) Respelling of German HAMBRECHT.

Hambrick (1527) Respelling of German HAMBRECHT.

Hambright (617) Americanized form of German HAMBRECHT.

Hamburg (801) German and Jewish (Ashkenazic): habitational name from the great city and port at the mouth of the river Elbe, named with the Germanic elements *ham* 'water meadow' + *burg* 'fortress', 'fortified town'.

Hamburger (656) German and Jewish (Ashkenazic): habitational name for someone from HAMBURG.
GIVEN NAMES Jewish 5%; German 4%. *Jakob* (2), *Avrohom, Isadore, Miriam, Myer, Nachman, Sol, Yaakov, Yehuda, Yisroel, Zvi; Kurt* (2), *Monika* (2), *Frieda, Siegmund, Viktor.*

Hamby (4857) **1.** English: habitational name from Hanby near Welton le Marsh, in Lincolnshire, which is named from the Old Norse personal name *Hundi* + Old Norse *býr* 'farmstead', 'settlement'. **2.** Perhaps an altered spelling of French **Hambye**, a habitational name from a place in Manche.

Hamdan (222) Muslim: from an Arabic personal name, *Ḥamdān* 'much praise', a derivative of HAMID. *Ḥamdān* was the name of a tribe in Arabia. The Hamdani dynasty ruled al-Jazira and Syria from 905 to 1004.
GIVEN NAMES Muslim 71%. *Ahmad* (8), *Khaled* (4), *Omar* (4), *Imad* (3), *Adham* (3), *Aiman* (2), *Ali* (2), *Hasan* (2), *Hassan* (2), *Maher* (2), *Mohammed* (2), *Nasser* (2).

Hamed (235) Muslim: see HAMID.
GIVEN NAMES Muslim 63%. *Mohamed* (4), *Ahmed* (3), *Ahmad* (2), *Amal* (2), *Hamed* (2), *Kamal* (2), *Karem* (2), *Khaled* (2), *Latif* (2), *Nader* (2), *Omar* (2), *Saade* (2).

Hameed (185) Muslim: see HAMID.
GIVEN NAMES Muslim 84%. *Abdul* (17), *Imran* (5), *Shahid* (4), *Akhtar* (3), *Mohammed* (3), *Tariq* (3), *Arshad* (2), *Azim* (2), *Faisal* (2), *Jameel* (2), *Khalid* (2), *Rashid* (2).

Hameister (154) North German: occupational name for a steward or manager of a farm or manor, from Middle Low German *hof* 'farmstead', 'manor farm' + *mēster* 'master'.

Hamel (4326) **1.** English, Scottish, and Irish: variant spelling of HAMILL. **2.** French: topographic name for someone who lived and worked at an outlying farm dependent on the main village, Old French *hamel* (a diminutive from a Germanic element cognate with Old English *hām* 'homestead'). **3.** German and Jewish (Ashkenazic): habitational name from the city of Hamlin, German *Hameln*, Yiddish *Haml*, where the Hamel river empties into the Weser. The name of the river probably derives from the Germanic element *ham* 'water meadow'. **4.** Dutch: metonymic occupational name for a shepherd, from

Middle Dutch *hamel* 'wether', 'castrated ram'.
FOREBEARS A Hamel from Normandy is documented in St. Jean et St. François, Quebec, in 1666.
GIVEN NAMES French 8%. *Armand* (17), *Lucien* (9), *Normand* (9), *Andre* (6), *Jacques* (6), *Fernand* (4), *Aime* (2), *Aubert* (2), *Cecile* (2), *Marcel* (2), *Michel* (2), *Raoul* (2).

Hamelin (436) French: diminutive of HAMEL 2.
FOREBEARS A Hamelin from the Anjou region of France is documented in Grondines, Quebec, in 1679, with the secondary surnames Grondines, Bellou, and Plagnol.
GIVEN NAMES French 9%. *Cecile, Dominique, Etienne, Jacques, Jean-Paul, Lucien, Monique, Normand, Renald.*

Hamelink (100) Dutch: patronymic derivative of the medieval personal name *Hamel*, a pet form of *Amalric*, composed of the Germanic elements *amal* 'strength', 'vigor' + *rīc* 'power'. Compare AMELUNG.

Hamell (111) Scottish, Irish, and English: variant spelling of HAMILL.

Hamer (2442) **1.** English: habitational name from a place in Lancashire named Hamer, from Old English *hamor* 'rock', 'crag'. **2.** English: possibly a metonymic occupational name for a smith or for a maker or seller of hammers, Middle English *hamer* (Old English *hamor*), or a habitational name for someone living at an inn or shop distinguished by the sign of a hammer. **3.** Dutch: from *hamer* 'hammer', hence a metonymic occupational name for a maker of hammers or a user of a hammer, for example a blacksmith. **4.** Jewish (Ashkenazic) and German: variant spelling of HAMMER. **5.** Slovenian: variant spelling of German HAMMER.

Hamernik (126) Slovak (**Hamerník**): occupational name for a smith, from Slovak *hámorník* 'smith'.
GIVEN NAMES German 5%. *Aloysius, Kurt.*

Hamersley (105) English: see HAMMERSLEY.

Hames (1409) English: habitational name from Hames Hall in Papcastle, Cumbria, named from the plural of northern Middle English *hame* 'homestead'.

Hamid (414) Muslim: from a personal name based on Arabic *ḥāmid* 'praising', 'praiser (of Allah)', or *ḥamīd* 'praised', 'praiseworthy'. *Al-Ḥamīd* 'the All-Laudable' is an attribute of Allah. The name *'Abd-ul-Hamīd* means 'servant of the All-Laudable'. The root *ḥmd* 'praise' is one of the most common elements in Arabic name forming; in addition to this name, it also lies behind names such as AHMAD and MUHAMMAD.
GIVEN NAMES Muslim 80%. *Abdul* (32), *Mohammed* (12), *Mohamed* (8), *Syed* (4), *Tariq* (4), *Bashir* (3), *Hamid* (3), *Mohammad* (3), *Rashid* (3), *Saeed* (3), *Zahid* (3), *Abdullah* (2).

Hamidi (167) Muslim: from an Arabic surname, *Ḥamīdī*, indicating descent from or association with someone called HAMID.
GIVEN NAMES Muslim 81%. *Ali* (5), *Mohammad* (5), *Aziz* (4), *Seyed* (3), *Abdul* (2), *Amanullah* (2), *Hamid* (2), *Hossein* (2), *Jafar* (2), *Jamal* (2), *Jamila* (2), *Majid* (2).

Hamiel (126) Origin uncertain. The name is recorded in northern France, Syria, Canada, and elsewhere. Perhaps a variant of Irish HAMILL through migration from Ireland to France and elsewhere.

Hamil (864) Irish: variant of HAMILL.

Hamill (2276) **1.** Scottish (of Norman origin): habitational name from Haineville or Henneville in Manche, France, named from the Germanic personal name *Hagano* + Old French *ville* 'settlement'. **2.** English (Yorkshire): nickname for a scarred or maimed person, from Middle English, Old English *hamel* 'mutilated', 'crooked'. **3.** Irish (Ulster): according to MacLysaght, a shortened Anglicized form of Gaelic **Ó hÁdhmaill** 'descendant of *Ádhmall*', which he derives from *ádhmall* 'active'.
FOREBEARS The first known bearer of the name in Scotland was a certain William, recorded variously as *de Hameville* and *de He(y)neuile* at the end of the 12th century. For long it was associated with Roughwood in Ayrshire. It has now more or less died out in Scotland, but is common in the north of Ireland, where its bearers can trace their ancestry to Hugh Hammill of Roughwood, who went to Ireland in the 15th century.

Hamilton (68294) Scottish and northern Irish: habitational name from what is now a deserted village in the parish of Barkby, Leicestershire. This is named from Old English *hamel* 'crooked' + *dūn* 'hill'. Hamilton near Glasgow was founded by the Hamiltons and named after them. In Ireland, this name may have replaced HAMILL in a few cases. It has also been used as the equivalent of the Irish (Cork) name **Ó hUrmholtaigh**.
FOREBEARS This name is borne by one of the most distinguished families of the Scottish nobility; they hold many titles, including the Marquessate and Dukedom of Hamilton, the Marquessate of Douglas, the Dukedom of Abercorn, and the Earldom of Haddington. They are descended from Walter FitzGilbert de Hameldone, a Norman baron who gave his support to Robert the Bruce in the 13th century. A member of this family was Sir William Hamilton (1730–1803), a British diplomat and archaeologist, whose wife, Lady Emma Hamilton (?1765–1815), became the mistress of Admiral Horatio Nelson. In the 16th century bearers of the name found their way to Russia, where they became naturalized; hence the Russian forms **Gamentov**, **Khamentov**, and **Khomutov** (the latter having been affected by folk etymological association with *khomut* 'horse

collar'). A branch of the family was established in Ireland by Sir Frederick Hamilton (died 1646), who served in the Swedish army of Gustavus Adolphus. He later became governor of Ulster, and his descendants were created Viscounts Boyne. The family have given their name to Newtownhamilton and Hamiltonsbaron in County Armagh. Another branch of the family was to be found in Denmark, where Henrik Albertsen Hamilton (1588–1648) was a noted Latin poet in his day. Debrabandere gives a 17th-century example of a Hamilton from Glasgow recorded in the Low Countries, where the name is found in the forms **Hamelton** and **Hammerton**.

Hamiter (155) German: topographic name from Middle High German *hamit*, *heimit* 'enclosure', 'clearing' + *-er* suffix denoting an inhabitant; also a habitational name for someone from any of several small places named *Hamet(en)* in Bavaria and Austria.
FOREBEARS The ancestor of the American Hamiter family, Thomas Hamiter, came from Baden-Württemberg in southern Germany to SC in 1752.

Hamlen (127) **1.** English and Irish: variant spelling of HAMLIN. **2.** Respelling of French HAMELIN.

Hamler (282) German: habitational name for someone from the city of Hameln (see HAMEL 3).

Hamlet (958) English: variant of HAMLETT.

Hamlett (1710) English (Gloucestershire): from the Norman personal name *Hamelet*, a double diminutive of the personal name *Haimo* (see HAMMOND).

Hamley (202) English: variant spelling of HAMBLY.

Hamlin (6268) **1.** English and Irish (of Norman origin): from the Norman personal name *Ham(b)lin*, *Hamelin*, a double diminutive of *Haimo* (see HAMMOND). This was the name of a prominent family in County Meath in Ireland in the 13th–18th centuries, but is now rare there. **2.** Variant of French HAMELIN.
FOREBEARS Both the personal name and the surname have always been common in Cornwall; bearers of the name Hamlin were recorded in Domesday Book as holding 23 manors in Cornwall.

Hamling (246) English: variant of HAMLIN.

Hamlyn (159) **1.** English (Devon) and Irish: variant of HAMLIN. **2.** Respelling of French HAMELIN. **3.** Jewish (Ashkenazic): Anglicized form of HAMEL.

Hamm (9637) **1.** English: topographic name from Old English *hamm*, denoting a patch of flat, low-lying alluvial land beside a stream (often a promontory or water meadow in a river bend), or a habitational name from any of numerous places named with this word, for example in Gloucestershire, Greater London, Kent, Somerset, and

Wiltshire. **2.** German: topographic name for someone who lived on land in a river bend, Old High German *ham* (see 1 above). **3.** German and Jewish (Ashkenazic): habitational name from Hamm, a city in Westphalia.

Hammac (197) Dutch: variant of HAMMACK.

Hammack (1962) Dutch: occupational name for a harness maker, from a shortened form of Middle Dutch *haemmaker*. Compare German HAMACHER.

Hammad (144) Muslim: from an Arabic personal name, *Ḥammād* 'much praising', an intensive form of HAMID.
GIVEN NAMES Muslim 77%. *Ahmad* (4), *Ahmed* (3), *Ali* (3), *Hammad* (3), *Hasan* (3), *Mohamad* (3), *Osama* (3), *Adnan* (2), *Belal* (2), *Issa* (2), *Jamal* (2), *Kamal* (2).

Hammaker (283) Americanized spelling of Dutch **Haemmaker** 'harness maker', from *haeme* 'horse collar,' or altered spelling of German **Hammacher**. Compare German HAMACHER.

Hamman (1478) Respelling of German HAMMANN.

Hammann (406) **1.** North German: from Middle Low German *hoveman*, status name for a farmer who owned his own land as opposed to holding it by rent or feudal obligation, from *hove* 'settlement', 'farm', 'court' + *man* 'man'. **2.** German: from an assimilated form of *Hanemann*, from an aphetic form of the personal name *Johann(es)* + Middle High German *man* 'man'.
GIVEN NAMES German 5%. *Detlef* (2), *Hans* (2), *Bernhard*, *Horst*, *Wilhelmina*.

Hammans (146) English: apparently a variant of HAMMONDS.

Hammar (457) Swedish: habitational name from a place named with Old Norse *hamarr* 'hammer', 'crag', 'cliff'.

Hammarstrom (136) Swedish (**Hammarström**): ornamental name from a place named with Old Norse *hamarr* 'hammer', 'crag' + *ström*.
GIVEN NAMES Scandinavian 18%. *Erik*, *Evald*, *Lars*, *Lennart*, *Sten*, *Sven*.

Hamme (276) Belgian and Dutch (**van Hamme**): habitational name from any of various places in Belgium, in the provinces of Brabant, Hainault, East Flanders, and Limburg, named with Middle Dutch *hamme* 'flood plain', 'water meadow', or 'land in a river bend'.

Hammel (1882) **1.** Scottish and English: variant spelling of HAMILL. **2.** North German: nickname or metonymic occupational name from Middle Low German *hamel* 'wether', 'castrated ram'. **3.** Jewish (Ashkenazic): variant spelling of HAMEL.

Hammell (501) Scottish and English: variant spelling of HAMILL.

Hammen (412) Dutch and North German: from a pet form of a Germanic personal name, such as *Hadumar* or *Hammingus*, or from *Hamo*, a short form of a name derived from an element cognate with Gothic *hamon* 'to cover', 'to clothe' and modern German *Hemd* 'shirt'.

Hammer (8969) **1.** German, English, and Jewish (Ashkenazic): from Middle High German *hamer*, Yiddish *hamer*, a metonymic occupational name for a maker or user of hammers, for example in a forge, or nickname for a forceful person. **2.** English and German: topographic name for someone who lived in an area of flat, low-lying alluvial land beside a stream, Old English *hamm*, Old High German *ham* (see HAMM) + the English and German agent suffix *-er*. **3.** Norwegian: variant of HAMAR.

Hammerbeck (104) German: unexplained; perhaps a habitational name from Hammerbrook (Hamburg) or Hammerbach (Bavaria).
GIVEN NAME German 5%. *Kurt*.

Hammerberg (137) Swedish: probably an ornamental name composed of the elements *hammer* 'hammer' (possibly taken from a place name) + *berg* 'mountain'.
GIVEN NAMES Scandinavian 7%; German 6%. *Knute; Frieda, Kuno*.

Hammerle (294) German (**Hämmerle**): diminutive of HAMMER.
GIVEN NAMES German 7%. *Kurt* (2), *Ewald, Fritz, Konrad, Waltraud*.

Hammerly (150) Americanized spelling of German HAMMERLE.

Hammerman (232) German (**Hammermann**) and Jewish (Ashkenazic): variant of HAMMER 2.
GIVEN NAMES Jewish 7%. *Chaim, Hillel, Miriam, Sheina, Sol*.

Hammermeister (143) German: occupational name for someone in charge of a hammer mill, from Middle High German *hamer* 'hammer' + *meister* 'master'.
GIVEN NAMES German 12%. *Frieda, Kurt, Manfred*.

Hammers (823) German: variant of HAMMER 2.

Hammerschmidt (482) German and Jewish (Ashkenazic): occupational name for a smith or for the owner of a forge, from Middle High German *hamer* 'hammer' + *smit* 'smith', German *Hammer* + *Schmidt*.
GIVEN NAMES German 7%. *Kurt* (4), *Christoph, Erwin, Hans, Heinz, Helmut, Matthias*.

Hammersley (395) English (Midlands): unexplained. Probably a habitational name from a lost or unidentified place.

Hammersmith (342) Anglicized form of German HAMMERSCHMIDT.

Hammerstein (123) **1.** German and Jewish (Ashkenazic): habitational name from any of various places called Hammerstein, from Old High German *hamar* 'rock', 'crag' + *stein* 'stone'. **2.** Jewish (Ashkenazic): ornamental name composed of German *Hammer* 'hammer' + *Stein* 'stone'.
FOREBEARS Hammerstein is the name of a Hanoverian family, which originated in a

small place of this name on the Rhine opposite Andernach. The most famous bearer of the name is Oscar Hammerstein (1895–1960), the Jewish-American song writer, whose surname is of ornamental origin. He was the grandson of Oscar Hammerstein (1848–1919), an operatic impresario who had made his fortune with a machine that rolled cigars.

Hammerstrom (280) Variant of Swedish **Hammarström** (see HAMMARSTROM).
GIVEN NAMES Scandinavian 5%. *Erik, Nels*.

Hammes (937) Dutch: from an altered form of *Hannes*, a short form of the personal name *Johannes* (see JOHN).

Hammett (2884) English (Devon): from a pet form of the Norman personal name *Hamo* (see HAMMOND 1).

Hammill (760) Scottish and English: variant spelling of HAMILL.

Hamming (120) English: from an Old English *hamming* 'dweller on a patch of land edged by water or marshland', from Old English *hamm* (see HAMM) + the suffix *-ing(as)*, denoting association with a person or place.

Hammitt (564) English: variant spelling of HAMMETT.

Hammock (2394) English: unexplained. This name is very common in GA and TN.

Hammon (1320) English: variant of HAMMOND.

Hammond (25102) English (of Norman origin): from a personal name, *Hamo(n)*, which is generally from a continental Germanic name *Haimo*, a short form of various compound names beginning with *haim* 'home', although it could also be from the Old Norse personal name *Hámundr*, composed of the elements *hár* 'high' + *mund* 'protection'. As an Irish name it is generally an importation from England, but has also been used to represent HAMILL 3 and, more rarely, McCAMMON.

Hammonds (3561) English (Midlands): patronymic form of HAMMOND.

Hammons (3696) English (Midlands and Wales): apparently a variant of HAMMONDS.

Hammontree (758) Origin unidentified. The surname has been recorded in VA since the 1690s and is probably of English or Scottish origin.

Hammoud (134) Muslim: from a personal name based on Arabic *ḥammūd* 'much praising', a derivative of *ḥmd* 'praise' (see HAMID).
GIVEN NAMES Muslim 84%. *Ali* (10), *Hassan* (8), *Ahmad* (3), *Jamal* (3), *Mohamad* (3), *Abdul* (2), *Ahmed* (2), *Ezzat* (2), *Fadi* (2), *Faisal* (2), *Fouad* (2), *Ibrahim* (2).

Hamner (1408) **1.** English (West Midlands): probably a metathesized form of **Hanmer**, a habitational name from Hanmer in Flintshire. **2.** Swedish (**Hamnér**): ornamental name from *hamn* 'harbor'

+ the surname suffix *-ér*, derived from the Latin adjectival ending *-er(i)us*.

Hamon (641) English, French, and Dutch: from the Norman personal name *Hamo(n)* (see HAMMOND, HAMMEN).

Hamons (111) English: patronymic from HAMON.

Hamor (217) English: probably a variant spelling of HAMER.

Hamp (405) **1.** English: unexplained; compare HEMP. **2.** German: variant of HAMPE.

Hampe (282) German: from the Germanic personal name *Hampo*, a short form of *Haginberht*, a compound of *hagan, hagin* 'enclosure', 'protected place' + *berht* 'bright', 'famous'. Compare HAMBRIGHT.
GIVEN NAMES German 6%. *Fritz* (2), *Kurt* (2).

Hampel (620) **1.** German: from a pet form of the personal name *Hampo* (see HAMPE). **2.** Jewish (Ashkenazic): variant of HEMPEL.
GIVEN NAMES German 8%. *Otto* (2), *Viktor* (2), *Erwin, Gerd, Helmut, Helmuth, Monika, Udo, Volker, Willi, Wolf, Wolfang*.

Hamper (144) **1.** English: occupational name for a maker or seller of goblets, from Old French *hanapier*. **2.** German and Dutch: from the Germanic personal name *Hambert*, composed of either *haim, heim* 'home' or *hagan* 'enclosure', 'protected place' + *berht* 'bright', 'famous'.

Hample (156) Respelling of German and Jewish HAMPEL.

Hampshire (527) English: **1.** regional name from the southern English county so called, which derives its name from *Hampton* (i.e. the port of Southampton) + Old English *scīr* 'division', 'district'. **2.** regional name from the area of Hallamshire in southern Yorkshire, named from HALLAM + Middle English *schir* 'division', 'administrative region' (Old English *scīr*). The surname is most common in Yorkshire, where this second derivation is most likely to be the source.

Hampson (1002) **1.** English (mainly Lancashire): patronymic from the Norman personal name *Hamo, Hamon* (see HAMMOND). **2.** Irish: shortened Anglicized form of Gaelic **Ó hAmhsaigh** 'descendant of *Amhsach*' a byname meaning 'mercenary soldier' or 'messenger', from the adjective *amhasach* 'aggressive'.

Hampton (19853) English and Scottish: habitational name from any of the numerous places called Hampton, including the cities of Southampton and Northampton (both of which were originally simply *Hamtun*). These all share the final Old English element *tūn* 'enclosure', 'settlement', but the first is variously *hām* 'homestead', *hamm* 'water meadow', or *hēan*, weak dative case (originally used after a preposition and article) of *hēah* 'high'. This name is also established in Ireland, having first been taken there in the medieval period.

FOREBEARS The descendants of the clergyman Thomas Hampton, resident at Jamestown, VA, in 1630, lived in VA through three generations, multiplying their homesteads as the colony expanded and then branched into SC. This very common English name was brought independently to North America by many other bearers.

Hamra (104) Jewish: ornamental name from Aramaic *chamra* 'wine'.
GIVEN NAMES Jewish 6%. *Izak, Yosef.*

Hamre (507) Norwegian: habitational name from numerous farmsteads, notably in western Norway, named Hamre, from the dative case of Old Norse *hamarr* 'cliff', 'rock'. See HAMAR.
GIVEN NAMES Scandinavian 5%. *Bjorn, Knute, Lars, Svein.*

Hamric (422) Respelling of German **Hämmerich** or HEMMERICH.

Hamrick (4663) Respelling of German **Hämmerich** or HEMMERICH.

Hamrock (167) Irish: MacLysaght describes this as an English toponym, known to have been in Ireland since the 16th century; the surname is extremely rare in England, however.
GIVEN NAMES Irish 5%. *Eamon, Jarlath.*

Hams (150) English: probably a variant of HAM.
GIVEN NAME French 4%. *Pierre.*

Hamsher (200) English: variant spelling of HAMPSHIRE.

Hamson (183) English: patronymic form of HAMMOND.

Hamstra (275) Frisian: topographic name for someone living on a flood plain or water meadow, or land in a river bend, from a locative agent noun derived from Middle Low German *ham* 'flood plain'. Compare HAMME.

Han (4837) **1.** Chinese 韩: from the name of a state of Han, which existed during the early part of the Western Zhou dynasty (1122–771 BC), in present-day Shaanxi province. This was the fief of a younger brother of Cheng Wang, second king of the Zhou dynasty. The state of Han was later annexed by the state of Jin, but the area was enfeoffed by the Jin ruler to Wu Zi, a descendant of Wen Wang. Wu Zi's descendants eventually adopted the name of the fief as their surname. **2.** Korean: there are two Chinese characters for the surname Han. However, one of these characters, meaning 'China', is extremely rare (only two households with this surname appeared in a recent census), so only the other will be considered here. Some records indicate that there are 131 clans of the Han family, but only one—the Han family of Ch'ǒngju, can be documented. Some sources name Han Ran as the founding ancestor of the Han family. Han Ran is recognized as one of the men who assisted the first Koryǒ king, Wang Kǒn, in setting up the Koryǒ kingdom in 918. More recent scholarship, however, postulates that the Ch'ǒngju Han clan's founding ancestor was U-P'yǒng, one of three sons of the fortieth generation descendant of Kija, the founder of the ancient Chosǒn kingdom (died 194 BC). The other two sons, U-sǒng and U-Kyǒng, founded the KI clan and the Sǒngan clans, respectively. **3.** French: of uncertain origin. In some cases at least it is from a Breton word meaning 'summer' or a topographic name from a place named with Gaulish *hafod* 'summer residence'. **4.** Dutch and Czech (**Hán**): from a reduced form of the personal name *Johann(es)* (see JOHN). **5.** Jewish: variant of HAHN.
FOREBEARS A bearer of the surname Han from the Poitou region of France was recorded in Repentigny, Quebec, in 1685 with secondary surnames Janhan and CHAUSSE.
GIVEN NAMES Chinese/Korean 61%. *Sang* (67), *Young* (65), *Sung* (36), *Yong* (31), *Kwang* (22), *Seung* (22), *Kyung* (21), *Dong* (20), *Jin* (18), *Jung* (18), *Myung* (15), *Song* (14); *Chong* (27), *Chang* (24), *Min* (11), *Myong* (11), *Byung* (8), *Chung* (8), *Moon* (7), *Chul* (6), *Hae* (5), *In Suk* (5), *Jeong* (5), *Kyung Soo* (5).

Hana (137) Muslim: from the Arabic female personal name *Hanā* 'bliss', 'happiness'.
GIVEN NAMES Muslim 29%. *Hani* (2), *Amad, Amir, Awni, Azhar, Aziz, Badr, Basima, Majid, Mamdoh, Milad, Nagi.*

Hanafin (161) Irish: shortened Anglicized form of Gaelic **Ó hAinbhthín** (modernized as **Ó hAinifín**) 'descendant of *Ainbhthín*', a personal name derived from *ainbhíoth* 'non-peace', 'storm'.

Hanagan (218) Irish: variant spelling of HANNIGAN.
GIVEN NAME Irish 6%. *Brennan.*

Hanahan (208) Irish (County Limerick): shortened Anglicized form of Gaelic **Ó hAnnacháin** 'descendant of *Annachán*', a diminutive of *Annach*, a byname of uncertain meaning.

Hanak (245) Czech (**Hanák**): **1.** regional name for someone from Haná, a region in central Moravia. **2.** from an aphetic pet form of the personal name *Johannes* (see JOHN).
GIVEN NAMES German 5%. *Alois, Horst, Otto.*

Hanan (530) Jewish: from the Biblical personal name *Hanan* or a short form of *Elchanan* or *Johanan* for example.

Hanania (110) Arabic: from a personal name based on Hebrew *Hananyah*, 'answered by the Lord'. This name was borne by various saints venerated in the Eastern Church. Compare ANANIA.
GIVEN NAMES Arabic 35%. *Ramzi* (2), *Abrahim, Amal, Farid, Fouad, Ghassan, Ibrahim, Issa, Jamal, Karimah, Khalil, Layla.*

Hanas (133) Greek: occupational name for an innkeeper, from Turkish *han* 'inn' + the Greek occupational ending *-as*.

Hanauer (319) German and Jewish (Ashkenazic): habitational name for someone from a place called Hanau in Hesse, named from Old High German *hano* 'rooster' + *ouwa* 'low-lying land', 'island'.

Hanavan (150) Irish: variant of HANAFIN or alternatively of the cognate **Hannavan**, a shortened Anglicized form of Gaelic **Ó Hainbheáin** occurring chiefly in County Monaghan.

Hanawalt (291) Americanized spelling of an unexplained German surname, **Hanewald**. This is a common name in the Rhineland.

Hanaway (237) Irish: reduced Anglicized form of Gaelic **Ó hAinbhith** (see HANVEY).

Hanback (263) Altered form of German HEIMBACH.

Hanberry (135) Altered spelling of English HANBURY.

Hanbury (280) **1.** English: habitational name from places in Staffordshire and Worcestershire named Hanbury, from Old English (*æt ðæm*) *hēan byrig* '(at the) high fortress'. In some cases it may also be from Handborough in Oxfordshire, which is named from the Old English byname *Hagena* or *Hana* + *beorg* 'hill'. **2.** Irish (mainly County Galway and County Clare): shortened Anglicized form of Gaelic **Ó hAinmhire** 'descendant of *Ainmhire*', a personal name meaning 'very wild', 'warlike'.

Hanby (420) English: variant of HAMBY.

Hance (1472) **1.** English: patronymic from the personal name HANN. **2.** English: plural form of HAND. **3.** Scottish: shortened form of **Machans**, an Anglicized form of Gaelic **Mag Aonghuis**, a patronymic from the personal name *Aonghus* (see ANGUS). Compare MCINNES. **4.** French: derivative of German HANS. **5.** Dutch: from an aphetic form of the personal name *Johannes* (see JOHN).

Hancey (123) English (Norfolk): unexplained.

Hancher (194) English (Staffordshire): unexplained.

Hanchett (542) English (Essex): unexplained.

Hanchey (329) Americanized spelling of a Swiss and southern German family name **Hantsche, Hansche,** or **Hentsche,** a metonymic occupational name for a glovemaker, from any of the variants **Hansche, Hantsche, Hentsche,** contracted forms of *Handschuh* 'glove', due to the loss of stress in the second syllable See HANDSCHUH. This name is found predominantly in LA and NC.
FOREBEARS Jacob Hanchey was a Swiss-German immigrant to SC from the Palatinate, Germany, in the 1740s.

Hancock (18615) **1.** English: from the Middle English personal name HANN + the hypocoristic suffix *-cok*, which was commonly added to personal names (see COCKE). **2.** Dutch: from Middle Dutch *hanecoc* 'winkle', 'periwinkle' (a type of shellfish), probably a metonymic occupational name for someone who gathered and sold shellfish.

FOREBEARS Thomas Hancock, the uncle of Declaration of Independence signatory John Hancock (1736/7–93), was among the foremost of 18th-century American businessmen. He was a descendant of Nathaniel Hancock, who was known to have been in Cambridge, MA, as early as 1634. Born in Braintree, MA, John Hancock was president of the Second Continental Congress and the first governor of the state of MA.

Hancox (251) English: patronymic from the personal name HANCOCK.

Hand (8372) **1.** English and German: nickname for someone with a deformed hand or who had lost one hand, from Middle English *hand*, Middle High German *hant*, found in such appellations as *Liebhard mit der Hand* (Augsburg 1383). **2.** Jewish (Ashkenazic): nickname from German *Hand* 'hand' (see 1). **3.** Irish: Anglicized form of Gaelic **Ó Flaithimh** (see GUTHRIE), resulting from an erroneous association of the Gaelic name with the Gaelic word *lámh* 'hand'. It is used as an English equivalent for several other names of Gaelic origin too, e.g. CLAFFEY, GLAVIN, and MCCLAVE. **4.** Dutch: from a variant of *hont* 'dog', 'hound', either a derogatory nickname, or a habitational name for someone living at a house distinguished by the sign of a dog.

Handa (239) **1.** Indian (Panjab): Hindu (Khatri) and Sikh name, probably from Panjabi *haṇa* 'cooking pot'. It is based on the name of a Khatri clan. **2.** Japanese: 'half of a rice paddy'. The name originated in Yamato and Kawachi (now Nara and Ōsaka prefectures), and is found mostly in the Tōkyō and Ōsaka areas, and the island of Okinawa.

GIVEN NAMES Indian 37%; Japanese 23%. *Ajay* (3), *Raj* (3), *Dev* (2), *Sanjiv* (2), *Sumeet* (2), *Suresh* (2), *Arun, Asha, Avtar, Balraj, Dhiraj, Harsha; Haruhisa* (2), *Yutaka* (2), *Akitoshi, Emiko, Harumi, Junya, Kats, Katsuhito, Kazuhiro, Kazuo, Kazuya, Keichi.*

Handal (151) **1.** Norwegian: habitational name from any of several farmsteads named Handal, probably from Old Norse *horn* 'horn' (denoting a sharp bend or angle in the landscape) + *dal* 'valley'. **2.** Arabic: from a descriptive epithet meaning 'dwarf'.

GIVEN NAMES Spanish 20%; Arabic 6%; French 4%. *Carlos* (4), *Alejandro* (2), *Jorge* (2), *Jose* (2), *Roxana* (2), *Salomon* (2), *Alberto, Ana, Domingo, Erlinda, Humberto, Manuel Dejesus; Shafiq* (3), *Imad, Issa, Jeries, Muna, Nasri; Michel, Remy.*

Handel (1013) **1.** German (also **Händel**) and Jewish: from a pet form of the personal name HANS. Sometimes this can be from a pet form of *Heinrich*, e.g. *Heindl, Haindl.* **2.** Jewish (Ashkenazic): metonymic occupational name for a merchant, German *Handel* 'trade', 'commerce'.

GIVEN NAMES German 4%. *Arno, Egon, Erwin, Ewald, Florian, Frieda, Hermann, Philo, Siegfried.*

Handeland (177) Norwegian: habitational name from any of several farmsteads in southwestern Norway. The first element is probably from Old Norse *hanga* 'to hang', with reference to a steep cliff or mountain with a farmstead (*land*) beneath.

GIVEN NAME Scandinavian 7%. *Einer.*

Handelman (446) Jewish (Ashkenazic): occupational name for a tradesman, merchant or dealer (see HANDEL).

GIVEN NAMES Jewish 8%. *Mayer* (3), *Avi, Emanuel, Hyman, Isadore, Mendel, Meyer, Sholom.*

Handelsman (208) Jewish (Ashkenazic): occupational name for a tradesman, merchant, or dealer (see HANDEL).

GIVEN NAMES Jewish 7%. *Moshe* (3), *Zahava.*

Handford (182) English: variant of HANFORD.

Handke (243) German: variant of HANKE.

Handleman (109) Jewish (American): Americanized spelling of HANDELMAN.

GIVEN NAMES Jewish 9%. *Avrom, Melech, Pola.*

Handler (1241) German (also **Händler**) and Jewish (Ashkenazic): variant of HENDLER.

GIVEN NAMES Jewish 6%. *Miriam* (3), *Moise* (3), *Isidor* (2), *Sol* (2), *Akiva, Aviva, Avrohom, Boruch, Chana, Mayer, Meyer, Mort.*

Handley (3734) English (chiefly central and northern), Scottish, and Irish: variant of HANLEY.

Handlin (286) Irish: probably a variant of HANLON.

Handlon (174) Irish: variant of HANLON.

Handlos (113) German: **1.** from *handlos*, literally 'handless', hence presumably a nickname for someone who had lost one or both of his hands. **2.** status name for a feudal tenant, who paid the so-called *hantloese* 'hand fee' for a noninheritable fief given to him for life; from Middle High German *hant* 'hand' + *loese* 'redemption in cash'.

GIVEN NAME German 6%. *Kurt* (2).

Handly (155) Irish: variant of HANLEY.

Handorf (104) German: habitational name from any of numerous places in northwestern Germany named Handorf.

Handrahan (152) Irish: variant of HANRAHAN, characteristic of some parts of southern County Tipperary.

Handrich (202) German: Sorbian form of ANDREAS.

Handrick (112) German: Sorbian form of ANDREAS.

GIVEN NAME German 4%. *Helmut.*

Hands (519) English (chiefly West Midlands): variant of HAND.

Handsaker (105) Altered spelling of Swiss German HUNZIKER.

Handschuh (113) German: metonymic occupational name for a maker or seller of gloves, or perhaps a nickname for someone who habitually wore gloves, from Middle High German *hantschuoch* 'glove', literally 'hand shoe'.

Handshoe (151) Literal translation of German HANDSCHUH 'glove'.

Handt (127) German: variant of HAND.

Handwerk (254) South German: metonymic occupational name for a craftsman or artisan (see HANDWERKER).

Handwerker (149) German, Dutch and Jewish (Ashkenazic): occupational name for a craftsman, from an agent derivative of German *Handwerk*, Middle High German *hantwërc* 'craft', Dutch *handwerk, hantwerk*.

GIVEN NAMES Jewish 6%; German 4%. *Haim, Rina, Sol; Kurt, Reinhard.*

Handy (4298) English: nickname from Middle English *hondi* 'skillful with one's hands', 'dextrous'.

Handyside (140) Scottish: habitational name from Handyside, a place in Berwickshire named with Middle English *hanging* + *side* 'slope', i.e. a natural shelf on a hillside, or possibly a place where executions were carried out.

Handzel (147) Polish form of German HANSEL.

GIVEN NAMES Polish 11%. *Casimier, Casimir, Jozef, Maciej, Stanislaw, Zbigniew.*

Hane (474) **1.** English: variant spelling of HAIN. **2.** Swiss German: probably a variant of HAHN 1.

Hanek (127) Czech (**Hánek**): from *(Jo)hánek*, Czech pet form of the German personal name JOHANN.

Hanel (420) German (**Hänel**): see HAENEL.

Haneline (248) Probably an Americanized spelling of German HEINLEIN.

Hanen (113) **1.** Scottish: unexplained. Possibly a variant of Irish HANNAN. **2.** German: from Middle High German: probably from a house name, *zem hanen* 'at the sign of the rooster' (see HAHN).

Hanenburg (121) Respelling of German **Hanenberg**, a habitational name from a place named Hanenberg or something similar, such as *Hahnenberg* in Rhineland-Palatinate or *Haneberg* in Bavaria (Allgäu).

Haner (690) **1.** German: altered spelling or variant of HAHNER, a habitational name for someone from any of the places named Hahn. **2.** German (**Häner**): variant of HANNER.

Hanes (3387) English and Welsh: variant spelling of HAYNES.

Haney (11850) **1.** English and Scottish: probably a variant of HANNEY. **2.** Scottish or Irish: reduced form of MCHANEY. **3.** Americanized spelling of Norwegian **Hanøy**, a habitational name from any of four farmsteads so named, from Old Norse *haðna* 'young nanny-goat' or *hani* 'cock' (probably indicating a crag or mountain resembling a cock's comb in shape) + *øy* 'island'. **4.** Jewish (American): Americanized form of various like-sounding Ashkenazic Jewish names.

Hanf (264) German: metonymic occupational name for a grower or seller of hemp, Middle High German *hanf*.
GIVEN NAMES German 5%. *Kurt* (2), *Hans*, *Horst*, *Ulrich*.

Hanford (745) English: habitational name from any of various places, such as Hanford in Staffordshire and Handforth in Cheshire, named from Old English *hān* 'stone' (used as a marker) or *hana* 'cock', 'male bird', perhaps used as a byname, + Old English *ford* 'ford'.

Hanft (284) German: variant of HANF, with the addition of an inorganic -*t*.

Hang (680) **1.** Chinese 杭: a comparatively rare surname in China, of later origin than most of the more common surnames. It was not until the Song dynasty (960–1279) that the current form of the character for the name became established, appearing in Hunan province after branching from a surname written with a similar character. **2.** Laotian or Cambodian: unexplained. **3.** Vietnamese: unexplained, **4.** South German and Swiss German: variant of HANK, a pet form of JOHANN or HEINRICH.
GIVEN NAMES Chinese 36%; Other Southeast Asian 15%; Vietnamese 9%. *Yee* (5), *Chang* (3), *Hong* (3), *Kang* (3), *Chen* (2), *Chue* (2), *Kao* (2), *Kaying* (2), *Leng* (2), *Mee* (2); *Vang* (9), *Doua* (4), *Pao* (4), *Chia* (3), *Chong* (3), *Pang* (3), *Shoua* (3), *Houa* (2), *Neng* (2), *Phoua* (2), *Sarin* (2), *Sou* (2), *Soua* (2); *Quang* (20), *Anh* (4), *Dang* (4), *Hoa* (4), *Huy* (4), *Ly* (4), *Mai* (4), *Minh* (4), *Nguyen* (4), *Phong* (4), *Lien* (3), *Loc* (3), *Thao* (3).

Hangartner (164) German: habitational name for someone from Hangard in the Saarland.
GIVEN NAMES German 4%. *Hans* (2), *Urs*.

Hangen (157) North German or Dutch: unexplained.

Hanger (753) English: topographic name from Middle English *hanger*, *hangre* 'wood on a steep hillside', or habitational name from a place named with this word, as for example Hanger in Netley Marsh, Hampshire.

Hanif (127) Muslim: from a personal name based on Arabic *hanif* 'upright', 'true believer'. The Qur'an (3: 67) mentions the Prophet Ibrahim (Abraham) as *hanif*: 'Ibrahim was not a Jew nor yet a Christian but he was an upright man who had surrendered to Allah accepting Islam.'
GIVEN NAMES Muslim 86%. *Mohammad* (16), *Mohammed* (11), *Mohamed* (8), *Muhammad* (5), *Ehtesham* (2), *Aamir*, *Abdelaziz*, *Abdul*, *Aleem*, *Amjad*, *Bibi*, *Faisal*.

Hanifan (155) Irish: variant of HANAFIN.

Hanifin (169) Irish: variant of HANAFIN.

Hanig (137) German (also **Hänig**): from a dialect variant of HENNING.

Hanigan (232) Irish: variant spelling of HANNIGAN.
GIVEN NAME French 4%. *Michel*.

Haning (329) Scottish: variant of HENNING.

Hanis (126) **1.** Hungarian: Magyarized spelling of German or Jewish HANISCH. **2.** Jewish (eastern Ashkenazic): metronymic from the personal name HANNA.

Hanisch (327) German (also **Hänisch**; of Slavic origin): variant of HANS.
GIVEN NAMES German 7%. *Gottfried*, *Gunther*, *Hans*, *Klaus-Dieter*, *Rainer*, *Wolf*, *Wolfgang*.

Hanish (190) Americanized spelling of German HANISCH.
GIVEN NAMES German 5%. *Gerhard*, *Kurt*, *Otto*.

Hank (480) **1.** German: from a pet form of HANS, itself a pet form of JOHANN. **2.** German (Alemannic): from a pet form of HEINRICH.

Hanka (106) **1.** North German and Czech: from a pet form of the personal name *Johan* (see JOHN). **2.** Finnish: unexplained.
GIVEN NAMES Hungarian 4%; Czech and Slovak 4%. *Etelka*, *Laszlo*; *Ladislav* (2).

Hanke (1525) **1.** North German and Dutch: from a pet form of the personal name *Johan* (see JOHN). **2.** English: from a medieval pet form of the personal name *Jehan* (see JOHN). **3.** English: in some cases, perhaps from Old Norse *Anki*, a pet form of a personal name with the first element *Arn-*, shortened from *arnar*, the genitive singular of *ǫrn* 'eagle'.
GIVEN NAMES German 5%. *Otto* (4), *Erwin* (3), *Lorenz* (3), *Claus*, *Dieter*, *Dietmar*, *Ernst*, *Frieda*, *Hans*, *Jurgen*, *Kurt*, *Lothar*.

Hankel (268) South German: from a pet form of HANKE.
GIVEN NAME French 4%. *Michel*.

Hanken (210) English and Scottish: variant spelling of HANKIN.

Hankerson (435) English (Warwickshire): probably a variant of HANKINSON.

Hankes (221) **1.** English: variant of HANKS. **2.** Jewish (eastern Ashkenazic): metronymic from *Khanke* (a pet form of the Yiddish female personal name *Khane*; see HANNA 1), with the Yiddish possessive suffix -*s*.

Hankey (637) English: from a pet form of HANKE.

Hankin (533) **1.** English (chiefly Lancashire) and Scottish: from the Middle English personal name *Hankin*, a pet form of HANN, with the addition of the hypocoristic suffix -*kin*. **2.** English: from Middle English *Handekin*, a diminutive of the nickname HAND. **3.** English: from Middle English *Hamekin*, a pet form of the personal name *Hamo*, *Hame* (see HAMMOND). **4.** Dutch: from a pet form of the personal name *Johann(es)* (see JOHN). **5.** Jewish (eastern Ashkenazic): metronymic from *Khanke* (a pet form of the Yiddish female personal name *Khane*; see HANNA), with the Slavic possessive suffix -*in*.
GIVEN NAMES Jewish 6%. *Yaron* (3), *Abbe*, *Isadore*, *Myer*, *Yitzhak*.

Hankins (6788) English: patronymic from HANKIN.

Hankinson (758) English (mainly Lancashire): patronymic from the personal name HANKIN.

Hankla (173) Origin unidentified.

Hanko (268) Polish: from a pet form of the personal name *Jan*, a vernacular form of Latin *Johannes* (see JOHN).

Hanks (6089) English (Gloucestershire): patronymic from the Middle English personal name *Hank*, a short form of HANKIN.

Hanlan (112) Irish: variant of HANLON.

Hanley (7144) **1.** Irish: shortened form of **O'Hanley**, an Anglicized form of Gaelic **Ó hÁinle** 'descendant of *Áinle*', a personal name meaning 'champion'. This is the name of a ruling family in Connacht; it is now common in southern Ireland. **2.** English: habitational name from any of various places, such as Handley in Cheshire, Derbyshire. Northamptonshire, and Dorset and Hanley in Staffordshire and Worcestershire, all from Old English *hēan*, the weak dative case (originally used after a preposition and article) of *hēah* 'high' + *lēah* 'wood', 'clearing', or from Handley Farm in Clayhanger, Devon, which is named from Old English *hān* '(boundary) stone' + *lēah*.
GIVEN NAMES Irish 6%. *Brendan* (2), *Conor*, *Declan*, *Donovan*, *Eamonn*, *John Patrick*.

Hanlin (855) Scottish and English: probably a variant spelling of Irish HANLON.

Hanline (153) Americanized spelling of German **Hänlein**, a habitational name from a place so named (now Hähnlein), in Hesse.

Hanlon (4318) Irish: shortened Anglicized form of Gaelic **Ó hAnluain** 'descendant of *Anluan*', a personal name from the intensive prefix *an*- + *luan* 'light', 'radiance' or 'warrior'. Occasionally *Hanlon* has been used to represent HALLINAN.
FOREBEARS Hanlon was the name of a ruling family in County Armagh in the 16th century.
GIVEN NAMES Irish 6%. *Brendan*, *Declan*, *Maeve*.

Hanly (334) English and Irish: variant spelling of HANLEY.

Hanmer (173) Welsh: habitational name from a place in Flintshire (now part of

Clwyd), named with the Old English personal name *Hagena* + *mere* 'lake', 'pond'. FOREBEARS An early ancestor of the Welsh family of this name was Sir David Hanmer, who was appointed a judge in the 14th century and whose daughter married the chieftain Owen Glendower (?1350–?1416), leader of a revolt against King Henry IV's rule in Wales.

Hann (1982) **1.** English: from the medieval personal name *Han(n)*, which is usually a short form of *Johan* (see JOHN). In some cases, however, it may be from HENRY and even RANDOLPH (for the replacement of *R*- by *H*- in Germanic names introduced by the Normans, compare HICK). **2.** German: from an aphetic form of the personal name *Johann* (see JOHN).

Hanna (13020) **1.** Irish (especially northeastern Ulster): shortened Anglicized form of Gaelic **Ó hAnnaigh** 'descendant of *Annach*', a byname of uncertain meaning. **2.** English: from the medieval female personal name *Hannah* or *Anna*, ultimately from Hebrew *Chana* 'He (God) has favored me' (i.e. with a child). The name is borne in the Bible by the mother of Samuel (1 Samuel 1: 1–28), and there is a tradition (unsupported by Biblical evidence) that it was the name of the mother of the Virgin Mary; this St. Anne was a popular figure in medieval art and legend. **3.** Scottish: variant of HANNAY. **4.** German: from a pet form of the personal name HANS.

Hannafin (109) Variant spelling of Irish HANAFIN.

Hannaford (552) English: variant of HANFORD.

Hannagan (210) Irish: variant spelling of HANNIGAN.

Hannah (6111) Scottish, northern Irish, and English: variant spelling of HANNA.

Hannahs (328) Scottish, northern Irish, and English: variant of HANNA.

Hannam (232) English: habitational name from a place called Hanham in Gloucestershire, which was originally Old English *Hānum*, dative plural of *hān* 'rock', hence '(place) at the rocks'. The ending *-ham* is by analogy with other place names with this very common unstressed ending.

Hannaman (175) Respelling of HANNEMANN.

Hannan (2386) **1.** Irish: Anglicized form of Gaelic **Ó hAnnáin** 'descendant of *Annán*', a contracted form of *Annach*, a byname of uncertain meaning. **2.** Muslim: from the Arabic personal name *Hannān* 'compassionate', 'merciful'.

Hannasch (144) German (Westphalia): from a pet form of the personal name *Johannes*.

Hannaway (117) Irish: reduced Anglicized form of Gaelic **Ó hAinbhith** (see HANVEY).

Hannay (217) Scottish: habitational name, probably from an unidentified place called Hannethe. FOREBEARS Gilbert de Hannethe or de Hahanith is recorded in Wigtownshire at the end of the 13th century. John of Hanna is recorded as the master of a ship belonging to the King of Scotland in 1424.

Hannegan (167) Irish: variant spelling of HANNIGAN.
GIVEN NAME Irish 4%. *Brendan*.

Hanneken (200) **1.** North German: patronymic from *Hanneke*, a pet form of HANS. **2.** Dutch: from a pet form of the personal name HAN.
GIVEN NAMES German 4%. *Horst*, *Ralf*.

Hannel (137) Americanized form of German HAENEL.

Hanneman (952) Americanized spelling of HANNEMANN.

Hannemann (321) German and Dutch: from a pet form of HANS.
GIVEN NAMES German 12%. *Ernst* (3), *Manfred* (2), *Wilhelm* (2), *Bernd*, *Erhard*, *Erwin*, *Gerhard*, *Helmuth*, *Kurt*, *Volker*.

Hannen (189) **1.** German: metronymic from the female Biblical name *Hanna* (see HANNA 2). **2.** Dutch and German: patronymic from a short form of the personal name *Johannes* (see JOHN).

Hanner (1234) **1.** English (mainly Norfolk): unexplained. **2.** German: from a pet form of *Hann*, short form of *Johann* (see JOHN).

Hanners (566) English (Kent): unexplained. Compare HANNER.

Hannes (223) German and Dutch: from an aphetic form of the personal name *Johannes* (see JOHN).
GIVEN NAMES German 8%. *Gunther* (2), *Kurt* (2), *Aloysius*, *Konrad*, *Wolfgang*.

Hanney (286) English: habitational name from East and West Hanney in southern Oxfordshire (formerly in Berkshire), named with Old English *hana* 'cock', 'male bird' + *ēg* 'island' or 'land between streams'.

Hanni (313) German (**Hänni**): from an aphetic pet form of the personal name *Johannes* (see JOHN).
GIVEN NAMES German 4%. *Erwin*, *Heinz*, *Kurt*, *Rudi*.

Hannibal (368) **1.** German: from a post-humanist personal name. **2.** English: from the personal name *Anabel*, an alteration of *Amabel*, a feminine name derived from Latin *amabilis* 'lovable'.

Hannig (242) Eastern German: from a dialect variant of the personal name HENNING.
GIVEN NAMES German 10%. *Franz* (2), *Dieter*, *Gerhard*, *Hans*, *Heinz*, *Inge*, *Kurt*, *Waltraud*.

Hannigan (1688) Irish: shortened Anglicized form of Gaelic **Ó hAnnagáin** 'descendant of *Annagán*', a pet form of the personal name *Annach* (see HANNA).
GIVEN NAMES Irish 5%. *Brendan* (2), *Liam*.

Hanninen (119) Finnish (**Hänninen**): probably from the German personal name *Johannes* (or a pet form such as *Hänschen*) + the common surname suffix *-nen*. German personal names were adopted in Finland during the Middle Ages; German influence was centered on the multi-cultural town of Viipuri in Karelia. This name is found typically in central and east-central areas of Finland.
GIVEN NAMES Finnish 17%; Scandinavian 4%. *Reino* (2), *Aarne*, *Jouni*, *Jyrki*, *Markku*, *Paavo*, *Pentti*, *Urho*; *Arni*.

Hanning (531) **1.** Scottish: habitational name from a place near Selkirk called Haining 'piece of enclosed ground'. The earliest known occurrence of the surname is around 1630. . **2.** Eastern German: variant of HANNIG.

Hannis (156) English (Gloucestershire): possibly a local variant of ANNIS.

Hanno (111) **1.** German: from a pet form of the personal name HANS. **2.** Perhaps also Greek (**Hannos**): from the vocabulary word *hannos* 'perch', used as a nickname for a gullible person.
GIVEN NAME French 4%. *Gabrielle* (2).

Hannold (181) Variant spelling of German HANOLD.

Hannon (4601) Irish: **1.** shortened Anglicized form of Gaelic **Ó hAinchín** 'descendant of *Ainchín*', a personal name possibly related to the personal name *Annach* (see HANNA), unless it is a variant of *ainghein* 'unborn'. **2.** shortened Anglicized form of Gaelic **Ó hAnnacháin** (see HANAHAN). **3.** shortened Anglicized form of Gaelic **Ó hAnnáin** (see HANNAN).

Hannula (233) Finnish: habitational name from a farmstead named for its owner, from the personal name *Hannu*, a derivative of German *Johannes* (see JOHN) + the local suffix *-la*. In the Middle Ages, *Johannes* was one of the most popular personal names in Finland.
GIVEN NAMES Finnish 8%. *Reino* (3), *Eino*, *Kauko*, *Oiva*, *Tarmo*, *Waino*.

Hannum (995) English: probably a variant spelling of HANNAM.

Hanny (139) **1.** Austrian and Swiss German: a variant spelling of **Hänni**, see HANNI. **2.** English: variant spelling of HANNEY.

Hano (137) Japanese: meaning 'leafy field'. This name is not common in Japan.
GIVEN NAMES Japanese 4%. *Kazu*, *Midori*.

Hanold (192) German: variant of HEINOLD.
GIVEN NAMES German 4%. *Claus*, *Kurt*, *Reinhardt*.

Hanon (133) **1.** Variant spelling of Irish HANNON. **2.** Possibly Dutch: from a pet form of HANS.

Hanover (553) German and Jewish (Ashkenazic): habitational name from the city of Hannover in Lower Saxony. The place name, first recorded in the form *Honovere*, is a compound of Middle Low German *hō*, *hŏch* 'high' + *ŏver* 'bank', 'shore'.

Hanrahan (2347) Irish: shortened Anglicized form of Gaelic **Ó hAnradháin** 'descendant of *Anradhán*', a personal name from a diminutive of *ánrad(h)* 'hero', 'warrior', 'champion', a title denoting the nobleman next in rank to the king in medieval Ireland. The title was also used to denote court poets of the second rank.
GIVEN NAMES Irish 5%. *Kieran* (3), *Brendan*, *Ciaran, Connor, Liam, Seamus, Sinead.*

Hanratty (445) Irish (chiefly counties Louth and Armagh): shortened Anglicized form of Gaelic **Ó hInreachtaigh** 'descendant of *Ionnrachtach*', a name meaning 'attacker'.

Hans (1439) **1.** German and Dutch: from a common and long-established vernacular personal name, an apheticy form of *Johannes* (see JOHN). The surname is also borne by Ashkenazic Jews, presumably as an adoption of the German or Dutch surname. **2.** Indian (Panjab): Hindu (Arora) and Sikh name, from Sanskrit *hamsa* 'swan', 'goose', based on the name of an Arora clan.
GIVEN NAMES Indian 4%; German 4%. *Ananta, Bhim, Chander, Gopal, Madhur, Malkit, Nirmal, Preet, Puneet, Ravi, Rohit, Roop; Erwin* (4), *Guenther* (2), *Helmut* (2), *Gerhard, Hermann, Klaus, Kurt, Manfred, Merwin.*

Hansard (692) English: metonymic occupational name for a cutler, from Old French *hansard, hansart* 'cutlass', 'dagger' (of Germanic origin, composed of elements meaning 'hand' and 'knife' (see SACHS)).
FOREBEARS This is the name of a family who have held land in Surrey and Sussex since the late 12th century. It has come to denote the official verbatim report of British parliamentary proceedings, first printed by Luke Hansard (1752–1828), who had left Norwich for London with one guinea in his pocket and a training as a journeyman printer. He himself believed (probably wrongly) that his surname came from German *Hanse* (Old High German *hansa* 'company', 'band'), as in the Hanseatic League, and that it was acquired by his ancestors through a connection with the East Anglian wool trade.

Hansberger (161) German: probably from a topographic name *Hansperger*, from a place in Bavaria or Austria named Hansperg.

Hansberry (393) **1.** English: variant spelling of HANSBURY. **2.** Possibly an Americanized spelling of German **Hansberg** (see HANSBERGER) or **Hansbruch** (see HANSBROUGH).

Hansbrough (274) Of uncertain origin: **1.** possibly an Americanized form of German **Hansbruch**, a habitational name from an unidentified place. **2.** perhaps also English, a variant of HANSBURY.

Hansbury (184) English and Irish: habitational name from an unidentified place. Possibly an altered form of HANBURY.

Hansch (139) German: from a pet form of the personal name HANS.
GIVEN NAMES German 17%. *Ernst* (2), *Otto* (2), *Dieter, Monika, Wilfried.*

Hanscom (813) Altered spelling of the English habitational name **Hanscomb(e)**, from Hanscombe End in Shillington, Bedfordshire, named from an Old English personal name *Hān* (from Old English *hān* '(boundary) stone') + *camp* 'enclosed land'.

Hanse (110) **1.** Dutch: variant of HANSEN. **2.** German: variant of HANS. **3.** German: habitational name for someone from a place called Hansen in Lower Saxony.

Hansel (1387) **1.** Dutch: from the personal name *Hansel* or *Ansel*, a pet form of *Anselm* (see ANSELMO). **2.** English: probably of Dutch origin (see 1). **3.** German (also **Hänsel**): from a pet form of the personal name HANS.

Hansell (733) **1.** English (Norfolk): variant spelling of HANSEL. **2.** In some cases probably a respelling of HANSEL 1 or 3.

Hanselman (587) German and Dutch: from a German personal name, *Hanselmann*, a pet form of HANS.

Hansen (56792) Danish, Norwegian, Dutch, and North German: patronymic from the personal name HANS.
FOREBEARS This name is recorded in Beverwijck in New Netherland in the mid 17th century, but it was also brought independently to North America by many other bearers from different parts of northwest Europe.
GIVEN NAMES Scandinavian 5%. *Erik* (111), *Lars* (28), *Nels* (27), *Niels* (25), *Thor* (18), *Jorgen* (14), *Knud* (14), *Holger* (11), *Morten* (8), *Nils* (8), *Einer* (7), *Johan* (7).

Hanser (246) South German: patronymic from the personal name HANS.

Hansford (1010) English (Dorset): habitational name from an unidentified place, possibly Ansford in Somerset, which is recorded in Domesday Book as *Almundesford*, from the genitive case of the Old English personal name *Ealhmund* (composed of the elements *ealh* 'temple' + *mund* 'protection') + Old English *ford* 'ford'.

Hanshaw (920) **1.** English: perhaps a variant of HENSHAW. **2.** Possibly also an Americanized spelling of German HANDSCHUH.

Hanshew (324) Americanized spelling of German HANDSCHUH.

Hansing (141) North German: patronymic from HANS.

Hansler (108) German (**Hänsler**): see HENSLER.
GIVEN NAMES German 4%. *Erwin, Kurt.*

Hansley (316) English: habitational name from Annesley Woodhouse in Nottinghamshire, or from Ansley in Warwickshire.

The first is named from an unattested Old English personal name *Ān* + *lēah* 'wood', 'clearing'. (The affix Woodhouse is a later, medieval addition.) The second is from Old English *ānsetl* 'hermitage' + *lēah*.

Hansman (211) Respelling of Dutch or German HANSMANN.

Hansmann (222) North German and Dutch: elaborated form of the personal name HANS.
GIVEN NAMES German 6%. *Fritz* (2), *Erwin, Kurt.*

Hanson (47293) **1.** English (chiefly Midlands and northern England, especially Yorkshire): patronymic from HANN or the byname HAND. **2.** Irish: shortened Anglicized form of Gaelic **Ó hAmhsaigh** (see HAMPSON 2). **3.** Irish: variant of MCKITTRICK. **4.** Respelling of Scandinavian HANSEN or HANSSON. **5.** Jewish (Ashkenazic): metronymic from the female personal name HANNA.
FOREBEARS A family by the name of Hanson was established in America by John Hanson, one of four brothers sent there by Queen Christina of Sweden in 1642. They were grandsons of an Englishman who had married into the Swedish royal family; he was descended from a certain Roger de Rastrick, who had lived in Yorkshire in the 13th century.

Hanssen (493) Danish, Norwegian, and North German: patronymic from the personal name HANS.
GIVEN NAMES Scandinavian 11%; German 5%. *Erik* (4), *Per* (2), *Alf, Maren, Nels, Tollef, Tor; Otto* (4), *Manfred, Monika.*

Hansson (238) **1.** Swedish: patronymic from the personal name HANS. **2.** Respelling of HANSSEN.
GIVEN NAMES Scandinavian 44%; Dutch 4%; German 4%. *Lars* (6), *Anders* (3), *Erik* (3), *Niels* (2), *Elof, Gudrun, Jarl, Lennart, Mats, Niklas, Per, Sten; Henrik; Hans* (5), *Elfriede, Kurt.*

Hanstad (100) Norwegian: habitational name from a place so called.

Hanten (177) **1.** Belgian and Luxembourgeois: unexplained. **2.** Possibly in some instances a variant spelling of English HANTON.

Hanthorn (171) English: unexplained. Compare HENTHORN.

Hantman (183) Jewish (Ashkenazic): nickname from Yiddish *hant* 'hand' + *man* 'man'.
GIVEN NAME Jewish 6%. *Shoshana.*

Hanton (146) **1.** Scottish: possibly, as Black postulates, a habitational name from a place recorded in 1661 as Hantestoun. **2.** English: variant of HAMPTON.

Hantz (237) German: from a variant spelling of the personal name HANS.

Hanus (612) **1.** Czech and Slovak (**Hanuš**): from the old personal name *Hanuš* or an aphetic form of *Johannes* (see JOHN). **2.** Dutch: from an aphetic form of the personal name *Johannes* (see JOHN).

Hanvey (419) Northern Irish: shortened Anglicized form of Gaelic **Ó hAinbhith** 'descendant of *Ainbhioth*', a byname meaning 'un-peace', 'stormy'.

Hanway (188) Northern Irish: variant of HANVEY.

Hanz (107) German: from a variant spelling of the personal name HANS.
GIVEN NAME German 5%. *Armin.*

Hanzel (331) German (also **Hänzel**), Czech, etc.: from the personal name *Hansel*, a pet form of the personal name *Johannes* (see JOHN).

Hanzlik (303) Czech (**Hanzlík**): pet form of HANZEL.

Hao (314) Chinese 郝: from the name of Hao village, in present-day Shanxi province. The penultimate king of the Shang dynasty, Di Yi (1191–1155 BC) granted this place to one of his sons. Descendants of this son eventually adopted Hao as their surname.
GIVEN NAMES Chinese 44%; Vietnamese 5%. *Ping* (4), *Hong* (3), *Ying* (3), *Chen* (2), *Chi* (2), *Chien* (2), *Jing* (2), *Li* (2), *Lian* (2), *Ming* (2), *Sheng* (2), *Wenjie* (2); *Chang, Hu, Min, Tam; Dinh, Ha, Le Van, Quan, Thi, Yen.*

Hapeman (185) Anglicized or Americanized form of German HAUPTMANN.

Hapgood (230) English: from Middle English *haue, habbe* '(may he/you) have' + *god* 'good', perhaps a nickname for someone who habitually used this phrase.

Hapke (206) North German: from a pet form of a Germanic personal name (see HAPPEL 1).
GIVEN NAMES German 7%. *Lothar* (2), *Herta, Lutz.*

Hapner (303) South German: variant of HAFNER or from **Höppner**, see HOEPPNER.

Happ (547) **1.** South German: metonymic occupational name for someone who made sickles or who used a sickle, from Middle High German *happe, heppe* 'sickle', 'vineyard worker's hook'. **2.** German: from a reduced form of the medieval German personal names *Hadebald* or *Hadebert* (see HAPPEL).

Happe (320) **1.** English: from Middle English *hap(pe)* 'chance', 'luck', 'fortune' (from Old Norse *happ*), applied as a nickname for someone considered fortunate or well favored. Compare CHANCE, FORTUNE. **2.** German, Dutch, and northern French (Picardy): from Middle Low German, Middle Dutch, Old French *happe* 'hook', 'hatchet', 'pruning hook', a metonymic occupational name for a maker of such implements or for someone who used one in his work. Compare HEPPE. **3.** German: from a reduced form of the me-

dieval German personal names *Hadebald* or *Hadebert* (see HAPPEL).

Happel (730) **1.** German: from a pet form of the medieval German personal names *Hadebald* or *Hadebert*, composed of the elements *had(u)* 'battle', 'strife' + *berht* 'bright', 'famous' or *bald* 'bold', 'brave'. **2.** Dutch: metonymic occupational name for a seller of apples, a variant of APPEL.

Happy (243) **1.** Americanized form of German, Dutch, or northern French HAPPE. **2.** English: nickname from the adjective *happy*.

Haq (317) Muslim: from a personal name based on Arabic *Haqq* 'true', 'truth', 'real'. *Al-Haqq* 'the Truth' is an attribute of Allah. The name is often found in combinations, for example *Abdul-Haqq* 'servant of the truth', *Nūr-ul-Haqq* 'light of the truth'.
GIVEN NAMES Muslim 90%. *Mohammed* (12), *Syed* (11), *Abdul* (10), *Ehsan* (10), *Mohammad* (8), *Anwar* (7), *Riaz* (7), *Muhammad* (6), *Zia* (6), *Ihsan* (4), *Nadeem* (4), *Ahsan* (3).

Haque (564) Muslim: see HAQ.
GIVEN NAMES Muslim 88%. *Mohammed* (47), *Syed* (27), *Mohammad* (20), *Shamsul* (7), *Anwarul* (6), *Muhammad* (6), *Abdul* (5), *Izhar* (5), *Badrul* (4), *Fazlul* (4), *Inam* (4), *Abu* (3).

Hara (668) **1.** Japanese: 'plain' or 'field'; variously written, taken from a place name in Musashi (now Tōkyō and Saitama prefectures), and perhaps from other similarly named localities, as well as in the Ryūkyū Islands. Listed in the Shinsen shōjiroku. **2.** reduced form of Irish O'HARA.
GIVEN NAMES Japanese 47%. *Mitsuo* (4), *Akira* (3), *Fusako* (3), *Hideaki* (3), *Kazuyoshi* (3), *Kenji* (3), *Naoto* (3), *Saburo* (3), *Daisuke* (2), *Hideki* (2), *Hideo* (2), *Hiroshi* (2).

Harada (666) Japanese: 'rice paddy on the plain'; topographic, mostly found in the island of Kyūshū and the Ryūkyū Islands.
GIVEN NAMES Japanese 55%. *Minoru* (5), *Akira* (3), *Hideo* (3), *Keiko* (3), *Masato* (3), *Nobuyuki* (3), *Takashi* (3), *Toru* (3), *Toshio* (3), *Yuji* (3), *Akiko* (2), *Hiroshi* (2).

Haraldson (154) **1.** Americanized spelling of Swedish **Haraldsson** or Norwegian **Haraldsen**, patronymics from the personal name *Harald*, Old Norse *Haraldr* (see HAROLD). **2.** Scottish: patronymic from the Scandinavian personal name *Harald*.

Haralson (994) Scandinavian: variant of HARALDSON.

Haran (346) **1.** Irish (especially Counties Clare and Connacht): variant of HAREN. **2.** Irish: reduced form of HANRAHAN. **3.** French: metonymic occupational name for a seller of herrings, from *hareng* 'herring'.
GIVEN NAME Irish 5%. *Fidelma.*

Harang (103) French (Lorraine): variant of Dutch **Hareng**.

Harari (205) Jewish (from southern France): habitational name for someone from Montpellier. The first part of this place name means 'mountain' in French; as a result in Jewish tradition the Jewish inhabitants of the city were called *charari*, from the Hebrew word literally meaning *mountaineer*.
GIVEN NAMES Jewish 21%. *Tzvi* (3), *Arnon, Avi, Azriel, Chaya, Dror, Galit, Meyer, Nurit, Oded, Ori, Rina.*

Harary (133) Jewish (from southern France): variant of HARARI.
GIVEN NAMES Jewish 13%. *Ilan* (2), *Moise* (2), *Eti, Zehava.*

Haraway (224) English: origin uncertain. Possibly a variant of HARROWER.

Harb (467) **1.** Arabic: from an ancient Arabic personal name based on the word *harb* 'war'. The Prophet Muhammad counseled against giving children names such as *Harb*, associated with violence. Nevertheless, the name has survived and flourishes in some places in the Arabic-speaking world. **2.** German: of uncertain derivation. Possibly a topographic name for someone living by a swamp, Old High German *hor*. It is also found in Switzerland, eastern Slovenia, and elsewhere.
GIVEN NAMES Arabic 36%. *Ali* (4), *Imad* (4), *Walid* (4), *Jamil* (3), *Mohamad* (3), *Sami* (3), *Youssef* (3), *Azizeh* (2), *Bassam* (2), *Bassem* (2), *Beshara* (2), *Elham* (2).

Harbach (180) **1.** South German: habitational name from any of several places named Harbach. **2.** English: probably from Old French, Middle English *herberge* 'hostel', 'shelter', hence a metonymic occupational name for a keeper of lodgings, or for a servant who worked there.

Harbaugh (1915) Americanized form of German HARBACH.

Harbeck (243) **1.** North German: habitational name from any of several places and streams called Harbeck 'marshy stream'. **2.** South German (Bavarian): variant of Harbach.
GIVEN NAME French 5%. *Camille.*

Harben (133) English: of uncertain derivation. The 18th-century parish registers of Marske, North Yorkshire, record the surname **Hartburn** with the variant **Harburn**; Harben may be a further variant of this. If so, its origin is probably topographic or habitational, from East Hartburn in Stockton-on-Tees or Hartburn in Northumberland, both named from Old English *heorot* 'hart' + *burna* 'steam'. However, this conjecture is not borne out by the distribution of the surname a century later, when it occurs chiefly in Cambridgeshire and London and also with a significant presence in the Channel Islands, perhaps suggesting that it could be a variant of HARPIN.
GIVEN NAME Welsh 4%. *Dwyn* (2).

Harber (1286) English: variant spelling of HARBOUR.

Harbers (123) North German and Dutch: patronymic form of HARBERT.

GIVEN NAMES German 6%. *Hans, Klaus, Reiner*.

Harbert (1175) Northern German, Dutch, French, English, and Scottish: variant of HERBERT.

Harberts (183) North German: patronymic form of HARBERT.

Harbeson (269) See HARBISON.

Harbin (2868) Irish (County Clare): variant of HERBERT.

Harbinson (126) English: variant of HARBISON.

Harbison (2325) English (chiefly northern Ireland): patronymic from the personal name HERBERT. (The change from *-er-* to *-ar-* was a common one in Old French and Middle English.)

Harbold (284) English: from a Norman personal name composed of the Germanic elements *hari, heri* 'army' + *bald, bold* 'bold', 'brave'.

Harbolt (114) English (Essex): variant of HARBOLD.

GIVEN NAME French 4%. *Camille*.

Harbor (323) English: variant spelling of HARBOUR.

Harbottle (141) English (Northumberland): habitational name from a place in the foothills of the Cheviots named Harbottle, from Old English *hȳra* 'hireling' (a derivative of *hȳr* 'wages', 'reward') + *bōtl* 'dwelling'.

Harbour (1641) **1.** English: metonymic occupational name for a keeper of a lodging house, from late Old English *herebeorg* 'shelter', 'lodging' (from *here* 'army' + *beorg* 'shelter'). (The change of *-er-* to *-ar-* is a regular phonetic process in Old French and Middle English.) **2.** Variant of French ARBOUR.

FOREBEARS A Harbour or Arbour, from Normandy, is documented in Quebec city in 1671.

Harbuck (332) Americanized form of German HARBACH.

Harclerode (199) Americanized spelling of German or Swiss German **Herkenrath**; variant of HARKLEROAD.

Harcourt (457) **1.** English (of Norman origin) and French: habitational name from places in Eure and Calvados named Harcourt, from Old French *cour(t)* (see COURT) with an obscure first element. **2.** English: habitational name from either of two places in Shropshire named Harcourt. The one near Cleobury Mortimer gets the name from Old English *heafocere* 'hawker', 'falconer' + *cot* 'hut', 'cottage'; the one near Wem has as its first element Old English *hearpere* (see HARPER).

FOREBEARS This is the name of a family of Norman origin with branches in France and England. Their name is derived from their lands in Normandy, held in 1024 by Turchetil, lord of Harcourt. They also held

lands in England, which were increased on the marriage of Sir Robert de Harcourt (died 1202), who acquired the manor of Stanton, Oxfordshire. The family seat is still at Stanton Harcourt.

Harcrow (255) Possibly English: unexplained. This name is concentrated in AL and TX.

Harcum (207) English: variant spelling of **Harcombe**, a habitational name from either of two places in Devon and Hampshire so named, probably from Old English *hara* 'hare' + *cumb* 'valley', or from various minor places named with this word, such as Harcomb Bottom in Devon and Gloucestershire, both named with Old English *heorot* 'hart' + *cumb*.

Harcus (100) Scottish: Orkadian form of **Harcarse**, a habitational name from the lands of Harcarse in Foro, Berwickshire, Scotland.

Hard (807) **1.** English: from the Old English personal name *Heard* or a Norman cognate *Hard(on)*, also of Germanic origin. This was a byname meaning 'hardy', 'brave', 'strong', but it also seems to have been used as a short form of the various compound names containing this as a first element. Occasionally this may also be a variant of HARDY. **2.** English, German, Dutch, and Swedish (**Hård**): nickname for a stern or severe man, from Middle English, Middle Low German *hard*, Middle Dutch *hart, hert*, Swedish *hård* 'hard', 'inflexible'. The Swedish name was probably originally a soldier's name. **3.** English: topographic name for someone who lived on a patch of particularly hard ground or one that was difficult to farm. Compare HARDACRE. **4.** Dutch: occupational name from Middle Dutch *harde, herde* 'herder'.

Hardacre (180) English (Lancashire and Yorkshire): topographic name for someone who lived on a patch of poor, stony land, from Middle English *hard* 'hard', 'difficult' + *aker* 'cultivated land' (Old English *æcer*), or a habitational name from Hardacre, a place in Clapham, West Yorkshire, which has this etymology.

Hardage (390) English: unexplained.

Hardaker (106) English: variant spelling of HARDACRE.

GIVEN NAME French 7%. *Michel* (2).

Hardaway (1320) English: perhaps a variant of **Hadaway**, itself a variant of HATHAWAY. In the U.S., this is name is concentrated in the south, in TX, TN, and GA.

Hardbarger (120) German: Americanized form of German **Hartberger**, a habitational name for someone from a place called Hartberg near Überlingen, Württemberg.

Hardcastle (1123) English (Yorkshire): habitational name from a place named with Middle English *hard* 'difficult', 'inaccessible', 'impregnable', or perhaps 'cheerless' + *castel* 'castle', 'fortress', 'stronghold' (see CASTLE), perhaps Hardcastle Garth in

North Yorkshire or Hardcastle Crags in West Yorkshire, although either or both of these could be from the surname. It has been suggested that the surname may come from a Roman fort forming part of Hadrian's Wall in northern England.

Hardebeck (229) German: habitational name from a place near Hamburg, whose name means 'dirty stream'.

Hardee (2418) Variant spelling of English HARDY.

Hardegree (208) Origin unidentified. This name is found chiefly in the south, in GA and TX. Compare HARDIGREE.

Hardeman (1258) **1.** English and Irish: variant of HARDIMAN. **2.** Dutch: from a Germanic personal name composed of the elements *hard* 'hardy', 'brave', 'strong' + *man* 'man'.

Harden (7886) **1.** English (mainly southeastern England): habitational name from Harden in West Yorkshire, which gets its name from Old English *hara* 'hare' or *hær* 'rock' + *denu* 'valley'. Harden in Staffordshire, recorded in the Middle Ages as *Haworthyn, Harwerthyn* (from Old English *hēah* 'high' + *worðign* 'enclosure'), was probably not reduced to its modern form early enough to lie behind any examples of the surname. **2.** Irish: reduced Anglicized form of Gaelic **Mac Giolla Deacair** (see HARDY). **3.** North German: patronymic from a short form of a Germanic personal name with the first element *hard* 'hardy', 'brave', 'strong'.

Hardenbergh (134) **1.** Dutch: old spelling of **Hardenberg**, a habitational name from Hardenberg in Overijssel, Netherlands or from a place in Germany. **2.** Variant (older spelling) of German **Hardenberg**, a habitational name from a place called Hardenberg, for example near Göttingen, or possibly from the place in the Netherlands of the same name.

Hardenbrook (322) Americanized form of German **Hardenbruch**, a topographic name from Middle High German *hart* 'firm ground', 'pasture' + *bruch* 'low lying, swampy land'.

Hardenburg (109) Respelling of **Hardenberg** (see HARDENBERGH).

Hardenburgh (100) Respelling of **Hardenberg** (see HARDENBERGH).

Harder (3935) **1.** English: occupational name for a hardener of metals or a baker, from an agent derivative of Middle English *harde(n)*; this verb is known to have been used with reference to metals and to heating dough. **2.** North German, Frisian, and Danish: from a personal name, *Harder, Herder*. **3.** South German: topographic name or habitational name from any of the places named with Middle High German *hart* 'woodland used as pasture'.

Harders (253) North German and Frisian: patronymic from the personal name HARDER 2.

Hardester (118) Altered form of English HARDESTY.

Hardesty (3971) English (Yorkshire): habitational name from Hardisty Hill in the parish of Fewston, North Yorkshire, recorded in 1379 as *Hardolfsty*, from the Old English personal name *Heardwulf* (composed of the elements *heard* 'hardy', 'brave', 'strong' + *wulf* 'wolf') + Old English *stīg* 'path'.

Hardey (168) English: variant spelling of HARDY.

Hardgrave (226) English: variant of HARGRAVE.

Hardgrove (360) English: variant of HARGROVE.

Hardick (143) English: perhaps a reduced form of HARDWICK.

Hardie (1554) **1.** Scottish: variant spelling of HARDY 1. **2.** Scottish: shortened form of **McHardie**, an Anglicized form of Gaelic **Mac C(h)ardaidh**, possibly 'son of the craftsman', from *ceardaiche*.

Hardigree (189) Variant of HARDEGREE, found chiefly in GA.

Hardiman (1304) **1.** English: nickname for a brave or foolhardy man, from Middle English *hardi* 'bold', 'courageous' + *man* 'man'. **2.** Irish: in addition to being an importation to Ireland of the English name, this is also found as an Anglicized form of Gaelic **Ó hArgadáin** (see HARGADON).

Hardimon (137) Variant of English and Irish HARDIMAN.

Hardin (14661) **1.** English: variant of HARDING. **2.** French: from a pet form of any of several Germanic compound personal names beginning with *hard* 'hardy', 'brave', 'strong'.

Hardina (111) Origin unidentified.

Harding (14400) **1.** English (mainly southern England and South Wales) and Irish: from the Old English personal name *Hearding*, originally a patronymic from HARD 1. The surname was first taken to Ireland in the 15th century, and more families of the name settled there 200 years later in Tipperary and surrounding counties. **2.** North German and Dutch: patronymic from a short form of any of the various Germanic compound personal names beginning with *hard* 'hardy', 'brave', 'strong'.

FOREBEARS Warren Gamaliel Harding (1865–1923), the 29th president of the U.S., was born on a farm in OH, of English and Scottish stock on his father's side. Early American bearers of this very common name include Joseph Harding who died at Plymouth in 1633. His great-great grandson Seth was a naval officer during the American Revolution.

Hardinger (196) Americanized variant of German HARTINGER.

Hardison (2772) English: probably a patronymic from HARDY, although the surname is rare in Britain.

Hardister (179) Probably a variant of English HARDESTY.

Hardisty (401) English (Yorkshire): variant spelling of HARDESTY.

Hardman (3284) **1.** English (chiefly Lancashire): occupational name for a herdsman, a variant of *Herdman* (see HEARD). (The change of *-er-* to *-ar-* was a regular phonetic pattern in Old French and Middle English.) **2.** English: from an unattested Old English personal name *Heardmann*, composed of the elements *heard* 'hardy', 'brave', 'strong' + *mann* 'man'. According to Reaney and Wilson, compound names with this second element became common in late Old English in eastern England. **3.** Irish: of English origin (see above), but sometimes confused with HARMAN. **4.** Dutch: variant of HARDEMAN 2. **5.** Americanized spelling of German HARTMANN.

Hardnett (265) Probably a variant of HARNETT. This surname occurs chiefly in GA.

Hardrick (311) Irish: unexplained.

Hards (107) English: from the possessive case of the personal name HARD, denoting a son or servant of someone called *Hard*.

Hardt (1071) **1.** German: topographic name for someone who lived by woods used as pasture, from Middle High German *hart*. **2.** German: from a short form of a Germanic compound personal name beginning with *hard* 'hardy', 'brave', 'strong'. **3.** Dutch: variant spelling of HARD 2. **4.** Jewish (Ashkenazic): variant spelling of HART.

GIVEN NAMES German 5%. *Otto* (5), *Ernst*, *Erwin*, *Frieda*, *Gerhard*, *Gottlieb*, *Gunther*, *Hans*, *Heinz*, *Reinhold*, *Udo*.

Hardtke (192) North German: from a pet form of a Germanic compound personal name beginning with *hard* 'hardy', 'brave', 'strong'.

GIVEN NAMES German 6%. *Arno* (2), *Erwin*, *Hans*.

Hardway (260) English: perhaps a variant of *Hadaway*, itself a variant of HATHAWAY. Compare HARDAWAY.

Hardwick (3680) **1.** English (Yorkshire): habitational name from any of numerous places, for example in South Yorkshire and Derbyshire, named Hardwick, from Old English *heorde* 'herd', 'flock' + *wīc* 'outlying farm'. **2.** German and French (Lorraine): from the Germanic personal name *Hardwic*, composed of the elements *hard* 'hardy', 'brave', 'strong' + *wīg* 'battle', 'combat'.

Hardwicke (131) English: variant spelling of HARDWICK.

GIVEN NAME Jewish 4%. *Mort*.

Hardy (25252) **1.** English, Scottish, and French: nickname for a brave or foolhardy man, from Old French, Middle English *hardi* 'bold', 'courageous' (of Germanic origin; compare HARD 1). **2.** Irish: in addi-

tion to being an importation of the English name, this is also found as an Anglicized form (by partial translation) of Gaelic **Mac Giolla Deacair** 'son of the hard lad'. **3.** Scottish: variant spelling of HARDIE 2.

FOREBEARS Bearers of the surname Hardy from Anjou and Normandy are documented in Quebec city in 1669. The secondary surnames Châtillon, JOLICOEUR, De Joncaire are documented.

Hardyman (127) English and Irish: variant spelling of HARDIMAN.

Hare (5912) **1.** Irish (Ulster): Anglicized form of Gaelic **Ó hÍr**, meaning 'long-lasting'. In Ireland this name is found in County Armagh; it has also long been established in Scotland. **2.** Irish: Anglicized form of **Ó hAichir** 'descendant of *Aichear*', a personal name derived from the epithet *aichear* 'fierce', 'sharp'. In Ireland this name is more commonly Anglicized as **O'Hehir**. **3.** English: nickname for a swift runner (possibly a speedy messenger) or a timorous person, from Middle English *hare* 'hare'. However, the surname AYER and its variants was sometimes recorded as *Hare*. **4.** English: topographic name from an Old English *hær* 'rock', 'heap of stones', 'tumulus'. **5.** French: according to Morlet, an occupational name for a huntsman, from a medieval French call used to urge on the hounds, or, in the form **Haré**, from the past participle of *harer* 'to excite, stir up (hounds in pursuit of a quarry)'.

Harel (160) Jewish (Israeli): ornamental name from *Harel*, a place name mentioned in the Bible.

GIVEN NAMES Jewish 38%. *Shimon* (2), *Uri* (2), *Yaron* (2), *Yossi* (2), *Aharon*, *Arie*, *Aron*, *Ayelet*, *Batya*, *Dov*, *Dvora*, *Eyal*.

Harelson (171) Variant of Scandinavian HARALDSON.

Haren (394) **1.** Irish (Counties Clare and Connacht): Anglicized form of Gaelic **Ó hEaghráin** 'descendant of *Eaghrán*', a diminutive of *Eaghra*, a personal name of unexplained origin. **2.** (County Fermanagh): Anglicized form of Gaelic **Ó hAráin** 'descendant of *Arán*', a name of unknown origin. **3.** (Armagh) Anglicized form of Gaelic **Ó hEaráin** (see HERRON). **4.** Dutch and Belgian: habitational name from a house named *Ten (H)aerne* ('At the Eagle'), in Bruges, Belgium, or from places called Haren in Brabant and North Brabant, or in Bommershoven in the province of Limburg.

Harer (267) South German: occupational name for a flax grower or dealer, from Middle High German *har* 'flax' + the agent suffix *-er*.

Hares (117) Muslim: from Arabic *ḥāris*, *ḥārith* 'provider', 'plowman', 'cultivator'.

GIVEN NAMES Muslim 6%. *Mohammed*, *Mustafa*, *Syed*, *Talha*, *Yahya*, *Ziad*.

Harewood (206) English: variant of HARWOOD.

GIVEN NAMES French 5%. *Maxime*, *Renald*.

Harford (682) **1.** English: habitational name from places called Harford, in Gloucestershire and Devon. The former is named from Old English *heorot* 'hart' + *ford* 'ford', the latter has as its first element Old English *here* 'army'. In some cases it may be an altered form of HEREFORD. **2.** Irish: mainly of English origin, an Anglo-Norman habitational name for someone from HEREFORD.

Harfst (112) North German and Dutch: from Middle High German *harfst* 'harvest'. See German HERBST.
GIVEN NAMES German 6%. *Gunter, Lutz.*

Hargadon (184) Irish: Anglicized form of Gaelic **Ó hArgadáin** 'descendant of *Argadán*', a personal name from a diminutive of *argad* 'silver'. In County Galway the surname *O'Hargadan* has tended to be replaced by HARDIMAN.
GIVEN NAME Irish 5%. *Liam.*

Hargan (187) Irish (Ulster): Anglicized form of Gaelic **Ó hArgáin** (see HORGAN).
GIVEN NAMES Irish 4%. *Fergus, Sorcha.*

Hargens (233) North German: variant of a Frisian patronymic surname, **Hergens**.
GIVEN NAMES German 5%. *Annice, Eldred, Kurt.*

Harger (924) English: from a Norman personal name composed of the Germanic elements *hari, heri* 'army' + *gār, gēr* 'spear', 'lance'.

Hargesheimer (103) German: habitational name for someone from Hargesheim, near Bingen in the Palatinate.

Hargest (87) Welsh: habitational name from Hergest in Radnorshire.

Hargett (1868) **1.** Variant of English **Hargate**, a habitational name from Harrogate in North Yorkshire, which is named with Old Norse *hórgr* 'cairn', 'heap of stones' + *gata* 'road'. **2.** variant of German HERGERT.

Hargis (3103) English: unexplained. **1.** Possibly a Huguenot name, a variant of GARGIS, which is an altered form of **Garrigus**, an Anglicized form of French GARRIGUES. **2.** Alternatively, it may be a variant of Scottish HARCUS.

Hargrave (2415) English: habitational names from any of a number of places called Hargrave or Hargreave, of which there are examples in Cheshire, Northamptonshire, and Suffolk; all are named with Old English *hār* 'gray' or *hara* 'hare' + *grāf* 'grove' or *græfe* 'thicket'.

Hargraves (1171) English: variant of HARGRAVE.

Hargreaves (1029) English: variant of HARGRAVE.

Hargroder (125) Americanized form of German **Hergenröder** or **Hergenrode**, habitational names from Hergenrode or Hergenroth in Hesse, or Herkenrath in the Rhineland (see HARKRIDER).

Hargrove (5824) English: variant of HARGRAVE.

Hargus (301) English: unexplained. See HARGIS.

Hari (209) **1.** Swiss German: probably a variant of HARIG. **2.** Slovenian: perhaps a derivative of the personal name *Zaharija* (see ZACHARIAS). **3.** Indian (southern states): Hindu name, from Sanskrit *hari* 'one who takes away (evil)', an epithet of the god Vishnu. It is only found as a male given name in India, but has come to be used as a surname in the U.S. among South Indians.
GIVEN NAMES Indian 24%. *Adarsh* (2), *Navnit* (2), *Anil, Ashwani, Bisram, Gopal, Hemanth, Hira, Kalpana, Krishan, Kumar, Lalitha.*

Harig (385) German: **1.** habitational name from any of several places named Haring(en). **2.** (also **Härig**) nickname for a hairy person, from Middle Low German *hārich* 'hairy'.

Haring (1138) **1.** Dutch, North German (**Häring**), and Jewish (Ashkenazic): from Middle Low German *hārinc* 'herring', German *Hering*, a metonymic occupational name for a seller of herrings. **2.** Dutch: also from a personal name, a variant of HERRING 3.

Hariri (119) Muslim: occupational name for a silk merchant, from Arabic *harīrī* 'related to or associated with silk'. Harir is also the name of an ancient region on the right bank of the Euphrates River in Syria. The Arabic scholar and writer Abū Muḥammad al-Qāsim ibn ʿAlī al-Ḥarīrī (1054–1152) was born, lived, and died in the city of Basra, in southern Iraq.
GIVEN NAMES Muslim 77%. *Ali* (3), *Mohammad* (3), *Abbas* (2), *Amir* (2), *Azadeh* (2), *Mojgan* (2), *Mustafa* (2), *Payam* (2), *Shahriar* (2), *Ahmad, Azim, Bachir.*

Harjes (118) Frisian: patronymic from a derivative of one of the Germanic personal names formed with *hari, heri* 'army' as the first element (see for example HERMAN, HERWIG).
GIVEN NAMES German 6%. *Hermann, Oskar.*

Harjo (311) **1.** American Indian (Creek): unexplained. **2.** American variant of Finnish HARJU.

Harju (415) Finnish: from *harju* 'ridge', either a topographic name from any of the numerous farmsteads named with this word, or a later ornamental adoption, one of the numerous names taken from the vocabulary of the natural landscape by Finns with Swedish names during the name conversion movement of the 19th and early 20th centuries.
GIVEN NAMES Finnish 12%. *Eino* (5), *Oiva* (3), *Timo* (3), *Tenho* (2), *Vaino* (2), *Wilho* (2), *Aarne, Erkki, Juhani, Onni, Toini, Toivo.*

Hark (191) **1.** English: perhaps a derivative of Middle English *herkien* 'to listen' (compare HARKER 2). **2.** Dutch and Belgian: habitational name from St-Lambrechts-

Herk or Herk-de-Stad in the Belgian province of Limburg, which take their names from the Herk river. **3.** Probably an altered spelling of German HARKE.
GIVEN NAME French 4%. *Andre.*

Harkavy (135) Jewish (from Belarus): nickname from Belorussian, *harkavyj* '(one) pronouncing uvular instead of dental *-r*'.
GIVEN NAME Jewish 4%. *Abbe.*

Harkcom (127) English: variant spelling of **Harcombe** (see HARCUM).

Harke (226) North German: **1.** from a Frisian personal name, a short form of any of the Germanic personal names with *hari, heri* 'army' as the first element (see for example HERMAN, HERWIG). **2.** possibly a nickname or metonymic occupational name from Middle Low German *harke* 'rake', or a topographic name from *herk, hark* 'marsh', 'bog'.
GIVEN NAMES German 5%. *Gitta, Guenter, Heinz.*

Harkema (156) Frisian: patronymic from the personal name *Hark* (see HARKE).

Harken (236) North German: patronymic from HARKE 1.

Harkenrider (107) Americanized form of German and Swiss German **Hergenreider** or **Hergenreiter**, variant of HARKLEROAD.

Harker (1904) **1.** English (mainly northeastern England and West Yorkshire): **2.** habitational name from either of two places in Cumbria, or from one in the parish of Halsall, near Ormskirk, Lancashire. The Cumbrian places are probably named from Middle English *hart* 'male deer' + *kerr* 'marshland'. The one in Lancashire has the same second element, while the first is probably Old English *hār* 'gray' or *hara* 'hare'. **3.** nickname for an eavesdropper or busybody, from an agent derivative of Middle English *herkien* 'to listen'.

Harkey (1273) English: probably from a pet form of a medieval personal name, probably either *Harry* or a derivative of HARD.

Harkin (478) **1.** Irish: Anglicized form of Gaelic **Ó hEarcáin** 'descendant of *Earcán*', a byname or personal name formed from a diminutive of *earc* 'red', 'bloody'; also meaning 'pig'. **2.** English: from a pet form of a medieval personal name (see HARKEY).
GIVEN NAMES Irish 6%. *Brendan, Cormac, Jarlath, Paddy.*

Harkins (4730) **1.** Irish: variant of HARKIN. **2.** English and Scottish: patronymic from the personal name HARKIN.

Harkleroad (491) Americanized spelling of German or Swiss German **Herkelrath** (also Americanized as HARCLERODE, **Harklerode**): a habitational name probably from the town of *Herkenrath* in the Rhineland. This is a PA name.

Harkless (452) English: unexplained. This name occurs mainly in OH and PA.

Harkness (2249) Scottish: apparently a habitational name from an unidentified

place (perhaps in the area of Annandale, with which the surname is connected in early records), probably so called from the Old English personal name *Hereca* (a derivative of the various compound names with the first element *here* 'army') + Old English *næss* 'headland', 'cape'. The surname is also established in northern Ireland, where it was taken in the 17th century by settlers from Dumfriesshire.
FOREBEARS A descendant of the Dumfriesshire family of this name was the founder of the Pilgrim Trust, Edward Stephen Harkness, born in Cleveland, OH, in 1874.

Harkrader (152) Americanized form of German and Swiss German **Hergenröder**: or **Hergenräder** or **Hergenreder**, a habitational name from a place named *Hergenrode* or *Herchenrode* in Hesse, or *Herkenrath* in the Rhineland.

Harkrider (209) Americanized form of German and Swiss German **Hergenreider** or **Hergenreiter**, a habitational name from a place named *Herchenrode* or *Herchenroth* or *Hergenrode* or *Hergenroth* in Hesse or *Herkenrath* in the Rhineland.
GIVEN NAMES French 4%. *Ancil* (2), *Chantal*, *Monique*.

Harl (239) German: variant or altered spelling of **Härle** (see HARLE).

Harlacher (197) German: habitational name for someone from Ober- or Unter-Harlachen, near Überlingen.
GIVEN NAME German 4%. *Kurt* (2).

Harlan (4305) Northern Irish (of English origin): altered form of HARLAND 1.
FOREBEARS Harlan County, KY, was named for Major Silas Harlan (died 1782).

Harland (820) 1. English (mainly northeastern): habitational name from any of various minor places (including perhaps some now lost) named from Old English *hār* 'gray', *hara* 'hare', or *hær* 'rock', 'tumulus' + *land* 'tract of land', 'estate', 'cultivated land', notably Harland in Kirkbymoorside, North Yorkshire, which is named from *hær* + *land*. This surname has been present in northern Ireland since the 17th century. 2. French (Normandy): nickname for someone given to stirring up trouble, from the present participle of medieval French *hareler* 'to create a disturbance'.
FOREBEARS George and Michael Harland were Quakers who emigrated from Durham, England, to Ireland. George went on to Delaware in 1687 and became governor in 1695, while Michael went to Philadelphia. George Harland's descendants, who dropped the final -d from their name, included a number of prominent American politicians, in particular James Harlan (1820–99), who became a senator and Secretary of the Interior.

Harle (283) 1. South German (**Härle**): nickname from a diminutive of Middle High German *hār* 'hair'. 2. Northern English and Scottish: habitational name from

Kirkharle and Little Harle in Northumberland (earlier simply *Herle*, *Harle*), possibly named from an Old English personal name *Herela* (a derivative of the various compound names with the first element *here* 'army') + Old English *lēah* 'wood', 'clearing'. 3. English: variant of EARL. 4. French (**Harlé**): topographic name from a derivative of *harle* 'ditch'.
GIVEN NAMES German 4%. *Dieter*, *Johann*, *Kurt*.

Harleman (123) German (**Harlemann**): variant or altered spelling of **Herlemann**, a habitational name for someone from any of several places called Herl.

Harler (100) English: unexplained.

Harless (2423) 1. German: unexplained. 2. English: probably a variant spelling of **(H)arliss**, a nickname from Middle English *earles* 'earless', probably denoting someone who was deaf rather than one literally without ears.

Harley (3488) 1. English (now mainly in Scotland; also West Midlands and Welsh border): habitational name from places in Shropshire and West Yorkshire, so named from Old English *hær* 'rock', 'heap of stones' or *hara* 'hare' + *lēah* 'wood', 'clearing'. In some cases the name may be topographic. 2. Irish: when not of English origin, this is an Anglicized form of Gaelic **Ó hEarghaile** 'descendant of *Earghal*', a variant of the personal name *Fearghal* without the initial *F*- (see FARRELL).

Harlin (578) 1. English and French: from a Norman personal name, *Herluin* or *Arluin*, composed of the Germanic elements *erl* 'nobleman', 'warrior' + *wini* 'friend'. 2. German (**Härlin**): variant of HARLE 1.

Harling (480) 1. English: variant of HARLIN. 2. English: habitational name from East Harling in Norfolk, named in Old English as '(settlement of) Herela's people'. 3. North German and Frisian: habitational name from the marsh area Harling in East Friesland or from the port of Harlingen in West Friesland. 4. German (**Härling**): nickname for an immature person, from Old High German *herling* '(sour) grape harvested before maturity'.

Harloff (133) North German: assimilated form of the personal name *Hardelof*, a variant of *Hardolf*, composed of the Germanic elements *hard* 'hardy', 'brave', 'strong' + *wolf*, *wulf* 'wolf'.

Harlos (125) German (Austria): a variant of **Haarlos**, a nickname for a person with little or no hair, from Middle High German *hār* 'hair' + *lōs* 'free of'.

Harlow (4648) English: 1. habitational name from any of various places called Harlow. One in West Yorkshire is probably named from Old English *hær* 'rock', 'heap of stones' + *hlāw* 'mound', 'hill'; those in Essex and Northumberland have Old English *here* 'army' as the first element, perhaps in the sense 'host', 'assembly'.

2. There is also a record of this name as a variant of Cornish PENHOLLOW.

Harlowe (136) English: variant spelling of HARLOW.

Harm (474) 1. English: nickname from Old English *hearm* 'evil', 'hurt', 'injury'. 2. English and North German: from a short form of HARMAN, HERMANN. 3. South German: nickname from Middle High German *harm* 'ermine'.

Harman (5734) 1. English (mainly southeast), French, German (**Harmann**) and Dutch: from a Germanic personal name composed of the elements *heri*, *hari* 'army' + *man* 'man' (see HERMANN). In England this name was introduced by the Normans. 2. Irish: generally of English origin (see 1); but sometimes also used as a variant of HARDIMAN, an Anglicized form of Gaelic **Ó hArgadáin** (see HARGADON). 3. Jewish (eastern Ashkenazic): of uncertain origin; perhaps a nickname for someone with a copious or noticeable head of hair (see HAAR).

Harmann (107) German: see HARMAN 1.
GIVEN NAME German 4%. *Eldor*.

Harmel (228) 1. Jewish (Ashkenazic): ornamental name from Yiddish *harml* 'ermine' (see HARMELING). 2. French: variant of the personal name *Armel*, derived from an Old Breton compound personal name, *Arthmael*, comprised of *arth*, *arzh* 'bear', 'warrior' + *mael*.

Harmeling (135) 1. Dutch: patronymic from a pet form of the personal name *Herman*, *Harman* (see HERMANN). 2. German: habitational name from Harmelingen near Soltau.

Harmelink (149) Dutch: variant of HARMELING.

Harmening (237) North German, Dutch, and Frisian: patronymic from HERMANN.
GIVEN NAMES German 4%. *Erwin*, *Klaus*, *Otto*.

Harmer (899) 1. English (mainly East Anglia and the southeast): from a Norman personal name composed of the Germanic elements *hari*, *heri* 'army' + *māri*, *mēri* 'famous'. 2. English: habitational name from Haremere Hall in Etchingham, Sussex, which is named from Old English *hār* 'gray' + *mere* 'pool'.

Harmes (211) 1. English: variant of HARM 2. 2. Dutch: patronymic from a short form of the personal name *Herman* (see HERMANN).

Harmeyer (435) German: variant of *Harmann* (see HARMAN) in which -*meyer* (see MEYER) was substituted for -*mann*.

Harmison (193) English (mainly northeast): hypercorrected spelling of **Armison**, a patronymic from the personal name *Ermin*, a short form of the various Germanic compound names beginning with this element (for example, *Ermenald*, *Ermingaud*).

Harmon (25857) 1. Irish (mainly County Louth): generally of English origin (see 1);

but sometimes also used as a variant of HARMAN or HARDIMAN, i.e. an Anglicized form of Gaelic **Ó hArgadáin** (see HARGADON). **2.** English: variant spelling of HARMAN 1.

Harmond (102) Irish and English: variant of HARMON.

Harmony (184) Origin unidentified. Examples of the name are found in both England and Hungary in the 19th century.

Harms (5743) North German, Dutch, Danish, and English: patronymic from a short form of the personal name *Herman(n)* (see HERMANN).

Harmsen (475) North German, Dutch, and Danish: patronymic from HARM.

Harn (608) English: variant of HEARN 4.

Harnack (270) **1.** German: nickname from Middle High German *hardenack* 'hard-nose', a tough, inflexible person. **2.** variant of HARNICK.

GIVEN NAMES German 5%. *Gerhard, Klaus, Kurt.*

Harnage (273) English: habitational name from Harnage in Shropshire, which has as its second element Old English *ecg* 'edge', 'steep ridge'; the first is uncertain but may be a derivative, *hæren* 'rocky', of an unrecorded Old English *hær* 'stone'. The surname now appears to be extinct in England; in the U.S. it is concentrated in FL and GA.

Harnden (612) English: probably a habitational name from a lost or unidentified place.

Harne (189) English: variant of HEARN 4. This is predominantly a MD name.

Harned (915) English or Irish: variant of HARNETT.

Harner (1578) German: of uncertain origin; probably a nickname for a noisy person, from Middle High German *har(e)n* 'call', 'shout' + *-er*, agent suffix.

Harness (1806) **1.** English: from a Norman personal name (Old German *Arn(e)gis*, Old French *Erneïs, (H)ernaïs*). **2.** English: occupational name for a maker of harness or suits of mail, from Middle English *harnais* 'harness' (Old French *harneis* 'equipment', 'accoutrements (of a soldier or horse)').

Harnett (562) **1.** Irish (County Limerick): variant of HARTNETT. **2.** English: variant of ARNOLD 1.

GIVEN NAMES Irish 4%. *Aileen, Fergus.*

Harney (1906) Irish: Anglicized form of Gaelic **Ó hAthairne** 'descendant of *Athairne*', a personal name from *athardha* 'paternal', which was borne by a famous Old Irish satirist.

Harnick (148) **1.** Jewish (Ashkenazic): unexplained. **2.** German: variant spelling of **Hasnick**, Sorbian form of ERNST.

GIVEN NAMES Jewish 5%; German 4%. *Emanuel, Myer, Nili; Kurt.*

Harnisch (246) **1.** German: metonymic occupational name for an armorer, from Middle High German *harnasch* 'iron

armor', from Old French *harneis* 'equipment', 'accoutrements (of a soldier or horse)'. **2.** variant of **Harnik** (see HARNICK).

GIVEN NAMES German 6%. *Fritz, Helmut, Matthias, Uwe.*

Harnish (1226) Americanized spelling of German HARNISCH.

Harnois (336) French: metonymic occupational name for a harness maker, saddler, or maker of armor, from Old French *harneis* 'equipment', 'accoutrements (of a soldier or horse)'.

FOREBEARS A Harnois from Normandy is recorded in St. Augustin, Quebec, in 1670.

GIVEN NAMES French 12%. *Armand* (3), *Mederic* (3), *Normand* (3), *Emile, Lucien.*

Harnsberger (119) German: probably a variant of HUNSBERGER.

Haro (1121) **1.** Spanish: habitational name from a place in the province of Logroño, so called from a North Castilian form of Spanish *faro* 'beacon'. **2.** French (Normandy): metonymic occupational name for a peddler, from an Old French cry used to hail someone or to attract attention.

GIVEN NAMES Spanish 48%. *Jose* (37), *Jesus* (14), *Juan* (14), *Luis* (11), *Salvador* (11), *Manuel* (10), *Carlos* (9), *Jorge* (9), *Miguel* (9), *Alberto* (7), *Francisco* (7), *Jaime* (6).

Harold (1827) **1.** English: from the Old English personal name *Hereweald*, its Old Norse equivalent *Haraldr*, or the Continental form *Herold* introduced to Britain by the Normans. These all go back to a Germanic personal name composed of the elements *heri, hari* 'army' + *wald* 'rule', which is attested in Europe from an early date; the Roman historian Tacitus records a certain *Cariovalda*, chief of the Germanic tribe of the Batavi, as early as the 1st century AD. **2.** English: occupational name for a herald, Middle English *herau(l)d* (Old French *herau(l)t*, from a Germanic compound of the same elements as above, used as a common noun). **3.** German: from a personal name equivalent to 1. **4.** Irish: this name is of direct Norse origin (see 1), but is also occasionally a variant of HARRELL and HURRELL.

Haroldson (303) Americanized spelling of Scandinavian HARALDSON.

GIVEN NAME Scandinavian 5%. *Helmer* (2).

Haroutunian (133) Armenian: patronymic from *Haroutun*, a personal name meaning 'resurrection'.

GIVEN NAMES Armenian 28%. *Haig* (3), *Aram* (2), *Vigen* (2), *Ashot, Garo, Grigor, Hagop, Haroutun, Norayr, Setrag, Tigran, Vahe.*

Harp (4598) **1.** English and Scottish: metonymic occupational name for a harpist (see HARPER), or occasionally a habitational name for someone living at a house distinguished by the sign of a harp. **2.** English: habitational name from a minor place such as Harp House in Eastwood, Essex, or South Harp in South Petherton,

Somerset, denoting a place where salt was produced, from Old English *hearpe* 'harp', an implement used in the processing of salt. Compare HARPHAM. **3.** German: metonymic occupational name for a harpist, from Middle High German *harpfe* 'harp'. **4.** German: variant of HARPE.

Harpe (543) German: **1.** from a short form of *Harprecht*, a Germanic personal name composed of the elements *hard* 'hard' + *brecht* 'bright', 'famous'. **2.** habitational name from a place so named on the Elbe river near Wittenberge.

Harpel (262) German: from a pet form of HARPE 1, or variant spelling of HERPEL.

Harpenau (195) North German: habitational or topographic name. Bearers of this name are concentrated in the area of Oldenburg and Damme, west and southwest of Bremen.

Harper (41293) English, Scottish, and Irish: occupational name for a player on the harp, from an agent derivative of Middle English, Middle Dutch *harp* 'harp'. The harper was one of the most important figures of a medieval baronial hall, especially in Scotland and northern England, and the office of harper was sometimes hereditary. The Scottish surname is probably an Anglicized form of Gaelic **Mac Chruiteir** 'son of the harper' (from Gaelic *cruit* 'harp', 'stringed instrument'). This surname has long been present in Ireland.

Harpham (179) English: habitational name from a place in East Yorkshire near Bridlington, so named from Old English *hearpe* 'harp' (the instrument or the device used for purifying sea salt) + *hām* 'homestead'.

Harpin (203) French (also found in England): occupational name for a player on the harp, from Old French *harpin* 'harper'.

FOREBEARS A Harpin or Herpin, also called Poitevin, from Poitiers is documented in St. Ours, Quebec, in 1689.

GIVEN NAMES French 15%. *Armand* (2), *Aime, Alain, Andre, Cecile, Donat, Emile, Laurent, Mathieu, Raoul.*

Harpine (110) Variant of French HARPIN.

Harple (108) Variant of English HARPOLE.

Harpold (273) Variant of English HARPOLE.

Harpole (524) English: habitational name from either of the places named Harpole, in Kent and Northamptonshire, from Old English *horu* 'dirt' + *pōl* 'pool'.

Harpring (114) Of German origin: unexplained.

Harps (163) German: patronymic from HARP 4.

Harpst (149) Americanized spelling of German HERBST.

Harpster (794) Americanized spelling of German HERBSTER.

Harr (1916) North German: from a Frisian short form of any of the Germanic personal names with the first element *hari*, *heri* 'army', for example, HERMANN, HERBERT.

Harrah (892) Origin unidentified.

GIVEN NAMES *Arbutus*, *Lakin*, *Xiomara*, *Mohamed*.

Harral (276) English: variant of HAROLD.

Harralson (139) Variant of Scandinavian HARALDSON.

Harre (228) **1.** North German: variant of HARR. **2.** English: from a pet form of HERBERT. **3.** English: nickname from Old English *hēarra* 'chief', 'lord'.

Harrel (422) English: variant of HAROLD.

Harreld (166) English: variant spelling of HAROLD.

Harrell (17053) **1.** English: variant of HAROLD. **2.** Irish: Anglicized form of Gaelic Ó hEarghail 'descendant of *Earghal*', a personal name with the same etymology as *Fearghal* (see FARRELL).

Harrelson (2941) Variant of Scandinavian and Scottish HARALDSON.

Harren (230) **1.** Irish: variant of HERRON. **2.** Dutch: unexplained.

GIVEN NAME Irish 5%. *Brigid*.

Harrer (406) South German: occupational name for a flax grower or seller, from Middle High German *har* 'flax' + the agent suffix *-er*.

Harrie (101) English: variant spelling of HARRY.

Harried (100) German: habitational name from a place called Harried in Bavaria.

GIVEN NAMES Scandinavian 5%. *Arnell*, *Hjalmer*.

Harrier (226) English and Scottish: **1.** nickname or occupational name for someone who hunted hares, or who was thought to resemble a breed of dog used in hunting hares. **2.** nickname for someone thought to resemble a harrier, a kind of hawk, Middle English *harrower*. **3.** nickname for a raider or plunderer, from an agent noun derived from Middle English *herian*, Old English *her(g)ian* 'to harry', 'plunder', 'ravage'.

Harries (388) **1.** Welsh: variant of HARRIS 1. **2.** North German (Frisian): variant of HARR, shortened from **Harringes**, see also HARJES.

GIVEN NAMES German 4%. *Kurt* (3), *Elfriede*, *Wolfgang*.

Harrigan (2189) Northern Irish: shortened Anglicized form of Gaelic Ó hArragáin, a variant of Ó hAnradháin (see HANRAHAN).

GIVEN NAME Irish 4%. *Donal*.

Harriger (350) German: probably an altered spelling of **Herriger**, variant of HERRIG. This name is found chiefly in PA.

Harrill (785) English (southwest): variant spelling of HARRELL.

Harriman (2011) English: occupational name for a servant (see MANN) of someone named HARRY.

Harring (300) **1.** North German and Dutch:

metonymic occupational name for a fisher or seller of herrings (see HARING). **2.** Dutch: from a personal name, a variant of HERRING 3. **3.** German: variant of HARIG.

Harrington (25087) **1.** English: habitational name from places in Cumbria, Lincolnshire, and Northamptonshire. The first gets its name from Old English *Haferingtūn* 'settlement (Old English *tūn*) associated with someone called Hæfer', a byname meaning 'he-goat'. The second probably meant 'settlement (Old English *tūn*) of someone called Hæring'. Alternatively, the first element may have been Old English *hæring* 'stony place' or *hāring* 'gray wood'. The last, recorded in Domesday Book as *Arintone* and in 1184 as *Hederingeton*, is most probably named with an unattested Old English personal name, *Heathuhere*. **2.** Irish (County Kerry and the West): adopted as an Anglicized form of Gaelic Ó hArrachtáin 'descendant of *Arrachtán*', a personal name from a diminutive of *arrachtach* 'mighty', 'powerful'. **3.** Irish (County Kerry): adopted as an Anglicized form of Gaelic Ó hIongardail, later Ó hUrdáil, 'descendant of *Iongardal*'. **4.** Irish: reduced Anglicized form of Gaelic Ó hOireachtaigh 'descendant of *Oireachtach*', a byname meaning 'member of the assembly' or 'frequenting assemblies'.

FOREBEARS Harington is the name of a family derived from the place in Cumbria. The earliest recorded bearer of the name was Robert de Heverington, living in the reign of Richard I (1189–99).

Harriott (312) English: variant of HERRIOTT 1.

GIVEN NAMES Irish 4%. *Donal*, *Donovan*.

Harris (185777) **1.** English and Welsh (very common in southern England and South Wales): patronymic from the medieval English personal name HARRY, pet form of HENRY. **2.** This name is also well established in Ireland, taken there principally during the Plantation of Ulster. In some cases, particularly in families coming from County Mayo, both **Harris** and **Harrison** can be Anglicized forms of Gaelic Ó hEarchadha. **3.** Greek: reduced form of the Greek personal name **Kharalambos**, composed of the elements *khara* 'joy' + *lambein* 'to shine'. **4.** Jewish: Americanized form of any of various like-sounding Jewish names.

Harrison (61639) Northern English: patronymic from the medieval personal name HARRY.

FOREBEARS Harrison is an extremely common surname in northern England. One important and influential American family of bearers is descended from Benjamin Harrison, who emigrated from England to VA in 1633 or 1634. Ancestors include another Benjamin Harrison (?1726–91), who was an activist in the American Revolution

and a signer of the Declaration of Independence. His son William Henry Harrison (1773–1841) and great-grandson Benjamin Harrison (1833–1901) both became presidents of the United States.

Harriss (400) English: variant spelling of HARRIS.

Harrity (293) Irish: Anglicized form of Gaelic Ó hOireachtaigh (see HARRINGTON).

Harrod (1840) English (East Anglia): **1.** derivative of the Scandinavian personal name *Harald* (see HAROLD). **2.** variant of HARWOOD. **3.** variant of HERROD 1.

Harrold (1750) Scottish and English: variant spelling of HAROLD.

Harron (260) **1.** Irish: Anglicized form of Gaelic Ó hEaráin (see HERRON). **2.** Muslim: variant of HARROUN.

Harrop (563) English (mainly south Lancashire): habitational name from any of several places in West Yorkshire or from one in Cheshire called Harrop, or from Harehope in Northumberland, all of which are named from Old English *hara* 'hare' + *hop* 'valley'.

Harroun (284) Muslim: from the Arabic personal name *Hārūn*, name of a prophet (see AARON), mentioned in the Qur'an (19: 53). It was also the name of a famous khalif, Hārūn ur-Rashīd (ruled 786–809).

Harrow (496) English and Scottish: habitational name from any of various places so named in England and Scotland, as for example Harrow in northwest London (*Herges* in Domesday Book), Harrow Head in Nether Wasdale, Cumbria, both named from Old English *hearg*, *hærg* '(pagan) temple', and Harrow near Mey, Caithness.

Harrower (186) Scottish (Fife) and English: occupational name for someone who harrowed cultivated land, perhaps someone who did this as a feudal service on manorial land, from an agent derivative of Middle English *harwen* 'to rake' (of Scandinavian origin).

FOREBEARS The first known Scottish bearer of this surname was William Harrower, recorded in Fife in the mid 14th century; he was also known as *Herwart*.

Harruff (100) German: Americanized spelling of *Hörauf* or its variant **Herauf**, from a Germanic personal name *Hariulf*, composed of the elements *hari* 'army', + *(w)ulf*, *wolf* 'wolf'.

Harrup (108) English: variant spelling of HARROP.

Harry (2634) **1.** English (mainly South Wales and southwestern England): from the medieval personal name *Harry*, which was the usual vernacular form of HENRY, with assimilation of the consonantal cluster and regular Middle English change of *-er*- to *-ar*-. **2.** French: from the Germanic personal name *Hariric*, composed of the elements *hari*, *heri* 'army' + *rīc* 'power(ful)'.

Harryman (427) English: variant spelling of HARRIMAN.

Harsch (537) **1.** North German: nickname for a stern or severe man, from Middle Low German *harsch* 'harsh', 'stern'. **2.** German: metonymic occupational name for a soldier, from Middle High German *harsch*, *harst* 'body of troops'.

GIVEN NAMES German 4%. *Erwin, Fritz, Gottlieb, Hans.*

Harsey (104) Probably a variant of Irish HERSHEY 2.

GIVEN NAMES Irish 4%. *Liam, Murphy.*

Harsh (1158) Americanized spelling of German HARSCH.

Harsha (281) English and Irish: variant of HARSHAW.

Harshaw (501) Northern Irish: unexplained. Perhaps a variant of English HERSHEY.

Harshbarger (1374) **1.** Altered form of German **Hirschberger**, a habitational name for someone from any of several places named HIRSCHBERG. **2.** Jewish (Ashkenazic): mainly an ornamental name composed of German *Hirsch* 'deer', 'hart' + *Berg* 'mountain', 'hill' + the agent suffix *-er*, but possibly habitational in some cases (see 1).

Harshberger (239) German: see HARSH-BARGER.

Harshfield (201) Americanized form of German HIRSCHFELD 2, found in PA.

Harshman (1375) Americanized form of German HIRSCHMANN.

Harsin (144) Variant of HERSON.

Harstad (480) Norwegian: habitational name from any of several farmsteads, notably in southeastern Norway, so named from the Old Norse personal name *Hǫrðr* (someone from Hǫrðaland) or *Hárekr* (from *Há* of unknown origin + *rekr* 'powerful', 'ruler') + *staðr* 'farmstead'.

Harston (257) English: habitational name from places so called in Cambridgeshire and Leicestershire, or from Harleston in Suffolk or Harlestone in Northamptonshire. The first was named in Old English possibly with an unattested personal name *Herel* + *tūn* 'enclosure', 'settlement'; the second is from *hār* 'gray' (or possibly 'boundary') + *stān* 'stone'. The two last were both named with the Old English personal name *Heoruwulf* (or *Herewulf*) + *tūn* 'enclosure', 'farmstead', 'settlement'.

Hart (50153) **1.** English and North German: from a personal name or nickname meaning 'stag', Middle English *hert*, Middle Low German *hërte, harte*. **2.** German: variant spelling of HARDT 1 and 2. **3.** Jewish (Ashkenazic): ornamental name or a nickname from German and Yiddish *hart* 'hard'. **4.** Irish: Anglicized form of Gaelic **Ó hAirt** 'descendant of *Art*', a byname meaning 'bear', 'hero'. The English name became established in Ireland in the 17th century. **5.** French: from an Old French word meaning 'rope', hence possibly a metonymic occupational name for a rope maker or a hangman. **6.** Dutch: nickname from Middle Dutch *hart, hert* 'hard', 'strong', 'ruthless', 'unruly'.

FOREBEARS This name was brought independently to New England by many bearers from the 17th century onward. Stephen Hart was one of the founders of Hartford, CT, (coming from Cambridge, MA, with Thomas Hooker) in 1635.

Hartbarger (117) German: American spelling of *Hartberger*, topographic name from a hill named *Hartberg* near Überlingen in Württemberg.

Harte (1053) **1.** Irish and English: variant spelling of HART. **2.** Dutch: variant of HART 6.

GIVEN NAMES Irish 4%. *Brendan, Sinead.*

Hartel (468) **1.** German (also **Härtel**): from a pet form of a Germanic compound personal name beginning with *hard* 'hardy', 'brave', 'strong'. **2.** French (Normandy): occupational name, a derivative of HART 5.

GIVEN NAMES German 5%. *Erwin* (2), *Erna, Gunter, Kurt, Lutz, Otto.*

Hartell (131) **1.** English (West Midlands): habitational name from any of the places called Harthill, named with Old English *heorot* 'hart' + *hyll* 'hill'. There are several places of this name, for example in Cheshire, Derbyshire, and South Yorkshire, but apparently none in the West Midlands. It is also possible that the surname represents a truncated derivative of Hartlebury in Worcestershire. This place name derives from the Old English personal name *Heortla* + Old English *burh* 'fort'. **2.** German: Americanized spelling of HARTEL or **Härtel**.

GIVEN NAME German 4%. *Theresia.*

Harten (196) **1.** North German: patronymic from HART 1. **2.** Dutch: from a derivative of a Germanic compound personal name beginning with *hard* 'hardy', 'brave', 'strong'. **3.** Dutch (**van Harten**): habitational name from a place so named near Renkum, Gelderland.

Hartenstein (286) **1.** German and Jewish (Ashkenazic): habitational name from any of several places named Hartenstein, in Saxony and Bavaria. **2.** Jewish (Ashkenazic): ornamental name composed of German *hart* 'hard' + *Stein* 'rock', 'stone'.

GIVEN NAMES German 4%. *Otto* (2), *Hermann, Reiner.*

Hartenstine (138) Americanized spelling of German and Jewish HARTENSTEIN.

Harter (4091) **1.** German (also **Härter**): variant of HARDER. **2.** South German and Tyrolean: habitational name for someone from Hart in Austria.

Hartfiel (189) German: occupational nickname for a file cutter, a maker of files, from Middle High German *hart* 'hard', + *file* 'file'.

GIVEN NAMES German 4%. *Fritz, Otto.*

Hartfield (861) **1.** English: habitational name from Hartfield in East Sussex, originally named with Old English *heorot* 'stag', 'hart' + *feld* 'open country'. **2.** Americanized form of German and Jewish HERZFELD.

Hartford (1602) English: habitational name from Hertford, or from either of two places called Hartford, in Cheshire and Cumbria; all are named with Old English *heorot* 'hart' + *ford* 'ford'.

Hartge (109) North German: from a pet form of a Germanic compound personal name beginning with *hart-* 'hardy', 'strong', for example *Hartwig* (see HARTWIG).

GIVEN NAMES French 5%; German 4%. *Emile; Erwin.*

Hartgraves (157) Variant of English **Hargraves** (see HARGROVE).

Hartgrove (326) English (Northampton): variant of HARGROVE.

Harth (358) **1.** German: variant of HARDT 1 and 2. **2.** Jewish (Ashkenazic): variant of HART.

Harthcock (117) Probably an altered form of English HEATHCOCK. Compare HATH-COCK.

Harthun (140) North German: of uncertain origin; perhaps a habitational name from Hartum near Minden in Westphalia.

GIVEN NAME German 4%. *Kurt.*

Hartig (775) **1.** German and Dutch: variant of HARTWIG. **2.** German: from a pet form of any of the various Germanic compound personal names beginning with *hard* 'hardy', 'strong', for example, HARTWIG. **3.** Dutch: variant of HARTOG.

GIVEN NAMES German 4%. *Gerhard* (2), *Franz, Helmut, Johann, Klaus, Kurt, Otto.*

Hartigan (1102) Irish: shortened Anglicized form of Gaelic **Ó hArtagáin** 'descendant of *Artagán*', a personal name from a double diminutive of *Art*, a byname meaning 'bear', 'hero'.

Hartill (127) English: variant of HARTELL.

Hartin (528) **1.** English: variant of HARTING. **2.** Irish: shortened Anglicized form of Gaelic **Ó hArtáin** 'descendant of *Artán*', a personal name formed from a diminutive of *Art*, a byname meaning 'bear', 'hero'.

Harting (778) **1.** English: habitational name from (East, South, and, formerly, West) Harting in West Sussex, named with an unattested Old English byname *Heort* 'hart' + *-ingas*, a suffix denoting 'family, dependants, or followers'. **2.** North German (also **Härting**): patronymic from HART or HARDT 2. **3.** German: habitational name from any of several places so named in Bavaria or from Hartingen, near Diepholz, Lower Saxony.

Hartinger (170) German: habitational name for someone from a place called Harting, Härting, or Hartingen (see HARTING 3).

Hartis (318) English (County Durham): variant of HARTS. In the U.S. this name is concentrated in NC.

Hartje (334) North German (Frisian) form of the personal name HARTKE.

Hartjes (121) North German (Frisian): patronymic from the personal name HARTKE.

Hartke (502) German: from a pet form HARTWIG, or of other Germanic compound personal names beginning with *hard* 'hardy', 'strong'.

Hartkopf (156) German: nickname for a thick-skulled or stubborn person, from Middle High German *harte* 'hard', 'strong' + *kopf* 'head'.

GIVEN NAMES German 7%; Scandinavian 6%. *Hans* (3), *Dieter, Fritz.*

Hartl (581) South German: variant of HARTLE.

GIVEN NAMES German 7%. *Erwin* (4), *Otto* (3), *Alois* (2), *Franz, Fritz, Hans, Kurt, Wenzel, Wolfgang.*

Hartlage (278) North German: habitational name from any of several places called Hartlage.

Hartland (251) English: habitational name from Hartland in Devon, named in Old English as 'estate (*land*) on the hart (*heorot*) peninsula (*teg*)'. The surname is now most frequent in the West Midlands and it may be that another, now lost, source is also involved.

Hartlaub (278) South German: from a Germanic personal name composed of the elements *hard* 'hardy', 'strong' + *wolf, wulf* 'wolf'.

Hartle (1092) **1.** German (also **Härtle**): from a pet form of the various Germanic compound names formed with *hard* 'hardy', 'brave', 'strong' as the first element. **2.** English: variant of HARTELL.

Hartleben (122) German: **1.** habitational name from Hartleb in Thuringia. **2.** patronymic from the Germanic personal name *Hartleip* (see HARTLIEB).

GIVEN NAMES German 7%. *Ewald, Frieda, Gerhard.*

Hartlein (104) South German (also **Härtlein**): from a pet form of the various Germanic compound names formed with *hard* 'hardy', 'brave', 'strong' as the first element.

Hartless (325) English (Midlands): unexplained.

Hartley (11654) **1.** English (mainly northern): habitational name from any of various places so called. Several, in particular those in Hampshire, Kent, and Devon, are named from Old English *heorot* 'hart', 'stag' + *lēah* 'wood', 'clearing'. One in Northumberland has as the second element Old English *hlāw* 'hill', and one in Cumbria contains Old English *clā* 'claw', in the sense of a tongue of land between two streams, + probably *heard* 'hard'. The surname is widely distributed, but most common in Yorkshire, where it arose from a

place near Haworth, West Yorkshire, also named with Old English *heorot* + *lēah*. As a Scottish name, it comes from the Cumbrian Hartley (see forebears note). **2.** Irish: shortened Anglicized form of surname adopted as equivalent of Gaelic **Ó hArtghaile** 'descendant of *Artghal*', a personal name composed of the elements *Art* 'bear', 'hero' + *gal* 'valor'.

FOREBEARS In the 13th century, Michael de Hardcla fled from Westmorland or Cumberland to Scotland after the execution of his brother, the Earl of Carlisle, for treason.

Hartlieb (149) German (southern and central): from a Germanic personal name composed of the elements *hard* 'hardy', 'brave', 'strong' + *lieb* 'live'.

GIVEN NAMES German 13%; Scandinavian 4%. *Gunther* (2), *Kurt* (2), *Hans, Willi.*

Hartline (1205) Americanized spelling of German HARTLEIN.

Hartling (207) German (also **Härtling**): patronymic from the personal name *Hartl(ein)* (see HARTLE).

Hartlove (107) Americanized form of German HARTLIEB.

Hartman (25552) **1.** Dutch: from a Germanic personal name composed of the elements *hard* 'hardy', 'strong' + *man* 'man'. **2.** Respelling of German HARTMANN. This name is also found in Slovenia and elsewhere in central Europe. **3.** Jewish (Ashkenazic): elaborated form of HART.

Hartmann (4641) **1.** North German and Danish: variant of HART 1. **2.** German: from a Germanic compound personal name composed of the elements *hard* 'hard', 'strong' + *man* 'man'. **3.** Jewish (Ashkenazic): see HARTMAN.

GIVEN NAMES German 8%. *Hans* (14), *Kurt* (11), *Otto* (9), *Erwin* (7), *Heinz* (6), *Helmut* (5), *Horst* (5), *Klaus* (4), *Manfred* (3), *Dieter* (2), *Dietrich* (2), *Franz* (2).

Hartnagel (129) German: metonymic occupational name for a nailsmith, from Middle High German *harte* 'hard' + *nagel* 'nail'.

Hartnell (214) English (mainly southwestern): habitational name from Hartnoll in Marwood, Devon, named from Old English *heor(o)t* 'hart', 'stag' + *cnoll* 'hilltop'.

Hartner (315) German: probably a habitational name for someone from any of several places named Harten, in Silesia and Württemberg.

Hartness (656) English (Cumbria): unexplained.

Hartnett (2600) Irish (especially County Cork): shortened Anglicized form of Gaelic **Ó hAirtnéada** 'descendant of *Airtnéad*', a personal name of uncertain origin. The first syllable is probably from *Art* 'bear', 'hero'.

Hartney (299) Irish: variant of HARNEY. This name has been confused with **Hartnane** (which is sometimes an Anglicized form of Gaelic **Ó hIfearnáin** (see HEFFERNAN), and sometimes an

Anglicized form of Gaelic **Ó hEarnáin** 'descendant of *Earnán*', a personal name derived from *earna* 'experienced' or perhaps from *iarn* 'iron').

Hartog (250) **1.** North German and Dutch: equivalent of HERZOG. **2.** Jewish (Ashkenazic): ornamental adoption of 1.

GIVEN NAMES German 4%; Dutch 4%. *Claus, Hans, Kurt; Dirk* (2), *Maurits* (2), *Cornie.*

Harton (541) **1.** English: habitational name from places so called in County Durham and North Yorkshire, and possibly also from the one in Shropshire. The first was named in Old English with *heorot* 'stag', 'hart' + *dūn* 'hill'; the second with *hær* 'rock' + *tūn* 'enclosure', 'farmstead', 'settlement'. **2.** Irish: variant spelling of HARTIN.

Hartong (168) Dutch: variant of HARTUNG.

GIVEN NAME Dutch 5%. *Hendrik* (3).

Hartpence (166) From a misdivision of the name of *Johannes Eberhart Pence*, living in Hunterdon County, NJ, in the 1730s. His name was no doubt originally German BENZ. See also PENCE.

Hartranft (503) German: descriptive nickname for a pauper, from Middle High German *harte* 'hard' + *ranft* 'rind', 'crust'.

Hartrick (134) German: an altered spelling of *Hartrich*, from a Germanic personal name composed of the elements *hard* 'hardy', 'strong' + *rīc* 'power', 'rule'.

FOREBEARS The name was brought from the Palatinate, Germany, to Co. Wexford, Ireland, in the early 18th century, and reached America from there a century later. It was brought to Canada independently in the 18th century.

Harts (192) **1.** Dutch: patronymic from a reduced and altered form of the personal names *Arnoud* (see ARNOLD), *Alaert*, or *Adriaan*. Compare ARTZ. **2.** English: patronymic from HART. **3.** Variant of German and Jewish HARTZ.

Hartsel (118) Americanized form of German HARTZEL.

Hartsell (1573) Americanized form of German HARTZEL. Hartsell is a particularly common name in NC.

Hartsfield (1346) **1.** Americanized form of **Harzfeld**, an Ashkenazic Jewish ornamental name formed with German HARZ + *Feld* 'field'. **2.** Americanized form of HERZFELD.

Hartshorn (1221) English: habitational name from Hartshorne in Derbyshire or Hartshorn in Northumberland, named from Old English *heorot* 'hart', 'stag' + *horn* 'horn', i.e. hill with some fancied resemblance to a hart's horn. Reaney suggests a further possibility: that it could come from the Middle English plant name *harteshorn* 'hartshorn', denoting either of two plants with leaves branched like a stag's antlers: *Senebiera coronopus* and *Plantago coronopus.*

Hartshorne (241) English: variant spelling of HARTSHORN.

Hartsock (1192) Probably an altered form of HERZOG.

Hartsoe (251) Perhaps an altered form of HERZOG.

Hartson (465) English: variant of HART-SHORN.

Hartsook (306) Americanized form of German HERZOG.

Hartsough (231) Americanized form of German HERZOG.

Hartstein (269) **1.** German and Jewish (Ashkenazic): habitational name from a place in Upper Silesia called Hartstein. **2.** German: nickname for a mean or harsh and inflexible person, from Middle High German *hart* 'hard' + *stein* 'stone'. **3.** Jewish (Ashkenazic): ornamental compound name from German *Hart* 'deer' + *Stein* 'stone'.
GIVEN NAMES Jewish 6%. *Ari, Ilan, Meir, Miriam, Moshe.*

Hartt (455) Respelling of HART.

Hartter (153) German: habitational name for someone from a place called *Hartte* in Brandenburg or a respelling of German HARTER.
GIVEN NAMES German 4%. *Juergen, Klaus.*

Hartung (2181) German, Dutch, and Danish: from a Germanic personal name, a derivative (originally a patronymic) of compound names beginning with *hart* 'hardy', 'strong'.
GIVEN NAMES German 4%. *Hans* (3), *Bernd, Elke, Ernst, Erwin, Ewald, Fritz, Georg, Gunter, Hermann, Ilse, Johannes.*

Hartvigsen (109) Scandinavian: patronymic from the Germanic personal name *Hartvig* (see HARTWIG).
GIVEN NAMES Scandinavian 6%. *Erik, Oluf.*

Hartwell (2458) English: habitational name from places in Buckinghamshire, Northamptonshire, and Staffordshire called Hartwell, from Old English *heorot* 'stag', 'hart' + *wella* 'spring', 'stream'. In some cases the surname may have arisen from Hartwell in Hartfield, Sussex or Hartwell in Lamerton, Devon.

Hartwick (945) Probably an altered spelling of HARTWIG.

Hartwig (2591) German (also **Härtwig**), Dutch, and Danish (**Hartvig**): from a Germanic personal name composed of the elements *hard* 'hardy', 'strong' + *wīg* 'battle', 'combat'.
GIVEN NAMES German 5%. *Kurt* (7), *Otto* (5), *Hans* (3), *Klaus* (2), *Lorenz* (2), *Alfons, Elfriede, Erna, Erwin, Ewald, Fritz, Gerhard.*

Harty (1523) **1.** Irish (chiefly Counties Tipperary and Cork): shortened form of **O'Harty**, an Anglicized form of Gaelic **Ó hAthartaigh, Ó hÁrtaigh** 'descendant of *Athartach* or *Artach*', variants of the personal name *Faghartach*, which is probably a derivative of *foghartach* 'noisy'.
2. Perhaps also English, a habitational name from the Isle of Harty in Kent, named in Old English as 'stag island', from *heorot* 'hart', 'stag' + *ēg* 'island'.
GIVEN NAMES Irish 4%. *Kieran, Ronan.*

Hartz (1769) German: **1.** topographic name, a variant of HARDT. **2.** from a short form of a Germanic compound name beginning with *hard* 'hardy', 'brave', 'strong'. **3.** North German: from a form of Low German HART 1 altered to the phonology of standard German. **4.** Jewish (Ashkenazic): ornamental name from Yiddish *harts* 'heart'.

Hartzel (229) Variant spelling of German **Herzel** (see HARTZELL).

Hartzell (2603) Americanized spelling of German **Herzel**, which Brechenmacher derives from the personal name *Harzelo*.

Hartzheim (145) German: habitational name from a place of this name.

Hartzler (685) German: probably an occupational name for a pitch or resin gatherer, from Middle High German *harz* 'resin' + agent suffix *-ler*.

Hartzog (1152) **1.** Americanized spelling of German HERZOG 1. **2.** Jewish (Ashkenazic): variant of HERZOG.

Harutunian (67) Armenian: variant of ARUTYUNYAN.

Harvan (106) Czech: metathesized form of HAVRAN.

Harvard (359) **1.** English: from the Old English personal name *Hereweard*, composed of the elements *here* 'army' + *weard* 'guard', which was borne by an 11th-century thane of Lincolnshire, leader of resistance to the advancing Normans. The Old Norse cognate *Hervarðr* was also common and, particularly in the Danelaw, it may in part lie behind the surname. **2.** Welsh: variant of HAVARD.
FOREBEARS John Harvard (1607–38), who gave his name to Harvard College, was the son of a London butcher. He inherited considerable property, and emigrated to MA in 1637. On his death he bequeathed half his estate and the whole of his library to the newly founded college at Cambridge, MA.

Harvat (108) Variant of Hungarian HORVATH or Croatian HORVAT.

Harvath (217) Variant of Hungarian HORVATH.

Harvel (329) English: variant spelling of HARVELL.

Harvell (1397) English (Dorset): probably a habitational name from either of the places mentioned at HAIRFIELD, or from Harvel near Rochester, Kent, named with Old English *heorot* 'hart', 'stag' + *feld* 'open country'.

Harvey (38284) **1.** English and Scottish: from the Breton personal name *Aeruiu* or *Haerviu*, composed of the elements *haer* 'battle', 'carnage' + *vy* 'worthy', which was brought to England by Breton followers of William the Conqueror, for the most part in the Gallicized form *Hervé*. (The change from *-er-* to *-ar-* was a normal development in Middle English and Old French.) Reaney believes that the surname is also occasionally from a Norman personal name, Old German *Herewig*, composed of the Germanic elements *hari, heri* 'army' + *wīg* 'war'. **2.** Irish: mainly of English origin, in Ulster and County Wexford, but sometimes a shortened Anglicized form of Gaelic **Ó hAirmheadhaigh** 'descendant of *Airmheadhach*', a personal name probably meaning 'esteemed'. It seems to be a derivative of *Airmheadh*, the name borne by a mythological physician. **3.** Irish (County Fermanagh): shortened Anglicized form of Gaelic **Ó hEarchaidh** 'descendant of *Earchadh*', a personal name of uncertain origin.

Harvick (137) Possibly an Americanized spelling of German **Harwig**, a variant of HERWIG and HARTWIG, or of HARWICK.

Harvie (339) Scottish: variant of HARVEY 1.

Harvill (722) English: variant spelling of HARVELL.

Harvilla (133) Slovak: metathesized form of HAVRILLA.

Harville (1398) **1.** Variant spelling of English HARVELL. **2.** Americanized spelling of Slovak HARVILLA. This is a common name in TN.

Harvin (632) Variant spelling of Dutch **Harvyn**, from the Germanic personal name *Herrewijn*, composed of the elements *hari* 'army' + *wini* 'friend'.

Harvison (298) English: patronymic from HARVEY.

Harward (666) English: variant of HARVARD.

Harwell (2875) English: habitational name from places called Harwell in south Oxfordshire (formerly part of Berkshire) and Nottinghamshire. The former was named in Old English as 'spring or stream by or from the gray one', from *Hāra* 'the gray' (here referring to a certain hill) + *wella*; while the latter was named from Old English *hēore, hȳre* 'pleasant' + *wella* 'stream'.

Harwick (401) **1.** English: probably a variant of **Horwick**, a topographic or habitational name from Old English *horh* 'muddy' + *wīc* 'outlying dairy farm'. **2.** German: habitational name from a place so called near Coesfeld, Westphalia.

Harwin (101) English (East Anglia): from the Old French personal name *Harduin*, composed of the Germanic elements *hard* 'hardy', 'brave' + *win* 'friend'.

Harwood (4586) English and Scottish: habitational name from any of various places, for example in the Scottish Borders and in Cheshire, Lancashire, Lothian, Northumberland, and North and West Yorkshire, called Harwood or Harewood from Old English *hār* 'gray' or *hara* 'hare' + *wudu* 'wood'. This name has also become established in Ireland.

Hary (118) Hungarian: unexplained.

GIVEN NAMES French 6%; Hungarian 6%. *Alexandre, Andre; Laszlo* (2), *Miklos.*

Harz (124) German and Jewish (Ashkenazic): variant of HARTZ.

GIVEN NAMES German 9%. *Kurt* (2), *Gunther.*

Hasan (1099) **1.** Muslim: from the Arabic personal name *Ḥasān* 'good', 'handsome'. Hasan (*c.*625–669) and his brother HUSAIN were sons of the khalif 'Alī ibn Abī Ṭālib (see ALI) and, through their mother Fatima, grandsons of the Prophet Muhammad. Shiite Muslims regard Hasan and his brother Husain as the true successors of Muhammad. The name is popular among Sunni Muslims as well as Shiites. **2.** Jewish: variant of HAZAN.

GIVEN NAMES Muslim 81%. *Syed* (79), *Mohammad* (22), *Mohammed* (15), *Ahmad* (9), *Ali* (7), *Muhammad* (7), *Omar* (7), *Abdul* (6), *Abul* (6), *Abdullah* (5), *Anwar* (5), *Masud* (5).

Hasbargen (133) Respelling of a German habitational name from a place named Hasbergen, for example in Hannover and Oldenburg.

Hasbrook (152) Americanized spelling of HASBROUCK.

Hasbrouck (768) French (Huguenot): habitational name from a place in French Flanders, spelled Hazebrouck in French, Hazebroek in Flemish, meaning 'hare fen'.

FOREBEARS In 1675–78 Abraham Hasbrouck and his brother Jean were among the founders of New Paltz, NY.

Hascall (251) English: variant spelling of HASKELL.

Hasch (150) German (of Slavic origin): from an aphetic form of the personal name *Johannes* (see JOHN).

Haschke (145) German (of Slavic origin): from a pet form of the personal name HASCH.

GIVEN NAMES German 15%. *Guenter* (2), *Dieter, Gerhard, Horst, Oskar, Otto.*

Hase (508) **1.** German: nickname for a swift runner or a timorous person, from Middle High German, Middle Low German *hase* 'hare'. **2.** Jewish (Ashkenazic): ornamental name from German *Hase* 'hare'. **3.** English: from a Middle English nickname, *Hase*, from Old English *hās* 'harsh, raucous, or hoarse voice'. **4.** Japanese: usually written with characters meaning 'long valley'; habitational name from a place in Yamato (now Nara prefecture). Listed in the Shinsen shōjiroku. Some bearers are descended from the TAIRA clan; they are found mainly in eastern Japan. Also pronounced **Nagaya** and **Nagatani**; the original pronunciation was *Hatsuse*, meaning 'beginning of the strait'.

GIVEN NAMES Japanese 7%; German 5%. *Keiko, Masafumi, Mitsunori, Miyo, Reiko, Rieko, Riko, Satoshi, Soichi, Tatsuo, Teruko, Yasuo; Volker* (3), *Ernst, Gerhard, Helmut, Klaus, Manfred, Siegfried.*

Hasegawa (580) Japanese: 'long valley river'; topographic name found in eastern Japan and the Ryūkyū Islands. It originated in the same place as HASE, therefore the actual meaning may be 'river at the beginning of the strait'. Several bearers descend from the MINAMOTO and FUJIWARA clans.

GIVEN NAMES Japanese 64%. *Akira* (9), *Hiroshi* (9), *Takashi* (5), *Kiyoshi* (4), *Toru* (4), *Kazuo* (3), *Takeshi* (3), *Yutaka* (3), *Chieko* (2), *Haruki* (2), *Hiroko* (2), *Hiromi* (2).

Hasek (163) Czech: **1.** (**Hásek**): from German, either from *Haase* 'hare' or from the personal name *Hartmann* (see HARTMANN 2). **2.** (**Hašek**): from a pet form of the personal name *Haštal* (Latin *Castulus*, from *castus* 'pure', 'chaste').

GIVEN NAMES Czech and Slovak 7%. *Ondrej* (2), *Vaclav.*

Haselden (409) English: habitational name from any of various places named from Old English *hæsel* 'hazelnut tree' (or the Old Norse cognate, *hesli*) + *denu* 'valley'. This surname is also established in Ireland.

Haseley (208) English: variant of HEASLEY.

Haselhorst (247) German: habitational name from any of several places called Haselhorst.

GIVEN NAME German 4%. *Otto.*

Haselhuhn (130) German: nickname for someone with gray hair, from Middle High German *haselhuon*, Middle Low German *haselhōn* 'hazel grouse', a game bird with gray plumage.

Haseltine (334) English: variant of HASELDEN.

Haselton (255) English: variant of HASELDEN.

Haselwood (123) English: variant spelling of HAZELWOOD.

Haseman (195) Respelling of German **Hasemann**.

Hasemann (105) German: habitational name for someone from the river *Hase* (tributary of the Ems) in Lower Saxony.

GIVEN NAMES German 8%. *Gunther, Heinz.*

Hasen (106) **1.** Northern Irish: probably a variant of HASSON. **2.** Muslim: variant of HASAN. **3.** Jewish: variant of HAZAN 'cantor'.

GIVEN NAMES Muslim 6%. *Ashraf* (2), *Ibrahim, Maher, Syed.*

Hasenauer (178) German: habitational name for someone from Hasenau in Silesia.

Hasenfus (100) Respelling of German **Hasenfuss**, literally 'hare foot', hence a nickname for a swift runner. See also HASE.

Hasenkamp (123) **1.** North German (Westphalia): from a field name derived from the genitive of Middle Low German *hase* 'hare' + *kamp* 'field', 'domain', or a habitational name from Hasenkamp, a place name near Minden, North Rhine-Westphalia, among others in Lower Saxony. **2.** Dutch: habitational name from

Hazenkamp in Gelderland, also meaning 'hare field'.

Hasenstab (104) German: originally **Haselstab**, literally 'hazel rod', taken as a symbol of judicial power, which then came to mean a certain area, a field where judicial decisions were made or actions taken.

GIVEN NAME German 5%. *Rainer.*

Haser (151) German: probably a habitational name for someone from a minor place named with Middle High German *hase* 'hare' + the suffix *-er* denoting an inhabitant.

Hash (1878) Americanized spelling of German HASCH.

Hashagen (165) North German (Bremen): habitational or topographic name from an abandoned place named Hashagen, from Middle Low German *hase* 'hare' + *hage(n)* 'woods'.

Hashbarger (115) Possibly a variant of HARSHBARGER or an Americanized form of German **Hasberger**, a habitational name for someone from a place called Hasbergen, earlier Hasberge. Compare HASBARGEN.

Hashem (272) Muslim: see HASHIM.

GIVEN NAMES Muslim 43%. *Mohamed* (8), *Abul* (4), *Ali* (4), *Ahmad* (3), *Mohammed* (3), *Sami* (3), *Abdul* (2), *Akil* (2), *Mohammad* (2), *Mustafa* (2), *Abdel, Abdo.*

Hashemi (226) Muslim: Arabic surname indicating descent from HASHIM, great-grandfather of the Prophet Muhammad.

GIVEN NAMES Muslim 80%. *Ali* (6), *Hamid* (4), *Majid* (4), *Amir* (3), *Hossein* (3), *Said* (3), *Forough* (2), *Hadi* (2), *Hashem* (2), *Hassan* (2), *Mehdi* (2), *Mohamad* (2).

Hasher (107) English: possibly a hypercorrected form of ASHER.

Hashim (200) Muslim: from an Arabic personal name, *Hāshim*, the byname of the great-grandfather of the Prophet Muhammad, who provided for pilgrims coming to the Ka'ba (the holy temple) in Mecca each year. *Hāshim* literally means 'crusher'. Hāshim, whose original name was 'Amr, initiated a twice-yearly caravan (trading expedition) to Yemen and the Levant. The story goes that he returned from one such expedition bringing with him bread, which he crushed and distributed, earning him the nickname 'the crusher'. The Kingdom of Jordan is known as 'Hashemite' because its rulers are descended from Hashim.

GIVEN NAMES Muslim 59%. *Mohammad* (4), *Ali* (2), *Hussain* (2), *Jamil* (2), *Junaid* (2), *Malik* (2), *Masih* (2), *Mohammed* (2), *Mohd* (2), *Mumtaz* (2), *Zaffar* (2), *Abdul.*

Hashimoto (854) Japanese: '(one who lives) near the bridge'; habitational name common throughout Japan. Some bearers are of samurai descent.

GIVEN NAMES Japanese 58%. *Hideo* (7), *Takashi* (6), *Akira* (5), *Hiroshi* (5), *Toshio*

(5), *Kenji* (4), *Kiyoshi* (4), *Makoto* (4), *Hiro* (3), *Kazuhiko* (3), *Kazuo* (3), *Keiko* (3).

Hashman (225) Americanized spelling of an unexplained German name, **Haschmann**.

Hashmi (189) Muslim: variant of HASHEMI. GIVEN NAMES Muslim 88%. *Syed* (18), *Shoaib* (5), *Muhammad* (4), *Asif* (3), *Raza* (3), *Abdul* (2), *Adnan* (2), *Amjed* (2), *Farooq* (2), *Fayyaz* (2), *Imran* (2), *Jawaid* (2).

Haskamp (121) German: variant of HASENKAMP.

Haske (228) German: from a pet form of a Germanic compound name formed with *hadu* 'fight', 'battle' as the first element.

Haskell (4067) **1.** English: from the Norman personal name *Aschetil*, from Old Norse *Ásketill*, *Áskell*, a compound *áss* 'god' + *ketill* 'kettle', 'helmet'. **2.** Jewish (Ashkenazic): from the personal name *Khaskl*, a Yiddish form of the Hebrew name *Yechezkel* (see EZEKIEL).

Haskett (851) English: from a pet form of the Norman personal name *Aschetil* (see HASKELL).

FOREBEARS Stephen Hasket, a soap boiler and merchant of Salem, MA, was a native of Henstridge, Somerset, England. He came to Salem from Exeter, Devon, about 1666. His son Elias, born at Salem, went on to become governor of New Providence, Bahamas, before the people there revolted and sent him back to NY.

Haskew (194) English (northern): hypercorrected form of ASKEW.

Haskin (1152) **1.** English: from the Norman personal name *Asketin*, a pet form of the Old Norse name *Ásketil* (see HASKELL). **2.** Irish: shortened Anglicized form of Gaelic **Ó hUiscín** 'descendant of *Uiscín*', apparently a diminutive of *uisce* 'water' (and thus the surname may be 'translated' WATERS), but possibly a corruption of a diminutive of *Fuarghus* meaning 'cold choice'. **3.** Jewish (from Ukraine): metronymic from Yiddish name *Khaske*, a pet form of *Khane* (see HANNA 1) + the Slavic possessive suffix *-in*.

Haskins (5651) **1.** English: patronymic form of HASKIN. **2.** Irish: variant of HASKIN 2.

Haslag (101) Origin unidentified.

Haslam (1012) English (especially Lancashire): topographic name for someone who lived 'by the hazels', or a habitational name from Haslam in Lancashire, in both cases from Old English *hæslum*, dative plural of *hæsel* 'hazel tree'. This surname was taken to Ireland in the 17th century.

Haslem (159) English: variant spelling of HASLAM.

Hasler (725) **1.** English (Essex) and German (also **Häsler**): topographic name from Middle English *hasel*, Middle High German *hasel* + the English and German agent suffix *-er*. **2.** English: habitational

name from Haselour in Staffordshire or Haselor in Warwickshire and Worcestershire, named with Old English *hæsel* 'hazel' + *ofer* 'hill', 'ridge'. **3.** Variant of German HASSLER. GIVEN NAMES German 4%. *Christoph, Erna, Florian, Fritz, Heinz, Helmut.*

Haslett (616) English and northern Irish: variant spelling of HAZLETT.

Hasley (532) English: variant spelling of HASELEY.

Haslinger (104) German (Austria): habitational name for someone from any of several places named *Hasling* in Bavaria. GIVEN NAME German 6%. *Wilfried.*

Haslip (129) English and northern Irish: variant of HYSLOP.

Hason (66) **1.** Scottish: see HASEN. **2.** Jewish (Sephardic): variant of HASSON.

Haspel (194) German, Dutch, and Jewish (Ashkenazic): from Middle High German, Middle Dutch *haspel*, German *Haspel* 'reel', 'winch', hence a metonymic occupational name for someone who wound thread into a skein from a bobbin or who operated a winch or who manufactured the implements.

Hasper (118) German: habitational name for someone from any of several places named Haspe, Hasper, or Hasperde, mostly in northern Germany. GIVEN NAMES German 14%. *Kurt* (3), *Udo* (2), *Wolfgang.*

Hass (2796) **1.** German and Dutch: from *Hasso*, a pet form of the Germanic personal name *Hadubert*, or of some other compound personal name beginning with *hadu* 'battle', 'strife'. **2.** German: nickname for a bitter and vicious man, from Middle High German *haz* 'hatred'. **3.** Jewish (Ashkenazic): from German *Hass* 'hatred', one of names selected from vocabulary words by government officials when surnames became compulsory.

Hassall (104) English: variant of HASSELL.

Hassan (2242) **1.** Muslim: from a personal name based on Arabic *hassan* 'beautifier'. The poet Hassan bin Sabit was a companion of the Prophet Muhammad. **2.** Muslim: variant spelling of HASAN. **3.** Irish (County Derry): shortened Anglicized form of Gaelic **Ó hOsáin** 'descendant of *Ósán*', a personal name formed from a diminutive of *os* 'deer'. GIVEN NAMES Muslim 65%. *Mohamed* (51), *Syed* (36), *Ali* (24), *Mohammad* (23), *Mohammed* (23), *Ahmed* (21), *Hassan* (18), *Mahmoud* (16), *Ibrahim* (10), *Mahmood* (10), *Mostafa* (9), *Omar* (9).

Hassard (148) Northern Irish: variant of HAZARD.

Hasse (821) **1.** German and Dutch: variant of HASS 1. **2.** English: topographic name from an unattested Old English word, *hasse* 'coarse grass', or a habitational name from a minor place, such as The

Hasse in Soham, Cambridgeshire, named from this word. GIVEN NAMES German 5%. *Otto* (3), *Erwin* (2), *Horst* (2), *Arno, Frieda, Gerhard, Gunter, Hans.*

Hassebrock (170) Dutch: variant of HASBROUCK.

Hassebroek (108) Dutch: variant of HASBROUCK.

Hassel (693) **1.** German: topographic name from *has* 'marsh' + *lo* 'wooded lowland', or a habitational name from a place so named (for example, in Hannover and Westphalia). **2.** Swedish (also **Hässel**): ornamental name from Swedish *hassel* 'hazel', or possibly a habitational name from a place name containing the element *Hassel* or *Hässel*. **3.** Belgian: habitational name from Hasselt in Belgian Limburg, Ophasselt in East Flanders, or Neerhasselt in Aalst, East Flanders; the place names denote the presence of hazel trees.

Hasselbach (175) German: habitational name from any of the places in various parts of Germany called Hasselbach. GIVEN NAMES German 7%. *Kurt* (2), *Karlheinz, Otto.*

Hasselbring (215) Dutch and North German: topographic name for someone who lived on the edge of a wood, from *Hassel* 'lowland wood' + Middle Low German *brink* 'edge', 'slope', 'grazing land' (see BRINK). GIVEN NAME German 4%. *Kurt.*

Hassell (2166) English: habitational name from Hassall in Cheshire, named from the genitive case of the Old English byname *Hætt* 'hat' (or possibly from Old English *hægtesse* 'witch') + Old English *halh* 'nook', 'recess'.

Hasselman (237) **1.** Altered spelling of German **Hasselmann**, a derivative of HASSEL 1. **2.** Dutch: either a variant of the habitational name **Hasselt** (see HASSEL 3), or a topographic name from *hasselt* 'hazelwood', 'place where hazels grow' + *man* 'man'. GIVEN NAME German 5%. *Kurt* (2).

Hassen (450) **1.** Muslim: see HASAN. **2.** Dutch: patronymic from HASS 2. GIVEN NAMES Muslim 18%. *Ahmed* (3), *Fareed* (3), *Mohamed* (3), *Mohammed* (3), *Abdul* (2), *Waleed* (2), *Abdu, Abdulkadir, Abed, Ahmad, Akil, Alia.*

Hasser (104) German: nickname from Middle High German *hassære* 'hater', 'adversary'. GIVEN NAMES German 4%. *Erhard, Hans.*

Hassett (1456) **1.** Irish: shortened Anglicized form of Gaelic **Ó hAiseadha** 'descendant of *Aisidh*', a personal name meaning 'discord', 'strife'. **2.** English and Irish: shortened form of the habitational name **Blennerhasset**, from a place in Cumbria, so named from Celtic *blain* 'summit' + an unexplained second element +

Old Scandinavian *hey* 'hay' + *sǽtr* 'shieling'.

GIVEN NAMES Irish 4%. *Brendan, Kaitlin, Siobhan.*

Hassey (198) Irish: variant of HUSSEY.

Hassig (166) **1.** German: derivative from a Germanic personal name, see HASS 1. **2.** German (**Hässig**): nickname from Middle High German *hazzec, hezzec* 'hostile', 'resentful'.

GIVEN NAMES German 7%. *Otto* (2), *Hermann.*

Hassing (204) **1.** German and Dutch: patronymic derivative from the Germanic personal name *Hasso* (see HASS). **2.** Danish: habitational name from any of numerous places named Hassing. The first element of the name probably means 'gray'.

GIVEN NAMES Scandinavian 5%. *Erik, Per.*

Hassinger (698) German: from a Germanic personal name derived from *Hasso*, a short form of several personal names composed with *hadu* 'strife', 'battle' as the first element.

Hassler (1690) German: topographic name for someone who lived in a place where hazels grew, from Middle High German *hasel* 'hazel' + the suffix *-er* denoting an inhabitant.

Hasslinger (115) German: habitational name for someone from any of several small places in Lower Saxony named *Hassling* or *Hasslingen.*

Hassman (304) **1.** German (**Hassmann**): patronymic from a short form of a Germanic personal name formed with *hadu* 'fight', 'battle' as the first element, or a regional name for someone from Hesse (HESS 1). **2.** Jewish (Ashkenazic): origin uncertain; perhaps a variant of HAUSMANN.

Hasson (1203) **1.** Scottish and northern Irish: patronymic from *Hal* (pet form of HENRY). **2.** French: from the Old French oblique case of the personal name *Hasso*, a variant of a name derived from *Hadizo*, an unattested short form of a compound names beginning with *hadu* 'battle', 'strife' **3.** Jewish (Sephardic): either a nickname from Hebrew *chason* 'strong', or from a cognate male personal name derived from an Arabic word meaning 'fortress'.

GIVEN NAMES Jewish 4%. *Morry* (2), *Golda, Meir, Mordechai, Moshe, Rina, Shimon, Shlomo, Shmuel, Yehoshua.*

Hast (239) **1.** German: probably a habitational name from Haste near Wunstorf or Osnabrück. **2.** Dutch: nickname from Middle Dutch *haest* 'hasty'. **3.** Swedish: soldier's name, from *hast* 'haste', 'hurry'. **4.** English (Lancashire and Yorkshire): reduced form of HAYHURST.

Haste (240) English and French: metonymic occupational name for a turnspit, i.e. a servant who turned the spit, from Old French *haste* '(roasting) spit'.

FOREBEARS A bearer of the name Haste from Paris is documented in Montreal in 1662.

Hasten (225) Shortened form of Dutch **van Hasten**, a habitational name for someone from Asten in North Brabant or Astene in the Belgian province of East Flanders, or a shortened form of **van (der) Hasten**, from Middle Dutch *a(e)st* 'drying room', 'drying kiln', as used in the manufacture of beer or the preparation of madder for dyeing.

Hastert (161) German: perhaps a nickname from *Ha(a)stert*, one of the many bynames from Middle High German and Middle Low German *hase* 'hare' + *stērt* 'tail'.

Hastey (168) English: variant spelling of HASTY.

Hastie (635) **1.** Scottish: variant of HASTY. **2.** Irish (Ulster): variant of HASTINGS.

Hasting (483) Scottish and northern English: patronymic from the comparatively rare Anglo-Norman French personal name *Hasten(c), Hastang*, assimilated to HASTINGS. The personal name is of Old Norse origin, composed of the elements *há* 'high' + *steinn* 'stone'.

Hastings (10836) **1.** English and Scottish: habitational name from Hastings, a place in Sussex, on the south coast of England, near which the English army was defeated by the Normans in 1066. It is named from Old English *Hǣstingas* 'people of Hǣsta'. The surname was taken to Scotland under William the Lion in the latter part of the 12th century. It also assimilated some instances of the native Scottish surname *Harestane* (see HAIRSTON). **2.** English: variant of HASTING. **3.** Irish (Connacht): shortened Anglicized form of Gaelic **Ó hOistín** 'descendant of *Oistín*', the Gaelic form of *Augustine* (see AUSTIN).

FOREBEARS Hastings was the family name of the Earls of Huntingdon. Their descent can be traced from Sir Henry de Hastings (died 1268). The family once held great power; by marriage they were related to the kings of Scotland, and John, 1st Lord Hastings (1262–1312), was one of the claimants to the Scottish throne in 1290.

Haston (565) English: according to Reaney, a habitational name from Haston in Shropshire, which is possibly named with Old English *hēafod* 'head' + *stān* 'stone'. However, the present-day concentration of the name in Scotland suggests that in some cases at least it could perhaps be from one of the places mentioned at HAIRSTON.

Hastreiter (151) South German: habitational name for someone from Hasreit in Austria.

GIVEN NAMES German 8%. *Hermann* (3), *Alois, Fritz.*

Hasty (2366) English: **1.** from the personal name *Asti*, a pet form of the Norman personal name *Asketin*, derived from Old Norse *Ásketill*, composed of the elements *áss* 'god' + *ketill* 'kettle', 'helmet'. Compare HASKELL. **2.** from Middle English, Old French *hasti* 'quick', 'speedy', a nick-

name for a brisk or impetuous person, or possibly for a messenger.

Haswell (433) English (chiefly Northumberland): habitational name from a place named Haswell, notably the one in County Durham, which is named from Old English *hǣsel* 'hazelnut tree' + *well(a)* 'spring', 'stream'.

Hasz (201) German: variant spelling of HASS.

Hata (222) Japanese: an ancient clan descended from the family and followers of Yuzuki no Kimi, a Korean prince who claimed descent from Qin Shihuangdi, the first Emperor of China (259–210 BC). According to the Nihon shoki, Yuzuki no Kimi migrated to Japan during the reign of Emperor Ōjin (late 4th century) with thousands of followers, many of whom were skilled silk producers and weavers; they were therefore given the name *Hata* meaning 'loom'. They settled in the Yamato-Yamashiro heartland, especially in the region of present-day Kyōto. The family later enjoyed very close relations with Prince Regent Shōtoku (564–622), a statesman and Sinophile known as the 'father of Japanese civilization'. Listed in the Shinsen shōjiroku, the name is related etymologically to HATTORI. Actually, the character *qin* (or *ch'in*) has nothing to do with weaving; it means 'flourishing rice plants'. As the name of the first clan to conquer and unify the rest of China, it is the source of the name *China*. It is most likely that the reading *hata* was arbitrarily applied by the newly literate Japanese to the character *qin* because the newly arrived weavers claimed Qin clan connections, or at least were 'Chinese'. Be that as it may, it is possible for some Qin refugees to have escaped to Korea after their empire fell in 206 BC, and for their descendants to have moved on to Japan during the 4th century, when the growing might of the Korean Shilla kingdom made life precarious for some in that peninsula. Other immigrant groups were also arriving in Japan at this time. See also HADA.

GIVEN NAMES Japanese 57%. *Yuko* (3), *Hiro* (2), *Nobuhiko* (2), *Takao* (2), *Takashi* (2), *Yoshio* (2), *Akemi, Akiko, Akinori, Akira, Arisa, Chisato.*

Hatala (306) Finnish (**Hätälä**): of uncertain origin; perhaps from a nickname based on *hätä* 'hurry', 'scurry' + the local suffix *-la*. Alternatively, the element *hätä* may be derived from a foreign personal name.

Hatanaka (120) Japanese: '(one who lives) in the midst of the fields'. This name is found mostly in western Japan.

GIVEN NAMES Japanese 44%. *Iwao* (2), *Katsuyoshi* (2), *Tatsuo* (2), *Teiko* (2), *Chieko, Etsuko, Hidekazu, Ichiro, Junji, Kazumi, Kenichi, Kikuyo.*

Hataway (328) English: variant of HATHAWAY.

Hatch (9827) English (mainly Hampshire and Berkshire): topographic name from Middle English *hacche* 'gate', Old English *hæcc* (see HATCHER). In some cases the surname is habitational, from one of the many places named with this word. This name has been in Ireland since the 17th century, associated with County Meath and the nearby part of Louth.

Hatchel (204) English: unexplained. Compare HATCHELL.

Hatchell (650) English: unexplained.

Hatcher (9657) Southern English: topographic name for someone who lived by a gate, from Middle English *hacche* (Old English *hæcc*) + the agent suffix *-er*. This normally denoted a gate marking the entrance to a forest or other enclosed piece of land, sometimes a floodgate or sluice-gate.

Hatchett (1676) English: from Old French *hachet* 'small axe', 'hatchet', hence a metonymic occupational name for a maker or user of such implements, or perhaps a nickname of anecdotal origin.

Hatem (330) **1.** Muslim: from an Arabic personal name, *Ḥātim*, literally 'decisive' or 'determined'. Ḥātim al-Ṭā'iy (died 605) was a personage living in Arabia immediately before the rise of Islam, famous for his benevolence and hospitality. The name is popular throughout the Muslim world. **2.** Dutch: habitational name from a place in Gelderland.

GIVEN NAMES Muslim 7%. *Fouad* (2), *Ahmed*, *Assem*, *Esam*, *Fadi*, *Ghaleb*, *Hatem*, *Issa*, *Majed*, *Marwan*, *Milad*, *Moneer*.

Hatfield (12167) English (mainly Yorkshire and central England): habitational name from any of the various places named Hatfield, for example in Yorkshire, Nottinghamshire, Herefordshire, Worcestershire, Hertfordshire, and Essex, from Old English *hǣð* 'heathland', 'heather' + *feld* 'pasture', 'open country'.

Hathaway (7110) **1.** English (mainly central southern England and South Wales): **2.** topographic name for someone who lived by a path across a heath, from Middle English *hathe* 'heath' + *weye* 'way'. **3.** from an (apparently rare) Old English female personal name, *Heaðuwīg*, composed of the elements *heaðu* 'strife', 'contention' + *wīg* 'war'.

Hathcoat (192) Probably an altered spelling of HEATHCOTE.

Hathcock (1310) English (Worcestershire): variant of HEATHCOCK.

Hatheway (248) English: variant spelling of HATHAWAY.

Hathorn (766) English and Scottish (chiefly northern Ireland): variant of HAWTHORNE.

Hathorne (193) English and Scottish (chiefly northern Ireland): variant of HAWTHORNE.

Hatke (113) Danish: unexplained.

Hatlen (110) Scandinavian: unexplained.

Hatler (229) Perhaps an altered spelling of

South and Swiss German **Hattler** (also **Hättler**), an occupational name for someone who raises goats, from dialect *hettel* 'goat' + the agent suffix *-er*.

Hatlestad (237) Norwegian: habitational name from any of several farmsteads in western Norway, so named from Old Norse *Atlastaðir*, from the personal name *Atli* (from Germanic *Attala* 'little father') + *staðir* 'place', 'farmstead'.

Hatley (2288) English: habitational name from any of a group of places in Bedfordshire and Cambridgeshire, named with Old English *hætt* 'hat', probably the name of a hill (see HATT) + *lēah* 'wood', 'clearing'.

Hatmaker (683) Translation of Swiss German HUTMACHER.

Hatridge (118) English: hypercorrected form of ATTRIDGE.

Hatt (856) **1.** English and Scottish: metonymic occupational name for a hatter or nickname for someone noted for the hat or hats that he wore. Some early forms such as Thomas del Hat (Oxfordshire 1279) and Richard atte Hatte (Worcestershire 1327) indicate that the word was also used of a hill or clump of trees; so in these cases the surname must have been topographic in origin. **2.** South German: from a short Germanic personal name, *Hatto* (derived from compound names with the first element *hadu* 'battle', 'strife'). **3.** Frisian: from a personal name, a short form of any of the various compound names formed with *Hade-* as the first element, for example *Hadebert*.

Hattabaugh (189) Americanized form of German **Hattenbach**, possibly from a stream so named in Württemberg, derived from *hatt*, *had* 'bog' + *bach* 'stream', or, more likely, a habitational name from a place so named near Bad Hersfeld.

Hattan (232) English and Scottish: apparently a variant spelling of HATTON.

Hattaway (654) English: variant of HATHAWAY.

Hatten (1733) **1.** English: variant spelling of HATTON. **2.** North German and Jewish (Ashkenazic): from the name of an area of marshland between Oldenburg and Bremen.

Hattendorf (133) German and Jewish (Ashkenazic): habitational name from places called Hattendorf, near Alsfeld and near Hannover. The element *hatt*, *had* means 'bog'.

GIVEN NAME German 6%. *Kurt*.

Hatter (1108) English: occupational name for a maker or seller of hats, Middle English *hatter(e)*.

Hattersley (126) English: habitational name from Hattersley in Cheshire, named from an unexplained first element (perhaps the genitive case of Old English *hēahdēor* 'stag') + Old English *lēah* 'wood'.

Hattery (170) English or Irish: unexplained.

Hatton (3868) **1.** English (mainly Lancashire): habitational name from any of the various places named Hatton, from Old English *hǣð* 'heathland', 'heather' (see HEATH) + *tūn* 'enclosure', 'settlement'. Examples of the place name are found in Cheshire, Derbyshire, Lincolnshire, West London, Shropshire, Staffordshire, and Warwickshire. **2.** French: from the Old French oblique case of the Germanic personal name *Hado*, *Hatto*, a short form of various compound names beginning with *hadu* 'strife'. **3.** Irish (Ulster) and Scottish: shortened Anglicized form of Gaelic **Mac Giolla Chatáin** (Irish), **Mac Gille Chatain** (Scottish) (see MCHATTON). **4.** Scottish: habitational name, perhaps in part of English origin (see 1), but perhaps also from a Scottish place name.

FOREBEARS The center of London's diamond trade is Hatton Garden, which was once an actual garden, granted by Elizabeth I to her favorite Sir Christopher Hatton (1540–91), whose chief attraction was said to be his graceful dancing. He came of a family which claimed to be of Norman lineage.

Hattori (222) Japanese: 'clothing guild'; an ancient family listed in the Shinsen shōjiroku as **Hatori**. They were a silkworm growers' guild, and were therefore of Korean or Chinese origin. See also HATA. The name is mostly found in eastern Japan and the Ryūkyū Islands.

GIVEN NAMES Japanese 64%. *Sachiko* (3), *Takashi* (3), *Akira* (2), *Hidefumi* (2), *Kiyo* (2), *Masayuki* (2), *Nob* (2), *Takeshi* (2), *Tomo* (2), *Tomoko* (2), *Yumiko* (2), *Ayumi*.

Hattrup (120) North German: probably from the (original) dialect form of the place named *Hattorf* (near Hannover), hence a habitational name.

Hatz (190) German (Bavaria): (also **Hätz**) nickname from a dialect word meaning 'magpie'.

Hatzenbuhler (113) German (**Hatzenbühler**): habitational name for someone from a place called Hatzenbühl, for example in Rhineland-Palatinate.

Hatzis (106) Greek: from the vocabulary word *khatzis* 'pilgrim (to Jerusalem)', from the Arabic *hajji* 'pilgrim (to Mecca)', borne originally by Greek Muslims. Having completed a pilgrimage to the Holy Land was a mark of high social distinction. Often, this surname is a reduced form of a surname with *Hatzi-* as a prefix to a patronymic, naming the ancestor who performed the pilgrimage; e.g. **Hatzimarkou** 'son of Mark the Pilgrim', *Hatzioannou* 'son of John the Pilgrim'.

GIVEN NAMES Greek 21%. *Andreas*, *Christos*, *Costas*, *Demetrios*, *Dimitris*, *Eleni*, *Ioannis*, *Kalliopi*, *Nikolaos*, *Vasilios*.

Hau (378) **1.** Vietnamese (**Hậu**): unexplained. **2.** Chinese 侯: variant of HOU. **3.** Chinese 郝: variant of HAO. **4.** French

(Gascony): topographic name from a local form of Occitan *fau* 'beech tree' (from Latin *fagus*). **5.** South German: topographic name from Middle High German *hou*, a measure of woodland.

GIVEN NAMES Vietnamese 12%; Chinese 11%. *Chau* (2), *Duc* (2), *Hoang* (2), *Kien* (2), *Toan* (2), *Vuong* (2), *Boi, Chinh, Ha, Hai, Hoa, Hung; Tat* (2), *Chak, Chan, Chi Wing, Dong, Fook, Foong, Hon, Kwai, Ming, Sang, Shui.*

Haub (237) South German: variant of HAU.

Hauber (509) German and Jewish (Ashkenazic): occupational name for a maker of headgear, from Middle High German *hūbe*, *hoube* 'cap', 'hood', 'helmet', German *Haube* + the agent suffix *-er*.

GIVEN NAMES German 5%. *Otto* (2), *Erwin, Franz, Gerhard, Hans, Juergen, Karl-Heinz, Wilhelm.*

Haubert (354) **1.** German: variant of HUBERT. **2.** French: from a personal name *Aubert*, a late medieval form of a Germanic compound name, *Adalberht* (see ALBERT). **3.** French: possibly a metonymic occupational name for someone who made or wore a mailcoat, Old French *halberc*, *hauberc*.

Haubner (189) German: occupational name for a maker of headgear, a variant of HAUBER, from the plural of Middle High German *hūbe*, *hoube* + the agent suffix *-er*.

GIVEN NAMES German 6%. *Otto* (2), *Fritz, Reinhard.*

Haubold (100) German: from a Germanic personal name composed of the elements *hugu* 'mind', 'sense', 'courage' + *bald*, *bold* 'bold', 'brave'.

GIVEN NAMES German 16%; Scandinavian 4%. *Achim* (2), *Bernd, Gerhard, Gunter; Niels.*

Haubrich (402) German and Dutch: variant of HUBERT.

GIVEN NAMES German 4%. *Hans* (2), *Gunter, Kurt, Lothar.*

Hauch (282) German: from the Germanic personal name *Hugo*. Compare HAUCK.

GIVEN NAMES German 4%. *Alois, Erna, Kurt, Otto.*

Hauck (3403) German: from a dialect variant of the Germanic personal name *Hugo* (see HUGH).

Hauenstein (466) German and Swiss German: habitational name from any of the places called Hauenstein, in the Palatinate, Bavaria, Baden-Württemberg, and also in Switzerland.

GIVEN NAMES German 4%. *Armin, Dieter.*

Hauer (1171) German: literally 'cutter' or 'chopper', Middle High German *houwer* (an agent derivative of *houwen* 'to chop'), an occupational name for a woodcutter, a butcher, or a stonemason.

GIVEN NAMES German 5%. *Erwin* (7), *Ewald* (2), *Wilhelm* (2), *Wolfgang* (2), *Claus, Florian, Henrich, Ingo, Jochen, Konrad, Kurt, Lorenz.*

Haueter (182) Swiss German (**Häuter**): occupational name for a skinner and/or dealer in skins and hides, from Middle High German *hūt* 'hide', 'skin' (modern German *Haut*) + *-er*, agent suffix.

GIVEN NAME German 4%. *Kurt.*

Hauf (364) German: variant spelling of HAUFF.

GIVEN NAMES German 5%. *Kurt* (2), *Otto* (2), *Erwin, Frieda, Manfred.*

Haufe (108) German: variant of HAUFF.

GIVEN NAMES German 7%. *Fritz, Gunther.*

Hauff (427) **1.** English: variant of HAUGH. **2.** German: topographic name from Middle High German *houfe* 'heap', e.g. of stones, or in southern Germany, a nickname from the same word in the sense 'crowd', 'group of soldiers'.

Haufler (142) German (also **Häufler**): occupational name for a farm laborer who heaped up crops such as hay or grain into piles or stacks, from Middle High German *houfeln* 'to heap'.

GIVEN NAMES German 14%; Scandinavian 4%. *Udo* (3), *Kurt* (2), *Otto; Hilmar.*

Haug (2056) **1.** German: from the Germanic personal name *Hugo* (see HUGH). Compare HAUCK. **2.** Norwegian: habitational name from any of numerous farmsteads named Haug, from the indefinite singular form of Old Norse *haugr* 'hill', 'mound'.

GIVEN NAMES German 4%; Scandinavian 4%. *Otto* (5), *Ernst* (3), *Ingeborg* (2), *Kurt* (2), *Albrecht, Arno, Eberhard, Hans, Hedwig, Helmuth, Siegfried, Wolfgang; Bjorn* (2), *Arlis, Erik, Helmer, Odvar, Paal, Selmer, Toril.*

Haugan (309) Norwegian: habitational name from any of numerous farmsteads named Haugan, from the definite plural form of Old Norse *haugr* 'hill', 'mound'.

GIVEN NAMES Scandinavian 6%; German 4%. *Juel, Morten, Oluf, Sig; Eldred.*

Hauge (1269) **1.** German and Dutch: from the Germanic personal name *Hugo* (see HUGH). **2.** Norwegian: habitational name from any of numerous farmsteads named Hauge, from the dative singular of Old Norse *haugr* 'hill', 'mound'. **3.** Danish: habitational name from a place so named or a topographic name from *have* 'garden' or Old Norse *hagi* 'enclosure'.

GIVEN NAMES Scandinavian 9%. *Erik* (4), *Hilmar* (2), *Knut* (2), *Thor* (2), *Anders, Erland, Knute, Morten, Per, Sven.*

Haugen (4045) **1.** Dutch: patronymic form of HAUGE. **2.** Norwegian: habitational name from any of numerous farmsteads named Haugen, from the definite singular form of Old Norse *haugr* 'hill', 'mound'.

GIVEN NAMES Scandinavian 6%. *Erik* (8), *Bjorn* (4), *Per* (4), *Helmer* (3), *Nels* (3), *Alf* (2), *Karsten* (2), *Lars* (2), *Nils* (2), *Nordahl* (2), *Obert* (2), *Anders.*

Hauger (627) **1.** South German: patronymic from the personal name *Haug*, a German

form of HUGH. **2.** Norwegian: habitational name from any of numerous farmsteads so named, from the indefinite plural form of Old Norse *haugr* 'hill', 'mound'.

Haugh (1379) **1.** Irish (mainly County Clare): shortened form of **O'Haugh**, an Anglicized form of Gaelic **Ó hEachach** 'descendant of *Eochu*', possibly a pet form of *Eochaidh, Eachaidh* (see HAUGHEY). **2.** English: topographic name from Middle English *haw, haugh* 'enclosure' (Old English *haga*), or a habitational name from a place named with this word such as Haugh in Lincolnshire. Compare HAW. **3.** English: topographic name for someone who lived in a nook or hollow, from Middle English *haulgh* 'nook', 'hollow', 'recess' (Old English *h(e)alh*; see HALE), or a habitational name from Haulgh in Lancashire, named from this word.

GIVEN NAMES Irish 4%. *Connor* (3), *Eamon.*

Haughey (658) Irish: shortened form of **O'Haughey**, an Anglicized form of Gaelic **Ó hEachaidh** 'descendant of *Eachaidh*', a byname meaning 'horseman', from *each* 'horse'.

Haughn (191) Variant spelling of Irish **Haughan**, a shortened Anglicized form of Gaelic **Ó hEacháin** 'descendant of *Eachán*', probably a diminutive of *Eachaidh* (see HAUGHEY).

Haughney (137) Irish: shortened form of **McHaughney**, an Anglicized form of Gaelic **Mac Fhachtna**, a patronymic from the personal name *Fachtna*, meaning 'malicious', 'hostile'.

Haught (1647) **1.** Probably an altered form of German HAUG or more likely of **Hacht**, a topographical name of uncertain origin. **2.** Possibly also English: unexplained. This is a common name in WV and OH.

Haughton (884) **1.** English: habitational name from any of various places called Houghton. Nearly all, including those in Cheshire, County Durham, Lancashire, Northumberland, Shropshire, and Staffordshire, are named from Old English *halh* 'nook', 'recess' + *tūn* 'enclosure', 'settlement'; however, in the case of one in Nottinghamshire, the first element is Old English *hōh* 'spur of a hill' (literally 'heel'). **2.** Irish: in many cases of English origin, but in some a shortened Anglicized form of Gaelic Ó hEacháin (see HAUGHN) or (in County Tipperary) of **Ó hEachtair** 'descendant of *Eachtair*', probably a Gaelic form of the personal name *Hector*.

Haugland (534) Norwegian: habitational name from any of numerous farmsteads so named, notably in southwestern Norway, from Old Norse *haugr* 'hill', 'mound' + *land* 'farmstead', 'land'.

GIVEN NAMES Scandinavian 12%. *Nels* (2), *Helmer, Magnar, Morten, Selmer, Sigfred, Svein.*

Haugrud (124) Scandinavian: unexplained.
GIVEN NAME Scandinavian 4%. *Gunhild.*

Haugstad (133) Scandinavian: unexplained.

Hauk (641) German: variant spelling of HAUCK.

Hauke (321) **1.** German: variant of HAUCK. **2.** English: variant of HAWK.

GIVEN NAMES German 4%. *Dieter, Guenter, Wolfgang.*

Haulk (134) Possibly a variant of German HAUCK.

Haulman (124) South German: a variant of German HAUMANN, from *Haule*, a dialect variant of *Hau*, see HAU 5.

Hauman (103) Respelling of German HAUMANN.

Haumann (104) German: probably a variant of HAU 5, a settler on a *Hau* when these units were changed to agricultural land; or an occupational name for a butcher, a woodcutter, or a stonemason, from Middle High German *houwen* 'to chop' + *man* 'man'. Compare HAUER.

GIVEN NAMES German 9%. *Helmut* (2), *Wilfried.*

Haun (2017) German: from a short form a the Germanic personal name formed with *Hun* 'Hun' (the people) or *hūn* 'bear cub' as the first element.

Haupert (365) German: variant of HUBERT.

Haupt (2293) German and Jewish (Ashkenazic): from Middle High German *houbet*, German *Haupt* 'head'; generally, a descriptive nickname for someone with a big head, or perhaps a designation of the head of a guild or other group. It is also recorded in the Upper Rhineland as a habitational name from a house sign.

Hauptman (669) Variant spelling of Jewish or German HAUPTMANN. This form is also found in Slovenia and elsewhere.

GIVEN NAMES German 4%. *Otto* (2), *Arno, Gunter, Kurt.*

Hauptmann (176) **1.** German: status name for a headman, leader, or captain, from Middle High German *houb(e)t, houpt* 'head' + *man* 'man'. This word denoted any of various civil and military officials at different times and places; it is found as a surname in many parts of central Europe. The first element represents the original Germanic word for 'head', but already during the Middle Ages it was being replaced in the literal sense by *Kopf*, so that today it is retained only in compounds such as this, where it has the transferred sense 'chief', 'principal'. **2.** Jewish: mainly an ornamental adoption of 1.

GIVEN NAMES German 13%; Polish 4%. *Arno, Dietmar, Erwin, Franz, Gerhard, Hans, Manfred; Jerzy* (2).

Hauri (128) Swiss German: nickname meaning 'crier', from Alemannic *hauren* 'to cry'.

Haury (306) **1.** Swiss German: variant spelling of HAURI. **2.** French (Gascony): topographic name or a metonymic occupational name for a blacksmith, from Gascon *haury* 'forge', 'smithy', from a derivative of Latin *fabrum*.

GIVEN NAMES German 4%. *Fritz, Kurt.*

Haus (663) German: topographic and occupational name for someone who lived and worked in a great house, from Middle High German, Middle Low German *hūs* 'house' (see HAUSMANN, and compare English HOUSE).

GIVEN NAMES German 6%. *Sigismund* (2), *Arno, Eldred, Erhard, Ewald, Franz, Hermann, Nikolaus.*

Hausauer (216) German: habitational name from a place called Hasau in the Upper Rhine area.

Hausch (157) German: from the Germanic personal name *Huso*, a short form of a compound name composed with *hūs* 'house', 'dwelling' as the first element.

GIVEN NAMES German 11%. *Otto* (4), *Kurt* (2).

Hauschild (501) German: nickname for a ferocious soldier: literally, 'hack the shield', from Middle High German *houw* (imperative of *houwen* 'to chop or hack') + *den* (accusative form of the definite article) + *schilt* 'shield'.

GIVEN NAMES German 7%. *Ernst* (2), *Hans* (2), *Jurgen, Kurt, Manfred, Otto.*

Hauschildt (227) German: variant of HAUSCHILD.

GIVEN NAMES German 7%. *Fritz, Gerhard, Ingo, Kurt.*

Hause (975) German: variant of HAUS.

Hausen (146) German and Jewish (Ashkenazic): habitational name from any of several places in central and southern Germany called Hausen.

Hauser (6697) **1.** German (also **Häuser**) and Jewish (Ashkenazic): from Middle High German *hūs* 'house', German *Haus*, + the suffix *-er*, denoting someone who gives shelter or protection. Compare HAUSMANN. **2.** variant of HAUSEN.

Hauserman (191) German: variant of HAUSMANN.

Hausfeld (185) North German (Oldenburg): habitational name from an unidentified place named with Middle Low German *hūs* + *velt* 'open country'.

Haushalter (139) German (also **Haushälter**): occupational name for the steward (administrator) of an estate, from Middle High German *hūs* 'house' + agent derivative of *halten* 'to hold or keep'. Compare HAUSMANN.

GIVEN NAME German 4%. *Kurt.*

Hauskins (113) Variant spelling of English HOSKINS.

Hausknecht (135) German: occupational name from Middle High German *hūs* 'house' + *knëcht* 'boy', 'servant', slao a town-hall messenger.

Hausladen (147) German: variant of **Hausloden**, metonymic occupational name manufacturer (weaver) of loden, a material officially designated as suitable for peasants' clothing; from Middle High German *hūs* 'house' + *lode* 'loden'.

GIVEN NAME German 4%. *Matthias.*

Hausler (493) **1.** South German (**Häusler**): from a diminutive of Middle High German *hūs* 'house' + the suffix *-er* denoting an inhabitant, hence a status name denoting the occupant of a small house with no land, a day laborer. **2.** Jewish (Ashkenazic): variant of HAUSER.

GIVEN NAMES German 7%. *Heinz* (2), *Kurt* (2), *Dieter, Gunter, Gunther, Hartmut, Herta.*

Hausman (1406) German and Jewish (Ashkenazic): variant spelling of HAUSMANN.

Hausmann (876) German and Jewish (Ashkenazic): from Middle High German *hūs* 'house' + *man* 'man', German *Haus* + *Mann*. In the Middle Ages the majority of the population lived in cottages or huts rather than houses, and in most cases this name probably indicates the steward of a great house or someone who had some other connection with the largest and most important building in a settlement. In some cases it may indicate a householder, someone who owned his own dwelling as opposed to being a tenant. Compare HAUSHALTER.

GIVEN NAMES German 6%. *Fritz* (3), *Gunther* (3), *Arno, Benno, Berthold, Dietmar, Hans, Helmut, Jutta, Kurt, Lieselotte, Monika.*

Hausner (397) German (also **Häusner**) and Jewish (Ashkenazic): variant of HAUSER.

GIVEN NAMES German 7%. *Frieda, Horst, Kurt.*

Hauss (219) German: variant spelling of HAUS.

GIVEN NAMES French 6%. *Jacques* (3), *Pierre.*

Hausser (182) German: variant of HAUSER.

Haussler (179) German (**Häussler**): variant of **Häusler** (see HAUSLER).

GIVEN NAMES German 12%. *Otto* (3), *Dieter, Erwin, Gunter, Wolfgang.*

Haussmann (110) German: variant of HAUSMANN.

GIVEN NAMES German 20%. *Dieter* (2), *Bernd, Friedrich, Hans, Ulrich.*

Hauswirth (228) German: status name from Middle High German *hūs* 'house' + *wirt* 'owner', 'master'.

GIVEN NAMES German 4%. *Aloys* (2), *Kurt.*

Haut (311) **1.** French: nickname from *haut* 'high' (Latin *altus* plus initial *h* said to be due to the influence of Frankish *hoh*), usually denoting a haughty or proud person, and occasionally a tall man. **2.** North German: metonymic occupational name for a hat maker, from Middle Low German *hōt* 'hat'. **3.** German (southern and central) and Jewish (Ashkenazic): metonymic occupational name for a dealer in skins, from Middle High German *hūt, hout*, German *Haut* 'skin', 'hide'.

Hautala (229) Finnish: from *hauta* 'pit' + the local suffix *-la*, either a topographic name or a habitational name from a farmstead so named, with reference to a nearby storage pit, cooking pit, tar pit, charcoal-burning pit, or animal trap. This is a common surname in Ostrobothnia.

GIVEN NAMES Finnish 8%; Scandinavian 5%. *Eino* (2), *Timo* (2), *Toivo* (2), *Arvo, Reino.*

Hauter (182) **1.** Dutch: from the Germanic personal name *Wouter* (see WALTER). **2.** German (**Häuter**) and Jewish (Ashkenazic): occupational name for a dealer in skins or hides, from an agent derivative of Middle High German *hūt* 'skin', 'hide', modern German HAUT.

Hauth (279) German: variant of HAUT.

Hauver (150) Dutch and Belgian (**van Hauwer**): habitational name from Houwaart in Brabant or from either of two places in East Flanders called Hauwaart.

Haux (147) Variant spelling of German **Haucks**, patronymic from HAUCK.

GIVEN NAME German 5%. *Franz.*

Havard (1130) Welsh: of uncertain origin. It is believed by some to be a habitational name from HEREFORD, while others favor a Norman origin, from the port of Le Havre.

FOREBEARS This name is found mainly in Breconshire, with a smaller cluster in Pembrokeshire. In the 12th century, the Norman conqueror of Brecon, Bernard de Neufmarché, granted the manor of Pontwilym to Sir Walter Havard, who established an important family in South Wales.

Havas (182) Hungarian: most probably a nickname from Old Hungarian *havas* 'sleepwalker', one of several Hungarian family names deriving from terms denoting illnesses. Less likely, but nevertheless possible, is derivation from a nickname for someone with prematurely white hair, from the Hungarian vocabulary word *havas* 'snowy', 'snow-covered'.

GIVEN NAMES Hungarian 10%. *Endre* (2), *Akos, Barna, Janos, Laszlo, Zoltan.*

Havel (819) **1.** Czech: from the personal name *Havel* (see GALL 2). **2.** French: metonymic occupational name from Old French *haf* 'hook', 'pickaxe'. **3.** Dutch: metonymic occupational name from Middle Dutch *houweel, hauweel* 'hoe', 'mattock', 'pick', diminutive of Old Dutch *hauwa.*

Havelka (364) Czech: from a pet form of the personal name HAVEL.

GIVEN NAMES French 4%. *Camille, Edouard.*

Haveman (336) Respelling of German HAVEMANN.

Havemann (144) North German: from Middle Low German *hove, have* 'farm', 'courtyard' + *man* 'man', hence an occupational name for a steward or overseer, equivalent to South German HOFFMANN, or for a farmer/peasant in the service of a manor.

GIVEN NAME German 7%. *Ernst* (3).

Haven (1449) **1.** English: topographic name from Middle English *haven* 'harbor', 'haven' (Old English *hæfen*). **2.** Irish (County Westmeath): variant of HEAVEN.

Havener (677) German (Saar): unexplained. Probably a variant of HAFNER.

Havens (4187) English: unexplained; possibly a variant of HAVEN or a hypercorrected form of **Avins**, which Reaney derives from the female personal name *Avina.* .

Haver (667) **1.** North German: metonymic occupational name for a grower of or dealer in oats, from Low German *Haver* 'oats'. Compare HAFER, HABER. **2.** Dutch: of uncertain derivation; possibly a Brabantine form of **de Hauwer**, an occupational name for a wood or stone cutter, Middle Dutch *hauwer(e)* 'cutter', 'hewer'. **3.** English: from Middle English *haver* 'oats', applied as a metonymic occupational name for a farmer who grew oats or for a grain merchant. **4.** English: possibly a nickname from Middle English *haver* 'buck', 'billy-goat'.

Haverfield (184) English: habitational name from a lost minor place named with Middle English *haver* 'oats' (Old Norse *hafri*) + *feld* 'field'.

Haverkamp (513) North German and Dutch: topographic name from Middle Low German *haver* 'oats' + *kamp* 'field', 'domain'.

Haverland (343) Dutch: topographic name from *haver* 'oats' + *land* 'land', 'field'.

Haverly (320) English: unexplained; probably a habitational name from a lost or unidentified place so named. There may be a connection with Haverley House in Co. Durham, England.

Haverstick (248) Possibly an Americanized form of German and Swiss German **Haberstich**, a topographic name from Middle High German *haber* 'oats' + *stich* 'steep slope', 'hill'.

Haverstock (228) Probably an Americanized form of German **Haberstock**, a topographic name from Middle High German *haber* 'oats' + *stock* 'stick', 'pole'.

Haverty (423) Irish: shortened Anglicized form of Gaelic Ó hÁbhartaigh 'descendant of *Ábhartach*', a personal name of unexplained origin.

Havey (541) English, Scottish, and Irish: possibly a variant spelling of HARVEY or an old spelling of Scottish **Hawey**, which Black records as an Ayrshire variant of HOWIE.

Havice (106) Origin unidentified. Perhaps a variant of English AVIS.

Haviland (1379) English: habitational name from Haveland in Membury, Devon, probably named in Old English with *hæfer* 'he-goat' + *land* 'tract of land', 'estate'.

Havill (194) English (of Norman origin): habitational name from two places in northern France, Hauville in Eure, and Hauteville la Guichard in La Manche.

Havins (181) English: variant spelling of HAVENS.

Havis (201) English (Essex): perhaps a variant spelling of **Havers** (see HAVER).

Havlicek (277) Czech (**Havlíček**): from a pet form of HAVEL.

Havlik (523) Czech (**Havlík**): from a pet form of HAVEL.

Havlin (178) **1.** Jewish (eastern Ashkenazic): metronymic from *Khavele*, a pet form of the Yiddish female personal name *Khave* (Hebrew *Chava*, English EVE). **2.** Irish (County Donegal): Anglicized form of an unidentified Gaelic name.

Havner (205) Variant of German HAFNER.

Havran (149) Czech: nickname for someone with black hair, from *havran* 'raven', 'rook'.

Havranek (221) Czech (**Havránek**): from a diminutive of HAVRAN.

Havrilla (382) Slovak: derivative of the Slovak form of the personal name GABRIEL.

Havron (164) **1.** Irish (County Down): shortened Anglicized form of Gaelic Ó hAmhráin 'descendant of *Amhrán*', a diminutive of *amhra* 'eminent', 'noble'. **2.** French: from an assimilated form of the word *haveron*, a diminutive from Old French *haf* 'hook', 'pickaxe' (see HAVARD).

Haw (254) **1.** English: topographic name from Middle English *haw, haugh* 'enclosure' (Old English *haga*), or a habitational name from a place named with this word such as The Haw in Tirley, Gloucestershire. Compare HAUGH 2. **2.** English: from a Middle English personal name, probably a back-formation from *Hawkin* (see HAWKINS). **3.** Scottish: habitational name from an unidentified place in lowland Scotland.

Hawbaker (471) Americanized form of German HABECKER.

Hawe (168) **1.** English: variant of HAW. **2.** Irish: variant of HAUGH.

Hawes (3710) English (southern): **1.** patronymic from HAW 2. **2.** from a Norman female personal name, *Haueis*, from Germanic *Haduwidis*, composed of the elements *hadu* 'strife', 'contention' + *widi* 'wide'.

Hawk (6214) English (Devon): **1.** from Middle English *hauek* 'hawk', applied as a metonymic occupational name for a hawker (see HAWKER), a name denoting a tenant who held land in return for providing hawks for his lord, or a nickname for someone supposedly resembling a hawk. There was an Old English personal name (originally a byname) *H(e)afoc* 'hawk', which persisted into the early Middle English period as a personal name and may therefore also be a source. **2.** topographic name for someone who lived in an isolated nook, from Middle English *halke* (derived from Old English *halh* + the diminutive suffix *-oc*), or a habitational name from some minor place named with this word, such as Halke in Sheldwich, Kent.

Hawke (714) English: variant spelling of HAWK.

Hawken (216) English (Devon): from a Middle English personal name (see HAWKINS).

GIVEN NAME French 4%. *Monique.*

Hawker (805) English: occupational name for someone who bred and trained hawks, Middle English *haueker* (an agent derivative of *haueke* 'hawk'). Hawking was a major medieval sport, and the provision and training of hawks for a feudal lord was a not uncommon obligation in lieu of rent. The right of any free man to keep hawks for his own use was conceded in Magna Carta (though social status determined what kind of bird someone could keep, the kestrel being the lowest grade).

Hawkes (2101) English (mainly central and southeastern England): patronymic from a personal name (see HAWK 1), or a variant of HAWK 2.

Hawkey (416) English (Devon): nickname meaning 'hawk eye'.

Hawkins (44465) **1.** English: patronymic from the Middle English personal name *Hawkin*, a diminutive of HAWK 1 with the Anglo-Norman French hypocoristic suffix *-in*. **2.** English: in the case of one family (see note below), this is a variant of **Hawkinge**, a habitational name from a place in Kent, so called from Old English *Hafocing* 'hawk place'. **3.** Irish: sometimes used as an English equivalent of Gaelic Ó hEacháin (see HAUGHN).

FOREBEARS Sir John Hawkyns (1532–95) was a renowned English naval commander who was knighted for his services against the Spanish Armada in 1588. Until recent times the family still used the spelling *Hawkyns*. They had been established in Plymouth as far back as 1480, when a certain John Hawkyns held land there. They were originally a branch of a Kentish family from the village of Hawkinge (see 2 above), but the name had early on become assimilated to the form of the more common patronymic.

Hawkinson (1369) English: patronymic from the personal name *Hawkin* (see HAWKINS 1).

Hawks (3372) English: variant of or patronymic from HAWK.

Hawksley (154) English: topographic name from Middle English *hauk*, *hauek* 'hawk' + *ley(e)* 'open country', 'grassland', 'field', or a habitational name from Hawkesley Hall in King's Norton, Worcestershire, named from the Old English personal name *Heafoc* or Old English *heafoc* 'hawk', 'clearing' + *lēah* 'wood', 'clearing'.

Hawksworth (161) English (chiefly South Yorkshire): habitational name from a place called Hawksworth; there is one in West Yorkshire, named from the Old English personal name *Hafoc* 'hawk' + Old English *worð* 'enclosure'; another, in Nottinghamshire, is probably named from the Old English personal name *Hoc* + *worð*.

Hawley (7335) English and Scottish: habitational name from any of various places called Hawley. One in Kent is named with Old English *hālig* 'holy' + *lēah* 'wood', 'clearing', and would therefore have once been the site of a sacred grove. One in Hampshire has as its first element Old English *h(e)all* 'hall', 'manor', or *healh* 'nook', 'corner of land'. However, the surname is common in South Yorkshire and Nottinghamshire, and may principally derive from a lost place near Sheffield named Hawley, from Old Norse *haugr* 'mound' + Old English *lēah* 'clearing'.

Hawn (1392) Altered spelling of Dutch HAAN.

Haworth (2054) English (mainly Lancashire) and Scottish: **1.** habitational name from Haworth in West Yorkshire, named with Old English *haga* 'enclosure' (here perhaps with the sense 'hedge') + *worð* 'enclosure'. **2.** variant of HOWARTH.

Hawrylak (102) Ukrainian and Polish (**Hawryłak**): patronymic from the personal name, *Hawryło*, East Slavic form of GABRIEL. Compare GABRYS.

GIVEN NAMES Polish 7%. *Tadeusz, Wasyl.*

Hawryluk (140) Ukrainian: patronymic from the personal name *Havrylo*, the Ukrainian equivalent of GABRIEL.

Haws (1408) **1.** Possibly an altered spelling of HAAS. **2.** English: variant spelling of HAWES.

Hawse (145) **1.** Possibly an altered spelling of HAAS(E). **2.** English: variant spelling of HAWES.

Hawthorn (329) English and Scottish: variant spelling of HAWTHORNE.

Hawthorne (5281) English and Scottish: topographic name for someone who lived by a bush or hedge of hawthorn (Old English *haguþorn*, *hægþorn*, i.e. thorn used for making hedges and enclosures, Old English *haga*, *(ge)hæg*, or a habitational name from a place named with this word, such as Hawthorn in County Durham. In Scotland the surname originated in the Durham place name, and from Scotland it was taken to Ireland. This spelling is now found primarily in northern Ireland.

FOREBEARS The American novelist Nathaniel Hawthorne (1804–64) was a direct descendant of Major William Hathorne, one of the English Puritans who settled in MA in 1630, and whose son John Hathorne was one of the judges in the Salem witchcraft trials. The writer's father was a sea captain, as was his grandfather, the Revolutionary war hero Daniel Hathorne (1731–96). The spelling of the surname was altered by the novelist himself.

Hawver (274) Americanized form of Dutch HAVER.

Hawxhurst (127) Probably an altered form of **Hawkhurst**, an English habitational name from Hawkhurst, a place in Kent, named from Old English *hafoc* 'hawk' + *hyrst* 'wooded hill'.

Haxby (101) English: habitational name from Haxby in Lincolnshire, named from the Old Scandinavian personal name *Hákr* + Old English *ēg* or Old Norse *ey* 'island', 'dry ground in marsh'.

Haxton (419) Scottish (Fife): reduced form of **Halkerston**, a habitational name from a place so named in Lothian, originally called *Hawkerton*, from Middle English *haueker* 'hawker' + *toun* 'village', 'town', i.e. land held by the king's falconer.

Hay (6779) **1.** Scottish and English: topographic name for someone who lived by an enclosure, Middle English *hay(e)*, *heye* (Old English *(ge)hæg*, which after the Norman Conquest became confused with the related Old French term *haye* 'hedge', of Germanic origin). Alternatively, it may be a habitational name from any of various places named with this word, including Les Hays and La Haye in Normandy. The Old French and Middle English word was used in particular to denote an enclosed forest. Compare HAYWOOD. This name was taken to Ireland (County Wexford) by the Normans. **2.** Scottish and English: nickname for a tall man, from Middle English *hay*, *hey* 'tall', 'high' (Old English *hēah*). **3.** Scottish and English: from the medieval personal name *Hay*, which represented in part the Old English byname *Hēah* 'tall', in part a short form of the various compound names with the first element *hēah* 'high'. **4.** French: topographic name from a masculine form of Old French *haye* 'hedge', or a habitational name from Les Hays, Jura, or Le Hay, Seine-Maritime. **5.** Spanish: topographic name from *haya* 'beech tree' (ultimately derived from Latin *fagus*). **6.** German: occupational name from Middle High German *heie* 'guardian', 'custodian' (see HAYER). **7.** Dutch and Frisian: variant of HAYE 1.

FOREBEARS The surname Hay is particularly common in Scotland, where it has been established since 1160. The principal family of the name are of Norman origin; they trace their descent from William de la Haye, who was Butler of Scotland in the reign of Malcolm IV (1153–65). They hold the titles Marquess of Tweeddale, Earl of Kinnoul, and Earl of Erroll. The Earl of Erroll also holds the hereditary office of Constable of Scotland, first bestowed on the family by Robert I in 1314. A bearer of the name Hay from Burgundy, is documented in Boucherville, Quebec, in 1689.

Hayakawa (163) Japanese: 'fast river'; found mostly in eastern Japan and the Ryūkyū Islands.

GIVEN NAMES Japanese 74%. *Hiroshi* (3),

Kazuo (3), *Eriko* (2), *Fumio* (2), *Katsumi* (2), *Masako* (2), *Masazumi* (2), *Noboru* (2), *Satoshi* (2), *Shigekazu* (2), *Goro*, *Hajime*.

Hayashi (1083) Japanese: 'forest'; variously written, found mostly in western Japan and the Ryūkyū Islands. Listed in the Shinsen shōjiroku. One family produced several noted scholars during the Tokugawa era (1600–1867).

GIVEN NAMES Japanese 58%. *Nobuo* (8), *Koji* (5), *Shigeo* (5), *Shigeru* (5), *Takashi* (5), *Yuzo* (5), *Hideki* (4), *Hiroshi* (4), *Masaki* (4), *Susumu* (4), *Toshio* (4), *Yoshio* (4).

Hayashida (226) Japanese: 'forest rice paddy'; mostly found in the island of Kyūshū. Some bearers are descended from the MINAMOTO clan.

GIVEN NAMES Japanese 42%. *Akiko* (2), *Akira* (2), *Hideki* (2), *Hiroshi* (2), *Kazuo* (2), *Akinori*, *Akio*, *Akiyoshi*, *Hirokazu*, *Hirotaka*, *Juro*, *Kazu*.

Haycock (491) English (West Midlands): from a medieval personal name, a pet form of HAY 3, formed with the Middle English hypocoristic suffix *-cok* (see COCKE).

Haycook (126) English: variant of HAYCOCK.

Haycox (139) English: patronymic form of HAYCOCK.

Haycraft (491) English: topographic name from Middle English *hay, hey* 'hay' + *croft* 'field attached to a house', 'paddock', or a habitational name from a minor place named with these elements, such as Haycroft in Swyncombe, Oxfordshire or Haycroft in Gloucestershire.

Haydel (555) Variant spelling of Swiss German **Heydel**, which is perhaps a pet form of HEIDRICH.

GIVEN NAMES French 10%. *Andre* (2), *Gaston* (2), *Honore* (2), *Alberic*, *Camile*, *Cecile*, *Celina*, *Clothilde*, *Emile*, *Leonce*, *Marie Therese*, *Oneil*.

Hayden (13650) **1.** Irish: reduced form of **O'Hayden**, an Anglicized form of Gaelic **Ó hÉideáin** and **Ó hÉidín** 'descendant of *Éideán*' or 'descendant of *Éidín*', personal names apparently from a diminutive of *éideadh* 'clothes', 'armor'. There was also a Norman family bearing the English name (see 2 below), living in County Wexford. **2.** English: habitational name from any of various places called Hayden or Haydon. The three examples of Haydon in Northumberland are named from Old English *hēg* 'hay' + *denu* 'valley'. Others, for example in Dorset, Hertfordshire, Somerset, and Wiltshire, get the name from Old English *hēg* 'hay' (or perhaps *hege* 'hedge' or *(ge)hæg* 'enclosure') + *dūn* 'hill'. **3.** Jewish: see HEIDEN.

Haydock (233) English: variant of HADDOCK 2.

Haydon (881) English and Irish: variant of HAYDEN.

Haydt (150) German: variant of HEID.

Haydu (223) Hungarian: variant of HAJDU.
GIVEN NAMES Hungarian 4%. *Zoltan* (2), *Janos*, *Sandor*.

Hayduk (275) Americanized spelling of Polish HAJDUK.

Haye (365) **1.** Dutch and Frisian: from a personal name, Frisian *Hajo*, Germanic *Haio*; or from a short form of the feminine name *Hadewig*, composed of the elements *hadu* 'battle', 'strife' + *wīg* 'war'. **2.** German: variant of HEY 4, 5. **3.** French: topographic name from Old French *haye* 'hedge'. **4.** Scottish and English: variant spelling of HAY 1–3.
GIVEN NAMES German 4%. *Hans*, *Helmut*, *Willi*.

Hayek (618) Altered spelling of Czech **Hájek**, a topographic name for someone living by a copse or small wood, *hájek*.
GIVEN NAMES French 4%. *Antoine* (3), *Jacques*, *Pierre*.

Hayen (186) Dutch and Frisian: patronymic from HAYE 1.
GIVEN NAMES French 4%; German 4%. *Alphone*; *Heinz*, *Wilhelm*.

Hayenga (180) Frisian: derivative of the personal name *Hajo* (see HAYE 1).

Hayer (173) **1.** English: variant of AYER. **2.** English: topographic name for someone who lived by an enclosure, Middle English *hay* (see HAY 1) + the suffix *-er(e)* denoting an inhabitant. **3.** French: occupational name for a warder of woodland, from an agent derivative of Old French *haye* 'hedge', 'enclosed forest'. **4.** South German: from an agent derivative of Middle High German *heien* 'to guard or protect', hence an occupational name for a warden of woodland or crops. **5.** Indian (Panjab): Sikh name based on the name of a Jat clan, also called **Her**.

Hayes (64858) **1.** Irish: reduced Anglicized form of Gaelic **Ó hAodha** 'descendant of *Aodh*', a personal name meaning 'fire' (compare MCCOY). In some cases, especially in County Wexford, the surname is of English origin (see below), having been taken to Ireland by the Normans. **2.** English: habitational name from any of various places, for example in Devon and Worcestershire, so called from the plural of Middle English *hay* 'enclosure' (see HAY 1), or a topographic name from the same word. **3.** English: habitational name from any of various places, for example in Dorset, Greater London (formerly in Kent and Middlesex), and Worcestershire, so called from Old English *hǣse* 'brushwood', or a topographic name from the same word. **4.** English: patronymic from HAY 3. **5.** French: variant (plural) of HAYE 3. **6.** Jewish (Ashkenazic): metronymic from Yiddish name *Khaye* 'life' + the Yiddish possessive suffix *-s*.
FOREBEARS U.S. President Rutherford B. Hayes (1822–1893), born in Delaware, OH, was descended from old New England

families on both sides. Through the paternal line he was descended from George Hayes, who emigrated from Scotland in 1680 and settled in Windsor, CT.

Hayford (545) English: habitational name from several places called Heyford in Northamptonshire and Oxfordshire, or Hayford in Buckfastleigh, Devon, all named with Old English *hēg* 'hay' + *ford* 'ford'.

Haygood (1301) Altered form of English **Hawkwood**, a habitational name from a place called Hawkswood in Sible Hedingham, Essex, or from Hawkwood Farm in Gosfield, Essex. This is a common name in the South, notably in GA, TX, and AL.

Hayhurst (979) English (Cumbria and Lancashire): habitational name from Hay Hurst in the parish of Ribchester, Lancashire, so called from Old English *hæg* 'enclosure' (see HAY 1) or *hēg* 'hay' + *hyrst* 'wooded hill'.

Hayles (343) English and Irish: variant spelling of HALES.
GIVEN NAME French 4%. *Andre* (2).

Haylett (149) English (Norfolk): from a pet form of HAY 3.

Hayley (211) English: variant spelling of HALEY.
GIVEN NAMES French 5%. *Adrien*, *Yngve*.

Haylock (114) English (Cambridgeshire and Suffolk): possibly from an Old English personal name, *Hægluc*, a pet form of an unrecorded *Hægel*, found in various place names.

Haymaker (351) **1.** English: unexplained. **2.** Possibly an Americanized form of German HAMACHER.

Hayman (1808) **1.** English: topographic name for a man who lived by an enclosure, from Middle English *hay* (see HAY 1) + *man*. The term was in many cases effectively a synonym for HAYWARD. **2.** English: nickname for a tall man (see HAY 2). **3.** English: occupational name for the servant of someone called *Hai* (see HAY 3), with *man* in the sense 'servant'. **4.** English: occupational name for someone who sold hay. **5.** Jewish: variant of HEIMAN. **6.** Possibly an Americanized spelling of German HAMANN or HEUMANN.

Haymes (355) English: patronymic from the Norman personal name *Hamo* (see HAMMOND).

Haymon (384) French: variant of HAYMOND.

Haymond (474) French: from a personal name, *Haimon* (with excrescent *-d*), which was the Old French oblique case of the Germanic personal name *Haimo* (a short form of compound names with the first element *haim* 'home').

Haymore (276) English (chiefly South Wales): unexplained; possibly an altered form of HAMER or perhaps a habitational name from minor places in Cheshire and

Somerset called Haymoor or from Haymore Farm in Shropshire.

Hayn (164) **1.** English: variant spelling of HAIN 1–3. **2.** German: variant spelling of HAIN 4. **3.** Jewish: variant spelling of HAIN 6.

Hayne (429) English: variant spelling of HAIN 1–3.

FOREBEARS Isaac Hayne (1745–81) was an American Revolutionary militia officer, executed by the British for breaking parole. He owned an ironworks and was manufacturing ammunition for the American forces when he was caught. His grandfather had emigrated from England to SC in about 1700.

Hayner (713) German: probably a variant of HEINER.

Haynes (27037) **1.** English (Shropshire): from the Welsh personal name *Einws*, a diminutive of *Einion* (of uncertain origin, popularly associated with *einion* 'anvil'). **2.** English: patronymic from the medieval personal name HAIN 2. **3.** English: habitational name from Haynes in Bedfordshire. This name first appears in Domesday Book as *Hagenes*, which Mills derives from the plural of Old English *hægen*, *hagen* 'enclosure'. **4.** Irish: variant of HINES.

FOREBEARS The first governor of CT colony was John Haynes (?1594–1653). Earlier he had been governor of MA. He had emigrated from Essex, England, where his father was lord of the manor of Copford Hall near Colchester.

Haynesworth (157) Variant spelling of English HAINSWORTH.

GIVEN NAMES French 6%. *Celestine, Dominique.*

Haynie (2573) Variant of Irish HEANEY.

Hayre (114) **1.** English (Midlands): probably a hypercorrected spelling of AYER or a variant spelling of HARE. **2.** Indian: variant of HAYER.

GIVEN NAMES Indian 14%. *Sajjan* (2), *Jiwan, Raghbir, Sadhu.*

Hays (14030) Irish and English: variant spelling of HAYES 1–4.

Hayse (354) Variant of HAYS or HAYES.

Hayslett (478) Variant spelling of English HAZLETT.

Hayslip (542) English: variant of HYSLOP.

Hayter (681) English (Hampshire, Dorset, and Wiltshire): topographic name for someone who lived at the top of a hill or on a piece of raised ground, from Middle English *heyt* 'summit', 'height' + the agent suffix *-er*.

Hayton (419) English: habitational name from any of various places, in Cumbria, Nottinghamshire, Shropshire, East Yorkshire, and elsewhere, so called from Old English *hēg* 'hay' + *tūn* 'enclosure', 'farmstead', 'settlement'.

Hayward (5551) English: occupational name for an official who was responsible for protecting land or enclosed forest from damage by animals, poachers, or vandals, from Middle English *hay* 'enclosure' (see HAY 1) + *ward* 'guardian'.

Haywood (4792) English (Midlands): habitational name from any of various places, for example in Herefordshire, Nottinghamshire, Shropshire, and Staffordshire, so called from Old English *(ge)hæg* 'enclosure' + *wudu* 'wood'. It was a common practice in the Middle Ages for areas of woodland to be fenced off as hunting grounds for the nobility. This name may have been confused in some cases with HAYWARD and perhaps also with the name

Hogwood (of uncertain origin, possibly a habitational name from a minor place).

Hayworth (884) English: habitational name from Haywards Heath in Sussex, which was named in Old English as 'enclosure with a hedge', from *hege* 'hedge' + *worð* 'enclosure'. The modern form, with its affix, arose much later on (Mills gives an example from 1544).

Hazan (297) Jewish (Ashkenazic): status name for a cantor in a synagogue. Compare CHAZEN.

GIVEN NAMES Jewish 16%. *Isidor* (2), *Shalom* (2), *Sol* (2), *Uri* (2), *Avi, Barak, Gavriel, Haim, Ilan, Isadore, Mordechai, Ofer.*

Hazard (1575) English (also established in Ireland), French, and Dutch: nickname for an inveterate gambler or a brave or foolhardy man prepared to run risks, from Middle English, Old French *hasard*, Middle Dutch *hasaert* (derived from Old French) 'game of chance', later used metaphorically of other uncertain enterprises. The word derives from Arabic *az-zahr*, from *az*, assimilated form of the definite article *al* + *zahr* 'die'. It appears to have been picked up in the Holy Land and brought back to Europe by Provençal crusaders.

Haze (131) **1.** Dutch and Belgian: variant of HAAS. Debrabandere notes that in Flanders this is found as a shortened form of **Hazaert** (see HAZARD). **2.** English and Irish: variant spelling of HAYES or HAYS.

Hazekamp (104) Dutch: topographic name meaning 'hare field'. See HASENKAMP.

GIVEN NAME German 6%. *Kurt.*

Hazel (2461) **1.** English: topographic name for someone who lived near a hazelnut tree or grove, Middle English *hasel, hesel*, or perhaps a habitational name from a minor place named with this word such as Heazille Barton or Heazle Farm in Devon, or from Hessle in East Yorkshire and West Yorkshire, both named from Old English *hæsel* 'hazel' (influenced by Old Norse *hesli*). **2.** French: possibly a topographic name a diminutive of Old French *hase, haise* 'hedge'.

Hazelbaker (354) Americanized form of German **Hesselbacher**, a habitational name for someone from any of various places named Hesselbach, or of **Haselbacher**, a habitational name of any of nine places named Haselbach.

Hazelett (293) English: variant spelling of HAZLETT.

Hazelip (162) English: variant of HYSLOP.

Hazell (420) English (southern): variant spelling of HAZEL.

Hazelrig (100) Variant spelling of English HAZELRIGG.

Hazelrigg (310) English: habitational name from places so called in Cumbria, Lancashire, and Northumberland, all named from Old Norse *hesli* 'hazel' + *hryggr* 'ridge'.

Hazeltine (379) English: variant of HASELDEN.

Hazelton (1600) English: habitational name from either of two places called Hazleton in Gloucestershire, or from Hazelton Bottom in Hertfordshire, Hazelton Wood in Essex, or Hesselton in North Yorkshire. All are named from Old English *hæsel* 'hazel' + *denu* 'valley'. (The first element of Hesselton may be influenced by Old Norse *hesli*.) It is possible that there are other minor places elsewhere of this name, in which the second element is Old English *tūn* 'enclosure', 'settlement'. There has been considerable confusion of this name with HASELDEN.

Hazelwood (2225) English: habitational name from any of various places, for example in Devon, Derbyshire, Suffolk, Surrey, and West Yorkshire, so called from Old English *hæsel* (or Old Norse *hesli*) 'hazel (tree)' + *wudu* 'wood'; or a topographic name from this term.

Hazen (3078) Dutch: from *Hasin*, a pet form of a Germanic personal name, *Haso*, derived from *haswa* 'gray', 'black'; or from the plural of HAAS.

Hazle (151) English: variant spelling of HAZEL.

Hazleton (137) English: habitational name from any of various places named with this word: Hazleton Bottom (Hertfordshire), Hazleton Wood (Essex), or Hazelton (Gloucestershire), which is named from Old English *hæsel* 'hazel' + *tūn* 'farmstead', 'settlement'. The present-day distribution of the surname points to the places in Essex and Gloucester as the likely sources.

Hazlett (2058) English (now chiefly northern Ireland): **1.** topographic name for someone who lived by a hazel copse, Old English *hæslett* (a derivative of *hæsel* 'hazel'). **2.** habitational name from Hazelhead or Hazlehead in Lancashire and West Yorkshire, derived from Old English *hæsel* 'hazel' + *hēafod* 'head', here in the sense of 'hill'; also a topographic name of similar etymological origin.

Hazlewood (627) English: variant spelling of HAZELWOOD.

Hazley (122) English: variant of HEASLEY. Today the surname is found chiefly in northern Ireland and Scotland, but seems not to have a local source.

Hazuka (134) Czech: from *hazuka* 'tunic', 'habit', 'shirt', presumably a metonymic occupational name for a maker of such garments.

Hazzard (1353) English: variant spelling of HAZARD.

He (1307) **1.** Chinese 何: from a southern pronunciation of the name of the state of Han (in present-day Shaanxi province), which existed during the early stages of the Western Zhou dynasty (1122–771 BC). This was the fief of a younger brother of Cheng Wang, second king of the Zhou dynasty (see HAN). When the state of Han was later annexed by the state of Jin, the members of the royal family scattered. Those descendants who settled further south, in the area of the Yangtze and Huai rivers, found that the character for Han was pronounced *He* in this area, and so changed their name to a character more widely pronounced *He*. **2.** Chinese 賀: during the Eastern Han dynasty (25–220 AD), members of the Qing clan needed to change their surname, as Qing was the name of the emperor's father and so they were not permitted to use this name. They decided on *he*, which like *qing* means 'celebrate'. In modern Chinese these two characters have been compounded into one word, *qinghe*, which also means 'celebrate'. **3.** Chinese 和: from a word meaning 'and' in modern Chinese, which was part of the title *Xihe* 'astrologer'. Members of the He clan held this hereditary position and adopted their surname from the title.

GIVEN NAMES Chinese 75%; Vietnamese 5%. *Wei* (18), *Bin* (10), *Li* (10), *Ming* (9), *Ping* (9), *Yi* (8), *Jian* (7), *Min* (7), *Feng* (6), *Lei* (6), *Qing* (6), *Xin* (6), *Yan* (6), *Tian* (2), *Chang, Neng, Sha, Yiping, You*; *Hao* (3), *Huan* (3), *Cong* (2), *Lan* (2), *Hai, Hieu, Ngan, Nu, Pu, Quan*.

Heaberlin (302) Altered form of German **Haeberlein**, an alternate spelling of *Häberlein*, a variant of HEBERLEIN.

Heacock (882) English: variant spelling of HAYCOCK.

Heacox (260) English: patronymic from HEACOCK.

Head (9946) English (chiefly Kent): from Middle English *heved* 'head', applied as a nickname for someone with some peculiarity or disproportion of the head, or a topographic name for someone who lived on a hill or at the head of a stream or valley. This surname has long been established in Ireland.

Headd (101) Variant spelling of English HEAD.

GIVEN NAME French 4%. *Patrice*.

Headden (125) Scottish and English: variant spelling of HEDDEN.

Headen (503) Scottish and English: variant spelling of HEDDEN.

Headings (232) English: unexplained; perhaps an altered form of EDDINGS.

Headington (181) English: habitational name from Headington in Oxfordshire, named with the genitive of an unrecorded Old English personal name, *Hedena*, + *dūn* 'hill'.

Headland (110) English: topographic name for someone who lived by a headland, Middle English *hevedland*.

Headlee (522) Altered spelling of HEADLEY.

Headley (3107) English: **1.** habitational name from any of various places, for example in Hampshire, Surrey, Worcestershire, and West Yorkshire, so called from Old English *hǣð* 'heathland', 'heather' + *lēah* 'wood', 'clearing'. **2.** variant spelling of HEDLEY.

Headman (104) English: status name from Middle English *hefdman* 'chief', 'headman', 'leader' (Old English *hēfodman*).

Headrick (2101) Scottish: probably a habitational name from an unidentified minor place, named with Old English *headrig* 'ridge at the end of a field'.

Heady (912) English: possibly a hypercorrected form of EADY.

Heafner (269) Altered spelling of German **Häfner** (see HAFNER).

Heagerty (153) Irish: variant spelling of HAGGERTY.

Heagle (191) Possibly an altered form of German **Hägel**, with *Haegel* as an intermediate form (see HAGEL), or of HEGEL.

Heagney (190) Irish: reduced form of **O'Heagney**, an Anglicized form of Gaelic **Ó hÉignigh**, 'descendant of *Éigneach*', a byname meaning 'forceful'. The surname has often been simplified as **Ó hÉinigh** and Anglicized as HEANEY or BIRD, the latter because of the similarity to *éan* 'bird'.

Heagy (440) Americanized spelling of Swiss German **Haegi** (also **Hägi**, **Hägy**), or **Hegi**. See HAGY. This name is concentrated in PA.

Heal (573) English (chiefly southwestern): variant of HALE 1.

Healan (120) Irish: variant of HEELAN.

Heald (1582) English (Lancashire and Yorkshire): topographic name for someone who lived on a hillside, from Old English *helde, hælde, hielde* 'slope'.

Healey (4332) **1.** English: habitational name from Healey near Manchester, named with Old English *hēah* 'high' + *lēah* 'wood', 'clearing'. There are various other places in northern England, for example in Northumberland and Yorkshire, with the same name and etymology, and they may also have contributed to the surname. **2.** Variant of Irish HEALY.

Health (105) English and Scottish: perhaps a nickname from the vocabulary word

health, or a variant of HEATH, altered by folk etymology.

Healy (9001) Southern Irish: reduced form of **O'Healy**, an Anglicized form of Gaelic **Ó hÉilidhe** 'descendant of the claimant', from *éilidhe* 'claimant', or of Gaelic **Ó hÉalaighthe** 'descendant of *Éaladhach*', a personal name probably from *ealadhach* 'ingenious'.

GIVEN NAMES Irish 5%. *Brendan* (5), *Seamus* (4), *Kieran* (3), *Liam* (3), *Aileen* (2), *Brigid* (2), *Connor* (2), *Aidan, Colm, Conn, Eamonn, John Patrick*.

Heaney (1602) Irish: **1.** reduced Anglicized form of Gaelic **Ó hÉighnigh** 'descendant of *Éighneach*' (see HEAGNEY). **2.** Anglicized form of Gaelic **Ó hÉanna** 'descendant of *Éanna*', a very common personal name of uncertain meaning. It was borne by various early saints, most notably St. Éanna of Aran. The name has been erroneously understood as containing the element *éan* 'bird' and as a result the surname was sometimes Anglicized as BIRD.

GIVEN NAMES Irish 5%. *Aidan, Malachy, Nuala, Ronan*.

Heap (638) English (chiefly Lancashire): habitational name from Heap Bridge in Lancashire, or a topographic name for someone who lived by a hill or heap, from Old English *hēap* 'heap', 'mound', 'hill'.

Heape (267) English: variant of HEAP.

Heaphy (275) **1.** Irish (especially County Waterford): Anglicized form of Gaelic **Ó hÉamhthaigh** 'descendant of *Éamhthach*', an adjective meaning 'swift'. **2.** English: habitational name from Heapey in Lancashire, named in Old English as '(rose)hip hedge or enclosure', *hēope* 'hip' + *hege* 'hedge' or *gehæg* 'enclosure'.

Heaps (766) English (Lancashire and Yorkshire): variant of HEAP.

Heard (6361) English (chiefly southwest): occupational name for a tender of animals, normally a cowherd or shepherd, from Middle English *herde* (Old English *hi(e)rde*).

Heare (113) English: variant of HARE.

Hearin (100) Irish: variant spelling of HEARON.

GIVEN NAME French 5%. *Gervais*.

Hearing (173) **1.** English: unexplained. Probably a respelling of Irish HEARON. **2.** Possibly also an altered form of German **Haering** (see HERING).

Hearl (177) English: variant of EARL, with the addition of an inorganic initial *H-*.

Hearld (124) English: unexplained.

Hearn (5478) **1.** Irish: reduced Anglicized form of Gaelic **Ó hEachthighearna** 'descendant of *Eachthighearna*', a personal name meaning 'lord of horses', from *each* 'horse' + *tighearna* 'master', 'lord'. This name is most common in southwestern Ireland. **2.** Irish: Anglicized form of Gaelic **Ó hUidhrín** (see HERRON). **3.** English:

variant of HERON 1. **4.** English: topographic name for someone who lived by a bend in a river or in a recess in a hill, both of which are meanings of Middle English *herne* (Old English *hyrne*). It may also be a habitational name from any of the various places, such as Herne in Kent and Hurn in Dorset, which are named with the Old English word. Its exact original sense and its etymology are not clear; it may be a derivative of *horn* 'horn'. **5.** English: habitational name from Herne in Bedfordshire, so called from the dative plural (originally used after a preposition) of Old English *hær* 'stone'.

Hearne (1341) Irish and English: variant spelling of HEARN 1 and 4.

Hearns (390) Irish: patronymic from HEARN 1.

Hearnsberger (126) Respelling of German **Hirnsberger**, a habitational name for someone from Hirnsberg in Bavaria.

Hearon (609) Irish: variant of HEARN, HERON, or HAREN.

Hearrell (122) English and Irish: variant of HARRELL.

Hearron (155) Irish: variant of HEARN, HERON, or HAREN.

Hearst (393) **1.** English: variant spelling of HURST. **2.** Jewish: American adoption of the English name in place of some like-sounding Ashkenazic name such as HIRSCH.

Heart (179) English: variant spelling of HART.

Heartsill (115) Probably an Americanized spelling of English **Hartshill**, a habitational name from a place in Warwickshire named Hartshill, from the Old English personal name *Heardrēd* + Old English *hyll* 'hill'.

Hearty (146) Irish: Anglicized form of Gaelic **Ó hAghartaigh** (see HARTY).

Heary (136) Irish: variant of HEERY.

Heasley (780) English: habitational name from places in Oxfordshire, Warwickshire called Haseley, Heasley in the Isle of Wight, or North Heasley in North Molton, Devon, all named with Old English *hæsel* 'hazel' + *lēah* 'wood', 'glade'. The surname is now found predominantly in northern Ireland.

Heaslip (232) English (Ireland): variant of HYSLOP.

Heaster (135) English: unexplained; perhaps a hypercorrected form of EASTER.

Heaston (323) English: probably a variant of EASTON or HESTON.

Heater (1194) English: of uncertain origin, possibly a variant of HAYTER or HEATHER.

Heath (18433) English: topographic name for someone who lived on a heath (Middle English *hethe*, Old English *hǣð*) or a habitational name from any of the numerous places, for example in Bedfordshire, Derbyshire, Herefordshire, Shropshire, and

West Yorkshire, named with this word. The same word also denoted heather, the characteristic plant of heathland areas. This surname has also been established in Dublin since the late 16th century.

Heathcoat (109) English: variant spelling of HEATHCOTE.

Heathcock (342) English (Worcestershire): nickname from the 'heath cock', the black grouse.

Heathcote (277) English: habitational name from any of various places called Heathcote, for example in Derbyshire and Warwickshire, from Old English *hǣð* 'heathland', 'heather' + *cot* 'cottage', 'dwelling'.

Heathcott (131) English: variant of HEATHCOTE.

Heather (362) English: topographic name, a variant of HEATH with the addition of the habitational suffix *-er*. This surname is widespread in southern England, and also well established in Ireland.

Heatherington (207) English: variant spelling of HETHERINGTON.

Heatherly (1048) English: habitational name from Down Hatherley and Up Hatherley in Gloucestershire, or from Hatherleigh in Devon, all named from Old English *haguþorn* 'hawthorn' + *lēah* '(woodland) clearing'.

Heathman (401) English: topographic name for a heath dweller, a variant of HEATH with the addition of Middle English *man* 'man'.

Heatley (443) Northern English and Scottish: habitational name from any of various places so called, of which the most significant is in Cheshire. The place name is derived from Old English *hǣð* 'heath' + *lēah* 'wood', 'clearing'.

FOREBEARS The surname is well established in Scotland, the earliest recorded bearer being William de Hatteley, son of Sir Robert 'called de Hatteley', who held lands at Kelso in the early 13th century.

Heaton (5051) English (northern): habitational name from any of the numerous places so called, for example in Lancashire, Northumberland, and West Yorkshire, from Old English *hēah* 'high' + *tūn* 'enclosure', 'settlement'. This surname was taken to Ireland in the mid 17th century, and within Ireland is now mainly found in Ulster.

FOREBEARS A landowning family of this name, originally from Heaton in the parish of Lonsdale, Lancashire, can be traced to the 12th century. Another landowning family bearing the name can be traced to Heaton-under-Horwich in Lancashire in the 13th century.

Heatwole (456) Americanized spelling of German **Hütwohl**, possibly a nickname for a good shepherd or guard, from Middle High German *hüet* (imperative of *hüeten* 'to guard') + *wol* 'well'.

Heaven (152) **1.** Welsh: variant of EVAN, with the addition of an inorganic initial *H-*. **2.** Irish (County Offaly): Anglicized form of Gaelic **Ó hEimhín** 'descendant of *Eimhín*', possibly a diminutive of *éimh* 'swift', 'prompt', 'ready'.

Heavener (413) Probably an Anglicized variant of German **Häfner**, see HAFNER. The name is recorded in Ireland in the 19th century.

Heavey (365) Reduced and altered form of Irish **O'Heavy**, an Anglicized form of Gaelic **Ó hEamhaigh**, a cognate of HEAPHY.

GIVEN NAMES Irish 5%. *Eamon, Oonagh.*

Heavilin (138) Altered spelling of English EVELYN, with the addition of an inorganic *H-*.

Heavin (215) Possibly an altered spelling of Welsh EVAN.

Heavner (754) Probably an Anglicized form of German **Häfner** (see HAFNER). This name is found predominantly in SC. See also HEAVENER.

Heavrin (225) Probably a variant of Irish HAVRON.

Hebard (223) English: variant of HERBERT.

Hebb (676) **1.** English: from a short form of HERBERT. **2.** Dutch: from a pet form of the Germanic personal name *Herbrecht*, composed of the elements *hari*, *heri* 'army' + *berht* 'bright', 'illustrious'.

Hebbard (171) English: variant of HERBERT.

Hebbe (100) **1.** Dutch: variant of HEBB 2. **2.** North German (Frisian): from a short form of the Germanic personal name *Hadebert*, composed of the elements *hadu* 'strife' + *berht* 'bright'.

GIVEN NAME German 5%. *Hertha.*

Hebble (101) English: possibly a variant of **Hepple**, a habitational name from Hepple in Northumberland, named from Old English *hēope* 'rosehip' or *hēopa* 'bramble' + *halh* 'nook', 'hollow'.

Hebblethwaite (124) English: habitational name from a place called Heblethwaite in Cumbria, named with Old English *hēope* 'rosehip' or *hēopa* 'bramble' + Old Norse *þveit* 'clearing'.

Hebda (213) Polish: nickname from *chebda* 'elderberry'. This is found as a personal name in Old Polish.

GIVEN NAMES Polish 5%. *Piotr* (2), *Aniela, Casimir.*

Hebden (141) English (Yorkshire): habitational name from Hebden in North Yorkshire or Hebden Bridge in West Yorkshire, both named from Old English *hēope* 'rose-hip' + *denu* 'valley'.

FOREBEARS In 1120 the manor of Hebden was granted by Roger de Mowbray to Uctred de Hebden, a descendant of Uctred, Earl of Northumberland (died 1016). The lands descended in the Hebden family until the 15th century, when they were divided between the families of Tempest and

Dymoke as the result of the marriage of heiresses. The surname Hebden is also established in Scotland; one of the Orkney islands was owned by a Hebden family during the 19th century.

Hebdon (160) English: variant of HEBDEN.

Hebel (618) **1.** German: metonymic occupational name for a baker, from Middle High German *hebel* 'yeast'. **2.** French: nickname from the dialect word *ébeul* 'colt', 'foal' (Old Breton *ebol*).
GIVEN NAMES German 4%. *Kurt* (2), *Horst*, *Inge*, *Otmar*, *Otto*, *Wolf*.

Hebeler (142) South German: occupational name for a baker, from Middle High German *hebel* 'yeast' + agent suffix *-er*.

Hebenstreit (247) German: nickname for a quarrelsome person, from *heb* (imperative of *heben* 'to start') + the definite article (accusative) *(d)en* + *strīt* 'quarrel', 'fight'.
GIVEN NAMES German 5%. *Kurt*, *Otto*, *Wolf*.

Heber (357) **1.** German: occupational name for a carrier (someone who loaded or transported goods), from an agent derivative of Middle High German *heben* 'to lift'. **2.** French (**Héber**): from a Germanic personal name derived from *eber* 'boar'.
GIVEN NAMES German 5%. *Kurt* (2), *Erwin*, *Franz*.

Heberer (250) South German: variant of HABERER.

Heberle (224) German: diminutive of HABER. This name is also found in northern Slovenia.
GIVEN NAMES German 7%. *Erwin* (2), *Klaus* (2), *Alois*, *Gottfried*, *Juergen*.

Heberlein (281) South German: diminutive of HABER.
GIVEN NAMES German 5%. *Horst* (2), *Kurt*.

Heberling (554) South German: variant of HEBERLEIN.

Hebert (15430) **1.** French (**Hébert**) and Dutch: assimilated form of HERBERT. **2.** German: variant of HEBER 1. **3.** Dutch: from the personal name EGBERT.
FOREBEARS Louis Hébert (son of Nicolas, apothecary to the Queen, and grocer, and his wife Jacqueline Pajot) was in Acadia in 1606–1607 and again in 1611–1613; he arrived in Quebec city in 1617, and was the father of the first French child born in Quebec. The following secondary surnames are recorded: LECOMTE, from Normandy, documented in Quebec city in 1655; JOLICOEUR, documented in Montreal in 1653; Laverdure, from Paris, documented in Trois Rivières in 1666; DESLAURIERS, recorded in 1679; Larose, from Normandy, documented in Voucherville in 1679; and Minfret or LESPERANCE, from Normandy, recorded in 1701. The LA Hébert families trace their descent from Acadian descendants of Albert and Étienne Hébert who left their native village of La-Haye-Descartes, Touraine, circa 1640.

GIVEN NAMES French 8%. *Armand* (28), *Andre* (22), *Emile* (20), *Normand* (19), *Jacques* (14), *Marcel* (11), *Pierre* (11), *Lucien* (10), *Michel* (10), *Gaston* (9), *Alcide* (8), *Camille* (8).

Hebl (112) German: variant of HEBEL.

Hebner (363) Americanized form of German **Hübner** (see HUEBNER).

Hebrank (160) German: etymology uncertain; perhaps a nickname for a person who challenged someone physically or figuratively, from Middle High German *heben* 'lift' + *rank* 'bend', 'curve in a road', which subsequently came to mean 'rank'.

Hebron (400) **1.** English: habitational name from Hebron in Northumberland, which probably has the same origin as HEPBURN. **2.** Czech: from the Biblical place name.

Hechler (269) German: occupational name for a comber of flax, from an agent derivative of Middle High German *hechel*, *hachel* 'hackle', 'flax comb'.
GIVEN NAMES German 4%. *Hans*, *Otto*.

Hecht (3444) **1.** German and Dutch: from Middle High German *hech(e)t*, Middle Dutch *heect*, *hecht* 'pike', generally a nickname for a rapacious and greedy person. In some instances it may have been a metonymic occupational name for a fisher and in others it may be a habitational name from a house distinguished by a sign depicting this fish. **2.** Jewish (Ashkenazic): ornamental name from German *Hecht* or Yiddish *hekht* 'pike', one of the many Ashkenazic ornamental names taken from vocabulary words denoting wildlife.
GIVEN NAMES German 4%; Jewish 4%. *Manfred* (6), *Kurt* (5), *Otto* (5), *Arno* (2), *Erwin* (2), *Ingeborg* (2), *Reinhard* (2), *Ute* (2), *Ernst*, *Guenther*, *Gunter*, *Gunther*; *Mendel* (5), *Hyman* (4), *Emanuel* (3), *Sholem* (3), *Levi* (2), *Rivka* (2), *Shimon* (2), *Sol* (2), *Yehuda* (2), *Yisroel* (2), *Aryeh*, *Avrohom*.

Hechtman (145) Jewish (Ashkenazic): variant of HECHT.
GIVEN NAME Jewish 4%. *Tovah*.

Hecimovich (123) Of Slavic origin, but unexplained. IGI records only American bearers, so this name is no doubt an altered form of some other Slavic original. This name is found chiefly in WI and MN.

Heck (5517) **1.** English: topographic name for someone who lived by a gate or 'hatch' (especially one leading into a forest), northern Middle English *heck* (Old English *hæcc*), or a habitational name from Great Heck in North Yorkshire, which is named with this word. Compare HATCH. **2.** German: topographic name from Middle High German *hecke*, *hegge* 'hedge'. This name is common in southern Germany and the Rhineland. **3.** Possibly an Americanized spelling of French **Hec(q)**, a topographic name from Old French *hec* 'gate', 'barrier', 'fence' (compare 1), or a habitational name

from a place named with this word. **4.** Shortened form of the Dutch surname **van (den) Hecke**, a habitational name from any of several places called ten Hekke in the Belgian provinces of East and West Flanders.

Heckaman (181) German (**Heckemann**): variant of HECKMANN.

Heckard (285) Americanized spelling of French **Hécard**, **Hecquard**, a derivative of the topographic name *Hec* (see HECK 3).

Heckart (250) Variant of French HECKARD.

Heckathorn (456) Americanized form of German HECKENDORN.

Hecke (107) Dutch (**van den Hecke**) and North German: topographic name from Middle Low German *hecke* 'hedge', 'fence'.

Heckel (922) **1.** German: variant of **Häckel** (see HACKEL). **2.** Dutch: from Middle Dutch *eekel* 'acorn', possibly denoting someone who herded hogs in the forest, or who collected acorns as swine fodder.

Heckendorf (134) German: habitational name from an unidentified place, probably named with Middle High German *hecke* 'hedge', 'fence' + genitive or plural suffix *-n* + *dorf* 'hamlet', 'village'.
GIVEN NAMES German 5%. *Otto*, *Reinhold*.

Heckendorn (195) German: topographic name composed of Middle High German *hecke* 'hedge', 'fence' + genitive suffix *-n* + *dorn* 'thorn', or from Middle High German *heckedorn* 'hawthorn'.

Heckenlaible (132) South German: etymology uncertain; perhaps a topographic name for someone whose house was ditinguished by a hedge in the form of a bower or arbor, from Middle High German *hecke* 'hedge' + an unrounded diminutive form of *loube* (*löubelīn*) 'small bower'.

Hecker (2246) **1.** German: variant of HECK 2, with the addition of the suffix *-er*, denoting an inhabitant. **2.** German and Jewish (Ashkenazic): variant of HACKER 'butcher', 'woodcutter'.

Heckerman (102) German (**Häckermann**): occupational name for a butcher or woodcutter, an elaborated form of **Häcker** (see HACKER).

Heckert (685) **1.** German and Dutch: from a Germanic personal name composed of the elements *hagan* 'hedge' + *hard* 'hardy', 'brave', 'strong'. **2.** German: variant of **Häcker**, see HACKER.

Heckethorn (100) Of Swiss German origin: probably an Americanized form of HECKENDORN. Compare HECKATHORN.

Heckle (170) **1.** English (Cheshire): from Middle English *hekel* 'heckle', an implement for combing or scutching flax or hemp for spinning, hence a metonymic occupational name for someone who made or used heckles. **2.** French (Alsace; **Hecklé**): from a diminutive of German HECK 2.

Heckler (768) **1.** English: occupational name from an agent derivative of Middle

English *hekel* 'to comb (flax or hemp) with a heckle'. **2.** South German: occupational name for someone who used a small hoe, from a diminutive of Middle High German *hacke* hoe + the agent suffix *-er*. **3.** German: variant of **Häckler** (see HACKLER).

Heckman (3741) **1.** Dutch: topographic name for someone living near a hedge, from Middle Dutch *hecke, hegge* 'hedge', 'enclosure'. **2.** Altered spelling of German HECKMANN.

Heckmann (330) German: topographic name for someone who lived by a hedge or by the boundary of an enclosure or who owned an enclosed lot in the forest, from Middle High German *hecke, hegge* 'hedge' (see HECK 2) + *man* 'man'.
GIVEN NAMES German 10%. *Hans* (3), *Klaus* (2), *Dieter, Erwin, Ewald, Gerhard, Kurt, Manfred, Wilhelm.*

Hecksel (118) German: probably a variant of *Hexel*, from a short form of a Germanic personal name (*Hago, Hecco*) formed with *hag* 'enclosure', 'protected place' as the first element.
GIVEN NAMES German 6%. *Eldor, Otto.*

Heckstall (113) English (Leicestershire): habitational name from a lost or unidentified place.

Hecox (282) English: perhaps an altered spelling of HICKOX, but see also HEACOX.

Hector (1088) **1.** Scottish: Anglicized form of the Gaelic personal name *Eachann* (earlier *Eachdonn*, already confused with Norse *Haakon*), composed of the elements *each* 'horse' + *donn* 'brown'. **2.** English: found in Yorkshire and Scotland, where it may derive directly from the medieval personal name. According to medieval legend, *Britain* derived its name from being founded by *Brutus*, a Trojan exile, and *Hector* was occasionally chosen as a personal name, as it was the name of the Trojan king's eldest son. The classical Greek name, *Hektōr*, is probably an agent derivative of Greek *ekhein* 'to hold back', 'hold in check', hence 'protector of the city'. **3.** German, French, and Dutch: from the personal name (see 2 above). In medieval Germany, this was a fairly popular personal name among the nobility, derived from classical literature. It is a comparatively rare surname in France.

Hedberg (1159) Swedish: ornamental name composed of the elements *hed* 'heath', 'moor' + *berg* 'mountain', 'hill'.
GIVEN NAMES Scandinavian 6%. *Anders* (3), *Lars* (2), *Nels* (2), *Bjorn, Erik, Hilmer, Hjalmer, Mats, Nils.*

Hedden (1415) **1.** English: habitational name from various places such as Headon, Nottinghamshire, Hedon in East Yorkshire, and Heddon on the Wall and Black Heddon. Northumberland. The first is probably named from Old English *hēah* 'high' + *dūn* 'hill'; the others have the same second element, combined with Old

English *hǣþ* 'heath', 'heather'. **2.** North German (Frisian): variant of HADDEN.

Hedding (155) **1.** Scottish: probably a habitational name from any of the places mentioned at HEDDEN, especially one of those in Northumbria. **2.** North German: Frisian clan form (the *-ing* suffix denoting affiliation) of the Germanic personal name *Hatto* (see HADEL).
GIVEN NAMES German 4%. *Frieda, Kurt.*

Heddings (112) English: probably a hypercorrected form of EDDINGS.

Hedeen (263) Swedish (**Hedén**): ornamental name from *hed(e)* 'heath', 'moor' + the adjectival suffix *-én*, a derivative of Latin *-enius*.
GIVEN NAMES Scandinavian 4%. *Bjorn, Erik.*

Hedeman (108) Swedish: ornamental name from *hed(e)* 'heath', 'moor' + *man* 'man'.

Hedge (1248) English: topographic name for someone who lived by a hedge, Middle English *hegg(e)*. In the early Middle Ages, hedges were not merely dividers between fields, but had an important defensive function when planted around a settlement or enclosure.

Hedgecock (618) English: variant of HITCHCOCK, altered by folk etymology.

Hedgecoth (122) English: variant of HITCHCOCK. Compare HEDGECOCK.

Hedgepath (254) Variant of English HUDSPETH. Compare HEDGEPETH.

Hedgepeth (982) Variant of English HUDSPETH, altered by folk etymology. This name is particularly common in NC.

Hedger (619) English (mainly Sussex): variant of HEDGE, with the addition of agent suffix *-er*.

Hedges (3824) English: variant of HEDGE.

Hedgespeth (101) Variant of English HUDSPETH. Compare HEDGEPETH.

Hedglin (214) Probably a variant of English (Devon) **Hedgeland**, habitational name from a lost or unidentified place.

Hedgpeth (429) Variant of English HUDSPETH. Compare HEDGEPETH.

Hediger (224) Swiss German: variant of HEDINGER.
GIVEN NAMES German 6%. *Fritz* (2), *Erwin, Hans, Kurt.*

Hedin (684) **1.** Swedish: variant of HEDEEN. **2.** French: from a derivative of the Germanic personal name *Haido*, a short form of any of the various compound names beginning with *haid* 'heath' (i.e. wasteland, often with heather).
GIVEN NAMES Scandinavian 6%. *Sven* (3), *Lars* (2), *Algot, Dagny, Nels, Nils.*

Hedinger (155) Swiss German: habitational name from places called Hedingen or Hödingen (near Zürich, Sigmaringen, and Überlingen).
GIVEN NAME German 4%. *Kurt* (2).

Hedley (339) English and Scottish: **1.** habitational name from places in County Durham and Northumberland, so named

from Old English *hǣð* 'heathland', 'heather' + *lēah* 'wood', 'clearing'. **2.** variant spelling of HEADLEY.

Hedlund (1455) Swedish: ornamental name composed of the elements *hed* 'heath', 'moor' + *lund* 'grove'.
GIVEN NAMES Scandinavian 5%. *Erik* (2), *Britt, Lars, Mats, Nils.*

Hedman (802) Swedish: ornamental name composed of the elements *hed* 'heath', 'moor' + *man* 'man'.
GIVEN NAMES Scandinavian 5%. *Britt, Egil, Lars, Lennart.*

Hedquist (187) Swedish: ornamental name composed of the elements *hed* 'heath', 'moor' + *quist*, an old or ornamental spelling of *kvist* 'twig'.

Hedrich (214) **1.** German and Dutch: variant of HEIDRICH. **2.** from a Germanic personal name composed with the elements *hadu* 'strife' + *rīhhi* 'power(ful)', 'rich'.
GIVEN NAMES German 7%. *Hans* (2), *Konrad* (2), *Wilhelmina* (2), *Kurt.*

Hedrick (6950) Dutch: variant of HENDRICK.

Hedrington (110) English: possibly a habitational name from a lost or unidentified place.

Hedstrom (786) Swedish (**Hedström**): ornamental name composed of the elements *hed* 'heath', 'moor' + *ström* 'river'.
GIVEN NAMES Scandinavian 5%; German 4%. *Erik* (3), *Birgid, Iver, Lars, Lennart, Nils, Sven; Bernhard* (2), *Kurt* (2), *Eldred, Elke, Erna, Erwin.*

Hedtke (286) North German: from a pet form of the personal name HEIDRICH.

Hee (374) **1.** Danish: habitational name from any of several places so named from a word meaning 'shining', 'clear', with reference to a river. **2.** Norwegian: habitational name from any of several farmsteads in the county of Hedmark named He, from Old Norse *hæð* 'hill', 'mound'. **3.** Dutch: habitational name from the common place name ten Heede, meaning 'on the heath'.

Heeb (244) Swiss German: from *Habo*, a short form of several Germanic names formed with *hadu* 'strife' as the first element, see HAAB.
GIVEN NAMES German 6%. *Gunther* (2), *Wilhelm.*

Heebner (216) Americanized form of German HUEBNER.

Heefner (143) Variant of German **Hefner** (see HAFNER).

Heeg (251) **1.** German: variant of HEGE. **2.** Dutch: topographic name, a variant of HAAG, or a habitational name from a place so called in Friesland.

Heeke (163) German: habitational name from Heeke near Bramsche or Heek on the Dinkel river.

Heekin (145) Hypercorrected form of Irish EAKIN.
GIVEN NAME Irish 5%. *James Patrick.*

Heelan (148) Irish: Anglicized form of Gaelic **Ó hAoileáin**, from a form of *faolán* (without the initial *f-*), a diminutive of *faol* 'wolf'. Compare FELAN.
GIVEN NAME Irish 6%. *Brennan*.

Heemstra (194) Frisian: variant of HIEMSTRA.

Heenan (710) Irish: **1.** Anglicized form of Gaelic **Ó hÉanáin** 'descendant of *Éanán*'. Woulfe, however, believes it to be a form of **Ó hEidhneáin**, which he derives from a diminutive of *eidhean* 'ivy'. **2.** sometimes a reduced version of HENEGHAN.

Heeney (264) Irish: variant spelling of HEANEY.

Heep (111) **1.** English: variant spelling of HEAP. **2.** German: variant of HEEB.
GIVEN NAMES German 4%. *Hans, Siegfried*.

Heer (728) **1.** Frisian: from the Germanic personal name *Hero*, a short form of compound names with the first element *hari*, *heri* 'army', as, for instance, HERMANN. **2.** North German and Dutch: equivalent of HERR.
GIVEN NAMES German 5%. *Bernhard* (2), *Erwin* (2), *Hans* (2), *Alfons, Alois, Ewald, Kurt, Monika, Otto*.

Heerdt (128) Dutch: variant of HERD 2 or 3.

Heerema (117) Frisian: patronymic from the personal name HEER.
GIVEN NAME Dutch 6%. *Egbert* (2).

Heeren (608) **1.** Dutch: patronymic from HEER 2. **2.** Dutch: variant of HERRIN. **3.** Frisian: patronymic from HEER 1.

Heeringa (156) Frisian: patronymic from HEER 1.

Heermann (122) German: variant of HERMANN.
GIVEN NAME German 6%. *Reinhard* (2).

Heery (135) Irish: Anglicized form of Gaelic **Ó hÍoruaidh** 'descendant of *Íoruadh*', a personal name of unknown origin.

Hees (162) **1.** North German: habitational name from a place on the lower Rhine near Kevelaer, named with Low German *hees* 'brush'. **2.** Northern French (**Hées**): habitational name from a place in present-day Belgium or from any of the French villages so named, from Old French *haisi* 'bushy place'. **3.** Dutch: variant of HAAS. **4.** Shortened form of Dutch **van Hees**, a habitational name for someone from any of the places in the Netherlands and Belgium named Hees, for example in Drenthe, Utrecht, North Brabant, and Luxembourg.
GIVEN NAMES German 6%. *Dieter, Elfriede*.

Heesch (187) North German: **1.** from a short form of the female personal name *Heseke*, a pet form of *Hedwig*, composed of the Germanic elements *hadu* 'battle' + *wīg* 'fight'. **2.** nickname for a person with a rasping voice, from Middle High German *hēsch* 'hoarse'.
GIVEN NAMES German 5%. *Klaus, Otto*.

Heese (209) **1.** North German and Westphalian: topographic name from Low German *hees(e)* 'brush', 'scrub', or a habi-

tational name from places named with this word. **2.** Dutch: variant of HAAS.
GIVEN NAMES German 6%. *Ralf* (2), *Horst, Manfred*.

Heeter (730) **1.** North German: habitational name for someone from Heeten in the Netherlands near Deventer. **2.** English: unexplained; perhaps a variant of HAYTER. Compare HEATER.

Hefel (173) **1.** German: Swabian form of HEBEL. **2.** Perhaps altered form of HAEFELE.
GIVEN NAMES German 4%. *Gotthard, Hans, Kurt*.

Hefele (122) South German: variant of **Häfele**, see HAEFELE.
GIVEN NAMES German 4%. *Bernd, Eugen*.

Heffel (149) Dutch and Belgian (**van Heffel**): habitational name from Heffel in Brabant.
GIVEN NAMES German 5%. *Kurt, Otto*.

Heffelfinger (780) Swiss German: Americanized spelling of the habitational name **Häfelfinger**, for someone from a small place called *Häfelfingen* or *Häfelfing*.

Hefferan (161) Irish: variant of HEFFERON.

Hefferman (97) English: occupational name for a cowherd, from Middle English *heffre*, *heffour* 'young cow', 'heifer' + *man* 'man'.

Heffern (261) Irish: variant of HEFFERON.

Heffernan (2715) Irish: Anglicized form of Gaelic **Ó hIfearnáin** 'descendant of *Ifearnán*', a personal name from a diminutive of *ifreannach* 'demon' (from *ifreann* 'hell').
GIVEN NAMES Irish 5%. *Brendan* (2), *Siobhan* (2), *James Patrick, Sinead*.

Hefferon (183) Irish: **1.** (Mayo) Anglicized form of Gaelic **Ó Éimhrín** 'descendant of *Éimhrín*', diminutive of the female personal name *Éimhear* (still in use as *Emer*). **2.** Anglicized form of Gaelic **Ó hUidhrín** (see HERON 3).

Heffington (424) English: unexplained; perhaps an altered spelling of **Evington**, habitational name from places so named in Gloucestershire and Leicestershire. The first is named with the Old English personal name *Geofa* + *-ing-* (denoting association) + *tūn*; the second with the Old English personal name *Eafa* + *-ing-* + *tūn*.

Heffler (229) Variant spelling of German HEFLER, itself a variant of HEFNER 'potter'.

Heffley (445) See HEFLEY. This name occurs mainly in PA and TX.

Heffner (2709) German (southwestern) and Jewish (Ashkenazic): occupational name for a potter (see HAFNER).

Heffron (1041) Irish: reduced form of HEFFERON.

Hefler (168) German: variant of HEFFNER.

Hefley (792) Probably an Americanized spelling of the Swiss family names **Haefely**, **Häfeli**, **Häffele** or **Hefele**, of unexplained origin.

Heflin (2660) Probably an Americanized spelling of the Swiss family name **Häfelin**.

Hefner (3086) German and Jewish (Ashkenazic): occupational name for a potter (see HAFNER).

Heft (565) German: metonymic occupational name for a maker of hilts, clasps, and handles (for knives, swords, etc.), Middle High German *hefte*.

Hefter (290) **1.** German: occupational name from Middle High German *hefte* 'hilt', 'handle', 'clasp' + *-er* agent suffix (see HEFT). **2.** Jewish (Ashkenazic): occupational name for an embroiderer, from an agent derivative of Yiddish *heftn* 'to embroider'.
GIVEN NAMES Jewish 5%. *Arie, Aron, Isidor, Malkiel, Tzvi*.

Hefti (160) Swiss German: spelling variant of HEFTY, from Middle High German *heftec*, *heftic* 'durable', 'strong', later 'severe', 'violent'.
GIVEN NAMES German 4%. *Hans, Heinrich, Mathias*.

Hefty (480) **1.** French (Alsatian) form of German *heftig* 'fierce', 'irascible'. **2.** Probably an altered spelling of HEFTI.

Hegarty (1363) Irish: variant of HAGGERTY.
GIVEN NAMES Irish 7%. *Brendan* (2), *Donal* (2), *Aidan, Declan, Kieran, Liam*.

Hegdahl (137) Norwegian: habitational name from any of several farmsteads named *Heggdal*, from *hegg* 'bird cherry (tree)' + *dal* 'valley'.

Hegde (127) Indian (Karnataka); pronounced as *heg-day*: Hindu (Brahman, Bunt) and Jain name, from Kannada *hegga e*, Old Kannada *pergae*, meaning 'chief', 'headman' (from *per* 'great' + *kae* 'end', 'limit').
GIVEN NAMES Indian 98%. *Shankar* (4), *Dinesh* (3), *Kiran* (3), *Narayan* (3), *Subhash* (3), *Asha* (2), *Damodar* (2), *Dayanand* (2), *Deepak* (2), *Ganesh* (2), *Gopal* (2), *Jairaj* (2).

Hege (570) German: habitational name from Hege in Bavaria or from any of several places in Switzerland named Hegi; or a topographic name from Middle High German *hac* 'enclosed wood'.

Hegedus (690) Hungarian (**Hegedüs**) and Jewish (from Hungary): occupational name for a player on the fiddle, Hungarian *hegedü*, of unexplained origin.
GIVEN NAMES Hungarian 12%. *Laszlo* (7), *Tibor* (6), *Gabor* (3), *Zoltan* (3), *Geza* (2), *Lajos* (2), *Sandor* (2), *Attila, Denes, Ferenc, Imre, Istvan*.

Hegel (318) South German: **1.** topographic name from a diminutive of Middle High German *hac* 'hedge'. **2.** from a pet form of the personal name *Hugo* (see HUGH). **3.** diminutive form of a metonymic occupational name for the owner or keeper of a breeding bull, Middle High German *hagen*.

GIVEN NAMES German 4%. *Bernd, Gerhard, Hermann, Wilhelm.*

Hegeman (426) **1.** Dutch: habitational name for someone from a place called Hegge(n) or ter Hegge(n), derived from a word meaning 'hedge'. **2.** Altered spelling of German **Hegemann**, a Westphalian topographic name for someone who lived in an enclosed (i.e. fenced) area, Middle High German *hagen* + *man* 'man'.

Hegemann (107) German: topographic name for someone who lived by a hedge or by the boundary of an enclosure (see HECKMANN).

GIVEN NAMES German 5%. *Bernd, Ingeborg.*

Heger (643) **1.** German: occupational name for a forest warden, from an agent derivative of Middle High German *hegen* 'to mind, take care (of)'. **2.** North German: status name denoting a minor tenant, Middle Low German *heger.*

GIVEN NAMES German 6%. *Armin* (2), *Heinz* (2), *Kurt* (2), *Erwin, Hans, Lothar, Siegfried, Ulrich, Wilhelm, Wilhelmina.*

Hegewald (119) German (common in Saxony): topographic name denoting an enclosed part of a forest, from *Hege* (see HEGE) + *Wald* 'forest'. It may also be a metonymic personal name denoting a forest warden.

GIVEN NAMES German 12%. *Erwin, Hans, Heinz, Johannes, Markus, Siegfried.*

Hegg (570) **1.** Norwegian: habitational name from any of several farmsteads so named, from *hegg* 'bird cherry (tree)'. **2.** Respelling of Swedish **Hägg**, an ornamental name of the same etymology as 1. **3.** Swiss German: spelling variant of HECK 2.

GIVEN NAMES Scandinavian 4%. *Erik* (2), *Johan, Peer.*

Hegge (509) **1.** Dutch: from a short form of a Germanic personal name with the first element *agi* 'edge', 'blade' (see, e.g., EGBERT). **2.** Norwegian: habitational name from any of several farmsteads so named, either from Old Norse *Heggvin* from *heggr* 'bird cherry (tree)' + *vin* 'meadow', or from *hegg* (indefinite plural of *heggr*) alone. **3.** Variant spelling of Swedish **Hägge** (see HAGG).

GIVEN NAMES Scandinavian 4%. *Nels, Niels.*

Heggem (129) Norwegian: habitational name from a farmstead so named from the dative plural of *hegg* 'bird cherry (tree)'.

GIVEN NAME Scandinavian 5%. *Nils.*

Heggen (326) **1.** Dutch: patronymic from HEGGE. **2.** Norwegian: habitational name from any of several farmsteads so named, either from the dative singular of *hegg* 'bird cherry (tree)' or from Old Norse *Heggvin* (see HEGGE).

GIVEN NAMES Scandinavian 10%. *Odvar* (2), *Selmer* (2), *Bernt, Erik, Nels.*

Hegger (138) Dutch: from a Germanic personal name composed of the elements *agi* 'edge', 'blade' + *hari, heri* 'army'.

GIVEN NAMES German 7%. *Dieter, Hilde, Horst, Kurt.*

Heggie (401) Scottish: reduced form of **MacKeggie**, an Anglicized form probably of Gaelic **Mac Adhamh, Mac Edhamh**, patronymics from the Gaelicized form of ADAM.

Heggins (106) Scottish: Anglicized form of Irish Gaelic **Ó hUiginn** (see HIGGINS).

Heggs (108) English (Leicester): perhaps a variant of HIGGS.

Hegland (349) Norwegian: habitational name from any of several farmsteads, notably in Agder and southwestern Norway, named *Heggland* in Old Norse, from *heggr* 'bird cherry (tree)' + *land* 'land'.

GIVEN NAMES Scandinavian 7%. *Erik, Gudrun, Hjalmer, Sig, Tor.*

Heglar (109) Probably an altered form of German **Hägler** (see HAGLER).

Hegle (104) Americanized form of German HEGEL.

Hegler (305) **1.** Swiss German: topographic name for someone who lived by a hedge or enclosure, variant spelling of **Hägler** (see HAGLER). **2.** South German: from Middle High German *hagen* 'breeding bull', an occupational nickname for the owner of such an animal. **3.** North German: habitational name for someone from Hegel near Oldenburg.

Heglin (117) South German and Swiss German: in some cases an occupational nickname from Middle High German *hegelīn* 'occasional poet', 'speaker'.

Heglund (181) **1.** Norwegian: habitational name from any of several farmsteads so named, from *heggr* 'bird cherry (tree)' + *lund* 'grove'. **2.** Variant spelling of Swedish **Hägglund** (see HAGGLUND).

Hegman (109) **1.** Dutch: variant of HEGEMAN. **2.** Americanized spelling of Swedish **Häggman**, an ornamental name from *hägg* 'bird cherry (tree)' + *mann* 'man'.

Hegna (193) Norwegian: habitational name from any of numerous farmsteads, notably in the county of Telemark, so named from *hegne* 'enclosure'.

Hegner (232) **1.** German: variant of HEGER. **2.** German: habitational name from Hegnau near Zurich, or Hegne on Lake Constance. **3.** Danish: topographic name from *hegen* 'hedge' + agent suffix *-er.*

GIVEN NAMES German 6%. *Erwin, Manfred.*

Hegstad (128) Norwegian: habitational name from any of several farmsteads so named, from Old Norse *Heggsstaðir*, probably from the personal name *Heggr* (from *heggr* 'bird cherry (tree)') + *staðir* 'farmstead', 'settlement'.

GIVEN NAME Scandinavian 6%. *Toralf.*

Hegstrom (223) Variant of Swedish **Häggström** (see HAGGSTROM).

GIVEN NAME Scandinavian 5%. *Erik* (2).

Hegwood (598) Perhaps a part-translation of HEGLUND.

Hegyi (166) Hungarian: unexplained.

GIVEN NAMES Hungarian 13%; Jewish 4%. *Attila* (2), *Laszlo* (2), *Geza, Imre, Kalman, Karoly.*

Hehir (200) Irish: Anglicization of Gaelic **Ó hAichir** (see HARE).

GIVEN NAMES Irish 10%. *Brendan* (2), *Brighid.*

Hehl (208) German: **1.** from a medieval personal name, a short form of various Germanic personal names. **2.** German: nickname for an unctuous person, from Middle High German *hæl(e)* 'secret', 'smooth'. **3.** North German: nickname for a secretive or reclusive person, or topographic name for someone who lived at a remote or concealed spot, from Middle Low German *hēle* 'secret', 'concealed'.

GIVEN NAME German 4%. *Kurt.*

Hehman (160) North German (**Hehemann**): Westphalian variant of HEIDEMANN.

Hehn (427) German (Saxony): from a dialect variant of HEINE.

GIVEN NAMES German 6%. *Guenther, Gunther, Helmuth, Milbert.*

Hehr (246) German: mostly a variant of HEER but in some instances a nickname either from *hëher* 'jay', or from Middle High German *hēr* 'distinguished', 'proud'.

GIVEN NAMES German 5%. *Elfriede, Erhart, Horst, Milbert.*

Heibel (294) South German: metonymic occupational name for a maker of caps and bonnets, from an unrounded diminutive form of Middle High German *hūbe, hoube* 'bonnet'.

Heiberg (201) **1.** Norwegian (also found in Sweden and Denmark): topographic name from *hei* 'heath', 'moor' + *berg* 'hill', 'mountain' or habitational name from any of several farmsteads so named. **2.** German: dialect variant of **Heuberg**, a common topographic name composed of Middle High German *höu* 'hay' + *berg* 'hill', or a habitational name from any of several places named Heiberg. **3.** Dutch: habitational name from a place so called in Veldhoven in North Brabant.

GIVEN NAMES Scandinavian 10%; German 4%. *Alf, Ejnar, Gunn, Lars.*

Heiberger (232) German: derivative of HEIBERG 2 + the suffix *-er* denoting an inhabitant. Compare HEUBERGER.

Heichel (240) German: presumably from a pet form of the personal name *Hugo* (see HUGH), but also a variant of HEICK and HEIKE.

Heichelbech (118) German: habitational name from a lost or unidentified place.

Heick (227) North German: from a short form of a Germanic personal name formed with *hag* 'enclosure', 'fenced area' as its first element.

GIVEN NAMES German 4%. *Hanns, Rainer.*

Heid (931) **1.** German and Jewish (Ashkenazic): topographic name from Middle High German *heide*, German *Heide* 'heath', 'moor'. Compare HEATH. **2.** German: from the medieval personal name *Haido*.

GIVEN NAMES German 4%. *Dieter* (2), *Eckhart, Gerd, Gotthilf, Heinz, Klaus, Konrad, Kurt, Manfred, Ralf, Uli.*

Heidbreder (233) North German: habitational name for someone from Heitbrede in Westphalia, maed with Middle Low German *heide* 'uncultivated land' + *brēde* 'width', 'breadth'.

Heidbrink (149) Dutch and North German: topographic name from Middle Low German *heide* 'heath', + *brink* 'edge', 'grazing land', or 'village green', or a habitational name from any of several places so named in Lower Saxony.

Heide (770) **1.** German and Jewish: variant of HEID. **2.** Dutch and Danish: topographic name for a dweller on moorland, from Middle Dutch *heede, heyde*, Danish *heyde* 'heath', 'heather'. **3.** Norwegian: habitational name from any of several farmsteads named Heie, from Old Norse *heiðr* 'heath', 'moor'.

GIVEN NAMES German 5%. *Kurt* (3), *Claus, Eberhard, Hans, Juergen, Markus, Wolfgang.*

Heidebrecht (162) German: from a Germanic personal name composed of the elements *heid* 'heath' + *berht* 'bright', 'famous'.

GIVEN NAMES German 4%. *Arno, Erna.*

Heidebrink (124) Dutch and North German: variant of HEIDBRINK.

GIVEN NAMES Dutch 4%. *Harm, Onno.*

Heidecker (219) South German and Swiss German: habitational name from any of the various places in Germany called Heideck or from Heidegg near Zurich. All of them get their names from Middle High German *heide* 'heath' + *egge, ecke* 'corner' (see ECK).

Heidel (570) German: from a pet form of the personal name HEIDRICH or another name with the same first element, for example HEIDEBRECHT.

Heidelberg (402) German and Jewish (Ashkenazic): habitational name from any of the places named Heidelberg, of which the best-known example is in Baden.

Heidelberger (216) German and Jewish (Ashkenazic): habitational name for someone from any of the places named HEIDELBERG.

Heideman (773) German and Jewish: variant of HEIDEMANN.

Heidemann (528) German and Jewish (Ashkenazic): topographic name for a heathland dweller, from *Heide* 'heath' (see HEID) + *mann* 'man'.

GIVEN NAMES German 6%; Scandinavian 5%. *Johannes* (2), *Gerda, Gerhard, Hans,* *Hermann, Juergen, Klaus, Otto, Siegfried; Jorgen* (2), *Anders.*

Heiden (1092) **1.** German: habitational name from any of several places so named, for example in Westphalia and Switzerland. **2.** German: nickname from Middle High German *heiden* 'heathen', Old High German *heidano*, apparently a derivative of *heida* 'heath', modeled on Latin *paganus* (see PAINE). The nickname was sometimes used to refer to a Christian knight who had been on a Crusade to fight in the Holy Land. **3.** Jewish (Ashkenazic): of uncertain origin; possibly a shortened form of any of various ornamental names formed with German *Heide-* 'heath', for example *Heidenberg, Heidenkorn, Heidenkrug, Heidenwurzel.* **4.** English: variant spelling of HAYDEN. **5.** Dutch: shortened form of VANDERHEYDEN.

GIVEN NAMES German 4%. *Erwin* (4), *Kurt* (2), *Dietmar, Hannelore, Lorenz, Siegfried, Wolfgang.*

Heidenreich (944) German: from the medieval personal name *Heidenrich*, ostensibly composed of the elements *heiden* 'heathen', 'infidel' (see HEIDEN 2) + *rīc* 'power', 'rule', but probably in fact a variant by folk etymology of HEIDRICH. The name was popular at the time of the Crusades, the sense 'power over the heathens' being attributed to it.

GIVEN NAMES German 5%. *Hans* (3), *Fritz* (2), *Ute* (2), *Deiter, Dieter, Diether, Heinrich, Heinz, Kurt, Otto.*

Heider (1021) German: topographic name for a heath dweller, a variant of HEIDE + the *-er* suffix denoting an inhabitant; or a habitational name for someone from any of the various places called Heide or Heidau (named with the same term); the place name is common in Silesia, Saxony, and Bohemia.

GIVEN NAMES German 4%. *Erwin* (2), *Otto* (2), *Fritz, Gunter, Johann, Konrad, Kurt, Matthias, Willibald.*

Heidinger (271) South German: probably a habitational name for someone from a lost or unidentified place called Heiding.

GIVEN NAMES German 6%. *Kurt* (2), *Ewald, Gernot, Manfred.*

Heidkamp (129) German: habitational name for someone from any of several places so named in northwest Germany, from Middle Low German *heide* 'heath', 'uncultivated land' + *kamp* '(enclosed) field', 'domain'.

Heidlebaugh (106) Americanized form of German **Heidelbach**, near Alsfeld in Hesse.

Heidler (237) South German: **1.** derivative of the personal name *Heidel*, a pet form of HEIDRICH. **2.** topographic name for a heath dweller, from Middle High German *heide* 'heath' + *-(l)er* suffix denoting an inhabitant.

Heidmann (129) German: variant of HEIDEMANN.

GIVEN NAMES German 13%. *Armin, Ilse, Juergen, Kurt, Ralf, Ulrike, Wolfgang.*

Heidner (112) German: a topographic name, variant of HEIDER.

Heidorn (273) North German: variant of HAGEDORN.

GIVEN NAMES German 5%. *Ewald, Kurt.*

Heidrich (391) German and Dutch: from the medieval personal name *Heidrich*, which is in some instances a variant of *Heinrich* (see HENRY) with *Heidenrich* as an intermediary form (see HEIDENREICH) or is composed of the elements *haidu* 'appearance', 'personality' + *rīh* 'power', 'rule'.

GIVEN NAMES German 8%. *Dieter* (2), *Hans* (2), *Jochen, Kurt, Lutz, Uwe.*

Heidrick (222) Dutch: variant of HEIDRICH.

Heidt (882) German: variant of HEID.

Heidtke (149) German: from a pet form of the personal name HEID 2.

GIVEN NAMES German 6%. *Fritz, Siegfried.*

Heidtman (127) German (**Heidtmann**): variant of HEIDEMANN.

GIVEN NAME German 6%. *Kurt* (2).

Heien (152) **1.** Norwegian: habitational name from any of numerous farmsteads, notably in Agder and southwestern Norway, so named from the definite singular form of *hei* 'heath', 'moor'. **2.** German: from a short form of any of the Germanic compound personal names formed with *hag* 'enclosure', 'fenced area' as the first element.

Heier (704) **1.** South German: generally a variant of HAUER, but in some cases an occupational name from Middle High German *heie* 'ranger', 'guard'. **2.** Norwegian: habitational name from any of several farmsteads so named in the Oslofjord region. The place name is from the plural of Old Norse *heiðr* 'heath', 'moor'. **3.** Dutch and German: variant of HEYER 3–5.

GIVEN NAMES German 4%. *Kurt* (4), *Otto* (2), *Erwin, Helmut, Wilfried.*

Heifetz (199) Jewish (from Belarus and Lithuania): ornamental name from Hebrew *chefets* 'delight', 'pleasure'.

GIVEN NAMES Jewish 13%. *Eliezer* (2), *Gilad* (2), *Chayim.*

Heifner (336) German: probably Americanized spelling of of **Hüfner**, a variant of **Hübner**, see HUEBNER.

Heigel (105) German: variant of HEIGL.

Heiges (169) German: topographic name for someone who lived by a watercourse that was usually dry, from Middle High German *heige* 'dry', 'without water'.

Height (323) English: variant spelling of HIGHT.

Heighton (116) English (Midlands): apparently a habitational name from South Heighton in East Sussex, named from Old English *hēah* 'high' + *tūn* 'farmstead', 'settlement'. However, the high concentration of the modern name in the Midland region suggests that in many cases it is likely to be a variant of HAYTON, specifically from the places so named in Nottinghamshire and East Yorkshire.

Heigl (169) South German and Bavarian: from a pet form of the personal name *Hugo* (see HUGH).
GIVEN NAMES German 5%. *Helmuth, Monika.*

Heike (106) **1.** North German: variant of HEICK. **2.** Common Sino-Japanese reading of the characters meaning 'Taira family'. They are sometimes called the **Heishi**, with the same meaning.
GIVEN NAME French 6%. *Patrice.*

Heiken (174) North German and Dutch: patronymic from a pet form of the Germanic personal name *Haio*, a short form of a compound personal name formed with *hag-* 'enclosure', 'fenced area' as the first element.

Heikes (423) **1.** North German: patronymic from **Heike** (see HEICK). **2.** Jewish (eastern Ashkenazic): metronymic from the Yiddish female personal name *Khayke*, a pet form of *Khaye*, 'life', with the addition of the Yiddish possessive suffix *-s*.

Heikkila (572) Finnish (**Heikkilä**): from the personal name *Heikki* (derived from German *Heinrich*; see HENRY) + the local ending *-la*, denoting someone from a household headed by someone called *Heikki*. This personal name was very popular during the Middle Ages, St. Henry being the patron saint of Finland.
GIVEN NAMES Finnish 8%; Scandinavian 5%. *Eino* (4), *Reino* (4), *Pentti* (2), *Sulo* (2), *Wilho* (2), *Armas, Arvo, Onni, Tapani, Tauno, Toivo, Waino; Alvar, Nels.*

Heikkinen (482) Finnish: from the personal name *Heikki* (see HEIKKILA) + the common surname suffix *-nen*. Heikkinen is the eleventh most common surname in Finland.
GIVEN NAMES Finnish 9%; Scandinavian 4%. *Eino* (3), *Reino* (2), *Risto* (2), *Toivo* (2), *Antti, Arvo, Eero, Runo, Vaino, Veikko, Vieno, Vilho; Gunhild, Hjalmer, Iver, Sven.*

Heil (3223) **1.** German: from a pet form of HEINRICH. **2.** Dutch and North German: from a short form of the Germanic female personal name *Heila*, derived from *hail* 'whole'.

Heiland (379) South German: from Middle High German *heilant* 'savior', 'Christ', presumably either a name given to someone who had played the part of Christ in a mystery play or an occupational name for a healer, from Middle High German *heilen* 'to heal', 'save'.
GIVEN NAMES German 4%. *Kurt* (2), *Gerhard, Gunter, Gunther.*

Heilbron (107) Variant of German or Jewish *Heilbronn*, a habitational name from the city of Heilbronn in Württemberg.
GIVEN NAME German 5%. *Fritz.*

Heilbrun (165) German and Jewish (Ashkenazic): variant spelling of HEILBRUNN.

GIVEN NAMES German 8%. *Eugen, Gerd, Kurt, Lothar.*

Heilbrunn (100) German and Jewish (Ashkenazic): habitational name from the city of Heilbronn in Württemberg, where there was once a large Jewish community. The city is named from Old High German *heil(ag)* 'holy' + *brunno* 'spring', 'well'. See also HALPERN.
GIVEN NAMES German 8%. *Gerda, Gunther, Kurt.*

Heileman (138) German (**Heilemann**): in part a variant of HEILER, and in part an assimilated derivative of HEINRICH.
GIVEN NAME German 4%. *Kurt.*

Heiler (176) South German: occupational name for someone who castrated animals, from an agent derivative of *heilen* 'to cut'.

Heilig (780) German and Jewish (Ashkenazic): from Middle High German *heilec*, German *heilig* 'holy', a nickname for a pious person or someone with a trusting temperament.

Heiliger (132) German and Jewish (Ashkenazic): nickname for someone of a religious disposition or with a with a pious or saintly temperament, from Middle High German *heiliger* 'saint', 'holy one', 'pious one'.

Heilman (2738) **1.** Dutch: metronymic from HEIL 2. **2.** Variant of German and Jewish HEILMANN.

Heilmann (422) **1.** German: occupational name for someone who castrated animals (see HEILER). **2.** German: derivative of the personal name HEINRICH. Compare HEIMANN. **3.** German and Jewish (Ashkenazic): from a Germanic personal name composed of the elements *heil* 'healthy' + *man* 'man', also used by Ashkenazic Jews.
GIVEN NAMES German 15%. *Kurt* (5), *Otto* (3), *Gerhard* (2), *Helmut* (2), *Volker* (2), *Dieter, Eberhard, Gottfried, Gunther, Hans, Klaus, Manfred.*

Heim (4209) **1.** South German: from the Germanic personal name *Haimo*. Compare English HAMMOND. **2.** Jewish (Ashkenazic): from the Yiddish personal name *Khayim*, from Hebrew *chayim* 'life'. **3.** Norwegian: habitational name from a farmstead named Heim, from Old Norse *heimr* 'home', 'farmstead', 'settlement', or in some cases a more recent ornamental formation from *heim* 'home'.

Heiman (1340) **1.** Jewish: from the Yiddish personal name *Khayman*, a variant of *Khayem* (see HEIM). **2.** Altered spelling of German HEIMANN.

Heimann (919) German: **1.** from a pet form of HEINRICH. **2.** topographic name for someone who lived by a hedge or enclosure, from *Hei* 'hedge', 'enclosure'. Compare HAGEMANN.
GIVEN NAMES German 7%. *Kurt* (4), *Fritz* (2), *Klaus* (2), *Otto* (2), *Alois, Ewald, Friedrich, Gerhard, Guenther, Hans, Heinz, Jurgen.*

Heimark (113) Norwegian: habitational name from a farm in Hordaland, named with Old Norse *heiðr* 'moor', 'heath' + *mark* 'forest'.

Heimbach (659) German: habitational name from any of numerous places called Heimbach.

Heimbaugh (122) Americanized spelling of German HEIMBACH.

Heimberg (139) German: habitational name for someone from any of numerous places in Bavaria, the Rhineland, and Württemberg named Heimberg.
GIVEN NAMES German 6%. *Kurt, Manfred.*

Heimberger (162) German and Jewish (Ashkenazic): **1.** habitational name for someone from any of numerous places named Heimberg. **2.** variant of HEIMBURGER.
GIVEN NAMES Jewish 4%. *Herschal, Hirsch.*

Heimbigner (176) Variant of South German **Heimbiechner** or **Heimbüchner**, habitational name for someone from a place called Heimbuch, or from a field name, *Heimbüchen*, composed of Middle High German *hac, hagen* 'enclosure', 'hedge' + *büchen* or *biechen*, dative plural of Middle High German *buoche* 'beech tree'.
GIVEN NAMES German 5%. *Fritz, Hans, Kurt.*

Heimbuch (169) German: habitational name from any of several places so named.
GIVEN NAME French 4%. *Andre.*

Heimburger (147) **1.** German (**Heimbürger**): status name for a village headman, Middle High German *heimbürge*, a compound of *heim* 'homestead', 'settlement' + *bürge* 'guardian'. This was the title regularly used for the office of village headman in Franconia. Compare GRAF, HOFFMANN, MEYER, SCHULTZ, and VOGT. **2.** German and Jewish (Ashkenazic): habitational name for someone from any of several places named Heimburg.
GIVEN NAMES German 5%. *Arno, Hans.*

Heimer (608) North German: from the personal name *Heimbert*, composed of the Germanic elements *heim* '(farm) house', 'home' + *berht* 'bright', 'illustrious'.
GIVEN NAMES Scandinavian 4%. *Knut* (2), *Erik, Hakon, Lennart.*

Heimerdinger (137) German and Jewish (western Ashkenazic): habitational name for someone from Heimerdingen in Württemberg.
GIVEN NAMES German 7%. *Friedrich, Uli, Ulrich.*

Heimerl (329) German (Bavarian): from a pet form of the personal name *Heimeran*, derived from a Germanic compound name composed of the elements *heim* 'home' + *hraban* 'raven', or a variant of HEIMER.

Heimerman (169) German (**Heimermann**): elaborated derivative of HEIMER, with the addition of *Mann* 'man'.

Heimes (127) Dutch: variant of HEIMS.
GIVEN NAMES German 4%. *Hans, Otto.*

Heimgartner (116) German (**Heimgärtner**): topographic name for a person from a house with a *Heimgarten* 'house garden', an enclosed, fenced garden, with the special meaning 'leisurely gathering', 'social get-together', from Middle High German *heim* 'house' + *garten* 'garden'.

Heimlich (369) German and Jewish (Ashkenazic): nickname for a secretive person, from Middle High German *heimelich*, German *heimlich* 'confidential', 'secret'.
GIVEN NAMES Jewish 4%. *Mendel* (2), *Moshe, Shaya, Tova.*

Heims (228) North German and Dutch: patronymic from a short form of the personal name *Heimbert* (see HEIER).
GIVEN NAMES German 4%. *Kurt* (2), *Otto.*

Heimsoth (196) German (also **Heimsöth**): habitational name from Heimsath in Westphalia, an abandoned settlement.

Hein (5248) German, Dutch, Danish, and Jewish (Ashkenazic): from a short form of the Germanic personal name *Heinrich* (see HENRY 1).
GIVEN NAMES German 4%. *Erwin* (8), *Egon* (4), *Kurt* (4), *Manfred* (3), *Wolfgang* (3), *Gerd* (2), *Ilse* (2), *Jurgen* (2), *Klaus* (2), *Matthias* (2), *Otto* (2), *Siegfried* (2).

Heinbach (107) German: topographic name from Middle High German *hagen* 'shrub', 'thorn bush' + *bach* 'small stream'.

Heinbaugh (228) Partly Americanized form of German HEINBACH (compare HINEBAUGH).

Heindel (415) South German: from a pet form of the personal name HEINRICH.

Heindl (329) South German: variant of HEINDEL.
GIVEN NAMES German 5%. *Phares* (2), *Alfons, Alois, Friedrich, Rainer.*

Heine (2190) German, Dutch, and Jewish (Ashkenazic): from a short form of the personal name HEINRICH.
GIVEN NAMES German 5%. *Kurt* (4), *Erwin* (3), *Hans* (3), *Fritz* (2), *Uwe* (2), *Armin, Eldor, Ernst, Eugen, Gebhard, Gerhard, Gunter.*

Heineck (110) Variant of German HEINECKE. This spelling of the name is found mainly in Hungary.
GIVEN NAME French 12%. *Joffre* (4).

Heinecke (411) North German: from a pet form of HEINRICH.
GIVEN NAMES German 5%. *Erwin* (3), *Eberhard, Kurt, Monika.*

Heineman (949) 1. Dutch, German, and Jewish (Ashkenazic): variant of HEINE, with the addition of *man* 'man'. 2. respelling of German HEINEMANN.
GIVEN NAMES German 4%. *Manferd* (2), *Erna, Fritz, Herta, Horst, Kurt, Otto.*

Heinemann (983) German and Jewish (Ashkenazic): elaborated derivative of HEINE, with the addition of *Mann* 'man'.
GIVEN NAMES German 9%. *Klaus* (4), *Fritz* (3), *Hans* (3), *Manfred* (3), *Heinz* (2),

Bernd, Dieter, Gunther, Hermann, Inge, Juergen, Kurt.

Heinemeyer (142) German: distinguishing nickname for a farmer called Heine, from the personal name HEINE + Middle High German *meier* 'tenant farmer' (see MEYER).
GIVEN NAMES German 6%. *Benno, Helmuth, Otto.*

Heinen (1404) North German and Dutch: patronymic from HEIN.

Heiner (616) German: patronymic from a short form of HEINRICH.

Heinert (143) South German: 1. variant of HEINER. 2. in some instances from the Germanic personal name *Heinhard*, from *hagin* 'enclosure', 'protected place' + *hard* 'strong', 'hardy'.
GIVEN NAMES German 4%. *Hans, Klaus.*

Heines (131) Dutch: patronymic from HEINE.

Heiney (462) Americanized spelling of the Swiss family name **Heini**, a variant of German HEINE.

Heinicke (183) North German, Dutch, and Danish: variant of HEINECKE.
GIVEN NAMES German 16%. *Kurt* (3), *Otto* (2), *Christoph, Gerhard, Joerg, Lothar, Willi.*

Heinig (180) German and Dutch: from a pet form of the personal name HEINRICH.
GIVEN NAMES German 5%. *Arno, Franz, Lutz.*

Heiniger (122) German: variant of HEINIG.

Heininger (237) 1. German: variant of HEINIG. 2. German: habitational name denoting someone from any of the places in Württemberg and Hannover called Heiningen, or from Heining in Bavaria.
GIVEN NAMES German 6%. *Erwin, Klaus, Oskar.*

Heinisch (145) German (of Slavic origin): from a pet form of the personal name HEINRICH.
GIVEN NAMES German 13%. *Gerhard* (2), *Reinhard* (2), *Heinz.*

Heinitz (142) German and Jewish (Ashkenazic): habitational name from a place in Saxony called Heinitz, a place name of Slavic form.

Heinke (192) German: from a pet form of the personal name HEINRICH.
GIVEN NAMES German 7%. *Erwin, Kurt, Wilhelm.*

Heinkel (185) German: from a pet form of the personal name HEINRICH.
GIVEN NAMES German 6%. *Erwin* (3), *Otto.*

Heinl (173) South German: variant of HEINLE.

Heinle (443) South German: from a pet form of the personal name HEINRICH.
GIVEN NAMES German 5%. *Gunther* (2), *Konrad* (2), *Otto.*

Heinlein (761) German: from a pet form of the personal name HEINRICH.
GIVEN NAMES German 4%. *Armin, Herta, Horst, Kurt, Manfred.*

Heinlen (180) Variant of German HEINLEIN.

Heinly (180) Variant of South German HEINLE.

Heinmiller (113) Part-translation of German **Heinmüller**, a distinguishing nickname for a miller called Hein, from the personal name HEIN + Middle High German *mülnære* 'miller'; compare HEINEMEYER.

Heino (305) 1. Finnish: either from a Finnish form of the Germanic personal name *Heinrich* (see HENRY) or an ornamental name from *heinä* 'hay'. During the name conversion movement in the 19th and early 20th centuries, many Finnish families with Swedish names such as **Hahl**, **Hammar**, and **Henriksson** adopted the name Heino. In the U.S. it is also found as a shortened form of HEINONEN. 2. German and Jewish (Ashkenazic): from a pet form of HEINRICH.
GIVEN NAMES Finnish 10%; German 4%. *Arvo* (3), *Reino* (3), *Kalervo* (2), *Armas, Eero, Irja, Jorma, Onni; Arno, Otto.*

Heinold (320) German: from a Germanic personal name, *Haginold*, composed of the elements *hagin* 'enclosure', 'hedge' + *wald* 'rule'.

Heinonen (222) Finnish: variant of HEINO + the common surname suffix *-nen*. This is the fifteenth most common surname in Finland. In the U.S. it has sometimes been shortened to HEINO.
GIVEN NAMES Finnish 9%; Scandinavian 5%. *Erkki* (2), *Eero, Hannu, Juha, Kauko, Pasi, Waino; Erik, Evald, Olle, Viljo.*

Heinrich (3458) German and Jewish (Ashkenazic): from personal name *Heinrich*, composed of the Germanic elements *haim*, *heim* 'home' + *rīc* 'power'. In the Middle Ages this was the most popular of personal names in Germany. See also HENRY.
GIVEN NAMES German 8%. *Kurt* (18), *Erwin* (8), *Helmut* (5), *Manfred* (4), *Otto* (4), *Dieter* (3), *Hans* (3), *Christl* (2), *Ewald* (2), *Gerd* (2), *Gerhard* (2), *Guenter* (2).

Heinrichs (879) German: patronymic from HEINRICH.

Heinritz (123) German: from a contracted form of the Germanic personal name *Haganrich*, composed of the elements *hagin* 'enclosure' + *rīc* 'power(ful)'.
GIVEN NAMES German 5%. *Dietrich, Kurt.*

Heins (1591) North German, Dutch, Frisian, and Jewish (Ashkenazic): patronymic from HEIN.
GIVEN NAMES German 4%. *Arno, Claus, Georg, Hans, Helmut, Johann, Kurt, Otto, Wilfried.*

Heinsen (110) Danish: patronymic from a short form of the personal name *Hein*, short form of HEINRICH.
GIVEN NAMES German 7%; Spanish 6%. *Christl, Erna, Hans; Jose* (2), *Auturo, Elva, Lourdes, Reynaldo.*

Heinsohn (347) North German: patronymic from the personal name *Hein*, short form of HEINRICH.

GIVEN NAMES German 6%. *Gerd* (2), *Claus, Elfriede, Gerhard, Jutta, Katharina, Klaus.*

Heintschel (107) German: from a pet form of **Heintzsch** (Saxony; see HEINZ) or **Heinzel** (Silesia; see HENSCHEL).

Heintz (2431) German: variant spelling of HEINZ.

Heintze (112) German: variant of HEINZ.

GIVEN NAMES German 19%; Scandinavian 4%. *Achim* (4), *Siegfried* (2), *Arno, Erwin.*

Heintzelman (747) German (**Hein(t)zelmann**): from a pet form of HEINRICH, with the addition of -*mann* 'man'.

Heintzman (189) German (**Heinzmann**): from a pet form of HEINRICH, with the addition of -*mann* 'man'.

Heiny (246) Variant of Swiss German HEINEY.

Heinz (3351) German and Jewish (Ashkenazic): from a pet form of the personal name HEINRICH.

GIVEN NAMES German 4%. *Kurt* (8), *Otto* (5), *Hans* (4), *Erwin* (2), *Bernd, Dieter, Franz, Frieda, Guenter, Gunter, Harro, Hedwig.*

Heinze (1103) German and Jewish (Ashkenazic): variant of HEINZ.

GIVEN NAMES German 8%. *Horst* (4), *Otto* (3), *Bernd* (2), *Dieter* (2), *Gunter* (2), *Kurt* (2), *Reinhold* (2), *Udo* (2), *Hans, Heinz, Jochen, Lorenz.*

Heinzel (185) South German: from a pet form of the personal name HEINRICH.

GIVEN NAMES German 10%. *Gunther* (2), *Kurt* (2), *Johann, Math.*

Heinzelman (212) German (**Heinzelmann**): see HEINTZELMAN.

Heinzen (341) German: patronymic from HEINZ.

Heinzer (105) German: derivative of HEINZ.

GIVEN NAMES German 5%. *Dieter, Hans.*

Heinzerling (123) South German: patronymic from a pet form of the personal name HEINZ.

GIVEN NAME German 5%. *Sieglinde.*

Heinzman (368) Variant of German HEINZMANN.

Heinzmann (166) South German: from the personal name HEINZ, with the addition of *Mann* 'man': either a pet form or an occupational name meaning 'servant of Heinz'.

GIVEN NAMES German 10%. *Dieter* (2), *Fritz, Gottlieb, Kurt.*

Heiple (214) Americanized spelling of German **Heipel**; unexplained.

Heird (108) Scottish: probably a variant spelling of HEARD.

Heironimus (160) Altered spelling of HIERONYMUS.

Heis (110) **1.** South German (Bavarian and Swabian): from a short form of the personal name *Matheis* (see MATTHIAS). **2.** North German: variant of HEISE.

Heise (1723) **1.** North German: from a short form of the personal name HEIDRICH. **2.** Dutch: from the Germanic personal name *Haiso.*

GIVEN NAMES German 6%. *Otto* (4), *Kurt* (3), *Ewald* (2), *Klaus* (2), *Rudi* (2), *Wolfgang* (2), *Alphons, Arno, Berthold, Fritz, Hans, Heinz.*

Heisel (404) **1.** South German and Austrian: from a pet form of HEISS. **2.** South German: topographic name meaning 'little house', an unrounded form of **Häusel**, diminutive of HAUS.

Heiser (2464) **1.** South German and Austrian: variant of **Häuser** (see HAUSER). **2.** nickname for a person with a rasping voice, from Middle High German *heiser* 'hoarse'.

Heiserman (246) German (**Heisermann**): variant of HEISER, reinforced by the addition of -*mann* 'man'.

Heisey (864) Altered spelling of German or Dutch HEISE, written thus to preserve the second syllable.

Heishman (462) German (**Heischmann**): habitational name for someone from a place called Heisch in Holstein.

Heisinger (175) German: habitational name from any of several places named Heising or Heisingen.

Heiskell (260) English: variant of HASKELL.

Heisler (2327) German: variant of **Häusler** (see HAUSLER).

Heisner (237) German: variant of HAUSNER.

Heiss (838) **1.** South German and Austrian: variant of **Hiess**, which is from an aphetic short form of the personal name *Mathies* (see MATTHEW). **2.** South German and Austrian: variant of HEUSS. **3.** Jewish (Ashkenazic): ornamental from German *heiss* 'hot'.

GIVEN NAMES German 4%. *Kurt* (4), *Ernst, Gerhard, Guenther, Herta, Hertha, Otto, Reinhold.*

Heisser (138) German: variant of HAUSER.

GIVEN NAMES German 5%. *Fritz, Kurt.*

Heisserer (110) German: probably a habitational name for someone from Heissen in the Ruhr region.

Heist (601) German: habitational name for someone from a place so named near Hamburg.

Heistand (312) German: probably an altered spelling of German **Hiestand**, of uncertain origin and meaning. In Swabian-Bavarian *Hie-* is often a reduced form of *Hieb-* or *Hüb-*, but if this is a variant of **Hübstand**, the meaning is equally unexplained.

Heister (313) North German and Dutch: variant of HESTER 1.

Heit (537) German: **1.** from a short form of a Germanic personal name formed with *heid* 'heath' as the first element, or derived from Old High German *heit* 'specimen', 'being', 'character'. **2.** habitational name from a place so named, near Bremervörde in Lower Saxony.

Heiter (131) South German: variant of HEIDER.

GIVEN NAMES German 9%. *Gerhard, Heinz, Kurt.*

Heithoff (141) North German: habitational name from any of several places called Heidhof in northern Germany, named with Middle Low German *heide* 'heath' + *hof* 'farmstead', 'manor farm'.

Heiting (121) German: from a short form of a Germanic personal name composed with *heida* 'heath', 'open field' or *heit* 'nature (of a person)'.

Heitkamp (518) North German: variant of HEIDKAMP.

GIVEN NAMES German 4%. *Erwin* (2), *Florian, Fritz, Kurt, Othmar.*

Heitland (112) North German: topographic name from Middle Low German *heide* 'heath', 'wasteland' + *land* 'land'.

Heitman (1349) Dutch, Danish, and German: see HEITMANN.

Heitmann (580) German, Dutch, and Danish: topographic name for someone who lived on a heath from Middle Low German *heide* 'heath', 'moor' + *mann* 'man' (see HEID).

GIVEN NAMES German 9%; Scandinavian 4%. *Kurt* (4), *Dieter* (2), *Gunter* (2), *Fritz, Hans, Horst, Juergen, Jurgen, Klaus, Otto, Uwe; Erik* (2), *Lars.*

Heitmeyer (194) German: distinguishing nickname for a farmer whose land included heathland, from Middle Low German *heide* 'heath', 'wasteland' + MEYER.

GIVEN NAMES German 5%. *Kurt, Monika.*

Heitner (225) German: habitational name for someone from any of several places named HEIDEN.

GIVEN NAMES German 4%. *Erna, Frieda, Hilde.*

Heitz (1055) South German and Swiss German: from a dialect variation of the personal name HEINZ.

Heitzenrater (165) Americanized spelling of German **Heitzenröther**, a surname of unexplained etymology found chiefly in the Rhineland and Württemberg.

Heitzman (816) Variant of German HEITZMANN.

Heitzmann (156) South German: from an elaborated dialect variation of the personal name HEINZ (see HEITZ) + *Mann* 'man'.

Heizer (355) German: occupational name for someone whose job was to tend a stove or fire, Middle High German *heizer* 'heater', an agent derivative of *heizen* 'to heat'.

Hejduk (108) Czech: status name denoting an armed retainer of a nobleman. The term was borrowed from Hungarian (see HAJDU).

Hejl (280) Czech: from *hejl, hýl* 'bullfinch', a nickname either for someone with a red nose or for a greenhorn.

Hejna (140) Polish: from a Polonized form of the Germanic personal name HEINE (see HEINRICH, HENRY).

GIVEN NAMES Polish 6%. *Jerzy, Krzysztof, Tadeusz.*

Hejny (128) Czech (**Hajný**): variant of **Hajný** (see HAJNY).

Helander (199) Swedish: of uncertain origin. It is either from an unidentified first element *He-* + *-lander* 'inhabitant' (from *land* 'country', 'land'), or from an unidentified first element *Hel-* + *-ander* (a common Swedish surname suffix based on Greek *-andros* 'man'). This surname is also found in Finland.

GIVEN NAMES Scandinavian 9%; Finnish 4%. *Per* (2); *Orvo, Seppo, Terttu.*

Helber (144) **1.** South German: occupational name for a thresher, from Middle High German *helwe* 'chaff' + the agent suffix *-er*; alternatively, it could be a habitational name from a place called Helba near Meiningen. **2.** Dutch: variant of HELBERT 2 and 3.

GIVEN NAME German 5%. *Markus.*

Helberg (453) **1.** German and Jewish (Ashkenazic): habitational name from any of various places called Hel(l)berg or in Lower Rhine-Westphalia, Lower Saxony, and Bavaria. **2.** Jewish (Ashkenazic): variant spelling of HELLBERG. **3.** Norwegian: habitational name from any of several farmsteads so named, either from the female personal name *Helga* or from Old Norse *heilagr* 'holy', 'sacred', or *hella* 'flagstone' + *berg* 'rock', 'mountain'.

Helbert (332) **1.** North German: variant of HILBERT, or from another Germanic compound personal name, *Helmbert*, composed of the elements *helm* 'helmet', 'protection' + *berht* 'bright', 'illustrious'. **2.** French and Dutch: from a Germanic personal name composed of the elements *heil* 'healthy' + *berht* 'bright', 'illustrious'. **3.** Dutch: hypercorrected form of ELBERT.

Helbig (569) German and Dutch: from the medieval personal name *Heilwig, Helwig* (see HELWIG).

GIVEN NAMES German 9%. *Franz* (2), *Hans* (2), *Heinz* (2), *Kurt* (2), *Erna, Ernst, Erwin, Gunther, Jutta, Manfred, Otto, Rudi.*

Helbing (246) German: variant of HELBIG.

GIVEN NAMES German 6%. *Claus* (3), *Siegfried.*

Helbling (463) South German: from Middle High German *helbling* 'halfpenny', applied as a nickname for a weak man, or for someone who paid this amount in rent or taxes, or for a stingy person.

Held (3821) **1.** German, Dutch, and Jewish (Ashkenazic): nickname from Middle High German, Middle Dutch, Yiddish *held* 'hero'. As a Jewish name, it is often ornamental. **2.** German: from a short form of any of the Germanic personal names formed with *hild* 'strife' as the first element. **3.** English: variant of HEALD.

Heldenbrand (207) Variant of German HILDEBRAND, in which the first element has been altered by folk etymology to a form of *Held* 'hero'.

Helder (270) **1.** Dutch and German: from a Germanic personal name, *Halidher*, composed of the elements *halið* 'hero' + *hari, heri* 'army', or from another personal name, *Hildher*, composed of the elements *hild* 'strife', 'battle' + the same second element. **2.** Dutch and North German: topographic name for someone living on a slope, from Middle Dutch *helldinge* 'slanting surface'. Compare HALDER. **3.** English: from an agent derivative of Old English *healdan* 'to hold', hence a name denoting an occupier or tenant. Compare HOLDER. **4.** English: variant of HILDER. **5.** English: possibly a variant of ELDER, with the addition of an inorganic initial *H-*.

GIVEN NAMES Dutch 6%. *Reinard* (3), *Ceciel, Dirk, Jaap.*

Helderman (242) German (**Heldermann**): topographic name for someone living on a slope (see HELDER).

Heldman (334) German (**Heldmann**) and Jewish (Ashkenazic): nickname from Middle High German, Yiddish *held* 'hero' + *man(n)* 'man'. As a Jewish name, it is often ornamental.

Heldreth (248) English: variant of HILDRETH.

Heldt (743) **1.** German and Dutch: variant of HELD 1. **2.** German: variant of HELD 2.

Helf (233) South German: metonymic occupational name for an assistant of some kind, or nickname for a helpful person, from an agent noun based on Middle High German *helf* 'help'.

GIVEN NAMES German 4%. *Klaus, Kurt, Monika.*

Helfand (379) Jewish (eastern Ashkenazic): ornamental name or nickname from Yiddish *helfand* 'elephant'.

GIVEN NAMES Jewish 7%. *Sol* (4), *Leibish, Mordechai, Mort, Zeev, Zolman.*

Helfenstein (115) German: habitational name from a place called Helfenstein.

GIVEN NAMES German 5%. *Franz, Otto.*

Helfer (558) South German: metonymic occupational name for an assistant of some kind, or nickname for a helpful person, from Middle High German *hëlfære*, German *Helfer* 'helper', 'assistant'.

Helferich (110) German: variant of HELFRICH.

Helfert (116) German: variant of HELFER.

GIVEN NAME French 4%. *Jacques.*

Helfgott (160) German and Jewish (Ashkenazic): from a reduced form of *helfe mir Gott* 'God help me', a nickname for someone who habitually used the expression.

GIVEN NAMES Jewish 10%. *Meyer* (2), *Batsheva, Simcha, Vered.*

Helfman (207) German (**Helfmann**) and Jewish (Ashkenazic): variant of HELFER.

GIVEN NAMES Jewish 8%. *Samoil, Sol.*

Helfrich (1491) German and French: from a Germanic personal name composed of the elements *helfe* 'help' + *rīc* 'power', 'rule'. One of the early medieval kings of the Franks bore this name, in the form *Chilperic*, and *Helferich* was also the name of a character in a medieval heroic epic.

Helfrick (139) Respelling of HELFRICH.

Helgason (112) Scandinavian: unexplained.

GIVEN NAMES Scandinavian 11%. *Hilmar, Kristinn.*

Helgeland (124) Norwegian: habitational name from any of numerous farmsteads so named, notably in the county of Rogaland. In most cases, the name is derived from Old Norse *Helgaland*, from *heilagr* 'holy', 'sacred' + *land* 'land' (see HELLAND).

GIVEN NAME Scandinavian 6%. *Selmer.*

Helgerson (472) Swedish (**Helgersson**): patronymic from the personal name *Helger* (see HELGESEN).

GIVEN NAMES Scandinavian 5%. *Erik* (3), *Nels, Nordahl, Ordell.*

Helgesen (298) Danish and Norwegian: patronymic from the personal name *Helge*, Old Norse *Helgi*, literally 'holiness', a derivative of the adjective *heilagr* 'holy', 'sacred'.

GIVEN NAMES Scandinavian 10%. *Erik* (2), *Lars* (2), *Alf, Oddvar, Thor.*

Helgeson (1571) Americanized spelling of HELGESEN.

GIVEN NAMES Scandinavian 4%. *Lars* (4), *Erik* (2), *Helmer* (2), *Nels, Obert, Peer, Selmer.*

Helget (259) German (common in the Czech Republic): from the medieval personal name *Helgoth, Helgath*, Germanic *Hildegaud*, composed of *hild* 'strife' + *got*, of uncertain meaning (perhaps from the same word as *Goth*).

Helgren (222) Swedish (**Hellgren**): ornamental name composed of the elements *häll* 'stone', 'rock' + *gren* 'branch'; the first element is unexplained.

Helie (139) French: **1.** (**Hélie**): from a medieval personal name derived from the Biblical name *Elijah* (see ELLIS). **2.** (**Helié**): from a vernacular form of the Latin personal name *Hilarius* (see HILLARY).

GIVEN NAMES French 10%. *Jacques, Leopaul, Ovila.*

Helin (256) **1.** Swedish (also frequent in Finland): ornamental name from an unexplained first element + the suffix *-lin* or *-in*, common suffixes of surnames. **2.** French (**Hélin**): from a pet form of *Hélie* (see HELIE 1). **3.** French (**Hélin**): from the Germanic personal name *Heilin*, a short form of any of various compound names with the first element *heil* (see HEILMANN 2). **4.** English: variant of HILLIAN.

GIVEN NAMES Finnish 5%; Scandinavian 4%. *Rauni* (2), *Toivo* (2), *Osmo.*

Heling (147) North German: habitational name, probably from Hehlingen near Wolfsburg.

Helinski (192) Polish: habitational name for someone from a place called Helin in Skierniewice voivodeship, named with the personal name *Hela* (*Helena*).
GIVEN NAMES Polish 5%. *Janusz, Pawel, Zigmund.*

Helke (168) North German (Frisian): variant of HILKE.

Hell (105) **1.** English: variant of HILL, from southeastern Middle English *hell* 'hill', a dialect form characteristic of Kent and Sussex. **2.** English: from a personal name, *Helle*, which may have been a variant of *Elie* (a Middle English form of *Elias*), or perhaps a short form of a personal name formed with *Hild-* as the first element (see HILLIARD for example), or perhaps from the female personal name *Helen*. **3.** German: nickname from Middle High German *hell* 'bright', 'shining'. **4.** German: variant of HELLE 3.

Hellams (154) English: variant of HELMS. This name occurs predominantly in SC.

Helland (1000) Norwegian: habitational name from any of numerous farmsteads so named, notably in the counties of Rogaland and Hordaland, mostly from Old Norse *Helgaland* (see HELGELAND), but in some cases from Old Norse *hella* 'flat stone', 'flagstone', 'flat mountain' or *hellir* 'cave' + *land* 'country', 'land'.
GIVEN NAMES Scandinavian 6%. *Erik* (2), *Alfhild, Lars, Oivind, Sig, Sigvard.*

Hellard (309) French: from the Germanic personal name *Hailhard*, composed of *hail* 'hale', 'healthy' + *hard* 'hardy', 'brave', 'strong'.

Hellberg (182) **1.** North German and Norwegian: variant spelling of HELBERG. **2.** Swedish: ornamental name from *häll* 'stone', 'rock' + *berg* 'mountain'. **3.** Jewish (Ashkenazic): ornamental name composed of German *hell* 'light', 'bright' + *Berg* 'mountain', 'hill'.
GIVEN NAMES Scandinavian 14%; German 8%. *Lars* (2), *Per; Kurt* (2), *Eldred.*

Hellbusch (169) North German: probably a topographic name composed of Middle Low German *helle* 'hollow', 'precipitous place' (see also HELLE 3) + *busch* 'small woods'.

Helle (525) **1.** Norwegian and Swedish: from Old Norse *hella* 'flat stone', 'flagstone', 'flat mountain' or *hellir* 'cave'. As a Nowegian name this is generally a habitational name from any of numerous farmsteads so named. As a Swedish name, it is generally ornamental. **2.** English: variant spelling of HELL 1. **3.** German: topographic name from Middle High German *helle* 'hell' (modern German HÖLLE), used (often in field names) in a topographic sense to denote a hollow or a wild, precipitous place.
GIVEN NAME Scandinavian 4%. *Erik.*

Hellem (119) Norwegian: habitational name from any of several farmsteads so named from Old Norse from Old Norse *hella* 'flat stone', 'flagstone', 'flat mountain' or *hellir* 'cave' + the element *-em*, which may come from Old Norse *heimr* 'farmstead'.
GIVEN NAME Scandinavian 8%. *Magnar.*

Hellems (118) Variant of Norwegian HELLEM.

Hellen (254) **1.** Swedish: ornamental name formed with *häll* 'rock', 'stone' + the adjectival suffix *-én*, a derivative of Latin *-enius.* **2.** English: variant of ELLEN 1 (with inorganic initial *H-*). **3.** English: variant of HILLIAN. **4.** Irish (west Cork): variant of HEELAN.

Hellenbrand (265) North German and Dutch: variant of HILDEBRAND.

Heller (11061) **1.** German: nickname from the small medieval coin known as the *häller* or *heller* because it was first minted (in 1208) at the Swabian town of (Schwäbisch) Hall. Compare HALL. **2.** Jewish (Ashkenazic): habitational name for someone from Schwäbisch Hall. **3.** German: topographic name for someone living by a field named as 'hell' (see HELLE 3). **4.** English: topographic name for someone living on a hill, from southeastern Middle English *hell* + the habitational suffix *-er*. **5.** Dutch: from a Germanic personal name composed of the elements *hild* 'strife' + *hari, heri* 'army'. **6.** Jewish (Ashkenazic): nickname for a person with fair hair or a light complexion, from an inflected form, used before a male personal name, of German *hell* 'light', 'bright', Yiddish *hel*.

Hellerman (153) **1.** South German (**Hellermann**): variant of HELLER. **2.** Jewish (Ashkenazic): nickname for a person with fair hair or a light complexion, a derivative of HELLER 6.

Hellerud (111) Norwegian: unexplained.

Hellickson (173) Americanized spelling of Swedish **Helliksson** and Norwegian **Helliksen**, patronymics from the Old Norse personal name *Herleikr*, composed of the elements *her* 'army' + *leikr* 'battle', 'fight'.

Hellier (103) English: variant spelling of HILLIER 1.

Helling (610) **1.** English: habitational name from Healing in northeastern Lincolnshire, named in Old English as '(settlement of) the family or followers of *Hægel*' (an unattested Old English personal name). **2.** English: variant of HILLIAN. **3.** German and Dutch: nickname from Middle Low German *hellin*, Middle Dutch *hellinc, hallinc* 'halfpenny'. Compare HELBLING. **4.** German: habitational name from any of various places named Helling or Hellingen.
GIVEN NAMES German 6%. *Kurt* (2), *Manfred* (2), *Wilhelm* (2), *Bernd, Bernhard, Detlef, Eberhard, Franz, Friedhelm, Guenther, Hans.*

Hellinger (302) German: habitational name for someone from a place called Helling or Hellingen.
GIVEN NAMES German 8%. *Kurt* (2), *Mathias* (2), *Fritz, Hans, Heinz, Wolfgang.*

Hellings (137) **1.** English (Devon): variant of HILLIAN. The surname is associated chiefly with Devon, where the family held land at Upton Hellions from the 13th century onward. **2.** North German and Dutch: patronymic from a short form of any of various Germanic personal names composed with *hild* 'strife' (see HILD, HILDEBRAND).

Helliwell (122) English (Yorkshire): habitational name from any of several places named with Old English *hǣlig* 'holy' (a mutated variant of *hālig*) + *well(a)* 'well', 'spring', in particular Helliwell in Worsborough, South Yorkshire, or Holywell (earlier *Helliwell*) in Stainland, West Yorkshire. Compare HOLLOWELL.

Hellman (1784) **1.** English: topographic name for a hill dweller (see HELLER). **2.** Jewish (Ashkenazic): variant of HELLERMAN. **3.** Dutch: variant of HELMAN. **4.** German: see HELLMANN.

Hellmann (745) **1.** North German: topographic name from Middle Low German *helle* 'precipitous terrain', 'steep slope' + *Mann* 'man'. **2.** German: nickname for a hellraiser, from HELLE 3.
GIVEN NAMES German 7%. *Kurt* (3), *Aloysius, Dieter, Gerhardt, Gunther, Hannes, Hans, Heinrich, Heinz, Ingo, Klaus, Manfred.*

Hellmer (165) North German: variant of HILLMER.
GIVEN NAMES German 8%. *Angelika, Gerhard, Kurt.*

Hellmers (138) North German: patronymic from HELLMER.
GIVEN NAMES German 5%. *Aloysius, Kurt.*

Hellmich (138) North German: variant spelling of HELMICH.
GIVEN NAMES German 5%. *Klaus, Kurt.*

Hellmuth (222) German: variant spelling of HELMUTH.
GIVEN NAMES German 5%. *Eckhard, Erwin, Kurt.*

Hellner (133) German: variant of HILLNER.
GIVEN NAMES German 5%. *Arno, Dieter.*

Hellriegel (109) German: nickname from Middle High German *helleriegel* 'bolt to lock hell', also meaning 'the Devil' and 'a devil of a man'. Among other things, this denoted someone who played the devil in a Shrovetide play.
GIVEN NAMES German 14%. *Dieter, Ernst, Hans, Jurgen, Otto, Wolf.*

Hellstern (119) German: from German *Hellstern* 'bright star', i.e. the star of Christian faith. In some cases this was from a house name; in others it was used as a nickname for a baptized Jew.
GIVEN NAME German 6%. *Fritz.*

Hellstrom (226) Swedish (**Hellström**): ornamental name composed of the elements *häll* 'stone', 'rock' + *ström* 'river'.

GIVEN NAMES Scandinavian 19%. *Lars* (3), *Lennart* (2), *Anders*, *Mats*, *Nels*, *Nils*, *Sigfrid*, *Sven*.

Hellums (334) English: probably a variant of HELMS.

Hellweg (116) **1.** German: habitational name typical of the Ruhr region and Westphalia, from any of several places so named there; also frequent as a topographical name, especially as the name of the east-west trade route that ran north of the central German mountain range from the Rhine to the Elbe, the Hellweg, ostensibly from elements literally meaning 'light way'. However, the real etymology remains unclear; for one possibility, see HELL-WEGE. **2.** Dutch: variant of HELLWEGE or HELWIG.

GIVEN NAMES German 6%. *Gerhard*, *Kurt*.

Hellwege (125) German: habitational name from any of several places so named, from *hel*, an old word meaning 'bog', + Middle High German *weg* 'way', or a topographic name with the same meaning.

GIVEN NAMES German 5%. *Otto*, *Reinhold*.

Hellwig (552) Dutch: variant of HELWIG.

GIVEN NAMES German 7%. *Helmut* (2), *Kurt* (2), *Otto* (2), *Bernhard*, *Juergen*, *Jutta*, *Oskar*, *Wolfgang*.

Hellyer (457) English: variant spelling of HILLIER 1.

Helm (6273) **1.** English (chiefly Lancashire): topographic name for someone who lived by or worked at a rough temporary shelter for animals, Middle English *helm* (Old Norse *hjalmr*, related to the Old English and Old High German words in 2 below), or a habitational name from a minor place named Helm or Helme from this word, as for example in County Durham, Northumberland, and West Yorkshire. **2.** English, German, and Dutch: metonymic occupational name for a maker of helmets, from Middle English, Middle High German, Middle Dutch *helm*. **3.** German and Dutch: from a medieval personal name, a short form of any of the various compound names formed with *helm* 'helmet'. Compare, e.g., HELMBRECHT. **4.** Scottish: habitational name from Helme in Roxburghshire (Borders). **5.** Jewish (Ashkenazic): ornamental name from German *Helm* 'helmet'.

Helman (1294) **1.** Jewish (Ashkenazic): nickname for a person with fair hair or a light complexion, a derivative of HELLER 5. **2.** Altered spelling of German HELL-MANN. **3.** Dutch: from a Germanic personal name composed of the elements *hild* 'strife' + *man* 'man'.

Helmandollar (123) Americanized form of German **Helmenthaler**, habitational name from place called Helmenthal.

GIVEN NAME French 5%. *Gabrielle* (2).

Helmbrecht (282) German (especially Franconia and Bavaria): from a personal name composed of the elements *helm* 'hel-

met', 'protection' + *brecht* 'bright', 'illustrious'.

Helme (147) **1.** English (Cumbria and Lancashire): variant spelling of HELM 1. **2.** German: variant of HELM 2 and 3. .

Helmer (1983) **1.** South German: occupational name for a helmet-maker, from Middle High German *helm* 'helmet' + the agent suffix *-er*. **2.** German and Dutch: from a Germanic personal name composed of the elements *helm* 'helmet', 'protection' + *heri*, *hari* 'army'; or from one composed of the elements *hail* 'whole', 'sound' + *mari*, *meri* 'renowned'; or from one composed of the elements *helm* 'helmet' + *hard* 'hardy', 'brave', 'strong'. **3.** Jewish (Ashkenazic): ornamental name, a derivative of HELM.

Helmers (496) North German and Dutch: patronymic from HELMER 2.

Helmes (168) German: patronymic from HELM 3.

GIVEN NAMES German 4%. *Beate*, *Hans*, *Kurt*.

Helmich (247) German: from the Germanic personal name *Helmwig*, composed of the elements *helm* 'helmet' 'protection' + *wīg* 'fight', 'battle', 'fight'.

GIVEN NAMES German 5%. *Erwin*, *Frieda*, *Reinhold*.

Helmick (1775) German: **1.** Americanized spelling of German HELMICH. **2.** from an Old Prussian name, *Helmik*.

Helmig (217) German: variant of HELMICH.

Helming (237) **1.** North German: patronymic from HELM 3. **2.** Bavarian: habitational name from any of several places called Helming.

GIVEN NAMES German 4%. *Kurt*, *Willi*.

Helminiak (239) Polish: patronymic from the Germanic personal name *Helmin* (see HELMAN).

GIVEN NAMES Polish 6%. *Casimir*, *Zigmund*, *Zigmunt*.

Helminski (133) Polish: derivative of the Germanic personal name *Helmin* (see HELMAN) + the Polish surname suffix *-ski*.

Helmkamp (195) North German: probably a variant of **Hellenkamp**, a name composed of Middle Low German *Helle* 'hollow', 'precipitous place' + *kamp* 'enclosed field', 'domain'.

Helmke (469) North German: from a pet form of HELM 3.

GIVEN NAMES German 4%. *Beate*, *Bernd*, *Eldor*, *Otto*, *Reinhart*.

Helmle (134) South German: from a pet form of HELM 3.

GIVEN NAMES German 9%. *Alfons*, *Juergen*, *Ottmar*.

Helmlinger (139) German: habitational name for someone from any of several places called Helmlingen, for example on the Rhine opposite Strassburg.

Helmly (128) Variant of German HELMLE.

Helmreich (130) German: from the Germanic personal name *Helmrich*, composed of *helm* 'helmet' + *rīc* 'power', 'rule'.

GIVEN NAMES German 14%. *Erwin* (2), *Wolf* (2), *Ernst*, *Kurt*, *Otto*.

Helmrich (134) German: variant of HELM-REICH.

Helms (11487) **1.** English: variant of HELM 1. **2.** North German and Dutch: patronymic from HELM 2–3.

Helmstetter (254) German: habitational name for someone from any of several places called Helmstedt, especially one near Brunswick.

Helmus (134) Dutch and German: from an aphetic form of the personal name *Wilhelmus* (see WILLIAM).

Helmuth (718) German: from a Germanic personal name composed of *heil* 'wholeness' or *helm* 'helmet' + *mut* 'craving', 'mind'; compare HELWIG.

Helper (101) **1.** Jewish (Ashkenazic): see HALPERN. **2.** North German form of HELFER.

Helsel (1208) Americanized form of South German HOELZEL.

Helser (288) Americanized form of German **Hölzer** (see HOLZER).

Helseth (242) Norwegian: habitational name from any of several farmsteads, most of them named with Old Norse *Helgasetr*, *Helgusetr*, from the male personal name *Helgi* and the female personal name *Helga* respectively; both names are derived from *heilagr* 'holy', 'sacred'. In some cases, other personal names, for example *Herleifr* or *Herlaugi*, are the source of the first element, and in other cases it is derived from *hella* 'flat stone', 'flat mountain'. The second element, *-seth*, is derived from *setr* 'farmstead', 'dwelling'.

GIVEN NAMES Scandinavian 4%. *Petter*, *Thor*, *Tryg*.

Helsing (137) **1.** Norwegian: habitational name from a farmstead named Helsing. The origin of the farm name is uncertain; possibly it indicated that the occupant was someone from Helsingland in Sweden. **2.** Swedish: possibly a habitational name for someone from Helsingland (Swedish *Häsingland*). **3.** German: possibly a habitational name from Helsungen in the Harz Mountains.

GIVEN NAMES Scandinavian 12%; German 5%. *Knud*, *Lennart*, *Nils*; *Kurt* (2).

Helsley (519) Americanized form of German HOELZLE.

FOREBEARS Bearers of this name are mostly descended from Hans Jacob Helzele, usually known as Jacob Helsley Sr., who came to VA from PA in the late 1750s.

Helstrom (262) Swedish (**Hellström**): see HELLSTROM.

GIVEN NAMES German 4%. *Kurt*, *Otto*.

Helt (747) **1.** German and Dutch: variant of HELD 1. **2.** Danish: from a byname, *Helt*, meaning 'hero'.

Heltemes (109) German: unexplained.

Helton (8167) English: habitational name from Helton in Cumbria, named in Old English probably with *helde* 'slope' + *tūn* 'farmstead', 'settlement', or possibly a variant of HILTON. This is a common name in TN, KY, OH, TX, and GA.

Heltsley (240) Americanized form of German HOELZLE.

Heltzel (358) German and Jewish (Ashkenazic): Americanized spelling of HOELZEL.

Helveston (163) Probably English, a habitational name from an unidentified place.

Helvey (593) French or Americanized form of German HELWIG.

Helvie (201) Variant of HELVEY.

Helvig (113) Scandinavian: from the personal name *Helvig*, composed of the Germanic elements *hel* 'luck' + *wīg* 'war'. Compare German HELWIG.
GIVEN NAME Scandinavian 4%. *Jorgen*.

Helwig (1238) German and Dutch: from the medieval personal name *Heilwig*, *Helwig* (female and male), composed of the Germanic elements *heil* 'luck' + *wīg* 'war'.

Helzer (520) Americanized spelling of German **Hölzer** (see HOLZER).

Hem (156) Cambodian or other Southeast Asian: unexplained.
GIVEN NAMES Cambodian 11%; Other Southeast Asian 9%. *Sophany* (2), *Vuthy* (2), *Chham, Chhem, Hoeun, Somaly, Sovann; Ly* (2), *Nhong, Phan, Phon; Chea, Hong, Ong, Soeun, Sun; Sarath, Sareth*.

Heman (135) Altered spelling of German HEMANN or HEMMANN.

Hemann (379) North German: variant of HAMANN.

Hemauer (124) German: habitational name for someone from Heman near Regensburg, Bavaria.

Hemberger (300) German: habitational name for someone from any of several places called Hemberg (also in Switzerland) or Hembergen.
GIVEN NAMES German 6%. *Fritz* (2), *Helmut, Klaus, Siegfried, Wilhelm*.

Hembree (2320) **1.** Altered spelling of English **Hembr(e)y**, a variant of *Amery* with excrescent *H-* (see EMERY). **2.** Possibly a variant of German HEMBERGER. This is a common name in the southern states, notably TN and GA.

Hembrough (116) English: habitational name from Emborough in Somerset (see EMBURY).

Hemby (491) English: most probably a habitational name from a lost or unidentified place, presumably named with Old Norse *býr* 'farmstead' and an unexplained first element.

Hemenway (1122) English: variant of HEMINGWAY.

Hemeon (137) Origin unidentified.

Hemesath (129) North German: **1.** nickname for a settler on a new farm, from Middle Low German *heme* 'home', 'farm' + *sate* 'one who sits', 'settler'. **2.** variant of HEIMSOTH.

Heming (264) English and German: variant spelling of HEMMING.

Heminger (426) Variant spelling of German HEMMINGER.

Hemingway (1657) English (Yorkshire): apparently a habitational name from a lost or unidentified minor place in West Yorkshire, probably in the parish of Halifax, to judge by the distribution of early occurrences of the surname.

Hemken (128) **1.** German: patronymic from HEMME 1. **2.** German: habitational name for someone from Hemke near Osnabrück.
GIVEN NAMES German 6%. *Heinz* (2), *Otto*.

Hemker (278) German: **1.** variant of HEMME 1. **2.** variant of HEMKEN 2.
GIVEN NAME German 4%. *Fritz*.

Hemler (217) German: occupational name for a castrator of rams, from Middle High German *hamel* 'ram' + the agent suffix *-er*.

Hemm (188) German: **1.** habitational name from a place so called near Stade. **2.** variant of HEMME.

Hemmann (120) North German: from an elaborated form of the personal name HEMME.
GIVEN NAMES German 11%. *Folker* (2), *Beate, Gerhard, Reinhold*.

Hemme (332) German (Frisian): **1.** from a short form of the personal name *Hemmert* derived from a Germanic compound name formed with *heim* 'home' + *berht* 'bright', 'illustrious'. **2.** possibly a habitational name from a place called Hemme in Holstein.

Hemmelgarn (311) German (Westphalia): topographic name meaning 'Paradise', from Low German *Hemmelgarn*, from *hemmel* (standard German *Himmel*) 'heaven', 'sky' + *garn* 'garden' (equivalent of standard German *Garten*).

Hemmen (244) North German and Dutch: metronymic from the female Germanic personal name *Imma, Emma*.
GIVEN NAMES German 5%. *Frieda, Gerhard, Heinz*.

Hemmer (939) **1.** German: habitational name from Hemmern in Westphalia or Hemmen in Hesse. **2.** Dutch: from a Germanic personal name composed of *haim* 'home' + *hari, heri* 'army'.

Hemmerich (143) **1.** German: habitational name from Hemmerich in the Rhineland, or from any of several places called Hemberg or Heimberg, with dialect alteration. **2.** German and Dutch: from a Germanic personal name composed of the elements *haim* 'home' + *rīc* 'power', 'rule'.
GIVEN NAMES German 11%. *Ilse* (2), *Helmut, Kurt*.

Hemmerle (116) German: diminutive of HAMMER. In the French province of Alsace this takes the form **Hemmerlé**.

Hemmerling (182) **1.** German: diminutive of HAMMER. **2.** Dutch: derivative of HEMMERICH 2.
GIVEN NAMES German 4%. *Hartmut, Klaus*.

Hemmerly (100) Americanized spelling of German HEMMERLE.

Hemmert (276) German: possibly from the personal name *Heinprecht*, from a Germanic personal name composed with *hag* 'bush', 'woods' + *berht* 'bright', 'illustrious'.

Hemmes (116) Dutch: habitational name from a place called Hemme, named with the Germanic element *hamm, hemm* 'water meadow'.
GIVEN NAMES Dutch 7%. *Cornelis* (2), *Diederik*.

Hemming (629) **1.** English (chiefly West Midlands), Scottish, and Swedish: from the Old Norse personal name *Hemingr*, of uncertain origin, apparently related to *hemingr* 'skin on the hind legs of an animal'. **2.** German (Frisian): patronymic from HEMME 1. **3.** French: habitational name from Heming in Moselle.

Hemminger (633) German: habitational name for someone from any of several places called Hemmingen, for example near Stuttgart and near Hannover.

Hemmings (420) English: patronymic from HEMMING.

Hemmingsen (262) Danish and Norwegian: patronymic from HEMMING.

Hemmingson (169) Respelling of Swedish **Hemmingsson** or Danish and Norwegian HEMMINGSEN, patronymics from HEMMING.
GIVEN NAME Scandinavian 5%. *Lars*.

Hemmingway (149) English: variant of HEMINGWAY.

Hemond (195) French (**Hémond**): from *Haimon*, oblique case of the Germanic personal name *Haimo* (see HAMMOND).
GIVEN NAMES French 12%. *Lucien* (2), *Andre, Fernand, Gaetan, Lucienne, Marcel*.

Hemp (323) **1.** German: variant of HAMPE. **2.** English: unexplained; compare HAMP.

Hempe (100) German: variant of HAMPE.
GIVEN NAMES German 6%. *Juergen, Kurt*.

Hempel (1048) German and Jewish (Ashkenazic): variant of HAMPEL.
GIVEN NAMES German 5%. *Kurt* (3), *Otto* (2), *Ewald, Frieda, Gunther, Helmut, Ilse, Lothar, Siegfried*.

Hempen (185) Dutch: patronymic from a pet form of the Germanic personal name *Imbert*.

Hemperly (125) Americanized spelling of German **Hemperle**, from a pet form of the personal name *Haginbert*.

Hempfling (192) German: from Middle High German *henfelinc* 'linnet', probably applied as a nickname for someone thought to resemble the bird in some way or as a metonymic occupational name for a bird-catcher.

Hemphill (4460) Northern Irish, originally Scottish: habitational name from a place near Galston in Ayrshire, apparently so named from Old English *henep* 'hemp' + *hyll* 'hill'.

Hemple (116) **1.** English and Scottish: reduced form of HEMPHILL. **2.** German: variant of HEMPEL, or in some instances probably an Americanized spelling of the same name.

Hempstead (472) English: habitational name from any of various places so called, most of which were originally named with Old English *hāmstede* or *hæmstede* 'homestead'. One Hempstead in Norfolk derives its name from Old English *hænep* 'hemp' + *stede* 'place', while Hempsted in Gloucestershire was originally 'high homestead' (Old English *hēah* + *hāmstede*).

Hemric (167) Altered form of German HEMMERICH.

Hemrich (105) Variant of German HEMMERICH.

Hemrick (186) Altered form of German HEMMERICH.

Hemry (152) Perhaps an altered form of German HEMMERICH.
GIVEN NAME German 4%. *Kurt.*

Hemsath (126) German: habitational name from Heimsath in Westphalia, an abandoned settlement (see HEIMSOTH).
GIVEN NAMES German 8%. *Armin, Klaus, Otto.*

Hemsley (314) English: habitational name from either of two places in North Yorkshire called Helmsley. The names are of different etymologies: the one near Rievaulx Abbey is from the Old English personal name *Helm* + Old English *lēah* 'wood', 'clearing', whereas Upper Helmsley, near York, is from the Old English personal name *Hemele* + Old English *ēg* 'island', and had the form *Hemelsey* till at least the 14th century.

Hemstreet (311) Americanized form of Dutch **Heemstraat**, a habitational name from a place named in Dutch with *heem* 'farmyard' + *straat* 'street', 'road'.

Hemsworth (118) English (Yorkshire): habitational name from Hemsworth in West Yorkshire, named from an unattested Old English personal name, *Hymel*, + *worð* 'enclosure'.

Henagan (117) Irish: variant spelling of HENEGHAN.
GIVEN NAMES Irish 7%. *Murphy, Seumas.*

Henager (110) Variant of German HENNIGER.
GIVEN NAME French 6%. *Patrice* (2).

Henao (253) Spanish: habitational name from the Belgian province of Hainault. In the 16th century this province was part of the area of the Netherlands controlled by Spain.
GIVEN NAMES Spanish 53%. *Jose* (6), *Luis* (6), *Carlos* (5), *Gustavo* (5), *Jairo* (5), *Jorge* (4), *Bernardo* (3), *Francisco* (3),

Javier (3), *Juan* (3), *Adriana* (2), *Alfonso* (2); *Dario* (2), *Carlo, Silvio.*

Henard (230) French (**Hénard**) and German: from the Germanic personal name *Hainhard*, composed of the elements *hagin* 'enclosure', 'safe place' + *hard* 'strong', 'hardy'.

Henault (375) French and Swiss French (**Hénault**): from the Germanic personal name *Haginwald*, composed of the elements *hagin* (see HENARD) + *wald* 'rule'.
GIVEN NAMES French 18%. *Armand* (5), *Andre* (2), *Emile* (2), *Lucien* (2), *Martial* (2), *Pierre* (2), *Camille, Fernand, Laurier, Monique, Normand, Philippe.*

Henbest (104) English (Hampshire): unexplained.

Hence (158) **1.** Americanized spelling of German HENZ. **2.** English: possibly a variant of HINCE.
GIVEN NAME French 4%. *Andre.*

Hench (326) English: possibly a variant of HINCH.

Henchey (114) Irish (County Clare): Anglicized form of Gaelic **Ó hAonghusa** (see HENNESSY).

Henck (141) German: from a reduced form of HEINRICH.

Henckel (195) German: from a pet form of HENCK.

Hency (114) Possibly an Americanized spelling of German HENZE.

Hendee (321) Variant spelling of HENDY.

Hendel (488) **1.** German and Dutch: variant of HANDEL. **2.** Jewish (Ashkenazic): variant of HANDLER. **3.** Jewish (Ashkenazic): from the female personal name *Hendl*, a pet form of HANNA.
GIVEN NAMES Jewish 5%; German 4%. *Menachem* (2), *Miriam, Mordechai, Shaul, Zevi; Hans* (4), *Rudi* (2), *Hanni, Inge, Konrad, Kurt.*

Henderlight (109) Americanized form of German **Hinterleitner**, a topographic name for someone who lived 'at the farther slope (into the valley)', 'behind the mountain spur', from Middle High German *hinter* 'behind' + *līte* 'mountain spur', 'slope' (see LEITNER).
FOREBEARS Bearers of this surname trace their ancestry to Johann Caspar Hinterleitner (1709–80), who emigrated from Dietfurt, Bavaria, Germany, to Marborough township, Montgomery Co., PA.

Hendershot (2040) Americanized form of German **Hinderschied**, a habitational name from an unidentified place (probably in the Middle Rhine area).
FOREBEARS Bearers of this name are descended from Michael Henneschied (1674–1749), who came to New York aboard the *Lyon* from Munich, Germany, and settled in New Germantown (now Oldwick), NJ.

Hendershott (486) Of German origin: see HENDERSHOT.

Henderson (69047) Scottish and northern Irish: patronymic from *Hendry*, a chiefly Scottish variant of the personal name HENRY 1. Some Scottish families with this name have ancestors whose name was *Henryson.*

Hendler (430) German and Jewish (Ashkenazic): occupational name for a merchant or trader, Middle High German *hendeler*, German *Händler.*
GIVEN NAMES Jewish 6%. *Sol* (3), *Chaim, Chana, Hyman, Mayer, Shaya, Zvi.*

Hendley (1203) English: apparently a habitational name, probably a variant of HENLEY or HAN(D)LEY.

Hendon (1101) English: habitational name from places so named in County Durham and Middlesex. The former was named with Old English *hind* 'hind', 'female deer' + *denu* 'valley', and the latter with Old English *hēan* (dative case of *hēah* 'high') + *dūn* 'hill'.

Hendren (1354) Scottish: variant spelling of HENDRON.

Hendrich (162) German: from the personal name *Hendrich*, a variant of HEINRICH (see HENRY).

Hendrick (2978) Dutch, Scottish, and English: from the personal name *Hendrick* (see HENRY).

Hendricks (15083) Dutch, German, and English: patronymic from the personal name HENDRICK.

Hendricksen (362) German: variant spelling of HENDRIKSEN.
GIVEN NAMES Scandinavian 5%; German 4%. *Alf, Erik; Bernhard, Erwin.*

Hendrickson (11922) **1.** Americanized spelling of Dutch HENDRIKSEN. **2.** Scottish and English: patronymic from HENDRICK.

Hendrickx (134) Dutch and North German: patronymic from the personal name *Hendrik* (see HENRY 1).

Hendrie (247) Scottish: variant of HENRY 1.

Hendriks (230) Dutch and North German: patronymic from the personal name *Hendrik* (see HENRY 1).
GIVEN NAMES Dutch 6%. *Geert, Gerrit, Hendrik, Klaas.*

Hendriksen (152) Dutch, German (northwest), Danish, and Norwegian: patronymic from the personal name *Hendrik* (see HENRY 1).

Hendrix (12233) Dutch and German (northwest): patronymic from the personal name *Hendrik* (see HENRY 1).

Hendrixson (399) Altered spelling of Dutch HENDRICKSEN.

Hendron (158) English and Scottish (of Norman origin): from a derivative of HENRY 1 found predominantly in Ireland, in County Armagh.

Hendry (2180) English, Scottish, Dutch, and French: variant of HENRY 1. In Scotland this surname is common in the Ayr and Fife districts; in northern Ireland it is usually from the Scottish variant **Hendrie**, though some examples of the name were originally as at HENRY 3.

Hendryx (402) Variant spelling of HENDRIX.

Hendy (237) English (mainly West Country): nickname for a pleasant and affable man, from Middle English *hende* 'courteous', 'kind', 'gentle'. *Hendy* was also sometimes used as a personal name in the Middle Ages and some examples of the surname may derive from this rather than from the nickname. The surname is also found in Ireland.

Henegar (595) Variant of German HENNIGER. This name is found predominantly in TN.

Heneghan (458) Irish: Anglicized form of Gaelic **Ó hEidhneacháin** 'descendant of *Eidhneachán*', a personal name of uncertain origin. Heneghan is an important family name in County Mayo.
GIVEN NAMES Irish 9%. *Brendan* (3), *Liam*, *Padraic*, *Roisin*.

Henehan (239) Irish: variant of HENEGHAN.
GIVEN NAME Irish 5%. *Brendan*.

Henery (212) Irish: variant of HENRY 2.

Henes (203) Americanized spelling of German HEINZ.
GIVEN NAMES German 4%. *Ernst*, *Erwin*, *Ulrich*.

Heney (179) **1.** Irish: variant spelling of HEANEY. **2.** English: variant of HENNEY.
GIVEN NAMES Irish 4%. *Brigid*, *Niall*.

Heng (548) **1.** Cambodian or other Southeast Asian: unexplained. **2.** German: from a short form of HEINRICH. See also HENK.
GIVEN NAMES Southeast Asian 27%. *Kheng* (2), *Meng* (2), *Po* (2), *Seng* (2), *Chak*, *Chhay*, *Eng*, *Fook*, *Heang*, *Heng*, *Hieng*, *Ho*; *Huy* (3), *Leang* (3), *Ly* (3), *Mong* (2), *Sophal* (2), *Thong* (2), *Thy* (2), *Duong*, *Kieu*, *Kim Seng*, *Ky*, *Lac*.

Hengel (315) **1.** German: metonymic occupational name for a maker of handles, hooks, or hangers, from Middle High German *hengel* 'handle'. **2.** German: from a pet form of the personal name HENG. **3.** Shortened form of Dutch **van Hengel**, a habitational name for someone from Hengel, near Houthalen, in the Belgian province of Limburg.

Hengen (156) German and Dutch: patronymic from the personal name HENG.

Hengesbach (110) German: variant of **Hengsbach**, habitational name from a farm near Siegen, North Rhine-Westphalia.

Henggeler (153) Swiss German: from a pet form of HENG.

Hengst (432) German: metonymic occupational name for someone who worked with horses, or nickname for a lustful man or one who liked to boast about his sexual conquests, from Middle High German *heng(e)st* 'stallion', also 'gelding'.
GIVEN NAMES German 4%. *Erwin* (4), *Arno*.

Henig (175) Jewish (Ashkenazic) and German: variant of HOENIG.
GIVEN NAMES Jewish 7%. *Shloime*, *Sol*, *Yair*, *Yitshak*, *Yosef*.

Henigan (161) Irish: variant of HENEGHAN.

Henige (102) German: probably an altered spelling of **Hönicke**, from a shortened form of a Germanic personal name formed with *Hun* 'Hun'.

Heninger (322) German: variant spelling of HENNINGER.

Henington (115) English: habitational name, possibly a variant of **Hannington**, which is from places so named in Hampshire, Northamptonshire, or Wiltshire. The first and second are named from the Old English personal name *Hana* + -*ing*- denoting association with + *tūn* 'farmstead', 'settlement', while the one in Wiltshire is from Old English *hanena*, genitive plural of *hana* 'cock', 'male bird' or the Old English personal name *Hana* + *dūn* 'hill'.

Henion (237) Variant of Welsh HENNION.

Henjum (150) Norwegian: habitational name from a farmstead in Sogn, western Norway, so named from Old Norse *Heinvinjar*, a compound of *hein* 'whetstone' + *vinjar*, plural of *vin* 'meadow'.
GIVEN NAME Scandinavian 4%. *Nels*.

Henk (388) German and Dutch: variant of HENKE.

Henke (3193) **1.** German: from a pet form of the personal name HEINRICH. **2.** Dutch: variant of **Hanke**, a pet form of JOHANN.
GIVEN NAMES German 4%. *Kurt* (8), *Otto* (6), *Erwin* (3), *Gerhard* (3), *Heinz* (2), *Bernhard*, *Elke*, *Erhard*, *Franz*, *Fritz*, *Gerhardt*, *Gerhart*.

Henkel (2235) German: from a pet form of the personal name HEINRICH.
GIVEN NAMES German 5%. *Kurt* (5), *Hans* (3), *Wolfgang* (3), *Fritz* (2), *Klaus* (2), *Othmar* (2), *Otto* (2), *Ralf* (2), *Rudi* (2), *Bernd*, *Bodo*, *Dietrich*.

Henkelman (217) German (**Henkelmann**): pet form of HENKEL.

Henkels (211) German: patronymic from HENKEL.

Henken (235) North German and Dutch: patronymic from HENKE.

Henkes (205) Dutch: patronymic from a short form of HENNEKE.
GIVEN NAME French 4%. *Andre*.

Henkin (233) **1.** English: from a pet form of HENN 1. **2.** Dutch: from a pet form of HENNEKE. **3.** Jewish (eastern Ashkenazic): metronymic from *Khenke* (a pet form of the Yiddish female personal name *Khane*; see HANNA 2) + the Slavic possessive suffix -*in*.
GIVEN NAMES Jewish 8%. *Doron* (2), *Hyman*.

Henkle (456) Americanized spelling of German **Henkel**, a pet form of HENKE.

Henle (253) German: from a pet form of HANS or *Händel* (see HANDEL 1).
GIVEN NAMES German 4%. *Ernst*, *Kurt*.

Henley (7032) **1.** English: habitational name from any of the various places so called. Most, for example those in Oxfordshire, Suffolk, and Warwickshire, are named with Old English *héan* (the weak dative case of *hēah* 'high', originally used after a preposition and article) + Old English *lēah* 'wood', 'clearing'. Others, for example one near Ludlow in Shropshire, have as their first element Old English *henn* 'hen', 'wild bird'. Others still, for example those in Somerset and Surrey, are ambiguous between the two possibilities. **2.** In Ireland, Henley is used for HENNELLY, and sometimes for HANLEY. **3.** Possibly an Americanized spelling of German HENLE.

Henline (577) Americanized spelling of German **Henlein**, from a pet form of the personal names *Johann(es)* (see JOHN) or HEINRICH.

Henly (142) English: variant spelling of HENLEY.

Henman (170) English: probably an occupational name for someone who looked after poultry, from Middle English *hen(n)* 'hen' + *man* 'man', though in instances it may be a nickname from Middle English *hende* 'noble', 'courteous' + *man*.

Henn (1430) English (chiefly West Midlands): **1.** from the Middle English personal name *Henn(e)*, a short form of HENRY. **2.** from Middle English *hen(e)* 'hen' (Old English *henn*, related to *hana* 'cock'), applied as a metonymic occupational name for a keeper or seller of poultry or as a nickname, perhaps for a fussy man. **3.** Dutch: from a short form of the personal name *Johannes* (see JOHN); or a variant of HEIN. **4.** German: variant of HENNE 1 and 3.
GIVEN NAMES German 5%. *Helmut* (2), *Otto* (2), *Siegfried* (2), *Ulrike* (2), *Aloysius*, *Bernhard*, *Heinz*, *Hermann*, *Herta*, *Jurgen*, *Kurt*, *Manfred*.

Henne (828) **1.** North German (Hesse): from a pet form of HANS. **2.** German: nickname or metonymic occupational name for a poultry keeper from Middle High German *henne* 'hen', 'chicken'. **3.** German: from a pet form of the personal name HEINRICH. **4.** Dutch: variant of HENN 3.

Henneberg (141) German and Dutch: habitational name from any of several places so named.
GIVEN NAMES German 10%. *Beate*, *Ewald*, *Kurt*, *Ulrich*.

Henneberger (163) German: habitational name for someone from a place called HENNEBERG.
GIVEN NAMES German 7%. *Armin* (2), *Fritz*, *Gerhard*.

Henneberry (312) Americanized form of German and Dutch HENNEBERG.

Hennecke (119) Variant of North German and Dutch HENNEKE.
GIVEN NAMES German 10%; Scandinavian 4%. *Hans* (2), *Gerhardt*, *Juergen*.

Hennegan (111) Irish: variant spelling of HANNIGAN.

Henneke (266) **1.** North German and Dutch: from a pet form of HANS. **2.** Dutch: from a pet form of the personal name *Hendrik* (see HENRY).

Hennelly (264) Irish: Anglicized form of Gaelic **Ó hlonnghaile**, from a variant (without initial *F-*) of the personal name *Fionnghal*, which gave rise to **Ó Fionnghaile** (see FENNELLY). The surname is common in County Mayo.

Henneman (561) **1.** Dutch: from a pet form of the personal name HANS, or a derivative of the personal name *Hendrik* (see HENRY 1). **2.** Variant of German HENNEMANN.

Hennemann (128) German: elaborated form of the personal name HENNE 1.
GIVEN NAMES German 12%. *Erhard, Erna, Guenter, Kurt, Otto.*

Hennen (982) **1.** North German: patronymic from HENNE 1. **2.** Dutch: from a pet form of HENN 3.

Henner (167) **1.** English: habitational name from Hennor in Herefordshire or Heanor in Derbyshire, named in Old English with *hēan* (dative cases of *hēah* 'high') + *ofer* 'ridge'. **2.** German: patronymic from HENNE 1 and 3 or a variant of HENNE 2. **3.** German: habitational name from Hänner in Säckingen, Henne in Saxony, or Hennen in Westphalia.

Hennes (479) Dutch: patronymic from HENN 3.

Hennesey (100) Irish: variant of HENNESSY.

Henness (144) Probably an altered spelling of Dutch HENNES or English HENNIS.

Hennessee (514) Variant spelling of Irish HENNESSY.

Hennessey (3270) Irish: variant spelling of HENNESSY.
GIVEN NAMES Irish 5%. *Brendan* (2), *Brigid, Niamh, Thomas Patrick.*

Hennessy (3683) Irish: reduced form of **O'Hennessy**, an Anglicized form of Gaelic **Ó hAonghusa** 'descendant of *Aonghus*' (see ANGUS, and compare MCGINNIS).
GIVEN NAMES Irish 5%. *Kieran* (3), *Declan* (2), *Brendan, Dermot, Donal, Fidelma, Fintan, Liam, Mairead, Sean Patrick.*

Hennesy (148) Irish: variant spelling of HENNESSY.

Henney (381) English: habitational name from Great and Little Henny in Essex, named with Old English *hēan* (dative case of *hēah* 'high') + *ēg* 'island', 'land partly surrounded by water'.

Hennick (186) Variant spelling of North German and Dutch HENNIG.

Hennies (101) North German and Dutch: patronymic from the personal name HENNIG or HANS.

Hennig (991) German and Dutch: from a local form of HANS or HEINRICH.
GIVEN NAMES German 9%. *Kurt* (4), *Berthold* (2), *Fritz* (2), *Gerhard* (2), *Guenter* (2), *Ralf* (2), *Dietrich, Erwin, Guenther, Gunter, Heinz, Helmut.*

Hennigan (1000) Irish (County Mayo): variant spelling of HENEGHAN.

Hennigar (189) Slavic: variant of German HENNIGER.

Henniger (109) German: variant of HENNINGER.

Hennigh (152) Dutch and North German: variant of HENNIG.
GIVEN NAME German 5%. *Kurt* (2).

Henning (6474) **1.** North German, Dutch, and Danish: from a pet form of HANS or HEINRICH. **2.** English: in part the German, Dutch, or Danish name (see 1), but possibly in some cases a variant of Scottish HANNING. **3.** Norwegian: habitational name from a farm in Trøndelag. The first element is of uncertain origin, possibly from *hein* 'whetstone'; the second element is from Old Norse *vin* 'meadow'. **4.** Swedish: probably of the same origin as 1.

Henninger (1531) German: **1.** habitational name for someone from places called Henning or Heiningen, in Baden-Württemberg and Franconia. **2.** German: derivative of the personal name *Henning* (see HENNING 1).

Hennings (1114) North German and Danish: patronymic from HENNING 1.

Henningsen (723) North German, Danish, and Norwegian: patronymic from HENNING 1.
GIVEN NAMES German 5%. *Kurt* (2), *Otto* (2), *Gerhard, Guenter, Heinrich, Ingo, Klaus, Manfred.*

Henningson (125) Respelling of HENNINGSEN or the Swedish cognate **Henningsson**.
GIVEN NAMES Scandinavian 9%; German 4%. *Erik, Sven; Kurt.*

Hennington (271) Possibly of English origin: a variant of **Hannington**.

Hennion (122) **1.** Welsh: hypercorrected spelling of **Ennion**, a variant spelling of EYNON. **2.** Dutch: from an altered form of the personal names *Hans* (see JOHN) or HENNING.

Hennis (410) **1.** Possibly a hypercorrected form of Irish ENNIS. **2.** Dutch: patronymic from HENNIG.

Hennon (230) Dutch: variant of HANNON 4. This name is found chiefly in PA.

Henny (131) **1.** German and Swiss German: variant of HENNIG. **2.** French form of German HENNIG.

Henretty (118) Scottish: variant of HANRATTY.

Henri (225) French: variant of HENRY 1.

GIVEN NAMES French 12%. *Eloi, Gilles, Hermance, Hermite, Jacques, Jean Michel, Laurier, Luckner.*

Henrich (962) North German and Dutch: from the personal name (see HEINRICH).

Henrichs (975) North German and Dutch: patronymic from HENRICH.

Henrichsen (297) Danish and Norwegian: patronymic from the personal name *Henrich* (see HENRY).

Henrick (159) **1.** Dutch: variant of HENDRICK. **2.** Irish: Anglicized form of Gaelic **Mac Annraic**, a patronymic from a Norse personal name cognate with HENRY. **3.** Altered spelling of Polish **Henryk**, from the personal name, Polish form of HENRY.

Henricks (768) Scottish: patronymic from the personal name *Henrick*, an Americanized spelling of the Scandinavian name *Henrik* (see HENRY 1).

Henricksen (412) Altered spelling of HENRIKSEN.
GIVEN NAMES German 4%. *Kurt* (2), *Gerhard.*

Henrickson (852) Americanized spelling of Swedish **Henriksson** or Danish and Norwegian HENRIKSEN.

Henrie (688) Scottish: variant spelling of HENRY 1.
GIVEN NAMES French 4%. *Camille, Collette, Jean Claude, Pierre, Valmond.*

Henriksen (1200) Danish and Norwegian: patronymic from the personal name *Henrik* (see HENRY 1).
GIVEN NAMES Scandinavian 12%; German 4%. *Lars* (4), *Erik* (3), *Niels* (3), *Sven* (2), *Anders, Bente, Bjorg, Gunner, Iver, Ketil, Knud, Lief; Kurt* (6), *Hans* (2), *Hans Peter, Inge, Margrethe, Math, Philo.*

Henrikson (674) Probably a respelling of HENRIKSEN, or of the Swedish cognate **Henriksson**.
GIVEN NAMES Scandinavian 7%. *Erik* (5), *Bertel, Lars, Sig, Thor.*

Henrion (116) French: from a pet form of the personal name *Henri* (see HENRY 1).
GIVEN NAME French 6%. *Francois.*

Henriques (726) Portuguese: patronymic from the personal name *Henrique*, Portuguese form of HENRY.
GIVEN NAMES Spanish 18%; Portuguese 14%. *Jose* (15), *Manuel* (13), *Carlos* (4), *Luis* (4), *Fernando* (3), *Mario* (3), *Adolfo* (2), *Adriano* (2), *Americo* (2), *Augusto* (2), *Julio* (2), *Adelino; Joao* (4), *Joaquim* (4), *Aderito, Afonso, Agostinho, Duarte, Henrique, Paulo.*

Henriquez (1175) Spanish (**Henríquez**): variant of **Enríquez** (see ENRIQUEZ).
GIVEN NAMES Spanish 51%. *Jose* (49), *Juan* (22), *Luis* (20), *Carlos* (16), *Manuel* (14), *Ana* (13), *Francisco* (11), *Rafael* (10), *Mario* (9), *Miguel* (9), *Ricardo* (7), *Pedro* (6).

Henry (53692) **1.** English and French: from a Germanic personal name composed of the elements *haim*, *heim* 'home' + *rīc* 'power', 'ruler', introduced to England by the Normans in the form *Henri*. During the Middle Ages this name became enormously popular in England and was borne by eight kings. Continental forms of the personal name were equally popular throughout Europe (German *Heinrich*, French *Henri*, Italian *Enrico* and *Arrigo*, Czech *Jindřich*, etc.). As an American family name, the English form *Henry* has absorbed patronymics and many other derivatives of this ancient name in continental European languages. (For forms, see Hanks and Hodges 1988.) In the period in which the majority of English surnames were formed, a common English vernacular form of the name was *Harry*, hence the surnames HARRIS (southern) and HARRISON (northern). Official documents of the period normally used the Latinized form *Henricus*. In medieval times, English *Henry* absorbed an originally distinct Old English personal name that had *hagan* 'hawthorn'. Compare HAIN 2 as its first element, and there has also been confusion with **Amery**. **2.** Irish: Anglicized form of Gaelic **Ó hInnéirghe** 'descendant of *Innéirghe*', a byname based on *éirghe* 'arising'. **3.** Irish: Anglicized form of Gaelic **Mac Éinrí** or **Mac Einrí**, patronymics from the personal names *Éinrí*, *Einrí*, Irish forms of *Henry*. It is also found as a variant of MCENERY. **4.** Jewish (American): Americanized form of various like-sounding Ashkenazic Jewish names.

FOREBEARS A bearer of the name from the Touraine region of France is documented in Quebec city in 1667. Another (also called LAFORGE), from the Champagne region, is documented in Montreal in 1710. Other secondary surnames include **Berranger**, **Labori**, LIVERNOIS, **Madou**.

Hensarling (252) Americanized spelling of German *Henzerling*, a derivative of HENTZ or of HEINZERLING.

Hensch (185) German: from a pet form of the personal name *Johannes* (see HENSCHEL).

GIVEN NAMES German 5%. *Erwin* (2), *Kurt* (2).

Henschel (706) German and Jewish (Ashkenazic): from a pet form of the personal name *Johannes* (see JOHN), or in some cases from a pet form of HEINRICH.

GIVEN NAMES German 4%. *Erwin* (2), *Horst* (2), *Dieter*, *Fritz*, *Gerhard*, *Guenter*, *Inge*, *Kurt*.

Henschen (303) German: patronymic from HENSCH.

Hense (180) North German and Dutch: variant of HANS.

GIVEN NAMES German 7%. *Ernst*, *Fritz*, *Kurt*.

Hensel (2107) German and Jewish (Ashkenazic): from a pet form of the personal name HANS.

GIVEN NAMES German 4%. *Otto* (4), *Kurt* (3); *Klaus* (2), *Manfred* (2), *Arno*, *Dieter*, *Erwin*, *Ewald*, *Fritz*, *Hans*, *Helmut*, *Johannes*.

Henseler (148) German: variant of HENSLER.

GIVEN NAMES German 7%. *Udo* (2), *Fritz*, *Gerd*.

Hensell (120) English: **1.** habitational name from Hensall in North Yorkshire, originally named with the unattested Old English personal name *Hepīn* or Old Scandinavian *Hepinn* + Old English *halh* 'nook'. **2.** Huguenot surname, of unexplained origin, which was taken to England by a Protestant refugee who fled France after the Massacre of St. Bartholomew's Day (24 August 1572) and settled in Newcastle-upon-Tyne.

Hensen (430) Dutch, North German, and Danish: patronymic from the personal names HANS or HEINRICH.

Henshall (130) English: variant of HENSHAW.

Henshaw (1815) English (mainly north central England): **1.** habitational name from a place in Northumberland, so called from the genitive case of the Old English personal name *Heðīn* (from a short form of the rare compound names formed with *hǣð* 'heath' as the first element) + Old English *halh* 'nook', 'recess'. **2.** habitational name from a place in the parish of Prestbury, Cheshire, and from a lost place in southeastern Lancashire, both named from Middle English *hen* 'hen' + *shaw* 'wood'. The name *de Henneshagh* occurs at Rochdale as early as 1325.

Henslee (727) English: variant spelling of HENSLEY.

Hensler (896) German: from a derivative of the personal name HANS.

Hensley (16956) English: **1.** probably a habitational name from either of two places in Devon: Hensley in East Worlington, which is named with the Old English personal name *Hēahmund* + Old English *lēah* '(woodland) clearing', or Hensleigh in Tiverton, which is named from Old English *hengest* 'stallion' (or the Old English personal name *Hengest*) + *lēah*. **2.** possibly also a variant of HEMSLEY.

Henslin (108) Origin uncertain. Possibly a variant of Irish HESLIN.

Henson (15888) **1.** English: patronymic from the personal name *Henn(e)*, a short form of HENRY 1, *Hayne* (see HAIN 2), or HENDY. **2.** Irish: Anglicized form of Gaelic **Ó hAmhsaigh** (see HAMPSON 2).

Hentges (698) Dutch: patronymic from a short form of the personal name *Hendrik* (see HENRY 1), with the diminutive ending *-tje*.

Henthorn (765) English (Lancashire): unexplained.

Henthorne (352) English: unexplained. Compare HENTHORN.

Henton (592) English: habitational name from a place so called, probably either the one in Oxfordshire, which is named from Old English *hēan*, the weak dative case of *hēah* 'high' (originally used after a preposition and article), + Old English *tūn* 'enclosure', 'settlement', or the one in Somerset, which is from Old English *henn* 'hen' (perhaps a byname) + *tūn*. The surname, however, is now most common in Leicestershire and Nottinghamshire, and could be a variant of HINTON.

Hentschel (473) German: variant of HENSCHEL.

GIVEN NAMES German 15%. *Helmut* (5), *Fritz* (3), *Gerhard* (3), *Erwin* (2), *Hans* (2), *Kurt* (2), *Rainer* (2), *Dieter*, *Gunther*, *Heinz*, *Horst*, *Lutz*.

Hentz (635) German: from a dialect pet form of the personal names HEINRICH or HANS.

Hentze (111) German: from a dialect pet form of the personal names HEINRICH or HANS.

Henwood (430) English: habitational name from any of various places so named, as for example Henwood in Cornwall, in Linkinhorne parish, which is named from Old English *henn* 'hen', 'wild bird' + *wudu* 'wood', or Hen Wood in Wootton, Oxfordshire (formerly in Berkshire), which is named from Old English *hīwan* 'religious community' (genitive plural *hīgna*) + *wudu*.

Henz (110) German: variant of HENTZ.

GIVEN NAME German 4%. *Siegfried*.

Henze (646) North German and Dutch: from a pet form of the personal name HEINRICH (Dutch *Hendrik*) or from a variant of HANS.

GIVEN NAMES German 8%. *Kurt* (5), *Dieter* (2), *Fritz* (2), *Gerhardt*, *Heinrich*, *Heinz*, *Juergen*, *Matthias*.

Henzel (196) **1.** German: from a pet form of either HEINRICH (in part an altered spelling of an eastern German pet form, *Heintschel*) or *Johannes* (see JOHN). **2.** German: variant of HENDEL. **3.** Jewish (Ashkenazic): variant spelling of HENSEL.

Henzler (232) South German: derivative of HENZE, or equivalent of HENSLER.

GIVEN NAMES German 4%. *Kurt*, *Manfred*.

Heo (130) Korean: variant of Hŏ (see HO).

GIVEN NAMES Korean 83%. *Yong* (5), *Young* (4), *Nam* (3), *Sang* (3), *Chul* (2), *Chung* (2), *Jeong* (2), *Joon* (2), *Jung* (2), *Kyun* (2), *Kyung* (2), *Sun* (2), *Boksoon*, *Choon*, *Chung Ho*, *Eun Joo*, *Hoon*, *Hye Jung*, *Inchul*, *Jaeyoung*.

Heon (227) French (**Héon**): habitational name from a place called Eon in Burgundy.

GIVEN NAMES French 11%. *Andre*, *Emile*,

Laurette, Marcel, Normand, Raoul, Veronique.

Hepburn (1154) Northern English and Scottish: habitational name from HEBRON, or Hebburn in County Durham, so named from Old English *hēah* 'high' + *byrgen* 'burial mound', 'tumulus'.

Hepfer (193) Altered spelling of German **Höpfer** (see HOPFER).

Hephner (139) Altered spelling, under classical influence, of German and Jewish HEFFNER.

Hepker (184) Probably an altered spelling of **Höpcker** (see HOPKE).

Hepler (1725) Variant spelling of German HEPPLER.

Hepner (1196) German and Jewish (Ashkenazic): variant of HEPPNER.

Hepp (896) German: variant of HEPPE.
GIVEN NAMES German 4%. *Hans* (2), *Otto* (2), *Siegfried* (2), *Ernst, Ewald, Gerhard, Helmut, Johann, Rudi, Wilhelm.*

Heppe (238) German and Dutch: metonymic occupational name for a vineyard laborer, from Middle High German *hepe, heppe* 'curved knife used to cut grapes from the vine'.
GIVEN NAMES German 5%. *Erwin, Hans, Kurt, Wilhelm.*

Hepper (166) South German: from an agent noun based on Middle High German *hepe, heppe* 'curved knife or hook for cutting grapes from the vine', an occupational name for a vineyard laborer or for someone who made such implements.

Heppler (253) South German: occupational name for a vineyard laborer or a maker of implements for cutting grapes from the vine (see HEPPER).
GIVEN NAME German 4%. *Kurt.*

Heppner (636) **1.** German and Jewish (Ashkenazic): occupational name for a dealer in hops, variant of HOEPPNER. **2.** German: occupational name for a vineyard worker or for a maker of implements for cutting grapes from the vine (see HEPPER).

Hepting (100) German: habitational name from a place called Hepting (formerly Ewatingen).
GIVEN NAME German 7%. *Kurt* (2).

Hepworth (618) English (Yorkshire): habitational name from places so named, of which there is one West Yorkshire and another in Suffolk, both probably deriving their name from an Old English personal name *Heppa* + *worð* 'enclosure'. The surname is still found mainly in Yorkshire, so it seems that the first place is the more likely source of the surname.

Her (1007) **1.** Korean: variant of **Hŏ** (see HO). **2.** Laotian: unexplained. **3.** German and Jewish (Ashkenazic): variant spelling of HERR.
GIVEN NAMES Korean 45%; Other Southeast Asian 30%. *Yang* (9), *Chang* (8), *Chong* (8), *Pao* (20), *Vang* (16), *Chia* (14), *Chai*

(12), *Chue* (11), *Kao* (11), *Pang* (11), *Tong* (11), *Kou* (10), *Shoua* (10), *Neng* (9), *Yeng* (9), *Tou* (9), *Seng* (8), *Xai* (8), *Yee* (8), *Cheng* (7); *Toua* (8), *Blong* (7), *Yer* (7), *Youa* (7); *Mai* (8), *Dang* (5), *Long* (4), *Thao* (4), *Bao* (3), *Kha* (3), *Pha* (3), *Mang* (2), *Cao, Da, Dao, Khia.*

Herald (1387) English: variant of HAROLD 1 and 2.

Herard (105) French (**Hérard**): from a Germanic personal name composed of *heri* 'army' + *hard* 'strong', 'hardy'.
GIVEN NAMES French 25%. *Serge* (2), *Etienne, Gesner, Jean Michel, Maxime, Monique, Patrice, Pierre.*

Heras (150) Spanish: unexplained.
GIVEN NAMES Spanish 53%. *Jose* (6), *Arturo* (3), *Carlos* (3), *Jaime* (3), *Fernando* (2), *Jesus* (2), *Luis* (2), *Miguel* (2), *Sergio* (2), *Adolfo, Adriana, Alberto; Antonio, Cecilio, Filiberto, Marco.*

Heraty (124) Irish: variant of HARRITY.
GIVEN NAMES Irish 11%. *Cathal, Kieran.*

Herb (1174) **1.** South German: nickname for a harsh or rough person, from Middle High German *herb* 'severe', 'harsh'. **2.** German: from the personal name *Herpo*, a pet form of HERBERT.

Herbaugh (119) Americanized form of German HARBACH.

Herbeck (198) Belgian or French (**Herbecq(ue)**): habitational name from places called Herbeek in the Belgian provinces of Antwerp and Brabant, or from Herbecq, Herbecque, and Herbecques in Pas-de-Calais, France.
FOREBEARS A Herbecq from Flanders is documented in Quebec city in 1698.

Herbel (271) German: from a pet form of the Germanic personal name *Herbord*, composed of the elements *heri, hari* 'army' + *bord* 'shield rim', 'shield'.

Herber (769) German and Dutch: variant of HERBERT.

Herberg (281) German and Dutch: metonymic occupational name for a keeper of a lodging house, from Middle High German *herberge*, Dutch *herberg* 'inn', 'hostel'.

Herberger (313) German: occupational name for a keeper of a lodging house, from Middle High German *herberge* + agent suffix *-er.*

Herbers (240) German: patronymic from HERBERT.

Herbert (8899) **1.** German, Dutch, English, and French: from a Germanic personal name composed of the elements *heri, hari* 'army' + *berht* 'bright', 'famous'. In Britain, this Old French name, introduced by the Normans, reinforced the less common Old English cognate *Herebeorht*. The surname was taken to Ireland after the Anglo-Norman invasion and in the 16th century. **2.** Jewish (Ashkenazic): from the German personal name.

FOREBEARS This is the name of a great Welsh family, earls of Pembroke, who are descended from William Herbert (*d.* 1469).

Herbertson (107) English: patronymic from the personal name HERBERT.

Herbig (401) German and Dutch: variant of HERWIG.
GIVEN NAMES German 4%. *Hannelore, Jodel, Othmar.*

Herbin (224) French: from a pet form of HERBERT.

Herbison (239) English (northern Ireland): patronymic from a pet form of HERBERT.

Herbold (465) German and Dutch: from a Germanic personal name composed of the elements *heri, hari* 'army' + *bald* 'bold', 'brave'.

Herbolsheimer (113) German: habitational name for someone from either of two places called Herbolzheim, in Baden and Bavaria.
GIVEN NAMES German 5%. *Kurt, Lorenz.*

Herbst (3529) **1.** German: nickname from Middle High German *herb(e)st* 'harvest'. The modern German word *Herbst* has come to mean 'Fall', the time of year when the harvest takes place. The exact application of the nickname is not clear; perhaps it referred to a peasant who had certain obligations to his master at the time of the harvest, or it may have been acquired for some other anecdotal reason which is now lost. **2.** Jewish (Ashkenazic): ornamental name from modern German *Herbst* 'Fall', perhaps reflecting the season when the name was first taken or given. In some cases, it seems to have been one of the group of names referring to the seasons that were distributed at random by government officials when surnames became compulsory. Compare FRUHLING, WINTER, and SUMMER.

Herbster (300) German: probably an occupational name for a grape picker, from Middle High German *herb(e)st* '(grape) harvest' (see HERBST).

Herbstritt (131) German: **1.** probably an altered form of **Herbstreuth**, habitational name from a place so called near Bayreuth, Bavaria; the second element, denoting a clearing in the forest, has several variants in German: *-reuth, -rieth, -reith.* **2.** Alternatively, perhaps, it may be an altered form of HEBENSTREIT.

Herceg (164) Croatian (northwestern Croatia): nickname from *herceg* 'duke', from the Hungarian form of German HERZOG. *Herceg* was the title of the medieval feudal lords of Herzegovina.
GIVEN NAME South Slavic 4%. *Stanko.*

Hercules (367) **1.** English and Scottish: from a personal name of Greek origin, which was in use in Cornwall and elsewhere till the 19th century. *Hercules* is the Latin form of Greek *Hēraklēs*, meaning 'glory of Hera' (the queen of the gods). It was the name of a demigod in classical mythology, who was the son of Zeus, king of the gods, by a human woman. His outstanding quality was his superhuman strength. **2.** Scottish (Shetland): from a personal name adopted as an Americanized form of Old Norse *Hákon* (see HAAGENSEN).

GIVEN NAMES Spanish 12%. *Juan* (5), *Carlota, Deysi, Genoveva, Gerardo, Jose, Jose Alfonso, Jose Antonio, Jose Roberto, Juan Pablo, Juanita, Marcial.*

Herczeg (124) Hungarian form of German HERZOG.

GIVEN NAMES Hungarian 22%. *Imre* (4), *Laszlo* (2), *Tibor* (2), *Attila, Ferenc, Gaza, Istvan, Janos.*

Herd (1502) **1.** Scottish and English: variant spelling of HEARD. **2.** Dutch: variant of HERDER. **3.** Dutch: from Middle Dutch *hert, herte* 'hart', 'stag'; probably a nickname for someone who was fleet of foot, or a habitational name for someone who lived at a house distinguished by the sign of a deer.

Herda (269) **1.** Czech: nickname for a clumsy, noisy, or loutish person, from *herda* 'thump'. **2.** Swiss German: variant of HERDE.

GIVEN NAMES German 4%. *Erwin, Florian, Hans, Heinrich, Helmut.*

Herde (122) **1.** English and Scottish: variant spelling of HERD. **2.** German: from a short form of any of various Germanic personal names composed with *hard* 'strong', 'hardy'.

GIVEN NAME German 6%. *Otto.*

Herdegen (104) German: from a Germanic personal name composed of the elements *hard* 'bold', 'hardy' + *degen* 'hero'.

GIVEN NAME German 6%. *Gunther* (2).

Herder (476) **1.** English, Dutch, and German: occupational name for a herdsman, someone who tended a herd of domestic animals, Middle English *herder*, Middle Dutch *herder, harde(r)*, Middle High German *herder*. **2.** German: from the medieval German personal name *Herdher*, composed of the elements *hart* 'strong' + *heri, hari* 'army'. **3.** South German: habitational name from either of two places called Herdern: near Freiburg and near Winterthal in Switzerland.

Herdina (107) Czech (northern Bohemia): flattering or ironic nickname from *herdina*, dialect form of Czech *hrdina* 'hero'.

Herdman (650) **1.** English (chiefly Northumbria): occupational name for a tender of animals, normally a cowherd or shepherd, from Middle English *herde* + *man* 'man'. The surname is also found in Ireland, where it dates back to around the 14th century. **2.** Scottish: status name from Old English *hīredman* 'retainer', denoting a member of a lord's household and followers, the *hīred*. **3.** German (**Herdmann**): occupational name for a tender of animals (see HERDER).

Herdrich (129) German: from a Germanic personal name composed of the elements *hard* 'strong' + *rīc* 'power', 'rule'.

Herdt (333) **1.** South German: nickname from Middle High German *hert(e)* 'hard', 'coarse', 'crude'; perhaps occasionally also from a house name, from *herde* 'stove'. **2.** German: from a personal name, *Herto*, a short form of any of the Germanic compound names beginning with *hard* 'hardy', 'brave', 'strong'. **3.** Dutch: variant of HERD 3.

Heredia (1449) Basque: habitational name from any of various places, for example in the province of Araba, Basque Country, so named from the plural of Late Latin *heredium* 'hereditary estate' (a derivative of *heres*), i.e. one that could be passed on to the heirs of its tenant instead of reverting to the overlord.

GIVEN NAMES Spanish 48%. *Jose* (30), *Juan* (23), *Luis* (22), *Manuel* (21), *Jesus* (15), *Guillermo* (13), *Carlos* (12), *Armando* (10), *Miguel* (10), *Francisco* (9), *Ruben* (9), *Mario* (8); *Antonio* (9), *Heriberto* (4), *Lorenzo* (4), *Fausto* (3), *Leonardo* (2), *Adalgisa, Angelo, Constantino, Dante, Eliseo, Filiberto, Flavio.*

Hereford (731) English: habitational name from Hereford in Herefordshire, or Harford in Devon and Goucestershire, all named from Old English *here* 'army' + *ford* 'ford'.

Herek (111) Croatian: **1.** nickname from a derivative of the adjective *herav* 'slanted', 'bent', 'crooked', a word of Turkish origin. **2.** patronymic from the personal name *Hero*, a short form of German HERMANN. **3.** nickname for someone from Herzegovina.

Herendeen (340) Said to be a 17th-century New England variant of English HARRINGTON.

Hereth (134) German: **1.** from the Germanic personal name *Harihard*, composed of the elements *hari, heri* 'army' + *hard* 'strong', 'hardy'. **2.** habitational name for someone from a place called Herreth near Bamberg, Bavaria.

Herfel (110) German: probably a variant of **Herpel** or **Herbel**, short forms of **Herpold**, from a Germanic personal name composed of *heri, hari* 'army' + *bald* 'brave'.

Herford (172) **1.** English: variant of HEREFORD. **2.** German: variant of HERFURTH.

Herfurth (131) **1.** German: metonymic occupational name for a soldier, from Middle High German *hervart* 'campaign', 'military expedition' (from Old High German *heri* 'army' + *vart* 'journey'). **2.** German and Jewish (Ashkenazic): habitational name from Herford in Westphalia or Herfurth near Regensburg, or a topographic name from *herfurt* 'ford suitable for the passage of an army'.

Hergenrader (124) Respelling of German **Hergenröder**, a variant of HERGENROTHER.

Hergenreder (115) German: variant of **Hergenröder** (see HERGENROTHER).

Hergenrother (107) German (**Hergenöther**): habitational name for someone from Hergenroth near Limburg or from Hergenrode near Darmstadt, both in Hessen.

GIVEN NAME German 7%. *Kurt.*

Hergert (512) South German and Dutch: from a Germanic personal name, *Herger*, composed of the elements *heri, hari* 'army' + *gēr, gār* 'spear'.

GIVEN NAMES German 4%. *Kurt* (2), *Ernst, Otto.*

Herget (285) German: variant of HERGOTT.

Hergott (167) German: from Middle High German *herr got* 'Lord God'. The reasons for its application as a surname are uncertain. It may be an occupational name for a producer or seller of crucifixes or religious paintings. Alternatively, it may be a nickname, either for a frequent user of this expression as an oath, or for arrogant person who behaved 'like Almighty God'.

Heriford (126) Respelling of English HEREFORD.

Herin (161) Dutch: variant of HERRIN.

Hering (1255) **1.** German and Jewish (Ashkenazic): from Middle High German *hærinc* 'herring', German *Hering*, a nickname for someone supposedly resembling a herring or a metonymic occupational name for a fish seller. In some cases the Jewish surname is ornamental. **2.** English: variant spelling of HERRING.

GIVEN NAMES German 4%. *Hasso* (2), *Alfons, Alois, Arno, Ernst, Erwin, Florian, Gerhard, Guenther, Kurt, Ludwig, Manfred.*

Heringer (192) German: **1.** occupational name from Middle High German *hæringer* 'herring seller'. **2.** habitational name for someone from Hering, near Darmstadt, or from any of several places called Heringen, for example near Limburg and in Saxony.

Herington (278) English: probably a variant spelling of HERRINGTON, HARRINGTON or ERRINGTON.

Herink (124) North German and Dutch: variant of HERING, from Middle Low German *herink, harink.*

GIVEN NAME German 7%. *Reiner* (3).

Heriot (107) Scottish: variant spelling of HERRIOTT 2.

Heritage (517) English: status name for someone who inherited land from an ancestor, rather than by feudal gift from an overlord, from Middle English, Old French *(h)eritage* 'inherited property' (Late Latin *heritagium*, from *heres* 'heir').

FOREBEARS The first known bearers of the name are John Heritage of Oxfordshire and John Erytage of Huntingdonshire, both recorded in the Hundred Rolls for 1279. The name also occurs early in Warwickshire, near the Oxfordshire border, and at least one present-day family of this name probably goes back to that source. All

American bearers of the name seem to be descended from a single individual who emigrated from England in 1684.

Herkert (179) German: variant of **Herkner**, an unrounded form of the habitational name *Hörckner*, denoting someone from Horka in Silesia.

GIVEN NAMES German 5%. *Hans, Klaus, Ralf.*

Herko (122) Slovak: variant of HIRKO.

Herl (221) German: from a pet form of HERMANN.

Herlache (132) Dutch: habitational name from a place in North Brabant called Hierlaxhe (modern Herlaar).

Herlan (101) English and northern Irish: variant of **Harlan** (see HARLAND).

Herley (100) Irish: **1.** (County Cork): variant of HERLIHY. **2.** (Ulster): variant of HARLEY.

GIVEN NAMES Irish 4%. *Art, Cormac.*

Herlihy (1147) Irish: Anglicized form of Gaelic **Ó hIarfhlatha** 'descendant of *Iarfhlaith*', a personal name meaning 'lord of the west', sometimes Anglicized as **Jarlath**.

GIVEN NAMES Irish 5%. *Brendan* (4), *Eoin.*

Herling (277) **1.** German: habitational name from places called Herlingen (Saar) or Herrlingen (near Ulm). **2.** Dutch: patronymic from the Germanic personal name *Herilo*, originally a pet form of one of the compound names with the first element *hari, heri* 'army'. **3.** Jewish (Ashkenazic): ornamental name from German *Herling* 'unripe grapes'.

Herlinger (107) German and Jewish (Ashkenazic): habitational name for someone from Herrlingen near Ulm.

GIVEN NAMES German 10%. *Ernst, Erwin, Gerhard, Hans.*

Herlocker (143) Americanized form of German HORLACHER.

Herlong (256) Perhaps a variant of German or Dutch HERLING. This surname is found chiefly in SC.

Herm (136) **1.** North German: from a short form of HERMANN. **2.** South German: derisive nickname for a stiff, obstinate person.

GIVEN NAMES German 6%. *Hans* (2), *Rainer.*

Herman (17663) **1.** English, French, Dutch, Slovenian, Croatian, and Jewish (Ashkenazic): from a Germanic personal name composed of the elements *heri, hari* 'army' + *man* 'man'. As a Jewish surname this is no doubt an adoption of the German surname HERMANN. **2.** Respelling of the German cognate HERMANN.

Hermance (275) Altered spelling of HERMANNS. This is a surname found chiefly in NY.

Hermann (3798) German: from a Germanic personal name composed of the elements *heri, hari* 'army' + *man* 'man'. The surname is also borne by Ashkenazic Jews, probably as an adoption of the German surname.

GIVEN NAMES German 5%. *Kurt* (11), *Hans* (3), *Jurgen* (3), *Mathias* (3), *Gottlieb* (2), *Horst* (2), *Juergen* (2), *Klaus* (2), *Lorenz* (2), *Bernd, Dieter, Erwin.*

Hermanns (149) North German: patronymic from HERMANN.

GIVEN NAMES German 10%. *Egon, Erwin, Heida, Helmut, Horst, Otto.*

Hermans (342) North German and Dutch: patronymic from HERMAN.

GIVEN NAMES French 6%. *Albertine, Amiee, Anais, Andre, Emile, Michel.*

Hermansen (557) North German, Danish, and Norwegian: patronymic from the personal name HERMAN.

GIVEN NAMES Scandinavian 9%; German 4%. *Erik* (3), *Knud* (2), *Alf, Knut*; *Hans* (4), *Inge, Kurt, Markus.*

Hermanson (1556) Respelling of HERMANSEN, or of the Swedish cognate **Hermansson**.

GIVEN NAMES Scandinavian 4%. *Erik* (2), *Helmer* (2), *Anders, Bjorn, Per.*

Hermens (101) Dutch: **1.** variant of HERMANS. **2.** variant of **Ermens**, a metronymic from a short form of the female personal name *Ermelendis* or *Ermgart.*

Hermes (1583) **1.** French (**Hermès**) and Dutch: from the Greek name *Hermes*, name of a saint mentioned briefly in Paul's Epistle to the Romans. **2.** Dutch and North German: variant of **Ermens**, a metronymic from a short form of the female personal name *Ermelendis* or *Ermgart.* **3.** Dutch and German: patronymic from a short form of HERMAN. **4.** Southern French (**Hermès**): topographic name for someone who lived in a deserted spot or on a patch of waste land, from Occitan *erm* 'desert', 'waste' (Greek *erēmia*) + the local suffix *-ès.*

Hermesch (105) German: unexplained.

GIVEN NAME French 4%. *Colette.*

Hermida (130) Spanish: **1.** nickname from *eremita* 'hermit' (Greek *erēmitēs*), generally no doubt a nickname for someone living in an isolated spot (compare HERMES). **2.** Galician and Spanish: habitational name from any of various places, for example in the provinces of Lugo, Orense, and Pontevedra, named with Old Spanish and Galician *hermida* 'hermitage', 'shrine'.

GIVEN NAMES Spanish 47%. *Jose* (6), *Juan* (4), *Alfonso* (3), *Andres* (3), *Pedro* (3), *Avelino* (2), *Carlos* (2), *Alberto, Alejandro, Ana, Caridad, Cesar.*

Hermon (185) **1.** English: variant of HERMAN. **2.** Dutch: from a Germanic personal name composed of the elements *hari, heri* 'army' + *mund* 'protection'.

Hermosillo (496) Spanish: nickname for a dandy, from a diminutive of *hermoso* 'finely formed', 'handsome' (Latin *formosus*, from *forma* 'shape', 'form', 'beauty').

GIVEN NAMES Spanish 52%. *Jose* (14), *Juan* (7), *Manuel* (6), *Enrique* (5), *Felipe* (5), *Fernando* (4), *Gerardo* (4), *Guillermo* (4),

Miguel (4), *Rodolfo* (4), *Ruben* (4), *Carlos* (3); *Antonio* (3), *Federico* (2), *Carmela, Ceasar, Flavio, Heriberto, Julieta, Marco, Romeo.*

Hermreck (122) German: probably an altered form of HEINRICH.

Herms (160) **1.** Variant of HERMES. **2.** North German: patronymic from a short form of the personal name *Hermann* (see HERMAN).

Hermsen (483) North German and Dutch: patronymic from a short form of the personal name HERMAN.

Hern (857) English and Irish: variant spelling of HEARN.

Hernadez (245) Spanish (**Hernádez**): patronymic from a variant of the personal name *Hernando* (see FERNANDEZ).

GIVEN NAMES Spanish 56%. *Jose* (10), *Juan* (6), *Francisco* (3), *Mario* (3), *Roberto* (3), *Alejandra* (2), *Arturo* (2), *Carlos* (2), *Enrique* (2), *Gustavo* (2), *Ignacio* (2), *Jorge* (2).

Hernan (172) Spanish (**Hernán**): short form of the personal name *Hernando*, variant of FERNANDO.

Hernandes (202) Spanish and Portuguese: variant of HERNANDEZ.

GIVEN NAMES Spanish 55%. *Jose* (6), *Carlos* (4), *Juan* (3), *Francisco* (2), *Jorge* (2), *Jose Luis* (2), *Mario* (2), *Mercedes* (2), *Miguel* (2), *Rafael* (2), *Victoriano* (2), *Adan.*

Hernandez (73728) Spanish (**Hernández**) and Jewish (Sephardic): patronymic from the personal name *Hernando* (see FERNANDO). This surname also became established in southern Italy, mainly in Naples and Palermo, since the period of Spanish dominance there, and as a result of the expulsion of the Jews from Spain and Portugal at the end of the 15th century, many of whom moved to Italy.

GIVEN NAMES Spanish 51%. *Carlos* (705), *Manuel* (673), *Jesus* (659), *Luis* (625), *Francisco* (519), *Pedro* (461), *Miguel* (459), *Jorge* (405), *Mario* (391), *Raul* (358), *Ramon* (335), *Roberto* (332).

Hernando (128) Spanish: from the personal name *Hernando*, variant of FERNANDO.

GIVEN NAMES Spanish 47%. *Jose* (6), *Jorge* (3), *Mariano* (3), *Francisco Jose* (2), *Maximo* (2), *Abelardo, Alejandro, Ana, Anastacia, Benito, Bernardo, Carlos.*

Herndon (7350) English: probably a habitational name from a lost or unidentified place.

Herne (179) English: variant of HEARN 2 and 4.

Herner (240) North German: habitational name for someone from Herne in Westphalia.

Hernon (227) Irish: **1.** Anglicized form of Gaelic **Ó hIarnáin, Ó hEarnáin**, 'descendant of *Iarnán, Earnán*', possibly from *i-arn* 'iron'. **2.** reduced form of HEFFERNAN.

GIVEN NAMES Irish 8%. *Brendan, Colm.*

Hero (188) Greek: probably an Americanized form of a Greek surname sounding something like the English word 'hero', for example **Irodotou** 'son of Herodotus', or **Khiras** 'son of the widow'.

Herod (809) **1.** English (chiefly Nottinghamshire): nickname from the personal name *Herod* (Greek *Hērōdēs*, apparently derived from *hērōs* 'hero'), borne by the king of Judea (died AD 4) who at the time of the birth of Christ ordered that all male children in Bethlehem should be slaughtered (Matthew 2: 16–18). In medieval mystery plays Herod was portrayed as a blustering tyrant, and the name was therefore given to someone one who had played the part, or who had an overbearing temper. **2.** English: variant of HAROLD (1 or 2). **3.** Greek: shortened form of **Herodiadis**, a patronymic from the classical personal name *Hērodiōn*. This was the name of a relative of St. Paul and an early Bishop of Patras, venerated in the Orthodox Church. *Hērōdēs* 'Herod' is also found in Greek as a nickname for a violent man, but this is less likely to be the source of the surname.

Herold (2445) **1.** English: variant of HAROLD. **2.** German, Dutch, and French: from the Germanic personal name *Hari(o)wald* (see HAROLD 1). **3.** French (**Hérold**): status name for a herald, Old French *herau(l)t* (see HAROLD 2). **4.** Jewish (Ashkenazic): ornamental name from German *Herold* 'herald' (see 3).

Heron (1210) **1.** English and French (**Héron**): nickname for a tall, thin person resembling a heron, Middle English *heiroun*, *heyron* (Old French *hairon*, of Germanic origin). **2.** English: habitational name from Harome in North Yorkshire, named with Old English *harum*, dative plural of *hær* 'rock', 'stone'. This surname has evidently become confused with 1. **3.** Irish: reduced form of **O'Heron**, an Anglicized form of Gaelic **Ó hUidhrín** 'descendant of *Uidhrín*', a personal name from a diminutive of *odhar* 'dun', 'swarthy'. **4.** Irish: reduced Anglicized form of Gaelic **Ó hEaráin** (see HAREN). **5.** Irish: reduced Anglicized form of Gaelic **Mac Giolla Chiaráin** 'son of the servant of (Saint) *Ciarán*' (see KIERAN).

Heroux (593) French (**Héroux**): from the Germanic personal name *Hariwulf*, composed of the elements *heri*, *hari*, 'army' + *wulf* 'wolf'.

FOREBEARS A Hérou or Héroux, also called Bourgainville, from Normandy, is documented in Trois Rivières, Quebec, in 1674. GIVEN NAMES French 13%. *Armand* (3), *Normand* (3), *Pierre* (3), *Andre* (2), *Edouard* (2), *Aurore*, *Donat*, *Gaston*, *Gisele*, *Herve*, *Laurier*, *Marcel*.

Herpel (143) German (Middle Rhine): from a pet form of a Germanic personal name formed with *heri*, *hari* 'army' + *bald* 'bold', *ber(h)t* 'famous', or *bord* 'shield'. GIVEN NAME German 4%. *Helmut*.

Herpich (105) German: variant of HERBIG, itself a variant of HERWIG. GIVEN NAME German 4%. *Otto*.

Herpin (125) French: variant of HARPIN. FOREBEARS A Herpin, also called TOURANGEAU, from the Touraine region of France, is documented in Quebec city in 1669. GIVEN NAMES French 7%. *Aldes*, *Andre*.

Herr (4643) **1.** German and Jewish (Ashkenazic): from Middle High German *herre*, German *Herr* 'master', 'lord'; a nickname for someone who gave himself airs and behaved in a lordly manner, or an occupational name for someone in the service of the lord of the manor. As a Jewish surname it is often ornamental. **2.** Breton: variant of **Her**. **3.** Irish: variant spelling of HARE 4.

Herrada (122) Spanish: unexplained. GIVEN NAMES Spanish 54%. *Jesus* (4), *Juan* (4), *Jose* (3), *Manuel* (3), *Adan* (2), *Carlos* (2), *Raul* (2), *Angel*, *Armando*, *Aurelio*, *Bernardo*, *Berta*.

Herran (95) Spanish (**Herrán**): **1.** habitational name from Herrán, a village in the province of Burgos, named from Basque *erro* 'bramble' + suffix of location *-ain*, *-an*; or from a village of the same name in the province of Santander. **2.** from a derivative of *hierro* 'iron'. GIVEN NAMES Spanish 44%. *Francisco* (3), *Alberto* (2), *Sergio* (2), *Alvaro*, *Angel*, *Carlos*, *Elena*, *Emiliano*, *Getulio*, *Jaime*, *Jesus*, *Jose*.

Herrboldt (112) German: variant spelling of HERBOLD. GIVEN NAMES German 4%. *Ewald*, *Reinhold*.

Herre (181) **1.** German: variant of HERR 1 and 2. **2.** French (**Herré**): habitational name from a place in Landes. The place name is a Gascon form of *Ferré*, ultimately a derivative of Latin *ferrarium* 'worker in iron', 'smith'. **3.** Norwegian: habitational name from either of two farmsteads, so named either from Old Norse *herað* 'settlement', 'settled district', or from Old Norse *hár* 'high' + *ré* 'ridge'. GIVEN NAMES German 5%. *Dieter*, *Otto*.

Herreid (170) Americanized spelling of Norwegian **Hæreid**, a habitational name from any of several farmsteads so named in Hardanger and Sogn, from Old Norse *hæri* 'higher (up)' + *eið* 'isthmus'.

Herrel (109) **1.** Americanized form of German HERRLE. **2.** English and Irish: variant of HARRELL. GIVEN NAME German 4%. *Kurt*.

Herrell (1009) English and Irish: variant of HARRELL.

Herrema (118) Frisian: variant of HEEREMA.

Herren (1499) German: byname for someone in the service of a lord and his family, from a genitive plural form of Middle High German *her* 'nobleman', 'lord', as in **Herrendorf**, habitational name from a place near Küstrin; or the nickname **Herrenhans**, for someone named John in the

service of a nobleman; **Herrenknecht**, a servant in a noble family; or **Herrenschneider**, a tailor hired by a nobleman.

Herrera (17039) **1.** Spanish and Jewish (Sephardic): habitational name from villages so called in the provinces of Seville and Badajoz, from a word meaning 'iron smithy', 'blacksmith's forge' (a derivative of *hierro* 'iron', Latin *ferrum*). **2.** French: habitational name from the Gascon form of *Ferrière*, a place in Pyrénées-Atlantique. The place name is derived from Latina *ferraria* 'iron-mine', 'iron-forge'. GIVEN NAMES Spanish 47%. *Jose* (428), *Juan* (247), *Manuel* (184), *Carlos* (171), *Jesus* (123), *Luis* (122), *Jorge* (102), *Francisco* (93), *Raul* (93), *Rafael* (86), *Mario* (85), *Roberto* (76).

Herrero (284) Spanish: occupational name for a blacksmith, from an agent derivative of *hierro* 'iron' (Latin *ferrum*). GIVEN NAMES Spanish 42%. *Luis* (8), *Jose* (7), *Carlos* (3), *Eduardo* (3), *Juan* (3), *Manuel* (3), *Angel* (2), *Blanca* (2), *Emilio* (2), *Gustavo* (2), *Hermilo* (2), *Ignacio* (2).

Herres (150) German: this name is found Latinized as *Henrici*, so it presumably represents a patronymic based on a short form of HEINRICH.

Herriage (153) Probably an altered spelling of English HERRIDGE. This surname is found chiefly in TX.

Herrick (5139) **1.** English: from the Old Norse personal name *Eiríkr*, composed of the elements *eir* 'mercy', 'peace' + *rík* 'power'. The addition in English of an inorganic *H-* to names beginning with a vowel is a relatively common phenomenon. It is possible that this name may have swallowed up a less common Germanic personal name with the first element *heri*, *hari* 'army'. **2.** Dutch: from a Germanic personal name composed of the elements *heri*, *hari* 'army' + *rīc* 'power', or from an assimilated form of *Henrick*, a Dutch form of HENRY. **3.** Irish: Anglicized form of Gaelic **Ó hEirc** 'descendant of *Erc*', a personal name meaning 'speckled', 'dark red', or 'salmon'. There was a saint of this name. The surname is born by families in Munster and Ulster, where it has usually been changed to HARKIN.

FOREBEARS The English poet Robert Herrick (1591–1674) was from a prosperous family of goldsmiths, who had a long association with the city of Leicester. There is a family tradition that they were of Scandinavian origin, descended from Eric the Forester, who settled in the city in the 11th century. The initial aspirate came into the name in the late 16th century; the name of the poet's great-grandfather is recorded in the corporation books of the city of Leicester in 1511 as Thomas Ericke.

Herridge (187) English: possibly a habitational name from Eridge in East Sussex, so named from Old English *earn* 'eagle' +

hrycg 'ridge' or an altered form of **Harwich**, a habitational name from Old English *here* 'army' + *wīc* 'dwelling', 'camp'

Herrig (288) German: habitational name from any of several places named Herrig in the Rhineland or from Herringen in Westphalia. See also HERRING.

Herriges (187) German: from a short form of any of the many Germanic personal names composed with *hari, heri* 'army'.
GIVEN NAMES German 4%. *Gerhard, Mathias.*

Herriman (400) English: variant of HARRIMAN.

Herrin (2944) **1.** Dutch: from a pet form of any of various Germanic compound personal names with the first element *hari, heri* 'army'. **2.** English: probably a variant of HERRING.

Herring (13163) **1.** English, Scottish, Dutch, and German: metonymic occupational name for a herring fisher or for a seller of the fish, Middle English *hering*, Dutch *haring*, Middle High German *hærinc*. In some cases it may have been a nickname in the sense of a trifle, something of little value, a meaning which is found in medieval phrases and proverbial expressions such as 'to like neither herring nor barrel', i.e. not to like something at all. **2.** German: habitational name from Herringen in Westphalia. **3.** Dutch: from a personal name, a derivative of a Germanic compound name with the first element *hari, heri* 'army'. **4.** Jewish (Ashkenazic): variant spelling of HERING.

Herringshaw (158) English: habitational name from a lost or unidentified place, most probably in Lincolnshire or Leicestershire, named with Middle English *shaw*, Old English *skeaga* 'copse', as its second element.

Herrington (5128) English: **1.** habitational name from Herrington in County Durham, possibly so named from an unattested Old English personal name *Hȳra*(from Old Enlish *hȳra* 'servant') + *-ing-* denoting association + *denu* 'woodland', 'pasture'. **2.** Possibly a variant of HARRINGTON or a hypercorrected form of ERRINGTON.

Herriott (436) **1.** English and French: from a pet form (with the suffix *-ot*) of the medieval personal name *Herry*, HARRY (a variant of HENRY). **2.** Scottish: habitational name from a place, as for example Heriot to the south of Edinburgh, named with Middle English *heriot*, which denoted a piece of land restored to the feudal lord on the death of its tenant. The Middle English word is from Old English *heregeatu*, a compound of *here* 'army' + *geatu* 'equipment', referring originally to military equipment that was restored to the lord on the death of a vassal. **3.** English: habitational name from Herriard in Hampshire, which may have been named as 'army quarters' (Old English *here* 'army' + *geard*

'enclosure'), or possibly from the Celtic terms *hyr* 'long' + *garth* 'ridge'.

Herritt (123) Scottish: variant of HERRIOTT.

Herrity (144) Irish: Anglicized form of Gaelic **Ó hOireachtaigh** (see HARRINGTON).

Herrle (164) German: **1.** from a pet form of the personal name HERMANN. **2.** from a diminutive of HERR 1.

Herrling (102) German: variant of HERRLING.

Herrman (955) Dutch or German: variant spelling of HERMAN or HERMANN.
GIVEN NAMES German 4%. *Kurt* (3), *Aloysius, Armin, Arno, Bernhard, Fritz, Wendelin.*

Herrmann (5705) German: variant spelling of HERMANN.
GIVEN NAMES German 7%. *Kurt* (18), *Hans* (11), *Otto* (10), *Ernst* (6), *Siegfried* (6), *Erwin* (5), *Jurgen* (5), *Heinz* (4), *Manfred* (4), *Franz* (3), *Fritz* (3), *Gunther* (3).

Herro (181) Spanish: habitational name from a place called Hierro in the province of León, so named from *hierro* 'iron'.

Herrod (518) English: variant spelling of HEROD.

Herrold (511) English: variant of HAROLD 1 and 2.

Herron (8684) **1.** English: variant spelling of HERON. **2.** Irish: Anglicized form of Gaelic **Ó hEaráin** 'descendant of *Earán*', a personal name from a diminutive of *earadh* 'fear', 'dread', 'distrust'. **3.** Spanish (**Herrón**): unexplained.

Hersch (477) **1.** Jewish (Ashkenazic): Yiddish dialect variant of HIRSCH 2 and 3. **2.** German: variant of HIRSCH 1. **3.** German (under Slavic influence): from a pet form of the personal name HERMANN.

Herschbach (107) German: habitational name for someone from either of two places so called, one in the Westerwald area (Hesse), another in the Eifel (Rhineland-Palatinate).

Herschberger (178) German and Jewish (Ashkenazic): **1.** habitational name for someone from any of several places named Herschberg, for example one near Kaiserslautern. **2.** variant of HIRSCHBERG.

Herschel (110) German and Jewish (Ashkenazic): from a pet form of HIRSCH.
GIVEN NAME German 6%. *Kurt.*

Herscher (120) **1.** German: variant of **Harscher** (see HARSCH). **2.** Jewish (Ashkenazic): derivative of HERSCH. **3.** Jewish (Ashkenazic): ornamental name from modern German *Herrscher* 'ruler', 'sovereign'.

Herschman (100) Jewish: variant of HIRSCHMAN.
GIVEN NAMES Jewish 5%. *Aviva, Miriam.*

Hersey (1466) English: probably a variant of HERSHEY 2.

Hersh (1617) Jewish (Ashkenazic): Yiddish dialect variant of HIRSCH 2 and 3.
GIVEN NAMES Jewish 4%. *Ahron* (2), *Isadore* (2), *Miriam* (2), *Aharon, Aron, Chanie,*

Hyman, Isack, Itzhak, Mendel, Meyer, Mordechai.

Hershberg (127) Americanized spelling of German or Jewish variant spelling of **Herschberg** (see HERSCHBERGER) or HIRSCHBERG.
GIVEN NAMES Jewish 5%. *Hyman, Yehoshua.*

Hershberger (2386) Americanized spelling of German or Jewish variant spelling of HERSCHBERGER.

Hershey (2537) **1.** Jewish (American): Americanized form of various like-sounding Ashkenazic Jewish names, see for example HERSHKOWITZ. **2.** English (of Norman origin): habitational name from Hercé or Hercy in Mayenne, France.

Hershfield (124) Jewish: Americanized spelling of HIRSCHFELD.
GIVEN NAME Jewish 4%. *Elihu.*

Hershkowitz (382) Jewish (eastern Ashkenazic): patronymic from the personal name *Hershke*, a pet form of *Hersh* (see HIRSCH 2).
GIVEN NAMES Jewish 12%. *Emanuel* (3), *Isadore* (2), *Moshe* (2), *Chaim, Dvora, Haim, Mayer, Meyer, Nachman, Shlome, Yakov, Yosef.*

Hershman (790) **1.** Jewish (Ashkenazic): variant of HIRSCHMAN. **2.** Perhaps also an Americanized spelling of German HIRSCHMANN.
GIVEN NAMES Jewish 4%. *Hyman* (3), *Meyer, Miriam, Moshe.*

Hershner (172) Americanized spelling of German **Herschner**, a variant of *Harscher* (see HARSCH), that is now rare in Germany.

Herskovits (123) Jewish (eastern Ashkenazic): variant of HERSHKOWITZ.
GIVEN NAMES Jewish 23%; Hungarian 9%; Czech and Slovak 4%; German 4%. *Arie, Haya, Itzhak, Moishe, Moshe, Shimon, Shulem, Tema, Yossi, Zelig, Zvi; Zoltan* (2), *Kalman, Sandor, Tibor; Ignac, Vojtech; Erwin.*

Herskovitz (190) Jewish (eastern Ashkenazic): variant of HERSHKOWITZ.
GIVEN NAMES Jewish 12%; Hungarian 11%. *Zelig* (3), *Aron, Izak, Jakob, Meyer, Miriam, Nili; Sandor* (3), *Bela* (2), *Zoltan* (2), *Aladar, Miklos.*

Herskowitz (287) Jewish (eastern Ashkenazic): variant of HERSHKOWITZ.
GIVEN NAMES Jewish 17%. *Zvi* (3), *Moshe* (2), *Shraga* (2), *Sol* (2), *Avi, Avraham, Binyomin, Chaim, Channan, Eliezer, Hershel, Leibish.*

Hersman (275) Dutch (of German origin): variant of HIRSCHMANN, or possibly an Americanized form of the German name.

Hersom (329) English: nickname from Old French *hérisson* 'hedgehog'.

Herson (242) **1.** English: variant of HERSOM. **2.** Jewish: of uncertain origin; perhaps a reduced form of German

Herschsohn, a patronymic from HERSCH (Yiddish HERSH).
GIVEN NAMES Jewish 6%. *Mendel* (2), *Asher*, *Moshe*.

Herst (174) **1.** English: variant of HURST. **2.** Jewish (Ashkenazic): ornamental name or nickname from Polish *herszt* 'ringleader', 'chieftain'.

Herstein (123) German: habitational name from Herrstein in Rhineland-Palatinate.

Hert (365) **1.** German: variant of HERDT 2. **2.** Dutch: variant of HERD 3.

Hertel (1713) German: from a pet form of a personal name based on the Germanic element *hard* 'hardy', 'brave', 'strong'. Compare HARD 1.
GIVEN NAMES German 5%. *Kurt* (3), *Fritz* (2), *Gerhard* (2), *Gerhart* (2), *Hans Peter* (2), *Otto* (2), *Dieter*, *Eldred*, *Erwin*, *Ewald*, *Gerd*, *Guenter*.

Hertenstein (235) German and Swiss German: habitational name from various places so called in Switzerland, or from a castle so named near Sigmaringen in Germany.
GIVEN NAMES German 4%. *Frieda*, *Ulrich*.

Herter (435) German: occupational name for a herdsman, Middle High German *hertære*. Compare HEARD, HERDER.

Hertig (163) German (central eastern): variant of HERTWIG.
GIVEN NAMES German 5%; Scandinavian 4%. *Hans* (2), *Urs*; *Lars*.

Herting (158) German: variant of HERTIG.
GIVEN NAMES German 4%. *Hans*, *Horst*.

Hertle (122) German: variant of HERTLEIN.
GIVEN NAMES German 14%. *Frieda*, *Helmut*, *Ingo*, *Klaus*, *Otto*, *Xaver*.

Hertlein (283) German: from a pet form of a personal name (see HERDT 2 and HERTER; also compare HARD 1).

Hertler (106) German: patronymic from HERTEL or **Härtel** (see HARTEL 1).

Hertling (118) German: variant of **Härtling** (see HARTLING).
GIVEN NAMES German 5%. *Gunter*, *Heiner*.

Hertweck (128) Variant of German HARTWIG.
GIVEN NAMES German 7%. *Klaus*, *Wolfgang*.

Hertwig (105) German: variant of HARTWIG.
GIVEN NAMES German 13%; Scandinavian 6%. *Otto* (2), *Kurt*, *Ralf*, *Rudi*; *Erik*, *Gunner*.

Hertz (1869) **1.** German and Dutch: from a personal name derived from a short form of the various Germanic compound names with the first element *hard* 'hardy', 'brave', 'strong'. **2.** German: nickname for a stout-hearted or kind-hearted individual, from Middle High German *herze* 'heart'. **3.** Jewish (Ashkenazic): ornamental name from German *Herz* 'heart', Yiddish *harts*. **4.** Jewish (Ashkenazic): from the Yiddish personal name *Herts*, which is from Middle

High German *hir(t)z* 'deer', 'hart' (see HIRSCH). **5.** Dutch: variant of HIRSCH. **6.** Danish and Swedish: probably of German origin.

Hertzberg (521) **1.** German and Jewish (Ashkenazic): variant spelling of HERZBERG. **2.** Swedish: respelling of German HERZBERG.
GIVEN NAMES Jewish 4%. *Arie*, *Hyman*, *Meyer*.

Hertzler (498) South German: occupational name for a collector of resin (used for making pitch), from Middle High German *harz* 'resin'.

Hertzog (892) German and Jewish (Ashkenazic): variant spelling of HERZOG.

Hervey (962) English: variant of HARVEY 1.

Herwick (139) **1.** German: variant of HERWIG. **2.** Americanized spelling of Norwegian Hervik, a habitational name from any of three farmsteads so named from Old Norse *herr* 'army', 'large gathering' + *vik* 'bay' (perhaps referring to a meeting place for ships).

Herwig (471) German (central eastern) and Dutch: from a Germanic personal name, composed of the elements *heri*, *hari* 'army' + *wīg* 'war'.
GIVEN NAMES German 5%. *Arno*, *Gerhardt*, *Helmut*, *William Otto*.

Heryford (116) Altered spelling of English HEREFORD.

Herz (759) German, Dutch, and Jewish (Ashkenazic): variant spelling of HERTZ.
GIVEN NAMES German 11%. *Kurt* (4), *Erwin* (3), *Fritz* (2), *Gerhard* (2), *Hans* (2), *Helmut* (2), *Ilse* (2), *Arnd*, *Egon*, *Ewald*, *Heinz*, *Irmgard*.

Herzberg (866) **1.** German and Jewish (Ashkenazic): habitational name from any of numerous places named Herzberg. **2.** Jewish (Ashkenazic): ornamental compound name from German *Herz* 'heart' + *Berg* 'hill'.
GIVEN NAMES German 5%; Jewish 4%. *Kurt* (3), *Erwin* (2), *Fritz* (2), *Hans* (2), *Detlef*, *Ernst*, *Horst*, *Rainer*; *Moshe* (2), *Asher*, *Chanina*, *Esti*, *Hershel*, *Isadore*, *Myer*, *Nisson*, *Shlomo*, *Sunya*, *Yehuda*, *Zipora*.

Herzberger (146) German and Jewish (Ashkenazic): habitational name for someone from any of numerous places called HERZBERG.

Herzer (233) **1.** German (Thuringia): regional name for someone from the Harz Mountains. **2.** South German: occupational name for a gatherer of resin, from an agent derivative of Middle High German *herzen* 'to cover with resin or tar'. **3.** Jewish (Ashkenazic): derivative of HERTZ 3 and 4.
GIVEN NAMES German 4%. *Arno*, *Horst*.

Herzfeld (317) **1.** German and Jewish (Ashkenazic): habitational name from any of several places called Herzfeld or Herzfelde, mostly in northern German.

2. Jewish (Ashkenazic): ornamental name composed of German *Herz* 'heart' + *Feld* 'field'.
GIVEN NAMES German 7%. *Heinrich*, *Helmut*, *Manfred*, *Ulrich*, *Ute*, *Wolfgang*.

Herzig (618) **1.** German (eastern and central Germany and Silesia): variant of HERZOG. **2.** German: from a short form of any of several Germanic personal names composed with *hard* 'strong', 'hardy', for instance *Herto*. **3.** Jewish (Ashkenazic): ornamental name from German *herzig* 'delightful', 'lovely'.
GIVEN NAMES German 4%. *Erna*, *Fritzi*, *Hans*, *Horst*, *Markus*, *Monika*.

Herzing (248) German: affectionate pet name based on Middle High German *herze* 'heart'.

Herzog (4648) **1.** German: from the Middle High German title of nobility *herzoge* 'duke' (Old High German *herizoho*, from *heri* 'army' + *ziohan* 'to lead', a calque of the Byzantine title *stratēlatēs* 'general', 'commander', from Greek *stratos* 'army' + *elaunein* 'to lead'). The name is unlikely to refer to descent from an actual duke; it is normally an occupational name for the servant of a duke or a nickname for one who put on the airs and graces of a duke. **2.** Jewish (Ashkenazic): ornamental name from German *Herzog* 'duke'. Compare GRAF and KAISER.
GIVEN NAMES German 5%. *Hans* (11), *Erwin* (4), *Fritz* (4), *Heinz* (4), *Kurt* (4), *Otto* (4), *Wolfgang* (4), *Franz* (3), *Arno* (2), *Ernst* (2), *Hildegarde* (2), *Reinhold* (2).

Hesch (338) German: variant of HEESCH or **Hösch** (see HOSCH).

Heschke (110) German: from a pet form of the female personal name *Heseke* (see HEESCH).

Hescock (127) English: variant of HISCOCK.

Heselton (181) English: variant of HAZELTON.

Heser (128) German: variant of HASER or a habitational name for someone from Hees near Emmenrich in the Lower Rhine.

Hesketh (314) English (Lancashire): habitational name from places in Lancashire and North Yorkshire called Hesketh, or from Hesket in Cumbria, all named from Old Norse *hestr* 'horse', 'stallion' + *skeið* 'racecourse'. The ancient Scandinavians were fond of horse-racing and horse-fighting, and introduced both pastimes to England.
FOREBEARS A family named Hesketh originating at Hesketh, Lancashire, traces its descent from Sir William Hesketh, who was living in the reign of Edward I (1272–1307).

Heskett (661) English (Lancashire): variant of HESKETH.

Heskin (108) **1.** Irish: Anglicized form of Gaelic **Ó hUiscín**, which has also been

Anglicized as Waters, although it is unlikely to have been derived from *uisce* 'water'. **2.** Scandinavian: unexplained.

GIVEN NAME Scandinavian 7%. *Erik* (2).

Heslep (256) English: variant of HYSLOP.

Hesler (400) German: variant of HASLER 1.

Hesley (138) English: habitational name from either of two places so called, in Cumbria and Nottinghamshire, from Old English *hæsel* 'hazel' (influenced by Old Norse *hesli*) + Old English *lēah* 'wood', 'clearing'.

Heslin (521) Irish: reduced Anglicized form of Gaelic **Ó hEislin**, a reduced form of the older **Ó hEisleanáin** 'descendant of *Eisleanán*', probably from *éislinn* 'unsafe', 'weak'.

Heslip (118) Northern Irish: variant of Scottish HYSLOP.

Heslop (418) English (northeastern England and Scotland): variant of HYSLOP.

Hespe (111) German: habitational name from a place near Bückeburg.

Hess (23120) **1.** German, Dutch, Danish, and Jewish (Ashkenazic): regional name for someone from the territory of Hesse (German *Hessen*). **2.** South German: from a short form of the personal name *Matthäus* (see MATTHEW). **3.** German and Dutch: from the Germanic personal name *Hesso*.

Hesse (2545) German and Dutch: variant of HESS.

GIVEN NAMES German 5%. *Gerhard* (4), *Kurt* (4), *Hans* (3), *Erwin* (2), *Florian* (2), *Otto* (2), *Siegfried* (2), *Ullrich* (2), *Wilhelm* (2), *Wolfgang* (2), *Bernd*, *Bernhard*.

Hessel (597) **1.** German: from a pet form of HERMANN. **2.** Swedish: variant of HASSEL. **3.** English: variant of HAZEL. **4.** Dutch: from a derivative of a Germanic personal name, either from a compound name formed with *hadu* 'strife' as the first element, or from a derivative of *Hermann* (see HERMAN) or *Hendrik* (see HENRY 1).

Hesselgrave (113) English: habitational name from Hazel Grove in Greater Manchester (recorded in 1690 as Hesselgrove), which is named from Old English *hæsel* 'hazel(tree)' + *grāf* 'grove'.

Hesselink (140) Dutch: patronymic from HESSEL 4.

Hessell (100) **1.** English: probably a variant of HAZEL. **2.** variant spelling of German HESSEL.

GIVEN NAME German 4%. *Aloysius*.

Hesseltine (308) English: variant of HASELDEN.

Hessen (105) German: **1.** regional name for someone from the territory of Hesse (German *Hessen*). **2.** habitational name from a place so named near Wolfenbüttel in Lower Saxony.

GIVEN NAMES German 4%; Scandinavian 4%. *Erna*; *Hjalmer*.

Hesser (670) German: **1.** nickname from an agent derivative of Middle High German *hessen* 'to hound'. **2.** regional name for a person from Hesse.

Hessert (100) German: variant of HESSER.

Hessey (109) English: habitational name from Hessay in York, named from Old English *hæsel* 'hazel(tree)' + *sǣ* 'marshland' or *ēg* 'island'.

Hessing (142) Dutch and German: patronymic from HESS 3.

GIVEN NAME French 4%. *Toussaint*.

Hessinger (150) German (Rhineland and Frankfurt area): **1.** habitational name for someone from Hessingen near Brilon in Westphalia. **2.** possibly a variant of **Hassinger**, from the personal name *Hasso* (see HASSING).

Hession (607) Irish (Connacht): Anglicized form of Gaelic **Ó hOisín** 'descendant of *Oisín*', a personal name from a diminutive of *os* 'deer'.

GIVEN NAMES Irish 6%. *Conal* (2), *Brendan*, *Donal*, *Malachy*.

Hessler (1344) German (southern and central): topographic name from Middle High German *hasel*, *hesel* 'hazel', or a habitational name from places called Hesslar, Hessler, or Hässler in Thuringia, Franconia, Westphalia, and Hesse.

Hessling (224) German: **1.** habitational name from Hesslingen near Rinteln. **2.** variant of HESSING.

Hessman (158) German (**Hessmann**) and Dutch: **1.** nickname or occupational name for a chaser at a hunt, from Middle High German *hessen* 'to hunt with hounds'. **2.** from a derivative of the personal name *Hesso* (see HESS 3).

GIVEN NAMES Dutch 4%. *Dirk*, *Durk*.

Hesson (802) Scottish and northern Irish: unexplained.

Hessong (102) German: variant spelling of **Hessung**, a patronymic derivative of HESS 3.

Hestand (354) Variant spelling of an unexplained German name, HIESTAND.

Hester (11984) **1.** North German: topographic name for someone who lived by a conspicuous beech tree, Middle Low German *hēster*. **2.** Irish (mainly County Mayo): reduced Anglicized form of Gaelic **Ó hOistir** 'descendant of *Oistir*'.

Hesterberg (141) German: habitational name from a place near Hannover, so named from Middle Low German *hēster* 'beech tree' + *berg* 'hill'.

GIVEN NAMES German 6%. *Armin*, *Ernst*.

Hesterman (138) North German (**Hestermann**): topographic name for someone who lived by a conspicuous beech tree, Middle Low German *hēster* + *man* 'man'.

GIVEN NAME German 4%. *Otto*.

Heston (1045) English: habitational name from Heston, Middlesex, named with Old

English *hǣs* 'brushwood' + *tūn* 'farmstead', 'settlement'.

Hetchler (120) Americanized spelling of German HECHLER.

Heter (127) Variant of English HEATER.

Heth (398) Scottish: from an early Anglicized form of the Gaelic personal name *Aed*, meaning 'fire'.

Hetherington (1317) English (northern border counties): habitational name from a place so named in Northumberland, possibly from Old English *hēahdēor* 'stag', 'deer' or *hæddre* 'heather' + *-ing* 'characterized by' + *tūn* 'farmstead', 'settlement'. This surname has been established in Ireland since the 16th century.

Hetland (513) Norwegian: habitational name from any of several farmsteads, mostly in Rogaland, so named from Old Norse *Hesliland*, a compound of *hesli* 'place where hazel grows' + *land* 'land'.

Hetler (124) German: variant spelling of HETTLER.

GIVEN NAME German 5%. *Kurt* (2).

Hetman (139) **1.** Polish, German (**Hettmann**), and Jewish (eastern Ashkenazic): from Polish *hetman* 'military leader' (a derivative of German HAUPTMANN 'captain'), a status name for a military officer or for the elected leader of a community. In some cases, it may have been given as a nickname. As a Jewish name it is generally ornamental; the literal sense 'military leader' never applies. **2.** Frisian: variant of HETT.

Hetrick (2524) Scottish: variant of HEADRICK.

Hett (276) Frisian, North German, and Dutch: from a pet form of any of the many Germanic personal names formed with *hadu* 'strife' as the first element.

Hettel (159) South German: from *Hettel* 'goat', which still exists as a dialect word; hence either a nickname for someone thought to resemble a goat, or a metonymic occupational name for a goatherd.

GIVEN NAME German 5%. *Kurt* (2).

Hettenbach (108) Variant of German **Hattenbach** (see HATTABAUGH).

Hettich (300) German (also **Hättich**): from *Hattich*, a pet form of a Germanic personal name (see HATT 2).

GIVEN NAMES German 6%. *Manfred* (2), *Frieda*, *Gottlieb*, *Hermann*.

Hettick (162) Americanized spelling of German HETTICH.

Hettinga (133) Frisian: patronymic derivative of the personal name *Hatto*, short form of any of the many Germanic personal names composed with *hadu* 'strife' as the first element.

GIVEN NAME German 5%. *Kurt* (2).

Hettinger (1109) German: habitational name for someone from any of the places called Hettingen, for example near Heilbronn or near Ebingen in Swabia.

Hettler (236) South German: **1.** occupational name for a goatherd, from an agent derivative of the dialect word *Hettel* 'goat'. **2.** North German: nickname for a hateful or belligerent person, from Middle Low German *heteler* 'hater', 'enemy'.
GIVEN NAMES German 4%. *Fritz, Kurt, Ulrich.*

Hettrick (211) Scottish: variant of HEADRICK.

Hettwer (106) German: from the Germanic personal name *Hathuward*, composed of the elements *hadu* 'strife' + *ward* 'guard', 'protection'.
GIVEN NAME German 4%. *Erwin.*

Hetu (147) French (**Hétu**): unexplained.
FOREBEARS A Hétu from Normandy, with the secondary surname LAFLEUR, is recorded as arriving in Canada in 1685 and marrying at Boucherville, Quebec, in 1699. Other secondary surnames associated with Hétu are ETHIER, **Étié**, and **Étu**.
GIVEN NAMES French 20%. *Andre* (2), *Marcel* (2), *Jean-Guy, Michel, Normand, Raymonde.*

Hetz (211) German: **1.** from a pet form of HERMANN. **2.** in Bavaria, a variant of HATZ.
GIVEN NAMES German 4%. *Heinz, Hellmut, Kurt.*

Hetzel (1529) German: **1.** from a pet form of the personal name HERMANN. **2.** from a Germanic personal name, a pet form of a compound name formed with *haid* 'heath', 'wasteland' as the first element. **3.** from Middle High German *holz*, Middle Low German *holt* 'wood', a topographic name, an occupational name for someone who provided wood, or a nickname for a stubborn person.

Hetzer (371) German: occupational name for a hunter with hounds, Middle High German *hetzer*.

Hetzler (465) German: variant of HETZEL 3 or HETZER.
GIVEN NAMES German 4%. *Ernst, Horst.*

Hetzner (103) German: possibly a variant of HETZEL 3 or HETZER.
GIVEN NAMES German 12%. *Eldor* (3), *Otto.*

Heuberger (182) German and Jewish (Ashkenazic): habitational name for someone from a place called Heuberg, a common German place name, composed of Middle High German *höu* 'hay' + *berg* 'mountain', 'hill'.
GIVEN NAMES German 10%. *Hans* (2), *Jutta* (2), *Fritz, Helmut, Helmuth, Kurt, Manfred.*

Heuck (106) German: variant of HAUCK.
GIVEN NAMES German 6%. *Irmgard, Otto.*

Heuer (1771) **1.** German: variant of HAUER. **2.** German: occupational name from Middle High German *höuwer* 'mower', 'hay-maker'.
GIVEN NAMES German 4%. *Armin* (3), *Elke* (3), *Hans* (2), *Kurt* (2), *Otto* (2), *Ernst,*

Frieda, Gerhard, Gunther, Helmut, Hermann, Rainer.

Heuerman (204) Variant spelling of German HEUERMANN.

Heuermann (149) German: occupational name for a hired hand, a day laborer, from Middle High German *hüren* 'to hire' + *man* 'man'.
GIVEN NAME German 4%. *Kurt.*

Heuman (159) German and Jewish (Ashkenazic): see HEUMANN.
GIVEN NAMES German 6%. *Manfred, Wolfgang.*

Heumann (324) **1.** German and Jewish (Ashkenazic): occupational name for a grower or mower of grass, from Middle High German *höu* 'grass', 'hay' + *man* 'man', German *Heu* + *Mann*. **2.** German: from a pet form of the Germanic personal name *Hago* or a variant of HEINEMANN.
GIVEN NAMES German 6%. *Kurt* (2), *Otto, Wilhelm.*

Heun (286) **1.** German: nickname from Middle High German *hiune* 'giant' (see HUHN 1). **2.** German: variant of HEINE. **3.** Dutch: from a Germanic personal name, *Huno*.

Heupel (388) South German: from a pet form of a Germanic personal name composed of *hagin* 'enclosure', 'fenced area' + *berht* 'bright', 'illustrious', or of the elements *hugi* 'thinking mind' + *bald* 'bold', 'quick'.
GIVEN NAMES German 4%. *Otto* (3), *Frieda, Helmuth.*

Heuring (270) **1.** Dutch: habitational name from any of a number of places named with *horik* 'corner', 'hook', such as Horrink in Turnhout, in the Belgian province of Antwerp, or Hooring in Brabant. **2.** German: possibly from a Germanic personal name beginning with *hugi* 'thinking mind'.

Heusel (106) South German: **1.** variant of **Häusel**, a diminutive of HAUS. **2.** perhaps also from a Germanic personal name derived from *huso* 'house'.
GIVEN NAME German 4%. *Udo.*

Heuser (631) South German: variant of HAUSER.
GIVEN NAMES German 7%. *Hans* (2), *Klaus* (2), *Detlef, Dieter, Elfriede, Helmut, Inge, Kurt, Manfred, Otto.*

Heusinkveld (125) Dutch: habitational name from a place so called.

Heuss (123) German (Alemannic, Swabian): nickname from Middle High German *hiusse* 'lively', 'fresh'.
GIVEN NAMES German 5%. *Beate, Ernst.*

Heusser (172) South German: variant of HAUSER.
GIVEN NAMES German 4%. *Kurt, Monika.*

Heussner (117) German: status name for a day laborer with no land, a variant of **Häusler** (see HAUSLER).
GIVEN NAMES German 7%. *Helmut, Otto.*

Heustess (101) Variant of HEUSTIS.

Heustis (114) English: unexplained. Perhaps a variant of EUSTACE.

Heuston (145) Irish: variant of HOUSTON or HEWSON.

Heuton (131) **1.** Probably of Dutch origin, an altered form of Dutch **Houten** 'woods'. **2.** Perhaps also a variant of English HOOTON. This surname is found chiefly in IA.

Hevener (325) Probably an Anglicized form of German **Häfner** (see HAFNER). See also HEAVENER.

Heverly (355) Possibly an altered spelling of German HEBERLE.

Hevey (157) Altered spelling of French **Hévé**, a variant of the Normandy name **Dévé**, a nickname from *desvé* 'mad,' 'insane'.
FOREBEARS A Hévé from Normandy is documented in Quebec city in 1672.
GIVEN NAME French 4%. *Nicolle.*

Hevia (136) Asturian-Leonese: habitational name from a parish in Siero, in Asturies.
GIVEN NAMES Spanish 44%. *Manuel* (8), *Jose* (6), *Luis* (5), *Roberto* (5), *Jorge* (4), *Carlos* (3), *Rafael* (3), *Ramon* (3), *Armando* (2), *Sergio* (2), *Alfonso, Arnaldo.*

Hevner (130) Anglicized form of German **Häfner** (see HAFNER). See also HEAVENER.

Hew (190) **1.** Scottish: variant of HUGH. This was at one time the usual form of the personal name in Scotland. **2.** English: status name for a domestic servant, Middle English *hewe*, a singular form derived from a plural noun *hewen* (Old English *hīwan*) 'members of a household', 'domestic servants'.

Heward (209) English: variant of HOWARD 1.

Hewatt (143) English: variant of HEWITT.

Hewell (289) English: from a pet form of the personal name *Hugh*, *Hew* (see HUGH).

Hewes (802) English: patronymic from *Hew*, a variant of HUGH.

Hewett (2549) English: variant of HEWITT.

Hewey (175) Probably an altered spelling of HUEY.

Hewgley (160) Possibly of German origin: see HUGLEY.

Hewins (291) Scottish: patronymic from EWAN (with inorganic *H-* prefixed).

Hewitson (154) English (mainly Cumbria) and Scottish: patronymic from HEWITT 1.

Hewitt (11006) **1.** English, Welsh, and Scottish: from the medieval personal name *Huet*, a diminutive of HUGH. See also HEW. The surname has also long been established in Ireland. **2.** English: topographic name for someone who lived in a newly made clearing in a wood, Middle English *hewett* (Old English *hīewet*, a derivative of *hēawan* 'to chop', 'to hew').

Hewlett (1372) English (central western England): from the Middle English personal name *Huwelet, Huwelot, Hughelot*, a double diminutive of HUGH formed with the diminutive suffixes *-el* + *-et* and *-ot*. The surname is also established in Ireland.

Hewson (603) **1.** English (chiefly Lincolnshire): patronymic from *Hew* (see HUGH). **2.** Scottish and Irish: Anglicized form of Gaelic **Mac Aodha** (see McCOY).

Hext (160) English (Devon): nickname from Middle English *hext* 'tallest', 'highest' (Old English *hēhst*, superlative of *hēah* 'high').

Hexter (102) **1.** Jewish (Ashkenazic): unexplained. **2.** English (Devon and Cornwall): unexplained.
GIVEN NAMES Jewish 6%. *Shoshana, Simcha*.

Hexum (117) Scandinavian: unexplained.
GIVEN NAME Scandinavian 5%. *Bodil*.

Hey (758) **1.** English (Yorkshire): habitational name from a place called Hey. **2.** Dutch: topographic name for someone who lived on a heath, Dutch *hei, heide*. **3.** German: metonymic occupational name for a grower or mower of grass, from Middle High German *höu* 'grass', 'hay'. **4.** North German (Frisian) and Dutch: from a Germanic personal name formed with *hag* 'fence', 'enclosure' as the first element. **5.** South German: occupational name from Middle High German *heie* 'ranger', 'warden', 'guard' or a topographic name from Middle High German *haie* 'protected wood'.

Heyboer (204) Dutch: distinguishing nickname for someone whose farm was on or by heathland, from *hei* 'heath' + *boer* 'farmer'.

Heyd (241) German and Dutch: topographic name for someone who lived on a heath, a variant of HEID or HEIDE.
GIVEN NAMES German 4%. *Aloys, Erwin, Hans, Lorenz*.

Heyde (245) German and Dutch: topographic name for someone who lived on a heath, a variant of HEID or HEIDE.
GIVEN NAMES German 6%. *Achim, Dietrich, Helmut, Volker*.

Heyden (305) German: **1.** variant spelling of HEIDEN 2. **2.** topographic name shortened from *von der Heyden* 'of the heath' (see HEID 1).

Heyder (117) German: variant spelling of HEIDER.
GIVEN NAMES German 17%; Scandinavian 4%. *Dietrich, Ekkehard, Gerhard, Markus, Siegmund, Wolfgang; Bjoern*.

Heydinger (101) German: variant spelling of HEIDINGER.

Heydon (179) English: variant of HAYDEN 2.

Heydt (383) German: variant spelling of HEIDT, itself a variant of HEID.

Heye (165) **1.** English (chiefly Yorkshire and Lancashire): variant of HEY 1.

2. Dutch, Frisian, and North German: variant of HEY 4.

Heyen (366) German (Frisian) and Dutch: patronymic from HEYE 2.

Heyer (1303) **1.** English: variant of AYER 1. **2.** German: occupational name for a grower or reaper of grass for hay, from Middle High German *höu* 'grass', 'hay' + the agent suffix *-er*. **3.** German: variant spelling of HEIER 1. **4.** Dutch: from a Germanic personal name composed of the elements *hagi* 'enclosure', 'fenced area' + *hari, heri* 'army'. **5.** Dutch: nickname from Middle Dutch *(h)eiger, heeger, heger* 'heron'. Compare HERON 1.
GIVEN NAMES German 4%. *Kurt* (3), *Gerhart* (2), *Hans* (2), *Achim, Bernhardt, Dietrich, Gerhard, Hertha, Ilse, Ingeburg, Klaus*.

Heyes (140) English (Lancashire): variant spelling of HAYES.

Heying (375) German (Westphalia): from a short form of a Germanic personal name formed with *hagi* 'enclosure', 'fenced area' as the first element.

Heyl (531) German: from a pet form of the personal name *Heinrich* (see HENRY 1).

Heyliger (114) Variant spelling of German HEILIGER.

Heyman (1319) **1.** English: variant of HAYMAN. **2.** Dutch: variant of HEY 2. **3.** Jewish (Ashkenazic): variant of HEIMAN. **4.** Respelling of German HEYMANN.

Heymann (432) **1.** German: variant spelling of HEIMANN 1. **2.** Jewish (Ashkenazic): variant of HEIMAN.
GIVEN NAMES German 9%. *Hans* (5), *Dieter, Erwin, Hanns, Irmgard, Juergen, Kurt, Manfred, Otto*.

Heyn (447) German and Dutch: variant spelling of HEIN.
GIVEN NAMES German 4%. *Hans* (3), *Arno* (2), *Hermann, Kurt*.

Heyne (375) **1.** English: variant spelling of HAIN 1–3. **2.** Irish: variant of HINES. **3.** Dutch and German: variant of HEIN.
GIVEN NAMES German 5%. *Ewald, Gerda, Heinrich, Helmuth, Ingo, Klaus, Otto*.

Heynen (120) Dutch: variant of HEINEN.
GIVEN NAMES French 6%. *Henri, Remi*.

Heyob (102) German (Kaiserslautern): variant of *Hiob*, vernacular form of the Biblical name *Job*.

Heyrman (108) North German (also **Heyrmann**): variant of HEUERMANN.
GIVEN NAME German 6%. *Kurt* (2).

Heys (140) **1.** English (Lancashire): variant spelling of HAYES. **2.** Dutch: variant of HEISE 2.

Heyse (158) North German and Dutch: variant spelling of HEISE.
GIVEN NAMES German 9%. *Gunther* (2), *Bernd, Heinz*.

Heyser (163) South German and Austrian: variant spelling of HEISER.

Heyward (1009) English: variant spelling of HAYWARD.

Heywood (1122) English (chiefly Lancashire): habitational name from a place near Manchester, so named from Old English *hēah* 'high' + *wudu* 'wood'. There is also a place in Wiltshire so called, from Old English *(ge)hæg* 'enclosure' + *wudu*. Compare HAYWOOD, although this is probably not the source of the surname.

Hiatt (4124) English: variant spelling of HYATT.

Hibbard (2974) English: variant of HILBERT.

Hibben (169) German (Frisian) and Dutch: from *Hibbo*, a pet form of the Germanic personal name *Hildibrand*, composed of the elements *hild* 'strife', 'battle' + *brand* 'fire', 'sword'.

Hibberd (277) English: variant of HILBERT.

Hibbert (988) English: variant of HILBERT.

Hibbett (125) English: variant spelling of HIBBITT.

Hibbitt (103) English: **1.** from a pet form of the female personal name *Isabel* (see HIBBS 2). **2.** from a pet form of the personal name HILBERT.

Hibbitts (254) English: metronymic or patronymic from HIBBITT.

Hibbler (331) **1.** German: variant of **Hibbeler**, a derivative of the personal name *Hibbo*, a pet form of any of the many several Germanic personal names formed with *hild* 'strife' as the first element. **2.** North German: nickname for a fidgety person, from *hibbelen, hiwwelen* 'to act nervously'.

Hibbs (2195) English (chiefly south coast): **1.** patronymic from a short form of HIBBARD. **2.** metronymic from the medieval female personal name *Ibb*, a reduced form of *Isabel(le)* (see ISBELL).

Hibdon (433) Variant of English HEBDEN.

Hibler (611) South German (Bavaria, Tyrol): topographic name from a word preserved in dialect as *Hiebel* 'hill' + the agent suffix *-er*.

Hibma (145) Frisian: patronymic from the medieval personal name *Hibbo* (see HIBBEN).

Hibner (432) German: variant of **Hübner** (see HUEBNER).

Hibshman (171) **1.** Jewish (Ashkenazic): variant of HIPSHER. **2.** Americanized spelling of German **Hübschmann**, a variant of HUEBSCH.

Hice (691) Possibly an Americanized spelling of German and Jewish HEISS.

Hick (309) **1.** English: from the medieval personal name *Hicke*, a pet form of RICHARD. The substitution of *H-* as the initial resulted from the inability of the English to cope with the velar Norman *R-*. **2.** Dutch: from a pet form of a Germanic personal name, such as *Icco* or *Hikke* (a Frisian derivative of a compound name with the first element *hild* 'strife', 'battle').

3. East German: from a derivative of a Slavic pet form of HEINRICH. **4.** South German: from *Hiko*, a pet form of any of the Germanic personal names formed with *hild* 'strife', 'battle' as the first element.

Hickam (477) English: variant of HICKEN.

Hickcox (171) English: patronymic from HICKOK.

Hickel (312) German: pet form of HICK 4.

Hicken (364) English (West Midlands): from a pet form of HICK.

Hickenbottom (341) English: variant of HIGGINBOTHAM.

Hickernell (123) Origin unidentified.

Hickerson (1941) English: variant of HICKSON.

Hickey (11636) **1.** Irish (Munster): Anglicized form of Gaelic **Ó hÍceadh** 'descendant of *Ícidhe*', a byname meaning 'doctor', 'healer'. **2.** English: from a pet form of HICK.
FOREBEARS Irish bearers of the name claim descent from the hereditary physicians to the O'Brien kings of Thomond.
GIVEN NAMES Irish 4%. *Brendan* (7), *James Patrick* (2), *Marypat* (2), *Aileen*, *Bridie*, *Colm*, *Conn*, *Conor*, *Delma*, *Fergus*, *Kieran*, *Liam*.

Hickle (465) Possibly an Americanized spelling of German **Hickel**, which derives from a pet form of HICK 4.

Hicklin (464) English: variant of HICKLING.

Hickling (174) English (East Midlands): **1.** habitational name from either of two places called Hickling, in Nottinghamshire and Norfolk, from the Old English tribal name *Hicelingas* 'people of *Hicel(a)*', a personal name or byname of unknown origin. **2.** pet form of HICK.

Hickman (14143) English (chiefly West Midlands): occupational name denoting the servant (Middle English *man*) of a man called HICK. According to Reaney and Wilson, *Hickman* was also used as a medieval personal name. This surname has long been established in Ireland, notably in County Clare. In the U.S., it could be an altered spelling of German **Hickmann**, a variant of HICK 4.

Hickmon (215) English: variant of HICKMAN.

Hickmott (130) English: from the Middle English personal name HICK + Middle English *maugh*, *mough* 'relative' (from Old Norse *mágr* or Old English *magu*). The exact nature of the relationship is not clear; the Middle English word meant 'relative by marriage', but was also used occasionally of a female blood relation.

Hickok (1104) Altered spelling of English **Hickock**, from a pet form of HICK or a pet form of HAY 3.
FOREBEARS The family name made famous by the frontier marshal James Butler 'Wild Bill' Hickok (1837–76) was introduced to North America by his grandfather Otis Hickok, an emigrant from Ireland who

fought at Plattsburgh, NY, in the War of 1812 and started a family in Grand Isle Co., VT.

Hickory (109) English (Gloucestershire): unexplained.

Hickox (843) English: patronymic from HICKOK.

Hicks (49751) **1.** English: patronymic from HICK 1. This is a widespread surname in England, and is common in the southwest and southern Wales. **2.** Dutch and German: patronymic from HICK. Compare HIX.

Hickson (1616) English: patronymic from HICK. This surname has also been established in the Irish county of Kerry since the 17th century.

Hidalgo (2522) Spanish: from *hidalgo* 'nobleman' (attested in this form since the 12th century), a contraction of the phrase *hijo de algo* 'son of something'. The expression *hijo de* (Latin *filius* 'son' + *de* 'of') is used to indicate the abundant possession of a quality, probably influenced by similar Arabic phrases with *ibn*; *algo* (Latin *aliquid* 'something') is used in an elliptical manner to refer to riches or importance. As in the case of other surnames denoting high rank, the name does not normally refer to the nobleman himself, but is usually an occupational name for his servant or a nickname for someone who gave himself airs and graces.
GIVEN NAMES Spanish 40%. *Jose* (48), *Carlos* (30), *Juan* (23), *Manuel* (23), *Luis* (18), *Mario* (15), *Miguel* (14), *Jorge* (13), *Ricardo* (13), *Julio* (12), *Pedro* (12), *Ramon* (11).

Hiday (136) Origin unidentified. Perhaps an Americanized form of German HIDDE.

Hidde (144) German: from the medieval personal name *Hidde*, a reduced form of HILDEBRAND or a similar name containing the Old High German element *hild* 'battle', 'strife'.

Hidden (110) English: habitational name from Hidden in Berkshire or Clayhidon in Devon, recorded in Domesday Book as *Hidone*, from Old English *hī(e)g* 'hay' + *dūn* 'hill'.

Hider (196) English: variant spelling of HYDER.

Hidy (206) Hungarian: archaic form of *Hidi* (or *Hídi*), topographic name for someone living by a bridge, from *híd* 'bridge'.

Hieb (616) German: from *Hib(b)o*, a pet form of a Germanic personal name *Hildibert* (see HIEBERT).

Hieber (358) German: **1.** variant of HIEBERT. **2.** variant of **Hüber** (see HUEBER).
GIVEN NAMES German 6%. *Erwin* (4), *Fritz*, *Kurt*, *Ralf*.

Hiebert (976) German: from the Germanic personal name *Hildibert*, composed of the elements *hild* 'strife', 'battle' + *berht* 'bright', 'famous'.
GIVEN NAMES German 4%. *Kurt* (2), *Otto* (2), *Erwin*, *Franz*, *Gerhard*.

Hiegel (189) German and French (Alsace): from a pet form of HUGO.

Hielscher (107) German: variant of HILSCHER 1.

Hiemenz (141) German (Baden): unexplained.

Hiemstra (351) Frisian: topographic name from *hiem* '(farm)yard', 'area around a farmhouse' + the locative agent suffix *-stra*.

Hier (358) **1.** Welsh: descriptive nickname from Welsh *hir* 'long', 'tall'. **2.** South German: from a rare Germanic personal name composed with the unexplained element *hīr*, possibly related to Old Saxon *heru* 'sword'.

Hierholzer (225) South German: habitational name for someone from Hierholz, near St Blasien.
GIVEN NAME German 4%. *Otto* (2).

Hieronimus (104) Dutch and German: variant of HIERONYMUS.

Hieronymus (296) Dutch and German: from a humanistic personal name, a Latinized form of Greek *Hierōnymos*, composed of the elements *hieros* 'sacred' + *onyma* 'name'. See also JEROME, which is the vernacular English form of this name.

Hiers (1017) Dutch: occupational name for a grower or seller of millet, Middle Dutch *hirse*.

Hiestand (477) German (Baden) and Swiss German: unexplained.

Hiester (259) German (Rhineland): probably a habitational name from a place so named near Celle.

Hietala (289) Finnish: from *hieta* 'sand' + the local suffix *-la*, originally a habitational name from any of numerous farmsteads and villages so named, especially in western Finland; later, during the name conversion movement in the 19th and early 20th centuries, it was also adopted as an ornamental name, especially by Finns bearing Swedish names containing the element *sand*. It is now found throughout Finland.
GIVEN NAMES Finnish 5%; Scandinavian 4%. *Eino* (2), *Kaarlo* (2), *Arvo*, *Erkki*, *Toivo*.

Hietpas (376) Probably Dutch, but unexplained. In the U.S. this surname is found predominantly in WI.

Hiett (683) English: variant of HYATT.

Higa (1129) Japanese: written phonetically with characters meaning 'comparison' and 'praise'; the actual meaning, however, is unclear, although it is the name of several locations in Okinawa. The surname is most common in western Japan and the Ryūkyū Islands.
GIVEN NAMES Japanese 32%. *Isamu* (5), *Shigeru* (5), *Haruko* (4), *Kiyoshi* (4), *Shigeo* (4), *Toshio* (4), *Fumi* (3), *Masao* (3), *Masaru* (3), *Noboru* (3), *Take* (3), *Yoshi* (3).

Higareda (129) Hispanic (common in Mexico): unexplained.
GIVEN NAMES Spanish 53%. *Jose* (5), *Luis* (4), *Francisco* (3), *Sergio* (3), *Guadalupe*

(2), *Jose Luis* (2), *Rogelio* (2), *Adolfo*, *Adulfo*, *Alberto*, *Alejo*, *Alicia*; *Amadeo*, *Antonio*, *Clemente*, *Federico*, *Marco Antonio*.

Higashi (384) Japanese: 'east' (also read **Azuma**), a common place name in Japan, held as a surname by several different families.
GIVEN NAMES Japanese 42%. *Akira* (3), *Emiko* (2), *Masa* (2), *Toshio* (2), *Yoshio* (2), *Aki*, *Chieko*, *Chiyo*, *Chizuko*, *Eichi*, *Eiki*, *Fumiko*.

Higbee (1319) English: of unknown etymology. It looks like a habitational name, but no place of this name is known in Britain. The proposed etymology from an Old English personal name, *Higbert*, is equally doubtful.
FOREBEARS The name was brought to North America in the 1640s from Ivinghoe in Buckinghamshire, England.

Higbie (334) English: variant spelling of HIGBEE.

Higby (577) English: variant spelling of HIGBEE.

Higdon (3514) English: from the personal name *Hikedun*, a medieval pet form of RICHARD; it is apparently a variant of *Ricardun*, a form of *Ric(h)ard* with a diminutive ending; for explanation of the initial *H-*, see HICK.

Higgason (208) English (Hereford): unexplained. Compare HIGGERSON.

Higgenbotham (141) English: variant spelling of HIGGINBOTHAM.

Higgens (100) English and Irish: variant of HIGGINS.

Higgerson (191) English (Warwickshire): unexplained. Compare HIGGASON.

Higginbotham (5353) English (Lancashire and Yorkshire): habitational name from a place in Lancashire now known as Oakenbottom. The history of the place name is somewhat confused, but it is probably composed of the Old English elements *æcen* or *ācen* 'oaken' + *botme* 'broad valley'. During the Middle Ages this name became successively *Eakenbottom* and *Ickenbottom*, the first element becoming associated with the dialect word *hicken* or *higgen* 'mountain ash' or the personal name *Higgin*.

Higginbottom (357) Northern English: variant of HIGGINBOTHAM.

Higgins (29665) 1. Irish: Anglicized form of Gaelic **Ó hUiginn** 'descendant of *Uiginn*', a byname meaning 'viking', 'searover' (from Old Norse *víkingr*). 2. Irish: variant of HAGAN. 3. English: patronymic from the medieval personal name *Higgin*, a pet form of HICK.

Higginson (700) English (mainly Lancashire): patronymic from the medieval personal name *Higgin*, a pet form of HICK.
FOREBEARS The Higginson family of New England, which includes several prominent 17th and 18th century ministers and merchants, first appeared in America in 1629 with the Rev. Francis Higginson of Claybrooke, Leicestershire, England. He was a Puritan divine who emigrated to Salem, MA in that year.

Higgs (3352) English: patronymic from HICK.

High (4726) English (chiefly East Anglia and northern England): nickname for a tall man, from Middle English *hegh, hie* 'high', 'tall', Old English *hēah* (compare HAY 2), or a topographic name for a dweller on a hilltop or high place, from the same word used in a topographical sense. This second use is supported by early forms such as Richard *atte High* (Sussex 1332).

Higham (574) English (Lancashire): habitational name from any of the many places in England so called, of which the most likely source for present-day bearers is that near Burnley. The place name is from Old English *hēah* 'high' + *hām* 'homestead'.

Highbaugh (130) Altered spelling of German **Heibach**, a habitational name from a place so named in the Rhineland, near Lindlar.

Highberger (172) Americanized spelling of HEIBERGER.

Highfield (573) English: habitational name from any of the numerous minor places so called from Old English *hēah* 'high' + *feld* 'pasture', 'open country' (see FIELD).

Highfill (951) 1. Possibly an altered spelling of Dutch **Heuvel**, a nickname or topographic name from Middle Dutch *hoevel, heuvel* 'hump', 'mound'. 2. Possibly an altered form of HIGHFIELD.

Highland (983) 1. English, Scottish, and Irish: variant spelling of HYLAND. 2. Possibly an Americanized spelling of German HEILAND.

Highlander (212) Americanized spelling of German **Heilander**, probably a topographic name composed of Middle High German *höu* 'hay' + *land* 'land' + the agent suffix *-er*.

Highley (631) English: habitational name from any of several places so called, for example one in Shropshire, which was named in Old English as 'Hugga's woodland clearing', from an unattested personal name + *lēah* 'wood', 'glade'.

Highman (147) English: nickname for a tall man (see HIGH).

Highsmith (1351) English: occupational name for a smith, with the distinguishing epithet *high*, probably denoting one whose forge was at a higher location than another nearby smith.

Hight (2110) English: topographic name for someone who lived at the top of a hill or on a piece of raised ground, from Middle English *heyt* 'summit', 'height'.

Hightower (5968) English: perhaps an altered form of HAYTER (see HIGHT).

Higinbotham (233) English: variant spelling of HIGGINBOTHAM.

Higley (1627) English: variant of HIGHLEY.

Higman (235) English (chiefly Devon): variant of HICKMAN.

Hignight (138) Origin uncertain. 1. Possibly an altered spelling of English **Hignett**, which is from a pet form of the personal name HICK. 2. Alternatively, perhaps it may be an Americanized form of a German name ending with *-knecht*. Compare GOODNIGHT.

Hignite (270) Variant of HIGNIGHT.

Higson (115) English: variant of HICKSON.

Higuchi (270) Japanese: topographic name for someone who lived by a drain or water spout. Certain bearers of the surname descend from the Seiwa-Genji through the Tayaka family. The surname is most common in western Japan.
GIVEN NAMES Japanese 54%. *Kenji* (4), *Nobuhiro* (3), *Hirokazu* (2), *Kentaro* (2), *Kiyoshi* (2), *Masayuki* (2), *Nobuyuki* (2), *Tadashi* (2), *Yoshiyuki* (2), *Aiko*, *Akio*, *Ayako*.

Higuera (479) Spanish: habitational name from any of numerous places named Higuera, from *higuera* 'fig tree' (Latin *ficaria*).
GIVEN NAMES Spanish 39%. *Jose* (9), *Manuel* (9), *Juan* (6), *Jesus* (4), *Luis* (4), *Carlos* (3), *Guadalupe* (3), *Margarita* (3), *Raul* (3), *Adelina* (2), *Aurelio* (2), *Blanca* (2).

Hilaire (185) French: from the personal name, French form of HILLARY 1.
GIVEN NAMES French 33%. *Andre* (2), *Jacques* (2), *Pierre* (2), *Antoine*, *Chantal*, *Edeline*, *Georges*, *Luc*, *Maryse*, *Mimose*, *Serge*, *Yolaine*.

Hiland (340) 1. Variant spelling of HYLAND. 2. Altered spelling of German HEILAND.

Hilario (294) Portuguese (**Hilário**) and Spanish: from a personal name of the same origin as HILLARY 1.
GIVEN NAMES Spanish 46%; Portuguese 10%. *Julio* (5), *Alfredo* (4), *Luis* (4), *Abelardo* (3), *Arturo* (3), *Eduardo* (3), *Francisco* (3), *Juan* (3), *Mario* (3), *Pedro* (3), *Carlos* (2), *Cesar* (2); *Afonso*, *Joao*.

Hilber (135) German: variant of HILBERT.
GIVEN NAMES German 7%. *Alois*, *Hedwig*, *Niklaus*, *Ralf*.

Hilberg (162) German: habitational name from Hüllberg in the Ruhr, Hillenberg in Bavaria, or Hilburg in the Odenwald.

Hilbert (2127) English, French, Dutch, and German: from a Germanic personal name composed of the elements *hild* 'strife', 'battle' + *berht* 'bright', 'famous'.

Hilbig (149) German and Dutch: variant of HELWIG.
GIVEN NAMES German 11%. *Kurt* (3), *Manfred*.

Hilbish (116) Americanized form of German HILBIG.
GIVEN NAME German 4%. *Georg*.

Hilborn (398) English: variant of HILBURN.

Hilbrich (106) German: variant of HILBERT.
GIVEN NAME German 5%. *Otto* (2).

Hilbun (278) English: variant of HILBURN.

Hilburn (1481) English: habitational name from a lost or unidentified place.

Hilby (116) English: unexplained; possibly a habitational name from a lost or unidentified place.

Hild (752) **1.** German and Dutch: from a short form of HILDEBRAND or other compound names with the same initial element, *hild* 'strife', 'battle'. **2.** English: from the medieval female personal name *Hilda* (Old English *Hild*), representing a short form of compound names with the first element *hild* 'strife', 'battle'. Compare HILLIARD, for example.
GIVEN NAMES German 4%. *Helmut* (2), *Erna*, *Inge*, *Irmgard*, *Johann*, *Udo*, *Volker*.

Hildahl (132) Swedish: ornamental name from *dahl* 'valley' with an unidentified first element.
GIVEN NAMES Scandinavian 4%. *Erik*, *Selmer*.

Hilde (264) German and Dutch: variant of HILD 1.
GIVEN NAMES Scandinavian 7%. *Arlys*, *Erik*, *Iver*, *Juel*, *Selmer*.

Hildebran (212) Variant of German HILDEBRAND.

Hildebrand (4662) German, Dutch, French, and English: from a Germanic personal name composed of the elements *hild* 'strife', 'battle' + *brand* 'fire' 'sword'.

Hildebrandt (2110) German and Danish: variant of HILDEBRAND.
GIVEN NAMES German 7%. *Otto* (7), *Kurt* (6), *Hans* (4), *Erwin* (3), *Horst* (3), *Heinz* (2), *Konrad* (2), *Bernhard*, *Dieter*, *Dietrich*, *Fritz*, *Gerhard*.

Hildebrant (422) German and Dutch: variant of HILDEBRAND.

Hilden (392) German: habitational name from a place so called near Benrath.

Hildenbrand (640) German: variant of HILDEBRAND.

Hildenbrandt (109) German: variant of HILDEBRAND.
GIVEN NAMES German 7%. *Frederich*, *Kurt*.

Hilder (108) English (mainly Sussex and Kent): topographic name from Middle English *hilder* 'dweller on a slope' (from Old English *hylde* 'slope').

Hilderbrand (1054) English: variant spelling of HILDEBRAND.

Hilderbrandt (144) German: variant of HILDEBRAND.

Hilderman (111) Dutch: from a masculine personal name composed of the Germanic elements *hild* 'strife', 'battle' + *man* 'man'.

Hilding (133) **1.** Swedish: from the personal name *Hilding*, which was popularized in the 19th century thanks to the poem *Fritjofs saga* by Esaias Tegnér, who took it from Old Icelandic *Hildingr* (from *hildingr* 'chieftain'). **2.** Dutch: patronymic from the personal name HILD.

GIVEN NAME Scandinavian 8%. *Lennart*.

Hilditch (146) English: unexplained.

Hildman (106) German (**Hildmann**): elaborated form of the personal name HILD.
GIVEN NAMES German 6%. *Eberhard*, *Otto*.

Hildner (108) **1.** German: habitational name for someone from Hilden near Düsseldorf. **2.** South German: nickname from the dialect word *hilde* 'attic', denoting someone who lived at the top of an apartment block.
GIVEN NAMES German 8%. *Hermann*, *Klaus*.

Hildreth (2673) Northern English: probably from a Middle English personal name, perhaps a variant of ELDRIDGE.

Hile (1015) Americanized spelling of Dutch HEIL.

Hileman (1738) Americanized spelling of German HEILMANN.

Hiler (700) Americanized spelling of HEILER.

Hiles (1235) English: unexplained.

Hiley (234) English (mainly Yorkshire): possibly a variant spelling of HIGHLEY.

Hilferty (145) Irish: variant of HALFERTY.

Hilfiker (187) Swiss German: altered spelling of **Hilfinger**, patronymic derivative of the personal name *Hilfo*, *Helfo*, a short form of a Germanic personal name based on *helfe* 'helper'. Compare HELFRICH.
GIVEN NAMES German 5%. *Hans* (2), *Ernst*.

Hilgart (189) German: from a reduced form of the female Germanic personal name *Hildegard* (see HILLIARD).

Hilgeman (197) North German (**Hilgemann**): occupational name for a member of a church council, from Middle Low German *hilge* 'holy' (inflected form of *hillich*) + *man* 'man'.

Hilgenberg (260) North German: probably a habitational name from an unidentified place named with Middle Low German *hilge(n)* 'holy' (inflected form of *hillich*) + *berg* 'mountain'.

Hilgendorf (460) North German: habitational name from any of several places so named, from Middle Low German *hilge(n)* 'holy' (inflected form of *hillich*) + *dorp* 'village'.

Hilger (774) German, Dutch, French, and English: from a Germanic personal name composed of the elements *hild* 'strife', 'battle' + *gēr*, *gār* 'spear'. This name was taken to England by the Normans; however, in East Anglia the surname is from an Old Danish personal name of similar origin.

Hilgers (429) North German and Dutch: patronymic from HILGER.

Hilgert (222) German (eastern and central) and Dutch: variant of HILGER.

Hilinski (171) Variant of Polish **Chyliński**, a habitational name for someone from any of several places called Chylin or Chylyny.
GIVEN NAME Polish 6%. *Casimir* (2).

Hilke (234) North German, Frisian, and Dutch: usually from a pet form of *Hilde-*

gund, a Germanic female name composed of the elements *hild* 'strife' + *gund* 'battle'. The Dutch surname is sometimes derived from a masculine personal name such as HILDEBRAND or HILGER.
GIVEN NAMES German 5%. *Gernot*, *Jurgen*.

Hilker (537) **1.** North German and Frisian: variant of HILKE. **2.** German and Dutch: variant of HILGER.

Hilkert (123) German: variant of HILKER.

Hill (141823) **1.** English and Scottish: extremely common and widely distributed topographic name for someone who lived on or by a hill, Middle English *hill* (Old English *hyll*). **2.** English: from the medieval personal name *Hill*, a short form of *Hilary* (see HILLARY) or of a Germanic (male or female) compound name with the first element *hild* 'strife', 'battle'. **3.** German: from a short form of HILDEBRAND or any of a variety of other names, male and female, containing Germanic *hild* as the first element. **4.** Jewish (American): Anglicized form of various Jewish names of similar sound or meaning. **5.** English translation of Finnish **Mäki** ('hill'), or of any of various other names formed with this element, such as **Mäkinen, Heinämaki, Kivimäki**.

Hilla (177) Variant of German or Dutch HILLE.

Hillard (1759) **1.** English (mainly Wales): possibly a reduced form of HILLIARD. **2.** French: from a derivative (pejorative) of *Hilaire*, French form of HILLARY 1.

Hillary (323) English: **1.** from a medieval male personal name (from Latin *Hilarius*, a derivative of *hilaris* 'cheerful', 'glad', from Greek *hilaros* 'propitious', 'joyful'). The Latin name was chosen by many early Christians to express their joy and hope of salvation, and was borne by several saints, including a 4th-century bishop of Poitiers noted for his vigorous resistance to the Arian heresy, and a 5th-century bishop of Arles. Largely due to veneration of the first of these, the name became popular in France in the forms *Hilari* and *Hilaire*, and was brought to England by the Norman conquerors. **2.** from the much rarer female personal name *Eulalie* (from Latin *Eulalia*, from Greek *eulalos* 'eloquent', literally well-speaking, chosen by early Christians as a reference to the gift of tongues), likewise introduced into England by the Normans. A St. Eulalia was crucified at Barcelona in the reign of the Emperor Diocletian and became the patron of that city. In England the name underwent dissimilation of the sequence *-l-l-* to *-l-r-* and the unfamiliar initial vowel was also mutilated, so that eventually the name was considered as no more than a feminine form of *Hilary* (of which the initial aspirate was in any case variable).
GIVEN NAMES Irish 5%. *Caitlin*, *Ciaran*.

Hillberg (121) Variant of Swedish HELL-BERG.
GIVEN NAME Scandinavian 4%. *Lars*.

Hillberry (148) Americanized form of Swedish HELLBERG.

Hille (589) **1.** English: variant of HILL 1. **2.** North German: from the personal name *Hille*, a pet form of HILDEBRAND. **3.** Dutch: from the place name *ten Hulle*, from *hulle* 'hill', found in many parts of the Netherlands. **4.** Norwegian: habitational name from any of several farmsteads in southwestern Norway, mostly on islands, named Hille, from Old Norse *hilla* 'terrace', 'ledge'.
GIVEN NAMES German 5%; Scandinavian 4%. *Juergen* (2), *Darrold, Franz, Guenter, Karl Heinz, Klaus, Konrad, Monika*; *Erik* (2), *Johan, Sig*.

Hilleary (287) English and Scottish: variant spelling of HILLARY.

Hillebrand (620) North German and French: variant of HILDEBRAND.
GIVEN NAMES German 5%. *Ewald* (2), *Dieter, Gerhard, Hans, Horst, Otto, Siegfried*.

Hillebrandt (122) North German and Dutch: variant of HILDEBRAND.

Hillegas (389) German: variant of HILLE-GASS.

Hillegass (382) German: from a variant of the Germanic personal name *Hildegaud*, composed of *hild* 'strife', 'battle' + *got*, of uncertain meaning (perhaps the same word as *Goth*).

Hilleman (124) German: variant of HILL-MANN.
GIVEN NAME German 6%. *Kurt* (2).

Hillen (422) **1.** Swedish (**Hillén**): ornamental name composed of an unexplained first element + the adjectival suffix *-én*, from Latin *-enius*. **2.** Dutch and North German: from the personal name *Hillin*, a derivative of a Germanic personal name formed with *hild* 'strife', 'battle' as the first element. **3.** Scottish and northern Irish: variant of HILLING. **4.** English: variant of HILLIAN.

Hillenbrand (521) North German and Dutch: variant of HILDEBRAND.

Hillenburg (220) German: possibly a variant spelling of **Hellenberg**, a habitational name from a place so named near Dortmund.

Hiller (3360) **1.** Southern English: topographic name for someone living by a hill. See HILL 1. **2.** German: metronymic from *Hille*, a pet form of the female personal name *Hildegund* (see HILKE). **3.** North German, Frisian, and Dutch: from a masculine personal beginning with the Germanic element *hild* 'strife', 'battle'. **4.** German: variant of **Hüller** (see HULLER).

Hillerman (101) **1.** German and Dutch: elaborated form of HILLER. **2.** German: habitational name for someone from Hillern near Soltau.

Hillers (126) **1.** North German and Frisian: patronymic from HILLER 3. **2.** English: variant of HILLHOUSE.

Hillery (569) English: variant spelling of HILLARY. This name has long been established in Ireland.

Hillesheim (216) German (northern and central) and Jewish (western Ashkenazic): habitational name from the city of Hildesheim or from any of several places named Hillesheim in Hesse and the Rhineland. The place name is probably from the genitive case of a personal name derived from a short form of the various Germanic compound names with a first element *hild* 'strife', 'battle' + Old High German *heim* 'homestead'.

Hillesland (124) Scandinavian: unexplained.
GIVEN NAME Scandinavian 5%. *Lief*.

Hillestad (301) Norwegian: habitational name from any of several farmsteads named Hillestad, from the Old Norse female personal name *Hildr*, literally 'battle', or any of several other names beginning with *Hild-* (for example *Hildufr, Hildir*) + *staðir* 'farmstead', 'dwelling'. In one example in Hordaland county the last element is Old Norse *stǫð* 'landing place' (for boats).
GIVEN NAMES Scandinavian 5%. *Erik* (4), *Nils*.

Hilley (640) Northern Irish and Scottish: variant spelling of **Hilly**, an Anglicized form of Gaelic **Ó hIcheallaigh**, itself a variant of **Ó Fithcheallaigh** 'descendant of *Fithcheallach*' (see FEELEY).

Hillhouse (756) **1.** English: topographic name for someone who lived at a house on a hill, Middle English *hill* + *hus*. **2.** Scottish and northern Irish: habitational name from any of several minor places so called in Ayrshire.
FOREBEARS Rev. James Hillhouse, the first minister of Montville, CT, came to America from Co. Londonderry, Ireland, about 1720. His grandson James Hillhouse was a Federalist congressman from CT and treasurer of Yale College from 1782 to 1832.

Hillian (100) English (of Norman origin): habitational name from Helléan in Brittany, France. The name was taken to England by Tihel de Helion, who after the Norman conquest gave his name to the manor of Helions Bumpstead in Essex.

Hilliard (6724) English: from the Norman female personal name *Hildiarde, Hildegard*, composed of the Germanic elements *hild* 'strife', 'battle' + *gard* 'fortress', 'stronghold'. The surname has been in Ireland since the 17th century.

Hillier (1084) **1.** English (southwest): occupational name for a roofer (tiler or thatcher), from an agent derivative of Middle English *hele(n)* 'to cover' (Old English

helian). **2.** French: from the personal name *Hillier* (see HILLARY).

Hilligoss (331) German: variant of HILLE-GASS.

Hilliker (711) Dutch and German: from the Germanic female personal name *Hildiger*, composed of the Germanic elements *hild* 'strife', 'battle' + *gēr, gār* 'spear'.

Hillin (267) Scottish and English: variant of HILLING or HILLIAN.

Hilling (226) Scottish and English: **1.** topographic name from an unattested Old English word, *hylling* 'hill-dweller'. **2.** variant of HILLIAN.

Hillis (2150) English: **1.** variant of HILLS. **2.** variant of HILLHOUSE. In the British Isles, this name is now most frequent in northern Ireland and Scotland.

Hillman (5906) **1.** English: topographic name for someone who lived or worked in hilly country, from Middle English *hill* + *man* 'man'. **2.** English: occupational name for the servant (Middle English *man*) of someone called *Hild* (see HILD 2). **3.** Altered spelling of North German HILLMANN.

Hillmann (283) North German: from an elaborated form of the personal name *Hille* (a reduced form of HILDEBRAND) + *Mann* 'man'.
GIVEN NAMES German 12%. *Gerhard* (2), *Klaus* (2), *Bernd, Erwin, Friedrich, Gerhardt, Hermann, Kurt*.

Hillmer (331) North German: variant spelling of HILMER.

Hillner (124) **1.** German (Silesia): variant of HILLER 2 or 3. **2.** Danish (Tønder) and Swedish: probably of German origin.
GIVEN NAMES Scandinavian 9%. *Erik, Gunner*.

Hillock (332) English and Scottish: topographic name for someone living on a small hill, Middle English *hilloc, hillok*.

Hills (4441) English (southeastern): **1.** variant of HILL 1. **2.** patronymic from HILL 2.

Hillsman (308) Americanized spelling of German **Hillsmann** (see HILSMAN).

Hillson (194) English: metronymic or patronymic from HILL 2.

Hillstead (115) English: habitational name from a lost or unidentified place, named as 'the estate (see STEAD) on the hill'.

Hillstrom (441) Swedish: probably a respelling of **Hellström** (see HELLSTROM) or possibly HALLSTRÖM.

Hillyard (737) English: variant spelling of HILLIARD.

Hillyer (1003) English: variant spelling of HILLIER 1.

Hilman (126) English: variant spelling of HILLMAN.
GIVEN NAME French 4%. *Henri*.

Hilmer (289) **1.** North German and Dutch: from the Germanic personal name *Hildemar*, formed with *hild* 'strife', 'battle' + *mari* 'famous'. **2.** German (South

German and Austrian): contracted form of *Hillmeier*, which is a topographic name derived from Middle High German *hülwe* 'water-hole' + *meier* '(tenant) farmer'.
GIVEN NAMES German 6%. *Otto* (2), *Heinrich*, *Juergen*.

Hilmes (219) German: habitational name for someone from Hilmes near Hersfeld (Hesse) or from Hildesheim, which is called *Hilm(e)sen* in the local dialect.

Hilpert (245) German and Dutch: variant of HILBERT.
GIVEN NAME French 4%. *Alphonse*.

Hils (113) **1.** German (Lower Rhine-Westphalia) and French (Alsace): **2.** topographic name for someone who lived near a stand or grove of holly, from a dialect form of *hülse* 'holly' (*Ilex aquifolium*). Compare HULST. This is also the name of a range of wooded hills near Hildesheim. **3.** from a short form of a Germanic personal name with *hild* 'fight', 'battle' as the first element.
GIVEN NAMES French 5%; German 4%. *Gabrielle* (2), *Henri*; *Friedrich*.

Hilsabeck (257) Americanized spelling of German **Hilsenbeck**, a habitational name from a minor place named with *Hülse* 'holly' + *beck* 'brook'.

Hilscher (171) German: **1.** metronymic from a Slavic female personal name, *Helusch*, *Hilusch*, a vernacular derivative of *Elisabeth*. **2.** variant of **Hölscher** (see HOLSCHER).
GIVEN NAMES German 6%. *Bernd*, *Erwin*, *Juergen*.

Hilsinger (149) German: probably a habitational name for someone from Helsungen in the Harz Mountains. Compare HELSING.

Hilsman (143) German (**Hilsmann**): from the personal name *Hildo*, a pet form of a Germanic personal name formed with *hild* 'strife', 'battle' as the first element.

Hilson (502) English and Scottish: patronymic or metronymic from HILL 2.

Hilst (106) Dutch or North German: variant of HULST.

Hilt (1086) German: from a short form of HILDEBRAND or other compound Germanic names formed with *hild* 'strife', 'battle' as the first element.

Hiltbrand (119) German: variant of HILDEBRAND.
GIVEN NAME German 5%. *Ernst*.

Hilterbrand (125) Altered form of HILDEBRAND.

Hiltner (348) South German: probably a habitational name for someone from a place called Hilte or Hilde.

Hilton (10037) **1.** English (Lancashire) and Scottish: habitational name from any of various places so called. Most, including those in Cambridgeshire (formerly Huntingdonshire), Cleveland, Derbyshire, and Shropshire, get the name from Old English *hyll* 'hill' + *tūn* 'enclosure', 'settlement'. Others, including those in Cumbria

and Dorsetshire, have early forms in *Hel-* and probably have as their first element Old English *hielde* 'slope' or possibly *helde* 'tansy'. **2.** English: some early examples such as Ralph filius Hilton (Yorkshire 1219) point to occasional derivation from a personal name, possibly a Norman name *Hildun*, composed of the Germanic elements *hild* 'strife', 'battle' + *hūn* 'bear cub'. The English surname is present in Ireland (mostly taken to Ulster in the early 17th century, though recorded earlier in Dublin).
FOREBEARS A family bearing this name originated at *Hetton* in County Durham (from Old English *hēope* 'rosehip' + *dūn* 'hill'). The surname had already been assimilated to Hilton by the time of Robert de Hilton (died *c.*1309).

Hilts (565) Americanized spelling of HILTZ.

Hiltunen (213) Finnish: from a personal name derived from a short form of a Germanic compound name formed with *hild* 'battle', 'strife' (as for example HILDEBRAND) + the common surname suffix *-nen*.
GIVEN NAMES Finnish 7%; Scandinavian 7%. *Jorma*, *Reijo*, *Siiri*, *Sulo*, *Toivo*, *Waino*; *Jalmer*, *Jarl*, *Lars*.

Hilty (690) Swiss German: from a pet form of HILDEBRAND.

Hiltz (604) Altered spelling of South German **Hilz**, a variant of HILD 1.

Hilyard (361) English: variant spelling of HILLIARD.

Hilyer (278) English: variant spelling of HILLIER 1.

Hime (318) Americanized spelling of German or Jewish HEIM.

Himebaugh (245) Americanized spelling of German HEIMBACH.

Himel (385) Jewish (Ashkenazic): variant of HIMMEL.
GIVEN NAMES French 6%. *Oneil* (3), *Emile*, *Fernand*, *Yves*.

Himelfarb (131) Jewish (Ashkenazic): ornamental name composed of German *Himmel* 'heaven', 'sky' + *Farbe* 'color'.

Himelright (124) Americanized form of German HIMMELREICH.

Himelstein (105) Jewish (Ashkenazic): variant of HIMMELSTEIN.
GIVEN NAMES Jewish 6%. *Ephrain*, *Mandel*.

Himes (3190) Americanized spelling of German HEIMS.

Himler (120) German: variant of HIMMLER.

Himmel (530) **1.** German: topographic name from Middle High German *himel* 'heaven', 'paradise' (Old High German *himil* 'heaven', 'sky'), with reference to high altitude, pleasant situation, or the fruitfulness of the soil. **2.** Jewish (Ashkenazic): ornamental name from German *Himmel* 'heaven', selected because of the pleasant associations of the word.
GIVEN NAMES German 6%. *Hans* (3), *Ernst* (2), *Franz* (2), *Kurt* (2), *Reinhard*.

Himmelberg (143) German: see HIMMELBERGER.

Himmelberger (250) German: habitational name for someone from a place called Himmelberg, named with Middle High German *himel* 'heaven' + *bërc* 'hill', 'mountain'.

Himmelfarb (111) Jewish (Ashkenazic): ornamental name composed of German *Himmel* 'heaven', 'sky' + *Farbe* 'color'.
GIVEN NAMES Jewish 10%. *Sol* (2), *Hyman*.

Himmelman (135) Jewish (Ashkenazic): ornamental name from German *Himmel* 'heaven' (see HIMMEL) + *Mann* 'man'.
GIVEN NAMES Jewish 4%. *Doron*, *Hadar*, *Sol*.

Himmelreich (111) **1.** German: humorous topographic name, from a place so named as being at a high altitude, from Middle High German *himel* 'heaven' + *rīch(e)* 'empire'. **2.** Jewish (Ashkenazic): ornamental name composed of German *Himmel* 'heaven' + *Reich* 'empire'.

Himmelsbach (141) German: topographic name for someone living by a stream so named, from Middle High German *himel* 'heaven' + *bach* 'stream'.
GIVEN NAME German 5%. *Mathias*.

Himmelspach (109) German: variant of HIMMELSBACH.

Himmelstein (157) **1.** German: topographic name for someone living by a feature so named, from Middle High German *himel* 'heaven' + *stein* 'rock'. **2.** Jewish (Ashkenazic): ornamental name composed of German *Himmel* 'heaven' + *Stein* 'stone'.
GIVEN NAME Jewish 8%. *Meyer*.

Himmler (106) German: topographic name for someone living at a high altitude or in a pleasant place (see HIMMEL), the suffix *-er* denoting an inhabitant.
GIVEN NAMES German 12%. *Kurt* (2), *Dieter*, *Heinrich*, *Otto*.

Himsel (105) German: unexplained.
GIVEN NAME German 4%. *Erwin*.

Hincapie (117) Hispanic (Colombia): unexplained.
GIVEN NAMES Spanish 62%. *Diego* (4), *Carlos* (3), *Gustavo* (3), *Jose* (3), *Julio* (3), *Luis* (3), *Fernando* (2), *Marina* (2), *Alonso*, *Amparo*, *Ana*, *Ana Isabel*.

Hince (120) English: habitational name from either of two places in Staffordshire and Shropshire named Hints, from Welsh *hynt* 'road', 'path'.
GIVEN NAME French 5%. *Michel*.

Hinch (509) English: of uncertain origin; possibly from an unattested Old English person name *Hynci*.

Hinchcliff (173) English: variant spelling of HINCHCLIFFE.

Hinchcliffe (190) English (Yorkshire): habitational name from a place in West Yorkshire, so named from an unattested Old English element *henge* 'steep' + Old English *clif* 'cliff'.

Hinchee (145) Much altered variant of Irish HENNESSY.

Hinchey (576) Much altered variant of Irish HENNESSY.

Hinchliffe (324) English (Yorkshire): variant of HINCHCLIFFE.

Hinchman (491) English: unexplained.

Hinck (372) **1.** German and Dutch: variant of HINK 1. **2.** Dutch: variant of HINK 2.
GIVEN NAMES German 8%. *Claus* (3), *Helmut* (2), *Udo* (2), *Arno, Guenter, Otto*.

Hinckle (135) Americanized spelling of German HINKEL.

Hinckley (1634) English: habitational name from a place in Leicestershire, so called from the Old English byname *Hynca* (a derivative of *Hūn* 'bear-cub') + Old English *lēah* 'wood', 'clearing'.

Hincks (141) English: variant of HINKSON.

Hind (259) **1.** English (central and northern): nickname for a gentle or timid person, from Middle English, Old English *hind* 'female deer'. **2.** English and Scottish: variant of HINE 'servant', with excrescent *-d*.

Hinde (335) English: variant spelling of HIND.

Hinden (120) **1.** German: variant of HINDERER. **2.** Jewish (eastern Ashkenazic): variant of HINDIN.

Hinderer (274) South German: topographic name for someone who lived at the back of a village, or behind some prominent natural feature such as a mountain.
GIVEN NAMES German 6%. *Otto* (2), *Erwin, Gerhard*.

Hinderliter (475) Altered form of South German **Hinderleitner**, a topographic name from Middle High German *hinder* 'behind', 'beyond' + *līte* 'mountainside'.

Hinderman (167) German (**Hindermann**): variant of HINDERER.

Hinders (273) German: variant of HINDERER.

Hindes (344) **1.** English: variant spelling of HINDS. **2.** Jewish (eastern Ashkenazic): metronymic from the Yiddish female personal name *Hinde* 'hind', 'female deer'.

Hindin (121) Jewish (eastern Ashkenazic): variant of HINDES with the Slavic possessive suffix *-in*.

Hindle (433) English (Lancashire): **1.** topographic name from Old English *hind* 'female deer' + Old English *dæl* 'valley'. **2.** habitational name from a place in the parish of Whalley, Lancashire, so called from the same first element + Old English *hyll* 'hill'.

Hindley (244) English (Lancashire): habitational name from a place near Manchester, so named from Old English *hind* 'female deer' + *lēah* 'wood', 'clearing'.
FOREBEARS Richard de Hindele was a substantial landowner in Lancashire c. 1210–40. It seems likely that many modern bearers of the name may be descended from him.

Hindman (2234) Scottish: variant spelling of HYNDMAN.

Hindmarsh (139) English (Northumberland and Durham): probably a topographic name or a habitational name from a lost or unidentified place, most likely in northeastern England, where the name is still most frequent.

Hindmon (110) Variant of Scottish HYNDMAN.

Hinds (5037) **1.** English: patronymic from HIND. **2.** Irish: variant of HEYNE.

Hindsley (144) English: probably a rare variant of HINCKLEY.

Hindsman (103) Of uncertain origin: probably English: occupational name for a servant's servant, from HIND + *man*.

Hindson (106) English: patronymic from HIND.

Hine (1429) **1.** English (southwestern): occupational name for a servant, from Middle English *hine* 'lad', 'servant' (originally a collective term for a body of servants, from an Old English plural noun, *hīwan* 'household'). Later in the Middle English period, the word acquired an excrescent *-d* (see HIND). **2.** Americanized spelling of German HEIN.

Hinebaugh (222) Americanized form of German HEINBACH.

Hinegardner (129) Americanized spelling of German **Haingärtner**, habitational name for someone from a minor place named with Middle High German *hagen* 'shrub', 'thorn bush' + *garten* 'garden', 'yard'.

Hineline (302) Americanized spelling of German HEINLEIN.

Hinely (214) Possibly an Americanized spelling of German **Heinle**, a variant of HEINLEIN.

Hineman (311) Probably an Americanized spelling of HEINEMANN.
GIVEN NAMES German 4%. *Otto* (2), *Kurt*.

Hiner (1255) **1.** English (Suffolk): of uncertain origin, possibly an occupational name for a peasant or agricultural laborer, a variant of HINE, with the addition of the Middle English agent suffix *-er*. **2.** Americanized spelling of German HEINER.
FOREBEARS The earliest known bearer of the name is Philip Hyner, who was married on 25 July 1608 at Mildenhall, Suffolk. The name seems to have originated somewhere on the Cambridgeshire-Suffolk border.

Hinerman (343) Americanized spelling of German **Heinermann**, variant of HEINEMANN.

Hines (21968) **1.** Irish: Anglicized form of Gaelic Ó hEidhin 'descendant of *Eidhin*', a personal name or byname of uncertain origin. It may be a derivative of *eidhean* 'ivy', or it may represent an altered form of the place name Aidhne. The principal family of this name is descended from Guaire of Aidhne, King of Connacht. From the 7th century for over a thousand years they were chiefs of a territory in County Galway. **2.** English: patronymic from HINE.

3. Americanized spelling of German HEINS or HEINZ.

Hinesley (329) Possibly an Americanized spelling of South German **Heinzle**, a pet form of HEINZ. This surname is found chiefly in GA and NC.

Hiney (239) Irish: Anglicized form of Gaelic Ó hEidhnigh 'descendant of *Eidneach*' or Ó hAdhnaigh 'descendant of *Adhnach*'.

Hing (255) **1.** English: unexplained. **2.** East Asian: unexplained.
GIVEN NAMES Southeast Asian 5%. *Lam, Phal, Que, Sophal, Suong*.

Hinger (190) German: **1.** possibly a habitational name for someone from Hengen near Stuttgart. **2.** Alternatively, a Rhenish form of **Hinder**, variant of HINDERER.

Hingle (265) English: variant of INGLE.
GIVEN NAMES French 4%. *Landry, Leontine, Pierre*.

Hingson (136) English (Devon): probably a variant of HINGSTON. The name in this spelling has died out in England.

Hingst (169) North German form of HENGST.
GIVEN NAMES German 8%. *Gunther* (2), *Ewald, Hans, Klaus*.

Hingston (146) English (Devon): habitational name from any of three places so named. Hingston, Cornwall and Hingston Down in Moretonhampstead, Devon are both named from the Old English byname *Hengest* (or from Old English *hengest* 'stallion') + Old English *dūn* 'hill', while Hingston in Bigbury, Devon is named from Old English *hind* 'hind' + *stān* 'stone'.

Hingtgen (140) Dutch: probably from a derivative of the personal name *Hendrik*.

Hiniker (141) Dutch or North German: variant of HEINECKE.

Hink (414) German and Dutch: **1.** from a pet form of the personal name HEINRICH or HENDRICK. **2.** nickname for someone with a limp, from Middle Dutch *hinken* 'to limp'.

Hinke (132) Dutch and German: variant of HINK.

Hinkebein (100) Dutch and North German: nickname for someone with a limp, from Middle Low German *hinken* 'to limp' + *bein* 'leg'.

Hinkel (988) **1.** Dutch and North German: variant of HENKEL. **2.** German: nickname for a timid, fearful person, from dialect *hinkel* 'chicken'.

Hinkelman (190) German (**Hinkelmann**): elaborated variant of HINKEL, with the addition of Middle High German *man* 'man'.
GIVEN NAMES German 9%. *Kurt* (2), *Armin, Erwin, Otto*.

Hinken (140) Dutch and North German: patronymic from HINK.

Hinker (102) Dutch and North German: descriptive nickname for someone with a limp (see HINK).

Hinkle (8369) **1.** Americanized spelling of Dutch and German HINKEL. **2.** Variant spelling of English HINCKLEY.

Hinkley (1594) English: variant spelling of HINCKLEY.

Hinks (177) English (Midlands): patronymic from an unidentified medieval personal name (see HINKSON).

Hinkson (572) English: patronymic from an unidentified medieval personal name, perhaps a survival of Old English *Hȳnci* or *Hȳnca*. Compare HINCKLEY.

Hinman (2211) English (Midlands): probably a variant of HENMAN, or of INMAN, with the addition of an inorganic *H-*.

Hinnant (804) Origin uncertain; probably a variant of Dutch **Hinant**, from a personal name composed of the Germanic elements *hild* 'strife', 'battle' + *nand* 'bold', 'brave'.

Hinnenkamp (253) North German: topographic name for someone whose property lay at the back of a village or beyond the main settlement, from Middle Low German *hindene* 'behind' + *kamp* 'enclosed field', 'domain'.
GIVEN NAMES German 5%. *Alphons, Eberhard, Erwin, Klaus.*

Hinners (253) German (Frisian): patronymic from an equivalent of HENRY 1.

Hino (133) Japanese: 'sun field'; name of a noble family descended from the Fujiwara. Found mainly in eastern Japan, the name is habitational, from a place called Hinomura, near Kyōto. The family name is also found in Okinawa Island.
GIVEN NAMES Japanese 45%. *Hiro* (2), *Kenji* (2), *Toshiharu* (2), *Akira, Chisa, Chizuru, Hirofumi, Hiroshi, Hirotaka, Hisako, Kazutoshi, Keiko.*

Hinojos (472) Spanish: topographic name for someone who lived in a place where fennel grew in abundance, from *hinojo* 'fennel', or a habitational name from Hinojos in Huelva province, Andalusia.
GIVEN NAMES Spanish 45%. *Jose* (11), *Manuel* (6), *Jesus* (5), *Alberto* (3), *Alfonso* (3), *Angel* (3), *Armando* (3), *Efrain* (3), *Enrique* (3), *Juan* (3), *Ramon* (3), *Salvador* (3), *Adauto.*

Hinojosa (2972) Spanish: habitational name from any of the numerous places called Hinojosa, from a derivative of *hinojo* 'fennel'. See also FENNELL.
GIVEN NAMES Spanish 50%. *Jose* (83), *Juan* (51), *Manuel* (29), *Raul* (25), *Arturo* (20), *Pedro* (20), *Ricardo* (18), *Jesus* (17), *Ruben* (17), *Luis* (16), *Armando* (15), *Guadalupe* (15).

Hinote (307) Probably an Americanized form of **Hénault** (see HENAULT).

Hinrichs (2127) Dutch and North German: patronymic from the personal name *Hinrich* (see HEINRICH).
GIVEN NAMES German 5%. *Hans* (7), *Kurt* (6), *Erwin* (2), *Gerhard* (2), *Klaus* (2), *Otto* (2), *Arno, Benno, Erna, Fritz, Hermann, Inge.*

Hinrichsen (383) **1.** North German: variant of HINRICHS. **2.** Danish: patronymic from the personal name HEINRICH.
GIVEN NAMES German 10%; Scandinavian 4%. *Hans* (6), *Kurt* (3), *Ernst* (2), *Otto* (2), *Bernhard, Claus, Frieda, Fritz, Lorenz, Uwe; Erik* (2).

Hinsch (259) German (of Slavic origin) and Danish: from a pet form of the personal name HEINRICH.
GIVEN NAMES German 11%. *Heinrich* (2), *Kurt* (2), *Fritz, Gerhard, Gunter, Johann, Johannes.*

Hinsdale (216) English: perhaps a variant of HINDLE, a habitational name from a lost or unidentified place.

Hinsey (117) Irish: reduced form of HENNESSY.

Hinshaw (1909) Scottish: probably a variant of HENSHAW 1.

Hinsley (357) English: variant of HINCKLEY.

Hinson (7165) English: variant of HINKSON.

Hintermeister (105) German: topographic name for a master craftsman who lived at the back of a village, from *hinter* 'behind' + *Meister* 'master craftsman'.

Hinton (10500) English: habitational name from any of the numerous places so called, which split more or less evenly into two groups with different etymologies. One set (with examples in Berkshire, Dorset, Gloucestershire, Hampshire, Herefordshire, Somerset, and Wiltshire) is named from the Old English weak dative *hēan* (originally used after a preposition and article) of *hēah* 'high' + Old English *tūn* 'enclosure', 'settlement'. The other (with examples in Cambridgeshire, Dorset, Gloucestershire, Herefordshire, Northamptonshire, Shropshire, Somerset, Suffolk, and Wiltshire) has Old English *hīwan* 'household', 'monastery'. Compare HINE as the first element.

Hintz (2981) German and Danish: from a pet form of HEINRICH.
GIVEN NAMES German 4%. *Kurt* (8), *Otto* (8), *Erwin* (6), *Helmut* (3), *Florian* (2), *Alois, Eldor, Ewald, Gerhard, Jurgen, Lisel, Manfred.*

Hintze (701) German: Variant of HINTZ.
GIVEN NAMES German 5%. *Erwin* (2), *Hans* (2), *Kurt* (2), *Christoph, Fritz, Klein, Otto, Siegfried, Udo.*

Hintzen (103) German: patronymic from HINTZ.
GIVEN NAMES German 11%. *Heinz* (2), *Hans.*

Hintzman (154) German (**Hintzmann**): see HINZMANN.

Hinz (1939) German and Danish: from a pet form of HEINRICH.
GIVEN NAMES German 7%. *Kurt* (5), *Gerhard* (3), *Otto* (3), *Ulrich* (3), *Hans* (2), *Manfred* (2), *Siegfried* (2), *Armin, Bodo, Dietmar, Eldred, Elfriede.*

Hinze (851) German: variant of HINZ.

Hinzman (522) Variant of German HINZMANN.

Hinzmann (120) German: elaborated form of HINZ, a pet form of HEINRICH.
GIVEN NAMES German 10%. *Fritz* (2), *Otto* (2).

Hiott (481) Perhaps an altered form of HYATT. This is a common surname in SC.

Hipes (114) Variant of HYPES.

Hipke (132) German: probably a metonymic occupational name for a waffle baker, from a diminutive of Middle High German *hippe* 'waffle'.

Hipkins (259) English: patronymic from *Hipkin*, a pet form of the Middle English male or female personal name *Hibb* (see HIBBS).

Hipolito (195) Spanish and Portuguese (**Hipólito**): from the personal name *Hipolito* (see IPPOLITO).
GIVEN NAMES Spanish 45%. *Jose* (10), *Jesus* (3), *Emilio* (2), *Juan* (2), *Miguel* (2), *Rolando* (2), *Alexandrina, Alfredo, Araceli, Arsenio, Arturo, Beatriz.*

Hipp (1818) **1.** South German: metonymic occupational name for a baker of waffles, from Middle High German *hippe* 'waffle'. **2.** South German: from a short form of HUBERT, also spelled **Hüpp** (see HUPP). **3.** German and Dutch: from a short form of a Germanic name with the initial element *hild* 'strife', 'battle' and a second element beginning with *b-* (for example *Hildibald, Hildibrand*).

Hippe (216) **1.** German and Dutch: variant of HIPP 1 and 3. **2.** Norwegian: habitational name from a farmstead in Valdres named Hippe, from an unexplained first element + Old Norse *vin* 'meadow'. **3.** French: from a Germanic personal name, possibly of the same etymology as HIPP 3.

Hippen (212) German (Frisian): patronymic from HIPP 3.
GIVEN NAMES German 4%. *Erwin, Johann.*

Hippensteel (275) Americanized spelling of German **Hippenstiel**, a metonymic occupational name for a maker of handles for scythes, from Middle High German *heppe* 'scythe' + *stil* 'handle'.
GIVEN NAMES German 4%. *Kurt* (2), *Walther.*

Hippert (191) North German and Dutch: variant of HILBERT.

Hipple (610) Americanized spelling of German and Dutch **Hippel**: **1.** from a pet form of HIPP 3. **2.** from a pet form of HIPP 1 or 2. **3.** variant of **Hippel**, a short form of the personal name *Hippolyt* (see IPPOLITO).

Hippler (269) German: occupational name for a baker of waffles (see HIPP 1).
GIVEN NAMES German 4%. *Gerd, Otto, Rainer.*

Hipps (795) English: probably a variant of HIBBS.

Hipsher (409) Jewish (Ashkenazic): ornamental name from an inflected form of German *hübsch* 'handsome', 'nice'. The first syllable has been influenced in sound by the Yiddish word *hipsh* 'considerable', 'sizeable'.

Hipskind (156) German: nickname for a well-mannered young person, from a variant of Middle High German *hüebsch* (older *hövesch*) 'handsome', 'polite' + *Kind* 'child'.

Hipsley (141) English: possibly a habitational name from a lost or unidentified place.

Hipwell (177) English: habitational name from Hipswell in North Yorkshire, named in Old English possibly as 'stream with stepping stones'; the first element may be from an unattested noun derivative *hyppels* of the verb *hoppian* 'to hop', and the second is *wella*, *wiella* 'spring', 'stream'. The surname has been present in Ireland (County Leix) since the 17th century.

Hirabayashi (111) Japanese: 'peaceful forest'; the name is found mostly in central Japan. The same characters are also pronounced *Tairabayashi* by some families, perhaps denoting connections to the ancient TAIRA clan.
GIVEN NAMES Japanese 43%. *Shinichi* (2), *Ayano*, *Hisashi*, *Kanae*, *Kazuko*, *Kazuo*, *Kyo*, *Makoto*, *Manabu*, *Miyako*, *Osamu*, *Ryuichi*.

Hirai (289) Japanese: 'placid well'; a habitational name from Hiraimura in Settsu (now part of Hyōgo prefecture). Families bearing this name descend variously from the FUJIWARA, TAIRA, MINAMOTO, and other clans. The name is also found in the Ryūkyū Islands.
GIVEN NAMES Japanese 50%. *Akira* (3), *Fumio* (3), *Eiji* (2), *Koji* (2), *Minoru* (2), *Rie* (2), *Shinji* (2), *Tatsuya* (2), *Yutaka* (2), *Akane*, *Arata*, *Ayako*.

Hirano (380) Japanese: 'flat (or peaceful) field'; a common topographic and habitational name throughout Japan and the Ryūkyū Islands. One daimyō family descended from the ancient Kiyowara clan.
GIVEN NAMES Japanese 64%. *Kenji* (5), *Takashi* (5), *Atsushi* (2), *Hiroyuki* (2), *Ikuo* (2), *Junko* (2), *Kenichi* (2), *Kenichiro* (2), *Kiyoshi* (2), *Koichiro* (2), *Masako* (2), *Mitsuru* (2).

Hiraoka (128) Japanese: 'peaceful hill'; found mostly in western Japan and the Ryūkyū Islands. Some bearers of the name descend from the Kudō branch of the southern FUJIWARA, others from the Mizoguchi branch of the MINAMOTO.
GIVEN NAMES Japanese 58%. *Tadashi* (2), *Toshihiko* (2), *Toshiki* (2), *Atsushi*, *Chiaki*, *Hideaki*, *Hidenori*, *Hiroshi*, *Hiroyuki*, *Ichiro*, *Keiko*, *Kiyoshi*.

Hirata (489) Japanese: 'peaceful rice paddy'; there are several families, descended from the TAIRA, SASAKI, and Sakanoue clans. The family has several branches of its own. It is listed in the Shinsen shōjiroku, and is found throughout Japan and in the Ryūkyū Islands.

GIVEN NAMES Japanese 47%. *Hideo* (4), *Yoshio* (4), *Masao* (3), *Eiji* (2), *Hajime* (2), *Hiro* (2), *Kaoru* (2), *Katsumi* (2), *Kazuo* (2), *Kei* (2), *Makoto* (2), *Masaru* (2).

Hirayama (175) Japanese: 'peaceful mountain'; mostly found in eastern Japan and the Ryūkyū Islands. There are several unrelated families.
GIVEN NAMES Japanese 61%. *Masahiro* (3), *Megumi* (3), *Hiroshi* (2), *Nobuo* (2), *Osamu* (2), *Shiro* (2), *Akira*, *Asao*, *Chikako*, *Chikara*, *Goichi*, *Goro*.

Hirchert (104) German: possibly from a Sorbian form of the personal name *Georg* (see GEORGE).
GIVEN NAMES German 6%. *Georg*, *Kurt*.

Hird (494) English (chiefly Yorkshire and Northumbria), also Scottish: variant spelling of HEARD.

Hire (357) **1.** Americanized spelling of Dutch and German HEYER or HEIER. **2.** Welsh: variant of HIER.

Hires (482) Origin uncertain: perhaps a variant of Dutch or German HEYER or HEIER, with excrescent -*s*.

Hirko (108) Slovak: unexplained.

Hirn (189) German (Bavaria): topographic name from Old High German *horo* 'swamp', 'mire', or from Middle High German *horn* 'horn (of land)'.

Hirner (111) **1.** German: topographic name for someone who lived by a swamp, German *Hirn*, or on a horn (of land) (see HIRN). **2.** possibly a variant of **Hürner**, itself a variant of **Hörner** (see HORNER).
GIVEN NAME German 5%. *Franz*.

Hirning (126) South German: habitational name from a place in Swabia so named with Middle High German *hurn* 'mire', 'swamp' (see HIRN).
GIVEN NAME German 4%. *Reinhardt*.

Hironaka (133) Japanese: 'wide center'; name of a noble family of Suō (now part of Yamaguchi prefecture), as well as other families of Shimane and Hyōgo prefectures.
GIVEN NAMES Japanese 44%. *Masami* (3), *Noboru* (2), *Aiko*, *Atsushi*, *Eiji*, *Hajime*, *Hatsuo*, *Hiroshi*, *Kenji*, *Kuni*, *Makoto*, *Masaaki*.

Hirons (172) English (of Norman origin): **1.** patronymic from a nickname for a lively person, from Old French *hirond*, *arond* 'swallow' (the bird). **2.** patronymic from a nickname for a discontented individual, from a diminutive of Old French *hire* 'complaint' (of unknown origin).

Hirose (221) Japanese: 'wide strait'; a very common place name throughout Japan, variously written. The surname is listed in the Shinsen shōjiroku, but it is possible that not all bearers are related.
GIVEN NAMES Japanese 71%. *Akira* (4), *Yuki* (4), *Takashi* (3), *Yoshio* (3), *Yuka* (3), *Hideaki* (2), *Hitoshi* (2), *Ryozo* (2), *Takao* (2), *Toshiyuki* (2), *Yasuko* (2), *Akihide*.

Hirota (186) Japanese: 'wide rice paddy'; the name of an immigrant family from Paekche, an ancient Korean kingdom (15 BC–AD 663) with many close Japanese ties; also other families descended more recently from the SASAKI and Watarai clans. The name is mostly found in west-central Japan and the Ryūkyū Islands, and is listed in the Shinsen shōjiroku.
GIVEN NAMES Japanese 51%. *Akira* (2), *Hitoshi* (2), *Yoshikazu* (2), *Chiyoko*, *Hanayo*, *Harumi*, *Haruo*, *Hideo*, *Hideyuki*, *Junichi*, *Junko*, *Keiko*.

Hirsch (8214) **1.** German: from Middle High German *hir(t)z* 'deer', 'stag'; a metonymic occupational name for a keeper of deer, a nickname for someone thought to resemble a deer or stag, or a habitational name for someone who lived at a house distinguished by the sign of a stag. **2.** Jewish (Ashkenazic): from the Yiddish male personal name *Hirsh* 'deer', which is common because of the association of the deer with the Hebrew personal name *Naphtali*, deriving from the blessing by Jacob of his sons (Genesis 49: 21), in which Naphtali is referred to as 'a hind let loose'. **3.** Jewish (Ashkenazic): ornamental name from German *Hirsch* or Yiddish *hirsh* 'deer', one of the many Ashkenazic surnames taken from vocabulary words denoting wildlife.
GIVEN NAMES Jewish 4%; German 4%. *Sol* (9), *Miriam* (7), *Emanuel* (6), *Meyer* (6), *Shimon* (5), *Moshe* (4), *Josif* (3), *Yosef* (3), *Beril* (2), *Chaim* (2), *Elihu* (2), *Eliyohu* (2); *Kurt* (11), *Otto* (9), *Erwin* (6), *Hans* (4), *Heinz* (3), *Helmut* (3), *Beate* (2), *Fritz* (2), *Gunther* (2), *Hedwig* (2), *Hilde* (2), *Ilse* (2).

Hirschberg (422) **1.** German and Jewish (Ashkenazic): habitational name from any of several places named Hirschberg, from Middle High German *hirz* 'deer', 'stag' + *berg* 'hill', 'mountain', for example in Thuringia, North Rhine-Westphalia, or in western Poland (Jelenia Góra). In some instances the German surname may be topographic, from the same elements. **2.** Jewish (Ashkenazic): ornamental name composed of German *Hirsch* 'deer' + *Berg* 'mountain', 'hill' (see 1 above).
GIVEN NAMES German 7%; Jewish 4%. *Hanns* (2), *Manfred* (2), *Erwin*, *Gunter*, *Klaus*, *Raimund*; *Aharon*, *Emanuel*, *Naftoli*, *Noson*, *Yerachmiel*.

Hirschel (121) Jewish (Ashkenazic) and German: variant of HERSCHEL.
GIVEN NAMES French 4%; Jewish 4%. *Henri*; *Avi*.

Hirschey (141) **1.** German: variant of HIRSCHY. **2.** Jewish (American): variant spelling of HERSHEY.

Hirschfeld (645) **1.** Jewish (Ashkenazic): ornamental name composed of German *Hirsch* or Yiddish *hirsh* 'deer' + *Feld* 'field'. **2.** German: topographic name for someone who lived in an area of land frequented by deer (from Middle High German *hirz* 'deer' + *feld* 'open country') or where millet (Middle High German *hirs(e)*) grew.

GIVEN NAMES German 6%. *Kurt* (3), *Erna* (2), *Horst* (2), *Frieda, Gerhard, Gottlieb, Hans, Otto.*

Hirschfield (281) Partly Americanized form of HIRSCHFELD.

Hirschhorn (347) **1.** German and Jewish (Ashkenazic): habitational name from any of several places so named in Hesse, the Palatinate, and Bavaria. **2.** Jewish (Ashkenazic): ornamental name composed of German *Hirsch*, Yiddish *hirsh* 'deer' + *Horn* 'horn'.

GIVEN NAMES German 5%; Jewish 4%. *Kurt* (2), *Hans; Isidor.*

Hirschi (322) Swiss German: diminutive of HIRSCH.

Hirschler (180) **1.** German: occupational name for a keeper of deer, from Middle High German *hir(t)z* 'deer' + the agent suffix *-ler*. **2.** Jewish (Ashkenazic): patronymic from a pet form of HIRSCH 2.

GIVEN NAMES German 9%. *Gunter, Hartmut, Herta, Kurt, Otto, Wolf.*

Hirschman (538) **1.** Jewish (Ashkenazic): variant of HIRSCH 2 and 3. **2.** Altered spelling of German HIRSCHMANN.

GIVEN NAMES Jewish 4%. *Ari, Avrom, Kolman, Meyer, Mordechai, Shaya.*

Hirschmann (241) German: elaborated form of HIRSCH 1.

GIVEN NAMES German 19%. *Hans* (2), *Kurt* (2), *Viktor* (2), *Arno, Erwin, Frieda, Fritz, Gerd, Gunther, Helmut, Otto, Siegfried.*

Hirschy (229) Swiss German: diminutive of HIRSCH.

Hirsh (1139) **1.** Jewish (Ashkenazic): variant of HIRSCH. **2.** Americanized spelling of German HIRSCH.

GIVEN NAMES Jewish 4%. *Chaim, Emanuel, Gedaliah, Hyman, Myer, Sol.*

Hirshberg (263) Respelling of German or Jewish variant spelling of HIRSCHBERG.

GIVEN NAMES Jewish 4%. *Isadore* (2), *Sol* (2).

Hirshfield (141) Americanized form of HIRSCHFELD.

GIVEN NAMES Jewish 6%; German 5%. *Hyman; Gunter, Hans.*

Hirshman (196) **1.** Jewish (Ashkenazic): variant spelling of HIRSCHMAN. **2.** Americanized spelling of German HIRSCHMANN.

GIVEN NAMES Jewish 10%; German 5%. *Morry* (2), *Elisheva, Mort; Kurt.*

Hirst (1459) **1.** Northern English: variant spelling of HURST. **2.** German (**Hürst**): topographic name from Middle Low German *hurst* 'brushwood', 'wild place', cognate with English HURST and Low German HORST.

Hirt (1141) German: occupational name for a herdsman, Middle High German *hirt*, cognate with English HEARD.

Hirte (158) German: variant of HIRT.

GIVEN NAMES German 9%. *Klaus, Kurt, Meinhard, Otto.*

Hirth (522) German: variant spelling of HIRT.

GIVEN NAMES German 4%. *Gerhard* (2), *Alois, Erwin, Helmut, Theresia.*

Hirtle (171) South German (also **Hirtl**): diminutive of HIRT.

Hirtz (164) German: variant of HIRSCH 1.

Hirtzel (140) South German and Swiss German: from a diminutive of HIRTZ.

Hirzel (173) German: variant spelling of HIRTZEL.

GIVEN NAME German 6%. *Heinz.*

Hisaw (235) Origin unidentified.

Hiscock (363) English: from a pet form of HICK.

Hiscox (193) English (chiefly Bristol): patronymic from HISCOCK.

Hise (807) Probably an Americanized spelling of HEISE.

Hisel (329) Probably an altered spelling of German HEISEL.

Hiser (1034) Probably an Americanized form of German HEISER.

Hisey (487) Probably an Americanized form of German HEISE.

Hiskey (112) Irish: Anglicized form of Gaelic **Ó hUisce** 'descendant of *Uisce*'. Gaelic *uisce* means 'water', and for this reason the name has sometimes been Anglicized as WATERS. However, it is more likely to be an altered form of **Ó hUarghuis** 'descendant of *Uarghus*', a personal name composed of elements meaning 'cold' + 'vigor'.

Hisle (381) Possibly an Americanized spelling of HEISEL.

Hisler (129) Possibly an Americanized spelling of HEISLER.

Hislop (512) Scottish: variant spelling of HYSLOP.

Hiss (231) German: **1.** from a short form of the Germanic personal name *Hizo*, a short form of names with *hild* 'fight', 'battle' as the first element. **2.** South German: variant of HEISS 1.

Hissam (134) Origin unidentified.

Hissom (110) Origin unidentified. Compare HISSAM.

Hissong (371) Probably of German origin, a variant of HESSONG, a patronymic derivative of HESS 3.

Hitch (886) English: variant of HICK.

Hitchcock (5331) English (mainly southern): from a pet form of HICK, with the Middle English diminutive suffix *-cok*.

Hitchen (107) English (Lancashire): **1.** from a pet form of HITCH. **2.** in parts of the West Midlands this may have been a patronymic from HITCH, from an old genitive ending. **3.** habitational name from Hitchin in Hertfordshire, which is derived from the dative plural of the old tribal name *Hicce*, which itself may be derived from a Celtic river name meaning 'dry'.

Hitchens (812) English: patronymic from HITCHEN 1.

Hitchings (485) English: variant of HITCHENS.

Hitchins (172) English: variant of HITCHENS.

Hitchman (215) English (chiefly West Midlands): variant of HICKMAN.

Hitchner (278) Probably of English origin, but unexplained.

Hite (4487) **1.** English: variant spelling of HIGHT. **2.** Americanized spelling of German HEIT.

Hiter (120) Jewish (Ashkenazic): occupational or ornamental name from Yiddish *hiter* 'protector', an agent derivative of *hitn* 'to protect'.

Hites (399) Americanized spelling of German HEITZ.

Hitesman (116) Probably an Americanized spelling of German HITZEMANN.

GIVEN NAME German 5%. *Hans* (2).

Hitsman (181) Probably an Americanized spelling of German **Hitzmann**, a variant of HITZEMANN.

Hitson (235) English: unexplained; perhaps a metathesized form of **Histon**, a habitational name from Histon in Cambridgeshire. In the U.S., this is a southern surname, found chiefly in TN, AL, and GA.

Hitt (3046) **1.** Americanized form of German **Hütt** (see HUETT). **2.** German: occupational name in Westphalia for a goat dealer, from dialect *hitte* 'goat'. **3.** English (Devon): unexplained.

Hittinger (142) German: habitational name for someone from any of various places called Hitting.

Hittle (702) Americanized form of German **Hüttl** (see HUETTL).

Hittner (218) Americanized form of German **Hüttner** (see HUETTNER).

Hitz (615) German: from a pet form of a Germanic personal name formed with the first element *hild* 'strife', 'battle'.

Hitzeman (207) Variant of German HITZEMANN.

GIVEN NAMES German 6%. *Kurt* (3), *Erwin.*

Hitzemann (127) German: occupational name for a chaser at a hunt, from Middle High German *hetzen* 'to chase' + *man* 'man'.

GIVEN NAMES German 7%. *Erhardt, Hans, Kurt.*

Hively (908) Origin unidentified.

Hix (2045) **1.** English: variant of HICKS. **2.** German: from a pet form of a Germanic personal name formed with *hild* 'strife', 'battle' as the first element.

Hixenbaugh (416) Americanized form of German **Höchstenbach**, a habitational name from a place so called.

FOREBEARS The founder of the American family, Johannes Wilhelm Höchstenbach, emigrated from Germany to Baltimore MD in the 1760s.

Hixon (1896) English: variant spelling of HICKSON.

Hixson (2555) English: variant spelling of HICKSON.

Hiza (112) **1.** Altered spelling of Dutch HEISE. **2.** Portuguese: unexplained.

Hizer (227) Americanized spelling of German HEISER.

Hjelle (181) Norwegian: habitational name from any of numerous farmsteads, notably in western Norway, so named from Old Norse *hjallr* or *hjalli* 'terrace', 'ledge'.
GIVEN NAMES Scandinavian 8%. *Carsten, Helmer, Knute, Steinar.*

Hjelm (300) **1.** Swedish: probably a soldier's name from *hjälm* 'helmet'. **2.** Danish: habitational name from any of numerous farmsteads and islands so named from *hjälm* 'helmet'.
GIVEN NAMES Scandinavian 10%. *Erik* (3), *Alf, Klas, Lars, Mats, Nels.*

Hjelmstad (123) Scandinavian: unexplained.
GIVEN NAMES Scandinavian 10%. *Erik, Magnar, Thor.*

Hjerpe (143) Swedish: possibly a variant of **Järpe**, a soldier's name from *järpe* 'hazel grouse'.
GIVEN NAMES Scandinavian 7%; German 4%. *Erik, Gunhild; Kurt.*

Hjort (264) **1.** Swedish: ornamental name from *hjort* 'deer', 'stag'. **2.** Danish: from a nickname or byname from *hjort* 'deer', 'stag'.
GIVEN NAMES German 6%; Scandinavian 4%. *Erwin, Guenter, Hans, Kurt; Erik, Thor.*

Hjorth (151) Scandinavian: variant of HJORT.
GIVEN NAME German 4%. *Klaus.*

Hlad (187) Czech and Slovak: nickname for a thin or poor person, or possibly for a miser, from *hlad* 'hunger'. This surname occurs chiefly in OH and IL.

Hladik (295) Czech (**Hladík**): **1.** nickname for a clean-shaven or bald man, from *hladký* 'smooth' + the diminutive suffix *-ík*. **2.** occupational name for a finisher or polisher of furniture, from a derivative of *hladit* 'to polish or burnish', from *hladký*; the word *hladík* is also a technical term in carpentry denoting a kind of rasp or plane.

Hladky (249) Czech and Slovak (**Hladký**): nickname for an easy-going person, from *hladký* 'smooth'.

Hlavac (295) Czech and Slovak (**Hlaváč**): from *hlava* 'head', applied as a nickname for an important person, a clever one, or someone with a large head.

Hlavacek (277) Czech (**Hlaváček**): from a diminutive of **Hlaváč** (see HLAVAC).
GIVEN NAMES Czech and Slovak 5%. *Milos* (2), *Bohumil, Ladislav, Lubor, Milan.*

Hlavaty (346) Czech and Slovak (**Hlavatý**): nickname for someone with a large head, from an adjectival form of *hlava* 'head'.
GIVEN NAME Czech and Slovak 4%. *Vaclav* (4).

Hlavin (102) Czech: (**Hlavín**): from *hlava* 'head', a nickname for someone with a par-

ticularly large or otherwise remarkable head. This surname is found in OH and IL.

Hlavinka (161) Czech: from a diminutive of *hlava* 'head'. Compare HLAVIN.

Hlavka (134) Czech and Slovak (**Hlávka**): from *hlava* 'head', a nickname for someone with a particularly large or otherwise remarkable head.

Hnat (171) Czech and Slovak (**Hnát**): **1.** nickname for someone with long or bony limbs, from *hnát* 'bone', 'limb'. **2.** from a short form of the personal name *Ignát*, a vernacular form of *Ignatius* (see IGNACIO).

Hnath (103) Variant spelling of Slovak or Czech **Hnát** (see HNAT).

Ho (8218) **1.** Korean (**Hŏ**): there is only one Chinese character for the Hŏ surname. Some records indicate that there are fifty-nine Hŏ clans, but only four have been identified and documented. All four clans descend from the same founding ancestor. In AD 48, a sixteen-year-old Indian princess is said to have arrived by boat on the shores of Korea. The Karak Kingdom's King Suro married the woman, and out of respect for her origins allowed the second of their ten children to retain his mother's surname, Hŏ. The Hŏ surname is very common and is widely distributed throughout the Korean peninsula. **2.** Vietnamese (**Hồ**): unexplained. **3.** Chinese: variant of HE.
GIVEN NAMES Vietnamese 26%; Chinese/Korean 25%. *Hai* (31), *Thanh* (30), *Hung* (29), *Quang* (18), *Son* (18), *Tuan* (17), *Vinh* (17), *Anh* (16), *Tien* (16), *Binh* (15), *Hoa* (15), *Minh* (15); *Sang* (16), *Ming* (15), *Kam* (14), *Ching* (13), *Hong* (13), *Chan* (11), *Chin* (11), *Ho* (11), *Wai* (10), *Kin* (9), *Kwok* (9), *Ping* (9); *Tam* (16), *Nam* (13), *Chung* (12), *Phong* (8), *Chang* (7), *Tuong* (7), *Thai* (6), *Yiu* (6), *Thach* (5), *Chong* (4), *Kok* (4), *Pak* (3).

Hoad (136) English: topographic name for someone who lived on a heath, from Middle English *hōth* 'heath', Old English *hāð*, a byform of *hǣð* (see HEATH). This form was restricted in the Middle Ages to southeastern England, and the surname is still largely confined to Kent and Sussex. In some cases it may be a habitational name from the village of Hoath in Kent, which is named with this word.

Hoadley (912) English: habitational name from East or West Hoathly in Sussex, so named from Old English *hāð* (see HOAD 1) + *lēah* 'wood', 'clearing'.

Hoag (2828) **1.** variant of Scottish and English HOGG. **2.** possibly an altered spelling of Norwegian HAUG.

Hoage (142) **1.** variant of HOAG. **2.** variant of HAUGE.
GIVEN NAMES German 4%. *Frieda, Merwin.*

Hoagland (2371) Americanized form of Swedish **Högland** (see HOGLAND) or Norwegian HAUGLAND.

Hoaglin (253) Probably a variant of HOAGLAND or HOAGLUND.

Hoaglund (365) Americanized form of Swedish **Höglund** (see HOGLUND).

Hoak (614) Probably an Americanized form of Dutch **van (den) Hoek(e)**, a habitational name for someone from a place called Hoek (East Flanders and Zeeland) or Hoeke (West Flanders). This surname occurs chiefly in PA.

Hoang (3346) Vietnamese (**Hoàng**): unexplained.
GIVEN NAMES Vietnamese 68%; Chinese 15%. *Hung* (54), *Minh* (43), *Thanh* (41), *Dung* (37), *Thuy* (27), *Tuan* (26), *Cuong* (25), *Hoa* (25), *Anh* (23), *Long* (23), *Binh* (20), *Chau* (18), *Nam* (19), *Tam* (15), *Thai* (12), *Phong* (10), *Sinh* (10), *Chung* (9), *Tinh* (5), *Manh* (3), *Tuong* (3), *Uyen* (3), *Thach* (2), *Tham* (2), *Phoung* (2); *Chi* (19), *Hong* (17), *Sang* (12), *Man* (6), *Dong* (5), *Han* (5), *Ho* (4), *Lai* (3), *Chan* (2), *Chien* (2), *Kao* (2).

Hoar (756) English: **1.** nickname for an old man or someone with prematurely gray hair, from Middle English *hore*, Old English *hār* 'gray'. **2.** topographic name for someone who lived by a slope or shore, Old English *ōra*, or a habitational name from any of the places named with this word, as for example Oare in Kent, Berkshire, and Wiltshire.

Hoard (1345) English: variant of HEARD.

Hoare (272) English: variant spelling of HOAR.

Hoback (548) Americanized spelling of German **Hobach**, a habitational name from Hohebach near Künzelsau.

Hoban (1309) Irish (Mayo): Anglicized form of Gaelic **Ó hÚbáin** 'descendant of *Úbán*', a personal name of unknown origin.
GIVEN NAMES Irish 6%. *Seamus* (3), *Colm, Eamonn.*

Hobart (1346) English (especially East Anglia) and Dutch: variant of HUBERT.

Hobaugh (239) Americanized form of German **Hobach** (see HOBACK).

Hobbie (327) Scottish: from a pet form of the personal name *Robert* (see HOBBS).
GIVEN NAMES Irish 4%. *Conley* (2), *Aileen.*

Hobbins (238) English (mainly West Midlands): patronymic from a pet form of the medieval personal name *Hobb* (see HOBBS).

Hobbs (16948) English: patronymic from the medieval personal name *Hobb(e)*, a short form of ROBERT. For the altered initial, compare HICK.

Hobby (1045) English: **1.** nickname from Middle English *hobi* 'hobby', a small falcon, or from the same word denoting a small horse. **2.** habitational name from Hoby in Leicestershire, named with Old English *hōh* 'spur of a hill' + Old Norse *býr* 'farmstead', 'settlement'.

Hobday (251) English (mainly West Midlands): from the personal name *Hob* (see HOBBS) + Middle English *day* 'servant', i.e. either 'Hob the servant' or 'servant of Hob'.

Hobdy (270) English: variant of HOBDAY.

Hobel (112) North German (**Höbel**): topographic name for someone who lived on a hill, Middle Low German *hövel*.

Hoben (237) German and Dutch: patronymic from a short form of HUBERT.

Hober (126) **1.** German (**Höber**): occupational name for someone whose work involved lifting heavy loads, from an agent derivative of Middle High German *heben* 'to lift', or habitational name for someone from *Höver* near Ülzen. **2.** Jewish (Ashkenazic): metonymic occupational name or ornamental name from Yiddish *hober* 'oats'. Compare HABER.

Hoberg (364) **1.** German and Danish: habitational name from places with this name or a variant of it, for example Hohberg or Hoberge. **2.** Belgian: habitational name from places called Hoberg or Hogeberg, for example in the Belgian province of Antwerp, or from Opbergen or Obberge in Brabant.
GIVEN NAMES German 6%; Scandinavian 4%. *Elfriede, Gunter, Manfred, Otto, Wenzel, Wolfgang; Anders, Erik, Jorgen.*

Hoberman (227) **1.** German (**Höbermann**): occupational name for someone whose work involved lifting heavy loads (see HOBER) or habitational name for someone from *Höver* near Ülzen. **2.** Jewish (Ashkenazic): occupational name for a dealer in oats, from Yiddish *hober* 'oats' + *man* 'man'.
GIVEN NAMES Jewish 6%. *Chaim, Mayer, Sol, Zev.*

Hobert (289) German and Dutch: variant of HUBERT.

Hobgood (997) Apparently an altered form of HOPGOOD.

Hobin (201) Dutch: patronymic from a short form of HOBERT.

Hobkirk (100) Scottish (Roxburghshire): habitational name from a place near Hawick in Roxburghshire called Hopekirk.

Hobler (102) **1.** German and Czech: variant of German HOBER. **2.** English: unexplained.

Hoblit (141) Probably a variant spelling of English **Hoblet**, from *Hobelot*, a double diminutive of the personal name *Hobb* (see HOBBS). Neither Hoblit nor Hoblet occurs in present-day English records.

Hobson (5702) English (mainly Yorkshire): patronymic from the medieval personal name *Hobb(e)*, a short form of ROBERT. For the altered initial, compare HICK.

Hocevar (249) Slovenian (**Hočevar**): variant of **Kočevar** (see KOCEVAR).
GIVEN NAMES French 5%. *Michel, Toussaint.*

Hoch (2378) **1.** German: from Middle High German *hōch* 'high'; a habitational name from any of various places named Hoch, or a topographic name for someone who lived in an area of high land, or a descriptive

nickname for a tall man, from the same word. **2.** Jewish (Ashkenazic): nickname for a tall person, from German *hoch* 'tall', Yiddish *hoykh*. **3.** Czech: from a pet form of the personal name *Hodislav*, composed of the elements *hodi-* 'to be fit or suited' + *slav* 'glory', 'splendor'.

Hochberg (736) **1.** German: habitational name from any of various places so named, all in southern Germany. **2.** Jewish (Ashkenazic): ornamental name from German *hoch* 'high' + *Berg* 'mountain', 'hill'.
GIVEN NAMES Jewish 8%. *Sol* (3), *Shlomo* (2), *Yigal* (2), *Akiva, Dovid, Emanuel, Iren, Miriam, Reuven, Shaya, Zev.*

Hochgesang (108) South German: **1.** variant of **Hochsang**, topographic name for someone who lived in a high forest clearing made by burning, from Middle High German *hōhe* 'high' + *gesang*, collective noun from *sengen* 'to burn'. **2.** nickname meaning 'festival chorus'.

Hochhalter (399) German: topographic name for someone who lived by a meadow at a high altitude in the mountains, from Middle High German *hoch* 'high' + *halte* 'pasture' + the suffix *-er* denoting an inhabitant (see HALTER).
GIVEN NAMES German 5%. *Otto* (3), *Helmuth, Ilse, Konrad, Rainer, Reinhold.*

Hochhauser (172) South German and Jewish (Ashkenazic): topographic name for someone who lived in a tall house or a house built in a high place, from Middle High German *hōhe* 'high' (German *hoch*) + Middle High German *hūs* 'house' (German *Haus*) + the agent suffix *-er*.
GIVEN NAMES Jewish 10%; German 6%. *Avrohom, Chaim, Menachem, Meyer, Shalom; Gunther* (2), *Kurt.*

Hochheiser (104) Jewish (Ashkenazic): variant of HOCHHAUSER.
GIVEN NAMES Jewish 5%; German 4%. *Chaskel; Inge.*

Hochman (959) German (**Hochmann**) and Jewish (Ashkenazic): descriptive nickname for a tall man, from *hoch* 'tall' (see HOCH) + *Mann* 'man'.
GIVEN NAMES Jewish 6%. *Chaim* (2), *Boruch, Herschel, Hyman, Irina, Mendy, Sholom, Sol.*

Hochmuth (209) German and Jewish (Ashkenazic): nickname for a proud, arrogant, or high-spirited person, from Middle High German *hōher muot* 'pride', 'joy', or 'arrogance'.

Hochrein (114) German: of uncertain origin. Either a distinguishing name of a person named *Rein* (see REIN) living at a high location, from Middle High German *hōhe* 'high', or from a topographic name, which is more likely, denoting a high berm or embankment, from Middle Low German *rein* 'edge of a field', 'border', 'berm'.
GIVEN NAMES German 9%. *Erwin, Heinz, Otto.*

Hochreiter (148) South German: topographic name for someone who lived on or owned a piece of high-lying cleared land, from Middle High German *hōhe* 'high' + *riute* 'cleared land' + the agent suffix *-er*.
GIVEN NAMES German 9%. *Eugen, Hans, Heinrich, Hermann, Siegfried.*

Hochschild (109) German: nickname for a fighter or soldier, variant of *Hauschild* (see HAUSCHILD). *Hoch* reflects a Frankish dialect form of *hauen* 'to hit'.

Hochstadt (106) German (southern and central) and Jewish (Ashkenazic): habitational name from any of several places named Hochstadt.

Hochstatter (154) German (also **Hochstätter**): habitational name from a place called HOCHSTADT, or topographic name for someone who lived in a high location, from Middle High German *hōhe* + *stat* 'place', 'location' + the agent suffix *-er*.

Hochstedler (193) Swiss German: variant of HOCHSTETLER.

Hochstein (431) German: topographic name for someone who lived by a high rock, from Middle High German *hōhe* 'high' + *stein* 'rock', 'stone'.
GIVEN NAMES German 4%. *Kurt* (2), *Fritz.*

Hochstetler (959) Swiss German (**Hochstettler**): topographic name for someone living high on a mountainside, from Middle High German *hōhe* 'high' + *stat, stete* 'place' + the diminutive suffix *-l* + the agent suffix *-er*.

Hochstrasser (133) South German and Swiss German: topographic name for someone who lived by on a high-lying street, from Middle High German *hōhe* 'high' + *straze* 'street', 'road' + the agent suffix *-er*.

Hock (1899) **1.** German (Bavaria; **Höck**): topographic name for someone living by a hedge, from a dialect variant of HECK 2. **2.** German: occupational name from Middle High German *hocke* 'street trader'. **3.** South German form of HAACK 2. **4.** Dutch: from a short form of a Germanic name with the first element *hugi* 'mind', 'thought' (e.g. HUGH, HUBERT). **5.** Dutch: habitational or topographic name, a variant of HOEK. **6.** Jewish (Ashkenazic): when not of the same origin as 2 above, from a short form of the personal name ISAAC.

Hockaday (725) English: nickname from Middle English *Hocedei, Hokedey* 'Hockday', the second Tuesday after Easter. This was formerly a time at which rents and dues were paid, and from the 14th century it was a popular festival. The name possibly denoted someone born at this time of year.

Hockemeyer (136) German (northern and central): **1.** distinguishing name for a tenant farmer (see MEYER) who also ran a local general store, which was typically the case in rural communities in the 18th century, providing a service for the community and additional income for the owner.

2. possibly also an occupational name for a supervisor of small traders, from Middle High German *hocke* 'street trader' + *meier* 'official', 'steward'.

Hockenberry (1266) Americanized form of German **Hachenburger**, habitational name for someone from Hachenburg in the Westerwald (Hesse), or of *Hackenberger*, habitational name from any of several towns named *Hackenberg* in Bavaria, Rheinland-Westphalia, and Brandenburg, or from *Hachenberg* in the Rhineland.

Hockenbury (257) Americanized form of German **Hackenberger** (see HOCKENBERRY).

Hockensmith (506) Americanized form of German **Hackenschmidt**, an occupational name for a maker of hoes and axes, from Middle High German *hacke* 'hoe', 'ax' + *smit* 'smith'.

Hocker (1224) **1.** South German; North German (**Höcker**): variant of HAACK 2, with the addition of the agent suffix *-er*. **2.** German (also **Höcker**): from a Germanic personal name composed with *hugi* 'mind', 'spirit' + *gēr* 'spear'.

Hockersmith (271) See HOCKENSMITH.

Hockert (149) German (also **Höckert**): from a Germanic personal name composed of *hugi* 'heart', 'mind', 'spirit' + *hard* 'hardy', 'strong'.

Hockett (1176) English: from a Middle English pet form of the Old English personal name *Hocca*.

Hockey (233) English (Somerset): apparently a habitational name from an unidentified place, probably in southern England.

Hockin (170) English (chiefly Devon): variant of HOCKING 1.

Hocking (1134) **1.** English (chiefly Devon): from a Middle English pet form of the Old English personal name *Hocca*. **2.** Dutch: patronymic from HOCK 4.

Hockley (164) English (mainly Essex): habitational name from any of various places, for example in Essex and West Midlands. The former is so called from the Old English personal name *Hocca* or *hocc* 'mallow' + *lēah* 'wood', 'clearing'; the latter from the personal name *Hucca* + *hlāw* 'hill'.

Hockman (1024) **1.** North German and Dutch: topographic name for someone living on a corner. **2.** German: Americanized spelling of **Hochmann** (see HOCHMAN).

Hoctor (202) Irish: Anglicized form of Gaelic **Ó hEachtair** 'son of *Eachtar*', which may be a Gaelic form of the personal name HECTOR.

Hocutt (498) Variant of English **Howcutt**, of uncertain origin; possibly a variant of HOCKETT. In America this surname is found mainly in NC.

Hoda (136) Muslim: variant of HUDA.

GIVEN NAMES Muslim 24%. *Syed* (6), *Mohammed* (2), *Aminul, Amir, Arash, Asif,* *Badrul, Nadeem, Omar, Saiful, Tabassum, Zahra.*

Hodak (151) **1.** Croatian, Serbian, or Czech: from a short form of an Old Slavic personal name formed with *hod* 'good', as for example *Hodislav* or *Hoděmysl*. **2.** Polish and Jewish (Ashkenazic): probably from a variant spelling of *chodak* 'clog', 'wooden shoe', a metonymic occupational name for a clog maker.

Hodapp (577) **1.** South German: probably a nickname for a clumsy person, from Middle High German *hōh* 'high', 'tall' + the dialect word *dapp* 'fool'. **2.** possibly a short form of a Germanic personal name composed with *od* 'property', 'wealth', *Hot(t)op*, altered under Slavic influence.

Hodde (236) **1.** North German and Dutch: variant of OTTO. **2.** English: variant of HOOD 1.

GIVEN NAMES German 6%. *Erwin* (3), *Ernst, Fritz, Lorenz.*

Hodder (445) English: occupational name for a maker or seller of hoods, from a Middle English agent derivative of Old English *hōd* (see HOOD 1).

Hoddinott (118) English: variant of HODNETT.

Hodel (485) South German: occupational name for a trader in rags, from the dialect word *hodel, hudel* 'rag'.

Hodell (105) Americanized spelling of German HODEL.

Hoder (128) English: probably a variant spelling of HODDER.

Hodes (566) **1.** Jewish (Ashkenazic): from the Yiddish female personal name *Hodes* (Hebrew *Hadasa* 'myrtle'; English spelling *Hadassah*). **2.** Polish: from a variant of *Chodysz* or *Chadys*, pet forms of the eastern Slavic personal name *Chodor*. Compare HODOR. **3.** English: variant of HOOD 1.

GIVEN NAMES Jewish 5%. *Hyman* (2), *Meyer, Myer.*

Hodgden (110) Probably a respelling of English HODGDON.

Hodgdon (1040) English: variant of HODSDON.

Hodge (16622) English: **1.** from the medieval personal name *Hodge*, a short form of ROGER. (For the change of initial, compare HICK.) **2.** nickname from Middle English *hodge* 'hog', which occurs as a dialect variant of *hogge*, for example in Cheshire place names.

Hodgeman (128) English: variant spelling of HODGMAN.

Hodgen (267) English (northern Ireland): from a pet form of HODGE.

Hodgens (241) English: patronymic from HODGEN.

Hodges (24305) English: patronymic from HODGE.

Hodgetts (120) English: patronymic from a pet form of the personal name HODGE.

Hodgin (770) English: from a pet form of the personal name HODGE.

Hodgins (860) English (Ireland): patronymic from the personal name HODGIN.

Hodgkin (237) English: from a pet form of the personal name HODGE.

Hodgkins (1167) English (West Midlands): patronymic from the personal name HODGKIN.

Hodgkinson (495) Northern English: patronymic from the personal name HODGKIN.
FOREBEARS The name Hodgkinson has long had two main areas of concentration; in western Lancashire around Preston, and in northern Derbyshire around Ashover. It appears in the Preston Guild Rolls in 1582 in the spelling *Hogekynson*.

Hodgkiss (240) English: patronymic from a pet form of the personal name HODGE.

Hodgman (387) English: **1.** occupational name for the servant (Middle English *man*) of a man called HODGE. **2.** possibly an occupational name for a swineherd or shepherd, from Middle English *hoggeman*. Compare HODGE 2.

Hodgson (4146) English (northern): patronymic from HODGE.

Hodkinson (201) English (Lancashire): patronymic from *Hodkin*, a pet form of HUGH, or *Hodgkin*, a pet form of HODGE.

Hodnett (973) English (found chiefly in the West Midlands and in Ireland): habitational name from Hodnet in Shropshire, or any of various places called Hoddnant in Wales. The place names are from Welsh *hawdd* 'pleasant', 'peaceful' + *nant* 'valley', 'stream'.

Hodo (380) Probably a variant of Scottish HADDOW. This surname occurs chiefly in AL and GA.

Hodor (131) Polish and Slovak: from the eastern Slavic personal name *Chodor*, a vernacular form of *Teodor* (see THEODORE).

Hodsdon (339) English: habitational name from Hoddesdon in Hertfordshire, named in Old English with the personal name *Hod* + *dūn* 'hill'.
FOREBEARS The earliest known bearer of this name is Norman de Hoddesdon, recorded in 1165–6. The surname was taken to America by Nicholas Hodsdon in about 1628, from whom probably all current U.S. bearers of the name are descended.

Hodson (2361) English (mainly Lancashire and Staffordshire): patronymic from HODGE.

Hodum (100) German: southern dialect form of the personal name *Adam*; see ADAM.

GIVEN NAME French 4%. *Gaston.*

Hoe (177) English: topographic name for someone who lived by a spur of a hill, from the Old English dative case *hō(e)* (originally used after a preposition) of *hōh* 'spur of a hill' (literally 'heel'). In many cases the surname may be a habitational name from a minor place named with this element, for example one in Norfolk.

Hoechst (112) German: from a topographic name for someone who lived in a very high place (high on a mountainside or at the top of a tenement building), from the superlative form of Middle High German *hōhe* 'high' (modern German *hoch*).

GIVEN NAME German 7%. *Hartmut*.

Hoeck (230) **1.** German (**Höck**): see HOCK 1. **2.** German: variant of HAACK 2. **3.** Dutch: variant spelling of HOEK.

GIVEN NAMES German 4%. *Friedrich, Juergen, Wolfgang*.

Hoecker (204) German (**Höcker**): occupational name for a small trader, Middle High German *hocke*.

Hoefer (1000) **1.** German (also **Höfer**): variant of HOFER. **2.** German: habitational name for someone from any of several places called Hof.

GIVEN NAMES German 5%. *Kurt* (4), *Hans* (3), *Ernst, Frieda, Joerg, Karl-Heinz, Mathias, Meinhard, Monika, Wilhelmina*.

Hoefert (162) German (also **Höfert**): variant of HOFER.

GIVEN NAMES German 5%. *Kurt* (2).

Hoeffel (131) German (**Höf(f)el**): topographic name from a diminutive of Middle High German *hof* 'farmstead', 'manor farm', 'court'.

Hoeffner (272) German (**Höffner**): occupational name or status name for the owner or manager of an estate, from an agent noun from Middle High German *hof* 'farmstead', 'manor farm' (see HOFFMANN).

Hoefle (199) South German: diminutive of HOFF.

GIVEN NAME German 4%. *Heinz*.

Hoefler (499) German (**Höfler**): occupational name or status name for the owner or the manager of an estate, from an agent noun from Middle High German *hof* 'farmstead', 'manor farm' (see HOFFMANN).

GIVEN NAMES German 4%. *Ewald, Kurt, Otto, Wenzel, Wolfgang*.

Hoeflich (150) German (**Höflich**): nickname for someone who behaved in a courtly manner, from Middle High German *hovelīh* 'courtly', 'courteous'.

Hoefling (300) German (**Höfling**): **1.** nickname from Middle High German *hovelinc* 'member of a courtly household', 'person having a courtly manner'; or alternatively from the same word applied as a nickname for a bondsman or servant. **2.** habitational name from any of various places in Bavaria and Austria named Höfling.

GIVEN NAMES German 4%. *Franz, Kurt, Otto*.

Hoefner (104) German: variant of HOEFFNER.

Hoefs (371) **1.** Dutch and North German (**Höfs**): probably from Middle Low German *hovet*, *hōft* 'head', used as a nickname. **2.** Shortened form of Dutch **van Hoefs**, a variant of HOVE.

Hoeft (1316) **1.** North German (**Höft**): from

Middle Low German *hovet*, *höft* 'head', applied as a nickname or topographic name. **2.** German (**Höft**): habitational name from places named Höft in Westphalia or near Linz in Austria.

Hoeg (182) Danish (**Høeg**): nickname or metonymic occupational name for a falconer, from *høg* 'hawk' (see HAWK 1). This surname also occurs in Norway.

GIVEN NAMES Scandinavian 4%. *Erik, Ove*.

Hoeger (235) German (**Höger**): **1.** Bavarian variant of HEGER. **2.** North German: from a personal name, a variant of HOYER 2.

GIVEN NAMES Scandinavian 4%; German 4%. *Erik, Sven*; *Hans, Johann, Johannes, Kurt*.

Hoehl (110) German (**Höhl**): topographic name for someone living by a hole or cave, Middle High German *höl*.

GIVEN NAMES German 10%. *Otto* (2), *Brunhilde, Eberhard*.

Hoehn (1506) **1.** South German (**Höhn**): from an aphetic form of the personal name *Johann(es)* (see JOHN). **2.** North German: from a short form of a Germanic compound name formed with *hūn* 'bear cub' or *hun* 'giant' as the first element. **3.** German: habitational name from any of several places in Hesse and Bavaria called Höhn.

Hoehne (497) German: **1.** from a short form, *Huno*, of any of various Germanic personal names composed with *hun* 'giant' or *hūn* 'bear cub'. **2.** German (**Höhne**): nickname from Middle High German *hōnen* 'to get angry'.

GIVEN NAMES German 12%. *Kurt* (5), *Fritz* (3), *Franz, Gerhard, Hans, Helmut, Hermann, Horst, Ingo, Juergen, Klaus, Manfred*.

Hoehner (101) **1.** German: variant of HOEHN 3 and perhaps of HOEHNE 2. **2.** North German: reduced form of **Hövener**, variant of **Höfer** (see HOEFER).

GIVEN NAME German 7%; Scandinavian 4%. *Bernd* (2).

Hoek (246) Dutch: **1.** habitational name from places called Hoek, e.g. in Ghent or Zeeland, or from Hoeke in West Flanders, or a topographic name from *hoek* 'corner', 'nook'. **2.** variant of HOUCK 1.

GIVEN NAMES Dutch 4%. *Dirk, Hendrik, Jilles, Maarten*.

Hoekman (152) Dutch: variant of HOCKMAN.

GIVEN NAMES Dutch 4%. *Dirk, Gerritt*.

Hoeksema (328) Frisian: topographic name for someone living on a corner, Dutch *hoek*, or habitational name for someone from a place called Hoek(e) (see HOEK 1).

Hoekstra (1348) Frisian: topographic name for someone living on a corner or in a nook, or perhaps a habitational name for someone from a place named with this word (see HOEK 1).

Hoel (627) Norwegian: habitational name from any of numerous farmsteads, notably in southern Norway, named *Hol* from Old Norse *hóll* 'round hill', 'mound'.

GIVEN NAMES Scandinavian 7%. *Erik* (2), *Lars* (2), *Per* (2), *Berger, Kjersti, Oystein*.

Hoell (174) German (**Höll**): **1.** variant of HELL 3. **2.** habitational name from any of several places so named in Bavaria, Württemberg, and Baden.

GIVEN NAMES German 9%. *Manfred* (2), *Dieter, Gerda, Helmuth, Otto*.

Hoelle (141) German (**Höelle**): topographic name from a field name meaning 'hell' (see HELLE 3).

GIVEN NAMES German 7%. *Eberhard, Helmut, Kurt*.

Hoeller (100) German: topographic name from a field name meaning 'hell' (see HELLE 3) + *-er*, suffix denoting an inhabitant.

GIVEN NAMES German 9%. *Gerhard, Helmut, Winfried*.

Hoelscher (1366) North German (**Hölscher**): occupational name for a maker of clogs (wooden shoes), Middle Low German *holsche* (from Middle Low German *holt* 'wood' + *scho* 'shoe'), with the agent noun suffix *-er*.

Hoelter (100) German: habitational name from several places in Westphalia called Hölt and Holt.

GIVEN NAMES German 11%. *Kurt* (3), *Gerhard*.

Hoelting (210) German (**Hölting**): topographic name from Middle Low German *holting*, *holtink* 'wooded area'.

GIVEN NAME German 4%. *Kurt* (2).

Hoeltzel (110) German: variant spelling of HOELZEL.

GIVEN NAME German 4%. *Frederika*.

Hoelzel (278) South German (**Hölzel**): topographic name from a diminutive of HOLTZ.

GIVEN NAMES German 5%. *Gerhardt* (2), *Otto*.

Hoelzer (240) **1.** North German: occupational name for a lumberjack or woodcutter, from Middle High German *holz* 'wood' + *-er*, agent noun suffix. **2.** South German (**Hölzer**): topographic name from Middle High German *holz* 'wood', 'copse' + *-er* suffix denoting an inhabitant.

GIVEN NAMES German 4%. *Hans, Helmut, Ingeborg, Wolfgang*.

Hoelzle (116) South German (**Hölzle**): topographic name from a diminutive of HOLTZ.

GIVEN NAMES German 9%. *Urs* (3), *Erwin*.

Hoem (120) Norwegian: habitational name from any of eight farms, in particular in Møre og Romsdal, named in Old Norse as *Hóheimr*, from *hór* 'high (up)' + *heimr* 'home', 'farmstead', referring to a farm high up on a mountainside.

Hoemann (121) German: variant of HOMANN or its variant **Högemann**.

GIVEN NAME German 4%. *Kurt*.

Hoen (193) **1.** Dutch and German: nickname from *hoen* 'chicken', 'hen', perhaps denoting a silly person. **2.** Dutch: from the

Germanic personal name *Huno* (from *hūn* 'bear cub'). **3.** German: variant of **Höhn** (see HOEHN). **4.** Norwegian: habitational name from either of two farmsteads named *Hon*, from Old Norse *hundr* 'dog', or from *Hóvin*, a compound of *hór* 'high' + *vin* 'meadow'.

Hoene (249) German (**Höne**): variant spelling of **Höhne** (see HOEHNE).

Hoener (219) North German (**Höner**): variant spelling of HOEHNER.
GIVEN NAMES German 5%. *Dieter, Kurt, Monika, Wolfgang.*

Hoenes (124) German (Rhineland): variant of HOEHN or HOEHNE.

Hoenig (583) **1.** Eastern German (**Hönig**): variant of HEINIG. **2.** Jewish (Ashkenazic): from the personal name *Henich*, a form of the Biblical name *Hanoch*, *Henoch* (see ENOCH).
GIVEN NAMES German 4%. *Aloysius, Egon, Gerhard, Helmuth, Hermann, Kurt, Otto.*

Hoenshell (112) Probably an altered form of German HENSCHEL.

Hoeper (248) North German (**Höper**): topographic name from *hop(e)* 'raised ground in a bog', or 'bog', or a habitational name from any of various places named with this word.
GIVEN NAMES German 4%. *Friedrich, Hans, Klaus, Kurt.*

Hoepfner (196) German (**Höpfner**): occupational name for a grower of or dealer in hops, Middle High German *hopfener*. In some cases it may have been a metonymic occupational name for a brewer.
GIVEN NAMES German 12%. *Dietrich, Guenther, Gunter, Hans, Horst, Klaus, Otto, Ulrich.*

Hoepner (220) North German: variant of HOEPPNER.
GIVEN NAMES German 5%. *Otto (2), Erwin.*

Hoeppner (623) North German (**Höppner**): occupational name for a grower of or dealer in hops (see HOEPFNER).
GIVEN NAMES German 4%. *Egon, Elfriede, Ernst, Fritz, Hans, Heinz, Otto, Ralf.*

Hoerauf (126) German (**Hörauf**): ostensibly a nickname meaning 'stop it!' (German *Hör auf!*), but in fact it derives from the Low German place name Hörup near Flensburg.
GIVEN NAMES German 4%. *Erwin, Hans.*

Hoerig (168) German: **1.** (**Hörig**): variant of HERING. **2.** (of Slavic origin): topographic name from Sorbian *gorka* 'little mountain'.
GIVEN NAMES German 6%. *Helmut, Kurt.*

Hoerl (154) German (**Hörl**): variant of *Herl*, a pet form of HERMANN, found chiefly in Bavaria.
GIVEN NAMES German 7%. *Hermann, Monika, Theodor, Wilhelm.*

Hoerle (110) German (**Hörle**): variant of HERL, found chiefly in Bavaria.
GIVEN NAMES German 5%. *Arno, Hans.*

Hoerman (102) German: see HOERMANN.

GIVEN NAMES German 9%; Scandinavian 5%. *Hans (2), Klaus, Kurt; Tor.*

Hoermann (132) German (**Hörmann**): variant of HERMANN, found chiefly in Bavaria.
GIVEN NAMES German 12%. *Siegfried (2), Arno, Helmut.*

Hoerner (804) South German (**Hörner**): variant of HORNER.

Hoerning (120) German: **1.** (**Hörning**): variant of HORNING. **2.** (of Slavic origin): see HOERIG.
GIVEN NAMES German 5%. *Fritz, Udo.*

Hoerr (305) German (**Hörr**): possibly a derivative of Middle High German *hor* 'dirt', 'mire' (see HORR).

Hoerter (138) German (Bavaria; **Hörter**): variant of HERTER 'herdsman'.
GIVEN NAMES German 4%. *Erna, Otto.*

Hoerth (119) German: habitational name from either of two places, Hürth near Cologne or Hörth in the Palatinate.
GIVEN NAME German 5%. *Kurt.*

Hoes (173) **1.** English: topographic name for someone living between the spurs of two or more hills, from Old English *hōs*, plural of *hōh* 'spur of a hill' (literally 'heel'). **2.** German: unexplained.
GIVEN NAME German 5%. *Otto (2).*

Hoesch (117) German (**Hösch**): see HOSCH.

Hoeschen (174) German (**Höschen**): probably a standardized form of Low German *Hoeske*, diminutive of Middle Low German (Middle High German) *hose* 'hose', 'leggings', either a metonymic occupational name for a knitter or maker of hose or a topographic name from a field so named because of its shape.
GIVEN NAMES French 5%. *Andre, Colette, Raoul.*

Hoese (164) German (**Höse**): probably a variant of HOSE.

Hoesing (119) German (**Hösing**): unexplained; possibly a variant of HOSANG (recorded in 1457 in the form *Hoesang*).

Hoesly (202) Swiss German (**Hösly**): Alemannic diminutive of *Hose* 'hose', 'leggings', either from a metonymic occupational name for a maker of these garments or a topographic name from the shape of a field (see HOESCHEN).

Hoey (1626) **1.** Irish: Anglicized form of Gaelic **Ó hEochaidh** 'descendant of *Eochaidh*', a variant of *Eachaidh* (see HAUGHEY). **2.** Norwegian: habitational name from a farmstead named *Hoøy* from Old Norse *hór* 'high' + *ey* 'island'.
GIVEN NAMES Irish 7%. *Brendan (2), Caitlin, Conor, Declan, Thomas Patrick.*

Hoezee (104) Perhaps an altered spelling of Dutch **Hozzee**, from a diminutive of Old French *hose* 'stocking', 'boot', applied as a metonymic occupational name for a maker of such articles or possibly as a nickname for someone who wore flamboyant or otherwise remarkable leg wear.

Hof (360) German and Dutch: variant spelling of HOFF.
GIVEN NAME German 4%. *Helmut (2).*

Hofacker (361) German: topographic name from Middle High German *hof* 'farmstead', 'manor farm' + *acker* 'field', a very old field name in Württemberg, probably denoting a field owned by the feudal lord and cultivated on his behalf by his tenants. The surname would have denoted someone living by such a field.
GIVEN NAMES German 6%. *Elfriede, Hartmut, Ingo, Kurt, Otto, Wolfgang.*

Hofbauer (416) German: occupational name for a farmer (Middle High German *gebūr(e)*) who owned his farm, Middle High German *hof*, or who farmed in the service of a court, Middle High German *hof*.
GIVEN NAMES German 5%. *Egon (2), Bernd, Franz, Gerhard, Kurt, Manfred, Monika.*

Hofeldt (142) North German: topographic name composed of Middle Low German *hov, hof* 'manor farm', 'farmstead' + *velt* 'open country'. This and variants such as *Hofeld, Hoffeld(e)* are also common place names all over Germany (compare HOFACKER); the surname may be a habitational name from one of these.
GIVEN NAMES German 4%. *Hans (2), Irmgard.*

Hofer (2901) South German and Jewish (Ashkenazic): topographic name for someone who lived at, worked on, or managed a farm, from Middle High German *hof* 'farmstead', 'manor farm', 'court' + the agent suffix *-er*. Compare HOFFMANN.
GIVEN NAMES German 5%. *Franz (4), Kurt (4), Erwin (3), Florian (3), Hans (2), Heinz (2), Hermann (2), Johannes (2), Reiner (2), Ulli (2), Egon, Fritz.*

Hoff (7147) **1.** North German, Dutch, and Danish: topographic name or status name for the owner of a farm, or occupational name for someone who worked on the main farm in a community, from Middle High and Low German *hof* 'farmstead', 'manor farm', or habitational name from any of the many places named with this word. Compare HOFER. **2.** Norwegian: habitational name from any of numerous farmsteads named Hov, from Old Norse *hof* 'sacrificial temple'.

Hoffa (303) Altered form of German or Dutch HOFER.

Hoffacker (152) German: variant of HOFACKER.
GIVEN NAMES German 6%. *Hans, Kurt.*

Hoffard (109) Probably an Americanized form of German HOFFART.

Hoffart (373) **1.** German: nickname from Middle High German *hōchvart* 'pride', 'superciliousness'. **2.** Norwegian: habitational name from a farmstead in Buskerud named Hoffar, possibly from Old Norse *Hagfura*, composed of the element *hag* denoting an enclosure + *fura* 'fir tree'.

Hoffarth (251) German: variant of HOF-FART.
GIVEN NAMES German 4%. *Fritz, Monika, Otto.*

Hoffberg (103) **1.** German: habitational name from a place named as 'the farm on the mountain'. **2.** Jewish (Ashkenazic): variant of HOFFENBERG.

Hoffecker (177) German (Rhineland): variant of HOFACKER.

Hoffenberg (139) Jewish (Ashkenazic): ornamental elaboration of German *Hoffnung* 'hope', with *Berg* 'mountain', 'hill'. It may have been adopted as an expression of hope for a better future.
GIVEN NAMES Jewish 7%. *Miriam, Sol.*

Hoffer (2239) German and Jewish (Ashkenazic): variant of HOFER.

Hofferber (226) North German: variant of **Hofferbert**, from Middle Low German *hof* 'farmstead', 'manor farm' + the personal name *Herber(t)*, a short form of any of the Germanic names composed with *heri* 'army'.

Hoffert (674) **1.** German: variant of HOFER. **2.** German: from a Germanic personal name *Hoffred*, composed of *hōh* 'high' + *fridu* 'peace'.

Hoffland (113) Altered spelling of HOF-LAND.

Hoffler (161) German (**Höffler**): variant spelling of **Höfler** (see HOFER).

Hoffman (55227) **1.** German and Jewish (Ashkenazic): variant of HOFFMANN 'steward'. **2.** Dutch: occupational name for a farm laborer or a gardener, someone who worked at the *hof*, the manor farm.

Hoffmann (6994) German and Jewish (Ashkenazic): status name for a steward on an farm or estate, from German *hof(f)* 'manorfarm', 'courtyard' + *Mann* 'man'. Originally, this was a status name for a farmer who owned his own land as opposed to holding it by rent or feudal obligation, but the name soon came to denote the manager or steward of a manor farm, in which sense it is extremely frequent throughout central and eastern Europe; also among Jews, since many Jews held managerial positions on non-Jewish estates. This name is widespread throughout central and eastern Europe, not only in German-speaking lands.
GIVEN NAMES German 8%. *Kurt* (19), *Gerhard* (10), *Hans* (9), *Heinz* (9), *Otto* (9), *Dieter* (6), *Klaus* (6), *Wolfgang* (6), *Armin* (5), *Manfred* (5), *Ernst* (4), *Erwin* (4).

Hoffmaster (491) Partly Americanized form of German HOFMEISTER.

Hoffmeier (193) German: variant spelling of **Hofmeyer** (see HOFFMEYER).
GIVEN NAMES German 5%. *Gerhard, Hans, Lorenz.*

Hoffmeister (650) German: variant spelling of HOFMEISTER.
GIVEN NAMES German 4%. *Kurt* (3), *Gerd, Gerhart, Ulrich.*

Hoffmeyer (524) German (**Hofmeyer**): occupational name for the supervisor (see MEYER) of the manor farm on an estate, Middle High German *hof*. This surname is also found in Denmark.

Hoffnagle (105) Americanized spelling of North German **Hofnagel**, a variant of HUFNAGEL.

Hoffner (907) German and Jewish (Ashkenazic): **1.** status name for a steward on an farm or estate (see HOFFMANN). **2.** German (**Höffner**): status name for a prosperous small farmer, from an agent noun derivative of Middle Low German *huove*, a measure of land. Compare German HUBER. **3.** German: variant spelling of **Hofner**, habitational name from any of several places called Hof. **4.** Jewish (Ashkenazic): variant of HOPFER.

Hofford (111) English or Irish: probably a variant of HAFFORD, which is itself a variant of HARFORD or HEREFORD.

Hoffpauir (802) Americanized form of German HOFBAUER.

Hoffstetter (118) Swiss German: variant of HOFSTETTER.
GIVEN NAMES French 6%; German 4%. *Armand* (2); *Otto* (2).

Hofius (133) German, Dutch, and Scandinavian: humanistic name representing a partial Latinization of HOFER.

Hofland (278) **1.** Dutch: habitational name from a common place name denoting land adjacent to a lord's court. **2.** Norwegian: variant of HOVLAND.

Hofler (165) South German (**Höfler**): variant of HOFER.
GIVEN NAMES German 5%. *Gunther* (2), *Johann.*

Hofman (772) Dutch, North German, and Jewish (Ashkenazic): variant of HOFMANN (see HOFFMANN).
GIVEN NAMES German 6%; Dutch 5%. *Kurt* (3), *Bernd, Claus, Fritz, Hans, Henrich, Matthias, Otto, Volker, Waltraud, Wolf; Dirk* (3), *Marinus* (2), *Roelf* (2), *Cornelus, Gerrit, Gert, Harmen, Hendrick, Jilles, Willem, Willen, Wim.*

Hofmann (3869) German and Jewish (Ashkenazic): variant of HOFFMANN. The surname in this spelling is also found in Denmark.
GIVEN NAMES German 9%. *Hans* (13), *Otto* (10), *Ernst* (9), *Erwin* (6), *Kurt* (6), *Gerhard* (5), *Helmut* (4), *Klaus* (4), *Fritz* (3), *Heinz* (3), *Ruedi* (3), *Wilhelm* (3).

Hofmeister (1003) German: occupational name for the chamberlain in a noble household or an official with similar functions in a religious house, from Middle High German *hof* 'court', 'household' (originally 'settlement', 'manor farm') + *meister* 'master'. This name was also adopted as an ornamental name by Ashkenazic Jews.
GIVEN NAMES German 7%. *Kurt* (9), *Otto* (3), *Angelika, Franz, Gottfried, Hans, Inge, Klaus, Konrad, Ursel.*

Hofmeyer (128) German: see HOFFMEYER.

Hofrichter (154) German: occupational name for a judge at a manor court, Middle High German *hoverihter.*
GIVEN NAMES German 4%. *Hans, Willi.*

Hofstad (228) **1.** Dutch and Belgian: habitational name from the common place name Hofsta(d)t or Hofstade, meaning a place (*stad*) where there was a farmstead. **2.** Norwegian: habitational name from any of several farmsteads, most of them so named from Old Norse *hof* 'sacrificial temple' + *staðir* 'farmstead', 'dwelling'.
GIVEN NAMES Scandinavian 4%. *Erik, Helmer.*

Hofstetter (902) **1.** German: occupational or status name for someone who worked or lived at the principal farm on an estate, from Middle High German *hof* 'farmstead', 'manor farm' + *stete* 'place'. **2.** German and Jewish (Ashkenazic): habitational name for someone from any of various places called Hofstetten, in particular one in Bavaria.
GIVEN NAMES German 4%. *Hans* (3), *Kurt* (2), *Fritz, Gunter, Horst, Otmar.*

Hofstra (179) Frisian: topographic name for someone who lived by a garden or courtyard, or who worked at the main house on an estate, from an agent noun derived from HOF.

Hoft (112) German (**Höft**): see HOEFT.
GIVEN NAMES German 10%. *Christoph, Hartmut, Hermann.*

Hoga (24) Japanese (**Hōga**): 'respectful congratulations', found mostly in northeastern Japan.

Hogan (22955) Irish: Anglicized form of Gaelic Ó hÓgáin 'descendant of *Ógán*', a personal name from a diminutive of *óg* 'young', also 'young warrior'. In the south, some bearers claim descent from an uncle of Brian Boru. In northern Ireland a surname of the same form was Anglicized as HAGAN.

Hogancamp (139) Altered spelling of North German and Dutch **Hogenkamp**, a topographic name from Middle Low German *hoge*, Dutch *hoog* 'high' + *kamp* 'enclosed field'.

Hogans (273) Probably a variant of Irish HOGAN, with English patronymic -*s*.

Hoganson (183) Americanized spelling of Danish and Norwegian HAAGENSEN or Swedish **Håkansson** (see HAKANSON).

Hogard (126) English: variant of HOG-GARD.

Hogarth (395) English (northern borders) and Scottish: probably a variant of HOGGARD, but perhaps, as Black suggests, a habitational name from a lost or unidentified place named with the dialect word *hoggarth* 'lamb enclosure'.

Hogarty (180) Irish: Anglicized form of Gaelic Ó hÓgartaigh, a variant of FOGARTY (with loss of the initial *F*- of the personal name).

Hogate (142) English: apparently a variant of HOGGATT.

Hogberg (189) Swedish (**Högberg**): ornamental name composed of the elements *hög* 'high' + *berg* 'mountain', 'hill'.
GIVEN NAMES Scandinavian 8%; German 4%. *Erik, Nels, Nils; Hans.*

Hoge (1223) North German (Rhineland): nickname for a person of high status, from Middle Low German *hoge* 'high'. Compare HOCH.
GIVEN NAMES German 4%. *Kurt* (4), *Franz* (2), *Alfons, Erwin, Hermann, Otto, Reinhard, Reinhold.*

Hogeboom (120) Dutch and Belgian: variant spelling of **Hooge(n)boom** (see HOOGENBOOM).

Hogeland (304) Americanized spelling of Swedish **Högland** (see HOGLAND).

Hogen (148) Swedish (**Högen**): either a nickname from *hög* 'high', 'tall' + the adjectival suffix *-en* (from Latin *-enius*), or an ornamental name with the first element taken from a place name formed with *hög-* 'high'.
GIVEN NAMES Scandinavian 5%. *Erik, Hilma, Obert.*

Hogenmiller (120) Dutch: partly Americanized occupational name for a miller located in the upper part of a community, from Dutch *hoge* 'high' + an English translation of *molenaar* 'miller'.

Hogenson (293) Americanized spelling of Danish and Norwegian HAAGENSEN or its Swedish cognate **Håkensson** (see HAKANSON).

Hoger (150) **1.** German (also **Höger**): variant of HEGER. **2.** North German: from the Germanic personal name *Hucger*, composed of the elements *hug* 'head', 'mind', 'spirit' + *gēr* 'spear'. **3.** South German: nickname for a hunchback, from Middle High German *hoger* 'hump'. **4.** French: variant of OGIER.
GIVEN NAMES German 5%. *Arno, Ernst.*

Hogg (2862) **1.** Scottish and English: metonymic occupational name for a swineherd, from Middle English *hog(ge)* 'swine'. **2.** Scottish and English: metonymic occupational name for a shepherd, from Middle English *hogg* 'yearling sheep'. **3.** German (**Högg**): topographic name, a variant of HECK 2, found chiefly in Bavaria.

Hoggan (225) **1.** Irish: variant of HAGAN 1 or 2. **2.** Scottish: unexplained, possibly the same as 1.

Hoggard (1103) English: occupational name for a swineherd or shepherd, from Middle English *hog(ge)* 'hog', 'swine' or *hogg* 'yearling sheep' + *herd, hard* 'herdsman', but see also HOGARTH.

Hoggarth (135) English and Scottish: variant of HOGARTH.

Hoggatt (667) English (northern): probably a variant spelling of **Hoggett**, a variant of HOCKETT and HOGGARD.

Hogge (826) English and Scottish: variant spelling of HOGG.

Hoggle (136) Variant of HOGLE.

Hogland (187) **1.** Swedish: ornamental or topographic name from *hög* 'high' + *land* 'land'. **2.** Possibly an Americanized spelling of Norwegian HAUGLAND.

Hogle (675) Perhaps a respelling of German **Högel**, a habitational name from a place so named in Schleswig-Holstein, or alternatively of Dutch origin, but unexplained.

Hoglen (128) Origin unidentified.

Hoglund (786) Swedish (**Höglund**): ornamental or topographic name composed of the elements *hög* 'high' + *lund* 'grove'.
GIVEN NAMES Scandinavian 7%; German 4%. *Erik, Helmer; Ingeborg, Kurt.*

Hogrefe (256) North German: occupational and status name from Middle Low German *hogreve*, a compound of *hoch* 'high' + *grefe* 'lord', 'supervisor' (see GRAF).
GIVEN NAMES German 4%. *Hans* (2), *Bernd.*

Hogsed (230) **1.** Variant spelling of Norwegian **Høgset(h)** (see HOGSETT). **2.** English: Reaney and Wilson record a 17th-century example of this name in Devon. Evidently an uncomplimentary nickname meaning 'hog's head', it is no longer found in the British Isles.

Hogsett (355) Americanized spelling of Norwegian **Høgset(h)**, a habitational name from any of several farmsteads so named, mostly from Old Norse *Heggsetr*, a compound of *heggr* 'bird cherry (tree)' + *setr* 'farmstead', 'dwelling'.

Hogston (164) English: habitational name, possibly in part from Hogston in Angus, Scotland, named from Older Scots *hogg* 'young sheep', but the concentration of the name in the Midlands and southern England suggests that it is primarily from Hoggeston in Buckinghamshire, which is named from the Old English personal name *Hogg* + Old English *tūn*.

Hogue (5493) French (**Hogué**): topographic name from a diminutive of *hogue*, derived from Old Norse *haugr* 'hill', or a habitational name either from places in Calvados, Eure, and Manche called La Hogue or from Le Hoguet in Seine-Maritime.
FOREBEARS A bearer of the name from Picardy is documented in Montreal in 1672.

Hogwood (112) English (Kent): possibly a habitational name from places in Kent and West Sussex called Hog Wood.

Hoh (263) **1.** German (also **Höh**): topographic name or nickname from Middle High German *hōch, hō* 'high' (see HOCH). **2.** Chinese: variant of HU.

Hoheisel (203) German: topographic name from Middle High German *hōch* 'high' + a diminutive of Middle High German *hūs* 'house'.
GIVEN NAMES German 4%. *Dietmar, Franziska.*

Hohenberger (224) German: habitational name for someone from any of numerous places named Hohenberg, or a topographic name from Middle High German *hōhen*, an inflected form of *hōch* 'high' + *berg* 'mountain', 'hill'.
GIVEN NAMES German 5%. *Kurt, Maximilian, Rudi.*

Hohensee (374) German: habitational name from any of several places so named in Pomerania and East Prussia, or perhaps from Hohenseeden near Magdeburg.
GIVEN NAMES German 5%. *Heinz, Klaus, Kurt, Reinhard, Volker.*

Hohenstein (498) **1.** German and Jewish (Ashkenazic): habitational name from any of various places so named. **2.** German: topographic name composed of Middle High German *hōhen*, an inflected form of *hōch* 'high' + *stein* 'rock'.
GIVEN NAMES German 4%. *Erwin* (2), *Georg, Hans.*

Hohertz (100) **1.** German: variant of German **Hochherz**, literally 'high heart', nickname for a generous-spirited individual. **2.** perhaps from a Germanic personal name composed with *hōh* 'high' + *hard* 'strong'.

Hohimer (118) Altered form of German **Hochheimer**, habitational name for someone from a place called Hochheim.

Hohl (789) German (also **Höhl**): topographic name for someone who lived in or by a depression or low-lying spot, from Middle High German *hol* 'hollow', 'cave'.
GIVEN NAMES German 4%. *Hans* (2), *Kurt* (2), *Erwin, Fritz, Guenter, Heinrich, Heinz.*

Hohler (237) German: variant of HOHL, with the addition of the agent suffix *-er.*

Hohlt (162) **1.** North German: variant of North German HOLT with the additional *h* reflecting the lengthened vowel. **2.** Scandinavian: variant of HOLT.
GIVEN NAME Scandinavian 4%. *Ordell.*

Hohm (106) German: probably a variant of **Höhme**, a nickname for an unimportant person, from Middle High German *ome* 'chaff', 'negligible entity'.
GIVEN NAMES German 14%. *Otto* (3), *Gottfried* (2), *Ulrich.*

Hohman (1412) Altered spelling of HOHMANN.

Hohmann (726) German: variant of *Hochmann* (see HOCHMAN), itself a variant of HOCH.
GIVEN NAMES German 8%. *Heinz* (2), *Fritz, Hanns, Hans, Helmut, Horst, Kurt, Manfred, Nikolaus, Otto, Rainer, Volker.*

Hohn (972) **1.** North German: from Middle Low German *hōn* 'chicken', hence a nickname, or a metonymic occupational name for someone who raised poultry. **2.** North German: topographic name from an old word, *hon*, meaning 'bog'. **3.** North German: variant of HOEHN 2. **4.** South German (**Höhn**): variant of HOEHNE.

5. South German: from an aphetic form of the personal name *Johann(es)* (see JOHN).
GIVEN NAMES German 4%. *Arno* (3), *Hans* (3), *Fritz, Gunter, Helmut, Jutta, Kurt.*

Hohner (158) **1.** South German: variant of **Höhne** (see HOEHNE). **2.** North German (**Höhner**): topographic name for a marshland dweller, from *hon* 'bog', 'marsh' + *-er* suffix denoting an inhabitant.

Hohnstein (177) **1.** German: habitational name from a place so named near Dresden. **2.** variant of HOHENSTEIN.

Hoiland (269) Norwegian (**Høiland**): variant spelling of HOYLAND.
GIVEN NAMES Scandinavian 4%. *Gudrun, Sten.*

Hoilman (230) Origin uncertain. Perhaps an Americanized form of German HOLLMANN.

Hoing (123) German (**Höing**): habitational name from any of several places so named, for example near Hamm. In Germany this surname occurs chiefly in Westphalia.

Hoisington (903) Perhaps an altered form of **Horsington**, an English habitational name, from places so named in Somerset and Lincolnshire. The first is named from Old English *hors-þegn* 'horsekeeper', 'groom' + *tūn* 'farmstead', while the second is named in Domesday Book as *Horsintone* 'farmstead (Old English *tūn*) associated with (*-ing-*) a man called *Horsa*'.

Hoit (157) English: variant spelling of HOYT.

Hoium (167) Norwegian (**Høium**): habitational names from any of several farmsteads in Sogn and Østfold, so named from Old Norse *hár* 'high' + *heimr* 'home', 'farmstead'.

Hojnacki (386) Polish: variant of CHOJNACKI.

Hojnowski (109) Polish: variant of CHOJNOWSKI.

Hokama (100) Japanese: written with characters meaning 'other' and 'space'. This name is found mostly in the Ryūkyū Islands.
GIVEN NAMES Japanese 25%. *Goro, Isamu, Kameko, Kayo, Kiyoshi, Masaru, Shigeru, Shizuko, Takeo, Yoshimitsu, Yoshio, Yukiko.*

Hokanson (1098) Americanized spelling of Swedish **Håkansson** or **Håkanson** (see HAKANSON) or the Norwegian cognates **Håkensen** and **Håkonsen**.
GIVEN NAMES Scandinavian 5%. *Anders, Erik, Fritjof, Hjalmer, Hokan, Knute, Lars, Nels, Ragner.*

Hoke (3310) German **1.** (**Höke**) occupational name from Middle Low German *hoke, hake* 'small trader' (see HOCK). **2.** Americanized form of HAUCK.

Hokenson (220) Americanized spelling of Swedish **Håkansson** or **Håkanson** (see HAKANSON) or the Norwegian and Danish cognates **Håkensen** and **Håkonsen**.

Hokkanen (119) Finnish: from the Karelian personal name *Hokka* (a derivative of Russian *Foka*) + the common surname suffix *-nen*.
GIVEN NAMES Finnish 21%. *Oiva* (2), *Sulo* (2), *Aarne, Jarmo, Petri, Pirjo, Ritva, Toivo, Urho, Veikko.*

Holaday (459) English: variant spelling of HOLLADAY.

Holahan (309) Irish: variant of HOULIHAN.
GIVEN NAME Irish 5%. *Paddy* (2).

Holan (200) **1.** Czech: nickname from a derivative of *holý* 'naked', 'bare', or 'clean-shaven' (see HOLY). **2.** Norwegian: habitational name from any of several farms, chiefly in Trøndelag, so named from *hol*, definite plural form of Old Norse *hóll* 'round hill', 'mound'.

Holaway (181) English: variant spelling of HOLLOWAY.

Holbach (104) German: habitational name from any of several places so named in the Harz Mountains and Württemberg.
GIVEN NAME German 4%. *Gerhart.*

Holbeck (105) German: habitational name from a place so named south of Berlin, probably from a derivative of Sorbian *holb* 'dove', 'pigeon'.

Holbein (159) German: nickname for a bow-legged man, from Middle High German *hol* 'hollow' + *bein* 'leg'.

Holben (367) **1.** Dutch and German: variant of HOLBEIN. **2.** English: habitational name from either of two places named in Devon and Kent named Holbeam, from Old English *hol* 'hollow' + *bēam* 'tree', or from Holbeanwood in Ticehurst, a minor place in Sussex.

Holberg (206) **1.** German and Jewish (Ashkenazic): habitational name from a place so named, now part of Wuppertal. **2.** German: topographic name from Middle High German *hol* 'hollow', 'cave' + *berg* 'hill', 'mountain'. **3.** Norwegian: habitational name from farmsteads in the Trøndelag region and in Nordmøre, named in Old Norse as *Hólaberg*, probably from Old Norse *hóll* 'round hill' + *berg* 'hill', 'mountain'. This surname is also found in Denmark and Sweden.
GIVEN NAMES German 4%. *Dieter* (2), *Hans.*

Holbert (2162) English: from a Middle English personal name *Holbert*, which according to Reaney is probably a survival of an unrecorded Old English name *Holdbeorht*, composed of the Germanic elements *hold* 'friendly', 'gracious', or 'loyal' + *berht* 'bright', 'famous'.

Holbrook (8459) English: habitational name from any of various places, for example in Derbyshire, Dorset, and Suffolk, so called from Old English *hol* 'hollow', 'sunken' + *brōc* 'stream'. The name has probably absorbed the Dutch surname **van Hoobroek**, found in London in the early 17th century, and possibly a similar Low German surname (**Holbrock** or **Halbrock**). Several American bearers of the name in the 1880 census give their place of birth as Oldenburg or Hannover, Germany.
FOREBEARS This name was first taken to America by the brothers Thomas and John Holbrook, who emigrated to MA in the 17th century; their line can be traced back to Dundry, Somerset, in the first half of the 16th century. Other English bearers who started early lines of descent in the New World are Joseph Ho(u)lbrook of Warrington, Lancashire, who emigrated to MD as an indentured servant in the later 17th century; Randolph Holbrook, who was in VA in the 1720s but later returned to Nantwich, Cheshire; and Rev. John Holbrook, who emigrated from Handbury, Staffordshire, to NJ in about 1723. The spelling *Haulbrook* originated in GA in the 1870s, reflecting the southern U.S. pronunciation of the name.

Holbrooks (423) English: variant of HOLBROOK.

Holby (129) English: probably a variant of HOLTBY.

Holck (231) **1.** North German (**Hölck**): probably from an old personal name (see HILKE). **2.** Danish or Americanized spelling of German (Franconian) **Holch**, a nickname for a pious man, from Middle High German *heilec* 'holy'.
GIVEN NAME German 4%. *Manfred* (2).

Holcomb (10632) English: habitational name from any of various places, for example in Devon, Dorset, Gloucestershire, Greater Manchester, Oxfordshire, and Somerset, so named from Old English *hol* 'hollow', 'sunken', 'deep' + *cumb* 'valley'.

Holcombe (3154) English: variant spelling of HOLCOMB.

Hold (156) **1.** English: from Old Norse *hǫldr*, within the Danelaw (the region of pre-conquest England where Danish rule and custom was dominant) a rank of feudal nobility immediately below that of earl. **2.** German: nickname from Middle High German *holde* 'friend' or 'servant', 'vassal'. **3.** German (**Höld**): variant of *Held* 'hero' (see HELD 1), found chiefly in Bavaria.
GIVEN NAME French 4%. *Lucien.*

Holda (191) Polish (**Hołda**) or Ukrainian: variant of **Gołda** (see GOLDA).
GIVEN NAMES Polish 5%. *Krystyna* (2), *Franciszek, Janina.*

Holdaway (454) English: variant of HOLLOWAY.

Holdcraft (144) Variant of English HOLDCROFT.

Holdcroft (133) English: habitational name from Holcroft in Lancashire, so named from Old English *holh* 'hollow', 'depression' + *croft* 'paddock', 'smallholding', or from some other minor place named with the same elements.

Holdeman (527) German: variant of **Holderman** or HOLDMAN.

Holden (12446) **1.** English (mainly Lancashire): habitational name from places in Lancashire and West Yorkshire, both so named from Old English *hol* 'hollow', 'sunken', 'deep' + *denu* 'valley'. Compare HOLCOMBE. **2.** German: unexplained.

Holdener (146) Swiss German: unexplained.

GIVEN NAME German 4%. *Ludwina*.

Holder (11444) **1.** German: topographic name for someone who lived by an elder tree, Middle High German *holder*, or from a house named for its sign of an elder tree. In same areas, for example Alsace, the elder tree was believed to be the protector of a house. **2.** Jewish (Ashkenazic): ornamental name from German *Holder* 'elder tree'. **3.** English (chiefly western counties): occupational name for a tender of animals, from an agent derivative of Middle English *hold(en)* 'to guard or keep' (Old English *h(e)aldan*). It is possible that this word was also used in the wider sense of a holder of land within the feudal system. Compare HELDER.

Holderbaum (194) German: topographic name for someone who lived by an elder tree, a variant of HOLDER 1, with the addition of Middle High German *boum* 'tree' (see HOLDER, BAUM).

Holderby (250) Origin uncertain. **1.** Perhaps an altered form of English **Holdenby**, a habitational name from Holdenby in Northamptonshire, which is named with the Old Norse personal name *Halfdan* + Old Norse *býr* 'farmstead', 'settlement'. **2.** Alternatively, perhaps, an Americanized form of HOLDERBAUM.

Holderfield (402) Origin unidentified. This has the form of an English habitational name, but neither the place name nor the surname are now known in England. It may be a variant of HOLLIFIELD.

Holderman (696) German (**Holdermann**): variant of HOLDER 1.

Holderness (332) English: regional name from the coastal district of eastern Yorkshire (now Humberside), the origin of which is probably Old Norse *hǫldr*, within the Danelaw (the region of pre-conquest England where Danish rule and custom was dominant) a rank of feudal nobility immediately below that of earl, + *nes* 'nose', 'headland'.

Holding (520) English: variant of HOLDEN.

Holdman (239) **1.** English: occupational name for the servant (Middle English *man*) of a nobleman (Middle English *hold(e)*). **2.** English: variant of **Oldman**, derived from Old English *(e)ald* 'old' + *mann* 'man'. **3.** North German (**Holdmann**): topographic name from Middle Low German *holt* 'small wood' + *man* 'man'.

Holdorf (252) North German: habitational name from any of several places so named, all in northern Germany.

GIVEN NAMES German 6%. *Heinz* (2), *Armin*, *Kurt*.

Holdredge (106) English: probably a variant of ALDRIDGE, but see also HOLDRIDGE.

Holdren (996) English: unexplained.

Holdridge (743) English: possibly a habitational name from Holdridge in Devon, so named from Old English *heald* 'sloping' + *hrycg* 'ridge', but more likely a variant of ALDRIDGE.

Holdsworth (750) English (Yorkshire): habitational name from either of two places in West Yorkshire now called Holdsworth, both probably originally named with an Old English byname *Halda* 'bent' + *worð* 'enclosure'.

Holdt (132) North German: topographic name from Middle Low German *holt* 'small wood'.

Holdway (125) English: reduced form of **Holdaway**, itself a variant of HOLLOWAY.

Hole (631) **1.** English (mainly southwest England): topographic name for someone who lived by a depression or low-lying spot, from Old English *holh* 'hole', 'hollow', 'depression'. **2.** Norwegian: habitational name from any of numerous farmsteads, so named from the dative singular or indefinite plural form of Old Norse *hóll* 'round hill', 'mound'. **3.** Shortened form of Dutch **van (den) Hole**, a habitational name from the common place name Hol, meaning 'hollow', 'depression', 'valley', or a topographic name from the same term.

Holec (118) Czech: nickname for a beardless young man, from a noun derivative of *holý* 'naked', 'bare' (see HOLY).

Holecek (255) Czech (**Holeček**): from a diminutive of *holý* 'naked', 'bare', 'clean-shaven' (see HOLY).

Holeman (982) English and Dutch: variant of HOLMAN.

Holen (349) **1.** Norwegian: habitational name from any of numerous farmsteads, so named from the definite singular form of Old Norse *hóll* 'round hill', 'mound' (see HOLE). **2.** Shortened form of Dutch **van (den) Holen**, a variant of HOLE 2.

GIVEN NAMES Scandinavian 5%. *Lennart*, *Selmer*, *Sigfred*.

Holes (140) English: variant of HOLE 1.

Holewinski (303) Polish: variant of **Cholewiński** (see CHOLEWINSKI).

Holey (123) Irish: variant spelling of WHOLEY.

Holford (433) English: habitational name from any of various places named Holford, for example in Somerset, or from Holdforth in Durham, so named from Old English *hol* 'hollow', 'sunken', 'deep' + *ford* 'ford'.

Holgate (439) English (northern): habitational name from any of various places, for example in West Yorkshire, so called from Old English *hol* 'hollow', 'sunken' + Old Norse *gata* 'road'.

Holgerson (179) **1.** Frisian: patronymic from the personal name *Holger*. **2.** Respelling of Danish and Norwegian **Holgersen**, or Swedish **Holgersson**, a patronymic (cognate with 1) from the Old Danish and Swedish personal name *Holmger*, composed of the elements *holm* 'islet' + *-gēr*, 'spear'.

GIVEN NAMES Scandinavian 11%. *Olle* (2), *Britt, Erik, Klas, Nils*.

Holguin (1735) Spanish (**Holguín**): possibly from a derivative of *holgar* 'to enjoy oneself'.

GIVEN NAMES Spanish 43%. *Jose* (36), *Manuel* (20), *Jesus* (19), *Juan* (16), *Carlos* (14), *Raul* (13), *Luis* (12), *Ramon* (12), *Eduardo* (9), *Jaime* (9), *Roberto* (9), *Ruben* (9).

Holian (174) Irish: reduced Anglicized form of Gaelic **Ó hÓileáin** (see HOLLAND).

Holick (133) Germanized or Americanized spelling of Czech HOLIK.

Holiday (1420) English: variant spelling of HOLLADAY.

Holien (213) Norwegian: habitational name from farmsteads in Trøndelag and Valdres named Holien; the Trøndelag name is possibly from Old Norse *hór* 'high' + *lið* 'slope', 'mountain', while the Valdres one is from Old Norse *Holvin*, a compound of *hol* 'hollow', 'sunken', 'deep' + *vin* 'meadow'.

Holifield (1293) English (chiefly Oxfordshire): variant spelling of HOLLIFIELD.

Holihan (220) Irish: variant of HOULIHAN.

GIVEN NAMES Irish 4%. *Brendan, Sinead*.

Holik (172) Czech (**Holík**): nickname from a noun derivative of *holý* 'bald', 'bare', or 'clean-shaven' (see HOLY).

Holiman (311) English: variant of HOLLIMAN.

Holl (916) **1.** German and Dutch: topographic name from Middle High German, Middle Low German *hol* 'hollow', 'hole'. **2.** German: from a short form of HOLD. **3.** German (**Höll**): variant of HELLE 2, found chiefly in Bavaria.

GIVEN NAMES German 4%. *Erwin* (2), *Heinz* (2), *Erna, Fritz, Horst, Jurgen, Lorenz, Manfred, Otto*.

Hollabaugh (429) Americanized form of German HOLLENBACH.

Holladay (1960) English: from Old English *hāligdæg* 'holy day', 'religious festival'. The reasons why this word should have become a surname are not clear; probably it was used as a byname for one born on a religious festival day.

Hollahan (103) Variant of Irish HALLAHAN.

Hollan (369) English (Northumbria): apparently a variant spelling of HOLLEN.

Holland (36823) **1.** Irish: reduced Anglicized form of Gaelic **Ó hÓileáin**, a variant of **Ó hAoláin**, from a form of *Faolán* (with loss of the initial *F-*), a personal name representing a diminutive of *faol* 'wolf'. Compare WHELAN. **2.** English and Scottish: habitational name from Holland, a division of Lincolnshire, or any of the eight villages in various parts of England so called, from Old English *hōh* 'ridge' + *land* 'land'. The Scottish name may also be from places called Holland in Orkney, Houlland in Shetland, Hollandbush in Stirlingshire, and Holland-Hirst in the parish of Kirkintilloch. **3.** English, German, Jewish (Ashkenazic), Danish, and Dutch: regional name from *Holland*, a province of the Netherlands.

FOREBEARS This is the name of an important English landowning family, traceable to Upholland in Lancashire in the 13th century. The surname is particularly common in southern Lancashire.

Hollander (2671) German, English, Jewish (Ashkenazic), Dutch, and Swedish: regional name for someone from Holland (see HOLLAND 2).

Hollands (244) **1.** English: variant of HOLLAND 1. **2.** Dutch: variant of HOLLAND 2. **3.** Dutch: habitational name from places called Holland in northern France, named with Middle Dutch *onland(e)* 'marsh'.

Hollandsworth (745) Possibly an altered form of HOLLINGSWORTH. This surname is common in VA.

Hollar (1590) German: habitational name from a place so named, formerly Hunlar.

Hollars (344) German: variant of HOLLAR.

Hollas (118) Czech: unexplained.

Hollatz (192) German (of Slavic origin): nickname for someone with a bald head, based on Sorbian *holy* 'naked', 'bare'.

Hollaway (742) English: variant spelling of HOLLOWAY.

Holle (825) **1.** North German: habitational name from any of numerous places named Holle(n) (e.g. in Westphalia, Hannover, and Pomerania), from *hol* 'hollow', 'cave', 'bog'; or a topographic name from the same word. **2.** German (**Hölle**): variant of HELLE 2.

GIVEN NAMES German 4%. *Erwin* (2), *Armin*, *Eldred*, *Frieda*, *Fritz*, *Helmuth*, *Juergen*, *Raimund*.

Holleman (1217) English, German (**Hollemann**), and Dutch: variant of HOLLE, HOLMAN, or HOLLIMAN.

Hollen (742) English (chiefly Yorkshire): topographic name from Middle English *holin* 'holly tree', or a habitational name from any of the minor places named with this word, as for example Hollin and Holling in Worcestershire, or Hollins in West Yorkshire.

Hollenbach (554) German: habitational name from any of several places so named, for example in Bavaria.

Hollenback (440) Americanized form of German HOLLENBACH.

Hollenbaugh (359) Americanized form of German HOLLENBACH.

Hollenbeck (2283) North German: habitational name from a place so named near Hamburg or from Hollenbek near Ratzeburg.

Hollenberg (217) German and Dutch: habitational name from places so called in Gelderland, Bavaria, and Lower Rhine-Westphalia.

GIVEN NAMES German 4%. *Fritz, Kurt*.

Hollender (179) German: variant of HOLLANDER.

Hollenkamp (172) North German: topographic name formed with a first element of various origins + Middle Low German *kamp* 'enclosed or fenced field', 'domain'.

Hollenshead (143) Variant spelling of English HOLLINGSHEAD.

Holler (1865) **1.** English: topographic name for someone living in a hollow, from Middle English *hole* 'hollow'. **2.** German and Dutch: topographic name for someone living in a hollow or a wooded ravine, from Middle High German, Middle Low German *hol* (see HOLL 1). **3.** German and Danish: variant of HOLDER 1.

Holleran (764) Irish (Counties Galway and Mayo): variant of HALLORAN.

GIVEN NAMES Irish 4%. *Brigid, Declan*.

Hollerbach (173) German: habitational name from a place so named near Heilbronn, or a topographic name for someone who lived by an elder near a stream or by a stream in a hollow, a compound of HOLLER 2 or 3 + Middle High German *bach* 'stream'.

GIVEN NAMES German 8%. *Aloysius, Hans, Kurt, Rainer, Wolf*.

Hollern (191) English and Scottish: possibly a reduced form of HOLLERAN.

Hollers (107) English: variant of HOLLER.

Hollett (282) English: probably a variant of HULLETT, itself a variant of HEWLETT.

Holley (9783) English (chiefly Yorkshire): topographic name from Middle English *holin, holi(e)* 'holly tree'. Compare HOLLEN.

Hollibaugh (187) Possibly an altered spelling of German HOLLERBACH or HOLLENBACH.

GIVEN NAME German 4%. *Kurt* (2).

Hollick (169) English: unexplained; perhaps a variant of HILLOCK in which the vowels have been transposed.

Holliday (6931) English: variant of HOLLADAY.

Hollie (472) Variant spelling of Irish or English HOLLY.

Hollier (699) **1.** English and French: occupational name for a brothelkeeper, Middle English, Old French *holier, hollier* (a dissimilated variant of *horier* 'pimp', agent noun from *hore, hure* 'whore', of Germanic origin). It was probably also used as an abusive nickname. **2.** English: topographic name for someone who lived by a holly grove or conspicuous holly tree, from a derivative of Middle English *holi(e), holin* 'holly (tree)' (from Old English *hold(g)n*).

GIVEN NAMES French 4%. *Andre, Clovis, Easton, Nicolle, Pierre, Vernice*.

Hollifield (1421) English: habitational name from a place named in Old English with *hālig* 'holy' + Old English *feld* 'open country'. This may be Holyfield in Essex (which belonged to Waltham Abbey), but the present-day distribution of the name (mainly in the Midlands and Wales) suggests that another source may be involved.

Holliman (1258) English: nickname, perhaps ironic, from Middle English *holy* 'holy' + *man* 'man'.

Hollimon (241) English: variant of HOLLIMAN.

Hollin (272) English: variant spelling of HOLLEN.

Holling (266) **1.** English (chiefly Yorkshire): topographic name for someone who lived by a holly tree, variant of HOLLEN. **2.** German: habitational name from any of several places so named.

GIVEN NAMES German 5%. *Ilse* (2), *Inge* (2), *Hans, Otto*.

Hollinger (2081) **1.** South German and Jewish (Ashkenazic): habitational name for someone from places called Holling or Hollingen. **2.** English, northern Irish, and Scottish: topographic name from Middle English *holin* 'holly' + the suffix *-er* denoting an inhabitant.

Hollings (206) English (chiefly Yorkshire): topographic name for someone who lived among holly trees, from Middle English *holins*, a plural form from Old English *hollegn* 'holly'.

GIVEN NAMES French 7%. *Andre* (2), *Celestine, Jacques*.

Hollingshead (1333) English (northern): habitational name from a lost place in County Durham called Hollingside or Holmside, from Old English *hole(g)n* 'holly' + *sīde* 'hillside', 'slope'; there is a Hollingside Lane on the southern outskirts of Durham city. In some cases it may be from Hollinhead in Lancashire, so named from Old English *holegn* 'holly' + *hēafod* 'headland', 'ridge'.

Hollingshed (130) English: variant spelling of HOLLINGSHEAD.

Hollingsworth (8694) **1.** English and Irish: habitational name from places in Cheshire and Lancashire called Hollingworth, from Old English *hole(g)n* 'holly' + *worð* 'enclosure'. The surname was taken to Ireland in the 17th century. **2.** Jewish (American): presumably an Americanized form of some like-sounding Jewish name.

Hollingworth (288) English (mainly Yorkshire): variant of HOLLINGSWORTH.

Hollins (2049) English: plural variant of HOLLEN.

Hollinshead (277) English: variant of HOLLINGSHEAD.

Hollinsworth (163) English: variant of HOLLINGSWORTH.

Hollis (9112) English (mainly central): topographic name for someone who lived where holly trees grew, from Middle English *holi(n)s*, plural of *holin, holi(e)* (Old English *hole(g)n*).

Hollister (2279) English: occupational name for a brothelkeeper; originally a feminine form of HOLLIER.

Hollman (802) **1.** English: variant spelling of HOLMAN. **2.** Variant spelling of German HOLLMANN.

Hollmann (277) German: **1.** (**Höllmann**): variant of HELLMANN 2. **2.** (**Hollmann**): topographic name from *hol* 'hollow', 'cave', 'bog' (see HOLLE 2) + *Mann* 'man'.
GIVEN NAMES German 4%. *Erwin* (2), *Hans, Hellmuth.*

Hollo (152) Hungarian (**Holló**): nickname for a dark-haired person, from Hungarian *holló* 'raven'.
GIVEN NAMES Hungarian 4%. *Istvan, Magdolna, Timea.*

Hollobaugh (160) Altered form of German HOLLENBACH or HOLLERBACH. Compare HOLLABAUGH, HOLLIBAUGH.

Holloman (2151) English: variant of HOLLIMAN.

Hollomon (402) English: variant of HOLLIMAN.

Hollon (1161) Belgian French: habitational name from any of several places called Hollogne or Hologne.

Hollopeter (211) German: of uncertain origin; perhaps a distinguishing nickname *Hollepeter* 'helpful Peter'. (like **Hollefreund** and **Gutfreund**; see GOODFRIEND), from Middle Low German *holde, holt* 'friendly', 'helpful' + the personal name PETER.
GIVEN NAMES German 4%. *Kurt, Wolf.*

Holloran (298) Irish: variant of HALLORAN.
GIVEN NAME Irish 6%. *Brendan.*

Hollow (134) English: variant of HOLE.

Holloway (17682) English: habitational name from any of the numerous minor places so called, from Old English *hol* 'hollow', 'sunken' + *weg* 'way', 'path'. In Ireland, it has sometimes been Gaelicized as **Ó hAilmhic** (see HULVEY).

Hollowell (1881) English: habitational name from any of numerous places named with Old English *hālig* 'holy' + *well(a)* 'well', 'spring', such as Holwell in Dorset and Oxfordshire. (Reaney suggests it could also have been a topographic name with the same etymological origin.) However, the present-day concentration of the name in Northamptonshire would suggest that Holwell in Leicestershire, which has a different etymology, from Old English *hol* 'hollow' + *wella*, was most likely the primary source of this form of the surname. There is also a Holwell in Hertfordshire of the same derivation, as well as places called Halwill and Halwell in Devon, Holywell in Cambridgeshire, Cornwall, Clwyd, and Northumberland, and Halliwell near Man-

chester, all of which could have contributed to the surname.

Hollrah (135) Origin unidentified.

Hollstein (149) German: variant of HOLSTEIN, or perhaps a habitational name from Hollstein on the Werra River.
GIVEN NAMES German 16%. *Gerhard, Hans, Heinz, Klaus, Kurt, Otto, Ulrich.*

Holly (3020) **1.** Irish: part-translation of Gaelic *Mac Cuilinn* (see MCCULLEN) in County Kerry, and in Ulster sometimes a variant of MCQUILLAN, also an Anglicized form of *Mac Cuilinn*. It is rarely of English origin. **2.** English: variant spelling of HOLLEY. **3.** Possibly an altered spelling of Czech or Slovak **Holý** (see HOLY).

Hollyfield (200) English: variant spelling of HOLLIFIELD.

Hollywood (317) Irish: translation of Gaelic **Ó Cuileannáin** 'descendant of *Cuileannán*', a personal name from a diminutive of *cuileann* 'holly tree', which is more commonly Anglicized as CULLINAN.

Holm (5662) **1.** Northern English, German, and Scandinavian: topographic name for someone who lived on an island, in particular a piece of slightly raised land lying in a fen or partly surrounded by streams, Middle English, Middle Low German *holm*, Old Norse *holmr*, or a habitational name from a place named with this element. The Swedish name is often ornamental. **2.** English: topographic name for someone who lived where holly grew, from Middle English *holm*, a variant of *holin* 'holly', or possibly a habitational name from places called Holme (Dorset and West Yorkshire) or Holne (Devon), named with this word.
GIVEN NAMES Scandinavian 7%. *Erik* (8), *Lars* (7), *Anders* (4), *Thor* (4), *Holger* (3), *Nels* (3), *Nils* (3), *Sven* (3), *Helmer* (2), *Lennart* (2), *Niels* (2), *Vibeke* (2).

Holman (11151) **1.** English (chiefly southern) and Dutch: topographic name for a dweller in a hollow (see HOLE). **2.** English (chiefly southern): topographic name for a dweller by a holly tree or on an island, from Middle English *holm* (see HOLME) + *man*.

Holmbeck (112) Swedish: ornamental name composed of Swedish *holm* 'island' + *bäck* 'stream'.

Holmberg (2126) Swedish: ornamental name from *holm* 'island' + *berg* 'hill'.
GIVEN NAMES Scandinavian 7%. *Erik* (6), *Lars* (6), *Nels* (4), *Anders* (2), *Hartvig* (2), *Lennart* (2), *Per* (2), *Britt, Helmer, Johan, Sven, Tor.*

Holme (209) **1.** English (mainly Lancashire) and Scottish: topographic name for someone who lived by a holly tree, from Middle English *holm*, a divergent development of Old English *hole(g)n*; the main development was towards modern English *holly* (see HOLLIS). **2.** English and Scottish: topographic name or habitational name from northern Middle English *holm*

'island', Old Norse *holmr* (see HOLM 1).
3. Danish and Swedish: variant of HOLM 1.
4. Norwegian: habitational name from any of several farmsteads, so named from the dative singular of Old Norse *holmr* 'islet', 'low flat land beside a river'.
GIVEN NAME Scandinavian 7%. *Erik* (2).

Holmen (416) Scandinavian: variant of HOLM, from the definite singular form.
GIVEN NAMES Scandinavian 7%. *Britt* (2), *Agnar, Bjorn, Holger, Juel.*

Holmer (415) **1.** English: habitational name from Holmer in Buckinghamshire and Herefordshire, both named with Old English *hol* 'hollow' + *mere* 'pool'.
2. English: topographic name for someone who lived either on a piece of slightly raised land lying in a fen or partly surrounded by streams or where holly grew, from a derivative of Middle English *holm* (see HOLM 1 and 2). **3.** Swedish, Danish, and North German (Schleswig-Holstein): topographic name for someone who lived on an island (see HOLM).
GIVEN NAMES Scandinavian 5%; German 4%. *Algot, Erik, Nils; Hans* (3), *Otto* (2), *Reinhold.*

Holmes (48841) **1.** English (chiefly central and northern England): variant of HOLME. **2.** Scottish: probably a habitational name from Holmes near Dundonald, or from a place so called in the barony of Inchestuir. **3.** Scottish and Irish: Anglicized form of Gaelic **Mac Thomáis, Mac Thómais** (see MCCOMB). In part of western Ireland, **Holmes** is a variant of **Cavish** (from Gaelic **Mac Thámhais**, another patronymic from THOMAS).
FOREBEARS John Holmes came from England to Woodstock, CT, in 1686. His descendants include the Congregational clergyman and historian Abiel Holmes, born 1763 in Woodstock, and Abiel's son Oliver Wendell Holmes (1809–94).

Holmgren (1417) Swedish: ornamental name composed of the elements *holm* 'island' + *gren* 'branch'.
GIVEN NAMES Scandinavian 5%; German 4%. *Erik* (5), *Nels* (2), *Thor* (2), *Bjorn, Iver, Nils, Nyman; Kurt* (3), *Erhardt* (2), *Hans, Helmuth, Inge, Manfred.*

Holmlund (209) Swedish and Norwegian: ornamental name composed of the elements *holm* 'island' + *lund* 'grove'.
GIVEN NAME Scandinavian 4%. *Erik.*

Holmquist (1489) Swedish: ornamental name composed of the elements *holm* 'island' + *quist*, an old or ornamental spelling of *kvist* 'twig'.
GIVEN NAMES Scandinavian 6%. *Sven* (3), *Algot* (2), *Nils* (2), *Anders, Birgit, Elof, Erik, Eskil, Gunnel, Lars, Mats, Nels.*

Holms (112) English: variant of HOLM.

Holmstrom (923) Swedish (**Holmström**): ornamental name composed of the elements *holm* 'island' + *ström* 'river'.

Holness (191) English (Kent): **1.** habitational name, probably from a lost place, Holmherst in Smarden, Kent; Holnest in Dorset is another possibility. Both are named from Old English *holegn* 'holly' + Old English *hyrst* 'wooded hill'. **2.** reduced form of HOLDERNESS.

Holohan (291) Irish: variant of HOULIHAN.
GIVEN NAMES Irish 7%. *Brendan, Niall.*

Holoman (106) Apparently an altered spelling of English HOLLIMAN.
GIVEN NAME French 6%. *Octa.*

Holoubek (123) Czech: nickname from a diminutive of *holub* 'pigeon' (see HOLUB), denoting a mild-mannered person, also a lovely young person.
GIVEN NAMES Dutch 4%. *Dirk, Jet.*

Holroyd (465) English (Yorkshire): habitational name from any of various minor places in northern England so named from Old English *hol* 'hollow', 'sunken' + *rod* 'clearing' (see RHODES).

Holsapple (529) Americanized spelling of German HOLZAPFEL.

Holschbach (109) German: habitational name from a place so named near Koblenz.

Holscher (480) North German (**Hölscher**): see HOELSCHER.
GIVEN NAMES German 4%. *Franz* (5), *Rudi.*

Holschuh (139) German: metonymic occupational name for a clog maker, from Middle Low German *holt* 'wood' + *scho* 'shoe' (see HOELSCHER).
GIVEN NAME German 5%. *Albrecht.*

Holsclaw (413) Americanized spelling of German **Holzklau** (see HOLTZCLAW).

Holsen (142) Norwegian, Danish, and Dutch: patronymic of uncertain etymology; possibly a reduced form of HOLGERSON.

Holsey (420) English: of uncertain origin; perhaps a variant of HALSEY.

Holshouser (443) Americanized spelling of German HOLZHAUSER.

Holsing (103) German: probably a respelling of **Holzing** (see HOLZINGER).

Holsinger (1140) Respelling of German and Jewish HOLZINGER.

Holsman (124) Americanized form of German HOLZMANN.

Holsomback (269) Probably a variant of German **Huelsenbeck**, a habitational name from a place named Hülsenbecke in Westphalia or Brandenburg.

Holson (118) Origin unidentified. Compare HOLSEN.

Holsonback (181) Probably of German origin (see HOLSOMBACK).

Holsopple (264) Americanized form of German HOLZAPFEL.

Holst (1853) **1.** North German, Dutch, and Scandinavian: regional name for someone from HOLSTEIN, Danish *Holtsete* 'person from Holstein'. **2.** Dutch: habitational name from Holst in Limburg.

GIVEN NAMES Scandinavian 4%. *Jorgen* (3), *Erik* (2), *Vibeke* (2), *Anders, Carsten, Ludvig, Sven.*

Holstad (204) Norwegian: habitational name from any of several farmsteads named Holstad, from *Hol-* (probably derived from a personal name such as Old Norse *Hávarðr, Ólafr*) + *-stad* from *staðir* 'farmstead', 'dwelling'.
GIVEN NAMES French 4%; Scandinavian 4%. *Michel* (2); *Sophus, Tor.*

Holste (276) **1.** Variant of HOLST 1. **2.** Shortened form of Dutch **van Holste**, a variant of HOLST 3.
GIVEN NAMES German 4%. *Erwin, Gerhard, Hans, Rainer.*

Holstead (166) **1.** English: probably a variant of HALSTEAD. **2.** Possibly an altered form of Norwegian HOLSTAD.

Holsted (128) Probably a variant of English HALSTEAD, or an altered spelling of Norwegian HOLSTAD.

Holstein (1544) German: regional name from the province of Holstein, long disputed between Germany and Denmark. This gets its name from *holsten*, the dative plural, originally used after a preposition, of *holst*, from Middle Low German *holt-sate* 'dweller in the woods' (from Middle Low German *holt* 'wood' + *sate, sete* 'tenant'). The final syllable has been erroneously altered by analogy with North German *Steen* 'stone', which in South German and standard German has the form *Stein*.

Holsten (413) **1.** North German: variant of HOLSTEIN. **2.** Dutch: habitational name from Hoolsteen in Zonhoven, Belgium, from *hol* 'hollow' + *steen* 'stone'.

Holster (165) North German: probably a variant of HOLST (with the addition of the agent suffix *-er*), but perhaps a habitational name from Holsten near Hannover.

Holstine (343) Americanized spelling of German HOLSTEIN.

Holston (1172) **1.** English: probably a variant of **Halston**, which is partly a habitational name from Halston in Shropshire, possibly named with the Old English personal name *Ealh* + *tūn* 'settlement', and partly derived from the Old Norse personal name *Halsteinn*. Alternatively, it may perhaps be a habitational name from Holstone in County Durham, so named from Old English *hol* 'hollow' + *stān* 'stone'. **2.** Possibly an Americanized form of HOLSTEIN.

Holstrom (283) Swedish: ornamental name composed possibly of a shortening of *holm* 'island' + *ström* 'stream'.
GIVEN NAMES Scandinavian 4%. *Bjorg, Swen.*

Holsworth (209) English: variant of HOLDSWORTH.

Holt (31432) **1.** English, North German, Danish, and Norwegian: topographic name for someone who lived in or by a small wood, Middle English, Middle Low German, Danish, Norwegian *holt*, or a

habitational name from one of the very many places named with this word. In England the surname is widely distributed, but rather more common in Lancashire than elsewhere. **2.** Shortened form of Dutch **van Holt**, a habitational name from places named Holt (see 1).

Holtan (373) Norwegian: habitational name from any of numerous farmsteads, from the definite plural form of *holt* 'small wood' (see HOLT).

Holtby (103) English: habitational name from Holtby, a place near York, probably named with the Old Norse personal name *Holti* + *býr* 'farmstead', 'settlement'.

Holtcamp (110) Variant spelling of German HOLTKAMP.

Holte (724) **1.** North German: variant of HOLT. **2.** North German: habitational name from any of several places so named. **3.** Norwegian: habitational name from any of numerous farmsteads, most of them named from the dative singular of *holt* (see HOLT). **4.** Dutch: from a short form of a Germanic compound personal name with initial element *holt* 'loyal', 'friendly'.
GIVEN NAMES Scandinavian 6%. *Bjorg, Erik, Helmer, Hjalmer, Knute, Nels, Nordahl, Selmer, Swen, Thorvald.*

Holten (346) **1.** Dutch and German (also North German **von Holten**): habitational name from places so called, from Low German *holt* 'holt', 'copse', 'small wood'. There is one in the Dutch province of Overijssel and another near Oberhausen in the Rhineland. **2.** Danish: variant of HOLT. **3.** Norwegian: habitational name from any of several farmsteads so named, either from the definite singular form of *holt* 'holt', 'small wood' (see HOLT), or from *holt* 'hill', 'stony slope'. **4.** English: variant spelling of HOLTON.
GIVEN NAMES Scandinavian 4%. *Erik, Hjalmer, Lars, Nils.*

Holter (1038) **1.** English (Sussex): topographic name for someone who lived by a *holt*, a small wood, + the suffix *-er* denoting an inhabitant. **2.** North German (also **Hölter**): habitational name from places called Holter or Hölter. **3.** Norwegian: habitational name from any of several farmsteads in southeastern Norway, from the indefinite plural of *holt* 'holt', 'small wood' (see HOLT).
GIVEN NAMES Scandinavian 4%. *Erik* (3), *Selmer* (2), *Hilmar, Knute, Lars.*

Holterman (157) North German (**Holtermann, Höltermann**): variant of HOLTER 2, with the addition of Middle Low German *man* 'man'.

Holtermann (116) German: variant of **Haltermann** (see HALTERMAN).
GIVEN NAMES French 5%; German 5%. *Francois; Alphons.*

Holtgrave (102) North German: variant of HOLTGREWE.

Holtgrewe (140) North German: occupational name for a forest warden, Middle Low German *holtgreve*, a compound of *holt* 'small wood' + *greve* 'warden', related to High German GRAF.

Holthaus (952) North German: topographic name for someone who lived by a copse, from Middle Low German *holt* 'small wood' + *hūs* 'house'.

Holthouse (148) Americanized form of German HOLTHAUS.

Holthus (157) North German: variant of HOLTHAUS.
GIVEN NAME German 4%. *Kurt*.

Holthusen (112) North German: habitational name from a common place name, derived from Middle Low German *holt* 'small wood' + *husen*, dative plural of *hūs* 'house'.

Holtkamp (465) North German: topographic name, from Middle Low German *holt* 'wood' + *kamp* 'enclosure', 'fenced or hedged field', 'domain'. This surname is common in Westphalia.
GIVEN NAMES German 5%. *Hans, Jochem, Kurt, Ralf, Rudi*.

Holtman (634) Respelling of German HOLTMANN.

Holtmann (165) North German: variant of HOLT.
GIVEN NAMES German 10%. *Udo* (3), *Aloys, Hans, Heinz*.

Holtmeier (131) German: variant spelling of HOLTMEYER.
GIVEN NAMES German 7%. *Erwin, Kurt, Othmar, Wolfgang*.

Holtmeyer (179) North German: occupational name for a steward of woodland, or a tenant farmer (see MEYER) whose farm lay by a wood (Middle Low German *holt*).
GIVEN NAMES German 4%. *Kurt, Otto*.

Holton (4177) English: habitational name from any of the numerous places so called. The final syllable represents Old English *tūn* 'enclosure', 'settlement'. The first element has a wide variety of possible origins. In the case of three examples in Lincolnshire it is Old English *hōh* 'spur of a hill'; for places in Oxfordshire and Somerset it is Old English *halh* 'nook', 'recess'; for one in Dorset it may be Old English *holh* 'hollow', 'depression' or *holt* 'small wood'; for a further pair in Suffolk it may be *hola*, genitive plural of *holh* 'hollow', but more probably a personal name *Hōla*.

Holtorf (176) North German: habitational name from any of several places so named in northern Germany, or from Holtorp in Westphalia.
GIVEN NAME German 4%. *Uwe*.

Holtrop (192) North German: probably a habitational name from a place so named near Leer, or from any of several places called Holtrup, for example one near Vechta and another near Minden.

Holtry (184) Origin unidentified. This surname occurs chiefly in PA.

Holts (140) Americanized spelling of German and Jewish HOLTZ.

Holtsclaw (424) Americanized spelling of German **Holzklau** (see HOLTZCLAW).

Holtz (3850) **1.** German: topographic name from Middle High German *holz* 'small wood', 'copse'. **2.** Jewish (Ashkenazic): from German *Holz* 'wood', either an ornamental name or a metonymic occupational name for a woodcutter or someone who sold wood.

Holtzapple (241) Americanized form of German HOLZAPFEL.

Holtzclaw (953) Americanized spelling of German **Holzklau**, which translates into modern German as 'wood thief', but is probably a nickname for someone who gathered wood, from Middle High German *holz* 'wood' + a derivative of *klūben* 'to pick up', 'gather', 'steal'.

Holtzen (148) German: from an inflected form of HOLTZ 'wood'.

Holtzer (181) **1.** German: topographic name for someone who lived in a wood, from HOLTZ + the *-er* suffix denoting an inhabitant. **2.** Jewish (Ashkenazic): occupational name for a woodcutter or someone who sold wood, from an agent derivative of German *Holz* 'wood'.
GIVEN NAMES Jewish 8%. *Dov* (2), *Cheskel, Miriam, Shmuel*.

Holtzinger (184) German: variant spelling of HOLZINGER.

Holtzman (1412) **1.** Jewish (Ashkenazic): variant of HOLTZER. **2.** Variant of German HOLZMANN.
GIVEN NAMES Jewish 4%. *Hyman* (3), *Sol* (2), *Emanuel, Golda, Iren, Meyer, Miriam, Rina, Rivka, Shlomit, Zelig*.

Holub (1443) Czech, Slovak, Ukrainian, Belorussian, and Jewish (eastern Ashkenazic): nickname from Czech, Ukrainian, and Belorussian *holub* 'dove', ultimately related to Latin *columba* (see COLOMB), denoting a mild-mannered or peace-loving man. As a Jewish name it is mainly ornamental.

Holubec (121) Czech and Slovak: derivative of HOLUB.
GIVEN NAME Czech and Slovak 4%. *Bohdan* (2).

Holum (230) Norwegian: habitational name from any of several farmsteads named Holum, either from the dative plural of *hol* 'hollow', 'depression' or from *hol* + *heimr* 'home', 'farmstead'.
GIVEN NAMES Scandinavian 7%. *Knute* (3), *Morten, Thorvald*.

Holveck (110) French (Alsace): unexplained.

Holverson (232) Americanized spelling of Norwegian HALVORSON or Danish HALVORSEN.

Holway (283) English: variant of HOLLOWAY, possibly specifically from Holway in Somerset.

GIVEN NAMES Irish 4%. *Donal* (2), *Patrick James*.

Holweger (152) German: probably a topographic name for a person living by a high-sided road, from Middle High German *hol* 'hollow' + *weg* 'way' + the agent suffix *-er*.
GIVEN NAMES German 4%. *Eberhard, Kurt*.

Holwerda (191) Frisian: unexplained. In North America this surname is found mainly in Grand Rapids, MI.

Holy (393) Czech and Slovak (**Holý**): nickname from *holý* 'naked', 'bare', 'clean-shaven', in various senses: denoting either a young, beardless man, a bald or clean-shaven man, or a destitute person.

Holycross (298) **1.** Probably a translation of Italian **Santacroce**, Spanish **Santa Cruz** or some other southern European habitational name from a place so called, from Italian, Spanish *santa* 'holy' + *croce* (Italian), *cruz* (Spanish) 'cross'. **2.** There are a few places in England called Holy Cross (in County Durham, Tyne and Wear, Herefordshire), and so the surname could be an English habitational name from any of these places; however, it is not found in England.

Holyfield (535) English (Wales and the West Midlands): variant of HOLLIFIELD.

Holyoak (234) English: **1.** topographic name, from Middle English *holy* 'holy' + *oke* 'oak', for someone who lived near an oak tree with religious associations. This would have been one which formed a marker on a parish boundary and which was a site for a reading from the Scriptures in the course of the annual ceremony of beating the bounds. **2.** habitational name from the village of Holy Oakes in Leicestershire, recorded in Domesday Book as *Haliach*, and no doubt deriving its name as above, from Old English *hālig* 'holy' + *āc* 'oak'.

Holyoke (110) English: variant spelling of HOLYOAK.
FOREBEARS Edward Holyoke emigrated from England and settled in Lynn, MA, in 1638. His descendants include Rev. Edward Holyoke, president of Harvard College from 1737 to 1769, and other prominent educators.

Holz (1321) German and Jewish (Ashkenazic): variant spelling of HOLTZ.
GIVEN NAMES German 8%. *Kurt* (4), *Hans* (3), *Dieter* (2), *Erna* (2), *Fritz* (2), *Gunther* (2), *Manfred* (2), *Otto* (2), *Ulrich* (2), *Bernhard, Erhardt, Erwin*.

Holzapfel (433) German: from Middle High German *holzapfel* 'crab apple', a topographic name for someone who lived by a crab apple tree or perhaps a nickname for someone with a sour disposition.
GIVEN NAMES German 7%. *Hans* (2), *Claus, Fritz, Gerhart, Heinz, Hilde, Johann, Kurt*.

Holzberg (136) German: habitational name from any of various places called Holzberg, for example in Hesse and Silesia.

Holzberger (125) German: habitational name for someone from any of various places called HOLZBERG.

GIVEN NAMES German 9%. *Milbert* (2), *Franz*.

Holzem (172) German: habitational name from a place so called near Koblenz or from one in the Grand Duchy of Luxembourg.

Holzemer (113) German: **1.** habitational name for someone from HOLZEM. **2.** dialect variant of HOLZHEIMER.

Holzer (1695) German (also **Hölzer**) and Jewish (Ashkenazic): variant spelling of HOLTZER.

GIVEN NAMES German 6%. *Kurt* (5), *Siegfried* (4), *Franz* (3), *Hans* (3), *Helmut* (3), *Mathias* (2), *Alfons, Aloys, Frieda, Fritz, Guenter, Gunther*.

Holzhauer (375) German: occupational name for a wood cutter, Middle High German *holzhouwer*.

GIVEN NAMES German 4%. *Kurt* (2), *Heinrich*.

Holzhausen (130) South German: habitational name from any of the numerous places so called, from Old High German *holz* 'wood' + the plural of *hūs* 'house'.

GIVEN NAMES German 4%. *Kurt, Udo*.

Holzhauser (174) German (**Holzhäuser**): habitational name for someone from any of the numerous places called HOLZHAUSEN.

GIVEN NAME German 4%. *Kurt*.

Holzheimer (194) German: habitational name for someone from any of various places called Holzheim.

Holzinger (398) South German and Jewish (Ashkenazic): habitational name for someone from any of various places called Holzing or Holzingen.

GIVEN NAMES German 12%. *Kurt* (3), *Helmut* (2), *Lorenz* (2), *Ernst, Ewald, Franz, Hans-Peter, Heinz, Kaspar, Rainer, Rudi, Ulrich*.

Holzknecht (132) German: occupational name for a forester's or forest ranger's assistant, from Old High German *holz* 'wood' + *knecht* 'boy', 'apprentice', 'servant'.

Holzman (1114) **1.** Jewish (Ashkenazic): occupational name for a woodcutter or someone who sold wood, from German *Holz* 'wood' + *Mann* 'man'. **2.** Altered spelling of German HOLZMANN.

GIVEN NAMES Jewish 4%. *Dalit, Hyman, Miriam, Moishe, Ofer, Sol, Zev*.

Holzmann (200) **1.** German: topographic name for someone who lived in a wood, from HOLZ 'wood' + *Mann* 'man'. **2.** German and Jewish (Ashkenazic): occupational name for a woodman (see HOLTZER).

GIVEN NAMES German 5%. *Franz, Gerhard*.

Holzschuh (241) German: metonymic occupational name for a maker of wooden shoes (clogs), from Middle High German *holz* 'wood' + *schuoch* 'shoe'.

Holzwarth (384) German: occupational name for a forest warden, from Middle High German *holz* 'wood' + *wart* 'keeper', 'guardian'. Compare HOLTGREWE.

GIVEN NAMES German 5%. *Otto* (2), *Erna, Ernst, Guenther*.

Holzworth (397) Altered form of German HOLZWARTH.

Hom (1345) **1.** Dutch: unexplained. **2.** Danish: unexplained. **3.** Chinese 譚: Taishan spelling of of TAN 1.

GIVEN NAMES Chinese 10%. *Suey* (7), *Wing* (6), *Wah* (4), *Wai* (4), *Bock* (3), *Jue* (3), *Ting* (3), *Doo* (2), *Gim* (2), *Jin* (2), *Jing* (2), *Kwock* (2).

Homa (581) Variant spelling of Ukrainian and Polish CHOMA.

Homan (3548) **1.** Altered spelling of German HOMANN. **2.** English: variant of HOLMAN. This surname has been in Ireland since the 17th century. **3.** Dutch: status name from Middle Dutch *hovetman, hooftman* 'head man', 'leader', 'adviser'. **4.** Dutch: variant of HOFFMAN 2. **5.** Slovenian: unexplained.

Homann (319) North German: **1.** status name from Middle Low German *homan*, denoting someone of high social class (Middle Low German *hō* 'high' + *man* 'man'). **2.** variant of HOFFMANN 1.

GIVEN NAMES German 9%. *Fritz* (3), *Hans, Inge, Juergen, Kurt, Otto, Reinhart, Ursel, Wilhelm*.

Homans (134) English: possibly a variant of HUMAN.

Homberg (136) German and Jewish (Ashkenazic): **1.** habitational name from any of various German places so called. The name is derived from an inflected form of Old High German *hōh* 'high' + *berg* 'hill'. **2.** variant of HOMBURG.

GIVEN NAMES German 7%; Jewish 4%. *Otto* (2), *Fritz; Aron* (2).

Homburg (160) German and Jewish (Ashkenazic): habitational name from places in Hesse and Saarland called Homburg, from the weak dative case (originally used after a preposition and article) of Old High German *hōh* 'high' + *burg* 'fortress', 'fortified town'.

GIVEN NAMES German 9%. *Dieter, Hans, Otto*.

Home (234) English and Scottish: variant spelling of HOLME.

Homeier (132) German: variant spelling of HOMEYER.

Homen (171) Respelling of Portuguese **Homem**, from *homem* 'man' (Latin *homo*), possibly applied as a nickname with reference to the physical or mental attributes of a man.

GIVEN NAMES Spanish 10%. *Manuel* (3), *Jose* (2), *Amarildo, Armando, Dulce, Fernando; Antonio* (2).

Homer (2140) **1.** English (West Midlands): occupational name for a maker of helmets, from the adopted Old French term *he(a)umier*, from *he(a)ume* 'helmet', of Germanic origin. Compare HELM 2.
2. English: variant of HOLMER. **3.** Americanized form of the Greek family name **Homiros** or one of its patronymic derivatives (**Homirou, Homiridis**, etc.). This was not only the name of the ancient Greek epic poet (classical Greek **Homēros**), but was also borne by a martyr venerated in the Greek Orthodox Church. **4.** Slovenian: topographic name for someone who lived on a hill, from *hom* (dialect form of *holm* 'hill', 'height') + the German suffix *-er* denoting an inhabitant.

FOREBEARS The American painter Winslow Homer (1836–1910) was of old New England stock dating back to Captain John Homer, an Englishman who crossed the Atlantic in his own ship and settled in Boston about 1636.

Homes (318) English: variant of HOLM.

Homesley (184) Possibly an English habitational name from a minor place named Holmsleigh, Homesleigh (for example Homesleigh Green in Devon) or Holmsley (for example in Hampshire).

Homewood (240) English (Kent and Sussex): habitational name from any of various places of this name, in particular one in the parish of Perching, Sussex, recorded as *Homwood* in about 1280; there were others in Chailey and Forest Row in Sussex. All are probably named from Middle English *home* 'homestead', 'manor' + *wode* 'wood'.

Homeyer (293) German (Westphalia): status name from Middle Low German *hō* 'high' + *meier* 'headman', 'steward' (see MEYER).

Homick (122) Of uncertain origin; probably an Americanized form of a Slavic name. This surname occurs chiefly in PA.

Homme (242) **1.** Norwegian: habitational name from any of several farmsteads in Agder and Telemark, so named from Old Norse *hvammr* 'small valley'. **2.** French: nickname from Old French *homme* 'man' (compare MANN), or status name from the same word with the sense 'vassal', 'feudal tenant'. **3.** Northern French (**Hommé**): from a French form of the Germanic personal name *Autmar, Otmar*, composed of the elements *aud* 'wealth' + *meri, mari* 'renowned'.

GIVEN NAMES Scandinavian 10%. *Erik, Helmer, Knut, Knute, Morten, Obert, Thor*.

Hommel (540) **1.** German and Dutch: variant of HUMMEL 1. **2.** North German and Dutch: variant of HUMMEL 2. **3.** French: topographic name from a diminutive of *homme*, a variant of *orme* 'elm'.

Hommer (104) Dutch, North German, and French (Alsace): from the personal name *Hommer*, a reduced form of HUMBERT.

Hommerding (144) German (mainly Saarland): probably a variant of **Humperding**, patronymic (with the suffix *-ding*) from HUMBERT.

GIVEN NAME German 5%. *Otto*.

Hommes (182) Frisian: patronymic from HUMM 2.

GIVEN NAME German 4%. *Wolfgang*.

Homola (231) Czech: from *homole* 'cone', probably a nickname for someone with a pointed or cone-shaped head.

Homolka (217) Czech: from *homolka* '(cone-shaped lump of) cream cheese' (from a diminutive of *homole* 'cone'), possibly applied as a nickname for a mild or soft person, or a metonymic occupational name for a cheesemaker.

Homrich (197) German (central and northern): habitational name from either of two places called Hommerich, both in the Rhineland.

Homsey (159) English: unexplained.

Homsher (136) Perhaps an altered form of English HAMPSHIRE.

Homstad (131) Norwegian: habitational name from a farmstead in Trøndelag named Homstad, probably from the Old Norse personal name *Hámundr* or *Hamarr* + *staðir* 'farmstead', 'dwelling'.

GIVEN NAME German 4%. *Kurt* (2).

Homuth (157) German: nickname from Middle High German *hōch* 'high' + *muot* 'mind', 'will', 'spirit', denoting a noble-minded person, or an arrogant one.

GIVEN NAMES German 5%. *Arno*, *Ewald*.

Homza (101) Czech: unexplained.

Hon (744) **1.** Jewish (Ashkenazic): nickname or ornamental name from Yiddish *hon* 'cock'. **2.** Chinese 韩: variant of HAN 1.

Honaker (1734) German (**Honacker**): topographic name from Middle High German *hōch* 'high' (+ dative *-n*) + *acker* 'field'.

Honan (419) Irish: **1.** Anglicized form of Gaelic **Ó hEoghanáin** 'descendant of *Eoghanán*', a pet form of the personal name *Eógan*, meaning 'born of the yew'. **2.** variant of **Honeen**, an Anglicized form of Gaelic **Ó hUainín** 'descendant of *Uainín*', a personal name formed from a diminutive of *uaine* 'green'.

GIVEN NAMES Irish 7%. *Sean Michael* (2), *Brendan*.

Honda (653) Japanese: 'original rice paddy'; variously written, common throughout Japan and the Ryūkyū Islands. One daimyō family of Mikawa (now part of Aichi prefecture) is descended from the Fujiwara. Another family was samurai from Satsuma (now Kagoshima prefecture).

GIVEN NAMES Japanese 51%. *Yoshio* (5), *Hiroshi* (4), *Osamu* (4), *Koji* (3), *Mitsuo* (3), *Nami* (3), *Noboru* (3), *Toshio* (3), *Akira* (2), *Hatsue* (2), *Keiichi* (2), *Masako* (2).

Hondros (106) Greek: nickname from the vocabulary word *khondros* 'fat'. It is usually a reduced form of a surname beginning with *Hondro-* as a prefix, e.g. **Hondrogiannis** 'fat John'.

GIVEN NAMES Greek 11%. *Spiro* (2), *Dimitrios*, *Nickolaos*, *Stylianos*.

Hone (648) **1.** English: topographic name for someone who lived by a boundary stone or a prominent outcrop of rock, from Middle English *hōn* 'stone', 'rock'. This is the same word as modern English *hone* 'whetstone', and the surname may also be a metonymic occupational name for someone who used a whetstone to sharpen swords, daggers, and knives. **2.** Dutch and North German (**Höne**): from the Germanic personal name *Huno*, a short form of the various compound names with the first element *hūn*. Compare, for example, HUMPHREY. The exact meaning of this element is disputed, but it may be cognate with Old Norse *húnn* 'bear cub'.

FOREBEARS This surname has been established in Devon and Gloucestershire, England, since the 14th century. There are a number of Irish bearers of the name Hone who claim that it is an altered form of Welsh OWEN. One family in Ireland can be traced to Samuel Hone, who went to Ireland as a soldier in 1649, probably from the Netherlands, and settled in Dublin.

Honea (1176) Origin uncertain. Possibly an American variant spelling of English HONEY.

Honeck (167) German: **1.** topographic or habitational name from a place called Ho(he)neck. **2.** from a Germanic personal name based on *hūn* 'bear cub' (see HONE) + *-ke* diminutive suffix.

Honecker (108) German: variant of HONECK.

Honegger (168) German: habitational name from any of the various places (including one in Switzerland) that get their names from an uncertain first element + Old High German *ecka*, *egga* 'corner', 'bend', 'nook'.

GIVEN NAMES German 7%. *Franz*, *Otto*, *Ulrich*, *Willi*.

Honer (406) **1.** English: occupational name for someone who used a whetstone to hone (sharpen) swords, daggers, and knives (see HONE 1). **2.** North German (**Höner**): variant of HOHNER.

Honey (966) English (southern): metonymic occupational name for a beekeeper or a gatherer or seller of honey, Middle English *hony* (Old English *hunig*), or a nickname from the same word used as a term of endearment, a sense which was common in medieval England.

Honeycutt (5755) English: habitational name from either of two places in Devon named Hunnacott, from either the Old English personal name *Hunā* or Old English *hunig* 'honey' + *cot* 'cottage'. There is also a place named Huncoat in Lancashire, which has the same origin, but the distribution of the surname in England suggests that it probably did not contribute to the surname.

Honeyman (416) English: variant of HONEY, found chiefly in Scotland.

Honeywell (457) English: habitational name from any of several minor places in Devon so named, from Old English *hunig* 'honey' + *wella* 'spring', 'stream'.

Hong (5187) **1.** Chinese 洪: from a word meaning 'water' or 'flood'. During the time of the emperors Yao and Shun in the 23rd century BC, there was a clan known as the Gonggongshi. They took the name *Gong* as a surname, but in order to escape their enemies, needed to change the character for their surname; by the addition of a component meaning 'water', the name was changed to *Hong*. Another legend provides a more colorful account: the Gonggongshi were a warrior people, and were able to bring about a flood. However, the emperor Yu succeeded in establishing flood control, and he banished the Gonggongshi. Descendants, in order to commemorate the ability of their ancestors to cause floods, changed their name from *Gong* to the word for 'flood', *Hong*. **2.** Chinese 康: Cantonese variant of KANG 1. **3.** Chinese 项: variant of XIANG 2. **4.** Chinese 杭: variant of HANG 1. **5.** Korean: there is only one Chinese character for the Hong surname in Korea. Some sources indicate that there are 59 different Hong clans, but only four can be documented. Each of the four clans claim different founding ancestors. The oldest Hong clan's founding ancestor, Hong Ch'ŏn-ha, migrated to Koguryŏ, Korea, sometime in the first half of the seventh century. The Hong surname is a fairly common one and is found throughout the Korean peninsula.

GIVEN NAMES Chinese/Korean 49%; Vietnamese 10%. *Sung* (70), *Soon* (57), *Young* (47), *Jong* (27), *Jung* (24), *Song* (24), *Yong* (19), *Jin* (18), *Seung* (17), *Jae* (16), *Sun* (16), *Kyung* (14); *Chong* (17), *Chang* (14), *Min* (11), *Seong* (11), *Chung* (9), *Moon* (9), *Chul* (8), *Byung* (7), *Dae* (6), *Myong* (5), *Sa* (5), *Jung Hee* (4); *Thanh* (10), *Cuong* (8), *Quang* (8), *Son* (8), *Hung* (7), *Binh* (6), *Mai* (6), *Vinh* (6), *Hoa* (5), *Long* (5), *Minh* (5), *Nhi* (5).

Honick (115) **1.** Americanized spelling of German and Jewish HONIG. **2.** Possibly an altered spelling of German **Hönicke**, from a Germanic personal name composed with *hūn* 'bear cub' + *-k* diminutive (compare HUNEKE).

Honig (833) **1.** German and Jewish (Ashkenazic): metonymic name for a gatherer or seller of honey, from Middle High German *honec*, *honic* 'honey', German *Honig*. As a Jewish surname it is generally ornamental. **2.** German (**Hönig**, of Slavic origin): from a pet form of HEINRICH.

GIVEN NAMES Jewish 5%. *Benzion* (2), *Blima* (2), *Emanuel*, *Isadore*, *Isidor*, *Miriam*, *Pinchas*, *Shoshana*, *Sol*, *Yossi*.

Honigman (150) German (**Honigmann**) and Jewish (Ashkenazic): elaborated form of HONIG 1.

GIVEN NAME Jewish 4%. *Isrel*.

Honkala (111) Finnish: ornamental name from *honka* 'pine tree' + the local ending *-la*. This name occurs chiefly in central western Finland.
GIVEN NAMES Finnish 10%; Scandinavian 7%; German 4%. *Veikko* (2), *Rauni*, *Tauno*, *Toivo*; *Erik*; *Rudi*.

Honkomp (109) German: habitational name from a place in Westphalia called Honkamp.

Honn (394) English: probably a variant of HUNN.

Honnold (177) German (also **Hönnold**): variant spelling of HONOLD.

Honold (176) German and Dutch: from the Germanic personal name *Hunold*, composed of the elements *hun-* 'giant' or *hūn* 'bear cub' + *wald* 'rule'.
GIVEN NAMES German 5%. *Erwin*, *Gerhard*, *Kurt*.

Honomichl (102) Czech: from a contracted form of the German personal name *Johann Michael*.

Honor (200) **1.** English: habitational name from Honor End Farm in Hampden, Buckinghamshire, which is named from Old English *hān* 'hone', 'stone' + *ōra* 'slope', or possibly from Honer in Sussex, named from Old English *hol* 'hollow' + *ōra* 'shore'. **2.** In some cases probably an Americanized form of French **Honoré** (see HONORE).
GIVEN NAME French 4%. *Regine*.

Honore (426) French (**Honoré**): from a medieval personal name (Latin *Honoratus* 'honored'). The name was borne by a 5th-century bishop of Arles and a 6th-century bishop of Amiens, both of whom became popular minor saints and contributed to the frequency of the name in the Middle Ages. The surname was taken to Denmark by French Huguenots who migrated there in the 17th century.
GIVEN NAMES French 8%. *Pierre* (2), *Auguste*, *Chantal*, *Jacques*, *Magalie*, *Mathurin*, *Ovide*, *Phillippe*, *Remy*.

Honour (110) English: variant spelling of HONOR.

Hons (198) **1.** Dutch: plural variant of HOEN. **2.** Dutch: patronymic from a Germanic personal name (see HOEN 2). **3.** French: topographic name from the plural of *homme* 'elm' (Latin *ulmus*, standard French *orme*).

Honsberger (164) German and Swiss German: habitational name from a place called Honsberg near Wuppertal.
GIVEN NAME German 5%. *Kurt*.

Honse (152) German (Bavaria): variant of HANS.

Honsinger (194) German: variant of HUNTZINGER.

Honts (108) Variant spelling of HONTZ.

Hontz (316) Origin uncertain. It is said to be a German form of an unidentified Hungarian name, possibly KUNC.

Hoo (217) **1.** English (East Anglia and the south): topographic name for someone who lived on a spur of a hill, from the Old English dative case *hōe* (originally used after a preposition) of *hōh* 'spur of a hill'. The surname may also derive from any of the minor places named with this word, such as Hoo in Kent and Hooe in Devon and Sussex. **2.** Chinese 胡: see HU.
GIVEN NAMES Chinese 12%. *Chi* (2), *Wai Lam* (2), *Wing* (2), *Beng*, *Chin*, *Gan*, *Hing*, *Hui*, *Kee*, *Lai*, *Lai Ching*, *Mei-Mei*.

Hoober (100) Americanized spelling of German, Dutch, or Jewish HUBER.

Hoobler (390) Americanized spelling of German HUBLER.

Hoock (138) Americanized spelling of Dutch, Frisian, and North German HOUCK.
GIVEN NAMES German 5%. *Erwin*, *Gunther*, *Irmgard*.

Hood (19089) **1.** English and Scottish: metonymic occupational name for a maker of hoods or a nickname for someone who wore a distinctive hood, from Middle English *hod(de)*, *hood*, *hud* 'hood'. Some early examples with prepositions seem to be topographic names, referring to a place where there was a hood-shaped hill or a natural shelter or overhang, providing protection from the elements. In some cases the name may be habitational, from places called Hood, in Devon (possibly 'hood-shaped hill') and North Yorkshire (possibly 'shelter' or 'fortification'). **2.** Irish: Anglicized form of Gaelic **Ó hUid** 'descendant of *Ud*', a personal name of uncertain derivation. This was the name of an Ulster family who were bards to the O'Neills of Clandeboy. It was later altered to **Mac hUid**. Compare MAHOOD.

Hoodenpyle (119) Americanized form of an unexplained Dutch name.
FOREBEARS The name was brought to North America from the Netherlands in about 1781 by Philip Hoodenpyle (born *c*. 1756).

Hooe (141) English: variant spelling of HOO 1.

Hooey (171) Irish: variant of HOEY.

Hoof (124) **1.** Dutch and North German: variant of HOFF. **2.** North German: topographic name from a variant of HOFF. **3.** Dutch: nickname from *hoofd* 'head'. Compare English HEAD 1. **4.** English: variant spelling of HUFF.

Hoofnagle (136) Americanized spelling of German HUFNAGEL.

Hoog (243) **1.** Swedish (**Höög**): nickname for a tall person from *hög* 'high', 'tall', possibly a soldier's name. **2.** Dutch (**de Hoog**) and North German: nickname from Middle Dutch, Middle Low German *hooch* 'high', in the sense of 'noble', 'proud', 'of high status'.

Hooge (167) Dutch and North German: variant of HOOG.

Hoogenboom (110) Dutch: **1.** topographic name for someone living by a tall tree, or

possibly a nickname for a tall man, literally meaning 'tall tree'. **2.** Belgian: habitational name from places called Hoogboom and Hogenboom in the Belgian province of Antwerp, named with the same elements as 1.
FOREBEARS The name **Hoogeboom** is recorded in Beverwijck in New Netherland (Albany, NY) in the mid 17th century.
GIVEN NAMES Dutch 7%; German 4%. *Dirk* (2), *Gerrit* (2); *Kurt*.

Hoogendoorn (171) Dutch: reinterpreted form of HAGEDORN.
GIVEN NAMES Dutch 4%. *Cor*, *Cornelis*.

Hoogerhyde (135) Altered spelling of Dutch **Hoogerheide**, a topographic name from Middle Dutch *hooch* 'high' + *heyde* 'heath'.

Hoogeveen (126) Dutch: habitational name from a place in Drenthe province called Hoogeveen.

Hoogland (229) Dutch: topographic name for someone who lived on a piece of raised land, from Middle Dutch *hooch* 'high' + *land* 'land'.
GIVEN NAMES Dutch 7%. *Dirk* (4), *Gerrit* (2), *Roelof*.

Hook (5054) **1.** English (southern): from Middle English *hoke*, Old English *hōc* 'hook', in any of a variety of senses: as a metonymic occupational name for someone who made and sold hooks as agricultural implements or employed them in his work; as a topographic name for someone who lived by a 'hook' of land, i.e. the bend of a river or the spur of a hill; or as a nickname (in part a survival of an Old English byname) for someone with a hunched back or a hooked nose. A similar ambiguity of interpretation presents itself in the case of CROOK. In some cases the surname may be habitational from any of various places named Hook(e), from this word, as for example in Devon, Dorset, Hampshire, Surrey, Wiltshire, and Worcestershire. **2.** Swedish (**Hö(ö)k**): nickname or a metonymic occupational name from *hök* 'hawk', a soldier's name.

Hooke (213) English: variant spelling of HOOK.

Hooker (5425) English (mainly southeastern): variant of HOOK (in the occupational or topographic and habitational senses), with the addition of the agent suffix *-er*.
FOREBEARS Congregational clergyman Thomas Hooker (1586?–1647) sailed from England with John Cotton and Samuel Stone and arrived in Boston in 1633. He led the 1635 migration of most of his congregation to Hartford in the Connecticut Valley. Thomas is the earliest known entrant, but the name Hooker is common and was also introduced independently by others during the 17th and 18th centuries.

Hooks (4821) English: variant of HOOK, either in the topographic sense or a patronymic from the nickname. This surname is also established in northern Ireland.

Hoole (155) English (mainly Yorkshire): variant of HOOLEY.

GIVEN NAME French 4%. *Michel.*

Hooley (632) English (northern England): habitational name from places called Hoole, in Cheshire and Lancashire. The former is so called from the Old English dative case *hole* of *holh* 'hollow', 'depression'; the latter from Middle English *hule* 'hut', 'shelter' (Old English *hulu* 'husk', 'covering'). In both cases the final -*e* is now silent in the place name, but has been retained in the surname, with consequent alteration in the spelling.

Hoolihan (147) Irish: variant spelling of HOULIHAN.

Hoon (335) Dutch (**de Hoon**): nickname from Middle Dutch *hoon*, *hone* 'dangerous', 'deceitful', 'treacherous' + the definite article *de*.

Hoop (319) **1.** Dutch (**de Hoop**): metonymic occupational name for a cooper, from Middle Dutch *houp* 'hoop'. **2.** Dutch (**van (der) Hoop**): habitational name from De Hoop in Gelderland or Hoop in Overijssel, or Ter Hope in Gistel, West Flanders (Belgium). **3.** North German: topographic name for someone who lived on a raised piece of land in a bog, *hop*, or a habitational name from a place named with this word.

Hooper (12528) English: occupational name for someone who fitted wooden or metal hoops on wooden casks and barrels, from an agent derivative of Middle English *hoop* 'hoop', 'band'.

Hoopes (1261) Probably a variant of Dutch HOOP 1.

Hoopingarner (327) North German and Dutch: Americanized form of **Hoppe(n)-gartner**, a topographic or occupational name referring to an enclosed plot where hops were grown.

Hoople (106) English (Devon): variant of **Hupple**, recorded in 1327 as *Uppehull*, a topographic name for someone who lived 'up the hill'.

Hoopman (125) Dutch: from Middle Dutch *houp* 'hoop', occupational name for someone who fitted wooden or metal hoops on wooden casks and barrels.

Hoops (792) **1.** Dutch: variant of HOOP 1. **2.** North German: variant of HOOP 3.

Hoos (280) **1.** Dutch: from Middle Dutch *hose* 'hose', 'stocking', hence a metonymic occupational name for a knitter of hose (garments for the legs), or a nickname for someone who wore a striking style of hose. **2.** Dutch: nickname from *hoofse* 'courtly', 'mannered', 'well-bred'.

Hoose (482) **1.** Scottish and English: variant of HOUSE 1. **2.** German: variant of HOSE 3. **3.** Dutch: variant of HOOS.

Hooser (378) Probably a variant of English HOSIER.

Hoosier (408) English: variant of HOSIER.

Hoot (338) **1.** North German: variant of HOTH. **2.** Dutch: variant of HOUT.

Hooten (1498) Variant of the Dutch topographic name **Houten** 'woods'.

Hootman (305) Variant spelling of Dutch HOUTMAN.

Hooton (528) **1.** English (mainly central and northwestern England): habitational name from Hooton in Cheshire, or from Hooton Levitt, Hooton Pagnell, or Hooton Roberts in South Yorkshire, all named with Old English *hōh* 'spur of land' + *tūn* 'farmstead'. **2.** See HOOTEN.

Hoots (722) Dutch: possibly an altered form of **van Houts**, a topographic name for someone who lived by a wood (*hout*).

Hooven (379) Shortened form of Dutch **ten Hooven** or **van den Hooven**, a topographic name for someone who lived by some gardens.

Hoover (21384) Dutch: from Middle Dutch *huve*, a measure of land area (compare German HUBER) + -*er*, suffix of agent nouns; a status name for a landowner or a prosperous small farmer.

Hoovler (151) Dutch and Low German: topographic name from Middle Low German *huvel* 'hill'. Compare HUBLER.

Hooyman (156) Dutch: occupational name for someone who mowed or sold hay, Dutch *hooi*.

Hop (206) **1.** Dutch: variant of HOPP 2 and 3. **2.** German: variant of HOOP 3.

Hope (5665) **1.** Scottish and English: topographic name for someone who lived in a small, enclosed valley, Middle English *hop(e)*, or a habitational name from a place named with this word, of which there are examples in North Yorkshire, Lancashire, Derbyshire, Cheshire, Shropshire, Clwyd, Devon, Herefordshire, Kent, Sussex, and elsewhere. The surname is most common in Scotland and northern England, and it is also established in Ireland. **2.** Norwegian: habitational name from any of several farmsteads, notably in Hordaland, so named from Old Norse *hóp* 'narrow bay'.

Hopes (218) English and Scottish: variant of HOPE.

Hopewell (552) English (East Midlands): habitational name from Hopwell in Derbyshire, named with Old English *hop* 'valley' + *well(a)* 'spring', 'stream'.

Hopf (592) German: metonymic occupational name for a grower of hops or dealer in hops, or a metonymic occupational name for a brewer, from the use of hops in the manufacture of beer, from Middle High German *hopfe* 'hops'.

GIVEN NAMES German 6%. *Gerhard* (2), *Kurt* (2), *Ernst, Georg, Gunther, Hans, Hartmut, Wolfgang.*

Hopfensperger (212) South German: apparently a topographic or habitational name of undetermined derivation.

Hopfer (215) German (Bavaria; also **Höpfer**) and Jewish (Ashkenazic): metonymic occupational name for a grower of hops or dealer in hops, from Middle High German *hopfe* 'hops', German *Hopfen* + the agent suffix -*er*.

GIVEN NAMES German 6%. *Arno, Kurt, Lorenz, Ulrich.*

Hopfinger (145) German (**Höpfinger**): habitational name for someone from Höpfingen near Heilbronn.

GIVEN NAME German 6%. *Otto* (2).

Hopgood (218) English (southern counties): apparently a variant of HAPGOOD.

Hopke (201) North German (Westphalia; **Höpke**): topographic name from *hop*, denoting a raised piece of land in a bog, or a habitational name of similar origin.

Hopkin (263) English: from a medieval personal name, a pet form of *Hobb*, a pet form of ROBERT (see HOBBS). This form is also common in Wales.

Hopkins (33897) **1.** English: patronymic from HOPKIN. The surname is widespread throughout southern and central England, but is at its most common in South Wales. **2.** Irish (County Longford and western Ireland): Anglicized form of Gaelic **Mac Oibicín**, itself a Gaelicized form of an Anglo-Norman name. In other parts of the country this name is generally of English origin.

FOREBEARS Stephen Hopkins (*c*.1580–1644) was a pilgrim on the *Mayflower* in 1621 and one of the founders of Plymouth Colony. At his death he left seven children and eighteen grandchildren.

Hopkinson (546) English (chiefly Yorkshire): patronymic from HOPKIN.

Hopko (104) Ukrainian: nickname from Ukrainian *hopka* 'child', a term of endearment.

GIVEN NAME French 4%. *Andre.*

Hopler (135) Swiss German (**Hoppler**): nickname for a person with an irregular gait, who jumped or limped, from Middle High German *hoppeln* 'to jump or leap' + -*er* suffix.

Hopley (103) Americanized form of Swiss German **Hoppler** (see HOPLER).

Hopman (246) North German (**Hopmann**), Dutch, and Jewish (Ashkenazic): from Middle Low German, Middle Dutch *hoppe*, Yiddish *hopn* 'hop(s)' + *man* 'man', an occupational name for a grower or seller of hops.

Hopp (1724) **1.** English: from the medieval personal name *Hobb(e)* (see HOBBS). **2.** Dutch: from Middle Dutch *hoppe* 'hops', hence a metonymic occupational name for a grower or seller of hops. **3.** Dutch: from a pet form of the personal name *Hubrecht* (see HUBERT). **4.** South German: variant of HOPPE 3. **5.** North German form of HOPF.

Hoppa (188) Variant spelling of German HOPPE.

Hoppe (3790) **1.** North German and Dutch: variant of HOPP. **2.** South German: nickname from dialect *hoppen* 'to hop' (a variant of standard German *hüpfen*). This name is widespread throughout central Europe. **3.** Danish: from North German HOPP (see HOPF), or the Danish byname *Hoppe* 'horse', 'mare'. **4.** English: metonymic form of HOPPER 1.

GIVEN NAMES German 5%. *Kurt* (10), *Hans* (5), *Gerhard* (3), *Helmut* (3), *Erwin* (2), *Fritz* (2), *Klaus* (2), *Otto* (2), *Sieg* (2), *Siegfried* (2), *Wolfgang* (2), *Erna*.

Hoppel (234) German: variant of **Hoppler** or Swiss **Höppli** (see HOPLER).

Hoppenrath (104) German: habitational name from a place so named in the Lower Rhine region, or from Hoppenrade in Mecklenburg.

Hopper (10114) **1.** English and Scottish: occupational name for a professional tumbler or acrobat, or a nickname for a restless individual with plenty of energy, Middle English *hoppere*, an agent derivative of Old English *hoppian* 'to hop'. **2.** German: nickname from an agent derivative of Middle High German, Middle Low German *hoppen* 'to limp or stumble'. **3.** Dutch: occupational name for a hop grower or seller, from Middle Dutch *hoppe* 'hop(s)' + the agent suffix *-er*.

Hoppert (163) South German: variant of HUBERT.

GIVEN NAMES Scandinavian 6%; German 5%. *Bernt* (2); *Kurt, Otto*.

Hoppes (726) Dutch: metonymic occupational name for a hop grower or seller, from Middle Dutch *hoppes* 'hop(s)'.

Hoppin (121) English: variant of HOPPING.

Hopping (454) English and Scottish: probably from an unattested Middle English word *hoping*, denoting a dweller in a valley (see HOPE).

Hopple (353) Americanized spelling of German HOPPEL.

Hoppman (142) North German: variant of **Hopmann** (see HOPMAN).

Hoppmann (116) North German: variant of **Hopmann** (see HOPMAN).

GIVEN NAMES German 6%. *Kurt, Leonhard*.

Hoppock (120) Origin unidentified. The name has been established in Hunterdon, NJ, since at least the 1730s.

Hopps (306) English: variant of HOBBS, found chiefly in the northeast of England.

Hopson (3435) English: variant of HOBSON.

Hopton (243) English: habitational name from any of various places, for example in Derbyshire, Herefordshire, Shropshire, Staffordshire, Suffolk, and West Yorkshire, so named from Old English *hop* 'valley among hills' + *tūn* 'enclosure', 'settlement'.

Hopwood (975) English (Lancashire): habitational name from a place in Lancashire, so named from Old English *hop* 'valley among hills' + *wudu* 'wood'. There is a Hopwood in Worcestershire, identical in

meaning, which may also have given rise to the surname in some instances.

Hoque (186) Muslim: variant of HAQ.

GIVEN NAMES Muslim 82%. *Mohammed* (19), *Mohammad* (9), *Enamul* (5), *Akm* (3), *Azizul* (3), *Fazlul* (3), *Abul* (2), *Anwarul* (2), *Kazi* (2), *Mahbubul* (2), *Samsul* (2), *Shahidul* (2).

Hora (434) **1.** Czech and Slovak: topographic name from *hora* 'mountain', 'hill', earlier 'forest'. **2.** Irish: variant of O'HARA. **3.** Indian (Panjab): Sikh name based on the name of a Jat tribe. **4.** Japanese: 'preserve good'. The name is Ryūkyūan in origin and is also pronounced *Bora* and *Yasura*.

GIVEN NAMES Indian 5%; Japanese 4%. *Kiran, Manohar, Neeraj, Priya, Rajiv, Saloni, Sundeep; Masuo* (2), *Hiro, Hisako, Masao, Sadao, Toshio, Yoshio*.

Horace (301) English: from the personal name *Horace*, Latin *Horatius*, a Roman family name of unknown origin, associated chiefly with the name of the poet Quintus Horatius Flaccus (65–8 BC).

Horacek (307) Czech (**Horáček**): from a diminutive of **Horák** (see HORAK).

Horack (135) Germanized or Americanized spelling of Czech HORAK.

Horak (1091) Czech and Slovak (**Horák**): topographic name for someone who lived in the mountains, from a noun derivative of *hora* 'mountain'.

Horan (4371) Irish: **1.** (Connacht) Anglicized form of Gaelic **Ó hUghróin** 'descendant of *Ughrón*', a personal name from *ughrach* 'warlike'. **2.** Anglicized form of Gaelic **Ó hOdhráin** 'descendant of *Ódhrán*', a personal name (borne, according to legend, by St. Patrick's charioteer) from *odhar* 'dun-colored'. **3.** reduced form of HANRAHAN.

GIVEN NAMES Irish 7%. *Brendan* (5), *Aileen* (2), *Dermot* (2), *Brennan, Brigid, Dymphna, Kieran*.

Horath (116) **1.** Hungarian **2.** German (also **Hörath**): habitational name from places so named in Westphalia and the Rhineland.

Horch (136) **1.** Jewish (Ashkenazic): origin uncertain; perhaps a habitational name from Horchheim in the Rhineland, named from Middle High German *hork, horec* 'dirt' + *heim* 'home', 'dwelling place'. **2.** German: topographic name for someone who lived in a swampy place, from Middle High German *hor* 'mire', 'mud'. **3.** German: nickname for an eavesdropper, from Middle High German *horchen* 'to listen'.

Horchler (104) German: probably a variant of HORCH 3.

GIVEN NAMES German 5%. *Hans, Helmut*.

Hord (1287) **1.** English: variant of HERD. **2.** Respelling of Swedish **Hård** (see HARD 2).

Horejsi (158) Czech (**Hořejší**): topographic name for someone who lived in the upper

part of a village or on an upper story of an apartment house, from Czech *hořejš* 'upper', 'higher', applied as a distinguishing epithet where there were two or more bearers of the same personal name in the community.

Horen (202) **1.** German (**Hören**): habitational name from Höri, a peninsula on Lake Constance. **2.** Dutch: variant of HORNE 2. **3.** Jewish (Ashkenazic): variant of HORN.

Horenstein (195) Jewish (Ashkenazic): variant of HORNSTEIN.

GIVEN NAMES Jewish 9%. *Isadore* (2), *Avraham, Avrom, Miriam*.

Horgan (1546) Irish: **1.** shortened Anglicized form of Gaelic **Ó hAragáin**, a reduced form of **Ó hAnradgáin** (see HANRAHAN). **2.** (County Cork): shortened Anglicized form of Gaelic **Ó hArgáin** 'descendant of *Argán*'. 1 and 2 are related, but arose from variants that existed in Irish before Anglicization.

GIVEN NAMES Irish 5%. *Dermot* (2), *Brendan, Bridie*.

Horgen (135) Norwegian: habitational name from any of several farmsteads, notably in southeastern Norway, so named from Old Norse *horgr* 'steep mountainside', 'sanctuary', or 'naked rock' + *vin* 'meadow'.

GIVEN NAMES Scandinavian 11%. *Alf, Erik*.

Horger (182) German: **1.** (Württemberg): habitational name from Horgen near Rottweil, or perhaps from either of the places called Horgau, in Swabia and Switzerland. **2.** (Bavaria; **Hörger**): variant of *Herger* (see HERGERT).

GIVEN NAMES German 4%. *Otto* (2), *Frieda*.

Hori (287) Japanese: 'moat'; found mostly in central Japan and the Ryūkyū Islands. One noble family, descended from the FUJIWARA, resided in Mino (now part of Gifu prefecture).

GIVEN NAMES Japanese 61%. *Kazuo* (3), *Osamu* (3), *Hiroshi* (2), *Kazutoshi* (2), *Kotaro* (2), *Makoto* (2), *Mayumi* (2), *Satoru* (2), *Takayuki* (2), *Takeo* (2), *Tsugio* (2), *Yoshihiro* (2).

Horie (108) Japanese: 'moat river'; the name is found mostly in the Tōkyō and Ōsaka regions.

GIVEN NAMES Japanese 72%. *Maki* (2), *Shinobu* (2), *Atsushi, Harue, Hideki, Hidenori, Hideo, Hiroaki, Hiroshi, Hitoshi, Kaoru, Kazuaki*.

Horigan (145) Irish: variant of HORGAN.

Horine (484) Probably an altered spelling of Czech **Hořín**, a habitational name from a place so named in central Bohemia. In the U.S. the surname occurs most frequently in IN, MO, and KY.

Horinek (167) Czech (**Hořínek**): diminutive of **Hořín** (see HORINE).

Horiuchi (243) Japanese: topographical name meaning '(one who lives) within the moat'; it is also (less commonly) pronounced **Horinouchi**. Some bearers

descend from the Seiwa-Genji though the Funaki family; others from the Kumano family. The surname is found throughout Japan.
GIVEN NAMES Japanese 56%. *Atsushi* (3), *Takashi* (3), *Hiroaki* (2), *Kazuo* (2), *Kenji* (2), *Kensuke* (2), *Koji* (2), *Takeshi* (2), *Aki*, *Akira*, *Chiye*, *Eiji*.

Horkan (148) Irish: **1.** shortened anglicized form of Gaelic **Ó hAnradháin** (see HAN-RAHAN). **2.** (County Mayo): variant of HARKIN 2.
GIVEN NAME Irish 7%. *Aidan*.

Horkey (176) Americanized spelling of Czech HORKY.

Horky (217) Czech (**Horký**, **Hořký**): nickname from Czech *horký* 'hot' or *hořký* 'bitter'.

Horlacher (307) German: habitational name for someone from Horlach in Bavaria or Horlachen in Württemberg, both so called from Old High German *hor* 'mud', 'marsh' + *lahha* 'pool', 'pond'; the latter place retains traces of an inflected ending.

Horlick (169) English: nickname for someone with a patch of gray in his hair, from Old English *hār* 'gray' + *locc* 'lock of hair'.

Horman (456) Americanized spelling of German HORMANN.
GIVEN NAMES German 4%. *Phares* (2), *Dietrich*, *Otto*.

Hormann (305) German: **1.** reduced form of **Hornemann**, a habitational name from any of places in northern Germany called Horn. **2.** (Bavaria; **Hörmann**): variant of HERMANN.
GIVEN NAMES German 5%. *Bernd*, *Erwin*, *Heinz*, *Helmut*.

Hormel (146) German: variant of **Hörmle**, a South German pet form of HERMANN.
GIVEN NAME German 4%. *Heinz*.

Hormell (110) Variant spelling of German HORMEL.

Horn (19755) **1.** English, Scottish, German, and Dutch: from Middle English, Middle High German, Middle Dutch *horn* 'horn', applied in a variety of senses: as a metonymic occupational name for someone who made small articles, such as combs, spoons, and window lights, out of horn; as a metonymic occupational name for someone who played a musical instrument made from the horn of an animal; as a topographic name for someone who lived by a horn-shaped spur of a hill or tongue of land in a bend of a river, or a habitational name from any of the places named with this element (for example, in England, Horne in Surrey on a spur of a hill and Horn in Rutland in a bend of a river); as a nickname, perhaps referring to some feature of a person's physical appearance, or denoting a cuckolded husband. **2.** Norwegian: habitational name from any of several farmsteads so named, from Old Norse *horn* 'horn', 'spur of land'. **3.** Swedish: ornamental or topographic name from *horn*

'horn', 'spur of land'. **4.** Jewish (Ashkenazic): presumably from German *Horn* 'horn', adopted as a surname for reasons that are not clear. It may be purely ornamental, or it may refer to the ram's horn (Hebrew *shofar*) blown in the Synagogue during various ceremonies.

Hornack (97) Germanized or Americanized spelling of Czech and Slovak **Hornák** (see HORNAK).

Hornaday (426) Origin unidentified. This name is found mainly in NC, where it has been established since the early 18th century.

Hornak (364) Czech (**Horňák**), Slovak (**Horniak**), and German (of Slavic origin): topographic name for someone who lived in the mountains, in particular a part of Moravia so named.

Hornbacher (141) German: habitational name for someone from any of various places called Hornbach.
GIVEN NAMES German 4%. *Bernd*, *Erwin*.

Hornback (1034) Americanized spelling of German **Hornbach**, a habitational name from any of various places so named.

Hornbaker (398) Americanized spelling of HORNBACHER.

Hornbeak (154) See HORNBECK.

Hornbeck (1227) Americanized spelling of Dutch **Hornbeek**, a habitational name from a place named as 'horn creek'.

Hornberger (1169) German: habitational name for someone from Hornberg, a common place name composed of Old High German *horn* 'horn' + *berg* 'hill'.

Hornbostel (160) North German: habitational name from a place so called near Celle.
GIVEN NAMES German 5%; Scandinavian 4%. *Hans* (3), *Eldred*; *Sig*.

Hornbrook (236) English: habitational name from Hornbrook in Kelly, Devon, so named from Old English *horn* 'hill spur' + *brōc* 'book', 'stream'.

Hornbuckle (786) English (chiefly North Midlands): variant of ARBUCKLE.

Hornburg (179) German: habitational name from any of numerous places so named.
GIVEN NAMES German 4%. *Fritz*, *Kurt*.

Hornby (389) English (chiefly Lancashire): habitational name from any of various places in northern England so called. Those in Lancashire and near Bedale in North Yorkshire are from the Old Norse personal name *Horni* 'horn' + Old Norse *býr* 'farm', 'settlement'. One in the parish of Great Smeaton, North Yorkshire, is recorded in Domesday Book as *Horenbodebi* and probably has as its first element an Old Norse personal name composed of the elements *horn* 'horn' + *boði* 'messenger'.

Horne (12658) **1.** English, Scottish, and Dutch: variant of HORN 1–4. **2.** Norwegian: habitational name from any of several farmsteads mostly so named from the da-

tive singular of *horn* (see HORN). **3.** Swedish: variant of HORN.

Hornecker (135) German: habitational name denoting someone from any of various places called Horneck.

Horner (9391) **1.** English, Scottish, German, and Dutch: from HORN 1 with the agent suffix *-er*; an occupational name for someone who made or sold small articles made of horn, a metonymic occupational name for someone who played a musical instrument made from the horn of an animal, or a topographic name for someone who lived at a 'horn' of land. **2.** habitational name from Horner in Diptford, Devon, which is named from Old English *horn* 'horn of land' + *ora* 'hill spur', 'ridge'. **3.** Jewish (Ashkenazic): variant of HORN 4.

Horney (539) **1.** German: Eastphalian or Americanized form of a personal name composed of the Germanic elements *hard* 'hardy', 'brave', 'strong' + *nit* 'battle fury', 'eagerness to fight', or a habitational name from a place so called in Brandenburg or in the Rhineland. **2.** English: probably a derivative of HORN.

Hornick (815) Germanized or Americanized spelling of Czech **Horník** (see HOR-NIK).

Hornig (258) **1.** Eastern German: from Sorbian or Czech *horník* 'miner' (see HOR-NIK). **2.** Jewish (Ashkenazic): see HORNIK 3.
GIVEN NAMES German 7%. *Kurt* (4), *Winfried*.

Hornik (224) **1.** Czech and Slovak (**Horník**): occupational name from *horník* 'miner'. **2.** Czech (**Horník**): habitational name for someone from Kutná Hora, so named for its silver mine. **3.** Polish: variant of **Górnik** (see GORNIK). **4.** Jewish (Ash-kenazic): origin uncertain; possibly an occupational name for a miner (see 1 above).
GIVEN NAMES Polish 4%. *Boleslaw*, *Jacek*, *Jozef*, *Kazimierz*.

Horning (2579) German: **1.** nickname from *Hornung* 'February', with reference to a tax obligation or some other association with that month, for example being born in February. **2.** from a personal name, *Hornunc*. **3.** North German: nickname for a person born out of wedlock, Middle Low German *hornink*, with reference to parentage by a cuckold, traditionally symbolized by horns. **4.** topographic name referring to the location or shape of a farming property (see HORN).

Hornish (130) Americanized spelling of German **Hornisch** or **Hörnisch**, a nickname from Middle High German *horniz*, *hornuz* 'hornet', probably denoted an uncontrolled or bad-tempered man.

Hornor (207) English: variant spelling of HORNER.

Hornsby (2553) English: habitational name from a place in Cumbria, so called from the genitive case of the Old Norse byname *Ormr* 'serpent' (see ORME 1) + Old Norse *býr* 'farm', 'settlement'. The form of the name seems to have been influenced by confusion with HORNBY. The surname is widespread in northern England.

Hornstein (561) **1.** German: habitational name from places so named near Sigmaringen and in Bavaria. **2.** Jewish (Ashkenazic): ornamental compound of German *Horn* 'horn' + *Stein* 'stone'.
GIVEN NAMES Jewish 6%. *Hyman* (2), *Aron*, *Chaim*, *Dafna*, *Sol*, *Yetta*.

Hornstra (103) Frisian: topographic name for someone who lived by a horn-shaped field, a horn-shaped spur of a hill, or a tongue of land in a bend of a river, from an agent noun derived from Middle Low German *horn* 'horn'.

Hornung (1204) German: variant of HORN-ING 1 and 2.
GIVEN NAMES German 4%. *Helmut* (3), *Dieter* (2), *Erwin*, *Franz*, *Guenther*, *Hans*, *Horst*, *Kurt*, *Rudiger*.

Hornyak (619) Americanized spelling of Czech **Horňák** or Slovak **Horniak** (see HORNAK).

Horovitz (190) Jewish (Ashkenazic): variant of HOROWITZ.
GIVEN NAMES Jewish 20%. *Zvi* (3), *Doron* (2), *Arieh*, *Arye*, *Avrohom*, *Bracha*, *Devorah*, *Hadar*, *Hillel*, *Merav*, *Miriam*, *Moshe*.

Horowitz (4739) Jewish (Ashkenazic): habitational name from Hořovice in central Bohemia, now in the Czech Republic, which is named with a short form of a personal name formed with *Hoř*, as for example *Hořimir*, *Hořislav*.
GIVEN NAMES Jewish 10%. *Sol* (12), *Gershon* (6), *Hyman* (6), *Naftali* (6), *Mayer* (5), *Baruch* (4), *Meyer* (4), *Miriam* (4), *Moshe* (4), *Shlomo* (4), *Yaakov* (4), *Avram* (3).

Horr (273) German (**Hörr**): unexplained; possibly a derivative of Middle High German *hor* 'dirt' (see HOERR).

Horrall (123) English: variant of HORRELL.

Horrell (835) English (mainly Devon): unexplained.

Horrigan (746) Irish: **1.** reduced Anglicized form of Gaelic **Ó hAnradháin** (see HANRAHAN). **2.** (in counties Cork and Kerry) variant of HORGAN.
GIVEN NAMES Irish 6%. *Aileen*, *Brendan*, *Kieran*, *Patrick Sean*.

Horrocks (837) English (chiefly Lancashire): habitational name from Great or Little Horrocks in Greater Manchester, so named from the plural of the dialect term *hurrock* 'heaped-up pile of loose stones or rubbish' (of uncertain origin).

Horry (101) English: variant of HURRY.

Horsburgh (116) Scottish: according to Black, from 'the old ten pound land of the same name' in Innerleithen parish, Peeblesshire.
GIVEN NAME Scottish 4%. *Iain*.

Horsch (364) German (also **Hörsch**): topographic name from a dialect form of Middle High German *horst*, *hurst* 'under-

growth', 'brushwood', of Slavic origin in eastern regions, e.g. the place name Horscha (Lausitz).
GIVEN NAMES German 5%. *Klaus* (2), *Dieter*, *Kurt*, *Siegmar*, *Volker*.

Horseman (320) English: variant spelling of HORSMAN.

Horsey (455) English: habitational name from places in Norfolk, Somerset, and Sussex, so named from Old English *hors* 'horse' (perhaps a byname) + *ēg* 'island', 'low-lying land'.

Horsfall (370) English (Yorkshire): habitational name from Horsefall in West Yorkshire, so named from Old English *hors* 'horse' (perhaps a byname) + *fall* 'clearing', 'place where the trees have been felled' (from *fellan* 'to fell', causative of *feallan* 'to fall').

Horsfield (127) English (Yorkshire and Lancashire): either a variant of HORSFALL, or else a habitational name from an unidentified place named with Old English *hors* 'horse' (perhaps a byname) + *feld* 'pasture', 'open country'.

Horsford (121) English: habitational name from places so named, for example in East Worlington, Devon, Norfolk, and West Yorkshire. The two last are named from Old English *hors* 'horse' + *ford* 'ford', because they lay at fords that could only be crossed on horseback.
GIVEN NAME Jewish 4%. *Miriam* (2).

Horsley (2088) English: habitational name from any of various places, for example in Derbyshire, Gloucestershire, Northumberland, Staffordshire, and Surrey, so named from Old English *hors* 'horse' + *lēah* 'wood', 'clearing'. The reference is probably to a place where horses were put out to pasture. The surname is widespread in north-central England.

Horsman (646) English (Yorkshire): occupational name for a stable worker, from Old English *hors* 'horse' + *mann* 'man'. It is unlikely to have been a nickname for a skilled rider, for in the Middle Ages the maintenance and use of a horse was far beyond the means of the mass of common people.

Horst (3205) North German and Dutch: **1.** topographic name from Middle Low German *hurst*, Middle Dutch *horst* 'undergrowth', 'brushwood', 'wild place'. More specifically, the term was also used to denote a crow's or similar large bird's nest, a raised area in surrounding marshland, or an area of uncleared woodland, all of which meanings could have contributed to the surname. **2.** habitational name from any of numerous places named with this word.
GIVEN NAMES German 4%. *Kurt* (7), *Otto* (4), *Phares* (3), *Alois*, *Armin*, *Fritz*, *Hans*, *Inge*, *Manfred*, *Monika*, *Reinhold*.

Horstman (1410) **1.** Dutch: topographic name, a variant of HORST, with the addition of *man* 'man'. **2.** Altered spelling of the German cognate HORSTMANN.

Horstmann (550) North German: topographic name, a variant of HORST, with the addition of Middle German *man* 'man'.
GIVEN NAMES German 6%. *Theodor* (2), *Bernhard*, *Dieter*, *Fritz*, *Heinz*, *Kurt*, *Otto*, *Uwe*.

Horstmeyer (121) North German: distinguishing nickname for a tenant farmer (see MEYER) who lived on wild overgrown land (see HORST).
GIVEN NAME Scandinavian 4%. *Thora*.

Hort (153) **1.** South German and Austrian: variant of HARDT 1. **2.** English: variant of HART 1.

Horta (374) Catalan and Portuguese: from *horta* 'garden' (Latin *hortus*), hence a topographic name for someone who lived by an enclosed garden or a metonymic occupational name for a gardener.
GIVEN NAMES Spanish 51%. *Jose* (14), *Juan* (7), *Carlos* (6), *Roberto* (5), *Jesus* (4), *Manuel* (4), *Miguel* (4), *Armando* (3), *Arturo* (3), *Orlando* (3), *Pablo* (3), *Ricardo* (3).

Horten (112) English: variant spelling of HORTON.

Horter (158) **1.** Southern German (mainly Austria): variant of HARTER 1. **2.** German (Bavaria; **Hörter**): occupational name, a variant of HERDER 1. **3.** Dutch (**de Horter**): nickname from an agent derivative of Middle Dutch *horten*, *hurten* 'to jolt, knock, or jerk' + the definite article *de* 'the'.

Horth (126) German: **1.** nickname from Middle High German *hort* 'treasure', 'wealth'. **2.** (**Hörth**): probably a habitational name from a place such as Hürth near Cologne or Hördt in the Palatinate. **3.** variant of HARTH 1.

Hortin (137) English: variant of HORTON.

Hortman (338) **1.** German (**Hortmann**): variant of HORT 1. **2.** possibly also a variant spelling of HARTMANN.

Horton (28501) English: habitational name from any of the various places so called. The majority, with examples in at least fourteen counties, are named from Old English *horh* 'mud', 'slime' or *horn* 'dirt' + *tūn* 'enclosure', 'settlement'. One in southern Gloucestershire, however, is named from Old English *heorot* 'hart' + *dūn* 'hill'.

Horvat (679) **1.** Croatian (northern and eastern Croatia): ethnic name for a Croat (see HORVATH). In particular, this term was used to denote Croatian refugees from the Ottoman Empire who settled in the eastern and northern parts of Croatia. When Hungarian officials could not spell the Slavic name of such refugees, they would simply write them down as *Horvat(h)* 'Croatian'. **Horvat** is now the most frequent surname in Croatia. **2.** Slovenian: nickname for someone from Croatia, in particular a refugee from the Ottoman Empire in the 15th and 16th centuries, from

an old spelling of *Hrvat*, ethnic name for a Croat. The surname **Horvat**, together with its variant **Hrovat**, is the second most frequent surname in Slovenia. **3.** Hungarian (**Horvát**) and Jewish (from Hungary): ethnic name for a Croat (see HORVATH).
GIVEN NAMES South Slavic 5%. *Bozidar* (3), *Branko* (2), *Alojz, Davor, Drago, Drazen, Marko, Vinko, Zarko.*

Horvath (5888) Hungarian (**Horváth**) and Jewish (from Hungary): ethnic name for a Croat, from Hungarian *Horvát* (Croatian *Hrvat*). Compare HORVAT. Additionally, this is found as a nickname for a Hungarian who lived in Croatia, who had dealings with Croatia, or who often traveled there. The Croats were one of the Slavic peoples who settled in what was then the Roman province of Pannonia in the 7th century AD. From 1091 to 1526 Croatia was under Hungarian rule. As a Jewish name, this indicates provenance from Croatia.
GIVEN NAMES Hungarian 7%. *Laszlo* (24), *Zoltan* (18), *Tibor* (16), *Sandor* (15), *Geza* (11), *Bela* (8), *Lajos* (8), *Kalman* (7), *Imre* (6), *Istvan* (6), *Attila* (5), *Gyula* (5).

Horvitz (280) Jewish (Ashkenazic): variant of HOROWITZ.
GIVEN NAMES Jewish 8%. *Dvora, Ephraim, Hava, Hyman, Isadore, Meir.*

Horwath (595) Hungarian and Jewish (from Hungary): variant spelling of HORVATH.

Horwedel (109) German: topographic name for someone who lived by a swampy ford, from *hor* 'dirt' + *wede* 'woods'.

Horwich (148) English: habitational name from Horwich in Lancashire, so named from Old English *hār* 'gray' + *wice* 'wych elm'.

Horwitz (1857) Jewish (Ashkenazic): variant of HOROWITZ.
GIVEN NAMES Jewish 5%. *Sol* (4), *Hyman* (2), *Isadore* (2), *Avi, Channa, Elihu, Emanuel, Mandel, Mayer, Meyer, Miriam, Yetta.*

Horwood (112) English: habitational name from Great and Little Horwood in Buckinghamshire, named from Old English *horu* 'dirty', 'muddy' + *wudu* 'wood', or from Horwood in Devon, which may be of the same derivation or may have Old English *hār* 'gray' as the first element.

Hosack (361) **1.** Scottish: unexplained; possibly a habitational name from an unidentified place. **2.** Americanized form of Czech and Slovak **Husák** (see HUSAK).

Hosang (114) German: of uncertain origin; possibly a nickname for a pious person from Middle High German *hōch sanc* 'chanting', 'songs of praise'.

Hosbach (118) German: habitational name from Hosbach near Sontra.
GIVEN NAME German 5%. *Gunter.*

Hosch (603) German (**Hösch**): **1.** (North German): nickname from a reduced form of Middle Low German *hovesch* 'courtly', a derivative of *hof* 'court' (see HOFF). **2.** (South German): probably a nickname

for a scornful person, from Middle High German *hoschen* 'to mock', *hosche* 'mockery'. **3.** (eastern German, of Slavic origin): from a pet form of the personal name *Johannes* (see JOHANN, JOHN).

Hose (624) **1.** English: topographic name from Middle English *hose, huse* 'brambles', 'thorns'. **2.** English: habitational name from a place in Leicestershire, named from Old English *hōs*, plural of *hōh* 'spur of land' (literally 'heel'), or a topographic name with the same meaning. **3.** English and German: metonymic occupational name from Middle English, Middle Low and High German *hose* 'hose', 'leggings', denoting a knitter or seller of hose, or a nickname for someone who habitually wore noticeble legwear. **4.** German (Upper Saxony): apparently from a Czech personal name, *Hos*, a reduced form of *Johannes* (see JOHN).

Hosea (547) English: from the Biblical personal name *Hosea*.

Hosein (200) Muslim: variant of HUSAIN.
GIVEN NAMES Muslim 55%. *Ali* (2), *Ayub* (2), *Azim* (2), *Jamal* (2), *Khalid* (2), *Khalil* (2), *Mohamed* (2), *Shiraz* (2), *Zul* (2), *Aftab, Ahamad, Aleem.*

Hosek (336) Czech (**Hošek**): from a pet form of the personal name *Hodislav*.

Hoselton (248) Probably an altered form of HAZELTINE.

Hosey (1138) Irish: variant of HUSSEY.

Hosfeld (103) **1.** German: of uncertain origin; possibly a habitational name from a place named Hosenfeld near Fulda (Hesse), or a topographic name (**Hossfeld**), a derivative of *Hose* 'hose', denoting a field shaped like a leg or a pair of legs (see HOSE). **2.** Possibly an altered spelling of English HORSFIELD.

Hosfield (106) English: variant of **Horsefield**, a topographic or occupational name for someone who lived or worked at an enclosure for horses, from Old English *hors* 'horse' + *falod* 'enclosure', or a variant of the habitational name HORSFALL.

Hosford (900) English: variant of HORSFORD. The surname was taken to Ireland in the 17th century.

Hoshaw (146) Origin unidentified. **1.** It is said to be an altered form of the Alsatian name **Hoschar**, which is probably a nickname from German *Hoscher* 'mocker' (see HOSCH). **2.** Alternatively, it may be an altered spelling of Slavic *Hascha*, a short form of JOHANNES, popular in Saxony, Silesia, and Bohemia.

Hoshino (195) Japanese: 'star field'; habitational name adopted by a family of Shintō priests of the Atsuta Shrine in Owari (now part of Aichi prefecture). Other families descend from the TAIRA and MINAMOTO clans. The name is also found in the Ryūkyū Islands.
GIVEN NAMES Japanese 66%. *Kenji* (3), *Osamu* (3), *Akio* (2), *Hiroaki* (2), *Itsuki* (2),

Kazunari (2), *Mutsuo* (2), *Saburo* (2), *Takashi* (2), *Takayuki* (2), *Takeshi* (2), *Yoko* (2).

Hosick (189) **1.** Scottish: variant of HOSACK, now found chiefly in northern Ireland. **2.** Possibly an altered spelling of Czech **Hošik**, a nickname from a diminutive of *hoch* 'boy'.

Hosie (177) Scottish form of Irish HUSSEY.

Hosier (818) English: occupational name for a maker or seller of leggings, from an agent derivative of Middle English *hose* (Old English *hosa*). *Hose* was the regular term for garments worn on the legs until the 18th century.

Hosken (107) English: variant spelling of HOSKIN.

Hoskin (702) English: from the Middle English personal name *Osekin*, a pet form of the various personal names with an Old English first element *ōs* 'god'. Compare, for example, OSBORN, OSGOOD, and OSMOND, or its Old Norse cognate *ás*. For the inorganic initial *H-*, compare HERRICK.

Hosking (641) English: variant of HOSKIN.

Hoskins (7547) **1.** English: patronymic from HOSKIN. **2.** Variant of Dutch **Hosekin**, a metonymic occupational name for a maker or seller of hose (garments for the legs), from Middle Low German *hose* 'hose'.

Hoskinson (847) English: patronymic from HOSKIN.

Hosler (1006) **1.** German (**Hösler**): occupational name for a maker of hose (garments for the legs), from Middle High German *hose* (see HOSE 3) + the agent suffix *-r*. **2.** German (**Hösler**): habitational name for someone from Hösel near Düsseldorf. **3.** English: occupational name for a fowler, a variant of OSLER, or for an innkeeper, a reduced form of OSTLER. In both cases, the initial *H-* is inorganic.

Hosley (422) Americanized spelling of Swiss German **Hösli** or **Hösly**, or Swabian **Hösle**, metonymic occupational name for a maker of hose or leggings (see HOSE 3), from a diminutive of Middle High German *hose*.

Hosman (343) German (**Hosmann**): possibly a variant of HOSE 3, in eastern Germany related to the Czech personal name *Hos*.

Hosmer (1024) English: variant of OSMER with an inorganic initial *H-*.

Hosner (161) German (**Hosner, Hösner**): occupational name for a knitter of hose (garments for the legs), from the plural form of Middle High German *hose* + the agent suffix *-er* (see HOSE 3).

Hosp (103) German: from Latin argot *hospes*, originally 'innkeeper', later used in the sense 'strange guy', 'odd bird'.

Hospodar (113) Czech (**hospodář**): status name from *hospodář* 'farmer', 'husbandman'.

Hoss (827) German (**Höss**): variant of HESS.

Hossack (129) **1.** Scottish: variant of HOSACK. **2.** Germanized form of Czech **Husák** (see HUSAK).

Hossain (640) Muslim: variant of HUSAIN.
GIVEN NAMES Muslim 88%. *Mohammed* (66), *Mohammad* (40), *Anwar* (12), *Syed* (12), *Zakir* (12), *Kazi* (9), *Abul* (5), *Akram* (5), *Showkat* (5), *Ahmed* (4), *Akhtar* (4), *Amir* (4).

Hosseini (238) Muslim: from an Arabic surname indicating descent from or association with HUSAIN.
GIVEN NAMES Muslim 77%. *Mohammad* (9), *Hossein* (6), *Hamid* (5), *Seyed* (4), *Ahmad* (3), *Ali* (3), *Mehdi* (3), *Mohsen* (3), *Mojtaba* (3), *Saeed* (3), *Bahram* (2), *Kamal* (2).

Hossfeld (127) German: variant of HOSFELD.

Hossler (288) South German (**Hössler**): variant of *Hässler*, a form of HASSLER 1.

Host (533) **1.** English: occupational name for an innkeeper, from Middle English, Old French *(h)oste* 'host', 'guest'. **2.** Danish (**Høst**): nickname from *høst* 'harvest', 'autumn' (see HERBST). **3.** French: from Old French *ost* 'army', hence an occupational name for a soldier. **4.** Dutch: from the Germanic personal name *Austa*, meaning 'east'. **5.** German: habitational name from either of two places called Host, near Koblenz and near Bitburg.

Hoster (211) **1.** English: occupational name for a maker or seller of hoods, from Middle English *hodestre*, a feminine form of HODDER. **2.** German (also **Höster**): habitational name for someone from either of two places called Host (see HOST 5).

Hosterman (286) German (**Hostermann**): elaborated form of HOSTER 2.

Hostetler (3256) Swiss German: variant of HOCHSTETLER.

Hostetter (1853) Swiss German: variant of HOCHSTETLER without the diminutive infix *-l-*.

Hostettler (293) Variant of Swiss German HOCHSTETLER.
GIVEN NAMES German 8%. *Phares* (2), *Bernhard*, *Hans*, *Kurt*, *Niklaus*, *Otto*.

Hostler (359) English: occupational name for the keeper of an inn or hostelry, a variant of OSTLER.

Hoston (116) English: probably a variant of northern Irish HOUSTON.

Hostutler (190) Variant of Swiss German HOCHSTETLER.

Hotaling (1022) Americanized spelling of Dutch **Hoogteijling**, an indirect occupational name for a productive farmer, from *hoogh* 'high' + *teling* 'cultivation', 'breeding'.

Hotard (409) French: unexplained. This name occurs almost exclusively in LA.

GIVEN NAMES French 4%. *Armand* (3), *Camille*, *Emile*.

Hotchkin (182) English: from a pet form of HODGE.

Hotchkiss (2296) English: patronymic from *Hodgkin*, a pet form of HODGE.

Hotelling (114) Dutch: see HOTALING.

Hoth (413) North German form of HUTH 1.

Hotham (131) English (Yorkshire): habitational name from Hotham in the East Riding of Yorkshire, named from a dative plural *hōdum* of an Old English *hōd* 'shelter'.

Hotop (120) Variant spelling of German HOTOPP.

Hotopp (96) North German: nickname from Middle Low German *hō* 'high', 'tall' + *top* 'braid' or 'head'.
GIVEN NAMES German 6%. *Kurt*, *Manfred*.

Hott (905) **1.** North German: possibly a nickname or metonymic occupational name from Middle Low German *hotte* 'coagulated milk'. **2.** South German: probably from a Germanic personal name (see HOTTMAN).

Hotte (130) **1.** German (**Hötte**): variant of **Hütte** (see HUETT 1) or a variant of HOTT. **2.** French: from French *hotte*, denoting a type of basket carried on the back, hence a nickname or metonymic occupational name for someone who carried or made these.
FOREBEARS An immigrant from Normandy, recorded as Hot and Hotte, is documented in Quebec city in 1666.
GIVEN NAMES French 18%. *Lucien* (3), *Adelard*, *Adrien*, *Jacques*, *Marcel*, *Pierrette*.

Hottel (271) German: habitational name from Hotteln near Hildesheim.

Hottenstein (259) German: topographic name from an uncertain element + Middle High German *stein* 'stone'.

Hottinger (474) German: habitational name for someone from Hotting in Bavaria or Hottingen near Waldshut in Baden.

Hottle (348) Americanized spelling of German HOTTEL.

Hottman (154) German (**Hottmann**): **1.** from a Germanic personal name formed from Germanic *hut* 'protection', 'helmet' (compare German *Hut* 'hat'). **2.** variant of HOTT.

Hotvedt (107) Norwegian: unexplained.

Hotz (852) **1.** German: from a Germanic personal name, *Hugizo* or *Huz o*, pet forms of a compound name formed with *hug-* as the first element (see, for example, HUBERT, HUGH). **2.** South German: possibly a nickname from Middle High German *hotzen* 'to run swiftly'.

Hotze (147) German: variant of HOTZ.

Hou (686) Chinese 侯: from a Chinese word denoting a feudal rank, often translated into English as 'marquis'. One known source of the surname is Marquis Hou Min

of the state of Jin in the Spring and Autumn period (722–481 BC).
GIVEN NAMES Chinese 40%. *Gang* (4), *Hong* (4), *Ching* (3), *Ping* (3), *Cheng* (2), *Cheng Hua* (2), *Feng* (2), *Fong* (2), *Lei* (2), *Ming* (2), *Ning* (2), *Shuling* (2).

Houchen (231) English: variant of HOUCHIN.

Houchens (541) English: patronymic from HOUCHEN.

Houchin (1007) Variant spelling under French influence of English HUTCHEON, a pet form of HUGH.

Houchins (778) English: patronymic from HOUCHIN.

Houck (5142) Dutch, Frisian, and North German: **1.** nickname from Middle Dutch *houck*, a marine fish, or from Middle Dutch *hoec*, *houck* 'buck'. **2.** variant of HOEK.

Houde (718) **1.** French: from the personal name *Heude*, *Houde*, derived from the Germanic name *Hildo* (see HILDEBRAND). **2.** French (**Houdé**): from the personal name *Oudet*, a Frenchified form of the Germanic name *Odo*, derived from the element *aud* 'wealth'.
FOREBEARS Bearers of the name from the Perche region of France are documented in 1665 in Quebec city. Recorded secondary surnames include BELLEFEUILLE, DESROCHERS, and Desruisseaux.
GIVEN NAMES French 17%. *Andre* (3), *Armand* (3), *Gilles* (3), *Normand* (3), *Adrien* (2), *Gaston* (2), *Ghyslaine* (2), *Herve* (2), *Jacques* (2), *Marcel* (2), *Michel* (2), *Yvan* (2).

Houdek (588) Czech: from a diminutive of HUDEC.

Houdeshell (158) Americanized form of Swiss German **Haudenschild** (see HAUSCHILD).

Houdyshell (113) Americanized form of Swiss German **Haudenschild** (see HAUSCHILD).

Houfek (128) Czech: nickname from *houfek* 'crow', 'flock'.

Houff (216) **1.** English: variant of HUFF. **2.** Altered spelling of German HAUFF.

Houg (195) **1.** Dutch: variant spelling of HOUGE 1. **2.** Norwegian: variant spelling of HAUG. **3.** Altered spelling of German HAUG.
GIVEN NAMES German 5%. *Kurt*, *Otto*.

Houge (276) **1.** Dutch: from the Germanic personal name *Hugo* (see HUGH). **2.** Norwegian: variant spelling of HAUGE.

Hougen (184) **1.** Dutch: patronymic from HOUGE. **2.** Norwegian: variant spelling of HAUGEN.
GIVEN NAMES Scandinavian 7%. *Erik*, *Oddvar*, *Tor*.

Hough (5916) **1.** English: habitational name from any of various places, for example in Cheshire and Derbyshire, so named from Old English *hōh* 'spur of a hill' (literally 'heel'). This widespread surname is especially common in Lancashire. **2.** Irish (County Limerick): variant of HAUGH 1.

Hougham (155) English: habitational name from Hougham, Kent, probably so named from an unattested Old English personal name, *Huhha*, or possibly *hōh* 'spur of a hill' (literally 'heel') + *hām* 'homestead'.

Houghland (161) **1.** Americanized spelling of Norwegian HAUGLAND. **2.** English: apparently a habitational name from a lost or unidentified place, though the existence of a variant, **Houghlan**, suggests that there may be a different origin.

Houghtaling (857) Dutch: see HOTALING.

Houghton (4654) English: habitational name from any of the various places so called. The majority, with examples in at least fourteen counties, get the name from Old English *hōh* 'ridge', 'spur' (literally 'heel') + *tūn* 'enclosure', 'settlement'. Haughton in Nottinghamshire also has this origin, and may have contributed to the surname. A smaller group of Houghtons, with examples in Lancashire and South Yorkshire, have as their first element Old English *halh* 'nook', 'recess'. In the case of isolated examples in Devon and East Yorkshire, the first elements appear to be unattested Old English personal names or bynames, of which the forms approximate to *Huhha* and *Hofa* respectively, but the meanings are unknown.

Hougland (362) Respelling of Norwegian HAUGLAND.

Houk (2227) Dutch (**de Houk**): variant of HOUCK 1, with the definite article, *de*.

Houlahan (132) Irish: variant spelling of HOULIHAN.

GIVEN NAME Irish 11%. *Padraig*.

Houle (3108) **1.** French: from a reduced form of the Germanic personal name *Hildo* (see HILDEBRAND, HOUDE). **2.** French: habitational name from any of several places in Normandy called La Houle or Les Houles, named in Old French with the singular or plural of *houle* 'cave'. **3.** English: variant of HOLE.

GIVEN NAMES French 13%. *Armand* (18), *Andre* (14), *Lucien* (10), *Normand* (9), *Fernand* (6), *Alcide* (5), *Emile* (5), *Marcel* (4), *Adrien* (2), *Alain* (2), *Alexandre* (2), *Benoit* (2).

Houlette (100) French: **1.** habitational name from either of two places in Normandy called Houlettes, named with a diminutive of *houle* 'cave' (see HOULE 2). **2.** from a diminutive of *houe* 'hoe', a metonymic occupational name for an agricultural worker or someone who made or sold hoes.

Houlihan (1671) Irish: Anglicized form of Gaelic **Ó hUallacháin** 'descendant of *Uallachán*', a personal name from a diminutive of *úallach* 'proud', 'arrogant'.

GIVEN NAMES Irish 6%. *Brendan* (2), *Aileen*.

Hoult (141) English: variant of HOLT.

Houlton (195) English: variant of HOLTON.

Hounsell (103) English (Dorset): unexplained.

Hounshell (326) **1.** English: variant of HOUNSELL. **2.** Americanized spelling of German **Hauenschild**, a variant of HAUSCHILD.

Houp (226) **1.** Scottish: variant of HOPE. **2.** Possibly also an Americanized spelling of German HAUB.

Houpt (571) Americanized spelling of German HAUPT.

Hourigan (509) Irish: variant of HORGAN.

GIVEN NAMES Irish 4%. *Brendan, Siobhan*.

Hourihan (429) Irish: variant of HANRAHAN.

GIVEN NAME Irish 6%. *Declan*.

Housand (144) Probably of Scottish origin, but unexplained. The surname was never common in Scotland and has now died out there.

Housden (251) English: probably a habitational name from Ousden in Suffolk, so named from Old English *ūf* 'owl' + *denu* 'valley'.

House (14628) **1.** English (southwestern): from Middle English *hous* 'house' (Old English *hūs*). In the Middle Ages the majority of the population lived in cottages or huts rather than houses, and in most cases this name probably indicates someone who had some connection with the largest and most important building in a settlement, either a religious house or simply the local manor house. In some cases it may be a status name for a householder, someone who owned his own dwelling as opposed to being a tenant, but more often it is an occupational name for a servant who worked in such a house, in particular a steward who managed one. **2.** English: respelling of HOWES. **3.** Translation of German HAUS.

Houseal (194) Variant of HOUSEL.

Householder (1453) Americanized form of German HAUSHALTER.

Houseknecht (410) Partly Americanized form of German **Hausknecht**, a status name from Middle High German *hūskneht* 'steward of a house'.

Housel (565) **1.** French (Lorraine): French spelling of German **Häusel**, a topographic name meaning 'small house', a diminutive of HAUS. **2.** Americanized spelling of German *Hausel*, a variant of HAUSCH, from the Germanic personal name *Husuald(us)*, composed of *hūs* 'house' + *walt* 'rule'.

Houseman (1158) **1.** English: occupational name for a servant who worked at a great house, or status name for a householder (see HOUSE). **2.** Americanized form of German HAUSMANN.

Housen (119) Americanized spelling of German HAUSEN.

Houser (7721) **1.** English: variant of HOUSE 1. **2.** Americanized spelling of German HAUSER.

Houseworth (311) Americanized form of HAUSWIRTH.

Housewright (342) Possibly an Americanized form of HAUSWIRTH.

Housey (141) Possibly an altered spelling of German HAUSE, written thus to preserve the second syllable.

GIVEN NAME French 4%. *Eugenie*.

Housh (367) Possibly an Americanized spelling of German HAUSCH.

Housholder (190) Americanized form of German HAUSHALTER.

Houska (360) Czech: metonymic occupational name for a baker, from *houska* 'bread roll' (literally 'gosling').

Housler (115) Scottish: unexplained.

Housley (1232) English (mainly South Yorkshire): habitational name from Housley Hall in Ecclesfield, South Yorkshire, a compound of Old English *hūs* 'house' + *lēah* 'wood', 'clearing'.

Housman (745) **1.** English: occupational name for a servant who worked at a great house, or status name for a householder (see HOUSE). **2.** Americanized form of German HAUSMANN.

Houston (16999) Northern Irish: **1.** habitational name from a place near Glasgow, Scotland, named with the genitive case of the medieval personal name HUGH + Middle English *tune*, *toun* 'settlement', 'village' (Old English *tūn* 'enclosure', 'settlement'). The landlord in question is a certain Hugo de Paduinan, who held the place *c*.1160. The Scottish surname is common in Ulster. **2.** Anglicized form of Gaelic **Mac Uisdein**, **Mac Uistein** (see MCCUTCHEON).

FOREBEARS In 1836 the newly founded city of Houston, TX, was named in honor of Sam Houston (1793–1836), soldier and statesman. His ancestors were Ulster Scots who had emigrated to Philadelphia earlier in the 18th century. As commander in chief of the Texan army he achieved Texan independence from Mexico by routing the army of the Mexican general Santa Ana.

Housworth (117) Americanized form of German HAUSWIRTH.

Hout (418) Dutch: topographic name for someone who lived in or by a wood or copse, Middle Dutch *hout*.

Houtchens (170) English: variant spelling of HOUCHENS.

Houtman (207) Dutch: variant of HOUT.

GIVEN NAMES Dutch 5%. *Dirk* (2), *Gerben, Hessel*.

Houts (531) **1.** Dutch (**van Houts**): variant of HOUT. **2.** Possibly also an altered spelling of German **Hautz** (see HOUTZ).

Houtz (798) German: **1.** Probably an altered spelling of **Hautz**, an argot word (thieves' slang) in Bavaria and Austria for a peasant farmer. **2.** from a short form of a Germanic personal name composed with *hug* 'mind' (see HUGO).

Houx (157) French: topographic name from *houx* 'holly', or a habitational name from places named with this word, for example in the Belgian province of Namur and the French department of Eure-et-Loir.
GIVEN NAME French 4%. *Adrien.*

Houy (173) French: habitational name from any of various places so named in Nord, or from Huy in the Belgian province of Liège. FOREBEARS Bearers of this name from the Orléanais region of France are recorded in Cap-Santé, Quebec, in 1689, with the secondary surname ST. LAURENT.

Houze (292) **1.** Possibly an Americanized spelling of German HAUSE. **2.** French (**Houzé**): metonymic occupational name for a maker or seller of boots and shoes or a nickname for someone noted for his footwear, from Old French *ho(u)se*, *heuse* 'boot', 'shoe'.

Hovan (258) **1.** Irish: unexplained. **2.** Americanized spelling of Czech and Slovak **Chovan**, a variant of *Chovanec* (see HOVANEC).

Hovanec (353) Americanized spelling of Czech and Slovak **Chovanec**, from *schovanec* 'fosterchild'. This name occurs mainly in PA and OH.

Hovanesian (66) Armenian: variant of **Ohanesian**.

Hovater (202) Variant of HOVATTER.

Hovatter (305) Probably of Dutch or North German origin, perhaps a status name for a person of high rank in a community, from *hoch* + *vater* 'father', 'senior person' (see VATER).

Hovda (179) Norwegian: habitational name from any of several farmsteads, so named from the dative singular of Old Norse *hófði* 'rounded peak', from *hǫfuð* 'head'.

Hovde (557) Norwegian: variant of HOVDA.

Hovden (159) Norwegian: variant of HOVDA, from the definite singular form.

Hove (629) **1.** North German and Dutch: topographic name from the plural of *hof* 'manor farm', 'court', 'garden', or a habitational name from places named with this word, for example in the Belgian provinces of Antwerp and Hainault. **2.** Norwegian: habitational name from any of numerous farmsteads named Hove, from the dative singular of Old Norse *hof* 'pagan temple', 'place of worship'.
GIVEN NAME Scandinavian 4%. *Helmer.*

Hovel (102) Scottish and English: variant of HAVILL.

Hoveland (130) Americanized spelling of Norwegian HOVLAND.

Hovell (128) English: variant of HAVILL.

Hoven (463) Dutch and North German: variant of HOVE.

Hover (931) **1.** Dutch: from a dialect variant of *haver* 'oats', either an occupational name for someone who grew or sold oats, or a habitational name (**van Haver**), from any of several minor places named with this word.

2. English: possibly a variant of OVER, with the addition of an inorganic *H-*.

Hovermale (283) Americanized spelling of North German or Dutch **Havermehl**, metonymic occupational name for a producer or seller of oatmeal (compare German HABERMEHL).

Hoverman (143) **1.** Americanized form of German **Havermann**, a variant of HABERMANN. **2.** German (**Hövermann**): habitational name for someone from either of two places called Höver, one near Hannover, the other near Ülzen.
GIVEN NAMES German 4%. *Aloysius, Gunther.*

Hoverson (211) Americanized form of Norwegian HALVORSON.

Hoversten (153) Probably an Americanized spelling of Norwegian **Håvastein**, a habitational name from a farmstead in Rogaland named Håvastein, from Old Norse as *Hávisteinn*, from *hár* 'high' + *steinn* 'stone', indicating a tall stone, such as a standing stone.
GIVEN NAMES Scandinavian 4%. *Erik, Knut.*

Hovet (132) Norwegian: unexplained.

Hovey (2130) **1.** Welsh: from the personal name *Hofa* or *Hwfa*, of unexplained origin. **2.** Americanized form of Dutch HOVE.

Hovick (110) Americanized spelling of Norwegian **Hovik**.

Hoving (143) **1.** Dutch: from a pet form of the Germanic personal name *Ovo*. **2.** Swedish: apparently an ornamental name formed from the place-name element *hov-*, with several different meanings (including 'pagan temple' and 'hill') + the suffix *-ing* (see ARNING).
GIVEN NAMES Dutch 5%; Scandinavian 4%. *Dirk, Gerrit, Willem; Hilmer, Thor.*

Hovious (186) Probably an American variant of Dutch HOVIS.

Hovis (1306) Latinized form of Dutch HOF or HOVE.

Hovland (952) Norwegian: habitational name from any of numerous farmsteads, named in Old Norse as *Hofland*, from *hof* 'pagan temple', 'place of worship' + *land* '(piece of) land'.
GIVEN NAMES Scandinavian 5%. *Gunhild* (2), *Selmer* (2), *Carsten, Hjalmer, Iver, Juel, Ottar, Thorleif.*

Hovorka (274) Czech: nickname for a talkative person, *hovorka*, from *hovor* 'talk', 'conversation'.

Hovsepian (287) Armenian: patronymic from the personal name *Hovsep*, classical Armenian *Yovsēp* (see JOSEPH).
GIVEN NAMES Armenian 31%. *Armen* (3), *Vartkes* (3), *Aram* (2), *Ohan* (2), *Ara, Arsen, Berge, Berj, Dickran, Ervand, Gagik, Garo.*

How (291) English: variant spelling of HOWE 1 and 2.

Howald (300) German: habitational name from any of several places so named, for example in Westphalia and Baden, or a

topographic name from Middle High German *hō* 'high' + *wald* 'forest'. This surname is also established in France.

Howard (84046) **1.** English: from the Norman personal name *Huard, Heward*, composed of the Germanic elements *hug* 'heart', 'mind', 'spirit' + *hard* 'hardy', 'brave', 'strong'. **2.** English: from the Anglo-Scandinavian personal name *Hāward*, composed of the Old Norse elements *há* 'high' + *varðr* 'guardian', 'warden'. **3.** English: variant of EWART 2. **4.** Irish: see FOGARTY. **5.** Irish (County Clare) surname adopted as an equivalent of Gaelic **Ó hÍomhair**, which was formerly Anglicized as **O'Hure**.
FOREBEARS The house of Howard, the leading family of the English Roman Catholic nobility, was founded by Sir William Howard or Haward of Norfolk (died 1308). The family acquired the dukedom of Norfolk by marriage. The first Duke of Norfolk of the Howard line was created Earl Marshal of England by Richard III in 1483, and this office has been held by his succeeding male heirs to the present day. They also hold the Earldoms of Suffolk, Berkshire, Carlisle, and Effingham. Henry VIII's fifth queen, Catherine Howard (?1520–42), was a niece of Thomas Howard, 3rd Duke of Norfolk.

Howarth (1564) English (chiefly south Lancashire): **1.** variant spelling of HAWORTH. **2.** habitational name from Howarth in the parish of Rochdale, Lancashire, apparently so called from Old English *hōh* 'mound' + *worð* 'enclosure'. However, if the 13th-century form *Halwerdeword* refers to this place, the first element may instead be Middle English *halleward* 'keeper of a hall' or represent a personal name such as Old English *Æðelweard* or Old Norse *Hallvarðr*.

Howat (213) Scottish: variant of HEWITT 1.

Howatt (233) Scottish: variant of HEWITT 1.

Howcroft (155) English (mainly south Lancashire): habitational name from some place named as a smallholding (see CROFT) on the spur of a hill (see HUFF), e.g. Howcroft in Rimington, West Yorkshire.

Howd (140) Americanized form of Norwegian **Hovd**, a habitational name from any of several farmsteads so named (see HOVDA).

Howden (394) **1.** Scottish: habitational name from a place so called near Kelso on the border with England. Early forms include *Hadden, Hauden*, and *Halden*; the place name is probably from Old English *halh* 'nook', 'recess' + *denu* 'valley'. **2.** English: habitational name from a place in East Yorkshire, so named from Old Norse *hǫfuð* 'head' (replacing Old English *hēafod*) + Old English *denu* 'valley'; the first element may have been used in the sense 'principal', 'top', or 'end'. **3.** Americanized form of Norwegian HOVDEN.

Howdeshell (158) Americanized form of Swiss German **Haudenschild** (see HAUSCHILD).

Howdyshell (261) Americanized form of Swiss German **Haudenschild** (see HAUSCHILD).

Howe (17043) **1.** English: topographic name for someone who lived by a small hill or a man-made mound or barrow, Middle English *how* (Old Norse *haugr*), or a habitational name from a place named with this word, such as Howe in Norfolk and North Yorkshire. **2.** English: variant of HUGH. **3.** Jewish (American): Americanized form of one or more like-sounding Jewish surnames. **4.** Americanized form of Norwegian HOVE.

Howell (39612) **1.** Welsh: from the personal name *Hywel* 'eminent', popular since the Middle Ages in particular in honor of the great 10th-century law-giving Welsh king. **2.** English: habitational name from Howell in Lincolnshire, so named from an Old English *hugol* 'mound', 'hillock' or *hūne* 'hoarhound'.

Howells (1161) Welsh: from HOWELL, with English patronymic *-s*.

Howen (142) English (Shropshire, Worcestershire): variant of Welsh OWEN.

Howenstine (143) Americanized spelling of German HAUENSTEIN.

Hower (1164) Probably an Americanized spelling of German HAUER. This is a common name in PA.

Howerter (161) Possibly an Americanized spelling of the Swiss family name **Haueter**; unexplained.

Howerton (2478) English: habitational name from an unidentified place.
FOREBEARS Thomas Howerton came from England in about 1663 to former Rappahannock County, VA.

Howery (493) English (County Durham): unexplained.

Howes (2787) English: **1.** topographic name from the plural of Middle English *how* 'barrow' (see HOWE 1) **2.** possibly a variant of HOUSE. **3.** patronymic from HUGH.

Howeth (263) English: apparently a variant spelling of HOWARTH.

Howett (129) English: variant of HEWITT 1.

Howey (886) **1.** Northern English and Scottish: variant of HOWIE. **2.** Irish: variant of HOEY.

Howick (135) English: habitational name from places in Lancashire and Northumberland. The former is named from Old English *hōh* 'spur of a hill' or *hōc* 'hook' + *wīc* 'outlying farm'; the latter probably originally had as its first element Old English *hēah* 'high', but was later influenced by *hōh*.
GIVEN NAME French 4%. *Romain*.

Howie (1557) Northern English and Scottish: from a medieval personal name, a pet form of HUGH.

Howington (766) Probably of English origin, a habitational name from an unidentified place.

Howison (165) Northern English and Scottish: patronymic from HOWIE.

Howitt (284) English (mainly East Midlands) and Scottish: variant of HEWITT 1.

Howk (285) Americanized spelling of German HAUCK.

Howland (3573) **1.** English: variant of HOLLAND 1. **2.** Americanized form of Norwegian HOVLAND.
FOREBEARS Howland was the name of three Quaker brothers, original settlers in Marshfield, MA. They were from Huntingdonshire, England. The eldest, John Howland (*c.*1593–1672) was a passenger on the *Mayflower*, servant to Governor John Carver, who died in the first winter at Plymouth Colony.

Howle (739) English (mainly Staffordshire): habitational name from Howle in Shropshire, named from Old English *hugol* 'hillock', 'mound'.

Howlett (1915) English (mainly East Anglia): variant of HEWLETT.

Howley (1036) **1.** English (chiefly Yorkshire): habitational name from any of various places so called, for example in Cheshire, Gloucestershire, and West Yorkshire. The first is from a lost place in Lower Bebington, named from Old English *hol* 'hollow' + *weg* 'way'; the second is from Old English *hol* + *lēah* 'woodland clearing'; and the last, Howley Hall in Moreley, is from Old English *hōfe* 'ground ivy' + *lēah*. **2.** Irish: Anglicized form of Gaelic **Ó hUallaigh** 'descendant of *Uallach*', a personal name or byname from *uallach* 'proud'.
GIVEN NAMES Irish 4%. *Bridie, Niall*.

Howman (104) English: variant of HUMAN.

Howorth (164) English: variant spelling of HOWARTH.

Howren (136) Origin unidentified.

Howrey (149) Variant spelling of English HOWERY.

Howry (218) Variant spelling of English HOWERY.

Howsare (153) Probably an Americanized spelling of German HAUSER.

Howse (702) English (mainly Oxfordshire and Berkshire): variant of HOWES.

Howser (689) Probably an Americanized spelling of German HAUSER.

Howson (353) English (mainly Yorkshire): patronymic from HUGH.

Howton (489) English: variant of HOUGHTON.

Howze (900) Possibly an Americanized spelling of German HAUSE.

Hoxie (721) Possibly an altered form of English **Hawksey**, a Lancashire name,

which Reaney believes may preserve an old form of **Hawkshaw**, a habitational name from Hawkshaw in Lancashire. Compare HOXWORTH.

Hoxsey (120) See HOXIE.

Hoxsie (144) See HOXIE.

Hoxworth (205) English (Cheshire): variant of HAWKSWORTH.

Hoy (3570) **1.** English (mainly East Anglia): metonymic occupational name for a sailor, from Middle Dutch *hoey* 'cargo ship'. **2.** Northern Irish: variant of HOWEY 2 and HAUGHEY. **3.** Scottish: habitational name from some unidentified minor place named Hoy, or from the Orkney island of Hoy, which was named in Old Norse as *Háey*, from *há* 'high' + *ey* 'island'. **4.** Danish (**Høy**): nickname for a tall person, from *høj* 'high'.

Hoye (770) **1.** English: variant spelling of HOY 1. **2.** Norwegian: habitational name from any of several farmsteads named Høye, from the dative singular of Old Norse *haugr* 'hill', 'mound'.

Hoyer (1409) **1.** North German and Danish: from a Germanic personal name *Hucger*, a compound of *hug* 'heart', 'mind', 'spirit' + *gēr* 'spear'. **2.** Danish (**Høyer, Højer**): variant of HOY 4.
GIVEN NAMES German 6%. *Kurt* (5), *Horst* (4), *Hans* (2), *Helmut* (2), *Johannes* (2), *Dieter, Egon, Ernst, Gerhard, Gerhardt, Heinz, Helmuth*.

Hoyes (136) English: variant of HOY 1.

Hoying (203) German (**Höying**): variant spelling of HÖING (see HOING).

Hoyland (173) **1.** English (South Yorkshire): habitational name from any of various places in South Yorkshire named with Old English *hōh* 'hill spur' + *land* '(cultivated) land'. **2.** English: variant of HOLLAND 1. **3.** Norwegian: habitational name from any of numerous farmsteads, notably in southwestern Norway, named in Old Norse as *Heyland*, from *hey* 'hay' + *land* '(piece of) land'.

Hoyle (3263) **1.** English (Yorkshire and Lancashire): topographic name for someone who lived by a depression or low-lying spot, from Old English *holh* 'hole', 'hollow', 'depression' (see HOLE). **2.** Irish: reduced Anglicized form of Gaelic **Mac Giolla Chomhghaill**, a patronymic from a personal name meaning 'devotee of (Saint) Comhghal' (see McCOOL). Woulfe, however, traces *Hoyle* (as well as **MacIlhoyle** and **McElhill**) to **Mac Giolla Choille** 'son of the lad of the wood', which has sometimes been translated as WOODS.

Hoyler (129) German (Swabian): variant of HEILER.

Hoylman (130) Variant of HOILMAN.

Hoyman (123) German (**Hoymann**): habitational name for someone from Hoya on the Weser river.
GIVEN NAME French 4%. *Julienne*.

Hoyne (169) Irish (Kilkenny): Anglicized

form of Gaelic *Ó hEoghain*, which is generally Anglicized as OWENS.

Hoyos (374) Spanish: habitational name from Hoyos in Cáceres province or one of the three places so named in Ávila province, from *hoyo* 'pit', 'hole', probably from Latin *fovea*.
GIVEN NAMES Spanish 57%. *Luis* (7), *Alberto* (5), *Carlos* (5), *Javier* (4), *Jorge* (4), *Luz* (4), *Miguel* (4), *Rafael* (4), *Alfredo* (3), *Fernando* (3), *Francisco* (3), *Hernando* (3); *Albertina, Aureliano, Guido, Julieta, Sal*.

Hoyt (8486) English: nickname for a tall, thin person, from Middle English *hoit* 'long stick'.

Hoyte (201) English: variant spelling of HOYT.
GIVEN NAME Scottish 4%. *Iain*.

Hoza (129) Czech: unexplained.

Hrabak (193) Czech and Slovak (**Hrabák**): nickname for a greedy or miserly person, from a derivative of *hrabat* 'to rake in or hoard'.

Hrabe (158) Czech (**Hrabě**): from *hrabě* 'count', either an occupational name for a servant of a count or an ironic nickname for someone who gave himself airs and graces.

Hrabik (122) Czech (**Hrabík**): metonymic occupational name for a gardener or agricultural worker, from *hraba* 'hoe'.

Hrabovsky (136) Czech: habitational name for someone from any of five places in Moravia called Hrabová.
GIVEN NAMES German 4%. *Alois, Aloysius, Bernhard*.

Hrbek (134) Czech: nickname for a hunchback, from a diminutive of *hrb* 'hump'.

Hrdlicka (385) Czech and Slovak (**Hrdlička**): from *hrdlička* 'turtle dove'; a nickname denoting someone with a mild, peaceable, or affectionate temperament, or metonymic occupational name for a keeper of doves.

Hreha (250) Czech: from a vernacular form of the personal name GREGORY.

Hren (319) Slovenian and Croatian (northern Croatia): nickname or topographic name from *hren* 'horseradish', a nickname for someone with an aggressive temperament or a sharp wit.

Hresko (114) Ukrainian: variant of **Hrechko**, a derivative of the personal name *Hrehor*, Ukrainian form of Latin *Gregorius* (see GREGORY).

Hribar (304) Slovenian: topographic name for a person who lived on a hill or in a hilly region, from *hrib* 'hill'.

Hricko (101) Ukrainian: variant of **Hritsko**, a pet form of the personal name *Hrehor*, Ukrainian form of Latin *Gregorius* (see GREGORY).

Hritz (387) Ukrainian: from the personal name *Hrits*, Ukrainian pet form of *Gregorius* (see GREGORY).

Hrivnak (206) Czech (**Hřivňák**) and Slovak (**Hrivnák**): **1.** nickname for an accomplished person, from *hřivna* 'talent'. **2.** from *hřivnáč* 'wood pigeon', 'ring dove', possibly a nickname for someone thought to resemble the bird in some way. **3.** nickname for someone with particularly luxuriant hair, from *hříva* 'mane'.

Hrncir (162) Czech (**Hrnčíř**): occupational name from *hrnčíř* 'potter', an agent derivative of *hrnec* 'pot'.
GIVEN NAMES German 5%. *Otto* (2), *Erwin*.

Hromadka (114) Czech (**Hromádka**): nickname from Czech *hromádka*, diminutive of *hromada* 'pile', 'heap'.

Hron (198) **1.** Czech: from a short form of *Hroznata*, an Old Czech personal name. **2.** Slovak: possibly a habitational name from a river so called in Slovakia.

Hronek (181) Czech (**Hroněk**): from a diminutive of HRON.

Hrovat (149) Slovenian: from an old spelling of *Hrvat*, ethnic name for a Croat, in particular a Croat refugee from the Turkish occupation of the Balkans in the 15th and 16th centuries.

Hrubes (152) Czech (**Hrubeš**): variant of **Hrubý** (see HRUBY).

Hruby (654) Czech and Slovak (**Hrubý**): nickname for a large individual, from *hrubý* 'big'.

Hruska (874) Czech and Slovak (**Hruška**): from *hruška* 'pear', a metonyic occupational name for a grower or seller of pears, or a nickname for someone with a pear-shaped head.

Hruza (127) Czech (**Hrůza**): **1.** nickname from *hrůza* 'horror'. **2.** from a short form of the personal name *Hroznata*.
GIVEN NAMES Czech and Slovak 4%. *Matej, Zdenek*.

Hsi (117) Chinese 羿: variant of XI.
GIVEN NAMES Chinese 10%. *Chen-Yu, Cheng, Kuo, Mei, Shu, Xiao Jun, Ya-Wen, Yu-Chung*.

Hsia (353) Chinese 夏: variant of XIA.
GIVEN NAMES Chinese 20%. *Ching* (2), *Chiu* (2), *Liang* (2), *Ming* (2), *Pei* (2), *Shu* (2), *Yuan* (2), *Chen, Chen-Li, Cheng, Chengyu, Cheung*.

Hsiao (615) Chinese 蕭: variant of XIAO.
GIVEN NAMES Chinese 24%. *Ting* (4), *Chih* (3), *Ching* (3), *Chien* (2), *Ping* (2), *Chan, Chao, Chen, Cheng, Chi, Chi Hung, Chia-Wei*.

Hsieh (1419) **1.** Chinese 謝: variant of XIE 1. **2.** Chinese 解: variant of **Xie** 2.
GIVEN NAMES Chinese 26%. *Wen* (10), *Ming* (9), *Cheng* (6), *Ching* (4), *Chin* (3), *Shih* (3), *Tseng* (3), *Tsung* (3), *Wing* (3), *Chen* (2), *Chi* (2), *Hui-Chen* (2).

Hsiung (218) Chinese 熊: variant of XIONG 1.
GIVEN NAMES Chinese 26%. *Ching Ming* (2), *Shang* (2), *Chao, Cheng, Cheng-Chung, Chia-Ling, Chieh, Chuan, Chuen, Chun, Chung-Chi, Fei*.

Hsu (3951) **1.** Chinese 徐: variant of XU 1. **2.** Chinese 許: variant of XU 2.
GIVEN NAMES Chinese 22%. *Cheng* (13), *Wen* (10), *Yung* (10), *Chin* (9), *Wei* (9), *Chen* (7), *Chien* (7), *Ming* (7), *Shih* (7), *Chun* (6), *Kuang* (6), *Kuo* (6).

Hsueh (242) Chinese 薛: variant of XUE.
GIVEN NAMES Chinese 36%. *Chung* (4), *Ping* (2), *Chao, Chi, Chia, Ching Ling, Feng, Hsing, Hsun, Hui, Jung, Kan, Kang, Yeh*.

Hu (2663) **1.** Chinese 胡: from *Hu*, a name bestowed posthumously on Gui Man, Duke of Chen. After conquering the Shang dynasty and becoming the first king of the Zhou dynasty in 1122 BC, Wu Wang searched for a descendant of the great ancient emperors to guard their memory and offer sacrifices, to help retain the mandate of heaven which was considered essential to remain in power. He found Gui Man, a descendant of the model emperor Shun (2257–2205 BC), and granted him the region of Chen (in present-day Henan province), along with one of his daughters in marriage and the title Marquis of Chen. Gui Man was posthumously named Hu, Duke of Chen, and some of his descendants adopted this name as their surname. **2.** Chinese 扈: from part of the name of the state of Youhu, which existed during the Xia dynasty (2205–1766 BC). Its residents subsequently adopted the second character of the name, Hu, as their surname. **3.** French: nickname from Old French *hu* 'outcry', 'noise' (the same word as gave rise to the English phrase 'hue and cry', which referred to a clamour raised when in pursuit of a criminal); compare HUARD 2. **4.** Mexican (Maya): nickname meaning 'iguana'.
GIVEN NAMES Chinese 44%. *Wei* (15), *Jian* (13), *Ming* (11), *Ping* (10), *Bin* (9), *Yi* (8), *Ying* (8), *Jing* (7), *Xiao* (7), *Qi* (6), *Yan* (6), *Chi* (5); *Chang* (3), *Chung* (3), *Min* (2), *Yiping* (2), *Chong, Chul, Hu, Jung Soo, Sang Hoon, Tian, Wook, Yiming*.

Hua (944) **1.** Hawaiian: unexplained. **2.** Vietnamese (**H{us'}a**): unexplained. **3.** Chinese 華: one source of the name is Hua mountain, from the time of the Xia dynasty (2205–1766 BC). Also, during the Zhou dynasty (1122–221 BC), a duke of the state of Song enfeoffed the city of Hua to his son, whose descendants adopted the name of the city as their surname. Hua also means 'China' or 'Chinese' in a broad sense, as in 'Chinese culture' or 'the Chinese people'. **4.** Chinese 花: there is another Chinese name romanized as *Hua*, whose origins are not clear, but it is apparent that the name came into common use beginning with the Tang dynasty (618–907). This character for Hua also means 'flower'. **5.** Chinese 滑: Wu Wang, who established the Zhou dynasty in 1122 BC, granted the state of Hua along with the title of Earl to a subject. Descendants of this Earl of Hua adopted Hua as their surname.

This character for Hua also means 'slippery' or 'smooth'.

GIVEN NAMES Vietnamese 43%; Chinese 28%. *Minh* (9), *Hung* (8), *Quang* (8), *Cuong* (7), *Khanh* (7), *Sinh, Tanh, Trung* (7), *Thanh* (6), *Huy* (5), *Ngoc* (5), *Phat* (5), *Son* (5), *Tri* (5); *Hua* (7), *Tuong* (5), *Jian* (4), *Ming* (4), *Wei* (4), *Chi* (3), *Fang* (3), *Cheng* (2), *Chin* (2), *Dong Keun* (2), *Hui* (2), *Lei* (2), *Li* (2), *Min* (2), *Phong* (2), *Tam* (2), *Tinh* (2), *Chung, Hoa Kim, Jih, Sa, Sha*.

Huang (9016) Chinese 黄 : from an ancient territory called Huang. Perhaps the most famous and revered of the ancient Chinese emperors is Huang Di (2697–2595 BC), considered father of the Chinese people. He is also known as 'the Yellow Emperor', since Huang also means 'yellow'. Surprisingly, though, Huang Di is not credited with being a direct source of the surname. A descendant of his was granted the fief of the territory of Huang, which later served as the surname for certain descendants of the ruling family.

GIVEN NAMES Chinese 47%. *Wei* (50), *Ming* (37), *Jian* (30), *Ying* (28), *Yi* (26), *Jing* (23), *Wen* (23), *Jin* (22), *Ping* (19), *Min* (18), *Yong* (18), *Cheng* (17), *Hong* (17), *Chong* (8), *Chang* (7), *Pao* (5), *Sha* (3), *Shen* (3), *Tun* (3), *You* (3), *Chung* (2), *Shiu* (2), *Ti* (2), *Tian* (2).

Huard (526) French: **1.** from the Germanic personal name *Huard*, composed of *hug* 'heart', 'mind', 'spirit' + *hard* 'hardy', 'brave', 'strong'. Compare HOWARD. **2.** nickname from Old French *huard* 'owl' (a derivative of *huer* 'to cry or howl'). There has probably also been some confusion with **Houard**.

FOREBEARS A Huard is documented in Quebec city in 1667; the secondary surnames LALIBERTE and DESILETS are also recorded.

GIVEN NAMES French 14%. *Aime* (3), *Adelard* (2), *Jacques* (2), *Jean-Pierre* (2), *Lucien* (2), *Marcel* (2), *Alcide, Amiee, Armand, Aurele, Clermont, Fernard*.

Huba (106) **1.** Dutch: from a short form of HUBERT. **2.** Czech and Slovak: nickname for a cheeky or sharp-tongued person, from *huba* 'mouth', 'muzzle'.

GIVEN NAME German 4%. *Kurt*.

Hubacek (105) Czech (**Hubáček**): nickname for a cheeky or sharp-tongued person, from a diminutive of HUBA.

Hubach (138) **1.** German: from a pet form of a Slavic equivalent of JACOB. **2.** German: habitational name from a lost place near Ahrweiler called Hubach. **3.** Possibly an Americanized spelling of Czech **Hubač**, a nickname for a loud mouth, from *huba* 'mouth', 'gob'.

GIVEN NAMES German 7%. *Kurt, Otto*.

Hubacher (101) German: habitational name for someone from Hubach (see HUBACH 2).

GIVEN NAME German 4%. *Fritz*.

Huband (113) English: patronymic from HUGH, the second element being Middle English *barn* 'child', a northern English word of Scandinavian origin.

Hubanks (152) Probably an altered form of EUBANKS. Compare HUGHBANKS.

Hubbard (23545) English (chiefly Leicestershire): variant of HUBERT.

Hubbart (215) English: variant of HUBBARD or HUBERT.

Hubbartt (135) English: variant spelling of HUBBART.

Hubbell (2555) English: variant spelling of HUBBLE.

Hubbert (722) English and North German: variant of HUBERT.

Hubble (1303) English (West Midlands): from the Norman personal name *Hubald*, composed of the Germanic elements *hug* 'heart', 'mind', 'spirit' + *bald* 'bold', 'brave'.

Hubbs (1445) English: probably a variant of HOBBS.

Hubby (109) **1.** English: apparently a variant of **Huby**, a habitational name from either of two places so called in North Yorkshire. Huby near Easingwold is named from Old English *hōh* + Old Scandinavian *bý* 'settlement', while Huby near Stainburn is name with the Old French personal name *Hu(gh)e* (see HUGH) + Old Scandinavian *bý*. **2.** Possibly an altered spelling of German **Hubbe**, a short form of HUBERT. In the U.S. it is found chiefly in TX and IN.

Hubel (159) **1.** French: from a pet form of HUBERT. **2.** German (**Hübel**): see HUEBEL.

GIVEN NAMES German 7%. *Gunther, Horst, Otto, Wenzel*.

Huben (100) English: possibly a variant spelling of **Huban**, a variant of HUBAND.

Hubenak (107) Czech (**Hubenák**): nickname from a noun derivative of *hubený* 'silly'.

GIVEN NAMES French 5%. *Arianne, Marcel*.

Huber (15240) **1.** German (also **Hüber, Hueber**): status name based on Middle High German *huobe*, a measure of land, varying in size at different periods and in different places, but always of considerable extent, appreciably larger than the holding of the average peasant. The surname usually denotes a holder or owner of this amount of land, who would have been a prosperous small farmer and probably one of the leading men of his village. This name is widespread throughout central and eastern Europe, not only in German-speaking lands. **2.** Slovenian (eastern Slovenia): status name of Franconian origin (see 1) for a peasant who had his own landed property, dialectally called *huba*. **3.** Dutch: variant of HUBERT. **4.** Jewish (Ashkenazic): from a southern Yiddish pronunciation of Yiddish *hober* 'oats' (see HABER).

GIVEN NAMES German 4%. *Otto* (17), *Kurt* (14), *Hans* (12), *Erwin* (10), *Franz* (7),

Alois (6), *Fritz* (6), *Helmut* (5), *Mathias* (4), *Oskar* (4), *Wilhelm* (4), *Dieter* (3).

Huberman (207) **1.** German (**Hubermann**): status name for a prosperous small farmer (see HUBER). **2.** Jewish (eastern Ashkenazic): elaborated form of HUBER 4.

GIVEN NAMES Jewish 5%. *Aba* (2), *Eliezer* (2), *Avi*.

Hubers (216) North German (Rhineland; **Hübers**) and Dutch: patronymic from a variant of the personal HUBERT.

Hubert (3534) German, Dutch, English, French, and Jewish (Ashkenazic): from a Germanic personal name composed of the elements *hug* 'heart', 'mind', 'spirit' + *berht* 'bright', 'famous'. The name was borne by an 8th-century bishop of Maastricht who was adopted as the patron of hunters, and helped to increase the popularity of the personal name, especially in the Low Countries.

FOREBEARS A Hubert, also called LA CROIX and Le grand Lacroix, of unknown origin, is documented in Montreal in 1656. Another, from Paris, is documented in Quebec city in 1669; the secondary surnames PARISIEN and Saint-Hubert are also documented.

GIVEN NAMES French 4%. *Lucien* (3), *Armand* (2), *Normand* (2), *Olivier* (2), *Adlore* (2), *Alphonse, Andre, Benoit, Camil, Camille, Fernand*.

Huberty (499) French: variant of HUBERT.

Hubka (206) Czech: nickname from a diminutive of HUBA.

Hubler (1069) German (also **Hübler**): topographic name from Middle High German *hübel* 'hill' + agent suffix *-er*.

Hubley (481) Americanized spelling of Swiss German **Hubli**, which is unexplained.

Hubner (526) German (**Hübner**): status name for a prosperous small farmer, from a variant of HUBER.

GIVEN NAMES German 6%. *Otto* (2), *Franz, Fritz, Gerhardt, Klaus*.

Hubscher (106) German (**Hübscher**): nickname for a well-educated or polite man, from an inflected form of the Middle High German adjective *hövesch, hübesch* 'courtly', 'polite', 'cultivated'.

GIVEN NAMES French 6%; German 4%. *Luc* (2); *Hedwig*.

Huch (156) North German and Dutch: from a Low German personal name equivalent to HUGH.

GIVEN NAMES German 8%. *Ernst, Erwin, Otto, Volker*.

Huck (1903) **1.** English: from the medieval personal name *Hucke*, perhaps from the Old English personal name *Hucca* or *Ucca*, which may in some cases be a pet form of Old English *Ūhtrǣd*. Later, however, this name fell completely out of use and the forms became inextricably confused with those of HUGH. **2.** German: topographic name from a term meaning 'bog'. **3.** German and Dutch: from a pet form of the personal name *Hugo* (see HUGH).

Huckaba (223) Variant of English HUCKABY.

Huckabay (487) Variant of English HUCKABY.

Huckabee (1121) Variant of English HUCKABY.

Huckabone (100) Probably a variant of English HUCKABY.

Huckaby (1578) English (rare in England): apparently a habitational name from Huccaby in Devon, possibly so named from Old English *woh* 'crooked' + *byge* 'river bend', or Uckerby in North Yorkshire, named with an unattested Old Norse personal name, *Úkyrri* or *Útkári*, + *býr* 'farmstead'.

Hucke (286) **1.** English: variant of HUCK 1. **2.** German: topographic name from *huck*, a dialect word meaning 'bog'. **3.** German: variant of HUCK 2 and 3. **4.** German (of Slavic origin): pet form of Sorbian *hui* 'uncle'.

GIVEN NAMES German 5%. *Berthold, Helmut, Kurt.*

Huckeba (228) Variant of English HUCKABY.

Huckeby (160) Variant of English HUCKABY.

Hucker (169) English (Somerset) and German (also **Hücker**): occupational name for a peddler or other tradesman, Middle English *hucker, hukker* (an agent derivative of *hukken* 'to hawk or trade'), Middle High German *hucker*.

Huckfeldt (127) German: topographic name from a dialect word, *huck* 'bog' + *feld* 'open country', 'field'.

Huckins (830) English: patronymic from a pet form of HUGH.

Huckle (141) **1.** English: from a pet form of the medieval personal name HUCK. **2.** German (North: **Huckel**; South: **Huckle**): topographic name from a dialect term *Huckel, Hückel* 'small hill'.

Huckleberry (305) Americanized form of German (Bavarian) name, **Hackelberg**, from a place called Hacklberg near Passau.

Hucko (107) Czech and Slovak (also **Hučko**): from a pet form of any of several personal names beginning with *Hu-*, for example *Hubert* or *Humprecht*.

Hucks (710) English: patronymic from HUCK.

Huckstep (235) English (Kent): unexplained.

Huda (164) Muslim: from an Arabic personal name based on Arabic *hūda* 'right guidance'.

GIVEN NAMES Muslim 62%. *Mohammed* (9), *Syed* (8), *Nurul* (4), *Shamsul* (4), *Akbar* (2), *Najmul* (2), *Omar* (2), *Abdul, Akm, Amir, Amjad, Anwarul.*

Hudack (134) Germanized or Americanized form of Czech and Slovak **Chudák** (see HUDAK).

Hudak (2185) Germanized or Americanized form of Czech and Slovak **Chudák**, a

descriptive nickname from *chudák* 'poor man'.

Huddle (596) English: from a pet form of the medieval personal name *Hudde* (see HUTT 1).

Huddleson (238) Northern Irish (of English origin): patronymic from HUDDLE.

Huddleston (6118) English: habitational name from Huddleston, a place in West Yorkshire named from the genitive case of an Old English personal name *Hūdel*, a derivative of *Hūda* (see HUTT 1) + Old English *tūn* 'enclosure', 'settlement'.

Huddlestun (144) Variant spelling of English HUDDLESTON.

Huddy (224) **1.** English (Devon and Cornwall): from a pet form of the medieval personal name *Hudde* (see HUTT). **2.** Irish: Anglicized form of Gaelic **Ó hUada** 'descendant of *Uada*', a personal name.

Hudec (313) Czech and Slovak: occupational name for a fiddler, *hudec*, a derivative of *housti* 'to play the fiddle'.

Hudecek (160) Czech (**Hudeček**): from a diminutive of HUDEC.

Hudek (171) Czech and Slovak: from a diminutive of HUDEC.

Hudelson (295) Perhaps a variant of HUDDLESON.

Hudepohl (108) North German: topographic name from *Hude*, probably meaning 'grazing spot', + Low German *Pohl* 'mud hole'.

Hudes (103) Jewish (eastern Ashkenazic): southern and central Yiddish dialect variant of HODES.

GIVEN NAME Jewish 7%; German 4%. *Siegfried.*

Hudgens (1748) English: variant of HUTCHENS.

Hudgeons (126) English: variant of HUTCHENS.

GIVEN NAME German 4%. *Kurt.*

Hudgins (4135) English: variant of HUTCHENS.

Hudkins (378) English: variant of HUTCHENS.

Hudler (261) South German: occupational name for a rag-trader, from an agent derivative of Middle High German *hudel* 'rag'.

Hudlow (229) Americanized form of German **Huttenloch**, a habitational name from a place in Württemberg, the second element being from the Middle High German *lōch* 'small woods', 'underbrush'.

Hudman (321) English: occupational name denoting the servant (Middle English *man*) of someone called *Hudde* (see HUTT).

Hudnall (1377) English: a habitational name from any of various place so called, such as Hudnall in Hertfordshire or Hudnalls in Gloucestershire, both named from the Old English personal name *Huda* (genitive *Hudan*) + Old English *healh* 'nook', 'corner of land'. This is a common name in TX.

Hudnell (209) English: variant of HUDNALL.

Hudnut (110) Variant of English **Hudnott**, itself a variant of HODNETT.

Hudock (636) Americanized form of an unidentified Czech name.

Hudon (416) French: from a pet form of HOUDE 1.

FOREBEARS A Hudon, also called BEAULIEU, from the Anjou region of France, is documented in Quebec city in 1666.

GIVEN NAMES French 17%. *Armand* (4), *Cecile* (2), *Henri* (2), *Marcel* (2), *Adrien, Alphege, Alphonse, Amedee, Andre, Antoine, Florent, Herve.*

Hudson (44641) English: patronymic from the medieval personal name *Hudde* (see HUTT 1). This surname is particularly common in Yorkshire and is also well established in Ireland.

Hudspeth (1762) English (northeastern counties): unexplained. Compare HEDGEPETH.

Hudy (213) **1.** Slovak and Ukrainian: nickname from *chudý, hudy* 'thin'. **2.** perhaps an Americanized variant of Czech **Chudý** 'poor' (see CHUDY).

Hudzik (167) **1.** Ukrainian: from *hudzyk* 'button' metonymic occupational name for a button maker or nickname for a small man. **2.** Slovak: nickname for a thin man, Slovak *chudzik*, from *chudý* 'thin'.

Hudzinski (113) Variant of Polish **Chudziński** (see CHUDZINSKI).

Hue (192) **1.** French: from the Old French personal name *Hue*, variant of *Hugues* (see HUGH). **2.** Vietnamese: unexplained.

GIVEN NAMES French 9%; Vietnamese 8%; Chinese 5%. *Pierre* (2), *Andre, Ludger, Ulysse; Au, Dao, Hoang Thi, Lam, Pham, Trung, Truong, Vo, Vuong; Sing* (2), *Chung Won, Dong Kyu, Shang, Shiao, Wai, Wong, Young.*

Huebel (160) German (**Hübel**): topographic name from Middle High German *hübel* 'hill'.

GIVEN NAME German 5%. *Claus.*

Hueber (234) South German: variant of HUBER.

GIVEN NAMES French 4%; German 4%. *Franz, Markus.*

Huebert (219) German (**Hübert**): variant of HUBERT.

Huebner (2946) German (**Hübner**): status name for a prosperous small farmer, from a variant of HUBER.

GIVEN NAMES German 5%. *Kurt* (8), *Otto* (5), *Fritz* (4), *Gerhard* (3), *Hans* (3), *Dieter* (2), *Ernst* (2), *Erwin* (2), *Heinz* (2), *Manfred* (2), *Wolf* (2), *Arno.*

Huebsch (308) German (**Hübsch**) and Jewish (Ashkenazic): nickname from Middle High German *hübesch* 'courtly', 'polite', 'refined', 'agreeable', German *hübsch*. The present-day sense of *hübsch*, 'pretty', 'handsome', 'nice', is a comparatively recent development and is unlikely to have affected the German surname, although it is the sense of the Jewish name, which is mainly ornamental.

Huegel (339) German (**Hügel**): **1.** from a pet form of the personal name *Hugo* (see HUGH). **2.** (North German): topographic name for someone who lived by a hill, from the vocabulary word *Hügel* 'hill'.
GIVEN NAMES German 4%. *Gerhard, Kurt, Otto, Wendelin.*

Huels (143) North German (**Hüls**): variant of HULSE.

Huelskamp (242) North German (**Hülskamp**): topographic name from Middle Low German *hüls* 'holly' (*Ilex aquifolium*) + *kamp* 'enclosed field', 'domain'.

Huelsman (435) Variant of German HUELSMANN.

Huelsmann (170) German (**Hülsmann**): topographic name from Middle Low German *huls* 'holly' (see HULSE).

Huemmer (100) South German (**Hümmer**): from a contracted form of **Huebmeyer**, a distinguishing name for a farmer whose farm consisted of a *huobe* (a particular measure of land; see HUBER).
GIVEN NAMES German 7%; Jewish 5%. *Alphons, Hans, Kurt; Rebekah* (2).

Huenefeld (134) German (**Hünefeld**): habitational name from a place called Hünfeld in Hesse, or from other places called Hünefeld.

Huenink (177) Probably an altered spelling of Dutch **Hoenink**, either from Middle Dutch *honich* 'honey' (a metonymic occupational name for a seller of honey, or a nickname), or a patronymic from a short form of a Germanic personal name formed with *hūn* 'bear cub' as the first element.

Huerta (3528) Spanish: habitational name from any of the numerous places named Huerta, from *huerta* 'vegetable garden' (Latin *hortus*). This is also a Sephardic Jewish surname.
GIVEN NAMES Spanish 54%. *Jose* (119), *Juan* (67), *Jesus* (35), *Manuel* (33), *Carlos* (29), *Francisco* (27), *Luis* (26), *Raul* (26), *Ruben* (25), *Pedro* (23), *Salvador* (23), *Javier* (21).

Huertas (434) Spanish: variant of HUERTA, from the plural form, found in numerous place names.
GIVEN NAMES Spanish 45%. *Jose* (12), *Luis* (8), *Carlos* (7), *Miguel* (6), *Angel* (5), *Pedro* (5), *Raul* (5), *Eduardo* (4), *Juan* (4), *Roberto* (4), *Ana* (3), *Enrique* (3); *Marco* (3), *Angelo* (2), *Antonio, Carmelo, Silvano.*

Huerter (190) German (**Hürter**): nickname for a stingy person, from Middle High German *hurtære* 'hoarder (of treasure)'.

Hueser (121) German: variant of HUSER.
GIVEN NAME German 4%. *Fritz.*

Hueske (104) North German: variant of **Hüseke**, from Middle Low German *hūs* 'house' + diminutive suffix *-ke*, topographical name for someone living in a small house.

Huesman (236) North German (**Hüsmann**): variant of HUSEMAN.

Huestis (350) Origin unidentified. Perhaps a variant of English EUSTACE. Compare HEUSTIS.

Hueston (264) English and northern Irish: variant spelling of HOUSTON.

Huet (157) **1.** English: variant spelling of HEWITT 1. **2.** French: from a pet form of the Old French personal name *Hue, Hughe* (see HUGH).
FOREBEARS A Huet from the Anjou region of France is recorded in Trois Rivières, Quebec, in 1666, with the secondary surname DULUDE.
GIVEN NAMES French 7%. *Marcel* (2), *Andre.*

Hueter (168) German: variant of HUETHER.
GIVEN NAMES German 8%. *Jochen, Ottmar, Uwe.*

Huether (482) German (**Hüther**): occupational name for a herdsman, guard, or guardian, Middle High German *hüetære*.
GIVEN NAMES German 6%. *Frieda* (2), *Ernst, Ewald, Klaus, Kurt, Lothar, Otto, Reinhold.*

Huett (406) **1.** English: variant spelling of HEWITT 1. **2.** German (**Hütt**): status name for someone living in a hut or owning a small shop, Middle High German *hütte*, or a habitational name from any of several places called Hütt or Hütte.

Huetter (152) German (**Hütter**): **1.** variant of **Hütt** (see HUETT 2), with the addition of the agent suffix *-er*. **2.** from the same word as an occupational name for someone who built huts or worked in one.
GIVEN NAMES German 8%. *Gerhard, Heinz, Kurt.*

Huettl (293) South German (**Hüttl**): diminutive of **Hütt** (see HUETT).
GIVEN NAMES German 6%. *Alfons* (3), *Erhard* (2), *Othmar.*

Huettner (193) German (**Hüttner**): habitational name for someone from any of various places called Hütten.
GIVEN NAMES German 6%. *Gunther, Juergen, Lothar.*

Huey (3539) **1.** English and northern Irish: from a pet form of HUGH. **2.** Irish: variant of HOEY.

Huezo (166) Hispanic (common in Mexico and El Salvador): unexplained.
GIVEN NAMES Spanish 60%. *Jose* (8), *Juan* (8), *Ana* (4), *Carlos* (3), *Luis* (3), *Blanca* (2), *Jorge* (2), *Miguel* (2), *Rafael* (2), *Raul* (2), *Adolfo, Agustin; Antonio* (2), *Angelo.*

Huff (19332) **1.** English: topographic name for someone who lived by a spur of a hill, Old English *hōh* (literally, 'heel'). **2.** German: from the Germanic personal name *Hufo*, a short form of a compound name formed with *hug* 'heart', 'mind', 'spirit' as the first element.

Huffaker (953) Altered spelling of German HOFACKER.

Huffer (978) **1.** English: possibly an unflattering nickname for a boastful, swaggering

person (one who huffs and puffs). **2.** German (**Hüffer**): from the Germanic personal name *Hugifrid*, composed of *hug* 'head', 'mind', 'spirit' + *frid* 'peace'. **3.** North German (**Hüffer**): status name for a prosperous small farmer. Compare South German HUBER. **4.** German: probably an American spelling of HOF or HOFF.

Huffhines (124) Of German origin: see HUFFINES.

Huffine (557) Of German origin: see HUFFINES.

Huffines (427) Americanized form of German **Hof(f)heinz**, originally a distinguishing name for a man called Heinz (see HEINZ) who lived on or was in charge of a farm or estate (see HOFF).

Huffington (102) English: habitational name, most likely Uffington in Lincolnshire, named with the Old English personal name *Uffa* + Old English *-ing-* denoting association + *tūn* 'settlement'. Other places so named are found in Shropshire and Oxfordshire, as well as Uffington Farm in Goodneston, Kent, which may also have contributed to the surname. The Oxfordshire place name is from the genitive form (*Uffan*) of the Old English personal name *Uffa* + *tūn*, while the other two are of the same derivation as the Lincolnshire place name.

Huffman (18899) Altered spelling of HOFFMANN.

Huffmaster (272) Americanized form of HOF(F)MEISTER.

Huffnagle (100) Americanized spelling of German HUFNAGEL.

Hufford (1434) English: variant of UFFORD with the addition of an inorganic *H-*.

Huffstetler (722) South German or Swiss German: occupational or status name for someone who worked or lived on a large farm or estate, from Middle High German *hof* 'farmstead', 'manor farm' + *stete* 'place'.

Huffstickler (121) Americanized form of German HUFFSTETLER.

Huffstutler (441) Americanized form of German HUFFSTETLER.

Huffstutter (118) Americanized form of German HOFSTETTER.

Hufham (101) Probably English, a variant of HOUGHAM.

Hufnagel (663) German: metonymic occupational name for a farrier, from Middle High German *hufnagel* 'horseshoe nail' (literally 'hoof nail').

Hufnagle (235) Americanized spelling of German HUFNAGEL.

Hufstedler (178) Variant of German HUFFSTETLER.

Hufstetler (263) Variant of German HUFFSTETLER.

Huft (106) Variant spelling of German HOFT.

Hug (832) **1.** English: variant of HUCK. **2.** German and Dutch: from the personal name *Hug* or *Hugo*, equivalent of English HUGH.
GIVEN NAMES German 4%. *Hans* (3), *Bernd, Eldred, Eugen, Kurt, Wolfgang.*

Huge (163) German (also **Hüge**) and Dutch: variant of HUG 2.

Hugel (148) German (**Hügel**): see HUEGEL.
GIVEN NAMES German 9%. *Dieter* (3), *Ulrich.*

Huger (124) German (also **Hüger**): from a derivative of the personal name *Hugo* (see HUGH), or a Germanic personal name composed of the elements *hug* 'heart', 'mind', 'spirit' + *hari, heri* 'army'.

Hugg (292) English (rare in England): variant of HUG 1.

Huggard (305) English: pejorative derivative of HUGH. This surname is also established in Ireland, where MacLysaght believes it to be in part of French (Huguenot) origin.

Hugger (133) German: variant of HUCKER 2.
GIVEN NAMES German 8%. *Fritz, Lothar, Uwe.*

Huggett (369) English (chiefly Sussex and Kent): **1.** from a pet form of HUGH. **2.** habitational name from Huggate in East Yorkshire, possibly named in Old Norse with *hugr* 'mound' (an unattested variant of *haugr*) + *gata* 'road'.

Hugghins (102) Variant spelling of English HUGGINS.
GIVEN NAME French 4%. *Clovis.*

Huggins (7138) English: patronymic from a pet form of HUGH.

Huggler (195) German and Swiss German: from a derivative of the personal name HUGO.

Hugh (361) **1.** English: from the Old French personal name *Hu(gh)e*, introduced to Britain by the Normans. This is in origin a short form of any of the various Germanic compound names with the first element *hug* 'heart', 'mind', 'spirit'. Compare, for example, HOWARD 1, HUBBLE, and HUBERT. It was a popular personal name among the Normans in England, partly due to the fame of St. Hugh of Lincoln (1140–1200), who was born in Burgundy and who established the first Carthusian monastery in England. **2.** In Ireland and Scotland this name has been widely used as an equivalent of Celtic *Aodh* 'fire', the source of many Irish surnames (see for example McCoy).

Hughart (373) Origin uncertain. Probably a northern Irish variant of Scottish URQUHART. The name is no longer found in Britain or Ireland.

Hughbanks (195) Probably an altered form of EUBANKS. Compare HUBANKS.

Hughen (128) Northern English and Scottish: derivative of a pet form of the personal name HUGH.

Hughes (84186) **1.** English (also common in Wales): patronymic from the Middle English and Anglo-Norman French personal name HUGH. **2.** Welsh: variant of HOWELLS. **3.** Irish and Scottish: variant Anglicization of Gaelic **Mac Aodha** (see McCoy).

Hughett (285) Altered spelling of HEWITT.

Hughey (2506) Irish: variant spelling of HUEY.

Hughlett (227) Altered spelling of HEWLETT.

Hughley (525) **1.** English: habitational name from a place so called in Shropshire, named in Old English with the element *lēah* 'wood', 'glade'; the Middle English personal name *Hugh* (see HUGH) was prefixed to this in the 12th century, to indicate ownership. **2.** Possibly an altered spelling of German **Hügli** (see HUGLEY).
GIVEN NAME French 4%. *Andre.*

Hughs (409) English: patronymic from HUGH.

Hughson (431) English and Scottish: patronymic from HUGH.

Hughston (177) English: of uncertain origin; it could be a Scottish habitational name from Hughston in the Highland region but is more likely a variant spelling of HOUSTON.

Hugill (227) English: habitational name from Howgill in Sedbergh or from Hugill, Cumbria. Howgill is named from Old Norse *hol* 'hollow' + *gil* 'ravine'; Hugill probably takes its name from Old Norse *hór* 'high' + *geil* 'ravine'.

Hugley (155) Possibly an altered form of (Swiss) German **Hügli**, from a pet form of HUGO 2.

Hugo (961) **1.** French and Dutch: from a Latinized form of the personal name HUGH, also found in England (Cornwall). **2.** German: from a short form of any of the Germanic compound personal names with the first element *hug* 'heart', 'mind', 'spirit' (see HUGH).

Huguenin (200) French: from a pet form of the Old French personal name *Hue, Hughe* (modern *Hugues*) (see HUGH).
GIVEN NAMES French 8%. *Andre, Gabrielle, Laurent, Marcel, Marcelle.*

Huguet (136) French and Catalan: from a pet form of the personal name *Hu(gh)e* or *Hugo* (see HUGH).
FOREBEARS A bearer of this name from the Poitou region of France is documented in Lachine, Quebec, in 1680, with the secondary surname LATOUR.
GIVEN NAMES Spanish 11%. *Blanca* (2), *Alfredo, Ana, Angel, Felipe, Gilberto, Juan, Lourdes, Oswaldo, Rey, Siria, Virgilio.*

Huguley (466) Americanized spelling of Swiss German **Hügli** (see HUGLEY).

Hugunin (143) Variant spelling of French HUGUENIN.

Hugus (181) Dutch: patronymic from the personal name *Hugo* (see HUGH).

Huh (436) Korean: variant of **Hŏ** (see HO).
GIVEN NAMES Korean 71%. *Young* (14), *Jung* (6), *Yoon* (6), *Joon* (5), *Kyung* (5), *Sung* (5), *Kwon* (4), *Won* (4), *Yong* (4), *In* (3), *Kwan* (3), *Kwang* (3); *Nam* (7), *Chang* (5), *Chul* (3), *Yeon* (3), *Choon* (2), *Dong Jin* (2), *Hae Jung* (2), *Jang* (2), *Min* (2), *Sik* (2), *Woon* (2), *Byung Ho.*

Huhn (1148) German: **1.** (also **Hühn**): nickname for a tall man, from Middle High German *hiune* 'giant', 'monster', 'bogeyman', from Middle High German *Hiune* 'Hun', a word probably ultimately of Turkic origin. **2.** (also **Hühn**): from an old personal name derived from the Germanic element *hūn* 'bear cub'. **3.** metonymic occupational name for a poultry keeper, from Middle High German *huon* 'hen'.

Huhta (199) Finnish: habitational name from a farmstead or village so named, from *huhta* 'glade', 'forest clearing', commonly denoting an area of land that had been cleared of forest in order to produce farmland. Compare AHO. Villages called Huhta, Huhtaa, and Huhti are found in western Finland. In some cases the American surname may be a shortened form of some other name formed with this word (for example, see HUHTALA).
GIVEN NAMES Finnish 6%. *Aino, Armas, Arvo, Jaakko, Rauha, Waino.*

Huhtala (125) Finnish: variant of HUHTA 'glade', with the local suffix *-la*. This name occurs mainly in Ostrobothnia, but is also common in western Finland.
GIVEN NAMES Finnish 12%; Scandinavian 4%. *Eino* (3), *Keijo, Petri, Reino, Taito; Erik.*

Hui (1169) **1.** Chinese 許: Cantonese variant of XU 1. **2.** Chinese 惠: the 18th king of the Zhou Dynasty is most commonly known to posterity by his posthumously given name, Hui Wang. His descendants adopted Hui as their surname.
GIVEN NAMES Chinese 29%. *Ming* (8), *Kwong* (6), *Man* (6), *Wing* (6), *Chee* (4), *Cheuk* (4), *Kwok* (4), *Wai* (4), *Kin* (3), *Kin Wah* (3), *Siu* (3), *Sun* (3), *Yiu* (3), *Chung* (2), *Pak* (2), *Hu, Yew, You.*

Huibregtse (178) Dutch: patronymic from the personal name *Hubrecht* (see HUBERT).

Huie (956) **1.** Variant of HUEY. **2.** Chinese: possibly a variant of HUI.

Huinker (148) Probably a North German variant of German HUNKER.

Huiras (150) German: unexplained; possibly a derivative of Sorbian *hui* 'uncle' or an altered spelling of Slavic JURAS.

Huisenga (135) Frisian: variant spelling of HUIZENGA.

Huish (194) English (also common in South Wales): habitational name from any of the places so called in Devon, Dorset, Somerset, and Wiltshire, named with Old English *hīwisc*, a measure of land considered sufficient to support a household.

Huisinga (139) Frisian: variant spelling of HUIZENGA.

GIVEN NAMES German 4%. *Gerhard, Theodor.*

Huisman (580) Dutch: status name for someone who lived in a house, as opposed to a cottage, or who owned his own house (see HOUSE 1), from *huis* 'house' + *man* 'man'.

Huitron (122) Hispanic (Mexico): unexplained.

GIVEN NAMES Spanish 66%. *Carlos* (3), *Efren* (2), *Francisco* (2), *Jose* (2), *Rafael* (2), *Salvador* (2), *Alberto, Alejandro, Alicia, Ambrocio, Antonieta, Bernarda.*

Huitt (486) English: variant spelling of HEWITT 1.

Huizar (495) Hispanic (Mexico): unexplained.

GIVEN NAMES Spanish 47%. *Jose* (9), *Salvador* (6), *Juan* (5), *Efrain* (4), *Javier* (4), *Mario* (4), *Alberto* (3), *Alfredo* (3), *Gonzalo* (3), *Jesus* (3), *Manuel* (3), *Pedro* (3); *Antonio* (4), *Sal* (2), *Aureliano, Eligio, Enedino, Flavio, Julieta, Lorenzo, Marco.*

Huizenga (773) Frisian: habitational name from Huizinge, in Groningen, named with *huis* 'house' (see HOUSE 1).

Huizinga (322) Frisian: variant of HUIZENGA.

Hukill (433) Altered form of English HUGILL, found predominantly in TX.

Hula (191) Czech (**Hůla**): nickname from a variant of *holý* 'bald', 'bare', or 'cleanshaven' (see HOLY).

GIVEN NAME German 4%. *Otto.*

Hulan (109) **1.** Czech (**Hulán**): occupational name for an uhlan (a member of a cavalry regiment armed with a lance), a word ultimately derived from Turkish *uğlan* 'servant', 'young man'. **2.** Probably also a variant of French HULIN.

GIVEN NAME French 6%. *Pierre.*

Hulbert (2013) **1.** English and German: from a Germanic personal name, *Holbert, Hulbert*, composed of the elements *hold, huld* 'friendly', 'gracious' + *berht* 'bright', 'famous'. **2.** German (**Hülbert**): topographic name for someone living by a pool or small pond, from Old High German *huliwa* 'pool'.

Hulburt (211) English: variant spelling of HULBERT.

Hulce (194) Americanized spelling of Dutch and North German HULSE.

Hulcher (128) German: probably an Americanized spelling of **Hultscher** or **Hülscher**, North German form of **Holzschuher, Holzschuhmacher**, occupational name for a clog maker (see HOELSCHER).

Hulen (502) English: variant spelling of HULIN.

Hulet (382) French: from a pet form of the personal name *Hue* (see HUGH).

Hulett (1575) **1.** French: variant spelling of HULET. **2.** English: variant spelling of HEWLETT.

Hulette (158) French: variant spelling of HULET.

GIVEN NAME French 5%. *Valere.*

Hulgan (167) Origin uncertain. Perhaps an Americanized form of Irish HALLIGAN. This name is found chiefly in AL.

Hulick (304) Americanized spelling of Czech **Hulík** (unexplained).

Hulin (552) **1.** English (Gloucestershire): from a pet form of the personal name HUGH. **2.** French: from a pet form of *Hue* (see HUGH). **3.** French: from a reduced form of *Hudelin*, a double diminutive of the personal name *Hude* (see HOUDE). **4.** Possibly Swedish: from an unidentified first element + the common ornamental suffix *-(l)in.* FOREBEARS A Hulin from the Brie region of France is recorded in Quebec city in 1659.

Huling (661) English: from a pet form of the personal name HUGH.

Hulings (212) English: patronymic from HULING.

Hulit (122) Variant spelling of English HEWLETT.

Hulka (93) Czech (**Hůlka**): nickname for a tall thin person, from *hůl* 'stick', 'cane'.

GIVEN NAMES German 7%. *Otto* (2), *Frieda.*

Hulke (146) German (of Slavic origin): descriptive nickname from a Slavic word meaning 'bald'.

Hull (16379) English: **1.** variant of HILL 1. **2.** from a pet form of HUGH.

Hullender (178) Variant spelling of HOLLANDER.

Huller (141) **1.** English: topographic name for someone who lived by a hill, from Middle English *hull* 'hill', a dialect form characteristic of southwestern England and the West Midlands. Compare HILLER. **2.** German (**Hüller**): occupational name for a tailor, from an agent derivative of Middle High German *hülle, hulle* 'cloak'.

Hullett (404) English: variant of HEWLETT.

Hulley (139) English (South Yorkshire): possibly a habitational name from Ulley in South Yorkshire, probably so named from Old English *ūle* 'owl' + *lēah* '(woodland) clearing'.

Hullihen (100) Americanized spelling of Irish HOULIHAN.

Hullinger (598) Variant spelling of German HOLLINGER.

Hullings (116) English: variant of HOLLINGS.

Hullum (157) Variant of English HALLAM.

Hulm (117) English: variant spelling of HOLM.

Hulme (824) English (mainly Lancashire) and Scottish: variant spelling of HOLME.

Hulon (185) Probably a variant of English HULIN. This is a predominantly southern name in the U.S., common in SC and NC.

Huls (703) Dutch and North German (**Hüls**): variant of HULSE.

Hulse (2538) **1.** Dutch and North German (**Hülse**): topographic name for someone who lived where holly grew, Middle Low German *huls, hüls.* **2.** English (mainly Lancashire): habitational name from a place in Cheshire, recorded in the mid 13th century in the forms *Holes, Holis,* and *Holys.* This probably represents a Middle English plural of Old English *holh* 'hollow', 'depression' (see HOLE).

Hulsebus (206) North German (**Hülsebus**) and Dutch: topographic name for someone who lived in an area where holly grew, from Middle Low German *huls, hüls* 'holly' + *bus, busch* 'scrub'.

Hulsey (3252) Of English origin: unexplained. It may be a variant of HALSEY. This is a very frequent name in GA, AL, and TX.

Hulsing (117) German: from a place so named in Lower Saxony.

GIVEN NAME German 4%. *Kurt.*

Hulsizer (224) Dutch: topographic name for someone who lived in a wooden house. Compare German HOLZHAUSER.

Hulslander (260) Dutch: habitational name from Hulsland, named as 'the place where holly grows'.

Hulsman (196) Dutch: topographic name for someone who lived by a holly tree or a holly grove, Middle Dutch *huls* 'holly' + *man* 'man'.

Hulst (349) **1.** North German (**Hülst**) and Dutch (**van der Hulst**): topographic name for someone living where holly grew, from *hulst* 'holly'. **2.** Dutch and Belgian (**van Hulst**): habitational name from Hulst in Zeeland, or from any of various other places so called, in Alsemberg (Brabant), Kortemark and Zonnebeke (West Flanders), and Scheldewindeke (East Flanders).

Hulstein (117) **1.** Respelling of Dutch **Hoolsteen**, habitational name from a place in Zonhoven. **2.** Respelling of Dutch **Hulsteyn**, a regional name for someone from Holstein, on the border between Denmark and northern Germany.

GIVEN NAMES Dutch 8%; German 5%. *Gerrit* (4), *Albertus, Kees.*

Hult (458) Swedish: ornamental or topographic name for someone who lived in or by a wood or copse, from *hult, holt* 'grove', 'copse' (Old Norse *holt*).

GIVEN NAMES Scandinavian 9%. *Nels, Sten.*

Hultberg (272) Swedish: ornamental name composed of the elements *hult* 'grove', 'copse' + *berg* 'mountain', 'hill'.

GIVEN NAME Scandinavian 4%. *Erik* (2).

Hultgren (776) Swedish: ornamental name composed of the elements *hult* 'grove', 'copse' + *gren* 'branch'.

GIVEN NAMES Scandinavian 6%. *Erland, Gunhild, Lars, Lennart, Nils, Sven.*

Hultin (162) Swedish: ornamental name from *hult* 'copse' + *-in*, a common suffix of

Swedish surnames, derived from Latin *-in(i)us* 'descendant of'.

GIVEN NAMES Scandinavian 10%; Dutch 4%; German 4%. *Johan* (3), *Lars, Ove*; *Frieda*.

Hultman (641) **1.** Dutch: possibly a habitational name for someone from Hulten in North Brabant. **2.** Swedish: ornamental or topographic name from *hult* 'grove', 'copse' + *man* 'man'.

GIVEN NAMES Scandinavian 5%. *Erik, Niklas, Nils, Sig*.

Hulton (148) English: habitational name from places in Lancashire and Staffordshire, so named from Old English *hyll* 'hill' + *tūn* 'enclosure', 'settlement'.

FOREBEARS A family of this name has been established at Hulton, near Bolton, Lancashire, since the 12th century, when Bleythin de Hulton was mentioned in records of the reign of Henry II (1154–89).

Hultquist (447) Swedish: ornamental name composed of the elements *hult* 'grove', 'copse' + *quist*, an old or ornamental spelling of *kvist* 'twig'.

Hults (519) Shortened form of Dutch **de Hults**, a variant of HULSE 1.

Hultz (276) Possibly an altered spelling of HOLTZ.

Hulvey (258) Altered spelling of Irish **O'Halvey**. In Counties Galway and Mayo this is an Anglicized form of Gaelic **Ó hAilmhic** 'descendant of *Ailmhac*', a personal name meaning 'noble son'. In Leinster, *Halvey* is found as an equivalent of HOLLOWAY.

Hum (241) **1.** English: variant spelling of HUMM 1. **2.** Swiss German: unexplained. **3.** Chinese 譚: Taishan spelling of of TAN 1. **4.** Other Southeast Asian: unexplained.

GIVEN NAMES Chinese 4%; Other Southeast Asian 4%. *Chi* (2), *Yi* (2), *Foo, Soo, Wing, Yee*; *Lih, Roeun, Shee*.

Human (525) **1.** English: partly from an unattested late Old English personal name, *Hygemann*, composed of the elements *hyge* 'mind' (cognate with the underlying Germanic element in HUGH) + *mann* 'man'. In some cases this may also have been an occupational name for a servant (Middle English *man*) of a man called HUGH. **2.** Perhaps an altered spelling of German HOMANN.

Humann (260) Apparently an altered spelling of German HOMANN.

GIVEN NAMES German 5%. *Otto* (2), *Heinz, Manfred*.

Humason (100) Origin unidentified.

Humbard (145) Variant of French, English, or German HUMBERT.

Humbarger (173) Probably an altered spelling of **Homberger**, a German and Ashkenazic Jewish habitational name for someone from Homberg (see HOMBERG 1).

Humber (387) English: habitational name from any of the various places so called from their situation on a stream with this name. *Humber* is a common prehistoric river name, of uncertain origin and meaning.

Humberson (150) See HUMBERTSON.

Humbert (1456) German, Dutch, and French: from a Germanic personal name composed of the elements *hun* 'Hun', 'giant' or *hūn* 'bear cub' + *berht* 'bright', 'famous'. This was particularly popular in the Netherlands and North Germany during the Middle Ages as a result of the fame of a 7th-century St. Humbert, who founded the abbey of Marolles in Flanders.

Humbertson (117) **1.** Patronymic from the personal name HUMBERT. **2.** In some cases it may be a metathesized variant of English **Humberston**, a habitational name from a place in Lincolnshire named Humberston, from the ancient pre-English river name *Humber* + Old English *stān* 'stone'. The surname occurs mainly in TX, PA, and OH.

Humble (1662) **1.** English (mainly northeast): nickname for a meek or lowly person, from Middle English, Old French *(h)umble* (Latin *humilis* 'lowly', a derivative of *humus* 'ground'). **2.** French (also **Humblé**): from a short pet form of the personal name HUMBERT.

Humbles (197) English: unexplained. Probably a metonymic occupational name for a venison butcher or sausage maker, from Middle English *umbels, numbels* 'offal' (of a deer), earlier 'loin or haunch' (of a deer), a word of Old French origin.

Humburg (158) German: perhaps an altered spelling of HOMBURG.

GIVEN NAMES German 4%. *Katharina, Kurt*.

Hume (2890) **1.** Scottish: habitational name from the barony of Home in Berwickshire. **2.** Scottish, English (East Anglia), and Irish: variant of HOLME, from Old Danish *hulm*.

Humenik (185) Czech and Slovak (**Humeník**): topographic name for someone who lived in the backyards of a village, from *humna* 'backyard'.

Humerickhouse (117) Americanized spelling of German **Homerighausen**, habitational name from a place near Berleburg (Westphalia).

Humes (1957) English (Cumbria): perhaps a variant of HOLME.

Humeston (105) Scottish: variant of HUMISTON.

Humfleet (100) Variant of English **Amphlett** (see UMFLEET).

Humiston (421) Scottish: habitational name from Humeston near Cumnock in Ayrshire.

Humke (166) **1.** German: habitational name from a place so called near Lippe, originally named *Hunebeke* 'dirty stream'. **2.** North German (Frisian): from a pet form of the personal name *Hummo*, a reduced form of the Germanic names *Hugimar* (composed of the elements *hugi* 'heart', 'mind', 'spirit' + *māri* 'great', 'famous') or

Hunmar (composed of the elements *hun* 'Hun', 'giant' + *mari* 'great', 'famous').

GIVEN NAMES German 5%. *Friedrich, Kurt*.

Huml (136) German: variant spelling of HUMMEL.

Humm (327) **1.** English (of Norman origin): nickname from Old French *homme* 'man' (Latin *homo*), representing an Anglo-Norman translation of German MANN. **2.** North German (Frisian): from a short form of HUMBERT or *Humbold* (a compound name with the same first element + *bald* 'bold', 'brave').

GIVEN NAMES German 4%. *Heinz, Inge, Kurt, Mathias*.

Hummel (5973) **1.** German and Dutch: from a pet form of HUMBERT or *Humbold* (a compound name with the same first element + *bald* 'bold', 'brave'). **2.** German, Dutch, and Danish (of German origin): nickname for a busy or bustling person, from Middle High German *hummel*, Middle Dutch *hommel* 'bee', of imitative origin. Compare English *humblebee*, which in modern English has become *bumblebee*.

Hummell (435) Variant spelling of German and Dutch HUMMEL.

Hummer (1329) German (Frisian): from a Germanic personal name composed of the elements *hugi* 'heart', 'mind', 'spirit' + *mari* 'famous'.

Hummert (151) German: variant of HUMBERT.

GIVEN NAME German 4%. *Aloys*.

Humpal (232) Czech: status name for an artisan who was not a member of a guild.

Humpert (193) Dutch and German: variant of HUMBERT.

Humphery (170) English and Irish: variant of HUMPHREY.

Humpherys (188) English: variant of HUMPHRIES.

Humphres (124) English: variant of HUMPHRIES.

Humphress (129) English: variant of HUMPHRIES.

Humphrey (16829) English: from the Old French personal name *Humfrey*, introduced to Britain by the Normans. This is composed of the Germanic elements *hūn* 'bear cub' + *frid, fred* 'peace'. It was borne by a 9th-century saint, bishop of Therouanne, who had a certain following in England among Norman settlers.

Humphreys (5683) English and Welsh: variant spelling of HUMPHRIES.

Humphries (6300) English and Welsh: patronymic from HUMPHREY.

Humphry (157) English: variant spelling of HUMPHREY.

GIVEN NAME French 4%. *Camille*.

Humphrys (106) English: variant spelling of HUMPHRIES.

Hund (432) German: variant of HUNDT.

Hundertmark (208) German: nickname for a wealthy man, from Middle High German *hundert* 'hundred' + *mark*, a denomination of coin.

GIVEN NAMES German 4%. *Erna, Kurt*.

Hundley (3192) English (Worcestershire): probably a variant of HINDLEY or HANDLEY.

Hundt (543) German: metonymic occupational name for a keeper of dogs for hunting or other purposes, or derogatory nickname, from Middle High German *hund* 'dog'.

GIVEN NAMES German 4%. *Dieter* (2), *Erwin, Otto*.

Huneke (279) German: from a pet form of the personal name *Huno*, derived from the Germanic element *hūn* 'bear cub'.

GIVEN NAMES German 5%. *Friedhelm* (2), *Kurt*.

Huner (114) German: variant of **Hühner**, a nickname meaning 'giant', 'monster' (see HUHN).

GIVEN NAME German 6%. *Eldor* (2).

Huneycutt (852) Variant spelling of English HUNNICUTT.

Hung (1454) **1.** Chinese 洪: variant of HONG 1. **2.** Chinese 孔: variant of KONG 2. **3.** Chinese 熊: variant of XIONG 1. **4.** Chinese 红: variant of HONG 5.

GIVEN NAMES Chinese 25%; Vietnamese 8%. *Ming* (7), *Ting* (5), *Chin* (3), *Ching* (3), *Hin* (3), *Ying* (3), *Chen* (2), *Cheng* (2), *Cheung* (2), *Chia-Ying* (2), *Chiming* (2), *Chiu* (2); *Tran* (11), *Nguyen* (7), *Bui* (3), *Hao* (3), *Huynh* (3), *Pham* (3), *Doan* (2), *Ly* (2), *Mai* (2), *Trinh* (2), *Truong* (2), *Cao*.

Hungate (431) English: habitational name from various minor places so called, in York, Lincoln, Market Weighton (East Yorkshire), Methley (West Yorkshire), and Sawley (West Yorkshire), all named from Old English *hund* 'hound' or Old Norse *hundr* + Old Norse *gata* 'road', 'street'.

Hunger (435) **1.** German and Dutch: from a Germanic personal name, *Hun(e)ger*, composed of the elements *hūn* 'bear cub' + *gēr, gār* 'spear'. **2.** German: ethnic name from *Ungar, Unger* 'Hungarian'. **3.** German: from Middle High German *hunger* 'hunger'; a nickname for a thin or undernourished person, or sometimes a topographic name from a piece of land named with this word with reference to the infertility of the soil. **4.** English: probably from an Old English personal name, *Hungār*.

GIVEN NAMES German 7%. *Hans* (2), *Helmuth* (2), *Armin, Florian, Franziska, Juerg, Kurt, Otto*.

Hungerford (1433) English: habitational name from Hungerford in Berkshire, named with Old English *hungor* 'hunger' (here probably denoting unproductive land) + *ford* 'ford'. This surname has been established in Ireland since the 17th century.

Hunke (196) German: from the personal name *Hunke*, a pet form of *Huno*, a short form of any of various compound Germanic names formed with *hun* 'Hun',

'giant' or *hūn* 'bear cub' as the first element.

Hunkele (158) German: from a pet form of the personal name HUNKE.

Hunker (247) German: from the Germanic personal name *Hungar*, composed of *hun* 'Hun', 'giant' or *hūn* 'bear cub' + *gēr, gār* 'spear'.

Hunkins (302) English: probably a variant of HANKINS.

Hunkler (100) Swiss German (**Hunkeler**): a derivative of **Hunkel**, from a short form (*Huno*) of a Germanic personal name composed with *hun* 'giant', 'Hun', or *hūn* 'bear cub' as the first element.

Hunley (1412) English: variant spelling of HUNDLEY. This is a common name in TN.

Hunn (600) **1.** English (mainly Norfolk): from an Old English personal name, *Hun(n)a*. **2.** English: from a nickname derived from Old Norse *húnn* 'bear cub'. **3.** German: from the personal name *Huno*, a short form of a Germanic compound name formed with *hun* 'Hun', 'giant' or *hūn* 'bear cub' as the first element.

Hunnell (187) Probably a reduced form of English HONEYWELL.

Hunnewell (313) Variant of English HONEYWELL.

Hunnicutt (1938) English: variant of HONEYCUTT.

Hunnings (108) English: patronymic from the Old English personal name *Hun(n)a*.

Hunsaker (1643) Variant spelling of Swiss German HUNZIKER.

Hunsberger (1058) German: habitational name for someone from a place called Hunsberg or Huntsberg.

Hunsicker (983) Altered spelling of Swiss German HUNZIKER.

Hunsinger (1029) German: variant of HUNTZINGER.

Hunsley (163) English: habitational name from High and Low Hunsley in East Yorkshire, named with an unattested Old English personal name *Hund* 'hound' + *lēah* 'wood', 'glade'.

Hunstad (153) Norwegian: habitational name from any of several farmsteads so named. The place name is derived either from Old Norse *Hunstad*, from the personal name *Huni* + *staðir* 'farmstead', 'dwelling', or from *Hundstad*, formed with the nickname *Hundr*, literally 'dog' + the same second element.

GIVEN NAME Scandinavian 5%. *Nels*.

Hunsucker (919) Variant of Swiss German HUNZIKER.

Hunt (54737) **1.** English: occupational name for a hunter, Old English *hunta* (a primary derivative of *huntian* 'to hunt'). The term was used not only of the hunting on horseback of game such as stags and wild boars, which in the Middle Ages was a pursuit restricted to the ranks of the nobility, but also to much humbler forms of pursuit

such as bird catching and poaching for food. The word seems also to have been used as an Old English personal name and to have survived into the Middle Ages as an occasional personal name. Compare HUNTINGTON and HUNTLEY. **2.** Irish: in some cases (in Ulster) of English origin, but more commonly used as a quasi-translation of various Irish surnames such as Ó Fiaich (see FEE). **3.** Possibly an Americanized spelling of German HUNDT.

Hunte (300) Variant spelling of English HUNT.

Hunter (51238) Scottish, English, and northern Irish: variant of HUNT, a Middle English secondary derivative formed with the addition of the agent noun suffix *-er*.

Hunting (413) English: occupational name from Old English *hunting*, a derivative of *huntian* 'to hunt'.

Huntington (2877) English: habitational name from any of several places so called, named with the genitive plural *huntena* of Old English *hunta* 'hunter' + *tūn* 'enclosure', 'settlement' or *dūn* 'hill' (the forms in *-ton* and *-don* having become inextricably confused). A number of bearers of this name may well derive it from Huntingdon, now in Cambridgeshire (formerly the county seat of the old county of Huntingdonshire), which is named from the genitive case of Old English *hunta* 'huntsman', perhaps used as a personal name, + *dūn* 'hill'.

FOREBEARS A prominent American family of this name was founded by Simon Huntington, who himself never saw the New World, for he died in 1633 on the voyage to Boston, where his widow settled with her children. Their descendants include Jabez Huntington (1719–86), a wealthy West Indies trader, and Samuel Huntington (1731–96), who was one of the signers of the Declaration of Independence. Collis Potter Huntington (1821–1900) was an American railway magnate. Beginning with little education or money, he made a huge fortune, some of which he left to his nephew, Henry Huntington (1850–1927), who used the money to establish the Huntington library and art gallery in CA.

Huntley (4312) **1.** English: habitational name from a place in Gloucestershire, so named from Old English *hunta* 'hunter' (perhaps a byname (see HUNT) + *lēah* 'wood', 'clearing'). **2.** Scottish: habitational name from a lost place called Huntlie in Berwickshire (Borders), with the same etymology as in 1. Huntly in Aberdeenshire was named for a medieval Earl of Huntly (who took his title from the Borders place); it is not the source of the surname.

Hunton (422) English: habitational name from places so called in North Yorkshire, Hampshire, and Kent. The Yorkshire place is named from the Old English personal name *Hūna* + *tūn* 'enclosure', 'settlement';

that in Hampshire from the genitive plural of *hund* 'hound' + *tūn* 'enclosure', 'settlement'; and the Kentish place from Old English *huntena*, genitive plural of *hunta* 'hunter' + *dūn* 'hill'. The present-day distribution shows clusters in North and South Yorkshire, and also in Norfolk.

Huntoon (645) Variant of English HUNTON.

Huntress (246) Scottish: apparently from the feminine form of HUNTER.

Huntsberger (153) German: variant of HUNSBERGER.

Huntsberry (114) Americanized form of German HUNSBERGER.

Huntsinger (392) Americanized spelling of German HUNTZINGER.

Huntsman (1306) English: occupational name for a hunter or a huntsman's servant. The second element is Middle English *man* 'man', 'servant', while the first is either from Old English *hunta* 'hunter' or Middle English *hunte* 'a hunt'. In some cases it is probably from an unattested Old English personal name, *Huntmann* (a compound of *hunta* 'hunter' + *mann* 'man').

Huntzinger (458) German: habitational name for someone from Hintschingen, earlier Huntzingen.

Hunzeker (195) Americanized spelling of Swiss German HUNZIKER.

Hunziker (694) Swiss German: habitational name for someone from either of the places called Hunzikon and Huntziken in Switzerland.
GIVEN NAMES German 4%. *Hans* (2), *Kurt* (2), *Fritz, Hanspeter, Markus, Otto*.

Huo (94) Chinese 霍: the sixth son of the virtuous duke Wen Wang was granted the State of Huo (in present-day Shanxi province) when the Zhou dynasty was established in 1122 BC. His descendants adopted Huo as their surname.

Huot (548) French: from a pet form of the Old French personal name *Hue, Hughe* (see HUGH).
FOREBEARS A Huot, with the secondary surname ST. LAURENT, is documented in Quebec city in 1662.
GIVEN NAMES French 12%. *Andre* (3), *Adelard* (2), *Lucien* (2), *Aime, Cecile, Emile, Germaine, Gilles, Jacques, Jean-Louis, Jean-Marie, Marcel*.

Huotari (149) Finnish: from the Finnish form of the Russian personal name *Fe(o)dor*, from Greek *Theodōros* (see THEODORE). As a family name it is first recorded in the Savo region in the 16th century.
GIVEN NAMES Finnish 8%. *Arvi, Kaisa, Keijo, Veikko, Waino*.

Hupe (186) North German and Dutch: from a short form of HUBERT.
GIVEN NAMES German 4%. *Kurt, Wessel*.

Hupf (105) German: variant of HUPFER.

Hupfer (201) South German (also **Hüpfer**): nickname for a restless individual or an occupational name for a fairground enter-

tainer, from German *Hüpfer* 'hopper', 'jumper' (at fairs), an agent derivative of Middle High German *hupfen* 'to hop, skip, or jump'.
GIVEN NAMES German 6%. *Kurt, Mathias, Merwin*.

Hupka (102) Czech: unexplained.
GIVEN NAME German 5%. *Achim*.

Hupman (115) Probably an altered spelling of German **Huppmann**, a variant of HUPP.

Hupp (1753) **1.** North German form of HUPFER. **2.** German: variant of HUPE. **3.** (**Hüpp**): variant of HIPP 2.

Huppe (136) **1.** French: from *huppe* 'hoopoe' (the bird), perhaps applied as a nickname for someone with hair resembling the hoopoe's crest or a with a long curved nose resembling its bill. **2.** German (also **Hüppe**): from a pet form (*Hubo*) of the personal name *Hugebert*, composed of *hug* 'spirit', 'thought' + *berht* 'bright', 'famous'.
GIVEN NAMES French 20%; Italian 5%. *Andre* (3), *Armand* (3), *Alain, Camille, Cecile, Fernand, Marcel*; *Romeo* (2), *Antonio, Sylvio*.

Huppert (572) German and Jewish (Ashkenazic): variant of HUBERT.

Huq (152) Muslim: variant of HAQ.
GIVEN NAMES Muslim 82%. *Syed* (9), *Abdul* (4), *Mohammad* (4), *Enamul* (3), *Mohammed* (3), *Abu* (2), *Ashraful* (2), *Shamim* (2), *Zahra* (2), *Ziaul* (2), *Anwarul, Asma*.

Hur (346) Korean: variant of **Hŏ** (see HO).
GIVEN NAMES Korean 57%. *Young* (8), *Jung* (5), *Jae* (3), *Kwang* (3), *Man* (3), *Sung* (3), *Jin* (2), *Jong* (2), *Joon* (2), *Kuk* (2), *Kyung* (2), *Won* (2), *Min* (4), *Nam* (3), *Woon* (3), *Chung* (2), *Beom, Byung, Chang, Cho, Choon, Chul, Dong Hoon, Dong Soo*.

Hurd (7237) English (chiefly Midlands): variant spelling of HEARD.

Hurdle (846) English: probably a metonymic occupational name for a hurdle maker, from Middle English *herdle, hurdel* 'hurdle'.

Hurford (240) English (chiefly southwestern England and South Wales): habitational name from an unidentified place, probably a variant of HARFORD or HEREFORD.

Hurlbert (674) English: variant of HURLBUT.

Hurlburt (1495) English: variant of HURLBUT.

Hurlbut (1028) English: nickname from a medieval throwing game, known as *hurlebat(te)*.

Hurlbutt (254) English: variant spelling of HURLBUT.

Hurless (220) English: variant of HARLESS. This name is found chiefly in OH.

Hurley (14991) **1.** Irish: variant of HERLIHY. **2.** Irish (Munster): Anglicized form of Gaelic **Ó hUrthuile** 'descendant of *Urthuile*'. **3.** Irish: Anglicized form of

Gaelic **Ó Murthuile**, 'descendant of *Murthuile*' (see MURLEY). **4.** English: habitational name from places in Berkshire and Warwickshire so named from Old English *hyrne* 'corner', 'bend' + *lēah* 'wood', 'clearing'.

Hurliman (152) Swiss German (**Hürlimann**): topographic name for someone from a place named with the field name *Hürnli* (see HORN 1).

Hurlock (295) English: variant of **Harlock**, a nickname for someone with gray hair, from Old English *hār* 'gray' + *locc* 'lock'.

Hurlocker (104) Americanized form of German HORLACHER.

Hurm (208) German (also **Hürm**): status name for a lowly farmer, one owning only a single strip of land, from *hurm* 'strip of land'.

Hurn (391) English: variant spelling of HEARN 4.

Hurney (190) Irish: Anglicized form of a Gaelic name, possibly **Ó hUrnaidhe** 'descendant of *Urnaidhe*', though MacLysaght considers this to be doubtful.

Huron (264) French: **1.** occupational name for a sapper, one who laid mines during a siege. **2.** nickname for someone with an untidy head of shaggy hair, from a diminutive of the past participle of Old French *hurer* 'to bristle', 'ruffle', 'stand on end' (a word of uncertain, possibly Germanic, origin). **3.** ethnic name for a member of an American Indian people who lived around the shores of Lake Ontario.
GIVEN NAMES Spanish 6%. *Ernesto* (2), *Adelita, Alfredo, Ana, Consuelo, Francisco, Juan, Juanita, Junita, Manuel, Margarita, Oralia*.

Hurr (121) English (Suffolk): unexplained.

Hurrell (237) **1.** English (of Norman origin): from a derivative of Old French *hurer* 'to bristle or ruffle', 'to stand on end' (see HURON). **2.** Irish: this may be an Anglicized form of Gaelic **Ó hEarghaill** 'descendant of *Earghall*', a variant of **Ó Fearghail** (see FARRELL).

Hurrle (132) South German (Baden-Württemberg; **Hürrle**): nickname for a busy, noisy, fast-moving person, from *hurren* 'to hurry' or 'rush about'.
GIVEN NAME German 4%. *Otto* (2).

Hurry (227) English (of Norman origin): from a Norman form of the Middle English personal name *Wol(f)rich* (with the addition of an inorganic initial *H-*) (see WOOLDRIDGE).

Hursey (554) English: habitational name from Hursey in Dorset, so named from the Old English personal name *Heorstān* + Old English *(ge)hæg* 'enclosure'.

Hursh (689) Americanized spelling of German and Jewish HIRSCH.

Hurst (16091) **1.** English: topographic name for someone who lived on a wooded hill, Old English *hyrst*, or habitational name from one of the various places named with this word, for example Hurst in Berkshire, Kent, Somerset, and Warwickshire, or Hirst in Northumberland and West Yorkshire. **2.** Irish: re-Anglicized form of **de Horsaigh**, Gaelicized form of the English habitational name HORSEY, established in Ireland since the 13th century. **3.** German: topographic name from Middle High German *hurst* 'woodland', 'thicket'.

Hurston (250) English: habitational name, probably from either of two places in Devon or one West Sussex so named. Hurston in Chagford, Devon is named with the Old English personal name *Heort* or *heort* 'hart' + *tūn* 'settlement'; Hurston in Whitestone, Devon has the same first element + *þorn* 'thorn tree'; and Hurston in Storrington, West Sussex is named from Old English *hyrst* 'wooded hill' + *tūn*.

Hurt (6749) **1.** English (chiefly Nottinghamshire): variant of HART. **2.** German: topographic name from Middle High German *hurt* 'hurdle', 'woven fence'. **3.** Dutch: nickname, presumably for a pugnacious or aggressive person, from Middle Dutch *hort*, *hurt* 'strike', 'blow', 'attack'.

Hurta (163) Czech: nickname for an aggressive person, from *hurt* 'attack'.

Hurtado (2535) Spanish: nickname from the past participle of *hurtar* 'to rob or conceal' (Late Latin *furtare*, from *furtum* 'theft', *fur* 'thief'). The reference was probably to an illegitimate child, whose existence was concealed, or to a kidnapped child.
GIVEN NAMES Spanish 51%. *Jose* (62), *Juan* (46), *Carlos* (33), *Manuel* (23), *Jorge* (20), *Rafael* (20), *Luis* (19), *Pedro* (19), *Raul* (19), *Jesus* (17), *Francisco* (16), *Salvador* (14).

Hurteau (192) French: from a diminutive derivative of Old French *hurter* 'to strike'.

Hurter (125) German: topographic name for someone living by a wattle fence or hurdle, from Middle High German *hurt* 'hurdle', 'woven fence'.
GIVEN NAME German 4%. *Otto*.

Hurtgen (118) **1.** German (**Hürtgen**): habitational name from a place so called near Düren, Rhineland. **2.** Rhenish pet form of HURT.

Hurtig (240) **1.** German and Jewish (Ashkenazic): nickname from Middle High German *hurtec*, German *hurtig* 'brisk', 'rapid'. **2.** Swedish: soldier's name or nickname from *hurtig* 'brisk', 'rapid'.
GIVEN NAME Scandinavian 7%. *Per*.

Hurtt (721) Respelling of HURT.

Hurtubise (180) Altered spelling of French **Heurtebise**, which may be a topographic name for someone living in an exposed situation, buffeted by the north wind, from Old French *hurte(r)* 'to collide, knock against' + *bise* 'north wind', both these elements being of Germanic origin; a related place name is Heurtevent in Calvados. It is also possible that it may have been a hu-

morous nickname for someone with a prominent nose.
FOREBEARS A bearer of this name from the Maine region of France is documented in Montreal in 1660; the name is recorded as both Hurtubise and Heurtebise.
GIVEN NAMES French 10%. *Francois*, *Marcel*, *Michel*, *Normand*, *Serge*, *Yvon*.

Hurvitz (157) Jewish (Ashkenazic): variant of HOROWITZ.
GIVEN NAMES Jewish 10%. *Hyman*, *Igal*, *Ilan*, *Isadore*, *Nachum*, *Sol*.

Hurwitz (1732) Jewish (Ashkenazic): variant of HOROWITZ.
GIVEN NAMES Jewish 7%. *Hyman* (4), *Sol* (3), *Emanuel* (2), *Mendel* (2), *Meyer* (2), *Miriam* (2), *Myer* (2), *Abbe*, *Alter*, *Ari*, *Aryeh*, *Avi*.

Husa (139) Czech: from *husa* 'goose'; a nickname, a metonymic occupational name for someone who reared geese, or a habitational name for someone who lived at a house distinguished by the sign of a goose.

Husain (498) Muslim: from the Arabic personal name *Ḥusayn*, a diminutive of *Ḥasan* 'good', 'handsome' (see HASAN). Husain (c. 626–680) and his elder brother Hasan were sons of the khalif 'Alī ibn Abī Ṭālib (see ALI) and, through their mother Fatima, grandsons of the Prophet Muhammad. The death of Husain in a massacre at Karbela signaled the beginning of a long period of internecine strife in the Muslim world. Shiite Muslims regard Hasan and his brother Husain as the true successors of Muhammad, and observe the day of his death as a day of mourning. The name is popular among Sunni Muslims as well as Shiites.
GIVEN NAMES Muslim 85%. *Syed* (47), *Mohammed* (7), *Iqbal* (6), *Akhtar* (4), *Ali* (4), *Bibi* (4), *Ishrat* (4), *Mohammad* (4), *Nasir* (4), *Abid* (3), *Arif* (3), *Arshad* (3).

Husak (324) Czech and Slovak (**Husák**): from a derivative of *husa* 'gander' (see HUSA, and compare GANDER).

Husar (227) **1.** Czech and Slovak (**Husár**): from Czech *husar* 'hussar' (see HUSZAR). **2.** Czech: (**Husař**): occupational name for a keeper of or dealer in geese, *husař*.

Husband (1132) English: occupational name for a peasant farmer, from Middle English *husband* 'tiller of the soil', 'husbandman'. The term (late Old English *hūsbonda*, Old Norse *húsbóndi*), a compound of *hús* 'house' + *bóndi* (see BOND) originally described a man who was head of his own household, and this may have been the sense in some of the earliest examples of the surname.

Husbands (401) English: patronymic from HUSBAND.

Husby (358) Norwegian: habitational name from any of numerous farmsteads so named, especially in central Norway (see HUSEBY).
GIVEN NAMES Scandinavian 8%. *Lars*, *Thor*.

Huscher (114) **1.** German: from the Germanic personal name *Huzo* (see HUSS 3). **2.** (Of Slavic origin) from Czech and Sorbian *hus* 'goose', a nickname with a similar application as GANS.

Huschka (150) **1.** East German: variant of HUSCHER. **2.** Germanized form of Czech **Huška**, from an aphetic pet form of the personal name *Bohuša*.
GIVEN NAMES German 5%. *Franz*, *Fritz*, *Mathias*.

Huse (812) North German: from Middle Low German *hūs* 'house' (see HOUSE 1), which may also refer to an important building such as the town hall, a castle, or a manor house, so that the name would indicate dwelling in close proximity to these, or perhaps it is an epithet for a servant who worked at a great house.

Huseby (489) Norwegian: habitational name from any of numerous farmsteads, notably in southeastern Norway, so named from Old Norse *Húsabýr* from *hús* 'house' + *býr* 'farmstead', 'settlement'.
GIVEN NAMES Scandinavian 5%. *Sven* (2), *Erik*, *Hilmer*, *Nord*, *Nordahl*.

Huseman (535) North German (**Husemann**): epithet for a servant or an administrator who worked at a great house, from Middle Low German *hūs* 'house' (see HOUSE 1, HUSE) + *man* 'man'.

Husen (184) German: habitational name from any of several places so called, for example near Paderborn.
GIVEN NAMES German 6%. *Bernhard*, *Kurt*.

Huser (516) **1.** North German form of HAUSER, from an agent derivative of Middle Low German *hūs* 'house', or a nickname from the same word in the sense 'provider of shelter', 'protector'. **2.** Germanized form of Slavic HUSAR.

Huset (124) Possibly a respelling of Norwegian HUSETH.

Huseth (170) Norwegian: habitational name from any of several farmsteads named Huseth, probably from the definite singular form of *hus* 'house'.

Hush (130) English and Scottish: unexplained.

Husk (468) English: unexplained.

Huska (184) **1.** Americanized spelling of Finnish **Huuska**, a name of uncertain etymology, common in north-central and eastern Finland. **2.** Czech (**Húska**): dialect variant of HOUSKA.

Huske (113) **1.** English: variant spelling of HUSK. **2.** East German: variant of HUSCHKA. **3.** German (**Hüske**): topographic name for someone who lived in a very small (stone) house, from the diminutive form of Middle Low German *hūs* 'house'.

Huskey (2361) **1.** English (Warwickshire) and Scottish (Stirling, Lanarkshire, West Lothian): unexplained. **2.** Americanized form of German HUSKE or HUESKE.

Huskins (588) English: variant of HOSKINS.

Huskisson (132) English: patronymic from HOSKIN.

Husky (98) English, Scottish, or German: variant of HUSKEY.

Husman (328) North German: variant of HUSEMAN.

Husmann (326) North German: variant of HUSEMAN.

GIVEN NAMES German 6%. *Otto* (2), *Elfriede*, *Gerhard*, *Konrad*, *Kurt*.

Huso (136) Norwegian: habitational name from a farmstead named Huso, probably from the dative plural of *hus* 'house'.

Huson (367) **1.** French: variant of HUSSON. **2.** English: patronymic from HUGH.

Huss (2472) **1.** North German: status name for a householder or for someone who lived or worked at a house, Middle Low German *hūs* 'house' (see HOUSE). **2.** Czech and Slovak (**Hus**), German, and Jewish (Ashkenazic): from Czech *husa* 'goose' (see HUSA). **3.** German: from the Germanic personal name *Huzo*, a short form of any of the various compound names formed with *hugi* 'heart', 'mind', 'spirit' as the first element. **4.** Swedish: most probably from German. **5.** Jewish (Ashkenazic): unexplained.

Hussain (1732) Muslim: variant spelling of HUSAIN.

GIVEN NAMES Muslim 88%. *Syed* (129), *Mohammed* (50), *Mohammad* (33), *Zahid* (22), *Altaf* (20), *Akhtar* (15), *Muhammad* (15), *Abid* (14), *Ali* (14), *Arshad* (13), *Iqbal* (12), *Manzoor* (12).

Hussar (182) Americanized form of Hungarian HUSZAR or Czech and Slovak HUSAR.

Hussein (509) Muslim: variant spelling of HUSAIN.

GIVEN NAMES Muslim 80%. *Ahmed* (13), *Mohamed* (12), *Ali* (9), *Mohammed* (8), *Hussein* (7), *Mohammad* (7), *Ahmad* (6), *Maged* (6), *Mohamad* (6), *Hassan* (4), *Jamal* (4), *Ibrahim* (3).

Husser (273) German: **1.** habitational name from Hussen in Westphalia. **2.** variant of HUSCHER.

GIVEN NAME French 4%. *Roch*.

Hussey (3470) **1.** Irish: reduced Anglicized form of Gaelic **Ó hEodhusa** 'descendant of *Eodhus*'; this was the name of a bardic family associated with the Maguires of Fermanagh, also Anglicized as OSWELL, OSWALD. **2.** English (of Norman origin): habitational name from Houssaye in Seine-Maritime, so called from a collective noun from Old French *hous* 'holly'. **3.** English: nickname for a woman who was mistress of her own household, from Middle English *husewif* (a compound of Old English *hūs* 'house' + *wīf* 'woman'). It was not until the 17th century that this word acquired pejorative connotations.

Hussman (125) North German (**Hussmann**): variant of HUSEMAN.

Husson (249) French: from a pet form of the Old French personal name *Hue* (see HUGH).

GIVEN NAMES French 6%. *Michel*, *Pierre*.

Hussong (303) Germanized spelling of French HUSSON.

Hust (457) German: habitational name from various places, for example Huste near Melle or Husten near Olpe.

Hustad (360) Norwegian: habitational name from any of several farmsteads, notably in Møre and Trøndelag, named in Old Norse either as *Húsastaðir* (from *hús* 'house' + *staðir* 'farmstead', 'dwelling') or as *Hústaðr* '(house)lot', 'site'.

GIVEN NAME Scandinavian 4%. *Sig*.

Hustead (262) Americanized spelling of **Hustedt** (see HUSTED).

Husted (1678) North German (**Hustedt**) and Danish: habitational name from any of several places named Hustedt.

Hustedt (106) North German and Danish: see HUSTED.

GIVEN NAMES German 6%; Scandinavian 4%. *Hans* (2), *Dietrich*.

Huster (264) **1.** German: habitational name for someone from any of several places called Husten in Westphalia. **2.** German: a nickname for someone with a cough, from *husten* 'to cough'. **3.** German: an occupational name for harvester of grass or grain, from Middle High German *hūsten* 'to set up sheaves of hay or grain'.

GIVEN NAMES German 4%. *Armin*, *Heinrich*, *Othmar*.

Huston (6277) Scottish: variant spelling of HOUSTON 1.

Huszar (128) Hungarian (**Huszár**): status name for a hussar, a member of a light, fast-riding cavalry regiment. The Hungarian vocabulary word is from Old Croatian *husar* 'robber', 'plunderer'.

GIVEN NAMES Hungarian 15%. *Attila* (2), *Gabor*, *Gyula*, *Istvan*, *Jozsef*, *Kalman*, *Tibor*, *Zoltan*.

Hutch (114) English: from the medieval personal name *Huche*, a pet form of HUGH.

Hutchcraft (326) English (Huntingdon): unexplained. Probably a habitational name from a lost or unidentified place named with the Middle English personal name HUTCH + *craft* 'mill' or *croft* 'paddock'.

Hutchcroft (130) English (Yorkshire): unexplained. Compare HUTCHCRAFT.

Hutchens (2944) English: patronymic from the medieval personal name *Huchin*, a pet form of HUGH (see HUTCHEON).

Hutcheon (153) English and Scottish: from the medieval personal name *Huchin*, a pet form of HUGH.

Hutcherson (2063) Scottish: variant of HUTCHISON.

Hutcheson (3356) Scottish: variant spelling of HUTCHISON.

Hutchings (2958) English (chiefly Devon and Somerset): patronymic from the

medieval personal name *Hutchin*, a pet form of HUGH.

Hutchins (9366) Southern English: patronymic from the medieval personal name *Hutchin*, a pet form of HUGH.

Hutchinson (16961) Northern English: patronymic from the medieval personal name *Hutchin*, a pet form of HUGH.

FOREBEARS Anne Marbury Hutchinson (1591–1643) and her husband William came from Lincolnshire, England, to MA in 1634. A religious dissident, she led the first attack on the Puritans and was banished from the Massachusetts Bay Colony. She moved to RI in 1638, and, after her husband's death in 1642, settled in NY, where the Hutchinson River was named in her honor. Ironically, the Hutchinson name stayed on in MA and one of her descendants, Thomas Hutchinson (1711–80), was royal governor of Massachusetts Bay Colony.

Hutchison (9195) Scottish: patronymic from the medieval personal name *Hutche*, a variant of HUGH.

Huter (120) German: **1.** occupational name for a hatter, Middle High German *huotære*, *huoter*. **2.** (**Hüter**): see HUETHER.

GIVEN NAMES German 8%. *Hans*, *Hermann*, *Manfred*, *Theodor*.

Huth (1554) German: metonymic occupational name for a maker of hats or a nickname for a wearer of distinctive hats, from Middle High German *huot* 'hat'. Compare the cognates HOOD and HATT.

GIVEN NAMES German 4%. *Hans* (5), *Otto* (4), *Kurt* (3), *Erwin* (2), *Egon*, *Ernst*, *Franz*, *Milbert*, *Oskar*.

Huther (125) German: variant of HUTER.

GIVEN NAMES German 6%. *Arno*, *Hans*, *Ralf*.

Hutmacher (198) German: occupational name for a hatmaker, Middle High German *hudemacher*.

Hutman (124) German (**Hutmann**): occupational name for a hatmaker, Middle High German *hudeman*.

Hutner (100) German: **1.** variant of HUTER. **2.** probably a variant of **Hüttner** (see HUETTNER).

Hutnick (139) Germanized or Americanized spelling of HUTNIK.

Hutnik (112) Czech, Polish, and Jewish (Ashkenazic): occupational name from Czech and Polish *hutnik* 'smelter'.

Hutsell (779) Possibly an altered spelling of HUTZEL. This is a frequent name in TN and MO.

Hutson (5677) English (mainly Lincolnshire): patronymic from the medieval personal name *Hudde* (see HUTT 1).

Hutt (1165) **1.** English: from the popular medieval personal name *Hudde*, which is of complex origin. It is usually explained as a pet form of HUGH, but there was a pre-existing Old English personal name, *Hūda*, underlying place names such as Huddington, Worcestershire. This personal name may well still have been in use at the time of the Norman Conquest. If so, it was absorbed by the Norman HUGH and its many diminutives. Reaney adduces evidence that *Hudde* was also regarded as a pet form of RICHARD. **2.** German: from a short form of a Germanic compound personal name formed with *hut* 'guard' as the first element. **3.** Variant spelling of German **Hütt** (see HUETT). **4.** Jewish (Ashkenazic): metonymic occupational name from Yiddish *hut*, German *Hut* 'hat' (see HUTH).

Hutter (1147) **1.** German and Jewish (Ashkenazic): occupational name for a hatter from an agent derivative of Middle High German *huot* 'hat'; Yiddish *hut*, German *Hut* 'hat'. **2.** German (**Hütter**): topographic name from Middle High German *hütte* 'hut'. **3.** English: when not of German origin (see above), perhaps a variant of **Hotter**, an occupational name for a basket maker, Middle English *hottere*; the same term also denoted someone who carried baskets of sand for making mortar. Alternatively it may have denoted someone who lived in a hut or shed, from a derivative of Middle English *hotte, hutte* 'hut', 'shed'.
GIVEN NAMES German 6%. *Kurt* (3), *Alois* (2), *Erwin* (2), *Heinz* (2), *Alfons, Ernst, Franz, Gerhard, Hedwig, Konrad, Otto, Reinhard.*

Huttner (230) German and Jewish (Ashkenazic): variant of HUTTER 1.

Hutto (3095) Origin unidentified. This is a frequent name in SC, TX, and GA.
FOREBEARS Isaac Hutto is recorded in Orangeburg county, SC, in 1735.

Hutton (6970) Scottish and northern English: habitational name from any of the numerous places so called from Old English *hōh* 'ridge', 'spur' + *tūn* 'enclosure', 'settlement'.

Hutzel (236) German: from a short form of a Germanic personal name, *Huzo*, composed with the element *hug* 'mind'.

Hutzell (271) Respelling of German HUTZEL.

Hutzler (403) South German: variant of HUTZEL.
GIVEN NAMES French 4%. *Dominique, Jacques, Patrice.*

Huval (399) Possibly an altered spelling of Dutch **Heuvel**, a nickname for a hunchback, from Middle Dutch *heuvel, ho(e)vel* 'hump', 'bump'.
GIVEN NAME French 4%. *Aurelien.*

Huver (127) Dutch and North German: status name for a prosperous small farmer. Compare South German HUBER.

Huwe (259) German: nickname from Middle High German *huwe* '(great horned) owl', or a habitational name from a house distinguished by the sign of an owl.
GIVEN NAMES German 6%. *Dieter, Eldor, Otto.*

Hux (608) German: probably from a topographic name Huck or Hucks, of uncertain

origin. It occurs in many place and field names.

Huxford (205) English: habitational name from a place in Devon called Huxford (preserved in the name of Huxford Farm), from the Old English personal name *Hōcc* or the Old English word *hōc* 'hook or angle of land' + *ford* 'ford'.

Huxhold (125) German: habitational name from Hoxhohl or Huxo in the Odenwald or Hüxholl in Westphalia, named in Middle Low German as *huckes hol* 'mud hole'.
GIVEN NAMES French 4%. *Amie, Germaine.*

Huxley (247) English (mainly Shropshire): habitational name from a place in Cheshire, which is probably so called from the genitive case of the Old English personal name *Hucc* or from Old English *husc, hux* 'insult', 'taunt' + *lēah* 'wood', 'clearing'.

Huxtable (303) English (mainly Devon): habitational name from a farm in North Devon on a spur of Exmoor, named with the Old English personal name *Hōc* or Old English *hōc* 'hook or spur of land' + *stapol* 'post'.

Huy (124) **1.** German: Sorbian kinship term meaning 'uncle'. **2.** East Asian: unexplained.
GIVEN NAMES Southeast Asian 17%. *Tran* (2), *Bui, Duong, Lam, Ly, Nga, Nguyen, Riem, Sambath, Saroeun, Thap.*

Huyck (458) Dutch: **1.** from *huik* 'hooded cloak'; a metonymic occupational name for a cloak maker or a nickname for someone who normally wore a cloak. **2.** variant of HUCK 3. **3.** (**van Huyck**): habitational name from any of various minor places called Huik.

Huyett (240) Variant spelling of French **Huyet**, a pet form of the personal name *Hugues*.
FOREBEARS A Huyet or Huguet from the Champagne region of France is recorded in Montreal in 1718. The secondary surnames **Poncelet** and **Champagne** also occur with this name.

Huyler (163) Probably of Dutch origin: unexplained. This name is found chiefly in NY and NJ.

Huynh (6111) Vietnamese (**Huỳnh**): unexplained.
GIVEN NAMES Vietnamese 57%; Chinese 19%. *Thanh* (103), *Minh* (69), *Hung* (68), *Hoa* (61), *Anh* (60), *Dung* (60), *Quang* (50), *Tam* (49), *Hai* (42), *Son* (40), *Long* (38), *Lan* (37), *Tuan* (37); *Hong* (32), *Sang* (21), *Chi* (20), *Phong* (18), *Tong* (16), *Dong* (13), *Lai* (11), *Ho* (8), *Sen* (7), *Chien* (6), *Han* (5), *Hon* (5), *Man* (5).

Huyser (291) Dutch: derivative of *huis* 'house' + the agent noun suffix *-er*, a status name for a householder (compare HUSEMAN) or possibly for an innkeeper.

Hwang (3272) **1.** Korean: there is one Chinese character for the Hwang surname. Some sources indicate that there are 163 Hwang clans, but only eleven can be posi-

tively documented. The founding ancestor of the Hwang clans was named Hwang Nak. He was a Chinese emissary who had been sent on a mission to Vietnam. Instead of going to Vietnam, however, he went to Korea and settled there in AD 23. Each of Hwang Nak's three sons were founding ancestors of their own clans, and some of their descendants founded additional Hwang clans. **2.** Chinese 黄: variant of HUANG.
GIVEN NAMES Chinese/Korean 53%. *Young* (31), *Sun* (21), *Yong* (18), *Jung* (14), *Jong* (13), *Kyung* (13), *Jae* (12), *Sung* (11), *In* (10), *Soo* (10), *Song* (9), *Ho* (8); *Chong* (16), *Chung* (9), *Chang* (7), *Myong* (7), *Chul* (6), *Byung* (5), *Dae* (5), *Seong* (5), *Kum* (4), *Hae* (3), *Hak* (3), *Jung Sook* (3).

Hy (114) **1.** Variant of English HIGH. **2.** Chinese 解: Taishan spelling of XIE 2. **3.** Vietnamese: unexplained.
GIVEN NAMES Chinese 22%; Vietnamese 18%. *Heng* (2), *Hong* (2), *Sang* (2), *Dong, Khin, Kin, Kong, Man, Sin, Yong; Soi* (2), *Cong, Dang, Dau, Duoc, Mui, Nhi, Phu, Quyen, Tau.*

Hyams (374) Jewish: Americanized form of any of the various Ashkenazic surnames derived from the Yiddish personal name *Khayem, Khayim* (see HEIM).

Hyatt (6828) **1.** English (mainly London and Surrey): possibly a topographic name from Middle English *hegh, hie* 'high' + *yate* 'gate'. **2.** Jewish (American): Americanized spelling of CHAIT.

Hybarger (108) Americanized form of German HEIBERGER or HEUBERGER.
GIVEN NAME French 4%. *Monique.*

Hyche (433) English: unexplained. Perhaps an altered form of **Hytch**, a variant spelling of HITCH (see RICHARD). This surname is found mainly in AL.

Hyde (11184) **1.** English: topographic name for someone living on (and farming) a hide of land, Old English *hī(gi)d*. This was a variable measure of land, differing from place to place and time to time, and seems from the etymology to have been originally fixed as the amount necessary to support one (extended) family (Old English *hīgan, hīwan* 'household'). In some cases the surname is habitational, from any of the many minor places named with this word, as for example Hyde in Greater Manchester, Bedfordshire, and Hampshire. The surname has long been established in Ireland. **2.** English: variant of IDE, with inorganic initial *H-*. Compare HERRICK. **3.** Jewish (American): Americanized spelling of HAID.

Hyden (918) **1.** English: possibly a habitational name from Clayhidon in Devon (recorded as *Hidon, Hydon* up to the end of the 15th century), which was originally named from Old English *hīeg* 'hay' + *dūn* 'hill', or from any of the places named Iden (see IDEN), of which there are two examples in Kent and one in East Sussex. In medieval records these all occur with the spelling *Hiden* or *Hyden*. **2.** German: unexplained. **3.** Altered spelling of German HEIDEN. **4.** Dutch (**van der Hyden**): topographic name for a moorland dweller (see HEIDE 2).

Hyder (1655) English: status name for someone who farmed a *hide* of land (see HYDE).

Hydock (154) **1.** Perhaps an Americanized form of Czech HEJDUK. **2.** Alternatively, perhaps, an altered spelling of the English habitational name HADDOCK. The name is found predominantly in PA.

Hydrick (295) Americanized spelling of Dutch HEIDRICH.

Hyer (1073) Americanized spelling of German HEIER, HAYER, or HEYER.

Hyers (223) **1.** English: unexplained. **2.** Variant of Dutch HIERS.

Hyett (111) English: variant spelling of HYATT.

Hyink (110) Dutch: unexplained.

Hyjek (104) Polish: nickname from the dialect word *chyjać* 'avoid', 'disappear', nickname for an escapee, deserter, or refugee.
GIVEN NAME Polish 4%. *Bronislaw*.

Hyke (102) Americanized spelling of German HEICK.
GIVEN NAME French 5%. *Vernice*.

Hykes (220) Czech (**Hykeš**): from the personal name *Hugo* (see HUGH).

Hylan (117) Variant of Scottish and English HYLAND.

Hyland (3166) **1.** Scottish and English: topographic name for someone who lived on high ground or by land where hay was grown, from Middle English *hegh*, *hie* 'high' or *heye* 'hay' + *land* 'land'. **2.** Irish: Anglicized form of Gaelic **Ó hAoileáin**, a variant of **Ó Faoláin** (see WHELAN). **3.** Swedish: possibly an ornamental name based on Greek *hulē* 'wood' + *land* 'land'.
GIVEN NAMES Irish 7%. *Brendan* (3), *Kieran*, *Parnell*, *Seamus*, *Siobhan*.

Hyle (226) Americanized spelling of Dutch HEIL.

Hylen (112) **1.** Swedish (**Hylén**): unexplained. **2.** Norwegian: habitational name from either of two farms, of uncertain etymology.
GIVEN NAMES Scandinavian 8%. *Knute*, *Niels*, *Swen*.

Hyler (428) Americanized spelling of German HEILER.

Hyles (131) English: variant of HILES.

Hylton (2586) English: variant spelling of HILTON.

Hyman (4618) **1.** Jewish (American): Americanized variant of HEIMAN. **2.** English: variant of HAYMAN. **3.** Americanized spelling of HEIMANN.

Hymas (343) English (chiefly Essex): unexplained; perhaps a variant of **Haymes**, from the Old French personal name *Haim*, of Germanic origin.

Hymel (772) Origin unidentified. Perhaps an altered form of German and Dutch HUMMEL, under French influence. This name is found mainly in LA.
GIVEN NAMES French 6%. *Albon* (2), *Octave* (2), *Andre*, *Angelle*, *Antoine*, *Dumas*, *Leonie*, *Leontine*.

Hymer (381) Americanized spelling of German HEIMER.

Hymes (587) Americanized spelling of German HEIMS.

Hymon (90) **1.** Polish: possibly a variant spelling of the Ukrainian patronymic **Hyman**, from the personal name *Hyma*. **2.** Possibly a variant spelling of American Jewish HYMAN.

Hymowitz (155) Jewish: Americanized spelling of HAIMOWITZ.
GIVEN NAMES Jewish 6%; German 4%. *Isadore*.

Hynd (121) Scottish: variant spelling of HIND.

Hyndman (473) **1.** Scottish: possibly a nickname from Middle English *hende* 'courteous' (see HENDY), or an occupational name for a deer-keeper, from Middle English *hind* 'female deer'. **2.** Jewish (Ashkenazic): metronymic from the female personal name *Hinde*.

Hynds (286) **1.** English: patronymic from HIND. **2.** Irish: variant of HINES.

Hynek (400) Czech: from a pet form of the German personal name *Heinrich* (see HENRY).

Hyneman (164) Americanized spelling of Dutch or German HEINEMAN.

Hynes (3187) **1.** Irish: variant spelling of HINES. **2.** English: patronymic from HINE. **3.** Possibly an Americanized spelling of German HEINS or HEINZ.
GIVEN NAMES Irish 7%. *Aidan*, *Conor*, *Dermot*, *Fintan*.

Hynson (435) English: perhaps a patronymic from HINE.

Hypes (440) Origin unidentified. Possibly a variant of English HIPPS or HEAPS. This is a common name in WV. Compare HIPES.

Hypolite (159) French: from the personal name *Hippolyte*, from Greek *Hippolytos*, composed of the elements *hippos* 'horse' + *lyein* 'to loose', 'release' (see IPPOLITO).

Hyppolite (147) French: variant spelling of HYPOLITE.
GIVEN NAMES French 39%. *Antoine*, *Dominique*, *Fernande*, *Franck*, *Herve*, *Jean Jacques*, *Jean-Claude*, *Lucienne*, *Maxime*, *Michel*, *Philomene*, *Pierre*.

Hyre (412) Americanized spelling of HEIER.

Hysell (595) Americanized spelling of German HEISEL.

Hyser (204) Americanized spelling of German HEISER.

Hyslop (528) Scottish and northern English: habitational name from an unidentified place in northern England, perhaps so called from Old English *hæsel* (or the Old Norse equivalent *hesli*) 'hazel' + *hop* 'enclosed valley'.

Hysmith (132) Variant spelling of English HIGHSMITH.

Hyson (446) English: evidently a patronymic, but unexplained; perhaps a variant of HEWSON.

Hysong (149) Of uncertain origin (see HUSSONG 1). The name occurs mainly in PA and IN.

Hyun (454) Korean (**Hyŏn**): there is one Chinese character for the surname Hyŏn. Some records indicate that there are 106 Hyŏn clans, but only four can be documented, and these all descend from the same founding ancestor. The Hyŏn clan founding ancestor was a Koryŏ general named Hyŏn Tam-yun, who lived during the latter part of the 12th century. Members of the Hyŏn clan can be found throughout Korea, with high concentrations in Kyŏngsang North province, Kyŏnggi province, Ch'ungch'ŏng South province, and Chŏlla South province.
GIVEN NAMES Korean 59%. *Young* (13), *Sung* (8), *Byung* (4), *Chang* (4), *Jung* (4), *Soon* (4), *Yun* (4), *Jae* (3), *Jong* (3), *Kyung* (3), *Myung* (3), *Sang* (3), *Chul* (2), *Chang Sup* (2), *Dong* (2), *Jang* (2), *Soo Jin* (2), *Chong*, *Chung*, *Deuk*, *Do Young*, *Dong Chul*, *Hee Sook*, *Hyunsook*.

Hyzer (147) Americanized spelling of German HEISER.

I

Iaccarino (114) Italian: from a pet form of the unexplained personal name *Iaccaro*.
GIVEN NAMES Italian 29%. *Antonio* (2), *Salvatore* (2), *Antonella, Camillo, Carlo, Ciro, Gennaro, Lorenzo, Mario, Raffaele, Sergio.*

Iacobelli (161) Italian: patronymic or plural form of the personal name *Iacobello*, a pet form of *Iacobo*, Latin *Iacobus* (see JACOB).
GIVEN NAMES Italian 32%. *Emilio* (2), *Grazio* (2), *Luciano* (2), *Aldo, Antonio, Carlo, Domenic, Domenico, Donato, Franco, Onofrio, Ottavio, Salvatore.*

Iacobucci (338) Italian: patronymic or plural form of the personal name *Iacobucco*, Latin *Iacobus* (see JACOB).
GIVEN NAMES Italian 26%. *Primo* (3), *Attilio* (2), *Antonio, Camillo, Carmine, Cesidio, Domenic, Donato, Emidio, Enzo, Gennaro, Guillermo, Livia, Mario, Orestes, Orlando, Renato, Santa, Teodoro.*

Iacona (167) Southern Italian: variant of IACONO.
GIVEN NAMES Italian 22%. *Salvatore* (3), *Vito* (3), *Angelo* (2), *Antonio, Gaetano, Pietro, Pino, Sal.*

Iacono (698) Southern Italian: **1.** according to Caracausi, this is from *iacono*, southern dialect form of *diacono* 'deacon', hence an occupational name for someone in the service of a deacon or a nickname for someone thought to resemble a deacon. **2.** Possibly from an augmentative of *Giacco*, a short form of the personal name GIACOMO.
GIVEN NAMES Italian 31%. *Mario* (7), *Salvatore* (6), *Giovanni* (5), *Sal* (5), *Vito* (4), *Angelo* (3), *Carmine* (3), *Gaetano* (3), *Gennaro* (3), *Giuseppe* (3), *Silverio* (3), *Aniello* (2), *Antonio* (2), *Leonardo* (2), *Pacifico, Rodolfo, Rosario, Salvadore, Ubaldo.*

Iacovelli (291) Italian: variant of IACOBELLI.
GIVEN NAMES Italian 12%; French 4%. *Sante* (2), *Domenic, Donato, Giacomo, Guido, Marco, Pasquale, Rosaria, Sal, Vito; Patrice* (2), *Jean-Claude.*

Iacovone (135) Italian: from an augmentative ('big Jacob') of the personal name *Iacovo*, from Latin *Iacobus* (see JACOB).
GIVEN NAMES Italian 24%. *Rocco* (3), *Angelo, Antonio, Bernardo, Domenic, Pietro, Vito.*

Iadarola (143) Italian: unexplained.
GIVEN NAMES Italian 9%. *Carmine* (2), *Antonio, Gilda, Umberto.*

Iadevaia (124) Italian: unexplained.

GIVEN NAMES Italian 41%. *Antonio* (2), *Carmine* (2), *Costantino* (2), *Domenic* (2), *Giuseppe* (2), *Luigi* (2), *Rocco* (2), *Vincenzo* (2), *Aniello, Camillo, Clemente, Domenico.*

Iafrate (192) Southern Italian: from a shortened form of the personal name IANNI + *frate* 'brother', i.e. 'brother Johnny'.
GIVEN NAMES Italian 33%. *Mario* (4), *Alessio* (2), *Dante* (2), *Geno* (2), *Marco* (2), *Pasco* (2), *Vito* (2), *Aldo, Alfredo, Angelo, Antonio, Arcangelo, Domenic, Enio, Gerardo, Orlando, Renato.*

Iams (285) Origin uncertain. Possibly a result of misdivision of the English surname WILLIAMS, taken as Christian name and surname: 'Will Iams'. Alternatively it may be an altered spelling of EAMES.

Iandoli (118) Southern Italian: patronymic or plural form of the personal name *Iandolo*, a variant of *Candolo*, ultimately of Germanic origin.
GIVEN NAMES Italian 12%. *Ciro* (2), *Donato, Salvatore.*

Iannaccone (208) Italian: variant of IANNACONE.
GIVEN NAMES Italian 21%. *Carmine* (5), *Ciro* (3), *Antonio* (2), *Luigi* (2), *Angelo, Constantino, Domenic, Gennaro, Lazzaro, Lorenzo.*

Iannacone (304) Southern Italian: of uncertain derivation; perhaps from an augmentative ('big John') of the personal name *Iannaco* (an elaborated form of IANNI), or from some other personal name.
GIVEN NAMES Italian 12%. *Domenic* (2), *Angelo, Carmine, Enrico, Giacomo, Giro, Guido, Quido, Rocco.*

Iannarelli (148) Italian: from a pet form of IANNI or GENNARO.
GIVEN NAMES Italian 15%. *Antonio* (4), *Angelo* (2), *Carmela, Domenic, Sal.*

Iannelli (370) Southern Italian: patronymic or plural form of IANNELLO.
GIVEN NAMES Italian 20%. *Sal* (3), *Pasquale* (2), *Silvio* (2), *Aldo, Amato, Angelo, Antonio, Carlo, Carmine, Francesco, Gaetano, Giacomo.*

Iannello (196) Italian: from the personal name *Iannello*, a pet form of IANNI.
GIVEN NAMES Italian 20%. *Salvatore* (5), *Angelo* (4), *Carmelo* (2), *Carmel, Caterina, Matteo, Nino, Pasquale.*

Iannetta (134) Italian: from a feminine pet form of IANNI.

GIVEN NAMES Italian 31%. *Domenic* (3), *Mario* (3), *Sal* (2), *Angelo, Camillo, Carmela, Emilio, Giorgio, Lodovico, Marco, Pasqualino, Piero, Rocco, Sabato, Virgilio.*

Ianni (298) Italian: central and southern form of the personal name GIANNI, from Greek *Iōannēs* (see JOHN).
GIVEN NAMES Italian 21%. *Dino* (5), *Ettore* (2), *Guido* (2), *Angelo, Antonio, Dante, Domenica, Emedio, Enrico, Enzo, Gildo, Giovanni.*

Ianniello (226) Italian: from a pet form of the personal name IANNI.
GIVEN NAMES Italian 27%. *Mario* (4), *Alicia,* (2), *Angelo* (2), *Clemente* (2), *Aniello, Carmella, Carmine, Isidoro, Natale, Olindo, Pasquale, Sal, Salvatore.*

Iannone (596) Italian: from an augmentative form ('big John') of the personal name IANNI.
GIVEN NAMES Italian 15%. *Salvatore* (3), *Angelo* (2), *Carmine* (2), *Luigi* (2), *Pasquale* (2), *Antonio, Carmel, Carmelo, Ciro, Corrado, Domenic, Franco.*

Iannotti (321) Italian: from a pet form of the personal name IANNI.
GIVEN NAMES Italian 15%. *Angelo* (2), *Domenic* (2), *Carmelo, Carmine, Gennaro, Rocco, Sal, Salvatore.*

Iannucci (496) Italian: from a pet form of the personal name IANNI.
GIVEN NAMES Italian 21%. *Angelo* (4), *Salvatore* (4), *Antonio* (3), *Donato* (3), *Vincenzo* (3), *Ciro* (2), *Dante* (2), *Dino* (2), *Agostino, Alessio, Carmine, Concetta.*

Iannuzzi (476) Italian: from a pet form of the personal name IANNI.
GIVEN NAMES Italian 18%. *Salvatore* (5), *Carmine* (4), *Antonio* (3), *Marcello* (2), *Pasquale* (2), *Sal* (2), *Attilio, Carlo, Cosimo, Domenic, Domenico, Elio.*

Iantosca (114) Italian: unexplained.
GIVEN NAMES Italian 24%. *Angelo* (5), *Armando* (3), *Mario* (3), *Antonio* (2), *Rocco, Sal, Umberto.*

Iaquinta (163) Italian: variant (feminine) of IAQUINTO.
GIVEN NAMES Italian 12%. *Antonio, Gaetano, Giovani, Lorenzo, Salvatore.*

Iaquinto (134) Southern Italian: from the personal name *Iaquinto*, a southern variant of GIACINTO. Compare Spanish JACINTO.
GIVEN NAME Italian 10%. *Salvatore* (2).

Iarussi (111) Italian: variant of **Giarrusso**, from a shortened form of the personal name IANNI + *russo* 'red'.
GIVEN NAMES French 4%; Italian 4%. *Luigi*, *Mauro*.

Iavarone (171) Southern Italian: possibly from a shortened form of the personal name IANNI + *varone*, a variant of *barone* 'baron'; literally 'baron John'.
GIVEN NAMES Italian 31%. *Antonio* (3), *Carmine* (2), *Pasquale* (2), *Aldo*, *Carmela*, *Egidio*, *Gaetano*, *Gianfranco*, *Gino*, *Guido*, *Riccardo*, *Salvatore*.

Ibach (335) German: habitational name from any of several places in Baden-Württemberg named Ibach.

Ibanez (822) Spanish (**Ibáñez**): patronymic from the personal name *Ibán*, a variant of *Juan*, a vernacular form of Greek *Iōhannēs* (see JOHN).
GIVEN NAMES Spanish 49%. *Jose* (23), *Carlos* (12), *Manuel* (11), *Jesus* (10), *Jorge* (9), *Angel* (6), *Enrique* (6), *Pedro* (6), *Luis* (5), *Miguel* (5), *Rafael* (5), *Raul* (5).

Ibarra (4323) Basque: habitational name from any of several places in the Basque Country named Ibarra, from *ibar* 'meadow' + the definite article *-a*.
GIVEN NAMES Spanish 56%. *Jose* (186), *Juan* (95), *Jesus* (57), *Francisco* (53), *Manuel* (51), *Carlos* (42), *Luis* (41), *Raul* (34), *Javier* (30), *Pedro* (30), *Roberto* (30), *Armando* (28).

Ibbotson (221) English: metronymic from the Middle English female personal name *Ibbot*, a pet form of *Isabel*.

Ibe (134) German and Dutch: probably from a variant of the personal name *Ivo*, which is ultimately derived from Old High German *īwa* 'yew'.
GIVEN NAMES Spanish 7%; French 5%; German 4%. *Alfonso*, *Cesar*, *Cruz*, *Felicitas*, *Javier*, *Juanito*, *Ruben*; *Cecile*, *Charlemagne*, *Laurette*; *Aloysius*, *Dieter*.

Ibrahim (1562) Muslim: from the personal name *Ibrāhīm*, Arabic form of ABRAHAM. In Islam, Ibrāhīm is identified as a prophet, the ancestor of all the Semitic peoples, both Hebrew and Arab, and the father of Ismā'īl (see ISMAIL) and Ishāq (see ISHAK).
GIVEN NAMES Muslim 75%. *Ibrahim* (44), *Mohamed* (40), *Hassan* (17), *Ahmed* (14), *Mohammad* (14), *Ashraf* (12), *Ali* (11), *Samir* (11), *Ismail* (10), *Mohammed* (9), *Abdul* (8), *Ahmad* (8).

Ibsen (295) Danish: patronymic from the personal name *Ib*, a Danish short form of JACOB.
GIVEN NAMES Scandinavian 12%; German 6%. *Niels* (2), *Erik*, *Lars*, *Thor*; *Kurt* (3), *Claus*, *Hans*, *Otto*.

Icard (223) See IKERD.

Ice (1406) Americanized spelling of German EIS.

Icenhour (273) Americanized spelling of German EISENHAUER.

Icenhower (183) Americanized spelling of German EISENHAUER.

Icenogle (284) Americanized spelling of German **Eisnagel** (see EISNAUGLE).

Ichikawa (214) Japanese: 'marketplace river'; variously written, a common place name throughout Japan. One branch of the TAIRA clan lived in a place called *Ichikawa-gō* in Kai (now Yamanashi Prefecture), and took that name. Found mostly in eastern Japan.
GIVEN NAMES Japanese 70%. *Hiroshi* (4), *Kiyoshi* (3), *Akira* (2), *Koji* (2), *Mitsuhiro* (2), *Nobuo* (2), *Rumi* (2), *Shoji* (2), *Yoko* (2), *Yoshio* (2), *Yukie* (2), *Ayako*.

Icke (105) English (West Midlands): variant of HICK.

Ickes (1043) **1.** German: unexplained. **2.** English: variant of HICKS.

Ida (204) **1.** English and German: from *Ida*, which is found as both a male and female personal name in English but only as a female name in German. This is of continental Germanic origin and was popular among the Normans, who brought it to England. Its etymology is disputed: it is thought by some to be of the same origin as *hild-* 'battle', 'strife'; by others to be of the same origin as Old High German *idis* '(wise) woman', or from Old Norse *idh* 'work', 'activity'. **2.** Japanese: 'rice paddy by the well'; habitational name from *Ida-mura* in Musashi (now Tōkyō and Saitama prefectures). Variously written and found mostly in eastern Japan and the Ryūkyū Islands.
GIVEN NAMES Japanese 18%. *Etsuko*, *Hajime*, *Kazu*, *Kazuhiro*, *Keizo*, *Kenji*, *Masaaki*, *Matsuo*, *Midori*, *Naohiro*, *Tadao*, *Takahiro*.

Iddings (432) English: from the Old Norse female personal name *Iðunn(r)*, probably composed of the elements *ið-* 'again', 'anew' + *unna* 'to love'. The name is often recorded in the Latin form *Idonea*, as a result of folk etymological association with the feminine form of Latin *idoneus* 'suitable'.

Ide (1186) **1.** English: variant of IDA. There is a place called Ide near Exeter in Devon; the etymology is obscure, perhaps from a pre-English river name; it does not seem to be connected with the surname. **2.** North German: variant of IHDE. **3.** Japanese: 'sluice', 'spillway'; a topographic name for someone who lived near a dam. Variously written, it originated in Echizen and Kaga (now Fukui and Ishikawa prefectures) and is found mostly in eastern Japan.
GIVEN NAMES Japanese 8%. *Haruyuki* (2), *Isao* (2), *Tadahiko* (2), *Takashi* (2), *Takayuki* (2), *Yoshihiro* (2), *Hideo*, *Hiroko*, *Hiromi*, *Hiroshi*, *Izumi*, *Junichi*.

Ideker (145) North German: from a pet form of the female personal name IDA + *-er* suffix denoting family association.

Idell (143) **1.** English: variant spelling of IDLE. **2.** Jewish (Ashkenazic): from the

Yiddish personal name *Idl*, a pet form of JUDE. **3.** Possibly a respelling of German EITEL.

Idema (125) Frisian: metronymic or patronymic from the personal name IDA.

Iden (367) **1.** English: habitational name from a place called Iden Green in Benenden, Kent, or Iden Manor in Staplehurst, Kent, or from Iden in East Sussex. All these places are named in Old English as 'pasture by the yew trees', from *īg* 'yew' + *denn* 'pasture'. **2.** North German: metronymic or patronymic from the personal name IDA.

Ideus (115) Origin unidentified. This name is common in TX and IL.

Idle (151) **1.** Welsh: from the Welsh personal name *Ith(a)el*, Old Welsh *Iudhail* 'bountiful lord'. **2.** English: habitational name from a place in West Yorkshire, which is probably named with a derivative of Old English *īdel* 'unused ground', 'patch of waste land'. **3.** English: derogatory nickname from Middle English *idel* 'idle', 'indolent', 'useless', 'worthless', 'devoid of good works'.

Idleman (182) Americanized spelling of Ashkenazic Jewish **Idelman**, a variant of IDELL.

Idler (177) English: nickname for a lazy person, from Middle English *idel* (see IDLE 2).

Idol (324) Variant spelling of Welsh IDLE.
GIVEN NAMES French 4%. *Amie*, *Monique*.

Idris (109) Muslim: from an Arabic personal name, *Idrīs*. Idrīs is mentioned in the Qur'an as a prophet, and many legends are related of him in Arabic folklore and literature. Linguistically, his name corresponds to Hebrew *Ezra*, Greek *Esdras*, but the Muslim figure is not the same person as the Biblical prophet of this name. Some legends about him correspond more nearly to those about the Biblical ENOCH. Idris ibn-Abdullah (died 793) was founder of the Idrisid dynasty which ruled Morocco from 789–926 AD.
GIVEN NAMES Muslim 77%. *Mohammad* (3), *Ahamed* (2), *Ahmed* (2), *Beshir* (2), *Farouk* (2), *Ismail* (2), *Jaafar* (2), *Mohamed* (2), *Omar* (2), *Abdalla*, *Abdulkader*, *Abubakar*.

Ierardi (182) Southern Italian: patronymic or plural form of the personal name *Ierardo*, southern form of *Gherardo* (see GERARD).
GIVEN NAMES Italian 12%. *Gennaro* (2), *Amedio*, *Pasquale*, *Rocco*, *Vitale*.

Iezzi (215) Italian: southern variant of GHEZZI.
GIVEN NAMES Italian 15%. *Angelo* (3), *Antonio* (2), *Vito* (2), *Eduardo*, *Enrico*, *Gaetano*, *Mariano*, *Orlando*, *Romolo*.

Iffland (135) Northern German: ethnic name for someone from Livonia (German *Livland*), the intial *l* having been lost through dissimilation.
GIVEN NAME German 4%. *Georg*.

Ifft (140) German: of uncertain origin; perhaps a habitational name from a place called Ifta near Eisbach in Thuringia.

Ifill (167) **1.** Americanized spelling of German **Eiffel** (see EIFLER). **2.** English: unexplained.

Igarashi (150) Japanese: 'fifty tempests'; the name is found mostly in eastern Japan.
GIVEN NAMES Japanese 80%. *Makoto* (3), *Masaru* (3), *Tsutomu* (3), *Akira* (2), *Kazunari* (2), *Kunihiro* (2), *Nobuyuki* (2), *Seiji* (2), *Yasuyuki* (2), *Akie*, *Chiye*, *Eriko*.

Ige (201) Japanese: variously written, possible meanings are '(one who lives) below the well' or 'lowest rank'. The name is not common in Japan.
GIVEN NAMES Japanese 23%. *Hiroshi* (2), *Takeo* (2), *Fusae*, *Katsumi*, *Kozo*, *Masaichi*, *Masao*, *Matsu*, *Minoru*, *Saburo*, *Tatsuo*, *Teruko*.

Igel (175) German and Jewish (Ashkenazic): nickname from Middle High German *igel*, German *Igel* 'hedgehog', given perhaps to a prickly or unapproachable person. There is a place near Trier called Igel, but it does not seem to have contributed to the surname. As a Jewish surname it is mainly ornamental.
GIVEN NAMES Dutch 6%. *Kort* (4), *Lous*.

Iglehart (316) Probably an Americanized form of German ENGELHARDT.

Igleheart (135) Probably an Americanized form of German ENGELHARDT.

Iglesia (128) Spanish: habitational name from any of countless places in Spain called Iglesia, named with *iglesia* 'church', or topographic name for someone living beside a church.
GIVEN NAMES Spanish 49%. *Jose* (5), *Carlos* (2), *Manuel* (2), *Margarita* (2), *Rogelio* (2), *Alejandrino*, *Avelino*, *Caridad*, *Dulce*, *Eduardo*, *Enrique*, *Fernando*.

Iglesias (1323) Spanish: habitational name from a place called Iglesias (from the plural of *iglesia* 'church'), in particular the one in Burgos province.
GIVEN NAMES Spanish 52%. *Jose* (52), *Carlos* (28), *Juan* (26), *Luis* (17), *Jesus* (14), *Manuel* (14), *Francisco* (12), *Jorge* (12), *Fernando* (11), *Rafael* (10), *Ramon* (10), *Roberto* (10); *Antonio* (8), *Aldo* (2), *Ciro* (2), *Dante* (2), *Elio* (2), *Silvio* (2), *Albertina*, *Carmelo*, *Claudina*, *Clementina*, *Franco*, *Heriberto*.

Ignacio (672) Spanish: from a Latinized form of the personal name *Íñigo*, which is of pre-Roman origin (recorded in classical times as *Enneco*). As a personal name it was not common in the Middle Ages; its comparative popularity in Catholic countries today is due to the fame of St. Ignatius of Loyola (Iñigo Yáñez de Oñaz y Loyola, 1491–1556), founder of the Society of Jesus (Jesuits).
GIVEN NAMES Spanish 35%. *Manuel* (7), *Jesus* (4), *Jose* (4), *Ramon* (4), *Adriana* (3), *Alejandro* (3), *Eduardo* (3), *Fortunato* (3), *Luis* (3), *Renato* (3), *Roberto* (3), *Rogelio* (3); *Romeo* (6), *Clemente* (3), *Dante* (3),

Antonio (2), *Dino*, *Giovani*, *Leonardo*, *Pio*, *Virna*.

Ignasiak (167) Polish: patronymic from *Ignacy*, a pet form of the personal name *Ignacy*, a vernacular form of *Ignatius* (see IGNACIO).
GIVEN NAMES Polish 4%. *Miroslaw*, *Tadeusz*.

Ignatius (115) From the Latin personal name *Ignatius* (see IGNACIO). This is found as a surname in the Netherlands, Finland, and Estonia, among other places.

Ignatowski (173) Polish: habitational name for someone from a place called Ignatów, in Chełm or Piotrków voivodeships, so named from the Polish personal name *Ignacy*, a vernacular form of *Ignatius* (see IGNACIO).
GIVEN NAMES Polish 4%. *Ignacy*, *Zygmunt*.

Igo (601) **1.** Scottish and Irish: unexplained. **2.** Hungarian (**Igó**): from a pet form of the personal name *Ignác*, a vernacular form of *Ignatius* (see IGNACIO).

Igoe (485) Scottish and Irish: variant of IGO.

Igou (266) Probably a variant spelling of Scottish and Irish IGO.

Iha (109) Japanese: written phonetically with characters meaning 'that' and 'waves', this name is habitational, from a place of this name in Okinawa.
GIVEN NAMES Japanese 35%. *Kazuo* (2), *Shigeru* (2), *Shizu* (2), *Akira*, *Fumio*, *Kame*, *Kenichi*, *Kiyoshi*, *Mieko*, *Seiko*, *Takeji*, *Tamae*.

Ihde (368) North German: from the Germanic personal name IDA, which was used for both men and women.

Ihle (390) **1.** North German: topographic name for someone who lived by or owned a piece of land by the Ihle River, a tributary of the Elbe northeast of Magdeburg. **2.** Norwegian: habitational name from any of several farmsteads in southeastern Norway named Ile, from Old Norse *íla* 'well', 'spring'.
GIVEN NAMES German 7%. *Hans* (2), *Franz*, *Fritz*, *Hedwig*, *Horst*, *Jochen*, *Jurgen*, *Karlheinz*, *Kurt*.

Ihlenfeld (127) German: variant of IHLENFELDT.
GIVEN NAMES German 8%. *Klaus*, *Mathias*, *Monika*, *Otto*.

Ihlenfeldt (144) North German: topographic name for someone who lived in open country adjacent to the Ihle river. Compare IHLE.

Ihm (137) German: **1.** from the personal name *Immo* (see IMMEL). which is in part derived from a short form of a personal name formed with *Irmin* (see IRMEN). **2.** habitational name from a place named Ihme, for example in Lower Saxony.

Ihnat (142) Belarus: from the personal name *Ihnat*, a vernacular form of *Ignatius* (see IGNACIO).

Ihnen (233) North German and Frisian: patronymic from a short form of a Germanic

compound name formed with *irmin-* 'great', 'powerful' as its first element.

Ihrig (509) German: from a variant of the unexplained Germanic personal name *Iring*.

Ihrke (249) North German: from a pet form of the unexplained Germanic personal name *Iring*.

Iiams (215) Origin unidentified, but see IAMS.

Iida (237) Japanese: written with characters meaning 'paddy of cooked rice', perhaps the original meaning was 'good rice paddy'. One family, descended from the TAKEDA family, lived in the village of Iida in Kai (now Yamanashi prefecture); another family, of Murakami descent, lived in a village by that name in Shinano (now Nagano prefecture). Both families are of the MINAMOTO clan. The name is also found on Okinawa Island.
GIVEN NAMES Japanese 59%. *Kenji* (4), *Satoshi* (3), *Hiroshi* (2), *Katsumi* (2), *Keisuke* (2), *Maki* (2), *Mieko* (2), *Naoki* (2), *Naoshi* (2), *Takashi* (2), *Tamotsu* (2), *Yasuo* (2).

Ijames (181) Origin unidentified; evidently an elaboration of English JAMES. It occurs chiefly in NC.

Ijams (112) Origin unidentified. Compare IJAMES. This name is common in MD and NC.

Ikard (217) Of German origin: see IKERD.

Ike (334) **1.** Japanese: 'lake'. Though listed in the Shinsen shōjiroku, this name is not common in the main Japanese islands and is found mostly in the Ryūkyū Islands. The word *ike* is more usually found in compound names such as IKEDA. **2.** Possibly an Americanized spelling of German EICH.
GIVEN NAMES Japanese 6%; French 4%. *Toshio* (2), *Atsushi*, *Haruo*, *Kazuo*, *Kiyoshi*, *Koichi*, *Yujiro*; *Andre*, *Camille*.

Ikeda (907) Japanese: 'rice paddy near the lake'; found throughout Japan and the Ryūkyū Islands, and variously written. One family, descended from the MINAMOTO, were daimyō of Ōmi (now Shiga prefecture). Listed in the Shinsen shōjiroku.
GIVEN NAMES Japanese 54%. *Hiroshi* (8), *Minoru* (6), *Hideo* (4), *Kazumi* (4), *Yuji* (4), *Atsushi* (3), *Hisashi* (3), *Kazumasa* (3), *Kazuo* (3), *Osamu* (3), *Toshio* (3), *Akira* (2).

Ikehara (110) Japanese: 'lake plain'; the name is not common in the main Japanese islands but is found mostly in the Ryūkyū Islands. Listed in the Shinsen shōjiroku.
GIVEN NAMES Japanese 33%. *Akira*, *Hanae*, *Hiroshi*, *Isao*, *Kazuo*, *Keiji*, *Kozo*, *Misao*, *Miyoshi*, *Seiko*, *Shizue*, *Tatsuo*.

Ikeler (111) Americanized spelling of German EICHLER.

Ikenberry (180) Americanized spelling of German EICHENBERG or **Eikenberg**, a North German form of this surname.

Ikerd (302) Americanized spelling of German EICHERT or **Eickert**, a North German form of this surname. Compare ICARD, IKARD.

Ikner (214) Americanized spelling of EICHNER, **Eickner** (a North German form of this surname), or EIGNER.

Ilacqua (120) Italian: from a reduced form of **di il Acqua**, presumably applied as a topographic name for someone who lived by a source or stretch of water, *acqua*.
GIVEN NAMES Italian 23%. *Antonio, Carmela, Elvira, Rosario.*

Ilagan (131) Filipino: unexplained.
GIVEN NAMES Spanish 45%. *Manuel* (6), *Nestor* (3), *Angelito* (2), *Cesar* (2), *Angel, Arturo, Aurelio, Conrado, Dominador, Emiliano, Estela, Fernando.*

Ilardi (196) Italian: from the personal name, possibly a derivative of the Germanic personal name *Adalhard*, or alternatively perhaps a southern form of GILARDI.
GIVEN NAMES Italian 27%. *Angelo* (2), *Luigi* (2), *Salvatore* (2), *Vito* (2), *Antonino, Carmelo, Francesco, Guiseppe, Ignazio, Marco, Margherita, Sal.*

Iler (634) Americanized spelling of German EILER.

Iles (971) English (mainly Somerset and Gloucestershire): topographic name from Anglo-Norman French *isle* 'island' (Latin *insula*) or a habitational name from a place in England or northern France named with this element.

Iley (108) **1.** English: habitational name from Illey in Worcestershire or from Brent or Monks Eleigh in Suffolk; the first is probably named with an Old English personal name *Illa* + Old English *lēah* 'woodland clearing'; the two last are from an unattested Old English personal name *Illa* + *lēah*. **2.** Perhaps an Americanized spelling of German ILLE or ILLIG.

Ilg (306) German and Swiss German: variant of ILLIG.
GIVEN NAMES German 7%. *Gerd* (2), *Fritz, Hans Peter, Matthias, Wilhelm.*

Ilgen (132) German: **1.** patronymic from *Ilg*. **2.** habitational name from a place so named in Bavaria, southwest of Munich.
GIVEN NAME German 4%. *Kurt* (2).

Ilgenfritz (232) German: compound patronymic, meaning 'Fritz, the son of Ilg'.

Ilic (142) Serbian and Croatian (**Ilić**): patronymic from the personal name *Ilija* (see ELIAS).
GIVEN NAMES South Slavic 64%. *Dusan* (3), *Miodrag* (3), *Davor* (2), *Gordana* (2), *Rajko* (2), *Slavko* (2), *Aleksandar, Bozidar, Branko, Dragan, Dragana, Dragica, Dragomir, Branislav* (2), *Janek, Milan, Mirko, Radmila.*

Ilich (102) Serbian and Croatian (**Ilić**): see ILIC.
GIVEN NAMES South Slavic 25%. *Milan* (2), *Dragan, Dragomir, Dusan, Dusanka,*

Dusko, Jakov, Miloje, Milorad, Obrad, Radomir, Vesna.

Iliff (499) English: from a Middle English personal name of Norse origin. Compare Old Norse *Eilífr*, composed of the elements *ei* 'alone', 'unique', 'outstanding' + *lífr* 'heir', 'descendant'.

Ill (108) Perhaps a respelling of German **Ihl**, a variant of IHLE.
GIVEN NAMES German 6%. *Kurt, Mathias.*

Ille (132) German: from the personal name *Ille*, a vernacular form of *Aegidius* (see GILES, and compare ILLIG).
GIVEN NAMES German 7%. *Gerhard, Guenter, Ralf.*

Illes (211) **1.** English: variant spelling of ILES. **2.** Hungarian (**Illés**): from the old ecclesiastical name *Illés*, variant of *Éliás*, Hungarian form of *Elijah*. **3.** German: patronymic from the personal name *Ille*, one of several vernacular forms of *Aegidius* (see GILES).
GIVEN NAMES Hungarian 11%. *Geza* (2), *Imre* (2), *Zoltan* (2), *Arpad, Gabor, Katalin, Sandor; Kieran* (2).

Illg (157) German: variant of ILLIG.
GIVEN NAMES German 5%. *Ernst, Friedrich.*

Illian (142) German and French (Alsace): unexplained; possibly from a short form of the Latin form (*Julianus*) of the personal name JULIAN.
GIVEN NAMES German 6%. *Friedhelm, Klaus, Otto.*

Illies (150) Origin unidentified.

Illig (435) German: from a vernacular form of a medieval personal name, the Latin form of which was *Aegidius* (see GILES).
GIVEN NAMES German 7%. *Kurt* (3), *Dieter* (2), *Ernst, Otto, Reinhold, Siegbert.*

Illing (128) English: from an Old English personal name, *Illing*.

Illingworth (378) English: habitational name from a place in West Yorkshire near Halifax, so called from Old English *Illingworð* 'enclosure associated with Illa', *Illa* being a short form of various personal names containing the first element *hild* 'strife', 'battle'.

Illsley (118) English: variant spelling of ILSLEY.

Ilse (116) German: habitational name for someone who lived by the Ilse river in the Harz Mountains.

Ilsley (125) English: habitational name from the villages of East and West Ilsley on the Berkshire Downs, named from Old English *Hild* (a short form of various personal names containing the first element *hild* 'strife', 'battle') + *lēah* 'woodland clearing'.

Im (846) Korean: there are two Chinese characters for this surname. The founding ancestors of all Korean Im clans were originally from China. Some sources indicate that there are 216 clans that use the most common character, but only two—the Naju Im family and the P'ŏngt'aek Im family—

have actually been documented. The founding ancestor of the P'yŏngt'aek Im family, Im P'algŭp, immigrated to Korea from China during the Tang Dynasty and settled in the P'yŏngt'aek area. The Naju Im clan is said to be descended from the P'ŏngt'aek Im clan. Members of the Im clans which use this more common character are found throughout the peninsula. Although some sources indicate that there are 120 clans that use the other Im character, only two of these are documented: the Im clan of Changhŭng and the Im clan of P'ungch'ŏn. The founders of these two clans are also from China. The founders of both the Changhŭng Im clan and the P'ungch'ŏn Im clan came to Korea during the Koryŏ period (AD 918–1392), the latter while escorting a princess bride to the Koryŏ court. About fifty percent of the Ims bearing the less common character as a surname live in South Ch'ungch'ŏng province.
GIVEN NAMES Korean 62%. *Sung* (10), *Chong* (9), *Young* (9), *Soon* (8), *Sang* (7), *Yong* (7), *Kwang* (6), *Myung* (6), *Chang* (5), *Chul* (5), *Jin* (5), *Chan* (4), *Dong* (4), *Hong* (4), *Hyun* (4), *Hyong* (3), *Jeong* (3), *Byung* (2), *Chung* (2), *Dae* (2), *Hyung Chul* (2), *Tae Hyun* (2), *Boksoon, Chong Man.*

Imada (115) Japanese: 'new rice paddy'. Two lines descend from the TAIRA clan: one of Bingo, the other of Aki (both now part of Hiroshima prefecture).
GIVEN NAMES Japanese 42%. *Katsumi* (2), *Masao* (2), *Junichi, Katsura, Kenji, Kinji, Masami, Masayuki, Michiko, Minori, Osamu, Takashi.*

Imai (363) Japanese: 'new residence', but mostly written with characters meaning 'new well'; also written with other characters, pronounced **Arai**, with the same meanings. Several families of MINAMOTO descent and one from the SASAKI line originated in villages of this name. The name is also found in the Ryūkyū Islands.
GIVEN NAMES Japanese 61%. *Hiroyuki* (4), *Ayako* (3), *Hideki* (3), *Hiroshi* (3), *Keiko* (3), *Kiyoshi* (3), *Hiro* (2), *Hitoshi* (2), *Kenichi* (2), *Masao* (2), *Mieko* (2), *Mitsuo* (2).

Imam (120) Muslim: status name from Arabic *imām*, literally 'one who leads the way', an honorific title for one who leads prayers in a mosque, also applied to the founders of Islamic law schools. Among Shiite Muslims the title *imām* is applied to the spiritual leaders descended from Fatima, daughter of the Prophet Muhammad, and her husband Ali, the fourth and last of the 'rightly guided' khalifs (see ALI).
GIVEN NAMES Muslim 87%. *Syed* (8), *Hussain* (3), *Mohammad* (3), *Ali* (2), *Ashraf* (2), *Hasan* (2), *Ibrahim* (2), *Khaled* (2), *Khalifa* (2), *Lubna* (2), *Mohamed* (2), *Mohmed* (2).

Imamura (235) Japanese: 'new village'; a common place name and surname throughout Japan and the Ryūkyū Islands.

GIVEN NAMES Japanese 54%. *Atsushi* (2), *Haruo* (2), *Hiroshi* (2), *Junko* (2), *Tomoko* (2), *Yoko* (2), *Yumiko* (2), *Atsuko*, *Chie*, *Fumie*, *Hideyuki*, *Hiroko*.

Iman (310) Muslim (widespread throughout the Islamic world): from a personal name based on Arabic *imān* 'belief', 'faith' (see the Qur'an 4:25).
GIVEN NAMES Muslim 10%. *Hasan* (2), *Syed* (2), *Abdolreza*, *Abdullah*, *Achmad*, *Ameen*, *Aqil*, *Bashir*, *Faruq*, *Fauzia*, *Hadi*, *Imran*.

Imber (275) **1.** English: habitational name from either of two places, one in Surrey, the other in Wiltshire. The former is named in Old English as 'Imma's enclosure' (see WORTH); the latter as 'Imma's lake' (from *mere* 'lake', 'pond'). **2.** Jewish (Ashkenazic): variant of INGBER, from Yiddish *imber* 'ginger'. **3.** German: nickname for an industrious person or metonymic occupational name for a beekeeper, from Middle High German *imbe*, *imme* 'bee'.
GIVEN NAMES Jewish 5%. *Emanuel*, *Etti*, *Hyman*, *Sol*, *Syma*.

Imbert (113) French and Catalan: from a Germanic personal name composed of a reduced form of *ermen*, *irmin* 'immense', 'vast' + *berht* 'bright', 'shining'.
GIVEN NAMES French 20%; Spanish 11%. *Charlet*, *Dominique*, *Jean Claude*, *Jean-Paul*, *Magloire*, *Marcel*, *Mirielle*, *Pascal*; *Rafael* (2), *Alberto*, *Ana*, *Cesar*, *Enrique*, *Ramon*.

Imbesi (112) Italian: from *in Besi* 'belonging to the **Besi** family'. *Besi* is an old Sicilian personal name derived from the Arabic personal name *'Abbās*.
GIVEN NAMES Italian 27%. *Angelo* (3), *Tino* (3), *Carmela*, *Carmelo*, *Domenica*, *Natale*, *Rocco*.

Imbimbo (136) Southern Italian (originally from Naples): from *bimbo*, a nickname derived from a variant of *bambino* 'baby', with the addition of the typically southern (especially Sicilian) prefix *in-* denoting 'belonging to the family of'.
GIVEN NAMES Italian 12%. *Dante*, *Lucio*, *Modestino*, *Remo*, *Salvatore*.

Imboden (375) South German, Austrian, and Swiss German: topographic name for someone who lived 'in the (valley) bottom', from Middle High German *bodem*, *boden* 'floor', 'bottom', 'ground' (cf. BODEN).
GIVEN NAMES German 4%. *Hilde* (2), *Katharina*, *Otto*.

Imbriale (100) Italian: unexplained.
GIVEN NAMES Italian 22%. *Rocco* (3), *Salvatore* (2), *Angelo*, *Carmine*, *Grazio*.

Imbrogno (186) Italian: of uncertain derivation; possibly from a derivative of *imbrogliare* 'to confuse or embroil', hence a nickname for a muddler. More likely perhaps (since there is no evidence for an older form *Imbroglio*), it may be from a variant of the personal name *Bruno* + the southern prefix *in-* 'of the family of' (see IMBIMBO).

GIVEN NAMES Italian 25%. *Armando* (2), *Mario* (2), *Orlando* (2), *Aurelio*, *Biagio*, *Carmine*, *Enrico*, *Gaetano*, *Giacomino*, *Gilda*, *Guilio*, *Vita*.

Imburgia (216) Italian: unexplained.
GIVEN NAMES Italian 20%. *Sal* (3), *Salvatore* (3), *Gaspare* (2), *Marco*.

Imdieke (111) German: unexplained; apparently a topographic name for someone who lives *im diecke* 'in (or 'at') the dike' (see DIECK).

Imel (701) Probably an altered spelling of German **Immel**, from a pet form of the personal name *Immo*, which is in part derived from a short form of a personal name formed with *Irmin* (see IRMEN).

Imes (776) **1.** English: unexplained. **2.** Americanized spelling of German **Eimes**, a patronymic from a short form of the Germanic personal name *Agimo*, formed with *agi* 'point (of a sword or lance)' (Old High German *ecka*).

Imfeld (139) German: topographic name meaning literally 'in the field', i.e. one who lived in open country, not in a village or town.
GIVEN NAMES German 9%. *Ernst* (2), *Erwin*, *Hans*, *Meinrad*.

Imgrund (144) German: topographic name for someone who lived at the bottom of a deep valley, a variant of GRUND, with the addition of the fused preposition and article *im* 'in the'.

Imhof (516) North German: variant spelling of IMHOFF.
GIVEN NAMES German 7%. *Hans* (3), *Otto* (3), *Bernhardt*, *Erhardt*, *Erwin*, *Kurt*, *Markus*, *Matthias*.

Imhoff (1518) North German (Westphalia): topographic name for someone who lived or worked 'at the manor farm', from Middle Low German *hof* 'farmstead', 'manor farm', 'court'.

Imholte (133) German: (plural) variant of **Im Holz**, a topographic name for someone who lived in a wood, itself a variant of HOLZ, with the addition of the fused preposition and definite article *im* 'in the'.

Imig (277) German: unexplained.

Imlay (325) Scottish: variant of **Imlach**, which is of unknown, probably Gaelic, origin. It is recorded as a surname in Aberdeen from 1402 onwards.

Imler (756) Americanized spelling of German **Immler**: **1.** perhaps an occupational name for a beekeeper, from Middle High German *imme* 'bee' + suffix *-ler* denoting occupation. **2.** alternatively, a metronymic from the female personal name *Imel*.

Imm (316) English and German: from the female personal name *Imma*, *Emma* or (in the case of the German name) from the male equivalent, *Immo*, short forms of various Germanic personal names formed with *irmin*, *ermen* 'whole', 'entire' (also the name of a Germanic deity). In Old English *Imma*, *Emma* was

borne by both males and females. Compare IMBER, but in Middle English, under Norman influence, it came to be used almost exclusively for women, being taken as a short form of *Ermingard*.

Immekus (120) German: unexplained.

Immel (925) North German: from a pet form of the Germanic personal name *Im(m)o* (see IMM).

Immer (110) German: habitational name for someone from a place named Immer near Oldenburg in Lower Saxony.
GIVEN NAMES German 6%. *Klaus*, *Wolfgang*.

Immerman (182) **1.** German (**Immermann**): habitational name for someone from a place named Immer near Oldenburg in Lower Saxony. **2.** Jewish (eastern Ashkenazic): from Yiddish *imerman* 'divorced husband'.
GIVEN NAMES Jewish 7%. *Faina*, *Sholom*, *Sima*.

Imming (134) North German: patronymic from the personal name *Im(m)o* (see IMMEL).

Imondi (156) Italian: probably a dialect form of **Gimondi**, from a germanic personal name.
GIVEN NAMES Italian 12%. *Antonio* (2), *Carmine* (2), *Carmino*, *Guido*, *Pasquale*, *Rocco*, *Sabatino*.

Imparato (122) Italian: either a variant of IMPERATO or a nickname from *imperato* 'clever', 'adept'.
GIVEN NAMES Italian 13%. *Angelo*, *Carmine*, *Gioacchino*, *Remo*.

Impastato (171) Italian (Sicily): nickname from Sicilian *mpastatu* 'dirty', 'filthy'.
GIVEN NAMES Italian 15%. *Salvatore* (3), *Vito* (2), *Concetta*, *Giuseppe*, *Natale*, *Sal*, *Saverio*.

Impellizzeri (126) Southern Italian: from the occupational name for a furrier **Pellizzeri** (from Old Italian *pellicière*, from Late Latin *pellicia* 'fur cloak', from Latin *pellis* 'hide'), with the addition of the southern prefix *in-* 'of the family of' (see IMBIMBO). This name is cognate with northern Italian **Pellicia** and French PELLISSIER.
GIVEN NAMES Italian 22%. *Francisco* (2), *Salvatore* (2), *Agatino*, *Antonio*, *Ignazio*, *Sal*, *Silvio*, *Vito*.

Imperato (326) Italian: from the personal name *Imperato*, from the past participle of *imperare* 'to rule or command'.
GIVEN NAMES Italian 10%; French 4%. *Ciro*, *Gaetano*, *Nino*, *Rocco*; *Jacques*, *Pierre*.

Imperatore (137) Italian: from a personal name or nickname from *imperatore* 'emperor'.
GIVEN NAMES Italian 5%. *Crispino*, *Giuseppina*, *Luciano*.

Imperial (312) Spanish and Portuguese: from the Italian surname IMPERIALE, which was taken from Genoa to Spain in the 16th century.

GIVEN NAMES Spanish 18%; French 4%. *Carlos* (3), *Manuel* (3), *Enrique* (2), *Ruben* (2), *Adolfo, Agustin, Alfonso, Alicia, Arsenio, Arturo, Carlito, Catalina*; *Aime, Mireille*.

Imperiale (195) Italian: from Latin *imperialis* 'imperial', either denoting someone of aristocratic lineage or a nickname for a haughty person.
GIVEN NAMES Italian 27%. *Carmine* (2), *Angelo, Antonio, Assunta, Betzaida, Biagio, Emidio, Francesca, Giuseppe, Guiseppe, Marco, Mario, Rino, Sergio, Vincenzo*.

Impson (180) English (Norfolk): patronymic from an unidentified personal name.
GIVEN NAME German 4%. *Eldred*.

Imre (89) Hungarian: from the personal name *Imre*, Hungarian equivalent of *Amery*.
GIVEN NAMES Hungarian 11%. *Zoltan* (2), *Attila, Tibor*.

Imrie (213) Scottish (of Norman origin): variant of AMORY or EMERY.

Imus (225) Origin unidentified.

Imwalle (106) Origin unidentified.

In (228) **1.** Korean: name of a family that migrated from China to Korea during the reign of Shilla's 3rd-century king Sok Yurye (284–298). The founding ancestor, In So, established a clan seat in the Kyodong area of Cholla North Province. Another clan seat was subsequently established by his descendent, In Pin, during the Koryo period. The surname is not common in Korea. **2.** Cambodian: unexplained.
GIVEN NAMES Chinese/Korean 45%. *Kyung* (3), *Sung* (3), *Chan* (2), *Duk, Eun Suk, Hee, Hyun, Hyung, Ik, Jae, Kon, Kwang Won*; *Chang* (2), *Chung* (2), *Chong, Hyun Jin, Inki, Jeong, Jin Tae, Joo, Myong, Ok Soon, Poon, Poong*; *Hung, Khen, My, Phan, Tek, Thang, Tok*.

Inaba (169) Japanese: 'leaves of the rice plant'; name of the daimyō of Mino (now southern Gifu prefecture, descended from Kōno Michitaka (died 1374), who was himself descended from Emperor Kanmu (736–805). Found mainly in eastern Japan.
GIVEN NAMES Japanese 57%. *Mitsuaki* (3), *Akira* (2), *Minoru* (2), *Nobuhiro* (2), *Yoshio* (2), *Akihiro, Akinobu, Ayako, Chika, Eiichiro, Etsuko, Fumi*.

Inabinet (288) Respelling of Swiss German **Imäbnit**: unexplained.

Inabinett (113) Swiss German: variant of INABINET.

Inabnit (146) Swiss German: variant of INABINET.

Inboden (176) Variant of German IMBODEN.

Inbody (194) Variant of German IMBODEN.

Ince (725) English: habitational name from either of two places, in Greater Manchester and Merseyside, named from Welsh *ynys* 'island', 'strip of land between two rivers' (cf. INNES).

Inch (279) Scottish: variant of INNES.

Incorvaia (190) Southern Italian: from *Corvaia*, a topographic name from *corvaia* 'place frequented by crows', with the addition of the southern prefix *in-* 'belonging to the family of' (see IMBIMBO).
GIVEN NAMES Italian 35%. *Angelo* (9), *Salvatore* (5), *Francesco* (2), *Santo* (2), *Vincenzo* (2), *Carmela, Gasper, Giuseppina, Nunzio, Rocco, Vito*.

Inda (196) Basque: topographic name from Basque *inda* 'path', 'lane'.
GIVEN NAMES Spanish 26%; French 4%. *Jose* (5), *Enrique* (2), *Jaime* (2), *Juan* (2), *Mercedes* (2), *Xavier* (2), *Araceli, Armida, Arnulfo, Caridad, Domitila, Iluminada*; *Marcel, Michel*.

Indelicato (394) Italian: from a nickname from *delicato* 'gentile', 'refined', with the addition of the southern prefix *in-* (see IMBIMBO).
GIVEN NAMES Italian 17%. *Salvatore* (6), *Sal* (4), *Angelo* (3), *Antonio* (3), *Carina, Domenic, Enrico, Gasper, Giovanni, Matteo, Pasquale, Rocco*.

Indorf (103) German: topographic name for someone who lived 'in the village', from Middle High German *dorf* 'village'.

Indovina (132) Italian: occupational name from *indovina* (feminine form) 'soothsayer', 'fortune teller', 'magician', 'wizard', and in Sicily 'praying mantis'.
GIVEN NAMES Italian 10%. *Mario, Salvatore*.

Ines (107) **1.** Scottish: variant spelling of INNES. **2.** German (Württemberg): unexplained. **3.** Portuguese and Spanish: unexplained.
GIVEN NAMES Spanish 37%; Italian 7%. *Doroteo* (2), *Acacio, Adolfo, Alejandro, Armando, Aura, Bernabe, Desiderio, Ernesto, Eustaquio, Gilberto, Jose*; *Antonio, Caesar, Eliseo, Emiliana, Quirino*.

Infante (1248) **1.** Spanish: from *infante* literally 'child', but in Spain also a title borne by the eldest sons of noblemen before they inherited, and in particular by the son of the king of Castile; thus the surname probably originated either as a nickname for one of a lordly disposition or as an occupational name for a member of the household of an infante. **2.** Italian: nickname for someone with a childlike disposition, from *infante* 'child' (Latin *infans*, literally 'one who cannot speak').
GIVEN NAMES Spanish 41%; Italian 7%. *Jose* (28), *Carlos* (13), *Pedro* (13), *Rafael* (12), *Manuel* (11), *Juan* (10), *Angel* (7), *Fernando* (7), *Ramon* (7), *Francisco* (6), *Ana* (5), *Eduardo* (5); *Antonio* (7), *Marco* (3), *Angelo* (2), *Aniello* (2), *Carmine* (2), *Leonardo* (2), *Adalgisa, Attilio, Carlo, Carmelo, Deno*.

Infanti (106) Italian: patronymic or plural form of INFANTE.
GIVEN NAMES Italian 17%. *Angelo* (2), *Ettore, Marco, Mario* (2), *Vittorio*.

Infantino (376) Italian (chiefly Sicilian): **1.** from a diminutive of INFANTE. **2.** in

some cases, a habitational name for someone from Infantino, a district of San Giovanni in Fiore in Cosenza province.
GIVEN NAMES Italian 18%. *Salvatore* (7), *Angelo* (5), *Rocco* (2), *Carlo, Carmelina, Carmelo, Carmine, Corrado, Gaspare, Palma*.

Infield (138) English: topographic name from Middle English *infeld* 'land near the homestead or village', or a habitational name from any of various minor places named with this term, for example In Field in Humberside or Infield House in Lancashire.

Infinger (282) Probably a respelling of Swiss **Infanger**, a topographic name for someone who lived in or owned an enclosed piece of land which also provided hunting or fishing, from the regional term *Fang, Fank* 'enclosure', 'weir', 'trap' (from *fangen* 'to catch').

Ing (509) **1.** English: from the Old Norse and Middle English personal name *Ing(a)*, a short form of various names with the first element *Ing-* (see INGLE). **2.** English: habitational name from an Essex place name, Ing, which survives with various manorial affixes in the names Fryerning, Ingatestone, Ingrave, and Margaretting, and which is probably from an Old English tribal name *Gēingas* 'people of the district'. **3.** Jewish (eastern Ashkenazic): nickname from Yiddish *ing* 'young'.

4. Chinese 吴: possibly a variant of WU 1.

5. Chinese 伍: possibly a variant of WU 4.

Inga (143) **1.** Spanish: unexplained. **2.** Italian: perhaps from Sicilian *inga* 'ink', a metonymic occupational name for a scribe.
GIVEN NAMES Spanish 45%. *Jose* (7), *Raul* (3), *Carlos* (2), *Juan* (2), *Luis* (2), *Manuel* (2), *Miguel* (2), *Pedro* (2), *Armando, Benigno, Gerardo, Gustavo*.

Ingalls (2770) English: patronymic from the Anglo-Scandinavian personal name *Ingell*, Old Norse *Ingjaldr* (see INGLE).

Ingalsbe (262) Altered spelling of **Ingoldsby**, an English habitational name from a place in Lincolnshire, so named from the Old Norse personal name *Ingjaldr* + Old Norse *býr* 'farmstead'.

Ingargiola (107) Italian: probably from a compound of *in-* 'of or belonging to' + *Gargiola*, probably a nickname from a diminutive of Sicilian *gargia* 'cheek', 'jaw'.
GIVEN NAMES Italian 32%. *Rosario* (3), *Francesca, Giorgio, Matteo, Onorato, Casimiro, Renato, Vito*.

Ingber (330) **1.** German and Jewish (Ashkenazic): metonymic occupational name for a dealer in spices, from Middle High German *ingeber* (from Old French *gingebre*), Yiddish *ingber*. The word is ultimately, like the spice, of Oriental origin. **2.** German: from the Germanic personal name *Ingobert*, formed with *Ing-* (see INGLE 3) + *berht* 'famous', 'shining'.

GIVEN NAMES Jewish 8%. *Hyman* (2), *Tsvi* (2), *Alter, Ari, Chaim, Noson, Sol*.

Inge (751) **1.** English: variant of ING. **2.** German: probably from the Germanic female personal name *Inga*.

Ingebretsen (118) Norwegian: patronymic from the German personal name ENGELBRECHT.

GIVEN NAMES Scandinavian 21%. *Erik* (3), *Lasse, Thorleif*.

Ingebretson (110) Norwegian: patronymic from the German personal name ENGELBRECHT.

Ingebritson (113) Norwegian: patronymic from the German personal name ENGELBRECHT.

Ingels (399) English: variant spelling of INGALLS.

Ingemi (129) Italian (Sicilian): variant of **Angemi**, itself a variant of GANGEMI (see CANGEMI). The loss of initial *g* is characteristic of the dialect of certain parts of Sicily.

GIVEN NAMES Italian 24%. *Antonio* (2), *Alessandra, Domenic, Pasquale*.

Ingenito (227) Italian: from *ingenito* 'innate', 'inborn', or 'not made', 'not created'; hence perhaps a nickname for a foundling.

GIVEN NAMES Italian 15%. *Gennaro* (2), *Aniello, Carmine, Ciro, Cosimo, Cosmo, Ettore, Lucio*.

Inger (107) Jewish (eastern Ashkenazic): nickname from an inflected form of Yiddish *ing* 'young'.

GIVEN NAMES Jewish 12%; Russian 7%. *Meyer, Polina, Yehudah*; *Mikhail* (2), *Anatoly, Boris, Sofiya*.

Ingerman (133) **1.** Jewish (from Ukraine and Poland): from southern Yiddish *inger man* 'younger man', perhaps a name taken by a younger son. **2.** Swedish and German (**Ingermann**): regional name for someone from Ingermanland (Ingria), a former province between Finland and Russia.

GIVEN NAMES Russian 8%; Jewish 6%. *Efim, Iosif, Lev, Mikhail, Vladimir, Yefim*; *Khana*.

Ingersoll (2579) English: habitational name from Inkersall in Derbyshire, recorded in the 13th century as *Hinkershil(l)* and *Hinkreshill*. The final element is Old English *hyll* 'hill'. The first may be the Old Norse personal name *Ingvarr* or an Old English byname *Hynkere* meaning 'limper'. Ekwall suggests that it may represent a contracted version of Old English *hīgna æcer* 'monks' field'.

FOREBEARS The Ingersoll name in America dates back to John Ingersoll, who emigrated to the Massachusetts Bay Colony in 1629. His descendants include lawyers, public officials, and politicians in CT and PA.

Ingerson (423) Swedish (**Ingersson**) and English: patronymic from the personal name *Inger*, from the Old Norse personal

name *Ingvard*, a compound of *Ing* (the name of a Norse god associated with fertility) + *vard* 'guardian'.

Ingham (1511) English (chiefly Yorkshire and Lancashire): habitational name from any of several places so called, of which the largest are in Lincolnshire, Norfolk, and Suffolk. The place name is from the Old English personal name *Inga* + *hām* 'homestead'. Some authorities believe the first element to be a word meaning 'the Inguione', from an ancient Germanic tribe known as the *Inguiones*.

Inghram (272) Variant spelling of English INGRAM.

Ingle (3894) **1.** English: from either of two Old Norse personal names: *Ingjaldr*, in which the prefix *in-* probably reinforces the element *-gjaldr*, related to Old Norse *gjalda* 'to pay or recompense', or *Ingólfr* 'Ing's wolf' (Ing was an ancient Germanic fertility god). **2.** English: habitational name from Ingol in Lancashire, which is named from the Old English personal name *Inga* + *holh* 'hollow', 'depression'. **3.** Probably a variant of German **Ingel**, from a short form of any of several Germanic personal names formed with *Ing-* (see 1 above).

FOREBEARS An early bearer, Richard Ingle (1609–*c*. 1653), was a rebel and a pirate who first came to the colonies in 1631 or 1632 as a tobacco merchant. He is known to have practiced piracy in MD.

Ingledue (105) English: variant of ENGLEDOW.

Ingles (852) Spanish (**Inglés**): ethnic term denoting someone of English origin, from Spanish *Inglés* 'English'.

Inglesby (101) English: of uncertain origin; probably a variant of **Ingleby**, a habitational name from either of two places called Ingleby, in Derbyshire or Lincolnshire, or from Ingleby Arncliffe or Ingleby Greenhow, both in North Yorkshire. All are named with the Old Scandinavian personal name *Englar* + Old Norse *býr* 'farmstead', 'settlement'.

Inglese (230) Italian: ethnic term denoting someone of English origin, from Italian *Inglese* 'English'.

GIVEN NAMES Italian 18%; French 5%. *Tullio* (3), *Antonino, Antonio, Calogero, Carmela, Ennio, Giovanni, Luigi, Pasquale, Remo, Sal, Salvatore*; *Camille, Pierre*.

Inglett (212) English: from the Middle English personal name *Ingelot*, a pet form of any of various names such as *Ingelbald* 'Angle bold', *Ingelbert* 'Angle bright', or *Ingelard* 'Angle hardy'. These were names of Germanic origin, introduced to Britain by the Normans or possibly by the Danish invaders a century earlier.

Inglis (1173) Scottish: from a term denoting an Englishman or an English speaker, in Gaelic-speaking areas denoting an English-speaking Scot. Compare ENGLISH.

Inglish (161) Scottish: variant of INGLIS.

Ingman (205) **1.** English: from a derivative of an Anglo-Scandinavian personal name, probably *Ingimund*, composed of elements meaning 'Ing protection'. **2.** German (**Ingmann**): unexplained. Perhaps a variant of ENGMAN(N), a variant of ENGE, with the addition of the personal suffix *-mann* 'man'.

GIVEN NAME Scandinavian 6%. *Lars* (2).

Ingmire (162) **1.** English (Kent): unexplained. **2.** perhaps an Americanized form of German **Engemeyer**, a topographic name for a tenant farmer who lived in a narrow place, i.e. a deep, narrow valley, from *eng* 'narrow' (see ENGE) + MEYER 'tenant farmer'.

Ingoglia (248) Southern Italian: from GOGLIA, with the addition of the southern prefix *in-* 'belonging to the family of' (see IMBIMBO).

GIVEN NAMES Italian 24%. *Salvatore* (4), *Angelo* (3), *Sal* (3), *Vito* (2), *Mario* (2), *Dino, Gaspare, Libero*.

Ingold (929) **1.** English: from the Anglo-Scandinavian personal name *Ingell*, Old Norse *Ingjaldr* (see INGLE). **2.** Swiss German: from the Germanic personal name *Ingwald*, formed with *Ing-* (see INGLE 1) + *walt(an)* 'to rule'.

Ingoldsby (140) English: habitational name from Ingoldsby in Lincolnshire, named from the Old Norse personal name *Ingjaldr* + *bý* 'farmstead', 'settlement'.

Ingraham (2553) English and Scottish: variant of INGRAM, influenced by GRAHAM.

Ingram (21896) English: from a common Norman personal name, *Ingram*, of Germanic origin, composed of the elements *Ing* (the name of a Germanic god) + *hraban* 'raven'.

Ingrao (148) Southern Italian: from a reduced form of *Ingarao*, composed of a Germanic personal name equivalent to GERALD, which was imported from Catalonia and Aragón in the form *Garau* with the addition of either the southern Italian prefix *in-* 'belonging to the family of' (see IMBIMBO) or Catalan *en* 'lord' (form of address).

GIVEN NAMES Italian 27%. *Angelo* (2), *Gaetano* (2), *Giuseppe* (2), *Carmela, Mario, Sal, Salvatore, Santino, Vito*.

Ingrassia (504) Southern Italian: possibly from Greek *enkarsios* 'slanting', 'diagonal' or alternatively from GRASSIA, with the southern prefix *in-* 'belonging to the family of' (see IMBIMBO).

GIVEN NAMES Italian 15%. *Angelo* (5), *Salvatore* (4), *Nunzio* (3), *Carmelo* (2), *Sal* (2), *Vito* (2), *Antonio, Biagio, Carmine, Domenic, Francesca, Gaeton*.

Ingrum (221) English: variant spelling of INGRAM.

Ingwersen (250) Danish and North German: patronymic from the Germanic personal name *Ingward*, composed of the name of the god *Ing* (see INGLE) + *ward* 'guardian'.

GIVEN NAMES German 6%; Scandinavian 4%. *Darrold, Erwin, Kurt, Ralf; Erik, Karsten, Niels.*

Ingwerson (104) Variant spelling of ING-WERSEN.

Iniguez (575) Spanish (**Íñiguez**): patronymic form of the personal name *Íñigo* (see IGNACIO), which was often bestowed in honor of Ignatius of Loyola, founder of the Jesuits.
GIVEN NAMES Spanish 60%. *Jose* (29), *Juan* (12), *Miguel* (12), *Jesus* (10), *Rafael* (8), *Luis* (7), *Javier* (6), *Ramon* (6), *Alfredo* (5), *Carlos* (5), *Enrique* (5), *Felipe* (4).

Inks (333) Variant of English **Ings**, a metronymic or patronymic from ING.

Inlow (424) English: perhaps a variant of ENSLOW. Compare ENLOE.

Inman (8454) English: occupational name for a keeper of a lodging house, Middle English *innmann*, from Old English *inn* 'abode', 'lodging' + *mann* 'man'. Until recently there was in England a technical distinction between an inn, where lodgings were available as well as alcoholic beverages, and a tavern, which offered only the latter.

Inmon (424) Variant of English INMAN.

Innamorato (118) Italian: nickname from *innamorato* 'lover', 'sweetheart'.
GIVEN NAMES Italian 25%. *Giuseppe* (2), *Annamarie, Benedetto, Cono, Cosimo, Cosmo, Donato, Emanuele, Gaetano, Lorenzo, Rocco, Saverio.*

Innes (1207) Scottish: **1.** habitational name from the barony of Innes in Moray, named from Gaelic *inis* 'island' or 'piece of land between two rivers'. **2.** reduced form of McINNIS.

Inness (149) Scottish: variant of INNES.

Innis (740) Scottish: variant of INNES.

Inniss (284) Scottish: variant of INNES.

Innocent (158) French: from the personal name *Innocent*, from Latin *Innocentius*, from *innocens* 'harmless', 'non-violent'.
GIVEN NAMES French 36%; German 7%. *Francois* (4), *Dominique, Flavie, Fresnel, Jean Claude, Jean-Robert, Magalie, Mathurin, Pierre, Regine, Remy, Reynald; Ernst, Fritz, Johann.*

Innocenti (209) Italian: **1.** patronymic from the personal name *Innocente* (Latin *Innocentius*), (see 2). This was borne by a 4th-century bishop of Tortona, several popes from the 5th century onwards, and a 6th-century bishop of Le Mans. **2.** from *innocente* 'innocent' (Latin *innocens*, literally 'not harming'). This was used as a nickname for a simpleton, following the Christian notion that simpletons, like children, were incapable of doing evil. The surname is found principally in Tuscany and neighboring regions and is extremely common in Florence, where it was given as a surname to the foundlings received into the *Spedale degli Innocenti*, an orphanage established in the 15th century.

GIVEN NAMES Italian 13%. *Aldo* (2), *Marino* (2), *Elio, Francesca, Livio, Primo, Remo, Silvano, Silvio, Umberto.*

Inocencio (172) Spanish and Portuguese: from the personal name *Inocencio*, Latin *Innocentius* (see INNOCENTI 1).
GIVEN NAMES Spanish 41%. *Carlos* (4), *Andres* (2), *Ernesto* (2), *Felipe* (2), *Gerardo* (2), *Maria Luisa* (2), *Alejandro, Alfredo, Amparo, Angelita, Esteban, Francisco.*

Inoue (507) Japanese (earlier pronounced **Inoe**); topographic name meaning 'above the well', found in western Japan and the Ryūkyū Islands. Some bearers were daimyō of Mikawa (now part of Aichi prefecture); others were samurai from western Honshū and southern Kyūshū.
GIVEN NAMES Japanese 87%. *Hiroshi* (7), *Tadashi* (6), *Takashi* (6), *Takeshi* (5), *Hideki* (4), *Kazuko* (4), *Kenji* (4), *Kunio* (4), *Akira* (3), *Fumio* (3), *Hiroyuki* (3), *Hitoshi* (3).

Inouye (903) Japanese: alternate Romanized spelling of INOUE. The -*ye* spelling represents a pronunciation no longer used in modern Japanese.
GIVEN NAMES Japanese 33%. *Masao* (5), *Kazuo* (4), *Hiroshi* (3), *Hisashi* (3), *Masato* (3), *Minoru* (3), *Shigeru* (3), *Kaoru* (2), *Kimiko* (2), *Kiyoshi* (2), *Masaru* (2), *Noboru* (2).

Insalaco (282) Italian (Sicily): of uncertain derivation; possibly from **Salaco**, an occupational name for a tanner, from Arabic *sallāq* with the addition of the southern prefix *in-* (see IMBIMBO).
GIVEN NAMES Italian 12%; French 5%. *Angelo* (4), *Antonio, Carmel, Carmine, Cosimo, Dino, Salvatore; Camille, Michelene, Monique.*

Insana (107) Italian: probably a derogatory nickname from Sicilian *insanu* 'insane', 'crazy'.
GIVEN NAMES Italian 20%. *Franco* (2), *Pietro* (2), *Tino* (2), *Elvira, Placido, Salvatore, Santo.*

Inscho (183) Variant of English INSCOE.
FOREBEARS Obadiah Inscho is recorded in Delaware in the late 18th and early 19th century. He is thought to have been an immigrant from Wales.

Insco (148) Variant of English INSCOE.

Inscoe (251) English (Staffordshire): unexplained.

Inscore (205) Probably a variant of English INSCOE.

Insel (102) German: topographic name for someone living on an island, German *Insel*.
GIVEN NAME German 5%. *Frieda.*

Inselman (132) German (**Inselmann**): topographic name for someone living on an island, German *Insel*, or a habitational name from any of several places called Insel, with the addition of Middle High German *man* 'man'.

Inserra (296) Italian: from the topographic element *serra* 'mountain' with the addition

of the southern prefix *in-* 'belonging to the family of' (see IMBIMBO).
GIVEN NAMES Italian 14%. *Carmine* (3), *Vito* (3), *Salvatore* (2), *Giuseppe, Luciano, Sal, Santo.*

Insinga (108) Italian: from a short form of the personal name *Bonansinga*, an omen name meaning 'good sign', 'good auspices'.
GIVEN NAMES Italian 18%. *Caterina, Liborio, Lucio, Mario, Paolo, Salvatore, Vito.*

Inskeep (679) English: habitational name from Inskip in Lancashire, of uncertain etymology. The first element of this place name has been tentatively connected with Welsh *ynys* 'island' (compare INCE); the second with Old English *cȳpe* 'keep' (noun) in the sense 'osier basket for keeping or trapping fish'.

Insko (156) Variant of English INSCOE.

Inslee (107) Respelling of English INSLEY.

Insley (612) English (Midlands): habitational name from an unidentified place, most probably in Staffordshire. It may be from a lost place named in Old English as *Inesleāh*, the first element being the Old English personal name *Ine* + Old English *leāh* 'woodland clearing'. Alternatively, it could be a variant of the Devon name ENDSLEY, although the distribution makes this unlikely.

Interiano (115) Spanish or Portuguese: unexplained.
GIVEN NAMES Spanish 51%. *Jose* (5), *Carlos* (3), *Juan* (3), *Marina* (3), *Miguel* (3), *Edgardo* (2), *Julio* (2), *Manuel* (2), *Roberto* (2), *Ana, Armando, Blanca.*

Interrante (174) Italian: of uncertain derivation. Caracausi suggests that it may be from a shortened form of **Interlandi**, formed from the surname LANDI, with the addition of *Inter-*, a prefix of surnames denoting 'belonging to the family of'.
GIVEN NAMES Italian 21%. *Angelina* (2), *Gaspar* (2), *Mario* (2), *Vito* (2), *Aurelio, Carlo, Ciro, Gaspare, Gasper, Ignazio, Pellegrino, Vincenzo.*

Inthavong (124) Laotian: unexplained.
GIVEN NAMES Southeast Asian 44%. *Khamphet* (2), *Amphone, Noi, Noy, Sombath, Sommay, Somphet, Soun, Souvanh; Bounkong, Kham, Khamphong, Sounthone, Soutchay, Xay.*

Intrieri (191) Italian: unexplained.
GIVEN NAMES Italian 15%. *Luigi* (2), *Salvatore* (2), *Carmine, Edvige, Gennaro, Rachele, Rocco, Sal.*

Inverso (132) Italian: possibly an altered form of **Inverno**, a habitational name from Inverno Pinascta in Torino province or the district of Inverno in Vico Canavese, in Turin province.
GIVEN NAMES Italian 12%. *Angelo, Cosmo, Donato.*

Inwood (158) English: topographic name for someone who lived by the 'inner wood', i.e. the wood nearest the home farm (the main farm) of an estate.

Inzer (153) Altered spelling of German **Inser** (unexplained) or of ENSER.

Inzerillo (130) Southern Italian: from *Zerillo*, a pet form of the personal name *Zero*, from Greek *xeros* 'dry', with the addition of the southern prefix *in-* 'belonging to the family of' (see IMBIMBO).
GIVEN NAMES Italian 22%. *Angelo, Biagio, Caesar, Matteo, Sal, Salvatore.*

Inzunza (100) most probably from a derivative of Basque *inza* 'reed bed'.
GIVEN NAMES Spanish 52%. *Jorge* (3), *Alfonso* (2), *Carlos* (2), *Felizardo* (2), *Gildardo* (2), *Miguel* (2), *Abelardo, Adela, Angel, Blanca, Catalina, Delfina; Heriberto.*

Ioannou (149) Greek: patronymic from the genitive case of the personal name *Iōannēs* (see JOHN). Patronymics formed with the genitive are typical of Cyprus.
GIVEN NAMES Greek 41%. *Ioannis* (5), *Evangelos* (3), *Christos* (2), *Demos* (2), *Yiannis* (2), *Andreas, Athanasios, Christakis, Constantine, Costas, Despina, Georgios.*

Iocco (111) Italian: probably from a pet name, the underlying personal name from which it developed being no longer discernable.
GIVEN NAMES Italian 38%. *Rocco* (3), *Domenico* (2), *Giovanni* (2), *Nicolo* (2), *Salvatore* (2), *Stefano* (2), *Vittorio* (2), *Antonio, Ettore, Luigi, Pasquale, Romano.*

Iodice (233) Southern Italian: occupational name for a judge, from a southern form of GIUDICE.
GIVEN NAMES Italian 26%; French 5%. *Gennaro* (4), *Salvatore* (3), *Angelo* (2), *Antonio* (2), *Sal* (2), *Agostino, Aniello, Carmine, Ciro, Dante, Domenico, Donato; Andre, Armand, Michel.*

Ioffe (153) Jewish (eastern Ashkenazic): variant of JAFFE, reflecting an Ashkenazic pronunciation of the Hebrew word.
GIVEN NAMES Russian 37%; Jewish 34%. *Boris* (7), *Mikhail* (7), *Igor* (6), *Leonid* (6), *Vladimir* (5), *Grigory* (2), *Michail* (2), *Oleg* (2), *Aleksandr, Aleksey, Alexei, Anatoliy; Naum* (4), *Ilya* (3), *Dveyra* (2), *Yakov* (2), *Aron, Basya, Fira, Irina, Leyb, Mendel, Mikhael, Rakhil.*

Ion (137) **1.** Romanian: from the personal name *Ion* (see JOHN). **2.** English: probably a variant of JOHN.
GIVEN NAMES Romanian 7%. *Alexandru, Constantin, Nistor, Petrica.*

Ionescu (198) Romanian: patronymic from the personal name *Ion* (see JOHN).
GIVEN NAMES Romanian 44%. *Nicolae* (7), *Alexandru* (5), *Dumitru* (5), *Florin* (5), *Mircea* (4), *Mihai* (3), *Constantin* (2), *Corneliu* (2), *Liviu* (2), *Mihaela* (2), *Costel, Eugeniu.*

Iorio (740) Southern Italian: from a central–southern form of the personal name GIORGIO (see GEORGE).
GIVEN NAMES Italian 18%. *Angelo* (4), *Carmine* (4), *Sal* (4), *Carlo* (3), *Biagio* (2), *Giuseppe* (2), *Pasquale* (2), *Amedeo, Aniello, Cosmo, Dante, Donato.*

Iosue (101) Italian: from the personal name *Iosue* (see JOSHUA).
GIVEN NAMES Italian 17%. *Carmine* (3), *Angelo, Antonio, Giovanni, Pasqule, Saverio.*

Iott (205) Origin unidentified.

Iovine (174) Southern Italian: variant of **Giovene**, a nickname meaning 'young', from Latin *juvenis*.
GIVEN NAMES Italian 21%. *Ciro* (2), *Gennaro* (2), *Carmine, Cosmo, Donato, Gino, Igino, Salvatore.*

Iovino (466) Southern Italian: **1.** (**iòvino**): variant of *Giovene* (see IOVINE). **2.** (**iovíno**): from the Latin personal name *Jovinus* a derivative of *Iovis* 'Zeus'.
GIVEN NAMES Italian 19%. *Vito* (3), *Angelo* (2), *Carlo* (2), *Filomena* (2), *Pasquale* (2), *Aniello, Antonio, Camillo, Carmela, Carmine, Domenic, Donato.*

Iozzo (120) Italian: from the personal name *Iozzo*, which is of uncertain, probably Germanic, origin.
GIVEN NAMES Italian 25%. *Angelo, Lorenzo, Natale, Paolo, Renato, Vito.*

Ip (437) Chinese 叶: variant of YE.
GIVEN NAMES Chinese 26%. *Kam* (7), *Chi* (2), *Chu* (2), *Chun Wah* (2), *Hon* (2), *Kwai* (2), *Lai* (2), *Ping* (2), *Pui* (2), *Chan, Cheng, Chi Keung.*

Ipock (425) Respelling of German IBACH.

Ippoliti (170) Italian: patronymic or plural form of the personal name IPPOLITO.
GIVEN NAMES Italian 24%. *Mario* (3), *Gino* (2), *Valeriano* (2), *Alfonse, Caesar, Fernando, Franco, Giuseppe, Orlando, Renzo, Sante.*

Ippolito (1503) Italian: from the personal name *Ippolito* (classical Greek *Hippolytos*, composed of the elements *hippos* 'horse' + *lyein* 'loose', 'release'). This was the name of various minor early Christian saints. (In classical mythology Hippolytos was a young man who rejected the incestuous advances of his stepmother Phaedra.)
GIVEN NAMES Italian 17%. *Angelo* (20), *Carmine* (6), *Salvatore* (6), *Sal* (4), *Vito* (3), *Concetta* (2), *Natale* (2), *Nunzio* (2), *Orazio* (2), *Pasquale* (2), *Ugo* (2), *Vincenzo* (2).

Ipsen (261) **1.** Danish: variant of IBSEN. **2.** German: from the Germanic personal name *Ivo* (see IWEN). **3.** English: when not of Danish or German origin, possibly a variant of **Ipstone**, a habitational name from Ibstones, a place in Staffordshire, or from Ipsden in Oxfordshire.

Ipson (123) English: probably a variant of **Ibson**, a metronymic from the female personal name *Ibb*, a reduced form of *Isabel*

(see ISABELL) or a patronymic from the same name as a reduced form of the personal name *Ilbert* (see HILBERT).

Iqbal (674) Muslim (especially common in Pakistan, India, and Bangladesh): from a personal name based on Arabic *'iqbāl* 'prosperity', 'success'. Allama Iqbal (1873–1938) was a great poet and philosopher in India.
GIVEN NAMES Muslim 89%. *Mohammad* (57), *Zafar* (41), *Mohammed* (31), *Javed* (30), *Muhammad* (21), *Javaid* (13), *Shahid* (12), *Syed* (12), *Asif* (9), *Arshad* (7), *Azhar* (7), *Tariq* (7).

Ira (118) Origin uncertain: perhaps of Basque origin, a topographic name for someone living in a bracken-covered region, from Basque *ira* 'bracken'.

Irace (136) Southern Italian: possibly a habitational name from Gerace in Reggio Calabria or (less probably) from Geraci Siculo in Palermo province, named with medieval Greek *ierakion* 'hawk'. See also GERACI.
GIVEN NAMES Italian 15%. *Gennaro* (3), *Silvio* (2), *Domenic, Pasquale, Pietro.*

Iraheta (181) Basque: variant of **Iraeta**, a Basque topographic name with *ira* 'fern' + the collective suffix *-eta*.
GIVEN NAMES Spanish 58%. *Jose* (9), *Carlos* (4), *Francisco* (4), *Juan* (4), *Julio* (3), *Abimael* (2), *Alfredo* (2), *Armando* (2), *Jesus* (2), *Luis* (2), *Marta* (2), *Raul* (2).

Irani (236) Muslim and Parsi: ethnic name for an Iranian, from Persian *irānī* 'of or relating to Iran'. This name is common in Gujarat and Bombay city.
GIVEN NAMES Muslim 46%; Indian 12%; Parsi 8%. *Farokh* (3), *Majid* (3), *Ali* (2), *Asgar* (2), *Jehangir* (2), *Rafic* (2), *Rohinton* (2), *Shirin* (2), *Adil, Ahmad, Alireza, Arash, Atallah; Behram* (4), *Freny, Keki, Maneck, Manek, Moti, Zubin; Mehernosh* (2), *Tehmina.*

Irby (3575) English: habitational name from any of various places in Lincolnshire, Cheshire, and North Yorkshire, named from Old Norse *Írabýr* 'settlement of the Irish'. Compare IRETON.

Iredale (122) English: habitational name from a lost hamlet in Cumbria, so named from Old Norse *Íradalr* 'valley of the Irish'. The surname is first recorded in the 16th century; until recently it was found almost exclusively in Cumbria.

Irelan (397) Variant of English and Scottish IRELAND.

Ireland (5609) English and Scottish: ethnic name for someone from Ireland, Old English *Íraland*. The country gets its name from the genitive case of Old English *Íras* 'Irishmen' + *land* 'land'. The stem *Ír-* is taken from the Celtic name for Ireland, *Èriu*, earlier *Everiu*. The surname is especially common in Liverpool, England, which has a large Irish population.

Irene (113) Spanish and Italian: from the female personal name *Irene*, from Greek *Eirēnē* 'peace'.
GIVEN NAMES Spanish 6%. *Juan* (2), *Angel*, *Jose*, *Manuel*.

Ireson (136) English: unexplained.

Ireton (372) English: **1.** habitational name from either of two places in Derbyshire called Ireton, or one in North Yorkshire called Irton. All of these are named from the genitive case of Old Norse *Íri* 'Irishmen' (see IRELAND) + *tūn* 'enclosure', 'settlement'. **2.** habitational name from *Irton* in Cumbria, named from the old river name *Irt*, which is of uncertain origin, + Old English *tūn*.

Irey (452) Origin unidentified. This name is common in PA and OH, and is probably of Dutch or German origin.

Iriarte (150) Basque: topographic name for someone who lived between two or more settlements, from Basque *iri* 'settlement', 'village' + *arte* 'between'.
GIVEN NAMES Spanish 44%. *Carlos* (4), *Cesar* (3), *Francisco* (3), *Alvaro* (2), *Javier* (2), *Juan* (2), *Alberto*, *Alfonso*, *Alfredo*, *Alonso*, *Angel*, *Arturo*.

Irick (669) Probably a respelling of German EIRICH or ERICH, or Scandinavian *Eirik* (see ERICKSON).

Irigoyen (138) Basque: habitational name from Irigoyen in Gipuzkoa province or a topographic name from Basque *iri* 'village' + *goi* 'superior', 'upper'.
GIVEN NAMES Spanish 50%. *Carlos* (4), *Mario* (4), *Jose* (3), *Juan* (3), *Guillermo* (2), *Leticia* (2), *Luis* (2), *Miguel* (2), *Salvador* (2), *Andres*, *Arturo*, *Eleazar*; *Marco* (2), *Angelo*, *Antonio*, *Enzo*.

Irion (507) German: from the personal name *Irion*, more usually known in the form *Gereon*, which was the name of a medieval martyr.

Irish (2913) English and Scottish: ethnic name for someone of Irish origin. Compare IRELAND.

Irizarry (1628) Respelling of Basque **Irizarri**, a variant of the Basque surname **Irizar** meaning 'ancient village', from *iri* 'village' + *zar* 'old', or a habitational name from a town called Irisarri in Nafarroa Beherea province, Basque Country.
GIVEN NAMES Spanish 38%. *Jose* (44), *Luis* (28), *Carlos* (17), *Pedro* (10), *Angel* (9), *Juan* (9), *Rafael* (8), *Ramon* (8), *Manuel* (7), *Miguel* (7), *Roberto* (6), *Ruben* (6).

Irland (138) Variant of English and Scottish IRELAND or Scandinavian ERLAND.

Irlbeck (226) German: topographic name for someone who lived near an alder-lined stream, from Middle High German *erle* 'alder' + *beck* 'brook'.

Irle (100) Variant spelling of German ERLE.

Irmen (133) German: from the short form of a Germanic personal name formed with *Irmin*, a mythological name meaning 'all-encompassing', 'universal'.

Irons (2474) English (of Norman origin): habitational name from Airaines in Somme, so named from Latin *harenas* (accusative case) 'sands'. The form of the name has been altered as a result of folk etymology, an association of the name with the metal.

Ironside (235) **1.** Scottish: habitational name from a place in the parish of New Deer in Aberdeenshire. This was probably named with the Old English elements *earn* 'eagle' + *sīde* 'side' (of a hill). **2.** English: possibly from Middle English *irenside* (Old English *īren* 'iron' + *sīde* 'side'), a nickname for an iron-clad warrior. The best-known bearer of this nickname (not as a surname) was Edmund Ironside, who was briefly king of England in 1016.
GIVEN NAME Scottish 4%. *Alastair*.

Irrgang (102) German: nickname for a wanderer, from Middle High German *irreganc* 'aimless, meadering, restless gait'.
GIVEN NAME German 4%. *Otto*.

Irvan (147) Irish: variant spelling of IRVIN.

Irvin (7066) Irish: reduced Anglicized form of Gaelic **Ó hEireamhóin** 'descendant of *Eireamhón*', a personal name of uncertain origin. See also IRWIN. There has also been some confusion with IRVINE.

Irvine (3752) Scottish, also common in northern Ireland: habitational name from Irvine in Ayrshire, which is named from a Celtic river, Welsh *ir*, *yr* 'green', 'fresh' + *afon* 'water'. There has been much confusion with IRVING and IRWIN.

Irving (4521) Scottish: habitational name from Irving in Dumfries and Galloway region, which has the same origin as IRVINE, with which it has become inextricably confused.
FOREBEARS The writer Washington Irving (1783–1859), who wrote the stories 'Rip Van Winkle' and 'The Legend of Sleepy Hollow', was born in NY. His father was Deacon William Irving (from a family also recorded as *Irvine*), who came to NY in 1763 from Orkney, Scotland, a former British packet officer, a patriot during the Revolution, and a successful merchant.

Irwin (14090) **1.** Northern Irish, Scottish, and English: variant of IRVIN. **2.** English: from the Middle English personal name *Irwyn*, *Erwyn*, or *Everwyn*, Old English *Eoforwine*, composed of the elements *eofor* 'wild boar' + *wine* 'friend'. **3.** From the Welsh personal name *Urien* (see UREN).

Isa (155) **1.** Arabic: variant of ISSA. **2.** Japanese: written with characters meaning 'that' and 'help'. The name is found mostly in the Ryūkyū Islands.
GIVEN NAMES Arabic 40%; Japanese 13%. *Mohammad* (6), *Ahmad* (3), *Muhammad* (2), *Sana* (2), *Abdallah*, *Abed*, *Ahmed*, *Anwar*, *Ayad*, *Aziz*, *Azmi*, *Faiz*; *Yoshinobu* (2), *Chiyoko*, *Fumi*, *Kumiko*, *Shigeru*, *Tooru*, *Toshiro*, *Wataru*, *Yaeko*, *Yoshiaki*.

Isaac (4002) Jewish, English, Welsh, French, etc.: from the Biblical Hebrew personal name *yishāq* 'he laughs'. This was the name of the son of Abraham (Genesis 21:3) by his wife Sarah. The traditional explanation of the name is that Abraham and Sarah laughed with joy at the birth of a son to them in their old age, but a more plausible explanation is that the name originally meant 'may God laugh', i.e. 'smile on him'. Like ABRAHAM, this name has always been immensely popular among Jews, but was also widely used in medieval Europe among Christians. Hence it is the surname of many gentile families as well as Jews. In England and Wales it was one of the Old Testament names that were particularly popular among Nonconformists in the 17th–19th centuries, which accounts for its frequency as a Welsh surname. (Welsh surnames were generally formed much later than English ones.) In eastern Europe the personal name in its various vernacular forms was popular in Orthodox (Russian, Ukrainian, and Bulgarian), Catholic (Polish), and Protestant (Czech) Churches. It was borne by a 5th-century father of the Armenian Church and by a Spanish saint martyred by the Moorish rulers of Cordoba in AD 851 on account of his polemics against Islam. In this spelling, the American family name has also absorbed cognates from other European languages, e.g. German ISAAK, Dutch **Izaac**, etc. (for the forms, see Hanks and Hodges 1988). It is found as a personal name among Christians in India, and in the U.S. is used as a family name among families from southern India.

Isaacks (186) English and Welsh: variant spelling of ISAACS.

Isaacs (5380) Mainly Jewish, but also English and Welsh: patronymic from ISAAC.

Isaacson (3473) Patronymic from ISAAC; this is both a Jewish and English form but has probably also assimilated cognate names from other languages as well.

Isaak (554) **1.** Jewish: variant spelling of ISAAC. **2.** German: from the personal name, German form of ISAAC.

Isabel (232) English, French, and Portuguese: from the female personal name *Isabel* (see ISBELL).
FOREBEARS Isabel and Isabelle are documented as family names in Trois Rivières, Quebec, in 1648. Other families, from Normandy, France, are documented in Sainte-Famille, Quebec, in 1669.
GIVEN NAMES Spanish 5%. *Alfonso*, *Alvarado*, *Augusto*, *Belia*, *Josefina*, *Juan*, *Manuel*, *Mario*, *Romero*, *Santa*.

Isabell (430) French and English: from the female personal name *Isabel* (see ISBELL).

Isabella (344) Italian, Spanish, and Portuguese: from the female personal name *Isabella* (see ISBELL).

GIVEN NAMES Italian 15%. *Carmine* (3), *Ennio* (2), *Angelo, Antonio, Concetta, Domenic, Francesco, Nunzio, Rocco, Sal, Salvatore.*

Isabelle (365) French and English: see ISBELL.

GIVEN NAMES French 17%. *Serge* (4), *Fernand* (2), *Marcel* (2), *Andre, Cecile, Edouard, Emile, Gaston, Jacques, Jean Marc, Jean Marie, Ludger.*

Isackson (175) Swedish: see ISAKSON.

GIVEN NAMES Scandinavian 5%. *Erik, Helmer, Iver.*

Isadore (131) French (also spelled **Isidore**): from a medieval personal name based on Greek *Isidōros* 'gift of Isis'. This was borne by at least three Christian saints venerated especially in the Orthodox Church. Compare ISIDRO. **Isidoros** is also found as a surname in Greek, along with patronymics such as **Sideropoulos** (see SIDERIS). Because of its perceived similarity to *Isaac* and *Israel*, it also became popular in modern times as a Jewish given name.

GIVEN NAME French 5%. *Easton.*

Isaksen (259) Norwegian and Danish: patronymic from the personal name *Isak* (see ISAAC).

GIVEN NAMES Scandinavian 20%. *Nils* (2), *Borg, Gunner.*

Isakson (553) **1.** Swedish (**Isaksson**): patronymic from the personal name *Isak* (see ISAAC). **2.** Respelling of Norwegian and Danish ISAKSEN.

GIVEN NAMES Scandinavian 6%. *Erik* (2), *Alf, Knut.*

Isaman (140) Americanized spelling of German *Eisermann*, see EISERMAN.

Isaza (107) possibly Basque: of uncertain derivation, perhaps a topographic name from Basque *isats* 'broom' (the plant) + the definite article *-a.*

GIVEN NAMES Spanish 52%. *Luis* (5), *Adriana* (3), *Fernando* (3), *Jesus* (2), *Jorge* (2), *Mario* (2), *Octavio* (2), *Ruben* (2), *Alfredo, Bernardo, Camilo, Carlos.*

Isbell (3524) English: from the female personal name *Isabel(l)(a)*. This originated as a variant of *Elizabeth*, a name which owed its popularity in medieval Europe to the fact that it was borne by John the Baptist's mother. The original form of the name was Hebrew *Elisheva* 'my God (is my) oath'; it appears thus in Exodus 6:23 as the name of Aaron's wife. By New Testament times the second element had been altered to Hebrew *shabat* 'rest', 'Sabbath'. The form *Isabella* originated in Spain, the initial syllable being detached because of its resemblance to the definite article *el*, and the final one being assimilated to the characteristic Spanish feminine ending *-ella*. The name in this form was introduced to France in the 13th century, being borne by a sister of St. Louis who lived as a nun after declining marriage with the Holy Roman Emperor. Thence it was taken to England, where it

achieved considerable popularity as an independent personal name alongside its doublet *Elizabeth.*

Isberg (115) **1.** Swedish: ornamental name composed of the elements *is* 'ice' + *berg* 'mountain'. **2.** Norwegian: habitational name from a farmstead in Hordaland named Isberg (see 1).

GIVEN NAME Scandinavian 8%. *Per* (2).

Isbill (193) English: variant of ISBELL.

Isbister (108) Scottish (Orkney): habitational name from any of several places in the Orkneys and Shetlands named Isbister.

Isch (258) Swiss German: from a shortened form of a compound Germanic personal name formed with *īsen-* 'iron' as its first element.

Iseli (101) Swiss German: variant of EISELE.

GIVEN NAMES German 16%. *Ernst* (2), *Hans, Kurt, Otto, Ulrich.*

Iselin (198) German and Swiss German: variant of EISELE.

Isely (131) Swiss German: variant of EISELE.

GIVEN NAME French 5%; Scandinavian 4%. *Alain.*

Iseman (281) Americanized spelling of German **Eismann** (see EISMAN) or of Swiss **Isenmann.**

Iseminger (237) Americanized spelling of German EISENMENGER.

Isenbarger (126) Respelling of German or Jewish EISENBERGER.

Isenberg (1710) **1.** Americanized spelling of German EISENBERG. **2.** Swedish: variant of ISBERG or an adoption of German EISENBERG.

Isenberger (139) Respelling of German or Jewish EISENBERGER.

GIVEN NAME German 4%. *Kurt.*

Isenburg (118) Respelling of German or Jewish EISENBERG.

Isenhart (293) Americanized spelling of German EISENHARDT.

Isenhour (699) Americanized spelling of German EISENHAUER.

Isenhower (328) Americanized spelling of German EISENHAUER.

Isensee (203) German: habitational name from Isensee, a place near Stade in Lower Saxony.

GIVEN NAMES German 4%. *Klaus, Reinhard.*

Iser (178) North German variant spelling of EISER.

Iseri (106) Japanese: written with characters meaning 'well' and 'parsley', the name is not common in Japan.

GIVEN NAMES Japanese 25%. *Chie* (2), *Hiroshi, Katsuo, Manabu, Nobu, Nobuhiro, Nobuo, Shig, Shigeru, Sueki, Tadashi, Teruo.*

Iserman (110) Americanized spelling of North German **Isermann** or of its cognate *Eiserman* (see EISERMAN).

Isett (119) English (Midlands): unexplained.

Isgett (120) Origin unidentified. This name is concentrated in SC.

Isgrig (115) Engish: variant of ISGRIGG.

Isgrigg (126) Northern English: habitational name from Eskrigg in Cumbria or Eskrigge in Lancashire (see ESKRIDGE).

Isgro (146) Southern Italian (**Isgrò**): variant of *Sgrò* 'curly (headed)' (see SGRO).

GIVEN NAMES Italian 31%. *Angelo* (3), *Biagio* (2), *Salvatore* (2), *Vito* (2), *Biago, Carmelo, Carmine, Francesco, Giuseppe, Nunzio, Santo, Vittoria.*

Ish (137) Americanized spelling of Swiss German ISCH.

Ishak (159) Muslim: from the Arabic personal name *'Isḥāq*. In Islam this is the name of a Prophet (Biblical ISAAC), the son of Ibrahim (Biblical ABRAHAM). See the Qur'an 37:112.

GIVEN NAMES Muslim 63%; French 4%. *Samir* (4), *Maher* (2), *Mohammed* (2), *Moussa* (2), *Raif* (2), *Waguih* (2), *Ahmed, Anwar, Ashraf, Azar, Azhar, Bahgat; Alphonse, Andre, Antoine.*

Isham (1371) English: habitational name from a place in Northamptonshire named Isham, from the river name *Ise* (of Celtic origin) + Old English *hām* 'homestead' or *hamm* 'promontory' or 'enclosure hemmed in by water'.

Ishee (367) Altered spelling of Swiss German **Ischi** or **Ischy**, variants of ISCH which occur mainly in the border area between French-speaking and German-speaking Switzerland.

Isherwood (414) English: habitational name from a lost place in the parish of Bolton-le-Moors, near Manchester, of uncertain etymology.

Ishibashi (188) Japanese: from a common place name meaning 'stone bridge'. People of this name who are from Yamanashi prefecture descend from the TAKEDA family; others descend from the ASHIKAGA. Both are branches of the MINAMOTO clan. The name is also found in the Ryūkyū Islands.

GIVEN NAMES Japanese 57%. *Haruyo* (2), *Kazunori* (2), *Koji* (2), *Masako* (2), *Masayuki* (2), *Naoki* (2), *Nobuyuki* (2), *Akitoshi, Atsushi, Hanako, Hideki, Hiroki.*

Ishida (448) Japanese: from a common place name meaning 'rocky rice paddy'. Some families of this name descend from samurai of Tosa (now Kōchi prefecture). The name is also found in the Ryūkyū Islands.

GIVEN NAMES Japanese 60%. *Akira* (3), *Hiroshi* (3), *Kenji* (3), *Susumu* (3), *Teruo* (3), *Fumiko* (2), *Katsumi* (2), *Kazuo* (2), *Kumiko* (2), *Megumi* (2), *Nobu* (2), *Norio* (2).

Ishihara (265) Japanese: from a common place name meaning 'rocky plain'. This is a frequent surname; one group of bearers, from Kai (now Yamanashi prefecture), is descended from the TAKEDA family; several others descend from other branches of the MINAMOTO clan. The name is pronounced **Ishibaru** in the Ryūkyū Islands.

GIVEN NAMES Japanese 64%. *Miyuki* (3), *Akira* (2), *Jiro* (2), *Junko* (2), *Saburo* (2), *Takeshi* (2), *Tosh* (2), *Yosh* (2), *Yukio* (2), *Chiemi, Eiji, Eriko.*

Ishii (634) Japanese: usually written with characters meaning 'rock well', also with characters meaning 'resides in a rocky place'; the latter is the original meaning. Mostly found in Chiba prefecture and the Tōkyō area, it is related to the name IWAI, which has a similar meaning. The name originated variously: in Shimotsuke (now Tochigi prefecture), from the Utsunomiya branch of the northern FUJIWARA, who dwelt there; from a branch of the TAIRA clan in Musashi (now Tōkyō and Saitama prefectures); and others. Bearers of the name Ishii are also found in the northeast, around the Inland Sea, and in the Ryūkyū Islands.

GIVEN NAMES Japanese 61%. *Hiroshi* (5), *Akira* (3), *Chikara* (3), *Fumiko* (3), *Kazuyoshi* (3), *Kimie* (3), *Kunio* (3), *Mamoru* (3), *Mitsuru* (3), *Shoji* (3), *Takayuki* (3), *Atsuko* (2).

Ishikawa (565) Japanese: 'rock river'; found mostly in eastern Japan and the Ryūkyū Islands. Listed in the Shinsen shōjiroku. One family, descended from Minamoto no Yoshitoki (11th–12th centuries), settled in Kawachi (now part of Ōsaka prefecture) and took the place name *Ishikawa* as their surname.

GIVEN NAMES Japanese 70%. *Hiroshi* (7), *Akira* (3), *Eiji* (3), *Hiroyasu* (3), *Hitoshi* (3), *Kiyoshi* (3), *Shigeru* (3), *Takashi* (3), *Tetsuya* (3), *Yoshihiro* (3), *Yuji* (3), *Hajime* (2).

Ishimoto (112) Japanese: '(one who lives) near the rock'. This name is found mostly in western Japan.

GIVEN NAMES Japanese 38%. *Eiko, Haruki, Hisao, Itsuko, Jitsuo, Kazuo, Kazuyuki, Kentaro, Kohei, Masao, Michi, Rikio.*

Ishler (169) See ISLER.

Ishmael (778) Muslim: see ISMAIL.

Ishman (267) English: unexplained. Possibly an altered form of ISHAM.

Isidro (117) Spanish: from a reduced form of the personal name *Isidoro*, Greek *Isidōros*, meaning 'gift of Isis'. (Isis was an Egyptian goddess, mother of Horus.) This name was borne by various Christian saints, including the great encyclopedist St. Isidore of Seville (*c.* 560–636).

GIVEN NAMES Spanish 51%. *Jose* (4), *Alfonso, Alfredo, Angel, Arnulfo, Beltran, Braulio, Cirilo, Corazon, Edgardo, Eleuteria, Enrique; Geronimo, Severino.*

Ising (125) North German: patronymic from a short form of a Germanic compound name formed with *isan-* 'iron' as its first element. Compare EISENHARDT.

GIVEN NAMES German 7%. *Konrad* (2), *Otto, Siegfried.*

Iskandar (104) Iranian: from the Persian form of ALEXANDER.

GIVEN NAMES Iranian and Arabic 51%. *Adly* (3), *Hany* (2), *Niveen* (2), *Samir* (2), *Samy* (2), *Amany, Atif, Gamil, Guirguis, Hamid, Ibrahim, Issa.*

Iskander (137) Iranian: variant of ISKANDAR.

GIVEN NAMES Iranian and Arabic 64%. *Hany* (4), *Atef* (3), *Moheb* (3), *Fayez* (2), *Nader* (2), *Raouf* (2), *Sameh* (2), *Samir* (2), *Amgad, Amir, Amira, Arif.*

Iske (124) Perhaps a reduced form of German **Isecke**, from a pet form of a personal name formed with Old High German *īs(an)* 'iron'.

Iskra (186) Polish and Slovenian: nickname for a sprightly person, from *iskra* 'spark'. Compare English SPARK.

GIVEN NAMES Polish 7%. *Danuta, Jadwiga, Jerzy, Radoslaw, Stanislawa.*

Islam (972) Muslim: from a personal name based on Arabic *islām* 'peace', the name of the religion of Muslims. *Islām* is mentioned in several places in the Qur'an, for example at 3:19 'Religion with Allah is Islām (peace)' and 5:3 'I have chosen for you Islām (peace) as religion'. This name is often found in combinations, e.g. **Nūr-ul-Islām** 'light of Islam'.

GIVEN NAMES Muslim 87%. *Mohammed* (81), *Mohammad* (52), *Nurul* (19), *Rafiqul* (18), *Nazrul* (17), *Muhammad* (15), *Shahidul* (15), *Saiful* (14), *Shafiqul* (13), *Kazi* (11), *Mohamed* (10), *Syed* (8).

Island (212) Norwegian: habitational name from any of four farmsteads so named. The origin of their name is not certain; it may be a compound of *is* 'ice' + *land* 'land' or from *Island* 'Iceland' (the name of the country).

Islas (535) Spanish: habitational name from a place called Islas (Málaga, Ciudad Real), or a topographic name meaning 'from the islands' (for example the Canaries), from the plural of *isla* 'island', from Latin *insula*.

GIVEN NAMES Spanish 54%. *Jose* (12), *Francisco* (9), *Jesus* (7), *Jorge* (6), *Luis* (6), *Alfredo* (5), *Carlos* (5), *Juan* (5), *Mario* (5), *Ruben* (5), *Enrique* (4), *Guadalupe* (4).

Isle (135) English: presumably a variant of ILES.

Isler (734) Variant spelling (mainly Swiss) of EISLER.

GIVEN NAMES German 4%. *Hans* (3), *Otto* (2), *Erna.*

Isles (225) English: variant spelling of ILES.

Isley (1354) **1.** English: unexplained. The connection with Isley Walton in Leicestershire is not clear. **2.** Possibly a respelling of German EISELE or Swiss ISLER.

Ismael (114) Muslim: variant of ISMAIL.

GIVEN NAMES Muslim 42%; Spanish 12%; French 5%. *Ahmed* (2), *Mohamed* (2), *Mohammad* (2), *Mohammed* (2), *Abdel, Abdirahman, Abou, Ahmad, Ali, Ashraf, Daud, Farook; Fernanda* (2), *Jose* (2),

Imelda, Martinez, Rafael, Ramirez, Reyes, Rolando, Santiago, Viviana; Romain, Yvon.

Ismail (667) Muslim: from an Arabic personal name, 'Ismā'īl, name of a Prophet (Biblical Ishmael), son of Ibrahim (Abraham). Ibrahim left his second wife Hajar (Hagar) and their small son Ismail in the wilderness outside Mecca with only a short supply of food and water. Allah took pity on them and caused the well of Zamzam to spurt up in that desolate place, which saved their lives. Later, Ibrahim sought out his son Ismail, and together they built the Ka'ba in Mecca, towards which all Muslims turn when praying. Arabs believe that Ismail was the founder of the Arab peoples, and for this reason Arabs are sometimes referred to as Ishmaelites. The term *Ismaeli* is of much more recent origin; it refers to a sect of Shiite Muslims headed by the Aga Khan, who claim descent from the Fatimid dynasty that ruled Egypt and North Africa from 909 to 1171. They take their name from Ismā'īl al-Ṭiddiq (699–765), son of the sixth Shiite imam, because they believe that the divine spirit passed to him and not to his brother Mūsa.

GIVEN NAMES Muslim 81%. *Mohammed* (23), *Mohamed* (19), *Mohammad* (19), *Ali* (16), *Ismail* (9), *Mohamad* (7), *Ahmed* (6), *Hassan* (6), *Ahmad* (5), *Ibrahim* (5), *Muhammad* (5), *Tarek* (4).

Ismay (42) English: see ESMAY.

Isner (345) Americanized spelling of German EISNER. It is concentrated in WV.

Isobe (104) Japanese: 'seashore'. The name is written in two different ways and is found mostly in eastern Japan and the Ryūkyūan island of Miyako.

GIVEN NAMES Japanese 67%. *Tomomi* (3), *Hideki* (2), *Isamu* (2), *Shinichi* (2), *Yuji* (2), *Atsuko, Daisuke, Hiroshi, Kanichi, Katsuji, Keisuke, Kenjiro.*

Isola (401) Italian: topographic name for someone who lived on an island, *isola*.

GIVEN NAMES Italian 10%. *Domenic* (2), *Anello, Angelo, Carlo, Carmine, Duilio, Gino, Lido, Palma, Santina, Ugo.*

Isom (2858) English: variant of ISHAM.

Ison (2110) English: patronymic or metronymic from the Middle English personal name IDA, which was used for both sexes.

Israel (3522) **1.** Jewish: from the Hebrew male personal name *Yisrael* 'Fighter of God'. In the Bible this is a byname bestowed on Jacob after he had wrestled with the angel at the ford of Jabbok (Genesis 32:24–8). **2.** name adopted by Jews with reference to the ancient Kingdom of Israel, destroyed by the Assyrians in 721 BC, or to the concept of Jewish nationhood, or, in modern times, to the state of Israel. **3.** Comparatively recent adoption of the Biblical name in Britain among Nonconformists, especially in Wales. **4.** altered form of EZELL.

GIVEN NAMES Jewish 4%. *Hyman* (7), *Sol* (6), *Faina* (2), *Shimon* (2), *Avi, Ehud, Elihu, Gerson, Isadore, Merav, Meyer, Miriam.*

Israelson (269) **1.** Jewish (Ashkenazic) and Swedish: patronymic from ISRAEL 1. **2.** Respelling of Swedish **Israelsson**, or Danish and Norwegian **Israelsen**, patronymics from ISRAEL.
GIVEN NAMES Scandinavian 6%; German 4%. *Nels; Fritzi.*

Isreal (196) Variant spelling of ISRAEL.

Issa (505) Arabic (mainly Lebanon and Syria): from the personal name *'Īsā*, Arabic form of Hebrew *Yeshua*, Greek *Iēsous* (see JESUS). This name is born by both Christian and Muslim Arabs. In Islam *'Īsā* is a prophet, 'a messenger of Allah and his word' (Qur'an 4:171). In the Qur'an 19:30, he proclaims, 'He (Allah) has given me the Book and established me as a Prophet.'
GIVEN NAMES Arabic 58%; French 4%. *Ali* (7), *Ahmad* (6), *Bassam* (5), *Nabil* (5), *Ahmed* (4), *Mohamad* (4), *Sami* (4), *Hani* (3), *Hassan* (3), *Ibrahim* (3), *Khalil* (3), *Mahmoud* (3); *Michel* (3), *Georges* (2), *Andre, Antoine, Jean-Pierre, Pierre.*

Issac (207) **1.** Indian (Kerala): derivative, alongside the more usual European form ISAAC, of the Hebrew personal name *yishāq* 'he laughs'. In Kerala this is used as a given name among Christians and in the U.S. it has come to be used as a last name among families from Kerala. **2.** French, English, Welsh, etc.: variant spelling of ISAAC.
GIVEN NAMES Indian 5%; French 5%. *Benoy, Leela, Varughese; Michel, Monique, Yanick.*

Issler (109) Swabian and Swiss German form of EISLER.

Istre (528) Norwegian: habitational name from either of two farmsteads so named.
GIVEN NAMES French 5%. *Camille, Celestin, Clovis, Onezime, Placide.*

Istvan (112) Hungarian: from the personal name *István*, Hungarian form of STEVEN.
GIVEN NAMES Hungarian 7%. *Dezso, Geza, Istvan.*

Iszler (117) German: unexplained.
GIVEN NAMES German 11%. *Otto* (2), *Gottieb, Helmuth, Reinhold.*

Italiano (404) Italian: ethnic name for an Italian, no doubt originating from an area in which many of the inhabitants were non-Italians.
GIVEN NAMES Italian 22%. *Sal* (3), *Salvatore* (3), *Mario* (2), *Nunzio* (2), *Americo, Angelo, Cosmo, Giuseppe, Guido, Pietro, Sebastiano, Stefano, Vito, Vittorio.*

Iten (213) Variant spelling of German **Ithen**, from a female personal name (see ITTNER).

Itkin (200) **1.** Jewish (eastern Ashkenazic): metronymic from the Yiddish female name *Itke*, a pet form of the biblical name *Judith* + the Slavic possessive suffix -*in*. **2.** English: from the Middle English personal name *Idkin*, a pet form of the personal name IDA.

GIVEN NAMES Russian 14%; Jewish 11%. *Boris* (2), *Dmitry* (2), *Mikhail* (2), *Aleksandr, Grigori, Igor, Leonid, Lyudmila, Oleg, Raisa, Vladimir, Vlagimir; Yehuda* (2), *Ilya, Isaak, Khaim, Meyer, Yakov.*

Ito (1454) Japanese (**Itō**): variously written; one of the ten most common Japanese surnames. The most usual rendering means 'Fujiwara of Ise' (*Ise no Fujiwara*); Ise is now part of Mie prefecture. These Itō claim descent from Fujiwara no Hidesato (10th century), of the northern branch of the clan. Another prominent Itō family (whose name means 'eastern Izu'), one-tenth as numerous, takes its name from a district now part of Shizuoka prefecture. They too are of Fujiwara descent, through Sukechika (d. 1181), a grandson of Kudō Ietsugu of the southern Fujiwara. Both Itō surnames are found in the Ryūkyū Islands.
GIVEN NAMES Japanese 66%. *Hiroshi* (14), *Takeshi* (12), *Takashi* (10), *Kenji* (7), *Koji* (7), *Isao* (6), *Kazuo* (6), *Shinichi* (6), *Yoshio* (6), *Hiroyuki* (5), *Tomoko* (5), *Yutaka* (5).

Itoh (100) Japanese: variant of ITO.
GIVEN NAMES Japanese 88%. *Hiroshi* (4), *Hitoshi* (2), *Kouichi* (2), *Minoru* (2), *Setsuo* (2), *Takashi* (2), *Tatsuya* (2), *Akemi, Atsushi, Chihiro, Hajime, Hirokazu.*

Ittner (265) Southern Germany: metronymic from a short form of a female compound personal name beginning with *Ita*- (of uncertain origin) + -*er* suffix.
GIVEN NAMES German 8%. *Klaus* (2), *Otto* (2), *Heinrich, Hermann, Lorenz.*

Iturralde (127) Basque: habitational name from Iturralde in Biscay province, Basque Country, so named from *iturri* 'spring' + *alde* 'near (to)'.
GIVEN NAMES Spanish 55%. *Alfredo* (4), *Jose* (4), *Manuel* (4), *Pablo* (3), *Santiago* (3), *Arturo* (2), *Carlos* (2), *Jesus* (2), *Jorge* (2), *Juan* (2), *Luis* (2), *Mario* (2); *Palma, Salvatore.*

Itzen (107) German and Danish: from a Frisian patronymic based on a personal name derived from *agi* '(sword) point'.

Itzkowitz (312) Jewish (eastern Ashkenazic): patronymic from the Yiddish personal names *Itsek, Itske*, variants of ISAAC.
GIVEN NAMES Jewish 13%; German 4%. *Chaim* (3), *Anshel, Avrum, Bentzion, Hershy, Hyman, Mendle, Rifka, Rivka, Ruchie, Sol, Yidel; Ignatz.*

Iuliano (201) Italian: from the southern form of GIULIANO.
GIVEN NAMES Italian 31%. *Carmine* (4), *Raffaele* (3), *Salvatore* (3), *Angelo* (2), *Aniello, Antonio, Biagio, Domenico, Donato, Giovanni, Giro, Giuseppe.*

Ivan (443) Romanian, Hungarian (**Iván**), and Slovak: from the personal name *Ivan*, eastern Slavic form of JOHN. It may also be a shortened form of a Slovenian or Croatian patronymic derived from the personal name *Ivan* (i.e. Slovenian **Ivanc, Ivančič**, or

Ivanjko; Croatian **Ivančić, Ivanić, Ivančević**).
GIVEN NAMES Romanian 4%. *Vasile* (2), *Constantin, Danut, Dumitru, Floarea, Gheorghe, Viorel.*

Ivancic (162) Croatian (**Ivančić**): patronymic from the personal name IVAN.
GIVEN NAMES South Slavic 8%. *Slavko* (2), *Stanko.*

Ivanoff (262) Russian, Belorussian, and Bulgarian: alternative spelling of IVANOV.
GIVEN NAMES Russian 5%. *Grigori, Oleg, Sergei, Vitali, Vladimir.*

Ivanov (438) Russian, Belorussian, and Bulgarian: patronymic from the personal name IVAN.
GIVEN NAMES Russian 39%; Czech and Slovak 5%; South Slavic 5%. *Vladimir* (16), *Igor* (8), *Sergey* (8), *Anatoly* (5), *Boris* (5), *Nikolay* (5), *Alexei* (4), *Alexey* (4), *Andrei* (4), *Dmitry* (4), *Oleg* (4), *Vasily* (4); *Pavel* (3), *Petr* (2), *Stanislav* (2), *Lubomir; Atanas* (3), *Apostol, Branko, Cvetko, Dimitar, Dragan, Kristo, Ratko, Srecko, Zarko.*

Ivans (154) Variant of Welsh EVANS.

Ivens (211) **1.** English: patronymic from the Old Norse personal name *Ívar* (see IVERSON). **2.** North German: variant of IVERSEN.

Ivers (871) **1.** Irish and English: patronymic from the Old Norse personal name *Ívar* (see IVERSON). **2.** North German: patronymic from the personal name *Ivar* (see IVERSEN).

Iversen (1118) **1.** Danish and Norwegian: patronymic from the personal name *Ivar*, from Old Norse *Ívarr*, a compound of either *ív* 'yew tree', 'bow' or *Ing* (the name of a god) + *ar* 'warrior' or 'spear'. **2.** North German (Frisian): patronymic from a Germanic personal name composed of the elements *īwa* 'yew (tree)' + *hard* 'strong', 'firm'. **3.** English: variant spelling of IVERSON.
GIVEN NAMES Scandinavian 10%. *Iver* (6), *Bernt* (3), *Erik* (3), *Niels* (2), *Svein* (2), *Alf, Anders, Bent, Bjorg, Einer, Gudmund, Jorgen.*

Iverson (6487) **1.** English and Scottish: patronymic from the Old Norse personal name *Ívarr*, a compound of either *ív* 'yew tree', 'bow' or *Ing* (the name of a god) + *ar* 'warrior' or 'spear'. **2.** Swedish equivalent of IVERSEN 1. **3.** Respelling of Danish, Norwegian, and North German IVERSEN.
GIVEN NAMES Scandinavian 4%. *Iver* (19), *Erik* (10), *Hjalmer* (3), *Lars* (2), *Selmer* (2), *Thor* (2), *Evald, Gunner, Helmer, Ingman, Jarl, Joneen.*

Ivery (416) English and Scottish: variant of IVORY.

Ives (3460) English (Norman) and French: from the Old French personal name *Ive* (modern French *Yves*), which is of Germanic origin, being a short form of various compound names containing the element *iv-*, *īwa* 'yew'. The final *-s* is the mark of the Old French nominative case.

Iveson (119) English (Yorkshire): patronymic from the Old French personal name IVE.

Ivester (718) English (Lancashire): unexplained. This name is common in GA and SC.

Ivey (7769) English (of Norman origin): habitational name from Ivoy in Cher, northern France.

Ivie (1560) English: variant spelling of IVY.

Ivins (674) Variant of Welsh EVANS.

Ivory (1598) **1.** English (of Norman origin): habitational name from Ivry-la-Bataille in Eure, northern France. **2.** Scottish: when not of the same origin as 1, an Anglicized form of Gaelic **Mac Iamharach** (see MCIVER).

Ivy (3753) English: variant spelling of IVEY.

Iwai (149) Japanese: 'stone well' or 'resides in a stony place', depending on the characters; a common place name. The first is found as a surname in western Japan, the second is more common in eastern Japan. Both are related to the name ISHII, which has similar meanings. In the Ryūkyūan island of Amami, the name is written with the character for 'celebrate'.
GIVEN NAMES Japanese 56%. *Makoto* (3), *Hiroshi* (2), *Kazuhiro* (2), *Shiro* (2), *Yoshio* (2), *Akira*, *Asako*, *Eiichi*, *Eiko*, *Haruhiko*, *Haruko*, *Hideko*.

Iwamoto (357) Japanese: '(one who lives) near the base of the stone'; common in west-central Japan and the Ryūkyū Islands. One family is named after *Iwamoto-mura* in Suruga (now part of Shizuoka prefecture); another descends from Minamoto no Yoshimitsu (1056–1127), an ancestor of several samurai families; still another family is of northern FUJIWARA descent.
GIVEN NAMES Japanese 53%. *Hiroshi* (5), *Shigeo* (3), *Kosuke* (2), *Masami* (2), *Masaru* (2), *Nobuo* (2), *Satoru* (2), *Shuhei* (2), *Toshihiko* (2), *Akio*, *Akira*, *Chika*.

Iwan (160) Polish spelling of the personal name *Ivan*, East Slavic form of *Jan* (see JOHN).
GIVEN NAMES Polish 5%. *Henryk*, *Karol*, *Malgorzata*.

Iwanicki (207) Ukrainian and Polish: habitational name for someone from Iwaniec (now Iwonicz) in Krosno voivodeship, or Iwanki, Iwanovice, or other places named with the personal name IWAN.
GIVEN NAMES Polish 11%; French 4%. *Andrzej*, *Bogdan*, *Casimir*, *Iwona*, *Janusz*, *Jozef*, *Miroslaw*, *Stanislaw*, *Tomasz*; *Celina*, *Jeanmarie*.

Iwanowski (116) Polish: habitational name for someone from Iwanowice in Suwałki voivodeship, or from Iwanowo in Częstochowa and Kalisz voivodeships, all named with the personal name IWAN.
GIVEN NAMES Polish 14%. *Boleslaw*, *Krystyna*, *Krzysztof*, *Tadeusz*, *Zygmunt*.

Iwanski (346) Polish (**Iwański**): habitational name for someone from Iwanie (now

Iwonie) in Sieradz voivodeship, a place named from the personal name IWAN.
GIVEN NAMES Polish 4%; German 4%. *Casimir*, *Danuta*, *Ryszard*; *Florian* (3), *Alois* (2), *Fritz*, *Kurt*.

Iwasaki (295) Japanese: 'stone cape'; variously written, also pronounced **Iwazaki** and **Iwagasaki**. A common place name throughout Japan, found as a surname in western Japan and the Ryūkyū Islands. One family was samurai of Tosa (now Kōchi prefecture).
GIVEN NAMES Japanese 66%. *Junichi* (4), *Hiroshi* (3), *Kazuo* (3), *Koji* (3), *Noriko* (3), *Takeshi* (3), *Masataka* (2), *Michiko* (2), *Miyo* (2), *Shota* (2), *Yoshio* (2), *Yuichi* (2).

Iwata (300) Japanese: 'stony rice paddy'; variously written. One family comes from *Iwata-mura* in Chichibu-gun, Musashi (now part of western Tōkyō). Another family is descended from the Sugawara family of Chikugo (now part of Saga prefecture).
GIVEN NAMES Japanese 53%. *Megumi* (3), *Toshio* (3), *Akiko* (2), *Hisashi* (2), *Koji* (2), *Mitsuo* (2), *Sachiko* (2), *Satoshi* (2), *Shigeru* (2), *Takashi* (2), *Yasushi* (2), *Yukio* (2).

Iwen (191) North German (Frisian): patronymic from the Germanic personal name *Ivo*, which is thought to be derived from *īwa* 'yew (tree)'.
GIVEN NAMES German 4%. *Heinz* (2), *Hans*.

Iwinski (144) Polish (**Iwiński**): habitational name for someone from Iwiny in Płock voivodeship, a place named from *Iwa*, a nickname meaning 'sallow'.
GIVEN NAMES Polish 7%. *Krzysztof*, *Lech*, *Zbigniew*.

Iyengar (160) Indian (Tamil Nadu): Hindu (Brahman) name, *aiyangār* in Tamil, from *aiyan* 'sage', 'priest', 'Brahman', 'lord' (from Indo-Aryan *ayya*, from Sanskrit *ārya* 'Aryan', 'master', 'preceptor', or 'father-in-law') + the Telugu honorific plural suffix *-gāru*. The Telugu form of the word is *ayyagāru*, meaning 'father', 'sir'. The Tamil word *ayyan* consists of the noun stem *ayya* + the masculine singular suffix *-n*. The Iyengar Brahmans are a prominent community from Tamil Nadu and votaries of the god Vishnu; only some members of the community use *Iyengar* as a surname.
GIVEN NAMES Indian 95%. *Arun* (4), *Krishna* (4), *Sampath* (3), *Vasuki* (3), *Giridhar* (2), *Murali* (2), *Raghu* (2), *Raj* (2), *Rama* (2), *Ranga* (2), *Rekha* (2), *Satish* (2).

Iyer (511) Indian (Tamil Nadu): Hindu (Brahman) name, *aiyar* in Tamil, composed of the noun stem *ayya* (see IYENGAR) + the honorific plural suffix *-r*. The Iyer Brahmans are a prominent community from Tamil Nadu.
GIVEN NAMES Indian 95%. *Ravi* (16), *Shankar* (12), *Sridhar* (7), *Hari* (6), *Krishna* (6), *Ramesh* (6), *Anand* (5), *Ganesh* (5), *Mani* (5), *Prakash* (5), *Raju* (5), *Shekhar* (5).

Izaguirre (404) Basque **Izagirre**, a variant of **Aizagirre**, a topographic name for someone who lived in a place exposed to the

wind, from Basque *aize* 'wind' + *ager*, *agir* 'visible', 'exposed.'
GIVEN NAMES Spanish 58%. *Jose* (15), *Juan* (12), *Carlos* (8), *Guadalupe* (6), *Ignacio* (5), *Alberto* (4), *Francisco* (4), *Jesus* (4), *Jorge* (4), *Javier* (3), *Juana* (3), *Manuel* (3).

Izard (272) **1.** English and French: from a Germanic female personal name composed of the elements *īs* 'ice' + *hild* 'strife', 'battle'. This was introduced into England by the Normans in the forms *Iseu(l)t* and *Isolde*. The popularity of the various versions of the legend of Tristan and Isolde led to widespread use of the personal name in the Middle Ages. **2.** French: from *Ishard*, a Germanic personal name composed of the elements *īs* 'ice' + *hard* 'hardy', 'brave', 'strong'.

Izatt (165) English: variant of IZARD.

Izbicki (121) Polish: habitational name for someone from any of several places called Izbica or Izbice, named with Polish *izba* 'room'.
GIVEN NAMES Polish 9%. *Agnieszka*, *Casimir*, *Karol*, *Krzysztof*.

Izer (116) Americanized spelling of German EISER.

Izquierdo (684) Spanish: nickname for a left-handed man, from Spanish *izquierdo* 'left' (a word of pre-Roman origin, akin to Basque *ezker*).
GIVEN NAMES Spanish 53%. *Jose* (28), *Juan* (12), *Julio* (12), *Carlos* (11), *Francisco* (8), *Manuel* (8), *Angel* (7), *Luis* (7), *Pablo* (7), *Pedro* (7), *Eduardo* (6), *Humberto* (6); *Antonio* (7), *Fausto* (3), *Angelo* (2), *Dario* (2), *Heriberto* (2), *Lucio*.

Izumi (196) Japanese: 'spring of water'; variously written. Listed in the Shinsen shōjiroku. The name written with two characters meaning 'harmonious spring' is more common in the Ōsaka area and eastern Japan; the version written only with the character for 'spring' is mostly found widely in northern Japan, the island of Kyūshū, and the Ryūkyū Islands.
GIVEN NAMES Japanese 57%. *Kiyoshi* (5), *Keiko* (3), *Hideki* (2), *Hiroshi* (2), *Hisae* (2), *Kazuhiko* (2), *Koji* (2), *Masashi* (2), *Toshiaki* (2), *Yoko* (2), *Akihiko*, *Akira*.

Izzard (215) English: variant spelling of IZARD.

Izzi (365) Italian: patronymic or plural form of IZZO.
GIVEN NAMES Italian 17%. *Antonio* (3), *Domenic* (3), *Angelo* (2), *Giulio* (2), *Pasquale* (2), *Aldo*, *Carmine*, *Gasper*, *Giacomo*, *Gino*, *Guiseppe*, *Lorenzo*.

Izzo (1742) Italian: nickname from Sicilian *izzu* 'slave' or directly from Latin *aegyptius* 'Egyptian', or from the same word in the sense 'dark-skinned'.
GIVEN NAMES Italian 16%. *Carmine* (11), *Angelo* (10), *Antonio* (8), *Salvatore* (7), *Domenic* (5), *Rocco* (5), *Pasco* (4), *Domenico* (3), *Francesco* (3), *Gaetano* (3), *Lorenzo* (3), *Nunzio* (3).

J

Jabara (151) Muslim: from Arabic *jabari* 'adherent of the doctrine of predestination'. *Al-Jabariya* was an early Islamic school of thought that denied free will and maintained determinism and the inescapability of fate.
GIVEN NAMES Muslim 12%. *Marwan* (3), *Haifa, Hassan, Ibrahim, Said, Sami, Yousef, Zaina, Ziad.*

Jabbar (101) Muslim: from a personal name based on Arabic *jabbār* 'powerful', 'mighty'. *Al-Jabbār* 'the All-Compelling' is an attribute of Allah.
GIVEN NAMES Muslim 80%. *Abdul* (18), *Ahmad* (2), *Farooq* (2), *Mohammad* (2), *Muhammad* (2), *Omar* (2), *Ali, Aziz, Fouzia, Hadi, Hossain, Husein.*

Jabbour (210) Muslim: variant of JABBAR.
GIVEN NAMES Muslim 29%; French 15%. *Salim* (4), *Nabil* (3), *Fadi* (2), *Halim* (2), *Kamal* (2), *Ramzi* (2), *Samer* (2), *Badia, Chafic, Ghassan, Hadi, Hala; Antoine* (3), *Emile* (3), *Michel* (2), *Andre, Dany, Marcell, Pierre, Rodolph, Serge.*

Jaber (447) Muslim: from a personal name based on Arabic *jābir* 'comforter', 'healer', 'bone-setter'. Jābir ibn 'Abdullah was one of the Companions of the Prophet Muhammad. Jābir ibn Hayyān (c. 721–c. 815) is known as the father of Arabic alchemy.
GIVEN NAMES Muslim 58%. *Ali* (13), *Ahmad* (5), *Ibrahim* (5), *Hussein* (4), *Mohamad* (4), *Mohamed* (4), *Mohammed* (4), *Amal* (3), *Imad* (3), *Khaled* (3), *Mahmoud* (3), *Abdul* (2).

Jablon (258) **1.** Polish: metonymic occupational name for a grower or seller of apples, from *jabłoń* 'apple tree'. **2.** Jewish (from Poland and Lithuania): ornamental name from Polish *jabłoń* 'apple tree', or a habitational name from any of the villages in Poland named Jabłoń from this word.

Jablonowski (244) Polish (**Jabłonowski**) and Jewish (from Poland): habitational name for someone from a place called Jabłonowo or Jabłonow; both place names are from *jabłoń* 'apple tree'.
GIVEN NAMES Polish 6%. *Ryscard* (2), *Andrzej, Dariusz, Wieslaw.*

Jablonski (2797) Polish (**Jabłoński**) and Jewish (eastern Ashkenazic): habitational name for someone from Jabłonka, Jabłonna, or Jabłonica, all places named with *jabłoń* 'apple tree', or the diminutive form *jabłonka.*

GIVEN NAMES Polish 6%. *Zygmunt* (4), *Aleksander* (2), *Casimir* (2), *Jerzy* (2), *Karol* (2), *Krzysztof* (2), *Ryszard* (2), *Stanislaw* (2), *Tadeusz* (2), *Zygmund* (2), *Alicja, Alojzy.*

Jablonsky (228) Jewish (eastern Ashkenazic): variant spelling of JABLONSKI.

Jabour (148) Muslim: variant of JABBAR.

Jabs (225) North German: patronymic from a Frisian pet name based on a Germanic personal name formed with *theud* 'people', 'race', or from *Gabo*, a short form of GEBHARDT or some other Germanic name having *geb* 'gift' as its first element.
GIVEN NAMES German 9%. *Armin* (2), *Bernhard, Dietmar, Elke, Ewald.*

Jacaruso (123) Italian: from a compound of *Ia-* (from the personal name *Ianni*) + southern Italian *caruso* 'lad', 'boy'.
GIVEN NAMES Italian 12%. *Donato* (2), *Nunzio, Sal.*

Jacek (111) Polish: from the personal name *Jacek*, a pet form of *Jacenty* (Latin *Hyacinthus*, Greek *Hyakinthos*). The personal name was popularized in Poland through the cult of St. Jacek, a 13th-century apostle and missionary who was sent to Kraków, where he established a Dominican friary. Compare Spanish JACINTO, Italian GIACINTO.
GIVEN NAMES Polish 7%. *Irena, Pawel, Wojciech.*

Jach (121) Polish, Czech, and German (of Slavic origin): from the personal name *Jach*, a pet form of various names beginning with *Ja-*, principally *Jan* (see JOHN), *Jakub* (see JACOB), and, in Polish, *Jacenty* (see JACEK).
GIVEN NAMES Polish 11%. *Andrzej, Jerzy, Tadeusz, Urszula.*

Jachim (176) German, Polish, and Jewish: variant of JOACHIM.
GIVEN NAMES Polish 5%. *Bogdan, Wieslawa, Witold.*

Jacinto (543) Spanish and Portuguese: from the personal name *Jacinto*, (Latin *Hyacinthus*, Greek *Hyakinthos*). This was the name of a 3rd-century saint who was martyred together with his brother Protus. He enjoyed a certain cult in Portugal. His name, which is almost certainly of pre-Greek origin, in classical times denoted a flower (not the modern hyacinth, but perhaps the martagon lily), and it was borne by a mythological character from whose blood the flower was supposed to have sprung up.

GIVEN NAMES Spanish 42%; Portuguese 9%. *Jose* (7), *Jesus* (6), *Juan* (6), *Arturo* (4), *Manuel* (4), *Alfonso* (3), *Carlos* (3), *Luis* (3), *Santiago* (3), *Alicia* (2), *Eduardo* (2), *Francisco* (2); *Joao* (2), *Agostinho, Albano, Amadeu; Antonio* (3), *Antonino, Bartolo, Cecilio, Eliseo, Lucio, Marco, Mario Antonio, Nino, Rossano, Sabastian, Salustiano.*

Jack (4442) **1.** Scottish and English: from a Middle English personal name, *Jakke*, from Old French *Jacques*, the usual French form of Latin *Jacobus*, which is the source of both JACOB and JAMES. As a family name in Britain, this is almost exclusively Scottish. **2.** English and Welsh: from the same personal name as 1, taken as a pet form of JOHN. **3.** German (also **Jäck**): from a short form of the personal name JACOB. **4.** Americanized form of one or more like-sounding Jewish surnames.

Jacka (166) **1.** English (Cornwall and Wales): variant of JACK. **2.** Czech (**Jačka**), Polish, and German (of Slavic origin): from a pet form (Czech *Jač*, Polish *Jacz*) of any of the various Slavic personal names beginning with *Ja-*, for example JAKUB, JAN, *Jacenty* (see JACEK).

Jackel (202) German (also **Jäckel**): from a pet form of the personal name JACOB. See also JAECKEL.

Jackels (100) German and French (Alsace): patronymic form of JACKEL.

Jackett (111) English: from a pet form of JACK. In the U.K. this surname is now found chiefly in Cornwall and Wales.

Jackiewicz (86) Polish: patronymic from a pet form of the personal name JACEK.
GIVEN NAMES Polish 18%. *Slawomir* (2), *Mariusz, Miroslaw, Pawel.*

Jackley (141) Americanized spelling of South German and Swiss **Jäckle, Jaeckly**, or any of the many variants of this name, which in origin are pet forms of JACOB. Compare JAECKEL.

Jacklin (353) **1.** English: from a pet form of JACK. **2.** South German and Swiss German (**Jäcklin**): from a pet form of *Jack*, a South German name based on JACOB. Compare JACKLEY.

Jackman (2585) **1.** English: occupational name for the servant of someone who bore the personal name JACK. **2.** English: Americanized form of French *Jacquème* (see JAMES). **3.** Americanized form of one or more like-sounding Jewish surnames.

4. Americanized spelling of German **Jachmann** or **Jackmann**, from a Czech pet form of a name ultimately from the Biblical name *Yochanam* (see JOHN) + Middle High German *man* 'man'.

Jacko (215) German: of undetermined, possibly Slavic, origin. It could also be an Americanized spelling of French JACOT or a short form of any of the various surnames beginning with the element *Jacko-* (see below), but the concentration of the name in OH, PA, and TX is suggestive of a German origin.

Jackovich (159) Americanized spelling of Polish **Jackowicz**, a patronymic from the personal name JACEK, or of a cognate name in another Slavic language.

Jackowiak (76) Polish: patronymic from the personal name JACEK.
GIVEN NAMES Polish 17%. *Beata, Bogdan, Casimir, Jozef, Witold, Wlodzimierz.*

Jackowski (525) Polish: habitational name for someone from Jacków, Jackowice, or Jackowo, places named with the personal name JACEK.
GIVEN NAMES Polish 7%. *Jerzy* (2), *Dariusz, Iwona, Janina, Kazimierz, Leszek, Piotr, Stanislaw, Zdzislaw, Zygmunt.*

Jacks (2207) English and North German: patronymic from JACK.

Jackson (184136) English, Scottish, and northern Irish: patronymic from JACK 1. As an American surname this has absorbed other patronymics beginning with *J-* in various European languages.
FOREBEARS This extremely common British name was brought over by numerous different bearers in the 17th and 18th centuries. One forebear was the father and namesake of the seventh U.S. president, Andrew Jackson, who migrated to SC from Carrickfergus in the north of Ireland in 1765. The Confederate General Thomas 'Stonewall' Jackson came from VA, where his great-grandfather John, likewise of Scotch–Irish stock, had settled after emigrating to America in 1748.

Jacky (118) Swiss German (also **Jäcky**): from a pet form of the personal name JACOB.

Jaco (554) Of uncertain origin. **1.** Perhaps Spanish and Portuguese (**Jacó**) or southern Italian (**Jacò**): from the personal name (see JACOB). **2.** Possibly a respelling of French JACOT.

Jacob (6682) Jewish, English, German, Portuguese, French, Dutch, and southern Indian: derivative, via Latin *Jacobus*, from the Hebrew personal name *ya'aqobh* (*Yaakov*). In the Bible, this is the name of the younger twin brother of Esau (Genesis 25:26), who took advantage of the latter's hunger and impetuousness to persuade him to part with his birthright 'for a mess of potage'. The name is traditionally interpreted as coming from Hebrew *akev* 'heel', and Jacob is said to have been born holding on to Esau's heel. In English *Jacob* and *James* are now regarded as quite distinct names, but they are of identical origin (see JAMES), and in most European languages the two names are not distinguished. It is used as a given name among Christians in India, and in the U.S. has come to be used as a surname among families from southern India.

Jacobe (154) Jewish: variant spelling of JACOBI.

Jacober (191) Jewish: patronymic from JACOB.
GIVEN NAMES German 4%. *Milbert, Wilhelm.*

Jacobi (1489) Jewish, English, Dutch, and North German: from the Latin genitive *Jacobi* '(son) of Jacob', Latinized form of English *Jacobs* and JACOBSON or North German JAKOBS(EN) and JACOBS(EN).
GIVEN NAMES German 5%. *Arno* (2), *Ernst* (2), *Erwin* (2), *Heinz* (2), *Helmut* (2), *Helmuth* (2), *Kurt* (2), *Christoph, Gerd, Hermann, Herta, Otto.*

Jacobitz (100) **1.** German (of Slavic origin): from a patronymic based on the Latin personal name *Jacobus* (see JACOB). **2.** Probably also a reduced form of Jewish JACOBOWITZ.

Jacobo (626) Spanish and Italian: from the Latin personal name *Jacobus* (see JAMES, GIACOMO).
GIVEN NAMES Spanish 56%. *Jose* (18), *Jesus* (12), *Francisco* (7), *Juan* (7), *Manuel* (7), *Miguel* (7), *Rafael* (7), *Alfredo* (6), *Luis* (6), *Carlos* (4), *Mario* (4), *Roberto* (4).

Jacobowitz (380) Jewish (eastern Ashkenazic): Germanized spelling of a Slavic patronymic from the personal name JACOB.
GIVEN NAMES Jewish 18%; German 4%. *Aron* (3), *Benzion* (3), *Aviva* (2), *Herschel* (2), *Hyman* (2), *Lipot* (2), *Shloma* (2), *Yosef* (2), *Bezalel, Emanuel, Mendel, Oded; Erna, Kurt, Wolf.*

Jacobs (43403) Jewish and English: patronymic from the personal name JACOB. As a Jewish surname it has also assimilated various other patronymics from the same personal name, as for example JACOBOWITZ.

Jacobsen (8356) Dutch, Danish, North German, and Norwegian: patronymic from JACOB.
GIVEN NAMES Scandinavian 7%. *Erik* (12), *Lars* (9), *Jorgen* (5), *Nils* (4), *Anders* (3), *Gudrun* (3), *Iver* (3), *Knud* (3), *Alf* (2), *Bjorn* (2), *Borge* (2), *Fredrik* (2).

Jacobsma (142) Frisian: patronymic from the personal name JACOB.

Jacobsmeyer (137) North German: habitational name from an estate so named.

Jacobsohn (118) German and Jewish (Ashkenazic): patronymic from the personal name JACOB.
GIVEN NAMES German 9%; Jewish 5%. *Erwin, Kurt, Ulrich; Reuven.*

Jacobson (21035) English: patronymic from JACOB. As an American surname this name has absorbed cognates from other languages, for example Danish, Norwegian, and Dutch JACOBSEN and Swedish **Jacobsson**.

Jacobucci (117) Italian: variant spelling of IACOBUCCI.
GIVEN NAMES Italian 6%. *Angelo, Pasquale.*

Jacobus (1057) Dutch and German: humanistic Latinate form of *Jakob*.

Jacoby (4061) Jewish, English, and German: variant spelling of JACOBI.

Jacocks (145) English: variant spelling of JAYCOX.

Jacome (238) Spanish and Portuguese (**Jácome**): from a variant of the personal name *Iacobus* (see JACOB).
GIVEN NAMES Spanish 40%. *Carlos* (5), *Jose* (4), *Luis* (4), *Rafael* (4), *Gonzalo* (3), *Manuel* (3), *Roberto* (3), *Enrique* (2), *Fernando* (2), *Mario* (2), *Pablo* (2), *Silvia* (2).

Jacot (251) French: from a pet form of JACQUES.
GIVEN NAMES French 5%. *Amie, Andre, Francoise, Henri, Pierre.*

Jacoway (105) English: altered form of the personal name JACQUE. Compare JAKEWAY.

Jacox (229) English: variant spelling of JAYCOX.

Jacquart (140) Variant spelling of French **Jacquard**, from a derivative of the personal name JACQUES.
GIVEN NAME French 6%. *Emile.*

Jacque (222) Variant of French and English JACQUES. As an English name, it is generally pronounced as two syllables.
GIVEN NAMES French 6%. *Andre, Emile, Germaine, Yvon.*

Jacquemin (114) French: from a pet form of the personal name JACQUES.
GIVEN NAMES French 12%. *Alain, Cecile, Philippe.*

Jacques (4496) French and English: from the Old French personal name *Jacques*, the usual French form of Latin *Jacobus* (see JACOB). The English surname is either a late introduction from France or a Frenchification of JAKES. In English this surname is traditionally pronounced as two syllables, *jay-kwez*.
FOREBEARS A bearer of the name from Picardy is recorded in Quebec city in 1688.
GIVEN NAMES French 12%. *Andre* (12), *Marcel* (6), *Armand* (5), *Emile* (5), *Normand* (5), *Pierre* (5), *Aime* (3), *Alain* (3), *Francois* (3), *Gaston* (3), *Germaine* (3), *Honore* (3).

Jacquet (306) French: from the personal name *Jacquet*, a pet form of JACQUES.
GIVEN NAMES French 18%. *Jacques* (2), *Alain, Andre, Antoine, Cecile, Christophe, Constant, Edwige, Henri, Irby, Jean-Paul, Lucien.*

Jacquez (514) Northern French: variant of JACQUET.
FOREBEARS A Jacquet, also called CHAMPAGNE, is documented in Quebec city in

1661. A Jacquet, Jacqueze, or Jacques, also called LEBLOND, from Brussels, is recorded in Montreal in 1715.
GIVEN NAMES Spanish 41%. *Jose* (9), *Manuel* (6), *Juan* (5), *Roberto* (5), *Carlos* (4), *Ricardo* (4), *Armando* (3), *Arturo* (3), *Francisco* (3), *Mario* (3), *Pedro* (3), *Rafael* (3).

Jacquin (181) French: from a pet form of the personal name JACQUES.
GIVEN NAMES French 8%. *Arnaud, Emile.*

Jacquot (255) French: from a pet form of the personal name JACQUES.
GIVEN NAMES French 7%. *Alain, Frederique, Jean Claude, Pierre, Serge.*

Jadin (121) French: from a diminutive of **Jade**, a metonymic occupational name for a maker or seller of bowls, from *jade*, a regional variant of *jatte*.

Jadwin (163) Origin unidentified. This name is common in OH.

Jaeckel (269) German (**Jäckel**): from a pet form of the personal name JAKOB.
GIVEN NAMES German 9%. *Kurt* (4), *Klaus* (2), *Karl Heinz, Manfred.*

Jaeckle (117) German (**Jäckle**): variant of JAECKEL.
GIVEN NAMES German 15%. *Kurt* (4), *Gerhardt* (2).

Jaecks (114) Swiss German and South German: patronymic from a pet form of the personal name JACOB.

Jaeger (5407) German (mostly **Jäger**) and Jewish (Ashkenazic): occupational name for a hunter, Middle High German *jēger(e)*, Middle Low German *jeger(e)* (agent derivatives of *jagen* 'to hunt'); as a Jewish surname, it is mainly ornamental, derived from German *Jäger*. The surname is also established in Scandinavia (Swedish **Jäger**; Danish and Norwegian **Jæger**) and has been Latinized as **Venator**.
GIVEN NAMES German 6%. *Kurt* (20), *Hans* (7), *Otto* (7), *Friedrich* (5), *Klaus* (5), *Fritz* (4), *Armin* (3), *Erwin* (3), *Helmut* (3), *Ralf* (3), *Alois* (2), *Gerhard* (2).

Jaegers (153) German (**Jägers**): Lower Rhine variant of **Jäger** (see JAEGER).
GIVEN NAMES German 6%. *Dieter, Helmut.*

Jaekel (157) German (**Jäkel**) and Danish: variant of **Jäckel** (see JAECKEL).
GIVEN NAMES German 11%; Scandinavian 6%. *Wolfgang* (2), *Hans, Otto, Reinhold, Siegfried.*

Jaenicke (131) German (**Jänicke**): from a pet form of the personal name *Johann(es)* (see JOHN).
GIVEN NAMES German 13%. *Kurt* (3), *Ingeborg, Juergen, Lutz.*

Jaeschke (134) German (of Slavic origin): from a pet form of the personal name *Johannes* (see JOHN).
GIVEN NAMES German 13%. *Horst* (2), *Ernst, Gerhard, Hartmut, Kurt.*

Jafari (177) Muslim: surname denoting someone associated with the school of Muslim law founded by Ja'far as-Sadiq

(699–765), sixth imam of the Shiite Muslims.
GIVEN NAMES Muslim 72%. *Ali* (4), *Mehdi* (3), *Abdullah* (2), *Behzad* (2), *Fariba* (2), *Hossein* (2), *Jafar* (2), *Jamal* (2), *Jehad* (2), *Kianoosh* (2), *Ladan* (2), *Masoud* (2).

Jaffa (130) Jewish: variant of JAFFE.
GIVEN NAMES Jewish 9%. *Noam, Sol, Yehuda, Zevi.*

Jaffe (3398) Jewish (Ashkenazic): from Hebrew *yafe* 'beautiful', 'pleasant', a surname recorded in Prague as early as the 16th century.
GIVEN NAMES Jewish 5%. *Hyman* (6), *Miriam* (4), *Sol* (4), *Hillel* (3), *Ari* (2), *Aron* (2), *Avi* (2), *Bentzion, Chaim, Dov, Elchonon, Este.*

Jaffee (447) Jewish: variant of JAFFE.
GIVEN NAMES Jewish 4%. *Sol* (2), *Gilat, Isadore, Meyer.*

Jaffer (165) Muslim: from a personal name based on Arabic *ja'far* 'spring', 'source', 'rivulet'. The warrior Ja'far ibn-Abī-Ṭālib died heroically at the Battle of Mota (629), holding aloft the Muslim banner proclaiming 'Paradise!'
GIVEN NAMES Muslim 77%. *Akbar* (3), *Amir* (3), *Mohamed* (3), *Abdul* (2), *Adil* (2), *Ali* (2), *Hyder* (2), *Khalid* (2), *Mohammed* (2), *Mohsin* (2), *Nazim* (2), *Sajjad* (2).

Jafri (152) Muslim: variant of JAFARI.
GIVEN NAMES Muslim 92%. *Syed* (25), *Ali* (7), *Amir* (3), *Aziz* (3), *Iftikhar* (3), *Ahmed* (2), *Hasan* (2), *Irshad* (2), *Jawed* (2), *Khalid* (2), *Muhammad Ali* (2), *Rafat* (2).

Jagels (126) German: probably a patronymic form from a voiced variant of the personal name **Jä(c)kel**, for instance **Jägel** (see JAECKEL).
GIVEN NAMES German 10%. *Erwin, Helmut, Kurt, Otto, Wilhelm.*

Jager (1193) **1.** Dutch: occupational name for a hunter, Middle Dutch *jagher*. **2.** German: variant of JAEGER 'hunter'. **3.** Slovenian: occupational name for a hunter, from German JAEGER.
GIVEN NAMES German 4%. *Bernhard, Dieter, Gunter, Hans, Irmgard, Kurt, Wilhelm, Wolfgang.*

Jagers (128) Dutch: patronymic from JAGER.
GIVEN NAMES German 4%. *Karlheinz, Kurt.*

Jaggard (119) English: from the personal name JACK + the pejorative suffix *-ard.*

Jaggars (122) English: variant of JAGGER.

Jagger (471) English (West Yorkshire): occupational name from Middle English *jagger* 'carter', 'peddler', an agent derivative of Middle English *jag* 'pack', 'load' (of unknown origin). All or most present-day bearers of this surname are probably members of a single family, which originally came from Staniland in the parish of Halifax. During the 16th century it spread through the Calder valley, and from there to other parts of England.

Jaggers (1012) English (West Yorkshire): variant of JAGGER.

Jaggi (135) **1.** Indian (Panjab): Hindu (Hazari) and Sikh name of unknown meaning. **2.** South German and Swiss German (also **Jäggi**): from a pet form of JACOB. Compare JAECKEL.
GIVEN NAMES Indian 21%; German 8%. *Bawa* (2), *Ajit, Arvind, Birendra, Narendra, Pran, Radhe, Rajiv, Saroj, Savita, Simmi; Hans* (2), *Erwin, Franz, Inge, Ulrich.*

Jagiello (155) Polish (**Jagiełło**): **1.** from the personal name *Jagiełło*, Polish form of Lithuanian *Jogaila*. The Jagiellonian royal house of Poland was founded by the Lithuanian Władysław Jagiełło (Vlodislav Jogaila; 1348–1434), whose dynasty ruled the Kingdom of Poland and the Grand Duchy of Lithuania from 1386 to 1572. In most cases *Jagiełło* was adopted by Poles as a family name to suggest a connection with the dynasty, or in honor of royalty and the glorious period of Polish history that they represent. **2.** habitational name for someone from Jagiełła in Przemyśl voivodeship, or Jagiełły (Jogiliai) in Lithuania.
GIVEN NAMES Polish 17%. *Jacek* (2), *Andrzej, Czeslaw, Jerzy, Krysztof, Malgorzata, Stanislaw, Zygmunt.*

Jagielski (290) Polish: habitational name for someone from an unidentified place, possibly Jagiele in Suwałki voivodeship. See also JAGIELLO.
GIVEN NAMES Polish 4%. *Henryk, Jerzy, Rafal.*

Jagla (104) Polish (**Jagła**): from Polish *jagła* 'millet', a nickname or occupational name for a seller of millet.
GIVEN NAMES Polish 11%; German 6%. *Aleksander, Andrzej, Krystyna, Krzysztof, Wojtek; Klaus, Reinhard.*

Jaglowski (104) Polish (**Jagłowski**): derivative of **Jagła** (see JAGLA) + the common surname ending *-owski.*
GIVEN NAMES Polish 7%. *Stanislaw, Zofia.*

Jagneaux (124) Possibly a reduced form of French **Jagueneau**, which may be from an equivalent of French *Jacques* (see JACK), such as Breton *Jagou.*
GIVEN NAMES French 11%. *Curley, Eloi, Emile, Julien, Theophile.*

Jago (225) **1.** German: variant of JAGOW. **2.** English (Cornwall): from a Cornish form of JACK.

Jagoda (238) Polish and Jewish (eastern Ashkenazic): from Polish *jagoda* 'berry', hence perhaps a nickname for someone thought to resemble a berry, a topographic name for someone who lived by berry-producing plants, a metonymic occupational name for someone who gathered and sold berries, or, among Jews, an ornamental name.
GIVEN NAMES German 4%; Jewish 4%. *Florian* (2), *Erwin, Kurt; Jechiel* (2), *Miriam.*

Jagodzinski (420) Polish (**Jagodziński**) and Jewish (from Poland): habitational name for someone from a place called Jagodziny, Jagodzinek, or Jagodziniec, all named with *jagoda* 'berry'.

Jagoe (111) English (Cornwall): variant spelling of JAGO.

Jagow (163) Eastern German: habitational name from a place named Jagow, for example in Pomerania and near Prenzlau in Brandenburg.

Jagusch (100) German (of Slavic origin): from a pet form of the Slavic form of the personal name JACOB.
GIVEN NAME German 7%. *Georg* (2).

Jahn (2114) **1.** German and Dutch: from a reduced form of the personal name *Johann(es)* (see JOHN). **2.** Eastern German: from the Czech personal name *Jan*, also a form of JOHN.
GIVEN NAMES German 7%. *Otto* (8), *Gerhard* (3), *Kurt* (3), *Gerlinde* (2), *Hans* (2), *Helmut* (2), *Horst* (2), *Othmar* (2), *Bernd*, *Bernhard*, *Bodo*, *Dietrich*.

Jahner (261) German (also **Jähner**): from a derivative of the personal name *Johann(es)* (see JOHN).

Jahnke (1774) Eastern German: from the Czech personal name *Janek*, a pet form of *Jan*, vernacular form of Latin *Johannes* (see JOHN).
GIVEN NAMES German 5%. *Otto* (4), *Erwin* (2), *Heinz* (2), *Kurt* (2), *Reinhart* (2), *Arno*, *Bernhard*, *Detlef*, *Dieter*, *Elfriede*, *Ernst*, *Frieda*.

Jahns (479) German: patronymic from the personal name JAHN.
GIVEN NAMES German 6%. *Otto* (3), *Dieter* (2), *Gunther* (2), *Hans*, *Orlo*, *Oskar*.

Jahoda (100) East German: variant of **Jagode**, from Czech *jahoda* 'strawberry' (Sorbian and Polish *jagoda* 'grape'), possibly applied as a metonymic occupational-name for someone who grew grapes or gathered and sold strawberries.
GIVEN NAMES German 11%. *Fritz* (2), *Franz*, *Kurt*.

Jahr (352) **1.** German: either a variant of GEHR or from a short form of a Slavic personal name beginning with *jar-* 'young', 'robust'. **2.** Norwegian: habitational name from any of three farmsteads named Jar, from Old Norse *jaðarr* 'edge', 'rim' (under a mountain or beside water).
GIVEN NAMES German 7%. *Armin* (2), *Gerhard*, *Kurt*, *Markus*, *Otto*, *Reiner*, *Ute*.

Jahraus (101) German: probably of Slavic origin, an altered spelling of *Gerasch*, *Jarrasch*, *Jarausch*, or *Jarasch*, all from the stem of *jary* 'lively', 'vehement', or possibly from *jar* 'young', 'early'. Compare Polish *Jarosław* (see JAROSZ). This is one of the German names that were established in Ukraine in the 19th century.

Jaillet (135) French: topographic name for someone who lived on marshy land, from a diminutive of Old French *jaille* 'marsh', 'mud', now a regional term found mainly in western France. It may also perhaps have

been a nickname with the sense 'muddy'; in the Jura the word is applied to a cow with dark patches on its flanks. In the U.S., Jaillet is concentrated in MA.
GIVEN NAME French 6%. *Normand*.

Jaime (1159) Spanish: from the personal name *Jaime*, Spanish equivalent of JAMES.
GIVEN NAMES Spanish 53%. *Jose* (30), *Jesus* (19), *Jorge* (17), *Juan* (15), *Manuel* (14), *Carlos* (10), *Javier* (9), *Arturo* (8), *Luis* (8), *Alfredo* (7), *Enrique* (7), *Miguel* (7).

Jaimes (885) Spanish: patronymic from the personal name JAIME.
GIVEN NAMES Spanish 60%. *Jose* (25), *Juan* (11), *Jesus* (8), *Luis* (8), *Pedro* (8), *Carlos* (7), *Miguel* (7), *Alejandro* (6), *Manuel* (6), *Francisco* (5), *Pablo* (5), *Angel* (4).

Jaimez (100) Spanish (**Jáimez**): variant of JAIMES.
GIVEN NAMES Spanish 38%. *Armando* (3), *Juan* (3), *Juana* (3), *Carlos* (2), *Gerardo* (2), *Jose* (2), *Luis* (2), *Alicia*, *Cristino*, *Elvira*, *Emilio*, *Fernando*.

Jain (1521) Indian (chiefly Rajasthan and Gujarat): Jain name from Sanskrit *jaina* 'derived from Jina' or 'follower of Jina'. *Jina*, meaning 'triumphant', is an epithet for a saint of the Jain religion.
GIVEN NAMES Indian 91%. *Sanjay* (28), *Ashok* (23), *Anil* (21), *Rakesh* (21), *Arun* (19), *Sunil* (18), *Ajay* (17), *Raj* (17), *Manoj* (16), *Vijay* (15), *Rajeev* (13), *Rajiv* (13).

Jakab (172) Hungarian: from the personal name *Jakab*, Hungarian form of JACOB.
GIVEN NAMES Hungarian 18%. *Laszlo* (4), *Sandor* (4), *Zoltan* (2), *Arpad*, *Imre*, *Lajos*, *Miklos*, *Tibor*.

Jake (163) Possibly a respelling of French JACQUES.
GIVEN NAME French 4%. *Curley* (2).

Jakel (195) South German: from a pet form of the personal name JAKOB.
GIVEN NAMES German 8%. *Gunther*, *Harro*, *Otto*, *Reiner*.

Jakeman (108) English: variant of JACK-MAN.

Jakes (370) **1.** English: patronymic from JACK 1. **2.** Czech (**Jakeš**): from a derivative of the personal name *Jakub*, Czech form of JACOB.

Jakeway (164) English: altered form of the personal name JACQUE.

Jakob (310) German, Hungarian (**Jákob**), and Slovenian: from the personal name, German and Slovenian *Jakob*, Hungarian *Jákob* (see JACOB).
GIVEN NAMES German 10%. *Hans* (2), *Klaus* (2), *Rainer* (2), *Fritz*, *Gerd*, *Hedwig*, *Oskar*.

Jakobsen (179) Variant spelling of JACOBSEN.
GIVEN NAMES Scandinavian 41%. *Bjorn* (2), *Lars* (2), *Anders*, *Bent*, *Gunner*, *Knut*, *Nels*, *Niels*, *Sven*, *Thor*, *Tor*.

Jakub (125) Jewish (Ashkenazic), Czech, and Slovak: from the personal name *Jakub*, from Hebrew *Jahaqóbh* (see JACOB).

Jakubczak (109) Polish: patronymic from a

pet form of the personal name *Jakub*, vernacular form of Latin *Jacobus* (see KUBEK).
GIVEN NAMES Polish 11%. *Janusz*, *Mieczyslaw*, *Miroslaw*, *Zdzislaw*.

Jakubec (100) Czech and Slovak: derivative of the personal name JAKUB.
GIVEN NAMES German 4%; Czech and Slovak 4%. *Otto*; *Milan*.

Jakubek (195) Polish and Czech: from a pet form of the personal name *Jakub*, vernacular form of Latin *Jacobus* (see JACOB).

Jakubiak (256) Polish: patronymic from the personal name *Jakub*, vernacular form of Latin *Jacobus* (see JACOB).
GIVEN NAMES Polish 13%. *Jerzy* (2), *Andrzej*, *Casimir*, *Janusz*, *Jozef*, *Kazimierz*, *Ludwik*, *Miroslaw*, *Ryszard*, *Tadeusz*, *Zbigniew*.

Jakubiec (130) Polish: from a derivative of the personal name *Jakub*, vernacular form of Latin *Jacobus* (see JACOB).
GIVEN NAMES Polish 11%. *Ignatius* (2), *Alicja*, *Henryk*, *Jacek*, *Ludwik*, *Stanislaw*.

Jakubik (215) Polish: from a derivative of the personal name *Jakub*, vernacular form of Latin *Jacobus* (see JACOB).
GIVEN NAMES Polish 6%. *Casimir*, *Ryszard*, *Zofia*.

Jakubowicz (185) Polish and Jewish (from Poland): patronymic from the personal name *Jakub*, vernacular form of Latin *Jacobus* (see JACOB).
GIVEN NAMES Jewish 9%; Polish 5%. *Doron*, *Icek*, *Mirjam*, *Rachmil*; *Andrzej*, *Witold*, *Zofia*.

Jakubowski (1299) **1.** Polish and Jewish (from Poland): habitational name for someone from Jakubów, Jakubowo, or Jakubowice, all places named with *Jakub*, vernacular form of Latin *Jacobus* (see JACOB). **2.** Jewish (from Poland): patronymic from the personal name *Jakub* (see JACOB).
GIVEN NAMES Polish 8%. *Andrzej* (3), *Janusz* (3), *Zbigniew* (3), *Grzegorz* (2), *Piotr* (2), *Boguslaw*, *Casimir*, *Czeslaw*, *Ewa*, *Ignacy*, *Jaroslaw*, *Krysztof*.

Jalali (122) Muslim: from an adjectival derivative of Arabic *jalāl* 'majesty', 'glory', or denoting a descendant of someone named with this word. It is also found in compound names such as *Jalāl ud-Dīn* 'Glory of Religion'. Jalāl ud-Dīn Rumi (1207–73) was a great Islamic mystic poet. Jalāl ud-Dīn Akbar (1556–1605) was one of the greatest of the Mughal emperors (see AKBAR).
GIVEN NAMES Muslim 78%. *Abdul* (2), *Ahmad* (2), *Alireza* (2), *Laleh* (2), *Saeed* (2), *Sahba* (2), *Abdullah*, *Aisha*, *Ali*, *Bahram*, *Batoul*, *Behnaz*.

Jalbert (916) French: from a Germanic personal name composed of the elements *galan* 'to sing' + *berht* 'bright', 'famous'.
GIVEN NAMES French 13%. *Armand* (7), *Marcel* (4), *Laurent* (3), *Andre* (2), *Fernand*

(2), *Normand* (2), *Pierre* (2), *Rosaire* (2), *Adelard, Aime, Alberie, Alderic.*

Jalil (104) Muslim: from a personal name based on Arabic *jalīl* 'great', 'exalted', 'magnificent'. *Jalīl* 'the Exalted' is an attribute of Allah. This name is found in combinations such as '*Abdul-Jalīl* 'servant of the Exalted'.
GIVEN NAMES Muslim 67%. *Abdul* (11), *Mohammed* (4), *Mohammad* (3), *Abdel* (2), *Adnan, Amir, Arshad, Asad, Asif, Athar, Aziza, Enamul.*

Jalloh (124) West African: probably a derivative of Arabic JALIL.
GIVEN NAMES Muslim 59%; African 16%. *Mohamed* (10), *Abdul* (5), *Ibrahim* (5), *Abou* (2), *Alusine* (2), *Ismail* (2), *Abrahim, Abu, Aisha, Alhaji, Essa, Isata; Amadu* (3), *Aminata* (3), *Fatmata* (3), *Mariama* (2), *Lansana.*

Jalomo (107) Hispanic (Mexico): unexplained.
GIVEN NAMES Spanish 48%. *Juan* (6), *Armando* (3), *Anselmo* (2), *Elpidio* (2), *Gilberto* (2), *Jose* (2), *Julio* (2), *Lupe* (2), *Santos* (2), *Armandina, Belia, Casimiro; Antonio, Leonardo, Marco Antonio.*

Jalufka (103) Origin unidentified.

Jama (140) Muslim: from a derivative of Arabic *jāmi'* 'author', 'writer' (literally 'gatherer'). Nur-ud-Dīn Abdur Rahman Jāmi' (1414–92) was a Persian Sufi poet.
GIVEN NAMES Muslim 69%; Indian 4%. *Mohamed* (6), *Mohamud* (4), *Ahmed* (3), *Ali* (3), *Omar* (3), *Said* (3), *Abdullahi* (2), *Amina* (2), *Hassan* (2), *Hibo* (2), *Issa* (2), *Abdi; Asha* (3).

Jamail (105) Muslim: North African variant of JAMAL.
GIVEN NAME French 8%. *Emile* (3).

Jamal (286) Muslim: from a personal name based on Arabic *jamāl* 'beauty', 'grace'. This name is also found in compounds such as *Jamāl ud-Dīn* 'Beauty of Religion'.
GIVEN NAMES Muslim 82%. *Mohammad* (7), *Mohammed* (6), *Syed* (6), *Abdul* (4), *Ali* (4), *Nasir* (4), *Salim* (4), *Tariq* (4), *Ahmad* (3), *Jamal* (3), *Sami* (3), *Akbar* (2).

Jamar (221) **1.** Probably an altered spelling of the French surname **Jamard**, from the Germanic personal name *Gamhard*, of which the first element *gam-* may be a shortened form of *gamal* 'old' or *gaman* 'joy'; the second element *hard* means 'hardy', 'strong'. **2.** Northern Slovenian: topographic name for someone who lived in a cave or pit, from an agent derivative of *jama* 'pit', 'cave', 'hole'.
GIVEN NAMES French 8%. *Andre* (4), *Benoit.*

Jambor (222) Hungarian (**Jámbor**): from *jámbor* 'godly', 'modest', 'well-disposed', hence a nickname for a humble and friendly person.

Jamerson (1304) Altered form of Scottish and northern Irish JAMESON.

James (70272) English: from a personal name that has the same origin as JACOB.

However, among English speakers, it is now felt to be a separate name in its own right. This is largely because in the Authorized Version of the Bible (1611) the form *James* is used in the New Testament as the name of two of Christ's apostles (James the brother of John and James the brother of Andrew), whereas in the Old Testament the brother of Esau is called *Jacob*. The form *James* comes from Latin *Jacobus* via Late Latin *Jac(o)mus*, which also gave rise to *Jaime*, the regular form of the name in Spanish (as opposed to the learned *Jacobo*). See also JACK and JACKMAN. This is a common surname throughout the British Isles, particularly in South Wales.

Jameson (4951) Scottish, northern English, and northern Irish: patronymic from JAMES.

Jamgochian (151) Armenian and Iranian: patronymic from Armenian *žamkoč'*, an occupational name for a muezzin, from *žam*, 'church', 'mosque' + *koč'*- 'call'.
GIVEN NAMES Armenian 17%. *Souren* (2), *Artin, Deran, Dicran, Hagop, Haig, Sarkis, Shake, Zaven.*

Jamieson (3096) Scottish and northern Irish: patronymic from JAMES.

Jamil (186) Muslim: from a personal name based on Arabic *jamīl* 'handsome', 'good-looking'.
GIVEN NAMES Muslim 79%. *Mohammad* (11), *Mohammed* (5), *Omar* (4), *Syed* (4), *Tariq* (4), *Arshad* (3), *Jamil* (3), *Khalid* (3), *Shabana* (3), *Shahid* (3), *Ali* (2), *Amjad* (2).

Jamison (8603) Scottish and northern Irish: patronymic from JAMES.

Jamrog (130) Polish: variant of JAMROZ.
GIVEN NAMES Polish 7%. *Boleslaw, Ignatius, Witold.*

Jamroz (151) Polish: from the personal name *Ambroży*, Polish form of Latin *Ambrosius* (see AMBROSE).
GIVEN NAMES Polish 19%. *Wieslaw* (2), *Bogdan, Janina, Jerzy, Mariusz, Marzena, Miroslaw, Tadeusz, Waclaw, Wieslawa, Zbigniew.*

Jan (437) **1.** Dutch, Danish, North German, English, Polish, etc.; Czech and Slovak (**Ján**): from the personal name *Jan*, a vernacular form of Latin *Johannes* (see JOHN). **2.** Slovenian: from a pet form of the personal name *Janez* (see JOHN). **3.** Muslim: unexplained. **4.** Chinese 詹: variant of ZHAN.
GIVEN NAMES Muslim 25%; French 4%. *Mohammad* (5), *Mohammed* (3), *Ferdous* (2), *Momin* (2), *Sultan* (2), *Ahmad, Altaf, Ameen, Amin, Amina, Arif, Arshad; Pierre* (2), *Andre, Marcel, Pascale.*

Janacek (158) Czech (**Janáček**): from a pet form of the personal name *Jan*, vernacular form of Latin *Johannes* (see JOHN).

Janak (510) Czech (**Janák**): from an augmentative form of the personal name *Jan*,

vernacular form of Latin *Johannes* (see JOHN).

Janas (383) Polish: from the personal name *Janas*, a derivative of *Jan*, vernacular form of Latin *Johannes* (see JOHN).
GIVEN NAMES Polish 6%. *Arkadiusz, Bogdan, Danuta, Genowefa, Irena, Janusz, Krzysztof, Witold, Zbigniew.*

Janca (203) **1.** Czech (**Janča**) and Slovak (**Janča, Jančo**): from *Janča*, a derivative of the personal name *Jan*, vernacular form of Greek *Iōannēs* (see JOHN). **2.** Americanized spelling of Hungarian JANKA or **Jancsa**, pet forms of the personal name *János*, Hungarian form of JOHN.
GIVEN NAME German 4%. *Otto* (2).

Janco (177) Americanized spelling of JANKO or of Hungarian **Jancsó**, also a derivative of the personal name *János*, Hungarian form of JOHN.

Janczak (262) Polish: patronymic from *Janek*, a pet form of the personal name JAN.
GIVEN NAMES Polish 9%. *Casimir* (3), *Edyta, Grzegorz, Jerzy, Wojciech, Zygmunt.*

Janczewski (116) Polish: habitational name for someone from Janczewo in Łomża voivodeship or Janczewice in Warszawa voivodeship.
GIVEN NAMES Polish 14%. *Andrzej, Grazyna, Jacek, Janusz, Miroslaw.*

Janda (890) Czech and Polish: from a derivative of the personal name JAN.

Jandl (106) South German (Austrian): from a pet form of the Slavic personal name JANDA, or from a Germanic personal name, probably *Gando*, a short form of a word possibly meaning 'magic', or, according to Finsterwalder, from JAN, a Tyrolean family name, a short form of JOHANN.

Jandreau (417) French: from a diminutive of *Jandier*, a derivative of the personal name JEAN.
GIVEN NAMES French 10%. *Clovis* (2), *Normand* (2), *Alberie, Alphie, Antoine, Aurel, Camille, Emile, Lucien, Oneil, Treffle, Valier.*

Jandro (121) Americanized spelling of French JANDREAU.

Jandt (167) German: from Czech JANDA or a Sorbian cognate.
GIVEN NAMES German 11%. *Arno, Erwin, Klaus, Kurt, Otto, Ralf, Ulrich.*

Jandura (106) Polish: from a derivative of the personal name JANDA.
GIVEN NAMES Polish 7%. *Janusz, Piotr, Tadek.*

Jane (236) **1.** English: variant spelling of JAYNE. **2.** Catalan (**Jané**): variant spelling of Catalan **Gener** 'January', from Latin *Januarius*.
GIVEN NAMES Spanish 7%. *Carlos* (2), *Jaime* (2), *Orlando* (2), *Alicia, Isidro, Julio, Miguel, Rafael.*

Janecek (526) Czech (**Janeček**): from *Janek*, a pet form of the personal name *Jan*, a vernacular form of Greek *Iohannēs* (see JOHN).

Janecka (140) Czech: from a pet form of *Janek*, itself a pet form of *Jan*, a vernacular form of Latin *Johannes* (see JOHN).
GIVEN NAME French 5%; German 4%. *Delphin* (2).

Janeczek (142) Polish: from a pet form of the personal name JAN.
GIVEN NAMES Polish 13%. *Bogdan, Grazyna, Halina, Henryk, Jerzy, Ryszard, Zigmund.*

Janeczko (173) Polish: from a pet form of the personal name JAN.
GIVEN NAMES Polish 7%. *Jaroslaw* (2), *Miroslaw.*

Janek (199) Czech and Polish: from a pet form of the personal name JAN.
GIVEN NAMES German 4%. *Erwin* (2), *Otto.*

Janelle (247) Probably an altered spelling of French **Janel**, from a pet form of *Jean*, French form of JOHN.
FOREBEARS A bearer of the name from Paris is documented in Baie-du-Febvre, Quebec, in 1730.
GIVEN NAMES French 17%. *Armand* (4), *Normand* (3), *Alphee* (2), *Adrien, Alcide, Calixte, Henri, Luc, Lucien.*

Janes (3294) **1.** English: patronymic from the personal name *Jan* (see JAYNE). **2.** Czech (**Janeš**): from a pet form of the personal name *Jan*, a vernacular form of Greek *Iōannēs* (see JOHN).

Janeski (113) Jewish (Ashkenazic): habitational name from the village of Janishki in the district of Vilnius in Lithuania.

Janet (147) English: from a pet form (not necessarily female) of the personal name *Jan* (see JAYNE).

Janeway (324) English: habitational name for someone from Genoa in Italy, from a medieval folk-etymological alteration of Italian *Geno(v)a* (see GANNAWAY).

Janey (208) English: from a pet form of the personal name *Jan* (see JAYNE).

Jang (1115) **1.** Chinese 张: variant of ZHANG 1. **2.** Korean: variant of CHANG.
GIVEN NAMES Chinese/Korean 59%. *Young* (13), *Jae* (8), *Soon* (8), *Sung* (8), *Dong* (6), *Hyun* (5), *Kwang* (5), *Sun* (5), *Ho* (4), *Jung* (4), *Yong* (4), *Han* (3); *Chang* (10), *Young Chul* (4), *Byung* (3), *Seong* (3), *Chong Tae* (2), *Dae* (2), *Jaeyoung* (2), *Nam* (2), *Sungwoo* (2), *Weon* (2), *Bae, Baek.*

Jangula (155) Ukrainian: nickname from *yangyola*, diminutive of *yangyul* 'angel'.

Jani (271) Indian (Gujarat): Hindu (Brahman) name, from Sanskrit *jñānī* 'knowing', 'learned'.
GIVEN NAMES Indian 76%. *Bharat* (5), *Anil* (3), *Yogendra* (3), *Dushyant* (2), *Harish* (2), *Harshad* (2), *Jitesh* (2), *Jyoti* (2), *Kishor* (2), *Pankaj* (2), *Rohit* (2), *Sonal* (2).

Janiak (325) Polish: patronymic from the personal name JAN.
GIVEN NAMES Polish 8%. *Andrzej, Boguslaw, Iwona, Janina, Jerzy, Krystyna, Tadek, Zdzislaw, Zygmunt.*

Janice (144) Possibly an altered spelling of

English **Jannis**, a patronymic from the personal name *Jan* (see JAYNE).

Janicek (279) Czech (**Janíček**): from a pet form of the personal name *Jan*, Czech form of JOHN.

Janick (162) **1.** German (of Slavic origin): see JANIK. **2.** Probably a respelling of *Janík* or JANIK.

Janicke (209) Eastern German (also **Jänicke**): from the personal name, a Polish form of JOHN.

Janicki (714) Polish: habitational name for someone from Janice in Płock voivodeship, named with the personal name JAN.
GIVEN NAMES Polish 9%. *Irena* (3), *Casimir* (2), *Jozef* (2), *Slawomir* (2), *Boleslaw, Bronislaw, Czeslaw, Dionizy, Dorota, Ignatius, Janusz, Mietek.*

Janiec (117) Polish: from a derivative of the personal name JAN.
GIVEN NAMES Polish 14%. *Janusz* (2), *Dorota, Krystyna, Tadeusz, Wiesia.*

Janiga (210) Polish: from the personal name JAN.
GIVEN NAMES Polish 9%. *Zofia* (2), *Cecylia, Jerzy, Karol, Stanislaw, Stanislawa, Witold.*

Janik (1089) Polish, Czech, and Slovak (**Janík**), and Hungarian: from a pet form of the personal name JAN.
GIVEN NAMES Polish 8%. *Leszek* (4), *Stanislaw* (4), *Andrzej* (2), *Casimir* (2), *Janusz* (2), *Aleksander, Bogdan, Czeslawa, Dorota, Elzbieta, Feliks, Janina.*

Janikowski (182) Polish: habitational name for someone from Janików, Janikowo, Janikowice, or other places named with the personal name JAN.
GIVEN NAME French 4%. *Michel.*

Janis (1232) **1.** English: perhaps a variant spelling of JANICE. **2.** French: unexplained. **3.** Latvian: from the first name *Jānis*, Latvian form of JOHN.
FOREBEARS A Janis from the Champagne region of France is documented in 1704 in Trois Rivières, Quebec, with the secondary surname SICARD.

Janisch (489) German (also **Jänisch**): from a Slavic personal name (see Polish JANUSZ).
GIVEN NAMES German 5%. *Kurt* (4), *Hans* (2), *Ludwina, Wilhelm.*

Janish (206) Americanized spelling of JANISCH.

Janisse (142) Possibly a respelling of French **Janisset**, from a pet form of *Jan*, a variant spelling of *Jean*, French equivalent of JOHN.
GIVEN NAMES French 13%. *Andre* (2), *Emile, Euclide, Marcel.*

Janiszewski (427) Polish: habitational name for someone from Janiszew in the voivodeships of Konin, Płock, and Radom, or Janiszów in the voivodeships of Lublin and Tarnobrzeg; both place names are from the personal name JAN.
GIVEN NAMES Polish 8%. *Leszek* (3), *Bogdan*

(2), *Bronislaw, Czeslaw, Danuta, Halina, Jadwiga, Kazimierz, Stanislaw.*

Jank (123) **1.** North German and Dutch: variant of JANKE. **2.** Hungarian (**Jánk**): from a pet form of the personal name *János*, Hungarian form of JOHN.
GIVEN NAMES German 8%. *Kurt, Wolfgang.*

Janka (175) **1.** Eastern German: variant of JANKE. **2.** Hungarian: from a pet form of the personal name *János*, Hungarian form of JOHN.

Jankauskas (105) Lithuanian form of Polish JANKOWSKI.
GIVEN NAMES Lithuanian 25%; Polish 5%. *Antanas* (2), *Kazys* (2), *Kestutis* (2), *Alfonsas, Algirdas, Arunas, Laima, Saulius; Casimir, Janina.*

Janke (1700) North German and Dutch: from a pet form of *Jan* (see JOHN).
GIVEN NAMES German 5%. *Erwin* (4), *Kurt* (4), *Lothar* (4), *Otto* (4), *Hans* (3), *Heinz* (2), *Udo* (2), *Dieter, Eldor, Hannelore, Helmuth, Manfred.*

Jankiewicz (220) Polish: patronymic from a pet form of the personal name JAN.
GIVEN NAMES Polish 13%. *Tomasz* (2), *Casimir, Grazyna, Janusz, Jerzy, Jolanta, Malgorzata, Mieczyslaw, Witold.*

Janko (223) **1.** Polish, Ukrainian, Czech, and Slovenian; Hungarian (**Jankó**): from a pet form of the Slavic personal name *Jan*, Slovenian *Janez*, Hungarian *János*, vernacular forms of Latin *Johannes* (see JOHN). **2.** Jewish (Ashkenazic): from a pet form of the personal name *Yakov* (see JACOB).

Jankovic (155) Croatian and Serbian (**Janković**); Slovenian, Czech, and Slovak (**Jankovič**): patronymic from the personal name *Janko*, a pet form of *Jan* (Slovenian *Janez*), from Latin *Johannes* (see JOHN).
GIVEN NAMES South Slavic 28%; Czech and Slovak 8%; Russian 6%; Jewish 6%. *Zarko* (3), *Dragan* (2), *Dragisa* (2), *Bojana, Djordje, Drago, Marko, Matija, Mihailo, Milenko, Momcilo, Nebojsa; Dusan* (2), *Jakub, Miroslava; Oleg* (4), *Vladimir* (2), *Igor, Luka; Izidor.*

Jankovich (190) Serbian and Croatian (**Janković**); Slovenian (**Jankovič**): see JANKOVIC.
GIVEN NAMES South Slavic 6%; Czech and Slovak 5%; Hungarian 4%. *Branko, Rade, Zarko; Milan* (3), *Milos* (2), *Dusan; Sandor* (2), *Geza, Tibor.*

Jankowiak (225) Polish: patronymic from *Janek* or *Janko*, pet forms of the personal name JAN.

Jankowski (3319) Polish: habitational name for someone from Janków, Jankowo, or Jankowice, places named with the personal name JANEK.
GIVEN NAMES Polish 6%. *Casimir* (6), *Piotr* (6), *Tadeusz* (5), *Witold* (4), *Henryk* (3), *Krzysztof* (3), *Andrzej* (2), *Czeslaw* (2), *Jerzy* (2), *Karol* (2), *Thadeus* (2), *Zygmunt* (2).

Jann (231) North German: from the personal name *Jann*, a reduced form of JOHANN.

Janney (956) English: from a pet form of the medieval personal name *Jan* (see JAYNE).

Janning (167) Dutch and North German: patronymic from a reduced form of the personal name *Johann* (see JOHN).

Jannusch (128) Eastern German: from a pet form of the personal name *Jan* (see JOHN).

Janoff (156) **1.** Alternative spelling of Jewish JANOW. **2.** Shortened form of any of various names formed with *Janow* or *Janov*, as for example JANOWSKI, JANOWICZ, or JANOVSKY.

Janofsky (105) Respelling of Polish and Jewish JANOWSKI.

Janos (357) **1.** Hungarian (**János**): from the personal name *János*, vernacular form of Latin *Johannes* (see JOHN). **2.** Czech (**Jánoš**), Slovak (**Janoš**), and Polish (**Janosz**): from a derivative of the personal name JAN.

Janosik (210) **1.** Slovak (**Jánošík**): from a pet form of the personal name JAN. **2.** Polish: from a derivative of the personal name JAN.

Janoski (245) Polish: **1.** habitational name for someone from Janoszyce in Płock voivodeship. **2.** from a derivative of the personal name *Janosz* (see JANOS).

Janosko (181) Slovak (**Janoško**): from a derivative of the personal name JANOS.

Janosky (145) Czech: from a derivative of the personal name JANOS.

Janota (167) **1.** Czech: from the personal name *Jan* (Czech form of JOHN), with the augmentative ending *-ota*. **2.** Portuguese: nickname from *janota* 'chic', 'elegant'.

Janousek (398) Czech (**Janoušek**): from a pet form of *Jan*, Czech form of JOHN.

Janovsky (188) Jewish (eastern Ashkenazic): variant spelling of JANOWSKI.

Janow (183) Polish (**Janów**): habitational name from Janów, a place named with the personal name JAN.

Janowiak (260) Polish: patronymic from the personal name JAN.

GIVEN NAMES Polish 4%. *Grzegorz, Ignacy, Stanislaw.*

Janowicz (219) **1.** Polish: patronymic from the personal name JAN. **2.** Jewish (from Poland and Belarus): habitational name for someone from a place named Janowice, Janowo, or Janów. Compare JANOWSKI.

GIVEN NAMES Polish 8%; German 4%. *Beata, Jacek, Janina, Mariusz, Tadeusz, Walenty; Otto* (2), *Erwin.*

Janowitz (195) German and Jewish (Ashkenazic): Germanized spelling of Polish JANOWICZ.

GIVEN NAME Jewish 6%. *Haim.*

Janowski (801) Polish and Jewish (eastern Ashkenazic): habitational name for someone from Janów, Janowo, or Janowice, all places named with the personal name JAN.

GIVEN NAMES Polish 9%. *Piotr* (3), *Aleksander* (2), *Andrzej* (2), *Henryk* (2), *Zbigniew* (2), *Zigmunt* (2), *Bogdan, Casimir, Czeslaw, Ignacy, Janina, Kazimierz.*

Janowsky (102) Variant spelling of Jewish and Polish JANOWSKI.

GIVEN NAMES German 6%. *Fritz, Kurt.*

Jans (459) **1.** Dutch and North German: patronymic from the personal name JAN; or a reduced form of JOHANNES. **2.** English: patronymic from the personal name *Jan* (see JAYNE).

GIVEN NAMES German 5%. *Hans, Johannes, Klaus, Kurt, Matthias, Otto.*

Jansa (166) Slovenian (**Janša**): respelled derivative of the personal name *Janž*, an old spelling of *Janez*, Slovenian form of JOHN.

Jansen (6490) Danish, Norwegian, North German, and Dutch: patronymic from the personal name *Jan*, a vernacular form of *Johannes* (see JOHN).

Jansing (129) Dutch and North German (Westphalia): patronymic from the personal name *Jans*, a reduced form of *Johannes* (see JOHN).

Jansky (447) Czech (**Janský, Jánský**): from the personal name *Jan*, Czech form of JOHN.

Jansma (334) Frisian: patronymic from the personal name *Jan*, Frisian form of JOHN.

GIVEN NAMES German 5%. *Erwin* (2), *Kurt.*

Janson (1455) **1.** Americanized spelling of JANSEN, JANSSEN, and JANSSON. **2.** English: patronymic from the personal name *Jan*, a medieval form of JOHN.

FOREBEARS A Janson with the secondary surname Lapalme, from Paris, is documented in Quebec city in 1688.

GIVEN NAMES Scandinavian 5%; German 4%. *Nils* (3), *Lars* (2), *Anders, Helmer, Jan-Erik, Johan, Sven; Kurt* (3), *Otto* (2), *Reinhard* (2), *Ernst, Gerhard, Gotthard, Hans, Juergen, Siegfried, Udo.*

Jansons (109) Latvian derivative of Scandinavian JANSEN or JANSSON.

GIVEN NAMES Latvian 53%; Scandinavian 5%. *Juris* (4), *Andrejs* (2), *Arvids* (2), *Dace* (2), *Peteris* (2), *Uldis* (2), *Aleksandrs, Andris, Ansis, Arnolds, Edgars, Edvins, Eriks, Ernests, Ilga, Karlis, Maris, Martins, Olgerts, Vilis; Erik* (2), *Maija.*

Janssen (4672) Dutch, North German, and Danish: patronymic from *Jan*, a vernacular form of the personal name *Johannes* (see JOHN).

GIVEN NAMES German 4%. *Kurt* (8), *Erwin* (4), *Benno* (3), *Hans* (3), *Heinrich* (3), *Claus* (2), *Fritz* (2), *Gerhard* (2), *Gunter* (2), *Helmut* (2), *Hermann* (2), *Klaus* (2).

Janssens (222) Dutch and North German: variant of JANSSEN.

GIVEN NAMES French 12%; German 4%. *Amedee, Andre, Florent, Gaetan, Jacques, Luc, Monique, Pierre, Thierry; Ilse, Wieland.*

Jansson (495) **1.** Swedish: patronymic from the personal name *Jan*, a reduced

form of *Johannes* (see JOHN). **2.** Americanized spelling of JANSEN.

GIVEN NAMES Scandinavian 23%; German 6%. *Erik* (2), *Lars* (2), *Lennart* (2), *Mats* (2), *Nils* (2), *Per* (2), *Alf, Anders, Berger, Bjorn, Holger, Jan Erik; Rainer* (2), *Ralf* (2), *Gunther, Hans.*

Jantz (1141) North German: patronymic from the personal name *Jan*, a reduced form of *Johann(es)* (see JOHN).

Jantzen (672) North German and Danish: patronymic from the personal name *Jan*.

GIVEN NAMES German 4%. *Franz, Gerhard, Hans, Heino, Klaus, Kurt, Manfred.*

Jantzi (158) German: from a pet form of JANTZEN.

January (659) **1.** Americanized form of the Latin personal name *Januarius* or its Italian derivative GENNARO, which was borne by a number of early Christian saints, most famously a 3rd-century bishop of Benevento who became the patron of Naples. **2.** English: altered form of JANEWAY. **3.** In New England, a translation of French JANVIER.

Janulewicz (102) Polish: patronymic from *Janul(a)*, a pet form of the personal name JAN.

GIVEN NAMES Polish 5%. *Casimir, Krzysztof.*

Janulis (109) Lithuanian: patronymic from Polish *Janul(a)*, pet form of the personal name JAN.

GIVEN NAMES Lithuanian 6%. *Bronislaus* (2), *Kazys.*

Janus (818) Polish: from the personal name *Janus*, a derivative of JAN.

GIVEN NAMES Polish 5%; German 4%. *Alicja, Dorota, Elzbieta, Irek, Irena, Janina, Jaromir, Jozef, Ryszard, Slawomir, Wladyslaw, Zdzislaw; Manfred* (3), *Alois, Erna, Ernst, Frieda, Lutz, Otto.*

Janusz (433) Polish: from the personal name *Janusz*, a derivative of JAN.

GIVEN NAMES Polish 9%. *Stanislaw* (2), *Andrzej, Casimir, Eugeniusz, Ewa, Kazimierz, Krystyna, Miroslaw, Ryszard, Zdzislaw.*

Januszewski (224) Polish: habitational name for someone from Januszewo or Januszewice, both named with the personal name JANUSZ.

GIVEN NAMES Polish 8%. *Halina, Janusz, Ludwik, Tadeusz, Zygmunt.*

Janvier (165) French: from the personal name *Janvier* 'January' (see JANUARY 1).

FOREBEARS A bearer of the name from the Poitou region of France is documented in Quebec city in 1680.

GIVEN NAMES French 34%; Jewish 4%. *Jacques* (2), *Michel* (2), *Arsene, Etienne, Luc, Marcelin, Maxime, Myrtha, Pierre, Raymonde, Renel, Yolette; Miriam* (2), *Moise.*

Janvrin (210) French: from a diminutive of **Janvre**, which Morlet suggests may have been a nickname for the youngest son or child in a family, from *jenvre*.

FOREBEARS A bearer of the name from the Poitou region of France is documented in Quebec city in 1680.

Janz (524) North German and Dutch: patronymic from the personal name *Jan*, a reduced form of *Johann(es)* (see JOHN).
GIVEN NAMES German 4%. *Gerhard* (2), *Armin, Franz, Guenter, Siegfried.*

Janzen (1266) North German: variant spelling of JANTZEN.
GIVEN NAMES German 5%. *Bernd* (2), *Ernst* (2), *Erwin* (2), *Claus, Erna, Fritz, Heinz, Hertha, Juergen, Klaus, Kurt, Reinhild.*

Janzer (105) North German: derivative of JANZ.
GIVEN NAME German 4%. *Kurt.*

Japhet (106) From the Biblical name *Japhet.*

Japp (120) **1.** German (Hesse, the Rhineland): from a short form of JACOB. **2.** German: from a short form of a Germanic personal name composed with *geba* 'gift' (see GAPP 2). **3.** of uncertain origin: Bahlow asserts that it is Frisian *Tjappen*, but equally it may be the Biblical name JAPHET.
GIVEN NAMES German 5%. *Gerhard, Heinz.*

Jaqua (249) Origin uncertain. **1.** Most probably a respelling of the English personal name JACQUE. **2.** Possibly an Americanized form of French JAQUET.

Jaquay (176) See JAQUA.

Jaques (1040) English: from the Old French personal name *Jaques*, a vernacular form of Latin *Jacobus* (see JACOB). In English this surname is traditionally pronounced as two syllables, *jay-kwez*. Compare JACQUES.

Jaquess (176) English: variant spelling of JAQUES.

Jaquet (98) **1.** French: from a pet form of the French personal name JACQUES. **2.** English: variant of JACKETT, under French influence.
GIVEN NAMES French 5%; German 4%. *Pierre; Udo.*

Jaquette (146) French: Canadian form of JAQUET.

Jaquez (692) Spanish (**Jáquez**): patronymic based on the Latin personal name *Jacobus* (see JACOB).
GIVEN NAMES Spanish 47%. *Jose* (16), *Manuel* (11), *Jesus* (10), *Juan* (8), *Juana* (6), *Luis* (6), *Rafael* (6), *Ruben* (6), *Francisco* (4), *Gerardo* (4), *Julio* (4), *Ramona* (4).

Jaquish (252) Altered form of English JAQUES.

Jaquith (409) English: probably an altered form of JAQUES.

Jara (755) Spanish: habitational name any of the various places in southern Spain named Jara or La Jara, from *jara* 'rockrose', 'cistus'.
GIVEN NAMES Spanish 47%. *Jose* (17), *Carlos* (14), *Juan* (13), *Manuel* (10), *Luis* (9), *Ruben* (9), *Miguel* (8), *Raul* (7), *Jesus* (6), *Cesar* (5), *Francisco* (5), *Javier* (5).

Jaracz (102) Polish: derivative of the personal name *Horacy*, Polish form of Latin *Horatius* (see HORACE).
GIVEN NAMES Polish 9%. *Grzegorz, Henryk, Stanislaw.*

Jaramillo (4159) Spanish: habitational name from either of two places in the Burgos province: Jaramillo de la Fuente or Jaramillo Quemada.
GIVEN NAMES Spanish 37%. *Jose* (62), *Manuel* (36), *Carlos* (33), *Juan* (33), *Jorge* (21), *Jesus* (19), *Luis* (19), *Francisco* (14), *Jaime* (13), *Miguel* (13), *Mario* (12), *Orlando* (12).

Jarboe (1048) Probably an Americanized form of French **Charbon**, nickname for a man with dark hair or a swarthy complexion (see CHARBONNEAU).

Jarchow (281) German: habitational name Jarchau (earlier Jarchow), a place near Stendal.

Jardin (304) French and English: from Old French *jardin* 'enclosure', 'garden', hence a topographic name for someone who lived by a garden or a metonymic occupational name for someone who worked in one. Compare English GARDNER.
GIVEN NAMES Spanish 8%. *Manuel* (7), *Mario* (2), *Alvaro, Armando, Augusto, Dulce, Edgardo, Francisco, Isaura, Luis, Rosario.*

Jardine (1300) English: variant of JARDIN.

Jardon (146) French: variant of JARDIN.
GIVEN NAMES Spanish 14%. *Sergio* (3), *Mario* (2), *Roberto* (2), *Alicia, Arturo, Cesar, Jesus, Jose, Ladislao, Miguel, Milagros, Orlando.*

Jarecki (378) Polish: habitational name for someone from a place called Jarki in Bydgoszcz voivodeship.
GIVEN NAMES Polish 6%. *Stanislaw* (2), *Alicja, Andrzej, Bogdan, Janusz.*

Jared (499) English: variant of GARRETT.

Jarema (219) Frisian: unexplained.

Jares (148) Czech (**Jareš**): variant of **Jaroš** (see JAROS).

Jarka (125) German (of Czech or Sorbian origin): from a pet form of the Slavic personal name *Jaroslav.*
GIVEN NAMES German 5%. *Florian, Horst.*

Jarman (2205) English (of Norman origin): from an Old French personal name, *Germain* (see GERMAN).

Jarmer (105) **1.** North German and Frisian: variant of **Garmer**, from a personal name composed of the Germanic elements *gār, gēr* 'spear', 'lance' + *māri* 'famous'. **2.** East German: from a short form of the Slavic personal name *Jaromir.* **3.** habitational name from a place called Jarmer near Stettin (Polish Szczecin).
GIVEN NAMES German 5%. *Alois, Wolfgang.*

Jarmin (110) English: variant spelling of JARMAN.

Jarmon (653) English: variant of JARMAN.

Jarnagin (752) Variant spelling of English JERNIGAN.

Jarnigan (221) Variant spelling of English JERNIGAN.

Jarnot (158) French: spelling variant of GARNEAU. This name is concentrated in MN and NY.
GIVEN NAME French 5%. *Alphonse.*

Jaroch (100) Czech: derivative of the personal name *Jaroš* (see JAROS).

Jarocki (147) Polish: habitational name for someone from a place called Jarocin in Ciechanów voivodeship.
GIVEN NAMES Polish 15%. *Casimir, Henryka, Janusz, Jarek, Jerzy, Ryszard, Teofil, Wieslaw.*

Jaros (680) **1.** Czech and Slovak (**Jaroš**): from a short form of a personal name formed with *jaro* 'young', 'lively', for example *Jaroslav, Jaromír, Jarohněv.* **2.** Polish: variant of JAROSZ. **3.** Hungarian (also **Jaross**): from a pet form of the personal name *Gyárfás* (alternative form *Járfás*).

Jarosch (104) German spelling of Polish JAROSZ or Czech and Slovak *Jaroš* (see JAROS).
GIVEN NAME German 4%. *Kurt.*

Jarosh (122) Partly Americanized spelling of Hungarian JAROS, German JAROSCH, Polish JAROSZ, or Czech and Slovak **Jaroš** (see JAROS).

Jarosinski (123) Polish (also **Jaroszyński**): habitational name for someone from a place called Jaroszyn in Konin voivodeship.
GIVEN NAMES Polish 7%. *Iwona, Ryszard, Tadeusz.*

Jarosz (931) Polish: **1.** from a short form of the personal name *Jarosław* (composed of the elements *jaro-* 'young', 'robust' + *-sław* 'glory'), or from some other personal name formed with *jaro-*, or from a dialect form of the personal name *Hieronim*, Polish form of Greek *Hierōnymos* (see JEROME). **2.** in some cases it may have originated as a nickname for a vigorous young man, from the adjective *jary.*
GIVEN NAMES Polish 9%. *Danuta* (2), *Henryk* (2), *Stanislaw* (2), *Zigmund* (2), *Alicja, Andrzej, Aniela, Beata, Bogumil, Boleslaw, Casimir, Elzbieta.*

Jaroszewski (170) Polish: habitational name for someone from Jaroszewo or Jaroszowce, places named with the personal name JAROSZ.
GIVEN NAMES Polish 6%. *Andrzej, Janusz.*

Jarquin (210) Spanish (**Jarquín**): ethnic name for someone from the east, from *jarqui*, from Arabic *sharqī* 'eastern'. This name is common in Mexico.
GIVEN NAMES Spanish 56%. *Jose* (8), *Luis* (4), *Manuel* (4), *Alvaro* (3), *Carlos* (3), *Jorge* (3), *Juan* (3), *Raul* (3), *Camilo* (2), *Edmundo* (2), *Eduardo* (2), *Emilia* (2).

Jarrard (768) English: variant of GARRETT 1.

Jarratt (457) English: variant of GARRETT.

Jarreau (495) French: from a diminutive of Old French *garra* 'crock or jar for oil', presumably a metonymic occupational name for a maker of such crocks or for a producer or seller of aromatic or comestible oils. This name is concentrated in LA.

FOREBEARS The Jarreau families of LA trace their descent from two men from Bordeaux: Pierre Jarreau and Jacques Jarreau, possibly Pierre's nephew, who arrived in the 1760s and 1780s. Their descendants have long been concentrated in Pointe Coupee parish and Baton Rouge.
GIVEN NAMES French 6%. *Andre, Julien, Kearney, Lucien, Marcel, Ovide.*

Jarred (136) English: variant of GARRETT.

Jarrell (4567) English: probably a variant of GERALD.

Jarrells (238) English: patronymic from JARRELL.

Jarrett (7103) English: variant of GARRETT.

Jarriel (188) Probably a variant of English JARRELL.

Jarry (173) **1.** Southern French: topographic name for someone who lived by an oak tree or oak grove, from Occitan *garric* (masculine) 'kermes oak' or *garrique* (feminine) 'grove of kermes oaks'. **2.** English (Norfolk): variant of GEARY 2.
FOREBEARS A bearer with the secondary surname LAHAYE, from the Perche region of France, is documented in Montreal in 1654.
GIVEN NAMES French 13%. *Andre* (2), *Pierre* (2), *Cecile, Jacques, Normand.*

Jarvela (130) Finnish (**Järvelä**): topographic name from *järvi* 'lake' + the local suffix *-la.* This was also commonly adopted as an ornamental name during the name conversion movement at the beginning of the twentieth century. It occurs throughout Finland.
GIVEN NAMES Finnish 9%. *Eino, Mikko, Teuvo, Toivo, Waino.*

Jarvey (120) Scottish: variant spelling of JARVIE.

Jarvi (542) Finnish (**Järvi**): topographic or ornamental name from *järvi* 'lake'. During the name conversion movement in the 19th and early 20th centuries, **Järvi** was widely adopted as an ornamental replacement by Finns with Swedish surnames. It is also found as a Finnish American abbreviation of names such as **Järviluoma** and **Sikojärvi**.
GIVEN NAMES Finnish 11%; Scandinavian 5%. *Veikko* (3), *Arvo* (2), *Eero* (2), *Eino* (2), *Reino* (2), *Weikko* (2), *Aimo, Annikki, Armas, Esa, Juhani, Mikko; Erik* (3), *Alvar* (2), *Jalmer.*

Jarvie (307) Scottish: **1.** pet form of the Norman personal name JARVIS 1. **2.** variant of GARVIE.

Jarvinen (137) Finnish (**Järvinen**): topographic or ornamental name from **Järvi** (see JARVI) + the common surname suffix *-nen*. This name is found mainly in western Finland.
GIVEN NAMES Finnish 20%. *Tauno* (2), *Aarne,*

Eino, Juha, Markku, Pekka, Seppo, Urho, Vilho, Wilho.

Jarvis (12391) English: from the Norman personal name *Gervase*, composed of the Germanic element *gār, gēr* 'spear' + a second element of uncertain meaning and original form. The name was borne by a saint, martyred under the Roman Emperor Domitian, who became one of the patrons of Milan.

Jarzombek (166) Polish: variant spelling of **Jarząbek**, from *jarząbek* 'grouse', presumably a nickname for someone thought to resemble the bird.

Jarzynka (148) Polish: nickname from *jarzynka*, a diminutive of *jarzyna* 'vegetable'.
GIVEN NAMES Polish 6%. *Beata, Jerzy.*

Jasa (109) Czech (**Jaša**): from the personal name *Jan*, Czech form of JOHN.

Jasek (237) Czech (**Jašek**) and Polish (**Jaszek**): from a pet form of the personal name JACH, or directly from JAN.
GIVEN NAMES Polish 4%. *Lucyna* (2), *Andrzej, Dorota.*

Jasin (113) Origin unidentified. Possibly a variant spelling of English JASON.

Jasinski (1334) Polish (**Jasi(e)ński**): habitational name for someone from Jasień, Jasionna, or Jasionka, all of which are named with *jasień* 'ash tree' (later *jesion*).
FOREBEARS The names Jasieński and Jasiński were borne by many Polish noble families and can be traced back to the 14th century.
GIVEN NAMES Polish 5%. *Ireneusz* (2), *Jozef* (2), *Krystyna* (2), *Piotr* (2), *Andrzej, Darek, Dariusz, Elzbieta, Grzegorz, Janusz, Marcin, Slawomir.*

Jaskiewicz (253) Polish (**Jaśkiewicz**): patronymic from *Jasiek*, a pet form of JAN.
GIVEN NAMES Polish 11%. *Andrzej* (2), *Maciej* (2), *Ewa, Halina, Jerzy, Teofil, Zofia, Zygmund.*

Jasko (168) Polish (**Jaśko, Jaszko**): from a pet form of JAN, *Jaczemir, Jaromir*, or some other personal name starting with *Ja-*. This name is also established in Hungary.
GIVEN NAMES Hungarian 4%. *Arpad, Attila, Dezso.*

Jaskolka (118) Polish (**Jaskółka**): nickname from Polish *jaskółka* 'swallow'.
GIVEN NAME Polish 4%. *Zygmond.*

Jaskolski (228) Polish (**Jaskólski**): habitational name for someone from a place called Jaskółki, from *jaskółka* 'swallow'.
GIVEN NAMES Polish 10%. *Tadeusz* (2), *Jacek, Jaroslaw, Kazimierz, Ryszard, Slawomir.*

Jaskot (149) Polish: nickname for a noisy person, from a derivative of the Polish dialect verb *jaskotać* 'to clamor'.
GIVEN NAMES Polish 9%. *Andrzej, Tadeusz, Zbigniew.*

Jaskowiak (219) Polish (**Jaśkowiak**): patronymic from the personal name *Jasiek* or *Jaśko*, pet forms of *Jan, Jaczemir, Jaromir*, or any of various other personal names starting with *Ja-*.

Jaskowski (106) Polish (**Jaśkowski, Jaszkowski**): habitational name for someone from any of several places in Poland called Jaszkowice or Jaśków.
GIVEN NAMES Polish 12%. *Dariusz, Krystyna, Mieczyslaw, Stanislawa.*

Jaskulski (139) Polish: variant of **Jaskólski** (see JASKOLSKI). This name is also found in German-speaking lands.

Jaslow (106) Origin unidentified.

Jasman (122) German (**Jasmann**): of Slavic origin but unexplained etymology.

Jasmer (178) North German: unexplained.

Jasmin (421) **1.** French: topographic name for someone who lived in an area where jasmine grew, *jasmin*, from Arabic *yasmūn*. **2.** Possibly in some cases Spanish: from the female personal name *Jasmín*, which, like 1 above, is from the name of the plant.
GIVEN NAMES French 12%. *Andre, Armand, Ferrier, Francois, Gaetan, Luc, Lucienne, Magalie, Normand, Placide, Serge, Urgel.*

Jasmine (105) French: variant of JASMIN.
GIVEN NAME French 6%. *Yanick.*

Jaso (224) Basque: perhaps a habitational name from a place named from Basque *jats, yats* 'sorghum' + the collective suffix *-zu.*
GIVEN NAMES Spanish 21%. *Narciso* (2), *Santiago* (2), *Adela, Angel, Carlos, Cirildo, Concha, Hermelinda, Herminia, Jose, Juan Manuel, Juanita; Donato* (3), *Angelo, Antonio, Heriberto.*

Jason (1218) **1.** English: probably a patronymic from JAMES or any of various other personal names beginning with *J-*. **2.** Possibly also Greek: shortened and Americanized form of **Iassonides**, patronymic from the personal name *Iasōn*, which is derived from the Greek vocabulary word *iasthai* 'to heal'. This was borne by a saint mentioned in St. Paul's Epistle to the Romans, traditionally believed to have been martyred. In classical mythology this is the name (English *Jason*) of the leader of the Argonauts, who captured the Golden Fleece with the aid of Medea, daughter of the king of Colchis.

Jasper (3136) **1.** North German: from a variant of the personal name KASPAR. **2.** English (Devon and Cornwall): from the personal name *Jasper*, cognate with 1.

Jaspers (244) North German: patronymic from JASPER.

Jasperson (339) Probably of Scandinavian origin, a patronymic from the personal name JASPER.

Jass (192) German: probably a shortened form of Polish *Jasínski* (see JASINSKI) or other Polish names beginning with *Jas-*.
GIVEN NAMES German 5%. *Erwin, Otto.*

Jasso (1146) **1.** possibly Basque: variant spelling of JASO. **2.** In some cases possibly an altered spelling of French **Jassot**, a topographic name from a derivative of *jas* 'resting place for animals'.
GIVEN NAMES Spanish 51%. *Jose* (28), *Juan* (25), *Manuel* (17), *Jesus* (12), *Armando*

(9), *Javier* (8), *Mario* (8), *Pedro* (8), *Carlos* (7), *Luis* (7), *Miguel* (7), *Arturo* (6).

Jaster (446) North German (Frisian): from a Germanic personal name, a variant of GASTER.
GIVEN NAMES German 5%. *Erwin, Gunther, Heinz, Helmut, Herta, Otto, Reinhard, Siegfried.*

Jastrzebski (143) Polish (**Jastrzębski**): habitational name for someone from any of several places in Poland called Jastrzębie or Jastrząbki, named with Polish *jastrząb* 'goshawk'.
GIVEN NAMES Polish 28%. *Andrzej* (2), *Bogdan* (2), *Janusz* (2), *Tadeusz* (2), *Beata, Dorota, Eugeniusz, Jacek, Jaroslaw, Lucjan, Piotr, Witold.*

Jauch (263) **1.** South and Swiss German: topographic name from Middle High German *jūch*, a unit of measurement of land. **2.** Eastern German: from a shortened form of the personal name JOACHIM.
GIVEN NAMES German 11%. *Fritz, Gerhard, Heinz, Helmut, Johann, Kurt, Mathias.*

Jaudon (248) Origin uncertain; possibly an altered spelling of JORDAN.

Jauquet (112) French: variant of JACQUET.

Jauregui (1022) Basque: Castilianized form of **Jauregi**, a habitational name from any of several places in the Basque Country called Jauregi, from Basque *jauregi* 'palace', 'manor house'.
GIVEN NAMES Spanish 50%. *Jose* (25), *Luis* (14), *Juan* (12), *Francisco* (11), *Alfredo* (9), *Jesus* (9), *Miguel* (9), *Salvador* (9), *Enrique* (8), *Manuel* (8), *Raul* (8), *Carlos* (7).

Javed (145) Muslim (especially common in Pakistan): from a personal name based on Persian *jāved* 'eternal'.
GIVEN NAMES Muslim 90%. *Muhammad* (9), *Khalid* (8), *Mohammed* (8), *Tariq* (8), *Mohammad* (7), *Amjad* (4), *Arshad* (3), *Masood* (3), *Mian* (3), *Asif* (2), *Azhar* (2), *Baber* (2).

Javens (122) English: variant of JAVINS.

Javid (110) Muslim: variant of JAVED.
GIVEN NAMES Muslim 70%. *Ali* (2), *Bahram* (2), *Massoud* (2), *Mohammed* (2), *Anis, Arshad, Asif, Baha, Fiaz, Hassan, Jamileh, Khalid.*

Javier (820) Spanish: from a personal name or religious byname bestowed in honor of St. Francis Xavier (1506–52), Jesuit missionary to the Far East. He was a member of a noble family who took their name from the castle of Xabier in Navarre, where he was born. The place name **Xabier** is of Basque origin (see ECHEVERRIA).
GIVEN NAMES Spanish 45%. *Jose* (14), *Manuel* (7), *Carlos* (6), *Ernesto* (6), *Francisco* (6), *Miguel* (5), *Rafael* (5), *Ramon* (5), *Renato* (5), *Arturo* (4), *Domingo* (4), *Fernando* (4); *Antonio* (2), *Marino* (2), *Angelo, Dario, Franco, Lia, Lirio, Lorenzo, Nazareno, Romeo, Saturnina.*

Javins (136) English: variant of English **Jeavons**, a distinguishing epithet from Old French *jovene* 'young', Latin *juvenis*.

Javor (132) Hungarian (**Jávor**); Croatian, Serbian, Slovenian, and Bosnian: from South Slavic *javor* 'maple tree', which is also found as a Slavic loanword in Hungarian. This is found as a topographic name for someone living near a maple tree, a habitational name from a place named with this word, a personal name, and a nickname.
GIVEN NAMES South Slavic 8%; Hungarian 4%. *Mladen* (2), *Slobodan, Zvonko; Karoly, Vilmos.*

Javorsky (160) **1.** Czech and Slovak (**Javorský**): topographic name for someone who lived by a maple or sycamore tree, Czech *javor*. **2.** Jewish (from Belarus): habitational name from the village of Yavor in Belarus. Compare Polish JAWORSKI.

Jaworowski (188) Polish and Jewish (eastern Ashkenazic): habitational name for someone from any of various places in Poland called Jawory or Jaworów or Jaworówka, all named with Polish *jawor* 'sycamore', 'maple'.
GIVEN NAMES Polish 12%. *Andrej, Grzegorz, Jacek, Jadwiga, Janusz, Jaroslaw.*

Jaworski (1855) Polish and Jewish (eastern Ashkenazic): habitational name for someone from any of numerous places named Jawory or Jaworze, named with Polish *jawor* 'maple', 'sycamore'.
GIVEN NAMES Polish 6%. *Andrzej* (4), *Jacek* (2), *Tadeusz* (2), *Tomasz* (2), *Zigmund* (2), *Zygmunt* (2), *Basia, Bogdan, Bronislaw, Casimir, Czeslaw.*

Jax (110) Variant spelling of English JACKS or possibly of English and French JACQUES.
GIVEN NAME French 6%. *Alphonse* (2).

Jay (3786) English and French: nickname from Middle English, Old French *jay(e), gai* 'jay' (the bird), probably referring to an idle chatterer or a showy person, although the jay was also noted for its thieving habits.
FOREBEARS The name is associated with a Huguenot family from La Rochelle, who settled in New Amsterdam.

Jayaraman (116) Indian (Kerala, Tamil Nadu): Hindu name from Sanskrit *jaya* 'victory' + *rāma* 'pleasing' (name of an incarnation of the god Vishnu), + the Tamil-Malayalam third-person masculine singular suffix *-n*. This is only a given name in India, but has come to be used as a family name in the U.S. among families from South India.
GIVEN NAMES Indian 99%. *Krishna* (5), *Ganesh* (3), *Shyam* (3), *Krishnamurthy* (2), *Narayanan* (2), *Ramesh* (2), *Rao* (2), *Shankar* (2), *Suresh* (2), *Arjun, Arul, Arun.*

Jaycox (416) English: patronymic from a pet form of JACK 1.

Jaye (386) English: variant spelling of JAY.

Jayne (1197) English: from the Middle

English personal name *Jan*, a variant of JOHN. (As a personal name, *Jane* was not specialized as a female form until the 17th century.)

Jaynes (2159) English: patronymic from JAYNE.

Jayroe (245) Americanized form of French GEROU or GIRAUD, or of a variant of either.

Jayson (178) Variant spelling of English JASON.

Jazdzewski (103) Polish (**Jażdżewski**): habitational name for someone from a place named with Polish *jażdż* or *jaszcz*, denoting a species of fish.

Jazwinski (101) Polish (**Jaźwinski**): habitational name for someone from any of several places in Poland called Jaźwiny, named with *jaźwa* 'cave'.
GIVEN NAMES Polish 8%. *Gustaw, Irena, Jerzy.*

Jean (3593) **1.** French: from the personal name *Jean*, French form of JOHN. **2.** English: variant of JAYNE.
FOREBEARS A Vivien Jean, recorded in Canada in 1681, was also known as VIEN; some descendants adopted that surname and are now called Vien or Viens. Another Jean, from the Saintonge region of France, is documented in Quebec city in 1655 with the secondary surname DENIS. Other secondary surnames associated with this name include LAFOREST, Godon, TOURANGEAU, VINCENT, and Pierrejean.
GIVEN NAMES French 22%. *Pierre* (15), *Francois* (8), *Marcel* (7), *Yves* (7), *Andre* (6), *Jacques* (6), *Georges* (5), *Michel* (5), *Philippe* (5), *Serge* (5), *Yvon* (5), *Cecile* (4).

Jean-Baptiste (551) French: from the personal name, a compound of *Jean* (see JOHN) and BAPTISTE. This saint's name was especially frequent as a secondary surname in French Canada.
GIVEN NAMES French 42%. *Herve* (4), *Nesly* (4), *Yves* (4), *Marielle* (3), *Cecile* (2), *Michel* (2), *Pierre* (2), *Raymonde* (2), *Serge* (2), *Andre, Antoine, Armelle.*

Jean-Charles (102) French: from the personal name, a compound of *Jean* (see JOHN) and CHARLES.
GIVEN NAMES French 33%. *Jean Robert* (2), *Andre, Armand, Carmelle, Chantal, Jacques, Mathieu, Pierre, Rolande, Victoire, Yves.*

Jeane (208) Variant spelling of French JEAN. This name is concentrated in LA.

Jeanes (413) English: patronymic from the personal name *Jean* (not necessarily female) (see JAYNE).

Jeanette (118) North American form of French **Jeanet**, a pet form of *Jean*, French form of JOHN.

Jeanfreau (106) French: from the Germanic personal name *Gantfrid*, composed of *gant* 'wild goose' + *frid* 'peace'.
GIVEN NAMES French 20%. *Lucien* (4), *Andre* (2), *Marcel.*

Jean-Jacques (107) French: from the personal name, a compound of *Jean* (see JOHN) + JACQUES.
GIVEN NAMES French 38%; German 8%. *Serge* (3), *Etienne* (2), *Evens, Ghislaine, Julienne, Ketly, Marcellin, Oge, Oliva, Pascal, Ricot; Ernst* (2), *Fritz.*

Jean-Louis (348) French: from the personal name, a compound of *Jean* (French form of JOHN) + LOUIS.
GIVEN NAMES French 44%. *Pierre* (4), *Andre* (2), *Francois* (2), *Mirlande* (2), *Odette* (2), *Pascal* (2), *Serge* (2), *Yolette* (2), *Alcide, Antoine, Brunel, Calix.*

Jeanneret (129) French: derivative of or nickname from the personal name *Jean* (French form of JOHN).
GIVEN NAMES French 7%; German 6%. *Andre* (2), *Raoul; Fritz, Mathias.*

Jeannette (155) Altered spelling, reflecting Canadian pronunciation, of the French surname **Jeannet**, from a pet form of *Jean*, French form of JOHN.
GIVEN NAME French 5%. *Girard.*

Jeannotte (152) Altered spelling, reflecting Canadian pronunciation, of the French surname **Jeannot**, from a pet form of *Jean*, French form of JOHN.
GIVEN NAMES French 6%. *Antoine, Cecile.*

Jean-Pierre (337) French: from the personal name, a compound of *Jean* (French form of JOHN) + *Pierre* (French form of PETER).
GIVEN NAMES French 38%. *Jacques* (3), *Pascal* (3), *Andre* (2), *Antoine* (2), *Claudel* (2), *Emile* (2), *Michel* (2), *Pascale* (2), *Yves* (2), *Daphnee, Flore, Francoise.*

Jeans (606) English and Scottish: patronymic from the personal name *Jean* (see JAYNE).

Jeanson (105) Variant of JEANSONNE.

Jeansonne (533) Acadian form of English JOHNSON.
FOREBEARS This surname was taken to Acadia in the early 18th century by an English bearer whose descendants were dispersed with the rest of the Acadians by the English in the 1750s. The name is especially frequent in LA.
GIVEN NAMES French 4%. *Andre* (2), *Numa* (2), *Camille, Celina, Girard.*

Jeanty (172) Perhaps an altered spelling of French **Gentil** (compare Italian GENTILE).
GIVEN NAMES French 37%. *Yves* (2), *Altagrace, Andre, Anselme, Berard, Emile, Giraud, Jean-Baptiste, Jean-Marie, Lucien, Marcel, Maryse.*

Jech (180) Czech and Eastern German: from a derivative of any of various Slavic personal names beginning with *J-*, for example JAN or JACEK.
GIVEN NAMES German 6%. *Helmut, Lorenz, Otto.*

Jeck (130) **1.** South German: variant of *Jäck* (see JACK 3). **2.** Americanized spelling of German or Slavic JECH.
GIVEN NAMES German 7%. *Fritz, Kurt, Reinhart.*

Jedlicka (490) Czech and Slovak (**Jedlička**): nickname for a tall, well-built man, from a diminutive of *jedle* 'spruce', 'fir'.

Jedynak (103) Polish: descriptive epithet from *jedynak* 'only child'.
GIVEN NAMES Polish 16%; German 4%. *Bazyli, Beata, Danuta, Henryk, Jacek, Wieslaw, Zbigniew; Adelheid.*

Jee (235) **1.** English: variant spelling of GEE. **2.** Korean: variant of CHI.
GIVEN NAMES Korean 30%. *Hyung* (2), *Jong* (2), *Kan* (2), *Shew* (2), *Chor, Ding, Eunyoung, Hyang, Hyeong, Hyun, In Hwan, Jae; Moon* (4), *Chong* (2), *Dae, Sang Hoon, Sang Wook, Wee, Yoo.*

Jefcoat (276) English: variant of JEFFCOAT.

Jeff (205) English: from a short form of the personal name JEFFREY.

Jeffcoat (1416) English: from a pet form of the personal name JEFFREY.

Jefferies (1560) English: patronymic from JEFFREY.

Jefferis (470) English: variant of JEFFERIES.

Jeffers (5869) English: variant of JEFFERSON.

Jefferson (11909) English: patronymic from JEFFREY.
FOREBEARS The third U.S. president, author of the Declaration of Independence, and VA statesman Thomas Jefferson relates in his memoirs a family tradition that he was descended from Welsh stock on his father's side, while noting the relative infrequency of the name Jefferson in Wales. It is a characteristically northern English name. A Jefferson was among the burgesses who attended the first representative assembly at Jamestown, VA, in 1619.

Jeffery (2958) English: variant of JEFFREY.

Jefferys (244) English: patronymic from JEFFERY.

Jeffords (820) Perhaps a variant of the English surname GIFFORD 1. It is very frequent in SC.

Jeffres (118) English: variant of JEFFRESS.

Jeffress (416) English: patronymic from JEFFREY.

Jeffrey (3828) English: from a Norman personal name that appears in Middle English as *Geffrey* and in Old French as *Je(u)froi*. Some authorities regard this as no more than a palatalized form of GODFREY, but early forms such as *Galfridus* and *Gaufridus* point to a first element from Germanic *gala* 'to sing' or *gawi* 'region', 'territory'. It is possible that several originally distinct names have fallen together in the same form.

Jeffreys (1188) English: variant spelling of JEFFRIES.

Jeffries (7505) English: patronymic from JEFFREY.

Jeffs (443) English: patronymic from a short form of the personal name JEFFREY.

Jeffus (187) Probably an altered form of English JEFFS.

Jeglum (102) Norwegian: unexplained.

GIVEN NAME Scandinavian 5%; German 4%. *Hilma.*

Jehl (113) Variant of German JEHLE.
GIVEN NAME French 5%. *Etienne.*

Jehle (282) German: topographic or status name related to Old High German *ōdal, uodal* 'inherited property', 'ancestral home', or from a pet form (*Udo, Udilo*) of any of various Germanic personal names formed with this element, as for example *Uodelrich, Ulrich.*
GIVEN NAMES German 8%. *Hans* (5), *Alois, Eberhard, Hermann, Kurt, Seigfried.*

Jehn (136) German: variant of JAHN 1.

Jekel (176) Jewish (Ashkenazic): from the Yiddish personal name *Yekl*, a pet form of JACOB.
GIVEN NAMES German 5%. *Fritz, Gitta, Kurt.*

Jelen (241) Polish (**Jeleń**), Czech, Slovak (**Jeleň**), Slovenian, and Jewish (Ashkenazic): nickname or ornamental name from Slavic *jelen* 'stag'. Among Jews this was also widely adopted as a translation of HIRSCH.
GIVEN NAMES Polish 6%; French 5%. *Henryk, Jerzy, Jozef, Lucyna, Stanislaw; Alphonse, Fabienne, Ignace.*

Jelinek (1264) Czech (**Jelínek**) and Jewish (from Bohemia and Moravia): from a diminutive of JELEN. As a Jewish name it is mainly a translation of the Yiddish personal name *Hirsh* (see HIRSCH).

Jelinski (194) Polish (**Jeliński**): habitational name for someone from a place called Jelna in Lithuania, named with Polish *jedla, jodła* 'fir tree'.
GIVEN NAMES German 4%. *Johannes, Klaus, Wolf.*

Jelks (449) English: variant of GILKES.

Jelle (112) **1.** English, Scottish, and northern Irish: probably a variant of JELLEY. **2.** German and Frisian: from a Germanic personal name composed with *gelt-*, cognate with the verb *gelten* 'sacrifice', 'repay'. **3.** Norwegian: unexplained.
GIVEN NAMES German 5%; Scandinavian 5%. *Erwin, Jurgen; Jorgen, Obert.*

Jelley (264) English, Scottish, and northern Irish: Anglicized form of French GILES. This is believed to be a Huguenot name.

Jellinek (113) Germanized spelling of Czech JELINEK.
GIVEN NAMES German 6%. *Kurt* (2), *Hans.*

Jellison (1009) English: patronymic from *Gelis*, a variant of GILES, or possibly a patronymic or metronymic from a short form of JULIAN.

Jellum (125) Norwegian: unexplained.
GIVEN NAME Scandinavian 7%. *Erik.*

Jelsma (112) Frisian: unexplained.
GIVEN NAMES Dutch 4%. *Henk, Wiebe.*

Jemison (1010) English: patronymic from JAMES.

Jemmott (172) English: variant spelling of **Jemmett**, from a pet form of *Jem*, a short form of JAMES.

GIVEN NAMES Spanish 8%. *Alicia* (2), *Armando, Dionicio, Gregoria, Guillermo, Roberto, Rosita, Ruperto.*

Jen (327) **1.** English, Danish, Dutch, etc.: variant of JAN. **2.** Chinese 任: variant of REN 1.

GIVEN NAMES Chinese 14%. *Li* (2), *Chao, Chen-Chen, Chien, Chih, Chin, Hsing, Jin, Kuo, Li-Ping, Liwei, Man.*

Jencks (265) English: variant of JENKS.

Jendro (156) Americanized spelling of French GENDRON 'son-in-law'. Compare JOHNDROW.

Jeng (206) Chinese 郑: variant of ZHENG.

GIVEN NAMES Chinese 11%. *Ching Yu, Chun, Guey, Hsing, Shien, Shu, Tsung, Weiwen, Wenwei, Yi, Yi-Chun.*

Jenifer (110) Probably a variant spelling of English **Jennifer**, from the Welsh female personal name *Gwenhwyfar*, a compound of *gwen* 'fair', 'white' + *(g)wyf* 'smooth', 'yielding' + *fawr* 'large'.

Jenison (285) English: patronymic from the medieval personal name *Jan* (see JAYNE).

Jenke (109) German: from a Slavic pet form of the personal name JOHANNES, or a variant of **Jänke**, a Low German pet form of *Jan*, a short form of JOHANN.

GIVEN NAMES German 11%. *Rainer* (2), *Erwin.*

Jenkin (360) English (chiefly Devon): from the Middle English personal name *Jenkin*, a pet form of JOHN with the addition of the suffix *-kin* (of Low German origin).

Jenkins (66617) English: patronymic from JENKIN. *Jenkins* is one of the most common names in England, especially southwestern England, but is also especially associated with Wales.

Jenkinson (708) English: patronymic from JENKIN. Compare JENKINS. The form *Jenkinson* is rather more common in Lancashire and southern Yorkshire.

Jenks (2905) English (also found in Wales): patronymic from the Middle English personal name *Jenk*, a back-formation from JENKIN with the removal of the supposed Anglo-Norman French diminutive suffix *-in*.

FOREBEARS Joseph Jenks (1602–83), the descendant of an old Welsh family, was born in England and traveled to Saugus, near Lynn, MA, in 1642 to assist in the development of America's first iron works. His son, Joseph Jenckes (sic), followed in 1650, founded Pawtucket, RI, and raised four sons who held places of respect and distinction in RI, including one who served as governor for five years.

Jenne (634) **1.** English: variant of JAYNE. **2.** South German: from a reduced form of the personal name *Johannes* (see JOHN).

Jennelle (116) Origin unidentified.

Jenner (940) **1.** English (chiefly Kent and Sussex): occupational name for a designer or engineer, from a Middle English reduced form of Old French *engineor* 'contriver' (a

derivative of *engaigne* 'cunning', 'ingenuity', 'stratagem', 'device'). Engineers in the Middle Ages were primarily designers and builders of military machines, although in peacetime they might turn their hands to architecture and other more pacific functions. **2.** German: from the Latin personal name *Januarius* (see JANUARY 1). *Jänner* is a South German word for 'January', and so it is possible that this is one of the surnames acquired from words denoting months of the year, for example by converts who had been baptized in that month, people who were born or baptized in that month, or people whose taxes were due in January.

Jenness (592) **1.** English: patronymic from the Middle English personal name *Jan* (see JAYNE). **2.** Possibly an Americanized form of French LAJEUNESSE.

Jennett (357) **1.** English: from a pet form of the personal name *Jan* (see JAYNE). **2.** Variant spelling of French JEANNETTE.

Jennette (485) French: variant spelling of JEANNETTE.

Jennewein (126) South German and Austria: from the Latin personal name *Ingenuinus*, meaning 'true-born', borne by a 7th-century saint, bishop of Brixen in southern Tyrol.

GIVEN NAME German 4%. *Manfred.*

Jenney (425) **1.** English: unexplained. **2.** Altered spelling of German JENNY, or perhaps of JENNE.

Jenni (113) Swiss German: variant spelling of JENNY.

GIVEN NAMES German 8%. *Hans, Kurt, Markus.*

Jenniges (157) German (Rhineland): from a variant of a reduced form of the personal name *Johann(es)* (see JOHN).

GIVEN NAMES German 5%. *Mathias* (2), *Kurt.*

Jenning (143) German: patronymic from or pet form of a reduced form of the personal name *Johann(es)* (see JOHN).

Jennings (30656) **1.** English: patronymic from the Middle English personal name *Janyn, Jenyn*, a pet form of JOHN. **2.** German: patronymic from a pet form of the personal name *Johannes* (see JOHN).

Jennison (553) English: patronymic from the Middle English personal name *Jen, Jan* (see JAYNE).

Jenny (579) **1.** Swiss German: from a pet form of *Jähn*, Alsatian and Swiss form of the personal name JOHANNES (see JOHN). **2.** English: variant spelling of JENNEY.

GIVEN NAMES German 4%. *Hans* (4), *Dietrich* (3), *Otto* (2).

Jenrette (150) French: variant of *Jeaneret*, a pet form of *Jean*, French form of John.

Jens (339) North German: from the personal name *Jens*, a reduced form of *Johannes* (see JOHN).

Jenschke (144) Eastern German: from a Slavic pet form of *Johannes* (see JOHN).

GIVEN NAMES German 10%. *Benno* (2), *Erwin* (2), *Alois, Kurt.*

Jensen (46691) Danish, Norwegian, and North German: patronymic from the personal name *Jens*, a reduced form of *Johannes* (see JOHN). This is Denmark's most frequent surname.

GIVEN NAMES Scandinavian 6%. *Erik* (92), *Nels* (40), *Niels* (34), *Lars* (26), *Holger* (18), *Einer* (15), *Jorgen* (15), *Bent* (13), *Knud* (10), *Per* (10), *Ove* (9), *Morten* (8).

Jenson (2786) **1.** English: perhaps an altered spelling of JANSON. **2.** Respelling of Danish, Norwegian, and North German JENSEN.

Jenssen (146) Danish, Norwegian, and North German: variant of JENSEN.

GIVEN NAMES Scandinavian 13%; German 5%. *Carsten* (2), *Bjorn, Lars, Nels*; *Hans* (2).

Jent (486) English: variant spelling of **Gent** (see GENTRY).

Jentsch (188) Eastern German: from a Slavic short form of *Johannes* (see JOHN).

GIVEN NAMES German 7%. *Gerhard, Gerhardt, Hans, Kurt.*

Jentz (228) North German: variant of JANTZ.

Jentzen (124) North German: variant of **Jantzen** (see JANTZ).

GIVEN NAME German 4%. *Erwin.*

Jentzsch (122) German: from a pet form of the personal name *Janš*, Sorbian form of JOHANNES.

GIVEN NAMES German 25%. *Dieter* (3), *Gunther* (2), *Klaus* (2), *Kurt* (2), *Gertraud, Rainer, Ulrich.*

Jeon (421) Korean: variant of CHON.

GIVEN NAMES Korean 66%. *Young* (7), *Kwang* (5), *Sang* (3), *Yong* (3), *Yun* (3), *Chan* (2), *Chi* (2), *Hong* (2), *Joong* (2), *Kyung* (2), *Seong Ho* (2), *Soon* (2); *Byung* (4), *Chang* (2), *Eun Sook* (2), *Jeong* (2), *Jong Keun* (2), *Kiho* (2), *Kwang Soo* (2), *Yeong* (2), *Young Chul* (2), *Chang Hyun* (2), *Chang Jin, Chong.*

Jeong (603) Korean: variant of CHONG.

GIVEN NAMES Korean 60%. *Jin* (5), *Dong* (4), *Sang* (4), *Sung* (4), *Hong* (3), *In* (3), *Jae* (3), *Byeong* (2), *Haeng* (2), *Hee* (2), *Hyeon* (2), *In Young* (2); *Byung* (7), *Chang* (4), *Jeong* (3), *Eun Soo* (2), *Hye Young* (2), *Min* (2), *Myong* (2), *Seong* (2), *So Young* (2), *Yoomi* (2), *Baek, Chang Hyun.*

Jepperson (118) Danish: patronymic from a pet form of the personal name *Jakob* (see JEPSON, JACOB).

Jeppesen (506) Danish: variant of JEPSEN.

GIVEN NAMES Scandinavian 5%; German 5%. *Ejner, Jeppe, Jorgen, Karsten*; *Hans* (3), *Kurt* (2), *Gerhardt.*

Jeppsen (149) Danish: variant spelling of JEPSEN.

Jeppson (394) Variant spelling of Danish JEPPSEN or English JEPSON.

Jepsen (1134) Danish and North German: patronymic from *Jep(pe)*, a pet form of the personal name *Jakob* (see JACOB).

GIVEN NAMES Scandinavian 6%. *Anders* (4),

Ejner (2), *Erik* (2), *Gudmund* (2), *Arnell, Gudrun, Holger, Lars, Niels, Nils, Thor.*

Jepson (1297) **1.** Americanized spelling of Danish and North German JEPSEN. **2.** English: patronymic from a short form of JEFFREY.

Jerabek (277) Czech (**Jeřábek**): nickname for a tall, gangling person, from a pet form of *jeřáb* 'crane'; cognate with Polish *Żuraw* (see ZURAW).

Jeralds (101) Variant spelling of GERALDS.

Jerauld (144) Variant spelling of French **Gérauld** (see GERALD).

Jerde (269) Respelling of Norwegian GJERDE.

Jerdee (135) Americanized spelling of Norwegian GJERDE.

Jerden (145) Scottish: variant of JARDIN.

Jereb (148) Slovenian: from *jereb* 'partridge', either a nickname or perhaps for someone living in a house distinguished by the sign of a partridge.

Jeremiah (351) From the Hebrew name *Yirmeyahu* (meaning 'appointed by God' in Hebrew), borne by a Biblical prophet of the 7th–6th centuries BC, whose story, prophecies of judgement, and lamentations are recorded in the book of the Bible that bears his name.

Jeremias (100) Mainly Jewish: variant of JEREMIAH.
GIVEN NAMES Jewish 14%. *Lipot* (2), *Mayer* (2), *Shraga, Yanky, Zev.*

Jerez (352) Spanish: habitational name from places in the provinces of Badajoz and Cadiz called Jerez. The former, now known in full as Jerez de los Caballeros, was the birthplace of the explorer Vasco Núñez (*c.*1475–1519); the latter, Jerez de la Frontera, was an important center for the manufacture of sherry (named in English from the place) and brandy.
GIVEN NAMES Spanish 56%. *Jose* (10), *Carlos* (8), *Jorge* (7), *Juan* (6), *Luis* (5), *Ramon* (5), *Manuel* (4), *Alvaro* (3), *Ana* (3), *Francisco* (3), *Javier* (3), *Libia* (3); *Antonio* (4), *Heriberto* (2), *Carmin, Gabino, Leonardo, Lorenzo, Luciano, Marco, Romano.*

Jerge (134) German: from a dialect form of the personal name *Georg* (see GEORGE).

Jergens (201) North German and Dutch: patronymic from a vernacular form of the personal name *Georg* (see GEORGE), or from Latvian **Jirgens**, of the same etymology.

Jergenson (204) Respelling of Scandinavian *Jørgensen* or North German *Jörgensen* (see JORGENSEN), or of German *Jürgensen* (see JURGENSEN).
GIVEN NAME Scandinavian 4%. *Obert.*

Jerger (280) South German (Württemberg): patronymic from *Jerg*, a vernacular form of *Georg* (see GEORGE).
GIVEN NAMES German 4%. *Lorenz, Siegfried, Wilhelm.*

Jerke (162) German and Dutch: from a vernacular form of *Georg* (see GEORGE).
GIVEN NAMES German 5%. *Milbert, Otto.*

Jerkins (421) English: unexplained.

Jerles (100) Origin unidentified.

Jermain (100) English: variant spelling of GERMAIN.

Jerman (497) **1.** Slovenian: probably from a medieval form of the personal name *Herman*, from German HERMANN. **2.** English: variant spelling of GERMAN.

Jermyn (218) English: variant spelling of GERMAN.

Jernberg (239) Swedish (also **Järnberg**): ornamental name composed of the elements *järn* 'iron' + *berg* 'mountain'.

Jernigan (5475) English (Suffolk): variant spelling of English **Jernegan**, which is of uncertain derivation. Reaney believes it to be of Breton origin, probably identical with the Old Breton personal name *Iarnuuocon* 'iron famous', taken to East Anglia by Bretons at the time of the Norman Conquest.
FOREBEARS Thomas Jernigan was granted land at Somerton, VA, in 1668. Many of his descendants were sea captains. His son, also called Thomas, settled on Martha's Vineyard, MA, in 1712.

Jerome (2722) **1.** French (**Jérôme**) and English: from the medieval personal name *Jérôme* (French), *Jerome* (English), from Greek *Hierōnymos* (see HIERONYMUS). This achieved some popularity in France and elsewhere, being bestowed in honor of St Jerome (?347–420), creator of the Vulgate, the standard Latin version of the Bible. **2.** English (of Norman origin): from a personal name, *Gerram*, composed of the Germanic elements *gār, gēr* 'spear' + *hraban* 'raven'.
FOREBEARS A Jerome is recorded in Montreal in 1655 with the secondary surnames **Beaune** and **Leblanc**. Another bearer of the name, from Brittany, is recorded in Montreal in 1705 with the secondary surname LATOUR.
GIVEN NAMES French 4%. *Emile* (2), *Andre, Armelle, Dominique, Edmound, Francois, Georges, Herve, Jean Robert, Lucien, Lucienne, Marcel.*

Jeronimo (105) **1.** Portuguese: from the personal name *Jeronimo*, from Greek *Hierōnymos* (see HIERONYMUS). **2.** Probably an Americanized spelling of Spanish **Gerónimo** or Italian GERONIMO, equivalents of 1.
GIVEN NAMES Spanish 54%. *Carlos* (2), *Francisco* (2), *Jose* (2), *Miguel* (2), *Alejandro, Avelino, Delfina, Elvira, Evaristo, Guadalupe, Gustavo, Jacinto.*

Jerrell (358) Slavic?

Jerrett (141) English: variant of GARRETT.

Jerry (697) **1.** English (Norfolk): from a pet form of the Norman personal name GERALD. **2.** Probably also an altered

spelling of Scottish **Gerrie, Gerry**, shortened forms of **Garioch**.

Jersey (212) English: ethnic name for someone from Jersey in the Channel Islands.

Jerue (140) Americanized form of the French Huguenot surname **Girou**, a widespread variant of **Geroul**, based on the Germanic root elements *ger(i)* 'lance' + *wulf* 'wolf'.

Jervey (128) Scottish: variant of JARVIE.

Jervis (650) English: variant of JARVIS.

Jerzak (168) Polish: from a pet form or patronymic form of the personal name *Jerzy*, a vernacular form of Greek *Geōrgios* (see GEORGE).
GIVEN NAMES Polish 4%. *Katarzyna, Zigmund.*

Jesberger (121) German (Rhineland): habitational name for someone from Jesberg in Hesse.
GIVEN NAMES German 5%. *Kurt, Otto.*

Jeschke (401) German (of Polish origin) and Polish: Slavic-German hybrid, from *Jasiek*, a pet form of the personal name *Jan* (see JOHANNES).
GIVEN NAMES German 14%. *Otto* (3), *Ralf* (3), *Heinz* (2), *Lothar* (2), *Reinhard* (2), *Erwin, Helmut, Johann, Kurt, Manfred, Reiner, Wilhelm.*

Jesionowski (116) Polish: habitational name for someone from Jesionowo, a place named with *jesion* 'ash tree'.
GIVEN NAME Polish 7%. *Kazimierz.*

Jeska (128) Polish: from a pet form of the personal name *Jan* (see JOHN).

Jeske (1254) Eastern German (of Slavic origin): from a pet form of the personal name *Jan* or *Johannes* (see JOHN).
GIVEN NAMES German 5%. *Otto* (4), *Alois* (2), *Hans* (2), *Horst* (2), *Kurt* (2), *Bernhardt, Erna, Ernst, Erwin, Ewald, Florian, Friedrich.*

Jesko (147) Polish: from a pet form of the personal name *Jan* (Latin *Johannes*; see JOHN).

Jesmer (143) Origin unidentified.

Jespersen (539) Danish and North German: patronymic from the personal name *Jesper*, Danish and Low German form of KASPAR.
GIVEN NAMES Scandinavian 8%; German 4%. *Aksel, Eilif, Jorgen, Maija, Niels, Sigfred, Sten; Otto* (4).

Jesperson (138) Respelling of JESPERSEN or the Swedish cognate **Jespersson**.

Jess (514) English: variant of JESSE.

Jesse (1307) **1.** North German: from a short form of the personal name *Jesper*, a Low German form of KASPAR. **2.** South German: from a reduced form of the personal name *Johannes* (see JOHN). **3.** Eastern German (of Slavic origin): topographic name from Czech *jes(en)* 'ash tree'. **4.** English: from a short form of JESSUP. **5.** French: from Old French *jaisse* 'chick pea'; probably a metonymic occupational name for a grower of chick peas or a topographic name.

Jessee (1522) Variant spelling of English or respelling of German JESSE.

Jessel (148) **1.** English: from a pet form of JESSUP. **2.** German: probably a topographic name from Czech *jes(en)* 'ash tree'.
GIVEN NAMES German 6%. *Kurt* (2), *Heinz*.

Jessen (1838) **1.** Danish and North German: patronymic from the North German personal name *Jess*, a variant of JENS. **2.** German: habitational name from any of various places named Jessen, mostly in eastern Germany. **3.** German: variant of JESSEL.
GIVEN NAMES Scandinavian 5%; German 4%. *Erik* (3), *Gudmund* (2), *Nels* (2), *Carsten, Holger, Niels, Sten, Sven, Thorvald*; *Hans* (6), *Gerhard* (3), *Otto* (2), *Elke, Frieda, Georg, Johannes, Kurt, Rainer, Wilhelm*.

Jesser (230) East German: habitational name for someone from any of several places called Jessen, which derives from Czech *jes(en)* 'ash tree'.

Jessie (929) English: presumably a variant spelling of **Jessey**, which, as Reaney suggests, may be a metonymic occupational name for a maker of jesses for hawks, Middle English *jesse*.

Jesson (158) English: patronymic from a short form of *Jessup*, a variant of JOSEPH.

Jessop (790) English: variant spelling of JESSUP.

Jessup (2761) English: from the personal name, a variant of JOSEPH, representing the usual pronunciation of the name in the Middle Ages.

Jester (2759) **1.** English: occupational name for a jester, Middle English *gester*. **2.** German: from the Germanic personal name *Gastharo*, composed of the elements *gast* 'warrior' + *heri* 'army'.

Jestice (122) English: variant of JUSTICE.

Jesus (226) Spanish (**(de) Jesús**) and Portuguese: either from the personal name *Jesú*, taken in honor of Christ, or from a short form of compound name composed of a personal name + *de Jesús*. The name *Jesus* is from the Greek form, *Iēsous*, of Aramaic *Yeshua*, from Hebrew *Yoshua*, a byform of *Yehoshuah* (English *Joshua*) 'may Jehovah help him'.
GIVEN NAMES Spanish 37%; Portuguese 16%. *Manuel* (10), *Jose* (5), *Angel* (2), *Fernando* (2), *Gilberto* (2), *Juan* (2), *Lopez* (2), *Mario* (2), *Adelina, Adelino, Alicia, Alonzo*; *Catarina, Joao, Joaquim, Paulo, Vanderlei*; *Antonio* (4), *Carmela, Carmelo, Filomena*.

Jeter (3640) **1.** French: perhaps a variant of **Jetté** (see JETTE). **2.** Perhaps also German, a variant of JETTER. Compare YATER.
FOREBEARS According to family historians, John Jeter was one of a group of Huguenots who came from England to VA in 1700.

Jett (3804) German: variant of JETTE.

Jette (614) **1.** French **Jetté**: surname bestowed on a foundling, from *jeté* 'thrown out'. It is Americanized sometimes as TROW and also as STAY. **2.** German: from a short form of a Germanic personal name with a first element related to Middle High German *gate* 'companion'.
FOREBEARS A Jetté from the Anjou region of France is documented in Montreal in 1659 with the secondary surname Durivage.
GIVEN NAMES French 8%. *Armand* (2), *Alcide, Alphee, Andre, Cecile, Emile, Fernand, Gilles, Laurent, Pierre Paul*.

Jetter (412) German: occupational name from an agent derivative of Middle High German *jĕten* 'to weed'.

Jetton (787) English: unexplained.

Jeune (120) French: distinguishing epithet meaning 'young'.
GIVEN NAMES French 34%. *Dominique* (3), *Pierre* (2), *Astride, Gardy, Julien, Maxime, Michaud, Rosemene*.

Jeung (150) Chinese (Cantonese): **1.** variant of CHANG 1. **2.** variant of CHANG 3. 章
GIVEN NAMES Chinese 23%. *Hoon* (2), *Sheung* (2), *Young* (2), *Young Ju* (2), *Bo Young, Eunkyung, Hing, Jae, Kam, Myung Ok, Sang, Sang Woon*; *Hyun Jong, Yeun, Yiu*.

Jevne (126) German: unexplained.
GIVEN NAME German 7%. *Franz* (3).

Jew (390) **1.** English: ethnic name for a Jew, from Middle English *jeu* 'Jew', Old French *giu*. **2.** English: from a short form of JULIAN. **3.** Chinese 周: possibly a variant of ZHOU. **4.** Chinese 赵: possibly a variant of ZHAO.
GIVEN NAMES Chinese 12%. *Ming* (5), *Jung* (2), *Sing* (2), *Wai Mun* (2), *Wing* (2), *Choi, Chun, Chun Mei, Chun Ying, Fong, Gong, Kam Oi*.

Jewart (109) See DEWART.

Jewel (211) English: variant spelling of JEWELL.

Jewell (8232) English (of Breton or Cornish origin): from a Celtic personal name, Old Breton *Iudicael*, composed of elements meaning 'lord' + 'generous', 'bountiful', which was borne by a 7th-century saint, a king of Brittany who abdicated and spent the last part of his life in a monastery. Forms of this name are found in medieval records not only in Devon and Cornwall, where they are of native origin, but also in East Anglia and even Yorkshire, whither they were imported by Bretons after the Norman Conquest.

Jewett (3461) English: from the Middle English personal name *Juwet, Jowet* (feminine *Juwette, Jowette*). These originated as pet forms (with the Anglo-Norman French suffix *-et(te)*) of *Juwe, Jowe*, variants of *Jull*, a short form of JULIAN, which was borne by both men and women.

Jewison (106) English: patronymic from the personal name *Juwet* (see JEWETT).

Jewitt (125) English: variant spelling of JEWETT.

Jewkes (228) English: patronymic from a short form of a Celtic personal name, Old Breton *Iudicael* (see JEWELL).

Jex (249) **1.** English: probably a variant of JACKS. **2.** German: unexplained; perhaps a patronymic from the personal name JECK.

Jez (122) Polish (**Jeż**) and Slovenian (**Jež**): from *jeż* (Polish), *jež* (Slovenian) 'hedgehog', probably a nickname for a prickly or disobliging individual.
GIVEN NAMES Polish 15%. *Bogdan, Boguslaw, Jaroslaw, Mariusz, Stanislaw, Wladyslaw, Zbigniew*.

Jezek (326) Czech and Slovenian (**Ježek**): from *ježek* 'hedgehog', probably a nickname for a prickly or unapproachable man.

Jezewski (169) Polish (**Jeżewski**): habitational name for someone from any of various places named Jeżewo, named with *jeż* 'hedgehog'.
GIVEN NAMES Polish 4%. *Jozef, Piotr*.

Jezierski (224) Polish: habitational name for someone from Jezioro, Jeziory, Jeziora, or Jezierzyce, all places named with *jezioro* 'lake'.
GIVEN NAMES Polish 5%. *Andrzej, Jacek, Wojciech*.

Jeziorski (210) Polish: variant of JEZIERSKI.
GIVEN NAMES Polish 6%. *Krystyna* (2), *Andrzej, Casimir, Tomasz*.

Jezowski (85) Polish: variant of **Jeżewski** (see JEZEWSKI).
GIVEN NAME Polish 4%. *Thadeus*.

Jha (123) Indian (northern states): Hindu (Brahman) name, from a much reduced form of Sanskrit *upādhyāya* 'teacher'.
GIVEN NAMES Indian 94%. *Anil* (3), *Manoj* (3), *Rajesh* (3), *Ashok* (2), *Indra* (2), *Pran* (2), *Sanjay* (2), *Shashi* (2), *Sunil* (2), *Aditya, Alok, Amar*.

Jhaveri (162) Indian (Gujarat and Bombay city): Hindu (Vania) and Parsi name meaning 'jeweler', 'appraiser of precious stones' in Gujarati, from Arabic *jawharī*.
GIVEN NAMES Indian 87%. *Ramesh* (5), *Bharat* (3), *Bhasker* (3), *Dilip* (3), *Raj* (3), *Arun* (2), *Aswin* (2), *Deepak* (2), *Geeta* (2), *Kamlesh* (2), *Mukesh* (2), *Nayana* (2).

Ji (408) The Romanization **Ji** represents at least seven different Chinese surnames, some of them of extremely ancient origin. **1.** Chinese 纪: from the title Marquis of Ji, which was awarded to a descendant of an ancient emperor. In due course his descendants adopted Ji as their surname. This character also means 'write down' or 'record'. **2.** Chinese 季: from a term meaning 'youngest brother', which was also used as a personal name. The descendants of some of these youngest brothers adopted Ji as their surname. **3.** Chinese 姬: there are two sources of this character as a surname. The first is from Bo Shu, a great-grandson of the legendary emperor Huang Di (2697–2595 BC). He was given an honorary surname, Ji, which was adopted by his descendants and later slightly altered to another character for *Ji* (a prescient decision, as the older character now means 'prostitute' in modern Chinese, while the altered form means 'auspicious'). The second source is from Manchuria. **4.** Chinese 冀: from the state of Ji during the Zhou dynasty (1122–221 BC). **5.** Chinese 姬: from a byname of the legendary emperor Huang Di (2697–2595 BC), who supposedly acquired the name from the Ji river, by which he lived as a boy. A branch of his descendants kept the surname, and it was from this branch that the rulers of the Zhou dynasty (1122–221 BC) claimed descent. **6.** Chinese 籍: from one of the characters in the word *dianji* 'library', 'collection of classical books and historical records'. In the state of Jin during the Spring and Autumn period (722–481 BC), there existed an official in charge of classical books and historical records. Descendants of at least one such official adopted this character as their surname. **7.** Chinese 稽: from part of the name of an area called Huiji. A king of the Xia dynasty (2205–1766 BC) granted this area to his son, and its name was subsequently adopted by the son's descendants as their surname. At the beginning of the Han dynasty (206 BC–220 AD) a branch of this clan move to an area in present-day Anhui province called Ji Mountain. The characters for *Ji* in the names Huiji and 'Ji mountain' are very similar and are pronounced the same; this branch of the family modified the surname to correspond to the name of their new home in Ji mountain. GIVEN NAMES Chinese 72%. *Hong* (4), *Sang* (4), *Yong* (4), *Kyung* (3), *Wei* (3), *Young* (3), *Yuhe* (3), *Chen* (2), *Dong* (2), *Fang* (2), *Guoping* (2), *Hongbin* (2); *Chang* (5), *Dae* (2), *Min* (2), *Bok Nam*, *Byung*, *Do Young*, *Dong Sik*, *Hak*, *Jong Won*, *Jung Hwan*, *Jung Ok*, *Kwang Sun*.

Jia (185) Chinese 贾: from the place name Jia. The third king of the Zhou dynasty, Kang (1078–1053 BC), made a grant of the fief of Jia. When the state of Jin later conquered Jia, the former ruling class adopted the place name Jia as their surname.
GIVEN NAMES Chinese 72%. *Wei* (5), *Ho* (3), *Hong* (3), *Li Ping* (3), *Tao* (3), *Ying* (3), *Bei* (2), *Hang* (2), *Jian* (2), *Lei* (2), *Aijun*, *Anning*; *Yiping*.

Jian (93) Chinese 简: name borne by descendants of Xu Jianbo, a senior official of the state of Jin during the Spring and Autumn period (722–481 BC).

Jiang (1514) **1.** Chinese 纪: from the name of an area known as the Jiang Hills, which in ancient times was granted to a descendant of the legendary emperor Zhuang Xu. Later, during the Spring and Autumn period (722–481 BC), when the Jiang Hills

administration was defeated by the state of Chu, the defeated ruling class took Jiang as their surname. **2.** Chinese 蒋: from the name of the state of Jiang, in present-day Henan province. The Duke of Zhou was the younger brother and chief adviser of Wu Wang, who established the Zhou dynasty in 1122 BC; his third son, Bo Ling, was granted lordship of the state of Jiang. Bo Ling's descendants eventually adopted Jiang as their surname. **3.** Chinese 姜: from the name of the Jiang Creek, a tributary of the Wei river in Shaanxi province. This surname goes back 4700 years to Shen Nong, a legendary emperor (2734–2697 BC). Shen Nong was raised beside Jiang Creek, and adopted Jiang as one of his names.
GIVEN NAMES Chinese 70%; Vietnamese 5%. *Hong* (22), *Wei* (12), *Tao* (10), *Ying* (10), *Yong* (10), *Jing* (9), *Yang* (9), *Hua* (8), *Jian* (8), *Ming* (8), *Fan* (7), *Feng* (7), *Min* (4), *Tian* (3), *Chang*, *Chong*, *Hu*, *Neng*; *Hao* (9), *Lan* (4), *Hai* (2), *Long* (2), *Quan* (2), *Du*, *Huan*, *Nien*, *Tan*.

Jiao (72) Chinese 焦: from the name of the ancient state of Jiao, in present-day Henan province. After conquering the Shang dynasty and becoming the first king of the Zhou dynasty in 1122 BC, Wu Wang granted the state of Jiao to a descendant of Shen Nong, a legendary emperor (2734–2697 BC). Later descendants adopted the name of the state as their surname.

Jicha (151) Czech (**Jícha**): **1.** from a pet form of the personal name *Jan*, vernacular form of Latin *Johannes* (see JOHN). **2.** from *jícha* 'liquid manure', 'soup', 'gravy', presumably applied as a derogatory nickname.

Jiggetts (162) Probably an altered form of English CHECKETTS.

Jilek (397) Czech (**Jílek**): from a pet form of *Jiljí*, a vernacular form of Latin *Aegidius* (see GILES).

Jiles (990) English: variant spelling of GILES.

Jillson (415) Probably an altered spelling of the English surname *Gilson*, a patronymic from GILES.

Jim (358) Chinese 詹: Cantonese variant of ZHAN. This name is common in Hawaii.

Jimenez (17046) Spanish (**Jiménez**): patronymic from the medieval personal name *Jimeno*, which is of pre-Roman origin.
GIVEN NAMES Spanish 51%. *Jose* (523), *Juan* (264), *Luis* (173), *Manuel* (167), *Carlos* (165), *Jesus* (157), *Francisco* (131), *Miguel* (111), *Pedro* (98), *Mario* (96), *Rafael* (95), *Raul* (95).

Jimerson (836) Variant of Scottish and northern English JAMESON, based on a pet form of the personal name.

Jiminez (754) Spanish (**Jimínez**): variant of Spanish **Jiménez** (see JIMENEZ).
GIVEN NAMES Spanish 44%. *Jose* (25), *Manuel* (9), *Juan* (8), *Pedro* (8), *Francisco*

(7), *Luis* (7), *Rafael* (7), *Jesus* (6), *Miguel* (6), *Roberto* (6), *Ernesto* (5), *Cesar* (4); *Antonio* (6), *Marco Antonio* (2), *Angelo*, *Benigna*, *Camillo*, *Carmelo*, *Cecilio*, *Guido*, *Lorenzo*, *Luciano*, *Marino*, *Rinaldo*.

Jimison (400) English (County Durham): variant of JAMESON.

Jimmerson (535) Variant of Scottish and northern English JAMESON, based on a pet form of the personal name *James*.

Jin (1034) **1.** Chinese 金: from the honorary surname, *Jin Tianshi* of Shao Hao, a son of the legendary emperor Huang Di of the 26th century BC. The character for *jin* also means 'gold' or 'metal'. Some later descendants of Shao Hao adopted *Jin* as their surname. **2.** Chinese 靳: from the name of Jin Shang, a chief official in the state of Chu during the Zhou dynasty (1122–221 BC). Some of his descendants adopted this surname. **3.** Chinese 晋: from the name of the Jin river. Wu Wang, the first king of the Zhou dynasty (1122–16 BC), granted the state of Tang to his third son. Since the Jin river flowed through it, the name of the state was later changed to Jin. Descendants of the third son adopted the new name of the state name as their surname. **4.** Korean: variant of CHIN 4. **5.** Japanese: 'ranks' or 'battle array'. The name is not common in Japan.
GIVEN NAMES Chinese/Korean 66%; Japanese 4%. *Young* (10), *Wei* (9), *Yi* (8), *Sung* (7), *Yan* (7), *Hong* (6), *Jian* (6), *Jin* (6), *Li* (6), *Dong* (5), *Lei* (5), *Peng* (5); *Byung* (2), *Chang* (2), *Chang Hyun* (2), *Chul* (2), *Dae* (2), *Hak* (2), *Jeong* (2), *Seong* (2), *Tian* (2), *Yiping* (2), *Young Woo* (2), *Byung Soon*; *Yu* (3), *Kaoru* (2), *Yue* (2), *Akiko*, *Chiaki*, *Hiroshi*, *Kyo*, *Naohiro*, *Susumu*, *Takashi*, *Yumi*.

Jindra (388) Czech: from the personal name *Jindra*, a pet form of *Jindřich* (see JINDRICH).

Jindrich (59) Czech (**Jindřich**): from the personal name *Jindřich*, Czech form of German *Heinrich* (see HENRY).

Jines (318) Origin unidentified. Perhaps a variant of English JONES or JAYNES. Compare JOINES. The name in this spelling is well established in Mexico.

Jing (116) **1.** Chinese 景: a common surname among royalty in the state of Chu during the Zhou dynasty (1122–221 BC). **2.** Chinese 荆: from the place name Jingzhou, denoting an area which later became the state of Chu during the Spring and Autumn period (722–481 BC). **3.** Chinese 井: from a character that means '(water) well'. This originated with the Earl of Jing, a senior adviser in the state of Yu during the Zhou dynasty (1122–221 BC). **4.** Chinese 金: from the name of the Marquis Jing of the state of Wei, who lived during the Warring States period (403–221BC).
GIVEN NAMES Chinese 69%. *Ming* (4), *Jin*

(2), *Junping* (2), *Ning* (2), *Tao* (2), *Gang, Guoping, Hong, Jian, Jung, Li, Liang, Min.*

Jinkerson (106) English (East Anglia): patronymic from the Middle English personal name JENKIN.

Jinkins (249) English: variant of JENKINS.

Jinks (965) English: variant of JENKS.

Jinright (194) Americanized spelling of Czech **Jindřich**, from the personal name *Jindřich*, Czech form of HENRY.

Jipson (201) English: variant of JEPSON.

Jirak (196) Czech (**Jirák**): patronymic from the personal name *Jiři*, vernacular form of Greek *Geōrgios* (see GEORGE).

Jirik (223) Czech (**Jiřík**): from a pet form of *Jiři*, vernacular form of Greek *Geōrgios* (see GEORGE).

Jiron (347) Spanish (**Jirón**): variant of the habitational name **Girón** (see GIRON).
GIVEN NAMES Spanish 22%. *Juan* (3), *Armando* (2), *Carlota* (2), *Claudio* (2), *Guillermo* (2), *Orlando* (2), *Rafael* (2), *Sergio* (2), *Ada Luz, Ana Silvia, Angelina, Candido.*

Jirsa (167) Czech: from a pet form of the personal name *Jiři*, vernacular form of Greek *Geōrgios* (see GEORGE).

Jiskra (104) Czech: unexplained.
GIVEN NAMES German 6%. *Otto* (2), *Florian.*

Jividen (400) Origin unidentified.

Jo (511) **1.** Chinese and Korean: variant of CHO. **2.** Japanese(**Jō**): 'castle'. The same character is also pronounced SHIRO. A noble family in Echigo (now Niigata prefecture) named Jō was descended from the TAIRA clan. Another name pronounced similarly, written with the character meaning 'emotion', is found in Okinawa. **3.** Hungarian (**Jó**): nickname from *jó* 'good'.
GIVEN NAMES Chinese/Korean 51%; Japanese 8%. *Young* (5), *Jae* (4), *Kyung* (4), *Sung* (4), *Chun* (3), *Heon* (3), *Yong* (3), *Dong* (2), *Han* (2), *Ho* (2), *Won* (2), *Yoon* (2); *Chang* (4), *Byung* (3), *Jang* (2), *Wonho* (2), *Woong* (2), *Cheol, Chul, Dong Hyun, Eun Hee, Ho Soon, Hyun Sook, Hyun Young; Kyu* (4), *Hiroshi* (3), *Satoru* (2), *Shingo, Tadao, Tadashi, Taisuke, Takao, Yoshi.*

Joa (100) **1.** Dutch and German: unexplained. **2.** perhaps Catalan: possibly a nickname or metonymic occupational name from *joa*, a variant of Catalan *joia* 'jewelery' (compare JOYA).
GIVEN NAMES Spanish 20%; German 5%; Scandinavian 4%. *Argentina, Armando, Carlos, Damaso, Francisco, Jacinto, Josefina, Juana, Miguel, Miguelito, Ramon, Ruben; Detlef; Alf, Nils.*

Joachim (739) German, French, and English: from the Hebrew personal name *Yoyakim* 'God has granted (a son)', which occurs in the Bible (Nehemiah 12:10) and was also borne, according to medieval legend, by the father of the Virgin Mary.
FOREBEARS A bearer of the name from the Dordogne region of France who arrived in

Canada in 1665 is documented in Trois Rivières, Quebec, in 1679, with the secondary surname Laverdure.
GIVEN NAMES French 6%; German 4%. *Normand* (2), *Pierre* (2), *Colette, Etienne, Herve, Jean Claude, Serge, Yva; Kurt* (2), *Erwin, Gernot, Heinrich, Otto, Ralf, Siegbert.*

Joanis (129) Southern French: patronymic from the personal name *Joan*, Occitan form of Latin *Johannes* (see JOHN).
GIVEN NAMES French 9%. *Chantal* (2), *Pierre* (2).

Joaquim (103) Portuguese and Catalan: from the personal name *Joaquim* (see JOACHIM).
GIVEN NAMES Spanish 23%. *Manuel* (7), *Jose* (4), *Albino, Alfredo, Armando, Carlos, Domingos, Mario, Raul.*

Joaquin (437) Spanish (**Joaquín**): from the personal name, Spanish equivalent of JOACHIM.
GIVEN NAMES Spanish 28%. *Manuel* (8), *Jose* (6), *Juan* (5), *Gilberto* (3), *Alejandro* (2), *Ana* (2), *Carlos* (2), *Eduardo* (2), *Leticia* (2), *Miguel* (2), *Natividad* (2), *Santiago* (2).

Job (850) English, French, German, and Hungarian (**Jób**): from the personal name (Hebrew *Iyov*) borne by a Biblical character, the central figure in the Book of Job, who was tormented by God and yet refused to forswear Him. The name has been variously interpreted as meaning 'Where is the (divine) father?' and 'Persecuted one'. It does not seem to have been used as a personal name in the Middle Ages: the surname is probably a nickname for a wretched person or one tormented with boils (which was one of Job's afflictions).
GIVEN NAMES French 4%. *Andre* (2), *Christophe, Damien, Laure, Michel.*

Jobe (3067) English: **1.** variant spelling of JOB. **2.** nickname from Old French *job, joppe* 'sorry wretch', 'fool' (perhaps a transferred application of the name of the Biblical character). **3.** from Middle English *jubbe, jobbe* 'vessel containing four gallons', hence perhaps a metonymic occupational name for a cooper. It could also have been a nickname for a heavy drinker or for a tubby person. **4.** metonymic occupational name for a maker or seller (or nickname for a wearer) of the long woolen garment known in Middle English and Old French as a *jube* or *jupe*. This word ultimately derives from Arabic.

Jobes (582) English: patronymic from JOB or JOBE.

Jobin (375) French: from a pet form of JOB 1 and 2.
FOREBEARS A Jobin from Normandy is recorded in Quebec city in 1669.
GIVEN NAMES French 14%. *Fernand* (3), *Emile* (2), *Armand, Benoit, Camille, Henri, Leonce, Normand, Patrice, Rosaire, Serge, Yves.*

Jobson (403) English: patronymic from JOB.

Jobst (233) German: from the Biblical name JOB, influenced by *Jost* (see JOOST).
GIVEN NAMES German 7%. *Bernd* (2), *Gernot, Hans, Kurt.*

Jocelyn (138) English: variant spelling of JOSLIN.
GIVEN NAMES French 12%. *Antoine* (2), *Mireille* (2), *Jean Raymond, Marthe, Solange.*

Jochem (191) German: variant of JOACHIM.
GIVEN NAME German 4%. *Otto* (2).

Jochim (406) German and French: variant of JOACHIM.

Jochimsen (155) North German and Danish: patronymic from the personal name JOCHIM.
GIVEN NAMES German 4%. *Hans* (3), *Kurt.*

Jochum (421) German: variant of JOACHIM.
GIVEN NAMES German 6%. *Otto* (2), *Bernhard, Gottfried, Helmut, Klaus, Konrad, Oskar.*

Jock (393) German (also **Jöck**): from a short form of the personal name JAKOB.

Jockisch (108) German: from a West Slavic pet form of the personal name *Jakob* (see JACOB).
GIVEN NAME French 5%. *Camille.*

Jodoin (385) Variant spelling of French **Jaudouin**, from the Germanic personal name *Gaudwin*, a compound of the tribal name *Gaut* (see JOSLIN) + *wini*, 'friend'.
FOREBEARS A bearer of the name from the Poitou region of France is documented in Montreal in 1666.
GIVEN NAMES French 14%. *Adelard* (3), *Marcel* (2), *Michel* (2), *Adrien, Camille, Denys, Eugenie, Julien, Lucien, Ovide, Philias, Urbain.*

Jodon (113) Variant of French **Jaudouin** (see JODOIN).

Jodrey (115) Probably a variant of English **Godrey**, a reduced form of GODFREY.

Joe (1398) **1.** Chinese and Korean: variant of CHO. **2.** English: from a short form of JOSEPH.

Joeckel (116) German: pet form of *Jakob* (see JAKOB).

Joel (453) **1.** English: variant of JEWELL. **2.** French, German, and English: from the Biblical personal name *Joel*.
GIVEN NAMES German 4%. *Manfred* (2), *Hans, Helmut, Helmuth, Ilse.*

Joelson (132) Northern English: patronymic from JOEL.

Joens (311) Swedish, Danish, and North German (**Jöns**): from a vernacular form of *Johannes* (see JOHN).
GIVEN NAMES German 4%. *Claus* (3), *Hans.*

Joerg (135) German (**Jörg**): from the personal name *Joerg*, a German vernacular form of GEORGE.
GIVEN NAMES German 9%. *Bernd, Hans, Heinrich, Wilhelm, Wolf.*

Joerger (278) South German (**Jörger**):

patronymic from *Jörg*, a German vernacular form of Greek *Geōrgios* (see GEORGE).
GIVEN NAMES German 5%. *Otto* (2), *Bernhard*.

Joers (145) North German (**Jörs**): from a dialect variant of **Jürgens** (see JURGENS).

Joffe (532) Jewish (eastern Ashkenazic): variant of JAFFE, reflecting an Ashkenazic pronunciation of the Hebrew word.
GIVEN NAMES Jewish 5%. *Chayim* (2), *Jakob* (2), *Sol* (2), *Ilan*, *Isak*, *Tova*, *Zalman*.

Joffrion (256) Variant spelling of French GEOFFRION.
GIVEN NAMES French 5%. *Emile*, *Landry*, *Monique*.

Joh (148) **1.** German: unexplained. **2.** Korean: variant of CHO.
GIVEN NAMES Korean 43%. *Shin* (4), *Young* (3), *Sung* (2), *Sungwook* (2), *Yoon* (2), *Choong*, *Dae Hyun*, *Eunyoung*, *Gwang*, *Jae Ho*, *Jung*, *Junhee*; *Choon*, *Hak*, *Jang*, *Joo Young*, *Moon*, *Myung Kyu*, *Sung-Ho*.

Johal (124) Indian: Sikh name of unknown meaning, based on the name of a tribe in the Jat community.
GIVEN NAMES Indian 82%. *Sukhi* (2), *Avtar*, *Buta*, *Gurmukh*, *Lakhbir*, *Mahavir*, *Mohan*, *Raju*, *Ranvir*, *Resham*, *Sardara*, *Sati*.

Johanek (145) Czech (**Johánek**): from a pet form of the German personal name JOHANN.

Johann (360) German: from the personal name *Johann*, a vernacular form of Latin *Johannes* (see JOHN).
GIVEN NAMES German 4%. *Franz*, *Kurt*, *Otto*.

Johannes (1245) German: from the personal name *Johannes* (see JOHN).

Johannesen (376) Danish and North German: variant of JOHANSEN.
GIVEN NAMES Scandinavian 10%; German 4%. *Lars* (2), *Ingard*, *Iver*, *Morten*, *Thora*; *Otto* (2), *Fritz*.

Johannessen (397) Danish, Norwegian, and North German: variant of JOHANSEN.
GIVEN NAMES Scandinavian 31%. *Erik* (5), *Thor* (5), *Bjorn* (2), *Sven* (2), *Aase*, *Alf*, *Anders*, *Erlend*, *Gorm*, *Johan*, *Knut*, *Lars*.

Johanning (292) North German: patronymic from *Johann*, German form of JOHN.
GIVEN NAMES German 4%. *Alois*, *Erna*, *Fritz*, *Kurt*.

Johanns (190) North German and Latvian (**Johans**): patronymic from the personal name *Johann*, *Johannes* (see JOHN).

Johannsen (1096) North German and Danish: patronymic from the personal name *Johann*, German and Danish form of JOHN.
GIVEN NAMES Scandinavian 4%; German 4%. *Carsten* (2), *Birgit*, *Hiltrud*, *Holger*, *Nels*, *Ove*, *Sven*, *Thorwald*; *Hans* (8), *Willi* (2), *Arno*, *Dieter*, *Fritz*, *Ingeborg*, *Johann*, *Johannes*, *Kurt*, *Otto*.

Johansen (4018) North German, Danish, and Norwegian: patronymic from the personal name *Johann* (Scandinavian), *Johann*

(German), vernacular forms of *Johannes* (see JOHN).
GIVEN NAMES Scandinavian 12%. *Erik* (15), *Per* (10), *Niels* (5), *Nils* (5), *Thor* (5), *Johan* (4), *Bjorn* (3), *Lars* (3), *Oluf* (3), *Borge* (2), *Holger* (2), *Jarl* (2).

Johanson (2194) Respelling of JOHANSSON or JOHANSEN.
GIVEN NAMES Scandinavian 11%; German 4%. *Erik* (7), *Sven* (7), *Lars* (4), *Anders* (2), *Helmer* (2), *Mats* (2), *Alf*, *Alvar*, *Astrid*, *Einer*, *Eskil*, *Fritjof*; *Kurt* (3), *Gerhard* (2), *Otto* (2), *Fritz*.

Johansson (955) Swedish: patronymic from the personal name *Johan*, Scandinavian form of JOHN.
GIVEN NAMES Scandinavian 37%; German 6%. *Lars* (14), *Anders* (12), *Erik* (12), *Nils* (8), *Lennart* (6), *Per* (3), *Alf* (2), *Bjorn* (2), *Mats* (2), *Sven* (2), *Alarik*, *Bernt*; *Hans* (6), *Kurt* (4), *Alfons*, *Heimo*, *Ulrika*.

John (7161) English, Welsh, German, etc.: ultimately from the Hebrew personal name *yōḥānān* 'Jehovah has favored (me with a son)' or 'may Jehovah favor (this child)'. This personal name was adopted into Latin (via Greek) as *Johannes*, and has enjoyed enormous popularity in Europe throughout the Christian era, being given in honor of St. John the Baptist, precursor of Christ, and of St. John the Evangelist, author of the fourth gospel, as well as others of the nearly one thousand other Christian saints of the name. Some of the principal forms of the personal name in other European languages are Welsh *Ieuan*, *Evan*, *Siôn*, and *Ioan*; Scottish *Ia(i)n*; Irish *Séan*; German *Johann*, *Johannes*, *Hans*; Dutch *Jan*; French *Jean*; Italian *Giovanni*, *Gianni*, *Ianni*; Spanish *Juan*; Portuguese *João*; Greek *Iōannēs* (vernacular *Yannis*); Czech *Jan*; Russian *Ivan*. Polish has surnames both from the western Slavic form *Jan* and from the eastern Slavic form *Iwan*. There were a number of different forms of the name in Middle English, including *Jan(e)*, a male name (see JANE); *Jen* (see JENKIN); *Jon(e)* (see JONES); and *Han(n)* (see HANN). There were also various Middle English feminine versions of this name (e.g. *Joan*, *Jehan*), and some of these were indistinguishable from masculine forms. The distinction on grounds of gender between *John* and *Joan* was not firmly established in English until the 17th century. It was even later that *Jean* and *Jane* were specialized as specifically feminine names in English; bearers of these surnames and their derivatives are more likely to derive them from a male ancestor than a female. As a surname in the British Isles, **John** is particularly frequent in Wales, where it is a late formation representing Welsh *Siôn* rather than the older form *Ieuan* (which gave rise to the surname EVAN). As an American family name this form has absorbed various cognates from continental European languages. (For forms, see Hanks

and Hodges 1988.) It is used as a given name among Christians in India, and in the U.S. has come to be used as a surname among families from southern India.

Johncox (116) English: from a pet form of JOHN, with the Middle English suffix *-cok* (see COCKE).

Johndro (117) Americanized spelling of French GENDRON 'son-in-law'.
GIVEN NAME French 4%. *Cyr*.

Johndrow (191) Americanized spelling of French GENDRON 'son-in-law'.

Johner (109) **1.** habitational name for someone from Jonen in Switzerland. **2.** South German: occupational name for a reaper, from a noun derivative of Middle High German *jān* 'row of mown grass or cereal'.

Johnes (105) English and German: variant spelling of JOHNS or JONES. This spelling is also found in Finland.

Johnk (111) North German (also **Jöhnk**): from a pet form of JOHN.
GIVEN NAME German 5%. *Fritz*.

Johnke (122) North German (also **Jöhnke**): from a pet form of JOHN.
GIVEN NAMES German 4%. *Hans*, *Otto*.

Johns (16386) **1.** English and German: patronymic from JOHN. As a German name it may also be a reduced form of JOHANNES. **2.** Americanized form of Swiss German SCHANTZ.

Johnsen (3193) Danish, Norwegian, and North German: patronymic from the personal name *Jo(h)n*, *Johann(es)* (see JOHN).
GIVEN NAMES Scandinavian 10%. *Erik* (10), *Niels* (4), *Johan* (3), *Knut* (3), *Per* (3), *Alf* (2), *Anders* (2), *Bjorg* (2), *Carsten* (2), *Kerstin* (2), *Lars* (2), *Ove* (2).

Johnsey (256) English: from a pet form of JOHN.

Johnson (610104) English and Scottish: patronymic from the personal name JOHN. As an American family name, *Johnson* has absorbed patronymics and many other derivatives of this name in continental European languages. (For forms, see Hanks and Hodges 1988.)
FOREBEARS Johnson is the second most frequent surname in the U.S. It was brought independently to North America by many different bearers from the 17th and 18th centuries onward. Andrew Johnson (1808–75), 17th president of the U.S., was born in Raleigh, NC, the younger son of Jacob Johnson and Mary (or Polly) McDonough. Little is known of his ancestors. The 36th president, Lyndon B. Johnson, dates his American forebears back seven generations to James Johnston (sic) (b. about 1662) who lived at Currowaugh, Nansemond, and Isle of Wight Counties, VA. Noted early bearers also include Marmaduke (d. 1674), a printer who came from England to MA in 1660; Edward (1598–1672), a colonial chronicler who was baptized at St. George's parish, Canterbury, England, and

emigrated to Boston in 1630; and Sir Nathaniel (*c.* 1645–1713), a colonial governor of Carolina, who came from County Durham, England.

Johnsrud (322) Norwegian: habitational name from any of numerous farmsteads in southeastern Norway, so named from the personal name *Jon* (Scandinavian form of JOHN) + Old Norse *ruð* 'clearing'.
GIVEN NAMES Scandinavian 4%. *Erik, Selmer.*

Johnston (53969) Scottish: **1.** habitational name, deriving in most cases from the place so called in Annandale, in Dumfriesshire. This is derived from the genitive case of the personal name JOHN + Middle English *tone, toun* 'settlement' (Old English *tūn*). There are other places in Scotland so called, including the city of Perth, which used to be known as *St. John's Toun,* and some of these may also be sources of the surname. **2.** variant of *Johnson* (see JOHN), with intrusive *-t-*.
FOREBEARS As far as can be ascertained, most Scottish bearers of this surname are descendants of a certain John, probably a Norman baron from England, who held lands at Johnstone in Annandale from the Bruce family in the late 12th century. His son Gilbert was the first to take the surname Johnstone and their descendants later held the earldom of Annandale.

Johnstone (3026) Scottish: variant of JOHNSTON.

Joice (160) English: variant spelling of JOYCE.

Joiner (5146) English: occupational name for a maker of wooden furniture, Anglo-Norman French *joignour* (Old French *joigneor,* from *joinre* 'to join', 'to connect', Latin *iungere*).

Joines (825) English: probably a variant of JONES. Compare JOYNES.

Jojola (216) Hispanic: unexplained.
GIVEN NAMES Spanish 14%. *Jose* (3), *Carlos* (2), *Mario* (2), *Delfino, Estevan, Felicita, Josefa, Juan, Juanita, Leandro, Manuel, Marcelina.*

Jokela (188) Finnish: from *joki* 'river' + the local suffix *-la*, originally a habitational name from any of various farmsteads named for their riverside location. During the name conversion movement from Swedish in the 19th and early 20th centuries, it was adopted as a replacement by Finns with Swedish surnames, especially those containing Swedish *ström* 'river'.
GIVEN NAMES Finnish 11%. *Reino* (3), *Arvo, Eino, Juha, Jukka, Vaino, Veikko.*

Jokerst (203) German: unexplained.

Joki (186) Finnish: topographic name from *joki* 'river'. During the name conversion movement in the 19th and early 20th centuries, Joki was adopted as a replacement by Finns with Swedish surnames, especially those containing Swedish *ström* 'river'. In some cases it may have been adopted as

a topographic name by someone who lived by a river.
GIVEN NAMES Finnish 12%. *Pekka* (2), *Arvo, Niilo, Olavi, Reino, Urho, Weikko, Wilho.*

Jokinen (215) Finnish: variant of JOKI 'river' + the common surname suffix *-nen*. In some instances *Jokinen* arose as a family name from the farm name JOKELA. Later, during the name conversion movement of the 19th and early 20th centuries, it was widely adopted as an ornamental name by Finns, especially as a replacement for Swedish surnames ending in *-ström* 'river'.
GIVEN NAMES Finnish 9%; Scandinavian 6%. *Reino* (2), *Armas, Eino, Esko, Martti, Senja, Taisto, Toivo; Erik* (2), *Walfrid.*

Joles (262) Jewish (Ashkenazic): patronymic from the Hebrew personal name *Yoel* (Joel), born by a Biblical prophet.

Jolicoeur (422) French: nickname for a cheerful person, from Old French *joli* 'joyful', 'cheerful' + *cuer* 'heart'. This was a frequent secondary surname in French Canada, and was often Americanized as Hart.
GIVEN NAMES French 15%. *Jacques* (3), *Emile* (2), *Lucien* (2), *Pierre* (2), *Aime, Andre, Armand, Gaston, Herve, Normand, Renaud, Yvon.*

Jolie (120) French: variant of JOLY.

Jolin (476) French and English: from a pet form of a Celtic personal name, *Jol,* reduced form of Breton *Iudicael* (see JEWELL).
GIVEN NAMES French 9%. *Adelard, Aime, Armand, Camille, Emile, Fernand, Lucien, Marcel, Pierre, Raoul, Simmone, Yvan.*

Jolivet (124) French: from a diminutive of JOLLY. This name occurs chiefly in LA and TX.
GIVEN NAMES French 15%. *Pierre* (2), *Damien, Landry, Michel, Normand.*

Jolivette (279) Altered spelling, reflecting the Canadian pronunciation, of JOLIVET.
GIVEN NAMES French 4%. *Cecile, Fabien, Jean-Paul.*

Jolles (113) English: from the personal name *Jolle, Jull,* a short form of JULIAN.

Jolley (3321) English: variant spelling of JOLLY.

Jollie (154) English (mainly Scotland): variant spelling of of JOLLY.

Jolliff (756) English: variant of JOLLY.

Jolliffe (449) English: variant of JOLLY.

Jolls (103) English: variant of JOLLES.

Jolly (5276) English, Scottish, and French: nickname for someone of a cheerful or attractive disposition, from Middle English, Old French *joli(f)* 'merry', 'happy'.

Joly (509) French: variant spelling of JOLLY.
FOREBEARS A bearer of the surname Joly from Brittany is documented in Quebec city in 1670. Another, from Flanders, is documented in Quebec city in 1673 with the secondary surname Delbec. A third

line, of Norman origin, is recorded in Montreal in 1681; and another, of unknown origin, is documented in Sorel, Canada, in 1698 with the secondary surname LAFOREST.
GIVEN NAMES French 18%. *Lucien* (7), *Armand* (4), *Pascal* (2), *Philippe* (2), *Pierre* (2), *Alain, Alberic, Alphonse, Anatole, Andre, Christophe, Frederique.*

Jon (112) Korean: variant of CHON.
GIVEN NAMES Korean 9%; Spanish 8%. *Eun, Jeon, Won, Young Hee, Yung; Domingo* (2), *Carlos, Maria Luisa, Ruben.*

Jonaitis (134) Lithuanian: from the personal name *Jonas,* Lithuanian form of *Johannes* (see JOHN).
GIVEN NAMES Lithuanian 6%. *Aldona, Antanas, Kazys, Vytautas.*

Jonak (132) **1.** Polish (**Jonák**): patronymic from the personal name *Jon,* a dialect form of JAN, or *Jonasz.* **2.** Czech and Slovak (**Jonák**): from a pet form of the personal name *Jonáš* (see JONAS).
GIVEN NAMES Polish 5%; German 4%. *Grazyna* (2), *Waclaw; Hermann, Johann.*

Jonas (3241) **1.** English, German, French, Jewish (Ashkenazic), Lithuanian, Czech, and Slovak (**Jonáš**), and Hungarian (**Jónás**): from a medieval personal name, which comes from the Hebrew male personal name *Yona,* meaning 'dove'. In the book of the Bible which bears his name, Jonah was appointed by God to preach repentance to the city of Nineveh, but tried to flee instead to Tarshish. On the voyage to Tarshish, a great storm blew up, and Jonah was thrown overboard by his shipmates to appease God's wrath, swallowed by a great fish, and delivered by it on the shores of Nineveh. This story exercised a powerful hold on the popular imagination in medieval Europe, and the personal name was a relatively common choice. The Hebrew name and its reflexes in other languages (for example Yiddish *Yoyne*) have been popular Jewish personal names for generations. There are also saints, martyrs, and bishops called *Jonas* venerated in the Orthodox Church. **Ionas** is found as a Greek family name. **2.** Jewish (Ashkenazic): respelling of *Yonis,* with Yiddish possessive *-s*.

Jonason (119) Americanized spelling of JONASSON or JONASSEN.

Jonassen (137) German, Danish, and Norwegian: patronymic from the Biblical personal name JONAS.
GIVEN NAMES Scandinavian 35%; German 8%. *Sven* (3), *Bjorg, Johan, Jorgen, Lars, Tor; Hans* (3), *Otto* (2).

Jonasson (150) **1.** Swedish: patronymic from the Biblical personal name JONAS. **2.** Respelling of JONASSEN.
GIVEN NAMES Scandinavian 18%; German 6%. *Anders* (2), *Erik, Klas, Lars, Per; Ernst.*

Jonathan (131) Jewish and Gentile (from northern Europe to South India): from the

Biblical name *Jonathan*, meaning 'God has given' in Hebrew. In the Bible this is the name of a son of King Saul, the close friend of the young David, whose friendship persisted even when Saul and David are themselves at loggerheads (1 Samuel 31; 2 Samuel 1:19–26). In South India, this is found as a personal name among Christians, and in the U.S. it has come to be used as a family name among South Indian Christians.

GIVEN NAMES Jewish 5%; Indian 5%. *Kaplan*, *Mayer*; *Basdeo*, *Sampath*.

Joncas (159) Southern French: topographic name from Occitan *jouncas* 'place where there is an abundance of reeds'.

FOREBEARS A Joncas from Gascony is documented in Sainte-Famille, Quebec, in 1672, with the secondary surname LAPIERRE.

GIVEN NAMES French 13%. *Armand* (3), *Adelard*, *Chanel*, *Emile*, *Jacques*, *Luc*.

Jone (149) English: from a medieval form of the personal name JOHN.

Jones (432177) English and Welsh: patronymic from the Middle English personal name *Jon(e)* (see JOHN). The surname is especially common in Wales and southern central England. In North America this name has absorbed various cognate and like-sounding surnames from other languages. (For forms, see Hanks and Hodges 1988).

Jong (275) **1.** Dutch, Frisian, and North German: distinguishing name, from Middle Dutch *de jonc* 'the young', for the younger of two bearers of the same name, usually a son who bore the same name as his father. **2.** Korean: variant of CHONG. **3.** Chinese: see ZHONG.

GIVEN NAMES Chinese/Korean 16%. *Gwo* (2), *Lei* (2), *Soo* (2), *Cheong*, *Chun Ming*, *Haewon*, *Huimin*, *In*, *Jung*, *Keun*, *Min Young*, *Myong Ja*; *Chang*, *Pak*, *Tuong*.

Jongsma (134) Frisian: patronymic from JONG.

GIVEN NAMES Dutch 5%. *Cornelus*, *Harm*, *Hendrik*.

Jonke (105) German: **1.** nickname from a diminutive of Middle High German *junc*, Middle Low German *junk* 'young'. **2.** (also **Jönke**): from a pet form of *Jo(h)n*, a reduced form of *Johannes* (see JOHN).

GIVEN NAMES German 19%; Scandinavian 5%. *Alois* (2), *Guenter* (2), *Erna*, *Erwin*, *Frieda*, *Otto*; *Johan*.

Jonker (271) Dutch and North German: from Middle Dutch *jonghheer* 'young nobleman' (a compound of *jong(h)* 'young' + *herr* 'master', 'lord'). The term was used of a member of the nobility who had not yet assumed knighthood.

GIVEN NAMES Dutch 7%. *Bartel* (2), *Berend*, *Henk*, *Martien*, *Nelvie*, *Willem*.

Jons (153) **1.** Dutch, North German, Danish, and Swedish (**Jöns**): from a reduced form of the personal name *Johannes*

(see JOHN). **2.** reduced form of Latvian **Jonas**.

GIVEN NAMES German 4%. *Claus*, *Otto*.

Jonson (379) **1.** English: patronymic from JOHN. **2.** Respelling of Swedish JONSSON.

GIVEN NAMES Scandinavian 8%. *Erik* (4), *Lars*, *Sven*.

Jonsson (462) Swedish: patronymic from the personal name *Jon*, Scandinavian form of JOHN.

GIVEN NAMES Scandinavian 44%; German 6%. *Nils* (5), *Lars* (3), *Lennart* (3), *Thor* (3), *Alf* (2), *Anders* (2), *Arni* (2), *Erik* (2), *Jorgen* (2), *Mats* (2), *Olafur* (2), *Per* (2); *Hans* (3), *Kurt* (2), *Egon*, *Hannes*, *Johann*, *Johannes*.

Joo (516) **1.** Chinese and Korean: variant of CHU. **2.** Hungarian: archaic spelling variant of **Jó** (see JO).

GIVEN NAMES Chinese/Korean 60%. *Sung* (10), *Young* (6), *Jae* (4), *Sun* (4), *Yong* (4), *Dong* (3), *Han* (3), *Jung* (3), *Sang* (3), *Yoon* (3), *Young Sook* (3), *Hyun* (2); *Byung* (2), *Chang* (2), *In Suk* (2), *Sunyoung* (2), *Young Kun* (2), *Beom*, *Byung Hee*, *Chong*, *Chong Sun*, *Chul*, *Chung*, *Dae*.

Joos (509) **1.** Dutch, South and Swiss German: variant of JOST. **2.** Hungarian: archaic form of the family name *Jós* meaning 'fortune teller'.

Joost (225) **1.** Dutch, South and Swiss German: variant of JOST. **2.** Hungarian: variant of JOOS.

GIVEN NAMES German 7%. *Lorenz* (2), *Horst*, *Wilhelm*.

Joosten (199) Dutch and German: patronymic form of JOST.

Joplin (731) English: patronymic from the Biblical personal name JOB.

Jopling (168) English: variant of JOPLIN.

Jopp (159) **1.** English: variant of JOB. **2.** South German: from the personal name, either a derivative of *Hiob*, the German form of JOB, or a reduced form of JAKOB.

GIVEN NAMES German 9%. *Erwin* (2), *Detlef*, *Gerhard*, *Hannelore*, *Willi*.

Jordahl (465) Norwegian: habitational name from any of several farmsteads; the name is a compound of an unidentified word (probably a river name meaning 'the shining river', Old Norse *Hjó*) + Old Norse *dalr* 'valley'.

GIVEN NAMES Scandinavian 7%. *Erik* (2), *Juel*, *Lars*.

Jordal (104) Variant of Norwegian JORDAHL.

GIVEN NAMES German 7%. *Kurt* (2), *Otto*.

Jordan (63950) English, French, German, Polish, and Slovenian; Spanish and Hungarian (**Jordán**): from the Christian baptismal name *Jordan*. This is taken from the name of the river Jordan (Hebrew *Yarden*, a derivative of *yarad* 'to go down', i.e. to the Dead Sea). At the time of the Crusades it was common practice for crusaders and pilgrims to bring back flasks of water from the river in which John the

Baptist had baptized people, including Christ himself, and to use it in the christening of their own children. As a result *Jordan* became quite a common personal name.

Jorde (152) Norwegian: habitational name from any of numerous farmsteads so named, from Old Norse *gerði* 'enclosed land', 'field'.

GIVEN NAMES German 5%; Scandinavian 4%. *Klaus*, *Ulrich*; *Bjorn*.

Jorden (480) **1.** English: variant spelling of JORDAN. **2.** North German (mostly **Jörden**): probably a variant of JORDAN.

Jordison (118) Northern English: patronymic from a pet form of the personal name JORDAN.

Jordon (1668) English and French: variant spelling of JORDAN.

Jorge (779) Spanish and Portuguese: from the personal name *Jorge*, a borrowing of French (and English) GEORGE.

GIVEN NAMES Spanish 47%; Portuguese 17%. *Jose* (33), *Manuel* (17), *Carlos* (12), *Juan* (11), *Luis* (8), *Fernando* (7), *Jorge* (6), *Mario* (6), *Miguel* (6), *Pedro* (6), *Francisco* (5), *Mercedes* (5); *Joao* (5), *Amadeu*, *Anabela*, *Duarte*, *Joaquim*, *Serafim*.

Jorgensen (8606) Danish, Norwegian (**Jørgensen**), and North German (**Jörgensen**): patronymic from the personal name *Jörgen*, a vernacular form of Greek *Geōrgios* (see GEORGE).

GIVEN NAMES Scandinavian 8%. *Erik* (29), *Jorgen* (10), *Nels* (9), *Lars* (8), *Niels* (7), *Holger* (6), *Anders* (3), *Borge* (3), *Einer* (3), *Folmer* (3), *Morten* (3), *Bjorn* (2).

Jorgenson (3041) Respelling of *Jørgensen* or *Jörgensen* (see JORGENSEN) or the Swedish cognate **Jörgens(s)on**.

GIVEN NAMES Scandinavian 4%. *Nels* (4), *Alf* (3), *Erik* (2), *Iver* (2), *Jorgen* (2), *Dagny*, *Einer*, *Helmer*, *Hjalmer*, *Holger*, *Knute*, *Ove*.

Jorissen (113) Dutch: patronymic from the personal name *Joris*, a vernacular form of GEORGE.

GIVEN NAME French 4%. *Andre*.

Jorn (107) North German (**Jörn**): from a short form of *Jörgen*, a variant of *Jürgen*; a German form of GEORGE.

Jorns (132) North German (**Jörns**): patronymic from the personal name *Jörn* (see JORN).

Jorstad (285) Norwegian: habitational name from any of seven farmsteads named Jørstad, from the Old Norse personal names *Jǫrundr* (composed of elements meaning 'battle' + 'winner', 'victor') or *Jórulfr* ('wild boar (helmet)' + 'wolf') + *staðr* 'farm'.

GIVEN NAMES Scandinavian 10%. *Lars*, *Ottar*, *Sig*.

Jory (201) Southern French: from the personal name, the Occitan form of GEORGE.

Jose (1293) **1.** Spanish, Portuguese, French (**José**): from the personal name

José, equivalent to JOSEPH. **2.** English: variant of JOYCE.

GIVEN NAMES Spanish 22%; Portuguese 5%. *Manuel* (9), *Francisco* (6), *Ernesto* (5), *Jose* (5), *Joselito* (4), *Rogelio* (4), *Armando* (3), *Luis* (3), *Mario* (3), *Roberto* (3), *Aurelio* (2), *Bernardo* (2); *Caetano*, *Henrique*, *Ilidio*.

Joseph (19388) English, German, French, and Jewish: from the personal name, Hebrew *Yosef* 'may He (God) add (another son)'. In medieval Europe this name was borne frequently but not exclusively by Jews; the usual medieval English vernacular form is represented by JESSUP. In the Book of Genesis, Joseph is the favorite son of Jacob, who is sold into slavery by his brothers but rises to become a leading minister in Egypt (Genesis 37–50). In the New Testament Joseph is the husband of the Virgin Mary, which accounts for the popularity of the given name among Christians. FOREBEARS A bearer of the name Joseph with the secondary surname **Langoumois** (and therefore presumably from the Angoumois) is documented in Quebec city in 1718.

GIVEN NAMES French 7%. *Pierre* (32), *Andre* (16), *Jacques* (14), *Francois* (13), *Antoine* (10), *Emile* (9), *Michel* (7), *Serge* (7), *Solange* (7), *Marcel* (6), *Etienne* (5), *Lucien* (5).

Josephs (862) English, German, and Jewish: patronymic from JOSEPH.

Josephsen (124) North German and Danish: patronymic from the personal name JOSEPH.

GIVEN NAMES German 4%; Scandinavian 4%. *Hans, Ute*.

Josephson (1700) **1.** English: patronymic from JOSEPH. **2.** Americanized spelling of Swedish **Josefsson** or Danish JOSEPHSEN.

Josey (1226) English: from a pet form of JOSEPH.

Joshi (1098) Indian: Hindu (Brahman) name, from Sanskrit *jyotiṣī* 'astrologer'.

GIVEN NAMES Indian 93%. *Ramesh* (13), *Vijay* (13), *Arun* (12), *Anil* (11), *Bharat* (10), *Prakash* (10), *Mahesh* (9), *Sanjay* (9), *Kirit* (7), *Rakesh* (7), *Satish* (7), *Arvind* (6).

Joshua (473) Jewish and Gentile (from northern Europe to South India): from the Biblical name, Hebrew *Yehoshuah*, meaning 'may Jehovah help him'. It was borne by the Israelite leader who took command of the children of Israel after the death of Moses and led them to take possession of the promised land. In Britain this was a popular name among Nonconformists from the 17th century onward; as a result, it is a typically Welsh surname, since Welsh surnames were comparatively late in formation. It is also used as a personal name among Christians in India, and in the U.S. has come to be used as a family name among families from southern India.

GIVEN NAMES French 6%; Jewish 5%; Indian

4%. *Camile, Camille, Celina, Curley, Emile, Lucien, Oliva; Moshe* (2), *Nadav* (2), *Ayal, Cohen; Baskaran, Ranjan, Sarath, Sudhir, Suresh, Vijay*.

Joslin (2632) English: from an Old French personal name imported into England by the Normans in the forms *Goscelin, Gosselin, Joscelin*. For the most part it is from the Germanic personal name *Gauzelin*, a diminutive from a short form of the various compound names having as their first element the tribal name *Gaut* (apparently the same word as Old English *Gēatas*, the Scandinavian people to which Beowulf belonged, and also akin to the ethnic name *Goth*). However, the name also came to be considered as a pet form of Old French *Josse* (see JOYCE).

Joslyn (1027) English: variant spelling of JOSLIN.

Joss (348) English and German: from the Breton personal name *Iodoc* (Latinized as *Jodocus*) (see JOYCE).

GIVEN NAMES German 5%. *Erwin, Fritz, Kurt, Otto*.

Jossart (109) French (mainly Belgium): variant of GOSSARD.

Josselyn (275) English: variant spelling of JOSLIN. FOREBEARS The Josselyn name appears in Black Point (now Scarborough, ME) before 1638, when the author John Josselyn came to visit his brother Henry, who was for many years a principal representative in eastern New England of the interests of the Mason and Gorges heirs, which were endangered by the Massachusetts Bay colony's expansion into Maine. Their father was Sir Thomas Josselyn, of Torrell's Hall in Willingale, Essex, England.

Josserand (112) French: from a Germanic personal name composed of the tribal name *Gaut* + *hramn* 'crow'.

GIVEN NAMES French 6%. *Henri, Pierre*.

Jost (1675) Dutch and German: from a personal name, a derivative of the Breton personal name *Iodoc* (see JOYCE), or from the personal name *Just* (see JUST).

GIVEN NAMES German 4%. *Gerhard* (2), *Hans* (2), *Aloys, Erna, Erwin, Hans Peter, Heinz, Inge, Jurgen, Mathias, Reinhart*.

Jostad (100) Scandinavian: unexplained.

GIVEN NAMES Scandinavian 10%; German 4%. *Berger* (3), *Helmer*.

Josten (170) Dutch and German: patronymic from the personal name JOST.

Jostes (153) Dutch and North German: patronymic form from JOST.

Joswiak (143) Polish: variant spelling of **Jóźwiak** (see JOZWIAK).

Joswick (227) Americanized form of Polish JOZWIAK or of its German (Sorbian) cognate **Joswig**.

Jou (147) Chinese and Korean: variant of CHU.

GIVEN NAMES Chinese/Korean 22%. *Wen-Chin* (2), *Chi-Chang, Ching, Ding, Heng,*

Hong, Kuang, Pei, Sen, Shu-Ping, Tsung, Wen.

Joubert (976) Southern French and English (of Norman origin): from a Germanic personal name of uncertain origin. The first element is probably the tribal name *Gaut* (see JOSLIN); the second is *berht* 'bright', 'famous'. FOREBEARS The name is documented in 1665 in Trois Rivières, Quebec, with the secondary surname Desfontaines. A bearer from the Poitou region of France is recorded in 1669 in Quebec city. The secondary surname Chety is recorded in 1709.

GIVEN NAMES French 10%. *Lucien* (3), *Normand* (3), *Ulysse* (2), *Alphege, Andre, Andree, Etienne, Eugenie, Gabrielle, Gervais, Ivelisse, Jean-Paul*.

Jouett (171) Variant spelling of English JEWETT.

Jourdain (195) English and French: variant of JORDAN. FOREBEARS A Jourdain from the Saintonge region of France is recorded in Quebec city in 1676. Another, from the Savoie, is documented in 1688 in Lachine, Quebec, with the secondary surname Lafrizade. A third, from Provence, is documented in Champlain in 1688; and another, also called Labrosse, in Montreal in 1696. Other secondary surnames include BELLEROSE, LAFRANCE, and Saint-Louis.

GIVEN NAMES French 12%; German 4%. *Henri* (2), *Pierre* (2), *Jacques; Fritz, Hans, Rommel*.

Jourdan (831) English and French: variant of JORDAN. FOREBEARS A Jourdain from the Saintonge region of France is recorded in Quebec city in 1676. Another, from the Savoie, is documented in 1688 in Lachine, Quebec, with the secondary surname Lafrizade. A third, from Provence, is documented in Champlain in 1688; and another, also called Labrosse, in Montreal in 1696. Other secondary surnames include BELLEROSE, LAFRANCE, and Saint-Louis.

GIVEN NAMES French 4%. *Dominique, Gabrielle, Henri, Lucien, Pierre, Raoul, Yves*.

Jourden (106) Variant spelling of French JORDAN.

GIVEN NAMES French 4%. *Gaile, Ghislaine*.

Journey (384) **1.** English: unexplained; possibly of French origin (see 2). Compare JURNEY. **2.** Anglicized spelling of French **Journet** or **Journée**, from Old French *jornee*, a measure of land representing an area that could be ploughed in a day; hence a name for someone who owned or worked such an area.

Jovanovic (292) Serbian (**Jovanović**): patronymic from the personal name *Jovan*, vernacular form of Greek *Iōannēs* (see JOHN).

GIVEN NAMES South Slavic 59%. *Dusan* (5), *Goran* (5), *Slobodan* (4), *Petar* (3), *Milan*

(3), *Dejan* (2), *Dragutin* (2), *Drasko* (2), *Lazar* (2), *Ljubisa* (2), *Mile* (2), *Milorad* (2), *Predrag* (2), *Vladan* (2), *Milos*, *Miroslav*, *Radmila*.

Jovanovich (217) Serbian (**Jovanović**): see JOVANOVIC.
GIVEN NAMES South Slavic 12%. *Darinka*, *Dejan*, *Dragan*, *Marko*, *Milorad*, *Miodrag*, *Radovan*, *Slobodan*, *Stojan*, *Zivan*.

Jovel (137) Catalan: Castilianized form of Catalan **Jovell**, a metonymic occupational name for a maker of yokes or possibly for a plowman, from a diminutive of Catalan *jou* 'yoke'.
GIVEN NAMES Spanish 61%. *Jose* (7), *Ana* (3), *Carlos* (3), *Alfredo* (2), *Jesus* (2), *Juan* (2), *Juan Jose* (2), *Luis* (2), *Marcos* (2), *Margarita* (2), *Miguel Angel* (2), *Ana Gladys*.

Jow (97) Chinese 周: variant of ZHOU.
GIVEN NAMES Chinese 10%. *Hong*, *Kwok*, *Shee*, *Wai Lan*, *Wing*, *Yan*.

Jowdy (104) Origin unidentified.
GIVEN NAME French 6%. *Camille* (2).

Jowell (124) English: variant of JEWELL.

Jowers (1090) English: from Old French *jour* 'day', hence a nickname for a journeyman or day laborer.

Jowett (217) English: variant of JEWETT.

Joy (4807) English: nickname for a person of a cheerful disposition, from Middle English, Old French *joie*, *joye*. In some cases it may derive from a personal name (normally borne by women) of this origin, which was in sporadic use during the Middle Ages.
FOREBEARS Thomas Joy (*c.* 1610–78), an architect and builder born probably in Hingham, Norfolk, England, appears in land records in Boston, MA, in 1636. He had a considerable influence on Boston architecture.

Joya (169) Catalan: possibly a variant of HOYOS.
GIVEN NAMES Spanish 55%. *Jose* (8), *Juan* (4), *Pedro* (3), *Alejandro* (2), *Ana Julia* (2), *Carlos* (2), *Jorge* (2), *Jose Raul* (2), *Luis* (2), *Manuel* (2), *Mauricio* (2), *Rafael* (2).

Joyal (576) French: perhaps related to *joyau* 'jewelry'.
FOREBEARS A Joyal or Joyel from the Périgord region of France is recorded in 1676 Trois Rivières, Quebec, with the secondary surname Bergerac. Another, also called Saint-Quentin, is documented in Saint-François-du-Lac, Quebec, in 1716.
GIVEN NAMES French 9%. *Marcel* (3), *Armand* (2), *Euclide* (2), *Achille*, *Alcide*, *Collette*, *Fernand*, *Julien*, *Monique*, *Rosaire*.

Joyce (13460) English and Irish: from the Breton personal name *Iodoc*, a diminutive of *iudh* 'lord', introduced by the Normans in the form *Josse*. *Iodoc* was the name of a Breton prince and saint, the brother of *Iudicael* (see JEWELL), whose fame helped to spread the name through France and western Europe and, after the Norman Conquest, England as well. The name was occasionally borne also by women in the Middle Ages, but was predominantly a male name, by contrast with the present usage.
FOREBEARS The name Joyce was introduced to Ireland in the 12th century by Normans from Wales. A certain Thomas de Joise married the daughter of the prince of Thomond. It has been Gaelicized as **Seoighe** and is found mainly in Connemara.
GIVEN NAMES Irish 8%. *Brendan* (9), *Bridie* (3), *Declan* (2), *Eamon* (2), *Kieran* (2), *Liam* (2), *Brian Patrick*, *Conor*, *Cormac*, *John Patrick*, *Nuala*, *Siobhan*.

Joye (440) English: variant spelling of JOY.

Joyner (8871) English: variant spelling of JOINER.

Joynes (289) English: probably a variant of JONES. Compare JOINES.

Joynt (354) English: presumably from Old French *joint* 'united', 'joined'. The application as a surname is unclear.

Jozefowicz (84) Polish (**Józefowicz**): patronymic form the personal name *Józef* (see JOSEPH).
GIVEN NAMES Polish 11%. *Bronislaw*, *Danuta*, *Zygmunt*.

Jozwiak (789) Polish (**Józwiak**): patronymic from the personal name *Józwa*, a pet form of *Józef* (see JOSEPH).
GIVEN NAMES Polish 7%. *Jerzy* (2), *Pawel* (2), *Zygmunt* (2), *Andrzej*, *Beata*, *Danuta*, *Ewa*, *Janina*, *Janusz*, *Jozefa*, *Leslaw*.

Ju (373) **1.** Chinese 鞠: surname borne by descendants of a man named Ju, who lived during the early part of the Zhou dynasty (1122–221 BC). **2.** Chinese 朱: variant of ZHU 1. **3.** Korean: variant of CHU.
GIVEN NAMES Chinese/Korean 43%. *Young* (6), *Hong* (3), *Jae* (2), *Kil* (2), *Kong* (2), *Kyoung* (2), *Young Soo* (2), *Bu*, *Chang Ho*, *Chi*, *Chiping*, *Chun Hui*; *Jeong* (3), *Byung* (2), *Hyun Tae* (2), *Chang*, *Eun Young*, *Hyun Sun*, *Hyung Joon*, *In Suk*, *Jin-Young*, *Jong Sook*, *Jung Woo*, *Ki Hwan*.

Juaire (119) French: unexplained; perhaps a respelling of **Jouar**, from the Germanic personal name *Gauthard*, from the tribal name *Gaut* + *hard* 'hardy', 'strong'.
GIVEN NAMES French 7%. *Adelard*, *Armand*.

Juan (564) Spanish: from the personal name *Juan*, Spanish equivalent of JOHN.
GIVEN NAMES Spanish 40%. *Francisco* (6), *Juan* (5), *Domingo* (4), *Jose* (4), *Manuel* (4), *Alberto* (3), *Andres* (3), *Roberto* (3), *Santos* (3), *Alfredo* (2), *Carlos* (2), *Cesar* (2); *Antonio* (7), *Dario* (2), *Cesario*, *Clemente*, *Eligio*, *Leonardo*, *Lorenzo*, *Marino*, *Romeo*, *Sabastian*, *Severino*, *Siriaco*.

Juarez (6366) Spanish (**Juárez**): regional variant of **Suárez** (see SUAREZ).
GIVEN NAMES Spanish 50%. *Jose* (181), *Juan* (104), *Jesus* (61), *Manuel* (58), *Carlos* (57), *Francisco* (47), *Benito* (40), *Luis* (38), *Mario* (37), *Miguel* (34), *Raul* (33), *Armando* (31); *Antonio* (59), *Lorenzo* (10), *Leonardo* (7), *Marco* (7), *Heriberto* (4), *Luciano* (4), *Ciro* (3), *Filiberto* (3), *Lucio* (3), *Marco Antonio* (3), *Romeo* (3), *Amadeo* (2).

Juba (185) **1.** English (Leicestershire): possibly a variant spelling of **Jubber**, an occupational name for a maker either of woolen garments, from an agent derivative of Middle English *jube*, or of large vessels, from Middle English *jobbe*. Alternatively, it may derive from the personal name JOUBERT. **2.** Japanese (**Jūba**): 'ten places'. The name is not common in Japan.
GIVEN NAMES Japanese 4%. *Hisashi*, *Taka*.

Jubb (204) English: variant of JOB.

Jubert (155) **1.** French: variant spelling of JOUBERT. **2.** German:unexplained.
GIVEN NAME French 5%. *Andre* (2).

Jubinville (104) French: habitational name from Jubainville in the Vosges.
GIVEN NAMES French 18%. *Adrien*, *Alcide*, *Germain*, *Jacques*, *Pierre*.

Juby (125) English (East Anglia): variant of JOBE.

Juckett (188) Altered spelling of French CHOQUETTE.

Jud (129) **1.** Swiss German and Slovenian: ethnic name or nickname meaning 'Jew'. **2.** English: variant spelling of JUDD.
GIVEN NAMES German 11%. *Franz* (2), *Gerhard*, *Guenter*.

Juda (164) Jewish, German, and French: variant of JUDE.
GIVEN NAMES Polish 4%. *Janusz*, *Stanislawa*.

Judah (404) Jewish: variant of JUDE 1.
GIVEN NAME Jewish 4%. *Aviva*.

Juday (218) Origin unidentified. Compare JUDY.

Judd (6694) **1.** English: from a short form of JORDAN. **2.** German: variant of JUDE.

Jude (689) **1.** English, French, and German: from the vernacular form of the Hebrew personal name *Yehuda* 'Judah' (of unknown meaning). In the Bible, this is the name of Jacob's eldest son. It was not a popular name among Christians in medieval Europe, because of the associations it had with Judas Iscariot, the disciple who betrayed Christ for thirty pieces of silver. Among Jews, however, the Hebrew name and its reflexes in various Jewish languages (such as Yiddish *Yude*) have been popular for generations, and have given rise to many Jewish surnames. **2.** French: name for a Jew, Old French *jude* (Latin *Iudaeus*, Greek *Ioudaios*, from Hebrew *Yehudi* 'member of the tribe of Judah'). **3.** English: from a pet form of JORDAN.

Judge (3817) **1.** English: occupational name for an officer of justice or a nickname for a solemn and authoritative person thought to behave like a judge, from Middle English, Old French *juge* (Latin *iudex*, from *ius* 'law' + *dicere* to say), which replaced the Old English term *dēma*. Compare DEMPSTER. **2.** Irish: part translation of Gaelic **Mac an Bhreitheamhain**, later **Mac an Bhreithimh** 'son of the judge (*breitheamhnach*)'. Compare BRAIN.

Judice (426) **1.** Portuguese (**Júdice**): from the Italian occupational name GIUDICE 'judge'. **2.** In some cases, an American respelling of the Italian surname.
GIVEN NAMES French 5%. *Alcide, Angelle, Monique, Odette, Pierre, Remi, Roch*; *Murphy* (2), *Delma*.

Judkins (1861) English: possibly a patronymic from a pet form (with intrusive *d*) of *Juk*, a reduced form of the Breton personal name *Iudicael* (see JEWELL).

Judson (1724) English: patronymic from a short form of JORDAN.

Judy (2648) Perhaps an Americanized spelling of the French surname **Judet**, from a pet form of JUDE.

Jue (420) **1.** Possibly a respelling of English and Welsh DEW. **2.** Korean: variant of CHU. **3.** Chinese 阚: possibly a variant of QUE 4.
GIVEN NAMES Chinese/Korean 5%. *Dok, Fong, Foong, Haw, Hing, Jin, Jung, Leung, Li, Lim, Wah, Wing*.

Juedes (218) German (**Jüdes**): patronymic form of a personal name composed with *Jut*, from the ethnic name of the Jutes, a Germanic tribe of Denmark and northern Germany.

Juel (210) Danish and Norwegian: variant of JUHL.
GIVEN NAMES Scandinavian 4%. *Folmer, Johan, Niels, Thora*.

Juelfs (103) Frisian (**Jülfs**): related to **Jolfs**, a patronymic from the personal name *Jolleff*, a variant of *Godlef*.

Juenemann (181) German (**Jünemann**): habitational name for someone from Jühnde near Göttingen.

Juengel (97) German (**Jüngel**): nickname for a young person, from Middle High German *junc* 'young' + the diminutive suffix *-el*.

Juenger (254) German (**Jünger**): see JUNGER.

Juengling (111) German: nickname from German *Jüngling* 'youth', 'young man'.
GIVEN NAMES German 15%; French 8%. *Dietrich, Fritz, Hans, Heinz, Otto; Camille*.

Juergens (791) German (**Jürgens**): see JURGENS.
GIVEN NAMES German 5%. *Hans* (3), *Kurt* (2), *Bernhard, Detlef, Dieter, Gerhardt, Heinz, Otto*.

Juergensen (141) North German and Danish (**Jürgensen**): patronymic from the personal name *Jürgen*, Low German and Danish form of GEORGE.
GIVEN NAMES German 8%; Scandinavian 5%. *Hans* (3), *Gerd, Klaus, Kurt; Erik*.

Juers (120) **1.** North German and Frisian (**Jürs**): patronymic form from a northern form of the personal name *Georg* (see

GEORGE). Compare JURGENS. **2.** English: variant of JOWERS.
GIVEN NAMES German 6%. *Claus, Uwe*.

Juett (211) English: variant spelling of JEWETT.

Juhas (133) Americanized spelling of Hungarian **Juhász** (see JUHASZ).
GIVEN NAMES Hungarian 5%. *Attila, Ferenc, Gabor*.

Juhasz (499) Hungarian (**Juhász**): occupational name for a shepherd, from *juh* 'sheep' + the occupational suffix *-ász*.
GIVEN NAMES Hungarian 17%. *Bela* (8), *Tibor* (4), *Attila* (3), *Laszlo* (3), *Zoltan* (3), *Andras* (2), *Arpad* (2), *Barna* (2), *Imre* (2), *Sandor* (2), *Istvan, Janos*.

Juhl (906) **1.** Danish and Norwegian: nickname for someone who was born on Christmas Day or had some other connection with this time of year, from Old Norse *jól*. This was originally the name of a pagan midwinter festival, which was later appropriated by the Christian Church for celebration of the birth of Christ. **2.** German: in North Germany, an adoption of the Danish surname; elsewhere a nickname or topographic name from a Slavic stem *gol* 'naked', 'barren'.
GIVEN NAMES German 4%. *Ernst* (3), *Arno* (2), *Erwin, Heinz, Kurt*.

Juhlin (158) Swedish: ornamental name composed of an unexplained first element + *-(l)in*, a common suffix of Swedish surnames.
GIVEN NAME Scandinavian 7%; German 4%. *Nils*.

Juhnke (325) German: from Czech *Junek*, a diminutive of JUN.

Juillerat (127) French: from a derivative of *juillet* 'July', probably bestowed on someone born or baptized in July or on a foundling discovered in that month.

Jukes (205) English: patronymic from a short form of a Celtic personal name, Old Breton *Iudicael* (see JEWELL).

Jules (304) **1.** French: from a personal name (Latin JULIUS). The name was borne in the Middle Ages in honor of various minor Christian saints. **2.** English: patronymic or metronymic from a short form of JULIAN.
GIVEN NAMES French 27%. *Jacques* (3), *Andre* (2), *Celestin* (2), *Dominique, Emile, Etienne, Eugenie, Francois, Herve, Jean Robert, Lucien, Lude*.

Julia (154) Catalan (**Julià**): from the personal name *Julià*, Catalan form of JULIAN.
GIVEN NAMES Spanish 26%. *Juan Carlos* (2), *Luis* (2), *Miguel* (2), *Aida, Altagracia, Ana, Carlos, Conchita, Garcia, Gregorio, Gustavo, Jaime*.

Julian (4991) English (common in Devon and Cornwall), Spanish (**Julián**), and German: from a personal name, Latin *Iulianus*, a derivative of *Iulius* (see JULIUS), which was borne by a number of early saints. In Middle English the name was

borne in the same form by women, whence the modern girl's name *Gillian*.

Juliana (140) Spanish, Catalan, and southern Italian: feminine form of JULIANO.
GIVEN NAMES Spanish 6%. *Lopez, Mario, Marita*.

Juliano (1597) Catalan and southern Italian: from the personal name *Juliano* (see JULIAN). As an Italian name, it is a variant spelling of GIULIANO.
GIVEN NAMES Italian 10%. *Angelo* (10), *Antonio* (4), *Rocco* (4), *Salvatore* (3), *Amato* (2), *Carmela* (2), *Domenic* (2), *Pasquale* (2), *Amelio, Carmine, Domenica, Domenico*.

Julich (142) German: **1.** of the same origin as JUHL. **2.** (**Jülich**): habitational name for someone from Jülich in the Rhineland.
GIVEN NAMES German 8%. *Kurt* (3), *Otto*.

Julien (1242) **1.** French: from the personal name, French form of JULIAN. **2.** English: variant spelling of JULIAN.
FOREBEARS From the Dauphiné region of France, a Julien, also called Vantabon, is documented in Quebec city in 1654. A Julien or Jullien, from Poitou, is recorded in Quebec city in 1665. Other secondary surnames associated with this name include LeDragon and Saint-Julien.
GIVEN NAMES French 12%. *Pierre* (6), *Andre* (5), *Jacques* (3), *Michel* (3), *Antoine* (2), *Lucien* (2), *Marcel* (2), *Adelard, Ancil, Anite, Armand, Aubert*.

Julin (199) Swedish: probably a variant spelling of JUHLIN.
GIVEN NAMES Scandinavian 7%. *Erik, Helmer, Johan, Mats, Nils*.

Julio (192) Spanish and Portuguese (**Júlio**), and Italian: from the personal name *Julio*, a vernacular form of Latin JULIUS.
GIVEN NAMES Spanish 19%; Italian 8%. *Humberto* (2), *Adriano, Ambrocio, Americo, Amparo, Demetrio, Edilberto, Enedina, Francia, Jose, Luis, Luz; Antonio* (3), *Angelo, Lorenzo, Palma, Rocco*.

Julius (1172) From the Latin personal name *Julius*, an aristocratic Roman family name made famous by Julius Caesar, the first Roman emperor. The personal name was borne in the Middle Ages by various minor Christian saints, and was nearly as popular as its derivative JULIAN. As a modern surname it is found in various European languages, generally as a humanistic name or a re-Latinization of a vernacular form such as French JULES.

Julson (305) **1.** Norwegian: unexplained. **2.** English: patronymic from a short form of JULIAN.

July (160) Translation French **Juillet**, from the name of the month 'July', probably applied as a nickname for someone born or baptized in that month or for a foundling discovered in July.
FOREBEARS A Juillet, also called **Avignon**, and presumably from that city, is recorded in Trois Rivières, Quebec, in 1651.

Jumonville (229) French: altered form of a habitational name, perhaps from Jumeauville in Yvelines or Gémonville in Meurthe-et-Moselle.
GIVEN NAMES French 7%. *Alcee* (2), *Jean-Paul, Marcel*.

Jump (1349) English (Lancashire): unexplained.

Jumper (1055) English: unexplained.

Jun (671) **1.** Korean: variant of CHONG. **2.** Czech: nickname for a lively young man, *juný* (ultimately cognate with French JEUNE and English YOUNG).
GIVEN NAMES Korean 65%. *Soo* (9), *Yong* (9), *Young* (9), *Sung* (7), *Byung* (6), *Woo* (6), *Chol* (5), *Sang* (5), *Seong* (5), *Hyun* (4), *Hyung* (4), *Jong* (4), *Chang* (3), *Choon* (3), *In* (3), *Jung* (3), *Kwang* (3), *Kyung Soo* (3), *Jungwon* (2), *Ki Hwan* (2), *Min* (2), *Moon* (2), *Woon* (2), *Chong*.

Junck (106) Dutch: variant of DE JONG.

Juncker (139) German: variant spelling of JUNKER.
GIVEN NAMES German 6%. *Gunther, Klaus, Kurt*.

Junco (213) **1.** Spanish: topographic name for someone who lived where reeds grew, Spanish *junco*, from Latin *iuncus*. **2.** Asturian-Leonese: Castilianized form of **Xuncu**, a habitational name from either of two places in Asturies named with this word, especially the one in the district of Ribesella. **3.** Galician: Castilianized form of **Xunco**, a habitational name from a town of this name in Galicia.
GIVEN NAMES Spanish 44%. *Roberto* (5), *Carlos* (4), *Manuel* (4), *Ramon* (4), *Blanca* (3), *Jose* (3), *Ricardo* (3), *Alejandro* (2), *Ana* (2), *Francisco* (2), *Jorge* (2), *Juan* (2); *Antonio* (3), *Constantino, Maurio, Pio*.

Jundt (296) German (Upper Rhine and Switzerland): metronymic from a derivative of the female personal names *Junta* (from *Judinta*) or *Judith*.

June (1138) **1.** English: from French *jeune* 'young', a distinguishing name for the younger of two bearers of the same personal name. Compare YOUNG. **2.** Translation of French **Juin**, name of the month of June, probably applied as a nickname for someone born or baptized in that month or for a foundling discovered in June. This name is very frequent in LA.
FOREBEARS A Juin from La Rochelle is recorded in Saint-Jean, Quebec, in 1666.

Juneau (1115) French: probably from a derivative of *jeune* 'young'.
GIVEN NAMES French 8%. *Andre* (3), *Emile* (3), *Armand* (2), *Camille* (2), *Gaston* (2), *Jacques* (2), *Normand* (2), *Achille, Cecile, Dominique, Germaine, Irby*.

Junek (148) Czech: from a pet form of the personal name JUN.

Jung (5367) **1.** German: distinguishing epithet, from Middle High German *junc* 'young', for the younger of two bearers of the same personal name, usually a son who

bore the same name as his father. **2.** Jewish (Ashkenazic): from German *jung* 'young', given to or assumed by people who were young at the time when surname became obligatory. **3.** Chinese 容, 荣, 戎: variant of RONG. **4.** Chinese 钟, 仲, 钟: variant of ZHONG. **5.** Korean: variant of CHONG.
GIVEN NAMES Chinese/Korean 12%; German 5%. *Young* (22), *Sung* (12), *Kwang* (9), *Dong* (8), *Myung* (8), *Sun* (8), *Han* (7), *Ho* (7), *Jae* (7), *Hong* (6), *Jin* (6), *Kyung* (6); *Hans* (8), *Gerhard* (7), *Kurt* (7), *Erwin* (6), *Heinz* (4), *Otto* (4), *Lothar* (3), *Reinhold* (3), *Bernd* (2), *Dieter* (2), *Ernst* (2), *Fritz* (2).

Jungbluth (185) German: nickname for a young or impetuous man, from Middle High German *junc* 'young' + *bluot* 'blood'.
GIVEN NAME German 4%. *Achim*.

Junge (704) **1.** German and Jewish (Ashkenazic): variant of JUNG. **2.** Scandinavian: from an Old Danish personal name *Odhinkar*, composed of the elements *Óðinn* (the god) + *kárr* 'strong'.
GIVEN NAMES German 7%. *Claus* (4), *Fritz* (2), *Helmut* (2), *Kurt* (2), *Hans, Hartmut, Heinz, Jurgen, Otto, Wolfgang*.

Jungels (138) German (also **Jüngels**): common name in the Rhineland, a patronymic form of **Jüngel**, a pet form, according to Brechenmacher, of a Germanic personal name *Junk, Jungo* 'young', found as an element of place names and recorded sporadically up to the 15th century.

Junger (173) **1.** German (**Jünger**): distinguishing name, from Middle High German *jünger* 'younger', for the younger of two bearers of the same personal name, usually a son who bore the same name as his father. It is also found in eastern Slovenia. **2.** German and Jewish (Ashkenazic): descriptive nickname from Middle High German *junger*, German *Junger* 'young man'.
GIVEN NAMES French 7%; German 6%; Scandinavian 5%. *Marcel* (2), *Jacques, Pascal, Sylvain; Kurt, Wolfang; Anders*.

Jungers (334) Derivative of German JUNGER.

Junghans (144) German: distinguishing name (a compound of Middle High German *junc* 'young' + the personal name HANS) for the younger of two bearers of the same personal name, often a son who bore the same name as his father. Compare JUNG, JUNGER.
GIVEN NAMES German 7%; Scandinavian 4%. *Heinz, Lothar, Natascha; Helmer* (2).

Jungles (100) Probably an altered form of German JUNGELS or a variant spelling of **Junglas**, a compound of *jung* 'young' + *Clas*, a short form of *Claus* (see NIKOLAUS), literally 'young Claus', distinguishing junior from senior.

Jungling (147) German (**Jüngling**) and Jewish (Ashkenazic): nickname from German *Jüngling* 'youth', 'young man'.

Jungman (206) German and Jewish (Ashkenazic): variant of JUNGMANN.

Jungmann (143) German and Jewish (Ashkenazic): from German *Jung* 'young' + *Mann* 'man'.
GIVEN NAMES German 5%. *Erwin, Uwe*.

Jungwirth (329) German: distinguishing name, from Middle High German *junc* 'young' + *wirt* 'husband', 'master of the house', for a son or son-in-law. *Wirt* also came to mean 'innkeeper' and in some cases may have been applied in this sense.

Juniel (102) North German: perhaps a reduced form of **Jungnickel**, equivalent to *Nikolaus* junior, a distinguishing name (see NIKOLAUS).

Junior (415) **1.** Portuguese (**Júnior**): from a personal name, from Latin *junior*, comparative of *juvenis* 'young'. **2.** In some cases this may be a translation of for example German JUNG(ER).

Junk (531) South German: variant of JUNG.

Junker (1113) German: from Middle High German *junc herre* 'young nobleman' (literally 'young master'). In the Middle Ages the term denoted a member of the nobility who had not yet assumed knighthood.
GIVEN NAMES German 5%. *Kurt* (4), *Hans* (2), *Manfred* (2), *Bernhard, Detlef, Ernst, Gerhardt, Otto, Wilhelm*.

Junkin (477) Irish: reduced form of McJUNKIN, which is a patronymic based on the Middle English personal name JENKIN.

Junkins (672) **1.** English: variant of JENKINS. **2.** Irish: reduced form of McJUNKINS.

Juno (155) Origin unidentified. Possibly an altered form of French JUNOD or a much altered form of Italian GIOVANNI.
GIVEN NAMES Italian 4%. *Canio, Carlo*.

Junod (238) French: from a diminutive of **Jeune** (see LEJEUNE).
GIVEN NAMES French 5%. *Henri* (2), *Laurent*.

Junot (109) French: variant spelling of JUNOD.

Juntunen (450) Finnish: from a diminutive or genitive form of the personal name *Juntti* or *Juntto* (Finnish forms of *Johannes*; see JOHN) + the common surname suffix *-nen*.
GIVEN NAMES Finnish 4%. *Arvo, Eino, Ensio, Esa, Risto, Sulo, Tauno, Waino*.

Jupin (194) French: from a diminutive of Old French *jupe*, a term denoting a long woolen garment, hence a metonymic occupational name for a maker or seller (or a nickname for a wearer) of such garments. This word ultimately derives from Arabic.

Jupiter (186) Jewish (eastern Ashkenazic): ornamental name from German *Jupiter* 'Jupiter'.
GIVEN NAME Jewish 4%. *Oded* (2).

Jura (146) **1.** Romanian, Polish, and Czech (Moravian): from the Slavic personal name *Jura*, a vernacular form of Greek *Geōrgios* (see GEORGE). **2.** Croatian: from a short form of the personal name *Juraj*, a vernacular form of Greek *Geōrgios* (see GEORGE).

GIVEN NAMES Romanian 6%; Polish 4%. *Ionel* (2), *Vasile* (2); *Janusz, Jerzy*.

Juracek (101) Czech (Moravian; **Juráček**): from a pet form of the personal name JURA, Moravian form of *Jiří*, Old Czech *Juřie*.

GIVEN NAMES German 6%. *Kurt, Otto, Rudie*.

Jurado (812) Spanish and Portuguese: occupational name for any of various officials who had to take an oath that they would perform their duty properly, from *jurado* 'sworn', past participle of *jurar* 'to swear' (Latin *iurare*).

GIVEN NAMES Spanish 47%. *Jose* (15), *Manuel* (12), *Carlos* (10), *Francisco* (6), *Jaime* (6), *Jesus* (6), *Ricardo* (6), *Juan* (5), *Rafael* (5), *Alfonso* (4), *Armando* (4), *Jorge* (4).

Juran (265) Czech and Slovak (**Juraň**, **Juráň**) and Croatian: from a derivative of the personal name, Czech (Moravian dialect) *Jura*, Croatian *Juraj*, vernacular forms of Greek *Geōrgios* (see GEORGE).

GIVEN NAMES German 4%. *Erwin, Florian*.

Juranek (144) Czech (**Juránek**): from a pet form of the personal name *Jura*, a Moravian variant of the personal name *Jiří*, vernacular form of Greek *Geōrgios* (see GEORGE).

Juras (160) Czech (Moravian), Slovak (**Juráš**), and Polish: from a pet form of a personal name *Jura*, an old or dialect vernacular form of Greek *Geōrgios* (see GEORGE).

Jurasek (132) Czech (**Jurásek**; Moravian): from a pet form of *Jura* (see JURANEK).

Jurczak (230) Polish: from a pet form of the personal name JUREK (see JURA).

GIVEN NAMES Polish 6%. *Franciszek, Jozef, Krzysztof, Wieslawa*.

Jurczyk (191) Polish: from a pet form of the personal name JUREK (see JURA).

GIVEN NAMES Polish 11%; German 7%. *Casimir, Jolanta, Karol, Krzysztof, Miroslaw, Stanislaw, Thadeus, Waclaw; Willi* (2), *Helmut, Volker*.

Jurek (737) Polish: from a pet form of the personal name JURA.

GIVEN NAMES Polish 4%. *Andrzej, Genowefa, Irena, Jozef, Ryszard, Stanislaw, Teofil, Wladyslaw, Zdzislaw*.

Jurewicz (349) Polish: patronymic from the personal name JURA.

GIVEN NAMES Polish 6%. *Witold* (2), *Mieczyslaw, Stanislaw, Waclaw, Zygmunt*.

Jurgens (1400) North German (**Jürgens**) and Dutch: patronymic from the personal name *Jürgen*, a vernacular form of the Greek Christian name *Geōrgios* (see GEORGE).

Jurgensen (781) North German (**Jürgensen**) and Scandinavian: patronymic from *Jürgen, Jørgen*, equivalents of GEORGE.

GIVEN NAMES Scandinavian 5%; German 4%. *Erik* (3), *Aagot, Niels; Hans, Hilde, Kurt, Uwe*.

Jurgenson (173) Scandinavian variant spelling or respelling of JURGENSEN.

GIVEN NAME German 5%. *Kurt* (2).

Jurica (199) **1.** Czech and Sovak: from a pet form of the personal name *Jura*, Moravian variant of *Jiři*, Czech form of Greek *Geōrgios* (see GEORGE). **2.** Southern Slavic: from a pet form of *Juraj, Jurij*, or *Jurije*, vernacular forms of Greek *Geōrgios* (see GEORGE). **3.** Americanized spelling of Hungarian *Gyurica*, pet form of the personal name *György*, vernacular form of Greek *Geōrgios* (see GEORGE).

Jurich (248) Croatian (**Jurić**); Slovenian **Jurič**: patronymic from the personal name *Juraj*, a vernacular form of Greek *Geōrgios* (see GEORGE).

GIVEN NAMES South Slavic 6%. *Rade* (2), *Marija, Slavko*.

Jurick (134) Germanized or Americanized spelling of Slovak JURIK.

Jurik (139) Slovak (**Jurík**): from a pet form of the personal name *Juri*, a vernacular form of Greek *Geōrgios* (see GEORGE).

Juris (193) Latvian, Czech, Slovak (**Juriš**), Sorbian, and Eastern German: derivative of the personal name *Juris* (Latvian) or *Jura* (Slavic), from Greek *Geōrgios* (see GEORGE).

Jurist (119) Americanized variant of JURIS.

Jurkiewicz (294) Polish: patronymic from the personal name JUREK, a pet form of JURA.

GIVEN NAMES Polish 5%. *Boleslaw, Genowefa, Iwona, Janusz, Kazimierz*.

Jurkovich (153) Croatian (**Jurković**) and Slovenian (**Jurkovič**): patronymic from the personal name *Jurko*, pet form of *Juraj* and *Jurij*, Croatian and Slovenian forms respectively of GEORGE.

Jurkowski (376) Polish: habitational name for someone from Jurkowo, Jurków, Jurkowice, or other places named with the personal name JUREK.

GIVEN NAMES Polish 9%. *Bronislaw, Franciszek, Grzegorz, Halina, Piotr, Ryscard, Stanislaw, Tomasz, Wieslaw, Zbigniew*.

Jurman (110) Slovenian: derivative of the personal name *Jurij*, Slovenian form of GEORGE, formed with the suffix *-man* 'man'. See also YURMAN.

Jurney (208) See JOURNEY. This name is found mainly in NC and TX.

Jurrens (128) North German (**Jürrens**): altered form of JURGENS.

Jurs (167) **1.** Danish and North German (**Jürs**): patronymic from a vernacular form of GEORGE. **2.** Latvian: variant of JURIS.

Jury (812) English: habitational name from Middle English, Old French *ju(ie)rie* 'Jewish quarter', often denoting a non-Jew living in the Jewish quarter of a town, rather than a Jew. Most medieval English cities had their Jewish quarters, at least until King Edward I's attempted expulsion of the Jews from England in 1290. This did not succeed in expelling the Jews, but it did

give a license to persecution and so broke up many of the old Jewish quarters.

Jusino (174) Hispanic (Puerto Rico): unexplained.

GIVEN NAMES Spanish 42%. *Jose* (6), *Juan* (6), *Carlos* (4), *Luis* (4), *Angel* (2), *Cesar* (2), *Efrain* (2), *Jaime* (2), *Pablo* (2), *Pedro* (2), *Ramon* (2), *Santiago* (2).

Juska (108) Lithuanian: from a pet form of the personal name *Justus* (see JUST).

GIVEN NAMES Lithuanian 13%. *Aldona, Alfonsas, Algimantas, Arunas, Birute, Gintaras, Vilius*.

Jusko (151) Polish (**Juszko**): from a pet form of any of the personal names JUST, *Justyn* (see JUSTIN), or JULIAN.

GIVEN NAMES Polish 4%. *Franciszek, Jolanta*.

Just (1620) **1.** French, English, German, Danish, Catalan, Polish, Czech, Slovak, and Hungarian: from a personal name, a vernacular form of Latin *Justus* meaning 'honorable', 'upright'. There were several early saints of this name, among them a 4th-century bishop of Lyon and a 6th-century bishop of Urgell in Catalonia. **2.** South and eastern German: variant of JOST.

GIVEN NAMES German 4%. *Kurt* (4), *Erwin* (2), *Christoph, Ernst, Gerhart, Heinz, Helmut, Hildegarde, Horst, Otto, Reinhard, Reinhold*.

Justen (244) German (also **Jüsten**): **1.** variant of JUST 1. **2.** variant of JOSTEN.

GIVEN NAMES German 8%. *Christoph* (2), *Frieda* (2), *Heinz, Kurt, Wolfgang*.

Juster (142) English: occupational name or nickname from Anglo-Norman French *justour* 'jouster', Old French *justeor*.

GIVEN NAME French 4%. *Alain*.

Justesen (256) Danish: patronymic from JUST.

GIVEN NAMES Scandinavian 10%. *Erik* (3), *Palle*.

Justi (105) Finnish: from a Finnish form of the personal name *Justus* (see JUST).

Justice (10175) English: nickname for a fair-minded man, from Middle English, Old French *justice* 'justice', 'equity', Latin *iustitia*, a derivative of *iustus* (see JUST). It may also have been an occupational name for a judge, since this metonymic use of the word is attested from as early as the 12th century.

Justin (754) French, English, Slovenian, etc.: from a medieval personal name, Latin *Justinus*, a derivative of *Justus* (see JUST). This name was borne by various early saints, including a 3rd-century Parisian martyr and the first archbishop of Tarbes.

Justiniano (224) Spanish: from the personal name, *Justiniano*, Latin *Justinianus*, a derivative of *Justinius*, from *justus* 'just', 'fair'.

GIVEN NAMES Spanish 39%. *Jose* (4), *Luis* (3), *Adalberto* (2), *Emilio* (2), *Juan* (2), *Manuel* (2), *Miguel* (2), *Pablo* (2), *Ramon* (2), *Ricardo* (2), *Roberto* (2), *Rogelio* (2).

Justis (548) Variant spelling of English JUSTICE.

Justiss (201) Variant spelling of English JUSTICE.

Justman (248) **1.** German (**Justmann**): elaborated form of JUST. **2.** Jewish (Ashkenazic): ornamental name from a German or Polish spelling of Yiddish *yust man* 'well-to-do man'.
GIVEN NAME German 4%. *Arno* (2).

Justo (172) Spanish and Portuguese: from the personal name *Justo*, Latin *Justus*, meaning 'honorable', 'upright' (see JUST).
GIVEN NAMES Spanish 40%; Portuguese 13%. *Jose* (4), *Eduardo* (2), *Emilio* (2), *Fernando* (2), *Manuel* (2), *Pedro* (2), *Adelino*, *Amado*, *Angel*, *Apolonio*, *Aurelio*, *Belen*; *Joao*, *Joaquim*; *Antonio* (3), *Carmelo*, *Paolo*.

Justus (2314) German: humanistic adoption of the Latin form of the personal name JUST.

Juszczak (117) Polish: patronymic from the personal name *Justek*, a pet form of JUST.
GIVEN NAMES Polish 30%. *Leszek* (2), *Agnieszka, Andrzej, Bronislaus, Eugeniusz, Iwan, Janina, Jerzy, Jozef, Krzysztof, Piotr, Slawomir.*

Jutila (113) Finnish: from the personal name *Jut(t)i*, a derivative of *Johannes* (see JOHN) + the local suffix *-la*. This name is found chiefly in central Finland.
GIVEN NAMES Finnish 7%. *Eino* (2), *Waino*.

Jutras (380) French: unexplained.
FOREBEARS A Jutras from Paris, with the secondary surname **Lavallé** is documented in Trois Rivières, Quebec, in 1657; a brother is documented with the secondary surname in Sorel in 1684.
GIVEN NAMES French 14%. *Armand* (3), *Andre* (2), *Adelard, Aime, Alphonse, Aurore, Benoit, Colombe, Donat, Germain, Laurent, Lucien.*

Jutte (170) German (**Jütte**): from a derivative of the female personal name *Juditha*, a variant of the Biblical name *Judith*.
GIVEN NAMES German 4%. *Aloys* (2), *Hans* (2).

Juul (246) Danish and Norwegian: variant of JUHL.
GIVEN NAMES Scandinavian 22%. *Einer* (2), *Erik* (2), *Niels* (2), *Sten* (2), *Sven* (2), *Nels, Ove.*

Juve (173) **1.** Norwegian: habitational name from any of several farmsteads so named, from *juv* 'gorge', 'ravine', a word of disputed origin. **2.** Catalan (**Juvé**): occupational name for a maker of yokes, Catalan *jover* (Latin *iugarius*, a derivative of *iugum* 'yoke'). This word was apparently also used as an occupational name for an oxherd.
GIVEN NAME Scandinavian 7%. *Selmer*.

K

Kaake (111) **1.** Dutch: perhaps an altered form of Dutch **Kaak**, from Middle Dutch *cake* 'jaw' or 'cheek', hence a descriptive nickname alluding to some facial peculiarity. **2.** Dutch: from Dutch *kaag* (earlier *kaack*), the same word as English *keg*. A *bierkaacker* was someone who used a beer hoist to carry and deliver kegs of beer. There was a Marten Hendricksz de Bierkaacker at Beverwijck (Albany) in the 17th century. **3.** North German: occupational name for a cook, from *Kaack(er)*, Low German equivalent of German KOCH.

Kaas (268) **1.** Dutch and North German: metonymic occupational name for a maker or seller of cheese, *kaas*. **2.** Norwegian: variant of KAASA, from the indefinite singular form. **3.** Danish: habitational name from a common place name or a topographic name from *kaas* 'landing place', 'quay'.
GIVEN NAMES Scandinavian 5%. *Erik* (2), *Ove*.

Kaasa (138) Norwegian: habitational name from any of various farmsteads named Kaasa, notably in Telemark, from the definite singular form of *kås*, from Old Norse *kǫs* 'heap', 'pile' (from cleared woodland).

Kaase (114) Scandinavian and North German: variant of KAAS.
GIVEN NAMES German 7%. *Erhard, Erwin*.

Kaatz (400) Jewish (Ashkenazic): variant of KATZ.
GIVEN NAMES German 6%. *Otto* (4), *Eldor, Gerda*.

Kaba (224) **1.** Muslim: from a personal name based on Arabic *ka'b* 'fame', 'glory'. This was the name of the ancestors of two different tribes in Mecca, Ka'b bin Rabiah and Ka'b bin Kilāb. The ka'ba is an Islamic sacred shrine in Mecca, and the personal name may also have been chosen with reference to this. **2.** Muslim: possibly also from a personal name based on Arabic *ka'ba* 'sorrow'. **3.** Japanese: 'birch tree'. The name is not common in Japan. **4.** Czech (**Kába**): from the personal name *Kába*, a derivative of the Biblical name GABRIEL. **5.** Hungarian: from *kaba* 'falcon', from Serbian and Croatian *koba*, *kobac* 'sparrowhawk', hence a nickname for someone thought to resemble a falcon, or a metonymic occupational name for a falconer. Alternatively, it may be a nickname for a slow-witted person, from *kába* 'slow', 'lethargic'. It could also be a habitational name from places so called in Szabolcs county in northern Hungary and in former Kűlső Szolnok county, now in Romania.
GIVEN NAMES Muslim 34%; Japanese 4%. *Karim* (3), *Lamine* (3), *Mohammed* (3), *Ibrahima* (2), *Mohamed* (2), *Abdoulaye, Amir, Fawaz, Khalil, Mahmoud, Mohamad, Moussa; Mamady* (7), *Amadou* (2), *Fatoumata, Mamadou, Oumar, Sekou; Masa, Shigeru, Yae*.

Kabacinski (110) Polish (**Kabaciński**): **1.** habitational name for someone from a place called Kabaty, in Warszawa voivodeship (see KABAT). **2.** from a derivative of the nickname KABAT.
GIVEN NAMES Polish 5%. *Alicja* (2), *Janina*.

Kabat (520) Polish, Ukrainian, Sorbian, Czech, Slovak, and Hungarian (**Kabát**): from Polish and Sorbian *kabat*, Czech, Slovak, and Hungarian *kabát* 'coat', 'jerkin', also 'military uniform', hence a metonymic occupational name for a maker of short coats or a nickname for a soldier. In Ukrainian the Polish loanword *kabat* also means 'skirt', and may have been applied as a nickname for an effeminate man.
GIVEN NAMES Polish 5%. *Irena* (3), *Ludwik, Ryszard, Slawomir, Tadeusz, Zbigniew, Zosia*.

Kabel (243) **1.** German: from Middle High German *kabel* 'rope', 'cable', hence a metonymic occupational name for a rope maker. The surname is found mainly in the North Sea ports. **2.** German: topographic name from Middle Low German *kabel* 'lot field'. This alludes to the custom in North Rhine-Westphalia of alloting communally-owned plots of land to individual farmers by the drawing of lots. **3.** Czech and Slovak (**Kabela**): nickname for a loud or boastful person, a big mouth, from *kabela* 'satchel', 'leather bag'.

Kaber (103) Muslim: variant of KABIR.

Kabir (200) Muslim: from a personal name based on Arabic *kabīr* 'splendid', 'magnificent'. *Al-Kabīr* 'the Magnificent' is an attribute of Allah.
GIVEN NAMES Muslim 85%. *Humayun* (16), *Mohammed* (16), *Mohammad* (9), *Syed* (4), *Alamgir* (3), *Ahmed* (2), *Khairul* (2), *Mohamed* (2), *Mohmmad* (2), *Muhammed* (2), *Abdul, Abu*.

Kable (187) Variant of German KABEL.

Kabler (192) Probably an eastern German variant of GABLER.

Kacer (168) **1.** Czech (**Kačer**), Slovak (**Káčer**), and Jewish (Ashkenazic): from Czech *kačer* 'drake', probably applied as a nickname for someone with some fancied resemblance to a drake, or perhaps a metonymic occupational name for a poultry seller. As a Jewish surname it is mainly ornamental. **2.** Hungarian (**Kacér**): nickname from *kacér* 'immoral', 'narcissistic', 'seductive' (from Middle High German *kether, ketzer, katzer* 'heretic', 'sodomite').

Kach (122) German: nickname for someone with a loud laugh, from a noun derivative of Middle High German *kachen* 'to laugh'.

Kachel (319) German and Jewish (Ashkenazic): metonymic occupational name for a potter, from Middle High German *kachel* 'pot', 'earthenware vessel'. The surname is common in the Alemannic and Swabian regions. The modern German sense 'glazed tile' is a fairly recent development, and probably has not contributed to the surname. Compare EULER, HAFNER, and **Töpfer** (see TOEPFER).

Kacher (132) **1.** German: nickname for someone with a loud laugh, from an agent derivative of Middle High German *kachen* 'to laugh'. **2.** Americanized spelling of KACER, KACHUR, or KACZOR. **3.** Jewish (from Ukraine): ornamental name from Yiddish *katsher* 'drake'. Compare KACER.
GIVEN NAMES Russian 9%; Czech and Slovak 4%; Jewish 4%. *Betya, Dmitriy, Gennady, Yefim, Yeva; Petr* (2); *Genya, Josif, Semen*.

Kachmar (197) Americanized spelling of a Slavic surname meaning 'innkeeper', for example Czech **Kačmář**, **Krčmář**, Slovak **Krčmár**, or Polish **Ka(r)czmarz** (see KACZMAR). Compare German KRETSCHMER.

Kachur (195) Ukrainian and Jewish (from Ukraine): from Ukrainian *kachur* 'drake', applied as a nickname, a metonymic occupational name for a fowler, or (among Jews) an ornamental name (see KACER, and compare Polish KACZOR).

Kackley (274) Probably an Americanized spelling of German **Kächele**, **Kachler** or **Kächler**, occupational names for a potter, from Middle High German *kachel* 'pot', 'earthenware vessel' + the agent suffix *-er* (see KACHEL).

Kaczanowski (105) Polish: habitational name for someone from any of various places called Kaczanów or Kaczanowo, named with Polish *kaczan* 'cob'.
GIVEN NAMES Polish 11%. *Ewa, Jozefa, Krystyna, Witold*.

Kaczka (120) Polish: nickname from *kaczka* 'duck'.

GIVEN NAME Polish 5%. *Krzysztof*.

Kaczkowski (115) Polish: habitational name for someone from any of various places in Poland called Kaczków or Kaczkowice, named with Polish *kaczka* 'duck'.

GIVEN NAMES Polish 15%. *Basia, Casimir, Halina, Karol, Pawel, Stanislaw, Zbigniew*.

Kaczmar (99) Partly Americanized spelling of Polish **Kaczmarz** 'innkeeper'. The Polish name is itself an altered form of the older Polish word *karczmarz*.

Kaczmarczyk (414) Polish: from a diminutive of *ka(r)czmarz* 'innkeeper' (see KACZMAR).

GIVEN NAMES Polish 11%. *Casimir* (3), *Wieslaw* (2), *Andrzej, Franciszek, Janusz, Jozef, Lucjan, Maciej, Mariusz, Miroslaw, Stanislaw, Wladyslaw*.

Kaczmarek (1539) Polish: from a pet form or patronymic from *ka(r)czmarz* 'innkeeper' (see KACZMAR).

GIVEN NAMES Polish 5%. *Elzbieta* (3), *Boleslaw* (2), *Piotr* (2), *Zygmund* (2), *Casimir, Ewa, Franciszek, Jacek, Jadwiga, Janina, Jaroslaw, Kazimierz*.

Kaczmarski (247) Polish: occupational name from *ka(r)czmarz* 'innkeeper' + the common surname suffix *-ski*.

GIVEN NAMES Polish 5%. *Janusz, Mariusz, Wojciech*.

Kaczor (593) **1.** Polish and Jewish (from Poland): from Polish *kaczor* 'drake', applied either as a nickname or (especially among Jews) as an ornamental name. **2.** Hungarian: nickname from Slovak *kocúr* 'tom cat'; alternatively it may be from Hungarian *kacor* 'curved knife' (from Southern Slav *koser, kosir, kosor*), perhaps as a metonymic occupational name for a maker or user of such knives.

GIVEN NAMES Polish 10%. *Jozef* (2), *Krystyna* (2), *Mieczyslaw* (2), *Ryszard* (2), *Andrzej, Bronislaw, Casimir, Franciszek, Irena, Jadwiga, Jerzy*.

Kaczorowski (302) Polish: habitational name for someone from any of various places called Kaczorów, Kaczorowo, or Kaczorowice, named with *kaczor* 'drake' (see KACZOR).

GIVEN NAMES Polish 9%. *Zygmunt* (2), *Bronislawa, Casimir, Henryka, Jerzy, Pawel, Tadeusz, Waclaw, Zofia*.

Kaczynski (534) Polish (**Kaczyński**) and Jewish (eastern Ashkenazic): habitational name for someone from a place called Kaczyn, Kaczyna, or Kaczyniec in Poland.

GIVEN NAMES Polish 9%. *Czeslaw* (2), *Jozef* (2), *Krzysztof* (2), *Casimir, Henryk, Jacek, Jaroslaw, Piotr, Stanislaw, Tadeusz, Tomasz, Wieslaw*.

Kadakia (124) Indian (Gujarat): Hindu (Vania) name of unknown meaning.

GIVEN NAMES Indian 95%. *Ajay* (4), *Ashok* (3), *Rajesh* (3), *Sailesh* (3), *Sunil* (3), *Geeta*

(2), *Jayant* (2), *Mitesh* (2), *Mohit* (2), *Pratish* (2), *Rajendra* (2), *Rakesh* (2).

Kadar (209) **1.** Hungarian (**Kádár**) and Slovak (**Kadár**): occupational name for a cooper, from Hungarian *kádár*, a Slavic loanword. **2.** Hungarian: from a personal name in Hun mythology. In 19th-century Hungarian romantic literature this was taken as a common noun meaning 'judge' or 'chieftain', from the time of the Magyar conquest of the Carpathian Basin. **3.** Jewish: in some cases an adoption of the Hungarian name; in others a variant of KADER.

GIVEN NAMES Hungarian 14%. *Sandor* (4), *Geza* (2), *Laszlo* (2), *Arpad, Miklos, Zoltan, Zsuzsanna*.

Kade (162) **1.** German: habitational name for someone from a place called Kade near Magdeburg, Kaaden (German name of *Kadeň* in North Bohemia), or Kaden in Westerwald. **2.** Czech (**Káde**): nickname for a fat man, from *kád'* 'tub', 'vat'. **3.** Indian (Maharashtra); pronounced as two syllables: Hindu (Maratha) name of unknown meaning.

GIVEN NAMES Indian 6%; German 6%. *Nirmal* (2), *Hemant; Joerg* (2), *Helmut*.

Kadel (408) South German and Austrian: **1.** from a pet form of the personal name *Konrad*. **2.** metonymic occupational name for a chimneysweep, from Middle High German *kadel* 'soot', 'dust', a word of Slavic origin.

Kaden (229) German: habitational name for someone from Kaaden (Czech Kadeň) in North Bohemia, or any of several other places called Kaden, examples of which are found in Schleswig-Holstein and in the Westerwald, near Koblenz.

GIVEN NAMES German 6%. *Ewald, Reinhard, Ute*.

Kader (283) **1.** Muslim: from a personal name based on Arabic *qādir* 'powerful' or *qadīr* 'able', 'capable'. Both *Al-Qādir* 'the All-Powerful' and *Al-Qadīr* 'the Capable' are attributes of Allah. *Qādir* is found in combinations such as *'Abd-ul-Qādir* 'servant of the All-Powerful' or *Nur-ul-Qādir* 'light of the All-Powerful'. 'Abdul-Qādir al-Jīlānī (1077–1166) was one of the most celebrated Sufis in Islam. **2.** Jewish (eastern Ashkenazic): occupational name from Hebrew *qador* 'potter'. **3.** Czech (**Kaděr**): nickname for someone with curly hair, from *kadeř* 'curl', now a rather old-fashioned term. Compare KUDRNA. **4.** German: perhaps from the Germanic personal name *Cado*.

GIVEN NAMES Muslim 31%. *Abdul* (5), *Gihan* (3), *Ahmed* (2), *Fuad* (2), *Mohamed* (2), *Mohammed* (2), *Nabil* (2), *Abdullah, Adbul, Ahmad, Aiman, Amer*.

Kadera (104) Czech (**kadeřa**): nickname for a man with curly hair, from *kadeř* 'curl'.

Kaderabek (123) Czech (**kadeřabek**): nickname for a man with curly hair, from a derivative of *kadeř* 'curl'.

GIVEN NAME German 5%. *Otto* (2).

Kadin (129) Jewish (from Belarus): habitational name from the village of Kadino in eastern Belarus.

GIVEN NAMES Jewish 14%. *Sol* (2), *Aron, Bezalel, Nachum, Simcha, Yosef*.

Kading (388) Americanized spelling of German **Käding** (see KAEDING).

Kadinger (105) German (**Kädinger**): regional name for someone from Kehdingen (see KAEDING).

Kadis (122) **1.** Swiss German: unexplained. **2.** Jewish: variant of KADISH.

GIVEN NAMES Jewish 8%. *Irina, Mindel, Myer*.

Kadish (369) **1.** Jewish (eastern Ashkenazic): from the Yiddish personal name *kadish*, derived from Hebrew *qadish* 'prayer for the dead', 'heir'. **2.** German: from the old personal name *Cado*.

Kadlec (757) Czech: occupational name for a weaver, *(t)kadlec*.

Kadow (203) German: habitational name from a place of this name in Mecklenberg.

Kadrmas (229) Origin unidentified. In the U.S. this name is found almost exclusively in ND.

Kady (183) English: unexplained; perhaps a respelling of CADDY.

Kaechele (104) German (**Kächele**): variant of KACHEL.

GIVEN NAME German 7%. *Friedrich*.

Kaeding (252) German (**Käding**): **1.** regional name for someone from Kehdingen, an area on the Lower Elbe near Hamburg. **2.** possibly a patronymic from the old personal name *Cado*.

GIVEN NAMES German 7%. *Detlef* (2), *Erwin, Helmuth, Horst, Kurt*.

Kaefer (123) German (**Käfer**): see KAFER.

GIVEN NAME German 8%. *Kurt*.

Kaegi (113) South German and Swiss (**Kägi**): topographic name from Middle High German *gehage, gehegi* 'hedge', 'fence' (see KAGE).

GIVEN NAMES German 4%. *Armin, Erwin*.

Kaehler (374) North German (**Kähler**): occupational name from Low German *Kähler* 'charcoal burner'. Compare High German KOEHLER.

GIVEN NAMES German 4%. *Frieda, Hans, Uwe*.

Kaelber (112) German (**Kälber**): **1.** occupational name for someone who raised calves, from an agent derivative of Middle High German *kalp* 'calf'. **2.** topographic name for someone who lived by the Kalbe river in the Harz mountains.

GIVEN NAMES German 7%. *Kurt, Lutz*.

Kaelin (968) South German (also **Kälin**): of uncertain origin. Perhaps a nickname from Swiss German *chäli* 'weak old man with an unsteady gait'.

Kaercher (323) German (**Kärcher**; mainly Baden-Württemberg and Alsace): variant of KARCHER.

Kaeser (322) German: occupational name for a maker or seller of cheese, from an agent derivative of Middle High German *kæse* 'cheese'.
GIVEN NAMES German 6%. *Hans* (2), *Fritz, Kurt, Manfred*.

Kaestner (324) German: see KASTNER.
GIVEN NAMES German 6%. *Gottfried* (2), *Hellmut, Kurt, Uli, Wolfgang*.

Kaetzel (130) Jewish (Ashkenazic): diminutive of KATZ.

Kafer (316) **1.** German (**Käfer**): nickname from Middle High German *keveor* 'bug', 'beetle'. **2.** Possibly an altered spelling of German **Köfer**, from Low German *küfe* 'hut', 'pen', hence a nickname for someone living in a hut.

Kaffenberger (142) German: habitational name from a minor place called Kaffenberg, named with southern German dialect *kapf* 'mountain top' + *Berg* 'mountain', 'hill'.
GIVEN NAMES German 8%. *Ernst* (2), *Kurt*.

Kafka (725) **1.** Czech and Jewish (from Bohemia): nickname from *kavka* 'jackdaw', applied as a nickname, ornamental name, or habitational name for someone who lived at a house distinguished by the sign of a jackdaw. **2.** Jewish (from Bohemia): from a pet form of the personal name *Jakov* (see JACOB).

Kagan (1445) Jewish (eastern Ashkenazic): one of the many forms of COHEN.
GIVEN NAMES Jewish 13%; Russian 9%. *Yakov* (7), *Ilya* (4), *Ari* (3), *Dov* (3), *Meir* (2), *Myer* (2), *Naum* (2), *Shaul* (2), *Aron, Baruch, Basya, Elik*; *Boris* (15), *Vladimir* (7), *Leonid* (6), *Mikhail* (6), *Lev* (4), *Yefim* (3), *Michail* (2), *Mikhall* (2), *Savely* (2), *Sofiya* (2), *Alik, Anatoliy*.

Kagarise (124) Origin unidentified.

Kagawa (172) Japanese: 'fragrant river'; held by two families, one from *Kagawa* in Sagami (now Kanagawa prefecture), descended from the Kamakura branch of the TAIRA clan. The other family originated in Kagawa in Aki (now part of Hiroshima prefecture). In Okinawa, the name is written with characters meaning 'deer river'.
GIVEN NAMES Japanese 31%. *Hiroshi* (2), *Masaru* (2), *Hiromi, Kenso, Kiyomi, Kiyoshi, Mayumi, Mitsuyo, Mutsumi, Noboru, Norio, Osamu*.

Kage (184) German: of uncertain origin; perhaps a topographic name from a reduced form of Middle High German *gehage* 'hedge', 'fence', a term denoting an enclosed settlement in otherwise wild terrain; alternatively, it may be from a southern dialect word *Kage* 'cabbage stalk' and hence a metonymic occupational name for a cabbage grower. Cabbage was an important winter staple until recent times and was grown by some farmers mostly for seed. A third possible source is Middle Low German *koge, kage*, a term denoting a contagious (lung?) disease.
GIVEN NAMES German 6%. *Claus, Hermann, Wilhelm*.

Kagel (258) **1.** German: metonymic occupational name for a maker of hoods or hooded robes and cloaks, from Low German *Kogel, Kagel* (from Latin *cuculla* 'sphere'). **2.** German: variant of **Kögel** (see KOGEL).

Kagen (122) Jewish (eastern Ashkenazic): one of the many forms of COHEN.
GIVEN NAMES Jewish 7%; French 4%. *Hershel* (2); *Francoise, Laure*.

Kagey (147) Americanized form of South German and Swiss **Kägi** (see KAEGI).

Kagle (126) Americanized form of KEGEL, KAGEL, or **Kögel** (see KOGEL).

Kagy (154) Americanized form of the South German and Swiss surname **Kägi**, a topographic name from *Gehegi*, from Middle High German *gehage* 'hedge', 'fence' (see KAGE).
GIVEN NAMES French 5%. *Edmound, Serge*.

Kahan (920) Jewish (eastern Ashkenazic): one of the many forms of COHEN.
GIVEN NAMES Jewish 16%. *Yudel* (7), *Cheskel* (5), *Aron* (3), *Chaim* (3), *Mendel* (3), *Meyer* (3), *Moshe* (3), *Osher* (3), *Sol* (3), *Dov* (2), *Jenoe* (2), *Mayer* (2).

Kahana (115) Jewish (from Romania): variant of COHEN.
GIVEN NAMES Jewish 32%. *Emanuel* (3), *Nachman* (2), *Rivka* (2), *Zvi* (2), *Alter, Aron, Chavie, Dovid, Hershy, Menachem, Pesach, Yigal*.

Kahane (136) Jewish (eastern Ashkenazic): one of the many forms of COHEN.
GIVEN NAMES Jewish 9%; German 4%. *Dov, Hinda, Izak, Sol, Zvi*; *Manfred*.

Kahanek (128) Origin uncertain. **1.** Possibly Czech, a diminutive of an unidentified personal name. **2.** Alternatively, perhaps Jewish (eastern Ashkenazic): from a Slavic diminutive of KAHAN. This name is found mainly in Texas.

Kahl (2257) German: nickname from Middle High German *kal* 'bald'.
GIVEN NAMES German 4%. *Kurt* (7), *Heinz* (3), *Manfred* (2), *Otto* (2), *Dieter, Eberhardt, Erna, Friedrich, Fritz, Hans, Helmuth, Matthias*.

Kahle (1315) German: variant of KAHL.
GIVEN NAMES German 4%. *Dieter* (2), *Kurt* (2), *Reichard* (2), *Detlef, Heinz, Hermann, Mathias, Otto, Wolfgang*.

Kahler (2492) German: **1.** nickname meaning '(the) bald one', from an agent derivative of Middle High German *kal* 'bald'. Compare KAHL. **2.** Americanized spelling of **Kähler** (see KAEHLER).

Kahley (148) Americanized spelling of German KAHLE, KAHLER, or **Kähler** (see KAEHLER).

Kahmann (100) German: reduced form of *Kagemann* (see KAGE 1).
GIVEN NAMES German 6%. *Heinz, Uwe*.

Kahn (7657) **1.** North German: occupational name for a bargee, from Low German *kane* 'boat'. **2.** German: from a short form of the Germanic personal name *Cagano*, itself a short form of a personal name formed with *gagan, gegen* 'against'. **3.** Jewish (Ashkenazic): one of the many variants of COHEN.
GIVEN NAMES Jewish 4%. *Miriam* (8), *Hyman* (6), *Emanuel* (5), *Sol* (5), *Isadore* (4), *Aron* (3), *Avrohom* (3), *Avrum* (3), *Meyer* (3), *Chaim* (2), *Kopel* (2), *Mayer* (2).

Kahnke (101) German: from a diminutive of KAHN.

Kahoe (108) Irish: variant of KEOUGH.

Kahoun (107) Irish: variant of Scottish COLQUHOUN.

Kahr (102) **1.** German: probably a short form of the medieval personal name *Makarius*, from Greek *makarios* 'blessed'. **2.** German: variant of KAHRE. **3.** Swedish: unexplained. **4.** Danish: habitational name from a place called Kahr.
GIVEN NAMES Scandinavian 9%; German 6%. *Astrid*(2); *Hans, Otto*.

Kahre (195) German: of uncertain origin; perhaps a topographic name, either from the South German dialect word *kar* 'bowl-shaped valley', (from Middle High German *kar* 'bowl', 'basket', 'vessel'), or alternatively from *kār* '(sharp) turn or bend in the road'.
GIVEN NAMES German 8%. *Bernhardt, Frieda, Friedhelm, Kurt, Otto*.

Kahrs (349) German: short form of the medieval personal name *Makarius*, from Greek *makarios* 'blessed'. Compare KARES.
GIVEN NAMES German 4%. *Hans* (2), *Fritz, Heinz*.

Kai (288) **1.** Dutch and North German: topographic name for someone living by a quayside, from Dutch *kaai* 'quay', German *Kai* (which was borrowed from the Dutch). **2.** Danish and Frisian: from the Danish personal name *Kai, Kaj, Kay*, which is of uncertain origin, most likely from Frisian or Latin *Caius*. **3.** Japanese: the original meaning is probably 'shell', but the name is written phonetically with two characters meaning 'first class' or 'shell', plus 'beauty'. Though the surname is found mostly in the island of Kyūshū, some families could have connections with the ancient province of Kai (now Yamanashi prefecture) in the mountains of central Honshū.
GIVEN NAMES Japanese 22%. *Ritsuko* (3), *Takashi* (2), *Akiko, Chitose, Hidetaka, Hisashi, Kaoru, Kumiko, Mamoru, Masakazu, Masaru, Masayuki*.

Kaigler (168) Americanized spelling of KEGLER.

Kail (602) Perhaps an Americanized spelling of KEHL.

Kaim (151) Jewish (Ashkenazic): **1.** variant of HEIM. **2.** variant of KEIM.

Kain (1882) **1.** Variant spelling of Irish Kane; also a variant of Coyne. **2.** Jewish (Ashkenazic): variant of Cohen. This was the family name of the first Chief Rabbi of Berlin.

Kaine (205) **1.** Variant spelling of Irish Kane; also a variant of Coyne. **2.** Jewish (Ashkenazic): variant of Cohen.

Given name Irish 5%. *Paddy.*

Kainer (231) Jewish (Ashkenazic): habitational name for someone from a place called Kajnary in Moldova.

Given names German 4%. *Erwin* (2), *Alfons.*

Kainz (279) Austrian: Tyrolean dialect form of Kuntz.

Given names German 5%. *Franz, Hanns, Helmut, Kurt.*

Kairis (142) **1.** Lithuanian (**Kairys**) and Jewish (eastern Ashkenazic): nickname from Lithuanian *kairys* 'left-handed'. **2.** Jewish (eastern Ashkenazic): habitational name from Kajry (Kairiai), a village in Lithuania, or a nickname for a left-handed person, 'left'. **3.** Greek: of uncertain etymology. In Crete it is a nickname for a stingy or avaricious person. It may also be a nickname from Turkish *kahır* 'rage' or 'sorrow', a word of Arabic origin.

Kaiser (13621) **1.** German: from Middle High German *keiser* 'emperor', from the Latin imperial title *Caesar*. This was the title borne by Holy Roman Emperors from Otto I (962) to Francis II (who relinquished the title in 1806). Later, it was borne by the monarch of Bismarck's united Germany (1871–1918). It is very common as a German surname, originating partly as an occupational name for a servant in the Emperor's household, partly as a nickname for someone who behaved in an imperious manner, and partly from a house sign. **2.** Jewish (Ashkenazic): ornamental name from German *Kaiser* 'emperor', adopted (like Graf, Herzog, etc.) because of its aristocratic connotations. **3.** Muslim: from Arabic *qayṣar* 'emperor', which, like 1, is of Latin origin, from the imperial title in the Roman Empire.

Given names German 4%. *Kurt* (34), *Otto* (14), *Hans* (7), *Erwin* (4), *Manfred* (4), *Wolfgang* (4), *Arno* (3), *Franz* (3), *Gunter* (3), *Klaus* (3), *Bernd* (2), *Florian* (2).

Kaiserman (117) Jewish (Ashkenazic): ornamental name from German Kaiser 'emperor' + *man* 'man'.

Given names Jewish 9%. *Moshe* (2), *Gerson, Shoshana.*

Kaitz (117) Origin unidentified.

Kajiwara (110) Japanese: written with characters meaning 'oar' and 'plain', this name is found mostly in western Japan.

Given names Japanese 46%. *Akira, Hisano, Hisao, Ichiro, Kazuo, Kazuto, Kenji, Michio, Mitsuo, Mutsuko, Nobuyoshi, Sadako.*

Kakar (104) Indian (Panjab): Hindu (Khatri) and Sikh name based on the name

of a Khatri clan of the Bahri subdivision. The same clan is also called Seth.

Given names Indian 53%; Muslim 29%. *Anand* (2), *Deepak* (2), *Jaideep* (2), *Ramesh* (2), *Rani* (2), *Sudhir* (2), *Amit, Anil, Bharat, Darshan, Gautam; Abdul* (3), *Mohammed* (2), *Tamim* (2), *Arifa, Farida, Fatima, Haji, Hassan, Hayat, Khair, Mahmood, Mohammad.*

Kakos (127) **1.** Greek: Reduced form of surnames prefixed with the epithet *kakos* 'bad', 'mean', for example, **Kakopetros** 'Peter the mean'. **2.** Iranian: from a Persian personal name, *Kaykaus*, meaning 'just', 'noble'. This was the name of a king of Iran (died 1058). **3.** Hungarian: habitational name from a place in Szatmár county. **4.** Hungarian: variant spelling of **Kakas**, from *kakas* 'rooster', hence a nickname for someone thought to resemble a rooster or a metonymic occupational name for a farmer who kept chickens.

Given names Greek 4%; Muslim 4%. *Demetrios, Spiros; Ezzat, Habib, Issam, Jamila, Najib, Talal.*

Kala (100) **1.** Indian (Andhra Pradesh): Hindu name from Sanskrit *kalā* with several meanings, including 'art', 'skill', and 'a part of division of something'. **2.** Indian (Panjab): Hindu (Brahman) name of unknown origin. **3.** Indian (Kashmir): variant of Kalla. **4.** Polish: see Kalis.

Given names Indian 20%; Polish 4%. *Ajit, Anjali, Daya, Gurbux, Kiran, Padam; Zbyszek.*

Kalafut (191) Dutch and North German: from *kal(e)fat* 'oakum', 'tow', 'calk' (loose fibers of rope used to caulk a ship's seams and make her watertight), hence a metonymic occupational name for a calker, someone who specialized in making ships watertight. The word is ultimately from Arabic *qalafa*; it is also found in 17th-century English in various spellings, mainly *calf(r)et.*

Kalahar (104) Origin unidentified.

Kalajian (148) Armenian: patronymic from the Turkish occupational name *kâlâci* 'merchant', from *kâlâ* 'silk' cloth', 'goods', 'furniture' (from Persian) + the occupational suffix *-ci.*

Given names Armenian 21%; French 5%. *Vartan* (3), *Berge* (2), *Krikor* (2), *Anahid, Ara, Arax, Armen, Garbis, Gevork, Karapet, Mihran, Sirvard; Armand* (2), *Henri.*

Kalal (242) Czech (**Kálal**): occupational name for a woodcutter, from a Moravian dialect derivative of *kálat* 'to hew', 'to cut (a block of wood)'.

Kalan (179) **1.** Slovenian: habitational name for someone from any of numerous places called Kal, or a topographic name for someone who lived near a pool or swampy place, Slovenian *kal.* **2.** Czech (**Kalán**): nickname from Moravian dialect

galán 'young man', 'lover'. **3.** Czech: from the personal name *Kála* (see Kalis).

Kalar (152) Slovenian: topographical name, an agent noun for someone who lived near a pool or swampy place, from Slovenian *kal.*

Kalas (245) **1.** Hungarian (**Kalász**): ethnic name for a member of a Turkic people known as the *Kaliz.* **2.** Czech and Slovak (**Kalaš**): from the personal name *Kála* (see Kalis). **3.** Finnish: unexplained.

Kalata (214) **1.** Polish: variant of Kaleta. **2.** Czech: from a derivative of the personal name *Kála* (see Kalis).

Kalb (1155) **1.** German and Jewish (Ashkenazic): from Middle High German *kalp* 'calf', German *Kalb*, hence either a metonymic occupational name for someone who reared calves or a nickname for a meek or foolish person. **2.** Arabic: from *kalb* 'dog'; one of several Arabic protective names that were supposed to frighten the jinn.

Kalbach (271) German: habitational name from any of various places named for a stream, named as 'the cold stream' (from *kalt*) or the 'bleak stream' (from *kahl* 'bleak') + *Bach* 'stream'.

Given names German 5%. *Kurt* (2), *Otto.*

Kalbaugh (155) Americanized form of German Kalbach.

Kalberer (154) German (also **Kälberer**): occupational name for someone who reared calves; a variant of Kalb, with the addition of the agent suffix *-er.*

Given names German 13%. *Kurt* (4), *Gottlob, Otto.*

Kalberg (101) **1.** Norwegian and Danish: habitational name from a farm name composed of an uncertain first element (possibly *kald* 'cold') + *berg* 'mountain'. **2.** Swedish: ornamental name from a placename element *Kal(l)-* (from *Karl-* 'man' or *Kall-* 'cold', among other possibilities) + the common second element *berg* 'mountain'.

Given names Scandinavian 7%. *Erik, Nels.*

Kalbfleisch (290) German and Jewish (Ashkenazic): literally 'calf meat', hence a metonymic occupational name for a veal butcher.

Given names German 4%. *Kurt* (2), *Erwin.*

Kalchik (103) Slavic: unexplained.

Given names Russian 6%. *Aleksandr, Anatoly, Vladimir.*

Kaldenberg (119) North German: variant **Kaltenberg**, a habitational name for someone from a place literally named 'cold mountain', for example near Düsseldorf.

Kaldor (141) Hungarian (**Káldor**) and Jewish (from Hungary): from a Magyarized form of German Kalter.

Given names Hungarian 5%. *Sandor* (2), *Istvan.*

Kale (1095) **1.** Dutch: nickname from *kaal* 'bald'. **2.** English: habitational name from the villages of East and West Keal in Lincolnshire, which are named from Old

Norse *kjǫlr* 'ridge'. **3.** Perhaps an altered spelling of German **Köhl** (see KOHL). **4.** Indian (Maharashtra); pronounced as two syllables: Hindu descriptive nickname from Sanskrit *kāla* 'black', found among Brahmans, Marathas, and other communities. The Konkanasth Brahmans have a clan called Kale.
GIVEN NAMES Indian 11%. *Vasant* (3), *Alka* (2), *Anil* (2), *Jayant* (2), *Narendra* (2), *Vijay* (2), *Abhay*, *Ajita*, *Alok*, *Amod*, *Aniruddha*, *Anjali*.

Kaleel (138) Muslim: variant spelling of KHALIL.

Kalemba (110) Polish (also **Kalęba**): nickname from Polish dialect *kalęba* 'scraggy old cow'.
GIVEN NAMES Polish 8%. *Jozef* (2), *Maciej*.

Kalen (156) **1.** German: habitational name of Slavic origin from a place so named in Mecklenburg. **2.** Altered spelling of German **Kahlen**, a variant of KAHL, or a habitational name from either of two places so named in northern Germany.
GIVEN NAMES Irish 5%; German 4%. *Delma*; *Bodo*, *Erna*.

Kaler (521) **1.** German: variant spelling of KAHLER or **Köhler** (see KOEHLER). **2.** Probably an Americanized form of German KEHLER.

Kales (111) Czech (**Kaleš**): from a vernacular form of the Latin personal name *Calixtus* (see KALISTA).

Kaleta (323) Polish: from *kaleta* 'leather purse', either a metonymic occupational name for a maker of such purses or a nickname for someone who habitually carried one.
GIVEN NAMES Polish 8%. *Bogdan*, *Genowefa*, *Halina*, *Janusz*, *Leszek*, *Pawel*, *Tadeusz*, *Zbigniew*.

Kaley (332) **1.** Americanized spelling of German KAHLE. Compare KAHLEY or **Köhler** (see KOHLER). **2.** English and Manx: variant spelling of CALEY.

Kalfas (121) **1.** Greek: status name for an apprentice, from Greek *kalfas* 'apprentice', Turkish *kalfa*. **2.** Czech: from *kalfas* 'large pot', presumably a metonymic occupational name for a potter or a nickname for someone with a pot belly.
GIVEN NAMES Greek 11%. *Kyriacos* (2), *Sotirios* (2), *Kyriakos*.

Kalich (139) **1.** Altered spelling of German **Kahlich**, an occupational name for a lime burner (see KALK, KALKBRENNER). **2.** German: topographic name for someone living in a dwelling on piles in a marshy region, from Sorbian *kolik*, diminutive of *kol* 'pile', 'stake'. **3.** Czech: from *kalich* 'chalice', possibly a nickname for a protestant. **4.** Perhaps an altered spelling of Czech or Slovak **Kaleš**, **Kališ** (see KALES, KALIS).
GIVEN NAME German 4%. *Wilhelm*.

Kalil (461) Muslim: variant spelling of KHALIL.

Kalin (697) **1.** Slovenian: nickname from *kalin* 'bullfinch', probably denoting someone living in a house identified by the sign of a bullfinch or a nickname for someone thought to resemble a bullfinch in some way. **2.** Jewish (eastern Ashkenazic): variant of KALINA.

Kalina (833) **1.** Polish, Czech, and German: from the personal name *Kalina*, derivative of various personal names, in particular Latin *Calixtus* (see KALISTA) or *Aquilinus* (see AQUILINO). **2.** Polish, Czech, and Jewish (eastern Ashkenazic): from Slavic *kalina* 'guelder rose', 'snowball tree'. As a Polish and Czech name it is probably topographic; as a Jewish name it is more likely ornamental. **3.** Jewish (eastern Ashkenazic): habitational name from a place called Kalina or Kalino.

Kalinoski (271) Variant of Polish and Jewish KALINOWSKI.

Kalinowski (1357) Polish and Jewish (from Poland): habitational name for someone from places called Kalinowa, Kalinowo, Kalinów, named with Polish *kalina* 'snowball tree', 'guelder rose' (a species of viburnum). See also KALINA.
GIVEN NAMES Polish 11%. *Janusz* (4), *Wieslaw* (4), *Jerzy* (3), *Piotr* (3), *Tadeusz* (3), *Andrzej* (2), *Casimir* (2), *Jaroslaw* (2), *Krzysztof* (2), *Miroslaw* (2), *Stanislaw* (2), *Bogdan*.

Kalinski (186) **1.** Polish (**Kaliński**) and Jewish (eastern Ashkenazic): **2.** habitational name for someone from a place called Kalina, named with Polish *kalina* 'snowball tree', 'guelder rose'. **3.** habitational name for someone from a place called Kaliń, now Kaleń, named with *kaleń* 'pool', 'puddle'.
GIVEN NAMES Polish 10%. *Andrzej* (3), *Czeslawa*, *Pawel*, *Wieslaw*.

Kalinsky (136) Jewish (eastern Ashkenazic): variant spelling of KALINSKI.
GIVEN NAMES Jewish 11%; Russian 4%. *Hershel* (2), *Ilissa*, *Sol*; *Iosif*, *Semyon*, *Yevgeny*.

Kalis (426) **1.** Dutch, Czech, and Slovak (**Kališ**): from the Latin personal name *Calixtus* (see CALIXTO, KALISTA). **2.** Latvian: of uncertain etymology, perhaps of the same origin as 1. **3.** Hungarian: from a pet form of the Hungarian personal name KALMAN.

Kalisch (138) **1.** Germanized spelling of Czech or Slovak **Kališ** (see KALIS). **2.** Jewish (Ashkenazic): habitational name for someone from Kalisz in Poland (see KALISZ).
GIVEN NAMES German 5%; Jewish 4%. *Gerhard*; *Menachem*.

Kalish (988) Americanized spelling of Czech or Slovak **Kališ** (see KALIS), Hungarian KALIS, or German and Jewish KALISCH.
GIVEN NAMES Jewish 4%. *Gerson* (2), *Arnon*, *Avram*, *Hyman*, *Mandel*, *Meyer*, *Miriam*, *Sol*.

Kalista (127) Czech and Polish: from the medieval western Slavic personal name *Kalist*, Late Latin *Calixtus* (from Latin *calix* 'cup', specifically the cup containing the wine of the Christian sacrament). The name was borne by three popes, including a 3rd-century saint (d. 222); it became especially popular in Bohemia among members of a Hussite sect who called themselves Calixtines, referring to Latin *calix* 'cup': they believed that wine as well as bread should be given to the laity in the Eucharist.
GIVEN NAME French 4%. *Camille*.

Kalisz (200) Polish and Jewish (eastern Ashkenazic): habitational name from Kalisz in west central Poland, which probably derives its name from Old Polish *kał* 'muddy place', 'slough'.
GIVEN NAMES Polish 7%. *Dariusz*, *Henryk*, *Jacek*, *Leszek*.

Kaliszewski (177) Polish and Jewish (eastern Ashkenazic): habitational name, probably for someone from KALISZ.

Kalita (137) **1.** Polish: variant of KALETA. **2.** Indian (Assam): Hindu name of unknown origin.
GIVEN NAMES Polish 14%; Indian 6%. *Jerzy* (3), *Janusz*, *Mariusz*, *Wieslaw*; *Jugal*, *Lalita*.

Kalivas (109) Greek: topographic name for someone living in a hut, from *kaliva* 'hut' (classical Greek *kalybē*).
GIVEN NAMES Greek 7%. *Nikolaos*, *Spero*.

Kalivoda (146) Czech: habitational name from Kalivoda near Mělnik, so named from *kalit* 'to stir' + *voda* 'water'. It may also be a nickname for a troublemaker, someone who stirred the waters.
GIVEN NAME German 5%. *Kurt* (2).

Kalk (269) **1.** German and Dutch: metonymic occupational name for a lime burner, from Middle High German *kalc* 'lime' (a loanword from Latin *calx*), Middle Dutch *calk*. Lime is a white calcium oxide obtained by heating limestone (see KALKBRENNER). **2.** German: of Slavic origin; unexplained.

Kalka (264) **1.** Polish (also **Kałka**): nickname for a dirty man, from *kalać*, *kalić* 'to soil', 'make dirty', or perhaps a topographic name from Old Polish *kał* 'muddy place', 'slough'. **2.** Perhaps a respelling of German **Kalker**, occupational name for a lime burner, from KALK + the agent suffix *-er*.

Kalkbrenner (222) German: occupational name for a lime burner, from Middle High German *kalc* 'chalk', 'lime' (see KALK) + *brenner* 'burner'. Lime (calcium carbonate) is a product of some historical importance, obtained from limestone by heating ('burning'). It had various agricultural, domestic, and industrial applications, including fertilizing soil, treating furniture, bleaching, and making mortar.
GIVEN NAME German 5%. *Kurt* (2).

Kalkman (129) German and Dutch: occupational name for a lime burner, literally 'lime man' (see KALK).

GIVEN NAMES Dutch 5%. *Cees, Gerrit, Willem.*

Kalkowski (106) Polish (**Kałkowski**): habitational name for someone from places called Kalków in Kielce, Opole, and Radom voivodeships.

Kalkstein (131) German and Jewish (Ashkenazic): habitational name from a place so named (probably *Kalckstein* in former East Prussia).

GIVEN NAME Jewish 4%. *Avi.*

Kalkwarf (138) North German: topographic name for someone who lived by a slack heap produced from lime burning, from *Kalk* 'lime' (see KALKBRENNER) + *Warf* 'mound with a dwelling'.

Kall (277) **1.** Swedish (**Käll**): ornamental name from *källa* 'spring', 'source' (Old Norse *kelda*). **2.** German: habitational name from a place in the Rhineland named Kall or a topographic name from Slavic *kal* 'bog', 'marshland'.

Kalla (174) Indian (Kashmir): Hindu (Brahman) name of unknown meaning.

GIVEN NAMES Indian 10%; German 4%. *Ashwani, Hari, Keshav, Radhika, Rashmi, Ravi, Sunil, Vijay; Erwin* (2), *Alois, Kurt.*

Kallal (169) Variant of Czech KALAL.

Kallam (245) Perhaps an altered spelling of English KELLAM.

Kallas (665) **1.** Greek: see CALLAS. **2.** Estonian (**Kállass**): topographic name for someone living by the shore of the sea or a lake. **3.** Polish: of uncertain origin; possibly a topographic name from Old Polish *kał* 'muddy place'.

Kallay (160) Hungarian (**Kállay**) and Jewish (from Hungary): habitational name for someone from a place called Kálló or Kallo in Nógrád county, or from the provincial town of Nagykálló in Szabolcs county. The Kállay family of Szabolcs county were one of Hungary's oldest noble families, descendants of the Bolok-Simian clan, one of the 108 ancient clans mentioned in the Chronicle of Simon Kézai.

GIVEN NAMES Hungarian 7%. *Attila, Kalman, Katalin, Laszlo.*

Kallberg (145) Swedish (**Källberg**): ornamental name from *källa* 'spring', 'source' + *berg* 'mountain', 'hill'.

GIVEN NAMES Scandinavian 7%. *Erik, Jarl.*

Kallen (195) **1.** Swedish (**Källén**): ornamental name from *källa* 'spring', 'source' + the adjectival suffix *-én*, a derivative of Latin *-enius*. **2.** German: from the medieval personal name *Gallus* (see GALL). **3.** Dutch: variant of CALLENS.

Kallenbach (360) German: habitational name from places in Thuringia and Westphalia, probably named with an old word, *kalle* 'muddy water' + *Bach* 'stream' (see BACH).

Kallenberg (111) **1.** Swedish (**Källenberg**): ornamental name from *källa* 'spring', 'source' + *berg* 'mountain'. **2.** German: habitational name from Kallenberg, name of a farmstead near Lennep (near Düsseldorf), which is probably named with *kalne, kalle* 'muddy water' + *Berg* 'mountain', 'hill' (see BERG). **3.** German: habitational name from any of several places so named in Westphalia, Saxony, Bavaria, and Württemberg.

GIVEN NAME Scandinavian 7%; German 6%. *Kurt.*

Kallenberger (188) German: habitational name for someone from KALLENBERG.

GIVEN NAMES German 6%. *Bernd, Hans, Heinz, Klaus.*

Kaller (122) **1.** German: habitational name for someone from a place called Kall (south of Düren, Rhineland) or Kalle (near Meppen, Lower Saxony). **2.** German and Dutch: from Middle High German *kallen*, Middle Dutch *callen* 'to shout', 'to speak loudly', hence perhaps a nickname for a chatterbox, or someone with a loud voice.

Kallestad (115) Norwegian: habitational name from various farmsteads in Hordaland named Kallestad, from the Old Norse personal name *Karli*, a compound of *karl* '(free) man', or a river name derived from *kaldr* 'cold' + *staðir* 'farmstead', 'dwelling'.

GIVEN NAME Scandinavian 7%. *Thor.*

Kallevig (110) Norwegian: unexplained.

GIVEN NAME Scandinavian 4%. *Joneen.*

Kallgren (103) Swedish (**Källgren**): ornamental name composed of the elements *källa* 'spring', 'source' + *gren* 'twig'.

GIVEN NAMES Scandinavian 8%; German 4%. *Johan; Monika.*

Kallhoff (149) German: Westphalian variant of **Kalkhof**, a topographic name for someone who lived or worked at a lime works (Middle High German *kalc* 'lime', 'chalk' + *hof* in the sense 'courtyard').

Kallies (110) German: habitational name from Kallies, a place in Pomerania.

GIVEN NAME German 5%. *Kurt.*

Kallin (113) Swedish: ornamental name from the place-name element *Kal-* (see KALBERG) + the common surname suffix *-in*, from the Latin adjectival ending *-inius* 'relating to'.

GIVEN NAMES Scandinavian 7%; German 6%. *Anders, Lars, Per, Sven; Fritz, Karl.*

Kallio (443) Finnish: topographic name from *kallio* 'rock'. This is an old surname that dates back to the 16th century; it was also widely adopted during the name conversion movement in the 19th and early 20th centuries, and was one of the many words denoting natural features taken by Finns to replace Swedish surnames, in this case, particularly Swedish surnames containing the elements *-berg* or *-sten*.

GIVEN NAMES Finnish 16%. *Toivo* (5), *Reino* (3), *Eino* (2), *Veikko* (2), *Alpo, Arvo, Eero, Erkki, Heikki, Hilja, Jorma, Jukka.*

Kallis (186) **1.** Greek: from a shortened form of the personal name *Kallistos* 'best' or a reduced form of a patronymic formed from it. **2.** variant spelling of Hungarian KALIS.

GIVEN NAMES Greek 4%. *Apostolos, Konstantinos, Kyriakos.*

Kallman (390) **1.** Variant spelling of KALMAN. **2.** Swedish (**Källman**): ornamental name composed of the elements *källa* 'spring', 'source' + *man* 'man'. **3.** Americanized spelling of German **Kallmann**, from the medieval personal name *Gallus* (see GALL).

GIVEN NAMES German 4%. *Gunther, Klaus, Kurt.*

Kallmeyer (170) German: from Slavic *kal* 'marshland', 'bog' + Middle High German *meier* 'farmer', 'steward', hence a distinguishing nickname for a farmer whose farm lay on marshy land.

Kalloch (105) German: unexplained.

Kallsen (125) German: habitational name for someone from either of two places named Kalsen: near Plön, Holstein, and in fomer West Prussia. Alternatively, it may be a patronymic from KARL.

Kallstrom (231) Swedish (**Källström**): ornamental name composed of the elements *källa* 'spring', 'source' + *ström* 'river'.

GIVEN NAMES German 4%. *Erwin, Jutta, Kurt.*

Kallus (191) **1.** German: from Slavic *kal* 'marsh'. **2.** German: variant of **Gallus** (see GALL). **3.** Jewish (from Ukraine): habitational name for someone from a place called Kalyus in Podolia, Ukraine.

GIVEN NAMES German 4%; Jewish 4%. *Gerhard, Klaus, Markus; Avrohom* (2).

Kalm (132) **1.** Swedish and Finnish: unexplained. **2.** German: perhaps a habitational name from a place named Kalme near Brunswick.

Kalman (963) **1.** Hungarian (**Kálmán**): from the old Hungarian personal name *Kálmán*, meaning 'remainder' (from Turkic *kal* 'to remain'), hence a protective name, which was given to infants to ward off evil and harmful spirits. In medieval times the name became particularly popular because it was confused with a Christian name of Irish origin; St. Colmán (see COLEMAN) was an influential Irish missionary to Central Europe in the early 7th century. **2.** Jewish (Ashkenazic): from the Yiddish personal name *Kalmen*, an everyday form of *Kloynemes* (from Hebrew *Kalonimos*, which is from Greek *kalos* 'lovely' or *kallos* 'beauty' + *onyma* 'name'). This Hebrew name is first recorded in the Talmud and has been used continuously since then. Among Hungarian Jews, it was sometimes confused with 1 above.

GIVEN NAMES Hungarian 6%. *Bela* (5), *Gabor* (5), *Sandor* (3), *Imre* (2), *Lajos* (2), *Geza*, *Gyula*, *Katalin*, *Zoltan*.

Kalmar (251) **1.** Swedish: habitational name from the seaport of Kalmar, which is situated opposite the island of Öland. **2.** Hungarian (**Kalmár**): occupational name from *kalmár* 'merchant' (from Middle High German *kram* 'trading post', 'tent').
GIVEN NAMES Hungarian 4%. *Attila*, *Gaza*, *Miklos*.

Kalmbach (401) German: habitational name from Kalmbach an der Enz in southwest Germany, probably so named from Old High German *galm* 'loud noise' + *bah* 'creek', 'stream' (see BACH).
GIVEN NAMES German 4%. *Kurt* (2), *Ewald*, *Fritz*, *Klaus*, *Otto*.

Kalmer (99) German: **1.** perhaps a nickname from Thuringian dialect *galmer* 'yellowhammer', equivalent to **Goldammer** in standard German, which is found as a surname in eastern parts of the country. **2.** Alternatively it could be a habitational name for someone from Kalme near Wolfenbüttel, Lower Saxony. **3.** Perhaps an altered spelling of KALMAR.

Kalmes (113) German and Luxembourgeois: variant of KALMUS.
GIVEN NAME French 5%. *Yves*.

Kalmus (179) **1.** Polish, Czech, German, Estonian, Jewish (Ashkenazic), and Luxembourgeois: **2.** metonymic occupational name for a herbalist, from *kalmus* 'calamus', a plant with medicinal properties, a kind of reed or cane. **3.** from the personal name *Kalmus*, related to KALMAN.
GIVEN NAMES German 5%. *Kurt*, *Wilhelm*.

Kalnins (187) Latvian (**Kalniņš**): topographic name from *kalns* 'mountain', or habitational name from a place named with this word.
GIVEN NAMES Latvian 57%. *Andris* (3), *Arturs* (3), *Atis* (3), *Eriks* (3), *Imants* (3), *Juris* (3), *Karlis* (3), *Valdis* (3), *Arvids* (2), *Eduards* (2), *Ivars* (2), *Viesturs* (2), *Vilis* (2), *Andrejs*, *Arnolds*, *Edgars*, *Elmars*, *Fricis*, *Guntis*, *Gunars*, *Harijs*, *Ilmars*, *Indulis*.

Kalous (154) Czech: from *kalous* 'horned owl', evidently a nickname for someone thought to resemble the bird.

Kaloustian (123) Armenian: patronymic from the personal name *Kaloust*, classical Armenian *Galust*, 'coming', which is probably short for *Hsgegalust* 'good coming', 'good arrival', a calque on Italian BONAVENTURA.
GIVEN NAMES Armenian 34%. *Ara* (2), *Maral* (2), *Sarkis* (2), *Aram*, *Boghos*, *Diran*, *Garabed*, *Garabet*, *Hagop*, *Kaloust*, *Kevork*, *Kohar*.

Kalp (181) German and Jewish (Ashkenazic): from Middle High German *kalp* 'calf', German *Kalb*, probably applied as a metonymic occupational name for someone who reared calves (see KALB).

Kalra (174) India (Panjab): Hindu (Arora) and Sikh name, based on the name of a clan in the Arora community, of unexplained etymology.
GIVEN NAMES Indian 96%. *Sanjay* (5), *Jyoti* (4), *Sanjeev* (4), *Ajay* (3), *Arun* (3), *Krishan* (3), *Prem* (3), *Rajesh* (3), *Satish* (3), *Satya* (3), *Sudhir* (3), *Vivek* (3).

Kalscheur (162) North German: variant spelling of *Kalscheuer*, probably a variant of *Kaltscheuer*, a nickname for a conspicuous building, from Middle High German *kalt* 'cold' + *schiur* 'barn'.

Kalt (236) German and Swiss German: from Middle High German *kalt* 'cold', probably applied as a nickname for someone who felt the cold or for someone with an unfriendly disposition.
GIVEN NAMES German 6%. *Christoph*, *Erwin*, *Frieda*, *Ruedi*, *Ulrike*.

Kaltenbach (512) German: habitational name from any of various places named as 'the cold brook', from Old High German *kalt* 'cold' + *bah* 'stream', 'brook'.
GIVEN NAMES German 4%. *Hans* (2), *Alois*, *Frieda*, *Hedwig*, *Konrad*, *Kurt*, *Markus*.

Kaltenbaugh (116) Respelling of German KALTENBACH.

Kalter (244) German and Jewish (Ashkenazic): **1.** metonymic occupational name for a vintner or someone who worked in a vineyard, from Middle High German *kalter*, *kelter* 'wine press'. **2.** possibly a nickname meaning 'the cold one', from KALT + the agent suffix *-er*.
GIVEN NAMES Jewish 7%. *Moshe* (3), *Aron*, *Hadassa*, *Naftali*.

Kalthoff (153) German (Westphalian): habitational name from a place named as 'the cold farm', from Middle High German *kalt* + *hof* 'farmstead', 'manor farm', 'court'.
GIVEN NAMES German 6%. *Florian*, *Klaus*, *Ulrich*.

Kaltman (100) German: probably a nickname for a cool, unfriendly person, from Middle High German *kalt* 'cold' + *mann* 'man'.

Kaltreider (109) **1.** Altered form of German **Kaltreuter**, a topographic name from Middle High German *kalt* 'cold' + *riute* 'clearing for settlement or farming'. **2.** Probably an altered spelling of **Kaltreuther**, a topographic name from *kalt* 'cold' + REUTER, or a habitational name for someone from Kalkreuth in Silesia or Saxony.
GIVEN NAME German 6%. *Erwin*.

Kaltz (113) Eastern German: occupational name from Sorbian *tkac* 'weaver'.
GIVEN NAMES German 8%. *Dieter*, *Kurt*.

Kaluza (260) Polish (**Kałuża**) and Slovenian (**Kaluža**): from Polish *kałuża*, Slovenian *kaluža* 'puddle', 'slough', hence a topographic name for someone who lived near a puddle or a nickname for a muddy person.

GIVEN NAMES German 6%; Polish 6%. *Bernd* (2), *Ruediger* (2), *Alfons*; *Krzysztof* (2), *Andrzej*, *Malgorzata*.

Kaluzny (164) Ukrainian, Polish (**Kałużny**), and Jewish (from Ukraine): from Ukrainian *kalyuzhnyj*, Polish *kałużny* 'muddy' (derivative of *kałuża* 'puddle'), a nickname for a muddy person or perhaps a topographic name for someone who lived in a muddy spot.
GIVEN NAMES Polish 6%; German 4%. *Zbigniew*, *Zygmunt*; *Alfons*, *Alois*.

Kam (922) **1.** Dutch and Jewish (Ashkenazic): from Dutch and Yiddish *kam* 'comb', hence a metonymic occupational name either for a comb maker or for a wool comber or fuller. **2.** Reduced form of Dutch **van der Kam**, from Middle Dutch **kamme** 'brewery', hence a topographic name for someone who lived by a brewery or a metonymic occupational name for someone who worked in one. **3.** Reduced form of Dutch **van Kam**, a habitational name for someone from Chaam (formerly Kam) near Breda. **4.** Chinese 甘: variant of GAN 1. **5.** Chinese 金: variant of JIN 1.
GIVEN NAMES Chinese 5%. *Chi* (2), *Chun* (2), *Ho* (2), *Kam* (2), *Kwong* (2), *Ming* (2), *Cheung*, *Chi Leung*, *Chi Ping*, *Chun Hung*, *Eng*, *Hong*.

Kamal (344) **1.** Muslim: from a personal name based on Arabic *kamāl* 'perfection', 'integrity'. It is found in compound names such as *Kamāl ud-Dīn* 'perfection of religion'. **2.** Hindu name found among people from Sind, Pakistan, which goes back to the personal name of an ancestor, derived from Sanskrit *kamala* 'lotus'. The personal name is common in India, and has become a family name in the U.S. among South Indians.
GIVEN NAMES Muslim 72%; Indian 6%. *Syed* (11), *Mostafa* (9), *Mohammed* (8), *Mustafa* (7), *Ahmed* (6), *Ahmad* (5), *Ali* (5), *Mohammad* (5), *Abu* (4), *Amin* (3), *Anwer* (3), *Mounir* (3); *Indar* (2), *Anupam*, *Arvind*, *Darshan*, *Deepti*, *Gagan*, *Raj*, *Rajiv*, *Sajjan*, *Saroj*, *Seema*.

Kamali (108) Muslim: adjectival derivative of KAMAL, meaning 'pertaining to perfection' or 'descended from someone called Kamāl'.
GIVEN NAMES Muslim 64%; Armenian 4%. *Saeed* (3), *Ali* (2), *Aslan* (2), *Kaan* (2), *Mohammad* (2), *Aghdas*, *Ahmed*, *Alireza*, *Ezat*, *Farideh*, *Fatemeh*, *Kayhan*; *Garnik*, *Knarik*.

Kaman (189) Jewish (Ashkenazic): variant spelling of KAMMAN.
GIVEN NAMES German 5%. *Gerhard*, *Hans*, *Helmut*, *Otto*.

Kamara (421) **1.** Muslim: from a personal name based on Arabic *qamar* 'moon'. **2.** Hungarian: from *kamara* 'little room', from Latin *camera* or *camara* 'house', 'room', 'royal treasury'. The most common Hungarian variant of this surname,

Kamarás, is a status name for the treasurer of a court or of the royal household, or alternatively for a chamberlain. Compare German KAMMERER.

GIVEN NAMES Muslim 36%; African 22%. *Abu* (9), *Mohamed* (7), *Abdul* (6), *Hassan* (6), *Ibrahim* (6), *Zainab* (6), *Mohammed* (3), *Musa* (3), *Abass* (2), *Abdulai* (2), *Dauda* (2), *Fatima* (2); *Isatu* (8), *Fatmata* (5), *Aminata* (4), *Foday* (4), *Idrissa* (3), *Kadijatu* (3), *Siaka* (3), *Alimamy* (2), *Amadu* (2), *Ansumana* (2), *Mamadou* (2), *Mariama* (2).

Kamath (205) India (Goa and Karnataka): Hindu (Brahman) name found among the Saraswat Brahmans of Goa, and particularly in coastal Karnataka. It is from Old Konkani *kāmati*, *kāmatī* 'cultivator', from *kāmata* 'cultivation', 'cultivated land' (a derivative of Sanskrit *karma* 'work') + the agent suffix *-i*, *-ī*. In Kannada, *kamata* denoted in particular cultivation which a landowner carried out using his own stock but the labor of others.

GIVEN NAMES Indian 94%. *Ramesh* (7), *Laxman* (6), *Arvind* (4), *Satish* (4), *Vivek* (3), *Ashok* (2), *Deepak* (2), *Ganesh* (2), *Manjunath* (2), *Poornima* (2), *Prakash* (2), *Praveen* (2).

Kamber (164) **1.** German: occupational name for a comb maker, from Middle High German *kambe* 'comb' + *-er*, agent suffix. **2.** Greek: short for **Kamberakis, Kamberoglou, Kamberidis**, etc., patronymics from *kamberis* 'devoted servant', from a Turkish and Arabic word meaning literally 'one born in the house of his master'. It may also be a reduced form of **Kamberis** itself, which is also a Greek surname. **3.** Jewish (Ashkenazic): unexplained; perhaps an adoption of the German name.

GIVEN NAMES Jewish 5%. *Batya, Emanuel, Shira.*

Kamdar (145) Indian (Gujarat, Maharashtra): Hindu name meaning 'government servant' or 'official', from modern Indo-Aryan *kam* 'work' + the Persian agentive suffix *-dar*.

GIVEN NAMES Indian 75%; Muslim 8%. *Mahendra* (4), *Bharat* (3), *Manoj* (2), *Rashmi* (2), *Vijay* (2), *Yogesh* (2), *Ajay, Ankur, Ashesh, Ashvin, Ashwin, Bhakti; Rizwan* (3), *Iqbal, Khodadad, Mehul, Neela, Sadruddin, Samir.*

Kamei (114) Japanese: 'turtle well'. The name is found mostly in western Japan. One noble family, descended from the MINAMOTO, first settled in Izumo (now part of Shimane prefecture), and later in Inaba (now part of Tottori prefecture).

GIVEN NAMES Japanese 66%. *Itsuo* (2), *Kazuo* (2), *Kenzo* (2), *Midori* (2), *Takayuki* (2), *Asao, Chiyoko, Daisuke, Eiji, Eiko, Emiko, Haruko.*

Kamel (277) **1.** Muslim: from a personal name based on Arabic *kāmil* 'perfect', 'complete'. Compare KAMAL. **2.** German, Dutch, and Jewish (Ashkenazic): from *kamel* 'camel' (Latin *camelus*, Greek *kamēlos*; cf. Hebrew *gamal*). This was a common house sign in central Europe in the later Middle Ages, and the surname generally denoted someone who lived in a house bearing this sign. It may also have been a nickname for an ill-tempered or clumsy person, or as a Jewish name it was probably ornamental.

GIVEN NAMES Muslim 61%. *Ahmed* (10), *Mohamed* (9), *Emad* (4), *Hassan* (4), *Nagui* (3), *Alaa* (2), *Atef* (2), *Hany* (2), *Hussein* (2), *Ibrahim* (2), *Kamel* (2), *Maged* (2).

Kamen (478) Slavic (e.g. Czech **Kámen** or Slovak **Kameň**), German, and Jewish (Ashkenazic): from a Slavic word meaning 'stone' or 'rock' (see KAMIN), either directly, as a nickname, topographic name, or ornamental name, or indirectly as a habitational name for someone from Chemnitz (Slavic *Kamenice*), near the Czech border with Germany, or from one of the many other places in eastern Europe named with this word.

Kamens (179) **1.** German: variant of KAMEN. **2.** Americanized form of some like-sounding Jewish or Slavic name, for example KAMINSKI.

Kamensky (120) Jewish (eastern Ashkenazic): variant spelling of KAMINSKI.

GIVEN NAMES Jewish 7%; Russian 6%. *Hadassa, Yakov, Yehoshua; Lev, Valeri, Yury.*

Kamer (339) **1.** Reduced form of Dutch **van der Kamer** or **Verkamer**: from *kamer* 'room', 'chamber', hence either a status name for a chamberlain or a topographic name for someone who lived in a single-room dwelling. **2.** Swiss German: variant of KAMMER. **3.** Jewish (Ashkenazic): from German *Kammer* 'room', 'chamber'.

Kamerer (210) German: variant spelling of KAMMERER.

Kamerman (134) Dutch: status name for a chamberlain (see KAMER).

Kamholz (124) German: from a name ending in *holz* 'wood', with an unexplained first element.

Kamienski (121) Polish: variant of KAMINSKI.

GIVEN NAME Polish 4%. *Andrzej.*

Kamin (707) **1.** German and Jewish (Ashkenazic): variant of KAMEN. **2.** German: topographic name for someone who lived at a house with a stove, Middle High German *kamin*, *kemin* 'chimney', 'fireplace', 'stove' (Latin *caminus*). **3.** German: probably a metonymic occupational name for a spice dealer, from Middle Low German *kamin* 'caraway'.

Kaminer (241) Jewish (from Poland and Ukraine): habitational name for someone from any of various places in Poland and Ukraine named with Polish *kamień* or Ukrainian *kamin* 'stone', 'rock'.

GIVEN NAMES Jewish 10%. *Miriam* (2), *Noam* (2), *Amnon, Dror, Esfir, Mendel, Nachum, Smadar.*

Kamins (211) German and Jewish (Ashkenazic) (of Slavic origin): variant of KAMENS.

Kaminska (103) Polish: feminine of KAMINSKI.

GIVEN NAMES Polish 17%. *Agnieszka, Ewa, Genowefa, Grazyna, Izabela, Jadwiga, Jozef, Krystyna, Malgorzata.*

Kaminskas (120) Lithuanian form of Polish **Kamiński** (see KAMINSKI).

GIVEN NAMES Lithuanian 4%. *Saulius; Vito* (2).

Kaminski (5284) **1.** Polish (**Kamiński**): habitational name for someone from any of more than 60 villages and towns named Kamień, from Polish *kamień* 'stone', 'rock'. **2.** Jewish (eastern Ashkenazic): habitational name from any of the places mentioned at 1 or from places in Ukraine named Kamiń, from Ukrainian *kamiń* 'stone'. **3.** Jewish (eastern Ashkenazic): habitational name for someone from any of various places named Kamionka in Polish or Kaminka in Ukrainian.

GIVEN NAMES Polish 6%. *Andrzej* (6), *Casimir* (6), *Jerzy* (6), *Krzysztof* (6), *Kazimierz* (4), *Tadeusz* (3), *Wieslaw* (3), *Zbigniew* (3), *Zygmund* (3), *Aleksander* (2), *Bogdan* (2), *Czeslaw* (2).

Kaminsky (1794) Jewish (eastern Ashkenazic) and German: variant spelling of KAMINSKI.

GIVEN NAMES Jewish 5%. *Ilya* (5), *Chaim* (2), *Hyman* (2), *Sol* (2), *Avram, Gavriel, Hershel, Hillel, Inna, Isadore, Isak, Liuba.*

Kamiya (158) Japanese: 'divine valley'; also pronounced *Kamitani, Kamegai,* and *Kabeya.* A habitational name; one family, descendants of the Iwaki branch of the TAIRA clan, took the name from Kamiya-mura in Iwaki (now part of Fukushima prefecture). Other families descend from the northern FUJIWARA through the Utsuno-miya family, and through Fujiwara no Hidesato (10th century) by his descendant Iga and Satake families. The pronunciation *Kamiya* is mostly found in eastern Japan and the Ryūkyū Islands; the pronunciation *Kamitani* in western Japan.

GIVEN NAMES Japanese 59%. *Akira* (3), *Keiko* (2), *Sanae* (2), *Tomoko* (2), *Akihide, Eiichi, Fumiaki, Genichi, Hideaki, Hiroaki, Hiroko, Hirotsugu.*

Kamke (168) Eastern German: habitational name of Slavic origin, possibly from a place named Kamminke, on the island of Usedom, Pomerania.

Kamler (159) Altered spelling of German **Kammler**, occupational name for a comb maker or more probably a wool comber (see KAMM). It has been suggested that it may also be an agent noun from Middle High German *kamin* 'chimney', 'stove', hence an occupational name for a stove and chimney fitter. The surname **Kamsetzer** undoubtedly has this sense, but it is not clear whether Kamler does.

Kamm (965) German and Jewish (Ashkenazic): from Middle High German *kamb(e)*, *kam(me)*, German *Kamm*, Yiddish *kam* 'comb', hence a metonymic occupational name for a comb maker or more probably a wool comber or fuller. *Kamm* is also used to mean the crest of a mountain range, but it seems unlikely that the name is topographic.

GIVEN NAMES German 4%. *Dieter* (3), *Dietrich*, *Georg*, *Gerhard*, *Gunter*, *Kurt*, *Matthias*, *Otto*, *Wilhelm*.

Kamman (239) **1.** Reduced form of German KAMPMANN. **2.** Jewish (Ashkenazic): occupational name for a comb maker or wool comber, from Yiddish *kam* 'comb' + *man* 'man'.

Kammann (109) German: reduced form of KAMPMANN.

GIVEN NAMES German 11%. *Kurt* (2), *Bernhard*, *Gerhard*.

Kammer (913) South German: **1.** from *Kammer* 'chamber', 'storage chamber', 'treasury', hence an occupational name for a chamberlain or treasurer (see KAMMERER). **2.** (**Kämmer**) occupational name for a comb maker or a wool comber or fuller, from an agent derivative of Middle High German *kam(b)*, *kam(me)* 'comb'.

Kammeraad (102) German: of uncertain origin. Either a metonymic occupational name from Middle High German *kamprat* 'cogwheel (in a mill)' (see KAMPRATH) or a nickname from French *camarade*, Italian *camerata* 'comrade', 'companion'.

GIVEN NAME German 6%. *Kurt*.

Kammerdiener (113) German: occupational name meaning 'chamber servant'.

Kammerer (1327) German (**Kämmerer**; South German **Kammerer**): from Middle High German *kamerære* 'chamberlain' (from *kamer(e)* 'chamber'), a status name for the treasurer of a court, a great household, or a city.

GIVEN NAMES German 4%. *Kurt* (4), *Otto* (4), *Berthold* (2), *Konrad* (2), *Aloysius*, *Gottlieb*, *Hans*, *Heinz*, *Kaspar*.

Kammerman (151) German (**Kammermann**) and Jewish (Ashkenazic): variant of KAMMER.

GIVEN NAME Jewish 5%. *Hyman*.

Kammerzell (149) German: habitational name from a place named Kämmerzell, near Fulda in Hesse.

GIVEN NAME German 4%. *Kurt*.

Kammeyer (281) German: distinguishing name denoting a tenant farmer whose farm was on a mountain crest, from Middle High German *kamb(e)*, *kam(me)* 'comb', by extension 'crest of a mountain range' + *meier* 'tenant farmer' (see MEYER).

GIVEN NAMES German 4%. *Armin*, *Gerhart*, *Hans*, *Kurt*.

Kamp (1513) **1.** Dutch and German: from Low German *kamp* 'enclosed, fenced, or hedged piece of land', 'field' (from Latin *campus* 'plain'), hence a topographic name

for someone who lived by a field. **2.** Dutch: from Middle Low German *kampe* 'warrior', 'combatant', applied as a nickname or an occupational name, or from a Germanic personal name based on this element. Compare German KAMPE, KAMPF. **3.** Dutch: metonymic occupational name for a hemp grower, from Middle Dutch *kanep* 'hemp'. **4.** South German: from the Austrian dialect word *Kamp* 'comb', hence a metonymic occupational name for a comb maker or a wool comber, or a topographic name for a mountain dweller, from the same word in the sense 'mountain ridge'. Compare KAMM.

Kampa (438) Eastern German variant of KAMPE.

Kampe (315) German: **1.** habitational name from any of several places called Kamp(e), in Pomerania, in Hessen, and near Düsseldorf. **2.** status name for a peasant farmer or serf (see KAMP 1). **3.** (**Kämpe**): occupational name for a champion (see KAMPF).

GIVEN NAMES German 7%. *Ernst* (2), *Kurt* (2), *Bernd*, *Johannes*, *Otto*.

Kampen (211) **1.** Reduced form of Dutch **van Kampen**, a habitational name from the city of Kampen in the Netherlands, on the east coast of the Ijsselmeer in the province of Overijssel. **2.** North German: Kampen is also the name of a village on the island of Sylt in Schleswig-Holstein. However, the German name is more likely to be a topographic name, from the plural or an inflected from of Low German *kamp* 'enclosed field' (see KAMP 1). **3.** Norwegian: habitational name from any of numerous farmsteads in southeastern Norway named Kampen, from the definite singular form of *kamp* 'round hill top', 'boulder'.

Kamper (334) **1.** German (Westphalia): topographic or status name for a peasant farmer or serf, from an agent derivative of KAMP 1. **2.** North German variant of **Kämpfer** (see KAMPFER).

Kampf (420) German and Jewish (Ashkenazic): from Middle High German *kampf*, German *Kamf* 'fight', 'struggle', hence an occupational name for a champion, a professional fighter (see KEMP), or a nickname for someone with a pugnacious temperament. As a Jewish name it can be ornamental.

Kampfer (155) German (**Kämpfer**): occupational name for a fighter or champion, from an agent derivative of Middle High German *kampf* 'fight' (see KAMPF and KEMP).

GIVEN NAMES German 4%. *Hans*, *Kurt*, *Rainer*.

Kamphaus (204) North German: topographic name for someone who lived in a house (*-haus*) by an enclosed field, Low German *Kamp* 'enclosed field', or a habitational name from a minor place so named, for example in Lower Saxony. It may be a

standardized German form of Low German **Kamphus** or Dutch KAMPHUIS.

Kamphuis (155) Dutch: topographic name for someone who lived in a house by a field, from *kamp* 'enclosed field' + *huis* 'house'.

Kampman (145) Variant spelling of KAMPMANN.

GIVEN NAMES German 6%. *Armin*, *Claas*, *Kurt*.

Kampmann (188) **1.** North German: status name for a smallholder, usually with just one field to work, from Low German *Kamp* 'enclosed field' (see KAMP 1) + *Mann* 'man'. **2.** occupational name for a champion (see KAMPF, and compare English KEMP).

GIVEN NAMES Scandinavian 4%. *Niels* (2), *Lars*.

Kampmeier (117) North German: distinguishing name for a tenant farmer with just one field to work, from Low German *Kamp* 'enclosed field' (see KAMP 1) + MEYER 'tenant farmer'.

GIVEN NAME German 4%. *Heinz*.

Kamprath (105) German: from Middle High German *kamprat* 'cogwheel (in a mill)', hence a metonymic occupational name for a maker of cogwheels or possibly for a miller.

Kamps (717) German: derivative of KAMP 1.

Kampwerth (117) German: topographic name composed of *Kamp* (from Middle Low German *kamp* 'enclosed field for cultivation', 'pasture') + *wert* (from Middle High German, Middle Low German *wert* 'island', 'peninsula'), denoting someone who lived on or owned a field surrounded by water.

GIVEN NAME French 5%. *Marcel* (2).

Kamradt (135) German: of uncertain origin. It could be an occupational nickname for a miller, from Middle High German *kamprat*, Low German *kamrat* 'cogwheel (in a mill)'. Alternatively, it could be a variant of **Gamradt**, **Gamroth**, an eastern German name of Slavic origin denoting a type of drinking vessel. It has also been suggested that an old personal name *Gamerat* (reflected for instance in *Gahmuret*, the name of Parzifal's father in the courtly epic by Wolfram von Eschenbach) could be the source. A fourth possibility is the vocabulary word *Kamerad* 'comrade', a 16th-century loanword from French *camarade*, from Italian *camerata*, originally someone who shared the same room or quarters.

Kamrath (342) German: of uncertain origin. It could be an occupational nickname for a miller, from Middle High German *kamprat*, Low German *kamrat* 'cogwheel (in a mill)'. Alternatively, it could be a variant of **Gamradt**, **Gamroth**, an eastern German name of Slavic origin denoting a type of drinking vessel. It has also been suggested that an old personal name *Gamerat* (reflected for instance in *Gahmuret*, the name of Parzifal's father in the courtly epic by Wolfram von Eschenbach) could be the source. A fourth possible source is the vocabulary word *Kamerad* 'comrade', a 16th-century loanword from French *camarade*, from Italian *camerata*, originally someone who shared the same room or quarters.

Kamrowski (138) Polish: unexplained.

Kamstra (171) Frisian: topographic name for someone living by an enclosed field, from an agent noun derived from Low German *kamp* 'enclosed field'.

Kan (700) **1.** Chinese 简: spelling variant of JIAN. **2.** Chinese 阚: from the name of a place called Kan which existed during the Spring and Autumn period (722–481 BC) in the state of Lu, in present-day Shandong province. Some residents adopted the place name as their surname. **3.** Chinese 甘: variant of GAN 1. **4.** Czech (**Káň**): from *kanit* meaning 'to slobber or slaver' and by extension 'to gossip', hence a nickname for a gossip. **5.** Czech: nickname from *káně* 'buzzard'. **6.** German: derivative of the personal name KONRAD. **7.** Jewish (Ashkenazic): one of the many forms of COHEN. **8.** Dutch: from Middle Dutch *kan(ne)*, *can(ne)* 'tankard', 'flagon', 'pitcher', hence a metonymic occupational name for a maker of such vessels: a potter or a pewterer. **9.** Reduced form of Dutch **van de Kan**: habitational name for someone from De Kan in Veurne or a place called Kanne.

GIVEN NAMES Chinese 19%. *Wai* (5), *Kam* (3), *Chan* (2), *Chi* (2), *Hsin* (2), *Lai* (2), *Ming* (2), *Chai, Chao, Chea, Chen, Cheng.*

Kana (220) **1.** Czech (**Káňa**): variant of KAN. **2.** Bulgarian (**Kána**): reduced form of **Balkána**, a regional name for a woman from the Balkans.

Kanaan (110) Arabic: from a personal name based on *kan'ān* 'beauty', or from a personal name bestowed with reference to the land of Canaan in the Bible.

GIVEN NAMES Arabic 48%; French 6%. *Ahmad* (2), *Azzam* (2), *Amin, Ammar, Baha, Charbel, Fouad, Hassan, Hisham, Hussein, Issam, Jubran; Antoine, Camille, Michel.*

Kanady (189) **1.** Hungarian (**Kanády**): habitational name from an unidentified place called Kand. **2.** Perhaps also an Americanized spelling of the Scotch–Irish name KENNEDY.

Kanagy (194) Altered spelling of Swiss German **Gnaegi** or **Gnagy**, a topographic name, composed of the prefix *ge-* + Latin *in agro* 'in the field', denoting someone who lived in or by his field(s) as opposed to in a village.

Kanai (118) Japanese: 'gold well'. The name is found mostly in the Tōkyō area and the Ryūkyū Islands.

GIVEN NAMES Japanese 55%. *Akira, Hidehiro, Hideki, Hideo, Hiromitsu, Hiroto, Junichi, Kazunori, Keiichi, Kenichi, Kimio, Kiyoshi.*

Kanak (161) Czech (**Kaňák**): nickname for a gossip (see KAN 1).

Kanaley (134) Reduced and altered form of Irish MCNALLY.

Kanaly (112) Reduced and altered form of Irish MCNALLY.

GIVEN NAME Irish 5%. *Briana.*

Kanan (159) Muslim: variant of KANAAN.

GIVEN NAMES Muslim 10%. *Ahmad* (2), *Mohammad* (2), *Ahmed, Ameneh, Ayman, Fadi, Ibtesam, Majdi, Sayel.*

Kanarek (190) Polish and Jewish (from Poland): from Polish *kanarek* 'canary', hence a nickname for someone thought to resemble the bird in some way, for example with cheerful singing, or, among Jews, an ornamental name.

GIVEN NAMES Jewish 14%. *Reuven* (2), *Baruch, Hershel, Mendel, Rivka, Shlomo, Sol, Yael.*

Kanas (137) **1.** Lithuanian: nickname for a miser, Lithuanian *kanas*. **2.** Greek: unexplained.

Kanatzar (106) Origin unidentified.

Kanda (213) **1.** Japanese: from a common place name throughout Japan meaning 'divine rice paddy'; also pronounced *Kamita* and *Kōda*. The more prominent families of this name are descended either from the notorious 10th-century rebel Taira no Masakado, or from the MINAMOTO clan through the Matsuura family. **2.** Indian (Panjab): Sikh name based on the name of a Jat clan. The word *kaṇā* means 'thorn' in Panjabi. **3.** Czech: nickname from dialect *kandat* 'prattler', 'chatterer'.

GIVEN NAMES Japanese 46%; Indian 8%. *Hiroshi* (4), *Mamoru* (3), *Iwao* (2), *Masami* (2), *Masato* (2), *Akihiro, Chie, Hideki, Hikaru, Katsushi, Katsuto, Katsuya; Atma, Som, Subhash, Usha, Vikas.*

Kandel (639) **1.** German and Jewish (Ashkenazic): from Middle High German *kandel*, German *Kandel* 'pitcher', hence a metonymic occupational name for a maker or seller of these. **2.** German: habitational name from either of two places so named: in the Rhineland-Palatinate and in the Black Forest.

GIVEN NAMES Jewish 4%. *Arie* (2), *Anat, Aron, Bronya, Emanuel, Leyb, Meyer, Shmuel.*

Kandell (129) Variant spelling of German KANDEL.

Kandle (107) Americanized spelling of German KANDEL.

Kandler (220) German (also **Kändler**): **1.** occupational name for a potter or pewterer, from an agent derivative of Middle High German *kandel* 'pitcher'. **2.** occupational name for a maker of (wooden) gutters and drainage ducts, from an agent derivative of Middle High German *kanel* 'pipe', 'gutter' (from Latin *canalis*). **3.** habitational name for someone from Kändler near Chemnitz in Saxony.

GIVEN NAMES German 9%. *Kurt* (4), *Frieda, Hans.*

Kandt (158) German: probably from Middle High German *kant* 'jug' (from Latin *olla cannata* 'pot with one spout') and hence an occupational name for a maker or seller of jugs, a variant of KANNE.

Kane (20131) **1.** Irish (Ulster): reduced Anglicized form of Gaelic **Ó Catháin** 'descendant of *Cathán*' (see O'KANE). Compare KEANE. **2.** Scottish: reduced form of MCKEAN. **3.** Jewish (Ashkenazic): altered spelling of COHEN. **4.** Jewish (eastern Ashkenazic): variant spelling of KANNE. **5.** Probably also an Americanized spelling of German **Köhn** (see KOHN).

GIVEN NAMES Irish 8%. *Brendan* (5), *Aileen* (3), *Padraic* (2), *Brennan, Declan, Donovan, Fergus, James Patrick, Keelin, Kieran, Siobhan.*

Kaneko (343) Japanese: 'golden (or metal) child'; variously written. Bearers of the name are not numerous, but there are several places of this name. It apparently derives from gold dust or iron ore dust found in streams or sand banks; the character representing *kane* means 'gold' and is also the generic term for metal. The surname is mostly found in the Tōkyō area and Okinawa Island, and one family is descended from the ancient Mononobe clan.

GIVEN NAMES Japanese 64%. *Minoru* (4), *Toshio* (4), *Akira* (3), *Kazuo* (3), *Masahiro* (3), *Mitsue* (3), *Fujio* (2), *Fumiyo* (2), *Hajime* (2), *Hideo* (2), *Isamu* (2), *Kenji* (2).

Kanelos (104) Greek: nickname for someone with fair or red hair, from *kanela* 'cinnamon', from Italian *cannella*.

Kanemoto (107) Japanese: topographic name meaning '(one who lives) near where gold (or any metal) is found'. Found in the island of Okinawa, where it is variously written.

GIVEN NAMES Japanese 32%. *Chiyo, Fumio, Iwao, Kazuko, Kenzo, Kumiko, Masaji, Masao, Masaru, Misako, Nobuo, Reiji.*

Kaner (240) **1.** Jewish (Ashkenazic): variant spelling of KANNER. **2.** Possibly a respelling of German KANNER or **Köhner** (see KUEHNER).

GIVEN NAMES Jewish 9%; Russian 4%. *Avi, Berka, Gitla, Hymen, Isadore, Semen, Yakov, Yossi; Arkady, Boris, Lyubov, Yevgeny.*

Kaneshiro (698) Japanese: 'golden castle'; also pronounced *Kinjo*, and found mostly in western Japan. In the Ryūkyū Islands, the name is pronounced *Kanegushiku*.

GIVEN NAMES Japanese 32%. *Seichi* (5), *Shigeru* (5), *Kiyoshi* (4), *Hideo* (3), *Isamu* (3), *Masao* (3), *Seiko* (3), *Eichi* (2), *Hiroshi* (2), *Kame* (2), *Kazuo* (2), *Masaichi* (2).

Kanevsky (103) Jewish (from Ukraine): habitational name for someone from the town of Kanev in Ukraine.
GIVEN NAMES Russian 27%; Jewish 23%. *Leonid* (3), *Vladimir* (3), *Boris* (2), *Semyon* (2), *Dmitry, Enya, Fenya, Grigory, Igor, Lev, Oleg, Pesya; Aharon, Aron, Avram, Bluma, Isaak, Isadore, Rakhil, Sura.*

Kaney (216) Possibly an Americanized spelling of German **Köhner** (see KUEHNER) or of **König** (see KOENIG).

Kanfer (108) Jewish (eastern Ashkenazic): ornamental name from Yiddish *kanfer* 'camphor'.
GIVEN NAMES Jewish 7%; Russian 4%. *Sol; Serafima, Yevsey.*

Kang (5003) **1.** Chinese 康: from the name of Kang Shu, the eighth son of Wen Wang, who was granted the state of Wei (see WEI 3) soon after the founding of the Zhou dynasty in 1122 BC. Many of his descendants later adopted Kang as their surname. Another source of the name comes from the Kang Ju tribe, who moved into China from central Asia during the Han dynasty (206 BC–220 AD), and adopted their tribal name, Kang, as their surname. **2.** Chinese 耿: variant of GENG 2. **3.** Korean: there are five Chinese characters for the surname Kang. Some records indicate that there are as many as one hundred separate Kang clans, but only four have actually been documented. There is one Chinese character for each clan. The fifth character is an alternate character for the smallest of the Kang clans, and is the result of a scribal error which was introduced in 1908. That segment of the smaller Kang clan which was labeled with the alternate character still uses it and recognizes it as the character for their surname. The largest clan, the Kang family of Chinju, first appears in the historical record in AD 597. Many members of the largest Kang clan still live in the area of Chinju of Kyŏngsang Province. The second Kang clan is centered on Cheju Island. The two smaller Kang clans have only a few households in all of Korea.
GIVEN NAMES Chinese/Korean 64%. *Young* (94), *Sung* (68), *Yong* (38), *Jung* (36), *Shin* (26), *Sang* (24), *Kyung* (23), *Hyun* (19), *Sun* (19), *Myung* (18), *Soon* (18), *Jae* (16); *Chang* (31), *Min* (20), *Dae* (19), *Myong* (17), *Moon* (13), *Byung* (12), *Chong* (12), *Seong* (12), *Jeong* (7), *Chung* (6), *Young Woo* (6), *Chul* (5).

Kangas (1712) Finnish: from *kangas* 'pine heath', a habitational name from a farmstead so named; traditionally this was convenient terrain for siting a farm, and the oldest holdings date back to the medieval period. Kangas was also widely adopted as an ornamental name during the name conversion movement in the 19th and early 20th centuries. It is found mainly in Ostrobothnia.
GIVEN NAMES Finnish 8%. *Eino* (11), *Reino* (8), *Waino* (6), *Toivo* (5), *Tauno* (4), *Oiva*

(3), *Sulo* (3), *Arvi* (2), *Hilja* (2), *Kalevi* (2), *Niilo* (2), *Aimo.*

Kania (1094) Polish and Jewish (Ashkenazic): Polish nickname or Jewish ornamental name, from Polish *kania* 'kite'.
GIVEN NAMES Polish 9%. *Zygmunt* (3), *Jozef* (2), *Zbigniew* (2), *Zdzislaw* (2), *Zofia* (2), *Boguslaw, Casimir, Danuta, Edyta, Ignacy, Jacek, Janusz.*

Kaniecki (114) Polish: habitational name for someone from Kanice in Piotrków voivodeship, named with Polish *kania* 'kite'.

Kaniewski (155) Polish: habitational name for someone from Kaniewo in Włocławek voivodeship, named with Polish *kania* 'kite'.
GIVEN NAMES Polish 19%; German 4%. *Wojciech* (2), *Andrzej, Bogdan, Boguslaw, Darek, Kazimierz, Maciej, Marcin, Tomasz, Zdzislaw; Kurt.*

Kanipe (301) Americanized spelling of German KNEIP. This name is concentrated mainly in NC.

Kanis (146) **1.** Dutch and North German: altered spelling of **Canis**, a humanistic Latinization of Dutch **de Hond(t)**, German **Hundt**, nicknames meaning 'dog'. **2.** German: variant of KANITZ.

Kanitz (188) German and Jewish (Ashkenazic): habitational name for someone from Kanitz in Saxony, or from one of the similar place names in Germany and Bohemia; in some cases Czech *kanec* 'boar' may be the source of the name.
GIVEN NAMES German 4%. *Arno, Heinz.*

Kann (622) **1.** German, Danish, and Jewish (Ashkenazic): from Middle High German, Middle Low German, Danish *kanne*, German *Kanne* 'jug', 'flagon' (Latin *canna*), hence a metonymic occupational name for a maker or seller of jugs, or in some cases possibly a habitational name for someone who lived at a house or tavern distinguished by the sign of a flagon. **2.** German (Austria): from a short form of the personal name *Candidus*. **3.** Jewish (Ashkenazic): one of the many forms of COHEN.

Kannady (135) Americanized form of Irish–Scottish KENNEDY.

Kannan (166) Indian: variant of KRISHNAN.
GIVEN NAMES Indian 59%. *Ramesh* (3), *Ravi* (3), *Suresh* (3), *Hari* (2), *Kesavan* (2), *Murugan* (2), *Narasimhan* (2), *Sridhar* (2), *Sridharan* (2), *Vijay* (2), *Akila, Arun.*

Kanne (274) German, Danish, and Jewish (Ashkenazic): variant of KANN 1.

Kannel (103) Origin unidentified.

Kannenberg (279) German: habitational name from Kannenberg (literally 'jug mountain') near Magdeburg.
GIVEN NAMES German 5%. *Eldor, Ilse, Konrad.*

Kanner (492) **1.** German and Jewish (Ashkenazic): occupational name for a maker of jugs, from an agent derivative of Middle High or Middle Low German *kanne* 'jug',

'tankard', German *Kanne* (see KANN). **2.** German: occupational name for a maker of gutters and drainage pipes, Middle High German *kaner*. Compare KANDLER.
GIVEN NAMES Jewish 12%. *Mayer* (3), *Aron* (2), *Chaim* (2), *Isak* (2), *Zvi* (2), *Abbe, Heskel, Meni, Moshe, Pinchas, Reuven, Shlomo.*

Kanney (129) Scottish, Irish, or English: unexplained; perhaps a variant of KEANEY.

Kanning (135) German and Frisian: **1.** patronymic from the personal name *Kanke*, a short form of *Johannes* or *Johanna*, the feminine form; both are still common personal names in present-day Dutch Friesland. **2.** nickname for someone who habitually pretended to be unable to do something, with the sense of 'cannot' in Low German, or alternatively a nickname for someone thought to resemble a rabbit in some way, from the word *Kaninchen*.
GIVEN NAMES German 6%. *Otto* (2), *Markus.*

Kanno (156) Japanese: mostly written with characters meaning 'deity' and 'field'. It is prounced *Kanno* or *Kamino* in western Japan and *Jinno* along the eastern seaboard.
GIVEN NAMES Japanese 57%. *Yasuhiro* (3), *Hiroshi* (2), *Takashi* (2), *Yoshihiro* (2), *Eiji, Eriko, Hifumi, Hiroaki, Hiromi, Hisashi, Ikumi, Katsuya.*

Kano (195) **1.** Japanese: 'harvested field'; variously written, with such variation in the characters used for the second syllable that the name can be pronounced either *Kano* or *Kanō*. There are several place names of both pronunciations throughout Japan. One Kano family was descended from the Itō branch of the southern Fujiwara. A Kanō family was descended from daimyō of Suruga (now part of Shizuoka prefecture), and another from the Matsudaira family of *Kanō-mura* in Mikawa (now part of Aichi prefecture). **2.** Jewish (Ashkenazic): see COHEN.
GIVEN NAMES Japanese 55%. *Yoshio* (4), *Shigeo* (2), *Tetsuro* (2), *Tomohisa* (2), *Akihiro, Atsushi, Ayako, Fusako, Hayato, Hideaki, Hideki, Hideo.*

Kanode (203) Possibly an Americanized spelling of German KNOTH or of **Kanold**, from a Germanic personal name, probably based on *gan* 'magic'.

Kanoff (130) Probably Bulgarian (**Kanov**), a patronymic from the personal name *Kano*, a short form of *Balkan* or *Lukan*.

Kanouff (104) Variant spelling of KANOFF.

Kanouse (259) Americanized form of German KNAUS.

Kanoy (121) Respelling of Swiss German **Kneu**, a topographic name from *kneu* 'hill', 'bend'.

Kanski (105) Polish: habitational name for someone from any of several places named with Polish *kania* 'kite'.

Kant (301) **1.** German: topographic name for a person living on the edge of a settlement or in a corner, from Middle Low

German *kant(e)* 'edge', 'corner'. **2.** German: habitational name from any of various places called Kant in Prussia, or from Kanth, near Wrocław (Breslau) in Silesia. **3.** Indian (northern states): Hindu name from Sanskrit *kānta* 'beloved'. This occurs frequently as the final element of compound given names such as *Lakshmikant* 'beloved of Lakshmi' (an epithet of the god Vishnu) and *Rajanikant* 'beloved of the night' (an epithet of the moon).
GIVEN NAMES Indian 10%; German 7%. *Ravi* (3), *Shashi* (3), *Arun* (2), *Avinash, Chander, Krishna, Rishi*; *Horst* (2), *Erwin, Hedwig, Otto*.

Kanter (1393) **1.** German and Jewish (Ashkenazic): variant of KANTOR. **2.** German: topographic name for someone living at the edge of a settlement or in a corner, or habitational name for someone from a place called Kant (see KANT). **3.** German: from the medieval personal name *Ganthart*.
GIVEN NAMES Jewish 4%. *Isadore* (2), *Mayer* (2), *Ari, Herschel, Miriam, Shira, Sol, Yakov*.

Kantner (451) German: **1.** habitational name from either of the places named Kanten, in former East Prussia or Silesia. **2.** occupational name for someone who made wooden racks or trestles for beer and wine barrels, from an agent derivative of Middle High German *ganter, kanter* 'barrel rack'.

Kantola (239) Finnish: from *kanto, kanta* 'stump', 'base' + the local suffix *-la*, applied originally as a topographic name or a habitational name from a farm so named. Later, during the name conversion movement of the 19th and early 20th centuries, it was adopted as an ornamental name by Finns bearing Swedish surnames.
GIVEN NAMES Finnish 6%. *Reino* (3), *Eino, Raimo, Risto*.

Kantor (1927) **1.** Jewish (Ashkenazic): occupational name for a cantor, an official of a synagogue whose duty is to sing liturgical music and leads prayers, from Latin *cantor* 'singer', a derivative of *canere* 'to sing'. **2.** German, Czech, Slovak, and northern Croatian; Hungarian (**Kántor**): occupational name for a choirmaster or village schoolmaster.
GIVEN NAMES Jewish 7%. *Yakov* (4), *Hyman* (3), *Ilya* (2), *Miriam* (2), *Mort* (2), *Aron, Avi, Avrum, Chana, Doron, Eitan, Faina*.

Kantrowitz (348) Jewish (eastern Ashkenazic): Germanized spelling of a Slavic patronymic meaning 'son of the cantor' (see KANTOR 2).
GIVEN NAMES Jewish 11%. *Hyman* (6), *Ari, Emanuel, Meyer, Miriam, Shlomo*.

Kantz (316) German: **1.** from a pet form of the personal name KONRAD. **2.** nickname for someone with a bull neck, from the dialect word *kanz* 'upper part of the neck', 'scruff'.

Kanz (219) German: variant of KANTZ.

Kanzler (286) German: from Middle High German *kanzler* 'chancellor' (Latin *cancellarius*), hence a nickname for someone in the employ of a chancellor or possibly an occupational name for the man himself.
GIVEN NAMES German 9%. *Kurt* (3), *Helmut, Juergen, Manfred, Reinhart, Reinhold, Siegfried*.

Kao (1352) Chinese 高: variant of GAO.
GIVEN NAMES Chinese 22%. *Cheng* (6), *Chi* (4), *Chia* (3), *Ching* (3), *Ming* (3), *Ting* (3), *Yuan* (3), *Chen* (2), *Chien Chung* (2), *Chih* (2), *Hsiang* (2), *Hsiao* (2).

Kapadia (428) Indian (Gujarat, Bombay city, Rajasthan): Hindu (Bania, Vania) and Parsi name meaning 'cloth merchant' in Gujarati, from *kapǝ* 'cloth' (Sanskrit *karpaṭa*) + the adjectival suffix *-ya*.
GIVEN NAMES Indian 74%; Muslim 11%. *Dinesh* (7), *Dilip* (6), *Bharat* (4), *Atul* (3), *Deepak* (3), *Divya* (3), *Hitesh* (3), *Mahendra* (3), *Mahesh* (3), *Naresh* (3), *Rajesh* (3), *Sudhir* (3); *Abdul* (4), *Shabbir* (4), *Aslam* (2), *Abbas, Aliasghar, Altaf, Anwar, Ashraf, Bashir, Chirag, Farid, Hashim*.

Kapala (152) Polish (also **Kapała**): nickname from a derivative of *kapać* 'to drip'.
GIVEN NAMES Polish 8%. *Halina, Jacek, Karol, Ryszard, Stanislaw*.

Kapaun (177) German: nickname from *Kapaun* 'capon', 'castrated cock'.

Kapel (101) **1.** Polish: variant of KAPELA. **2.** Slovenian (**Kapel** and **Kapelj**): unexplained.
GIVEN NAMES Polish 5%. *Andrze, Lucyna*.

Kapela (124) Polish: occupational name for a musician, from Polish *kapela* 'music band', 'court orchestra'.
GIVEN NAME Polish 5%. *Wojciech*.

Kaper (126) **1.** Dutch: variant of CAPERS. **2.** Dutch: from *kaper* 'pirate' or 'privateer'. **3.** German: from Czech *kapr* 'carp', hence a nickname for someone thought to resemble the fish.

Kapfer (197) German: **1.** topographic name for a dweller near the top of a mountain, from southern German *Kapf* 'peak'. **2.** from an agent derivative of Middle High German *kapfen* 'to stare or keep watch', hence a nickname for an alert or watchful person, or an occupational name for a guard or watchman.

Kapinos (267) Ukrainian and Polish: compound name meaning 'run, nose!', an example of a peculiar brand of humorous Ukrainian family names, in which an imperative is followed by a noun in the nominative or vocative case.
GIVEN NAMES Polish 7%. *Fryderyk, Janusz, Karol, Mieczyslaw, Wladyslaw*.

Kapitan (178) German, Polish, and Hungarian (**Kapitán(y)**): status name from a word meaning 'captain' (Late Latin *capitaneus* 'chief', 'principal' from *caput* 'head'). This title was used in various senses, for example the master of a ship and

as an official rank in the army. This may also be a reduced form of Greek **Kapetanos** or of its numerous patronymic and other derivatives (**Kapetanakis, Kapetanopoulos, Kapetanoglou, Kapetanellis**, etc.). As a Greek surname, it derives from Italian (Venetian) *capitano*.

Kapke (146) German: altered spelling of western Slavic **Kapka**, nickname for a heavy drinker.
GIVEN NAMES German 4%. *Benno, Kurt*.

Kapla (114) Slovenian (also **Kaplja**): perhaps a nickname from the noun *kaplja* 'drop', 'raindrop'.

Kaplan (16223) **1.** Jewish (Ashkenazic): surname used as a translation of COHEN, from German *Kaplan* or Polish *kapłan* 'chaplain', 'curate'. **2.** German, Swedish, Czech, and Slovenian; Slovak **Kaplán**, Polish (**Kapłan**); Hungarian (**Káplán**): status name for a deacon, chaplain, or curate (ultimately from Late Latin *capellanus* (see CHAPLIN 1), or a nickname for someone resembling a clergyman). **3.** Turkish: from *kablan* 'tiger', hence a nickname for someone thought to resemble a tiger, typically in having indomitable courage or spirit. In the form **Kaplanis**, this is also found as a Greek surname, with various patronymic and other derivatives (**Kaplanidis, Kaplanoglou, Kaplanellis**, etc.)
GIVEN NAMES Jewish 7%. *Sol* (31), *Meyer* (30), *Hyman* (28), *Isadore* (17), *Miriam* (10), *Emanuel* (5), *Yitzchok* (5), *Ari* (4), *Morty* (4), *Yakov* (4), *Batya* (2), *Binyomin* (2).

Kaple (123) Probably an Americanized spelling of German **Göbel** (see GOEBEL).

Kapler (172) **1.** German: variant spelling of KAPPLER. **2.** Hungarian: Germanized form of Hungarian *Káplár* or *Kaplár*, status name for a corporal. It is disputed whether the Hungarian word *káplár* was borrowed from Italian or German, but it ultimately derives from Latin *caput* 'head'. The Kapler noble family, identified as Hungarian, was registered in Pozsony (German Pressburg, Slovak Bratislava) as early as the 15th century, but their ancestors were German, and their original name was *Kaplitz*.

Kaplin (222) Jewish (eastern Ashkenazic): variant spelling of KAPLAN.

Kaplon (114) **1.** Polish (**Kapłon**): nickname from *kapłon* 'capon'. **2.** Jewish (Ashkenazic): variant spelling of KAPLAN. **3.** Hungarian: habitational name from a place so named in Nógrád county in northern Hungary or from Kaplony in former Szatmár county. Both places were named with Turkic *kaplon* 'tiger', probably indicating that these villages were established by a clan of Kalizes, Uzes, Pechenegs, Cumanians, or some other extinct Turkic people whose totemic animal was the tiger.
GIVEN NAMES Polish 8%. *Ludwik, Pawel, Stanislaw*.

Kaplow (153) Jewish (Ashkenazic): shortened form of KAPLOWITZ.

Kaplowitz (316) Jewish (Ashkenazic): Germanized spelling of the Polish-Jewish surname **Kaplowicz**, a patronymic from the personal name KAPEL.
GIVEN NAMES Jewish 8%. *Sol* (3), *Hyman, Shimon, Toba, Yocheved*.

Kaplun (145) Jewish (eastern Ashkenazic): variant of KAPLAN.
GIVEN NAMES Russian 41%; Jewish 23%. *Leonid* (5), *Arkadiy* (3), *Lev* (3), *Raisa* (3), *Aleksandr* (2), *Igor* (2), *Mikhail* (2), *Vladimir* (2), *Aleks, Anatoliy, Boris, Fania; Irina* (3), *Yakov* (3), *Esfir, Isaak, Isak, Marat, Rakhil, Sima, Yankel, Zinaida*.

Kapner (161) Jewish (Ashkenazic): of uncertain origin; perhaps an occupational name from Yiddish *kape* 'bedspread' + the agent suffix *-ner*.

Kapolka (102) Polish (**Kapołka**): nickname or metonymic occupational name from Polish dialect *kapałka* 'whey'.
GIVEN NAMES Polish 7%. *Jozef, Lukasz, Stanislaw*.

Kapoor (555) Indian (Panjab): Hindu (Khatri) and Sikh name of a clan in the Khatri community, whose ancestor is said to have been called Kapoor Chand. The derivation is from a personal name meaning 'camphor' (Sanskrit *karpūra*). In Sanskrit literature, it is quite common as a personal name, and there is also a feminine form, *karpūrikā*. Many compound names are also found with *karpūa* as the first element: masculine names such as *Karpuravarsha, Karpurasena*, as well as feminine names such as *Karpuratilaka* and *Karpuramanjari*.
GIVEN NAMES Indian 90%. *Ashok* (13), *Vijay* (13), *Anil* (10), *Raj* (10), *Rakesh* (9), *Vinod* (9), *Sanjay* (8), *Deepak* (6), *Ajay* (5), *Amit* (5), *Atul* (5), *Sunil* (5).

Kapp (1600) German: **1.** from Middle High German *kappe* 'hooded cloak', hence a metonymic occupational name for a maker of hoods and hooded cloaks or a nickname for someone who habitually wore such a garment. **2.** nickname for a man with a high voice, from Middle High German *kappe* 'capon'. **3.** from a variant of the personal name KASPAR.

Kappas (106) Greek: reduced form of a surname beginning with the prefix *Kapa-, Kamba-,* or *Kapo-*, from Turkish *kaba* 'large', 'coarse', for example **Kapogiannis** 'John the coarse'. It is unlikely to be from Latin *cappa* 'cape'.
GIVEN NAMES Greek 5%. *Anthi, Panagiota, Sotos*.

Kappel (866) **1.** German and Dutch: topographic name for a person living near a chapel, from Middle High German *kap(p)elle, kappel* 'chapel'. This is a loanword from Late Latin *cap(p)ella*, a diminutive of *cappa* 'hooded cloak', the first building to be so called having housed a cloak that reputedly belonged to St. Martin of Tours. **2.** German and Dutch: habitational name from a place named with this word, of which there are many examples in northwestern Germany. **3.** German (**Käppel**): diminutive of KAPP.
GIVEN NAMES German 4%. *Otto* (3), *Hans* (2), *Kurt* (2), *Alois, Franz, Friedrich, Viktor*.

Kappeler (146) German: variant of KAPPLER.

Kappelman (176) German (**Kappelmann**): habitational name for someone from any of various places called Kappel, Cappel, or Kappeln (see KAPPEL).
GIVEN NAME German 4%. *Kurt*.

Kappen (144) German: most likely a shortened form of **Kappenmacher**, an occupational name for a maker of hoods and hooded cloaks (see KAPP), or of **Kappenberg**, a habitational name from a place so named near Minden, Westphalia.
GIVEN NAME German 5%. *Ernst* (2).

Kappenman (119) German (**Kappenmann**): probably a nickname for someone who wore a hood or a coat with a hood, from Middle Low German *kappe* 'long outer garment', 'overcoat', 'robe' (typically one made of high quality material) (see KAPP).

Kapper (171) **1.** North German and Dutch: from a variant of the personal name KASPAR. **2.** German: occupational name, from an agent derivative of Middle High German *kappen* 'to caponize or castrate (chickens)'. **3.** Dutch: variant of KAPER.

Kappers (107) **1.** Dutch (also **Cappers**): occupational name for a hood maker or nickname for someone who habitually wore a hood, from an agentderivative of Middle Dutch *cappe* 'hood'. **2.** Dutch and North German: patronymic form of a variant of the personal names GEBHARDT or KASPER (see also KASPAR).
GIVEN NAME German 4%. *Erwin*.

Kappes (640) German: variant of KAPPUS.

Kapple (123) Americanized spelling of German KAPPEL.

Kappler (519) German: **1.** occupational name for a clergyman bound to a chapel and living in its vicinity (i.e. a chaplain or a chaplain's assistant), from Latin *capellarius*. **2.** habitational name for someone from a place named Kappel or topographic name for someone who lived by a chapel, Middle High German *kappel(le)* (see KAPPEL).
GIVEN NAMES German 5%. *Otto* (2), *Erwin, Fritz, Hermann, Kurt, Willi, Wolfgang*.

Kappus (202) German: metonymic occupational name for a cabbage farmer, from Middle High German *kabess* 'cabbage head' (a loanword from Latin *caput* 'head').
GIVEN NAMES German 7%. *Hans-Peter, Kurt, Ulrich, Wilfried*.

Kapral (219) **1.** Polish: from *kapral* 'corporal' (ultimately from Latin *caput* 'head'), hence a status name for a corporal in the army. **2.** Reduced form of Greek **Kapralos**, which may also be a military status name meaning 'corporal', derived from Italian *caporale*, but is more probably related to Albanian *kapruall, kaproll* 'roebuck' or Aromanian *caprã* 'goat'.

Kaprelian (106) Armenian: unexplained.
GIVEN NAMES Armenian 9%. *Hagop, Karekin, Raffi, Satenig, Vahe*.

Kaprielian (119) Armenian: patronymic from the personal name *Kapriel* (see GABRIEL).
GIVEN NAMES Armenian 33%. *Ara* (4), *Aram* (2), *Hratch* (2), *Agop, Arakel, Armen, Armenag, Arshag, Artin, Kapriel, Kevork, Raffi*.

Kaps (175) **1.** German: reduced form of KAPPUS. **2.** Slovenian (**Kapš**): probably a shortened and metathesized form of the personal name *Kašper*, an old vernacular form of *Gašper* (see CASPAR).
GIVEN NAMES German 8%. *Erwin* (2), *Franz, Fritz, Gottfried*.

Kapsch (104) German: **1.** Probably a metonymic occupational name for a cabbage farmer or a nickname for a poor person, from Middle High German *kabez* (from Latin *caput* 'head', 'head of [white] cabbage'). **2.** (**Käpsch**): from a short form of a Germanic personal name formed with *geba* 'gift' as the first element, as in GEBHARDT.

Kapsner (139) Origin unidentified.

Kapur (350) Indian: variant spelling of KAPOOR.
GIVEN NAMES Indian 91%. *Krishan* (6), *Sanjay* (6), *Ashok* (5), *Vivek* (5), *Arun* (4), *Kailash* (4), *Ramesh* (4), *Rohit* (4), *Sunil* (4), *Vijay* (4), *Anil* (3), *Deepak* (3).

Kapuscinski (192) Polish (**Kapuściński**): habitational name for someone from Kapuścin or Kapuścino, placed named with *kapusta* 'cabbage'.
GIVEN NAMES Polish 12%; French 5%. *Zdzislaw* (2), *Andrzej, Beata, Casimir, Jaroslaw, Pawel, Stanislaw, Zygmunt; Ignace, Jacques*.

Kapusta (347) Polish, Czech, and Slovak: from *kapusta* 'cabbage', hence a metonymic occupational name for a cabbage grower or a nickname for someone with a peculiarity of the head.
GIVEN NAMES Polish 8%. *Janusz* (2), *Kazimierz* (2), *Andrzej, Jolanta, Leszek, Stanislaw, Wladyslaw, Zigmund, Zygmunt*.

Kapustka (142) Polish and Czech: from a diminutive of KAPUSTA.
GIVEN NAMES Polish 8%. *Bronislaw, Janusz, Karol, Zofia*.

Kar (149) **1.** Indian (Bengal) and Bangladeshi: Hindu (Kayasth) name, probably from Sanskrit *kara* 'doer', 'hand'. **2.** Jewish: origin uncertain; perhaps a nickname from Hebrew *kar* 'cold'.
GIVEN NAMES Indian 43%; Jewish 4%. *Dilip* (2), *Tapas* (2), *Amit, Anil, Ashok, Bharati,*

Dev, Dulal, Gautam, Gopal, Jayashree, Kalpana; Ziva (2), Binyamin, Hillel, Pincus, Yoel.

Kara (375) **1.** Indian (Gujarat): Hindu (Bhatia) name of unknown meaning. **2.** Polish: nickname from *karać* 'to punish'. **3.** Czech, Slovak, and Hungarian: from a pet form of a personal name: Czech *Karel*, Slovak *Karol*, Hungarian *Károly*, vernacular forms of *Carolus* (see CHARLES). **4.** Czech: metonymic occupational name for a carter, from *kára* 'hand cart'. **5.** Greek: see CARAS.

GIVEN NAMES Muslim 12%; Indian 5%. *Ali (2), Salim (2), Sultan (2), Alkarim, Amin, Fayez, Halim, Hamza, Kader, Maher, Malika, Munzer; Ashok (2), Dhirajlal, Jitendra, Murthy, Ramnik, Seema.*

Karaba (115) Slovak: unexplained. All American bearers of this name apparently originate from the village of Drahovce in Slovakia.

Karabin (170) **1.** Jewish (Ashkenazic): ornamental name from Russian *karabin* 'carbine' (see CARBINE). **2.** Perhaps also a reduced form of Greek **Karabinos** or **Karabineris**, or a derivative of these such as the patronymic **Karabinidis**, from Greek *karabina* 'carbine', 'musket used by cavalry', Italian *carabina*. This was also used as an unflattering nickname for a lazy or opportunistic person and for a tight player at cards.

Karaffa (211) Germanized spelling of Italian **Caraffa**, from *caraffa* 'carafe', 'water jug' (probably a derivative of Arabic *gharrāf* 'water wheel'). The Italian surname has cognates in several other European languages, e.g. Spanish **Garrafa**, German **Karaffe**, and any of these could lie behind the American family name.

Karahalios (100) Greek: from Turkish *karahal*, a kind of bird of prey. *Karahal* is also found as a surname in Turkish.

GIVEN NAMES Greek 24%. *Vasilios (2), Andreas, Angelos, Christos, Dimitrios, Efstathios, Fotios, Spiro, Vasiliki.*

Karalis (157) Greek: **1.** from the Turkish personal name *Kara Ali* 'Black (or Moody) Ali'. **2.** from the Slavic personal name *Kral* 'king'.

GIVEN NAMES Greek 18%. *Despina (3), Dimitrios (2), Constantine, Costas, Fotios, Ioannis, Panagiotis, Spiro, Stavros.*

Karam (889) Muslim: from a personal name based on Arabic *karam* 'generosity', 'bounty'. In Arabic this name is usually used in combination with other words, e.g. **Karamullah** (*Karam Allah* 'bounty of Allah').

GIVEN NAMES Muslim 13%; French 6%. *Samir (4), Issa (3), Karam (3), Karim (3), Ali (2), Halim (2), Maher (2), Majed (2), Nasr (2), Walid (2), Abdallah, Abdel; Andre (5), Antoine (4), Emile (3), Clovis, Michel, Micheline, Pierre.*

Karan (231) **1.** Indian (Bengal, Orissa) and Bangladeshi: Hindu (Kayasth) name, from the name of a subgroup in the Kayasth community, derived from Sanskrit *karaṇa* 'writer', 'scribe'. **2.** Jewish (Eastern Ashkenazic): variant of KORAN.

GIVEN NAMES Indian 12%; Jewish 5%; Russian 4%. *Deo (2), Divya, Hemant, Pankaj, Rajesh, Rajnish, Renuka, Shashi, Umesh; Faina, Ilya, Yakov, Zalmon; Aleksandr, Boris, Leonid, Vladimir, Yefim.*

Karapetian (140) Armenian: patronymic from the classical Armenian personal name *Karaped*, from a word meaning 'leader'.

GIVEN NAMES Armenian 56%; Russian 4%. *Armen (2), Gaiane (2), Grigor (2), Haik (2), Minas (2), Samvel (2), Vahe (2), Akop, Anik, Ara, Armenak, Arusyak; Fanya, Garri, Grisha.*

Karapetyan (107) Armenian: variant spelling of KARAPETIAN.

GIVEN NAMES Armenian 57%. *Sarkis (4), Oganes (3), Gegam (2), Naira (2), Alvard, Ambartsum, Aramais, Armen, Ashot, Azat, Gayane, Gevorg.*

Karas (1847) **1.** Polish (**Karaś**); Hungarian (**Kárász**); Czech, Slovak, Croatian, Slovenian (Prekmurje), and Jewish (Ashkenazic): from Slavic *karas* 'crucian carp', hence a metonymic occupational name for a carp fisher or possibly a nickname for someone with a fishlike appearance. As a Jewish name it is mainly an ornamental name. **2.** Greek: from a nickname meaning 'black' (see CARAS). **3.** Hungarian: topographic name for someone living by the Karas river, a tributary of the river Danube, named with Turkish *kara* 'black' + *suğ* 'water'. **4.** German: from a short form of the personal name ZACHARIAS or of the Greek saint's name *Makarios*, meaning 'blessed one'.

Karasek (319) Polish and Jewish (from Poland): from a diminutive of KARAS.

GIVEN NAME French 4%. *Patrice.*

Karash (127) **1.** Jewish (eastern Ashkenazic): ornamental name from Polish *karaś* 'carp'. **2.** Americanized spelling of Hungarian KARAS 4.

GIVEN NAME German 4%. *Fritz.*

Karasik (213) **1.** Jewish (eastern Ashkenazic) and Czech: from a diminutive of *karas* 'crucian carp' (see KARAS), presumably a metonymic occupational name for a carp fisher or a nickname for someone thought to resemble the fish. As a Jewish name it is mainly an ornamental name. **2.** Czech: from a derivative of the personal name KAREL.

GIVEN NAMES Russian 16%; Jewish 16%. *Boris (6), Leonid (2), Mikhail (2), Yefim (2), Aleksandr, Anatoly, Arkady, Dmitriy, Lev, Semyon, Vladimir, Vladmir; Isak (2), Fira, Hillel, Hyman, Iren, Isaak, Marat, Miriam, Naum, Shira.*

Karasinski (127) Polish (**Karasiński**): habitational name for someone from any of various places called Karaś, named with Polish *karaś* 'crucian carp'.

GIVEN NAMES Polish 14%. *Dariusz, Leszek, Maciej, Pawel, Piotr, Stanislaw.*

Karau (160) German: variant of KARAS 1.

GIVEN NAMES German 4%. *Arno, Hans.*

Karban (128) **1.** Czech: nickname for a gambler, from *karban* 'to gamble'. **2.** Polish: nickname for an overseer, from *karb* 'notch', 'nick'.

Karber (209) **1.** German: unexplained; perhaps from an agent derivative of Middle High German *karwe* 'field caraway'. **2.** German: probably a habitational name for someone from either Grosskarben or Kleinkarben in Hesse.

Karbowski (294) Polish: habitational name for someone from Karbowo in Toruń voivodeship, a place so named from Polish *karbowy* 'overseer (of farm laborers)', from *karbować* 'to make notches', i.e. to keep records.

GIVEN NAMES Polish 5%. *Izydor, Slawomir.*

Karch (704) **1.** Jewish (Ashkenazic): Americanized spelling of KARCZ. **2.** German: metonymic occupational name for a carter, from Middle High German *karrech* 'barrow', 'two-wheeled cart'. **3.** northern or central German variant of KARG.

Karcher (1155) German (also **Kärcher**): occupational name for a carter; an agent derivative of KARCH 2.

Karchner (121) German (**Kärchner**): variant of KARCHER, an occupational name from Middle High German *karrecher*, *kercher* 'porter'.

Karcz (234) Polish and Jewish (Ashkenazic): from Polish *karcz* 'stump', presumably a nickname, or among Jews an ornamental name.

GIVEN NAMES Polish 11%. *Andrzej (2), Genowefa, Janina, Marzenna, Miroslaw, Piotr, Stanislaw, Witold.*

Karczewski (407) Polish and Jewish (from Poland): habitational name for someone from Karczew, named with Polish *karcz* 'stump'.

GIVEN NAMES Polish 5%. *Bogdan (2), Casimir, Elzbieta, Irena, Jerzy, Jozef.*

Kardas (141) **1.** Polish (**Kardasz**), Czech and Slovak (**Kardaš**): from an old Slavic word meaning 'brother' or 'kinsman', probably denoting a member of a junior branch of an important noble family. **2.** Perhaps also Greek, a reduced form of **Kardassis** 'brother', from Turkish *kardaş* 'brother, comrade' or from a patronymic derivative of this, e.g. **Kardassakis**, **Kardassiadis**, **Kardassopoulos**.

GIVEN NAMES Polish 12%. *Aleksander (2), Irena, Jaroslaw, Maciej, Pawel, Stanislaw.*

Kardash (107) **1.** Jewish (from Ukraine): habitational name from Kardash, a village in Rovno district, Ukraine. **2.** Americanized spelling of Slavic KARDAS 1.

GIVEN NAMES Russian 5%; Jewish 4%. *Nadezhda, Vitaly; Aron, Irina.*

Kardell (188) **1.** Altered spelling of German **Kardel**, a metonymic occupational name for a wool carder, from a Rhineland dialect word, *Karde* 'thistle', dried thistle heads having originally been used to comb and clean (i.e. card) wool. **2.** topographic name from *Kardel*, Rhineland dialect for a steep hillside path hewn out of the rock.
GIVEN NAMES German 4%. *Franz, Hans, Kurt.*

Kardon (166) Jewish (from Ukraine): from Russian *kordon* 'border'.
GIVEN NAME French 4%. *Cecile.*

Kardos (502) **1.** Hungarian and Jewish (from Hungary): from *kard* 'sword', hence a metonymic occupational name for a warrior or a status name for a swordsman, i.e. a nobleman who had the right to wear a sword. As a Jewish surname it was ornamental. **2.** Czech (**Kardoš**): variant of KARDAS.
GIVEN NAMES Hungarian 9%. *Bela* (4), *Laszlo* (3), *Gabor* (2), *Andras, Geza, Gyula, Janos, Jeno, Kalman, Laszio, Zsolt.*

Karel (382) Dutch, German, Czech, and Slovenian: from the personal name *Karel* (see CHARLES).

Karels (336) Dutch: patronymic from KAREL.

Karem (124) Origin unidentified.

Karen (191) Czech: from *Kara* or *Kára*, derivatives of the personal name *Karel* (see CHARLES).
GIVEN NAMES Jewish 6%. *Ari, Aron, Gidon, Shoshana.*

Kares (103) **1.** Czech: from *Kara* or *Kára*, derivatives of the personal name *Karel*, Czech form of CHARLES. **2.** German: from a reduced form of the Greek personal name *Makarios* (see MACARIO).
GIVEN NAME French 5%. *Marcel.*

Karg (497) **1.** German: nickname from Middle High German *karc* 'cunning' 'sly', 'tricky'. **2.** Jewish (Ashkenazic): nickname for a mean person, from Yiddish *karg(er)* 'stingy', 'niggardly' (from Middle High German *karc* 'cunning').
GIVEN NAMES German 7%. *Manfred* (2), *Otto* (2), *Alois, Gunter, Kurt, Wolfgang.*

Karge (128) German (also found in Poland): variant of KARG 1.
GIVEN NAMES German 5%. *Bodo, Kurt.*

Karger (366) **1.** German: nickname for a sly, tricky, or unreliable man (see KARG). **2.** Jewish (Ashkenazic): variant of KARG 2. **3.** German and Czech: habitational name for someone from a place called Kargen in Bavaria.

Karges (203) German: from the personal name *Karges*, a derivative of ZACHARIAS, or a pet form of *Makarios* (see MACARIO).

Karhoff (123) German: topographic name from Middle High German *kar* 'bowl', 'hollow', for a farm or house on low-lying ground, or from *kār* 'turn', 'switchback', for someone living on a bend or turn in a road.

Kari (272) **1.** Finnish: topographic and ornamental name from *kari* 'small island', 'stony rapids', 'sandbar', or 'rocky place in a field'. This name is found throughout Finland. **2.** German: from a Carinthian pet form of the personal name ZACHARIAS. **3.** Hungarian: from a pet form of the personal name *Károly*, Hungarian form of CHARLES. **4.** Indian (Maharashtra): Hindu (Maratha) name of unknown meaning.
GIVEN NAMES Finnish 7%; Indian 4%. *Pentti* (2), *Ahti, Armas, Eino, Tauno, Toini, Waino*; *Prasad* (2), *Ramesh, Suresh, Uday.*

Karim (714) Muslim: from a personal name based on Arabic *karīm* 'kind', 'generous'. *Al-Karīm* 'the Generous' is an attribute of Allah. The word is found in compound names such as *'Abdul-Karīm* 'servant of the Most Generous'.
GIVEN NAMES Muslim 78%. *Abdul* (32), *Mohammad* (16), *Mohammed* (9), *Fazal* (8), *Syed* (8), *Rezaul* (7), *Aziz* (6), *Aminul* (5), *Anwar* (5), *Iqbal* (5), *Muhammad* (5), *Ali* (4).

Karimi (298) Muslim: adjectival derivative of KARIM, meaning 'relating to Karim'.
GIVEN NAMES Muslim 80%. *Ali* (10), *Majid* (7), *Hamid* (6), *Hossein* (5), *Mohammad* (5), *Simin* (3), *Afsaneh* (2), *Ahmad* (2), *Akhtar* (2), *Amir* (2), *Amirali* (2), *Bijan* (2).

Karis (252) German and Dutch: **1.** variant of KARAS. **2.** from *Karius*, a reduced form of the personal name *Makarios* (see MACARIO).
GIVEN NAME German 5%. *Kurt* (2).

Karjala (140) Finnish: from *karja* 'cattle' + the local suffix *-la*, or possibly from a word of Germanic origin, *harja-* 'host', 'crowd', Old Swedish *haer*. Historic records suggest that the Germanic inhabitants of the area around Lake Ladoga (in present-day Russia) used this term to refer to the Finns who once lived there.
GIVEN NAMES Finnish 7%. *Eino, Urho, Waino, Wilho.*

Kark (126) **1.** Possibly a variant spelling of German **Karg** or **Karch**, a nickname from Middle High German *karc* in any of its various senses: 'clever', 'crafty', 'sly'; 'strong', 'violent'; 'mean', or 'barren'. **2.** Low German variant of KIRCH.
GIVEN NAMES German 7%. *Gerhard* (2), *Otto.*

Karl (2490) German, Dutch, Scandinavian, and eastern and southern Slavic: from the personal name *Karl*, from a common Germanic word, Old High German *karl* 'man', 'husband', 'freeman'. See also CARL and CHARLES. The popularity of this name and its cognates in central and northern Europe was greatly enhanced by its status as a royal and imperial name; in particular it was bestowed in honor of the Frankish emperor Charlemagne (in Latin, *Carolus Magnus*).
GIVEN NAMES German 4%. *Hans* (5), *Lothar* (4), *Erwin* (3), *Erhard* (2), *Georg* (2), *Otto*

(2), *Bernd, Bernhard, Ernst, Gerhard, Hartmut, Heinz.*

Karlberg (140) Swedish: variant spelling of CARLBERG.

Karle (468) German (Schleswig-Holstein and East Prussia) and Swiss German: variant of KARL.

Karlen (454) **1.** German and Swiss German: derivative of KARL. **2.** Swedish: variant spelling of CARLEN.

Karlik (177) **1.** Czech (**Karlík**) and Slovak: from a form of the Slavic personal name *Karel* or *Karol*, vernacular forms of the Latin name *Carolus* (see KARL, CHARLES). **2.** Polish, Ukrainian, and Jewish (from Poland and Ukraine): nickname from eastern Slavic and Yiddish *karlik* 'dwarf'.
GIVEN NAMES Russian 4%. *Semyon* (2), *Yefim.*

Karlin (896) **1.** Jewish (eastern Ashkenazic): habitational name for someone from Karlin, a suburb of Pinsk in Belarus, in which the Jews formed the majority of the population until the Holocaust. A well-known Hasidic sect originated in Karlin and at one time it attracted so many followers that a (now obsolete) Russian word for 'Hasid' was *Karliner* (of Yiddish origin). It is possible that at least some people taking this surname did so because they were members of this sect and not because they were born or lived in Karlin. **2.** German (also **Kärlin**) and Southern Slavic: from the personal name KARL (Slavic *Karlo*). See also CHARLES. **3.** Swedish: variant spelling of CARLIN. **4.** Western Slavic: habitational name from places in Poland and Bohemia. **5.** Altered spelling of Russian *Karélin*, ethnic name for someone from Karelia (see KARJALA). **6.** Altered spelling of German GERLING.

Karlovich (157) Croatian (**Karlović**) and Slovenian (western Slovenia; **Karlovič**): patronymic from the personal name *Karlo* (Croatian) or *Karel* (Slovenian), of Germanic origin (see KARL, CHARLES).

Karls (461) German: patronymic from KARL.

Karlsen (254) Danish, Norwegian, North German, and Dutch: patronymic from the personal name *Karl* (see CHARLES).
GIVEN NAMES Scandinavian 29%; German 8%. *Anders* (2), *Bjorn, Britt, Erik, Holger, Knut, Magnar, Oddvar, Oyvind, Per, Svein, Thor*; *Bernhardt, Ernst, Fritz, Kurt.*

Karlson (772) **1.** Respelling of a Scandinavian patronymic derived from the personal name KARL, i.e. Swedish KARLSSON or Danish and Norwegian KARLSEN. **2.** German: patronymic from the personal name KARL. See also CHARLES.
GIVEN NAMES Scandinavian 12%; German 5%. *Algot* (2), *Lars* (2), *Nils* (2), *Eskil, Holger, Knute, Lennart, Sven*; *Kurt* (2), *Hans, Otto.*

Karlsson (326) Swedish: patronymic from the personal name *Karl* (see CHARLES).

GIVEN NAMES Scandinavian 46%; German 9%; Dutch 4%. *Lars* (7), *Anders* (5), *Alf* (2), *Bjorn* (2), *Erik* (2), *Kerstin* (2), *Agust*, *Elnar*, *Fritjof*, *Gudmundur*, *Johan*, *Kristinn*; *Hans* (5), *Kurt* (2), *Egon*, *Ernst*, *Matthias*; *Henrik* (2), *Marten* (2).

Karlstad (127) **1.** Swedish: habitational name from Karlstad in western Sweden. **2.** Norwegian: habitational name from any of several farms in southeastern Norway called Karlstad, from the personal name *Karl* + *stad* 'farm', 'place'. **3.** Respelling of German and Ashkenazic Jewish **Karlstadt**, a habitational name from places so named in Franconia and Croatia.
GIVEN NAMES Scandinavian 10%. *Carsten*, *Erland*, *Hjalmer*, *Lief*.

Karm (116) Swedish: of uncertain origin; possibly a soldier's name from *karm* meaning, among other things, 'covered wagon'.

Karman (239) **1.** Dutch: occupational name for a carter, Middle Dutch *kerreman*. **2.** Hungarian (**Kármán**): from *kármány*, ethnic name for the Turkish people of southern Anatolia's Karaman region, which was famous for its silk and leather products. The Hungarian name is probably derived via medieval Latin *Caramanus*, *Carmanus*, not directly from Turkish. **3.** Jewish (from Hungary): adoption of 2. **4.** Jewish (eastern Ashkenazic): from Russian *karman* 'bag', 'pocket', presumably applied as a metonymic occupational name for a maker of such articles. **5.** Altered spelling of German KARMANN.

Karmann (113) **1.** North German: occupational name for a carter, Middle Low German *karman*. **2.** South German: from Middle High German *kar* 'container', 'bowl', 'grain measure' + *-man* 'man', hence an occupational name for a maker of such utensils. **3.** German (Tyrolean): topographic name for someone who lived in a *kar*, a bowl-shaped valley bottom.

Karmazin (111) Ukrainian and Czech; Hungarian (**Karmazsin**); and Jewish (from Ukraine and Poland): from *karmazin* (Czech *karmazín*) 'dark red cloth' (ultimately from Arabic *qirmizī* 'crimson'), probably a metonymic occupational name for a dyer or a producer of dyestuffs.

Karmel (142) Jewish (from Poland): **1.** ornamental name from Polish *karmel* 'caramel', 'burnt sugar'. **2.** Jewish (Israeli): modern Hebrew name from Mount Carmel, mentioned in the Bible (1 Kings 18:19).
GIVEN NAMES Jewish 15%. *Miriam* (2), *Zvi* (2), *Leibel*, *Mazal*, *Menashe*, *Shaul*.

Karn (740) **1.** Irish: variant of KERN, a reduced and altered form of MCCARRON. **2.** German (**Kärn**): variant of KERN.

Karnatz (108) German: **1.** habitational name for someone from a place in eastern Germany named Karnatz. **2.** variant of **Kornatz**, from Slavic *kornac* 'hornblower',

an occupational name for a musician employed by a town or court.
GIVEN NAMES German 8%. *Hertha*, *Kurt*, *Otto*.

Karner (416) German: **1.** from South German dialect *Karner* 'charnel house', hence a metonymic occupational name for an undertaker. **2.** in northern Germany, a metonymic occupational name for a peddler who used a handcart or barrow, from *Karren* 'cart' + the *-er* agent suffix. **3.** possibly a variant of KERNER or **Körner** (see KOERNER) or an altered spelling of GARNER, GERNER.
GIVEN NAMES German 4%. *Kurt* (2), *Erwin*, *Gunther*.

Karnes (2103) **1.** Irish: variant of KEARNS. **2.** perhaps also an Americanized spelling of Polish **Karniesz**, a noun derivative of the adjective *karny* 'obedient'.

Karney (278) Irish: reduced form of MCCARNEY.

Karnik (150) **1.** Czech (**Kárník**): occupational name for a user or maker of hand carts (see KARA). Alternatively, it may be a nickname for a convicted offender, from *kárat* 'to punish or scold'. **2.** Indian (Karnataka, Maharashtra): Hindu (Brahman, Kayasth Prabhu) name, ultimately from Sanskrit *karaṇa* 'writer', 'scribe'. This name is found among the Havyaka Brahmans in Karnataka and the Kayastha Prabhus of Maharashtra.
GIVEN NAMES Indian 48%. *Satish* (6), *Rahul* (3), *Ashok* (2), *Dilip* (2), *Jayant* (2), *Ajit*, *Arvind*, *Ash*, *Ashutosh*, *Chandan*, *Ganesh*, *Kanchan*.

Karnitz (140) Variant of German KARNATZ.
GIVEN NAMES German 7%. *Armin*, *Eldred*, *Erwin*.

Karnopp (141) North German: variant of **Karnap**, from Middle Low German *karnap* 'oriel window', 'bay window'; hence probably a habitational name for someone who lived at a house distinguished by such a window or at a place named with this word. Karnap is also found in topographic and habitational names, such as Karnap near Essen.

Karnowski (172) Polish (also **Karniowski**) and Jewish (eastern Ashkenazic): habitational name for someone from a place called Karniów, in Kraków voivodeship, or Karniewo, in Ciechanów voivodeship.

Karns (1402) Irish: variant of KEARNS.

Karo (145) **1.** Bulgarian (**Káro**): from the Turkish loanword *kara* 'black'. **2.** Jewish (Sephardic, also Ashkenazic): nickname from Spanish *caro* 'dear'. The surname is recorded in Toledo, Spain, in the 14th century. The Ashkenazic branch is ultimately of Sephardic origin. **3.** Slovenian: unexplained.
GIVEN NAMES German 4%. *Kurt*, *Wolf*.

Karol (474) **1.** Western Slavic: from the personal name *Karol* (see CHARLES). **2.** Jewish: possibly a shortened form of

some Ashkenazic name, as for example **Karolinski**, a habitational name for someone from the town of Karolin, in Poland and Belarus.
GIVEN NAMES Jewish 4%. *Hyman* (2), *Isak*, *Mendel*.

Karoly (157) Hungarian: **1.** from the personal name *Károly*, Hungarian form of CHARLES. **2.** habitational name from a place so named in Bihar County. **3.** possibly from *karuly*, variant of *karvaly* 'sparrow-hawk', a symbolic name from a totemic animal of an ancient Hungarian tribe.
GIVEN NAMES Hungarian 5%. *Ferenc* (2), *Laszlo*.

Karon (160) **1.** Dutch and French (Picardy): variant spelling of CARON 3. **2.** Jewish (from Belarus): unexplained.

Karow (382) German (of Sorbian origin): habitational name for someone from Carow in Mecklenburg, or any of several places in eastern Germany named Karow.

Karp (2904) **1.** German, Polish, and Jewish (eastern Ashkenazic): from Middle High German *karp(f)e*, Middle Low German *karpe*, or Slavic (Russian and Polish) and Yiddish *karp* 'carp', hence a metonymic occupational name for a carp fisherman or seller of these fish, or a nickname for someone thought to resemble the fish. As a Jewish surname it is often of ornamental origin. **2.** Polish, Russian, and German: from a reduced vernacular form of the Greek saint's name *Polykarpos* (meaning 'rich in fruit'), or *Karponios* (from Greek *karpos* 'fruit', a word with mystical connotations among early Christians). This was the name of an early Christian leader said to have known the Apostle John. In the Orthodox Church he is believed to have been a bishop and is revered as a saint.
GIVEN NAMES Jewish 4%. *Miriam* (5), *Sol* (3), *Chaim* (2), *Isadore* (2), *Abbe*, *Aron*, *Avrum*, *Cyla*, *Eliyahu*, *Ephraim*, *Golde*, *Hyman*.

Karpe (101) **1.** Indian (Maharashtra); pronounced as *cur-pay*: Hindu (Maratha) name, from Marathi *kərpa* 'burned', 'scorched'. **2.** Possibly also an American variant of KARP.
GIVEN NAMES Indian 6%. *Pratima*, *Yatin*.

Karpel (199) **1.** German and Polish: from a personal name, a diminutive of KARP 2. **2.** Jewish (Ashkenazic): from the Yiddish personal name *karpl*, a pet form of KARP 1. **3.** Altered form of Polish **Karpiel** 'rutabago', a metonymic nickname for a peasant farmer.
GIVEN NAMES Jewish 7%; German 4%. *Ari*, *Ephraim*, *Miriam*, *Zev*, *Zvi*; *Theodor*.

Karpen (202) German: from central or northern German dialect *Karpe(n)* 'carp', hence a metonymic occupational name for a carp fisherman or a seller of these fish, or a nickname for a person with fishlike features. The standard modern German form of the word is **Karpfen**.

Karpenko (110) Ukrainian: patronymic from KARP 2.

GIVEN NAMES Russian 13. *Leonid* (2), *Igor, Mikhail, Nikolay, Raissa, Yana.*

Karper (148) German and Jewish (from Poland and Germany): a derivative of KARP.

Karpf (226) German and Jewish (Ashkenazic): from Middle High German *karpfe*, German *Karpfen*, a metonymic occupational name for a carp fisherman or seller of these fish, or a nickname for someone with a fishlike appearance (see KARP 1). As a Jewish name it is mainly of ornamental origin.

GIVEN NAMES Jewish 4%. *Sol, Yitzchok.*

Karpiak (128) Polish: patronymic derivative of KARP 2.

Karpinski (1068) Polish (**Karpiński**) and Jewish (eastern Ashkenazic): habitational name for someone from either of the places named Karpin, in the voivodeships of Łódź and Ostrołęka, or from some other place named with *karp* (see KARP 1).

GIVEN NAMES Polish 6%. *Zygmunt* (3), *Slawomir* (2), *Andrzej, Boguslaw, Casimir, Dariusz, Halina, Irena, Jozef, Krzystof, Lech, Rafal.*

Karpman (103) Jewish (eastern Ashkenazic): elaborated form of KARP 1.

GIVEN NAMES Jewish 13%; Russian 11%. *Ephraim, Feyga, Ilya, Itzhak, Marat, Moisey, Sarra; Boris* (2), *Aleksandr, Leonid, Lev, Natalya.*

Karpovich (149) **1.** Jewish (eastern Ashkenazic): patronymic from KARP 1. **2.** Eastern Slavic: patronymic from KARP 2. **3.** Jewish (eastern Ashkenazic): habitational name for someone from the village of Karpovichi in Belarus.

GIVEN NAMES Russian 5%; Jewish 5%; French 4%. *Igor, Leonid, Sergey, Vladimir; Esfir, Yakov; Serge* (2).

Karpowich (123) Variant spelling of Slavic and Jewish KARPOVICH.

Karpowicz (254) Polish and Jewish (from Poland): patronymic from KARP.

GIVEN NAMES Polish 10%. *Tadeusz* (2), *Andrzej, Henryk, Jadwiga, Janusz, Lucjan, Mieczyslaw, Walentyna.*

Karr (3843) German: shortened form of KARREN or KARRER.

Karraker (226) **1.** Variant spelling of Scottish **Kerracher**, a reduced form of **MacKerracher**. **2.** Americanized form of KARRIKER.

Karras (553) **1.** Greek: occupational name for a carter, from *karro* 'cart' + the occupational suffix -*as*. **2.** Greek: nickname from *karas* 'black', 'dark', a variant spelling of CARRAS. **3.** German: variant spelling of KARAS 1.

GIVEN NAMES Greek 9%. *Andreas* (3), *Dimitrios* (3), *Kostas* (2), *Spiros* (2), *Constantine, Costas, Evangelos, Georgios, Taso, Thanos, Xenophon.*

Karre (103) **1.** German: probably a variant of *Karremann*, an occupational name for a carter (see KARMAN 1). Middle Low German *kar(re)* is an early loanword from Latin *carrus* 'cart', 'wagon'. **2.** Dutch: occupational name for a cart or wagon driver.

Karrels (122) Origin unidentified.

Karren (234) German: from Middle High German *karre* 'cart', 'barrow' (Latin *carrus*), hence a metonymic occupational name for a carter or cart maker.

Karrer (285) German and Swiss German: metonymic occupational name for a carter or cartwright, from Middle High German *karre* 'barrow' + -*er* agent suffix.

GIVEN NAMES German 8%. *Ulrich* (2), *Erna, Heinz, Kurt, Urs.*

Karrick (236) **1.** Variant of Scottish CARRICK or reduced form of Irish MCCARRICK. **2.** Possibly also German: metonymic occupational name for a carter or cartwright, from Middle High German *karrech* 'cart', from Latin *carruca*. Compare KARCHER.

Karriker (203) Probably an altered spelling of Irish CARRAHER.

Karsch (129) **1.** German: nickname for a cheerful vivacious person, from Middle Low German *karsch* 'lively', 'merry'. **2.** Jewish (Ashkenazic): Germanized spelling of KARSH.

GIVEN NAME German 5%. *Gunter* (2).

Karschner (109) German: habitational name for someone from Karrasch in former West Prussia.

Karsh (247) **1.** Jewish (Ashkenazic): ornamental name from Yiddish *karsh* 'cherry'. **2.** Americanized spelling of German KARSCH, KIRCH, or KIRSCH.

GIVEN NAMES Jewish 6%. *Bentzion, Hymen.*

Karshner (151) **1.** Americanized spelling of German KARSCHNER or possibly KIRCHNER. **2.** variant of the Jewish surname KURSCHNER.

Karsky (100) German (of Slavic origin).

GIVEN NAME German 4%. *Otto.*

Karson (223) **1.** English: possibly an altered spelling of northern Irish CARSON. **2.** Swiss German: unexplained.

Karst (739) German: from Middle High German *karst* 'mattock', 'hoe', hence a metonymic occupational name for a maker or user of such tools.

GIVEN NAMES German 5%. *Kurt* (4), *Otto* (2), *Frieda, Hertha, Reinhard, Ulrike.*

Karsten (821) Scandinavian (especially Denmark): variant spelling of CARSTEN.

GIVEN NAMES German 6%. *Kurt* (7), *Erhardt, Ernst, Hans, Helmut, Horst, Klaus, Orlo, Siegfried.*

Karstens (321) Patronymic from KARSTEN. The spelling *Carstens* is more common.

GIVEN NAMES French 4%. *Michel, Vernice.*

Karstetter (183) German: habitational name for someone from a place called Karstädt in Mecklenburg or Prignitz region.

Kartchner (267) Perhaps an Americanized variant of German KIRCHNER.

Karten (131) Jewish (Ashkenazic): from German *Karten* 'playing cards', hence most probably a nickname for a gambler.

GIVEN NAME Jewish 9%. *Sol* (2).

Karter (175) German: occupational name for a carder (someone who prepares wool for spinning), from Middle High German *karter.*

Kartes (196) Altered spelling of German KORDES or GERDES.

Kartman (113) Jewish (Ashkenazic): from German *Karte* 'playing card' + *Mann*; possibly a nickname for a gambler.

Karvonen (188) Finnish: **1.** most probably from a Germanic personal name such as *Garuward* or *Garufrid*. **2.** alternatively, perhaps from *karva* 'fur', 'hair' (possibly applied as a nickname) + the common surname suffix -*nen*.

GIVEN NAMES Finnish 12%. *Aaro, Eino, Mauno, Petri, Reino, Sulo, Tauno, Waino.*

Karwacki (143) Polish: habitational name for someone from Karwacz in Ostrołęka voivodeship, named with *Karw*, a nickname from the dialect word *karw* 'ox'.

Karwoski (378) Polish: variant of KARWOWSKI.

Karwowski (268) Polish: habitational name for someone from Karwowo, or other places named with the dialect word *karw* 'ox'.

GIVEN NAMES Polish 19%. *Jerzy* (3), *Zbigniew* (2), *Zygmunt* (2), *Aleksander, Andrzej, Elzbieta, Genowesa, Henryk, Iwona, Lech, Marcin, Ryszard.*

Kary (362) Irish: variant spelling of CAREY.

Kasa (141) Hungarian (**Kása**); Czech and Slovak (**Kaša**): from a Slavic word meaning 'porridge' (Czech *kaše*, Slovak *kaša*), probably applied as a nickname for a poor farmer. Compare Polish KASZA.

GIVEN NAMES Hungarian 7%. *Jeno* (2), *Zoltan* (2).

Kasai (115) Japanese: in the Tōkyō area and the Ryūkyū Islands, the name is written with characters meaning 'bamboo hat' and 'well'. In western Japan, and in the name of a village east of Tōkyō, it is written with characters meaning 'west of the river', and this latter is pronounced *Kawanishi* by some. Other variants exist as well.

GIVEN NAMES Japanese 65%. *Katsumi* (2), *Kazuhiko* (2), *Minako* (2), *Ryo* (2), *Akihiro, Akio, Ayako, Ayumu, Eiji, Etsuko, Hideo, Hidetoshi.*

Kasak (102) Polish: nickname from Old Polish *kasać się* 'to gird oneself'.

GIVEN NAMES Polish 8%; Russian 5%. *Andrzej, Malgorzata, Stanislaw; Nikolai* (2).

Kasal (205) Czech: nickname for a weak person, someone who was bullied, from *kasal* 'bullied', passive of *kasat se* 'to bully' (see KASA).

Kasarda (123) Origin unidentified.

Kasch (356) German: **1.** variant of KARSCH. **2.** occupational name for a cook, from a Sorbian or other Slavic word related to Czech *kaša* 'porridge'. **3.** from an unexplained medieval personal name, *Cazo*.

Kaschak (215) Slavic: from the personal name *Kaschak*, a short form of *Lukaschek*, a pet form of LUCAS.

Kasdan (129) Jewish (from Belarus): acronymic name from a Talmudic Aramaic expression *Kaheney Shluchey DeRachamona Ninhu* 'they are messengers of the Merciful' (see COHEN).
GIVEN NAMES Jewish 7%. *Asher, Menachem, Miriam.*

Kasdorf (167) **1.** In all probability a Germanized spelling of **Karsdorp**, the name of a prominent Dutch Mennonite family in Leiden, some of which reportedly moved to Hamburg, Germany. **2.** German: habitational name from places in Saxony or former West Prussia called Kasdorf or Kastorf, named with the Rhineland dialect word *Kas, Kos* 'copse of young oaks' + Old High German *dorf, thorf* 'village'. **3.** (**Käsdorf**): habitational name from any of several places in Lower Saxony named Käsdorf.
GIVEN NAMES German 7%. *Kurt* (3), *Frieda, Hans.*

Kase (635) **1.** German (**Käse**): metonymic occupational name for a cheese maker or cheese merchant, from Middle High German *kæse* 'cheese'. **2.** German: topographic name from Rhineland dialect *Kas* 'thicket of young oak trees'. **3.** German: from an unexplained medieval personal name, *Cazo*. **4.** Slovenian (**Kaše**): nickname for a very small man, from the dialect word *keše* 'dwarf'. **5.** Japanese: written with characters meaning 'add' and 'strait'. This name is found mostly in the Tōkyō area.
GIVEN NAMES Japanese 4%. *Akira, Asao, Hiroshi, Isao, Kiyoshi, Nobuyuki, Shuichi, Suguru, Tatsuo, Yu.*

Kasel (258) Americanized spelling of German **Kösel** (see KOSEL).

Kaseman (171) German (**Käsemann**): **1.** occupational name for someone who made or sold cheese, or a topographic name for someone who lived by an oak grove (see KASE). **2.** from an unexplained Germanic stem (see KASE 3).
GIVEN NAME German 4%. *Gottlieb* (2).

Kasen (106) Jewish: variant of KASSIN.
GIVEN NAMES Jewish 7%. *Hyman* (2), *Eliezer.*

Kaser (746) Swiss and German: **1.** (also **Käser**) occupational name for a cheese maker or a cheese merchant, from an agent derivative of Middle High German *kæse* 'cheese'. **2.** topographic name for some-

one who lived by a summer dairy in the Alps, from a Tyrolean dialect word derived from Ladin *casura*.

Kasey (245) Altered spelling of German **Käse** (see KASE).

Kash (570) **1.** Jewish (Ashkenazic): unexplained; perhaps an acronym. **2.** Americanized spelling of KASCH. **3.** Possibly an Americanized spelling of German KIRCH or KIRSCH.

Kashani (169) Iranian: habitational name for someone from the city of Kashān.
GIVEN NAMES Muslim 77%. *Ali* (9), *Amir* (5), *Ahmad* (3), *Hamid* (3), *Saeed* (3), *Afshin* (2), *Haleh* (2), *Hossein* (2), *Mahmoud* (2), *Massoud* (2), *Mehrdad* (2), *Naseer* (2).

Kashner (184) Perhaps an Americanized spelling of German KIRCHNER.

Kashuba (183) Americanized spelling of Polish KASZUBA (German **Kaschuba, Kaschube**).
GIVEN NAMES German 4%. *Kurt, Mathias.*

Kashyap (107) Indian (northern states): Hindu name based on the name of a gotra (an exogamous group among Brahmans and some other communities) called Kashyap. It was the name of a celebrated Hindu sage, from Sanskrit *kaśyapa*, a word with many meanings, including 'tortoise' and 'deer'.
GIVEN NAMES Indian 96%. *Anil* (5), *Kapil* (2), *Krishna* (2), *Narendra* (2), *Neera* (2), *Rajnish* (2), *Vikas* (2), *Vivek* (2), *Yogesh* (2), *Akash, Amit, Arun.*

Kasik (230) Czech and Slovak (**Kasík, Kašík**): from *Kaš*, a pet form of the personal name *Lukáš* (see LUCAS).

Kasinger (206) German (**Käsinger**): variant of **Kiesinger** (see KESINGER).

Kask (114) Swedish (also common in Finland): soldier's name from *kask* 'helmet'.
GIVEN NAMES Scandinavian 6%; German 5%. *Aksel, Erik; Eugen, Hans, Inge.*

Kaska (219) **1.** Czech: from a pet form of the personal name *Kazimír* (see KAZMIERCZAK). **2.** Czech and Slovak (**Kaška**): variant of **Kaša** (see KASA 2). **3.** German: variant of KASKE.
GIVEN NAMES German 4%. *Alfons, Horst.*

Kaske (135) German: **1.** from a Silesian pet form of the Slavic personal name *Lukášek*, Slavic pet form of LUCAS. **2.** (Silesian and East Prussian) from a Slavic word meaning 'duck' (Polish *kaczka*; Czech *kačka*), hence a nickname for someone thought to resemble a duck, or a metonymic occupational name for a breeder or keeper of ducks.
GIVEN NAMES German 10%. *Otto* (2), *Gerhard, Klaus.*

Kaskel (101) German: from a pet form of the personal name KASKE.

Kaskey (108) **1.** Reduced form of Scottish and Irish MCCASKEY. **2.** Americanized spelling of German KASKE. **3.** Possibly also an altered form of Polish KOSKI.

Kaskie (112) **1.** Reduced form of Scottish and Irish MCCASKEY. **2.** Americanized spelling of German KASKE. **3.** Possibly also an altered form of Polish KOSKI.

Kasko (121) Origin unidentified.

Kasler (169) Altered spelling of German KASSLER.
GIVEN NAMES German 5%. *Franz, Kurt.*

Kaslow (132) Origin unidentified.

Kasman (115) Jewish (Ashkenazic): variant of KASSMAN 3.
GIVEN NAMES Russian 5%; Jewish 5%. *Efim, Semyon; Mort* (2).

Kasmer (134) From the Slavic personal name *Kazimir* (see CASIMIR). Possibly also an altered spelling of Hungarian *Kázmér*.
GIVEN NAME French 5%. *Chantal.*

Kasner (342) **1.** Variant of German KASTNER or respelling of KASSNER. **2.** Czech: topographic name for someone who lived on a street, from a derivative of German *Gasse* 'street', or possibly from German KASTNER. **3.** Jewish (Ashkenazic): occupational name for a community treasurer, from German *Kastner* or alternatively from German *Kasse* 'cash(box)', 'coffer' + the agent suffix *-ner*.
GIVEN NAMES German 4%. *Kurt, Otto, Raimund.*

Kasowski (108) Polish (**Kaszowski**): habitational name for someone from either of two places called Kaszów, in Kraków and Radom voivodeships, named with *kasza* 'cereal'.
GIVEN NAME Polish 5%. *Stanislaw.*

Kaspar (724) German, Czech (**Kašpar**), Slovak (**Gašpar**) and Slovenian (**Kaspar** and **Kašpar**): from the personal name *Kaspar, Kašpar*, which was especially popular in central Europe up to the 18th century. From Persian *kaehbaed, khazana-dar*, or *ganjvaer*, all meaning 'treasure bearer', it was ascribed by popular tradition in Europe to one of the three Magi. The supposed remains of the Magi were taken in the 12th century from Constantinople to Cologne, where they became objects of veneration. See also BALTAZAR and MELCHIOR.

Kasparek (285) Czech (**Kašpárek**): from a pet form of the personal name *Kašpar* (see CASPER). Kašpárek is the Czech name of the marionette character known as Punch in English.

Kaspari (100) Dutch; humanistic patronymic from the personal name KASPAR.
GIVEN NAME French 5%. *Alphonse.*

Kasparian (310) Armenian: patronymic from the personal name KASPAR.
GIVEN NAMES Armenian 28%; French 6%. *Aram* (3), *Hagop* (3), *Kevork* (3), *Avedis* (2), *Haig* (2), *Haik* (2), *Hovannes* (2), *Meline* (2), *Souren* (2), *Vahe* (2), *Varant* (2), *Vartan* (2); *Armand* (2), *Girard* (2), *Andre, Francoise, Gaspard.*

Kasper (4094) German, Danish, Czech, and Polish; Slovenian (also **Kašper**): see KASPAR.

Kasperek (201) Polish: from a pet form of the personal name *Kasper* (see KASPAR).
GIVEN NAMES Polish 14%. *Janina* (2), *Bogdan, Boguslaw, Casimir, Janusz, Kazimierz, Mieczyslaw, Stanislaw, Wieslaw, Zbigniew*.

Kasperski (164) Polish and Jewish (from Poland): **1.** habitational name for someone from Kaspry in Olsztyn voivodeship, one of the six Lithuanian villages called Kasperyszki (Lithuanian *Kasperiškiai*), or any of several other places named with the personal name *Kasper, Kaspar* (see CASPER). **2.** patronymic from the personal name *Kasper*, used in Poland by both Christians and Jews.

Kasprowicz (175) Polish: patronymic from the personal name *Kasper* (see KASPAR).
GIVEN NAMES Polish 8%. *Andrzej, Boguslaw, Janusz, Leszek, Wojtek*.

Kasprzak (519) Polish: patronymic from the personal name *Kasper* (see KASPAR).
GIVEN NAMES Polish 8%. *Grzegorz* (2), *Agnieszka, Andrzej, Bronislaw, Czeslawa, Ewa, Henryk, Janusz, Jerzy, Jozef, Kazimierz, Tadeusz*.

Kasprzycki (75) Polish: habitational name for someone from a place called Kasprzyki (see KASPRZYK).
GIVEN NAMES Polish 10%; German 4%. *Ignacy, Stanislaw; Alois, Florian*.

Kasprzyk (369) Polish: derivative of the personal name *Kasper* (see KASPAR).
GIVEN NAMES Polish 8%. *Casimir, Czeslaw, Elzbieta, Janina, Jozef, Leszek, Stanislaw, Walenty, Wiktor*.

Kass (1698) **1.** Eastern German (also **Käss**): nickname from Czech *kos* 'blackbird', 'shrewd person' (see KOS). **2.** Eastern German: from the personal name *Cazo*. **3.** Jewish (Ashkenazic): unexplained. **4.** Possibly an Americanized form of Czech **Káš** (see KASA) or German KASE.
GIVEN NAMES Jewish 5%. *Miriam* (3), *Shaya* (3), *Sol* (3), *Hyman* (2), *Amram, Aron, Mayer, Meyer, Mort, Morty, Nachum, Rivka*.

Kassa (238) **1.** Ethiopian: unexplained. **2.** Hungarian: habitational name from a place so named, which was established by Saxon settlers in Abauj county in former Upper Hungary, now part of Slovakia (Košice).
GIVEN NAMES Ethiopian 30%. *Abraha* (2), *Alemayehu* (2), *Getachew* (2), *Mekonnen* (2), *Theodros* (2), *Abera, Aklilu, Berhan, Berhane, Dawit, Hailemariam, Kassa*.

Kassab (266) Arabic and Jewish (Sephardic): occupational name from Arabic *qaṣṣāb* 'butcher'.
GIVEN NAMES Arabic 26%; Jewish 4%. *Jamal* (3), *Sabri* (2), *Samir* (2), *Akram, Amir, Bachar, Bashir, Daoud, Fadi, Fadia, Fahima, Faris; Emanuel, Heskel, Nissim, Sasson, Smadar*.

Kassabian (139) Armenian: patronymic meaning 'son of the butcher', from Turkish *kasab* 'butcher', from Arabic *qaṣṣāb*.
GIVEN NAMES Armenian 49%; French 4%. *Vahan* (5), *Mihran* (4), *Aram* (3), *Ara* (2), *Garo* (2), *Kourken* (2), *Krikor* (2), *Raffi* (2), *Seta* (2), *Vasken* (2), *Armen, Artin; Andre, Georges*.

Kassay (173) Hungarian: habitational name for someone from a place called Kassa, now Košice in Slovakia.
GIVEN NAMES Hungarian 4%. *Zoltan* (2), *Dezso*.

Kassebaum (226) North German variant of KIRSCHBAUM.

Kassel (629) German: habitational name from a place of this name in northeastern Hesse, so named from Frankish *castella, cassela* 'fortification', a military term from Late Latin *castellum* 'fortified position', 'fort', or a topographic name from the same word.

Kasselman (100) German (**Kasselmann**) and Belgian: habitational name for someone from Kassel in Hesse or from Cassel in French Flanders.

Kassem (155) Muslim: from a personal name based on Arabic *qāsim* 'distributor', 'divider'. This was the name of a son of the Prophet Muhammad.
GIVEN NAMES Muslim 76%. *Ahmed* (4), *Mohamed* (4), *Khaled* (3), *Khalil* (3), *Sami* (3), *Abbas* (2), *Ahmad* (2), *Ali* (2), *Mohamad* (2), *Mohammad* (2), *Moustapha* (2), *Walid* (2).

Kassen (142) German: habitational name from a place so named.

Kasser (115) German and Swiss German (**Kässer**): probably a variant of *Käser, Kaser*, an occupational name for a maker and seller of cheese, from Middle High German *kaeser*, which also denotes an Alpine place for making cheese, a dairy hut.
GIVEN NAMES German 4%. *Gerlinda, Kurt*.

Kassin (201) Jewish: unexplained.
GIVEN NAMES Jewish 6%. *Meyer* (2), *Miriam*.

Kassing (209) German: patronymic from KERSTEN or possibly from KARSTEN.

Kassinger (102) German (**Kässinger**): variant spelling of KESSINGER.

Kassis (222) **1.** Arabic: from Arabic *qisīs* 'priest' (see CASSIS). **2.** Jewish (Sephardic): status name (from Arabic *qisīs* 'priest'), designating a Jewish community leader in North Africa.
GIVEN NAMES Arabic 27%; French 6%. *Aziz* (2), *Fayek* (2), *Marwan* (2), *Salim* (2), *Sami* (2), *Adib, Adnan, Afif, Ayoub, Basim, Bassam, Fadi; Camille* (2), *Antoine, Michel*.

Kassler (132) German: habitational name for someone from KASSEL.

Kassman (132) **1.** German (**Kassmann**): of uncertain origin. **2.** Possibly an altered form of GASSMANN. **3.** Jewish (Ashkenazic): possibly an occupational name for a

treasurer, from German *Kasse* 'cash(box)' + *Mann* 'man'.
GIVEN NAMES Jewish 6%. *Ari* (2), *Mayer*.

Kassner (376) German: **1.** habitational name for someone from a placed called Kassen. **2.** variant of KASTNER in either of its senses ('steward' or 'joiner'). **3.** variant of GASSNER.
GIVEN NAMES German 6%. *Heinz, Klaus, Kurt, Otto, Reinhold*.

Kasson (349) Perhaps an altered spelling of the Hungarian habitational name **Kászon**, from a place so named, also the name of the river on which it stands, from Slavic *kvasn* 'sour'.

Kast (845) **1.** North German: variant of KARST. The dropping of 'r' before 's' is a regular feature of some north and central German dialects. **2.** German: from an Alemannic short form of the medieval personal name ARBOGAST. **3.** variant of GAST.

Kastan (119) **1.** German: probably a respelling of **Kasten**, either a habitational name from a place so named, for example in Styria and Upper Austria, or from the Frisian personal name *Karsten*, equivalent to CHRISTIAN. **2.** German: variant of KESTEN 1; also of Sorbian origin.
GIVEN NAMES German 5%. *Bernhard, Hans*.

Kaste (171) German: **1.** from *Karsten*, a pet form of the personal name *Christianus* (see CHRISTIAN). **2.** metonymic occupational name in northern Germany for a treasurer or a furniture maker, from Middle Low German *kaste* 'box', 'chest (of drawers)', also 'shrine'. **3.** from the personal name *Kast*, an Alemannic short form of ARBOGAST.
GIVEN NAME German 4%. *Otto*.

Kastel (187) German: topographic name for someone living near a castle or fort, from *Kastell* 'fort', 'citadel' (Latin *castellum*). Equally, the surname could come from any of the numerous places in Germany so named (more usually written *Kastell*).
GIVEN NAME German 4%. *Bernhard*.

Kastelic (318) Slovenian: from a derivative of *kastel* '(small) castle', 'fort' (formed with the obsolete suffix *-ic* instead of standard *-ec*), a topographic name for someone who lived in or near a castle or a fort.

Kasten (1658) **1.** Dutch and North German: from a vernacular personal name, a variant of KARSTEN. **2.** German: from Middle High German *kasten* 'chest', 'coffer' or *kornkasten* 'grain bin', hence a metonymic occupational name for the manager of a granary, and later for the treasurer of an estate or guild. See also KASTNER. **3.** South German (Bavaria): topographic name from the dialect word *Kasten* 'crag', 'steep rock'. **4.** Swedish (**Kastén**): from an unexplained first element, perhaps part of a place name, + the adjectival suffix *-én*, a derivative of Latin *-enius*.

GIVEN NAMES German 4%. *Erwin* (2), *Kurt* (2), *Aloysius, Armin, Arno, Dietrich, Eldor, Ernst, Klaus, Otto, Wilhelm.*

Kastens (220) Dutch: patronymic from KASTEN.

GIVEN NAMES German 5%. *Dietrich, Ernst, Hans, Ulrike.*

Kaster (742) German: **1.** habitational name from Caster in Rhineland. **2.** (also **Käster**): variant of KASTEN 2 or a metonymic occupational name for a joiner or furniture maker, from Middle High German *kasten* 'box', 'chest', 'shrine'.

Kasting (123) German: variant of KASTNING.

GIVEN NAME German 4%. *Kurt.*

Kastl (272) German (also **Kästl**): **1.** from a pet form of the saint's name *Castulus*, itself a diminutive of the Latin adjective *castus* 'chaste'. **2.** habitational name from any of various places so named in Bavaria. **3.** from an old personal name related to Old High German, Middle High German *gast* 'guest', earlier 'foreign warrior'.

Kastle (134) **1.** German: from an Alemannic pet form of KAST 2. **2.** Respelling of KASTEL.

Kastler (212) German: **1.** habitational name for someone from a place called Kastel or Castel. **2.** see KASTNER. **3.** variant of KASTL 3.

GIVEN NAME German 4%. *Otto* (2).

Kastner (1752) **1.** German (also **Kästner**): from Middle High German *kastner, kestner*, an occupational name for the steward of a granary (*kornkasten*) and hence, since general taxation developed from taxes on grain, a steward or treasurer responsible for financial matters at a court, monastery, or other institution. **2.** German (also **Kästner**) and Jewish (Ashkenazic): metonymic occupational name for a joiner or furniture maker, from South German *Kasten* 'box', 'chest'. Compare KISTNER.

GIVEN NAMES German 4%. *Kurt* (5), *Ilse* (2), *Manfred* (2), *Wilhelm* (2), *Alois, Armin, Arno, Friedrich, Hedwig, Jurgen, Otto.*

Kastning (123) North German: patronymic from the personal name *Karsten* (see KERSTEN).

GIVEN NAMES German 5%. *Ernst, Erwin.*

Kastor (128) German: from the Roman personal name *Castor* (meaning 'beaver'). It was the name of the patron saint of Koblenz, a 4th century priest and missionary who worked in the area of the Mosel.

Kasun (171) German: probably a habitational name from a place named Kassuhn (of Slavic origin) in the Altmark region near Salzwedel.

Kasza (219) **1.** Polish: nickname for a peasant farmer, from *kasza* 'cereal', 'porridge'. Compare KASA. **2.** Polish: from a short form of any of several personal names beginning *Ka-*, in particular *Kasper* and *Kazimierz*. **3.** Hungarian: metonymic occupational name for a tool maker, from the

Slavic loanword word *kasza* 'sickle' (from Slovak *kosa*). **4.** Hungarian: habitational name from a place so named (sometimes spelled Kaza or Kasa) in Arad county, now in Romania.

GIVEN NAMES Polish 7%; Hungarian 5%. *Zdzislaw* (2), *Bronislaw, Dariusz, Pawel; Imre* (3), *Bela, Karoly.*

Kaszuba (207) Polish: ethnic name for a Kashubian (Polish *Kaszuba*). The Kashubians are a Slavic people with their own distinctive dialect and customs, living in northern Poland to the southwest and west of Gdańsk.

GIVEN NAMES Polish 12%. *Jozef* (2), *Krystyna* (2), *Andrzej, Bogdan, Dariusz, Jaroslaw, Katarzyna, Waclaw, Wieslaw.*

Kaszynski (130) **1.** Polish (**Kaszyński**): habitational name from Kaszyno (now in Lithuania). **2.** derivative of the nickname KASZA 'porridge'.

GIVEN NAMES Polish 7%. *Casimir, Piotr, Tadeusz.*

Kata (128) **1.** Polish, Slovak, and Hungarian: from *Kata*, a vernacular short form of the female personal name CATHERINE (Polish *Katarzyna*, Hungarian *Katalin*). **2.** Indian (Andhra Pradesh): Hindu name of unknown meaning.

GIVEN NAMES Polish 7%; Indian 6%. *Piotr, Stanislaw, Zofia; Rao, Srinivas.*

Kataoka (169) Japanese: 'hill on the side'; listed in the Shinsen shōjiroku. One family of Ōmi (now Shiga prefecture) is descended from the MINAMOTO clan.

GIVEN NAMES Japanese 63%. *Shigeru* (2), *Tatsuya* (2), *Yoichi* (2), *Atsuo, Ayako, Chie, Harumi, Hidetsugu, Hiroe, Hiroko, Hiroshi, Hisashi.*

Katayama (224) Japanese: 'mountain on the side'; a common place name throughout Japan. The surname is also found in the Ryūkyū Islands.

GIVEN NAMES Japanese 54%. *Mitsuru* (2), *Yoshio* (2), *Akio, Atsuko, Ayako, Daisuke, Emiko, Hajime, Hikaru, Hiromu, Hiroyoshi, Hitoshi.*

Katch (105) **1.** Jewish (Ashkenazic): probably a variant of *Katsch*, from Polish *tkacz* 'weaver'. **2.** German: variant spelling of **Kätsch**, a habitational name from Ketsch in the Palatinate.

GIVEN NAMES Jewish 5%; German 5%. *Avron* (2); *Kurt, Mathias.*

Katcher (350) German (**Kätcher**): metonymic occupational name for a fisherman or net maker, from Middle Low German *kesser* 'net', in particular the type of net used by fisherman in the North or Baltic Sea.

Katen (185) North German: possibly a derivative of KATER 1.

Kater (205) **1.** Dutch and North German: nickname from Middle Dutch *cater, kater* 'tomcat'. **2.** Dutch: occupational name from Middle Dutch *cater* 'provisioner'. **3.** North German: status name for a cot-

tager, from an agent derivative of Middle Low German *kate* 'small house', 'hut'.

Kates (1379) Dutch: **1.** variant spelling of **Kattes**, patronymic from the personal name *Kat(t)e* (see KATT 1). **2.** from the possessive case of *kat* 'cat' as a nickname (see KATT 2).

Kath (400) **1.** North German: from Middle Low German *kate, kot(e)* 'small tenanted dwelling', 'hut', hence a topographic name for a person living in such a dwelling. **2.** variant spelling of KATT 1 and 2.

Kathan (160) German: occupational name for the constable of a castle, from Italian *cattano* 'captain'.

Kathman (219) North German (**Kathmann**): topographic name or status name for someone living in a small cottage, from Middle Low German *kate, kote* 'hut', 'cottage' + *-man* 'man'. Compare KATER 3.

Kathol (175) **1.** North German: unexplained. **2.** Possibly an altered spelling of Irish **Cathal**.

Katich (192) Serbian and Croatian (**Katić**): from a pet form of the female personal name *Katarina* (see CATHERINE).

Katko (107) Hungarian: from a pet form of the female personal name *Katarina* (see CATHERINE).

GIVEN NAMES Russian 6%. *Aleksandr* (2), *Yelena.*

Kato (1460) **1.** Japanese (**Katō**): variously written; most bearers descend from the Fujiwara of Kaga (*Kaga no Fujiwara*). Kaga is now part of Ishikawa prefecture. Mostly found along the southeastern seaboard and in the Ryūkyū Islands. One family was daimyō of Hizen (now Nagasaki prefecture). **2.** Hungarian (**Kató**): from a pet form of the female personal name *Katalin* (see CATHERINE).

GIVEN NAMES Japanese 59%. *Hiroshi* (13), *Kazuo* (10), *Akira* (8), *Akiko* (7), *Takashi* (7), *Hiroko* (6), *Hiroyuki* (5), *Ichiro* (5), *Yoshio* (5), *Yuko* (5), *Chiaki* (4), *Hiroki* (4).

Katon (157) Jewish (Ashkenazic): nickname from Hebrew *qoton* 'small'.

Katona (542) Hungarian: occupational name from *katona* 'soldier' (from Byzantine Greek *katouna* 'tent', 'camp').

GIVEN NAMES Hungarian 6%. *Laszlo* (4), *Antal, Gaza, Geza, Imre, Istvan, Lajos, Sandor, Tibor, Zsuzsa.*

Kats (501) **1.** Jewish (eastern Ashkenazic): variant of KATZ. **2.** Dutch: patronymic from the personal name *Kat* (see KATT).

GIVEN NAMES Russian 29%; Jewish 20%. *Boris* (12), *Mikhail* (11), *Leonid* (6), *Vladimir* (6), *Lev* (5), *Yefim* (5), *Aleksandr* (4), *Iosif* (4), *Konstantin* (3), *Semyon* (3), *Yuriy* (3), *Alik* (2), *Ilya* (4), *Irina* (4), *Semen* (4), *Mikhael* (3), *Yakov* (3), *Aron* (2), *Isaak* (2), *Naum* (2), *Ahron, Basya, Erez, Filipp.*

Katsaros (173) Greek: from a nickname meaning 'curly-haired', ultimately from *akanthēros* 'thorny'.

GIVEN NAMES Greek 12%. *Apostolos, Dimitrios, Eleni, Ioannis, Konstantinos, Kyriakos, Stilianos, Vasilis.*

Katsnelson (115) Jewish (from Belarus): patronymic from KATZENELLENBOGEN (see KATZEN 2) + German *Sohn* 'son'.

GIVEN NAMES Jewish 34%; Russian 33%. *Ilya* (3), *Naum* (3), *Yakov* (3), *Isaak* (2), *Jakov* (2), *Esfir, Faina, Gersh, Khaim, Mariya, Mikhael, Moysey*; *Boris* (5), *Leonid* (5), *Mikhail* (3), *Galina* (2), *Lev* (2), *Yefim* (2), *Aleksandr, Aleksey, Arkady, Emiliya, Fanya, Gennadiy.*

Katt (381) North German and Dutch: **1.** from a Germanic personal name, *Katt*, of obscure origin. **2.** from Middle Low German *katte* 'cat', Middle Dutch *catte*, hence a nickname conferred with reference to some attribute of the animal, such as independence or light-footedness.

GIVEN NAMES German 4%. *Otto* (3), *Erwin, Kurt.*

Kattan (145) **1.** Arabic: perhaps from *quṭn* 'cotton', a metonymic occupational name for a cotton merchant. **2.** Jewish (Sephardic and Israeli): nickname from Hebrew *katan* 'small'. As an Israeli name, in some cases it represents a translation of Ashkenazic KLEIN.

GIVEN NAMES Arabic 17%; Jewish 9%; French 6%; Spanish 5%. *Mourad* (2), *Osama* (2), *Sami* (2), *Azar, Basim, Bilal, Fadi, Fuad, Hadi, Imad, Rahamin, Samir; Amnon, Meyer, Mordechai, Shlomy; Camille, Emile, Marcel, Marcelle; Jose* (2), *Jacobo, Jorge, Juan.*

Katter (143) German: **1.** variant of KATER 3, in the sense 'cottager'. **2.** Perhaps also a variant of KATER 1.

Kattner (233) German: variant of KATER 3.

GIVEN NAMES German 4%. *Fritz, Horst.*

Katz (16467) **1.** Jewish (Ashkenazic): acronym from the Hebrew phrase *kohen tsedek* 'priest of righteousness' (see COHEN). **2.** German: nickname from *Katz(e)* 'cat'. Compare English CATT.

GIVEN NAMES Jewish 8%. *Hyman* (35), *Sol* (28), *Isadore* (17), *Miriam* (14), *Meyer* (13), *Moshe* (11), *Chaim* (8), *Emanuel* (8), *Aron* (7), *Mayer* (7), *Shoshana* (6), *Zev* (6).

Katzen (315) Jewish (Ashkenazic): **1.** variant of KOTZEN. **2.** shortened form of **Katzenellenbogen**, a habitational name from Katzenelnbogen in Hesse-Nassau. The place name is probably derived from a Celtic tribal name, *Chattimelibochi*, but was altered by folk etymology as if it meant 'cat's elbow'. The earliest known bearer of this name is Meir Ben Yitschak (*c*.1480–1565), Chief Rabbi of the Venetian Republic, who was born in Katzenellenbogen.

GIVEN NAMES Jewish 7%. *Isadore* (2), *Chani, Emanuel, Hirsh, Rina, Sol, Zalman.*

Katzenberg (120) **1.** German: habitational name from places in Hesse and Saxony (see KATZENBERGER). **2.** Jewish (Ashkenazic):

ornamental elaboration of KATZ, from German *Katze* 'cat' + *Berg* 'hill'.

GIVEN NAME French 5%. *Lucien* (2).

Katzenberger (316) **1.** German: habitational name from minor places so called in Hesse and Saxony. **2.** Jewish (Ashkenazic): variant of KATZENBERG, with the suffix *-er* making the name look as if it were habitational.

GIVEN NAMES German 5%. *Georg, Heinz, Kurt.*

Katzenmeyer (153) **1.** German: topographic name for the owner or tenant of the *Katzenhof* 'cat farm', from Middle High German *katze* 'cat' + *meier* 'farmer' (Latin *major domus*, literally 'keeper of the household'). **2.** variant of **Casimir** (see KAZMIERCZAK), which in German- and Yiddish-speaking environments produced forms such as **Kasem(e)ier** and **Katzemeier**.

GIVEN NAME German 4%. *Fritz* (2).

Katzenstein (246) **1.** German: topographic name for someone living at a castle known as 'Cat Rock', from Middle High German *katze* 'cat' + *stein* 'stone', 'crag', 'rocky peak'. **2.** Jewish (Ashkenazic): ornamental name elaboration of KATZ, from German *Katze* 'cat' + *Stein* 'stone' (see 1).

GIVEN NAMES German 13%; Jewish 5%. *Ernst* (2), *Bernhard, Friedrich, Hans, Heinz, Kurt, Sigfried*; *Chaya, Moshe, Pinchas.*

Katzer (364) German: **1.** perhaps a derivative of the Old High German personal name *Cazo*, of uncertain origin (see KASE 1). **2.** Silesian (also **Ketzer**): from Middle High German *ketzer* 'heretic', 'freethinker'. **3.** Germanized form of Sorbian *kacor* or Czech *kačer* 'drake' (see KASKA 2).

GIVEN NAMES German 4%. *Kurt, Rainer, Wolfgang.*

Katzin (126) Jewish: nickname from Hebrew *katsin* 'rich man'.

GIVEN NAMES Jewish 11%. *Aryeh, Emanuel, Nissim, Ori, Ronit.*

Katzman (1010) Jewish (Ashkenazic) and German (**Katzmann**): elaboration of KATZ.

GIVEN NAMES Jewish 9%. *Moshe* (4), *Eliezer* (3), *Sol* (3), *Aron* (2), *Elihu* (2), *Herschel* (2), *Miriam* (2), *Mordechai* (2), *Zelig* (2), *Batya, Charna, Doron.*

Kau (276) **1.** South German: from Middle High German *gehau* '(mountain) clearing', hence a topographic name for a mountain dweller or possibly an occupational name for a logger. **2.** South German: topographic name for someone who lived by a mineshaft, from Middle High German *kouw(e)* 'mining hut'. **3.** Chinese 高: possibly a variant of GAO.

Kauble (112) Americanized spelling of German KABEL.

Kaucher (162) German: nickname for an asthmatic or someone habitually out of breath, from an agent derivative of Middle

High German *kuchen* 'to breathe (heavily)', 'to wheeze'. See also KEICHER.

GIVEN NAMES German 6%. *Erwin* (3), *Hans.*

Kauer (246) German: **1.** topographic name, a variant of KAU. **2.** from Middle High German *gou* 'province', 'region' + *-er* suffix denoting an inhabitant, hence a nickname for a country dweller, as opposed to someone who lived in a city. **3.** from a short form of the personal name KONRAD.

GIVEN NAMES German 4%. *Gottlieb, Hermann, Urs.*

Kaufenberg (118) German: unexplained; probably a habitational name from a lost or unidentified place.

GIVEN NAME French 4%. *Serge.*

Kaufer (287) German (also **Käufer**) and Jewish (Ashkenazic): occupational name for a trader or shopkeeper, from Middle High German *koufer, köfer*, German *Kaufer* 'seller', 'trader'. The base form *kouf* (from Latin *caupo* 'merchant') already had this meaning but was subsequently augmented by various suffixes: *-er, -el, -man.*

Kauffman (8028) Variant spelling of German and Ashkenazic Jewish KAUFMANN.

Kauffmann (451) Variant spelling of German and Ashkenazic Jewish KAUFMANN.

GIVEN NAMES German 4%; French 4%. *Fritz* (2), *Reinhard*; *Jacques, Olivier, Sylvie, Thierry.*

Kaufhold (276) German: topographic name from a Middle Low German field name composed of the elements *kouf* 'trade' + *holt* 'forest' denoting a location which was connected with the primary local trade (e.g. mining, salt extraction, etc.). By a process of folk etymology the second element was modified to *-hold* 'loyal', a common element of personal names.

GIVEN NAMES German 4%. *Kurt* (2), *Hans.*

Kaufman (16694) **1.** Respelling of German and Jewish (Ashkenazic) KAUFMANN. **2.** Jewish (Ashkenazic): from the personal name *Kaufman*, Yiddish *koyfman*, meaning 'merchant'.

GIVEN NAMES Jewish 4%. *Sol* (13), *Miriam* (9), *Hyman* (8), *Meyer* (7), *Chaim* (5), *Emanuel* (4), *Moshe* (4), *Eytan* (3), *Herschel* (3), *Zvi* (3), *Ari* (2), *Aron* (2).

Kaufmann (3039) **1.** German and Jewish (Ashkenazic): occupational name for a merchant or wholesaler (see KAUFER). **2.** Jewish (Ashkenazic): variant spelling of KAUFMAN.

GIVEN NAMES German 7%. *Kurt* (10), *Erwin* (4), *Hans* (4), *Franz* (3), *Manfred* (3), *Otto* (3), *Berthold* (2), *Gerhard* (2), *Gerhart* (2), *Siegbert* (2), *Alois, Beate.*

Kauk (237) **1.** Possibly an altered spelling North German **Kauke**, from Middle Low German *koke* 'cake' (dialect *Kauke*), hence a metonymic occupational name for a baker or confectioner or a nickname for a cake lover. **2.** Perhaps an altered spelling of

Dutch *Kaak* or North German *Kaack* (see KAAKE).

GIVEN NAMES German 4%. *Otto* (2), *Bernhard, Erwin*.

Kaul (1027) **1.** German: habitational name from any of three places in Rhineland named Kaul. **2.** North German (Westphalian): topographic name from *Kaul* 'pit', 'pond'. Compare KUHL. **3.** Indian (Kashmir): Hindu (Brahman) name, from Sanskrit *kaula* 'well-born' (from Sanskrit *kula* 'family'). According to Koul (1994), the surname *Kaul* is derived from *Mahakaul* meaning 'the great Kaul', which is an epithet of the god Shiva. Kashmiri Hindus are votaries of Shiva.

GIVEN NAMES Indian 21%. *Ajay* (4), *Anil* (4), *Sanjay* (4), *Ashok* (3), *Renuka* (3), *Sandeep* (3), *Sunil* (3), *Surendra* (3), *Deepak* (2), *Pushkar* (2), *Rajeev* (2), *Rajiv* (2).

Kaun (124) **1.** North German: from a short form of KONRAD. **2.** German: possibly from a Silesian short form of *Kaunath* or *Kaunert*, derivatives of the Old High German personal name *Chunihard*, meaning 'strong tribe'.

GIVEN NAMES German 6%. *Kurt, Otto*.

Kaup (514) North German form of KAUFER.

Kaupp (230) North German form of KAUFER.

GIVEN NAMES German 5%. *Dieter, Franz, Otto*.

Kauppi (145) Finnish: from a short form of the personal name *Jakaupr* (Scandinavian form of JACOB). This was a common personal name in the medieval period, when it was also used by Finns to denote a foreign merchant.

GIVEN NAMES Finnish 13%; Scandinavian 4%. *Eino* (2), *Tauno* (2), *Arvo, Niilo, Olavi, Wilho*; *Erik*.

Kauppila (148) Finnish: from KAUPPI + the local suffix -*la* (i.e. 'Jacob's place'). This name is found mainly in western Finland.

GIVEN NAMES Finnish 5%; Scandinavian 4%. *Eino, Ensio, Oiva, Vaino*; *Nels*.

Kaur (604) Indian (chiefly Panjab): term used by Hindu and Sikh women either as the final element of a compound personal name or as a last name. It cannot be regarded as a true surname or family name. It goes back to Sanskrit *kumārī* 'girl', 'daughter', which was reduced to *kuar* and then changed into *kaur* by metathesis. Among Sikhs, female names are often derived from male names by the addition of *Kaur* to the male name: e.g. *Mahinder Kaur*, from the male name *Mahinder*.

GIVEN NAMES Indian 95%. *Amrit* (8), *Balwinder* (4), *Nirmal* (4), *Amar* (3), *Balvir* (3), *Pritam* (3), *Charan* (2), *Darshan* (2), *Gursharan* (2), *Nasib* (2), *Prem* (2).

Kaus (343) German: from a regional (Hessian) variant of the habitational name **Kues**, from a place on the Mosel river, probably so named from Late Latin *covis*

'field barn', 'rack' and earlier recorded as *Couese, Cobesa*.

Kausch (151) German: **1.** pet name derived from the Old High German personal name *Gozwin*, of uncertain origin. **2.** from a medieval form of the Old High German personal name *Chuzo*. **3.** variant of KAUTZ or KAUS.

GIVEN NAMES German 6%. *Kurt, Uwe*.

Kaut (110) German: **1.** metonymic occupational name for a flax grower or dealer, from Middle High German *kūte*. **2.** from *Kaut(e)* 'male dove', hence a metonymic occupational name for the owner or keeper of a dovecote. **3.** topographic name from the Franconian dialect word *Kaut(e)* 'hollow', 'pit', 'den'.

Kauth (316) German: variant of KAUT.

Kautz (1581) German: **1.** nickname for a shy or strange person, from Middle High German *kūz* 'screech owl'. **2.** possibly a variant of KAUT or KAUSCH 2.

Kautzer (148) **1.** German: variant of KAUTZ. **2.** German: perhaps a habitational name for someone from Kautzsch near Leipzig or from Gautzsch near Dresden.

Kautzman (394) German (**Kautzmann**): variant of KAUTZ, with the addition of Middle High German *man* 'man'.

Kauzlarich (278) Croatian and/or Bosnian: unexplained.

Kava (150) **1.** Czech: nickname from *kavka* 'jackdaw'. **2.** Jewish (Ashkenazic): from Polish *kawa* 'coffee', probably an ornamental name but possibly a metonymic occupational name for a coffee merchant.

Kavan (182) Origin unidentified. Possibly a reduced form of KAVANAGH.

GIVEN NAME French 4%. *Lucien*.

Kavanagh (2046) Irish: **1.** in Wexford, an Anglicization of Gaelic **Mac Caomhánach** 'son of *Caomhán*' (see KEVIN). MacLysaght says that this is a famous branch of the MacMurroughs. The name is said to have been acquired from the first Kavanagh having been fostered by a follower of St. Caomhán. **2.** Anglicization of Gaelic **Mac an Mhanaigh** 'son of the monk', from *manach* 'monk', a rare Mayo surname.

GIVEN NAMES Irish 7%. *Aidan, Aileen, Brendan, Cathal, Conor, Eamon, Keelin, Liam, Michael Sean, Niall, Ronan, Sean Patrick*.

Kavanaugh (2394) Irish: variant of KAVANAGH.

GIVEN NAMES Irish 5%. *Brendan, Oonagh*.

Kaveney (144) Variant of Irish KAVANAGH 2.

Kawa (380) Polish: nickname from *kawka* 'jackdaw'.

GIVEN NAMES Polish 7%. *Janina* (2), *Bogdan, Bogumil, Boguslaw, Bronislaw, Danuta, Jerzy, Krystyna, Leszek, Lucja, Zofia*.

Kawabata (140) Japanese: 'side or bank of the river'; written two ways, with two different characters for *kawa* 'river'. One family is descended from the northern

FUJIWARA through the Saionji family; the other from the SASAKI family. The name is also found in Okinawa Island.

GIVEN NAMES Japanese 63%. *Hiroshi* (2), *Kohei* (2), *Osamu* (2), *Yasuhiro* (2), *Akira, Fumihiko, Hideo, Hiroki, Hiroko, Hiroyuki, Kazumi, Kazuto*.

Kawaguchi (375) Japanese: 'mouth of the river'; found throughout Japan and the Ryūkyū Islands. One prominent family of Kii (now Wakayama prefecture) were samurai.

GIVEN NAMES Japanese 65%. *Haruhiko* (48), *Isamu* (3), *Kenji* (3), *Masashi* (3), *Toshiaki* (3), *Yoshihiro* (3), *Aki* (2), *Akira* (2), *Hiro* (2), *Kazuo* (2), *Kohei* (2), *Mitsuo* (2).

Kawahara (256) Japanese: 'river plain'; written two ways with the same meaning. One is mostly found in eastern Japan; the other is more common in the Kyōto–Ōsaka region.

GIVEN NAMES Japanese 43%. *Takeshi* (3), *Nobuo* (2), *Shigeo* (2), *Yoshio* (2), *Chikashi, Hideaki, Hideki, Hidenori, Hideo, Hiroshi, Hiroyuki, Hitoshi*.

Kawai (249) Japanese: variously written, the original meaning is 'meeting of (two) rivers'. An ancient family by this name is listed in the Shinsen shōjiroku. The most usual renderings are found mostly in eastern Japan; families in different localities seem to have their own different ways of writing the name. In Okinawa Island, it is written with characters meaning 'river well'.

GIVEN NAMES Japanese 72%. *Hideki* (4), *Kiyoshi* (4), *Takashi* (3), *Taro* (3), *Yumiko* (3), *Atsushi* (2), *Hideo* (2), *Hiroshi* (2), *Koji* (2), *Noriko* (2), *Satoshi* (2), *Shoji* (2).

Kawakami (402) Japanese: 'above the river'; found throughout Japan and the Ryūkyū Islands. Two families from villages of that name, in Iwami (now part of Shimane prefecture) and Shimotsuke (now Tochigi prefecture), descend from the SASAKI and northern FUJIWARA respectively. Another samurai family is of Satsuma (now Kagoshima prefecture). The characters are sometimes pronounced *Kawanoe* or *Kawaue*. A less usual rendering is with characters meaning 'river deity'. Listed in the Shinsen shōjiroku.

GIVEN NAMES Japanese 53%. *Yoji* (5), *Kenji* (3), *Takeo* (3), *Atsushi* (2), *Hiroshi* (2), *Ichiro* (2), *Katsunori* (2), *Kazuo* (2), *Kiyoshi* (2), *Masako* (2), *Mikio* (2), *Noboru* (2).

Kawalec (116) Polish: from Old Polish *kawałec*, modern *kawałek* 'piece', a nickname for someone who had only a small piece of something such as land or bread.

GIVEN NAMES Polish 12%; German 4%. *Andrzej, Danuta, Karol, Stanislaw, Zdzislaw*; *Alois*.

Kawamoto (480) Japanese: written two ways, both meaning 'source of the river'; found mostly in western Japan.

GIVEN NAMES Japanese 43%. *Masayoshi* (3), *Noboru* (3), *Takeshi* (3), *Tomoko* (3), *Toshio* (3), *Yoshio* (3), *Yukio* (3), *Hajime* (2), *Haruo* (2), *Hiroshi* (2), *Kinya* (2), *Masao* (2).

Kawamura (442) Japanese: 'river village'; found throughout Japan and the Ryūkyū Islands. One family of samurai is from Satsuma (now Kagoshima prefecture). Written two ways, one way is more common in west-central Japan.

GIVEN NAMES Japanese 57%. *Hiroshi* (3), *Masako* (3), *Masao* (3), *Masaru* (3), *Seiji* (3), *Shigemasa* (3), *Shoji* (3), *Toshio* (3), *Toyo* (3), *Haruo* (2), *Hiroaki* (2), *Katsumi* (2).

Kawano (231) Japanese: 'river field'; mostly found in western Japan, the island of Shikoku, and the Ryūkyū Islands. Written two ways, of which one can also be pronounced *Kōno*.

GIVEN NAMES Japanese 50%. *Kenji* (3), *Takashi* (3), *Masato* (2), *Shuichi* (2), *Yoshio* (2), *Akifumi*, *Atsushi*, *Chika*, *Eisuke*, *Hanako*, *Hidehiro*, *Hideo*.

Kawasaki (401) Japanese: 'river cape'; found mainly in eastern Japan and the Ryūkyū Islands.

GIVEN NAMES Japanese 53%. *Hiroshi* (3), *Akira* (2), *Atsushi* (2), *Hideki* (2), *Hiro* (2), *Hiroki* (2), *Isamu* (2), *Isao* (2), *Kaori* (2), *Kaoru* (2), *Keisuke* (2), *Kenichi* (2).

Kawashima (196) Japanese: 'river island'; mostly found in eastern Japan and the Ryūkyū Islands.

GIVEN NAMES Japanese 69%. *Hidenori* (3), *Hiroshi* (3), *Makoto* (2), *Masako* (2), *Mikio* (2), *Satoru* (2), *Yoko* (2), *Akihiro*, *Akio*, *Fujio*, *Hanako*, *Hideo*.

Kawata (115) Japanese: 'rice paddy near the river'; the version of this name written with the more common character for 'river' is found in the Tōkyō and Ōsaka areas; the version with the traditional character for 'river' is found mostly in western Japan and the Ryūkyū Islands.

GIVEN NAMES Japanese 52%. *Akihiko*, *Ayumi*, *Ayumu*, *Hajime*, *Hideo*, *Hiro*, *Hiroshi*, *Hiroyuki*, *Hisato*, *Kaz*, *Kiku*, *Kiyoshi*.

Kawczynski (118) Polish (**Kawczyński**): habitational name for someone from Kawczyn or Kawczyno, both named from *kawka* 'jackdaw'.

GIVEN NAMES Polish 9%; German 5%. *Bronislaus*, *Jerzy*, *Zygmund*; *Kurt*.

Kawecki (240) Polish: habitational name for someone from any of various places called Kawcze or Kawki, named with *kawka* 'jackdaw'.

GIVEN NAMES Polish 7%. *Bronislaus*, *Jerzy*, *Krzystof*, *Stanislaw*, *Witold*.

Kay (9760) **1.** English: nickname from Middle English *ca* 'jackdaw', from an unattested Old Norse *ká*. See also DAW. **2.** English: nickname from Middle English *cai*, *kay*, *kei* 'left-handed', 'clumsy'. **3.** English: metonymic occupational name

for a locksmith, from Middle English *keye*, *kaye* 'key'. Compare CARE, KEAR. **4.** English: topographic name for someone living on or near a quay, Middle English *kay(e)*, Old French *cay*. **5.** English: from a Middle English personal name which figures in Arthurian legend. It is found in Old Welsh as *Cai*, Middle Welsh *Kei*, and is ultimately from the Latin personal name *Gaius*. **6.** Scottish and Irish: reduced form of MCKAY. **7.** French: variant of QUAY, cognate with 2. **8.** Much shortened form of any of various names, mostly Eastern European, beginning with the letter *K-*. **9.** Variant of Danish and Frisian KAI.

Kaya (247) **1.** Japanese: 'miscanthus reed'; rare as a surname in Japan. In America the name may be the result of shortening any of several other names beginning with *kaya*, such as *Kayashima*, none of which is common by itself. **2.** Turkish and Greek: from a personal name based on Turkish *kaya* 'rock', or nickname for a tough or obstinate person.

GIVEN NAMES Japanese 19%; Muslim 15%; Armenian 4%. *Hideo* (2), *Kazumasa* (2), *Asami*, *Chikara*, *Fumie*, *Hisao*, *Iwao*, *Kimiyo*, *Kiyoshi*, *Masayoshi*, *Setsuo*, *Shingo*; *Azmi* (3), *Huseyin* (2), *Ismail* (2), *Salih* (2), *Ahmet*, *Ali*, *Aydin*, *Bedri*, *Esin*, *Ibrahim*, *Mustafa*, *Muzaffer*; *Agavni*, *Alpaslan*, *Avedis*, *Bedros*, *Hagop*.

Kaye (4365) English: variant spelling of KAY 4 and 5.

Kayes (195) English: patronymic from KAY 5.

Kayl (108) German and Luxembourgeois: probably a variant of KEIL.

Kayler (110) See KAYLOR.

Kaylor (1842) **1.** Variant of Scottish KEILLOR. **2.** Americanized form of German **Köhler** (see KOHLER).

Kayne (237) English: elaborated spelling of CAIN.

Kays (1105) English: patronymic from KAY.

Kaysen (111) Danish: patronymic from the personal name *Kay*, variant of KAI.

Kayser (1507) **1.** German and Dutch: variant spelling of Dutch KEIZER and German KAISER. **2.** Jewish (Ashkenazic): variant of KAISER.

GIVEN NAMES German 4%. *Erwin* (2), *Hans* (2), *Kurt* (2), *Aloysius*, *Frieda*, *Fritz*, *Gunther*, *Helmut*, *Horst*, *Katharina*, *Wendelin*, *Wieland*.

Kayton (142) English: possibly a variant of the habitational name CAYTON or a variant spelling of KEETON. Compare KEYTON.

Kaz (139) Jewish (Ashkenazic): variant of KATZ.

GIVEN NAMES Jewish 6%; Russian 5%. *Ari*, *Irina*, *Moisey*; *Boris*, *Mikhail*, *Semyon*, *Yana*.

Kazan (203) **1.** Jewish (eastern Ashkenazic): from Hebrew *chazan*, an occupational name for a cantor in a synagogue.

2. Ukrainian, Belorussian, and Jewish (eastern Ashkenazic): from a Turkish loanword in eastern Slavic languages *kazan* 'kettle', 'boiler', 'furnace'. **3.** Greek: reduced form of **Kazandzis**, occupational name for a maker of cauldrons or for someone who used a cauldron for the distillation of ouzo or raki, from Turkish *kazancı* 'cauldron worker' or 'furnace worker', from *kazan* 'cauldron' + the agent noun suffix *-cı*, or of a patronymic derivative of this, e.g. **Kazandzakis**, **Kazandzoglou**.

FOREBEARS The film director Elia Kazan (b. 1909) was of Greek origin, born in Asia Minor. His original family name was **Kazandzoglou**.

Kazanjian (331) Armenian: patronymic from Turkish *kazancı*, an occupational name for a maker or seller of cauldrons or kettles, from *kazan* 'cauldron', 'kettle'.

GIVEN NAMES Armenian 23%. *Aram* (3), *Vahe* (3), *Hagop* (2), *Raffi* (2), *Antranik*, *Ara*, *Armen*, *Arsen*, *Garabed*, *Garabet*, *Haig*, *Harout*.

Kazar (103) Shortened form of Armenian KAZARIAN.

Kazarian (313) Armenian: patronymic from the personal name *Kazar*, variant of *Ghazar*, itself a variant of *Łazar* (see LAZAR). It is possible, but less likely, that the name is an ethnic name for a Kazar, a member of a people living in the southern Caucasus in the Middle Ages.

GIVEN NAMES Armenian 17%. *Sarkis* (4), *Kazar* (3), *Aram* (2), *Garnik* (2), *Haig* (2), *Adrine*, *Ara*, *Artour*, *Gegam*, *Grigor*, *Nubar*, *Nvard*.

Kazda (183) Czech: **1.** from a pet form of the personal name *Kazimír* (see CASIMIR). **2.** variant of GAZDA.

Kazee (270) Altered spelling of German **Käse** (see KASE).

Kazemi (145) Muslim: from an Arabic name denoting a follower of Mūsā al-Kāzim (died 1183), the seventh imam of the Shiite Muslims, who is revered as a saint. *Kāzim* means 'one who controls his anger'.

GIVEN NAMES Muslim 76%. *Ali* (6), *Abbas* (3), *Ahmad* (3), *Hamid* (3), *Mohammad* (3), *Hossein* (2), *Maryam* (2), *Masoud* (2), *Mehdi* (2), *Saeed* (2), *Shirin* (2), *Abol*.

Kazen (166) Jewish (Ashkenazic): **1.** variant of KAZAN. **2.** variant of KATZEN.

GIVEN NAMES Jewish 4%. *Sol*, *Zalman*.

Kazi (140) Muslim: variant spelling of QAZI 'judge'.

GIVEN NAMES Muslim 75%; Indian 4%. *Abdul* (5), *Syed* (3), *Ahmed* (2), *Farid* (2), *Mohammad* (2), *Shakeel* (2), *Showkat* (2), *Abdul Majid*, *Abdullah*, *Abul*, *Afaq*, *Ahmad*; *Shaji*, *Shital*, *Sushama*.

Kazimer (105) German and Dutch: variant of KAZIMIR.

Kazimir (102) German, Dutch, and Polish: from the personal name *Kazimir*, a name of Slavic origin meaning 'destroyer of peace' (see CASIMIR, and compare Polish KAZMIERCZAK).

Kazlauskas (210) Lithuanian form of Polish KOZLOWSKI.

GIVEN NAMES Lithuanian 6%. *Vitas* (2), *Algirdas, Brone, Vytas.*

Kazmaier (104) German: variant of KAZIMIR.

GIVEN NAME German 6%. *Kurt.*

Kazmer (145) Hungarian (**Kázmér**): from the personal name *Kázmér*, Hungarian form of *Casimir* (see CASIMIR and compare Polish KAZMIERCZAK).

Kazmi (135) Muslim: variant of KAZEMI.

GIVEN NAMES Muslim 87%. *Syed* (25), *Saeed* (3), *Farrukh* (2), *Mehmood* (2), *Rumana* (2), *Abrar, Afzal, Ahmad, Ahsan, Aijaz, Ali, Ambreen.*

Kazmierczak (637) Polish (**Kaźmierczak**): patronymic from the personal name *Kazimierz*, a compound of Polish *kazić* 'to destroy' + the Old Slavic element *mir* 'peace', 'quiet', 'esteem'. This was a traditional name of Polish kings in the Middle Ages.

GIVEN NAMES Polish 5%. *Andrzej, Bogdan, Bogumil, Casimier, Henryk, Jadwiga, Jerzy, Karol, Kazimierz, Krystyna, Leszek, Zofia.*

Kazmierski (345) Polish (**Kaźmierski**): habitational name for someone from the numerous places in Poland named with the personal name *Kazimierz* (see KAZMIERCZAK, CASIMIR).

Ke (217) **1.** Chinese 柯: from the name of a prince of the state of Wu (see WU1) named Ke Lu. **2.** Chinese 葛, 戈: see GE.

GIVEN NAMES Chinese 51%; Vietnamese 9%. *Heng* (3), *Yong* (3), *Bin* (2), *Song* (2), *Yan* (2), *Zhi* (2), *Cheng, Chih-Ming, Chun-Yen, Fan, Fong, Gang; Lan* (2), *Hai, Hoa, Le Van, Mui, Tuy.*

Kea (374) Scottish and Irish: variant of KEY.

Keach (415) English: variant spelling of KEECH.

Keadle (203) **1.** Variant of English **Kiddle** (see KIDWELL). **2.** Perhaps also an Americanized spelling of German **Küderle**, a variant of KUDER.

Keady (310) Irish: reduced Anglicized form of Gaelic **Mac Céadaigh** 'son of *Céadach*', a personal name based on *céad* 'hundred'.

GIVEN NAMES Irish 6%. *Brendan, Eamonn.*

Keagle (296) Americanized form of German KEGEL.

Keagy (271) Altered spelling of Swiss German **Kägi** or **Kägy** (see KAEGI).

Keahey (317) Irish: Anglicized form of Gaelic **Mac Eachaidh** (see KEOGH).

Keal (173) **1.** English: variant spelling of KEEL. **2.** Perhaps an Americanized spelling of German KEHL or **Kühl** (see KUHL).

Kealey (312) **1.** English and Irish: variant spelling of KEELEY. **2.** Americanized spelling of German **Kühle**, variant of **Kühl** (see KUHL).

GIVEN NAME Irish 7%. *Brendan.*

Kealoha (143) Hawaiian: unexplained.

Kealy (336) **1.** Irish: variant of KEELEY. **2.** Americanized spelling of German **Kühle**, variant of **Kühl** (see KUHL).

GIVEN NAME Irish 6%. *Kieran.*

Kean (1545) **1.** Irish: variant spelling of KEANE. **2.** English: variant spelling of KEEN.

Keane (4227) **1.** Southern Irish: Anglicized form of Gaelic **Ó Catháin** 'descendant of *Cathán*', a personal name from a diminutive of *cath* 'battle'. Compare KANE. **2.** Irish: occasionally an Anglicized form of **Ó Céin** 'descendant of *Cian*', a personal name meaning 'distant', 'long'. **3.** English: variant spelling of KEEN. **4.** Americanized spelling of German *Kühn(e)* (see KUEHN).

GIVEN NAMES Irish 7%. *Brendan* (4), *Aisling* (2), *Conor* (2), *Fergus* (2), *Seamus* (2), *Aidan, Bridie, Ciaran, Declan, Dermot, Donal, Liam.*

Keaney (414) Irish: possibly an Americanized form of **Ó Cianaigh**, from *cianach*, a derivative of *cian* 'distant', 'long', or **Ó Caoinnigh**, a variant of **Ó Coinnigh** (see KENNY).

GIVEN NAMES Irish 7%. *Brendan, Kieran.*

Kear (554) English: occupational name for a locksmith, Middle English *keyere, kayer*, Old English *cǣgere*, from *cǣg* 'key' (see CARE).

Kearbey (158) Variant of English KIRBY.

Kearby (186) Variant of English KIRBY.

Kearl (157) Americanized spelling of German KERL.

Kearley (263) English (mainly Dorset and Hampshire): unexplained; perhaps a variant of CURLEY.

Kearn (180) **1.** Irish: variant of KERN, a reduced and altered form of McCARRON. **2.** Americanized spelling of German KERN.

Kearnes (122) Variant spelling of Irish KEARNS.

Kearney (7586) Irish: Anglicized form of Gaelic **Ó Catharnaigh** 'descendant of *Catharnach*', a byname meaning 'warlike' or 'soldier', and **Ó Cearnaigh**, from *cearnach* 'victorious'. Both surnames were widely distributed and are now very difficult to disentangle.

FOREBEARS Many present-day bearers of this name are descended from Tadhg Ó Catharnaigh, killed in battle in 1084. He was nicknamed *An Sionnach* 'the Fox', and for this reason the surname has sometimes been Anglicized as FOX. Denis Kearney, born in Oakmont, Ireland, in 1847, was a major U.S. labor movement leader.

GIVEN NAMES Irish 8%. *Brendan* (5), *Seamus* (2), *Caitlin, Declan, Dermot, Donovan, Eamonn, Liam.*

Kearns (5845) Irish: Anglicized form of Gaelic **Ó Céirín** 'descendant of *Céirín*', a

personal name from a diminutive of *ciar* 'dark', 'black'. English patronymic *-s* has been added superfluously.

Kearse (541) Irish: variant of KEIRSEY.

Kearsley (167) English: habitational name for someone from Keresley in Warwickshire, probably so named from the Old English personal name *Cēnhere* + *lēah* 'woodland clearing'.

Keary (147) Irish: Anglicized form of Gaelic **Ó Ciardha** (from a personal name based on *ciar* 'black'), now generally Anglicized as CAREY.

GIVEN NAME Irish 6%. *Dermot.*

Keas (184) Americanized spelling of German KIES.

Keasey (104) English (Midlands): possibly a variant of Irish CASEY.

Keasler (435) Americanized spelling of German KIESLER.

Keasling (201) Americanized spelling of German KIESSLING.

Keast (404) Cornish: nickname for a fat man, from Cornish *kest* 'paunch'.

Keaster (105) Americanized form of Dutch KEISTER.

Keath (150) Scottish: variant spelling of KEITH.

Keathley (840) English: variant of KEIGHLEY.

Keating (7143) **1.** English: from an Old English personal name *Cȳting*, a derivative of *Cȳta* (see KITE). **2.** Irish (of Norman origin): Americanized form of **Céitinn**, a Gaelicized form of **de Ketyng** (probably a habitational name), which was taken to southern Ireland by Anglo-Norman settlers.

GIVEN NAMES Irish 7%. *Brendan* (3), *Connor* (2), *Finola, Kieran, Niall, Padraic.*

Keatley (223) English: variant of KEIGHLEY.

Keaton (2769) English: variant spelling of KEETON.

Keator (232) Probably an Americanized spelling of German **Küter** (see KUTER).

Keats (326) English (chiefly West Midlands): patronymic from **Keat**, a variant of KITE.

Keatts (345) English: variant spelling of KEATS.

Keaveney (256) Irish: variant spelling of KEAVENY.

GIVEN NAMES Irish 9%. *Declan, Dermot, Kieran, Kiernan.*

Keaveny (240) Irish: Anglicized form of Gaelic **Ó Géibheannaigh** 'descendant of *Géibheannach*' and **Mac Géibheannaigh** 'son of *Géibheannach*' (see GUINEY).

Keay (258) English and Scottish: variant of KAY.

Keays (143) English: variant of KAY.

Kebede (204) Ethiopian: unexplained.

GIVEN NAMES Ethiopian 67%; African 6%. *Alemayehu* (5), *Abebe* (3), *Frehiwot* (3), *Genet* (3), *Tesfaye* (3), *Ermias* (2), *Fasil*

(2), *Girma* (2), *Henock* (2), *Lemlem* (2), *Tessema* (2), *Zewdu* (2); *Almaz* (2), *Lishan*.

Keber (111) Slovenian: nickname from the colloquial word *keber* 'beetle', 'chafer', of German origin (see KAFER).

Kebler (108) South German: variant spelling of KEEBLER.

Keck (4493) **1.** English: from the Old Norse personal name *Keikr* (from Old West Scandinavian *keikr* 'bent backwards'). **2.** German: nickname from Middle High German *kec* 'lively', 'active' (cognate of English *quick*), which later changed its meaning to 'bold', 'forward', 'fresh'.

Keckler (354) Altered spelling of German **Kechler**, occupational name for a potter, from an agent derivative of Middle High German *kachel* 'clay pot', 'tile'. Later it came to denote a stove fitter who built the typical Bavarian and Austrian tile stoves.

Keddie (140) Scottish: variant spelling of KEDDY.

Keddy (233) Scottish and northern Irish: **1.** reduced Anglicized form of Gaelic **Mac Adaidh**, a patronymic from a Gaelic form of the personal name ADAM. **2.** Anglicized form of Gaelic **Mac Conduibh** (see McADOO).

Keding (127) German: variant of **Käding** (see KAEDING).
GIVEN NAMES German 10%. *Willi* (2), *Konrad, Kurt, Ulrich*.

Kedrowski (179) Polish (**Kędrowski**): from a derivative of *kędra* 'lock of hair', *kędrawy* 'long-haired' (see KEDZIOR).

Kedzierski (225) Polish (**Kędzierski**): derivative of KEDZIOR, with the addition of *-ski*, suffix of surnames.
GIVEN NAMES Polish 17%. *Aleksander, Andrzey, Bogdan, Eugeniusz, Jacek, Jerzy, Leszek, Mariusz, Mieczyslaw, Pawel, Rafal, Taddeus*.

Kedzior (109) Polish (**Kędzior**): from *kędzior* 'lock of hair', hence a nickname for someone with long hair.
GIVEN NAMES Polish 24%. *Pawel* (2), *Zbigniew* (2), *Kazimierz, Leslaw, Ryszard, Slawomir, Waclaw, Zdzislaw*.

Kee (2381) **1.** Irish: reduced form of McKEE. **2.** Korean: variant of KI.

Keebaugh (131) Americanized form of German **Kühbach**, a habitational name from any of various places in Bavaria and Austria, so named from Old High German *kuo* 'cow' + *bah* 'stream'.

Keeble (422) **1.** English: variant of KIBBLE. **2.** Americanized spelling of South German **Kübel**, a metonymic occupational name for a cooper, from Middle High German *kübel* 'tub', 'vat'.

Keebler (478) Americanized spelling of German KIEBLER or **Kübler** (see KUEBLER).

Keech (898) English: from Middle English *keech* 'lump', 'fat', hence an unflattering nickname for a fat, lumpish person.

Keedy (250) **1.** English (Durham and North Yorkshire): unexplained; perhaps an altered spelling of Scottish and northern Irish **Keddy**. **2.** Irish: variant spelling of KEADY.

Keef (281) Irish: reduced form of O'KEEFE.

Keefauver (117) Americanized form of German **Kiefhaber**. See KEFAUVER.

Keefe (4795) Irish: reduced form of O'KEEFE.
GIVEN NAMES Irish 4%. *Brendan* (2), *Aileen, Thomas Patrick*.

Keefer (3707) Americanized spelling of KIEFER.

Keeffe (191) Irish: variant spelling of KEEFE.

Keefner (119) Americanized spelling of German **Küfner**, a variant of **Küfer** (see KIEFER).
GIVEN NAME German 4%. *Kurt*.

Keefover (114) Americanized spelling of South German **Kiefhaber** (see KEFAUVER).

Keegan (4039) Irish: reduced Anglicized form of Gaelic **Mac Aodhagáin** 'son of *Aodhagán*', a personal name that is a pet form of the ancient Irish personal name *Aodh* 'fire' (see McKAY).
GIVEN NAMES Irish 5%. *Brendan* (4), *Eamonn* (3), *Liam* (2), *Bridie, Colum, Fintan, Francis Pat, Kieran, Niall*.

Keehan (227) Irish: reduced form of McKEEHAN.

Keehn (805) **1.** Variant of Irish KEEHAN. **2.** Americanized spelling of German **Kühn** (see KUEHN).

Keehner (221) Americanized spelling of German **Kühner** (see KUHNER).

Keel (2940) **1.** English: habitational name from Keele in Staffordshire, named from Old English *cȳ* 'cows' + *hyll* 'hill', or from East and West Keal in Lincolnshire, which are named from Old Norse *kjǫlr* 'ridge'. **2.** Irish: reduced form of McKEEL. **3.** Swiss German: probably a variant of KEHL 2. **4.** Americanized spelling of German **Kühl** (see KUHL) or **Kiehl, Kiel** (see KIEL).

Keelan (356) **1.** Irish: reduced form of **Keelahan**, an Anglicized form of Gaelic **Ó Céileacháin**, from *céileachán*, a diminutive of *céile* 'companion'. **2.** Welsh: habitational name for someone from any of various townships called Cilan, especially one in Llanair Dyffryn Clwyd, Denbighshire.

Keele (1108) English and possibly also Irish: variant spelling of KEEL.

Keelen (111) **1.** Dutch: habitational name for someone from a place called Keel or Kel. **2.** Irish: variant spelling of KEELAN.

Keeler (4432) **1.** English: occupational name for a boatman or boatbuilder, from an agent derivative of Middle English *kele* 'ship', 'barge' (from Middle Dutch *kiel*). **2.** Americanized spelling of German **Kühler**, from a variant of an old personal name (see KEELING) or a variant of KUHL.

Keeley (2046) **1.** Irish: reduced Anglicized form of Gaelic **Ó Caollaidhe** 'descendant of *Caollaidhe*', a personal name based on *caol* 'slender', 'graceful'. **2.** English: variant of KEIGHLEY. **3.** Americanized spelling of German **Kühle**, variant of **Kühl** (see KUHL) or of **Kühling** (see KEELING).
GIVEN NAMES Irish 7%. *Brendan* (6), *Eamonn, Colum, Fintan, Francis Pat, Kieran, Niall*.

Keelin (188) Variant of Irish or English KEELING.

Keeling (2961) **1.** Irish: see KEELEY. **2.** English: nickname from Middle English *keling* 'young codfish'. **3.** Americanized spelling of German **Kühling**, a patronymic from *Colo*, probably a short form of an old personal name meaning 'helmet'.

Keels (586) Dutch: from a reduced form of KEGEL.

Keely (656) Irish: variant spelling of KEELEY.

Keen (6265) **1.** English: from *Kene*, a short form of the Old English personal name *Cēn* or *Cyne*, based on Old English *cēne* 'wise', 'brave', 'proud'. **2.** Americanized spelling of German **Kühn** (see KUEHN).
FOREBEARS Robert Keayne (d. 1655) was one of the founders of Boston MA, and is buried in the King's Chapel Burying Ground there.

Keena (319) Irish: possibly an Anglicized form of Gaelic **Ó Caoinnigh**, a variant of **Ó Coinnigh** (see KENNY).
GIVEN NAMES Irish 6%. *Brendan, Brigid*.

Keenan (7867) Irish: Anglicized form of Gaelic **Ó Cianáin** 'son of *Cianán*', a personal name from a diminutive of *cian* 'distant', 'long', or possibly of **Mac Fhinghin** 'fair offspring'.
GIVEN NAMES Irish 4%. *Brendan* (8), *Colm* (2), *Aileen, Declan, Fergal, Mairead, Paddy, Roisin, Siobhan*.

Keene (6423) **1.** English: variant spelling of KEEN. **2.** Americanized spelling of German **Kühne** (see KUEHN).

Keenen (131) Variant spelling of Irish KEENAN.

Keener (4685) Americanized spelling of KIENER or **Kühner** (see KUEHNER).

Keeney (3609) **1.** Irish: variant spelling of KEANEY. **2.** Americanized spelling of Swiss German **Kühni, Kühne** (see KUEHN), or German KIENE or KIENER.

Keenum (401) Variant of Irish KEENAN.

Keeny (162) Irish: variant spelling of KEANEY.

Keep (383) **1.** English: occupational name for a jailer or someone employed at a keep or castle, Middle English *kepe*. **2.** Americanized spelling of German **Kiep**, from a short form of the old personal name *Gebolf*, from a Germanic personal name composed of the elements *geb* 'gift' + *wolf* 'wolf'. Compare GEBHARDT.

Keepers (252) Americanized spelling of Dutch KUIPERS or North German

(Rhenish) **Küppers**, a variant of **Küpper** (see KUEPPER).

Keer (140) **1.** English: variant spelling of KEAR. **2.** Indian (Maharashtra): Hindu name, probably from Marathi *kir* 'parrot'. **3.** Indian (Panjab): Sikh (Khatri) name of unknown meaning.
GIVEN NAMES Indian 4%. *Dilip, Mahesh.*

Keeran (274) Probably an altered spelling of Irish KIERAN.

Kees (800) German: **1.** from a vernacular form of the Roman family name CORNELIUS. **2.** variant of KASE 2 or possibly 1. **3.** Americanized spelling of German KIES and *Kiese*, from an old personal name, *Giso*, of uncertain etymology.

Keese (503) German: variant of KEES.

Keesecker (144) German: of uncertain origin. There are two possibilities: **1.** altered spelling of **Kiesecker**, which may have arisen as a nickname from Middle Low German *kīf–sake* 'legal dispute' or alternatively as a topographic name from *Kies* 'gravel', 'coarse sand' + *Ecke* 'corner' or *-ecker*, from *Acker* 'field'. **2.** variant of GIESECKE.

Keesee (1200) Altered spelling of **Keese**, a North German form of KASE, or GIESE, also a German surname.

Keesey (280) Altered spelling of **Keese**, a North German form of KASE, or GIESE, also a German surname.

Keesler (574) Americanized spelling of German KIESLER.

Keesling (591) Americanized spelling of German KIESSLING.

Keetch (157) English: variant spelling of KEECH.

Keeter (914) Altered spelling of German **Küter** (see KUETER).

Keeth (323) Probably an altered spelling of KEITH.

Keeton (3029) English: habitational name from a place called Ketton in Durham or one in Rutland or from Keaton in Ermington, Devon. The first is named from the Old English personal name *Catta* or the Old Norse personal name *Káti* + Old English *tūn* 'settlement'; the second is probably from an old river name or tribal name *Cētan* (possibly a derivative of Celtic *cēd* 'wood') + Old English *ēa* 'river'; and the last possibly from Cornish *kee* 'hedge', 'bank' + Old English *tūn*.

Keeven (165) Variant spelling of Irish **Keevan**, which is an Anglicized form of Gaelic **Ó Ciabháin** 'descendant of *Ciabhán*', a personal name or byname based on *ciabhach* 'having long locks of hair', or **Ó Caomháin** 'descendant of *Caomhán*', a diminutive of *caomh* 'pleasant'; this is the name of an important Mayo family.

Keever (1111) Irish: reduced form of MCKEEVER (see MCIVER).

Keezer (232) Respelling of German KIESER.

Kefalas (128) Greek: nickname from a derivative of the vocabulary word *kephalē* 'head', in either of two senses: 'big-headed' or 'obstinate'.
GIVEN NAMES Greek 15%. *Constantine* (2), *Costas, Despina, Kimon, Kostas, Panagiotis, Panayiotis, Spiros, Vassilis.*

Kefauver (181) **1.** Americanized spelling of South German **Kiefhaber**, probably from Middle High German *kifen* 'to gnaw or chew' + *haber* 'oats' and hence a nickname for a poor person or an oats farmer. **2.** An alternative etymology has it as a topographic name, from Middle Low German *kīf* 'feud' + *haber* 'oats', denoting an oats field that had been the subject of a dispute.

Keffeler (124) Probably Dutch or North German: probably a nickname for a contentious person, from Middle Low German *kevelen* 'to argue', 'squabble'.

Keffer (1277) Dutch: nickname meaning 'bug' or 'beetle'.

Kegel (432) German: from Middle High German *kegel* 'skittle', 'pin', hence a nickname for an inveterate skittles or bowls player. The term also denoted an illegitimate child (hence the phrase (still current) *mit Kind und Kegel* 'with all the family') and in early New High German (15th century) took on the meaning 'uncouth person'.
GIVEN NAMES German 4%. *Gunter* (2), *Franz, Fritz, Grete, Ute, Wilhelm.*

Kegerreis (155) German: variant of **Kägersch**, Swabian nickname for a petty thief or pilferer, one of numerous derivations from Middle High German *kagelster* 'magpie'.

Kegg (199) Manx: reduced form of Gaelic **Mac Thaidhg** (see MCCAIG).

Kegler (414) German: nickname for a skilled or enthusiastic skittles player, from an agent derivative of Middle High German *kegel* 'skittle', 'pin'.

Kegley (1164) Irish: Anglicized form of Gaelic **Ó Coigligh** (see QUIGLEY).

Kehl (1047) German: **1.** habitational name from various places so named, notably the town across the Rhine from Strasbourg. **2.** from Middle High German *kel(e)* 'throat', hence a nickname possibly for someone with a goiter or perhaps with a distinctively throaty voice. **3.** variant of **Köhl** (see KOHL). **4.** from a northern German field name of unknown etymology.

Kehler (537) German: **1.** habitational name from a place called KEHL. **2.** variant of **Köhler** (see KOHLER).

Kehm (313) German: **1.** probably a variant of *Gehm*, from an old personal name based on Old High German *gam* 'joy', 'play'. **2.** variant of *Köhm*, a Low German variant of **Kümmel** (see KIMMEL).

Kehn (359) German: variant of **Köhn** (see KOHN).

Kehoe (3349) **1.** Irish: variant of KEOGH. **2.** English (of Norman origin): habitational name from Caieu, a lost place near Boulogne-sur-Mer, Pas-de-Calais. Compare CAHOW.
GIVEN NAMES Irish 4%. *Brendan* (2), *Cormac* (2), *Aidan, Eithne, Sinead, Siobhan.*

Kehr (664) German: **1.** from Middle High German *kere* 'bend', 'corner', hence a topographic name for someone living near a bend in a road or near a field named with this word. The name is common in Tyrol (where it is also a place name from which the surname may have arisen) and in adjoining parts of Switzerland. **2.** possibly a short form of a personal name, *Kehri* or *Kehrein*, derived from the Roman personal name *Quirinus*, which was borne by several early Christian martyrs.
GIVEN NAMES German 4%. *Manfred* (2), *Ewald, Franz, Wilhelm, Wolfgang.*

Kehrer (451) German: **1.** topographic name for someone living by a bend in a road, from a derivative of KEHR 1. **2.** occupational name for a cleaner, from an agent derivative of Middle Low or Middle High German *kēren* 'to sweep'. Compare FEGER.
GIVEN NAMES German 4%. *Erwin, Franz, Helmut, Willi, Wolfgang.*

Kehres (258) German: probably from a Germanic personal name, a variant form of GEHRES.

Kehrli (166) Swiss German: diminutive of KERL.

Kehs (120) Variant of German **Käse**, a metonymic occupational name for a maker or seller of cheese, more often Americanized as CASE.

Keibler (130) Americanized spelling of South German KIEBLER, occupational name for a cooper (see KUEBLER).

Keicher (166) German: **1.** from the East Prussian dialect word *Keicher* 'small cake', 'pastry', hence a metonymic occupational name for a pastrycook. **2.** South German: from Middle High German *kīchen* 'to gasp for breath', hence a nickname for an asthmatic or someone perpetually out of breath. Compare KAUCHER. **3.** habitational name for someone from a place called Kaichen in Hesse.

Keidel (288) South German: from Middle High German *kīl* 'wedge', applied as a nickname for a ruffian or someone who was misshapen.
GIVEN NAMES German 5%. *Kurt* (3), *Ernst.*

Keifer (920) **1.** Altered spelling of German KIEFER. **2.** German: nickname for someone who was quarrelsome, from an agent of Middle High German *kīben, kīven* 'to quarrel'.

Keiffer (483) **1.** Variant spelling of German KEIFER. **2.** Altered spelling of German **Kieffer** (see KIEFER).

Keigher (128) English (Lancashire, Cheshire): unexplained; perhaps of Irish origin, a variant of **Kehir**, **Keher**, Munster

and Connacht variants of **Cahir**, an Anglicized form of Gaelic **Ó Cathaoir**, from an old Irish personal name.
GIVEN NAME Irish 6%. *Liam.*

Keighley (126) **1.** English: habitational name from a place so named in West Yorkshire, recorded in Domesday Book as *Chichelai*, apparently named with an Old English personal name *Cyhha* + Old English *lēah* 'woodland clearing'. **2.** Americanized spelling of German **Kiechle** (see KUECHLE) or **Kiechler** (see KUECHLER).

Keightley (131) **1.** English: variant of KEIGHLEY. **2.** Irish: also found in Ireland as an equivalent of GATELY.
GIVEN NAME French 5%. *Cecile.*

Keigley (188) Origin uncertain. **1.** Perhaps an altered spelling of German **Kügele** (see KUGLER). **2.** Alternatively, perhaps a variant of English KEIGHLEY.

Keil (2292) **1.** German: from Middle High German *kīl* 'wedge', 'wooden peg', hence possibly a metonymic occupational name for a maker of such pegs or for a wood chopper. Alternatively, it may be nickname for an uncouth or misshapen person (compare KEIDEL) or a topographic name for someone who lived on or near a wedge-shaped plot of land. **2.** Altered spelling of German **Geil**, nickname from Middle High German *geil* 'boisterous', 'mischievous', later 'horny'.
GIVEN NAMES German 5%. *Otto* (5), *Hans* (4), *Fritz* (3), *Klaus* (3), *Dieter* (2), *Gerhard* (2), *Juergen* (2), *Kurt* (2), *Alfons*, *Armin*, *Egon*, *Erna.*

Keilen (114) Dutch: reduced form of **Van der Keilen**, a variant of KEELEN.

Keiler (126) German: **1.** occupational name for a maker of wooden pegs and wedges or a woodchopper, from an agent derivative of Middle High German *kīl* 'wedge', 'wooden peg'. **2.** possibly a derivative of **Geil** (see KEIL 2).
GIVEN NAME German 4%. *Franz.*

Keilholtz (106) **1.** German: probably a metonymic occupational name for a joiner or cabinet maker, from the name of a woodworking tool derived from Middle High German *kil* 'wedge', 'peg'. **2.** German: nickname for a crude person, from a technical term for knotty wood, which must be worked with a *Keil* 'wedge'.

Keillor (182) Scottish: habitational name from a place in Angus called Keilor.

Keilman (371) German: topographic name for someone who lived on or by a wedge-shaped piece of land, from KEIL 1 + -*man* 'man'.

Keilty (146) Irish: variant of KIELTY.

Keily (123) Irish: variant of KIELY.

Keim (2391) **1.** Jewish (Ashkenazic): from the Yiddish personal name *kayem*. This is an apotropaic name, given to a sickly child, based on the Hebrew adjective *qayom* 'tough', 'enduring'. **2.** German (Bavaria, Baden-Württemberg): from Middle High

German *kīme* 'sprout', 'shoot', 'offspring', sometimes used as a personal name, or from a pet form of JOACHIM.

Keimig (194) German: nickname from *keimig* 'fruitful', 'fertile', or possibly from a reduced form of the personal name *Keimling*, from the same word.

Keinath (228) German: **1.** possibly a variant of **Keinrath**, from the personal name *Konrad* (see KONRAD). **2.** (Swabian) from medieval Latin *caminata* (*camera*) 'room with a fireplace (in medieval castles)', which by extension came to a freestanding stone building for storage or a hostelry and hence a topographic name. In Germany a much more common form is **Kemnat(h)**, also a common place name.
GIVEN NAMES German 7%. *Gunter* (2), *Arno*, *Frieda*, *Wolfgang.*

Keiner (181) German: from a reduced form of the personal name *Kagenher*, from Old High German *gagan* 'against' + *heri* 'army'.
GIVEN NAMES German 4%. *Adelheid*, *Mathias.*

Keip (109) **1.** Northeastern German: topographic name, from the East Prussian dialect term *keip* 'weir' (fish trap). **2.** German: variant of *Keip*, a nickname for a quarrelsome person, from Middle High German *kīp*.

Keiper (765) German: **1.** occupational name for a fisherman, from Middle High German *keiper* 'fisherman', 'fish netter', found in the Upper German dialects, but also in Prussian, *keip* 'weir' (fish trap) (see KEIP) may be the source of the name. **2.** variant of **Keuper**, itself a variant of **Käufer** (see KAUFER) or of **Küpper** (see KUPPER); this is a frequent surname in the lower Rhine area.

Keir (341) Scottish: habitational name from a place north of Dunblane in Stirlingshire called Keir.

Keirn (263) **1.** Irish: variant of KERN, a reduced and altered form of MCCARRON. **2.** Possibly also an Americanized spelling of German KERN.

Keirns (196) Probably a variant spelling of KEARNS.

Keirsey (159) Irish (of Norman origin): topographic name dating back to the 13th century.

Keirstead (134) Americanized spelling of Dutch **Kierstede** (see KIERSTEAD).

Keiser (2795) Dutch or German: variant spelling of KEYSER or KAISER.

Keisler (452) German: occupational name for a kettle or cauldron maker, from an agent derivative of Middle High German *kezzel* 'kettle'.

Keisling (296) Altered spelling of German KIESLING.

Keister (1436) Dutch: from Middle Dutch *keisterlinc* 'pastry', hence an occupational name for a pastrycook.

Keita (120) West African: unexplained.

GIVEN NAMES African 42%; Muslim 36%. *Mamadou* (4), *Djibril* (2), *Aboubacar*, *Amadou*, *Bakary*, *Boubacar*, *Cheikh*, *Mahamadou*, *Mamady*, *Modibo*, *Oumar*, *Ousman*; *Ibrahima* (2), *Mahamed* (2), *Mohammed* (2), *Moussa* (2), *Abdoul*, *Abdoulaye*, *Abou*, *Abrahim*, *Fatima*, *Ibrahim*, *Issa*, *Lamine.*

Keitel (224) **1.** German: of uncertain origin. It may be a variant spelling of KEIDEL, a variant spelling of the unexplained Prussian name **Keytel**, or a derivative of the South German dialect word *Geitel* 'duck' (and so a metonymic occupational name for a rearer of ducks or possibly a nickname for someone thought to resemble a duck). Alternatively the name may be derived from the Langobardic word *gaida* 'spike (of a lance)'. **2.** Jewish (Ashkenazic): metonymic occupational name from Yiddish *keytl* 'small chain', 'hook'.
GIVEN NAMES German 6%; Jewish 4%. *Ernst*, *Gunther*, *Hans*; *Miriam* (2), *Herschel.*

Keiter (429) German: of uncertain origin; possibly a South German derivative of KAUT.

Keith (16834) **1.** Scottish: habitational name from the lands of Keith in East Lothian. In the 17th century numerous bearers of this name settled in Ulster. **2.** German: nickname from Middle High German *kīt* 'sprout', 'offspring'.
FOREBEARS George Keith (*c.* 1638–1716), born at Peterhead, Aberdeenshire, Scotland, came to NJ in or before 1685. In 1689 he settled in Philadelphia, where he became headmaster of the school now called the William Penn Charter School. He came into sharp collision with the Quaker leaders in PA and formed a separatist party known as the Christian Quakers, popularly known as 'Keithians'.

Keithley (825) English: variant of KEIGHLEY.

Keithly (158) English: variant of KEIGHLEY.

Keitt (273) Possibly an altered spelling of German KEITH 2 (in order to retain the original pronunciation).
GIVEN NAME French 4%. *Marcell.*

Keitz (123) German: from a Germanic personal name based on *gaida* 'point (of a lance)' (see KEITEL).

Keizer (364) Dutch: modern spelling of KEYSER.

Kelbaugh (200) Americanized spelling of the North German **Kelbach**, a topographic name from *kel* 'swamp' + *Bach* 'brook', 'creek'.

Kelber (159) German: **1.** shortened form of **Kelberer**, occupational name for someone who reared calves, from Middle High German *kalb*, *kalp* (plural *kelber*) + the agent suffix -*er*. **2.** habitational name for someone from a place called Kelbra on the Unstrut river.
GIVEN NAMES German 7%. *Hermann, Udo.*

Kelch (828) German: **1.** nickname from Middle High German *kelch* 'double chin', 'goiter'. **2.** from another meaning of Middle High German *kelch* 'glass', 'chalice', hence a metonymic occupational name for a chalice maker or a habitational name for someone living at a house distinguished by the sign of a chalice.

Kelchner (393) German: occupational name or habitational name, from a derivative of Middle High German *kelch* 'chalice' (see KELCH 2).

Kelder (176) Dutch: from Middle Dutch *kelder* 'cellar', hence a metonymic occupational name for a keeper of a cellar, especially a wine cellar, or a waiter in one. Compare KELLNER.
GIVEN NAME German 6%. *Kurt* (2).

Kelderman (157) Dutch: occupational name for the keeper of a wine cellar. Compare KELDER.

Keleher (562) Irish: variant spelling of KELLEHER.
GIVEN NAME Irish 4%. *Siobhan*.

Keleman (123) Altered spelling of Hungarian KELEMEN.
GIVEN NAMES Hungarian 4%. *Lajos, Laszlo*.

Kelemen (484) Hungarian: from the personal name *Kelemen*, Hungarian form of CLEMENT.
GIVEN NAMES Hungarian 10%. *Andras* (4), *Gabor* (2), *Geza* (2), *Imre* (2), *Laszlo* (2), *Tibor* (2), *Bela, Gyula, Istvan, Jozsef, Karoly, Leszlo*.

Keliher (120) Irish: variant spelling of KELLEHER.

Kelker (133) German: occupational name for a painter (someone who applied lime wash), from an agent derivative of Middle High German *kelken* 'to whitewash', 'to lime' or for a lime burner (see KALK-BRENNER).

Kell (1923) German: **1.** from Middle High, Middle Low German *kelle* 'trowel', hence a metonymic occupational name for a maker or user of such tools. **2.** habitational name from any of the places, especially in Rhineland, named Kell, from Middle Low German *kel* (a field name denoting swampy land), or from *kelle* 'steep path', 'ravine' (see KELLE).

Kellam (1465) English: habitational name for someone from Kelham in Nottinghamshire, so named from the dative plural of Old Norse *kjǫlr* '(place at) the ridges'.

Kellams (295) Variant of English KELLAM.

Kellar (1638) **1.** English and Scottish: variant of KEILLOR. **2.** German: variant of KELLER.

Kellas (133) Scottish (Aberdeenshire): habitational name from Kellas, a village in the parish of Dallas in Morayshire.

Kelle (121) German: topographic name from the dialect word *Kelle* 'steep path', 'ravine'.
GIVEN NAMES German 4%. *Bernhard, Klaus*.

Kelleher (4280) Irish: Anglicized form of Gaelic Ó Céileachair 'son of *Céileachar*', a personal name meaning 'companion-dear', i.e. 'lover of company'.
GIVEN NAMES Irish 6%. *Brendan* (6), *Aidan* (3), *Siobhan* (2), *Colm, Dermod, Donal, Donovan, Niall, Sean Patrick*.

Kellem (133) Variant spelling of English KELLAM.

Kellems (281) Variant of English KELLAM.

Kellen (535) German: habitational name from a place so named in Rhineland (see KELL 2).

Kellenberger (435) German: habitational name for someone from a place called Kellenberg in Rhineland (see KELL 2).

Keller (38840) **1.** German: from Middle High German *kellaere* 'cellarman', 'cellar master' (Latin *cellarius*, denoting the keeper of the *cella* 'store chamber', 'pantry'). Hence an occupational name for the overseer of the stores, accounts, or household in general in, for example, a monastery or castle. Kellers were important as trusted stewards in a great household, and in some cases were promoted to ministerial rank. The surname is widespread throughout central Europe. **2.** English: either an occupational name for a maker of caps or cauls, from Middle English *kellere*, or an occupational name for an executioner, from Old English *cwellere*. **3.** Irish: reduced form of KELLEHER. **4.** Scottish: variant of KEILLOR.

Kellerhals (114) German and Swiss German: from Middle High German *keller* 'cellar' + *hals* 'neck', perhaps a nickname for someone with a peculiarity of the neck.

Kellerman (1348) Altered spelling of German KELLERMANN.

Kellermann (265) German: occupational name for a man who worked in a cellar (see KELLER).
GIVEN NAMES German 7%. *Goetz, Gottfried, Helmut, Horst, Ingeborg, Uwe*.

Kellett (1295) English: habitational name from Nether or Over Kellet in Lancashire or Kelleth in Cumbria, named from Old Norse *kelda* 'spring' + *hlíth* 'slope'.

Kelley (52553) Irish, Scottish, and English: variant spelling of KELLY.

Kellie (121) Scottish: variant spelling of KELLY.

Kelliher (929) Irish: variant spelling of KELLEHER.
GIVEN NAMES Irish 5%. *Brendan* (2), *Malachy*.

Kelling (561) German: **1.** from Middle Low German *Kelling* 'pain'. **2.** variant of **Kellmann** (see KELLMAN).

Kellis (331) **1.** Scottish: patronymic based on KELLY as a personal name. Compare KELLISON. **2.** Greek: descriptive nickname for a bald man, from *kelis* 'bald', a word of Turkish origin.
FOREBEARS As a family name of Scottish

origin, this has been established in NC since the 18th century.

Kellison (433) Scottish: patronymic based on KELLY as a personal name.

Kellman (512) **1.** German (**Kellmann**): elaborated variant of KELL, with the addition of *man* 'man'. **2.** Jewish (Ashkenazic): variant of KALMAN.
GIVEN NAMES Jewish 6%. *Ari, Chaya, Meyer, Miriam, Yaakov*.

Kelln (122) German: variant of KELLNER.
GIVEN NAME German 4%. *Merwin*.

Kellner (1895) German, Dutch, and Jewish (Ashkenazic): occupational name from Middle High German *kelnære*, Middle Dutch *kel(le)nare*, German *Kellner* 'cellarman'. This term developed various specialized senses: a steward, an overseer in a castle, monastery, or the like, and in modern usage, a wine waiter.
GIVEN NAMES German 4%. *Hans* (5), *Kurt* (4), *Erwin* (2), *Manfred* (2), *Gottfried, Guenther, Gunther, Hermann, Uwe, Willi*.

Kello (107) Variant spelling of English and Scottish KELLOW.

Kellogg (6328) **1.** Scottish: of uncertain origin. Early forms such as *de Kellock, de Keloche* are evidently habitational names, perhaps from Keiloch in Aberdeenshire or Killoch in Ayrshire (see KILLOUGH). **2.** Scottish and northern English: from the Old Norse personal name *Kjallákr*, which is a borrowing of Irish *Ceallach* (see KELLY).
FOREBEARS Daniel Kellogg (1630–88), from Great Leighs, Essex, England, settled in Norwalk, CT, in 1656. His son, Edward (1790–1858), was a financial reformer and the intellectual father of Greenbackism (a movement favoring promotion of economic growth by increasing the paper money supply, regardless of the inflationary side effects).

Kellom (100) Probably a variant spelling of English KELLAM.

Kellough (269) Variant of Scottish KELLOGG.

Kellow (234) **1.** Cornish: habitational name from a minor place named Kellow, from Cornish *kellow*, plural of *kelli* 'wood', 'grove'. **2.** English: habitational name from Kelloe in Durham, named from Old English *celf* 'calf' + *hlāw* 'hill'. **3.** Scottish: from the lands of Kelloe in Berwickshire, or in some cases possibly a variant of KELLOGG.

Kells (481) Scottish and Irish: from Old Norse *kaetil* 'cauldron'; in Scotland of topographic origin.

Kellum (1748) English: variant spelling of KELLAM.

Kelly (94726) Irish: Anglicized form of Gaelic Ó Ceallaigh 'descendant of *Ceallach*', an ancient Irish personal name, originally a byname meaning 'bright-headed', later understood as 'frequenting churches' (Irish *ceall*). There are several early Irish saints who bore this name. *Kelly* is now the most common of all Irish family names in Ireland.

GIVEN NAMES Irish 4%. *Brendan* (55), *Kieran* (15), *Aileen* (12), *John Patrick* (11), *Siobhan* (9), *Liam* (7), *Brigid* (6), *Donovan* (6), *Eamon* (6), *Parnell* (5), *Aidan* (4), *Clancy* (4).

Kelm (1114) Germanized form of Polish **Chełm** 'peak', 'hill', a topographic name for someone who lived by a hill with a pointed summit, or habitational name from a city in eastern Poland or any of various other places named with this word.

GIVEN NAMES German 5%. *Otto* (4), *Erwin* (3), *Gerhard* (2), *Gunter* (2), *Theresia* (2), *Hedwig, Helmut, Wilhelm, Wolfgang.*

Kelman (529) **1.** Scottish: according to Black, a habitational name from a place in Aberdeenshire named Kelman. **2.** English: occupational name for a maker of caps or cauls, from Middle English *kelle* + *man*. **3.** English: perhaps an occupational name for a bargeman, from Middle English *kele* 'ship', 'barge'. Compare KEELER. **4.** Americanized spelling of German KELLMAN. **5.** Jewish (Ashkenazic): from the male personal name *Kelman*, a variant of KALMAN.

GIVEN NAMES Jewish 9%. *Leib* (2), *Sol* (2), *Ari, Aron, Baruch, Gitel, Hyman, Izya, Mayer, Mort, Moshe, Shalom.*

Kelner (272) **1.** English: variant of KILNER. **2.** German, Dutch, and Jewish (Ashkenazic): variant spelling of KELLNER, in any of its senses: 'cellarman', 'steward', 'overseer', or 'waiter'. In this spelling it is also found as a Czech name. **3.** Jewish (Ashkenazic): occupational name from modern German *Kellner* or Yiddish *kelner* 'waiter'.

GIVEN NAMES Jewish 5%. *Aron, Sarra, Yakov.*

Kelnhofer (211) German (**Kelnhöfer**): status name for the tenant or manager of a *Kelnhof*, a farm (Middle High German *hof*; see HOFF) to which an overseer (see KELLNER) has been assigned on behalf of the landlord.

Kelp (118) English (Norfolk): possibly a metonymic occupational name for someone who collected and burnt kelp (seaweed) for use in soap and glass making, Middle English *culp(e)*.

Kelsall (157) English: habitational name from a place in Cheshire named Kelsall, from the Middle English personal name *Kell* + Old English *halh* 'nook or corner of land', or possibly from Kelshall in Hertfordshire, which is named with an Old English personal name *Cylli* + Old English *hyll* 'hill', or even Kelsale in Suffolk, named with an Old English personal name *Cēl(i)* or *Cēol* + Old English *halh*.

Kelsay (459) Probably a variant spelling of KELSEY.

Kelsch (633) Partly Americanized form of German KOELSCH.

Kelsey (5057) **1.** English: habitational name from North or South Kelsey in Lincolnshire, so named from *Cēol*, an Old English personal name, or alternatively from an unattested Old Scandinavian word, *kæl* 'wedge-shaped piece of land', + *ēg* 'island', 'area of dry land in a marsh'. **2.** Possibly also an Americanized form of German **Gelzer**.

FOREBEARS William Kelsey was one of the founders of Hartford, CT, (coming from Cambridge, MA, with Thomas Hooker) in 1635.

Kelsh (122) Americanized spelling of German KOELSCH.

Kelso (3206) Scottish: habitational name from Kelso on the river Tweed in Roxburghshire, perhaps so named from Old English *cealc* 'chalk' + *hōh* 'ridge', 'spur'.

Kelsoe (187) Scottish: variant spelling of KELSO.

Kelson (559) **1.** Jewish (eastern Ashkenazic): metronymic from the Yiddish female personal name *Keyle*, of uncertain origin. **2.** Probably in some cases of Scandinavian origin, an Americanized form of a patronymic from the Old Norse personal name *Ketill* meaning 'kettle', 'helmet' (see for example KETELSEN).

Kelter (196) German: from Middle High German *kelter, kalter* 'wine press' (Latin *calcatura*), hence a topographic name or a metonymic occupational name for a vintner or the overseer of a wine press.

Kelting (140) German: probably from a field name or place name in northern Germany.

GIVEN NAMES German 8%. *Ernst, Kurt, Otto, Siegfried.*

Keltner (1079) German: occupational name for a vintner or the overseer of a wine press from KELTER + the agent suffix *-(n)er*.

Kelton (1017) Scottish: habitational name from the village of Kelton in the parish of the same name in Kirkcudbrightshire.

Kelty (669) Scottish: habitational name from the old lands of Keltie near Callander, Perthshire, or from Keltie in Fife.

GIVEN NAMES Irish 5%. *Conley, Pegeen.*

Keltz (332) South German: nickname for someone in the habit of shouting or boasting, from Middle High German *kelz* 'loud talk', 'bragging', a noun derivative of *kelzen* 'to shout or boast'.

Kelzer (115) German: **1.** habitational name for someone from Kelze in Hesse, or Kelzin North Rhine-Westphalia. **2.** Variant of **Gelzer** (see GELTZ).

Kem (213) German: occupational name for a comb maker, from Middle High German *kam* 'comb' (see KAMM) or a variant of KEMME.

Kembel (148) German: from Middle High German *kembel* 'camel'. The surname arose from the name of a house or inn *zum kembel* 'at the (sign of the) camel'. *Zum*

Kämbel is still found as an inn name in Zürich.

Kemble (615) **1.** Welsh: from an Old Welsh personal name, *Cynbel*, composed of the elements *cyn* 'chief' + *bel* 'war'. This was borne by Welsh chieftain in Roman times whose name is recorded in a Latinized form as *Cunobelinus*; he provided the inspiration for Shakespeare's Cymbeline. **2.** English: habitational name from a place in Gloucestershire, so named from a Celtic word related to Welsh *cyfyl* 'border'. **3.** Possibly also a variant of English KIMBALL or KIMBLE. **4.** It is also quite likely that this name has assimilated some instances of German KEMBEL.

Kemen (118) Hungarian: variant of KEMENY.

GIVEN NAME German 8%. *Aloysius.*

Kemeny (147) Hungarian (**Kemény**): nickname from *kemény* 'hard', 'tough'.

GIVEN NAMES Hungarian 14%. *Zoltan* (4), *Gabor* (3), *Lorant.*

Kemerer (300) German: variant of *Kämmerer*; KAMMERER.

Kemerling (132) German: variant spelling of KEMMERLING.

Kemery (219) English (Avon): perhaps a variant of **Kembery** or **Cambrey**, a Norman habitational name from any of four places in northern France called Cambrai.

Kemler (215) Altered spelling of German **Kemmler** or **Kämmler**, occupational name for a comb maker or a wool comber, from Middle High German *kamb(e)* 'comb' + the agent suffix *-(l)er*. Compare KAMLER.

Kemme (133) German: habitational name from Kemme near Hildesheim.

GIVEN NAMES German 7%. *Friedrich, Hermann, Kurt.*

Kemmer (603) German: **1.** variant spelling of **Kämmer** (see KAMMER 2). **2.** from a variant of *Kammer* 'chamber', 'store', 'treasury', hence an occupational name for a chamberlain or treasurer (see KAMMERER). **3.** habitational name for someone from KEMME.

Kemmerer (913) German: variant of **Kämmerer** (see KAMMERER 1).

Kemmerlin (110) German: variant of KEMMERLING.

Kemmerling (235) German: status name from Middle High German *kemerlinc* 'chamberlain', either denoting a court official or used in the original sense of personal servant or valet.

GIVEN NAMES German 6%. *Kurt* (3), *Bernhard.*

Kemmet (106) Irish or English: unexplained.

GIVEN NAME Irish 4%. *Delma.*

Kemmis (106) Irish: according to MacLysaght, a Monmouthshire surname associated with Ireland since the late 17th century. The etymology is unexplained.

Kemna (167) German: variant spelling of **Kemnah**, habitational name from any of several places named Kemnat(h). See also KEINATH 2.

Kemner (162) **1.** German: reduced form of **Kemenater**, from Latin *caminata* 'with a fireplace or chimney', hence a nickname for someone who lived in a house with a chimney or a house made of stone. **2.** Danish: occupational name from *kemner* 'rent collector', 'chamberlain'.

Kemnitz (409) German (of Slavic origin): habitational name from any of various places (e.g. Chemnitz in Saxony), named with the Slavic word *kamien* 'stone'.
GIVEN NAMES German 4%. *Erwin* (2), *Detlef, Heino, Kurt, Leonhard.*

Kemp (15666) **1.** English, Scottish, Dutch, and North German: status name for a champion, Middle English and Middle Low German *kempe*. In the Middle Ages a champion was a professional fighter on behalf of others; for example the King's Champion, at the coronation, had the duty of issuing a general challenge to battle to anyone who denied the king's right to the throne. The Middle English word corresponds to Old English *cempa* and Old Norse *kempa* 'warrior'; both these go back to Germanic *campo* 'warrior', which is the source of the Dutch and North German name, corresponding to High German KAMPF. **2.** Dutch: metonymic occupational name for someone who grew or processed hemp, from Middle Dutch *canep* 'hemp'.

Kempa (259) **1.** Polish (also **Kępa**): from *kępa* 'islet'. The same word is also applied to isolated clumps of trees and to tufts of grass; hence a topographic name for someone who lived on a small island or by an isolated clump of trees. **2.** German: variant of KEMPE or KEMPEN.

Kempe (378) **1.** English, Scottish, Dutch, and North German: variant of KEMP 'champion'. **2.** Dutch: variant of KEMPEN 1.
GIVEN NAMES German 4%; Scandinavian 4%. *Erna, Ilse; Detlev, Gunhild.*

Kempel (173) German: diminutive of KEMP.

Kempen (288) **1.** German: topographic names from any of various places called Kempen, in the Rhineland, in the Ruhrgebiet, and Schleswig-Holstein, or from Kempno in Poland (Polish *Kępno*). **2.** Belgian: regional name for someone from Kempen, a region in Brabant.

Kemper (4002) **1.** German: status name denoting a peasant farmer or serf, an agent noun derivative of KAMP 1. **2.** Dutch: agent noun derivative of KEMP, i.e. an occupational name for someone who grew, processed, or used hemp. **3.** German (possibly also Dutch): habitational name from any of the twelve places named Kempen in the Dutch-German border area.

Kempf (2502) German: variant of **Kämpf** (see KAMPF).

Kempfer (269) German: variant of **Kämpfer** (see KAMPFER).

Kemph (164) Classicized spelling of German **Kämpf** or **Kempf** (see KAMPF).

Kempinski (123) Polish (**Kępiński, Kempiński**): habitational name for someone from Kępina, Kępino, Kępiny, Kępno or other places named with Polish *kępa* 'islet' (see KEMPA).
GIVEN NAMES Polish 11%. *Tomasz* (2), *Bronislaw, Casimir, Wladyslaw.*

Kempisty (100) Polish: unexplained.

Kempka (115) Variant of German KEMPKE.

Kempke (149) North German: topographic name from a diminutive of KAMP 1.

Kempker (298) German: **1.** diminutive of KEMP. **2.** North German: occupational name for a bucket maker, from an agent derivative of the dialect word *Kimke* 'wooden bucket'.

Kempkes (113) German: variant of KEMPKE.

Kemple (300) **1.** Altered spelling of South German **Kempfle**, a Swabian pet form of KEMPF. **2.** Possibly Americanized spelling of KEMPEL.

Kempler (154) Jewish (Ashkenazic): occupational name from southern German *Kampel* 'comb' + the agent suffix *-er.*
GIVEN NAMES Jewish 11%; German 4%. *Hyman* (2), *Ari, Ilan, Nachman, Naftoli; Bernhard* (2), *Oskar.*

Kemplin (166) German: probably a spelling variant of **Kempflin**, a Swabian or Alemannic dialect variant of **Kempfle** (see KEMPLE).

Kempner (267) **1.** German: occupational name for a champion at jousting or wrestling, from *Kempner*, agent derivative of *Kempe* 'fight' (see KEMP). **2.** German: habitational name, with agent suffix *-er*, for someone from any of various places called Kempen (notably in the Ruhrgebiet) or from Kempno near Poznan, Poland.

Kemppainen (206) Finnish: of uncertain origin. **1.** Possibly from an old Swedish personal name, *Kaempe* (from Swedish *kämpe* 'soldier', 'hero') + the common surname suffix *-nen.* **2.** Alternatively, it may be from a nickname based on *kempas, kemppi,* denoting a small insect, in particular the plant louse *Psyllida* + the common surname suffix *-nen.*
GIVEN NAMES Scandinavian 8%; Finnish 5%. *Nels* (2); *Eino* (2), *Tauno, Tyyne, Wilho.*

Kemps (153) German: variant of KEMP.
GIVEN NAMES German 4%. *Bernd, Kurt.*

Kempski (131) Polish (**Kępski**): habitational name for someone from any of various places called Kępa, from *kępa* 'islet' (see KEMPA).

Kempson (157) English: patronymic from KEMP, meaning 'son of the champion'.

Kempster (132) English: occupational name for a wool or flax comber, Middle English *kem(be)stere* (an agent derivative of Old English *cemban* 'to comb'). Although this was originally a feminine form of the masculine *kembere,* by the

Middle English period the suffix *-stre* had lost its feminine force, and the term was used to refer to both sexes. Compare BAXTER, BREWSTER, DEXTER.
GIVEN NAME German 4%. *Kurt.*

Kempter (140) German: **1.** habitational name from Kempten in the Allgäu (Bavaria). **2.** variant of **Kemter**, a reduced form of the topographic name **Kemenater** (see KEMNER).
GIVEN NAMES German 6%. *Gerhard, Kurt.*

Kempton (1143) English: **1.** habitational name from a place called Kempton in Shropshire, named from an Old English personal name *Cempa* (or the Old English vocabulary word *cempa* 'warrior') + *tūn* 'farmstead', 'settlement'. **2.** variant of KIMPTON.

Ken (85) **1.** English: habitational name for someone from either of two places named Kenn, in Devon and Avon, both of which take their name from the streams on which they stand. **2.** English: from Anglo-French *ken, chen* 'dog' (Old French *chien*), possibly applied as a nickname or as a metonymic name for someone who kept hunting dogs. **3.** Perhaps also a respelling of German **Kenn**, either from a short form of the personal name KONRAD or a habitational name from Kenn, near Trier.

Kenady (133) Americanized form of Irish–Scottish KENNEDY.

Kenagy (248) Swiss German: variant of KANAGY.

Kenan (269) Altered spelling of Irish KEENAN.

Kenaston (128) Altered spelling of English KENNISTON.

Kendall (11384) **1.** English: habitational name from Kendal in Cumbria, recorded in 1095 as *Kircabikendala* 'village with a church in the valley of the Kent river'. **2.** From an Anglicized form of the Welsh personal name *Cynddelw,* which was borne by a famous 12th-century Welsh poet. It probably derives from a Celtic word meaning 'exalted', 'high' + *delw* 'image', 'effigy'.

Kendell (219) English: variant of KENDALL.

Kender (211) Hungarian: from *kender* 'hemp', from Old Turkish *kändir,* hence a metonymic occupational name for someone who grew hemp or used it to make ropes and sacks, or a topographic name for someone who lived near a field of hemp.

Kenderdine (119) English (Staffordshire): unexplained. Probably a habitational name from a lost or unidentified place.

Kendig (581) Altered spelling of German KINDIG.

Kendle (358) **1.** English: variant spelling of KENDALL. **2.** South German: possibly from *Kindel* or *Kindl* (from a diminutive of Middle High German *kint* 'child'), a nickname for a childish or childlike person. **3.** Possibly an altered spelling of German **Kendler**, variant of KANDLER.

Kendra (289) Polish: nickname for a long-haired man, variant of **Kędzior** (see KEDZIOR).

Kendrick (8733) **1.** Welsh: from the Welsh personal name *Cyn(w)rig, Cynfrig*, of unexplained origin. **2.** Scottish: reduced form of McKENDRICK. See also McHENRY. **3.** English: from the Middle English personal name *Cenric, Kendrich*, Old English *Cynerīc*, composed of the elements *cyne* 'royal' + *rīc* 'power'.

Kendricks (324) English: patronymic from KENDRICK 3.

Kendrix (127) English: patronymic from KENDRICK 3.

Kendzierski (203) Polish: see KEDZIERSKI.

Kendzior (151) Polish: see KEDZIOR.
GIVEN NAME Polish 5%. *Stanislaw*.

Kendziorski (115) Polish: see KEDZIERSKI.
GIVEN NAME Polish 6%. *Casimir* (2).

Kenealy (307) Irish: variant spelling of KENNEALLY.

Kenefick (356) Irish (from Welsh): Anglicized form of Gaelic **Cinipheic**, a habitational name from Kenfig in mid-Glamorgan, Wales, (Welsh *Cynffig*); the name was taken to Ireland by Norman settlers in the 13th century.

Keneipp (119) Altered spelling of South German KNEIP.

Kenerly (124) English: variant spelling of KENNERLY.

Kenerson (174) English: probably an altered spelling of Scottish KENISON.
GIVEN NAME Irish 4%. *Aileen*.

Kenfield (219) English: apparently a habitational name from a place called Kenfield Hall in Kent, so named from Old English *cyning* 'king' (genitive plural *cyninga* 'of the kings') + *feld* 'open country'.

Keng (108) **1.** Chinese 耿: variant of GENG 2. **2.** Korean: variant of KANG. **3.** Other Southeast Asian: unexplained.
GIVEN NAMES Southeast Asian 8%. *Da, Nen, Saroeun*.

Kenimer (123) Origin unidentified.

Kenison (451) Scottish: variant of *Cunieson*, meaning 'the son of Conan'.

Keniston (426) English: possibly a habitational name from a lost or unidentified place, most likely in Dorset or Somerset, where the surname occurs most frequently. Alternatively, it may be from the Old English personal name *Cynestān*.

Kenkel (288) South German: possibly a variant of **Gengel**, deriving either from Old High German *gang* 'go', an element in many personal names, or from Middle High German *gengeler* 'street seller', 'seller of haberdashery'; alternatively, it may be a topographic name from Middle High German *kengel* 'gutter' or a shortened form of Swabian **Kenkelin**, a variant of **Künkelin**, a pet form of the personal name KONRAD or *Kuno*, or alternatively a

diminutive of KUNKEL, a nickname for a tall lanky man.

Kenley (453) **1.** Scottish: reduced form of **McKenley**, a variant of McKINLEY, an Anglicized form of Gaelic *Mac Fionnlaigh*. **2.** English: habitational name from places in Shropshire and Greater London (formerly Surrey), so named from the Old English personal name *Cēna* + *lēah* 'woodland clearing'.

Kenly (119) Variant spelling of KENLEY.

Kenna (621) Irish and Scottish: reduced form of McKENNA.

Kennamer (300) Dutch: habitational name from a place so named in North Holland.

Kennan (236) Scottish: reduced form of **McKennan** (see KENNY).

Kennard (1658) English: from the Old English personal name *Cēnweard* 'bold guardian' or *Cyneweard* 'royal guardian'.

Kenne (143) English: variant spelling of KEN.

Kenneally (496) Irish: Anglicized form of Gaelic **Ó Cionnfhaolaidh** 'descendant of *Cionnfhaoladh*', a personal name derived from *ceann* 'head' + *faol* 'wolf'.
GIVEN NAMES Irish 7%. *Brendan, Paddy*.

Kennealy (104) Irish: variant spelling of KENNEALLY.

Kennebeck (188) Probably of German origin: **1.** from a topographic name composed of the elements *Kenn*, the name of a place near Trier, + *beck* 'stream' (BACH). **2.** alternatively, from **Kennebeck**, an occupational name for a potter, from Middle Low or Middle High German *kanne* 'jug', 'pitcher' + *beck*, variant of *Bäcker* 'baker'.

Kennebrew (124) Variant of Scottish KINNEBREW.

Kennedy (64834) Irish and Scottish: Anglicized form of Gaelic **Ó Ceannéidigh** 'descendant of *Ceannéidigh*', a personal name derived from *ceann* 'head' + *éidigh* 'ugly'. FOREBEARS Kennedy ancestral lands are found both in Ireland and in Scotland, where the family's medieval ancestral seat is sited on the Ayrshire coast, facing the Irish Sea. The great-grandparents of U.S. President John Fitzgerald Kennedy (1917–63) came to North America as immigrants from Ireland in the 1840s. His paternal great-grandparents were Patrick Kennedy (1823–58), born in Dunganstown, County Wexford, Ireland, and Bridget Murphy, who was born probably in Owenduff, County Wexford, Ireland in about 1827; they came to Boston, MA, in 1849. His maternal great-grandparents were Thomas Fitzgerald (1823–85), who was born in Bruff, County Limerick, Ireland, and Rose Anna Cox, who was born probably in Tomregan or Kinawley, County Cavan, Ireland, in about 1835; they came to Boston, MA, in 1857. An early Scottish Kennedy forebear of a quite different family was British colonial official Archibald Kennedy (1685–1763), the son of Alexander Kennedy of

Craigoch, who emigrated to NY about 1710.

Kennel (400) Swiss German: topographic name for a person living near a water channel, (dialect variants *Channel, Känel*).

Kennell (632) Respelling of German KENNEL.

Kennelly (996) Irish: variant spelling of KENNEALLY.
GIVEN NAME Irish 5%. *Michael Sean*.

Kennemer (478) Origin uncertain. Perhaps English (see KENNEMORE) or Dutch, an altered spelling of KENNAMER.

Kennemore (182) Perhaps an altered spelling of English **Kenmore**, from Old English *Cynemǣr*, a personal name found in several early place names, but recorded only in the reign of Edward the Confessor as the name of a moneyer. It appears also as the name of a 12th century cowman.

Kennemur (105) Origin uncertain. See KENNEMER.

Kennen (143) Variant spelling of Irish KENNAN.

Kenner (1295) **1.** German and Jewish (Ashkenazic): from *Kenner* 'connoisseur' (from *kennen* 'know'), hence a nickname for someone considered to be knowledgeable or an expert of some kind; it may also have been used ironically to denote a 'know-all'. **2.** German: habitational name for someone from Kenn, near Trier. **3.** German: topographic name for someone living near a water pipe or channel, from Middle High German *kener* 'water channel', 'drainage pipe'.

Kennerly (604) English: according to Reaney, a habitational name from Kennerleigh in Devon, so named from the Old English personal name *Cyneweard* + Old English *lēah* 'woodland clearing'. However, the surname is found predominantly in Cheshire and Lancashire, suggesting that a more likely source is Kinnerley in Shropshire, which is named with the Old English personal name *Cyneheard* + *lēah*. **Kennerley** is the much commoner spelling in the U.K.

Kennerson (187) Possibly English: unexplained.

Kenneson (102) Probably Scottish: a variant spelling of KENISON.

Kenneth (207) Scottish: from a Gaelic personal name (*Coinneach*) meaning 'handsome', now generally Anglicized as *Kenneth*, although this was originally the Anglicized form of *Cionaodh* (see McKINNEY). Etymologically, this surname is equivalent to KENNY (which can arise from either personal name) and McKENZIE (which is from *Coinneach*).

Kennett (897) English: habitational name for someone from places so named in Wiltshire and Cambridgeshire. Both are named from the rivers on which they stand: the Kennet in Wiltshire and Kennett in

Kent, an old British or Celtic name of uncertain origin.

Kenney (11093) Irish and Scottish: see KENNY.

Kennicott (101) English (Devon): habitational name from Kennicott in Devon.

Kenning (333) **1.** English: **2.** German: from the personal name *Keno*, derivative of KONRAD. **3.** German: patronymic from the Frisian personal name *Keno*; alternatively, but less likely, from a derivation of the old Nordic root *gan* 'spell', 'magic', which was used in personal names.
GIVEN NAMES German 5%. *Kurt* (2), *Gunter*, *Helmut*.

Kennington (619) English: habitational name for someone from a place called Kennington in Greater London (formerly in Surrey), Oxfordshire, or Kent. The first two are from the Old English personal name *Cēna* + *-ing-* (a connective particle denoting association with) + *tūn* 'farmstead', 'settlement'. The place in Kent is named from Old English *cyne-* 'royal' + *tūn*.

Kennis (126) **1.** Irish and Manx: reduced form **Mac Aenghuis** 'son of *Aenghus*' (see ANGUS). **2.** Jewish (eastern Ashkenazic): metronymic from the Yiddish female personal name *Kene* (of uncertain origin) + the Yiddish possessive suffix *-s*.
GIVEN NAME Jewish 5%. *Abbe* (2).

Kennison (700) Scottish and English: patronymic from KENNY or variant spelling of KENISON.

Kenniston (156) English: variant spelling of KENISTON.

Kennon (1238) Irish and Scottish: reduced form of MCKENNON.

Kenny (6467) **1.** Irish and Scottish: Anglicized form of Gaelic **Ó Coinnigh** 'descendant of *Coinneach*', an Old Irish personal name equivalent to Scottish KENNETH. This was borne by a 6th-century monk and saint who gave his name to the town of *Kilkenny* 'church of Coinneach'. **2.** Irish: possibly an Anglicized form of Gaelic **Ó Cionaodha** 'descendant of *Cionaodh*', a personal name of unexplained etymology.
GIVEN NAMES Irish 6%. *Brendan* (7), *Liam* (4), *Declan* (3), *Dermot* (2), *Fergus* (2), *Caitlin, Clodagh, Colm, Eilis, Fergal, Finbarr, Finola.*

Kenoyer (250) Respelling of German **Kneuer**, a variant of KNAUER.

Kenrick (140) English, Welsh, and Irish: variant of KENDRICK.

Kensinger (470) Swiss German: habitational name from Kenzingen (near Emmendingen). See also KINSINGER.

Kensler (161) Americanized spelling of the German name **Kenzler**, from Middle High German *kenzeler, kanzelære* 'chancellor', hence an occupational name for a chancellor (in a law office) or, more likely, a nickname for someone in his service.

Kent (16654) English: habitational name for someone from Kent, an ancient Celtic

name. The surname is also frequent in Scotland and Ireland. In Irrerwick in East Lothian, English vassals were settled in the middle of the 12th century and in Meath in Ireland in the 13th century.

Kenter (136) German: variant of KANTNER.

Kentner (264) German: variant of KANTNER.

Kenton (615) English: habitational name from any of various places so named, for example in Devon, Greater London (formerly Middlesex), and Suffolk. All have as the second element Old English *tūn* 'farmstead', 'settlement'. The first element of the place in Devon is a pre-English river name; the place in London is named with the Old English personal name *Cēna*; and the place in Suffolk is named either with *Cēna* or more probably with Old English *cyne-* 'royal'.

Kenward (152) English: variant of KENNARD.

Kenworthy (1246) English: habitational name from a place in Cheshire, apparently so called from the Old English personal name *Cēna* + *worðig* 'enclosure'.

Kenyon (5206) **1.** English (Lancashire): habitational name from a place near Warrington, which is of uncertain etymology. There was formerly an ancient burial mound there and Ekwall has speculated that the name is a shortened form of a British name composed of the elements *crūc* 'mound' + a personal name cognate with Welsh *Einion* (see EYNON). **2.** Irish: Anglicized form of Gaelic **Mac Coinín** 'son of *Coinín*', a byname based on a diminutive of *cano* 'wolf', also Anglicized as CUNNEEN. The similarity to *coinín* 'rabbit', a later borrowing, has also caused it to be 'translated' as rabbit.

Keo (349) **1.** Cambodian: unexplained. **2.** Hawaiian: unexplained.
GIVEN NAMES Southeast Asian 18%; Vietnamese 13%; Cambodian 13%. *Heng* (2), *Chan, Chor, Eng, Kin, Meng, Peng, Sin, Sok; Sambath* (2), *Thy* (3), *Mang* (2), *Phal* (2), *Phan* (2), *Khen, Leang, Long, Roeun, Rong, Samnang, Saroeun, Sophal, Sophea, Tha; Chheang* (2), *Pheap* (2), *Savoeun* (2), *Sopheap* (2), *Sovann* (2), *Chamroeun, Chay, Chhorn, Choun, Noy, Oeung, Phoeun; Kalyan, Sarath, Sareth, Thara; Pao.*

Keogh (1150) Irish: variant spelling of KEOUGH.
GIVEN NAMES Irish 6%. *Declan* (2), *Eamonn, Seamus, Sinead.*

Keohane (479) Irish (Cork): reduced Anglicized form of Gaelic **Mac Eocháin** 'son of *Eochán*', a diminutive of the personal name *Eochaidh* (see KEOGH).
GIVEN NAMES Irish 6%. *Brendan* (2), *Donal, Padraic.*

Keon (163) Irish: see KEOWN.

Keough (1795) Irish and Scottish: reduced Anglicized form of Gaelic **Mac Eochaidh**

'son of *Eochaidh*', a personal name based on *each* 'horse'. Compare MCGAHAN.

Keown (1097) Irish: reduced Anglicized form of Gaelic **Mac Eoghain** (in Connacht) and **Mac Eoin** (in east Ulster), both meaning 'son of John', and possibly also of **Ó Ceantháin** in Co. Fermanagh.

Kepes (111) Hungarian: unexplained.
GIVEN NAME Hungarian 4%. *Gyorgy* (2).

Kepford (122) Americanized spelling of Swiss German **Göpfert** (see GOEPFERT).

Kephart (1865) Americanized spelling of German GEBHARDT.

Keplar (125) Slavic variant of the German surname KEPLER.

Kepler (1226) German: occupational name for a maker of cloaks and hoods, from an agent noun from Middle High German *kappe* 'hooded cloak' (see KAPP).

Kepley (632) Perhaps an Americanized form of German KEPLER.

Keplinger (718) Americanized spelling of German **Köpplinger**, a habitational name for someone from a place called Köpplingen.

Kepner (887) **1.** South German: occupational name for a maker of cloaks and hoods, a variant of KEPLER. **2.** Americanized spelling of **Göppner** (see GEPNER).

Kepp (139) **1.** German: from the personal name KASPAR. **2.** Probably an altered spelling of German **Köpp(e)** (see KOEPP).

Keppel (554) **1.** German: variant of **Käppel** (see KAPPEL). **2.** Altered form of **Köppel** (see KOEPPEL).

Keppen (112) **1.** Altered spelling of Dutch **Keppene, Keepen** or **Keppenne**, nickname from Middle Dutch *kippin* 'new-born calf' or from Flemish *keppe* 'pampered child'. **2.** Respelling of German **Köppen** (see KOEPPEN).

Kepple (548) Americanized spelling of German KEPPEL or **Köppel** (see KOEPPEL).

Keppler (772) German: variant spelling of KEPLER.
GIVEN NAMES German 4%. *Dieter* (2), *Dietmar, Ernst, Kurt.*

Ker (207) **1.** English and Scottish: variant of CARR. **2.** Hungarian (**Kér**): one of the eight ancient Hungarian tribal names from the Magyar conquest of the Carpathian basin. The *Kér* tribe, led by a chief called Vata settled in what is now known as Békés county, but King Steven I resettled the tribe in royal estates, far away from their original residence. Thus the 42 villages named after the *Kér* tribe are scattered around in Hungary.

Keranen (231) Finnish (**Keränen**): possibly from *Keräpää*, a nickname for a bald person or someone with a round head and/or with closely cropped hair, + the common surname suffix *-nen*. In eastern Finland the name dates back to the 16th century.
GIVEN NAMES Finnish 7%. *Arvo* (2), *Toivo* (2), *Eero, Tauno.*

Kerans (140) Irish: probably a variant of KIERAN, with English patronymic -s.

Kerbaugh (110) Perhaps of French (Huguenot) origin, an altered form of French **Corbeille** (see CORBELL) or or **Corbeau** (see CURBOW).

Kerbel (204) Americanized spelling of German **Körbel** (see KORBEL).

Kerber (1093) German: variant of **Körber** (see KORBER) or GERBER.

Kerbo (115) Of French (Huguenot) origin: variant of CURBOW.

Kerbow (177) Of French (Huguenot) origin: variant of CURBOW.

Kerbs (345) Perhaps a metathesized spelling of KREBS.

Kerby (1477) English: variant spelling of KIRBY.

Kerce (194) Origin unknown.

Kerch (103) German: variant spelling of KIRCH.

Kercher (545) **1.** Southern German variant of KARCHER. **2.** Altered spelling of German KIRCHER.

Kercheval (210) Probably an altered spelling of German **Kirchenwall**, a topographic name from Middle High German *kirche* + *wal* 'dike', 'embankment'.

Kerchner (430) German: variant of KIRCHNER.

GIVEN NAMES German 4%. *Christoph* (2), *Kurt*.

Kerekes (489) Hungarian and Jewish (from Hungary): metonymic occupational name for a wheelwright, from *kerék* 'wheel' a derivative of *kerek* 'round'.

GIVEN NAMES Hungarian 6%. *Zoltan* (3), *Attila, Csaba, Gabor, Imre, Istvan, Karoly, Sandor, Tibor.*

Kerestes (154) Hungarian (**Keresztes**): **1.** from a personal name, the Hungarian form of CHRISTIAN. **2.** habitational name from any of the many places in Hungary, for example Mezőkeresztes, named with *kereszt* 'cross', a loanword from one of the Slavic languages.

Kerfoot (375) English (Lancashire): habitational name from an unidentified place, perhaps named from Middle English *kerr* 'wet ground' + *fote* 'foot', 'bottom' (of a hill).

Kerin (361) Irish: see KIERAN.

GIVEN NAMES Irish 5%. *Brendan, Dermot.*

Kerins (377) Irish: see KIERAN.

Kerker (261) **1.** South German: variant of **Kercher** (see KARCHER), but also from the dialect word *Kerker* 'prison' (Latin *carcer*), hence a metonymic occupational name for a prison warder or possibly a topographic name. **2.** North German: topographic name for someone who lived near a church, from Low German *kerke* 'church', or possibly an occupational name from a reduced form of Low German **Kerkener** 'sexton'. **3.** Sorbian topographic name for someone living near bushes, from Sorbian *kerk*

'bush', 'undergrowth'. **4.** Dutch: topographic name for someone who lived by a dungeon, Dutch *kerker*.

Kerkes (100) Czech: unexplained.

Kerkhoff (327) **1.** Dutch: topographic name for someone who lived by a churchyard, Middle Dutch *kerchof*, or (with the preposition *van*) a habitational name, from any of various places named with this word. **2.** North German form of KIRCHHOFF, cognate with 1.

Kerkman (213) **1.** Dutch: from Middle Dutch *kercman* 'clergyman'. **2.** North German: from Low German *kerke* 'church', hence an occupational name for a sexton or a parishioner.

GIVEN NAME French 4%. *Marcell* (2).

Kerkstra (120) Frisian: habitational name for someone living by a church, from Middle Low German *kerke* 'church' + the agent noun suffix *-stra*.

GIVEN NAMES Dutch 9%; German 4%. *Joris* (2), *Gerritt, Hendrik; Otto* (2).

Kerl (298) German: status name from Middle Low German *kerl* '(free)man (of non-aristocratic descent)', Middle High German *kerl(e), karl(e)* 'man', 'lover', 'chap'.

GIVEN NAMES German 9%. *Hanns* (2), *Klaus* (2), *Frieda, Helmut, Helmuth, Otto.*

Kerley (1707) **1.** Americanized spelling of German and Swiss KEHRLI or **Kerle**, a variant of KERL. **2.** Irish: variant spelling of CURLEY (see MCCURLEY).

Kerlin (784) **1.** Irish: see CARLIN. **2.** South German and Swiss German: variant of KERL.

Kerman (378) Jewish (Ashkenazic): unexplained.

GIVEN NAMES Jewish 4%. *Hyman, Ilan, Ilya, Sol.*

Kermode (130) Irish: reduced Anglicized form of Gaelic *Mac Dhiarmada*, with lenited initial *D* (see MCDERMOTT).

Kern (11505) **1.** Irish: reduced form of MCCARRON. **2.** German, Dutch, and Jewish (Ashkenazic): from Middle High German *kerne* 'kernel', 'seed', 'pip'; Middle Dutch *kern(e), keerne*; German *Kern* or Yiddish *kern* 'grain', hence a metonymic occupational name for a farmer, or a nickname for a small person. As a Jewish surname, it is mainly ornamental. **3.** English: probably a metonymic occupational name for a maker or user of hand mills, from Old English *cweorn* 'hand mill', or a habitational name for someone from Kern in the Isle of Wight, named from this word.

Kernaghan (154) Irish: Anglicized form of Gaelic **Ó Cearnacháin** 'descendant of *Cearnachán*', a personal name based on *cearnach* 'victorious' + the diminutive ending *-án*.

Kernan (1090) Irish: **1.** reduced form of MCKIERNAN. **2.** reduced and altered form of KERNAGHAN.

GIVEN NAMES Irish 4%. *Eamon, Teague.*

Kernell (114) **1.** Swedish: ornamental name formed with the common surname suffix *-ell*. The first element is unexplained, possibly from a place-name. **2.** English, Scottish, and northern Irish: unexplained; possibly a respelling of Scottish **Kerneil**, a habitational name from Carneil in Carnock, Fife.

GIVEN NAME Irish 9%. *Liam* (3).

Kernen (231) Dutch: variant of KERN.

Kerner (1546) **1.** German and Jewish (Ashkenazic): occupational name for a farmer or a nickname for a small person, from an agent derivative of Middle High German *kerne* 'kernel', 'seed', 'pip', German *Kern* or Yiddish *kern* 'grain'. **2.** German: occupational name for a carter, from *Karren* 'cart' (see KARNER). **3.** Alemannic occupational name for a baker using spelt (a type of wheat) or for a spelt dealer. **4.** German: variant of **Körner** (see KORNER).

Kernes (141) Irish: variant spelling of KEARNS.

Kerney (330) Irish: variant of KEARNEY.

Kernodle (333) Possibly an altered spelling of German **Knödel** (see KNODEL) or of **Kerndl**, a diminutive of KERN.

Kerns (5585) **1.** Irish: variant of KEARNS. **2.** Dutch: variant of KERN.

Kerper (188) **1.** German: habitational name for someone from one of the places, in the Rhineland and former East Prussia, called Kerpen. **2.** German: variant of **Körper** (see KORBER). **3.** Jewish (Ashkenazic): see KARP.

Kerr (17727) **1.** English and Scottish: topographic name for someone who lived by a patch of wet ground overgrown with brushwood, northern Middle English *kerr* (Old Norse *kjarr*). A legend grew up that the Kerrs were left-handed, on theory that the name is derived from Gaelic *cearr* 'wronghanded', 'left-handed'. **2.** Irish: see CARR. **3.** This surname has also absorbed examples of German KEHR.

Kerrick (376) English: from Old English *Cyneríc* 'family ruler'.

Kerridge (101) English: variant of KENDRICK.

Kerrigan (2130) Irish: Anglicized form of Gaelic **Ó Ciaragáin** 'descendant of *Ciaragán*', a byname from a double diminutive of *ciar* 'black', 'dark'.

GIVEN NAMES Irish 5%. *Brendan* (2), *Aileen, Brigid, Eamonn, Malachy, Murph.*

Kerry (624) Welsh: habitational name from *Ceri*, an ancient commot of central Wales.

Kersch (168) **1.** German and Jewish (Ashkenazic): variant of KIRSCH. **2.** German: from a metathesized short form of CHRISTIAN.

GIVEN NAMES German 4%. *Franz, Kurt.*

Kerschen (141) Luxembourgeois: unexplained; possibly a shortened form of a family name formed with *Kirschen* 'cherries' (see, for example KIRSCHENBAUM, KIRSCHENMANN).

Kerscher (176) German: **1.** habitational name from a place called Kirsch or Körsch. **2.** occupational name for a grower or seller of cherries, from an agent derivative of Middle High German *kirs(ch)e, kerse* 'cherry'.
GIVEN NAMES German 4%. *Gunther, Leonhard.*

Kerschner (433) German: variant of **Kürschner** (see KURSCHNER).

Kersey (2754) English: habitational name from Kersey in Suffolk, recorded in Domesday Book as *Careseia*, probably from Old English *cærs* 'watercress' + *ēg* 'island', 'area of dry land in a marsh'.

Kersh (523) **1.** Jewish (Ashkenazic): see KIRSCH. **2.** Americanized spelling of German KERSCH or KIRCH.

Kershaw (1760) English: habitational name from Kirkshaw in the parish of Rochdale, Lancashire, so named from northern Middle English *kirk* 'church' + *shaw* 'grove'. There are two minor places in West Yorkshire called Kershaw, which may be of the same origin and may also lie behind the surname, but on the other hand they may themselves derive from the surname. In some cases the name may be topographic for someone who lived near the 'church grove'.

Kershner (1432) **1.** Respelling of German and Ashkenazic Jewish KERSCHNER or **Kürschner** (see KURSCHNER). **2.** German: variant of KIRCHNER.

Kerslake (118) English (Devon): topographic name for someone who lived by a stream where cress grew, from Old English *cærse* 'watercress' + *lacu* 'stream'.

Kerst (167) German: **1.** from a short form of KERSTEN. **2.** southern variant of GERST. **3.** variant of CHRISTIAN.

Kerstein (255) **1.** German: variant of the personal name CHRISTIAN, with metathesis of the *-r-* and a folk-etymological component *-stein* 'stone', influenced by names such as *Kirschstein* 'cherry stone'. **2.** Jewish (Ashkenazic): variant of KIRSTEIN.
GIVEN NAMES Jewish 5%. *Golde, Itzhak, Moshe.*

Kersten (1363) North German: from the personal name *Kersten*, a Low German derivative of *Christian* (from Latin *Christianus*) (see CHRISTIAN).
GIVEN NAMES German 4%. *Erwin* (3), *Gerhard* (3), *Kurt* (2), *Otto* (2), *Ewald, Hans, Udo.*

Kerstetter (954) Altered form of German **Kirchstetter**, habitational name for someone from a place called Kirchstätt in Upper Bavaria, or from Kirchstetten.

Kerstiens (146) Probably an altered spelling of Dutch **Kersteyns, Kersteens**, a patronymic from the personal name *Christianus* (see CHRISTIAN).

Kersting (584) German: patronymic from the personal name *Kerst*, a short form of KERSTEN.

Kerswell (36) English: habitational name from places in Devon and Worcestershire, named from Old English *cærse* '(water)cress' + *well(a)* 'spring', 'stream'.

Kertes (101) Americanized spelling of Hungarian or Jewish KERTESZ.

Kertesz (234) Hungarian (**Kertész**) and Jewish (from Hungary): occupational name for a gardener, *kertész*, from *kert* 'garden', a derivative of one of three Hungarian verbs *kerül* 'to go around or avoid', *kerít* 'to encircle', or *kering* 'to go around in circles'.
GIVEN NAMES Hungarian 11%; French 4%. *Imre* (3), *Tibor* (2), *Arpad, Attila, Csaba, Istvan, Laslo, Sandor, Zoltan; Francois* (2), *Patrice.*

Kerth (164) German: from a reduced and altered form of the personal name *Gerhard* (see GERHARDT).
GIVEN NAME German 4%. *Gunter.*

Kertis (141) Altered spelling of Hungarian KERTESZ.

Kertz (235) German: **1.** from *Gero, Kero*, a reduced and altered form of the personal name *Gerhard* (see GERHARDT), or sometimes a nickname for a greedy person, from Middle High German *gere* 'greed'. **2.** from Middle High German *kerze* 'candle', applied as a habitational name for someone living at a house distinguished by the sign of a candle or as a metonymic occupational name for a candle maker. **3.** from Polish **Kierz**, a topographic name from *kierz* 'small bush'.

Kervin (335) **1.** English: probably a variant of Irish KIRWAN. Like KERWIN, this name is concentrated in the Liverpool area of England. **2.** Americanized spelling of Dutch **Kervijn**, a habitational name for someone from a place called Carvin, Pas-de-Calais, France.

Kerwick (129) Irish: variant Anglicized form of Gaelic **Ó Garmhaic**, more commonly Anglicized as KIRBY.

Kerwin (1493) **1.** Irish: variant spelling of KIRWAN. **2.** Variant spelling of German GERWIN. **3.** Americanized spelling of Dutch **Kerwyn**, a variant of **Kervijn** (see KERVIN).
GIVEN NAMES Irish 4%. *Delma, Killian.*

Kerwood (202) English and Scottish: variant of KIRKWOOD.

Kerzman (112) South German (**Kerzmann**): occupational name for someone who made or sold candles, from Middle High German *kerze* 'candle' + *man* 'man'.

Kerzner (202) South German and Jewish (Ashkenazic): occupational name for a candlemaker, from Middle High German *kerze* 'candle', German *Kerze* + the agent suffix *-(n)er*.
GIVEN NAMES Jewish 5%. *Rina* (2), *Rivkah.*

Kes (104) Dutch and North German: variant of KESS.

Kesecker (156) German: variant of KEESECKER.

Kesel (161) Dutch and North German: topographic name for someone living on gravelly land. Compare German KIESEL.
GIVEN NAMES German 5%. *Frieda, Kurt.*

Keser (102) **1.** Dutch: from Low German *K(i)eser* 'inspector of foodstuff', from Middle Low German *kiesen* 'to examine'. **2.** North German: occupational name for a cheese maker, an agent noun from Low German *kese* (a loanword from Latin *caseus* 'cheese').

Keshishian (251) Armenian: patronymic from Turkish *keşiş* '(Christian) priest', 'monk', a term that came to be used as a distinguishing name for a Christian.
GIVEN NAMES Armenian 46%. *Ara* (3), *Garnik* (3), *Rouben* (3), *Anahid* (2), *Andranik* (2), *Armen* (2), *Kevork* (2), *Razmik* (2), *Serjik* (2), *Vahe* (2), *Vahik* (2), *Vahram* (2).

Keshishyan (102) Armenian: variant of KESHISHIAN.
GIVEN NAMES Armenian 69%; Russian 6%. *Arutyun* (2), *Edik* (2), *Grigor* (2), *Sarkis* (2), *Yervand* (2), *Agavni, Akop, Anahit, Ara, Aram, Ararat, Artin, Arusyak, Siranush; Grisha* (2), *Svetlana.*

Kesinger (166) South German: variant of **Kiesinger**, a habitational or topographic name, presumably of Württemberg origin, or from a derivative of the old personal name *Giso*.

Keske (189) German: variant of KASKE.

Keslar (252) Altered spelling of German *Kessler* or Jewish (Ashkenazic) **Keslyar** or **Kesler** (see KESSLER).

Kesler (2367) German and Jewish (Ashkenazic): variant of KESSLER.

Kesling (323) North German: variant of **Keseling** (see KIESEL 2).

Kesner (719) German: variant of KASTNER.

Kess (139) Dutch and North German: unexplained.

Kessel (1628) **1.** English: variant of KESTEL. **2.** German: from Middle High German *kezzel* 'kettle', 'cauldron', hence a metonymic occupational name for a maker of copper cooking vessels, or alternatively a topographic and habitational name, from the same word in the sense '(ring-shaped) hollow'. **3.** Dutch and Belgian: habitational name from any of the places so named in the Belgian provinces of Antwerp and Limburg or the Dutch province of North Brabant.

Kessell (279) **1.** English: variant of KESSEL. **2.** Altered spelling of German or Dutch KESSEL.

Kesselman (359) **1.** Jewish (Ashkenazic): occupational name for a coppersmith or maker of copper cooking vessels, from German KESSEL 'kettle', 'cauldron' + the agent suffix *-man(n)*. **2.** German (**Kesselmann**): habitational name from any of several places named Kessel in Bavaria, Rhineland, Pomerania, or Silesia (see KESSEL).

GIVEN NAMES Jewish 9%. *Avraham, Dov, Irina, Meyer, Moshe, Shmuel, Sol.*

Kesselring (421) German: occupational name for a maker of copper cooking vessels, from Middle High German *kezzel* 'kettle', 'cauldron' + *rinc* 'ring'.

Kessen (195) **1.** Scottish: Anglicized form of Gaelic **Cessán**, a byform of *Cessóg*, a personal name of unknown origin, borne by a 6th-century bishop and martyr. **2.** Dutch and German: from a pet form of the personal name CHRISTIAN.

Kessenich (229) German: habitational name from Kessenich near Bonn.
GIVEN NAMES French 4%. *Romain* (2), *Patrice.*

Kessinger (1328) **1.** German: from the personal name *Cazo.* **2.** variant spelling of KISSINGER.

Kessler (12392) German, Dutch, and Jewish (Ashkenazic): occupational name for a maker of copper cooking vessels, from an agent derivative of Middle High German *kezzel* 'kettle', 'cauldron', Middle Dutch *ketel*, modern German *Kessel.*

Kessner (218) German: variant of **Kestener** (see KASTNER 1).
GIVEN NAMES German 6%. *Kurt* (2), *Otto.*

Kestel (170) **1.** English: habitational name from Kestle, a place in Cornwall, so named from Cornish *castell* 'castle', 'village', 'rock'. **2.** German: habitational name from a place so called in Upper Franconia. **3.** Dutch: variant of KESSEL.

Kesten (223) German: **1.** from the personal name *Kesten*, a short form of CHRISTIAN. **2.** habitational name from a place near Wittlich on the Mosel river. **3.** shortened form of KESTENBAUM.

Kestenbaum (321) German and Jewish (Ashkenazic): from German dialect *Kästenbaum* (Latin *Castanea*), a topographic name for someone living near a horse-chestnut tree. As a Jewish name it is mainly of ornamental origin.
GIVEN NAMES Jewish 15%. *Moshe* (3), *Ilan* (2), *Shulem* (2), *Zwi* (2), *Bernat, Boruch, Chaim, Eran, Hyman, Miriam, Morty, Yehuda.*

Kester (2582) Perhaps Dutch: see KEISTER.

Kesterson (1103) Patronymic from KESTER.

Kesting (167) Dutch and German: from *Kersting*, a derivative of the personal name *Christianus* (see CHRISTIAN).
GIVEN NAMES German 4%. *Urs, Walther.*

Kestler (514) German: variant of KASTNER.
GIVEN NAMES German 4%. *Hans* (2), *Adelheid, Franz, Matthias, Otto, Wolfgang.*

Kestner (854) German: variant of KASTNER.

Keszler (108) Hungarian spelling of German KESSLER.
GIVEN NAMES German 8%. *Milbert* (2), *Lorenz.*

Ketch (239) English: variant of **Kedge**, a nickname from Middle English *kedge* 'brisk', 'lively', a dialect term confined to East Anglia (probably of Old Norse origin).

Ketcham (1765) English: perhaps a habitational name from Kitcham in Devon, but more likely a reduced form of **Kitchenham**, a habitational name from a place so named in East Sussex.
FOREBEARS Edward Ketcham (d. 1655) immigrated from Cambridge, England, to Massachusetts Bay Colony in about 1629–30, and subsequently moved to Stratford, CT.

Ketchel (130) Origin unidentified.

Ketchem (272) English: variant of KETCHAM.

Ketchen (147) Scottish: perhaps a variant of KITCHEN.

Ketcher (263) English: from Middle English *cachere* 'one who always chases or drives', 'huntsman'. It is probably also used in the same sense as the diminutive *cacherel*, which is common both as a name of office and as a surname in Norfolk.

Ketchersid (127) Variant spelling of English KETCHERSIDE.

Ketcherside (280) English: Altered form of **Kitcherside**, a habitational name of unexplained origin. The final element is presumably Middle English *side* 'hillside', 'slope'.

Ketchie (149) Americanized form of German **Goetchen** or Swiss German **Göttschi** (see GOETSCH).

Ketchmark (136) Americanized form of German **Kretzschmar** (see KRETSCHMER).

Ketchum (3089) English: variant of KETCHAM.

Ketelhut (142) German: metonymic occupational name for a maker of helmets or perhaps a nickname for someone who wore a helmet. In form the name is a cross between **Kesselhut** (the standard German form, from Middle High German *hut* 'helmet') and **Ketelhot** (from Low German *ketel* 'pot' + *hot* 'hat', 'helmet').
GIVEN NAMES German 7%. *Dieter, Kurt.*

Ketelsen (443) Danish, Norwegian, and North German: patronymic from a personal name derived from Old Norse *Ketill*, from *ketill* 'kettle', 'cauldron'.
GIVEN NAMES German 5%. *Hans* (2), *Kurt* (2), *Gerhardt, Otto.*

Ketler (146) German: variant spelling of KETTLER.

Ketner (712) German: variant spelling of KETTNER.

Keto (158) Finnish: from *keto* 'meadow', 'grassy field', originally a habitational name from a farmstead so named; it was also adopted during the name conversion movement in the 19th and early 20th centuries by Finns with Swedish surnames.
GIVEN NAMES Finnish 5%; Scandinavian 4%. *Aaro, Eino, Toivo; Erland.*

Ketola (244) Finnish: topographic name from KETO + the local suffix *-la*. This name occurs chiefly in western Finland.
GIVEN NAMES Finnish 13%. *Heikki* (3), *Reino* (3), *Arvo, Eeva, Eino, Esa, Esko, Tauno, Timo, Toivo, Veikko.*

Ketring (164) Variant of English KETTERING.

Ketron (591) Americanized form of English KETTERING.

Kett (248) **1.** German: topographic name for someone living near a water channel or water source, from the Bavarian dialect word *Kett* 'water channel', 'spring'. **2.** English: Norfolk variant of KITE.

Kettel (107) **1.** German: variant of KESSEL. **2.** English: variant spelling of KETTLE.
GIVEN NAMES French 6%; German 6%; Scandinavian 4%. *Ewald, Kurt; Morten.*

Kettell (185) **1.** English: variant spelling of KETTLE. **2.** Altered spelling of German KETTEL.

Ketter (562) **1.** German: metronymic from a pet form of the female personal name *Katharina.* **2.** German: nickname from Low German *Ketter* 'heretic' (standard German *Ketzer*). **3.** German: Austrian variant of the topographic name **Köther**, from Middle High German *kote* 'hut', 'cottage of a day laborer' (see KOTH). **4.** German: possibly a derivative of Middle High German *keten(e)* 'chain' (see KETTERER). **5.** Dutch: nickname from Middle Dutch *catter* 'heretic'. Compare 2 above.

Ketterer (771) German: **1.** occupational name for a chain maker, from an agent derivative of Middle High German *keten(e)* 'chain' (Latin *catena*). **2.** metronymic from *Ketter*, a pet form of the personal name *Katharina* (see CATHERINE).

Ketterhagen (139) **1.** German (**Käterhagen**): habitational name from a place so named in Mecklenburg-West Pomerania. **2.** Probably a topographic or habitational name from *Ketter*, a variant of *Kötter* 'someone living in a small house' (from Middle High German *kote* 'small house') + *Hagen* 'hedge' (from Middle High German *hag* 'scrub', 'enclosure', 'hedge' (see also KITTERMAN).

Kettering (490) **1.** English: habitational name from a place in Northamptonshire, recorded in Domesday Book as *Cateringe*, probably from an unattested Old English personal name *Cytra* + *-ingas*, a suffix denoting 'family or followers of'. **2.** Possibly an altered spelling of German KETTERLING.

Ketterling (421) North German: variant of **Kesselring**, from Low German *Kettel* 'kettle' + *-ring* 'ring', 'hob', hence an occupational name for a maker of iron rings.

Ketterman (560) German (**Kettermann**): **1.** occupational name for a chain maker, from Middle High German *keten(e)* 'chain' + *man* 'man'. **2.** metronymic from the female personal name *Ketter*, a pet form of *Katharina* (see CATHERINE).

Kettinger (120) German: habitational name from a place named Kettingen.

Kettle (512) **1.** English: from the Old Norse personal name *Ketill*, from *ketill* 'kettle', '(sacrificial) cauldron'. **2.** English translation of German KESSEL.

Kettler (997) **1.** Americanized form of German KESSEL. **2.** South German variant of KETTNER 1. **3.** Jewish (Ashkenazic): occupational name from German *Kette* 'chain' + the agent suffix *-ler*.
GIVEN NAMES German 5%. *Kurt* (6), *Horst* (2), *Inge*, *Otto*, *Rudi*, *Wolf*.

Kettles (185) English and Scottish: patronymic from KETTLE.

Kettleson (124) English: patronymic from the Old Norse personal name *Ketill* (see KETTLE).

Kettlewell (235) English: habitational name from Kettlewell in North Yorkshire, recorded in Domesday Book as *Cheteleuuelle*, from Old English *cetel* 'deep valley' + *wella* 'spring', 'stream'.

Kettner (525) **1.** South German: variant of KETTERER, occupational name for a chain maker. **2.** German: habitational name for someone from any of several places in Germany named Ketten. **3.** German: variant of the Austrian topographic name **Köther**, from Middle High German *kote* 'hut', 'day laborer's cottage' (see KOTH, KOTT). **4.** Czech: from German *Kettner*, or *Kötner*, or alternatively a habitational name for someone from a place called Chotyně (German Ketten).
GIVEN NAMES German 7%. *Erwin* (2), *Helmut* (2), *Otto* (2), *Alfons*, *Detlef*, *Johann*, *Kurt*.

Ketz (149) German: **1.** modern reflex of the Old High German personal name *Cazo*, which derives from the unexplained root *kad-*. **2.** from Middle High German *katze* 'cat'; probably short for a more usual derivative such as *Ketzel*, a nickname for a cat-lover or breeder, or for someone with feline qualities, or **Kätzmayr** (see KATZENMEYER). **3.** nickname from Middle High German *ketzer* 'heretic', 'free-thinker'.

Keuler (131) Possibly German: from an agent derivative of *keule* 'stick', 'club', 'bat', hence possibly an occupational name for someone who made or used such implements, or alternatively a habitational name for someone from Keula in Thuringia.
GIVEN NAME French 4%. *Gisele*.

Keune (175) German: variant of **Köhne** (see KOHNE).
GIVEN NAMES German 7%. *Manfred* (3), *Reinhard*.

Keup (165) Dutch: from a short form of the personal name *Jacop* (see JACOB).
GIVEN NAMES German 7%. *Erwin* (3), *Erna*, *Gunter*.

Keusch (125) German and Swiss German: nickname from Middle High German *kiusche* 'pure', 'chaste'; given the word's

more extensive meaning in the Middle Ages, 'gentle', 'moderate', 'good tempered', a religious purity may well have been implied.

Kever (171) Dutch: nickname from Middle Dutch *kever* 'beetle'.

Kevern (115) Cornish: unexplained.

Keville (148) English: habitational name for someone from a place called Keevil in Wiltshire, recorded in the Domesday book as *Chivele*, probably from Old English *cȳf* 'hollow' + *lēah* 'woodland clearing'.
GIVEN NAME German 5%. *Kurt* (2).

Kevin (159) Irish: Anglicized form of **Ó Caoimhín** 'descent of *Caoimhín*' (Kevin), a byname representing a diminutive of Gaelic *caomh* 'comely', 'beloved'. This was the name of a 7th-century saint who is one of the patrons of Dublin.

Kevorkian (249) Armenian: patronymic from the western Armenian personal name *Kevork*, classical Armenian *Geworg* (see GEORGE).
GIVEN NAMES Armenian 22%; French 4%. *Vasken* (3), *Aram* (2), *Armen* (2), *Berge* (2), *Krikor* (2), *Sarkis* (2), *Agop*, *Ararat*, *Armine*, *Artine*, *Avedis*, *Boghos*; *Girard* (2), *Henri*.

Kew (160) **1.** English: occupational name for a cook, Anglo-Norman French *k(i)eu* (from Latin *coquus*). **2.** English (of Norman origin): habitational name from Caieu, a lost place near Boulogne in Northern France. **3.** English: habitational name from a place in Middlesex, now part of Greater London, probably named with Old English *cǣg* 'key', 'projection' + *hōh* 'spur of land'. **4.** Irish: Ulster variant of McHUGH.

Kewley (198) English: variant of COWLEY.

Key (10827) **1.** English and German: variant of KAY. **2.** Irish: reduced form of McKAY.

Keyes (5443) **1.** English: variant of KAY. **2.** English (of Norman origin): habitational name from Guise in Aisne, Picardy, which is first recorded in the 12th century as *Gusia*; the etymology is uncertain. **3.** Irish: Anglicized form of Gaelic **Mac Aodha** (see McKAY).

Keylon (210) Probably of German origin, but unexplained. Perhaps an altered form of KEYLOR.
GIVEN NAME German 4%. *Dieter*.

Keylor (107) Possibly an Americanized form of German **Köhler** (see KOHLER).

Keys (5266) English and Irish: variant spelling of KEYES.

Keyser (3111) Dutch: from *keyser* 'emperor', modern Dutch *keizer* (from Latin *Caesar*). **Keyser** is a 17th-century spelling. Compare German KAISER. In addition to the meanings of the German name (nickname, house name, etc.), this was also a status name for the head of a society of marksmen.

Keysor (170) Altered spelling of Dutch KEYSER.

Keyt (122) English: variant spelling of KITE.

Keyte (106) English: variant spelling of KITE.

Keyton (191) English (Kent): possibly a variant of the habitational name CAYTON or a variant spelling of KEETON.
GIVEN NAMES French 4%. *Henri*, *Monique*.

Keyworth (196) English: habitational name from a place in Nottinghamshire, recorded as *Caworde* in Domesday Book; the first element is thought to be from a personal name, the second from Old English *worð* 'enclosure'.

Keyzer (110) Dutch (also **de Keyzer**): variant of KEYSER.
GIVEN NAMES Dutch 15%. *Pieter* (3), *Willem* (2), *Corniel*, *Laurens*.

Kezar (169) Possibly an altered spelling of German KIESER or Dutch **Kezer**, a Dutch form of the same name.

Kezele (106) Dutch: reduced variant of **de Kesele**, a nickname from Middle Dutch *kezel* 'pebble', 'boulder', with the definite article *de*, presumably denoting someone with a rotund figure.

Kezer (114) Dutch: variant of KESER.

Keziah (256) Origin unidentified.

Kha (163) Vietnamese: unexplained.
GIVEN NAMES Vietnamese 51%; Chinese 19%. *Hung* (5), *Long* (3), *Thanh* (3), *Dang* (2), *Duc* (2), *Nghia* (2), *Quoc* (2), *Tai Van* (2), *Trung* (2), *Anh*, *Chuoi*, *Chuong*, *Cui*; *Han*, *Hong*, *Hui*, *Kao*, *Man*, *Sen*, *Vang*, *Xai*, *Yia*, *Ying*.

Khalaf (172) Muslim: from the Arabic personal name *Khalaf*, literally 'successor', which is often used in combination with the father's or the grandfather's name. Khalaf bin Ahmad, an amir of the 10th century, was noted as a generous patron of learning.
GIVEN NAMES Muslim 57%. *Samir* (4), *Ali* (2), *Kamel* (2), *Khalil* (2), *Mohamed* (2), *Sami* (2), *Abdul Aziz*, *Adiba*, *Ahmad*, *Ahmed*, *Amin*.

Khalid (248) Muslim: from a personal name based on Arabic *khālid* 'eternity', 'eternal', 'remaining'. Khālid ibn-al-Walīd (d. 642) was the Muslim military leader who brought about the defeat of the Byzantine Empire and its expulsion from Syria. The Prophet Muhammad called him *Sayf-ullah* 'sword of Allah'.
GIVEN NAMES Muslim 86%. *Mohammad* (19), *Mohammed* (9), *Muhammad* (7), *Abdul* (5), *Syed* (5), *Ali* (3), *Irfan* (3), *Mahmood* (3), *Mohamed* (3), *Sheikh* (3), *Zafar* (3), *Fawad* (2).

Khalifa (135) Muslim: status name or honorific title from Arabic *khalīfah* 'successor', 'regent', 'viceroy', in English often transliterated as *caliph*. This was the title adopted after the death of Muhammad in 632 by his successor Abu-Bakr. The caliphs ruled in Bahgdad until 1258, then in Egypt until the Ottoman conquest (1517). The title was then held by the Ottoman sultans in Istanbul until it was abolished by Kamal Atatürk in 1924.

GIVEN NAMES Muslim 80%. *Ahmed* (10), *Mohamed* (6), *Ibrahim* (3), *Ismail* (3), *Ammar* (2), *Gulam* (2), *Hesham* (2), *Mahmoud* (2), *Mohammed* (2), *Nagib* (2), *Omar* (2), *Abdullah*.

Khalil (835) Muslim: from a personal name based on Arabic *khalīl* 'friend'. *Khalīl-ullah* 'friend of Allah' is an honorific title given to the Prophet Ibrahim (Abraham). See the Qur'an 4:125: 'Allah took Abraham as his friend.'

GIVEN NAMES Muslim 72%. *Mohamed* (11), *Samir* (8), *Ali* (7), *Khalil* (7), *Mohammad* (7), *Ahmed* (5), *Ashraf* (5), *Hussein* (5), *Jamal* (5), *Khalid* (5), *Maged* (5), *Mohammed* (5).

Khalili (194) Muslim: surname denoting descent from or association with someone called KHALIL.

GIVEN NAMES Muslim 75%. *Hamid* (5), *Nader* (4), *Ebrahim* (3), *Hossein* (3), *Arsalan* (2), *Bahram* (2), *Faezeh* (2), *Koroush* (2), *Ladan* (2), *Mahmoud* (2), *Mohammad* (2), *Mohammed* (2).

Khalsa (554) Indian (Panjab): Sikh name, from Arabic *khālis* 'pure'. A Sikh brotherhood called Khalsa was established by Guru Gobind (1666–1708).

GIVEN NAMES Indian 81%; Scandinavian 4%. *Amrit* (8), *Dharma* (4), *Hari* (4), *Atma* (3), *Avtar* (3), *Darshan* (3), *Daya* (3), *Dharm* (3), *Guru* (3), *Ajeet* (2), *Balwinder* (2), *Dharam* (2).

Khan (8093) Muslim: from a personal name or status name based on Turkish *khan* 'ruler', 'nobleman'. This was originally a hereditary title among Tartar and Mongolian tribesmen (in particular Genghis Khan, 1162–1227), but is now very widely used throughout the Muslim world as a personal name. In Iran and parts of the Indian subcontinent it is used as an honorific title after a person's personal name.

GIVEN NAMES Muslim 82%. *Mohammad* (228), *Mohammed* (190), *Abdul* (136), *Muhammad* (97), *Mohamed* (63), *Bibi* (43), *Tariq* (43), *Ali* (38), *Asif* (37), *Khalid* (37), *Amir* (36), *Saeed* (36).

Khang (161) Laotian or other Southeast Asian: unexplained.

GIVEN NAMES Southeast Asian 75%. *Ying* (4), *Leng* (3), *Nhia* (3), *Chue* (2), *Sung* (2), *Tong* (2), *Yang* (2), *Chee, Chi, Chia, Chin, Chou*; *Neng* (3), *Pang* (2), *Shoua* (2), *Yer* (2), *Youa* (2), *Blong, Chong, Chong Neng, Chung, Houa, Khoua, Moua*; *Khue, Mai, Nguyen, Tran*.

Khanna (518) Indian (Panjab): Hindu (Khatri) and Sikh name based on the name of a clan found in the Khatri community who are said to be the descendants of a certain Khan Chand.

GIVEN NAMES Indian 89%. *Ashok* (10), *Rajiv* (10), *Deepak* (7), *Pradeep* (7), *Rakesh* (7),

Sunil (6), *Vijay* (6), *Rajeev* (5), *Tarun* (5), *Ajay* (4), *Anil* (4), *Mohan* (4).

Khare (100) Indian (Maharashtra); pronounced as two syllables: Hindu (Brahman) name, from Marathi *khǝra* 'true', 'genuine', found among Konkanasth Brahmans.

GIVEN NAMES Indian 77%. *Alok* (3), *Vijay* (3), *Yogesh* (3), *Anand* (2), *Atul* (2), *Jitendra* (2), *Milind* (2), *Rahul* (2), *Sandeep* (2), *Amita, Anil, Ashok*.

Khatib (223) Muslim: status name based on Arabic *khattīb* 'orator', 'preacher', 'speaker', bestowed as an honorific title on someone who delivers a sermon (*khutba*) on a Friday during the Jum'a prayers.

GIVEN NAMES Muslim 77%. *Khaled* (5), *Ahmad* (3), *Nabila* (3), *Nassim* (3), *Omar* (3), *Osamah* (3), *Samir* (3), *Ziad* (3), *Abd* (2), *Ali* (2), *Aziz* (2), *Bassam* (2).

Khatri (205) Indian (chiefly Panjab): Hindu (Khatri) and Sikh name based on the name of a prominent mercantile community in the Panjab. It is from Sanskrit *kṣatriya* 'member of the warrior class', derived from *kṣatra* 'dominion', 'power'. As their name suggests, the Panjabi Khatris claim to be of Kshatriya origin. They have been prominent in civil administration from the time of the Mughal emperors. Several well-known Sikh gurus, including Guru Nanak, the founder of the Sikh religion, have come from the Khatri community. The vast majority of the Khatris are, however, Hindus.

GIVEN NAMES Indian 67%; Muslim 22%. *Dilip* (4), *Hiralal* (3), *Jayesh* (3), *Mahesh* (3), *Vijay* (3), *Vinod* (3), *Alkesh* (2), *Anil* (2), *Jagdish* (2), *Manilal* (2), *Mukesh* (2), *Nandlal* (2); *Mohammed* (3), *Faiz* (2), *Ibrahim* (2), *Nisar* (2), *Saleem* (2), *Yusuf* (2), *Abdul, Abid, Afzal, Ahmed, Anwer, Ayub*.

Khawaja (175) Muslim: from an honorific title based on Persian *khawāja* 'lord', 'master'.

GIVEN NAMES Muslim 87%. *Mohammad* (6), *Tariq* (5), *Shahid* (4), *Abdul* (3), *Anjum* (2), *Imran* (2), *Irfan* (2), *Khalid* (2), *Majeed* (2), *Naeem* (2), *Nasim* (2), *Sadruddin* (2).

Kho (176) Chinese 高: variant, common in Indonesia, of GAO.

GIVEN NAMES Chinese 41%; Spanish 4%. *Jong* (2), *Young* (2), *Choon, Chung, Eng, Hwa, Kyung, Pheng, Ping, Pui, Seng, Sook Hee, Sook Ja, Sung, Teck, Wonkyu, Xeng*; *Ana, Corazon, Estrella, Rodrigo, Rogelio*.

Khong (111) **1.** Vietnamese: unexplained. **2.** Cambodian: unexplained. **3.** Indonesian or Malaysian: unexplained.

GIVEN NAMES Vietnamese 42%; Other Southeast Asian 32%. *Hanh* (3), *Thanh* (3), *Duc* (2), *Ha* (2), *Hinh* (2), *Tuan* (2), *Vien* (2), *An Van, Anh Ngoc, Bao, Bao Van, Binh*; *Han, Hong, Jee, Ling, Ying*; *Chong, Chung, Nam*.

Khoo (195) Chinese 邱: variant, common in Malaysia, of QIU 1.

GIVEN NAMES Chinese 8%. *Soo* (2), *Cheng, Eng, Heang, Mei, Shih, Ting, Yong, Yoon*.

Khosla (154) Indian (Panjab): Hindu (Khatri) and Sikh name based on the name of a Khatri clan. This clan belongs to the Sarin subgroup of the Khatri community.

GIVEN NAMES Indian 88%. *Ramesh* (4), *Vijay* (4), *Ashok* (3), *Sandeep* (3), *Suman* (3), *Achal* (2), *Anand* (2), *Dinesh* (2), *Lalit* (2), *Prem* (2), *Rajesh* (2), *Sandip* (2).

Khouri (376) Arabic (Lebanon and Syria): variant of KHOURY.

GIVEN NAMES Arabic 33%; French 10%. *Samir* (4), *Farid* (3), *Hassan* (3), *Walid* (3), *Issa* (2), *Issam* (2), *Khalil* (2), *Nabil* (2), *Nagi* (2), *Riad* (2), *Samer* (2), *Yousef* (2); *Antoine* (4), *Michel* (4), *Emile* (2), *Jacques* (2), *Andre, Georges, Patrice, Philippe, Rodolph*.

Khoury (1483) Arabic (Lebanon and Syria): from Arabic *khūrī* 'priest', in particular a Christian priest.

GIVEN NAMES Arabic 29%; French 6%. *Nabil* (14), *Sami* (13), *Samir* (9), *Issa* (7), *Ibrahim* (6), *Ramzi* (6), *Bassam* (4), *Fouad* (4), *Habib* (4), *Issam* (4), *Jamil* (4), *Riad* (4); *Michel* (7), *Antoine* (6), *Emile* (6), *Pierre* (4), *Andre* (2), *Camille, Clemence, Clovis, Georges, Gisele, Henri, Jacques*.

Khurana (183) Indian (Panjab): Hindu (Arora) and Sikh name of unknown meaning, based on the name of a clan in the Arora community.

GIVEN NAMES Indian 92%. *Sanjay* (6), *Anil* (4), *Ram* (4), *Ramesh* (4), *Sanjeev* (4), *Saroj* (4), *Ritu* (3), *Satish* (3), *Aruna* (2), *Jyoti* (2), *Krishan* (2), *Pradeep* (2).

Khuu (268) Vietnamese: unexplained.

GIVEN NAMES Vietnamese 78%. *Linh* (7), *Hung* (6), *Hue* (5), *Loi* (4), *Thanh* (4), *Thien* (4), *Dinh* (3), *Dung* (3), *Hien* (3), *Khanh* (3), *Son* (3), *Anh* (2); *Dong, Hon, Jung, Ke, Tong*; *Tam* (3), *Phong* (2), *Nam, Thai, Tham, Uyen*.

Ki (86) Korean: there are two Chinese characters for the surname Ki, but one is extremely rare. Only the common one is discussed here. Only one Ki clan uses this other character, the Haengju Ki clan. The founder of the Haengju Ki clan, U-Sŏng, is said to have been one of three sons of the 40th generation descendant of Kija, the founder of the ancient Chosŏn kingdom in about 194 BC. The other two sons, U-P'yŏng and U-kyŏng, founded the HAN clan and the Sŏn'gan clan respectively.

Kiah (136) Origin unidentified.

Kiang (167) Chinese 紀: variant of JIANG 1.

GIVEN NAMES Chinese 13%. *Ching-Hwa, Chuang, Hsing, Kang, Kwai, Miu, Pei, Tseng, Wei, Yun, Zang*.

Kibbe (751) **1.** English: according to Reaney this is a nickname from an unattested Old English word *cybbe* meaning 'clumsy' or 'thickset'. Reaney's speculation is apparently based on taking the Middle

English word *kibble* 'cudgel' as a diminutive of an unattested Old English word. Corresponding personal names have been postulated for the place names Kibworth ('enclosure of a man called *Cybba*') and Kibblesworth ('enclosure of a man called *Cybbel*'); so, in theory, the surname could be a reflex of these Old English personal names. **2.** North German: nickname for a cantankerous person, from Middle Low German, Middle High German *kiven* 'to quarrel'.

Kibbee (213) **1.** Respelling of German **Kibi**, an Alemannic form of KIBBE, or possibly of **Kibbe** itself. **2.** Probably also a respelling of English KIBBY.

Kibbey (301) English: variant spelling of KIBBY.

Kibble (290) **1.** English: from Middle English *kibble* 'cudgel', hence a nickname for a heavy, thickset man or for a belligerent individual. **2.** Altered spelling of German **Kibbel** or **Kübel**, a metonymic occupational name for a cooper, from Middle High German *kübel* 'vat', from Latin *cupella* 'drinking vessel', 'grain measure'. Compare KIBLER.

Kibby (454) **1.** Americanized spelling of German **Kibi** (see KIBBEE) or KIBBE. **2.** Anglicized spelling of Welsh **Cybi**, probably a habitational name from Caergybi, the Welsh name of Holyhead. The surname is common in Somerset and Wiltshire, England.

Kibe (100) **1.** Japanese: habitational name from the village of Kibe in Ōmi (now Shiga prefecture), usually written with characters meaning 'tree' and 'department'. A family descended from the FUJIWARA directed the Buddhist temple there and took the name as their own. **2.** Indian (Maharashtra, Goa); pronounced as two syllables: Hindu (Brahman) name of unknown meaning, found among Saraswat Brahmans.
GIVEN NAMES Japanese 8%; Indian 7%. *Akihiro, Haruki, Junko*; *Madhavi, Sujata.*

Kibel (121) German: unrounded form of **Kübel**, a metonymic occupational name for a cooper, from Middle High German *kübel* 'vat', 'tub'.
GIVEN NAME German 4%. *Frieda.*

Kibler (2145) Austrian, Swiss, and South German: variant of KUEBLER.

Kiblinger (111) German: possibly a derivative of KIBLER.

Kibodeaux (269) Partly Americanized spelling of French QUEBEDEAUX or altered form of THIBODEAUX.
GIVEN NAMES French 8%. *Andrus* (2), *Curley, Gaston, Lucien.*

Kice (100) German: Americanized form of **Keis**, which is probably of Slavic origin, or from **Keiss**, from a pet form of a Germanic personal name composed with *gīs(il)*, as in GIESBRECHT.
FOREBEARS This family is believed to have been founded by a certain Peter Kice, a

Hessian mercenary fighting for the British during the Revolutionary War. Eventually, he deserted and settled in Wharton, NJ.

Kichler (108) German: occupational name for a baker of cookies and small cakes, an agent derivative of Middle High German *küechel(in)* 'small cake' (see KUCHLER).
GIVEN NAME French 4%. *Pascale.*

Kichline (178) Americanized spelling of South German **Kiechlein**, a dialect variant of German **Küchlein** 'little cake', a metonymic occupational name for a pastrycook.

Kicinski (143) Polish (**Kiciński**): habitational name for someone from *Kicino* in Ostrołęka voivodeship, named with Polish *kita* 'fluffy tail' (for example, a fox's brush).
GIVEN NAMES Polish 8%. *Jacek, Mariusz, Tomasz.*

Kick (489) **1.** English (Somerset and Wiltshire): possibly a derivative of Middle English *kiken* 'to watch', 'to spy'. Compare KICKER. **2.** German: variant of KECK. **3.** Dutch: probably a nickname, from a derivative of *kikken* 'to kick'.

Kicker (122) English: occupational name or nickname from a noun derivative of Middle English *kiken* 'to watch', 'to spy'.

Kicklighter (527) Americanized spelling of German **Kückleiter**, literally 'chicken ladder', probably a nickname for a chicken farmer.

Kida (186) Japanese: 'rice paddy near a tree'; found in western Japan and the Ryū kyūan island of Yaeyama.
GIVEN NAMES Japanese 24%. *Yoji* (3), *Akiyoshi* (2), *Eiko* (2), *Koji* (2), *Akiko, Haruo, Hiroyuki, Jitsuo, Keiichi, Koichi, Masatoshi, Reiko.*

Kidane (152) Ethiopian: unexplained.
GIVEN NAMES Ethiopian 64%; African 5%; Jewish 4%. *Afeworki* (3), *Abraha* (2), *Alem* (2), *Assefa* (2), *Dawit* (2), *Ghenet* (2), *Mekonnen* (2), *Mesfin* (2), *Saba* (2), *Tirhas* (2), *Zekarias* (2), *Theodros* (2); *Almaz*; *Berhe, Yosef.*

Kidd (10829) **1.** Scottish: from a medieval personal name *Kid*, a variant of *Kit*, a pet form of CHRISTOPHER. **2.** English: from Middle English *kid(e)* 'young goat', hence a nickname for a frisky person or a metonymic occupational name for a goatherd. **3.** English: metonymic occupational name for a seller of faggots, from Middle English *kidde* 'faggot' (of unknown origin).

Kidder (2777) English: possibly an occupational name from early modern English *kidd(i)er* 'badger', a licensed middleman who bought provisions from farmers and took them to market for resale at a profit, or alternatively a variant of KIDMAN.

Kiddoo (131) Reduced form of Irish McADOO. Compare KIDDY, KEDDIE.

Kiddy (271) Variant of Scottish KEDDIE.

Kidman (198) English: occupational name, probably for a goatherd (from Middle English *kid(e)* 'young goat' + *man* 'man'), but

possibly also for a cutter of faggots (from Middle English *kidde* 'faggot').
GIVEN NAMES German 4%. *Georg, Kurt.*

Kidner (116) English (Somerset): unexplained.

Kidney (490) Irish: from a mistranslation of Gaelic **Ó Dubháin** 'descendant of *Dubhán*', a byname from a diminutive of *dubh* 'black' (see DEVINE). This was confused with the Gaelic word *dubhán* 'kidney', which is in fact a derivative of *dubh* 'black'.

Kido (162) Japanese: variously written, usually with characters meaning 'wooden door'. A less usual rendering is 'castle door'. It is found in western Japan. One family of samurai came from Suō (now part of Yamaguchi prefecture).
GIVEN NAMES Japanese 50%. *Fumi* (2), *Hiroshi* (2), *Satoshi* (2), *Atsuo, Atsushi, Chieko, Fumiko, Fumio, Hiro, Hirofumi, Hiromitsu, Hisao.*

Kidwell (3319) English: possibly a habitational name from Kiddal in Barwick in Elmet, West Yorkshire, which is probably so named from the Old English personal name *Cydda* + Old English *halh* 'nook or corner of land'. However, the surname occurs predominantly in Devon, suggesting another, unidentified source may be involved. Alternatively, it could be a variant of **Kiddle**, a topographic name for someone living by (or making his living from) a fish weir, Middle English *kidel* (Old French *cuidel, quidel*, a word of Breton origin).

Kiebler (125) Austrian, Swiss, and South German: occupational name for a cooper, a variant of **Kübler** (see KUEBLER).

Kiecker (122) German: **1.** habitational name for someone from a place called Kieck near Potsdam. **2.** from an agent derivative of Low German *kieken* 'to look'.

Kiedaisch (103) German (Swabian): nickname meaning 'cow dung' (from Middle High German *teisch* 'dung'), probably denoting a peasant.

Kiedrowski (230) Polish: habitational name for someone from Kiedrowo in Piła voivodeship, perhaps named with Polish *kędra* 'lock of hair' (see KEDZIOR).

Kief (211) North German: probably a nickname for a quarrelsome person, from Middle Low German *kīf* 'quarrel'.
GIVEN NAMES German 6%. *Hans* (2), *Helmut, Kurt.*

Kiefer (4332) **1.** German: occupational name for a cooper or the overseer of a wine cellar, from an agent derivative of Middle High German *kuofe* 'vat', 'barrel' (from Latin *cupa*). **2.** from an agent derivative of Middle High German *kiffen* 'to quarrel', hence a nickname for a bickerer. **3.** Jewish (Ashkenazic): ornamental name from German *Kiefer* 'pine tree'. This word, which is first attested in the early 15th century, is a blend of *kien* and *forhe*, both meaning 'pine'. The two elements still have a separate existence: *kieboom* is the Dutch term for a pine tree, while in many parts of Germany the word for the tree is *Föhre*.

GIVEN NAMES German 4%. *Kurt* (15), *Franz* (5), *Erwin* (3), *Heinz* (3), *Dieter* (2), *Fritz* (2), *Alois*, *Aloys*, *Claus*, *Ernst*, *Florian*, *Frieda*.

Kieffer (2607) German and Jewish (Ashkenazic): variant spelling of KIEFER.

Kiefner (123) German: variant of KIEFER 1.

Kieft (220) Dutch: variant of KIEVIT, from a dialect variant of the vocabulary word found in Twente and eastern Gelderland.

FOREBEARS Willem Kieft, born in Holland, was governor of New Netherland 1638–1645.

Kiehl (799) German: **1.** from Middle Low German *kīl* 'wedge', applied as a metonymic occupational name or as a pejorative nickname for a ruffian. **2.** possibly a habitational name from Kiel in Schleswig-Holstein, from Dutch and Frisian *kil* 'stagnant water' (see KIEL). **3.** South German: variant of **Kühl** (see KUEHL). **4.** from a pet form of the personal name *Kilian*. **5.** in Bavaria, a nickname for a fool, probably from Middle High German *kīl* 'wedge', used figuratively for a bumbler.

Kiehn (347) **1.** South German (Bavaria, Austria, Saxony): from the personal name *Kiehn*, a variant of KUEHN. **2.** North German: topographic name for someone who lived by a standing of pines, from Middle Low German *kien* 'pinewood spill', 'pine cone', or alternatively a metronymic from the female personal name *Kunigunde*.

Kiehne (184) German: variant of KIEHN.

GIVEN NAMES German 4%. *Otto*, *Wolfgang*.

Kieke (127) North German: shortened form of any of various compound names with this as the first element, as for example *Kieckebusch* or *Kiekhöfer*.

GIVEN NAME German 5%. *Ewald*.

Kiel (1667) **1.** German (common in the north of Germany and around Hamburg): in some cases probably a habitational name from the city of Kiel in Schleswig-Holstein, but more likely a topographic name for someone living by a long narrow bay or area of sheltered water, from Middle Low German *kil* 'wedge', the word from which the city derives its name. Alternatively, it may be from the same word applied as a nickname to denote a crude person. **2.** North German: possibly an occupational name for a ship's captain, short for Low German *Kilmester* (Middle Low German *kil* 'keel', 'boat' + *mester* 'master', 'skipper'). **Kilmester** is attested as a surname near Rostock in the 13th century. **3.** German: from a pet form of the personal name KILIAN. **4.** Dutch: from Middle Dutch *kidel*, *kedel* 'smock', hence a metonymic occupational name for someone who make such garments or perhaps a nickname for someone who habitually wore one. **5.** Dutch: habitational name from a place so

named in Antwerp or from the German city (see 1). **6.** Jewish (Ashkenazic): variant of KIL. **7.** Polish (**Kieł**): from *kieł* 'tooth', 'fang', hence a nickname for someone with bad or protruding teeth.

Kielar (185) Polish: occupational name for a cellarman, a borrowing of German KELLER 'cellar'.

GIVEN NAMES Polish 13%. *Jolanta* (2), *Tadeusz* (2), *Boleslaw*, *Czeslaw*, *Elzbieta*, *Matylda*, *Thadeus*, *Zbigniew*.

Kielb (150) Polish (**Kiełb**): nickname from *kiełb* 'gudgeon'.

GIVEN NAMES Polish 6%. *Leslaw*, *Leszek*.

Kielbasa (233) Polish (**Kiełbasa**): from *kiełbasa* 'sausage', hence either a metonymic occupational name for a seller of sausages or a nickname bestowed on someone with a fancied resemblance to a sausage.

GIVEN NAMES Polish 4%. *Janusz*, *Stanislaw*, *Wieslaw*.

Kieler (246) North German and Danish: topographic name for someone living by a long narrow bay or habitational name for someone from the city of Kiel in Schleswig-Holstein (see KIEL).

GIVEN NAMES Scandinavian 4%. *Erik* (2), *Morten*.

Kieliszewski (119) Polish: possibly a derivative of a Polish nickname based on *kielich* 'drinking glass', 'punch bowl', or a habitational name from an unidentified place named with this word.

Kielman (172) **1.** German (**Kielmann**): variant of KIEL 1, with the addition of -*man(n)* 'man'. **2.** German (**Kielmann**): possibly a variant of KILIAN. **3.** Swedish: ornamental name from the place-name element *kil*- 'wedge' + *man* 'man'.

GIVEN NAMES Scandinavian 6%; German 4%. *Bjorn* (2); *Otto*.

Kielty (329) Irish: reduced Anglicized form of Gaelic **Ó Caoilte**, 'descendant of Caoilte', a personal name, probably based on *caol* 'slender', though 'hard' has been suggested.

Kieltyka (114) Polish (**Kiełtyka**): nickname for Polish dialect *kiełtyka* 'swinger', probably with reference to a peculiarity of gait.

GIVEN NAME Polish 4%. *Jozef*.

Kiely (1241) Irish: **1.** Americanized form of **Ó Cadhla** 'descendant of *Cadhla*', a personal name meaning 'graceful'. **2.** variant of KEELEY.

GIVEN NAMES Irish 5%. *Finbarr*, *Mavourneen*, *Niamh*.

Kien (105) **1.** German and Dutch: variant of KUHN. **2.** Vietnamese: unexplained.

GIVEN NAMES Vietnamese 16%; Chinese 7%; German 6%; Dutch 5%. *Diem*, *Duc*, *Duong*, *Hoang*, *Huy*, *Huynh*, *Khanh*, *Kinh*, *Quoc*, *Rinh*, *Thanh*, *Tri Minh*; *Hong* (2), *Hon*; *Erwin*, *Klaus*; *Pieter* (2).

Kienast (245) **1.** German and Swiss German: topographic name from the Slavic element *chojnasti* 'rich in conifers' (hence

the place name Kynast, which could also be a source of the surname). **2.** Jewish (Ashkenazic): ornamental name composed of German KIENE 'pine' + *Ast* 'branch'.

GIVEN NAMES German 7%. *Kurt* (2), *Dieter*, *Gunter*, *Horst*, *Ilse*.

Kienbaum (141) German or Jewish (Ashkenazic): ornamental name from Low German *Kienbaum* 'Scots pine', originally denoting any species or variety of pine tree.

Kiene (222) South German: **1.** from a dialect form of *kühn* 'bold' (Middle High German *küene*). This is found as an element in Germanic personal names such as KONRAD. Compare KUEHN. **2.** altered spelling of **Keine**, a variant of KEINER.

GIVEN NAMES German 4%. *Fritz*, *Klaus*.

Kiener (183) **1.** South German: inflected form of KIENE. **2.** Swiss German: nickname derived from the dialect verb *chienen* 'to whimper'. **3.** Variant spelling of KEINER.

Kienholz (152) German: **1.** habitational name from a place so named in Bavaria. **2.** topographic name for someone living near a stand of fir trees, from Middle High German *kien* 'pine', 'pine wood shavings' + *holz* 'wood', 'lumber'.

Kienitz (313) German: **1.** habitational name from a place so named in Brandenburg. **2.** possibly from the Germanic personal name *Chunizo*, formed with *kuoni* 'daring', 'experienced', or *chunni*, *kuni* 'race', 'people'. Compare KUNTZ, KONRAD.

GIVEN NAMES German 7%. *Helmut* (2), *Kurt* (2), *Otto* (2), *Ernst*.

Kienle (200) German: from a pet form of KIENE, common especially in Austria and Swabia.

GIVEN NAMES German 13%. *Juergen* (2), *Otto* (2), *Gerhard*, *Hans*, *Hilde*, *Kurt*, *Rainer*.

Kienlen (120) German: variant of KIENLE.

Kientz (200) German: variant of **Künz** (see KUNTZ).

Kienzle (483) South German: variant of KUENZEL.

GIVEN NAMES German 4%. *Monika* (3), *Kurt* (2), *Frieda*.

Kieper (163) German: **1.** from the medieval personal name *Kiepert*, an altered form of GEBHARDT. **2.** It has also been suggested that it is from an agent derivative of Low German *Kiep(e)*, which denotes a basket designed to be carried slung across the back, hence an occupational name for a basket maker or peddler.

Kier (730) **1.** Austrian: occupational name for a cowherd, *Chüyger* in the Tyrolean dialect, from *Kühe* 'cows' (plural of *Kuh*) + -*er* suffix of agent nouns. **2.** English and Scottish: possibly a variant spelling of KEAR.

Kieran (152) Irish: Anglicized form of Gaelic **Ó Ciaráin** 'descendant of *Ciarán*', a byname from a diminutive of *ciar* 'dark', 'black-haired'. It was borne by two Irish saints, a hermit of the 5th century and the founder of the monastery at Clonmacnoise (d. 547).

Kierce (118) English: perhaps an altered spelling of Irish **Kierse**, itself a variant, found in County Clare, of **(Mac) Kerrisk**, Anglicized form of Gaelic **Mac Fhiarais** 'son of *Fiaras*', Gaelic form of *Piers*. Compare FERRICK.
GIVEN NAME Irish 11%. *Brendan* (2).

Kiernan (2410) Irish: reduced form of McKIERNAN, an Anglicized form of Gaelic **Mac Thighearnáin** 'son of *Tighearnan*' (see TIERNAN).
GIVEN NAMES Irish 6%. *Brendan* (3), *Brian Patrick, Dermot, Eamon, Finbarr, Patrick Michael.*

Kierstead (401) Altered spelling of the Dutch surname **Kierstede**, probably from a place in the Netherlands so named. *Kier* means 'chink' or 'crack', as in a slightly opened door.
FOREBEARS Hans Kierstede was a barber-surgeon in New Amsterdam in the 17th century.

Kies (618) German: from Middle High German *kis* 'gravel', 'low grade iron ore', hence probably a topographic name for someone living on land characterized by coarse sand and pebbles or an occupational nickname for an iron smelter.

Kieschnick (181) Eastern German: 1. from Sorbian *khěžnik* 'cottager', either a topographic name for someone who lived in a cottage or a byname denoting the feudal status of a cottager. 2. topographic name from Slavic *kierz* 'bush'.
GIVEN NAMES German 5%. *Fritz, Kurt.*

Kiesel (760) German: 1. from the Germanic personal name *Gisilo* (see GIESEL). 2. topographic name for someone who lived on a patch of gravelly land, from Middle High German *kisel* 'pebble', 'gravel'. There are also several minor places named with this word, and the surname may be a habitational name from any of them. See also KIESLING.
GIVEN NAMES German 7%. *Kurt* (3), *Otto* (3), *Frieda* (2), *Armin, Bernhardt, Bodo, Erwin, Juergen, Klaus, Reinhardt, Wolf.*

Kieser (413) German: from an agent derivative of Middle High German *kiesen* 'to choose, examine, or inspect', an occupational name for an official inspector of food or beverages.
GIVEN NAMES German 4%. *Kurt* (3), *Manfred.*

Kiesewetter (201) German (found mainly in Saxony and Silesia): apparently from Middle High German *kiesen* 'to choose or test' (see KIESER) + *wetter* 'weather', hence a nickname for someone who forecast the weather.

Kiesler (175) German: topographic name for someone who lived on a patch of gravelly land (see KIESEL), or habitational name for someone from a place named with this word.

GIVEN NAMES German 10%. *Detlef, Dieter, Hedwig, Reinhard, Siegfried.*

Kiesling (510) German: topographic name for someone who lived in an area of gravelly land, from Middle High German *kiselinc* 'gravel', a derivative of Old High German *kisil* 'pebble', 'gravel' (see KIESEL). There are various minor places named with this word, and the surname may also be a habitational name from any of these.
GIVEN NAMES German 7%. *Kurt* (2), *Bernhardt, Ernst, Erwin, Gerhard, Heinz, Helmut, Horst, Otto.*

Kiesow (308) German: habitational name from Kiesow, a place near the Baltic port of Stralsund.
GIVEN NAMES German 5%. *Kurt* (2), *Ernst, Lutz, Ulrich.*

Kiess (228) German: variant spelling of KIES.
GIVEN NAMES German 5%. *Erwin, Klaus, Kurt, Manfred.*

Kiessling (386) German: variant spelling of KIESLING.
GIVEN NAMES German 11%. *Kurt* (3), *Bodo* (2), *Otto* (2), *Bernhard, Dieter, Gerd, Gerhard, Hans, Hermann, Wolf.*

Kiester (236) Possibly a variant of German KISTER.

Kietzman (226) 1. German (**Kietzmann**; found mainly in Brandenburg and eastern Germany generally): 2. topographic name for someone living in a (fisherman's) cottage, or (by extension) an occupational name for a fisherman, from Sorbian *kyza* '(fisherman's) hut'. 3. habitational name from any of the places in eastern Germany named Kietz, from Sorbian *kyza* 'hut', 'dwelling' (see 1 above). 4. in Western Germany, perhaps also an occupational name for a basketmaker or for a peddler carrying a basket, from the dialect word *Kieze* 'basket'.

Kieu (125) Vietnamese: unexplained.
GIVEN NAMES Vietnamese 69%; Chinese 11%. *Thanh* (4), *Trang* (3), *Trinh* (3), *Hanh* (2), *Lan* (2), *Lien* (2), *Loi* (2), *Oanh* (2), *Thang* (2), *Thao* (2), *Thuan* (2), *Tu* (2), *Cho, Phong, Tam, Tap; Chen, Dong, Hang, Ho, Kan, Lung, Sang.*

Kievit (188) 1. Dutch: nickname from *kievit* 'peewit', 'lapwing' (of onomatopoeic origin), an extremely common bird of coastal marshlands. 2. Altered spelling of German cognates **Kiewitt** or **Kiwitt**.

Kifer (596) Dutch, German, and Jewish (Ashkenazic): variant of KIEFER.

Kiff (162) German: topographic name from a Westphalian dialect *Kiff* 'outhouse', 'tied cottage', 'shack'.

Kiffmeyer (104) North German (Westphalia): distinguishing name for a tenant farmer (see MEYER) who lived in a decrepit cottage, from dialect (*kiff* 'shack').
GIVEN NAMES German 9%. *Kurt* (3), *Fritz.*

Kiger (1527) Variant of German GEIGER.

Kiggins (360) Irish: reduced Anglicized form (with redundant English patronymic -*s*) of Gaelic **Mag Uiginn** 'son of the Viking' (see HIGGINS).

Kight (1779) Americanized spelling of German KEITH.

Kightlinger (290) Americanized form of German **Keitlinger**, habitational name for someone from a place with some such name as Keitlingen. Keitlinghausen is the name of a place near Gütersloh in Westphalia, and may be the source.

Kihara (123) Japanese, meaning 'plain of the trees'; found in western Japan. Listed in the Shinsen shōjiroku.
GIVEN NAMES Japanese 42%. *Akinori* (2), *Kenji* (2), *Shinichi* (2), *Atsushi, Eiko, Hayato, Hitoshi, Isamu, Kohei, Koichi, Naoto, Naoya.*

Kihm (134) Swiss German: probably a variant of **Kiem**, an Alemannic variant of KEIM.
GIVEN NAME French 4%. *Emanuelle.*

Kihn (159) German and Jewish (Ashkenazic): variant of **Kühn** (see KUEHN) or KIENE.
GIVEN NAMES German 4%. *Erwin* (2), *Hans.*

Kijak (113) Polish: patronymic from *Kij*, a nickname based on *kij* 'stick'.
GIVEN NAMES Polish 6%. *Krzysztof, Ryszard.*

Kijek (125) Polish: nickname from *kijek* 'little stick'.
GIVEN NAMES Polish 6%. *Janina, Katarzyna.*

Kijowski (172) Polish: habitational name for someone from Kijów in Częstochowa voivodeship, or from Kijowice, or sometimes possibly from the city of Kiev (Polish *Kijów*), now the capital of Ukraine, all named with Polish *kij* 'stick'.
GIVEN NAMES Polish 4%. *Grazyna, Wojciech.*

Kikel (109) German: unexplained.
GIVEN NAMES German 10%. *Alois, Erwin, Hans.*

Kiker (953) Perhaps an altered spelling of German GIGER or of **Kiecker**, a habitational name for someone from a place called Kieck near Potsdam or, more likely, from an agent derivative of Low German *kieken* 'to look', hence a nickname for an inquisitive person.

Kikta (132) Polish: probably a nickname from *kik, kikut* 'stump', as a topographic name or a nickname.

Kikuchi (351) Japanese: 'chrysanthemum pond' (also read **Kikuike**); found mostly in western Japan. Another rendering, substituting the character 'ground' for 'pond' (both *chi*), is found in northeastern Japan and the island of Kyūshū. An ancient variant, *Kukuchi* of Higo (now Kumamoto prefecture), is listed in the Shinsen shōjiroku.
GIVEN NAMES Japanese 67%. *Takashi* (4), *Hideo* (3), *Hiroshi* (3), *Kazuo* (3), *Masato* (3), *Minoru* (3), *Satoshi* (3), *Tadashi* (3), *Chihiro* (2), *Hideki* (2), *Hiromi* (2), *Isamu* (2).

Kil (165) 1. Korean: There is one Chinese character for the Kil surname. In the 1930

census, there was a significantly larger number of Kils living in Korea; it was the 62nd most common name in Korea. In a census taken after the Korean War, however, it had dropped to 72nd. The postwar census includes only South Korea, so it can be assumed that a relatively large number of Kils live in North Korea. There is only one Kil clan, Haep'yŏng. The origins of the surname are uncertain; it is believed to have originated in China. The surname Kil appears in Shilla period records, and so it is known to be old and well established. **2.** Jewish (Ashkenazic): of uncertain origin; perhaps a nickname from Yiddish *kil* 'cool'.
GIVEN NAMES Korean 55%. *Young* (4), *Eun* (2), *Joon* (2), *Yong* (2), *Byung, Chan, Chang, Chin, Chol Ho, Duck, Hee Ok, Hyun, Hyung, Hyun Ju, Hyung Wook, Ja Young, Ik Soo, Moon, Sun Cha, Sung Kwon, Taesik, Yong Sung, Young Hwan.*

Kilbane (392) Irish: Anglicized form of Gaelic **Mac Giolla Bháin** 'son of the fair-haired lad' (see BAIN).
GIVEN NAMES Irish 10%. *Brendan, James Patrick.*

Kilbarger (119) Probably an Americanized form of Jewish or German **Kilberger**.

Kilber (131) German: metonymic occupational name for a sheep breeder, from *kilber* 'female lamb'.
GIVEN NAMES German 7%. *Armin, Eldor, Erhard.*

Kilberg (103) Jewish (Ashkenazic): ornamental name compound from German *kühl* 'cold' + *Berg* 'hill'.
GIVEN NAMES Jewish 5%. *Hyman, Mordechai.*

Kilborn (363) English: variant spelling of KILBURN.

Kilbourn (494) English: variant spelling of KILBURN.

Kilbourne (641) English: variant spelling of KILBURN.

Kilbride (492) **1.** Irish and Scottish: Anglicized form of Gaelic **Mac Giolla Brighde** (Irish) or **Mac Gille Brighde** (Scottish) 'son of the servant of (Saint) Brigit', more often Anglicized as MCBRIDE. The name *Brighid* (modern *Brigit*) means 'exalted'. Brighid was probably originally a pagan fire goddess, many of whose attributes became attached to the historical figure of St. Brigit of Kildare (452–523), founder of the first Irish convent. **2.** Scottish: habitational name from any of the various places with this name, from Gaelic *cill Brighde* 'church of St. Brigit' (*cill* being from Latin *cella* 'room', 'cell').
GIVEN NAMES Irish 7%. *Kieran* (2), *Aidan.*

Kilburg (297) Swedish: from any of the various places in Sweden called Kilberg, meaning 'wedge mountain'. This name is found chiefly in IA.

Kilburn (1510) English: habitational name from a place in North Yorkshire or one in Derbyshire, both of uncertain etymology. They are possibly named from an Old English personal name *Cylla* or Old English *cyl(e)n* 'kiln' + *burna* 'stream'. The place of this name in London has apparently not contributed to the surname.

Kilbury (141) Probably a respelling of Swedish KILBURG.

Kilby (1577) English: habitational name from a place in Leicestershire, recorded in Domesday Book as *Cilebi*. It was probably originally named with the Old English elements *cild* (see CHILD) + *tūn* 'enclosure', 'settlement'. Compare CHILTON. The second element was then replaced some time after the Danish invasions by the Old Norse form *býr*.
FOREBEARS Christopher Kilby (1705–71), merchant and government contractor of the colonial era, was born in Boston, MA, as was his father, John. According to family tradition, his grandfather John was born in 1632 in Hertfordshire, England.

Kilcoyne (551) Irish: Anglicized form of Gaelic **Mac Giolla Chaoin** 'son of the servant of St. *Caoin*' or 'son of the gentle lad'. *Caoin* is a personal name or adjective meaning 'gentle'.
GIVEN NAMES Irish 9%. *Brendan* (5), *Aidan.*

Kilcrease (446) Americanized form of Scottish GILCHRIST.
FOREBEARS Robert Kilcrease (c. 1750–1808) came from Scotland (probably Kilmarnock) to Edgefield, SC, in about 1770.

Kilcullen (249) Irish: Anglicized form of Gaelic **Mac Giolla Coileáin** or **Mac Giolla Cuilinn**, both of which Woulfe believes originally referred to St. Caillín, i.e. 'son of the servant of St. *Caillín*'. Compare KILGALLON.

Kildahl (108) Norwegian: unexplained.

Kilday (327) Irish: Anglicized form of Gaelic **Mac Giolla Dhé** 'son of the servant of God', from *Dia* 'God'. The name originated with a monastic family in Donegal in the 11th century and has always been more or less confined to northwestern Ireland, where it is usually written **Kildea**.
GIVEN NAME Irish 4%. *Kieran.*

Kildow (291) Irish: variant of KILDUFF. In the modern pronunciation of Irish Gaelic, final -*bh* is often silent.

Kilduff (527) Irish (Connacht): Anglicized form of Gaelic **Mac Giolla Duibh** 'son of the black-haired lad', from *dubh* 'dark', 'black-haired', a very common name and name-forming element in Gaelic.
GIVEN NAMES Irish 6%. *Kieran, Liam.*

Kile (1864) **1.** Norwegian: habitational name from any of thirteen farmsteads name Kile, from Old Norse *kíll* 'wedge', by extension 'narrow bay', 'inlet'. **2.** Topographic name of Dutch origin denoting someone who lived close by a salt-water creek or area of sheltered water, *kil*. **3.** Respelling of German KEIL.

Kilen (185) Norwegian: habitational name from any of several farmsteads named Kilen, from the singular definite form ('the inlet') of KILE.
GIVEN NAME Scandinavian 6%. *Anders.*

Kiley (2271) Irish: see KIELY.
GIVEN NAMES Irish 4%. *Brendan* (2), *James Patrick.*

Kilfoyle (160) Irish: Anglicized form of Gaelic **Mac Giolla Phóil**, patronymic from the personal name *Giolla Phóil* 'servant of (Saint) Paul'.

Kilgallen (197) Irish: variant spelling of KILGALLON.
GIVEN NAME Irish 10%. *Cormac.*

Kilgallon (152) Irish: Anglicized form of Gaelic **Mac Giolla Chaillín** 'son of the servant of St. *Caillín*'. Compare KILCULLEN.

Kilgo (407) American variant of Scottish KILGORE. This name is concentrated in AL.

Kilgore (7389) Scottish: habitational name from Kilgour in Fife, named in Gaelic as 'goat wood', from *coille* 'wood' + *gobhar, gabhar* 'goat'.

Kilgour (226) Scottish: variant spelling of KILGORE.
GIVEN NAME Scottish 4%. *Hamish.*

Kilgus (222) German: from an altered form of the personal name *Kilius*, a Latinate form of KILIAN.

Kilian (1158) German, Dutch, Polish, and Czech (**Kilián**): from the Irish personal name *Cillín* (see KILLEEN). The Irish missionary St. Kilian is the patron saint of Würzburg.
GIVEN NAMES German 4%. *Hans* (3), *Arnd, Fritz, Gunter, Heinz, Helmut, Klaus, Lutz, Otto, Ulrich.*

Kilinski (132) Polish (**Kiliński**): **1.** from the personal name *Kilian*, which is from the Irish personal name *Cillín* (see KILLEEN). St. Kilian was a 7th-century Irish missionary to Franconia and Thuringia, martyred c. 698 at Würzburg, hence the popularity of the personal name in medieval central Europe. **2.** habitational name for someone from a place called Kiliany, named for this saint.

Kilkelly (134) Irish: Anglicized form of Gaelic **Mac Giolla Ceallaigh** 'son of the devotee of (Saint) Ceallach' (see KELLY).
GIVEN NAME Irish 6%. *Bridie.*

Kilkenny (504) Irish: Anglicized form of Gaelic **Mac Giolla Chainnigh** 'son of the devotee of (Saint) Cainneach'.
GIVEN NAMES Irish 8%. *Colm* (2), *Kieran.*

Kilker (250) Probably an altered spelling of Swiss **Kilcher**, which is the Alemannic form of KIRCHER.

Kill (469) **1.** German and Dutch: possibly from a short form of KILIAN. **2.** German: habitational name from the village of Kill in the Eifel. **3.** Jewish: of uncertain origin; perhaps a nickname from Yiddish *kil* 'cool'.

GIVEN NAMES German 5%. *Mathias* (5), *Aloysius*.

Killam (662) Altered spelling of the English habitational name **Kil(l)ham**, from places in Northumberland and East Yorkshire, so named from Old English *cylnum* '(at) the kilns', dative plural of *cyln*.

Kille (228) **1.** English: from a Middle English personal name *Kille*, which is probably of Scandinavian origin. **2.** German: variant of KILIAN.

Killebrew (1023) Evidently an altered form of Cornish **Killigrew**, a habitational name from a place in St. Erme parish, Cornwall, probably named in Cornish as 'hazelnut grove', from *kelly* 'grove' + *cnow* 'hazel trees'.

Killeen (1307) Irish: from an Anglicized form of the Gaelic personal name *Cillín*, a pet form of *Ceallach* (see KELLY). The name was borne by various early Irish saints, including the leader of a 7th-century mission to Franconia and Thuringia, hence the popularity of the personal name *Kilian* in medieval central Europe.
GIVEN NAMES Irish 7%. *Brendan, Donovan, Kieran, Liam*.

Killelea (131) Irish: variant spelling of KILLILEA.

Killen (1497) Irish: Anglicized form of Gaelic **Mac Coilín** 'son of Colin'. According to MacLysaght, the name was that of a gallowglass family from Scotland taken to Ireland by the O'Donnells.

Killens (103) Scottish and Irish: variant of KILLEN, with English patronymic -*s*.

Killey (145) Perhaps an altered spelling of Irish **Kiley** (see KIELY) or Swiss **Kille(r)**, variants of KILIAN or derivatives of the Germanic personal name *Gelther* (cognate with modern *(ver)gelten* 'to repay').

Killgore (504) Scottish: variant spelling of KILGORE.

Killian (4549) **1.** Irish: variant of KILLEEN, found in counties Clare and Galway. **2.** German and Dutch: variant spelling of KILIAN.

Killilea (179) Irish: reduced Anglicized form of Gaelic **Mac Giolla Leith** 'son of the gray lad'.

Killin (141) **1.** Scottish: perhaps a habitational name from Killin in Perthshire. **2.** Irish: variant of KILLEEN. **3.** According to Reaney and Wilson, a variant of **Killing**, a habitational name from Kelling in Norfolk or Nunkeeling in Humberside.

Killingbeck (197) English: habitational name from a place in Seacroft, West Yorkshire, most probably named from an Old Norse personal name *Killing* + Old Norse *bekkr* 'stream'.

Killinger (682) German: **1.** habitational name from Killingen, a place near Ellwangen (Baden-Württemberg), thought to be so named from association with Saint KILIAN. **2.** from a short form of a Germanic personal name cognate with GILBERT (see KILLEY).

Killings (155) **1.** German: from **Killing**, a variant of KILIAN or **Kille** (see KILLEY). **2.** Possibly an altered form of Swiss German **Külling**, a variant of **Küllig**, itself a derivative of **Kille** (see KILLEY), or a topographic name from South German *gülle* 'swamp', 'dung puddle'.

Killingsworth (1704) English: habitational name probably from Killingworth in Tyne and Wear, so named from an Old English personal name *Cylla* + -*ing*- 'associated with' + *worð* 'enclosure'.

Killion (1785) Irish: variant of KILLEEN, found chiefly in Westmeath and Roscommon.

Killip (105) Irish: reduced form of McKILLIP.

Killips (114) Irish: variant of KILLIP, with English patronymic -*s*.

Killman (316) **1.** Respelling of German **Killmann**, probably a derivative of KILIAN. **2.** English: variant of GILLMAN.

Killmer (321) German: variant spelling of KILMER.

Killmeyer (130) German: probably from a variant of KILIAN + Middle High German *meier* 'farmer'.

Killmon (156) Variant of German KILLMAN or English GILLMAN.

Killoran (397) Irish (Sligo): Anglicized spelling of Gaelic **Mac Giolla Luaighrinn** 'son of a devotee of (Saint) *Luaighreann*'.

Killoren (101) Irish: variant of KILLORAN.

Killough (985) Northern Irish variant of a Scottish surname, probably **Killock**, which is from the village of Killoch in Ayrshire. The possibility that it is a variant of **Kelloch** (see KELLOGG) cannot be ruled out.

Killpack (235) English (Midlands): unexplained.

Kilman (272) **1.** Jewish (Ashkenazic): nickname from Yiddish *kil* 'cool' + *man* 'man'. **2.** Scottish: variant of KELMAN. **3.** Possibly an altered spelling of German **Killmann** (see KILLMAN).

Kilmartin (408) Irish: reduced Anglicized form of Gaelic **Mac Giolla Mhartain**, 'son of the servant of (Saint) Martin', sometimes further shortened to MARTIN.
GIVEN NAMES Irish 8%. *Cliona, Declan, Eamonn, Fergus*.

Kilmer (2060) German: variant of GILMER, from the medieval personal name *Gildemir* or *Gilmar*.

Kilmon (121) **1.** Variant of German KILLMAN. **2.** Variant of English GILLMAN.

Kilner (152) English: occupational name for a potter or lime burner, from an agent derivative of Old English *cylen(e)* 'kiln'.

Kilpatrick (5145) **1.** Irish: reduced Anglicized form of Gaelic **Mac Giolla Phádraig** 'son of the servant of (Saint) Patrick' (Irish *Pádraig*). **2.** Scottish: habitational name from any of various places named in Gaelic as *cill Padraig* 'church of (Saint) Patrick'.

Kilpela (121) Finnish (**Kilpelä**): From *kilpi* 'shield' + the local suffix -*la*. Found chiefly in northeastern Finland.

Kilroy (957) Irish: Anglicized form of Gaelic **Mac Giolla Ruaidh** 'son of the red-haired lad'. Compare ROY 1.
GIVEN NAME Irish 4%. *Lorcan*.

Kilsdonk (117) Reduced form of Dutch **van Kilsdonck**, a habitational name for someone from a place in North Brabant called Kilsdonk or Keldonk.

Kilton (158) English: habitational name from a place named Kilton, probably the one in Somerset, from Old English *cylfe* 'club-shaped hill' + *tūn* 'settlement', 'enclosure'. There are other places similarly named in Nottinghamshire and North Yorkshire (Cleveland), which probably have different etymologies.

Kilts (215) Americanized spelling of German **Kilz**, a habitational name from a place named Kilz, or possibly from a field name, possibly of Slavic origin (see KILZER).

Kilty (224) Irish: see KIELTY.

Kilzer (229) German: **1.** variant spelling of **Kelzer**, habitational name for someone from a place called Kilz near Serno, Saxony-Anhalt, district of Zerbst. Several field names composed with a variant, *Kilitz*, in an area once populated by Slavic tribes lend proof to the Slavic origin of this name. **2.** nickname for a noisy person, from an agent derivative of Middle High German *kelzen* 'to shout'.

Kim (43413) **1.** Korean: there is one Chinese character for the surname Kim. Kim is the most common Korean surname, comprising about 20 percent of the Korean population. According to some sources, there are over 600 different Kim clans, but only about 100 have been documented. Kims can be found in virtually every part of Korea. The two largest Kim clans, the Kim family of Kimhae and the Kim family of Kyŏngju, are descended from semi-mythological characters who lived two thousand years ago. According to legend, the Kimhae Kim family founder, Kim Suro, came in answer to a prayer offered by the nine elders of the ancient Karak Kingdom. In 42 AD, these elders met together to pray for a king. In answer to their prayer, they were sent a golden box containing six golden eggs. From the first egg emerged King Su-ro, Karak's first king. The other five eggs became the five kings of Karak's neighboring kingdom, Kaya. The founder of the Kim family of Kyŏngju, Kim Al-ji, had similar origins. In 65 AD the king of Shilla, T'alhae, heard a strange sound from a forest near the Shilla capital, Kyŏngju. On investigation he found a crowing white rooster standing next to a golden egg. From this egg emerged Al-ji, founder of the Kyŏngju Kim family and subsequent king of the Shilla Kingdom. Because Al-ji emerged from a golden egg, King T'alhae bestowed upon the child the surname *Kim*, which means 'gold'. It is estimated that about half of the one hundred or so Kim clans of modern Korea are descended from the Kyŏngju Kim clan. **2.** Swiss German: unexplained.

GIVEN NAMES Korean 67%. *Young* (875), *Yong* (447), *Sung* (374), *Chong* (310), *Jung* (261), *Sang* (256), *Jong* (252), *Jin* (233), *Chang* (218), *Kyung* (214), *Dong* (197), *Kwang* (196), *Jae* (179), *Myung* (155), *Byung* (113), *Chung* (100), *Dae* (75), *Chul* (68), *Myong* (65), *Moon* (64), *Nam* (61), *Seong* (61), *Jeong* (57), *Min* (57).

Kimak (124) Origin unidentified.

Kimball (9743) **1.** English: from the Middle English personal name *Kimbel*, Old English *Cynebeal(d)*, composed of the elements *cyne-* 'royal' + *beald* 'bold', 'brave'. **2.** English: variant spelling of KIMBLE.

Kimbel (328) **1.** English: variant spelling of KIMBALL or KIMBLE. **2.** German: from the medieval personal name *Gimboldt*. Compare KIMPEL.

Kimbell (677) **1.** English: variant spelling of KIMBALL or KIMBLE. **2.** Respelling of German KIMPEL.

Kimber (952) **1.** English: probably a habitational name from East and West Kimber in the parish of Northlew in Devon, so named from Old English *cempa* 'warrior' (or the Old English personal name *Cempa*) + *bearn* 'grove', 'wood'. It may also be an altered form of KIMBROUGH. **2.** Jewish (Ashkenazic): variant of KINBERG.

Kimberley (212) English: habitational name from any of three places so named, in Nottinghamshire, Warwickshire, and Norfolk. The one in Nottinghamshire, *Chinemarelie* in Domesday Book, is 'woodland clearing of Cynemær', from an Old English personal name composed of the elements *cyne-* 'royal' + *mær* 'fame', with *lēah* 'clearing'. The one in Warwickshire, recorded in 1311 as *Kynebaldeleye*, is 'Cynebald's clearing' (see KEMBLE). The one in Norfolk, *Chineburlai* in Domesday Book, is 'Cyneburh's clearing' (see KIMBROUGH).

Kimberlin (875) Variant of South German **Kümperling** or **Gemperlein**, from Middle High German *gampen* 'to jump', hence a nickname for an acrobat or juggler, or from a Germanic personal name based on Old High German *gund* 'battle'.

Kimberling (478) Variant of German KIMBERLIN.

Kimberly (675) English: variant spelling of KIMBERLEY.

Kimble (5277) **1.** English: variant spelling of KIMBALL. **2.** English: habitational name from Great or Little Kimble in Buckinghamshire, named in Old English as 'the royal bell' (*cynebelle*), referring to the shape of a local hill. **3.** Americanized

spelling of German **Gimbel** (see GIMBLE) or KIMBEL.

Kimbler (421) Americanized form of German **Kimmler** (see KIMLER).

Kimbley (169) English: reduced form of KIMBERLEY.

Kimbrel (393) Cornish: variant of KIMBRELL.

Kimbrell (2195) Cornish: unexplained.

Kimbriel (106) Probably a variant of Cornish KIMBRELL.

Kimbro (964) English: variant spelling of KIMBROUGH.

Kimbrough (3502) English: from the female personal name *Kynborough*, recorded in Suffolk, England, as late as the 16th and 17th centuries. Although there is no Middle English evidence for it, this probably represents a survival of Old English female personal name *Cyneburh*, composed of the elements *cyne-* 'royal' + *burh* 'fortress', 'stronghold'. This was the name of a daughter of the 7th-century King Penda of Mercia, who, in spite of her father's staunch opposition to Christianity, was converted and founded an abbey, serving as its head. She was venerated as a saint, and gave her name to the village of Kimberley in Norfolk. The surname is now almost extinct in England, but continues to flourish in the U.S.

Kime (1134) **1.** Americanized spelling of German KEIM. **2.** Bulgarian (**Kimé**): southern variant of *Kímo*, a pet form of *Jakim* or *Kimon*, from the personal name *Joakim* (see JOACHIM).

Kimel (189) Variant of German and Jewish (Ashkenazic) KIMMEL.

Kimelman (104) Jewish (Ashkenazic): elaborated form of KIMEL.

GIVEN NAMES Jewish 15%. *Hyman* (2), *Gerson, Hava, Nili, Reuven, Yaron.*

Kimery (221) English: variant of KEMERY.

Kimes (1000) English or Scottish: unexplained.

Kimler (229) German: reduced form of **Kimmeler**, an occupational name for a spicer, from KIMMEL + the agent suffix *-er*.

Kimm (334) **1.** English: from a Middle English personal name, *Kymme*, which Reaney regards as a pet form of the Old English female personal name *Cyneburh* (see KIMBROUGH). **2.** Reduced form of Scottish McKIM. **3.** German: probably a metonymic occupational name for a cooper, from Middle High German *kimme*, a term denoting the notch in the staves of a barrel where the base is seated; by extension it also has the meaning 'edge', 'horizon' and in this sense may also have given rise to a topographic name.

Kimmel (4018) German and Jewish (Ashkenazic): from Middle High German *kumin*, German **Kümmel** 'caraway' (related to Latin *cuminum*, a word of Oriental origin, like the plant itself), hence a metonymic occupational name for a spicer, literally a

supplier of caraway seeds. Compare CARAWAY, also LORBER and ZIMÊT.

Kimmell (485) Altered spelling of KIMMEL.

Kimmelman (221) Jewish (Ashkenazic): occupational name for a spicer (see KIMMEL).

GIVEN NAMES Jewish 8%; German 5%. *Meyer; Fritz, Ilse, Kurt.*

Kimmer (178) German: **1.** occupational name for a cooper, from an agent derivative of Middle High German *kimme* 'rim', 'flange (on a tub)' (see KIMM 2). **2.** from a short form of the Germanic personal name *Chunibald*, formed with *chunni* 'race', 'people' or *kuoni* 'daring', 'experienced', + *bald* 'bold', 'brave'.

Kimmerle (206) German (Swabian): **1.** probably from **Kümmerle**, a diminutive of *Kummer* 'grief', 'trouble' (see KUMMER). As a name, this probably has the force of a nickname meaning 'miserable creature'. **2.** variant of KIMMER 3.

GIVEN NAMES German 5%. *Horst, Kurt.*

Kimmerling (101) German: variant of KIMMERLE.

GIVEN NAME German 4%. *Kurt.*

Kimmerly (135) South German: variant of KIMMERLE.

Kimmes (183) Dutch: from a Latinized form of *keim* 'way', 'street'.

Kimmet (251) Perhaps a derivative of the obsolete German personal name *Kümmet*, *Kühnemut*, Old High German *Cunimund* 'strong guardian' or 'guardian of the tribe'; the first element is *chunni* or *kuoni*, as in KONRAD; the second is *mund* 'guardian'.

Kimmey (401) Scottish: habitational name for someone from Kemnay in Aberdeenshire.

Kimmich (192) German (Swabian) and Swiss German: from the Alemannic dialect word *Kim(m)ich* 'cumin', 'caraway', hence a metonymic occupational name for a spicer. See KIMMEL.

GIVEN NAMES German 12%. *Erwin* (2), *Otto* (2), *Christoph, Dietrich, Kurt, Ulrich.*

Kimmick (117) **1.** Scottish: reduced form of **McKimmick**, a pet form of Gaelic **Mac Shimidh**, patronymic from *Simidh*, Gaelic form of SIMON (see McKIMMY). **2.** German: variant of **Kimmig** (see KIMMICH).

Kimminau (125) German: habitational name from Kemmenau in the Rhineland-Palatinate.

Kimmins (160) Scottish and Irish: variant of KIMMONS.

GIVEN NAME Irish 6%. *Brendan.*

Kimmons (551) Scottish and Irish: Anglicized form of Gaelic **Mac Shiomóin** 'son of Simon' (Gaelic *Sh-* is pronounced as *H-*). The *K-* in this name represents the Gaelic patronymic form *Mac*, while the final *-s* represents an English patronymic ending.

Kimoto (139) Japanese: '(one who lives) beneath the trees'; found in western Japan.

GIVEN NAMES Japanese 47%. *Takashi* (2), *Atsushi, Hanayo, Hayato, Isami, Isao,*

Itaru, Junji, Kazushi, Kenji, Mamoru, Masahiro.

Kimpel (430) Jewish (Ashkenazic) and German: variant of GIMPEL.

Kimple (191) Americanized spelling of KIMPEL.

Kimpton (198) English: **1.** habitational name from places in Hertfordshire and Hampshire, both named from the Old English personal name *Cȳma* + Old English *tūn* 'settlement'. **2.** variant of KEMPTON.

Kimrey (477) Perhaps an altered form of English KIMBROUGH or KEMERY.

Kimsey (1015) English: habitational name from a place called Kempsey in Worcestershire, recorded in Domesday Book as *Chemesege*, from an Old English personal name *Cymi* + *ēg* 'island', 'area of dry land in a marsh'.

Kimura (1308) Japanese: very common place name and surname, especially in western and northeastern Japan. Variously written, the original meaning is 'tree village'. Some bearers are descended from the FUJIWARA, Mononobe, and other noble families.
GIVEN NAMES Japanese 57%. *Hiroshi* (11), *Shigeru* (10), *Kazuo* (7), *Takeshi* (7), *Shigeo* (6), *Yoshio* (6), *Akira* (5), *Hideo* (5), *Kaz* (5), *Makoto* (5), *Noriko* (5), *Toyoshi* (5).

Kimzey (364) Apparently an altered spelling of English KIMSEY.

Kin (397) **1.** English: from a Middle English personal name, *Kin, Kinna*, which is a shortened form of any of various Old English names beginning with *Cyne* 'royal', for example *Cynesige* (see KINSEY). **2.** Dutch: nickname for someone with a pointed or jutting chin. **3.** Dutch: from Middle Dutch *kinne* 'kin'. **4.** Hungarian: nickname from *kín* 'pain'. **5.** Variant of Korean KIM.
GIVEN NAMES Korean 33%. *Sang* (4), *Young* (4), *Chong* (2), *Chun* (2), *Hak* (2), *Kwang* (2), *Song* (2), *Tae Wan* (2), *Yong* (2), *Yung* (2), *Aeja, Chin, Chul, Dong Joo, Dongil, Doo, Eng, Hee Chul, Hyeok, Hyung Joon, In-Young, Jong Woo, Min, Moon*.

Kinahan (127) Irish: Anglicized form of Gaelic **Ó Coinneacháin**, from the personal name *Coinneachan*, pet form of *Coinneach* (see KENNETH).
GIVEN NAMES Irish 11%. *Caitlin, Eoin*.

Kinane (110) Irish: variant of KINAHAN.

Kinard (2204) Scottish: variant of KINNAIRD.

Kinberg (104) Jewish (Ashkenazic): ornamental name from a compound of German *Kien* 'pine' + *Berg* 'mountain', 'hill'.
GIVEN NAMES Jewish 5%. *Aron, Dovid, Yoram*.

Kincade (912) Scottish: variant spelling of KINCAID.

Kincaid (6576) Scottish: habitational name from a place near Lennoxtown, north of Glasgow, which is first recorded in 1238 as *Kincaith* and in 1250 as *Kincathe*. The for-

mer spelling suggests derivation from Gaelic *ceann* 'head', 'top' + *càithe* 'pass', whereas the latter would point to *cadha* 'quagmire' as the second element.

Kincaide (125) Scottish: variant spelling of KINCAID.

Kincannon (450) Irish: variant of CONCANNON.

Kincer (483) Slavic spelling of German KINTZER.

Kinch (653) **1.** English: of uncertain origin; perhaps a shortened form of KINCHEN. **2.** Irish: reduced form of the Gaelic patronymic **Mac Aonghuis** 'son of Angus' (see McGINNIS). **3.** Anglicized spelling of South German **Kintsch**, a variant of **Künz** (see KUNTZ).

Kincheloe (711) Americanized form of Irish KINSELLA. In this form, it is a very common surname among African Americans, originating on a plantation in Virginia.

Kinchen (747) **1.** English: of uncertain origin; it may be from the thieves' slang term *kinchin* 'child', which is probably a derivative of German *Kindchen*, diminutive of *Kind* 'child'. **2.** Americanized form of **Kindchen** or more probably of Rhenish **Kindgen** (pronounced 'kintshen'), both diminutives of KIND.

Kincy (142) **1.** Variant of English KINSEY. **2.** Variant of German KINZIE.
GIVEN NAME French 5%. *Autrey*.

Kind (598) **1.** German and Jewish (Ashkenazic): from Middle High German *kint*, German *Kind* 'child', hence a nickname for someone with a childish or naive disposition, or an epithet used to distinguish between a father and his son. In some cases it may be a short form of any of various names ending in *-kind*, a patronymic ending of Jewish surnames. **2.** Dutch: variant spelling of KINT, cognate with 1, also found in such forms as **'t Kind** and compounds such as JONGKIND. **3.** English: nickname from Middle English *kind* (Old English *gecynde*) in any of its many senses: 'legitimate', 'dutiful', 'benevolent', 'loving', 'gracious'.
GIVEN NAMES German 6%. *Otto* (2), *Uwe* (2), *Juergen, Klaus, Kurt, Reinhart, Siegfried, Volker*.

Kindall (272) English: variant of KENDALL.

Kindberg (162) **1.** Danish: habitational name from a place called Kindbjerg. **2.** Swedish: ornamental name formed with the place-name element *kind-* 'family', 'tribe' + *berg* 'mountain'. **3.** Possibly Ashkenazic Jewish, an ornamental name from German *Kind* 'child' + *Berg* 'mountain', 'hill': possibly an allusive nickname for someone with many children.
GIVEN NAME German 7%; Scandinavian 7%. *Fritz*.

Kindel (361) German: **1.** diminutive of KIND. **2.** altered spelling of *Kiendl*, a pet form of the personal name KONRAD.

Kindell (330) **1.** English: variant of KENDALL. **2.** Americanized spelling of German KINDEL. **3.** Swedish: ornamental name formed with the place-name element *kind-* 'family', 'tribe' + the adjectival suffix *-ell*, taken from the Latin adjectival ending *-elius*.

Kinder (3818) **1.** English: habitational name from a place in Derbyshire, of unknown etymology (probably a pre-English hill name, but the form is obscure). **2.** German: from the genitive plural of *Kind* 'child', possibly denoting someone who had a lot of children, as in *Hans der Kinder* 'Hans of the children' (Eisleben 15th century), or short for some compound such as **Kindervater** 'male midwife' or **Kinderfreund** 'one who likes children'. **3.** German: variant of **Günther** (see GUENTHER).

Kinderknecht (141) German: probably an occupational name for a servant in charge of the children at a manor, from *Kinder*, the plural of *Kind* 'child' + *Knecht* 'servant'. Compare the surnames **Herrenknecht** 'lords' servant', **Frauenknecht** 'ladies' servant'.

Kinderman (322) **1.** Americanized spelling of German **Kindermann**, or Jewish (Ashkenazic): occupational name for a schoolteacher, literally 'children man'. **2.** It may also be an altered form of the German surname **Kunterman**, a derivative of the personal name *Günther* (see GUENTHER).

Kindig (568) German: nickname from *kündig* or *kundig* (later *kindig*) 'skillful', 'knowledgeable', 'clever'.

Kindl (109) German: variant spelling of KINDEL.
GIVEN NAMES German 7%; Czech and Slovak 4%. *Dietrich, Siegbert, Siegfried; Ladislav, Ludvik*.

Kindle (1148) **1.** English: variant of KENDALL. **2.** Variant of German KINDEL.

Kindler (485) **1.** German: from an agent derivative of the obsolete verb *kindeln* 'to beget children', hence a nickname for someone who had a lot of children. **2.** Jewish (Ashkenazic): from German *Kind* 'child' + the agent suffix *-ler*, most likely an occupational name for a schoolteacher.
GIVEN NAMES German 6%. *Fritz* (3), *Hans* (2), *Erwin, Heinz, Klaus, Manfred, Mathias, Willi*.

Kindley (304) **1.** Americanized spelling of southern German and Swiss **Kindle**, earlier **Kindeli**, a diminutive of KIND (compare KINDEL). **2.** Americanized spelling of German KINDLER.

Kindred (1634) English: probably a variant of KENDRICK.

Kindrick (327) English, Scottish, Irish, and Welsh: variant of KENDRICK.

Kindschi (131) South German: variant of *Kintschi*, a pet form of the personal name KONRAD.

Kindt (616) Variant spelling of German and Jewish (Ashkenazic) KIND or Dutch KINT.

GIVEN NAMES German 4%. *Kurt* (3), *Hans* (2), *Fritz*.

Kindy (173) Probably an altered spelling of German KINDIG or Swiss German **Kündig** (see KUNDINGER).

Kiner (451) **1.** Jewish (Ashkenazic): metonymic occupational name for a violinist, from Hebrew *kinoyr* 'violin'. **2.** Altered spelling of German KEINER.

Kines (303) **1.** Jewish (Ashkenazic): unexplained. **2.** Americanized spelling of Austrian German **Kainz**, from a Tyrolean dialect pet form of KONRAD.

King (153615) **1.** English and Scottish: nickname from Middle English *king*, Old English *cyning* 'king' (originally merely a tribal leader, from Old English *cyn(n)* 'tribe', 'race' + the Germanic suffix *-ing*). The word was already used as a byname before the Norman Conquest, and the nickname was common in the Middle Ages, being used to refer to someone who conducted himself in a kingly manner, or one who had played the part of a king in a pageant, or one who had won the title in a tournament. In other cases it may actually have referred to someone who served in the king's household. The American surname has absorbed several European cognates and equivalents with the same meaning, for example German **König** (see KOENIG), Swiss German **Küng**, French LEROY. It is also found as an Ashkenazic Jewish surname, of ornamental origin. **2.** Chinese 金: variant of JIN 1. **3.** Chinese 景, 荆, 井, 金: see JING.

Kingan (133) Scottish: variant of Irish Gaelic **Ó Cuineáin** (see QUEENAN).

Kingcade (103) Variant of Scottish KINCAID.

Kingdom (101) English: variant of KINGDON.

Kingdon (284) English (Devon): habitational name from Higher Kingdon in Alverdiscott, Devon, or from Kendon in North Bovey, Devon. Both are named in Old English as 'the king's hill', from *cyning* (see KING) or *cyne-* 'royal' + *dūn* 'hill'.

Kingen (145) Scottish: variant of KINGAN.

Kingery (1737) Swiss German: Americanized form of GINGRICH.

Kingham (192) English: habitational name from a place in Oxfordshire, named in Old English as *Cǣgingahām*, 'homestead (Old English *hā*) of Cǣga's people'.

Kinghorn (445) Scottish: habitational name from Kinghorn in Fife. This is recorded as *Kyngorn* in 1374; it is named in Gaelic from *ceann* 'head', 'height' + *gronna* 'bog'. The modern spelling is the result of folk etymology.

Kingma (240) Frisian: patronymic from the personal name *Kinge*.

GIVEN NAMES Dutch 6%. *Cornelis* (2), *Dirk, Gerben, Gerrit, Marten*.

Kingman (642) English: status name denoting a servant of the king, a member of the king's household.

Kingrey (343) Americanized form of Swiss German GINGRICH.

Kingry (205) Americanized form of Swiss German GINGRICH.

Kings (123) English: variant of KING.

Kingsberry (129) English: variant of KINGSBURY.

Kingsbury (2674) English: habitational name from any of several places, for example in northwest London (formerly Middlesex), Somerset, and Warwickshire. These are mostly named in Old English as *cyninges burh* 'the king's stronghold', but the last mentioned is *Cynesburh* 'stronghold of Cyne'. *Cyne* is a short form of any of various compound names with *cyne-* 'royal' as the first element.

Kingsford (165) English: habitational name from any of various places named Kingsford, for example in Essex, Devon, Warwickshire, and Worcestershire. The name ostensibly means 'the king's ford', but the one in Worcestershire is named as *Cēningaford* 'ford of Cēna's people'.

Kingsland (358) English: **1.** habitational name from any of ten or more minor places known as 'the king's land', such as Kingsland in South Molton, Devon, or Kingsland in Hackney, Greater London (formerly Middlesex), both named from Middle English *kingis* 'of the king' + *land* 'land'. **2.** habitational name from Kingsland in Herefordshire near Leominster, which is named as 'the king's estate in Leon'. *Leon* is the old Celtic name for the district, meaning 'at the streams'.

Kingsley (3183) English: habitational name from any of the places so called, in Cheshire, Hampshire, and Staffordshire. These are all named in Old English as *cyningeslēah* 'the woodland clearing (Old English *lēah*) of the king (*cyning*)'.

Kingsmore (123) English: probably a habitational name from any of several places named Kingsmoor or King's Moor, in Somerset, Sussex, and Essex.

Kingsolver (148) Altered form of English **Consolver**, which is unexplained. Compare KINSOLVING.

FOREBEARS Charles Consolver, of Albemarle Co., VA, in the 1770s, had two sons: James started the Kinsolving family; his brother, Martin, started the Kin(g)solver family.

Kingston (2482) English: habitational name from any of the numerous places throughout England called Kingston or Kingstone. Almost all of them, regardless of the distinction in spelling, were originally named in Old English as *cyningestūn* 'the king's settlement', i.e. royal manor. However, Kingston upon Soar in Nottinghamshire is named as 'royal stone', while

Kingstone in Somerset is 'king's stone'; both probably being named for some local monument.

Kington (178) English: habitational name from any of the various places so called, in Dorset, Herefordshire, Warwickshire, Wiltshire, and Worcestershire. These are named from Old French *cyne-* 'royal' (replaced by Old English *cyning* 'king') + *tūn* 'settlement'.

Kinion (302) Irish and Scottish: reduced Americanized form of **Mac Fhionghuin** (see MCKINNON).

Kiniry (173) Irish: reduced form of MCENERY, an Americanized form of **Mac Innéirghe** 'son of *Innéirghe*'.

Kinkade (1016) Northern Irish: variant of KINCAID.

Kinkaid (318) Scottish and northern Irish: variant of KINCAID.

Kinkead (776) Northern Irish: variant of KINCAID.

Kinkel (294) German: variant of **Künkel** (see KUNKEL).

GIVEN NAMES German 4%. *Konrad* (2), *Erna, Erwin, Otto*.

Kinker (208) Dutch: **1.** nickname from an agent derivative of *kincken, kichen* 'to gasp or wheeze' or of *kinken* 'to sound'. **2.** spelling variant of Middle Dutch *quinker*, nickname for someone who darted around, from *quinken* 'to move quickly, dart', 'to flicker or twinkle'. **3.** Austrian German: from a derivative of *Kink*, a variant of *Königer*, from a Germanic personal name based on *kuoni* 'daring', 'experienced' or *chunni, kuni* 'race', 'people'.

Kinkle (147) Americanized spelling of German KUNKEL.

Kinlaw (634) Irish: variant of Scottish KINLEY.

Kinler (120) Irish: variant of Scottish KINLEY.

GIVEN NAMES French 5%; Welsh 4%. *Emile; Rhys*.

Kinley (1054) Reduced form of Scottish MCKINLEY.

Kinloch (215) Scottish: habitational name from any of various places that derive their names from Gaelic *ceann* 'head(land)' + *loch* 'loch'. The most likely source of the surname is Kinloch at the head of Loch Rossie (now drained) in Fife, where a certain John Kinloch is recorded in charters dating from around 1240.

GIVEN NAMES Scottish 4%. *Alastair, Iain*.

Kinman (804) **1.** English: either an occupational name for a cowherd, from Middle English *kineman* 'cattle man' (not recorded except as a surname), or more probably from a Middle English survival of the Old English personal name *Cynemann* 'royal man', i.e. the king's man. **2.** Scottish: according to Black, a reduced form of **Kininmonth**, a habitational name from either of two places so named in Fife; alternatively, it may be a variant of **Kinmont**, a habitational name from a place named Kinmont, in Annandale in the Borders. **3.** Jewish (Ashkenazic): see KIN. **4.** Altered spelling of German **Kinmann** (see KUEHN).

Kinn (358) **1.** English: from a Middle English personal name, which originated as a short form of any of various Old English personal names beginning with *Cyne-* 'royal'. **2.** German: nickname for someone with a prominent chin, from Middle High German *kinne* 'chin', or from an Old High German personal name formed with the element *kuoni* 'bold' or *chunni* 'race', 'people'. Compare KONRAD. **3.** Norwegian: habitational name from any of several farmsteads named Kinn, from Old Norse *kinn* 'chin' with reference to the land formation.

Kinna (110) Irish and Scottish: reduced form of MCKENNA.
GIVEN NAME Irish 4%. *Brendan*.

Kinnaird (581) Scottish: habitational name from a place so called in Perthshire, which is named in Gaelic from *ceann* 'head' + *aird* 'height', i.e. 'summit', 'peak'.

Kinnaman (569) Respelling of German **Kinnemann**, a variant of **Kinmann** (see KUEHN).

Kinnamon (459) German: see KINNAMAN.

Kinnan (284) Irish: reduced Anglicized form of Gaelic **Mac Fhionnáin** 'son of *Fionnán*', a pet form of FINN, or of **Ó Cianáin** (see KEENAN), **Ó Cuinneáin**, or **Ó Cuineáin** (see CUNNEEN).

Kinnane (110) Irish: reduced Anglicized form of Gaelic **Ó Cuinneáin** 'descendant of *Cuinneán*' (see GUINAN).
GIVEN NAME Irish 7%. *Brendan*.

Kinnard (895) Scottish: variant of KINNAIRD.

Kinne (944) **1.** German: from the female personal name *Kinne*, a Silesian pet form of Middle High German *Kunigunde*, composed of the Old High German elements *kuoni* 'brave' + *gund* 'battle'. **2.** Dutch: from Middle Dutch *kinne* 'relative', possibly denoting someone who was the relative of a prominent person.

Kinnear (677) Scottish: habitational name from Kinneir in Fife, first recorded at the beginning of the 13th century as *Kyner*, apparently from Gaelic *ceann* 'head(land)' + *iar* 'west'.

Kinnebrew (176) Americanized form of Scottish **Kinniburgh**, from the female personal name *Kynborough*, a survival of Old English female personal name *Cyneburh*. Compare English KIMBROUGH.
GIVEN NAME French 4%. *Easton* (2).

Kinnee (155) Variant of Scottish KINNEY.

Kinneer (128) Respelling of Scottish KINNEAR.

Kinneman (126) **1.** Variant of North German **Kennemann**, a derivative of the Frisian personal name *Keno*. **2.** German: see KINNAMAN and KINMAN 4. **3.** Possibly also an old spelling of English KINMAN.

Kinner (575) **1.** German: variant of KINDER 2. **2.** German: habitational name for someone from a place called Kinne, near Bissingen. **3.** Perhaps also a reduced form of Irish KINNEAR; the name is found in this spelling in northern Ireland and England.

Kinnett (451) English: from a Middle English personal name, *Kinnet*, *Kynot*, pet forms of *Kine* (see KINN).

Kinney (12002) Scottish: reduced form of MCKINNEY.

Kinnick (251) Scottish: Anglicized form of the Gaelic personal name *Coinneach* (see KENNETH).

Kinnie (153) Scottish: variant spelling of KINNEY.

Kinnison (693) Scottish: **1.** variant of **Cunieson**, a patronymic from the personal name *Conan*, which was borne by an illegitimate son of Henry, Duke of Atholl, from whom many bearers are descended. **2.** patronymic from an Anglicized form of the Gaelic personal name *Coinneach* (see KENNETH).

Kinnon (111) Scottish: reduced form of MACKINNON.
GIVEN NAME French 6%. *Patrice*.

Kinnunen (295) Finnish: of uncertain origin. Possibly a derivative of Swedish *skinn* '(animal) skin' + the common surname Finnish suffix *-nen*. This is a common name in the east-central region of Finland, particularly in Kainuu.
GIVEN NAMES Finnish 9%. *Reino* (6), *Markku*, *Timo*, *Toivo*, *Waino*, *Wilho*.

Kinoshita (428) Japanese: meaning '(one who lives) under a tree'; the surname is found throughout Japan and the Ryūkyū Islands. The most famous bearer of this name, Kinoshita Tōkichi, used several names throughout his career and is best remembered as Toyotomi Hideyoshi, the brilliant general who unified Japan at the end of the 16th century. It is doubtful, however, that anyone named Kinoshita is his descendant.
GIVEN NAMES Japanese 53%. *Keiji* (3), *Koichi* (3), *Masao* (3), *Takashi* (3), *Yoshito* (3), *Fumio* (2), *Hide* (2), *Hiromi* (2), *Ichiro* (2), *Kazunori* (2), *Kazuo* (2), *Noboru* (2).

Kinsel (465) **1.** Americanized form of the German family names KINZEL or **Künzel** (see KUENZEL). **2.** Perhaps also an Americanized form of Irish KINSELLA.

Kinsell (144) See KINSEL.

Kinsella (1551) Irish (Wexford): Anglicized form of Gaelic **Uí Ceinnsealaigh** 'descendant of *Cinnsealach*', a personal name probably meaning 'chief warrior'.
GIVEN NAMES Irish 6%. *Brendan* (2), *Ciaran*, *Donal*, *Finbar*, *Fintan*.

Kinser (1826) Americanized spelling of German KINZER or **Kintzer** (see KINTZ).

Kinsey (5396) **1.** English: from the Middle English personal name *Kynsey*, a survival of Old English *Cynesige*, composed of the elements *cyne* 'royal' + *sige* 'victory'.

2. This name may also have assimilated some cases of Scottish MACKENZIE, with the *Mac* prefix omitted. **3.** Possibly an Americanized spelling of Swiss German **Künzi** (see KUENZI).
FOREBEARS The paternal grandfather of NJ and PA legislator John Kinsey (1693–1750) was one of the commissioners sent out from England in 1677 by the West Jersey proprietors to buy land from the Indians and to lay out a town. John was the leader of the Quaker party in the PA assembly and chief justice of the PA supreme court.

Kinsinger (393) Swiss German: variant of KENSINGER. This is the name of a Swiss Mennonite family whose name appears in several other forms: **Kenzinger, Kentzinger, Kinnzinger, Kitzinger**.

Kinsler (555) Americanized form of German **Künzler** (see KUNZLER).

Kinsley (1071) **1.** English: habitational name from Kinsley in West Yorkshire, recorded in Domesday Book as *Chineslai* 'woodland clearing (Old English *lēah*) of a man called Cyne'. **2.** Probably also an altered spelling of various like-sounding German names, such as KINZLER, **Kinseli, Künzli** or **Künzle** (see KUENZLI).

Kinslow (775) **1.** English: perhaps a habitational name from a minor place in Derbyshire named Kenslow, though the surname is now found in Kent rather than Derbyshire. **2.** Possibly also an Americanized form of German KINZLER.

Kinsman (1010) English: from Middle English *kinnesman*, 'kinsman', 'relative', probably denoting a kinsman of some important noble or royal personage.

Kinsolving (106) Altered form of English **Consolver**, which is unexplained.

Kinson (114) English (now chiefly Leicestershire): habitational name from either of two places called Kinson, one in Shropshire and the other in Dorset, which is named from the Old English personal name *Cynestān* + Old English *tūn*.
GIVEN NAME French 6%. *Henri* (2).

Kinstle (125) Americanized form of German **Künstle** or **Künstel**, from a pet form of the personal name KONRAD.

Kinstler (243) Americanized form or Jewish (Ashkenazic) form of German **Künstler** (see KUENSTLER).

Kint (179) **1.** Dutch: nickname from Middle Dutch *kint* 'child'. **2.** German: variant of KIND, possibly derived from pet forms *Kintlein* or *Kintling* 'little child'.
FOREBEARS A Hendrick Pietersz Kint also known as Kint int Water, 'child in the water,' occurs in New Amsterdam.

Kinter (427) **1.** German: possibly a derivative of Middle High German *kint* 'child', or alternatively from *Kinter*, a regional variant of the personal name *Günther* (see GUENTHER). **2.** Czech: from the German personal name *Günther* (see GUEN-THER).

Kintigh (168) Americanized spelling of German **Kündig**, a pet form of KONRAD, or an altered spelling of KINDIG.

Kintner (548) Probably an altered spelling of **Günthner** (see GUENTHER).

Kinton (202) English: habitational name from Kinton in Herefordshire, Kineton in Warwickshire (both named with Old English *cyne-* 'royal' + *tūn* 'settlement'), or Kineton in Gloucestershire, which is named with Old English *cyning* 'king' + *tūn*.

Kintop (102) German: variant spelling of **Kientop(f)** or **Kühntop(f)**, habitational names from a place called Köntopf in Pomerania.

Kintz (684) German: from a South German or Silesian variant of the personal name **Küntz** (see KUNTZ).

Kintzel (151) German: from a South German or Silesian variant of the personal name **Küntzel** (see KUENZEL).

GIVEN NAMES German 6%. *Bernd, Willi.*

Kintzer (116) German: variant of KINTZ.

Kinville (112) Respelling of French QUENNEVILLE.

Kinworthy (107) Variant of English KEN-WORTHY.

Kinyon (542) English: variant of KENYON.

Kinzel (556) German: variant spelling of **Kintzel** (see KINTZ).

GIVEN NAMES German 7%. *Otto* (4), *Florian* (2), *Franz* (2), *Dietmar, Heinz, Juergen, Kurt, Wolfgang.*

Kinzer (1091) South German: variant of **Kintzer** (see KINTZ) or **Künzer** (see KUN-ZER).

Kinzey (168) **1.** Scottish: variant of MCKENZIE. **2.** English: variant of KINSEY.

Kinzie (565) Scottish: variant of MCKEN-ZIE.

FOREBEARS John Kinzie (1763–1828), a fur trader, was born at Quebec, where his father, John McKenzie, had come over as a surgeon with the British army. The younger John changed his name to Kinzie and began trading with Indians on the Maumee and St. Joseph rivers after 1781. In or after 1804 he moved to what is now Chicago, where there are a subdivision and a street bearing his name.

Kinzler (389) German: variant of KINTZ or **Künzler** (see KUNZLER).

Kio (103) Origin unidentified.

Kious (174) Probably an Americanized form of German **Kiausch**, of uncertain origin.

FOREBEARS Bearers of this name are said to be descended from Johann Kowes, a Hessian mercenary fighting for the British during the Revolutionary War, who changed sides and fought against the British, and changed his name to **Kious**.

Kip (102) Dutch: metonymic occupational name for a basketmaker, from Middle Dutch *kiepe* 'basket', 'pannier'.

FOREBEARS This name is recorded in Beverwijck in New Netherland (Albany, NY) in the mid 17th century.

Kipe (139) Scottish: this form may well have the same origin as **Kipp**, which according to Black is a habitational name from a small place named Kype in the parish of Avondale in Lanarkshire.

Kiper (428) **1.** Americanized spelling of Dutch KUIPER or North German **Keuper**, occupational name for a cooper. **2.** Altered form of East Prussian **Keiper**, occupational name for someone who caught fish in a trap, from an agent derivative of *keip* 'fish trap', 'weir'. **3.** Altered form of German KAUFER 'merchant'. **4.** Jewish (from Poland and Ukraine): metonymic occupational name for a coppersmith, from central and southeastern Yiddish *kiper* 'copper'. In some instances it may have been adopted as an ornamental name.

Kipfer (263) **1.** Swiss German: topographic name for someone living on or near a peak or summit, from *Kipf* 'edge', 'verge', 'point'. **2.** German: from a derivative of the personal name *Giebfried*, from Old High German *geba* 'gift' + *fridu* 'protection', 'peace'. **3.** South German: from the dialect word *Kipf* or *Kipferl* 'croissant', 'crescent-shaped roll', hence a metonymic occupational name for a baker or pâtissier. **4.** Respelling of Swiss German **Küpfer** (see KUPFER).

Kiphart (110) **1.** German: perhaps an altered form of **Kipphaut**, a North German name meaning 'pointed hat', presumably applied as a nickname for someone who habitually wore one or as a metonymic occupational name for a maker of such hats. **2.** German: probably a respelling of GEBHARDT.

Kipling (143) Northern English: from a minor place in the old East Riding of Yorkshire named Kipling.

Kiplinger (180) German: unexplained.

Kipnis (304) Jewish (from Ukraine): perhaps a nickname from Ukrainian *kyrponis* 'flat-nosed'.

GIVEN NAMES Jewish 13%; Russian 12%. *Faina, Gersh, Leizer, Mariya, Mikhael, Miriam, Naum, Rakhil; Leonid* (5), *Boris* (3), *Mikhail* (3), *Igor* (2), *Lev* (2), *Aleksandr, Alexey, Arkadiy, Arkady, Lyudmila, Michail, Reyzya.*

Kipp (2415) **1.** English: from Middle English *Kipp*, perhaps a byname for a fat man, from an unattested Old English form *Cyppe*, which according to Reaney is from the Germanic root *kupp* 'to swell'. **2.** German: topographic name for someone living on a hill, from *Kippe* 'edge', 'brink'. **3.** German: from Sorbian *kipry* 'weak' (Czech *kyprý*).

Kippen (124) Scottish: habitational name from a place so named in Stirlingshire.

Kipper (380) **1.** German: variant of KIPP. **2.** German: habitational name for someone from a place called Kipper in Westphalia. **3.** Eastern German: from Sorbian *kipry* 'weak', hence a nickname for a frail or weak-willed person. **4.** German: from Middle High German *kipper* 'unfair fighter', hence a nickname for a person of no standing. **5.** Jewish (Ashkenazic): variant of KIPER 4.

GIVEN NAMES Jewish 4%. *Avi, Avram, Berish, Hyman, Meyer.*

Kippes (173) **1.** English: variant of KIPPS. **2.** German: from a Rhenish pet form of the personal name **Gerhard** (see GERHARDT).

Kipping (134) German: habitational name from a place named with Middle High German *kip* 'point', 'peak' or from Kippingen in the Rhineland.

GIVEN NAMES German 5%. *Hans* (3), *Gerhard.*

Kipple (109) South German: **1.** topographic name from dialect *Kipp* 'point' denoting someone who owned or farmed a piece of land with a sharp angle. **2.** from a pet form of a Germanic personal name formed with *geba* 'gift', as in GEBHARDT.

Kipps (141) English: patronymic from KIPP.

Kiracofe (223) **1.** Altered spelling of Dutch **Kircove** or German **Kirchhof**, topographic names for someone living by the church-yard. **2.** Altered spelling of Bulgarian **Kirákov** 'son of Kira', a feminine form of the personal name *Kiro*, a pet form *Kyril*.

Kiraly (412) Hungarian (**Király**): nickname from *király* 'king', from western Slavic *kral* (Czech *král*), derivative of the personal name *Karl* 'Charles', the name of the Frankish king and Holy Roman Emperor Charlemagne (Latin *Carolus Magnus*).

GIVEN NAMES Hungarian 9%. *Zoltan* (4), *Jolan* (2), *Miklos* (2), *Attila, Dezso, Gaza, Imre, Jozsef, Laszlo, Lorant.*

Kirby (19656) **1.** English: habitational name from any of the numerous places in northern England called Kirby or Kirkby, from Old Norse *kirkja* 'church' + *býr* 'settlement'. **2.** Irish: adopted as an English equivalent of Gaelic **Ó Garmhaic** 'descendant of *Ciarmhac*', a personal name meaning 'dark son'. Compare KERWICK.

Kirch (664) German: from Middle High German *kirche* 'church', hence a topographic name for someone living by a church or a occupational nickname from someone employed by the church.

Kirchberg (168) German: **1.** habitational name for someone from one of the various places called Kirchberg in Rhineland, Saxony, or Württemberg. **2.** topographic name for someone living at a church on a hill or on a hill so named, from Middle High German *kirche* 'church' + *berc* 'hill', 'mountain'. **3.** Jewish (Ashkenazic):

ornamental name from German *Kirchberg* 'church mountain'.

Kirchen (206) German: habitational name from Kirchheim, a place name common in the Roman Catholic regions of southern Bavaria and Upper Austria, or from a compound place name containing the element *Kirchen*, as for example *Altenkirchen*. See also KIRCH.

Kircher (1307) German: from Middle High German *kirchner* 'minister', 'sexton', 'patron', hence an occupational name for a priest or a church assistant.

Kirchgessner (257) German: topographic name for an inhabitant of a street called *Kirchgasse* 'church lane'.

Kirchhof (101) German: variant spelling of KIRCHHOFF.

GIVEN NAMES German 11%. *Bernd, Kurt, Lorenz*.

Kirchhofer (159) German: topographic name for someone living near a churchyard, or habitational name for the proprietor or tenant of a farm named as 'Church Farm', from Middle High German *kirche* 'church' + *hof* 'farmstead', 'manor farm'.

Kirchhoff (832) German: from Middle High German *kirche* 'church' + *hof* 'court', 'yard', hence a topographic name for someone dwelling near a churchyard or at a farm situated by a church or owned by the Church.

GIVEN NAMES German 4%. *Kurt* (2), *Ernst, Erwin, Hans, Harro, Joerg, Klaus, Siegfried*.

Kirchman (262) Respelling of German KIRCHMANN.

Kirchmann (102) German: from Middle High German *kirche* 'church' + *man* 'man', hence an occupational name for someone working in the service of the church or possibly a topographic name for someone living near a church.

GIVEN NAME German 7%. *Gerhardt* (2).

Kirchmeier (160) German: from Middle High German *kirche* 'church' + *meier* 'steward' or 'tenant farmer', hence an occupational name for an administrator of church property, the tenant farmer of a church, or a farm laborer on church land, a glebe farmer.

GIVEN NAME German 6%. *Otto* (2).

Kirchner (3878) **1.** German: from Middle High German *kirchenaere* 'sexton', hence an occupational name for a priest, an assistant at a church, or the administrator of church property and possessions. **2.** German and Czech: habitational name for someone from a place called Kirchen.

Kirchoff (901) Altered spelling of German KIRCHHOFF.

Kirgan (161) Irish: probably a variant of KIRWAN.

Kirk (19695) Scottish and northern English, and Danish: from northern Middle English, Danish *kirk* 'church' (Old Norse *kirkja*), a

topographic name for someone who lived near a church.

Kirkbride (711) Scottish and northern English: habitational name from a place in Cumbria near Carlisle, so named from having a church (see KIRK) dedicated to St. Bride or Brigid (cf. KILBRIDE).

Kirkby (203) English: variant of KIRBY.

Kirkeby (253) Danish and Norwegian: habitational name from a place named Kirkeby (or, in the case of the Norwegian name, from any of ten farmsteads so named), from Old Norse *kirkja* 'church' + *býr* 'settlement'.

Kirkegaard (144) Danish: topographic name for someone living near a churchyard, from *kirke* church *gaard* 'yard'.

GIVEN NAMES Scandinavian 12%. *Knud, Sven*.

Kirkendall (1045) Altered spelling of Dutch **Kerkendal**, a topographic name for someone who lived by a church in a valley. It is found chiefly in OH.

Kirkendoll (362) Variant of Dutch KIRKENDALL.

Kirker (510) **1.** Irish: of uncertain origin; perhaps an Anglicized form of Gaelic **Mac Fhearchair**, which was usually Anglicized as **Carragher** (see CARRAHER). **2.** Perhaps also a variant spelling of German KIRCHER.

Kirkes (159) Possibly a reduced form of English **Kirkhouse**, an occupational name for someone employed at the church house.

Kirkey (190) Probably an Americanized spelling of German KIRCHER or of **Gehrke** or **Gierke** (see GEHRKE).

Kirkham (1612) **1.** Northern English: habitational name from places in Lancashire and North Yorkshire named Kirkham, which is a scandinavianized form of Old English *ciric-hām*, from *cirice* 'church' + *hām* 'homestead'. **2.** Possibly a respelling of German **Kirchham**, a habitational name from either of two places named Kirchham, in Austria or Bavaria.

Kirkhart (204) Respelling of German **Kirchhardt**, from an old personal name, a compound of *kirche* 'church' + *hart* 'strong'.

Kirkland (9572) English (now mainly East Midlands) and Scottish: topographic name for someone who lived on land belonging to the Church, from northern Middle English *kirk* 'church' + *land* 'land'. There are several villages named with these elements, for example in Cumbria, and in some cases the surname will have arisen from these. Exceptionally, Kirkland in Lancashire has as its second element Old Norse *lundr* 'grove'.

Kirkley (809) English: habitational name from Kirkley in Northumberland, found in early records as *Crekellawe*. The element *Crekel* is from Celtic *crūg* 'hill' + Old English *hyll* 'hill', to which the tautologous addition (Old English *hlā* 'hill', 'mound') was later made. There is also a Kirkley in

Suffolk, named from Old Norse *kirkja* 'church' + Old English *lēah* 'woodland clearing', which may also have contributed to the surname.

Kirklin (306) Origin uncertain. **1.** Perhaps a variant of English KIRKLAND. **2.** Alternatively, a respelling of German **Kerkeling**, a Low German form of KIRCHNER.

Kirkman (2237) **1.** Northern English: from northern Middle English *kirk* 'church' + *man* 'man', hence an occupational name for a man who looked after a church. **2.** German (**Kirkmann**): see KIRCHMAN.

Kirkner (166) Altered spelling of German KIRCHNER.

Kirkpatrick (10646)` Scottish and North Irish: habitational name from any of various places so called from the dedication of their church (see KIRK) to St. Patrick. The order of the elements is the result of Gaelic influence.

Kirks (209) Variant of KIRK.

Kirksey (1543) English: probably a habitational name from a lost or unidentified place.

FOREBEARS According to family lore, this name was brought to the southern States by a certain Isaac I. Kirksey in the second half of the 17th century. He is believed to have been born in about 1660, probably in one of the midland counties of England.

Kirkwood (2740) Scottish: habitational name from any of several places named as being a wood belonging to the Church or situated by a church (see KIRK). There are places so called in Ayrshire, Dumfries, and Lanarkshire.

Kirley (218) Irish: variant spelling of CURLEY (see MCCURLEY).

Kirlin (317) Irish: variant spelling of CARLIN.

Kirmse (114) German: from Middle High German *kir(ch)messe* '(church) fair', 'kermis', probably applied as a nickname for someone who traded at such occasions.

Kirn (556) German: **1.** habitational name for someone from Kirn, a small town in Rhineland-Palatinate, the name of which probably derives from Middle High German *kürne* 'mill'. **2.** in eastern Germany, possibly from a Sorbian word meaning 'ravine' or 'drain', related to Czech *krn* 'ravine', *krne* 'gutter', 'water channel', 'drain'.

Kirner (161) German: **1.** from an agent derivative of Middle High German *kürne* 'mill', hence an occupational name for a miller or a topographic name for someone living near a mill. **2.** regional variant of KERNER.

GIVEN NAME German 4%. *Kurt*.

Kirouac (197) French: most probably a habitational name from an unidentified Breton place name formed with *kaer, caer* 'fortified settlement' + a personal name.

GIVEN NAMES French 21%. *Andre* (2), *Rolande* (2), *Camille, Emile, Fernand*,

Jacques, Laurien, Marielle, Michel, Normand, Philippe, Rejean.

Kirsch (3839) **1.** German: topographic name from Middle High German *kirse* 'cherry (tree)'. It may also have been a metonymic occupational name for a grower or seller of cherries or a nickname for a man with a ruddy complexion. **2.** Jewish (Ashkenazic): ornamental name from German *Kirsche* 'cherry', one of the many names taken from words for trees and other features of the natural world. The surname is from either the German or the northeastern or western Yiddish form of the word. Compare KARSH.

Kirschbaum (801) **1.** German: topographic name from *Kirschbaum* 'cherry tree'. **2.** Jewish (Ashkenazic): ornamental name with the same meaning.

Kirschenbaum (487) German and Jewish (Ashkenazic): variant of KIRSCHBAUM.
GIVEN NAMES Jewish 9%. *Ari* (6), *Arie, Baruch, Chaim, Hyman, Moisei, Sol, Zvi.*

Kirschman (145) Respelling of German KIRSCHENMANN.

Kirschenmann (185) German: from Middle High German *kirs(ch)e* 'cherry' + *man* 'man', an occupational name for a grower or seller of cherries or a topographic name.
GIVEN NAMES German 8%. *Reinhold* (2), *Erwin, Helmuth, Klaus.*

Kirschke (113) German: **1.** Silesian variant of KIRSCH with the Slavic *-ke* suffix. **2.** from a pet form of the personal name *Krischan* (see CHRISTIAN).
GIVEN NAMES German 7%. *Gerhard, Juergen.*

Kirschling (119) German: possibly a variant of **Kirsching**, with a folk etymological interpretation of the name KIRST (see also KIRSCHT).
GIVEN NAME German 7%. *Kurt* (2).

Kirschman (234) German (**Kirschmann**): variant of KIRSCHENMANN.

Kirschner (1843) German and Jewish (Ashkenazic): Saxon or Silesian form of **Kürschner** (see KURSCHNER).

Kirscht (100) South German: from a dialect pronunciation of a short form (*Kirst*) of the personal name *Christianus* (see CHRISTIAN).

Kirsh (275) Jewish or Americanized spelling of German KIRSCH.
GIVEN NAMES Jewish 9%. *Devorah, Hyman, Meir, Mendy, Moshe, Tsila.*

Kirshbaum (127) Variant spelling of Ashkenazic Jewish KIRSCHBAUM.
GIVEN NAMES French 4%; Jewish 4%. *Patrice* (2); *Meyer.*

Kirshenbaum (278) Variant of German and Jewish KIRSCHENBAUM.
GIVEN NAMES Jewish 8%. *Ari, Feivel, Isidor, Miriam, Rivka, Yitty.*

Kirshner (458) Variant spelling Ashkenazic Jewish KIRSCHNER or an Americanized spelling of the German name.

GIVEN NAMES Jewish 6%. *Fira, Jefim, Mayer, Noam, Pola, Shosh, Sol, Yacov.*

Kirsner (126) Jewish: variant of KIRCHNER.
GIVEN NAMES Jewish 13%. *Hyman* (3), *Myer, Shira.*

Kirst (476) North German: from a short form of *Kirsten*, a vernacular form of the personal name CHRISTIAN.

Kirstein (412) **1.** German: from a derivative of the Latin personal name *Christianus* (see CHRISTIAN). **2.** Jewish (Ashkenazic): ornamental name from German *Kirsch* 'cherry' + *Stein* 'stone'.
GIVEN NAMES German 12%. *Franz* (3), *Klaus* (2), *Kurt* (2), *Raimund* (2), *Volker* (2), *Fritz, Guenther, Ulrich, Willi, Wolfgang.*

Kirsten (261) North German: from the personal name *Kirsten*, a vernacular form of CHRISTIAN.
GIVEN NAMES German 9%; Scandinavian 6%. *Oskar* (2), *Gerd, Horst, Kurt, Otto, Wolf, Sven.*

Kirt (159) English: variant of KIRK.

Kirtland (335) English: variant of KIRKLAND.

Kirtley (1019) English: variant of KIRKLEY.

Kirton (503) Northern English: habitational name from any of various places, for example in Lincolnshire, Nottinghamshire, and Staffordshire, named with Old English *cirice* or Old Norse *kirkja* 'church' + Old English *tūn* 'enclosure', 'settlement'.

Kirts (254) Probably a variant of German KIRTZ.

Kirtz (165) German: patronymic from a pet form of the personal name *Gero* or *Gier* derived from either of the Old High German roots *gār, gēr* 'spear' or *giri* 'desire', 'greed'.

Kirvan (100) Irish: variant of KIRWAN.

Kirven (404) Irish: variant of KIRWAN.

Kirvin (102) Irish: variant of KIRWAN.

Kirwan (919) Irish: Anglicized form of Gaelic **Ó Ciardhubháin** 'descendant of *Ciardhubhán*', a personal name composed of the elements *ciar* 'dark' + *dubh* 'black' + the diminutive suffix *-an*.
GIVEN NAMES Irish 7%. *Donal* (2), *Brendan, Ronan.*

Kirwin (500) Irish: variant spelling of KIRWAN.

Kisamore (201) Americanized spelling of German **Geismar**, a habitational name from any of several places so named in Hesse and Lower Saxony.

Kisch (217) Czech and Jewish (from Bohemia): habitational name for someone from a place called Chýše (German *Chiesch*).
GIVEN NAMES German 4%. *Horst, Wolfgang.*

Kise (237) Norwegian: habitational name from any of four farmsteads named Kise, from Old Norse *Kísi*, which is probably related to German *Kies* 'gravel'.

Kisel (119) Variant spelling of KISSEL.

Kiser (6737) Dutch: see KEYSER.

Kish (3133) **1.** Americanized spelling of Hungarian KISS. **2.** Jewish (Ashkenazic): variant spelling of KISCH.

Kishbaugh (305) Americanized spelling of German **Kirchbach**, a habitational name from any of numerous places in Germany and Austria named *Kirchbach* 'church stream'.

Kishel (137) Jewish (Ashkenazic): variant of KUSEL.

Kishi (154) Japanese: 'shore'; topographic name found throughout Japan. Written two ways; the older, phonetic rendering is listed in the Shinsen shōjiroku.
GIVEN NAMES Japanese 52%. *Hajime* (2), *Miyoshi* (2), *Haruo, Hideya, Hiromi, Hiroshi, Hisashi, Junji, Junko, Kanji, Kazu, Kazuhiro.*

Kishimoto (115) Japanese: '(one who lives) near the shore'; found mostly in western Japan and the Ryūkyū Islands.
GIVEN NAMES Japanese 53%. *Chizuko, Hiro, Hiroshi, Ichiro, Iwao, Izumi, Kazuo, Kiyoshi, Kyoko, Makoto, Masahiro, Masaru.*

Kishpaugh (139) See KISHBAUGH.

Kisiel (280) Polish: **1.** from *kisiel* 'fruit jelly', perhaps applied as a nickname for someone with a passion for this type of confection or some perceived likeness to it. **2.** topographic name, a variant of German KIESEL 'gravel'.
GIVEN NAMES Polish 9%. *Stanislaw* (2), *Aleksander, Jacek, Jerzy, Kazimier, Witold, Zdzislaw, Zygmund.*

Kisielewski (105) Polish: habitational name for someone from Kisiele in Piotrków voivodeship, Kisielewo in Płock and Włocławek voivodeships, or Kisielów in Bielsko-Biała and Przemyśl voivodeships.
GIVEN NAMES Polish 9%. *Andrzej, Casimir, Szczepan.*

Kisker (115) German: habitational name for someone from Kisker in Westphalia.

Kisler (181) German: **1.** see KISSLER. **2.** possibly a variant spelling of KISTLER.

Kisling (519) Variant spelling of German KISSLING or KIESLING.

Kisner (1242) German: variant of KISTNER.

Kisor (314) Probably an altered spelling of German KAISER or Dutch KEYSER. Compare KISER.

Kispert (168) German: from *Kisebert*, a variant of the German personal name *Gisibert*, from *gis-* 'offshoot' + *berht* 'bright', 'famous'.

Kiss (1159) **1.** Hungarian: from *kis* 'small', applied as a nickname for a person of small stature or the younger of two bearers of the same personal name. **2.** English: from Anglo-Norman French *cuisse* 'thigh' (from Latin *coxa*), applied as a metonymic occupational name for a maker of leg armor, which was normally of leather. **3.** German: variant of KISCH (of Czech origin).

GIVEN NAMES Hungarian 23%. *Laszlo* (15), *Zoltan* (11), *Sandor* (9), *Bela* (7), *Gabor* (7), *Tibor* (7), *Attila* (6), *Imre* (5), *Istvan* (4), *Miklos* (4), *Arpad* (3), *Ferenc* (3).

Kissack (177) Scottish: reduced form of McKISSACK.

Kissam (162) Probably an altered form of Irish KISSANE.

Kissane (378) Irish: Anglicized form of Gaelic **Ó Casáin** 'descendant of *Casán*', a diminutive of *cas* 'curly', or of **Ó Ciosáin**, which Woulfe believes to be a variant.

Kissee (255) Altered spelling of German **Kisse** (see KISSEL).

Kissel (1441) **1.** German: from a pet form of the Germanic personal name *Gisulf*. **2.** Jewish (Ashkenazic): variant of KUSEL.

Kisselburg (103) German: Americanized form of **Kesselburg**, a habitational name from any of several places called Kesselberg in the Rhineland, Bavaria, and Baden.

Kissell (805) Variant spelling of German and Jewish KISSEL.

Kissick (372) Scottish: reduced form of McKISSACK.

Kissinger (1924) German and Jewish (from Germany): habitational name from Kissingen in Franconia or Kissing in Bavaria, both of which, according to Bahlow, are named with a lost element *kis(s)* 'marsh', 'swamp', although Berger favors a Slavic origin, from *kisač* 'to make acid'.

Kissler (283) German: from an agent derivative of Middle High German *kis* 'gravel', 'low grade iron ore' (Old High German *kisil* 'pebble'); probably a topographic name for someone living in an area of poor land covered with coarse sand and pebbles or an occupational name for an iron worker.

Kissling (391) German: from the Germanic personal name *Gisilo* (see GIESEL).

Kissner (440) Americanized spelling of German KISTNER.

GIVEN NAMES German 4%. *Kurt* (2), *Fritz*, *Georg*, *Gerhard*.

Kist (418) German: **1.** habitational name for someone from Kist near Würzburg in Bavaria. **2.** Westphalian variant of KIRST.

GIVEN NAMES German 4%. *Hans* (2), *Otto*.

Kister (321) German: **1.** habitational name for someone from KIST. **2.** variant of KISTNER. **3.** from *Kirst*, a pet form of the personal name CHRISTIAN. **4.** variant of **Küster** 'sexton' (see KUSTER).

GIVEN NAMES German 7%. *Helmut* (3), *Kurt* (3).

Kistler (2370) German: occupational name for a joiner or cabinet maker, Middle High German *kisteler*. Compare KISTNER.

Kistner (1061) German: occupational name for a cabinet maker or carpenter, from an agent derivative of Middle High German *kiste* '(clothes) chest'. Compare KASTNER.

Kita (282) **1.** Japanese: 'north'; variously written, found mostly in western Japan and Okinawa Island. In America, some instances of the name may be the result of shortening other names beginning with *Kita*. **2.** Polish: nickname from Polish *kita* 'brush' (as in a fox's brush), 'crest'.

GIVEN NAMES Japanese 20%; Polish 5%. *Kenji* (2), *Nobuo* (2), *Eriko, Hirohito, Hitoshi, Ichiro, Kanae, Kazuo, Makoto, Masato, Nobuyuki, Sadao*; *Andrzej, Czeslaw, Lukasz, Stanislaw, Zdzislaw.*

Kitagawa (254) Japanese: 'northern river'; found mostly in western Japan and Okinawa Island.

GIVEN NAMES Japanese 55%. *Kenji* (3), *Yoshito* (3), *Keigo* (2), *Kumiko* (2), *Mitsuo* (2), *Mutsuo* (2), *Shuichi* (2), *Akiko, Akio, Akira, Chiaki, Chie.*

Kitamura (197) Japanese: 'northern village'; mostly found in western Japan and the Ryūkyū Islands.

GIVEN NAMES Japanese 69%. *Hiroshi* (3), *Toshio* (3), *Kenji* (2), *Masako* (2), *Noriko* (2), *Shinkichi* (2), *Takaaki* (2), *Takashi* (2), *Takayuki* (2), *Yoshiyuki* (2), *Bunji, Eiko.*

Kitay (115) Jewish (Ashkenazic): from Polish or Ukrainian *kitaj* 'buckram' or 'canvas', hence probably a metonymic occupational name for a linen trader or perhaps a nickname.

GIVEN NAMES Jewish 9%; German 4%. *Moshe, Shlomo, Zvi*; *Otto.*

Kitch (450) **1.** English (Somerset): unexplained. **2.** Perhaps an Americanized form of German **Kitsche**, a Silesian and Saxon pet form of CHRISTIAN.

Kitchel (273) Variant of English KITCHELL.

Kitchell (547) English: from Middle English *kichel*, a diminutive of *kake* 'cake', probably applied as a metonymic occupational name for a baker of small cakes of a kind given by godparents to their godchildren when they asked for a blessing.

Kitchen (4850) **1.** English and Scottish: from Middle English *kychene* 'kitchen', hence an occupational name for someone who worked in or was in charge of the kitchen of a monastery or great house. **2.** Scottish and northern Irish: variant of McCUTCHEON.

Kitchener (122) English and Scottish: variant of KITCHEN.

Kitchens (3802) English: variant of KITCHEN, with possessive -*s*, i.e. 'of the kitchen'.

Kitchin (484) English and Scottish: variant spelling of KITCHEN.

Kitching (213) English and Scottish: variant spelling of KITCHEN.

Kitchings (234) English and Scottish: variant spelling of KITCHEN.

Kite (1987) English (chiefly West Midlands): from Middle English *kete*, *kyte* 'kite' (the bird of prey; Old English *cȳta*), a nickname for a fierce or rapacious person.

Kitelinger (118) Americanized form of German **Geitlinger**: **1.** most probably a habitational name for someone from a lost or unidentified place with a name such as Geitlingen. **2.** alternatively, perhaps, a nickname based on Middle Low German *geidlink* 'thrush'. **3.** a third possibility is a patronymic derivative from *Geith* or *Geidel*, personal names based on Langobardic *gaida* 'point (of a lance or spear)'.

Kithcart (155) Variant of English CATHCART.

Kitko (160) Ukrainian: nickname from a diminutive of *kit* 'tomcat'.

Kitner (193) Jewish (Ashkenazic): habitational name for someone from a place called Kutno in Poland.

Kitowski (133) Polish and Jewish (Ashkenazic) (**Kitovskij**): habitational name for someone from Kitów in Zamość voivodeship.

GIVEN NAMES French 4%; Polish 4%. *Czeslaw, Zigmond.*

Kitsmiller (96) Variant of German KITZMILLER.

Kitson (683) Scottish and northern English: patronymic from the Middle English personal name *Kit*, a pet form of CHRISTOPHER.

Kitt (638) English: **1.** from the Middle English personal name *Kit*, a pet form of CHRISTOPHER. **2.** metonymic occupational name for a maker or seller of wooden tubs and pails made of staves held together by a hoop, Middle English *kitte*. **3.** German: perhaps from Middle High German *kīt* 'offshoot', 'sprout', applied as a nickname for a junior member of a family; alternatively it may be from the old personal name *Giddo*.

Kittel (480) **1.** German: from Middle High German *kit(t)el* 'smock', 'shirt-like garment', hence a metonymic occupational name for a maker of such garments or a nickname for someone who habitually wore one. **2.** English: variant of KETTLE.

GIVEN NAMES German 6%. *Otmar* (2), *Armin, Erwin, Guenter, Hans, Manfred, Otto.*

Kittell (403) **1.** English: variant of KETTLE. **2.** Americanized spelling of German KITTEL.

Kittelson (606) Americanized spelling of Danish KETELSEN or its Norwegian variant **Kittelsen**.

Kitten (154) **1.** Reduced form of Irish or Scottish **McKitten**, of uncertain etymology; perhaps a variant of **Mac Curtáin** (see McCURTAIN). **2.** Possibly a variant of German **Gitten**, from a medieval personal name *Giddo*, or an altered spelling of German **Kütten**, of unexplained origin.

Kitterman (655) German: altered spelling of **Kettermann**, in the south a metronymic from *Ketter*, a short form of *Katharina*; in the north a nickname for a heretic or godless person, from Middle Low German *ketter* (modern German *Ketzer*) 'heretic' + *man* 'man'.

Kittinger (342) German: **1.** possibly from a Germanic personal name with the initital element *Gid-*, cognate with Old English *gidd* 'song'. **2.** variant of **Kettinger**, from Middle High German *kote* 'cottage', hence a topographic name or an indirect occupational name for a day laborer.

Kittle (1462) **1.** English: variant of KETTLE. **2.** Americanized spelling of German KITTEL or Swiss German **Küttel**, which is perhaps a variant of KITTEL.

Kittler (209) German: **1.** from an agent derivative of Middle High German *kit(t)el* 'smock', 'shirt-like garment', hence an occupational name for a maker of such garments. **2.** variant of **Küttler** (see KUTTLER).
GIVEN NAMES German 9%; Irish 4%. *Gerhard, Herta, Kurt, Reinhold.*

Kittles (134) English: variant of KETTLES.
GIVEN NAME French 4%. *Camille.*

Kittleson (679) **1.** Northern English: patronymic from the Norse personal name *Kittel* (see KETTLE). **2.** Norwegian: variant spelling of KITTELSON.

Kittner (160) German: **1.** patronymic, more common in Silesia than elsewhere, derived from the Sorbian personal name *Kittan*, an equivalent of CHRISTIAN. **2.** Silesian variant of *Küttner*; KUTTNER. **3.** variant of KETTNER.
GIVEN NAMES German 4%. *Erwin, Johannes, Wolfang.*

Kitto (269) **1.** Cornish: from the personal name *Kitto*, Cornish equivalent of Welsh GRIFFITH. **2.** German (of Slavic origin): from a pet form of CHRISTIAN.

Kittredge (809) English (East Anglian): from a Middle English personal name, *Keterych*. Reaney suggests this is a blend of the Old Norse name *Ketill* (see KETTLE) with the common Old English name element *rīc*, as in BURRIDGE.

Kittrell (1332) English: probably a variant of COTTRELL.

Kittridge (128) English: variant spelling of KITTREDGE.
GIVEN NAME French 5%. *Camille.*

Kitts (1394) **1.** English: patronymic from the Middle English personal name *Kit* (see KITT). **2.** Perhaps also an Americanized form of German KITZ.

Kitz (190) German: **1.** from the Austrian dialect word *Kitz* 'kid', 'fawn', hence a metonymic occupational name for someone who raised or tended goats. **2.** from a German personal name beginning with *Gid-*, cognate with Anglo-Saxon *gidd* 'song'.

Kitzerow (108) **1.** Respelling of German **Kutzerow**, a habitational name from a place so named in Mecklenburg–West Pomerania. **2.** German: habitational name from a place so called (Polish Kiczarowo), formerly in Pomerania, now in Poland.

Kitzinger (149) German and Jewish (from Germany): habitational name for someone from a place in Franconia named Kitzingen, from the personal name *Chitzo*.
GIVEN NAME German 4%. *Ernst.*

Kitzman (525) Americanized spelling of German KITZMANN.

Kitzmann (129) German: **1.** occupational name or byname for someone who raised goats, from *Kitz* 'kid'. **2.** variant of **Kietzmann** (see KIETZMAN).
GIVEN NAME German 6%. *Otto* (2).

Kitzmiller (875) Americanized form of German **Kitzmüller**, literally 'kid miller' (see KITZ + MULLER), a nickname for a miller who kept goats; alternatively, the first element may be from a personal name formed with the Germanic element *Gid-*, cognate with Old English *gidd* 'song'.

Kivel (111) English: variant of KEVILLE.

Kivela (165) Finnish (**Kivelä**): from *kivi* 'stone' + the local ending *-la, -lä*, originally a habitational name from a farmstead so named. It was also adopted during the name conversion movement in the 19th and early 20th centuries by Finns with Swedish surnames, especially those formed with Swedish *sten* 'stone', such as **Stenvall**, **Stenroos**, and STENBERG.
GIVEN NAMES Finnish 6%. *Armas, Eino, Mauno, Sulo, Veikko.*

Kivett (605) **1.** Reduced form of Irish **McKivett**, which is probably a metathesized form of **McKevitt**, an Anglicized form of Gaelic **Mac Daibhéid** (see MCDEVITT). **2.** Americanized of Dutch KIEVIT or the German cognate **Kiewitt**.

Kivi (233) Finnish: topographic or ornamental name from *kivi* 'stone', 'rock'. As a topographic name this dates back to the 16th century; it was also adopted during the name conversion movement in the 19th and early 20th centuries by Finns with Swedish surnames, especially those formed with Swedish *sten* 'stone', such as **Stenvall**, **Stenroos**, and STENBERG. **Kivi** is sometimes a shortened form of various other Finnish names formed with this word.
GIVEN NAMES Finnish 7%. *Aarre, Aino, Arvi, Olavi, Reino, Toivo, Tyyne.*

Kivisto (130) Finnish (**Kivistö**): variant of KIVI, with the addition of the local suffix *-stö*.
GIVEN NAMES Finnish 14%; German 4%. *Eino, Jorma, Juhani, Markku, Paavo, Reino, Sirpa, Toivo; Erwin, Kurt.*

Kiyabu (118) Japanese: written with characters meaning 'joy', 'room', and 'warrior', this name is found mostly in the Ryūkyū Islands.
GIVEN NAMES Japanese 33%. *Sachiko* (2), *Shoichi* (2), *Yukio* (2), *Akira, Goro, Kiyoshi, Kosei, Nobuichi, Sakae, Seiichi, Shinichi, Tadashi.*

Kizer (1773) **1.** Americanized form of Dutch KEYSER or German KAISER. **2.** Jewish (from Ukraine): habitational name for someone from the village of Kizya, now in Ukraine.

Kizziah (217) Origin unidentified. Compare KIZZIAR, KIZZIRE. This name is found mainly in AL.

Kizziar (152) Origin unidentified. Compare KIZZIAH, KIZZIRE.

Kizzire (119) Origin unidentified. Compare KIZZIAH, KIZZIAR.

Kjar (206) **1.** Swedish: ornamental name from *kärr* 'brushwood' (from Old Norse *kjarr*). **2.** Respelling of various variants of 1 or cognates in other Scandinavian languages, such as **Kjaer**, **Kjärr**, **Kjær**, or **K(i)ær**.
GIVEN NAMES Scandinavian 5%. *Erik* (2), *Juhl.*

Kjelland (132) Norwegian: unexplained.

Kjellberg (160) **1.** Norwegian: habitational name from a farmstead named Kjellberg, from Old Norse *kelda* 'spring' + *berg* 'hill', 'mountain'. **2.** Swedish: ornamental name composed of the elements *källa* 'spring' + *berg* 'hill', 'mountain' (see KALL).
GIVEN NAMES Scandinavian 11%. *Bent, Nels, Sten.*

Kjos (411) Norwegian: habitational name from any of several farmsteads, especially in southeastern Norway, named Kjos, from Old Norse *kjóss* 'narrow bay or inlet', 'narrow valley'.
GIVEN NAMES Scandinavian 6%. *Alf, Anders, Selmer.*

Klaas (511) North German and Dutch: from a reduced form of the personal name *Nikolaus, Niklaas*, vernacular forms of the Greek name *Nikolaos* (see NICHOLAS).
GIVEN NAMES German 4%. *Hermann* (2), *Aloys, Elfriede, Erwin, Hans, Otto.*

Klaasen (103) Dutch: patronymic from KLAAS.

Klaassen (383) Dutch: patronymic from KLAAS.

Klabunde (360) German: variant of **Klawund(e)**, **Klawohn**, from a Baltic composite name meaning 'son of Nicholas'.
GIVEN NAMES German 6%. *Erwin* (3), *Ulrich* (2), *Erna, Fritz, Otto, Rinehart.*

Klaes (112) North German and Dutch: from a reduced form of *Niklaas*, vernacular form of the Greek personal name *Nikolaos* (see NICHOLAS).

Klages (367) North German: from a pet form of the medieval personal name KLAUS.

Klahn (406) North German (**Klähn**): topographic name from Lower Saxony field names *Klähn* or *Klähn*, of unknown meaning.

Klahr (276) **1.** German and Jewish (Ashkenazic): variant spelling of KLAR. **2.** German: (**Klähr**): from a short form of the Latin personal name *Hilarius* (see HILLARY). This surname is also found in Sweden, probably originally taken there from Germany.
GIVEN NAMES Jewish 7%. *Aryeh* (2), *Shifra* (2), *Chanina, Meyer, Sol, Zelig.*

Klaiber (356) German: see KLEIBER.
GIVEN NAMES German 4%. *Fritz, Kurt, Wolfang.*

Klain (112) Variant spelling of German and Jewish KLEIN.

GIVEN NAMES Jewish 6%; German 4%. *Volf* (2); *Kurt*.

Klamer (154) German: **1.** variant of KLAMMER. **2.** from the medieval personal name *Clamer* (*Clamor*), which was popular in patrician families in the 16th and 17th centuries.

Klamm (312) German: topographic name for someone living in or near a gorge or ravine, from Middle High German *klamm* 'gorge', 'ravine', 'pass'.

GIVEN NAMES German 4%. *Egon, Konrad, Rommel, Ullrich.*

Klammer (235) German: topographic name for someone living in or near a gorge or ravine (see KLAMM).

GIVEN NAMES German 8%. *Siegfried* (2), *Erhard, Franz.*

Klang (268) **1.** Swedish: soldier's name from *klang* 'clang', 'ringing noise'. **2.** Possibly also German: from an altered and reduced form of the personal name *Nikolaus*, vernacular form of Greek *Nikolaos* (see NICHOLAS).

GIVEN NAMES Scandinavian 7%. *Hilmer, Sven, Thor.*

Klann (346) German: probably a topographic name of West Slavic origin from a word meaning 'maple' (compare Polish *klon*). This is an element contained in numerous field names in the formerly Slavic-speaking areas of northeastern Germany.

GIVEN NAMES German 7%. *Kurt* (2), *Erwin, Gerhard, Gerhardt, Hildegarde, Juergen, Manfred, Otto.*

Klaphake (124) German: variant of **Klaphek, Klaphecke**, topographic names for someone living near a trapdoor or a gate in the village fence, from *klappen* 'to clap', 'slam' + *hecke* 'hedge', 'fence'.

GIVEN NAMES German 7%. *Florian, Kurt, Math.*

Klapp (305) German: nickname for a gossip or a slanderer, from Middle High German *klapf, klaff* 'prattle', 'malicious gossip'.

Klapper (469) German and Jewish (Ashkenazic): from an agent derivative of Middle High German *klappern* 'chatter', 'rattle', hence a nickname for a talkative person or a gossip or a metonymic occupational name for a night watchman, a reference to the clapper used for making announcements. As a Jewish name it could be a metonymic occupational name for someone who called people to the synagogue.

GIVEN NAMES Jewish 4%. *Meir* (2), *Aryeh, Avrohom, Miriam.*

Klapperich (262) German: from a derivative of Middle High German *klapf, klaff* 'prattle', 'malicious gossip', hence a nickname for a prattler, or possibly for a bony man, someone with clanking bones.

GIVEN NAME German 4%. *Kurt* (3).

Klar (530) **1.** German: nickname from Middle High German and Middle Low German *klār* 'pure', 'beautiful', 'clear'. **2.** German: metronymic from the female

personal name *Klara*, equivalent of *Clara* (see CLAIR and SINCLAIR). **3.** German: from a short form of the Latin personal name *Hilarius* (see HILLARY). **4.** Jewish (Ashkenazic): ornamental name from German *Klar* 'clear', 'beautiful'. **5.** This surname is also found in Sweden, probably originally taken there from Germany.

GIVEN NAMES Jewish 5%; German 5%. *Ezriel* (2), *Tzvi* (2), *Baruch, Devorah, Isadore, Miriam, Nachman, Yitzchok; Gerhard* (2), *Johann* (2), *Erhard, Kurt, Willibald.*

Klare (227) German: variant of KLAR 2, 3.

Klarich (223) Croatian (**Klarić**) and Slovenian (**Klarič**): metronymic from the female personal name *Klara* (see CLAIRE).

Klarman (142) **1.** Jewish: variant of KLAR 4. **2.** Americanized spelling of the German surname **Klarmann**, from Middle High German *klar* 'pure', 'clear', 'sensible', a nickname for an honorable man, also used as a personal name.

GIVEN NAME Polish 4%. *Casimir.*

Klas (192) **1.** North German: variant spelling of KLASS. **2.** Czech: from Czech *klas* 'ear of a cereal plant'. See also KLESS. **3.** Czech and Slovak: from a short form of the personal name *Nikolas* (see NICHOLAS). **4.** Jewish (Ashkenazic): unexplained.

Klase (159) German: variant of KLASS.

Klasen (217) Dutch and North German: variant of KLASSEN.

Klasing (114) North German and Dutch: variant of KLAUSING.

Klass (646) **1.** North German: from the personal name *Klass*, a Low German reduced form of *Nikolaus* (see NICHOLAS). Compare Dutch CLAES. **2.** Jewish (Ashkenazic): variant of KLAS 4.

GIVEN NAMES Jewish 4%. *Moshe* (2), *Hyman, Isadore, Miriam, Rebekah, Sol.*

Klassen (1343) North German: patronymic from *Klass*, a Low German reduced form of *Nikolaus* (see NICHOLAS).

Klassy (118) Origin unidentified.

Klatt (1796) German: **1.** from Middle Low German *klatte* 'rag', 'low-grade wool'; also 'tousled hair', hence a nickname for someone with untidy hair. **2.** Silesian variant of **Klette** (see KLETT 1).

GIVEN NAMES German 4%. *Manfred* (4), *Erwin* (2), *Klaus* (2), *Egon, Erna, Georg, Gerhard, Gertraud, Lothar, Monika, Otto, Reinhold.*

Klatte (112) German: variant of KLATT.

Klauber (172) German: **1.** from a pet form of the personal name *Nikolaus* (see NICHOLAS). **2.** from an agent derivative of Middle High German *klūben* 'to pick' 'gather', hence a nickname for a thief or an occupational name for a person who sorted out ore-containing rocks. **3.** variant of **Kleuber**, an occupational name for a stone cutter or mason, from an agent derivative of Middle High German *kliuben* 'to split'.

GIVEN NAME German 4%. *Erwin* (2).

Klauck (117) North German: variant of KLUG.

GIVEN NAME German 5%; Scandinavian 4%. *Uwe.*

Klaudt (134) German: from a short form of any of the Germanic personal names composed with (h)*lut* 'clear' (modern German *laut*) or with *liut*- 'people', as in LUDWIG.

GIVEN NAMES German 4%. *Milbert, Otto.*

Klauer (210) German: **1.** occupational name for a bailiff, later a servant in general, Middle Low German *klüver* (from *kluven* 'to put someone in chains or handcuffs'). **2.** in northern Germany, from *klaue* 'claw', a nickname for a quick, agile man. **3.** habitational name for someone from a place called Klauen near Hildeshiem or from Klau near Aachen. **4.** in nautical slang an occupational name for someone who repaired cracked and leaking boats. **5.** in Hessen and the central Rhine area, a metonymic occupational name for someone who bred oxen, from a dialect word *Klauer* 'breeding bull'.

Klaus (2238) German: from the personal name *Klaus*, a reduced form of *Nikolaus* (see NICHOLAS).

GIVEN NAMES German 5%. *Kurt* (10), *Angelika* (2), *Ernst* (2), *Guenther* (2), *Bernhard, Christl, Eberhard, Erwin, Friedrich, Fritz, Gerhard, Guenter.*

Klausen (134) Danish and North German: patronymic from the personal name *Klaus*, a reduced form of *Nikolaus* (see NICHOLAS).

GIVEN NAMES Scandinavian 17%; German 4%. *Aksel, Espen, Lars, Niels; Theresia.*

Klauser (167) **1.** Swiss German: patronymic from the personal name *Klaus*, a reduced form of *Nikolaus* (see NICHOLAS). **2.** German: variant of KLAUSNER.

GIVEN NAMES German 11%. *Markus* (2), *Gunther, Heinz, Horst, Maximilian.*

Klausing (219) German: Westphalian patronymic from the personal name *Klaus*, reduced form of *Nikolaus* (see NICHOLAS).

GIVEN NAMES German 4%. *Dieter, Horst.*

Klausman (122) **1.** Swiss German (**Klausmann**): patronymic from the personal name KLAUS or occupational name meaning 'servant of KLAUS '. **2.** German (**Klausmann**): elaborated form of KLAUS + *man* 'man'.

GIVEN NAMES German 6%. *Frieda, Gerhard.*

Klausner (460) **1.** German and Jewish (Ashkenazic): from Middle High German *klōsenære, klūsenære* and German *Klausner* 'hermit' (from Latin *clausum* 'cell', 'shut-away place'), hence a topographic name for someone living by a hermit's cell or a byname for a hermit. The reasons of its adoption by Jews are uncertain. **2.** Austrian and Swiss German: topographic name from *Klause* 'narrow pass', 'defile'.

GIVEN NAMES Jewish 5%. *Sol* (2), *Bracha, Meyer, Miriam, Mirra, Yitzhak.*

Klauss (126) German: variant spelling of KLAUS.
GIVEN NAMES German 13%. *Rudi* (2), *Dieter, Ernst, Gerd, Gunter, Helmut, Rainer.*

Klaver (306) Dutch: from *klaver* 'clover', hence a topographic name for someone living near a field of clover, or an occupational name for someone who grew clover to feed cattle.

Klawiter (130) Eastern German: variant of KLAWITTER.
GIVEN NAMES German 5%. *Reiner, Wolf.*

Klawitter (513) Eastern German: **1.** habitational name for someone from a place named with Lithuanian *klava* 'maple'. **2.** Germanized form of the Latvian patronymic **Klevas**, a derivative of the forename *Klāvs*, a pet form of *Nikolaus* (see NICHOLAS).
GIVEN NAMES German 5%. *Erwin* (2), *Wolfram* (2), *Ewald, Florian, Helmut, Kurt, Otto.*

Klay (149) German and Swiss German (also **Kläy**): variant of KLEY.
GIVEN NAMES German 4%. *Gunther, Othmar.*

Klayman (268) **1.** German (**Klaymann**): variant of KLAY. **2.** Jewish (from Poland): variant of KLEIMAN.
GIVEN NAMES Jewish 7%. *Bernat, Meyer.*

Kleban (193) **1.** Jewish (Ashkenazic): habitational name for someone from a place called Kleban in Ukraine. **2.** Perhaps a shortened form of KLEBANOFF. **3.** German: from Sorbian *khleb* 'bread' (Polish *chleb*), hence probably a metonymic occupational name for a baker.

Klebanoff (112) Jewish: alternative spelling of **Klebanov**, habitational name from a village named Kolybanovo in eastern Belarus.
GIVEN NAME Jewish 6%. *Hyman.*

Klebba (233) Polish: Germanized derivative of Polish dialect *chlebdać się* 'be half open', 'leave (a door) half open'.

Klebe (231) German: **1.** see KLEBER. **2.** (of Slavic origin) variant of *Clewi* or *Klewe*, Sorbian short forms of the personal name *Nikolaus* (see NICHOLAS).
GIVEN NAMES German 7%. *Kurt* (3), *Egon, Franziska, Wolfgang.*

Kleber (455) German **1.** from an agent derivate of *kleben* 'to bind or stick', hence an occupational name for someone who applied clay daub on buildings or, in Swabia, for someone who applied whitewash. **2.** habitational name from various occurrences of *Kleber* as a field name; the etymology is uncertain. **3.** perhaps a habitational name for someone from Cleve in Westphalia (see KLEVE).

Klecha (111) Polish: nickname from *klecha* 'shaven-headed person'.
GIVEN NAMES Polish 10%; German 4%. *Janina, Janusz, Katarzyna, Wladyslawa.*

Kleck (147) German: variant of **Klöck**, itself a variant of **Glöck** (see GLOCK).
GIVEN NAMES German 4%. *Benno, Gerhardt, Katharina.*

Klecka (189) Czech (**Klečka**): nickname for a lame person, from Old Czech *klecavý* 'to hobble'.

Klecker (231) German: variant of **Klöcker**, itself a variant of **Klöckner** (see KLOECKNER).

Kleckley (146) Respelling of German **Klöckler**, a variant of **Klöckner** (see KLOECKNER).

Kleckner (912) Respelling of German **Klöckner** (see KLOECKNER).

Kleczka (103) Polish: nickname or occupational name from *kleczka* 'rattle'.

Klee (978) German: **1.** apparently from Middle High German *klē* 'clover', either a topographic name for someone who lived near a field of clover or a metonymic occupational name for someone who grew clover to feed cattle. **2.** from a shortened form of the personal name KLEMENS.
GIVEN NAMES German 5%. *Ernst, Hans, Hellmut, Helmut, Horst, Kurt, Manfred, Otmar, Otto, Wolfgang.*

Kleeman (628) **1.** German (**Kleemann**) and Jewish (Ashkenazic): literally 'clover man', perhaps a topographic name. As a Jewish name, it is mainly ornamental. **2.** German (**Kleemann**): altered form of the personal name KLEMENS.
GIVEN NAMES German 4%. *Ewald, Kurt, Otto, Sigi.*

Kleemann (135) German and Jewish (Ashkenazic): see KLEEMAN.
GIVEN NAMES German 14%; Scandinavian 5%. *Hans* (2), *Achim, Erwin, Gunter, Johann, Kurt.*

Kleen (231) North German form of KLEIN.

Klees (314) German and Dutch: from a short form of German *Nikolaus*, Dutch *Nik(o)laas* (see NICHOLAS).

Kleffman (141) **1.** North German: topographic name from Middle Low German *clēf, cleff* 'cliff', 'precipice' + *man* 'man'. **2.** German: habitational name for someone from Cleve (now *Kleve*) or from any of various places, also in the Rhineland, called Kleff.

Kleffner (170) **1.** North German: topographic name from Middle Low German *clēf, cleff* 'cliff', 'precipice'. **2.** German: nickname for a prattler or gossip, from Middle High German, Middle Low German *kleffer(er)*.
GIVEN NAME French 4%. *Alouis.*

Klehm (107) North German: from a short form of the personal name *Klement* (see CLEMENT).

Klehr (129) **1.** Respelling of German **Klähr**, a variant of KLAR. **2.** North German: of uncertain origin. Either from the medieval personal name *Hilarius* or from an old German personal name formed with a derivative of Latin *clarus* 'famous' (see KLAR).
GIVEN NAMES German 7%. *Heinz, Ilse, Math.*

Kleiber (472) German: **1.** from an agent derivative of Middle High German *kleben* 'to stick or bind', an occupational name for a builder working with clay or, in Swabia, for someone who applied whitewash. **2.** in Bavaria and Austria, an occupational name for a shingle maker, from Middle High German *klieben* 'to split (wood or stone)'. Compare KLAUBER.
GIVEN NAMES German 7%. *Gottfried* (2), *Otto* (2), *Florian, Frieda, Guenter, Kaspar, Margrethe.*

Kleid (101) Jewish (Ashkenazic): metonymic occupational name for a tailor, from Yiddish *kleyd*, German *Kleid* 'garment', 'dress'.
GIVEN NAME Jewish 4%. *Sol.*

Kleier (242) North German: **1.** topographic name for a farmer who worked on the heavy clay soil typical of low-lying areas of northern Germany, from Middle Low German *klei* 'clay'. **2.** habitational name for someone from a place called Klei or Kley (Westphalia, Schleswig-Holstein).

Kleiman (1070) **1.** German and Jewish (Ashkenazic): nickname from a reduced form of German KLEINMANN 'small man' or a variant of the Yiddish form, *klayman*. **2.** North German (**Kleimann**): topographic name for a farmer who worked on heavy clay soil (see KLEIER).
GIVEN NAMES Jewish 8%. *Sol* (4), *Ari* (2), *Boruch* (2), *Miriam* (2), *Shlomo* (2), *Shulem* (2), *Ephraim, Hyman, Irina, Irit, Izak, Mayer.*

Klein (36412) German, Dutch (also **de Klein(e)**) and Jewish (Ashkenazic): from Middle High German, Dutch, German *klein* 'small', or Yiddish *kleyn*. This was a nickname for a person of small stature, but is also often found as a distinguishing name for a junior male, usually a son, in names such as KLEINHANS and KLEINPETER. This name is common and widespread throughout central and eastern Europe.

Kleinberg (569) **1.** Jewish: ornamental name from German *klein* 'small' + *Berg* 'mountain', 'hill'. **2.** German: topographic name of the same meaning as 1, from Middle High German *klein* + *berc*.
GIVEN NAMES Jewish 5%. *Gerson, Hershel, Hyman.*

Kleindienst (151) German: from German *klein* 'small' + *Dienst* 'service', an occupational name for a farmhand or laborer who was second in line to a more highly paid class of servant (see also KLEINKNECHT). The term also denoted a particular kind of tax levied in the Middle Ages, hence the surname may be a metonymic name for a collector of such taxes or for someone who had to pay such a tax.
GIVEN NAMES German 6%; Polish 5%. *Helmut, Manfred; Kazimierz, Tadeusz.*

Kleindl (101) South German: from a diminutive of KLEIN.
GIVEN NAME German 6%. *Gerhard* (2).

Kleine (673) German: from an inflected form of KLEIN 'small'.

GIVEN NAMES German 6%. *Erwin* (2), *Bernhard, Detlef, Dietrich, Ernst, Friedrich, Georg, Juergen, Klaus, Kurt, Otto, Siegfried.*

Kleiner (1018) German, Swiss, Dutch, and Jewish (Ashkenazic): nickname from an inflected form of KLEIN 'small'.

GIVEN NAMES German 6%; Jewish 5%. *Kurt* (4), *Erwin* (2), *Otto* (2), *Alois, Erna, Fritz, Hermann, Lothar, Reinhold, Wilhelmina, Wolf; Shmuel* (2), *Chaim, Jakov, Marat, Morry, Zelik.*

Kleinert (389) German: 1. variant of KLEIN. 2. from a reduced form of the medieval personal name *Kleinhart*, from Middle High German *klein* 'small' + *hart* 'strong'.

GIVEN NAMES German 8%. *Ernst* (2), *Fritz* (2), *Kurt* (2), *Erwin.*

Kleinfeld (197) 1. German: habitational name from a place in Mecklenburg, but more often a topographic name for someone who worked a smallholding, from Middle High German *klein* 'small' + *velt* 'open country'. 2. Jewish (Ashkenazic): ornamental name from German *klein* 'small' + *feld* 'field' (Yiddish *kleynfeld*).

GIVEN NAMES Jewish 5%; German 4%. *Kieve* (2); *Erwin, Volker.*

Kleinfelder (118) German: topographic name for someone who worked a smallholding, or habitational name from Kleinfeld in Mecklenburg (see KLEINFELD).

Kleinfeldt (134) Variant spelling of German KLEINFELD.

Kleinfelter (227) Variant spelling of German KLEINFELDER.

Kleingartner (102) German: topographic name for someone who worked a small plot of land or a small vineyard, from Middle High German *klein* 'small' + *garten* 'enclosure' + the agent suffix *-er*.

Kleinhans (531) German: from a nickname or term of endearment meaning 'small Johnny', 'John the younger', from *klein* 'small' + *Hans*, a pet form of the personal name *Johannes*, German form of JOHN.

GIVEN NAMES German 7%. *Kurt* (10), *Gerhard, Inge, Lothar.*

Kleinheksel (109) 1. Dutch and North German: unflattering nickname for a worthless person, from *klein* 'small' + *heksel* 'chaff'. 2. German: possibly from a nickname composed of *klein* 'small' or 'young' (see KLEIN) + *hexel*, a short form of a Germanic personal name composed with *hag* 'enclosure', as in HAGEMAN.

Kleinhenz (299) German: variant of KLEINHANS, possibly from the pet form *Kleinhensel*; alternatively it may be an altered spelling of *Kleinhenze*.

Kleinjan (112) Dutch: distinguishing name, literally 'little Jan', for the smaller or younger (*klein*) of two bearers of the personal name JAN.

GIVEN NAMES Dutch 4%. *Leendert, Teunis.*

Kleinke (157) German: derivative of KLEIN.

GIVEN NAMES German 7%. *Hans* (2), *Arno, Klaus, Siegfried.*

Kleinknecht (153) German: occupational name for a secondary hired hand, a *Kleinknecht* as opposed to a *Grossknecht*. Compare KLEINDIENST.

GIVEN NAMES German 5%. *Fritz, Hans.*

Kleinman (1618) German (**Kleinmann**) and Jewish (Ashkenazic): descriptive nickname for someone of small stature, from German KLEINMANN 'small man'.

GIVEN NAMES Jewish 7%. *Sol* (4), *Aron* (2), *Ronen* (2), *Shlomo* (2), *Yair* (2), *Ari, Avrum, Dov, Dovid, Erez, Heshy, Isador.*

Kleinmann (118) German and Jewish: see KLEINMAN.

Kleinow (139) German: 1. habitational name Kleinow in Mecklenburg. 2. Americanized spelling of the German surname **Kleinau**, possibly a topographic name for someone living on the *kleine Aue* 'small meadow'.

GIVEN NAME German 5%. *Kurt* (2).

Kleinpeter (284) German: from a compound name composed of the elements *klein* 'little' + the personal name *Peter*, hence 'little Peter', a term of endearment, or simply 'Peter the younger'.

GIVEN NAMES German 5%. *Gunther, Klein, Kurt.*

Kleinsasser (286) German (Austrian): from Middle High German *klein* 'small' + *sāze* 'sitter', 'occupant', hence a nickname for someone renting or dwelling on a small plot of land.

Kleinschmidt (1227) German and Jewish (Ashkenazic): occupational name for a maker of small forged items and metal hand tools, literally 'small smith'.

GIVEN NAMES German 6%. *Kurt* (8), *Otto* (3), *Frieda* (2), *Hans* (2), *Erwin, Franz, Gerhard, Hermann, Hertha, Johannes, Lorenz, Ralf.*

Kleinschmit (148) German and Jewish (Ashkenazic): variant of KLEINSCHMIDT.

Kleinsmith (274) Part-translation of German KLEINSCHMIDT.

Kleinsorge (131) German: 1. Nickname for a carefree person, from Middle High German *klein* 'small', 'little' + *sorge* 'worry', 'concern'. 2. Habitational name from Kleinsorge in the former East Prussia, named as a resort meaning 'few worries', 'without a care'.

GIVEN NAMES German 7%. *Kurt* (2), *Dietmar.*

Kleintop (145) Altered form of **Kleintopf**, a hybrid of Low and High German falsely suggesting the meaning 'small pot' but actually meaning 'small braid or plait', possibly applied as a nickname for a short person.

Kleis (298) German: from the personal name *Kleis*, a South German variant of KLAUS.

GIVEN NAMES German 5%. *Kurt* (3), *Manfred, Mathias.*

Kleiser (136) German: patronymic from KLEIS.

Kleiss (162) German: variant spelling of KLEIS.

GIVEN NAMES German 6%. *Aloys, Ewald, Kurt.*

Kleist (590) German: probably a habitational name of Slavic origin, from a place near Köslin in Pomerania.

Klem (804) German: 1. from a short form of the personal name *Klemens* (see CLEMENT). 2. respelling of KLEMM.

Klema (164) Czech and Serbian: from a pet form of the personal name *Klement*, a vernacular form of *Clemens* (see CLEMENT).

Kleman (466) Probably an altered form of German KLEMENS.

Klemann (203) Probably an altered form of German KLEMENS.

Klemens (207) German: from the personal name *Klemens*, a variant spelling of *Clemens* (see CLEMENT).

GIVEN NAMES German 6%. *Claus, Eberhard, Kaethe, Kurt.*

Klement (448) North German: variant of KLEMENS.

GIVEN NAMES German 4%. *Gerd, Gerda, Gerhard, Hilde, Klaus, Kurt.*

Klemish (106) Probably an Americanized form of German **Kle(m)mig**, **Kleinmisch**, a reduced form of *Klein Michel*, a distinguishing name for the smaller or younger of two bearers of the personal name *Michel* (see KLEIN, MICHAEL).

Klemm (1245) German: 1. from Middle High German *klem* 'narrow', 'tight', 'scarce', hence a nickname for a thin or inhibited person, or alternatively a topographic name for someone living in a narrow, precipitous place, from the Middle High German noun form *klemme* 'constriction'. 2. short form of the personal name KLEMENS.

GIVEN NAMES German 9%. *Gerhard* (6), *Kurt* (5), *Hans* (4), *Heinz* (4), *Otto* (3), *Gerd* (2), *Helmut* (2), *Horst* (2), *Siegfried* (2), *Bernhard, Detlef, Ewald.*

Klemme (589) German: variant of KLEMM.

GIVEN NAMES German 5%. *Kurt* (4), *Armin, Erwin, Fritz, Gerhard, Manfred, Uwe.*

Klemmer (330) 1. German: nickname from an inflected form of Middle High German *klem* 'narrow', 'tight', 'scarce', or a topographic name *klemme* 'constriction', the suffix *-er* denoting an inhabitant (see KLEM 1). 2. (in northern Germany) occupational name for someone who worked with clay (i.e someone who applied the daub infill on timber-framed houses), Middle High German *klemer*. 3. in various German dialects the word (an agent derivative of *klemmen* 'to pinch, squeeze, or claw') denotes a bird of prey and hence an uncouth young woman or a penny pincher (Tyrol).

GIVEN NAMES German 4%. *Kurt* (2), *Hans.*

Klemp (499) German: from Middle High German *klambe* 'clamp', 'pliers'; hence a metonymic occupational name for a maker or user of such tools.

Klempner (159) North German and Jewish (Ashkenazic): occupational name for a tin smith, from an agent derivative of *klempern* 'to hammer tin'.

GIVEN NAMES Jewish 10%; German 4%. *Bentsion, Doron, Hyman; Erwin, Viktor.*

Klemz (177) German: reduced form of *Klemenz*, a German form of CLEMENT.

Klenk (558) **1.** German: nickname from Middle High German *glenke* 'nimble', 'alert'. **2.** from Middle High German *klenken* 'to cause something to sound or ring', hence a nickname for a gossip. **3.** Czech: topographic name for someone living near a maple tree, from *klen* 'maple'.

GIVEN NAMES German 4%. *Hans* (2), *Fritz, Helmut, Juergen, Lorenz, Wilhelm.*

Klenke (404) Variant of German and Czech KLENK.

GIVEN NAMES German 4%. *Othmar* (2), *Helmut.*

Klenz (102) German: habitational name from a place so named in Mecklenburg, of Slavic origin.

Klepac (192) **1.** Czech and Slovak (**Klepáč**): from *klepáč* 'small water mill', a derivative of *klepat* 'to tap'. **2.** Croatian (**Klepac** or **Klepač**): a nickname from *klepati* 'to beat or sharpen with a hammer', in a figurative sense probably denoting a talkative person.

Klepacki (142) Polish: **1.** habitational name for someone from Klepacze in Białystok voivodeship. **2.** occupational name for a smith, from *klepacz* 'smith', a variant of *klepać* 'to hammer'.

GIVEN NAMES Polish 10%. *Boguslawa, Dariusz, Karol, Krystyna, Witold, Zygmunt.*

Klepfer (182) German: **1.** see KLOPFER. **2.** (southern Germany and Tyrol) variant spelling of **Klapfer**, a topographic name, from an agent derivative of Middle High German *klapf* 'rock'.

Klepinger (143) Variant of German KLEPPINGER.

Klepp (118) **1.** Eastern German: nickname from Middle High German *klapp* 'malicious gossip', 'idle chatter'. Compare KLEPPER. **2.** Norwegian: habitational name from any of seventeen farmsteads named Klepp, notably in Agder and Vestlandet, from Old Norse *kleppr* 'bluff', 'cliff'.

GIVEN NAMES Scandinavian 11%; German 4%. *Erik* (2), *Alf, Knut; Inge, Johann.*

Kleppe (331) **1.** Eastern German: variant of KLEPP. **2.** Norwegian: habitational name from any of over twenty farmsteads named Kleppe, from the singular dative case of KLEPP.

GIVEN NAMES German 4%; Scandinavian 4%. *Kurt* (2), *Frieda, Hans; Lars* (2), *Hedvig.*

Klepper (847) **1.** Eastern German (mainly Silesian): from a dialect variant of **Klöpfer** (see KLOPFER). **2.** German: nickname for a gossip, from Middle High German *klep-*

pern, klappern 'to blabber, chatter, or gossip'. **3.** German: from the rare Middle High German word *klepper* 'knight's horse', probably originally a metonymic occupational name for someone who tended or bred such animals. From the 16th century, however, the term came to denote a low-grade horse, a 'nag', and also someone who castrated horses. **4.** Jewish (Ashkenazic): occupational name for someone who called people to the synagogue by rattling a stick, from an agent derivative of Yiddish *klepn* 'to stick'.

Kleppinger (224) German: from **Klöppinger**, which is either a patronymic from an old personal name formed with Old High German, Middle High German *liut* 'people', 'clan'; or from Middle Low German *kloppen* 'to knock, pound, or beat', which in place names also denoted 'defense'.

FOREBEARS Johann Georg and Anna Margaretta Schreiner Klöppinger emigrated from Pfungstadt, Hesse, in 1737, and settled in PA. Three of their sons spelled their name Kleppinger; two others adopted the spelling Clippinger.

Kless (182) German: from the personal name *Kless*, a pet form of *Niklaus*, a German form of NICHOLAS.

Klessig (144) German: variant of NIKOLAUS.

GIVEN NAMES German 7%. *Ernst, Helmuth, Kurt.*

Klett (537) German: **1.** topographic name from Bavarian dialect *glet* 'smallholding' (a word of Slavic origin). **2.** variant of KLETTE.

GIVEN NAMES German 6%. *Helmut* (2), *Otto* (2), *Rainer* (2), *Hans, Kurt.*

Klette (120) German: **1.** unflattering nickname for an annoyingly persistent person, from Middle High German *klette* 'burr', by extension 'nuisance'. **2.** nickname from Middle Low German *klatte* 'tatter', 'rag'. **3.** from a byname for a social climber or upstart, related to *klettern* 'to climb'. **4.** topographic name for someone who lived in a hovel, from a Slavic word meaning 'hovel' or 'shed', e.g. Polish *kléta, klete* 'shack'.

Kletter (118) **1.** Dutch and North German: variant of KLETTE. **2.** North German: habitational name from a place named Klett in Brandenburg, or a topographic name from Middle Low German *klēt* 'cottage', both of Slavic origin.

Kleve (254) **1.** German: habitational name from Kleve (earlier Cleve) in Rhineland. The place name probably derives from an old topographic term *cleve* 'swamp'. **2.** variant of KLEVER 2 and 3. **3.** Norwegian: habitational name from any of numerous farmsteads named Kleiva, from Old Norse *kleif, klif* 'cliff', 'rocky ascent with a road or path'.

Kleven (673) **1.** German: habitational name for someone from a place called Klevenow.

2. German: variant of KLEVE. **3.** Norwegian: habitational name from any of numerous farmsteads all over Norway named Kleven, from the definite singular form of KLEVE.

GIVEN NAMES Scandinavian 5%. *Erik* (2), *Berger, Hjalmer, Jalmer, Knute, Maren, Obert, Thor, Thorval.*

Klever (191) German: **1.** habitational name for someone from Kleve in the Rhineland (see KLEVE 1). **2.** German: nickname for a complainer, from Middle High German *klewen* 'to whine'. **3.** German: possibly from Middle Low German *klēver* 'clover', also 'resin', 'turpentine', hence a metonymic occupational name either for a farmer who grew clover or perhaps for someone who collected and distilled turpentine. In the Alemannic area this was also a nickname for a bungler.

GIVEN NAMES German 6%. *Otto* (2), *Kurt, Ulrike.*

Kley (193) German: **1.** topographic name for someone living on heavy soil, from Middle Low German *klei* 'clay'. **2.** habitational name from any of various places named Kley or Klei, notably in Westphalia, of uncertain origin. **3.** from the personal name *Kley*, a Franconian derivative of the saint's name *Eligius*, or alternatively from a Rhenish short form of the personal name *Nikolaus*. **4.** Americanized spelling of KLEE.

Kleyman (153) Jewish (eastern Ashkenazic): variant of KLEIMAN.

GIVEN NAMES Russian 34%; Jewish 31%. *Boris* (6), *Vladimir* (4), *Aleksandr* (3), *Igor* (3), *Mikhail* (3), *Svetlana* (3), *Anatoly* (2), *Arkadiy* (2), *Grigory* (2), *Sergey* (2), *Yefim* (2), *Aleksey; Irina* (3), *Yakov* (2), *Aron, Avi, Elik, Faina, Genya, Haya, Ilya, Isaak, Mikhael, Moisey.*

Kleyn (111) Jewish (eastern Ashkenazic) and Dutch: variant spelling of KLEIN.

GIVEN NAMES Russian 14%; Jewish 11%; Dutch 6%; German 5%. *Aleksandr, Boris, Gennady, Grigory, Maryana, Mikhail, Svetlana, Veniamin, Yelena, Yeva; Arie, Ilya, Mendel, Semen, Yakov; Dirk* (2), *Cornelis; Florian, Hans, Otto.*

Kleypas (113) North German (East Prussia): Americanized form of *Kleophas*, the name of one of the two disciples who met Jesus on the way to Emmaus and adopted as the patron saint of the Teutonic Order.

Klich (187) **1.** German and western Slavic: from a Slavic short form of the personal name *Kliment* (see CLEMENT). **2.** Respelling of German **Klitsch**, a variant of **Klisch** (see KLISH).

GIVEN NAMES Polish 7%. *Andrzej, Waclaw, Wieslawa, Wojciech.*

Klick (617) German: **1.** topographic name from Low German *Klick* 'clay soil'. **2.** variant of GLICK.

Klicker (104) North German: topographic name for someone who lived on clayey soil, from Middle Low German *klick* 'clay'.
GIVEN NAME German 4%. *Kurt.*

Kliebert (163) German: occupational name for a woodsman or woodworker, from an agent derivative of Middle High German *klieben* 'to cleave or split'.
GIVEN NAMES French 6%. *Alcee* (2), *Anicet, Benoit.*

Klien (141) Eastern German: from Slavic *klin* 'nook', 'corner', 'wedge (of an axe)', hence a topographic name or a metonymic occupational name for an axe-maker.
GIVEN NAMES German 8%. *Wolfgang* (2), *Otto.*

Klier (421) Czech: from a derivative of German **Klieber** (see KLIEBERT).

Kliethermes (223) North German: probably a variant of **Klütermes**, a metonymic occupational name for an inspector in the wool trade, from dialect *klüter* 'wool weight (22 lbs.)' + *mes(se)* 'weight' (a lump of metal), 'measure'.

Kliewer (680) German: **1.** from the Dutch family name **Kluiver, Kluyver, Cluyver**, occupational name for a court official, originally a hangman or torturer. Some Mennonites so named migrated to West Prussia in the 17th century. **2.** North German: topographic name from *cleve* 'swamp'. Compare KLEVER 1.

Kliger (104) Jewish (from Ukraine and Poland): nickname from an inflected form of Yiddish dialect *klig* 'clever', 'wise'.
GIVEN NAMES Jewish 11%; Russian 7%; Irish 4%. *Arie, Yonah; Iosif, Leyzer, Mikhail, Yefim, Yelena.*

Kligerman (121) Jewish (from Ukraine and Poland): elaborated form of KLIGER.
GIVEN NAMES Jewish 8%. *Abbe, Sol.*

Kligman (132) Jewish (from Poland and Ukraine): nickname from Yiddish dialect *klig* 'clever', 'wise' + *man* 'man'.
GIVEN NAME Jewish 7%. *Myer.*

Klika (126) Czech: from a pet form of the personal name *Klimeš, Kliment, Klemens* (see CLEMENT).

Klim (280) **1.** Polish and Sorbian: from a short form of the personal name *Kliment, Klemens*, from the Latin personal name *Clemens* (see CLEMENT). **2.** Perhaps also a variant of South German **Klimm**, a topographic name from Middle High German *klimme* 'height', 'hill'. **3.** nickname for a fearful person, from Middle High German *klimpfen* 'to press', 'to oppress'.
GIVEN NAMES Polish 7%. *Danuta, Irena, Karol, Krzysztof, Leszek, Lucjan, Stanislaw, Tadeusz.*

Klima (754) Czech (**Klíma**) and southeastern German: from a vernacular form of the personal name *Kliment* or *Klemens*, Latin *Clemens* (see CLEMENT).
GIVEN NAMES German 4%. *Otto* (4), *Gunter, Kurt, Monika, Uwe.*

Kliman (100) Czech: from a variant of the personal name KLIMENT, from Latin *Clemens* (see CLEMENT).

Klimas (389) Polish (**Klimasz**): from the personal name *Klimas*, a vernacular form of Latin *Clemens* (see CLEMENT).
GIVEN NAMES Polish 4%. *Henryk, Janina, Jaroslaw, Zbigniew.*

Klimaszewski (179) Polish: habitational name for someone from Klimaszewnica or Klimasze in Łomża voivodeship, so called from the personal name *Klimasz*, a pet form of *Klemens*, from the Latin personal name *Clemens* (see CLEMENT).
GIVEN NAMES Polish 8%; French 6%. *Andrzej, Krzysztof, Piotr, Waclawa, Wieslaw; Celine, Marcel, Michel.*

Klimczak (212) Polish and eastern Slavic: patronymic from the personal names *Klim* or *Klima*, short forms of *Klemens*, from the Latin personal name *Clemens* (see CLEMENT).
GIVEN NAMES Polish 11%. *Ewa, Irena, Jaroslaw, Maciej, Stanislaw, Zdzislaw, Zofia, Zygmunt.*

Klimek (1330) Polish, Czech (**Klímek**), and Sorbian: from the personal name *Klim*, short form of *Kliment* or *Klemens*, from the Latin personal name *Clemens* (see CLEMENT).
GIVEN NAMES Polish 4%. *Krzysztof* (2), *Boleslaw, Casimir, Elzbieta, Halina, Jozefa, Mariusz, Marzena, Ryszard, Slawomir, Szymon, Tomasz.*

Kliment (137) Czech: from the personal name *Kliment*, from Latin *Clemens* (see CLEMENT).
GIVEN NAME German 4%. *Kurt.*

Klimko (136) Polish and eastern Slavic: from a pet form of the western Slavic personal name *Klemens* or eastern Slavic *Klymentij*, from the Latin personal name *Clemens* (see CLEMENT).

Klimkowski (112) Polish: habitational name for someone from Klimków in the southern borderland of Poland.

Klimowicz (140) Polish: **1.** patronymic from the personal name *Klim*, short form of the personal name *Klement* (see CLEMENT). **2.** habitational name for someone from any of three villages in Poland called Klimowicze.
GIVEN NAMES Polish 13%. *Agnieszka, Andrzej, Elzbieta, Waclaw, Wieslaw, Zbigniew, Zygmunt.*

Klinck (183) German: variant spelling of KLINK.

Klindt (243) North German: topographic name from Middle Low German *klin(d)t* 'steep bank', 'cliff' or a habitational name from places in Schleswig-Holstein and Hannover named Klint.
GIVEN NAMES German 4%. *Hans, Otto.*

Klindworth (146) Variant of German KLINTWORTH.

Kline (17769) **1.** Americanized spelling of Dutch, German, and Jewish KLEIN.

2. Slovenian (eastern Slovenia): probably a nickname or topographic name from *klin* 'wedge', 'wooden peg'.

Klinedinst (434) Americanized spelling of German KLEINDIENST.

Klinefelter (563) Americanized spelling of German KLEINFELDER.

Kliner (107) Dutch: variant of KLEINER.

Kling (3020) **1.** Swedish: soldier's name from *kling(a)*, from Swedish *klinga* 'blade'. **2.** German, Danish, and Dutch: variant of KLINGE.

Klingaman (356) **1.** German: habitational name for someone from Klinga in Saxony. **2.** Probably an altered spelling of **Klingemann**, variant of KLINGE.

Klingbeil (568) German: from Middle High German *klingen* 'to ring or sound' + *bīl* 'axe', literally 'sound the axe', an occupational nickname for a journeyman, carpenter, shipwright (or any occupation involving the use of an axe). Journeymen's names often contained a humorous element, as they were bestowed at merry promotion parties or 'christenings' held to celebrate the recipients successful completion of their apprenticeship.
GIVEN NAMES German 5%. *Kurt* (4), *Gerda, Hans, Manfred, Reinhold, Ulrich.*

Klingberg (177) German: variant of KLINGENBERG.
GIVEN NAMES German 4%. *Detlef, Wilfried.*

Klinge (363) **1.** German: topographic name for someone who lived in a valley or ravine, or near a mountain stream, Middle High German *klinge* 'murmuring brook'. There are many places named with this word, and the surname may also be a habitational name from any of them. **2.** North German: topographic name for someone living near a ford or on boggy moorland, from Low German *klinge* 'ford', 'muddy heath', or a habitational name from Klinge in Schleswig-Holstein, Klingen, or any of several other places containing the element *klinge* 'ford'. **3.** German and Danish: metonymic occupational name for a cutler or swordsmith, from Middle High German *klinge* 'metal blade', 'sword' (a later imitative derivative of *klingen* 'to ring or clatter'). **4.** Dutch and Belgian: topographic name meaning 'valley' or habitational name from places named Klinge in East Flanders and Zeeland. **5.** Swedish: variant of KLING.

Klingel (296) German: from *Klingel* 'small bell', hence a metonymic occupational name for a maker of handbells or alternatively a nickname for an incessant chatterer.

Klingele (178) German: variant of KLINGEL.

Klingenberg (500) **1.** German: habitational name from places so called in Schleswig-Holstein, Saxony, and Franconia. **2.** Scandinavian: either of German origin (see 1) or an ornamental name.

GIVEN NAMES German 7%. *Klaus* (3), *Erwin* (2), *Hans* (2), *Kurt* (2), *Grete, Juergen, Otto.*

Klingensmith (1189) Partly Americanized form of the German surname **Klingenschmidt**, an occupational name for a swordsmith or cutler, from Middle High German *klinge* 'blade', 'sword' + *smit* 'smith'.

Klinger (3498) **1.** German and Czech: derivative of KLINGE. **2.** German: see KLINGLER.

GIVEN NAMES German 4%. *Kurt* (5), *Otto* (4), *Heinz* (3), *Erwin* (2), *Benno, Brunhilde, Dieter, Eldor, Erhard, Ernst, Ewald, Fritz.*

Klingerman (233) German (**Klingermann**): variant of KLINGER.

Klinginsmith (129) Americanized form of German **Klingenschmidt** (see KLINGENSMITH).

Klingler (1391) German: **1.** in southern Germany and Austria, a topographic name from the field name **Klingle**, a diminutive of KLINGE. **2.** nickname for a gossip, from Middle High German *klingelen* 'to chat'. **3.** in southwestern Germany, an occupational name for town crier or a nickname for a beggar, from an agent derivative of *klingeln* 'to ring a bell'.

Klingman (505) German (**Klingmann**): elaborated form of KLINGE.

Klingner (101) German: occupational name for a swordsmith, from an agent derivative of Middle High German *klinge* 'sword blade'.

GIVEN NAME German 9%. *Kurt* (2).

Klingshirn (101) German: nickname for a rabble rouser or trouble maker, from Middle High German *klingen* 'to make ring or sound' + *hirn* 'brain'.

GIVEN NAME German 4%. *Otto.*

Klingsporn (125) German: nickname for a horseman, literally 'sound the spur (*Sporn*)'.

GIVEN NAMES German 9%. *Horst, Manfred, Wilfried.*

Klink (1369) **1.** German: topographic name from Slavic *klink*, a diminutive of *klin* 'nook', 'corner', 'wedge'. **2.** German: topographic name (see KLINGE 1, 2). **3.** German: habitational name from places named Klink or Klinke in Rhineland, Mecklenburg, Silesia, or East Prussia. **4.** German: metonymic occupational name for a maker of door fittings or for a border or customs officer, from Middle High German, Middle Low German *klinke* 'barrier', also 'latch', 'door handle'. **5.** Dutch: metonymic occupational name for a maker of iron door latches and the like, from Middle Dutch *clinke* 'bolt', 'strap', 'door handle'. Compare 5 above.

Klinke (193) German: variant of KLINK.

GIVEN NAMES German 8%. *Gerd, Gerhard, Horst, Manfred, Otto, Ulrich.*

Klinkenberg (150) German: variant of KLINGENBERG.

Klinker (416) **1.** German: topographic or habitational name, a variant of KLINK, the *-er* suffix denoting an inhabitant. **2.** Dutch: metonymic occupational name for a road paver, from Middle Dutch *clinkaert* 'brick', 'clinker paving'.

Klinkhammer (302) **1.** Dutch: metonymic occupational name for a blacksmith, probably a journeyman's name, meaning literally 'sound the hammer'. **2.** German: variant of **Klinghammer**, cognate with 1. Compare KLINGBEIL.

GIVEN NAMES German 4%. *Kurt, Ulrich.*

Klinkner (205) German: **1.** variant of **Klingner**, an occupational name for a blade maker or swordsmith, from Middle High German *klinge* 'metal blade', 'sword' + *-er* agent suffix. **2.** Alternatively it may be a habitational name from places named Klingen in Bavaria, the Palatinate, and elsewhere, or from Klingnau in the northern Swiss canton of Aargau.

Klinner (103) German: occupational name for a builder working with clay, from an agent derivative of Middle High German *klenen* 'to stick', 'to spread or smear'. Compare KLEIBER.

Klint (165) German: variant of KLINDT.

GIVEN NAMES Scandinavian 10%. *Erik, Lars.*

Klintworth (175) North German: topographic name from Middle Low German *klindt* 'steep bank', 'cliff' + Middle Low German *wort* 'raised land with a farmstead'.

Klinzing (157) Altered spelling of German **Klinzig**, nickname for a tiny person.

Klipfel (248) German: from Middle High German *klüpfel, klöpfel, klüppel* 'mallet', 'cudgel', 'clapper (of a bell)', hence a metonymic occupational name for a maker of cudgels and mallets or clappers for bells or a metonymic occupational name for a butcher, a stone-breaker. This name also became established in Greece by followers of King Otto, of Bavarian origin.

Klipp (221) North German: **1.** topographic name from Middle Low German *klif* 'steep hill', 'river bank'. **2.** metonymic occupational name for a shoemaker, from Middle Low German *klipp* 'low shoe', 'clog'.

Klippel (290) North German variant of KLIPFEL.

GIVEN NAMES German 6%. *Bernhardt, Kurt, Wolfgang.*

Klipper (103) **1.** North German: variant of KLIPPERT. **2.** Jewish (Ashkenazic): ornamental name from German *Klippe* 'cliff', 'rock' + the agent suffix *-er*.

GIVEN NAMES Jewish 5%; German 4%. *Shmuel, Uri; Erwin, Ilse.*

Klippert (145) North German: **1.** occupational name for a maker of clogs, from a derivative of Middle Low German *klipp* 'low shoe', 'clog' (plural *klippen*). **2.** from Middle Low German *klipper* 'wooden stick', 'clapper', presumably a metonymic occupational name for someone who used such a

tool in his work. **3.** occupational nickname for a plumber, from *klipperer*, an agent derivative of *klippen* 'to clap'.

GIVEN NAME German 4%. *Otto.*

Klipstein (120) Altered spelling of German **Klippstein**, in northern Germany an metonymic occupational name for a stone mason, from Low German *klipstein* 'recycled stone'.

GIVEN NAME German 4%. *Kurt.*

Klise (120) Probably an Americanization of German KLEIS.

Klish (146) Americanized spelling of German **Klisch**: **1.** from Old Polish *kleć* 'shabby room' or 'gossip', or from Upper Sorbian *kletka* 'smallholding', 'tumbledown house' (from Old Slavic *kleti* 'house'). **2.** alternatively, it may be from the Slavic personal name *Klich*, a derivative of the personal name *Kliment* (see CLEMENT).

GIVEN NAME German 4%. *Otto* (2).

Klitz (140) German: from an eastern German or Slavic pet form of the personal name *Kliment*, from Latin *Clemens* (see CLEMENT).

Klitzke (363) German: from a pet form of KLITZ.

GIVEN NAMES German 4%. *Kurt* (3), *Otto.*

Kloberdanz (175) Altered form of North German **Klobedanz**, a nickname for a killjoy or spoilsport, from Middle Low German *kloven* 'to cleave' + *danz* 'dance', i.e. 'one who breaks up the dance'.

Klobuchar (124) Slovenian, Croatian, and Serbian (all **Klobučar**): occupational name for a hatter, from the vocabulary word *klobučar* 'hatter', itself derived from *klobuk* 'hat'.

Kloc (265) Polish: from *kloc* 'log', 'block', 'trunk', nickname for a clumsy or awkward man. Compare German KLOTZ.

GIVEN NAMES Polish 6%. *Andrzej, Bronislaw, Jerzy, Jolanta, Karol.*

Klocek (273) Polish: nickname from *klocek* 'chock', diminutive of KLOC.

GIVEN NAMES Polish 7%; German 4%. *Andrzej* (2), *Karol* (2), *Kazimierz* (2); *Eldred, Florian, Manfred.*

Klock (1012) Dutch and North German: **1.** nickname from Middle Dutch or Low German *cloec, clo(o)c* 'deft', 'skillful', 'clever'. **2.** habitational name from a house distinguished by the sign of a bell, Middle High German *glocke*, Middle Dutch *clocke*. In some instances this may also have been a metonymic occupational name for a bell maker or bell ringer. **3.** nickname from *de Kloke* 'the wise one', from Middle Low German *kloke* 'wise person'.

FOREBEARS Abraham Clock was one of the first carpenters in New Amsterdam in the 17th century.

Klocke (486) North German and Dutch: variant of KLOCK.

Klocko (126) Polish and Ukrainian: from *kloc* 'log', 'chunk', 'block of wood', nickname for a clumsy or awkward man.

Klockow (105) German: habitational name from any of the places in Pomerania, Mecklenburg, and Uckermark called Klockow.
GIVEN NAME German 5%. *Kurt* (2).

Kloeckner (134) North German, Rhineland, and Westphalian (**Klöckner**): occupational name for a bell ringer, sexton, or the like, from an agent derivative of KLOCK.
GIVEN NAMES German 6%. *Frieda, Kurt, Ullrich.*

Kloehn (228) German (**Klöhn**): variant of **Klähn** (see KLAHN).
GIVEN NAMES German 4%. *Hans, Kurt.*

Kloepfer (279) German (**Klöpfer**): see KLOPFER.
GIVEN NAMES German 5%. *Gottlieb, Hans, Heinz.*

Kloeppel (227) German (**Klöppel**): from *Klöppel* 'bell-clapper', hence a metonymic occupational name for a bell-ringer or a craftsman using a clapper-like instrument in his work. Compare KLOPFER. The same word was also used to denote a clumsy youth and the surname could equally have arisen from a nickname with this sense.

Kloepper (127) Central or northern German variant of **Klöpfer** (see KLOPFER).
GIVEN NAME German 5%. *Udo.*

Kloepping (125) North German: from a derivative of KLOPP.

Kloes (135) German: from a short form of the personal name *Nikolaus* (see NICHOLAS).

Kloesel (114) German (**Klösel**): from a pet form of *Kloss*, a medieval short form of the personal name *Nikolaus* (see NICHOLAS).
GIVEN NAMES German 7%. *Franz, Kurt.*

Klohr (104) **1.** German: origin uncertain; perhaps a variant of KLAHR. **2.** German: variant of the medieval personal name *Hilarius*.
GIVEN NAME French 4%. *Camille.*

Kloiber (235) German: variant of KLEIBER.

Kloke (123) North German: from Middle Low German *klōk* 'quick', 'clever', 'wily', 'skillful'.
GIVEN NAME German 4%. *Otto.*

Klomp (175) Dutch: **1.** nickname for a burly, stockily-built person, from Middle Dutch *clomp* 'lump', 'block'. **2.** metonymic occupational name for a clog maker, from *klomp* 'clog'.
GIVEN NAMES Dutch 5%; German 5%. *Gerrit* (3); *Johannes, Manfred.*

Klonowski (240) Polish and Jewish (from Lithuania): habitational name for someone from a place called Klonów, named with Polish *klon* 'maple tree' + the possessive suffix -*ów*.

Klontz (171) Eastern German: **1.** topographic name from Slavic *klon* 'maple'. **2.** alternatively, perhaps, an altered form of GLANZ. Compare CLAUNCH.

Kloos (397) Dutch and North German: variant of Dutch *Claes*, German *Klaus*, from a

short form of the personal name *Niklaas, Nikolaus* (see NICHOLAS).

Klooster (223) Dutch: topographic name for someone living by or working in a monastery, Middle Dutch *kloestere*.

Kloosterman (193) Dutch: topographic name for someone living by or working in a monastery, from Middle Dutch *kloestere* + *man* 'man'.
GIVEN NAMES Dutch 4%. *Pieter* (2), *Gerrit.*

Klopf (176) German (also **Klöpf**): metonymic occupational name from a noun derivative of Middle High German *klopfen* 'to pound, bang, or hammer' (see KLOPFER).

Klopfenstein (669) German: occupational name for a quarryman or stone mason, from *klopfen* '(to) strike or knock' + *Stein* 'stone', literally 'strike the stone'.

Klopfer (389) South German (also **Klöpfer**) and Jewish (Ashkenazic): occupational name from Middle High German *klopfære*, German *Klöpfer*, a noun derivative of Middle High German *klopfen* 'to pound, bang, or hammer'; this could denote someone working in the wool, hemp, or millinery trades, a miner, metal worker, or hunter.
GIVEN NAMES German 5%. *Ulrike* (2), *Erwin, Hans, Kurt.*

Klopp (868) German: **1.** habitational name from a place called Kloppe. **2.** short form of any of the compound names formed with *Klopp-* or *Klopf-*, from Middle Low German *klopper* 'clapper', 'bobbin', 'hammer'. **3.** from the medieval personal name *Chlodobert*.

Kloppenburg (184) German: habitational name from Cloppenburg near Oldenburg, probably named from Middle Low German *kloppen* 'to hit or beat', 'to beat up', one of several so-called 'defying names' in this area.
GIVEN NAMES German 7%. *Erwin, Heinz, Kurt, Otto.*

Klos (770) **1.** Dutch and German: variant spelling of KLOSS. **2.** Polish: from a short form of *Miklos*, variant of the personal name *Mikołaj*, the Polish form of NICHOLAS. **3.** Polish (**Kłos**): probably also a nickname for a small person, from *kłos* 'ear or spike of cereal'.
GIVEN NAMES German 8%; Polish 6%. *Kurt* (2), *Alfons, Bernd, Hans, Otto, Wolfgang; Andrzej, Danuta, Janina, Jerzy, Lucyna, Piotr, Ryszard, Wladyslaw.*

Klose (658) German and Western Slavic: from the pet name *Klose*, a Silesian derivative of the personal name *Nikolaus* (see KLOS and NICHOLAS).
GIVEN NAMES German 8%. *Hans* (4), *Gerhard* (3), *Dieter* (2), *Heinz* (2), *Erwin, Gerd, Guenter, Gunther, Kurt, Rudi, Ute.*

Klosek (100) Polish (also **Kłosek**): from a diminutive of KLOS.
GIVEN NAMES Polish 9%. *Marcin, Tomasz, Wojciech.*

Klosinski (167) Polish (**Kłosiński**): habitational name for someone from Kłosin in Kraków voivodeship, a place so named from *kłos* 'ear of a cereal plant' or from a short form of the personal name *Mikołaj* (see KLOS).
GIVEN NAMES Polish 6%. *Andrzej, Bronislaw.*

Klosky (115) Eastern German and Czech: **1.** habitational name from a place so named from Slavic *klos* (Czech *klas*) 'ear of a cereal plant'. **2.** patronymic from a short form of the personal name *Mikolas, Mikuláš*, Slavic equivalents of NICHOLAS (see KLOS).

Klosowski (272) Polish (**Kłosowski**): habitational name for someone from a place called Kłosów or Kłosowo (see KLOS).
GIVEN NAMES Polish 10%. *Zdzislaw* (2), *Andrzej, Beata, Czeslaw, Ewa, Feliks, Kazimierz, Miroslaw.*

Kloss (1132) German: **1.** from the south and eastern German personal name *Kloss*, a short form of *Nikolaus*, German form of NICHOLAS. Compare KLOS. The form **Klöss** is found in Württemberg and Rhineland. **2.** nickname from Sorbian *klos* 'lanky child' (literally 'stalk').

Klossner (230) German: variant of KLAUSNER.
GIVEN NAMES German 5%. *Hans* (2), *Erwin, Fritz.*

Kloster (651) **1.** German: from Middle High German *klōster* (Old High German *klōstar*, from Late Latin *clostrum* 'monastic cell'), hence a topographic name for someone who lived by a monastery or a metonymic occupational name for a servant in a monastery. **2.** Dutch: variant of KLOOSTER, cognate with 1.
GIVEN NAMES Scandinavian 4%. *Erik* (2), *Alf, Iver, Per.*

Klosterman (982) Americanized spelling of German KLOSTERMANN or Dutch KLOOSTERMAN.

Klostermann (233) German: occupational name for a servant in a monastery or for a lay member of a monastic community, from Middle High German *klōster* monastery (see KLOSTER) + *man* 'man'. The surname may also have denoted someone who farmed land belonging to a monastery and who paid rent in the form of provisions for the monks.
GIVEN NAMES German 4%. *Erwin, Heinz, Kurt.*

Kloth (306) North German: from *kloth* 'clump' or alternatively a short form of *Schneekloth* 'heap of snow', hence possibly a nickname for a fat and clumsy person.
GIVEN NAMES German 7%. *Erwin, Friedrich, Hans, Heinz, Kurt, Rainer, Reiner, Wolfgang.*

Klotz (2532) **1.** German: nickname for a clumsy, awkward man, from Middle High German *klotz* 'lump', 'block', cognate with modern English *clot*, which is similarly used in a transferred sense to denote a stupid person. **2.** Jewish (Ashkenazic): cognate of 1, from modern German *Klotz* 'lump', 'block', or Yiddish *klots*.

Klotzbach (196) German: topographic name from a common fieldname around Brunswick (Braunschweig).
GIVEN NAME German 4%. *Kurt.*

Klouda (170) Czech: from *Kloud*, a short form of the Latin personal name *Claudius* (see CLAUD).
GIVEN NAMES German 4%. *Georg, Viktor.*

Klover (100) German (**Klöver**): variant of **Klüver** (see KLUVER).

Kluck (825) German: **1.** variant of GLUCK. **2.** Germanized form of Czech **Kluk**, a nickname meaning 'lad', 'boy', in German also having the sense 'rogue'.

Kludt (222) German: probably from Middle Low German *klūte* 'lump', 'clod', a nickname for a loutish or clumsy person. Compare KLOTH.

Kluender (237) German (**Klünder**): variant of KLUNDER.

Kluesner (453) North German (**Klüsner**): Low German variant of KLAUSNER 1.

Kluever (235) German: variant spelling of **Klüver** (see KLUVER).
GIVEN NAMES German 6%. *Gerda, Guenter, Kurt, Lorenz, Otto.*

Klug (2634) **1.** German: nickname from eastern Middle High German *klūc* 'wise', 'prudent', or from the western form *kluoc*, which had the sense 'noble', 'refined'; the word came into German from Middle Dutch *cloec* (see KLOCK) via Middle Low German *klōk* (see KLOKE). **2.** Jewish (Ashkenazic): nickname from German and Yiddish *klug* 'clever', 'wise'.
GIVEN NAMES German 4%. *Erwin* (8), *Otto* (4), *Hans* (3), *Achim, Alois, Berthold, Dieter, Erhard, Gunter, Hannelore, Hertha, Ingo.*

Kluge (970) German: nickname from Middle High German *kluoc* 'noble', 'gentle', 'refined'. Later the meaning changed to 'understanding', 'learned', 'experienced', and subsequently 'clever'.
GIVEN NAMES German 9%. *Kurt* (5), *Gerhard* (4), *Heinz* (2), *Otto* (2), *Armin, Dieter, Eldor, Ernst, Ewald, Gerhart, Gunther, Hans.*

Kluger (275) **1.** German (**Klüger**): nickname meaning '(the) refined one', '(the) clever one', from an agent derivative of Middle High German *kluoc* (see KLUGE). **2.** Jewish (Ashkenazic): nickname from an inflected form of German and Yiddish *klug* 'clever', 'wise'.
GIVEN NAMES German 10%; Jewish 6%. *Kurt* (3), *Fritz* (2), *Bernhard, Horst, Markus, Otto, Willi; Avi, Miriam, Sol.*

Klugh (228) Variant spelling of German KLUG.

Klugman (243) German (**Klugmann**) and Jewish (Ashkenazic): elaborated form of KLUG.

GIVEN NAMES Jewish 9%; German 4%. *Ahron, Avrohom, Elchonon, Hyman, Ilya, Nosson, Toba, Yetta; Hertha.*

Kluk (101) Polish: from *kluka* 'hook', probably applied as a nickname for someone with a hooked nose. This name is concentrated in IL and OH.

Klukas (173) **1.** Ukrainian and Moldovan: nickname from Slavic *klujka* 'gossip', 'tale-telling'. **2.** Lithuanian: unflattering nickname from Lithuanian *klukius* 'foolish man', or possibly from *kliukis* 'chatterer', 'blabberer'.
GIVEN NAMES German 8%. *Kurt* (3), *Berthold, Otto.*

Klumb (388) German: variant of KLUMP.

Klump (612) German: nickname for a clumsy, crude, or fat person, a South German form of KLOMP.

Klumpp (525) German: variant spelling of KLUMP.

Klun (134) Slovenian: nickname for someone with a beak-shaped nose, from *kljun* 'beak', 'bill' (old spelling *klun*).

Klunder (239) German (also **Klünder**): nickname a small or dirty person, from Low German *klunter* 'small lump of dirt', or alternatively for a loud person or a trouble maker, from a noun derivative of Middle Low German *klunderen* 'to make noise'.
GIVEN NAMES German 8%. *Kurt* (2), *Wilhelm* (2), *Ewald, Hans, Otto.*

Klundt (227) German: probably a variant of KLUNDER.

Klunk (383) German: from *Klunker* 'tassel', later 'rag', a metonymic occupational name for a tassel-maker or, in its later sense, perhaps a nickname for a slow-witted person.

Klus (213) **1.** Polish: from a pet form of the personal name *Mikołaj*, Polish form of NICHOLAS. Compare KLOS. **2.** Polish (**Kłus**): nickname from *kłus* 'trot', *kłusak* 'trotter'. **3.** North German: topographic name from Middle Low German *kluse* 'monk's cell', 'narrow passage'. Compare KLAUSNER.
GIVEN NAMES Polish 4%. *Boleslaw, Wladyslawa.*

Kluska (119) Polish, Jewish (from Poland), and German: from Polish *kluska* 'dumpling', a nickname for a thick-set, rotund person.
GIVEN NAMES Polish 6%. *Jozef, Ryszard.*

Klusman (234) North German (**Klusmann**): habitational name for someone from a place in northern Germany named Kluse or Klus, from Middle Low German *kluse* 'monk's cell', 'narrow passage'.

Klusmeyer (123) North German: distinguishing name denoting a tenant farmer (see MEYER) whose farm was situated near a hermit's cell or a narrow passageway (see KLUS 3).
GIVEN NAMES German 5%. *Dieter, Dietrich.*

Klute (206) Americanized form of German KLUTH.
GIVEN NAMES German 5%. *Eldred, Ernst, Kurt.*

Kluth (489) **1.** North German: from Middle Low German *klūt(e)* 'lump of earth', 'sod', 'clod', hence nicknames for an ungainly, clumsy, or uncouth person; in some cases they may have been applied as a metonymic occupational name for a farmer. See also KLOTH, KLOTZ. **2.** North German: habitational name from, for example, places called Klut near Hamelin or Detmold. **3.** Probably also a variant of Dutch **Kloot(e)** or **Kloet**, cognates of 1, from Middle Dutch *cloot* 'clog', 'clod', 'lump'.
GIVEN NAMES German 7%. *Kurt* (5), *Dietmar* (2), *Erwin* (2), *Gerhard, Wolfgang.*

Kluthe (132) German: variant of KLUTH.
GIVEN NAME German 4%. *Alfons.*

Klutts (320) **1.** Apparently an Americanized spelling of KLUTZ. **2.** Possibly a variant of German **Klutt**, from a short form of a Germanic personal name based on *hlōd* 'clear', used in the sense 'famous' in personal names (Old High German *hlut*).

Kluttz (555) Altered spelling of KLUTZ.

Klutz (191) **1.** German (**Klütz**): habitational name from a place near Wismar named Klutz. **2.** German: from Sorbian *kluc* 'bubbling water', probably a topographic name for someone who lived by a spring. **3.** Dutch: from German KLOTZ.

Kluver (406) German (**Klüver**): from an agent derivative of *Kluven* 'split wooden block' (related to Middle Low German *kluven* 'to split or cleave'), hence an occupational name for an official whose responsibilities included putting prisoners into the stocks.

Kluz (134) Polish: derivative of Old Polish *kluza* 'shutter', a nickname for someone who was in jail.
GIVEN NAMES Polish 4%. *Czeslawa, Leszek.*

Klyce (116) Americanized spelling of German KLEIS.

Klym (163) Probably a respelling of KLIM.

Klyn (124) Reduced form of Dutch **de Klyn** 'the little one' (see KLEIN).
GIVEN NAME German 4%. *Reinold.*

Kmet (137) Slovenian, Serbian, and Croatian; Slovak (**Kmeť**): status name for a type of peasant. In Slovenia this denoted a peasant who had his own landed property. In Serbia and elsewhere it was a status name for a feudal peasant farmer who cultivated the land of his lord instead of paying rent or doing military service. In Croatia it was also a term denoting a village headman.

Kmetz (682) Germanized form of the Slavic surname **Kmetec**, a diminutive of KMET, with the diminutive suffix *-ec*.

Kmiec (393) Polish (**Kmieć**): status name for a peasant farmer who owned his own land, from Old Polish *kmieć*.

GIVEN NAMES Polish 4%. *Bogumil, Malgorzata, Stas, Zofia.*

Kmieciak (112) Polish: patronymic from **Kmieć** 'peasant farmer' (see KMIEC).

GIVEN NAMES Polish 6%. *Jaroslaw, Zbigniew.*

Kmiecik (292) Polish: from a diminutive of **Kmieć** 'peasant farmer' (see KMIEC).

GIVEN NAMES Polish 9%. *Casimir, Dariusz, Jadwiga, Jozef, Mieczyslaw, Stanislaw, Walenty, Wlodzimierz, Zygmunt.*

Knaack (505) North German: from Low German *knaak* 'bone', hence an occupational nickname for a butcher or possibly for a knacker, or a nickname for a bony, stocky, or crude person. Compare South German KNOCH.

GIVEN NAMES German 4%. *Erwin* (2), *Jurgen, Kurt.*

Knaak (346) North German: variant spelling of KNAACK.

GIVEN NAMES German 7%. *Fritz, Gerd, Hannelore, Hans, Ingo, Kurt, Otto, Wilfried.*

Knab (387) German: variant of KNABE.

GIVEN NAMES German 4%. *Alois, Erwin, Ilse, Klaus, Kurt.*

Knabb (142) German: variant of **Knabbe**, a northwestern form of KNABE.

Knabe (482) German: status name for a young man or a page, from Middle High German *knabe*. In aristocratic circles this term denoted a page or squire (a youth destined to become a knight), while among artisans it referred to a journeyman's assistant or (as a short form of *Lehrknabe*) 'apprentice'. In the 15th century a semantic split between *Knabe* and its variants *Knape, Knapp(e)* resulted in *Knabe* meaning 'boy' and *Knapp(e)* 'servant', 'apprentice', and 'miner' in modern German.

GIVEN NAMES German 4%. *Erna, Gerhard, Helmut, Volker.*

Knabel (112) South German (also **Knäbel**): from a diminutive of KNABE.

Knable (281) South German (**Knäble**): from Middle High German *knebel*, a diminutive of *knabe* 'boy' (see KNABE).

Knack (360) German: **1.** variant of KNAACK. **2.** nickname for a crude person or someone with a thick neck, from Bavarian *genack* 'neck'. **3.** shortened form of **Knacker**.

Knackstedt (168) German: euphemistic form of **Knackster(d)t**, a nickname for a bony boy, from Low German *Knack* (*Kochen*) 'bone' + *Stert* 'tail'.

GIVEN NAMES German 5%. *Heinz, Kurt.*

Knadler (148) South German: topographic name for someone living on a mountainside, from Middle High German *genade* 'mountainside', 'slope' + *-(l)er* suffix denoting an inhabitant.

Knaebel (111) South German **Knäbel**: from a diminutive of KNABE.

GIVEN NAMES French 5%; Scandinavian 4%. *Alban; Nelle.*

Knaff (101) Dutch and North German: perhaps, as Debrabandere suggests, from a Low German form of KNAPP 2.

Knaggs (315) Northern English: topographic name for someone who lived by a geographical feature named with the Middle English word *knagg*, which had various senses, including 'stunted dead branch', 'jagged crag', and 'outcrop of rock'.

Knake (149) German: variant spelling of **Knaake** or **Knacke**, variants of KNAACK.

Knape (216) German: variant of KNAPP.

Knapek (120) Czech: from a diminutive of *knap* 'page boy', 'armor bearer' (see KNAPIK).

Knapik (586) **1.** Polish: occupational name from a diminutive of *knap* 'weaver'. **2.** Czech: occupational name for a page boy or armor bearer, from a diminutive of early modern German *Knape* (see KNAPP).

GIVEN NAMES Polish 7%. *Casimir* (2), *Jozef* (2), *Dariusz, Ewa, Grazyna, Henryk, Jerzy, Kazimierz, Krystyna, Miroslawa, Stanislaw, Wieslaw.*

Knapke (264) German: from a pet form of KNAPP.

GIVEN NAMES German 5%. *Aloys* (2), *Florian.*

Knapp (16951) **1.** German: occupational name or status name from the German word *Knapp(e)*, a variant of KNABE 'young unmarried man'. In the 15th century this spelling acquired the separate, specialized meanings 'servant', 'apprentice', or 'miner'. **2.** German: in Franconia, a nickname for a dexterous or skillful person. **3.** English: topographic name for someone who lived by a hillock, Middle English *knappe*, Old English *cnæpp*, or habitational name from any of the several minor places named with the word, in particular Knapp in Hampshire and Knepp in Sussex. **4.** German and western Slavic: variant of KNABE.

Knappe (101) German: variant of KNAPP.

GIVEN NAMES German 13%. *Klaus, Rainer, Siegfried, Wolf.*

Knappenberger (312) German: habitational name for someone from Knappenberg in Schleswig-Holstein.

Knapper (287) **1.** English: topographic name for someone who lived by a hillock (see KNAPP), or habitational name for someone from a place named with this word. **2.** English: possibly a variant spelling of **Napper**, a variant of NAPIER. **3.** German (also **Knäpper**): habitational name from either of two places in Westphalia named Knapp. **4.** German (**Knäpper**): unflattering nickname from an agent derivative of *knappen* 'to be stingy' or, in some places, 'to grab or snatch'.

Knapton (276) English: habitational name from either of two places so called, in Norfolk and North Yorkshire, named from Old English *cnapa* 'servant' or the Old

English personal name *Cnapa* + Old English *tūn* 'settlement'.

Knarr (535) Dutch: variant of KNORR.

Knaub (593) Altered spelling of German KNAUP.

Knauber (120) German: variant, found in the Saar Palatinate, of KNAUER.

Knauer (979) German (also **Knäuer**): **1.** (Silesian) nickname for a gnarled person, from Middle High German *knūr(e)* 'knot', 'gnarl'. **2.** habitational name for someone from either of two places in Thuringia called Knau.

GIVEN NAMES German 4%. *Erwin* (2), *Helmut, Jurgen, Kurt, Otto, Phares, Siegfried.*

Knauf (588) German: nickname for a short, chubby man, from Middle High German *knouf* 'knob', 'button', 'pommel'.

Knauff (486) German: variant spelling of KNAUF.

Knaup (191) German: nickname for a gnarled man, from Middle High German *knūpe* 'knot (in wood)', related to *knaupeln* 'to gnaw on something', 'to untie a knot'.

Knaus (828) German: **1.** from Middle High German *knūz* 'proud', 'arrogant', 'daring', hence a nickname for a haughty person. **2.** in Württemberg *knaus* (and in Switzerland *knūs*) also meant 'gnarl', hence a nickname for a short, fat, gnarled person. **3.** topographic name for someone living on a hillock, from *knaus* 'hillock' in the Swabian and Alemannic dialects of German.

GIVEN NAMES German 4%. *Kurt* (3), *Bernhard, Heimo, Rainer, Wolfgang.*

Knauss (978) German: variant of KNAUS.

Knaust (100) German: standardized form of KNUST.

GIVEN NAMES German 9%. *Helmut, Kurt.*

Knauth (134) German: variant of KNOTH.

GIVEN NAMES German 11%. *Kurt* (3), *Monika, Otto.*

Kneale (201) Manx: reduced Anglicized form of Gaelic **Mac Néill** (see MCNEIL).

Knebel (693) German: **1.** from Middle High German *knebel* 'peg', 'stake' and, by extension 'ankle', 'uncouth person', this latter connotation is found particularly in southeast German and Silesian dialects. **2.** diminutive of KNABE.

Knecht (2173) German and Swiss German: occupational name for a journeyman, from Middle High German *kneht*, Middle Low German *knecht* 'knight's assistant', 'lad', 'servant', 'hired hand', 'apprentice', 'helper'.

Knechtel (236) German: diminutive of KNECHT.

GIVEN NAMES German 7%. *Kurt, Otto, Waldron.*

Knee (566) **1.** Irish and Manx: reduced form of MCNEE. **2.** English (Wiltshire): nickname for someone with some peculiarity of the knee(s), Middle English *kne* (Old

English *cnēow*). **3.** German: altered spelling of *knie* 'knee', a topographic name for an odd-shaped piece of land, or a nickname for someone with an unusual or injured knee.

Kneebone (205) English: from Middle English *kne* 'knee' (Old English *cnēow*) + *bone* 'bone' (Old English *bān*), presumably a nickname for someone with nobbly knees.

Kneece (258) Americanized spelling of German KNIESS or Slovenian and Croatian KNEZ.

Kneedler (146) Probably an altered spelling of English **Needler**, a variant of NADLER.

Kneeland (900) Scottish and northern Irish: probably an Anglicized form of Gaelic **Ó Nialláin** (see NEALON).

FOREBEARS Family tradition holds that John Kneeland, born in 1575 in Glasgow, Scotland, came with his brother Edward to Massachusetts Bay about 1630 on board one of his father's vessels freighted with provisions for the Pilgrims, and that he settled near Boston. His grandson Samuel Kneeland (1697–1769) was a printer who published the Boston Gazette from 1741 to 1755.

Kneen (121) Manx: probably an Anglicized form of Gaelic **Mac Niadháin**, from a pet form of the personal name *Nia* (see McNEE).

Kneer (229) **1.** German: Swabian nickname for a poor person scratching a living, from Middle High German *ner* 'salvation', 'rescue' with the intensifying prefix *ge-*. **2.** German: from the early medieval personal name *Chnodomar*. **3.** Manx: variant of KNEEN.

Kneifl (158) German: from a dialect diminutive form of KNAUF.

Kneip (319) South German: from Middle High German *knīp* 'knife', in particular a cobbler's knife, and hence probably an occupational nickname for a shoemaker.
GIVEN NAMES French 4%. *Lucien* (2), *Jeremie, Marcel.*

Kneipp (131) German: metonymic occupational name for someone who made or sold knives or who used one in their work, from Middle High German *knīp* 'knife'.

Kneisel (199) South German: variant of **Knäusel**, a diminutive of KNAUS.
GIVEN NAMES German 6%. *Otto* (2), *Jochen.*

Kneisley (199) Americanized spelling of German **Kneissle** (see KNEISEL).

Knell (494) **1.** English: topographic name for someone living by a knoll or hilltop, from Middle English *knelle* (Old English *cnyll(e), cnell(e)*, a derivative of Old English *cnoll*), or a habitational name from a minor place named with this word, for example Knell or Knelle in Sussex. **2.** South German: from Middle High German *knellen* 'to cause to explode', 'to snap one's fingers', hence a nickname for a noisy,

loud-mouthed person, or in Swabia and Bavaria for someone who cursed a lot.

Kneller (388) German: nickname for a loud or noisy person, from an agent derivative of Middle High German *knellen* 'to cause to explode', 'to snap one's fingers'.

Knepp (1131) German: variant of KNOPP.

Knepper (1333) **1.** German: from German KNAPP or KNOPF. **2.** German: nickname from a dialect word meaning 'stork' in Uckermark region. **3.** Jewish (Ashkenazic): from Yiddish *knop* 'large button' + the agent suffix *-er*.

Knepshield (119) Americanized form of German *Knippschild*, a nickname for a brave fighter, from Low German *knippen* 'to shoot', 'flick' + *schild* 'shield', or for a tavern owner or a beer drinker, from the same word denoting a light beer (*Weissbier* 'wheat beer').

Knerr (620) German: variant of **Knörr** (see KNORR).

Knesek (110) From a pet form of Slavic *knez* 'prince', 'ruler', 'headman'. See KNEZ.

Kness (284) Germanized or Americanized form of Slavic KNEZ.

Knetter (104) German: of uncertain origin. Probably an occupational nickname for a baker, an agent noun from Middle High German *kneten* 'to knead'.

Knez (135) Croatian and Slovenian: from *knez* 'prince', 'lord', 'chief', a status name for a dignitary, applied also to the headman of a village. As a surname it may also be an ironic or figurative nickname.
GIVEN NAMES French 4%; South Slavic 4%. *Celina, Jacques; Predrag, Srecko.*

Knezevich (247) Serbian and Croatian (**Knežević**): patronymic from *knez* 'chief', i.e. the headman of a village or small district.
GIVEN NAMES South Slavic 6%. *Bosko, Marija, Milorad, Predrag, Srecko.*

Knibbs (141) English (Midlands): unexplained.

Kniceley (123) Americanized spelling of German **Kneissle** (see KNEISEL).

Knicely (382) Americanized spelling of German **Kneissle** (see KNEISEL).

Knick (391) German: from *Knick* 'hedge', 'boundary', hence a topographic name for someone living near a hedge or hedged enclosure or a metonymic occupational name for someone who lays hedges. Hedging is a characteristic feature of the pastureland of Holstein, Mecklenburg, Westphalia, and Lower Saxony.

Knickerbocker (1131) Americanized spelling of the Dutch occupational name **Knickerbacker** 'marble baker', i.e., a baker of children's clay marbles. This lowly occupation became synonymous with the patrician class in NYC through Washington Irving's attribution of his *History of New York* (1809) to a fictitious author named Diedrich Knickerbocker. By the late 1850s

the term had also come to denote a type of loose breeches gathered below the knee, evidently because of the resemblance of the garment to the breeches of the Dutchmen in Cruikshank's illustrations to Irving's book.

Knickrehm (123) North German: of uncertain derivation; possibly related to Low German *reme* 'strap', 'belt', or a topographic name from Middle Low German *knick* 'scrub' + *rīm* 'enclosure'.
GIVEN NAMES German 8%. *Hans, Kurt, Otto, Ralf.*

Knief (148) German: variant of KNEIP.
GIVEN NAME German 4%. *Kurt.*

Kniep (162) German: variant of KNEIP.
GIVEN NAME German 5%. *Ulrich* (2).

Knier (184) German: probably a variant of **Knürr** or KNORR (see KNORR).
GIVEN NAMES German 4%. *Wenzel* (2), *Aloysius.*

Knieriem (232) German: metonymic occupational name for a leather worker or cobbler, from Middle High German *knierieme* '(leather) knee strap'.

Knierim (409) German: metonymic occupational name for a leather worker or cobbler, from Middle High German *knierieme* '(leather) knee strap'.

Knies (342) German: see KNIESS.

Kniess (158) German: Germanized form of Slovenian or Croatian KNEZ; also a habitational name from a place in Mecklenburg, which is named with the same word.
GIVEN NAMES German 6%. *Erwin, Gerhard, Kurt.*

Kniffen (382) Probably an altered form of Dutch or North German KNUEVEN.

Kniffin (355) Probably an altered form of Dutch or North German KNUEVEN.

Knigge (316) North German: variant of KNICK.
GIVEN NAMES German 5%. *Kurt* (3), *Erwin, Hans, Waltraut.*

Knight (45435) **1.** English: status name from Middle English *knyghte* 'knight', Old English *cniht* 'boy', 'youth', 'serving lad'. This word was used as a personal name before the Norman Conquest, and the surname may in part reflect a survival of this. It is also possible that in a few cases it represents a survival of the Old English sense into Middle English, as an occupational name for a domestic servant. In most cases, however, it clearly comes from the more exalted sense that the word achieved in the Middle Ages. In the feudal system introduced by the Normans the word was applied at first to a tenant bound to serve his lord as a mounted soldier. Hence it came to denote a man of some substance, since maintaining horses and armor was an expensive business. As feudal obligations became increasingly converted to monetary payments, the term lost its precise significance and came to denote an honorable estate conferred by the king on men of noble birth who had served him well. Knights in this last sense normally belonged to ancient noble families with distinguished family names of their own, so that the surname is more likely to have been applied to a servant in a knightly house or to someone who had played the part of a knight in a pageant or won the title in some contest of skill. **2.** Irish: part translation of Gaelic **Mac an Ridire** 'son of the rider or knight'. See also MCKNIGHT.

Knighten (953) English: variant spelling of KNIGHTON.

Knightly (236) English: habitational name from Knightley in Staffordshire, named in Old English as 'the wood or clearing of the retainers', from *cnihtā*, genitive plural of *cnihta* 'servant', 'retainer' + *lēah* 'wood', 'clearing'.

Knighton (1500) English: habitational name from any of the numerous places named with Old English *cnihta*, genitive plural of *cniht* 'servant', 'retainer' + *tūn* 'enclosure', 'settlement'.

Knights (633) English: from the genitive singular of KNIGHT, hence a name for a son or a retainer of a knight.

Knill (157) **1.** English: variant of KNELL. **2.** German and Swiss German: variant of KNELL.

Knipe (643) **1.** English: unexplained. **2.** Americanized spelling of German KNEIP.

Knipfer (194) German: occupational name for a knitter, net maker, or button maker, from an agent derivative of Middle High German *knüpfen* 'to tie or knot'.

Knipp (903) **1.** German and Dutch: metonymic occupational name for someone whose work involved clipping or snipping. **2.** German: nickname for an unimportant person, from Middle Low German *knippe* 'snap of the fingers', 'trick'.

Knippa (158) Variant of German KNIPPER.
GIVEN NAME German 4%. *Otto* (2).

Knippel (279) Variant of German **Knüppel** (see KNUEPPEL).

Knippen (102) Dutch: of uncertain origin. Apparently from the verb *knippen* 'to clip or snip' or 'to blink', or possibly from *knijpen* 'to pinch'. Alternatively, it may be a shortened form of KNIPPENBERG.

Knippenberg (172) German: habitational name from a place formerly so named in North Rhine-Westphalia, north of Essen.

Knipper (308) Dutch or German: **1.** metonymic occupational name for someone whose worked involved clipping or snipping. **2.** habitational name from a farm named Knippen near Mülheim, Cologne.

Knippers (127) German: variant of KNIPPER.

Knipple (231) Americanized spelling of German **Knüppel** (see KNUEPPEL).

Kniseley (109) See KNISELY.

Knisely (663) Americanized spelling of German **Knäusle** (or of the variants

Kneuss(e)l, **Kneisel**, or **Kneissl**), diminutives of KNAUS.

Kniskern (186) German: nickname for a bon vivant, from *geniess gern* 'like(s) to enjoy'.

Knisley (1127) Respelling of **Knüsli**, Swabian-Alemannic (Swiss), from a diminutive of KNAUS.

Knispel (166) German: habitational name from a place in Upper Saxony formerly called Kniespol (Czech Knežpole) 'princely land', now in the Czech Republic.
GIVEN NAMES German 10%. *Heinz* (2), *Erna*, *Ewald*, *Reinhardt*.

Kniss (317) **1.** Americanized spelling of German KNIESS. **2.** Possibly a shortened form of German **Knüsli** (see KNISLEY).

Knittel (519) German and Jewish (Ashkenazic): from a dialect variant of *Knüttel* 'club', 'cudgel', hence a metonymic occupational name for a maker of these or possibly a nickname for a crude, loutish individual.
GIVEN NAMES German 4%. *Otto* (3), *Wolfgang*.

Knitter (312) German: variant spelling of **Knütter**, an occupational name for someone who fashioned materials by knotting or knitting, from Low German *knütten* 'to tie, knot, or knit'.

Knittle (377) Altered spelling of KNITTEL.

Knobbe (284) North German: nickname for an uncouth, stupid, or stingy person, from Middle Low German *knobbe* 'knot', 'lump'. Compare KNAUF, South German KNOPF.

Knobel (439) **1.** German and Swiss German (also **Knöbel**): from Middle High German *knübel*, probably a nickname in the sense 'ankle'. However, the term also denotes a rounded elevation and may therefore also be a topographic name for someone who lived by a knoll. *Knöbel* is also an archaic word for a servant. **2.** Jewish (Ashkenazic): ornamental name from German *Knobel* 'knot', 'node'. **3.** Jewish (eastern Ashkenazic): from Yiddish *knobl* 'garlic'.
GIVEN NAMES Jewish 4%. *Aba*, *Meyer*, *Miriam*, *Toba*, *Yakov*.

Knoblauch (659) German and Danish: **1.** metonymic occupational name for a grower or seller of garlic, or possibly a nickname for someone who ate or prepared food with copious amounts of garlic, Middle High German *knobelouch*. **2.** habitational name from any of several places so named in Saxony and Brandenburg.
GIVEN NAMES German 4%. *Kurt* (2), *Erwin*, *Gerhard*, *Hans*, *Otto*, *Wolfram*.

Knoble (282) Americanized spelling of German and Jewish KNOBEL.

Knoblich (100) German: variant of KNOBLAUCH.
GIVEN NAMES German 8%. *Bernhard*, *Frieda*, *Gottlieb*.

Knobloch (751) German: variant of KNOBLAUCH.

Knoblock (540) Americanized spelling of German KNOBLAUCH.

Knoch (381) German: variant of KNOCHE.

Knoche (448) German: from Middle High German *knoche* 'bone', also 'knot (on a tree)', 'snag (on a tree)', applied as an occupational nickname for a butcher or possibly for a knacker, or a nickname for a bony, stocky, or crude person. Compare North German KNAACK.

Knochel (127) German (**Knöchel**): from a diminutive of KNOCHE.
GIVEN NAME German 4%. *Kurt*.

Knock (322) **1.** North German form of KNOCHE. **2.** German: possibly a habitational name from Knock near Emden. **3.** English: topographic name for someone living by a hill, from Middle English *knocke* 'hill' (Old English *cnoc*).

Knocke (118) **1.** German and English: variant of KNOCK. **2.** South German: topographic name from *Knock* 'hill'.
GIVEN NAMES German 4%. *Erna*, *Erwin*.

Knode (301) South German: nickname for a coarse, unrefined person, from Middle High German *knode* 'knot'.

Knodel (465) **1.** German (**Knödel**): diminutive of KNODE. **2.** German: from the medieval personal name *Knodel*, a short form of *Chnodomar*.
GIVEN NAMES German 4%. *Erwin* (3), *Arno*, *Gerhardt*, *Wilhelm*.

Knodle (148) Americanized spelling of German **Knödel** (see KNODEL).

Knoebel (350) German (**Knöbel**): **1.** see KNOBEL. **2.** variant of **Knäbel** (see KNAEBEL).

Knoedler (215) South German (**Knödler**): occupational name, probably for someone who made dumplings, from an agent derivative of Middle High German *knödel*.
GIVEN NAMES German 7%. *Gunther*, *Heinz*, *Helmut*, *Manfred*, *Otto*.

Knoell (214) German (**Knöll**): nickname for a peasant or for a crude uncouth person, from Middle High German *knolle* 'sod', 'lump of earth' (with diminutive unlaut, typical of some dialects).

Knoff (219) Altered spelling of German KNOPF or KNAUFF.

Knoke (317) German: variant of KNOCHE or KNAACK.

Knoles (272) English: variant spelling of KNOWLES.

Knoll (3945) **1.** English and German: topographic name for someone living near a hilltop or mountain peak, from Middle English *knolle* 'hilltop', 'hillock' (Old English *cnoll*), Middle High German *knol* 'peak'. In some cases the English name is habitational, from one of the many places named with this word, for example Knole in Kent or Knowle in Dorset, West Midlands, etc. **2.** German and Jewish (Ashkenazic): nickname for a peasant or a crude clumsy person, from Middle High

German *knolle* 'lump', 'clod', German *Knolle*.

Knolle (118) German: variant of KNOLL 1.
GIVEN NAMES German 8%. *Kurt* (2), *Ernst*.

Knollenberg (163) German: habitational name from a place in Württemberg called Knollenberg.

Knollman (108) German (**Knollmann**): topographic name for someone living near the summit of a hill or mountain (see KNOLL 1).
GIVEN NAME German 4%. *Dieter*.

Knoop (623) English, German, and Dutch: variant of KNOPP.
GIVEN NAMES German 4%. *Hans* (2), *Erwin*, *Guenter*, *Klaus*, *Manfred*.

Knop (747) **1.** English, German, and Dutch: variant spelling of KNOPP. **2.** Polish: occupational name for a weaver, Polish *knap* (see KNAPIK). **3.** Jewish (Ashkenazic): metonymic occupational name from Yiddish *knop* 'button' (see KNOPF).
GIVEN NAMES German 4%. *Kurt* (4), *Otto* (2), *Franz*, *Gunter*, *Rudi*, *Wolfgang*.

Knope (194) **1.** English: variant of KNOPP. **2.** Altered spelling of German **Knoop** or **Knoppe**, variants of KNOPF.

Knopf (1208) German (also **Knöpf**) and Jewish (Ashkenazic): from Middle High German *knopf* 'swelling', 'lump', 'knob', 'button', 'glob', modern German *Knopf*, hence a metonymic occupational name for a maker of buttons, normally of horn; a nickname for a small, rotund man (especially in Swabia, where the term also has the sense 'dumpling'); or a topographic name for someone who lived by a rounded hillock.
GIVEN NAMES German 4%. *Annice*, *Fritz*, *Gunter*, *Helmuth*, *Kurt*, *Manfred*, *Otto*, *Siegfried*.

Knopik (149) Polish: variant of KNAPIK 'weaver'.

Knopp (1593) **1.** German and Dutch: from Middle Low German, *knōp*, Middle Dutch *cnoop*, *cnop(pe)* 'swelling', 'lump', 'knob', 'button', 'glob', hence a metonymic occupational name for a maker of buttons, normally of horn; a nickname for a small, rotund man; or a topographic name for someone who lived by a rounded hillock. **2.** English: from Middle English *knop(pe)* 'knob', 'protuberance', presumably applied as a nickname for someone with a noticeable wart or carbuncle or with knobbly knees or elbows, or possibly to someone who was small and chubby. **3.** Jewish (Ashkenazic): variant of KNOP 3.

Knops (144) Dutch: variant of KNOPP.

Knorr (1724) German and Dutch: from Middle High, Middle Low German *knorre*, Middle Dutch *cnorre* 'knot', 'gnarl', 'protuberance', hence a nickname for a gnarled person.

Knost (138) German: probably an altered spelling of **Knaust**, a South German nickname for a stocky person, derivative of

KNUST; or an altered form of **Knast**, nickname for a gnarled or crude person, from Low German *Knast* 'gnarl', 'knot'.

Knotek (183) Czech: nickname for a man of small stature, from a diminutive of Czech and Sorbian *knot* 'mole', 'wick', 'little fellow'.
GIVEN NAME French 4%. *Marcel*.

Knoth (334) German: nickname for a gnarled or crude person, from Middle High German *knode*, *knote* 'knot'. Compare KNOLL, KNORR.
GIVEN NAMES German 4%. *Erwin*, *Frieda*, *Georg*.

Knothe (102) **1.** German: variant of KNOTH. **2.** North German: nickname for a partner or companion, from Low German *genōte* 'companion'.

Knott (5270) **1.** English: from the Middle English personal name *Knut*, of Scandinavian origin. **2.** German: variant of KNOTH.

Knotts (2489) English: patronymic from KNOTT.

Knouff (151) Americanized spelling of German KNAUF(F).

Knous (175) Americanized spelling of German KNAUS.

Knouse (614) Americanized spelling of German KNAUS.

Knowland (103) Irish: variant of NOLAN.

Knowlden (125) English: probably a variant of KNOWLTON.

Knowles (10731) **1.** English: topographic name for someone who lived at the top of a hill or by a hillock, from a genitive or plural form of Middle English *knoll* 'hilltop', 'hillock' (Old English *cnoll*; see KNOLL), or habitational name from any of the many places named with this word. **2.** Irish: Anglicized form of Gaelic **Ó Tnúthghail** (see NEWELL).

Knowlton (3243) English: habitational name from either of two places so named, one in Dorset and the other in Kent. Both are named in Old English as 'the settlement (*tūn*) by the hilltop (*cnoll*)'.

Knox (14847) **1.** Scottish, northern English, and northern Irish: from a genitive or plural form of Old English *cnocc* 'round-topped hill', hence a topographic name for someone who lived on a hilltop, or a habitational name from one of the places in Scotland and northern England named with this element, now spelled *Knock*, in particular one in Renfrewshire. **2.** The surname is also borne by eastern Ashkenazic Jews as an Americanized form of one or more like-sounding Jewish surnames.

Knoy (151) Altered spelling of Swiss German **Kneu** (see KANOY).

Knuckles (628) English: presumably a nickname for someone with noticeable knuckles, or someone who was able to crack his knuckles loudly.

Knudsen (3816) Danish, Norwegian, and German: patronymic from a personal name

derived from Old Norse *Knútr* meaning 'knot' (Danish *Knud*, Norwegian *Knut*, German *Knuth*). This was a Danish royal name, Latinized as *Canutus*.
GIVEN NAMES Scandinavian 9%. *Erik* (9), *Knud* (7), *Niels* (7), *Holger* (3), *Jorgen* (3), *Ove* (2), *Alf*, *Alfhild*, *Anders*, *Baard*, *Berger*, *Einer*.

Knudson (3274) Americanized spelling of KNUDSEN.
GIVEN NAMES Scandinavian 4%. *Erik* (10), *Knute* (8), *Lars* (4), *Iver*, *Knud*, *Nels*, *Nils*, *Obert*, *Sigvald*, *Sven*.

Knudsvig (110) Norwegian and Danish: habitational name from a place named with the personal name *Knut* (see KNUDSEN) + *vig*, Danish spelling of *vik* 'bay', 'inlet'.
GIVEN NAMES Scandinavian 5%. *Arlys*, *Helmer*.

Knudtson (708) Scandinavian: see KNUDSEN.

Knue (117) North German: of uncertain origin.

Knueppel (203) German (**Knüppel**): from Low German *knüppel* 'cudgel', 'cleaver', hence a nickname for a peasant or a coarse man; or possibly a metonymic occupational name for a maker of (metal) billets.
GIVEN NAMES German 7%. *Ernst*, *Helmut*, *Hermann*, *Kurt*.

Knueven (141) Dutch and North German (**Knüven**): nickname from *knuffen* 'to push or thump'.

Knull (111) German: variant of KNOLL 1.
GIVEN NAMES German 8%. *Erhard*, *Kurt*, *Manfred*.

Knupp (651) German: variant of KNAPP or KNOPP.

Knuppel (124) German (**Knüppel**): see KNUEPPEL.
GIVEN NAMES German 7%. *Inge*, *Kurt*, *Manfred*.

Knust (305) North German: from *knust* 'knot', 'crust (of a loaf)', hence possibly a nickname for a stocky person or a tough character.
GIVEN NAMES German 8%. *Reinhold* (2), *Eldred*, *Fritz*, *Kurt*, *Udo*.

Knuteson (151) German and Scandinavian: patronymic from a personal name derived from the personal name *Knut*, Old Norse *Knútr* (see KNUDSEN).
GIVEN NAME Scandinavian 4%. *Helmer*.

Knuth (1595) German and Scandinavian: **1.** from the personal name *Knut*, Old Norse *Knútr* (see KNUDSEN). **2.** North German: variant of KNOTH.
GIVEN NAMES German 4%. *Kurt* (5), *Hans* (3), *Arno*, *Claus*, *Erwin*, *Ewald*, *Frieda*, *Hans-Peter*, *Heinz*, *Jurgen*, *Klaus*, *Lorenz*.

Knutsen (934) Norwegian, Danish, and German: see KNUDSEN.
GIVEN NAMES Scandinavian 13%; German 5%. *Erik* (3), *Knute* (3), *Gunner* (2), *Aksel*, *Anders*, *Berent*, *Berger*, *Jarl*, *Knut*, *Lars*, *Nels*, *Nils*; *Hans* (4), *Bernhard* (2), *Kurt* (2), *Gerd*, *Kaspar*, *Konrad*, *Oskar*, *Otto*.

Knutson (7541) Respelling of any of the Scandinavian patronymics from the personal name *Knut* (see KNUTH), for example KNUDSEN.

GIVEN NAMES Scandinavian 4%. *Erik* (10), *Knute* (8), *Selmer* (3), *Ingard* (2), *Jarl* (2), *Jorgen* (2), *Juel* (2), *Nels* (2), *Obert* (2), *Tryg* (2), *Algot*, *Egil*.

Knutzen (289) German and Scandinavian: patronymic from KNUTH.

GIVEN NAMES Scandinavian 8%; German 4%. *Nels* (2), *Anders*, *Asmund*, *Egil*, *Einer*, *Erik*; *Erwin* (2), *Hans*, *Horst*, *Otto*.

Ko (2365) **1.** Chinese 柯: Min (Taiwanese) form of KE. **2.** Chinese 高: Cantonese variant of GAO. **3.** Chinese 葛: variant of GE 1. **4.** Chinese 戈: variant of GE 2. **5.** Korean: there is only one Chinese character for the surname *Ko*. There are ten different Ko clans, but they are all descended from the Ko clan of Cheju Island. There is no historical information regarding the founder of this clan, but there is a legend which tells of three men who appeared from a cave on the north side of Cheju Island's Halla Mountain. These three men were the founders of the Yang clan, the Pu clan, and the Ko clan, the latter being named Ko Ŭl-la. Some days after the three men emerged from the cave, a box was washed up on the shore of the island. In the box were three women, horses, cows, and agricultural seed. From these beginnings, the three established Cheju Island's T'amnaguk kingdom and ruled peacefully. Ko is a common surname found throughout the Korean peninsula. Approximately ten percent of Cheju Island's present-day population consists of members of the Ko family. **6.** Hungarian (**Kő**): from *kő* 'stone', a word from the ancient Finno-Ugric word stock of Hungarian (cognate with Finnish *kivi*, Estonian *keve*), hence a topographic name for someone who lived on stony ground or by a notable outcrop of rock, or alternatively a metonymic occupational name for a mason or stonecutter.

GIVEN NAMES Chinese/Korean 52%. *Young* (19), *Kwang* (15), *Yong* (13), *Sung* (12), *Jae* (11), *Eun* (7), *Hyun* (7), *Myung* (7), *Jung* (6), *Kyong* (6), *Sang* (6), *Wing* (6); *Chang* (18), *Chong* (13), *Chung* (5), *Byung* (3), *Byung Soo* (3), *Hak* (3), *Jeong* (3), *Kwang Soo* (3), *Min* (3), *Myong* (3), *Pak* (3), *Sinae* (3).

Koba (155) Czech: **1.** from a pet form of the personal name *Jakub* (see JACOB). **2.** nickname from Slavic *koba* 'raven'. **3.** Japanese: 'small place', found mostly in the Ryūkyū Islands.

GIVEN NAMES Japanese 11%. *Akira*, *Kaz*, *Kazumi*, *Koichi*, *Sadamu*, *Shinji*.

Koback (118) **1.** Perhaps a respelling of German **Kubach**, a habitational name from any of various places named Kubach, for example in Hesse. **2.** German (Palatine): of uncertain origin.

Kobak (158) **1.** Polish: patronymic from a reduced form of Polish *Jakub* (see JACOB). **2.** Hungarian: from a Turkish loanword *kobak* 'head', 'forehead' (from Cumanian and Pechenegg *quabaq* or Ottoman Turkish *kabak* 'pumpkin'), hence a nickname for an unsophisticated person or someone with a bald or big head.

GIVEN NAMES Polish 4%. *Aniela*, *Jerzy*.

Kobal (100) **1.** Slovenian and Croatian (northwestern Croatia): unexplained. **2.** German: perhaps a variant of **Kubal**, from Sorbian *kowal* 'blacksmith'.

GIVEN NAME German 4%; South Slavic 4%. *Branko*.

Kobashigawa (122) Japanese: 'river with a small bridge', found mostly in the Ryūkyū Islands.

GIVEN NAMES Japanese 35%. *Isamu* (2), *Noboru* (2), *Atsuo*, *Katsuhiro*, *Katsuyoshi*, *Kiichi*, *Masaichi*, *Masako*, *Masao*, *Masashi*, *Matsue*, *Nobu*.

Kobayashi (1311) Japanese: 'small forest'; one of the ten most common Japanese surnames, found especially in central Japan; the different families bearing this name are not all related. The name is also found in the Ryūkyū Islands.

GIVEN NAMES Japanese 69%. *Takashi* (11), *Hiroshi* (9), *Toshio* (7), *Akira* (6), *Hisako* (6), *Hitoshi* (6), *Makoto* (6), *Hideaki* (5), *Hideo* (5), *Hisashi* (5), *Kazuo* (5), *Nobuo* (5).

Kobbe (136) German: **1.** from a pet form of the personal name *Jakob* (see JACOB). **2.** habitational name from a field name common in Westphalia, which is of uncertain etymology.

GIVEN NAME Scandinavian 5%. *Lars* (2).

Kobe (332) **1.** Japanese (**Kōbe**): habitational name which began as occupational, meaning the private residence of a chief priest of a Shintō shrine; it could also indicate others who lived near his residence. The name is mostly found in eastern Japan, but because of the importance of the western port city of *Kōbe*, some emigrants from the city may have taken their surnames from it. More correctly pronounced *Kanbe*; other alternate pronunciations are *Jinbe* and *Kamito*. **2.** German, Slovenian, and Jewish (Ashkenazic): from a pet form of the personal name JAKOB.

Kobel (364) German: **1.** topographic name from Middle High German *kobel* 'rock', 'gorge'. **2.** eastern German habitational name for someone from any of several places, mainly in Silesia, of Slavic origin, e.g. Kobel, Kobeln, Koblau, which are named from Slavic *kobyla* 'mare'. **3.** from *Kobel* 'laborer's cottage', 'hut', hence, by metonymy, a bondsman or serf.

Kober (939) **1.** German and Jewish (Ashkenazic): from a derivative of the personal name *Jakob* or *Yakov* (see JACOB). **2.** German and Jewish (Ashkenazic): from German *Kober* 'basket', Middle High German

kober, hence a metonymic occupational name for a basket maker or perhaps a nickname for someone who carried a basket on his back. **3.** German (**Köber**): habitational name for someone from a place called Köben. **4.** Germanized form of Czech **Kovář** (see KOVAR) 'blacksmith' or a cognate in another western Slavic language. **5.** Czech: nickname for a fat man, from *kobero* 'pot belly'.

GIVEN NAMES German 5%. *Otto* (3), *Bernhard* (2), *Angelika*, *Dieter*, *Ernst*, *Erwin*, *Gottlieb*, *Konrad*, *Manfred*, *Reinhold*, *Sepp*, *Wolfgang*.

Koberstein (179) German: probably a habitational name from a place in eastern Germany.

GIVEN NAMES German 6%. *Erna*, *Erwin*, *Manfred*, *Raimund*.

Kobes (158) German (also **Köbes**): from a pet form of the personal name *Jakob* (see JACOB).

Koble (232) Americanized spelling of German KOBEL.

Kobler (218) German (also **Köbler**): from *Kobel* 'cottage', hence a topographical name or status name for someone who lived in a cottage (see KOBEL 3). It is also found as a Slovenian surname, with the variant **Koblar**.

GIVEN NAMES German 11%. *Helmut* (2), *Johann* (2), *Otto* (2), *Ewald*, *Fritz*, *Theresia*.

Kobliska (118) Slavic: unexplained.

Koblitz (102) German (**Köblitz**): habitational name from Köblitz in Oberlausitz or Saxony, or from Köbbelitz in the Altmark area, of Slavic origin.

GIVEN NAMES German 10%. *Kurt* (2), *Heinz*.

Kobold (113) German: nickname meaning 'goblin', 'sprite', from Middle High German *kobolt* 'household spirit'.

GIVEN NAME German 4%. *Klaus*.

Kobos (113) Polish: variant of KOBUS.

GIVEN NAMES Polish 16%. *Casimir*, *Dariusz*, *Feliks*, *Fryderyk*, *Irena*, *Krzysztof*, *Zygmunt*.

Kobrin (246) Jewish (from Belarus): habitational name from Kobrin, now in Belarus.

GIVEN NAMES Jewish 6%. *Faina* (2), *Emanuel*, *Isadore*.

Kobs (441) German: from a pet form of the personal name *Jakob* (see JACOB).

Kobus (460) **1.** Polish, Czech, Dutch, and German: from a pet form of the personal name *Jakobus* (Czech *Jakub*) (see JACOB). **2.** Polish and Jewish (from Poland): nickname from *kobus* 'falcon'.

GIVEN NAMES Polish 5%; German 4%. *Casimir* (3), *Piotr* (2), *Janina*, *Mieczyslaw*, *Zbigniew*; *Gerhard*, *Joerg*, *Kurt*, *Reinhold*, *Rudi*, *Wilhelm*.

Koby (280) Origin unidentified.

GIVEN NAMES French 4%. *Micheline*, *Pierre*.

Kobylanski (68) Polish (**Kobylański**): habitational name for someone from a place called Kobylany, named with *kobyła* 'mare'.

GIVEN NAMES Polish 12%; French 7%. *Andrzej, Grazyna, Zbigniew; Andre* (2).

Kobylarz (183) Polish: occupational name for a horse butcher, Polish *kobylarz* 'horse butcher', 'knacker'.

GIVEN NAMES Polish 5%. *Jerzy, Katarzyna.*

Kobylinski (151) Polish (**Kobyliński**): habitational name for someone a place called from Kobylin, so named from *kobyła* 'mare'.

GIVEN NAMES Polish 17%. *Andrzej* (2), *Karol* (2), *Franciszek, Jerzy, Leszek, Ryszard, Zdzislaw.*

Kobza (245) Czech, Slovak, and Hungarian: from Czech *kobos*, Hungarian *koboz*, a term denoting a kind of musical instrument resembling a lute (Turkish *qopuz*), hence a metonymic occupational name for a lutenist or a troubadour. The instrument was first introduced into eastern and central Europe by the Cumanian and Pecheneg people, and its use became widespread during the Turkish occupation of the region.

Koc (127) **1.** Turkish: nickname meaning 'little'. **2.** Polish: nickname from *koc* 'blanket' or possibly from the verb *kocić się* 'to behave like a kitten'.

GIVEN NAMES Muslim 21%; Polish 16%. *Ali* (3), *Aydin, Emine, Fatih, Harun, Hasan, Huseyin, Mustafa, Yener; Henryk* (2), *Andrzej, Czeslaw, Jerzy, Maciej, Tadeusz, Wieslaw, Zdzislaw.*

Koca (117) Turkish: variant of KOC or KOCAK.

Kocak (165) Turkish (**Koçak**): nickname from **Koçak** 'brave' or 'generous'.

GIVEN NAMES Muslim 10%. *Huseyin* (2), *Adnan, Ali, Ibrahim, Ismail, Kemal, Mahmut, Refik.*

Kocan (149) **1.** Polish, Czech, and Slovak: from a pet form of an Old Slavic personal name, *Chotimir*, Polish *Chocimir*, or possibly from *kocan* 'cob' (Polish *kaczan*). **2.** Slovenian (**Kočan**): topographic or status name for someone who lived in a cottage, from *koča* 'cottage'.

Koch (21108) **1.** German and Jewish (Ashkenazic): occupational name from Middle High German *koch*, German *Koch* 'cook' (cognate with Latin *coquus*). The name in this sense is widespread throughout eastern and central Europe, and is also well established in Denmark. **2.** Czech and Slovak: from a pet form of any of several medieval personal names beginning with Ko-, for example *Kochan, Kocián, Kojata,* and *Kosmas.* **3.** Polish: nickname from *kochać* 'to love' (see KOCHAN).

GIVEN NAMES German 4%. *Kurt* (23), *Hans* (22), *Otto* (21), *Erwin* (16), *Klaus* (9), *Helmut* (8), *Fritz* (7), *Heinz* (6), *Gerhard* (5), *Wolfgang* (5), *Ernst* (4), *Florian* (4).

Kochan (560) **1.** Czech, Slovak, and eastern German (Sorbian): from the old personal name *Kochan* 'beloved' (i.e.. by God), a calque on Latin *Amatus* 'beloved', i.e. by God. Compare AMATO. **2.** Polish: nick-

name for an attractive man, from *kochan, kochanek,* a term of endearment meaning 'darling', 'beloved', from *kochać* 'to love'. **3.** Americanized spelling of Slovenian **Kočan** (see KOCAN 2).

GIVEN NAMES Polish 6%. *Casimir* (2), *Genowesa, Ireneusz, Jacek, Jerzy, Jozef, Kazimierz, Piotr, Stanislaw, Tadeusz, Waclaw.*

Kochanek (146) Polish: nickname from *kochanek* 'darling', 'dear', 'lover', from *kochać* 'to love' (see KOCHAN).

GIVEN NAMES Polish 7%. *Jozef, Piotr, Stanislaw.*

Kochanowski (183) Polish and Jewish (from Poland and Belarus): habitational name for someone from Kochanów or Kochanowo, both named from Polish *kochać* 'to love' (*kochany* 'dear').

GIVEN NAMES Polish 9%. *Bogumil, Boguslaw, Boleslaw, Jacek, Jerzy.*

Kochanski (340) Polish (**Kochański**) and Jewish (from Poland): habitational name for someone from a place called Kochań, in Siedlce voivodeship, or Kochany, now in Belarus.

GIVEN NAMES Polish 6%. *Piotr* (2), *Boleslaw, Ewa, Jacek.*

Kochel (256) German (**Köchel**): habitational name from any of the numerous minor place names in Bavaria and the Tyrol that get their name from *Köchel*, a dialect term denoting an island of raised land surrounded by marsh.

Kochenderfer (114) German: variant spelling of **Kochendörfer**, a dialect variant of KOCHENDORFER.

GIVEN NAMES German 9%. *Ottmar* (2), *Kurt.*

Kochendorfer (151) German: habitational name for someone from any of several places called Kochendorf in Württemberg, Schleswig-Holstein, and Bohemia.

GIVEN NAME German 4%. *Wilhelm.*

Kocher (2275) **1.** German (**Köcher**): from Middle High German *kochaere* 'vessel', 'container (for transporting fish)', 'quiver', hence a metonymic occupational name maker of these. **2.** German and Jewish (Ashkenazic): occupational name for a cook, from an agent derivative of German *kochen* 'to cook'. Compare KOCH. **3.** Jewish (Ashkenazic): ornamental name from Yiddish *kacher* 'drake'. **4.** Jewish (eastern Ashkenazic): from Yiddish *kochere* 'poker', 'fork'.

Kochersperger (118) **1.** German and French (Alsatian): habitational name for someone from either of two places in Alsace called Kochenberg: Dossenheim-Kochersberg and Wintzenheim-Kochersberg. **2.** German: probably also a habitational name for someone from a small place called Kochersperg, most likely in Bavaria or Austria.

Kochert (140) German: variant of KOCHER 2.

Kochevar (330) **1.** Slovenian (**Kočevar**): habitational name for someone from the city of Kočevje or from Kočevsko region in south central Slovenia. **2.** Czech (**Kočvar**): metonymic occupational name for a potter, from *kočvar* 'big pot', 'jar'.

Kochis (452) Americanized spelling of Hungarian KOCSIS.

Kochman (327) German (**Kochmann**) and Jewish (Ashkenazic): occupational name for a cook; a variant of KOCH with the addition of -*man* 'man'.

GIVEN NAMES Jewish 6%; German 5%. *Doron, Gilad, Hyman, Isadore, Menachem; Frederika, Heinz, Kurt, Manfred, Otto.*

Koci (234) Czech (**Kočí**) and Hungarian (**Kocsi**): metonymic occupational name for a coachman or coachbuilder, from Czech *kočí* 'coach', Hungarian *kocsi.*

Kocian (466) **1.** Czech and Slovak (**Kocián**) and Hungarian (**Kócián**): from a personal name, from Latin *Cassianus*, a derivative of the old Roman family name *Cassius.* **2.** Altered form of Slovenian and Croatian **Kocjan** or **Kocijan**, vernacular forms of the personal name *Kancijan*, Latin *Cantianus.* Saint Cantianus was a martyr under the Roman emperor Diocletian. He died together with his brother and sister in S. Canzian d'Isonzo (Slovenian *Škocjan*) in Friuli, in northeastern Italy. He was one of the most popular Catholic saints in Slovenia and Croatia in the Middle Ages and many places bear his name (*Škocjan* 'Saint Kocjan'). The American surname **Kocian** may also be a reduced form of the Slovenian patronymics **Kocjančič** or **Kocijančič**.

Kocik (132) **1.** Polish and Czech (**Kocík**): from a pet form of the Old Slavic personal name *Chotimir*, Polish *Chocimir*. **2.** nickname from a diminutive of *kot* 'cat', 'kitten'.

GIVEN NAMES Polish 4%. *Jerzy, Wojciech.*

Kocinski (143) Polish: (**Kociński**): habitational name for someone from a village called Kocin in Bydgoszcz voivodeship, or various places called Kocina in Kalisz, Kielce or Sieradz voivodeships, all named with *kot* 'cat'.

Kocis (228) Slovak (**Kočiš**) variant of Hungarian KOCSIS.

Kock (408) **1.** Dutch (**De Kock**) and German: occupational name for a cook, Middle Dutch, Middle Low German *kok.* **2.** German (**Köck**): Bavarian variant of **Keck**, a nickname from Alemannic *kech* 'lively', 'bold'.

GIVEN NAMES German 7%. *Gerhard* (3), *Dieter, Elfriede, Erhard, Fritz, Hans, Helmut, Kurt, Orlo, Reinhard.*

Kocon (132) Polish: variant of KOCAN.

GIVEN NAMES Polish 8%. *Andrzej, Piotr, Stanislawa.*

Kocourek (224) Czech: nickname for a promiscuous man, from a diminutive of *kocour* 'tom cat'.

Kocsis (674) Hungarian: occupational name for a coachman or coachbuilder, from

Hungarian *kocsi* 'coach', 'wagon', originally *kocsi szekér* 'Kocs cart', from the village of Kocs, where in the 15th century this type of conveyance, with springs, was first made. The modern English word *coach* and French *coche* are derived from this Hungarian word, as well as German *Kutsche* and Czech *koči*.

GIVEN NAMES Hungarian 6%. *Balint* (2), *Imre* (2), *Istvan* (2), *Laszlo* (2), *Atilla, Bela, Geza, Jolan, Kalman, Nandor, Tamas, Tibor.*

Kocur (273) Polish: nickname for a promiscuous man, from *kocur* 'tom cat'.

GIVEN NAMES Polish 5%. *Bogdan, Genowefa, Wojciech, Zbigniew.*

Kocurek (297) Polish: diminutive of KOCUR, meaning 'little tom cat'.

Koda (141) Japanese (**Kōda**): 'rice paddy of happiness'; also pronounced *Sakita* and *Yukita,* found mostly in western Japan.

GIVEN NAMES Japanese 30%. *Akihiko, Akihiro, Fujie, Haruhisa, Hironobu, Hiroyuki, Isao, Kazuhide, Kenji, Koji, Maki, Michio.*

Kodama (332) Japanese: 'small ball'; habitational name of an important family from *Kodama-gun,* in a part of Musashi now in Saitama prefecture. Another family, of TAIRA descent, from Kodama-mura in Shinano (now Nagano prefecture), writes the name with a different first character.

GIVEN NAMES Japanese 48%. *Terue* (4), *Hiroshi* (3), *Takashi* (3), *Hiroki* (2), *Masako* (2), *Nobuko* (2), *Reiko* (2), *Seiji* (2), *Akihiko, Azusa, Chiyoko, Etsuko.*

Koder (129) Slovenian: nickname for a person with a curly hair, from *koder* 'curl'.

Koebel (328) German (**Köbel**): from a pet form of the personal name *Jakob* (see JACOB).

Koebler (103) German: status name for day laborer dwelling in a cottage, *Kobel.*

Koecher (101) German (**Köcher**): from Middle High German *kocher* 'container', 'quiver', 'pouch', presumably a metonymic occupational name for a maker of such articles or possibly for an archer, fisherman, etc.

Koeck (170) German: see KOCK.

Koegel (303) German: alternative spelling of **Kögel**, a Bavarian variant of KEGEL.

Koegler (255) German (**Kögler**): Bavarian variant of KEGLER.

GIVEN NAMES German 11%. *Kurt* (4), *Bernd* (2), *Heinz* (2), *Hans, Lieselotte.*

Koehl (674) South German (**Köhl**): Alemannic variant of KOHL.

Koehler (8265) German: see KOHLER.

GIVEN NAMES German 5%. *Kurt* (32), *Otto* (7), *Erwin* (6), *Hans* (6), *Wolfgang* (5), *Ernst* (4), *Heinz* (4), *Klaus* (4), *Dieter* (3), *Eckhard* (3), *Fritz* (3), *Helmut* (3).

Koehn (3341) North German (**Köhn**): variant of KUEHN.

GIVEN NAMES German 4%. *Kurt* (11), *Frieda* (2), *Helmut* (2), *Reinhold* (2), *Alois, Benno,*

Bernhard, Ernst, Gerhard, Hans, Hilde, Klaus.

Koehne (377) North German (**Köhne**): variant of KUEHNE.

Koehnen (193) North German (**Köhnen**): patronymic from a short form of the personal name KONRAD or alternatively a metronymic from a short form of the female personal name *Kunigunde.*

Koehnke (143) North German (**Köhnke**): variant of **Köneke** (see KOENEKE).

GIVEN NAMES German 4%. *Claus, Lothar.*

Koehnlein (103) German (**Köhnlein**): from a pet form of the personal name *Köhn,* a short form of KONRAD.

GIVEN NAME German 4%. *Otto.*

Koel (120) **1.** Dutch: variant spelling of **Coel,** itself a variant of KOOL. **2.** German: variant spelling of **Köhl** (see KOHL 1).

Koelbl (107) German (**Kölb(e)l**): **1.** nickname for a fat or coarse man, from a diminutive of Middle High German *kolbe* 'club', 'cudgel' (see KOLB). **2.** nickname for a slow, relaxed man, from early modern High German *kölbeln* 'to stroll', 'to amble'.

GIVEN NAMES German 5%. *Erna, Markus.*

Koelker (152) German: variant of **Kalker** (see KALK, KALKBRENNER).

Koelle (166) German (**Kölle**): **1.** from the Germanic personal name *Kolo* or from a pet form of *Nikolaus* (see NICHOLAS). **2.** habitational name from the city of Cologne (German *Köln*) or places so named near Berlin, in Saxony, Pomerania, or the Palatinate.

GIVEN NAMES German 4%. *Hans, Kurt.*

Koeller (609) German (**Köller**): variant of KELLER.

GIVEN NAMES German 4%. *Klaus, Kurt, Reinhard, Wolfram.*

Koelliker (105) Swiss German (**Kölliker**): habitational name from Kölliken in Aargau, Switzerland.

Koelling (511) German (**Kölling**): from the Germanic personal name *Kolo* + the suffix *-ing* denoting affiliation.

GIVEN NAMES German 4%. *Dieter, Franz, Lorenz, Otto.*

Koellner (135) German (**Köllner**): habitational name for someone from the city of Cologne (German *Köln,* Latin *Colonia*).

GIVEN NAMES German 6%. *Alois, Hans, Manfred.*

Koelsch (453) German: from the adjective *kölsch,* denoting someone from Cologne (German *Köln*).

Koelzer (263) German: **1.** from a noun derivative of *Kolzen* 'ankle boots' (Latin *calceus* 'half-boot', 'walking shoe'), hence an occupational name for a bootmaker or cobbler. **2.** habitational name for someone from a place called Kölzen near Merseburg.

Koen (527) **1.** Dutch: nickname from Middle Dutch *coen(e)* 'bold', 'daring' or personal name *Cono* with the same mean-

ing. **2.** Jewish (Ashkenazic): one of the many forms of COHEN.

Koenecke (117) German (**Könecke**): variant of **Köneke** (see KOENEKE).

Koeneke (120) **1.** German (**Köneke**): from a pet form of the personal name KONRAD. **2.** Dutch: diminutive of KOEN.

GIVEN NAMES German 6%. *Franz, Otto.*

Koeneman (191) **1.** Variant of North German **Köhnemann** (see KOENEMANN). **2.** Dutch: variant of KOEN, with the addition of *man* 'man'.

Koenemann (112) North German (**Könemann**): variant of **Köhnemann,** a derivative of the personal name KONRAD.

GIVEN NAMES German 10%. *Bernd, Ewald, Jurgen.*

Koenen (447) **1.** Dutch: patronymic from KOEN. **2.** Variant of German KOEHNEN.

GIVEN NAMES German 6%. *Kurt* (3), *Rudi* (2), *Guenter, Heinrich.*

Koenig (9380) German (**König**) and Jewish (Ashkenazic): from Middle High German *kūnic,* German *König* 'king', hence a German nickname for a servant or retainer of a king (for example, a farmer on a royal demesne); or alternatively a status name for the head of a craftmen's guild, or a society of sharpshooters or minstrels. As a Jewish surname, it was ornamental, one of several such Ashkenazic names based on European titles of nobility or royalty.

GIVEN NAMES German 5%. *Kurt* (24), *Otto* (14), *Hans* (9), *Erwin* (7), *Dieter* (5), *Frieda* (4), *Monika* (4), *Reinhard* (4), *Egon* (3), *Fritz* (3), *Heinz* (3), *Wilhelm* (3).

Koenigs (303) German: derivative of KOENIG.

GIVEN NAMES German 4%. *Achim, Florian, Kurt.*

Koenigsberg (366) German and Jewish (Ashkenazic): see KONIGSBERG.

GIVEN NAMES Jewish 5%. *Sol* (3), *Mordecai* (2), *Avi, Yaakov.*

Koeninger (111) German (**Königer**): occupational name denoting a member of a king's household.

Koenning (138) Probably a respelling of Dutch **Koening,** either from *koning* 'king' or a derivative of KOEN, or of German **Könning** (see KOENIG).

GIVEN NAME German 4%. *Otto.*

Koep (195) German (**Köp(p)**): variant of **Köpp** (see KOEPP).

GIVEN NAMES German 5%. *Wendelin* (2), *Armin, Florian.*

Koepf (101) German: variant of KOPF.

GIVEN NAME German 7%. *Ulrich* (2).

Koepke (1345) German (**Köpke**): from a pet form of **Köpp** (see KOEPP).

Koepnick (148) Altered spelling of German **Köpenick,** a habitational name from a former place so named near Berlin or from Köpernick in Saxony.

GIVEN NAMES German 5%. *Kurt, Lutz.*

Koepp (758) German (**Köpp**): variant of KOPP 1.

GIVEN NAMES German 5%. *Erwin* (4), *Armin* (2), *Guenther* (2), *Ewald*, *Guenter*, *Klaus*, *Kurt*, *Reinhart*, *Theodor*, *Ulrich*.

Koeppe (257) German (**Köppe**): variant of KOPP 1.

GIVEN NAMES German 5%. *Kurt*, *Otto*, *Wolfram*.

Koeppel (562) **1.** German (**Köppel**) and Jewish (Ashkenazic): from a pet form of the personal name *Jakob* (see JACOB). **2.** Silesian: nickname, probably for someone with a small head, from a diminutive of German *Kopf* (Low German *Kopp*) 'head'.

GIVEN NAMES German 4%. *Gerhard*, *Hans*, *Kurt*, *Merwin*, *Urs*.

Koeppen (519) German (**Köppen**): patronymic from the personal name *Köpp* (see KOEPP).

GIVEN NAMES German 5%. *Fritz* (3), *Arnulf*, *Bernhardt*, *Christoph*, *Erna*, *Horst*, *Otto*.

Koepsel (162) German (**Köpsel**): from a pet form of the personal name *Jakobus* (see JACOB).

GIVEN NAMES German 5%. *Eldred*, *Erwin*, *Hans*, *Kurt*.

Koepsell (231) Altered spelling of German **Köpsel** (see KOEPSEL).

GIVEN NAMES German 6%. *Erna*, *Erwin*, *Ewald*, *Gunter*, *Markus*.

Koerber (727) German (**Körber**) and Jewish (Ashkenazic): occupational name for a basket maker, from an agent derivative of Middle High German *korp*, German *Korb* 'basket'.

GIVEN NAMES German 6%. *Lorenz* (2), *Otto* (2), *Theodor* (2), *Bernd*, *Erwin*, *Florian*, *Frieda*, *Inge*, *Ingeborg*, *Kurt*.

Koering (109) **1.** German: variant of **Küring**, a personal name from Latin *Quirinus*. **2.** German: variant of KOHRING.

Koerner (2356) German (**Körner**): **1.** occupational name for a grain merchant or possibly for the administrator of a granary, Middle High German *körner*. **2.** nickname for a miller, from a noun derivative of Middle High German *kürne* 'mill'. **3.** from the personal name *Kor(de)ner*, a derivative of KONRAD, which was altered to *Körner*.

GIVEN NAMES German 5%. *Hans* (5), *Kurt* (5), *Ernst* (2), *Heinz* (2), *Horst* (2), *Otto* (2), *Angelika*, *Claus*, *Dieter*, *Erhardt*, *Eugen*, *Ewald*.

Koerper (107) German: variant of **Körber** (see KOERBER).

GIVEN NAMES Scandinavian 6%. *Nels*, *Wulf*.

Koerth (123) German (**Körth**): from the personal name *Kort*, a short form of KONRAD.

GIVEN NAMES German 9%. *Orlo* (2), *Kurt*, *Otto*.

Koester (2966) North German (**Köster**): **1.** Low German form of **Küster** 'sexton' (see KUSTER). **2.** variant of KOSTER.

GIVEN NAMES German 4%. *Hans* (5), *Hermann* (3), *Kurt* (3), *Otto* (3), *Gerhard* (2), *Helmut* (2), *Bernhard*, *Berthold*, *Elke*, *Frieda*, *Fritz*, *Gerhardt*.

Koesters (178) North German (**Kösters**): variant of **Köster** (see KOESTER).

GIVEN NAMES German 8%. *Christoph*, *Kurt*, *Ulrich*, *Willi*.

Koestler (183) German: **1.** topographic name from Latin *costa* 'rocky ledge'. **2.** variant of KOSTER.

GIVEN NAMES German 6%. *Kurt* (2), *Otto*, *Reinhold*.

Koestner (250) **1.** North German: variant of **Köster** (see KOSTER). **2.** German: habitational name for someone from a place called Kösten, near Bamberg, or Köstenberg.

GIVEN NAMES German 4%. *Kurt*, *Otto*.

Koeth (125) German (**Köth**): **1.** habitational name for someone from a place in Saxony called Köthen. **2.** from an old personal name formed with Old High German *got* 'god' or *guot* 'good'. Compare GOTT. **3.** variant of KOTH.

Koether (108) German (**Köther**): variant spelling of **Kötter** (see KOETTER).

GIVEN NAME German 5%. *Gerhard*.

Koetje (186) Dutch: apparently a nickname meaning 'little cow' or 'coot'.

Koets (101) Probably Dutch and German (Frisian).

Koetter (279) German (**Kötter**): status name for a farm laborer who lived in a cottage or hovel with no land, from an agent derivative of Middle High German and Middle Low German *kote* 'cottage', 'hovel' (see KOTH).

GIVEN NAMES German 8%. *Dieter*, *Franz*, *Gunter*, *Hans*, *Heinz*, *Juergen*, *Kurt*, *Othmar*.

Koetting (240) German (**Kötting**): from an old personal name formed with Old High German *got* 'god' or *guot* 'good'.

Koetz (147) German (**Kötz**): see KOTZ.

Koff (311) **1.** Jewish (Ashkenazic): ornamental name from the nineteenth letter in the Hebrew alphabet. **2.** Jewish (Ashkenazic): metonymic occupational name for a merchant or trader, from German *Kauf* 'purchase'. **3.** Americanized spelling of German **Kauf**, an occupational name for a trader, Old High German *koufo*. Compare Low German KOOP.

GIVEN NAMES Jewish 8%. *Zvi* (2), *Yitzchok*.

Koffel (139) **1.** South German: topographic name from *Kofel* 'rounded hilltop or mountain summit'. **2.** Respelling of German **Kofahl**, an occupational name for a blacksmith, from Sorbian *kowal*.

Koffler (383) South German (also **Köf(f)ler**): topographic name for someone living by a rounded hilltop (see KOFFEL).

Koffman (286) **1.** German and Jewish (Ashkenazic): variant of KAUFMANN. **2.** German: nickname for a cottager, from Low German *kaben*, *küfe* 'hut', 'stable'.

GIVEN NAMES Jewish 6%. *Yetta* (2), *Feyga*, *Mordechai*, *Sima*.

Kofford (157) Possibly an Americanized spelling of German **Kauffert**, an occupa-

tional name for a trader, Middle High German *koufer*, plus excrescent *-t*.

Kofler (157) German (**Köfler**): **1.** variant of KOFFLER. **2.** old form of **Käufler**, an occupational name for a trader or salesman.

GIVEN NAMES German 7%. *Ernst*, *Otto*, *Wolfgang*.

Kofman (255) Jewish (Ashkenazic): variant of KAUFMAN.

GIVEN NAMES Jewish 28%; Russian 27%. *Ilya* (3), *Isaak* (2), *Mendy* (2), *Naum* (2), *Semen* (2), *Aron*, *Basya*, *Faina*, *Feyga*, *Genya*, *Irina*, *Izak*; *Boris* (8), *Mikhail* (3), *Vladimir* (3), *Yefim* (3), *Aleksandr* (2), *Igor* (2), *Leonid* (2), *Lev* (2), *Masha* (2), *Semyon* (2), *Arkady*, *Asya*.

Kofoed (284) **1.** Altered spelling of Dutch **Koefoed** or **Koevoet**, literally 'cow's foot', hence a nickname for someone with a club foot or other deformity of the foot, or a habitational name for someone living at a house distinguished by the sign of a cow's foot (presumably a butcher's shop). The term also denotes a crowbar (because it is cleft like a cow's hoof), and the name may also have arisen as a metonymic occupational name for a maker or user of such tools. **2.** Danish: nickname with the same meaning as 1, from *ko* 'cow' + *fod* 'foot'.

GIVEN NAMES Scandinavian 4%. *Anders* (2), *Nanna*.

Kofron (179) Czech (**Kofroň**): nickname from Gafron, the name of a place whose inhabitants were reputed to pontificate on matters they did not understand.

Kofsky (148) Shortened form of any of various Jewish (eastern Ashkenazic) surnames ending with *-kovski* or *-kowski*.

GIVEN NAME Jewish 6%. *Hyman*.

Koga (382) Japanese: 'old river'; variously written, with one ancient variant of imperial descent pronounced *Kuga*; other alternate readings are FURUKAWA or *Kogawa* and are derived from a village named *Koga* in Shimōsa (now Chiba prefecture). The most common Koga name is mostly found in Kyūshū, and is descended from the TAKEDA family. The name is also found in the Ryūkyū Islands.

GIVEN NAMES Japanese 44%. *Toshio* (3), *Akira* (2), *Hiroshi* (2), *Masao* (2), *Yoshio* (2), *Yoshitaka* (2), *Chiyoko*, *Emiko*, *Hajime*, *Harumi*, *Hideko*, *Hideo*.

Kogan (1169) Jewish (from Ukraine and Bessarabia): one of the many forms of COHEN. This spelling represents the Russian form of the Jewish name, with *h* (absent in Russian) replaced by *g*.

GIVEN NAMES Russian 27%; Jewish 22%. *Boris* (39), *Leonid* (20), *Mikhail* (19), *Iosif* (12), *Yefim* (12), *Igor* (11), *Vladimir* (10), *Lev* (9), *Aleksandr* (5), *Gennady* (5), *Grigory* (5), *Anatoly* (4); *Yakov* (12), *Ilya* (11), *Aron* (4), *Inna* (3), *Irina* (3), *Izrail* (3), *Marat* (3), *Meyer* (3), *Naum* (3), *Sarra* (3), *Semen* (3), *Tsilya* (3).

Kogel (159) German: as a northern name, a metonymic occupational name for a maker of hooded cloaks or cowels, Middle Low German *kogel* 'hood' (Late Latin *cuculla*); as a southern German and Austrian name, a topographic or habitational name from the dialect word *kogel* 'mountain top'. In the form **Kögel**, it may be a variant of KEGEL.
GIVEN NAMES German 6%. *Gottlieb* (2), *Jutta*.

Kogen (101) Jewish (from Ukraine and Moldava): variant of COHEN.
GIVEN NAMES Jewish 18%; Russian 7%. *Aron, Avram, Ben Zion, Ilya, Mariya, Meyer, Noam, Zeev; Boris* (3), *Yuriy*.

Koger (1272) South German: occupational name for a knacker, from an agent derivative of *koge* 'carrion'.

Kogler (241) German: from KOGEL + the agent or habitational suffix *-er*. This name is also found in Hungary and eastern Slovenia.
GIVEN NAMES German 6%; Hungarian 4%. *Kurt* (2), *Alois, Hans, Klaus; Geza* (2), *Aladar, Bela*.

Koglin (136) Origin uncertain. Perhaps an altered spelling of Irish COUGHLIN or of Swiss German **Köglin**.

Kogut (632) Polish, Ukrainian, and Jewish (Ashkenazic): nickname from Polish *kogut* or Ukrainian *kohut* 'rooster'. Compare KOHUT, KOHOUT.
GIVEN NAMES Polish 7%. *Casimir* (2), *Andrzej, Grzegorz, Jaroslaw, Karol, Kazimierz, Krzysztof, Malgorzata, Mikolaj, Stanislawa, Tadeusz, Zbigniew*.

Koh (773) **1.** Chinese and Korean: variant of KO. **2.** Filipino: unexplained.
GIVEN NAMES Chinese/Korean 46%. *Young* (10), *Kwang* (7), *Kyung* (6), *Jong* (5), *Soon* (5), *Hyun* (4), *Sang* (4), *Sung* (4), *Jae* (3), *Soo* (3), *Yong* (3), *Yung* (3); *Chang* (4), *Byung* (2), *Chong* (2), *Jong Man* (2), *Woon* (2), *Dae, Dong Hun, Dong Jin, Eun Hee, Eunmi, Hae, Hyonsuk*.

Kohan (383) Jewish (Sephardic and eastern Ashkenazic): one of the many forms of COHEN.
GIVEN NAMES Muslim 7%. *Ebrahim* (3), *Bijan* (2), *Abbas, Aman, Aziz, Haleh, Homa, Jalil, Keyvan, Mahnaz, Niloofar, Rahmat*.

Kohanski (105) Polish and Jewish (from Poland): variant of KOCHANSKI.

Kohel (134) Czech: unexplained.

Kohen (284) Jewish (Ashkenazic): variant spelling of COHEN.
GIVEN NAMES Jewish 19%. *Yehuda* (2), *Amnon, Ari, Bruria, Chiam, Ilya, Izhak, Meier, Moche, Mordechai, Moshe, Ofer*.

Kohl (3916) **1.** German (also **Köhl**): from Middle High German *kōl, köl* 'cabbage', 'cabbage head' (ultimately from Latin *caulis* 'stalk'), hence a metonymic occupational name for a grower or seller of cabbages. **2.** from the Germanic personal name *Kolo*.

Kohlbeck (234) German: variant of KOLBECK 1.

Kohlberg (106) **1.** German: habitational name from any of several places called Kohlberg. **2.** German and Jewish: variant of KOHLENBERG.
GIVEN NAME German 5%. *Helmut*.

Kohlenberg (180) **1.** German: habitational name from an area in Kassel called Kohlenberg. **2.** Jewish (Ashkenazic): ornamental name composed of German *Kohle* 'coal' + *Berg* 'mountain', 'hill'.

Kohler (6548) German: occupational name for a charcoal burner, from Middle High German *kol* '(char)coal' + the agent suffix *-er*. The form **Kohler** is South German; elsewhere it is usually written **Köhler**.
GIVEN NAMES German 4%. *Kurt* (15), *Otto* (9), *Erwin* (6), *Hans* (6), *Fritz* (3), *Gunter* (3), *Heinz* (3), *Arno* (2), *Georg* (2), *Gerhard* (2), *Irmgard* (2), *Konrad* (2).

Kohles (201) German: occupational name for a wheelwright or cartwright, from Sorbian and Czech *kolař*.
GIVEN NAMES German 4%; Irish 4%. *Kurt* (2), *Hans*.

Kohlhaas (146) German: apparently a nickname from Middle Low German *kōlhase*, literally 'cabbage rabbit'.
GIVEN NAMES German 7%. *Otto* (2), *Uli*.

Kohlhepp (216) German: of disputed origin; thought either to be from Middle Low German *kōlhupper* 'grasshopper', and hence a nickname for an agile person; or alternatively from Middle High German *kōl* 'cabbage' + *heppe* 'garden knife', and hence an occupational nickname for a cabbage grower.

Kohlhoff (181) German: **1.** metonymic occupational name for a market gardener, from Middle High German *kōlhof* 'vegetable garden'. **2.** habitational name from a farm so named or from a hamlet near Speyer in the Palatinate.
GIVEN NAMES German 6%. *Siegfried, Wilhelm*.

Kohli (478) **1.** Swiss German (also **Köhli**): from a pet form of an old personal name formed with the element *Colo-* (cognate with Old Norse *kollir* 'helmet'). **2.** Indian (Panjab): Hindu (Khatri) and Sikh name of unknown etymology. It is based on the name of a clan in the Khatri community.
GIVEN NAMES Indian 60%. *Vijay* (5), *Anil* (4), *Ravi* (4), *Poonam* (3), *Sanjay* (3), *Anand* (2), *Ashok* (2), *Ashu* (2), *Chhaya* (2), *Deepak* (2), *Harsh* (2), *Manish* (2).

Kohlman (572) Jewish (Ashkenazic) or Americanized spelling of German KOHLMANN.

Kohlmann (298) **1.** German and Jewish Ashkenazic: from a compound Middle High German *kol* 'coal', German *Kohle* or *kōl*, German *Kohl* 'cabbage' + Middle High German *man*, German *Mann* 'man', hence an occupational name for a coal miner or for a cabbage farmer. **2.** German (Austria):

from the personal name *Koloman*, which was borne by an 11th century saint.
GIVEN NAMES German 8%. *Gerhard* (4), *Benno* (2), *Siegbert, Wilhelm*.

Kohlmeier (251) German: variant spelling of KOHLMEYER.

Kohlmeyer (381) German: distinguishing name for a tenant farmer who grew cabbages, from Middle High German *kōl* 'cabbage' + *meier* 'tenant farmer' (see MEYER).
GIVEN NAMES German 4%. *Kurt* (3), *Ewald*.

Kohls (958) German: **1.** patronymic from KOHL 2. **2.** variant of Kols (see KOLZ).
GIVEN NAMES German 4%. *Erwin* (3), *Eldor* (2), *Elke, Ewald, Fritz, Lothar, Otto*.

Kohman (122) North German (**Kohmann**): occupational name for a cowherd, Low German *Kohmann*.

Kohn (4057) **1.** Jewish (Ashkenazic): variant of COHEN. **2.** North German (also **Köhn**): from the personal name *Kohn* or *Köhn*, former Low German short forms of KONRAD.
GIVEN NAMES Jewish 6%; German 4%. *Meyer* (8), *Chaim* (6), *Miriam* (6), *Aron* (4), *Moshe* (4), *Chaya* (3), *Emanuel* (3), *Mendel* (3), *Amron* (2), *Gitty* (2), *Leib* (2), *Mayer* (2); *Kurt* (6), *Fritz* (5), *Erwin* (4), *Gunther* (4), *Manfred* (4), *Gerhard* (3), *Bernhard* (2), *Erna* (2), *Hans* (2), *Armin, Egon, Eldred*.

Kohne (263) German: **1.** variant of KOHN. **2.** (**Köhne**): from a Low German short form of the personal name KONRAD or of the female personal name **Kunigunde**. It is also found in eastern Slovenia.

Kohnen (350) German (**Köhnen**): variant of **Köhn** (see KOHN 2).

Kohner (153) Jewish (Ashkenazic): variant of COHEN.

Kohnert (107) German: from a derivative of the personal name KONRAD.
GIVEN NAMES German 12%. *Ernst, Hans, Klaus, Kurt*.

Kohnke (341) German (also **Köhnke**): from **Kohnke** or **Köhnke**, pet forms of **Kohn** or **Köhn** (see KOHN 2).
GIVEN NAMES German 5%. *Rudi* (2), *Fritz, Otto*.

Kohorst (135) German: habitational name from Kuhhorst, northwest of Berlin, a place named with Low German *kō, kau* 'cow' + *horst* 'group of trees'.

Kohout (597) Czech: nickname from Czech *kohout* 'rooster'. Compare KOHUT, KOGUT.

Kohoutek (100) Czech: from a diminutive of KOHOUT.

Kohr (604) North German: from a short form of the personal name *Cordes* (see KORDES).

Kohring (160) North German or Westphalian (**Köhring**): patronymic from *Kohrt*, a Low German pet form of the personal name KONRAD.
GIVEN NAMES German 6%. *Claus, Heinz, Otto*.

Kohrman (133) **1.** German: possibly a habitational name for someone from Kohren in Saxony, which was earlier called *Kohr(e)*. **2.** German (**Kohrmann**): of uncertain origin. Either a variant of **Kuhrmann**, itself a variant of KUHR, or a reduced form of **Kornmann**, an occupational name for the manager of a granary, from Middle High German *korn* 'grain' + *man* 'man'.

Kohrs (311) German: patronymic from KOHR.

Kohrt (132) North German: from a Low German pet form of the personal name KONRAD.

Kohtz (107) German: variant spelling of KOTZ.

Kohut (859) Ukrainian, Polish, and Jewish (eastern Ashkenazic): nickname from *kohut* 'rooster'. Compare KOGUT, KOHOUT.

Kohutek (120) Polish: nickname from a diminutive of Polish dialect *kohut* 'rooster'.

Koike (181) Japanese: meaning 'small lake'. Some families descend from the TAIRA clan, some from the northern FUJIWARA, and others from the Seiwa-Genji. The surname is found chiefly in eastern Japan and also in the Ryūkyū Islands.
GIVEN NAMES Japanese 75%. *Hideo* (7), *Hitoshi* (2), *Kazunari* (2), *Kazuo* (2), *Masami* (2), *Osamu* (2), *Satoshi* (2), *Shigeo* (2), *Shinichi* (2), *Toshio* (2), *Tsuyoshi* (2), *Yasuo* (2).

Kois (145) Polish (**Koisz**): nickname for a peace maker, from a derivative of *koić* 'to calm'.
GIVEN NAMES Polish 7%. *Andrzej, Czeslawa, Ryszard, Wladyslaw.*

Koistinen (146) Finnish: from the forename *Koisti*, Karelian form of *Konstantin* (see CONSTANTINE), + the common surname suffix *-nen*. This name is found chiefly in Eastern Finland, in the Savo region.
GIVEN NAMES Finnish 6%; Scandinavian 4%. *Pentti, Pertti, Rauni, Seppo; Erik.*

Koivisto (243) Finnish: from *koivu* 'birch tree' + the local suffix *-sto*, i.e. 'birch wood or forest', originally a habitational name dating back to the 15th century, from a farm so named for its location; later it was also adopted as a translation of Swedish names such as **Björklund** (see BJORKLUND).
GIVEN NAMES Finnish 8%. *Eino* (3), *Olli* (2), *Toivo* (2), *Jorma.*

Koizumi (139) Japanese: found mostly in eastern Japan, but a common topographic name nationwide; its meaning is 'small spring'. Several samurai families of various lineages took this surname from a number of villages by this name.
GIVEN NAMES Japanese 65%. *Hiroshi* (2), *Hisako* (2), *Keiko* (2), *Koichi* (2), *Tadao* (2), *Takeshi* (2), *Yoko* (2), *Akira, Chiyo, Hiromichi, Hiroyuki, Ikuko.*

Kojima (315) Japanese: 'small island'; mostly found along the coast between Tōkyō and Kyōto and in the Ryūkyū Islands; an alternate reading found farther east is *Ojima*. Another Kojima with a different first character but similar meaning is found in western Japan.
GIVEN NAMES Japanese 76%. *Akira* (5), *Hiroshi* (5), *Kenji* (5), *Takashi* (4), *Junichi* (3), *Kentaro* (3), *Makoto* (3), *Masaru* (3), *Masayuki* (3), *Mieko* (3), *Toru* (3), *Toshio* (3).

Kok (517) Dutch: **1.** occupational name for a cook, Middle Dutch *coc*. **2.** occupational name from Middle Dutch *(scarp)coc* 'executioner', 'hangman'.
GIVEN NAMES Dutch 5%. *Frans* (3), *Dirk, Jeroen, Klaas, Martinus, Willem, Wolter.*

Kokal (123) Slovenian: nickname or topographic name from *kokalj* 'corn cockle' (also *kokolj*, old spellings *kokal* and *kokol*) (the plant Agrostemma githago), a weed of cereal crops. Compare KONKOL.

Koke (240) North German and Westphalian: occupational name for a cook, Middle Low German *kok*; perhaps also a metonymic occupational name for a pastrycook, from the dialect word *koke(n)* 'cake'.
GIVEN NAMES German 4%. *Kurt, Lothar.*

Koker (214) Dutch: **1.** from Middle Dutch *coker* 'case', 'sheath', 'cover', perhaps a metonymic occupational name for a maker of such articles or for a messenger or official who carried letters or documents in a case. **2.** occupational name for a cook, from an agent derivative of *coken* 'to cook'.

Kokes (154) **1.** Czech (**Kokeš**): nickname from *kokeš* 'rooster'. **2.** Greek (also **Kokis**): variant of **Gogas**.

Kokesh (199) Americanized spelling of Czech **Kokeš** (see KOKES).

Kokinda (157) Origin unidentified.

Kokko (107) Finnish: from a personal name based on *kotka* 'eagle'. This surname is found throughout Finland.
GIVEN NAMES Finnish 12%; German 6%; Scandinavian 4%. *Eino, Juha, Timo, Waino, Yalmer, Yrjo; Kurt; Erik.*

Kokoska (128) Variant of Polish KOKOSZKA.

Kokoszka (277) Polish: nickname for a fussy or broody person, from *kokoszka* 'laying hen'.
GIVEN NAMES Polish 10%. *Czeslaw* (2), *Henryk, Irena, Jerzy, Jolanta, Mariusz, Piotr.*

Kokot (108) Slovenian (eastern Slovenia): nickname from the dialect word *kokot* 'rooster', 'cock'.

Kolacki (88) Polish (**Kołacki**): habitational name for someone from a place called Kołaty, Kołacin, or Kołacinek (see KOLAK).

Kolacz (103) Polish (**Kołacz**): from *kołacz* 'wedding cake', presumably a metonymic occupational name for a patissier or confectioner.
GIVEN NAMES Polish 14%. *Arkadiusz, Jerzy, Piotr, Szczepan.*

Kolak (88) **1.** Croatian or Serbian: a nickname of Turkish origin, denoting someone who had lost a hand. **2.** Polish (**Kołak**): probably from a pet form of the personal name *Mikołaj*, Polish form of NICHOLAS.
GIVEN NAME South Slavic 4%. *Davor.*

Kolakowski (513) Polish (**Kołakowski**): habitational name for someone from Kołaki, Kołakowo, or Kołaków.
GIVEN NAMES Polish 7%. *Jaroslaw, Jerzy, Kazimierz, Leszek, Stanislaw, Tadeusz, Waclaw, Wieslaw, Wojiech, Zdzislaw, Zygmunt.*

Koland (102) Origin unidentified.

Kolander (260) German: variant of **Kalander**, a status name for the chairman or a member of a religious or other fraternity that held meetings on the first of each month, from Latin *ad calendas*. This name is often Americanized as CALENDER.

Kolanko (111) **1.** Polish: nickname for someone with a deformed knee, from a diminutive of KOLANO. **2.** Ukrainian: from a pet form of the personal name *Mikolai*, Ukrainian form of NICHOLAS.
GIVEN NAMES Polish 10%. *Jacek, Jaroslaw, Kazimierz.*

Kolano (106) Polish: descriptive nickname for someone with some deformity or peculiarity of the knee, from *kolano* 'knee'.
GIVEN NAMES Polish 12%. *Andrzey, Stanislaw, Wojciech, Zbigniew.*

Kolanowski (112) Polish: habitational name for someone from either of two places called Kolanów, in Kraków and Tarnów voivodeships.

Kolar (1527) Czech and Slovak (**Kolár**; Czech also **Kolář**); Serbian, Croatian, and Slovenian: occupational name from Czech *kolář* and South Slavic *kolar* 'wheelwright', 'cartwright', agent noun from *kola* 'cart'.

Kolarik (374) Czech (**Kolařík**) and Slovak **Kolárik**): from a pet form of KOLAR 'wheelwright' or 'cartwright'.

Kolasa (276) Polish: from *kolasa* 'wagon', 'carriage', hence a metonymic occupational name for a cartwright or coachman.
GIVEN NAMES Polish 6%. *Beata, Boguslaw, Irena, Krystyna, Stanislaw, Zbigniew.*

Kolasinski (227) Polish (**Kolasiński**): habitational name for someone from Kolasa in Sieradz voivodeship.
GIVEN NAMES Polish 5%. *Casimir, Mariusz, Tadeusz, Zdzislaw.*

Kolb (4954) German: from Middle High German *kolbe* in various meanings. The main sense is 'mace' or 'cudgel', which was both a weapon and part of an official's insignia, in some cases the insignia of a jester. It may also be a house name: there is also record of a house named 'zum Kolben' in Strasbourg. In Silesia the term denoted a shock of hair or a shorn head. Any of these senses could have given rise to the surname.
FOREBEARS Dielman Kolb (1691–1756), a

Mennonite preacher who arrived in America in 1717 and assisted Swiss and German emigration to America, was born in the Palatinate, Germany, and migrated to PA, following two of his brothers who were also Mennonite preachers. Some of the family settled in Germantown, PA.

Kolba (119) Czech and Polish: **1.** from *kolba* 'corn cob' or 'butt end of a rifle', perhaps an indirect occupational name for a soldier. **2.** adaptation of the German surname KOLB.

GIVEN NAMES Polish 6%. *Jadwiga, Krzysztof, Zdzislaw.*

Kolbe (828) German: variant of KOLB.

GIVEN NAMES German 6%. *Arno, Bernhard, Hans, Helmut, Hermann, Horst, Kurt, Liesl, Marliese, Otto, Wolfgang.*

Kolbeck (293) **1.** German: possibly a habitational name from an abandoned settlement called Colbeck, in the district of Wernigerode, in the Harz Mountains. **2.** Scandinavian: from Old Norse *kaldr* 'cold' + *bekkr* 'stream', hence presumably either an ornamental name or a topographic name for someone who lived near a cold stream.

Kolber (239) German: **1.** (also **Kölber**): from an agent derivative of Middle High German *kolbe* 'club', 'cudgel', hence an occupational name for a person who made wooden clubs, later for an armorer. **2.** (**Kölber**): habitational name for someone from Kolben in Württemberg or Cölbe in Hessen.

Kolberg (530) **1.** German and Jewish (Ashkenazic): habitational name from Kolberg in Pomerania, or from various places formerly named Kohlberg or Colberg and now spelled Kolberg. **2.** Jewish (Ashkenazic): variant of KOHLENBERG or GOLDBERG. **3.** Norwegian: habitational name from any of numerous farmsteads in eastern Norway, so named from *kol* 'charcoal' + *berg* 'mountain'. **4.** Swedish: ornamental name from the same elements as in the Norwegian name.

GIVEN NAMES German 6%. *Aloysius* (2), *Erwin* (2), *Franz* (2), *Otto* (2), *Erhardt, Kurt, Sieglinde.*

Kolbert (132) German: variant of KOLBER.

GIVEN NAMES German 5%. *Erna, Johann.*

Kolbo (139) German: possibly a habitational name from Kolbow in Mecklenburg.

GIVEN NAME Scandinavian 4%. *Juel* (2).

Kolbus (101) German: Latinized form of KOLB.

GIVEN NAME German 4%. *Ilse.*

Kolby (112) Americanized spelling or variant of German **Kolbe**, a variant of KOLB.

GIVEN NAMES German 7%. *Kurt, Maximilian.*

Kolczynski (86) Polish (**Kolczyński**): habitational name for someone from either of two places called Kolczyn, in Lublin or Płock voivodeships, named with Old Polish *kolcza* 'chain armor'.

Kolden (209) **1.** German: from Middle Low German *kolt, kolde* 'cold', a nickname for an unfriendly person; alternatively, it may be a habitational name, a shortened form of **Koldenhof** 'cold farm' in Mecklenburg (standardized form: *Kaltenhof*, a frequent place name in northern Germany, East Prussia, Bavaria, and Württemberg). **2.** Norwegian: habitational name from a farm called Kolden, from Old Norse *kollr* 'rounded mountain top'.

Kole (508) Perhaps an Americanized spelling of German KOHL.

Kolek (225) **1.** Polish and Czech: from a pet form of Polish *Mikołaj* or Czech *Mikoláš*, vernacular forms of the Greek personal name *Nikolaos* (see NICHOLAS). **2.** Polish (**Kołek**): nickname for a solitary person, from *kołek* 'peg'.

Kolenda (386) Polish: **1.** from a pet form of the personal name *Mikołaj*, Polish form of NICHOLAS. **2.** from *kolęda* 'Christmas carol', also denoting a collection of donations at Advent and Christmas, from Latin *Calendae* 'first days of the month'. Compare KOLANDER.

GIVEN NAMES Polish 5%. *Zygmunt* (2), *Grazyna, Jolanta, Stanisław.*

Koler (126) **1.** German: variant of KOHLER. **2.** Slovenian: variant of KOLAR.

Koles (116) Origin unidentified. Probably a respelling of German KOLZ or its variants **Kols** or **Kohls**, or of KOHLES.

Kolesar (757) Serbian, Croatian; Slovak (**Kolesár**): metonymic occupational name for a cartwright, from *kolesa* 'two- or four-wheeled cart', from *kolo* 'wheel'.

Koleszar (104) Hungarian form of Slavic KOLESAR.

GIVEN NAMES Hungarian 7%. *Miklos* (2), *Zoltan.*

Kolich (160) **1.** German: from a pet form of *Kol*, a short form of the personal name *Nikolaus* (see NICHOLAS). **2.** Polish: pet form of the personal name *Mikołaj* (see NICHOLAS).

Kolin (141) Czech (**Kolín**) and Jewish (from Bohemia): habitational name for someone from Kolín in central Bohemia.

GIVEN NAMES Jewish 6%. *Isak, Mendel.*

Kolinski (238) **1.** Polish (**Koliński**) and Jewish (from Poland): habitational name from any of numerous places called Kolno. **2.** Czech: variant of KOLINSKY.

GIVEN NAMES Polish 6%. *Casimir, Dorota, Jerzy, Stanisław, Zygmunt.*

Kolinsky (136) **1.** Czech (**Kolínský**) and Jewish (Ashkenazic): habitational name from Kolín in central Bohemia (see KOLIN). **2.** Jewish: variant spelling of KOLINSKI.

Kolis (116) Czech (**Koliš**): from a pet form of the personal name *Mikoláš*, a vernacular form of Greek *Nikolaos* (see NICHOLAS).

Kolk (240) **1.** Dutch and North German: topographic name for someone living near

a hollow or gully, or (in Dutch) a pool. **2.** North German: variant of KALK.

GIVEN NAMES Dutch 4%. *Dirk* (2), *Herm.*

Kolka (138) Czech: from a pet form of **Kola**, a short form of the personal name *Mikoláš*, Czech form of NICHOLAS.

Kolker (371) **1.** Jewish (from Ukraine): habitational name for someone from a place called Kolki in Ukraine. **2.** German (also KOELKER): occupational name for a lime burner, a variant of **Kalker** (see KALK, KALKBRENNER).

GIVEN NAMES Jewish 5%; Russian 4%. *Chaim, Dov, Rakhmil; Leonid* (2), *Arkady, Boris, Iosif, Mikhail, Nadejda, Reyza, Yefim.*

Kolkman (120) **1.** Dutch and North German: variant of KOLK, with the addition of *-man* 'man'. **2.** South German (**Kolkmann**): variant of **Kalkmann** (see KALKMAN).

GIVEN NAMES Dutch 4%. *Cornelis, Hendrik.*

Koll (594) **1.** German (also **Kölle**): from a short form of the old personal name *Colo*, or in Austria of *Koloman*, which is of the same origin (see KOLLING 1). **2.** German: nickname from Middle Low German *kolle* 'head'.

Kollar (1101) Slovak and Hungarian (**Kollár**; Slovak also **Kolár**): variant of KOLAR.

Kollars (126) German (Austrian): occupational name from Czech *kolář* 'cartwright'.

Kollasch (201) German: **1.** from a Slavic-influenced short form of the personal name *Nikolaus* (see NICHOLAS). **2.** from Czech *koláč* 'bread bun', 'cake', hence a metonymic occupational name for a baker.

Kollath (155) German (Sorbian): from a Slavic short form of the personal name *Nikolaus* (see NICHOLAS).

Kolle (195) German: variant of KOLL.

GIVEN NAMES German 5%; Scandinavian 4%. *Ernst, Margarethe, Otto; Jorgen, Thor.*

Koller (2388) **1.** South German: variant of the occupational name KOHLER. **2.** South German: from Middle High German *kolli(e)r* 'leather harness', 'horse collar', 'neck piece of garment of armor', hence a metonymic occupational name for a harness maker or armorer. **3.** German (**Köller**): Westphalian habitational name for someone from Cologne (German *Köln*); *Kölle* is the Rhenish dialect form of the place name.

GIVEN NAMES German 4%. *Franz* (4), *Kurt* (4), *Alois* (3), *Erwin* (3), *Hans* (2), *Mathias* (2), *Otto* (2), *Ernst, Helmut, Horst, Manfred, Reinhard.*

Kollias (119) Greek: variant of COLLIAS.

GIVEN NAMES Greek 15%. *Spiro* (3), *Anastasios, Kostas, Paraskevi, Vassilios.*

Kollin (132) German: habitational name from Collin in Brandenburg or Pomerania, Kolline in Silesia, or Kolin in Bohemia.

GIVEN NAME French 4%. *Emile.*

Kolling (327) North German: **1.** (**Kölling**): from the Germanic personal name *Kolo*, *Colo* + the suffix *-ing* denoting affiliation. **2.** topographic name from Middle Low German *kolinge*, a term denoting an area of forest to be cut for charcoal burning.

Kollman (488) Variant of German KOLL-MANN or Jewish or Slavic KOLMAN.

Kollmann (278) German: variant of KOHL-MANN.
GIVEN NAMES German 7%. *Kurt* (4), *Manfred*.

Kollmar (119) German: habitational name from Colmar in Alsace.

Kollmeyer (156) German: variant spelling of KOHLMEIER.
GIVEN NAMES German 6%. *Erwin, Kurt*.

Kollmorgen (109) German: variant of **Kallmorgen**, from a field name.
GIVEN NAME German 5%. *Kurt*.

Kollock (112) Variant spelling of German (Sorbian) **Kollack**, from a Slavic short form of the personal name *Nikolaus* (see NICHOLAS).

Kolm (134) German: habitational name from Kollm or Kulm, both in Saxony, so named from Slavic *kholm*, *hlumu* 'small hill'.
GIVEN NAME German 4%. *Arno*.

Kolman (495) **1.** Jewish (Ashkenazic): variant of KALMAN. **2.** Jewish (eastern Ashkenazic): variant of KOHLMANN. **3.** Czech and Slovenian: from the medieval personal name *Kolman*, derived from the name of St. Columban, an Irish missionary to Europe (see COLEMAN). **4.** Austrian German (**Kolmann**): from the medieval personal name *Coloman*, altered at a later period by folk etymology to *Kohlmann*, as though derived from German *Kohl* 'cabbage' + *Mann* 'man'.
GIVEN NAMES Jewish 4%. *Isadore* (2), *Mendel* (2), *Faivel, Lipot, Zeev*.

Kolo (147) Tongan: unexplained.

Kolodny (231) Jewish (from Belarus): habitational name for someone from a place called Kolodnoe in Belarus.
GIVEN NAMES Jewish 12%; French 5%. *Bentsion, Chaim, Menachem, Moshe, Shimon, Shlomo, Sol, Yosef; Armand* (4), *Anatole*.

Kolody (140) Americanized form of a Slavic occupational name for a wheelwright.

Kolodziej (822) Polish (**Kołodziej**): occupational name for a wheelwright, Polish *kołodziej*.
GIVEN NAMES Polish 11%. *Tadeusz* (5), *Irena* (2), *Ireneusz* (2), *Zosia* (2), *Andrzej, Boguslaw, Casimir, Czeslawa, Dariusz, Eugeniusz, Feliks, Genowefa*.

Kolodziejczyk (121) Polish: pet form or patronymic from KOLODZIEJ.
GIVEN NAMES Polish 27%. *Wieslaw* (2), *Alicja, Czeslawa, Elzbieta, Jacek, Jerzy, Kazimir, Malgorzata, Mariusz, Mieczyslaw, Piotr, Walenty*.

Kolodziejski (167) Polish: habitational name for someone from any of several places called Kołodzieje, named with KOLODZIEJ 'wheelwright'.
GIVEN NAMES Polish 12%. *Lucjan* (2), *Gerzy, Ireneusz, Janusz, Tadeusz, Tomasz*.

Koloski (212) Polish: **1.** habitational name for someone from a place called Kołosice (now Kołoszyn) in Sieradz voivodeship.

Kolosky (115) Variant of Polish KOLOSKI.

Kolp (343) German: variant of KOLB.

Kolpack (131) German: of Slavic, possibly Polish, origin.
GIVEN NAME French 4%. *Armand*.

Kolpin (125) **1.** Jewish (from Belarus): habitational name for someone from Kolpin or Kolpino, now in Belarus. **2.** German: habitational name from places called Kolpin or Kolpien, in eastern Germany.
GIVEN NAMES French 5%. *Olivier, Thierry*.

Kolsky (142) Czech (**Kolský**): habitational name for someone from a place called Koloveč near Kdyně in Bohemia.

Kolson (101) German: patronymic from KOLL.

Kolsrud (102) Scandinavian: unexplained.
GIVEN NAME Scandinavian 5%. *Lars*.

Kolstad (614) **1.** Norwegian: habitational name from any of numerous farmsteads especially in Østlandet, named Kolstad, from the Old Norse personal name *Kolr* meaning 'coal', 'black' or *Kollr* meaning 'round skull', 'bald head' + *staðr* 'farmstead', 'dwelling'. **2.** Altered spelling of German **Kohlstädt**, a habitational name from a place so named near Paderborn in Westphalia.
GIVEN NAME Scandinavian 4%. *Thor*.

Kolter (168) German: **1.** metonymic occupational name for a quilt maker, from an agent derivative of Middle High German *kulter, kolter* 'quilt' (Latin *culcitra*). **2.** from Middle High German, Middle Low German *kolter* 'plowshare' (Latin *culter*), hence a metonymic occupational name for a maker of plows, a plowman, or possibly for an arable farmer.

Kolterman (151) German (**Koltermann**): occupational name, a variant of KOLTER, with the addition of *-mann* 'man' (Middle High German *man*).
GIVEN NAMES Scandinavian 4%. *Hilmer, Swen*.

Koltes (133) German: unexplained; perhaps a respelling of KOLZ.
GIVEN NAME French 5%. *Colette*.

Kolthoff (118) Variant of German KALTHOFF or **Koldenhof** (see KOLDEN 2).
GIVEN NAME Dutch 4%. *Marinus*.

Kolton (197) Polish (**Kołton**) and Jewish (eastern Ashkenazic): variant of KOLTUN.
GIVEN NAMES Polish 4%. *Henryk, Jerzy, Zygmunt*.

Koltun (159) Polish (**Kołtun**), Ukrainian, and Jewish (eastern Ashkenazic): nickname for someone with a tangled mass of hair, from Polish *kołtun* 'elf-lock', Yiddish *koltn*.

GIVEN NAMES Russian 7%. *Igor* (2), *Dmitry, Gennady, Lev, Leya, Nelya*.

Koltz (184) **1.** German: variant of KOLZ. **2.** German (**Költz**): variant of KELTZ. **3.** Hungarian: variant of **Kótz** (see KOTZ).

Kolz (120) North German: nickname for a talkative person, from Middle Low German *kolz* 'talk', 'chatter'.
GIVEN NAMES German 15%. *Manfred* (4), *Arno* (2), *Gerd*.

Koman (192) **1.** Jewish (from Ukraine): unexplained. **2.** Dutch: possibly a reduced form of KOOPMAN. **3.** Slovenian: unexplained.

Komar (636) Ukrainian, Polish, Czech and Slovak (**Komár**), Slovenian, and Jewish (eastern Ashkenazic): from *komar* 'gnat', 'mosquito', hence a nickname for a small, insignificant, or annoying person.

Komara (138) Polish, Ukrainian, and Czech: variant of KOMAR 'gnat'.

Komarek (273) Czech (**Komárek**) and Polish: nickname from a diminutive of *komár* 'mosquito', 'gnat' (see KOMAR).

Komatsu (212) Japanese: 'small pine tree'; found mostly in west-central Japan, the island of Shikoku, and the Ryūkyū Islands; an alternate reading found farther east is *Omatsu*. Several samurai families of various lineages took this surname from any of the various villages of this name.
GIVEN NAMES Japanese 66%. *Kiyoshi* (4), *Hiroshi* (3), *Isao* (2), *Kazuko* (2), *Satoshi* (2), *Susumu* (2), *Aiko, Akane, Akio, Atsushi, Chizu, Eiji*.

Komenda (122) Czech and Polish: nickname for a domineering person, from Italian *commendatore* 'commander'.
GIVEN NAMES Polish 4%. *Irena, Miroslaw*.

Komer (193) Jewish (eastern Ashkenazic): variant of KOMAR.

Kominek (125) Polish and Czech (**Komínek**): metonymic occupational name for a chimneysweep, from Polish *kominek* 'chimney'.
GIVEN NAMES Polish 4%. *Alojzy, Krystyna*.

Kominsky (130) Czech: metonymic occupational name for a chimneysweep, from Slavic *komin* 'chimney'.

Komisar (159) Jewish (eastern Ashkenazic): status name from eastern Slavic *komis(s)are* 'commissary', 'commissioner', Latin *commissarius*, an agent noun from *com* 'with' + *missus* 'sent'.

Komm (124) **1.** Jewish (from Belarus): unexplained. **2.** German: respelling of **Kumm**, a topographic name for someone who lived in a dale. **3.** German: of uncertain origin. Possibly a habitational name from Commen on the Mosel river or from Kommen in East Prussia; or a topographic name from Slovenian *kom* 'hill', 'peak'.
GIVEN NAMES Russian 11%; German 8%; Jewish 5%. *Anatoliy* (2), *Boris* (2), *Aleksandr, Yekaterina, Yelena, Yuriy; Gerhard, Reinhard; Revekka*.

Kommer (197) German and Dutch: **1.** occupational name for a maker of kettles and buckets, from an agent derivative of Middle Low German *komp* 'bowl'. **2.** variant of KAMMER.

GIVEN NAMES German 5%. *Aloysius, Franz, Wolfgang.*

Komoroski (128) Variant of Polish KOMOROWSKI.

Komorowski (357) Polish and Jewish (from Polish): habitational name for someone from Komorowo or Komorów, both places named from Old Polish *komor* 'mosquito'.

GIVEN NAMES Polish 7%. *Stanislaw* (2), *Andrzej, Boguslaw, Henryk, Jadwiga, Jozef, Zbigniew.*

Komp (201) **1.** North German: from Low German *komp* 'dish', 'bowl', hence a metonymic occupational name for a maker of these. **2.** Hungarian: metonymic occupational name for a ferryman, from *komp* 'ferry'. **3.** Jewish (Ashkenazic): habitational name for someone from Kampiai in Lithuania.

Komperda (124) From a Polish altered form of the German personal name *Gumprecht.*

GIVEN NAMES Polish 21%. *Stanislaw* (3), *Stanislawa* (2), *Darek, Janina, Janusz, Jozef, Kazimierz, Tadeusz.*

Kon (228) **1.** Japanese (rare in Japan): the most usual rendering is 'gold'; bearers are most likely descended from immigrants named KIM, from the ancient Korean Shilla kingdom. **2.** Jewish (eastern Ashkenazic): one of the many forms of COHEN. **3.** Polish (**Koń**): from *koń* 'horse', hence a metonymic occupational name for someone who bred or cared for horses or a nickname for someone thought to resemble a horse.

GIVEN NAMES Japanese 17%; Jewish 5%. *Hideo* (2), *Masayuki* (2), *Akio, Atsushi, Hideaki, Hiroshi, Kinuko, Kumiko, Masao, Megumi, Sadao, Shigenori; Basya, Dov, Henia, Isak, Zalman.*

Konarski (174) **1.** Polish and Jewish (from Poland): habitational name for someone from any of various places called Konary, from Polish *konarze* 'grooms'. **2.** Polish: occupational name for a horse breeder or for someone who worked with horses, from Old Polish *konarski* 'groom', a derivative of *koń* 'horse'.

GIVEN NAMES Polish 12%; German 4%. *Ryszard* (2), *Tadeusz* (2), *Dariusz, Leszek, Pawel; Gerhard.*

Konczal (149) Polish (**Kończal**): from *koniec* 'end', 'finish', probably a nickname for someone who brought something to a conclusion.

Konda (113) **1.** Indian (Andhra Pradesh): Hindu name meaning 'hill' in Telugu. **2.** Japanese: written with characters meaning 'now' and 'rice paddy', this version of the name is found mostly in eastern Japan. In western Japan it is pronounced *Imata.*

3. Slovenian (southern half of central Slovenia): pet form of the personal name *Kondrad* (see KONRAD).

GIVEN NAMES Indian 23%; Japanese 11%. *Santha* (2), *Brahma, Kishan, Ramakrishna, Ramesh, Shri, Srikanth, Suresh, Vandana, Vijayakumar; Katsuya, Keiichi, Masaaki, Muneo, Shigeto, Shunji.*

Kondas (142) Hungarian (**Kondás**): occupational name from *konda* 'swineherd'.

Kondo (456) Japanese (**Kondō**): variously written, the most usual form being with characters meaning 'nearby wisteria', and actually designating 'Fujiwara of Ōmi' (Ōmi no Fujiwara). *Kon* ('near') is the Sino-Japanese pronunciation of *chika*, as in Chika-tsu-awa-umi ('Nearer Lake', now Shiga prefecture). The name refers to Lake Biwa and was shortened by usage to Ōmi. The surname is mostly found in the Tōkyō area.

GIVEN NAMES Japanese 67%. *Kenji* (7), *Hiroshi* (5), *Koji* (5), *Yoko* (5), *Hiroki* (4), *Makoto* (4), *Takashi* (4), *Akihiro* (3), *Michi* (3), *Akihiko* (2), *Ayako* (2), *Kazuhiro* (2).

Kondor (119) Hungarian: nickname for someone with curly hair, from *kondor* 'curly'.

Kondos (119) Greek: variant of KONTOS.

GIVEN NAME Greek 6%. *Pericles.*

Kondracki (173) Polish: habitational name for someone from a place called Kondraty, e.g. in Zamość voivodeship, named with the personal name KONDRAT.

GIVEN NAMES Polish 10%. *Bogdan, Grzegorz, Krzysztof, Marinna, Witold.*

Kondrat (184) Polish and Czech (**Kondrát**): from the personal name KONRAD.

Kone (215) **1.** African: unexplained. **2.** Americanized spelling of German KUHN or Dutch KOEN.

GIVEN NAMES African 21%; Muslim 9%. *Yaya* (4), *Mamadou* (3), *Oumar* (2), *Siaka* (2), *Aliou, Alou, Amadou, Amadu, Aminata, Boubacar, Brahima, Fatoumata; Issa* (3), *Moussa* (3), *Abdoulaye* (2), *Karim* (2), *Hassan, Ibrahima, Mohamed, Souleymane.*

Konecky (120) Czech and Slovak (**Konecký**): variant of KONECNY.

Konecny (425) Czech and Slovak (**Konečný**): from *konečný* 'final', 'ultimate', perhaps a nickname for the youngest son of a family, a topographic name for someone who lived at the end of a settlement, or a nickname for someone who brought something to a conclusion.

Konefal (135) Polish: occupational name for a farrier or horse doctor, Polish dialect *konefal*, a variant of *konował* 'farrier'.

GIVEN NAMES Polish 11%. *Boleslaw, Ignacy, Stanislaw.*

Konen (525) Altered spelling of German *Köhnen* or KOEHNEN.

Konesky (133) Czech: variant of KONECKY.

Kong (2169) **1.** Korean: There are two Chinese characters for the surname Kong.

One of these is borne by only one clan, the other by two clans. One of the Kong clans claims Confucius as its ancestor, the 53rd ancestor of Confucius having migrated from his home in China to Koryǒ and settled in Ch'angwǒn, where his grave can still be seen today. The other two Kong clans, the Kimhae Kong and the Munch'ǒn Kong clans both sprang from descendants of a famous T'ang Chinese scholar, Kong Yun-po. A man named Kong Myǒng-nye founded the Kimhae Kong clan when he was exiled to Kimhae during the reign of Chosǒn King Sǒngjong in the latter half of the fifteenth century. The founder of the Munch'ǒn Kong clan, Kong Chin-ǒn, was banished to Munchǒn in Hamgyǒng province during the reign of Chosǒn King Sejong during the first half of the fifteenth century. **2.** Chinese 孔: Cheng Tang was the first king of the Shang dynasty, founded in 1766 BC. Although now known as Cheng Tang, his surname was Zi, and he had a 'style name' (given around age 20) of Tai Yi. Later descendants of his combined the character for Zi with the character for Yi, creating the character for Kong, and adopted the latter as their surname. The *Con* in 'Confucius' represents this surname. **3.** Chinese 纪: variant of JIANG 1. **4.** Chinese 龚: variant of GONG 1. **5.** Cambodian: unexplained. **6.** Danish: nickname from Danish *kong* 'king', or occupational nickname for someone in the service of the king.

GIVEN NAMES Chinese/Korean 36%; Other Southeast Asian 5%. *Jin* (7), *Sung* (7), *Kam* (5), *Kan* (5), *Wai* (5), *Byong* (4), *Chi* (4), *Chin* (4), *Kin* (4), *Seng* (4), *Shing* (4), *Xiang* (4); *Chang* (9), *Chul* (3), *Blia* (2), *Chang Sik* (2), *Chong* (2), *Chung* (2), *Jang* (2), *Pang* (2), *Seong* (2), *Tam* (2), *Woon* (2); *Lam* (4), *Dung* (3), *Lap* (3), *Mai* (3), *Hung* (2), *Sophal* (2), *Soua* (2), *Tha* (2), *Dat, Gam, Hoan, Hoi, Lan.*

Konicek (201) Czech (**Koníček**): **1.** nickname from *koníček* 'horsey', a hypocoristic form of *kůn* 'horse'. **2.** habitational name for someone from a place in Moravia called Konice.

Konicki (230) Polish (also **Kanicki**): habitational name for someone from a place called Kanice in Piotrków voivodeship, named with Polish *kania* 'kite'.

Konieczka (189) Polish: from a derivative of KONIECZNY.

GIVEN NAME Polish 5%. *Casimir* (2).

Konieczny (641) Polish: topographic name for somebody who lived at the edge of a village, from Old Polish *konieczny* 'final', 'ultimate'.

GIVEN NAMES Polish 5%. *Andrzej* (3), *Bronislaw, Janusz, Jerzy, Wieslaw, Zbigniew, Zigmund, Zygmunt.*

Konig (322) German (**König**) and Jewish (Ashkenazic): see KOENIG.

GIVEN NAMES German 8%; Jewish 5%. *Markus* (2), *Erna, Florian, Fritz, Gunther, Ilse, Manfred, Otto; Chaim, Moishe, Moshe, Rozalia, Shmuel.*

Konigsberg (230) **1.** Jewish (Ashkenazic) and German (**Königsberg**): habitational name from any of the twenty or more places in Germany, Austria, Bohemia, Moravia, and elsewhere named Königsberg in German, literally 'king's mountain'. The most famous of these is the city of Königsberg (now Kaliningrad), in former East Prussia, the home of the philosopher Immanuel Kant. **2.** Jewish (Ashkenazic): ornamental name from German *Königsberg* 'king's mountain'.

GIVEN NAMES Jewish 6%; German 4%. *Chaim, Eph, Moshe, Shmuel; Gunter, Otto.*

Konik (139) **1.** Polish, Czech, and Slovak (**Koník**): from *koník* 'pony' (a diminutive of Polish *koń*, Czech *kůň* 'horse'), a nickname for someone thought to resemble a pony in some way, for example in short stature or docile temperament. **2.** Jewish (Ashkenazic): variant of KOENIG. **3.** Dutch: variant of KONING.

GIVEN NAMES Polish 13%. *Elzbieta, Ignacy, Lech, Ludwika, Miroslaw, Stanislaw, Wladyslawa.*

Koning (558) Dutch and German: from Middle Dutch *coninc*, Middle Low German *konink* 'king' (see KOENIG).

GIVEN NAMES German 4%. *Erwin* (2), *Otto* (2), *Rainer.*

Konishi (202) Japanese: 'small west'; habitational name from Konishisato in Kazusa (now part of Chiba prefecture). Most bearers are descended from the CHIBA branch of the TAIRA clan. Mostly found in western Japan.

GIVEN NAMES Japanese 59%. *Toru* (3), *Akira* (2), *Hiroko* (2), *Masayuki* (2), *Megumi* (2), *Mika* (2), *Setsuko* (2), *Shigeo* (2), *Yasuo* (2), *Akiko, Chiemi, Fusao.*

Konitzer (188) German (also **Könitzer**) and Jewish (western Ashkenazic): habitational name for someone from any of several places called Konitz in Pomerania, Moravia, and West Prussia, or **Könitzer** from Könitz in Thuringia, both of Slavic origin.

GIVEN NAMES German 5%. *Dieter* (2), *Kurt* (2).

Konkel (623) **1.** Dutch: from Middle Dutch *konckel, kunkel* 'distaff', hence a metonymic occupational name for a maker of distaffs or for a flax spinner. **2.** German: variant of KUNKEL. **3.** German: habitational name from Kankel in Mecklenburg or near Posen (now Poznan).

Konkle (408) Americanized spelling of KONKEL.

Konkler (134) German: variant of KUNKLER.

Konkol (469) **1.** Polish (**Kąkol**) and Hungarian (**Konkoly**): nickname meaning 'corn cockle', a weed of cereal crops, Polish *kąkol*, Hungarian *konkoly*, the latter

a loanword from Slovenian *kokolj* (see KOKAL), hence a topographic name for someone who lived on a weed-covered plot of land, or a nickname for a poor farmer or someone who was not highly thought of. **2.** German: variant of KONKEL 3.

Konno (106) Japanese: variously written, most usually with characters meaning 'now' or 'near' and 'field'. Found mostly in eastern Japan, farther to the northeast it is pronounced *Imano*.

GIVEN NAMES Japanese 55%. *Masaru* (2), *Fumiko, Hiroki, Hiroshi, Junichi, Kazunori, Kazuyuki, Keiji, Keisuke, Kuniko, Mamoru, Masae.*

Kono (442) Japanese: probably *Kōno*, an alternate reading of the characters for the name KAWANO. Another *Kōno* is a western Japanese reading of the characters pronounced as TAKANO in eastern Japan.

GIVEN NAMES Japanese 49%. *Toru* (4), *Hiroshi* (3), *Kenji* (3), *Takashi* (3), *Yoshiko* (3), *Yutaka* (3), *Ichiro* (2), *Kazuhiro* (2), *Makoto* (2), *Masamichi* (2), *Masashi* (2), *Motoko* (2).

Konold (169) German: from an old personal name *Kuniald* or presumably a variant of **Kanold**, from a Germanic personal name based on *gan* 'magic'.

GIVEN NAMES German 4%. *Gunter, Kurt.*

Konop (316) Polish: from *konopie* 'hemp', perhaps an occupational name for a grower or processor of hemp or a maker of ropes, or a nickname for someone who acted thoughtlessly.

Konopa (118) Polish: variant of KONOP.

GIVEN NAMES Polish 6%. *Janusz, Wojciech.*

Konopacki (143) Polish: habitational name from any of various places named with *konopie* 'hemp', for example Konopaty or Konopki.

GIVEN NAMES Polish 6%. *Pawel, Piotr, Zofia.*

Konopasek (134) Czech (**Konopásek**): from *konopa* 'hemp', probably an occupational name for a rope maker.

Konopka (894) **1.** Polish, Czech, Slovak (**Konôpka**), and Jewish (eastern Ashkenazic): nickname for an active person, from *konopka* 'linnet'. **2.** Polish and Jewish (from Poland): habitational name from some place named with *konopie* 'hemp', for example Konopki.

GIVEN NAMES Polish 8%. *Janina* (3), *Dariusz* (2), *Stanislaw* (2), *Alicja, Andrzej, Ewa, Jaroslaw, Jozef, Piotr, Rafal, Stanislawa, Waclaw.*

Konow (136) German: habitational name from any of several places so named in Mecklenburg.

GIVEN NAMES German 6%. *Kurt, Otto.*

Konrad (1239) German: from the Germanic personal name *Konrad*, composed of the elements *kuoni* 'daring', 'experienced' + *rād, rāt* 'counsel'. This fell together at an early date with another Germanic name, of which the first element was *chunni, kuni* 'race', 'people'. *Konrad* was extremely

popular as a personal name in central Europe during the Middle Ages, being a hereditary name in several princely families as well as enjoying widespread popularity among the people at large. It was also adopted as a surname by Ashkenazic Jews, Slovenians, and others.

GIVEN NAMES German 9%. *Hans* (6), *Kurt* (4), *Otto* (4), *Erwin* (3), *Franz* (3), *Horst* (3), *Gerhard* (2), *Armin, Arno, Bernhard, Ernst, Florian.*

Konrath (274) German: variant of KONRAD.

GIVEN NAMES German 5%. *Kurt* (2), *Florian, Otto, Wilhelm.*

Kontny (106) Polish (**Kątny**): nickname for someone who resided in a corner of a locality or for one who sheltered under somebody else's roof, from Polish *kąt* 'corner'.

Kontos (433) **1.** Greek: nickname for a short man, from *kontos* 'short'; also a reduced form of any of various surnames formed with *Konto-* as a prefix, e.g. **Kontogiannis** 'short John'. **2.** Hungarian (**Köntös**): from *köntös* 'gown', 'short fur coat', hence a metonymic occupational name for a furrier or a maker of coats.

GIVEN NAMES Greek 13%. *Evris* (4), *Spero* (3), *Demos* (2), *Evangelos* (2), *Alexandros, Christos, Constantine, Constantinos, Costas, Dimitrios, Panagiota, Panagiotis.*

Kontz (178) German: variant spelling of KONZ or KUNTZ.

Konvicka (115) Czech (**Konvička**): metonymic occupational name for a potter, from *konvička* 'jug', a derivative of *konvice* 'pot'.

Konwinski (185) Polish (**Konwiński**): probably a habitational name, but from an unidentified place; perhaps from a place named with Old Polish *konwa* 'watering can', modern Polish *konew.*

Konya (125) **1.** Hungarian (**Kónya**): nickname from *konya* 'lop-eared', a derivative of *konyul* 'to curve or hang'. **2.** Japanese: written with characters meaning 'dark blue room'. The name is not common in Japan.

GIVEN NAMES Hungarian 8%; Japanese 6%. *Bela* (2), *Antal, Gabor; Hideo, Megumi, Tosh.*

Konz (477) German: **1.** from the pet name *Konz*, a variant of KUNTZ. **2.** habitational name from Konz near Trier or Konzen near Aachen.

Konzen (172) German: from a derivative of KONZ.

Koo (925) **1.** Chinese 顧: variant of GU 1. **2.** Chinese 谷: variant of GU 2. **3.** Chinese 古: variant of GU 3. **4.** Korean: see KU.

GIVEN NAMES Chinese/Korean 32%. *Young* (8), *Kyung* (7), *Jae* (4), *Myung* (4), *Dong Hee* (3), *Haeng Ja* (3), *Kwok* (3), *Sang* (3), *Sing* (3), *Chi* (2), *Dong* (2), *Hoon* (2); *Chul* (2), *Myung Sook* (2), *Tae Hwan* (2), *Chang, Choon, Eun Ha, Eunmi, Hae Soo, Jang, Jeong, Jong Ok, Joo.*

Koob (458) German: from a pet form of the personal name *Jakobus* (see JACOB).

GIVEN NAMES German 4%. *Gunther, Hans, Hermann, Otto.*

Koogle (103) Americanized spelling of German KUGEL.

Koogler (321) Americanized spelling of German KUGLER.

Kooi (260) Dutch: from Middle Dutch *kooye* 'decoy', 'cage', 'fold', a metonymic occupational name for a maker of cages or decoys or for someone who caught ducks by decoying them.

Kooiker (183) Dutch: occupational name for a decoy man, someone who caught ducks by decoying them.

Kooima (100) Frisian: occupational name for a decoy man, from an agent derivative of Middle Dutch *kooye* 'decoy'.

Kooiman (267) Dutch: **1.** occupational name for a decoy man, from Middle Dutch *kooye* 'decoy'. **2.** patronymic from *Koye*, a reduced form of a personal name such as *Alecoya, Odecoia.*

Kooistra (354) Frisian: occupational name for a decoy man, from an agent derivative of Middle Dutch *kooye* 'decoy'.

GIVEN NAMES Dutch 4%; German 4%. *Gerrit, Hendrik, Hessel, Pieter; Dietmar, Erna, Erwin, Johannes, Kurt.*

Kook (165) **1.** Dutch: occupational name for a baker or cook, from a shortened form of *koekenbakker* 'pastrycook'. **2.** Jewish (American): respelling of KUK. **3.** Korean: variant of KUK. **4.** Chinese 鞠: variant of JU 1.

GIVEN NAMES Chinese/Korean 7%. *Hong Sik* (3), *Dae Hyun, Ji, Joong, Jung, Kwang, Kyung Ho, Seung, Sun, Yung.*

Kooken (188) Dutch: occupational name for a pastrycook, a variant of KOOK.

Kooker (177) Jewish (American): respelling of KUKER.

Kool (233) Dutch: from a reduced form of the personal name *Nikoolaas, Nikolaus,* Dutch forms of NICHOLAS.

Koon (2113) Americanized spelling of German KUHN or Dutch KOEN.

Koonce (1948) Americanized spelling of German KUNTZ or Dutch **Koens**, a patronymic from KOEN.

Koone (159) Americanized form of German KUHN or Dutch KOEN.

Koons (2183) **1.** Americanized form of Dutch **Koens**, a patronymic from KOEN. **2.** Americanized form of German KUNTZ or KUHNS.

Koonts (146) Americanized form of German KUNTZ.

GIVEN NAME French 4%. *Jeanmarie.*

Koontz (4092) Americanized spelling of German KUNTZ.

Koonz (119) Americanized spelling of KUNTZ or KUNC.

Koop (963) German and Dutch: **1.** occupational name for a trader, from Low German *kōpen* 'to buy', from an early Latin loanword, *caupo* meaning 'tavern owner',

'small trader'. **2.** from the Frisian personal name *Koop*, a short form of *Jakob* (see JACOB).

GIVEN NAMES German 4%. *Dietrich, Erwin, Ewald, Hans, Heinrich, Heinz, Jurgen, Klaus, Kurt, Meinard.*

Koopman (1006) **1.** Dutch: occupational name for a buyer or merchant, Middle Dutch *coepman*. **2.** Altered spelling of North German KOOPMANN.

Koopmann (210) North German: occupational name for a buyer or wholesaler, a Low German form of KAUFMANN.

GIVEN NAMES German 12%. *Gerhard, Kurt, Meinhard, Otto, Reinhardt, Udo, Uwe.*

Koopmans (152) **1.** Dutch: patronymic from KOOPMAN. **2.** North German: Rhineland dialect equivalent of KAUFMANN.

GIVEN NAMES Dutch 5%. *Klaas, Pieter.*

Koops (174) German and Dutch: patronymic from a short form of *Jakob* (see JACOB).

GIVEN NAMES German 9%. *Uwe* (2), *Helmuth, Kurt, Otto.*

Koors (190) Variant of Dutch KORS.

Koos (386) **1.** German: habitational name from Koos in Pomerania. **2.** Dutch: nickname for a flatterer or persuasive talker, from Middle Dutch *cose* 'flattery', a noun derivative of *cosen* 'to fondle or caress', 'to smooth talk'. **3.** Hungarian (**Koós**): variant of **Kós** (see Kos).

GIVEN NAMES Hungarian 5%. *Laszlo* (4), *Bela, Istvan, Sandor, Tibor.*

Kooser (179) German: habitational name for someone from KOOS in Pomerania.

Kooy (215) Dutch: variant spelling of KOOI.

Kooyman (197) Dutch: variant spelling of KOOIMAN.

GIVEN NAMES Dutch 5%. *Bastiaan, Dirk.*

Kopa (78) **1.** Polish: nickname from *kopa* 'dozens', 'stack'. **2.** Polish: occupational name for someone who cleared woodland for cultivation, from a derivative of *kopać* 'to dig'. **3.** Czech, Slovak, and Eastern German: from a pet form of the personal name *Jakob* (see JACOB).

Kopack (142) German or American derivative of Slovenian **Kopač**, occupational name for a digger, in particular for someone who cleared land for cultivation, from *kopač* 'digger', from *kopati* 'to dig', or from a cognate term in some other Slavic language.

GIVEN NAME German 4%. *Kurt.*

Kopacz (476) Polish: occupational name for someone who cleared land for cultivation, Polish *kopacz*, from *kopać* 'to dig'.

GIVEN NAMES Polish 7%. *Zbigniew* (3), *Jerzy* (2), *Jozef* (2), *Andrzej, Czeslawa, Karol, Krystyna, Miroslaw.*

Kopanski (105) Polish (**Kopański**): habitational name for someone from Kopana in Warszawa voivodeship.

GIVEN NAMES Polish 4%. *Jacek.*

Kopas (166) **1.** Americanized spelling of Hungarian **Kopasz**, a nickname from *kopasz* 'bald'. **2.** Polish: occupational

name for an agricultural laborer, from a derivative of *kopać* 'to dig'. **3.** German, of Slavic origin: occupational name for someone who cleared land for cultivation (see KOPACK).

Kopchak (114) From a pet form of *Kop*, a short form of the Slavic personal name *Prokop* (see PROKOP) or of a variant of JAKOB.

Kopcho (122) Bulgarian (**Kópčo**): from a short form of the personal name *Prokópi* (see PROKOP).

Kopczynski (294) **1.** Polish (**Kopczyński**): habitational name for someone from Kopczyn, named with Polish *kopka* 'little stack'. **2.** Jewish (from Poland): habitational name from an unidentified place, possibly in northeastern Poland.

GIVEN NAMES Polish 6%. *Jerzy* (2), *Casimir, Zygmunt.*

Kope (204) Hungarian: **1.** (**Kópé**): from *kópé* 'funny', 'outlandish', hence a nickname for a wicked but clever and humorous person. **2.** (**Köpe**): from the old secular personal name *Köpé.*

Kopec (905) **1.** Polish (**Kopeć**): from Polish *kopeć* 'smoke', 'soot', probably a nickname for a dirty or swarthy person; or alternatively a metonymic occupational name for a chimneysweep or for someone who worked in a smokehouse. **2.** Variant of Hungarian **Köpeci**, a habitational name for someone from Köpec or Kepecz; or alternatively a topographic name from the archaic Székely dialect word *göbec* 'pit', 'river bed'.

GIVEN NAMES Polish 12%. *Jerzy* (3), *Jozef* (3), *Stanislaw* (3), *Boguslaw* (2), *Ewa* (2), *Henryk* (2), *Jacek* (2), *Janina* (2), *Lucyna* (2), *Ludwik* (2), *Aniela, Elzbieta.*

Kopecki (109) Polish: habitational name for someone from any of numerous places called Kopiec, or a topographic name from *kopiec* 'hill' or 'pile of earth'.

Kopecky (836) Czech (**Kopecký**): topographic name for someone living by a hill, from *kopec* 'hill', or habitational name for someone from a place named with this word.

Kopel (308) **1.** Dutch: from Middle Dutch *coppel* 'measure of dry goods', possibly a metonymic occupational name for a merchant. **2.** Dutch: from Middle Dutch *coppel* (Middle Low German *koppel*) 'common pasture', probably a topographic name for someone who lived by common land. **3.** Jewish (Ashkenazic): from the Yiddish personal name *kopl*, from the German form of the Biblical name JACOB.

Kopelman (234) **1.** Dutch: variant spelling of KOPPELMAN. **2.** Jewish (Ashkenazic): from the Yiddish personal name **Koplman**, a variant of *kopl* (see KOPEL), with the addition of -*man* 'man'.

GIVEN NAMES Jewish 9%. *Arie* (5), *Miriam, Ori, Rozalya, Semen.*

Koper (273) **1.** Polish: from *koper* 'dill', 'fennel', a metonymic occupational name for a grower or seller of herbs and spices. **2.** German (also **Köper**): occupational name from Middle Low German *kopere* 'salesman', 'dealer', 'merchant'. **3.** German (**Köper**): variant of **Küpper** (see KUPPER). **4.** Dutch: metonymic occupational name for a coppersmith, from Dutch *koper* 'copper'.

Kopera (164) Polish: **1.** topographic name, from *koper* 'dill'. **2.** occupational name for a coppersmith, from a derivative of *kopr* 'copper'.

Kopernik (21) Polish: **1.** occupational name for a copper miner or copper smelter, Old Polish *kopernik*. **2.** habitational name for someone from Koperniki in Opole voivodeship, named with *kopr* 'copper'.

FOREBEARS The Polish astronomer Mikołaj Kopernik (1473–1543), better known by his Latin name *Copernicus*, established that the earth revolves around the sun and prompted the eventual rejection of geocentric cosmology.

Koperski (180) Polish: derivative of *koper* 'dill' or *kopr* 'copper'.

Kopetsky (113) Germanized or Americanized form of Czech **Kopecký** (see KOPECKY).

Kopf (1061) **1.** German: metonymic occupational name for a maker or seller of cups or flasks, from Middle High German *kopf* 'flask' (from Late Latin *cuppa* 'cask'). **2.** German and Jewish (Ashkenazic): nickname for someone with some noticeable peculiarity or deformity of the head, from Middle High German *kopf* (the same word as in 1, used in a transferred sense which during the Middle Ages gradually ousted the earlier word *houbet* 'head'), German *Kopf*.

GIVEN NAMES German 6%. *Kurt* (5), *Otto* (4), *Helmut* (2), *Arno, Dieter, Erwin, Gerhard, Heinz.*

Kopfer (104) German (**Köpfer**): occupational name for a maker and seller of mugs, cups, etc. (see KOPF 1), or for a person (a barber, for instance) who applied cupping glasses (to bleed people).

GIVEN NAME German 5%. *Kurt.*

Kopinski (180) Polish (**Kopiński**) and Jewish (from Poland): habitational name for someone from a village called Kopin or Kopino.

Kopischke (160) German: from a Slavicized variant of eastern German **Kopisch**, a derivative of the personal name *Jakob* (see JACOB).

Kopitzke (157) German: derivative of **Kopatz**, an occupational name for someone who cleared woodland for cultivation, from Czech *kopáč* 'digger'.

Kopka (291) Eastern German (under Slavic influence): from a reduced pet form of the personal name *Jakob* (see JACOB).

GIVEN NAMES German 6%. *Helmut, Wilhelm, Willi.*

Kopke (181) North German (**Köpke**): from a Low German pet form of the personal name *Jakob* (see JACOB).

GIVEN NAMES German 4%. *Gerhard, Hans, Helmut.*

Kopko (242) Ukrainian: from a reduced pet form of the personal name PROKOP.

Koplin (330) **1.** German: habitational name from a place near Teltow named Koplin, or possibly from Kapliai in Lithuania. **2.** Jewish (Ashkenazic): patronymic from the Yiddish personal name *kople*, *kopl* (see KOPEL).

GIVEN NAMES German 4%. *Arno, Dietrich, Gerd, Gerda.*

Koplowitz (100) Jewish (eastern Ashkenazic): patronymic from the Yiddish personal name *kopl* (see KOPEL).

GIVEN NAMES Jewish 21%. *Hyman, Kopel, Mendy, Miriam, Moshe, Zev.*

Kopman (122) Jewish (eastern Ashkenazic): nickname for a clever person, from Yiddish *kop* 'head' + *man* 'man'.

GIVEN NAMES Jewish 13%; Russian 6%. *Herschel* (2), *Naum, Yakov; Igor* (3), *Leonid* (2), *Yefim.*

Kopp (4634) **1.** German (also **Köpp**): from a North German pet form of *Jakob* (see JACOB). **2.** German: nickname for someone with a noticeable deformity or peculiarity of the head, from Low German *Kopp* 'head'. **3.** German: from the South German dialect word *Kopp* (also *Kapp*) 'young cock', 'capon', hence possibly a nickname for a young upstart or a metonymic occupational name for a keeper or breeder of poultry or game cocks. **4.** German: habitational name from a place so called in the Eifel Mountains. **5.** Hungarian: habitational name from a place so named near Naszvad. The place name is of German origin. A small plot of land near village was named *Vábrikkenkopp* (from German *Weg Brückenkopf*) by a Hungarian soldier in the Habsburg Army, who used to stand on watch at the bridge across the Vág river. The locals had difficulty with the name and later shortened it to *Kopp*.

Koppa (156) Polish: variant of KOPA.

GIVEN NAME French 4%. *Prosper.*

Koppang (116) Norwegian and Swedish: habitational name from any of several places named with Old Norse *kaupangr* 'market town'.

Koppe (162) North German: from Low German *Köppe*, a pet form of *Jakob*, German form of JACOB.

Koppel (655) **1.** North German: from Middle Low German *koppel* 'enclosed common pasture', hence a topographic name for someone living near such pasture, or possibly a status name for a commoner, i.e. someone who had the right to use such land for his livestock. **2.** German: from the Silesian dialect word *Köppel* 'head', a

nickname for someone with a visible deformity or peculiarity of the head. **3.** Jewish (Ashkenazic): from the Yiddish personal name *kopl*, a pet form of *Jakob* (see JACOB).

GIVEN NAMES German 4%; Jewish 4%. *Erwin* (2), *Erna, Ernst, Gerd, Hanni; Morty, Uri, Yakov, Yetta, Zalmen.*

Koppelman (406) **1.** Dutch: from *coppel* 'yoke', 'band', 'tie' + *man* 'man', an occupational name for a yoke maker or perhaps a nickname for a matchmaker. **2.** North German (**Koppelmann**) and Dutch: from a derivative of KOPPEL 'common land'. **3.** Jewish (Ashkenazic): elaborated form of KOPPEL, with Yiddish *man* 'man'.

GIVEN NAMES Jewish 5%. *Hyman* (2), *Chaim, Meyer, Sol.*

Koppen (237) North German (also **Köppen**): **1.** patronymic from a reduced pet form of the personal name *Jakob* (see JACOB). **2.** habitational name from any of several places named Koppen.

GIVEN NAMES German 4%. *Otto, Reinhard, Rudiger.*

Koppenhaver (346) **1.** Probably an altered spelling of German **Kobenhauer**, an occupational name for a cooper, from Middle High German *kope* 'vat', 'large barrel' + *hauer* 'chopper', from *hauen* 'to chop', 'to make or construct from wood'. **2.** Alternatively, it may be a habitational name for someone from Copenhagen (Danish *København*).

Kopper (213) **1.** German: from Low German *Kopper* 'copper', hence a metonymic occupational name for a copper dealer or coppersmith. **2.** German: occupational name, from Low German *Köpper* 'bloodletter', i.e. someone who applied cups in order to effect a bleeding. **3.** German: from Slavic *kopr* 'dill', 'fennel', hence a topographic name or a metonymic occupational name for a herb grower or dealer. Compare KOPER. **4.** German: habitational name for someone from any of the places called KOPPEN. **5.** Dutch: variant of KOPER.

Kopperud (132) Norwegian: habitational name from any of several farmsteads in southeastern Norway, named Kopperud, from Old Norse *koppari* 'a maker of cups' + *ruð* 'clearing'.

Koppes (265) Dutch: patronymic from a reduced form of the personal name *Jakob* (see JACOB).

Koppinger (111) **1.** German: probably a variant of **Kuppinger**, a habitational name for someone from Kuppingen in Baden-Württemberg. **2.** German (**Köppinger**): unexplained.

Kopplin (316) German: **1.** variant spelling of KOPLIN. **2.** Possibly a shortened form of **Köpplinger** (see CAPLINGER).

Koppy (112) Origin unidentified. Possibly a respelling of German KOPPE.

Kopriva (219) Czech (**Kopřiva**) and Slovenian: from *kopřiva* 'nettle', either a topographic name for someone who lived at a place overgrown with nettles or a nickname for someone who was unapproachable.

Koprowski (293) **1.** Polish: habitational name for someone from a lost place called Koprów or Koprowo, or from Koporów, now Kaporovka in Belarus. **2.** Jewish (from Poland): metonymic occupational name for a coppersmith, from Polish *koprowy* 'of copper'.

GIVEN NAMES Polish 6%. *Henryk, Irena, Piotr, Witold, Zdzislaw, Zigmund.*

Kops (190) **1.** Dutch: metonymic occupational name for a maker of cups and plates, from Middle Dutch *cop(pe)* 'cup', 'dish'. **2.** German and Dutch: patronymic from a short form of the personal name *Jakob* (see JACOB).

Kor (155) **1.** Scottish: unexplained. Perhaps a respelling of **Caw**, a reduced form of MCCAW. **2.** Possibly a variant of German **Kur**, an occupational name from Middle High German *kure* 'officialinspector' or Middle Low German *kur(e)* 'scout', 'lookout'. **3.** Dutch: unexplained. **4.** Polish: perhaps an altered form of a topographic or habitational name from any of various places named with Slavic *gora* 'mountain'.

GIVEN NAMES Polish 4%; German 4%. *Jozefa* (2), *Bogumil; Claus, Klaus.*

Korab (142) Polish and Czech (**Koráb**): from *koráb* 'boat', 'ship', a metonymic occupational name for someone who worked on a river boat or a ship, or a habitational name for someone who lived at a house distinguished by the sign of a ship or boat. As a Polish name, it may also be from a coat of arms bearing the sign of a ship. An earlier meaning of the word was 'old tree', and in some cases the surname may have arisen as a topographic name from this sense.

GIVEN NAMES French 5%. *Gabrielle, Pierre.*

Korach (112) **1.** Jewish (eastern Ashkenazic): occupational name from Hebrew *korach* 'bookbinder'. **2.** Serbian and Croatian (**Korać**): nickname from *korać* 'horseshoe hammer', from Greek *korakion*, literally 'raven'.

GIVEN NAMES Jewish 5%; South Slavic 4%. *Shlomo, Yosef; Dmitar, Milovan.*

Koral (188) **1.** Polish and Jewish (Ashkenazic): from Polish *koral* 'coral', 'coral bead', applied as a nickname, an ornamental name, or an occupational name for someone who worked or sold coral. **2.** Possibly also a short form of Greek *Koralis*, nickname from Greek *koralli* 'coral', applied as a nickname for someone wiht a red face or red hair.

Koralewski (110) Polish: habitational name for someone from a place called Koralewo in Ciechanów voivodeship.

GIVEN NAMES Polish 7%. *Casimir* (2), *Ludmilla.*

Koran (364) **1.** Czech (**Kořán**): metonymic occupational name for a herbalist or spicer,

from the southern dialect word *kořán* 'root'. **2.** Jewish (from Belarus): habitational name from the village of Korany, now in Belarus.

Koranda (278) Czech: from the personal name *Kornel*, a vernacular form of Latin CORNELIUS, or the German personal name KONRAD.

Korando (109) Czech: variant of KORANDA.

Korb (1101) German and Jewish (Ashkenazic): from Middle High German *korb*, German *Korb* 'basket', applied as a metonymic occupational name for a basketmaker or for a peddler who carried his wares around in a basket. In Bavaria it also denoted the occupant of a laborer's cottage built with wattle (i.e. interwoven twigs) and daub.

Korba (253) **1.** Czech: metonymic occupational name for a basketmaker, from German *Korb* 'basket'. **2.** Greek (**Korbas**): nickname for a person with black hair, from Albanian *korbë* 'crow'.

Korbel (308) **1.** South German (**Körbel**): from *Körbel*, a diminutive of *Korb* 'basket'. **2.** Czech: metonymic occupational name for a maker of drinking vessels, from *korbel* 'tankard'.

Korber (216) German (also **Körber**) and Jewish (Ashkenazic): occupational name for a basketmaker, from an agent derivative of KORB.

Korby (181) Americanized form of Finnish KORPI.

GIVEN NAMES Finnish 5%. *Erkki* (2), *Aino, Aune.*

Korch (106) Polish: nickname from *korch*, variant of *karch*, from *karchut* 'left hand'.

Korczynski (103) Polish (**Korczyński**): habitational name for someone from a place called Korczyn in Kielce voivodeship.

GIVEN NAMES Polish 13%. *Andrzej* (2), *Franciszek, Ludwik, Zbigniew.*

Korda (168) **1.** Hungarian, Polish, and Jewish (from Hungary and Poland): from *korda* 'rope' (Latin *corda* 'rope'). This was used as a nickname in various senses (including 'monk', with reference to the rope used by monks as belts). It may also have been a metonymic occupational name for a monk. **2.** Czech: from a pet form of the Old Czech personal name *Kornel*, a vernacular form of Latin CORNELIUS.

Kordes (121) **1.** German: reduced and altered form of **Konerding**, a patronymic derived from any of several Low German personal names cognate with KONRAD, such as *Kohnert*. **2.** Polish: variant of KORDUS.

GIVEN NAMES German 6%. *Alois, Ewald, Uwe.*

Kordich (102) Jewish: variant of KORDISH.

GIVEN NAME Jewish 4%. *Jakov.*

Kordish (121) Jewish (from Ukraine): habitational name for someone from the village of Kordyshev(ka) in Ukraine.

Kordsmeier (126) German: distinguishing nickname for a tenant farmer, from a farm

named with a first element, *Kord*, of uncertain origin.

Kordus (124) Polish: nickname from a derivative of *kord* 'sword'.

Korell (185) **1.** German: from an altered form of the personal name *Kornel* (see CORNELIUS). **2.** German: nickname for a humble or modest person, from a Slavic word, *kořil*, meaning 'humble'.

Koren (740) **1.** Jewish (Ashkenazic): variant of KORN. **2.** Dutch and North German: from a short form of *Cornelis* or CORNELIUS. This name was also established in Norway from the 16th century onward. **3.** Slovenian: nickname from *koren* 'root'.

GIVEN NAMES Jewish 7%. *Emanuel* (2), *Arie, Avi, Chaja, Eliahu, Eliya, Haim, Hyman, Meyer, Miriam, Moshe, Ofer.*

Korenek (186) Czech (**Kořenek**): nickname meaning 'ruddy fellow', a variant of **Kořínek** (see KORINEK).

Koretz (126) Origin unidentified.

Korey (166) Origin unidentified. Compare KORY.

Korf (359) **1.** German: metonymic occupational name for a basketmaker, from Low German *Korf* 'basket'. **2.** Jewish (from Ukraine): unexplained.

GIVEN NAMES Jewish 7%. *Benzion* (2), *Mendel* (2), *Menachem, Mordechai, Sholom, Yossi.*

Korff (323) German: variant of KORF.

GIVEN NAMES German 5%. *Elfriede, Elke, Gunter, Konrad, Otto.*

Korfhage (164) **1.** German: probably an occupational name for a peddler who carried his wares in a basket, from Low German *Korf* 'basket' + *Hake* 'huckster', or a topographic name for someone living near a woven fence, from *Hag* 'hedge', 'fence', 'enclosure'. **2.** Dutch: from a builder's term for the basket frame (literally 'basket hedge') used to hold hardcore in front of breastworks.

GIVEN NAMES German 8%. *Kurt* (2), *Franz, Milbert.*

Korhonen (245) Finnish: from the descriptive nickname *korho* 'deaf person', + the common surname suffix *-nen*. The term was used to denote not only a deaf person but also someone who was elderly, aloof, clumsy, silly, or foolish.

GIVEN NAMES Finnish 10%. *Reino* (2), *Esko, Hannu, Pentti, Petri, Sirkka, Toivo, Veijo, Vesa.*

Korin (119) Jewish: variant of KORN.

GIVEN NAMES Jewish 11%; Russian 6%; German 4%. *Hillel, Hyman, Izhak, Polina, Samoil, Yael; Boris, Dmitriy, Nikolay; Theodor.*

Korinek (304) Czech (**Kořínek**): nickname from *kořínek* 'ruddy fellow'.

Korkowski (113) Polish: surname coined to look like a habitational name, but in fact a nickname from *korek* 'cork (in a bottle)'.

GIVEN NAME French 4%. *Monique.*

Korman (1224) **1.** Dutch: occupational name for a grain dealer, Middle Dutch *cornman*. **2.** German (**Kormann**) and Jewish (Ashkenazic): see KORMANN.
GIVEN NAMES Jewish 6%. *Sol* (4), *Chaim* (2), *Hyman* (2), *Fishel, Hinda, Ilya, Jakob, Miriam, Nechama, Shaul, Shlomo, Sira.*

Kormanik (140) Czech: occupational name for an overseer of a granary, from a Czech pet form of German KORMAN.

Kormann (102) German and Jewish (Ashkenazic): variant of **Kornmann**, an occupational name for the overseer of a granary, a grain dealer, or a farmer.
GIVEN NAMES German 9%. *Erhard, Gunther, Kurt.*

Kormos (179) **1.** Hungarian: from *korom* 'soot', 'black dust', 'dirt', 'darkness', from Old Turkish *qurun*, hence a nickname for a poorly dressed or dirty person, or for someone with black hair or a dark face. **2.** Hungarian (**Körmös**): nickname for someone with long or dirty nails or an aggressive manner, from *köröm* 'nail'. **3.** Greek: nickname for a stocky man, from Greek *kormos* 'tree trunk', 'torso'.
GIVEN NAMES Hungarian 5%. *Balint* (2), *Arpad, Geza.*

Korn (2481) **1.** German: from Middle High German *korn* 'grain', a metonymic occupational name for a factor or dealer in grain or a nickname for a peasant. **2.** Dutch and German: from a short form of the personal name *Cornelis* or CORNELIUS. **3.** Jewish (Ashkenazic): from German *Korn* (Yiddish *korn*) 'grain', a metonymic occupational name as in 1, or an ornamental name. **4.** Czech: from a short form of the Czech personal name *Kornel*, a vernacular form of CORNELIUS.

Kornacki (257) Polish: habitational name from Kornaty in Konin voivodeship, probably named with *korny* 'humble', or from the use of this adjective as a nickname.
GIVEN NAMES Polish 8%. *Zbigniew* (2), *Jacenty, Malgorzata, Teofil, Walerian.*

Kornberg (199) **1.** German: habitational name from any of the various places so named in Hessen and Baden-Württemberg. **2.** Jewish (Ashkenazic) and Swedish: ornamental name meaning 'grain hill', from German *Korn* 'grain' + *Berg* 'mountain', 'hill', or Swedish *korn* + *berg*.
GIVEN NAMES Jewish 5%; German 5%; Scandinavian 4%. *Avram; Hans, Markus; Knud.*

Kornblatt (110) Jewish (Ashkenazic): ornamental name from German *Korn* 'grain' + *Blatt* 'leaf'.
GIVEN NAME Jewish 10%. *Hyman.*

Kornbluh (104) Jewish (Ashkenazic): ornamental name, probably from German *Korn* 'grain' + *blau* 'blue'.
GIVEN NAMES Jewish 16%. *Chaim* (2), *Sol* (2), *Eliahu, Hyman.*

Kornblum (293) Jewish (Ashkenazic): ornamental name from Yiddish *kornblum* (German *Kornblume*) 'cornflower'.

GIVEN NAMES Jewish 6%. *Sol* (2), *Avi, Miriam, Shalom, Yigal, Yoel.*

Kornbluth (177) Jewish (Ashkenazic): ornamental name from German *Kornblüte* 'grain blossom'.
GIVEN NAMES Jewish 6%; German 4%. *Emanuel* (2), *Aharon, Mendel; Kurt, Siegfried.*

Kornegay (1509) Probably an altered spelling of German **Kornegger**, a topographic name for someone who lived by a cornfield, from Middle High German *korn* 'grain' + *acker* 'field'.

Kornely (105) German: from Latin *Cornelii*, genitive form of the humanistic name CORNELIUS.

Korner (267) German (also **Körner**): see KOERNER.
GIVEN NAMES German 5%. *Markus, Otto.*

Kornfeld (582) **1.** German: habitational name from any of several places in former Silesia and East Prussia named Kornfelde or topographic name for someone who lived by a cornfield, from Middle High German *korn* 'grain' + *veld* 'open country', 'field'. **2.** Jewish (Ashkenazic): ornamental name from German *Kornfeld* 'cornfield'.
GIVEN NAMES Jewish 6%; German 4%. *Sol* (3), *Ari* (2), *Devorah, Emanuel, Meyer, Morty, Nachum, Noam, Ronen; Frieda* (2), *Erwin, Hans, Kurt.*

Kornhauser (159) German and Jewish (Ashkenazic): occupational name for the manager of a granary, from Middle High German *kornhūs*, German *Kornhaus* '(communal) granary' + the agent suffix *-er*. As a Jewish name it can also be ornamental name.
GIVEN NAMES Jewish 5%; German 4%. *Ari* (2), *Uzi; Arno.*

Kornick (117) **1.** German: habitational name from Kórnik in Poznan, Poland. **2.** East German: probably a habitational name from Körnik in Holstein, or a nickname from a Slavic word, for instance Czech *krne*, meaning 'weak', 'ailing', or 'wretched'.
GIVEN NAME German 4%. *Kurt.*

Kornman (121) German (**Kornmann**): occupational name for a corn merchant, from Middle High German *korn* 'corn' + *man* 'man'.

Kornreich (182) Jewish (Ashkenazic): ornamental name from German *kornreich*, literally 'rich in grain'.
GIVEN NAMES Jewish 8%. *Chana, Eliezer, Hirsch, Yaakov.*

Korns (145) Dutch: patronymic from KORN.

Korol (202) Ukrainian and Jewish (from Ukraine): Ukrainian nickname and Jewish ornamental name from Ukrainian *korol* 'king' (see KRAL).
GIVEN NAMES Russian 15%; Jewish 11%; Polish 7%. *Sergey* (2), *Svetlana* (2), *Aleksandr, Arkadiy, Boris, Fanya, Fruma, Gennady, Khayka, Lev, Leyzer, Nikolai; Avram, Ber, Etya, Polina, Volf, Yakov;*

Casimir (2), *Janina, Oleksa, Slawomir, Zbigniew.*

Koroma (142) Muslim (from West Africa): unexplained.
GIVEN NAMES Muslim 39%; African 9%. *Mohamed* (4), *Abu* (3), *Ibrahim* (3), *Abdul* (2), *Abdulai, Essa, Fatima, Isata, Ishmeal, Issa, Mohammed, Mohomed; Alieu* (2), *Fatmata* (2), *Foday, Kadiatu, Kadijatu.*

Korona (226) Hungarian, Czech, and Slovak: from *korona, koruna* 'crown' (from Latin *corona* 'garland', 'chaplet', 'diadem'). The application as a surname is unclear: it may be a nickname for someone who lived in a house distinguished by this sign, or one who lived on a royal estate. Alternatively, it may be from the monetary unit *korona* 'crown'.

Korosec (115) Slovenian (**Korošec**): habitational name for someone from Carinthia (Slovenian *Koroška*), a region now divided between Austria and Slovenia. The name of the region in Latin is *Carantania* (Old Slovenian *Korotan*); it was an early medieval Slovenian state on the territory of present-day Carinthia and Styria.
GIVEN NAMES French 5%. *Franck, Gabrielle.*

Korp (103) German: variant spelling of KORB.
GIVEN NAME German 5%. *Otto.*

Korpal (117) Indian (Panjab): Hindu (Brahman) name of unknown origin.
GIVEN NAMES Indian 6%. *Rakesh* (2), *Dev.*

Korpela (259) Finnish: habitational name from a farm so named for its situation, from *korpi* 'remote forest' + the local suffix *-la*. The surname has been traced back to the 16th century. It is a typical western Finnish surname.
GIVEN NAMES Finnish 10%; German 5%. *Tauno* (2), *Waino* (2), *Arvo, Juha, Paavo, Seppo, Toivo, Wiljo; Hans, Heino, Kurt, Otto.*

Korpi (469) Finnish: topographic or ornamental name from *korpi* 'remote forest'. In the U.S. it may also be a shortened form of KORPELA or **Korpinen**.
GIVEN NAMES Finnish 6%. *Eino* (4), *Irja, Kalevi, Niilo, Onni, Orvo, Pentti, Sulo, Tauno, Toimi, Toini.*

Kors (111) Dutch: patronymic from a short form of the personal name *Korsten* (Latin *Christianus*; see CHRISTIAN) or *Cornelis*.
GIVEN NAMES Dutch 14%. *Cornelis* (4), *Pieter* (2).

Korsak (102) **1.** Polish and eastern Slavic: nickname from *korsak* 'steppe fox', a Turkish loanword in various Slavic languages. **2.** Belorussian (**Kórsak**): nickname for someone thought to resemble a hawk, from *kóršak* 'kite'.
GIVEN NAMES German 6%; Polish 4%. *Georg; Witold.*

Korsmo (150) Norwegian: habitational name from any of several farmsteads in southeastern Norway named Korsmo, from *korz* 'cross(roads)' + *mo* 'plain', 'sandy meadow'.

Korson (199) Origin unidentified.

Korst (124) German: from a metathesized short form of the personal name *Christianus* (see CHRISTIAN).

Kort (490) **1.** Dutch: nickname for a short person, from Dutch *kort* 'short'. **2.** German: from a pet form of the personal name KONRAD. **3.** Jewish (eastern Ashkenazic): metonymic occupational name for a weaver or cloth dealer, from Polish or Yiddish *kort* 'cord'. **4.** Jewish (eastern Ashkenazic): nickname for a gambler, from Yiddish *kort* 'card'.

Kortan (155) Czech (**Kortán**): from a pet form of the Old Czech personal name *Kornel*, a vernacular form of Latin CORNELIUS.

Kortas (103) Polish: nickname from the dialect verb *kortać* 'to plow over a second time', also 'to tan somebody's hide'.

Korte (1771) **1.** Dutch and North German: nickname for a short person, from Middle Dutch, Middle Low German *kort* 'short'. **2.** German (**Körte**): Westphalian variant of the personal name KURT. **3.** German: from Sorbian *khort* 'hunting dog', hence possibly a nickname for someone resembling the animal in some way or for someone who kept hunting dogs. **4.** Hungarian (**Körte**): from *körte* 'pear', a metonymic occupational name for a grower or seller of the fruit.
GIVEN NAMES German 4%. *Kurt* (5), *Fritz* (2), *Hans* (2), *Otto* (2), *Aloysius*, *Christoph*, *Florian*, *Folker*, *Heimo*, *Heinrich*, *Klaus*, *Matthias*.

Korth (1047) German: **1.** variant of KORTE 1. **2.** from the personal name *Kord*, a Low German derivative of KONRAD.
GIVEN NAMES German 4%. *Otto* (4), *Fritz* (2), *Arno*, *Ewald*, *Heinz*, *Juergen*, *Othmar*.

Korthals (192) Dutch and North German: descriptive nickname for someone with a short neck (*kort hals*).
GIVEN NAMES German 7%. *Fritz*, *Heinz*, *Kurt*.

Kortman (181) Dutch and North German (**Kortmann**): descriptive nickname for a short (*kort*) man.
GIVEN NAMES German 6%. *Dieter*, *Hildegarde*.

Kortright (131) Americanized spelling of Dutch **Kortrijk** (see COURTRIGHT).
GIVEN NAMES Spanish 6%. *Jose* (2), *Aurelio*, *Eduardo*, *Enrique*, *Ernesto*, *Julio*, *Manuel*, *Miguel*.

Kortum (172) German: from a nickname for an agile, nimble, decisive person, from Low German *kortum*, literally 'turn round quickly', standard German *kurzum* 'in short'.

Kortz (281) German: **1.** variant of KURZ. **2.** from a short form of the personal name KONRAD.
GIVEN NAMES German 4%. *Aloys*, *Ulrich*.

Korus (160) Czech: from the Old Czech personal name *Kornel*, a vernacular form of Latin CORNELIUS.

Korver (195) **1.** German (**Körver**): occupational name for a basketmaker, from an agent derivative of KORF. **2.** Dutch: occupational name for a herring fisher, Middle Dutch *corvenaer*.
GIVEN NAMES German 5%. *Kurt* (2), *Johannes*, *Otto*.

Kory (167) Origin unidentified. Compare KOREY.

Korzeniewski (133) Polish: variant of KORZENIOWSKI.
GIVEN NAMES Polish 11%. *Casimir*, *Jerzy*, *Jozef*, *Kazimierz*, *Tadeusz*, *Zbigniew*.

Korzeniowski (145) Polish: habitational name for someone from any of various places called Korzeniów, for example in the voivodeships of Lublin or Tarnów; the place name is from *korzeń* 'root'.
FOREBEARS This name, borne by several Polish noble families, dates back to the 14th century. One member of the family was the novelist Józef Korzeniowski (1862–1924), better known by his Anglicized name of Joseph Conrad.
GIVEN NAMES Polish 15%. *Jozef* (2), *Tomasz* (2), *Andrzej*, *Bogdan*, *Elzbieta*, *Zbigniew*, *Zdzislaw*, *Zygmund*.

Kos (630) **1.** Slovenian, Croatian, Czech, and Polish: nickname from *kos* 'blackbird', denoting someone thought to resemble the bird in some way, for example someone with a good singing voice. This is a very common surname in Slovenia and Croatia. **2.** Czech and Sorbian (**Koš**): metonymic occupational name for a basketmaker, from *koš* 'basket'. **3.** German (**Kös**): possibly a nickname for a gossip or a smooth-talker, from Middle High German *kōse*, *koese* 'talk', 'chat'. Compare KOSER. **4.** Jewish (Ashkenazic): of uncertain origin. It may be an ornamental name from Slavic *kos* 'blackbird', as in 1, or alternatively it may be from Hebrew *kos* 'drinking glass' or Yiddish *kos* 'goblet', 'cup', probably applied as a metonymic occupational name for someone who made glasses or cups. **5.** Dutch: from a Zeeland personal name derived from *Constantius* (see CONSTANT). **6.** Hungarian (**Kós**): from a Turkish loanword *kos* 'ram' (from Old Turkish *qoč*, Ottoman Turkish *qoç*); perhaps a metonymic occupational name for a shepherd but more probably a nickname for someone thought to resemble the animal.

Kosa (232) **1.** Hungarian, Czech, and Slovak (**Koša**): from a pet form of any of various personal names beginning with *Ko-*, e.g. *Kornel* (see CORNELIUS). **2.** Czech, Polish, and Sorbian: from *kosa* 'scythe', a metonymic occupational name for a maker of scythes or a metonymic occupational name for a reaper. **3.** Czech, Polish, and Sorbian: variant of KOS.

Kosak (249) **1.** Czech and Slovak (**Kosák**): from a diminutive of KOS or KOSA. **2.** Slovenian (**Košak**): nickname from a simplified form of *koščak*, denoting a kind of nut tree with very hard nuts, probably denoting a strong, vigorous man. Also found as **Koščak**.

Kosakowski (320) Polish (also **Kossakowski**), Ukrainian, and Jewish (from Ukraine): habitational name for someone from any of various places laces named with *kos* 'blackbird', including Kossaki in Łomża voivodeship or Kosakowo in Konin voivodeship, or from the village of Kossakovka, now in Ukraine.
GIVEN NAMES Polish 7%. *Czeslaw*, *Jacek*, *Janusz*, *Jozefa*, *Mieczyslaw*, *Tadeusz*, *Witold*.

Kosanke (196) Eastern German (Pomerania) and Moldavian: probably a pet form of *Kosan*, a personal name of Slavic origin, but the details are unexplained.

Kosanovich (169) Serbian (**Kosanović**): patronymic from the personal name *Kosan*.
GIVEN NAMES South Slavic 6%. *Branko*, *Lazo*, *Vuk*.

Kosar (294) **1.** Czech (**Kosař**): from an agent noun derivative of *kosa* 'scythe', hence a metonymic occupational name for a maker of sickles and scythes or a metonymic occupational name for a reaper. **2.** Hungarian (**Kosár**): from the southern Slavic loanword *kosár* 'basket', hence a metonymic occupational name for a basketmaker. **3.** Bulgarian and Macedonian: from *kosar*, *koser* 'beehive', hence a metonymic occupational name for someone who made skeps or produced and sold honey.

Kosarek (106) Czech (**Kosárek**): occupational name for a maker of scythes or a reaper, from a diminutive of *kosař* (see KOSAR). This word also denoted a kind of plum typical of Moravia.

Kosch (302) Eastern German: **1.** probably from a short form *Mikusch* or *Nikusch*, Slavic forms of NICHOLAS, or a short form of *Jakusch*, a Slavic form of JACOB. **2.** metonymic occupational name for a basketmaker, from Sorbian *koš* 'basket'.

Koschak (110) Germanized spelling of Polish **Koszak** or Slovenian **Košak** (see KOSAK).

Koscielniak (193) Polish (**Kościelniak**): patronymic from the occupational name *kościelny* 'sacristan', 'churchwarden'.
GIVEN NAMES Polish 12%. *Dariusz*, *Janusz*, *Jozefa*, *Kazimierz*, *Tadeusz*, *Waclaw*, *Wlodzimierz*, *Zbigniew*.

Koscielski (104) Polish (**Kościelski**): habitational name for someone from any of many places called Kościelec or Kościół, named with *kościół* 'church'.
GIVEN NAME Polish 7%. *Casimir* (2).

Koscinski (185) Polish (**Kościński**): **1.** habitational name for someone from any of several places called Kościan. **2.** nickname from a derivative of Polish *kość* 'bone' + the common surname suffix *-ski*. **3.** perhaps from a derivative of the personal name *Konstanty* (see CONSTANT).

Kosciolek (117) Polish: topographic name for someone who lived by a church, from a diminutive of *kościół* 'church'.
GIVEN NAMES Polish 8%. *Bogdan, Casimir, Thadeus.*

Kosco (186) Variant spelling of KOSKO.

Kosek (443) **1.** Polish and Czech: nickname from a diminutive of KOS 'blackbird'. **2.** Polish and Czech (**Košek**): nickname or metonymic occupational name from a diminutive of *kosa* 'scythe'. **3.** Czech: from a pet form of the personal name **Koša** (see KOSA).
GIVEN NAMES Polish 5%. *Stanislaw* (2), *Andrzej, Grazyna, Jozef, Wojciech.*

Kosel (259) **1.** German (also **Kösel**): habitational name from places named Kosel, in eastern Germany and Schleswig-Holstein. **2.** German: variant of KUSEL 1, a nickname meaning 'spinning top'. **3.** Eastern German (of Slavic origin): from a Slavic word meaning 'he-goat', e.g. Polish dialect *kozieł*. Compare KOZIOL
GIVEN NAMES German 7%. *Helmut* (2), *Egon, Erwin, Hans, Horst, Kurt, Otto.*

Koser (563) South German: from an agent derivative of Middle High German *kōsen* 'to talk or discuss'; later 'to chat up', 'to caress'; possibly a nickname for a talker but more likely for a smooth-talker, a lady's man.

Kosh (169) Americanized spelling of KOS or KOSCH.

Koshak (119) Americanized spelling of Slovenian **Košak** (see KOSAK).

Koshy (240) Indian (Kerala): from a pet form of the personal name JOSHUA, found as a personal name among Christians in Kerala (southern India) and in the U.S. used as a last name among families from Kerala.
GIVEN NAMES Indian 37%. *Oommen* (4), *Ninan* (2), *Shaji* (2), *Soman* (2), *Ajay, Babu, Eapen, Lalitha, Mathai, Pramila, Raji, Shibu.*

Kosiba (296) Polish: possibly a metonymic occupational name for a reaper, from Polish *kosa* 'scythe'.
GIVEN NAMES Polish 7%. *Dariusz* (2), *Boguslawa, Kazimierz, Wiktor, Zygmunt.*

Kosich (108) **1.** Serbian (**Kosić**): from a pet form of the personal name *Kostadin*, Serbian form of CONSTANTINE. **2.** Croatian (**Kosić**) and Slovenian (**Kosič**): from a patronymic or diminutive form of KOS.
GIVEN NAME South Slavic 4%. *Obren.*

Kosick (115) Germanized or Americanized spelling of Slavic KOSIK.

Kosier (254) Origin unidentified.

Kosik (332) **1.** Czech (**Kosík**), Slovak, Polish, and Sorbian: nickname from western Slavic *kos* 'blackbird' (see KOS). **2.** Czech and Slovak (**Košík**): metonymic occupational name for a basketmaker, from *košík*, a derivative of *koš* 'basket'.

Kosin (144) Jewish (Ashkenazic): habitational name for someone from a place called Kossy, now in Belarus.

Kosinski (1004) Polish (**Kosiński**): habitational name for someone from Kosina, a place named with Polish *kosa* 'scythe'.
GIVEN NAMES Polish 6%. *Krzysztof* (2), *Wieslaw* (2), *Bronislaus, Casimir, Ignatius, Jerzy, Kazimierz, Mariola, Slawomir, Stanislaw, Tadeusz, Witold.*

Kosior (134) Polish: nickname from Polish dialect *kosior* 'fire rake', 'broom'.
GIVEN NAMES Polish 12%. *Zbigniew* (2), *Ignatius, Jozef, Mariusz, Urszula.*

Kosiorek (136) Polish: nickname from a pet form of KOSIOR.
GIVEN NAMES Polish 8%; German 4%. *Alicja, Kazimierz, Wladyslaw; Florian.*

Koska (190) Polish: nickname from a diminutive of *kosa* 'scythe'.

Koske (135) German (of Slavic origin): from a diminutive of western Slavic *kosa* 'scythe' (see KOSA) or *kos* 'blackbird' (see KOS).

Koskela (297) Finnish: ornamental name from *koski* 'waterfall', 'rapids' + the local suffix *-la*. In many cases it was probably adopted as an equivalent of Swedish **Forström** (see FORSTROM), **Grönfors**, **Stenfors**, etc.
GIVEN NAMES Scandinavian 5%; Finnish 4%. *Nels; Eino, Juha, Vaino, Waino.*

Koskey (163) Americanized spelling of KOSKI or KOSKE.

Koski (2408) **1.** Finnish: ornamental name from *koski* 'waterfall', 'rapids'. This was one of the many words denoting natural features that were used in the formation of Finnish surnames during the name conversion movement in the 19th and early 20th centuries. In the U.S. this is sometimes a shortened form of other Finnish surnames formed with this element, e.g. **Kalliokoski**, **Ylikoski**. **2.** Polish: habitational name from any of several places called Koski, named with *kos* 'blackbird'.
GIVEN NAMES Finnish 4%. *Eino* (7), *Tauno* (4), *Arvo* (3), *Toini* (3), *Aarne* (2), *Armas* (2), *Ensio* (2), *Mikko* (2), *Reijo* (2), *Reino* (2), *Toivo* (2), *Eero.*

Koskie (138) **1.** Reduced and altered form of Irish **McCuskey**, a variant of MCCASKEY. **2.** Americanized spelling of KOSKI or KOSKE.
GIVEN NAMES Irish 4%. *Aileen, Kieran.*

Koskinen (223) Finnish: variant of KOSKI + the common surname suffix *-nen*.
GIVEN NAMES Finnish 16%; Scandinavian 4%; German 4%. *Timo* (3), *Esko, Heikki, Jarmo, Juhani, Jussi, Mikko, Onni, Pekka, Toini, Toivo, Tuula; Erik; Kurt* (3).

Kosko (377) **1.** Ukrainian (**Kosko**) and Jewish (from Ukraine): nickname for a squint-eyed person, from Ukrainian *kosyj* 'squint' + *-ko*, suffix of Ukrainian sur-

names. **2.** Greek (**Koskos**): nickname for a bony person, from Albanian *koskë* 'bone'.

Koskovich (140) Origin unidentified.

Kosky (303) Americanized spelling of Finnish KOSKI.

Kosloske (124) Germanized spelling of Polish and Jewish KOSLOWSKI.

Kosloski (326) Polish and Jewish: variant of KOSLOWSKI.

Koslosky (231) Jewish: variant of KOSLOWSKI.

Koslow (339) **1.** Germanized or Americanized spelling of Polish **Kozłów** (see KOZLOW) or of a Sorbian cognate. **2.** Jewish (eastern Ashkenazic): habitational name from a place called Kozlovo or Kozly in eastern Galicia, now in Belarus (German name *Kossow*, Polish *Kozlów*), named with *kozioł* 'he-goat'.

Koslowski (287) Polish and Jewish (eastern Ashkenazic): variant of KOZLOWSKI.
GIVEN NAMES German 7%. *Gerda, Hans, Klaus, Kurt, Otto.*

Koslowsky (110) Jewish (Ashkenazic): variant of KOZLOWSKI.
GIVEN NAMES German 6%; Irish 4%; Russian 4%. *Dieter, Kurt; Konstantin, Raisa.*

Kosmalski (95) Polish: **1.** nickname from *kosmała* (a derivative of *kosmaty* 'shaggy', 'hairy'; see KOSMATKA) + -*ski* suffix of surnames. **2.** from a derivative of the personal name *Kosmas* (see KOSMAN) + the common surname suffix *-ski*. This name is also established in German-speaking lands.
GIVEN NAME German 5%; Polish 4%. *Wojciech.*

Kosman (301) **1.** Czech and Polish: from an altered form of the Greek personal name *Kosmas* (a derivative of Greek *kosmos* 'order', 'universe'), borne by an early Christian saint martyred in Cilicia in AD 303 under the emperor Domitian, together with his brother Damian (see DAMIAN). **2.** Jewish (Ashkenazic): from the Jewish personal name *Kosman*, borrowed from German Christians. **3.** Jewish (Ashkenazic): occupational name for someone who made glasses or cups, from Hebrew *kos* 'drinking glass' or Yiddish *kos* 'goblet', 'cup' + *man* 'man'. See also KOS.

Kosmatka (150) Polish: nickname for a shaggy, unkempt individual, from *kosmaty* 'shaggy', 'hairy'.

Kosmicki (224) Polish (**Kośmicki**): variant of **Koźmicki**.

Kosnik (109) Polish (**Kośnik**): occupational name from dialect *kośnik* 'mower' (standard Polish *kosiarz*).
GIVEN NAMES Polish 6%. *Jerzy, Zygmunt.*

Kosobucki (125) Polish: habitational name for someone from Kossobudy in Ciechanów voivodeship.
GIVEN NAMES Polish 4%. *Andrzej, Casimir.*

Kosowski (185) Polish (also **Kossowski**) and Jewish (eastern Ashkenazic): habitational name for someone from any of various places called Kosowa, Kos(s)ów,

Kos(s)owo, or Kossewo, named with *kos* 'blackbird'.

GIVEN NAMES Polish 8%. *Andrzej, Benedykt, Henryk, Teofil, Wladyslaw.*

Koss (2043) **1.** Germanized spelling of Czech, Polish, Slovenian, and Jewish KOS. **2.** Eastern German: from a short form of the personal name *Kosmas* (see KOSMAN), popular mainly in Slavic-speaking regions. **3.** German: from an altered form of an old personal name formed with Old High German *got* 'god'. **4.** Norwegian: habitational name from a farm so named, from Old Norse *kǫs* 'mound', 'heap'.

Kossack (118) German: **1.** Germanized spelling of Slavic KOZAK, either an ethnic name for a Cossack, or a nickname for an aggressive or ferocious person. **2.** in northern Germany, probably also a folk-etymological adaptation of the Low German term *Kotsasse* 'cottager' (see KOTZ) to the Slavic ethnic name *Kossack* (see KOZAK).

GIVEN NAMES German 19%. *Hartmut* (4), *Gunther, Hermann, Reinhard.*

Kossak (108) **1.** Polish (**Kosak**): patronymic from the nickname *kos* 'blackbird' (see KOS). **2.** Polish and Ukrainian: variant of KOSAK.

GIVEN NAMES Polish 7%; Czech and Slovak 4%. *Teofil; Bohdan.*

Kosse (115) German: variant of KOSS.

GIVEN NAMES German 6%. *Angelika, Gunter, Karl-Heinz.*

Kossler (111) German: **1.** (**Kössler**): variant of KESSLER. **2.** Habitational name for someone from Koslar near Jülich.

Kossman (217) **1.** Jewish (Ashkenazic): variant spelling of KOSMAN. **2.** German: variant spelling of KOSSMANN.

GIVEN NAMES German 4%. *Dietmar, Gottlieb.*

Kossmann (103) German: variant of KOSMAN.

GIVEN NAMES German 7%; Scandinavian 4%. *Hans, Ingeborg, Otto; Britt.*

Kossoff (116) Jewish: alternative spelling of eastern Ashkenazic **Kossov**, habitational name for someone from a place called Kossovo, now in Belarus.

GIVEN NAME Jewish 5%. *Sol.*

Kossow (224) Jewish: German and Polish spelling of eastern Ashkenazic **Kossov** (see KOSSOFF).

GIVEN NAME German 5%. *Lorenz.*

Kost (1361) **1.** German, Dutch, Czech, etc.: from the personal name *Kost*, a vernacular short form of the Latin personal name *Constantius* or *Constantinus* (see CONSTANT, CONSTANTINE). **2.** Polish, Czech, and German (of Slavic origin): from Slavic *kost* 'bone', 'knucklebone', probably a nickname for a thin, angular person. **3.** Jewish (Ashkenazic): metonymic occupational name for a grocer, from German *Kost* 'provisions', 'food'.

Kosta (243) **1.** Greek: variant of KOSTAS. **2.** Czech: nickname for a bony person, from *kost* 'bone' (see KOST 2).

Kostal (198) Czech (**Košťál**) and Slovak (**Koštial**): nickname from *košt'ál* 'stalk'.

Kostas (169) Greek: from the personal name *Kostas*, a pet form of *Konstantinos* (see CONSTANTINE).

GIVEN NAMES Greek 11%. *Constantine, Dimitrios, Spiro, Spiros, Stergios, Stratis.*

Kostecki (351) Polish: habitational name for someone from a place called Kostki in Kielce or Siedlce voivodeships.

GIVEN NAMES Polish 6%. *Zbigniew* (2), *Jarek, Maciej, Malgorzata, Stanislaw, Tadeusz, Teofil.*

Kostek (178) Polish: from a pet form of the personal name *Konstanty* (see CONSTANT).

GIVEN NAMES Polish 8%. *Bronislaw, Ewa, Kazimierz, Stanislaw, Zbigniew.*

Kostelac (117) Czech: variant of KOSTELNIK.

Kostelecky (314) Czech: habitational name for someone from any of the many places in Bohemia and Moravia called Kostelec, named from *kostel* 'church'.

Kostelnik (337) Czech (**Kostelník**): status name for a sacristan, from an agent noun based on *kostel* 'church'.

Kosten (148) **1.** German: from Middle High German *kost* 'provisions', 'board', 'livelihood', but in some cases probably a shortened form of KOSTENBADER. **2.** German: habitational name from a place so named in Tyrol. **3.** Dutch: from a reduced vernacular form of the personal name *Konstant* or *Konstantin* (see CONSTANT, CONSTANTINE).

Kostenbader (108) German: occupational name for someone who owned or worked in a bathhouse or spa, from *Koste(n)* 'bath apron' + *Bader* 'spa or bathhouse attendant'. This is the name of a Palatine immigrant family.

Kostenko (110) Ukrainian: patronymic from a pet form of the personal name *Konstanty* (see CONSTANT, CONSTANTINE).

GIVEN NAMES Russian 21%; Jewish 5%. *Yury* (2), *Anatoly, Fedor, Galina, Lyubov, Nicoli, Sergei, Sergey, Valeriy, Yevgeniya; Inna, Irina, Polina.*

Koster (2434) **1.** Dutch and North German: status name for a sexton, Middle Dutch *coster(e)*. Compare German KUSTER. **2.** North German (**Köster**): occupational nickname or status name for a day laborer who owned no land, from Middle Low German *koster*, from *kossater* 'cottager'. **3.** South German: occupational name for a wine taster, from *kosten* 'to taste'. **4.** Jewish (Ashkenazic): occupational name for a grocer or provisioner, from German *Koster* 'provisions', 'foodstuffs' + the agent suffix *-er*.

Kosterman (127) **1.** Jewish (Ashkenazic): occupational name for a grocer or provisioner, elaborated form of KOSTER 4. **2.** German (**Kostermann**): elaborated form of KOSTER 2.

Kosters (152) Dutch and North German (**Kösters**): patronymic from KOSTER 1 and 2.

GIVEN NAMES Dutch 4%. *Egbert, Gerrit.*

Kostic (173) Serbian (**Kostić**): patronymic from *Kosta*, a pet form of the personal name *Konstantin* (see CONSTANTINE).

GIVEN NAMES South Slavic 22%. *Miodrag* (2), *Nenad* (2), *Dejan, Dragan, Dragana, Dusan, Milan, Milivoje, Milomir, Milorad, Predrag.*

Kostick (331) Probably a Germanized or Americanized spelling of Ukrainian KOSTIUK or some other Slavic derivative of the Latin personal name *Constantius* or *Constantinus* (see CONSTANT, CONSTANTINE).

Kostiuk (126) Ukrainian: patronymic from a pet form of the personal name *Konstanty* (see CONSTANT, CONSTANTINE).

Kostka (525) Polish and Czech: **1.** possibly a nickname for a bony, angular person, from a derivative of *kost* 'knucklebone'. **2.** more probably a derivative of the Latin personal name *Constantius* or *Constantinus* (see KOST, CONSTANT, CONSTANTINE).

GIVEN NAMES Polish 4%. *Jaromir, Jerzy, Karol, Radoslaw, Stanislaw, Wieslaw, Zofia.*

Kostman (111) German (**Kostmann**): variant of KOSMAN. Compare KOSSMANN.

GIVEN NAME German 4%. *Kurt.*

Kostner (148) **1.** German (**Köstner**) occupational name from the Bavarian, Franconian dialect word *Köstner* 'granary administrator', 'treasurer'. **2.** German (**Köstner**): habitational name for someone from either of two places: Kösten near Bamberg, or Köstenberg. **3.** German: topographic name for someone living on a 'shelf' in the mountains, from Latin *costa* 'rib', 'side', 'flank'.

Kostoff (170) Bulgarian: alternative spelling of **Kostov**, a patronymic from the Bulgarian personal name *Kostadin* (see CONSTANTINE).

Kostopoulos (136) Greek: patronymic from the personal name KOSTAS + the patronymic ending *-poulos*, derived from Latin *pullus* 'nestling', 'chick'. This ending is found mainly in the Peloponnese.

GIVEN NAMES Greek 13%. *Andreas* (2), *Demetrios, Efstathios, Kostas, Nichlos, Nikolaos, Ourania.*

Kostrzewa (164) Polish: topographic name or perhaps a nickname, from *kostrzewa* 'fescue grass' (from *kostra* 'spike').

GIVEN NAMES Polish 8%. *Bogdan, Jozef, Stanislawa, Waclaw, Zofia, Zygmunt.*

Kostrzewski (153) Polish: habitational name for someone from a place called Kostrzewice in Sieradz voivodeship or Kostrzewy in Kalisz voivodeship, both named with *kostrzewa* 'fescue grass'.

GIVEN NAMES German 5%; Polish 5%. *Hans* (2), *Alphons; Stanislaw, Witold.*

Kostuch (106) Polish: **1.** from a pet form of the personal name *Konstanty*, Latin *Constantius* or *Constantinus* (see KOST, CONSTANT, CONSTANTINE). **2.** from a derivative of *kość* 'knucklebone' (see KOST). GIVEN NAMES Polish 6%; German 5%. *Marcin, Tadeusz; Erna, Kurt.*

Kosty (122) Probably an Americanized spelling of Czech *kost'*, a nickname meaning 'bone'.

Kostyk (113) Ukrainian: from a pet form of CONSTANTINE.

Kosub (138) Polish: variant of KOZUB.

Kot (431) Polish, Slovak, Czech, Belorussian, Jewish (eastern Ashkenazic), and German (of Slavic origin): from a personal name or nickname based on Slavic *kot* 'tom cat'. As a Jewish name it is generally an ornamental name. GIVEN NAMES Polish 13%; Jewish 4%. *Czeslawa* (2), *Zbigniew* (2), *Zygmunt* (2), *Bogdan, Boguslaw, Danuta, Dariusz, Dymitr, Elzbieta, Halina, Janina, Janusz; Shlomo* (2), *Avraham.*

Kota (105) Indian (Andhra Pradesh): Hindu name meaning 'fort' in Telugu. GIVEN NAMES Indian 52%. *Chandrasekhar* (3), *Ananda* (2), *Ranga* (2), *Shyam* (2), *Srinivas* (2), *Subu* (2), *Gowri, Kishore, Madhu, Madhuri, Mehar, Murali.*

Kotalik (117) Czech (**Kotalík**): nickname meaning 'roller', from a derivative of the verb *kotálet se* 'to roll'.

Kotar (106) Slovenian: **1.** topographic or status name for someone who lived in a cottage, from Middle High German *kote* 'cottage', formed with an agent noun suffix *-ar*. **2.** topographic name for someone who lived in a corner of a valley or plain, from *kot* 'corner', or a habitational name for someone from any of the numerous places called Kot, named with this word. GIVEN NAME French 4%. *Serge.*

Kotara (184) **1.** Polish: nickname from *kotara* 'curtain'. **2.** Czech (**Kot'ara**): nickname for a lame person, from the Czech dialect word *kot'ara* 'leg'. **3.** Czech: from the personal name *Chtěbor*. **4.** Possibly also a reduced form of Greek **Kotaras** or **Kotaridis**, derivatives of the personal name *Kotas*, a pet form of *Konstantinos* (see CONSTANTINE), + the augmentative suffix *-aras*. GIVEN NAMES Polish 7%. *Karol* (2), *Malgorzata, Piotr, Slawomir, Zigmunt.*

Kotarski (280) Polish: habitational name for someone from a place called Kotarczyn in Płock voivodeship, Kotary in Częstochowa voivodeship, or Kotarz in Bielsko-Biała voivodeshop. . GIVEN NAMES Polish 5%. *Ignatius, Jaroslaw, Wieslaw, Zbigniew.*

Kotas (246) **1.** Polish: derivative of KOT 'cat'. **2.** Czech: from a pet form of the personal name *Chotěbor*, meaning 'warlike'. **3.** Greek: with the stress on the first syllable, this is from a pet form of the personal

name *Konstantinos* (see CONSTANTINE, and compare KOSTAS). **4.** Greek: with the stress on the second syllable, it is an occupational name for a poulterer, from *kota* 'hen' + the occupational suffix *-as*. GIVEN NAMES Slavic 4%. *Jozef, Justyna, Piotr, Wojciech.*

Kotch (462) Americanized form of Hungarian KOCI 'coach' or its Czech cognate **Kočí**.

Kotcher (120) Jewish (Ashkenazic): variant of KOCHER 3, an ornamental name meaning 'drake'.

Kotecki (330) Polish: habitational name for someone from Kotki in Kielce voivodeship, named with Polish *kotek* 'little cat, kitten'.

Kotek (175) Czech and Polish: nickname from Western Slavic *kotek* 'kitten' or 'little tom cat', diminutive of *kot* 'cat'.

Koteles (131) Hungarian (**Köteles**): **1.** occupational name for a rope maker, from *kötél* 'rope'. **2.** possibly a nickname for someone with some particular moral or legal obligation, from *köteles* 'obliged' (a derivative of *kötél* 'rope').

Koterba (114) Polish: nickname from *kotarba*, variant of *kocierba* 'bird cherry'.

Koth (510) **1.** German (also **Köth**): from Middle High German, Middle Low German *kote* 'cottage', 'hovel', a status name for a day laborer who lived in a cottage and owned no farmland. Compare KOTZ. **2.** German: from a short form of any of various personal names formed with Old High German *got* 'god', for example *Gottfried*. **3.** Jewish (eastern Ashkenazic): variant spelling of KOT. GIVEN NAMES German 5%. *Otto* (3), *Kurt* (2), *Gerhard, Lorenz, Oskar.*

Kothari (345) Indian (Gujarat, Rajasthan): Hindu (Bania, Vania) and Jain name meaning 'storekeeper' in Gujarati, from *kotha* 'granary', 'store' (Sanskrit *koṣṭhaka*). Several Bania communities have clans called Kothari. GIVEN NAMES Indian 92%. *Sanjay* (8), *Ashok* (7), *Pravin* (7), *Vinay* (6), *Bharat* (5), *Pankaj* (5), *Suresh* (5), *Ajay* (4), *Anil* (4), *Jagdish* (4), *Arun* (3), *Atul* (3).

Kothe (367) German: variant of KOTH 1. GIVEN NAMES German 7%. *Heinz* (3), *Manfred, Otto.*

Kothmann (142) German: probably a variant of **Kotmann**, a topographic name or nickname, from Middle High German *kāt* 'dung' + *man* 'man'. GIVEN NAME German 4%. *Konrad.*

Kotila (177) Finnish: **1.** habitational name from any of various farms named with Finnish *koti* 'home' + the locative suffix *-la*. **2.** Alternatively, it may be from a farm name based on an ancient Scandinavian personal name, *Gote* or *Goti*, presumably the naem of the proprietor. GIVEN NAMES Scandinavian 5%; Finnish 5%. *Nels; Reino* (2), *Waino.*

Kotkin (104) Jewish (from Belarus): unexplained. GIVEN NAMES Jewish 8%. *Meyer, Mort.*

Kotkowski (51) Polish and Jewish (from Poland): habitational name for someone from Kotkowo in Bydgoszcz or Katowice voivodeships, or Kotków in Konin or Piotrków voivodeships. GIVEN NAMES Polish 10%; Jewish 9%. *Bogdan, Zygmunt; Doron, Miriam.*

Kotlar (118) Variant spelling of Jewish and Ukrainian KOTLYAR. GIVEN NAMES Jewish 5%. *Irina, Isadore; Simeone* (2).

Kotlarz (152) Polish and Jewish (from Poland): occupational name for a boiler maker or coppersmith, Polish *kotlarz*. GIVEN NAMES Polish 6%. *Mieczyslaw, Ryszard, Witold.*

Kotler (390) **1.** German: variant of **Kötter** (see KOETTER). **2.** Jewish (Ashkenazic): occupational name for a coppersmith, Yiddish *kotler*. GIVEN NAMES Jewish 10%. *Aryeh, Baruch, Hyman, Isser, Meyer, Miriam, Moisha, Shmuel, Shraga, Sol.*

Kotlinski (48) Polish (**Kotliński**): habitational name for someone from any of several places called Kotlin, Kotlina, or Kotliny, named with *kotlina* 'dale'. GIVEN NAMES Polish 5%; Scandinavian 5%. *Tomasz; Sig.*

Kotlowski (107) Polish (**Kotłowski**): habitational name for someone from a place called Kotłów, named with *kocioł* 'kettle', 'boiler'. GIVEN NAME Polish 5%. *Radoslaw.*

Kotlyar (184) Jewish (from Ukraine) and Ukrainian: occupational name for a boiler maker or coppersmith, Ukrainian *kotlyar*. GIVEN NAMES Russian 37%; Jewish 28%. *Vladimir* (8), *Boris* (4), *Igor* (4), *Yefim* (4), *Aleksandr* (3), *Leonid* (3), *Mikhail* (3), *Aleksey* (2), *Arkady* (2), *Oleg* (2), *Semyon* (2), *Sergey* (2); *Faina* (2), *Yakov* (2), *Busya, Gersh, Gitel, Ilya, Inna, Isaak, Moysey, Naum, Rivka, Tsilya.*

Kotnik (136) Slovenian: topographic name for someone who lived in a corner of a valley or plain, from *kot* 'corner', or a habitational name for someone from any of the numerous places called Kot, named with this word.

Kotowicz (112) Polish and Jewish (from Poland): patronymic from the personal name KOT. GIVEN NAMES Polish 15%. *Czeslaw, Kazimierz, Krzysztof, Szczepan, Wladyslaw, Zdzislaw.*

Kotowski (492) Polish and Jewish (Ashkenazic): habitational name for someone from places called Kotów, Kotowy, or Kotowice, named with *kot* 'cat'. GIVEN NAMES Polish 11%. *Tadeusz* (3), *Casimir* (2), *Jacek* (2), *Wieslaw* (2), *Alicja, Andrzej, Boguslaw, Henryk, Jadwiga, Janusz, Jaroslaw, Lech.*

Kotrba (138) Czech: probably a nickname for a stubborn person, from *kotrba* 'head', 'pate'.

Kott (702) **1.** German: variant of KOTH or KOTZ. **2.** Polish and Czech: variant of KOT.

Kotter (262) German: **1.** habitational name for someone from any of several places in Germany named Kotten. **2.** variant of **Kötter** (see KOETTER).

GIVEN NAMES German 4%. *Dietmar, Kurt.*

Kottke (596) German: from a diminutive of KOTT.

GIVEN NAMES German 5%. *Kurt* (3), *Egon, Erwin, Ewald, Helmut, Konrad.*

Kottler (183) **1.** German: variant of **Köttler**, itself a variant of **Kötter** (see KOETTER). **2.** North German: occupational name for a butcher, from Middle Low German *koteler* 'preparer of entrails' (compare KUTTLER). **3.** Jewish (Ashkenazic): variant of KOTLER.

GIVEN NAMES Jewish 6%; Russian 4%. *Ilan; Misha* (2), *Iosif.*

Kottman (136) German (**Kottmann**): status name for a farm laborer who lived in a cottage (see KOETTER).

Kottwitz (260) German: habitational name from Katowice (German *Kottwitz*) in Silesia.

Kotula (376) **1.** Polish and Czech: nickname from *kot* 'tom cat'. **2.** Czech: nickname for someone with a rolling gait, from *kotoulet* 'to roll'.

GIVEN NAMES Polish 6%. *Dariusz, Dorota, Janina, Leszek, Stanislawa, Tadeusz, Wieslaw.*

Kotz (562) **1.** German: status name for a cottager or day laborer, from German *Kotsasse, Kotsate*, literally 'inhabitant of a cottage'. **2.** German and Jewish (Ashkenazic): from Middle High German, Middle Low German *kotze* (or Polish *koc*) 'blanket', 'horsecloth', 'coarse woolen cloth or garment', hence a metonymic occupational name for a maker of such cloth or a nickname for a poorly dressed person. **3.** German (**Kötz**): from a pet form of the personal name KONRAD. **4.** Hungarian (**Kótz**) and German: nickname from the Slavic loanword *kóc* 'untidy hair', 'hair of corn'.

Kotzen (122) **1.** German: habitational name from a place so named in Brandenburg. **2.** Jewish (Ashkenazic): nickname from Hebrew *katsin* 'rich man', pronounced as *kotsn* by Ashkenazic Jews.

Kotzur (144) Romanian: unexplained.

Kou (142) **1.** Chinese 寇: from the title of an important official in ancient China, the Sikou, who was in charge of criminal investigation and punishment. During the Zhou dynasty (1122–221 BC), the descendants of several Sikou adopted the second character of the title, Kou, as their surname. **2.** Chinese 高: variant of GAO. **3.** Cambodian or other Southeast Asian: unexplained.

GIVEN NAMES Chinese 22%; Other Southeast Asian 16%. *Hong* (2), *Chen-Chen, Chi, Hui, Kou, Kuei, Mei Juan, Qing, Yang; Koua, Hop, Samnang, Sau, Yen.*

Kouba (605) Czech: from a pet form of the personal name *Jakub*, Czech form of JACOB.

Koubek (152) Czech: from a pet form of the personal name *Jakub*, Czech form of JACOB.

Koudelka (197) Czech: **1.** nickname for someone with tow-colored hair, from a derivative of *koudel* 'tow'. **2.** habitational name for someone from a village in Moravia called Koudelov.

GIVEN NAME German 4%. *Otto.*

Kough (253) Irish: variant spelling of KEOUGH.

Kouns (401) Dutch: from a medieval personal name, usually taken as a pet form of KONRAD, but see KUNTZ.

Kountz (297) Dutch and North German: from a medieval personal name, usually taken as a pet form of KONRAD, but see KUNTZ.

Koupal (127) Czech: occupational name for a merchant.

Kouri (344) **1.** Variant of Greek KOURIS. **2.** Arabic: variant of KHOURY.

Kouris (101) Greek: topographic name for someone who lived in a forest, from northern Greek *kouri* 'small forest' or Aromanian *curie* 'forest', both from Turkish *koru* 'small forest'.

GIVEN NAMES Greek 9%. *Andreas* (2), *Kostas* (2), *Ilias.*

Koury (756) Arabic: variant of KHOURY.

Koutnik (110) Czech (**Koutník**): **1.** habitational name for someone from a place called Kouty. **2.** topographic name for someone who lived on a corner, Czech *kout*.

Kovac (1013) Czech (Moravian) and Slovak (**Kováč**), Slovak, Slovenian, Serbian, and Croatian (all **Kovač**): occupational name from Slavic *kovač* 'smith'.

Kovacevic (204) Serbian and Croatian (**Kovačević**): patronymic from *kovač* 'smith' (see KOVAC).

GIVEN NAMES South Slavic 33%. *Nebojsa* (3), *Radovan* (3), *Dejan* (2), *Dragan* (2), *Dzevat* (2), *Miodrag* (2), *Slavica* (2), *Blazo, Dinko, Dragoljub, Ljiljana, Marija; Mirko* (3), *Milan* (2), *Miroslav* (2), *Milos.*

Kovacevich (317) Serbian and Croatian (**Kovačević**): see KOVACEVIC.

GIVEN NAMES South Slavic 5%. *Dinko, Dmitar, Dragan, Momir, Velimir.*

Kovach (3529) Americanized spelling of Hungarian **Kovács** (see KOVACS) or Slavic KOVAC, meaning 'smith'.

Kovacic (421) Croatian and Serbian (**Kovačić**); Slovenian (**Kovačič**): patronymic from *kovač* 'blacksmith'.

GIVEN NAMES South Slavic 5%. *Bozidar, Marijan, Petar, Simo, Slavko, Zivko, Zvonko.*

Kovacich (198) Serbian and Croatian (**Kovačić**); Slovenian **Kovačič**: see KOVACIC.

Kovacik (230) Slovak (**Kováčik**): from a pet form of *kováč* 'smith' (see KOVAC).

Kovack (222) Americanized spelling of Slovak and Czech **Kováč** (see KOVAC); Croatian, Serbian, and Slovenian **Kovač**; or Hungarian *Kovács*. All of them mean 'smith'. See KOVACS.

Kovacs (3246) Hungarian (**Kovács**): occupational name for a blacksmith, Hungarian *kovács*, a loanword from Slavic.

GIVEN NAMES Hungarian 15%. *Laszlo* (24), *Sandor* (17), *Gabor* (12), *Tibor* (12), *Zoltan* (12), *Bela* (11), *Imre* (10), *Istvan* (9), *Arpad* (8), *Andras* (7), *Lajos* (7), *Miklos* (7).

Koval (1572) Ukrainian, Belorussian, Czech dialect, and Jewish (eastern Ashkenazic): occupational name for a blacksmith, from the vocabulary word *koval*.

Kovalchick (154) Americanized spelling of **Kovalchik** (see KOVALCHIK) or Czech and Slovak **Kovalčík** (see KOVALCIK), both meaning 'smith'.

Kovalchik (162) Belorussian: from a diminutive of Belorussian *koval* 'smith'.

Kovalcik (294) Czech (**Kovalčík**): from a diminutive of Czech *koval* 'smith'. Compare KOVAC.

Kovalenko (136) Ukrainian and Jewish (from Ukraine): patronymic from *koval* 'smith'.

GIVEN NAMES Russian 30%; Jewish 15%. *Vladimir* (5), *Mikhail* (2), *Oleg* (2), *Anatoliy, Boris, Grigory, Leonid, Nikolaj, Nikolay, Sergey, Serguei, Vasily; Heshy, Irina, Leibel, Mordechai, Yakov.*

Kovaleski (322) Belorussian: habitational name for someone from any of several places called Kovali in Belarus, or perhaps Kavoliai in Lithuania, named with a derivative of *kavalj* 'smith'.

Kovalick (118) Germanized spelling of Czech **Kovalík** (see KOVALIK).

GIVEN NAME German 4%. *Kurt* (2).

Kovalik (216) Czech (**Kovalík**), Ukrainian, and Belorussian: from a diminutive of *koval* 'smith'. Compare KOVAC.

Kovalski (135) Ukrainian, Belorussian, and Jewish (eastern Ashkenazic): variant of KOVALSKY.

Kovalsky (196) Ukrainian, Belorussian, and Jewish (eastern Ashkenazic): habitational name for someone from any of various places called Kovali, named with eastern Slavic *koval* 'smith'. Compare Polish KOWALSKI.

GIVEN NAME Jewish 5%. *Rakhil.*

Kovanda (125) Czech: nickname for a person of good breeding, from *kovaný* 'true-born'.

Kovar (1025) Czech and Slovak (**Kovář**): occupational name from Czech *kovář* 'smith'.

Kovarik (620) Czech (**Kovářík**): occupational name for a blacksmith, from a pet form of **Kovář** (see KOVAR).

Kovash (141) Americanized spelling of Czech **Kovař** (see KOVAR), Slovak **Kováč** (see KOVAC), or Hungarian **Kovács** (see KOVACS).

Kovatch (414) Americanized spelling of Hungarian **Kovács** (see KOVACS), Slovak **Kováč** (see KOVAC), or Slovenian **Kovač** (see KOVAC).

Kovats (145) Americanized spelling of Hungarian **Kovács** (see KOVACS).
GIVEN NAMES Hungarian 17%. *Gabor* (2), *Zsolt* (2), *Bela, Geza, Istvan, Jolan, Laszlo, Sandor, Zoltan.*

Kovel (134) Germanized spelling of Slavic KOVAL.
GIVEN NAME German 4%. *Wolf.*

Koven (188) Jewish: shortened form of eastern Ashkenazic **Kovenski** or **Kovensky**, a habitational name from Kaunas in Lithuania, from its Yiddish name, *kovne* (*Kovno* in Russian).
GIVEN NAME Jewish 4%. *Sol.*

Kover (166) **1.** Hungarian (**Kövér**): nickname from *kövér* 'fat'. **2.** German (**Köver**): variant of **Küver**, a Low German form of KUPER, an occupational name for a cooper or tubmaker.
GIVEN NAMES Hungarian 4%. *Arpad, Janos, Laszlo.*

Kovich (227) Slovenian (central Slovenia; **Kovič**): probably a derivative of *kov* 'hammering' or *kovač* 'smith'.

Kovitz (100) Jewish (Ashkenazic): variant spelling of KOWITZ.
GIVEN NAME Jewish 7%. *Avraham.*

Kovner (126) Jewish (eastern Ashkenazic): habitational name for someone from Kaunas in Lithuania, from its Yiddish name, *kovne* (*Kovno* in Russian).
GIVEN NAMES Jewish 6%; Russian 5%. *Basya, Hyman; Vladimir* (2), *Alexei.*

Kowal (1696) Polish, Jewish (from Poland), and German (of Slavic origin): occupational name for a blacksmith, Polish and Sorbian *kowal*.
GIVEN NAMES Polish 5%. *Jerzy* (3), *Kazimierz* (3), *Stanislaw* (3), *Jaroslaw* (2), *Wasyl* (2), *Casimir, Danuta, Elzbieta, Ewa, Genowefa, Irena, Jacek.*

Kowalchuk (245) Ukrainian, Belorussian, and Jewish (eastern Ashkenazic): patronymic from eastern Slavic *kowal, koval* 'smith' (see KOWAL).

Kowalczyk (1875) Polish: from a derivative of KOWAL 'smith'.
GIVEN NAMES Polish 10%. *Tadeusz* (5), *Bogdan* (4), *Casimir* (4), *Andrzej* (3), *Elzbieta* (3), *Jacek* (3), *Janina* (3), *Piotr* (3), *Zbigniew* (3), *Bronislaw* (2), *Henryk* (2), *Janusz* (2).

Kowaleski (422) **1.** Belorussian: see KOVALESKI. **2.** Polish: variant of KOWALEWSKI.

Kowalewski (1031) **1.** Polish: habitational name for someone from places called Kowalew or Kowalewo, named with *kowal* 'smith'. **2.** Jewish (from Poland): occupational name from the vocabulary word *kowal* 'smith', with the addition of the common surname ending *-ewski*.
GIVEN NAMES Polish 8%. *Casimir* (3), *Tadeusz* (2), *Bogdan, Danuta, Ewa, Halina, Jacek, Janusz, Jerzy, Kazmierz, Krzystof, Mariusz.*

Kowalick (107) Germanized or Americanized spelling of Polish KOWALIK.

Kowalik (505) Polish: from a diminutive of *kowal* 'smith' (see KOWAL), or nickname from *kowalik* in the sense 'woodpecker'.
GIVEN NAMES Polish 11%. *Janina* (2), *Jerzy* (2), *Alicja, Casimir, Danuta, Ewa, Halina, Henryk, Jacek, Jacenty, Lucyna, Malgorzata.*

Kowalke (229) German (of Slavic origin): from a diminutive of Sorbian KOWAL 'smith'.
GIVEN NAMES German 4%. *Gerhard, Helmut, Otto.*

Kowalkowski (240) Polish: habitational name for someone from any of several places called Kowalki or Kowaliki, named with *kowalik* (see KOWALIK).
GIVEN NAMES Polish 7%. *Andrzej, Janina, Janusz, Jozef, Ludwik, Zbigniew.*

Kowall (167) German (of Slavic origin): occupational name for a blacksmith, from Sorbian and Polish *kowal*.

Kowalske (114) German: occupational name for a blacksmith, from Sorbian and Polish *kowal*.

Kowalski (6710) **1.** Polish: habitational name for someone from Kowalskie in Poznań voivodeship or a place called Kowale. **2.** Polish and Jewish (from Poland): patronymic from KOWAL, an occupational name from *kowal* 'smith', with the addition of the common surname suffix *-ski*.
GIVEN NAMES Polish 6%. *Casimir* (13), *Andrzej* (7), *Zbigniew* (7), *Halina* (5), *Henryk* (5), *Jacek* (5), *Lech* (5), *Zygmunt* (5), *Bogdan* (4), *Janusz* (4), *Jerzy* (4), *Kazimierz* (4).

Kowalsky (582) Jewish (Ashkenazic): variant spelling of KOWALSKI.
GIVEN NAMES Jewish 4%. *Eluzer* (2), *Miriam* (2), *Sholem* (2), *Avrum.*

Kowatch (151) Americanized spelling of German **Kowatsch**, itself a Germanization of Hungarian **Kovács** (see KOVACS) or Slovenian **Kovač** (see KOVAC).

Kowis (107) German: unexplained; perhaps a variant of KOWITZ.

Kowitz (248) German and Jewish (Ashkenazic): Germanized form of Slavic *kovač* 'smith'.

Kownacki (136) Polish and Jewish (from Poland): habitational name for someone from any of various places called Kownatki or Kownaty, named with Old Polish *kownata* 'palatial room'.
GIVEN NAME Polish 6%. *Zygmunt.*

Kowski (101) Polish: unexplained.

Koy (144) German: unexplained.
GIVEN NAMES German 6%. *Ernst, Kuno.*

Koyama (272) Japanese: 'small mountain'. Another common pronunciation is OYAMA. Both are found throughout Japan, as are several locations by this name. Many descend from Fujiwara no Hidesato (10th century), of the northern branch of the FUJIWARA clan.
GIVEN NAMES Japanese 64%. *Masaaki* (3), *Takashi* (3), *Hiroyuki* (2), *Junichi* (2), *Kazuo* (2), *Masako* (2), *Tetsuo* (2), *Yoshito* (2), *Yuji* (2), *Yuki* (2), *Yuzo* (2), *Akira.*

Koyanagi (106) Japanese: 'small willows'; the name is found mostly in eastern Japan; some families pronounce the name *Oyanagi.*
GIVEN NAMES Japanese 38%. *Akira, Ikuko, Junichi, Kaoru, Kenji, Kosaku, Masaaki, Masaru, Mitsue, Mitsuhiro, Mitsuji, Shinichi.*

Koyle (136) Irish: variant of COYLE.

Koza (594) Polish, Czech, Slovak, and Jewish (eastern Ashkenazic): from western and eastern Slavic *koza* 'nanny goat', probably applied as a nickname for someone thought to resemble a goat, or alternatively as a metonymic occupational name for a goatherd.
GIVEN NAMES Polish 5%. *Casimir* (3), *Aleksander, Augustyn, Janina, Malgorzata, Wincenty.*

Kozak (2848) **1.** Ukrainian, Polish, Sorbian; Czech, Slovak, and Hungarian (**Kozák**): ethnic name for a Cossack, a member of a people descended from a group of runaway serfs who set up a semi-independent military republic in Ukraine in the 15th and 16th centuries. The Cossacks became noted for their military prowess. The word *Cossack* is of Turkic origin, but most European languages borrowed it from eastern Slavic (Russian, Ukrainian *kazák*, *kozák*). This term also came to be used as a nickname for a pert fellow, a devil-may-care blusterer. **2.** Polish and Czech (**Kozák**): metonymic occupational name for a goatherd, from a diminutive of KOZA. **3.** Jewish (Ashkenazic): nickname from Yiddish *kozak* 'warrior', 'brave man' (a Ukrainian loanword), a derivative of 1.

Kozakiewicz (167) Polish: patronymic from KOZAK.
GIVEN NAMES Polish 9%. *Alicja, Darek, Irena, Jerzy, Leszek, Piotr.*

Kozan (132) Slovenian: unexplained.

Kozar (533) **1.** Czech (**Kozař**), Slovak (**Koziar**), Slovenian, Serbian, and Croatian: from an agent noun from Slavic *koza* 'nanny goat', either an occupational name for a goatherd or a nickname for an impoverished farmer who had only goats, because he could not afford cows. **2.** Slovenian and Croatian (**Kožar**): from *kožar*, an occupational name for a skinner or a dealer in skins, from *koža* 'skin', 'hide' + the agent noun suffix *-ar*.

Kozel (635) **1.** Ukrainian, Belorussian, Czech, Slovenian, and Jewish (eastern Ashkenazic): from Slavic *kozel* 'buck', 'billy goat', hence a nickname for someone thought to resemble a buck or a goat, or else a metonymic occupational name for a goatherd. **2.** Americanized form of Slovenian **Koželj** or **Kožel**, a nickname or occupational name from *koželj* 'upper part of a spindle' (part of a spinning wheel).

Kozelka (121) Czech: from a diminutive of Kozel.

Kozera (112) Polish: nickname for a gambler, from *kozera* 'cause', 'good reason', also meaning 'trumps'.
GIVEN NAMES Polish 12%. *Jerzy* (2), *Casimir*, *Genowesa, Stanislaw.*

Koziara (105) Polish: nickname from a derivative of *koza* 'nanny goat' (see KOZA).
GIVEN NAMES Polish 12%. *Stanislawa* (2), *Casimir, Ewa, Kazimierz.*

Koziatek (114) Polish: nickname from a diminutive of *koza* 'nanny goat' (see KOZA).
GIVEN NAMES Polish 7%. *Jozef, Stanislaw.*

Kozicki (310) Polish: habitational name for someone from any of several places called Kozice, named with *koza* 'nanny goat' (see KOZA).
GIVEN NAMES Polish 9%. *Casimir* (2), *Tadeusz* (2), *Andrzej, Halina, Miroslaw, Piotr, Radoslaw, Zigmond.*

Koziel (266) Polish: from an Old Polish and dialect variant of *kozioł* 'goat' (see KOZIOL).
GIVEN NAMES Polish 10%. *Jacek, Janina, Miroslaw, Stanislaw, Stanislawa, Wiktor, Witold, Wojciech, Zygmunt.*

Kozik (390) **1.** Czech (**Kožík**): metonymic occupational name for a tanner or a leather merchant, from *kůže* 'skin', 'leather'. **2.** Polish: from a pet form of *kozia* 'nanny goat' (see KOZA). **3.** Polish: possibly also from *kozik* 'clasp knife'.
GIVEN NAMES Polish 6%. *Miroslaw* (2), *Dionizy, Krystyna, Mariusz, Wieslaw, Wladyslawa, Zophia.*

Kozikowski (268) Polish: habitational name for someone from Koziki in Ostrołęka and Łomża voivodeships.
GIVEN NAMES Polish 11%. *Tadeusz* (2), *Andrzej, Boguslaw, Bronislaw, Kazimierz, Waclaw, Wladyslawa, Wojciech.*

Kozinski (173) Polish (**Koziński**) and Jewish (from Poland): habitational name for someone from any of various places called Kozina, Kozińce, or Kozino, named with *koza* 'nanny goat'.
GIVEN NAMES Polish 9%. *Boleslaw, Dariusz, Iwona, Janusz.*

Koziol (1125) Polish (**Kozioł**): from *kozioł* 'billy goat', hence a metonymic occupational name for a goatherd or a nickname for someone thought to resemble a goat, in particular a pert or devil-may-care fellow.

GIVEN NAMES Polish 11%. *Jozef* (4), *Kazimierz* (4), *Stanislaw* (4), *Zbigniew* (4), *Tadeusz* (3), *Andrzej* (2), *Halina* (2), *Janina* (2), *Janusz* (2), *Mieczyslaw* (2), *Piotr* (2), *Bernadeta.*

Kozisek (140) Czech (**Kožíšek**): From Czech *kožich* 'fur coat', either a nickname for someone who habitually wore a fur coat, or a metonymic occupational name for someone who traded in furs.

Kozlik (199) Polish (**Koźlik**) and Czech (**Kozlík**): from a pet form of *kozioł* 'goat' (see KOZIOL).
GIVEN NAME French 4%. *Laurette.*

Kozloff (129) Jewish (eastern Ashkenazic) and Russian: alternative spelling of **Kozlov**, a patronymic form derived from eastern Slavic *koziol* 'goat'. As a Jewish name, this generally represents a habitational name from any of various places named with this word.

Kozloski (328) Polish: variant of KOZLOWSKI.

Kozlovsky (124) Jewish (eastern Ashkenzazic), Russian, and Ukrainian: habitational name from any of various places named with *koziol* 'goat'. Compare Polish KOZLOWSKI. The Russian and Ukrainian names can also be directly derived from a nickname meaning 'goat'.
GIVEN NAMES Jewish 8%; German 4%; Russian 4%. *Meir, Menachem, Rakhil; Viktor; Vladimir* (2), *Grigory, Lyudmila.*

Kozlow (151) Polish (**Kozłów**): habitational name from any of various places so called, named with a possessive derivative of Polish *kozioł* 'goat' (see KOZIOL), or perhaps an occupational name from a goatherd.

Kozlowski (3766) Polish (**Kozłowski**): **1.** habitational name for someone from any of various places named Kozłów (see KOZLOW) + *-ski* suffix of surnames. **2.** possibly also a variant of KOZIOL with the addition of the common surname ending *-owski.*
GIVEN NAMES Polish 7%. *Jerzy* (5), *Kazimierz* (4), *Stanislaw* (4), *Elzbieta* (3), *Krzysztof* (3), *Ryszard* (3), *Tadeusz* (3), *Wojciech* (3), *Zbigniew* (3), *Andrzej* (2), *Czeslaw* (2), *Ignatius* (2).

Kozma (499) **1.** Hungarian: from a short form of *Kozmás*, vernacular form of COSMA. **2.** Czech, Slovak, and Polish: from the personal name *Kosma* (Polish *Koźma*), vernacular forms of Greek *Kosmas* (see COSMA). **3.** Jewish (from Poland): ornamental adoption of the Slavic personal name (see 2). **4.** possibly also Greek (**Kozmas**): variant of **Kosmas** (see COSMA 2).
GIVEN NAMES Hungarian 5%. *Gabor* (2), *Janos* (2), *Sandor* (2), *Andras, Endre, Jozsef, Nandor, Tibor.*

Kozminski (131) Polish (**Koźminski**) and Jewish (from Poland): habitational name for someone from any of various places in

Poland called Koźmin, named with the personal name *Koźma* (see KOZMA).
GIVEN NAMES Polish 9%. *Jacek, Krzysztof, Tadeusz, Wojciech.*

Kozub (234) Polish and Slovak: metonymic occupational name for a fireplace maker, from western Slavic *kozub* 'fireplace'.
GIVEN NAMES Polish 6%. *Cecylia* (2), *Stanislaw, Stanislawa.*

Kozuch (228) Polish (**KOZUCH**), Ukrainian, Belorussian, and Jewish (from Ukraine and Poland): metonymic occupational name for a furrier, Polish *kożuch*, Ukrainian and Belorussian *kozhukh* 'fur', 'sheepskin'.
GIVEN NAMES Polish 8%. *Alicja, Beata, Bogdan, Ignatius, Janusz, Tadeusz, Zdzislaw.*

Kozy (112) Origin unidentified. Probably an altered form of a Slavic surname, e.g. Polish KOZA.

Kozyra (100) Polish: variant of KOZERA.
GIVEN NAMES Polish 13%; German 5%. *Halina* (2), *Tadeusz* (2), *Casimir; Kurt.*

Kraai (204) Dutch: from Middle Dutch *craie* 'crow', hence a nickname for someone thought to resemble a crow, such as chattering or having a raucous voice. Compare English CROW.
GIVEN NAMES German 6%. *Kurt* (2), *Fritz.*

Kraak (103) **1.** Dutch: from Middle Dutch *crake, craek* 'ship','galleon', presumably applied as a metonymic occupational name for a ship builder or a mariner. **2.** German: habitational name from a place so named in Mecklenburg.
GIVEN NAMES Dutch 4%; German 4%. *Roelof, Wim.*

Kraatz (392) German: **1.** habitational name from a place in Brandenburg named Kraatz. **2.** variant of KRATZ 1.

Krabbe (252) **1.** North German: from Middle Low German *krabbe* 'small crab', 'shrimp', 'prawn', hence a metonymic occupational name for someone who caught or sold shellfish or a nickname for a lively person. **2.** Dutch, Danish, and Swedish: from Middle Dutch *crabbe*, Old Norse *krabbi* 'crab', hence a metonymic occupational name for someone who caught or sold shellfish or perhaps a nickname for someone with a peculiar gait.
GIVEN NAMES German 6%; Scandinavian 4%. *Otto* (2), *Erwin, Kurt; Erik, Niels.*

Krabbenhoft (228) North German (**Krabbenhöft**): nickname for a quirky person, literally 'crab head'.
GIVEN NAMES German 5%. *Erwin* (2), *Erhardt, Kurt.*

Krabill (199) Americanized form of German **Krähenbühl** (see KRAHENBUHL).

Krach (214) German: **1.** from *krachen* 'to make a loud noise', 'to explode', hence a nickname for noisy person or a trouble maker. **2.** southern nickname for a feeble person, from Middle High German *krach* 'crack', 'weakness'.

Kracht (482) North German and Dutch: from Middle Low German *kracht*, Middle Dutch *cracht* 'power', hence a nickname for a strong person. Compare South German KRAFT.

GIVEN NAMES German 5%. *Otto* (3), *Klaus* (2), *Hans, Wilhelm.*

Krack (166) **1.** Dutch: from Middle Dutch *crake, craek* 'carrack' (a type of large merchant ship), hence a metonymic occupational name for the master or owner of such a ship. **2.** German: topographic name from Middle Low German *krack* 'underbrush' or from Middle High German *krac* 'crevice', or alternatively, a nickname for someone with a harsh raucous voice, from *krack* 'crow'.

Kracke (231) German: **1.** variant of KRACK. **2.** from *Kracke* 'bad horse', 'nag', probably applied as a derogatory nickname for a horse dealer with a questionable reputation, or for a small crippled child, or for a weak old person, especially a woman.

GIVEN NAMES German 6%. *Fritz, Kurt, Otto.*

Kracker (106) **1.** Probably an Americanized spelling of German **Kräger** (see KRAGER). **2.** German (**Kräcker**): nickname for a complainer, from Middle Low German *kraken* 'to grumble', 'whine'. **3.** German: nickname for a noise maker, from Middle High German *krach* 'bang', 'noise'.

Kraeger (200) German (**Kräger**): see KRAGER.

Kraemer (3288) German (**Krämer**), Jewish (Ashkenazic), Danish, and Dutch: see KRAMER.

GIVEN NAMES German 5%. *Klaus* (6), *Kurt* (6), *Hans* (3), *Erwin* (2), *Frieda* (2), *Helmut* (2), *Otto* (2), *Wolfgang* (2), *Armin, Bernd, Bernhard, Dieter.*

Krafft (493) German and Swedish: variant spelling of KRAFT.

GIVEN NAMES German 5%. *Fritz, Gottfried, Kurt, Otto, Reinhard.*

Krafka (109) Origin unidentified.

Kraft (9065) German (also **Kräft**), Danish, Swedish, and Jewish (Ashkenazic): nickname for a strong man, from Old High German *kraft*, German *Kraft* 'strength', 'power'. The Swedish name probably originated as a soldier's name. In part the German and Danish names possibly also derive from a late survival of the same word used as a byname, Old High German *Chraft(o)*, Old Norse *Kraptr.*

Krag (110) Danish, Norwegian, and North German: from *krage* 'collar', either a metonymic occupational name for a maker of collars or a nickname for someone who wore a distinctive collar. Collars were worn by wealthy people, and in Denmark at least this also seems to have been a nickname for a nobleman or a courtier.

GIVEN NAMES Scandinavian 12%; German 6%. *Erik* (4), *Niels; Manfred* (2).

Krage (198) German (also **Kräge**): **1.** from Middle High German *krage* 'neck', 'collar', hence a metonymic occupational name for a maker of collars or someone who wore a distinctive collar. **2.** nickname from *krage* 'simpleton', 'fool'. **3.** in the Rhineland, a variant of **Krähe** (see KRAY).

Krager (317) German (**Kräger**): occupational name for a maker of collars or someone who wore a distinctive collar, from an agent derivative of KRAGE.

Kragh (177) Danish: variant of KRAG.

GIVEN NAMES Scandinavian 7%. *Borge, Jorgen, Lars, Niels.*

Kragness (177) Norwegian: habitational name from any of numerous farms called Kragnes or Kraakenes, mainly in Western Norway, named with Old Norse *kráka* 'crow' + *nes* 'headland', 'promontory'.

Kragt (151) Dutch: variant spelling of KRACHT.

Krah (166) German: variant of KRAY.

Krahe (116) German (also **Krähe**): nickname from Middle High German *krāe* 'crow', applied as a nickname for someone with dark hair or a dark complexion or for someone thought to resemble the bird in some other way.

GIVEN NAMES German 5%. *Klaus, Otto.*

Krahenbuhl (208) South German and Swiss German (**Krähenbühl, Krayenbühl, Kreyenbühl**): habitational name for someone from a place so named; the place name means 'crow hill'.

GIVEN NAMES German 4%. *Ulrich* (2), *Frieda.*

Krahl (216) German: variant of KREUL or a Germanized spelling of Slavic KRAL.

GIVEN NAMES German 6%. *Fritz, Hans, Kurt, Reinhold.*

Krahling (154) German: **1.** derivative of KRAHL. **2.** (**Krähling**): habitational name, perhaps from Krehlingen in Rhineland, or Krelingen in Lower Saxony.

Krahmer (133) German: variant of KRAMER.

Krahn (989) German: nickname for a slim or long-legged person, from Middle Low German *krane* 'crane'. Compare KRANICH.

GIVEN NAMES German 6%. *Kurt* (5), *Eldred, Gerd, Gerhard, Hans, Hans-Peter, Horst, Irmgard, Mathias, Otto, Wilhelm, Willi.*

Kraig (107) Variant spelling of CRAIG.

Krajewski (1307) Polish: habitational name for someone from any of several places called Krajewo, so named from *kraj* 'border area'.

GIVEN NAMES Polish 5%. *Witold* (2), *Andrzej, Boguslaw, Casimir, Iwona, Jacek, Jerzy, Kazimierz, Krzysztof, Mariusz, Miroslaw.*

Krajicek (135) Czech (**Krajíček**): nickname for a miser or a poor man, from *krajíček* 'small piece or slice of bread'.

GIVEN NAME German 4%. *Kurt* (2).

Krajnak (105) Polish: patronymic from *krajny*, an adjectival derivative of *kraj* 'end', 'border'. Compare KRAJNIK.

Krajnik (128) Polish; Ukrainian (**Krajnyk**); Czech and Slovak (**Krajník**); and Slovenian: topographic name for someone who lived on the edge of a village, from Slavic *krajny*, an adjectival derivative of *kraj* 'end', 'border'.

GIVEN NAMES Polish 4%. *Elzbieta, Stanislaw.*

Krakauer (152) German and Jewish (Ashkenazic): habitational name for someone from the Polish city of Kraków, from its German name *Krakau.*

Krake (166) North German: variant of KRACKE or KRAGE.

Kraker (330) Dutch (**de Kraker**): **1.** nickname for a noisy person, from *kraken* 'to make noise'. **2.** Debrabandere also suggests that it may be an occupational name for a hangman, from a derivative of Middle Dutch *craghe* 'neck'.

GIVEN NAMES German 5%. *Alois* (3), *Hans* (2), *Erwin, Fritz, Otto.*

Krakow (215) Jewish (eastern Ashkenazic): habitational name from the city of Kraków in Poland.

GIVEN NAMES French 4%; Jewish 4%. *Collette, Jeremie; Doron, Hyman, Sol.*

Krakower (169) Jewish (Ashkenazic): habitational name for someone from the city of Kraków in Poland (see KRAKOW).

GIVEN NAME Jewish 4%. *Hyman.*

Krakowiak (131) Polish: habitational name for someone from the city of Kraków.

GIVEN NAMES Polish 11%. *Andrzej, Jadwiga, Krzysztof, Merek, Stanislaw.*

Krakowski (364) Polish and Jewish (eastern Ashkenazic): habitational name for someone from the city of Kraków in Poland.

GIVEN NAMES Polish 5%; German 4%. *Aleksander, Janusz, Piotr, Stanislaw, Tadeusz; Fritz* (2), *Wolf* (2), *Aloysius.*

Kral (1194) **1.** Czech (**Král**), Slovak (**Kráľ**), and eastern German (of Slavic origin): from the western Slavic word *kral* 'king', a derivative of the personal name *Karl* 'Charles', the name of the Frankish king and Holy Roman Emperor Charlemagne (?742–814; Latin name *Carolus Magnus*). The word *kral* as a generic term meaning 'king' became widespread throughout eastern Europe in the Middle Ages; in Byzantium it generally denoted the kings of Serbia. As a surname, it generally arose either as an occupational name for a servant of the king or as an ironic nickname for one who gave himself regal airs. The surname is also found in German, often in the spelling **Krahl**. **2.** Americanized form of Slovenian, Croatian, or Serbian **Kralj** 'king', of the same origin as 1. Compare KRALY.

Kralicek (147) Czech (**Králíček**): nickname for a timid man, from a diminutive of *králík* 'rabbit'.

GIVEN NAME German 4%. *Otto* (2).

Kralik (382) Czech (**Králík**): nickname for a timid man, from *králík* 'rabbit'.

Krall (1466) **1.** Germanized or Americanized spelling of KRAL. **2.** Germanized form of Slovenian **Kralj** (see KRALY). **3.** German: nickname for a lively person, from Low German *krall* 'lively', 'cheerful'. **4.** German: habitational name from a farmstead so named near Meppen, Westphalia.

Kraly (125) **1.** Americanized form of the Slovenian, Croatian, and Serbian surname **Kralj**, an ironic or figurative nickname from *kralj* 'king'. The word is derived from the name of the Frankish king and Holy Roman Emperor Charlemagne (?742–814; Latin name *Carolus Magnus*). **2.** Perhaps also an Americanized form of Hungarian **Király**, from *király* 'king'. See also KRAL.
GIVEN NAME German 4%. *Kurt*.

Kram (410) German, Czech (**Krám**), Polish, and Jewish (Ashkenazic): metonymic occupational name for a shopkeeper, from Middle High German, Middle Low German *krām* 'tent', 'booth' or the Slavic derivative *kram* 'shop', 'store'. Compare KRAMER.

Kramar (199) **1.** Czech (**Kramář**), Slovak (**Kramár**), Ukrainian, Belorussian, and Jewish (eastern Ashkenazic): occupational name for a shopkeeper, Czech *kramař*, Ukrainian *kramar*, from *kram* 'store', from Old High German *crām* 'tent', 'trading post'. **2.** Slovenian: occupational name for a peddler or hawker, from *krama* 'cheap goods', a word of German origin. See 1, and compare KRAMER.
GIVEN NAMES Czech and Slovak 4%. *Jaroslav* (2), *Lubomir*.

Kramarz (102) Polish and German: occupational name for a shopkeeper (see KRAMAR).
GIVEN NAMES Polish 13%; German 9%. *Wojciech*(2), *Janina*, *Ludwik*, *Piotr*; *Kurt*, *Wolf*.

Kramb (100) **1.** German: variant of KRAMP or KRAMPE. **2.** German: topographic name meaning 'edge'; the word also appears in place names.

Krambeck (109) German (Schleswig-Holstein): habitational name from a place so named.

Krambeer (119) North German: from *Kranichbeere*, 'juniper' or *Kronsbeere* 'cranberry', presumably applied as a metonymic occupational name for someone who grew or collected the berries or as a topographic name for someone who lived in a place where they grew.

Kramer (26928) German (also **Krämer**), Dutch, and Jewish (Ashkenazic): occupational name for a shopkeeper, peddler, or hawker, from an agent derivative of Middle High German, Middle Low German *krām* 'trading post', 'tent', 'booth'. This name is widespread throughout central and eastern Europe.

Kramlich (202) German: variant spelling of GRAMLICH.
GIVEN NAMES German 7%. *Reinhold* (2), *Ewald*, *Milbert*, *Otto*.

Kramm (205) German: variant of KRAM or KRAMME.
GIVEN NAMES German 12%. *Otto* (2), *Ernst*, *Hans*, *Johann*, *Ludwing*, *Manfred*.

Kramme (173) German: **1.** from an old personal name formed with Old High German *hrabo* 'raven'. **2.** habitational name for someone from a place called Cramme near Salzgitter.
GIVEN NAME German 4%. *Erwin* (2).

Krammer (127) **1.** Dutch and Jewish (Ashkenazic): variant of KRAMER. **2.** German: from an old personal name formed with Old High German *hrabo* 'raven'. **3.** Possibly a variant of German KRAMER.
GIVEN NAMES German 22%. *Raimund* (3), *Kurt* (2), *Otto* (2), *Alois*, *Franz*, *Wilhelm*, *Xaver*.

Krammes (211) German: of uncertain origin. Perhaps a familiar form of KRAMM; in southwestern German dialects *-es* often denotes a jocular kind of endearment.
GIVEN NAMES German 5%. *Kurt* (2), *Armin*.

Kramp (438) **1.** German: from Middle Low German *krampe* 'hook', 'staple'; either a nickname for someone with a hooked nose or a hunched back or a metonymic occupational name for a locksmith. **2.** German: variant of KRAMPE 2. **3.** Dutch: according to Debrabandere, possibly a nickname for someone who suffers from cramps, from Middle Dutch *crampe* 'cramp'.
GIVEN NAMES German 4%. *Kurt* (2), *Heinz*, *Manfred*.

Krampe (149) **1.** German and Dutch: variant of KRAMP. **2.** German: habitational name from any of various places named Krampe (Schleswig and Pomerania) or Crampe (Pomerania and Brandenburg).
GIVEN NAMES German 5%. *Armin*, *Fritz*, *Hans*.

Krampf (103) **1.** German: variant of KRAMP. **2.** German: habitational name from a place so named near Liegnitz, Silesia. **3.** German: nickname for a deformed person, from Middle High German *krampf* 'cramp'.
GIVEN NAME French 4%. *Elcie*.

Krampitz (111) German: nickname from Polish *krępy* 'stocky', 'thickset'.
GIVEN NAMES German 6%. *Reinhardt*, *Reinhold*.

Krane (334) **1.** Dutch: nickname for a long-legged or tall thin man, from Middle Dutch *crane* 'crane'. **2.** North German: variant of KRAHN.
GIVEN NAMES German 4%. *Klaus* (2), *Franz*.

Kraner (238) German (Austria) and Slovenian: Germanized form of the Slovenian habitational name **Kranjec** (also found in the forms **Krajnc** and **Kranjc**), denoting someone from Kranjska province (Latin name *Carniola*, German *Krain*), a historical name for the central part of medieval Slovenia. The name was also used as a term denoting a Slovenian.

Kranich (242) German: nickname for a long-legged or tall and slender person, from Middle High German *kranech* 'crane'.

Kranick (136) Americanized form of German KRANICH.

Kraning (110) **1.** German: probably a habitational name from either Krinning or Kröning, both in Bavaria. **2.** German: possibly a variant of **Kranig**, from a house name due to a sign or picture of a crane (bird), or a nickname for a tall person or for someone with a proud or dignified gait.

Kranitz (110) Jewish (Ashkenazic) and German: unexplained.
GIVEN NAMES Jewish 7%. *Herschel*, *Mort*.

Krank (136) **1.** North German: nickname from Middle Low German *kraneke*, a diminutive of *krān* 'crane' (see KRAHN). **2.** German: nickname for a feeble person, from Middle High German *kranc* 'feeble'.

Krans (159) **1.** Dutch: from Middle Dutch *crans* 'wreath', 'garland', 'crown'; hence a metonymic occupational name for a maker of wreaths and garlands, a habitational name for someone who lived at a house distinguished by the sign of a garland, or a nickname for someone whose hair was tonsured. **2.** German: nickname from Middle High German *grans* 'beak'. Compare SCHNABEL.

Krantz (2575) German and Dutch: variant spelling of KRANZ.

Kranz (2020) **1.** German: from Middle High German *kranz* 'garland', 'wreath'; a metonymic occupational name for a maker of chaplets and wreaths, a habitational name for someone who lived at a house distinguished by the sign of a garland, or a nickname for someone whose hair was tonsured. **2.** Dutch: variant spelling of KRANS, cognate with 1. **3.** In some cases it may also be one of the several German spellings of the Slovenian habitational name **Kranjec** (also found as **Krajnc** or **Kranjc**), denoting someone from Kranjska province (Latin *Carniola*, German *Krain*), an old name for the historical central part of Slovenia. **4.** Jewish (Ashkenazic): ornamental name from German *Kranz* or Yiddish *krants* 'wreath', 'garland'.

Kranzler (165) German: occupational, habitational name, or nickname from a derivative of KRANZ.

Krape (112) Possibly an altered spelling of **Krappe**, the North German equivalent of KRAPF, or alternatively a nickname from Middle Low German *krape* 'carp', a variant of *karpe* (see KARP).

Krapf (561) German: nickname for a small malformed individual, from Middle High German *krapfe* 'hook'. In southern Germany the word was also applied to a type of crescent-shaped pastry, and the surname may thus also have been a metonymic occupational name for a baker.

Krapfl (133) South German: from a diminutive of KRAPF.

Krapp (136) **1.** German: variant of RAPP. **2.** Dutch: variant of KRABBE.
GIVEN NAMES German 4%. *Otmar, Winfried.*

Kras (149) **1.** Polish: from *kras* 'beauty', 'good looks', a nickname for a handsome person (see KRASNY). **2.** Dutch: nickname from Old French *cras* 'fat'.
GIVEN NAMES Polish 17%; German 4%. *Casimir* (4), *Czeslawa, Gustaw, Jacek, Janina, Jozef, Tadeusz; Aloysius* (2).

Krase (108) Americanized form of Polish KRAS.

Krasinski (311) **1.** Polish (**Krasiński**): habitational name for someone from Krasne in Ciechanów voivodeship, named with a derivative of *krasny* 'beautiful'. **2.** Ukrainian, Belorussian, and Jewish (eastern Ashkenazic): habitational name from any of various places in Ukraine, and Belarus called Krasnaya, Krasna, or Krasnoe (cognate with the Polish name). Compare KRASNER.
FOREBEARS This is the surname of a very large and well-known Polish family, with numerous branches, the oldest of which can be traced back to the 15th century. The Romantic poet Zygmunt Krasiński (1812–59) was a member of this family.
GIVEN NAMES German 4%. *Kurt, Sigismund.*

Kraska (282) **1.** Polish and Jewish (eastern Ashkenazic): from Polish *kraska* 'European roller' (a species of bird of the crow family, noted for its fine feathers, also for its loud and persistent cry), hence (in Polish) a nickname for a garrulous person. As a Jewish name it is mainly ornamental. **2.** Jewish (eastern Ashkenazic): metonymic occupational name for a dyer, from Belorussian *kraska* 'dye'. **3.** Jewish (eastern Ashkenazic): ornamental name from Belorussian and Ukrainian *kraska*, denoting a kind of flower.
GIVEN NAMES German 6%. *Johann, Juergen, Kurt, Reinhold, Sigismund.*

Krasne (117) Jewish (Ashkenazic): variant of KRASNY.
GIVEN NAME Jewish 6%. *Mordechai.*

Krasner (534) **1.** German: nickname for a handsome man, from Slavic *krasny* 'beautiful', 'handsome', 'brightly colored' (see KRASNY). **2.** Jewish (eastern Ashkenazic): habitational name from any of various places in Poland, Ukraine, and Belarus called Krasne in Polish (Krasnaya, Krasna, or Krasnoe in Russian).
GIVEN NAMES Jewish 8%; Russian 5%. *Ilya* (2), *Meyer* (2), *Fayna, Inna, Mordechai, Naum, Rivka, Semen, Shimon, Sol, Sura, Yakov; Semyon* (2), *Leonid, Lev, Michail, Shura, Yefim, Yelena, Yosif, Yuriy.*

Krasnoff (150) Russian and Jewish (from Ukraine): alternative spelling of **Krasnov**, a patronymic from the vocabulary word *krasny* 'beautiful' (see KRASNY).

Krasnow (313) Jewish: Polish or German spelling of KRASNOFF.
GIVEN NAMES Jewish 8%. *Hershel* (2), *Avi, Azriel, Miriam, Moshe, Shlomo.*

Krasny (171) Czech (**Krásný**), Slovak (**Krásny**), Polish, and Jewish (eastern Ashkenazic): nickname from the common Slavic word *krasny* 'handsome', 'beautiful', 'colorful', and (in modern Russian) 'red'.
GIVEN NAMES Jewish 5%. *Hyman, Isaak, Yakov.*

Krason (123) Polish (**Krasoń**): nickname for a beautiful person or for someone with red hair (see KRASNY).
GIVEN NAMES Polish 9%. *Ewa, Piotr, Stanislaw, Tadeusz.*

Krasowski (191) Polish and Jewish (from Poland): habitational name for someone from the villages of Krasowa, Krasów, or Krasowa.
GIVEN NAMES Polish 21%. *Janusz* (3), *Krzysztof* (2), *Boguslaw, Casimir, Danuta, Ignacy, Kazimierz, Malgorzata, Miroslaw, Remigiusz, Stanislaw, Tadeusz.*

Krass (320) **1.** German: from *krasse*, which in Middle Low German meant 'shrimp', 'prawn', but in early modern German came to denote the gudgeon; it may therefore have been a nickname for someone who was small and active or stubborn and thick-headed. **2.** German (**Kräss**): from the Slavic personal name *Kres*.

Krassner (104) German: variant of KRASNER.

Kraszewski (206) Polish: habitational name for someone from places called Kraszew or Kraszewo, both named with the personal name *Krasz*, from *krasić* 'to add color or seasoning'.
GIVEN NAMES Polish 12%. *Andrzej, Boleslaw, Kazimierz, Lech, Maciej, Tadeusz, Wieslaw, Zbigniew.*

Kratky (237) Czech (**Krátký**) and Slovak (**Krátky**): nickname for a short man, from Czech *krátký* 'short'.

Kratochvil (510) Czech (**Kratochvíl**): nickname for an idle pleasure seeker, from Czech *kratochvíle* 'pastime'.

Kratovil (102) Altered form of Czech KRATOCHVIL.

Kratt (264) German: metonymic occupational name for a basketmaker, from Middle High German *kratte* 'basket'.

Kratz (1718) German: **1.** from a short form of the medieval personal name *Pankratz*, a vernacular form of Latin *Pancratius* (see PANKRATZ), bestowed in honor of St. Pancras, one of the three 'ice saints' martyred under Diocletian. **2.** variant of KRAATZ 1. **3.** from an old personal name formed with Old High German *grātag* 'greedy'.
GIVEN NAMES German 4%. *Kurt* (3), *Ruediger* (3), *Hans* (2), *Bernd, Erwin, Frieda, Gerhardt, Hermann, Ignaz, Ilse, Konrad, Otto.*

Kratzer (1411) **1.** German and Jewish (Ashkenazic): occupational nickname for a wool carder or a barber from an agent derivative of Middle High German, German *kratzen*, Yiddish *kratsn* 'to scratch'. **2.** patronymic from KRATZ 1. **3.** German: patronymic from KRATZ.

Kratzke (173) German: from a pet form of KRATZ.
GIVEN NAMES German 6%. *Erwin, Kurt.*

Krauel (101) German: from Middle High German *kröuwel, krewel* 'fork with hooked tines', 'claw', applied as a nickname for a brusque or curtperson, or a house name.
GIVEN NAME German 5%. *Heinz.*

Kraus (7848) German and Jewish (Ashkenazic): nickname for someone with curly hair, from Middle High German *krūs* 'curly', 'crinkly', German *kraus*.
GIVEN NAMES German 4%. *Kurt* (12), *Otto* (11), *Hans* (5), *Erwin* (4), *Franz* (4), *Gerhard* (3), *Heinz* (3), *Wilhelm* (3), *Bodo* (2), *Egon* (2), *Gunther* (2), *Rainer* (2).

Krause (14780) **1.** German and Jewish (Ashkenazic): variant of KRAUS. **2.** German: from Middle High German *krūse* 'pitcher', 'jug'; a metonymic occupational name for a maker or seller of jugs or a nickname for a heavy drinker.
GIVEN NAMES German 5%. *Kurt* (33), *Otto* (26), *Erwin* (13), *Hans* (12), *Heinz* (8), *Horst* (7), *Fritz* (6), *Gerhard* (6), *Dieter* (4), *Manfred* (4), *Arno* (3), *Bernd* (3).

Krauser (246) German and Jewish (Ashkenazic): nickname for someone with curly hair, from a derivative of Middle High German *krūs* 'curly', 'crinkly', German *kraus*.

Kraushaar (323) German and Jewish (Ashkenazic): nickname for someone with curly hair, from Middle High German *krūs* 'curly', 'crinkled' + *hār* 'hair'; German *kraus* + *Haar*.
GIVEN NAMES German 5%. *Otto* (3), *Kurt.*

Krauskopf (160) German and Jewish (Ashkenazic): nickname for someone with curly hair, from Middle High German *krūs* 'curly', 'crinkled' + *kopf* 'head'; German *kraus* + *Kopf*.
GIVEN NAME German 4%. *Kurt.*

Krausman (147) Jewish (Ashkenazic) and German (**Krausmann**): nickname for someone with curly hair, from German *kraus* 'curly', 'crinkled' + *Mann* 'man'; Middle High German *krūs* + *man*.
GIVEN NAME German 4%. *Ernst.*

Krauss (2919) German and Jewish (Ashkenazic): variant spelling of KRAUS.
GIVEN NAMES German 6%. *Otto* (7), *Kurt* (6), *Siegfried* (5), *Heinz* (4), *Hans* (3), *Helmut* (3), *Ernst* (2), *Erwin* (2), *Gerhard* (2), *Inge* (2), *Karl-Heinz* (2), *Theodor* (2).

Krausse (128) German: variant of KRAUSE.
GIVEN NAMES German 12%. *Kurt* (2), *Dieter.*

Krausz (242) Hungarian and Jewish (from Hungary): Hungarian spelling of German KRAUS.
GIVEN NAMES Jewish 11%; German 6%. *Chaim* (2), *Ari, Bernat, Mendel, Miriam, Mordchai, Moshe, Shimon, Shlomo, Shmuel; Fritz, Hermann, Ignatz.*

Kraut (579) **1.** German: metonymic occupational name for a market gardener or a herbalist, from Middle High German *krūt* 'herb', 'plant', 'cabbage'. It is also found in eastern Slovenia. **2.** Jewish (Ashkenazic): ornamental or metonymic occupational name from German *Kraut* 'herb', 'cabbage'.

GIVEN NAMES German 4%; Jewish 4%. *Gerhard, Hans, Helmut, Kurt, Wolfgang; Yehuda* (2), *Zev* (2), *Aron, Hershel.*

Krauter (315) **1.** German (also **Kräuter**) and Jewish (Ashkenazic): occupational name for a grower or seller of herbs, from an agent derivative of KRAUT. **2.** German: nickname for a grumpy old man, an old fogey.

GIVEN NAMES German 4%. *Fritz, Hans, Kurt, Orlo.*

Krauth (351) German: variant spelling of KRAUT.

Krautheim (111) German: habitational name from any of various places called Krautheim, for example in Baden-Württemberg, Bavaria, and Thuringia.

Krautkramer (168) German (**Krautkrämer**) and Jewish (Ashkenazic): occupational name for a seller of herbs, from Middle High German *krūt* 'herb' + *krämer* 'shopkeeper', 'trader'; German *Kraut* + *Krämer*.

Kravec (135) Ukrainian, Belorussian, and Jewish (eastern Ashkenazic): variant of KRAVETS 'tailor'.

GIVEN NAME Slavic 4%. *Mihajlo* (2).

Kravets (207) Ukrainian, Belorussian, and Jewish (eastern Ashkenazic): occupational name from Ukrainian and Belorussian *kravets* 'tailor', a derivative of Old Slavic *kravati* 'to cut'.

GIVEN NAMES Russian 35%; Jewish 23%. *Vladimir* (7), *Leonid* (4), *Mikhail* (4), *Boris* (3), *Igor* (3), *Lev* (3), *Anatoly* (2), *Arkady* (2), *Galina* (2), *Nikolay* (2), *Sergey* (2), *Zinovy* (2); *Aron* (2), *Yakov* (2), *Fayvel, Hyman, Ilya, Irina, Mikhael, Naum, Polina, Sima, Tsilya.*

Kravetz (412) Jewish (eastern Ashkenazic): variant of KRAVETS.

Kravitz (1370) Jewish (eastern Ashkenazic): occupational name from Slavic *kravets* 'tailor' (see KRAVETS).

GIVEN NAMES Jewish 7%. *Hyman* (4), *Meyer* (3), *Sol* (3), *Emanuel, Haim, Irina, Isadore, Menachem, Miriam, Moshe, Sima, Yehuda.*

Krawchuk (146) Ukrainian and Jewish (eastern Ashkenazic): variant spelling of **Kravchuk**, a patronymic derivative of Ukrainian *kravets* 'tailor' (see KRAVEC).

Krawczak (135) Polish: patronymic from a derivative of *krawiec* 'tailor' (see KRAWIEC).

GIVEN NAMES Polish 5%. *Jacek, Janina, Miroslawa.*

Krawczyk (1330) Polish and Jewish (from Poland): occupational name from a diminu-tive of *krawiec* 'tailor', possibly in the sense 'tailor's apprentice'.

GIVEN NAMES Polish 10%. *Tadeusz* (5), *Bogdan* (4), *Ignatius* (4), *Wieslaw* (3), *Jadwiga* (2), *Jozef* (2), *Krzysztof* (2), *Miroslaw* (2), *Stanislaw* (2), *Alicja, Andrzej, Beata.*

Krawiec (444) Polish and Jewish (from Poland): occupational name for a tailor, Polish *krawiec*, from Old Slavic *kravati* 'to cut'.

GIVEN NAMES Polish 9%. *Zbigniew* (2), *Bronislaw, Czeslawa, Henryk, Mariusz, Piotr, Tadeusz, Wieslawa, Wlodzimierz, Wojciech, Zygmunt.*

Krawitz (164) Jewish (eastern Ashkenazic): variant of KRAVETS.

GIVEN NAMES Jewish 5%; German 5%. *Isadore; Gerhart, Kurt.*

Kray (332) **1.** German: nickname for someone thought to resemble a crow in some way, from Middle High German *krā, krei(g)e* 'crow'. **2.** German: habitational name from a place called Kray, near Essen.

Kraybill (119) Americanized form of German and Swiss **Krähenbühl** (see KRAHENBUHL, KREHBIEL).

Krayer (138) German: habitational name for someone from KRAY.

Kraynak (347) Americanized spelling of Slovak **Krajňák**, a topographic name for someone who lived on the edge of a village, from *kraj* 'end', 'border'.

Kraynik (118) Americanized spelling of the Slavic name KRAJNIK.

Kreager (369) Americanized spelling of German and Jewish (Ashkenazic) KRIEGER or possibly **Krüger** (see KRUEGER).

Kreamer (397) Altered spelling of German **Krämer** (see KRAMER) or the variant KREMER.

Krebbs (163) German: variant spelling of KREBS.

Krebs (4709) **1.** German and Swiss German: metonymic occupational name for a catcher or seller of crabs or shellfish or a nickname for someone thought to resemble a crab, perhaps because they had a peculiar gait. The name was certainly standardized from older variants like *Krevetes* or *Krebiss* which reflect Middle Low German *crevet* 'crab', 'shrimp', as well as Middle High German *krebez*. **2.** Jewish (Ashkenazic): ornamental name from German *Krebs* 'crab' (see 1). **3.** Danish: from *krebs* 'crayfish'.

GIVEN NAMES German 4%. *Kurt* (9), *Hans* (5), *Gerhard* (3), *Arno* (2), *Bernd* (2), *Dieter* (2), *Erwin* (2), *Franz* (2), *Fritz* (2), *Heinz* (2), *Helmut* (2), *Irmgard* (2).

Krebsbach (578) German: habitational name from an unidentified place named as 'crab stream' (see KREBS, BACH).

Krech (359) **1.** German: habitational name for someone from a place called Graicha, near Altenburg in Thuringia. The Middle German form *Krech* derives from *Krai-chen*, the old spelling of GRAICHEN. **2.** German: metonymic occupational name for a maker of jugs and pitchers or a nickname for a heavy drinker, from a variant (plural in form) of KRUG. **3.** Czech: nickname from German *Krähe* 'crow'.

GIVEN NAMES German 5%. *Kurt* (3), *Otto, Siegfried.*

Kreeger (358) Americanized spelling of German and Jewish (Ashkenazic) KRIEGER or **Krüger** (see KRUEGER).

Kreft (481) German: **1.** from Middle Low German *krevet* 'crab', 'crayfish' (see KREBS), a metonymic occupational name for a catcher or seller of these shellfish or a nickname for someone thought to resemble a crab. **2.** variant of KRAFT.

Kregel (182) German: nickname from Middle Low German *kregel* 'ready to fight', 'tenacious', which in modern Low German came to mean 'lively', 'vivacious'.

Kreger (1448) German: **1.** nickname for someone with a croaky voice, from a noun derivative of Middle Low German *kregen* or *kreigen* 'to crow'. **2.** possibly an altered spelling of KRIEGER.

Kreh (177) German: **1.** variant of KRAY. **2.** shortened form of KREHBIEL.

Krehbiel (714) Swiss German: variant of **Krähenbühl** (see KRAHENBUHL).

Kreher (222) German: variant of KREGER 1.

GIVEN NAMES German 6%. *Kurt* (2), *Erhard, Gerhardt, Otto.*

Kreibich (103) Probably a variant of German **Kreibig**, a habitational name from Kreibig in Silesia.

Kreider (1947) German: topographic name for someone who lived on newly cleared land, from Middle High German *geriute* 'clearing', 'woodland cleared for settlement or cultivation', 'assart'.

Kreidler (466) **1.** German and Jewish (Ashkenazic): occupational name for someone who gathered or sold chalk, from Middle High German *krīde*, German *Kreide* 'chalk' + the agent suffix *-ler*. **2.** German: habitational name for someone from Kreidel in Silesia. **3.** South German: variant of KREUTER.

Kreie (136) German: variant of KREY.

GIVEN NAMES German 4%. *Gunther, Otto.*

Kreifels (212) German: topographic name for someone who lived by a field or area of open country frequented by crows, from Middle Low German *kreie* 'crow' + *fels*, a Rhenish form of *Feld* 'field', 'open country' (Middle Low German *velt*). The Rhenish city of Krefeld has the same etymology.

Kreig (134) Variant of German KRIEG.

GIVEN NAMES French 4%; German 4%. *Alphonse; Lorenz, Ulrike.*

Kreiger (446) **1.** German and Dutch: variant of KREGER. **2.** German: Americanized spelling of KRIEGER.

GIVEN NAMES German 4%. *Kurt* (2), *Mathias, Otto.*

Kreighbaum (145) Altered spelling of German **Kriechbaum** (see KRICHBAUM).

Kreikemeier (146) German (Westphalia): distinguishing name for a tenant farmer (see MEYER) whose farm produced plums or was characterized by blackthorn (wild plum) trees (Low German *kre(i)ke*).
GIVEN NAMES German 5%. *Kurt, Otto.*

Kreil (124) German: variant of KREUL.

Kreiling (249) German: probably a variant of **Greuling**, a nickname for a man with gray hair, a gray beard, or a gray robe (i.e. a monk), from a derivative of Middle High German *grā* 'gray'.

Kreimer (173) Jewish (from Ukraine and Poland): occupational name from Yiddish dialect *kreymer* 'shopkeeper' (see KREMER).
GIVEN NAMES German 8%. *Hermann* (2), *Fritz, Heinz.*

Krein (483) Western German: from the personal name *Quirinus*, a name borne by several early Christian saints.
GIVEN NAMES German 5%. *Milbert* (2), *Otto* (2), *Bernhardt, Hans, Theodor.*

Kreinbring (101) Variant of German KREINBRINK.
GIVEN NAMES Scandinavian 4%; German 4%. *Erik; Kurt.*

Kreinbrink (127) Reduced form of German **Krei(g)enbrink**, a habitational name from a place named with Middle High German *krei(g)e* 'crow' + *brink* 'slope', 'edge', 'grazing land'.

Kreiner (529) **1.** German: variant of KREIN or GREINER. **2.** Jewish (eastern Ashkenazic): metronymic from the Yiddish female personal name *kreyne*, of German origin. **3.** Jewish (from Poland): habitational name for someone from Krajno in Poland or Krajna in Ukraine.
GIVEN NAMES German 4%. *Hans, Helmut, Kurt, Leonhard, Mathias, Otto.*

Kreis (747) **1.** German: nickname for a noisy person, from Middle High German *kreiss, kreisch* 'cry', 'noise'. **2.** German: topographic name for someone who lived by a circular feature, from Middle Low German *kreis* (Middle High German *kreiz*) 'circle'. **3.** Jewish (Ashkenazic): from German *Kreis* 'circle', 'circular field', 'border'.

Kreisberg (151) German and Jewish (Ashkenazic): habitational name for someone from Kreisberg (now Hafka) in Slovakia or, in the case of the German name, a topographic name from a field name in Uelzen, Lower Saxony. In many cases the Jewish name may simply be ornamental, from German *Kreis* 'circle' + *Berg* 'mountain', 'hill'.
GIVEN NAME Jewish 5%. *Meyer.*

Kreischer (277) German: **1.** habitational name for someone from a place called Kreische, Kreischa, or Kreischau in Saxony. **2.** nickname from an agent derivative of Middle High German *krīschen* 'to shriek or cry' or a metonymic occupational name for a torturer, from an agent deriva-

tive of Middle High German *kreischen* 'to make someone shriek (in pain)'.

Kreisel (246) German and Jewish (Ashkenazic): nickname for a perpetually active and somewhat disorganized person, from Middle High German *kriusel*, German *Kreisel*, Yiddish *krayzl* 'spinning top'; or alternatively a nickname for someone with curly hair from the same word in the sense 'spiral', 'curl'.
GIVEN NAMES German 6%. *Erhard, Erna, Frieda, Gerda, Kurt.*

Kreiser (608) **1.** German: habitational name for someone from a place named Kreisau. **2.** German: occupational name for a forest warden or a guard protecting crops from birds and thieves, from an agent derivative of *kreisen* 'to circulate', 'to go round'. **3.** German (in Tyrol): habitational name for someone from St. Quirinus. **4.** Jewish (Ashkenazic): of uncertain origin; perhaps a derivative of KREIS.

Kreisher (192) Variant spelling of German KREISCHER.

Kreisler (251) German and Jewish (Ashkenazic): derivative of KREISEL, with the agent suffix *-er*.
GIVEN NAMES Jewish 5%; German 4%. *Chana, Dorit, Myer; Fritz, Kurt.*

Kreisman (141) Jewish (Ashkenazic): elaborated form of KREIS.
GIVEN NAMES Jewish 6%; German 5%. *Emanuel, Moshe; Erwin, Kurt, Wolfgang.*

Kreiss (214) German and Jewish (Ashkenazic): variant spelling of KREIS.
GIVEN NAMES German 4%. *Fritz, Heinz, Kurt.*

Kreiter (239) **1.** German: from Middle Low German *kreter* 'quarreler', 'argumentative person', 'legal counsel', a derivative of Middle Low German *krēte* 'discord', hence a nickname for a quarrelsome person or an occupational name for a legal representative. **2.** German: variant of KREIDER. **3.** Jewish (eastern Ashkenazic): metronymic occupational name for a seller of herbs, from Yiddish *krayter* 'herbs' (see KRAUT).

Kreitler (168) German: variant of KREITER.
GIVEN NAME German 4%. *Kurt.*

Kreitman (182) **1.** Jewish (Ashkenazic): occupational name from Yiddish *krayt* 'chalk' + *man* 'man'. **2.** German (**Kreitmann**): variant of KRAUTER.
GIVEN NAMES Jewish 4%. *Emanuel, Isador.*

Kreitner (141) **1.** Jewish (Ashkenazic): occupational name from Yiddish *krayt* 'chalk' + the agent suffix *-ner*. **2.** German and Jewish (Ashkenazic): variant of KRAUTER.

Kreitz (360) German: **1.** variant of KREUTZ. **2.** habitational name for someone from a place called Kreitz near Neuss on the Rhine.

Kreitzer (611) German and Jewish (Ashkenazic): variant of KREUTZER.

Kreitzman (108) Jewish (Ashkenazic): possibly a derivative of German *Kreuz* 'cross' + *Mann* 'man'.
GIVEN NAME Jewish 5%. *Chaim.*

Krejci (784) Czech (**Krejčí**): occupational name for a tailor, *krejčí.*

Kreke (130) **1.** North German: nickname or metonymic occupational name for a grower of soft fruits, from Low German *Kreke* 'plum'. **2.** Dutch: topographic name from Dutch *kreek* 'creek', 'bay'.

Krekel (112) **1.** German: habitational name from a place so named near Aachen. **2.** German: nickname for a cantankerous person, from Low German *kräkeln* 'to quarrel'. **3.** Dutch: nickname for someone thought to resemble a cricket, from Middle Dutch *crekel, criekel* 'cricket'.

Krekeler (118) German: probably a habitational name from Krekler, a plateau near Höxter, or from Krekel, near Aachen.
GIVEN NAMES German 5%. *Aloysius, Otto.*

Krell (996) **1.** German: nickname for a brusk person, from Middle High German *krellen* 'to claw'. **2.** German: variant of KREUL or KARL. **3.** Jewish (Ashkenazic): ornamental name from Yiddish *krel* 'coral'.

Kreller (126) German: from an agent derivative of Middle High German *krellen* 'to scratch', 'to scrape', hence probably a nickname for an unfriendly person.

Kremen (129) **1.** Czech (**Křemen**) and Slovak (**Kremeň**): nickname for a hard man, from Czech *křemen* 'quartz', 'flint', of proverbial hardness. **2.** Jewish (eastern Ashkenazic): ornamental name or metonymic occupational name from Ukrainian *kremin* 'pebble', 'flint' (Russian *kremen*).
GIVEN NAME Jewish 7%. *Aron.*

Kremer (3065) German, Dutch, and Jewish (Ashkenazic): variant of KRAMER. Compare Yiddish *kremer* 'shopkeeper'.
GIVEN NAMES German 4%. *Kurt* (7), *Otto* (4), *Erwin* (2), *Gerhard* (2), *Horst* (2), *Juergen* (2), *Ulrich* (2), *Wilhelm* (2), *Aloysius, Arno, Bernhard, Erna.*

Kremers (256) Variant of German KREMER.

Kremin (118) Jewish (eastern Ashkenazic): variant of KREMEN.
GIVEN NAME German 4%. *Grete* (2).

Krempa (167) Polish: variant spelling of **Krępa**, descriptive nickname from *krępy* 'squat', 'square-built'.
GIVEN NAMES Polish 5%. *Agnieszka, Casimir.*

Krempasky (185) Czech or Slovak (**Krempaský**): descriptive nickname from *krępy* 'squat', 'square-built'.

Kren (189) **1.** Austrian German and Czech (**Křen**): from Czech *křen* 'horseradish', hence a nickname for a keen, fit person, or possibly an occupational name for a dealer in spices and condiments. **2.** Jewish (from Belarus): unexplained. **3.** Slovenian: altered form of HREN.

Krenek (454) Czech (**Křenek**): diminutive of KREN.

Krengel (195) **1.** German: probably an occupational name for a baker, from Middle High German *krengel* 'doughnut'. **2.** Dutch: nickname for someone with curly hair, from Middle Dutch *cringel* 'curl'.

3. Jewish (eastern Ashkenazic): ornamental name from Polish *kr(e,)giel* 'skittle'. **4.** Jewish (eastern Ashkenazic): from German *Kringel* '(cake) ring', either an ornamental name or a metonymic occupational name for a pastrycook.

GIVEN NAMES German 5%; Jewish 5%. *Arno, Guenter, Otto*; *Shalom* (2), *Moshe*.

Krenik (181) Variant spelling of German **Krenig**, itself a variant of KRANICH.

Krenitsky (107) Germanized or Americanized form of Czech **Křenický**, habitational name for someone from either of two villages in Bohemia called Křenice.

Krenke (184) German: probably a nickname for a sickly person from Middle High German *krenke* 'weakness', 'deficiency'.

Krenn (210) South German: apparently a noun derivative of *(ge-)rinnen* 'to flow or run', applied as a metonymic occupational name for someone who made or installed wooden drainage channels and gutters.

GIVEN NAMES German 8%. *Alois* (2), *Fritz, Johann, Kurt, Matthias*.

Krentz (418) German: variant spelling of KRENZ.

Krenz (713) German: **1.** habitational name from any of various place called Kreinitz, Krenitz, or Krensitz, so named from Middle High German *greniz(e)* 'boundary', 'border' (of Slavic origin), modern German *Grenze*. **2.** German: variant of KRANZ.

GIVEN NAMES German 4%. *Erna, Gerhard, Horst, Kurt, Otto, Rudi, Wolfgang*.

Krenzel (126) South German: diminutive of KRANZ.

GIVEN NAMES German 7%. *Florian, Otto*.

Krenzer (222) German: **1.** topographic name for someone living near a border, or habitational name for someone from any of various place called Kreinitz, Krenitz, or Krensitz (see KRENZ). **2.** probably from Middle High German *grans* 'beak', 'muzzle', hence a nickname for someone with a protruding mouth or a topographic name for someone who lived by a beak-shaped plot of land.

Krenzke (130) German (of Slavic origin): from a derivative of KRENZ.

Krepp (127) German: **1.** Bavarian topographic name for someone living in a hollow ('in der Greppen'). **2.** from a Slavic personal name meaning 'firm'.

Krepps (452) German, Czech, and Jewish (Ashkenazic): variant of KREBS or KREPS.

Kreps (818) Czech and Jewish (Ashkenazic): from German *Krebs* 'crab' or Yiddish *kreps* 'crayfish'. As a Jewish name it is of ornamental origin; otherwise it was probably a nickname for someone with a peculiar gait.

Kresch (102) **1.** German and Jewish (Ashkenazic): unexplained; perhaps an altered form of **Krat(z)sch**, a habitational name from Kratschütz, recorded in 1378 as Kracz. **2.** German: from a personal name cognate with Old High German *grātag*

'greedy'. **3.** German: from the Czech personal name *Kreč* (Kretsch).

GIVEN NAMES Jewish 6%. *Ari, Mendel*.

Kresge (776) Probably of German origin: **1.** variant of **Kreske**, from an old personal name formed with Old High German *grātag* 'greedy'. **2.** variant of KRESSE. **3.** altered spelling of **Grazke**, a topographic name, from the Slavic stem *grad* 'castle', 'town'.

Kresin (135) Jewish (from Lithuania): **1.** habitational name for someone from a place called Kresy. **2.** metronymic from the Yiddish female personal name *kresye*, of uncertain origin.

GIVEN NAMES Russian 5%; German 4%. *Vitaly* (2), *Vladimir*; *Elke* (2).

Kresl (125) Respelling of German **Kressl**, from a pet form of KRESS.

Kress (2926) German: **1.** from a much altered pet form of the personal name *Erasmus*, a Latinized form of Greek *erasmos* 'loved' (see RASMUS). **2.** from a much altered pet form of the personal name CHRISTIAN. **3.** from Middle High German *kresse* 'gudgeon', hence probably a nickname for someone thought to resemble the fish in some way or a metonymic occupational name for a fisherman. **4.** unflattering nickname for a greedy person, from Old High German *krāssig, grātag* 'greedy'.

Kresse (320) German: **1.** variant of KRESS. **2.** variant of **Krätsch**, a derivative of *Křes*, an Old Czech personal name.

GIVEN NAMES German 6%. *Gerhard, Herta, Kurt, Mathias, Wolfgang*.

Kresser (177) German: variant of KRESS 4.

GIVEN NAMES German 6%. *Helmut, Hermann, Kurt*.

Kressin (281) Jewish (eastern Ashkenazic): variant spelling of KRESIN.

Kressler (185) German: habitational name for someone from Kressel in Baden.

GIVEN NAME German 4%. *Otto* (2).

Kressley (138) Probably an Americanized spelling of German KRESSLER or **Kressle**, from a much altered short form of the medieval personal name *Erasmus* (see KRESS 1).

Kresta (109) Czech: **1.** habitational name for someone from any of several villages in Bohemia named with the vocabulary word *krs* 'cross'. **2.** possibly a derivative of the Old Czech personal name *Krs*.

Kret (127) Polish: nickname from *kret* 'mole'.

GIVEN NAMES Polish 12%. *Stanislaw* (2), *Irena, Kazimierz, Tadeusc, Tadeusz*.

Kretchman (144) Americanized spelling of German **Kretschmann**, a partly Germanized form of KRETSCHMER.

Kretchmar (130) Americanized spelling of German KRETSCHMER.

Kretchmer (191) Americanized spelling of German KRETSCHMER.

Kretlow (106) German: probably a habitational name from **Kartlow**, the name of two places in Mecklenburg-West Pomerania.

Kretsch (201) Shortened form of German KRETSCHMER.

GIVEN NAMES German 4%; Irish 4%. *Armin* (2), *Hans, Theresia*.

Kretschman (106) German: variant of KRETSCHMER.

GIVEN NAME German 7%. *Bodo*.

Kretschmar (209) German: variant of KRETSCHMER.

Kretschmer (435) Eastern German: occupational name for an innkeeper, Middle High German *kretschmar*. The word is of Slavic origin. Compare Czech *krčmář* 'innkeeper'.

GIVEN NAMES German 15%. *Klaus* (4), *Gerhard* (2), *Hans* (2), *Horst* (2), *Achim, Erna, Gerda, Gerhart, Guenter, Kurt, Matthias, Otto*.

Kretz (492) **1.** German: from the medieval personal name *Krezzo*. **2.** German: from a reduced pet form of the personal name PANKRATZ.

Kretzer (413) German: **1.** nickname for a juror or a collector of legal fines. **2.** occupational name for a basketmaker or a peddler, from an agent derivative of Middle High German *kretze* 'basket'. **3.** habitational name for someone from Kretz, near Mayen in the Eifel Mountains. **4.** Jewish (Ashkenazic): variant of KRATZER.

GIVEN NAMES German 4%. *Otto* (2), *Dietrich*.

Kretzschmar (311) German: variant of KRETSCHMER.

GIVEN NAMES German 12%. *Erwin* (2), *Kurt* (2), *Wolfgang* (2), *Arno, Florian, Gunther, Hanns, Hans, Heinrich, Johann, Otto, Uli*.

Kreuger (159) German: variant of **Krüger** (see KRUGER).

GIVEN NAME German 5%. *Kurt* (3).

Kreul (189) German: from Middle High German *kröuwel* 'claw', 'hook', 'three-pronged fork', apparently a nickname for someone who used such an implement or perhaps a metonymic occupational name for someone who made them.

Kreuscher (115) German: unexplained.

Kreuser (305) Jewish (Ashkenazic): variant of KRAUSER.

Kreuter (265) German: **1.** topographic name for someone who lived on or worked newly cleared land, from an agent derivative of *gereute*, a late medieval form of Middle High German *geriute* (see KREIDER). **2.** variant of **Kräuter** (see KRAUTER).

GIVEN NAMES German 7%. *Kurt* (2), *Manfred, Urs*.

Kreutz (412) German: topographic name for someone who lived near a cross set up by the roadside, in a marketplace, or as a field or boundary marker, from Middle High German *kriuz(e)* 'cross'.

GIVEN NAMES German 5%. *Kurt* (4), *Bernhard, Gottfried, Orlo, Reinhold*.

Kreutzberg (100) German: habitational name from any of various place in Germany and Austria called Kreuzberg.

Kreutzer (940) **1.** German and Swiss German: topographic name for someone who lived near a cross set up by the roadside or in a marketplace, from Middle High German *kriuz(e)* 'cross' + the suffix *-er* denoting an inhabitant. **2.** German: habitational name for someone from a place called Krögis (recorded as *Creuz* in 1186), or from some other place similarly named. **3.** German: in some cases, possibly from Middle High German *kriuzære, kriuzer*, a term denoting a crusader or Teutonic Knight, an allusion to the symbol of the cross worn on the tunic by such knights. **4.** German: possibly also a metonymic occupational name for a coiner, from the same word denoting a small coin marked with the symbol of a cross (in full *kriuzerpfenninc*). **5.** Jewish (Ashkenazic): ornamental name from *Kreutzer*, the name of the coin (see 4).

Kreuz (128) German: variant spelling of KREUTZ.

Kreuzer (364) German: variant spelling of KREUTZER.

GIVEN NAMES German 10%. *Otto* (3), *Dietmar, Hans, Heinrich, Horst, Reiner, Wilhelm, Willi, Wolfgang.*

Krewson (401) Origin unidentified.

Krey (375) German: **1.** nickname from Middle Low German *krege* 'crow'. Compare KRAY. **2.** occupational name for a watchman, Middle High German *krai*, a loanword from French *cri* 'shout', 'cry'.

GIVEN NAMES German 5%. *Kurt* (3), *Benno, Gerhard, Johann.*

Kreyer (105) German: occupational name (especially in Austria) for a herald or town crier, from an agent derivative of Middle High German *krai* 'shout' (see KREY). Compare KRIER.

Kreyling (131) German: probably a nickname from a diminutive of Middle Low German *krege* 'crow'.

Kribbs (105) Possibly a variant of German KREBS.

Kribs (196) German: variant of KREBS.

GIVEN NAMES French 6%. *Lucien, Romain.*

Krich (101) Origin uncertain. Possibly a shortened form of German KRICHBAUM or a respelling of **Kriech**, a topographic name for someone who lived by a blackthorn or wild plum tree.

Krichbaum (228) German: topographic name for someone who lived near a wild plum tree (blackthorn), Low German *Kreke, Krike.*

Krick (1154) German: **1.** probably an altered spelling of **Krich**, a dialect plural of *Krug* 'pitcher', 'jug', probably applied as a metonymic occupational name for a maker or seller of such vessels. **2.** habitational name from a place called Krickau. **3.** nickname for someone who walked with a

crutch, from *Krick* 'crutch', dialect form of *Kruücke*.

Krider (604) Altered spelling of German KREITER, KREUTER, or **Kräuter** (see KRAUTER).

Kridler (150) Altered spelling of German and Jewish KREIDLER.

Kriebel (577) German: **1.** variant of **Kreuel**, itself a variant of KREUL. **2.** variant of **Kribel**, earlier **Crebel**; unexplained.

Krieg (1759) **1.** Swiss, German, and Jewish (Ashkenazic): nickname for an argumentative person, from Middle High German, Middle Low German *kriec*, German *Krieg* 'strife', 'conflict', 'squabble' (Yiddish *krig*). **2.** German: variant of KRUG.

Kriegel (563) **1.** South German: from a diminutive of KRIEG 2. **2.** Jewish (eastern Ashkenazic): metonymic occupational name for a potter, from Yiddish *krigl* 'small jug'. Compare KRUG 1.

GIVEN NAMES German 4%. *Armin, Balzer, Erwin, Frieda, Fritz, Heinz.*

Krieger (4937) **1.** Swiss German, German, and Dutch: occupational name for a mercenary soldier, Middle High German *krieger* (possibly from Late Latin *(miles) gregarius* 'common soldier', from *grex* 'herd', 'flock', 'crowd'). This name, in various spellings, is found throughout western and central Europe. **2.** German and Jewish (Ashkenazic): nickname for a quarrelsome person (see KRIEG). **3.** Jewish (Ashkenazic): variant of KRUGER.

GIVEN NAMES German 4%. *Kurt* (15), *Fritz* (5), *Hans* (3), *Bernhard* (2), *Erwin* (2), *Otto* (2), *Dietrich, Erdmann, Frieda, Gerhardt, Guenther, Heinz.*

Kriegler (111) German: variant of **Krügler**, an occupational name for a maker or seller of stoneware jugs and mugs, from an agent derivative of Middle High German *kruoc* 'pitcher', 'drinking vessel'.

GIVEN NAMES German 5%. *Franz, Kurt.*

Kriegshauser (119) German: probably a habitational name for someone from an unidentified place called Kriegshaus, literally 'war house'.

GIVEN NAMES German 8%. *Berthold, Otto.*

Kriel (120) German: habitational name from a place called Kriele, near Rathenow.

GIVEN NAME French 5%. *Andre.*

Krienke (235) German: habitational name for someone from a place called Krienke, on Usedom, an island in western Pomerania.

GIVEN NAMES German 6%. *Ernst* (2), *Ingeborg* (2), *Erwin, Frieda.*

Krier (1030) German: occupational name from Middle High German *krier* 'herald'. Compare KREY.

Kries (116) German: from Middle High German *kriese* 'cherry', hence a metonymic occupational name for a seller of soft fruits or a topographic name for someone who lived near a cherry tree.

Kriese (172) German: **1.** variant of KRIES. **2.** probably also a variant of GRIESE.

GIVEN NAMES German 4%. *Gerda, Otto.*

Kriesel (331) **1.** German: from a diminutive of KRIES(E). **2.** Possibly a respelling of German KREISEL.

Krieser (123) German: variant of GRIESER.

GIVEN NAMES German 14%. *Kurt* (5), *Siegfried.*

Kriete (185) German: nickname for a quarrelsome man, from Middle Low German *krēte* 'discord'. Compare KREITER 1.

GIVEN NAMES German 6%. *Fritz, Otto.*

Krietemeyer (153) German: distinguishing nickname for a farmer who cultivated newly cleared land, from Middle High German *geriute* 'woodland cleared for cultivation or settlement', 'assart' + *meier* 'farmer', 'steward'.

Krigbaum (269) Variant spelling of German KRICHBAUM.

Kriger (280) **1.** German, Dutch, Danish, Jewish (Ashkenazic), etc.: variant spelling of German KRIEGER. **2.** German: from the personal name *Krigar*, a pet form of *Gregor* (see GREGORY).

Krikorian (506) Armenian: patronymic from the western Armenian personal name *Krikor*, classical Armenian *Grigor* (see GREGORY).

GIVEN NAMES Armenian 22%; French 5%. *Krikor* (8), *Haig* (3), *Sarkis* (3), *Anoush* (2), *Hagop* (2), *Kevork* (2), *Kirkor* (2), *Sahag* (2), *Antranik, Aram, Arshak, Artin; Serge* (3), *Jacques* (2), *Andre, Jean-Marc.*

Kriley (124) Probably a respelling of Irish CRILLY.

Krill (552) German: **1.** nickname for a lively, cheerful person, from Low German *krill* 'lively', 'healthy'. **2.** variant spelling of **Krüll** (see KRULL). **3.** from an East Prussian pet form of KARL.

Krim (184) **1.** German: probably a variant of GRIMM. **2.** German: variant of KRIMM. **3.** Jewish (from Poland and Ukraine): nickname from Yiddish dialect *krim* 'crooked', 'bent' (see KRUM).

GIVEN NAMES Jewish 4%. *Meyer, Sol.*

Krimm (131) German: **1.** habitational name from any of the places named Krimm or Krim, in Schleswig-Holstein, Mecklenburg, former East Prussia, and Bavaria. **2.** variant of GRIMM. **3.** North German: nickname for a hunched or bent person, from Low German *krimpen* 'to crimp or shrivel'.

GIVEN NAMES German 4%. *Hans* (2), *Gunter.*

Krimmel (181) German: variant of **Krümmel** (see KRUMMEL).

Krimmer (122) **1.** German: from an agent derivative of Middle High German *krimmen* 'to pinch', 'to flex (the claws)', a term used to denote a hawk or falcon and hence a nickname for someone thought to resemble a bird of prey or a metonymic occupational name for a falconer. **2.** Jewish (from

Poland and Ukraine): inflected form of KRIM.

GIVEN NAMES German 5%. *Erwin, Friedl, Fritz.*

Kriner (591) Altered spelling of German and Jewish KREINER.

Kring (742) **1.** German: topographic name for someone living by a round village green field or a metonymic occupational name for a baker of round pastries, from Middle High German *kring(e)* 'ring', 'circle'. **2.** German: from the name of St. Quirin(us), especially in Rhineland. **3.** Danish: from *kring* 'circle (of people)'; also a nickname meaning 'kind' or 'quick'. **4.** Swedish: probably a soldier's name from Old Swedish or dialect *kring* 'quick', 'lively'.

Kringen (122) Norwegian: unexplained.

Kringle (125) Respelling of German **Kringel**, a variant of KRENGEL.

Krings (347) **1.** German (Rhineland and Bavaria): from a reduced vernacular form of the medieval personal name *Quirinus*, a name borne by several early Christian saints. **2.** Dutch: topographic name for someone who lived by a circular path or waterway.

Krinke (186) German: **1.** variant spelling of KRIENKE. **2.** metonymic occupational name from Slavic *krinka* 'pot'.

GIVEN NAMES German 7%. *Kurt* (2), *Egon, Erhard.*

Krinsky (454) Jewish (from Belarus): habitational name for someone from places called Krynki (Krinki), now in Belarus.

GIVEN NAMES Jewish 7%. *Levi* (3), *Mendel* (3), *Menachem, Miriam, Yehuda.*

Krippner (159) Variant of German **Kreppner**, probably a topographic name from Bavarian dialect *greppe* 'hollow'.

Krisch (162) German: **1.** from a short form of the personal name *Krischan*, a Slavic variant of CHRISTIAN. **2.** nickname for a loud person from Slavic *krič* 'crier' or a topographic name from Slavic *křiž*.

GIVEN NAMES German 5%. *Hans, Jurgen, Rudiger.*

Krise (430) **1.** Altered spelling of German and Jewish KREIS. **2.** German: variant of KRIES.

Krish (112) Indian (southern states): shortened form of KRISHNA or of any other name beginning with *Krishna* (such as KRISHNAN, **Krishnaswami**, KRISHNA-MURTHY, etc.), used in the U.S. by families from southern India. It is not in use in India.

GIVEN NAMES Indian 11%. *Rajesh, Ravishankar, Shankar, Vijay.*

Krisher (298) Americanized form of **Krischer**, a Palatinate dialect of German KREISCHER, from the dialect word *Krisch* 'cry', 'shout'.

Krishna (215) Indian (southern states): Hindu name from Sanskrit *kṛṣṇa* 'black', an epithet of the eighth incarnation of the god Vishnu. Among Tamil and Malayalam

speakers who have migrated from their home states it is a variant of KRISHNAN. It is found only as a male given name in India, but used a family name in the U.S. among South Indians.

GIVEN NAMES Indian 91%. *Gopal* (10), *Murali* (8), *Hari* (4), *Anand* (3), *Arvind* (3), *Radha* (3), *Raj* (3), *Rama* (3), *Sanjay* (3), *Shailendra* (3), *Suresh* (3), *Vijay* (3).

Krishnamurthy (224) Indian (southern states): Hindu name from Sanskrit *kṛṣṇamūrti* meaning 'manifestation of the god Krishna', from *krisna* 'black' (epithet of an incarnation of the god Vishnu) + *murti* 'image', 'manifestation'. It is only a given name in India, but has become a family name in the U.S. among South Indians.

GIVEN NAMES Indian 94%. *Ramesh* (4), *Ravi* (4), *Bala* (3), *Ganesh* (3), *Karthik* (3), *Narayanan* (3), *Sridhar* (3), *Vasanth* (3), *Arvind* (2), *Ashok* (2), *Mohan* (2), *Sharada* (2).

Krishnan (493) Indian (Kerala, Tamil Nadu): Hindu name from Sanskrit *kṛṣṇa* 'black' (see KRISHNA) + the Tamil-Malayalam third-person masculine singular suffix *-n*. This is only a given name in India, but has come to be used as a family name in the U.S.

GIVEN NAMES Indian 92%. *Radha* (8), *Ramesh* (8), *Ram* (7), *Suresh* (7), *Mahesh* (6), *Murali* (6), *Raj* (5), *Rajesh* (5), *Ravi* (5), *Anand* (4), *Anantha* (4), *Rama* (4).

Kriska (106) Slavic: from a derivative of the Greek personal name *Khristophoros* (see CHRISTOPHER).

Krisko (187) Ukrainian: from the personal name *Krisko*, Ukrainian form of CHRISTO-PHER.

Kriss (476) German: probably a variant of Swiss German **Kries**, Alemannic form of KIRSCH 'cherry'.

Krist (423) North German: from a short form of the personal name *Kristen* or one of its variants, North German form of CHRISTIAN.

Kristal (156) **1.** Jewish (Ashkenazic), Czech (**Křistál**), and Hungarian (**Kristály**): ornamental name from German *Kristall* 'crystal'. **2.** Czech and Hungarian: possibly also from a personal name, an adjectival derivative of CHRISTOS 'Christ'.

GIVEN NAMES Jewish 7%. *Elihu, Emanuel.*

Kristan (129) **1.** Slovenian: from *Kristan*, a medieval Slovenian form of the personal name *Kristjan*, Latin *Christianus* (see CHRISTIAN). **2.** German: variant of **Christan** (see CHRISTIAN).

Kristek (113) Czech: **1.** from the personal name *Kristián* (see CHRISTIAN). **2.** (**Křistek**) nickname for a mischievous person, from *skřítek* 'goblin', 'sprite', 'fairy'.

GIVEN NAME German 4%. *Otto.*

Kristensen (468) Norwegian and Danish: patronymic from the personal name *Kristen* (see CHRISTIAN).

GIVEN NAMES Scandinavian 30%; German 6%. *Erik* (7), *Jorgen* (2), *Ove* (2), *Peer* (2), *Sven* (2), *Vibeke* (2), *Bent, Bjorn, Carsten, Hilmar, Juhl, Karsten; Hans* (3), *Kurt* (2), *Benno, Bernhard, Claus, Georg, Gerda, Jutta, Konrad, Wolfgang.*

Kristiansen (366) Norwegian and Danish: patronymic from the personal name *Kristian* (see CHRISTIAN).

GIVEN NAMES Scandinavian 39%; German 6%. *Erik* (9), *Nils* (2), *Alf, Bent, Britt, Egil, Gunvor, Karsten, Lars, Morten, Per, Petter; Hans* (2), *Fritz, Inge, Kurt, Oskar, Otto, Wilhelm.*

Kristof (256) Hungarian (**Kristóf**); Czech, Slovak, and Slovenian (**Krištof**): from the personal name, a vernacular form of Greek *Khristophoros* (see CHRISTOPHER).

GIVEN NAMES Hungarian 4%. *Dezso, Gabor, Karoly, Zoltan.*

Kristoff (430) **1.** Altered form of Bulgarian **Hristov**, a patronymic from the personal name *Hristo*, Bulgarian form of CHRISTO-PHER. **2.** Russian: patronymic from a Russian form of the personal name CHRISTO-PHER. **3.** variant spelling of Hungarian KRISTOF.

Kriston (129) **1.** Hungarian: from a derivative of the personal name *Kristóf*, Hungarian form of CHRISTOPHER. **2.** German: variant of KRISTAN or of *Kristen, Christa(h)n,* or *Christen,* all variants of the personal name CHRISTIAN.

Kristy (118) Origin unidentified.

Kritikos (146) Greek: ethnic name for a Cretan, someone from the island of Crete, from an adjectival derivative of *Kriti* 'Crete'. In the Ionian islands the ethnic name acquired the secondary meaning 'good-for-nothing', 'scrounger', after the large number of refugees who came to the islands from Crete following its conquest by the Ottoman Turks.

GIVEN NAMES Greek 33%. *Christos* (5), *Dimitrios* (3), *Antonios, Demetrios, Diamantis, Kosta, Kostas, Nicolaos, Panagiota, Panagiotis, Sevasti, Sophocles.*

Kritz (256) **1.** German: metonymic occupational name for a gristmiller, from Middle High German *grütze* 'grits'. **2.** German: from a Slavic form of the personal name *Christian,* possibly from Czech **Kříž** (see KRIZ). **3.** German: from a dialect variant of KREUTZ. **4.** Jewish (from Ukraine): nickname or occupational nickname for a wool carder or barber, from Yiddish *krits* 'scratch'. Compare KRATZER.

Kritzer (346) **1.** South German: probably an occupational name for a coiner, from *krüzer* 'kreutzer' (the coin), a dialect variant of KREUTZER. **2.** Jewish (Ashkenazic): variant of KRETZER. **3.** Jewish (Ashkenazic): variant of KRATZER, from Yiddish *kritsn* 'to scratch'.

Kritzman (123) **1.** German (**Kritzmann**): topographic name for someone living near a cross (see KREUTZER). **2.** German and

Jewish (Ashkenazic): occupational name for a gristmiller, from Middle High German *grütze*, Yiddish *grits* 'grits' + Middle High German, Yiddish *man* 'man'. **3.** Jewish: elaborated form of KRITZ.

Krivanek (172) Czech (**Křivánek**): nickname for a cheerful or singing person, from Czech *(s)křivánek* 'skylark'.

Kriz (649) **1.** Czech (**Kříž**) and Slovak (**Kríž**): from the old personal name *Kříž* (literally 'cross') or a short form of *Kristián* (see CHRISTIAN). **2.** Slovenian (**Križ**): nickname or topographic name from *križ* 'cross', 'crucifix'.

Krizan (394) **1.** Czech and Slovak (**Křižan**): habitational name for someone from a place called Křižany, named with *kříž* 'cross'. **2.** Croatian (**Križan**): from a short form of the personal names *Kristofor* (see CHRISTOPHER) or *Kristijan* (see CHRISTIAN). **3.** Slovenian (**Križan**): habitational name for a person from any of the many places called Križ, named with *križ* 'cross', or a nickname derived from this word. **4.** Hungarian (**Krizsán**): from the personal name *Krizsán* (see CHRISTIAN).

Krizek (222) Czech (**Křížek**): from a pet form of the personal name *Kříž* (see KRIZ).

Krizman (159) **1.** Slovenian (**Križman**): of uncertain origin. It may be a derivative of the personal name *Kristjan*, Latin *Christianus*, formed with the suffix *-man* (equivalent of German *-mann*), or a nickname or topographic name from the dialect plant name *križman* 'milkwort' (German *bittere Kreuzbume*, Latin *Polygala amara*), which was noted for its medicinal properties. It could also be derived from the archaic adjective *križman* 'anointed', from *križmati* 'to anoint' (derivative of Latin *chrisma* 'unction'). **2.** Jewish (Ashkenazic): variant of KRITZMAN.

Krob (228) German: nickname for a boorish individual, from Middle High German *g(e)rop*, German and Yiddish *grob* 'coarse', 'crude'.

Kroboth (211) German: ethnic name for a Croat, from an altered form of Slavic *Hrvat* (see HORVATH).

GIVEN NAMES German 5%. *Fritz, Kurt.*

Krochmal (149) Polish: from *krochmal* 'starch', a nickname for a stiff person.

GIVEN NAME Polish 5%; German 4%. *Zygmunt.*

Krock (263) **1.** German: habitational name for someone from the city of Kraków in Poland, from a shortened form of **Kraker**, a Silesian variant of German **Krakauer**. **2.** Germanized variant of Polish KROK. **3.** North German (also **Kröck**): topographic name from Low German *krock* 'crack', 'crevice' (plural *kröcke*). **4.** Dutch: nickname for someone with long, curly, or thick hair, from Middle Dutch *crook, croke* 'curly locks', 'mop (of hair)'. **5.** Jewish: variant spelling of KROK.

Krocker (107) German: habitational name for someone from the city of Kraków in Poland (see KROCK 1).

Krodel (164) German (**Krödel**): from an old personal name, related to *Ruhm* 'fame'.

GIVEN NAMES German 7%. *Gerhard, Gottfried, Hans, Kurt.*

Kroeger (1895) German (**Kröger**): variant of **Krüger** (see KRUEGER).

GIVEN NAMES German 4%. *Kurt* (7), *Heinz* (4), *Otto* (3), *Erwin* (2), *Hans* (2), *Juergen* (2), *Guenter, Theodor.*

Kroeker (506) German: Rhenish variant of **Kröger** (see KRUEGER).

Kroemer (142) Variant of German **Kröhmer**, a variant of **Krämer** (see KRAMER).

GIVEN NAMES German 7%. *Erhard, Friedrich, Kurt.*

Kroener (160) German (**Kröner**): see KRONER.

GIVEN NAMES German 9%. *Helmut, Hermann, Horst, Otto.*

Kroening (673) German (**Kröning**): **1.** from an old personal name based on Old High German *gruoni* 'green'. **2.** probably a habitational name for someone living at a house distinguished by the sign of a crown, Sorbian *krona*.

GIVEN NAMES German 5%. *Kurt* (2), *Armin, Erwin, Ewald, Frederich, Juergen, Otto.*

Kroenke (183) German (**Krönke**): diminutive of KROHN.

GIVEN NAMES German 6%. *Klaus, Kurt, Willi.*

Kroeplin (119) German (**Kröplin**): habitational name from a place in Mecklenburg called Kröpelin.

Kroes (217) Dutch: **1.** metonymic occupational name for a potter, from Middle Dutch *croes(e), cruese* 'stone jar', 'drinking vessel'. **2.** nickname for someone with curly hair, from Middle Dutch *croes* 'curly', 'crinkly'.

GIVEN NAMES German 4%; Dutch 4%. *Johannes, Monika; Cor* (2), *Gerrit, Jaap.*

Kroese (185) Dutch: **1.** metonymic occupational name for a potter, from Middle Dutch *croes(e), cruese* 'stone jar', 'drinking vessel'. **2.** nickname for someone with curly hair, from Middle Dutch *croes* 'curly', 'crinkly'.

GIVEN NAME German 4%. *Kurt* (2).

Kroeze (212) Variant spelling of Dutch KROESE.

GIVEN NAMES Dutch 4%. *Dirk, Gerritt, Marinus.*

Kroft (272) Czech form of the German KRAFT 'strength', 'power'.

Krog (256) Scandinavian (mainly Denmark): habitational name from places named with *krog* 'corner', 'bend'.

Kroger (623) German (also **Kröger**): occupational name for an innkeeper, a variant of **Krüger** (see KRUEGER).

GIVEN NAMES German 6%. *Otto* (3), *Dieter, Erwin, Fritz, Hannelore, Hanns, Hilde, Inge, Kurt, Manfred.*

Krogh (769) Scandinavian (mainly Denmark): **1.** variant of KROG. **2.** from *crock* 'inn', hence a metonymic occupational name for an innkeeper.

GIVEN NAMES Scandinavian 7%. *Nels* (3), *Knud* (2), *Borge, Dagny, Egil, Erik, Gudrun.*

Krogman (516) Variant of German KROGMANN.

Krogmann (108) German: occupational name for an innkeeper, Middle Low German *krūch, krōch*. Compare KROGER.

GIVEN NAMES German 7%. *Ernst, Johannes, Otto.*

Krogstad (374) Norwegian: habitational name from various farmsteads named Krokstad, especially in southeastern Norway, from the Old Norse personal name *Krókr* denoting a crooked person + *staðr* 'farm'.

Kroh (430) German: nickname for someone thought to resemble a crow in some way, from Middle High German *krā* 'crow'. Compare KRAGE.

GIVEN NAMES German 4%. *Otto* (2), *Gunther, Wolfgang.*

Krohmer (112) South German and Silesian: variant of KRAMER.

GIVEN NAMES German 5%. *Eberhard, Helmut.*

Krohn (2664) **1.** German (also **Kröhn**): nickname for a tall, thin person with long legs, from Middle High German *krān, krōn* 'crane'. Compare KRAHN. **2.** German: from an old personal name based on Old High German *gruoni* 'green'. **3.** Jewish (Ashkenazic): variant spelling of KRON.

GIVEN NAMES German 5%. *Otto* (6), *Hans* (5), *Kurt* (5), *Erwin* (3), *Claus* (2), *Eldor* (2), *Gerhard* (2), *Guenther* (2), *Klaus* (2), *Uwe* (2), *Armin, Ewald.*

Krohne (111) German: variant of KROHN.

GIVEN NAMES German 11%. *Kurt* (3), *Gerhardt.*

Krok (208) **1.** Polish: nickname for someone with an unusual walk, from Polish *krok* 'gait', 'step'. **2.** German and Dutch: variant spelling of KROCK. **3.** Perhaps also a Swedish soldier's name from *krok* 'crook', 'bend'.

GIVEN NAMES Polish 7%. *Casimir, Ewa, Henryk, Jozef, Zofia.*

Krol (1291) **1.** Dutch: variant spelling of KROLL. **2.** Polish (**Król**) and Jewish (from Polish): from Polish *król* 'king', a Polish nickname for someone with a superior manner or for a leader in a community, or a metonymic occupational name for someone who worked in a royal household. As a Jewish name it is an ornamental adoption. Compare KRAL. **3.** Polish and Jewish (eastern Ashkenazic): nickname or ornamental name from Polish *król* 'rabbit', Ukrainian *krol*. See also KROLIK.

FOREBEARS The Dutch colonial official Bastiaen Jansen Krol (1595–1674) was born at Harlingen in Friesland. He emigrated to New Netherland in 1626 with authority to perform the ceremonies of baptism and marriage. At various times from 1626 to 1643 he was commissary and director at Fort Orange (Albany), NY.

GIVEN NAMES Polish 13%. *Casimir* (7), *Jerzy* (4), *Ryszard* (4), *Andrzej* (3), *Bogdan* (3), *Kazimierz* (3), *Zofia* (3), *Ewa* (2), *Krzysztof* (2), *Leszek* (2), *Lucyna* (2), *Alojzy*.

Krolak (207) Polish (**Królak**): patronymic from the nickname *Król* 'king' or 'rabbit' (see KROL, KROLIK).

GIVEN NAMES Polish 7%. *Andrzej, Casimir, Jaroslaw, Slawomir, Zbigniew*.

Krolczyk (234) Polish (**Królczyk**): derivative of the nickname *Król* 'king' or 'rabbit' (see KROL, KROLIK).

Krolick (159) Germanized or Americanized spelling of KROLIK.

Krolik (132) **1.** Polish (**Królik**): from a diminutive of Polish *król* 'king' (see KROL). **2.** Polish: nickname from *królik* 'rabbit'. This originated as an attempted calque on Low German dialect *Kuniklīn* 'rabbit', being misinterpreted as a diminutive of *König*, although in fact it is from the unrelated Latin word *cuniculus*. **3.** Jewish (eastern Ashkenazic): ornamental name from Russian and Yiddish *krolik* 'rabbit' (see 2 above).

GIVEN NAMES Polish 8%. *Bogdan, Janusz, Rafal, Zdislaw*.

Krolikowski (337) Polish (**Królikowski**): habitational name for someone from places called Królikowo or Królików.

GIVEN NAMES Polish 8%; German 4%. *Andrzej, Jaroslaw, Miroslaw, Ryszard, Stanislaw, Tomasz, Witold; Alfons, Alois, Ignatz*.

Kroll (4407) **1.** German and Dutch: nickname for someone with curly hair, from Middle High German *krol* 'curly', Middle Low German *krulle* 'ringlet', 'curl', Middle Dutch *croel, crul* (apparently a loanword from German). **2.** German and Polish: variant of KROL. **3.** German: (also **Kröll**): from the Germanic personal name *Rollo*, based on *hrōd* 'renown', 'victory'. **4.** Jewish (Ashkenazic): variant spelling of KROL.

Krom (598) **1.** Dutch: nickname for a hunchback, from Middle Dutch *crom* 'crooked'. **2.** Jewish (Ashkenazic): from Yiddish *krom* 'shop', 'store', hence a metonymic occupational name for a retailer.

Krome (146) **1.** German: see KROMER. **2.** Perhaps an altered spelling of Dutch KROM.

Kromer (921) German (also **Krömer**): occupational name for a small retailer, a variant of **Krämer** (see KRAMER).

Kromm (157) Variant spelling of German KRUMM or Dutch KROM.

Kron (888) **1.** German, Dutch, and Swedish: from Middle High German *krōn(e)* 'garland', 'chaplet', 'diadem', Swedish *krona* (from Latin *corona*). As a German

surname it may have been a habitational name for someone who lived in a house with this sign or a nickname for a bald or tonsured man. The Swedish surname, on the other hand, is probably an ornamental name. **2.** Jewish (Ashkenazic): variant of KRONE. **3.** Jewish (Ashkenazic): metronymic from the Yiddish personal name *kroyne*, a derivative of Yiddish *kroyn* 'crown'.

GIVEN NAMES German 6%. *Fritz* (2), *Helmut* (2), *Otto* (2), *Gerhard, Gunther, Hermann, Kurt, Manfred, Othmar, Siegfried, Winfried*.

Kronberg (329) **1.** German: habitational name from any of the places named Kronberg, near Frankfurt, in Hesse, and (commonly) in Bavaria. **2.** Jewish (Ashkenazic) and Swedish: ornamental name from German *Krone*, Swedish *kron* 'crown' + German *Berg*, Swedish *berg* 'mountain'.

GIVEN NAMES German 4%; Scandinavian 4%. *Kurt* (2), *Orlo* (2), *Alfons*.

Kronberger (128) German and Jewish (Ashkenazic): habitational name for someone from any of the various places named KRONBERG.

GIVEN NAME German 4%. *Fritz* (2).

Kroncke (107) Respelling of German **Kröhnke**: from a diminutive of Middle Low German *krōn, krān* 'crane'.

GIVEN NAMES German 13%. *Fritz* (2), *Hans, Kurt*.

Krone (990) **1.** German: variant of KRON. **2.** Jewish (Ashkenazic): from German *Krone* 'crown', probably as an ornamental name. **3.** German: nickname for a slender, long-legged individual, from a dialect form of KRANICH. **4.** Altered spelling of Dutch KROON.

GIVEN NAMES German 4%. *Heinz* (2), *Helmut* (2), *Kurt* (2), *Dieter, Merwin, Otto, Reinhart*.

Kronebusch (131) German: unexplained.

Kronen (105) Dutch: variant of KROON.

Kronenberg (448) **1.** German and Swiss German: habitational name from a place called Kronenberg (there is one near Wuppertal), or possibly from any of the places called Kronberg (see KRONBERG). **2.** Jewish (Ashkenazic): ornamental name from German *Krone* 'crown' + German *Berg* 'mountain', 'hill'.

Kronenberger (215) German and Swiss German: habitational name for someone from KRONENBERG.

GIVEN NAMES German 5%. *Gunter* (2), *Gerhard*.

Kronenwetter (118) German: habitational name for someone from any of numerous places in Bavaria and Austria named Kranewitt, from Old High German *kranaw-itu* 'juniper tree', or possibly a topographic name for someone who lived by a juniper, Middle High German *kranewite*.

Kroner (479) German (also **Kröner**): **1.** habitational name for someone from a

place called Kronau, near Bruchsal. **2.** from a noun derivative of Middle Low German *kronen* 'to grumble', hence a nickname for a cantankerous person. **3.** from an old personal name based on Old High German *gruoni*, Old Saxon *grōni* 'green' in the sense of 'fresh new life'. **4.** habitational name for someone who lived at a house distinguished by the sign of a crown, from Middle High German *krōne*.

GIVEN NAMES German 6%. *Kurt* (3), *Klaus* (2), *Aloysius, Georg*.

Krones (103) German: probably a patronymic from KRON or KRONE.

Kronfeld (104) Jewish (Ashkenazic): ornamental name from German *Krone* 'crown' + *Feld* 'field'.

GIVEN NAMES Jewish 8%. *Chana, Yakov*.

Kronholm (111) **1.** Swedish: ornamental name composed of the elements *kron* 'crown' + *holm* 'inlet', 'island'. **2.** Danish: habitational name from a farm named with the same elements as in 1.

GIVEN NAME Scandinavian 8%; German 6%. *Kurt*.

Kronick (246) Jewish (from Lithuania): habitational name for someone from a place called Kroni.

Kroninger (100) German (**Kröninger**): habitational name for someone from Kröning in Bavaria.

Kronk (293) German: **1.** nickname for a sickly person, from Middle High German *kranc* 'physically weak'. **2.** from Low German *Kraneke* 'crane' (see KRAHN).

Kronmiller (106) Americanized spelling of German **Kromüller**, a habitational name for someone from a place called Kronmühle 'crown mill'.

Krontz (144) Variant spelling of German KRANTZ.

Krook (159) **1.** Dutch: nickname for someone with long curly hair, from Middle Dutch *crook* 'curly'. **2.** Swedish (also found in Finland): variant of KROK. **3.** Respelling of Polish and Ashkenazic Jewish KRUK.

GIVEN NAMES Scandinavian 8%; Finnish 6%; German 5%. *Evald, Lennart, Oluf; Eero, Jorma, Orvo, Saara; Kurt* (2).

Kroon (467) **1.** Dutch: from Middle Dutch *croen(e)*, a habitational name for someone living at a house distinguished by the sign of a crown, or a topographic name from a common field name from this word. **2.** Swedish: see KRON.

Kropf (835) German and Swiss German: **1.** from Middle High German *kropf* 'goiter', hence a nickname for a person with a conspicuous crop due to goiter. **2.** nickname for a person of short stature (see KROPP).

GIVEN NAMES German 4%. *Siegfried* (2), *Alois, Aloys, Arno, Jurgen, Liesl, Matthias*.

Kropidlowski (101) Polish: habitational name for someone from Kropidło in Kielce voivodeship, named with kropidło 'aspergillum'.

GIVEN NAME German 4%. *Hedwig.*

Kropp (1465) **1.** German and Dutch: nickname for a person with a conspicuous crop due to goiter, from Middle High German *kropf* 'goiter', Middle Dutch *crop* 'crop', 'gizzard', 'maw'. **2.** North German: from Middle Low German *krūp* 'small farm animals'; possibly a nickname for a small farmer. **3.** German: nickname for a person of short stature, a cripple, or a midget, from Middle Low German *krop* 'torso'. **4.** German: habitational name from a place called Kropp in Schleswig.

GIVEN NAMES German 4%. *Heinz* (3), *Ernst* (2), *Kurt* (2), *Erwin, Gunter, Helmut, Inge, Klaus, Manfred, Otto, Reinhold.*

Krosch (102) German: **1.** variant of GROSCH. **2.** perhaps also a variant of German **Krösche**, from Middle Low German *krōseke* 'pitcher'.

Kroschel (122) South German (**Kröschel**): variant of **Gröschel** (see GROESCHEL).

GIVEN NAME German 10%. *Kurt* (4).

Kross (377) German: **1.** metonymic occupational name for a maker of mugs and jugs, from Middle Low German *krūs, kros* 'pitcher', 'ceramic drinking vessel'. **2.** (**Kröss**): variant of KRESS 2.

Kroth (130) German: **1.** from a Germanic personal name formed with an element cognate with Gothic *hrōtheigs* 'fame', 'victory'. Compare KRAUT, KRUPP. **2.** respelling of KRAUTH.

Krotz (258) **1.** German: from a short form of any of various Germanic personal names formed with *hrōd* 'renown', 'victory'. **2.** German: from Alemannic **Grotz**, meaning 'shrimp', possibly a nickname for a little man. **3.** Possibly a respelling of German KRATZ.

GIVEN NAMES German 4%. *Achim, Florian, Kurt, Otto.*

Krotzer (244) German: derivative of KROTZ.

Kroupa (442) Czech: from *kroupa* 'pearl barley', probably a metonymic occupational name for someone who worked in a mill or for a grain dealer.

Krouse (1176) Americanized form of German KRAUS.

Krout (690) Americanized form of German and Jewish KRAUT.

Kruchten (232) Dutch: habitational name from Krochten in North Brabant, Cruchten in Luxembourg, or Kruchten-Maasbracht in Limburg.

GIVEN NAMES French 4%. *Alban, Jean-Claude.*

Kruck (201) **1.** German (also **Krück**): topographic name for someone who lived by a field named with Middle Low German *krucke* 'crooked piece of wood', 'crutch', 'crosier'. **2.** German (also **Krück**): metonymic occupational name for a maker of jugs, from Low German *Kruke* 'jug'.

3. Dutch: nickname for someone who used a crutch or walking stick, Middle Dutch *crucke, cricke*. **4.** Respelling of Polish and Jewish KRUK.

GIVEN NAMES German 7%. *Ewald, Hans.*

Kruckeberg (199) German (**Krückeberg**): habitational name from a place so named near Herford, Westphalia.

Kruckenberg (334) German (**Krückenberg**): habitational name for someone from a place so named in Bavaria.

GIVEN NAMES German 4%. *Kurt* (2), *Erhardt, Lorenz.*

Kruczek (239) Polish and Jewish (from Poland): nickname for someone with black hair, from a Polish diminutive of *kruk* 'raven' (see KRUK).

GIVEN NAMES Polish 6%. *Cecylia, Henryk, Ignacy, Leszek.*

Krueger (16176) German (**Krüger**) and Jewish (Ashkenazic): **1.** occupational name for a maker or seller of stoneware mugs and jugs, from an agent derivative of Middle High German *kruoc* 'jug', 'pitcher', German *Krug*. **2.** occupational name from *Krüger* 'innkeeper', an agent derivative of *Krug* 'inn', 'tavern', from Middle Low German *krūch, krōch* (probably originally a different word from 1, with which it has subsequently fallen together).

GIVEN NAMES German 5%. *Kurt* (64), *Otto* (33), *Erwin* (22), *Gerhard* (8), *Fritz* (6), *Heinz* (6), *Ewald* (5), *Hans* (5), *Dieter* (4), *Manfred* (4), *Ernst* (3), *Guenter* (3).

Kruel (107) German (**Krül**): variant of KROLL 1.

GIVEN NAMES German 5%. *Kurt, Manfred.*

Kruer (199) North German (**Krüer**): **1.** occupational name for a herb or vegetable dealer or a maker of herbal medicines, from a contracted form of Low German **Krüder**, an agent noun from Middle Low German *krut* 'green plant', '(medicinal) herb', 'spice'. **2.** from an old personal name denoting 'fame', 'victory'.

GIVEN NAMES French 5%; German 5%. *Alban* (2); *Hans.*

Krug (3281) **1.** German and Jewish (Ashkenazic): metonymic occupational name for a maker or seller of mugs and jugs, from Middle High German *kruoc* 'jug', 'drinking vessel'; alternatively, mostly in southern and eastern Germany, a nickname for a heavy drinker. **2.** occupational nickname for a tavern keeper, from *Krug* 'inn', 'tavern', especially in northern Germany.

Kruger (5622) German (**Krüger**) and Jewish (Ashkenazic): see KRUEGER.

GIVEN NAMES German 5%. *Kurt* (23), *Hans* (7), *Otto* (6), *Gerhard* (3), *Klaus* (3), *Konrad* (2), *Arno* (2), *Dieter* (2), *Elke* (2), *Erwin* (2), *Ewald* (2), *Fritz* (2).

Kruggel (114) Possibly a respelling of German **Krugel** or **Krügel**, from a diminutive of KRUG.

GIVEN NAMES German 10%. *Kurt* (2), *Ulrich.*

Krugh (201) Variant spelling of German KRUG.

Krugman (370) German (**Krugmann**) and Jewish (Ashkenazic): occupational name for a tavern keeper or a maker or seller of mugs and jugs, a variant of KRUEGER.

GIVEN NAMES Jewish 4%. *Faina, Hyman, Meyer.*

Kruis (120) **1.** Dutch (**van de Kruis**): topographic name for someone who lived by a village or roadside cross, from Dutch *kruis* 'cross'. **2.** German: nickname meaning 'crab', from Middle High German *kruiz.*

GIVEN NAME Dutch 4%. *Derk.*

Kruizenga (105) Dutch: unexplained.

GIVEN NAMES Dutch 4%. *Gerrit, Gerritt.*

Kruk (582) **1.** Polish and Jewish (Ashkenazic): nickname (Polish) or ornamental name (Jewish), from Polish *kruk* 'raven'. **2.** Dutch: variant spelling of KRUCK.

GIVEN NAMES Polish 9%. *Danuta* (2), *Stanislaw* (2), *Andrzej, Beata, Edyta, Henryk, Irena, Jadwiga, Jaroslaw, Jolanta, Jozef, Karol.*

Krukowski (379) Polish: habitational name for someone from any of various places called Kruki, Kruków, or Krukowo, named with *kruk* 'raven'.

GIVEN NAMES Polish 7%. *Stanislaw* (2), *Andrzej, Czeslaw, Franciszek, Henryk, Marcin, Ryszard.*

Krul (184) **1.** Dutch: nickname for a person with a curly hair, from Dutch *krul* 'curl' (see KROLL). **2.** Jewish (eastern Ashkenazic): variant of KROL 1.

Krull (1643) **1.** German and Dutch: variant of KROLL 1. **2.** Jewish (Ashkenazic): variant of KROL 1.

Krum (745) **1.** German: variant spelling of KRUMM. **2.** Jewish (Ashkenazic): nickname from German *krumm* 'crooked', 'deformed'. **3.** Scandinavian: of uncertain origin, probably German.

Krumenacker (135) German: habitational name from a lost or unidentified place.

Krumholz (272) German and Jewish (Ashkenazic): from *Krumbholz* 'bent timber', 'mountain pine', hence probably a metonymic occupational name for a cartwright or wheelwright. As a Jewish surname it is ornamental.

Krumins (125) Latvian (**Krūmiņš**): topographic name from *krūms* 'bush'.

GIVEN NAMES Latvian 42%; German 7%; Scandinavian 4%. *Arvids* (2), *Aivars, Aleksandrs, Arturs, Egons, Eriks, Girts, Verners, Voldemars; Andris* (2), *Juris* (2), *Karlis* (2), *Atis, Laimonis, Maris, Modris, Peteris, Uldis, Valdis; Bernhard, Egon, Herta, Viktor; Nils; Miriam, Sol.*

Krumm (981) German: nickname from Middle High German *krum* 'crooked', 'deformed'; it may have been applied in the literal sense to a hunchback or cripple, but equally it may have denoted someone who was 'bent' in the abstract sense, i.e. 'dishonest' or 'false'.

Krumme (164) German: **1.** variant of KRUMM. **2.** topographic name for someone who lived at a bend in the road, from Middle High German, Middle Low German *krumme* 'bend'.
GIVEN NAMES German 8%. *Gunter, Klaus, Reiner, Ulrich, Ursel.*

Krummel (335) German (**Krümmel**): **1.** nickname for a crippled person (see KRUMM). **2.** habitational name for someone from one of the various places called Krümmel, for example near Koblenz.

Krummen (100) German and Swiss German: unexplained.

Krumnow (112) Possibly a German habitational name from Kromnów in Poland.
GIVEN NAME German 5%. *Otto* (2).

Krump (160) German: **1.** variant of KRUMM. **2.** from an old personal name formed with Old High German *hruom* 'fame'.

Krumrey (186) **1.** North German: variant of **Krumreihn**, from Middle Low German *krum* 'bent', 'crooked' + *rein* 'ridge', 'margin of a field', hence a topographic name for someone who lived by a bend in the bank or edge of a field or by a field with a crooked boundary. **2.** German: from an old personal name, from Old High German *hruom* 'fame'.
GIVEN NAMES German 4%. *Dietmar, Ulrike.*

Krumwiede (343) North German: topographic name for someone who lived by gnarled old willow tree, from Middle Low German *krum* 'bent', 'crooked' + *wiede* 'willow'.
GIVEN NAMES German 5%. *Kurt* (3), *Armin, Arno, Erwin, Lorenz.*

Krupa (1406) **1.** Polish, Slovak, and eastern German (of Slavic origin): from Polish, Sorbian *krupa* 'barley', hence a metonymic occupational name for a dealer in barley. **2.** Czech: variant of KROUPA.
GIVEN NAMES Polish 7%. *Zofia* (4), *Andrzej* (3), *Casimir* (3), *Halina* (3), *Grzegorz* (2), *Stanislaw* (2), *Wladyslaw* (2), *Aleksander, Bogdan, Dariusz, Elzbieta, Ewa.*

Krupicka (170) Czech and Slovak (**Krupička**): nickname meaning 'little pearl barley', a pet form of KROUPA.

Krupinski (398) Polish (**Krupiński**) and Jewish (eastern Ashkenazic): habitational name for someone from Krupin in Suwałki voivodeship, or any of various other places named with *krupa* 'barley'.
GIVEN NAMES Polish 7%. *Witold* (2), *Boguslawa, Henryk, Ignatius, Jerzy, Kazimerz, Wieslaw.*

Krupka (350) **1.** Polish, Czech, eastern German, and Jewish (from Poland): metonymic occupational name for a grain dealer, from Slavic *krupka* 'grain'. **2.** Czech and German: nickname for an ill-mannered person, from old Czech *krupy* 'crude'. **3.** Jewish (from Belarus): habitational name for someone from a place called Krupka, now in Belarus.

GIVEN NAMES Polish 5%. *Jacek* (4), *Aniela, Stanislaw.*

Krupke (131) German (also **Krüpke**): metonymic occupational name for a grain dealer, from a Germanized form of Slavic **krupka**.
GIVEN NAMES German 5%. *Fritz, Wilhelm.*

Krupnick (214) Jewish (eastern Ashkenazic): Germanized or Americanized spelling of KRUPNIK.

Krupnik (133) Czech (**Krupník**), Polish, and Jewish (eastern Ashkenazic): from a noun derivative of *kroupa* 'pearl barley'. This may have been an occupational name for a dealer in barley, or a nickname with any of various applications. Yiddish *krupnik* also means 'pearl barley soup', and the Jewish name may also be ornamental.
GIVEN NAMES Russian 18%; Jewish 17%; Polish 4%. *Grigory* (2), *Leonid* (2), *Aleksandr, Arkadiy, Gennadiy, Mikhail, Raisa, Vladimir, Vyacheslav, Yasha, Yekaterina, Yevgeniya; Baruch, Chanie, Eliezer, Gersh, Meir, Moysey, Rozalia, Shlomo; Casimir.*

Krupp (1257) German: **1.** nickname for a disabled person, from a derivative of Middle Low German *krupen* 'to creep'. **2.** from a Germanic personal name formed with an element cognate with Gothic *hrōtheigs* 'fame', 'victory' 'fame'. Compare KRAUT, KROTH.

Kruppa (170) Eastern German: **1.** nickname for an ill-mannered person, from Czech *krupy* 'crude'. **2.** nickname for a grain dealer, from Slavic *krupa* 'grain'. Compare Czech KROUPA.
GIVEN NAMES German 8%. *Horst, Otto, Wolfgang.*

Krupski (315) Polish, Belorussian, and Jewish (eastern Ashkenazic): habitational name for someone from Krupy in Poland, Krupiai or Kruopiai in Lithuania, or Krupka or Krupa in Belarus, all named with *krupa* 'barley'.

Krus (173) German: variant of KRAUS.

Kruschke (183) German: derivative of **Krusch**, from Sorbian *kruscha* 'pear tree'; a topographic name for someone who lived by a pear tree or perhaps a metonymic occupational name for a fruit seller.

Kruse (8482) **1.** German and Danish: nickname for someone with curly hair, a Low German variant of KRAUS. **2.** German: from Middle High German *kruse* 'pitcher', 'ceramic drinking vessel'; a metonymic occupational name for a maker or seller of jugs or a nickname for a heavy drinker.

Krusemark (196) German: habitational name from a place called Krusemark, near Magdeburg.

Krusen (102) Probably an Americanized spelling of Dutch **Cruyssen** (see CRUSAN), or a North German cognate of this.
GIVEN NAME German 6%. *Kurt* (2).

Kruser (180) German: see KRUSE

Krusinski (149) Polish (**Krusiński**): habitational name for someone from a place called Krusin.

Kruszewski (309) Polish: habitational name for someone from any of the places called Kruszew or Kruszewo. For the etymology of the place names, see KRUSZYNSKI.
GIVEN NAMES Polish 14%. *Wieslaw* (2), *Zygmunt* (2), *Andrzej, Casimir, Czeslaw, Jacek, Jadwiga, Jaroslaw, Leszek, Mieczyslaw, Ryszard, Tomasz.*

Kruszka (150) Polish: nickname for a small or insignificant person, from *kruszek* 'crumb', 'fragment'.

Kruszynski (135) Polish (**Kruszyński**): habitational name for someone from any of various places called Kruszyn, Kruszyna, or Kruszyny. These place names are probably from Polish dialect *krusza* 'pear tree' or from a derivative of *kruszyć* 'to crumble', 'fragment', or from a derivative of *kruch* 'block', 'lump'.
GIVEN NAMES German 4%; French 4%. *Kurt; Alphonse, Camille.*

Kruth (110) German: unexplained.

Krutsch (127) German: from Slavic *křz* 'block of wood', 'piece of cleared land', hence a metonymic occupational name for a forester or a topographic name for someone who lived on or farmed land that had recently been cleared.
GIVEN NAME German 4%. *Kurt.*

Krutsinger (252) Respelling of German **Kreuziger**, a variant of KREUTZER 1 and 3.

Krutz (280) German (**Krütz**): variant of KREUTZ.

Kruzan (130) Probably an Americanized spelling of Dutch **Cruyssen** (see CRUSAN), or a North German cognate of this.

Kruzel (280) Polish (**Krużel**): metonymic occupational name for a potter, from *krużel* 'small clay utensil', 'pot'.
GIVEN NAMES Polish 9%. *Katarzyna* (2), *Andrzej, Casimir, Ignatius, Jacek, Kazimierz, Mateusz, Waclaw, Zofia.*

Kruzich (108) Croatian (**Kružić**): of uncertain origin. Perhaps a derivative of *krug* 'circle', 'ring', and so a nickname for a fat person.

Krych (151) Polish: from a pet form of the personal name *Krystian* (see CHRISTIAN).

Kryder (178) Variant spelling of German **Krüder, Krüter** (see KRUER).

Kryger (248) **1.** Dutch and Danish: occupational name for a soldier, from Middle Dutch *criger*, German *Krieger* 'warrior'. **2.** Polish and Jewish (Ashkenazic): Polish spelling of German KRIEGER 'soldier'. **3.** Polish and Jewish (Ashkenazic): Polish spelling of German KRUEGER 'innkeeper'.

Krygier (228) Polish and Jewish: variant of KRYGER.

Krygowski (109) Polish: habitational name from a place called Kryg.
GIVEN NAMES Polish 7%. *Casimir, Karol, Kazimierz.*

Krynicki (102) Polish: habitational name from any of numerous places called Krynica, named with *krynica* 'spring', 'well'. GIVEN NAMES Polish 13%. *Andrzej, Bogdan, Lukasz, Miroslaw, Witold.*

Krysiak (305) Polish: patronymic from a pet form of the personal name *Krzysztof* (see CHRISTOPHER) or *Krystian* (see CHRISTIAN).
GIVEN NAMES Polish 17%. *Tadeusz* (3), *Andrzej* (2), *Elzbieta* (2), *Lech* (2), *Zofia* (2), *Casimir, Henryk, Karol, Ryszard, Stanislaw, Sylwester, Thadeus.*

Krysinski (128) Polish (**Krysiński**): habitational name for someone from a place called Kryszyń or Krysin.
GIVEN NAMES Polish 6%. *Andrzej, Boguslaw.*

Kryszak (106) Polish: from a pet form of the personal name *Krzysztof* (see CHRISTOPHER).
GIVEN NAME Polish 4%. *Zigmund.*

Krzemien (102) Polish (**Krzemień**): from the vocabulary word *krzemień* 'flint', either a topographic name for someone living in a flinty place or a nickname for a hard man.
GIVEN NAMES Polish 15%. *Bogdan, Casimir, Ewa, Jolanta, Jozef, Marcin, Zbigniew.*

Krzeminski (338) Polish (**Krzemiński**): habitational name for someone from any of numerous places named with Polish *krzemień* 'flint'.
GIVEN NAMES Polish 7%. *Bogdan* (3), *Boguslaw, Dariusz, Dorota, Jacek, Pawel, Zdzislaw.*

Krzeszewski (23) Polish: habitational name for someone from places called Krzeszew, Krzeszów, or Krzeszowice, named with the Polish personal name *Krzesz*, a short form of *Krzesisław*, composed of the Slavic elements *krzesić* 'raise' + *slav* 'glory'.

Krzycki (101) Polish: habitational name for someone from Krycko in Leszno voivodeship.

Krzykowski (105) Polish: habitational name for someone from a place called Krzykosy, from the nickname *Krzykos* 'shouter', from *krzyk* 'shout'.
GIVEN NAME Polish 6%. *Waclaw.*

Krzywicki (199) Polish: habitational name for someone from Krzywica or Krzywice, both so named from Polish *krzywy* 'crooked'.
GIVEN NAMES Polish 6%. *Czeslaw, Halina.*

Krzyzaniak (120) Polish (**Krzyżaniak**): patronymic from the personal name *Krzyżan*, a derivative of *kryż* 'cross'.
GIVEN NAME Polish 5%. *Urszula.*

Krzyzanowski (227) Polish (**Krzyżżanowski**): habitational name for someone from Krzyżanów in Piotrków or Płock voivodeships, Krzyżanowo in Płock or Poznań voivodeships, or various places in Poland called Krzyżanowice, all named with *krzyż* 'cross'.
GIVEN NAMES Polish 16%. *Andrzej* (2), *Jacek* (2), *Ludwik* (2), *Czeslaw, Danuta, Jerzy, Kazimierz, Ryszard, Slawomir, Wlodzimierz.*

Ksiazek (194) Polish (**Książek**): **1.** nickname meaning 'little priest' or possibly a patronymic for an illegitimate son of a priest, from *ksiądz* 'priest' + the diminutive suffix -*ek*. **2.** nickname meaning 'little prince', from a diminutive of *książę* 'prince'.
GIVEN NAMES Polish 10%. *Tadeusz* (2), *Boleslaw, Bronislaus, Grazyna, Kazimierz, Thadeus, Waclaw.*

Ku (872) **1.** Chinese 顾: variant of GU 1. **2.** Chinese 谷: variant of GU 2. **3.** Chinese 古: variant of GU 3. **4.** Korean: there are three Chinese characters for the surname Ku. The most common of the three claims thirty-two clans, but only two can be documented. The other two Ku surnames each have one clan, with its own Chinese character. All four of the Ku clans immigrated from China. The clans that use the more common character came in two waves: the first settled in the Nŭngsŏng sometime before 945, and the second, which settled in Ch'angwŏn, arrived in 1224. The name of the immigrant who founded the first of these two clans has been lost; but the name of the second is Ku Chon-yu. Members of these two clans can be found throughout the Korean peninsula, but 45 percent of them live in Kyŏngsang South province, while 20 percent of them live in Seoul and Kyŏnggi province. The founder of the clan that uses the other Ku character was named Ku T'ae-rim. He was an emissary for Tang China on his way to Japan when a storm blew his ship onto the shores of Koguryŏ Korea in 663. He settled in Koguryŏ territory and subsequently held a post in that government. Koguryŏ was a Korean kingdom which existed in the northern part of the Korean peninsula from 37 BC to AD 668. Its territory was incorporated into Shilla when the peninsula was unified in 668. Most of the modern-day members of this clan live in Ch'ungch'ŏng province. Very little is known of the origins of the clan which uses the third Ku character. There are only a few families which still use this character in Korea; they live in Kyŏngsang province and Kangwŏn province.
GIVEN NAMES Chinese/Korean 33%. *Sung* (4), *Yong* (4), *Chen* (3), *Kyung* (3), *Mei* (3), *Chan* (2), *Hyon* (2), *Kyong* (2), *Pei* (2), *Pin* (2), *Sen* (2), *Wei Chun* (2); *Jeong* (2), *Seong* (2), *Yiming* (2), *Chang, Chol, Chong, Chong Sik, Choon, Hae, Jin Soon, Pai, Pak.*

Kuan (281) **1.** Chinese 关: variant of GUAN 1. **2.** Chinese 管: variant of GUAN 2. **3.** Filipino: unexplained.
GIVEN NAMES Chinese 24%; Spanish 12%. *Beng* (2), *Hang* (2), *Wai* (2), *Wang* (2), *Chee, Chen, Cheng, Hsiang, Hsien, Hui, In, Jeng*; *Caridad* (2), *Jose* (2), *Leandro* (2), *Luis* (2), *Anthonio, Arturo, Augustina, Joaquin, Lourdes, Marina, Mario, Rafael.*

Kuang (392) **1.** Chinese 邝: from Kuang Chengzi, a legendary figure from the time of the legendary emperor Huang Di (2697–2595 BC). **2.** Chinese 匡: from a city called Kuang that existed in the state of Lu during the Zhou dynasty (1122–221 BC).
GIVEN NAMES Chinese 64%. *Jian* (3), *Mei* (3), *Fu* (2), *Guang* (2), *Guo* (2), *Guo Rong* (2), *Hong* (2), *Hui* (2), *Jian Ming* (2), *Lei* (2), *Li* (2), *Ping* (2).

Kuba (399) **1.** Dutch, Polish, Czech, Slovak, and Jewish (Ashkenazic): from *Kuba*, a pet form of the personal name *Jakub* (see JACOB). **2.** Japanese: written with characters meaning 'long time' and 'method', this name is found mostly in the Ryūkyū Islands.
GIVEN NAMES Japanese 4%. *Fumiko, Masayuki, Misako, Shizuko, Tadashi, Yasuki, Yoshio, Yoshiya, Yoshiyuki.*

Kubach (103) German (of Slavic origin): from a derivative of *Kuba*, a pet form of the personal name *Jakub* (see JACOB).
GIVEN NAMES German 12%. *Lorenz* (3), *Reinhold.*

Kubacki (394) Polish: habitational name for someone from Kubaczyn in Poznań voivodeship, a place so named from *Kuba*, a pet form of the personal name *Jakub* (see JACOB).
GIVEN NAMES Polish 5%. *Zbigniew* (2), *Andrzej, Bronislaw, Wojciech.*

Kubal (134) Polish, Czech, Slovak, and German: from a derivative of *Kuba*, a pet form of the personal name *Jakub* (see JACOB).

Kubala (513) Polish, Czech, Slovak, and German: from a derivative of *Kuba*, a pet form of the personal name *Jakub* (see JACOB).
GIVEN NAMES Polish 4%. *Stanislaw* (2), *Casimir, Teofil, Zbigniew, Zygmunt.*

Kuban (184) **1.** Polish, Czech, and Slovak (**Kubáň**): from a derivative of *Kuba*, a short form of the personal name *Jakub* (see JACOB). **2.** Polish: nickname for a fixer or a corrupt official, from *kuban* 'gratification', 'bribe'.

Kubas (236) **1.** Polish, Czech, and Slovak (also **Kubaš**): from a derivative of the personal name *Kuba*, a pet form of *Jakub* (see JACOB). **2.** Polish: nickname from *kubas* 'mug', 'tumbler'.

Kubat (460) Polish and Czech (**Kubát**): from a derivative of the personal name *Kuba*, a pet form of *Jakub* (see JACOB).

Kube (445) German (of Slavic origin): from the personal name *Kuba*, a pet form of *Jakub* (see JACOB).
GIVEN NAMES German 5%. *Kurt* (2), *Lutz, Manfred, Otto, Wolfram.*

Kubeck (137) Germanized or Americanized form of KUBEK.

Kubecka (137) German form of Polish **Kubeczka**, from a derivative of the personal name *Kuba*, a pet form of *Jakub* (see JACOB).
GIVEN NAME German 5%. *Otto* (2).

Kubek (128) Polish, Czech, and German: from a pet form of *Kuba*, itself a pet form of the personal name *Jakub* (see JACOB).
GIVEN NAME Polish 4%. *Casimir.*

Kubena (179) Czech (**Kuběna**): **1.** from a derivative of the personal name *Kuba*, a pet form of *Jakub* (see JACOB). **2.** perhaps also a nickname from Old Czech *kuběna* 'concubine'.

Kubera (115) Polish and Czech: from a derivative of the personal name *Kuba*, a pet form of the personal *Jakub* (see JACOB).
GIVEN NAMES German 5%. *Alois, Fritz, Hedwig.*

Kuberski (146) Polish: habitational name for someone from Kubery in Sieradz voivodeship.

Kubes (293) Czech (**Kubeš**): from a derivative of the personal name *Kuba*, a pet form of the personal name *Jakub* (see JACOB).

Kubesh (129) Americanized spelling of Czech **Kubeš** (see KUBES).

Kubiak (1349) Polish: patronymic from KUBA.

Kubic (201) Polish and Czech (**Kubič**): from a derivative of the personal name *Kuba*, a pet form of *Jakub* (see JACOB).

Kubica (194) Polish and Czech: from a derivative of the personal name *Kuba*, a pet form of *Jakub* (see JACOB).
GIVEN NAMES Polish 6%. *Casimir, Ewa, Irena, Wladyslaw.*

Kubicek (498) Czech (**Kubíček**): from a double diminutive of the personal name *Kuba*, itself a pet form of *Jakub* (see JACOB).

Kubick (158) Germanized or Americanized spelling of Czech and Polish KUBIK.

Kubicki (393) Polish: habitational name for someone from Kubice in Ciechanów voivodeship, so named from the personal name KUBA.
GIVEN NAMES Polish 7%. *Dariusz* (3), *Andrzej, Boguslaw, Janusz, Rafal, Tadeusz, Wieslaw, Zofia.*

Kubik (1167) Polish, Czech, and Slovak (**Kubík**): from a pet form of the personal name *Kuba*, itself a pet form of *Jakub* (see JACOB).
GIVEN NAMES Polish 4%. *Piotr* (2), *Beata, Grzegorz, Halina, Jerzy, Lech, Leslaw, Malgorzata, Rafal, Ryszard, Tadeusz, Tomasz.*

Kubilus (116) Lithuanian: derivative of the personal name *Jakub* (see JACOB).

Kubin (254) Czech (**Kubín**): from a derivative of the personal name *Kuba*, a pet form of *Jakub* (see JACOB).
GIVEN NAME German 5%. *Otto* (2).

Kubina (123) Polish: from a derivative of the personal name *Kuba*, a pet form of *Jakub* (see JACOB).

Kubinski (266) Polish (**Kubiński**): from a derivative of *Kuba*, a pet form of the personal name *Jakub* (see JACOB), with the addition of the common surname ending -*iński.*

Kubis (257) Polish (also **Kubiś, Kubisz**), Latvian, and Lithuanian (**Kubys**): from a derivative of the personal name *Kuba*, a pet form of *Jakub* (see JACOB).
GIVEN NAMES Polish 5%. *Andrzej* (2), *Bogdan, Gustaw.*

Kubisiak (179) Polish: patronymic from *Kubis*, a pet form of the personal name *Jakub* (see JACOB).

Kubista (143) Czech (**Kubišta**): from a derivative of *Kuba*, a pet form of the personal name *Jakub* (see JACOB).

Kubit (144) Polish: from a derivative of *Kuba*, a pet form of the personal name *Jakub* (see JACOB).
GIVEN NAMES Polish 5%. *Andrzej, Jozef.*

Kubitz (255) Eastern German: from a Polish, Czech, or other Slavic pet form (e.g. KUBIT) of *Jakub* (see JACOB).
GIVEN NAMES German 6%. *Frieda, Fritz, Kurt, Lothar.*

Kubler (206) German: **1.** variant of **Kübler** (see KUEBLER). **2.** metonymic occupational name for a farmer, from Sorbian *kublo* 'farm'.
GIVEN NAMES German 10%. *Klaus* (3), *Ekkehard, Friedrich, Hans, Horst, Manfred.*

Kubly (214) South German and Swiss German: from a pet form of **Kübel** (see KUEBLER).

Kubo (384) **1.** Japanese: 'sunken ground'; variously written, mostly with characters used phonetically. Found mostly in western Japan, apparently taken from several habitational names. Many unrelated families descend from various branches of the TAIRA, MINAMOTO, and other great families. **2.** Czech and Slovak: from a variant of the personal name *Kuba*, a pet form of *Jakub* (see JACOB).
GIVEN NAMES Japanese 55%. *Hiroshi* (5), *Hayato* (4), *Kazuya* (3), *Koichi* (3), *Takayuki* (3), *Tetsuo* (3), *Aki* (2), *Masao* (2), *Masayuki* (2), *Ryu* (2), *Sadao* (2), *Shigeo* (2).

Kubota (458) **1.** Japanese: 'sunken rice paddy'; variously written, most usually with characters used phonetically; found throughout Japan and the Ryūkyū Islands. **2.** Czech: from a derivative of *Kuba*, a pet form of the personal name *Jakub* (see JACOB).
GIVEN NAMES Japanese 62%. *Hideo* (4), *Miho* (3), *Shiro* (3), *Tadashi* (3), *Takayuki* (3), *Hajime* (2), *Hiromi* (2), *Hiroshi* (2), *Kaoru* (2), *Kazuo* (2), *Keiko* (2), *Kenichiro* (2).

Kuc (171) Polish: nickname from *kuc* 'pony', applied as a nickname to a short man.
GIVEN NAMES Polish 17%. *Wiktor* (2), *Czeslaw, Danuta, Genowefa, Henryka, Janina, Leszek, Stanislaw, Tadeusz, Wasyl, Zofia.*

Kucera (1892) Czech and Slovak: nickname for someone with curly hair, from *kučera*

'curl'. This is the eighth most common Czech surname. Other Czech surnames with the same meaning are **Kudrna** and **Kadeř**.

Kuch (462) German: metonymic occupational name for a pastry cook, from German *kuchen* 'cake', or simply a variant of KOCH 'cook'.

Kuchan (121) Slovenian and Croatian (**Kučan**): unexplained. The Slovenian surname originates from the Goričko region.

Kuchar (500) **1.** Czech (**Kuchař**) Slovak (**Kuchár**) and Polish (**Kucharz**): occupational name for a cook (from Middle High German *koch* 'cook' + -*ař* Czech suffix of agent nouns). **2.** Americanized spelling of Slovenian and Croatian KUHAR.

Kucharczyk (128) Polish: from a diminutive of **Kucharz** 'cook' (see KUCHAR), or from the vocabulary word *kucharczyk* 'cook's apprentice'.
GIVEN NAMES Polish 19%. *Maciej* (2), *Stanislaw* (2), *Casimir, Jerzy, Waclawa, Wojciech, Zbyszek.*

Kucharek (118) Polish: from a diminutive of **Kucharz** 'cook' (see KUCHAR).
GIVEN NAME French 4%. *Andre.*

Kucharski (904) Polish: habitational name for someone from any of the various places in Poland called Kuchary, named with *kucharz* 'cook'.
GIVEN NAMES Polish 10%. *Janusz* (3), *Zbigniew* (3), *Casimir* (2), *Lech* (2), *Piotr* (2), *Tomasz* (2), *Andrzej, Basia, Bogdan, Boguslaw, Czeslaw, Ewa.*

Kuchenbecker (244) German: occupational name for a pastry cook, from Middle High German *kuoche* 'pastry' + *becker, bäcker* 'baker'.
GIVEN NAMES German 5%. *Erwin, Gerhard, Otto.*

Kuchenbrod (102) German: literally 'kitchen bread'.

Kuchenmeister (122) German: occupational name for a master cook (literally 'kitchen master'), a court official.
GIVEN NAME German 7%. *Wolfgang* (2).

Kucher (186) **1.** German: occupational name for a pastry cook, from an agent derivative of Middle High German *kuoche* 'cake', 'pastry'. **2.** German: habitational name for someone from Kuchen (Geislingen-Steig) in Württemberg. **3.** German: Germanized variant of Slavic KUCHAR 'cook'. **4.** German: (**Kücher**): of uncertain origin. **5.** Jewish (Ashkenazic): variant of KUTSCHER.
GIVEN NAMES Russian 7%; Jewish 5%; German 4%. *Lev* (2), *Aleksandr, Igor, Leonid, Sergey, Svetlana, Vladimir; Ilya; Lutz, Markus.*

Kuchera (294) Americanized spelling of Czech and Slovak **Kučera** (see KUCERA).

Kuchinski (262) Americanized spelling of Polish **Kuczyński** (see KUCZYNSKI) or **Kuciński** (see KUCINSKI).

Kuchinsky (138) **1.** Americanized spelling of Polish **Kuczyński** (see KUCZYNSKI) or **Kuciński** (see KUCINSKI). **2.** Jewish (from Belarus): habitational name for someone from Kuchin, now in Belarus.

GIVEN NAME Polish 5%. *Casimir* (2).

Kuchler (252) South German: **1.** (also **Küchler**): occupational name for a pastry cook, from an agent derivative of Middle High German *kuoche* 'cake', 'pastry'. **2.** (**Küchler**): occupational name for a pastry cook, from *Küchle*, a southern diminutive of *Kuchen* 'cake' (Middle High German *kuoche*). **3.** in Austria, occupational name for someone who worked in a kitchen, from Bavarian-Austrian *Kuchel* 'kitchen'.

GIVEN NAMES German 4%. *Frederich, Gunther.*

Kuchta (733) Polish and Czech: occupational name or nickname for a worker in a kitchen, from *kuchta* 'scullery maid', 'skivvy'.

Kucinski (282) **1.** Polish (**Kuciński**) and Jewish (from Poland): habitational name for someone from a place called Kuciny. **2.** Polish: variant of **Kuczyński** (see KUCZYNSKI).

GIVEN NAMES Polish 4%. *Karol, Zdzislaw, Zigmund.*

Kuck (745) **1.** German (**Kück**): nickname meaning 'chicken' (see KUECK). **2.** German: derivative of Slavic *kukol* 'weed', probably a nickname for a farmer who neglected his land.

GIVEN NAMES German 6%. *Kurt* (3), *Otto* (3), *Ernst* (2), *Ewald* (2), *Horst* (2), *Wilhelm.*

Kuczek (147) Polish: nickname from Polish dialect *kuczek* 'squat, crouching person', from *kucić* 'to squat or crouch'.

GIVEN NAMES Polish 12%. *Casimir, Czeslaw, Dariusz, Genowefa, Grazyna, Malgorzata.*

Kuczkowski (108) Polish: habitational name habitational name from any of numerous places called Kuczki, Kuczkowo, or Kuczków, named with the old personal name *Kucz*, diminutive *Kuczka*, or from the Old Polish words *kucza* or *kuczka* 'shed', 'shelter'.

GIVEN NAME French 4%. *Camille.*

Kuczmarski (133) Polish: of uncertain origin; probably from the Old Polish word *kuczmar* 'fur cap', a borrowing from Hungarian. This word is found in descriptions of Polish armorial bearings.

Kuczynski (533) **1.** Polish (**Kuczyński**) and Jewish (from Poland): habitational name for someone from any of various places called Kuczyn, Kuczyna, or Kuczyny. **2.** Jewish (from Poland): variant spelling of KUCINSKI.

GIVEN NAMES Polish 12%; German 4%. *Bogdan* (2), *Andrzej, Casimir, Henryk, Janina, Janusz, Jaroslaw, Krzysztof, Maciej, Mieczyslaw, Mieczyslawa; Kurt* (3), *Alois, Aloysius, Erwin, Frieda.*

Kudelka (101) Czech: variant of KOUDELKA.

Kuder (425) South German: **1.** metonymic occupational name for someone who worked or dealt with tow (hemp, broken strands of flax), early modern German *kuder*. **2.** nickname from the southern dialect term *Kuder* 'wildcat'.

GIVEN NAMES German 4%. *Horst* (2), *Armin, Franz, Klaus.*

Kudla (386) **1.** Polish (**Kudła**), Czech, and Jewish (eastern Ashkenazic): nickname from Polish *kudły*, Czech and Ukrainian *kudla* 'mop of hair'. **2.** Czech: from *kudla* 'clasp knife', 'little knife', a nickname for a small but powerfully built person.

GIVEN NAMES Polish 8%. *Leszek* (2), *Bronislaw, Casimir, Janina, Jozef, Stas, Tadeusz, Wasil, Wladyslaw.*

Kudo (172) Japanese (**Kudō**): 'potter'; some bearers descend from a branch of the southern FUJIWARA based in Izu (now part of Shizuoka prefecture). The name is found mostly in northeastern Japan.

GIVEN NAMES Japanese 76%. *Yasuhiro* (3), *Fumio* (2), *Isao* (2), *Kunio* (2), *Masaaki* (2), *Mitsuyuki* (2), *Takashi* (2), *Akihiro, Akio, Atsuko, Goro, Hideki.*

Kudrick (122) Americanized spelling of Czech **Kudřík**, a diminutive of KUDRNA.

Kudrna (326) Czech: nickname for a curly-haired person, from *kudrna* 'curly'. Compare KADER.

Kudron (119) Czech: derivative of KUDRNA 'curly'.

Kue (130) **1.** Hawaiian: unexplained. **2.** Laotian: unexplained. **3.** English: probably a variant of KEW.

GIVEN NAMES Southeast Asian 69%. *Yer* (4), *Youa* (4), *Yeng* (3), *Chia* (2), *Chue* (2), *Kao* (2), *Mee* (2), *Toua* (2), *Xee* (2), *Yee* (2), *Yia* (2), *Ying* (2), *Blong, Chai, Chong, Chou, Chung, Foung, Her, Neng, Ngia, Pao, Pheng, Phoua, Thao.*

Kuebel (123) German: occupational name for a cooper, from Middle High German *kübel* 'tub', 'barrel', or possibly a nickname for a fat man, one 'round as a barrel'.

GIVEN NAMES German 7%; Scandinavian 4%. *Klaus* (2), *Fritz; Hilmar* (2).

Kueber (114) German: occupational name for a cooper, from an agent derivative of KUEBEL 'tub', 'vat', 'barrel'.

Kuebler (970) German (**Kübler**): occupational name for a cooper, from an agent derivative of Middle High German *kübel* 'tub', 'vat', 'barrel'. Alternatively, but less likely, it may be a derivative of the Franconian dialect word *Kobel* 'hut', 'dovecote', here denoting a farm laborer's cottage, and hence a name for a cotter (a peasant occupying a tied cottage belonging to a farm).

GIVEN NAMES German 5%. *Kurt* (5), *Erwin* (2), *Wilhelm* (2), *Fritz, Konrad, Reinhold, Theresia.*

Kuechenmeister (132) German (**Küchenmeister**): occupational name for a chief cook, the person in charge in the kitchen of a great house, Middle High German *küchenmeister.*

GIVEN NAME German 4%. *Kurt.*

Kuechle (164) South German (**Küchle**): metonymic occupational name for a pastry cook, from *Küchle* 'cookie', 'little cake' (see KUCHLER 2).

Kuechler (166) German and Swiss German (**Küchler**): see KUCHLER 1, 2.

GIVEN NAMES German 6%. *Kurt, Lorenz.*

Kueck (138) German (**Kück**): from Middle Low German *küken* 'chicken', possibly a nickname for someone thought to resemble chicken in some way or alternatively a metonymic occupational name for someone who kept poultry.

GIVEN NAMES German 13%. *Dieter, Fritz, Gerhard, Hans, Helmut, Hermann, Klaus.*

Kuecker (218) German: unexplained; perhaps a nickname for someone with a habit of peering about from side to side, from a noun derivative of *kuecken* 'to peer'.

Kuefler (105) German (**Küfler**): occupational name for a cooper or for the keeper of a winecellar, from a derivative of Middle High German *kuofe* 'vat', 'barrel'.

Kuehl (2179) German (**Kühl**): see KUHL.

GIVEN NAMES German 4%. *Hans* (5), *Otto* (3), *Claus* (2), *Dieter* (2), *Frieda* (2), *Klaus* (2), *Kurt* (2), *Armin, Eldred, Ernst, Guenter, Guenther.*

Kuehler (244) German (**Kühler**): **1.** topographic name for someone living by a quarry, from a derivative of Middle High German *küle*, Middle Low German *kule* 'quarry', 'pit'. **2.** derivative of an old personal name formed with a German cognate of Old Norse *kollir* 'helmet'.

Kuehn (3182) German: **1.** from a short form of any of the medieval German names containing as a first element Old High German *kuoni* 'bold', 'daring', 'experienced', or *chunni* 'tribe', 'race', 'people'. The distinction became blurred at an early date. By far the most common such name is KONRAD. **2.** In some cases, no doubt, it is a nickname derived directly from Middle High German *küene* 'bold'.

GIVEN NAMES German 6%. *Kurt* (6), *Otto* (6), *Erwin* (3), *Fritz* (3), *Heinz* (3), *Juergen* (3), *Klaus* (3), *Guenter* (2), *Horst* (2), *Reinhold* (2), *Bernd, Bernhard.*

Kuehne (652) German: variant of KUEHN.

GIVEN NAMES German 8%. *Otto* (3), *Kurt* (2), *Christoph, Dieter, Erwin, Friedrich, Gerhard, Horst, Ilse, Inge, Wilhelm, Willi.*

Kuehnel (184) German (**Kühnel**): from a pet form of the personal name *Kuno*, a short form of KONRAD.

GIVEN NAMES German 8%. *Eberhard, Gerhard, Kurt, Manfred.*

Kuehner (479) German (**Kühner**): from a noun derivative of KUEHN 2.

GIVEN NAMES German 7%. *Kurt* (2), *Bernhard, Dieter, Helmut, Rudi.*

Kuehnert (128) German (**Kühnert**): from a medieval personal name, a variant of

KONRAD influenced by the form of the word *kuehn* 'bold' (see KUEHN), from which it is derived.

GIVEN NAMES German 9%. *Kurt, Volker.*

Kuehnl (107) German (**Kühnl**): from a pet form of the personal name KUHN.

Kuehnle (222) German (**Kühnle**): see KUHNLE.

GIVEN NAME German 6%. *Manfred* (2).

Kueker (229) German: variant of KUECKER.

GIVEN NAMES German 5%. *Erhardt, Erwin, Helmut, Hermann.*

Kuempel (110) German (**Kümpel**): nickname for a short stout man, from a diminutive of Middle High German *kumpf* 'pouch'.

Kuennen (232) German (**Künnen**): metronymic from a short form of the female personal name *Kunigunde*, composed of the Old High German elements *kunni* 'clan' + *gund* 'battle'. This was a popular name among the nobility from the 11th century.

Kuenning (118) German: unexplained.

Kuenstler (187) German (**Künstler**): nickname from Middle High German *kunster, künst(en)er* 'knowledgeable or skilled man', specifically an able trader or merchant.

Kueny (160) Swiss German: unexplained.

GIVEN NAMES French 4%. *Jacques, Marcel.*

Kuenzel (218) South German (**Künzel**): from a pet form of the personal name KUNTZ.

GIVEN NAMES German 13%. *Kurt* (4), *Fritz* (3), *Rainer* (2), *Hans, Ingo.*

Kuenzi (281) South German, Swiss, and Austrian (**Künzi**): from a pet form of the personal name KUNTZ.

GIVEN NAMES German 4%. *Hans* (2), *Franz.*

Kuenzli (195) Swiss German (**Künzli**): from a pet form of the personal name KUNTZ.

Kuepper (144) German (**Küpper**): see KUPPER.

GIVEN NAMES German 6%. *Hans* (2), *Ernst.*

Kues (107) North German and Dutch: habitational name from Cues, now part of Bernkastel-Kues in the Rhineland Palatinate.

Kuester (928) German (**Küster**): status name for a sexton (see KUSTER).

GIVEN NAMES German 6%. *Ernst, Ewald, Fritz, Hans, Helmuth, Johann, Jurgen, Klaus, Kurt, Manfred, Monika, Ulrich.*

Kueter (184) German (**Küter**): see KUTER.

GIVEN NAMES German 5%. *Kurt* (2), *Klaus.*

Kuethe (126) German (**Küthe**): topographic name from *Kute, Kaute* 'quarry', 'pit', 'depression' (see KUETHER).

Kuether (304) German (**Küther**): 1. topographic name from *Kute, Kaute* 'quarry', 'pit', 'depression'. 2. variant of KUETER.

GIVEN NAMES German 5%. *Helmut, Kurt, Ulrich.*

Kufahl (188) German: occupational name for a blacksmith, Germanized spelling of Slavic KOVAL.

GIVEN NAMES German 7%. *Eldred* (2), *Uwe* (2).

Kuffel (236) German (also **Küffel**): metonymic occupational name for a cooper or for the keeper of a winecellar, from a diminutive of Middle High German *kuofe* 'vat', 'barrel'.

Kuffner (116) German (**Küffner**): occupational name for a maker of tubs, Middle High German *kuofener, küefer.*

GIVEN NAMES German 9%. *Erik, Herta, Kurt, Ulrich.*

Kugel (482) 1. German and Jewish (Ashkenazic): nickname for a rotund person, from Middle High German *kugel(e)*, German *Kugel* 'ball', 'orb'. The term also denoted a hooded cloak or round-topped mountain, and in some cases the surname may have arisen from either of these senses. 2. Jewish (eastern Ashkenazic): from Yiddish *kugl*, a term denoting various kinds of pudding.

GIVEN NAMES Jewish 5%; German 4%. *Shlomo* (3), *Chaim, Ilya, Moshe, Yakov; Erhard* (2), *Kurt, Wilhelm, Wolfgang.*

Kugelman (171) Jewish (western Ashkenazic): elaborated form of KUGEL.

GIVEN NAMES Jewish 15%. *Sholom* (2), *Avrohom, Chaim, Elimelech, Hyman, Miriam, Yehoshua.*

Kugler (1703) 1. German and Swiss German (also **Kügler**): occupational name for a maker of hooded coats or cowls, Middle High German *gugler*. 2. Jewish (Ashkenazic): variant of KUGEL with the addition of the agent suffix *-er*.

GIVEN NAMES German 4%. *Kurt* (4), *Ernst* (3), *Hans* (3), *Heinz* (2), *Herta* (2), *Eldor, Hermann, Nikolaus, Oskar, Rudi.*

Kuh (121) Jewish (from Bohemia and Silesia): habitational name from a butcher's shop distinguished by the sign of a cow, German *Kuh*.

GIVEN NAMES German 7%. *Kurt* (2), *Erwin, Math.*

Kuhar (455) Slovenian and Croatian: occupational name for a cook, from *kuhar*, an agent derivative of *kuhati* 'to cook'.

Kuhel (106) Slovenian (also **Kuhelj**): apparently a nickname or occupational name from the dialect word *kuhelj*, denoting a kind of doughnut.

Kuhl (2404) German (also **Kühl**): 1. topographic name for someone who lived by a hollow or depression, Middle High German *küle*, Middle Low German *kule* or habitational name from one of the numerous minor places in North Germany named with this word. The spelling *Kühl* results from a folk-etymological association with High German *kühl* 'cool' (Middle High German *küel(e)*) (see 2). 2. (**Kühl**): nickname from Middle High German *küel* 'cool', 'calm'. 3. from a short form of a Germanic personal name formed with an element cognate with Old Norse *kollir* 'helmet'.

GIVEN NAMES German 4%. *Kurt* (5), *Otto* (3), *Berthold* (2), *Aloys, Armin, Benno, Eldred, Erwin, Fritz, Gerhardt, Guenter, Heinz.*

Kuhle (154) German (**Kühle**): variant of KUHL.

Kuhlman (2583) Respelling of German KUHLMANN.

Kuhlmann (1234) German (also **Kühlmann**): nickname from Middle High German *küel* 'cool', 'calm' (see KUHL 2).

GIVEN NAMES German 7%. *Kurt* (6), *Erwin* (4), *Hans* (4), *Horst* (4), *Otto* (3), *Dietrich, Friedrich, Fritz, Hermann, Joerg, Klaus, Theodor.*

Kuhn (13111) 1. German: from the personal name *Kuno*, a short form of *Kunrat* (see KONRAD). The German word *kühn*, meaning 'bold', may have influenced the popularity of this short form, but is not necessarily the immediate source of it. 2. German: variant spelling of **Kühn(e)** (see KUEHN). 3. Jewish (Ashkenazic): ornamental name from German *kühn* 'bold', but in some cases an altered spelling of **Cohn** or **Kohn** (see COHEN).

GIVEN NAMES German 4%. *Kurt* (22), *Otto* (10), *Hans* (9), *Wolfgang* (6), *Fritz* (5), *Gerhard* (5), *Manfred* (5), *Dieter* (4), *Erwin* (4), *Helmut* (4), *Arno* (3), *Gunther* (3).

Kuhne (314) German and Jewish (Ashkenazic): variant of KUHN.

GIVEN NAMES German 8%. *Kurt* (3), *Bernhard, Heinz, Wolf.*

Kuhnel (153) German (**Kühnel**): see KUEHNEL.

Kuhner (230) German (also **Kühner**): derivative of *Kuhn*, a short form of KONRAD.

GIVEN NAMES German 6%. *Gerhard* (2), *Heinz.*

Kuhnert (307) German (also **Kühnert**): from a variant of the personal name *Kuhnhart*, a variant of *Kunrat* (see KONRAD).

GIVEN NAMES German 9%. *Klaus* (2), *Gotthard, Hans, Helmut, Jurgen, Manfred, Otto, Siegfried.*

Kuhnke (163) German: from a pet form of *Kunat(h)*, an eastern German form of *Kunrat* (see KONRAD).

GIVEN NAMES German 14%. *Horst* (2), *Kurt* (2), *Erwin, Fritz, Gunter, Otto.*

Kuhnle (233) German (**Kühnle**): from a pet form of *Kuno*, a short form of KONRAD.

GIVEN NAMES German 11%. *Kurt* (3), *Otto* (2), *Wilhelm* (2), *Erwin, Fritz, Hans.*

Kuhns (2474) Although in German-speaking countries, this surname arose either as a patronymic from KUHN or a habitational name from a place so named in former Silesia, in the majority of instances in the U.S. it is a Pennsylvania form of German KUNTZ, the other common spelling being KOONS.

Kuhr (440) North German: 1. occupational name for a guard or watchman on a tower, Middle Low German *kure*. 2. from a short form of *Kunrat* (see KONRAD).

GIVEN NAMES German 7%. *Dietmar* (2), *Gerhard* (2), *Ernst, Hans, Heinrich, Horst, Johannes, Jurgen, Reiner, Wolfgang.*

Kuhrt (153) German: **1.** nickname for a short man, from Middle Low German *kort* 'small', 'short'. **2.** variant of *Kord* or *Kurd*, short forms of KONRAD.

Kuhs (126) German: from Middle Low German *kuse* 'cudgel', 'club', probably applied as a metonymic occupational name for a maker of clubs or as a nickname for a stocky person.

Kuiken (258) Dutch (**van der Kuiken**): occupational name for a cook or kitchen servant, from Dutch *kuiken* 'kitchen'.

GIVEN NAME German 4%. *Siebert.*

Kuiper (897) Dutch: occupational name for a cooper, Middle Dutch *cup(e)re.*

GIVEN NAMES Dutch 4%. *Gerrit* (4), *Hendrik* (2), *Willem* (2), *Harm, Klaas, Kort, Marinus, Nicolaas, Wouter.*

Kuipers (593) Dutch: patronymic from KUIPER.

Kujala (207) Finnish: habitational name from *kuja* 'lane' + the local suffix *-la*, denoting a farm or house that was located by one of the lanes that were formed by parallel fences constructed to protect the arable fields on either side from roaming cattle.

GIVEN NAMES Finnish 10%. *Eino* (3), *Onni* (2), *Waino* (2), *Arvo, Olli.*

Kujath (114) Polish or eastern German (of Slavic origin): probably a derivative from a base *kuj-* (Polish *kuć*) 'to forge', 'to hammer', hence an occupational name for a smith.

Kujawa (1143) Polish: from the district Kujawy, on the west bank of the Vistula, bounded by the Vistula and Noteć rivers and Lake Gopło.

Kujawski (479) Polish: regional name for someone from Kujawy (see KUJAWA) or from a village called Kujawy, for example in Sielce voivodeship.

GIVEN NAMES Polish 4%. *Casimir, Ewa, Janina, Jerzy, Kazimierz, Zygmunt.*

Kuk (227) **1.** Dutch and North German: occupational name for a pastrycook. See also KOOK. **2.** Korean: there are three Chinese characters for this surname, used by three different clans. Two of them are very rare; only the Tamyang Kuk clan will be considered here. This is said to have originated in Song China. The clan's founding ancestor, Kuk Ryang, held a government post during the early 12th century, in the Koryǒ period. Kuk Ryang's ancestors are said to have come from Song China. **3.** Chinese 鞠: variant of JU 1.

GIVEN NAMES Korean 7%; German 5%. *Song* (2), *Hyung, Jae, Kam, Keum, Man, Min Soo, Myung Ho, Seung, Soon, Sun, Sung; Siegfried* (2), *Horst, Otto.*

Kuka (117) **1.** German: unexplained. Probably a variant of KUK 'pastry cook'. **2.** Dutch: variant of **Kuke** or KOK 'cook'. **3.** Tongan: unexplained.

Kuker (153) Dutch and North German: occupational name for a pastrycook (see KUK).

GIVEN NAMES German 4%. *Erwin, Otto.*

Kukla (681) Polish (also **Kukła**) and Czech: from *kukla* 'cowl', 'hood', 'mask', probably a nickname bestowed on an habitual wearer of a hood or perhaps a metonymic occupational name for a hood or cowl maker. In Polish *kukla, kukła* also means a kind of bread roll and a puppet. This surname is also found in German-speaking countries.

GIVEN NAMES German 4%; Polish 4%. *Aloysius, Erwin, Eugen, Kurt, Otto; Andrzej, Boguslaw, Casimir, Ewa, Maciej.*

Kuklinski (358) **1.** Polish: habitational name for someone from Kukle in Suwałki voivodeship or Kuklin in Ciechanów voivodeship, both named with *Kukla* 'cowl' (see KUKLA). **2.** Jewish (from Belarus): habitational name for someone from the village of Kukli in Belarus.

GIVEN NAMES Polish 6%. *Bronislaus, Casimir, Kazimierz, Piotr, Stanislaw.*

Kuklis (106) **1.** Czech (**Kukliš**): diminutive of KUKLA. **2.** Latvian and Lithuanian (also **Kuklys**): of uncertain etymology. **3.** Jewish (from Ukraine): habitational name for someone from Kulky in Ukraine.

Kukowski (313) Polish: habitational name for someone from a place called Kukowo in Włoławek voivodeship or Kuków in Bielsko-Biała voivodeship, named with *kuk*, the cry of the cuckoo.

Kukuk (267) German: from Middle High German *kukuk*, hence a nickname for someone thought to resemble a cuckoo or a topographic name for somebody who lived in a place frequented by cuckoos.

Kukulka (117) Polish (**Kukułka**): nickname from *kukułka* 'cuckoo'.

GIVEN NAMES Polish 11%; German 4%. *Pawel* (2), *Ewa, Zigmund; Alois.*

Kukulski (117) Polish: habitational name for someone from a place named with *kukułka* 'cuckoo', or alternatively a nickname for someone thought to resemble the bird.

GIVEN NAMES Polish 12%. *Cecylia* (2), *Zygmunt* (2), *Grzegorz, Pawel.*

Kukura (140) **1.** Ukrainian: unexplained. This surname is associated particularly with the town of Nizankowice (formerly part of Poland, now in Ukraine). **2.** Slovak: unexplained.

Kula (789) **1.** Polish, Czech, Slovak, and Jewish (from Poland): nickname for a rotund person, from Polish *kula* 'ball', Czech dialect *kula* (standard Czech *koule*). **2.** Czech: from a short form of the personal name *Mikuláš*, Czech form of NICHOLAS. **3.** Jewish (from Belarus): habitational name from Kulya, now in Belarus.

GIVEN NAMES Polish 7%. *Czeslaw* (2), *Halina* (2), *Jozef* (2), *Krzysztof* (2), *Witold* (2),

Zbigniew (2), *Casimir, Grzegorz, Janusz, Jozefa, Kazimierz, Ludwik.*

Kulaga (186) Ukrainian and Polish (**Kułaga**): from the dialect word *kułága* denoting a kind of gruel. In some places this is a synonym of KULESZA. As a surname, it may be a nickname for a fat man or for an impoverished person who could eat only gruel.

GIVEN NAMES Polish 15%. *Ewa* (2), *Zygmunt* (2), *Henryk, Jozefa, Krzysztof, Mikolaj, Thadeus, Zbigniew.*

Kulak (373) **1.** Polish (**Kułak**): nickname from an eastern Slavic word meaning 'fist'. **2.** Jewish (from Belarus): habitational name from Kulaki, now in Belarus.

GIVEN NAMES Polish 8%. *Henryk* (2), *Casimir, Danuta, Jerzy, Jozef, Krystyna, Mieczyslaw, Piotr.*

Kulakowski (223) Polish (**Kułakowski**): habitational name for someone from Kułaki in Łomża voivodeship or Kułakowice in Zamość voivodeship.

GIVEN NAMES Polish 7%. *Boguslaw, Jerzy, Kazimierz, Piotr, Tomasz.*

Kulas (728) Czech: from a short form of the personal name *Mikuláš*, Czech form of NICHOLAS.

Kulbacki (112) Polish: habitational name for someone from a place called Kulbaki (now in Belarus), named with Polish *kulbaka* 'saddle'.

GIVEN NAMES Polish 7%. *Casimir, Jaroslaw.*

Kulberg (103) **1.** Swedish (also common in Finland): probably a variant of KOLBERG. **2.** Jewish (eastern Ashkenazic): variant spelling of KOLBERG.

GIVEN NAMES Russian 5%. *Leonid, Semyon.*

Kulcsar (122) Hungarian (**Kulcsár**): occupational name for a wine butler, treasurer, caretaker, warder, or keeper of keys, from a derivative of *kulcs* 'key', a southern Slavic loanword.

GIVEN NAMES Hungarian 14%. *Attila* (2), *Gyula, Istvan, Laszlo, Zoltan.*

Kulczycki (115) Polish: habitational name for someone from Kulczyce (now in Ukraine), named with *kulczyk* 'goldfinch'.

GIVEN NAMES Polish 7%. *Halina, Stanislaw.*

Kulczyk (116) Polish: nickname from *kulczyk* 'goldfinch'.

GIVEN NAME Polish 10%. *Leszek* (3).

Kulesa (312) Americanized spelling of Polish KULESZA.

GIVEN NAME Polish 4%. *Casimir.*

Kulesza (391) Polish: from *kulesza* 'gruel', a dish normally made with corn flour; probably a nickname for someone who habitually cooked or was fond of this dish.

GIVEN NAMES Polish 17%. *Jerzy* (3), *Janina* (2), *Kazimierz* (2), *Urszula* (2), *Andrzej, Bogdan, Czeslaw, Jacek, Jadwiga, Jolanta, Jozef, Jozefa.*

Kulhanek (338) Czech (**Kulhánek**): nickname for a lame man, from a derivative of *kulhat* 'to limp'.

Kulich (128) **1.** Czech: nickname from Czech *kulich* 'little owl'. **2.** Altered spelling of German **Kühlich**, a derivative of a Germanic personal name formed with a cognate of Old Norse *kollir* 'helmet'. **3.** Respelling of German **Küllich**, a topographic name for someone living near a dung pit, cesspool, or stagnant water, Middle High German *hülwe, hü(e)l*.

Kulick (744) **1.** Americanized spelling of Polish, Czech, and Jewish KULIK. **2.** Altered spelling of German **Kühlich** or **Küllich** (see KULICH).

Kulig (437) Polish: **1.** variant of KULIK 'curlew'. **2.** from *kulig* 'carnival', 'sledging cavalcade', perhaps a nickname for someone who organized or took place in such a cavalcade.
GIVEN NAMES Polish 8%. *Bronislawa* (2), *Jozef* (2), *Beata, Bogdan, Boguslawa, Casimir, Karol, Michalina, Miroslaw, Urszula, Wieslaw, Zbigniew.*

Kuligowski (191) Polish: habitational name for someone from any of several places called Kuligów, Kuligowo, or Kuligi, named with *kulig, kulik* 'curlew'.
GIVEN NAMES Polish 7%; German 4%. *Eugeniusz, Leszek, Miroslaw, Piotr; Florian* (3), *Erwin.*

Kulik (806) **1.** Polish, Jewish (eastern Ashkenazic), and German (of Slavic origin): nickname from Slavic *kulik* 'curlew'. **2.** Czech (**Kulík**): from a short form of the personal name *Mikuláš*, Czech form of NICHOLAS. **3.** Jewish (from Belarus): habitational name from Kuliki, now in Belarus.

Kulikowski (398) Polish: habitational name for someone from Kulików in Zamość voivodeship, named with *kulik* 'curlew'.
GIVEN NAMES Polish 8%. *Franciszek, Halina, Henryk, Lech, Lucjan, Mariusz, Stanisław, Tadeusz, Zygmunt.*

Kulinski (290) **1.** Polish (**Kuliński**) and Jewish (from Poland): habitational name for someone from a place called Kulin in Dobrzyn region, named with *kula* 'ball'. **2.** Jewish (eastern Ashkenazic): habitational name for someone from Kuleni in Belarus or Kulna in Ukraine.
GIVEN NAMES Polish 5%. *Leszek* (2), *Lech.*

Kulis (253) **1.** Polish: nickname from a derivative of *kula* 'ball' (see KULA, KULKA). **2.** Czech (**Kuliš**): from a short form of the personal name *Mikuláš*, Czech form of NICHOLAS. **3.** Latvian and Lithuanian (also **Kulys**): descriptive epithet for a lame person, from *kulys* 'lame'.
GIVEN NAMES Polish 9%. *Zbigniew* (2), *Jozef, Jozefa, Krystyna, Stanislaw, Wieslaw.*

Kulish (187) Ukrainian and Jewish (eastern Ashkenazic): nickname from Ukrainian and Yiddish *kulish* 'thin gruel', 'potato soup'.
GIVEN NAME German 4%. *Kurt* (2).

Kulka (317) **1.** Polish: nickname for a short, round person, from Polish, Czech *kulka* 'ball', a diminutive of *kula* (see KULA).

2. Czech: from a short form of the personal name *Mikuláš*, Czech form of NICHOLAS.
GIVEN NAMES Polish 4%. *Casimir, Czeslaw, Grzegorz.*

Kulkarni (488) Indian (Maharashtra, Karnataka): Hindu (usually Brahman) name, from Marathi *kuḷkərṇi* 'village clerk' (from Sanskrit *kula* 'family', 'community' + *karaṇa* 'writer' or *karṇī* 'helmsman'). The kulkarni was a village official under the patel or village headman; he kept the accounts of the cultivators for the government and also the public records. The office of kulkarni was hereditary. As a rule, a Brahman was appointed to this office. He received some land rent free and was paid an annual salary.
GIVEN NAMES Indian 94%. *Arun* (7), *Pradeep* (7), *Deepa* (6), *Prakash* (6), *Ravi* (6), *Sunil* (6), *Ajit* (5), *Anil* (5), *Ashok* (5), *Sandeep* (5), *Sudhir* (5), *Ajay* (4).

Kull (970) German: **1.** from a short form of KULLMANN. **2.** from a short form of a Germanic personal named based on a cognate of Old Norse *kollir* 'helmet'.

Kulla (224) Variant spelling of Polish and Czech KULA.

Kullberg (190) **1.** Swedish: probably an ornamental name composed of the elements *kull* 'round hilltop' + *berg* 'mountain'. **2.** German: possibly an altered form of **Küllenberg**, a habitational name from a farmstead near Solingen or from a place name related to it.
GIVEN NAMES Scandinavian 8%. *Lennart* (2), *Lars.*

Kuller (166) North German (**Küller**): topographic name for someone who lived by in a depression or hollow, Middle Low German *kule.*

Kullman (483) Americanized or Jewish variant spelling of KULLMANN.

Kullmann (140) **1.** German: from a personal name, a derivative of a Germanic cognate of Old Norse *kollir* 'helmet', or alternatively a derivative of the personal name KONRAD, especially in central western Germany. **2.** German: variant of KUHLMANN. **3.** Jewish (Ashkenazic): unexplained.
GIVEN NAMES German 8%. *Bernhard, Heinz, Udo.*

Kulm (134) German: habitational name from a place so named in Nieder Lasitz (now in Poland) or possibly others also named with the Slavic loanword *kholm* 'hill', 'mountain top'.

Kulman (132) **1.** Americanized or Jewish variant spelling of KULLMANN. **2.** Respelling of German KUHLMANN.

Kulon (36) Polish: **1.** nickname from *kulon* 'stone curlew', sometimes used as a nickname for a townsman. **2.** descriptive nickname for someone with a large visible growth, from Polish dialect *kulon* 'swelling', 'callosity', 'excrescence'.

Kulow (280) German: habitational name from Kuhlow near Schwerin, Mecklenburg.

GIVEN NAMES German 6%. *Kurt* (2), *Frieda, Gerhard, Volkmar.*

Kulp (1813) **1.** Variant of German KOLB or KALB. **2.** German: habitational name from Kulpin in Mecklenburg.

Kulpa (432) Polish and Lithuanian: nickname from Latin *culpa* 'fault', 'guilt', a nickname for an apologetic person who frequently used the Latin expression *mea culpa* 'my fault'.
GIVEN NAMES Polish 7%. *Stanislaw* (2), *Tadeusz* (2), *Bronislaw, Malgorzata, Pawel, Ryszard, Wladyslawa; Kestutiss, Vytautas.*

Kult (111) Swiss German: unexplained.

Kultgen (133) German: unexplained.

Kulwicki (168) Polish: habitational name for someone from a place called Kulwa, or perhaps from Kulwa (Kulva) in Lithuania.

Kulzer (222) German: **1.** habitational name for someone from either of two places named Külz, near Koblenz or Stettin (now Szczeszin in Poland). **2.** variant spelling of **Kolzer**, nickname for a chatterer, from an agent derivative of Middle Low German *kolz* 'talk', 'chatter'.
GIVEN NAMES German 5%. *Kurt* (2), *Heinrich.*

Kumagai (188) Japanese: 'bear valley'; also pronounced *Kumatani, Kumaya,* and *Kumagaya,* a habitational name from the town of Kumagaya, in a part of Musashi now part of Saitama prefecture. The earliest bearers were of TAIRA descent. Found in northeastern and western Japan.
GIVEN NAMES Japanese 56%. *Akira* (3), *Akiko* (2), *Kazuo* (2), *Tomoyuki* (2), *Toshimi* (2), *Yoshio* (2), *Yuriko* (2), *Akihiko, Atsushi, Chiharu, Chizuko, Harumi.*

Kumar (3083) **1.** Indian: Hindu name found in several communities, from Sanskrit *kumāra* 'child', 'son', 'prince'. It is also an epithet of the god Kartikeya, the son of Shiva. It commonly occurs as the final element of compound given names, and sometimes as a personal name in its own right. **2.** Slovenian: either a variant spelling of KUMER or a variant of **Humar**, a topographic name for someone who lived on a hill, from *holm* (dialectally *hum* 'hill', 'height').
GIVEN NAMES Indian 92%. *Ashok* (92), *Vijay* (66), *Anil* (51), *Arun* (48), *Raj* (45), *Sunil* (34), *Suresh* (34), *Rakesh* (31), *Ajay* (29), *Satish* (29), *Vinod* (28), *Sanjay* (27).

Kumer (133) **1.** Slovenian: nickname from the archaic word *kumer* 'scrawny fellow', a derivative of the adjective *kumrn* 'lean', 'thin'. **2.** Indian: variant of KUMAR.
GIVEN NAMES Indian 10%. *Ashok, Keshava, Mukesh, Rahul, Ram, Sushil.*

Kumler (172) German (**Kümmler**): occupational name for a spicer, literally a supplier of caraway seeds, German *Kümmeler,* from a derivative of Middle High German *kumin* 'caraway', from Latin *cuminum.*

Kumm (467) **1.** North German: metonymic occupational name from Middle Low

German *kum(p)* 'bowl'. **2.** Swiss German: topographic name for someone living in a valley, from Swiss German *kumme* 'hollow'.

GIVEN NAMES German 4%. *Jochen, Reinhold.*

Kummer (1209) German: **1.** from Middle High German *kummer, kumber* 'grief', 'distress', 'trouble', hence a byname for someone who had suffered some loss or other misfortune; or alternatively a topographic name of the same origin for a person living near a rubble heap. *Kummer* is also a slang word for a penitentiary, and in some instances the surname may have arisen as nickname for a prisoner or a jailer. **2.** possibly a derivative of the medieval personal name *Kunemar*, of which the first element is from Old High German *kuoni* 'bold' or *chunni* 'people' (see KONRAD); the second is from Old High German *māri* 'fame', 'glory'.

Kummerer (134) German: variant of KUMMER 'trouble', with the addition of the agent noun suffix *-er*.

Kummerow (103) German: habitational name from any of various places in Brandenburg and Mecklenburg called Kummerow.

GIVEN NAME German 5%. *Ulrike.*

Kumor (129) Polish: nickname for a small, insignificant, or annoying person, from a dialect variant of KOMAR 'mosquito', 'gnat'.

GIVEN NAMES Polish 11%; German 4%. *Alicja, Dariusz, Ignacy, Leslaw.*

Kump (616) German: **1.** metonymic occupational name for a bowl maker, from Middle Low German *kump* '(wooden) bowl'. **2.** habitational name from a place so named in Westphalia. **3.** variant spelling of KUMPF.

GIVEN NAMES German 5%. *Erwin* (3), *Mathias* (3), *Alois, Gerhard, Traude.*

Kumpe (106) German: variant of KUMP.

GIVEN NAME German 4%. *Klaus.*

Kumpf (411) **1.** South German: variant of KUMP. **2.** German: nickname for a short stout man, from Middle High German *kumpf* '(small) measure of grain', 'pouch (for whetstones)'.

GIVEN NAMES German 5%. *Hermann, Kurt, Otto.*

Kumpula (134) Finnish: ornamental name composed of *kumpu* 'grassy mound' + the local suffix *-la*. It was first recorded in the 17th century and is found chiefly in northern Finland.

GIVEN NAMES Finnish 4%. *Reino, Taisto.*

Kun (216) **1.** Hungarian: ethnic name for a member of a Turkic people known in English as the Cumanians (Hungarian *kún*). **2.** Jewish (from Hungary): adoption of 1, replacing the Jewish homophone KUHN. **3.** Jewish (eastern Ashkenazic): variant of KUHN.

GIVEN NAMES Jewish 6%; Hungarian 6%; Russian 5%. *Khaim, Rozalia, Sarra; Istvan*

(2), *Laszlo* (2), *Balazs, Zoltan; Boris* (2), *Betya, Liliya, Milya, Vladimir, Yefim, Yelizaveta, Zoya.*

Kuna (241) **1.** Polish, Czech, Slovak, Hungarian, and Jewish (from Poland): nickname for a quick-tempered or aggressive person, from Slavic *kuna* 'marten', 'weasel'. This is also found as a German surname, of Slavic origin. **2.** Czech: also from the old personal name *Kuna*, a pet form of *Kunrat* (see KONRAD).

Kunath (224) Eastern German: from a Sorbian form of KONRAD.

GIVEN NAMES German 9%. *Erwin* (2), *Dieter, Gerhard, Gunter, Heinz, Manfred.*

Kunau (109) German: habitational name from any of various places named Kunhau.

Kunc (103) **1.** Polish, Czech, Slovak, and Hungarian spelling of German KUNTZ. **2.** Slovenian: short form of the medieval personal name *Kunrad* or *Kunrat* (see KONRAD), formed with the diminutive suffix *-c*. **3.** Slovenian: alternatively, perhaps a nickname from an old spelling of *kunec* 'coney', 'rabbit'.

GIVEN NAME Polish 4%. *Zofia.*

Kunce (298) Americanized spelling of KUNC or KUNTZ.

Kunda (190) **1.** Polish: nickname from a derivative of *kunda* 'marten'. **2.** Polish: from a pet form of the personal name KONRAD. **3.** Jewish (Ashkenazic): variant of KUNDE. **4.** Indian (Gujarat): Hindu (Lohana) name of unknown meaning.

GIVEN NAMES Indian 9%; Polish 5%. *Anand, Asim, Manoj, Prabha, Purna, Ramachandra, Sastry, Usha; Kazimir, Stanislaw.*

Kunde (531) German and Jewish (Ashkenazic): eastern variant of KUHN or alternatively a nickname from Middle High German *kunde* 'native'.

Kundert (453) Swiss German: from the Alemannic form of KONRAD.

Kundinger (184) German and Swiss German (**Kündinger**): **1.** occupational name for a town crier, Middle High German *kündigære*. **2.** habitational name for someone from Kunding in Bavaria. **3.** possibly a nickname for a knowledgeable person, from Middle High German *kündic* 'known', 'intelligent'.

Kundrat (216) German: variant of **Kunrat** (see KONRAD).

Kunert (285) German: variant of **Kunrat** (see KONRAD).

GIVEN NAMES German 5%. *Hans* (2), *Erhardt, Erwin, Frieda, Kurt.*

Kunes (262) **1.** Czech (**Kuneš**): from the old personal name *Kuneš*, a pet form of *Kunrat* (see KONRAD). **2.** Jewish (eastern Ashkenazic): metronymic from a short form of the German female personal name *Kunigunde* (see KUENNEN). **3.** Possibly a respelling of German KUHNS or KUNTZ.

Kunesh (209) **1.** Americanized spelling of Czech **Kuneš** (see KUNES). **2.** Altered

spelling of German **Kunisch**, from a Slavic pet form of *Kuno*, a short form of KONRAD.

Kuney (147) Americanized spelling of German **Kühne**, variant of **Kühn** (see KUEHN).

Kung (709) **1.** Chinese 龔, 宮, 巩, 公, 弓: see GONG. **2.** Chinese 孔: variant of KONG 2. **3.** South German (**Küng**): variant of **König** (see KOENIG).

GIVEN NAMES Chinese 22%. *Ching* (4), *Fu* (3), *Wing* (3), *Chi* (2), *Chun* (2), *Chung Jen* (2), *Fan* (2), *Hin* (2), *Ling* (2), *May Ling* (2), *Wai Chung* (2), *Wen Wei* (2).

Kunicki (110) Polish: habitational name for someone from a place called Kunice (formerly Kończyce), named either with *Kon* (a short form of the personal name KONRAD) or from *kuna* 'marten'.

GIVEN NAMES Polish 9%. *Boleslaw, Wojciech.*

Kunik (129) Jewish (from Belarus): from a Slavic pet form of the Yiddish female name *Kune* (see KUNIN).

Kunin (249) Jewish (from Belarus): metronymic from the Yiddish female name *Kune*, a pet form of the German female personal name *Kunigunda* (see KUENNEN).

GIVEN NAMES Jewish 11%; Russian 11%. *Aron, Basya, Isaak, Mendel, Mikhael, Naum, Revekka; Boris* (2), *Igor* (2), *Lev* (2), *Vladimir* (2), *Galina, Grigory, Leonid, Matvey, Mikhail, Nison, Sergei, Sergey.*

Kunis (127) **1.** Dutch and German: from a derivative of the personal name KONRAD. **2.** Jewish (eastern Ashkenazic): metronymic from the Yiddish female name *Kune* (see KUNIN).

GIVEN NAMES Jewish 5%. *Emanuel, Naum.*

Kunka (176) Respelling of German **Kunke**, from a diminutive of KUNA.

Kunkel (3889) German: **1.** from Middle High German *kunkel* 'spindle', 'distaff' (from Late Latin *conicula, conucula* diminutive of *conus* 'cone', 'peg'), hence a metonymic occupational name for a maker of spindles or a spinner or alternatively a nickname for a tall thin person. **2.** from a medieval German personal name, a pet form of *Kuno* (see KUHN). **3.** possibly from Low German *kunkel* 'dugout', 'shelter', or 'deep water', of uncertain application: perhaps a topographic name. **4.** (**Künkel**): habitational name from a manor near Eisenack (Thuringia) or Erkelenz (Westphalia).

Kunkle (1907) Americanized spelling or variant of KUNKEL.

Kunkler (307) German (also **Künkler**): occupational name for a spinner or spinster, i.e. someone who spins wool or flax, from an agent derivative of Middle High German *kunkel* 'spindle', 'distaff'. *Kunkler* also denoted a gossipmonger, and in some cases the surname may have arisen from this sense.

Kuno (123) **1.** Japanese: not common in Japan, this name can be written with characters meaning either 'nine fields' or 'long time' and 'field'. **2.** German: habitational name from places in Pomerania and Brandenburg called Kunow.

GIVEN NAMES Japanese 33%. *Kei* (2), *Susumu* (2), *Akemi, Chikako, Goro, Haruo, Hiroyuki, Kazuo, Kenichiro, Koichi, Masako, Mitsugu.*

Kuns (238) Probably an altered spelling of German KUHNS, KUNTZ, or KONZ.

Kunselman (329) Americanized spelling of German **Kunzelmann**, from a pet form of the personal name KONRAD.

Kunsman (287) Probably an altered form of German **Kunstmann** (see KUNSTMAN).

Kunst (468) **1.** German, Czech (**Kunšt**), and Jewish (Ashkenazic): from Middle High German *kunst* 'wisdom', 'skill', in German-speaking communities a nickname for a knowledgeable or skillful person. Among Jewish communities, this was adopted as an ornamental name in the sense 'knowledge', 'wisdom', 'dexterity', or 'art'. In Slavic regions, the word acquired negative connotations, 'trickery', 'sleight of hand', and hence 'ridicule', 'scorn', or 'mockery'. **2.** German: from a short form of the personal name *Konstantin*, German form of CONSTANTINE. **3.** German: from the personal name *Kunz*, a short form of KONRAD.

GIVEN NAMES German 7%. *Gerhard* (3), *Kurt* (2), *Otto* (2), *Alfons, Alois, Franz, Ilse.*

Kunstman (150) German (**Kunstmann**): occupational name for an artisan, from Middle High German *kunst* 'knowledge', 'skill' + *man* 'man'. Compare KUENSTLER.

Kuntz (4401) German: from the old personal name *Chunizo*, formed with Old High German *kuoni* 'bold', 'brave', 'experienced', or possibly *chunni* 'race', 'people'. It is sometimes taken as a pet form of KONRAD. The expression *Hinz und Kunz* was a German equivalent of 'every Tom, Dick, and Harry'.

Kuntze (144) North German: variant of KUNTZ.

GIVEN NAMES German 10%. *Otto* (2), *Erhard, Gunter, Hans, Hartmut.*

Kuntzman (217) German (**Kuntzmann**) and Jewish (Ashkenazic): variant of KUNZMAN.

Kunz (3950) German: variant spelling of KUNTZ.

GIVEN NAMES German 5%. *Hans* (8), *Otto* (5), *Alois* (3), *Erwin* (3), *Kurt* (3), *Wolfgang* (3), *Fritz* (2), *Gerhard* (2), *Heinz* (2), *Rainer* (2), *Arno, Dieter.*

Kunze (1417) North German: from a Low German pet form of KONRAD. See KUNTZ.

GIVEN NAMES German 7%. *Kurt* (7), *Gerhard* (3), *Hans* (3), *Horst* (2), *Lutz* (2), *Otto* (2), *Arno, Fritz, Heinrich, Helmut, Ingo, Jurgen.*

Kunzelman (126) German (**Kunzelmann**): from a pet form of the personal name KONRAD.

Kunzer (127) German (also **Kuenzer**): variant of KUNTZ, the *-er* suffix denoting affiliation.

Kunzler (227) German (**Künzler**): nickname for a flatterer, from an agent derivative of Middle High German *künzen* 'to flatter'.

GIVEN NAMES German 6%. *Kurt, Markus, Wilhelm.*

Kunzman (291) **1.** German (**Kunzmann**; also **Künzmann**): from a short form of the personal name KONRAD. **2.** Jewish (Ashkenazic): nickname from Yiddish *kunts* 'trick', 'feat'.

GIVEN NAMES German 4%. *Helmut, Kurt.*

Kuo (1809) Chinese 郭, 国, 过: see GUO.

GIVEN NAMES Chinese 20%. *Shu* (6), *Cheng* (5), *Ming* (5), *Lih* (4), *Wen* (4), *Chia-Ming* (3), *Chien* (3), *Ching* (3), *Li* (3), *Yi-Chun* (3), *Chao* (2), *Chia* (2).

Kupec (215) **1.** Czech, Slovak, Slovenian, and Hungarian: occupational name from *kupec* 'merchant', 'shopkeeper', a derivative of the Slavic verb *kupit* 'to buy'. **2.** Czech: from a reduced pet form of *Jakub*, Czech form of JACOB.

Kuper (681) **1.** North German (also **Küper**): occupational name for a cooper, from Middle Low German *kuper* 'cooper'. **2.** Swiss German: nickname for a sulky person, from Swiss German *kupen* 'to sulk', 'to pout'. **3.** Jewish (eastern Ashkenazic): from Yiddish *kuper* 'copper' (or a Yiddishized form of German *Kupfer*), hence a metonymic occupational name for a coppersmith or an ornamental name.

Kuperman (239) Jewish (Ashkenazic): occupational name for a cooper; alternatively a metonymic occupational name for a coppersmith, from Yiddish *kuper*, or a Yiddishized form of German KUPFERMAN.

GIVEN NAMES Jewish 18%; Russian 13%. *Arie, Chaim, Gilad, Icek, Ilya, Mayer, Menachem, Mirra, Moysey, Naum, Rakhmil, Semen*; *Boris* (4), *Mikhail* (3), *Igor* (2), *Yefim* (2), *Arkady, Fenya, Gennadiy, Grigory, Leonid, Lev, Maksim, Misha.*

Kupersmith (144) Partial Americanized form of German and Ashkenazic Jewish **Kupferschmidt**, an occupational name for a coppersmith.

GIVEN NAMES Jewish 4%; German 4%. *Hyman*; *Kurt.*

Kupetz (109) Jewish (eastern Ashkenazic): occupational name for a merchant, Russian *kupets*, Polish *kupiec*.

GIVEN NAMES Jewish 4%. *Chaim, Sol.*

Kupfer (514) German (**Küpfer**) and Jewish (Ashkenazic): metonymic occupational name for a worker or trader in copper, Middle High German *kupfer*, German *Kupfer* 'copper'. As a Jewish name it is often an ornamental name.

GIVEN NAMES Jewish 6%; German 4%. *Boruch* (2), *Moshe* (2), *Avi, Chana, Dov,*

Mascha, Pinhas, Zelman, Zvi; *Kurt* (2), *Fritz, Hans, Manfred, Otto.*

Kupferberg (166) **1.** German: habitational name from any of three places named Kupferberg, in Bavaria (near Bayreuth), Rhineland, or the Czech Republic. **2.** Jewish (Ashkenazic): ornamental name composed of German *Kupfer* 'copper' + *Berg* 'mountain', 'hill'.

GIVEN NAMES German 5%; Jewish 4%. *Kurt, Siegmund.*

Kupferer (104) German and Jewish (Ashkenazic): occupational name for a coppersmith (see KUPFERMAN).

Kupferman (158) German (**Kupfermann**) and Jewish (Ashkenazic): occupational name for a coppersmith or someone in the copper trade, from Middle High German *kupfer*, German *Kupfer* 'copper' + Middle High German *man*, German *Mann* 'man'.

GIVEN NAMES Jewish 8%; German 6%. *Meyer* (2), *Bronia, Hagit, Jakob, Zelig*; *Ilse, Kurt.*

Kupiec (352) Polish: occupational name from Polish *kupiec* 'merchant' (from a derivative of *kupić* 'to buy').

GIVEN NAMES Polish 13%. *Jerzy* (3), *Janusz* (2), *Tadeusz* (2), *Arkadiusz, Halina, Jacek, Krzystof, Mariusz, Wieslawa, Zbigniew, Zosia.*

Kupka (331) Polish, Ukrainian, Jewish (eastern Ashkenazic), and German (of Slavic origin): nickname from Polish and Ukrainian *kupka* 'small heap', a diminutive of *kupa* 'pile'.

GIVEN NAMES German 4%. *Elfriede, Wenzel, Wilhelm, Wolfgang.*

Kupp (119) Swiss German: unexplained.

Kupper (398) **1.** German (**Küpper**): Rhenish dialect variant of KUPER 1. **2.** German: central variant of KUPFER. **3.** Swiss German: topographic name from *Kuppe* 'hill', 'elevation'. **4.** Swiss German: occupational name for a potter, from an agent derivative of Rhaeto-Romansh *cuppa* 'bowl', 'dish'. **5.** Jewish (Ashkenazic): variant of KUPER.

GIVEN NAMES German 4%. *Helmut, Otto, Udo.*

Kupperman (130) Jewish (Ashkenazic): variant of KUPERMAN.

GIVEN NAMES Jewish 12%. *Aron, Chaim, Elchanan, Golda, Moishe, Pinchas.*

Kuramoto (132) Japanese: '(one who lives) near the storehouse'; there are three main variants of the name as written in characters, all with the same meaning. All are found throughout Japan and on Okinawa island.

GIVEN NAMES Japanese 43%. *Hiroshi* (2), *Akira, Hideyuki, Junji, Kanji, Kazuhiko, Kazuhiro, Kenji, Masaharu, Masako, Masao, Masatake.*

Kuras (366) **1.** Polish: nickname from Polish dialect *kurasz, kuraś* 'big fat rooster', a derivative of *kur* 'rooster'. **2.** Czech (**Kuraš**): from an altered form of the personal name *Kornel*, Czech form of

Cornelius (see Cornell). **3.** Jewish (from Belarus): perhaps a habitational name for someone from the village of Kurashi in Belarus.

GIVEN NAMES Polish 8%. *Andrzej* (2), *Janusz* (2), *Darek*, *Henryk*, *Jadwiga*, *Jozef*, *Krzysztof*.

Kurata (130) Japanese: there are two forms of this name, both written with characters meaning 'storehouse' and 'rice paddy'. The more frequent version is found mainly in western Honshū and the Kyōto-Ōsaka area, and its bearers are descended from the Abel clan through the Sasaki family.

GIVEN NAMES Japanese 45%. *Kenichi* (2), *Morio* (2), *Akiko*, *Akira*, *Chiyono*, *Etsuko*, *Hanako*, *Haruo*, *Hiromichi*, *Hiroshi*, *Juro*, *Kanji*.

Kurcz (100) Polish: nickname from Old Polish *kurcz*, a kind of dog race, or from *kurczyć się* 'to shrink'.

GIVEN NAMES Polish 7%. *Casimir*, *Mateusz*.

Kurczewski (121) Polish: habitational name for someone from a place called Kurczew in Kalisz voivodeship, or Kurczewo or Kurczów in Bydgoszcz voivodeship.

GIVEN NAME Polish 4%. *Danuta*.

Kurdziel (179) Polish: unflattering nickname from Polish dialect and Old Polish *kurdziel* 'abscess on an animal's tongue'.

GIVEN NAMES Polish 8%. *Halina*, *Jozef*, *Lucja*, *Tadeusz*, *Zbigniew*.

Kure (113) Japanese: though written with the character for 'give' or 'present', the original meaning may actually be 'sunset'. The name is listed in the Shinsen shōjiroku and is no longer common in Japan, but there is a city by that name in Hiroshima prefecture and the area may have ancient connections with the family.

GIVEN NAMES Japanese 9%. *Kohji* (2), *Miyako*, *Tatsuo*, *Yoshio*.

Kurek (619) Polish: nickname from *kurek* 'cockerel', a Polish diminutive of *kur* 'rooster'.

GIVEN NAMES Polish 6%. *Jozef* (2), *Malgorzata* (2), *Stanislaw* (2), *Agnieszka*, *Andrzej*, *Bogdan*, *Miroslaw*, *Waclaw*.

Kurgan (140) Jewish (eastern Ashkenazic): habitational name for someone from a place called Kurgany in Belarus.

GIVEN NAMES Jewish 6%. *Hyman*, *Myer*.

Kuri (111) **1.** Variant of German Kury. **2.** New Zealand (Maori): unexplained.

GIVEN NAMES Spanish 12%. *Carlos* (3), *Eduardo*, *Jose*, *Luis*, *Miguel*, *Pedro*, *Ruben*.

Kurian (320) Indian (Kerala): name in the Christian community, a derivative of the Greek personal name *Kyriakos* 'of the Lord' (equivalent to Dominic), with the Tamil-Malayalam third personal singular suffix *-n*. It is found only as a given name in Kerala, but in the U.S. has come to be used as a family name among families from Kerala.

GIVEN NAMES Indian 36%. *Mohan* (3), *Varughese* (3), *Babu* (2), *Manju* (2), *Mathai* (2), *Raju* (2), *Shibu* (2), *Sobha* (2), *Anil*, *Biju*, *Binoy*, *Lal*.

Kuriger (145) German (**Küriger**): from Middle High German *kurc* 'distinct', 'excellent', 'chosen'; possibly applied as a nickname for someone with exceptional personal qualities or talents.

Kurihara (200) Japanese: meaning 'chestnut plain'; the surname is borne by several different families. One is descended through the Nakatomi clan from a family of the ancient Korean kingdom of Paekche and is listed in the Shinsen shōjiroku. Another is descended from the Seiwa-Genji through the Takeda family, and a third from the Taira clan through the Chiba family. There are other bearers of this surname, which is found chiefly in Tōkyō area, whose origins are unclear.

GIVEN NAMES Japanese 60%. *Toru* (3), *Hirofumi* (2), *Masaki* (2), *Mika* (2), *Naoto* (2), *Rokuro* (2), *Tatsuo* (2), *Aiko*, *Akinori*, *Akira*, *Atsushi*, *Ayumi*.

Kurilla (179) German: probably of eastern Slavic origin, from the personal name *Kyril* 'Cyril'.

Kurk (120) **1.** German: unexplained. Perhaps a Germanized form of Czech Kurka. **2.** English: variant spelling of Kirk.

Kurka (185) Czech: nickname for someone thought to resemble a hen, from a diminutive of *kura* 'hen', 'domestic fowl'.

Kurkjian (173) Armenian: patronymic from Turkish *kürkçü* 'furrier', from *kürk* 'fur' + the occupational suffix *-ci*.

GIVEN NAMES Armenian 18%. *Ara* (3), *Garbis* (2), *Garo*, *Haig*, *Hrand*, *Nerses*, *Sarkis*, *Satenig*, *Vahan*.

Kurkowski (383) Polish: habitational name for someone from Kurkowo in the voivodeships of Bydgoszcz or Łomża, named with *kurek* 'cockerel' (see Kurek).

GIVEN NAMES Polish 4%. *Wojciech* (2), *Basia*, *Stanislaw*.

Kurland (643) Jewish (eastern Ashkenazic): regional name for someone from Kurland, a region, now in Latvia, named for the Kurs, a Baltic people who once lived here.

GIVEN NAMES Jewish 4%. *Dov*, *Hyman*, *Yakov*, *Zelig*.

Kurlander (159) Jewish (eastern Ashkenazic): regional name for someone from Kurland.

Kurle (101) Probably a respelling of South German and Austrian **Kerle**, a variant of Karl.

Kurman (155) **1.** German (**Kurmann**) and Jewish (Ashkenazic): occupational name for an inspector of food, wine, etc., derived from Middle High German *kiesen* 'to choose, test, or inspect'. Compare Kyser. **2.** Jewish (Ashkenazic): possibly from German *Kur*, Yiddish *kur* 'cure', presumably a nickname for some sort of healer.

GIVEN NAMES Jewish 8%. *Froim*, *Mort*, *Sima*.

Kurnik (103) Austrian (Styria) and Slovenian: topographic name for someone who lived by a piece of ground that had been cleared by fire, from *kuriti* 'to make a fire', formed with the agent noun suffix *-nik*.

Kuroda (196) Japanese: 'black rice paddy', denoting an old field; mostly found in western Japan and the island of Okinawa. Also sometimes pronounced *Kurota* and *Kuruta*, it is a habitational name taken from many locations throughout Japan.

GIVEN NAMES Japanese 66%. *Hideo* (3), *Yasumasa* (3), *Yutaka* (3), *Hiroshi* (2), *Ichiro* (2), *Kazuo* (2), *Masaru* (2), *Setsu* (2), *Shinichi* (2), *Akira*, *Chiaki*, *Eiji*.

Kurokawa (128) Japanese: 'black river'; the name is found as a surname mostly on the island of Kyūshū, though several places elsewhere in Japan bear the name.

GIVEN NAMES Japanese 54%. *Takayoshi* (3), *Masato* (2), *Akemi*, *Haruo*, *Hidemi*, *Jiro*, *Katsuyoshi*, *Kazuo*, *Kazutoshi*, *Kazuya*, *Keiji*, *Kenichi*.

Kurowski (638) Polish: habitational name for someone from a place called Kurowo or Kurów, named with *kur* 'rooster'.

GIVEN NAMES Polish 6%. *Andrzej*, *Boguslaw*, *Grzegorz*, *Gustaw*, *Ireneusz*, *Jolanta*, *Krzysztof*, *Leszek*, *Stanislaw*, *Tadeusz*, *Zdzislaw*.

Kurpiel (102) Polish: **1.** nickname from *kurpiel* 'rude', 'uncouth', 'ill-mannered'. **2.** metonymic occupational name for a clog maker, from Polish dialect *kurpiel* 'clog', 'bast shoe'.

GIVEN NAME Polish 4%. *Stanislaw*.

Kurpiewski (114) Polish: habitational name for someone from a place called Kurpiewo (modern *Kurpie*) in Ostrołenka voivodeship.

GIVEN NAMES Polish 27%. *Zygmunt* (2), *Boguslaw*, *Casimir*, *Henryk*, *Ireneusz*, *Janusz*, *Jerzy*, *Stanislaw*, *Zigmunt*.

Kurr (128) **1.** German: unexplained; perhaps of Slavic origin (see 2) or a shortened form of **Kurrer**, from an agent derivative of Middle High German *kurren* 'to grunt'. **2.** Perhaps an Americanized spelling of Polish **Kur**, nickname from *kur* 'rooster'. See Kurek.

Kurre (101) German: unexplained. Compare Kurr.

Kurschner (137) German (**Kürschner**): occupational name for a furrier, Middle High German *kürsenære*, from Middle High German *kürsen* 'fur coat'.

GIVEN NAMES German 5%. *Hans* (2), *Hermann*, *Jurgen*.

Kurszewski (111) Polish: unexplained. Possibly a variant of Kruszewski.

Kurt (437) **1.** German: from the personal name *Kurt*, a reduced form of Konrad. **2.** Hungarian (**Kürt**): from an ancient Magyar clan name, from *kürt* 'horn', possibly from the symbol of the tribe.

Kurta (134) **1.** Hungarian: nickname from German Kurtz 'short'. **2.** Jewish (eastern

Ashkenazic): from Polish, Ukrainian, Belorussian *kurta* 'short overcoat', applied as a metonymic occupational name for someone who made such garments or possibly a nickname for someone who habitually wore a coat of this kind.

Kurtenbach (280) German (**Kürtenbach**): probably a habitational name from Rhineland, where Kürten is recorded as a place name meaning 'creek'.

Kurth (1913) German: variant spelling of KURT.
GIVEN NAMES German 4%. *Otto* (4), *Hans* (2), *Heinz* (2), *Bernhard, Erwin, Franz, Manfred, Matthias, Wilhelm, Wolfgang.*

Kurtin (140) Croatian (from Zadar on the Adriatic coast): Slavicized form of Italian CURTO 'short'.
GIVEN NAMES South Slavic 6%; Jewish 5%. *Bozidar, Dragan, Sime; Sol* (3).

Kurtis (122) Jewish (Ashkenazic): unexplained.

Kurtti (123) Finnish: from the personal name *Kurtti*, a Finnish form of German KURT. This surname is found chiefly in northern Finland.
GIVEN NAME Scandinavian 4%. *Helmer.*

Kurtyka (125) Polish: **1.** from a pet form of the German personal name KURT. **2.** nickname from a derivative of *kurta* 'short coat'.
GIVEN NAMES Polish 8%. *Wojciech* (2), *Bogdan, Wieslaw.*

Kurtz (9542) German and Jewish (Ashkenazic): nickname for someone who was short in stature, from Middle High German *kur(t)z*, German *kurz* 'short'.

Kurtzer (133) German and Jewish (Ashkenazic): nickname from an inflected form of KURTZ 'short'.
GIVEN NAME Jewish 4%. *Sol.*

Kurtzman (410) German (**Kurtzmann**) and Jewish (Ashkenazic): nickname for someone who was short in stature, a variant of KURTZ.
GIVEN NAMES Jewish 4%. *Hyman* (2), *Miriam, Sol.*

Kurtzweil (106) German and Jewish (Ashkenazic): variant spelling of KURZWEIL.

Kuruc (115) Variant of Hungarian KURUCZ.

Kurucz (132) Hungarian: from *kuruc* (from German KREUZ 'cross'), a term denoting the army in general or an individual soldier of the Hungarian anti-Habsburg resistance, a Magyar freedom fighter. This was originally a derogative nickname given by the Austrians to the Hungarian soldiers of Imre Thököly at the end of the 17th century and the anti-Habsburg rebels of Ferenc Rákóczi at the beginning of the 18th century.
GIVEN NAMES Hungarian 4%. *Bela, Tibor.*

Kurutz (111) Germanized spelling of Hungarian KURUCZ.

Kuruvilla (130) Indian (Kerala): elaborated form of KURIAN.
GIVEN NAMES Indian 41%. *Varughese* (3), *Anand* (2), *Thampi* (2), *Ashok, Bose, Lali,*

Mohan, Omana, Prakash, Prasad, Sheela, Suresh.

Kury (128) German and Swiss German (also **Küry**): from a short form of the medieval personal name *Quirinus.*

Kuryla (114) Variant of Ukrainian KURYLO.

Kurylo (139) Ukrainian: from the personal name *Kurýlo*, a Ukrainian form of the ancient Slavic name *Kiril*, from Greek *Kyrillos*, a derivative of *kyrios* 'lord'. This was the name of the saint and missionary of the Orthodox Church (826–869) who, together with his brother Methodios, brought Christianity to the Slavs. The Cyrillic alphabet is named for him.
GIVEN NAMES Polish 6%; German 5%. *Jerzy, Jolanta; Kurt* (2).

Kurz (1723) German and Jewish (Ashkenazic): variant spelling of KURTZ.
GIVEN NAMES German 5%. *Erna* (2), *Hans* (2), *Jutta* (2), *Armin, Benno, Fritz, Gunter, Heinz, Hermann, Horst, Manfred, Otto.*

Kurzawa (133) Polish: nickname from *kurzawa* 'whirling cloud of dust'.
GIVEN NAMES Polish 8%. *Boleslaw, Jerzy, Wieslaw, Wincenty.*

Kurzman (111) Variant of German **Kurtzmann** and Jewish KURTZMAN.

Kurzweil (173) German and Jewish (Ashkenazic): nickname for a joker, from German *Kurzweil* 'pastime', 'amusement', 'entertainment', a compound of *kurz* 'short' + *Weile* 'while', 'short time'.

Kus (302) **1.** Polish: descriptive nickname from *kus, kusy* 'short', 'cropped (hair)', 'bob-tailed' (see KUSY). **2.** Slovenian and Czech: nickname from *kus*, an old spelling of *kos* 'blackbird' (see KOS), perhaps applied to someone with a good singing voice. **3.** Hungarian: from Slavic *kus* 'falcon'. This was a totemic symbol of an ancient Hungarian clan, hence a protective name for a member of the tribe. **4.** German: variant of KUSS.
GIVEN NAMES Polish 7%; German 4%. *Andrzej, Boguslaw, Krystyna, Ludwik, Miroslaw, Tadeusz, Tadusz; Florian, Otto, Winfried.*

Kusch (327) German: **1.** probably from a short form of either of two germanicized Slavic personal names *Jakusch* (see JACOB) and *Mikusch* (see NICHOLAS). **2.** from a pet form of *Godizo*, from a Germanic personal name, formed with *god, got* 'god', which intertwined very early with *gōd* 'good'.

Kuschel (312) **1.** German: from a pet form of either of the personal names *Jacob* and *Nicholas* (see KUSCH). **2.** German: variant of KUSCH 2. **3.** Jewish (Ashkenazic): from the Yiddish personal name *kushl*, a pet form of the Biblical name *Yekuthiel*.

Kuse (153) **1.** German: from Middle Low German *kuse* 'club', 'cudgel'. **2.** German: from a pet form of the personal name *Cuonrad* (see KONRAD). **3.** Japanese: not common in Japan, this name is usually

written with characters meaning 'long time' and 'generation'.
GIVEN NAMES Japanese 5%. *Isamu, Koichi, Takashi.*

Kusek (312) Polish: nickname from Polish dialect *kusek* 'a bite to eat', 'a little bit'; or perhaps a derivative of *kusy* 'short' (see KUS).
GIVEN NAMES Polish 4%. *Casimir, Eugeniusz, Wladyslaw.*

Kusel (154) **1.** North German (also **Küsel**): nickname for a squat but agile person, from Middle Low German *kusel* 'spinning top'. **2.** South German: nickname from Middle High German *kuose* 'female calf' or 'sheep'. **3.** German: habitational name for someone from Kusel in Palatinate or Küsel near Magdeburg. **4.** German: metonymic occupational name for someone who made or used sickles, from Sorbian *kósa* 'sickle'. **5.** Jewish (Ashkenazic): from the Yiddish personal name *kusl*, a pet form of the Biblical name *Yekuthiel*.
GIVEN NAME German 4%. *Heinz.*

Kuser (140) German and Swiss German: **1.** metronymic from a short form of the female personal name *Kunigunde* (see KUENNEN). **2.** habitational name, perhaps for someone from Kues on the Mosel, alternatively from some other place similarly named.

Kush (598) Respelling of German KUSCH.

Kushman (131) Origin unidentified.

Kushner (2012) Jewish (eastern Ashkenazic): occupational name from Belorussian *kushner* 'furrier', a word of German origin (see KURSCHNER).
GIVEN NAMES Jewish 5%. *Sol* (4), *Hyman* (3), *Meyer* (2), *Emanuel, Mascha, Meir, Miriam, Mort, Moshe, Naum, Ruvim, Semen.*

Kushnir (312) Ukrainian and Jewish (from Ukraine): occupational name for a furrier, Ukrainian *kushnir*, a word of German origin (see KURSCHNER).
GIVEN NAMES Russian 27%; Jewish 20%. *Mikhail* (6), *Leonid* (5), *Boris* (4), *Aleksandr* (3), *Efim* (3), *Lev* (2), *Sofya* (2), *Svetlana* (2), *Yuriy* (2), *Anatolij, Anatoly, Arkadiy; Yakov* (4), *Ilya* (3), *Moysey* (3), *Naum* (3), *Froim, Genya, Isaak, Marat, Mariya, Polina, Rina, Ruvim.*

Kusiak (236) Polish: nickname or patronymic from *kusy* 'short' or 'poor', or from *kusić* 'to tempt'.
GIVEN NAMES Polish 9%. *Casimir, Feliks, Stanislaw, Wieslaw, Zigmund, Zygmont.*

Kuska (100) Probably a respelling of German KUSKE.

Kuske (269) German (of Slavic origin): a reduced form of the personal name *Markus*.

Kuskie (108) Origin unidentified.

Kusler (233) Altered spelling of North German **Kuseler** or **Küseler**, a nickname for an agile, restless person, from an agent derivative of Middle Low German *kuselen* 'to spin (like a top)'.

Kusner (124) Jewish (eastern Ashkenazic): variant of KUSHNER.

Kuss (621) **1.** German: from *Kunz*, a pet form of KONRAD. **2.** Eastern German (of Slavic origin): nickname from Polish *kusy* 'short'. **3.** German: habitational name from Bernkastel-Kues on the Mosel river. **4.** from the personal name *Kus*, a pet form of *Markus* (see MARK) or *Dominikus* (see DOMINIQUE).
GIVEN NAMES German 5%. *Gerhard* (2), *Kurt* (2), *Erwin, Helmut, Otto, Willi.*

Kussman (210) German: variant of KUSS.
GIVEN NAME German 4%. *Otto* (2).

Kussmaul (110) German: apparently from *Kuss* 'kiss' + *Maul* 'mouth', but actually a Germanized form of Czech *kosmatý* 'shaggy-haired'.
GIVEN NAMES German 5%; Dutch 5%. *Willi; Rud* (2).

Kussow (101) German: habitational name from places called Kussow or Kossow, both in Mecklenburg.

Kust (156) Czech: **1.** dialect variant of a nickname from Czech *kůst*, a dialect form of *kost* 'bone'. **2.** from the German personal name KUNST 2 or 3.

Kuster (816) **1.** German (also **Küster**): status name for a sexton or churchwarden, Middle High German *kuster* (Late Latin *custor* 'guard', 'warden'). The umlaut of the modern form is due to association with other agent nouns in *-er*, from Old High German *-āri* (Latin *-arius*). **2.** Slovenian (**Kušter**): nickname for a person with disheveled hair, from *kušter* 'tuft of hair', 'towhead'.
GIVEN NAMES German 4%. *Kurt* (2), *Armin, Eldor, Hans, Heinz, Horst, Ulrich.*

Kusterer (101) German: from an agent derivative of KUSTER.
GIVEN NAMES German 7%. *Helmut, Wilhelm.*

Kustra (186) Polish: unflattering nickname for a slow, indolent person, from Polish dialect and Old Polish *kustrać się* 'to dawdle'.
GIVEN NAMES Polish 6%. *Boleslaw, Danuta, Jozef, Zbigniew.*

Kusumoto (108) Japanese: '(one who lives) near the camphor tree'. This name is found mostly in the Ōsaka area and Okinawa.
GIVEN NAMES Japanese 53%. *Katsumi* (2), *Takashi* (2), *Hiro, Hiroki, Isao, Jiro, Kazuhiro, Kazuhito, Kikuko, Masami, Masayuki, Minoru.*

Kusy (141) Czech and Slovak (**Kusý**), Polish, and Jewish (from Poland): nickname for a person of short stature, from Polish *kusy* 'short', Czech *kusý* 'incomplete', 'unfinished', 'truncated'.
GIVEN NAMES Polish 7%; German 4%. *Jozef* (3), *Ludwika; Monika.*

Kusz (125) Polish: from a short form of the personal name *Jakusz*, a pet form of **Jakob** (see JACOB).
GIVEN NAME Polish 5%. *Janusz* (2).

Kuszmaul (105) Hungarian spelling of German KUSSMAUL.

Kuta (412) **1.** Polish: nickname from *kuty* 'wrought', 'forged', also used in the sense 'cunning', 'shrewd', or 'wily'. **2.** Czech: nickname from *kutý* 'well wrought', 'well versed'.
GIVEN NAMES Polish 5%; German 4%. *Beata, Ignacy, Stanislaw, Zbigniew, Zofia; Kurt* (2), *Konrad, Monika.*

Kutach (112) German: unexplained.
GIVEN NAMES German 9%. *Otto* (2), *Alois.*

Kutch (400) Americanized variant of German KUTSCH.

Kutcher (455) Americanized variant of German and Jewish KUTSCHER.

Kuter (109) **1.** German (**Küter**): occupational name for a butcher or sausage maker, from Middle High German, Middle Low German *kuter* 'butcher' (from *kut* 'entrails', 'tripe'). **2.** Jewish (eastern Ashkenazic): unexplained.

Kutil (128) Czech: unexplained.

Kutler (124) Jewish (Ashkenazic): possibly a variant of KOTLER.
GIVEN NAMES Jewish 7%. *Sol* (3), *Meyer.*

Kutner (421) **1.** German: variant spelling of KUTTNER. **2.** Jewish (from Poland): habitational name for someone from Kutno in central Poland.
GIVEN NAMES Jewish 4%. *Ephraim* (2), *Ari, Shifra, Sol.*

Kutney (115) Origin uncertain; probably an Americanized form of German KUTNER.

Kutsch (287) German: **1.** topographic name of Slavic origin, from Sorbian *kut* 'corner', 'nook'. **2.** variant of **Kutsche**, metonymic occupational name for a coachman or coachbuilder, from the Hungarian loanword *kocsi* (see KOCSIS).

Kutscher (184) German and Jewish (Ashkenazic): occupational name for a coachman or coachbuilder, from a derivative of the 16th-century Hungarian loanword *kocsi* 'coach', German *Kutsche*. The German *-u-* vowel comes from Slavic (Polish *kucer*).
GIVEN NAMES German 5%. *Hans, Kurt, Lothar.*

Kutter (225) German: **1.** variant of **Küter** (see KUTER). **2.** habitational name for someone from Kottern in Bavaria. **3.** occupational name from *kutten* 'to rummage through spoil heaps from mining'.
GIVEN NAMES German 7%. *Hans, Klaus, Monika, Wolf, Wolfgang.*

Kuttler (147) German (also **Küttler**): occupational name for a butcher who prepared and sold offal for making into sausage meat, Middle High German *kuteler*. Compare KUTER.

Kuttner (164) South German (also **Küttner**): nickname from Middle High German *kuttener* 'robe wearer', 'monk'.
GIVEN NAMES German 12%. *Fritz, Gerhard, Hanns, Heinz, Irmgard.*

Kutz (1714) German: **1.** habitational name for someone from Kuhz, near Prenzlau.

2. from a pet form of the personal name KONRAD. **3.** Germanized form of Polish KUC 'pony', 'short person'.

Kutzer (186) German: **1.** occupational name for a coachman or a coach builder, from a derivative of the Hungarian loanword *kocsi* 'coach' (see KOCSIS). **2.** variant of KUTSCHER. **3.** (**Kützer**): nickname for a miser, Middle High German *kützer*.
GIVEN NAMES German 5%. *Gerhard, Otto.*

Kutzke (113) German: diminutive of KUTZ.

Kutzler (156) German (**Kützler**): **1.** probably a variant of KUTZER. 3 **2.** metonymic occupational name for an upholsterer, from Rhenish dialect *kützel* 'cushion'.

Kutzner (146) German: occupational name for a blanket maker, from Middle High German *kotze* 'coarse shaggy woolen cloth', 'blanket or garment made of such material'. In Bavaria and Austria *kotze* is still used to denote the woolen cloth more widely known as *Loden*.
GIVEN NAMES German 10%. *Arno, Horst, Inge, Kurt, Wolfgang.*

Kuusisto (105) Finnish: topographic name from *kuusi* 'spruce' + the local ending *-sto*. This name is found chiefly in western and central Finland.
GIVEN NAMES Finnish 19%. *Pekka* (2), *Urho* (2), *Arvo, Jaakko, Waino, Wiljo.*

Kuwahara (170) Japanese: 'mulberry plain'; also pronounced *Kuwabara*. One family of *Kuwahara-gō* in Yamato (now Nara prefecture) claims descent from ancient Chinese immigrants, which is feasible because silk culture was imported from China and Korea, and silkworms eat mulberry leaves. Other families have taken the name from similarly named locations throughout Japan.
GIVEN NAMES Japanese 41%. *Akio* (2), *Hideo* (2), *Kenji* (2), *Toshio* (2), *Akihiro, Etsuko, Fuji, Fumio, Hideaki, Hiro, Hiroko, Hitoshi.*

Kuykendall (3603) Variant of Dutch **Kerkendal** (see KIRKENDALL).

Kuyper (295) Dutch: variant spelling of KUIPER.
GIVEN NAMES Dutch 4%. *Pieter* (2), *Derk, Dirk.*

Kuypers (120) Dutch: variant of KUIPER.
GIVEN NAMES Dutch 10%. *Cor, Derk, Frans, Maarten, Pieter.*

Kuzara (113) Polish: from a variant of *koziarz* 'goatherd'.
GIVEN NAME Polish 4%. *Leszek.*

Kuzel (184) Czech (**Kužel**): from *kužel* 'distaff', 'cone', either a descriptive nickname for someone with a cone-shaped head or an unflattering nickname for an unstable, inconstant person, one who was easliy moved around.

Kuzia (115) Polish: **1.** unflattering nickname from Polish dialect *kuza* 'old cow'. **2.** from *kuzia*, an expression used to drive away horses.

GIVEN NAMES Polish 10%. *Leslaw* (2), *Bogdan, Halina.*

Kuzio (115) Polish: variant of KUZIA.

Kuzma (1005) **1.** Ukrainian and Belorussian: from the personal name *Kuzma*, Greek *Kosmas*, a derivative of *kosmos* 'universe', '(ordered) arrangement'. St. Cosmas, martyred with his brother Damian in Cilicia in the early 4th century AD, came to be widely revered in the Eastern Church. **2.** Slovenian (also **Küzma**): from the personal name *Kuzma, Küzma*, dialect forms of *Kozma*, Greek *Kosmas* (see 1 above). The spelling **Küzma** come from easternmost Slovenia.

Kuzmich (149) **1.** Ukrainian: patronymic from the personal name KUZMA. **2.** Slovenian (**Kuzmič, Küzmič**): patronymic from the personal name *Kuzma, Küzma* (see KUZMA 2). The form **Küzmič** comes from easternmost Slovenia.

GIVEN NAMES Russian 5%. *Aleksandr, Vasiliy, Vasily.*

Kuzminski (166) **1.** Polish (**Kuźmiński**) and eastern Slavic: from the personal name *Kuźma* (see KUZMA). **2.** Polish, Ukrainian, and Jewish (from Ukraine): habitational name for someone from Kuźmina in Przemyśl voivodeship or from Kuzmin or Kuzmintsy in Ukraine.

GIVEN NAMES Polish 4%. *Casimir, Piotr.*

Kuznetsov (120) Russian and Jewish (from Belarus): patronymic form of an occupational name meaning 'smith' in Russian.

GIVEN NAMES Russian 61%; Jewish 14%. *Vladimir* (7), *Boris* (5), *Igor* (5), *Aleksandr* (4), *Sergei* (4), *Gennadiy* (3), *Anatoliy* (2), *Galina* (2), *Grigoriy* (2), *Oleg* (2), *Anatoly, Andrei; Faina, Mikhael, Yakov; Alexandr* (2), *Pavel* (2), *Vladislav* (2).

Kuznia (170) Polish (**Kuźnia**): metonymic occupational name for a smith, from *kuźnia* 'smithy', 'forge'.

Kuzniar (221) Polish (**Kuźniar**): occupational name for a smith, from an agent noun derived from *kuźnia* 'smithy', 'forge'.

GIVEN NAMES Polish 7%. *Janusz, Krystyna, Slawomir, Tadeusc.*

Kuznicki (203) Polish (**Kuźnicki**): habitational name for someone from any of various places called Kuźnica or Kuźnice, named with Polish *kuźnia* 'smithy', 'forge'.

GIVEN NAMES Polish 6%. *Jacek, Jaroslaw, Stanislaw.*

Kuznik (111) **1.** Polish (**Kuźnik**): occupational name for a blacksmith, from a diminutive of *kuźnia* 'smithy', 'forge' (see KUZNIA). **2.** Slovenian (central Slovenia; **Kužnik**): unflattering nickname from the archaic word *kužnik* 'person with bubonic plague', a derivative of the adjective *kužen* 'pestilential', from *kuga* '(bubonic) plague'.

GIVEN NAME Dutch 4%. *Dirk.*

Kvale (186) Norwegian: habitational name from any of numerous farmsteads named

Kvåle, from the dative singular of Old Norse *hváll* 'knoll'.

GIVEN NAMES Scandinavian 15%. *Erik, Knut, Lars, Oddvar, Selmer.*

Kvalheim (105) Scandinavian: unexplained.

GIVEN NAMES Scandinavian 21%. *Per* (3), *Nels* (2), *Erik.*

Kvam (239) Norwegian: habitational name from any of numerous farmsteads named Kvam from Old Norse *hvammr* 'small valley'.

GIVEN NAMES Scandinavian 10%; German 4%. *Erik* (2), *Halvar, Lars, Sig, Thor; Kurt* (2).

Kvamme (249) Norwegian: habitational name from any of numerous farmsteads, especially in Vestlandet, named Kvamme, from the dative singular of Old Norse *hvammr* 'little valley'.

GIVEN NAMES Scandinavian 11%. *Torvald* (2), *Lief, Sig.*

Kvapil (102) Czech: nickname for a quick, hasty person, from a derivative of the verb *kvapit* 'be in a hurry'.

Kvasnicka (223) Czech (**Kvasnička**): from *kvasnička* 'sour cherry', applied as a nickname.

GIVEN NAMES Czech and Slovak 6%. *Ladislav, Ludmila, Milan.*

Kveton (134) Czech (**Květoň**): from the personal name *Květoň*, a derivative of *květ* 'flower', adopted as a vernacular equivalent of *Florián*, Latin *Florianus* (see FLORIAN).

Kvidera (117) Czech: unexplained.

Kvistad (100) Swedish: habitational name from a place called *Kvistad* or perhaps a reduced form of the ornamental name **Kviststad**, from *kvist* 'twig' + *stad* 'town'.

GIVEN NAME Scandinavian 5%. *Elert.*

Kwak (877) Korean: there is only one Chinese character used for the surname Kwak. Some sources list 52 clans for Kwak, but only two clans can be documented. The founder of the Ch'ŏngju Kwak family was an official during the reign of Shilla King Hŏn'gyŏng (875–886) named Kwak Sang. The founder of the other Kwak clan, the Hyŏnp'ung clan, was named Kwak Kyŏng, and migrated to Korea from Song China in 1133.

GIVEN NAMES Korean 53%. *Young* (12), *Sang* (10), *Sung* (7), *Jung* (6), *Dong* (5), *Yong* (5), *Doo* (3), *Han* (3), *Kyung* (3), *Seung* (3), *Soon* (3), *Yoon* (3); *Chang* (8), *Byung* (4), *Chong* (4), *Chul* (3), *Sinae* (3), *Soon Ok* (3), *Dong Soo* (2), *Hae* (2), *Han Young* (2), *Kum* (2), *Min* (2), *Byung Ho.*

Kwan (1747) **1.** Chinese 关: variant of GUAN 1. **2.** Chinese 管: variant of GUAN 2. **3.** Korean: variant of KWON.

GIVEN NAMES Chinese/Korean 33%. *Wing* (20), *Chun* (12), *Wai* (9), *Kin* (7), *Yuk* (7), *Chi* (6), *Kam* (6), *Man* (6), *Wah* (6), *Ming* (5), *Hong* (4), *Shui* (4); *Chung* (10), *Pak* (4), *Yiu* (4), *Cho* (2), *Chun Ho, Hosang, Kum, Moon, Shiu, Sik, Toy, Woon.*

Kwasniewski (246) Polish (**Kwaśniewski**): **1.** habitational name for someone from Kwaśno in Płock voivodeship or Kwaśniów in Katowice voivodeship, named with *kwaśny* 'sour', probably referring to the quality of the soil. **2.** possibly a derivative of *kwaśny* as an unflattering nickname for a sour-faced man.

GIVEN NAMES Polish 4%. *Izydor, Jacek.*

Kwasnik (192) Polish (**Kwaśnik**): nickname for someone with an acerbic manner, from *kwas* 'acid'.

GIVEN NAMES Polish 12%. *Andrzey, Elzbieta, Ewa, Janusz, Krystyna, Miroslaw, Stanislaw, Wladyslaw.*

Kwasny (240) Polish (**Kwaśny**): nickname for a sour-faced individual, from *kwaśny* 'sour', 'peevish', from *kwas* 'acid'.

GIVEN NAMES Polish 6%. *Krzysztof* (2), *Boguslaw, Iwona.*

Kwiat (129) Polish and Jewish (from Poland): from Polish *kwiat* 'flower', a metonymic occupational name for a florist or a gardener. As a Jewish name, this is generally of ornamental origin.

Kwiatek (210) Polish and Jewish (from Poland): from a diminutive of *kwiat* 'flower', a metonymic occupational name for a grower or seller of flowers. As a Jewish name it is generally ornamental.

GIVEN NAMES Polish 6%. *Malgorzata, Marzena, Witold.*

Kwiatkowski (2224) Polish and Jewish (from Poland): habitational name from any of various places called Kwiatków, Kwiatkowo, or Kwiatkowice, named with Polish *kwiatek* 'flower'.

GIVEN NAMES Polish 8%. *Bogdan* (4), *Janusz* (3), *Jaroslaw* (3), *Andrzej* (2), *Boguslaw* (2), *Halina* (2), *Henryk* (2), *Jerzy* (2), *Kazimierz* (2), *Stanislaw* (2), *Witold* (2), *Wojciech* (2).

Kwiecien (159) Polish (**Kwiecień**): from Polish *kwiecień* 'April', given to someone who was baptized in that month.

GIVEN NAMES Polish 16%. *Danuta, Jacek, Kazimierz, Krystyna, Lucyna, Piotr, Tadeusz, Thadeus, Wladyslaw, Zigmund.*

Kwiecinski (263) Polish (**Kwieciński**) and Jewish (from Poland): habitational name for someone from a place called Kwiecin (now in Lithuania), named with *kwiat* 'flower'. As a Jewish name, it is of ornamental origin.

GIVEN NAMES Polish 9%. *Pawel* (2), *Jerzy, Maciej, Mariusz, Wieslaw, Zbigniew, Zosia.*

Kwock (116) **1.** Chinese 郭: variant of GUO 1. **2.** Chinese 国: variant of GUO 2. . **3.** Korean: variant of KWAK. **4.** Hawaiian: unexplained.

GIVEN NAMES Chinese/Korean 6%. *Chan, Chi Ming, Fook, Sau Ying, Yick.*

Kwok (1062) **1.** Chinese 郭: variant of GUO 1. **2.** Chinese 国: variant of GUO 2. **3.** Korean: variant of KWAK.

GIVEN NAMES Chinese/Korean 25%. *Choi* (5), *Chun* (5), *Kam* (5), *Ching* (4), *Ping* (4), *Sai* (4), *Sun* (4), *Kwong* (3), *Pui* (3), *Cheng* (2), *Chi* (2), *Fei* (2).

Kwolek (204) Altered form, under German influence, of Polish **Chwałek** (see CHWALEK).

GIVEN NAMES Polish 4%. *Czeslaw, Zygmund.*

Kwon (2132) **1.** Korean (**Kwŏn**): there is only Chinese character for the Kwŏn surname. Some sources list as many as 56 clans, but only two are documented. One of these, the Andong Kwŏn clan, was founded by a Shilla aristocrat named Kim Shin who helped Wang Kŏn, the founder of the Koryŏ kingdom, establish himself as ruler in 918. The new king bestowed upon Kim Shin a new surname: Kwŏn, meaning 'authority'. The Andong Kwŏn clan has one of the oldest extant printed genealogies in Korea. The Yech'ŏn Kwŏn clan's original surname was **Hŭn**. However, the name Hŭn was chosen for the Koryŏ king Myŏngjong's posthumous name in 1197. To avoid having living people using a king's posthumous name, the Hŭn family were directed to change their name to Kwŏn. The head of the Hŭn clan at this time became Kwŏn Sŏ, the founding ancestor of the Yech'ŏn Kwŏn clan. Approximately two thirds of all present-day Kwŏn clan members live in the Kyŏngsang provinces. **2.** Chinese 关: variant of GUAN 1. **3.** Chinese 管: variant of GUAN 2.

GIVEN NAMES Korean 68%. *Young* (82), *Yong* (25), *Soon* (21), *Oh* (18), *Jung* (14), *Sang* (14), *Sung* (14), *Hyuk* (13), *Sun* (12), *Hee* (8), *Kyung* (8), *Suk* (8), *Byung* (6), *Chang* (5), *Young Hwa* (5), *Chong* (4), *Chung* (4), *Hak* (4), *Moon* (4), *Seok* (4), *Sung Hee* (4), *Hyong* (3), *Taek* (3), *Wook* (3).

Kwong (1169) **1.** Chinese 邝: variant of KUANG 1. **2.** Chinese 匡: variant of KUANG 2.

GIVEN NAMES Chinese 30%. *Wing* (7), *Kin* (6), *Kam* (5), *Wah* (5), *Wai* (5), *Yuk* (5), *Wun*

(4), *Cheung* (3), *Fung* (3), *Kwok* (3), *Mei* (3), *Ming* (3), *Pak* (3), *Shiu* (3), *Moon* (2), *Yiu* (2), *Chung, In Sung, Kok, Sik, Woon.*

Ky (141) Vietnamese: unexplained.

GIVEN NAMES Vietnamese 57%; Other Southeast Asian 14%. *Hoa* (3), *Hong* (2), *Sun* (2), *Bau, Cau, Chanh, Dieu, Duc, Dung, Duong, Dzung, Hoang, Hung, Hung Quoc, Pheng; Chin, Chou, Kam, Lim, Pao, Sang, Song, Teng, Tuong.*

Kyburz (109) Swiss German: unexplained.

GIVEN NAME German 5%. *Helmut.*

Kydd (146) Scottish: variant spelling of KIDD.

Kye (151) **1.** English: unexplained; possibly a respelling of KAY 6, a shortened form of Scottish and Irish MCKAY. **2.** Korean: There is only one Chinese character and one clan for the Kye family name. According to the Kye family genealogy, the clan was founded by a Ming Dynasty government official named Kye Sŏk-son who migrated to Koryŏ and settled in today's Suan County of Hwanghae Province. The majority of bearers of the Kye family name today live in North Korea.

GIVEN NAMES Korean 31%. *Kwang* (5), *Young* (3), *Hoon* (2), *Yong* (2), *Dong, Ho, Ho Joon, Hyun, Jihong, Jin, Junghee, Jung Hee, Kiho, Min, Myong Ho, Song, Sun Ja, Taek, Wonkyu.*

Kyer (254) Americanized spelling of German GEIER.

GIVEN NAME German 5%. *Fritz* (4).

Kyes (200) Probably an Americanized spelling of German GEIS.

Kyger (260) Possibly a respelling of German (Alemannic) **Keiger**, a nickname from an agent derivative of Middle High German *kegen* 'to shuffle'.

Kyker (318) Dutch: perhaps a nickname from *kijker* 'spectator'.

Kyle (6379) **1.** Scottish and northern Irish: regional name from a district in Ayrshire called Kyle, named for the British chieftains who ruled it in the 5th century, the

Coel Hen. **2.** Scottish and northern Irish: habitational name from any of the numerous Scottish places named Kyle from Gaelic *caol* 'narrow', also *caolas* 'narrows', 'strait'. Compare KYLES.

Kyler (550) German (of Slavic origin): from a derivative of the Irish personal name *Kilian* (see KILIAN, KILLEEN).

Kyles (851) **1.** Scottish and northern Irish: habitational name from any of various minor places named with Gaelic *caolas* 'narrows', 'strait'. Compare KYLE. **2.** Czech (**Kyleš**): from a personal name derived from Irish *Kilian* (see KILIAN, KILLEEN).

Kyllo (256) Finnish (**Kyllö**): from the old Finnish personal name *Kyllä, Kyllöi,* or *Kylliä.* In America it may also be a shortened form of **Kyllönen** (see KYLLONEN).

Kyllonen (225) Finnish (**Kyllönen**): from the old Finnish personal name *Kyll(i)ä, Kyllö,* + the common surname suffix *-nen.* This name occurs chiefly in eastern and central Finland (Savo), where it has been recorded since the 16th century.

GIVEN NAMES Finnish 9%. *Tauno* (2), *Aune, Eino, Jussi, Toimi, Toivo, Wilho.*

Kynard (127) Possibly an altered spelling of German **Kühnhard**, a variant of KUEHNERT.

Kyne (203) Irish: variant of COYNE.

Kysar (208) Dutch: variant of KYSER.

Kyser (1059) **1.** Dutch: from an old spelling of *keizer* 'emperor', 'czar'; either as a nickname or as the title of the head of a sharpshooting club. **2.** German (**Kyser**): occupational name for an inspector of food, wine, etc., from Middle High German *kiesen* 'to choose', 'test', or 'inspect'. **3.** Jewish: Americanized spelling of KAISER 2.

GIVEN NAMES Jewish 8%. *Froim, Mort, Sima.*

Kyte (506) English: variant spelling of KITE.

Kyzar (192) Dutch: variant of KYSER.

Kyzer (524) Dutch: variant of KYSER.

L

La (687) Vietnamese (**La** and **Lã**): two Vietnamese names, both unexplained.
GIVEN NAMES Vietnamese 49%; Chinese 19%. *Hung* (15), *Cuong* (9), *Anh* (8), *Thanh* (8), *Ha* (5), *Hoang* (5), *Tuan* (5), *Chau* (4), *Hao* (4), *Hien* (4), *Hoa* (4), *Hue* (4); *Nam* (3), *Phong* (2), *Sinh* (2), *Tuong* (2), *Min, Tam, Tanh, Thai, Tham, Tinh, Yeong; Hong* (4), *Hang* (2), *Sang* (2), *Tong* (2), *Chan, Chi, Hwa Ja, Hyung, Kam, Ki Bong, Kin, Man.*

Laabs (699) North German: habitational name from some eastern German place name (of Slavic origin), such as Labes in Pomerania.
GIVEN NAMES German 4%. *Armin* (3), *Erwin, Frieda, Gerhardt, Kurt, Otto.*

Laack (155) North German: topographic name for someone living in a swampy or wetland area, Middle Low German *lake*, or a habitational name from Laak on the Orte river in Lower Saxony.

Laake (202) **1.** North German: variant of LAACK. **2.** Norwegian: habitational name from either of two farmsteads near Oslo named Låke, possibly from a river name from Old Norse *leka* 'drip', 'leak'.
GIVEN NAME German 4%. *Otto* (2).

Laakso (298) Finnish: from *laakso* 'valley', generally an ornamental name adopted during the name conversion movement of the 19th and early 20th centuries. Often, it was adopted by Finnish bearers of Swedish names containing the Swedish element *dal* 'valley'.
GIVEN NAMES Finnish 12%; Scandinavian 8%. *Toini* (3), *Eino* (2), *Aarre, Arvo, Eero, Jorma, Olavi, Tarja, Tauno, Toivo, Veikko; Erik, Hilma, Nels, Viljo.*

Laas (136) **1.** Eastern German: habitational name of Slavic origin, from a town so named in Saxony, from Slavic *laz* 'uncultivated land', 'clearing'. **2.** North German (Hamburg): possibly a metonymic occupational name for a fisherman, from Middle Low German *las* 'salmon' (see LAX 1).
GIVEN NAMES German 6%. *Heino, Otto.*

Laatsch (269) North German: regional nickname for a person with a slouching gait, then for a limp, listless person, from the adjective *latsch*, with the above meaning (see LASCH).

Lab (136) German: perhaps a habitational name for someone from Labe in Bohemia or Laabe in Bavaria, both named with German *Lab* 'rennet'.

Laba (167) Polish (**Łaba**): nickname from Polish dialect *łaba* 'paw', standard Polish *łapa.*
GIVEN NAMES Polish 8%. *Zbigniew* (2), *Mieczyslaw, Teofil.*

Labadie (586) **1.** Southern French: topographical name from Occitan *l'abadie* 'the abbey' (see ABADIE). **2.** In some cases, possibly Italian (Sicily), of the same origin as 1.
GIVEN NAMES French 7%. *Emile* (5), *Antoine* (2), *Fabien, Jeanpaul, Monique.*

Labahn (127) German (Pomerania): habitational name from any of various place names such as Labehn, Labahn, all of Slavic origin.
GIVEN NAME French 4%. *Albert Louis.*

Laban (135) **1.** North German: variant of LABAHN. **2.** Possibly an altered spelling of Hungarian **Labanc**, a nickname for a pro-Austrian soldier who fought against the Hungarians in the independence wars in the late 17th and early 18th centuries. This derogatory nickname derived from the Hungarian *lobonc* 'unkempt hair', referring the long hair of the Habsburg soldiers. Later the name became a vocabulary word denoting a foot soldier or a rough strong man. See also KURUCZ.

Labar (728) French: variant spelling of LABARRE.

La Barbera (903) Italian (Sicily, southern Calabria): from *barbiera*, a term used to denote both the wife of a barber and a prostitute.
GIVEN NAMES Italian 15%. *Sal* (7), *Salvatore* (7), *Vito* (5), *Angelo* (4), *Ciro* (3), *Francesca* (2), *Giuseppe* (2), *Vincenzo* (2), *Antonio, Carmine, Cataldo, Domenico.*

La Barca (109) **1.** Spanish: habitational name from any of several places called La Barca (see BARCA). **2.** Southern Italian: probably a topographic or metonymic occupational name for a sailor or the owner of a boat (see BARCA).
GIVEN NAMES Spanish 21%; Italian 15%. *Carlos* (2), *Ramon* (2), *Jose, Luis, Marcelo, Pedro, Raul, Sergio, Wilfredo; Carmine, Ciro, Giovanni, Salvatore, Vito.*

Labare (119) French (Belgium): variant spelling of LABARRE.

Labarge (1115) French: see BARGE.
GIVEN NAMES French 4%. *Andree* (2), *Pierre* (2), *Alphonse, Andrus, Marcel, Michel, Monique, Napoleon.*

Labarr (277) French: variant spelling of LABARRE.

Labarre (790) French: topographic name for someone who lived by a gateway or barrier, from Old French *barre* 'bar', 'obstruction' (of obscure origin, possibly akin to the Celtic element *barr* 'height'), or a habitational name from Barre-en-Ouche in Eure or Barre-de-Semilly in Manche, both named with this word.
GIVEN NAMES French 7%. *Pierre* (2), *Alain, Andre, Armand, Aurore, Fernande, Gilles, Herve, Laure, Michel, Urbain.*

Labash (101) **1.** Americanized form of Polish **Łabasz**, a variant of **Łaba** (see LABA). **2.** Americanized form of Czech **Lubaš** (see LUBAS).

Labat (332) Southern French: **1.** from Occitan *l'abat* 'the priest'. Compare LABBE. **2.** topographic name for someone who lived in a valley, from Gascon dialect *la bat* 'the valley', equivalent of French LAVALLE.
FOREBEARS A bearer of the name from Bordeaux, France, was established at Trois Rivières, Quebec, by 1653.
GIVEN NAMES French 8%. *Emile* (2), *Chanel, Germain, Lucien, Michel, Monique, Ulysse.*

Labate (343) Italian (**L'Abate**): variant of ABATE 'priest', with the definite article *l(o).*
GIVEN NAMES Italian 21%. *Angelo* (3), *Salvator* (2), *Salvatore* (2), *Aldo, Antonino, Antonio, Carmelo, Carmine, Domenic, Domenico, Francesco, Gaetano.*

Labauve (242) Of French origin: unexplained. Compare LABOVE. This name occurs chiefly in Louisiana.

Labay (252) Americanized spelling of French LABBE 'the priest'.

Labbate (109) Italian: variant of **Abbate** (see ABATE), with the definite article *l(o).*
GIVEN NAMES Italian 28%. *Angelo* (2), *Benedetto, Dante, Dino, Matteo, Olympia, Rocco, Salvatore, Saverio.*

Labbe (1625) French (**Labbé**): from Old French *l'abe(t)*, 'the priest'; an occupational name for someone employed in the household of a priest, or in some cases perhaps for the priest himself.
FOREBEARS A bearer of the name from Maine, France, was established in Orleans Isle, Quebec, by 1672.
GIVEN NAMES French 15%. *Marcel* (8), *Andre* (6), *Armand* (6), *Fernand* (5), *Lucien* (5), *Normand* (5), *Aime* (3), *Camille* (3), *Emile* (3), *Laurent* (3), *Marielle* (2), *Raoul* (2).

Labbee (119) French: variant of **Labbé** (see LABBE).

GIVEN NAMES French 11%. *Fernand, Gilles, Marcel.*

Labby (110) French: variant of **Labbé** (see LABBE).

Labeau (365) Variant of French LEBEAU 'the handsome (man)'. In Canada and New England, the masculine definite article is often replaced by the feminine.

GIVEN NAMES French 4%. *Alain, Amiee, Phillippe, Pierre.*

Labell (204) French: variant spelling of LABELLE.

GIVEN NAMES French 6%. *Andre, Donat, Emile.*

La Bella (775) Italian (**La Bèlla, Labèlla**): nickname from *La Bèlla*, literally 'the beautiful (female)' (see BELLA).

GIVEN NAMES Italian 18%. *Angelo* (4), *Rocco* (4), *Sal* (4), *Salvatore* (4), *Vito* (4), *Luigi* (3), *Antonio* (2), *Carmine* (2), *Marco* (2), *Dante, Domenico, Donato.*

Labelle (2198) French: metronymic from *La Belle*, literally 'the beautiful (woman)' (Old French *beu, bel* 'fair', 'lovely').

GIVEN NAMES French 6%. *Andre* (4), *Gilles* (3), *Armand* (2), *Emile* (2), *Marcel* (2), *Alcide, Amie, Collette, Dominique, Elzear, Etienne, Fernand.*

Labenz (124) German: habitational name from places so named in Holstein, Brandenburg, and Pomerania, or from Labens in former East Prussia.

GIVEN NAME German 5%. *Kurt* (2).

Laber (436) German: topographic name for someone living near the Laber river in Bavaria.

Laberge (634) Variant of French LABARGE (see BARGE).

GIVEN NAMES French 16%. *Marcel* (5), *Pierre* (3), *Armand* (2), *Laurent* (2), *Lucien* (2), *Amie, Andre, Benoit, Emile, Fernand, Ferrier, Germain.*

La Bianca (136) Italian: nickname from *la bianca*, literally 'the white (female) one', or possibly a metronymic from the personal name BIANCA.

GIVEN NAMES Italian 25%. *Giuseppe* (2), *Angelo, Gaspare, Gennaro, Lorenzo, Mario, Nunzio, Rocco.*

Labiche (122) French (eastern): nickname for a gentle or timid person, from *la biche* or *la bisse* 'the hind', 'the doe'.

GIVEN NAMES French 8%. *Alphonse, Franck, Numa.*

Labine (215) Southern French: topographic name from Occitan *labine* 'land cut by ravines', 'small stony ravine'.

GIVEN NAMES French 7%. *Armand* (2), *Aldor, Fernand, Gabrielle.*

Labit (123) French: habitational name from places in Eure, Charente, Mayenne, Manche, and Sarthe named L'Habit, from Old French *l'habit* 'the hermitage' (derived from Latin *habitus*), or a topographic name from the same word.

FOREBEARS A bearer of the name from Gascony, France, is recorded in Montreal from 1758.

GIVEN NAME French 6%. *Oneil.*

Lablanc (205) Variant of French LEBLANC. In Canada and New England, the masculine definite article is often replaced by the feminine.

GIVEN NAMES French 6%. *Aurele, Elodie, Jean-Guy.*

Labo (147) Americanized spelling of French LEBEAU.

Laboda (156) Hungarian: **1.** from the Slavic loanword *labud* 'swan'. **2.** from a place name, a derivative of 1.

Labombard (400) French: soldier's nickname for an artilleryman (see BOMBARD). It is sometimes found alternating with BOMBARDIER as a surname for the same individual.

Labonte (1731) French: nickname for a wealthy man, from *la* 'the' *bonté* 'goodness', 'wealth'. This is a frequent secondary surname in Canada.

GIVEN NAMES French 11%. *Armand* (6), *Lucien* (5), *Aime* (4), *Adelard* (2), *Camille* (2), *Marcel* (2), *Napoleon* (2), *Normand* (2), *Andre, Arsene, Benoit, Clermont.*

Labor (203) Variant spelling of French LABARRE.

Laborde (1433) French: occupational or status name for a tenant farmer, from *borde* 'small farm' (from Frankish *bord* 'plank') + the definite article *la*.

GIVEN NAMES French 9%. *Pierre* (4), *Henri* (3), *Armand* (2), *Camille* (2), *Irby* (2), *Lucien* (2), *Marcel* (2), *Philippe* (2), *Amedee, Andre, Dominique, Easton.*

Labore (182) North American variant spelling of French LABARRE.

GIVEN NAME French 4%. *Andre.*

Labossiere (351) French (**Labossière**): **1.** Norman habitational name from a common village name La Boissière, meaning 'wooded area', from *bois* 'wood'. **2.** possibly a metronymic, from a feminine derivative of BOSSIER 'cooper', denoting the 'wife of the cooper'.

GIVEN NAMES French 17%. *Emile* (2), *Girard* (2), *Pierre* (2), *Armand, Georges, Jacques, Jean Claude, Lucien, Luckner, Maxime, Valmore, Vilaire.*

Labounty (645) Americanized form of French **Labonté** (see LABONTE).

Labove (166) French: possibly an altered spelling of French LEBOEUF. Compare LABAUVE.

GIVEN NAMES French 4%. *Emile, Ulysse.*

Labovitz (143) Partially Americanized spelling of Jewish LEIBOWITZ.

Laboy (478) Hispanic (Puerto Rico): unexplained. Compare LAMBOY.

GIVEN NAMES Spanish 44%. *Jose* (18), *Juan* (9), *Ramon* (7), *Miguel* (6), *Angel* (5), *Domingo* (5), *Francisco* (4), *Luis* (4), *Mario* (4), *Jorge* (3), *Julio* (3), *Roberto* (3).

Labra (108) Castilianized form of Asturian-Leonese **Llabra**, habitational name from the town of Llabra, in Asturies.

GIVEN NAMES Spanish 52%. *Arturo* (3), *Luis* (3), *Tito* (3), *Fernando* (2), *Jose* (2), *Juan* (2), *Manuel* (2), *Miguel* (2), *Adelaido, Agapito, Alfredo, Armando; Antonio* (3), *Lorenzo.*

Labrada (157) Spanish: habitational name for a place called Labrada, of which there are several examples in Galicia, probably named from *(terra) labrada* 'cultivated (land)', from *labrar* 'to cultivate'.

GIVEN NAMES Spanish 45%. *Carlos* (5), *Jose* (5), *Armando* (4), *Manuel* (4), *Luis* (3), *Ernesto* (2), *Jesus* (2), *Jorge* (2), *Orlando* (2), *Adela, Alberto, Alicia; Antonio* (2), *Dario, Lorenzo.*

Labrador (294) Spanish: occupational name for a laborer who worked the land, from an agent derivative of *labrar* 'to cultivate (land)'.

GIVEN NAMES Spanish 37%. *Jose* (5), *Luis* (4), *Raul* (3), *Alfredo* (2), *Angel* (2), *Carlos* (2), *Cesar* (2), *Juan* (2), *Miguel* (2), *Orlando* (2), *Pablo* (2), *Pedro* (2).

Labrake (188) Americanized spelling of French LABRECQUE.

Labranche (407) French: secondary surname, found as a primary name since 1717, from *la branche* 'the twig', 'the branch'. In LA, German ZWEIG was translated as Labranche, and the name survives in this form.

GIVEN NAMES French 13%. *Celina* (2), *Emile* (2), *Marcel* (2), *Pierre* (2), *Herve, Jacques, Jean Pierre, Laurette, Lucien, Ovide.*

Labrec (118) Variant spelling of French LABRECQUE.

Labreche (161) French (**Labrèche**): from Old French *la brèche* 'the breach', 'the gap', hence a topographic name for someone who lived by a gap in the hills or a breach in a wall. See also LABRECQUE.

GIVEN NAMES French 10%. *Fernand, Gaston, Laurette, Laurier.*

Labreck (155) Americanized spelling of French LABRECQUE.

Labrecque (1122) French (**La Brècque**): habitational name from La Brèque in Seine-Maritime, named with the Norman form of *brèche* (see LABRECHE). It may also be a Norman topographic name for someone living by a gap or breach of some kind.

GIVEN NAMES French 17%. *Normand* (8), *Armand* (6), *Andre* (4), *Emile* (4), *Marcel* (4), *Fernand* (3), *Lucien* (3), *Renald* (3), *Adrien, Aime, Alain, Alphe.*

Labree (276) Americanized spelling of French LABRIE.

Labrie (1246) French: topographic name from *l'abri* 'the shelter', or a habitational name from a place named with this word.

GIVEN NAMES French 13%. *Armand* (6), *Andre* (4), *Marcel* (4), *Normand* (3), *Adrien* (2), *Aime* (2), *Fernand* (2), *Jacques* (2), *Zoel* (2), *Alcide, Alphonse, Antoine.*

Labriola (412) Italian: habitational name for someone from a place in Potenza called Abriòla. The surname is widespread in Campania and Basilicata.
GIVEN NAMES Italian 11%. *Donato* (5), *Carmine* (4), *Rocco* (3), *Antonio, Domenico, Mauro, Pasquale.*

Labrosse (204) French: topographic name for someone who lived in a scrubby area of country, from Old French *broce* 'brushwood', 'scrub' (Late Latin *bruscia*). Occasionally it may be a metonymic occupational name for a brush maker, from the same word in the sense 'brush'.
GIVEN NAMES French 12%. *Jacques* (3), *Andre* (2), *Etienne, Luc, Pierre.*

Labrum (298) New England variant of French LEBRUN, with typical North American use of the feminine article *la* in place of the masculine *le*.

Labruyere (129) French: see BRUYERE.
GIVEN NAMES French 7%. *Camille, Jean-Philippe.*

Labruzzo (121) Italian: regional name for someone from the Abruzzi (see ABRUZZO).
GIVEN NAMES Italian 26%. *Vito* (6), *Gino* (2), *Domenico, Igino, Rocco, Salvatore, Santo.*

Labs (177) North German: variant of LAABS.
GIVEN NAME German 4%. *Gerhardt.*

Labuda (455) Polish: 1. unflattering nickname for a moaner, from a derivative of *labiedzić* 'to complain'. 2. (**Łabuda**): nickname for an impoverished person, from a derivative of *łabudać* 'to scrape (things) together', 'be hard up'.

Labudde (102) Germanized spelling of Polish LABUDA.
GIVEN NAME German 4%. *Otto.*

Labue (101) Altered form of Italian **Lo Bue**, a nickname meaning 'the ox' (*lo* 'the' + *bue* 'ox') or of the feminized form **La Bua**.
GIVEN NAME Italian 7%. *Salvatore.*

Labus (217) 1. Polish (**Łabus**): nickname from *łaba* 'paw'. 2. German: a habitational name from any of several places so named in Pomerania and Mecklenburg.
GIVEN NAMES German 6%. *Ignatz, Otto, Rainer.*

Lac (106) Vietnamese: unexplained.
GIVEN NAMES Vietnamese 40%; Chinese 19%. *Mai* (4), *Chau* (2), *Muoi* (2), *Thuan* (2), *Anh Quoc, Cau, Cong, Cuong, Dam Van, Dung Tien, Ha, Khanh*; *Hong* (2), *Ming, Sang, Song, Tong.*

Lacasse (1250) 1. French: topographic name from *la casse* 'the oak' (a word of Gaulish origin). 2. French: metonymic occupational name for box maker, *la casse* 'the box'.
GIVEN NAMES French 15%. *Andre* (5), *Normand* (5), *Marcel* (4), *Pierre* (4), *Emile* (3), *Rejean* (3), *Armand* (2), *Fernand* (2), *Jacques* (2), *Raoul* (2), *Sylvain* (2), *Alain.*

La Cava (437) 1. Italian: habitational name from any of the Italian places called (La) Cava, from *cava* 'hole, cellar' with the def-inite article *la*, or a topographic name for someone who lived by, worked in, or owned a quarry, Italian *cava*, or perhaps a habitational name from a place named with this word. 2. Spanish, habitational name from either of the two places called La Cava in Attargona and Alicante provinces.
GIVEN NAMES Italian 13%; Spanish 6%. *Carmine* (2), *Rocco* (2), *Salvatore* (2), *Antonio, Domenic, Gaetano, Luigi, Marco, Santina, Saverio*; *Cesar, Gonzalo, Mario, Oswaldo, Salvador.*

Lacayo (353) Spanish: occupational name from *lacayo* 'foot soldier' or 'lackey'.
GIVEN NAMES Spanish 43%. *Jorge* (6), *Jose* (4), *Julio* (4), *Luis* (4), *Roberto* (4), *Alberto* (3), *Carlos* (3), *Fernando* (3), *Gustavo* (3), *Ronaldo* (3), *Alejandro* (2), *Alvaro* (2).

Lacaze (405) Southern French: from Occitan *la caze* 'the house' (Latin *casa*), hence perhaps a status name for someone living or working in a distinguished house, as opposed to a *mas* 'ordinary household'.
GIVEN NAMES French 5%. *Pierre* (3), *Francoise, Jean Michel, Octave.*

Lace (189) 1. Welsh: Anglicized form of Welsh *glas* 'gray', 'green', 'blue', probably denoting someone with silver-gray hair. Compare GLASS. 2. English: metonymic occupational name for a maker of cord and string, from Middle English *lace* 'cord' (Old French *laz, las*).

Lacefield (449) English: variant of LASWELL, which is of unknown origin. It may be a variant of LASCELLES.

Lacek (168) Slovak and Czech (Moravian): from a pet form of the personal name *(V)ladislav* (see LASZLO).

Lacelle (100) French: habitational name from Lacelle in Corrèze or numerous minor places called La Celle, all named for a monastic cell or hermitage in their vicinity.
GIVEN NAMES French 16%. *Alain, Andre, Aurele, Benoit, Cecile, Marcel, Marie Paule.*

Lacer (155) English: occupational name for a maker of cord and string, derived from Middle English *lace* 'cord' (Old French *laz, las*).

Lacerda (186) Portuguese and Spanish: nickname for someone with remarkably thick or long hair, or with an unusually hairy back or chest. From Spanish and Portuguese *la cerda* 'the lock (of hair)'.
GIVEN NAMES Spanish 25%; Portuguese 13%. *Carlos* (4), *Jose* (4), *Manuel* (3), *Roberto* (2), *Sergio* (2), *Arnaldo, Edmundo, Evaristo, Fernando, Geraldo, Horacio, Lauro*; *Joao* (3).

Lacerte (183) French: secondary surname with *Vacher*, found as a primary name since 1685. It may derive from Old French *lacerte* 'muscle'.
GIVEN NAMES French 19%. *Gilles* (2), *Marcel* (2), *Armand, Dominique, Emile, Jacques, Luc, Serge.*

Lacewell (200) English: variant spelling of LASWELL.

Lacey (6122) English: variant spelling of LACY.

Lach (854) 1. Ukrainian, Belorussian, and Polish: ethnic name from eastern Slavic *Lach* 'Pole'. This term is used in Czech to denote the inhabitants of the northeastern part of Moravia, near the Polish border. 2. Slovak, Czech (Moravian), and German (of Slavic origin): from the personal name *Lach*, a short form of Czech and Slovak *(V)ladislav* (see LASZLO). 3. Germanized spelling of Slovenian **Lah**, derivative of *Vlah* 'Wallachian', 'Vlach', 'Romanian', or more generally denoting any person of foreign origin.
GIVEN NAMES Polish 5%. *Cazimir, Danuta, Eugeniusz, Ignatius, Jozef, Jozefa, Krystyna, Mieczyslaw, Ryszard, Slawomir, Wladyslawa, Wojtek.*

Lachance (2304) French: secondary surname for PEPIN, from *la chance* 'luck', hence a nickname for a lucky person (or ironically, an unlucky one).
GIVEN NAMES French 15%. *Emile* (10), *Marcel* (9), *Armand* (8), *Normand* (6), *Andre* (5), *Pierre* (4), *Benoit* (3), *Cecile* (3), *Fernand* (3), *Gregoire* (3), *Monique* (3), *Napoleon* (3).

Lachapelle (1065) French: topographic name from *la chapelle* 'the chapel'. This is common as a secondary surname in Canada.
GIVEN NAMES French 12%. *Andre* (4), *Marcel* (3), *Normand* (3), *Aurele* (2), *Gaston* (2), *Mignonne* (2), *Simonne* (2), *Adrien, Aime, Andree, Armand, Chantelle.*

Lacharite (145) French (**La Charité**): 1. secondary surname occurring with many primary names and used as a primary name since 1669, from *la charité* 'charity'; probably a nickname for a person of generous nature. 2. habitational name from La-Charité-sur-Loire.
GIVEN NAMES French 15%. *Marcel* (2), *Alain, Andre, Pierre, Rejean.*

Lachat (140) French: 1. habitational name from Lachat in Savoy. 2. possibly from French *l'achat*, literally 'the purchase'; a nickname denoting someone who acquired property by a purchase (within a family), as opposed to an inheritance. 3. possibly a variant of **Lechat**, a nickname from *le chat* 'the cat'.
GIVEN NAMES French 5%. *Alain, Remy.*

Lacher (689) German: topographical name for someone living in a muddy place near a pond, from Middle High German *lache* 'pond', 'lake'.
GIVEN NAMES German 4%. *Egon, Ewald, Heinz, Kurt, Wilfried.*

Lachman (645) 1. Jewish (Ashkenazic): from the Yiddish personal name *lakhman*, a variant of NACHMAN. 2. Dutch: of uncertain origin. Compare German LACHMANN. 3. Guyanese and Trinidadian name found among people of Indian origin: from the Hindu personal name *Lakshman*, from Sanskrit *lakṣmaṇa* 'one who has auspicious marks'. See LAKHANI.

GIVEN NAMES Indian 5%; Jewish 5%. *Anil* (3), *Ajeet, Ishwar, Mohan, Parbatee, Parbatie, Prem, Rajdai, Rohan, Sumintra*; *Mort* (4), *Elkan, Gerson, Meyer, Sol, Tzvi*.

Lachmann (135) **1.** South German: topographic name for someone who lived near a pond or lake, Middle High German *lache* + *man* 'man'. **2.** German: topographic name for someone who lived by the boundary of a parish or other administrative unit, from Middle High German *lāche* 'boundary stone'. **3.** German (of Slavic origin): from LACH 1 or 3. **4.** Jewish (Ashkenazic): variant spelling of LACHMAN.

GIVEN NAMES German 15%. *Arno, Dieter, Gerd, Heinz, Klaus, Reiner.*

Lachner (132) German: **1.** occupational name for a physician, Middle High German *lachenære* 'healer' (see LEACH 1). **2.** topographic name for someone who lived by a pond or lake, from Middle High German *lache*.

GIVEN NAME German 5%. *Fritz.*

Lachney (306) Americanized spelling of the Swiss and Austrian family name **Lachnicht**, apparently a nickname for a miserable person, meaning 'does not laugh'. In the U.S., this is a southern name, found almost exclusively in LA.

GIVEN NAMES French 4%. *Camile, Camille.*

Lachowicz (172) Polish: patronymic from LACH.

GIVEN NAMES Polish 9%. *Lech, Pawel, Piotr, Stanislaw, Zbigniew.*

Lachowski (93) Polish: habitational name for someone from Lachów in Łomża voivodeship, named with the personal name LACH.

GIVEN NAMES Polish 11%. *Andrzej, Dymitr, Stanislaw.*

Lachut (123) Polish (also **Łachut**): **1.** derivative of LACH. **2.** nickname from a derivative of *łach* 'rag', *łachy* 'rags', 'old clothes'.

GIVEN NAMES Polish 8%. *Genowefa, Jerzy, Stanislaw.*

Lacina (337) Czech: nickname from *lacino* 'cheaply', apparently bestowed on someone who drove a hard bargain.

La Civita (184) Italian: from the feminine definite article *la* + the place name *Civita* (from Latin *civitas* 'town'), the name of various places, notably in central Italy, such as Civita Castellana in Viergo, Civitaluparella (Chieti), Civitavecchia (Rome). The surname is either a habitational name from one of these place or a topographic name for someone who lived in a city.

GIVEN NAMES Italian 10%. *Angelo* (4), *Francesco, Tullio.*

Lack (1010) **1.** English: variant of LAKE. **2.** North German: variant of LAACK.

3. Hungarian: from a short form of the personal name *László* (see LASZLO).

Lackey (6557) Northern Irish form of the Scottish habitational name LECKIE.

Lackie (296) Scottish: variant of either LECKIE or **Lachie**, an Anglicized form of Gaelic **Lachaidh**, a pet form of *Lochlann*, meaning 'stranger' (see LAUGHLIN).

Lackland (114) English: in all probability an English variant of Scottish **Lachlan** (see McLACHLAN), altered through folk etymology. However, Black cites one *John sine terra* (c. 1180–1214), suggesting that the surname could have arisen quite literally as a nickname for a man with no land.

Lackman (277) **1.** Americanized spelling of German LACHMANN. **2.** German (**Lackmann**): variant of LAACK.

Lackner (480) **1.** South German: habitational name for someone from any of various minor places in Bavaria and Austria called Lacken. **2.** Americanized spelling of German LACHNER.

GIVEN NAMES German 9%. *Franz* (2), *Kurt* (2), *Matthias* (2), *Ernst, Erwin, Gernot, Hans, Heinz, Klaus, Markus, Otto, Willi.*

Lacko (210) **1.** Hungarian (**Lackó**): from a pet form of the personal name *László* (see LASZLO). **2.** Slovak, Czech (Moravian), Slovenian, and Croatian: from the personal name *Lacko*, a local form of *(V)ladislav*. Compare LASZLO.

Lacks (396) German and Jewish (Ashkenazic): variant spelling of **Lachs** (see LAX 1).

Laclair (966) North American variant of French LECLAIR, with use of the feminine article in place of the masculine that is characteristic of French surnames in Canada and New England.

Laclaire (123) French: variant spelling of LACLAIR.

Lacock (189) **1.** English: variant spelling of LAYCOCK. **2.** Americanized form of French LECOCQ, with the feminine definite article that is characteristic of French surnames in Canada and New England.

Lacoe (132) Americanized spelling of Hungarian **Lacó**, or **Laczó**, from the personal name *László* (see LASZLO).

GIVEN NAME German 4%. *Kurt* (2).

Lacomb (239) Variant of French LACOMBE.

Lacombe (1535) French (western and southwestern): topographic name for someone living in or near a ravine, from *la combe* 'the ravine' (a word of Gaulish origin, related to English COMBE).

FOREBEARS Jean Lacombe (or Lacomble) was married to Marie Charlotte Millet on 20 June 1678 in Notre Dame, Montréal, Quebec. The family originated from St. Cybranet in the Dordogne, France.

GIVEN NAMES French 8%. *Armand* (6), *Fernand* (4), *Andre* (2), *Cecile* (2), *Pierre* (2), *Yves* (2), *Alcide, Aldea, Alphee, Andrus, Colette, Curley.*

Laconte (195) Variant of French LECONTE, with the use of the feminine article that

is characteristic of French surnames in Canada and New England.

GIVEN NAMES Italian 7%. *Carmine* (2), *Angelo.*

La Corte (367) Italian: topographic name from *corte* 'court', 'small town', or a habitational name from any of the places named with this word. See CORTE.

GIVEN NAMES Italian 15%. *Salvatore* (4), *Antonino* (2), *Santo* (2), *Antonio, Carlo, Concetta, Cosimo, Fiore, Giacomo, Pasquale, Vincenzo, Vito.*

Lacoss (188) French: North American variant of LACASSE.

Lacosse (186) French: North American variant of LACASSE.

Lacoste (759) French: see COSTE.

GIVEN NAMES French 10%. *Emile* (3), *Laurent* (2), *Lucien* (2), *Aime, Andre, Armand, Etienne, Francois, Gaspard, Germaine, Huguette, Jean-Charles.*

Lacount (407) New England variant of French LECONTE. Use of the feminine article (*la*) for the masculine (*le*) and translation of the noun are both common features of New England family names of French origin.

Lacour (1154) French: topographic or occupational name for someone who lived at or was employed at a manorial court (see COURT).

GIVEN NAMES French 5%. *Andre* (2), *Jacques* (2), *Alphonse, Antoine, Francoise, Girard, Lucien, Ovide, Pierre.*

Lacourse (569) French: secondary surname for DAVID and GELINAS, from *la course*, literally 'the course' or 'the race' and also 'privateering', hence perhaps denoting a runner, gambler, or privateer.

GIVEN NAMES French 10%. *Lucien* (5), *Armand* (2), *Julien* (2), *Aime, Cecile, Germain, Herve, Ludger, Marcel, Mechelle, Yvon.*

Lacoursiere (189) French (**Lacoursière**): secondary surname for RIVARD. It is of uncertain origin; the French word *coursier* means 'messenger', and *la coursière* is 'the female messenger'. There may be some reference to privateering (see LACOURSE).

GIVEN NAMES French 6%. *Colette, Fabien, Lucien, Marcel.*

Lacouture (176) French: topographic name from *couture* 'cultivated field' + the definite article *la* (from Latin *cultura*).

GIVEN NAMES French 12%. *Adelard, Alain, Andre, Emile, Lucien, Patrice.*

Lacovara (101) Italian: from the medieval Greek surname **Lagodares**, a nickname from *lagōdarion* 'leveret'.

GIVEN NAMES Italian 9%. *Lorenzo, Nichola.*

Lacoy (106) French: nickname for a quiet and unassuming person, from Old French *coi* 'calm', 'quiet' (Latin *quietus*).

GIVEN NAMES French 6%. *Amie, Normand.*

Lacroix (2982) French: topographic name for someone who lived near a cross set up by the roadside or in the marketplace, from

French *la croix* 'the cross' (Latin *crux, crucis*). In some cases the surname may have denoted one who carried the cross in church processions. Compare the English equivalent, CROSS. It is a very frequent French Canadian secondary surname, perhaps for a person who swore by the cross, and has also been used independently since 1670.

GIVEN NAMES French 12%. *Andre* (12), *Marcel* (7), *Armand* (6), *Normand* (6), *Lucien* (5), *Emile* (3), *Pierre* (3), *Rosaire* (3), *Amelie* (2), *Benoit* (2), *Edouard* (2), *Gabrielle* (2).

Lacross (448) Part translation of French LACROIX.

Lacrosse (414) Part translation of French LACROIX.

Lacson (150) Filipino: unexplained.

GIVEN NAMES Spanish 40%; Italian 8%. *Jose* (4), *Eduardo* (3), *Atilano* (2), *Carolina* (2), *Francisco* (2), *Leticia* (2), *Mario* (2), *Renato* (2), *Aida, Amalia, Amante, Arsenio; Dante, Ernani, Luigi.*

Lacy (7640) English and Irish (of Norman origin): habitational name from Lassy in Calvados, named from a Gaulish personal name *Lascius* (of uncertain meaning) + the locative suffix *-acum*. The surname is widespread in Britain and Ireland, but most common in Nottinghamshire. In Ireland the family is associated particularly with County Limerick.

Lad (78) **1.** Indian (Gujarat): Hindu (Vania) name, which is said to be from Sanskrit *lāṭa*, denoting an area of southern Gujarat. **2.** Indian (Maharashtra): Hindu (Brahman, Maratha) name, possibly of the same origin as the Gujarati name. The Marathas have a clan called Lad.

GIVEN NAMES Indian 75%. *Amrut* (2), *Mahesh* (2), *Abhay, Arun, Babu, Bhavesh, Chiman, Deepak, Gopal, Gulab, Harish, Hasmukh.*

Lada (286) **1.** Polish (also **Łada**) and Czech (Moravian): from a pet form of the personal name *Lada*, a short form of Polish *Władysław, Ładysław*, or Czech *(V)ladislav* (see LASZLO). **2.** Czech: topographic name from *lada* 'heath'. **3.** Hungarian (**Láda**): metonymic occupational name for a joiner, from Hungarian *láda* 'box', from Middle High German *lade* 'box', 'coffin'. **4.** Hungarian: from *Lad(a)* a short form of the personal name *Ladomér*, a Hungarian form of Slavic *Vladimir*.

GIVEN NAMES Polish 5%. *Andrzej, Grzegorz, Irena, Lucyna, Witold.*

Ladage (133) Origin uncertain. In spite of the French form of the name, early American bearers appear to have been of Dutch or German origin and the name is not found in French records. It may have been a Huguenot importation to the Netherlands and Germany of a French name such as **Ladigue**, a habitational name from a place named La Digue, examples of

which are found in Finistère and Loire-Atlantique, or from a district of Jumièges in Seine-Maritime.

Ladas (161) **1.** Greek: occupational name for a seller of olive oil, from *ladi* 'oil' (classical Greek *eladion*, pet form of *elea* 'oil') + the occupational suffix *-as*. **2.** Hungarian (**Ládas**): from a pet form of the personal name *Ladomér* (from the form *Ladamér*), Hungarian form of Slavic *Vladimir*.

GIVEN NAMES Greek 6%. *Dimitrios, Dionisios, Gerasimos.*

Laday (110) Hungarian (**Láday**): habitational name for someone from a place called Láda in former Sáros county.

Ladd (6354) English: occupational name for a servant, Middle English *ladde*. The word first appeared in the 13th century, with the meaning 'servant' or 'man of humble birth', the modern meaning of 'young man', 'boy' being a later shift.

FOREBEARS Most American bearers of this name trace their ancestry to a certain Daniel Ladd, who emigrated from London to Ipswich, MA, in 1634.

Lade (389) **1.** Norwegian: habitational name from any of several farmsteads, so named from Old Norse *hlað* 'pile or stack' (for example, of wood or stones) or 'pavement'. **2.** North German: short form of LADWIG, a variant of LUDWIG. **3.** English: topographic name for someone living by a road, path, or watercourse, Middle English *lade, lode* (Old English *(ge)lād*).

Ladeau (118) Canadian French: unexplained.

GIVEN NAME French 6%. *Andre* (2).

Ladehoff (115) German (Westphalia): habitational name from a farmstead named with *lad, lod* 'murky water' + *hof* 'farm.'

GIVEN NAME French 5%. *Mechelle* (2).

Laden (305) German: **1.** shortened form of *Ladengast* 'invite the guest', nickname for an innkeeper. **2.** from *von der Laden*, occupational name for a joiner or nickname for the keeper of a shrine or the chest of a guild, from Middle Low German *lade* 'chest'.

Lader (188) **1.** Variant of German and Jewish LEDER. **2.** German: occupational name for a cargo handler, from an agent derivative of Middle High German *laden* 'to load', 'to fill'.

GIVEN NAMES Jewish 5%; German 4%. *Hyman; Otto.*

Laderman (116) Jewish: probably an Americanized spelling of **Leyderman**, a metonymic occupational Ashkenazic name (from Ukraine and Poland) for a leather worker, from Yiddish dialect *leyder* 'leather' + *man*.

GIVEN NAME Jewish 7%. *Zev.*

Ladewig (235) North German: variant of LUDWIG.

GIVEN NAMES German 4%. *Kurt, Manfred.*

Ladig (103) German: possibly from a variant of the personal name LUDWIG. Compare LADWIG.

Ladin (163) Jewish: unexplained.

GIVEN NAME Jewish 4%. *Zvi.*

Ladley (186) English: probably a habitational name from a lost or unidentified place.

Ladner (2416) **1.** German: occupational name for a joiner who made *Laden* 'chests', 'wardrobes' (also 'armor'), from a derivative of Middle Low German, Middle High German *lade* 'chest', '(wooden) container'. **2.** Jewish (Ashkenazic): occupational name for a shopkeeper, from a derivative of *Laden* 'shop'.

Ladnier (311) Swiss French (Grisons): unexplained. In the U.S., this name occurs chiefly in MS.

Ladouceur (444) French: from *douceur* 'sweetness', presumably denoting a person of sweet disposition. It has been used independently as a surname since 1724.

GIVEN NAMES French 9%. *Yves* (2), *Armand, Camille, Cecile, Fernand, Henri, Jean-Luc, Ludger, Philippe, Rejean.*

Ladow (185) Variant of French LEDOUX. See also LADUE.

Ladson (560) English: patronymic from LADD.

La Duca (242) Italian: occupational name for a member of the household of a duke (see DUCA).

GIVEN NAMES Italian 20%. *Salvatore* (7), *Angelo* (3), *Carmelo* (2), *Cosimo, Francesco, Gaspare, Lucio, Sal.*

Ladue (897) Americanized form of French LEDOUX, with the use of the feminine article in place of the masculine that is characteristic of family names in Canada and New England.

FOREBEARS Pierre Ladoue was in New Rochelle, NY, by 1698. In the census of 1698 he is recorded as aged 36.

Laduke (908) Americanized form of French LEDUC. Use of the feminine article (*la*) for the masculine (*le*) and translation of the noun are common features of New England family names of French origin.

Ladwig (953) North German variant of LUDWIG.

Lady (407) **1.** English: from Middle English *lady* 'lady', 'female head of a household', hence a nickname for a woman who was ladylike or the head of a household or for an effeminate man. **2.** Polish: variant of LADA. **3.** Hungarian (**Ládi**): habitational name for someone from Lád in Borsod county or Lad in Somogy county.

Ladzinski (102) Polish (**Ladziński, Ładziński**): habitational name, probably from one of the places called Lady, now in Ukraine.

GIVEN NAME Polish 6%. *Leszek.*

Laehn (104) German (**Lähn**): see LAHN.

Laessig (135) German (**Lässig**): **1.** topographic name for someone living in or near a wood, from Sorbian, Czech *les*, Polish *las* 'woods', 'forest', or habitational name from a place called Lässig, near Frankfurt-on-Oder, named with this word. **2.** nickname meaning 'tired' or 'lazy', from Middle High German *laz* 'slow'.

La Falce (148) Italian: metonymic occupational name for a harvester or user of a sickle, from the definite article *la* + *falce* 'sickle', 'scythe' (Latin *falx*).
GIVEN NAMES Italian 12%. *Carmela, Carmelo, Carmine, Santo.*

Lafarge (104) French: variant of LAFORGE.
GIVEN NAME French 4%. *Gedeon.*

Lafargue (159) Southwestern French: variant of LAFORGE. In Canada this is secondary surname for many primary names.
GIVEN NAMES French 8%. *Camille, Emile, Gabrielle, Laurent, Phillippe.*

Lafary (104) French: perhaps an Americanized form of LAFORGE or LEFEVRE.
FOREBEARS According to family historians, four LaFary brothers came from Lorraine, France, to North America before 1770, and settled in Ripley Co., IN.

La Fata (446) Italian: from the feminine definite article *la* + the personal name *Fata*, feminine form of *Fato*, a reduced form of *Bonifato* or a similar name.
GIVEN NAMES Italian 33%. *Salvatore* (13), *Vito* (6), *Antonio* (3), *Gaspar* (3), *Gasper* (2), *Matteo* (2), *Angelo, Attilio, Carmine, Dino, Giovanni, Guiseppe, Leonarda, Leticia, Marco, Mario, Ninfa, Rosalia, Salvadore.*

La Fauci (169) Italian (Sicily): metonymic occupational name from the definite article *la* + Sicilian *fauci* 'sickle'. Compare LA FALCE.
GIVEN NAMES Italian 20%. *Salvatore* (7), *Angelo, Cosmo, Gino, Pietro, Saverio.*

Lafave (1290) North American variant of French LEFEVRE, the most common name in French-speaking Canada. As the vocabulary word *fèvre* 'smith' was replaced by *forgeron*, the meaning of the old word became opaque, and the name was reinterpreted by French Canadian immigrants as *Lafève*, from *fève* '(fava) bean' (see BEAN). *Lafève* would be heard as Lafave by English ears.

Lafaver (131) Americanized form of French Lefèvre (see LEFEVRE, LAFAVE), with the generalized use of the feminine article in family names that is characteristic of Canada and New England.

Lafavor (200) Americanized form of French Lefèvre (see LEFEVRE), with the generalized use of the feminine article in family names that is characteristic of Canada and New England.

Lafayette (762) Southern French: diminutive of **Lafaye**, a topographic name for someone living near a beech tree or beech wood, from Old French *fage*, variant of *fou* 'beech' (Latin *fagus*).
FOREBEARS Marie Joseph Paul Yves Roch Gilbert du Motier, marquis de Lafayette (1757–1834), was a rich French aristocrat and soldier who allied himself with the cause of liberty, religious toleration, and the abolition of slavery. He came to North America in 1777 and played a major part in securing George Washington's victory over the British.
GIVEN NAMES French 4%. *Camille, Jean Marie.*

La Fazia (122) Italian: from the definite article *la* + a second element which is probably the personal name *Fazia*, a feminine form of FAZIO.
GIVEN NAMES Italian 5%. *Domenic, Santo.*

La Femina (130) Italian: nickname for an effeminate man, from the definite article *la* + *femmina* 'female'.
GIVEN NAMES Italian 8%. *Aldo, Rocco.*

Laferriere (647) French (**Laferrière**): habitational name from a number of places so called, indicating the presence of iron mines or ironworking forges, from *fer* 'iron'. Compare Portuguese FERREIRA, Spanish HERRERA.
GIVEN NAMES French 14%. *Andre* (6), *Armand* (3), *Laurent* (2), *Lucien* (2), *Normand* (2), *Aurele, Cecile, Elphege, Henri, Luc, Raoul, Serge.*

Laferty (131) Irish: variant spelling of LAFFERTY.

Lafever (745) Variant of French **Lefèvre** (see LEFEVRE).

Lafevers (187) Of French origin: variant of LEFEVERS (see LEFEVER).

Laffan (103) Irish: variant of LAVIN.
GIVEN NAME Irish 10%. *Kieran.*

Lafferty (3658) Irish (mainly northern Ireland): reduced Anglicized form of Gaelic **Ó Fhlaithbheartaigh** or **Mac Fhlaithbheartaigh** 'descendant (or 'son') of *Flaithbheartach*', a personal name composed of the elements *flaith* 'prince', 'ruler' + *beartach* 'doer of valiant deeds'. See also FLAHERTY.

Laffey (628) Irish and Scottish: reduced Anglicized form of Gaelic **Ó Laithimh**, from the earlier form **Ó Flaithimh**, from *flaitheamh* 'ruler'.
GIVEN NAME Irish 6%. *Brendan.*

Laffin (325) Irish: variant of LAVIN.

Laffitte (176) French: variant spelling of LAFITTE.
GIVEN NAMES Spanish 6%. *Raul* (2), *Jorge, Juan, Lazaro, Pastora, Sergio.*

Laffoon (586) Southern French (possibly Huguenot): topographic name for someone living near a spring or well; an Americanized form of a southern French pronunciation of LAFONT.

Lafitte (281) French: topographic name for someone who lived near a boundary mark, Old French *fitte* (Late Latin *fixta petra* 'fixed stone', from the past participle of *figere* 'to fix or fasten'), or habitational name from any of several places in western France named with this word.

GIVEN NAMES French 7%. *Armand, Benoit, Henri, Jacques, Pierre, Pierrette.*

Laflam (224) Variant of French LAFLAMME.
GIVEN NAMES French 5%. *Armand, Jean-Paul, Valmore.*

Laflamme (1519) French: nickname, or perhaps an occupational name for a torch bearer, from *flamme* 'fire' + the definite article *la*.
GIVEN NAMES French 16%. *Pierre* (9), *Andre* (8), *Marcel* (6), *Armand* (5), *Adrien* (4), *Jacques* (4), *Raoul* (4), *Emile* (3), *Normand* (3), *Dominique* (2), *Fernand* (2), *Gaston* (2).

Lafleche (173) French: metonymic occupational name for an arrowsmith, from Old French *flèche* 'arrow' + the definite article *la*; also a French Canadian secondary surname, used independently since 1746.
GIVEN NAMES French 20%. *Andre* (3), *Armand* (2), *Rejean* (2), *Alphonse, Aurele, Gaston, Jacques, Marcel.*

Lafler (236) German and Jewish (Ashkenazic): anglicized spelling of German LOEFFLER, an occupational name for a maker or seller of spoons.

Lafleur (3284) French: ornamental surname borne by servants or soldiers in feudal France, from Old French *flor* 'flower' + the definite article *la*. Perhaps the most common of the distinguishing names in French Canada, it is associated as a secondary surname with some sixty family names and has been used independently since 1705.
GIVEN NAMES French 7%. *Armand* (5), *Emile* (5), *Antoine* (3), *Laurent* (3), *Adelard* (2), *Andre* (2), *Curley* (2), *Marcel* (2), *Napoleon* (2), *Pierre* (2), *Sylvie* (2), *Alcide.*

Laflin (281) **1.** English (Suffolk): unexplained. This appears to be a variant of **Lafflin**, which Reaney and Wilson believe to be of Irish origin (see 2), but the high concentration of the modern name in Suffolk suggests that a different source is probably involved. **2.** Respelling of Irish LAUGHLIN.

Lafoe (162) Origin unidentified.

Lafollette (1124) French: variant of FOLLETTE, with the definite article *la*.

Lafon (610) French: variant of LAFONT. Compare LAFFOON.
GIVEN NAMES French 4%. *Pierre* (2), *Jean Louis, Jean-Baptiste.*

Lafond (1509) French: variant of LAFONT.
GIVEN NAMES French 10%. *Marcel* (7), *Armand* (4), *Andre* (3), *Donat* (3), *Yves* (3), *Benoit* (2), *Gilles* (2), *Jacques* (2), *Pierre* (2), *Aurel, Cecile, Colombe.*

Lafont (262) French: topographic name for someone living near a spring or well (see FONT).
GIVEN NAMES French 8%. *Emile* (2), *Armand, Eustache, Jean-Luc, Pascal, Patrice.*

Lafontaine (1289) French: topgraphic name for someone who lived near a spring or well, a variant of FONTAINE, with the definite article *la*.

GIVEN NAMES French 8%. *Normand* (6), *Andre* (4), *Fernand* (3), *Herve* (2), *Jacques* (2), *Marcel* (2), *Rosaire* (2), *Valmore* (2), *Alcide, Jean-Jacques, Jeannot, Laurier.*

Lafontant (128) French: probably an altered form of LAFONTAINE.

GIVEN NAMES French 36%; German 5%. *Julien* (2), *Yves* (2), *Antoine, Ghislaine, Jean Claude, Jean-Philippe, Josee, Ketly, Lucien, Lucrece, Marie Ange, Pascal; Fritz* (2).

Lafoon (116) Variant of French LAFFOON.

Laforce (545) French: topographic name for someone who lived by a fortress or stronghold; a variant of FORCE, with the definite article *la*.

GIVEN NAMES French 5%. *Pierre* (3), *Jean Marc, Monique.*

Laforest (606) **1.** French: topographic name for someone who lived in or near a royal forest, or a metonymic occupational name for a keeper or worker in one, from Old French *forest*, with the definite article *la*. Unlike modern French *forêt, forest* was not simply a word for extensive woodland, but referred specifically to large, partly or mainly wooded areas reserved by law for the king and his nobles to hunt in. **2.** Americanized form of French **La Forêt**, a modern spelling of 1, here translated into English with the article left intact. Compare LAFONTAINE.

GIVEN NAMES French 12%. *Gilles* (2), *Pierre* (2), *Aime, Alphonse, Armand, Colette, Flore, Georges, Gisele, Guillaume, Herard, Jean-Claude.*

Laforge (797) French: topographic name for someone who lived by a forge or a metonymic occupational name for someone who worked in one; a variant of FORGE, with the definite article *la*.

GIVEN NAMES French 5%. *Emile* (2), *Alban, Alphonse, Armand, Camille, Lucien.*

La Forgia (140) Italian: from a noun derivative of *forgiare* 'to forge', a topographic name for someone who lived by a smithy or a metonymic occupational name for someone who worked in one.

GIVEN NAMES Italian 28%. *Vito* (3), *Antonio* (2), *Sal* (2), *Benito, Cosmo, Lucio, Mario, Michelina, Salvatore.*

La Forte (222) Italian: altered form of **Lo Forte**, a nickname meaning 'the strong one'. The feminine form is probably due to the influence of the Italian word *famiglia* 'family'.

GIVEN NAMES Italian 8%. *Carmine* (2), *Liberato, Sal, Salvatore, Vito.*

Lafortune (457) French: from *fortune* + the definite article *la*, a nickname for a lucky individual (see FORTUNE).

GIVEN NAMES French 15%. *Andre* (2), *Jacques* (2), *Jean-Claude* (2), *Normand* (2), *Antoine, Armand, Chantel, Clovis, Colombe, Jean-Paul, Jean-Yves, Ketly.*

Lafosse (184) French: topographic name for someone who lived by a ditch, a variant of FOSSE, with the definite article *la*.

GIVEN NAMES French 9%. *Aime* (2), *Andre, Armand, Olympe.*

Lafountain (1044) Partly Americanized form of French LAFONTAINE.

Lafountaine (201) Partly Americanized form of French LAFONTAINE.

Lafoy (173) French: nickname for a pious person, a variant of FOY, with the definite article *la*.

Laframboise (378) French: from *framboise* 'raspberry' + the definite article *la*, hence a nickname for someone with a ruddy complexion or for someone who grew raspberries.

GIVEN NAMES French 8%. *Aime, Armand, Aurel, Gilles, Jean-Claude, Luc, Lucien, Marcel, Philippe, Viateur.*

Lafrance (1787) French: habitational name given to someone from France, at the time when the name only applied to those lands belonging to the French king (excluding many areas of what is now France), or from the Île de France, a region centered on Paris. It was a surname given to soldiers in the feudal period. In French Canada it is a secondary surname, which has also been used alone since 1714. .

GIVEN NAMES French 10%. *Lucien* (5), *Pierre* (5), *Armand* (4), *Andre* (3), *Marcel* (3), *Yvon* (3), *Emile* (2), *Gaetan* (2), *Jacques* (2), *Michel* (2), *Normand* (2), *Achille.*

La Franchi (109) Italian Swiss (Ticino): derivative of FRANCO, the feminine definite article no doubt being due to the influence of the Italian word *famiglia* 'family'.

La Fratta (100) Italian: possibly a topographic name formed with *fratta* 'shrub', 'bramble', also 'deforested place'.

GIVEN NAMES Italian 11%; French 7%. *Angelo* (2), *Nicola; Camille* (2).

Lafrenier (103) Variant of French **Lafrenière** (see LAFRENIERE).

Lafreniere (852) French (**Lafrenière**): topographic name from *frenière* 'place of ash trees'. This is a secondary surname particularly associated with the name FOISY, although also used independently since 1749. It is often Americanized as FREEMAN.

GIVEN NAMES French 8%. *Marcel* (2), *Monique* (2), *Andre, Benoit, Gilles, Jacques, Laurette, Napoleon, Normand, Ovide, Pascal, Pierre.*

Lafrentz (102) German: see LAFRENZ.

Lafrenz (225) German: variant of the personal name *Laurenz* (see LAWRENCE).

GIVEN NAMES German 6%. *Juergen* (2), *Arno, Hans, Otto.*

Lafromboise (100) French: literally 'the strawberry'; either an occupational name for a grower or seller of strawberries, or a nickname for someone with a strawberry nose (a red, distended nose due to the effects of hard liquor).

Lafuente (157) Spanish: topographic name for someone living near a spring or well, *fuente*, with the definite article *la*.

GIVEN NAMES Spanish 44%. *Juan* (4), *Manuel* (4), *Javier* (3), *Lupe* (3), *Raul* (3), *Alfonso* (2), *Jose* (2), *Alfredo, Angelita, Arnulfo, Arturo, Cristina.*

Lagace (245) French: variant spelling of LAGASSE. Written **Lagacé** or **Lagasse**, it occurs as a secondary surname for Mignier, established in Canada by 1668.

GIVEN NAMES French 19%. *Andre* (2), *Jean-Guy* (2), *Laurent* (2), *Armand, Colombe, Constant, Gaetan, Gilles, Mireille, Olivier, Yvon.*

Lagan (135) Irish: **1.** reduced form of McLAGAN. **2.** variant of LOGAN.

Lagana (463) **1.** Southern Italian (**Laganà**): occupational name for a grower or seller of vegetables, *lagana, lacana* (from Greek *lakhanas*). **2.** Greek (**Laganas**): occupational name for a baker, from *lagana* 'unleavened bread', 'flatbread'.

GIVEN NAMES Italian 34%. *Salvatore* (5), *Rocco* (4), *Angelo* (3), *Santo* (3), *Aldo* (2), *Domenic* (2), *Domenico* (2), *Sal* (2), *Alicia, Benito, Bernardino, Carlo, Elio, Filomena, Fortunato.*

Lagarde (388) French: habitational name from any of various places, in Ariège, Gers, Moselle, Vaucluse, for example, named in Old French with *garde* 'watch', 'protection', with the definite article *la*. This is found as a French Canadian secondary surname, which has also been used independently since 1733.

GIVEN NAMES French 8%. *Andre, Celine, Chanel, Emile, Francois, Jacques, Lucien, Raoul.*

Lagasse (1074) French: nickname from Old French *agace, agasse* 'magpie' + the definite article *l'*.

GIVEN NAMES French 10%. *Armand* (8), *Herve* (2), *Normand* (2), *Andre, Aurele, Camille, Carmelle, Celine, Clovis, Colombe, Emile, Fernand.*

La Gattuta (145) Southern Italian: origin uncertain. *Gattuta* is apparently a feminine derivative of *gatto* 'cat'.

GIVEN NAMES Italian 15%. *Sal* (3), *Carmello, Enrico, Luciano, Salvatore.*

Lage (693) **1.** Portuguese and Galician: habitational name from any of the several places called Lage in Galicia and Portugal, named with *lage, laxe* 'flat rock or slab of stone', or a topographic name for someone who lived by such a rock. **2.** French: habitational name from any of a number of places named L'Age, *age* being a regional variant of French *haie* 'hedge'. **3.** Danish: from the personal name *Laghi*, Old Norse *Lage* (see LAGESON). **4.** North German, Dutch, and Danish: habitational name from any of several places named Lage or Laage, all in northern Germany. The name denotes a free, open space between wooded areas.

GIVEN NAMES Spanish 6%; Portuguese 4%. *Manuel* (7), *Jose* (4), *Alicia* (2), *Americo* (2), *Carlos* (2), *Conchita* (2), *Fernanda* (2), *Acacio*, *Aida*, *Albino*, *Aleida*, *Ana*; *Joao*, *Marcio*.

Lageman (116) Dutch and North German: **1.** occupational name for a highwayman (see LAGER). **2.** possibly also a variant of LACHMAN.
GIVEN NAME German 5%. *Gunther*.

Lagemann (127) North German: **1.** topographic name for someone living by a wood or brushland, Middle Low German *lage* 'brushwood' + *man* 'man'. **2.** occupational name for a highwayman (see LAGER).
GIVEN NAMES German 5%. *Benno*, *Manfred*.

Lager (638) **1.** Swedish: ornamental name from *lager* 'laurel', 'bay', a common element of ornamental compound names. **2.** Dutch and North German: from the vocabulary word *lager* 'highwayman', 'bandit'.
GIVEN NAME Scandinavian 4%. *Alf*.

Lagergren (162) Swedish: ornamental name composed of the elements *lager* 'laurel' + *gren* 'branch'.
GIVEN NAME Scandinavian 11%. *Johan*.

Lagerman (112) **1.** Swedish: ornamental name composed of the elements *lager* 'laurel' + *man* 'man'. **2.** Dutch: apparently from the vocabulary word *lager* 'highwayman', 'bandit'.
GIVEN NAMES Scandinavian 5%. *Brigid*; *Lars* (2).

Lagerquist (266) Swedish: ornamental name composed of the elements *lager* 'laurel' + *quist*, an old or ornamental spelling of *kvist* 'twig'.
GIVEN NAMES Scandinavian 6%; German 4%. *Erik*, *Helmer*; *Kurt*.

Lagerstrom (182) Swedish (**Lagerström**): ornamental name composed of the elements *lager* 'laurel' + *ström* 'river'.
GIVEN NAME Scandinavian 6%. *Holger*.

Lageson (129) Norwegian and Swedish: patronymic from *Lage*, a personal name meaning 'friend', which is of the same origin as *-lagi* in Old Norse *félagi* 'comrade', 'partner'; compare English *fellow*.
GIVEN NAME Scandinavian 4%. *Knute*.

Lagesse (184) French: unexplained. Possibly from *gesse*, denoting a type of pea, and hence a topographic or metonymic occupational name.

Laginess (114) Americanized form of French LAJEUNESSE.
GIVEN NAME French 4%. *Pierre*.

Lagle (172) **1.** variant spelling of German **Lägel**, metonymic occupational name for a barrel maker, from *Lägel* 'small barrel'. (see LEGLER). **2.** Perhaps a respelling of French **Laigle**, a nickname from the definite article *l'* + *aigle* 'eagle' (from Latin *aquila*).

Lagman (121) **1.** Filipino: unexplained. **2.** Swiss German: variant of LACHMANN.

3. Swedish: from the old personal name *Lagman*, from Old Norse *Lǫgmaðr*, composed of *lǫg* 'laws' + *maðr*, 'man' (genitive *manns*). Compare Scottish LAMONT.
GIVEN NAMES Spanish 29%. *Diosdado*, *Eufrosina*, *Jesus*, *Justina*, *Lamberto*, *Marcelino*, *Mario*, *Mercedes*, *Nestor*, *Norberto*, *Ramon*, *Ruben*.

L'Agnese (122) Southern Italian (also **Lagnese**): from the female personal name *Agnese*, Italian form of *Agnes* (see ANNIS).

Lago (591) Spanish and Portuguese: topographic name for someone living by a lake, from *lago* 'lake' (from Latin *lacus*), or habitational name from any of the many places named with this word.
GIVEN NAMES Spanish 35%. *Jose* (14), *Manuel* (11), *Francisco* (7), *Juan* (6), *Ramon* (6), *Carlos* (4), *Agustin* (3), *Angel* (3), *Jesus* (3), *Josefina* (3), *Luis* (3), *Pedro* (3); *Antonio* (6), *Delio* (2), *Flavio* (2), *Aldo*, *Bruna*, *Dino*, *Philomena*, *Rinaldo*, *Salvatore*, *Silvio*, *Vita*.

Lagomarsino (300) Italian: habitational name from a minor place so named in the province of Genoa.

Lagorio (117) Italian (**Lagòrio**): nickname from the Ligurian dialect word *lagö* 'green lizard'. This name is also established in Argentina.
GIVEN NAMES Italian 9%; Spanish 7%. *Angelo* (5); *Juan Carlos* (2), *Juan*, *Venecia*.

Lagos (405) **1.** Spanish, Galician, and Portuguese: habitational name from any of the numerous places named Lagos, especially in Galicia. **2.** Greek: nickname for a timid person or a fast runner, from Greek *lagos* 'hare', or a reduced form of a patronymic based on such a nickname, such as **Lagoudakis**.
GIVEN NAMES Spanish 28%; Greek 5%. *Carlos* (8), *Jose* (7), *Luis* (4), *Manuel* (3), *Raul* (3), *Alba* (2), *Alberto* (2), *Araceli* (2), *Benito* (2), *Eduardo* (2), *Enrique* (2), *Gerardo* (2); *Kiriakos* (2), *Panos* (2), *Voula* (2), *Constantine*, *Costas*, *Haralambos*, *Taso*.

Lagow (141) Polish (**Łagów**): variant of **Łagówski** (see LAGOWSKI).

Lagowski (106) Polish (**Łagówski**): habitational name from a place called Łagów, named with Polish *łao*, a derivative of Old Polish *łagoda* 'order', 'quiet'.
GIVEN NAMES Polish 11%. *Jacek*, *Wiktor*, *Zbigniew*.

Lagoy (157) French Canadian: unexplained.

Lagrand (114) Canadian and New England variant of French LEGRAND, with the generalization of the feminine article characteristic of the region.

Lagrange (869) French: topographic name for someone who lived by a granary, a variant of GRANGE, with the definite article *la*.
FOREBEARS This name is recorded in Beverwijck in New Netherland (Albany, NY) in the mid 17th century.

GIVEN NAMES French 5%. *Lucien* (2), *Andre*, *Ignace*, *Jacques*, *Josee*, *Laurier*, *Thierry*, *Veronique*.

Lagrave (108) French: **1.** habitational name from someone from Lagrave (Hautes-Alpes) named with *grave* 'gravel', or topographic name from this word. **2.** nickname for a solemn person, from French *grave* 'solemn', 'serious'.
GIVEN NAMES Spanish 6%. *Carlos* (2), *Emilio*, *Gustavo*.

La Greca (330) Italian (also **La Greca**): from the definite article *la* + *Greca*, ethnic name denoting someone whose family was Greek. Compare GRECO.
GIVEN NAMES Italian 17%. *Angelo* (6), *Salvatore* (6), *Antonio* (3), *Bartolo*, *Dario*, *Fedele*, *Gaetano*, *Nunziato*, *Philomena*, *Sal*, *Vito*.

Lagree (122) **1.** Canadian and New England variant of French **Legris** (see LEGREE), with generalized use of the feminine definite article that is characteristic of the region. **2.** French (**Lagrée**): topographic name for someone living in a stony place, or a habitational name from any of several places named La Grée or from one called La-Grée-Saint-Laurent.
GIVEN NAME French 5%. *Sebastien*.

Lagrone (779) Americanized form of French LAGRAND.

Lagrow (208) Americanized form of LEGROS, with the use of the feminine definite article that is characteristic of Canada and New England.

Laguardia (380) **1.** Spanish: habitational name from Laguardia in Araba province, Basque Country, or Vitoria province. **2.** Italian (**La Guardia**): from the definite article *la* + *guardia* 'lookout (tower)', a topographic name for someone who lived near a watchtower or an occupational name for someone who kept watch.
GIVEN NAMES Spanish 12%; Italian 7%. *Jose* (5), *Carlos* (2), *Alberto*, *Anabella*, *Andres*, *Armando*, *Efrain*, *Elvira*, *Emilia*, *Evelio*, *Fernando*, *Genaro*; *Antonio*, *Cono*, *Enrico*, *Rocco*, *Sal*, *Santo*.

Lague (338) French: **1.** (**Lagüe**): Gascon topographic name for someone who lived by a lagoon, from a local dialect form of French *lagune* 'lagoon'. **2.** (**Lagué**): habitational name from a minor place so named in Lot-et-Garonne.
GIVEN NAMES French 13%. *Normand* (4), *Andre* (3), *Laurette*, *Marie-Ange*, *Yvon*.

Laguerre (273) French: nickname for a belligerent person or for a valiant soldier, from Old French *guerre* 'war' (of Germanic origin). This is a French Canadian secondary surname, which has also been used independently since 1717.
GIVEN NAMES French 40%; German 4%. *Andre* (4), *Pierre* (4), *Magalie* (2), *Antoine*, *Edwige*, *Ermite*, *Francois*, *Gardy*, *Gracien*, *Herve*, *Jacques*, *Lucrece*; *Fritz*, *Muller*.

Lagueux (152) French: unflattering nickname from *le gueux* 'the rogue'.
GIVEN NAMES French 19%. *Gilles* (2), *Benoit, Emile, Julien, Laurent, Monique, Placide, Rejean, Viateur.*

Laguna (558) Spanish: habitational name from any of the numerous places named Laguna, from *laguna* 'pool', 'pond' (from Latin *lacuna* 'hollow', 'hole').
GIVEN NAMES Spanish 42%. *Jose* (16), *Juan* (7), *Manuel* (5), *Guadalupe* (4), *Jorge* (4), *Pedro* (4), *Alberto* (3), *Cesar* (3), *Francisco* (3), *Pablo* (3), *Adolfo* (2), *Agustin* (2).

Lagunas (300) Spanish: from the plural of *laguna* 'pool', 'pond' (see LAGUNA).
GIVEN NAMES Spanish 54%. *Juan* (8), *Francisco* (7), *Jose* (6), *Luis* (5), *Pedro* (5), *Miguel* (4), *Ramon* (3), *Ricardo* (3), *Santiago* (3), *Abelardo* (2), *Alejo* (2), *Armando* (2); *Antonio* (4), *Heriberto* (2), *Carmelo, Ciro, Constantino, Dario, Leonardo, Marco, Severino.*

Lahaie (304) **1.** French: variant spelling of LAHAYE. **2.** In Canada, many of this name descend from an Irishman, John Leahy, who married in Quebec in 1697.
GIVEN NAMES French 9%. *Adelore, Aime, Andre, Jacques, Lucien, Solange, Yannick, Yvon.*

Laham (174) **1.** English: unexplained. If it survives at all in England, the name is now very rare there. **2.** Muslim: unexplained.
GIVEN NAMES Muslim 10%. *Riad* (2), *Samir* (2), *Abir, Amin, Hala, Jamil, Nadim, Soad, Walid, Wedad.*

Lahart (141) Irish (Kilkenny and Tipperary): variant of **Laherty**, itself a variant of McLAFFERTY.

Lahaye (306) French: topographic name, from Old French *haye* 'hedge', with the definite article *la*.
GIVEN NAMES French 6%. *Gilberte, Landry, Laurent, Marcel, Ovide.*

Lahey (1071) Altered form of LEAHY.
GIVEN NAMES Irish 4%. *Brendan, Padraic.*

Lahiff (141) Irish: reduced Anglicized form of Gaelic **Ó Laithimh** (see LAFFEY).

Lahm (289) German: **1.** habitational name from any of several places so named, all in southern Germany. **2.** nickname for someone who was slow or lame, from Middle High German *lam* 'lame'.
GIVEN NAMES German 4%. *Gunther* (2), *Otto.*

Lahman (410) Altered spelling of German LAHMANN.

Lahmann (199) North German: variant of LOHMANN.

Lahn (176) German: habitational name from places so called in northern Germany near Meppen, in Bavaria, or in Hungary.

Lahner (118) German and Hungarian: habitational name for someone from any of various places called Lahn in Hungary and Germany. In southern Germany and Austria, *Lahn* denotes a place where there had been an avalanche or landslide, from Middle High German *laen, lēne* 'avalanche'.
GIVEN NAME Hungarian 4%. *Bela* (2).

Lahood (208) Americanized form of French Canadian **Lahoud**, of unexplained origin.
GIVEN NAMES French 4%. *Emile, Michel.*

Lahr (1359) German: **1.** habitational name from any of several places so named, from Old High German *(h)lār* 'grazing area'. **2.** in the Lower Rhine area, from a short form of the saint's name *Hilarius* (see HILLARY).

Lahrman (127) North German: variant of LAHR 1, with the addition of *man* 'man'.

Lahti (884) Finnish: from *lahti* 'bay', 'cove', generally an ornamental name that was frequently adopted during the name conversion movement in the 19th and early 20th centuries. It is particularly common in southwestern Finland.
GIVEN NAMES Finnish 10%. *Eino* (7), *Toivo* (7), *Arvo* (5), *Reino* (3), *Waino* (3), *Jukka* (2), *Aarre, Esko, Jorma, Martti, Mikko, Sulo.*

Lahue (379) Origin unidentified. Probably an altered form of a French name.

Lai (3602) **1.** Chinese 赖: from the name of a state called Lai (in present-day Henan province), which existed during the Spring and Autumn period (722–481 BC). Descendants of the ruling class of this state adopted its name as their surname. **2.** Chinese 黎: Cantonese variant of LI 2. **3.** Vietnamese: unexplained. **4.** Polish: dialect variant of the personal name *Lew* 'lion' (see LEW 2).
GIVEN NAMES Chinese 22%; Vietnamese 13%. *Ching* (10), *Kwok* (9), *Ming* (9), *Wing* (8), *Wai* (7), *Wen* (7), *Chi* (5), *Chun* (5), *Ho* (4), *Kam* (4), *Man* (4), *Yee* (4); *Hung* (15), *Thanh* (10), *Tuan* (5), *Hoa* (4), *Ky* (4), *Lan* (4), *Thang* (4), *Tien* (4), *Trang* (4), *Tu* (4), *Yen* (4), *Anh* (3).

Laib (241) German: metonymic occupational name for a baker, from Middle High German *leip* 'loaf'.

Laible (228) German: from a diminutive of LAIB.

Laich (103) South German: topographic name from *lai*, a secondary form of Old High German *lōh*, Middle High German *lōch* 'leafy woodland', 'former wooded area'.
GIVEN NAME German 6%. *Kurt.*

Laiche (197) Swiss German: variant of LAICH.
GIVEN NAMES French 10%. *Anicet* (2), *Emile, Ignace, Leonce, Numa, Pierre, Raoul.*

Laidig (165) German: variant of LEIDIG.
GIVEN NAMES German 5%. *Kurt, Manfred.*

Laidlaw (791) Scottish: Border surname found mainly around Selkirk and the vales of Ettrick and Yarrow. Family tradition has it that the name comes from LUDLOW in Shropshire, England, but this is doubtful.

Laidler (174) **1.** Scottish: variant of LAIDLAW. **2.** Northern English and Scottish:
perhaps also an occupational name for a maker of ladles, from an agent derivative of Middle English *ladel(e)* 'ladle'.

Laidley (144) Scottish: variant of LAIDLAW.

Laier (120) **1.** Dutch: from a reduced form of the personal name *Hilaire*, Latin *Hilarius* (see HILLARY). **2.** German: topographic name for someone who lived in a wood, from an agent noun derived from *lai* 'wood' (see LAICH).
GIVEN NAMES German 4%. *Alois, Otto.*

Lail (1440) Americanized form of German LEHL or **Loehl**. In either case, the name is a spelling variant of **Lehle** or **Löhle**, pet forms of the personal name LEONHARDT.
FOREBEARS The Loehl family came to North America in 1737. Another branch of the family came to North America from Germany via Russia. They settled in southern Russia in the mid 18th century, but kept their German identity. Both branches have adopted the American form Lail as a family name.

Lain (875) **1.** English: variant spelling of LANE. **2.** Reduced form of Scottish and northern Irish McLAIN (see McLEAN).

Laine (1350) **1.** Northern Irish: reduced form of Scottish McLEAN. **2.** English: perhaps a variant spelling of LANE. **3.** Finnish: ornamental name from *laine* 'wave'. This is one of the most common names among those that were derived from words denoting natural features when hereditary surnames were adopted in Finland in the beginning of the 20th century. This name is found chiefly in southern Finland. **4.** French: metonymic occupational name for a worker or dealer in wool, from Old French *la(i)ne* 'wool' (Latin *lana*).
GIVEN NAMES Finnish 6%; French 4%. *Eino* (5), *Reino* (5), *Antti* (2), *Armas* (2), *Arvo* (2), *Tauno* (2), *Torsti* (2), *Waino* (2), *Ahti, Eero, Ilkka, Jussi; Alphonse, Andre, Armand, Camille, Emile, Francoise, Germain, Gisele, Marie Flore, Philippe, Serge, Sylvain.*

Lainez (190) Spanish (**Laínez** or **Líinez**): patronymic from the personal name *Laín*.
GIVEN NAMES Spanish 59%. *Carlos* (7), *Jose* (7), *Angel* (2), *Arturo* (2), *Jesus* (2), *Jorge* (2), *Juan* (2), *Juan Jose* (2), *Julio* (2), *Luis* (2), *Manuel* (2), *Marina* (2).

Laing (2364) Scottish spelling of LANG.

Lainhart (309) Americanized spelling of German LENHARDT.

Laino (340) **1.** Italian (**Laìno**): habitational name from Laìno in Calabria, or a topographic name derived from medieval Greek *lainos* 'from the river Lao'. **2.** possibly also Spanish, from the medieval personal name *Laíno*, from Latin *Flavinus*.
GIVEN NAMES Italian 9%. *Angelo* (2), *Rocco* (2), *Cesare, Pasquale.*

Lair (1394) Possibly an Americanized spelling of German LEHR or **Löhr** (see LOEHR).

Laird (7195) Scottish and northern Irish: status name for a landlord, from northern Middle English *laverd* 'lord'.

Lairmore (146) Variant of English and Scottish LORIMER.

Lairson (190) Americanized spelling of Danish and Norwegian LARSEN or Swedish LARSSON, established in North America from the late 17th century.

Lais (206) German; of uncertain origin: **1.** perhaps a nickname from a variant of Middle High German *linse* 'gentle', 'forbearing'. **2.** alternatively, from a short form of the personal name *Nikolaus* (see NICHOLAS). This name is found chiefly in MN.

Laisure (117) Americanized spelling of the French names LEGER (also *Legère*) or LESUEUR. Compare LEASURE, LEISURE.
GIVEN NAME French 4%. *Marcelle*.

Laitinen (273) Finnish: from the personal name *Laiti*, of Germanic origin, + the common surname suffix *-nen*. This name is found mainly in eastern and central Finland.
GIVEN NAMES Finnish 5%. *Juhani, Mikko, Pekka, Reino, Seppo, Toivo*.

Laity (153) English: nickname for a trustworthy person, from Old French *léauté* 'loyalty' (Latin *legalitas*, a derivative of *legalis* 'legal', 'by law').

Laizure (104) Americanized form of the French names LEGER (also *Legère*) or LESUEUR. Compare LEASURE, LEISURE.

Lajaunie (122) Probably a respelling of French **Lajeunie**, which Morlet describes as a topographic name relating to the estate of a family called JEUNE.
GIVEN NAMES French 4%. *Philippe, Phillippe*.

Lajeunesse (527) French: secondary surname, also used independently since 1706, from *la jeunesse* 'youth', hence a nickname for someone especially young, fresh, or naive. It is often translated as YOUNG.
GIVEN NAMES French 9%. *Rollande* (2), *Yves* (2), *Alphonse, Andre, Aurele, Berthe, Brunel, Fernand, Lucien, Marcel, Michel, Pierre*.

Lajiness (116) Americanized spelling of French LAJEUNESSE.

Lajoie (1247) French Canadian: common secondary surname, also used independently since 1784, from *la joie* 'joy', hence a nickname for a happy, cheerful person.
GIVEN NAMES French 11%. *Armand* (5), *Marcel* (4), *Herve* (3), *Normand* (3), *Andre* (2), *Cecile* (2), *Jacques* (2), *Pierre* (2), *Adrien, Alcide, Alphonse, Andree*.

Lakatos (435) Hungarian: occupational name for a locksmith, *lakatos*, a derivative of *lakat* 'lock' (from Old French *loquet*). This is a common family name among Hungarian gypsies.
GIVEN NAMES Hungarian 7%. *Miklos* (3), *Andras* (2), *Tibor* (2), *Barna, Csaba, Dezso, Elek, Janos, Jolan, Zoltan*.

Lake (11536) **1.** English (chiefly West Country): topographic name for someone who lived by a stream, Old English *lacu*, or a habitational name from a place named with this word, for example in Wiltshire and Devon. Modern English *lake* (Middle English *lake*) is only distantly related, if at all; it comes via Old French from Latin *lacus*. This meaning, which ousted the native sense, came too late to be found as a place name element, but may lie behind some examples of the surname. **2.** Part translation of French BEAULAC.

Lakeman (260) **1.** English: variant of LAKE. **2.** Dutch: topographic name for someone who lived by a lake or pond.

Laker (275) English (Sussex and Kent): topographic name for someone who lived by a stream, from Old English *lacu* 'stream' (see LAKE) + the suffix *-er* denoting an inhabitant.

Lakes (779) English: variant of LAKE.

Lakey (1248) English: unexplained.

Lakhani (281) Muslim and Hindu name found in Gujarat, India, and among people from Sind, Pakistan, meaning '(descendant) of Lakh'. *Lakh* is most probably a shortened form of an ancestral name, perhaps *Lakhman*, which goes back to Sanskrit *lakṣmaṇa* 'one who has auspicious marks'. In the Sanskrit epic *Ramayana*, this is the name of Rama's brother.
GIVEN NAMES Muslim 66%; Indian 24%. *Abdul* (7), *Amin* (6), *Karim* (5), *Iqbal* (4), *Mohammed* (4), *Ali* (3), *Noorali* (3), *Saleem* (3), *Ahmed* (2), *Akber* (2), *Aziz* (2), *Badruddin* (2); *Arvind* (2), *Dilawar* (2), *Dinesh* (2), *Harshad* (2), *Pankaj* (2), *Priti* (2), *Ramesh* (2), *Arun, Ashok, Bansi, Bhupendra, Chandu*.

Lakin (1337) **1.** Americanized spelling of Jewish **Leykin** (from Belarus), a metronymic from *Leyke*, a pet form of the Yiddish female personal name *Leye*, from the Hebrew female personal name *Lea*, from which English *Leah* is derived (see Genesis 29: 16) + the Slavic possessive suffix *-in*. **2.** English: from a medieval personal name, a diminutive of LAWRENCE. Compare LAW 1 and LARKIN.

Lakins (190) English: patronymic from LAKIN 2.

Lakis (122) Latvian (**La{k̦,}is**): unexplained.

Lakner (122) Germanized form of Slovenian **Lokar**, a topographic name for a person who lived by a water meadow, from an agent derivative of *loka* 'water meadow', phonetically Germanized as *Lack* or *Lacke*. This is also found as a Swiss family name.
GIVEN NAME French 5%. *Armand* (2).

Laks (159) Jewish (Ashkenazic): variant spelling of LAX.
GIVEN NAMES Jewish 9%. *Hillel* (2), *Doron, Dov, Meyer, Rivka*.

Lakso (118) Finnish: variant spelling of LAAKSO.

Lal (551) Indian (northern states): Hindu name found in several communities, meaning 'darling', from Sanskrit *lāla* 'cajoling' (related to Sanskrit *lālana* 'caressing'). In several modern Indian languages *lāl* is a term of endearment for a child; it is also an epithet of the god Krishna. There is also a homonymous word *lāl* in Hindi, from Persian meaning 'ruby', 'red', which may have increased the popularity of this name. It occurs more commonly as the final element of a compound personal name, as in *Brajlal* (*Braj* being the name of the place where the god Krishna is supposed to have lived as a child) and *Motilal* (Hindi *motī* 'pearl').
GIVEN NAMES Indian 79%. *Sohan* (11), *Madan* (9), *Mohan* (9), *Tarsem* (9), *Ram* (8), *Manohar* (7), *Anil* (6), *Brij* (5), *Jagdish* (4), *Krishan* (4), *Moti* (4).

Lala (328) **1.** Indian (northern states): Hindu name (Bania, Kayasth), from Hindi *lālā*, a term of respect, used especially for members of Vaisya and Kayasth communities; typically bankers, merchants, tradesmen, schoolmasters, and clerks. It is probably related to LAL. **2.** Southern Italian: from modern Greek *Lalas*; the frequency of the name in the parochial records of Piana degli Albanesi leads Caracausi to suggest it may have been taken to Italy by Albanian settlers.
GIVEN NAMES Indian 16%; Italian 6%. *Vinod* (3), *Padma* (2), *Ramesh* (2), *Amitabha, Amrita, Asha, Gopal, Kanayo, Kantilal, Kirit, Kishor, Kishore*; *Angelo, Carlo, Ciro, Sal, Salvatore*.

Lalama (117) Italian, Spanish, and Portuguese: topographic name for someone living by a marsh, or Spanish habitational name for someone from any of the numerous places called (La) Lama, especially La Lama in Pontevedra province. See LAMA.
GIVEN NAMES Italian 21%; Spanish 11%; Jewish 4%. *Domenic* (2), *Attilio, Donato, Ettore, Gino, Giuseppe, Maddalena, Marcello, Remo*; *Angel* (2), *Aida, Carlos, Elena, Jorge, Luis*; *Isadore, Miriam*.

Lalande (202) French: habitational name from two places named Lalande or from La Lande, a more common place name, both referring to a place near a heath, Old French *la(u)nde* (see LAND 2).
GIVEN NAMES French 9%. *Antoine, Emile, Fernande, Jean Claude, Jean-Pierre*.

Lalani (129) **1.** Muslim and Hindu name found in Gujarat, India, and among people from Sind, Pakistan, meaning 'descended from Lal (or Lala)' (the name of an ancestor). **2.** Bangladeshi: name adopted by followers of the mystic philosophy of the Bengali poet and mystic Lalan (died 1890).
GIVEN NAMES Muslim 79%; Indian 8%. *Amin* (3), *Sadrudin* (3), *Salim* (3), *Amirali* (2), *Anwar* (2), *Badruddin* (2), *Hadi* (2), *Inayat* (2), *Karim* (2), *Nawaz* (2), *Nizar* (2), *Saleem* (2); *Atul, Bhupat, Govind, Jayantilal, Manoj, Sunil*.

Lalanne (145) French: habitational name from places so called in Gers and Haut-Pyrénées, a southern form of LALANDE.
GIVEN NAMES French 26%. *Serge* (2), *Chantal, Jacques, Jean-Claude, Lucien, Marie Ange, Michel, Philippe, Pierre, Rosemene, Yves.*

Laliberte (1283) French Canadian (**La Liberté**): secondary surname for many names, especially Colin (see COLLINS), from *liberté* 'freedom', with the definite article *la*; it has also been used independently since 1743.
GIVEN NAMES French 19%. *Armand* (9), *Marcel* (9), *Andre* (8), *Normand* (6), *Emile* (4), *Michel* (4), *Camille* (3), *Jacques* (3), *Adelard* (2), *Chantal* (2), *Eloi* (2), *Fernand* (2).

Laliberty (132) French Canadian: variant of LALIBERTE.
GIVEN NAME French 7%. *Lucien* (2).

Lalich (107) Serbian (**Lalić**): patronymic from the personal name *Lala*, a pet form of LAZAR.
GIVEN NAMES South Slavic 6%. *Ljubica, Marko.*

Lalime (100) Canadian French: unexplained.
GIVEN NAMES French 11%. *Alexina, Yves.*

Lall (327) Indian: variant spelling of LAL.
GIVEN NAMES Indian 61%. *Mohan* (5), *Onkar* (3), *Raj* (3), *Sanjay* (3), *Satish* (3), *Amrit* (2), *Deo* (2), *Drupatie* (2), *Indra* (2), *Mahendra* (2), *Pooran* (2), *Rajendra* (2).

Lalla (180) **1.** Italian (chiefly Apulia): from a feminine form of LALLO. **2.** Indian: variant of LALA. **3.** Guyanese and Trinidadian name found among people of Indian origin.
GIVEN NAMES Indian 14%; Italian 7%. *Ashram, Deepa, Deepak, Ishwar, Jagdish, Mohanie, Narine, Ramesh, Sailesh, Satnarine, Sunil; Donato* (2), *Rocco.*

Lalley (353) **1.** Irish: reduced form of **Mullalley** (see MULLALLY). **2.** French: see LALLY 2.

Lalli (554) Italian (chiefly Abruzzo): patronymic or plural form of the personal name LALLO.
GIVEN NAMES Italian 12%. *Cosmo* (2), *Lorenzo* (2), *Remo* (2), *Alberico, Amedeo, Antimo, Antonio, Concetta, Domenic, Gennaro, Gilda.*

Lallier (307) French: probably an occupational name, a variant of *aillier* 'grower or seller of garlic', with the definite article *l'*.
FOREBEARS Lalliers have been recorded in Deschambault, Quebec, since 1750.
GIVEN NAMES French 12%. *Armand* (2), *Napoleon* (2), *Pierre* (2), *Emile, Fernand, Gilles, Herve, Jean-Guy, Philias.*

Lallo (139) Southern Italian (mainly Campania): from a nursery pet form of various personal names.

Lally (2307) **1.** Irish: reduced form of MULLALLY. **2.** French (**L'Ally**): habitational name for someone who came from either of two places called Ally. **3.** French: vari-

ant of **Laly**, a habitational name from a place so named.
GIVEN NAMES Irish 5%. *Brendan* (5), *Aine, Kieran.*

Lalonde (1974) French (Normandy): habitational name from any of various places in Normandy, so named from Old Norse *lundr* 'grove', with the definite article *la*.
GIVEN NAMES French 8%. *Marcel* (6), *Jacques* (3), *Pierre* (3), *Raoul* (3), *Rejean* (3), *Gilles* (2), *Leonce* (2), *Achille, Aime, Alcee, Andre, Antoine.*

Lalone (389) Probably an Americanized spelling of LALONDE.
GIVEN NAMES French 4%. *Romain* (2), *Marcel.*

Lalor (365) Irish: variant of LAWLER.
GIVEN NAMES Irish 6%. *Brendan* (2), *Fintan.*

Lalumiere (128) French (**La Lumière**): from *lumière* 'lamp', 'torch', with the definite article *la*, probably applied as an occupational name for a cleric who was responsible for lighting a church or a scriptorium.
GIVEN NAMES French 15%. *Normand* (3), *Armand, Jacques, Philippe, Yves.*

Laluzerne (137) French: habitational name from places in Eure and Manche named La Luzerne, from Old French *lucerne* 'torch', 'lantern' (typically, one lit outside a monastery).

Lam (8937) **1.** Chinese 林: variant of LIN 1. **2.** Chinese 蓝: variant of LAN. **3.** Vietnamese (**Lâm**): unexplained. **4.** Dutch and North German: from a short form of the personal name LAMBERT. **5.** Danish: nickname for a gentle person, from Old Norse *lamb* 'lamb', or possibly for a lame man, Old Norse *lami*.
GIVEN NAMES Vietnamese 26%; Chinese/Korean 22%. *Thanh* (53), *Minh* (39), *Hung* (36), *Anh* (31), *Hoa* (31), *Vinh* (29), *Quang* (26), *Duc* (25), *Dung* (25), *Cuong* (22), *Hai* (20), *Son* (20); *Hong* (32), *Wing* (24), *Chi* (22), *Kin* (20), *Wai* (20), *Kwok* (18), *Chun* (16), *Kam* (16), *Sang* (16), *Ching* (13), *Man* (13), *Chan* (10); *Nam* (15), *Chung* (14), *Tam* (13), *Phong* (9), *Thai* (9), *Pak* (6), *Tuong* (6), *Yiu* (6), *Hoa Kim* (4), *Sik* (4), *Sinh* (4), *Woon* (4).

Lama (373) **1.** Spanish, Portuguese, and Italian: topographic name for someone who lived by a marsh, *lama* (from Latin *lama*). In some cases the Italian and Spanish name may be habitational, from any of numerous places named with this word. **2.** Buddhist name found among people from Tibet and Nepal, from Tibetan *blama* 'priest', 'monk'.
GIVEN NAMES Spanish 17%; Italian 5%; Indian 4%. *Carlos* (4), *Miguel* (3), *Jacobo* (2), *Jose Luis* (2), *Luis* (2), *Mario* (2), *Aleida, Beatriz, Catalina, Eduardo, Francisca, Gustavo; Luciano* (2), *Aldo, Antonio, Elio, Ezio, Guido, Nunzio, Salvatore; Amar, Basant, Hemant, Rakesh, Shyam, Sujay, Uday.*

La Macchia (283) Italian: topographic name from the definite article *la* + *macchia* 'thicket', 'scrub'. Scrub country was notorious as a hiding place for bandits, and this may be the true meaning of the surname. The phrase *alla macchia* means 'secretly' or 'clandestinely'.
GIVEN NAMES Italian 15%. *Placido* (2), *Rocco* (2), *Antonio, Carmela, Carmelo, Cosmo, Giuseppe, Santo.*

La Madrid (143) Spanish: habitational name for someone from Lamadrid in Santander province, or from the city of Madrid.
GIVEN NAMES Spanish 42%; Italian 7%. *Carlos* (5), *Luis* (4), *Jose* (3), *Fernando* (2), *Jorge* (2), *Juan* (2), *Sergio* (2), *Alberto, Ana, Diego, Esperanza, Francisco; Lorenzo* (6), *Marino.*

Lamagna (209) Italian: ethnic name for a member of the Alemanni, a Germanic people inhabiting what is now southern Germany, from a reduced form of **Alamagna** 'Alemannia', i.e. 'land of the Alemanni'. Compare LAMANNA.
GIVEN NAMES Italian 13%; Spanish 7%. *Carmine* (2), *Attilio, Carlo, Cataldo, Enrico, Gaetano, Gennaro, Rocco, Sal; Alfonso, Glicerio, Liborio, Luzviminda.*

Lamalfa (127) Southern Italian (Sicily): variant of **Malfa**, most probably a habitational name for someone from Malfa on the island of Salina (Messina), although the name has also been linked with Amalfi in Salerno and Melfi in Potenza.
GIVEN NAMES Italian 14%. *Salvatore* (2), *Carmelo, Giuseppe, Mario.*

Laman (428) Possibly a variant spelling of Dutch LEEMAN.

Lamanna (972) Southern Italian: **1.** (**La Manna**): from the definite article *la* + *manna*, denoting a type of ash tree. **2.** from a reduced form of **Alamanna**, an ethnic name from the Germanic tribal group, the Alemanni. The name is widespread in southern Italy. Compare LAMAGNA.
GIVEN NAMES Italian 13%. *Rocco* (8), *Carlo* (3), *Carmine* (3), *Vito* (3), *Luigi* (2), *Pasquale* (2), *Sal* (2), *Amedeo, Anella, Angelo, Carmelo.*

Lamantia (723) Southern Italian (also **La Mantia**): habitational name from Amantea in Cosenza.
GIVEN NAMES Italian 14%. *Angelo* (6), *Salvatore* (5), *Sal* (4), *Antonio* (2), *Raffaello* (2), *Rocci* (2), *Santo* (2), *Carmela, Cosmo, Giuseppe, Giuseppi, Nichola.*

Lamar (3379) **1.** Possibly a variant spelling of French LAMARRE. **2.** Possibly also Spanish: habitational name for someone from either of the two places called Mar in Asturias, probably named with *mar* 'sea' and the article *la*.

Lamarca (650) Catalan: **1.** topographic name for someone who lived near a boundary. **2.** metonymic nickname for someone with a noticeable birthmark or scar, from *marca* 'scar'. Compare French LAMARQUE.

GIVEN NAMES Italian 16%. *Angelo* (7), *Gino* (3), *Salvatore* (3), *Carmelo* (2), *Cataldo* (2), *Pasquale* (2), *Sal* (2), *Aldo*, *Carlo*, *Carmine*, *Cosimo*, *Domenic*.

Lamarche (808) French: topographic name or habitational name, a variant of LAMARQUE 1.

GIVEN NAMES French 13%. *Marcel* (4), *Fernand* (2), *Jacques* (2), *Lucien* (2), *Normand* (2), *Rosaire* (2), *Yvon* (2), *Andre*, *Aurore*, *Bibiane*, *Cecile*, *Flore*.

Lamark (109) Americanized form of French LAMARQUE.

Lamarque (112) French: **1.** topographic name for someone who lived near a boundary, Old French *marque* (Germanic *marca*); or a habitational name from places named Lamarque or La Marque. **2.** metonymic nickname for someone with a noticeable birthmark or scar, or for someone who had been disfigured by branding (a relatively common medieval punishment), from Old French *marque* 'mark' (a transferred use of 1).

GIVEN NAMES French 18%; Spanish 10%. *Emile* (2), *Adrien*, *Andre*, *Jean-Francois*, *Jean-Louis*, *Maryse*, *Yolaine*; *Ana*, *Arturo*, *Ezequiel*, *Francisco*, *Juan*, *Ramon*, *Ruben*.

Lamarr (298) Respelling of French LAMARRE.

Lamarre (704) French: habitational name from any of the places in Normandy called La Mare, from Old Northern French *mare* 'pool', 'pond' (Old Norse *marr*).

GIVEN NAMES French 17%. *Pierre* (8), *Andre* (2), *Jacques* (2), *Normand* (2), *Serge* (2), *Yves* (2), *Adrien*, *Alphonse*, *Antoine*, *Armand*, *Chantal*, *Hugues*.

La Martina (176) Italian: metronymic from the female personal name *Martina*, feminine form of *Martino* (see MARTIN), or name for someone belonging to 'the Martin family', the feminine form no doubt being due to the influence of the Italian word *famiglia* 'family'.

GIVEN NAMES Italian 11%. *Angelo* (3), *Salvatore* (2).

Lamas (516) Castilianized form of Asturian-Leonese **Llames**, **Llamas** or **L.lamas**, habitational names from any of the numerous places named Llames, Llamas, or L.lamas, in Asturies.

GIVEN NAMES Spanish 50%. *Jose* (20), *Carlos* (14), *Manuel* (8), *Fernando* (5), *Jesus* (5), *Jorge* (5), *Eduardo* (4), *Humberto* (4), *Jaime* (4), *Luis* (4), *Pedro* (4), *Alberto* (3).

Lamaster (316) Americanized form of French **Lemestre** (see LEMAITRE), with the generalized use of the feminine definite article and translation of the noun that are characteristic of New England.

GIVEN NAME French 4%. *Jacques*.

Lamastus (124) Probably of French (Huguenot) origin, an irregularly altered form of **Lemestre** (see LEMAITRE, LAMASTER).

Lamattina (154) Italian: possibly from a female pet form of the personal name *Matto*, which may derive from *matto* 'crazy', or alternatively from an old Germanic personal name.

GIVEN NAMES Italian 28%. *Angelo* (4), *Domenico* (2), *Rocco* (2), *Salvatore* (2), *Antonio*, *Benedetto*, *Carlo*, *Carmine*, *Gaetano*, *Girolamo*.

Lamay (515) French Canadian form of French LEMAY, with generalized use of the feminine definite article *la* in place of the masculine *le*, characteristic of Canada and New England.

Lamb (22273) **1.** English: from Middle English *lamb*, a nickname for a meek and inoffensive person, or a metonymic occupational name for a keeper of lambs. See also LAMM. **2.** English: from a short form of the personal name LAMBERT. **3.** Irish: reduced Anglicized form of Gaelic **Ó Luain** (see LANE 3). MacLysaght comments: 'The form **Lamb(e)**, which results from a more than usually absurd pseudo-translation (*uan* 'lamb'), is now much more numerous than **O'Loan** itself.' **4.** Possibly also a translation of French *agneau*.

Lambdin (667) English: habitational name from Lambden in Berwickshire.

Lambe (459) Irish and English: variant spelling of LAMB.

GIVEN NAMES Irish 4%. *Brendan*, *Ciaran*, *Ethna*.

Lamberg (207) **1.** German: habitational name from any of several places so called in Bavaria, Westphalia, and Schleswig-Holstein. **2.** Dutch: variant of LAMBERT. **3.** Swedish: probably of German origin, but perhaps an ornamental name composed of an unexplained first element + *berg* 'mountain'.

GIVEN NAME Scandinavian 4%. *Erik*.

Lambers (101) Dutch: patronymic from the personal name LAMBERT.

Lamberson (975) Americanized form of Dutch LAMBERTSEN.

FOREBEARS Cornelius Lambertsen came from Utrecht, Holland arriving at New Amsterdam in 1642. Later the family are found in NJ, and from there spread throughout the rest of the country.

Lambert (33046) English, French, Dutch, and German: from a Germanic personal name composed of the elements *land* 'land', 'territory' + *berht* 'bright', 'famous'. In England, the native Old English form *Landbeorht* was replaced by *Lambert*, the Continental form of the name that was taken to England by the Normans from France. The name gained wider currency in Britain in the Middle Ages with the immigration of weavers from Flanders, among whom St. Lambert or Lamprecht, bishop of Maastricht in around 700, was a popular cult figure. In Italy the name was popular-

ized in the Middle Ages as a result of the fame of Lambert I and II, Dukes of Spoleto and Holy Roman Emperors.

FOREBEARS The name Lambert is found in Quebec City from 1657, taken there from Picardy, France. There are also Lamberts from Perche, France, by 1670.

Lamberth (715) English: probably a variant of LAMBERT.

Lamberti (530) Italian: patronymic from the personal name *Lamberto*, Italian equivalent of LAMBERT.

GIVEN NAMES Italian 15%. *Antonio* (2), *Carlo* (2), *Gaetano* (2), *Luciano* (2), *Amedeo*, *Angelo*, *Biagio*, *Domenic*, *Donato*, *Enrico*, *Gino*, *Iolanda*.

Lamberton (414) English: habitational name from the barony of Lamberton in Berwickshire, or in some instances possibly from Lamerton in Devon, named from Old English *lamb* 'lamb' + *burna* 'stream' + *tūn* 'farmstead', 'settlement', i.e. 'farmsead on the lamb stream'.

Lambertsen (105) Dutch, Danish, and Norwegian: patronymic from LAMBERT.

GIVEN NAME Scandinavian 7%. *Erik*.

Lambertson (453) English and Scandinavian: patronymic from LAMBERT.

Lambertus (119) Dutch or German: humanistic name, from a Latinized form of LAMBERT.

Lamberty (272) German: altered form of **Lamberti**, Latin patronymic derivative of LAMBERTUS.

GIVEN NAMES Spanish 7%. *Ana* (2), *Dimas* (2), *Jose* (2), *Juan* (2), *Altagracia*, *Angel*, *Blanca*, *Efrain*, *Fernando*, *Jaime*, *Ramon*.

Lambertz (136) North German: patronymic from LAMBERT.

GIVEN NAMES German 11%. *Heinz* (2), *Erna*, *Johann*, *Ralf*.

Lambeth (1453) English: habitational name from Lambeth, now part of Greater London, named in Old English as 'lamb hithe', from Old English *lamb* 'lamb' + *hȳth* 'hithe', 'landing place', i.e. a place where lambs were put on board boat or taken ashore, no doubt in order to supply the meat markets of London on the other side of the river Thames.

Lambiase (201) Southern Italian: unexplained.

GIVEN NAMES Italian 8%. *Antonio* (2), *Angelo*, *Gilda*, *Stefano*.

Lambie (417) English: **1.** from a pet form of LAMB 1 and 2. **2.** from an Old Norse personal name *Lambi*, from *lamb* 'lamb'.

Lambing (247) Probably a North German and Dutch patronymic from a short form of LAMBERT.

Lambirth (101) English: probably a variant of LAMBERT. Compare LAMBERTH.

Lambo (122) Italian (Puglia): unexplained.

GIVEN NAMES Italian 12%. *Angelo* (2), *Antonio*, *Vito*.

Lamborn (466) English: habitational name from Lambourn in Berkshire or Lambourne in Essex, both of which were probably named in Old English as 'lamb stream', from *lamb* 'lamb' + *burna* 'stream', i.e. a place where lambs were washed.

Lamboy (126) Apparently of Hispanic origin: unexplained. This name is also found in France.
GIVEN NAMES Spanish 29%. *Juan* (3), *Aida, Carlos, Cristobal, Dominga, Eladio, Eliud, Fermin, Gaspar, Jose, Juanita, Luis.*

Lambrecht (1415) German and Dutch: variant of LAMBERT.
GIVEN NAMES German 4%. *Heinz* (2), *Kurt* (2), *Otto* (2), *Ernst, Erwin, Gerhardt, Konrad, Nikolaus, Theodor, Wolf.*

Lambright (941) Americanized form of German or Dutch LAMBRECHT or LAMPRECHT.

Lambrix (126) Dutch: patronymic from the personal name *Lambrick*, a variant of LAMBERT.

Lambros (395) Greek: from a personal name based on classical Greek *lampros* 'brilliant', 'radiant', 'luminous'. This name is given to commemorate Easter, which is known colloquially as *Lambri* 'the bright (day)'. This form may also represent a reduction of patronymics based on this personal name, such as **Lambropoulos**.
GIVEN NAMES Greek 10%. *Demetrios* (3), *Lambros* (3), *Athanasios, Constantine, Costas, Despina, Dimitrios, Kyriacos, Spyro, Toula, Xenophon, Yiannis.*

Lambson (229) English: patronymic from LAMB 2.

Lame (153) Possibly French **L'Amé**, a nickname from a variant of *l'aimé* 'the loved one', from the past participle of *aimer* 'to love'.

Lamendola (456) Italian (also **La Mendola**): nickname or more often a habitational name from places named with the dialect term *amendola, mendola, mendula* 'almond' (also 'almond tree'). This name is widespread in the south and in Sicily.
GIVEN NAMES Italian 14%. *Salvatore* (5), *Angelo* (3), *Saverio* (3), *Carlo* (2), *Carmelo* (2), *Antonio, Camillo, Gino, Giovanni, Giuseppe, Lorenzo, Nino.*

Lamer (320) French (Burgundian): habitational name from a place called La Mer, from French *mer* 'sea'. It is found as a French Canadian secondary surname for Rapidiou, present since 1701.

Lamere (716) French: possibly from *la mère* 'the mother'.

Lamers (482) Variant spelling of German LAMMERS.
GIVEN NAMES German 4%. *Gerhardt, Gottfried, Klaus.*

Lamey (560) **1.** English: from an Old Norse personal name, *Lambi.* **2.** French and English: nickname from Old French *amis, ami* 'friend' or *amé(e)* 'beloved', with the definite article *l'.*

Lamia (152) Southern Italian: topographic name from *lamia* 'ravine', 'gorge', or a

habitational name from any of the places named Lamia from this word.
GIVEN NAMES Italian 13%. *Angelo, Carmela, Salvatore, Santo, Vincenzo.*

Lamica (250) Apparently Italian, from *l'amica* 'the (female) friend'. However, there is some evidence that it may be a variant of French **L'Amitie** 'friendship'. This name is found predominantly in NY.

Lamie (318) **1.** English: variant spelling of LAMEY 1. **2.** Possibly French (**L'Amie**), from *l'amie* 'the (female) friend'.
GIVEN NAMES French 4%. *Armand, Laurier, Normand, Odette, Valere.*

Laminack (230) Americanized form of German **Lamenich**, which is itself a variant of the nickname *Laminich* or *Laminit*, a sentence name meaning 'don't leave me' (Middle High German *lâ mi nit*, modern German *lass mich nicht*).
FOREBEARS Jacob Laminack, also called Lamenck and Lamenich, arrived in Philadelphia on the *Samuel* on 27 August 1739. The family moved to SC in the 1760s.

Lamirand (100) French: variant spelling of LAMIRANDE.

Lamirande (148) French: topographic name from *mirande* 'lookout point' or 'fortified house'. This has been documented as an Acadian name since 1759.
GIVEN NAMES French 12%. *Andre* (2), *Almira, Eloi, Marcel, Normand, Pierre.*

Lamison (170) English: patronymic from LAMB 2.

Lamke (256) North German: from a pet form of LAMBERT.

Lamkin (1252) English: from a pet form of LAMB 1 and 2.

Lamkins (123) English (Kent): variant or patronymic form of LAMKIN.

Lamm (2590) **1.** English and German: from Middle English *lamb*, Middle High German *lamp* 'lamb'; a nickname for a meek and inoffensive person, or a metonymic occupational name for a keeper of lambs. As a German name particularly, it may also have been a habitational name for someone who lived at a house distinguished by the sign of the paschal lamb. **2.** English: from a short form of the personal name LAMBERT.

Lamme (130) Dutch: from a short form of the personal name *Lambrecht* or LAMBERT.
GIVEN NAME French 5%. *Etienne.*

Lammers (1966) North German and Dutch: patronymic from the personal name LAMBERT.

Lammert (518) English and North German (also **Lämmert**): variant of LAMBERT.

Lammey (167) English (also found in Ireland): from a pet form of LAMB 1 and 2.

Lammi (186) Finnish: variant of LAMPI, found chiefly in western Finland.
GIVEN NAMES Finnish 10%. *Eino* (2), *Reino* (2), *Arvo, Taisto, Toivo, Waino.*

Lammon (162) Variant of English LEMON.

Lammons (126) Variant of English LEMONS.

Lamon (679) **1.** French: variant of LAMONT. **2.** Possibly a variant of English LEMON.

La Monaca (100) Southern Italian: nickname (possibly also bestowed on a man), from *monaca* 'nun', with the definite article *la.*
GIVEN NAMES Italian 27%. *Caesar* (3), *Guido* (3), *Donato* (2), *Vito* (2), *Domenico, Gasper, Luca, Romano.*

Lamond (393) **1.** Scottish and northern Irish: variant of LAMONT. **2.** French Canadian: secondary surname of Couture.

La Monda (109) Italian: nickname meaning 'the pure' (see MONDA).

La Monica (840) Italian: **1.** metronymic from the female personal name MONICA. **2.** Alternatively, perhaps a nickname from a variant of *monaca* 'nun'.
GIVEN NAMES Italian 14%. *Salvatore* (8), *Angelo* (4), *Vito* (3), *Dino* (2), *Franco* (2), *Lorenzo* (2), *Sal* (2), *Aldo, Carmela, Domenic, Filomena, Gasper.*

Lamons (304) Variant of English LEMONS.

Lamont (2510) **1.** Scottish and northern Irish: from the medieval personal name *Lagman*, which is from Old Norse *Lǫgmaðr*, composed of *lǫg*, plural of *lag* 'law' (from *leggja* 'to lay down') + *maðr*, 'man' (genitive *manns*). **2.** French: habitational name from places called Amont, in Haute-Saône and Haute-Vienne.

Lamontagne (1402) French: from *montagne* 'mountain', with the definite article *la*, either a habitational name for someone who lived on a mountain or perhaps a nickname for a very large man.
GIVEN NAMES French 15%. *Armand* (10), *Lucien* (6), *Marcel* (5), *Emile* (4), *Pierre* (4), *Aime* (3), *Andre* (3), *Fernand* (3), *Normand* (3), *Gaston* (2), *Ovide* (2), *Achille.*

Lamonte (102) Variant spelling of Scottish LAMONT.

La Monte (334) Italian: topographic name for someone living on a mountain, Italian *monte.*
GIVEN NAMES Italian 4%. *Angelo* (2), *Ciro, Gino, Salvatore, Vincenzo.*

Lamora (168) Spanish: habitational name from any of the several places called La Mora, named with *mora* 'mulberry' (see MORA and MOREIRA).

Lamore (349) **1.** French (**Lamoré**): nickname for a lover or ladykiller, from *amoré* 'beloved', with the definite article *l'.* **2.** Irish: reduced and altered form of McLEMORE.
GIVEN NAMES French 5%. *Aime, Rejeanne, Sylviane.*

Lamoreaux (920) French: variant of LAMOUREUX.
GIVEN NAMES French 4%. *Andre* (2), *Amie, Berard, Colette, Etienne.*

Lamoree (100) French: nickname meaning 'the loved one'.

Lamoreux (187) French: variant of LA-MOUREUX.

La Morte (313) Italian: nickname literally meaning 'death', perhaps a nickname acquired by someone who had played the part of the personified figure of Death in a pageant or play, or for someone with a gloomy disposition.
GIVEN NAMES Italian 12%. *Vito* (3), *Angelo* (2), *Antonio* (2), *Donato* (2), *Pasquale* (2), *Salvatore* (2), *Carmine*.

Lamos (150) Hungarian: nickname from the archaic word *lamos* 'hairy'.

Lamothe (1142) French: topographic name for someone who lived by a fortified stronghold, Old French *motte*, a word of Gaulish origin denoting a hillock or mound (see MOAT), with the definite article *la*. The surname is also a habitational name from any of several places named with this word.
GIVEN NAMES French 14%. *Marcel* (6), *Andre* (3), *Jacques* (3), *Pierre* (3), *Donat* (2), *Francois* (2), *Lucien* (2), *Odette* (2), *Adrien, Andree, Armand, Armande*.

Lamott (153) Variant spelling of French **Lamotte** (see LAMOTHE).

La Motta (151) Italian: topographic name from *la motta* 'the fortified stronghold' (compare French LAMOTHE), or habitational name from a placed named with this word.
GIVEN NAMES Italian 16%; *Enrique* (2). *Gaetano, Giovanni, Mario, Ricardo*.

Lamotte (690) French: see LAMOTHE.
GIVEN NAMES French 5%. *Andre* (2), *Armand, Berthe, Gaston, Laurent, Nicolle, Philippe*.

Lamountain (243) Americanized form of French LAMONTAGNE.

Lamour (170) French: nickname meaning 'love'.
GIVEN NAMES French 32%. *Andre, Armand, Dominique, Ermite, Evens, Gabrielle, Ghislaine, Jacques, Marcel, Marie Nicole, Maryse, Mireille*.

Lamoureaux (230) French: variant of LAMOUREUX.

Lamoureux (1350) French: secondary surname, a nickname for an affectionate man or a philanderer, from Old French *amoureux* 'loving', 'amorous' (Latin *amorosus*, a derivative of *amor* 'love'), with the the definite article *l'*.
FOREBEARS A bearer of this name is recorded in Longueil, Quebec, in 1664; another, from Poitou, was there by 1681.
GIVEN NAMES French 17%. *Normand* (8), *Marcel* (7), *Lucien* (6), *Andre* (5), *Alcide* (4), *Emile* (4), *Jacques* (3), *Laurent* (3), *Pierre* (3), *Alain* (2), *Cecile* (2), *Donat* (2).

Lamp (1375) North German: from a short form of LAMBERT.

Lampa (104) **1.** Swedish: unexplained. **2.** Hispanic: apparently an occupational nickname from *lampa* 'hoe'. This name is found in Bolivia and Peru, but not in Spain or Portugal.

GIVEN NAMES Spanish 6%. *Emilio* (2), *Jose, Josefina, Teresita, Wilfrido*.

Lamparter (148) German: nickname for a banker or moneylender, derived from the ethnic name from *Lamparten* 'Lombardy' (see LOMBARD).
GIVEN NAMES German 8%. *Kurt* (2), *Bernd, Lutz*.

Lampe (2005) **1.** North German: from a pet form of LAMBERT. **2.** French: metonymic occupational name for someone who cast metal lamps and candlesticks, Old French *lampe*. **3.** Slovenian: from a short form of the medieval personal names *Lampret* or *Lampreht*, derivatives of the German personal name *Lamprecht*, Latin *Lambertus* (see LAMBERT). **4.** German: from a house name in Trier, where a prominent lamp or sign of a lamp gave rise to the name.

Lampel (124) Jewish (Ashkenazic): possibly, from German *Lammpelz* 'lamb's fur', a metonymic occupational or ornamental name.
GIVEN NAMES Jewish 8%. *Zvi* (2), *Sol*.

Lampen (129) English: from a pet form of LAMB 1 and 2.

Lamper (114) English (Sussex): unexplained.

Lampert (1369) English, North German, and Hungarian (**Lampért**): variant of LAMBERT.

Lamphear (265) Variant spelling of Cornish LANFEAR.

Lamphere (781) Variant spelling of Cornish LANFEAR.

Lamphier (489) Cornish: variant of LANFEAR.

Lampi (241) Finnish: ornamental name from *lampi* 'pond', which was widely adopted during the name conversion movement in the 19th and early 20th centuries. It is found predominantly in central and eastern Finland. In the U.S. it is also found as an abbreviation of other Finnish surnames such as **Sankilampi**.
GIVEN NAMES Finnish 9%. *Toivo* (2), *Armas, Olavi, Rauno, Reino, Taisto, Tauno, Urho, Wilho*.

Lampinen (150) Finnish: variant of LAMPI + the common surname suffix *-nen*. This name is recorded from the 16th century and occurs mainly in eastern Finland.

Lamping (509) North German and Dutch: patronymic from the personal name *Lampe*, a short form of LAMPERT, a variant of LAMBERT.

Lampkin (1361) English: from a pet form of LAMB 1 and 2.

Lampkins (361) English: patronymic from LAMPKIN.

Lampl (192) South German: from a pet form of LAMBERT.
GIVEN NAMES German 4%. *Hans* (2), *Manfred*.

Lampley (863) English: probably a habitational name from Lamplugh in Cumbria, an

ancient Celtic name meaning 'bare valley', from *nant* 'valley' + *bluch* 'bare'.

Lampman (945) German (**Lampmann**): from a short form of the personal name LAMBERT + Middle High German *man* 'man'.

Lampo (146) **1.** Italian: from a short form of **Alampo**, from the Greek personal name *Eulampios*, adjectival derivative of *eulampēs* 'most splendid'. **2.** Finnish: variant of LAMPI.
GIVEN NAMES Italian 4%. *Pasquale* (2), *Ciro*.

Lamport (147) English: probably a variant of LAMBERT.

Lampp (141) Variant of German LAMP.

Lamprecht (522) German: from a Germanic personal name composed of the elements *land* 'land', 'territory' + *berht* 'bright', 'famous'. Compare LAMBERT.
GIVEN NAMES German 9%. *Harro* (2), *Johann* (2), *Alois, Detlef, Dietrich, Egon, Eldred, Fritz, Hannes, Kurt*.

Lamprey (148) English: nickname for someone thought to resemble the fish in some way, Middle English *lampreye*.

Lampron (262) Canadian French: unexplained.
GIVEN NAMES French 13%. *Cecile* (2), *Adelard, Alyre, Andre, Armand, Jean-Claude, Leo-Paul, Marcel, Renald, Rudolphe*.

Lampros (172) Greek: see LAMBROS.
GIVEN NAMES Greek 5%. *Panos, Spiro*.

Lampshire (121) English (Cornwall): unexplained.

Lampson (402) English: patronymic from LAMB 2.

Lampton (488) English: habitational name from Lampton in Greater London (formerly Middlesex) or Lambton in County Durham, named in Old English as 'farm or settlement where lambs were reared', from *lamb* 'lamb' + *tūn* 'farmstead', 'settlement'.

Lamson (1203) English: patronymic from LAMB 2.

Lamunyon (161) From Irish MUNYON under French influence, prefixed with the French definite article *la*.

Lamy (501) French: nickname from Old French *amis, ami* 'friend', with the definite article *l'*. Compare LAMEY 2.
GIVEN NAMES French 19%. *Andre* (3), *Marcel* (3), *Michel* (3), *Pierre* (3), *Armand, Clovis, Emile, Gabrielle, Gislaine, Jacques, Julien, Laure*.

Lan (478) **1.** Chinese 蓝: from a place named Lan-tian (meaning 'blue field') in Guangdong province. **2.** Polish (**Łan**): perhaps from the vocabulary word *łan* 'plowland', 'soil'. **3.** Polish (**Łań**): alternatively, perhaps a nickname from a derivative of *łania* 'hind', 'doe'.
GIVEN NAMES Chinese 31%. *Feng* (4), *Hongjie* (2), *Jianqing* (2), *Jin* (2), *Wei* (2), *Xiao* (2), *Chan, Chi, Chi Keung, Chieh, Chung-Wen, Dong; Bui, Buu, Dung,*

Duong, Ha, Hao, Hoa, Hung, Lan, Mai, Nguyen, Nho.

Lana (155) **1.** Spanish and Italian: from *lana* 'wool', probably a metonymic occupational name for a wool merchant. **2.** Polish: derivative of LAN.

GIVEN NAMES Italian 9%; Spanish 7%. *Alberto, Salvatore* (2), *Claudio, Fernando, Stefano; Angel, Josefina, Juan, Libertad.*

Lanagan (184) Irish: either a reduced and altered form of MCCLANAHAN or a variant of LANIGAN.

Lanahan (402) Irish: either a reduced and altered form of MCCLANAHAN or a variant of LANIGAN.

La Nasa (274) Southern Italian: from a slang (feminine) form of *naso* 'nose', with the feminine definite article *la*. The feminine form is probably due to the influence of the Italian word *famiglia* 'family'.

GIVEN NAMES Italian 9%. *Salvatore* (2), *Santo* (2), *Vito.*

Lancaster (11909) English: habitational name from Lancaster in northwestern England, named in Old English as 'Roman fort on the Lune', from the Lune river, on which it stands, + Old English *cæster* 'Roman fort or walled city' (Latin *castra* 'legionary camp'). The river name is probably British, perhaps related to Gaelic *slán* 'healthy', 'salubrious'.

Lance (4255) **1.** English: from the Germanic personal name *Lanzo*, originally a short form of various compound names with the first element *land* 'land', 'territory' (for example, LAMBERT), but later used as an independent name. It was introduced to England by the Normans, for whom it was a popular name among the ruling classes, perhaps partly because of association with Old French *lance* 'lance', 'spear' (see 2). **2.** French: metonymic name for a soldier who carried a lance, or a nickname for a skilled fighter, from Old French *lance*.

Lancellotti (117) Italian: patronymic or plural form from the personal name *Lancellotto*, Italian form of *Lancelot*.

GIVEN NAMES Italian 28%. *Carmine* (2), *Luca* (2), *Agostino, Angelo, Bartolomeo, Carlo, Gaetano, Guido, Luco, Rocco.*

Lancer (111) Jewish (from Poland): ornamental name from German *Lanze* 'lance', 'spear' + the agent suffix *-er*.

GIVEN NAMES Jewish 4%; Irish 4%. *Bronia, Rebekah.*

Lancey (139) English: unexplained. The form **De Lancey** is also found in British records; it may well be a habitational name from Lancey in Isère, France.

Lanci (118) Italian: variant of LANCIA.

GIVEN NAMES Italian 21%. *Gerardo* (2), *Aida, Alda, Angelo, Ennio, Ettore, Marino, Rosaria, Rosario.*

Lancia (224) Italian: metonymic occupational name for an armorer or for a soldier who carried a lance, *lancia* (Latin *lancea*).

GIVEN NAMES Italian 30%. *Agostino* (3), *Mario* (3), *Bernardino* (2), *Gabriele* (2), *Lino* (2), *Maurizio* (2), *Orlando* (2), *Angelo, Claudio, Cosmo, Francesco, Gilda, Giulio, Giuseppe, Nino, Olinto, Santino.*

Lanclos (364) French: from Old French *enclus* 'anchorite', 'religious recluse', with the definite article *l'*, either a nickname for someone of reclusive habits, or a topographic name for someone living near a religious retreat.

GIVEN NAMES French 6%. *Antoine, Curley, Damien, Monique, Numa, Yves.*

Lancon (210) Possibly an altered form of LINCOLN, under French influence.

GIVEN NAMES French 6%. *Curley, Ovide.*

Lancour (275) French Canadian spelling of French LINCOURT.

Lancto (117) French Canadian: variant of LANCTOT.

Lanctot (342) French Canadian: perhaps related to **Lanctin**, a reduced form of *L'Anquetin*, itself a variant of the Norman personal name *Anquetil*.

FOREBEARS In the form **Lanqueteau**, the name has been found in Canada at least since 1654.

GIVEN NAMES French 12%. *Aldor* (2), *Adrien, Alphonse, Andre, Armand, Edouard, Gilles, Jean Guy, Leonide, Lucien.*

Land (7544) **1.** English and German: topographic name from Old English *land*, Middle High German *lant*, 'land', 'territory'. This had more specialized senses in the Middle Ages, being used to denote the countryside as opposed to a town or an estate. **2.** English: topographic name for someone who lived in a forest glade, Middle English, Old French *la(u)nde*, or a habitational name from Launde in Leicestershire or Laund in West Yorkshire, which are named with this word. **3.** Norwegian: habitational name from any of three farmsteads so named, from Old Norse *land* 'land', 'territory' (see 1 above).

Landa (1049) **1.** Norwegian: habitational name from any of several farmsteads in southwestern Norway, so named from the plural of *land* (see LAND 1). **2.** Czech: from a short form of the personal name *Mikulanda*, a derivative of *Mikuláš*, Czech form of Greek *Nikolaos* (see NICHOLAS). **3.** Polish: nickname for a persistent and irritating person, from a derivative of the dialect verb *landzić* 'to ask insistently', 'badger someone'. **4.** Jewish (eastern Ashkenazic): variant of LANDAU. **5.** Spanish and Basque: topographic name from the Basque *landa* 'meadow'. There is a place of this name in Álava province, Basque Country, and the surname may in fact be a habitational name from this place.

GIVEN NAMES Spanish 31%. *Carlos* (12), *Jorge* (9), *Jose* (8), *Luis* (7), *Juan* (6), *Manuel* (6), *Enrique* (4), *Jesus* (4), *Julio* (4), *Mario* (4), *Roberto* (4), *Miguel* (3).

Landaker (117) German (**Landacker**): altered form either of **Landegger**, a topographic name meaning 'owner of fields of a certain territory', or of **Landecker**, a habitational name from any of several places in Germany and Austria called Landeck (see LANDECK). This name was prominent among Salzburg Protestants who settled in East Prussia.

Landau (2314) German and Jewish (Ashkenazic): habitational name from either of two places called Landau, in the Palatinate and in Alsace, named with Old High German *lant* 'land', 'territory' + *auwa* 'damp valley'. According to family history, the Jewish surname originated from the Palatinate.

GIVEN NAMES Jewish 11%. *Chaim* (6), *Emanuel* (6), *Aron* (5), *Avi* (4), *Zev* (4), *Miriam* (3), *Shulem* (3), *Yaakov* (3), *Zvi* (3), *Ari* (2), *Hyman* (2), *Meyer* (2).

Landauer (277) German and Jewish (Ashkenazic): habitational name for someone from either of two places called LANDAU.

GIVEN NAMES German 5%. *Alois, Hans Peter, Heinz, Konrad.*

Landaverde (220) Spanish: topographic name from *landa* 'meadow' + *verde* 'green'.

GIVEN NAMES Spanish 57%. *Jose* (12), *Ana* (6), *Roberto* (5), *Juan* (4), *Francisco* (3), *Josefina* (3), *Julio* (3), *Mario* (3), *Bernardo* (2), *Carlos* (2), *Concepcion* (2), *Luis* (2); *Antonio* (3), *Eligio, Filiberto, Franco, Giovanni, Severiano.*

Landay (116) English: unexplained.

Landberg (217) Swedish: ornamental name composed of the elements *land* 'land' + *berg* 'mountain', 'hill'.

GIVEN NAME Scandinavian 5%. *Erik.*

Lande (583) **1.** French: topographic name for someone living on a heath, *lande* (from Gaulish *landa* 'space', 'land'), or a habitational name from any of numerous minor places named La Lande from this word. **2.** Norwegian: habitational name from any of several farmsteads, so named from either the dative singular or the plural form of *land* (see LAND 3). **3.** Jewish (eastern Ashkenazic): Yiddish variant of LANDAU.

Landeck (167) Dutch: habitational name from places so called near Klingenmünster and Teningen; it is also a quite common place name in Alsace-Lorraine.

GIVEN NAMES French 5%; German 4%. *Vernice; Kurt, Manfred.*

Landeen (144) Swedish: variant of LANDEN.

Landefeld (154) German: habitational name from a place so named in Hesse.

GIVEN NAMES German 4%. *Bernhard, Hans, Kurt.*

Landen (403) **1.** Swedish (**Landén**): ornamental name composed of the elements *land* 'land', 'territory' + the suffix *-én*, from the Latin adjectival ending *-enius*.

2. Belgian: habitational name from Landen in Brabant.

Landenberger (224) Swiss German: habitational name for someone from any of several places called Landenberg in Switzerland.
GIVEN NAMES German 4%. *Kurt* (2), *Erna*.

Lander (1959) **1.** German and Jewish (Ashkenazic): topographic name from Middle High German *lant*, German *Land* 'land', 'territory' (see LAND 1), used originally to denote either someone who was a native of the area in which he lived, in contrast to a newcomer (see NEUMANN), or someone who lived in the countryside as opposed to a town. **2.** Jewish (Ashkenazic): habitational name from either of two places called Landau (see LANDAU), *Lande* in Yiddish. **3.** Dutch: from a Germanic personal name formed with *land* 'land' + *hardu* 'strong'. **4.** English: variant of LAVENDER. **5.** Americanized form (translation) of French TERRIEN, found in New England.

Landerman (134) Jewish (Ashkenazic) and German (**Landermann**): **1.** altered form of LENDERMAN. **2.** altered form of **Lantermann** (see LANTERMAN).

Landeros (695) Spanish: topographic name for someone who lived by an oak wood, from a Castilianized form of Galician *landeiros*, from *landeiro* 'oak producing many acorns'.
GIVEN NAMES Spanish 54%. *Jose* (17), *Jesus* (13), *Juan* (8), *Manuel* (8), *Miguel* (8), *Raul* (8), *Carlos* (7), *Pedro* (7), *Mario* (6), *Francisco* (5), *Jorge* (5), *Luis* (5).

Landers (6687) Dutch: patronymic from LANDER.

Landes (1874) French: variant of LANDE 1 (specifically also a habitational name from any of numerous places named Landes or Les Landes) and 2.

Landesman (245) Jewish (eastern Ashkenazic): variant of LANDSMAN.
GIVEN NAMES Jewish 7%. *Avrom* (2), *Emanuel*, *Leib*, *Schlomo*.

Landess (339) Possibly an altered spelling of LANDIS.

Landfair (174) Apparently a translation of French TERREBONNE, a common name in LA.

Landfried (155) South German: from a Germanic personal name composed of the elements *land* 'land', 'territory' (see LAND) + *fred, frid* 'peace'.
GIVEN NAME French 7%. *Chantel* (3).

Landgraf (748) German and Dutch: status name for a royal judge and administrator of a province (Middle High German *lant* + *grāve*), or a nickname for a servant in the household of one.
GIVEN NAMES German 5%. *Kurt* (3), *Gerhard* (2), *Hans* (2), *Otto*.

Landgrebe (232) German: variant of LANDGRAF.

GIVEN NAMES German 7%. *Bernhard* (2), *Erwin*, *Fritz*.

Landgren (257) Swedish: ornamental name composed of the elements *land* 'land' + *gren* 'branch'.
GIVEN NAME Scandinavian 4%. *Knute*.

Landherr (126) German: **1.** from the personal name *Lanthar*, from *land* 'land' + *hari* 'army'. **2.** status name from Middle High German *lantherre* (*lant* 'land' + *herre* 'lord'), denoting an overlord, i.e. someone who had land in his gift.
GIVEN NAMES German 6%. *Erna*, *Klaus*, *Kurt*.

Landi (701) Italian: patronymic or plural form of the personal name LANDO.
GIVEN NAMES Italian 16%. *Angelo* (4), *Antonio* (2), *Dante* (2), *Dino* (2), *Florio* (2), *Luigi* (2), *Oreste* (2), *Romeo* (2), *Salvatore* (2), *Bruna, Carmine, Ciro*.

Landin (750) **1.** Swedish: ornamental name composed of the elements *land* 'land' + *-in*, a common suffix of Swedish surnames derived from Latin *-in(i)us* 'descendant of'. **2.** Spanish (mainly Galicia; **Landín**): habitational name from Landín in A Coruña province. The place name derives from the Germanic personal name *Nandinus*.
GIVEN NAMES Spanish 20%. *Luis* (7), *Carlos* (5), *Jose* (5), *Juan* (5), *Alicia* (3), *Lupe* (3), *Angel* (2), *Araceli* (2), *Criselda* (2), *Evaristo* (2), *Francisco* (2), *Herlinda* (2).

Landing (154) English: unexplained.

Landingham (148) Dutch: see VAN LANDINGHAM.

Landini (164) Italian: patronymic or plural form of the personal name LANDINO.
GIVEN NAMES Italian 10%. *Gino, Guido, Luigi, Paolo, Primo*.

Landino (278) Italian: from a pet form of the personal name LANDO.
GIVEN NAMES Italian 8%. *Angelo* (3), *Antonio, Pasquale, Vincenzo*.

Landis (7374) German and Swiss German: nickname for a highwayman or for someone who lays waste to the land, Middle High German *landoese*.

Landman (762) **1.** Dutch: variant of LANDSMAN. **2.** Jewish (Ashkenazic): variant of LANDER.
GIVEN NAMES Jewish 4%. *Chana* (2), *Haim, Ilya, Naum, Sol, Uzi, Yomtov, Zvi*.

Landmann (127) German and Jewish (Ashkenazic): variant of LANDER 1.
GIVEN NAMES German 5%. *Benno, Wolf*.

Landmark (145) Altered form of French **Lamarque** (see LAMARCHE).

Landmesser (156) German: occupational name for a land surveyor, from Middle High German *lant* 'land', 'territory' + an agent derivative of *mezzen* 'to measure'.
GIVEN NAMES German 4%. *Egon, Ralf*.

Lando (307) **1.** Italian: from the personal name *Lando*, a reduced form or short form of any of various personal names formed with the Germanic element *land* 'land', 'territory', for example ORLANDO,

ROLANDO, or *Landolfo* (see LANDOLFI). **2.** Hungarian (**Landó**): from a pet form of the old secular personal name *Lándor*. **3.** Jewish (eastern Ashkenazic): variant of LANDAU.
GIVEN NAMES Italian 7%; Jewish 4%. *Remo* (2), *Salvatore* (2), *Cosmo, Nicoletta, Salvator, Sandro; Chayim* (2), *Miriam* (2), *Mariya, Pinchas*.

Landolfi (252) Italian: patronymic or plural form of the personal name *Landolfo*, from a traditional Langobardic personal name, *Landulf*, composed of the Germanic elements *land* 'land', 'territory' + *wulf* 'wolf'.
GIVEN NAMES Italian 14%. *Pasquale* (2), *Angelo, Domenico, Liberato, Lorenzo, Maurizio, Pasco*.

Landoll (109) **1.** variant of German LANDOLT. **2.** perhaps also from English **Landell**, a topographic name for someone who lived in a glade, from a diminutive of Old French *launde* 'forest glade'.

Landolt (316) South German: from a Germanic personal name composed of the elements *land* 'land', 'territory' + *walt* 'power', reign.

Landon (3245) **1.** English or Scottish: unexplained. Possibly, as Black suggests, a reduced form of LANGDON. **2.** French: from the old Germanic personal name element *Lando* (see LAND), via the oblique case, *Landonis*.

Landor (116) **1.** Hungarian (**Lándor**): from the old secular personal name *Lándor*. **2.** English: possibly a variant spelling of LANDER.
GIVEN NAMES French 6%; Jewish 5%. *Alphonse, Oneil; Miriam*.

Landow (139) Americanized spelling of Ashkenazic Jewish LANDAU.
GIVEN NAME Scottish 4%; Jewish 4%. *Sol*.

Landowski (286) **1.** Polish (also **Ladowski**): habitational name from any of various places called Ląd and Lądy, named with Polish *ląd* 'land'. **2.** Jewish (from Poland): Polonized form of LANDAU.

Landram (100) Variant of LANDRUM.

Landreneau (293) Of French origin: unexplained. This is a Louisiana name.
GIVEN NAMES French 5%. *Aldes, Cyprien, Eulalie*.

Landress (237) Anglicized form of either of two Dutch names. **1.** possibly from **Landries**, a variant of **Langendries**, habitational name from any of various places so named in the Netherlands. **2.** alternatively, from **Landresse**, derivative of French **Landrieu**, a patronymic from the personal name *Andrieu* (see ANDREAS).

Landreth (1719) English (mainly northeastern) and Scottish: unexplained.

Landreville (168) French: habitational name from Landreville in Aube; in Canada, it was a secondary surname for GAUTIER.
GIVEN NAMES French 16%. *Lucien* (3), *Cecile, Huguette, Luc, Marcel, Pierre*.

Landrey (130) Variant spelling of LANDRY.

Landrigan (251) Irish: reduced Anglicized form of Gaelic **Ó Longargáin** (see LONERGAN).

Landrith (184) Variant spelling of LANDRETH.

Landrum (4017) Possibly of northern Irish or Scottish origin: unexplained. This is a common name in GA. There is said to be a Cherokee connection.

Landrus (176) Variant of LANDRESS.

Landry (14247) French (also English, imported to Britain by the Normans): from the Germanic personal name *Landric*, a compound of *land* 'land' + *rīc* 'powerful', 'ruler'.
FOREBEARS The name has been recorded in Quebec City since 1659, taken there from Perche, France. In LA, Landry families of Acadian origin are numerous.
GIVEN NAMES French 7%. *Armand* (16), *Lucien* (16), *Pierre* (12), *Emile* (11), *Andre* (9), *Fernand* (9), *Oneil* (9), *Marcel* (7), *Antoine* (6), *Benoit* (6), *Camille* (6), *Raoul* (6).

Lands (495) English: variant of LAND.

Landsberg (342) **1.** German and Jewish (Ashkenazic): habitational name from any of several places so named. **2.** Swedish: ornamental name composed of the possessive case of *land* 'land', 'country' + *berg* 'mountain', or an adoption of the German name (see 1).
GIVEN NAMES German 7%; Jewish 4%. *Klaus* (2), *Kurt* (2), *Fritz*, *Gunther*, *Hans*; *Eliyahu*, *Ephraim*, *Gilad*, *Isadore*, *Meyer*, *Yetta*.

Landsberger (165) German: habitational name for someone from a place called LANDSBERG.
GIVEN NAME German 6%. *Kurt* (3).

Landsiedel (127) German: nickname for a person living in the country, from Middle High German *lant* 'land' + *sidile* 'occupant'.

Landsman (633) German, Dutch, and Jewish (Ashkenazic): variant of LANDER 1, from Middle High German, Middle Dutch *lantsman*, German *Landsmann* or Yiddish *landsman* 'countryman' or 'fellow countryman'.
GIVEN NAMES Jewish 5%. *Miriam* (2), *Sol* (2), *Emanuel*, *Israil*, *Lasar*, *Mandel*, *Mascha*, *Mayer*.

Landstrom (267) Swedish (**Landström**): ornamental name composed of the elements *land* 'land' + *ström* 'river'.
GIVEN NAMES Scandinavian 8%. *Holger*, *Sven*.

Landsverk (138) Norwegian: habitational name from any of about 25 farmsteads in Telemark, Buskerud, and Agden called Landsverk, from the genitive of *land* 'land', 'field' + *verk* 'work', i.e. clearing or cultivating the land.
GIVEN NAME Scandinavian 9%. *Obert*.

Landt (232) German: variant of LAND 1.

Landucci (128) Italian: patronymic from a pet form of the personal name LANDO.
GIVEN NAMES Italian 17%. *Dino* (3), *Dante* (2), *Canio*, *Umberto*.

Landuyt (135) Belgian: habitational name from any of a number of places called Landuit in East Flanders and Brabant. The name may have developed from a word meaning 'country exit', that is, a border area.

Landwehr (980) German: from a Germanic personal name, *Lantwer*, composed of the elements *lant* 'land' + *wer* 'defender'.

Landy (941) French: habitational name from any of the places called (Le) Landy.

Lane (47026) **1.** English: topographic name for someone who lived in a lane, Middle English, Old English *lane*, originally a narrow way between fences or hedges, later used to denote any narrow pathway, including one between houses in a town. **2.** Irish: reduced Anglicized form of Gaelic **Ó Laighin** 'descendant of *Laighean*', a byname meaning 'spear', or 'javelin'. **3.** Irish: reduced Anglicized form of Gaelic **Ó Luain** 'descendant of *Luan*', a byname meaning 'warrior'. **4.** Irish: reduced Anglicized form of Gaelic **Ó Liatháin** (see LEHANE). **5.** Southern French: variant of LAINE. **6.** Possibly also a variant of Southern French LANDE.

Lanehart (159) Americanized spelling of German LENHARDT.

Laner (114) **1.** German and Hungarian: variant of LAHNER. **2.** Possibly also an Americanization of LEHNER.
GIVEN NAME German 6%. *Manfred* (2).

Lanes (177) English: variant of LANE.
GIVEN NAMES German 5%. *Kurt*, *Trud*.

Lanese (272) Italian: habitational name from a place named Lana, from an adjectival form of the place name, though probably not the one in Bolzano province, since the surname occurs chiefly in Molise.
GIVEN NAMES Italian 8%. *Nicola* (2), *Angelo*, *Domenico*, *Gaeton*, *Lucio*, *Pasquale*.

La Neve (164) Italian: nickname literally meaning 'the snow', probably applied to someone with snowy white hair.
GIVEN NAMES Italian 8%. *Antonio*, *Cosmo*, *Natale*.

Laney (3671) Irish: probably a reduced and altered form of MCELHINNEY.

Lanfear (150) English (Cornish): habitational name from a place named with Cornish *lan* 'church'. In England this surname is now found chiefly in the southern counties of Wiltshire and Hampshire, and Berkshire; it has no doubt moved there from Cornwall.

Lanford (821) English: habitational name, probably from Landford, Wiltshire, which was originally *Laneford*, from Old English *lane* 'narrow way' + *ford* 'ford'.

Lang (23405) **1.** Scottish, English, Dutch, German, Danish, Swedish, and Jewish (Ashkenazic): nickname for a tall person, from Older Scots, Middle English, Middle Dutch, Middle German, and Danish *lang* 'long', Swedish *lång*. **2.** Hungarian: from *láng* 'flame', hence probably a nickname for a passionate person, or a man with a fighting spirit. Alternatively it may be an indirect occupational name for a smith or someone who worked with fire. **3.** Chinese 郎: from the name of a place called Lang City in the state of Lu, founded during the Spring and Autumn period (722–481 BC) by a grandson of the ruler. His descendants lived there and adopted **Lang** as their surname. **4.** Vietnamese (**Lăng**): unexplained.

Langa (114) **1.** Spanish: habitational name for someone from one of the places called Langa in Ávila, Soria, and in particular Zaragoza provinces. **2.** Variant of German LANGE. .

Langager (124) **1.** German: variant of **Langacker**, topographic name for a farmer who cultivated a long field, from Middle High German *lang* 'long' + *ecker*, *egger* 'field', 'acre'. **2.** Danish or Norwegian: variant of LONGAKER.
GIVEN NAMES German 5%; Scandinavian 4%. *Eldor*, *Otto*.

Langan (1860) Irish: reduced Anglicized form of Gaelic **Ó Longáin** 'descendant of *Longán*', a personal name probably derived from *long* 'tall', or perhaps from the homonymous *long* 'ship' (and so originally a byname for a seafarer). Sometimes LEONARD is used as an equivalent.
GIVEN NAMES Irish 4%. *Brendan*, *Declan*.

Langbehn (198) North German: variant of LANGBEIN.
GIVEN NAME German 4%. *Kurt* (2).

Langbein (155) German: nickname for a person with long legs, from Middle High German *long* + *bein* 'leg'.

Langberg (117) **1.** German: topographic name for someone living by a long mountain, from Middle High German *lang* 'long' + *berc* 'hill', 'mountain'. **2.** Jewish (Ashkenazic) and Swedish: ornamental name meaning 'long mountain'.
GIVEN NAMES Jewish 9%; Scandinavian 5%; German 4%. *Aron*, *Sol*; *Lars*.

Langdale (262) **1.** English: habitational name from Langdale, Cumbria, named in Old Norse as 'long valley', from *lang* 'long' + *dalr* 'valley'. **2.** Possibly an Americanized form of Norwegian **Langdal**, **Langdalen**, **Langdahl**, habitational names from any of numerous farmsteads named Langdal(en), having the same etymology as 1.

Langdon (3583) English: habitational name from any of various places, for example in Devon, Dorset, Essex, Kent, and Warwickshire, so named from Old English *lang*, *long* 'long' + *dūn* 'hill'.
FOREBEARS Samuel Langdon, Harvard College president in 1774–80, was born in Boston, MA, in 1723 but lived out his years in Hampton Falls, NH. Three of his

children left descendants. His grandfather Philip (b. 1646) had came from Braunton in Devon, England, and was married in Andover, Essex Co., MA, in 1684, according to family historians. Another early Langdon immigrant was Tobias Langdon, who came to America before 1660 and settled in Portsmouth, NH. His great-grandson John was a revolutionary war leader, U.S. senator, and NH governor.

Lange (12885) **1.** German and Scandinavian: variant of LANG. **2.** French (**L'Ange**): nickname from *ange* 'angel', with the definite article *l'*.

FOREBEARS There was a L'Ange in Quebec as early as 1613.

GIVEN NAMES German 5%. *Kurt* (25), *Hans* (19), *Erwin* (11), *Heinz* (9), *Horst* (7), *Otto* (7), *Wolfgang* (5), *Ernst* (4), *Helmut* (4), *Hermann* (4), *Manfred* (4), *Reinhold* (4).

Langel (458) **1.** Swiss German and eastern German: from the nickname *Langel* 'the tall one', a diminutive of LANG. **2.** German: habitational name from any of several places called Langel.

Langeland (185) Norwegian: habitational name from any of about 25 farmsteads, most in western Norway, named from *lang* 'long' + *land* '(piece of) land', 'farmstead'.

GIVEN NAMES Scandinavian 17%. *Erik* (2), *Borge*, *Per*, *Tor*.

Langelier (251) French: from the personal name *Angelier*, with the definite article *l'*. This is in origin a Germanic personal name *Angilhari*, *Angalhari*, composed of the elements *angil*, *angal* (of uncertain origin) + *hari* 'army'. The first element may be an augmentation of *ango* 'point (of a sword)', 'lance', or an ethnic term for the Angles.

FOREBEARS The name L'Angelier has been found in Quebec City since 1665, taken there from Normandy, France.

GIVEN NAMES French 12%. *Andre*, *Armand*, *Lucien*, *Normand*, *Solange*, *Valmore*, *Yvan*.

Langell (110) Variant of German LANGEL.

Langella (163) Italian: variant of **Lancella**, from a diminutive of LANCIA.

GIVEN NAMES Italian 17%. *Alessandro*, *Annamarie*, *Carmine*, *Domenic*, *Emanuele*, *Gennaro*.

Langen (329) German: habitational name from any of several places so named.

GIVEN NAMES German 4%. *Bodo*, *Gunther*, *Heinz*, *Rainer*.

Langenbach (212) German: habitational name from any of several places so named, from Old High German *lang* + dative ending -*en* + *bah* 'stream'.

GIVEN NAMES German 10%. *Kurt* (2), *Gerhard*, *Klaus*, *Uwe*.

Langenberg (324) German and Dutch: habitational name from various places in Germany and one in the province of Antwerp, so named from Old High German *lang* + dative ending *en* + *berg* 'mountain', 'hill'.

Langenderfer (189) Americanized spelling of German *Langendörfer*, a habitational name from any of various places called LANGENDORF.

GIVEN NAME French 4%. *Romain* (2).

Langendorf (138) German: habitational name from any of several places so called from Old High German *lang* 'long' + dative ending *en* + *dorf* 'village'.

GIVEN NAME German 4%. *Dieter*.

Langenfeld (463) German: habitational name from any of several places so called from Old High German *lang* 'long' + the dative ending -*en* + *feld* 'open country', 'field', or a topographic name, based on the same elements, for the owner of a long piece of land.

Langenkamp (115) Dutch and North German: habitational name from places so called in Schleswig-Holstein, Lower Saxony, and North-Rhine Westphalia, or a topographic name for someone who lived by a long field, *kamp* being the North German word for 'field' or 'domain'. Compare LANGENFELD.

Langer (3072) German, Dutch, Danish, and Jewish (Ashkenazic): nickname for a tall man, from an inflected form of LANG. According to Gottschald, in the Franconian dialect of German this was also a term for an unskilled laborer (more fully, **Handlanger**).

GIVEN NAMES German 6%. *Hans* (4), *Horst* (4), *Kurt* (4), *Otto* (4), *Dieter* (3), *Franz* (3), *Gerhard* (3), *Manfred* (3), *Fritz* (2), *Siegfried* (2), *Alois*, *Angelika*.

Langerman (171) German (**Langermann**), Dutch, and Jewish (Ashkenazic): nickname for a tall man, from *lang(er)* 'long', 'tall' + *Mann* 'man'.

Langerud (156) Norwegian: habitational name from a farm named with *lang* 'long' + *rud* 'clearing'.

GIVEN NAMES Scandinavian 8%. *Selmer* (2), *Hjalmer*, *Lars*.

Langevin (1189) French: ethnic name for an Angevin (someone from Anjou), with the definite article *l'*. This is a frequent secondary surname in French Canada. The name is sometimes found as BERGEVIN.

FOREBEARS Langevin is first found in Quebec City in 1654, where there is Langevin also called LACROIX.

GIVEN NAMES French 10%. *Armand* (6), *Normand* (5), *Andre* (3), *Henri* (3), *Jean-Louis* (2), *Pierre* (2), *Adelard*, *Emile*, *Gaston*, *Leodore*, *Lucien*, *Marcel*.

Langfeldt (151) German: variant of LANGENFELD.

GIVEN NAME German 4%. *Kurt* (2).

Langfield (119) English: topographic name from Old English *lang* 'long' + *feld* 'stretch of open country', or a habitational name from a place so named, such as Langfield in Kent.

Langfitt (148) Probably an altered form of English LANGFORD.

Langford (6896) English: habitational name from any of the numerous places named in Old English as 'long ford', from *lang*, *long* 'long' + *ford* 'ford', except for Langford in Nottinghamshire, which is named with an Old English personal name *Landa* or possibly *land*, here used in a specific sense such as 'boundary' or 'district', with the same second element.

Langguth (130) German: **1.** habitational name from places in Württemberg and East Prussia. **2.** nickname for a slow but dependable person, from Middle High German *lang* 'long' + *guot* 'good'.

GIVEN NAMES German 10%. *Arno*, *Fritz*, *Gerhard*, *Ingeborg*.

Langham (1290) English: habitational name from any of various places so called. Most, as for example those in Dorset, Norfolk, Rutland, and Suffolk, were named from Old English *lang* 'long' + *hām* 'homestead', 'enclosure'; but one in Essex is recorded in Domesday Book as *Laingaham*, from Old English *Lāhhingahām* 'homestead of the people of *Lahha*', and one in Lincolnshire originally had as its second element Old Norse *holmr* 'island'.

Langhans (190) German and Dutch: distinguishing nickname for a tall man (see LANG) called Hans.

GIVEN NAMES German 8%. *Markus* (2), *Helmut*, *Wilhelm*.

Langhoff (253) North German (Westphalia) and Danish: habitational name from a farm (Middle Low German *hof*), probably one with a long, narrow shape (Middle Low German *lank* 'long') or situated at the side (Middle Low German *lanke*) of a river or hill.

GIVEN NAMES German 5%. *Reinhard*, *Volker*, *Wolfgang*.

Langholz (124) North German and Danish: habitational name from Langholz near Eckernförde or Langholt near Leer.

GIVEN NAMES German 6%. *Armin* (2), *Kurt*.

Langhorn (107) English: variant spelling of LANGHORNE.

Langhorne (335) **1.** Northern English: probably a habitational name from a minor place in Soulby, Cumbria, called Longthorn, from Old English *lang* 'long' + *horn* 'projecting headland', or a topographic name with the same meaning. **2.** English: nickname from Middle English *lang*, *long* 'long' + *horn* 'horn', with various possible applications; it could have denoted a horn blower or possibly a cuckhold, or it may have referred to some physical characteristic; there is some suggestion that *horn* in some names may mean 'head' or otherwise 'phallus'. **3.** Danish: habitational name from Langhorn. **4.** Dutch: nickname for someone with long ears.

Langhorst (220) North German: habitational name from any of several places so named in northern Germany.

GIVEN NAMES German 9%. *Eldor* (2), *Gerhard*, *Kurt*, *Lorenz*, *Otto*.

Langill (212) Variant of French LANGILLE.

Langille (351) French: nickname for a chatterbox from Old French *langille* 'little tongue'.

Langin (128) **1.** Irish: variant of LANGAN. **2.** French (Burgundy): nickname for a cunning, crafty man, from Old French *engin* 'cunning', 'deftness', with the definite article *l'*.

Langlais (589) French: ethnic name for an Englishman, from French *anglais* 'English(man)', with the definite article *l'*. This name is sometimes Americanized as LANGLEY.

FOREBEARS There was a Langlais also called Laperaille, from Normandy, France, in Quebec in 1634.

GIVEN NAMES French 15%. *Lucien* (3), *Pierre* (3), *Emile* (2), *Marcel* (2), *Normand* (2), *Albertine*, *Armand*, *Cecile*, *Enoil*, *Herve*, *Jacques*, *Laurent*.

Langland (312) **1.** English and Scottish: topographic name, from Old English *lang*, *long* 'long' + *land* 'land', 'territory'. **2.** Norwegian: variant of LANGELAND.

Langley (9630) English: **1.** habitational name from any of the numerous places named with Old English *lang* 'long' + *lēah* 'wood', 'glade'; or a topographic name with the same meaning. **2.** English: from the Old Norse female personal name *Langlíf*, composed of the elements *lang* 'long' + *líf* 'life'. **3.** Americanized spelling of French LANGLAIS.

Langlie (151) Norwegian: habitational name from any of several farmsteads named Langli, from *lang* 'long' + *li* 'hillside'.

GIVEN NAME Scandinavian 8%. *Selmer* (2).

Langlinais (296) Of French origin: unexplained; possibly a habitational name.

GIVEN NAMES French 7%. *Raoul* (2), *Minos*, *Norvin*, *Ulysse*.

Langlitz (114) German: distinguishing name for a tall man called **Litz**, a pet form of LUDWIG, variant of LUTZ.

Langlois (2885) French: variant of LANGLAIS.

FOREBEARS This name was found in Quebec City from 1634, taken there from Normandy, France, and in Trois Rivières, Quebec, from 1660, taken there from Paris.

GIVEN NAMES French 12%. *Armand* (8), *Pierre* (8), *Lucien* (7), *Marcel* (7), *Andre* (6), *Normand* (6), *Gaston* (4), *Henri* (4), *Jacques* (4), *Monique* (4), *Emile* (3), *Camille* (2).

Langmaid (155) English: nickname for a tall girl or an effeminate man, from Middle English *lang*, *long* 'long' + *maide* 'maid', 'girl'.

Langman (306) English, German (**Langmann**) and Jewish (Ashkenazic): nickname for a tall person (see LANG).

GIVEN NAMES Jewish 4%. *Hymie*, *Irina*, *Yaron*.

Langner (649) **1.** German: habitational name from any of several places called Langen or Langenau in Germany, Bohemia, and Silesia. **2.** English: habitational name from any of four places in Shropshire and Staffordshire called Longner or Longnor. Longner and Longnor in Shropshire are from Old English *lang* 'long' + *alor* 'alder tree', 'alder copse', as is Longnor near Penkridge, Staffordshire. But Longnor, Staffordshire is from Old English *lang* (genitive *langan*) + *ofer* 'ridge'.

GIVEN NAMES German 7%. *Horst* (2), *Otto* (2), *Rudi* (2), *Ernst*, *Guenther*, *Hans*, *Heinz*, *Oskar*, *Ute*, *Wolfgang*.

Langness (139) Norwegian: habitational name from any of several farmsteads named Langnes, from *lang* 'long' + *nes* 'headland', 'point'.

GIVEN NAME Scandinavian 6%. *Sig*.

Lango (150) **1.** Americanized form of Norwegian **Langøy** or **Langø**, habitational names from any of several farmsteads named *Langøy*, from *lang* 'long' + *øy* 'island'. **2.** Hispanic (Mexico and Venezuela): unexplained; possibly a variant of LANGA.

GIVEN NAMES German 5%; Scandinavian 4%; Spanish 4%. *Kurt*, *Udo*; *Lars*, *Soren*; *Armida*, *Felipe*, *Jose*, *Juanita*, *Luis*.

Langolf (124) German (Alsatian): from the Germanic personal name *Langwulf*, composed of the elements *lang* 'long' + *wulf* 'wolf'.

GIVEN NAMES German 5%. *Otto*, *Reinhart*.

Langone (425) Italian: unexplained.

GIVEN NAMES Italian 9%. *Carmine* (3), *Rocco*, *Vito*.

Langowski (210) Polish (**Łęgowski**): habitational name for someone from a place called Łęg, Łęgi, or Łęgowo, named with Polish *łęg* 'water meadow'.

GIVEN NAMES Polish 6%. *Andrzej*, *Bronislaw*, *Faustyn*, *Krzysztof*.

Langreck (148) German: altered spelling of the habitational name **Längericht** or LENGERICH.

GIVEN NAMES Irish 5%; German 4%. *Florian*, *Math*.

Langrehr (206) German: habitational name from Langreder, near Hannover.

Langridge (178) English: habitational name from any of the various places named with Old English *lang* 'long' + *hrycg* 'ridge', for example in Somerset, or a topographic name with the same meaning.

Langs (113) German: of Slavic origin, a topographic name from Slavic *lanka* 'meadow', 'swamp'.

Langsam (222) German and Jewish (Ashkenazic): nickname from Middle High German *lancsam*, German *langsam* 'slow'.

GIVEN NAMES Jewish 15%. *Aron* (3), *Pesach* (2), *Arie*, *Chaya*, *Izchak*, *Miriam*, *Noach*, *Shimon*, *Shulem*, *Sol*, *Yehuda*.

Langsdorf (199) German: habitational name from any of several places named Langsdorf.

Langseth (263) Norwegian: habitational name from any of several farmsteads named Langset, from *lang* 'long' + *set* 'farmstead'.

GIVEN NAMES Scandinavian 6%. *Ordell*, *Petter*.

Langstaff (322) English: apparently an occupational name for a tipstaff or beadle who carried a long staff as a badge of office; perhaps also a nickname for a very tall, thin man, or even an obscene nickname for a man with a long sexual organ. The surname is found chiefly in northeastern England.

Langston (6521) English (mainly West Midlands): habitational name from any of various places, for example Langstone in Devon and Hampshire, named with Old English *lang* 'long', 'tall' + *stān* 'stone', i.e. a menhir.

Langstraat (120) Dutch: habitational name for someone from a place named as the 'long street'.

Langton (872) English: habitational name from any of numerous places so called from Old English *lang* 'long' + *tūn* 'enclosure', 'settlement'. (Langton in County Durham, however, has the same etymology as LANGDON).

Langtry (145) English: habitational name from places in Devon, Oxfordshire, and Lancashire called Langtree, from Old English *lang*, *long* 'long', 'tall' + *trēow* 'tree'.

Langwell (190) English (rare; mainly northeastern): variant of LONGWELL.

Langworthy (693) English (Devon): habitational name from either of two places in Devon called Langworthy, from Old English *lang* 'long' + *worðig* 'enclosure'.

Lanham (3419) English (Suffolk and Essex): variant of LANGHAM.

Lanich (102) Perhaps a variant of Czech (Moravian) LANIK.

Lanier (7208) **1.** French, Dutch, and English: occupational name for someone involved in the wool trade, from an agent derivative of Old French *la(i)ne* 'wool'. **2.** French and Dutch: occupational name, with the definite article, for a pack driver, from French *âne* 'ass', 'donkey' (Latin *asinus*). **3.** French and Dutch: nickname for a falconer, from Old French *lanier*, *lenier*, a kind of falcon. **4.** French and Dutch: nickname for a lazy, slow, timid, or cowardly person, from Old French *lanier*, *lenier*.

Lanigan (942) Irish: reduced Anglicized form of Gaelic **Ó Lonagáin** 'descendant of *Lonagán*', apparently a double diminutive of *lon* 'blackbird', but possibly a variant of FLANAGAN with lenited initial *F*.

GIVEN NAMES Irish 5%. *Brendan*, *Oonagh*, *Patrick Michael*.

Lanik (110) Czech (Moravian; **Láník**): status name from Czech *láník* 'comparatively weathy farmer', from *lán*, a comparatively large measure of land. A *láník*, the Moravian equivalent of the western Czech *sedlák* (see SEDLAK), was a farmer who farmed one or more lán.

Laning (281) English: variant spelling of LANNING.

Laningham (173) Dutch: see VAN LANDINGHAM.

Lanius (235) Dutch: Latinized form of the occupational name **De Vleeschauwer** 'the butcher'.

Lank (333) **1.** English: nickname for someone tall and thin, from Old English *hlanc* 'long', 'narrow'. **2.** North German: topographic name for some living at the side of a hill or river for example, from Middle Low German *lanke* 'side', 'flank'.

Lanka (112) **1.** Indian (Andhra Pradesh): Hindu name of unknown meaning. **2.** Lithuanian and Latvian: probably a shortened form of Lithuanian **Lankauskas**.
GIVEN NAMES Indian 32%; Latvian 4%. *Anuradha* (2), *Murali* (2), *Sambasiva* (2), *Srinivas* (2), *Surya* (2), *Anupama*, *Prasad*, *Rajaram*, *Rao*, *Ravi*, *Satyanarayana*, *Srini*; *Alfreds*, *Vitauts*.

Lankenau (147) German: habitational name from a place so named near Bremen.
GIVEN NAMES German 6%. *Helmut*, *Kurt*.

Lankford (4433) English: apparently a variant of LANGFORD.

Lankton (116) Probably a variant of English LANGTON.

Lanman (429) English (Welsh borders): unexplained.

Lann (293) **1.** English: unexplained. In part, possibly a shortened form of Scottish and Irish **McLann**, also unexplained. **2.** German: from a short form of a Germanic personal name composed with *land* 'land' as the first element, for example *Lannhardt*, from *Landohard*.

Lannan (376) Irish: variant of LENNON.

Lannen (222) Irish: variant of LENNON.

Lanners (227) Dutch: variant of LANIER.
GIVEN NAME French 4%. *Chantale*.

Lannert (113) Dutch: variant of LENNERT.

Lanni (430) Southern Italian: variant of LANDI.
GIVEN NAMES Italian 12%. *Angelo* (7), *Antonio* (3), *Carmine* (2), *Carmino*, *Domenico*, *Francesco*, *Gennaro*, *Luigi*, *Pasquale*, *Philomena*, *Vincenzo*, *Vittorio*.

Lannigan (144) Irish: variant spelling of LANIGAN.

Lannin (155) Irish: variant of LENNON.

Lanning (3196) **1.** English (Dorset and Somerset): unexplained. **2.** Dutch: patronymic from a short form of the personal name *Julianus* (see JULIAN).

Lannom (346) Possibly an altered spelling of **Lanham** (see LANGHAM) or LANNON. This is a frequent name in TN.

Lannon (821) Irish: variant of LENNON.
GIVEN NAMES Irish 5%. *Brighid*, *Padraic*.

Lannoye (104) French (Belgium): habitational name from either of two places named Lannoy, in Nord and Oise.

Lano (188) Italian (Piedmont): perhaps a short form of a personal name ending with *-lano*.

Lanoue (690) French: habitational name from places called La Noue, this name being derived from a Gaulish word *nauda* 'water meadow', 'boggy place'. This is a Canadian secondary surname for Laigu, Laleu, and Robutel, recorded there since 1687.
GIVEN NAMES French 10%. *Andre* (4), *Alcide* (2), *Emile* (2), *Normand* (2), *Pierre* (2), *Armand*, *Fernand*, *Henri*, *Hilaire*, *Jacques*, *Jean Robert*, *Marcel*.

Lanouette (193) French Canadian: secondary surname for RIVARD, perhaps a diminutive of LANOUE. It has been recorded in Canada since the 17th century.
GIVEN NAMES French 5%; Irish 4%. *Fernand*, *Rejean*.

Lanoux (129) Variant of French LANOUE.
GIVEN NAMES French 9%. *Marcel* (2), *Andre*, *Leonie*.

Lanphear (579) Variant spelling of Cornish LANFEAR.

Lanpher (277) Variant spelling of Cornish LANFEAR.

Lanphere (321) Variant spelling of Cornish LANFEAR.

Lanphier (284) Variant spelling of Cornish LANFEAR.

Lans (115) Dutch, North German, and Swedish: from the personal name *Lans*, a short form of *Lambrecht* (see LAMBERT).
GIVEN NAMES German 6%. *Hedda*, *Theresia*.

Lansaw (104) Apparently of English, Scottish or Irish origin, but unexplained.
FOREBEARS This surname is attested in WV in 1807.

Lansberry (320) English: habitational name from a lost or unidentified place.

Lansdale (255) English: variant of LONSDALE.

Lansdell (242) English: variant of LONSDALE.

Lansden (126) Probably a variant of English LANSDOWN.

Lansdon (103) Probably a variant of English LANSDOWN.

Lansdown (209) English: habitational name from places in Somerset and Dorset (now part of Bournemouth), probably named with Old English *langet* 'long strip of ground', 'long ridge' + *dūn* 'hill'.

Lansdowne (242) English: variant spelling of LANSDOWN.

Lanser (328) German: habitational name from any of several places called Lans, Lanz, or Lanze (see LANS).

Lansford (629) English: habitational name probably from Langsford in Petertavy, Devon, so named from Old English *landscearu* 'boundary' + *ford* 'ford'.

Lansing (1266) **1.** Dutch: patronymic from the personal name *Lans* (Germanic *Lanzo*). **2.** English: habitational name from Lancing in West Sussex, so named from an Old English personal name *Wlanc* + *-ingas* 'family or followers of'.
FOREBEARS This was the most frequent name in New Netherland in the 17th century. Among others, Gerrit Frederickse Lansing and his wife, Elizabeth Hendrix, came to America with their European-born children during the late 1640s. There is a waterway near Utica, NY called Lansingkill, named for a family with this surname.

Lansky (206) **1.** Czech (**Lánský**) and Slovak (**Lánsky**): topographic name from a derivative of Old Czech *lán* 'large field' (see LANIK). It may also be a habitational name from any of several places called Lány, named with this element. **2.** Jewish (from Belarus): habitational name for someone from the village of Lan or Lanskaya, now in Belarus.
GIVEN NAMES Jewish 8%. *Avram*, *Dvorah*, *Isador*, *Meyer*.

Lant (235) English: perhaps a habitational name for someone who lived by a long strip of ground, Middle English *langet* (a derivative of *lang* 'long').

Lantagne (168) Possibly an altered form of French **Lantaigne**, **Lantenne**, a nickname for a miller, derived from Latin *antenna*, a term used to denote the sails of a windmill.
GIVEN NAMES French 13%. *Lucien* (2), *Alphe*, *Armand*, *Cecile*, *Emile*, *Oneil*, *Philippe*.

Lanter (527) Swiss German: possibly from the personal name *Lanthar*.

Lanterman (281) German (**Lantermann**): **1.** from a Germanic personal name *Lanthar* (from *land* 'land' + *hari* 'army') + *man* 'man'. **2.** habitational name from a farm name near Elberfeld, in North Rhine-Westphalia.

Lanthier (292) French: from the personal name *Lantier*, *Lantiez*, composed of the Germanic elements *land*, 'country', and *heri*, 'army'.
FOREBEARS In the form Lantié, this name is recorded in Montreal in 1694, taken there from Poitou, France.
GIVEN NAMES French 16%. *Andre* (7), *Camile*, *Gilles*, *Jacques*, *Jean-Guy*, *Lucien*, *Ludger*, *Yves*.

Lantier (152) French: variant of LANTHIER.
GIVEN NAMES French 8%. *Antoine*, *Raoul*.

Lantigua (214) Spanish: habitational name from any of several farms and other places named as *la antigua*, 'the old place'.
GIVEN NAMES Spanish 50%. *Jose* (7), *Ana* (4), *Jesus* (4), *Juan* (4), *Rafael* (3), *Carlos* (2), *Domingo* (2), *Enrique* (2), *Josefina* (2), *Luis* (2), *Manuel* (2), *Mercedes* (2); *Antonio* (2), *Bartolina*, *Carmelina*, *Dario*, *Heriberto*, *Leonardo*, *Marcello*.

Lanting (153) Dutch: patronymic from an old personal name, Latin *Lanterus*, of uncertain origin, perhaps *Landher* (see Lanthier).

Lantis (307) **1.** Variant of Swiss German Landis. **2.** Possibly a Germanized or Americanized form of Latvian **Lantiņš**.

Lantrip (412) Perhaps an altered form of English **Langthorpe**, a habitational name from a place so called in North Yorkshire. This name occurs chiefly in TX.

Lantry (206) English: variant of Langtry.

Lantz (4600) **1.** South German: from the Germanic personal name *Lanzo*, originally a short form of various compound names with the first element *land* 'land', 'territory', but later used as an independent name. **2.** German: habitational name from any of several places called Lanz.

Lantzer (111) German: variant of Lanzer.

Lantzy (249) Possibly an altered spelling of a German family name.

Lanum (240) Possibly an altered spelling of **Lanham** (see Langham).

Lanyi (114) Hungarian (**Lányi**): habitational name for someone from a place called *Lány*.

GIVEN NAMES Hungarian 7%. *Gabor, Geza, Janos.*

Lanyon (201) Cornish: habitational name from a place in Madron parish near Penzance, named in Cornish as 'cold pool', from *lyn* 'pool' + *yeyn* 'cold'.

Lanz (777) German: variant spelling of Lantz.

GIVEN NAMES German 4%. *Otto* (4), *Gebhard* (3), *Hans, Sepp.*

Lanza (1654) **1.** Italian: from a dialect or old form of Lancia. **2.** Italian: from a short form of a personal name formed with the suffix *-lanza* or *-lancia*, as for example *Francalanza* and *Giallanza*. **3.** Spanish: from *lanza* 'lance', either a nickname for a soldier (lancer) or occupational name for a lance maker.

GIVEN NAMES Italian 12%; Spanish 9%. *Salvatore* (13), *Sal* (5), *Carlo* (3), *Giovanni* (3), *Santo* (3), *Umberto* (2), *Virna* (2), *Aldo, Alfio, Angelo, Antonio, Calogero*; *Jose* (8), *Mario* (4), *Rosario* (4), *Jorge* (3), *Luis* (3), *Ernesto* (2), *Gerardo* (2), *Joaquin* (2), *Julio* (2), *Miguel* (2), *Otilio* (2), *Rafael* (2).

Lanzer (172) German: habitational name for someone from any of several places called Lanz or Lanze.

Lanzetta (239) Italian: from a diminutive of Lanza.

GIVEN NAMES Italian 13%. *Angelo* (2), *Dante* (2), *Antonio, Concetta, Domenica, Donato, Franco, Giuseppe, Sal.*

Lanzi (231) Northern Italian: patronymic or plural form of Lanzo.

GIVEN NAMES Italian 13%. *Angelo* (2), *Gino* (2), *Enrico, Gaetano, Italo, Leno, Luigi, Vincenzo.*

Lanzillo (154) Italian: from a derivative of Lanzo.

GIVEN NAMES Italian 12%. *Angelo* (2), *Pasquale* (2), *Vito.*

Lanzo (143) **1.** Italian: probably from the old Germanic personal name *Lanzo* or from a derivative of the occupational name *lancere* 'lance maker', 'lancer'. **2.** Spanish: nickname from *lanzo* 'a throw', a derivative of the verb *lanzar* 'to throw'.

GIVEN NAMES Italian 9%; Spanish 9%. *Antonio* (2), *Agostino, Biagio, Franco, Luigi*; *Miguel* (2), *Alfonso, Christiano, Gabina, Luis, Mario, Reinaldo.*

Lanzone (114) Italian: from an augmentative of Lanzo.

GIVEN NAMES Italian 19%. *Angelo* (3), *Vito* (2).

Lao (672) **1.** Chinese 刘: a Cantonese form of Liu 1. **2.** Chinese 劳: probably from the name of Lao Mountain in Shandong province, adopted as a surname most likely during the Zhou dynasty (1122–221 BC). **3.** Chinese 柳: a Cantonese form of Liu 3. This name is also found in the Philippines. **4.** Laotian: unexplained. **5.** Tongan: unexplained.

GIVEN NAMES Chinese 21%; Vietnamese 8%; Spanish 12%. *Ying* (5), *Chhay* (2), *Chue* (2), *Kong* (2), *Lai* (2), *Mee* (2), *Peng* (2), *Seng* (2), *Song* (2), *Tong* (2), *Yong* (2), *Zhi* (2); *Fernando* (3), *Jose* (3), *Wilfredo* (3), *Alberto* (2), *Beatriz* (2), *Carlos* (2), *Eduardo* (2), *Juanita* (2), *Julio* (2), *Manuel* (2), *Nestor* (2), *Ramon* (2); *Sanh* (5), *Mai* (3), *Hung* (2), *Huy* (2), *Dao, Dung, Ha, Hoc, Huan, Huong, Khang, Kinh*; *Chong* (2), *Moua* (2), *Cho, Koua, Nam, Neng, Vang Pao, Yuet.*

Lapa (102) **1.** Polish and Jewish (from Poland): nickname from Polish *łapa* 'paw', 'flipper', 'mutton fist'. **2.** Portuguese and Galician: habitational name for someone from any of the numerous places called Lapa, from *lapa* 'cavern', or from the Marian name *Senhora da Lapa*.

GIVEN NAMES Jewish 11%; Spanish 6%; Polish 4%. *Eliyahu* (2), *Nachman, Nechama, Tzvi*; *Frederico, Juan, Leandro, Marilia, Miguel, Ricardo*; *Pawel.*

La Padula (119) Italian: topographic name for someone who lived by a marsh or swamp, from *padula*, a metathesized variant of *palude*.

GIVEN NAMES Spanish 9%; Italian 7%. *Enrique* (3), *Angel, Cristina, Jose*; *Angelo, Carmine, Pasquale.*

Lapage (219) French Canadian: variant of Lepage. The use of the feminine definite article as a generic, i.e. *la famille Page*, is characteristic of New England and Canada.

GIVEN NAMES French 5%. *Fernand, Jacques, Serge.*

La Paglia (286) Italian: nickname literally meaning 'the straw', probably applied as an occupational nickname for someone who worked with straw, or perhaps as a nickname for someone with blond hair.

GIVEN NAMES Italian 12%. *Angelo* (2), *Pasquale* (2), *Vito.*

GIVEN NAMES Italian 15%. *Angelo* (3), *Salvatore* (3), *Rocco* (2), *Sal* (2), *Calogero, Carmelo, Giovanna, Luigi, Pasquale.*

Lapalme (168) French Canadian: nickname meaning 'the palm tree', a secondary surname for Gaboriau and Janson.

GIVEN NAMES French 18%. *Jacques* (2), *Andre, Armand, Benoit, Philias, Pierre, Regean.*

Lapan (427) **1.** New England form of French **LePin**, **LesPins**, from *pin*, 'pine tree', with the article *le*, plural *les*. This name illustrates the characteristic North American tendency to Americanize the spelling of French names and use the feminine definite article as a generic, i.e. *la famille Pin*. **2.** Slovenian: nickname from *lapati* 'to babble', from Slovenian dialect *lap* 'throat'.

Lape (831) **1.** German: Americanized spelling of Laib. **2.** German: Americanized spelling of Lapp. **3.** Perhaps a variant of Polish **Łapa** (see Lapa).

Lapeer (104) Americanized form of French Lapierre.

La Penna (253) Italian: topographic name from Latin *penna* 'pinnacle', 'battlement' (original meaning 'feather').

GIVEN NAMES Italian 12%. *Rocco* (2), *Vito* (2), *Dino, Fausto, Filomena, Luciano, Pasqualino.*

La Penta (208) Italian: variant of **La Pinta**, a nickname from the feminine form of *pinto* 'painted', 'flecked', 'two-tone'.

GIVEN NAMES Italian 23%. *Rocco* (13), *Angelo, Giovanni.*

La Pera (220) Italian: perhaps from *pera* 'pear'.

GIVEN NAMES Italian 10%. *Alphonso, Levia, Ricardo, Sal, Salvatore.*

Laperle (284) French Canadian: secondary surname, meaning 'pearl', which has also been used independently since 1721.

GIVEN NAMES French 19%. *Adrien* (3), *Fernand* (2), *Marcel* (2), *Alphonse, Armand, Arsene, Emile, Gilles, Luc, Normand, Philippe, Renald.*

Laperriere (147) French (**Laperrière**): topographic name from Old French *perriere* 'quarry' (Latin *petraria*), with the definite article *la*; or a habitational name from a place named with this word, as for example Laperrière-sur-Saône or La Perrière.

GIVEN NAMES French 15%. *Marcel* (3), *Andre, Aurele, Pierre.*

La Petina (124) Italian: unexplained.

GIVEN NAMES Italian 11%. *Amedeo, Gerardo, Mauro, Rocco.*

Lapeyrouse (162) French: habitational name from places called Lapérouze, in Ain, Drôme, Haute-Garonne, Puy-de-Dôme, a form of *la pierreuse* 'stony place'.

FOREBEARS As Lapérouse, the name has been found in Canada since 1756, with the secondary surname Vadeboncoeur.

GIVEN NAMES French 11%. *Emile* (3), *Armand, Camille.*

Lapham (1048) English: apparently a habitational name from a lost or unidentified place, possibly in Somerset or Wiltshire, where the surname is clustered, but perhaps a variant of **Lopham**, a habitational name from a place in Norfolk, so named from an Old English personal name *Loppa* + *hām* 'homestead'.

La Piana (176) Italian: topographic name for someone who lived on a plain or plateau, Italian *piana* (Latin *planum*, from the adjective *planus* 'flat', 'level'), or a habitational name from a place named with this word.
GIVEN NAMES Italian 17%. *Salvatore* (5), *Emilia, Gasper, Lia, Nicola, Rosario, Sal, Salvator.*

Lapides (233) Jewish (Ashkenazic): variant of LAPIDUS.
GIVEN NAMES Jewish 9%. *Syma* (2), *Isidor, Myer, Sol, Yitzchok.*

Lapidus (552) Jewish (eastern Ashkenazic): from the Hebrew personal name *Lapidoth*, borne in the Bible by the husband of Deborah (Judges 4: 4).
GIVEN NAMES Jewish 8%; Russian 4%. *Meyer* (2), *Sol* (2), *Yakov* (2), *Emanuel, Ilya, Mariya, Mort, Semen, Tsipa; Mikhail* (3), *Artem, Boris, Dmitriy, Fanya, Iosif, Lev, Vladimir, Yefim.*

Lapier (205) Altered spelling of French LAPIERRE.

Lapierre (1758) French: topographic name for someone who lived on a patch of stony soil or by a large outcrop of rock, from Old French *pierre* 'stone', 'rock' (Latin *petra*, from Greek), with the definite article *la*, or a habitational name from various places named Lapierre or La Pierre, with the same meaning. It may also have been a metonymic occupational name for a quarryman or stone carver. In the U.S. it is often translated as STONE.
GIVEN NAMES French 14%. *Marcel* (10), *Armand* (7), *Andre* (6), *Lucien* (4), *Normand* (4), *Adrien* (3), *Alcide* (2), *Aristide* (2), *Arnaud* (2), *Julien* (2), *Pierre* (2), *Aime.*

La Pietra (138) Italian: **1.** from *pietra* 'stone', 'rock', with the definite article *la* (Latin *petra*, from Greek); probably a topographic name for someone who lived by a prominent rock or on stony ground, or perhaps a metonymic occupational name for a quarryman or stone carver. **2.** from feminine form of PIETRO, the feminine form probably being due to the influence of the Italian word *famiglia* 'family'.
GIVEN NAMES Italian 34%. *Angelo* (2), *Pasquale* (2), *Raffaele* (2), *Antonio, Attilio, Clemente, Constantino, Costantino, Emilio, Federico, Francesco, Franco, Gennaro, Virgilio.*

Lapin (485) **1.** Jewish (from Belarus): habitational name for someone from the village of Łapy in northeastern Poland or Lapino in Belarus. **2.** Polish (**Łapin**): from a possessive form of *Łapa* 'paw', 'mutton fist' (see LAPA).
GIVEN NAMES Jewish 9%; Russian 4%. *Avrum* (2), *Chanie* (2), *Sol* (2), *Hayim, Hymie, Miriam, Yakov; Vitaly* (2), *Vladimir* (2), *Anatoly, Arkady, Gennady, Mikhail, Nikolai.*

Lapine (417) **1.** Americanized form of Jewish or Polish LAPIN. **2.** New England form of French **Lepin**, with *pin* translated as 'pine' and the feminine article *la* replacing the masculine form.

Lapinski (799) Polish (**Łapiński**) and Jewish (eastern Ashkenazic): habitational name for someone from any of various places in Poland and Belarus called Łapino, Łapin, Łapy, or Lapy, named with the nickname *Łapa*, from Polish *łapa*, Belorussian *lapa* 'paw'.
GIVEN NAMES Polish 10%. *Henryk* (3), *Stanislaw* (3), *Janusz* (2), *Jerzy* (2), *Slawomir* (2), *Tadeusz* (2), *Andrzej, Andrzey, Bronislawa, Czeslaw, Franciszek, Jacek.*

Lapinsky (186) Jewish (eastern Ashkenazic): variant spelling of LAPINSKI.

Lapka (187) Polish (**Łapka**): from a diminutive of **Łapa** 'paw', 'mutton fist' (see LAPA).

La Placa (368) **1.** Italian: topographic name from *placa* 'flat smooth rock', (from medieval Greek *plaka*). **2.** Possibly from an Italianized form, *placa*, of Albanian *plak*, a nickname meaning 'old'.
GIVEN NAMES Italian 17%. *Salvatore* (4), *Angelo* (3), *Dante* (2), *Calogero, Cosimo, Gandolfo, Lorenzo, Pasqualina, Salvator.*

Laplace (222) French: topographic name for someone who lived in the main market square of a town or village, Old French *place* (Late Latin *platea (via)* 'broad street', from Greek *platys*, feminine *plateia* 'broad', 'wide').
GIVEN NAMES French 9%. *Andre* (2), *Germain, Jacques, Odile, Remi.*

Laplant (853) Respelling of French LAPLANTE.

Laplante (2747) French (mainly Poitou), and French Canadian: topographic name for someone who lived by a nursery or plantation (often one planted with vines), from French *plant* '(nursery) plantation (of trees, bushes)'; or a habitational name from places in Loire and Vienne called La Plante.
GIVEN NAMES French 10%. *Emile* (9), *Pierre* (8), *Armand* (6), *Marcel* (4), *Andre* (3), *Lucien* (3), *Michel* (3), *Monique* (3), *Normand* (3), *Ovila* (3), *Chanel* (2), *Clovis* (2).

Laplume (199) French: from *plume* 'down' (soft feathers), with the definite article *la*; perhaps a metonymic occupation name for a seller of down and feathers; also a habitational name from a place so named in Lot-et-Garonne.
GIVEN NAMES French 17%. *Andre* (4), *Normand* (2), *Herve, Marcel, Rosaire, Yvan.*

Lapoint (994) Respelling of French LAPOINTE.

Lapointe (3318) French: apparently a nickname for a soldier, from Old French *pointe* 'point (of a lance)'. Compare LANCE. In Canada this is recorded as a secondary surname (from 1693 in Montreal), which has also been used independently since 1710.
GIVEN NAMES French 13%. *Emile* (14), *Andre* (9), *Armand* (9), *Marcel* (9), *Fernand* (6), *Normand* (6), *Michel* (5), *Gilles* (4), *Lucien* (4), *Aime* (3), *Cecile* (3), *Herve* (3).

Lapole (104) English: unexplained; probably of Norman origin.

La Polla (271) Italian: topographic name from *polla* 'vein (thin stream) of water', or a habitational name from a place in Salerno province named with this word.
GIVEN NAMES Italian 12%. *Angelo* (3), *Antonio, Cosmo, Nicola, Rocco, Saverio, Vito.*

Laport (118) Respelling of French LAPORTE.

Laporta (608) Italian (**La Porta**), Catalan, and Aragonese: topographic name for someone who lived near the gates of a fortified town (and often was in charge of them; thus in part a metonymic occupational name), from *porta* 'gateway', 'door', 'entrance' (Latin *porta*, 'door', 'entrance'), with the definite article *la*. This is a common name among Sephardic Jews in Catalonia.
GIVEN NAMES Italian 14%. *Angelo* (5), *Carlo* (4), *Vito* (3), *Pasquale* (2), *Sal* (2), *Salvatore* (2), *Biagio, Carmelo, Carmine, Clemente, Cosmo, Fabrizio.*

Laporte (2518) French: topographic name for someone who lived near the gates of a fortified town (and often was in charge of them; thus in part a metonymic occupational name), from Old French *porte* 'gateway', 'entrance' (from Latin *porta*, 'door', 'entrance'), with the definite article *la*. In French Canada it is a secondary surname, which has also been used alone since 1670.
GIVEN NAMES French 7%. *Andre* (10), *Pierre* (7), *Emile* (4), *Lucien* (4), *Cyprien* (2), *Flavien* (2), *Marcel* (2), *Rosaire* (2), *Sylvain* (2), *Adrien, Antoine, Armand.*

Lapp (1986) German: **1.** from Middle High German *lap(pe)* 'cloth', 'patch', 'rag'; a metonymic occupational name for a mender of clothes or shoes, or a nickname for a simple-minded person. **2.** ethnic name for a Lapp, someone from Lapland.

Lappe (367) German: **1.** nickname meaning 'spark', 'dandy'. **2.** variant of LAPP.

Lappen (192) German: variant of LAPPE.

Lappin (826) **1.** English and Irish: nickname for a timid person, from Old French *lapin* 'rabbit'. **2.** Polish and Jewish (eastern Ashkenazic): variant of LAPIN.

Lapping (123) English and Irish: probably a hypercorrected form of LAPPIN.

Laprad (150) Respelling of French LAPRADE.

Laprade (751) Southern French: topographic name for someone who lived near a meadow, Occitan *prada* (Latin *pratum*; the feminine forms are from Late Latin *prata*, originally the plural of this word), or a habitational name from any of the numerous minor places named with this word. In French Canada, this is a secondary surname, which is rarely seen alone.
GIVEN NAMES French 10%. *Andre* (6), *Marcel* (3), *Lucien* (2), *Adelard*, *Adrien*, *Aime*, *Alain*, *Elphege*, *Euclide*, *Herve*, *Jean-Paul*, *Michel*.

Laprairie (185) French Canadian: **1.** part translation of **La Pré** (see LAPRE). **2.** perhaps a habitational name from Laprairie in Quebec.
GIVEN NAME French 5%. *Pierre*.

Lapre (166) French (**Lapré**): habitational name from Laprée or Lapraye, places so named from Old French *pred* 'meadow' (see LAPRADE). It is a secondary surname for PETIT in French Canada.
GIVEN NAMES French 9%. *Normand* (2), *Aurore*, *Germain*.

Laprise (201) French Canadian: secondary surname, which has been used independently since 1734, from *prise* 'catch,' 'taking', with the definite article *la*; perhaps a nickname for a hunter or a soldier. It is sometimes rendered **La Priest**.
GIVEN NAMES French 12%. *Armand*, *Gisele*, *Herve*, *Jean-Yves*, *Marcel*, *Monique*, *Renaud*, *Roch*, *Serge*.

Lapsley (312) English and Scottish: habitational name, in part possibly from Lapley in Staffordshire, so named from Old English *læppa* 'end of a parish' + *lēah* 'woodland clearing', although the frequency of the surname in Scotland suggests another, unidentified source may also be involved.

Laqua (157) Swiss French and Alsatian: topographic name for someone living by water, from *acqua* 'water'.

Laque (104) Catalan (**Laqué**, variant **Llaqué**): possibly a variant of **Laquet**, **Llaquet**, a topographic name from a diminutive of *llac* 'pond'.
GIVEN NAMES Spanish 5%. *Arturo*, *Jaime*, *Leticia*, *Ruben*.

Laquerre (136) Probably of French origin: unexplained. Perhaps a reduced form of **Laquerrière**, a habitational name from an estate named La Quérière-Bertin, which was probably in the vicinity of Longueville-sur-Scie. This name has been recorded in Canada since 1700.
GIVEN NAMES French 23%. *Emile* (3), *Armand*, *Emilien*, *Fernand*, *Henri*, *Laurent*, *Marcel*, *Marie-Anne*, *Normand*, *Raoul*.

Lara (6460) Spanish: habitational name from a place named Lara de los Infantes in Burgos province.
GIVEN NAMES Spanish 50%. *Jose* (191), *Juan* (96), *Manuel* (61), *Francisco* (56), *Carlos* (53), *Jorge* (46), *Luis* (45), *Pedro* (45),
Jesus (44), *Roberto* (37), *Rafael* (32), *Mario* (31).

Larabee (483) English: variant of LARRABEE.

Laracuente (127) Hispanic (mostly Caribbean): unexplained.
GIVEN NAMES Spanish 42%. *Aurea* (2), *Mario* (2), *Rafael* (2), *Altagracia*, *Angel*, *Carlos*, *Domingo*, *Ignacio*, *Jaime*, *Javier*, *Jorge*, *Juanita*.

La Raia (210) Italian: from *raia* 'ray', 'skate' (the fish), also denoting a type of plant.
GIVEN NAMES Italian 14%. *Rocco* (5), *Sal*.

Laramee (357) French: Canadian secondary surname, which has also been used independently since 1736, a topographic name from *la ramée* 'canopy of leafy boughs'.
GIVEN NAMES French 15%. *Armand* (2), *Adrien*, *Alphonse*, *Andre*, *Camille*, *Emile*, *Eugenie*, *Florent*, *Gaetan*, *Jean-Paul*, *Lucien*, *Marcel*.

Laramie (427) French: variant of LARAMEE.
GIVEN NAMES French 5%. *Desire*, *Rosaire*, *Theophile*.

Laramore (406) English and Scottish: variant of LORIMER.

Laraway (341) English (Lancashire): unexplained.

Larch (228) German: topographic name for someone who lived by a larch tree or a stand of larches, Middle High German *larche*. The surname is also found in England, probably taken there from Germany, since the tree was not introduced into England until the mid 16th century.

Larche (122) French: topographic name for someone living by a bridge, from *l'arche* 'the arch', 'the bridge'.
GIVEN NAMES French 8%. *Alcide*, *Herve*, *Lucien*.

Larcher (106) French and English (of Norman origin): variant of ARCHER, with the French definite article *l(e)*.
GIVEN NAMES French 8%. *Emile*, *Gaston*, *Michel*.

Larcom (200) English: habitational name from Larcombe in Devon, so named from Old English *læfer* 'rush', 'reed' or *lāwerce* 'lark' + Old English *cumb* 'valley'.

Lard (357) French: metonymic occupational name for a pork butcher, from Old French *lard* 'lard', 'bacon fat'.
FOREBEARS There are Lart in St. Nicolas, Quebec, from 1699.

Lardie (131) French: variant of LARDY.

Lardinois (171) Possibly a respelling of French **Lardenois**, a regional name for a man from the Ardennes, *l'Ardenois*.

Lardner (215) English: metonymic occupational name for a servant in charge of a larder or storeroom for provisions, from Anglo-Norman French, Middle English *lardiner*, an altered form of Anglo-Norman French *larder* (Late Latin *lardarium*, a derivative of *lar(i)dum* 'bacon fat'). According to Reaney, the name **Lard(i)ner** was also given to a servant who oversaw the pannage of hogs in the forest.

Lardy (129) French: habitational name from places named Lardy in Seine-et-Oise, Essonne, and Dordogne.
GIVEN NAMES French 5%; German 4%. *Jean Claude*, *Philippe*; *Gotthard*, *Kurt*.

Lare (294) Dutch and Belgian (**van Lare**): habitational name from a common place name, Laar (places in North Brabant, Limburg, Gelderland, Utrecht, and Overijssel, and the Belgian province of Liège), meaning 'woodland clearing', 'marshy land', or a topographic name with the same meaning.

Lareau (637) Canadian French: unexplained. Bearers of the name have transformed it variously into **Laraue**, **De La Raue**, **Larue** ('the street'), **L'Heureux** ('the happy one'), which becomes LOWRY, and **L'Héraut** ('the herald').
GIVEN NAMES French 12%. *Andre* (4), *Normand* (3), *Alain* (2), *Armand* (2), *Camille* (2), *Marcel* (2), *Emile*, *Fabien*, *Florent*, *Francois*, *Germain*, *Lucien*.

Laredo (146) Spanish: habitational name from a place called Laredo in Santander province.
GIVEN NAMES Spanish 43%. *Jose* (4), *Josue* (4), *Octavio* (3), *Rafael* (3), *Carlos* (2), *Domingo* (2), *Fernando* (2), *Luis* (2), *Ramon* (2), *Ruben* (2), *Alfredo*, *Berta*.

Lares (309) Spanish: probably a topographic name from Estremadura, from the plural of *lar* 'farm'. Compare LAREZ.
GIVEN NAMES Spanish 37%. *Jose* (7), *Carlos* (4), *Alfredo* (3), *Francisco* (3), *Manuel* (3), *Delfino* (2), *Eduardo* (2), *Fernando* (2), *Gilberto* (2), *Jesus* (2), *Jose Luis* (2), *Juan* (2).

Larese (117) Italian: unexplained; rare in Italy, it could possibly be a habitational name from a lost or unidentified place.
GIVEN NAMES Italian 11%. *Geno* (2), *Aldo*, *Angelo*, *Gino*, *Lorenzo*.

Larew (218) Of French origin: either an altered spelling of LARUE or a variant of LAREAU.

Larez (103) Spanish (**Lárez**): **1.** probably variant of LARES. **2.** alternatively, perhaps a patronymic from LARA.
GIVEN NAMES Spanish 32%. *Pedro* (2), *Adolfo*, *Alicia*, *Armando*, *Ascencion*, *Conrado*, *Fortino*, *Guadalupe*, *Juan*, *Juana*, *Leandro*, *Lino*.

Largay (108) Origin unidentified. Compare LARGEY.

Large (2453) English and French: nickname (literal or ironic) meaning 'generous', from Middle English, Old French *large* 'generous', 'free' (Latin *largus* 'abundant'). The English word came to acquire its modern sense only gradually during the Middle Ages; it is used to mean 'ample in quantity' in the 13th century, and the sense 'broad' first occurs in the 14th. This use is probably too late for the surname to have originated as a nickname for a fat man.

Largen (296) Origin uncertain; perhaps an altered spelling of LARGENT.

Largent (1435) **1.** English (Suffolk, of Norman origin): nickname for someone with silvery hair, a variant of ARGENT, with the French definite article *l(e)*. **2.** French: metonymic occupational name for a silversmith, from French *argent* 'silver'.

Larger (112) German: topographic name for someone living near a larch tree or a stand of larches, from Middle High German *larche* 'larch'.
GIVEN NAMES German 5%. *Aloys, Markus.*

Largey (117) Variant spelling of Scottish **Largie**, a habitational name from Largie in Aberdeenshire.

Largin (114) Origin uncertain. Possibly a variant of LARGENT.

Largo (135) Spanish: nickname from *largo* 'large'; 'tall' or 'broad'.
GIVEN NAMES Spanish 14%. *Manuel* (2), *Alfonso, Angel, Asuncion, Cesar, Isidro, Jose, Leovigildo, Mario, Paulino, Remigio, Ricardo.*

Lariccia (135) Italian: of uncertain etymology; possibly from *riccia* 'ruff', with the definite article *la*, or from a female form of RICCIO. Alternatively, it could be a habitational name from Ariccia in Rome province, which was known as L'Ariccia until the beginning of the 20th century, or alternatively from *riccia* 'ruff', with the definite article.
GIVEN NAMES Italian 14%. *Rocco* (2), *Angelo.*

Larick (114) Origin unidentified. Perhaps an Americanized spelling of Polish **Larysz** (see LARISH).

Larimer (1008) English and Scottish: occupational name for a maker and seller of spurs, bits, and other small metal attachments to harness and tackle. Compare LORIMER.

Larimore (931) Scottish and northern Irish: variant of LORIMER.

Larin (135) Spanish (Santander): unexplained.
GIVEN NAMES Spanish 31%; French 5%. *Jose* (5), *Alfredo* (2), *Benito* (2), *Cesar* (2), *Eduardo* (2), *Lino* (2), *Alonzo, Beatriz, Carlos, Emilia, Enrique, Isaura*; *Pierre, Yvon.*

Larios (733) Spanish: habitational name from Larios in the province of Cádiz or Larios y San Gil in Cáceres province.
GIVEN NAMES Spanish 52%. *Jose* (27), *Antonio* (12), *Juan* (11), *Manuel* (8), *Carlos* (7), *Francisco* (7), *Luis* (7), *Miguel* (6), *Jesus* (5), *Jorge* (5), *Ramon* (5), *Gilberto* (4), *Margarita* (4).

Laris (127) **1.** Spanish (from Basque): from Basque *Lariz* 'oak', topographic name for someone who lived by an oak wood or habitational name from Lariz in Bilbao province. **2.** Polish: Americanized form of **Larysz** (see LARISH).

GIVEN NAMES Spanish 20%. *Jorge* (3), *Jose* (2), *Everardo, Francisco, Guadalupe, Guillermo, Javier, Jesus, Jose Jesus, Josefina, Lourdes, Mario.*

Lariscy (150) Probably an Americanized spelling of Polish **Larysz** (see LARISH).

Larish (107) **1.** Americanized spelling of Polish **Larysz**, a pet form of the personal name *Hilary* (see HILLARY). **2.** Jewish (Ashkenazic): unexplained.
GIVEN NAME Jewish 4%. *Naftali* (2).

Larison (455) Americanized spelling of Norwegian and Danish LARSEN or Swedish LARSSON, established in North America from the late 17th century.

Larive (123) French: topographic name for someone who lived on a bank (of a river or the like), Old French *rive* 'bank' (from Latin *ripa*), with the definite article *la*, or a habitational name from any of various places called Rive or La Rive, named with this word.

Larivee (296) French: variant of **Larrivée** (see LARRIVÉE).
GIVEN NAMES French 9%. *Armand* (2), *Laurent, Luc, Lucien, Normand, Serge.*

Lariviere (1008) French (**Larivière**): habitational name from any of various places in northern France called Rivière, from the plural form of Old French *rivière* 'river' (originally meaning 'riverbank', from Latin *riparia*, a derivative of *ripa* 'bank'), with the definite article *la*; also a topographic name from the same word. This is a frequent secondary surname in Canada, used to distinguish a branch of a particular family living near a river, as opposed to those living on higher ground (**Lamont**) or on a hill (**Descoteaux**); it has also been used independently since 1749.
GIVEN NAMES French 15%. *Lucien* (6), *Normand* (5), *Fernand* (4), *Marcel* (3), *Adelard* (2), *Andre* (2), *Gaston* (2), *Philibert* (2), *Aime, Alcide, Alphonse, Antoine.*

Lark (981) English: **1.** nickname for a merry person or an early riser, from Middle English *lavero(c)k, lark* (Old English *lāwerce*). It was perhaps also a metonymic occupational name for someone who netted the birds and sold them for the cooking pot. **2.** from a medieval personal name, a byform of LAWRENCE, derived by back-formation from LARKIN.

Larke (214) English (mainly Norfolk): variant of LARK 1.

Larkey (304) English: unexplained. It is found predominantly in Liverpool and Wales and is possibly a shortened form of **McLarkey**, an unexplained Irish and Scottish name or of Irish MULLARKEY.

Larkin (9188) **1.** English: from a medieval personal name, a pet form of LAWRENCE, formed with the addition of the Middle English suffix *-kin* (of Low German origin). **2.** Irish: reduced Anglicized form of Gaelic **Ó Lorcáin** 'descendant of *Lorcán*',

a personal name from a diminutive of *lorc* 'fierce', 'cruel', which was sometimes used as an equivalent to Lawrence.

Larkins (1886) English: patronymic from LARKIN 1.

Larman (136) English: unexplained.

Larmer (167) **1.** Northern Irish: variant of Scottish LORIMER. **2.** English: occupational name for a maker of arms, Anglo-Norman French *armer* (Old French *armier*), with the definite article *l'*.

Larmon (199) Probably a variant of English LARMAN.
GIVEN NAME Irish 5%. *Conley.*

Larmore (267) Scottish and northern Irish: variant of LORIMER.

Larmour (103) Northern Irish: variant of Scottish LORIMER.

Larned (265) Variant of LEARNED, which is itself a variant of LEONARD.

Larner (478) English: **1.** variant of LERNER. **2.** In the case of a Suffolk family who bore this name by the 16th century, ancestors are recorded in the forms *Lawney* (1381) and *de Lauuenay* (1327); this is therefore probably a variant of DELANEY.

Larney (154) Reduced form of Irish McLARNEY.

Laro (104) Probably a variant of French LAROUX or LHEUREUX.

Larocca (1577) Southern Italian (also **La Rocca**): habitational name from any of various places throughout Italy, so named from *rocca* 'fortress'.
GIVEN NAMES Italian 15%. *Salvatore* (11), *Angelo* (7), *Antonio* (5), *Carlo* (3), *Vito* (3), *Carmine* (2), *Dante* (2), *Flavio* (2), *Francesco* (2), *Marino* (2), *Saverio* (2), *Alfio.*

Larocco (635) Probably of Italian origin, most likely an altered form of LAROCCA or LA ROCCA.
GIVEN NAMES Italian 10%. *Angelo* (5), *Rocco* (2), *Salvatore* (2), *Vito* (2), *Gasper, Mafalda, Nunzio, Salvato.*

Laroche (1954) French: habitational name from any of numerous places so named, from Old French *roche* 'rocky crag', 'stony outcrop', or a topographic name from the same word. In Canada it is a frequent secondary surname, which has also been used independently since 1683; it is often translated as ROCK.
GIVEN NAMES French 11%. *Andre* (5), *Armand* (4), *Fernand* (4), *Normand* (4), *Pierre* (4), *Jacques* (3), *Laurent* (3), *Adrien* (2), *Cecile* (2), *Germain* (2), *Marcel* (2), *Oneil* (2).

Larochelle (946) French (also **La Rochelle**): habitational name from any of a number of places with this name, especially the port in Charente-Maritime. It occurs as a secondary surname in French Canada.
GIVEN NAMES French 20%. *Armand* (7), *Marcel* (6), *Fernand* (5), *Andre* (4), *Cecile* (3), *Jacques* (3), *Normand* (3), *Pierre* (3), *Adelard* (2), *Gilles* (2), *Julien* (2), *Lucien* (2).

Larock (853) French Canadian: part translation of LAROCHE or an Americanized spelling of LAROCQUE.

Larocque (1090) French: habitational name from any of the numerous places called La Roque or Laroque, from a southern and Picard form of *roche* 'rock' (see LAROCHE). In Canada, it is a frequent secondary, which has also been used independently since 1717; it is sometimes translated as ROCK. GIVEN NAMES French 12%. *Andre* (6), *Armand* (6), *Fernand* (4), *Henri* (2), *Marcel* (2), *Normand* (2), *Valmore* (2), *Yves* (2), *Achille, Amie, Donat, Emile.*

Laroe (276) Americanized spelling of French Canadian LAREAU.

Laroque (218) French: variant spelling of LAROCQUE. GIVEN NAMES French 5%. *Collette, Yves.*

La Rosa (1951) **1.** Southern Italian: from *rosa* 'rose', a topographic name for someone living by a prominent rose bush (see ROSA). **2.** Spanish: habitational name from any of the places called La Rosa in southern Spain, or short form of the family name **de la Rosa** (see ROSA). GIVEN NAMES Italian 14%; Spanish 9%. *Salvatore* (13), *Sal* (9), *Angelo* (7), *Antonio* (7), *Domenic* (4), *Gasper* (3), *Giacomo* (2), *Giuseppe* (2), *Pasquale* (2), *Pietro* (2), *Salvator* (2), *Santo* (2); *Mario* (8), *Alberto* (4), *Jose* (4), *Pablo* (4), *Alfredo* (3), *Carlos* (3), *Jesus* (3), *Julio* (3), *Rosario* (3), *Benito* (2), *Domingo* (2), *Fernando* (2).

Larose (2491) French: topographic name for someone who lived at a place where wild roses grew; or a habitational name from a town house bearing the sign of a rose. It may also have been a nickname for a man with a 'rosy' complexion, as well as a nickname of a soldier. In Canada it is a frequent secondary surname, which has also been used independently since 1704, and often translated as ROSE in English. GIVEN NAMES French 8%. *Marcel* (6), *Jacques* (4), *Pierre* (4), *Alphonse* (3), *Armand* (3), *Andre* (2), *Cecile* (2), *Henri* (2), *Normand* (2), *Prosper* (2), *Rosaire* (2), *Adrien.*

La Rossa (111) Italian: nickname meaning 'the red' (see ROSSO), the feminine form no doubt being due to the influence of the Italian word *famiglia* 'family'. GIVEN NAMES Italian 9%. *Donato, Ferdinando.*

Larouche (219) French Canadian: probably a variant of LAROCHE, used as a secondary surname for GAUTIER since 1743. GIVEN NAMES French 18%. *Armand* (2), *Gaston* (2), *Amie, Camille, Cecile, Francois, Huguette, Jean-Guy, Philomene, Pierrette, Remi, Sylvain.*

Laroux (113) French: variant of LEROUX.

Larowe (176) Americanized spelling of French Canadian LAREAU.

Laroy (140) Canadian and New England form of French LEROY, with the general-ized use of the feminine definite article in place of the masculine that is characteristic of this region. This name is sometimes translated as KING.

Larr (133) Origin unidentified. This name occurs chiefly in MI and OH.

Larrabee (1601) English: origin uncertain; probably from an unidentified English place name formed with the Old Norse element *by* 'farmstead', 'settlement'. FOREBEARS Greenfield Larrabee was a mariner who arrived in New Haven, CT, from England in 1647.

Larralde (107) Basque: topographic name for someone who lived by a patch of meadowland, from *larre* 'pasture', 'meadow' + *-alde* 'next to'. GIVEN NAMES Spanish 31%; French 7%. *Juan* (2), *Ovidio* (2), *Adolfo, Alejandro, Bernardo, Concepcion, Eduardo, Eloisa, Enedina, Guadlupe, Ivette, Javier; Gregoire, Michel.*

Larranaga (147) Basque (**Larrañaga**): topographic name for someone who lived by or worked at an area used as a threshing yard, from *larrin, larrein* 'threshing yard' + the locative suffix *-aga*. GIVEN NAMES Spanish 35%; French 5%. *Juan* (4), *Javier* (2), *Jorge* (2), *Jose* (2), *Abran, Alba, Alejandrina, Andres, Angelina, Efren, Eloy, Elvira; Andre, Fernand, Gaston.*

Larrance (119) Possibly an altered form of LAWRENCE.

Larrea (243) Basque: habitational name for someone from one of the places in the Basque Country called Larrea, from *larre* 'pasture', 'meadow' + the definite article *-a*. GIVEN NAMES Spanish 42%. *Jose* (10), *Luis* (6), *Fernando* (3), *Francisco* (3), *Gustavo* (3), *Javier* (3), *Pablo* (3), *Alberto* (2), *Armando* (2), *Ernesto* (2), *Guillermo* (2), *Maria Dolores* (2).

Larrick (524) Origin unidentified. See LARICK. This name is found predominantly in OH.

Larrieu (140) French (Occitan): topographic name for someone who lived by a stream, from the Occitan word *rieu* 'stream', with the definite article *la*. GIVEN NAMES French 9%; Spanish 4%. *Fernand, Francois, Henri, Remi; Hortensia, Jorge, Luis, Marta, Miguel.*

Larrimore (463) Scottish and northern Irish: variant of LORIMER.

Larrison (486) Americanized form of Danish and Norwegian LARSEN or Swedish LARSSON.

Larrivee (254) French Canadian: secondary surname from *l'arrivée* 'the arrival' or 'one who has arrived', i.e. a newcomer. FOREBEARS This name is first found in Boucherville, Quebec, in 1673, taken there from Saintonge, France. GIVEN NAMES French 15%. *Lucien* (2), *Yvon* (2), *Adrien, Armand, Francois, Marcel, Normand, Oneil, Onile, Simonne.*

Larrow (232) Probably an Americanized form of French LAREAU.

Larry (1119) English: from the personal name *Larry*, a pet form of LAWRENCE.

Larscheid (113) German: variant of **Lorscheid**, habitational name from several places so named in the middle Rhine area and near Trier.

Larsen (22594) Danish and Norwegian: patronymic from the personal name *Lars*, Scandinavian equivalent of LAWRENCE. GIVEN NAMES Scandinavian 7%. *Erik* (62), *Lars* (42), *Nels* (16), *Niels* (13), *Sven* (10), *Thor* (10), *Knud* (9), *Nils* (9), *Per* (9), *Jorgen* (8), *Alf* (7), *Bjorn* (7).

Larsh (249) Americanized spelling of German **Larsch**, a vernacular short form of the personal name **Laurentius** (see LAWRENCE).

Larson (53532) **1.** Americanized form of Swedish LARSSON, Danish and Norwegian LARSEN. **2.** English: patronymic from a pet form of LAWRENCE. GIVEN NAMES Scandinavian 4%. *Erik* (73), *Lars* (36), *Nels* (20), *Nils* (16), *Helmer* (14), *Lennart* (13), *Selmer* (9), *Sven* (9), *Iver* (7), *Thor* (7), *Alf* (5), *Erland* (5).

Larsson (483) Swedish: patronymic from the personal name *Lars*, Scandinavian equivalent of LAWRENCE. GIVEN NAMES Scandinavian 34%; German 5%. *Lars* (9), *Erik* (5), *Anders* (2), *Fredrik* (2), *Nels* (2), *Nils* (2), *Olle* (2), *Per* (2), *Sten* (2), *Algot, Birgit, Bjorn; Bernhard, Hans, Markus, Oskar.*

Larter (121) English (East Anglia): unexplained. There is a Larter Farm in Norfolk, but whether the place name gave rise to the surname or vice versa is not clear.

Lartigue (138) Southern French: habitational name from any of a number of places so called, from Occitan *artiga*, a term denoting freshly broken up or cleared land, or a topographic name with the same meaning. FOREBEARS A Lartigue from Gascony, France, was in Montreal by 1766. GIVEN NAMES French 17%. *Emile* (2), *Armand, Herve, Honore, Jean-Claude, Michel, Pierre.*

Larue (4309) French: topographic name for someone who lived beside a road, track, or pathway, Old French *rue* (Latin *ruga* 'crease', 'fold'), with the definite article *la*.

La Ruffa (103) Italian: probably a nickname for someone from a family with red hair (see RUFFO). GIVEN NAMES Italian 19%. *Cesare, Eduardo, Italia, Silvio.*

La Russa (328) Southern Italian: nickname for someone from a family with red hair, from a variant spelling of *rossa*, feminine form of *rosso* 'red', the feminine form probably being due to the influence of the Italian word *famiglia* 'family'.

GIVEN NAMES Italian 15%. *Salvatore* (3), *Angelo* (2), *Biagio, Gino, Giuseppe, Rocco, Sal, Vincenzo.*

La Russo (299) Altered form of Italian LA RUSSA.

GIVEN NAMES Italian 16%. *Salvatore* (7), *Angelo* (2), *Carmela* (2), *Vito* (2), *Lucrezia, Nichola.*

Lary (589) **1.** French: from a reduced form of *Hilary*, the southern form of the personal name *Hilaire* (see HILLARY) or possibly a habitational name from places called Saint-Lary. **2.** French: reduced form of the personal name ALARIE. **3.** Polish: from a pet form of the personal name *Hilary* (see LARISH).

Larzelere (156) Americanized form of French **La Resiliere**, which may perhaps be a habitational name from la Roussillière in Rhône.

FOREBEARS Bearers of this name are descended from Jacques La Resiliere (*c.*1640–*c.*1687), a French Huguenot in the Netherlands. His son Nicholas (1668–99) came to Staten Island, NY, in the early 1690s.

La Sala (499) **1.** Italian: topographic name for someone who lived by or worked at a manor house, from *sala* 'hall', with the definite article *la*, or a habitational name from any of the many places named with this word, as for example Sala Baganza (Parma), Sala Biellese (Biella), Sala Bolognese (Bologna), Sala Comacina (Como), Sala Consilina (Salerno), or Sala Monferrato (Alessandria). **2.** Spanish and Catalan: habitational name from one of the places called La Sala in Barcelona, Tarragona, Oviedo, or Huesca provinces.

GIVEN NAMES Italian 18%; Spanish 5%. *Salvatore* (3), *Vito* (3), *Dino* (2), *Sal* (2), *Angelo, Antonio, Calogero, Carmelo, Domenic, Margherita, Mario, Matteo, Pasquale, Roberto, Rosita, Rufino, Teodoro*; *Adan, Felipe, Gaspar, Manuel, Pablo.*

Lasalle (1121) French: **1.** local name or occupational name for someone who lived or worked at a manor house, from Old French *sal(e)* 'hall' (modern French *salle*; see also SALE 1), with the definite article *la*. **2.** habitational name from a place named Lasalle or La Salle, as for example Lasalle in Gard, likewise from Old French *sale* 'hall'.

GIVEN NAMES French 5%. *Andre* (3), *Michel* (2), *Emile, Gaston, Gisele, Jean-Louis, Normand.*

Lasater (1167) Variant of English **Lassiter** (see LESTER).

La Scala (277) Italian: from *scala* 'ladder', 'flight of steps', with the definite article *la*, a topographic name for someone who lived by a flight of steps or on terraced land.

GIVEN NAMES Italian 12%. *Salvatore* (2), *Faust, Natale, Nicola, Silvio.*

Lascano (152) Spanish (form Basque): variant spelling of LAZCANO.

GIVEN NAMES Spanish 48%. *Jose* (3), *Juan* (3), *Angel* (2), *Carlos* (2), *Fernando* (2), *Miguel* (2), *Raul* (2), *Roel* (2), *Alfonso, Armando, Arturo, Cesar*; *Antonio* (2), *Ceasar, Valentino.*

Lascelles (100) English (of Norman origin): habitational name from Lacelle in Orne, France.

Lasch (439) German: byname for a poor or untidy person from Middle High German *lasche* 'rag', 'patch'.

GIVEN NAMES German 5%. *Klaus* (2), *Otto* (2).

Lasco (175) Italian (Sicily): nickname from Sicilian dialect *lascu* 'sluggish', 'workweary', 'miserable'.

La Scola (276) Italian: from *scola*, a dialect form of *scuola* 'school', either a topographic name for someone living by a school or working in one, or possibly for a member of a brotherhood.

GIVEN NAMES Italian 7%. *Angelo* (2), *Antonio, Carina, Pietro, Sal.*

Lasecki (209) Polish: habitational name for someone from a place called Lasek or Laski, named with Polish *lasek*, diminutive of *las* 'forest'.

Lasee (111) Probably a variant spelling of English or Irish LACY.

Lasek (206) **1.** Polish (**Łasek**): nickname from *łasy* 'fond', 'keen'. **2.** Polish: topographic name for someone who lived in a forest, from a diminutive of *las* 'forest'. **3.** Czech (Moravian; **Lašek**): from a pet form of the personal name *(V)ladislav* (see LASZLO). **4.** Czech: diminutive of LACH, in the sense 'Pole' or 'northeast Moravian'.

GIVEN NAMES Polish 11%. *Andrzej, Czeslaw, Dorota, Jozef, Katarzyna, Krzysztof, Stanislaw, Tadeusz.*

Lasell (122) **1.** Probably an Americanized spelling of French **Lacelle**, a habitational name from Lacelle in Corrèze or from any of numerous places called La Celle, for example in Aisne, Cher, and Marne, all named with Old French *celle* 'hermitage', 'monastic cell', with the definite article *la*. **2.** It may also be a variant of LASALLE.

FOREBEARS A bearer of the name from Paris was in Montreal by 1698.

Laser (319) German: **1.** Americanized spelling of LOESER 2. **2.** variant of LAZAR.

GIVEN NAMES German 6%. *Kurt* (4), *Erwin, Franz.*

Laseter (227) Variant of English **Lassiter** (see LESTER).

Lash (2543) Origin uncertain. **1.** Possibly a shortened form of Scottish or Irish McLEISH. **2.** Americanized spelling of German LASCH or **Läsch**.

Lashbrook (602) English: habitational name from Lashbrook in Oxfordshire, named in Old English as 'boggy stream', from *læcc* 'stream flowing through boggy land', 'bog' + *brōc* 'brook', 'stream' (with a more ancient meaning of 'marsh').

Lasher (1719) **1.** English (Sussex): unexplained. **2.** Americanized form of German **Löscher** (see LOESCHER). **3.** Jewish (eastern Ashkenazic): habitational name for someone from the village of Lasha, now in Belarus.

Lashinsky (127) Jewish (eastern Ashkenazic): habitational name for someone from the village of Losha, now in Belarus, possibly also from Łasin in Toruń voivodeship, Poland.

GIVEN NAMES Jewish 8%. *Hyman, Isadore.*

Lashlee (147) Variant of English LASHLEY.

Lashley (1942) English: habitational name from Lashley Hall in Lindsell, Essex, or from Latchley in Cornwall, both named from Old English *læcc* 'boggy stream' + *lēah* 'woodland clearing'.

Lashomb (243) Americanized form of French Canadian **Lajambe** 'the leg' (a nickname for someone with some peculiarity of the leg), or *Lachamp* 'the field'. Compare DESCHAMPS. This name is found chiefly in NY.

Lashua (276) Americanized form of French LAJOIE.

Lashway (262) Americanized form of French LAJOIE.

Lasich (119) **1.** Croatian (**Lasić**): probably a nickname from *laso* 'white-haired'. **2.** Croatian (**Lasić**): alternatively, possibly a nickname from *lasica* 'weasel'. **3.** Slovenian (**Lašič**): patronymic from the nickname *Lah*, a variant of *Vlah* 'Wallachian' (see VLACH), denoting a person of foreign origin or a Romanized person.

Lasiter (475) Variant of English **Lassiter** (see LESTER).

Lask (142) Jewish (Ashkenazic): habitational name from Polish Łask, formerly Łasko, a place in Sieradz voivodeship.

GIVEN NAMES Jewish 8%. *Moshe, Reuven, Ronit.*

Laska (534) **1.** Polish (also **Łaska**) and Jewish (eastern Ashkenazic): from Polish *łaska*, 'grace', 'favor', or from a homonym meaning 'weasel'. As a Polish name, this is a nickname; as a Jewish name it is generally ornamental. **2.** Polish: from *laska* 'stick', 'walking stick', metaphorically a nickname for a tall, thin man. **3.** Czech (Moravian; **Laška**): from a pet form of *Lád*, a short form of the personal name *(V)ladislav* (see LASZLO). **4.** Czech and Slovak (**Láska**): nickname from *láska* 'love'. **5.** Hungarian: from the Slavic loanword *laska* 'pastry' (probably a metathesized form of Slovak *lokša* or Ukrainian *lókša*), hence a metonymic occupational name for a pastry cook. In Hungarian *laska* also denotes a type of mushroom, and in some cases the surname may have arisen as a nickname from this sense.

GIVEN NAMES Polish 5%. *Tadeusz* (2), *Casimir, Henryka, Ireneusz, Jadwiga, Jozef, Kazimierz, Urszula, Zygmund.*

Laskaris (146) Greek: occupational name from ancient and medieval Greek *laskaris*, a kind of soldier, from Persian *laeshkaer* 'army'. This is the same word as Urdu *lascar* 'sailor' and Arabic *el-askari* 'the army', 'the troops'.

GIVEN NAMES Greek 6%. *Demetrios, Dimitrios, Panos.*

Laske (234) **1.** German: topographic name of Slavic origin, from Slavic *laz* 'uncultivated land or clearing', or a habitational name from a place so named in eastern Germany. **2.** Jewish (eastern Ashkenazic): variant of LASKA.

GIVEN NAMES German 5%. *Kurt* (2), *Hans, Otto.*

Lasker (481) Jewish (eastern Ashkenazic): variant of LASK or LASKI, + the Yiddish suffix *-er* denoting an inhabitant.

GIVEN NAMES Jewish 8%. *Mayer* (2), *Miriam* (2), *Aryeh, Hyman, Izya, Liat, Meir, Moshe, Samoil, Shmuel.*

Laskey (869) **1.** English: variant of LASKY 2. **2.** Americanized spelling of Jewish LASKI.

Laski (242) **1.** Polish (**Łaski**) and Jewish (from Poland): habitational name from Łasko (now Łask) in Sieradz voivodeship, named with *łaz, łazy* 'clearing in a forest'. **2.** Hungarian: habitational name for someone from a place called Lask in Zemplén county, near the northeastern border of Hungary.

GIVEN NAMES Polish 5%. *Arkadiusz, Janusz, Rafal, Teofil.*

Laskin (287) **1.** Russian and Belorussian: nickname from Russian and Belorussian *laska* 'favor'; 'weasel' + the eastern Slavic possessive suffix *-in*. **2.** Jewish (from Belarus): either of the same origin as 1, or from the personal name Laske, a pet form of the Biblical name Elazar (see LAZAR).

GIVEN NAMES Jewish 11%. *Hyman* (3), *Ilya, Meyer, Miriam, Nochum, Yitzchak, Yoav, Yochanan.*

Lasko (656) **1.** Polish (**Łasko**): from a place called Łasko (now Łask) in Sieradz voivodeship. **2.** Jewish (Ashkenazic): variant of LASKA. **3.** Greek: nickname for a work-weary person, from *laskos*, from Italian *lasco* 'loose'.

Laskoski (115) Polish: variant of LASKOWSKI.

Laskowski (1568) Polish and Jewish (eastern Ashkenazic): habitational name from any of several places called Lasków, Laskowa, or Laskowo, named with Polish *lasek*, a diminutive of *las* 'forest'.

GIVEN NAMES Polish 5%. *Jerzy* (3), *Janusz* (2), *Wojciech* (2), *Andrzej, Bogdan, Casimir, Czeslaw, Dariusz, Iwona, Jozef, Karol, Krzysztof.*

Lasky (1511) **1.** Jewish (eastern Ashkenazic): variant spelling of LASKI. **2.** English:

habitational name from either of two places in Cornwall named Lesquite; one, in Lanivet, is named from Cornish *lost* 'tail' + *cos* 'wood'; the other, in Pelynt, is from Cornish *is* 'below' + *cos*.

Lasley (1498) Variant of Scottish LESLIE.

Laslie (129) Variant of Scottish LESLIE.

Laslo (203) Variant spelling of Hungarian LASZLO.

Lason (66) Polish (**Lasoń**): from the medieval personal name *Lasoń*, a derivative of Polish *las* 'wood', 'forest' (see LASOTA).

La Sorsa (172) Italian: nickname for a small man, literally 'the mouthful'.

GIVEN NAMES Italian 25%. *Santo* (2), *Gaetano, Giuseppe, Luigi, Nicola, Nicoletta, Reno, Saverio, Savino, Vincenzo, Vito.*

Lasota (406) Polish: from the medieval personal name *Lasota* (from Polish *las* 'wood', 'forest'), adopted as an equivalent of the Latin personal name *Sylvester* (which is from Latin *silva* 'wood', 'forest').

GIVEN NAMES Polish 7%. *Irena* (2), *Ewa, Feliks, Henryk, Jacek, Janina, Janusz, Jerzy, Jolanta, Wieslaw, Zbigniew.*

La Spada (109) Italian: from *spada* 'sword', a metonymic occupational name for a sword maker, or possibly in some cases a nickname.

GIVEN NAMES Italian 15%. *Carmelo, Giacomo, Salvator, Salvatore.*

La Spina (279) Southern Italian (**La Spina**): **1.** from *spina* 'thorn' (Latin *spina*), with the definite article *la*, applied as a topographic name for someone who lived by a thorn bush or in an area of scrubland, or (in a transferred sense) for someone who lived by the crest or ridge of a hill. It could also be a nickname for a tall, thin, spiky person. **2.** from a short form of a personal name formed with this word for its Christian associations, for example *Fiordespina, Despina,* MALASPINA.

GIVEN NAMES Italian 19%. *Sal* (5), *Angelo* (4), *Mario* (3), *Rosario* (2), *Sebastiano* (3), *Carmelo, Gino, Giuseppe, Ignazio, Javier, Orazio, Salvatore.*

Lass (643) **1.** North German variant of LAAS 2. **2.** Jewish (Ashkenazic): unexplained. **3.** English: nickname from Middle English *lesse, lasse* 'smaller' (from Old English *lǣssa* 'less'), perhaps also used in the sense 'younger'.

Lassa (124) Origin unidentified.

Lassalle (128) **1.** French: variant spelling of LASALLE. **2.** Jewish: Frenchified spelling of **Lossal**, a habitational name from *Loslau*, the German name of Włodisław Śląski in Silesia.

GIVEN NAMES French 11%; Spanish 4%. *Marcel* (3), *Pierre; Jose* (2), *Beatriz, Wilfredo, Zoraida.*

Lasseigne (388) Variant of French **Lassaigne**, a habitational name from places in Allier, Cantal, and Nièvre called La Saigne, from Latin *sagna* 'marsh'.

GIVEN NAMES French 6%. *Jacques* (2), *Alphie, Camille, Monique, Romain.*

Lassen (730) **1.** Danish and Norwegian: patronymic from *Lasse*, a pet form of *Lars*, Scandinavian form of LAWRENCE. **2.** North German: assimilated form of Danish **Larssen**.

GIVEN NAMES Scandinavian 8%; German 5%. *Anders* (2), *Erik* (2), *Svein* (2), *Sven* (2), *Thor* (2), *Hilmar, Lasse, Niels; Hans* (2), *Lorenz* (2), *Erwin, Manfred, Otto, Uwe.*

Lasser (340) **1.** German: occupational name for a physician, from Middle High German *lāzer* 'one who lets blood'. **2.** German: occupational name for a hunter, from Middle High German *lūzen* 'to lie in wait (for game)'. **3.** Southern French: according to Morlet, an occupational name for a net maker, from a southern form of *lacet* 'lace'.

Lassere (107) Respelling of French **Lasserre**, a habitational name from any of various places named La Serre, for example in Aude, Haute-Garonne, and Lot-et-Garonne.

GIVEN NAME French 7%. *Jacques.*

Lasseter (564) English: variant of **Lassiter** (see LESTER).

Lassetter (271) English: variant of **Lassiter** (see LESTER).

Lassig (102) German (**Lässig**): see LAESSIG 1.

GIVEN NAMES German 19%. *Reiner* (2), *Erwin, Gunter, Klaus, Kurt, Manfred, Reinhard.*

Lassila (188) Finnish: from the Swedish personal name *Lasse* or *Lassi* + the local suffix *-la*, i.e. 'Lasse's place'. This name is found throughout Finland.

GIVEN NAMES Finnish 10%; Scandinavian 4%. *Eino* (2), *Aarne, Juha, Lempi, Oiva, Reino, Sulo; Walfrid.*

Lassiter (4284) English: habitational name from the city of Leicester (see LESTER). This name has been long established in North America, and occurs in a wide variety of forms.

Lassley (117) Probably an altered spelling of LASLEY (see LESLIE).

Lassman (212) German: **1.** variant of LASS. **2.** from a form of the personal name *Ladislav* (of Slavic origin).

GIVEN NAMES German 4%. *Kurt, Wolf.*

Lasso (166) Spanish: **1.** variant spelling of Spanish **Laso**, a nickname from *laso* 'weak', 'exhausted'. **2.** variant spelling of LAZO.

GIVEN NAMES Spanish 27%. *Carlos* (3), *Jose* (3), *Angel* (2), *Manuel* (2), *Adolfo, Alberto, Ana, Bolivar, Catalina, Diego, Elena, Humberto; Fausto, Giovanni, Marco, Mauro.*

Lassonde (119) Variant of French **Lasonde**.

GIVEN NAMES French 5%; Czech and Slovak 4%. *Andre, Pierre; Antonin* (2).

Lasswell (319) English: variant spelling of LASWELL.

Last (787) **1.** English (East Anglia): metonymic occupational name for a cobbler, or perhaps a metonymic occupational name for a maker of cobblers' lasts (see LASTER). **2.** German and Jewish (Ashkenazic): metonymic occupational name for a porter, from Middle High German *last*; German *Last* or Yiddish *last* 'burden', 'load'. **3.** Dutch: metonymic occupational name as in 2, from Middle Dutch *last* 'load', 'burden'; or a nickname for an awkward character, from Dutch *last* 'trouble', 'nuisance'. **4.** French: habitational name from a place so named in Puy-de-Dôme.

La Stella (105) Italian: see STELLA.
GIVEN NAMES Italian 22%. *Rocco* (2), *Federico, Filiberto, Laurina, Mario, Nino, Savino.*

Laster (2435) English (East Anglia): **1.** variant of LESTER. **2.** occupational name for a maker of cobblers' lasts, from Middle English *last, lest, the.wooden* form in the shape of a foot used for making or repairing shoes (Old English *lǣste* from *lāst* 'footprint').

Lastinger (264) German: probably a habitational name from an unidentified place.

Lastra (227) Spanish: habitational name from any of the various places called Lastra in Lugo (Galicia) or Oviedo (Asturias), or La Lastra (numerous places in northern Spain), named with *lastra* 'flat slab of rock'.
GIVEN NAMES Spanish 48%. *Jose* (5), *Juan* (5), *Cesar* (4), *Luis* (4), *Manuel* (4), *Alfonso* (3), *Carlos* (2), *Eduardo* (2), *Enrique* (2), *Francisco* (2), *Jaime* (2), *Margarita* (2); *Aldo* (5), *Guido.*

Lastrapes (181) Probably French: perhaps related to *trappe* 'trap'? This name occurs most commonly in LA.
GIVEN NAMES French 5%. *Andre, Camille.*

Lasure (250) French: occupational name for a shoemaker (see LESURE).

Laswell (450) English: unexplained. Possibly an altered form of LASCELLES. This name is also found as LACEFIELD.

Lasyone (127) Origin unidentified.

Laszewski (171) Polish: (**Łaszewski**): habitational name for someone from any of various places called Łaszewo, named either with the Old Polish noble personal name *Łaszcz* (a derivative of Polish *łaska* 'favor') or with a form of the personal name *Lazarz* (see LAZAR).
GIVEN NAMES Polish 5%. *Marzena* (2), *Zofia.*

Laszlo (321) Hungarian (**László**): from the personal name *László*, Hungarian form of an old Slavic name composed of the elements *volod* 'rule' + *slav* 'glory', which was Latinized as *Ladislaus* and is found in Czech as *Vladislav*, in Polish as *Władysław.*
GIVEN NAMES Hungarian 20%. *Bela* (3), *Ferenc* (3), *Attila* (2), *Janos* (2), *Laszlo* (2),

Miklos (2), *Sandor* (2), *Zoltan* (2), *Andras, Barna, Emese, Imre.*

Lata (183) **1.** Polish (**Łata**): nickname from *łata* 'patch'. **2.** Indian (Rajasthan): Hindu (Brahman) name of unknown meaning. **3.** Galician: habitational name from either of two places called Lata in A Coruña province (Galicia).
GIVEN NAMES Polish 7%; Indian 7%; Spanish 5%. *Tadeusz* (2), *Bogdan, Jadwiga, Stanislaw; Sneh* (2), *Suman* (2), *Mehta, Pushpa, Som; Carlos, Erlinda, Francisco, Juan, Manuel, Marcela, Otilia, Ramon.*

Lataille (124) French: from *taille* 'cutting', 'hewing', with the definite article *la*, hence presumably a metonymic occupational name for a woodcutter or woodworker.
FOREBEARS This name was established in Quebec from 1746.
GIVEN NAMES French 20%. *Normand* (3), *Aime* (2), *Aldor, Armand, Emile, Solange.*

Latch (280) English: **1.** variant of LEACH 2. **2.** topographic name from an Old English element *læcc, lecc* 'boggy stream', or a habitational name from a place named with this word, such as Lach Dennis or Lache in Cheshire.

Latchaw (180) Probably of Swiss origin (see LATSHAW). This name is found chiefly in PA and MI.

Latchford (187) English: habitational name from any of various places, for example in Cheshire and Oxfordshire, named in Old English as 'stream ford', from *læcc* 'boggy stream' + *ford* 'ford'.

La Tella (206) Italian: family name based on the male personal name *Tello*, a reduced form of a name such as *Donatello, Otello*, or MOSCATELLO. The feminine form is probably due to association with the Italian word *famiglia* 'family'.

Latendresse (170) French Canadian: secondary surname associated with FREMONT, **Lagnier**, and **Poitevin**, from *tendresse* 'gentleness', 'tenderness', with the definite article *la*, applied to a person with these qualities, or perhaps ironically to someone spectacularly lacking in them.
GIVEN NAMES French 7%. *Armand, Fernand.*

Later (149) Dutch (**de Later**): occupational name for a physician or surgeon, from *(bloed)later* '(blood)letter'.

Laterza (171) Italian: habitational name from a place in Taranto province named Laterza.
GIVEN NAMES Italian 21%. *Marco* (3), *Caesar* (2), *Agostina, Alfonso, Antonio, Carlo, Carmel, Cesar, Cosmo, Giacomo, Giuseppe, Lorenzo, Luigi, Orlando.*

Latessa (145) Italian: of uncertain derivation. Possibly from a reduced form of the female medieval personal name *Contessa*, with addition of the definite article *la*.
GIVEN NAMES Italian 15%. *Umberto* (2), *Antonio, Elio, Gino, Remo.*

Latham (7521) English: habitational name from any of the various places in northern

England named with the dative plural form (used originally after a preposition) of Old Norse *hlaða* 'barn' (dative plural *hlǫðum*, i.e. 'at the barns'), as for example Latham in West Yorkshire, Lathom in Lancashire, and Laytham in East Yorkshire.

Lathan (870) English (mainly northeastern counties): variant of LATHAM.

Lathe (115) English (Staffordshire): variant of LEATH.

Lathem (384) English: variant spelling of LATHAM.

Lather (127) **1.** South German: occupational name for a maker of slats or laths (see LATTNER). **2.** English: perhaps a variant of LEATHER.
GIVEN NAMES German 7%. *Dieter* (2), *Otto.*

Lathers (190) English: perhaps a variant of LEATHERS.

Lathon (119) Probably an altered spelling of LATHAN.

Lathrom (121) Origin unidentified.
GIVEN NAMES French 5%. *Clovis, Eugenie.*

Lathrop (3074) English: probably a variant of LOTHROP. Alternatively, it may be a habitational name from Layerthorpe in York, which is named from Old Norse *leirr* 'clay' or *leira* 'clayey place' + *þorp* 'outlying farmstead'.

Latif (270) Muslim: from a personal name based on Arabic *latīf* 'kind', 'gentle'. *Al-Latīf* 'the Kind' is an attribute of Allah. This name is found in combinations such as *'Abd-al-Latīf* 'servant of the Kind'.
GIVEN NAMES Muslim 79%. *Abdul* (17), *Mohammad* (11), *Shahid* (8), *Khalid* (5), *Muhammad* (5), *Mohammed* (4), *Hamid* (3), *Javed* (3), *Malik* (3), *Mohamed* (3), *Aamer* (2), *Amer* (2).

Latimer (3687) English: occupational name for a Latinist, a clerk who wrote documents in Latin, from Anglo-Norman French *latinier, latim(m)ier*. Latin was more or less the universal language of official documents in the Middle Ages, displaced only gradually by the vernacular—in England, by Anglo-Norman French at first, and eventually by English.

Latimore (504) English: variant of LATIMER.

Latin (212) English: metonymic occupational name for a Latinist, a clerk or keeper of Latin records, from Middle English *Latyn, Latin*. Compare LATIMER.

Latina (151) Italian: from a feminine form of LATINO.
GIVEN NAMES Italian 12%; Spanish 9%. *Salvatore; Alfonzo, Alina, Mario, Virgilio.*

Latini (263) Italian: patronymic or plural form of the personal name LATINO.
GIVEN NAMES Italian 17%. *Angelo* (3), *Fiore* (3), *Tommaso* (2), *Carlo, Carmela, Carmine, Ezio, Fausto, Fortunata, Pierino, Pietro.*

Latino (436) Italian: from the medieval personal name *Latino*, originally an ethnic

name for someone of Latin as opposed to Germanic, Byzantine or Slavic descent.
GIVEN NAMES Italian 19%; Spanish 5%. *Roberto* (2), *Sal* (2), *Silvio* (2), *Annamaria*, *Baldassare*, *Carlo*, *Carmine*, *Ignacio*, *Mario*, *Octavio*, *Ramona*, *Ricardo*, *Rocco*, *Salvatore*, *Vito*; *Armida*, *Juan*, *Manuel*, *Salvador*.

La Tiolais (591) French: unexplained.
FOREBEARS This name is particularly associated with LA, where the progenitor was an early 18th century colonist, Raymond-Guillaume Coquelis de la Tiolais, from Vichy, France.
GIVEN NAMES French 5%. *Antoine* (3), *Curley* (2), *Andre*, *Benoit*, *Clovis*.

Latka (192) Polish: nickname from Polish *lato* 'summer' (see LATO), or from a derivative of the verb *latać* 'to flutter', or from *łatka*, a diminutive of *łata* 'patch'.

Latkowski (63) Polish: habitational name for someone from places called Latków, in the voivodeships of Radom and Skierniewice.

Latner (155) English: **1.** variant of LATIMER. **2.** occupational name for a worker in or maker of latten or brass, from Middle English *latoun* 'brass' (from Old French *laton*).

Lato (203) **1.** Hungarian (**Látó**): from *látni* 'to see', hence a nickname for a wise person or an occupational name for a clairvoyant, or possibly for an official who checked the quality of products at markets. **2.** Polish: nickname for someone who was born or baptized in summer, from *lato* 'summer'. **3.** Italian: unexplained.
GIVEN NAME Italian 6%. *Angelo* (2).

Laton (159) **1.** Polish (**Latoń**): nickname from a derivative of LATO 'summer'. **2.** Dutch and Belgian: habitational name from Latem in Brabant, St-Maria-Latem, or St-Martens-Latem; or from Lathum in Gelderland.

La Tona (513) Italian: variant of **Tona**, from a short form of the personal name *Anton(i)a*, feminine form of ANTONIO.
GIVEN NAMES Italian 13%. *Angelo* (6), *Salvatore* (4), *Sal* (3), *Antonio*, *Caterina*, *Gaetano*, *Gino*, *Matteo*, *Santo*, *Vita*.

La Torre (828) Spanish and Italian (mainly southern): habitational name from any of various places in Spain and Italy named La Torre or Torre, from *torre* 'watchtower', 'defensive fortification', with the definite article *la*.
GIVEN NAMES Spanish 22%; Italian 9%. *Jose* (11), *Alberto* (5), *Carlos* (5), *Fernando* (4), *Jorge* (4), *Angel* (3), *Juan* (3), *Luis* (3), *Manuel* (3), *Ricardo* (3), *Roberto* (3), *Alvaro* (2), *Rocco* (7), *Vito* (5), *Angelo* (2), *Antonio* (2), *Salvatore* (2), *Carmelo*, *Cosimo*, *Dante*, *Eligio*, *Ferdinando*, *Lorenzo*, *Pasquale*.

Latos (100) Polish (**Latosz**): from a derivative of *lato* 'summer' (see LATO).
GIVEN NAMES Polish 6%. *Czeslawa*, *Henryk*.

Latour (1104) French: topographic name for someone who lived near a tower, usually a defensive fortification or watchtower, from Old French *tūr*; or a habitational name from various places called Latour or La Tour. This is a French Canadian secondary surname, which has also been used independently since 1705.
GIVEN NAMES French 8%. *Emile* (3), *Andre* (2), *Antoine* (2), *Gaston* (2), *Marcel* (2), *Pierre* (2), *Armand*, *Cecile*, *Fernand*, *Jacques*, *Jean-Claude*, *Laurent*.

Latourelle (111) French: probably from a diminutive of Old French *tūr* 'watchtower' (see LATOUR).

Latourette (249) French: diminutive of LATOUR.

Latronica (138) Italian: habitational name, a variant of **Latronico**, from the place so name in Potenza province. This name is found chiefly in NY.
GIVEN NAMES Italian 15%. *Vito* (4), *Dino*, *Rocco*.

Latsch (163) German: variant of LAATSCH.

Latsha (144) Of Swiss German origin: variant of LATSHAW.

Latshaw (606) Americanized spelling of Swiss German **Latscha** (unexplained). This is a Pennsylvania name; compare LATSHA.

Latsko (139) Origin unidentified.

Latson (354) English: probably a variant of LETSON. This name is found chiefly in TX.

Latt (113) **1.** Swedish, Finnish, and German: ethnic name for a Latvian. **2.** Possibly a German nickname for a tall, thin man, from Middle High German *late* 'slat'.
GIVEN NAME German 5%; Jewish 4%. *Kurt*.

Latta (2151) Scottish: Black identifies this as a habitational name from Laithis in Ayrshire, a minor place of uncertain etymology, now lost.

Lattanzi (330) Italian: variant of LATTANZIO.
GIVEN NAMES Italian 12%. *Attilio* (3), *Gino* (2), *Battista*, *Carlo*, *Guido*, *Ilario*, *Lorenzo*, *Ottavio*, *Querino*, *Ricci*, *Romolo*, *Vito*.

Lattanzio (419) Italian: from the personal name *Lattanzio*, a humanistic revival of the Latin name *Lactantius*, which was perhaps from *Lactans*, the name of the Roman god of vegetation.
GIVEN NAMES Italian 16%. *Rocco* (4), *Aldo* (2), *Angelo* (2), *Nunzio* (2), *Antonio*, *Cesidio*, *Corrado*, *Dario*, *Francesco*, *Gino*, *Guido*, *Italia*.

Latter (231) **1.** English: occupational name for a worker in wood or a nickname for a thin person, from an agent derivative of Middle English *latt* 'thin narrow strip of wood', 'lath' (Old English *lætt*). **2.** Jewish (eastern Ashkenazic): occupational name for a cobbler, tinker, or the like, from an agent derivative of Yiddish *laten* 'to patch', 'to repair'.

Latterell (181) **1.** Probably an Americanized form of French LATOURELLE. **2.** Alter-

natively, perhaps a variant of English LUTTRELL.

Lattimer (612) English: variant spelling of LATIMER.

Lattimore (1090) English: variant of LATIMER.

Lattin (596) English: variant spelling of LATIN. The name has also been established in Ireland (County Kildare) since the 14th century.

Latting (124) Possibly a hypercorrected spelling of LATTIN.

Lattner (171) **1.** English: variant of LATIMER, or possibly of LATTER 2. **2.** German: occupational name for someone who prepared or used laths or slats, from Middle High German *latte* 'slat', 'lath' + -*n* (plural suffix) + the agent suffix -*er*.

Latto (103) Scottish: variant of LATTA.

Lattuca (138) Italian (Sicily): metonymic occupational name for a grower or seller of lettuces, from Sicilian *lattuca* 'lettuce' (Italian *lattuga*, Latin *lactuca*).
GIVEN NAMES Italian 18%. *Rosario* (5), *Carmelo* (2), *Angelo*, *Gaetano*, *Salvatore*.

Latty (194) Swiss French: unexplained. Perhaps a variant spelling of **Laty**, a habitational name from any of various minor places in Puy-de-Dôme so named.

Latulippe (264) Canadian form of French **La Tulipe**, a soldier's secondary surname (from French *tulipe* 'tulip', with the definite article *la*), used as a primary name since 1712.
GIVEN NAMES French 20%. *Lucien* (3), *Marcel* (3), *Aime* (2), *Armand*, *Cecile*, *Chantal*, *Francois*, *Gilles*, *Girard*, *Jacques*, *Leandre*, *Leodore*.

Latus (145) **1.** Polish (**Latuś**): from a derivative of *lato* 'summer' (see LATO). **2.** English: unexplained.
GIVEN NAME French 4%. *Francoise*.

Latvala (147) Finnish: topographic name from *latva* 'top' (in particular, in the sense 'source of a river') + the local suffix -*la*, or habitational name from a farm or village so named. More recently, it is an ornamental adoption dating from the period of name conversion from Swedish in the 19th and early 20th centuries.
GIVEN NAMES Finnish 18%; Scandinavian 6%. *Eino* (3), *Alpo* (2), *Arvo*, *Eero*, *Hannu*, *Reino*, *Veikko*, *Wilho*; *Aksel*, *Lasse*.

Latz (287) German: from a short form of the Slavic personal name *(W)ladislaw* (see LASZLO).

Latzke (121) German: from a pet form of LATZ.
GIVEN NAMES German 9%. *Gerhard*, *Heinz*, *Wilhelm*.

Lau (7350) **1.** German: nickname for a physically strong person, from Middle High German *louwe*, *lauwe* 'lion'. In some cases the surname may have been originally from a house sign. **2.** North German: topographic name for someone living in a bush-covered area or clearing, Middle Low German *lo*, *loch*, *lage*. **3.** North German and Dutch: from a vernacular short form of the personal name *Laurentius* (see LAWRENCE). **4.** Dutch: nickname from Middle Dutch *laeu* 'lazy', 'indifferent', 'faint-hearted'. **5.** Chinese 刘: Cantonese form of LIU 1. **6.** Chinese 柳: Cantonese form of LIU 3. **7.** Chinese 劳: variant of LAO 2.

GIVEN NAMES Chinese 14%. *Wai* (30), *Wing* (29), *Kam* (20), *Kwok* (18), *Ming* (15), *Chi* (14), *Yuk* (14), *Chun* (12), *Kin* (9), *Ching* (8), *Kwan* (8), *Man* (8).

Laub (1306) German: **1.** habitational name from any of several places so named. **2.** topographic name from Middle High German *loup* 'foliage', 'grove of trees'.

Laubach (1027) German (Rhineland and Alsace): habitational name from any of several places so named, from Middle High German *lō* 'wood', 'grove' + *bach* 'stream'.

Laubacher (175) German and Alsatian: habitational name for someone from a place called LAUBACH.

Laube (558) **1.** German (chiefly eastern) and Jewish (Ashkenazic): habitational name from any of several places called Lauba, Lauban, Laube, or Lauben, all names of Slavic origin. **2.** Jewish (Ashkenazic): ornamental from German *Laube* 'summerhouse', 'arbor'.

GIVEN NAMES German 6%. *Otto* (5), *Erna*, *Erwin*, *Gerhard*, *Gottfried*, *Hannes*, *Hans*.

Laubenstein (248) **1.** Jewish (Ashkenazic): ornamental name composed of German *Laub* 'leaves', 'foliage', or *Laube* 'summerhouse', 'arbor' + *Stein* 'stone'. **2.** German: variant of **Lauenstein**, habitational name from any of three places named Lauenstein.

GIVEN NAMES German 7%. *Erhart*, *Gerhard*, *Horst*, *Siegfried*.

Laubenthal (157) German: habitational name from a place so named near Eichstätt in Bavaria.

Lauber (1023) South German: habitational name for someone from any of various places called LAUB, LAUBE, or a similar name.

Laubert (102) German: variant of LAUBER, with excrescent -*t*.

GIVEN NAMES German 6%; French 5%. *Gerhard* (2); *Jacques* (2).

Laubhan (156) German: from Middle High German *loup* 'foliage' + *Han* (short form of JOHANN) or possibly *han* 'rooster' (which would be a nickname for a person with a crowing or cackling voice).

GIVEN NAME German 5%. *Reinhold*.

Laubscher (278) Eastern German: habitational name for someone from a place called Laubusch, near Hoyerswerda in Silesia, which is of Slavic origin.

GIVEN NAMES French 4%. *Andre*, *Andree*, *Esme*.

Lauby (165) Swiss: unexplained. Perhaps an altered form of **Laubach**, a habitational name from any of various places in Germany (and one in Alsace, France) so named.

Lauck (707) German: **1.** from the personal name *Lukas* (see LUCAS), or from the female personal name *Liutgard* (from Old High German *liut* 'people' + *gard* 'protection'). The latter was a popular name in medieval times; among others it was the name of the daughter of emperor Otto I and the wife of Charlemagne. **2.** short form of the personal name *Laurentius* (see LAWRENCE), of Slavic origin.

Laucks (104) German: variant of LAUCK, a contraction of the personal name *Lucas*.

Laudadio (116) Central and southern Italian: from the personal name *Laudadio*, a devotional name meaning 'praise to God', or else a nickname for someone who used this expression frequently for emphasis.

GIVEN NAMES Italian 23%. *Rocco* (3), *Tommaso* (2), *Carlo*, *Dante*, *Marino*, *Paolo*, *Sante*.

Laudano (150) Italian: possibly from *laudano* 'laudanum'.

GIVEN NAMES Italian 16%. *Cosmo* (3), *Rocco* (2), *Antonio*, *Salvatore*.

Laudato (105) Italian: from a personal name meaning 'praised'.

GIVEN NAMES Italian 26%. *Rocco* (2), *Carmine*, *Dino*, *Domenico*, *Gaetano*, *Guiseppe*.

Laude (171) **1.** German and Dutch: perhaps from the Germanic personal name *Lūdo*. **2.** Dutch: perhaps from a short form of the personal name *G(e)laude*, *Claude*. **3.** French: metonymic occupational name given to a singer or cantor who regularly sang the *Lauds* (Latin *laudes* 'praises'), the second part of the divine office.

GIVEN NAME French 6%. *Olivier*.

Laudeman (142) Variant of German **Lüdemann** (see LUEDEMAN).

GIVEN NAME French 4%. *Patrice*.

Laudenbach (132) German: habitational name from any of several places so named.

Laudenslager (408) Americanized spelling of German **Lautenschläger** (see LAUTENSCHLAGER).

Lauder (605) Scottish (Borders): habitational name from Lauder in Berwickshire, originally a river name. Compare LAUDERDALE.

Lauderback (265) Americanized spelling of German LAUTERBACH.

Lauderbaugh (188) Americanized spelling of German LAUTERBACH.

Lauderdale (1369) English: habitational name from the valley of Lauderdale, named from LAUDER + Old Norse *dalr* 'valley' (Old Danish *dal*, Old English *dæl*).

Lauderman (106) German: altered spelling of **Lautermann**, a habitational name from

any of several places called Lauter in Bavaria, Hesse, and Saxony or from Lauta in Brandenburg + *man* 'man'.

Laudermilch (132) Part-Americanized form of German **Lautermilch** (see LAUDERMILK).

Laudermilk (134) Americanized form of German **Lautermilch**, a metonymic occupational name for a dairy farmer, from Middle High German *lūter* 'clear', 'pure' + *milch* 'milk'.

Laudicina (134) Italian: from a pet form of the personal name *Laudice*, *Laodice*, Greek *Laodikē*, from *laos* 'people' + *dikē* 'judgement'.

GIVEN NAMES Italian 28%. *Vito* (7), *Antonino* (2), *Sal* (2), *Enza*, *Nicola*, *Salvatore*.

Laudick (145) German: altered spelling of **Laudig**, from a pet form of the personal name LUDWIG.

Laudon (166) German (Austria): of Slavic origin, from a personal name based on Old Slavic *ljudu* 'people'. The Austrian family Laudon had its ancestral home in Livonia on the Baltic.

Laue (542) North German: variant of LAU 1.

GIVEN NAMES German 6%. *Juergen* (3), *Gerhard* (2), *Johannes*, *Kurt*, *Udo*.

Lauer (4602) **1.** German, Alsatian, and Jewish (Ashkenazic): nickname from Middle High German *lūre*, German *Lauer* 'crafty or cunning person', 'cheat' (apparently originally 'one with narrowed eyes'). **2.** German: occupational name for a tanner, Middle High German *lōwer*, from *lō* 'tannin', which is extracted from the bark of trees. **3.** South German: habitational name from Lauer in Franconia, named from the stream on which it stands.

Lauerman (233) German (**Lauermann**): variant of LAUER.

Lauersdorf (134) German: presumably a habitational name from an unidentified place so named.

GIVEN NAMES German 4%. *Ernst*, *Otto*.

Lauf (206) German: habitational name from any of several places named Lauf, Laufin, or Lauffen in Baden-Württemberg and Bavaria, all name from the Middle High German word *loufe* 'rapids'.

GIVEN NAMES German 8%. *Otto* (2), *Erna*, *Heinz*, *Kurt*.

Laufenberg (508) German: habitational name from Laufenburg, Switzerland, which was formerly called Laufenberg.

Laufer (1151) **1.** German: habitational name for someone from a place called LAUF. **2.** German (**Läufer**) and Jewish (Ashkenazic): occupational name for a messenger or a nickname for a fast runner, from an agent derivative of Middle High German *loufen*, German *laufen* 'to run'. **3.** English: variant of LAVER.

GIVEN NAMES Jewish 12%; German 4%. *Berish* (4), *Mayer* (4), *Sol* (4), *Chaim* (3), *Leibish* (3), *Ari* (2), *Hyman* (2), *Miriam* (2), *Moishe* (2), *Moshe* (2), *Myer* (2), *Pinchas*

(2); *Hans* (5), *Armin, Berthold, Erwin, Frieda, Fritz, Fritzi, Ilse, Mathias, Otto, Siegmund, Wolfgang.*

Lauff (106) German: variant of LAUF.
GIVEN NAMES German 13%; Jewish 4%. *Otto* (2), *Ilse, Kurt; Miriam* (2).

Lauffer (554) German: variant of LAUFER.

Laufman (140) German (**Laufmann**) or Jewish (Ashkenazic): variant of LAUFER.
GIVEN NAMES French 6%; Jewish 4%. *Gabrielle* (2), *Laurien; Ofer, Yael.*

Laug (125) German: variant of LAUCK.

Laugen (123) Norwegian: habitational name from a farmstead in Buskerud, named from Old Norse *laug* 'bathwater', 'washing water'.

Laughead (140) Variant spelling of Scottish LOCHHEAD.

Laughery (380) Possibly a variant spelling of LOUGHREY. It is found chiefly in OH and Washington.

Laughinghouse (178) Probably an Americanized form of **Lefringhaus**, a habitational name from a place called Lefringhausen in northern Hesse, near Waldeck.

Laughlin (6629) Irish: reduced Anglicized form of Gaelic **Ó Lochlainn** 'descendant of *Lochlann*', a personal name meaning 'stranger', originally a term denoting Scandinavia (a compound of *loch* 'lake', 'fjord' + *lann* 'land'). Many Irish bearers of the name claim descent from Lochlann, a 10th century lord of Corcomroe, County Clare.

Laughman (444) Americanized form of German LACHMANN.

Laughner (229) Americanized form of German LACHNER.

Laughon (109) Origin unidentified. Perhaps a variant of English LAUGHTON.

Laughrey (142) Irish: variant spelling of LOUGHREY.
GIVEN NAME Irish 5%. *Donal.*

Laughridge (216) Variant spelling of northern Irish LOUGHRIDGE.

Laughter (568) **1.** English (Norfolk): of uncertain origin; perhaps a nickname for a jolly, laughing person, from the vocabulary word *laughter*. **2.** Possibly also an Americanized form of Dutch **Lachter**, an unflattering nickname from Middle Low German *lachter* 'shame', 'disgrace'. This is a common name in NC.

Laughton (363) English: **1.** habitational name from any of the numerous places in England so called. Most of them, as for example those in Leicestershire, Lincolnshire (near Gainsborough), Sussex, and West Yorkshire, are named with Old English *lēac* 'leek' + *tūn* 'enclosure'. The compound was also used in the extended sense of a herb garden and later of a kitchen garden. Laughton near Folkingham in Lincolnshire, however, was probably named as *loctūn* 'enclosed farm' (see LOCK 2). **2.** variant spelling of LAWTON.

Lauinger (197) German: habitational name for someone from any of several places called Lauingen.

Laukaitis (142) Lithuanian: **1.** derivative of a nickname based on *laukas* 'bald' or 'having a white forehead'. **2.** possibly a topographic name from *laūkas* 'field'.
GIVEN NAMES Lithuanian 4%. *Alphonsus, Kazys, Kestutis.*

Lauletta (131) Italian: habitational name for someone from Auletta in Salerno province (Campania). In this area family names formed by the addition of the definite article (Lo, La, Le, Li) to a place name are very common.
GIVEN NAME Italian 7%. *Angelo.*

Lauman (241) **1.** Dutch: occupational name for a servant of someone called *Lau*, a short form of LAWRENCE. **2.** Americanized spelling of German LAUMANN.

Laumann (300) German: variant of LAU.
GIVEN NAMES German 5%. *Heinz, Kurt, Manfred, Otto, Wilhelm.*

Laumer (109) German: from a short form of a Germanic personal name *Leudomar*, composed with Old High German *leod* 'people' + *mar-* 'famous'.
GIVEN NAMES German 8%; Scandinavian 5%. *Helmut, Otto; Ordell.*

Laun (259) German: habitational name from Laun (Czech name *Louny*) on the Eger river (Czech *Ohře*), northwest of Prague.
GIVEN NAMES German 5%. *Gerhard, Johannes, Wilhelm.*

Launder (140) English: variant of LAVENDER.

Launderville (108) Americanized spelling of French LANDREVILLE.

Laundry (110) English (Cornwall): **1.** metonymic occupational name for someone who worked in wash house, Middle English *lavendrie*. **2.** from the Old French personal name *Landri*, from a Germanic name composed of the elements *land* 'land' + *rīc* 'power'.

Launer (294) habitational name for someone from LAUN.

Launius (250) Lithuanian: perhaps a nickname from Lithuanian *launys* 'hornless'.

Lauper (108) **1.** Swiss German: from the short form of a Germanic personal name composed of the elements *liut* 'people', 'tribe' + *berht* 'famous'. **2.** topographic name for someone who lived at a *Lauben*, a row of houses and stores with an arcade in front, from Middle High German *loube* 'arbor', 'bower', 'gallery'.
GIVEN NAMES German 5%. *Ernst, Guenter.*

Laur (295) **1.** French: topographic name for someone who lived by a conspicuous laurel tree, Old French *laur* (Latin *laurus*). **2.** French: from a personal name of the same etymology, borne by various minor early saints, including a hermit, a martyr, and an abbot. **3.** German: variant of LAUER.

Laura (343) **1.** Italian: either from the female personal name *Laura* or a topographic name from Latin *laurea* 'laurel (bush or crown)'. **2.** Spanish: of uncertain derivation; in some cases, possibly a habitational name from Laura in Badajoz province.
GIVEN NAMES Spanish 7%. *Jorge* (4), *Adelio* (2), *Efrain, Jaime, Luis, Maria Emilia, Miguel, Ruiz, Sixto, Socorro.*

Laurain (115) French: **1.** from a diminutive or pet form of LAUR 1 and 2. **2.** variant spelling of LORRAIN.

Laurance (183) English: variant spelling of LAWRENCE.

Laureano (378) Spanish: from the personal name *Laureano* (derived from Latin *laurus* 'laurel'), which was borne by a 6th-century martyr from Seville.
GIVEN NAMES Spanish 49%. *Jose* (10), *Juan* (5), *Luis* (5), *Alberto* (4), *Francisco* (4), *Manuel* (4), *Angel* (3), *Carlos* (3), *Luz* (3), *Pablo* (3), *Ramon* (3), *Reynaldo* (3).

Laurel (413) Spanish: topographic name for someone who lived by a laurel tree, Spanish *laurel* (Latin *laurus*), or a habitational name from Laurel in the Canary Islands.
GIVEN NAMES Spanish 29%. *Carlos* (4), *Angel* (3), *Jesus* (3), *Ruben* (3), *Adolfo* (2), *Alfredo* (2), *Alonzo* (2), *Araceli* (2), *Armando* (2), *Humberto* (2), *Jorge* (2), *Leticia* (2).

Lauren (266) Swedish (**Laurén**; also found in Finland): from a Swedish vernacular form of the personal name *Laurentius* (see LAWRENCE, LAURI).

Laurence (1066) **1.** English: variant spelling of LAWRENCE. **2.** French: from the female personal name *Laurence*, a feminine equivalent of LAWRENCE.
GIVEN NAMES French 4%. *Andre, Marcel, Normand, Patrice, Raymonde, Serge.*

Laurendeau (138) French: from a pet form of *Laurand*, a French form of LAWRENCE.
GIVEN NAMES French 19%. *Dominique, Emile, Gaetan, Jacques, Michel, Normand, Philippe, Sylvain.*

Laurens (137) Dutch, French, and English: from the personal name *Lorens* (see LAWRENCE).

Laurent (1771) French: from a vernacular form of the Latin personal name *Laurentius* (see LAWRENCE).
GIVEN NAMES French 12%. *Pierre* (6), *Marcel* (4), *Andre* (3), *Armand* (3), *Chantal* (3), *Benoit* (2), *Herve* (2), *Jacques* (2), *Jean-Pierre* (2), *Leonce* (2), *Marcelle* (2), *Michel* (2).

Laurenti (115) Italian: variant of LORENZI.
GIVEN NAMES Italian 19%. *Dante* (2), *Mario* (2), *Anselmo, Dino, Luigi, Primo, Tito.*

Laurenzi (135) Italian: variant of LORENZI.
GIVEN NAMES Italian 12%. *Dino* (2), *Ezio* (2), *Domenic, Francesca, Luigi, Martino, Romolo.*

Laurenzo (118) Italian: from a variant of the personal name *Lorenzo* (see LAWRENCE).

GIVEN NAMES Italian 11%. *Dante* (2), *Antonio, Gino.*

Lauri (144) **1.** Italian: from a patronymic or plural form of the personal name LAURO. **2.** Finnish: from the personal name *Lauri*, vernacular form of Latin *Laurentius* (see LAWRENCE). In America, it may be a shortened form of LAURILA.

GIVEN NAMES Italian 14%. *Angelo* (2), *Gaeton* (2), *Aniello, Giorgio.*

Lauria (866) Italian (Basilicata): habitational name from Lauria in Potenza.

GIVEN NAMES Italian 23%; Spanish 7%. *Angelo* (8), *Rocco* (8), *Salvatore* (5), *Alberto* (3), *Carmelo* (3), *Carmine* (3), *Mario* (3), *Valentina* (3), *Antonio* (2), *Domenic* (2), *Amedeo, Biagio, Calogero, Carmela, Carmelina*; *Andres, Carlos, Domingo, Isidoro, Jose.*

Lauricella (454) Italian: from a pet form of LAURA.

GIVEN NAMES Italian 18%. *Salvatore* (9), *Angelo* (5), *Carmine* (2), *Gaetano* (2), *Marino* (2), *Sal* (2), *Antonino, Antonio, Arcangelo, Gerlando, Luigi, Santo.*

Laurich (250) **1.** Slovenian (**Lavrič**): patronymic from *Lavre*, an Old Slovenian short form of the Latin personal name *Laurentius* (see LAWRENCE). **2.** German: from a short form of the personal name *Laurentius* (see LAWRENCE) or of a personal name composed of Old High German *(h)lūt* 'clear', 'loud' + *rīhhi* 'powerful', 'rich', 'splendid'.

GIVEN NAMES German 4%. *Bernhard, Hermann.*

Lauridsen (261) Norwegian and Danish: patronymic from the personal name *Laurids*, a vernacular form of *Laurentius* (see LAWRENCE).

GIVEN NAMES Scandinavian 7%; German 6%. *Halvar, Morten*; *Hans* (3), *Kurt, Otto.*

Laurie (1269) **1.** Scottish and English: from a pet form of LAWRENCE. **2.** French: habitational name from a place in Cantal, derived from Latin *laurus* 'laurel', with the suffix *-ea.*

Laurila (144) Finnish: topographic and ornamental name composed of the personal name LAURI + the local suffix *-la*, i.e. 'Lauri's place'. This name occurs in eastern and western Finland.

GIVEN NAMES Finnish 12%. *Mauno* (2), *Arvo, Eino, Marketta, Tapio, Wilho.*

Laurin (545) **1.** French: diminutive or pet form of LAUR 1 and 2. **2.** It may also be a reduced and altered form of Scottish MCLAREN. **3.** Possibly also an Americanized spelling of Slovenian **Lavrin**, derivative of the personal name *Lavrencij*, Latin *Laurentius* (see LAWRENCE).

GIVEN NAMES French 12%. *Andre* (2), *Emile* (2), *Marcel* (2), *Michel* (2), *Pierrette* (2), *Alphonse, Armand, Germain, Herve, Jacques, Jean-Marc, Luc.*

Laurino (233) Italian: **1.** habitational name from Laurino in Salerno province. **2.** from a pet form of the personal name LAURO.

GIVEN NAMES Italian 22%. *Angelo* (3), *Bruna* (2), *Mario* (2), *Sabino* (2), *Vito* (2), *Alfonse, Alfonso, Cosmo, Enrico, Ersilia, Lorenzo, Luigi, Pasquale, Rocco.*

Laurion (135) Probably a variant of French **Laurian**, from the personal name, a vernacular form of Latin *Laurianus.*

GIVEN NAMES French 11%. *Andre, Gabrielle, Lucien, Monique, Serge.*

Laurita (119) Italian: feminine form of LAURITO. The feminine form is probably due to the influence of the Italian word *famiglia* 'family'.

Laurito (131) Italian: habitational name from a place in Salerno province called Laurito.

GIVEN NAMES Italian 14%. *Angelo, Antonio, Biagio, Domenic, Gennaro, Rocco, Salvatore, Santo.*

Lauritsen (405) Norwegian and Danish: variant of LAURIDSEN.

GIVEN NAMES Scandinavian 6%. *Alf, Peer, Thor, Viggo.*

Lauritzen (597) Norwegian, Danish, and North German: patronymic from a personal name equivalent to LAWRENCE.

GIVEN NAMES Scandinavian 7%. *Gorm* (2), *Nels* (2), *Astrid, Bent, Erik, Folmer, Hjalmer, Niels, Tor.*

Lauro (614) Italian: **1.** from the personal name *Lauro* (from Latin *Laurus*, meaning 'laurel'). **2.** habitational name from Lauro in Avellino province, or possibly from either of two districts so called: one in Diamante (Cosenza), the other in Sessa Aurunca (Caserta).

GIVEN NAMES Italian 27%. *Salvatore* (7), *Angelo* (4), *Vito* (3), *Carmine* (2), *Amedeo, Americo, Antonio, Ciro, Florindo, Francesco, Gaetano, Gerardo, Gilda, Mario, Orlando, Placido, Rico.*

Laursen (730) Norwegian, Danish, and North German: patronymic from *Laur*, a short form of LAWRENCE.

GIVEN NAMES Scandinavian 8%. *Erik* (4), *Aksel, Bent, Birgit, Kresten.*

Laury (322) **1.** Northern Irish: variant spelling of LAURIE. **2.** French: Latinized form of LAUR 1 and 2. **3.** Americanized spelling of French LAREAU.

Lausch (265) German and Alsatian: nickname for an eavesdropper or nosy person, from Middle High German *lūsche.*

Lause (127) North German and Dutch: from a short form of the personal name *Nikolaus* (see NICHOLAS).

GIVEN NAMES German 5%. *Aloys* (2), *Jurgen.*

Lauser (101) **1.** German: from a short form of the personal name *Nikolaus* (see NICHOLAS). **2.** German: nickname for a hunter, from Middle High German *lūzen* 'to lie in wait'. **3.** German: habitational name for someone from any of several places called Laus or Lausa.

GIVEN NAME German 4%. *Otto.*

Lausier (179) French: variant spelling of LOSIER, a secondary surname in French Canada for PINARD and Roy-Desjardins.

GIVEN NAMES French 19%. *Pierre* (2), *Alcide, Celine, Emile, Emilien, Fernand, Laurien, Luc, Lucien, Monique, Urbain.*

Lauster (137) German: nickname for an eavesdropper or nosy person, from an agent derivative of Middle High German *lüstern* 'to eavesdrop'.

Laut (148) **1.** German: from a reduced pet form of the personal name LUDWIG. **2.** French: from a personal name of Germanic origin, *Lauto* (the name of a 6th-century saint, a bishop of Coutances). The element *laut-* is related to Gothic *lauths* 'big' or *laudi* 'figure' or 'face'.

Lauten (162) Dutch: variant of LATON 2.

Lautenbach (254) German: habitational name from Lautenbach (Upper Rhine), which is named with the Germanic elements *hlutra* 'pure', 'clear' + *bach* 'stream'.

GIVEN NAMES German 7%. *Kurt* (3), *Ewald, Konrad, Reinhart.*

Lautenschlager (311) German and Alsatian (usually **Lautenschläger**): occupational name for a player on the lute, Middle High German *lūtenslaher.*

GIVEN NAMES German 4%. *Ernst, Johann, Kurt.*

Lauter (305) German and Alsatian: topographic name and habitational name, from a common stream name meaning 'clear', from Middle High German *hlutra.*

GIVEN NAMES German 6%. *Ernst, Erwin, Kurt, Sigismund, Wolf.*

Lauterbach (786) German: habitational name from any of numerous places so named, compare LAUTER, + Middle High German *bach* 'stream'.

GIVEN NAMES German 7%. *Armin* (2), *Gunter* (2), *Hans* (2), *Heinz* (2), *Kurt* (2), *Arno, Dieter, Heinrich, Jochen, Reinhard, Rudie.*

Lauth (368) German: from a Germanic personal name, *Luto*, a pet form of compound names with the Germanic element *lut, hluda* 'clear', 'fame'. Compare LUDWIG.

Lautner (252) **1.** German: habitational name from any of various places called Lauten. **2.** variant of **Lautenschläger** (see LAUTENSCHLAGER).

Lautt (117) German: variant spelling of LAUT.

Lautz (126) German: variant of LOTZ.

Lautzenheiser (271) Americanized spelling of German **Lautzenhäuser**, a habitational name for someone from Lautzenhausen in the Rhineland, near the Mosel river.

Lauve (106) **1.** French: unexplained. This name occurs chiefly in Louisiana. **2.** Norwegian: unexplained. **3.** Possibly a respelling of North German **Lauwe**, a variant of LAU 1.

GIVEN NAME French 8%. *Pierre.*

Lauver (609) Americanized form of Dutch **Lauwer**, occupational name for a tanner or leather worker.

Laux (1456) South German: from a vernacular form of the personal name LUCAS.

Lauzier (110) French: occupational name for a slater or worker in a slate quarry, from a derivative of a Gallic word *lausa* 'slate'.
GIVEN NAMES French 31%. *Gaston* (3), *Adelard, Alphonse, Cyrille, Edouard, Jacques, Jean-Paul, Lucien, Normand, Odette, Oneil.*

Lauzon (760) French: from a diminutive of **Lauze**, a metonymic occupational name for a slater, derived from Gaulish *lausa* 'slate', 'roofing stone'.
FOREBEARS The first Lauzon to arrive in North America came as governor of New France, in 1651. Other Lauzon families came from Le Mans, France, to Montreal (1656), and from Normandy, France, to Montreal (1656). They are also recorded as LAURENT, Loreau-Florentin, LOZON, and VADEBONCOEUR.
GIVEN NAMES French 15%. *Marcel* (5), *Pierre* (4), *Andre* (2), *Gilles* (2), *Jacques* (2), *Lucien* (2), *Michel* (2), *Normand* (2), *Adelard, Alain, Armand, Damien.*

Lavalette (123) French: topographic name for someone who lived in a valley, from a diminutive of Old French *val*.
GIVEN NAMES French 5%. *Alide, Henri.*

La Valla (114) Italian: topographic name for someone who lived in a valley.

Lavalle (839) French: topographic name for someone who lived in a valley (see LAVALLEE) or a habitational name from any of various places called Laval.
GIVEN NAMES Italian 7%. *Angelo* (5), *Dino* (3), *Santo* (3), *Antonio* (2), *Salvatore* (2), *Aldo, Carmel, Duilio, Egidio, Enrico, Luigi.*

Lavallee (1949) **1.** French and Canadian (**Lavallée**): topographic name for someone who lived in a valley, Old French *val* (Latin *vallis*), with the definite article *la*; or a habitational name from any of numerous places called Lavallée. **2.** French Canadian: secondary surname, used to distinguish a branch of a family (for example the Paquettes) living in a valley, as opposed to others, for example those living by a river (Paquette dit LaRivière).
GIVEN NAMES French 13%. *Normand* (6), *Armand* (5), *Andre* (4), *Marcel* (4), *Pierre* (4), *Adrien* (3), *Lucien* (3), *Julien* (2), *Laurent* (2), *Michel* (2), *Raoul* (2), *Achille.*

Lavalley (1254) Part translation of French Canadian **Lavallée** (see LAVALLEE), frequent in New England.

Lavallie (134) Part translation of French Canadian **Lavallée** (see LAVALLEE), frequent in New England.

Lavan (371) **1.** Jewish: nickname meaning 'white' in Hebrew. **2.** Vietnamese: unexplained.

GIVEN NAMES Vietnamese 5%. *Binh* (2), *Anh, Dac, Danh, Hoa, Hung, Quang.*

Lavanway (145) Americanized spelling of French LIVERNOIS.

Lavarnway (154) Americanized spelling of French LIVERNOIS.

Lavasseur (106) Respelling of French **Levasseur**, a status name from Old French *vasseor* 'vassal' (a short form of *vavasseur*), with the generalized use of the feminine definite article *la* in place of the masculine *le*, which is characteristic of Canada and New England.
GIVEN NAMES French 7%. *Alphy, Jacques.*

La Vecchia (224) Southern Italian: nickname from *la vecchia* 'the old', applied to a person of either gender, either as a nickname for a man who fussed like an old woman or for someone from an old family, the feminine form probably being due to the influence of the Italian word *famiglia* 'family'.
GIVEN NAMES Italian 22%. *Angelo* (2), *Gioacchino* (2), *Sal* (2), *Salvatore* (2), *Vittorio* (2), *Attilio, Carmela, Domenico, Francesca, Gaetano, Orest, Pasquale.*

Laveck (119) Possibly an Americanized spelling of French **Levêque** ('the bishop'), a variant of LEVESQUE.

Lavell (200) Irish and English: variant spelling of LAVELLE.

Lavelle (2312) **1.** Irish: adopted as an English equivalent of Gaelic **Ó Maoil Fhábhail** 'descendant of *Maolfhábhail*', a personal name meaning 'fond of movement or travel'. **2.** English: from the common French place name Laval, from Old French *val* 'valley'. This is also a Huguenot name (with the same etymology), taken to England by Etienne-Abel Laval, a minister of the French church in Castle Street, London, around 1730. **3.** French: habitational name from Lavelle in Puy-de-Dôme or various other, smaller places so named.
GIVEN NAMES Irish 4%. *Brendan* (2), *Colum, John Patrick.*

Lavely (315) Variant of French LAVALLEE.

Laven (281) Dutch: from a derivative of a Germanic personal name such as *Lavoldus* or from a derivative of a vernacular form of the Latin personal name *Laurentius* (see LAWRENCE).
GIVEN NAMES German 5%. *Otto* (3), *Hans, Kurt.*

Lavender (2563) English and Dutch: occupational name for a washerman or launderer, Old French, Middle Dutch *lavendier* (Late Latin *lavandarius*, an agent derivative of *lavanda* 'washing', 'things to be washed'). The term was applied especially to a worker in the wool industry who washed the raw wool or rinsed the cloth after fulling. There is no evidence for any direct connection with the word for the plant (Middle English, Old French *lavendre*). However, the etymology of the plant name is obscure; it may have been named

in ancient times with reference to the use of lavender oil for cleaning or of the dried heads of lavender in perfuming freshly washed clothes.

Lavene (105) French Canadian: secondary surname, which has been used independently since 1763; a nickname for an adventurer, traveler, or someone very lucky. Associated names include Hus, Nus, and MACE.

Laventure (221) French: nickname for a lucky or fortunate person, from Old French *adventure* 'fate', 'destiny' (Latin *adventura*).
GIVEN NAMES French 14%. *Andre* (2), *Marcel* (2), *Andrus, Henri, Lafontant, Laurent, Mireille, Philippe, Sauveur.*

Laver (250) English: **1.** occupational name for a washerman, Anglo-Norman French *laver* (an agent derivative of Old French *laver* 'to wash', Latin *lavare*). **2.** habitational name from High, Little or Magdalen Laver in Essex, named from Old English *lagu* 'flood', 'water' + *fær* 'passage', 'crossing'. **3.** topographic name for someone living where bulrushes or irises grew, Old English *læfer*.

Laverde (134) Spanish: topographic or habitational name, apparently from *verde* 'green'.
GIVEN NAMES Spanish 30%. *Jorge* (2), *Juan* (2), *Manuel* (2), *Adriana, Alvaro, Bernardo, Elena, Ezequiel, Francisca, Francisco, Jaime, Liliana; Dario, Leonardo, Salvatore.*

Laverdiere (306) French (**Laverdière**): habitational name from any of various places named La Verdière, for example in Nièvre and Gironde, or an altered form of the occupational and habitational name **Leverdier**, variant of VERDIER. Tanguay records Laverdière as a secondary surname for Cauchon from 1670 on.
GIVEN NAMES French 20%. *Armand* (3), *Lucien* (3), *Andre* (2), *Normand* (2), *Pierre* (2), *Adrien, Aime, Aurele, Carmeline, Gilles, Laurier, Luc.*

Laverdure (183) French: habitational name from either of two places called La Verdure, meaning 'greenness', 'greenery' (from Latin *viridis* 'green'). In French Canada, it is a secondary surname for ETHIER, Rithier, and Riquier.
GIVEN NAMES French 13%. *Jacques* (2), *Andre, Fernand, Gilles, Jean-Michael, Rosaire.*

Lavere (211) Probably a New England form of French LEVERT, with characteristic generalized use of the feminine article in place of the masculine.
GIVEN NAMES French 5%. *Francois, Michel.*

Lavergne (1127) French: topographic or habitational name from any of the numerous places named with the Gaulish element *ver(n)* 'alder'.
GIVEN NAMES French 9%. *Vernice* (3), *Andre* (2), *Monique* (2), *Nolton* (2), *Pierre* (2),

Alphe, Armand, Berchman, Donat, Dumas, Easton, Gabrielle.

Laverne (148) French: variant spelling of LAVERGNE.

GIVEN NAME French 5%. *Michel.*

Lavers (145) English (chiefly Devon and Cornwall): variant of LAVER, which was also used as a personal name in the 17th century.

Lavertu (132) French: nickname for a strong or upright person, from Old French *vertu* 'strength', 'vigor', 'wisdom'.

GIVEN NAMES French 14%. *Emile, Gaston, Marcel, Patrice, Pierre.*

Laverty (1052) Irish: variant of LAFFERTY.

Lavery (1440) Irish (chiefly northern Ireland): reduced Anglicized form of Gaelic **Ó Labhradha** 'descendant of *Labhraidh*', a byname meaning 'spokesman'. Three branches of the sept are sometimes distinguished as **Baun-Lavery** (from *bán* 'white'), **Roe-Lavery** (from *rua* 'red') and **Trin-Lavery** (from *tréan* 'strong'). Some of this last group have been 'translated' as ARMSTRONG (as if from *lámh* 'hand', 'arm').

Lavey (362) **1.** English: unexplained. **2.** Irish (Westmeath): probably a local variant of LEAVY (see DUNLEAVY).

La Via (103) Italian: topographic name for someone who lived by a main street or thoroughfare, from *via* 'main street', 'main road', with the definite article *la.*

Laviano (101) Italian: habitational name from Laviano in Salerno.

GIVEN NAMES Italian 23%. *Mario* (3), *Angelo, Carlo, Giuseppe, Pasquale, Salvatore, Vito.*

Lavier (79) French: occupational name for someone who quarried a kind of flat sandstone called *lave* (from Latin *lapis*), which was used for roofing.

Lavigna (144) Italian (also **La Vigna**): topographic name for someone who lived by a vineyard, Italian *vigna* (Latin *vinea*, a derivative of *vinum* 'wine').

GIVEN NAMES Italian 14%. *Angelo* (2), *Domenic, Donato, Rocco, Vito.*

Lavigne (2684) French: from Old French *vi(g)ne* 'vineyard' (Latin *vinea*, a derivative of *vinum* 'wine'), hence a topographic name for someone who lived near a vineyard; a metonymic occupational name for a vine dresser or the owner of a vineyard; or a habitational name from any of numerous places so named. In Canada, this is a frequent secondary surname, which has also been used alone since 1708.

GIVEN NAMES French 9%. *Andre* (8), *Armand* (6), *Jacques* (5), *Marcel* (5), *Normand* (5), *Lucien* (4), *Emile* (3), *Gilles* (3), *Francois* (2), *Germain* (2), *Michel* (2), *Ovila* (2).

Lavin (2510) **1.** Irish (Connacht): reduced Anglicized form of Gaelic **Ó Láimhín**, a reduced form of **Ó Flaithimhín** 'descendant of *Flaithimhín*', a personal name from a diminutive of *flaith* 'prince', 'ruler'. This name is sometimes translated HAND, from the similarity of the reduced form to *lámh* 'hand'. **2.** English: from the medieval female personal name *Lavin(a)* (from Latin *Lavinia*, of unknown origin) . **3.** Spanish (**Lavín**): habitational name from Lavin, a place so named in the Santander province. **4.** Respelling of French LAVIGNE.

GIVEN NAMES Irish 4%. *Thomas Patrick* (3), *Eamon* (2), *Brendan, Donovan, Kieran, Padraig.*

Lavinder (172) English: variant spelling of LAVENDER.

Lavine (1255) **1.** English: variant of LAVIN 2. **2.** Altered spelling of French LAVIGNE.

La Viola (101) Italian: unexplained.

GIVEN NAMES Italian 20%. *Angelo, Donato, Guido, Luigi, Philomena, Pierluigi.*

Laviolette (706) French: secondary surname, associated with some forty family names in Canada and also used independently since 1698, a nickname from the flower *violette* 'violet', with the definite article *la*. In feudal France it was a name given to soldiers and domestic servants.

GIVEN NAMES French 6%. *Marcel* (2), *Alphe, Andre, Antoine, Camile, Cecile, Pierre.*

Lavis (163) **1.** English (chiefly West Country): patronymic from LAVER. **2.** German: unexplained. **3.** French: nickname for someone living at a house with a spiral staircase, Old French *lavis.*

Lavoie (3889) French: topographic name for someone who lived by a road, French *voie* (Latin *via*). This is a very common secondary surname in Canada; it was first seen in Cap Rouge in 1667, taken there from Charente Maritime, and has also been used independently since 1690.

GIVEN NAMES French 16%. *Normand* (19), *Armand* (18), *Andre* (12), *Lucien* (11), *Fernand* (9), *Marcel* (9), *Adrien* (7), *Benoit* (5), *Emile* (5), *Pierre* (5), *Herve* (4), *Jacques* (4).

Lavorgna (191) Italian: unexplained.

GIVEN NAMES Italian 11%. *Antonio* (2), *Attilio, Carmine, Dante, Giovanni, Luigi, Mafalda.*

Lavoy (430) Variant of French LAVOIE.

Lavy (267) English: see LAVEY.

Law (10924) Scottish and northern English: **1.** from a Middle English short form of LAWRENCE. **2.** topographic name for someone who lived near a hill, northern Middle English *law* (from Old English *hlāw* 'hill', 'burial mound').

FOREBEARS Richard Law emigrated from England to America in 1638. In 1641 he was one of the founders of Stamford, CT. Others of the Law family were born in Milford, CT: Jonathan (b. 1674), who was governor 1741–50, Richard (b. 1733), a revolutionary patriot and jurist; and Andrew (b. 1748/49), a composer of sacred music.

Lawall (160) Americanized form of **Lawal**, a Germanized or Polonized spelling of French LAVALLE. This name is found chiefly in PA and NY.

Lawder (101) Scottish and northern English: variant spelling of LAUDER.

Lawerence (105) English: variant of LAWRENCE.

GIVEN NAME French 4%. *Pierre.*

Lawes (191) English (chiefly southern): patronymic from LAW 1.

GIVEN NAMES French 4%. *Donat, Odette.*

Lawhead (536) Probably Scottish: from any of various places named Lawhead ('hill head') in Fife, Lothian, and Strathclyde, which could have given rise to the surname, although there is no evidence of the surname in present-day Scotland.

Lawhon (1058) Northern Irish: variant of LAWHORN.

Lawhorn (1602) Northern Irish: probably a reduced Americanized form of Gaelic **Mac Labhrainn** 'son of *Labhrann*' (see McLAREN).

Lawhorne (397) Northern Irish: variant of LAWHORN.

Lawhun (125) Northern Irish: variant of LAWHORN.

Lawing (842) Origin uncertain. Perhaps an altered form of LEWIN. This name is found predominantly in NC.

FOREBEARS The immigrant William Lawing was born in 1725 in either England or the Palatinate, Germany, and died about 1825.

Lawler (5696) Irish (Ulster, Leinster, and Kerry): reduced Anglicized form of Gaelic **Ó Leathlobhair** 'descendant of *Leathlobhar*', a personal name composed of the elements *leath* 'half' (i.e. 'somewhat', 'fairly') and *lobar* 'leprous', 'sick'. The name seems to have been originally a byname for a man of unhealthy constitution.

Lawless (3551) Scottish, Irish, and English: nickname for an unbridled and licentious man, from Middle English *laghless, lawelas* (a compound of late Old English *lagu* 'law' (from Old Norse) + the native suffix *-l(ē)as* 'without', 'lacking'). Reaney suggests additionally that this name may have referred to an outlaw (i.e. one from whom the protection of the law had been withdrawn), but this seems unlikely.

Lawley (879) English (chiefly West Midlands): habitational name from Lawley in Shropshire, named in Old English as 'Lafa's wood', from a personal name *Lāfa* (from *lāf* 'remnant', 'survivor') + *lēah* 'wood', 'glade'.

Lawlis (214) Scottish, Irish, and English: variant spelling of LAWLESS.

Lawlor (2245) Irish: variant spelling of LAWLER.

GIVEN NAMES Irish 6%. *Brendan* (5), *Niall* (2), *Brigid, Cormac, John Patrick, Niamh, Siobhan.*

Lawman (127) Scottish and northern Irish: variant of LAMONT.

Lawn (357) English: variant of LAND 2.

Lawniczak (157) Polish (**Ławniczak**): patronymic from *Ławnik*, a status name for a town councilor, from Polish *ławnik* (from *ława* 'bench').

Lawrance (167) English: variant spelling of LAWRENCE.

GIVEN NAME French 5%. *Camille*.

Lawrence (44221) English: from the Middle English and Old French personal name *Lorens*, *Laurence* (Latin *Laurentius* 'man from *Laurentum*', a place in Italy probably named from its laurels or bay trees). The name was borne by a saint who was martyred at Rome in the 3rd century AD; he enjoyed a considerable cult throughout Europe, with consequent popularity of the personal name (French *Laurent*, Italian, Spanish *Lorenzo*, Catalan *Llorenç*, Portuguese *Lourenço*, German *Laurenz*; Polish *Wawrzyniec* (assimilated to the Polish word *wawrzyn* 'laurel'), etc.). The surname is also borne by Jews among whom it is presumably an Americanized form of one or more like-sounding Ashkenazic surnames.

Lawrenson (148) **1.** English: patronymic from LAWRENCE. **2.** Americanized form of any of various like-sounding Jewish surnames, as for example LEVENSON.

Lawrenz (320) North German: variant of LORENZ.

GIVEN NAMES German 6%. *Dietrich, Ewald, Gerhardt, Hans, Wolfgang*.

Lawrie (506) Scottish: from a pet form of LAWRENCE.

Lawrimore (142) English and Scottish: see LORIMER.

Lawry (505) Northern Irish and English: from a pet form of LAWRENCE.

Laws (4622) **1.** English (chiefly southern): patronymic from the personal name LAW (pet form of LAWRENCE). **2.** Perhaps a reduced form of Scottish or Irish MCLEISH. Compare MCLAWS.

Lawshe (142) Probably a reduced form of Scottish or Irish MCLEISH. Compare MCLAWS.

Lawson (38208) **1.** Scottish and northern English: patronymic from LAW 1. **2.** Americanized form of Swedish LARSSON.

Lawter (258) Scottish and northern English: variant of LAUDER.

Lawther (201) Scottish, northern Irish, and northern English: variant of LAUDER.

Lawton (5018) English: **1.** habitational name, common in Lancashire and Yorkshire, from Buglawton or Church Lawton in Cheshire, or Lawton in Herefordshire, named in Old English as 'settlement on or near a hill', or 'settlement by a burial mound', from *hlāw* 'hill', 'burial mound' + *tūn* 'enclosure', 'settlement'. **2.** variant spelling of LAUGHTON.

Lawver (498) Anglicized form of Dutch **Lauwer**, occupational name for a tanner or leather worker.

Lawwill (110) Variant of Irish LAVELLE.

Lawyer (1458) Anglicized form of Dutch **Lauwer**, occupational name for a tanner or leather worker.

Lax (906) **1.** German and Danish: metonymic occupational name for a salmon fisher or a seller of salmon, Middle High German *lahs* 'salmon'. **2.** English (northeastern counties) and Danish: from an Old Norse nickname, *Lax*, meaning 'salmon'. **3.** Jewish (Ashkenazic): ornamental name from German *Lachs* 'salmon', Yiddish *laks*, one of the many Ashkenazic surnames taken from words denoting fish, birds, and animals.

GIVEN NAMES Jewish 8%. *Chaim* (5), *Arie* (3), *Emanuel* (2), *Sol* (2), *Aron, Chain, Chaya, Hershel, Irit, Lazer, Menachem, Mordechai*.

Laxson (362) Danish and North German: patronymic from LAX.

Laxton (709) English: habitational name from places called Laxton, in East Yorkshire, Nottinghamshire, and Northamptonshire. The Northamptonshire place name is formed from an Old English personal name *Leaxa* + *tūn* 'enclosure', 'settlement'. The other examples were named with *Leaxa* + -*ing*- (denoting association with) + *tūn*.

Lay (5651) **1.** English: variant of LEE. **2.** Scottish: reduced variant of MCCLAY. **3.** French: habitational name from places so named in Loire, Meurthe-et-Moselle, and Pyrénées-Atlantique. **4.** German: habitational name from places so named, in the Rhineland near Koblenz and in Bavaria, named with *lay(h)*, a word meaning 'stone', 'rock', 'slate'.

Laybourn (114) English: habitational name from Leyburn in North Yorkshire, so named from an uncertain first element (possibly Old English *hlēg* 'shelter') + Old English *burna* 'stream'. Leybourne in Kent, which is named from an Old English personal name *Lytta* + *burna*, may also have contributed to the surname to some extent, although it is a predominantly northern name.

Laycock (693) English (chiefly Yorkshire): habitational name from Laycock in West Yorkshire or possibly from Lacock in Wiltshire. Both are recorded in Domesday Book as *Lacoc* and seem to be named with a diminutive of Old English *lacu* 'stream'.

Layden (678) Irish: variant spelling of **Leyden** (see LYDON).

GIVEN NAMES Irish 4%. *Brendan, Brigid, Kieran*.

Laye (201) English: variant of LEE.

Layer (503) **1.** English: habitational name from any of three places in Essex – Layer Breton, Layer de la Haye, and Layer Marney – all named from a river name, *Leire*, or from Leire in Leicestershire, also named from an identical river name. The river name is of Celtic origin and is probably the base of the tribal name *Ligore*, found in the place name Leicester. **2.** English: nickname or status name from Anglo-Norman French *le eyr* 'the heir'. Compare AYER. **3.** English: occupational name for a stone layer, Middle English *leyer*; the job of the layer was to position the stones worked by the masons. **4.** German: habitational name for someone from any of the various placed named LAY, in the Rhineland and Bavaria.

GIVEN NAMES German 4%. *Otto* (3), *Franz, Hans*.

Layfield (863) English: topographic name for someone who lived by a field that was untilled or used for pasture, from Middle English *leye* 'meadow', 'pasture', 'fallow' + *feld* 'open country', 'field', or a habitational name from Leyfield in Nottinghamshire, which has the same meaning.

Layher (160) **1.** German: variant of LAYER 4. **2.** Perhaps also a Germanized spelling of Hungarian **Lehár**.

GIVEN NAME German 4%. *Kurt* (2).

Layland (223) English (chiefly Lancashire): habitational name from Leyland in Lancashire (recorded in Domesday Book as *Lailand*), or from Laylands in Yorkshire; both are named from Old English *lǣge* 'untilled ground' + *land* 'land', 'estate'. In some cases the name may be topographical.

Layman (4014) **1.** English: topographic name for someone who lived near a meadow, pasture, or patch of (fallow) arable land, Middle English *leye*. **2.** Americanized spelling of German LEHMANN. **3.** German: variant of LAY 3.

Laymance (135) Origin unidentified. This name is found chiefly in TX.

Laymon (725) Variant of English LAYMAN.

Layne (4431) English: variant spelling of LANE.

Layng (132) English (south and south Midlands): variant spelling of LAING.

Layson (264) English (Kent): unexplained; possibly a variant of LEESON.

Layton (7005) English: habitational name from any of various places so called, for example in Lancashire (near Blackpool) and in North Yorkshire. The former was named in Old English as 'settlement by the watercourse', from Old English *lād* 'watercourse' + *tūn* 'enclosure', 'settlement'; the latter as 'leek enclosure' or 'herb garden', from *lēac* 'leek' + *tūn*. Compare LEIGHTON.

Laza (110) Galician: habitational name from Laza, a town in Galicia, in northwest Spain.

GIVEN NAMES Spanish 14%. *Adriano, Beatriz, Blanca, Jaime, Julio, Luz, Miguel, Noemi, Pedro, Rogelio*.

Lazar (2428) **1.** Jewish, German, Hungarian (**Lázár**), Slovenian, and Polish: from a personal name of Aramaic origin, a reduced form of the Hebrew male personal name *Elazar*, composed of the elements *El* 'God' + *azar* 'help', and meaning 'may God help him' or 'God has helped (i.e., by granting a son)'. This was well established in central Europe as a Jewish name, but was also popular among Christians because it is recorded in the New Testament. *Lazaros* is the New Testament Greek form of the name of the brother of Martha and Mary, who was restored to life by Christ (John 11: 1–44). As a non-Jewish name it was also used as a nickname for a beggar or an outcast leper; this use arises from the parable of Dives and Lazarus (Luke 16: 19–31). It may also be Greek, a shortened form of a patronymic based on this name, for example **Lazarakis**, **Lazaridis**, **Lazaroglou**, **Lazaropoulos**. **2.** Slovenian: topographic name for someone who lived in a area of cleared woodland, from *laz* 'cleared woodland' + the agent noun suffix *-ar*.

GIVEN NAMES Jewish 4%. *Meyer* (4), *Moshe* (3), *Yonah* (2), *Amnon, Chaim, Ilanit, Miriam, Naama, Naum, Semen, Shimon, Shira*.

Lazard (207) French: variant of the personal name LAZAR.

GIVEN NAMES French 13%. *Alain* (2), *Monique* (2), *Andre, Jacques, Marcell, Octave, Yanick*.

Lazare (211) French: from the Biblical personal name (see LAZAR).

GIVEN NAMES French 7%. *Marcel* (2), *Michel, Remy*.

Lazaro (738) Spanish and Portuguese (**Lázaro**): from the Biblical personal name *Lazaro* (see LAZAR).

GIVEN NAMES Spanish 41%. *Jose* (14), *Manuel* (8), *Jorge* (6), *Pablo* (5), *Carlos* (4), *Ernesto* (4), *Francisco* (4), *Juan* (4), *Luis* (4), *Alberto* (3), *Mario* (3), *Miguel* (3).

Lazaroff (223) Bulgarian, Russian (**Lazarev**), and Jewish (eastern Ashkenazic): alternative spelling of **Lazarov**, a patronymic from the personal name LAZAR.

GIVEN NAMES Jewish 8%. *Chaim, Chana, Eliezer, Shimon, Yisroel*.

Lazarski (169) Polish (**Łazarski**): habitational name for someone from a place called Łazarz or Łazarze, named with the personal name *Łazarz*, Polish form of LAZAR.

GIVEN NAMES Polish 6%. *Andrzej, Ewa, Janusz*.

Lazarus (2074) Jewish (western Ashkenazic) and German: variant of LAZAR.

GIVEN NAMES Jewish 4%. *Avi* (2), *Aviva, Baruch, Chaya, Hyman, Isador, Mendel, Morty, Moshe, Naftali, Shula, Sol.*

Lazarz (201) Polish (**Łazarz**): from the personal name *Łazarz*, Polish form of LAZAR.

GIVEN NAMES Polish 8%. *Casimir, Grazyna, Henryka, Janina, Stanislaw, Wladyslaw*.

Lazcano (199) Spanish (from Basque): habitational name from Basque Lazkao, a town in Gipuzkoa province.

GIVEN NAMES Spanish 59%. *Jose* (8), *Juan* (5), *Jorge* (4), *Luis* (4), *Armando* (3), *Enrique* (3), *Fernando* (3), *Francisco* (3), *Jesus* (3), *Carlos* (2), *Ernesto* (2), *Gerardo*

(2); *Antonio* (3), *Federico, Gasper, Heriberto, Marco Antonio, Severiano*.

Lazear (226) Apparently an altered spelling of LAZAR. It is found chiefly in OH and WV.

Lazenby (924) Northern English: habitational name from Lazenby in Redcar and Cleveland or Lazonby in Cumbria, both named in Old Norse as 'freedman's farm', or 'Freedmen's farm', from *leysingi* 'freedman' (also used as a nickname and personal name; see LEISING) + *býr* 'farm', 'settlement'.

Lazer (153) **1.** German and Jewish (Ashkenazic): variant of LAZAR. **2.** French: southern form of LAZARE. **3.** French: habitational name from a place in Haute-Alpes, the place name being derived from the personal name.

GIVEN NAMES Russian 4%; Jewish 4%. *Misha* (2), *Zoya; Anat, Simcha*.

Lazich (107) Serbian (**Lazić**): patronymic from the personal name *Laza*, a short form of the personal name LAZAR.

GIVEN NAMES South Slavic 8%. *Bozidar, Milovan, Radovan*.

Lazier (147) Apparently an altered spelling of LAZAR. See also LAZEAR.

Lazio (113) Italian: **1.** from a short form of the personal name *Alazio*, of Germanic origin. **2.** habitational name for someone from Lazio.

GIVEN NAME Italian 5%. *Ignazio*.

Lazo (1206) **1.** Galician: habitational name from Lazo in A Coruña province. **2.** Spanish: nickname from Spanish *lazo* 'hair ribbon', 'shoe lace'.

GIVEN NAMES Spanish 49%. *Jose* (37), *Luis* (19), *Juan* (16), *Carlos* (14), *Jorge* (9), *Manuel* (9), *Roberto* (9), *Ana* (7), *Jaime* (7), *Miguel* (7), *Cesar* (5), *Pedro* (5).

Lazor (392) Variant of LAZAR. It is found predominantly in PA.

Lazos (127) **1.** Spanish: from the plural of *lazo* 'hair ribbon', 'shoe lace', presumably applied as a metonymic nickname for a haberdasher. **2.** Greek: from the personal name *Lazos*, a pet form of *Lazaros* (see LAZAR).

GIVEN NAMES Spanish 35%; Greek 12%. *Arturo* (2), *Ernesto* (2), *Jose* (2), *Luis* (2), *Roel* (2), *Ruben* (2), *Benigno, Concepcion, Efrain, Erasmo, Esperanza, Francisco; Spiros* (3), *Christos, Panagiotis, Stavros, Theoharis, Vasilios*.

Lazowski (105) Polish (**Łazowski**): habitational name for someone from any of various places called Łazy, Łazow, or Łazowa, named with *łazy* 'clearing in a forest'.

Lazur (165) Apparently an altered or variant spelling of LAZAR. It is found chiefly in PA.

Lazzara (515) Italian: possibly from a feminine form of the personal name LAZZARO, but more likely a derivative of **l'Azzàra**, from *azzàra* 'flower', 'blossom', from Arabic *azzaharah*.

GIVEN NAMES Italian 27%. *Angelo* (6), *Salvatore* (6), *Gasper* (4), *Sal* (3), *Giuseppe* (2), *Ignazio* (2), *Santo* (2), *Vincenza* (2), *Agostino, Antonio, Attilio, Carmelo*.

Lazzari (333) Italian: patronymic or plural form of the personal name LAZZARO.

GIVEN NAMES Italian 10%. *Angelo* (2), *Alessandro, Cataldo, Gino, Giovanni, Luciano, Luigi, Pietro, Reno, Romano, Salvatore*.

Lazzarini (145) Italian: patronymic or plural form of the personal name *Lazzarino*, a pet form of LAZZARO.

GIVEN NAMES Italian 13%. *Marco* (2), *Aldo, Angelo, Dario, Francesco, Guido, Luigi, Renzo, Ricci*.

Lazzaro (723) Italian: from the personal name *Lazzaro* (see LAZAR).

GIVEN NAMES Italian 24%. *Salvatore* (5), *Carmelo* (3), *Angelo* (2), *Pasquale* (2), *Aldo, Domenic, Francesco, Gianluca, Giovanna, Giuseppe, Guido, Lorenzo, Rosario*.

Lazzeri (110) Italian: Tuscan variant of LAZZARI.

GIVEN NAMES Italian 6%. *Alessio, Nino, Rino*.

Le (11326) Vietnamese (**Lê**): a royal or aristocratic name, the family name of the Lê Dynasty.

GIVEN NAMES Vietnamese 61%. *Thanh* (155), *Hung* (145), *Minh* (100), *Dung* (98), *Tuan* (86), *Hai* (75), *Hoa* (73), *Thuy* (73), *Son* (72), *Anh* (65), *Long* (64), *Hoang* (63); *Hong* (57), *Sang* (27), *Chi* (19), *Dong* (18), *Tong* (17), *Lai* (16), *Hang* (15), *Man* (15), *Han* (11), *Ho* (11), *Phoung* (10), *Chan* (9); *Tam* (78), *Phong* (46), *Nam* (29), *Thai* (18), *Tuong* (13), *Chung* (12), *Thach* (12), *Tinh* (11), *Manh* (10), *Tham* (10), *Uyen* (10), *Vang* (9).

Lea (3513) **1.** English: variant spelling of LEE. **2.** Dutch: patronymic from a Germanic personal name formed of the elements *liut* 'people', 'tribe' + *hardi* 'strong'.

Leabo (180) Americanized spelling of French LEBEAU.

Leach (15956) English: **1.** occupational name for a physician, Old English *lǣce*, from the medieval medical practice of 'bleeding', often by applying leeches to the sick person. **2.** topographic name for someone who lived by a boggy stream, from an Old English *lǣcc*, or a habitational name from Eastleach or Northleach in Gloucestershire, named with the same Old English element.

Leachman (586) English: occupational name for a physician's servant, from LEACH 1 + Middle English *man* 'manservant'.

Leacock (248) English: variant of LAYCOCK.

Leadbeater (133) English: variant spelling of LEDBETTER.

Leadbetter (451) English: variant spelling of LEDBETTER.

Leader (1272) English: **1.** occupational name for someone who led a horse and cart conveying commodities from one place to another, Middle English *ledere*, an agent noun from Old English *lǣdan* 'to lead'. The word may also sometimes have been used to denote a foreman or someone who led sport or dance, but the name certainly did not originate with *leader* in the modern sense 'civil or military commander'; this is a comparatively recent development. **2.** occupational name for a worker in lead, from an agent derivative of Old English *lēad* 'lead'.

Leaders (142) **1.** English: patronymic from LEADER. **2.** Probably an Americanized spelling of German **Lüders** (see LUEDERS). GIVEN NAMES German 4%. *Frieda, Otto.*

Leadingham (208) **1.** English: habitational name, perhaps from Leadenham in Lincolnshire, which is probably so named from an Old English personal name, *Lēoda* + *hām* 'homestead'. **2.** Scottish: unexplained. Compare LEDINGHAM. **3.** Perhaps a variant of Dutch VAN LANDINGHAM.

Leadley (125) English (North Yorkshire): habitational name, apparently from Leathley in North Yorkshire, so named from Old English *hlith* 'slope' (genitive plural *hleotha*) + *lēah* 'woodland clearing'.

Leady (125) Probably a variant of Irish LEDDY.

Leaf (1220) **1.** English: from the Old English personal names *Lēofa* (masculine) and *Lēofe* (feminine) 'dear', 'beloved'. These names were in part short forms of various compound names with this first element, in part independent affectionate bynames. **2.** English: apparently a topographic name for someone who lived in a densely foliated area, from Middle English *lēaf* 'leaf'; a certain *Robert Intheleaves* is recorded in London in the 14th century. **3.** Americanized form of Swedish **Lö(ö)f, Löv**, an ornamental name from *löv* 'leaf'. **4.** English translation of the Ashkenazic Jewish ornamental surname BLATT.

League (635) English (Hereford and Worcester): unexplained; perhaps a variant of LEAKE.

Leahey (495) Irish: variant spelling of LEAHY.

Leahy (4559) Irish: reduced Anglicized form of Gaelic **Ó Laochdha** 'descendant of *Laochdha*', a personal name derived from *laoch* 'hero'.
FOREBEARS In Quebec, some families named Lahaie or Lahaye are descended from a Teague Leahy from Dublin, Ireland. GIVEN NAMES Irish 5%. *Brendan* (2), *Clancy, Conn, Connor, Kevin Patrick, Niall, Thomas Patrick.*

Leak (1199) English: variant of LEAKE.

Leake (2398) Northern English: **1.** topographic name for someone who lived by a stream, from Old Norse *lœkr* 'brook'. There are also a number of places named with this word—such as Leake in North Yorkshire, Lincolnshire, and Nottinghamshire, Leek in Staffordshire, and Leck in Lancashire—and the surname may also be from any of these. Compare southern English LEACH 2. **2.** possibly also a metonymic occupational name for a grower or seller of leeks, from Old English *lēac*.

Leakey (147) English (Somerset): unexplained. Compare LUKEY.

Leaks (199) English: variant of LEAKE.

Leal (4342) English, Spanish, and Portuguese: nickname for a loyal or trustworthy person, from Old French *leial*, Spanish and Portuguese *leal* 'loyal', 'faithful (to obligations)', Latin *legalis*, from *lex*, 'law', 'obligation' (genitive *legis*). GIVEN NAMES Spanish 43%; Portuguese 10%. *Jose* (99), *Manuel* (61), *Juan* (50), *Carlos* (35), *Raul* (31), *Luis* (29), *Jorge* (25), *Pedro* (24), *Roberto* (24), *Jesus* (23), *Francisco* (19), *Mario* (18); *Joao* (2), *Amadeu, Joaquim, Lidio, Nelio, Serafim.*

Leaman (931) **1.** English: from the Middle English personal name or nickname *Lefman* (see LEMON). **2.** Perhaps also an Americanized spelling of German LEHMANN.

Leamer (234) Americanized form of German LEHMER.

Leaming (282) English: variant of LEEMING.

Leamon (579) English: variant of LEAMAN.

Leamons (127) English: patronymic from LEAMON (see LEMON). GIVEN NAME French 4%. *Andre.*

Leamy (285) English: unexplained.

Lean (248) **1.** English (chiefly Devon): nickname for a thin or lean person, from Middle English *lene* 'lean' (Old English *hlǣne*). **2.** Irish: reduced Anglicized form of Gaelic **Ó Liatháin** (see LEHANE). **3.** Reduced form of Scottish MCLEAN.

Leander (329) German, Dutch, Danish, and Swedish: humanistic form of VOLKMANN, a graecized form based on the Greek personal name *Leandros* (see LEANDRO). GIVEN NAMES Scandinavian 8%. *Erik, Lars, Per, Pontus, Sven.*

Leandro (174) Italian and Spanish: from the personal name *Leandro*, Greek *Leandros*, which is composed of the elements *leon* 'lion' + *anēr* (genitive *andros*) 'man'. In Greek legend, Leander is the name of a hero who swam across the Hellespont every night to visit his beloved, Hero, and back again in the morning, but was eventually drowned during a violent storm. In Christian times, the name was borne by a 6th-century saint, who was a leading ecclesiastical figure of his day, a friend of Gregory the Great, and became archbishop of Seville. **Leandros** is also found as a Greek family name. GIVEN NAMES Spanish 26%; Portuguese 12%. *Jose* (11), *Manuel* (4), *Jorge* (2), *Luis* (2), *Sergio* (2), *Silverio* (2), *Alfonso, Ana, Angel, Blanca, Carlos, Eduardo*; *Joaquim, Serafim*; *Angelo* (2), *Giovanna, Sebastiano.*

Leanna (119) Origin unidentified.

Leano (128) **1.** Spanish (**Leaño**): probably a variant of **Liaño**, a habitational name from a place so called in Santander province. **2.** Italian: from a short form of the personal name *Eleano, Eliano*, from Latin *Helianus* or *Aelianus*. GIVEN NAMES Spanish 40%; Italian 9%. *Nestor* (3), *Alfredo* (2), *Ernesto* (2), *Javier* (2), *Jose* (2), *Luis* (2), *Ricardo* (2), *Alba, Araceli, Basilio, Bonifacio, Epifanio*; *Antonio* (6), *Leonardo, Romeo.*

Leanos (140) Spanish (common in Bolivia and Mexico; **Leaños**: presumably a derivative of **Leaño** (see LEANO). GIVEN NAMES Spanish 51%. *Jose* (4), *Jaime* (3), *Salvador* (3), *Alvaro* (2), *Fidel* (2), *Javier* (2), *Jesus* (2), *Sergio* (2), *Alejandro, Angel, Carlos, Domingo.*

Leanza (155) Southern Italian: **1.** from Old Italian *leanza* 'loyalty'. **2.** from a reduced form of the female personal name *Allegranza*. GIVEN NAMES Italian 22%. *Vito* (5), *Salvatore* (3), *Carmello* (2), *Alfredo, Carmelo, Francesco, Mario, Orlando, Ricardo.*

Leap (535) Scottish and English: metonymic occupational name for a basketmaker, from Old English *lēap* 'basket'. Compare LEEPER.

Leaper (127) English and Scottish: variant spelling of LEEPER.

Leaphart (284) Americanized spelling of German LIEBHART.

Leapley (132) Americanized spelling of German LIEBLICH.

Lear (2776) **1.** English: habitational name from any of various places in northern France named with the Germanic element *lār* 'clearing'. **2.** English: variant of LAYER. **3.** English: nickname from Old English *hlēor* 'cheek', 'face'. **4.** Irish: reduced Anglicization of Gaelic **Mac Giolla Uidhir** 'son of the swarthy lad' or 'son of the servant of *Odhar*', a byname from *odhar* (genitive *uidhir*) 'dun-colored', 'weatherbeaten'. Compare MCALEER.

Leard (428) Possibly a variant spelling of Scottish or northern Irish LAIRD.

Learman (165) Americanized spelling of German LEHRMANN.

Learn (639) English: possibly a reduced and altered form of Scottish MCLAREN.

Learnard (103) Variant of LEONARD.

Learned (756) **1.** Variant, due to folk etymology, of LEONARD. **2.** Possibly also a translation of French LESAGE.
FOREBEARS William Learned was admitted to the First Church in Charlestown, MA, in 1632, and in 1640 was one of the first settlers of Woburn, MA. One of his better known descendants, Ebenezer, a revolutionary war officer, was born at Oxford, MA, in 1728.

Learner (103) English, German, and Jewish: altered spelling of LERNER. GIVEN NAME Jewish 4%. *Avi.*

Leary (5914) Irish: reduced Americanized form of **Ó Laoghaire**, 'descendant of *Laoghaire*' (see O'LEARY).
GIVEN NAMES Irish 4%. *Brendan* (2), *Brigid*, *Liam*, *Oona*, *Padraic*.

Leas (601) **1.** Scottish and Irish: possibly a reduced and altered form of MCLEISH. **2.** English: see LEES 2. **3.** Americanized form of German LASCH.

Lease (1415) **1.** Scottish and Irish: possibly a reduced and altered form of MCLEISH. **2.** English: see LEES 2.

Leask (261) Scottish: habitational name from a place, now called Pitlurg, in the parish of Slains, Aberdeen. The name is first recorded in 1380 in the form Lask, but its origin is not known.

Leason (177) English: metronymic from LEES 3.

Leasure (1460) Americanized spelling of the French names LEGER (also **Legère**) or LESUEUR.

Leath (1078) English: topographic name for someone who lived by or worked at a barn, Middle English *lathe*, from Old Norse *hlaða*.

Leatham (353) English (West Yorkshire): variant of LATHAM.

Leathem (157) Northern Irish: variant of LATHAM.

Leather (187) English (chiefly Lancashire and Yorkshire): metonymic occupational name for a leatherworker or seller of leather goods, from Middle English *lether*, Old English *leþer* 'leather'.

Leatherberry (166) Variant of English LEATHERBURY.

Leatherbury (210) English (Lancashire): habitational name from an unidentified place. There is a hill in Somerset called Leather Barrow.
FOREBEARS Thomas Leatherbury (1622–73), from Ormskirk, Lancashire, England, arrived in MD in or before 1645, and settled in Accomack Co., VA.

Leatherman (2017) **1.** Jewish (Ashkenazic): Americanized form of **Lederman**, an occupational name for a leather worker or seller of leather goods. **2.** English: occupational name for a leatherworker (see LEATHER).

Leathers (1944) English: patronymic from LEATHER.

Leatherwood (1526) English: perhaps a deliberate alteration of **Leatherhead**, a habitational name from Leatherhead in Surrey, which is named from Celtic *lēd* 'gray' + *rïd* 'ford', or alternatively a habitational name from Lythwood in Shropshire, which is named from Old English *hlið* 'slope' + *wudu* 'wood'.
FOREBEARS Zachariah Leatherwood, son of John Leatherwood, was born in Prince William Co., VA, about 1735. After the revolutionary war, he settled in Spartanburg Co., SC, with his second wife, Jane Calvert, and many of his fourteen children.

Leaton (214) English: habitational name from Leaton in Shropshire. The first element is uncertain, but may be Old English *hlēo* 'shelter' or *(ge)lǣt* 'watercourse' (modern English 'leat'). The second element is Old English *tūn* 'enclosure', 'settlement'.

Leavell (928) Probably a variant of English or French LEVELL.

Leavelle (157) Probably a variant of English or French LEVELL.

Leavens (465) English: variant spelling of LEVENS.

Leavenworth (263) English: habitational name from a lost or unidentified place, possibly Leavenheath in Suffolk.

Leaver (586) English: variant spelling of LEVER.

Leaverton (244) English: variant spelling of LEVERTON.

Leavey (211) **1.** Irish: reduced form of DUNLEAVY. **2.** English: from the Middle English personal name *Lefwi*, Old English *Lēofwīg*, composed of the elements *lēof* 'dear', 'beloved' + *wīg* 'war'.
GIVEN NAMES Irish 4%. *Brendan*, *Kieran*.

Leavins (142) English: variant spelling of LEVINS.

Leavitt (5182) English: **1.** (of Norman origin) nickname from Anglo-Norman French *leuet* 'wolf cub' (see LOW 3). **2.** habitational name from any of the various places in Normandy called Livet. All are of obscure, presumably Gaulish, etymology. **3.** from the Middle English personal name *Lefget*, Old English *Lēofgēat*, composed of the elements *lēof* 'dear', 'beloved' + the tribal name *Gēat* (see JOCELYN). **4.** possibly from an unrecorded Middle English survival of the Old English female personal name *Lēofgȳð*, composed of the elements *lēof* 'dear', 'beloved' + *gȳð* 'battle'.
FOREBEARS Early American Leavitts include John Leavitt, who was born 1608 in England and married in Hingham, MA, in 1637. His descendants spread to NH.

Leavy (738) Reduced form of Irish DUNLEAVY.

Leazenby (133) Variant of English LAZENBY.

Leazer (296) Of French origin: see LEASURE.

Lebar (236) Slovenian: unexplained. Perhaps an altered spelling of German LIEBER.

Lebaron (719) French (**Le Baron**): status name from *baron*, 'vassal', 'nobleman', from Germanic (Frankish) *ber* 'man', 'warrior', that is, a knight who owed service. This name would also have denoted a servant in the household of a baron. The term *baron* was also used in the sense 'husband (of)', and some instances of the surname may be derived from this meaning.

Lebarron (271) Respelling of LEBARON.

Lebeau (1748) French: nickname for a handsome man (perhaps also ironically for an ugly one), from Old French *beu*, *bel* 'fair', 'lovely' (Late Latin *bellus*), with the definite article *le*. Compare BEAU, LEBEL.
GIVEN NAMES French 8%. *Armand* (7), *Normand* (5), *Andre* (3), *Pierre* (3), *Fernand* (2), *Gaston* (2), *Solange* (2), *Adelard*, *Baptiste*, *Cecile*, *Chantel*, *Donat*.

Lebeck (228) German: **1.** habitational name for someone from a place so named near Flensburg in Schleswig-Holstein. **2.** perhaps also from a pet form of a Slavic (Sorbian) personal name formed with *lub-* 'love', 'liking', for example, *Lubomir* or *Luboslav*.

Lebeda (208) Czech: nickname from *lebeda* 'orache' (a plant of the genus *Atriplex*, a fast-growing vegetable grown as a substitute for spinach). This nickname is associated with various idioms in Czech, for example *lebedit si* 'to feel nice and cozy' or 'to have a cushy job', or *dát si do lebedy* 'to tuck into the orache', i.e. 'to eat heartily'.

Lebel (1004) French: variant of LEBEAU.
GIVEN NAMES French 18%. *Andre* (5), *Lucien* (4), *Alphonse* (3), *Armand* (3), *Marcel* (3), *Emile* (2), *Leonce* (2), *Marise* (2), *Monique* (2), *Normand* (2), *Ovila* (2), *Rejean* (2).

Leben (153) **1.** German: of uncertain origin, possibly a habitational name from places called Lebehn in eastern Mecklenburg and Pomerania. **2.** Dutch: from a pet form of the Germanic personal name *Liebrecht* (composed of the elements *liut* 'people', 'tribe' + *berhta* 'bright'). **3.** Altered form of Slovenian **Leban**, which is probably a nickname derived from the archaic word *leb* 'forehead', 'skull'.
GIVEN NAME German 4%. *Kurt*.

Lebens (141) **1.** German: probably a variant of **Lebentzig**, from Middle High German *lebendic* 'alive', a nickname for a lively person. **2.** Dutch: patronymic from a pet form of the Germanic personal names LIEBRECHT or LIEBOLD.

Lebeouf (137) Variant spelling of French LEBOEUF.
GIVEN NAME German 4%. *Kurt*.

Leber (1081) **1.** German: of uncertain origin; possibly a topographic name from Middle High German *lē* (genitive *lēwes*) 'hill', or a northern nickname for a brave or healthy man, from Middle Low German *lēbar(e)* 'leopard'. Compare LEBERT. **2.** Dutch: habitational name from places called Le or Lew, meaning 'hill', from the same word as 1. **3.** Slovenian: unexplained.

Lebert (286) **1.** German: from Middle High German *lēbart* 'leopard', most probably a habitational name for someone living at a house distinguished by the sign of a leopard. **2.** French: from the personal name *Bert*, a short form of any of the Germanic compound names with the final element *berhta* 'bright'.
GIVEN NAMES French 4%. *Alphonse*, *Herve*.

Leblanc (15662) French: variant of BLANC 1 ('white', 'blond', 'pale'), with the definite article *le*.
GIVEN NAMES French 9%. *Armand* (26), *Pierre* (23), *Andre* (20), *Emile* (17), *Jacques* (17), *Camille* (11), *Marcel* (11), *Lucien* (10), *Normand* (9), *Alcide* (8), *Gaston* (8), *Leonce* (8).

Leblang (121) **1.** German and Jewish (Ashkenazic): ornamental name composed of German *leb* 'live' (single imperative form of *leben* 'to live') + *lang* 'long'. **2.** Altered form of French LEBLANC.

Lebleu (352) French: from *bleu* 'blue', with the definite article *le*, a nickname with various senses, in particular a person who habitually wore blue clothes, a person with blue eyes, or a person with a bluish complexion resulting from poor circulation.
GIVEN NAMES French 7%. *Julien* (2), *Pascal* (2), *Aime, Alain, Andre, Olivier, Silton*.

Leblond (348) French: variant of BLOND ('blond', 'fair'), with the definite article *le*.
GIVEN NAMES French 17%. *Andre* (5), *Emile* (2), *Marcel* (2), *Alphonse, Antoine, Benoit, Cecile, Clemence, Germaine, Laurette, Lucien, Normand*.

Lebo (926) Possibly an altered spelling of French LEBEAU.

Leboeuf (1304) French: nickname for a powerfully built man, from *boeuf* 'bull', with the definite article *le*. In some cases it may have been originally a metonymic occupational name for a herdsman. Compare BOUVIER.
GIVEN NAMES French 8%. *Pierre* (5), *Armand* (4), *Camille* (3), *Normand* (3), *Andre* (2), *Emile* (2), *Henri* (2), *Herve* (2), *Camile, Ghislaine, Gilles, Gillis*.

Lebold (187) German: probably an altered form of French **Lebaud** 'the lively (one)', a variant (with fused definite article *le*) of *Baud* (see BAULT).

Lebon (212) French: variant of BON ('good'), with the definite article *le*.
GIVEN NAMES French 17%. *Jacques* (2), *Andre, Armelle, Colette, Hilaire, Luc, Marceau, Reynald, Serge*.

Lebouef (439) Altered spelling of French LEBOEUF.
GIVEN NAMES French 7%. *Albon, Andrus, Easton, Emile, Julien, Lucien, Marcelin, Numa*.

Lebourgeois (105) French: status name for a burgess, a variant of BOURGEOIS, with the definite article *le*.
GIVEN NAMES French 16%; German 4%. *Benoit, Camille, Dreux, Jacques, Julien; Arno*.

Lebovits (125) Jewish (Ashkenazic): variant of LEIBOWITZ.
GIVEN NAMES Jewish 45%; German 7%. *Aron* (3), *Moishe* (3), *Moshe* (3), *Yechiel* (2), *Yehuda* (2), *Yitzchok* (2), *Anchel, Arje, Benzion, Berish, Bernat, Chaim; Benno* (3), *Ignatz*.

Lebovitz (317) Jewish (Ashkenazic): variant of LEIBOWITZ.
GIVEN NAMES Jewish 12%; German 4%. *Miriam* (2), *Aviva, Chaim, Hershel, Hyman, Kopel, Moshe, Sholem, Yehuda, Zvi; Wolf* (3), *Rudie*.

Lebow (659) Americanized spelling of French LEBEAU.

Lebowitz (759) Jewish (Ashkenazic): variant of LEIBOWITZ.
GIVEN NAMES Jewish 10%. *Meyer* (3), *Chaim* (2), *Elimelech* (2), *Miriam* (2), *Arieh, Aron, Asher, Hyman, Leizer, Mayer, Moshe, Naftali*.

Lebrecht (155) German: from a Germanic personal name composed of the elements *liut* 'people', 'tribe' + *berht* 'bright', 'shining'.
GIVEN NAMES German 9%. *Horst* (2), *Hans, Klaus, Kurt*.

Lebreton (185) French: ethnic name for a Breton, a variant of BRETON, with the definite article *le*.
GIVEN NAMES French 9%. *Gilles, Jean-Michael, Jean-Michel, Laurent, Pierre, Serge*.

Lebron (953) Spanish (**Lebrón**): nickname from *lebrón*, an augmentative of *liebre* 'hare' (Latin *lepus*), applied in the sense 'cowardly', 'timid'.
GIVEN NAMES Spanish 44%. *Jose* (26), *Juan* (17), *Carlos* (16), *Luis* (12), *Angel* (9), *Jorge* (7), *Pedro* (7), *Ramon* (7), *Julio* (6), *Miguel* (6), *Ana* (5), *Jesus* (5).

Lebrun (1221) French: variant of BRUN ('brown'), with the definite article *le*. This is a name associated with the Huguenots in the U.S.
GIVEN NAMES French 13%. *Pierre* (7), *Fernand* (5), *Normand* (5), *Andre* (3), *Emile* (2), *Herve* (2), *Lucien* (2), *Michel* (2), *Yves* (2), *Adelard, Dominique, Edouard*.

Lebsack (259) German: of uncertain origin. **1.** possibly from an altered form of a Slavic personal name. **2.** alternatively, perhaps, an altered form of the sentence name **Lebsacht**, North German equivalent of **Lebsanft** 'live pleasantly'.

Lebsock (123) Variant of German LEBSACK.

Lebus (98) German: habitational name from a place in Brandenburg named Lebus.

Lecates (213) English: variant of **Lecatt**, which is most probably a variant of LEGGETT.
FOREBEARS John Lecatt was born in VA during 1642. His descendants have borne the surnames **Lecatt, Lecat, Lecate, Lecates, Lecato, Lekate, Lekates, Lekites**, and **Legates**. The family lived first in Accomack Co., VA. By the 1790s most had moved north to MD and DE.

Lecce (136) Italian: habitational name from any of the places called Lecce, notably the city in Apulia.

GIVEN NAMES Italian 22%. *Gino* (2), *Vito* (2), *Angelo, Filippo, Lucio, Luigi, Maddalena, Orazio, Rocco, Vincenzo, Vittorio*.

Leccese (191) Italian: ethnic name denoting a person from LECCE.
GIVEN NAMES Italian 22%. *Cosmo* (3), *Salvatore* (3), *Gaetano* (2), *Pasquale* (2), *Alessandro, Libero, Vito*.

Lech (499) **1.** Polish and Czech: from the personal name *Lech*, often chosen as a patriotic name among Poles. According to Slavic legend, three brothers, *Lech, Czech*, and *Rus*, founded the nations of the Poles, Czechs, and Russians respectively. In Czech the term *Lech* denotes a Pole. **2.** North German: from a byname for a mean person, from Middle Low German *lēch* 'low', 'bad', 'mean'.
GIVEN NAMES Polish 8%; German 4%. *Agnieszka* (2), *Miroslaw* (2), *Piotr* (2), *Alicja, Andrzej, Irena, Kazimierz, Ryszard, Szczepan, Wieslaw, Zdzislaw; Klaus* (2), *Monika, Otto*.

Lecher (266) Americanized form of German **Löcher** (see LOCHER).

Lechleitner (118) **1.** South German: habitational name for someone from Lechleiten in Tyrol, Austria. **2.** Variant of LEGLEITER.

Lechler (153) German and Alsatian: nickname for a man with a crafty or cunning smile, Middle High German *lechelaere*.

Lechman (230) Variant spelling of German **Lechmann**, a variant of LEHMANN 1.

Lechner (1682) German: **1.** status name for a feudal tenant or vassal, Middle High German *lēhenære* 'feudal tenant', 'vassal'. Compare LEHMANN. **2.** habitational name for someone from any of several places called Lehen, especially in Bavaria.
GIVEN NAMES German 5%. *Kurt* (5), *Alois* (2), *Johann* (2), *Christoph, Erna, Ewald, Franz, Hans, Hartmut, Inge, Manfred, Otto*.

Lechowicz (146) Polish: patronymic from the personal name LECH.
GIVEN NAMES Polish 8%. *Andrzej, Leszek, Stanislawa, Wieslaw*.

Lechtenberg (260) Americanized spelling of German LICHTENBERG.
GIVEN NAMES German 4%. *Kurt* (2), *Fritz*.

Lechuga (343) Spanish (southeast Spain): metonymic occupational name for a grower or seller of lettuces, from *lechuga* 'lettuce' (Latin *lactuca*).
GIVEN NAMES Spanish 52%. *Jesus* (10), *Juan* (6), *Carlos* (5), *Jose* (5), *Manuel* (5), *Alfredo* (4), *Luis* (4), *Armando* (3), *Eusebio* (3), *Jaime* (3), *Mario* (3), *Miguel* (3); *Carmela* (2), *Antonio, Carmelo, Cecilio, Eliseo, Heriberto, Luciano*.

Leck (391) **1.** English: variant of LEAKE. **2.** German: habitational name from a place so named in Schleswig-Holstein. **3.** German: probably an altered spelling of LECH.

Lecker (157) German: derogatory nickname a sycophant or sponger, from an agent derivative of *lecken* 'to lick'.

Leckey (211) Northern Irish spelling of LECKIE.

Leckie (441) **1.** Scottish: habitational name from a place in the parish of Gargunnock, in Stirlingshire, so called from Gaelic *leac* 'flagstone' + the locative suffix *-ach* (i.e. 'place of flagstones'). **2.** Americanized spelling of Polish **Łęcki**.

Leckner (127) Altered spelling of German LECHNER.

Leckrone (294) Origin unidentified. Compare LECRONE.

Lecky (131) Northern Irish spelling of LECKIE.

Leclair (3179) **1.** French: from the adjective *clair* 'bright', 'light'. Generally this would have been a nickname for a cheerful individual, although derivation from the personal name *Clair* (see CLARE) is also possible. **2.** North American spelling variant of LECLERC.
GIVEN NAMES French 7%. *Marcel* (10), *Andre* (4), *Armand* (4), *Emile* (4), *Normand* (4), *Gaston* (3), *Adrien* (2), *Antoine* (2), *Lucien* (2), *Monique* (2), *Philias* (2), *Camille*.

Leclaire (1012) Respelling of French LECLAIR.
GIVEN NAMES French 7%. *Lucien* (4), *Andre* (2), *Marcel* (2), *Alban*, *Alphonse*, *Armand*, *Cyrille*, *Laurent*, *Leontine*, *Normand*, *Raymonde*, *Reynald*.

Leclear (103) Part-translation of French LECLAIR.

Leclerc (1238) **1.** French: from *le clerc* 'the clerk', occupational name for a scribe or secretary (see CLERC, CLARK). **2.** North American spelling variant of LECLAIR, LECLERF.
GIVEN NAMES French 20%. *Armand* (6), *Andre* (5), *Jacques* (5), *Normand* (5), *Adrien* (3), *Alain* (3), *Gilles* (3), *Laurier* (3), *Serge* (3), *Cecile* (2), *Colette* (2), *Francois* (2).

Leclercq (196) French: variant spelling of LECLERC.
GIVEN NAMES French 15%. *Pierre* (2), *Francois*, *Honore*, *Jacques*, *Laurent*, *Lucien*, *Toussaint*.

Leclere (244) **1.** French (**Leclère**): metronymic from a female personal name from the dialect word *clère* 'clear' (modern French *clair(e)*), with the definite article *le*, which was feminine in the old Picard dialect. The surname may also be derived from a place in Seine-Maritime called Clère, which comes from the name of a river which rises there, La Clères 'clear river'. **2.** North American spelling variant of LECLAIR or LECLERC.

Lecocq (157) French: nickname from *cocq* 'cock', 'cockerel' (see COCKE), with the definite article *le*.
GIVEN NAMES French 5%. *Cecile*, *Emile*.

Lecompte (1103) French: variant of LECONTE.
GIVEN NAMES French 7%. *Andrus* (2), *Easton* (2), *Emile* (2), *Adelard*, *Armand*, *Elrick*,

Julien, *Laurent*, *Leonce*, *Marcel*, *Monique*, *Normand*.

Lecomte (298) French: variant of LECONTE.
GIVEN NAMES French 17%. *Monique* (2), *Normand* (2), *Alain*, *Armand*, *Cecile*, *Dominique*, *Francois*, *Germain*, *Gilles*, *Gregoire*, *Huguette*, *Pierre*.

Leconte (189) French: from the Old French title of rank *conte* 'count', either a nickname or an occupational name for a servant in the household of a count.
GIVEN NAMES French 18%; German 4%. *Andre*, *Herve*, *Jean Louis*, *Pierre*, *Raoul*, *Raynald*, *Wesner*, *Yves*; *Fritz*, *Rommel*.

Lecoq (116) French: nickname for a vain, strutting man, from *coq* 'rooster' (from Old French *coc*), with the definite article *le*.
GIVEN NAMES French 8%; Irish 6%. *Jacques*, *Jean-Marc*, *Philippe*.

Lecount (302) Americanized form of French LECONTE.

Lecours (158) Probably an altered spelling of French **Lecourt**, a nickname for a small man, or ironically for a large man, from Old French *cort* 'short', with the definite article *le*; alternatively, it could be a respelling of LACOUR.
GIVEN NAMES French 21%. *Aime*, *Alain*, *Andre*, *Emile*, *Jean Guy*, *Jean Louis*, *Liette*, *Marcel*, *Michel*, *Normand*, *Pierre*.

Lecrone (281) Origin unidentified. Compare LECKRONE.

Lecroy (642) Probably an Americanized spelling of LACROIX.

Lecuyer (545) French (**Lécuyer**): from *écuyer*, originally meaning 'shield-bearer' (Latin *scutarius*, a derivative of *scutum* 'shield'). This became a status name for a man belonging to the social rank immediately below that of knight. The surname came to America with the Huguenots. It is sometimes translated as COOK; the original term having lost transparency of meaning, it was taken as a derivative of *cuire* 'to cook'.
GIVEN NAMES French 10%. *Alcide* (2), *Jacques* (2), *Marcel* (2), *Alain*, *Armand*, *Aurele*, *Emile*, *Laure*, *Lucienne*, *Michel*, *Monique*, *Pierre*.

Lecy (192) Probably an altered form of Irish LACY.

Leday (187) **1.** Irish: variant of LEDDY. **2.** Americanized spelling of French **Le Dé** (see LEDET).
GIVEN NAMES French 8%. *Alcide*, *Curley*, *Murphy*.

Ledbetter (7031) English: occupational name for a worker in lead, Middle English *ledbetere*, from Old English *lēad* 'lead' + the agent noun from *bēatan* 'to beat'.

Ledden (175) English: variant spelling of LEDDON.

Leddon (147) English: habitational name from Leadon or Upleadon in Herefordshire, or Highleadon or Upleadon in Gloucestershire, all named from the Leadon

river, which derives its name from British *litano-* 'broad'.
GIVEN NAMES Scandinavian 4%. *Bjorn*, *Hilmer*.

Leddy (1009) Irish: reduced Anglicized form of Gaelic **Ó Lideadha** 'descendant of *Lideadh*', a personal name of unexplained origin.
GIVEN NAMES Irish 5%. *Brendan* (4), *Liam*.

Ledeboer (103) Dutch: according to Debrabandere, a habitational name from Ledeburg in Hannover, Lower Saxony.

Leder (651) **1.** German and Jewish (Ashkenazic): metonymic occupational name for a tanner or leatherworker, from Middle High German and Yiddish *leder*, German *Leder* 'leather'. **2.** Hungarian (**Ledér**): nickname from the archaic Hungarian word *ledér* 'frivolous'.
GIVEN NAMES Jewish 4%. *Emanuel* (3), *Miriam* (3), *Arie*, *Hershy*, *Mandel*, *Shalom*.

Lederer (1156) South German, Alsatian, and Jewish (Ashkenazic): occupational name for a tanner or leatherworker, Middle High German *lēderære*, German *Lederer*.
FOREBEARS The first known immigrant bearing this name, John (Johannes) Lederer, was a traveler and explorer who came to VA from Germany in 1668. He was ill-treated by the inhabitants of VA and fled for his life to MD, where he was naturalized in 1671.
GIVEN NAMES German 5%. *Kurt* (3), *Otto* (3), *Alois*, *Ernst*, *Gerda*, *Helmut*, *Horst*, *Monika*, *Walther*.

Lederle (122) South German: diminutive of LEDER.
GIVEN NAME German 4%. *Bernd*.

Lederman (1221) German (**Ledermann**), Dutch, and Jewish (Ashkenazic): occupational name for a leatherworker or seller of leather goods, from Middle High German, Middle Dutch *leder*, German *Leder* 'leather' + *-man(n)* 'man'.
GIVEN NAMES Jewish 6%. *Sol* (4), *Emanuel* (2), *Meyer* (2), *Zev* (2), *Dvora*, *Irit*, *Kopel*, *Leib*, *Moshe*, *Surie*, *Zelik*.

Ledermann (110) German: see LEDERMAN.
GIVEN NAME German 6%. *Ernst* (2).

Ledesma (1932) Spanish: habitational name from any of the places called Ledesma, in the provinces of Logroño, Salamanca, and Soria. The place name is ancient and probably derives from a superlative form of a Celtic adjective meaning 'broad', 'wide'.
GIVEN NAMES Spanish 45%. *Jose* (51), *Juan* (25), *Jesus* (21), *Manuel* (17), *Miguel* (15), *Luis* (14), *Salvador* (14), *Javier* (13), *Mario* (12), *Carlos* (9), *Rafael* (9), *Alberto* (8).

Ledet (1342) Americanized spelling of French **Le Dé**, a nickname for a gambler, meaning 'the die'.
FOREBEARS The LA Ledets trace their ancestry perhaps to J.-F. Le Dée, who emigrated from Lille, France, c.1750. Another branch

is descended from an Antoine Le Dé of west-central France (1780).

GIVEN NAMES French 8%. *Cecile* (4), *Emile* (4), *Leonce* (4), *Angelle*, *Antoine*, *Aurelie*, *Camille*, *Curley*, *Etienne*, *Ferrel*, *Gillis*, *Gisele*.

Ledezma (438) Spanish: variant spelling of LEDESMA.

GIVEN NAMES Spanish 59%. *Jose* (14), *Jesus* (12), *Juan* (12), *Manuel* (8), *Ruben* (7), *Pedro* (6), *Arturo* (5), *Carlos* (5), *Francisco* (5), *Guadalupe* (4), *Raul* (4), *Emilio* (3).

Ledford (6275) English: habitational name, probably from either of two places called Lydford, in Devon and Somerset. The first is named with the river name *Lyd* (from Old English *hlȳde* 'noisy stream') + Old English *ford*, i.e. 'ford over the Lyd river'. Lydford in Somerset was named 'ford over the noisy stream', from Old English *hlȳde* + *ford*.

Ledger (749) English: **1.** from a Norman personal name, *Leodegar*, Old French *Legier*, of Germanic origin, composed of the elements *liut* 'people', 'tribe' + *gēr*, *gār* 'spear'. The name was borne by a 7th-century bishop of Autun, whose fame contributed to the popularity of the name in France. (In Germany the name was connected with a different saint, an 8th-century bishop of Münster.) **2.** variant of LETCHER, in part a deliberate alteration to avoid the association with Middle English *lecheor* 'lecher'.

Ledgerwood (579) Scottish: habitational name from a place so named in Berwickshire.

Ledin (271) Swedish: ornamental name composed of an unidentified first element + the suffix *-in*, from Latin *-in(i)us* 'descendant of'.

Ledingham (125) Scottish (Aberdeen): probably a local habitational name from an unidentified place, possibly Ledikin in Culsalmond, which is recorded in 1600 as *Ledinghame*. Compare LEADINGHAM.

Ledington (103) English: habitational name, probably from places called Liddington, in Wiltshire and Rutland. The first is named fom Old English *hlȳde* 'loud, noisy stream' + *tūn* 'farmstead'.

Ledlow (321) Variant of English LUDLOW or Scottish LAIDLAW.

Ledman (125) Swedish: ornamental name from an unidentified first element + *man* 'man'.

Ledo (158) **1.** Spanish, Galician, and Portuguese: nickname from *ledo* 'happy', 'joyful' (Latin *laetus*). **2.** Catalan: variant spelling of **Lledó**, a habitational name from Lledó d'Empordà in Girona province.

GIVEN NAMES Spanish 28%. *Jose* (5), *Manuel* (4), *Juan* (3), *Dalia* (2), *Gustavo* (2), *Miguel* (2), *Ramon* (2), *Alfonso*, *Amado*, *Emilio*, *Felipe*, *Jorge*.

Le Donne (407) Italian: from the plural of *la donna* 'the woman', in the sense 'from

the house of the women', probably an occupational name for someone who worked at a convent.

GIVEN NAMES Italian 13%. *Gino* (5), *Emelio* (2), *Sal* (2), *Salvatore* (2), *Angelo*, *Antonio*, *Costantino*, *Erminio*, *Fiore*, *Gennaro*, *Italo*.

Ledoux (2209) French: nickname from *le doux* 'the sweet (one)' (from Old French *dolz*, *dous*). This name is often translated as SWEET, and translations to **Fresh** are also attested. See also LADUE.

GIVEN NAMES French 8%. *Marcel* (5), *Andre* (4), *Armand* (4), *Pierre* (4), *Gabrielle* (3), *Lucien* (3), *Camille* (2), *Colette* (2), *Donat* (2), *Normand* (2), *Adrien*, *Aime*.

Ledsome (122) English: habitational name from either of two places, in Cheshire and West Yorkshire, called Ledsham. The first is named with the Old English personal name *Lēofede* + Old English *hām* 'homestead' and the second is recorded in Domesday Book as *Ledesham* 'homestead within the district of Leeds'.

GIVEN NAME German 5%. *Otto*.

Leduc (1694) French: nickname for someone who gave himself airs and graces, from the Old French title of rank *duc* 'duke' (from Latin *dux* 'leader', genitive *ducis*), or else an occupational name for a servant employed in a ducal household.

GIVEN NAMES French 13%. *Marcel* (7), *Gilles* (6), *Andre* (3), *Emile* (3), *Henri* (3), *Jacques* (3), *Michel* (3), *Monique* (3), *Pierre* (3), *Cecile* (2), *Evariste* (2), *Alcid*.

Ledvina (236) Origin unidentified; perhaps Slavic, from the vocabulary word *ledvo* 'hardly'.

Ledwell (205) English: habitational name from Ledwell in Oxfordshire, named in Old English as 'loud spring' or 'loud stream', from *Hlȳde* (a river-name derived from *hlūd* 'loud', i.e. 'roaring stream', 'torrent') + *wella* 'well', 'spring', or 'stream'.

Ledwith (276) English: probably a derivative of the old personal name *Lutwidge* (Latin *Lodovicus*) (see LUDWIG). This name is also established in Ireland.

Ledyard (262) English: variant of LIDDIARD.

FOREBEARS Revolutionary soldier William Ledyard was born at Groton, CT, in 1738, a descendant of John Ledyard who sailed from Bristol, England, and settled in CT. The celebrated traveler John Ledyard (1751–89) was William's nephew and was also born in Groton.

Lee (180338) **1.** English: topographic name for someone who lived near a meadow or a patch of arable land, Middle English *lee*, *lea*, from Old English *lēa*, dative case (used after a preposition) of *lēah*, which originally meant 'wood' or 'glade'. **2.** English: habitational name from any of the many places named with Old English *lēah* 'wood', 'glade', as for example Lee in Buckinghamshire, Essex, Hampshire, Kent, and Shropshire, and Lea in Cheshire,

Derbyshire, Herefordshire, Lancashire, Lincolnshire, and Wiltshire. **3.** Irish: reduced Americanized form of **Ó Laoidhigh** 'descendant of *Laoidheach*', a personal name derived from *laoidh* 'poem', 'song' (originally a byname for a poet). **4.** Americanized spelling of Norwegian LI or LIE. **5.** Chinese 李: variant of LI 1. **6.** Chinese 黎: variant of LI 2. **7.** Chinese 利: variant of LI 3. **8.** Korean: variant of YI.

FOREBEARS Lee is a prominent VA family name brought over in 1641 by Richard Lee (d. 1664), a VA planter and legislator. His great-grandsons included the brothers Arthur, Francis L., Richard Henry, and William Lee, all prominent American Revolution legislators and diplomats. The Civil War Confederate General Robert E. Lee was the son of Henry 'Lighthorse Harry' Lee (1756–1818), another revolutionary war hero.

GIVEN NAMES Chinese/Korean 7%. *Young* (497), *Sang* (324), *Jae* (214), *Jong* (210), *Jung* (208), *Sung* (206), *Yong* (205), *Kyung* (159), *Seung* (145), *Dong* (130), *Kwang* (122), *Myung* (105).

Leeb (175) **1.** South German: from Middle High German *lewe* 'lion', dialect *lēb*, used either as a nickname for a brave or regal person, or as a habitational name from a house sign. **2.** Americanized spelling of LIEB or LOEB.

GIVEN NAMES German 7%. *Franz*, *Franziska*, *Gunter*, *Lothar*.

Leece (198) English: **1.** from a medieval female personal name, *Lece*, a short form of *Lettice* (Latin *Laetitia*, meaning 'happiness', 'gaiety'). **2.** variant of LEES.

Leech (2042) **1.** English: variant spelling of LEACH. **2.** Irish (Galway): English name adopted as equivalent of Gaelic **Ó Maol Mhaodhóg** (see LOGUE).

Leed (255) English: topographic name for someone who lived near a loud, rushing stream, Old English *hlȳde*, or a habitational name from Lead in West Yorkshire, which is named from Old English *lǣd* 'water course' or Old English *hlēda* 'ledge'.

Leeder (309) English (Norfolk): variant spelling of LEADER 1.

Leedham (129) English: variant of LATHAM.

Leedom (469) English: variant of LATHAM.

Leeds (1749) English: habitational name from the city in West Yorkshire, or the place in Kent. The former is of British origin, appearing in Bede in the form *Loidis* 'People of the *Lāt*', (*Lāt* being an earlier name of the river Aire, meaning 'the violent one'). Loidis was originally a district name, but was subsequently restricted to the city. The Kentish place name may be from an Old English stream name *hlȳde* 'loud, rushing stream'.

FOREBEARS Daniel Leeds (1652–1720) was born in England, probably in Nottinghamshire, and emigrated to America with his father, Thomas, some time in the third quarter of the 17th century. The family settled in Shrewsbury, NJ, in 1677. Daniel made almanacs and was surveyor general of the Province of West Jersey in 1682. He was married four times and had numerous children.

Leedy (1187) Americanized spelling of Swiss German (Alemannic) **Lüthi**, **Lüdy**, or **Lüty**, pet forms of the personal name *Lüthold* (see LUTHI).
FOREBEARS The surname Leedy was brought to OH from Switzerland in 1744 by Johann (John) Leedy.

Leef (131) English: variant spelling of LEAF.
GIVEN NAME French 4%. *Andre*.

Leek (1073) **1.** English: variant spelling of LEAKE. **2.** Dutch (**de Leek**): nickname for an uneducated or ignorant person, from Dutch *leek* 'layman'.

Leeke (109) Northern English: variant spelling of LEAKE.

Leeks (130) Northern English: variant of LEAKE.

Leeman (1042) **1.** Dutch: status name for a feudal tenant or vassal, *leenman*. Compare LEHMANN 1. **2.** English: variant of LEAMAN.

Leeming (175) English: habitational name from either of two places, in West Yorkshire near Keighley and in North Yorkshire near Northallerton. Both are named with a river name, derived from the Old English word *lēoma* 'gleam', 'sparkle'.

Leemon (171) English and Dutch: variant of LEEMAN.

Leen (370) English: **1.** probably a habitational name from 'The Leen' (earlier *Leon*, 'at the streams') in Hereford or the Leen river in Nottinghamshire. Both are derived from a Celtic root verb *lei-* 'flow' (for example as in Welsh *lliant* 'stream'). **2.** variant spelling of LEAN.

Leenhouts (116) Dutch: from Middle Dutch *leenhouder* 'vassal', 'feudal tenant'. Compare LEEMAN 1.
GIVEN NAMES Dutch 5%. *Pieter*, *Willem*.

Leep (320) Of uncertain origin; perhaps an English and Scottish metonymic occupational name for a basket maker, from Old English *lēap* 'basket' (see LEEPER).

Leeper (2418) English and Scottish: **1.** from Middle English *le(a)pere*, an occupational name for a basket maker (from Old English *lēap* 'basket'). **2.** occupational name or nickname for a dancer, runner, or courier (Old English *hlēapere*).

Leer (463) **1.** Dutch: from a reduced form of the personal name *Hilaire* (Latin *Hilarius*). **2.** Danish: habitational name from a place so called in northern Germany, near Oldenburg. **3.** Danish: from *ler* 'clay', possibly a topographic name for someone who lived on clay or an occupational name for someone who extracted or used it.

Lees (2276) **1.** English and Scottish: topographic name from Middle English *lees*

'fields', 'arable land', plural of *lee* (see LEE), or from Middle English *lese* 'pasture', 'meadow' (Old English *lǣs*). **2.** English: habitational name from Leece or Lees in Lancashire, or Leese in Cheshire, all named from Old English *lēas* 'woodland clearings' (plural of *lēah*), or from Leece in Cumbria, which was probably named with a Celtic word, *liss* 'hall', 'court', 'the principal house in a district'. **3.** English: variant spelling of LEECE 1. **4.** Scottish: reduced form of GILLIES. **5.** Scottish and Irish: reduced and altered form of MCLEISH. **6.** Dutch: variant of LEYS.

Leese (647) **1.** Variant spelling of English and Scottish LEES. **2.** German: habitational name from a place so named near Hannover.

Leeser (193) German: habitational name for someone from LEESE.
GIVEN NAME German 4%. *Fritz*.

Leesman (123) Possibly an altered spelling of German **Leesemann**, a variant of LEESER.

Leeson (721) English (chiefly Northamptonshire): metronymic from LEECE 1.

Leet (762) English: topographic name for someone who lived by a watercourse or road junction, Old English *gelǣt*, or a habitational name from Leat in Devon, or The Leete in Essex, named with this element.

Leetch (198) English: variant spelling of LEACH 1.

Leete (333) English: variant of LEET.
FOREBEARS An early American bearer of this name was one of the founders of Guilford, CT. William Leete (*c.* 1613–83), a colonial governor of New Haven colony and CT, was born at Dodington, Huntingtonshire, England. He converted to Puritanism and sailed for America to escape persecution in May 1639.

Leeth (427) Variant spelling of Scottish LEITH.

Leever (250) Dutch (**de Leever**): unexplained.

Leezer (126) Probably of French origin. See LEASURE.

Lefave (229) **1.** Variant of French LEFEVRE, altered by folk etymology as if it were from *fave* 'bean' (see LAFAVE). **2.** Italian (Sicily; **Le Fave**): from *le fave*, plural of *fava* 'broad bean' (see FAVA).

Lefcourt (118) Origin unidentified.

Lefeber (299) Americanized spelling of French LEFEBRE.

Lefebre (185) French: variant of LEFEVRE.
GIVEN NAME French 4%. *Amedee*.

Lefebure (97) French (**Lefébure**): variant of LEFEBVRE. This form arose from the interchangeability of *u* and *v* in the written and printed word throughout the Middle Ages and Renaissance.
GIVEN NAMES French 7%. *Armand*, *Henri*.

Lefebvre (2568) French: variant of LEFÈVRE. The *-b-* occurs in this form of the

name by reason of hypercorrection influenced by the Latin word *faber* 'craftsman'.
GIVEN NAMES French 16%. *Andre* (13), *Armand* (10), *Lucien* (9), *Jacques* (8), *Normand* (8), *Yvon* (8), *Marcel* (7), *Pierre* (4), *Gaston* (3), *Gilles* (3), *Henri* (3), *Philippe* (3).

Lefever (1281) **1.** New England and Canadian form of LEFEVRE. **2.** English form of LEFEVRE, transmitted through Anglo-Norman French.

Lefevers (264) Variant of LEFEVER.

Lefevre (2052) French (**Lefèvre**): occupational name for an ironworker or smith, Old French *fevre*. One of the most common names in France from an early date, this was taken to Britain and Ireland by the Normans, by the French to Canada, and by the Huguenots (with the variant form **Lefebre**) to colonial America and elsewhere. In Canada, there were so many bearers of this name that many nicknames and epithets (secondary surnames or 'dit' names) were employed to distinguish between one family and another. Thus, for example, the Lefevre called *Descoteaux* became HILL by translation, and the Lefevre called *Boulanger* became BAKER. Since *fevre* 'smith' had ceded as a general vocabulary word to *forgeron* in French, the meaning of the name was no longer understood; in some cases it was reconstructed as *Lafeve* (Latin *faba*) and translated as BEAN.
GIVEN NAMES French 6%. *Andre* (3), *Emile* (2), *Jacques* (2), *Joffre* (2), *Luc* (2), *Adrien*, *Antoine*, *Armand*, *Camille*, *Eunide*, *Francois*, *Germaine*.

Leff (1159) Americanized spelling of Jewish LEV.
GIVEN NAMES Jewish 4%. *Miriam* (2), *Sol* (2), *Avraham*, *Hyman*, *Isadore*, *Mort*, *Shira*, *Yaakov*.

Leffel (665) German and Jewish (Ashkenazic): metonymic occupational name for a maker or seller of spoons, Middle High German *leffel*, Yiddish *lefl* 'spoon'.

Leffelman (128) Jewish (Ashkenazic): metonymic occupational name for a maker or seller of spoons, an elaborated form of LEFFEL.

Leffers (106) Dutch and German: variant of LEFFERTS.
GIVEN NAME German 5%. *Kurt* (2).

Leffert (236) **1.** Dutch and North German: nickname for someone thought to resemble a leopard, from Dutch *lefert* 'leopard'. **2.** Dutch, North German, and Frisian: short form from the Germanic personal name *Liubhart*, composed of *liob* 'dear' + *hart* 'strong'.

Lefferts (243) Dutch or North German: patronymic from LEFFERT.

Leffew (364) Probably of French origin, a much altered form of Lafoy (see FOY). This is a frequent name in LA.

Leffingwell (497) English: habitational name from a lost place in Essex (probably near Pebmarsh) recorded in Domesday Book as *Liffildeuuella* 'spring or stream (Old English *wella*) of a woman named Lēofhild'.

Leffler (2007) German: occupational name for a maker or seller of spoons, a variant of LOEFFLER.

Lefko (132) Jewish (eastern Ashkenazic): from the personal name *Lewko* (see LEWKOWICZ).

Lefkowitz (1298) Jewish: Germanized spelling of LEWKOWICZ.
GIVEN NAMES Jewish 13%. *Miriam* (7), *Sol* (6), *Chaim* (4), *Emanuel* (3), *Hyman* (3), *Aron* (2), *Hershel* (2), *Moshe* (2), *Aba*, *Aharon*, *Akiva*, *Avi*.

Lefler (1426) Jewish (Ashkenazic): variant of LOEFFLER.

Leflore (533) French: unexplained; perhaps an altered form of German LEFFLER or **Löffler** (see LOEFFLER).
FOREBEARS Antoine Leflore (b. *c.* 1763 in Alsace-Lorraine) was a fur trader who migrated from France to Canada, and from there to New Orleans, then up the Mississipi River to Ste. Genevieve Co., Mo.

Lefor (114) Most probably a variant of French LEFORT.

Leforce (145) Variant of French LAFORCE.

Lefort (416) French and English: from Old French *fort* 'strong', 'brave' (see FORT), with the definite article *le*.
GIVEN NAMES French 11%. *Julien* (2), *Michel* (2), *Arsene*, *Camille*, *Emile*, *Etienne*, *Laurent*, *Leonce*, *Ludger*, *Monique*, *Normand*, *Pierre*.

Lefrancois (290) French (**Lefrançois**): 1. literally 'the French' or 'the Frenchman', probably a regional name for someone who came from the Île de France. In the Middle Ages the French king held sway over a smaller territory than present-day France, and its boundaries tended to vary, but the Île de France was always at its center. 2. from the personal name *François*, Latin *Franciscus* (see FRANCIS).
GIVEN NAMES French 20%. *Camille* (2), *Adelard*, *Alphonse*, *Andre*, *Armand*, *Cecile*, *Donat*, *Emile*, *Francoise*, *Gaetan*, *Gilles*, *Henri*.

Lefton (253) English: 1. habitational name, perhaps from Lepton in West Yorkshire, which is named from Old English *hlēp* 'leap' (hence 'cliff', 'steep slope') + *tūn* 'enclosure', 'settlement'. 2. probably a variant of LEVERTON.
GIVEN NAME Jewish 6%. *Mendy*.

Leftridge (186) English: possibly a variant of **Lefridge**, from the Middle English personal name *Lefric*, Old English *Lēofrīc*, a compound of *lēof* 'dear', 'beloved' + *rīc* 'power'.

Leftwich (1294) English: habitational name from Leftwich in Cheshire, so named from the Old English female personal name *Lēoftǣt* + *wīc* 'dairy farm', 'settlement'.

Legacy (226) Origin unidentified.

Legall (105) Respelling of French **Légal**, a nickname for a loyal person, from a variant of Old French *leial*.
GIVEN NAMES French 24%. *Yves* (2), *Aliette*, *Francois*, *Jean Luc*, *Michel*, *Mireille*.

Legan (409) English: unexplained.

Legard (155) 1. English (Yorkshire): from a Norman female personal name, *Legard*, derived from the Germanic name *Liutgard* (borne by Charlemagne's wife), composed of the elements *liut* 'people', 'tribe' + *gard* 'enclosure'. 2. French: metonymic occupational name for a gardener, or status name for someone who owned garden, from Old French *gard* 'garden' with the definite article *le*.

Legare (501) French (**Legaré**): nickname from the past participle of Old French *esgarer* 'to be troubled or abandoned'.
GIVEN NAMES French 9%. *Armand* (3), *Adrien*, *Andre*, *Gisele*, *Jean-Jacques*, *Lucien*, *Philippe*, *Pierre*.

Legaspi (347) Basque (**Legazpi**): topographic name from Basque *le(g)a* 'gravel', 'pebble' + *azpi* 'lower part', or habitational name from a place called Legazpi in Gipuzkoa.
GIVEN NAMES Spanish 38%. *Jaime* (3), *Luis* (3), *Ruben* (3), *Angel* (2), *Arturo* (2), *Ernesto* (2), *Francisco* (2), *Isidro* (2), *Jesus* (2), *Jose* (2), *Manuel* (2), *Milagros* (2); *Dante* (2), *Romeo* (2), *Antonio*, *Ernani*, *Lorenzo*, *Quirino*.

Legate (384) 1. English: variant spelling of LEGGETT. 2. English: from a medieval personal name, a variant of LEGARD 1 or LEGER 1. 3. French (Breton): nickname from Breton *gad* 'hare', with the *le*.

Legates (147) English: variant of LEGGETT. Compare LECATES.

Legato (129) Italian: from *legato* 'legate', 'envoy of the Roman Catholic Church', presumably either a nickname for one who gave himself the air of a papal legate, or an occupational name for someone in the service of a legate.
GIVEN NAMES Italian 10%. *Antonio*, *Carmelo*, *Luciano*, *Rocco*, *Salvatore*.

Legault (740) French: topographic name from Old French *gaut* 'wood', or a habitational name from any of various places named with this word, for example in Loir-et-Cher, Marne, and Eure-et-Loire.
GIVEN NAMES French 13%. *Marcel* (3), *Yves* (3), *Jacques* (2), *Jean-Francois* (2), *Laurent* (2), *Andre*, *Berthe*, *Cecile*, *Celine*, *Emile*, *Etienne*, *Gaetan*.

Lege (304) French: of uncertain origin. With two syllables (**Legé**), it may be a variant of French **Le Gai**, a nickname for a cheerful person (see GAY, DUGAY).
GIVEN NAMES French 9%. *Alphie*, *Emile*, *Gaston*, *Henri*, *Leonce*, *Minus*, *Numa*, *Pierre*, *Raywood*, *Rodolph*.

Legel (106) Probably an Americanized form of French LEGAULT.

Legendre (642) French: status name from Old French *gendre* 'son-in-law', with the definite article *le*. See also GENDRON. This is a Huguenot name.
GIVEN NAMES French 12%. *Emile* (2), *Henri* (2), *Norvin* (2), *Oneil* (2), *Aime*, *Alain*, *Alberic*, *Alcide*, *Alphonse*, *Andre*, *Armand*, *Gabrielle*.

Leger (3256) 1. French (**Léger**) and English: from the Germanic personal name *Leodegar* (see LEDGER). 2. French: nickname from *léger* 'light', 'superficial'. 3. English: see LETCHER. 4. Dutch (also **de Leger**): occupational name from Middle Dutch *legger*, *ligger* 'bailiff', 'tax collector'.
FOREBEARS A Leger from Normandy, France, was in Quebec City by 1644; another was in Montreal by 1659. One from Limousin, France, was in Quebec City by 1691; another, from Paris, was there by 1706; and a third, from Poitou, France, arrived in 1711.
GIVEN NAMES French 10%. *Andre* (7), *Camille* (7), *Lucien* (4), *Pierre* (4), *Yvon* (4), *Antoine* (3), *Aurele* (3), *Emile* (3), *Jacques* (3), *Marcel* (3), *Zoel* (3), *Adelard* (2).

Legere (828) French (**Légère**): from a *légère*, feminine form of LEGER 2.
GIVEN NAMES French 10%. *Emile* (6), *Armand* (3), *Normand* (3), *Aurele* (2), *Jacques* (2), *Adelard*, *Alban*, *Antoine*, *Desire*, *Eloi*, *Monique*, *Yvon*.

Legerski (120) Polish: derivative of Old Polish *legier* 'camp', 'warehouse', a derivative of German LAGER.

Legette (449) Variant spelling of English LEGGETT.

Legg (3698) English (chiefly West Country): metonymic nickname for someone with some malformation or peculiarity of the leg, or just with particularly long legs, from Middle English *legg* (Old Norse *leggr*).

Leggat (124) Scottish spelling of LEGGETT.

Legge (834) English: variant spelling of LEGG.

Leggett (4197) English: occupational name for an ambassador or representative, from Middle English and Old French *legat*, Latin *legatus*, 'one who is appointed or ordained'. The name may also have been a pageant name or given to an person elected to represent his village at a manor court.

Leggette (178) Variant spelling of English LEGGETT.

Leggiero (100) Southern Italian: derogatory nickname from Sicilian *leggeru*, *leggiu* 'light', in the sense 'superficial', 'vain' 'irresponsible'.
GIVEN NAMES Italian 14%. *Angelo* (2), *Luigi*, *Pierino*, *Raffaele*.

Leggins (114) English: variant of LIGGINS.

Leggio (349) Italian (**Lèggio**): nickname for someone who was superficial, vain, or irresponsible, from Sicilian *liggeru* 'light(weight)' or *leggiu*.

GIVEN NAMES Italian 16%. *Salvatore* (5), *Angelo* (2), *Sal* (2), *Vito* (2), *Aldo*, *Francesco, Lorenzo, Matteo, Saverio, Vita*.

Leggitt (225) English: variant spelling of LEGGETT.

Legleiter (126) German (Austrian): status name for a feudal tenant whose land lay on sloping ground, from Middle High German *lēgen* (southern dialect variant of *lēhen* 'to hold land as a feudal tenant') + *līte* 'slope'. Compare LEGNER, LECHNER.

GIVEN NAMES German 6%. *Kurt* (2), *Florian*.

Legler (611) German: **1.** occupational name for a maker of small barrels, from Middle High German *lēgel* 'small barrel' + the agent suffix *-er*. **2.** Variant of LEGNER (see LECHNER).

GIVEN NAMES German 4%. *Kurt* (3), *Erwin*, *Heinz, Katharina, Viktor*.

Legner (196) South German: variant of LECHNER.

GIVEN NAMES German 6%. *Kurt* (2), *Hans*, *Hartmut*.

Legnon (115) French: unexplained; perhaps a habitational name from Leignon in Namur, in French-speaking Belgium. This name occurs chiefly in Louisiana.

GIVEN NAME French 4%. *Antoine*.

Lego (311) Americanized form of French LEGAULT.

Legore (171) Possibly Italian, a nickname for a fleet-footed or timid person, from a northern variant of standard Italian *lepre* 'hare'. However, only the plural form **Legori** is attested in Italian records.

Legrand (1681) French and English: nickname from Old French *grand, grant* 'tall', 'large' (occasionally used to denote seniority rather than size), with the French definite article *le*. It was taken to the U.S. also as Huguenot name.

GIVEN NAMES French 7%. *Pierre* (5), *Georges* (2), *Jean-Marie* (2), *Marcel* (2), *Michel* (2), *Philippe* (2), *Altagrace, Andre, Camille, Cecile, Clemence, Edouard*.

Legrande (382) French and English: variant of LEGRAND.

Legree (141) Americanized spelling of French **Legris**, a variant of *gris* 'gray', with the definite article *le*.

Legro (124) Americanized spelling of French LEGROS.

Legros (423) French: nickname from Old French *gros* 'large', with the the definite article *le*.

GIVEN NAMES French 13%. *Emile* (5), *Aime*, *Dominique, Dreux, Franck, Georges, Jacques, Laurent, Marcel, Martial, Mercel, Monique*.

Legrow (134) Americanized spelling of French LEGROS.

Legum (105) Origin unidentified.

Leh (230) Of German origin: perhaps an altered spelling of **Löh**, a habitational name from any of numerous places named Löh or Löhe. This name is found chiefly in PA.

Lehan (361) Irish: variant of LEHANE.

GIVEN NAMES Irish 4%. *Aisling, John Patrick*.

Lehane (290) **1.** Irish: reduced Anglicized form of Gaelic **Ó Liatháin** 'descendant of *Liathán*', a personal name from a diminutive of *liath* 'gray'. **2.** Dutch: nickname for a conceited person or a dandy, from *haan* 'cock'.

GIVEN NAMES Irish 4%. *Eoin, Seumas*.

Lehde (110) German: habitational name from any of several places so called in Brandenburg and Saxony.

GIVEN NAMES German 5%. *Berthold, Erwin*.

Lehenbauer (177) South German: occupational name for a tenant farmer in the feudal system, from Middle High German *lēhen* 'to hold land as a feudal tenant' + *buwære* 'peasant', 'farmer'.

Lehew (399) Possibly an altered form of French **Lehu(e)**, **Leheu**, **Leheut**, or **Leheux**, a nickname or metonymic occupational name, from Old French *hos, hues* 'boot', with the suffix *le*.

Lehigh (275) Irish: variant of LEAHY.

Lehl (185) German: variant of **Lehle** or **Löhl**, pet forms of the personal name LEONHARDT.

Lehman (12980) German and Jewish (western Ashkenazic): see LEHMANN.

Lehmann (3902) **1.** German: status name for a feudal tenant or vassal, Middle High German *lēheman, lēnman* (from *lēhen* 'to hold land as a feudal tenant' + *man* 'man'). The tenant held land on loan for the duration of his life in return for rent or service, but was not free to transfer or divide it. **2.** Jewish (western Ashkenazic): from an identical Jewish personal name of uncertain origin, perhaps related to LEO 3.

GIVEN NAMES German 9%. *Kurt* (14), *Heinz* (11), *Hans* (9), *Otto* (7), *Erwin* (6), *Fritz* (6), *Klaus* (5), *Gerhard* (4), *Arno* (3), *Gunter* (3), *Juergen* (3), *Almut* (2).

Lehmberg (127) German: habitational name from any of several minor places so named.

Lehmer (210) **1.** German: habitational name from any of several places named Lehm. **2.** North German: occupational name for a worker with clay, from Middle Low German *lēm* 'clay' + the agent suffix *-er*.

Lehmkuhl (492) North German: topographic or occupational name for someone working or living by a clay pit, from Middle Low German *lēm* 'clay' + *kule* 'pit', habitational name from any of several places named with this term, for example Lehmkuhlen near Kiel. Compare South German LEIMKUEHLER.

Lehn (598) German: status name for a feudal tenant or vassal, from Middle High German *lēhen* 'to hold land as a feudal tenant' (see LEHMANN).

Lehne (181) **1.** German: variant of LEHN. **2.** Norwegian: variant of **Leine**, a habitational name from any of several farmsteads so named (see LEIN 3).

Lehnen (259) German: variant of LEHN.

Lehner (1364) **1.** German: status name for a feudal tenant or vassal, from an agent derivative of Middle High German *lēhen* 'to hold land as a feudal tenant'. **2.** variant of LEONHARDT.

GIVEN NAMES German 5%. *Franz* (2), *Kurt* (2), *Otto* (2), *Alois, Christoph, Dieter, Franziska, Fritz, Hans, Heinz, Helmut, Juergen*.

Lehnert (570) North German: variant of LEONHARDT.

GIVEN NAMES German 8%. *Kurt* (2), *Uwe* (2), *Franz, Guenther, Hans, Ingeborg, Joerg, Klaus, Otto*.

Lehnertz (122) North German: patronymic from LEHNERT.

Lehnhardt (112) German: from the personal name *Leonhard* (see LEONARD).

GIVEN NAMES German 6%. *Otto* (2), *Hermann, Kurt, Urs*.

Lehnhoff (171) German (Westphalia): habitational name from a place in the Ruhr, named with Middle Low German *lēn* 'loan(ed land)' + *hof* 'farmstead', 'manor farm'.

GIVEN NAMES German 6%. *Hans* (2), *Fritz, Kurt, Wolfgang*.

Lehning (151) German and Alsatian: habitational name from a place called Lehningen near Pforzheim in Baden.

Lehouillier (103) French: occupational name, with the definite article *le*, for a maker or seller of wine, from a derivative of *ouiller* 'to fill a wine barrel up to the bung hole' (Old French *euiller*).

GIVEN NAMES French 22%. *Armand* (2), *Alain, Camille, Emile, Gilles, Lucien, Philippe*.

Lehr (2742) German: topographic name for someone who lived in a marshy area. There are a number of minor places, mostly in southern Germany, named with this element, and the surname may also come from any of them.

Lehrer (921) **1.** Jewish (Ashkenazic): occupational name for a teacher, from modern German *Lehrer*, Yiddish *lerer* 'teacher'. **2.** German: variant of LEHR.

GIVEN NAMES Jewish 5%; German 4%. *Miriam* (3), *Ephraim, Haskel, Meyer, Nachman, Shlomo*; *Otto* (3), *Bernhard, Erwin, Horst, Klaus, Reinhold, Ute*.

Lehrke (226) German: nickname for a person resembling a lark, possibly a good singer or someone with a cheerful disposition, from Middle High German *lēke, lērche* 'lark'.

GIVEN NAMES German 4%. *Bernd, Fritz*.

Lehrman (580) Variant spelling of German and Jewish LEHRMANN.

GIVEN NAMES Jewish 4%. *Sol* (2), *Hyman*, *Jakob, Meyer*.

Lehrmann (164) **1.** German: habitational name for someone from any of several places named Lehr (see LEHR). **2.** Jewish (Ashkenazic): occupational name for a teacher, a synonym of LEHRER, from German *lehren* 'to teach' + *Mann* 'man'.

GIVEN NAMES German 7%. *Otto* (2), *Ernst, Kurt*.

Lehtinen (233) Finnish: ornamental name from Finnish *lehti* 'leaf' + the common surname suffix *-nen*. This is the twelfth most common family name in Finland. Surnames formed with *Lehti-* are generally rather new southwestern Finnish surnames. Often, they are translations of Swedish names containing the elements *löf* or *blad* 'leaf'.

GIVEN NAMES Finnish 23%. *Merja* (3), *Waino* (3), *Eino* (2), *Sulo* (2), *Wilho* (2), *Aune, Esko, Jaana, Jyrki, Kauko, Olavi, Osmo*.

Lehto (640) Finnish: from *lehto* 'grove'; either a habitational name, recorded since the 17th century, from any of the farms in eastern Finland named for their location by a grove, or in other cases a more recent ornamental adoption. In the U.S. this may also be a shortened form of LEHTONEN, which is a more frequent form in Finland.

GIVEN NAMES Finnish 6%. *Reino* (4), *Toivo* (3), *Tyyne* (2), *Arvo, Aune, Kalevi, Oiva, Rauno, Tauno, Timo*.

Lehtola (109) Finnish: variant of LEHTO, with the local suffix *-la*, a habitational name from any of various farms so named in western Finland.

GIVEN NAMES Finnish 10%. *Ilmari, Jorma, Reino, Timo, Wilho*.

Lehtonen (178) Finnish: variant LEHTO + the common surname suffix *-nen*. This is a relatively new family name, occurring chiefly in western Finland.

GIVEN NAMES Finnish 17%; Scandinavian 4%. *Eino* (2), *Heikki, Jarmo, Jukka, Olavi, Pentti, Reino, Sirkka, Sulo, Toini, Toivo; Johan*.

Lei (864) **1.** Chinese 雷: said to be from a modified form of the name of Lei Zu, principal wife of the legendary emperor Huang Di (2697–2595 BC) and the first woman to be designated empress. **2.** Chinese 李: Cantonese variant of LI 1. **3.** Dutch: nickname for a lazy person, from Middle Dutch *lei* 'lazy'.

GIVEN NAMES Chinese 48%. *Ming* (6), *Li* (3), *Pei* (3), *Rong* (3), *Xun* (3), *Zhao* (3), *Chun* (2), *Da* (2), *Han* (2), *Hong* (2), *Jian Hua* (2), *Jian Sheng* (2), *Qi* (2). *Yong Kun* (2), *Huan, Lam, Lan, My, Yaping, Yen*.

Leib (872) **1.** Jewish (Ashkenazic): from the Yiddish personal name *Leyb*, meaning 'lion', traditional Yiddish translation equivalent of the Hebrew name *Yehuda* (Judah), with reference to the Old Testament description of Judah as 'a lion's whelp' (Genesis 49: 9). **2.** French (Alsace): from a

Germanic personal name *Leibo* (from an earlier form *Laibo*), the element *laib-* being related to Gothic *laiba* 'remnant', Old High German *leipa* 'relic', 'memento (of a family)'. **3.** Altered spelling of German LIEB.

Leibel (257) Jewish (Ashkenazic): from the Yiddish personal name *Leybl*, a pet form of *Leyb* (see LEIB).

GIVEN NAMES Jewish 4%. *Arye* (2), *Miriam, Sol*.

Leibensperger (166) South German: presumably a habitational name from an unidentified place called Leibensperg.

FOREBEARS The surname is recorded originally in Württemberg; by the 18th century it had spread to Alsace and Thurgau, Switzerland. John George Leibensperger emigrated to North America in 1732.

Leiber (226) South German: **1.** from the Germanic personal name *Liutbert*, a compound of *liut* 'people' + *bercht* 'bright', 'shining'. **2.** variant of LIEBER.

Leibert (179) German: variant of LIEBHART.

Leibfried (225) German: from the Germanic personal name *Liutfrid*, a compound of *liut* 'people' + *fridu* 'protection', 'peace'.

Leible (153) South German: variant of LAIBLE.

Leibman (194) **1.** Jewish (eastern Ashkenazic): elaborated form of the Yiddish male personal name *Leyb* 'lion'. **2.** Altered spelling of German LIEBMANN.

GIVEN NAMES Russian 7%; French 4%. *Genrikh, Leonid, Liliya, Lyubov, Matvei, Vladimir; Alain, Jacques*.

Leibold (544) German: from the Germanic personal name *Leibwald*, from *laib-* (see LEIB 2) + *waldan* 'rule'.

Leibovitz (180) Jewish (Ashkenazic): variant spelling of LEIBOWITZ.

GIVEN NAMES Jewish 6%. *Arie, Iren, Isadore*.

Leibowitz (1378) Jewish (Ashkenazic): patronymic from LEIB 1. The suffix *-owitz* represents a Germanized form of the eastern Slavic patronymic suffix *-ovich*, Polish *-owicz*.

GIVEN NAMES Jewish 6%. *Sol* (3), *Emanuel* (2), *Hyman* (2), *Shira* (2), *Syma* (2), *Boruch, Devorah, Elihu, Labe, Miriam, Sholem, Simcha*.

Leibrock (126) German: metonymic occupation name for a tailor, from Middle High German *līprock* 'coat' or 'vest'.

Leiby (669) Americanized spelling of German LIEBE or LIEBIG.

Leicher (103) German: occupational name for a fairground entertainer, from Middle High German *leich* 'dance', 'melody'.

GIVEN NAME German 4%. *Juergen*.

Leichliter (212) South German (**Leichleiter**): topographic name, probably from Middle High German *laich* 'copse' + *līte* 'mountain slope'. The first element may alternatively be *lēgen*, southern dialect variant of *lēhen* 'to hold land as a feudal tenant' (see LEGLEITER).

Leichner (145) German: topographic name for someone who lived in a copse, from an agent noun based on the dialect term *laich* 'copse'.

GIVEN NAMES French 4%; German 4%. *Desire; Fritz*.

Leicht (645) German and Dutch: nickname from Middle High German *līht*, Middle Dutch *līcht* 'light(weight)', 'nimble', 'quick', probably applied to a busy and active person, or to someone frivolous.

Leichter (244) German: occupational name for someone who gelded animals, from an agent derivative of Middle High German *līhten* 'to castrate'.

GIVEN NAMES German 8%. *Franz* (3), *Kurt* (2), *Eward*.

Leichtman (136) Jewish (Ashkenazic): nickname from Yiddish *laykht* 'light', 'not weighty' + *man* 'man'.

Leichty (239) Altered spelling of the Swiss German family name LIECHTI.

Leick (261) Dutch: from a Germanic personal name *Lideco*, itself an old diminutive of any of various compound names formed with *liut* 'tribe', 'people'.

GIVEN NAMES German 4%. *Alois, Aloys, Eldor, Hermann*.

Leid (164) German: a nickname for an unpleasant person, from Middle High German *leit* 'disagreeable'.

Leidecker (117) Dutch: occupational name for a slater, Dutch *leidekker*.

FOREBEARS In the spelling **Leydecker**, this was a prominent New Netherland name.

Leidel (132) German: pet form of the personal name *Liudulf*, composed of the Germanic elements *liut* 'people' + *wolf* 'wolf'.

GIVEN NAMES German 7%. *Dieter, Kurt, Manfred*.

Leider (423) **1.** German: variant of LEDER, from the Eastern Middle German word *leyder* 'leather'. **2.** North German: nickname for a courageous person or a leader, from Middle Low German *leider, lēder* 'leader'.

Leiderman (132) North German (**Leidermann**): variant of *Leider* 2, with *mann* 'man'.

Leidig (258) German: **1.** from a short form of any of several Germanic personal names composed with the first element *liut* 'people', 'tribe'. **2.** nickname for a disagreeable, cantankerous person, from Middle High German *leidic* 'disagreeable', 'tiresome'.

Leiding (141) German: **1.** from *Leiting*, a patronymic from the Germanic personal name *Laitho*. **2.** variant of LEIDIG. **3.** habitational name from any of several places called Leiding (Lower Saxony) or Leidingen (Saarland).

Leidner (266) German: variant of LEITNER.

GIVEN NAMES German 5%. *Berthold, Ernst, Otto, Ralf*.

Leidy (560) Americanized spelling of Swiss German LEIDIG.

Leiendecker (108) German: variant of LEYENDECKER.

GIVEN NAMES German 6%. *Erwin* (2), *Kurt*.

Leier (309) German (Rhineland): habitational name from any of several places named with Middle Low German *leie* 'rock', or a topographic name for someone living near a rock or in a rocky area.

GIVEN NAMES German 5%. *Kurt* (3), *Otto*.

Leif (178) **1.** Scandinavian: from the Old Norse personal name *Leifr*. **2.** Variant spelling of English LEAF or variant Americanization of Swedish **Lö(ö)f**, **Löv** (see LEAF 3).

Leifer (535) **1.** German and Jewish (Ashkenazic): variant of LAUFER 2. **2.** German: habitational name from a place called Leiferde, of which there are two examples in Lower Saxony.

GIVEN NAMES Jewish 12%. *Elihu* (3), *Mayer* (3), *Meyer* (2), *Avrum*, *Beril*, *Hersh*, *Hyman*, *Lasar*, *Miriam*, *Moshe*, *Rivka*, *Rochel*.

Leiferman (169) Jewish (eastern Ashkenazic): occupational name from Yiddish *leyfer* 'messenger' (see LAUFER).

Leifeste (151) North German or Dutch: probably from a topographic name, **Leinfest** or **Leinfeste**, derived from late Middle Low German *leine* 'grazing land with wide ditches' + *vēste* 'administrative district', hence a name for a farmer who farmed an area of low-lying land or who was entrusted with maintaining the ditches in a district.

GIVEN NAME German 6%. *Fritz* (2).

Leifheit (241) German: from a Germanic female name consisting of the elements *liub* 'beloved' + *heid* 'entity'.

Leigh (3859) English: habitational name from any of the numerous places (in at least sixteen counties, but especially Leigh in Lancashire) named either with the nominative case of Old English *lēah* 'woodland clearing' (see LEE) or with *lēage*, a late dative form of this word (see LYE).

Leight (390) Variant of German LEICHT or English LIGHT.

Leighton (3564) English: habitational name from any of various places so called. Most, as for example those in Bedfordshire, Cambridgeshire, Cheshire, Lancashire, and Shropshire, are named with Old English *lēac* 'leek' + *tūn* 'settlement'. Compare LAYTON.

Leighty (800) Perhaps an altered spelling of the English family name LAITY.

Leija (506) Hispanic (Mexico): unexplained; possibly a Castilianized spelling of the Catalan family name **Leixà**.

GIVEN NAMES Spanish 52%. *Jose* (13), *Juan* (11), *Mario* (7), *Javier* (5), *Manuel* (5), *Margarita* (5), *Carlos* (4), *Pedro* (4), *Ruben* (4), *Alicia* (3), *Amado* (3), *Jaime* (3).

Leik (111) Of German origin: possibly an altered spelling of **Liek**, which Bahlow derives from *liek* 'wet(ness)', and hence presumably a topographic name for someone living in a marshy area.

Leikam (209) Probably of Dutch or German origin: **1.** an altered form of German **Leinkamp**, a topographic name composed of Middle Low German *lein(e)* 'grazing land with wide ditches' (see LEIFESTE) + *kamp* 'field'. **2.** alternatively, perhaps, an altered form of **Leinkamp** 'flax field', from Middle High German *līn* 'flax', 'canvas', 'linen', + *kamp* 'field'.

Leiker (710) **1.** Origin uncertain. This name is found among Germans living in Russia in the 19th century. **2.** It may be an altered form of LEICHER. **3.** Alternatively, perhaps it is from a pet form of the personal name *Liutgard*, composed of the elements *liut* 'people', 'tribe' + *gard* 'settlement'.

Leiman (155) **1.** Jewish (eastern Ashkenazic): from the Yiddish male personal name *Leyman*, of uncertain origin. **2.** Jewish (eastern Ashkenazic): metronymic from the Yiddish female name *Leye* (English *Leah*) + *man* 'husband of'. **3.** Jewish (eastern Ashkenazic): metonymic occupational name from Yiddish *leym* 'clay' + *man* 'man'. **4.** Swedish: ornamental name composed of an unidentified first element + *man* 'man'.

GIVEN NAMES Jewish 7%. *Menashe*, *Shoshi*, *Sol*, *Yehoshua*.

Leimbach (359) German and Alsatian: habitational name from any of several places called Leimbach, from Middle High German *leim* 'mud', 'silt', 'clay' + *bach* 'stream'.

Leimer (197) German: **1.** occupational name for a worker with clay, from an agent derivative of Middle High German *leim* 'clay'. **2.** habitational name from any of several places called Leimen in the Palatinate and Baden.

Leimkuehler (133) German: topographic name for someone living by a clay pit, from Middle High German *leim* 'clay' + *küle* 'pit'.

Lein (725) Dutch: **1.** from a short form of the personal name *Gelein*, from French *Ghi(s)lain*, a Latinization of a Germanic personal name built on the element *gīsil* 'pledge' (see GIESEL). **2.** German: occupational name for a grower of or dealer in flax, from Middle High German *līn* 'flax'. **3.** Norwegian: habitational name from any of several farmsteads in Trøndelag, so named from Old Norse *lein* 'slope'.

GIVEN NAMES German 4%. *Erwin*, *Juergen*, *Kurt*, *Oskar*, *Otto*.

Leinart (149) German and Dutch: from a variant of the personal name LEONHART (see LEONARD, LEHNERT).

Leinbach (509) German: topographic name from any of several streams called *leinbach*, from Middle High German *līn* 'flax' or Middle Low German *leie* (genitive *leien*) 'rock', 'stone' + *bach* 'stream'.

Leinberger (211) German: **1.** perhaps an altered form of **Leinburger**, a habitational name for someone from places called Leinburg in Holstein and Bavaria. **2.** Alternatively, perhaps a habitational name for someone from an unidentified place named with Middle High German *līn* 'flax' + *berg* 'mountain'.

GIVEN NAMES German 4%. *Erwin*, *Lothar*, *Otto*.

Leindecker (150) German: variant of LEYENDECKER.

GIVEN NAME German 4%. *Kurt* (2).

Leinen (405) German: probably a metonymic occupational name for a linen weaver or someone who grew flax or sold linen, from *Leinen* 'linen', 'flax' (Middle High German *līn*), possibly shortened from **Leinenweber**, formed with *weber* 'weaver'.

Leinenbach (135) German: probably a topographical name from a creek so named, a variant of LEINBACH.

Leiner (358) **1.** English: variant of LANIER 1. **2.** Dutch: variant of LEONARD. **3.** Jewish (western Ashkenazic): name taken by someone who was good at chanting the Pentateuch at public worship in the synagogue or who regularly did so, from West Yiddish *layner* 'reader' (a derivative of West Yiddish *laynen* 'to read', which comes ultimately from Latin *legere* 'to read'). **4.** Jewish (Ashkenazic): occupational name for a flax grower or merchant, from German *Lein* 'flax' + agent suffix *-er*.

GIVEN NAMES Jewish 5%. *Haya*, *Herschel*, *Isack*, *Noson*.

Leingang (337) German: Alemannic-Swabian nickname for a pussyfoot, from *leins* (for *leise*) 'soft' + *gang* 'step', 'gait' (see LEINS).

Leininger (1679) German: habitational name from any of several places called Leiningen.

Leino (248) Finnish: **1.** associated with the adjective *leina leini*, *leino* meaning 'sad', 'weak'. This surname was originally found in Karelia but gained popularity during the name conversion movement in the 19th and early 20th centuries. It is now common in southern Finland. **2.** Perhaps also a derivative of a Germanic personal name.

GIVEN NAMES Finnish 12%. *Armas*, *Arto*, *Arvo*, *Eino*, *Jorma*, *Paavo*, *Pekka*, *Reijo*, *Vieno*.

Leinonen (171) Finnish: variant of LEINO + the common surname suffix *-nen*. In the 16th century this name was associated mainly with the Savo region; now it occurs throughout central and northern Finland.

GIVEN NAMES Finnish 11%. *Arvo* (2), *Toivo* (2), *Eino*, *Ensio*, *Seppo*, *Vieno*.

Leins (152) **1.** German: byname for a quiet or slow person, from Middle High German *līse*, *linse* 'quiet', 'soft', 'slow'. **2.** Latvian: unexplained.

GIVEN NAMES German 6%. *Helmut* (2), *Alfons*.

Leinwand (130) German and Jewish (Ashkenazic): metonymic occupational name for someone who made or sold linen, from German *Leinwand* 'linen'.
GIVEN NAME Jewish 6%. *Isidor*.

Leinweber (416) German: occupational name for a linen weaver, from Middle High German *līn* 'flax', 'linen', 'canvas' + *webære, weber* 'weaver'.
GIVEN NAMES German 5%. *Kurt* (3), *Eldred* (2), *Hans*.

Leiper (142) Scottish: variant of LEEPER 1.

Leiphart (207) Variant of German LIEBHART.

Leipold (258) German: variant of LEOPOLD.
GIVEN NAMES German 11%. *Hans* (3), *Horst* (2), *Kurt* (2), *Klaus, Matthias, Siegfried*.

Leipzig (149) German and Jewish (Ashkenazic): habitational name from the city of Leipzig in eastern Germany, which is named with the Slavic word *lipa* 'linden tree'.
GIVEN NAMES Jewish 5%. *Hava* (2), *Hyman*.

Leis (1061) **1.** Dutch: from a reduced form of the personal name *Laurei(n)s* (see LAWRENCE). **2.** German: nickname for a soft-spoken, quiet person, from Middle High German *līse* 'quiet'.
GIVEN NAMES German 4%. *Kurt* (3), *Hans* (2), *Helmut* (2), *Wilhelm* (2), *Erwin, Konrad, Manfred*.

Leischner (169) German: variant of LEUSCHNER.
GIVEN NAMES German 5%. *Erwin* (2), *Kurt, Otto*.

Leise (222) **1.** Dutch: from a female personal name such as *Lijse, Alice*, or *Aleidis*. **2.** German: nickname for a soft-spoken, quiet person, from Middle High German *līse* 'quiet'.

Leisen (102) German: probably a topographic name from Middle High German *leis* 'rut', or a habitational name from a place named Leisen near Hannover.

Leisenring (163) German (Saxony): metonymic occupational name for a maker of the iron rings used to secure loads on a farm vehicle, from a word related to the German dialect word *Leuchse* 'stake (on a vehicle)', 'tailboard' + Middle High German *ring* 'ring'.

Leiser (605) **1.** German: topographic name from Middle High German *leise* 'rut', or from an area name with this word. **2.** nickname for a soft-spoken, quiet person, from an inflected form of Middle High German *līse* 'quiet'. **3.** Jewish (Ashkenazic): from the Yiddish personal name *Leyzer*, from the Biblical name *Eliezer* (Genesis 15: 2).
GIVEN NAMES German 5%; Jewish 4%. *Erna, Fritz, Ilse, Kurt, Manfred, Reinhold; Chaim* (2), *Alter, Ari, Jakob, Leibish, Mandel, Mayer*.

Leisey (158) Altered spelling of the Swiss family name **Leisi** (see LEISE).

Leisher (133) Americanized spelling of German **Leischer**, a habitational name for someone from places called Leische (near Fallersleben) or Leisch (near Dannenberg). Both are of Slavic origin.

Leishman (543) Scottish: occupational name meaning 'servant of *Leish*', a reduced form of the personal name GILLIES.

Leising (248) **1.** English: from an Old Norse personal name or nickname, *Leysingi*, from *leysingi* 'freedman'. Compare LAZENBY. **2.** South German: habitational name from Leising in Bavaria.
GIVEN NAMES German 4%. *Armin, Erwin, Otto*.

Leisinger (186) South German: habitational name for someone from LEISING.

Leisner (222) German: habitational name for a person from any of several places in East Prussia and elsewhere in central Europe, called Leissen in German, or from Leissenau near Colditz in eastern Germany.

Leiss (286) South German: nickname from Middle High German *līse* 'quiet', 'soft', 'slow'.
GIVEN NAMES German 5%. *Ernst, Fritz, Kurt*.

Leissner (102) Variant of LEISNER.
GIVEN NAMES German 7%; Scandinavian 4%. *Bernd, Erwin, Ottmar; Britt, Hilmer*.

Leist (875) German: metonymic occupational name for a maker of lasts or a cobbler, from Middle High German *leist* 'last'.

Leisten (140) German: variant of LEIST.
GIVEN NAMES German 4%. *Karl-Heinz, Rudi*.

Leister (1202) **1.** English: variant of LESTER. **2.** German: occupational name for a maker of lasts or a cobbler, from Middle High German *leist* + the agent suffix *-er*.

Leistikow (157) German: of Slavic origin, a habitational name from either of two names so named in Pomerania.
GIVEN NAMES German 6%. *Kurt* (2), *Ralf*.

Leistner (212) German: variant of LEISTER.
GIVEN NAMES German 6%. *Armin, Erwin, Heinz, Kurt*.

Leisure (500) Probably of French origin: see LEASURE.

Leisy (156) Swiss German: unexplained.

Leitao (141) Portuguese (**Leitão**): metonymic occupational name for a keeper of pigs, or nickname meaning 'piglet', from Portuguese *leitão* '(suckling) pig'.
GIVEN NAMES Spanish 28%; Portuguese 21%; French 4%. *Manuel* (7), *Carlos* (3), *Jose* (3), *Adelino* (2), *Francisco* (2), *Pedro* (2), *Acacio, Adriana, Amancio, Arcenio, Augusto, Dimas; Joaquim* (3), *Vasco* (2), *Conceicao, Marcio, Pinto; Francoise, Jacques, Lucien*.

Leitch (1281) Scottish: occupational name for a physician (see LEACH 1).

Leite (616) **1.** Portuguese: nickname from *leite* 'milk' (Late Latin *lacte*), probably denoting someone with a particularly pale complexion. **2.** German and Dutch: from the female personal name *Aleit(e)*, a short form of a Germanic name, *Adelheid*, formed of the elements *adal* 'noble' + *heid* 'kind', 'sort', '(human) being'. **3.** Norwegian: habitational name from any of several farmsteads in western Norway named Leite or Leitet, from Old Norse *leiti* 'hill', 'elevation'.
GIVEN NAMES Spanish 21%; Portuguese 15%. *Jose* (13), *Manuel* (8), *Mario* (7), *Carlos* (6), *Luis* (5), *Eduardo* (4), *Pedro* (4), *Ana* (3), *Luiz* (3), *Miguel* (3), *Fernando* (2), *Marcos* (2); *Paulo* (6), *Joaquim* (3), *Marcio* (2), *Adao, Albano, Altair, Ilidio, Joao*.

Leiter (969) **1.** German: from *Leiter* 'leader', status name for a foreman or for the leader of a military expedition, from Middle High German *leiten* 'lead'. **2.** German and Jewish (Ashkenazic): variant of LEITNER.

Leiterman (194) German or Jewish (Ashkenazic): elaborated form of LEITER.

Leitgeb (109) South German: occupational name for someone who owned or worked in a tavern, Middle High German *lītgebe*, from *līt* 'punch' (the drink, a kind of spiced wine) + *gebe* 'giver', 'pourer'.

Leith (905) Scottish: habitational name from the port near Edinburgh, which takes its name from the river at whose mouth it stands. The river name is of Celtic origin, meaning 'flowing water'.

Leithauser (100) South German (**Leithäuser**): **1.** occupational name from an agent noun based on Middle High German *līthūs* 'tavern', an occupational name for an owner or operator of a tavern. **2.** habitational name from a place called Leitenhausen in Bavaria or Thuringia. (The former is more likely).

Leithead (118) Scottish: habitational name from a farm at the head of the Water of Leith, which flows through Edinburgh.

Leitheiser (132) German: variant of **Leithäuser** (see LEITHAUSER).

Leiting (140) German: from a patronymic derivative of any of the various Germanic personal names composed with Old High German *leod, liud* 'people' (see, for example, LUDWIG).

Leitman (150) Jewish (Ashkenazic): occupational name from Yiddish *leytn* 'to solder' + *man* 'man'.
GIVEN NAMES Jewish 8%. *Chaim, Isak, Yehuda, Yoel*.

Leitner (1548) **1.** German (Bavaria, Austria) and Jewish (Ashkenazic): topographic name for someone who lived by a mountain spur or on a slope of a mountain, from Middle High German *līte* 'mountain slope', 'spur' + the suffix *-(n)er*, denoting an inhabitant. **2.** Jewish (Ashkenazic): occupational name from Yiddish *leytn* 'to solder' + the agent suffix *-ner* (see LEITMAN).

Leitschuh (115) German: metonymic occupational name from an industrial tool (a guide rail that directs a mine cage) or an iron ruler used for keeping writing straight, from *leiten* 'to direct' + *Schuh* 'shoe'.

Leitz (480) German and Dutch: from the personal name *Leutz*, a pet form of any of various Germanic compound names formed with *liut* 'tribe', 'people'.

Leitzel (340) German: from a pet form of LEITZ.

Leitzell (110) Americanized spelling of German LEITZEL.

GIVEN NAME German 4%. *Kurt*.

Leitzke (242) German: **1.** habitational name from Leitzkau near Magdeburg. **2.** from a pet form of LEITZ.

Leiva (679) Spanish: habitational name a place called Leiva, chiefly the one in La Rioja province and to a lesser extent the one in Murcia.

GIVEN NAMES Spanish 50%. *Jose* (17), *Jorge* (12), *Carlos* (11), *Rolando* (8), *Fernando* (7), *Francisco* (7), *Juan* (7), *Julio* (7), *Manuel* (6), *Pedro* (6), *Ricardo* (6), *Blanca* (5).

Leja (326) Polish: nickname for a blabbermouth or chatterbox, someone unable to hold his tongue, from *lać* 'to pour'.

GIVEN NAMES Polish 15%. *Andrzej* (4), *Boguslaw* (2), *Jozef* (2), *Kazimierz* (2), *Stanislaw* (2), *Boguslawa*, *Bronislaw*, *Elizbieta*, *Franciszek*, *Jerzy*, *Karol*, *Michalina*.

Lejeune (1894) French: variant of JEUNE ('young'), with the definite article *le*. This name was also taken to Germany by Huguenot refugees. It is often translated as YOUNG.

GIVEN NAMES French 7%. *Curley* (3), *Monique* (3), *Irby* (2), *Roch* (2), *Alain*, *Armand*, *Camille*, *Colette*, *Damien*, *Dupre*, *Emile*.

Lekan (104) Origin unidentified.

Lekas (190) Greek: from the Albanian personal name *Leka*, an Albanian form of ALEXANDER.

GIVEN NAMES Greek 4%. *Fotis*, *Panos*.

Leland (1949) Scottish and Irish: reduced form of MCCLELLAN or MCLELLAND.

Leleux (252) French (Picardy): nickname for a crafty or dangerous person, from Old French *lou*, *leu* 'wolf' (Latin *lupus*).

GIVEN NAMES French 4%. *Dominique*, *Matilde*, *Numa*, *Vernice*.

Lelievre (138) French (**Lelièvre**): nickname for a fleet-footed or timid person, from Old French *le levre* 'the hare'. It may also have been a metonymic occupational name for a hunter of hares.

GIVEN NAMES French 16%. *Marcel* (2), *Emilien*, *Laurier*, *Napoleon*, *Normand*, *Sylvie*.

Lell (104) German: descriptive nickname from the Swabian word *lell*, *läll* 'twisted mouth'.

GIVEN NAME German 4%. *Otto*.

Lella (114) Italian: variant (feminine in form) of LELLO.

GIVEN NAMES Italian 11%. *Angelo*, *Antonio*, *Rocco*.

Lelli (131) Italian (**Lèlli**): patronymic or plural form of the personal name LELLO.

GIVEN NAMES Italian 14%. *Antonio* (2), *Corrado* (2), *Carmine*, *Enrico*, *Geno*.

Lello (100) Italian: from a short form of the personal name *Angiolello*, a pet form of the personal name ANGELO.

GIVEN NAMES Italian 10%. *Marco* (2), *Salvatore* (2), *Francesca*.

Lem (334) **1.** Dutch and Scandinavian: from a short form of the personal name *Lambrecht* or *Lempert* (see LAMBERT). **2.** English: probably a variant of LIMM (see LUM). **3.** Southeast Asian: unexplained.

GIVEN NAMES Southeast Asian 10%. *Wing* (4), *Wah* (3), *Hing* (2), *Hong* (2), *Lok* (2), *Yee* (2), *Chheng*, *Chiu*, *Chu*, *Hang*, *Jee*, *Jung*.

Lema (526) Spanish (mainly Galicia): habitational name from Lema in A Coruña province.

GIVEN NAMES Spanish 26%. *Manuel* (12), *Luis* (11), *Jose* (8), *Segundo* (5), *Miguel* (4), *Arturo* (3), *Juan* (3), *Roberto* (3), *Angel* (2), *Fernando* (2), *Florencio* (2), *Francisco* (2).

Lemacks (102) English: variant of LOMAX (see LOOMIS).

Lemahieu (113) French: nickname for someone named *Mahieu*, a vernacular (Norman and Picard) form of MATTHEW, literally 'the Matthew'.

Lemaire (1006) French: status name for a local magistrate or official (see MAIRE), with the definite article *le*.

GIVEN NAMES French 12%. *Andre* (4), *Fernand* (3), *Dominique* (2), *Marcel* (2), *Raywood* (2), *Armand*, *Auguste*, *Aurelien*, *Chantel*, *Constant*, *Cyrille*, *Emile*.

Lemaitre (145) French (**Lemaître**): from Old French *maistre* 'master', hence a nickname for someone who behaved in a masterful manner, or an occupational name for someone who was master of his craft.

GIVEN NAMES French 19%. *Lucien* (2), *Jean-Marie*, *Laurent*, *Olivier*, *Pierre*, *Yves*.

Leman (482) **1.** Dutch: variant of LEEMAN 1. **2.** English: variant of LEAMAN. **3.** Polish spelling of German LEHMANN.

Lemanski (684) Polish (**Lemański**): habitational name for someone from any of various places called Leman or Lemany, named with German LEHMANN.

GIVEN NAMES Polish 4%. *Aloisius*, *Boleslaw*, *Casimir*, *Krzysztof*, *Tadeusz*.

Lemar (367) French: probably a variant of LAMOUR.

Lemarr (200) French: variant of LEMAR.

Lemaster (2461) Americanized form of French **Lemestre** (see LEMAITRE).

Lemasters (896) Americanized form of French **Lemestre** (see LEMAITRE).

Lemay (3243) **1.** French: habitational name from Lemay in Maine-et-Loire. **2.** English: nickname from Middle English *may*

'young lad' or 'girl', with the Old French definite article *le*.

GIVEN NAMES French 9%. *Normand* (9), *Armand* (8), *Marcel* (8), *Emile* (4), *Andre* (3), *Gaston* (3), *Pierre* (3), *Benoit* (2), *Cecile* (2), *Fernand* (2), *Germain* (2), *Lucien* (2).

Lembcke (232) North German: variant of LEMKE.

Lembeck (163) **1.** German: habitational name from any of several places so named in Westphalia and Hesse. **2.** Belgian and Dutch: habitational name from places called Lembeke in East and West Flanders, and in Tielt, Ooigem, Sint-Baafs-Vijve, and Wielsbeke, or from Lembeek in Brabant.

Lemberg (288) **1.** Jewish (Ashkenazic): habitational name from the city of Lviv in Ukraine, from its German name *Lemberg*. **2.** German: habitational name from a place called Lemberg in Silesia (originally *Löwenberg*, from Middle High German *lewe*, *löwe* 'lion' + *berg* 'mountain'). There are other places so named in various parts of Germany.

GIVEN NAMES Russian 7%; Jewish 5%. *Vladimir* (2), *Lev*, *Lyubov*, *Michail*, *Mikhail*, *Sosya*, *Vyacheslav*, *Yefim*, *Yuliy*; *Hyman*, *Ilya*, *Isaak*, *Pinkhas*, *Zipporah*.

Lemberger (277) German: habitational name for someone from any of the various places called LEMBERG.

GIVEN NAMES German 4%. *Erwin*, *Reiner*.

Lembke (519) North German: variant of LEMKE.

Lembo (601) Southern Italian: from a hypercorrected form of *Lemmo*, a pet form of *Guglièlmo*, Italian equivalent of WILLIAM.

GIVEN NAMES Italian 15%. *Salvatore* (5), *Angelo* (2), *Carmelo* (2), *Domenic* (2), *Pietro* (2), *Alfio*, *Amelio*, *Antonio*, *Biagio*, *Dante*, *Giovani*, *Giovanni*.

Lemburg (166) Possibly a U.S. variant of LEMBERG.

Lemcke (288) North German: variant spelling of LEMKE.

GIVEN NAMES German 6%. *Dieter*, *Eberhard*, *Ewald*, *Gerhard*, *Kurt*.

Lemelin (350) Canadian French: unexplained. Possibly a variant of Breton **Melin**, a metonymic occupational name for a miller.

FOREBEARS A Lemelin, called le Tourangeau, from Chartres, France, was in Quebec City from 1658.

GIVEN NAMES French 13%. *Normand* (3), *Monique* (2), *Alcide*, *Armand*, *Damien*, *Emile*, *Gaston*, *Marcel*, *Rosaire*.

Lemelle (230) French: respelling of either **Lemerle**, a nickname from *merle* 'blackbird', or of **Lemesle**, a topographic name for someone who lived by a medlar tree, *mesle*.

GIVEN NAME French 5%. *Antoine*.

Lemen (421) Dutch: variant of LEEMAN.

Lemer (132) French (**Le Mer**): possibly a status name or occupational name for a mayor, Old French *mair(e)*, with the definite article *le*, or a nickname for someone thought to resemble a mayor (see MAIRE).

Lemere (306) Origin uncertain; perhaps an altered spelling of French LEMAIRE.

Lemerise (113) Canadian French: unexplained.

Lemert (129) German: **1.** nickname for a person having a fief, from a derivative of Middle High German *lēhen* 'to hold a fief as a feudal tenant' + *-ert*, agent suffix. **2.** variant of LAMBERT.

Lemery (316) French (**Lémery**): from the French personal name *Hemery*, with the definite article *l'*.

GIVEN NAMES French 8%. *Aldege, Andre, Armand, Colette, Marcel, Rejean, Rosaire.*

Lemieux (2985) French (**Lémieux**): habitational name from Leymieux, Loire. It is sometimes translated as BETTER or BETTERS, association with French *mieux* 'better'.

GIVEN NAMES French 12%. *Armand* (15), *Pierre* (12), *Normand* (9), *Andre* (7), *Laurent* (5), *Gilles* (4), *Jacques* (4), *Marcel* (4), *Adrien* (2), *Aime* (2), *Elzear* (2), *Emile* (2).

Leming (704) English: variant of LEEMING.

Lemire (1361) French: occupational name for a physician, Old French *mire* (from Latin *medicus*), with the definite article *le*.

GIVEN NAMES French 12%. *Armand* (8), *Jacques* (3), *Adrien* (2), *Aime* (2), *Germain* (2), *Marcel* (2), *Michel* (2), *Normand* (2), *Ovila* (2), *Pierre* (2), *Alphie, Anatole.*

Lemke (4324) North German: from a pet form of the personal name LEMERT (see LAMBERT).

GIVEN NAMES German 4%. *Kurt* (9), *Otto* (6), *Erwin* (5), *Klaus* (4), *Hans* (3), *Fritz* (2), *Heinz* (2), *Helmut* (2), *Arno, Dieter, Erhardt, Ewald.*

Lemler (239) German (**Lemmler**): habitational name from Lemmel near Hude in Oldenburg.

Lemley (1751) Of uncertain origin; perhaps an altered spelling of English LUMLEY.

Lemly (119) Variant of LEMLEY.

Lemm (363) **1.** North German: from a short form of LAMBERT. **2.** English: from *Lemme*, a pet form of an Old English personal name, either *Lēodmǣr* or *Lēofmǣr* (see LEMMER).

Lemma (176) Italian: from the personal name *Lemma*, feminine equivalent of LEMMO, from *Guglielma*.

GIVEN NAMES Ethiopian 24%; Italian 12%; African 4%. *Bekele* (2), *Mengistu* (2), *Seble* (2), *Aklilu, Amare, Ayele, Derege, Getachew, Girmai, Hirut, Kebede, Mekonnen; Cosmo* (2), *Massimo* (2), *Angelo, Carmine, Nicola, Sisto, Valentino; Almaz.*

Lemme (303) **1.** Italian (central–southern): metronymic from the female personal name LEMMA. **2.** North German: variant of LEMM.

GIVEN NAMES Italian 6%; German 5%. *Antonio* (2), *Pasquale* (2), *Angelo, Carmelo, Carmine, Cosmo, Rocco, Santino; Albrecht, Helmut, Ingo, Kurt, Wolfgang.*

Lemmen (182) North German: **1.** patronymic from a short form of LEMERT. **2.** from a short form of *Adelem*, from a Germanic personal name composed of the elements *adal* 'noble' + *helm* 'helmet', 'protection'.

Lemmer (575) **1.** English: from an Old English personal name, either *Lēodmǣr* or *Lēofmǣr*, from *lēod* 'people', 'tribe' or *lēof* 'beloved' + *mǣr* 'famous'. **2.** German: from the personal name LAMBERT.

GIVEN NAMES German 4%. *Arno, Heinz, Kurt, Ulrich.*

Lemmerman (203) German (**Lemmermann**): from a pet form of the personal name LEMMER.

GIVEN NAME German 4%. *Kurt.*

Lemming (157) Danish: habitational name from any of several places named Lemming, named with *lem*, either 'lamb' or 'limb', 'twig' + the suffix *-ing* denoting a place, i.e. 'the place with the lambs or twigs'.

Lemmo (219) Italian: from the personal name *Lemmo*, a pet form of *Guglielmo*, Italian equivalent of WILLIAM. Compare LEMBO.

GIVEN NAMES Italian 7%. *Angelo, Donato, Gino.*

Lemmon (2329) English: variant spelling of LEMON.

Lemmond (312) **1.** English: variant of LEMON. **2.** Scottish: variant of LAMONT.

Lemmons (1100) English: patronymic from LEMON.

Lemoi (108) French: variant spelling of **Lemoy**, a habitational name for someone from Moy in Aisne.

GIVEN NAMES French 11%. *Aime, Armand, Normand, Philias.*

Lemoine (2368) French: from Old French *moine* 'monk' (Latin *monacus*), with the definite article *le*, probably an occupational name for a servant at a monastery or a nickname for someone of monkish behavior or appearance.

GIVEN NAMES French 8%. *Andre* (4), *Armand* (4), *Emile* (4), *Normand* (4), *Jacques* (3), *Jean-Pierre* (3), *Lucien* (3), *Pierre* (3), *Aime* (2), *Clovis* (2), *Gaston* (2), *Marcel* (2).

Lemon (4618) **1.** English: from the Middle English personal name *Lefman*, Old English *Lēofman*, composed of the elements *lēof* 'dear', 'beloved' + *mann* 'man', 'person'. This came to be used as a nickname for a lover or sweetheart, from Middle English *lem(m)an*. There is no connection with the word denoting the citrus fruit (which is of Persian origin). **2.** Scottish and northern Irish: variant of LAMONT.

Lemond (362) Scottish: variant of LAMONT.

Lemonds (431) Scottish: variant of LAMONT, with English patronymic *-s*.

Lemons (4032) English: patronymic from the Middle English personal name *Lefman* (see LEMON).

Lemont (145) **1.** Scottish: variant of LAMONT. **2.** French: habitational name from Le Mont in Vosges or possibly other minor places so named from Old French *mont* 'mountain'.

GIVEN NAME German 4%. *Orlo* (2).

Lemos (945) Galician and Portuguese: habitational name from a place in Lugo province, Galicia. It is probably from a name recorded in Latin sources as *Lemavos*, apparently a derivative of the Celtic element *lemos, limos* 'elm'.

GIVEN NAMES Spanish 20%; Portuguese 6%. *Carlos* (8), *Jose* (8), *Manuel* (8), *Francisco* (4), *Marcos* (4), *Ruben* (3), *Alvaro* (2), *Armando* (2), *Bernardo* (2), *Guadalupe* (2), *Jaime* (2), *Jesus* (2); *Afonso, Duarte, Joaquim, Marcio.*

Lemp (221) German: **1.** habitational name from any of several places called Lempe or Lempen. **2.** alternatively, from an altered spelling of **Lempp** or **Lemppe**, a metonymic occupational name for a farmer who raised and sold lambs, from Middle High German *lamp* 'lamb' **3.** from a short form of LAMBERT.

GIVEN NAMES German 5%. *Bernhard, Hans, Kurt.*

Lempert (180) **1.** Jewish (eastern Ashkenazic): ornamental name from Yiddish *lempert* 'leopard'. **2.** German and Dutch: variant of LAMBERT.

GIVEN NAMES Jewish 9%; Russian 5%. *Fira, Marat, Sol, Yakov, Yonah; Aleksandr, Arkadiy, Boris, Vladimir.*

Lempka (114) Variant, under Slavic influence, of LEMPKE.

Lempke (199) North German: variant of LEMKE.

Lemus (1577) Galician: probably a variant spelling of LEMOS.

GIVEN NAMES Spanish 57%. *Jose* (63), *Juan* (24), *Jesus* (22), *Carlos* (21), *Manuel* (19), *Francisco* (16), *Jorge* (16), *Luis* (13), *Rafael* (13), *Ana* (12), *Mario* (12), *Miguel* (10).

Len (265) **1.** Polish and Jewish (eastern Ashkenazic): metonymic occupational name for a flax grower or merchant, from Polish *len* 'flax'. **2.** Polish (**Leń**): nickname from Polish *leń* 'lazybones'. **3.** Polish: from a short form of the personal name LEON or LENART (see LEONARD).

GIVEN NAMES Polish 4%. *Zbigniew* (2), *Jozef, Karol.*

Lena (244) **1.** Italian: from the female personal name *Lena*, a short form of *Maddalena* or *Helena*. **2.** Spanish: habitational name from a place called Lena in Asturies.

GIVEN NAMES Italian 18%; Spanish 7%. *Paolo* (2), *Emilio, Francesco, Giorgio, Giuseppe, Mariano, Mario, Vito; Manuel* (4), *Cesar, Maribel, Salvador.*

Lenahan (982) Irish: reduced Anglicized form of Gaelic **Ó Leanacháin** 'descendant of *Leanachán*', a personal name, probably derived from *leann* 'cloak'. (Derivation from *léanach* 'sorrowful' is phonologically unlikely).
GIVEN NAMES Irish 4%. *Brigid, Maeve.*

Lenane (111) Irish: variant of LENAHAN.

Lenard (972) French (**Lénard**), English, German, Dutch, and Hungarian (**Lénárd**): from a Germanic personal name (see LEONARD).

Lenart (581) **1.** Polish, Czech, and Slovenian; Slovak (**Lenárt**): from the personal name *Lenart* (see LEONARD). **2.** Hungarian (**Lénárt**): from the Hungarian personal name *Lénárt*, Hungarian form of LEONARD.
GIVEN NAMES Polish 6%. *Agnieszka, Bronislawa, Henryk, Henryka, Jacek, Janina, Leslaw, Stanislaw, Tadeusz, Witold, Zofia.*

Lenarz (180) Variant of German LENNARTZ.

Lence (131) **1.** Galician: habitational name from any of four places called Lence. **2.** Variant of Polish LENSKI. **3.** Possibly an Americanized spelling of Hungarian **Lencse**, meaning 'lentil', or **Lenke**, from a pet form of *Lénárt* (see LEONARD).
GIVEN NAMES Spanish 11%. *Joaquin (2), Caridad, Carmella, Delfina, Domingo, Fidelia, Marta, Roberto, Sergio.*

Lenci (135) Italian: patronymic from a personal name *Lencio*, probably a variant of a short form of LORENZO.
GIVEN NAMES Italian 28%. *Reno (2), Romano (2), Sal (2), Enio, Giorgio, Guido, Marina, Mario, Marisa, Tullio.*

Lencioni (243) Italian: patronymic from a personal name *Lencione*. Compare LENCI.
GIVEN NAMES Italian 10%. *Angelo (2), Oreste (2), Attilio, Dante, Dario, Dino, Giovanni, Silvestro.*

Lenda (102) Polish (also **Lęda**): variant of LANDA.

Lender (251) **1.** German (Rhineland): from a Germanic personal name, *Landher*, composed of the elements *land* 'land' + *her* 'army'. **2.** Jewish (Ashkenazic): unexplained.
GIVEN NAMES Jewish 4%. *Hymen (2), Menahem (2), Polina.*

Lenderman (396) German (**Lendermann**): probably an elaborated form of LENDER, with the addition of Middle High German *man* 'man'.

Leneave (120) French: unexplained.

Lenehan (293) Irish: variant spelling of LENAHAN.

Lenertz (174) North German: patronymic from LENARD.

Lenfest (112) Variant of German **Leinfest** (see LEIFESTE).

Lenfestey (111) French (Channel Islands): nickname from Norman French *enveisié* 'playful', 'merry' (see VEAZEY).
GIVEN NAME French 7%. *Pierre.*

Leng (288) **1.** English: nickname for the taller of two men with the same name, from Old English *leng(ra)* 'longer', 'taller', comparative of *lang* (see LANG). **2.** German: variant of LANG. **3.** Chinese 冷: from an ancient official title, *Lingguan*, denoting a court official in charge of music. The character for *Ling* is written similarly to that for *Leng* (冷), and the surname evolved to the latter form. **4.** Cambodian: unexplained.
GIVEN NAMES Chinese 12%; Cambodian 12%. *Chu (2), Chan, Chea, Chi-Cheng, Gang, Heang, Kao, Leung, Oi, Ping, Shek; Sophal (2), Chhay (2), Chhun, Da, Hoa, Khuon, Linh, Long, Thao; Loeuth, Oeun, Pheap, Sokheng, Sovann.*

Lengacher (208) Americanized spelling of German **Langacker** (see LANGAGER).

Lengel (463) Americanized spelling of Hungarian LENGYEL.

Lenger (182) German: nickname for a tall man; a variant of LANG.

Lengerich (108) German: habitational name from a place so named near Münster in Westphalia.

Lengle (135) **1.** South German: topographic name from a field or other place named with Middle High German *lange, lenge* 'long'. **2.** Altered form of Hungarian LENGYEL.
GIVEN NAMES German 4%. *Johannes, Kurt.*

Lengyel (696) Hungarian and Jewish (from Hungary): ethnic name for a Pole, *lengyel* 'Polish'. The name was used to denote not only ethnic Poles but also Polish speakers and people who had lived in Poland. The family name is fairly frequent amongst western Ashkenazic Jews from the former Austro-Hungarian province of Galicia.
GIVEN NAMES Hungarian 9%. *Istvan (4), Attila (2), Bela (2), Geza (2), Imre (2), Sandor (2), Zoltan (2), Arpad, Csaba, Endre, Karoly, Katalin.*

Lenhard (329) Dutch and North German: from the personal name *Leonhard* (see LEONARD).
GIVEN NAMES German 6%. *Otto (2), Hermann, Kurt, Urs.*

Lenhardt (623) North German: from the personal name *Leonhardt* (see LEONARD).
GIVEN NAMES German 5%. *Franz (3), Erwin, Lorenz, Lothar, Otto.*

Lenhart (1907) Dutch, North German, and Czech: from the personal name *Leonhard* (see LEONARD, LENART).

Lenhoff (151) German: variant spelling of German LEHNHOFF.

Lenig (179) Eastern German (of Slavic origin): status name for a feudal tenant (see LEHN, LENNICK).
FOREBEARS This name has been prominent in the Mohawk Valley of NY from an early date. A Lenig family are also found in PA, especially Lebanon Co., beginning in the 18th century.

Lenihan (870) Irish: variant of LENAHAN.
GIVEN NAMES Irish 5%. *Niall, Sinead.*

Lenington (138) English: habitational name from a lost or unidentified place.

Lenius (211) German or Dutch: Latinized (masculine) form of the metronymic **Lehn**, from the female personal name *Magdalene* (see MAUDLIN).

Lenk (425) South German: nickname from Middle High German *lenke* 'flexible', 'agile'.
GIVEN NAMES German 6%. *Guenther, Gunter, Johannes, Otto, Reinhard, Siegfried, Wolfgang.*

Lenke (148) **1.** German: variant of LENK. **2.** Hungarian: from a pet form of the personal name *Lénárd* (see LEONARD).
GIVEN NAMES German 5%. *Juergen, Otto.*

Lenker (483) German: nickname for an agile person (see LENKE).

Lenkiewicz (111) Polish: patronymic from the personal name *Lenek*, a pet form of *Lenart* (see LEONARD) or *Leon* 'lion' (see LEON).
GIVEN NAMES Polish 9%. *Bogdan (2), Lech, Yolanta.*

Lenn (161) **1.** English and Scottish: variant of LYNN. **2.** Jewish (Ashkenazic): variant spelling of LEN.

Lennard (238) Variant of LEONARD or LENNERT.

Lennartz (177) Dutch: patronymic from **Lennart**, variant of LENNERT.
GIVEN NAME German 4%. *Manfred.*

Lennert (140) Danish, Dutch and North German: from a Germanic personal name composed of the elements *leo* 'lion' + *hard*, 'hardy', 'brave', 'strong' (see LEONARD).

Lenney (147) Northern Irish or Scottish: variant spelling of LENNIE.

Lennick (101) Eastern German (of Slavic origin): status name for the tenant of a fief, from Czech or Polish *len(n)ik*, from Middle High German *lēhen* 'to hold land as a feudal tenant' (see LEHN) + the Slavik agent suffix *-ik*.
GIVEN NAME German 6%. *Armin (2).*

Lennie (124) Scottish: probably a habitational name from Lenzie near Kirkintilloch (formerly pronounced 'Lenyie'), or from Leny in the parish of Callander in Perthshire. The latter is named in Gaelic with *lánaigh* 'damp meadow' + the locative suffix *-ach*.

Lenning (312) German: habitational name from Lenningen in Württemberg.

Lennon (3953) Irish: **1.** reduced Anglicized form of Gaelic **Ó Leannáin** 'descendant of *Leannán*', a byname meaning 'little cloak' (less likely, 'sweetheart'). **2.** reduced Anglicized form of Gaelic **Ó Lonáin** 'descendant of *Lonán*', a personal name from a diminutive of *lon* 'blackbird'.
GIVEN NAMES Irish ^%. *Aidan (2), Aileen, Brendan, Colm, Finian, John Patrick, Kieran, Ronan.*

Lennox (1407) Scottish and northern Irish: habitational name from the district near Dumbarton, recorded in 1174 in the form

Leuenaichs and in the following year as *Levenax*. Apparently it is named from Gaelic *leamhan* 'elm' + the locative suffix *-ach* + English *-s*.

Leno (399) **1.** English: unexplained. **2.** Perhaps an Americanized form of German LIENAU.

Lenoir (937) French: nickname for a dark-haired or swarthy individual, from *noir* 'black' with the definite article *le*.

GIVEN NAMES French 4%. *Philippe* (2), *Blanchard, Cecile, Jacques, Margaux, Pascal, Pierre, Pierrette, Serge.*

Lenon (282) Irish: variant spelling of LENNON.

Lenox (1079) Scottish and northern Irish: variant spelling of LENNOX.

Lensch (144) North German: from a short form of the personal name LORENZ.

GIVEN NAMES German 10%; Scandinavian 8%. *Hans* (2), *Bernhard, Franz, Gerhard, Klaus, Otto; Anders, Erik, Juel.*

Lenser (148) German: habitational name for someone from any of several places called Lens.

GIVEN NAMES German 10%. *Kurt* (2), *Horst, Rinehart, Rudi.*

Lensing (333) German: **1.** habitational name, possibly from Lenzing in Austria. **2.** pet form of the personal name *Laurentius* (see LAWRENCE).

Lenski (110) Polish (**Leński**): habitational name from places called Leńce in Białystok voivodeship or Leńcze in Bielsko-Biała voivodeship.

GIVEN NAMES Irish 5%; German 5%. *Brendan; Gerhard.*

Lent (1750) **1.** Dutch (**van Lent**): habitational name from Lent in Elst, Gelderland, meaning a place where lime trees grew; or from a lost place, Leent. **2.** Perhaps an Americanized spelling of German LENTH.

Lenth (134) German: **1.** habitational name from Lenthe near Hannover. **2.** short form of a Germanic personal name formed with *land* 'land' as the first element.

GIVEN NAME German 4%. *Lorenz.*

Lentine (347) Italian (Sicily): variant of LENTINI.

GIVEN NAMES Italian 10%. *Sal* (5), *Santino* (2), *Gaspare, Gasper, Ignazio.*

Lentini (696) Italian (Sicily): habitational name from Lentini in Siracusa province, Sicily.

GIVEN NAMES Italian 21%. *Salvatore* (12), *Vito* (6), *Alfio* (2), *Angelo* (2), *Antonio* (2), *Biagio* (2), *Carlo* (2), *Carmine* (2), *Natale* (2), *Nino* (2), *Bartolomeo, Caesar.*

Lentner (163) German (Austrian Tyrol): **1.** topographic name from Middle High German *lende* 'area', 'land'. **2.** nickname for a neighbor, from Middle High German *lenten* 'to border'.

GIVEN NAMES German 4%. *Florian, Kurt.*

Lento (262) Italian: nickname from *lento* 'slow'.

GIVEN NAMES Italian 9%. *Carmelo* (2), *Gasper, Salvatore.*

Lenton (202) English: habitational name from Lenton in Nottinghamshire, which is named from the river on which it stands, the Leen (see LEEN) + Old English *tūn* 'settlement', 'enclosure'. There is also a Lenton in Lincolnshire; however, up to the 18th century it was known as Lavington and probably therefore did not contribute to the surname.

Lents (342) Possibly an Americanized spelling of LENZ.

Lentsch (249) North German: from a short form of the personal name LORENZ.

Lentz (5956) German: variant spelling of LENZ.

Lenz (4654) **1.** German: from a personal name, in which two originally distinct names have fallen together: a pet form of the personal name LORENZ, and the Germanic personal name *Lanzo*, which was originally a short form of any of several compound names with *land* 'land' as the first element, e.g. **Lambrecht** (see LAMBERT). **2.** German: nickname from Middle High German *lenz e* 'spring' from *lang* 'long', since in this season the days grow longer. The name may also have been bestowed on someone who was born in the spring or who owed rent or service at that time of year, or it may have denoted someone who was of a sunny and spring-like disposition. **3.** German: habitational name from any of several places named Lenz. **4.** Jewish (Ashkenazic): from German *Lenz* 'spring' (see 2), one of the class of ornamental names adopted from words denoting the seasons. Compare SUMMER, WINTER, HERBST, FRUHLING.

GIVEN NAMES German 4%. *Otto* (8), *Erwin* (6), *Kurt* (6), *Gerhard* (4), *Hans* (3), *Frieda* (2), *Hannelore* (2), *Heinz* (2), *Helmut* (2), *Horst* (2), *Aloys, Baerbel.*

Lenza (114) Italian: variant (feminine in form) of LENZO.

GIVEN NAMES Italian 15%. *Americo, Carmine, Mario, Querino, Sergio, Salvatore.*

Lenze (147) German: variant of LENZ.

GIVEN NAME German 7%. *Othmar* (2).

Lenzen (394) German habitational name from any of several places so named in various parts of Germany.

GIVEN NAMES German 4%. *Heinz, Kurt, Reiner, Theodor.*

Lenzi (512) Italian: patronymic or plural form of LENZO.

GIVEN NAMES Italian 11%; French 4%. *Ennio* (2), *Geno* (2), *Marco* (2), *Marino* (2), *Pasquale* (2), *Philomena* (2), *Salvatore* (2), *Aldo, Angelo, Aniello, Dante, Deno; Armand, Camille, Patrice.*

Lenzini (182) Italian: patronymic from a pet form of LENZO.

GIVEN NAMES Italian 11%. *Amedeo, Angelo, Carlo, Corrado, Fosco, Luciano, Luigi, Mauro, Pasquale.*

Lenzmeier (115) German: habitational name for a tenant farmer at a farm named LENZ.

Lenzner (161) German: habitational name for someone from any of several places named Lenz or Lenzen.

Lenzo (153) Italian: from a reduced form of the personal name LORENZO.

GIVEN NAMES Italian 11%. *Carmelo, Carmine, Giuseppe, Pino.*

Leo (2634) **1.** Southern Italian: nickname for a fierce or brave warrior, from Latin *leo* 'lion'. **2.** Italian: from a short form of the personal name PANTALEO. **3.** Jewish: from the personal name *Leo* (from Latin *leo* 'lion'), borrowed by Christians as an equivalent of Hebrew Yehuda (see LEIB 3). **4.** English: from the Old French personal name *Leon* 'lion' (see LYON 2). **5.** Spanish: variant or derivative of the personal name LEON. **6.** Dutch: from Latin *leo* 'lion', applied either a nickname for a strong or fearless man or a habitational name for someone living at a house distinguished by the sign of a lion; or alternatively from a personal name of the same derivation. **7.** German and Hungarian (**Leó**): Latinized form of **Löwe** (see LOEWE).

GIVEN NAMES Italian 10%. *Salvatore* (10), *Rocco* (8), *Antonio* (7), *Angelo* (5), *Domenic* (5), *Enrico* (4), *Luigi* (3), *Pasquale* (3), *Carlo* (2), *Carmine* (2), *Cosmo* (2), *Damiano* (2).

Leombruno (119) Italian: from a personal name, a compound of LEONE + BRUNO.

GIVEN NAMES Italian 14%. *Oreste* (2), *Salvatore* (2), *Antonio, Carlo, Guerino.*

Leon (8817) **1.** Spanish (**León**): habitational name from León, a city in northwestern Spain, named with Latin *legio*, genitive *legionis* 'legion', a division of the Roman army. In Roman times the city was the garrison of the 7th Legion, known as the *Legio Gemina*. The city's name became reduced from *Legion(em)* to *Leon(em)*, and in this form developed an unetymological association with the word for 'lion', Spanish *león*. **2.** Spanish: from the personal name *León*, from Greek *leōn* 'lion' (see LYON 2). **Leon** is also found as a Greek family name. **3.** Spanish: nickname for a fierce or brave warrior, from *león* 'lion'. **4.** French (**Léon**) and English: variant of LYON.

GIVEN NAMES Spanish 41%. *Jose* (174), *Juan* (89), *Luis* (89), *Manuel* (67), *Carlos* (58), *Pedro* (55), *Jesus* (54), *Jorge* (52), *Francisco* (51), *Rafael* (41), *Miguel* (39), *Raul* (36).

Leonard (33985) **1.** English and French (**Léonard**): from a Germanic personal name composed of the elements *leo* 'lion' (a late addition to the vocabulary of Germanic name elements, taken from Latin) + *hard* 'hardy', 'brave', 'strong', which was taken to England by the Normans. A saint of this name, who is supposed to have lived in the 6th century, but about whom nothing is known except for a largely fictional life dating from half a millennium later, was popular throughout Europe in the early Middle Ages and was regarded as the patron of peasants and horses. **2.** Irish (Fermanagh): adopted as an English equivalent of Gaelic **Mac Giolla Fhionáin** or of LANGAN. **3.** Americanized form of Italian LEONARDO or cognate forms in other European languages.

FOREBEARS The French Léonard family were at Château Richer, Quebec, by 1698, having come from Maine, France.

Leonardi (890) Italian: patronymic or plural form of the personal name LEONARDO.

GIVEN NAMES Italian 16%. *Angelo* (6), *Guido* (4), *Vito* (4), *Ezio* (3), *Gino* (3), *Salvatore* (3), *Alfio* (2), *Dante* (2), *Franco* (2), *Lido* (2), *Aldo*, *Attilio*.

Leonardis (173) Italian: variant of LEONARDO.

GIVEN NAMES Italian 21%. *Angelo* (2), *Gino* (2), *Pasquale* (2), *Alfonse*, *Ettore*, *Santo*.

Leonardo (1001) Italian, Spanish, and Portuguese: from the Germanic personal name *Leonhard*, formed from the elements *leo* 'lion' + *hard*, 'hardy', 'brave', 'strong'; this was an early medieval saint's name (see LEONARD).

GIVEN NAMES Spanish 17%; Italian 7%; Portuguese 5%. *Manuel* (11), *Jose* (7), *Fernando* (4), *Carlos* (3), *Ernesto* (2), *Felipe* (2), *Guillermo* (2), *Julio* (2), *Luz* (2), *Mario* (2), *Alberto*, *Altagracia*; *Antonio* (7), *Angelo* (4), *Carmelo* (2), *Dario*, *Ercole*, *Filomena*, *Giuseppe*, *Marco*, *Mauro*, *Oreste*, *Pasco*, *Quintino*; *Joao* (2), *Paulo*.

Leonards (129) English and Scottish: patronymic from LEONARD. It is probably also an adoption of a cognate in other European languages.

Leonardson (116) Americanized form of Norwegian **Leon(h)ardsen**, a patronymic from the personal name LEONARD.

GIVEN NAMES Scandinavian 6%; German 4%. *Sven*; *Otto*.

Leone (5665) Italian (**Leóne**): from a personal name based on a nickname for a fierce or brave warrior, from *leone* 'lion' (Latin *leo*, genitive *leonis*).

GIVEN NAMES Italian 16%. *Angelo* (27), *Salvatore* (27), *Vito* (18), *Antonio* (17), *Rocco* (13), *Aldo* (9), *Sal* (9), *Carlo* (8), *Pasquale* (8), *Giovanni* (7), *Luigi* (5), *Carmela* (4).

Leonelli (150) Italian (**Leonelli**, **Leonetti**): from a patronymic or plural form of *Leonello*, a pet form of LEO or LEONE.

GIVEN NAMES Italian 10%. *Antimo*, *Ermanno*, *Remo*, *Sal*.

Leonetti (509) Italian (**Leonelli**, **Leonetti**): from a patronymic or plural form of *Leonetto*, a pet form of LEO or LEONE.

GIVEN NAMES Italian 13%. *Angelo* (3), *Antonio* (3), *Gennaro* (2), *Salvatore* (2), *Aldo*, *Carlo*, *Domenico*, *Gino*, *Giuseppe*, *Luigi*, *Pasquale*, *Reno*.

Leong (2302) Chinese 梁: variant of LIANG.

GIVEN NAMES Chinese 12%. *Wai* (7), *Wing* (7), *Sang* (6), *Yin* (5), *Hing* (4), *Kam* (4), *Lai* (4), *Cheng* (3), *Kee* (3), *Kin* (3), *Ping* (3), *Sing* (3).

Leonhard (515) German and Dutch: variant of LEONHARDT.

Leonhardt (1437) German and Dutch: from the Germanic personal name *Leonhard*, composed of the elements *leo* 'lion' + *hard*, 'hardy', 'brave', 'strong'.

GIVEN NAMES German 5%. *Kurt* (5), *Erwin* (2), *Heinz* (2), *Manfred* (2), *Armin*, *Fritz*, *Guenther*, *Gunter*, *Gunther*, *Otto*, *Ute*.

Leonhart (258) German and Dutch: variant of LEONHARDT.

Leoni (372) **1.** Italian (**Leóni**): patronymic from LEONE. **2.** Catalan: probably an altered form of Catalan *lleoní* a nickname meaning 'like a lion'.

GIVEN NAMES Italian 22%; French 5%; Spanish 5%. *Angelo* (3), *Orlando* (3), *Gino* (2), *Mario* (2), *Ricardo* (2), *Roberto* (2), *Alfredo*, *Armando*, *Carmine*, *Dante*, *Enrico*, *Francesca*, *Giovanni*, *Leno*, *Reno*, *Rocco*, *Romolo*; *Gaston* (2), *Luc*, *Serge*; *Juan*, *Lourdes*, *Rodolfo*.

Leonti (101) Italian (Sicily): from the Greek personal name or nickname *Léon*, *Léontos* 'lion' (equivalent of Latin *Leo*, *Leonis*).

GIVEN NAMES Italian 9%. *Domenic*, *Salvatore*.

Leopard (726) English: from Middle English, Old French *lepard* 'leopard' (from Late Latin *leopardus*, a compound of *leo* 'lion' + *pardus* 'panther'), probably applied as a nickname or as a habitational name for someone who lived at a house distinguished by the sign of a leopard.

Leopold (1640) French (**Léopold**), German, and Dutch: from a Germanic personal name, *Luitpold*, composed of the elements *liut* 'people' + *bald* 'bold', 'brave'. The form of the first element has been influenced by LEONARD. The surname is also borne by Ashkenazic Jews, in which case it is an adoption of the German forename as a surname.

GIVEN NAMES German 5%. *Otto* (4), *Kurt* (3), *Gunter* (2), *Lorenz* (2), *Alois*, *Aloysius*, *Franz*, *Fritz*, *Gerhard*, *Heinz*, *Hermann*, *Herta*.

Leos (652) **1.** variant spelling of Spanish **Leoz**, a habitational name of Basque origin, from Leotz in Navarre province. **2.** Greek: from the personal name *Leos*, pet form of LEON.

GIVEN NAMES Spanish 43%. *Jose* (12), *Pedro* (8), *Francisco* (6), *Manuel* (6), *Ruben* (6), *Carlos* (5), *Juan* (5), *Santos* (5), *Jesus* (4), *Pablo* (4), *Raul* (4), *Alfonso* (3).

Leotta (135) Southern Italian: from the personal name *Leotta*, a pet form of LEO.

GIVEN NAMES Italian 27%. *Salvatore* (4), *Rosario* (2), *Sal* (2), *Benedetto*, *Carmela*, *Carmelo*, *Carmine*, *Mario*.

Lepage (1556) French: occupational name for a young servant, Old French *page*, with the definite article *le*. The word came from Italian *paggio*, apparently ultimately from Greek *paidion*, diminutive of *pais* 'boy', 'child'.

GIVEN NAMES French 11%. *Armand* (7), *Marcel* (4), *Andre* (3), *Fernand* (3), *Pierre* (3), *Raoul* (3), *Adelard* (2), *Alcide* (2), *Christophe* (2), *Lucien* (2), *Normand* (2), *Adrien*.

Lepak (525) Polish: nickname from a derivative of *lepić* 'to mould', 'model', or 'glue'.

Lepard (356) English: variant spelling of LEOPARD.

Lepe (273) Spanish: habitational name from Lepe in the province of Seville.

GIVEN NAMES Spanish 61%. *Jose* (15), *Juan* (5), *Mario* (4), *Andres* (3), *Manuel* (3), *Miguel* (3), *Pedro* (3), *Ramon* (3), *Raul* (3), *Roberto* (3), *Salvador* (3), *Adriana* (2).

Lepera (220) Italian (Sicilian): dialectal topographic name for someone who lived by 'the pear tree'.

GIVEN NAMES Italian 8%. *Cosmo*, *Domenic*, *Salvatore*.

Lepere (175) French (**Lepère**): from French *le père* 'the father'; the name was taken to the U.S. by the Huguenots.

GIVEN NAMES French 5%. *Pierre*, *Thierry*.

Lepine (515) French (**Lépine**): topographic name from Old French *espine* 'thorn bush' (Latin *spina*); or a habitational name from any of several places called Épine or l'Épine, named with this word. Occasionally the name may derive from the same word used in a transferred sense of the crest or ridge of a hill.

GIVEN NAMES French 16%. *Armand* (4), *Andre* (3), *Marcel* (3), *Emile* (2), *Jacques* (2), *Donat*, *Fernand*, *Gaston*, *Gilfred*, *Gilles*, *Henri*, *Normand*.

Lepinski (167) Polish (**Lepiński**): habitational name for someone from Lepinie or Lepino, now in Ukraine.

GIVEN NAME German 4%. *Kurt* (2).

Lepisto (191) Finnish (**Lepistö**): from the plural of *leppä* 'alder tree' + the locative or collective ending *-sto*. It is recorded from the 15th century in north-central and eastern Finland, and was later adopted as an ornamental name during the name conversion movement in the 19th and early 20th centuries.

GIVEN NAMES Finnish 13%; Scandinavian 4%. *Eino* (2), *Toimi* (2), *Antti*, *Esko*, *Lempi*, *Reino*, *Seija*, *Toivo*, *Veikko*; *Helmer* (2).

Lepkowski (295) Polish (**Łepkowski**, **Łebkowski**): habitational name for someone from Łepki in Tarnobrzeg voivodeship or any of the many places named Łebki in other voivodeships, named with Polish *łepek* or *łebek* 'little head'.

GIVEN NAMES Polish 8%. *Casimir* (2), *Jerzy*, *Kazimierz*, *Stanislaw*, *Zbigniew*.

Lepley (932) Americanized spelling of South German **Lepple**: **1.** a byname for a cobbler. **2.** a pet form of LAPP.

Lepore (1651) Southern Italian: nickname for a fleet-footed or timid person, from *lepore* 'hare', a dialect form of *lepre* (Latin *lepus*, genitive *leporis*).
GIVEN NAMES Italian 17%. *Vito* (10), *Rocco* (9), *Antonio* (6), *Angelo* (5), *Carmine* (5), *Dante* (5), *Pasquale* (4), *Guido* (3), *Aldo* (2), *Carmela* (2), *Enrico* (2).

Lepp (355) German: **1.** unflattering nickname from Middle High German *lappe* 'coxcomb', 'puppy' (modern German *Laffe*). **2.** habitational name from a place so named near Neuss in the Rhineland.

Leppanen (172) Finnish (**Leppänen**): topographic name from Finnish *leppä* 'alder tree' + the common surname suffix *-nen*. This name is recorded from the 16th century in eastern and western Finland; it was also adopted as an ornamental name during the name conversion movement of the late 19th and early 20 centuries, and is now found chiefly in western Finland. In the U.S. it has sometimes been translated as ALDER.
GIVEN NAMES Finnish 16%; Scandinavian 8%. *Runo* (3), *Wilho* (3), *Reino* (2), *Eino*, *Ilkka*, *Kauko*, *Wiljo*; *Einer*, *Erik*, *Lasse*.

Leppard (117) English: variant spelling of LEOPARD.

Leppek (137) Polish: **1.** nickname from a derivative of *lepić* 'to mould', 'model', or 'glue' (see LEPAK). **2.** nickname for a coxcomb, from a diminutive of German LEPP.

Lepper (727) **1.** German and Dutch: occupational name from an agent derivative of Middle High German *lappe* 'rag', 'cloth', apparently denoting a cobbler. **2.** German: habitational name for someone from LEPP. **3.** English: nickname for a person with leprosy, Middle English *lepre* 'leper'.

Leppert (676) **1.** German: variant of LEPPER with excrescent *-t*. **2.** English: variant of LEOPARD.

Leppla (181) Probably an altered spelling of German **Lepple** (see LEPLEY).
GIVEN NAMES German 5%. *Franz*, *Gunter*, *Otto*.

Leppo (253) Finnish: unexplained.

Lepre (271) **1.** Italian: nickname for a fleet-footed or timid person, from *lepre* 'hare' (from Latin *lepus* 'hare', genitive *leporis*). **2.** French (**Lepré**): topographic name for someone who lived by a meadow or field, Old French *pred*, with the definite article *le*.
GIVEN NAMES Italian 11%. *Aniello* (2), *Antonio* (2), *Gennaro* (2), *Biagio*, *Egidio*, *Stefano*.

Lequire (225) French: Huguenot variant of LECUYER.

Leray (122) French: topographic name for someone who lived by a spring, Old French *rai*, with the definite article *le*.
GIVEN NAMES French 11%; Irish 6%. *Pierre* (3), *Christophe*, *Nolton*; *Fitzroy* (2).

Lerch (1495) German and Jewish (Ashkenazic): from Middle High German *lerche*, German *Lerche* 'lark', probably a nickname for someone with a good singing voice, or a metonymic occupational name for a bird-catcher. As a Jewish surname, it is most probably ornamental.
GIVEN NAMES German 4%. *Franz* (2), *Hans* (2), *Horst* (2), *Arno*, *Egon*, *Erwin*, *Gerhard*, *Guenter*, *Gunter*, *Helmut*, *Ingeborg*, *Karl-Heinz*.

Lerche (139) **1.** Danish: from *Lærkia*, a medieval nickname meaning 'lark'. **2.** Danish: habitational name from a place in Westphalia, Germany. **3.** German: variant of LERCH.
GIVEN NAMES German 10%. *Erwin* (4), *Deitrich*, *Gunter*, *Otto*.

Lerer (144) Jewish (Ashkenazic): altered spelling of LEHRER.
GIVEN NAMES Jewish 9%. *Avi*, *Hagai*, *Hyman*, *Shifra*, *Sol*.

Lerette (151) Probably a variant form of French LIRETTE.

Lerew (186) Perhaps an altered spelling of French LARUE.

Leriche (105) French: nickname for a rich man, a variant of RICHE with the the definite article *le*.
GIVEN NAMES French 17%; German 4%. *Armand* (4), *Andre* (2), *Benoit* (2), *Cecile*; *Manfred*.

Lerma (1325) Spanish: habitational name from Lerma, a little town in Burgos province.
GIVEN NAMES Spanish 47%. *Jose* (29), *Juan* (22), *Manuel* (21), *Jesus* (12), *Carlos* (10), *Pedro* (10), *Jorge* (9), *Miguel* (9), *Armando* (8), *Javier* (7), *Lupe* (7), *Alfredo* (6).

Lerman (1088) Jewish (eastern Ashkenazic): variant of LEHRMAN.
GIVEN NAMES Jewish 9%; Russian 5%. *Sol* (3), *Gershon* (2), *Menachem* (2), *Simcha* (2), *Aryeh*, *Avrohom*, *Baruch*, *Benyamin*, *Eran*, *Golda*, *Herschel*, *Hyman*; *Leonid* (4), *Boris* (3), *Grigory* (3), *Mikhail* (3), *Yefim* (2), *Aleksandr*, *Arcady*, *Arkadiy*, *Gennady*, *Igor*, *Lyubov*, *Oleg*.

Lerner (4010) **1.** English: occupational name for a scholar or schoolmaster, from an agent derivative of Middle English *lern(en)*, which meant both 'to learn' and 'to teach' (Old English *leornian*). **2.** South German: habitational name for someone from Lern near Freising. **3.** South German: nickname from Middle High German *lerner* 'pupil', 'schoolboy'. **4.** Jewish (Ashkenazic): occupational name from Yiddish *lerner* 'Talmudic student or scholar'.
GIVEN NAMES Jewish 9%. *Sol* (9), *Ilya* (5), *Miriam* (5), *Yakov* (5), *Aron* (4), *Emanuel* (4), *Isadore* (4), *Meyer* (4), *Hyman* (3), *Moisey* (3), *Shlomo* (3), *Yaacov* (3).

Lero (115) Origin unidentified.

Le Rose (190) Italian: topographic name for someone who lived among roses, from the plural of LA ROSA.
GIVEN NAMES Italian 8%. *Enrico*, *Gaetano*.

Leroux (1073) French: nickname for a person with red hair, from Old French *rous* 'red(-haired)' (Latin *russ(e)us*), with the definite article *le*. This name is associated with the Huguenots in British America; notably, with silversmiths in SC and NY.
GIVEN NAMES French 16%. *Andre* (7), *Pierre* (5), *Jacques* (4), *Lucien* (4), *Marcel* (4), *Alain* (3), *Armand* (3), *Alcide* (2), *Donat* (2), *Ludger* (2), *Yves* (2), *Adrien*.

Leroy (2629) French: from Old French *rey*, *roy* 'king' (from Latin *rex*, genitive *regis*), with the definite article *le*. It may have been an occupational name for someone in the service of the king, or a nickname for someone who behaved in a regal fashion or who had earned the title in some contest of skill or by presiding over festivities. The name is associated with Huguenots in British America, having been brought by them to MA from La Rochelle.
GIVEN NAMES French 5%. *Pierre* (5), *Jacques* (4), *Marcel* (4), *Alain* (2), *Henri* (2), *Alphonse*, *Andre*, *Antoine*, *Christophe*, *Franck*, *Hugues*, *Jean Michel*.

Lerro (219) Italian: unexplained.
GIVEN NAMES Italian 19%. *Romeo* (4), *Mario* (2), *Angelo*, *Eduardo*, *Elina*, *Emilio*, *Pasquale*, *Rafael*.

Lersch (155) German and Dutch: metonymic occupational name for a maker of leather pants, stockings, and boots, from Middle Low German *lērse*, contracted form of *lederse* 'made of leather', adjective from *Leder* 'leather'.

Lerud (123) Norwegian: habitational name from a farmstead in eastern Norway named from Old Norse *leira* 'clay' + *ruð* 'clearing'.

Lerum (152) Norwegian: habitational name from any of several farmsteads named Lærum or Lerum, from Old Norse *Leirheimr*, a compound of *leira* 'clay' + *heimr* 'farmstead', 'dwelling'.
GIVEN NAMES Scandinavian 6%. *Erik*, *Nordahl*, *Vidar*.

Les (119) Polish: topographic name for someone who lived in a forest, Polish *les*, dialect form of standard Polish *las* 'forest'.
GIVEN NAMES Polish 9%. *Jadwiga*, *Janusz*, *Jerzy*, *Tadeusz*.

Lesage (788) French: nickname for a wise man, from Old French *sage* 'wise', 'shrewd', 'prudent' (Late Latin *sapius*, from *sapere* 'taste', 'discern', 'discriminate'), with the definite article *le*.
GIVEN NAMES French 9%. *Laurent* (3), *Andre* (2), *Armand* (2), *Jacques* (2), *Philippe* (2), *Pierre* (2), *Albertine*, *Allain*, *Francois*, *Germaine*, *Herve*, *Lucien*.

Lesak (132) Polish: from a derivative of *les* 'forest', either a variant of LESIAK or a patronymic meaning 'son of the forester'.

Lesane (187) French: variant of LESESNE.
GIVEN NAME French 5%. *Patrice*.

Lesar (103) Slovenian: from *lesar*, occupational name for a woodman, derived from *les* 'wood' + the agent noun suffix *-ar*.

Lescarbeau (113) Canadian French: unexplained.

GIVEN NAME French 6%. *Gilles.*

Lescault (100) Possibly a respelling of southern French **Lescaut**, a metonymic occupational name for a wool winder, from an Old Occitan word meaning 'ball (of thread)', 'skein'.

GIVEN NAMES French 17%. *Jean Marc* (2), *Cecile, Eloi, Pierre, Rejean.*

Lesch (635) German: variant of LOESCH.

Lescher (150) German: probably a metonymic occupational name for a mediator or arbitrator, or possibly for a fireman, from Middle High German *leschære* 'extinguisher'.

GIVEN NAMES German 4%. *Hans, Klaus, Ulrich.*

Lese (137) Origin uncertain. Said to be an Americanized form of Polish LIS.

Leseberg (124) German: habitational name from a former medieval town in central Germany, of uncertain etymology.

Leseman (105) Dutch (**Lesemann**): occupational name for a teacher, a variant of LESMEISTER.

Leser (222) **1.** German: occupational name for a reader at a church or school, from Middle High German *lesaere* 'reader'. **2.** occupational name for a picker of grapes or a gleaner of grain, from the same word in the sense 'gatherer'. **3.** Jewish (Ashkenazic): variant of LAZAR.

GIVEN NAMES Jewish 10%; German 5%. *Nisan* (3), *Yitzchok* (2), *Aron, Benzion, Berish, Naftali, Shulim; Ernst* (2), *Hellmut, Waltraud.*

Lesesne (260) French: respelling of **Lesaisne**, an ethnic name from Old French *saisne* 'Saxon'. This name occurs chiefly in SC.

Lesh (844) Americanized spelling of German **Lesch** (see LOESCH).

Lesher (1489) Americanized spelling of German LESCHER.

Leshin (107) Jewish (eastern Ashkenazic): unexplained.

GIVEN NAMES Jewish 10%. *Meyer, Sol.*

Leshko (120) Americanized spelling of Polish **Leszko** (see LESKO).

GIVEN NAME Polish 6%. *Jaroslaw* (3).

Leshner (152) German (**Leschner**): habitational name for someone from any of various places called Leschen (Saxony, Silesia), Leschna (Silesia), or Leschnau (East Prussia).

Lesiak (215) **1.** Polish: from dialect *lesiak* 'forester'. **2.** Slovenian: topographic name for someone living in a forest or woodland, from *les* 'forest', 'scrub'. **3.** Slovenian: possibly also a respelling of **Lisjak**, a nickname for a cunning person, from *lisjak* 'fox'.

GIVEN NAMES Polish 8%. *Casimir* (2), *Grzegorz, Jerzy, Leszek.*

Lesieur (221) French: from Old French *sieur* 'lord' (Latin *senior* 'elder'). This was either an occupational name for someone in the service of a great lord or a derisive nickname for a person who gave himself airs and graces.

GIVEN NAMES French 9%. *Alphonse, Andre, Antoine, Fernande, Henri, Jean-Paul, Normand.*

Lesikar (106) Apparently Czech: unexplained.

Lesinski (352) Polish (**Lesiński**): habitational name for someone from places called Lesin, Lesina, or Leśna, named with *les*, dialect form of standard Polish *las* 'forest'.

GIVEN NAMES Polish 5%. *Casimir, Danuta, Janina, Janusz, Kazimierz, Zigmund.*

Leske (204) German (of Slavic origin): topographic name for someone who lived in a forest or occupational name for a forester, from Slavic *les* 'forest'. Compare Polish LESIAK.

GIVEN NAMES German 8%. *Erwin, Georg, Helmuth, Kurt, Reinhold.*

Lesko (1420) Polish (also **Leśko**, **Leszko**): **1.** habitational name for someone from a place called Lesko, named with Polish *les*, dialect form of standard Polish *las* 'forest'. **2.** from the personal name *Leszko*, a pet form of LECH.

Lesky (148) Czech (**Leský**): from an adjectival form of Czech *les* 'forest', a topographic name for someone living in a forest, an occupational name for a woodman, or a habitational name for someone from any of the many places in Bohemia named with this word.

Lesley (960) Scottish and northern Irish: variant spelling of LESLIE.

Leslie (8850) **1.** Scottish: habitational name from a barony in Aberdeenshire, which is first recorded *c.*1180 in the form *Lesslyn*, of obscure origin. Leslie in Fife is said to be named for this place; in some cases the surname may come from there. **2.** English: possibly from a double diminutive of the personal name *Lece* (see LEECE), thus *Lecelin*.

Lesmeister (328) Dutch: occupational name from Middle Dutch *lesemeester*, *lesmeister* 'teacher', 'priest who taught theology and philosophy to monks'.

Lesner (144) Variant spelling of German **Lessner**, a habitational name from any of various places in eastern Germany called Lessen, all named with Slavic *les* 'forest'.

Lesniak (931) **1.** Polish (**Leśniak**): occupational name for a woodman or forester, a derivative of *les* 'forest'. **2.** Altered spelling of Slovenian **Lesnjak**, topographic name from *les* 'forest', 'bushes', or of *Lešnjak*, nickname from an archaic spelling of *lešnik* 'hazelnut'.

GIVEN NAMES Polish 6%. *Zbigniew* (3), *Stanislaw* (2), *Boguslaw, Ewa, Irena, Jerzy, Kazimierz, Krystyna, Lech, Miroslaw, Slawek, Wieslaw.*

Lesnick (343) **1.** Americanized spelling of Polish **Leśnik** (see LESNIK). **2.** Americanized spelling of Slovenian LESNIK 2 or 3.

Lesniewski (338) Polish (**Leśniewski**): habitational name for someone from Leśniewo Górne or Leśniewo Dolne in Ciechanów voivodeship, named with *les*, dialect form of standard Polish *las* 'forest'.

GIVEN NAMES Polish 8%; German 4%. *Dariusz, Ignacy, Jerzy, Rajmund, Ryscard, Witold; Alfons, Alois, Eldred, Florian.*

Lesnik (145) **1.** Polish (**Leśnik**): occupational name for a forester, Polish *leśnik*, an agent noun derived from *les*, dialect form of standard Polish *las* 'forest'. **2.** Slovenian: topographic name from *les* 'forest', 'bushes'. **3.** Slovenian (**Lešnik**): nickname or topographic name from *lešnik* 'hazelnut' or *lešje* 'hazel trees', or a habitational name for someone from a place called Lešje, named with this word.

GIVEN NAMES Polish 5%. *Alojzy, Piotr.*

Lesperance (987) French Canadian: common secondary surname, used to distinguish different branches of the same family; from French *espérance* 'hope', with the definite article *le*, it could designate an optimistic person, or ironically, a pessimist. It is translated as HOPE.

GIVEN NAMES French 10%. *Andre* (4), *Pierre* (4), *Armand* (3), *Edouard, Fernand, Francois, Gaston, Gilles, Jeannot, Laurette, Marie Therese, Maxime.*

Less (388) **1.** Probably a shortened form of an unidentified Jewish surname. **2.** English: variant of LASS 3.

Lessa (128) Portuguese: variant of **Leça**, a habitational name from various places in northern Portugal called Leça.

GIVEN NAMES Spanish 11%; Italian 7%. *Fabio* (2), *Jose* (2), *Claudio, Eduardo, Fernanda, Gustavo, Maria Jose, Pedro, Roberto; Domenic, Francesca, Rocco.*

Lessard (2250) French: topographic name for someone who lived in a clearing, Old French *essart* (Late Latin *exsartum*, past participle of *exsarire* 'to weed out', 'grub up'), with the definite article *l'*, or a habitational name from various places named Lessard or Lessart from this word.

FOREBEARS A bearer of the name from Normandy, France, was in Quebec City by 1652.

GIVEN NAMES French 17%. *Andre* (9), *Lucien* (9), *Pierre* (9), *Marcel* (7), *Emile* (4), *Laurent* (4), *Michel* (4), *Normand* (4), *Adrien* (3), *Aime* (3), *Camille* (3), *Laurier* (3).

Lesser (1827) **1.** German: habitational name for someone from any of several places named Lesse, for example in Lower Saxony. **2.** German: variant of LESER. **3.** Dutch: occupational name for a fireman, from an agent derivative of Middle Dutch *lesschen*, *lessen* 'to extinguish'.

Lessig (388) German (of Slavic origin): Germanized form of Slavic *lěsnik* 'forest dweller' (see LESNIAK).

Lessin (156) Possibly an altered spelling of LESSING.

Lessing (247) German (of Slavic origin): variant of LESSIG.

Lessley (307) English (Norfolk): variant of LESLIE.

Lesslie (132) Scottish: variant of LESLIE.

Lessman (315) German (**Lessmann**): variant of LESSER.

Lessner (385) German: habitational name for someone from any of several places named Lessen.

Lessor (168) Origin unidentified.

Lestage (134) French (southwestern): topographic name from Occitan *estatge*, Old French *estage* 'place of residence'; or a habitational name from places called Lestage (Landes, Lot-et-Garonne) or Lestages (Gironde).

FOREBEARS A Lestage from Gascony, France, was in Quebec City before 1691.

GIVEN NAMES French 8%. *Armand, Emile, Marceau.*

Lester (14897) **1.** English: habitational name from Leicester, named in Old English from the tribal name *Ligore* (itself adapted from a British river name) + Old English *ceaster* 'Roman fort or walled city' (Latin *castra* 'legionary camp'). **2.** English (of Norman origin): habitational name from Lestre in Normandy. **3.** English and Scottish: variant of LISTER.

Lestina (110) Origin unidentified.

Leston (102) **1.** Spanish (**Lestón**): habitational name from any of four places called Lestó in A Coruña province, Galicia. **2.** English: unexplained; perhaps a habitational name from Leiston in Suffolk, so named from Old English *lēg* 'beacon fire' + *tūn* 'farmstead', 'settlement'.

GIVEN NAMES Spanish 16%. *Jose* (4), *Manuel* (4), *Ernesto* (2), *Evaristo, Faustino, Josefa.*

Lestrange (167) French and English: from Old French *estrange*, Middle English *strange* 'foreign' (from Latin *extraneus*, from *extra* 'outside'), with the French definite article *le*, hence a nickname for a newcomer to an area.

Lesuer (145) Respelling of French LESUEUR.

Lesueur (388) French and Channel Islands (Jersey): occupational name for a shoemaker or cobbler (rarely a tailor), from Old French *sueur* 'one who sews' (from Latin *sutor*), with the definite article *le*.

Lesure (243) French: occupational name for a shoemaker (see LESUEUR).

Leszczynski (393) **1.** Polish (**Leszczyński**) and Jewish (from Poland): habitational name for someone from any of various places (Leszczyna, Leszczyno, Leszczyny, or Leszczynek) named with Polish *leszczy-*

na 'hazel'. **2.** Polish: habitational name for someone from Leszno in central Poland.

GIVEN NAMES Polish 15%. *Leszek* (4), *Andrzej* (2), *Janusz* (2), *Stanislaw* (2), *Bogdan, Ewa, Gerzy, Ireneusz, Jerzy, Ryszard, Tadeusz, Walenty.*

Letarte (205) Canadian French: unexplained.

GIVEN NAMES French 11%. *Laurier* (2), *Andre, Armand, Donat, Jacques, Normand.*

Letbetter (101) Respelling of English LEDBETTER.

Letcher (623) **1.** English: topographic name for someone who lived beside a stream, from Old English *lœcc, lœce* (see LEACH) + the suffix *-er* denoting an inhabitant. **2.** English: unflattering nickname for a lecher, Middle English *lech(o)ur* (Old French *leceor*). Reaney comments: 'The surname is rare, probably usually disguised as LEGER'. **3.** German (**Letscher**): habitational name for someone from Letsch, near Bensberg, Rhineland, or various other places such as Letsche, Letschin, Letschow, etc. See also LETSCH.

Letchworth (356) English: habitational name from Letchworth, Hertfordshire, probably so named from an Old English *lycce* 'enclosure' (related to Old English *loc* 'enclosure') + *worþ* '(enclosure round a) homestead'.

Letellier (328) French (Normandy and Picardy): occupational name for a weaver, Old French *telier, tellier*, with the definite article *le*.

GIVEN NAMES French 7%. *Alcide, Alphonse, Fernand, Jean-Marie, Leandre, Leonie, Marcel, Simonne.*

Letendre (783) French: from Old French *tendre* 'tender', 'gentle', a nickname perhaps for someone who was in love or for someone young, in the bloom of youth, possibly the youngest member of a group of workers, for instance.

GIVEN NAMES French 14%. *Armand* (4), *Fernand* (4), *Normand* (3), *Andre* (2), *Benoit* (2), *Cecile* (2), *Emile* (2), *Marcel* (2), *Alcide, Alphonse, Camille, Cyrille.*

Leth (181) Danish: nickname from *lœt* 'light (in weight)'; equivalent to LIGHT 2.

Lethbridge (155) English (Devon): habitational name from a lost or unidentified place, probably in southwestern England, where the surname is most common.

Lethco (134) Perhaps an altered form of LITHGOW. This name occurs chiefly in TN.

Letizia (350) Italian: from a female personal name derived from the Latin name *Laetitia*, meaning 'happiness', 'gaiety' (from *laetus* 'joyous', 'happy').

GIVEN NAMES Italian 15%; French 4%. *Angelo* (2), *Concetta* (2), *Enzo* (2), *Gaetano* (2), *Rocco* (2), *Antonio, Cono, Erminio, Gino, Italo, Paolo, Salvator; Germain, Monique.*

Letner (258) Perhaps an altered spelling of LEITNER. This name is found mainly in TN and OH.

Leto (712) Italian: from the personal name *Leto*, from Latin *Laetus* meaning 'happy', 'joyful'.

GIVEN NAMES Italian 19%. *Salvatore* (13), *Antonio* (4), *Sal* (4), *Angelo* (3), *Vito* (3), *Carlo* (2), *Giovanni* (2), *Luigi* (2), *Alfonse, Benedetto, Carmela, Cesare.*

Letourneau (1998) French (**Létourneau**): from Old French *estournel* 'starling' (Late Latin *sturnellus*, a diminutive of classical Latin *sturnus*), with the definite article *l'*, hence a nickname for a chattering, gregarious person or a metonymic occupational name for a birdcatcher.

GIVEN NAMES French 11%. *Marcel* (10), *Andre* (6), *Armand* (5), *Normand* (5), *Gilles* (3), *Pierre* (3), *Emile* (2), *Fernand* (2), *Laurent* (2), *Adrien, Alcide, Alphonse.*

Letsch (151) **1.** South German and Swiss: nickname for someone with a large, drooping lower lip, or a slouching gait, cognate with the Swabian dialect word *lätsch* 'flabby', 'drooping', 'slouching'. **2.** German: habitational name from any of the places mentioned at LETCHER 3.

Letsche (117) German: variant of LETSCH 1.

GIVEN NAME German 6%. *Kurt.*

Letsinger (243) Americanized form of German **Lutzinger**, a habitational name from a place called Lutzingen near Donauwörth in Bavaria.

Letson (827) English and Scottish: metronymic from LETT.

Lett (1844) **1.** English: from a short form of the medieval female personal name *Lettice* (see LEECE 1). **2.** German: from Middle High German *lette* 'clay', 'clayey soil', hence a topographic name for someone who farmed on fertile clay soil.

Lettau (173) Northeastern German: habitational name from a place so named in former East Prussia (Slavic *Lettow*) or from Lettow in Bohemia.

GIVEN NAMES German 14%. *Ulrich* (3), *Bernhard, Hans, Heinz, Katharina, Klaus, Kurt, Markus.*

Letter (149) English: unexplained.

Letterman (588) **1.** Dutch: nickname for a short person, from Middle Dutch *luttel, littel, lettel* 'small'. **2.** German (**Lettermann**): elaborated form of LETT 2. **3.** German (**Lettermann**): habitational name for someone from Letter, near Hannover.

Lettiere (146) Italian: **1.** from the personal name *Lettiere*, a derivative of *Eleuterio*, from Greek *eleutheros* 'free'. **2.** alternatively, from the Sicilian personal names *Letterio* (male) and *Letteria* (female), given in honor of the Madonna della Lettara, patron saint of Messina.

GIVEN NAMES Italian 15%. *Rocco* (3), *Angelo* (2).

Lettieri (391) Italian: patronymic or plural form of LETTIERE.

GIVEN NAMES Italian 16%. *Salvatore* (6), *Vito* (3), *Carmine* (2), *Donato, Eliseo, Giovanni, Nichola, Pasquale, Primo, Sabato, Sal, Saverio*.

Lettow (116) Northeastern German, also found elsewhere in central Europe: variant of LETTAU.

GIVEN NAMES German 12%. *Kurt* (3), *Wolfgang*.

Letts (756) **1.** English: metronymic from LETT 1. **2.** Americanized spelling of German LETZ.

Letz (187) German: **1.** nickname for someone awkward and clumsy, from Middle High German *letz* 'upside down', 'opposite'. **2.** from a derivative of any of various Germanic compound personal names with a first element *liut* 'tribe', 'people'.

Leu (803) North German and Dutch: from Middle Low German *lēwe* 'lion', a nickname for a brave or regal person, or a habitational name from a house distinguished by the sign of a lion.

GIVEN NAMES German 4%. *Erwin* (2), *Frieda, Hedwig, Manfred, Matthias, Otto*.

Leubner (123) German: habitational name for someone from any of several places in Saxony called Leuba or Leuben.

GIVEN NAMES German 12%; Czech and Slovak 4%. *Horst* (2), *Gerhard, Ingo, Rainer, Wolfgang*; *Milos* (2).

Leuck (242) **1.** Dutch: from a vernacular form of LUCAS. **2.** French: possibly a habitational name from Leuc in Aude.

Leuenberger (321) German: habitational name for someone from any of several places named Leuenberg, as for example one in Brandenburg, named with LEU ('lion') as the first element.

GIVEN NAMES German 7%. *Hans* (5), *Niklaus* (2), *Urs* (2), *Joerg, Kurt*.

Leuer (139) German: from a personal name, from which **Lüder** (see LUEDER) and LUTHER are also derived.

GIVEN NAMES German 4%. *Benno, Gerhard*.

Leugers (182) German: patronymic from **Leuger**, a short form of a Germanic name composed of *liod* 'people', ' tribe' + *gār, gēr*, 'spear'.

GIVEN NAMES German 5%. *Aloys, Gerhard, Othmar*.

Leung (4423) Chinese 梁: variant of LIANG.

GIVEN NAMES Chinese 33%. *Wing* (26), *Wai* (23), *Siu* (17), *Kam* (16), *Chi* (14), *Kwok* (14), *Kwan* (13), *Chung* (12), *Kin* (12), *Yuk* (12), *Ming* (11), *Man* (10), *Yuen* (10), *Pak* (11), *Yiu* (7), *Yuet* (5), *Kwok Fai* (3), *Kwok Wai* (3), *Shiu* (3), *Min* (2), *Poon* (2), *Poy* (2), *Sik* (2), *Woon* (2).

Leupold (219) German: variant of LEOPOLD.

GIVEN NAMES German 9%. *Arno, Bernd, Dieter, Mathias, Oskar*.

Leupp (101) Swiss German: most probably a short form of **Leupi**, a Swiss pet form of LEOPOLD.

Leuschen (132) German: probably a metronymic from the genitive case, *Luschen*, of *Lusche*, a pet form of the female personal name *Gertrud* (see TRUDE).

Leuschner (188) Eastern German: metronymic from the female personal name *Lusche*, ultimately from *Gertrud* (see TRUDE, LEUSCHEN), with the genitive *-er*.

GIVEN NAMES German 14%. *Heinz* (3), *Eberhard* (2), *Horst, Kurt, Manfred*.

Leuthauser (115) German: variant of LEITHAUSER.

Leuthner (110) German: habitational name for someone from Leuthen in Niederlausitz, eastern Germany.

Leuthold (305) Swiss German: from a Germanic personal name formed with the elements *leud, liut* 'people', 'tribe' + *walt* 'rule', 'reign'.

Leuty (149) **1.** Swiss German: Americanized form of **Lüthy** (see LUTHI). **2.** English: variant of LAITY.

Leutz (110) German: variant (rounded) of LEITZ.

GIVEN NAME German 4%. *Otto*.

Leutzinger (108) Swiss German: probably from *Leutz*, a pet form of any of several Germanic personal names formed with *liut* 'people', 'tribe' + *-inger*, a suffix of affiliation.

GIVEN NAME German 7%. *Kurt* (2).

Leuzinger (114) Swiss German: variant of LEUTZINGER.

Leuzzi (105) Italian: of uncertain etymology; possibly from a pet form of the personal name LEO.

GIVEN NAMES Italian 24%. *Angelo* (2), *Mario* (2), *Orlando* (2), *Domenic, Giuseppe, Martino, Pasquale, Rocco*.

Lev (531) Jewish (eastern Ashkenazic): **1.** from Slavic *lev* 'lion', which was used as an equivalent of the Yiddish personal name *leyb* (see LEIB 1). **2.** shortened form of LEVY.

GIVEN NAMES Jewish 18%; Russian 5%. *Shraga* (3), *Yehuda* (3), *Iser* (2), *Ovadia* (2), *Shlomo* (2), *Uri* (2), *Aaron David, Anat, Avi, Berish, Chaim, Doron*; *Igor* (3), *Boris* (2), *Dmitry, Oleg, Semion, Semyon, Sergey, Vladimir, Yefim, Yevgeniy, Yury*.

Leva (279) **1.** Possibly Italian, also found in Spain: unexplained. **2.** French: from Old Occitan *leva* 'import levy', hence a metonymic occupational name for a collector of such duties. **3.** Greek: of uncertain origin; possibly from the Italian exclamation *leva!* 'lift!', used as a metonymic nickname for a sailor.

GIVEN NAMES Italian 13%. *Antonio* (6), *Egidio* (2), *Carmine, Dino, Domenico, Ercole, Gennaro, Nicola, Sal, Salvatore*.

Levalley (332) Part translation of French **Lavallée** (see LAVALLEE).

Levan (1669) French (Belgium): nickname for someone who was fleet of foot, from French *le vent* 'the wind'.

Levander (134) Swedish (also common in Finland): ornamental name of various origins. One 19th century bearer of the name, a priest, took it from the name of his home farm, Hjärtungen, translating Swedish *hjärta* 'heart' into Hebrew *lev* and adding the suffix *-ander*, a derivative Greek *andr-* 'man'. In another example, the surname was taken from Levene, a place in Västergötland province.

GIVEN NAMES Finnish 4%; Scandinavian 4%. *Aarne, Veikko*; *Nils*.

Levandoski (358) Altered spelling of Polish LEWANDOWSKI.

Levandowski (368) Altered spelling of Polish LEWANDOWSKI.

Levangie (199) Canadian French: unexplained.

Levant (119) French (Brittany, Touraine): from French *levant* 'east', a topographic name for someone who lived in the eastern part of a town or settlement, or outside it to the east; or a regional name for someone who had migrated westward (and so was regarded as coming from the east). It may also denote someone from the Levant, the eastern Mediterranean (see LEVENTIS).

Levar (138) Slovenian: unexplained.

Levario (204) Hispanic (Mexico): possibly of Italian origin, but unexplained.

GIVEN NAMES Spanish 42%. *Carlos* (5), *Juan* (5), *Manuel* (5), *Horacio* (2), *Humberto* (2), *Jaime* (2), *Jesus* (2), *Odila* (2), *Albaro, Alfonso, Alfredo, Alicia*.

Levasseur (1605) French: status name from Old French *vasseor*, a short form of *vavasour*, a term of the feudal system for a tenant ranking immediately below a baron. Such a tenant would have been a prosperous man, and the surname may have been used for someone in his service more often than for the man himself. The term is probably derived from medieval Latin *vassus vassorum* 'vassal of vassals', i.e. vassal-in-chief.

GIVEN NAMES French 10%. *Armand* (5), *Emile* (4), *Lucien* (4), *Andre* (3), *Camille* (3), *Jacques* (2), *Oneil* (2), *Pierre* (2), *Sylvian* (2), *Alain, Alphonse, Cyr*.

Levatino (137) Italian: of uncertain etymology; it may be from the personal name *Levatino*, from *levatino* 'Levantine', or alternatively it could be a nickname from Sicilian *livantinu* 'moody', 'capricious', 'frivolous'.

GIVEN NAMES Italian 15%. *Sal* (3), *Salvatore* (3), *Angelo, Vita*.

Levay (238) Hungarian (**Lévay**): habitational name for someone from a place called Léva in former Bars county.

GIVEN NAMES Hungarian 6%. *Vilmos* (2), *Katalin, Laszlo, Tibor, Zoltan*.

Leve (158) **1.** Jewish: variant of LEV or LEVY. **2.** French: variant of LEVEE.

Leveck (110) Americanized spelling of French **Levêque** ('the bishop'), a variant of LEVESQUE.

Levee (207) French (**Levée**): **1.** from *levée* 'raised (ground)', 'bank', hence a topographic name for someone who lived on a piece of high ground. **2.** metonymic occupational name for a tax-collector, from *levée (d'impôts)* 'tax levy'. **3.** Americanized spelling of French **Léveillé** (see LEVEILLE).

Leveille (656) French (**Leveillé**, **L'Eveillé**, **Léveillé**): nickname from French *l'éveillé* 'the awake', 'the alert'. One VT Civil War soldier so named used the translation 'Wideawake' for his surname.
GIVEN NAMES French 13%. *Armand* (2), *Jacques* (2), *Louiselle* (2), *Raoul* (2), *Yves* (2), *Alexandre*, *Andre*, *Chantal*, *Claudelle*, *Germaine*, *Henri*, *Jean Claude*.

Leveillee (114) Of French origin: probably an altered spelling of **Leveillé**, a nickname meaning 'the alert one' (French *l'eveillé*).
GIVEN NAMES French 26%. *Herve* (3), *Pierre* (3), *Ghislaine*, *Jean Guy*, *Lucien*, *Marcel*, *Normand*.

Level (220) Eastern French: from Old French *veel* 'calf', with the definite article *le*; apparently a nickname for an indolent person (from its colloquial sense of 'lump', 'clod').

Levell (222) **1.** English: from a late Old English personal name *Lēofweald*, composed of the elements *lēof* 'dear', 'beloved' + *weald* 'power', 'rule'. **2.** French: variant spelling of LEVEL.

Leven (322) **1.** Jewish (Ashkenazic): variant spelling of LEVIN. **2.** English, North German, and Dutch: from the Germanic personal name represented by Old English *Lēofwine*, Saxon *Liafwin*, composed of the elements *lēof* 'dear', 'beloved' + *wine* 'friend'. **3.** English and Scottish: habitational name from places called Leven in East Yorkshire, Fife, and Renfrew. The first is probably from a stream name, possibly derived from a Celtic word meaning smooth (as in Welsh *llyfyn*). The Scottish place name is from a Gaelic river name meaning 'elm river'. **4.** Dutch and North German: from a Flemish saint's name, *Lefwin* (*Lieven*), the patron saint of Ghent (see LEWIN 2).
GIVEN NAMES German 4%. *Gerd*, *Inge*, *Merwin*, *Wilhelm*.

Levenberg (194) **1.** Jewish (eastern Ashkenazic): variant of LOWENBERG. **2.** Dutch and Belgian (**Levenbergh**): habitational name from Lewenborg in Groningen, or from Leeuwenbergh or Leyenburg, both in South Holland, or from Leeuwenburg in West Flanders, Belgium.
GIVEN NAMES Jewish 10%. *Ilya*, *Shoshana*, *Yehuda*, *Yetta*, *Zvi*.

Levendoski (112) Americanized spelling of LEWANDOWSKI.

Levendusky (146) Americanized spelling of LEWANDOWSKI.

Levene (310) **1.** Jewish (eastern Ashkenazic): variant of LEVIN. **2.** English: variant of LEVEN 3. **3.** Breton (**Lévéné**): from an old female personal name derived from Old Breton *louuinid* 'joy', 'gaiety'. The name gained popularity as it belonged to the mother of a Breton saint, Gwenael. **4.** Altered spelling of French LAVIGNE, LAVIN, LAVINE, LEVIN, or various other like-sounding surnames.

Levengood (433) **1.** Americanized form of a German name of uncertain origin. It is most probably from **Liebengut**, a nickname meaning 'dear and good' (*lieb und gut*). **2.** An alternative possibility is German **Leibengut**, a status name for a person bonded to an ecclesiastical estate, from Middle High German *līp* 'body', 'life' + *und* 'and' + *guot* 'goods', 'possessions'.

Levenhagen (198) German: habitational name from a place so named in Pomerania.

Levens (495) **1.** English: habitational name from a place in Cumbria, so named from the Old English personal name *Lēofa* (genitive form) + *næss* 'promontory'. **2.** North German: patronymic from LEVEN 2.

Levenson (1395) Jewish (Ashkenazic): variant of LEVINSON.

Levenstein (173) Jewish (Ashkenazic): ornamental name, or perhaps an ornamental elaboration associated with the name *Leyb*; from Middle High German *lēwe* 'lion', translating the Yiddish male personal name *Leyb* (see LOW 3) + German *stein* 'stone', 'rock'. There may have been some confusion between the first element and the personal name *Levi* (see LEVY).

Leventhal (1028) Jewish (Ashkenazic): ornamental name like LEVENSTEIN, but with German *thal* 'valley' as its second element.
GIVEN NAMES Jewish 4%. *Sol* (4), *Emanuel* (2), *Avrohom*, *Myer*.

Leventis (132) Greek: from Italian *levanti* 'Levantine', 'people from the East', i.e. the eastern Mediterranean, in particular armed sailors or pirates during the Middle Ages. In Italian the word took on a negative connotation and came to mean 'pirate' and hence 'undisciplined youth', but in Greek the term has positive connotations of fearlessness and gallantry. It is also a reduced form of surnames with *Levento-* as a prefix, e.g. **Leventogiannis** 'John the gallant'.
GIVEN NAMES Greek 5%. *Costas*, *Kostas*.

Leveque (521) French (also **Levêque**, **Lévêque**): variant of LEVESQUE.
GIVEN NAMES French 10%. *Marcel* (3), *Henri* (2), *Andre*, *Antoine*, *Auguste*, *Edouard*, *Emile*, *Germaine*, *Lucien*, *Marie-France*, *Yves*.

Lever (759) English (of Norman origin): **1.** nickname for a fleet-footed or timid person, from Old French *levre* 'hare' (Latin *lepus*, genitive *leporis*). It may also have been a metonymic occupational name for a hunter of hares. **2.** topographic name for someone who lived in a place thickly grown with rushes, from Old English *læfer* 'rush', 'reed', 'iris'. Compare LAVER 3. Great and Little Lever in Greater Manchester (formerly in Lancashire) are named with this word (in a collective sense) and in some cases the surname may also be derived from these places. **3.** possibly from an unrecorded Middle English survival of an Old English personal name, *Lēofhere*, composed of the elements *lēof* 'dear', 'beloved' + *here* 'army'.

Levere (124) Italian: nickname for a fleet-footed or timid person, from *levere*, variant of *lepre* 'hare' (see LEPRE).

Leverenz (513) North German: from a personal name derived from *Laurentius* (see LAWRENCE).

Leverett (1291) English: **1.** diminutive of LEVER 1. **2.** from the Middle English personal name *Lefred*, Old English *Lēofrǣd*, composed of the elements *lēof* 'dear', 'beloved' + *rǣd* 'counsel'.

Leverette (719) Apparently a respelling of LEVERETT.

Leverich (294) English: from the Middle English personal name *Lefric*, Old English *Lēofrīc*, composed of the elements *lēof* 'dear', 'beloved' + *rīc* 'power'.
GIVEN NAME French 4%. *Pierre*.

Leveridge (132) English: variant of LEVERICH.

Levering (614) English (Devon): unexplained. This is a frequent name in OH.

Leverone (143) Italian: augmentative form of LEVERE.

Leveroni (101) Italian: from a patronymic or plural form of LEVERONE.
GIVEN NAMES Italian 4%. *Mario*, *Roberto*.

Levers (150) English: patronymic from LEVER 3.

Leverson (188) English: patronymic from LEVER 3.
GIVEN NAMES Scandinavian 6%. *Erik*, *Sven*.

Levert (259) French: from Old French *verd* 'green', with the definite article *le*, presumably a nickname for someone who habitually dressed in this color.
FOREBEARS A Levert from Rouen was in Island of Orleans, near Quebec City, by 1669.
GIVEN NAMES French 6%. *Jacques* (2), *Jean-Guy*, *Jean-Pierre*.

Leverton (297) English: habitational name from any of several places so called. One in Berkshire is named with the Old English female personal name *Lēofwaru* (composed of the elements *lēof* 'dear', 'beloved' + *waru* 'care') + Old English *tūn* 'enclosure', 'settlement'; one in Lincolnshire has as its first element Old English *læfer* 'rush', 'reed' (see LEVER 2). North and South Leverton in Nottinghamshire may contain a river name identical to that in LEAR 2.

Levesque (4503) French: from Old French *eveske* 'bishop', Latin *episcopus* (see

BISHOP), with the definite article *l(e)*, hence an occupational name for a member of a bishop's household, or a nickname for a solemn person. This is the most frequent of several alternative spellings in French Canada.

GIVEN NAMES French 18%. *Andre* (16), *Normand* (16), *Armand* (14), *Lucien* (13), *Marcel* (11), *Rosaire* (9), *Emile* (8), *Gilles* (8), *Pierre* (8), *Jacques* (7), *Adrien* (6), *Raoul* (6).

Levett (223) English: variant spelling of LEAVITT.

Levey (1074) **1.** Jewish: variant spelling of LEVY. **2.** English: variant spelling of LEAVEY.

Levi (2379) Jewish (Sephardic and Ashkenazic): see LEVY.

GIVEN NAMES Jewish 8%. *Amnon* (4), *Meir* (4), *Moshe* (4), *Arie* (3), *Avi* (3), *Dror* (3), *Haim* (3), *Yehuda* (3), *Doron* (2), *Dov* (2), *Haskel* (2), *Ilan* (2).

Levick (334) **1.** English: nickname from Anglo-Norman French *l'eveske* 'the bishop' (see BISHOP). **2.** English: from the Middle English personal name *Lefeke*, Old English *Lēofeca*, a derivative of *Lēofa* (see LEAF). **3.** Jewish (eastern Ashkenazic): from Yiddish *Leyvik*, a pet form of the personal name *Leyvi*, itself a pet form of the Biblical name *Levi* (see LEVY).

Levie (276) Jewish: variant spelling of LEVY.

Levien (197) Altered spelling of French LAVIGNE.

Levier (135) Breton: occupational name for a guide or sea or river pilot.

Levin (10321) **1.** Jewish (mainly from Lithuania and Belarus): Slavicized form of LEVY. **2.** Jewish (Ashkenazic) and German: from the personal name *Levin*, which was also used by German Christians as a derivative of *Liebwin*. As a Jewish name it sometimes represents a pet form of western Yiddish 'lion' (see LOEWE 2). **3.** Russian: patronymic of *Lëva*, a pet form of the personal name *Lev* + the Russian possessive suffix *-in*.

GIVEN NAMES Jewish 7%. *Meyer* (13), *Sol* (13), *Moshe* (9), *Aron* (7), *Emanuel* (7), *Ilya* (7), *Miriam* (7), *Yakov* (7), *Hyman* (6), *Isadore* (6), *Doron* (5), *Batya* (4).

Levina (113) Jewish (eastern Ashkenazic): from the Russian feminine form of LEVIN.

GIVEN NAMES Russian 36%; Jewish 24%. *Lyubov* (3), *Galina* (2), *Sofiya* (2), *Asya*, *Gitya*, *Inessa*, *Khasya*, *Liliya*, *Lubov*, *Lyudmila*, *Masha*, *Raisa*; *Mariya* (4), *Faina* (2), *Irina* (2), *Khana* (2), *Polina* (2), *Sarra* (2), *Golda*, *Khanna*, *Miriam*, *Tsilya*.

Levine (19087) **1.** Jewish (Ashkenazic): variant of LEVIN. **2.** Altered spelling of French LAVIGNE.

GIVEN NAMES Jewish 5%. *Sol* (27), *Hyman* (24), *Meyer* (16), *Isadore* (12), *Miriam* (10), *Hillel* (5), *Yetta* (5), *Abbe* (4), *Mort* (4), *Aron* (3), *Chaim* (3), *Herschel* (3).

Leviner (295) Origin unidentified. This name occurs chiefly in NC and SC.

Levinger (104) Jewish (Ashkenazic): ornamental extension of LEVY; the ending *-inger* being common in German surnames derived from place names.

GIVEN NAMES Jewish 9%; Russian 4%. *Ari*, *Isaak*, *Menachem*, *Mort*, *Zeev*; *Dmitry*, *Semyom*.

Levings (266) **1.** North German: variant of the habitational name **Lewing**, from a place near Stade in Lower Saxony. **2.** North German: patronymic from a personal name (*Lehwing* or *Lewien*), formed with Middle Low German *lev* 'dear' + *win* 'friend'. **3.** English: perhaps a habitational name from Levens in Cumbria, probably so named from the Old English personal name *Lēofa* (+ genitive *n*) + *næss* 'promontory', 'headland'. **4.** Possibly a hypercorrected spelling of Irish **Levens**, a County Louth name, which Woulfe interprets as an Anglicized form of Gaelic **Mac Dhuinnshlébhín**, a variant of DUNLEAVY.

GIVEN NAMES German 4%. *Brunhilde*, *Helga*, *Hildegarde*.

Levingston (466) Scottish and northern Irish: variant of LIVINGSTONE.

Levins (702) **1.** English: patronymic from the Middle English personal name *Leving*, Old English *Lēofing*, based on *lēof* 'dear'. Compare LOVING. **2.** Latvian (**Leviņš**): Latvianized form of Jewish LEVIN.

Levinsky (227) Jewish (eastern Ashkenazic): patronymic from LEVY or LEVIN.

GIVEN NAMES Jewish 6%. *Meyer*, *Mort*.

Levinsohn (147) Jewish (Ashkenazic): variant of LEVINSON.

GIVEN NAMES Jewish 4%. *Sol*, *Tzivia*.

Levinson (3005) Jewish (Ashkenazic): patronymic from the personal names LEVIN or LEVY.

GIVEN NAMES Jewish 5%. *Sol* (6), *Hillel* (4), *Aviva* (2), *Gershon* (2), *Ilya* (2), *Meyer* (2), *Naum* (2), *Bina*, *Blume*, *Elad*, *Esfir*, *Hyman*.

Levis (611) **1.** Jewish: Americanized form of some like-sounding Ashkenazic surname such as LEVY or LEVINSON. **2.** French: habitational name from Levis, Yonne. **3.** French (Artois): from Old French *vis* '(spiral) staircase', with the Old Picard feminine article *le*; perhaps a nickname for someone whose house had such a feature.

Levison (369) Jewish (Ashkenazic): patronymic from LEVY.

Levit (335) **1.** Jewish (Ashkenazic): from German *Levit* 'Levite' (see LEVY). **2.** English: variant spelling of LEAVITT.

GIVEN NAMES Russian 16%; Jewish 14%. *Mikhail* (7), *Boris* (4), *Igor* (4), *Aleksandr* (2), *Leonid* (2), *Yury* (2), *Beyla*, *Dmitriy*, *Feiga*, *Gennady*, *Iosif*, *Jenya*; *Kopel* (2), *Sol* (2), *Golda*, *Herschel*, *Itzhak*, *Moisey*, *Revekka*, *Shai*, *Shmuel*.

Levitan (626) Jewish (eastern Ashkenazic): from Polish *Lewita* 'Levite' + the Slavic noun suffix *-an* (see LEVY).

GIVEN NAMES Jewish 8%; Russian 4%. *Miriam* (3), *Meyer* (2), *Ari*, *Dovid*, *Esfir*, *Moisey*, *Mort*; *Leonid* (2), *Vladimir* (2), *Yury* (2), *Arkady*, *Dmitry*, *Iliya*, *Lev*, *Leyzer*, *Lyudmila*, *Svetlana*, *Yelena*, *Yevgeniya*.

Levitas (153) Jewish (eastern Ashkenazic): from the Greek form of the Biblical name LEVY.

Levitch (133) Jewish (from Ukraine): patronymic from LEVY.

GIVEN NAME Jewish 8%; German 4%. *Mort* (2).

Levitin (170) Jewish (from Belarus): from eastern Slavic *levit* 'Levite' + the possessive suffix *-in* (see LEVY).

GIVEN NAMES Jewish 24%; Russian 14%. *Sholom* (3), *Binyomin*, *Chaya*, *Ilya*, *Moisey*, *Moshe*, *Naum*, *Reuven*, *Sarra*, *Shai*; *Boris* (3), *Mikhail* (3), *Svetlana* (2), *Vladimir* (2), *Anatoly*, *Genady*, *Igor*, *Lev*, *Sergei*, *Yuriy*.

Leviton (206) Jewish (eastern Ashkenazic): variant of LEVITAN.

Levitsky (320) Russian, Ukrainian, and Jewish (from Ukraine and Belarus): from the eastern Slavic adjective *levitskij* 'Levitical'. As a Jewish name it denotes members of the hereditary caste of Levites (see LEVI). As a Slavic name it is an ornamental name with Biblical associations, which was adopted mainly by students of religious high schools.

GIVEN NAMES Russian 11%; Jewish 8%. *Boris* (3), *Leonid* (2), *Lyubov* (2), *Mikhail* (2), *Vladimir* (2), *Arkady*, *Daniil*, *Gleb*, *Guennadi*, *Nikolay*, *Oleg*, *Sergey*; *Yakov* (3), *Asher* (2), *Irina*, *Isaak*.

Levitt (2614) **1.** English: variant spelling of LEAVITT. **2.** Jewish (Ashkenazic): variant spelling of LEVIT.

GIVEN NAMES Jewish 5%. *Sol* (8), *Miriam* (3), *Hyman* (2), *Isador* (2), *Isadore* (2), *Ari*, *Batya*, *Hersh*, *Mayer*, *Meyer*, *Rina*.

Levitz (332) Jewish (Ashkenazic): Germanized variant of LEVITCH.

GIVEN NAMES Jewish 5%. *Miriam* (2), *Ephraim*, *Isadore*, *Shoshana*.

Levron (119) Of French origin: unexplained. This is a South Carolina name.

GIVEN NAMES French 8%. *Alcee*, *Alphonse*, *Emile*.

Levy (17391) Jewish (Ashkenazic and Sephardic): from the Biblical personal name *Levi*, from a Hebrew word meaning 'joining'. This was borne by a son of Jacob and Leah (Genesis 29: 34). Bearers of this name are Levites, members of the tribe of Levi, who form a hereditary caste who assist the *kohanim* (see COHEN) in their priestly duties.

GIVEN NAMES Jewish 7%. *Hyman* (26), *Miriam* (19), *Sol* (16), *Meyer* (13), *Moshe* (13), *Emanuel* (11), *Avi* (9), *Shlomo* (7), *Isadore* (6), *Meir* (6), *Nissim* (6), *Ofer* (6).

Lew (2100) **1.** Polish: from the personal name *Lew* 'lion', adopted as a translation of *Leon* (see LYON 2). **2.** Jewish (Ashkenazic): variant spelling of LEV. **3.** English: topographic name for someone who lived by a hill or burial-mound, Old English *hlēw*, or a habitational name from Lew in Oxfordshire, named with this word. **4.** Chinese 刘: variant of LIU 1.
GIVEN NAMES Chinese 9%. *Wing* (13), *Yuen* (7), *Fook* (4), *Jung* (3), *Ying* (3), *Young* (3), *Yung* (3), *Bin* (2), *Foon* (2), *Hong* (2), *Kam* (2), *Koon* (2).

Lewallen (1677) Americanized form of Welsh LLEWELLYN.

Lewan (173) Polish (also **Lewań**): derivative of the personal name LEW 1.

Lewand (100) Polish: nickname from the vocabulary word *lewanda*, *lawanda* 'lavender'.

Lewandoski (206) Polish: variant of LEWANDOWSKI.

Lewandowski (4329) Polish: habitational name for someone from a place called Lewandów in Warszawa voivodeship, named with the vocabulary word *lewanda*, *lawenda* 'lavender'.
GIVEN NAMES Polish 5%. *Casimir* (9), *Andrzej* (4), *Danuta* (3), *Krzysztof* (3), *Zygmunt* (3), *Benedykt* (2), *Janusz* (2), *Stanislaw* (2), *Witold* (2), *Zdzislaw* (2), *Zyg* (2), *Bogdan*.

Lewark (137) North German: from Middle Low German *lēwerk* 'lark', hence a nickname for a merry person or an early riser, or a metonymic occupational name for someone who caught and sold birds for food.

Lewellen (1241) Americanized spelling of Welsh LLEWELLYN.

Lewelling (192) Americanized spelling of Welsh LLEWELLYN.

Lewellyn (576) Americanized spelling of Welsh LLEWELLYN.

Lewer (106) English: variant of LOWER.

Lewerenz (119) North German: from a personal name derived from *Laurentius* (see LAWRENCE).
GIVEN NAMES German 7%. *Kurt*, *Lutz*.

Lewers (174) English: variant of LOWERS.

Lewey (269) English: variant of LEAVEY.

Lewicki (468) **1.** Polish: habitational name for someone from either of two places called Lewiczyn, in the voivodeships of Ciechanów or Radom. **2.** Jewish (from Poland): from Polish *lewicki* 'of the Levites' (see LEVY).
GIVEN NAMES Polish 11%. *Jerzy* (2), *Pawel* (2), *Andrzej*, *Casimir*, *Czeslaw*, *Czeslawa*, *Jacek*, *Janusz*, *Jaroslaw*, *Kazimierz*, *Miroslaw*, *Ryszard*.

Lewin (2070) **1.** Jewish (Ashkenazic): German and Polish spelling of LEVIN. **2.** English, Dutch, and North German: from the Old English personal name *Lēofwine*, composed of the elements *lēof* 'dear', 'beloved' + *wine* 'friend'. This was the name borne by an English missionary who became the

patron saint of Ghent, and the personal name was consequently popular in the Low Countries during the Middle Ages. **3.** Irish and Manx: reduced Anglicized form of Gaelic **Mac Giolla Guillin** 'son of the servant of William'.
GIVEN NAMES German 4%. *Kurt* (6), *Hans* (2), *Alphons*, *Dieter*, *Egon*, *Ernst*, *Gerhard*, *Heinz*, *Hellmut*, *Ilse*, *Klaus*, *Lothar*.

Lewing (159) English: variant of LOVING.

Lewinski (265) **1.** Polish (**Lewiński**): habitational name for someone from a place called Lewin, Lewino, or Lewiny. **2.** Jewish (eastern Ashkenazic): patronymic from the personal name *Levin*, a derivative of LEVY.
GIVEN NAMES Polish 7%. *Grzegorz*, *Mariusz*, *Stanislaus*, *Zygmund*.

Lewinter (118) Jewish (Ashkenazic): of uncertain origin; possibly an ornamental extension of LEVY.
GIVEN NAMES Jewish 6%; German 4%. *Sol*, *Tovah*; *Bernhard*.

Lewis (166842) **1.** English (but most common in Wales): from *Lowis*, *Lodovicus*, a Norman personal name composed of the Germanic elements *hlod* 'fame' + *wīg* 'war'. This was the name of the founder of the Frankish dynasty, recorded in Latin chronicles as *Ludovicus* and *Chlodovechus* (the latter form becoming Old French *Clovis*, *Clouis*, *Louis*, the former developing into German *Ludwig*). The name was popular throughout France in the Middle Ages and was introduced to England by the Normans. In Wales it became inextricably confused with 2. **2.** Welsh: from an Anglicized form of the personal name *Llywelyn* (see LLEWELLYN). **3.** Irish and Scottish: reduced Anglicized form of Gaelic **Mac Lughaidh** 'son of *Lughaidh*'. This is one of the most common Old Irish personal names. It is derived from *Lugh* 'brightness', which was the name of a Celtic god. **4.** Americanized form of any of various like-sounding Jewish surnames.
FOREBEARS This name was brought independently to New England by many bearers from the 17th century onward. William Lewis was one of the founders of Hartford, CT, (coming from Cambridge, MA, with Thomas Hooker) in 1635. The explorer Meriwether Lewis (1774–1809) was a native of Albemarle Co., VA, where he was a neighbor of the Jeffersons, Randolphs, and other prominent families. His family also had plantations on the Broad River in Oglethorpe Co., GA. The Lewis family in VA date back to Robert Lewis, a native of Brecon, Wales, who settled in what is now Gloucester Co., VA, about 1635. Another early bearer of this very common British surname is Francis Lewis, a New York merchant and signer of the Declaration of Independence, who was born in 1713 in Llandaff, Glamorganshire, Wales.

Lewison (384) **1.** Welsh and English: patronymic from LEWIS. **2.** Jewish (Ashke-

nazic): patronymic from the personal name *Lewi*, Polish spelling of LEVY. **3.** Adoption of the Welsh and English surname as a sound-alike equivalent of Greek **Iliopoulos**, patronymic from ELIAS.

Lewitt (115) Jewish (Ashkenazic): variant of LEVIT.
GIVEN NAMES Jewish 5%. *Sol* (2), *Meyer*.

Lewkowicz (172) **1.** Polish and Jewish (from Poland): patronymic from the personal name *Lewek*, a pet form of *Lew*, meaning 'lion' (see LYON 2). As a Jewish personal name it was used as a Polish equivalent of Yiddish *leyb* (see LEIB 1). **2.** Polish: perhaps also a patronymic from the nickname *Lewek* 'left-handed', a diminutive of LEWY 1.
GIVEN NAMES Polish 8%; Jewish 6%. *Jerzy*, *Krystyna*, *Piotr*, *Tadeusz*; *Hershel*, *Leib*.

Lewman (293) Possibly an Americanized spelling of German **Lühmann** (see LUHMANN).

Lewter (479) English? This name occurs chiefly in NC, AL, and TN.

Lewton (295) English (Gloucestershire): habitational name from a lost or unidentified place.

Lewy (151) **1.** Polish: nickname for a left-handed person, from Polish *lewy* 'left'. **2.** Jewish (Ashkenazic): variant of LEVY.
GIVEN NAMES German 11%; Polish 4%. *Berthold*, *Gerda*, *Guenter*, *Hans*, *Ilse*, *Siegfried*, *Winfried*; *Janusz*, *Lucja*.

Lex (418) German and Dutch: from a short form of the personal name *Alexius*, ALEXIS.
GIVEN NAMES German 4%. *Kurt*, *Markus*.

Lexa (132) Czech and Slovak: from a reduced form of ALEXANDER.
GIVEN NAME French 4%. *Michel*.

Ley (1720) **1.** English: variant of LYE. **2.** French: habitational name from Ley in Moselle. **3.** French and German: from a medieval personal name, *Eloy* (Latin *Eligius*, a derivative of *eligere* 'to choose or elect'), made popular by a 6th-century saint who came to be venerated as the patron of smiths and horses. **4.** German (Rhineland): topographic name from Middle High German *leie* 'rock', 'stone', 'slate', or a habitational name from any of several places named with this word. Compare LEIER.

Leyba (688) Spanish: variant of LEIVA.
GIVEN NAMES Spanish 21%. *Luis* (6), *Jose* (5), *Ramon* (5), *Manuel* (4), *Orlando* (4), *Cayetano* (3), *Guillermo* (3), *Juan* (3), *Adolfo* (2), *Aurelio* (2), *Jesus* (2), *Lupe* (2).

Leyda (207) Origin unidentified.

Leyden (632) **1.** Irish: variant spelling of LYDON. **2.** Dutch (**van Leyden**): habitational name for someone from the city of Leiden.
GIVEN NAMES Irish 5%. *Brendan*, *Connor*, *Donovan*.

Leydig (133) Variant spelling of German LEIDIG.

Leydon (143) Irish: variant spelling of LYDON.

Leyendecker (294) German: occupational name for a slater, from Middle High German (Rhenish) *leie* 'stone', 'slate' (genitive *leien*) + an agent derivative of *decken* 'to cover'.

Leyes (101) **1.** German: perhaps a variant of **Leies**, a variant of ELIAS. **2.** German (Rhenish): patronymic from LEY. **3.** Scottish and English: unexplained. Possibly a variant of LEE.

Leyh (208) German: variant of LEY 3 and 4.

Leyland (217) English: variant spelling of LAYLAND.

Leyman (102) English: variant of LAYMAN.

Leyrer (154) German: occupational name for a player on the lyre, from an agent derivative of Middle High German *līre* 'lyre' (from Latin *lyra*, from Greek). Subsequently, this came to be a nickname for a slow, boring person.

Leys (193) **1.** French: habitational name from Leys in Saône-et-Loire. **2.** Dutch: patronymic from a reduced form of the personal name *Laurei(n)s* (see LAWRENCE). **3.** Scottish: habitational name from a place in Aberdeenshire called Leys, named with Old English *lǣse* 'pasture', 'meadow' (see LEES).
GIVEN NAMES French 7%. *Benoit, Monique, Patrice, Yanick.*

Leyton (145) **1.** English: variant spelling of LAYTON. **2.** Galician and Portuguese: perhaps a variant spelling of **Leitón** or **Leitão** (Galician), a nickname meaning 'suckling pig'.
GIVEN NAMES Spanish 21%. *Jose* (2), *Juan* (2), *Juan Carlos* (2), *Alonso, Amalia, Ana, Carlos, Erasmo, Fernando, Jorge, Jose Carlos, Mauricio.*

Leyva (2119) Spanish: variant of LEIVA.
GIVEN NAMES Spanish 49%. *Jose* (41), *Jesus* (24), *Luis* (22), *Manuel* (22), *Jorge* (19), *Juan* (19), *Carlos* (18), *Mario* (18), *Miguel* (15), *Armando* (14), *Alfredo* (11), *Francisco* (11).

Lezak (123) Americanized variant of Polish LESAK.

Lezama (215) Basque: habitational name from Lezama in Araba province, Basque Country. It is well established in Peru and Venezuela.
GIVEN NAMES Spanish 55%. *Jose* (7), *Alfredo* (3), *Jesus* (3), *Luis* (3), *Alejandro* (2), *Armando* (2), *Arturo* (2), *Carlos* (2), *Javier* (2), *Juan* (2), *Manuel* (2), *Miguel* (2).

Lezcano (160) probably a variant spelling of Spanish LAZCANO, a habitational name from Basque *Lazkao*, a town in Gipuzkoa province.
GIVEN NAMES Spanish 52%. *Jose* (4), *Juan* (4), *Luis* (4), *Fernando* (3), *Pedro* (3), *Manuel* (2), *Ricardo* (2), *Sergio* (2), *Teofilo* (2), *Amado, Ana, Ana Luisa.*

Lezon (107) Polish: probably a nickname for someone with a shuffling gait, from *lezon* 'shuffler', derivative of *leźć* 'to shuffle'.

GIVEN NAMES Polish 7%. *Krystyna, Leszek, Piotr.*

Lezotte (204) Variant of French LIZOTTE.

Lhamon (108) Apparently a variant, with the definite article *l'*, of French HAMON.

Lheureux (916) French: nickname for someone who was characteristically happy, successful or lucky, Old French *heureux*, with the definite article *l(e)*. In New England, the English version of this name is LOWRY.
GIVEN NAMES French 15%. *Normand* (5), *Jacques* (4), *Marcel* (3), *Pierre* (3), *Raoul* (3), *Andre* (2), *Armand* (2), *Emile* (2), *Orille* (2), *Adrien, Aime, Alcide.*

Lhommedieu (219) French: from the phrase *l'homme de dieu* 'the man of God', probably adopted as a surname by Huguenots.

Lhotka (146) Czech: habitational name from any of various places called Lhotka, Lhota, or Lhotek.

Lhuillier (131) French: occupational name for someone who produced or sold oil, from an agent derivative (with the definite article *l'*) of *huile* 'oil' (Old French *oilie, uile*).

Li (10930) **1.** Chinese 李: from a character meaning 'minister'. This was part of the title of Gao Yao, a great-grandson of the legendary emperor Zhuan Xu, who became famous as a minister under the model emperors Yao and Shun in the 23rd century BC; he was the first to introduce laws for the repression of crime. His descendants adopted this part of his title as their surname. The use of this name continued for over a millennium to the twelfth century BC, down to the rule of the last king of the Shang dynasty, the despotic Zhou Xin. Li Zhi, the head of the Li clan at that time, displeased Zhou Xin and was executed, leaving the rest of the clan facing imminent disaster. They fled, and nearly starved to death, surviving only by eating a fruit called *mu zi*. When the characters for *mu* and *zi* are combined, they form the character for plum, pronounced *Li*. In token of this salvation, the clan changed their name to the current character for *li* 'plum'. **Li** is now the most common surname in China. Among the many famous bearers are Lee Kwan Yew, prime minister of Singapore from 1959 to 1990; Lee Teng-hui, president of Taiwan from 1988; Li Peng, prime minister of China from 1988; and Bruce Lee (1941–73), movie actor. **2.** Chinese 黎: from the name of a state of Li (in present-day Shanxi province), which existed during the Shang dynasty (1766–1122 BC). Descendants of the state's rulers adopted the name of the state as their surname. **3.** Chinese 利: this character for **Li** is an altered form of 1 above. **4.** Norwegian: habitational name from any of numerous farmsteads named Li, from Old Norse *hlíð* 'mountain slope', 'hillside'.

GIVEN NAMES Chinese 67%. *Wei* (75), *Ming* (71), *Li* (54), *Jian* (50), *Hong* (46), *Yan* (46), *Ping* (42), *Jing* (41), *Yong* (35), *Ying* (34), *Hui* (32), *Jin* (27), *Min* (14), *Chung* (11).

Lia (167) **1.** Southern Italian: from a short form of the personal name ELIA. **2.** French: occupational name for someone who tied up vines, from French *liat*, past participle of *lier* 'to tie'. **3.** Norwegian: habitational name from any of several farmsteads, so named from the definite singular form of LI 4.
GIVEN NAMES Italian 22%; French 4%. *Sal* (2), *Vito* (2), *Adelmo, Angelo, Emilio, Luigi, Paolo, Pasquale, Rocco, Santa; Camille, Patrice.*

Liakos (158) Greek: patronymic from the personal name *Lias*, short form of ELIAS. Patronymics ending in *-akos* are characteristic of the Mani peninsula in the southwestern Peloponnese.
GIVEN NAMES Greek 13%. *Stavros* (2), *Christos, Costas, Dimitrios, Konstantinos, Spiro.*

Lian (325) **1.** Norwegian: habitational name from any of numerous farmsteads in Trøndelag, named with the definite plural form of LI 4. **2.** Chinese 连: the main source of this surname is Lian Cheng, a senior minister for the state of Qi, located in present-day Shandong province. **3.** Chinese 廉: the name Lian is found in traditional accounts as long as 4500 years ago, part of the name of a descendant of the legendary emperors Huang Di and Zhuan Xu. Later descendants adopted Lian as their surname.
GIVEN NAMES Scandinavian 18%; Chinese 16%. *Bernt* (2), *Bjorn, Lars, Olaf; Teck* (3), *Li* (2), *Ming* (2), *Bin, Cheng, Chun, Dong, Eng, Guohua, Hui-Ming, Jeng, Jian Ping.*

Liang (2698) Chinese 梁: from the name of Liang Mountain in present-day Shaanxi province. During the reign of the Zhou dynasty emperor Xuan Wang (827–782 BC), Qin Zhong set out on an expedition to subdue the peoples to the west in Central Asia. Qin Zhong was killed, however, which caused his five sons to develop a bitter hatred of those tribes, and so they set out to avenge their father, eventually succeeding and defeating the peoples of the west. The emperor divided the area of Shang among them, and the second son received the area around Liang Mountain, from which his descendants developed the surname Liang. Subsequently, Liang was the name of two Chinese dynasties, the Earlier Liang Dynasty (502–557) and the Later Liang Dynasty (907–923).
GIVEN NAMES Chinese 53%. *Hong* (16), *Jian* (13), *Feng* (10), *Wen* (10), *Wei* (9), *Ping* (8), *Ying* (8), *Cheng* (7), *Guang* (7), *Jin* (7), *Jing* (7), *Liang* (7), *Chang* (4), *Chung* (3), *Hu* (2), *Nam* (2), *Pang* (2), *Jang, Min, Neng, Shen, Shiu, Sieu, Yeong.*

Liao (1268) Chinese 廖: from a person named Liao Shu'an in ancient China, about whom nothing more is known.
GIVEN NAMES Chinese 37%. *Wen* (8), *Jian* (5), *Xiang* (5), *Cheng* (4), *Ching* (4), *Wei* (4), *Hong* (3), *Hsiang* (3), *Ming* (3), *Ping* (3), *Sheng* (3), *Chi* (2).

Lias (248) **1.** Greek: from the personal name *Lias*, short form of ELIAS. **2.** Portuguese: from a short form of the personal name ELIAS.

Liaw (141) Chinese 廖: possibly a variant of LIAO.
GIVEN NAMES Chinese 24%. *Wen* (2), *Chi Yung, Feng, Hsu, Jiin, Nae, Shuming, Weicheng, Yee, Yoon, Yuan.*

Libbert (138) German: variant of LIEBERT or **Lübbert** (see LUEBBERT).

Libbey (541) English: variant spelling of LIBBY.

Libby (4459) English (mainly Devon): from a pet form of the female personal names *Elizabeth* or *Isabel*.

Libengood (129) Americanized form of German **Liebengut** or **Leibengut** (see LEVENGOOD).

Liber (138) **1.** Jewish (Ashkenazic): from Yiddish personal name *Liber*, a pet form of LIBERMAN. **2.** French (southeastern and southwestern): nickname for a freedman, Old French *libert*, from Latin *libertus*. **3.** German: variant of LIEBERT.
GIVEN NAMES Jewish 5%. *Sol* (2), *Myer, Yael.*

Libera (179) **1.** Polish: nickname meaning 'free', a derivative of Latin *liber* 'free'. **2.** Italian: of uncertain derivation, but apparently a derivative of Latin *liber* 'free'.
GIVEN NAMES Polish 4%. *Boguslaw, Tadeusz, Zbigniew, Zdzislaw.*

Liberati (234) Italian: patronymic or plural form of the personal name LIBERATO.
GIVEN NAMES Italian 22%; French 4%. *Anello* (2), *Quido* (2), *Salvator* (2), *Tullio* (2), *Angelo, Domenic, Domenico, Elio, Ferdinando, Gino, Guido, Umberto*; *Armand* (3).

Liberato (170) Spanish, Italian, and Portuguese: from the personal name *Liberato* (still found as an Italian personal name), from Latin *liberatus* 'freed man' (i.e., from slavery, or, in a Christian context, from sin or the devil).
GIVEN NAMES Spanish 18%; Italian 15%. *Armando* (2), *Jose* (2), *Alphonso, Anastacio, Andres, Delfino, Dulce, Emilio, Javier, Lourdes, Manuel, Pablo*; *Angelo* (3), *Antonio, Dante, Domenic, Gabino, Rocco.*

Liberatore (1000) Italian: from the personal name *Liberatore*, from Latin *liberator* 'liberator'.
GIVEN NAMES Italian 17%. *Angelo* (5), *Antonio* (4), *Dante* (4), *Domenic* (3), *Sal* (3), *Umberto* (3), *Aldo* (2), *Carmine* (2), *Ettore* (2), *Giacomo* (2), *Luigi* (2), *Palma* (2).

Liberi (119) Italian: patronymic or plural form of the personal name *Libero*, from Latin *liber* 'free'.
GIVEN NAMES Italian 14%. *Sal* (2), *Aldo, Dante, Dino, Ercole.*

Liberman (908) Jewish (Ashkenazic): from the Yiddish personal name *Liberman*, meaning 'beloved man'.
GIVEN NAMES Jewish 13%; Russian 11%. *Dov* (2), *Ilya* (2), *Meyer* (2), *Miriam* (2), *Semen* (2), *Zvi* (2), *Basya, Emanuel, Esfir, Faina, Genya, Izya*; *Mikhail* (7), *Boris* (5), *Vladimir* (5), *Leonid* (4), *Svetlana* (3), *Aleksandr* (2), *Aleksandra* (2), *Anatoly* (2), *Arkady* (2), *Yefim* (2), *Dmitry, Efim.*

Libert (262) **1.** French: probably from a short form of a Germanic personal name such as *Alibert*, or otherwise from the Latin personal name *Libertus*. **2.** Dutch and North German: from a Germanic personal name composed of the elements *liub* 'beloved', 'dear' + *hard* 'brave', 'strong'. Compare LIEBERT.

Liberti (285) Italian: patronymic or plural form of LIBERTO.
GIVEN NAMES Italian 28%; French 5%. *Antonio* (3), *Angelo* (2), *Calogero* (2), *Nunzio* (2), *Salvatore* (2), *Ugo* (2), *Carlo, Dino, Filomena, Francesco, Galdino, Lino, Mario, Pasquale, Sal*; *Camille, Chantal, Girard, Monique.*

Liberto (638) Italian: from the personal name *Liberto*, either from Latin *libertus* 'freed' or from a reduced form of the Germanic personal name *Aliberto*.
GIVEN NAMES Italian 14%. *Angelo* (3), *Nunzio* (3), *Salvatore* (3), *Carmelo* (2), *Cosimo* (2), *Sal* (2), *Santo* (2), *Antonio, Carmello, Giuseppe, Matteo, Paolo.*

Liberty (1125) Translation of the French Canadian surname **Laliberté** (see LALIBERTE), found predominantly in New England.

Libhart (102) Variant of German LIEBHART.

Libke (112) Americanized spelling of German **Lübke** (see LUEBKE).

Libman (317) Jewish (Ashkenazic): from the personal name, a variant of LIPMAN.
GIVEN NAMES Russian 12%; Jewish 11%. *Boris* (3), *Igor* (3), *Lev* (2), *Semyon* (2), *Asya, Dmitriy, Galina, Gennady, Iosif, Konstantin, Leonid, Raisa*; *Dovid, Irina, Marat, Miriam, Rakhil, Semen, Sol, Yakov.*

Libonati (105) Italian: possibly a habitational name from a place so named.
GIVEN NAMES Italian 11%. *Caesar, Geno, Mario, Roberto.*

Librizzi (217) Southern Italian: habitational name from Librizzi in Messina province, Sicily.

Liburd (142) Americanized spelling of French LIBERT or German LIEBERT.
GIVEN NAMES French 5%; German 4%. *Alexandrine, Vernice*; *Grethel.*

Liby (163) Probably an altered or variant spelling of LIBBY.

Licari (546) Southern Italian: occupational name from Greek *alykarios* 'salt worker'.
GIVEN NAMES Italian 20%. *Vito* (6), *Antonio* (4), *Salvatore* (4), *Angelo* (3), *Geno* (2), *Rocco* (2), *Sal* (2), *Vita* (2), *Antonino, Biagio, Carlo, Filippo.*

Licata (1295) Italian (Sicily): habitational name from Licata, in Agrigento province.
GIVEN NAMES Italian 19%. *Salvatore* (19), *Angelo* (17), *Antonio* (5), *Vito* (5), *Carmine* (4), *Sal* (4), *Gaetano* (2), *Agatino, Baldassare, Calogero, Camillo, Carmela.*

Li Causi (146) Italian (Sicily): nickname for someone noted for his pantaloons, variant of **Li Calzi**, **Li Calsi**, from Old Sicilian *calzi* 'pantaloons'.
GIVEN NAMES Italian 20%. *Angelo* (2), *Vito* (2), *Franca, Gaspare, Gasper, Mario, Tito.*

Li Cavoli (104) Italian: from *li cavoli* 'the cabbages', applied as a metonymic occupational name for a grower or seller of cabbages or possibly as a nickname.
GIVEN NAMES Italian 23%; French 4%. *Salvatore* (3), *Angelo, Filippo*; *Alphonse, Patrice.*

Licciardello (146) Italian (Neapolitan and Sicilian): from a pet form of LICCIARDI.
GIVEN NAMES Italian 31%. *Mario* (3), *Salvatore* (3), *Domenic* (2), *Santo* (2), *Vito* (2), *Antonio, Benito, Emilio, Mauro, Pasquale, Vincenzo.*

Licciardi (289) Italian (Neapolitan and Sicilian): according to Felice from a southern dialect form of RICCIARDI, but Caracausi derives it from French **Léchard**, a nickname from the dialect word *lichard* 'greedy'.
GIVEN NAMES Italian 20%. *Angelo* (5), *Rosario* (4), *Sal* (3), *Salvatore* (3), *Bartolo* (2), *Antonio, Assunta, Ciro, Franco, Gaetano, Giacomo, Nino, Orazio, Pina.*

Licea (228) Spanish (of Basque origin): topographic name from Basque *leze* 'abyss', 'chasm'.
GIVEN NAMES Spanish 59%. *Jose* (10), *Francisco* (7), *Rafael* (6), *Salvador* (5), *Carlos* (4), *Javier* (4), *Jesus* (4), *Juan* (4), *Ramiro* (3), *Roberto* (3), *Alejandro* (2), *Enrique* (2).

Lich (195) German: habitational name from any of several places so named, of which the largest is in Hesse.

Lichliter (128) Americanized form of German **Leichleiter** (see LEICHLITER).

Lichlyter (140) Americanized form of German **Leichleiter** (see LEICHLITER).

Licht (1103) **1.** German and Jewish (Ashkenazic): metonymic occupational name for a chandler, from Middle High German *lieht*, Yiddish *likht* 'candle', 'light'. In some instances the German name may have arisen as a nickname from the same word in the sense 'light', 'shining', and the Jewish name may have been ornamental. **2.** German: habitational name from places called Lichta or Lichte, both in Thuringia.

3. Dutch: nickname for a slight man, from *licht* 'light (in weight)'.

GIVEN NAMES German 5%. *Gerhard* (2), *Helmut* (2), *Lorenz* (2), *Bernd, Ernst, Florian, Gerda, Hans, Hedwig, Heinz, Meinhard, Otto.*

Lichte (162) Dutch: nickname for a slender, lightweight person. Compare English LIGHT 2.

GIVEN NAMES German 8%. *Erwin, Klaus, Kurt.*

Lichtenberg (613) **1.** German and Dutch: habitational name from any of numerous places called Lichtenberg in Germany or one in Dutch Limburg. **2.** Jewish (Ashkenazic): ornamental compound name formed with German *Licht* 'light' (genitive *Lichten*) + *berg* 'hill', 'mountain'.

GIVEN NAMES German 5%. *Kurt* (3), *Horst* (2), *Bernd, Heinz, Wilhelm.*

Lichtenberger (482) German and Dutch: habitational name for someone from any of the numerous places called LICHTENBERG.

GIVEN NAMES German 6%. *Bernd* (3), *Dieter* (2), *Horst, Kurt.*

Lichtenfeld (115) **1.** Jewish (Ashkenazic): ornamental name composed of German *Licht* 'light' + *Berg* 'hill'. **2.** German: habitational name for someone from any of several places so named in Germany.

GIVEN NAMES German 16%; Jewish 6%. *Kurt* (3), *Hans* (2), *Christoph, Erwin, Klaus; Pincus.*

Lichtenfels (146) German: habitational name from any of several places which are named for a castle named with Middle High German *lieht* 'bright' + *vels(e)* 'rock'.

Lichtenstein (1178) **1.** German: habitational name from any of several places named Li(e)chtenstein, from Middle High German *lieht* 'bright' + *stein* 'stone', 'rock'. All take their name from a castle which formed the original settlement. **2.** Jewish (Ashkenazic): ornamental name composed of German *Licht* 'light' + *Stein* 'rock', 'stone'.

GIVEN NAMES Jewish 11%; German 4%. *Sol* (4), *Hyman* (3), *Meyer* (3), *Gerson* (2), *Isidor* (2), *Mayer* (2), *Moshe* (2), *Pinchas* (2), *Aron, Avi, Benyamin, Benzion; Kurt* (2), *Gerhard, Grete, Hans, Heinz, Otto, Theodor, Ute.*

Lichtenwalner (183) German: variant of LICHTENWALTER.

Lichtenwalter (135) German and Swiss German: habitational name from places called Lichtenwald (near Esslingen) or Lichtenwalde (near Chemnitz).

Lichter (601) **1.** German and Jewish (Ashkenazic): occupational name for someone who made candles or possibly for someone who tended a light, from an agent derivative of from Middle High German *lieht*, Yiddish *likht* 'candle', 'light'. **2.** German (Rhineland): variant of LEICHTER. **3.** Dutch: from Middle Dutch *lichter* 'candlestick', 'chandelier', hence probably a

metonymic occupational name for a maker of such items or perhaps for someone who tended a light, from an agent derivative of *lichten* 'to make light'.

GIVEN NAMES Jewish 5%; German 4%. *Uri* (2), *Akiva, Aviva, Chaim, Isadore, Izidor, Mayer, Rina, Yehuda, Yidel; Horst* (2), *Kurt, Lutz, Wolf, Wolfgang.*

Lichterman (141) Dutch: elaborated form of LICHT or LICHTER.

Lichti (159) Swiss German: variant of LIECHTI.

FOREBEARS The Lichtis were an early Anabaptist family in Switzerland. After 1671, the name is found in the Palatinate and also in Holland. The first members arrived in Lancaster Co., PA, in 1750; later, they migrated into OH and IN.

GIVEN NAMES German 8%. *Ekkehard, Jurgen, Rudiger, Ulrike.*

Lichtman (672) **1.** Jewish (Ashkenazic): occupational name for a chandler, from Yiddish *likht* 'candle', 'light' + *man*. **2.** Dutch: variant of LICHTERMAN.

GIVEN NAMES Jewish 13%; French 4%. *Igal* (3), *Sol* (3), *Ari* (2), *Aron* (2), *Jenoe* (2), *Shimon* (2), *Akiva, Berish, Blima, Chaim, Eliezer, Liat; Armand* (2), *Andre, Roch.*

Lichty (778) Swiss German: variant of LICHTI.

Li Citra (144) Southern Italian: topographic name from the plural of Sicilian *citru* 'cedar'.

GIVEN NAMES Italian 29%. *Angelo* (3), *Carmelo* (3), *Mario* (3), *Emanuele* (2), *Lorenzo* (2), *Sal* (2), *Aldo, Carmine, Giorgio, Giovanni, Giuseppina, Raimondo, Salvatore.*

Lick (417) Dutch: from a short form of a Germanic personal name *Lideco*, itself a short or pet form of a compound name formed with *leud*, *liut* (see, for example, LEOPOLD).

Licker (125) North German: nickname for a gourmand, from an agent derivative of Middle Low German *licken* 'to lick'.

Lickert (108) **1.** German: altered spelling of **Leikert** or **Leikart**, unrounded forms of *Leukart* (see LUCKHARDT). **2.** Possibly English: unexplained.

Lickey (134) **1.** English: probably a topographic name for someone living in the Lickey Hills, southwest of Birmingham. **2.** Perhaps an altered spelling of Scottish LECKIE.

Licklider (210) Americanized form of German **Leichleiter** (see LEICHLITER).

Lickliter (145) Americanized form of German **Leichleiter** (see LEICHLITER).

Lickteig (330) German: **1.** apparently a jocular nickname for a greedy person or a baker, from Low German *licken* 'to lick' + *teig* 'dough', like **Lickefett** 'lick the fat', a jocular name for a cook. **2.** Alternatively, it may be an altered form of **Leichteig**, topographic name from Middle High German

laich 'light', 'clear' + *teig*, variant of *teich* 'pond'.

Lico (105) Southern Italian: from a personal name based on medieval Greek *lykos* 'wolf'.

GIVEN NAMES Italian 12%. *Pino* (2), *Carmine, Pasquale.*

Licon (327) Hispanic (Mexico): presumably a variant of LICONA.

GIVEN NAMES Spanish 46%. *Francisco* (5), *Carlos* (4), *Jose* (4), *Juan* (4), *Armando* (3), *Arturo* (3), *Manuel* (3), *Miguel* (3), *Octavio* (3), *Rafael* (3), *Ramon* (3), *Ricardo* (3).

Licona (113) Spanish (of Basque origin): habitational name from Basque Likoa, in Biscay province (Basque Country).

GIVEN NAMES Spanish 59%. *Carlos* (3), *Pablo* (3), *Alberto* (2), *Candida Rosa* (2), *Francisco* (2), *Guillermo* (2), *Jesus* (2), *Juan* (2), *Adan, Alfonso, Alfredo, Andres; Antonio, Leonardo, Marco Tulio.*

Licursi (131) Italian: **1.** occupational name from Albanian *likurës* 'tanner', a derivative of *likurë, lëkurë* 'skin'. **2.** possibly a plural (**Li Cursi**) of **Cursio**, from a short form of the personal name *Accursio*, from medieval Latin *Accursius* (see ACCURSO).

GIVEN NAMES Italian 13%. *Angelo, Antonio, Carmine, Gaetano, Luigi, Sandro.*

Lidberg (109) Swedish: unexplained.

Liddell (1460) Scottish and northern English: habitational name from any of various places in the Scottish Borders and Cumbria called Liddel, from the Old English river name *Hlȳde*, meaning 'loud', + Old English *dæl* 'valley'.

Liddiard (149) English: habitational name from Lydiard in Wiltshire or Lydeard in Somerset, both of which apparently preserve a British name composed of Celtic *garth* 'hill' with an uncertain first element, possibly *lē* 'gray'.

Liddick (224) Americanized form of German **Lüdecke** (see LUEDECKE) or its variant **Lüttich**.

Liddicoat (190) English (Devon and Cornwall): habitational name from any of various places in eastern Cornwall now known as Lidcott, Lydcott, Ludcott, and Lidcutt. All are named from Old Cornish *luit* 'gray' + *cuit* 'wood'.

Liddle (1210) Scottish and northern English: variant spelling of LIDDELL.

Liddy (426) Irish: variant of LEDDY.

Lide (264) Possibly an Americanized spelling of LEID, which, however, is of uncertain origin.

Liden (159) Swedish (**Lidén**): ornamental name, probably from the place name element *lid* 'hill' + the adjectival suffix *-én*, from Latin *-enius*.

GIVEN NAMES Scandinavian 11%. *Gunner, Lars, Sven.*

Lidster (124) English: occupational name for a dyer, Middle English *litster* (see LISTER).

Lidstone (122) English (Devon): habitational name. There is a Lidstone in Oxfordshire, but the concentration of the surname in Devon would suggest that this is not the source.

Lidstrom (130) Swedish (**Lidström**): ornamental name from the place name element *lid* 'hill' + *ström* 'river'.
GIVEN NAMES Scandinavian 10%. *Erik, Lasse, Nels.*

Lie (234) **1.** Norwegian: variant spelling of LI 4. In Norway this is the most frequent spelling. **2.** Dutch (**de Lie**): from a short form of the saint's name *Odilia*, the Latin form of a Germanic name Odela, from *ōthala* 'paternal inheritance or possession'. **3.** Variant of Korean LI.
GIVEN NAMES Scandinavian 20%; Korean 7%; French 4%; German 4%. *Erik* (2), *Oystein, Sven, Thor; Han* (4), *Chang Ho, Chen, Chun, Hok, Jung, Kam, Liang, Lie, Ling, Shuen, Yung; Antoine, Jean-Paul, Sylvie; Hans* (2), *Gunther, Hilde.*

Lieb (1342) **1.** German and Jewish (Ashkenazic): nickname for a pleasant or agreeable person, from Middle High German *liep* 'dear', 'beloved'; Yiddish *lib* or German *lieb*. This word was also used as a personal name, both alone (German) and in compounds (German and Jewish). **2.** German (of Slavic origin): from a short form of the various compound Slavic personal names formed with *lubo-* 'love' as the first element.

Liebau (123) German: habitational name from any of several places so named.
GIVEN NAME German 5%. *Otto* (2).

Liebe (264) **1.** German: variant of LIEB 1. **2.** Jewish (Ashkenazic): ornamental name from German *Liebe* 'love'.
GIVEN NAMES German 4%. *Hans* (2), *Alois, Detlef, Klaus, Kurt.*

Liebel (357) German: **1.** from a pet form of a medieval personal name with the first element *Lieb* (see LIEB 1 and 2). **2.** (Lausitz, Silesia): variant of LIEBELT.

Liebelt (271) German (Lausitz, Silesia): variant of **Liebolt** (see LIEBOLD).
GIVEN NAMES German 4%. *Erwin, Helmuth, Klaus.*

Liebenow (202) German: habitational name from any of several places so named, near Dresden, in Brandenburg, and Pomerania.
GIVEN NAME German 4%. *Kurt.*

Lieber (1266) **1.** German: variant of LIEB 1. **2.** German: variant of LIEBERT. **3.** Jewish (Ashkenazic): variant of LIBER.
GIVEN NAMES Jewish 6%. *Moshe* (6), *Chaim* (3), *Meyer* (3), *Miriam* (2), *Sol* (2), *Uri* (2), *Aharon, Batsheva, Herschel, Hershy, Hyman, Mayer.*

Lieberg (115) Norwegian: habitational name from a farmstead named with *lie* 'mountain slope', 'hillside' + *berg* 'mountain'.
GIVEN NAMES Scandinavian 9%; German 6%. *Thor* (2); *Bernd, Bernhard, Ulrich.*

Lieberman (4461) **1.** Jewish (Ashkenazic): variant of LIBERMAN. **2.** Respelling of German LIEBERMANN.
GIVEN NAMES Jewish 7%. *Sol* (8), *Ari* (5), *Chaim* (5), *Isadore* (5), *Meyer* (5), *Moshe* (5), *Miriam* (4), *Aron* (3), *Aryeh* (2), *Emanuel* (2), *Hinda* (2), *Hyman* (2).

Liebermann (183) **1.** German: variant of LIEB 1. **2.** Jewish (Ashkenazic): variant of LIBERMAN.
GIVEN NAMES German 11%. *Benno, Bernd, Erna, Hans, Hermann, Kurt.*

Liebert (613) German: from the medieval personal name *Liebert*, a variant of LIEBHART.

Liebeskind (124) Jewish (Ashkenazic): **1.** affectionate nickname, literally 'child of love' in German. **2.** metronymic from the Yiddish female name *Libe* 'love' + Yiddish *kind* 'child'.
GIVEN NAMES Jewish 6%; German 4%. *Arie; Gerhard.*

Liebhaber (103) Jewish (Ashkenazic): ornamental name from German *Liebhaber* 'lover'.

Liebhart (135) German: from a Germanic personal name, composed of the elements *liub* 'beloved', 'dear' + *hard* 'brave', 'strong'.
GIVEN NAME German 4%. *Gunther.*

Liebich (106) German: variant of LIEBIG.
GIVEN NAMES German 13%. *Fritz, Hedwig, Otto, Reinhold.*

Liebig (349) German: **1.** in the north, probably from a variant of **Liebing**, short form of a Germanic personal name formed with *liob* 'dear'. **2.** in Silesia, Lausitz, and Bavaria, from the Slavic personal name Libnik, from *ljub-* 'dear' + suffix, or from a place name Liebich in Bohemia.
GIVEN NAMES German 10%. *Fritz* (3), *Hans* (2), *Florian, Gerhard, Johann, Jurgen, Klaus, Otto, Wolfgang.*

Liebl (442) German: **1.** from a pet form of LIEB. **2.** variant of LIEBELT.
GIVEN NAMES German 7%. *Alois* (2), *Hans* (2), *Kurt* (2), *Aloys, Armin, Erwin, Helmut.*

Liebler (271) German: **1.** nickname for an amorous or affectionate man, from an agent noun based on Middle High German *liep* 'dear', 'beloved'. **2.** habitational name for someone from Liebel in Silesia or Liblar near Cologne.

Lieblich (106) Jewish (Ashkenazic): ornamental name from German *lieblich* 'charming', 'lovely'.
GIVEN NAMES Jewish 5%. *Asher* (2), *Hyman.*

Liebling (165) **1.** German: from *Liebling*, used as a pet form of a compound name formed with *Lieb-*, for example LIEBHART. **2.** Jewish (Ashkenazic): ornamental name from German *Liebling* 'darling' (see LIEB 1).
GIVEN NAMES Jewish 10%; German 4%. *Hyam* (2), *Abbe, Mordechai; Otto* (2).

Liebman (1093) **1.** Jewish (Ashkenazic): variant of LIBMAN. **2.** Altered spelling of German LIEBMANN.
GIVEN NAMES Jewish 4%. *Sol* (4), *Mayer* (3), *Emanuel, Heshy, Hyman, Meyer, Shaya.*

Liebmann (249) **1.** German: variant of LIEB 1. **2.** Jewish (Ashkenazic): variant of LIBMAN.
GIVEN NAMES German 14%. *Kurt* (3), *Wolfgang* (2), *Erhard, Ernst, Erwin, Gerd, Wilhelm, Willi.*

Liebold (149) German: from a Germanic personal name formed with *leud, liut* 'people', 'tribe' + *bald, bold* 'bold', 'brave'.
GIVEN NAMES German 9%. *Otto* (2), *Ernst, Frieda.*

Liebowitz (500) Jewish: Americanized spelling of LEIBOWITZ.
GIVEN NAMES Jewish 8%. *Sol* (2), *Hyman, Isadore, Moshe, Rifka, Yossi, Zev.*

Liebrecht (104) German: from a Germanic personal name formed with *liut* 'people', 'tribe' + *berht* 'shining', 'famous'.

Liebsch (129) German: from a pet form of any of numerous Slavic personal names beginning *Lib-*, from Old Slavic *l(j)ub* 'beloved', 'dear' (see LIEB 2).
GIVEN NAME German 5%. *Otto.*

Liebscher (106) German: from an inflected form of LIEBSCH.
GIVEN NAMES German 5%; Scandinavian 4%. *Hans, Reiner; Alf.*

Liechti (151) Swiss German: topographic name for someone who lived in a clearing, Swiss German *Liechti.*
GIVEN NAMES German 5%. *Arno, Dieter, Hans, Liselotte.*

Liechty (544) Swiss German: variant of LIECHTI.

Lied (115) **1.** German: probably an altered spelling of **Liedt**, a field name in the northwest meaning 'swampy terrain'. **2.** Norwegian: habitational name from a farmstead in western Norway so named, a variant of LI 4.
GIVEN NAMES Scandinavian 4%. *Alf, Astrid.*

Liedel (174) South German: from a pet form of a Germanic compound name formed with *leud, liut* 'people', 'tribe' as the first element.

Lieder (293) South German: **1.** habitational name from any of various places in Lower Saxony and Westphalia named Liedern. **2.** variant of **Lüder** (see LUEDER).
GIVEN NAMES German 6%. *Bernhard, Eldor, Franz, Heinz, Horst.*

Liedke (109) German: variant of **Lüdtke** (see LUEDTKE).

Liedl (100) German: variant of LIEDEL.

Liedtke (520) German (frequent in East and West Prussia): variant of **Lüdtke** (see LUEDTKE).
GIVEN NAMES German 10%. *Kurt* (5), *Hans* (3), *Klaus* (2), *Armin, Detlef, Fritz, Gunter, Inge, Karl-Heinz, Otto, Rainer, Wolfgang.*

Lief (204) **1.** English: variant spelling of LEAF. **2.** Dutch (**de Lief**): nickname from *lief*, 'dear', 'beloved', with the definite article *de*. **3.** Jewish: unexplained, possibly from the Netherlands, with the same etymology as 2.

GIVEN NAMES Jewish 4%. *Varda* (2), *Meyer*, *Miriam*.

Liefer (152) German or Dutch: possibly from a short form of a Germanic personal name composed with *liub* 'dear' + *hart* 'strong' or *her-* 'army'.

GIVEN NAMES German 5%. *Erwin*, *Otto*.

Liegel (135) German: **1.** presumably a topographic name from Liegelberg, name of a hill near Uelzen in Lower Saxony. **2.** alternatively, perhaps, a nickname for a liar, from Middle High German *liegen* 'to lie', 'fib'.

GIVEN NAMES German 4%. *Alois*, *Erwin*, *Florian*.

Liegl (100) German: variant of LIEGEL.

Liehr (106) German: variant of LIER.

Liem (198) **1.** Indonesian: unexplained. **2.** German: habitational name from Lieme in Eastphalia, named with *lim* 'mire'.

GIVEN NAMES Southeast Asian 6%. *Chandra* (3), *Tik* (3), *Fu*, *Heng*, *Hui*, *Kam*, *Song*, *Tang*.

Lien (2509) **1.** Norwegian: habitational name from any of numerous farmsteads named with the definite singular form of LI 4. **2.** Dutch: from the Middle Dutch personal name *Liedin*, a pet form of any of the various Germanic compound names beginning with *leud*, *liut* 'people', 'tribe', such as *Liedwin*. **3.** New England variant spelling of LYON. **4.** Chinese 连: variant of LIAN 2. **5.** Chinese 廉: variant of LIAN 2. **6.** Vietnamese: unexplained.

GIVEN NAMES Scandinavian 6%; Vietnamese 5%. *Nels* (2), *Ove* (2), *Thor* (2), *Alf*, *Astrid*, *Carsten*, *Erik*, *Helmer*, *Hilmer*, *Iver*, *Lars*, *Per*; *Minh* (5), *Ngo* (3), *Buu* (2), *Hoa* (2), *Hung* (2), *Khoa* (2), *Kien* (2), *Mai* (2), *Phat* (2), *Quan* (2), *Quang* (2), *Thanh* (2).

Lienau (204) German: habitational name from any of several places so named or from Lienow, all in northern and eastern Germany.

GIVEN NAMES German 7%. *Kurt* (3), *Erna*.

Lienemann (264) German: habitational name for someone from either of two places named Lienen, in Westphalia and near Bremen.

Lienhard (237) South German: from the Germanic personal name **Leonhard** (see LEONARD 1).

GIVEN NAMES German 8%. *Fritz* (2), *Otto* (2), *Hans*, *Kurt*.

Lienhart (164) German: variant of LIENHARD.

GIVEN NAMES German 8%. *Otto* (3), *Johann*.

Liepins (102) Latvian (**Liepiņš**): topographic name from Latvian *liepa* 'lime tree'.

GIVEN NAMES Latvian 53%. *Karlis* (4), *Andrejs* (2), *Aldis*, *Aleksandrs*, *Andris*, *Arnolds*, *Atis*, *Baiba*, *Dzintra*, *Egils*,

Ernests, *Gunars*, *Guntis*, *Ilmars*, *Ilze*, *Indulis*, *Ivars*, *Leonids*.

Lier (128) **1.** English: occupational name for a bookbinder, from Anglo-Norman French *liur*. **2.** English: possibly a topographic name (recorded in 1332 as *le Lyghere*) for someone who lived in a woodland clearing, from a derivative of Old English *lēah* 'woodland clearing'. **3.** German: short form of a Germanic personal name formed with *liut* 'people', 'tribe' + *hari* 'army'. **4.** German: possibly a topographic name formed with the element *lir* 'swamp', 'bog', or a habitational name from Lier, named with this word. **5.** Dutch: habitational name from Lier, in the Belgian province of Antwerp. **6.** Norwegian: habitational name from any of numerous farmsteads named with the indefinite plural form of *li* 'mountain slope', 'hillside' (see LI 4).

GIVEN NAMES German 6%; Scandinavian 6%; French 5%. *Otto* (2); *Erik*, *Gunn*; *Patrice*, *Pierre*.

Lierman (345) Altered spelling of German LIERMANN.

Liermann (214) North German: occupational name for a player, originally of the lute, later of any musical instrument, from Low German *lire* 'lyre' + *mann* 'man'.

GIVEN NAMES German 5%. *Armin*, *Guenter*, *Gunter*.

Lierz (117) German or Dutch: variant of **Lürz(e)** 'cheat', 'swindler' (see LURZ).

Lies (522) Dutch and North German: **1.** metronymic from a female personal name, a form of the Germanic personal name *Adelheid* (see LEITE). From this were derived Frenchified names such as *Adelis*, *Alisa*, *Alis*, and *Alice*, hence the surname. **2.** metronymic from a short form of the female personal name *Elisabeth*.

Liesch (158) German: topographic name for someone who lived in an area covered by reeds, Middle High German *liesche*, or a habitational name from a place near Trier named with this word.

GIVEN NAMES German 5%. *Helmut*, *Ulrich*.

Liese (217) **1.** North German: variant of LEISS and LEISE. **2.** German: topographic name for someone who lived in an area of reeds (see LIESCH). **3.** German: metronymic from *Elisabeth* (see LIES 2). **4.** Dutch: variant of LIES.

GIVEN NAMES German 6%. *Alfons*, *Ilse*, *Kurt*.

Lieser (373) German: probably an Americanized spelling of LEISER.

GIVEN NAMES German 4%. *Eldred*, *Math*, *Mathias*, *Walburga*.

Lieske (441) Eastern German: habitational name from a place so named near Cottbus or from any of several places named Lieskau.

Liess (115) Dutch: variant of LIES.

Lieto (105) Italian: probably a nickname from *lieto* 'happy', 'cheerful', or alterna-

tively from the personal name LETO, which has the same meaning.

GIVEN NAMES Italian 9%. *Natale*, *Romeo*.

Lietz (633) **1.** Eastern German: habitational name from any of several places in eastern Germany, for example Lietzen, Lietzau, Lietzow, etc., all of Slavic origin. **2.** Dutch: patronymic from a short form of a Germanic compound name beginning with *Lied-*.

GIVEN NAMES German 6%. *Erwin* (3), *Klaus* (2), *Kurt* (2), *Eldred*, *Erna*, *Gerhard*, *Hans*, *Heinz*, *Lorenz*, *Manfred*.

Lietzau (153) Eastern German: habitational name from Lietzau or Lietzow in eastern Germany.

Lietzke (183) Eastern German: variant of LIETZ 1, with addition of the Slavic diminutive suffix *-ke*.

Lieu (518) Vietnamese (**Liêu**): unexplained.

GIVEN NAMES Vietnamese 47%. *Minh* (11), *Hung* (5), *Anh* (4), *Dung* (4), *Lam* (3), *Lan* (3), *Quang* (3), *Thuy* (3), *Trung* (3), *Cuong* (2), *Duc* (2), *Ha* (2), *Phong* (2), *Sinh* (2), *Chong*, *Manh*, *Nam*, *Sieu*, *Thai*, *Tuong*.

Lieurance (221) Fanciful respelling of LAWRENCE.

Lievens (119) Dutch: patronymic from the old personal name *Lieven*, of Germanic origin, composed of the elements *lief* 'dear' + *wine* 'friend'.

Liew (199) Chinese 刘: probably a variant of LIU 1. This spelling is found mainly in Malaysia.

GIVEN NAMES Chinese 44%. *Chee* (3), *Seng* (3), *Hon* (2), *Wing* (2), *Chien*, *Chin*, *Chun*, *Kah*, *Kam*, *Khee*, *Kwang*, *Kwong*, *Bae*, *Chong*, *Dae*, *Jin Sook*, *Seong*, *Weng*; *Hung*, *Khiem*, *Kien*, *Lam*, *Tin*.

Life (253) English: variant of LEAF.

Liff (200) **1.** English: variant of LEAF. **2.** Jewish: variant of LIEF.

GIVEN NAMES French 4%; Jewish 4%. *Patrice* (2); *Yechiel* (2), *Chaim*, *Miriam*.

Liffick (107) North German: probably a variant of **Lifeke**, from a short form of the Germanic personal name *Lewald*, composed of the elements *liub* 'dear' + *walt* 'to reign', + *-eke*, diminutive suffix.

Liford (186) English: variant spelling of LYFORD.

Lifsey (202) English: variant of LIVESEY.

Lifshitz (130) Jewish (eastern Ashkenazic): variant spelling of LIPSCHUTZ.

GIVEN NAMES Jewish 25%; Russian 6%. *Moshe* (2), *Shlomo* (2), *Baruch*, *Hyman*, *Ilya*, *Meyer*, *Miriam*, *Ofer*, *Yakov*, *Yifat*; *Fima* (3), *Vladimir*.

Lifson (146) Respelling of Norwegian **Leifsen**, a patronymic from the personal name *Leif* (Old Norse *Leifr* meaning 'heir', 'descendant').

Lifton (185) English: habitational name from Lifton in Devon, named in Old English as 'farmstead (Old English *tūn*) on the Lew', a Celtic river name meaning 'the bright one'.

Ligas (138) Polish (also **Ligasz**): nickname from a derivative of Old Polish *ligać* 'to lie' or 'to kick up a fuss'.
GIVEN NAMES Polish 6%. *Halina, Jan, Jozef, Zofia.*

Liggett (1782) English (now found mainly in northern Ireland): topographic name from Middle English *lidyate* 'gate in a fence between plowed land and meadow' (Old English *hlid-geat* 'swing-gate'), or a habitational name from one of the places named with this word, as for example Lidgate in Suffolk or Lydiate in Lancashire.

Liggins (707) English (Warwickshire): unexplained. **1.** Probably a variant of LIGONS. **2.** alternatively possibly a variant of HIGGINS due to misdivision of some such name as *Al Higgins*.

Liggio (153) Italian: from a reduced form of the personal name *Eligio*, from Latin *Eligius* (from *eligere* 'to select', 'to choose').
GIVEN NAMES Italian 7%. *Vito* (3), *Biagio.*

Light (6582) English: **1.** nickname for a happy, cheerful person, from Middle English *lyght*, Old English *lēoht* 'light' (not dark), 'bright', 'cheerful'. **2.** nickname for someone who was busy and active, from Middle English *lyght*, Old English *līoht* 'light' (not heavy), 'nimble', 'quick'. The two words *lēoht* and *līoht* were originally distinct, but they were confused in English from an early period. **3.** nickname for a small person, from Middle English *lite*, Old English *lȳt* 'little', influenced by *lyght* as in 1 and 2.

Lightbody (384) Scottish and northern Irish: **1.** nickname for a cheerful person or a busy and active one, from Middle English *lyght* 'light' (see LIGHT 1 and 2) + *body* 'individual'. **2.** nickname for a small person, from Middle English *lite* 'little' (see LIGHT 3) + *body* 'individual'.

Lightcap (525) Americanized form of German LEITGEB 'tavern owner'.

Lightell (101) **1.** English (Durham): unexplained. **2.** Perhaps an Americanized form of German **Lichtel**, a habitational name from a place named Lichtel, recorded in 1224 as *Lihental*. This name occurs chiefly in LA.

Lighter (123) **1.** English: nickname for the smaller of two men with the same forename, from the comparative of LIGHT. **2.** Perhaps an Americanized spelling of German LEITER.

Lightfoot (2822) English (chiefly northern England, especially Liverpool): nickname for a messenger or for a fast runner, from Middle English *lyght* 'light', 'nimble', 'quick' (Old English *līoht*) + *fote* 'foot'.

Lighthall (241) English: possibly a habitational name from a place called Lightollars in Lancashire, so named from Old English *lēoht* 'light-colored' + *alor* 'alder'. The sur-

name, however, is not found in current English sources.

Lighthill (108) Variant of English LIGHTHALL.

Lightle (448) **1.** Probably an Americanized spelling of German **Lichtel** (see LIGHTELL). **2.** Perhaps a variant of English LIGHTHALL.

Lightman (153) **1.** Jewish: Americanized form of LICHTMAN. **2.** English: nickname from LIGHT (in any of its senses) + *man* 'man'.
GIVEN NAMES Jewish 10%. *Meyer* (2), *Ari, Chani, Mordecai.*

Lightner (1942) **1.** Americanized spelling of German LEITNER. **2.** Americanized spelling of German **Lichtner**, a habitational name from any of various places called Lichten or Lichtenau in southern Germany and Austria.

Lightsey (982) Probably an Americanization of German **Leutze** or **Leitze**, short forms of a Germanic personal name formed with *liut* 'people', 'tribe'.

Lighty (278) Americanized form of Swiss German LIECHTI.

Ligman (169) German: habitational name from any of the places named Lieck, Lieg, Liegau in the Rhineland and Saxony.

Ligocki (118) Polish: habitational name for someone from any of numerous places in Poland called Ligota, denoting a settlement that was exempt from paying tribute.

Ligon (2191) **1.** English: variant of **Lygon**, name of an aristocratic English family said to be of Norman origin. The name is of unknown etymology. According to Morlet it is a variant of *L'Higon*, a patronymic from *Higon*, a southern French variant of *Hugo*. This seems rather doubtful. **2.** Polish (also **Ligoń**): nickname from a derivative of Old Polish *ligać* 'to lie' or 'to kick up a fuss'.
FOREBEARS The first known Ligon immigrant to North America, Col. Thomas Lygon or Ligon, came to VA from England in 1640.

Ligons (121) English: variant of LIGON with excrescent patronymic *-s*.

Liguori (749) Italian: patronymic or plural form of the personal name *Ligorio* (Latin *Ligorius*).
GIVEN NAMES Italian 13%. *Cono* (2), *Gennaro* (2), *Giuseppe* (2), *Salvatore* (2), *Santo* (2), *Vito* (2), *Aniello, Carmine, Domenic, Donato, Italia, Luigi.*

Lijewski (210) Polish: habitational name for someone from a place called Lijewo in Włocławek voivodeship.
GIVEN NAMES German 4%. *Aloysius, Florian, Maximilian.*

Like (380) Probably an altered form of Dutch **Luik**, a habitational name from the city in Belgium; the sound *uy* in Dutch often becomes *ai* in American English pronunciation, as in STUYVESANT.

Likely (146) Origin uncertain. Possibly a variant of English **Lightly**, a surname of

unexplained origin, assimilated by folk etymology to the vocabulary word *likely*.

Likens (684) Dutch: patronymic from *Liedekin*, a pet form of a Germanic personal name beginning with *Lied-*.

Likes (444) **1.** Variant of Dutch LIKENS. **2.** Variant spelling of English LYKES, which is unexplained.

Likins (261) Variant of Dutch LIKENS.

Likness (104) Norwegian: habitational name from a farmstead in southwestern Norway, named from *lik*, from Old Norse *leikr* 'a place for games and dancing' + *nes* 'headland', 'promontory'.
GIVEN NAMES Scandinavian 4%; German 4%. *Erik; Wenzel.*

Lile (944) **1.** English: topographic name from Anglo-Norman French *del isle* 'of the island', or a habitational name from the common French place names Lisle or Lille, all derived from Old French *isle* (Latin *insula*) 'island'. **2.** French: habitational name from the city of Lille, Nord (see 1).

Liles (3746) Probably a variant spelling of the LYLES.

Liley (183) English: variant spelling of LILLY.

Lilien (129) Jewish (Ashkenazic): ornamental name from German *Lilien* 'lilies'.
GIVEN NAME Jewish 4%. *Morty.*

Lilienthal (510) **1.** German: habitational name from places called Lilienthal in Schleswig-Holstein, Lower Saxony, and Baden-Württemburg, named with Middle High German *liljen* 'lilies' + *tal* 'valley'. **2.** Jewish (Ashkenazic): ornamental name composed of German *Lilie* 'lily' + *Thal* 'valley'.
GIVEN NAMES German 4%. *Otto* (2), *Erwin, Guenther, Hans, Kurt.*

Lilja (354) Swedish: ornamental name from Swedish *lilja* 'lily'.
GIVEN NAMES Scandinavian 6%. *Sten* (3), *Erik* (2), *Nels.*

Liljedahl (142) Swedish: ornamental name composed of the elements *lilje* (a genitive form of *lilja* 'lily' used in compounds) + *dahl*, an ornamental (old) spelling of *dal* 'valley'.
GIVEN NAMES Scandinavian 14%. *Nels* (2), *Gurli, Sven, Tor.*

Liljegren (188) Swedish: ornamental name composed of the elements *lilje* (a genitive form of *lilja* 'lily' used in compounds) + *gren* 'branch'.
GIVEN NAMES Scandinavian 11%; German 6%. *Mauritz* (2), *Erik, Karsten, Sven; Otto* (2).

Liljenquist (126) Swedish: ornamental name composed of the elements *liljen* 'lilies' + *quist*, an old or ornamental spelling of *kvist* 'twig'.

Lill (501) North German: topographic name based on an old word meaning 'dirt', or related to Middle High German *lilje* 'lily'.

Lilla (217) **1.** Dutch: variant of LILLARD. **2.** Italian: from a feminine form of the personal name LILLO; alternatively, from a reduced form of a female personal name such as *Angelilla* (from *Angela*), or a short form of *Camilla*.

Lillard (1456) **1.** Belgian: habitational name from either of two places called *Li(e)laar*, in Gavere and Sint-Maria-Oudenhove, East Flanders. **2.** English: unexplained.

Lillegard (104) Norwegian: habitational name from *lille* 'little' + *gard* 'farm'.
GIVEN NAME Scandinavian 4%. *Erik*.

Liller (347) German: topographic name, a variant of LILL + the suffix *-er*, denoting an inhabitant.
GIVEN NAMES German 4%. *Helmut* (2), *Gerhard*, *Hans*.

Lilley (3064) English: variant spelling of LILLY.

Lillibridge (374) Probably English, a habitational name from a lost or unidentified place. However, the surname is not found in current British records.

Lillich (225) German: probably from Middle High German *lilje* 'lily', a habitational name from a house named from the sign of a lily (one is recorded, for example, in Freiburg).
GIVEN NAMES German 4%. *Helmut, Otto*.

Lillie (1557) English: variant spelling of LILLY.

Lillig (101) German: variant of LILLICH.

Lillis (847) **1.** Irish and English: metronymic from LILLY. **2.** Greek: from the personal name *Lili*, a pet form of **Vangelis** (see VANGEL, EVANGELISTA) or any of various other personal names ending in *-lis*, e.g. *Anatolis, Vassilis, Gavrilis*.
GIVEN NAMES Irish 4%. *Brendan, Ethna, Michael Patrick*.

Lillo (297) Italian: from a short form of various personal names formed with the hypocoristic suffix *-lillo*, as for example *Jacolillo* or *Paolillo*.
GIVEN NAMES French 4%; Italian 4%. *Gaston* (3), *Monique*; *Angelo* (3), *Dino*.

Lillquist (138) Swedish: ornamental name from *lill* 'little' + *quist*, an old or ornamental spelling of *kvist* 'twig'.

Lilly (7597) English: **1.** from a pet form of the female personal name *Elizabeth*. Compare HIBBS 2. **2.** nickname for someone with very fair hair or skin, from Middle English, Old English *lilie* 'lily' (Latin *lilium*). The Italian equivalent *Giglio* was used as a personal name in the Middle Ages. In English and other languages there has also been some confusion with forms of GILES. **3.** habitational name from places called Lilley, in Hertfordshire and Berkshire. The Hertfordshire place was named in Old English as 'flax-glade', from *līn* 'flax' + *lēah* 'woodland clearing'. The Berkshire name is from Old English *Lillinglēah* 'wood associated with *Lilla*', an Old English personal name.

Lillywhite (100) English: nickname for someone with a complexion that was as 'white as a lily' (Middle English *lilie*).

Lim (6197) **1.** English: variant of LUM. **2.** Dutch: perhaps from a short form of a Germanic personal name, *Lieman* or *Liemaar*. **3.** Korean: variant of IM. **4.** Chinese 林: Fujian variant of LIN 1. **5.** Filipino: unexplained.
GIVEN NAMES Chinese/Korean 33%. *Young* (42), *Jung* (20), *Sung* (19), *Yong* (19), *Jong* (16), *Dong* (14), *Eng* (14), *Sang* (12), *Seng* (11), *Ho* (10), *Hong* (9); *Byung* (22), *Chang* (20), *Chong* (19), *Jae* (18), *Siew* (8), *Moon* (7), *Chung* (6), *Myong* (5), *Sook* (5), *Choon* (4), *Jong Man* (4), *Kok* (4), *Yeong* (4).

Lima (2884) **1.** Spanish: of uncertain derivation; possibly from *lima* 'file'. **2.** Portuguese: topographic name for someone living on the banks of the river of this name (of pre-Roman origin, probably akin to a Celtic element *lemos, limos* 'elm').
GIVEN NAMES Spanish 29%; Portuguese 11%. *Jose* (53), *Manuel* (53), *Carlos* (38), *Mario* (16), *Luis* (14), *Juan* (12), *Raul* (10), *Ricardo* (10), *Roberto* (10), *Eduardo* (9), *Francisco* (9), *Pedro* (8); *Joao* (6), *Paulo* (6), *Duarte* (4), *Guilherme* (4), *Vasco* (4), *Joaquim* (2), *Albano, Catarina, Goncalo, Margarida, Terezinha*; *Antonio* (33), *Angelo* (6), *Marco* (4), *Sal* (4), *Salvatore* (4), *Gandolfo* (3), *Enio* (2), *Marcello* (2), *Natale* (2), *Augustino, Carlo, Clemente*.

Limas (247) Portuguese and Spanish: variant of LIMA.
GIVEN NAMES Spanish 51%. *Jose* (7), *Jesus* (5), *Manuel* (5), *Juan* (3), *Lupe* (3), *Raul* (3), *Ricardo* (3), *Ruben* (3), *Fernando* (2), *Francisco* (2), *Luis* (2), *Maria Del Rosario* (2).

Limb (206) English: variant of LUM.

Limbach (379) German: habitational name from any of numerous places in Germany so named with Germanic *lindo* 'lime tree' + *bach* 'stream'. Several of these places are in areas such as the Palatinate, which contributed heavily to early German immigration to America.
GIVEN NAMES German 5%. *Kurt* (2), *Guenter, Heinrich, Ute*.

Limbacher (143) German: habitational name from any of the various places called LIMBACH.
GIVEN NAMES German 4%. *Kurt, Lorenz*.

Limback (109) Altered spelling of German LIMBACH.

Limbaugh (618) Altered spelling of German LIMBACH.

Limberg (409) German: habitational name from any of several places so named.

Limbert (221) English: variant of LOMBARD.

Limbocker (111) Altered spelling of German LIMBACHER.

Limbrick (155) English (Gloucestershire): variant of **Lambrick**, from the late Old English personal name *Landbeorht*. This name is found mainly in TX.

Limburg (221) **1.** German: habitational name from any of several places so named, the largest being in Hesse. **2.** Dutch: habitational name from Limburg in the Belgian province of Liège or from Limbourg, in Haut-Rhin, France, both named with the Germanic elements *lindo* 'lime tree' + *burg* 'fortified place', or possibly also from the places mentioned at 1.

Lime (108) English: metonymic occupational name for a lime burner or for a whitewasher, from Old English *līm* 'lime'.

Limehouse (130) English: habitational name from Limehouse in Greater London, named in Old English as '(the) lime-kilns', from *līm* 'lime' + *āst* 'oast', 'kiln'.

Limer (114) English: occupational name for a whitewasher, Middle English *limer, lymer*, an agent derivative of Old English *līm* 'lime'.

Limerick (240) Irish: presumably a habitational name for someone from the city of Limerick in Ireland, although habitational surnames are unusual in Ireland.

Limes (162) Spanish (**Limés**): habitational name from Limés in Oviedo (Uviéu) province, northern Spain.

Liming (579) Possibly a variant of English LEEMING.

Limke (107) German: variant of **Limpke**, of uncertain origin. It may be a topographic name from *Limbeke*, a river name in the Harz Mountains, or from *Limp*, a short form of a Germanic personal name composed with *lint* 'snake' + *berht* 'shining' + *-ke*, diminutive suffix.

Limmer (332) **1.** English: occupational name for an illuminator of manuscripts, from Middle English *luminour, lymnour*, Old French *enlumineor, illumineor*. **2.** German: habitational name from any of several places so named in northern Germany or, in Bavaria, from Lindemer and Lindmaier (see LINDENMEYER). **3.** Dutch: from a Germanic personal name composed of *liut* 'people' + *mar* 'famous', 'renowned'. Compare LEMMER.
GIVEN NAMES German 4%. *Hans* (2), *Kurt*.

Limoges (258) French: **1.** habitational name from the southern city of Limoges (Haute-Vienne), or various other places so named. **2.** According to Debrabandere, this is also a nickname from Old French *limoge*, 'pheasant', or perhaps a metonymic occupational name for a poulterer.
FOREBEARS A Limoges from Bordeaux, France was in Montreal by 1698.
GIVEN NAMES French 13%. *Andre, Emile, Fernand, Gaston, Jacques, Monique, Muguette, Pierre, Rosaire*.

Limon (1164) **1.** Spanish (**Limón**): from Spanish *limón* 'lemon', hence possibly an occupational name for a grower or seller of

the fruit. **2.** English: variant of LEMON. **3.** French: habitational name from Limon in Nièvre, Limont-Fontaine in Nord, or Limont in the Belgian province of Liège.
GIVEN NAMES Spanish 47%. *Jose* (28), *Juan* (17), *Jesus* (16), *Manuel* (9), *Pedro* (9), *Ruben* (9), *Carlos* (7), *Enrique* (7), *Guadalupe* (7), *Jorge* (7), *Julio* (7), *Luis* (7).

Limones (110) Spanish: **1.** probably an altered form of **Citrones**, a habitational name from either of two places called Citrones in Málaga and Granada, Andalucia. **2.** possibly also from the plural of *limón* 'lemon' (see LIMON), an occupational name for a grower or seller of the fruit.
GIVEN NAMES Spanish 40%. *Pedro* (3), *Jesus* (2), *Jose* (2), *Alicia, Andres, Arturo, Evangelina, Felipe, Gilberto, Guadalupe, Juan, Juanita; Antonio, Carmelo, Filiberto.*

Limpert (227) North German form of LAMBERT.

Lin (10833) **1.** Chinese 林: from a word meaning 'forest'. Bi Gan was a half-brother to Zhou Xin, the cruel and corrupt last king (1154–1123 BC) of the Shang dynasty. Bi Gan criticized his half-brother's excesses, and for this he had his belly ripped open and his heart cut out. His wife fled to Chang Forest, where she gave birth to a son. When Zhou Xin was toppled by the new Zhou dynasty, the new Zhou ruler granted the son some land together with the name Lin. **2.** Chinese 连: variant of LIAN 1. **3.** Scottish and English: perhaps a variant of LYNN. **4.** Dutch: probably a variant of LYN.
GIVEN NAMES Chinese 36%. *Wen* (27), *Feng* (25), *Hong* (23), *Ming* (23), *Wei* (22), *Yi* (22), *Ping* (21), *Chin* (19), *Jian* (19), *Li* (19), *Cheng* (18), *Ching* (18).

Lina (105) **1.** Spanish: possibly a nickname from *liña* 'thread', or a variant of *línea* 'line'. **2.** Italian: probably a short form of a female personal name ending with *-lina*, for example *Carolina, Angelina.*
GIVEN NAMES Spanish 10%. *Eugenio, Juan, Manuel, Oswaldo, Patria.*

Linam (289) English and Irish: variant spelling of LYNAM.

Linan (129) Spanish **Liñán**: possibly a variant spelling of Catalan **Llinyà**. However, this name is found mainly in Basque Country.
GIVEN NAMES Spanish 40%. *Jose* (5), *Francisco* (2), *Luis* (2), *Manuel* (2), *Alberto, Andres, Carolina, Eduardo, Epifanio, Ernesto, Esmeralda, Garcia.*

Linard (114) **1.** French: habitational name from a place in Creuse, or possibly from Linards in Haut-Vienne or Linars in Charente and Haute-Loire. **2.** French: from the personal name *Linard*, a variant of LEONARD. **3.** Greek: shortened form of a patronymic (**Linardakos, Linardakis, Linardatos,** etc.) based on *Linardos,* Greek form of LEONARD.
GIVEN NAMES French 7%. *Etienne* (2), *Richet.*

Linares (1591) **1.** Spanish: habitational name from any of various places called

Linares, as for example in the provinces of Jaén, Seville, Salamanca, Cantabria, Burgos, and Soria, from the plural of *linar* 'flax field' (Latin *linare*, a derivative of *linum* 'flax'). **2.** Asturian-Leonese and Aragonese: Castilianized form of Asturian-Leonese **Llinares** (also **L.linares**), or Aragonese **Linars**, habitational names from the towns in Aragon named with the word *linars* 'flax fields'. **3.** Spanish (**Liñares**): occupational name for a linen merchant, Latin *linarius*.
GIVEN NAMES Spanish 54%; Portuguese 12%. *Jose* (49), *Luis* (31), *Carlos* (26), *Juan* (25), *Manuel* (22), *Jorge* (16), *Ramon* (16), *Jesus* (14), *Miguel* (13), *Francisco* (12), *Pedro* (11), *Eduardo* (10); *Calixtro.*

Linberg (131) Of uncertain origin: possibly a variant of Swedish LINDBERG or an altered form of Belgian **van Linberghe**, a habitational name for someone from Lemberge in East Flanders.

Lince (216) **1.** Spanish and Portuguese: nickname from *lince* 'lynx'. **2.** Dutch: from a short form of the personal name *Laure(i)ns* (see LAWRENCE).
GIVEN NAMES Spanish 7%. *Arturo* (2), *Alba, Ana, Ana Maria, Blanca, Jaime, Jorge, Jose, Jose Enrique, Juan, Manuel, Mario.*

Lincecum (169) Origin unidentified. This name occurs chiefly in TX and LA.

Linch (348) Irish and English: variant spelling of LYNCH.

Lincicome (166) Origin unidentified. Compare LINCECUM and LINTHICUM.

Linck (495) German and Dutch: variant of LINK.

Lincks (197) Americanized spelling of Dutch **Linckx**, a nickname from *links* 'left', 'left-handed', 'clumsy'.

Lincoln (5946) English: habitational name from the city of Lincoln, so named from an original British name *Lindo-* 'lake' + Latin *colonia* 'settlement', 'colony'. The place was an important administrative center during the Roman occupation of Britain and in the Middle Ages it was a center for the manufacture of cloth, including the famous 'Lincoln green'.
FOREBEARS Abraham Lincoln (1809–65), 16th president of the United States, was the son of an illiterate laborer, descended from a certain Samuel Lincoln, who had emigrated from England to MA in 1637.

Lincourt (120) Canadian French: possibly a habitational name from a lost or unidentified place.
GIVEN NAMES French 6%. *Adelard, Georges.*

Lind (6412) **1.** Scandinavian, English, Dutch, and Jewish (Ashkenazic): topographic name for someone who lived by a lime tree, Middle English *lind*. As a Jewish and Swedish name, it is often of ornamental origin. **2.** South German, and Jewish (Ashkenazic): nickname for a gentle, tolerant man, from Middle High German *lint*, *linde* 'gentle', 'mild'. **3.** North German and Danish: habitational name from any of various places named with *Lind* 'lime tree'.

Linda (194) **1.** German and Jewish: variant of LINDE. **2.** Eastern German: habitational name from places so named in Thuringia, Saxony, and Silesia.
GIVEN NAMES Jewish 7%. *Myers* (2), *Hyman, Irina.*

Lindahl (1464) Swedish: ornamental name composed of Swedish *lind* 'lime tree' + *dahl*, an ornamental (old) spelling of *dal* 'valley'.
GIVEN NAMES Scandinavian 5%. *Lennart* (4), *Alf, Alvar, Astrid, Erik, Jalmer, Knute, Lars, Lasse, Nils, Selmer.*

Lindaman (249) Americanized or variant spelling of LINDEMAN or LINDEMANN.

Lindamood (493) Americanized form of German LINDEMUTH.

Lindau (198) German: habitational name from Lindau, which is named with Old High German *linta* 'lime tree' + *ouwa* 'water meadow' or 'island'.
GIVEN NAMES Scandinavian 7%; German 4%. *Kurt.*

Lindauer (703) German: habitational name for someone from LINDAU.

Lindbeck (191) Swedish: ornamental name composed of the elements *lind* 'lime tree' + *bäck* 'stream'.
GIVEN NAMES Scandinavian 4%. *Berger, Nels, Nils.*

Lindberg (4382) **1.** Swedish: ornamental name composed of Swedish *lind* 'lime tree' + *berg* 'mountain', 'hill'. **2.** South German: habitational name from any of several places so named.
GIVEN NAMES Scandinavian 5%. *Erik* (8), *Algot* (2), *Anders* (2), *Alvar, Bertel, Britt, Gunner, Hilma, Hjalmer, Knute, Lars, Lennart.*

Lindblad (563) Swedish: ornamental name composed of the elements *lind* 'lime tree' + *blad* 'leaf'.
GIVEN NAMES Scandinavian 6%. *Erik* (3), *Alvar, Arlys, Bjorn, Lars.*

Lindblom (732) Swedish: ornamental name composed of the elements *lind* 'lime tree' + *blom* 'flower'.
GIVEN NAMES Scandinavian 9%. *Erik* (2), *Anders, Joakim, Kerstin, Lars, Nels, Sten, Sven, Thora.*

Lindbloom (348) Americanized form of Swedish LINDBLOM.

Lindbo (102) Swedish: ornamental name composed. of *lind* 'lime tree' + *bo* 'farm', 'dwelling'.

Lindborg (145) Swedish: ornamental name composed of the elements *lind* 'lime tree' + *borg* 'castle'.
GIVEN NAMES Scandinavian 5%; French 4%. *Erik, Nils; Camille, Laure.*

Lindburg (159) Perhaps an altered spelling of LINDBERG or LINDBORG.

Linde (1123) **1.** German, Dutch, and Scandinavian: topographic name for someone who lived by a conspicuous lime tree, Middle High German, Dutch *linde*, Scandinavian *lind*. There are several places, especial-

ly in North Germany, named with this word, and the name may be a habitational name from any of these. The word was also used in a number of Old High German women's personal names, with the meaning 'shield' or 'spear' (these being made from the hard wood of the lime); it is possible that the surname in some cases is from a short form of one of these. As a Swedish name it is often ornamental rather than topographic. **2.** Jewish (Ashkenazic): ornamental adoption of German *Linde* 'lime tree' (see 1). **3.** Spanish: topographic name for someone who lived on a boundary, from Spanish *linde* 'boundary', Latin *limes*, or habitational name from any of the places called La Linde in Oviéu (Oviéu) and Biscay provinces.
GIVEN NAMES Scandinavian 4%; German 4%. *Erik* (3), *Nels* (3), *Gunner, Lars; Kurt* (4), *Dieter, Erna, Fritz, Hasso, Markus, Otto, Ralf.*

Lindeen (171) Swedish (**Lindén**): ornamental name composed of the elements *lind* 'lime tree' + the common suffix of surnames *-én*, from the Latin adjectival suffix *-enius.*

Lindekugel (101) German: a hypercorrected form of **Linnekogel**, a descriptive epithet from Middle High German *līn* 'linen' + *kogel* 'hood' (attached to a coat; see KOGEL).
GIVEN NAME German 7%. *Otto.*

Lindell (1409) **1.** Swedish: ornamental name composed of the elements *lind* 'lime tree' + *-ell*, a common suffix of Swedish surnames, from the Latin adjectival suffix *-elius.* **2.** English: habitational name from Lindal, Cumbria (formerly in Lancashire) or Lindale, also in Cumbria; both are named from Old Norse *lind* 'lime tree' + *dalr* 'valley'.
GIVEN NAMES Scandinavian 4%. *Erik* (3), *Iver* (2), *Swen* (2), *Alvar, Astrid, Elof, Lennart, Nels, Per.*

Lindelof (113) Swedish: ornamental name composed of the elements *lind* 'lime tree' + *löf* 'leaf'.
GIVEN NAMES Scandinavian 11%. *Erland* (2), *Erik.*

Lindeman (1920) Dutch, Danish, Swedish, and Jewish (Ashkenazic): elaborated form of the topographic or ornamental name LINDE.

Lindemann (1830) German and Jewish (Ashkenazic): elaborated form of LINDE.
GIVEN NAMES German 6%. *Kurt* (5), *Erwin* (3), *Klaus* (3), *Otto* (3), *Hans* (2), *Helmut* (2), *Manfred* (2), *Eckhart, Elfriede, Gerd, Grete, Guenter.*

Lindemulder (109) Dutch: occupational name for a miller whose mill was by a lime tree, from *linde* 'lime tree' + *mulder* 'miller'.
GIVEN NAMES Dutch 7%. *Harm, Klaas.*

Lindemuth (306) German: byname for someone with a gentle disposition, from Middle High German *liude* 'soft', 'gentle' + *muot* 'disposition'.

Linden (2496) **1.** Dutch, German, and Jewish (Ashkenazic): variant (plural) of LINDE. **2.** English: variant spelling of LINDON. **3.** Belgian and Dutch (**van Linden**): habitational name from places called Linden in Brabant and North Brabant. **4.** Dutch (**van der Linden**): habitational name from any of numerous places called Ter Linde. **5.** Irish: reduced form of **McLinden**. **6.** Swedish (**Lindén**): ornamental name from *lind* 'lime tree' + the common suffix *-én*, from the Latin adjectival ending *-enius.*

Lindenbaum (348) **1.** German: topographic name for someone who lived by a lime tree, *Lindenbaum*, or a habitational name for someone living at a house distinguished by the sign of a lime tree. **2.** Jewish (Ashkenazic): ornamental adoption of 1.
GIVEN NAMES French 5%; Jewish Biblical 4%; German 4%; Jewish 4%. *Marcel* (4), *Armand; Erna, Kurt, Manfred; Ephraim* (2), *Yakov* (2), *Miriam.*

Lindenberg (485) **1.** German: habitational name from any of numerous places called Lindenberg, from Middle High German *linde* 'lime tree' + *berg* 'mountain', 'hill'. **2.** Dutch: habitational name from Lindeberghe in Malle, Antwerp. **3.** Jewish (Ashkenazic): ornamental name composed of German *Linde* 'lime tree' + *Berg* 'mountain', 'hill'.
GIVEN NAMES German 6%. *Kurt* (4), *Uwe* (2), *Horst, Klaus.*

Lindenberger (204) German: habitational name for someone from a place called LINDENBERG.

Lindenfelser (149) German: habitational name for someone from Lindenfels in Hesse (a place name meaning 'lime-trees crag').
GIVEN NAMES German 4%. *Eldred, Gunther.*

Lindenmayer (105) German: variant spelling of LINDENMEYER.

Lindenmeyer (152) German: habitational name for the tenant of a farm identified by a lime tree, from Middle High German *linde* 'lime tree' + *meier* 'tenant farmer'.

Lindenmuth (394) German: variant of LINDEMUTH, probably altered by folk etymology as a result of a confusion of *linde* 'soft', 'gentle' with *Linde* 'lime tree' (plural *Linden*). The second element, *muth*, is from Middle High German *muot* 'disposition'.

Linder (5194) **1.** Swedish: ornamental name from *lind* 'lime tree' + either the German suffix *-er* denoting an inhabitant, or the surname suffix *-ér*, derived from the Latin adjectival ending *-er(i)us.* **2.** English (mainly southeastern): variant of LIND 2. **3.** German: habitational name from any of numerous places called Linden or Lindern, named with German *Linden* 'lime trees'.

Linderer (100) German: variant of LINDER.

Linderman (1200) **1.** German (**Lindermann**): habitational name from any of several places called Lindern. **2.** Dutch: variant of LINDEMAN.

Linders (155) Dutch: **1.** patronymic from the personal name LEONARD. **2.** from a

Germanic personal name composed of the elements *linta* 'shield' or 'spear' (see LINDE 1) + *hari, heri* 'army'.
GIVEN NAMES French 4%. *Camille, Marcel.*

Lindert (134) **1.** North German: habitational name from Linderte, near Hannover. **2.** Dutch: from the personal name *Lindert*, a variant of LEONARD.

Lindfors (212) Swedish (also frequent in Finland): ornamental name composed of the elements *lind* 'lime tree' + *fors* 'waterfall'.
GIVEN NAMES Scandinavian 9%; Finnish 5%; German 4%. *Erik* (2), *Knute, Nils; Eino* (2), *Martta, Onni, Sulo; Wenzel.*

Lindgren (3234) Swedish: ornamental name composed of the elements *lind* 'lime tree' + *gren* 'branch'.
GIVEN NAMES Scandinavian 6%. *Sven* (9), *Erik* (5), *Holger* (2), *Nels* (2), *Anders, Arlys, Bent, Berndt, Bjorn, Disa, Erland, Evald.*

Lindh (286) Swedish: ornamental spelling of *lind* 'lime tree' (see LINDE).
GIVEN NAMES Scandinavian 6%; German 4%. *Eskil, Nels; Wolf* (2), *Hans.*

Lindholm (1427) Swedish: ornamental name composed of the elements *lind* 'lime tree' + *holm* 'island'.
GIVEN NAMES Scandinavian 6%. *Erik* (7), *Evald* (2), *Alf, Astrid, Einer, Fredrik, Holger, Johan, Per.*

Lindhorst (336) German: habitational name from any of several places so called.
GIVEN NAMES German 4%. *Klaus, Kurt, Willi.*

Lindig (153) German (Saxony, Thuringia): habitational name from a place so named.
GIVEN NAMES German 8%. *Ernst* (2), *Johann, Markus.*

Lindland (103) Swedish: ornamental name from *lind* 'lime tree' + *land* 'land'.

Lindle (135) German: topographic name for someone living near a small group of lime trees, from Middle High German *linde* 'lime tree' + the diminutive suffix *-le.*

Lindler (383) German: possibly a habitational name from a place called Lindlar, west of Cologne.

Lindley (4063) **1.** English: habitational name from either of two places in West Yorkshire called Lindley, or from Linley in Shropshire and Wiltshire, all named from Old English *līn* 'flax' + *lēah* 'wood', 'glade', with epenthetic *-d-*, or from another Lindley in West Yorkshire (near Otley), named in Old English as 'lime wood', from *lind* 'lime tree' + *lēah* 'woodland clearing'. Lindley in Leicestershire probably also has this origin, and is a further possible source of the surname. **2.** German: habitational name from places in Bavaria and Hannover called Lindloh, meaning 'lime grove', or a topographic name with the same meaning (see LINDE + LOH).

Lindloff (109) North German: topographic name from Middle Low German *lind* 'lime tree' + 'lôf' 'foliage'.

Lindly (115) English: variant spelling of LINDLEY.

Lindman (299) **1.** Jewish (Ashkenazic): nickname or ornamental from Yiddish *lind* 'mild' + *man* 'man'. **2.** Jewish (Ashkenazic): variant of LINDEMAN. **3.** Swedish: ornamental name composed of *lind* 'lime tree' + *man* 'man'.
GIVEN NAME Scandinavian 7%. *Nils.*

Lindmark (163) Swedish: ornamental name composed of the elements *lind* 'lime tree' + *mark* 'ground', 'land', 'country'.
GIVEN NAMES Scandinavian 10%. *Mauritz, Nelle, Sven.*

Lindner (3076) **1.** German and Jewish (Ashkenazic): habitational name from any of numerous places called Lindenau, Linde, Linden, or Linda. **2.** Jewish (Ashkenazic): ornamental name from German *Linde* 'lime tree' + the agent suffix *-ner*.
GIVEN NAMES German 6%. *Kurt* (7), *Fritz* (4), *Erwin* (3), *Hans* (3), *Heinz* (3), *Horst* (3), *Otto* (3), *Erna* (2), *Frieda* (2), *Klaus* (2), *Manfred* (2), *Reinhold* (2).

Lindo (568) Spanish and Portuguese: nickname from *lindo* 'lovely'.
GIVEN NAMES Spanish 12%. *Cesar* (3), *Enrique* (3), *Jose* (3), *Manuel* (3), *Arturo* (2), *Carlos* (2), *Roberto* (2), *Adelina, Amparo, Ana, Ana Cristina, Armando.*

Lindon (246) English: habitational name from places called Lindon in Lincolnshire, Linden End, Haddenham, in Cambridgeshire, or Lyndon, Rutland, all named from Old English *lind* 'lime tree' or *līn* 'flax' + *dūn* 'hill'.
GIVEN NAMES French 4%. *Camille, Chantel.*

Lindor (122) Probably of French origin: unexplained. Perhaps a respelling of LINDER, an Alsace name of German origin. In North America, this name is found mainly in LA.
GIVEN NAMES French 26%. *Alphonse, Emilienne, Germaine, Jacques, Lucien, Lucienne, Pierre, Raymonde, Regine, Yvan, Yves.*

Lindow (528) German: habitational name of Slavic origin from places so called in Brandenburg, Pomerania, and Mecklenburg.

Lindquist (5059) Swedish: ornamental name composed of the elements *lind* 'lime tree' + *quist*, an old or ornamental spelling of *kvist* 'twig'.
GIVEN NAMES Scandinavian 5%. *Erik* (12), *Lars* (6), *Nels* (4), *Sten* (3), *Knute* (2), *Lennart* (2), *Swen* (2), *Anders, Bertel, Birgit, Einer, Erland.*

Lindroth (219) Swedish: ornamental name composed of the elements *lind* 'lime tree' + *roth*, an ornamental spelling of *rot* 'root'.
GIVEN NAMES Scandinavian 10%. *Lars, Mats, Nils.*

Lindsay (11935) **1.** Scottish: habitational name from Lindsey in Lincolnshire, England. This is first found in the form *Lindissi*, apparently a derivative of the British name of LINCOLN. To this was later added the Old English element *ēg* 'island', since the place

was virtually cut off by the surrounding fenland. The surname was taken to Scotland at an early date and is the name of an important and powerful Scottish family. **2.** Irish: adopted as an equivalent of various Gaelic names (see LINDSEY).

Lindseth (203) Norwegian: habitational name from any of numerous farmsteads in central Norway, so named from *lind* 'lime tree', 'linden' + *set* 'farmstead', 'dwelling'.
GIVEN NAMES Scandinavian 10%. *Erik* (3), *Knute, Nels.*

Lindsey (19954) **1.** Variant spelling of Scottish LINDSAY. **2.** Irish: reduced and Anglicized form of various Gaelic surnames, as for example **Ó Loingsigh** (see LYNCH 1), **Mac Giolla Fhionntóg** (see McCLINTOCK), and **Ó Fhloinn** (see FLYNN). **3.** English: habitational name from Lindsey in Suffolk, named in Old English as 'island (Old English *ēg*) of *Lelli*', a personal name representing a byform of an unattested name *Lealla*.

Lindskog (187) Swedish: ornamental name composed of the elements *lind* 'lime tree' + *skog* 'wood', 'forest'.
GIVEN NAMES Scandinavian 7%; German 6%. *Lars, Per; Fritz, Ilse, Otto.*

Lindsley (1204) English (Durham and Yorkshire): unexplained; perhaps an altered form of LINDLEY.

Lindstedt (237) **1.** Swedish: ornamental name composed of the elements *lind* 'lime tree' + *stedt* 'place', 'homestead' (from German). **2.** German: habitational name from a place so named in Brandenburg.
GIVEN NAMES Scandinavian 5%. *Erik* (2), *Nils.*

Lindstrand (160) Swedish: ornamental name composed of the elements *lind* 'lime tree' + *strand* 'shore'.
GIVEN NAMES Scandinavian 8%. *Erik, Lennart.*

Lindstrom (4061) Swedish (**Lindström**): ornamental name composed of the elements *lind* 'lime tree' + *ström* 'river'.
GIVEN NAMES Scandinavian 6%. *Erik* (9), *Nils* (7), *Johan* (3), *Sven* (2), *Thor* (2), *Anders, Astrid, Bjorn, Britt, Erland, Helmer, Hilmer.*

Lindt (151) **1.** German: variant of LIND 3. **2.** Dutch: variant spelling of LINT.

Lindvall (252) Swedish: ornamental name composed of the elements *lind* 'lime (tree)' + *vall* 'bank'.

Lindvig (102) Norwegian: habitational name from any of several farmsteads named with *lind* 'lime tree' + *vik* 'bay', 'inlet'.
GIVEN NAME Scandinavian 7%. *Jorgen.*

Lindwall (151) Swedish: variant of LINDVALL.
GIVEN NAMES Scandinavian 9%. *Erik* (2), *Sten.*

Lindy (199) Possibly an Americanized spelling of German **Linde**, so written to preserve the second syllable.
GIVEN NAMES German 6%. *Kurt, Lisl.*

Line (1190) **1.** English: from the medieval female personal name *Line*, a reduced form of *Cateline* (see CATLIN) and of various other names, such as *Emmeline* and *Adeline*, containing the Anglo-Norman French diminutive suffix *-line* (originally a double diminutive, composed of the elements *-el* and *-in*). **2.** French (**Liné**): metonymic occupational name for a linen weaver or a linen merchant, from an Old French adjective *liné* 'made of linen'.

Lineback (326) Americanized spelling of LEINBACH.

Linebarger (407) Americanized spelling of German LEINBERGER or LEUENBERGER.

Linebaugh (453) Americanized spelling of German LEINBACH.

Lineberger (891) Americanized spelling of German LEINBERGER or LEUENBERGER.

Lineberry (1184) Americanized spelling of German **Leinberg**, a habitational name for someone from Leinburg in Bavaria, or a topographic name from Middle High German *līn* 'flax' + *berg* 'mountain'.

Linehan (1510) Irish: reduced Anglicized form of Gaelic **Ó Laidhghneáin** 'descendant of *Laidhghneán*', a personal name that occurs in Old Irish genealogies; it is perhaps a diminutive of *laidhghein* 'snowbirth' (from *ladhg* 'snow' + *gein* 'birth').
GIVEN NAMES Irish 5%. *Brendan* (3), *Liam* (3).

Lineman (156) **1.** Altered spelling of German **Leinemann**, a topographic name for someone from the river Leine (near Hannover). **2.** Possibly also an altered spelling of German **Linnemann**, a variant of LINDEMANN.

Linen (164) **1.** Scottish: unexplained. Perhaps a shortened altered form of McLENNAN. **2.** German and French (Alsace): probably a variant of LEINEN.
GIVEN NAMES French 5%. *Batiste, Camille, Celestine.*

Linenberger (200) Americanized spelling of German LEINBERGER.
GIVEN NAMES French 4%. *Alphone, Amie.*

Liner (935) Variant spelling of LEINER.

Lines (1224) English: metronymic from LINE.

Lineweaver (160) Americanized form of German LEINWEBER.

Linford (293) English: habitational name from Great and Little Linford in Buckinghamshire or Lynford in Norfolk. The former may have Old English *hlyn* 'maple' as its first element; the latter is more likely to contain *līn* 'flax'. The second element in each case is Old English *ford* 'ford'.

Ling (2334) **1.** English (mainly East Anglia): habitational name from Lyng in Norfolk, so named from Old English *hlinc* 'hillside', or from either of two places in Norfolk and Lincolnshire named Ling, from Old Norse *lyng* 'ling', 'heather'. There is also a Lyng in Somerset, so named

from Old English *lengen* 'long place'. **2.** German: variant of LINK. **3.** Chinese 凌 : from a word meaning 'ice'. In ancient times, the imperial palace was able to enjoy ice in the summer by storing winter ice in a cellar, entrusting its care to an official called the iceman. This post was once filled during the Zhou dynasty (1122–221 BC) by a descendant of Kang Shu, the eighth son of Wen Wang, who had been granted the state of Wei soon after the establishment of the Zhou dynasty. Descendants of this particular iceman adopted the word for ice, *ling*, as their surname.
GIVEN NAMES Chinese 7%. *Ping* (5), *Hong* (4), *Yun* (4), *Chun* (3), *Feng* (3), *Ling* (3), *Yee* (3), *Ching* (2), *Jian* (2), *Li* (2), *Mei* (2), *Shui* (2).

Lingafelter (153) Altered spelling of German **Lingenfelder** (see LINGENFELTER).

Lingard (248) English: habitational name from Lingart, Lancashire, or Lingards Wood in Marsden, West Yorkshire, both named from Old English *līn* 'flax' + *garðr* 'enclosure'.

Linge (121) **1.** English: variant spelling of LING 1. **2.** Norwegian: habitational name from any of several farmsteads in western Norway named with *lyng* 'heather', either on its own, or with the addition of *vin* 'meadow'. **3.** Dutch (**de Linge**) and North German: habitational name from a place named with Old Low German *linge* 'strip of land or water', or possibly with the river name Linge (this river flows through the Betuwe). See also LINGEN. **4.** Possibly French, from a metonymic occupational name from *linge* 'linen goods', but there is no evidence of surname in North America.
GIVEN NAMES German 5%; Scandinavian 4%. *Egon, Juergen*; *Iver*.

Lingel (161) **1.** German: possibly a shortened form of a habitational name from a place such as LINGELBACH. **2.** Perhaps a nickname from Middle High German *linge* 'hurried', for someone always in a hurry (related to modern German *gelingen*).

Lingelbach (176) German: habitational name from Lingelbach in Hesse.

Lingen (170) **1.** Dutch (**van Lingen**) and German: habitational name from Lingen on the Ems river in Lower Saxony, Westphalia, and the former East Prussia. **2.** English (Herefordshire): habitational name from a place in Herefordshire, so named from an old British stream name, Welsh *llyn* 'water' + possibly *cain* 'clear', 'beautiful'.
GIVEN NAME French 4%. *Nicolle*.

Lingenfelter (1201) Variant of German **Lingenfelder**, a habitational name for someone from Lingenfeld in the Palatinate.

Linger (635) **1.** English: variant of LINGARD. **2.** French: occupational name for a maker of or dealer in linen goods, from Old French *linge* 'linen (goods)' (see LINGE 1).

Lingerfelt (766) Americanized spelling of German **Lingenfeld**, a habitational name from a place so named in the Palatinate.

Lingg (225) South German: variant of LINK.

Lingle (1579) Possibly an altered spelling of German LINGEL.

Lingley (141) English: variant of LINDLEY.

Lingner (153) German: **1.** Habitational name from Lingen near Osnabrück. **2.** dialect variant of LINDNER.
GIVEN NAMES German 6%. *Gerhard, Gerhardt, Kurt*.

Lingo (1043) Most probably an altered form of Scottish **Lingoch**, a habitational name from the lands of Lingoch (now Lingo) in Carnbee, Fife.

Lingren (143) Swedish: variant of LIND-GREN.
GIVEN NAME Scandinavian 4%. *Erik* (2).

Linhardt (188) German: variant of LEONARD.

Linhares (227) Portuguese: habitational name from any of several places called Linhares, for example in Braganca, Guarda, and Vila Real, from the plural of *linhar* 'flax field' (Latin *linare*, a derivative of *linum* 'flax').
GIVEN NAMES Spanish 13%; Portuguese 10%. *Manuel* (8), *Jose* (4), *Alfonso, Domingos, Ernesto, Francisco, Helio, Inocencio, Luis, Luiz, Pedro, Renato*; *Joaquim*.

Linhart (640) Dutch and Czech: from the personal name, a variant of LEONARD.

Lininger (561) Americanized spelling of German LEININGER.

Link (8873) German, Dutch, and Jewish (Ashkenazic): nickname for a left-handed person, from Middle High German *linc*, Dutch *linker, links*, Yiddish *link* 'left (side)'. In Europe left-handed people were long regarded with suspicion as clumsy, awkward, deviant, and even untrustworthy.

Linke (796) German and Dutch: variant of LINK.
GIVEN NAMES German 6%. *Heinz* (4), *Reinhold* (2), *Brunhilde, Fritz, Gerhard, Hannes, Inge, Klaus, Manfred, Rudi, Uli*.

Linkenhoker (173) Possibly an altered spelling of **Linkenauger**, an apparently German but unexplained name found in the U.S.

Linker (1115) German, Dutch, and Jewish (Ashkenazic): nickname for a left-handed person, from an inflected form of LINK.

Linkhart (100) German: possibly an elaborated form of the German nickname **Linkert**, a variant of LINKER.

Linklater (102) Scottish (Orkney): habitational name from either of two places named Linklater (in South Ronaldsay and North Sandwick).

Linkletter (105) Scottish (Orkney): variant of LINKLATER.

Linko (120) Polish: nickname from *lin* 'tench'.
GIVEN NAME Polish 4%. *Wasil* (2).

Linkous (1118) Probably an Americanization of an unidentified German name. This is a common name in VA, TN, and OH.
FOREBEARS The American family of this name is said to be descended from Henry Linkous, a Hessian mercenary fighting for the British in the Revolutionary War, who settled in Blacksburg, VA.

Links (136) Dutch: variant of LINK.
GIVEN NAME French 4%. *Alain*.

Linley (358) English: variant spelling of LINDLEY.

Linman (120) Dutch: reduced form of LINDEMAN.

Linn (5184) **1.** Scottish: variant spelling of LYNN. **2.** Irish: reduced and altered form of McLEAN. Compare McLINN. **3.** German: habitational name from a place called Linn, named with *lin* 'swamp', 'bog', 'marsh'. **4.** German: from a Germanic personal name, *Linto*, formed with Old High German *lind(i)* 'soft'. **5.** Eastern German and Jewish (eastern Ashkenazic): from Slavic *lin* 'tench', a metonymic occupational name for someone who caught and sold tench or a nickname for someone thought to resemble a tench.

Linna (102) Finnish: from *linna* meaning either 'castle' or 'stony tract of land'. This is a common farm name throughout Finland.
GIVEN NAMES Finnish 18%. *Eino* (2), *Waino* (2), *Arvo, Jorma, Mauno, Vesa*.

Linnane (174) Irish: reduced Anglicized form of Gaelic **Ó Lionnáin**, a variant of **Ó Leannáin** (see LENNON).
GIVEN NAMES Irish 8%. *Brendan, Kieran*.

Linne (300) **1.** German: habitational name from Linne, or North German topographic name equivalent to LINDE 1. **2.** Swedish (**Linné**): from Latin *Linnaeus*. **3.** French (**Linné**): from various personal names formed with the double diminutive suffix *-linet*, for example *Paulinet, Colinet*.

Linnebur (147) German: probably an occupational nickname for a flax grower, from Middle Low German *līn* + *būr* 'grower', 'farmer'.

Linnehan (178) Irish: variant spelling of LINEHAN.

Linnell (649) English: unexplained.

Linneman (493) Variant of German LINNE-MANN.

Linnemann (180) North German and Danish: variant of LINDEMANN.
GIVEN NAMES German 7%. *Heinz* (2), *Ernst, Horst*.

Linnen (154) Scottish and northern Irish: apparently a variant of LINEN, possibly from an earlier spelling **Linning**, which is recorded in Lanarkshire in 1623.

Linner (115) **1.** German: habitational name for someone from any of various places called Linne in Lower Saxony, or Linnern in Bavaria. **2.** Swedish (also **Linnér**): ornamental name from the place-name element *Linn-* (from *lind-* 'maple') + the surname suffix -ér, derived from the Latin adjectival ending -er(i)us.

GIVEN NAMES Scandinavian 6%; German 5%. *Anders, Erik*; *Gerhard*.

Linney (367) English: from an Old English female personal name *Lindgifu*, *Lindgeofu*, composed of the elements *lind* 'lime (wood)', i.e. 'shield' (a transferred sense) + *gifu, geofu* 'gift'.

Lino (342) **1.** Spanish (**Liño**): perhaps a metonymic occupational name for a linen weaver, from *liño* 'linen'. **2.** Spanish and Portuguese: from the medieval personal name *Lino* (Latin *Linus*), or from a short form of a personal name ending with -*lino*.

GIVEN NAMES Spanish 28%. *Jose* (5), *Fernando* (3), *Francisco* (3), *Bartolome* (2), *Blanca* (2), *Luz* (2), *Manuel* (2), *Pedro* (2), *Roberto* (2), *Abelardo, Alfredo, Ana*.

Linquist (331) Swedish: variant of LINDQUIST.

GIVEN NAMES German 4%. *Fritz* (2), *Kurt*.

Lins (445) **1.** German: from Middle High German *lins(e)* 'lentil', presumably a metonymic occupational nickname for a grower of lentils. **2.** German: from a short form of a Germanic personal name formed with Old High German *lint* 'snake' or *linta* 'linden tree', 'shield'. **3.** English (Staffordshire): unexplained. Possibly a variant of LYNES. **4.** Latvian: possibly from *lins* 'flax'.

Linscheid (136) German: topographic name from *lin* denoting 'water' or 'swamp' + the place name suffix -*scheid* 'division', 'border', which is frequent in Rhineland and southern Westphalia.

GIVEN NAMES German 4%. *Erwin, Kurt*.

Linscomb (177) English: habitational name possibly from any of three places in Devon called Lincombe, named in Old English with *līn* 'flax' or *lind* 'lime tree' + *cumb* 'valley'.

Linscott (811) English: habitational name from Linscott in Moretonhampstead or Limscott in Bradworthy, both in Devon and so named from the Old English personal name *Lēofwine* + Old English *cot* 'cottage'.

Linse (253) German: variant of LINS.

GIVEN NAMES German 4%. *Frieda, Klaus, Otto*.

Linsenbigler (102) altered spelling of South German **Linsenbichler**, from a topographic name probably formed with LINS + *bichel*, Bavarian dialect for B[die]hel 'hill', or the first part is of some other origin.

Linsenmeyer (118) German: distinguishing name for a tenant farmer who grew lentils or a variant of **Linsenmann**, an occupational name for a grower and seller of lentils, from Middle High German *lins(e)* 'lentil'.

GIVEN NAMES German 10%. *Kurt* (2), *Fritz, Monika, Otto*.

Linsey (224) **1.** Scottish, Irish, or English: variant of LINDSAY or LINDSEY. **2.** Americanized form of German LINSE.

Linskey (208) Irish (Mayo, Galway): variant of LYNSKEY.

Linsky (318) **1.** Irish (Mayo, Galway): variant of LYNSKEY. **2.** Germanized or Americanized spelling of Polish **Liński**, a habitational name for someone from places called Linie or Linne.

Linsley (405) English (County Durham): most probably a habitational name from a lost or unidentified place in northern England.

Linson (399) English: unexplained. Perhaps related to LINS.

Linster (118) Dutch: habitational name from *Altlinster* and *Junglinster* in the Grand Duchy of Luxembourg.

GIVEN NAMES German 7%. *Kurt* (2), *Aloys*.

Linstrom (180) Variant of Swedish LINDSTROM.

Lint (782) **1.** English: metonymic occupational name for a dresser of flax, from Middle English *lynet, lynt* 'flax'. **2.** Dutch: from a short form of a Germanic name formed with *lind* (see LINDE 1). **3.** Dutch: metonymic occupational name for a linen weaver or merchant.

Linthicum (792) Origin unidentified. Compare LINCECUM, LINCICOME.

Lintner (661) German: Austrian variant of LINDNER.

Linton (4792) Scottish, northern Irish, and English: habitational name from any of the numerous places so called, found in the Scottish Borders and in various parts of England. The second element is in all cases Old English *tūn* 'enclosure', 'settlement'. In the case of Linton in Northumberland the first element is a British river name, *Lyne* (related to Welsh *lliant* 'stream'), while Linton in Kent is 'estate associated with a man called *Lill* or *Lilla*'. The other places of this name normally have as their first element Old English *lind* 'lime tree' or *līn* 'flax', but occasionally perhaps *hlynn* 'torrent' or *hlinc* 'hillside'. (On the basis of geographical situation the meaning 'torrent' would be appropriate to Linton near Skipton in West Yorkshire).

Lints (124) **1.** Dutch: variant of LINT. **2.** Dutch: variant spelling of LINTZ 1. **3.** Americanized spelling of German LINZ.

GIVEN NAME French 4%. *Thierry*.

Lintz (632) **1.** German and Dutch: from a derivative of a Germanic personal name formed with the initial element *lind* (see LINDE 1 and LINS 2). **2.** English: habitational name from Lintz, County Durham, so named from Old English *hlinc* 'hillside'. Compare LYNCH 3.

Linville (2695) Of English origin: probably a habitational name from a lost or unidentified place, perhaps in France. The surname is not found in present-day English records, but is recorded in Hampshire (also in the forms **Lenvill, Linvel**) in the 17th century. Perhaps it is an altered form of English **Lindfield** or **Lingfield**, habitational name from a place so called in Sussex, altered by

false analogy with the alternation in Norman names between -*ville* and -*field*.

Linwood (134) Scottish and English: habitational name from places in Scotland (near Glasgow), Lincolnshire, and Hampshire named Linwood, from Old English *lind* 'lime (tree)' + *wudu* 'wood'.

Linz (373) **1.** German: habitational name from either of two places called Linz: one in Germany and one in Austria. **2.** German and Dutch: variant spelling of LINTZ 1.

GIVEN NAMES German 6%. *Hans* (2), *Wolfgang* (2), *Gerhard, Katharina, Ute*.

Linza (100) Origin unidentified.

Linzer (180) German: habitational name for someone from either of the two places called LINZ.

Linzey (164) Variant spelling of Scottish, Irish, or English LINDSAY or LINDSEY.

Linzmeier (155) German: probably a variant of LINSENMEYER, or a distinguishing name composed of the personal name **Lintz** (see LINTZ 1) + MEIER.

GIVEN NAMES German 5%. *Franz, Ignatz, Ulrich*.

Linzy (300) Variant of Scottish, Irish, or English LINDSAY or LINDSEY.

Lio (127) **1.** Southern Italian: most likely a variant of LEO, from a local form (compare DE LEO), but possibly also from a reduced form of a name such as LEONARDO, *Leopardo*, or from Greek *leios* 'smooth', 'glossy', presumably applied as a nickname. **2.** Catalan (**Lió**): habitational name from Lió in Girona province or Lyon in France (see LYON).

GIVEN NAMES Italian 23%; Spanish 15%. *Salvatore* (2), *Antonio, Carmine, Dante, Enrico, Francesco, Gino, Giovanni, Pietro*; *Alicia* (4), *Mario* (2), *Salvadore* (2), *Alejandro, Angel, Armando, Jose, Manuel, Miguel, Ramon, Rosario*.

Lion (339) **1.** English: variant spelling of LYON 1–3. **2.** French: variant of LYON 1. **3.** French: habitational name from places in Calvados, Loire, and Meuse named with Lion.

Lionberger (181) Part translation of German **Löwenberger**, a habitational name for someone from **Löwenberg** (see LOWENBERG).

Lionetti (187) Italian: patronymic from a derivative of personal names such as *Lione, Lión, Lio*.

GIVEN NAMES Italian 18%. *Angelo* (2), *Antonio, Carmine, Dario, Giovanni, Luigi, Nicola, Rocco*.

Liotta (542) Italian: variant of LEOTTA.

GIVEN NAMES Italian 13%. *Salvatore* (7), *Angelo* (2), *Carmine* (2), *Antonio, Carmelo, Domenic, Erminio, Gasper, Gaspere, Gino, Leonardo, Piero*.

Liou (315) **1.** Chinese 刘: variant of LIU 1. **2.** French: from the personal names *Liaud* or *Lioud* (from the Germanic elements *liut* 'people' + *waldan* 'to rule') or *Lioux* (from *liut* 'people' + *wulf* 'wolf').

GIVEN NAMES Chinese 31%. *Ching Ping* (2), *Ming* (2), *Wen* (2), *Chan, Cheng, Chia-Wei, Chieh, Choa, Chun, Fei, Fong, Han.*

Lipa (180) **1.** Polish, Ukrainian, and Jewish (eastern Ashkenazic): topographic name for someone who lived by a lime tree, from *lipa* 'lime tree'. As a Jewish name, it is also of ornamental origin. **2.** Jewish (from Poland): habitational name for someone from the village of Lipa, in Poland, named with *lipa* 'lime tree'. **3.** Jewish (eastern Ashkenazic): from a personal name, variant of LIPE.

Li Pani (118) Italian (also **Lipani**): from the plural of PANE, with the definite article *li*.
GIVEN NAMES Italian 8%. *Angelo, Croce, Francesco.*

Lipari (634) Italian (Sicily): habitational name from Lipari in Messina, where the surname is common.
GIVEN NAMES Italian 14%. *Salvatore* (9), *Sal* (4), *Angelo* (2), *Lia* (2), *Antonino, Antonio, Dante, Luciano, Santo, Saverio, Vito.*

Lipe (957) **1.** Possibly an Americanized spelling of German **Leipe**, a habitational name from places named Leipe, Leippe, and Leipa, all in eastern Germany. **2.** Jewish (eastern Ashkenazic): from the Yiddish personal name *Lipe*, a short form of LIPMAN. **3.** Jewish (eastern Ashkenazic): Yiddishized or Germanized form of LIPA 2 or 3.

Lipes (129) Origin unidentified. This name occurs chiefly in VA.

Lipford (628) English: habitational name, possibly from Lipwood Hall or Farm in Northumberland, named from Old English *hlēp* 'steep slope' + *wudu* 'wood', or from a lost or unidentified place. The surname does not occur in current English records, although a bearer of the name Lepford is recorded in the census of 1881.

Lipham (347) English: habitational name from a lost or unidentified place, possibly in southwestern England.

Lipinski (1310) **1.** Polish (**Lipiński**) and Jewish (from Poland): habitational name for someone from Lipno, Lipin, Lipiny, or Lipino, or other places named with Polish *lipa* 'lime tree'. **2.** Jewish (from Belarus): habitational name for someone from a place called Lipinki, now in Belarus.
GIVEN NAMES Polish 5%. *Casimir, Eugeniusz, Feliks, Grazyna, Jacek, Jadwiga, Jaroslaw, Leszek, Maciej, Pawel, Stanislaw, Stas.*

Lipinsky (114) Variant of Polish and Jewish LIPINSKI.
GIVEN NAME Jewish 4%. *Rivka.*

Lipka (706) **1.** Ukrainian and Polish: topographic name for someone who lived by a lime tree, from *lipka*, diminutive of *lipa* 'lime tree' (see LIPA). **2.** Jewish (eastern Ashkenazic): from a pet form of the personal name LIPE. **3.** Jewish (eastern Ashkenazic): from a pet form of the female personal name *Libe*, derived from Yiddish *libe* 'love'. **4.** Polish and Jewish (from Poland

and Ukraine): habitational name for someone from villages called Lipka or Lipki in Poland and Ukraine. **5.** German: from a diminutive of LIPPE 4.
GIVEN NAMES German 4%; Polish 4%. *Elke, Helmut, Kurt, Otto; Andrzej, Henryka, Jerzy, Kazimierz, Ryszard, Stanislaw, Zygmund.*

Lipke (497) German (of Slavic origin): from a diminutive of LIPPE 5.

Lipkin (571) Jewish (from Belarus): **1.** patronymic from a pet form of the personal name *Lipe* (see LIPPE 1) + the eastern Slavic possessive suffix -*in*. **2.** metronymic from a pet form of the female personal name *Libe* (see LIPKA 3).
GIVEN NAMES Jewish 10%; Russian 6%. *Emanuel* (2), *Meyer* (2), *Yakov* (2), *Ilya, Inna, Irina, Isadore, Shimon, Sol, Yossi, Ziv; Vladimir* (6), *Boris* (2), *Lev* (2), *Anatoly, Dmitry, Efim, Grigoriy, Igor, Leonid, Valeriy, Zinovy.*

Lipko (103) Ukrainian, Polish, German (of Slavic origin), and Jewish (eastern Ashkenazic): variant of LIPKA.

Lipkowitz (106) Jewish (Ashkenazic): patronymic or metronymic from the personal name LIPKA.
GIVEN NAME French 4%. *Marcel.*

Lipman (1411) **1.** Dutch: patronymic from a short form of the personal name PHILIP. **2.** Jewish (Ashkenazic): from the Yiddish personal name *Lipman*, derived from Middle High German words *liep* 'dear', 'beloved' + *man* 'man'. **3.** Possibly a respelling of German LIPPMANN.
GIVEN NAMES Jewish 4%. *Mayer* (2), *Chaim, Dov, Isadore, Jakob, Meyer, Miriam, Pinchas.*

Lipner (151) Jewish (eastern Ashkenazic): habitational name from a place called Lipno, in Ukraine and Poland.
GIVEN NAMES Jewish 12%. *Pinchas* (2), *Abbe, Aviva, Meyer.*

Lipnick (143) **1.** Jewish (from Belarus and Poland; **Lipnik**): habitational name for someone from Lipniki, now in Belarus, and Lipnik, in Poland. **2.** Americanized spelling of Slovenian **Lipnik**, habitational name for a person from any of numerous places called Lipje or Lipe, named with *lipa* 'lime tree', 'linden', or a topographic name, denoting someone who lived by a place where lime trees grow.

Lipovsky (138) **1.** Russian, Belorussian, and Jewish (from Belarus): habitational name for someone from any of the numerous villages called Lipovki and Lipovka in Belarus or Russia, named with *lipa* 'lime tree'. **2.** Altered spelling of Polish and Jewish LIPOWSKI.
GIVEN NAMES Jewish 5%. *Yakov, Yuly.*

Lipowski (128) Polish and Jewish (Ashkenazic): habitational name for someone from any of various places called Lipowo, Lipowa, or Lipowe, named with an adjectival derivative of Polish *lipa* 'lime tree'.

GIVEN NAMES Polish 5%; Scandinavian 4%. *Henryk; Erik, Sig.*

Lipp (1341) **1.** English: metonymic nickname for someone with large lips or with some deformity of the lips, from Middle English *lippe* (Old English *lippa*). **2.** English: perhaps from a Middle English personal name, *Leppe* or *Lippe*, apparently a short form of an Old English personal name formed with *Lēof*- 'dear', such as *Lēofsige, Lēofstan*. **3.** German: from a pet form of the personal name *Philipp* (see PHILIP).
GIVEN NAMES German 4%. *Alois* (2), *Frieda* (2), *Hans* (2), *Wendelin* (2), *Franz, Konrad, Otto, Rainer, Ralf.*

Lippa (251) Italian: from a short form of the personal *Filippa*, feminine form of FILIPPO.

Lippard (425) **1.** English: variant of LEOPARD. **2.** German: possibly a variant of **Liebhardt** (see LIEBHART).

Lippe (416) **1.** German and Jewish (western Ashkenazic): habitational name from the duchy of Lippe, which became an independent state in the 12th century. **2.** German: variant of LIPP 3. **3.** German: topographic name for someone living on the banks of the Lippe river in Westphalia. **4.** German: topographic name (of Slavic origin) for someone who lived among lime trees, from *lipa* 'lime'. Compare LIPINSKI. **5.** Jewish (Ashkenazic): Germanized form of LIPE.

Lippencott (107) English: variant of LIPPINCOTT.

Lippens (153) Dutch: patronymic from a reduced form of the personal name PHILIP.
GIVEN NAMES German 5%; French 5%. *Alfons, Alphons; Andre* (2).

Lipper (206) **1.** South German: variant of LIPPERT. **2.** North German: habitational name for someone from a place called LIPP or LIPPE, or a topographic name for someone who lived among lime trees.
GIVEN NAMES German 6%. *Berthold, Helmuth.*

Lippert (2369) German and Dutch: from a Germanic personal name *Liubhard*, composed of the elements *leuba, liuba* 'dear', 'beloved' + *hard* 'brave', 'strong', or from *Liutberht*, a compound of *liut, leud* 'people', 'tribe' + *berht* 'shining', 'famous'.

Lippi (195) Italian (Tuscany): patronymic or plural form of *Lippo*, a reduced form of the personal name FILIPPO.
GIVEN NAMES Italian 10%. *Ettore* (2), *Angelo, Attilio, Enzo, Francesca, Paolo, Vittorio.*

Lippincott (1331) English: habitational name from some lost place, perhaps in Devon, named with Old English an uncertain first element + *cot* 'cottage'.

Lippitt (238) English: apparently a habitational name from Lipyeate in Somerset or Lypiatt in Gloucestershire, both named from Old English *hlīepgeat* 'leap-gate', a gate which was low enough to be jumped by horses and deer but presented an obstacle to sheep and cattle.

Lippman (1016) **1.** Dutch and Jewish (Ashkenazic): variant of LIPMAN. **2.** Altered spelling of German LIPPMANN.
GIVEN NAMES Jewish 4%. *Hyman, Iren, Isadore, Meyer, Sol.*

Lippmann (249) **1.** German (Saxony, Thuringia): regional form of LIEBMANN. **2.** German: variant of LIPPE 3 and 4. **3.** Jewish (Ashkenazic): variant spelling of LIPMAN.
GIVEN NAMES German 15%. *Kurt* (2), *Otto* (2), *Siglinde* (2), *Volkmar* (2), *Fritz, Gerhard, Hans, Heinz, Uwe, Wilfried.*

Lippold (517) German: variant of LEOPOLD.
GIVEN NAMES German 6%. *Klaus* (3), *Fritz* (2), *Dieter, Jutta, Monika.*

Lipps (1057) North German: from a reduced form of the personal name *Philipps* (see PHILIP).

Lippy (278) Probably an Americanized spelling of Dutch or German LIPPE.

Lips (285) Dutch and North German: from a reduced form of the personal name *Philips* (from *Philippus*) (see PHILIP).

Lipschitz (152) Jewish (Ashkenazic): variant of LIPSCHUTZ.
GIVEN NAMES Jewish 16%; German 6%. *Chaim* (2), *Chaskel* (2), *Asher, Fishel, Moshe, Sol; Frieda* (2).

Lipschultz (167) Jewish (Ashkenazic): variant of LIPSCHUTZ.
GIVEN NAMES Jewish 5%. *Hyman, Izak.*

Lipschutz (293) Jewish (Ashkenazic): habitational name from Liebschütz in Thuringia, Leobschütz in Upper Silesia, or Liebeschitz in Bohemia. The place names are of Slavic origin, from *lipa* 'lime tree'. See also LIPSETT.
GIVEN NAMES Jewish 18%. *Mendel* (3), *Naftali* (3), *Shulem* (2), *Benzion, Bina, Chaim, Hirsch, Meyer, Moishe, Pinchos, Riv, Rivka.*

Lipscomb (4105) English: habitational name of uncertain origin, perhaps a variant of LISCOMB.

Lipsett (227) Irish: according to MacLysaght this is an Anglicized form of German (or Jewish) **Lipsitz** (see LIPSCHUTZ), brought to Ireland before the 18th century and common in Donegal.

Lipsey (958) Origin uncertain; possibly an Americanized form of Hungarian **Lipcsey**, a habitational name for someone from any of various places called Lipcse in former Zólyom and Liptó counties of Hungary, now in Slovakia, and Máramaros, now in Romania.

Lipshutz (138) Jewish (Ashkenazic): variant spelling of LIPSCHUTZ.
GIVEN NAMES Jewish 7%. *Meyer, Myer.*

Lipsitz (255) Jewish (Ashkenazic): variant of LIPSCHUTZ.
GIVEN NAMES Jewish 7%. *Hyman, Mort, Oded.*

Lipski (450) Polish and Jewish (eastern Ashkenazic): habitational name for someone from any of various places called Lipie,
Lipsk, Lipsko, Lipy, etc., all named with Polish *lipa* 'lime tree'.
GIVEN NAMES Polish 10%. *Tadeusz* (3), *Jacek* (2), *Jerzy* (2), *Boguslaw, Jolanta, Lech, Lucjan, Piotr, Stanislaw, Witold, Wladyslaw, Zbigniew.*

Lipsky (666) Jewish (Ashkenazic): variant spelling of LIPSKI.
GIVEN NAMES Jewish 4%. *Arie, Rimma, Shira, Sol, Yaacov, Yaakov.*

Lipson (1025) **1.** Jewish (eastern Ashkenazic): variant of *Libson*, a metronymic from the Yiddish female personal name *Libe*, from Yiddish 'love'. **2.** Jewish (eastern Ashkenazic): patronymic from the Yiddish personal name *Lipe* (a short form of LIPMAN). **3.** English: patronymic from LIPP 2. **4.** English: habitational name from Lipson in Devon, which is possibly named from Old English *hlīep* 'leap', 'steep place' + *stān* 'stone'.
GIVEN NAMES Jewish 4%. *Myer* (2), *Sol* (2), *Hyman, Isadore.*

Lipstein (108) Altered spelling of German of **Liebstein**, a habitational name from a place so named in Silesia.

Liptak (795) **1.** Slovak and Hungarian (**Lipták**): habitational name for someone from Liptó, a former county of upper Hungary, now in Slovakia. **2.** Polish: habitational name for someone from places called Liptaki or Liptakówka in Nowy Sącz voivodeship.

Lipton (1370) English: habitational name from Lipton in East Allington, Devon, which is probably named from Old English *tūn* 'settlement' with an uncertain first element.

Liptrap (127) English (Lancashire): unexplained; in the UK, it occurs more frequently as **Liptrot**, and according to Harrison is from a Germanic personal name composed of *liob* 'dear' + *trūt* 'beloved'. It seems to be a comparatively recent importation into the UK.

Li Puma (178) Southern Italian: from the plural of *puma*, Sicilian variant of *poma* 'apple' (or 'fruit' in general), presumably applied as topographic name, a metonymic occupational name for a fruit grower or seller, or a nickname for someone thought to resemble an apple in some way.
GIVEN NAMES Italian 13%. *Salvatore* (6), *Sal.*

Liquori (245) Italian: variant of LIGUORI, altered by folk etymology by association with *liquori* 'liquors'.
GIVEN NAMES Italian 11%; French 4%. *Angelo, Camillo, Carmela, Filomena, Fiore, Marco, Nicola, Sandro; Alphonse* (2), *Camille.*

Lira (1318) Spanish: of uncertain derivation; probably a habitational name from one of the places in Galicia called Lira, in A Coruña and Pontevedra provinces.
GIVEN NAMES Spanish 46%. *Jose* (26), *Juan* (25), *Armando* (10), *Francisco* (10), *Jesus* (10), *Manuel* (10), *Carlos* (7), *Mario* (7),
Raul (7), *Salvador* (7), *Sergio* (7), *Arturo* (6).

Lirette (606) French: of uncertain derivation; possibly related to *loir*, 'dormouse', noted in folk belief for its laziness.
FOREBEARS The name is particularly associated with Terrebonne parish in LA, where bearers are apparently descended from a Jean-Pierre Lirette and Marie-Madeleine Durambourg, who came from Nantes, France, through Acadia, in the 1780s.
GIVEN NAMES French 5%. *Andre, Angelle, Armand, Aurele, Caliste, Gaston, Gisele, Octave.*

Liriano (228) Hispanic: unexplained.
GIVEN NAMES Spanish 57%. *Ana* (6), *Carlos* (5), *Juan* (5), *Aura* (3), *Francisco* (3), *Ramon* (3), *Amparo* (2), *Benigno* (2), *Jose* (2), *Juana* (2), *Lourdes* (2), *Luis* (2); *Clementina, Sal.*

Lis (844) **1.** Polish, Czech, and Jewish (eastern Ashkenazic): from Polish and Czech dialect *lis* 'fox', a nickname for a cunning person or, in the case of the Jewish name, an ornamental name. **2.** Czech: nickname for a man with a bald pate, from a variant of Czech *lysý* 'bald'. **3.** Dutch: metronymic from a short form of the personal female names *Alice* or *Elisabeth* (see LIES). **4.** Dutch (**van Lis**): habitational name from Lixhe in Belgium or Lieze in the Netherlands. **5.** French: perhaps a habitational name for someone who lived at a house distinguished by the sign of a lily, Old French *lis*.
GIVEN NAMES Polish 14%. *Stanislaw* (4), *Wladyslaw* (4), *Andrzej* (3), *Casimir* (2), *Ignatius* (2), *Malgorzata* (2), *Slawomir* (2), *Tadeusz* (2), *Tomasz* (2), *Boleslaw, Bronislaw, Darek.*

Lisa (406) **1.** Czech: variant of LIS. **2.** Italian: from a short form of *Elisa* (see DELISA) or *Luisa* (feminine form of LUISI).
GIVEN NAMES Italian 10%. *Cono* (2), *Antonio, Battista, Oresto, Pasquale, Rocco, Vito.*

Lisak (228) **1.** Czech (**Lišák**) and Slovak (**Lisák**): nickname meaning 'male fox', applied to a cunning person or a red-headed person (see LIS). **2.** Polish: patronymic from the nickname LIS.
GIVEN NAMES Russian 4%. *Vyacheslav* (2), *Aleksandr, Yevgeniya.*

Li Santi (186) Italian: from the plural of *santo* 'saint', with the plural definite article *li*, possibly applied as a topographic name for someone who lived by a place of worship, or possibly connected with the personal name SANTO.
GIVEN NAMES Italian 19%. *Emanuele, Giuseppe, Luigi, Mario, Pasquale, Pietro, Rocco, Sal, Salvatore.*

Lisbon (154) Jewish (Sephardic): Anglicized form of 'Lisbon', Portuguese *Lisboa* the capital city of Portugal. The name is first recorded in the Latin form *Olisipo* and is of uncertain, possibly Carthaginian, origin.
GIVEN NAMES French 4%. *Andre, Patrice.*

Lisby (194) **1.** Danish: habitational name from a place named Lisby. **2.** English: unexplained. Possibly a habitational name; it may be a variant of LUSBY or from a lost or unidentified place.

Lischer (103) German: probably a habitational name from any of several places named Lisch in Holstein or Lischau in the former East Prussia.

Liscio (167) Italian: probably from a pet form of the personal name ALOISIO.
GIVEN NAMES Italian 15%. *Rocco* (5), *Antonio, Carmine, Vito.*

Liscomb (117) English: habitational name from either of two places called Liscombe, in Devon and Somerset. The first is named from Old English *lycce* 'enclosure' + *cumb* 'valley', while Liscombe in Somerset is named with Old English *hlōse* 'pigsty' + *cumb*.

Lisenbee (247) Variant of English LAZENBY.

Lisenby (627) Variant of English LAZENBY.

Lish (520) English and Scottish: unexplained. Probably a shortened form of northern Irish and Scottish MCLEISH.

Lishman (147) English (Northumberland, Durham, Cumbria): northern variant of LEACHMAN.

Lisi (675) Italian: patronymic from a reduced form of the personal name ALOISIO.
GIVEN NAMES Italian 18%. *Antonio* (4), *Enrico* (3), *Gaetano* (3), *Giuseppe* (3), *Pierino* (3), *Salvatore* (3), *Angelo* (2), *Elio* (2), *Marco* (2), *Biagio, Camillo, Carlo.*

Lisiecki (214) Polish: habitational name for someone from Lisiec in Konin voivodeship or a place called Liszki, both named with *lis* 'fox' (see LIS).
GIVEN NAMES Polish 10%. *Andrzej, Genowesa, Irena, Piotr, Stanislaw, Urszula, Wieslaw, Wojciech.*

Lisiewski (105) Polish: habitational name for someone from Lisiewice in Skierniewice voivodeship, named with *lis* 'fox' (see LIS).
GIVEN NAME Polish 5%. *Slawomir.*

Lisk (781) **1.** English and Scottish: unexplained. The name has been recorded in Glastonbury, Somerset, since 1705. **2.** Perhaps a variant of Czech **Liška**, Slovak **Líška**, (see LISKA) or German LISKE.

Liska (899) Czech (**Liška**) or Slovak (**Líška**): from *liška* 'fox', a nickname for a cunning person or for a redhead.

Liske (304) Germanized form of Czech **Liška** or Slovak **Líška** (see LISKA) or Polish LISZKA.
GIVEN NAMES German 7%. *Otto* (4), *Erwin, Hans, Kurt, Reinhard.*

Lisker (103) Jewish (eastern Ashkenazic): habitational name from Lisko in Poland or Liski, now in Belarus.
GIVEN NAMES Jewish 7%. *Batya, Meshulam, Tova.*

Liskey (294) Americanized form of LISKE.

Lisko (212) **1.** Polish (also **Łysko**): nickname from a derivative of *łysek* 'bald man' or 'bald-faced animal'. **2.** Polish and Ukrainian: nickname for a cunning person, from *lis* 'fox'. **3.** Ukrainian: nickname from *lysyj* 'bald' + the noun suffix *-ko*.

Lisle (747) English (of Norman origin) and French: variant spelling of LYLE.

Lisman (190) **1.** Jewish (Ashkenazic): variant of **Listman**, an ornamental name, composed of German *List* 'cunning' or *Lust* 'joy', 'pleasure' (with the vowel change from *u* to *i* peculiar to the Yiddish dialect spoken in Poland) + *Mann* 'man'. **2.** Dutch: variant of LIES.

Lison (107) **1.** English (of Norman origin): habitational name from Lison in Calvados, France. **2.** Perhaps also Czech or Slovak, a derivative of *lis* 'fox' (see LIS).

Lisonbee (111) Variant of English LAZENBY.

Lisowe (104) Jewish (eastern Ashkenazic): topographic name from Ukrainian *lisovy* 'of the forest'.

Lisowski (620) Polish and Jewish (from Poland): habitational name for someone from a place called Lisowo, Lisów, Lisowa, Lisowice, or other places named with Polish *lis* 'fox'.
GIVEN NAMES Polish 6%. *Witold* (2), *Andrzej, Boleslaw, Henryk, Janusz, Karol, Lech, Ryszard, Tadeusz, Zbigniew.*

Liss (1625) Jewish (eastern Ashkenazic): variant spelling of LIS.
GIVEN NAMES Jewish 4%. *Avi* (2), *Morty* (2), *Hyman, Meyer, Mort, Sol, Zalman.*

Lissner (155) German: habitational name from places called Lissa in Saxony, Lausitz, and Silesia.
GIVEN NAMES German 4%. *Arno, Helmuth.*

Lissy (105) Americanized form of the Czech nickname **Lysý** 'bald'.

List (1618) **1.** German and Dutch: nickname for someone who was wise and knowledgeable, from Middle High German *list*, Dutch *list* 'wisdom', 'ingenuity'. **2.** Dutch: habitational name from Ter List, the name being derived from the plant *lis* 'iris', 'flag'. **3.** Americanized spelling of Hungarian **Liszt**, a metonymic occupational name for a miller, from *liszt* 'flour'.

Lista (123) **1.** Galician: habitational name from a place called Lista in A Coruña province. **2.** Southern Italian: from a short form of EVANGELISTA.
GIVEN NAMES Spanish 11%; Italian 10%. *Andres, Humberto, Leticia, Marina, Marta, Nestor, Virginio, Visitacion; Aldo* (2), *Carlo.*

Lister (2864) **1.** English: occupational name for a dyer, Middle English *litster*, an agent derivative (originally feminine; compare BAXTER) of *lit(t)e(n)* 'to dye' (Old Norse *lita*). This term was used principally in East Anglia and northern and eastern England (areas of Scandinavian settlement), and to this day the surname is found

principally in these regions, especially in Yorkshire. **2.** Scottish: Anglicized form of Gaelic **Mac an Fhleisdeir** 'son of the arrow maker'.

Liston (1859) **1.** English: habitational name from a place in Essex, so named from the Old English personal name *Lissa* (probably a pet form of *Lēofsige*; see LIVESAY 2) + *tūn* 'enclosure', 'settlement'. **2.** Scottish: habitational name from places in West Lothian and Midlothian, which probably have the same origin as in 1. This surname is also found in Ireland.

Lisy (104) Czech and Slovak: nickname from a variant of *lysý* 'bald' (see LIS 2).

Liszewski (304) Polish: habitational name for someone from any of various places called Lisewo (also Liszewo), named with Polish *lis* 'fox'.
GIVEN NAMES Polish 6%. *Janusz, Ryscard, Witold, Wojciech, Zygmund.*

Liszka (156) Polish: from Old Polish or Polish dialect *liszka* 'fox', a nickname for a cunning person or for a redhead (see LIS 1).
GIVEN NAMES Polish 13%. *Kazimierz* (2), *Beata, Czeslaw, Dorota, Halina, Tadeusz, Zofia.*

Litaker (223) Americanized form of German LEIDECKER.

Litalien (177) French (Lorraine): ethnic name for an Italian, French *italien*, with the definite article *l(e)*. This is not common in France as a surname; during the Middle Ages people from Italy living abroad were more usually referred to as LOMBARD.
GIVEN NAMES French 14%. *Alphonse, Florent, Gaston, Laurien, Marie Jean, Rodrigue, Yvon.*

Litch (123) Variant of Scottish LEITCH.
GIVEN NAMES French 4%. *Gisele, Jacques.*

Litchfield (1739) English: **1.** habitational name from Lichfield in Staffordshire. The first element preserves a British name recorded as *Letocetum* during the Romano-British period. This means 'gray wood', from words which are the ancestors of Welsh *llŵyd* 'gray' and *coed* 'wood'. By the Old English period this had been reduced to *Licced*, and the element *feld* 'pasture', 'open country' was added to describe a patch of cleared land within the ancient wood. **2.** habitational name from Litchfield in Hampshire, recorded in Domesday Book as *Liveselle*. This is probably from an Old English *hlīf* 'shelter' + Old English *scylf* 'shelf', 'ledge'. The subsequent transformation of the place name may be the result of folk etymological association with Old English *hlið*, *hlid* 'slope' + *feld* 'open country'.

Litchford (204) English: habitational name, possibly a variant of LITCHFIELD. The surname is not found in current English records, but of the 52 bearers recorded in the 1881 British Census, 28 were born in Kent, suggesting that a different, unidentified source could be involved.

Lite (115) English: unexplained; perhaps a variant spelling of LIGHT.

Liter (139) Origin unidentified. Perhaps an altered spelling of German LEITER or English LIGHTER.

Literski (113) Polish: derivative of the vocabulary word *litera* 'letter of the alphabet'. The application as a surname is unclear.

Lites (159) Americanized form of German LEITZ.

Litfin (138) German and Jewish (Ashkenazic): regional or ethnic name for someone from Lithuania (see LITWIN).

GIVEN NAMES German 6%. *Helmuth*, *Siegfried*.

Litherland (359) English: habitational name from the district so called near Liverpool, consisting of Uplitherland and Downlitherland. The place name is derived from Old Norse *hlíðar*, genitive of *hlíð* 'slope' + *land* 'land'.

Lithgow (186) Scottish: habitational name from Linlithgow, between Edinburgh and Falkirk, which was probably named with British words related to modern Welsh *llyn* 'lake', 'pool' + *llaith* 'damp' + *cau* 'hollow'. In the 13th and 14th centuries the name appears both with and without the first syllable. Originally, Lithgow was the name of the settlement and Linlithgow that of the lake. Lithgow was associated by folk etymology with Gaelic *liath* 'gray' + *cu* 'dog', and such a figure appears on the medieval borough seal.

Litka (126) German: eastern variant of LITKE.

Litke (576) German: from a pet form of any of various Germanic compound personal names formed with *liut* 'people' as the first element, or an Americanized spelling of **Lüdtke** (see LUEDTKE, LUTKE).

Litle (182) Swedish and English: nickname for a small person (see LITTLE).

Litman (718) **1.** Jewish (eastern Ashkenazic): variant of LITTMAN. **2.** Possibly also English, a variant of LIGHTMAN.

GIVEN NAMES Jewish 5%. *Haviva* (2), *Arie*, *Esfir*, *Hinda*, *Jakob*, *Josif*, *Moshe*, *Sol*.

Litscher (145) German: variant of **Litsch**, of Slavic origin, from Old Slavic *ljutu* 'wild', a nickname for a wild, unruly person.

GIVEN NAMES German 7%. *Kurt* (2), *Markus*.

Litsey (207) Probably an Americanized form of a German name, perhaps LITSCHER.

Litster (94) English: occupational name for a dyer, Middle English *litster* (see LISTER).

Litt (674) **1.** Jewish: shortened form of some Ashkenazic surname such as LITTMAN or LITWIN. **2.** English: variant of LIGHT 'little'. **3.** Dutch and North German: from a short form of a Germanic personal name formed with *liut* 'people', 'tribe' as the first element.

GIVEN NAMES Jewish 5%. *Mandel* (3), *Sol* (2), *Hymen*.

Littau (141) **1.** German and Jewish (Ashkenazic): regional name from *Littau* 'Lithuania' (see LITWAK). **2.** German (of Slavic origin): habitational name from a place so named in Moravia, or related to a Slavic personal name such as *Litomir* or *Litoslaw*, the first element being from Old Slavic *ljutu* 'furious', 'wild'.

GIVEN NAMES German 8%. *Erwin* (2), *Otto* (2), *Inge*.

Litteken (181) Dutch: from a pet form of LITT 3.

Littel (144) English: variant spelling of LITTLE.

GIVEN NAME French 5%. *Michel*.

Littell (865) English: variant spelling of LITTLE.

Litten (592) English: variant spelling of LITTON.

Litteral (472) Origin uncertain. **1.** Perhaps an altered spelling of English LUTTRELL. **2.** Alternatively, it may be an Americanized form of a French name, possibly LA-TOURELLE.

Litterer (116) German: probably from a Slavic place name Littau in Moravia or a variant of LITTIG.

GIVEN NAME German 4%. *Bernhard*.

Littig (126) German (of Slavic origin): most probably a derivative of the personal name *Litomir* or *Litoslaw*, formed with a first element from Old Slavic *ljutu* 'furious', 'wild'.

GIVEN NAME German 4%. *Otto*.

Little (35412) **1.** English: nickname for a small man, or distinguishing epithet for the younger of two bearers of the same personal name, from Middle English *littel*, Old English *lȳtel*, originally a diminutive of *lȳt* (see LIGHT 3). **2.** Irish: translation of Gaelic **Ó Beagáin** 'descendant of *Beagán*' (see BEGIN). **3.** Translation of French PETIT and *Lepetit*; also used as an English form of names such as **Jean-Petit** 'little John'. **4.** Translation of any of various other European name meaning 'little'.

Littlefield (4040) English: habitational name from any of various minor places named Littlefield, for example in Surrey and Berkshire, from Old English *lȳtel* 'little' + *feld* 'open country'.

Littleford (159) English (chiefly West Midlands): topographic name from Old English *lȳtel* 'small' + *ford* 'ford', or a habitational name from a minor place so named.

Littlehale (104) English: topographic name from Old English *lȳtel* 'small' + *halh* 'nook', 'hollow', or a habitational name from a minor place so named.

Littlejohn (3287) **1.** Scottish and English: distinguishing epithet for the smallest of two or more bearers of the common personal name JOHN. Compare MEIKLEJOHN. In some cases the nickname may have been bestowed on a large man, irrespective of his actual personal name, in allusion to the character in the Robin Hood legend, whose nickname was of ironic application. **2.** Translation of French **Jeanpetit**.

Littlepage (495) English: nickname from Middle English *littel* 'small' + Middle English, Old French *page* 'young servant' (see PAGE).

Littler (429) English: distinguishing epithet for the smaller of two men with the same personal name (see LITTLE).

Littles (579) English: patronymic from the nickname LITTLE.

Littleton (3400) English: habitational name from any of various places, mostly in southwestern England, named in Old English as 'small settlement', from *lȳtel* 'small' + *tūn* 'enclosure', 'settlement'.

Littlewood (258) English (chiefly Yorkshire): habitational name from any of several minor places so called, mostly in West Yorkshire, Littlewood in Wooldale being a well-recorded instance. They are named with Old English *lȳtel* 'small' + *wudu* 'wood'.

Littman (756) **1.** Jewish (eastern Ashkenazic): from the Yiddish male personal name *Litman*, a variant of LIPMAN. **2.** Possibly also English, a variant of LIGHTMAN.

GIVEN NAMES Jewish 5%. *Avrohom*, *Mayer*, *Meir*, *Miriam*, *Mordechai*, *Sima*, *Sol*.

Littmann (169) Jewish (Ashkenazic): variant of LITTMAN.

Litton (1740) English: habitational name from any of the places so called, as for example Litton Cheney in Dorset (named from Old English *hlȳde* 'torrent' (from *hlūd* 'loud', 'roaring') + *tūn* 'enclosure', 'settlement'), or Litton in Somerset (from Old English *hlid* 'slope' or 'gate' + *tūn*), Derbyshire and North Yorkshire (both probably from Old English *hlið* 'slope' + *tūn*).

Littrel (109) Variant of English LUTTRELL.

Littrell (1858) Variant of English LUTTRELL.

Litts (269) Scottish: probably a variant of LETTS.

Litty (142) Swiss German: from a pet form of the Germanic personal name *Liuto*, a short form of any of various names beginning with *liut-* 'people' (see LUTHI).

Litvak (348) Jewish (eastern Ashkenazic): variant of LITWAK.

GIVEN NAMES Russian 24%; Jewish 20%. *Vladimir* (7), *Boris* (6), *Mikhail* (5), *Leonid* (4), *Oleg* (4), *Dmitriy* (3), *Efim* (3), *Lev* (3), *Anatoly* (2), *Savely* (2), *Yevgeny* (2), *Aleksandr*; *Irina* (3), *Aron* (2), *Ilya* (2), *Khaim* (2), *Semen* (2), *Yakov* (2), *Zinaida* (2), *Batia*, *Etya*, *Iakov*, *Izrail*, *Khana*.

Litvin (275) Russian and Jewish (eastern Ashkenazic): from eastern Slavic *litvin*, an ethnic name for someone from Lithuania. Compare LITWAK.

GIVEN NAMES Russian 14%; Jewish 10%. *Mikhail* (4), *Boris* (3), *Fanya* (2), *Arkadi*,

Arkady, Asya, Dmitriy, Gitya, Lev, Lyubov, Sergei, Sergey; Isaak (2), *Avrohom, Baruch, Hyman, Isadore, Marat, Naum, Tsilya.*

Litwack (143) Jewish (eastern Ashkenazic): variant of LITWAK.

GIVEN NAMES Jewish 7%. *Hillel, Hyman, Myer.*

Litwak (178) Jewish (eastern Ashkenazic): regional nickname from Yiddish *litvak,* Polish *Litwak* 'Lithuanian' denoting a Jew who spoke the northeastern dialect of Yiddish, i.e. someone from the historical Grand Duchy of Lithuania (a region much larger than present-day Lithuania, for it included Belarus, parts of northeastern Poland, parts of northern Ukraine, and Latvia).

GIVEN NAMES Jewish 6%. *Emanuel, Gershon, Sol.*

Litwiller (374) Variant of German **Lütwiler,** a habitational name from a place called Leutwil.

Litwin (876) **1.** Polish, German, and Jewish (eastern Ashkenazic): from Polish *litwin,* an ethnic name for someone from Lithuania (Polish *Litwa,* Lithuanian *Lietuva,* a word of uncertain etymology, perhaps a derivative of the river name *Leità*). In the 14th century Lithuania was an independent grand duchy which extended from the Baltic to the shores of the Black Sea. It was united with Poland in 1569, and was absorbed into the Russian empire in 1795. The region referred to as *Lite* in Ashkenazic culture encompassed not only Lithuania but also Latvia, Estonia, Belarus, parts of northern Ukraine, and parts of northeastern Poland. **2.** English: from an Old English personal name, *Lēohtwine,* composed of the elements *lēoht* 'light', 'bright' + *wine* 'friend'.

Litynski (34) Polish (**Lityński**) and Ukrainian: habitational name for someone from the region of Litynia or Letynia, now in Ukraine.

Litz (1050) Eastern German: **1.** from a derivative of the Germanic personal name *Liuzo.* **2.** variant of LIETZ.

Litzau (146) German: habitational name from a place so named in Bavaria or from Lützow in Mecklenburg. See also LUTZOW.

Litzenberg (172) Altered spelling of German **Lützenburg,** variant of the habitational name LUXENBERG.

Litzenberger (313) Altered spelling of German **Lützenberger,** a variant of **Lützenburg** (see LITZENBERG).

Litzinger (530) German: habitational name for someone from Lutzingen in southern Germany.

Liu (10804) **1.** Chinese 刘: from the name of the state of Liu, which was granted to a descendant of the model emperor Yao (2357–2257 BC). **2.** Chinese 廖: variant of LIAO. **3.** Chinese 柳: from the name of an area called Liu Xia in the state of Lu (in present-day Shanxi province). During the Spring and Autumn period (722–481 BC), this was granted to a counselor famous for his high moral character. His descendants adopted the name of this area as their surname.

GIVEN NAMES Chinese 43%. *Wei* (50), *Jian* (46), *Hong* (38), *Ming* (38), *Li* (36), *Ping* (30), *Yan* (28), *Ying* (28), *Yi* (26), *Hui* (23), *Feng* (20), *Qing* (20), *Chang* (18), *Min* (18), *Chung* (16).

Liuzza (153) Italian (Sicily): from a pet form of the female personal name *Lia,* a reduced form of *Rosalia,* the name of the patron saint of Palermo.

GIVEN NAMES Italian 10%. *Santino* (2), *Gaspare, Vito.*

Liuzzi (145) Italian: patronymic or plural form of the personal name LIUZZO.

GIVEN NAMES Italian 23%. *Rocco* (4), *Salvatore* (2), *Domenic, Domenico, Donato, Marco, Pasquale, Vincenzo, Vito.*

Liuzzo (146) Italian: **1.** from a derivative of the personal name LIA or possibly LEO. **2.** masculinized form of LIUZZA.

GIVEN NAMES Italian 18%. *Annalisa* (2), *Antonio* (2), *Mario, Nunzio, Salvatore.*

Livas (141) **1.** Catalan and Spanish: possibly from a truncated form of Catalan *olives* or Spanish *olivas* 'olives', presumably applied as a metonymic occupational name for someone who worked cultivating olive trees, or curing and selling olives. **2.** Greek: nickname from the *livas* (classical Greek *lips*), the sirocco, a hot dust-laden wind originating in Libya. Since this wind is hot, the term was probably a nickname denigrating someone's temper.

GIVEN NAMES Spanish 15%; Greek 4%. *Eduardo* (3), *Juan* (2), *Angelina, Bernardo, Concha, Elena, Faustino, Gavino, Javier, Pablo, Renato; Dimitrios, Irakis, Kirikos.*

Livaudais (147) French: regional name for someone from the Swiss canton of Vaud.

GIVEN NAMES French 16%. *Jacques* (2), *Marcel* (2), *Andre, Octave.*

Li Vecchi (120) Italian: variant of **Vecchi** (with the addition of the definite article *li*), plural of **Vecchio,** from *vecchio* 'old man', from Latin *vetulus.*

Livelsberger (107) German: probably a variant of LEIBENSPERGER.

Lively (3931) English: nickname from Middle English *lifly* 'lively', 'nimble'.

Livengood (1686) Americanized form of German **Liebengut** or **Leibengut** (see LEVENGOOD).

Liverett (114) English: variant of LEVERETT.

Livergood (180) **1.** Most probably an Americanized spelling of German **Liebergott** 'dear God', a nickname for someone who used this phrase frequently as an invocation. This is recorded as a family name in the 16th century in Freiburg. **2.** possibly also a variant of LEVENGOOD.

Liverman (494) Americanized spelling of German LIEBERMANN.

Livermore (1256) English: probably a habitational name from Livermere in Suffolk. This is first found in the form *Leuuremer* (*c.*1050), which suggests derivation from Old English *lǣfer* 'rush', 'reed' + *mere* 'lake'. However, later forms consistently show *i* in the first syllable, suggesting Old English *lifer* 'liver', referring either to the shape of the pond or to the coagulation of the water.

Livernois (212) French: ethnic or habitational name, from the adjectival form of an undetermined place name.

GIVEN NAME French 6%. *Rosaire.*

Liverpool (116) English: habitational name from the city of this name.

Livers (442) Variant of Dutch **Lievers,** a patronymic from the old personal name *Liever,* of Germanic origin, composed of the elements *lief* 'dear' + *hari, heri* 'army'.

Livesay (1587) English (chiefly Lancashire): **1.** habitational name from a place in Lancashire, named from Old Norse *hlíf* 'protection', 'shelter' (or an unrecorded Old English cognate) + Old English *ēg* 'island'. **2.** possibly in a few cases from an Old English personal name composed of the *lēof* 'dear', 'beloved' + *sige* 'victory'.

Livesey (310) English: variant spelling of LIVESAY.

Livezey (282) Variant of English LIVESAY.

Livingood (314) Americanized form of German **Liebengut** or **Leibengut** (see LEVENGOOD).

Livings (167) **1.** English: patronymic from a variant of LEWIN 1. **2.** German: variant of LEVINGS.

Livingston (14947) **1.** Scottish: habitational name from a place in Lothian, originally named in Middle English as *Levingston,* from an owner called *Levin* (see LEWIN 1), who appears in charters of David I in the early 12th century. **2.** Irish: name adopted as equivalent of Gaelic **Ó Duinnshléibhe** and **Mac Duinnshléibhe** (see DUNLEAVY). **3.** Americanized form of Jewish LOWENSTEIN.

FOREBEARS This is the name of an influential family of colnial and postcolonial America. The founder was Robert Livingston (1654–1728), who was taken by his father to the Netherlands, where he grew up bilingual. This gave him a particular advantage in the former territory of New Netherland, to which he emigrated in 1673. Among other offices, he held that of commissioner of Indian affairs. He married Alida Schuyler, widow of Nicolaes van Rensselaer, which gave him access to the highest and most influential families of NY. He acquired huge land holdings along the Hudson River, upon which he served as lord of the manor. His grandsons were

Philip (1716–78), who signed the Declaration of Independence, and William (1723–90), first governor of NJ, who was a signer of the Constitution. A great-grandson, Robert R. Livingston (1746–1813), as minister to France, negotiated the purchase of LA in 1803.

Livingstone (1020) Scottish: variant spelling of LIVINGSTON.

Li Volsi (224) Southern Italian: from a shortened form of the omen name *Deu lu volsi*, Old Sicilian form of *Dio lo volle* 'God wanted him' (the son), or 'God willed it' (the event).

GIVEN NAMES Italian 17%. *Salvatore* (5), *Dino* (3), *Angelo, Carmelo, Pietro, Santo*.

Li Voti (165) Italian: possibly, as Caracausi suggests, a topographic name for someone who lived by a twisting road, track, or watercourse, from *volti*, plural of *volta*, in the sense 'curve', 'bend'; *li* is the plural definite article.

GIVEN NAMES Italian 23%. *Gino* (2), *Salvatore* (2), *Carmine, Domenic, Francesco, Gilda, Giovanni, Sebastiano*.

Livsey (279) English (Lancashire): variant of LIVESAY.

GIVEN NAMES French 6%. *Curley, Michel*.

Livshits (218) Jewish (eastern Ashkenazic): variant of LIPSCHUTZ.

GIVEN NAMES Russian 41%; Jewish 30%. *Mikhail* (13), *Leonid* (10), *Boris* (7), *Galina* (5), *Igor* (5), *Aleksandr* (4), *Grigoriy* (3), *Grigory* (2), *Lev* (2), *Oleg* (2), *Vladimir* (2), *Yefim* (2); *Yakov* (4), *Aron* (2), *Etya* (2), *Ilya* (2), *Isaak* (2), *Semen* (2), *Basya, Inna, Irina, Khaim, Khana, Marat*.

Lizak (253) Polish: nickname from *lizać* 'to lick'.

GIVEN NAMES Polish 12%. *Jerzy* (2), *Stanislaw* (2), *Beata, Bronislaw, Janusz, Ludwik, Maciej, Mieczyslaw, Thadeus, Zdzislaw*.

Lizama (227) Basque: variant spelling of LEZAMA.

GIVEN NAMES Spanish 39%. *Jose* (12), *Juan* (4), *Santos* (3), *Blanca* (2), *Felipe* (2), *Julio* (2), *Pedro* (2), *Roberto* (2), *Alfredo, Alvaro, Ana, Arnulfo*.

Lizana (211) Spanish: of uncertain origin; perhaps a variant of Basque LIZAMA.

GIVEN NAMES Spanish 4%. *Juan* (2), *Alejandro, Jaime, Jose, Luis, Pablo*.

Lizardi (161) Basque: topographic name for someone who lived by an ash wood, from Basque *lizarr* (or *le(i)zar*) 'ash tree' + -*di* 'abundancy'.

GIVEN NAMES Spanish 37%. *Jose* (3), *Alejandro* (2), *Jesus* (2), *Luis* (2), *Armando, Benito, Carlos, Cesar, Cruz, Eduardo, Felipe, Gabriela*; *Angelo, Antonio, Carmelo, Lorenzo, Marco*.

Lizardo (173) Spanish and Portuguese (common in Mexico): probably from a reduced and altered form of the personal name *Elisardo*.

GIVEN NAMES Spanish 53%. *Jose* (5), *Manuel* (3), *Rafael* (3), *Roberto* (3), *Jorge* (2),

Maria Elisa (2), *Ramona* (2), *Renato* (2), *Rodolfo* (2), *Agustin, Amantina, Argentina*.

Lizarraga (460) Basque: habitational name from any of three places called Lizarraga, in Navarra and Alava and Guipuzcoa provinces, which are named from Basque *lizar* (or *le(i)zar*) 'ash tree' + the locative suffix -*aga*.

GIVEN NAMES Spanish 52%. *Jose* (10), *Juan* (10), *Ernesto* (4), *Francisco* (4), *Jesus* (4), *Luis* (4), *Manuel* (4), *Mario* (4), *Miguel* (4), *Raul* (4), *Rodolfo* (4), *Alberto* (3).

Lizer (162) Americanized spelling of German LEISER.

Lizotte (1158) French: of uncertain derivation; perhaps a nickname from a regional word for the vine weevil; alternatively, it could be from a pet form of the personal names *Élise* or *Elizabeth*.

FOREBEARS A bearer of the name from Normandy, France, was in Quebec City by 1670.

GIVEN NAMES French 14%. *Lucien* (4), *Normand* (4), *Adrien* (3), *Armand* (3), *Marcel* (3), *Oneil* (3), *Andre* (2), *Fernand* (2), *Gilles* (2), *Hermel* (2), *Michel* (2), *Raoul* (2).

Lizza (163) Italian: feminine variant of LIZZI, the feminine form being explained by the influence of the Italian word *famiglia*.

GIVEN NAMES Italian 16%. *Tiberio* (4), *Elia* (2), *Emilio* (2), *Carlo, Mario*.

Lizzi (162) Italian: **1.** from a short form of a personal name ending in -*lizzi*, for example MICALIZZI. **2.** Alternatively, perhaps, a topographic name from the Salentino dialect word *lizzo*, plural *lizzi* 'holm oak', 'ilex'.

Lizzio (106) Italian: variant of LIZZI 1, treated as a personal name in its own right.

GIVEN NAMES Italian 14%. *Angelo* (3), *Salvatore*.

Llamas (928) **1.** Asturian-Leonese: habitational name from any of the places called Llamas in Asturies, apparently named with *llama* 'mud' (plural *llamas*). Compare LAMAS. **2.** Spanish: possibly a nickname from the plural of Spanish *llama* 'flame'.

GIVEN NAMES Spanish 55%. *Jose* (25), *Juan* (19), *Francisco* (12), *Jesus* (11), *Carlos* (7), *Luis* (7), *Mario* (7), *Miguel* (7), *Salvador* (7), *Alfredo* (6), *Jorge* (6), *Josefina* (6).

Llanas (179) **1.** Asturian-Leonese: habitational name from a place called Llanas (or also Llanes) in Asturies (see LLANES). **2.** Spanish: topographic name for someone who lived on a plain or plateau, Spanish *llana* 'plain', 'flat ground', from Latin *planum* (see PLAIN). **3.** Catalan: variant spelling of LLANES.

GIVEN NAMES Spanish 44%. *Jose* (4), *Ramon* (4), *Armando* (3), *Alberto* (2), *Eluterio* (2), *Enrique* (2), *Juan* (2), *Julio* (2), *Reynaldo* (2), *Alba, Amador, Andres*.

Llanes (520) **1.** Asturian-Leonese: habitational name from Llanes in Asturies. **2.** Catalan: from the plural of *llana* 'wool', probably a metonymic occupational name for a wool merchant.

GIVEN NAMES Spanish 52%. *Carlos* (13), *Jose* (11), *Juan* (9), *Pedro* (8), *Manuel* (6), *Alfredo* (5), *Armando* (5), *Alejandro* (4), *Enrique* (4), *Julio* (4), *Luis* (4), *Mario* (4).

Llano (199) Spanish: habitational name from any of the numerous places named Llano or El Llano, from *llano* 'flat', 'plain' (from Latin *planus*).

GIVEN NAMES Spanish 52%. *Jose* (6), *Manuel* (5), *Cesareo* (3), *Francisco* (3), *Jesus* (3), *Juan* (3), *Luis* (3), *Rosendo* (3), *Adolfo* (2), *Alicia* (2), *Amalia* (2), *Carlos* (2); *Antonio* (2), *Marino, Romeo*.

Llanos (325) Spanish: habitational name from any of the numerous places named Llanos or Los Llanos, from the plural of *llano* 'plain'.

GIVEN NAMES Spanish 49%. *Jose* (7), *Luis* (5), *Carlos* (4), *Juan* (4), *Julio* (4), *Miguel* (4), *Fernando* (3), *Jorge* (3), *Pedro* (3), *Raul* (3), *Alfredo* (2), *Ana* (2); *Antonio* (4), *Cira, Clemente, Dario, Donato, Fausto, Guido, Lia, Luciano, Marco Antonio*.

Llerena (255) Spanish: habitational name from Llerena in Cáceres province.

GIVEN NAMES Spanish 57%. *Jose* (9), *Luis* (8), *Pablo* (5), *Juan* (4), *Gustavo* (3), *Jorge* (3), *Marcos* (3), *Mario* (3), *Pedro* (3), *Roberto* (3), *Ana* (2), *Augusto* (2); *Antonio* (3), *Ciro, Franco, Giraldo, Heriberto, Silvio*.

Llewellyn (2304) Welsh: from the Welsh personal name *Llywelyn* (anciently *Lugobelinos*), probably derived from the element *llyw* 'leader', although the exact formation is unclear. This was the name of two princes of North Wales who held the Normans at bay for many years in the 13th century. Etymologically speaking, the form with a fourth -*l*- is an error, not found as an original Welsh name, but this is now much the most common spelling in the U.S.

Llewelyn (139) Welsh: the original Welsh spelling of LLEWELLYN.

Llorens (247) Catalan: **1.** habitational name from places called Lloréns in the provinces of Tarragona and Lleida. **1.** possibly also a variant spelling of the personal name *Llorenç*, a vernacular form of Latin *Laurentius* (see LAWRENCE).

GIVEN NAMES Spanish 38%. *Jose* (8), *Luis* (8), *Rafael* (5), *Jesus* (3), *Juan* (3), *Manuel* (3), *Alberto* (2), *Beatriz* (2), *Carlos* (2), *Miguel* (2), *Ramon* (2), *Rodrigo* (2).

Llorente (157) Spanish: from the personal name *Llorente*, vernacular form of Latin *Florentius* (see FLORENCE).

GIVEN NAMES Spanish 45%. *Rafael* (5), *Jorge* (3), *Miguel* (3), *Pablo* (3), *Fernando* (2), *Raul* (2), *Ricardo* (2), *Rodolfo* (2), *Adelaida, Adriana, Alberto, Angel*; *Antonio, Renzo*.

Lloyd (21923) Welsh: descriptive nickname from Welsh *llwyd* 'gray'. In Welsh the color term *llwyd* also includes shades of brown, and it is likely that, when used with reference to younger men, *llwyd* denoted brown or mouse-colored hair.

Lo (2959) **1.** Chinese 卢: variant of Lu 2. **2.** Chinese 罗: variant of Luo 1. **3.** Chinese 劳: variant of Lao 2. **4.** Vietnamese (**Lỗ, Lộ**): unexplained. **5.** Variant spelling of German LOH. **6.** Variant spelling of English Low. **7.** Swedish: unexplained.
GIVEN NAMES Chinese 29%; Vietnamese 8%. *Wai* (8), *Chao* (7), *Kam* (7), *Chun* (6), *Ming* (6), *Wei* (6), *Wing* (6), *Kin* (5), *Kwok* (5), *Wan* (5), *Ying* (5), *Chi* (4); *Chung* (7), *Pheng* (5), *Chong* (4), *Pao* (3), *Chang* (2), *Cho* (2), *Pak* (2), *Shoua* (2), *Thai* (2), *Toua* (2), *Yer* (2), *Blia*; *Hieu* (2), *Hung* (2), *Phuc* (2), *Thong* (2), *Tien* (2), *Vinh* (2), *Bao*, *Bien*, *Chanh*, *Chau*, *Coong*, *Dinh Van*.

Loach (110) English: nickname for someone thought to resemble the loach (a species of freshwater fish), Middle English *loche*.

Loader (221) English: variant spelling of LODER.

Loadholt (136) Americanized spelling of German LEUTHOLD.

Loafman (116) Americanized spelling of German **Laufmann** (see LAUFMAN).

Loaiza (257) Basque: topographic name from Basque *loa* 'mud', 'mire', with the suffix *-tza* denoting abundance. This name is now well established in Mexico and Colombia.
GIVEN NAMES Spanish 52%. *Jose* (6), *Luis* (6), *Francisco* (5), *Jesus* (5), *Carlos* (4), *Ivette* (4), *Amparo* (3), *Eduardo* (3), *Fernando* (3), *Juan* (3), *Raul* (3), *Alfonso* (2).

Loan (253) English: variant of LANE.

Loane (101) English, Scottish, and Irish: variant spelling of LOAN.

Loar (704) **1.** English and Scottish: unexplained. The name is recorded in both England and Scotland. It may be a variant of Scottish **Lour**, a habitational name from Lour, formerly a part of the parish of Meathielour. **2.** Possibly also German: unexplained.

Loayza (107) Basque: variant spelling of LOAIZA.
GIVEN NAMES Spanish 44%. *Jose* (3), *Roberto* (3), *Alberto* (2), *Alfonso* (2), *Efrain* (2), *Fabiola* (2), *Francisco* (2), *Humberto* (2), *Jorge* (2), *Miguel* (2), *Carlos*, *Celedonio*; *Domenico*, *Marco*.

Lobato (594) Spanish and Portuguese: nickname from *lobato* 'wolf cub' or from a medieval personal name based on this word. Compare Italian LOVATO.
GIVEN NAMES Spanish 20%. *Manuel* (9), *Jose* (7), *Emilio* (4), *Alfonso* (2), *Carlos* (2), *Francisco* (2), *Juan* (2), *Mario* (2), *Pablo* (2), *Ricardo* (2), *Rosario* (2), *Adelaida*.

Lobaugh (341) Probably an Americanized form of LAUBACH, this pattern of modification being typical among the names of early immigrants from the Rhineland. However, there are also places named Lobach in both northern and southern Germany, which could have given rise to this as a habitational name.

Lobb (771) English: habitational name from a place in Devon, recorded in Domesday Book as *Loba*, apparently a topographical term meaning perhaps 'lump', 'hill', the village being situated at the bottom of a hill. There is also a place of the same name in Oxfordshire (recorded in 1208 as *Lobbe*), but the historical and contemporary distribution of the surname (which is still largely restricted to Devon), makes it unlikely that it ever derived from this place, or from Middle English, Old English *lobbe* 'spider'.

Lobban (166) Scottish: probably a habitational name from some minor place named with Gaelic *làban* 'muddy place'.

Lobdell (1058) English: unexplained.

Lobe (189) **1.** German (**Löbe**): variant of LOEWE. **2.** German: metonymic occupational name for a tanner, from Middle High German *lō* 'tanning bark'. **3.** Slovenian: unexplained.
GIVEN NAMES German 7%. *Alois*, *Erwin*, *Horst*, *Otto*, *Winfried*.

Lobeck (141) North German: altered spelling of **Lohbeck**, a habitational name from either of two places so named, in Lower Saxony and in the Rhineland.
GIVEN NAME French 4%. *Gabrielle*.

Lobel (446) **1.** Jewish (Ashkenazic): of uncertain origin; perhaps a pseudo-Germanized form of the Yiddish personal name *Leybl*, a pet form of *Leyb* (see LEIB). **2.** German (**Löbel**): see LOEBEL. **3.** French: nickname for a deceitful individual or for a flatterer, from a diminutive of Old French *lobe* 'flattery' (of Germanic origin; compare Old High German *lob* 'praise').
GIVEN NAMES Jewish 6%; German 5%. *Chaim* (2), *Emanuel*, *Herschel*, *Nisan*, *Yehoshua*; *Siegfried* (2), *Erwin*, *Franz*, *Hans*, *Manfred*.

Lobell (176) Catalan: variant of **Llobell**, from *llobell* 'wolf cub', also found as a medieval personal name (Latin *Lupellus*).
GIVEN NAME French 5%. *Laurent*.

Lo Bello (357) Southern Italian: nickname from *bello* 'handsome', with the definite article *lo*.
GIVEN NAMES Italian 14%. *Salvatore* (3), *Luciano* (2), *Sal* (2), *Santo* (2), *Antonio*, *Domenic*, *Giuseppe*, *Nino*, *Pasquale*, *Vincenzo*, *Vito*.

Lober (358) German (also **Löber**): **1.** occupational name for a tanner, Middle High German *lōwer*. **2.** habitational name for someone from either of two places named Löbau or Löben in Saxony.

Loberg (513) **1.** Norwegian (**Løberg**): habitational name from any of several

farmsteads named from *løe* 'barn' (Old Norse *hlaða*) + *berg* 'mountain'. **2.** German: habitational name from any of several places named Lohberg in Pomerania, former East Prussia, the Rhineland, and Bavaria, or Lohbergen in Lower Saxony.
GIVEN NAMES Scandinavian 4%. *Erik* (2), *Lars*.

Loberger (118) Altered spelling of German **Lohberger**, a habitational name from a place called Lohberg or Lohbergen (see LOBERG 2).

Lo Bianco (314) Southern Italian: nickname for a man with white hair or pale skin, from *bianco*, with the definite article *lo*.
GIVEN NAMES Italian 18%. *Angelo* (4), *Sal* (4), *Salvatore* (2), *Antonio*, *Carmine*, *Gino*, *Marco*, *Riccardo*, *Salvator*, *Vincenzo*.

Lo Biondo (113) Italian: nickname for a man with fair hair, from *biondo* 'blond', 'flaxen', with the definite article *lo*.
GIVEN NAMES Italian 17%. *Gasper* (2), *Salvatore* (2), *Angelo*, *Carmin*, *Giacomo*.

Lobitz (117) German: habitational name from any of several places called Lobitz or Lobitsch in eastern Germany, of Slavic etymology.
GIVEN NAMES German 8%. *Heinz* (2), *Rainer*.

Lobley (114) English (Yorkshire): habitational name from Lobley Gate in West Yorkshire.

Lobner (119) German (also **Löbner**): habitational name for someone from places called Löben or Löbau in eastern Germany.

Lobo (754) Spanish and Portuguese: nickname from Spanish and Portuguese *lobo* 'wolf' (Latin *lupus*). This name is also found in western India, where it was taken by Portuguese colonists.
GIVEN NAMES Spanish 28%; Portuguese 9%. *Carlos* (11), *Jose* (10), *Luis* (9), *Jorge* (6), *Mario* (4), *Alfredo* (3), *Fernando* (3), *Francisco* (3), *Gonzalo* (3), *Guillermo* (3), *Manuel* (3), *Orlando* (3); *Anabela*, *Paulo*.

Lobos (140) Spanish and Portuguese: from *lobo* 'wolf', plural *lobos*. This is a frequent element in minor place names.
GIVEN NAMES Spanish 46%. *Jose* (6), *Jorge* (3), *Ricardo* (3), *Carlos* (2), *Juan* (2), *Luis* (2), *Alba*, *Alicia*, *Amalia*, *Angel*, *Aura*, *Cesar*.

Lo Bosco (240) Southern Italian: topographic name from *bosco* 'wood' (see BOSCO), with the definite article *lo*.
GIVEN NAMES Italian 25%. *Angelo* (7), *Carmine* (4), *Gennaro* (2), *Sal* (2), *Salvatore* (2), *Antonino*, *Nichola*, *Pasquale*, *Piera*, *Raffaela*, *Rocco*.

Lobsinger (137) Southern German and Swiss German: habitational name from a place named Lobsing in Bavaria.

Lo Bue (476) Italian (**Lo Bue**): nickname for a powerfully built man, from *bue* 'bull', a dialect form of *bòve* (Latin *bos*, genitive *bovis*). In some cases it may have been originally a metonymic occupational name for a herdsman.

GIVEN NAMES Italian 11%. *Sal* (3), *Salvatore* (3), *Ciro, Francesca, Francesco, Gaetano, Giorgio, Pietro.*

Lo Cascio (858) Southern Italian: **1.** from a dialect word, *cascio* 'cheese' (Italian *cacio*), with the definite article *lo*, presumably a metonymic occupational nickname for a maker or seller of cheese. **2.** according to some sources, from a possible Sicilian form of LO CASTRO.
GIVEN NAMES Italian 17%. *Salvatore* (15), *Sal* (6), *Ciro* (3), *Leonardo* (3), *Nino* (3), *Rocco* (3), *Santo* (2), *Vincenzo* (2), *Angelo, Antonino, Attilio.*

Lo Castro (255) Italian (**Lo Castro**): topographic name for someone who lived by a fortification, from *castro* 'fortification' (Latin *castrum* 'fort', 'Roman walled city'), with the definite article *lo*.
GIVEN NAMES Italian 19%; Spanish 5%. *Angelo* (4), *Sal* (3), *Armando, Ciro, Gerlando, Giuseppa, Ignazio, Silvio, Vito; Diego* (3), *Manuel.*

Locatelli (225) Italian: habitational name from Locatello in Bergamo, Lombardy, where the surname is most frequent.
GIVEN NAMES Italian 25%. *Mario* (4), *Battista* (3), *Giovanni* (2), *Aldo, Angelo, Antonio, Carlo, Dino, Luciano, Raffaello, Serafino, Tarcisio.*

Locati (112) Italian: habitational name from either of two place in Lombardy: Locate Varesino in Como province and Locate di Triulzi in Milan province.
GIVEN NAMES Italian 4%. *Angelo, Guido, Remo.*

Loccisano (113) Variant of Italian **Lucisano**, a habitational name for someone from a place called Cesano, specifically Cesano Boscone or Cesano Maderno in Milano province.
GIVEN NAMES Italian 45%. *Rocco* (10), *Guiseppe* (2), *Antonio, Caterina, Domenico, Giulio, Giuseppe, Natale, Salvatore, Silvio, Vincenzo.*

Locey (262) Variant of LOSEE, probably of Dutch origin. This name occurs chiefly in NY.

Loch (861) **1.** German: topographic name from Middle High German *loch* 'hollow', 'valley', 'hole'. **2.** Scottish: topographic name for someone who lived by a loch or lake, or, according to Black, specifically from Portmore Loch in Eddleston.
GIVEN NAMES German 4%. *Benno* (2), *Kurt* (2), *Gottfried, Hartmut, Helmut.*

Locher (700) South German (**Löcher**): habitational name for someone from any of several places in Bavaria and Austria named Lochen or Lohen.
GIVEN NAMES German 6%. *Kurt* (2), *Ernst, Eugen, Horst, Manfred, Maximilian, Uwe.*

Lochhead (154) Scottish: local name for someone who lived at the head of a loch. Compare KINLOCH.

Lochmann (121) German: **1.** topographic name for someone who lived by a hole or a

valley (see LOCH). **2.** in some cases a topographic name as a variant of LOHMANN, mostly in southern Germany.
GIVEN NAMES German 11%; Scandinavian 4%. *Hans* (2), *Bernhard, Gerhard, Lothar, Otto; Erik.*

Lochner (774) German: variant of LOCHER.
GIVEN NAMES German 5%. *Kurt* (2), *Lorenz* (2), *Egon, Erna, Erwin, Helmut, Horst, Irmgard, Uwe.*

Lochridge (319) Scottish: habitational name from Lochridge in Ayrshire, named with Scots *loch* + English *ridge.*

Lochte (112) Dutch: variant of LICHTE.

Lo Cicero (554) Italian: the word *cicero* means 'chickpea' (later 'pea'), and the name may have originated as an occupational name or nickname for someone who grew or sold chickpeas, but it is more likely to have been a more flattering nickname for someone regarded as resembling the Roman statesman Cicero in wisdom and statesmanship. See CICERO.
GIVEN NAMES Italian 22%. *Salvatore* (8), *Angelo* (7), *Sal* (4), *Mario* (2), *Alfio, Armando, Attilio, Carmine, Concetta, Cristina, Gasper, Gino, Giovanna, Guido, Orazio, Rosario, Santa.*

Lock (2358) **1.** English: metonymic occupational name for a locksmith, from Middle English, Old English *loc* 'lock', 'fastening'. **2.** English: topographic name for someone who lived near an enclosure, a place that could be locked, Middle English *loke*, Old English *loca* (a derivative of *loc* as in 1). Middle English *loke* also came to be used to denote a barrier, in particular a barrier on a river which could be opened and closed at will, and, by extension, a bridge. The surname may thus also have been a metonymic occupational name for a lock-keeper. **3.** English, Dutch, and German: nickname for a person with fine hair, or curly hair, from Middle English *loc*, Middle High German *lock(e)* 'lock (of hair)', 'curl'. **4.** Americanized spelling of German LOCH.

Lockaby (250) Scottish: variant spelling of LOCKERBY.

Lockamy (438) Origin unidentified. Possibly a variant of Scottish LOCKERBY. This name is found mainly in NC.

Lockard (2253) **1.** Scottish and English: variant of LOCKHART 1 and 2. **2.** English: from Middle English *Locward* 'keeper of the fold', from Old English, Middle English *loc* 'enclosure', 'fold' + Middle English *ward* 'guardian', 'keeper' (Old English *weard*)

Lockart (164) Scottish and English: variant of LOCKHART.

Locke (10096) **1.** English, Dutch, and German: variant of LOCK. **2.** Dutch (**van Locke**): habitational name from any of various places called Loock, from *look* 'enclosure'.

Locken (255) Probably an Americanized spelling of Norwegian **Løkken** (see LOKKEN).
GIVEN NAME Scandinavian 5%. *Lars.*

Locker (1094) English: **1.** occupational name for a locksmith, from an agent derivative of Middle English, Old English *loc* 'lock', 'fastening' (see LOCK). **2.** topographic name for someone who lived by a lock or enclosure, from a derivative of Middle English *loke* (see LOCK 2). **3.** variant of LUKER.

Lockerby (160) Scottish: habitational name from Lockerbie in Dumfries and Galloway.

Lockerman (170) **1.** Belgian: habitational name from a place called Lokeren in East Flanders. **2.** Altered spelling of North German **Lockemann**, a habitational name for someone from a place named with the element *Lock-*, for example Lockhausen.
FOREBEARS Govert Loockerman was a prominent trader and businessman in New Netherland, who had come over in 1646 as a representative of the Verbrugge family, a private trading company.

Lockert (169) German: variant of LOCKHART 3.

Lockett (3217) Northern English: from a pet form of LUCAS.

Lockey (364) Northern English and Scottish: **1.** pet form of LOCK. **2.** Scottish: from a pet form of LUCAS.

Lockhart (8739) **1.** Scottish: of uncertain origin, probably from a Germanic personal name composed of the elements *loc* 'lock', 'bolt' + *hard* 'hardy', 'brave', 'strong'. **2.** English: occupational name for a herdsman in charge of a sheep or cattlefold, from Old English *loc* 'enclosure', 'fold' + *hierde* 'herd(er)'. **3.** Americanized form of German LUCKHARDT.

Lockie (198) Scottish: from a pet form of LUCAS.

Locklair (193) English: variant of LOCKLEAR.

Locklar (160) English: variant of LOCKLEAR.

Locklear (4005) Probably a variant of English LOCKYER. This name occurs predominantly in NC.

Lockley (421) English (West Midlands): habitational name from some minor place, such as Lockleywood in Hinstock, Shropshire, which is named from Old English *loc(a)* 'enclosure' + *lēah* 'wood', 'glade'.

Locklin (456) Probably an altered spelling of LAUGHLIN.

Lockman (909) **1.** English: variant of LOCK 2. **2.** Dutch: variant of **van Locke** (see LOCKE 2).

Lockmiller (130) Americanized form of German **Lochmüller**, or the variant **Lochmöller**, a distinguishing name for a miller (see MUELLER) whose mill was in a valley or hollow (Middle High German *loch*).

Lockner (274) Altered spelling of German LOCHNER.

Lockrem (154) Possibly an altered spelling of LOUGHRAN.

Lockridge (1062) English: habitational name, probably from Lockeridge in Wiltshire, or Lockridge Farm in Devon, both named from Old English *loc(a)* 'enclosure', 'fold' (see LOCK 2) + *hrycg* 'ridge'.

Locks (187) Northern English: variant of LOCK.

Lockwood (7646) English: habitational name from a place in West Yorkshire, probably named in Old English as 'enclosed wood', from *loc(a)* 'enclosure' (see LOCK) + *wudu* 'wood'. It seems likely that all present-day bearers of the name descend from a single family which originated in this place. There is another place of the same name in Cleveland, first recorded in 1273 as *Locwyt*, from Old English *loc(a)* + Old Norse *viðr* 'wood', 'brake', but it is not clear whether it has given rise to a surname.

Lockyer (254) English (mainly Dorset): occupational name for a locksmith, from an agent derivative of Middle English, Old English *loc* 'lock', 'fastening' (see LOCK, and compare LOCKER).

Lo Coco (480) Southern Italian (Sicily): occupational name for a cook, *cuòco* (from Latin *coquus*), with the definite article *lo*.
GIVEN NAMES Italian 14%. *Angelo* (5), *Sal* (3), *Antonino* (2), *Gasper* (2), *Salvator* (2), *Corrado, Francesca, Francesco, Gaetana, Gaetano, Ignazio, Pasquale*.

Lo Conte (199) Southern Italian: from the title of rank *conte* 'count', with the definite article *lo*, applied as a metonymic occupational name for someone in the service of a count, or possibly a nickname for someone who gave himself airs.
GIVEN NAMES Italian 24%. *Rocco* (2), *Vito* (2), *Angelo, Biagio, Carmine, Francesco, Gino, Manlio, Pasquale, Vincenza*.

Lo Curto (160) Southern Italian (**Lo Curto**): nickname for a short man, from *curto* 'short', southern form of standard Italian *corto* (from Latin *curtus* 'curtailed', 'truncated', 'cut short', 'broken off'), with the definite article *lo*.
GIVEN NAMES Italian 26%. *Angelo* (4), *Salvatore* (4), *Marino* (2), *Alessio, Carmello, Domenico, Gaspare, Rosolino*.

Locust (117) Origin unidentified.

Locy (187) Variant of LOSEE.

Lodahl (110) Danish: from a place so named in Jutland.
GIVEN NAME Scandinavian 4%. *Ove*.

Lodato (407) Italian: from the personal name *Lodato*, from Latin *Laudatus* 'praised'.
GIVEN NAMES Italian 21%. *Vito* (5), *Salvatore* (4), *Mario* (3), *Americo* (2), *Alfonso, Angelo, Antonio, Franco, Gaspare, Gasper, Pietro, Raffaele, Rosario, Sabato*.

Loden (571) **1.** Dutch: from the Middle Dutch personal name *Lodin*, a pet form of *Lodewijk*, Dutch form of LUDWIG. **2.** Swedish (**Lodén**): ornamental name composed of an unidentified first element + the adjectival suffix *-én*, from Latin *-enius*.

Loder (661) **1.** English: either an occupational name for a carter, from an agent derivative of Middle English *lode* 'to load', or a topographic name from a derivative of Middle English *lode* 'path', 'road', 'watercourse'. **2.** German: occupational name for a weaver of woolen cloth (loden), Middle High German *lodære*. **3.** North German: nickname for a good-for-nothing, from Middle Low German *lod(d)er*.

Lodermeier (132) German: unflattering distinguishing nickname for a sloppy farmer, from Middle Low German *loder* 'sloppy person or worker' + *meier* 'tenant farmer'.

Lodes (266) English: topographic name for someone living by a path, road, or watercourse, Middle English *lode* (the usual form from Old English *gelād*; compare LADE), or a habitational name from any of several minor places named with this word, for example Load in Somerset or Lode in Cambridgeshire and Gloucestershire.

Lodge (1721) English: local name for someone who lived in a small cottage or temporary dwelling, Middle English *logge* (Old French *loge*, of Germanic origin). The term was used in particular of a cabin erected by masons working on the site of a particular construction project, such as a church or cathedral, and so it was probably in many cases equivalent to an occupational name for a mason. Reaney suggests that one early form, *atte Logge*, might sometimes have denoted the warden of a masons' lodge.
FOREBEARS Henry Cabot Lodge (1850–1924), the influential U.S. senator from MA, was born in Boston, the only son of John Ellerton Lodge, a prosperous merchant and owner of swift clipper ships engaged in commerce with China, one of several Lodges who emigrated from England in the 18th and 19th centuries.

Lodholz (107) Altered spelling of German **Leutholz**, a variant of LEUTHOLD.
GIVEN NAME German 4%. *Hans* (2).

Lodi (172) **1.** Italian: habitational name from Lodi in the province of Milan. **2.** Hungarian (**Lódi**): habitational name for someone from a place called Lód. **3.** Muslim (Indian subcontinent): probably from *Lodi*, name of a dynasty of the sultans of Delhi, who ruled from 1451–1536, until they were overthrown by the Mughals.
GIVEN NAMES Italian 7%; Muslim 4%. *Anello, Carlo, Edoardo, Eliseo, Oreste, Remo; Shakeel* (2), *Amir, Aslam, Fariha, Imran, Shazia*.

Lodico (220) Italian: from a reduced form of the Germanic personal name *Lodovico* (see LUDWIG).
GIVEN NAMES Italian 13%. *Salvatore* (3), *Gaetano* (2), *Alessandro, Angelo, Antonio, Carmela, Cosmo, Rocco*.

Lo Duca (115) Italian: literally 'the duke' (see DUCA), an occupational name denoting the servant of a duke, or possibly a nickname for someone who gave himself airs like a duke.
GIVEN NAMES Italian 30%. *Salvatore* (3), *Giuseppe* (2), *Vito* (2), *Concetta, Gaspare, Gino, Matteo, Nicolo, Pasquale, Rosolino*.

Lodwick (191) **1.** English: habitational name from Ludwick Hall in Bishops Hatfield, Hertfordshire (see LUDWICK). **2.** Dutch: from an Americanized form of the personal name *Lodewijk*. Compare LUDWIG.

Loe (962) **1.** Norwegian: habitational name from any of several farms named Lo, from Old Norse *Ló*, of uncertain etymology. **2.** Dutch: variant of LOO.

Loeb (1732) **1.** German (**Löb**) and Jewish (Ashkenazic): nickname for a strong man, from Middle High German *lebe, lewe* 'lion', or a habitational name for someone living at a house distinguished by the sign of a lion. **2.** Jewish (western Ashkenazic): variant of LEIB.
GIVEN NAMES German 5%. *Kurt* (5), *Manfred* (3), *Otto* (3), *Erwin, Fritz, Gerda, Hans, Heinz, Herta, Lorenz, Siegfried, Sigfried*.

Loebach (116) German (**Löbach**): habitational name, from a place so named in the Sieg area.

Loebel (119) German (**Löbel**): **1.** from a pet form of LOEB. **2.** (southeastern): from the personal name LEOPOLD.
GIVEN NAME German 8%. *Kurt* (3).

Loeber (296) German (**Löber**): see LOBER.
GIVEN NAMES German 4%. *Erwin, Franz, Hans, Wilhelm*.

Loebig (149) German (**Löbig**): of Slavic origin, from a short form of a personal name formed with Sorbian *luby* 'dear'.

Loebs (148) German and French (Alsace): variant of or patronymic from **Löb** (see LOEB).
GIVEN NAME French 4%. *Jacques*.

Loeffel (176) German (**Löffel**): metonymic occupational name for a spoon maker, from Middle High German *leffel, löffel* 'spoon' (see LOEFFLER).

Loeffelholz (269) German (**Löffelholz**): metonymic occupational name for a maker of wooden spoons, from Middle High German *leffel, löffel* 'spoon' + *holz* 'wood'.
GIVEN NAMES German 5%. *Kurt* (3), *Ralf*.

Loeffler (2363) German (**Löffler**) and Jewish (Ashkenazic): occupational name for a maker or seller of spoons, from an agent derivative of Middle High German *leffel, löffel* 'spoon'. In the Middle Ages spoons were normally carved from wood, or more rarely from bone or horn.

GIVEN NAMES German 5%. *Hans* (5), *Fritz* (4), *Otto* (4), *Erwin* (3), *Kurt* (3), *Heinz* (2), *Markus* (2), *Arno, Bernd, Bodo, Dieter, Franz.*

Loegering (115) Of German origin: unexplained.

Loehr (1153) German (**Löhr**): **1.** occupational name for a tanner, Middle High German, Middle Low German *lōer, lōwer.* **2.** short form of LORENZ or of a Germanic personal name formed with *(h)lūt* 'clear' + *rīh* 'powerful'.

Loehrer (106) German (**Löhrer**): occupational name for a tanner. See LOEHR.

Loehrke (103) German: diminutive of LOEHR 2.

GIVEN NAMES German 6%. *Eldor, Math.*

Loeper (168) Dutch and North German: occupational name for a messenger or one who made excursions into the woods (see LOOPER).

GIVEN NAME German 5%. *Dietrich.*

Loepp (102) Dutch: variant of LOOP.

Loera (1026) Spanish: variant spelling of LUERA. This spelling is found mainly in Mexico.

GIVEN NAMES Spanish 53%. *Jose* (39), *Jesus* (19), *Juan* (19), *Manuel* (9), *Arturo* (8), *Miguel* (8), *Francisco* (7), *Luis* (7), *Salvador* (7), *Pedro* (6), *Rafael* (6), *Roberto* (6); *Antonio* (11), *Eliseo* (2), *Marco* (2), *Constantino, Federico, Geronimo, Leonardo, Lorenzo, Lucio, Marco Antonio, Romolo.*

Loerch (115) Swiss German (**Lörch**): nickname for a left-handed or clumsy person, from Middle High German *lerz* 'left', East Franconian *lorz.*

Loertscher (101) German (**Lörtscher**): nickname for a left-handed or clumsy person (see LOERCH).

Loerzel (113) German (**Lörzel**): from a diminutive of **Lörtsch** (see LOERCH).

Loesch (1017) German (**Lösch**): metonymic occupational name from Middle High German *lösch* 'fine leather'.

GIVEN NAMES German 4%. *Reinhardt* (3), *Christoph* (2), *Alois, Armin, Arno, Erwin, Heinz, Joerg, Konrad, Kurt, Otto.*

Loesche (148) German (**Lösche**): **1.** variant of LOESCH. **2.** occupational name for a fireman, from Middle High German *leschen* 'to extinguish'.

GIVEN NAMES German 5%. *Kurt* (2), *Hans.*

Loescher (332) **1.** German (**Löscher**): occupational name for a fireman, from Middle High German *leschen* 'to extinguish'. **2.** variant of LOESCH. **3.** variant of LESCHER or a derivative of LOESCHE.

GIVEN NAMES German 6%. *Wolfgang* (2), *Eberhard, Friedhelm, Gottfried, Kurt.*

Loesel (129) German (**Lösel**): from a pet form of the personal name *Nikolaus*, German form of NICOLAS.

Loeser (413) German (**Löser**): **1.** habitational name from any of several places called Lösau, Losa, or Losau. **2.** status name for a tenant farmer who had bought off the feudal obligations on his land, from Middle High German *lōsen, lösen* 'to redeem'. **3.** variant of LAZAR.

GIVEN NAMES German 6%; Scandinavian 4%. *Hans* (2), *Guenter, Helmut, Herta, Ilse, Otto, Volker*; *Erik, Hilma.*

Loethen (120) German: unexplained.

Loetscher (110) German (**Lötscher**): habitational name from either of two places named Lötsch in the Rhineland.

GIVEN NAMES German 6%. *Franz, Otto.*

Loew (817) German (**Löw**): variant of LOEWE.

GIVEN NAMES German 4%. *Erwin* (2), *Eckhard, Fritz, Hans, Heinz, Hermann, Manfred, Raimund.*

Loewe (369) **1.** German (**Löwe**): from Middle High German *lēwe, löuwe* 'lion', hence a nickname for a brave or regal person. In some cases the surname may have been a habitational name, from a house distinguished by the sign of a lion. The surname in the sense 'lion' is also found in Dutch, Swedish, and Danish. **2.** Jewish (Ashkenazic; **Löwe**): ornamental name from German *Löwe* 'lion'. Compare LOWE. **3.** Jewish (western Ashkenazic): variant of LEVY.

GIVEN NAMES German 6%. *Hans* (2), *Armin, Gerhard, Helmuth, Klaus, Kurt.*

Loewen (882) Dutch: variant of LOEWE.

Loewenstein (341) German (**Löwenstein**) and Jewish (Ashkenazic): see LOWENSTEIN.

GIVEN NAMES German 9%. *Fritz* (3), *Ingeborg* (2), *Gerda, Kurt.*

Loewenthal (181) German (**Löwenthal**) and Jewish (Ashkenazic): see LOWENTHAL.

GIVEN NAMES German 16%. *Kurt* (3), *Hellmut* (2), *Egon, Ernst, Fritz, Gunter, Lothar.*

Loewer (148) German (**Löwer**) **1.** occupational name for a tanner, a variant of **Löber** (see LOBER 1). **2.** probably a habitational name for someone from any of several places called Löwen in Westphalia, Silesia, and Belgium.

GIVEN NAME German 5%. *Otto.*

Loewy (243) Swiss German (also **Löwy, Löwi**) and Jewish (western Ashkenazic): variant of LOEWE.

GIVEN NAMES German 7%. *Ernst, Gunter, Hans, Manfred, Otto.*

Lo Faro (260) Italian (**Lo Faro**): **1.** topographic name from *faro* 'lighthouse', with the definite article *lo*. **2.** habitational name from Faro Superiore, Messina, named with this word.

GIVEN NAMES Italian 28%. *Rocco* (6), *Mario* (3), *Sal* (2), *Antonio, Carmine, Domenica, Francesca, Francesco, Gaetano, Mariano, Nunziato, Vito.*

Lo Faso (173) Italian: unflattering nickname from *falso* 'false', with the definite article *lo.*

GIVEN NAMES Italian 23%. *Carmine* (5), *Sal* (3), *Salvatore* (2), *Carmelo, Domenic, Gaetano, Gaspare.*

Lofdahl (114) Swedish: variant of LOVDAHL.

GIVEN NAMES German 5%. *Ewald, Kurt.*

Loff (142) **1.** Swedish (**Löff**): ornamental name from *löv* 'leaf'. **2.** North German: from a reduced form of LUDOLPH.

Loffer (129) Origin unidentified.

Loffler (116) German (**Löffler**) and Jewish (Ashkenazic): variant of LOEFFLER.

GIVEN NAMES German 4%; Jewish 4%. *Hans, Otto*; *Chaim, Shmuel.*

Loffredo (506) Italian (**Loffrédo**): from the personal name *Loffrédo*, from a Germanic personal name composed of the elements *liut* 'people', 'tribe' + *frid* 'peace'.

GIVEN NAMES Italian 15%. *Angelo* (3), *Pasco* (2), *Rocco* (2), *Salvatore* (2), *Antonio, Carmel, Constantino, Fedele, Ferdinando, Giovanni, Giuseppe, Immacolata.*

Lofgren (1343) Swedish (**Löfgren**): ornamental name composed of the elements *löv* 'leaf' + *gren* 'branch'.

GIVEN NAMES Scandinavian 5%. *Evald* (2), *Lars* (2), *Per* (2), *Aase, Anders, Bjorn, Gunnel, Hilmer, Lennart, Nels.*

Lofink (129) German: nickname for a cheerful, independent person, like a finch in the woods, from Middle High German *lō* 'brush', 'woods' + *vinke* 'finch'.

GIVEN NAME German 4%. *Kurt.*

Lofland (514) Altered spelling of Norwegian **Løvland** or **Lauvland**, habitational names from any of several farmsteads so named from *lauv* 'leaf' + *land* 'land' (probably referring to a place where deciduous trees grew).

Loflin (845) Possibly a variant spelling of Irish LAUGHLIN. This is a common name in NC.

Lofquist (326) Swedish (**Löfquist**): ornamental name composed of the elements *löv* 'leaf' + *quist*, an old or ornamental spelling of *kvist* 'twig'.

GIVEN NAMES Scandinavian 4%. *Anders, Erik, Erland.*

Lofstrom (222) Swedish (**Löfström**): ornamental name composed of the elements *löv* 'leaf' + *ström* 'river'.

GIVEN NAMES Scandinavian 5%. *Erik, Helmer, Sven.*

Loft (259) **1.** English: from Middle English *lofte* 'upper chamber', 'attic', possibly bestowed on a household servant who worked in an upper chamber, or used in the same sense as LOFTUS. **2.** Danish: habitational name from a place called Loft.

Loften (114) Swedish (**Loftén**): ornamental name composed of an unidentified first element + the suffix *-én*, from Latin *-enius.* Compare LOFTIN.

Lofthouse (214) **1.** English (Yorkshire): habitational name from a place in West Yorkshire called Lofthouse (see LOFTUS).

2. Americanized form of the Norwegian cognate LOFTHUS.

Lofthus (177) **1.** Norwegian: habitational name from any of about 20 places so named for having a farmhouse with an upper story (see LOFTUS). **2.** English: variant of LOFTUS.

GIVEN NAME Scandinavian 5%. *Obert* (2).

Loftin (2527) Swedish: ornamental name composed of an unexplained first element + the suffix *-in*, from Latin *-in(i)us* 'descendant of'. Compare LOFTEN. This is a common name in TX and NC.

Loftis (2426) English: variant of LOFTUS.

Lofton (3453) English: unexplained. In the US this is a southern name, common in TX, MS, and LA.

Loftus (3250) **1.** English (Yorkshire): habitational name from Loftus in Cleveland, Lofthouse in West Yorkshire, or Loftsome in East Yorkshire. All are named from Old Norse *lopt* 'loft', 'upper storey' + *hús* 'house', the last being derived from the dative plural form, *húsum*. Houses built with an upper storey (which was normally used for the storage of produce during the winter) were a considerable rarity among the ordinary people of the Middle Ages. **2.** Irish: English surname adopted by certain bearers of the Gaelic surname Ó **Lochlainn** (see LAUGHLIN) or Ó **Lachtnáin** (see LOUGH).

GIVEN NAMES Irish 4%. *Dermot, Eamon*.

Lofty (122) English: unexplained.

Loga (118) **1.** Norwegian: habitational name from a farm in Agder named Loga, from *lok* 'shallow pond'. **2.** German: perhaps an altered form of **Legau**, a habitational name from Legau in Bavaria.

Lo Galbo (140) Italian: nickname from Latin *galbus* 'yellowish', denoting someone with fair hair or a yellowish complexion.

GIVEN NAMES Italian 24%. *Sal* (3), *Salvatore* (2), *Antonio, Domenico, Santo, Saverio*.

Logan (22269) **1.** Scottish and northern Irish: habitational name from any of the places in Scotland so called, principally that near Auchinleck. They all get their names from Gaelic *lagan*, a diminutive of *lag* 'hollow'. **2.** Irish: reduced Anglicized form of Gaelic Ó **Leocháin** 'descendant of *Leochán*' (earlier spelled *Lothchán*), a personal name of unexplained origin.

FOREBEARS James Logan (1674–1751), an Ulster Scot and a Quaker, born in Lurgan, Co. Armagh, Ireland, became secretary to William Penn and held high office in the state of PA. Among his descendants have been numbered several prominent statesmen. KY pioneer Benjamin Logan moved with his parents from West Pennsborough Township, Cumberland Co., PA, to Augusta Co., VA, in 1740.

Logar (153) Slovenian: from an agent noun derived from *log* '(small) wood', 'grove', hence either an occupational name for a woodman, a topographic name for someone who lived by a grove, or a habitational name for a person from any of several places called Log.

GIVEN NAMES German 5%. *Ignaz, Inge, Kurt*.

Loge (201) **1.** Dutch: nickname from Middle Dutch *logghe* 'heavy'. **2.** German: topographic name from *log* 'marshy ground', or a habitational name from Loga or Logum, derived from the same word. **3.** Possibly Norwegian, a habitational name from any of several farmsteads in southeastern Norway, from the earlier form *Leikvin* (see LOKEN). **4.** French: topographic name for someone living in a small cottage or temporary dwelling, from Old French *loge* 'lodge'. Stonemasons in particular lived in such dwellings while engaged on major construction projects such as churches or cathedrals, and the surname may therefore in some cases may have denoted a mason. **5.** French: habitational name from any of the places in northern France called La Loge or Les Loges, derived from a Germanic word *laubja* '(hut covered with) leaves'.

GIVEN NAME Scandinavian 4%. *Sig*.

Logel (127) German (**Loegel**): probably an occupational name for a cooper, a variant of **Legel** (see LEGLER), with a variant **Kleinlogel**.

Logeman (140) **1.** Dutch: perhaps a topographic name from Middle Dutch *loge*, *looch*, *loech* '(town) square', 'dwelling'. **2.** Altered spelling of German LOGEMANN.

Logemann (146) Dutch and North German: topographic name from Middle Low German *log(e)* 'swamp', 'grove', 'bushes'.

Loges (221) **1.** French: habitational name from any of various places called Les Loges (see LOGE 2). **2.** German (Hannover, Brunswick): from the genitive form **Lodwiges, Lodiges**, of the personal name *Lodwig*, a regional form of LUDWIG.

GIVEN NAMES German 4%. *Armin, Guenther*.

Loggains (102) Variant of Irish LOGGINS.

Loggins (1566) Altered form of Irish LOGAN, with English patronymic *-s*.

Loghry (220) Irish: variant spelling of LOUGHREY.

Logie (202) Scottish: habitational name from any of the various places so called, from Gaelic *lag* 'hollow' + the locative suffix *-ach*.

GIVEN NAMES French 4%. *Andre, Eugenie*.

Lo Giudice (374) Italian (also **Lo Giudice**): occupational name for a judge or for the servant of a judge, from *giudice* 'judge', with the definite article *lo*. In the Middle Ages the judicial role was less specialized than now, and would have included administrative, political, and even military functions.

GIVEN NAMES Italian 28%. *Salvatore* (6), *Sal* (4), *Sebastiano* (4), *Angelo* (2), *Calogero* (2), *Domenic* (2), *Luigi* (2), *Santo* (2), *Vito*

(2), *Alfonso, Antonio, Attilio, Camillo, Guerrino, Mario, Rosario*.

Logo (17) Greek: reduced form of **Logothetis**, status name in Byzantium for a high ecclesiastical dignitary or for the keeper of the emperor's seal, also the person who composed the emperor's speeches and wrote his decrees. The term is derived from Greek *logos* 'word', 'speech' + *thetēs*, an agent noun from *tithēmi* 'to put' This was also in use as a personal name, and there are patronymic forms such as **Logothetides** and **Logothetopoulos**.

Lo Grasso (201) Southern Italian: nickname for a fat man, from *grasso* 'fat', with the definite article *lo*.

GIVEN NAMES Italian 24%. *Salvatore* (4), *Angelo* (3), *Vito* (3), *Domenic, Ottavio, Pasquale, Rocco, Silvio*.

Logsdon (3695) English (Bedfordshire): habitational name from an unidentified place. In Tudor records, the surname is generally spelled *Logsden* or *Loggesden*. It may be a variant of **Loxton**, name of a place in Somerset, or possibly an irregularly altered form of **Roxton**, name of a place in Bedfordshire (see RUXTON).

FOREBEARS A William Logsden is recorded in Somerset Co., MD, tax rolls in the late 17th century.

Logston (353) Variant of English LOGSDON.

Logue (3057) Irish (chiefly northern Ireland): reduced Anglicized form of Gaelic Ó **Maol Mhaodhóg** (also Ó **Maolaodhóg**) 'descendant of the servant (devotee) of St. *Maodhóg*'. Compare MOLLOY.

Lo Guidice (190) Metathesized spelling of Italian LO GIUDICE.

GIVEN NAMES Italian 26%. *Carmine* (2), *Rosario* (2), *Angelo, Gasper, Giuseppe, Mario, Rico, Sabato, Sal, Salvatore, Sante, Vito*.

Logwood (152) Perhaps an altered form of LOCKWOOD.

Loh (666) **1.** North German: topographic name for someone living by a wood or brushland, Middle Low German *lo*, *loge*, *lage*. **2.** Chinese 罗: variant of LUO 1.

GIVEN NAMES Chinese 8%. *Boon* (2), *Leng* (2), *Teck* (2), *Chee, Cheng, Chia Cheng, Ching-Hui, Choi, Chow, Chun, Eng, Heng*.

Lohan (170) **1.** Irish: variant of LOGAN 2. **2.** German: altered form of **Lohans**, a compound of LOH + the personal name HANS.

GIVEN NAMES Irish 6%; German 4%. *Brendan; Gerhard, Hannelore*.

Lohman (1865) Altered spelling of North German **Lohmann**.

Lohmann (888) North German: elaborated form of LOH.

GIVEN NAMES German 6%. *Heinz* (2), *Otto* (2), *Wilhelm* (2), *Christoph, Egon, Gerhardt, Hans, Ingeborg, Kurt, Otmar, Reinhart, Rudiger*.

Lohmeier (221) German: variant of LOH-MEYER.

Lohmeyer (478) German: distinguishing name for a farmer (Middle High German *meier*) who had land in a wooded area (see LOH).

Lohmiller (102) German: distinguishing name for a miller (Middle High German *meier*) whose mill was in a wooded area (see LOH).

Lohn (236) German: **1.** habitational name from a place so named near Jülich in the lower Rhine. **2.** (**Löhn**) probably a topographic name (river name) from the Hannover area, from a word denoting a small, swampy area of woodland (see LOH, LAU 2).
GIVEN NAMES German 6%; Scandinavian 4%. *Alois* (2), *Otto* (2).

Lohner (185) German: **1.** occupational name for a day laborer or journeyman, Middle High German *lōner*. **2.** habitational name for someone from places in the Austrian Tyrol named Lon and Lona, or Lohn in Westphalia, or Lohnau or Lohne. **3.** (**Löhner**): status name for a feudal tenant or vassal, Middle High German *lēhenære*, *lēner*. See also LEHMANN, LEHNER.
GIVEN NAMES German 10%; Scandinavian 5%. *Bernd, Erwin, Hans, Hubertus, Klaus, Konrad.*

Lohnes (473) German: from a reduced form of the personal name *Apollonius*, the name of a 2nd-century martyr. The male and female names were especially popular in the Rhineland and north Germany, the female name in part because of the popularity of St. Apollonia, the patron saint of toothache.

Lohr (2711) German: **1.** from a short form of the personal name LORENZ. **2.** (also **Löhr**): see LOEHR. **3.** habitational name from any of several places called Lohr in Bavaria and the Rhineland.

Lohrenz (154) German: variant of LORENZ.
GIVEN NAME German 4%. *Otto.*

Lohrer (135) German: **1.** (**Löhrer**): occupational name for a tanner (see LOEHR). **2.** (**Lohrer**): habitational name for someone from a place called LOHR 3.
GIVEN NAMES German 6%. *Eldred, Hans, Hermann.*

Lohrey (210) **1.** German: variant of LOREY. **2.** Possibly an altered spelling of Irish LOUGHREY.
GIVEN NAMES German 4%. *Erwin, Rainer.*

Lohrke (108) German: spelling variant of **Löhrke** (see LOEHRKE).
GIVEN NAMES German 10%. *Arno, Horst, Otto.*

Lohrman (230) Respelling of German LOHRMANN.

Lohrmann (161) **1.** German: habitational name for someone from a place named Lohr (see LOHR 3). **2.** South German: from a short form of LORENZ with the suffix *-mann*.

GIVEN NAMES German 16%; Scandinavian 4%. *Kurt* (2), *Manfred* (2), *Albrecht, Dieter, Ulrich, Wolfgang.*

Lohse (889) **1.** North German: habitational name from any of several places called Loose, or from places called Loosen or Lohsa (see LOOS). **2.** German: short form of the personal name *Nikolaus*, the German form of NICHOLAS.
GIVEN NAMES German 6%. *Kurt* (3), *Klaus* (2), *Otto* (2), *Detlef, Egon, Eldor, Hans, Hertha, Ingo, Karl-Heinz, Reinhard.*

Loi (216) **1.** Italian (Sardinia): most probably from a short form of a personal name *Balloe*, or possibly a short form of the personal name *Aloi*, Sicilian form of *Eligio* (see ALOI). **2.** Vietnamese: unexplained.
GIVEN NAMES Vietnamese 57%. *Phat* (4), *Ha* (3), *Muoi* (3), *Phuc* (3), *Thanh* (3), *Vinh* (3), *Cau* (2), *Chan* (2), *Cuong* (2), *Giang* (2), *Hue* (2), *Ly* (2), *Phuoc* (2), *Ping* (2), *Sun* (2), *Choi, Hing, Hong, Hoon, Kam, Kan, Mee, Tong.*

Lo Iacano (127) Variant spelling of Italian LO IACONO.
GIVEN NAME Italian 6%. *Santina.*

Lo Iacono (570) Southern Italian: occupational name for a deacon or for someone in the service of a deacon, from the southern dialect word *iacono, jacono* 'deacon', derived from Late Latin *diaconus*, from Greek *diakonos* 'servant', with the definite article *lo*.
GIVEN NAMES Italian 33%. *Salvatore* (12), *Angelo* (3), *Julio* (3), *Mario* (3), *Sal* (3), *Carmine* (2), *Luigi* (2), *Rocco* (2), *Antonio, Carlo, Carmel, Dino, Enzo, Giacomo, Roberto, Sergio.*

Loibl (164) German (Bavarian): from a pet form of the personal name *Leupold* (see LEOPOLD).

Lois (202) **1.** Portuguese and Galician: from a local variant of the personal names LUIS or *Eloi* (see LOY). **2.** Greek (also **Loes**): from a Greek form of the French personal names LOUIS. The name is found especially in Cyprus, which was under French rule for a time in the Middle Ages. It may also be a shortening of **Loizos**, patronymic **Loizidis**, which have the same origin.
GIVEN NAMES Spanish 11%. *Carlos* (2), *Jose* (2), *Leonidas* (2), *Emilio, Felipe, Fernando, Francisco, Guillermo, Humberto, Juan, Manuel, Maximo.*

Loiseau (170) French: from *oiseau* 'bird', with the definite article *l(e)* (see LOISEL).
FOREBEARS A Loiseau from the Perche region of France, was in Trois Rivières, Quebec, by 1666; another, from Champagne, France, was in Boucherville, Quebec, by 1669.
GIVEN NAMES French 32%. *Pierre* (3), *Germain* (2), *Alain, Andre, Armand, Fernande, Ghislain, Jean-Claude, Jean-Robert, Lucien, Lucienne, Maryse.*

Loisel (152) French: from Old French *oisel* 'bird', with the definite article *l(e)*, proba-

bly a nickname for a small birdlike person, but possibly also a metonymic occupational name for a bird-catcher.
GIVEN NAMES French 8%. *Alcide, Jean Marie, Micheline.*

Loiselle (772) French: from a feminine form of LOISEL.
FOREBEARS A bearer of the name from Normandy, France, was in Montreal by 1648.
GIVEN NAMES French 12%. *Armand* (4), *Andre* (3), *Lucien* (3), *Alcide* (2), *Normand* (2), *Pierre* (2), *Valmore* (2), *Allain, Aurele, Elzear, Emile, Francois.*

Lojek (110) Polish (**Łojek**): from a diminutive of *łój* 'tallow', 'suet', either an occupational name for a seller of tallow or perhaps a nickname for a plump person.
GIVEN NAMES Polish 16%. *Thadeus* (2), *Zofia* (2), *Dariusz, Janina, Walenty.*

Lojewski (127) Polish (**Łojewski**): habitational name for someone from places called Łoje or Łojewo, named with *łój* 'tallow', 'suet'.
GIVEN NAMES Polish 7%. *Andrzej, Henryk, Jozef.*

Lojko (100) Polish: from a derivative of *łój* 'tallow', 'suet' (see LOJEK).
GIVEN NAMES Polish 8%. *Bronislaw, Kazimierz.*

Lok (319) **1.** Chinese 骆: variant of LUO 2. **2.** Chinese 雷: variant of LEI 1. **3.** Dutch: variant of LOCK 3.
GIVEN NAMES Chinese 31%. *Ping* (3), *Tat* (2), *Wing* (2), *Ying Lin* (2), *Chi Ming, Ching Wah, Chun, Chung Man, Han, Kam, Kam Tim, Kin.*

Loke (143) Indian (Maharashtra); pronounced as two syllables: Hindu (Maratha) name, probably from Sanskrit *loka* 'world'.
GIVEN NAMES Indian 6%. *Aravind* (2), *Mohan.*

Loken (671) Norwegian (**Løken**): habitational name from any of numerous (about 40) farmsteads in southeastern Norway, so named from *leik* 'game', 'play' + *vin* 'meadow'. This name also occurs in Sweden.

Loker (310) **1.** English: variant of LUKER. **2.** Belgian (**van Loker**): habitational name from Loker in West Flanders.

Lokey (625) Probably a variant of Scottish LOGIE. This is a southern U.S. name, found chiefly in TX, GA, and TN.

Lokken (581) Norwegian (**Løkken**): habitational name from any of numerous farmsteads called Løkken, from Old Norse *lykkja* 'enclosure'.
GIVEN NAMES Scandinavian 5%. *Lars* (2), *Karsten, Sig, Thorvald.*

Loll (215) English and Dutch: from a dialect form of the personal name LAWRENCE.
GIVEN NAMES German 4%. *Erwin, Hannelore, Mathias, Matthias.*

Lollar (952) Probably English, a variant of LOLLER.

Loller (119) English: **1.** nickname from Middle English *loller* 'indolent fellow', a derivative of *lolle* 'to droop, dangle, or loll'. **2.** nickname from Middle English *lollere* 'mumbler', bestowed on a pious person or on a Lollard (a follower of the 14th-century religious reformer John Wyclif).

Lolley (434) English: unexplained. In some cases, probably an altered form of Irish **Lally** (see MULLALLY). This name occurs chiefly in AL.

Lolli (196) Southern Italian: patronymic or plural form of **Lollo**, an offensive nickname from Sicilian *lollu* 'silly', 'stupid', from classical Greek *lōlos* 'mad'.
GIVEN NAMES Italian 24%. *Dino* (3), *Adelmo* (2), *Alessandro*, *Angelo*, *Emidio*, *Lino*, *Mario*, *Oswaldo*, *Piero*, *Silvio*.

Lollis (818) Reduced form of Italian **De Lollis**, a patronymic from the nickname *Lollo* (see LOLLI), in the broader sense 'of the Lolli family'. This is also found as a Greek family name, most probably of Italian origin.

Loman (645) Americanized spelling of the German name LOHMANN.

Lo Manto (123) Southern Italian: apparently a metonymic occupational name for a maker of cloaks, or possibly a nickname for a habitual wearer of a distinctive cloak, from *manto* 'cloak', with the definite article *lo*.
GIVEN NAMES Italian 20%. *Aldo* (2), *Giulio* (2), *Angelo*, *Concetta*, *Eduardo*, *Fernando*, *Sal*, *Salvatore*.

Lomas (914) **1.** Spanish: habitational name from any of several places called Lomas or Las Lomas, named with the form of *loma* 'hill', or topographic name for someone who lived by a hill. **2.** English: variant of LOOMIS.
GIVEN NAMES Spanish 17%. *Manuel* (7), *Raul* (5), *Angel* (4), *Miguel* (4), *Guadalupe* (3), *Jorge* (3), *Pedro* (3), *Ana* (2), *Armando* (2), *Baldo* (2), *Esteban* (2), *Jesus* (2).

Lomasney (159) Irish (Tipperary): reduced Anglicized form of Gaelic **Ó Lomasna**, a byname from *lom* 'bare' + *asna* 'rib'.

Lomax (2706) English: variant of LOOMIS.

Lomba (152) Portuguese and Galician: habitational name from any of several places called Lomba, from *lomba* 'mountain ridge' (compare LOMAS), or topographic name for someone living by a mountain ridge.
GIVEN NAMES Spanish 21%. *Jose* (4), *Manuel* (3), *Ana* (2), *Carlos* (2), *Andres*, *Beatriz*, *Eugenio*, *Fernando*, *Jorge*, *Juan*, *Marcelino*, *Nydia*.

Lombard (2364) French and English (also common in Ireland): ethnic name for someone from Lombardy in Italy. The region is named for the Germanic tribe which overran the area in the 6th century AD. Their name is attested only in the Latinized form *Langobardi*, but is clearly a Germanic name meaning 'long beards'. Early immigrants from Lombardy to London were often involved in banking and moneylending, and the name came to be used from the 14th century onward as a generic term for a financier.
FOREBEARS In Canada, the name is found in Quebec City, coming from Savoy, France, by 1722.

Lombardi (5389) Italian: patronymic or plural form of LOMBARDO.
GIVEN NAMES Italian 14%. *Angelo* (22), *Salvatore* (16), *Antonio* (14), *Rocco* (13), *Carmine* (11), *Domenic* (11), *Guido* (9), *Aldo* (8), *Sal* (8), *Pasquale* (7), *Luigi* (6), *Dino* (5).

Lombardino (106) Italian: from a diminutive of LOMBARDO.
GIVEN NAMES Italian 12%. *Enrico* (2), *Salvatore*.

Lombardo (5483) Italian, Spanish, and Portuguese: ethnic name for someone from Lombardy (see LOMBARD) specifically, or more generally for someone from northern Italy, as opposed to the south (i.e. the area once under Byzantine rule). In the form **Lombardos** it is also found as a Greek family name.
GIVEN NAMES Italian 17%. *Salvatore* (50), *Angelo* (30), *Sal* (21), *Vito* (19), *Rocco* (15), *Santo* (11), *Gaspare* (10), *Carmine* (8), *Antonio* (6), *Domenic* (6), *Aldo* (5), *Carmela* (5).

Lombardozzi (157) Italian: from a derivative of LOMBARDO.
GIVEN NAMES Italian 26%. *Cosmo* (4), *Angelo* (3), *Antonio* (2), *Carmela*, *Carmine*, *Dino*, *Enzo*, *Gaetano*, *Nunzio*.

Lombardy (108) Ethnic name for someone from Lombardy (see LOMBARDO); this form may be of English origin, or it may be a Latinized form of LOMBARD (originating in France), or an Americanized form of Italian LOMBARDI.
GIVEN NAME French 7%. *Damien*.

Lomeli (900) Mexican, probably via Catalan **Lomelí** from the Italian family name **Lomellino**, habitational name from Lomello, a town in Lombardy.
GIVEN NAMES Spanish 54%. *Jose* (40), *Manuel* (18), *Jesus* (14), *Juan* (13), *Francisco* (12), *Guadalupe* (10), *Luis* (9), *Ramon* (8), *Roberto* (8), *Javier* (7), *Salvador* (7), *Jose Luis* (6); *Antonio* (11), *Eliseo* (2), *Filiberto* (2), *Aldo*, *Angelo*, *Bartolo*, *Ceasar*, *Cecilio*, *Clemente*, *Heriberto*, *Leonardo*, *Lorenzo*.

Lomen (120) Norwegian: unexplained.
GIVEN NAME Scandinavian 6%. *Erik*.

Lommel (137) Dutch: habitational name from a place called Lommel in Limburg.

Lommen (177) Dutch: **1.** from a pet form of any of the Germanic personal names composed of the elements *liut* 'people' + a second element beginning with *m-*, such as *mund* 'protection'. **2.** habitational name from Lummen in the Belgian province of Limburg, or perhaps from Lummen in Brabant.

Lo Monaco (476) Southern Italian (**Lo Mònaco**): nickname meaning 'the monk', from *monaco* 'monk' (see MONACO).
GIVEN NAMES Italian 21%. *Salvatore* (9), *Vito* (6), *Sal* (4), *Agostino* (3), *Angelo* (3), *Carmine* (2), *Dino* (2), *Enrico*, *Filippo*, *Gasper*, *Salvator*, *Serafino*.

Lona (126) **1.** Spanish and Catalan: of uncertain origin, possibly a nickname or metonymic occupational name from *lona* 'canvas', a derivative of *Olonne*, name of a town on the Atlantic coast of France that was noted in the 17th century for its production of canvas. **2.** Italian: unexplained.
GIVEN NAMES Spanish 42%. *Jose* (4), *Salvador* (3), *Francisco* (2), *Guadalupe* (2), *Javier* (2), *Manuel* (2), *Saturnino* (2), *Alejandro*, *Alfredo*, *Arcelia*, *Enrique*, *Gaspar*.

Lonardo (226) Italian: variant of LEONARDO, characteristic of central–southern Italy.
GIVEN NAMES Italian 26%. *Angelo* (4), *Vito* (3), *Antonio* (2), *Domenic* (2), *Riccardo* (2), *Attilio*, *Carlo*, *Francesco*, *Fulvio*, *Guido*, *Lorenzo*, *Luigi*.

Lonas (210) Americanized form of German LOHNES.

Loncar (204) **1.** Slovenian, Croatian, and Serbian (all **Lončar**): occupational name from *lončar* 'potter', derived from Slovenian *lonec*, Croatian and Serbian *lonac* 'pot', + the agent noun suffix *-ar*. **2.** possibly also an Americanized form of German **Langhaar** (see LONGCOR).
GIVEN NAMES South Slavic 7%. *Ljubica* (2), *Branko*, *Pasko*.

Lonczak (102) Polish: unexplained.

Londeree (104) Americanized form of French LANDRY.

Londergan (105) Irish: Anglicized form of Gaelic **Ó Longargáin** (see LONERGAN).

Londo (256) Dutch: habitational name from a place called *Longdoz* near Liège, Belgium, named with Latin *longum dorsum* 'long back', i.e. a long, low ridge.

London (5078) English and Jewish (Ashkenazic): habitational name for someone who came from London or a nickname for someone who had made a trip to London or had some other connection with the city. In some cases, however, the Jewish name was purely ornamental. The place name, recorded by the Roman historian Tacitus in the Latinized form *Londinium*, is obscure in origin and meaning, but may be derived from pre-Celtic (Old European) roots with a meaning something like 'place at the navigable or unfordable river'.

Londono (408) Spanish (**Londoño**): habitational name from Londoño in A Coruña province, in Galicia.
GIVEN NAMES Spanish 57%. *Carlos* (12), *Luis* (11), *Jaime* (9), *Jorge* (9), *Juan* (8), *Jose* (6), *Francisco* (5), *Gustavo* (5), *Amparo* (4), *Diego* (4), *Fernando* (4), *Fabio* (3).

Lone (280) **1.** Norwegian: habitational name from any of several farmsteads in southwestern Norway, named with Old Norse *lón* 'calm, deep pool (in a river)'. **2.** English: variant of LANE. **3.** Muslim: unexplained.

GIVEN NAMES Muslim 6%; German 5%; Scandinavian 4%. *Munir* (2), *Naheed* (2), *Nasser* (2), *Aamer*, *Jamil*, *Kashif*, *Muhammad*, *Nasir*, *Riaz*, *Salim*, *Samie*, *Wasim*; *Wolf* (5); *Arlys*, *Juel*, *Tor*.

Loner (154) **1.** English: unexplained. It may be of the same origin as 2. **2.** Possibly an Americanized spelling of German LOHNER.

Lonergan (1492) Irish (Munster): reduced Anglicized form of Gaelic **Ó Longargáin**, from *lonn* 'strong' + *garg* 'fierce' + the diminutive suffix *án*.

GIVEN NAMES Irish 5%. *Donal* (2), *Kaitlin*, *Seamus*.

Lonero (150) Southern Italian (also **Lo Nero**): nickname for someone with dark hair or dark skin, from *nero* 'black', with the definite article *lo*. Compare NERO.

GIVEN NAMES Italian 10%. *Salvatore* (2), *Angelo*, *Giovanni*.

Lones (325) English: variant of LANE.

Loney (1230) Irish: variant of LOONEY.

Long (83277) **1.** English and French: nickname for a tall person, from Old English *lang*, *long*, Old French *long* 'long', 'tall' (equivalent to Latin *longus*). **2.** Irish (Ulster (Armagh) and Munster): reduced Anglicized form of Gaelic **Ó Longáin** (see LANGAN). **3.** Chinese 龙: from the name of an official treasurer called Long, who lived during the reign of the model emperor Shun (2257–2205 BC). his descendants adopted this name as their surname. Additionally, a branch of the Liu clan (see LAU 1), descendants of Liu Lei, who supposedly had the ability to handle dragons, was granted the name Yu-Long (meaning roughly 'resistor of dragons') by the Xia emperor Kong Jia (1879–1849 BC). Some descendants later simplified *Yu-Long* to *Long* and adopted it as their surname. **4.** Chinese 隆: there are two sources for this name. One was a place in the state of Lu in Shandong province during the Spring and Autumn period (722–481 BC). The other source is the Xiongnu nationality, a non-Han Chinese people. **5.** Chinese 郎: variant of LANG. **6.** Cambodian: unexplained.

Longacre (907) English: topographic name from Middle English *lang*, *long* 'long' + *aker*, *acre* 'piece of tilled land', or a habitational name from any of various minor places so named, such as Long Acre Farm, Tyne and Wear, or Long Acres Farm in North Yorkshire.

Longaker (178) Americanized form of Norwegian **Langåker** or Danish **Langager**, cognates of English LONGACRE.

Longan (232) Irish: variant of LANGAN.

Longanecker (217) Americanized spelling of German **Langenecker** (see LONGENECKER).

Longbine (100) Americanized form of German LANGBEIN.

Longbotham (107) English: variant of LONGBOTTOM.

Longbottom (171) English (West Yorkshire): topographic name for someone who lived in a long valley, from Middle English *long* + *botme*, *bothem* 'valley bottom'. Given the surname's present-day distribution, Longbottom in Luddenden Foot, West Yorkshire, may be the origin, but there are also two places called Long Bottom in Hampshire, two in Wiltshire, and Longbottom Farm in Somerset and in Wiltshire.

Longbrake (213) Americanized form of German LAMPRECHT.

Longcor (149) Americanized spelling of German **Langhaar**, a nickname for a man with long hair.

FOREBEARS Johann Wilhelm Langhaar came to Wantage, NJ, in 1749 with his family from Puderbach, in Neuwied, Rhineland, Germany.

Longcore (133) See LONGCOR.

Longcrier (100) Origin unidentified.

Longden (171) English: habitational name from any of various places, for example *Longden*, the Middle English form that underlies Longdendale in Cheshire and Derbyshire. This is a compound of Old English *lang*, *long* 'long' + *denu* 'valley'. A place called Longden in Shropshire, however, has the same origin as LANGDON, so there has clearly been some confusion between the two forms.

Longe (328) **1.** French and Dutch: variant of LONG 1. **2.** French (**Longé**): apparently a derivative of Old French *longe* '(leather) thong', used in a transferred sense as a topographic name for someone who lived on a long, narrow stretch of terrain.

Longenberger (133) Altered spelling of German **Langenberger**, a habitational name for someone from any of various places called Langenberg.

Longenecker (1004) Altered spelling of Swiss German **Langenecker**, a habitational name for someone from any of several places called Langeneck, from Old High German *lang* 'long' + *egga* 'corner'.

Longerbeam (187) Americanized spelling of German **Langerbein**, a variant of LANGBEIN.

Longest (435) English: possibly a reduced form of LONGHURST.

Longfellow (809) English: nickname for a tall (Middle English *long* 'long') person who was a good companion (*felagh*, *felaw* 'partner', 'comrade').

FOREBEARS The name made famous in America by poet Henry Wadsworth Longfellow (1807–82) of Portland, ME, was introduced to North America by William Longfellow of Yorkshire, England, who settled in Newbury, MA, about 1676.

Longfield (225) English: topographic name for someone who lived by an extensive (Middle English *long* 'long') piece of open country or pastureland (*feld(e)*). There is a place so named in Kent (from Old English *lang* + *feld*), recorded from the 10th century, and there are several in West Yorkshire, where the surname is common. Two places now called Longville in Shropshire also have this origin.

Longhenry (131) Americanized form of German **Langheinrich**, a nickname meaning 'tall Henry' (see HEINRICH).

GIVEN NAME German 4%. *Otto*.

Longhi (206) Italian: patronymic or plural form of LONGO.

GIVEN NAMES Italian 12%; French 5%. *Carmino* (3), *Angelo* (2), *Geno* (2), *Aldo*, *Dario*, *Nicola*, *Umberto*; *Yves* (2), *Gabrielle*.

Longhofer (170) Altered spelling of German **Langhofer**, a habitational name for someone from any of several places called Langhof.

Longhurst (268) English: habitational name from any of various places, such as Longhirst in Northumberland, named in Old English as 'long wooded hill', from *lang*, *long* 'long' + *hyrst* 'wooded hill'.

Longino (485) Italian: from the personal name *Longino*, from Latin *Longinus*, from *longus* 'long', 'tall'; the name is found mainly in northeastern Italy, which was the center of the cult of San Longino, a soldier who, according to legend, was martyred at Cappadocia. Medieval legend also had it that this was the name of the soldier who pierced Christ's side with a spear at the Crucifixion. In the form **Longinos** it is also found as a Greek family name.

Longley (1282) English (mainly Nottinghamshire and South Yorkshire): variant of LANGLEY.

Longman (440) English: variant of LONG 1.

Longmire (1010) English: habitational name from a minor place in the parish of Windermere, Cumbria, named in Middle English as *long* 'long' + *myre*, *mire* 'marsh', 'bog' (Old Norse *mýrr*).

Longmore (289) English (chiefly in the West Midlands): topographic name for someone who lived by an extensive (Middle English *long*) marsh or fen (Middle English *more*).

Longnecker (616) Altered form of German **Langenecker** (see LONGENECKER).

Longo (4484) Italian: nickname from *lóngo* 'tall', 'lanky', a dialect variant of *lungo* (from Latin *longus*). In some cases the surname may be Spanish or Portuguese, of the same derivation and meaning.

GIVEN NAMES Italian 16%. *Angelo* (26), *Rocco* (25), *Salvatore* (23), *Vito* (15), *Antonio* (10), *Carmine* (6), *Marco* (6), *Sal*

(6), *Biagio* (4), *Gino* (4), *Francesco* (3), *Gaetano* (3).

Longobardi (326) Southern Italian: **1.** patronymic or plural form of the ethnic name *Longobardo* 'Lombard' (see LOMBARD). **2.** habitational name from Longobardi in Cosenza province.

GIVEN NAMES Italian 23%. *Alfonso* (4), *Arturo* (2), *Ciro* (2), *Matteo* (2), *Pasquale* (2), *Adamo*, *Angelo*, *Antonio*, *Carmine*, *Domenic*, *Edmondo*, *Gennaro*, *Gino*, *Giuseppe*.

Longoria (2253) Asturian-Leonese: Castilianized form of **Llongoria**, a habitational name from a town called Llongoria in Asturies.

GIVEN NAMES Spanish 41%. *Jose* (43), *Manuel* (32), *Juan* (26), *Ruben* (16), *Raul* (15), *Luis* (14), *Pedro* (13), *Jesus* (12), *Guadalupe* (11), *Alicia* (9), *Ricardo* (9), *Alfredo* (8).

Longpre (165) French (**Longpré**): topographic name from *long* 'long' + *pré* 'meadow', or a habitational name from a place called Long Pré, of which there are many in Belgium.

GIVEN NAMES French 22%. *Andre*, *Fernand*, *Florent*, *Gilles*, *Henri*, *Herve*, *Jacques*, *Laurent*, *Luc*, *Lucien*, *Marcel*, *Monique*.

Longsdorf (101) Part-translation of German LANGSDORF.

Longshore (703) English: possibly an altered form of **Longshaw**, habitational name from Longshaw in Derbyshire, Greater Manchester, and Staffordshire, named from Middle English *lang*, *long* + *shaw* 'copse', 'small wood' (Old English *sceaga*).

Longstaff (189) English: apparently an occupational name for a tipstaff or beadle who carried a long staff as a badge of office; perhaps also a nickname for a very tall, thin man, or even an obscene nickname for a man with a long sexual organ. The surname is found chiefly in northeastern England.

Longstreet (622) **1.** English: topographic name from Middle English *lang*, *long* 'long' + *strete* 'road'. **2.** Translation of Dutch **Langestraet**, cognate with 1.

FOREBEARS The confederate general James Longstreet (1821–1904), was born in SC, came from an old Dutch family in New Netherland with the name *Langestraet*; he was the nephew of Augustus B. Longstreet, a Methodist clergyman born in Augusta, GA, in 1790.

Longstreth (560) Possibly a variant of LONGSTREET 2. It is found chiefly in OH.

Longsworth (199) English (Lancashire): variant of LONGWORTH.

GIVEN NAMES German 4%. *Elke*, *Franz*, *Kurt*.

Longtin (501) French: nickname from Old French *lontin*, *lointain* 'far', 'distant', or a habitational name from Longtain in the Belgian province of Hainault.

FOREBEARS A Widow Langtin is recorded in Montreal from 1666; her son, Jérôme, was the founder of the Canadian line, which also has the surname *Jerome*, from his given name.

GIVEN NAMES French 7%. *Lucien* (4), *Armand*, *Huguette*, *Jacques*, *Ludger*, *Marcel*, *Normand*, *Pierrette*, *Thaddee*.

Longtine (112) Americanized form of French **Lanctin** or **L'Anquetin**, variant of **L'Anquetil** (see ANCTIL).

Longton (162) English: habitational name from places so called in Lancashire and Staffordshire (see LANGTON).

Longway (137) English: possibly a topographic name from Middle English *long* 'long' + *weye* 'way', 'road', or a habitational name from some minor place so named; Longway Bank in Derbyshire, however, is named from Old English *lang* 'long' + *hōh* 'hill spur'.

Longwell (710) English: **1.** habitational name from any of various minor places, for example in Cumbria, Northumberland, and Gloucestershire, all named from Old English *lang* 'long' + *wella* 'spring', 'stream'. **2.** (of Norman origin): habitational name from Longueville-sur-Scie (formerly Longueville-la-Gifart) in Seine-Inférieure, France.

Longwith (134) Possibly of English origin, a habitational name from Langwith or Nether Langwith in Nottinghamshire, so named Old Scandinavian *langr* 'long' + *vath* 'ford'; or alternatively, a variant of LONGWORTH.

Longworth (836) English: habitational name from any of various places, for example in Oxfordshire (formerly in Berkshire) and Lancashire, so named from Old English *lang*, *long* 'long' + *worð* 'enclosure'.

Longyear (110) English (Hampshire): unexplained.

Lo Nigro (182) Southern Italian: nickname for someone with dark hair or skin, or for someone from Africa, from medieval Italian *négro*, *nigro* 'black', with the definite article *lo*.

GIVEN NAMES Italian 12%. *Antonio* (3), *Rocco* (2), *Vito* (2), *Aldo*, *Carmelo*, *Gilda*.

Lonn (119) Swedish: ornamental name from *lönn* 'maple tree', one of the many Swedish surnames taken in the 19th century from vocabulary words denoting features of the natural landscape.

Lonneman (142) Dutch and North German: unexplained.

Lonning (116) Norwegian: habitational name from any of several farmsteads in southwestern Norway called Lønning or Løyning, from *løyning* 'remote, concealed place'.

GIVEN NAMES Scandinavian 11%. *Thor* (2), *Lennart*, *Nels*.

Lonon (265) English: probably a variant of LONDON. This is a predominantly southern name in the U.S., found mainly in NC, SC, GA, and TX.

Lonsberry (107) English: variant of LANSBERRY.

Lonsdale (344) English: habitational name from places in Lancashire and southern Cumbria, named in Old English as *Lunesdæl*, from the river name *Lune* + *dæl* 'valley'. This ancient British river name is the same as in the first element in LANCASTER, through which city the river runs.

Lonsinger (107) German: habitational name for someone from Lonsingen in Swabia.

Lonski (129) Polish (**Łoński**): habitational name for someone from Łońsko in Piła voivodeship or Łono in Rzeszów voivodeship.

GIVEN NAMES Polish 5%. *Jerzy*, *Wieslaw*.

Lonsway (195) Americanized form of French LANGEVIN.

Lontz (128) **1.** North German or Dutch: vernacular derivative of the personal name *Apollonius* (see LOHNES). **2.** South German: variant of **Lunz** or **Luntz**, a nickname for a careless drifter, from Middle High German *lunzen* 'to doze'.

Lonzo (133) Reduced form of Italian ALONZO.

Loo (980) **1.** North German and Dutch: topographic name for someone living near a wood (Dutch *loo* 'wood', Middle Low German *lo*, *loge*), or a habitational name from places called Lo or Loh, named with this word. **2.** Chinese: variant of LU.

GIVEN NAMES Chinese 5%. *Sing* (4), *Ying* (4), *Wing* (3), *Ming* (2), *Siu* (2), *Boon*, *Bor*, *Chih-Chung*, *Chuan*, *Chun*, *Dong*, *Eng*.

Looby (343) Irish (mostly Tipperary): reduced Anglicized form of Gaelic **Ó Lúbaigh** 'descendant of *Lúbach*', a byname (literally 'looped') originally applied to a cunning person.

GIVEN NAMES Irish 4%. *Dermot*, *Finbar*.

Loock (145) Dutch: **1.** from *look* 'leek' or *(knof)look* 'garlic', hence a metonymic nickname for a grower or seller of leeks or garlic. **2.** (**van Loock**): see LOOK 2.

GIVEN NAMES German 5%. *Katharina*, *Kurt*.

Loofbourrow (111) Probably Dutch: unexplained.

Looft (101) **1.** Dutch: apparently a nickname meaning 'exhausted'. **2.** perhaps an altered spelling of German LUFT.

GIVEN NAMES German 7%. *Guenther*, *Theodor*.

Look (960) **1.** English (Somerset): habitational name from Look in Puncknowle, Dorset, named in Old English with *lūce* 'enclosure'. **2.** English: possibly a variant of LUCK 3. **3.** Northern English and Scottish: from a vernacular pet form of LUCAS. **4.** Dutch (**van Look**): topographic name from *look* 'enclosure' or habitational name from a place named with this word. FOREBEARS Thomas Look (b. *c.* 1622) was in Lynn, MA, by 1646. His son, also called Thomas (b. 1646), moved to Martha's Vineyard about 1670.

Lookabaugh (161) Americanized spelling of German LUCKENBACH.

Lookabill (151) Americanized spelling of German **Luginbühl** (see LUGINBUHL).

Looker (434) English: occupational name for someone who had to watch or look after something (see LUKER).

Lookingbill (154) Americanized spelling of German **Luginbühl** (see LUGINBUHL).

Looman (324) Altered spelling of German LOHMANN or LUHMANN.

Loomans (124) See LOOMAN, of which this is probably a variant.

Loomer (364) English: unexplained.

Loomis (6061) English: habitational name from a lost place near Bury in Lancashire, recorded in the Middle Ages as *Lumhalghs*, and apparently named with the Old English elements *lumm* 'pool' + *halh* 'nook', 'recess'.

Looney (4713) Irish (Munster): reduced Anglicized form of Gaelic **Ó Luanaigh** 'descendant of *Luanach*', a personal name derived from *luan* 'warrior'. Compare LANE 3 and LAMB 3. Woulfe distinguishes the Munster name **Ó Luanaigh** from the Ulster name **Ó Luinigh**, whence LUNNEY. However, many of the Anglicizations are the same.

Loop (861) Dutch: habitational name from de Loop (meaning 'the watercourse'), in the province of Antwerp.

Loope (137) Dutch: variant of LOOP.

Looper (1343) Dutch: literally 'runner', an occupational name for a messenger or for someone who made excursions into the woods. In New Netherland the term *Boschlooper* was used to denote traders who went out (sometimes literally by running) into the woods to intercept Indians bringing furs to Fort Orange (now part of Albany, NY). The practice was forbidden because of the use of coercion to secure a deal, as happened especially when the trader was on horseback.

Loos (1737) **1.** North German: habitational name from any of several places called Loose or Loosey. **2.** North German: from a short form of *Nikolaus*, German form of NICHOLAS. **3.** Dutch: nickname from the adjective *loos* 'cunning', 'artful', 'guileful'. **4.** English: variant spelling of LOOSE.

Loose (943) **1.** English: habitational name from Loose in Kent or Suffolk, both named from Old English *hlōse* 'pigsty'. **2.** Dutch: variant of LOOS 3. **3.** German: variant of LOOS 1.

Looser (128) German: nickname from the Middle High German and Middle Low German adjective *lōs* 'loose', 'free', also 'careless', 'cunning'.

GIVEN NAMES German 5%. *Heinrich, Manfred.*

Loosli (126) Swiss German: from a pet form of the personal name *Nikolaus* (see NICHOLAS).

GIVEN NAME French 4%. *Renette.*

Lootens (165) Dutch: metronymic from the female personal name *Lote*, a short form of any of various personal names with the suffix *-lote*, or a patronymic from a short form of the male personal name *Lanseloot*.

Lopardo (136) Italian: probably a variant of **Leopardo**, from a Germanic personal name composed of elements meaning 'dear' and 'hardy', 'strong'. The form *Lopardus* is recorded as early as the 8th century.

GIVEN NAMES Italian 15%. *Americo, Conio, Federico, Luciano, Marco, Mario, Sal, Silvio, Vito.*

Lopata (379) Polish (**Łopata**): nickname or occupational name from *łopata* 'shovel'.

GIVEN NAMES Polish 4%. *Casimir, Jaroslaw.*

Lopatin (176) **1.** Russian and Jewish (eastern Ashkenazic): occupational name from eastern Slavic *lopata* 'shovel' + the possessive suffix *-in*. **2.** Jewish (eastern Ashkenazic): habitational name for someone from either of two places called Lopatin, one now in Ukraine and one in Belarus.

GIVEN NAMES Russian 9%; Jewish 5%. *Oleg (2), Anatoli, Dmitry, Leonid, Nikolay, Sergei, Vladimir; Asher, Hyman, Isaak, Naum.*

Lopeman (180) Dutch: occupational name for a messenger or for someone who made excursions into the woods, from *lopen* 'to run' + *man* 'man'. Compare LOOPER.

Loper (2682) Dutch and North German (**Löper**): occupational name for a messenger or for someone who made excursions into the woods (see LOOPER).

Lopes (3458) Portuguese: patronymic from the medieval personal name *Lopo* (from Latin *lupus* 'wolf').

GIVEN NAMES Spanish 22%; Portuguese 14%. *Manuel (83), Jose (68), Carlos (28), Fernando (14), Luis (13), Julio (10), Mario (8), Americo (7), Armando (7), Jorge (7), Alvaro (6), Ana (6); Joao (20), Joaquim (9), Ilidio (3), Martinho (3), Paulo (3), Serafim (3), Anabela (2), Duarte (2), Mateus (2), Aderito, Afonso, Agostinho; Antonio (61), Luciano (3), Sal (3), Aureliano (2), Dario (2), Julieta (2), Lucio (2), Marco (2), Mauro (2), Silvio (2), Agnelo, Angelo.*

Lopez (72076) Spanish (**López**): patronymic from the medieval personal name *Lope* (from Latin *lupus* 'wolf'). This is one of the commonest of all Spanish surnames.

GIVEN NAMES Spanish 47%. *Juan (932), Manuel (727), Carlos (599), Luis (558), Jesus (527), Francisco (437), Pedro (393), Miguel (386), Jorge (348), Raul (323), Ramon (321), Mario (307).*

Lo Piano (114) Italian: nickname meaning 'the still one', from PIANO, with the addition of the definite article *lo*.

GIVEN NAMES Italian 16%. *Angelo (2), Salvatore (2), Luigi.*

Lo Piccolo (519) Southern Italian: from *piccolo* 'small', 'little', with the definite article *lo*, applied either as a nickname for a short person or as a term of endearment for a younger man. See also PICCOLO.

GIVEN NAMES Italian 31%. *Salvatore (16), Vito (4), Antonio (3), Angelo (2), Giuseppe (2) (2), Lorenzo (2), Rocco (2), Sal (2), Carlo, Carmelo, Caterina, Ellio, Lucindo, Mario, Marisa.*

Lo Pilato (125) Italian: see PILATO.

Lo Pinto (227) Southern Italian (Sicily): nickname meaning 'the mottled one' (see PINTO).

GIVEN NAMES Italian 23%. *Sal (3), Antonino (2), Aida, Carmine, Rosario, Salvadore, Vito.*

Lopp (425) German (**Löpp**): from a short form of the personal name *Loppo*.

Loppnow (198) German: habitational name from a place called Loppnow in Pomerania, formerly part of Prussia, now Lopianów in Poland.

Lo Presti (1087) Southern Italian: occupational name for someone in the service of priests, from the plural of Old Italian *preste* 'priest'. See also PRETE, PRESTI.

GIVEN NAMES Italian 16%. *Angelo (8), Salvatore (7), Antonino (3), Antonio (3), Carmine (2), Francesco (2), Luigi (2), Rocco (2), Sal (2), Santo (2), Vito (2), Carlo.*

Lo Presto (244) Southern Italian: variant of LO PRESTI.

GIVEN NAMES Italian 6%. *Angelo, Geno, Guido, Santo.*

Lo Prete (136) Southern Italian: variant of LO PRESTI.

GIVEN NAMES Italian 22%. *Rocco (3), Domenic, Elvira, Horacio, Melio, Sal.*

Lo Priore (112) Italian: occupational name for the servant of a prior (see PRIORE).

GIVEN NAMES Italian 18%. *Mario (4), Aldo, Angelo, Emilio, Fiore, Gennaro, Palma.*

Lopshire (115) Americanized form of German LAUBSCHER.

Lor (787) **1.** Laotian: unexplained. **2.** Hmong: variant of LO. **3.** Dutch: from a short form of *Lorent*, Dutch vernacular equivalent of LAWRENCE.

GIVEN NAMES Southeast Asian 74%. *Chao (9), Chue (8), Kao (8), Mee (8), Nou (8), Chai (7), Fong (6), Seng (6), Ying (6), Chou (5), Leng (5), See (5); Neng (18), Pao (14), Vang (9), Soua (8), Yer (8), Chong (7), Vue (7), Houa (6), Toua (6), Yeng (6), Youa (6), Blia (5); Mai (17), Bao (2), Da (2), Doa (2), Long (2), Thong (2), Dang, Hoa, Hue, Huong, Kha, Thao.*

Lora (555) **1.** Spanish: habitational name from Lora de Estepa or Lora del Río, both in Seville province. **2.** Hungarian (**Lóra**): from a pet form of the personal name *Lóránt* (see ROLAND).

GIVEN NAMES Spanish 51%. *Jose (19), Juan (9), Luis (8), Rafael (7), Ana (6), Ramon (6), Mercedes (5), Altagracia (4), Fernando (4), Carlos (3), Cesar (3), Ernesto (3); Antonio (5), Angelo, Carina, Ceasar,*

Dario, Fausto, Gino, Heriberto, Lorenzo, Marco, Marino, Neri.

Lorah (427) Americanized form of French **Loreau(x)**, from a variant of the personal name *Lorel*, a pet form of LAURENT. This is a frequent name in PA.

FOREBEARS Family historians report that the name was brought to North America from the Alsace-Lorraine region of France with the Marquis de Lafayette in 1777 by two brothers who came to fight in the American Revolution. They settled in Allentown PA, but subsequently the two branches of the family quarreled bitterly.

Loran (195) Irish (Ulster): variant of LOUGHRAN.

Lorance (453) English and French: variant of LAWRENCE.

Lorang (268) Altered spelling of French **Lor(r)ain**, **Lorein(g)**, regional names for someone from Lorraine, or possibly of French LAURENT or **Lorain**, a metonymic occupational name for a saddler, derived from Old French *lorain* 'tackle', 'harness'.

Loranger (486) French: topographic name from Old French *oranger* 'orange tree', with the definite article *l(e)*. This is a common name in French Canada.

FOREBEARS The name was first taken to Canada from Perche, France, by a Rivard-Loranger who settled in Cap-de-la-Madeleine.

GIVEN NAMES French 14%. *Fernand* (3), *Gaston* (3), *Lucien* (2), *Pierre* (2), *Adelard, Alberic, Andre, Armand, Emile, Gilles, Marcel, Normand.*

Lorber (519) **1.** German: occupational name for a grocer, a seller of herbs and spices, from Middle High German *lörber* 'laurel', 'bay (tree)'. **2.** Slovenian: nickname from *lorber*, an informal word meaning 'laurel', 'bay', of German origin (see 1 above).

Lorbiecki (107) Polish: unexplained; possibly a derivative of German *Lorbeer* 'laurel'.

Lorch (540) German: habitational name from any of several places called Lorch in the district of Wiesbaden, Hesse.

GIVEN NAMES German 5%. *Otto* (2), *Heinz, Helmut, Klaus, Kurt, Rainer.*

Lord (9684) **1.** English: nickname from the vocabulary word *lord*, presumably for someone who behaved in a lordly manner, or perhaps one who had earned the title in some contest of skill or had played the part of the 'Lord of Misrule' in the Yuletide festivities. It may also have been an occupational name for a servant in the household of the lord of the manor, or possibly a status name for a landlord or the lord of the manor himself. The word itself derives from Old English *hlāford*, earlier *hlāf-weard*, literally 'loaf-keeper', since the lord or chief of a clan was responsible for providing food for his dependants. **2.** Irish: English name adopted as a translation of the main ele-

ment of Gaelic **Ó Tighearnaigh** (see TIERNEY) and **Mac Thighearnáin** (see MCKIERNAN). **3.** French: nickname from Old French *l'ord* 'the dirty one'. **4.** Possibly an altered spelling of LAUR.

FOREBEARS The French name is particularly associated with Acadia in Canada, around 1760.

Lordan (150) Irish: reduced Anglicized form of Gaelic **Ó Lórdáin** 'descendant of *Lórdán*', a personal name of unknown origin. The surname is particularly common in the west of County Cork.

Lorden (301) Probably a variant spelling of LORDAN.

GIVEN NAME French 4%. *Chantelle.*

Lordi (188) Southern Italian: patronymic or plural form of a nickname or possibly a topographic name from Italian *lordo* or Sicilian *lordu* 'dirty', 'muddy', 'turbid (of water)'.

GIVEN NAMES Italian 11%. *Vito* (2), *Angelo, Onofrio, Salvatore.*

Lords (205) Presumably a variant of English or Irish LORD.

Lore (959) **1.** French (**Loré**): habitational name from Loré in Orne. **2.** Dutch (**de Lore**): metonymic occupational name for a rag merchant, from Middle Dutch *lore, luere* 'rag'. **3.** Hungarian (**Lőre**): from a pet form of the personal name *Lőrinc* (see LORINCZ).

GIVEN NAMES Italian 8%. *Vito* (4), *Salvatore* (3), *Angelo* (2), *Biagio* (2), *Francesco* (2), *Rocco* (2), *Corrado, Domenico, Gandolfo, Gasper, Gesualdo.*

Loredo (516) Spanish: habitational name from any of the places in the Basque Country and Santander province called Loredo, or Castilianized form of Asturian-Leonese **Lloredo**, in both cases from Latin *lauretum* 'place of laurels'.

GIVEN NAMES Spanish 55%. *Jose* (25), *Juan* (10), *Guadalupe* (5), *Jesus* (5), *Miguel* (4), *Raul* (4), *Alejandro* (3), *Alfredo* (3), *Jorge* (3), *Juan Carlos* (3), *Pedro* (3), *Rodolfo* (3); *Antonio* (4), *Marco* (3), *Lorenzo* (2), *Bruna, Carmela, Gabino, Mauro, Mirella, Quirino, Simitrio.*

Loree (283) French **Lorée**: topographic name from Old French *orée* (with the article *l(a)*) denoting the outer edge or margin of a wood or field.

Lorek (154) German (of Slavic origin): from a pet form of LORENZ.

Lorello (146) Italian: from the personal name *Lorello*, a variant of *Laurello*, a pet form of LAURO.

GIVEN NAMES Italian 10%. *Natale, Salvatore, Sebastiano.*

Loren (324) **1.** Spanish (**Lorén**): probably a variant of the personal name LLORENTE. **2.** Swedish (**Lorén**): ornamental name composed of an unidentified first element + the adjectival suffix -*én*, from Latin -*enius*.

Lorenc (305) Polish and Czech: from a derivative, influenced by German (see

LORENZ), of the Latin personal name *Laurentius* (see LAWRENCE). This is a parallel development to the vernacular forms, Polish *Wawrzyniec* (see WAWRZYNIAK) and Czech *Vavřín* (see VAVRA).

GIVEN NAMES Polish 10%. *Casimir* (3), *Andrej, Bronislaw, Iwona, Janina, Ryszard, Slawomir.*

Lorence (577) Variant of LAURENCE under the influence of Hungarian, Swedish, Danish, or some other European language.

Lorensen (243) Danish and North German: patronymic from the personal name *Lorens* (see LAWRENCE).

GIVEN NAMES German 4%. *Elke, Kurt, Monika.*

Lorenson (293) Scandinavian: variant of Danish LORENSEN or its Swedish cognate LORENTSON.

Lorentson (105) Swedish: patronymic from the personal name *Lorens* (see LAWRENCE).

GIVEN NAME Scandinavian 4%. *Astrid.*

Lorentz (1013) German and Dutch: variant spelling of LORENZ.

Lorentzen (618) North German, Dutch, Norwegian, and Danish: patronymic from LORENTZ.

GIVEN NAMES Scandinavian 12%; German 4%. *Oivind* (3), *Palle* (2), *Erik, Jorgen, Oyvind, Peer, Per*; *Hans* (4), *Elke, Friedrich, Fritz, Gerhard, Inge, Ingeborg.*

Lorenz (6046) German, Dutch, Spanish (northern Spain), Jewish: from a vernacular form (German *Laurenz*, Dutch *Laurens*, Catalan *Lorenç*) of the Latin personal name *Laurentius* (see LAWRENCE). As a Jewish surname, it is probably an Americanized form of one or more like-sounding Ashkenazic names.

GIVEN NAMES German 4%. *Kurt* (10), *Hans* (9), *Alois* (3), *Erwin* (3), *Juergen* (3), *Dieter* (2), *Fritz* (2), *Gerhard* (2), *Guenter* (2), *Helmut* (2), *Ilse* (2), *Klaus* (2).

Lorenzana (248) Spanish: habitational name from Lorenzana in Lugo province, Galicia, which was named in Latin as *Laurentiana*, after its original proprietor *Laurentius*.

GIVEN NAMES Spanish 36%. *Jose* (6), *Rafael* (4), *Jorge* (3), *Luis* (3), *Carlos* (2), *Manuel* (2), *Mario* (2), *Agustin, Ana, Angel, Bernabe, Candelaria.*

Lorenzen (1644) North German, Dutch, Danish, and Norwegian: patronymic from the personal name LORENZ.

GIVEN NAMES German 6%. *Kurt* (7), *Hans* (2), *Lorenz* (2), *Ralf* (2), *Uwe* (2), *Bernhardt, Egon, Fritz, Gerhard, Gunther, Hartmut, Hedwig.*

Lorenzetti (226) Italian: patronymic from a pet form of the personal name LORENZO.

GIVEN NAMES Italian 22%. *Carlo* (4), *Dino* (3), *Caesar* (2), *Dario* (2), *Marco* (2), *Sal* (2), *Aldo, Domenica, Franco, Giulio, Lorenzo, Orlando, Osvaldo, Primo.*

Lorenzi (325) Italian: from the personal name *Lorenzo*, derived from the Latin personal name *Laurentius* (see LORENZ). This is also found as a Spanish family name, probably of Italian origin.
GIVEN NAMES Italian 11%; Spanish 9%. *Guido* (2), *Aldo, Angelo, Antonio, Dario, Elio, Gino, Giovanni, Reno, Renzo, Rino, Romolo; Alfonsina, Catalino, Jose, Juanita, Julio, Lesbia, Luz, Manuel, Maricruz, Pablo, Pedro, Raul.*

Lorenzini (265) Italian: patronymic from a pet form of the personal name LORENZO.
GIVEN NAMES Italian 11%. *Dino* (4), *Agostino, Aldo, Corrado, Domenico, Ettore, Gino, Guido, Marino, Massimiliano, Piero.*

Lorenzo (2537) Spanish and Italian: from the personal name *Lorenzo*, derived from the Latin personal name *Laurentius* (see LAWRENCE).
GIVEN NAMES Spanish 30%; Italian 6%. *Jose* (43), *Manuel* (20), *Juan* (18), *Luis* (14), *Carlos* (9), *Alfredo* (8), *Ana* (8), *Julio* (8), *Jorge* (7), *Orlando* (7), *Roberto* (7), *Sergio* (7); *Angelo* (16), *Antonio* (14), *Lorenzo* (5), *Luigi* (3), *Ottavio* (2), *Aldo, Amedio, Carmelo, Cecilio, Ciro, Dario, Dino.*

Loreto (147) Spanish, Portuguese, and Italian: from the Marian female personal name, Portuguese *Maria do Loreto*, Italian *Maria di Loreto*, from Loreto in Ancona province, Italy, the center of a cult of the Virgin Mary dating from the 15th century. Loreto is the site of the Santa Casa, the childhood home of the Virgin Mary, which according to legend was miraculously transported by angels from Nazareth to Loreto in the 13th century. The place name is from Latin *lauretum* 'place of laurels'. Compare LOREDO.
GIVEN NAMES Spanish 32%; Italian 10%. *Carlos* (3), *Javier* (2), *Pedro* (2), *Adelino, Agapito, Alejandro, Alfonso, Candelario, Cirilo, Consuelo, Eduardo, Ernesto; Albertina, Amedeo, Ciro, Filippo, Leonardo, Remo, Salvator.*

Loretta (113) Italian: variant of LORETO.

Lorette (144) **1.** French: habitational name from Lorette in the Loire, whose name is cognate with that of Loreto in Italy. **2.** French: from a French form of Italian LORETO, either a metronymic from the female personal name or the surname probably alludes to the Italian place name, possibly denoting someone who had been on a pilgrimage to Loreto. **3.** French and English: from a pet form of LAURA, a feminine form of LAWRENCE.

Loretto (125) Variant spelling of Italian LORETO.
GIVEN NAMES Italian 9%; Spanish 4%. *Angelo, Conio, Salvatore, Stefano; Andres, Ruben.*

Loretz (122) Variant of eastern German LORITZ (see LORENZ).
GIVEN NAME German 4%. *Erwin.*

Lorey (292) **1.** Variant of English LORY. **2.** German: pet form of the Germanic per-

sonal name *Chloderich*, formed with *(h)lūt* 'clear' + *rīh* 'powerful', 'rich' (see LORIG).

Lorge (258) French: from *l'orge* 'the barley', a metonymic occupational name for a grower or seller of barley, or a habitational name for someone living at a house distinguished by a sign depicting barley.
GIVEN NAMES German 4%. *Aloysius, Bernd, Heinz, Mathias.*

Lori (150) **1.** Swiss: variant spelling of LORY. **2.** Perhaps a respelling of Italian LAURI.
GIVEN NAMES Italian 5%. *Quinto* (2), *Angelo, Antonio, Loredana.*

Loria (518) **1.** Italian and Jewish (from Italy): variant of LAURIA. **2.** Jewish (western and eastern Ashkenazic): of uncertain origin; perhaps the same as 1. **3.** Spanish: unexplained.
GIVEN NAMES Italian 10%; Spanish 9%. *Angelo* (3), *Salvatore* (3), *Vita* (2), *Aldo, Antonio, Filippo, Natale, Nunzie, Pietro, Sal; Carlos* (2), *Jose* (2), *Luis* (2), *Alicia, Ana, Arturo, Basilio, Elvira, Estrella, Fermin, Francisco, Javier.*

Lorick (324) German: from an eastern German pet form of LORENZ.

Lorig (113) German: **1.** altered spelling of **Löhrig**, from a pet form of a Germanic personal name (see LOREY). **2.** perhaps a variant of LORICK.

Lorigan (112) Probably a variant of Irish LANIGAN.

Lorimer (464) Scottish: occupational name for a maker and seller of spurs, bits, and other metal attachments to harness and tackle, from Anglo-Norman French *lorenier, loremier* (an agent derivative of Old French *lorain* 'tackle', 'harness').

Lorimor (175) Variant of Scottish LORIMER.

Lorincz (171) Hungarian (**Lőrincz**): from the Hungarian ecclesiastical name *Lőrinc*, from Latin *Laurentius*, which was the name of an early Christian martyr (see LAWRENCE).
GIVEN NAMES Hungarian 8%; German 4%; Jewish 4%. *Akos, Ferenc, Jeno, Laszio, Rezso; Erwin* (2), *Otto; Chaim, Irina.*

Loring (1522) English: ethnic name from Old French *Lohereng* 'man from Lorraine' (see LORRAINE).

Lorino (194) Italian: variant of LAURINO.
GIVEN NAMES Italian 14%. *Gaeton* (2), *Saverio* (2), *Angelo, Gaspare, Pietro, Rocco, Santo.*

Lorio (315) **1.** French: from the bird name *loriot*, 'oriole'. This is a frequent name in LA. **2.** Italian: probably a topographic name from *rio* 'stream', 'brook', with the definite article *lo*.
FOREBEARS As **Loriot** or **Lauriot** this name has been recorded in Canada since 1670, taken there by immigrants from Limoges, France, who settled in Saint-François-de-Sales-de-Neuville, Quebec.
GIVEN NAMES French 5%. *Fernand* (2), *Chantal, Pierre.*

Loris (120) **1.** German (**Löris**): from the personal name LORENZ. **2.** Greek: possibly a nickname or metonymic occupational name for a seller of goat's cheese, from Turkish *lor* 'goat's cheese'.
GIVEN NAMES German 4%; Greek 4%. *Kurt; Anastasios* (2).

Loritz (138) Eastern German: altered form, under Slavic influence, of LORENZ.

Lorman (185) **1.** Dutch: derivative of the personal name LORENZ, or of the Germanic personal name *Loderic*. **2.** Americanized spelling of German LOHRMANN.
GIVEN NAME Jewish 5%. *Yakov* (2).

Lormand (248) Possibly French: habitational name from Le Lormand in the Pyrénées-Atlantique. This name is sometimes confused with NORMAN and **Lenormand**.
GIVEN NAMES French 4%. *Adrien, Eustache.*

Lorrain (106) French and English: variant spelling of LORRAINE.
FOREBEARS The name Lorrain was in Montreal by 1659.
GIVEN NAMES French 20%. *Adrien* (2), *Alban, Andre, Desire, Fernande, Philippe, Pierre.*

Lorraine (350) English and French: regional name from the border region of Lorraine in northeastern France, so called from the Germanic tribal name *Lotharingi* 'people of *Lothar*' (a personal name composed of the elements *hlod* 'famous', 'renowned' + *hari, heri* 'army').
GIVEN NAMES French 5%. *Armand, Emile, Perrine, Pierre.*

Lorson (227) French: nickname from *ourson* 'bear cub', with the definite article *l(e)*.

Lortie (272) French: topographic name or nickname from Old French *orttrie* 'nettle', with the definite article *l(a)*.
FOREBEARS In Canada, this has been found as a secondary surname for LAURENT since 1680, taken there from Bayonne, France.
GIVEN NAMES French 13%. *Armand* (2), *Marcel* (2), *Alcide, Andre, Colombe, Fernand, Gilles, Luc, Normand, Pierre, Reynald.*

Lorton (493) English: habitational name from places so named in Cumbria, probably so named from an Old English river name *Hlóra* nmeaning 'the roaring one' + Old English *tūn* 'settlement'.

Lorts (109) Dutch: from a reduced form of the personal name LORENZ.

Lortz (296) North German (also **Lörtz**) and Dutch: from a reduced form of the personal name LORENZ.

Lo Russo (815) Southern Italian (Apulia): nickname for someone with red hair, from *russo, rosso*, with the definite article *lo*. See RUSSO.
GIVEN NAMES Italian 20%. *Angelo* (8), *Vito* (8), *Rocco* (6), *Antonio* (3), *Domenico* (3), *Dante* (2), *Salvatore* (2), *Canio, Carmela, Carmine, Cosimo, Cosmo.*

Lory (219) **1.** Northern English, Scottish, and Irish: from a pet form of LAWRENCE.

Compare Lowry. **2.** South German and Swiss (also **Löry**): from a pet form of the personal name Lorenz. **3.** French: habitational name from either of two villages called Lory, in Loir-et-Cher and Lot, or from Lorry in Moselle.

FOREBEARS A Lory-Gargot from Poitou, France, was in Cap-de-la-Madeleine, Quebec City, by 1665; in Quebec city by 1666; and Becquet by 1670. A Francois Lory, born in Poitiers, France, died in Lachine, Quebec, in 1702.

GIVEN NAMES German 4%. *Eldred, Manfred.*

Los (327) **1.** Polish (**Łoś**): nickname for a large, ungainly person, from Polish *łoś* 'elk'. **2.** Dutch: nickname from Middle Dutch *losch* 'squinting'; 'cross-eyed'; 'one-eyed'.

GIVEN NAMES Polish 11%. *Jozef* (2), *Stanislaw* (2), *Tadeusz* (2), *Andrej, Bogdan, Czeslaw, Dorota, Edyta, Iwan, Jerzy, Ryszard, Wladyslaw.*

Lo Sacco (105) Italian: see Sacco.

GIVEN NAMES Italian 17%. *Dino* (2), *Antonio, Giuseppe, Mirella, Vito.*

Losada (173) Spanish and Portuguese: topographic name for someone who lived by an area paved with flagstones, Spanish *losada* (from *losar* 'to pave', a derivative of *losa*, a word of pre-Roman origin, meaning a flat stone slab).

GIVEN NAMES Spanish 50%. *Jose* (7), *Manuel* (5), *Fernando* (3), *Jorge* (3), *Juan* (3), *Luis* (3), *Alonso* (2), *Angel* (2), *Claudio* (2), *Enrique* (2), *Joaquin* (2), *Pilar* (2); *Lorenzo.*

Lo Sapio (109) Southern Italian: nickname for a wise man (see Sapio) or for the servant of a wise man.

GIVEN NAMES Italian 25%. *Mario* (3), *Mauro* (2), *Angelo, Filomena, Natale, Sal, Sergio.*

Lo Sasso (205) Southern Italian: ethnic name for a North German, literally 'the Saxon' (see Sasso).

GIVEN NAME Italian 5%. *Rocco* (2).

Lo Scalzo (253) Southern Italian: nickname for someone who habitually went barefoot (see Scalzo).

GIVEN NAMES Italian 15%. *Rocco* (4), *Vito* (2), *Donato, Giuliano, Pasquale.*

Losch (373) **1.** North German: metonymic occupational name for a maker of fine leather, from Middle Low German *losche* 'fine leather'. **2.** South German (**Lösch**): variant of Lesch (see Loesch).

Loschen (105) German: from a pet form of the personal name Ludwig.

Lo Schiavo (314) Italian: ethic name meaning 'the Slav' (see Schiavo).

GIVEN NAMES Italian 18%. *Sal* (3), *Salvatore* (3), *Angelo* (2), *Rafael* (2), *Antonio, Carmine, Domenico, Eliseo, Francesco, Vito.*

Losco (136) Southern Italian: nickname from *losco* 'sinister'.

GIVEN NAMES Italian 11%; French 5%. *Cosmo* (3), *Carlo, Giuseppina, Umberto; Maxime, Yves.*

Lose (288) **1.** North German: from a pet form of the personal name *Lodewig* (see Ludwig). **2.** In southern Germany, from a pet form of Nikolaus. **3.** Perhaps also Dutch, a variant of Losee.

Losee (684) Perhaps an Americanized spelling of **Lossie**, a vernacular derivative of the female personal name *Lucia*. Compare English Luce. This name was well established in the Hudson valley in the 18th century, which strengthens the likelihood that it is of Dutch origin.

Loseke (201) North German: from a pet form of the personal name *Lodewig* (see Ludwig).

Loser (352) German (**Löser**): variant of Loeser or Lazar.

GIVEN NAMES German 4%. *Alois* (2), *Helmut* (2), *Mathias.*

Losey (1217) Probably of Dutch origin: see Losee.

Losh (588) Americanized spelling of German Losch or Polish **Łoś** (see Los).

Losier (144) French: from Old French *osier* 'willow', 'osier'; a topographic name, or a metonymic occupational name for a basketmaker or for an osier grower.

GIVEN NAMES French 14%. *Albenie, Gaetan, Jean Michel, Julien, Michel, Pierre.*

Losinski (217) Polish (**Łosiński**) and Jewish (from Poland): habitational name for someone from any of various places named with Polish *łoś* 'elk' (Belorussian and Russian *los*), for example Łosie, Łosino, Łosiny, Łosiniec; or from Losi, now in Belarus.

Losito (254) Southern Italian: habitational name from Losito in Taranto province or Loseto in Bari.

GIVEN NAMES Italian 16%. *Vito* (6), *Antonio, Gaetano, Giacomo, Rocco, Salvatore, Vincenzo.*

Loso (204) Americanized form of French Lauzon.

Losoya (218) Variant spelling of Spanish Lozoya.

GIVEN NAMES Spanish 47%. *Jose* (7), *Juan* (5), *Eduardo* (3), *Ramon* (3), *Ruben* (3), *Guadalupe* (2), *Jesus* (2), *Juanita* (2), *Manuel* (2), *Ramiro* (2), *Santos* (2), *Agustina.*

Lo Squadro (100) Italian: nickname meaning 'the square one', from *(s)quadro* 'square', with the definite article *lo*.

GIVEN NAMES Italian 17%. *Luigi, Rocco.*

Loss (612) **1.** North German: topographic name from *los* 'marsh', or a habitational name from places named with this word, such as Losse and Lossa. **2.** German: pet form of the personal name Ludwig.

Lossing (214) German: habitational name, probably from Lossing in Bavaria.

Lo Surdo (156) Southern Italian: nickname for a deaf man, from *surdo* 'deaf', a dialect

form of standard Italian *sordo*, with the definite article *lo*.

GIVEN NAMES Italian 15%. *Vito* (2), *Angelo, Antonino, Carmine, Domenic.*

Loth (470) **1.** French: from the Biblical name *Lot*, which was the name of Abraham's nephew. Compare Lott 1. **2.** German: from a short form of the personal name Ludwig. **3.** German: habitational name from Lothe in eastern Westphalia. **4.** Possibly a habitational name from Loth, Orkney, Scotland.

GIVEN NAMES French 4%. *Michel, Renald.*

Lothamer (149) Possibly an altered form of German (Bavarian) **Lotthammer**, a habitational name for someone from Lottheim (named with the dialect word *lott* 'mud').

Lothian (159) Scottish: regional name from the region so named in southeastern central Scotland. The place name is very ancient and is of unknown origin.

Lothridge (131) Northern Irish: variant of Loughridge.

Lothrop (412) English: habitational name from **Lowthorpe** in East Yorkshire, named with the Old Norse personal name *Logi* or *Lági* + *þorp* 'outlying farmstead'

FOREBEARS In 1634 the name was brought to North America by the Rev. John Lathrop (b. 1584 in Etton, Yorkshire, England), a Puritan preacher fleeing religious persecution. He arrived at Plymouth Colony and lived in Scituate, MA until 1639, then moved to Barnstable MA, where his Bible can still be seen.

Lo Tito (362) Italian: see *Tito*.

GIVEN NAMES Italian 12%. *Ciro* (3), *Rocco* (3), *Domenico, Luigi, Nino, Vito.*

Lotspeich (278) German: **1.** possibly from Bavarian *lott* 'mud' + *speich* 'spittle', 'moist dirt', either a topographic name for someone who lived on land in a muddy area or a nickname for someone who had a dirty appearance. **2.** alternatively, a metonymic occupational nickname for a wheelwright who made sloppy spokes, from Middle High German *loter* 'loose' + *speich* 'spoke (of a wheel)'.

Lott (8342) **1.** English: from a medieval personal name brought to England by the Normans, of uncertain origin. It may be the Hebrew personal name *Lot* 'covering', which was relatively popular in northern France, or a reduced form of various names formed with the diminutive suffix *-lot* (originally a combination of *-el* + *-ot*), commonly used with women's names. **2.** English: from Middle English *lot(t)e* 'lot', 'portion' (Old English *hlot*), in the sense of an allotted share of land, hence a status name for someone who held such a plot. **3.** Dutch: metonymic occupational name for a plumber or lead roofer, from *lood* 'lead'. **4.** German: from a pet form of Ludwig. **5.** German: topographic name from the dialect word *lott* 'mud', 'dirt'.

Lotter (261) German: from Middle High German *lotter* 'rascal', 'juggler'; either a nickname for a good-for-nothing or possibly an occupational name for a minstrel or entertainer.
GIVEN NAMES German 8%. *Alfons, Fritz, Juergen, Klaus, Otto, Raimund.*

Lottes (218) German: patronymic from a short form of the personal name LUDWIG.

Lotti (160) Italian: patronymic or plural form of the personal name LOTTO.
GIVEN NAMES Italian 12%. *Angelo* (2), *Quinto* (2), *Antonio, Benedetto, Romano.*

Lottman (185) German (**Lottmann**): **1.** habitational name from Lotte near Osnabrück or Lotten near Meppen. **2.** from a short form of the personal name LUDWIG + *man* 'man'.

Lotto (148) Italian: from the personal name *Lotto*, a short form of a pet name formed from the hypocoristic suffix *-lotto*, for example *Bertolotto, Angelotto.*

Lotts (328) **1.** English: patronymic or metronymic from LOTT 1. **2.** Possibly an altered spelling of German LOTZ.

Lotz (1578) German: from a medieval pet form of the personal name LUDWIG.
GIVEN NAMES German 4%. *Benno* (3), *Armin* (2), *Wolfgang* (2), *Erna, Erwin, Georg, Gerhard, Gunther, Helmut, Johann, Otto, Reinhard.*

Lotze (171) German: variant of LOTZ.
GIVEN NAMES German 6%. *Heinz* (2), *Hans.*

Lotzer (113) German: habitational name from either of two places called Lotzen, near Dresden and Landsberg.

Lou (578) **1.** Chinese 娄: from a character in the name of the state of Zhu Lou, which existed during the Zhou dynasty. After Wu Wang established the dynasty in 1122 BC, he granted Zhu Lou to a descendant of the legendary emperor Zhuan Xu. Later descendants took the character for *Lou* from the place name as their surname. **2.** Chinese 卢: variant of LU 2. **3.** Dutch (**de Lou**): variant of LAU. **4.** Scottish: unexplained.
GIVEN NAMES Chinese 24%; Vietnamese 4%. *Ching-Yun* (3), *Jian* (3), *Wei* (3), *Chi* (2), *Hong* (2), *Jing* (2), *Jong* (2), *Kwan* (2), *Ting* (2), *Wai Keung* (2), *Zheng* (2), *Bin; Son* (2), *Cao, Hao, Khanh Thi, Ly, Rung, Tien, Tin.*

Louallen (151) Americanized spelling of Welsh **Llewelyn** (see LLEWELLYN).

Loubier (137) Southern French: occupational name for an official in charge of wolf hunts at a royal court, Occitan *loubier* 'wolf'. Compare LOUVIER.
GIVEN NAMES French 11%. *Fernande, Laurier, Lucien, Sylvain.*

Louch (110) English: unexplained. Perhaps a variant of LOACH.

Louck (157) Dutch: variant spelling of LOOCK 1.

Loucks (2027) Dutch (**Louckx**): **1.** variant of LOOCK 1. **2.** patronymic from a pet form

of the personal name *Lodewijk* (see LUDWIG).

Loud (570) English: **1.** nickname for a noisy person, from Middle English *lude* 'loud' (Old English *hlūd*), perhaps in part preserving the Old English byname *Hlūda* that Ekwall postulates to explain the place names Loudham (Suffolk) and Lowdham (Nottinghamshire). **2.** topographic name for someone who lived by a roaring stream, Old English *hlūde* or *hlȳde* literally 'the loud one', or a habitational name from any of the places named from *hlȳde*, for example Lyde in Herefordshire and Somerset. **3.** variant of LOUTH.

Louden (1318) **1.** Scottish: habitational name from Loudoun near Cunningham in Ayrshire, named in Celtic as *Lugūnon* 'fort of Lugus' (see LYON 2). **2.** Scottish and English (chiefly Northumbria): variant of LOTHIAN.

Loudenback (122) Americanized spelling of German LAUDENBACH.

Loudenslager (259) Americanized spelling of German **Lautenschläger** (see LAUDENSLAGER).
GIVEN NAMES German 5%. *Kurt* (2), *Fritz.*

Louder (370) Possibly an Americanized form of German LAUTER.

Louderback (520) Americanized form of German LAUTERBACH.

Loudermilk (1493) Americanized form of German **Lautermilch** (see LAUDERMILK).

Loudin (277) **1.** French: from a pet form of the personal name *Oude*, a variant of *Houde*, with the definite article. **2.** In some cases, possibly a variant spelling of Scottish LOUDEN.

Loudon (729) Scottish: variant spelling of LOUDEN.

Loudy (107) Irish: variant of LEDDY.
GIVEN NAME Irish 6%. *Clancy.*

Louer (112) Probably a variant of English **Lower**.

Lougee (334) Probably an Americanized form of French **Louge**, habitational name from a place so named in Haute-Garonne.

Lough (1357) Irish: reduced Anglicized form of Gaelic **Ó Lachtnáin** 'descendant of *Lachtnán*', a personal name from *lachtna* 'gray'. This is the name of several families in Ireland, and has more often been Anglicized as LOUGHLIN or LOUGHRAN, and in County Cork as LAWTON.

Loughead (146) Variant spelling of Scottish LOCHHEAD.

Lougheed (249) Variant of Scottish LOCHHEAD.

Loughery (235) Variant of Irish LOUGHREY.

Loughlin (1463) Irish: **1.** reduced and altered form of MCLAUGHLIN. **2.** reduced form of O'LOUGHLIN, an Anglicized form of Gaelic **Ó Lachtáin** (see LOUGH).
GIVEN NAME Irish 5%. *Brendan.*

Loughman (431) **1.** American variant of an Irish name, perhaps LOUGHNANE. **2.** Perhaps also an Americanized spelling of German LACHMANN.
GIVEN NAMES Irish 4%. *Kieran* (2), *Brendan.*

Loughmiller (246) Americanized form of German **Lachmüller**, a distinguishing name for a miller (Middle High German *mülnære*) whose mill was by a pond or lake (Middle High German *lache*).

Loughnane (101) Irish: reduced Anglicized form of Gaelic **Ó Lachtnáin** 'descendant of *Lachtnan*', a personal name from *lachtna* 'gray'.
GIVEN NAME Irish 7%. *Eamon.*

Loughner (231) Americanized spelling of German LACHNER.

Loughney (235) Irish: reduced form of **Mulloughney**, an Anglicized form of Gaelic **Ó Maolfhachtna** ('devotee of St. Fachtna'), a Tipperary surname usually assimilated to **Moloney** (see MALONEY); or of **O'Loughney**, an Anglicized form of Gaelic **Ó Lachtna**, from *lachtna* 'gray'.

Loughran (1062) Irish: reduced Anglicized form of Gaelic **Ó Luchaireáin** 'descendant of *Luchaireán*', a pet form of a personal name from *luchair* 'radiance'. Compare LOUGHREY.
GIVEN NAMES Irish 5%. *Eamon* (2), *Brendan, Fergus, Siobhan.*

Loughrey (384) Irish: reduced Anglicized form of Gaelic **Ó Luachra** 'descendant of *Luachra*', a personal name derived from *luachair* 'light'. The name is often translated, RUSH from a Gaelic homonym, *luachair* meaning 'rush'.

Loughridge (386) Northern Irish: altered form of LOUGHREY.

Loughry (333) Northern Irish: variant of LOUGHREY.

Loui (126) Possibly a respelling of French LOUIS or **Loué**, a nickname from Old French *loé* 'famous', 'renowned', or a habitational name from a place in Sarthe named Loué, from the Romano-Gallic estate name *Laudiacum.*
GIVEN NAME French 6%. *Camille* (2).

Louie (2234) **1.** Americanized spelling of French LOUIS. **2.** Scottish and English: unexplained. **3.** Chinese 雷: variant of LEI 1. **4.** Chinese 吕: variant of LU 1.
GIVEN NAMES Chinese 15%. *Wing* (14), *Ming* (9), *Wai* (9), *Kam* (7), *Gim* (5), *Kin* (5), *Kwok* (5), *Shew* (4), *Sing* (4), *Yuk* (4), *Chun* (3), *Ho* (3).

Louis (3991) French: from the personal name *Louis*, derived from a Germanic personal name (the name of the founder of the Frankish dynasty) composed of the elements *hlod* 'fame' + *wīg* 'war'. This is recorded in Latin chronicles as *Ludovicus* (see LUDWIG), and *Chlodovechus*, which became Old French *Clovis, Clouis, Louis*, a name borne by many French kings.
GIVEN NAMES French 15%. *Pierre* (13), *Andre* (5), *Antoine* (5), *Francois* (5),

Jacques (5), *Jean Claude* (5), *Michel* (5), *Jean Robert* (4), *Ghislaine* (3), *Jeannot* (3), *Mireille* (3), *Raoul* (3).

Louise (235) French: from the personal name *Louise*, feminine form of LOUIS.

Louison (121) English: apparently a variant spelling of LEWISON.

Louissaint (130) French: apparently from elements meaning 'St. Louis', but perhaps an altered form of a habitational name from Luisant in Eure-et-Loir.

GIVEN NAMES French 42%; German 5%. *Andre, Cyr, Ermite, Ghislaine, Islande, Jean-Claude, Laurette, Lucienne, Monique, Pierre, Renold, Sauveur; Ernst.*

Louk (427) Dutch: from the personal name *Louk*, a Dutch vernacular form of LUCAS.

Loukas (117) Greek: from the personal name *Loukas*, Greek form of LUCAS.

GIVEN NAMES Greek 15%. *Spero* (2), *Christos, Dimitrios, Gerasimos, Kostas, Loukas, Pantelis.*

Louks (279) Dutch: patronymic from LOUK. See also LOUCKS.

Lounds (100) English: 1. variant spelling of LOWNDES. 2. variant of **Lound**, a topographic name from Old Norse *lundr* 'grove', or a habitational name from various places named with this word: Lound in Lincolnshire, Nottinghamshire, and Suffolk; Lund in North Yorkshire and the East Riding; Lunt in Merseyside.

Lounsberry (347) English: variant of LOUNSBURY.

Lounsbery (170) English: variant of LOUNSBURY.

Lounsbury (972) English: probably a respelling of **Lownsbrough**, a habitational name from Londesborough in the East Riding of Yorkshire, which is named with the Old Norse personal name *Lothinn* + Old English *burh* 'stronghold'.

Loup (170) French: 1. from a personal name from Latin *Lupus* (meaning 'wolf'), which derived its popularity from a 5th-century bishop of Troyes, who repulsed Attila the Hun. 2. nickname from Old French *lou, leu* 'wolf' (modern French *loup*; from Latin *lupus*). This surname is frequently translated as WOLF or WOLFE.

FOREBEARS This surname has been established in Canada since 1687; it was identified in early records as Polish (perhaps a variant of a Polish name such as LUBA or LUBY).

GIVEN NAMES French 7%. *Francois, Georges.*

Loupe (451) French: 1. habitational name from Loupes in Gironde, or La Loupe in Eure-et-Loir. 2. possibly a nickname from Old French *loupe* 'grimace', 'sticking-out tongue', denoting, Morlet suggests, someone who mocked other people by grimacing.

GIVEN NAMES French 5%. *Emile* (2), *Sylvain* (2), *Monique.*

Louque (261) French: variant spelling of **Luc** (see LUKE), found predominantly in LA.

Loureiro (246) Portuguese and Galician: topographic name for someone who lived by a conspicuous laurel tree, *loureiro* (from Latin *laurus*).

GIVEN NAMES Spanish 37%; Portuguese 15%. *Manuel* (8), *Jose* (7), *Julio* (3), *Orlando* (3), *Agustin* (2), *Esteban* (2), *Gustavo* (2), *Jesus* (2), *Jorge* (2), *Luciana* (2), *Luiz* (2), *Raul* (2); *Duarte, Ilidio, Joao, Joaquim, Paulo; Antonio* (11), *Fausto* (2), *Leonardo.*

Lourenco (378) Portuguese (**Lourenço**): from the personal name *Lourenço*, Latin *Laurentius* (see LAWRENCE).

GIVEN NAMES Spanish 33%; Portuguese 22%. *Jose* (22), *Manuel* (17), *Carlos* (6), *Francisco* (5), *Fernando* (4), *Abilio* (3), *Mario* (3), *Albino* (2), *Armando* (2), *Luis* (2), *Luiz* (2), *Adalberto; Joaquim* (4), *Joao* (2), *Adauto, Anabela, Duarte, Goncalo, Leao, Paulo, Valentim; Antonio* (16), *Caesar* (2), *Filomena.*

Lourie (277) 1. Northern English, Scottish, and Irish: variant of LOWRY. 2. Jewish: variant of LORIA.

GIVEN NAMES Jewish 6%; French 4%. *Isadore* (3), *Barak; Jacques* (2), *Laure.*

Louro (123) Portuguese and Galician: nickname for someone with blonde or light chestnut hair, *louro* (probably a derivative, with altered meaning, of Latin *laurus* 'laurel').

GIVEN NAMES Spanish 27%; Portuguese 20%; Italian 7%. *Manuel* (10), *Silvia* (3), *Jorge* (2), *Jose* (2), *Alberto, Armindo, Carlos, Joaquin, Mario, Ruben, Salvador; Joaquim* (2), *Joao; Antonio* (4), *Angelo.*

Lout (123) Possibly an altered spelling of LOUD or LOUTH.

Louth (188) 1. English: habitational name from Louth in Lincolnshire, so called from its position on the river Lud (Old English *Hlūde*, meaning 'the loud one'). 2. Irish: when not of English origin (see 1), probably a reduced and altered form of MCLEOD. Compare MCLOUTH.

Louthan (447) Variant of Scottish LOTHIAN.

Louttit (109) Scottish (Orkney; of Norman origin): habitational name from a place in Seine-Maritime, France called Louvetot.

Loutzenhiser (229) Americanized form of German **Lautzenhäuser** (see LAUTZENHEISER).

Louvier (152) French: occupational name for a wolf-hunter, *louvier.*

Louviere (866) French: topographic name for someone who lived by a wolf's lair, *louvière.*

GIVEN NAMES French 4%. *Anatole, Andre, Antoine, Curley, Desire, Monique, Silton, Ulysse.*

Louwagie (109) Belgian French: of uncertain origin. It is probably an altered form, under Dutch influence, of French **Louage**, from *le gage* 'the pledge', hence a meto-

nymic occupational name for a bailiff who enforced debt collection or possibly for a pawnbroker.

GIVEN NAME French 5%. *Marcel.*

Loux (568) Variant spelling of Dutch LOUCKS.

Lovaas (189) Norwegian (**Løvaas**): habitational name from any of numerous farmsteads so named, from Old Norse *lauf* 'leaf', 'foliage' + *áss* 'hill'.

GIVEN NAME Scandinavian 5%. *Baard.*

Lo Vallo (230) Southern Italian: probably a topographic name for someone who lived by a wall or fortification, *vallo*, with the definite article *lo*.

GIVEN NAMES Italian 15%. *Angelo* (2), *Vito* (2), *Canio, Donato, Rocco.*

Lovan (390) 1. Dutch: variant of LOVEN. 2. Southeast Asian: unexplained.

GIVEN NAMES Southeast Asian 7%. *Nien* (2), *Anh, Banh, Bao, Cau, Chanh, Diem, Dzung, Ha, Hoa, Lieng, Mai.*

Lovas (355) 1. Hungarian: occupational name from *lovas* 'rider' (a derivative of *ló* 'horse'); this may have denoted a messenger or a mounted soldier. 2. Norwegian (**Løvås**): variant of LOVAAS.

GIVEN NAMES Hungarian 4%. *Andras, Arpad, Istvan, Laszio, Laszlo, Sandor.*

Lovato (1562) 1. Northern Italian: from the Late Latin personal name *Lupatus*, a derivative of Latin *lupus* 'wolf'. This is one of several medieval personal names which became popular under the influence of Germanic compound personal names formed with *wolf-* 2. Spanish: variant of LOBATO.

GIVEN NAMES Spanish 17%. *Manuel* (8), *Jose* (7), *Juan* (6), *Juanita* (5), *Alfonso* (4), *Eloy* (4), *Ruben* (4), *Carlos* (3), *Mario* (3), *Ramon* (3), *Salomon* (3), *Amado* (2).

Lovdahl (111) Norwegian (**Løvdahl**): habitational name from any of numerous farmsteads named with Old Norse *lauf* 'leaf', 'foliage' + *dalr* 'valley'.

GIVEN NAME Scandinavian 7%. *Erik.*

Love (24844) 1. English: from a Middle English personal name derived from the Old English female personal name *Lufu* 'love', or the masculine equivalent *Lufa*. Compare LEAF 2. 2. English and Scottish: nickname from Anglo-Norman French *lo(u)ve* 'female wolf' (a feminine form of *lou*). This nickname was fairly commonly used for men, in an approving sense. No doubt it was reinforced by crossing with post-Conquest survivals of the masculine version of 1. 3. Scottish: see MCKINNON. 4. Dutch (**de Love**): respelling and reinterpretation of **Delhove**, a habitational name from Hove and L'Hoves in Hainault, for example.

Loveall (600) English: presumably a variant of LOVELL, or possibly a habitational name from Lovehall in Tayside.

Lo Vecchio (186) Southern Italian (also **Lovecchio**): nickname for an old man, from *vecchio* 'old (man)', with the definite article *lo*. Compare VECCHIO.

GIVEN NAMES Italian 26%. *Angelo* (3), *Cosmo* (3), *Vito* (3), *Salvatore* (2), *Santo* (2), *Antonio*, *Carlo*, *Constantino*, *Matteo*, *Nicola*, *Sal*, *Trifone*.

Loveday (877) English: **1.** from the Middle English female personal name *Loveday*, Old English *Lēofdæg*, composed of the elements *lēof* 'dear', 'beloved' + *dæg* 'day'. **2.** nickname for someone who had some particular association with a 'loveday'. According to medieval custom this was a day set aside for the reconciliation of enemies and amicable settlement of disputes.

Lovegren (117) Americanized form of Swedish LOFGREN.

GIVEN NAMES Scandinavian 5%. *Nels*, *Sven*.

Lovegrove (264) English (Berkshire): habitational name from an unidentified place, possibly named with the Old English personal name *Lufa* (see LOVE 1) + Old English *grāf* 'grove', 'thicket'.

Lovejoy (2882) English: nickname from Middle English *love(n)*, *luve(n)* 'to love' (Old English *lufian*) + Middle English *joie* 'joy' (Old French *joie*).

Lovekamp (105) most probably an Americanized form of North German **Loofkamp**, a topographic name from Middle Low German *lōf* 'lee side' (or *love* 'foliage'; see LAUB) + *kamp* 'field', 'domain'.

GIVEN NAME German 4%. *Kurt.*

Lovel (101) English: variant spelling of LOVELL.

Lovelace (4657) English: variant of LOVELESS. The spelling is apparently the result of folk etymology, which understood the word as a nickname for a dandy fond of lace. The modern sense of this word is, however, not attested until the 16th century and at the time of surname formation it meant only 'cord' or 'shoelace'.

Lovelady (1351) English: nickname from Middle English *love(n)*, *luve(n)* 'to love' + *lavedi* 'lady'. Reaney describes this as an obvious nickname for a philanderer; but perhaps it denoted a man who loved a woman above his social status, given the connotation of high status carried by the word *lavedi*.

Loveland (2119) **1.** English: habitational name from Loveland in Devon, possibly named with the Old English personal name *Lufa* + Old English *land* 'cultivated land', 'estate'. **2.** Probably an Americanized spelling of Norwegian **Løvland**, **Lauvland** (see LOFLAND).

Loveless (3330) English: **1.** nickname from Middle English *loveles* 'loveless', 'without love', probably in the sense 'fancy free'. **2.** some early examples, such as Richard Lovelas (Kent 1344), may have as their second element Middle English *las(se)* 'girl', 'maiden'.

Lovell (7673) English: nickname from Anglo-Norman French *lo(u)ve* 'female wolf' (feminine form of *lou*, from Latin *lupus*) + the diminutive suffix *-el*.

Lovellette (118) French: variant of LAVIOLETTE.

Lovely (1301) **1.** English: nickname for an amiable person, also perhaps sometimes given in an ironical sense, from Middle English *luvelich*, *loveli* (Old English *luflic*). During the main period of surname formation the word was used in an active sense, 'loving', 'kind', 'affectionate', as well as the passive 'lovable', 'worthy of love'. The meaning 'attractive', 'beautiful' is not clearly attested before the 14th century, and remained rare throughout the Middle Ages. **2.** New England Americanized form of French **Lavallée** (see LAVALLEE) or a similar name.

Loveman (115) English: from the Middle English personal name *Lefman* (see LEAMAN, LEMON).

Loven (406) **1.** English: variant of LOWN. **2.** Dutch: habitational name for someone from Leuven in Belgium.

GIVEN NAMES Scandinavian 5%. *Ludvig*, *Nils*, *Selmer.*

Lover (137) English: nickname from Middle English *lovere* 'lover', 'sweetheart'.

Lovera (107) Italian and Spanish: from Italian *lovera*, Spanish *lobera* 'wolf pack' or 'wolves' lair'. In Spain this family name, also spelled **Lobera**, is also a habitational name from any of several places called Lobera or La Lobera.

GIVEN NAMES Spanish 35%; Italian 10%. *Carlos* (2), *Juan* (2), *Pedro* (2), *Raul* (2), *Angelita*, *Cesar*, *Clodomiro*, *Eneida*, *Ezequiel*, *Florencio*, *Gerardo*, *Guadalupe*; *Lorenzo* (3), *Angelo*, *Dante.*

Lo Verde (256) Southern Italian (**Lo Verde**): from *verde* 'green' + the definite article *lo*; presumably a nickname for someone who habitually wore green.

GIVEN NAMES Italian 20%. *Salvatore* (4), *Francesco* (2), *Vito* (2), *Antonio*, *Filomena*, *Gaspare*, *Giuseppe*, *Nichola*, *Nino*, *Santo*, *Vincenzo.*

Loveridge (382) English: variant of LEVERICH.

Lovering (489) English: from an unattested Old English personal name *Lēofhering*, *Lēofring* 'son of *Lēofhere*', a personal name composed of the elements *lēof* 'dear', 'beloved' + *here* 'army'.

Lovern (518) English: from the Middle English personal name *Loverun*, Old English *Lēofrūn*, composed of the elements *lēof* 'dear' + *rūn* 'rune'.

Lovett (5997) **1.** English (of Norman origin) and French: from Anglo-Norman French *lo(u)vet*, a nickname meaning 'wolf cub', 'young wolf' (see LOVE, LOW). **2.** Scottish: variant of **Lovat**, a habitational name for a sept of the Frasers from Lovat near Beauly in Inverness-shire, so named from Gaelic *lobh* 'rot', 'putrefy' + the locative suffix *-aid*.

Lovette (763) French: variant of LOVETT.

Lovewell (187) English (Norfolk): possibly a nickname for a philanderer, from Middle English *love(n)* 'to love' + *well*, or alternatively a variant of LOVELL, altered through folk etymology.

Lovgren (286) Swedish (**Lövgren**): variant of LOFGREN.

GIVEN NAMES Scandinavian 7%. *Erik*, *Holger*, *Knute*, *Per.*

Lovick (278) **1.** English (Norfolk): from the Middle English personal name *Loveke*, Old English *Lufeca*, a derivative of *Lufa* (see LOVE 1), or *Lēofeca*, a derivative of *Lēofa* (see LEAF 2). **2.** English: perhaps a habitational name from places in Cumbria and Northumberland called Lowick, or Lowich in Northamptonshire. The first is from Old Norse *lauf* 'leaf' + *vík* 'creek'; the second is from the river name *Low* (possibly from Old English *luh* 'pool') + Old English *wīc* 'dairy farm', 'dwelling'; and the third from an unattested Old English personal name, *Luffa*, or *Luhha* + *wīc*. **3.** Probably a respelling of LOVIK.

Lovig (123) Norwegian: variant of LOVIK.

GIVEN NAMES German 6%. *Hans*, *Otto.*

Lovik (130) Norwegian (**Løvik**): habitational name from any of numerous farmsteads, so named from *løe* 'barn' (from Old Norse *hlaða*) + *vik* 'bay', 'inlet'.

Lovin (624) English: variant of LOVEN or LOVING.

Loving (2172) **1.** English: from a Middle English personal name *Lyfing*, Old English *Lēofing*, based on *lēof* 'dear'. **2.** Swedish: apparently an ornamental name formed from the place-name element *lov-*, meaning unknown, + the suffix *-ing* (see ARNING).

Lovinger (171) Jewish (Ashkenazic): variant of LEVINGER.

GIVEN NAMES German 4%; Jewish 4%. *Henrich*, *Kurt.*

Lovinggood (110) Americanized form of German **Liebengut** or **Leibengut** (see LEVENGOOD).

Lovingood (344) Americanized form of German **Liebengut** or **Leibengut** (see LEVENGOOD).

Lovings (234) English: patronymic from the Middle English personal name *Lyfing* (see LOVING).

Lovins (755) **1.** Dutch: variant of **Lovens**, patronymic from LOVEN. **2.** English: variant of LOVINGS.

Lovitt (601) Scottish and English: variant spelling of LOVETT.

Lovitz (116) Jewish (Ashenazic): habitational name from the town of Łowicz in Poland.

GIVEN NAME Jewish 5%. *Hyman.*

Lovorn (129) Origin unidentified. According to family historians, it is one of many variants of LOVING. It may equally well be a variant of LOWHORN (see LAWHORN).

Lovoy (100) Origin unidentified.

Lo Vullo (112) Italian: nickname meaning 'the childless one' or 'the mutilated one', from VULLO, itself a variant of GULLO, with the addition of the definite article.

GIVEN NAMES Italian 11%. *Angelo* (3), *Pasquale*, *Salvatore*.

Lovvorn (544) Origin unidentified. It may be one of many variants of LOVING, or a variant of LOWHORN (see LAWHORN).

Low (4591) **1.** English and Scottish: topographic name for someone who lived near a tumulus, mound or hill, Middle English *lowe*, from Old English *hlāw* (see LAW 2). **2.** Scottish and English: nickname for a short man, from Middle English *lah*, *lowe* (Old Norse *lágr*; the word was adopted first into the northern dialects of Middle English, where Scandinavian influence was strong, and then spread south, with regular alteration of the vowel quality). **3.** English and Scottish (of Norman origin): nickname for a violent or dangerous person, from Anglo-Norman French *lou*, *leu* 'wolf' (Latin *lupus*). Wolves were relatively common in Britain at the time when most surnames were formed, as there still existed large tracts of uncleared forest. **4.** Scottish: from a pet form of LAWRENCE. Compare LOWRY 1. **5.** Americanized spelling of Jewish LOWE.

Lowary (138) Variant of northern Irish, Scottish, and northern English LOWERY.

Lowden (789) English (chiefly County Durham) and Scottish: variant spelling of LOUDEN.

Lowder (2036) **1.** Scottish, northern Irish, and northern English: variant of LAUDER. **2.** Americanized spelling of German LAUTER.

Lowdermilk (412) Americanized form of German **Lautermilch** (see LAUDERMILK).

Lowe (31213) **1.** English and Scottish: variant spelling of LOW. **2.** German (**Löwe**): see LOEWE. **3.** Jewish (Ashkenazic; **Löwe**): ornamental name from German *Löwe* 'lion'. **4.** Jewish (Ashkenazic): Germanized form of LEVY.

Lowell (2887) English: variant of LOVELL, derived from Anglo-Norman French *lou* 'wolf' + the diminutive suffix -*el*.

FOREBEARS Lowell is the surname of one of America's most distinguished New England families, which have been prominent for over 200 years. Its founder, John Lowell (1743–1802), was a legislator and judge. The city of Lowell, MA was named in honor of his son Francis Cabot Lowell (1775–1817), a textile manufacturer.

Lowen (447) **1.** English: variant of LEWIN 1. **2.** This name is also found in the Netherlands, and in Sweden as **Löwen**, **Löwén**, **Lövén**, in both cases presumably derived from the German surname **Löwe** (see LOEWE), although the Swedish forms could equally be ornamental names from *löv* 'leaf'.

Lowenberg (289) **1.** German (**Löwenberg**): habitational name from any of several places called Löwenberg. **2.** Jewish (Ashkenazic) and Swedish (**Löwenberg**): ornamental name composed of German *Löwe* 'lion' + *Berg* 'mountain', 'hill'; in some cases the Jewish name would have been an ornamental elaboration associated with the personal name *Levi* (see LEVY) or with the personal names meaning 'lion'.

GIVEN NAMES German 4%. *Hans, Heinrich, Kurt.*

Lowenstein (789) **1.** German (**Löwenstein**): habitational name from any of several places called Löwenstein. **2.** Jewish (Ashkenazic) and Swedish (**Löwenstein**): ornamental name composed of German *Löwe* 'lion' + *Stein* 'stone'; in some cases the Jewish name is an ornamental elaboration associated with the personal names *Levi* (see LEVY) or *Lew* 'lion'.

GIVEN NAMES Jewish 5%; German 5%. *Bronia, Emanuel, Hadassah, Lipot, Menachem, Miriam, Mordechai, Mort, Myer, Yehuda; Bodo* (2), *Erwin* (2), *Siegfried* (2), *Balzer, Gerhard, Klaus, Manfred, Otto.*

Lowenthal (723) **1.** German (**Löwenthal**): habitational name from any of various places called Löwenthal. **2.** Jewish (Ashkenazic) and Swedish (**Löwenthal**): ornamental name composed of German *Löwe* 'lion' + *T(h)al* 'valley'; in some cases the Jewish name would have been an ornamental elaboration associated with the personal name LEVY or with personal names meaning 'lion'.

GIVEN NAMES Jewish 6%; German 4%. *Herschel* (2), *Moshe* (2), *Sol* (2), *Abbe, Gerson, Meier, Mort, Zvi; Ernst, Erwin, Gerhard, Hanni, Hans, Hermann, Kurt.*

Lower (1878) **1.** English (of Norman origin): occupational name denoting a servant who carried the ewer to guests at table so that they could wash their hands, Anglo-Norman French and Middle English *ewerer* (related to *ewere* 'jug'), with the French definite article *l'*. **2.** Cornish: variant of FLOWER 4.

Lowers (361) Patronymic from LOWER.

Lowery (13470) **1.** Irish: reduced Anglicized form of Gaelic **Ó Labhradha** (see LAVERY). **2.** Northern English and Scottish: from a pet form of LAWRENCE. **3.** Southwestern English: habitational name from Lowery in Devon, named with the Old English personal name *Lēofa* or *Lufa* + Old English *worðig* 'enclosure'.

Lowes (451) English: **1.** patronymic from Low 3 and 4. **2.** topographic name from the plural of Middle English *lowe* 'mound', 'hill' (see LOW 1).

Lowey (170) Manx: unexplained.

Lowhorn (135) Origin unidentified. It seems clear that it is a variant of LAWHORN.

Lowing (146) Perhaps an altered spelling of LEWIN. It is found predominantly in MI.

Lowinger (147) Jewish (Ashkenazic): variant of LEVINGER.

GIVEN NAMES Jewish 7%. *Jakob* (2), *Meyer* (2), *Shulamith.*

Lowitz (124) German: habitational name from any of a number of places so named in Pomerania.

Lowman (2647) English: from the Middle English personal name *Lefman* (see LEAMAN, LEMON).

Lowmaster (111) Americanized form of German **Lohmeister**, occupational name for a master tanner, from Middle High German *lō*, *lōh* 'tanner' + *meister* 'master'.

Lown (503) English: **1.** from the Middle English personal name *Lovin*, Old English *Lēofhūn*, composed of the elements *lēof* 'dear', 'beloved' + *hūn* 'bear cub'. **2.** habitational name from the city of Louvain in Belgium (Dutch Leuven).

Lowndes (237) English: patronymic from LOWN 1.

Lownes (126) English: patronymic from LOWN 1.

Lowney (496) Irish: variant of LOONEY.

GIVEN NAME Irish 6%. *Brendan* (2).

Lowrance (1220) English: variant spelling of LAWRENCE.

Lowrey (2306) Northern Irish, northern English, and Scottish: from a pet form of LAWRENCE.

Lowrie (925) Scottish and northern Irish: from a pet form of LAWRENCE.

Lowrimore (214) Variant of English and Scottish LORIMER.

Lowry (9821) Northern English, Scottish, and Irish: from a pet form of LAWRENCE.

Lowther (1434) English: habitational name from a place in Cumbria, so called from the river on which it stands. The place name is of obscure etymology, perhaps of ancient Welsh origin (compare LAUDER), or from Old Norse *lauðr* 'froth', 'foam' + *á* 'river'.

Lowy (582) **1.** Jewish (Ashkenazic): variant of LEVY. **2.** Dutch: from a Dutch adaptation of the French personal name LOUIS. **3.** Variant of Swiss German and Jewish (Ashkenazic) LOEWE (see LOEWY).

GIVEN NAMES Jewish 8%; German 5%. *Ephraim* (2), *Shimon* (2), *Avram, Hershel, Mendel, Pincus, Shimshon, Shlomo, Yisroel, Zvi; Ernst* (2), *Gerhard* (2), *Ignatz, Otto.*

Loxley (106) English: habitational name from any of various minor places named Loxley, as for example one in Warwickshire, which is named with the Old English personal name *Locc* + *lēah* 'woodland clearing'.

Loy (3334) **1.** German (south and Rhineland) and Dutch: from a reduced form of the medieval personal name *Eloy* (Latin *Eligius*, a derivative of *eligere* 'to choose or elect'), popularized a 6th-century saint who came to be venerated as the patron of smiths and horses. **2.** German: habitational name from Loy in Oldenburg. **3.** Dutch: variant of LOWY. **4.** Italian (Sardinian): from the personal name *Loi*, a short form of *Balloi*, a pet form of *Salvatóre*. **5.** Spanish and Italian: possibly from a reduced form of the personal name *Eloy* (see 1 above), of which the Italian form is *Eligio*. **6.** French (Picardy): nickname for someone who was quick to have recourse to the law: a frequent or vexatious litigant, or perhaps a metonymic occupational name for a lawyer.

Loya (1363) Spanish: habitational name from Loya in Navarra, Basque Country.
GIVEN NAMES Spanish 43%. *Jose* (26), *Manuel* (23), *Jesus* (15), *Carlos* (14), *Juan* (13), *Luis* (9), *Javier* (7), *Mario* (7), *Roberto* (7), *Arturo* (5), *Cesar* (5), *Edmundo* (5).

Loyal (136) **1.** French: nickname from *loyal* 'faithful', 'honest'. **2.** Indian (Maharashtra): Hindu (Brahman) name of unknown meaning, found among the Konkanasth Brahmans of Maharashtra.
GIVEN NAMES Indian 6%. *Shamsher, Sushil.*

Loyall (109) Variant spelling of LOYAL.

Loyd (4497) Respelling of Welsh LLOYD.

Loye (114) **1.** French: metonymic occupational name for a keeper of geese, from French *oie* 'goose' (Old French *o(u)e*), with the article *l(a)*. **2.** Dutch: variant of LOWY.
GIVEN NAME French 4%. *Jean Baptiste.*

Loyer (315) **1.** French: occupational name for a keeper of geese, *oier*. **2.** Dutch (**(de) Loyer**): occupational name for a tanner, Dutch *looier*.
FOREBEARS A bearer of the name from Anjou, France, was in Quebec City before 1653.
GIVEN NAMES French 4%. *Emile, Marcel, Pascal.*

Loyola (311) Spanish form of Basque **Loiola**: habitational name from Loiola in Guipúzcoa and Biscay provinces, named from Basque *loi* 'mud' + the locative suffix *-ola*.
GIVEN NAMES Spanish 45%. *Carlos* (5), *Jose* (5), *Juan* (5), *Luis* (4), *Alfredo* (3), *Benito* (3), *Cesar* (3), *Guadalupe* (3), *Manuel* (3), *Alberto* (2), *Ana* (2), *Angel* (2); *Leonardo* (2), *Cecilio, Donato, Guido.*

Loza (693) **1.** Spanish (also **de la Loza**): habitational name from any of several places named Loza (in Galicia, Asturias, and the Basque Country), probably named with *loza* 'clay, earthenware'. **2.** in some cases Castilianized form of Asturian-Leonese **Lloza**, a habitational name from a town called Lloza in Asturies.
GIVEN NAMES Spanish 53%. *Jose* (25), *Juan* (11), *Miguel* (10), *Jesus* (8), *Rafael* (7), *Luis* (6), *Salvador* (6), *Francisco* (5), *Jaime* (5), *Lupe* (5), *Raul* (5), *Alfredo* (4).

Lozada (785) Spanish: southern variant of LOSADA.
GIVEN NAMES Spanish 47%. *Jose* (19), *Carlos* (13), *Angel* (11), *Juan* (7), *Luis* (7), *Jaime* (5), *Elba* (4), *Francisco* (4), *Javier* (4),

Jesus (4), *Manuel* (4), *Miguel* (4); *Antonio* (9), *Leonardo* (2), *Marco* (2), *Romeo* (2), *Ciro, Fausto, Federico, Heriberto, Italo.*

Lozano (5616) Spanish: nickname for an elegant or haughty person, from *lozano* 'splendid', later 'good-looking'.
GIVEN NAMES Spanish 48%. *Jose* (124), *Juan* (91), *Jesus* (62), *Manuel* (57), *Carlos* (54), *Luis* (44), *Francisco* (41), *Raul* (35), *Pedro* (33), *Roberto* (33), *Arturo* (27), *Jorge* (27).

Lozeau (174) Americanized spelling of French LOISEAU.
GIVEN NAMES French 13%. *Armand, Aurele, Emile, Herve, Jean Marc, Laurent, Remi.*

Lozen (118) Origin unidentified. Possibly an altered spelling of English LAWSON.

Lozier (983) French: variant spelling of LOSIER.

Lozinski (169) Polish (**Łoziński**), Ukrainian, and Jewish (eastern Ashkenazic): habitational name for someone from Łozin or Łozina, now in Ukraine, or Łozinki, now in Belarus, named with *łoz(in)a* 'osier'.
GIVEN NAMES Polish 10%. *Andrzej, Feliks, Karol, Kazimierz, Leszek, Zbigniew.*

Lo Zito (163) Southern Italian (also **Lozito**): nickname from *zito* 'boy', 'husband', with the definite article *lo*.
GIVEN NAMES Italian 13%. *Angelo* (2), *Antonio, Nunzio, Vito.*

Lozon (215) **1.** French: variant spelling of LAUZON. **2.** Spanish (**Lozón**): unexplained. This name is concentrated in Biscay province.

Lozowski (111) Polish (**Łozowski**): habitational name for someone from a place called Łoza in Białystok voivodeship, named with *łoza* 'osier', 'wicker'.
GIVEN NAMES Polish 16%; German 4%. *Karol, Stanislaw, Tomasz, Wladyslaw, Zbigniew, Zygmunt.*

Lozoya (299) Spanish: habitational name from Lozoya in Madrid province.
GIVEN NAMES Spanish 56%. *Jose* (9), *Jesus* (7), *Manuel* (6), *Juan* (5), *Ramon* (5), *Alberto* (4), *Luis* (4), *Ruben* (4), *Blanca* (3), *Guadalupe* (3), *Mario* (3), *Miguel* (3).

Lozzi (108) Italian: variant of LUZZI 2.
GIVEN NAMES Italian 11%. *Donato, Geno.*

Lu (4618) **1.** Chinese 吕: from the name of the ancient state of Lu, in present-day Henan province. This is one of the oldest Chinese surnames, going back well over 4000 years to an adviser of the founding emperor of the Xia dynasty, Yu (2205–2198 BC). The adviser was enfeoffed with the state of Lu, and the family held it throughout the Xia, Shang, and Western Zhou dynasties, eventually adopting the name of the state, Lu, as their surname. **2.** Chinese 卢: from area called Lu, in present-day Shandong province. During the Warring States period (403–221 BC), a descendant of previous dukes of the state of Qi became the high counselor of that state, and was granted the area of Lu. His descendants later adopted the place name Lu as their

surname. **3.** Chinese 陆: from the name of the city of Lu in the state of Qi. During the Zhou dynasty (1122–221 BC). The youngest son of a duke of Qi was granted the city of Lu, and his descendants adopted the place name Lu as their surname. **4.** Chinese 鲁: from the name of a different state of Lu, a large area covering parts of present-day Anhui, Jiangsu, and Shandong provinces. This was granted to Zhou Gong, Duke of Zhou, a famous figure in Chinese history, as he was revered by Confucius as the prototypical good adviser. The fourth son of Wen Wang, Zhou Gong was the younger brother and chief adviser of Wu Wang, the founder of the Zhou dynasty. After Wu Wang died in 1116 BC, his 13-year old son succeeded him, but actual power was held by Zhou Gong, acting as regent. Zhou Gong's descendants later adopted the name of the state as their surname. **5.** Chinese 路: from the name of the Lushui river. The characters for the river name contained a written component meaning 'water'; this component was dropped, leaving only the current character for *Lu*, which means 'street'. **6.** Chinese 鹿: from the name of an area known as Wulu 'Five Deer', which was granted to a senior adviser of the state of Wei. His descendants adopted Lu as their surname.
GIVEN NAMES Chinese 41%; Vietnamese 16%. *Hong* (23), *Wei* (22), *Ming* (19), *Jian* (18), *Min* (17), *Ping* (16), *Li* (14), *Yi* (14), *Feng* (13), *Ling* (12), *Hung* (11), *Minh* (11), *Nu* (11), *Gang* (10), *Ha* (10), *Muoi* (10), *Cheng* (9), *Chi* (9), *Hoa* (8), *Tan* (8), *Cuong* (7), *Ha To* (7), *Dung* (6), *Hai* (6), *Lan* (6), *Chung* (5), *Phong* (4), *Tuong* (4), *Tam* (3), *Chang* (2), *Manh* (2), *Shen* (2), *Tian* (2), *Tinh* (2), *You* (2), *Chong.*

Lua (213) **1.** Spanish and Galician (**Lúa**): habitational name from a place called Lúa in Lugo province (Galicia). This name is common in Mexico. **2.** Tongan: unexplained. **3.** Hawaiian: unexplained. **4.** Chinese: possibly a variant of LAI 1.
GIVEN NAMES Spanish 54%. *Jose* (10), *Francisco* (5), *Jesus* (5), *Juan* (3), *Dalia* (2), *Fernando* (2), *Ignacio* (2), *Jose Luis* (2), *Josefina* (2), *Luis* (2), *Manuel* (2), *Mario* (2).

Luallen (271) Americanized form of Welsh LLEWELLYN.

Luba (183) Polish and Czech: from a pet form of any of various Old Slavic personal names (for example, *Lubomir, Luboslav, Lubogost*) formed with *lub-* 'love', 'liking'.
GIVEN NAMES Polish 4%. *Eugeniusz, Zofia.*

Lubahn (122) Germanized form of a Slavic or Old Prussian name formed with *lub-* 'love', 'dear' (see LUBA).

Lubar (101) **1.** Polish and Czech: from a derivative of the personal name LUBA. **2.** Polish: possibly a habitational name for someone from places called Lubar or Lubarka in Lithuania.

Lubarsky (159) Ukrainian and Jewish (from Ukraine): habitational name for someone from Lyubar in Volhynia in Ukraine, or Lubarka in Lithuania.
GIVEN NAMES Russian 8%; Jewish 7%. *Anatoly, Efim, Grigory, Leonid, Lev, Mikhail, Svetlana; Ari, Inna.*

Lubas (226) Polish (**Lubaś, Lubasz**) and Czech (**Lubaš**): from a pet form of any of various Old Slavic personal names (for example, *Lubomir, Luboslav, Lubogost*) formed with *lub-* 'love', 'liking'.
GIVEN NAMES Polish 7%. *Casimir, Eugeniusz, Jerzy, Tadeusz, Wladyslaw.*

Lubash (102) Americanized variant of Polish **Lubasz** or Czech **Lubaš** (see LUBAS).

Lubbe (113) Dutch and North German (**Lübbe**): **1.** variant of LUBBEN. **2.** Germanized form of a Slavic or Old Prussian name formed with *lub-* 'love', 'dear' (see LUBA).
GIVEN NAMES German 5%. *Dieter, Kurt.*

Lubben (381) **1.** Dutch and North German (**Lübben**): patronymic from German *Lübbe*, Dutch *Lubbe*, short forms of the personal names LEOPOLD and *Lübbert* (see LUEBBERT). **2.** Dutch: from a pet form of the Germanic personal name *Lodebert*, a compound of *hlod* 'famous' + *berht* 'bright'.

Lubbers (770) Dutch and North German (**Lübbers**): patronymic from the personal name *Lübbert*, Dutch *Lubbert* (see LUEBBERT).

Lubbert (112) Dutch and North German (**Lübbert**): see LUEBBERT.

Lubeck (368) North German (**Lübeck**) and Dutch: habitational name from the city of Lübeck in Schleswig-Holstein.

Lubell (246) **1.** Swedish: ornamental name from an unexplained first element + the common surname suffix *-ell*, from the Latin adjectival ending *-elius*. **2.** Perhaps an altered spelling of French LABELLE.

Luber (497) German: habitational name from places called Luben in the Posen area, West and East Prussia, and near Hannover.
GIVEN NAMES German 6%. *Mathias* (3), *Kurt* (2), *Franz, Helmut, Otto.*

Lubert (121) Dutch and North German: **1.** variant of **Lübbert** (see LUEBBERT). **2.** Germanized form of a Slavic or Old Prussian name formed with *lub-* 'love', 'dear' (see LUBA).

Luberto (123) Italian: from the Germanic personal name *Liutberht* (see LUEBBERT), or from the personal name *Lubertu*, Calabrian form of ROBERT.
GIVEN NAMES Italian 17%. *Gabriele, Liberato, Matteo.*

Lubic (125) Americanized form of Serbian and Croatian **Ljubić**, patronymic or metronymic from the personal names *Ljubo* (male), *Ljuba* (male or female), or *Ljubica* (female), all from the adjective *ljub* 'dear', feminine *ljuba*.

Lubich (118) Americanized spelling of Serbian and Croatian **Ljubić** (see LUBIC).

Lubin (1313) **1.** French: from the Germanic personal name *Leobin*, a pet form of any of the compound names formed with *leub, liup, liob* 'dear', 'beloved' as the first element. St. Leobin was a bishop of Chartres in the 6th century (whence the name's popularity in the Middle Ages), and several places were named Saint-Lubin after him, as for example in Eure, Eure-et-Loir, and Loir-et-Cher. **2.** Jewish (from Belarus): habitational name for someone from Lyubin and Lyubny, now in Belarus. **3.** Jewish (from Belarus): metronymic from the Yiddish personal name *Lube*, from eastern Slavic 'love'.
GIVEN NAMES French 6%; Jewish 5%. *Pierre* (6), *Monique* (2), *Alain, Andree, Jean Charles, Jean-Claude, Julienne, Marie Ange, Michel, Micheline, Regine, Solange; Hyman* (4), *Emanuel* (3), *Meyer* (2), *Moshe* (2), *Shmuel* (2), *Dovid, Isador, Moise, Myer, Riv, Shlomo, Sol.*

Lubinski (466) Polish (**Lubiński**) and Jewish (from Poland): habitational name for someone from places called Lubin, Lubiń, or Lubiny.

Lubinsky (198) Jewish (from Poland): variant of LUBINSKI.
GIVEN NAMES Jewish 5%. *Chaim, Miriam, Pesach.*

Lubitz (286) Eastern German: habitational name from a place so named or from any of several places similarly named, all of Slavic origin.

Lubke (204) North German (**Lübke**): see LUEBKE.

Lublin (208) Polish: habitational name from the city of Lublin, named from the personal name *Lub(l)a*, a derivative of an Old Slavic compound personal name such as *Lubomir* or *Lubogost*.

Lubliner (126) Jewish (Ashkenazic) and German: habitational name for someone from the city of Lublin in Poland.
GIVEN NAMES Jewish 6%; German 4%; Scottish 4%. *Sol, Uri.*

Lubold (103) German: from the personal name *Lubold*, a variant of LEOPOLD.

Lubow (209) **1.** Jewish (eastern Ashkenazic): habitational name from Lubowo in Lithuania. **2.** Shortened form of various eastern Ashkenazic Jewish surnames, as for example **Lubowitz**, a metronymic from the Yiddish female personal name *Lube*, from Slavic 'love', or **Lubowski**, a habitational name (see 1 above).
GIVEN NAMES Jewish 4%. *Miriam* (2), *Sol.*

Lubrano (359) Italian (Naples): unexplained.
GIVEN NAMES Italian 28%. *Carlo* (4), *Antonio* (3), *Benito* (2), *Giuseppe* (2), *Alfonso, Benedetto, Biagio, Carmelo, Ciro, Cosmo, Domenic, Domenico, Emilio, Flavio, Franco, Julio.*

Luby (805) **1.** Irish: reduced Anglicized form of Gaelic **Ó Lúbaigh**, from *lúbach*

'cunning'. **2.** Polish: nickname from the adjective *luby* 'pleasant', 'beloved'.

Luc (363) **1.** French: from the personal name *Luc*, a vernacular form of LUCAS. **2.** French: topographic name from Latin *lucus* 'wood', or a habitational name from places in Aveyron and Lozère named with this word. **3.** Vietnamese: unexplained.
GIVEN NAMES Vietnamese 33%; French 8%. *Anh* (4), *Minh* (4), *Mui* (4), *Duong* (3), *Hong* (3), *Hung* (3), *Nu* (3), *Thanh* (3), *Duc* (2), *Dung* (2), *Hoa* (2), *Huu* (2), *Long* (2), *Hang, Heung, Tong; Pierre* (2), *Jean, Gabrielle, Germain, Sylvain.*

Luca (541) **1.** Italian: from the personal name *Luca*, from Latin LUCAS. **2.** Southern Italian (**Lucà**): possibly from a short form of Greek *Loukanos*, denoting an inhabitant of Lucania (see LUCAS). **3.** Dutch: variant of LUCAS. **4.** Hungarian: from *Luca*, a pet form of the personal name *Lucia*, feminine form of *Lucio*, from Latin *Lucius*.
GIVEN NAMES Italian 24%. *Rocco* (4), *Adolfo* (2), *Antonio* (2), *Carmine* (2), *Gasper* (2), *Giacomo* (2), *Mario* (2), *Rosario* (2), *Sal* (2), *Aldo, Antonino, Domenic, Domenico, Dominico, Guido.*

Lucado (165) Origin unidentified. Compare LUCKADOO.

Lucarelli (611) Italian: patronymic or plural form of a derivative of LUCA.
GIVEN NAMES Italian 16%. *Angelo* (4), *Dino* (2), *Domenic* (2), *Franco* (2), *Olindo* (2), *Rocci* (2), *Rocco* (2), *Aldo, Carlo, Caterina, Chiara, Domenico.*

Lucas (33656) **1.** English, French, Spanish, Portuguese, Dutch, etc.: from the Latin personal name *Lucas* (Greek *Loukas*) 'man from Lucania'. Lucania is a region of southern Italy thought to have been named in ancient times with a word meaning 'bright' or 'shining'. Compare LUCIO. The Christian name owed its enormous popularity throughout Europe in the Middle Ages to St. Luke the Evangelist, hence the development of this surname and many vernacular derivatives in most of the languages of Europe. Compare LUKE. This is also found as an Americanized form of Greek LOUKAS. **2.** Scottish: reduced Anglicized form of Gaelic **Mac Lùcais** (see MCLUCAS).
FOREBEARS As a French name Lucas has been recorded in Canada since 1653, taken to Trois Rivières, Quebec, by one Lucas-Lépine from Normandy.

Lucca (311) **1.** habitational name from Lucca Sicula in Agrigento province, Sicily, which was called simply Lucca until 1863. It was probably originally named with a Celtic element meaning 'marshy'. **2.** mainly northern variant of LUCA 1.
GIVEN NAMES Italian 17%; Spanish 9%. *Sal* (3), *Salvatore* (2), *Aldo, Angelo, Carlo, Dino, Domenic, Franco, Geno, Giuseppe,*

Livio, Marco; *Luis* (2), *Ana, Jose, Juan, Julio, Manuel, Orfilia*.

Lucchese (327) Italian (Sicily): ethnic name for someone from Lucca (see LUCCA 2), from an adjectival form of the place name.
GIVEN NAMES Italian 17%. *Salvatore* (4), *Santo* (3), *Cosimo* (2), *Gino* (2), *Ciro, Enrico, Nunzio, Sal, Vincenzo, Vita, Vito*.

Lucchesi (884) Italian (Tuscany): patronymic or plural form of LUCCHESE.
GIVEN NAMES Italian 13%. *Angelo* (5), *Dino* (5), *Gino* (4), *Guido* (3), *Reno* (3), *Ignazio* (2), *Oreste* (2), *Salvatore* (2), *Vito* (2), *Aldo, Carlo, Cesare*.

Lucchetti (168) Italian: probably a variant of LUCHETTI.
GIVEN NAMES Italian 21%. *Mario* (3), *Amato, Duilio, Gino, Pasquale, Pietro, Remo, Renaldo, Ricardo, Stefano, Tino*.

Lucci (590) Italian: patronymic or plural form of *Luccio*, a reduced form of a personal name formed with this suffix.
GIVEN NAMES Italian 17%. *Domenic* (3), *Luigi* (3), *Angelo* (2), *Attilio* (2), *Guido* (2), *Marco* (2), *Pasquale* (2), *Rocco* (2), *Aldo, Antonio, Biagio, Carlo*.

Luce (3821) English (Gloucestershire and South Wales): **1.** most probably from the Norman personal name *Luce* (a vernacular form of Latin *Lucia* or *Lucius*). This is generally a female name, although male bearers are found in France. It was borne by a young Sicilian maiden and an aged Roman widow, both of whom were martyred under Diocletian and are venerated as saints. **2.** Alternatively, the surname may be a variant of LEWIS.
FOREBEARS American bearers of this surname are descended from Henry Luce (1640–c.1688), who came to Scituate, MA, from south Wales in or before 1666, and moved to Martha's Vineyard, MA, in about 1670. He had many prominent descendants.

Lucena (136) Spanish: habitational name from Lucena in Andalusia.
GIVEN NAMES Spanish 44%. *Juan* (4), *Jose* (3), *Manuel* (3), *Angel* (2), *Bernardo* (2), *Ernesto* (2), *Josefina* (2), *Alberto, Amalia, Ana, Avelino, Carlos*; *Antonio* (2), *Heriberto, Luciano, Primo*.

Lucente (478) Italian: from the personal name *Lucente* 'shining'.
GIVEN NAMES Italian 22%. *Rocco* (7), *Salvatore* (4), *Angelo* (3), *Luca* (3), *Antonio* (2), *Domenico* (2), *Giuseppe* (2), *Marco* (2), *Vito* (2), *Agostino, Alessandra, Cesare*.

Lucero (6106) Spanish: nickname from *lucero*, a derivative of *luz* 'light', which has variety of meanings including 'morning or evening star', 'star or blaze marking on a horse'.
GIVEN NAMES Spanish 25%. *Jose* (51), *Manuel* (47), *Juan* (31), *Carlos* (26), *Luis* (25), *Ruben* (16), *Jesus* (14), *Francisco* (13), *Orlando* (13), *Alfonso* (11), *Eloy* (11), *Ramon* (11).

Lucey (1179) **1.** Irish: reduced Anglicized form of Gaelic **Ó Luasaigh**, an altered form of **Mac Cluasaigh**, a Cork name meaning 'son of *Cluasach*', a byname originally denoting someone with large or otherwise noticeable ears (from *cluas* 'ear'). **2.** English and Irish (of Norman origin), French: habitational name from any of various places in Normandy and northern France originally named with the Latin personal name *Lucius* + the locative suffix *-acum*. **3.** English: variant of LUCE 1.
GIVEN NAMES Irish 5%. *Maeve, Niall*.

Luchetti (159) Italian: patronymic or plural form of a pet form of LUCA.
GIVEN NAMES Italian 23%. *Everardo* (2), *Dante, Gino, Italo, Marco, Mario, Olindo, Ottavio, Rocco, Umberto*.

Luchini (276) Italian: patronymic or plural form of a derivative of LUCA.
GIVEN NAMES Italian 8%. *Oriano* (2), *Reno* (2), *Aldo, Angelo, Delio, Guido, Livio, Ottavio, Primo, Remo, Romano*.

Luchs (157) German: nickname for someone with keen sight, from Middle High German *luhs* 'lynx'.
GIVEN NAME French 4%. *Donat*.

Luchsinger (429) Swiss German: habitational name for someone from Luchsingen near Glarn.

Lucht (803) **1.** North German: nickname from Middle Low German *lucht* 'clumsy', 'left-handed'. **2.** North German: topographic name from Middle Low German *lucht* 'elevated spot' 'loft'. **3.** German and Dutch: topographic name from *Lucht* 'cleared area', related to Middle High German *liuhten* 'to shine', 'be bright'. **4.** Dutch: nickname for a lightweight person, from *lucht* 'air'.
GIVEN NAMES German 4%. *Otto* (3), *Erwin* (2), *Alois, Armin, Reinhardt*.

Lucia (1407) **1.** Spanish (**Lucía**) and southern Italian: from the female personal name *Lucia*, feminine derivative of Latin *lux* 'light'. **2.** English: from a Latinized form of LUCE. **3.** Respelling of French LUSSIER.
GIVEN NAMES Italian 7%. *Angelo* (6), *Rocco* (3), *Domenic* (2), *Francesco* (2), *Marcello* (2), *Pietro* (2), *Sal* (2), *Agostino, Biagio, Carmine, Cesare, Ferdinando*.

Lucian (120) **1.** English: from the personal names *Lucian* and *Luciana*, derived from the Latin personal names *Lucianus* and *Luciana* (see LUCIANO). **2.** Southern French: local (Occitan) variant of LUCIEN. **3.** Italian: Venetian variant of LUCIANO.
GIVEN NAMES Italian 8%. *Rocco* (3), *Aldo, Italo*.

Luciani (509) Italian: patronymic or plural form of LUCIANO.
GIVEN NAMES Italian 15%. *Dante* (2), *Giuseppe* (2), *Guerino* (2), *Nicola* (2), *Angelo, Antonio, Domenico, Donato, Emidio, Ettore, Gildo, Gioacchino*.

Luciano (1750) Italian, Spanish, and Portuguese: from the personal name *Luciano*,

Latin *Lucianus* (adjectival derivative of LUCIUS), borne by a number of minor early Christian martyrs. In the form **Loukianos** it is also found as a Greek family name.
GIVEN NAMES Spanish 16%; Italian 10%. *Jose* (11), *Carlos* (9), *Rafael* (5), *Francisco* (4), *Juan* (4), *Manuel* (4), *Pedro* (4), *Angel* (3), *Juana* (3), *Mario* (3), *Marisol* (3), *Ricardo* (3); *Antonio* (10), *Pasquale* (6), *Salvatore* (6), *Angelo* (3), *Carmine* (3), *Lorenzo* (3), *Rocco* (2), *Vito* (2), *Carlo, Carmela, Carmino, Cosmo*.

Lucibello (109) Italian: from a personal name meaning 'beautiful light'.
GIVEN NAMES Italian 16%; Spanish 5%. *Salvatore* (2), *Antonio, Pasquale*; *Alfonso* (3), *Maria Rosa, Mario*.

Lucich (166) **1.** Croatian and Serbian (**Lučić**): patronymic from the personal name *Luka* (see LUCAS). **2.** Croatian (**Lucić**): from the female personal name *Luce*, pet form of *Lucija* 'Lucy'.
GIVEN NAMES South Slavic 4%. *Marko, Petar*.

Lucid (101) Irish (County Kerry): of uncertain derivation; perhaps a variant of LUCEY.

Lucidi (100) Italian: patronymic or plural form of LUCIDO.
GIVEN NAMES Italian 13%. *Enrico, Gino, Sante*.

Lucido (657) Italian and Spanish (also **Lucído**): from the personal name *Lucido*, from Latin *lucidus* 'lucid', 'shining'. It could also be a nickname for a clear, lucid thinker.
GIVEN NAMES Italian 22%; Spanish 5%. *Sal* (9), *Salvatore* (8), *Angelo* (3), *Vito* (3), *Baldassare* (2), *Giovanna* (2), *Marco* (2), *Mario* (2), *Pietro* (2), *Calogero, Carlo, Carmela, Cesare*; *Cesar, Epifanio, Manolito, Manolo, Marcela, Nestor*.

Lucien (223) French: from a personal name derived from Latin *Lucianus* (from LUCIUS).
GIVEN NAMES French 22%. *Andre* (2), *Pierre* (2), *Serge* (2), *Bernadin, Luckner, Michel, Monique, Wesner, Yvon*.

Lucier (1150) French: variant spelling of LUSSIER 2.
GIVEN NAMES French 6%. *Armand* (5), *Adelard, Alain, Alphonse, Amie, Andre, Colette, Collette, Fernand, Herve, Monique, Normand*.

Lucio (857) **1.** Portuguese (**Lúcio**) and Italian: patronymic from the Latin personal name LUCIUS, a derivative of *lux* 'light'. **2.** Galician: habitational name from Lucio in Pontevedra province, Galicia.
GIVEN NAMES Spanish 41%. *Jose* (13), *Juan* (11), *Luis* (8), *Francisco* (7), *Jesus* (7), *Manuel* (7), *Pedro* (5), *Angel* (4), *Enrique* (4), *Felipe* (4), *Fernando* (4), *Guadalupe* (4).

Lucius (629) **1.** German: Latinized form of LUTZ. **2.** Dutch: from the personal name *Lucius* (Latin *Lucius*, an ancient Roman personal name probably derived from *lux* 'light', genitive *lucis*).

Luck (2306) **1.** English and German (also found in Alsace): variant of English LUKE, German LUKAS. **2.** German (also **Lück**): from a short form of *Lüdeke*, a pet form of LUDOLPH (compare LIEDTKE 2) or occasionally from LUDWIG or LUCAS. **3.** Dutch (**van Luck**) and English: habitational name from Luik, the Dutch name of the Belgian city of Liège. **4.** Translation of the French Canadian secondary surnames LACHANCE and LAFORTUNE.

Luckadoo (157) Origin unidentified. Possibly an altered form of Irish MCADOO, with an extraneous first element. This name occurs chiefly in NC.

Lucke (515) German (**Lücke**): variant of LUCK 2.
GIVEN NAMES German 4%. *Jochen* (2), *Erwin, Kurt, Ralf.*

Lucken (177) **1.** North German (**Lücken**): patronymic from the personal name *Lück* (see LUCK 2). **2.** English: variant of **Lovekin**, from a pet form of LOVE 1 or 2.

Luckenbach (207) German: habitational name from a place so named in the Rhineland, or a topographic name from any of several streams so named in the Rhineland and Württemberg.

Luckenbaugh (200) Americanized spelling of German LUCKENBACH.

Luckenbill (304) Americanized spelling of German **Luginbühl** (see LUGINBUHL).

Lucker (253) **1.** South German: from the personal name *Liutger*, derived from a Germanic personal name composed of the elements *liut* 'people' + *gār, gēr* 'spear'. **2.** North German (**Lücker**): patronymic from a reduced form of the personal name *Lüdeke* (see LUEDECKE).

Luckert (102) German: variant of LUCKER.
GIVEN NAME German 5%. *Otto.*

Luckett (1959) English: from a pet form of the personal name LUCK, variant of LUKE.

Luckey (1522) Irish spelling of Scottish LUCKIE.

Luckhardt (165) German: metronymic from the Germanic female personal name *Liutgard*, a compound of *liut* 'people' + *gard* 'protective enclosure', 'yard'.
GIVEN NAME French 4%. *Colette.*

Luckie (444) Scottish: reduced Anglicized form of a pet form of Gaelic **Mac Lùcais** (see MCLUCAS).

Lucking (177) English: from Old English *Lēofecing*, a patronymic from *Lēofeca* (see LEVICK 2), or possibly, as Reaney suggests, a late derivative of **Lovekin** (see LUCKEN).

Luckman (254) **1.** English: nickname or occupational name for a servant of someone called *Luck* (a variant of LUKE). **2.** North German (**Luckmann**): topographic name from the dialect term *luke* 'hollow', 'hole'. **3.** Dutch: derivative of the personal name *Luc* (see LUCAS). **4.** Dutch: habitational name for someone from Luik,

the Dutch name of Liège in Belgium.

Luckner (121) German (Saxony): habitational name from Luckenau near Zeitz.
GIVEN NAME German 5%. *Kurt.*

Luckow (269) **1.** Polish (**Łuków**) and Jewish (eastern Ashkenazic): habitational name from places called Łuków in Siedlce or Katowice voivodeship. **2.** Jewish (eastern Ashkenazic): from villages in Ukraine and Belarus named Lukov and Lukovo.

Lucks (187) **1.** English: patronymic from LUCK 1. **2.** Dutch (**Luckx**): patronymic from LUCAS. **3.** Possibly an altered spelling of German LUCHS.
GIVEN NAMES German 4%. *Kurt, Udo.*

Lucky (703) Probably a variant spelling of LUCKIE.

Lucore (122) English: unexplained. The name was established in MA at an early date. It was also spelled **Lacore**, **Lackor**, **Lecore**, and **Locker**, and may have been an Anglicized spelling of French LACOUR, which was brought to the US via England.

Lucus (273) Altered spelling of LUCAS, found chiefly in TX.

Lucy (1072) Irish, English, and French: variant spelling of LUCEY.

Luczak (498) Polish (**Łuczak**): **1.** derivative of *łuk* 'bow', a metonymic occupational name for a bow maker or an archer. **2.** from a vernacular form of the Latin name LUCAS.
GIVEN NAMES Polish 4%. *Jadwiga* (2), *Dariusz, Ewa, Hieronim, Irena, Mariusz, Wieslaw.*

Luczynski (114) Polish (**Łuczyński**): habitational name for someone from places called Łuczyna or Łuczynów.
GIVEN NAMES Polish 9%. *Boleslaw, Kazimierz, Piotr, Wojciech.*

Ludden (458) Irish: according to Mac-Lysaght, a variant of of LYDON, occurring in counties Galway and Mayo.

Luddy (251) Irish (Cork): variant of LEDDY. It occurs chiefly in CT and MA.

Ludeke (126) German (**Lüdeke**): see LUEDECKE.
GIVEN NAMES French 5%; German 5%. *Fritz, Otto.*

Ludeman (360) Americanized spelling of German **Lüdemann** (see LUDEMANN).

Ludemann (244) German (**Lüdemann**): from a pet form of the personal name *Ludolf* (see LUDOLPH) or LUDWIG.
GIVEN NAMES German 4%. *Eward, Fritz, Klaus.*

Ludens (110) German: patronymic from **Luden**, which is itself apparently a patronymic from the personal name *Lude*, a central and upper German short form of LUDWIG or *Ludolf* (see LUDOLPH).

Luders (123) North German (**Lüders**): see LUEDERS.
GIVEN NAME German 4%. *Hans* (2).

Ludewig (231) German: variant of LUDWIG.

GIVEN NAMES German 9%. *Otto* (3), *Erwin, Guenter, Gunther, Hermann, Joerg.*

Ludgate (128) English: habitational name probably from Ludgate in London, so named from Old English *ludgeat* 'back gate', 'postern', or possibly from Ludgate in Kent or Lidgate in Suffolk, both named from Old English *hlidgeat* 'swing gate'.

Ludin (100) German (also **Lüdin**): from a pet form of the personal name LUDWIG.
GIVEN NAME German 8%. *Reinhard* (2).

Ludington (554) English: habitational name from a place called Lutton in Northamptonshire named in Old English as *Ludingtūn* (see LUTTON) or from Luddington in Lincolnshire, recorded in Domesday Book as *Ludintone*, both named from the Old English personal name *Luda* + *-ing-* denoting association with + *tūn* 'estate', 'settlement'.

Ludka (110) Probably a variant, under Slavic influence, of German LUDKE.

Ludke (190) German (**Lüdke**): variant of LUEDECKE.
GIVEN NAMES German 5%. *Heinz, Kurt, Reinhard.*

Ludlam (419) English: possibly a habitational name from a lost place in Derbyshire or South Yorkshire, where the name is now most frequent.

Ludlow (1412) **1.** English: habitational name from a place in Shropshire, so named from the Old English river name *Hlūde* (from *hlūd* 'loud', 'roaring') referring to the Teme river + *hlāw* 'hill'. See also LAIDLAW. **2.** Dutch: from the personal name LUDOLPH.

Ludlum (461) Altered or variant spelling of LUDLAM.

Ludolph (211) German: from a Germanic personal name composed of the elements *leud, liut* 'famous' + *wulf* 'wolf'.

Ludovici (103) Italian: from a patronymic or plural form of LUDOVICO.
GIVEN NAMES Italian 13%. *Domenic, Giustino, Sabatino.*

Ludovico (113) Italian: from the personal name *Ludovico*, Italian equivalent of German LUDWIG.
GIVEN NAMES Italian 21%. *Dino* (2), *Rocco* (2), *Vito* (2), *Donato, Pasquale.*

Ludtke (363) German (**Lüdtke**): see LUEDTKE.

Ludvigsen (179) Danish and Norwegian: patronymic from the personal name *Ludvig* (see LUDWIG).
GIVEN NAMES Scandinavian 14%. *Thor* (2), *Vidar* (2), *Erik, Lars.*

Ludvigson (160) Variant spelling of Danish and Norwegian LUDVIGSEN or of the Swedish cognate **Ludvigsson**.
GIVEN NAME Scandinavian 5%. *Lars.*

Ludvik (130) Czech (**Ludvík**): from the personal name *Ludvík*, Czech form of LUDWIG.

Ludwick (1324) **1.** Americanized spelling of German LUDWIG, Czech **Ludvík**, Polish **Ludwik**, or cognates in other European languages. **2.** English: habitational name from Ludwick Hall in Bishops Hatfield, Hertfordshire, probably named from the Old English personal name *Luda* + Old English *wīc* 'outlying (dairy) farm'.

Ludwiczak (101) Polish: patronymic from the personal name *Ludwik*, Polish form of German LUDWIG.
GIVEN NAME French 5%. *Henri.*

Ludwig (9134) German and Dutch: from a Germanic personal name composed of the elements *hlod* 'fame' + *wīg* 'war'. This was the name of the founder of the Frankish dynasty, recorded in Latin chronicles as *Chlodovechus* (see LOUIS), and *Ludovicus*, which became German *Ludwig*. This became a hereditary name in the Wittelsbach family, the royal family of Bavaria.
GIVEN NAMES German 4%. *Kurt* (20), *Otto* (7), *Erwin* (6), *Ernst* (5), *Hans* (5), *Fritz* (4), *Klaus* (4), *Franz* (3), *Guenter* (3), *Horst* (3), *Claus* (2), *Erna* (2).

Ludwigsen (108) Dutch and North German: patronymic from the personal name LUDWIG.
GIVEN NAME German 5%. *Kurt.*

Ludwigson (110) Americanized spelling of a Scandinavian, Dutch, or North German patronymic from LUDWIG. Compare Danish and Norwegian LUDVIGSEN, Swedish **Ludvigsson**.

Ludwin (137) German and Polish: derivative, under Slavic influence, of the personal name *Ludwik*, Slavic form of LUDWIG.

Ludy (330) Southwestern German and Swiss (also **Lüdy**): from a pet form of LUDWIG.

Lue (249) Perhaps an altered form of the Dutch and North German name LOO, which is also established in northern France.
GIVEN NAMES French 4%. *Marcel* (2), *Camille.*

Luebbe (312) North German (**Lübbe**): from the personal name *Lübbe* (see LUEBKE 1).

Luebben (108) North German and Dutch: see LUBBEN.
GIVEN NAME German 4%. *Detlef.*

Luebbering (110) North German (**Lübbering**): reduced form of **Lübberding**, patronymic from the personal name *Lübbert* (see LUEBBERT).

Luebbers (318) North German (**Lübbers**): patronymic from the personal name *Lübbert* (see LUEBBERT).
GIVEN NAMES German 4%. *Gerhard* (2), *Hans.*

Luebbert (399) North German (**Lübbert**): from the personal name *Liutbert*, composed of the Germanic elements *liut* 'people' + *berht* 'bright'.

Luebke (1018) North German (**Lübke**): **1.** from a pet form of the personal name

Lübbe (see LUBBEN). **2.** habitational name from Lübbecke in Westphalia.
GIVEN NAMES German 4%. *Erwin* (4), *Kurt* (3), *Fritz, Gerhard, Hermann, Manfred, Otto.*

Luecht (114) **1.** German (**Lücht**): habitational name from Lüchte near Minden. **2.** German (**Lücht**): from Middle Low German *luchte* 'lantern', 'light', hence a metonymic occupational name for someone who made lanterns or tended a light, or possibly a nickname. **3.** Dutch: from a Middle Dutch personal name.

Lueck (1566) **1.** German (**Lück**): habitational name from any of several places so named. **2.** German (**Lück**): from the personal name *Lüdeke* (see LUEDECKE). **3.** Dutch: from the personal name *Lueck*, a vernacular form of LUCAS.
GIVEN NAMES German 5%. *Kurt* (5), *Erna* (2), *Horst* (2), *Otto* (2), *Aloysius, Armin, Dieter, Erwin, Ewald, Fritz, Guenter, Hans.*

Luecke (576) North German (**Lücke**): variant of **Lück** (see LUECK).
GIVEN NAMES German 4%. *Kurt* (3), *Erwin, Gerhard, Hans, Heinrich, Hertha.*

Luedecke (194) North German: from a pet form of the personal name *Ludolf* (see LUDOLPH) or of a short form of another Germanic personal name formed *leud, liut* 'people', 'tribe' (see LUETH) as the first element.
GIVEN NAMES German 9%. *Rainer* (3), *Heinz, Monika, Rudi.*

Luedeke (144) German: variant of LUEDECKE.
GIVEN NAMES German 6%. *Otto* (2), *Gerhard.*

Luedeman (159) German (**Lüdemann**): variant of LUDEMANN.

Lueder (219) Dutch and North German (**Lüder**): from a Germanic personal name (see LUTHER).

Lueders (625) Dutch and North German (**Lüder**): patronymic from LUEDER.
GIVEN NAMES German 4%. *Hans* (2), *Eldor, Erhart, Erna, Kurt, Willi, Wolfram.*

Luedke (704) North German: variant of LUEDTKE.
GIVEN NAMES German 6%. *Otto* (5), *Fritz* (2), *Kurt* (2), *Egon, Erna, Ewald, Gerhard, Willi.*

Luedtke (1568) North German (**Lüdtke**): from a pet form of the personal name *Ludolf* (see LUDOLPH). This is a frequent name in East and West Prussia and the Ruhr.
GIVEN NAMES German 5%. *Kurt* (8), *Erwin* (2), *Hans* (2), *Otto* (2), *Dietrich, Eldor, Gerhardt, Guenter, Manfred, Rainer.*

Luehring (177) North German (**Lühring**): patronymic from the personal name *Lüder* (see LUEDER).

Luehrs (258) North German (**Lührs**): patronymic from a reduced form of the personal name *Lüder* (see LUEDER).

GIVEN NAMES German 7%. *Armin* (2), *Hans, Helmut, Klaus.*

Lueke (143) Dutch and North German (**Lüke**): from a reduced form of the personal name *Lüdeke* (see LUEDECKE). See also LUECK.

Lueken (263) Dutch: from a pet form of the personal name *Ludo, Lode*, or a pet form of a Germanic name formed with the initial element *liut* or *hlod* (e.g. LUDOLPH).
GIVEN NAMES German 8%. *Kurt* (3), *Alois, Behrend, Eckhart, Othmar.*

Lueker (138) Dutch and North German (**Lüker**): from a derivative of the personal name *Lüdeke* (see LUEDECKE).
GIVEN NAMES German 7%. *Erwin* (2), *Kurt.*

Lueking (131) Dutch and North German (**Lüker**): from a derivative of the personal name *Lüdeke* (see LUEDECKE).

Luellen (350) Americanized form of Welsh LLEWELLYN.

Luepke (253) German (**Lüpke**): variant of **Lübke** (see LUEBKE).
GIVEN NAMES German 4%. *Eldor, Erwin, Otto.*

Luer (114) Origin unidentified. In part, possibly a respelling of German LOHR. However, the form **McLuer** is also found, suggesting that it could also be a shortened form of Scottish **Macleur** (see MCCLURE).

Luera (358) Castilianized form of Asturian-Leonese **Lluera**, habitational name from the village of Lluera in Asturies (northern Spain), named from or associated with the Marian name *Nues(tr)a Señora de Lluera* 'Our Lady of the Light'.
GIVEN NAMES Spanish 35%. *Manuel* (8), *Domingo* (3), *Luis* (3), *Lupe* (3), *Alicia* (2), *Andres* (2), *Armando* (2), *Cruz* (2), *Fernando* (2), *Jose* (2), *Jose Luis* (2), *Juan* (2).

Lueras (149) Castilianized form of Asturian-Leonese **Llueres**, topographic name for someone who lived close to a mountain called *Pico de Llueres* in Asturies, northern Spain.
GIVEN NAMES Spanish 12%. *Benito, Carlos, Emiliano, Esperanza, Macario, Manuel, Marina, Matias, Ricardo.*

Luers (277) German (**Lüers**): variant of **Lührs** (see LUEHRS).

Lueth (340) North German (**Lüth**): from a short form of a Germanic personal name formed with *leud, liut* 'people', 'tribe' as the first element.
GIVEN NAMES German 5%. *Juergen* (2), *Fritz, Klaus, Otto.*

Luetjen (109) Dutch and North German (**Lütjen**): see LUTGEN.
GIVEN NAME German 5%. *Kurt* (2).

Luetkemeyer (179) North German (**Lütkemeyer**): distinguishing name either for a tenant farmer (see MEYER) whose name was *Lüdeke* (see LUEDECKE) or for one of diminutive stature (from Middle Low German *luttik* 'small', 'little').

Luevano (502) Hispanic (Mexico): perhaps a misspelling of **Cuévano**, from *cuévano* 'basket'. This surname is not found in Spain.
GIVEN NAMES Spanish 50%. *Jose* (14), *Jesus* (9), *Juan* (7), *Miguel* (5), *Pablo* (5), *Raul* (5), *Armando* (4), *Arnoldo* (4), *Carlos* (4), *Eduardo* (4), *Alfredo* (3), *Fernando* (3).

Luevanos (114) Hispanic: plural form of LUEVANO.
GIVEN NAMES Spanish 60%. *Juan* (5), *Jesus* (4), *Rafael* (3), *Jose* (2), *Luis* (2), *Miguel Angel* (2), *Ramon* (2), *Augustina*, *Blanca*, *Dora Alicia*, *Elia*, *Emilio*.

Luff (627) **1.** English, Scottish, and Irish: variant of LOVE 1–3. **2.** Dutch: from *Luffo*, a pet form a personal name such as LUDOLPH.

Luffman (427) English: from the Middle English personal name *Lefman* (see LEAMAN, LEMON, LOVEMAN).

Lufkin (536) English: from a pet form of LOVE.

Luft (1124) German: **1.** from Middle High German *luft* 'air', of uncertain application, either a topographic name for someone who lived in an exposed place or a nickname for a happy-go-lucky fellow. **2.** variant spelling of **Lufft**, short form of the personal names *Liutfrid* or *Lotfrid*, composed of the elements *liut* 'people', 'tribe' or *hlōd* 'fame', + *frid* 'peace'.
GIVEN NAMES German 4%. *Kurt* (2), *Alois*, *Dieter*, *Guenther*, *Hans*, *Heinrich*, *Johann*, *Johannes*, *Siegfried*, *Ulrich*.

Luftig (104) German: nickname for a carefree fellow, from Middle High German *luft* 'air' (see LUFT) + *-ig*, adjectival ending.
GIVEN NAME German 7%. *Ernst* (2).

Lugar (371) **1.** English: from the Middle English personal name *Leugar*, *Levegar*, Old English *Lēofgār*, composed of the elements *lēof* 'dear' + *gār* 'spear'. **2.** Galician and Spanish: habitational name from any of several places in Galicia called Lugar, from *lugar* 'place', 'village', or a topographic name from this word.

Luger (321) **1.** German: habitational name for someone from Lugau in Saxony and Brandenburg (of Slavic origin, from a word meaning 'swamp'), or from any of several places named with Middle High German *luoc* 'hiding place', 'ambush'. *Lueg* is a common place name in the Tyrol, and the surname is particularly frequent in Bavaria and Austria. **2.** Jewish (Ashkenazic): unexplained.
GIVEN NAMES Jewish 4%. *Chaim*, *Mendel*, *Mordechai*, *Sol*.

Lugg (131) English (Devon): probably from a local vernacular derivative of LUCAS. However, Reaney posits an Old English personal name, *Lugga*, from which this name could be derived.

Luginbill (199) Americanized spelling of German **Luginbühl** (see LUGINBUHL).

Luginbuhl (163) South German (**Luginbühl**): topographic name from Middle High German *luogen* 'to watch or (lie in) wait' + *bühel* 'hillock'.

Lugo (3716) Galician and Spanish: habitational name from Lugo, a city in Galicia. This was a Roman settlement under the name of *Lucus Augusti* 'grove or wood of Augustus', but that may have been no more than an adaptation of an earlier name derived from that of the Celtic god *Lugos*.
GIVEN NAMES Spanish 45%. *Jose* (104), *Carlos* (50), *Juan* (39), *Manuel* (36), *Luis* (33), *Miguel* (27), *Jesus* (21), *Jorge* (19), *Francisco* (17), *Pedro* (17), *Rafael* (17), *Julio* (16).

Luh (111) German: from a short form of the personal name *Ludolf* (see LUDOLPH).

Luhman (345) Altered spelling of German LUHMANN.

Luhmann (198) **1.** North German: topographic name for someone who lived by the Luhe river, south of Hamburg. **2.** German (**Lühmann**): reduced form of **Lüdemann** (see LUDEMANN).
GIVEN NAMES German 11%. *Kurt* (3), *Ewald*, *Heinz*, *Lutz*, *Otto*.

Luhn (263) North German: topographic name for someone who lived by the Luhn river in East Friesland, or possibly a habitational name from Luhnau near Schleswig.

Luhr (160) North German (**Lühr**): reduced form of **Lüder** (see LUEDER).
GIVEN NAMES German 4%. *Alois*, *Uwe*.

Luhring (160) North German (**Lühring**): patronymic from **Lühr** (see LUHR).
GIVEN NAMES German 4%. *Johannes*, *Kurt*.

Luhrs (346) North German (**Lührs**): patronymic from **Lühr** (see LUHR).
GIVEN NAMES German 8%. *Otto* (3), *Gunther* (2), *Bernd*, *Kurt*.

Luhrsen (109) North German (**Lührsen**): patronymic from **Lühr** (see LUHR).

Lui (1321) **1.** Chinese 呂: variant of LU 1. **2.** Chinese 雷: variant of LEI 1. **3.** Hawaiian: unexplained. **4.** Italian: unexplained.
GIVEN NAMES Chinese 30%. *Chun* (6), *Kam* (6), *Yau* (6), *Chi* (4), *Kin* (4), *Ming* (4), *Shui* (4), *Wah* (4), *Wai* (4), *Mei* (3), *Cheuk* (2), *Chi Man* (2), *Chung* (3), *Yiu* (3), *Nam* (2), *Pak* (2), *Cho*, *Kwok Fai*, *Yeung*, *You*, *Yuet*.

Luick (182) Dutch: variant of LUECK.

Luikart (234) Possibly an altered spelling of German LUCKHARDT. It occurs chiefly in OH and WV.

Luis (1004) Portuguese (**Luís**) and Spanish: from the personal name *Luís* or *Luis*, from French LOUIS.
GIVEN NAMES Spanish 37%; Portuguese 13%. *Jose* (38), *Manuel* (21), *Mario* (9), *Luis* (8), *Carlos* (6), *Miguel* (6), *Fernando* (5), *Humberto* (5), *Alberto* (4), *Armando* (4), *Jorge* (4), *Juan* (4); *Joao* (3), *Duarte* (3), *Joaquim*, *Vasco*, *Wenceslao*.

Luisi (438) Italian: reduced form of ALOISI.
GIVEN NAMES Italian 15%. *Angelo* (5), *Enrico* (2), *Vito* (2), *Carlo*, *Carmine*, *Gennaro*, *Giuseppe*, *Italo*, *Luciano*, *Michelangelo*, *Nunzie*, *Rocco*.

Luiz (352) Portuguese and Spanish: variant spelling of LUIS.
GIVEN NAMES Spanish 14%; Portuguese 8%. *Manuel* (14), *Jose* (4), *Alvaro* (2), *Francisco* (2), *Carlos*, *Carolina*, *Eleazar*, *Florencio*, *Francisca*, *Jacinto*, *Juan*, *Luciana*; *Joaquim*.

Lujan (3095) Spanish (**Luján**): habitational name from Luján in Huesca province.
GIVEN NAMES Spanish 33%. *Jose* (46), *Manuel* (37), *Carlos* (22), *Juan* (19), *Jesus* (18), *Ruben* (17), *Luis* (14), *Ramon* (13), *Armando* (12), *Arturo* (10), *Javier* (9), *Mario* (9).

Lujano (135) Spanish: variant of **Luján** (see LUJAN).
GIVEN NAMES Spanish 49%. *Jose* (4), *Guadalupe* (3), *Armando* (2), *Isidro* (2), *Jose Luis* (2), *Manuel* (2), *Maria Guadalupe* (2), *Alonso*, *Ambrosio*, *Angel*, *Bonifacio*, *Conception*; *Antonio*, *Gino*, *Heriberto*, *Saturnina*.

Luk (410) **1.** Dutch: from a vernacular form of the personal name LUCAS. **2.** Chinese 陆: Cantonese variant of LU 3. **3.** Chinese 鹿: Cantonese variant of LU 6.
GIVEN NAMES Chinese 28%. *Kin* (4), *Choi* (3), *Siu* (3), *Wing* (3), *Cheung* (2), *Hing* (2), *Kwok* (2), *Chan*, *Chi*, *Chi Chung*, *Chiu*, *Chun Wah*.

Luka (209) **1.** Dutch: from a vernacular form of the personal name LUCAS. **2.** Czech, Polish (**Łuka**), and Hungarian: from a short form of Czech *Lukáš*, Polish *Łukasz*, Hungarian *Lukács*, vernacular forms of LUCAS.

Lukac (147) **1.** Slovenian, Serbian and Croatian (**Lukač**): from an old form or pet form of the personal name *Luka* (see LUCAS). **2.** Americanized spelling of Hungarian **Lukács** (see LUKACS).
GIVEN NAMES South Slavic 8%. *Djordje*, *Milan*, *Milos*, *Pavel*, *Zeljko*.

Lukach (217) Americanized spelling of Hungarian **Lukács** (see LUKACS) or Serbian, Croatian, and Slovenian **Lukač** (see LUKAC).

Lukacs (381) Hungarian (**Lukács**): from the personal name *Lukács*, Hungarian form of LUCAS. Where this name is borne by Jews, it is an adoption of the Hungarian name.
GIVEN NAMES Hungarian 21%. *Laszlo* (7), *Zoltan* (3), *Bela* (2), *Csaba* (2), *Jozsef* (2), *Andras*, *Antal*, *Barna*, *Csilla*, *Endre*, *Ferenc*, *Gabor*.

Lukas (1657) German, Dutch, Lithuanian, Czech and Slovak (**Lukáš**), etc.: from the personal name *Lukas* (see LUCAS).
GIVEN NAMES German 4%. *Kurt* (3), *Klaus* (2), *Erwin*, *Hedwig*, *Heinz*, *Helmut*, *Horst*, *Juergen*, *Jurgen*, *Markus*, *Monika*, *Ralf*.

Lukasiewicz (274) Polish (**Łukasiewicz**): patronymic from the personal name *Łukasz* (see LUCAS).

GIVEN NAMES Polish 6%. *Zofia* (2), *Ewa, Mieczyslaw, Ryszard, Zygmund.*

Lukasik (542) Polish (**Łukasik**) and Czech (**Lukašík**): from a pet form of *Łukasz* or *Lukáš*, Polish and Czech forms respectively of LUCAS.

GIVEN NAMES Polish 8%. *Janusz* (2), *Tomasz* (2), *Boleslaw, Czeslaw, Eugeniusz, Jaroslaw, Krystyna, Krzysztof, Leslaw, Tadeusz, Thadeus.*

Lukaszewicz (136) Polish (**Łukaszewicz**): patronymic from the personal name *Łukasz* (see LUCAS).

GIVEN NAMES Polish 21%. *Danuta, Grzegorz, Jadwiga, Lukasz, Miroslawa, Ryszard, Tadeusz, Waclaw, Wladyslaw, Zbigniew, Zdzislaw.*

Lukaszewski (259) Polish (**Łukaszewski**): habitational name for someone from Łukaszew or Łukaszewo, so named from the personal name *Łukasz* (see LUCAS).

GIVEN NAMES Polish 7%. *Casimir, Krystyna, Krzysztof, Mariusz, Witold.*

Luke (5873) **1.** English: from a derivative of LUCAS. This was (and is) the common vernacular form of the name, being the one by which the author of the fourth Gospel is known in English. **2.** English: habitational name for someone from Liège in Belgium (Dutch *Luik*). **3.** North German (**Lüke**): from a short form of *Lüdeke*; LUEDECKE.

Lukefahr (113) German: of uncertain origin.

FOREBEARS The Lukefahrs are concentrated in Missouri. Henry Lukefahr was born in Germany in 1816; several bearers of the name came to the U.S. in the 19th century.

Lukehart (302) Americanized form of German LUCKHARDT.

Luken (546) Dutch: variant of LUEKEN.

Lukenbill (174) Americanized spelling of German **Luginbühl** (see LUGINBUHL).

Lukens (1381) Altered spelling of Dutch **Luikens** (see LUEKEN), or German **Lückens**, a patronymic from the personal name *Lüdeke* (see LUEDECKE).

Luker (1608) English: **1.** habitational name from Lucker in Northumberland, probably named from Old English *luh* 'pool' + Old Norse *kjarr* 'marsh'. **2.** occupational name for someone who had to watch or look after something, typically a watchman or a keeper of animals, Middle English *lokere* (a derivative of Middle English *loke(n), luke(n)* 'to look', Old English *lōcian*).

Lukes (683) Czech (**Lukeš**): from the personal name *Lukáš*, Czech form of LUCAS.

Luketic (104) Croatian and Serbian (**Luketić**): patronymic from the personal name *Luketa*, a derivative of *Luka* (see LUCAS).

GIVEN NAMES South Slavic 9%; German 5%. *Velimir* (2), *Darko, Davor.*

Lukey (102) English (Devon and Cornwall): unexplained; most probably a pet form of LUKE. See also LEAKEY.

Lukin (179) **1.** Russian (**Lukín**): patronymic from the personal name *Luká*, a vernacular form of LUCAS. **2.** Jewish (from Belarus): habitational name for someone from Luki or Luka, villages now in Belarus. **3.** Serbian and Croatian: from the personal name *Lukin*.

GIVEN NAMES Russian 8%; Jewish 4%. *Aleksandr, Gennady, Iosif, Kirill, Lyubov, Sergey, Vladimir; Hyman.*

Lukins (183) **1.** English: variant of LUF-KIN. **2.** Latvian (**Lūkins**): patronymic from the Slavic personal name *Luk* (see LUKE, LUCAS).

GIVEN NAME French 4%. *Andre* (2).

Lukomski (128) Polish (**Łukomski**): habitational name for someone from a place called Łukomie in Płock voivodeship.

GIVEN NAMES Polish 9%. *Dariusz, Slawomir, Tomasz, Zbigniew.*

Lukowski (435) Polish (**Łukowski**): habitational name for someone from places called Łuków, Łukowa, or Łukowe, named with the personal name *Łukasz* (see LUCAS).

Luks (159) **1.** Dutch: patronymic from LUK. **2.** Czech: from a reduced form of the personal name *Lukáš*, Czech equivalent of LUCAS. **3.** Jewish (eastern Ashkenazic): ornamental name from German *Luchs* 'lynx'.

GIVEN NAMES German 4%; Jewish 4%. *Erna; Zalman.*

Lulay (146) German: nickname for a lazy or idle man, from Dutch *luilak* 'shepherd', a shepherd's life being considered an easy one.

Lulich (117) Serbian and Croatian (**Lulić**): probably a patronymic from the personal name *Lule*, a pet form of *Luka* (see LUCAS). It could also be from *lula* 'pipe', a word of Turkish origin.

Lull (477) **1.** English: from an Old English personal name, *Lulla*. **2.** German (**Lüll**): from a short form of any of the Germanic personal names formed with *liut-* 'people' as the first element. **3.** Catalan (also **Llull**): from the personal name *Lullus*, probably of Germanic origin.

Lullo (134) Italian: variant of *Lollo* (see LOLLI).

GIVEN NAMES Italian 15%. *Macario* (2), *Alina, Angelo, Emilio, Vito.*

Lum (2609) **1.** English: habitational name from places in Lancashire and West Yorkshire called Lumb, both apparently originally named with Old English *lum(m)* 'pool'. The word is not independently attested, but appears also in LOMAX and LUMLEY, and may be reflected in the dialect term *lum* denoting a well for collecting water in a mine. In some instances the name may be topographical for someone who lived by a pool, Middle English *lum(m)*. **2.** English: variant of LAMB. **3.** Chinese 林: variant of LIN 1. **4.** Chinese 蓝: possibly a variant of LAN.

Luma (100) Origin unidentified.

GIVEN NAMES French 7%. *Josephe, Solange.*

Lumadue (168) Americanized form of the French Huguenot surname LHOMMEDIEU.

GIVEN NAMES French 4%. *Amie, Verdun.*

Luman (572) **1.** Altered spelling of German LUHMANN or LOHMANN. **2.** English: unexplained.

Lumb (253) English: variant spelling of LUM.

Lumbard (174) English: variant spelling of LOMBARD.

Lumbert (279) Variant of LAMBERT.

Lumbra (190) Altered spelling of French Canadian LAMBERT.

Lumetta (110) Italian: possibly from a pet form of the Marian name **Lume**, from *La Madonna del Lume* 'Our Lady of the Lamp' (from *lume* 'light', 'lamp').

GIVEN NAMES Italian 20%. *Sal* (4), *Salvatore* (3), *Vito* (2).

Lumia (192) Italian (Sicily): from Sicilian *lumia* 'lemon', 'lemon tree', presumably a metonymic occupational name for a grower or seller of lemons, or possibly a topographic name.

GIVEN NAMES Italian 8%. *Gaetano, Salvatore, Santo.*

Lumley (1071) Northern English: habitational name from Lumley, a place in County Durham, so named from Old English *lum(m)* 'pool' (see LUM 1) + *lēah* 'woodland clearing'.

Lumm (165) German: of uncertain origin; possibly a nickname for a weak or listless person from the Hessian dialect word *lumm* 'soft', 'slack', 'limp'.

Lummis (163) English: variant of LOOMIS.

Lummus (538) English: variant spelling of LOOMIS.

Lumpkin (2893) English: from a pet form of LAMB 1 and 2.

Lumpkins (665) English: patronymic from LUMPKIN.

Lumpp (122) German and French (Alsace-Lorraine): nickname for a poor person clad in ragged clothes, from German *Lumpen* 'rags'.

Lumsden (1038) Scottish: habitational name from a place in the parish of Coldingham, Berwickshire. The first element of the place name is of uncertain origin, apparently the genitive case of a personal name; the second is probably Old English *denu* 'valley'.

Luna (9722) **1.** Spanish: habitational name from places called Luna in Zaragoza, Araba, and Lleón provinces. **2.** Jewish (Sephardic): from the female personal name *Luna* (Spanish *luna* 'moon').

GIVEN NAMES Spanish 43%. *Jose* (196), *Juan* (127), *Manuel* (83), *Luis* (66), *Carlos* (65), *Jesus* (58), *Raul* (51), *Jorge* (50), *Pedro* (50), *Miguel* (48), *Ruben* (43), *Mario* (38).

Lunceford (777) Variant of the English surname LUNSFORD.

Lund (10638) Scandinavian, German, and English: topographic name for someone who lived by a grove, Old Norse *lundr*; the word was adopted into northern dialects of Middle English and also into Anglo-Norman French. There are a number of places in England named with this word, as for example Lund in Lancashire, East Yorkshire, and North Yorkshire, Lunt in Merseyside, and Lound in Lincolnshire, Nottinghamshire, and Suffolk, and the surname may derive from any of these. The Swedish surname is probably more usually ornamental. When surnames became obligatory in Sweden in the 19th century, this was one of the most popular among the many terms denoting features of the natural landscape which were adopted as surnames, usually compounded with some other such term.
GIVEN NAMES Scandinavian 5%. *Erik* (26), *Anders* (4), *Lars* (4), *Nils* (4), *Thor* (4), *Iver* (3), *Nels* (3), *Obert* (3), *Berger* (2), *Einer* (2), *Knute* (2), *Morten* (2).

Lundahl (354) Swedish: ornamental name composed of the elements *lund* 'grove' + *dahl*, an ornamental spelling of *dal* 'valley'.

Lunday (297) Variant spelling of Scottish and northern Irish LUNDY. This name is found chiefly in TX.
GIVEN NAMES German 4%. *Otto* (2), *Georg*.

Lundberg (3527) Swedish: ornamental name composed of the elements *lund* 'grove' + *berg* 'mountain', 'hill'.
GIVEN NAMES Scandinavian 6%. *Erik* (6), *Nils* (4), *Lennart* (3), *Anders* (2), *Bjorn* (2), *Britt* (2), *Knut* (2), *Algot*, *Bernt*, *Fredrik*, *Helmer*, *Holger*.

Lundblad (368) Swedish: ornamental name composed of the elements *lund* 'grove' + *blad* 'leaf'.
GIVEN NAMES Scandinavian 4%; German 4%. *Nels* (2); *Kurt* (3), *Frieda*.

Lundborg (180) Swedish: ornamental name composed of the elements *lund* 'grove' + *borg* 'castle'.
GIVEN NAMES Scandinavian 6%. *Erik* (2), *Bernt*, *Walfrid*.

Lunde (1286) Norwegian: habitational name from any of numerous (about 70) farmsteads named Lunde, from either the plural or the dative singular of Old Norse *lundr* 'grove'.
GIVEN NAMES Scandinavian 10%. *Erik* (6), *Nels* (2), *Anders*, *Bjorn*, *Einer*, *Hedvig*, *Iver*, *Morten*, *Ove*, *Tor*.

Lundeen (1468) Swedish: ornamental name composed of the elements *lund* 'grove' + the adjectival suffix *-een*, from Latin *-enius*.

Lundell (741) Swedish: ornamental name from *lund* 'grove' + the common suffix *-ell*, taken from the Latin adjectival ending *-elius*.

GIVEN NAMES Scandinavian 5%. *Anders*, *Erik*, *Holger*, *Thora*.

Lunden (253) **1.** Swedish (**Lundén**): variant of LUNDEEN. **2.** Norwegian: habitational name from any of numerous farmsteads, so named from the definite singular form of *lund* 'grove'. **3.** German: habitational name from Lunden in Holstein.
GIVEN NAME Scandinavian 5%. *Anders*.

Lunder (159) Norwegian: habitational name from any of about 10 farmsteads named Lunder, from the indefinite plural form of *lund* 'grove'.
GIVEN NAME Scandinavian 6%. *Bjorn*.

Lundergan (107) Irish: Anglicized form of Gaelic Ó Longargáin (see LONERGAN).

Lundgren (3180) Swedish: ornamental name composed of the elements *lund* 'grove' + *gren* 'branch'.
GIVEN NAMES Scandinavian 6%. *Erik* (5), *Lars* (3), *Thor* (3), *Knute* (2), *Nils* (2), *Per* (2), *Sten* (2), *Algot*, *Anders*, *Bernt*, *Einer*, *Evald*.

Lundholm (229) Swedish: ornamental name composed of the elements *lund* 'grove' + *holm* 'island'.
GIVEN NAMES Scandinavian 4%. *Kerstin*, *Ove*.

Lundie (161) **1.** Scottish and northern Irish: variant spelling of LUNDY. **2.** Possibly an Americanized form of LUNDE.
GIVEN NAME French 4%. *Armand*.

Lundin (1433) Swedish: ornamental name from *lund* 'grove' + the adjectival suffix *-in*, from Latin *-in(i)us*.
GIVEN NAMES Scandinavian 8%. *Erik* (5), *Lars* (4), *Nels* (2), *Erland*, *Holger*, *Lennart*, *Mats*, *Nils*.

Lundmark (273) Swedish: ornamental name composed of the elements *lund* 'grove' + *mark* 'land'.
GIVEN NAME Scandinavian 8%. *Erik* (2).

Lundon (100) English: variant spelling of LONDON.

Lundquist (3108) Swedish: ornamental name composed of the elements *lund* 'grove' + *quist*, an old or ornamental spelling of *kvist* 'twig'.
GIVEN NAMES Scandinavian 5%. *Erik* (9), *Nils* (2), *Sven* (2), *Alf*, *Gunhild*, *Gunnel*, *Holger*, *Lars*, *Maren*, *Sten*, *Thor*.

Lundrigan (143) Irish: Anglicized form of Gaelic Ó Longargáin (see LONERGAN).

Lundry (103) Americanized spelling of French LANDRY.

Lundstedt (136) Swedish: ornamental name composed of the elements *lund* 'grove' + *stedt* 'place', 'homestead' (from German).
GIVEN NAMES Scandinavian 13%. *Erik*, *Sven*.

Lundsten (152) Swedish: ornamental name composed of the elements *lund* 'grove' + *sten* 'stone'.
GIVEN NAME Scandinavian 6%. *Nels*.

Lundstrom (1102) Swedish (**Lundström**): ornamental name composed of the elements *lund* 'grove' + *ström* 'river'.

GIVEN NAMES Scandinavian 6%. *Lennart* (3), *Lars* (2), *Arlis*, *Bertel*, *Elof*, *Johan*, *Ove*.

Lundt (167) German: variant of LUND.

Lundvall (147) Swedish: ornamental name composed of the elements *lund* 'grove' + *vall* 'bank' or 'pasture'.

Lundwall (123) Altered spelling of LUNDVALL.

Lundy (4870) **1.** Scottish and northern Irish: habitational name from any of several places called Lundie, for example one near Doune in Perthshire. **2.** Irish: according to MacLysaght, from Norman *de la Lounde*, a name recorded in medieval documents in counties Tipperary and Kilkenny.

Luneau (170) French: habitational name from Luneau in Allier.
GIVEN NAMES French 7%. *Andre*, *Armand*, *Emilien*, *Patrice*.

Lunetta (195) Italian: from the personal name *Lunetta*, a pet form of *luna* 'moon'.
GIVEN NAMES Italian 9%. *Biaggio* (2), *Angelo*, *Carmine*.

Lung (817) **1.** English: variant of LONG 1. **2.** German and French (Alsace–Lorraine): from Middle High German *lunge* 'lung', presumably applied as a nickname. **3.** Chinese 龙: variant of LONG 3. **4.** Chinese 隆: variant of LONG 4.

Lunger (403) Jewish (Ashkenazic): from German *Lunge* 'lungs' + the agent suffix *-er*, most likely one of the surnames selected at random from vocabulary words by government officials at the time when surnames became compulsory.
GIVEN NAMES Jewish 5%. *Chaim*, *Chaya*, *Cheskel*, *Feige*, *Mordechai*, *Shaya*, *Yaakov*, *Yacov*, *Yechezkel*, *Yechiel*.

Lungren (177) Variant of Swedish LUNDGREN.
GIVEN NAMES German 4%. *Kurt*, *Otto*.

Luning (145) North German (**Lüning**): nickname from Middle Low German *lunink* 'sparrow'.

Lunn (1590) English, Norwegian, and Danish: variant of LUND.

Lunney (338) Irish (Ulster): reduced Anglicized form of Gaelic Ó Luinigh. Compare LOONEY.
GIVEN NAMES Irish 4%. *Colm*, *Padraic*.

Lunning (149) **1.** Americanized form of German LUNING. **2.** Variant of LANNING.

Lunny (162) Irish: variant of LUNNEY.

Lunsford (5723) English: habitational name, probably from Lundsford in East Sussex, so named from an Old English personal name *Lundrǣd* + Old English *ford* 'ford', or possibly from Lunsford in Kent, although this was earlier called *Lullesworthe* (from the Old English personal name *Lull* + *worð* 'enclosure'); it is not certain whether the development to Lunsford took place early enough to have produced the surname.

Lunt (1140) Northern English: topographic name for someone who lived by a grove, from Old Norse *lundr* (see LUND).

Luntz (128) German: variant of LUNZ.

Lunz (219) German: **1.** nickname for a careless or slovenly person, from Middle High German *lunzen* 'to doze'. **2.** habitational name from Lunz in Tyrol.

Lunzer (109) German (**Lünzer**): habitational name for someone from Lunz in Tyrol or from Lünzen near Soltau, Lower Saxony.

Luo (922) Chinese: **1.** Chinese 罗: from the name of the state of Luo during the Zhou dynasty (1122–221 BC). This was granted to a descendant of Zhu Rong, a son of Zhuan Xu, legendary emperor of the 26th century BC. Subsequently, his descendants adopted the state name as their surname. **2.** Chinese 骆: from the personal name of Jiang Luo, a son of the grand duke of the state of Qi during the Spring and Autumn period (722–481 BC). His descendants adopted his given name, Luo, as their surname. This character also means 'camel'.
GIVEN NAMES Chinese 66%. *Wei* (12), *Jian* (10), *Yi* (10), *Ping* (6), *Yong* (6), *Zhen* (6), *Feng* (5), *Hong* (5), *Ming* (5), *Jin* (4), *Bin* (3), *Chen* (3), *Hai* (2), *Lan* (2), *Min* (2), *Huan, Hung, Shen, Tian.*

Luoma (786) Finnish: topographic name from *luomi* 'creek', 'small river'. Common in central-western Finland.
GIVEN NAMES Finnish 6%; Scandinavian 4%. *Reino* (4), *Toivo* (4), *Arvo* (2), *Eino* (2), *Onni* (2), *Aarne, Aatos, Aune, Lempi, Veikko, Weikko; Nels.*

Luong (1742) Vietnamese: unexplained.
GIVEN NAMES Vietnamese 73%. *Thanh* (24), *Vinh* (20), *Cuong* (17), *Hung* (17), *Ha* (16), *Hoa* (16), *Muoi* (16), *Dung* (15), *Quang* (15), *Minh* (14), *Tu* (12), *Tan* (11), *Chi* (8), *Phong* (7), *Hong* (6), *Dong* (4), *Ho* (3), *Chan* (2), *Chu* (2), *Han* (2), *Hon* (2), *Man* (2), *Sang* (2), *Tong* (2), *Yee* (2); *Nam* (6), *Sieu* (4), *Tuong* (4), *Tam* (3), *Sinh* (2), *Thai* (2), *Chong, Manh, Pom, Sa, Tay.*

Luongo (1021) Italian: Neapolitan form of LONGO.
GIVEN NAMES Italian 19%. *Angelo* (11), *Vito* (7), *Antonio* (5), *Rocco* (5), *Salvatore* (5), *Carmine* (4), *Rino* (3), *Cosmo* (2), *Giuseppe* (2), *Nicola* (2), *Pasquale* (2), *Carmela.*

Lupa (150) Polish: **1.** unflattering nickname from a Polish dialect word, *lupa* 'foolish man', 'blockhead'. **2.** (**Łupa**) nickname from Polish *łupa* 'peel'.
GIVEN NAMES Polish 10%. *Andrzej* (2), *Andrzey, Kazimierz, Michalina, Waclaw.*

Lupardus (109) Dutch or North German: humanistic name from a Latinized form of Dutch **Luypaert** or Low German **lupart** 'leopard', probably a habitational name for someone who lived at a house bearing the sign of a leopard.

Luper (639) Altered spelling of Dutch LOOPER.

Lupercio (159) Spanish and Portuguese (**Lupércio**): from the personal name *Lupercio* (Latin *Lupercius*), a derivative of *lupus* 'wolf'.
GIVEN NAMES Spanish 53%. *Francisco* (4), *Jose* (4), *Jesus* (3), *Ramon* (3), *Ana* (2), *Carlos* (2), *Gerardo* (2), *Javier* (2), *Pedro* (2), *Roberto* (2), *Trini* (2), *Adolfo; Antonio.*

Lupfer (152) German: habitational name from Lupfen, a lost place near Tuttlingen.

Lupi (254) Italian: patronymic or plural form of the personal name LUPO.
GIVEN NAMES Italian 11%; French 4%. *Massimo* (2), *Aldo, Amedeo, Antonio, Carmine, Elio, Grazia, Nino, Romeo; Armand* (2), *Antoine.*

Lupia (150) Italian: probably a habitational name from a place named Lupia, possibly the locality so named in Scigliano in Cosenza province. *Louppiai* is the Greek name for Lecce, and this may also be the source of the surname.
GIVEN NAMES Italian 10%. *Angelo, Fiorino, Gino, Serafino.*

Lupica (230) Italian: nickname from a dialect form of *upupa* 'bird', with the article *l'*.
GIVEN NAMES Italian 15%. *Salvatore* (5), *Angelo, Biagio, Domenico, Gaetano, Saverio.*

Lupien (321) French: from the personal name *Loupien*.
FOREBEARS The Lupien family of Canada trace their origin to Nicolas Barron-Lupien, whose father's first name was Loupien. The name was taken from Champagne, France, to Montreal before 1676.
GIVEN NAMES French 11%. *Armand* (2), *Gilles* (2), *Jacques* (2), *Gillis, Henri, Marcel, Pierre, Yves.*

Lupinacci (242) Italian: from a derivative of the personal name LUPO.
GIVEN NAMES Italian 10%. *Antonio, Carmine, Geno, Luigi, Romeo, Silvio.*

Lupinski (187) Polish (**Łupiński**): habitational name for someone from Łupin in Siedlce voivodeship.
GIVEN NAMES Polish 17%. *Andrzej* (2), *Jerzy* (2), *Bogdan, Czeslaw, Eugeniusz, Ireneusz, Kazimierz, Miroslaw, Stanislaw.*

Lupkes (111) German: derivative of the personal name *Lüpke*, variant of LUEBKE.

Luplow (106) German: habitational name from a place called Luplow near Malchin in Mecklenburg.

Lupo (1954) Italian: from the personal name *Lupo*, in part a continuation of the Latin personal name *Lupus* 'wolf', and in part a medieval revival under the influence of Germanic personal names formed with *wulf* 'wolf'. In some cases the surname may derive from a nickname for a violent, predatory person, from the vocabulary word *lupo* 'wolf'.
GIVEN NAMES Italian 12%. *Salvatore* (13), *Angelo* (7), *Giuseppe* (5), *Sal* (5), *Gasper* (4), *Carmine* (3), *Antonio* (2), *Benedetto* (2), *Pietro* (2), *Rocco* (2), *Santo* (2), *Saverio* (2).

Lupold (136) Possibly an altered spelling of German **Luppold**, a variant of LEOPOLD.

Lupoli (137) Italian (**Lùpoli**): patronymic from a pet form of LUPO.
GIVEN NAMES Italian 17%. *Domenic* (3), *Salvatore* (2), *Angelo, Antonio, Giovanna, Livio, Nicola.*

Luppino (320) Italian: from a pet form of *Luppo*, a northern variant of LUPO.
GIVEN NAMES Italian 33%. *Antonio* (6), *Rocco* (6), *Angelo* (4), *Vito* (4), *Carmelo* (3), *Cosimo* (2), *Domenic* (2), *Emilio* (2), *Matteo* (2), *Sal* (2), *Caterina, Fortunato, Francesco, Giovanni, Mario, Ninfa, Rosario.*

Luptak (140) Polish and Slovak (**L'upták**): variant of LIPTAK.
GIVEN NAME French 5%. *Andre.*

Lupton (1144) English: habitational name from a place in Cumbria (Westmorland). The place name is recorded in Domesday Book as *Lupetun*, and probably derives from an Old English personal name *Hluppa* (of uncertain origin) + Old English *tūn* 'enclosure', 'settlement'.
FOREBEARS The name was brought to America by John Lupton, who sailed from Gravesend, England, on the *Primrose* in 1635, and is recorded in VA three years later. On 24 October 1635 Davie Lupton set off on the *Constance* bound for VA, but there is no record of his arrival in the New World. A Christopher Lupton is recorded in Suffolk Co., Long Island, NY, *c*.1635, and a large number of Luptons in NC descend from him. An American family of the name settled in the area of Winchester, VA, in the mid18th century; they can be traced back to Martin Lupton, who was married in 1630 in the parish of Rothwell, Yorkshire, England.

Lupu (141) **1.** Romanian: nickname from *lupu* 'wolf', from Latin *lupus*. **2.** Jewish (from Romania): from Romanian *lupu* 'wolf', a translation of the personal name WOLF.
GIVEN NAMES Romanian 24%. *Cornel* (2), *Florin* (2), *Mihai* (2), *Petru* (2), *Traian* (2), *Viorel* (2), *Alejandro, Corina, Costica, Elena, Ilie.*

Luque (299) Spanish: habitational name from Luque in Córdoba.
GIVEN NAMES Spanish 36%. *Jose* (5), *Carlos* (4), *Mario* (4), *Enrique* (3), *Luis* (3), *Celestino* (2), *Ernesto* (2), *Francisco* (2), *Hernando* (2), *Jesus* (2), *Jorge* (2), *Pedro* (2).

Luquette (188) **1.** Canadian form of French **Luquet**, from a pet form of the personal name LUC 1. **2.** Variant of French **Loquet**, a metonymic occupational name for a locksmith.
GIVEN NAMES French 11%. *Irby* (2), *Alphe, Clovis, Emile, Onezime, Raywood.*

Lura (131) Norwegian: habitational name from a farmstead in Rogaland named Lura, from Old Norse *Lúðrar*, from the plural of *lúðr* 'trough', referring to a bay or inlet.

Luria (244) Jewish: variant of LORIA.
GIVEN NAMES Jewish 7%. *Chaim, Emanuel, Mendel, Moshe, Schmuel, Yitzchock.*

Lurie (1157) **1.** Scottish: variant of LOWRIE. **2.** Jewish (eastern Ashkenazic): variant of LORIA.
GIVEN NAMES Jewish 4%. *Leib* (2), *Ranan* (2), *Ari, Doron, Isadore, Meyer, Mordecai, Shmuel, Sol, Vered, Yocheved.*

Lurvey (274) Anglicized spelling (in the 17th century) of German or Jewish LOEWE.
FOREBEARS Peter Lurvy, the immigrant ancestor of this family, was in Ipswich, MA, by 1679.

Lurz (181) German: **1.** nickname for a clumsy person, from Middle High German *lurz* 'left-handed', 'clumsy'. **2.** (**lürz**) unflattering nickname from *Lürze* 'cheat', 'swindler'.

Lusardi (284) Italian: according to Caracausi this is a patronymic from a Genoese equivalent of **Luxardo**, linked with the Sardinian personal name *Luxorio*, *Lussorio*, which was borne by a soldier martyred during the persecution of Diocletian; San Lussorio is the patron of numerous places in the provinces of Nuoro and Oristano.
GIVEN NAMES Italian 11%. *Remo* (2), *Alessandro, Angelo, Annamaria, Guido, Luca, Luigi, Primo, Vincent Joseph.*

Lusby (859) English: habitational name from Lusby in Lincolnshire, named in Old Norse as 'Lútr's farmstead or settlement', from the Old Norse personal name *Lútr* (also a nickname meaning 'stooping') + *býr* 'farmstead', 'settlement'.

Lusch (186) German (**Lüsch**): habitational name from any of several places called Lüsche, for example near Celle and near Cloppenburg, or a topographic name from Middle High German *liesche* 'reeds'.

Luschen (103) North German (**Lüschen**): from a derivative of **Lüsch** (see LUSCH).

Luscher (196) German (**Lüscher**): habitational name for someone from any of the various places called Lüsche (see LUSCH), or topographic name for someone living among reeds.
GIVEN NAMES German 6%. *Erna, Erwin, Rudie, Ulrich.*

Lusco (124) **1.** Italian (Sicilian): nickname from Sicilian *luscu* 'myopic', 'short-sighted'. **2.** Possibly also Spanish or Portuguese: nickname from *lusco* 'cross-eyed', 'squinting'.
GIVEN NAMES Italian 11%; Spanish 4%. *Santo* (5), *Santi; Salvador* (5).

Luscomb (105) English (Devon): variant spelling of LUSCOMBE.

Luscombe (242) English (Devon): habitational name from any of the five villages of this name in Devon or from Loscombe in Powerstock, Dorset, all probably named from Old English *hlōse* 'pigsty' + *cumb*

'valley' (see COOMBE).

Luse (622) Probably an altered or variant spelling of LUCE.

Lush (497) **1.** English (Hampshire, Dorset, and Wiltshire): unexplained. According to MacLysaght this name, which is also found in Ireland, is akin to USHER (compare LUSHER). **2.** Probably an Americanized spelling of German **Lüsch** (see LUSCH).

Lushbaugh (118) Americanized form of German **Lüschbach**, a habitational name from a place so called, named with Middle Low German *lüsch* 'reed' (Middle High German *liesche*) + *bach* 'creek', 'stream'.

Lusher (475) **1.** English, Scottish, and Irish: variant of USHER 1, with the Old French definite article prefixed. **2.** Translation of French LUSSIER, **L'Huissier** with the French definite article retained. Compare LAFONTAINE. **3.** Americanized spelling of German **Lüscher** (see LUSCHER).

Lusignan (200) French: habitational name from a place near Poitiers.
FOREBEARS A De Lusignon from La Rochelle, France, was in Champlain, Quebec, by 1689. A family called **de Lusignan** became enormously powerful in the eastern Mediterranean during the Middle Ages. Guy de Lusignan (1129–94) bought the island of Cyprus from the Templars. Hugues III de Lusignan-Poitou (king of Cyprus 1267–84) was crowned king of Jerusalem in 1269. During the 14th century, De Lusignans became kings of the Armenian kingdom of Cilicia. This family are sometimes known by the alternative name of ZENO, due to their medieval connections with Cyprus. It has been suggested that they were in fact of Armenian origin, the name being an assimilation to French from Armenian **Lusinian**, a patronymic from a personal name based on Armenian *lusin* 'moon'.
GIVEN NAMES French 12%. *Normand* (2), *Andre, Francois, Lucien, Marcel.*

Lusk (4564) Scottish: probably a variant of LEASK.

Luskey (125) Reduced form of Irish MCCLUSKEY.
GIVEN NAME Irish 5%. *Brigid.*

Luskin (202) Jewish (from Belarus): habitational name for someone from Luski, a village now in Belarus.
GIVEN NAMES Russian 5%; Jewish 4%. *Anatoly, Boris, Fanya, Semyon, Vitaly, Vlad; Kaplan.*

Lusky (154) **1.** Jewish (from Belarus): habitational name from the town of Luzhki or the village of Luski, now in Belarus. **2.** Perhaps also a reduced form of Irish MCCLUSKEY.
GIVEN NAMES Jewish 6%; German 4%. *Naum* (3); *Kurt.*

Lussier (1862) French: **1.** occupational name from Old French *uissier* 'usher', 'doorkeeper', with the definite article *l(e)*. **2.** occupational name from Old French

huchier 'carpenter', 'joiner', 'cabinet-maker'.
FOREBEARS A bearer of the name from Paris was in Quebec City by 1669.
GIVEN NAMES French 15%. *Armand* (10), *Normand* (9), *Marcel* (6), *Laurent* (5), *Cecile* (4), *Michel* (4), *Andre* (3), *Gilles* (3), *Jacques* (3), *Pierre* (3), *Aime* (2), *Camille* (2).

Lust (581) **1.** German: nickname for a pleasant person, from Middle High German *luste* 'pleasant', 'lovely'. **2.** German: habitational name from any of several places so named in northern Germany. **3.** Dutch: nickname for a bon viveur, from Middle Dutch *lust* 'pleasure', 'desire'.
GIVEN NAMES German 4%. *Franz, Hannelore, Kurt.*

Luster (1931) **1.** German: habitational name for someone from a place called LUST. **2.** Perhaps also English, a variant of LESTER.

Lustgarten (210) Jewish (Ashkenazic): ornamental name from German *Lustgarten* 'pleasure garden' (a compound of *Lust* 'enjoyment', 'pleasure' + *Garten* 'garden'), perhaps a reference to the Garden of Eden.
GIVEN NAMES Jewish 9%; German 4%. *Avrom, Miriam, Morty, Shai, Sol; Kurt* (2).

Lustig (1269) German, Dutch, and Jewish (Ashkenazic): nickname for a person of a cheerful disposition, from Middle High German *lustig* 'merry', 'carefree', Middle Dutch *lustighe*, German *lustig*. As a Jewish name it is mainly ornamental.

Lusty (178) English: nickname for a person of a cheerful disposition, from Middle English *lusti* 'joyful', 'lively'.

Lute (564) English: from an Old Norse personal name and byname *Lútr* (meaning 'stooping').

Luten (136) Dutch: **1.** metronymic from the personal name *Luite*, a short form of *Lu(i)tgard* (see LUCKHARDT). **2.** from *Luttin*, a pet form of *Lutto*, a pet form of a Germanic personal name formed with *hlod-* as the first element.

Luter (293) **1.** English: occupational name for a player on the lute, Middle English *lutar*, an agent derivative of *lute*. **2.** English: metonymic occupational name for an otter hunter, from Old French *loutre* 'otter'. **3.** Dutch: variant of LUTHER 1.

Lutes (1530) English: apparently a patronymic from LUTE.

Lutey (128) Possibly an Americanized spelling of the Swiss German family name LUTHI.

Lutgen (313) Dutch and North German (**Lütgen**): from a pet form of a Germanic personal name formed with *liut-* 'people' or *hlod-* 'famous' as the first element (see for example LUTHER, LUDWIG).

Luth (453) German (**Lüth**): see LUETH.

Luthe (113) German (**Lüthe**): variant of **Lüth** (see LUETH).

Luther (5404) **1.** German: from a Germanic personal name composed of the elements *liut* 'people', 'tribe' + *heri, hari* 'army'. **2.** English: nickname from Middle English *luther(e), lither(e)* 'bad', 'wicked', 'base' (from Old English *lȳðre*).

Luthi (349) Swiss German (**Lüthi**): from a pet form of a Germanic personal name formed with *liut-* 'people' as the first element.
GIVEN NAMES German 9%. *Ernst* (3), *Heinz* (2), *Franz, Liesl, Lorenz, Otto.*

Luthman (127) Swedish: ornamental name, of which the first element is probably an Old Swedish nickname *Lut* 'the crooked one', which occurs in the 17th century in Sweden as a family name, + *-man* 'man'.
GIVEN NAME Scandinavian 5%. *Nels* (2).

Luthra (111) Indian (Panjab): Hindu (Arora) and Sikh name based on the name of an Arora clan.
GIVEN NAMES Indian 92%. *Annu* (3), *Madhu* (3), *Sanjay* (3), *Vinay* (3), *Sanjiv* (2), *Vineet* (2), *Ajay, Amar, Amit, Amrish, Anil, Arun.*

Luthy (395) Swiss German (**Lüthy**): variant spelling of LUTHI, also found in Alsace. In Switzerland the more usual spelling is *Lüthi.*

Lutjen (136) Dutch and North German (**Lütjen**): variant of LUTGEN.
GIVEN NAMES German 4%. *Gernot, Otto.*

Lutke (136) North German (**Lütke**): from a pet form of the personal name *Ludolf* (see LUDOLPH) or of a short form of another Germanic personal name formed *leud, liut* 'people', 'tribe' (see LUETH) as the first element. Compare LUEDECKE.

Lutkus (102) Lithuanian: patronymic from a pet form of the personal name *Ludolf* (see LUDOLPH).

Lutman (263) English and German: variant of LUTTMAN.

Lutomski (101) Polish: habitational name for someone from a place called Lutom in Poznań voivodeship.
GIVEN NAMES Polish 11%. *Pawel* (2), *Czeslaw, Halina.*

Luton (477) English: habitational name from the place in Bedfordshire (named in Old English as 'settlement (Old English *tūn*) on the (river) *Lea*'), or, more plausibly in view of the pattern of distribution, from Luton in Devon (near Teignmouth), named in Old English as 'Lēofgifu's settlement' (from an Old English female personal name composed of the elements *lēof* 'dear', 'beloved' + *gifu* 'gift'). A further possible source of the name is Luton in Kent, named as the 'settlement of *Lēofa*'.

Lutrick (126) Origin unidentified.

Lutsch (117) **1.** North German: from a pet form of LUDWIG. **2.** (also **Lütsch**) from the personal name *Liuzo* (see LUTZ 2).
GIVEN NAMES German 9%. *Franz* (2), *Mathias, Nikolaus.*

Lutsky (154) Jewish (eastern Ashkenazic) and Ukrainian: habitational name for someone from Lutsk, Volhynia, now in Ukraine.
GIVEN NAMES Jewish 9%; Russian 4%. *Aron, Irina, Meyer, Sol; Anatoly, Rukhlya, Vitaly.*

Lutter (363) **1.** Dutch and English: variant of LUTER. **2.** German: habitational name from any of several places so called, for example near Hannover.
GIVEN NAMES German 7%. *Kurt* (3), *Gerhardt* (2), *Gerd, Helmut, Horst, Klaus.*

Lutterman (214) German (**Luttermann**): variant of LUTTER.

Luttman (165) **1.** North German (**Lüttmann**): variant of **Lüdemann** (see LUDEMANN). **2.** North German (**Lüttmann**): nickname for a small man, from Low German dialect *lütt* 'small'. **3.** English: nickname for a small, light man (see LIGHT).
GIVEN NAMES German 5%. *Erwin, Otto.*

Lutton (512) English (now found mainly in northern Ireland): habitational name from any of the various places so called, in Northamptonshire, Devon, Lincolnshire, and elsewhere. The one in Northamptonshire is Old English *Ludingtūn* 'settlement (*tūn*) associated with *Luda*' (a personal name of uncertain origin); that in Cornwood, Devon, is Old English *Ludantūn* 'Luda's settlement'; that in Lincolnshire is 'pool settlement', from Old English *luh* 'pool', and Lutton in North Yorkshire is 'settlement on the river *Hlūde*' (see LOUD) or 'Luda's settlement'.

Luttrell (3383) English (of Norman origin): from a diminutive of Old French *loutre* 'otter' (Latin *lutra*), applied as a nickname for someone thought to resemble an otter, or a metonymic occupational name for someone who hunted otters (for their pelts). Compare LUTER.

Luttrull (218) Variant of English LUTTRELL.

Lutts (133) **1.** Americanized spelling of German LUTZ. **2.** English: patronymic from *Lutt*, a medieval personal name which probably preserves an Old English byname *Lutt(a)*, derived from *lȳt* 'small' (see LIGHT 3).

Luty (173) **1.** English: variant of LAITY. **2.** Americanized spelling of the Swiss family name **Lüthi** or **Lüthy** (reflecting the pronunciation of *th* as *t* in German) (see LUTHI).
GIVEN NAMES German 4%. *Fritz, Markus.*

Lutz (13162) **1.** German: from a short form or pet form of LUDWIG. **2.** South German (**Lütz**): from a short form of a name *Luizo, Liuzo*, derived from a Germanic name formed with *liut-* 'people' as the first element. **3.** French: habitational name from Lutz-en-Dunois in Eure-et-Loir. This is a common name in PA and OH.

Lutze (221) German: variant of LUTZ.
GIVEN NAMES German 6%. *Erwin* (2), *Hans* (2), *Gerhard, Horst, Inge.*

Lutzke (212) German: from a pet form of LUTZ.

Lutzker (100) Jewish (eastern Ashkenazic): habitational name for someone from Lutsk, Volhynia (now in Ukraine).
GIVEN NAMES Jewish 7%. *Dov, Meyer.*

Lutzow (107) German (**Lützow**): habitational name from Lützow in Mecklenburg. The place name is of Slavic origin.

Luu (1954) Vietnamese (**L{us}u**): unexplained.
GIVEN NAMES Vietnamese 75%. *Thanh* (35), *Hung* (27), *Minh* (22), *Vinh* (20), *Duc* (19), *Anh* (17), *Ha* (17), *Cuong* (15), *Hien* (14), *Hoa* (14), *Quang* (13), *Chi* (10), *Phat* (10), *Tam* (9), *Nam* (7), *Sang* (7), *Hong* (6), *Tuong* (6), *Thai* (5), *Tong* (5).

Lux (2151) **1.** German and Dutch: patronymic from a vernacular form of LUCAS. **2.** German: variant of LUCHS. **3.** French: habitational name from places so named in the Côte-d'Or, Haute-Garonne, and Saône-et-Loire.

Luxenberg (137) German and Jewish (Ashkenazic): habitational name from any of various places named Luxenberg, Luxemberg, Luxenburg, or Luxembourg, as well as the Grand Duchy of Luxembourg.
GIVEN NAME Jewish 4%; German 4%. *Frieda.*

Luxford (111) English: habitational name from Luxford in Crowborough, Sussex.

Luxon (100) English (Cornwall and Devon): possibly a variant of LUXTON.

Luxton (226) English: habitational name from a minor place, probably one of two in Devon, so called from the possessive form of the Middle English personal name or surname *Lugg* (from Old English *Lugga*) + Middle English *tune, tone* 'settlement' (Old English *tūn*).

Luy (115) **1.** German: unexplained. Possibly an altered spelling of French LOUIS. **2.** Spanish: probably a variant spelling of the Catalan family name **Lluí**, which is most probably derived from an old personal name based on Latin *Lucinus.*
GIVEN NAMES Spanish 8%. *Eduardo, Enrique, Ernesto, Jose, Julio, Leoncio, Ricardo.*

Luyster (152) Dutch (**van de Luyster**): habitational name, probably from Lijster, a place name which occurs in Beernem and Emelgem.

Luz (338) **1.** Spanish and Portuguese: religious byname from a title of the Virgin Mary, Spanish *María de la Luz*, Portuguese *Maria da Luz* 'Mary of Light' (from Latin *lux*, genitive *lucis*). **2.** German: variant of LUTZ. **3.** Jewish (Israeli): ornamental name from Hebrew *luz* 'almond', a translation of MANDEL.
GIVEN NAMES Spanish 24%; Portuguese 8%; German 4%. *Manuel* (10), *Jose* (4), *Agustin* (3), *Alicia* (3), *Consuelo* (2), *Luis* (2), *Virgilio* (2), *Aida, Benilda, Deodoro, Efrain, Enrique; Joao; Antonio* (6), *Eligio, Romeo, Rosangela, Viterbo; Matthias* (2), *Friedrich, Fritz, Hans, Otto.*

Luzadder (126) Jewish (Sephardic): variant of LUZADER.

Luzader (254) Jewish (Sephardic): altered form of Portuguese **Lousada**, a habitational name from a place in Portugal so called, probably named for its flagstones. Compare LOSADA.

FOREBEARS According to family historians the family bearing this name came to New York early in the 18th century from England, having previously come to England from Portugal via Holland.

Luzar (133) Slovenian (**Lužar**): topographic name for a person who lived near a pool, from *luža* 'pool', 'puddle' + the suffix *-ar* denoting an inhabitant.

Luzi (104) **1.** Italian: patronymic from the personal name *Luzio*, a variant of LUCIO. **2.** Possibly a respelling of French **Luzy**, a habitational name from places in Nièvre, Haute-Marne, and Meuse named Luzy, from a Romano-Gallic estate name.
GIVEN NAMES Italian 20%; French 9%. *Gino* (2), *Marcello* (2), *Reno* (2), *Duilio*, *Enio*, *Livio*, *Luciano*; *Armand* (4), *Patrice*.

Luzier (353) French: habitational name from places so named in Savoy and the Dordogne.

Luzzi (431) Italian: **1.** habitational name from Luzzi in Cosenza province. **2.** patronymic from a reduced pet form of a personal name ending in *-lo*, as for example *Angelo*.
GIVEN NAMES Italian 18%. *Angelo* (4), *Dino* (4), *Salvatore* (4), *Aldo* (2), *Carlo* (2), *Biaggio*, *Carmine*, *Domenic*, *Egidio*, *Federico*, *Fiore*, *Giovanni*.

Ly (3700) **1.** Vietnamese (**Lý**) and Hmong: unexplained. **2.** English: variant of LYE.
GIVEN NAMES Vietnamese 73%. *Hung* (51), *Minh* (44), *Thanh* (43), *Cuong* (35), *Hoa* (28), *Anh* (25), *Long* (25), *Binh* (23), *Chau* (20), *Kiet* (18), *Lan* (18), *Vinh* (18), *Hong* (16), *Tam* (14), *Chi* (12), *Sang* (11), *Nam* (10), *Man* (8), *Chan* (7), *Heng* (7), *Phong* (7), *Seng* (7), *Sinh* (7), *Thai* (6).

Lyall (589) Scottish: probably from an Old Norse personal name *Liulfr*, composed of an uncertain first element + *úlfr* 'wolf', although Reaney gives this as a pet form of *Lyon* or *Lionel*.

Lybarger (713) Americanized spelling of German LEINBERGER.

Lybbert (132) Dutch: variant of LIBERT.

Lybeck (185) Norwegian, Danish (**Lybæk**), or Swedish (**Lübeck**): habitational name from Lübeck in Schleswig-Holstein.
GIVEN NAMES Scandinavian 4%. *Anders*, *Nels*.

Lybrand (483) Americanized spelling of the Swiss family name **Leibbrand**, from the Germanic personal name *Liutbrand*, a compound of the elements *liut* 'people' + *brand* 'sword'. In North America, this name occurs chiefly in NC.

Lybrook (128) Americanized form of German LEIBROCK.

Lycan (218) Origin unidentified. Perhaps a variant of LEIKAM, which is likewise of unidentified origin.

Lycans (106) Origin uncertain. Perhaps a variant of English **Lysons**, **Licence**, variants of LISON. The spelling **Lycens** is recorded in 1524.

Lycett (109) English: variant of the habitational name **Lissett**, from Lissett in the East Riding of Yorkshire, which is named from Old English *læs* 'meadow', 'pasture' + *(ge)set* 'dwelling'.

Lyda (772) Polish (**Łyda**): descriptive nickname from an augmentative form of Polish *łydka* 'calf', 'lower leg', presumably applied to someone with long or otherwise noticeable calves.

Lyday (355) Probably an Americanized form of German LEIDIG.

Lyddon (124) English: possibly a habitational name from Lydden in Kent, named from Old English *hlēo* 'shelter' + *denu* 'valley'.

Lyde (207) English: **1.** topographic name from Old English *hlið*, *hlid*, Old Norse *hlíð* 'slope'. **2.** habitational name from places so named in Shropshire, Herefordshire, or Somerset, or on the island of Orkney. The Herefordshire and Somerset places are named with the Old English river name *Hlȳde* (see LOUD). **3.** from a medieval byname derived from Old English *līðe* 'mild', 'gentle'.

Lydecker (130) Dutch: occupational name for a slater, *leidekker*. Compare LEIDECKER.
GIVEN NAME Dutch 4%; German 4%. *Gerrit* (2).

Lyden (677) Irish: variant spelling of LYDON.
GIVEN NAME Irish 6%. *Cahal* (3).

Lydic (350) Americanized form of German LEIDIG.

Lydick (479) Americanized form of German LEIDIG.

Lydon (1599) Irish: reduced Anglicized form of Gaelic **Ó Loideáin** 'descendant of *Loideán*', a personal name of uncertain origin. This surname is found chiefly in western Ireland.
GIVEN NAMES Irish 6%. *John Patrick*, *Padraic*.

Lydy (111) Probably an Americanized form of German LEIDIG. Compare LYDAY.

Lye (131) **1.** English: topographic name for someone who lived near a meadow, pasture, or patch of arable land, Middle English *l(e)ye* (late Old English *lēage*, dative of *lēah* 'wood', 'glade'); or a habitational name from Lye in Herefordshire (with the same etymology). **2.** French: habitational name from Lye in Indre. **3.** French (**Lyé**): habitational name from places called Lié in Deux-Sèvres and Vendée. **4.** Norwegian: habitational name from a farmstead in Rogaland named Lye, Old Norse *Lýgi* meaning 'alliance', 'covenant', used to de-

note a place sanctified by such an agreement, such as a court or council meeting place.

Lyell (340) Scottish: variant spelling of LYALL.

Lyerla (203) Presumably a variant of LYERLY.

Lyerly (555) Origin unidentified. This is a frequent name in NC.

Lyford (515) English: habitational name from Lyford in south Oxfordshire (formerly in Berkshire), named in Old English as 'flax-ford', from *līn* 'flax' + *ford* 'ford'.

Lyga (136) Polish: probably from from a derivative of the dialect verb *ligać* 'to buck', 'to kick'.

Lyke (540) Possibly an altered spelling of Dutch **Lijcke**, from the Germanic personal name *Lideco*.

Lykens (182) Variant spelling of Dutch LIKENS. It occurs chiefly in PA.

Lykes (229) English: unexplained. This is a southern name, found chiefly in AL, SC, and FL.

Lykins (1458) Variant spelling of LIKENS. This is a frequent name in OH and KY.

Lykken (130) Norwegian: variant of LOKKEN.

Lyle (5063) **1.** Scottish and English (of Norman origin): topographic name for someone who lived on an island, Old French, Middle English *isle* (Latin *insula*). **2.** Scottish, English (of Norman origin) and French: habitational name for someone from the French city of Lille, or from various localities called Lisle, in Dordogne, Loir-et-Cher, Meuse, and Tarn, all of which derive their names from Old French *isle* (see 1). **3.** Scottish: variant of LYALL.

Lyles (4355) English and Scottish: variant of LYLE 1 or 2.

Lyman (4579) **1.** English: topographic name for someone who lived near a meadow or a patch of arable land (see LAYMAN). **2.** Dutch: from a Germanic personal name composed of the elements *liut* 'people', or possibly *liub* 'dear', 'beloved' + *man* 'man'. **3.** Americanized form of German **Leimann**, Americanized form of **Leinemann**, habitational name for someone from Leine in Pomerania, or for someone who lived by either of two rivers called Leine, near Hannover and in Saxony.

Lymburner (106) Translation into English of German KALKBRENNER.

Lymon (114) Variant of English or Dutch LYMAN.

Lyn (216) **1.** Scottish and English: variant of LYNN. **2.** Dutch: probably an altered form of Dutch **van der Li(j)n** (see VANDERLINDEN 3). **3.** Southeast Asian: unexplained.
GIVEN NAMES Southeast Asian 6%. *Ding*, *Fatt*, *Tov*, *Yol*, *Yun*.

Lynam (830) **1.** English: habitational name from places in Devon, Oxfordshire, and

Wiltshire named Lynam, from Old English *līn* 'flax' + *hām* 'homestead' or *hamm* 'enclosure hemmed in by water'. **2.** Irish: English surname adopted as an equivalent of Gaelic **Ó Laidhghneáin** (see LINEHAN).

Lynaugh (189) Irish: Anglicized form of Gaelic **Laighneach** 'Leinsterman'.

Lynch (44057) **1.** Irish: reduced Anglicized form of Gaelic **Ó Loingsigh** 'descendant of *Loingseach*', a personal name meaning 'mariner' (from *long* 'ship'). This is now a common surname in Ireland but of different local origins, for example chieftain families in counties Antrim and Tipperary, while in Ulster and Connacht there were families called **Ó Loingseacháin** who later shortened their name to **Ó Loingsigh** and also Anglicized it as **Lynch**. **2.** Irish (Anglo-Norman): Anglicized form of Gaelic **Linseach**, itself a Gaelicized form of Anglo-Norman French **de Lench**, the version found in old records. This seems to be a local name, but its origin is unknown. One family of bearers of this name was of Norman origin, but became one of the most important tribes of Galway. **3.** English: topographic name for someone who lived on a slope or hillside, Old English *hlinc*, or perhaps a habitational name from Lynch in Dorset or Somerset or Linch in Sussex, all named with this word.

FOREBEARS This name was brought independently from Ireland to North America by many bearers. Jonack Lynch emigrated from Ireland to SC shortly after the first settlement of that colony in 1670. His grandson Thomas Lynch, born in 1727 in Berkeley Co., SC, was a member of both Continental Congresses, and his great-grandson, also called Thomas Lynch, born 1749 in Winyaw, SC, was a signer of the Declaration of Independence.

GIVEN NAMES Irish 6%. *Brendan* (32), *Liam* (7), *Kieran* (6), *Dermot* (5), *Donovan* (4), *Brigid* (3), *Caitlin* (3), *Siobhan* (3), *Aileen* (2), *Colm* (2), *Conley* (2), *Conor* (2).

Lynd (594) English: variant spelling of LIND 2.

Lyndaker (139) Probably a variant of Dutch LEIDECKER 'slater'.

Lynde (433) English: variant spelling of LIND 2.

Lyndon (164) English (Midlands): variant spelling of LINDON.

Lynds (243) English (Kent): unexplained.

Lyne (500) **1.** English: variant of LIND 2 and LINE 1. **2.** Irish: variant of LANE 2. **3.** Scottish: habitational name from places so named in Ayrshire, Peebles-shire, and Wigtownshire.

GIVEN NAMES Irish 4%. *Dermot*, *Niall*.

Lynes (514) English: metronymic from LINE 1.

Lyness (250) Northern English and Irish: in part at least, probably a variant spelling of LINES. It was taken to County Armagh, Ireland, in the 17th century and is now found chiefly in counties Antrim and Down, where it is sometimes used for **Mac Aleenan**.

Lyng (271) **1.** Danish: ornamental name from *lyng* 'heather' (Old Norse *lyng*). **2.** Norwegian: habitational name from either of two farmsteads in Trøndelag named with the same word.

Lynk (258) Apparently an altered or variant spelling of LINCK or LINK.

Lynn (14342) **1.** Irish: reduced Anglicized form of Gaelic **Mac Fhloinn** and **Ó Fhloinn** (see FLYNN). **2.** Scottish: variant of LYNE 3. **3.** English: habitational name from any of several places so called in Norfolk, in particular King's Lynn, an important center of the medieval wool trade. The place name is probably from an Old Welsh word cognate with Gaelic *linn* 'pool', 'stream'.

Lynne (382) Scottish or English: variant of LYNN.

Lynott (292) Irish: Anglicized form of **Lionóid**, a Gaelicization of a Norman family name brought to Ireland from Wales in the 12th century.

Lynskey (263) Irish (Mayo, Galway): reduced Anglicized form of Gaelic **Ó Loingscigh**, a variant of **Ó Loingsigh** (see LYNCH).

GIVEN NAMES Irish 6%. *Brigid*, *Seamus*.

Lynum (102) Respelling of English LYNAM.

Lyon (11853) **1.** Scottish, English and French: from Old French, Middle English *lion* (Latin *leo*, genitive *leonis*), hence a nickname for a fierce or brave warrior, or a habitational name for someone living at a house distinguished by the sign of a lion. **2.** Scottish, English, French, and Dutch: habitational name from the city of Lyon in south central France (English name: *Lyons*), or from the smaller Lyons-la-Forêt in Eure, Normandy. The name of the former is recorded in the 1st century BC as *Lugdunum* and is from the name of a Celtic god *Lug* (or this as a personal name, from a word meaning 'brightness') + *dunon* 'hill fort'. **3.** Scottish and English: from the name *Leo(n)* (from Latin *leo* 'lion', or the cognate Greek *leōn*), borne by numerous early martyrs and thirteen popes. **4.** Irish: reduced Anglicized form of Gaelic **Ó Laighin** (see LANE 2).

Lyons (29539) **1.** English: variant of LYON 3. **2.** Irish: variant of LYON 4.

Lysaght (229) Irish: reduced Anglicized form of Gaelic **Mac Giolla Iasachta** 'son of the foreign lad or servant', from the gen-itive of *iasacht* 'borrowing', used as an adjective meaning 'foreign'.

GIVEN NAMES Irish 4%. *Aidan*, *Colm*.

Lysak (101) Jewish (Eastern Ashkenazic): nickname for a bald man, Ukrainian *lysak*.

GIVEN NAMES Russian 4%; Jewish 4%. *Lev*, *Zoya*.

Lysek (106) Polish: nickname for a man with a bald pate, from a diminutive of Polish *łysy* 'bald' (see LYSIAK).

GIVEN NAMES Polish 10%. *Jacek, Janusz, Ryszard*.

Lysiak (133) Polish (**Łysiak**): nickname for a man with a bald pate, from Polish *łysy* 'bald' + the noun suffix *-ak*.

GIVEN NAMES Polish 4%. *Ewa, Jozef*.

Lysinger (146) Americanized spelling of German LEISINGER.

Lysne (255) Norwegian: habitational name from farmsteads in southwestern Norway named *Ljøsne*, from Old Norse *Ljósnar*, plural of *ljósn*, related to *ljóss* 'light'. The name may denote a forest clearing or glade.

GIVEN NAMES Scandinavian 9%. *Johan* (2), *Per* (2), *Sigfred*.

Lyson (103) **1.** English: variant spelling of LISON. **2.** Possibly also an Americanized spelling of German LEISEN.

GIVEN NAME German 4%. *Alfons*.

Lyssy (199) Altered form of Czech and Slovak **Lysý** 'bald', nickname for a man with a bald pate.

GIVEN NAMES French 4%. *Clemence* (2), *Prosper*.

Lystad (110) Norwegian: habitational name from any of seven farms of this name in Norway. The first element of the place name is probably a river, either from Old Norse *hlýr* 'warm', 'mild' or, in another case, *Lýsa* 'the shining one' + *staðir*, plural of *staðr* 'dwelling', 'farmstead'. The surname has spread into Sweden.

Lyster (352) English and Scottish: variant of LISTER.

Lyter (221) Perhaps an altered spelling of LEITER. Compare LITER, LIGHTER. It occurs predominantly in PA.

Lythgoe (165) Scottish (now commonly found in Lancashire): variant spelling of LITHGOW.

Lytle (4923) English, Scottish, and Irish (chiefly northern Ireland): variant of LITTLE.

Lyttle (675) English, Scottish, and Irish (chiefly northern Ireland): variant of LITTLE.

Lytton (501) English: variant spelling of LITTON.

Lyvers (195) Variant spelling of Dutch **Lievers**, a patronymic from a Germanic personal name formed with *liub* 'dear', 'beloved' + *heri, hari* 'army'.

M

Ma (3986) **1.** Chinese 马: from an honorific title borne by a prince of the state of Zhao during the Warring States period (403–221 BC). He was awarded the title Noble Ma Fu after repeatedly distinguishing himself as a general, and subsequently, his descendants adopted part of the honorific title, Ma, as their surname. **2.** Korean: there are two Chinese characters for the surname Ma, only one of which is frequent enough to be treated here. Two clans use this character: the Mokch'ŏn clan and the Changhŭng clan. The founding ancestor of the Korean Mokch'ŏn Ma clan migrated to Korea from China during the Han Commanderies period (1st century BC). The Ma clans played fairly important roles in the formation of the pre-Shilla Paekche kingdom. The records are not consistent, but it seems that originally the Ma surname was Yŏng and that either the Koryŏ king T'aejo (941–943) or the Shilla king Kyŏngsun (927–935) changed the name to Ma. **3.** Cambodian: unexplained. **4.** Hawaiian: unexplained. **5.** Tongan: unexplained.
GIVEN NAMES Chinese/Korean 39%; Other Southeast Asian 10%. *Jian* (12), *Li* (11), *Hong* (10), *Hung* (10), *Wing* (10), *Wai* (9), *Wei* (9), *Ying* (9), *Ming* (8), *Ping* (8), *Chi* (7), *Cuong* (7), *Dong* (7), *Jin* (7), *Lan* (7), *Minh* (6), *Thanh* (6), *Lien* (5), *Trung* (5), *Binh* (4), *Hao* (4), *Phat* (4), *Quan* (4), *Quang* (4); *Chung* (7), *Chang* (4), *Phong* (4), *Sha* (2), *Tam* (2), *Tian* (2), *Cho, Chong, Chul, Dae Yong, Eun Hee, In Sook*; *Cuong* (7), *Dong* (7), *Minh* (6), *Thanh* (6), *Lien* (5), *Trung* (5), *Binh* (4), *Phat* (4), *Quan* (4), *Quang* (4).

Maack (330) Dutch and North German: variant of MACK 2.
GIVEN NAMES German 4%. *Hans, Horst, Kurt, Otto, Uwe.*

Maag (916) Dutch and German (southwestern and Switzerland): from Middle Dutch *maech, mage*, Middle High German *māc, māge* 'relative', 'kinsman'.

Maahs (364) Variant of MAAS.
GIVEN NAMES German 6%. *Kurt* (2), *Frieda, Gerda, Gerhardt, Horst, Otto.*

Maalouf (114) Arabic (mainly North African): variant of MALOOF.
GIVEN NAMES Arabic 28%; French 19%. *Sami* (3), *Ali* (2), *Ramzi* (2), *Antoun, Anwar, Assaad, Bechara, Chafic, Fadi, Hani, Jamal, Nabil*; *Alain, Andre, Antoine, Emile, Georges, Michel, Odette, Pierre.*

Maas (3798) Dutch and North German: from a short form of THOMAS.

Maaske (128) North German: from a pet form of MAAS.

Maass (858) Dutch and North German: variant of MAAS. The additional *s* could indicate a patronymic.
GIVEN NAMES German 6%. *Fritz* (2), *Gerhard* (2), *Hans* (2), *Kurt* (2), *Manfred* (2), *Otto* (2), *Claus, Dieter, Erwin, Hedwig, Helmut, Inge.*

Maassen (267) Dutch and North German: patronymic from MAAS.

Maat (104) Dutch: from the personal name *Maat*, a short form of *Mathias* (see MATTHEW) or, with loss of -*r*-, of MARTIN.

Mabb (105) English: from a short form of the female personal name *Mabel* (see MAPP).

Mabbitt (136) English: from a pet form of the medieval female personal name *Mab(be)*, a short form of Middle English or Old French *Amabel* (from Latin *amabilis* 'lovable'). This has survived into the 20th century as a personal name in the short form *Mabel*.

Mabe (2402) **1.** Dutch: from the medieval female personal name *Mabe*, a short form of *Mabelie*, derived from a Latin personal name and saint's name *(A)mabilia*. Compare MABBITT. **2.** Jewish (eastern Ashkenazic): unexplained.

Mabee (471) **1.** Variant spelling of MABEY. **2.** Dutch: this is a prominent Dutch family name in the Schenectady area of NY, where a Mabee Farmhouse still survives from the late 17th century. The name is derived from French MABIL(L)E, and came from Valenciennes in France, to the Netherlands in the 1580s, and thence to New Netherland in the 1650s. Mabee is the most common form, but it probably developed through **Mabie**, as a phonetic spelling, in the Netherlands, into its present form in Schenectady, where spelling was influenced by English conventions.

Maben (339) Scottish: from the medieval personal name *Maban, Mabon*, which is from an ancient British personal name (Old Welsh *Maponos* 'great son'). This is found as an element in Scottish place names of Brythonic origin.

Maberry (590) English and Irish: variant spelling of MAYBERRY.

Mabery (249) English and Irish: variant spelling of MAYBERRY.

Mabey (364) **1.** English (Hampshire): of uncertain origin. It could be from a pet form of a Middle English female personal name, *Mab(be)* (see MABBITT). Alternatively, it may be an altered form of MOWBRAY. **2.** French: from the personal name *Amable* (from Latin *Amabilis* meaning 'loveable').

Mabie (555) Scottish: **1.** habitational name from a place so named in the parish of Troqueer in Kirkcudbrightshire, which Black quotes as confirmed to Durand filius Christin by Alan filius Roland, constable of Scotland, in c. 1200–34. **2.** variant of MABEY.

Mabile (189) French: from the female personal name *Mabille*, derived from Latin *Amabilia*, a variant of *Amabilis* (see MABBITT).
GIVEN NAMES French 13%. *Pierre* (3), *Chantel, Emile, Gervais, Honore, Leonie, Lucien, Odile.*

Mabin (157) Scottish: variant spelling of MABEN.

Mable (152) English: from the female personal name *(A)mabel* (see MABBITT).
GIVEN NAME Irish 6%. *Donal* (2).

Mabon (212) **1.** Scottish: variant spelling of MABEN. **2.** French (Breton): ultimately of the same origin as the Scottish name. It is also found as an element in Breton place names, for example, in Kermabon.

Mabray (115) English and Irish: variant spelling of MAYBERRY.

Mabrey (769) English and Irish: variant spelling of MAYBERRY.
GIVEN NAME French 4%. *Jacques* (2).

Mabry (4518) English and Irish: variant spelling of MAYBERRY.

Mabus (222) German: variant of German **Mebes**, pet form of the personal name *Bartholomäus* (see BARTHOLOMEW).
FOREBEARS Christoph Maibus came to Charleston, SC, in 1833 with his two sons Rhinehart and Eustace. Many present-day American bearers of this name are descended from them.

Mac (385) **1.** Vietnamese: unexplained. **2.** Shortened form of any of the many Scottish and Irish surnames formed with Gaelic *mac* 'son of'.
GIVEN NAMES Vietnamese 20%. *Cuong* (3), *Minh* (3), *Lien* (2), *Muoi* (2), *Thanh* (2), *Tho* (2), *Tieu* (2), *Vinh* (2), *Anh, Beo, Binh, Chau.*

MacAdam (262) Scottish and Irish: see MCADAM.

MacAdams (144) Scottish and Irish: see MCADAMS.

MacAfee (108) Scottish and northern Irish: see MCAFEE.

Macak (102) Polish: patronymic from a pet form of the personal name *Maciej* (see MATTHEW).

GIVEN NAMES Polish 10%. *Katarzyna, Leszek, Maciej.*

MacAllister (399) Scottish and northern Irish: see MCALLISTER.

MacAlpine (157) Scottish: see MCALPINE.

Macaluso (1633) Italian (Sicily): from a personal name based on Arabic *makhlūṣ* 'freed', 'liberated'.

GIVEN NAMES Italian 21%. *Salvatore* (13), *Mario* (7), *Angelo* (6), *Rosario* (4), *Antonio* (3), *Gaetano* (3), *Giuseppe* (3), *Marco* (3), *Pietro* (3), *Sal* (3), *Santo* (3), *Calogero* (2), *Gandolfo* (2), *Alfonso, Armando, Benedetto, Gustavo, Mariano, Sergio.*

Macaraeg (132) Filipino: unexplained.

GIVEN NAMES Spanish 40%. *Pedro* (2), *Anacleta, Angelina, Angelita, Arsenio, Aureo, Catalino, Clarita, Dionisio, Dominga, Edmundo, Eduardo*; *Antonio* (4), *Dante, Romeo.*

Macari (278) Italian: **1.** patronymic or plural form of MACARIO. **2.** (Sicily): possibly also from Arabic *Maqqarī*, a habitational name for someone from the Algerian city of Maqqarah, or a habitational name from a place in Italy named Maccari from this word.

GIVEN NAMES Italian 11%. *Alessandra, Angelo, Edo, Leonardo, Pasco, Rocco.*

Macario (129) Italian, Spanish, and Portuguese: from the personal name *Macario*, from Greek *makarios* 'blessed'.

GIVEN NAMES Spanish 32%; Italian 9%; Portuguese 6%. *Alberto* (2), *Carlos* (2), *Orlando* (2), *Anastacio, Angel, Cesar, Elena, Evencio, Isidro, Jesus, Juan, Luis*; *Angelo, Cosmo, Dante*; *Joao.*

MacArthur (1642) Scottish and northern Irish: see MCARTHUR and ARTHUR.

MacArtney (181) Scottish and Irish: see MCCARTNEY.

MacAskill (154) Scottish and Irish: see MCCASKILL.

MacAulay (996) Scottish: see MCCAULEY.

GIVEN NAME Scottish 4%. *Alastair.*

MacAuley (775) Scottish: see MCCAULEY.

MacBain (132) Scottish: see MCBAIN.

MacBeth (467) Scottish: see MCBETH.

MacBride (408) Irish and Scottish: see MCBRIDE.

MacCallum (422) Scottish: see MCCALLUM.

Maccarone (326) Southern Italian: from *maccaroni* 'macaroni', hence perhaps an occupational name for a maker of pasta, or a Neapolitan nickname for a simpleton from the same word in the sense 'lump', 'clot'.

GIVEN NAMES Italian 23%. *Biagio* (4), *Salvatore* (3), *Angelo* (2), *Matteo* (2), *Rocco* (2), *Alfio, Antonio, Benedetto, Carmelo, Carmine, Concetta, Gaetano.*

MacCarthy (239) Irish: see MCCARTHY.

GIVEN NAME Irish 7%. *Donal.*

MacCartney (114) Irish: see MCCARTNEY.

Macchi (243) Italian: **1.** from a variant of the old personal name *Macco*, from Latin *Maccus*, which occurs frequently in medieval documents. **2.** possibly a variant of MACCHIA.

GIVEN NAMES Italian 11%. *Carlo* (3), *Angelo* (2), *Oreste* (2), *Aldo, Amadeo, Attilio, Dario, Domenico, Gabriele, Giuseppe, Silvio.*

Macchia (430) Italian: topographic name from *macchia* 'thicket', 'scrub' (from Latin *macula*), or a habitational name from any of various places named with this word, as for example Macchia in Trapani province, Sicily.

GIVEN NAMES Italian 24%. *Rocco* (7), *Carmine* (4), *Angelo* (3), *Gaetano* (3), *Antonio* (2), *Raffaele* (2), *Salvatore* (2), *Vito* (2), *Carlo, Domenica, Domenico, Italo.*

Macchio (160) Italian: variant of MACCHIA.

GIVEN NAMES Italian 15%. *Angelo, Carmine, Rocco, Sal, Vito.*

Macchione (120) Italian: **1.** from an augmentative of MACCHIA. **2.** in some cases, a habitational name from various places so named in Campania and Puglia.

GIVEN NAMES Italian 13%. *Natale* (2), *Giovanni, Giuseppe.*

Maccini (126) Italian: from a pet form of the personal name *Maccio*, a short form of a pet name formed with this suffix, as for example *Giacomaccio* (from GIACOMO) or *Guglielmaccio* (from GUGLIELMO).

GIVEN NAME French 5%. *Patrice.*

MacConnell (373) Scottish and Irish: see MCCONNELL.

MacCormack (270) Scottish and Irish: see MCCORMACK.

GIVEN NAMES Irish 5%. *Brendan, Dermot, Fintan, Niall.*

MacCracken (141) Northern Irish and Scottish: see MCCRACKEN.

MacCubbin (120) Scottish: see MCCUBBIN.

MacDermott (187) Irish: see MCDERMOTT.

GIVEN NAME Irish 5%. *Kieran.*

MacDiarmid (138) Scottish: see MCDIARMID.

MacDonald (20497) Scottish: see MCDONALD.

MacDonell (326) Irish: see MCDONNELL.

GIVEN NAME German 4%; Scottish 4%. *Eldred* (3).

MacDonnell (323) Irish: see MCDONNELL.

GIVEN NAME Irish 5%. *Brendan* (2).

MacDonough (144) Irish: see MCDONOUGH.

MacDougal (240) Scottish: see MCDOUGALL.

MacDougall (1878) Scottish: see MCDOUGALL.

MacDowell (612) Irish: see MCDOWELL.

MacDuff (221) Scottish and Irish: see MCDUFF.

Mace (4370) **1.** English: from a medieval personal name, a survival of Old English *Mæssa*, which came to be taken as a pet form of MATTHEW. **2.** English: possibly a metonymic occupational name for a mace-bearer, from Old French *masse* 'mace'. **3.** English: habitational name from Macé in Orne, France. **4.** French (**Macé**): variant of MASSEY; also a vernacular form of the personal name *Mathieu* (see MATTHEW).

MacEachern (387) Scottish and Irish: see MCEACHERN.

Macedo (833) **1.** Galician: habitational name from Macedo, a village in Lugo province, Galicia. **2.** Portuguese: topographic name from *macedo* 'apple grove', a derivative of *maça* 'apple'.

GIVEN NAMES Spanish 33%; Portuguese 13%. *Manuel* (21), *Jose* (18), *Carlos* (12), *Roberto* (6), *Fernando* (4), *Francisco* (4), *Javier* (3), *Juan* (3), *Pablo* (3), *Rafael* (3), *Ruben* (3), *Sergio* (3); *Manoel* (3), *Joao* (2), *Joaquim* (2), *Marcio* (2), *Paulo* (2), *Afonso, Albano, Caetano, Goncalo, Guilherme, Mateus.*

Macek (660) **1.** Czech: from the personal name *Macek*, a pet form of the personal name *Matěj*, from Latin *Mathias* or *Matthaeus* (see MATTHEW). **2.** Slovenian (**Maček**): from *maček* 'cat', hence probably a nickname denoting a cautious or handy, skillful person.

Macera (187) **1.** Southern Italian: topographic name from old central-southern Italian *macera* 'dry-stone wall', 'pile of stones (collected from cultivated land)', 'stone ruins'. **2.** Southern Spanish: habitational name either from La Macera in Cáceres province or, more likely, from a Spanish form of the common Galician and Portuguese place name Maceira, from *maceira* 'apple tree'.

GIVEN NAMES Italian 36%. *Mario* (7), *Pasco* (3), *Alfonso* (2), *Angelo* (2), *Antonio* (2), *Giuseppe* (2), *Pasquale* (2), *Armando, Basilio, Carmine, Cosmo, Dario, Modesto, Nunzio, Pietro, Ricci, Rosaria.*

MacEwan (163) Scottish: see MCEWEN.

GIVEN NAME Scottish 6%. *Hamish.*

MacEwen (225) Scottish: see MCEWEN.

Macey (936) **1.** English: variant of MASSEY. **2.** Ukrainian: from the personal name *Matei* (see MATTHEW).

MacFadden (196) Scottish and Irish: see MCFADDEN.

MacFadyen (159) Scottish and Irish: variant of MCFADDEN.

MacFarland (835) Northern Irish: see MCFARLAND.

MacFarlane (1964) Scottish: see McFAR-LANE.

MacGeorge (120) Scottish: see McGEORGE.

MacGibbon (127) Scottish and Irish: see McGIBBON.

MacGill (135) Scottish and Irish: see McGILL.

MacGillivray (404) Scottish: see McGILLI-VRAY.

MacGowan (258) Scottish and Irish: see McGOWAN.
GIVEN NAME Scottish 4%. *Evander* (2).

MacGregor (2371) Scottish: see McGRE-GOR.
GIVEN NAMES Scottish 5%. *Callum* (2), *Dugald, Iain, Murdo.*

MacGuire (100) Irish and Scottish: see McGUIRE.

Mach (1474) **1.** Czech, Polish, Ukrainian, and eastern German (of Slavic origin): from the personal name *Mach*, a pet form of a vernacular derivative of Latin *Matthaeus* or *Mathias* (Czech *Matěj*, Polish *Maciej*, etc. (see MATTHEW)). In some cases, the Czech and Polish names represent pet forms of other names beginning with *Ma-*, for example *Marek* (see MARK) or MARTIN. **2.** possibly also an Americanized spelling of Hungarian **Mács**, from a pet form of *Máté* or *Mátyás*, Hungarian forms of *Matthew*. **3.** Jewish (Ashkenazic): unexplained. **4.** Vietnamese, Cambodian, or other Southeast Asian: unexplained.
GIVEN NAMES Vietnamese 7%. *Huy* (4), *Minh* (4), *To* (4), *Hoa* (3), *Hung* (3), *Muoi* (3), *Quang* (3), *Tan* (3), *Anh* (2), *Binh* (2), *Chau* (2), *Chuc* (2).

Macha (422) **1.** Czech (**Mácha**), Polish, and eastern German: variant of MACH 1. **2.** Americanized spelling of Hungarian **Mácsa**, from a pet form of *Máté*, or *Mátyás*, Hungarian forms of *Matthew*, or alternatively a habitational name for someone from a place called Mácsa.

Machac (100) Czech (**Macháč**): from a pet form of the personal name *Mach* (see MACH 1).

Machacek (387) Czech (**Macháček**): from a pet form of **Macháč** (see MACHAC).

Machado (4140) Spanish and Portuguese: from Spanish and Portuguese *machado* 'hatchet' (a derivative of MACHO 2), probably a nickname, but possibly also a habitational name, as this word is also a common element of place names.
GIVEN NAMES Spanish 30%; Portuguese 12%. *Jose* (107), *Manuel* (103), *Carlos* (41), *Luis* (32), *Juan* (22), *Jorge* (19), *Julio* (16), *Francisco* (14), *Fernando* (13), *Mario* (13), *Pedro* (11), *Rafael* (10); *Joao* (11), *Paulo* (3), *Henrique* (2), *Joaquim* (2), *Manoel* (2), *Agostinho, Albano, Amadeu, Duarte, Ilidio, Ligia, Lourenco.*

Machak (136) **1.** Polish: patronymic from MACH. **2.** Americanized spelling of Slovak **Mačák**, a derivative of the personal name *Mach* (see MACH 1). **3.** Americanized

spelling of Croatian **Mačak**, nickname from the vocabulary word *mačak* 'cat', hence probably denoting a cautious or handy, skillful person.

Machala (166) **1.** Czech and Polish (**Machała**): from a derivative of the personal name *Mach* (see MACH 1). **2.** Polish (**Machała**): perhaps also a derivative of the verb *machać* 'swing', 'sway'.

Machamer (252) German: from a Germanic personal name composed of *magan* 'might' or *māg* 'kinsman' + *māri, mēri* 'famous'.
FOREBEARS Johan Philip and Johannes Magemer settled in Berks Co., PA, in 1744.

Machan (151) Czech (**Macháň**) and Slovak: from a derivative of the personal name *Mach* (see MACH 1).
GIVEN NAMES Czech and Slovak 8%. *Alois; Zdenka.*

Machart (131) **1.** Czech: from the Germanic personal name *Markhart*, composed of the elements *marka* 'frontier' + *hart* 'hard', 'strong'. **2.** Dutch: from a Germanic personal name composed of the elements *mag* 'relative', 'kinsman' + *hard* 'hardy', 'brave', 'strong'.

Machemer (111) Variant of German MACHAMER.

Machen (722) English: occupational name for a stonemason, Anglo-Norman French *machun*, a Norman dialect variant of Old French *masson* (see MASON).

Macher (155) German: **1.** habitational name for someone from any of several places called Machern, for example near Leipzig. **2.** from a Germanic personal name formed with *māg* 'kinsman' or *magan* 'might' + *hari* 'army'.

Machi (156) **1.** Italian (Sicily): unexplained. It may be from the Albanian personal name *Maqo*. Derivation from a Greek name ending in *-akis*, which has been suggested, is implausible. **2.** Japanese: 'town' or 'street', not common in Japan. Some occurrences in America could be shortened versions of longer names beginning with this element.
GIVEN NAMES Italian 22%; Japanese 4%. *Salvatore* (3), *Vito* (3), *Mario* (2), *Alfio, Carmelo, Domenic, Maximo, Sal; Tetsuji* (2), *Junji.*

Machia (182) Variant of Italian MACCHIA.

Machida (119) Japanese: 'rice paddy near the town'; the name is found mostly in eastern Japan and the Ryūkyū Islands.
GIVEN NAMES Japanese 59%. *Hiroko* (2), *Hitoshi* (2), *Jiro* (2), *Akemi, Akihiro, Chiyo, Eiko, Goro, Hideaki, Hiroshi, Kaz, Kazuko.*

Machin (435) **1.** English: variant spelling of MACHEN. **2.** Spanish (**Machín**): probably a nickname from *machín* 'boor', 'lout', often applied to a blacksmith's apprentice. **3.** French: nickname from Old French *machin* 'scheming'.
GIVEN NAMES Spanish 25%. *Manuel* (8), *Juan* (7), *Jose* (5), *Carlos* (3), *Jorge* (3), *Mario*

(3), *Miguel* (3), *Pedro* (3), *Blanca* (2), *Diego* (2), *Luis* (2), *Ramon* (2).

Machnicki (40) Polish: habitational name for someone from Machnice in Wrocław voivodeship.

Machnik (215) Polish, Ukrainian (**Machnyk**), Czech (**Machník**), and Slovak (**Machnič**): from a derivative of the personal name *Mach* (see MACH).

Macho (176) **1.** Spanish: nickname from *macho* 'mule', applied either to denote an idiot or alternatively a virile, strong man (Latin *masculus*). **2.** Spanish: possibly a nickname for a forceful person or a metonymic occupational name for a smith, from *macho* 'sledgehammer' (Latin *marculus* 'hammer'). **3.** Hungarian (**Macsó**): from the old secular personal name *Macsó*. The spelling is either Americanized, or an archaic form. In 15th- and 16th-century documents the family name is recorded in the form *Macho*, in which form the name is also found in Slovakia.

Machon (124) **1.** Polish (**Machoń**) and Czech (**Machoň**): derivative of the personal name *Mach* (see MACH 1). **2.** English and French (Normandy): occupational name for a mason (see MACHEN).
GIVEN NAMES Polish 5%; German 4%. *Jarek, Miroslaw, Zbigniew; Lutz, Otto.*

Machovec (131) Czech and Slovak: patronymic from the personal name *Mach* (see MACH 1).

Machowski (148) Polish: habitational name for someone from a place called Machów, Machowa, or Machowo, named with the personal name *Mach* (see MACH 1).
GIVEN NAMES Polish 6%. *Beata, Casimir.*

Macht (232) **1.** German: from a Germanic personal name formed with *macht* 'might', 'power' as the first element. **2.** Jewish (Ashkenazic): ornamental name or nickname from German *Macht* 'power'.

Machuca (436) Spanish and Portuguese: from *machucar, machacar* 'to squash', 'to crush', probably applied as a nickname for someone who was obstinate.
GIVEN NAMES Spanish 56%; Portuguese 15%. *Jose* (16), *Manuel* (10), *Carlos* (9), *Juan* (8), *Miguel* (8), *Francisco* (7), *Luis* (6), *Javier* (5), *Ramon* (5), *Alberto* (4), *Julio* (4), *Arturo* (3); *Catarina.*

Machuga (156) Eastern German (of Slavic origin), Polish (**Maczuga**), or Slovak (**Mačuga**): nickname from a Slavic word meaning 'mace', 'club', or 'cudgel' (from Latin *mattea* 'stick'), a medieval weapon also used as a ceremonial symbol of office.

Macia (143) **1.** Catalan (**Macià**): variant of the personal name *Maties*. **2.** Spanish (**Macía**): variant of **Macías** (see MACIAS).
GIVEN NAMES Spanish 35%. *Jose* (7), *Narciso* (3), *Alberto* (2), *Felipe* (2), *Mirta* (2), *Alejandro, Amparo, Camilo, Carlos, Eduardo, Elena, Enrique; Federico* (5), *Antonio, Domiciano, Leonardo, Margherita.*

Maciag (240) Polish (**Maciąg**): from a derivative of the personal name *Maciej* (see MATTHEW).
GIVEN NAMES Polish 12%. *Zbigniew* (2), *Boguslaw, Casimir, Ryszard, Tadeusz, Thadeus.*

Macias (5129) Spanish (**Macías**) and Portuguese: from a variant of the personal name *Matías* (see MATTHEW).
GIVEN NAMES Spanish 52%; Portuguese 12%. *Jose* (146), *Juan* (75), *Jesus* (69), *Manuel* (60), *Carlos* (46), *Raul* (43), *Francisco* (40), *Luis* (39), *Mario* (31), *Ruben* (27), *Jorge* (26), *Roberto* (26); *Paulo, Valentim.*

Macie (140) Variant of Polish MACIEJ.

Maciej (115) Polish: from the personal name *Maciej*, vernacular derivative of Latin *Matthaeus* (see MATTHEW).
GIVEN NAMES Polish 5%. *Ludwik, Wladyslaw.*

Maciejewski (919) Polish: habitational name for someone from any of various places called Maciejowa, Maciejów, or Maciejowice, all named with the personal name *Maciej* (see MATTHEW).
GIVEN NAMES Polish 7%. *Jerzy* (3), *Andrzej, Bogdan, Bronislaus, Casimir, Henryk, Jaroslaw, Kazimierz, Krzysztof, Lucjan, Mariusz, Pawel.*

Maciel (1112) **1.** Portuguese and Galician: of uncertain derivation; possibly from a derivative of *maça* 'apple'. **2.** Polish: from a derivative of the personal name *Maciej* (see MATTHEW).
GIVEN NAMES Spanish 35%; Portuguese 11%. *Jose* (30), *Manuel* (16), *Francisco* (8), *Jesus* (7), *Juan* (7), *Luis* (7), *Carlos* (6), *Ignacio* (6), *Javier* (6), *Jorge* (5), *Rafael* (5), *Ramon* (5); *Adauto, Joao, Paulo.*

Macik (222) Czech (**Macík**), Slovak, and Ukrainian: from a Slavic derivative of the personal name *Matthaeus* or *Mathias* (see MATTHEW), e.g. Czech *Matěj.* See also MACEK.

Macina (122) **1.** Italian: topographic name from *màcina* 'millstone', 'grindstone' or a habitational name from a place named with this word. **2.** Italian: from a pet form of the personal name *Maci* (see MACHI 1). **3.** Polish: derivative of the personal name *Maciej* (see MATTHEW).
GIVEN NAMES Italian 16%. *Corrado, Domenic, Domenica, Ferruccio, Marco, Orest, Vito.*

MacInnes (474) Scottish: see MCINNIS.

MacInnis (502) Scottish: see MCINNIS.

MacIntire (129) Scottish: see MCINTYRE.

MacIntosh (819) Scottish: see MCINTOSH.

MacIntyre (1104) Scottish: see MCINTYRE.
GIVEN NAMES Scottish 4%. *Alasdair* (2), *Alastair, Dugald, Iain.*

Macioce (182) **1.** Italian (southern Lazio): unexplained. **2.** Altered form of Polish *Maciocha*, a derivative of the personal name *Maciej* (see MATTHEW).
GIVEN NAMES Italian 24%. *Mario* (4), *Domenic* (3), *Valerio* (2), *Angelo, Mauro, Pasquale, Vito.*

Maciolek (219) Polish (**Maciołek**): from a pet form of the personal name *Macioł*, a derivative of *Maciej* (see MATTHEW).
GIVEN NAMES Polish 6%. *Aniela, Jozef, Leslaw, Miroslaw, Wladyslaw.*

MacIsaac (438) Scottish: see MCISAAC.
GIVEN NAME Irish 4%. *Donal.*

MacIver (390) Scottish and northern Irish: see MCIVER.
GIVEN NAME Scottish 7%. *Murdo* (3).

Mack (20386) **1.** Scottish (Berwickshire) and Irish: from the Old Norse personal name *Makkr*, a form of MAGNUS (Old Irish *Maccus*). **2.** North German, Dutch, and French (Alsace): from the Germanic personal name *Macco, Makko*, a pet form of a compound name with the initial element *māg-* 'kinsman'. **3.** Shortened form of any of the many Scottish and Irish names beginning *M(a)c-.*

Mackall (343) Scottish: Anglicized form of Gaelic **Mac Cathail** 'son of *Cathal*' (see CAHILL). Compare Irish MCCALL.

MacKay (4090) Scottish and Irish: see MCKAY.
GIVEN NAMES Scottish 4%. *Alastair* (2), *Callum* (2), *Iain* (2), *Murdo* (2), *Alasdair, Dougal.*

Macke (777) Dutch and German: variant of MACK 2.

MacKechnie (125) Scottish: see MCKECHNIE.

Mackel (175) Dutch and German: from a pet form of MACK 2 or a related personal name such as *Markward* or *Markhart* (*Mackart*).

Mackell (100) Dutch and German: variant spelling of MACKEL.

MacKellar (172) Scottish: see MCKELLAR.

Macken (361) **1.** Irish: shortened Anglicized form of Gaelic **Ó Maicín, Ó Macáin**, or **Mac Maicín** (see MACKIN). **2.** Dutch: variant of MACK 2.
GIVEN NAMES Irish 8%. *Colm, Jarlath, Niall.*

Mackenthun (107) German: habitational name from a place so called near Hannover.
GIVEN NAMES German 9%. *Kurt, Lorenz, Otto.*

MacKenzie (5839) Scottish: see MCKENZIE.
GIVEN NAMES Scottish 5%. *Alastair* (4), *Murdo* (3), *Calum, Dougal, Dugald, Ewan, Iain.*

Macker (101) German: variant of MARKWARDT.

Mackert (192) German: variant of MARKWARDT.

Mackes (136) North German and Dutch: patronymic from the Germanic personal name *Macco* (see MACK 2).
GIVEN NAME Jewish 4%; German 4%. *Kurt* (2).

Mackey (10550) **1.** Pronounced with the stress on the first syllable, this is Irish, an Anglicized form of Gaelic **Ó Macdha** 'descendant of *Macdha*', a personal name meaning 'virile', 'manly'. **2.** With the

stress on the second syllable, it is a variant of Scottish and Irish MCKAY.

Mackie (2401) Scottish: Anglicized form of Gaelic **Mac Aodha** 'son of *Aodh*'. Compare MCKAY.

Mackiewicz (536) Polish: patronymic from *Maciek*, a pet form of *Maciej* (see MATTHEW).

MacKillop (122) Scottish: see MCKILLOP.

Mackin (1571) **1.** Irish: Anglicized form of Gaelic **Ó Macáin, Ó Maicín** 'descendant of *Maicín*', or **Mac Maicín** 'son of *Maicín*', a personal name or byname from *mac* 'son', 'youth'. **2.** Dutch: from a pet form of the Germanic personal name *Macco* (see MACK 2).
GIVEN NAME Irish 4%. *Dermot.*

MacKinney (119) Scottish and northern Irish: see MCKINNEY.

MacKinnon (1851) Scottish: see MCKINNON.
GIVEN NAME Scottish 4%. *Alasdair.*

Mackintosh (476) Scottish: see MCINTOSH.

Macklem (153) Irish or Scottish: unexplained. Perhaps a variant of MACKLIN or MCLEAN.

Mackler (272) Jewish (Ashkenazic) and South German (Americanized form of **Mächler**): occupational name from Yiddish *makler* and Middle High German *mecheler* 'broker', 'middleman'.
GIVEN NAMES Jewish 4%. *Sol* (2), *Hyman, Isadore.*

Mackley (428) **1.** English: habitational name from Mackley in Derbyshire, which may have been named in Old English as 'Macca's forest', from an unattested personal name + *lēah* 'woodland clearing', 'glade'. **2.** Scottish: Anglicized form of Gaelic **Mac Donnshleibhe** 'son of *Donnshleibhe*', a personal name literally meaning 'brown hill'. **3.** Probably also an Americanized form of German **Mä(g)gli** (see MAGLEY).

Macklin (1880) **1.** English: unexplained. It occurs chiefly in Hampshire and Wiltshire. **2.** It is also established in Ireland, where it may be an Anglicized form of Gaelic **Mac Giolla Eóin** (see MCLEAN).

MacKnight (252) Irish and Scottish: see MCKNIGHT.

Macko (642) Polish (**Maćko**), Ukrainian, and Slovak: from a pet form of Polish *Maciej*, Slovak *Matej*, or some other Slavic form of MATTHEW.
GIVEN NAMES Polish 4%. *Andrzej, Casimir, Dymitr, Jerzy, Kazimierz, Ryszard, Witold.*

Mackowiak (333) Polish (**Maćkowiak**): patronymic from the personal name *Maciek*, a pet form of *Maciej* (see MATTHEW).
GIVEN NAMES Polish 6%. *Jerzy, Leszek, Maciej, Tadeusz, Wladyslaw, Wojciech.*

Mackowski (171) Polish (also **Maćkowski**): habitational name from any of various places called Maćki, Maćkowo, or

Maćkowy, named with derivatives of the personal name *Maciej* (see MATTHEW).

Mackrell (157) English: **1.** nickname from Old French *maquerel* 'bawd'. **2.** from Middle English *makerel* 'mackerel' (the fish), hence a metonymic occupational name for a fisherman or a seller of these fish. **3.** Possibly also from Middle English *mackerel* 'red scorch marks (on the skin)', perhaps a descriptive nickname for someone with a noticeable birthmark.

Macks (174) North German and Dutch: patronymic from the personal name *Macco* (see MACK).

MacLachlan (510) Scottish: see MCLAUGHLIN.
GIVEN NAMES Scottish 5%. *Calum, Mairi.*

MacLaren (601) Scottish: see MCLAREN.
GIVEN NAME Scottish 4%. *Iain.*

MacLaughlin (447) Scottish: see MCLAUGHLIN.

MacLay (243) Scottish: see MCCLAY.

Maclay (243) Scottish: see MCCLAY.

MacLean (3253) Scottish and Irish: see MCLEAN.
GIVEN NAMES Scottish 5%. *Alasdair, Hamish, Iain.*

MacLeay (102) Scottish: see MCCLAY.

MacLellan (508) Scottish and Irish: see MCCLELLAN.

MacLennan (595) Scottish: see MCLENNAN.
GIVEN NAMES Scottish 6%. *Alastair* (2), *Murdo.*

MacLeod (3518) Scottish: see MCLEOD.
GIVEN NAMES Scottish 6%. *Murdo* (9), *Iain* (2), *Alastair.*

Maclin (673) Variant spelling of Scottish and Irish MCLEAN. See also MACKLIN.

MacMahon (248) Irish: see MCMAHON.
GIVEN NAMES Irish 6%. *Dermot, Peadar.*

MacManus (160) Irish: see MCMANUS.
GIVEN NAMES Irish 10%; French 5%. *Declan, James Patrick, Padraig, Siobhan; Armand, Camille.*

MacMaster (319) Scottish: see MCMASTER.

MacMichael (132) Scottish: see MCMICHAEL.

Macmillan (2520) Scottish: see MCMILLAN.

MacMillen (101) Northern Irish: see MCMILLAN.

MacMullen (194) Scottish: variant of MCMILLAN.

MacMurdo (105) Scottish: see MCMURDO.

MacMurray (262) Irish: see MCMURRAY.

MacNab (210) Scottish and northern Irish: see MCNABB.

MacNair (206) Scottish and Irish: see MCNAIR.

MacNamara (312) Irish: see MCNAMARA.
GIVEN NAMES Irish 5%. *Eamon, Sinead.*

MacNaughton (393) Scottish: see MCNAUGHTON.

MacNeal (235) Irish and Scottish: see MCNEIL.

MacNeil (1220) Irish and Scottish: see MCNEIL.

MacNeill (656) Irish and Scottish: see MCNEIL.

Macom (104) Variant of Scottish MCCOMB or possibly of MALCOLM.

Macomb (106) Variant of Scottish MCCOMB.

Macomber (1541) Irish: variant of MCCOMBER.

Macon (1817) French: **1.** (**Mâçon**): occupational name for a mason, French *maçon*. **2.** habitational name from places so called in Saône-et-Loire, Allier, Aube, the Côte d'Or, Gers, and Deux-Sères. **3.** from the old oblique form of a Germanic personal name *Mako*, from *Mago*, a short form of a compound name formed with *maht* 'strength', 'power' as the first element.

MacPhail (363) Scottish and Irish: see MCPHAIL.
GIVEN NAME Scottish 8%. *Alasdair.*

MacPhee (502) Scottish and Irish: see MCPHEE.

MacPherson (2488) Scottish: see MCPHERSON.
GIVEN NAMES Scottish 5%. *Iain* (3), *Ewan* (2), *Alasdair, Alastair.*

MacQuarrie (339) Scottish: see MCQUARRIE.

MacQueen (442) Scottish: see MCQUEEN.
GIVEN NAME Scottish 6%. *Ewan* (2).

MacRae (1066) Scottish: see MCRAE.

Macri (963) **1.** Italian: patronymic or plural form of the nickname *macro* 'lean', 'thin' (Latin *macer*). **2.** Southern Italian: descriptive nickname derived from medieval Greek *makri* 'tall', 'long' (classical Greek *makros*).
GIVEN NAMES Italian 20%. *Rocco* (13), *Angelo* (4), *Carmelo* (3), *Pasquale* (3), *Antonio* (2), *Carlo* (2), *Domenic* (2), *Franco* (2), *Gaetano* (2), *Salvatore* (2), *Vincenzo* (2), *Agostino.*

Macrina (139) Southern Italian: derivative of MACRI.
GIVEN NAMES Italian 12%. *Domenic* (2), *Angelo, Antonio, Francesco, Vito.*

Macris (142) Greek: see MAKRIS.
GIVEN NAMES Greek 14%. *Constantine* (2), *Demetrios* (2), *Spiros* (2), *Kimon, Panagiota, Spiro, Spyridon.*

MacTaggart (179) Scottish and northern Irish: see MCTAGGART.
GIVEN NAME Scottish 4%. *Iain.*

MacTavish (159) Scottish: see MCTAVISH.

Macumber (180) Irish: variant of MCCOMBER.

MacVicar (150) Scottish and northern Irish: see MCVICAR.
GIVEN NAME Scottish 6%. *Alastair.*

MacWilliams (341) Scottish: see MCWILLIAMS.

Macy (2302) English: variant of MASSEY.

Maczko (162) Polish (also **Mączko**): **1.** from *mąka* 'flour', presumably a metonymic occupational name for a miller or a nickname for someone with a very pale complexion. **2.** nickname from a diminutive of *mak* 'poppy'.

Maczynski (28) Polish (**Mączyński**): habitational name for someone from Mąka in Piotrków voivodeship or Mąki in Kalisz or Suwalki voivodeships, all named with *mąka* 'flour'.

Madan (323) **1.** Indian (Kashmir): Hindu (Brahman) name, probably from an ancestral personal name *Madan* (from Sanskrit *madana* 'god of love, or infatuation'). **2.** Indian (Panjab): Hindu (Arora) and Sikh name based on the name of an Arora clan, probably from Persian *maidān* 'field'. The name from the Panjab is pronounced *mədān*. **3.** English: habitational name from Mathon in Herefordshire, or Mattins Farm, Radwinter, in Essex, or Martinfield Green, Saffron Walden, in Essex. The first of these is named with Old English *māthm* 'treasure', 'gift'.
GIVEN NAMES Indian 59%. *Rajesh* (5), *Arun* (4), *Shashi* (4), *Ajay* (3), *Ashok* (3), *Rajiv* (3), *Sunil* (3), *Vikram* (3), *Anil* (2), *Atul* (2), *Dilip* (2), *Manish* (2).

Madani (100) Muslim: from Arabic *Madani*, a term denoting a follower of a Sufi order, *Madaniyya*, established by Muhammad Hasan ibn Hamza al-Madani (died 1846). The word *madani* literally means 'citizen', 'townsman', or 'polite', 'sociable', 'urbane'.
GIVEN NAMES Muslim 84%. *Mohammad* (4), *Syed* (3), *Hassan* (2), *Majid* (2), *Nabil* (2), *Seyed* (2), *Shirin* (2), *Abdelkader, Ahmed, Ali, Ebrahim, Elahe.*

Madar (237) **1.** Hungarian (**Madár**) and Jewish (from Hungary): from *madár* 'bird', hence a metonymic occupational name for a fowler, or alternatively a nickname for someone thought to resemble a bird. **2.** Slovak (**Maďar**): ethnic name for a Hungarian (see MAGYAR).
GIVEN NAMES Jewish 6%. *Yoav* (2), *Igal, Mordechai, Ravit, Yardena.*

Madara (268) Southern Italian: topographic name from medieval Greek *madara*, feminine of *madaros* 'bald', in Ancient Greek also 'humid', 'wet', or from a byname, *Madaras*, from the same word with the suffix *-as*.

Madaras (151) Hungarian: occupational name for a fowler, from *madár* 'bird' (see MADAR). This is also a common Hungarian place name, and in the form **Madarasi**, the surname may be a habitational name for someone from Madaras in Bács-Kiskun county or from any of various Szekler villages so called in Transylvania.
GIVEN NAME Hungarian 4%. *Laszlo.*

Madariaga (112) Basque: habitational name from any of various places in

Gipuzkoa named Madariaga, from Basque *madari* 'pear tree' + *-aga* 'place'.

GIVEN NAMES Spanish 41%. *Juan* (3), *Jose* (2), *Luis* (2), *Ramon* (2), *Ricardo* (2), *Ana, Celso, Corazon, Eduardo, Fidel, Francisco, Gonzalo.*

Madaris (162) **1.** Probably an Americanized form of Portuguese MADEIRA. **2.** Possibly also an altered form of the Latvian family name **Madara**, from the personal name *Madari, Madara*, based on the name of a wild plant.

FOREBEARS This surname is recorded in VA at an early date. In 1658 Domingo **Madoras** (also spelled **Maderas** and **Mederis**) was a witness to a deed, and in 1668 he received a land grant in New Kent Co., VA. He died in or before 1687, whereupon there was a dispute over the inheritance of his land.

Madaus (114) German or Alsatian: variant of the personal name *Matthäus* (see MATTHEW).

Maday (453) Hungarian: variant of *Madai* or *Mádai*, habitational names for someone from a place called Mada in Szabolcs, or Szatmár county, or Máda in Bács or Hunyad county.

Maddalena (402) Italian and Dutch: from a female personal name taken from Mary *Magdalene*, i.e. Mary of Magdala, mentioned in the Gospels. See also MAUDLIN. In Italy the surname can also be habitational, from any of the numerous places so named from the personal name.

GIVEN NAMES Italian 10%. *Angelo* (3), *Antonio* (2), *Enzo* (2), *Guido* (2), *Aldo, Carmine, Pina, Salvatore.*

Maddalone (100) Italian: **1.** from an augmentative of the personal name *Mad(d)alo*, a derivative of the New Testament Greek personal name *Magdalēnē* (see MAUDLIN). **2.** variant of MADDALONI.

Maddaloni (136) Italian: habitational name from Maddaloni, a place in Caserta province.

GIVEN NAMES Italian 17%. *Aurelio, Claudio, Emilio, Fortunata, Gennaro, Giacinto, Italo, Marco.*

Madden (12997) Irish (Galway): shortened Anglicized form of Gaelic **Ó Madáin** 'descendant of *Madán*', a reduced form of *Madadhán*, from *madadh* 'dog' (see MADIGAN).

Maddern (122) English: nickname for a person with a ruddy complexion, from an adjective derivative of Middle English *mad(d)er* 'madder', the dye plant (see MADER 1), here used in a transferred sense.

Maddex (128) English (of Welsh origin): variant of MADDOX.

Maddin (112) Irish: variant of Irish MADDEN.

Madding (277) Probably a variant of Irish MADDEN.

Maddison (154) English: variant spelling of MADISON.

Maddix (271) English (of Welsh origin): variant of MADDOX.

Maddock (1000) English (of Welsh origin): from the Welsh personal name *Madog* (possibly a diminutive of *mad* 'fortunate', 'good').

Maddocks (471) English (of Welsh origin): variant of MADDOX.

Maddox (11984) English (of Welsh origin): patronymic from the Welsh personal name *Madog* (see MADDOCK).

Maddrey (121) Americanized form of Spanish MADERA.

Maddry (100) Of Spanish origin: see MADDREY.

Maddux (1932) English (of Welsh origin): variant of MADDOX.

Maddy (607) Welsh: from a pet form of the Welsh personal name *Madog* (see MADDOCK).

Madeira (383) **1.** Portuguese: metonymic occupational name for a carpenter, from *madeira* 'wood', 'timber' (Late Latin *materia*, from classical Latin *materies* 'material', 'substance'). **2.** local name from the island of Madeira, which was named with Portuguese *madeira* 'timber' because of the timber that grew there. The island was colonized in the 15th century under the patronage of Prince Henry the Navigator.

GIVEN NAMES Portuguese 17%; Spanish 17%. *Joaquim* (7), *Joao* (6); *Jose* (10), *Carlos* (5), *Manuel* (5), *Alfredo, Amancio, Amando, Ana, Anabel, Arlindo, Armando, Armindo, Augusto.*

Madeiros (122) Portuguese and Galician: variant of MEDEIROS.

GIVEN NAMES Spanish 5%. *Manuel* (2), *Graciela, Silvia.*

Madej (329) Polish: from a short form of the personal name *Amadej* or *Amadeusz* (from medieval Latin *Amadeus*, from *amare* 'to love' + *Deus* 'God'), or from a variant of *Matej* (see MATTHEW).

GIVEN NAMES Polish 18%. *Janusz* (3), *Tadeusz* (3), *Zdzislaw* (3), *Ewa* (2), *Boleslaw, Casimir, Danuta, Dariusz, Edyta, Grzegorz, Iwona, Jozefa.*

Madeja (103) Polish: from a derivative of MADEJ.

Madeley (120) English: habitational name from places so named in Shropshire and Staffordshire, named in Old English with the personal name *Māda* + *lēah* 'woodland clearing'.

GIVEN NAME Dutch 4%. *Algert.*

Maden (234) English (Lancashire): variant of Irish MADDEN.

Mader (2144) **1.** English: metonymic occupational name for a dyer or seller of dye, from Middle English *mad(d)er* 'madder' (Old English *mædere*), a pink to red dye obtained from the roots of the madder plant. **2.** German and Dutch (**Mader, Mäder**): occupational name for a reaper or mower, Middle High German *māder*, *mæder*, Middle Dutch *mader*. **3.** French

(southwestern and southeastern): metonymic occupational name for a carpenter.

Madera (852) **1.** Spanish and Asturian-Leonese: from *madera* 'wood', 'timber' (from Late Latin *materia*), probably applied as a topographic name or a habitational name from a place named with this word, as for example La Madera in Asturies. **2.** Czech (**Maděra**): ethnic name from an old word for a Hungarian (see MAGYAR).

GIVEN NAMES Spanish 43%. *Jose* (25), *Juan* (8), *Pedro* (7), *Miguel* (6), *Francisco* (5), *Lourdes* (5), *Manuel* (5), *Carlos* (4), *Enrique* (4), *Jesus* (4), *Luz* (4), *Alfonso* (3).

Madere (439) French (**Madère**): feminine form of MADER 3.

GIVEN NAMES French 8%. *Chantel* (2), *Antoine, Emile, Jacques, Leonce, Odette, Pierre.*

Madero (255) Spanish: from *madero* 'wood', 'trunk', probably applied as a nickname for a stupid person.

GIVEN NAMES Spanish 44%. *Manuel* (4), *Guillermo* (3), *Javier* (3), *Jose* (3), *Alejandro* (2), *Angel* (2), *Carlos* (2), *Fernando* (2), *Juan* (2), *Raul* (2), *Reyes* (2), *Ruben* (2).

Mades (104) German: variant of the personal name *Matthäus* (see MATTHEW).

Madewell (571) English: variant spelling of **Maidwell**, a habitational name from a place in Northamptonshire named Maidwell, from Old English *mægden* 'maidens' + *wella* 'spring', 'stream'.

Madey (154) Polish: Americanized spelling of MADEJ.

GIVEN NAMES Polish 7%. *Jozef, Rafal.*

Madia (216) Southern Italian: from a short form of the female personal name *Amadio* (see AMEDEO). Stressed *Màdia* (as opposed to *Madìa*) it is probably from a Apulian personal name, *Màdia*, popularized by the cult of Maria Santissima della Màdia.

GIVEN NAMES Italian 24%. *Angelo* (3), *Mario* (2), *Domenico, Emilio, Gaetano, Giuseppe, Tommaso, Valentino.*

Madigan (2364) Irish: Anglicized form of Gaelic **Ó Madagáin** 'descendant of *Madagán*', from *Madadhán*, a personal name meaning 'little dog'. This name occurs chiefly in western Ireland.

GIVEN NAMES Irish 5%. *Brendan, Conor.*

Madill (341) Irish (Monaghan and Cavan): **1.** when stressed on the first syllable, this is of Norman origin, from Old French *masle*, *madle* 'male'. **2.** With the stress on the second syllable, it is a variant of MADOLE.

Madison (8189) English: metronymic from the medieval female personal name *Madde*, a form of *Maud* (see MOULD 1) or *Magdalen* (see MAUDLIN).

FOREBEARS James Madison (1751–1836), 4th President of the U.S. (1809–17), was born in VA, the son of a planter. He was descended from John Madison, a ship's carpenter from Gloucester, England, who had settled in VA in about 1653.

Madkins (162) English: metronymic from a pet form of the personal name *Madde* (see MADISON).

Madl (185) **1.** German: habitational name from Madl in Bavaria, or a topographic name from Middle High German *māt* 'meadow', 'grassland'. **2.** Czech and Hungarian (**Mádl**): from German *Madel* or *Mädel* 'girl', nickname for someone thought to resemble a young girl.

Madland (133) Norwegian: habitational name from any of five farmsteads so named in southwestern Norway, which probably originally bore the Old Norse name *Matland* 'farmstead' from *mat* 'food' + *land* 'land', 'farmstead'.
GIVEN NAME Scandinavian 4%. *Thor.*

Madler (101) German: **1.** (also **Mädler**) habitational name from any of various small places in southern Germany and Austria with names such as Madl and Madlau. **2.** (**Mädler**) from a Germanic personal name composed of Old High German *mahal* 'traditional meeting place of a court' + *hari* 'army' (compare MEHLING).
GIVEN NAMES German 7%. *Achim, Hermann, Hildegard.*

Madlock (163) English: probably a variant of MATLOCK.

Madoff (100) Origin unidentified. Perhaps a variant of Bulgarian and Jewish (eastern Ashkenazic) MEDOFF.

Madole (323) Northern Irish: reduced form of McDOWELL.

Madonia (425) Southern Italian: habitational name from any of numerous places named Madonia, or a regional name for someone from Madonie in Sicily.
GIVEN NAMES Italian 20%. *Angelo* (6), *Salvatore* (3), *Gasper* (2), *Mario* (2), *Sal* (2), *Calogero, Carlo, Concetta, Elio, Enza, Ettore, Francesco, Gaspare.*

Madonna (595) Italian: from the person name *Madonna*, from *donna* 'lady', bestowed in honor of the Virgin Mary, or a habitational name from any of numerous places named with this word.
GIVEN NAMES Italian 10%. *Angelo* (2), *Aniello* (2), *Salvatore* (2), *Antonio, Augustino, Carlo, Carmel, Cosmo, Enrico, Pasquale, Plinio, Sante.*

Madore (931) French: apparently from a shortened form of the personal name *Amadour*, from Latin *Amator* meaning 'lover'.
GIVEN NAMES French 10%. *Armand* (5), *Eusebe* (2), *Fernand* (2), *Lucien* (2), *Normand* (2), *Adhemar, Adrien, Donat, Elzear, Francois, Gaetan, Gilles.*

Madray (127) Of Spanish origin: variant of MADDREY.

Madrazo (123) Spanish: unexplained.
GIVEN NAMES Spanish 24%; French 7%. *Jose* (5), *Alfredo* (2), *Carlos* (2), *Manuel* (2),

Armando, Corazon, Esteban, Felipe, Jorge, Julio, Rosa Maria.

Madren (119) English: probably a habitational name from Madron in Cornwall. Alternatively, possibly from Madryn in Gwynedd, Wales.

Madrid (3181) Spanish: habitational name from what is now Spain's principal city. Throughout the Middle Ages it was of only modest size and importance, and did not become the capital of Spain until 1561. Its name is of uncertain origin, most probably a derivative of Late Latin *matrix*, genitive *matricis* 'riverbed', much changed by Arabic mediation. Compare MADRIGAL. There are other, smaller places of the same name in the provinces of Burgos and Santander, and these may also be sources of the surname.
GIVEN NAMES Spanish 35%. *Jose* (40), *Manuel* (38), *Carlos* (25), *Jesus* (23), *Juan* (23), *Luis* (18), *Raul* (16), *Ruben* (13), *Mario* (11), *Pedro* (11), *Ramon* (10), *Armando* (9).

Madrigal (2069) Spanish: habitational name from any of various places, for example in the provinces of Avila, Burgos, Cáceres, and Guadalajara, apparently so called from Late Latin *matricale*, an adjective derivative of *matrix* 'womb', 'river bed'.
GIVEN NAMES Spanish 54%; Portuguese 12%. *Jose* (67), *Juan* (30), *Luis* (26), *Miguel* (26), *Carlos* (21), *Manuel* (20), *Francisco* (19), *Rafael* (17), *Jorge* (16), *Javier* (15), *Guadalupe* (13), *Ruben* (13); *Paulo.*

Madril (194) Origin uncertain. It occurs in Spain, chiefly in Valencia, and may be of Arabic origin.
GIVEN NAMES Spanish 26%. *Manuel* (2), *Angel, Armando, Arturo, Blanca, Carlos, Castro, Cipriano, Demetrio, Domingo, Edmundo, Ernesto.*

Madron (190) English (Cornwall): habitational name from Madron in Cornwall, named for the patron saint of its church, St. Madernus.

Madruga (260) Spanish and Portuguese: nickname for an early riser, from *madrugar* 'to get up early'.
GIVEN NAMES Spanish 22%; Portuguese 9%. *Luis* (5), *Manuel* (4), *Mario* (3), *Eugenio* (2), *Jaime* (2), *Jose* (2), *Pedro* (2), *Ana Maria, Angelina, Augusto, Candelaria, Carlos; Joao* (2).

Madry (233) Polish (**Mądry**): nickname from the vocabulary word *mądry* 'wise'.
GIVEN NAMES Polish 8%. *Kazimierz* (2), *Janusz, Miroslaw, Ryszard.*

Madsen (6816) Danish and Norwegian: patronymic from a pet form of *Mathias* (see MATTHEW).
GIVEN NAMES Scandinavian 7%. *Erik* (17), *Nels* (7), *Jorgen* (6), *Per* (6), *Viggo* (4), *Anders* (3), *Carsten* (3), *Niels* (3), *Thor* (3), *Alf* (2), *Einer* (2), *Jeppe* (2).

Madson (1282) **1.** English: variant of MADISON. **2.** Americanized spelling of

Danish and Norwegian MADSEN, possibly also of Swedish MATTSSON.

Madura (322) Polish: from a reduced derivative of the personal name *Amadeusz* (see AMADEO).

Maduro (124) Spanish and Portuguese: nickname from *maduro* 'ripe', which from the 12th century also had a figurative sense of 'mature', 'sensible'.
GIVEN NAMES Spanish 35%. *Carlos* (2), *Jorge* (2), *Jose* (2), *Raul* (2), *Roberto* (2), *Alvaro, Arturo, Carlota, Esperanza, Leonarda, Manuel, Marina; Antonio, Federico, Lorenzo.*

Mady (132) **1.** Hungarian (**Mády**): habitational name for someone from a place called Mád in Zemplén county, or Mad in Pozsony county, now in Slovakia. **2.** Muslim: variant of MAHDI.
GIVEN NAMES Muslim 5%. *Fathy* (3), *Nabil, Naeem, Zainab.*

Mae (149) **1.** Japanese: 'front' or 'before'; not common in Japan. Some occurrences in America could be shortened versions of longer names beginning with this element. **2.** Hawaiian: unexplained. **3.** English: variant of MAY.
GIVEN NAMES Japanese 14%. *Akihiro, Ichiro, Kenichiro, Wakako, Yoshikazu.*

Maeda (611) Japanese: 'front rice paddy'. It is found mostly on the island of Kyūshū and the Ryūkyū Islands.
FOREBEARS Two families of daimyō (Japanese feudal barons), called Maeda, both descended from the ancient Sugawara family, were prominent in the decades preceding the establishment of the Tokugawa Shogunate (1603–1867), which neither supported.
GIVEN NAMES Japanese 66%. *Yoshio* (7), *Hiroshi* (5), *Yoko* (4), *Akihiro* (3), *Akiko* (3), *Akira* (3), *Mayumi* (3), *Minoru* (3), *Susumu* (3), *Tatsuo* (3), *Hajime* (2), *Hirofumi* (2).

Maeder (399) German (**Mäder**) and Dutch: variant of MADER 2.

Maekawa (109) Japanese: 'river in front'. This name is found mostly in western Japan and the Ryūkyū Islands.
GIVEN NAMES Japanese 75%. *Kazuo* (2), *Koji* (2), *Aki, Akira, Atsushi, Eishi, Genji, Haruo, Hiro, Hiroaki, Hiroko, Hiromichi.*

Mael (145) Dutch (**van Mael**): see MALE.

Maenner (135) German (**Männer**): see MANER.

Maenza (177) Southern Italian: habitational name from Maenza in Latina province, probably so named from the Latin personal name *Magius* or *Maius*, or from any of various places so named, from medieval Latin *maiensis* '(payment) in the month of May', presumably denoting some sort of tax obligation.
GIVEN NAMES Italian 19%. *Salvatore* (4), *Saverio* (2), *Carlo, Carmine, Gaetano, Rocco.*

Maertens (172) **1.** Dutch: patronymic from *Maerten*, a variant of MARTIN. **2.** Americanized spelling of German **Märtens**, a variant of MARTENS.

Maertz (192) German (**Märtz**): **1.** variant of MAERZ. **2.** from a pet form of any of the personal names formed with *Mar-* or *Mark-*, for example *Marbod, Markward*.
GIVEN NAME German 5%. *Gunther*.

Maerz (230) German: from a nickname from the month of March, Middle High German *merze*, bestowed on someone born or baptized in March, or with some other particular connection with the month, perhaps a tax or feudal obligation owing then.
GIVEN NAMES German 7%. *Egon, Konrad, Otto, Siegfried, Volker, Willi.*

Maes (1553) **1.** Dutch: variant of MAAS 1. **2.** Spanish: unexplained; perhaps a variant of MAESE.
GIVEN NAMES Spanish 6%; French 4%. *Jose* (10), *Juan* (3), *Manuel* (3), *Margarito* (3), *Alfonso* (2), *Basilio* (2), *Eloy* (2), *Emilia* (2), *Miguel* (2), *Ruben* (2), *Adolfo, Agapito*; *Alphonse* (3), *Remy* (3), *Raoul* (2), *Alain, Andre, Cecile, Jacques, Luc, Marcel, Michel, Monique, Yolaine.*

Maese (252) **1.** Dutch: patronymic from MAES. **2.** Spanish: from *maese*, an obsolete form of *maestro* 'master', 'teacher' (from Latin *magister*).
GIVEN NAMES Spanish 29%. *Jose* (6), *Alfredo* (3), *Jesus* (3), *Armando* (2), *Edmundo* (2), *Manuel* (2), *Mario* (2), *Roberto* (2), *Salomon* (2), *Carlos, Efren, Emilia*; *Antonio* (2), *Lorenzo* (2), *Francesca.*

Maestas (1690) Hispanic: unexplained.
GIVEN NAMES Spanish 17%. *Jose* (19), *Juan* (14), *Manuel* (8), *Eloy* (6), *Ramon* (6), *Ruben* (5), *Carlos* (4), *Fidel* (4), *Orlando* (4), *Alfonso* (3), *Fermin* (3), *Miguel* (3).

Maestre (109) Portuguese and Spanish: status name from old Spanish and Portuguese *maestre* 'master', 'master craftsman', 'teacher' (Latin *magister*).
GIVEN NAMES Spanish 30%. *Jose* (5), *Fernando* (3), *Alfonso* (2), *Angel* (2), *Juan* (2), *Pedro* (2), *Adriano, Altagracia, Aura, Eduardo, Esperanza, Jorge*; *Antonio, Dante.*

Maestri (259) Italian: status name for a master craftsman or a scholar, from *maestro* 'master' (Latin *magister*).
GIVEN NAMES Italian 7%. *Angelo* (2), *Dante, Marcello, Marino, Santo.*

Maez (338) Spanish: perhaps a variant of MAES.
GIVEN NAMES Spanish 13%. *Manuel* (5), *Carlos* (2), *Adela, Alfonso, Aracely, Brijido, Catalina, Celestino, Domingo, Hilario, Jose, Juan.*

Maffei (826) Italian: patronymic or plural form of MAFFEO.
GIVEN NAMES Italian 12%. *Vito* (5), *Angelo* (3), *Carmine* (3), *Antonio* (2), *Sal* (2), *Agostino, Aldo, Carina, Cosmo, Dino, Domenico, Franco.*

Maffeo (302) Italian: from the personal name *Maffeo*, an old variant of *Matteo* (see MATTHEW).
GIVEN NAMES Italian 8%. *Angelo, Guilio, Salvatore, Silvio.*

Maffett (341) Scottish and northern Irish: variant of MOFFATT.

Maffia (209) Italian: variant of MATTIA.
GIVEN NAMES Italian 10%. *Romeo* (2), *Angelo, Carmine, Gennaro, Rinaldo, Salvatore.*

Maffucci (211) Italian: from a pet form of MAFFEO.
GIVEN NAMES Italian 12%. *Angelo* (2), *Gaetano* (2), *Canio, Salvatore, Vito.*

Maga (132) **1.** Polish: from Middle High German *mâge* 'blood relative' (literally 'belly'). **2.** Possibly also a Polish nickname from a derivative of the dialect word *magać* 'to wave'. **3.** Romanian (**Magă**): from Hungarian *mag* 'seed'.

Magaha (120) Irish: Anglicized form of Gaelic **Mac Eachaidh** (see McGAFFEY).

Magaldi (101) Italian: from the Germanic personal name *Magaldo*.
GIVEN NAME Italian 6%. *Angelo.*

Magalhaes (181) Portuguese or Galician: habitational name from any of various places named Magalhães.
GIVEN NAMES Spanish 35%; Portuguese 27%. *Manuel* (8), *Jose* (6), *Carlos* (5), *Fernando* (4), *Armando* (2), *Domingos* (2), *Helio* (2), *Mario* (2), *Sergio* (2), *Adriana, Alvaro, Ana*; *Joao* (5), *Joaquim, Paulo*; *Antonio* (11), *Ernani, Leonardo.*

Magallanes (642) Spanish: habitational name from the village of Magaláns (Castilian *Magalanes*) in Pontevedra province.
GIVEN NAMES Spanish 49%. *Jose* (25), *Juan* (10), *Jesus* (7), *Guadalupe* (6), *Luis* (6), *Francisco* (5), *Raul* (5), *Armando* (4), *Arturo* (4), *Fernando* (4), *Mario* (4), *Ricardo* (4).

Magallanez (134) Spanish: variant of MAGALLANES.
GIVEN NAMES Spanish 38%. *Arturo* (3), *Armando* (2), *Librado* (2), *Luis* (2), *Lupe* (2), *Manuel* (2), *Apolonio, Armida, Blanca, Bonifacio, Eduardo, Elida.*

Magallon (307) Spanish (**Magallón**): habitational name from a place called Magallón in Zaragoza province.
GIVEN NAMES Spanish 53%. *Jose* (13), *Francisco* (6), *Juan* (6), *Rafael* (5), *Javier* (4), *Leticia* (4), *Miguel* (4), *Carlos* (3), *Jesus* (3), *Manuel* (3), *Salvador* (3), *Alberto* (2); *Antonio* (4), *Leonardo* (3), *Dino, Julieta, Lorenzo, Marco, Sal.*

Magan (199) **1.** Spanish (**Magán**): habitational name from Magán, a village in Toledo province. **2.** German: from Old High German *magan* 'strength'.

Magana (2558) Spanish (**Magaña**): habitational name from either of the villages named Magaña, in Soria and Córdoba provinces.

GIVEN NAMES Spanish 56%. *Jose* (88), *Juan* (40), *Jesus* (37), *Luis* (32), *Francisco* (28), *Manuel* (26), *Jorge* (24), *Mario* (22), *Rafael* (21), *Salvador* (21), *Miguel* (19), *Ruben* (18).

Magann (149) Irish: **1.** variant of McGAHAN, with elision of the *h*. **2.** variant of McGANN.

Magar (155) **1.** Romanian: ethnic name for a Hungarian. **2.** Indian (Maharashtra): Hindu (Maratha) name meaning 'crocodile'.
GIVEN NAMES Indian 4%. *Ramesh, Sharad.*

Magarian (142) Armenian: perhaps a patronymic from a personal name derived from Greek *Makarios* 'blessed'.
GIVEN NAMES Armenian 11%; French 5%. *Aram, Arsen, Artin, Jirair, Krikor, Ohannes, Sedik, Vahag, Vahan*; *Alphonse, Michel.*

Magaro (158) Southern Italian: nickname from Sicilian *maggaru* 'sorcerer', 'wizard', from Latin *magus*, Greek *magos*.
GIVEN NAMES Italian 11%. *Dino, Guido, Marino, Remo, Salvatore.*

Magas (101) Dutch: unexplained. Probably a derivative of the female personal name *Marguerite* (see MARGESON).
GIVEN NAME Dutch 4%. *Gust* (2).

Magat (116) **1.** Jewish (eastern Ashkenazic and Sephardic): variant of MAGID 'preacher'. **2.** Filipino: unexplained.
GIVEN NAMES Spanish 25%; French 8%. *Abelardo, Alfredo, Andres, Carlos, Consuelo, Cornelio, Eduardo, Elvira, Fermin, Filomeno, Genaro, Gerardo*; *Pierre* (2), *Yves.*

Magaw (182) Scottish and Irish: see McCAW.
GIVEN NAME French 5%. *Camille* (2).

Magby (278) Probably a variant of Scottish or Irish McBEE, itself a shortened form of McBETH. In Gaelic, *-th-* is silent.
FOREBEARS This surname is borne mainly by African Americans.

Magda (333) Polish, Slovak, and Hungarian: from the female personal name *Magda*, a short form of Slavic *Magdalena*, Hungarian *Magdolna* (see MAUDLIN).
GIVEN NAMES Polish 6%. *Bogdan, Boguslaw, Bronislaw, Casimir, Jozef, Kazimierz, Wieslaw.*

Magdaleno (653) Spanish: from the personal name *Magdaleno*, masculine form of the Biblical name *Magdalena* (see MAUDLIN).
GIVEN NAMES Spanish 44%. *Jose* (26), *Manuel* (10), *Jesus* (8), *Jorge* (7), *Ramon* (6), *Rafael* (5), *Angel* (4), *Francisco* (4), *Ignacio* (4), *Javier* (4), *Juan* (4), *Miguel* (4); *Antonio* (3), *Geronimo* (2), *Albertina, Angelo, Eliseo, Heriberto, Lorenzo, Marco Antonio, Nino, Sal.*

Magee (9222) Scottish and Irish: Anglicized form of Gaelic **Mac Aodha** (see McGEE).

Magel (242) Dutch: from a female personal name derived from the Germanic female personal name *Machthild*, composed of the elements *macht* 'strength', 'might' + *hild* 'strife', 'battle'.
GIVEN NAMES German 8%. *Otto* (2), *Arno, Erna, Erwin, Klaus, Kurt, Reinhard.*

Magennis (114) Irish: variant of MCGINNIS.
GIVEN NAME Irish 8%. *Brendan.*

Mager (1215) **1.** Dutch and German: nickname for a thin man, Middle Dutch, Middle High German *mager*. This name also occurs frequently in western Slavic countries, especially Bohemia and Poland. **2.** English: variant of MAJOR. **3.** Czech: ethnic name for a Hungarian (see MAGYAR).

Magera (139) Czech: variant of MAGER.

Magers (1012) German, Dutch, and English: patronymic from MAGER.

Mages (291) German: probably a patronymic from a variant of the personal name MACK.
FOREBEARS The family of Wolfgang Mages (1784–1871) emigrated from Freihung, Bavaria, to Milwaukee, WI, in the early 19th century.
GIVEN NAMES French 4%. *Alphonse* (2), *Camille.*

Maggard (1943) English: from a pet form of the Middle English female personal name *Magge*, a short form of *Margaret* (see MARGESON).

Maggart (358) English: variant of MAGGARD.

Maggert (118) English: variant of MAGGARD.

Maggi (565) **1.** Italian and Swiss Italian: patronymic from MAGGIO. **2.** French (Savoy and eastern France): from a pet form of the Germanic personal name *Maggo*, a short form of compound names with the initial element *mag-* (from *magan* 'strength', 'might').
GIVEN NAMES Italian 23%. *Angelo* (5), *Aldo* (3), *Gino* (3), *Agostino* (2), *Alessio* (2), *Antonio* (2), *Guido* (2), *Sal* (2), *Sergio* (2), *Americo, Carmela, Deno, Decio, Elena, Elvira, Ennio, Fortunato, Giacomo, Julio, Luciana, Mario, Octavio.*

Maggiacomo (128) Italian (Sicily): compound of MAGGIO and GIACOMO.
GIVEN NAMES Italian 17%. *Antonio* (2), *Sal* (2), *Carmela, Concetta, Ennio, Gilda, Orlando, Piero, Salvatore, Sirio, Valentino.*

Maggio (2151) Italian: from a nickname or personal name from the month of May, *maggio*, from Latin *Maius (mensis)*, from *Maia*, a rather obscure goddess of fertility, whose name is derived from the same root as *maius* 'larger' and *maiestas* 'greatness'. This may have been bestowed on someone born or baptized in the month of May, or it may have been used to refer to someone of a sunny disposition, or who had some anecdotal connection with the month of May, such as owing a feudal obligation then. In Roman Catholicism, May is specially associated with the Virgin Mary, so the name may well have had a religious significance.
GIVEN NAMES Italian 13%. *Salvatore* (18), *Rocco* (8), *Angelo* (4), *Domenic* (3), *Nino* (3), *Sal* (3), *Santo* (3), *Vito* (3), *Gino* (2), *Ignazio* (2), *Marco* (2), *Pietro* (2).

Maggiore (403) Italian: from *maggiore* 'greater' (Latin *maior*), hence 'elder', applied as a distinguishing byname, particularly to denote the eldest son, or as an honorific title. It also denoted a rank of army officer, 'major'.
GIVEN NAMES Italian 16%. *Salvatore* (5), *Rocco* (3), *Angelo* (2), *Carmine, Enzo, Pasquale, Riccardo, Sal.*

Maggs (264) English (chiefly Somerset and Wiltshire): metronymic from the medieval female personal name *Mag(ge)*, a pet form of *Margaret* (see MARGESON).

Magid (458) Jewish (Ashkenazic): occupational name for a preacher, Hebrew *magid*, Yiddish *maged*.
GIVEN NAMES Jewish 9%; Russian 4%. *Meyer* (2), *Shaul* (2), *Hillel, Ilya, Nachum, Shaya, Sol, Zeev; Mikhail* (2), *Boris, Gennady, Igor, Iosif, Marima, Sofya.*

Magidson (132) Jewish (from Belarus): patronymic from MAGID.

Magie (152) Scottish and Irish: Anglicized form of Gaelic **Mac Aodha** 'son of *Aodh*' (see MCGEE).

Magiera (340) Polish: nickname from German *mager* 'lean', 'thin' (see MAGER).
GIVEN NAMES Polish 5%. *Grazyna, Jaroslaw, Kazimierz, Slawek, Tadeusz, Zygmont.*

Magill (2177) Scottish (Galloway) and Irish: **1.** Anglicized form of **Mac an Ghoill** 'son of the lowlander or stranger'. In Ireland the name was given to the descendants of early Anglo-Norman settlers. **2.** probably in some cases a short form of a surname beginning *Mac Giolla.*

Magin (391) Spanish (**Magín**): Castilian form of Catalan **Magí**, from the personal name *Maginus*, probably a variant of Latin *Maximus*. The name was borne by a minor Spanish saint from Tarragona, who was martyred at the beginning of the 4th century.

Maginn (223) Irish: see MCGINN.

Maginnis (450) Irish: see MCGINNIS.
GIVEN NAME Irish 5%. *Brendan.*

Magistro (167) Italian: occupational name for a teacher, or for a master of a craft or profession, or an expert scholar, from Latin *magister* 'master'.
GIVEN NAMES Italian 20%. *Angelo* (2), *Filippo* (2), *Sal* (2), *Dino, Donato, Nicola, Pasquale, Salvatore, Vito.*

Magleby (152) Danish: topographic name from places on the islands of Mon and Langeland, so named from *magle* 'large', 'big' + *by* 'farm', 'settlement'.
FOREBEARS American bearers of this surname are descended from Hans Olsen Magleby (1835–1903), who emigrated from Denmark to UT in 1859.

Magley (190) Americanized form of South German and Swiss German **Mäg(g)li**, from the Germanic personal name *Macco, Makko*, a pet form of a compound name with the initial element *māg-* 'kinsman'. Compare North German MACK.

Magliano (149) Italian: habitational name from any of eight places throughout Italy named with Magliano, in particular Magliano Vetere in Salerno and Magliano de Marsi in Aquila.
GIVEN NAMES Italian 11%. *Attilio, Rinaldo, Vito.*

Magliaro (129) Italian: occupational name for a maker or seller of fishing nets and traps or of chainmail, from an agent derivative of *maglia* 'mesh', 'net', 'mailcoat'.
GIVEN NAMES Italian 14%. *Angelo, Antonio, Camillo, Edoardo.*

Maglio (566) Italian: apparently from *maglio* 'wooden mallet (for killing cattle)' (from Latin *malleus* 'hammer'), hence presumably a nickname for a slaughterer. However, it may in fact be from an unidentified personal name.
GIVEN NAMES Italian 16%. *Angelo* (4), *Vito* (3), *Antonio* (2), *Francesco* (2), *Rocco* (2), *Sal* (2), *Silvio* (2), *Aldo, Biagio, Concetta, Gino, Luciano.*

Magliocca (104) Italian: variant (feminine in form) of **Magliocco**, from a diminutive of MAGLIO.
GIVEN NAME Italian 9%. *Santo.*

Magliocco (174) Southern Italian: from a diminutive of MAGLIO.
GIVEN NAMES Italian 22%. *Angelo* (2), *Luigi* (2), *Antonio, Cesare, Gino, Nicola, Pasquale, Quirino, Salvatore.*

Maglione (373) Italian: **1.** from an augmentative of MAGLIO, or a habitational name from a place in Turin, named with the same word. **2.** alternatively, perhaps from *maglione* 'castrated bull', 'steer', a derivative of *magliare* 'to hit with a hammer', 'to castrate'.
GIVEN NAMES Italian 19%. *Angelo* (4), *Rocco* (3), *Gennaro* (2), *Sal* (2), *Vito* (2), *Agostino, Antonio, Carmine, Giovanna, Giuseppe, Pasquale.*

Magliozzi (127) Italian: derivative of MAGLIO.
GIVEN NAMES Italian 19%. *Rocco* (3), *Cosmo* (2), *Oreste* (2), *Agostino, Angelo, Salvatore.*

Magloire (102) French: from the personal name *Maglorius*, of Gallic origin. The name was borne by a 6th century bishop of Dol.
GIVEN NAMES French 48%. *Jacques* (3), *Huguette* (2), *Serge* (2), *Achille, Aliette, Fernand, Gisele, Jean Robert, Jean-Robert, Ketly, Leandre, Maxime.*

Magnan (405) **1.** French: occupational name for a traveling tinker or locksmith, Old French *ma(i)gna(i)n*, literally 'worker', from a Late Latin derivative of *machina* 'work', 'trade', earlier 'contrivance', 'device'. This term also means 'silkworm', and the surname may also be an occupational name or nickname in this sense. **2.** Northern Italian: variant of MAGNANI.

FOREBEARS The name Magnan, from Normandy, France, is documented in Iroquois territory and at Quebec City in 1627. A Magnan or **Maigné**, from Poitou, France, is recorded in Quebec City in 1669. Another family called Magnan, also called LESPERANCE, from Berry, France, are documented in Montreal in 1672, and a **LeMagnan**, also called **LaGeauge**, of unknown origin, occurs in the documents of Sorel, Quebec, for 1675.

GIVEN NAMES French 7%. *Armand, Celine, Edeline, Euclide, Normand, Raoul, Valere, Yves.*

Magnani (418) Italian: patronymic or plural form of MAGNANO.

GIVEN NAMES Italian 26%. *Mario* (6), *Alberto* (3), *Aldo* (3), *Dante* (2), *Giorgio* (2), *Emilio, Enrico, Ercole, Evo, Gianluca, Gianni, Gino, Luciano, Matteo, Maurizio, Carlos, Manuel, Orlando, Roberto.*

Magnano (152) Italian: occupational name from the mainly northern regional term *magnano, magnàn* 'smith' or 'traveling tinker'. Compare French MAGNAN.

GIVEN NAMES Italian 22%. *Salvatore* (4), *Marco* (3), *Angelo* (2), *Margherita, Michelina.*

Magnant (188) Southern French: variant of MAGNAN 2.

Magner (1097) Irish: from a pet form of the Scandinavian name *Magnus*, in Ireland borne by both Vikings and Normans.

Magness (1180) English or Irish: probably a variant of MAGNUS.

FOREBEARS Perrygren (Peregrine) Magness was born in 1722 in Britain, and died in 1800 in Warren Co., KY.

Magni (131) Italian: patronymic or plural form of MAGNO.

GIVEN NAMES Italian 14%. *Riccardo* (2), *Tiziano* (2), *Angelo, Eliseo, Enrico, Enzo, Evo.*

Magnifico (122) Italian (Sicily): nickname from *magnifico* 'magnificent', used as a respectful term of address for a senior administrator, dean, etc.

GIVEN NAMES Italian 12%. *Orlando* (2), *Fiorino, Giuseppe, Adolfo.*

Magnin (143) French: occupational name for a traveling boilermaker.

GIVEN NAMES French 6%. *Laurent, Yves.*

Magno (515) Italian: **1.** from a short form of *Alamangno* meaning 'Germanic'. **2.** nickname or byname from *magno* 'fat'.

GIVEN NAMES Spanish 15%; Italian 13%. *Jose* (4), *Mario* (4), *Raymundo* (4), *Manuel* (3), *Manolo* (2), *Orlando* (2), *Sixto* (2), *Alfredo, Ana, Andres, Angel, Armando*; *Carlo* (7), *Angelo* (2), *Alessandro, Antonio,*

Cesare, Ciriaco, Enrico, Evangelio, Gaetano, Gilda, Giulio, Luigi.

Magnon (118) French: from the old oblique case of the Germanic personal name *Magino, -onis* (derived from Old High German *magan* 'strength', 'might').

Magnone (197) Italian: from an augmentative of MAGNO.

GIVEN NAMES Italian 24%. *Caesar* (2), *Carmine* (2), *Giuseppe* (2), *Angelo, Bonaventura, Dino, Domenic, Fiore, Guido, Matteo, Natale, Rinaldo.*

Magnotta (283) Southern Italian: from a diminutive of *Magna*, a feminine form of MAGNO 1, or a shortened form of the Lombardic female personal name *Alemagna* (see MAGNO 2).

GIVEN NAMES Italian 24%. *Rocco* (7), *Angelo* (3), *Mario* (3), *Alphonso* (2), *Amadeo, Amedeo, Antonio, Emilio, Gerardo, Livio, Luigi, Ugo.*

Magnotti (107) Italian: from a diminutive of MAGNO.

GIVEN NAMES Italian 9%. *Vito* (2), *Angelo.*

Magnus (917) English, Scottish, Swedish, Danish, Norwegian, German, and Dutch: from the Scandinavian personal name *Magnus*. This was borne by Magnus the Good (died 1047), king of Norway, who was named for the Emperor Charlemagne, Latin *Carolus Magnus* 'CHARLES the Great'. The name spread from Norway to the eastern Scandinavian royal houses, and became popular all over Scandinavia and thence in the English Danelaw. It has also been adopted as a Jewish name.

GIVEN NAMES German 4%. *Gerhard* (2), *Bernd, Egon, Erwin, Kurt, Otto, Reinhard, Volker, Wilhelm, Wolfgang.*

Magnusen (131) Variant of Danish and Norwegian MAGNUSSEN.

GIVEN NAME Scandinavian 4%. *Nels.*

Magnuson (3636) Americanized spelling of Swedish MAGNUSSON or Danish and Norwegian MAGNUSSEN.

GIVEN NAMES Scandinavian 5%. *Erik* (8), *Nels* (6), *Helmer* (4), *Sven* (3), *Kerstin* (2), *Alf, Anders, Hilma, Knut, Monrad, Thor.*

Magnussen (352) Danish, Norwegian, and North German: patronymic from MAGNUS.

GIVEN NAMES Scandinavian 15%. *Erik* (4), *Alf, Bjorn, Helle, Oivind.*

Magnusson (746) Swedish: patronymic from the personal name MAGNUS.

GIVEN NAMES Scandinavian 16%; German 4%. *Erik* (2), *Niels* (2), *Anders, Erland, Gisli, Kerstin, Lars, Nils, Ottar, Thor*; *Hans* (2), *Kurt* (2), *Fritz.*

Magoffin (100) Variant of northern Irish McGAFFIN.

Magoon (816) Probably an altered form of Scottish and Irish McGOWAN. Compare MAGOUN.

Magouirk (165) Irish and Scottish: variant of McGUIRK.

Magoun (101) Probably an altered form of Scottish and Irish McGOWAN. Compare MAGOON.

Magowan (210) Scottish and Irish: see McGOWAN.

Magrath (262) Irish: variant of McGRATH.

Magri (272) **1.** Italian: patronymic or plural form of MAGRO. **2.** Catalan (**Magrí**): from a diminutive of *magre* 'lean'.

GIVEN NAMES Italian 13%. *Angelo* (3), *Gino* (2), *Aldo, Antonino, Bruna, Carlo, Domenic, Pierina, Salvatore, Sebastiano.*

Magrini (150) Italian: from a diminutive of MAGRO.

GIVEN NAMES Italian 11%. *Aldo* (3), *Evo* (3), *Dino.*

Magrino (102) Italian: diminutive of MAGRO.

GIVEN NAME Italian 8%. *Rocco* (2).

Magro (380) Italian, Spanish, and Portuguese: nickname for a thin person, from Spanish, Portuguese, and Italian *magro* 'thin', 'lean', 'slender' (Latin *macer*).

GIVEN NAMES Italian 14%; Spanish 4%. *Salvatore* (5), *Alfonso* (2), *Dante* (2), *Eduardo* (2), *Valentino* (2), *Agostino, Alberto, Alfredo, Angelo, Carmela, Carmelo, Ignazio, Mario, Orlando, Paolo, Vito*; *Jose, Pablo, Valente.*

Magruder (1320) Scottish: variant spelling of McGRUDER.

Magrum (105) Scottish and northern Irish: variant of McCRUM.

Magsamen (119) German: from Middle High German *māgesāme* 'poppy seed', hence a metonymic occupational name for someone who milled oil.

Magstadt (130) German: habitational name from a place so called near Stuttgart.

GIVEN NAMES German 5%. *Helmuth, Kurt.*

Maguire (6914) Irish: see McGUIRE. In Ireland this is the usual spelling.

GIVEN NAMES Irish 5%. *Brendan* (4), *Liam* (2), *Siobhan* (2), *Brigid, Cathal, Ciaran, Connor, Conor, Eamonn, James Patrick, Niall, Seamus.*

Magwood (232) Origin uncertain. Most probably a northern Irish surname from a Scottish habitational name, from an unidentified place. The surname was brought to North America from Ireland, but it does not have an Irish etymology.

FOREBEARS William Magwood, born in 1794 in Clones, Monaghan, Ireland, emigrated to Leeds, Quebec, in the early 1830s.

Magyar (804) Hungarian: ethnic name from the vocabulary word *magyar* 'Hungarian'. The name was most often given to Hungarians who lived in nationally mixed rural areas, for example Transylvania. The ethnic name originates from the ancient *Megyer* tribe, one of the most powerful Hungarian clans which occupied the Carpathian basin in late Roman times. The Magyar people came originally from the Urals, but between the 5th and 9th cen-

turies they lived in the north Caucasus and were closely associated with the Turkic peoples there. They were forced to migrate westward and settled in their present territory at the end of the 9th century.
GIVEN NAMES Hungarian 5%. *Laszlo* (5), *Geza* (2), *Katalin* (2), *Miklos* (2), *Akos*, *Andras*, *Arpad*, *Attila*, *Balint*, *Bela*, *Gaza*, *Janos*.

Mah (628) Chinese and Korean: variant of MA.
GIVEN NAMES Chinese/Korean 17%. *Wing* (5), *Suey* (3), *Foon* (2), *Ke* (2), *Mei* (2), *Meng* (2), *Sun* (2), *Tsz* (2), *Wah* (2), *Chai*, *Chee*, *Cheng*.

Mahabir (176) Name found among people of Indian origin in Guyana and Trinidad: from a variant of the Indian personal name *Mahavir*, from Sanskrit *mahāvīra* 'great hero', from *mahā* 'great' + *vīra* 'hero'. The name of the founder of Jainism (6th century BC) was *mahāvīra*.
GIVEN NAMES Indian 43%. *Dindial* (2), *Indra* (2), *Kumar* (2), *Anand*, *Ashok*, *Dhanraj*, *Guru*, *Hemwattie*, *Kamaldai*, *Krishna*, *Lalita*, *Parbatee*.

Mahadeo (129) Name found among people of Indian origin in Guyana and Trinidad: from a variant of the Indian personal name *Mahadev*, from Sanskrit *mahādeva* 'the great god' (from *mahā* 'great' + *deva* 'god'), an epithet of the god Shiva.
GIVEN NAMES Indian 56%. *Ramdeo* (2), *Anand*, *Aruna*, *Bhim*, *Chandra*, *Deo*, *Deonarine*, *Hemchand*, *Indira*, *Indra*, *Indrani*, *Mohabir*.

Mahady (161) Irish: Anglicized form of Gaelic **Ó Moithide** 'descendant of *Moithide*', of unexplained origin. MacLysaght notes that this is a rare name in Ireland, found in the counties of Longford, Roscommon, and Westmeath.

Mahaffey (3094) Irish: Anglicized form of Gaelic *Mac Dhuibhshíthe* (see MCAFEE). In Ireland this name belongs mainly to County Donegal.

Mahaffy (296) Scottish and Irish: variant spelling of MAHAFFEY.

Mahajan (205) Indian (northern states): Hindu (chiefly Bania) name, from Hindi *məhājən* 'merchant', 'banker', 'money-lender', from Sanskrit *mahā* 'great' + *janas* 'person'.
GIVEN NAMES Indian 90%. *Vijay* (6), *Anil* (5), *Sanjeev* (4), *Satish* (4), *Suresh* (4), *Ajay* (3), *Naresh* (3), *Rajendra* (3), *Rakesh* (3), *Rohit* (3), *Subhash* (3), *Umesh* (3).

Mahal (150) Indian (Panjab): Sikh name based on the name of a Jat tribe.
GIVEN NAMES Indian 53%. *Jeet* (2), *Avtar*, *Karnail*, *Kishan*, *Mohan*, *Param*, *Pargat*, *Pradeep*, *Sridhar*.

Mahala (128) Origin unidentified. In part, at least, of Finnish origin.

Mahaley (109) Origin unidentified. Presumably a variant of MAHALA.

Mahan (5611) Irish: Anglicized form of Gaelic **Ó Macháin** 'descendant of *Machán*', which Woulfe suggests is a variant of *Mochán*, a diminutive of *moch* 'early', itself a short form of a name formed with this element, of which there are several, and a variant of MOHAN of Kilmacduagh in County Galway.

Mahana (124) Variant of Irish MAHONEY.

Mahanay (112) Variant of Irish MAHONEY.

Mahanes (160) Variant of Irish MAHONEY.

Mahaney (1075) Irish: variant of MAHONEY.
GIVEN NAME Irish 4%. *Brendan*.

Mahanna (127) Variant of Irish MAHONEY.

Mahannah (166) Variant of Irish MAHONEY.

Mahany (209) Irish: variant of MAHONEY.
GIVEN NAME Irish 4%. *Brendan*.

Mahar (1320) Irish: variant spelling of MAHER.
GIVEN NAMES Irish 4%. *Declan*, *Niall*.

Maharaj (376) Indian (north central): Hindu name, from Sanskrit *mahārāja* 'great king', derived from a title denoting an accomplished practitioner (a master) of a particular skill or craft (for example singing, drumming, dancing, cooking, etc.) or a religious guru.
GIVEN NAMES Indian 66%. *Krishna* (4), *Vishnu* (4), *Hardeo* (3), *Prakash* (3), *Ramsaran* (3), *Chandra* (2), *Geeta* (2), *Kishore* (2), *Mala* (2), *Rajendra* (2), *Ram* (2).

Maharrey (122) Altered form of an Irish name, most probably MCGARRY.

Mahdavi (110) Muslim: from Arabic *Madhdabī*, a term denoting a follower of a particular school of Islamic law.
GIVEN NAMES Muslim 85%. *Ali* (5), *Mohammad* (3), *Mehdi* (2), *Saeed* (2), *Alireza*, *Asghar*, *Esmaeil*, *Farnaz*, *Hassan*, *Hossein*, *Iradj*, *Latifeh*.

Mahdi (104) Muslim: from a personal name based on Arabic *mahdī* 'guided'. This was the name of the twelfth Shiite imam, who disappeared in mysterious circumstances in 939, giving rise to a belief that he will return and unite Muslims under his leadership, triumphing over injustice.
GIVEN NAMES Muslim 76%. *Syed* (6), *Ahmed* (2), *Mohamed* (2), *Muhammad* (2), *Mustafa* (2), *Talal* (2), *Abdal*, *Abdullahi*, *Ahmad*, *Akil*, *Alawi*, *Barakat*.

Maher (9486) Irish: Anglicized form of Gaelic **Ó Meachair** 'descendant of *Meachar*', a personal name meaning 'kindly', 'fine', 'majestic'.
GIVEN NAMES Irish 5%. *Brendan* (8), *Liam* (4), *Aidan* (2), *Aileen*, *Brigid*, *Ciaran*, *Declan*, *Delma*, *Dermot*, *Donal*, *Kieran*.

Maheras (123) Greek: occupational name for a knife maker, medieval Greek *makheras*, from an agent noun derivative of classical Greek *makhaira* 'knife'.

GIVEN NAMES Greek 16%. *Constantine*, *Constantinos*, *Konstantinos*, *Panagiotis*, *Spiros*, *Stylianos*.

Maheu (310) French: from the female personal name *Maheu(t)*, a cognate of *Mathilde*, from a Germanic personal name composed of the elements *maht*, *meht* 'might' + *hild* 'strife', 'battle'.
FOREBEARS A Maheu or Maheust from the Perche region of France is recorded in Acadia in 1610 and again in 1612; a marriage is recorded in Quebec City in 1639.
GIVEN NAMES French 7%. *Alphonse*, *Armand*, *Huguette*, *Jacques*, *Laurier*, *Lucienne*.

Maheux (154) French: variant of MAHEU.
GIVEN NAMES French 27%. *Alain* (2), *Armand* (2), *Laurier* (2), *Yoland* (2), *Alphonse*, *Benoit*, *Clermont*, *Gabrielle*, *Gedeon*, *Gilles*, *Laurent*, *Lucien*.

Mahfouz (158) Muslim: from a personal name based on Arabic *maḥfūẓ* 'safeguarded', 'well-protected'. This is a popular name throughout the Muslim world.
GIVEN NAMES Muslim 30%. *Afaf* (2), *Hussein* (2), *Nima* (2), *Tarek* (2), *Abdo*, *Ahmed*, *Amal*, *Ammar*, *Bechara*, *Faud*, *Fawaz*, *Ghazi*.

Mahieu (153) French: from a popular form of the personal name *Mathieu*, French equivalent of MATTHEW.
GIVEN NAMES French 13%. *Andre* (2), *Raoul* (2), *Armand*, *Pierre*.

Mahin (244) French: possibly from a pet form of the personal name MAHIEU, or of the female personal name *Mahaut* (see MAHEU).

Mahl (370) North German (**Mähl**): topographic name for someone who lived at a mill, or a metonymic occupational name for a miller or mill worker.

Mahlberg (139) Swedish: ornamental name probably composed of an unidentified first element (perhaps an ornamental spelling of the place name element *mal* meaning 'gravel', as in Malsta, but compare also MALSTROM) + *berg* 'mountain'.

Mahle (385) **1.** German (of Slavic origin): nickname for a small man (see MALY), or a child's pet name retained as a nickname in adult life. **2.** Possibly an Americanized spelling of Norwegian **Mæhle**, **Mæle** (see MEHLE 4).

Mahler (2210) German (also **Mähler**) and Jewish (Ashkenazic): occupational name for a painter, especially a painter of stained glass, from an agent derivative of German *malen* to paint (Middle High German *mālen*, Old High German *mālōn* 'to mark', from *māl* 'point', 'mark').
GIVEN NAMES German 4%. *Ernst* (3), *Kurt* (3), *Heinz* (2), *Aloysius*, *Claus*, *Franz*, *Gottfried*, *Guenther*, *Hans*, *Hermann*, *Ilse*, *Juergen*.

Mahlke (140) German (of Slavic origin): diminutive of MAHLE.

Mahlman (144) German: see MAHLMANN.
GIVEN NAMES German 5%. *Darrold*, *Otto*.

Mahlmann (103) German (**Mählmann**): occupational name for a miller's assistant, from Low German *Mähl, Möhl* 'mill' + *Mann* 'man'.
GIVEN NAMES German 13%. *Erwin, Gerhard, Heinz, Rainer.*

Mahlstedt (175) German: habitational name from any of several places named Mahlstedt or Malstetten.
GIVEN NAMES German 10%. *Dieter* (2), *Fritz, Ursel.*

Mahlum (363) Probably an altered spelling of Norwegian **Mæ(h)lum**, a habitational name from any of several farmsteads in southeastern Norway called *Meðalheimr* in Old Norse, i.e. 'the farm' (*heimr*) 'in the middle' (*meðal*).

Mahmood (678) Muslim: from a personal name based on Arabic *maḥmūd*, 'praiseworthy', 'commendable' (a derivative of *ḥamida* 'to praise'; compare MUHAMMAD). This is a popular name in all the countries of the Muslim world.
GIVEN NAMES Muslim 88%. *Khalid* (46), *Tariq* (41), *Arshad* (19), *Syed* (16), *Tahir* (16), *Shahid* (15), *Nasir* (14), *Arif* (8), *Zahid* (8), *Sultan* (7), *Zia* (7), *Asif* (5).

Mahmoud (362) Muslim: variant of MAHMOOD.
GIVEN NAMES Muslim 85%. *Mohamed* (13), *Mahmoud* (8), *Ahmed* (7), *Hassan* (7), *Ahmad* (5), *Ali* (5), *Mohammed* (4), *Naser* (4), *Salah* (4), *Tarek* (4), *Amin* (3), *Hisham* (3).

Mahmud (209) Muslim: variant of MAHMOOD.
GIVEN NAMES Muslim 89%. *Khalid* (9), *Shahid* (5), *Sultan* (5), *Ayaz* (3), *Syed* (3), *Abdullah* (2), *Arif* (2), *Bilal* (2), *Iffat* (2), *Ihsan* (2), *Jamil* (2), *Nasar* (2).

Mahn (508) North German: from a medieval short form of *Manegold* (see MANGOLD).
GIVEN NAMES German 8%. *Kurt* (3), *Ingo* (2), *Otto* (2), *Ulrich* (2), *Franz, Inge, Ralf.*

Mahnke (758) **1.** Northern German: from a medieval pet form of *Manegold* (see MANGOLD). **2.** Old Prussian name, originally **Man(e)ke**, of unexplained etymology.
GIVEN NAMES German 4%. *Kurt* (2), *Eldor, Erhard, Ernst, Heinz, Otto, Rainer.*

Mahnken (317) North German: patronymic from MAHNKE.
GIVEN NAMES German 4%. *Armin, Ernst, Jutta, Otto.*

Mahon (3596) **1.** Irish: reduced Anglicized form of Gaelic **Ó Mathghamhna** (see MAHONEY). **2.** Irish: variant of MAHAN and MOHAN. **3.** French: habitational name from Mahon in Gironde.
GIVEN NAMES Irish 4%. *Malachy* (3), *Brendan* (2), *Declan* (2), *Bridie, Brigid, Donal, Eamonn, Finbarr, James Patrick, Mahon, Moreen, Niamh.*

Mahone (896) Variant of Irish MAHONEY.

Mahoney (16119) Irish: Anglicized form of Gaelic **Ó Mathghamhna** 'descendant of

Mathghamhain', a byname meaning 'good calf'.
GIVEN NAMES Irish 5%. *Brendan* (7), *Donal* (3), *Kieran* (3), *Michael Patrick* (2), *Aileen, Clancy, Eamon, Mahon, Malachy, Murph, Parnell, Sean Patrick.*

Mahony (816) Irish: variant spelling of MAHONEY.
GIVEN NAMES Irish 8%. *Aileen, Brendan, Ciaran, Donal, Fergus.*

Mahood (407) Irish: Anglicized form of Gaelic **Ó hUid** 'descendant of *Ud*', in which *Ó* 'descendant' has been replaced by *Mac* 'son'. The family of Ó hUid were hereditary poets to the O'Neills in Ulster.

Mahorney (114) Irish: of uncertain origin; perhaps a variant of MCHENRY.

Mahowald (260) Luxembourgeois: topographic name meaning 'at the high forest', from German *(am) Hochwald.*
FOREBEARS Family tradition records that five Mahowald brothers came over from Luxembourg in 1852 and settled in MN.

Mahr (755) German: topographic name from Middle High German *mer, mar* 'lake', 'marsh'.
GIVEN NAMES German 4%. *Erwin* (2), *Franz* (2), *Eldred, Gerhard, Hans, Helmut, Ingo, Klaus, Reinhold.*

Mahrt (201) German: unexplained.

Mahurin (492) Origin unidentified. Possibly an altered form of French MATHURIN.

Mai (2104) **1.** Vietnamese: unexplained. **2.** Chinese 麦: origin unknown, although ancient accounts record its use in Guangdong and Henan provinces from an early date. The character for *Mai* also means 'wheat'. **3.** Dutch, Danish, German, and French: variant of MAY.
GIVEN NAMES Vietnamese 44%; Chinese 11%. *Hung* (25), *Thanh* (18), *Hoa* (16), *Son* (12), *Dung* (11), *Long* (11), *Binh* (10), *Minh* (10), *Thu* (10), *Hue* (9), *Huong* (9), *Thuy* (8); *Chi* (5), *Hong* (4), *Ho* (3), *Sang* (3), *Han* (2), *Hang* (2), *Jian* (2), *Li* (2), *Man* (2), *Mei* (2), *Sen* (2), *Wei* (2).

Maia (174) **1.** Portuguese: habitational name from any of several places named Maia, especially one in Porto. **2.** Catalan (**Maià**): habitational name from *Maià de Montcal*, a village in Girona, or any of several other places named with *Maià*, which is of pre-Roman origin.
GIVEN NAMES Spanish 36%. *Manuel* (7), *Julio* (3), *Alberto* (2), *Carlos* (2), *Hermilio* (2), *Jorge* (2), *Jose* (2), *Luis* (2), *Raul* (2), *Ronaldo* (2), *Ana, Armando; Antonio* (3), *Filippo, Giusto, Luciano.*

Maida (661) Southern Italian: habitational name from Màida in Catanzaro, Calabria.
GIVEN NAMES Italian 16%. *Salvatore* (5), *Angelo* (4), *Carmine* (2), *Franco* (2), *Pasquale* (2), *Pietro* (2), *Vito* (2), *Alfonse, Antonio, Carlo, Carmela, Concetta.*

Maiden (1065) English: nickname for a man of effeminate appearance, from Middle

English *maiden*, the usual word for a young girl (Old English *mægden*).

Maidens (106) English (Lincolnshire): occupational name for 'the servant of the MAIDEN'.

Maidment (149) English (Wiltshire): occupational name for a servant employed by a (young) woman or by nuns at a convent, from Middle English *maid(en)* + *man*. For the excrescent *-t*, compare DIAMOND.

Maiello (274) Southern Italian: from a pet form of MAIO.
GIVEN NAMES Italian 16%. *Angelo* (2), *Pasquale* (2), *Antonio, Salvatore.*

Maier (6227) **1.** German and Dutch: variant spelling of MAYER 2. This surname is also established in Italy. **2.** Jewish (Ashkenazic): variant spelling of MEYER 2.
GIVEN NAMES German 6%. *Kurt* (18), *Hans* (8), *Otto* (8), *Helmut* (7), *Manfred* (6), *Gerhard* (5), *Lothar* (5), *Armin* (4), *Erwin* (4), *Franz* (4), *Heinz* (4), *Rudi* (4).

Maiers (445) Jewish: patronymic from MAIER 2.

Maietta (354) Southern Italian: from a feminine pet form of MAIO.
GIVEN NAMES Italian 13%. *Luigi* (2), *Vincenzo* (2), *Angelo, Antonio, Baldassare, Carmela, Carmine, Lorenzo, Mauro, Raffaele, Romeo.*

Maijala (111) Finnish: **1.** topographic name from *maja* 'cottage', 'hut' + the local suffix *-la.* **2.** possibly also from the female name *Maija*, who would be the farm's hostess (farmer's wife), i.e. 'Maija's place'. Found chiefly in central and western Finland.
GIVEN NAMES Finnish 8%; German 7%; Irish 5%. *Reino* (2), *Jaakko, Sulo; Gerhart* (2), *Erwin; Aileen* (2).

Maike (101) German: from a pet form of MAY.
FOREBEARS Carl Maike (1853–1937) emigrated from Grabrow (Grabroh), Germany, to Alma, KS, in 1881.

Maikranz (101) German: nickname from a vocabulary word literally meaning, 'May garland', a crown of flowers worn by the *Maikönigin* (Queen of the May). The connection between this and the surname is not clear.

Mailand (127) German: habitational name for someone from the Italian city of Milan. See MAILANDER.

Mailander (134) German (**Mailänder**): habitational name for someone from Milan in Italy, from *Mailand*, the Germanic form of the place name (derived from Latin *Mediolanum* 'central plain').

Maile (331) German: variant of MAUL.
GIVEN NAMES German 4%. *Helmut, Hermann, Horst, Willi.*

Mailer (43) Scottish: **1.** occupational name for an enameler, Middle English *ameilleur*, Old French *esmaillier*. **2.** habitational name from Mailer in Perthshire.

Mailey (147) English: probably of Norman origin, a habitational name from any of the places in northern France called Mailly.

Mailhot (481) French: pejorative nickname from *maillet* 'mallet'.

FOREBEARS A bearer of this name from the Languedoc region of France is documented in Bequet, Quebec, in 1671, with the secondary surname LAVIOLETTE.

GIVEN NAMES French 16%. *Armand* (3), *Normand* (3), *Adrien* (2), *Andre* (2), *Emile* (2), *Alphonse, Benoit, Fernand, Georges, Henri, Honore, Jean Claude.*

Maillard (170) French: **1.** equivalent of MAILHOT. **2.** from a Germanic personal name: according to Morlet, *Magilhard*, composed of the elements *magil*, an augmented form of *magin, magan* 'strength', 'might' + *hard* 'hardy', 'brave', 'strong'. Debrabandere, however, derives it from the Germanic personal name *Madelhard*, from *madal* 'council' + *hard* 'hardy', 'brave', 'strong'. There are Huguenot families bearing this name.

GIVEN NAMES French 22%; Irish 6%. *Andre* (3), *Jean-Pierre* (2), *Philippe* (2), *Francoise, Jean-Marie, Julien, Michel, Yves*; *Aileen* (2), *Fitzgerald*.

Maille (168) French: from *maille*, the name of a small coin and by extension a feudal levy of this amount, hence possibly a nickname for someone who paid or collected this tax.

FOREBEARS A Maillé from Brittany, France, is documented in Lachine, near Montreal, in 1827.

GIVEN NAMES French 18%. *Emile* (3), *Alphonse, Andre, Armand, Gaston, Gilles, Jean Guy, Normand.*

Maillet (574) French: **1.** nickname from *maillet* 'mallet'. **2.** habitational name from places so named in Allier and Indre.

GIVEN NAMES French 16%. *Yvon* (4), *Emile* (3), *Ulysse* (3), *Alphee* (2), *Andre* (2), *Jean-Paul* (2), *Laurent* (2), *Normand* (2), *Alban, Alcide, Allain, Antoine.*

Mailliard (121) Probably a variant of French **Maillard**: **1.** occupational name for a collector of the tax known as *maille* (see MAILLE). **2.** derogatory nickname from a derivative of *maillet* 'mallet'. **3.** possibly from the Germanic personal name *Magilhard*.

Mailloux (830) Variant spelling of French **Maillou**, a dialect form of **Maillot** 'big mallet'. Compare MAILLET. Sometimes Anglicized as MAYHEW.

FOREBEARS A Mailloux from the Saintonge region of France is documented in Quebec City in 1670.

GIVEN NAMES French 8%. *Girard* (3), *Marcel* (3), *Adrien* (2), *Aime, Fernand, Herve, Michel, Normand, Pierre, Raoul, Serge, Ulderic.*

Mailman (241) Origin unidentified. Possibly an altered form (by folk etymology) of Jewish MAIMAN.

Maiman (123) Jewish (Ashkenazic): Yiddishized variant of the Sephardic name MAIMON.

GIVEN NAMES Jewish 10%. *Chuna, Hershel, Sol.*

Maimon (102) Jewish (Sephardic and Ashkenazic): from the male personal name *Maymon*, derived from Arabic *maymun* 'luck', 'good fortune'. Ashkenazic Jews started to use this personal name due to the fame of the medieval Sephardic religious scholar Moses ben Maimon (Maimonides).

GIVEN NAMES Jewish 29%. *Moshe* (3), *Nissim* (2), *Avshalom, Haim, Ravit, Uri.*

Maimone (332) Southern Italian: nickname from Arabic *maymūn* 'lucky', 'fortunate', or from a personal name from the same word.

GIVEN NAMES Italian 25%. *Mario* (3), *Sal* (3), *Angelo, Antonio, Camillo, Carmine, Dante, Giovanna, Giuseppe, Orazio, Pasquale, Pietro, Reginaldo, Rosalia, Rosario, Salvatore.*

Main (4909) **1.** Scottish: from a reduced form of the Scandinavian personal name MAGNUS. **2.** Scottish: topographic name for a farmer who farmed the main farm on an estate. **3.** Scottish, English (of Norman origin), and French: from the Continental Germanic personal name *Maino, Meino*, a short form of the various compound names with a first element *magin* 'strength', 'might'. **4.** Scottish and English (of Norman origin): regional name for someone from the French province of Maine. Compare MANSELL 1. **5.** Scottish and English (of Norman origin): nickname for a large man, from Anglo-Norman French *magne, maine* 'big'. **6.** Scottish, English (of Norman origin), and French: nickname for someone with a deformed or missing hand, from Old French *main* 'hand' (Latin *manus*).

Mainard (127) French: variant spelling of MAYNARD.

Maine (1246) **1.** French: topographic name from Old French *maine* 'dwelling', 'residence', 'abode', or a habitational name from any of numerous places so named. **2.** Scottish and English: variant spelling of MAIN. **3.** Catalan (**Mainé**): variant of MAINER.

Mainella (114) Italian: from a (feminine) pet form of the personal name MAINO. The feminine form is no doubt due to the influence of the Italian word *famiglia*.

GIVEN NAMES Italian 20%. *Domenic* (2), *Egidio* (2), *Alfonso, Filomena, Luigi, Nicola.*

Mainer (226) English and Catalan: from the Continental Germanic personal name *Maginhari*, composed of the elements *magin* 'strength', 'might' + *hari* 'army'.

Maines (1343) **1.** English and Scottish: variant spelling of MAINS. **2.** Catalan (**Mainés**): variant spelling of *Mainers*, plural form of MAINER.

Mainiero (110) Italian: from the personal name *Mainero*, from Frankish *Maginhari*, composed of the Germanic elements *magin* 'strength', 'might' + *hari, heri* 'army'.

GIVEN NAMES Italian 23%. *Rocco* (2), *Angelo, Antonio, Carmine, Gianni, Nicola, Pasquale, Salvatore.*

Mainini (110) Italian: from a pet form of the personal name MAINO.

GIVEN NAMES Italian 6%. *Angelo, Pino.*

Maino (162) Northern Italian: from the Germanic personal name *Maino*, a short form of compound names beginning with the element *magin* 'strength'.

GIVEN NAMES Italian 14%. *Elida* (2), *Angelo, Mario, Rodolfo, Vito.*

Mainor (302) Altered spelling of French **Ménard** (see MENARD).

Mainord (156) Altered spelling of French **Ménard** (see MENARD).

Mains (1359) **1.** Scottish and northern English: topographic name for a dweller at the chief farm (or home farm) on an estate, Scottish *mains*, or a habitational name from any of the various minor places named with this word (originally a shortened form of *domain*, later associated with the adjective *main* 'principal'). **2.** English and Scottish: variant of MAIN 1–4.

Mainville (314) French: habitational name from any of several places so called, in Aisne, Essonne, Loiret, and Moselle.

GIVEN NAMES French 8%. *Armand, Colette, Emile, Lucien, Normand, Rodolphe.*

Mainwaring (256) English (of Norman origin): habitational name from a lost place, of uncertain location, named in Anglo-Norman French as *mesnil Warin* 'domain of Warin' (see WARING). The surname has had a large number of variant spellings; it is normally pronounced 'Mannering'.

Mainz (111) German and Jewish (western Ashkenazic): habitational name from the city of Mainz in Germany.

GIVEN NAMES German 10%. *Erwin, Math, Otto, Siegbert, Walther.*

Mainzer (138) German and Jewish (western Ashkenazic): habitational name for someone from the city of Mainz in Germany.

GIVEN NAMES German 4%. *Fritz, Jurgen.*

Maio (591) Italian, Spanish, and Portuguese: from a nickname or personal name based on the word for the month of May, Latin *Maius* (see MAY 1).

GIVEN NAMES Italian 23%. *Angelo* (3), *Marco* (3), *Antonio* (2), *Carmela* (2), *Domenic* (2), *Rocco* (2), *Abilio, Attilio, Biagio, Carlo, Dante, Emilio, Francesco, Geremia, Gino, Rolando, Ruben.*

Maiocco (115) Italian: probably from a derivative of MAIO.

GIVEN NAMES Italian 16%. *Carmine* (2), *Egidio, Mario, Orlando, Salvatore.*

Maiolo (210) Italian: from a diminutive of MAIO.

GIVEN NAMES Italian 23%. *Isidoro* (2), *Salvatore* (2), *Domenic, Fortunato, Giovanni, Guido, Natale, Orlando, Paolo, Roberto.*

Maione (291) Southern Italian: from an augmentative of MAIO, or, more likely from an unattested personal name *Maione*.
GIVEN NAMES Italian 13%. *Angelo* (3), *Carlo, Enza, Gennaro, Guido, Natale, Nunzio, Pasquale, Raffaele, Romolo, Silvio.*

Maiorana (423) Southern Italian (common in Calabria and Sicily): topographic name from Sicilian *maiurana*, medieval Latin *majorana* 'marjoram'.
GIVEN NAMES Italian 21%. *Salvatore* (7), *Sal* (5), *Mario* (3), *Antonino, Antonio, Cosimo, Domenica, Gaetano, Gaspare, Gasper, Giuseppe, Lucio, Nunzio, Renato.*

Maiorano (451) Southern Italian: possibly a variant of MAIORANA, but more likely a habitational name from Maiorano di Monte, a locality of Dragoni in Caserta province.
GIVEN NAMES Italian 17%. *Angelo* (5), *Salvatore* (3), *Antonio* (2), *Gaetano* (2), *Rocco* (2), *Saverio* (2), *Serafino* (2), *Vito* (2), *Carmelo, Carmine, Domenico, Pasquale.*

Maiorino (176) Southern Italian: **1.** from a pet form of **Maiore**, a distinguishing nickname from Latin *maior* 'bigger', 'major'. **2.** possibly a habitational name for someone from Maiori in Salerno province, from an adjectival form of the place name.
GIVEN NAMES Italian 16%. *Salvatore* (3), *Alfonse, Angelo, Giancarlo, Pasquale, Sal.*

Mair (794) **1.** Scottish: occupational name for an officer of the courts whose functions resembled those of an English beadle (i.e. a minor official who dealt with petty offenders) and who was known as a *mair*. Compare MAYER 1. Reaney remarks that this title was used not only of the king's herald or sergeant but also of such officers as a head forester. **2.** Jewish: variant of MEYER 2.
GIVEN NAMES German 4%. *Franz* (2), *Alois, Benno, Egon, Hans, Hermann, Inge, Kurt, Othmar, Otto, Reinhard, Rudi.*

Maire (263) **1.** French: status name or occupational name for a *maire*, a title denoting a municipal magistrate or other local official (the role of the maire differed at different times at different places). It may also be a nickname for an officious or pompous person. **2.** French (**Mairé**): habitational name from Mairé in Vienne or from Mairél'Evescault in Deux-Sèvres.

Mairs (323) Scottish and Irish (chiefly northern Ireland): patronymic from MAIR 1.

Mais (239) **1.** German (**Maiss**): topographic name from Middle High German *meiz* 'cleared land'. **2.** Dutch: from a short form of the personal name THOMAS.

Maisano (352) Southern Italian: habitational name from a place in Calabria named Magisano (dialect forms *Maisano, Majisano*), from a Latin word, *Magisius* or

Magissius influenced by Calabrian *majisi* 'of (the month of) May'.
GIVEN NAMES Italian 28%. *Donato* (6), *Pasquale* (3), *Dino* (2), *Salvatore* (2), *Santo* (2), *Alfonso, Angelo, Carmelo, Concetta, Giovanni, Philomena, Sal, Vito.*

Maisch (236) North German: variant of MAIS.

Maisel (535) **1.** German and Jewish (Ashkenazic): variant spelling of MEISEL. This surname is widespread in eastern and central Europe. **2.** French: from Old French *maisel* 'slaughterhouse', 'butcher's shop', hence a topographic name for someone who lived by a butcher's shop or who worked in one.

Maish (204) Americanized spelling of German MAISCH.

Maison (236) French: probably a topographic name for someone who lived by an important house, Old French *maison*, from Latin *mansio* 'posting house', 'stage' 'halting place' (on a route). However, the centers of distribution in the U.S. (OH, PA, and NY) suggest that it is perhaps more likely to be an altered spelling of MASON.
GIVEN NAMES French 6%. *Andre, Marcel, Thierry.*

Maisonet (210) French (**Maisonnet**): diminutive of MAISON.
GIVEN NAMES Spanish 43%. *Luis* (9), *Jose* (5), *Carlos* (3), *Manuel* (3), *Angel* (2), *Emilio* (2), *Mario* (2), *Pedro* (2), *Aura, Catalina, Eduardo, Elba.*

Maisonneuve (102) French: habitational name for someone living at the 'new house'.
GIVEN NAMES French 24%. *Lucien* (2), *Armand, Laurent, Virginie, Yvan.*

Maisto (117) Italian: from a Campanese variant of *maestro* 'master' (Latin *magister*), probably a status name for a master craftsman or a scholar. Compare MAESTRI.
GIVEN NAMES Italian 18%. *Angelo* (3), *Pasquale, Remo.*

Maita (131) **1.** Southern Italian: probably a variant of **Màita** (see MAIDA). This name is now common in Peru, Bolivia, and Ecuador. **2.** Japanese: 'rice paddy'; found mostly in western Japan, it is also pronounced as YONEDA, **Kometa**, and **Maida**.
GIVEN NAMES Italian 15%; Spanish 7%; Japanese 4%. *Salvatore* (2), *Luciano, Vito; Jose, Luis, Manuel, Marianita, Milagros; Emiko, Nobuaki, Yosuke.*

Maitland (1232) Scottish and English: of uncertain origin, possibly a nickname for an ungracious individual, from Anglo-Norman French *maltalent, mautalent* 'bad temper' (Late Latin *malum* 'bad' + *talentum* 'inclination', 'disposition'). However, there is a place called Mautalant in Pontorson, France, which was named for its unproductive soil, and this may well be a partial source of the surname, particularly in Scotland where many historical exam-

ples of the name are written with the preposition *de*. The present spelling is the result of a contracted pronunciation and folk etymological identification with the common topographic element *land*.

Maitlen (122) Origin unidentified. Perhaps an altered form of Scottish and English MAITLAND.

Maitre (122) French (**Maître**): occupational name for one who was the head of a craft or trade guild, from Old French *maistre* 'master' (Latin *magister*).
GIVEN NAMES French 19%; German 7%. *Edouard, Jacques, Marie Josette, Philippe, Pierre, Raoul, Veronique; Juergen, Klaus, Ulrich.*

Maiuri (136) Southern Italian: habitational name from Maiori in Salerno province (from a dialect form), named from Latin *maior* 'bigger'.
GIVEN NAMES Italian 24%. *Angelo* (4), *Arduino* (2), *Dino, Luigi, Pio, Rocco.*

Maixner (124) German and Dutch: variant of MEISSNER.

Maize (402) Respelling of English **Mayze**, a patronymic or variant form of MAY.

Maizel (106) Jewish (eastern Ashkenazic): variant of MEISEL.
GIVEN NAMES Jewish 8%; Russian 7%. *Ilya; Anatoliy, Boris, Leonid, Yefim.*

Maj (113) Polish: surname adopted with reference to the month of May, Polish *maj* (see MAY). Surnames referring to months were sometimes adopted by Jewish converts to Christianity, with reference to the month in which they were baptized or in which the surname was registered.
GIVEN NAMES Polish 25%. *Agnieszka* (2), *Jaroslaw* (2), *Wieslaw* (2), *Augustyn, Janusz, Jozef, Katarzyna, Krystyna, Krzysztof, Maciej, Piotr, Tadeusz.*

Majano (114) Spanish: topographic name from *majano* 'pile of stones', 'cairn' (used as a boundary mark), or a habitational name from Majano in Toledo province.
GIVEN NAMES Spanish 63%. *Jose* (5), *Ana Cecilia* (2), *Carlos* (2), *Digna* (2), *Juan* (2), *Rosendo* (2), *Albania, Alicia, Andres, Antolin, Antolina, Bernadino.*

Majcher (234) Polish: from the personal name *Majcher*, a vernacular form of MELCHIOR.
GIVEN NAMES Polish 15%. *Grzegorz* (3), *Bronislaw, Danuta, Dorota, Janina, Ryszard, Stanislaw, Tadeusz, Zbigniew, Zygmunt.*

Majchrzak (288) Polish: patronymic from the personal name MAJCHER.
GIVEN NAMES Polish 10%. *Beata, Czeslaw, Henryk, Jaroslaw, Krzysztof, Marzena, Mieczyslaw, Tomasz.*

Majeed (158) Muslim: variant of MAJID.
GIVEN NAMES Muslim 85%. *Abdul* (12), *Tariq* (10), *Mohamed* (4), *Mohammad* (4), *Abdool* (3), *Ahad* (2), *Ali* (2), *Asif* (2), *Farhan* (2), *Iqbal* (2), *Kamal* (2), *Mian* (2).*

Majer (217) **1.** Polish, Czech, and Slovak: status name for a steward, bailiff, or tenant farmer, or a village headman, from German MEYER 1. **2.** Jewish (Ashkenazic): from a variant of the personal name *Meyer* (see MEYER 2). **3.** German: variant of MACHER 2.

GIVEN NAMES German 9%; Jewish 4%. *Armin, Erwin, Georg, Gerhard, Manfred, Ulrich, Wolfgang; Aron, Sol.*

Majerus (540) German and Swedish: humanistic name, a Latinized variant of MAJER.

Majeske (181) Germanized form of Polish MAJEWSKI.

Majeski (610) Polish: variant of MAJEWSKI.

Majesky (103) Jewish (Ashkenazic): variant spelling of Polish MAJEWSKI.

GIVEN NAME Jewish 6%. *Chaim.*

Majestic (167) Origin unidentified. It is almost certainly not a derivative of Latin *maiestatius* 'majestic'. It is perhaps an American altered form of a Slavic name such as Croatian **Majetić** (from the personal name *Majeta*), by folk-etymological association with the English adjective *majestic.*

Majette (208) Possibly French, metronymic from a pet form of the female personal name *Marguerite* (see MARGESON). However, the concentration of the name in OH, VA, and NC would suggest a different origin may be involved.

Majewski (1879) **1.** Polish and Jewish (from Poland): habitational name for someone from any of various places called Majewo. **2.** Jewish (from Poland): surname adopted with reference to the month of MAY, Polish *maj,* assimilated to the Polish surname.

GIVEN NAMES Polish 8%. *Casimir* (6), *Janusz* (4), *Jerzy* (4), *Zbigniew* (4), *Andrzej* (3), *Tadeusz* (3), *Jacek* (2), *Krzysztof* (2), *Mariusz* (2), *Stanislaw* (2), *Zofia* (2), *Bronislawa.*

Majid (161) Muslim: from a personal name based on Arabic *majīd* 'glorious', 'noble'. *Al-Majīd* 'the Glorious' is an attribute of Allah, and this name is found in combinations such as *'Abd-ul Majīd* 'servant of the All-Glorious'.

GIVEN NAMES Muslim 85%. *Abdul* (18), *Mohammed* (7), *Syed* (3), *Afzal* (2), *Noor* (2), *Umar* (2), *Yasmin* (2), *Abdool, Abdul Karim, Abir, Adil, Ahmad.*

Majka (589) Polish: **1.** nickname from a dialect variant of **Mańka** 'left-hander' (see MANKA). **2.** metronymic from a pet form of MARIA.

GIVEN NAMES Polish 6%. *Zbigniew* (2), *Beata, Ewa, Genowefa, Janina, Jaroslaw, Jozef, Sylwester, Tadeusz, Zdzislawa.*

Majkowski (170) Polish: habitational name for someone from any of various places called Majkowice or Majków, named with the personal name *Majek,* a pet form of MAJ.

GIVEN NAMES Polish 4%. *Bronislawa, Casimir, Kazimierz.*

Majkut (101) Polish: variant of **Mańkut**, from *mańkut* 'left-hander'.

GIVEN NAMES Polish 12%. *Alicja, Andrzej, Halina, Ignacy.*

Major (6590) **1.** English: from the Norman personal name *Malg(i)er, Maug(i)er,* composed of the Germanic elements *madal* 'council' + *gār, gēr* 'spear'. The surname is now also established in Ulster. **2.** Hungarian: from a shortened form of *majorosgazda* (see MAJOROS), or a derivative of German MEYER 1. **3.** Polish, Czech, and Slovak: from the military rank *major* (derived from Latin *maior* 'greater'), a word related to English *mayor* and the German surname MEYER. **4.** Catalan and southern French (Occitan): from *major* 'major' (Latin *maior* 'greater'), denoting a prominent or important person or the first-born son of a family. **5.** Jewish (eastern Ashkenazic): variant of MEYER 2.

Majoros (175) Hungarian: from a shortened form of *majorosgazda,* a status name for a senior tenant farmer or one who had been granted a particularly large land holding, Hungarian *major* (from Latin *maior* 'greater'). This name may also have been derived from German MEYER.

GIVEN NAMES Hungarian 4%. *Attila, Janos, Katalin.*

Majors (3162) English: patronymic from MAJOR 1.

Majumdar (104) Indian (Assam and Bengal) and Bangladeshi: Hindu (several communities) and Muslim name meaning 'record keeper', 'archivist', from Arabic *majmū'a* 'collection' + the Persian suffix *-dār* 'possessor'. The surname has evolved from an official title.

GIVEN NAMES Indian 83%. *Alok* (2), *Amitava* (2), *Bhaskar* (2), *Pradip* (2), *Aloke, Ananya, Anish, Arindam, Arjun, Arun, Arunava, Ashoke.*

Majure (158) Northern Irish: variant of MAJOR.

FOREBEARS According to family tradition John Majure came to North America from Ireland on the ship *Earl of Hillsborough* in 1767.

Mak (1072) **1.** Chinese 麦: Cantonese variant of MAI 2. **2.** Polish and Ukrainian: from a short form of the personal name *Makary, Makar,* or some other Slavic form of the Greek personal name *Makarios* 'blessed'. **3.** Polish, Jewish (Ashkenazic), and Slovenian: from *mak* 'poppy', a nickname for someone who grew poppies or (as a Jewish name) an ornamental name. **4.** Hungarian (**Mák**): from *Mák,* a short form of the ecclesistical personal name *Makár,* Hungarian form of Greek *Makarios* 'blessed'. **5.** Dutch: variant of MACK 2 and 3.

GIVEN NAMES Chinese 31%. *Chun* (6), *Kin* (6), *Wing* (6), *Kam* (4), *Wai* (4), *Chi* (3), *Chan* (2), *Chee* (2), *Chi Shing* (2), *Chik* (2), *Ching* (2), *Chun Wah* (2).

Maka (129) Polish (**Mąka**): from *mąka* 'flour', a metonymic occupational name for a miller or flour merchant.

GIVEN NAMES Polish 15%. *Jozef* (2), *Danuta, Kazimierz, Krystyna, Stanislaw, Wojciech, Zofia.*

Makar (423) Polish and Ukrainian: from the personal name *Makary* (Polish), *Makar* (Ukrainian), vernacular forms of the Greek ecclesiastical name *Makarios* meaning 'blessed'.

Makara (255) Polish, Ukrainian, and Slovak: derivative of MAKAR.

Makarewicz (264) Polish: patronymic from the personal name *Makary* (see MAKAR).

GIVEN NAMES Polish 11%. *Thadeus* (2), *Andrzej, Jadwiga, Jerzy, Jozef, Miroslaw, Stanislaw.*

Makela (545) Finnish (**Mäkelä**): ornamental name from *mäki* 'hill' + the local suffix *-la.*

GIVEN NAMES Finnish 10%; Scandinavian 4%. *Hannu* (3), *Reijo* (2), *Armas, Arvo, Eero, Eino, Kalervo, Kauko, Mauno, Onni, Osmo, Reino; Erik, Hjalmer, Nels, Walfrid.*

Makely (130) Probably an Americanized spelling of South German and Swiss **Mä(g)gli** (see MAGLEY).

Makepeace (271) English: nickname for a person known for his skill at patching up quarrels, from Middle English *make(n)* 'to make' (Old English *macian*) + *pais* 'peace' (see PACE).

Maker (575) Dutch: occupational name for someone who made or repaired things, from an agent derivative of Dutch *maken* 'to make or mend'.

Maki (3986) **1.** Finnish (**Mäki**): from Finnish *mäki* 'hill', originally a habitational name from a farm so named. From the late 19th century, when under the requirements of the Church people without surnames began to acquire them, this was one of the many words from nature that were adopted as surnames. During the name conversion movement in the 19th and early 20th centuries, Mäki was much used as a substitute for Swedish surnames formed with *berg* or *back* 'hill'. In the U.S. Maki may be a short form of **Mäkinen** (see MAKINEN) or other names based on this element. It has sometimes been translated as HILL. **2.** Japanese: 'pasture'; found in the island of Kyūshū, but not common in Japan proper, it appears to originate in the Ryū-kyūan island of Amami.

GIVEN NAMES Finnish 10%; Scandinavian 4%. *Eino* (33), *Toivo* (18), *Arvo* (11), *Reino* (11), *Waino* (9), *Tauno* (8), *Wilho* (8), *Oiva* (6), *Urho* (5), *Sulo* (4), *Taisto* (4), *Veikko* (4); *Erik* (7), *Nels* (4), *Viljo* (2), *Erland, Evald, Hjalmer, Kerstin, Sven, Swen.*

Makin (564) **1.** Northern English (Lancashire and Yorkshire): pet form (with the Middle English diminutive suffix *-kin*) of MAY 2. **2.** Northern English: nickname for an effeminate man, from Middle English *maid(en)* 'girl', 'young woman' (see MAIDEN) + the diminutive suffix *-kin*. It is possible, but unlikely, that it may also have been of more literal application as an occupational name for a female servant. **3.** Dutch: from a pet form of the Germanic name *Macco* (see MACK 2 and 3).

Makinen (236) Finnish (**Mäkinen**): variant of **Mäki** (see MAKI) + the common surname suffix *-nen*. For the most part this is a relatively recent ornamental adoption: it was particularly popular during the name conversion movement in the 19th and early 20th centuries, and is now the fourth most common name in Finland. However, examples of it are found dating back to the 16th century.
GIVEN NAMES Finnish 14%; Scandinavian 6%. *Reino* (3), *Eino* (2), *Antti, Jarmo, Kauko, Lempi, Marjatta, Mikko, Oiva, Tauno, Toivo*; *Erik*.

Makino (133) Japanese: 'pasture field'; the name is found mostly in central Japan and the Ryūkyū Islands. A noble family claiming descent from Takenouchi no Sukune bore the name; they resided in Mikawa (now part of Aichi prefecture).
GIVEN NAMES Japanese 83%. *Eiji* (3), *Kana* (2), *Kaoru* (2), *Koichi* (2), *Kyoko* (2), *Tomomi* (2), *Akihiro, Akira, Ayako, Chiho, Eiichi, Eijiro*.

Makins (116) **1.** Northern English (Lancashire and Yorkshire): patronymic from MAKIN 1. **2.** Dutch: patronymic from MAKIN 3.

Makinson (167) Northern English (Lancashire): patronymic from MAKIN 1.

Makley (132) Americanized form of South German and Swiss **Mäg(g)li** (see MAGLEY).

Mako (188) Hungarian (**Makó**): from a pet form of the ecclesiastical name *Makár*, from Greek *Makarios* 'blessed'. It may also be from a pet form of the personal name *Mátyás*, Magyar equivalent of MATTHEW.

Makos (155) **1.** Greek: origin uncertain. Possibly from Slavic *mak* 'poppy', or the Albanian personal name *Maqo*. **2.** Polish (**Makoś**) and Hungarian (**Mákos**): from *mak* 'poppy', occupational name for someone who grew poppies, or nickname meaning 'poppy'. **3.** Polish (**Makosz**) and Hungarian (**Mákos**): from the personal name *Makary* (Polish), *Makár* (Hungarian), vernacular forms of the Greek personal name *Makarios* 'blessed'.
GIVEN NAMES Greek 6%. *Kostas, Panagiotis*.

Makosky (124) Polish, Ukrainian, and Jewish (Ashkenazic): variant of MAKOWSKI.
GIVEN NAME Polish 5%. *Zygmunt*.

Makovec (127) Slovenian: topographic name or nickname from a derivative of *mak* 'poppy', perhaps denoting someone who grew poppies.

Makovsky (137) **1.** Czech and Slovak (**Makovský**): habitational name for someone from a place called Makov, named with *mak* 'poppy'. **2.** Jewish (eastern Ashkenazic): variant spelling of MAKOWSKI.

Makowski (1427) Polish, Ukrainian, and Jewish (Ashkenazic): habitational name for someone from any of various places called Maków, Makowa, or Makowo, all named from *mak* 'poppy'.
GIVEN NAMES Polish 6%. *Jacek* (3), *Janusz* (3), *Lech* (3), *Jerzy* (2), *Piotr* (2), *Ryszard* (2), *Tomasz* (2), *Wojciech* (2), *Bogdan, Casimir, Ewa, Henryka*.

Makowsky (213) Germanized spelling of Polish MAKOWSKI.
GIVEN NAME German 4%. *Otto*.

Makris (536) Greek: nickname for a tall man, from Greek *makri* 'tall' (ancient Greek *makros* 'long'). It is often found in combination with a personal name, e.g. **Makrigiannis** 'tall John', **Makrilias** 'tall Elias', **Makrimikhalis** 'tall Michael'.
GIVEN NAMES Greek 14%. *Costas* (4), *Constantine* (3), *Angelos* (2), *Dimitrios* (2), *Kostas* (2), *Nicholaos* (2), *Anastasios, Andreas, Antonios, Apostolos, Christos, Constantinos*.

Makuch (316) Polish, Ukrainian, and Jewish (from Ukraine): nickname from Ukrainian and Yiddish *makukh*, Polish *makuch* 'linseed oil cake'.
GIVEN NAMES Polish 8%. *Jozef* (2), *Aleksander, Danuta, Jolanta, Karol, Kazimierz, Stanislaw, Tadeusz, Teofil, Zbigniew*.

Malach (131) Jewish: ornamental name from Hebrew *malach* 'angel'.
GIVEN NAMES Jewish 8%. *Leib, Yosef*.

Malachi (112) Jewish: from the Hebrew name *Malachi*, name of a Biblical prophet, meaning 'my messenger'.

Malachowski (290) Polish (**Małachowski**): habitational name for someone from places called Małachowo, Małachów, or Małachowice.
GIVEN NAMES Polish 5%. *Andrzej, Bronislaw, Kazimierz, Zbigniew*.

Malady (145) Irish: variant of MELODY.

Malafronte (119) Southern Italian: nickname from *malo* (feminine *mala*) 'evil', 'wicked' + *fronte* 'brow', 'forehead'.
GIVEN NAMES Italian 16%. *Pasquale* (2), *Salvatore* (2), *Amato, Luigi*.

Malagon (213) Spanish (**Malagón**): habitational name from Malagón, a place in Ciudad Real, or from any of the other places so named in Galicia, in A Coruña, Lugo, and Orense provinces.
GIVEN NAMES Spanish 57%. *Jose* (13), *Carlos* (4), *Juan* (4), *Efren* (3), *Javier* (3), *Jorge* (3), *Miguel* (3), *Jesus* (2), *Juana* (2), *Leopoldo* (2), *Luis* (2), *Manuel* (2).

Malak (360) **1.** Polish (also **Małak**), Czech and Slovak (**Malák**): from a derivative of the common Slavic adjective *maly* 'small' (see MALY). **2.** As a Polish name it may

also be a derivative of the Old Polish personal name *Małomir*. **3.** Muslim: from a personal name based on Arabic *malak* 'angel'.
GIVEN NAMES Muslim 8%. *Mohamad* (3), *Mohammad* (2), *Sami* (2), *Amal, Asaad, Atef, Atta, Fadi, Fady, Faten, Fouad, Hamad*.

Malakoff (133) Jewish (eastern Ashkenazic): alternative spelling of **Malakov**, of uncertain origin; perhaps a shortened **Malakhovsky**, a habitational name from the village of Malakhovtsy in Belarus.
GIVEN NAME Jewish 8%. *Meyer* (2).

Malamud (188) Jewish (eastern Ashkenazic): variant of MELAMED 'teacher'.
GIVEN NAMES Jewish 25%; Russian 9%. *Moshe* (4), *Semen* (3), *Leyb* (2), *Mendel* (2), *Gitla, Isaak, Mariya, Moysey, Rimma, Yetta, Yisroel, Yossi*; *Arkadiy, Boris, Iosif, Mikhail, Raisa, Yafim*.

Malan (462) **1.** French: nickname from Old French *malan(t)* 'sore', 'ulcer' (Latin *malandria*). **2.** Czech and Slovak: nickname for a small man, a derivative of *malý* (see MALY).

Maland (166) Americanized spelling of Norwegian **Mæland** (see MELAND) or of **Maaland, Måland**, a habitational name, from a farm name composed of Old Norse *mór* 'moor', 'heath' + *land* 'land', 'farmstead'.

Malaney (220) Variant of Irish MALONEY.

Malanga (231) Southern Italian: according to Caracausi, perhaps from *malanga* 'tannia', a tall Caribbean plant of the arum family, with edible pear-shaped tubers, but how this could have translated into a European family name is difficult to envisage.
GIVEN NAMES Italian 16%. *Alfonso* (2), *Armando* (2), *Orlando* (2), *Americo, Angelo, Carmine, Guido, Nicola, Rocco, Vincenzo*.

Malanowski (171) Polish: habitational name for someone from places called Malanowo or Malanów.

Malara (166) **1.** Italian: perhaps from an unattested Latin word *malaria* 'apple tree'. **2.** Spanish: habitational name from either of two places named Malara, both in Málaga province. **3.** Polish: occupational name from a derivative of *malarz* 'painter'.
GIVEN NAMES Italian 16%; Spanish 9%. *Gino* (2), *Carmine, Domenic, Oreste, Santo*; *Elia* (4), *Demetrio*.

Malarkey (305) Irish: variant of MULLARKEY.

Malas (110) Turkish and Greek: from Turkish *mala* 'trowel' (see MALLAS) or *mal* 'property', both used metonymically.
GIVEN NAMES Muslim 29%; Greek 12%. *Amer* (2), *Mahmoud* (2), *Safwan* (2), *Ayman, Fatme, Haisam, Hassan, Iyad, Khaled, Marwan, Mazen, Nabil*; *Sotiris* (2), *Spiro* (2), *Panayiotis*.

Malaspina (164) Italian: habitational name from various places named Malaspina, from *malus* (feminine *mala*) 'bad' + *spina* 'thorn'.

FOREBEARS The Malaspina family were powerful in eastern Liguria and parts of Tuscany and Lombardy during the Middle Ages. In 1306 Franceschino Malespina offered refuge to the poet Dante during his exile.

GIVEN NAMES Italian 18%. *Tino* (2), *Aldo, Antonio, Carmella, Guido, Mario*.

Malatesta (516) Italian: nickname for a stubborn, malicious, or treacherous person, from *malus* (feminine *mala*) 'bad', 'evil' + *testa* 'head'. In the form **Malatestas**, this is also found as a Greek name.

FOREBEARS The Malatestas were a noble family who ruled Rimini during the Italian Renaissance. Sigismondo Malatesta (1417–68) is often regarded as the prototype of an Italian Renaissance prince. Ercole Malatesta was a soldier in the service of Venice in the 16th century; in 1582, as commander of the guard in Rethimno (Crete), he led an attack on the Turks in the Peloponnese.

GIVEN NAMES Italian 11%. *Dino* (2), *Luigi* (2), *Angelo, Antonio, Carmine, Ferdinando, Gabriele, Gino, Giuseppina, Massimo, Nicola, Nino*.

Malave (485) Spanish: probably a shortened form of Basque **Zumalabe, Zumalave**, a topographic name composed of the elements *zume* 'pasture' + *labe* 'oven'.

GIVEN NAMES Spanish 48%. *Luis* (13), *Carlos* (12), *Jose* (9), *Ramon* (8), *Angel* (6), *Francisco* (6), *Ruben* (6), *Pedro* (4), *Santos* (4), *Orlando* (3), *Alicia* (2), *Ana* (2).

Malay (245) French (Walloon): according to Debrabandere, a Walloon variant of **Mala(he)**, a nickname for a difficult, clumsy or maladroit person, from French *malaise* 'illness', 'sickness'; 'awkward', 'clumsy'.

Malberg (104) Swedish: ornamental name, from an unexplained first element + *berg* 'mountain'.

Malboeuf (140) French: from the Germanic personal name *Madalabod*, composed of *madal* 'council' + *bode* 'messenger'.

GIVEN NAMES French 11%. *Emile, Germain, Normand, Rejeanne*.

Malbon (132) English: unexplained. Probably of Anglo-Norman French origin; it is said to be from a place called Malbanc.

FOREBEARS Peter Malbone, born in 1633, married Sarah Godfrey in Norfolk Co., VA. The name **Mallabone** has been in Warwickshire, England, for over 400 years.

Malbrough (339) **1.** English: habitational name from Malborough (Devon) or Marlborough (Wiltshire). The Wiltshire place name is from an unattested Old English personal name *Mǣrla* or Old English *meargealla* 'gentian' + *beorg* 'hill', 'mound'. **2.** Irish: possibly a variant of the County Clare surname **Malborough, Marlborough**, which MacLysaght considers to be probably an Anglicization of

Gaelic **Ó Maoilbhearaigh** (see MULBERRY 2). **3.** Perhaps also an Americanized form of German MALBURG.

GIVEN NAMES French 7%. *Armand, Odile*.

Malburg (175) German: habitational name from a place so named in the Rhineland.

Malchow (503) German (Mecklenburg, Pomerania, and Brandenburg): habitational name from any of several places named Malchow; the *-ow* suffix indicates Slavic origin.

GIVEN NAMES German 4%. *Armin, Erhardt, Ernst, Kurt, Uwe*.

Malcolm (3468) **1.** Scottish: from the Gaelic personal name *Maol-Choluim* 'devotee of (Saint) Columba' (see COLOMB). **2.** Irish (Ulster): Anglicized form of Gaelic **Ó Maolcholuim** 'descendant of the devotee of St. *Columba*' (Irish *Colum Cille*, literally 'dove of the church'). In Ireland the personal name is often spelled *Colm*; in Scotland it has become *Calum*.

Malcom (1227) Scottish: variant spelling of MALCOLM.

Malcomb (291) Scottish: variant spelling of MALCOLM.

Malcomson (162) Scottish and Irish (chiefly northern Ireland): patronymic from MALCOLM.

Malczewski (179) Polish: habitational name for someone from a place called Malczewo in Poznań voivodeship, or Malczew in Radom voivodeship.

Malden (117) English: habitational name from Malden in Surrey (now part of Greater London) (see MAULDIN).

Maldonado (9881) Spanish and Portuguese: **1.** nickname for an ugly or stupid person, from Spanish *mal donado* 'ill-favored'. The phrase is a compound of *mal* 'badly' + *donado* 'given', 'endowed', past participle of *donare* 'to give', 'to bestow'. **2.** habitational name from Maldonado, a village in the province of Albacete.

GIVEN NAMES Spanish 48%; Portuguese 11%. *Jose* (281), *Juan* (147), *Luis* (109), *Carlos* (91), *Manuel* (74), *Francisco* (64), *Jesus* (64), *Jorge* (61), *Miguel* (57), *Angel* (55), *Pedro* (55), *Raul* (51); *Ligia, Omero, Wenceslao*.

Male (575) **1.** English: nickname for a virile man, from Middle English *male* 'masculine' (Old French *masle, madle*, Latin *masculus*). **2.** Belgian (**van Male**): habitational name from any of a number of places in Flanders named Male.

Malec (621) Polish, Czech, Slovak, Slovenian, and Croatian: nickname from a vocabulary word meaning 'small' (Czech *malý*, Polish *mały*, Slovenian and Croatian *mali*). Compare MALY.

GIVEN NAMES Polish 5%. *Beata, Casimir, Grzegorz, Jacek, Kazimier, Miroslaw, Piotr, Stanislaw, Tadeusz, Zosia*.

Malecek (126) Czech (**Maleček**): pet form from *malý* 'small' (see MALY).

Maіecha (358) Czech: **1.** nickname from a derivative of *malý* 'small' (see MALY). **2.** from a pet form of *Martin, Marek, Matěj*, or any other personal name beginning with *Ma-*.

Malecki (720) Polish (**Małecki**): habitational name for someone from places called Małki in the voivodeships of Ostrołęka and Toruń.

GIVEN NAMES Polish 7%. *Krzysztof* (2), *Zbigniew* (2), *Andrzej, Aniela, Bogdan, Boguslaw, Casimir, Jozef, Katarzyna, Teofil, Wieslaw, Zygmunt*.

Malek (1526) **1.** Polish (**Małek**), Czech, and Slovenian: from a pet form of a vocabulary word meaning 'small' (Polish *mały*, Czech *malý* 'small', Slovenian *mali*). Compare MALY. **2.** Czech: from a pet form of *Martin, Marek, Matěj*, or any other personal name beginning with *Ma-*. **3.** Polish: from a pet form of the personal name *Małomir*. **4.** Muslim: variant of MALIK.

GIVEN NAMES Muslim 9%; Polish 4%. *Abdul* (8), *Ahmad* (4), *Mohammed* (4), *Hani* (3), *Mansour* (3), *Mehrdad* (3), *Mohammad* (3), *Nabil* (3), *Shahram* (3), *Ali* (2), *Hany* (2), *Maged* (2), *Eugeniusz* (2), *Kazimierz* (2), *Stanislaw* (2), *Wladyslaw* (2), *Andrzej, Bronislawa, Danuta, Halina, Henryk, Jadwiga, Jerzy, Mieczyslaw*.

Malen (142) Jewish (Ashkenazic): perhaps a variant spelling of MALIN.

Malena (142) **1.** Italian: unexplained; perhaps from a female personal name. **2.** Czech: nickname derived from *malý* 'small' (see MALY).

GIVEN NAMES Italian 10%. *Oronzo, Rocco, Salvatore*.

Malenfant (273) French: nickname from the old adjective *mal* 'bad' + *enfant* 'child'.

GIVEN NAMES French 11%. *Armand* (2), *Rudolphe* (2), *Alain, Alcide, Camille, Pierre, Valmore*.

Maler (156) German and Jewish (Ashkenazic): variant of MAHLER.

GIVEN NAMES Jewish 4%. *Moshe, Shoshana*.

Malerba (171) Italian (mainly Liguria and Lombardy): from *mala* 'bad' + *èrba* 'grass', 'weed', applied in a transferred sense as a nickname for a wicked or dangerous person, or in some cases possibly a habitational name from any of various places so named; it is not clear whether the place name is a descriptive name or derives from the nickname.

GIVEN NAMES Italian 15%. *Rocco* (2), *Angelo, Aniello, Fiore, Franco, Guido*.

Males (285) English: variant of MALE.

Maleski (362) Polish: **1.** habitational name for someone from places called Malesin in Skierniewice voivodeship or Malesze in Białystok voivodeship. **2.** variant spelling of MALEWSKI.

Malesky (176) Probably a variant of Polish MALESKI.

Maletta (210) Italian: unexplained.

GIVEN NAMES Italian 8%. *Vito* (2), *Elio*, *Francesca, Silvo.*

Malette (156) French: from a diminutive of Old French *male* 'trunk', 'chest', 'coffer'. This may have been a metonymic occupational name for a maker of chests, or by extension for a carrier.

GIVEN NAMES French 12%. *Gaston* (4), *Alphonse, Francois, Jacques, Rejean, Serge.*

Malewski (76) Polish: habitational name for someone from any of the places called Malewo in the voivodeships of Ciechanów, Leszno, and Płock.

GIVEN NAMES Polish 6%. *Casimir, Florian.*

Maley (1772) **1.** Shortened and altered form of Irish O'MALLEY. **2.** Americanized form of Slovenian **Malej** 'small' or some other Slavic name meaning 'small' (see MALY and MALEC).

Malfitano (101) Italian: habitational name for someone from Amalfi, from an adjectival form of the place name.

GIVEN NAMES Italian 28%. *Sal* (2), *Angelo, Carmela, Domenic, Giorgio, Luciano, Ricardo, Rocco, Rosario, Salvatore, Santino.*

Malhotra (570) Indian (Panjab): Hindu (Khatri) name based on the name of a clan in the Khatri community. It is a modified form of **Mehrotra**, which is itself an extended form of MEHRA (Panjabi *mérā* 'chief', 'master'). The founder of the Malhotra clan is said to have been called Mehr Chand.

GIVEN NAMES Indian 94%. *Vinod* (13), *Raj* (11), *Sanjay* (11), *Anil* (8), *Rakesh* (8), *Sandeep* (8), *Ajay* (7), *Ashok* (7), *Ravi* (7), *Subhash* (7), *Vijay* (7), *Om* (6).

Malia (339) Southern Italian and Greek (**Malias**): habitational name from a place called Malia or Mallia.

Malich (100) Americanized spelling of Slovenian **Malič** and Croatian **Malić**: nickname for a small person, from the adjective *mali* 'small'. Compare MALEC, MALEK, and MALIK.

GIVEN NAMES Slavic 4%. *Oleg, Sava.*

Malick (536) **1.** Americanized spelling of a nickname derived from a diminutive of Ukrainian *malij*, Polish *mały* 'small'. **2.** Polish: from *Malik*, a pet form of the personal name *Małomir.*

Malicki (295) Polish: habitational name for someone from places called Malice, Malik, or Maliki.

GIVEN NAMES Polish 5%. *Jaroslaw, Jerzy, Mariusz, Stanislaw, Tomasz, Zbigniew.*

Malicoat (250) English: unexplained. Compare MALLICOAT.

Malik (2291) **1.** Muslim and Hindu (mainly Panjab): status name from a title meaning 'lord', 'ruler', 'chief', from Arabic *malik* 'king'. In the subcontinent this is often found as a title for the headman of a village. In Islam *Al-Malik* 'the King' is one of the attributes of Allah, regarded as 'the king of

mankind' (Qur'an 114:2), and this word is used in combination in names such as *'Abd-ul Malik* 'servant of the King'. This was the name of an Umayyad khalif (685–705). **2.** Czech, Slovak (**Malík**), and Slovenian: nickname for a small person, from a pet form of a vocabulary word meaning 'small' (Polish *mały*, Czech *malý* 'small', Slovenian *mali*). Compare MALY.

GIVEN NAMES Muslim 50%; Indian 11%. *Abdul* (33), *Mohammad* (33), *Khalid* (19), *Tariq* (17), *Muhammad* (16), *Ahmed* (14), *Shahid* (11), *Javed* (9), *Ali* (8), *Ghulam* (8), *Mohammed* (8), *Zafar* (8); *Krishan* (7), *Ashok* (6), *Chander* (4), *Rajesh* (4), *Ashish* (3), *Asim* (3), *Rajiv* (3), *Rohit* (3), *Sanjay* (3), *Arun* (2), *Kiran* (2), *Madan* (2).

Malikowski (125) Polish: habitational name for someone from a place called Malików or Malikowo.

Malin (1563) **1.** English: from the medieval female personal name *Malin*, a diminutive of MALL. **2.** French and Dutch: from the Germanic personal name *Madalin*, a short form of compound names with the initial element *madal* 'council'. **3.** Serbian: patronymic from *maly*, Serbian *mali* 'small'; compare MALY. **4.** Jewish (eastern Ashkenazic): metronymic from the Yiddish female personal name *Male* (a back-formation from MALKA as if it contained the Slavic diminutive suffix *-ke*) + the Slavic metronymic suffix *-in*. **5.** Jewish (eastern Ashkenazic): habitational name from Malin, a place in Ukraine.

Malina (347) **1.** Czech, Slovak, Polish, and Jewish (Ashkenazic): from the common Slavic word *malina* 'raspberry', used as a nickname for a pretty girl or an attractive person. As a Jewish surname it is generally ornamental. **2.** Polish: possibly also a nickname derived from *mały* 'small'.

Malinak (186) Czech (**Maliňák**) and Slovak (**Malinák**): **1.** from a derivative of *malý* 'small' (see MALY). **2.** from a derivative of MALINA.

Maline (177) **1.** Jewish (eastern Ashkenazic): variant spelling (under French influence) of MALIN 4 and 5. **2.** Jewish (eastern Ashkenazic): ornamental name from Ukrainian and Polish *malina* 'raspberry'. **3.** French (western and southwestern): metronymic from a feminine form of MALIN 4.

GIVEN NAME Jewish 4%. *Moshe.*

Maling (117) English: perhaps an altered form of MALIN.

GIVEN NAME French 4%. *Martial.*

Malinoski (209) Polish: variant spelling of MALINOWSKI.

Malinowski (2152) Polish, Ukrainian, and Jewish (eastern Ashkenazic): habitational name for someone from any of various places named in Polish as Malinów, Malinowo, or Malinówka, or in Ukrainian as Malinov, Malinovo, or Malinovka, all named with the common Slavic word *malina* 'raspberry'.

GIVEN NAMES Polish 8%. *Casimir* (5), *Stanislaw* (5), *Andrzej* (4), *Janusz* (3), *Jerzy* (3), *Lucjan* (3), *Zbigniew* (3), *Henryka* (2), *Jozef* (2), *Krzysztof* (2), *Miroslaw* (2).

Malinski (210) **1.** Polish (**Maliński**): habitational name for someone from places called Malin, Malina, Malinie, or Maliny, named either with *mały* 'small' or with *malina* 'raspberry'. **2.** Ukrainian and Jewish (from Ukraine): habitational name for someone from Malin, a place in Ukraine.

Malinsky (135) **1.** Ukrainian and Jewish (from Ukraine): variant spelling of MALINSKI. **2.** Czech (**Malínský**) and Slovak (**Malinksý**): habitational name for someone from a place called Malín in central Bohemia.

GIVEN NAMES Jewish 8%; Russian 8%; German 4%. *Irina, Sol; Igor* (2), *Leonid, Vladimir, Yefim; Kurt.*

Malis (262) **1.** Scottish: variant spelling of MALLIS. **2.** Polish (also **Malisz, Małys, Małysz**), Ukrainian; Czech, Slovak, and Croatian (**Mališ**); Slovenian; and Lithuanian(also **Malys**): from a derivative of a vocabulary word meaning 'small'. Compare MALY. **3.** Jewish (from Ukraine): metronymic, a variant of MALIN with the Yiddish possessive suffix *-s*.

GIVEN NAMES Polish 4%. *Aleksander, Casimir.*

Malish (101) Americanized spelling of Czech and Slovak **Mališ** (see MALIS).

Maliszewski (392) Polish: habitational name for someone from a place called Maliszew in Siedlce voivodeship, Maliszewo in Włocławek voivodeship, or Maliszów in Radom voivodeship.

GIVEN NAMES Polish 12%. *Bogdan, Grzegorz, Halina, Jaroslaw, Krzysztof, Leszek, Piotr, Tadeusz, Waclaw, Wincenty, Zbigniew, Zofia.*

Malito (124) Italian: habitational name from Malito in Cosenza province.

Malitz (106) German (of Slavic origin): from a diminutive of the Slavic adjective *maly* 'small'.

GIVEN NAMES German 5%. *Alois, Guenter.*

Malizia (348) Italian: nickname from *malizia* 'malice', 'spite'; 'mischievousness' (Latin *malitia*).

GIVEN NAMES Italian 14%. *Angelo* (2), *Natale* (2), *Carmela, Carmine, Domenic, Gaetano, Luigi, Rinaldo, Rino, Romolo, Santi, Valentino.*

Malka (136) Jewish (Ashkenazic and Sephardic): metronymic from the Yiddish female personal name *Malke* (from Hebrew *Malka* 'queen').

GIVEN NAMES Jewish 33%. *Moshe* (3), *Shlomo* (2), *Anat, Arye, Avi, Aviva, Doron, Eliyahu, Galit, Mordecai, Mordechai, Nadav.*

Malkasian (123) Armenian: patronymic from the personal name *Marxas*.

GIVEN NAMES Armenian 14%. *Zaven* (2), *Arad, Ararat, Armen, Dikran, Sarkis.*

Malkiewicz (139) Polish (**Małkiewicz**): patronymic from the nickname *Małek*, a diminutive of *mały* 'small'.
GIVEN NAMES Polish 6%. *Jolanta, Wladyslaw, Zdzislaw.*

Malkin (822) **1.** English: from a medieval female personal name, a diminutive of *Mal(le)*, a pet form of MARY (see MALL), with the hypocoristic suffix *-kin*. **2.** Jewish (from Belarus): metronymic from the Yiddish female personal name *Malke* (from Hebrew *Malka* 'queen') + the Slavic metronymic suffix *-in*.
GIVEN NAMES Jewish 6%. *Emanuel* (2), *Sol* (2), *Avram, Dov, Gersh, Meyer, Mort.*

Malko (103) Ukrainian: nickname from a noun derivative of Ukrainian *malyj* 'small'.
GIVEN NAMES French 6%; Russian 5%. *Berthe, Georges, Micheline; Tsilia, Vyacheslav.*

Malkowski (416) Polish (**Małkowski**): habitational name for someone from a place called Małkowo or Małków.
GIVEN NAMES Polish 7%. *Janusz* (2), *Casimir, Krystyna, Lech, Stanislaw, Tadeusz, Tomasz, Witold, Zbigniew.*

Malkus (121) **1.** Dutch and North German: variant of the Biblical personal name *Malchus* (in Christian tradition believed to be the name of the slave whose ear was cut off by Peter in the garden of Gethsemane). **2.** Polish (**Małkus**): nickname from the dialect word *małkus* 'stag which had shed its horns'. **3.** Jewish (eastern Ashkenazic): metronymic, a variant of MALKIN, with the Yiddish possessive suffix *-s*.
GIVEN NAMES German 6%; Dutch 4%. *Kurt; Willem.*

Mall (593) **1.** English: from the medieval female personal name *Mal(le)*, pet form of *Mary* (see MARIE). **2.** Indian (northern states): Hindu name found in several communities, from Sanskrit *malla* 'strongman', 'wrestler'.

Mallak (153) Polish, Czech, and Slovak: Americanized spelling of MALAK.

Mallard (1781) English: **1.** from the Old French personal name *Malhard*, composed of the Germanic elements *madal* 'council' + *hard* 'hardy', 'brave', 'strong'. This was introduced to Britain by the Normans. **2.** nickname for someone supposedly resembling a male wild duck, Middle English, Old French *malard.*

Mallari (206) Filipino: unexplained.
GIVEN NAMES Spanish 44%; Italian 7%. *Florentina* (2), *Jaime* (2), *Macario* (2), *Raymundo* (2), *Reynaldo* (2), *Adriano, Agapito, Alfonso, Angel, Arturo, Casimiro, Catalino; Antonio* (2), *Cesario, Eliseo, Geronimo, Julieta, Leonardo, Romeo.*

Mallary (117) English: variant spelling of MALLORY.
GIVEN NAME French 6%. *Narcisse.*

Mallas (138) Greek: metonymic occupational name for a bricklayer, from *mallas* 'trowel', from Turkish *mala.*

GIVEN NAMES Greek 4%. *Nikolaos, Spero, Spiros.*

Mallatt (102) English: variant spelling of MALLET.

Malle (106) **1.** French: metonymic occupational name for a mail carrier or person in charge of baggage animals, from *malle* 'baggage'. **2.** Perhaps also Spanish: unexplained.

Mallek (201) Of Slavic origin: respelling of **Malek** or **Malik**, derivatives of a diminutive of the common Slavic adjective *maly* 'small'.

Mallen (440) **1.** English: variant spelling of MALIN. **2.** Irish: variant of MELLON. **3.** Spanish (Aragonese **Mallén**): habitational name from Mallén in Zaragoza province.

Maller (242) **1.** Dutch: occupational name for a miller, from an agent derivative of Middle High German *maln* 'to grind'. **2.** German and Dutch: variant of MAHLER.
GIVEN NAMES Russian 4%. *Boris, Gennady, Mikhail, Svetlana.*

Mallernee (128) Origin unidentified.

Mallery (699) **1.** English: see MALLORY. **2.** French: from a Frenchified form of a Germanic personal name composed of the elements *madal* 'council' + *rīc* 'power'.

Malles (103) Scottish: variant spelling of MALLIS.

Mallet (494) **1.** French: from a pet form of the personal name *Malo* (see MALO 1). **2.** French: variant of MALETTE. **3.** French, Catalan and English: from French, English, and Catalan *mallet* 'hammer', Old French *ma(i)let*, diminutive of *ma(i)l* (Latin *malleus*) either a metonymic occupational name for a smith, or possibly a nickname for a fearsome warrior. **4.** French and English: nickname for an unlucky person, from Old French *maleit* 'accursed' (Latin *maledictus*, the opposite of *benedictus* 'blessed'). **5.** English: from the medieval female personal name *Malet*, a diminutive of *Mal(le)* (see MALL). **6.** English: variant of MALLARD 1.
GIVEN NAMES French 10%. *Jean-Yves* (2), *Adelard, Alain, Henri, Jacques, Leonce, Lucien, Monique, Philippe.*

Mallett (2109) Variant of MALLET.

Mallette (975) Variant spelling of French MALETTE.
GIVEN NAMES French 5%. *Marcel* (3), *Andre* (2), *Donat, Emile, Francois, Jacques, Laurent, Pierre, Rolande.*

Malley (1516) Irish: shortened form of O'MALLEY, Anglicized form of Gaelic *Ó Máille*.

Mallia (246) Southern Italian: variant of MALIA.
GIVEN NAMES Italian 10%; French 4%. *Salvatore* (3), *Carmel, Carmelo, Corrado, Palma; Pierre* (2), *Monique.*

Mallick (293) Indian (Bihar, Orissa, Bengal) and Bangladeshi: Hindu and Muslim name meaning 'lord', from Arabic *malik* 'king'. Compare MALIK.

GIVEN NAMES Indian 19%; Muslim 19%. *Rajiv* (2), *Ashish, Ashok, Babu, Bawa, Debashish, Deepa, Dhiraj, Dilip, Kalpana, Kaushik, Manish; Kamal* (2), *Mohammed* (2), *Abdur, Abid, Abida, Ali, Azhar, Farooq, Imtiaz, Irfan, Karem, Khalid.*

Mallicoat (240) English: unexplained. Compare MALICOAT.

Mallin (405) English: variant spelling of MALIN.

Mallinger (223) Dutch and German: habitational name from any of various places called Malling, for example in Bavaria.

Mallinson (248) English: metronymic from MALIN 1.

Mallis (171) Scottish (Perthshire): according to Black, a habitational name from lands called 'Malles infra Gowry'.

Mallison (215) English: metronymic either from MALIN 1 or MALLET 1.

Mallo (297) **1.** Italian (Sicily): from Italian *mallo* 'soft blanket' (from Latin *mallus* 'tuft of wool', from Greek *mallos* 'fleece'). Caracausi believes the surname may have arisen as a nickname for someone with curly hair. **2.** Asturian-Leonese: habitational name from a place called Mallo in Lleón province, Northwest Spain (probably from *mallo* 'threshing flail', 'mallet', or, alternatively, though less likely, from a pre-Roman territorial name).
GIVEN NAMES Spanish 13%. *Francisco* (3), *Jorge* (3), *Jose* (3), *Jesus* (2), *Manuel* (2), *Mario* (2), *Osvaldo* (2), *Angel, Braulio, Eduardo, Elva, Emilio.*

Malloch (217) Scottish: reduced Anglicized form of Gaelic *MacIain Mhalaich* 'son of Ian of the bushy eyebrows', which was the family name of the MacGregors of Balhaldie. The Ian from whom the name is derived died in the early 16th century.

Mallon (1947) Irish: probably a variant of MELLON.
GIVEN NAMES Irish 5%. *Brendan, Liam, Malachy.*

Mallonee (433) Possibly an altered spelling of Irish MALONEY.

Mallory (5745) English (of Norman origin): nickname for an unfortunate person, from Old French *malheure* 'unhappy', 'unlucky'. The etymology from *maloret* 'ill-omened' (Latin *male* 'badly' + *auguratus*) is less likely for the surname that has actually survived, although it does lie behind other medieval Norman surnames of this form, now defunct.

Mallow (804) German: variant spelling of **Malow**, a habitational name from Malow in Mecklenburg.

Malloy (5864) Irish: see MOLLOY.
GIVEN NAMES Irish 5%. *Brendan* (4), *Sheelagh* (2), *Brigid, Eamonn, James Patrick, Jarlath.*

Mallozzi (287) Italian: probably from a derivative of MALLO.
GIVEN NAMES Italian 26%. *Angelo* (4), *Antonio* (3), *Ottavio* (3), *Cosmo* (2),

Salvatore (2), *Domenic, Domenico, Giovanni, Marcello, Marco, Nicola, Pasquale.*

Mally (307) **1.** Irish: variant spelling of MALLEY, shortened form of O'MALLEY. **2.** French: from Old French *mal(l)ier* 'coach horse', 'draught horse', 'pack horse', hence a metonymic occupational name for a coachman, a carter, or a carrier.

Malm (943) Swedish: arbitrary or ornamental name from Swedish *malm* 'ore', adopted in some cases by people connected with the copper-mining industry.
GIVEN NAMES Scandinavian 7%. *Knute* (2), *Elof, Kerstin, Lars, Sigfrid.*

Malmberg (567) Swedish: ornamental name composed of the elements *malm* 'ore' + *berg* 'mountain', 'hill'.
GIVEN NAMES Scandinavian 8%; German 4%. *Nels* (2), *Lars, Olle; Claus, Hans.*

Malmborg (139) Swedish: ornamental name composed of the elements *malm* 'ore' + *borg* 'town'.
GIVEN NAMES Scandinavian 7%. *Fredrik, Knute.*

Malmgren (406) Swedish: ornamental name composed of the elements *malm* 'ore' + *gren* 'branch'.
GIVEN NAMES Scandinavian 4%. *Britt, Erland, Sven.*

Malmin (120) Norwegian: habitational name from either of two farmsteads in southwestern Norway, named *Malmheimr* in Old Norse, from *malmr* 'sand or gravel plain' + *heimr* 'homestead', 'farmstead'. Farmsteads such as these, established in Viking times, have since been broken up into many smaller farms; hence the proliferation of surnames based on what were originally very few named locations.
GIVEN NAME Scandinavian 14%. *Tor.*

Malmquist (448) Swedish: ornamental name composed of the elements *malm* 'ore' + *quist*, an old or ornamental spelling of *kvist* 'twig'.
GIVEN NAMES Scandinavian 5%. *Bertel, Bjorn.*

Malmstrom (391) Swedish (**Malmström**): ornamental name composed of the elements *malm* 'ore' + *ström* 'river'.
GIVEN NAMES Scandinavian 6%; German 4%. *Hans, Inge, Kurt.*

Malnar (233) Slovenian: occupational name from Slovenian *malinar*, archaic form of *mlinar* 'miller'. Compare MLINAR.
GIVEN NAME Scandinavian 4%. *Arnell* (3).

Malnati (134) Italian: habitational name from Malnate in Varese province; the *-i* (plural) ending is typical of Lombardic habitational names.

Malo (744) **1.** French: from the personal name *Malo*, which was relatively popular in Brittany in the Middle Ages, having been borne by a 6th-century Welsh missionary to the area. His name is also recorded in the Latinized form *Maclovius*, and perhaps has some connection with Celtic *megalos* 'chief', 'leader'. **2.** Spanish: nickname for

an unpleasant individual, from Spanish *malo* 'bad', 'evil' (Latin *malus*).
GIVEN NAMES French 9%. *Armand* (4), *Normand* (3), *Pierre* (2), *Aime, Andre, Cecile, Celine, Fernand, Germaine, Gilles, Gisele, Jean Guy.*

Malon (166) **1.** Polish (**Małoń**): nickname from a derivative of *mały* 'small' (see MALY). **2.** French: from the oblique case of the Germanic personal name *Madalo*, genitive *Madalonis*, a short form of compound names with the initial element *madal* 'council'. **3.** French: variant of MALO. **4.** French: habitational name from Saint-Melon-sur-Mela in Ille-et-Vilaine. **5.** Spanish and Aragonese (**Malón**): habitational name from Malón in Zaragoza province, Aragon.
GIVEN NAMES Polish 4%; German 4%. *Alicja; Aloysius.*

Malone (23182) Irish: Anglicized form of Gaelic **Ó Maoil Eoin** 'descendant of the devotee of (Saint) John'. This is the name of an ecclesiastical family at Clonmacnoise. MacLysaght states that this surname is now numerous in County Clare where it is pronounced Maloon and is probably really MULDOON.

Maloney (12480) Irish (Munster): Anglicized form of Gaelic **Ó Maol Dhomhnaigh** 'descendant of the devotee of the Church'. Compare MULDOWNEY.
GIVEN NAMES Irish 5%. *Donal* (5), *Brendan* (3), *Donovan* (2), *John Patrick* (2), *Kieran* (2), *Liam* (2), *Aileen, Bridie, Caitlin, Connolly, Fintan, James Patrick.*

Malonson (132) Variant spelling of MALLINSON.

Malony (100) Irish: variant spelling of MALONEY.
GIVEN NAME Irish 7%. *Aidan* (2).

Maloof (574) Arabic: the name of a well-known Christian clan in Lebanon and Syria, probably from Arabic *ma'lūf* 'fattened'.

Maloon (106) Variant of Irish MALONE.

Malott (1109) Variant of French **Marlet** (see MARLETT).

Malotte (132) Variant of French **Marlet** (see MARLETT).

Malouf (441) Arabic: variant spelling of MALOOF.
GIVEN NAMES French 7%; Arabic 7%. *Michel* (2), *Camil, Colette, Georges, Marthe, Philippe; Fouad* (2), *Khalil* (2), *Nawal* (2), *Riad* (2), *Said* (2), *Anis, Dalal, Faris, Fawzi, Fawzy, Haleem, Halim.*

Malouin (108) Respelling of French **Maluin, Maloin**, from the Germanic personal name *Madalwin*, a compound of *mahal* 'advice' + *win* 'friend'.
GIVEN NAMES French 10%. *Fabien, Normand.*

Maloy (1813) Variant spelling of Irish MOLLOY.

Malpass (577) English and Scottish (of Norman origin) and French: habitational

name from any of various places named Malpas, because of the difficulty of the terrain, from Old French *mal pas* 'bad passage' (Latin *malus passus*). It is a common French minor place name, and places in Cheshire, Cornwall, Gwent, and elsewhere in England were given this name by Norman settlers. A place in Rousillon (southeastern France) that had this name in the 12th century was subsequently renamed Bonpas for the sake of a better omen.

Malphrus (201) Variant of MALPASS.

Malphurs (110) Variant of MALPASS.
GIVEN NAME French 5%. *Colette.*

Malsam (169) Perhaps an altered form of MALSON. Compare MALSOM.

Malsbury (137) English: probably a variant of **Malmesbury**, a habitational name from a place of this name in Wiltshire, named in Old English as 'the stronghold (*burh*, *byrig*) of Maeldub', an ancient Celtic personal name.

Malsch (135) German: habitational name from any of several places, the largest being near Karlsruhe, which get their names from *malsk* 'muddy', 'boggy'.
GIVEN NAMES German 5%. *Klaus* (2), *Otto.*

Malsom (166) English: unexplained.

Malson (400) English: **1.** metronymic from the Middle English female personal name *Mal*, a pet form of the Norman name *Mathilde* (see MOULD 1). **2.** perhaps a habitational name from a place so named in Devon.
GIVEN NAMES French 4%. *Micheline, Monique.*

Malstrom (182) Swedish (**Mälström**): ornamental name composed of the elements *Mäl* (probably taken from the lake name *Mälar* in which *Mäl-* is a mutated form of *mal* 'gravel') + *ström* 'stream'.

Malta (221) **1.** Southern Italian, Spanish, and Portuguese: habitational name for someone from the Mediterranean island of Malta (Latin *Melita*, Greek *Melitē*). **2.** Dutch: habitational name from a place called Malta, near Zierikzee.
GIVEN NAMES Italian 12%; Spanish 10%. *Salvatore* (2), *Angelo, Carmela, Luigi, Palma, Sal, Vito; Alejandro, Luis, Luz, Mercedes, Ramon, Santiago.*

Maltais (202) French: ethnic name for a man from Malta, from *maltais* 'Maltese'.
GIVEN NAMES French 16%. *Pierre* (2), *Raoul* (2), *Adrien, Andre, Cecile, Colette, Emilien, Fernand, Francois, Phillippe, Rejean, Renald.*

Maltbie (191) Probably a respelling of MALTBY.

Maltby (802) English: habitational name from Maltby in Cleveland, Lincolnshire, and North and South Yorkshire, or Mautby in Norfolk, all named with the Old Norse byname *Malti* 'sharp', 'bitter' + Old Norse *býr* 'farm', 'settlement'.

Malter (231) **1.** English: occupational name for someone who produced or used malt for

brewing, from an agent derivative of Middle English *malt* 'malt', 'germinated barley' (Old English *mealt*). **2.** English (of Norman origin): according to Reaney, a habitational name from some place in France called Maleterre, from Old French *male terre* 'bad land' (Latin *mala terra*). **3.** German: metonymic occupational name for a grain measurer or a maker of grain measures, or for a miller, from Middle High German *malter*, a measure of grain. **4.** Jewish (Ashkenazic): unexplained.
GIVEN NAMES Jewish 4%. *Gili, Mort.*

Maltese (700) Italian: ethnic name for someone from the island of Malta.
GIVEN NAMES Italian 18%. *Salvatore* (6), *Carlo* (3), *Gaspare* (3), *Rocco* (3), *Angelo* (2), *Enzo* (2), *Giuseppe* (2), *Antonella, Antonio, Carmela, Carmelo, Caterina.*

Maltman (111) English: occupational name for someone who produced or used malt for brewing, from Middle English *malt* 'malt', 'germinated barley' + *man* 'man' (see MALTER).

Maltos (110) Hispanic (chiefly Mexico): unexplained.
GIVEN NAMES Spanish 55%. *Jose* (5), *Jose Luis* (3), *Humberto* (2), *Juan* (2), *Miguel* (2), *Alejandro, Alejo, Alfonso, Americo, Ana Maria, Arturo, Cosme.*

Maltsberger (109) German: habitational name from a place called Maltsberg.
FOREBEARS Johann (John) Maltsberger (1779–1854) emigrated from Germany and settled in Greene Co., TN, in the early 19th century.

Maltz (403) Jewish (Ashkenazic): metonymic occupational name from German *Malz*, Yiddish *malts* 'malt'.
GIVEN NAMES Jewish 7%. *Shira* (2), *Meyer, Miriam, Yaron.*

Maltzman (135) Jewish: elaborated form of MALTZ.

Malueg (204) German: unexplained. It looks like a Frenchified spelling of a German name such as **Malweg**, although the latter is not recorded as a German surname. Possibly it is from Malleck, name of a minor place near Emmendingen.

Malveaux (368) French: topographic name from a place known as Malvaux, from Latin *malus* 'bad' + *vallis* 'valley'.
GIVEN NAMES French 5%. *Antoine, Germaine, Vernice.*

Malvin (115) Possibly an altered form of MELVIN.

Malwitz (130) German: habitational name from an unidentified place.

Maly (963) Czech (**Malý**) and Polish (**Mały**): from the common Slavic adjective *maly* 'small' (Czech *malý*, Polish *mały*). This was both a nickname for a physically small man and a pet name for a child, which was sometimes retained into adult life. The cognate noun *malec* in Polish and Czech has the additional sense 'lad', which is probably also the origin of some surnames.

Malz (129) German: **1.** variant spelling of MALTZ. **2.** habitational name from a place so named in Brandenburg.
GIVEN NAMES German 8%. *Hans* (2), *Kurt, Manfred, Otto.*

Malzahn (203) North German: habitational name from Molzahn near Ratzeburg or Moltzahn in Pomerania.

Malzone (121) Italian: unexplained. This is a widespread name in Italy, occurring chiefly in Campania and to a lesser extent in Calabria.
GIVEN NAMES Italian 17%. *Gennaro* (2), *Alfonse, Grazio, Lorenzo, Pasquale.*

Mamer (140) Dutch: **1.** from the Latin personal name and saint's name *Mamerius* or *Mamertius*. **2.** habitational name from Mamer in the Grand Duchy of Luxembourg.

Mammano (128) Southern Italian: masculine form of **Mammana**, an occupational name for a midwife, Sicilian *mammana*.
GIVEN NAMES Italian 19%. *Salvatore* (2), *Angelo, Liborio.*

Mammen (349) **1.** German: East Frisian patronymic from the nursery name *Mamme*, linked to Middle High German *mamme, memme* 'mother's breast' (Latin *mamma*). **2.** English (of Norman origin): from the Old French personal name *Maismon, Maimon*, of unknown etymology. **3.** Indian (Kerala): variant of THOMAS among Kerala Christians, with the Tamil-Malayalam third person masculine singular suffix -*n*. It is only found as a personal name in Kerala, but in the U.S. has come to be used as a family name among Kerala Christians.
GIVEN NAMES Indian 9%. *Geetha* (2), *Mathai* (2), *Anil, Indira, Manoj, Priya, Satheesh.*

Mammenga (111) Frisian: patronymic from the personal name *Mamme*, which is said to be a masculine pet form ultimately derived from MARIA.

Mammone (126) Italian: variant of MAIMONE.
GIVEN NAMES Italian 22%. *Francesco, Nicola, Palma, Pasquale, Rocco, Sal, Salvatore, Silvio.*

Mamo (151) **1.** Ethiopian: unexplained. **2.** Italian and Maltese: unexplained. **3.** possibly Catalan (**Mamó**): variant spelling of *Maimó* (from Arab *Maymun* 'son of the fortunate one'), used in the Middle Ages to refer to unknown Muslims.
GIVEN NAMES Ethiopian 13%; Spanish 7%. *Yared* (2), *Bekele, Binyam, Eyob, Fetlework, Gashaw, Mulugeta, Tsegaye, Zewdu; Jose, Manuel, Ramona.*

Mamon (102) **1.** Spanish (**Mamón**): unexplained. **2.** Polish or other Slavic: unexplained.
GIVEN NAMES Spanish 5%; Polish 4%. *Octavio* (2), *Juan, Lordes; Kasimer* (2); *Wieslaw.*

Mamone (167) Southern Italian: variant of MAIMONE.

GIVEN NAMES Italian 27%. *Salvatore* (4), *Angelo, Concetta, Cosmo, Geno, Giuseppe, Rosaria, Vito.*

Mamula (264) Serbian and Croatian: nickname from *mamula*, a word denoting a type of cereal porridge, a word of Turkish origin.
GIVEN NAMES South Slavic 9%. *Milan* (6), *Branko* (2), *Rade.*

Man (588) **1.** Chinese 文: variant of WEN 2. **2.** Chinese 满: from a character in the personal name of Hu Gongman, a retainer of Wu Wang. After the latter established the Zhou dynasty in 1122 BC, he granted the state of Chen to Hu Gongman, whose descendants adopted the second character of his given name, Man, as their surname. This character also means 'Manchurian', but the name does not appear to be related to this meaning. **3.** Chinese 闻: variant of WEN 3. **4.** Chinese 万: variant of WAN 1. **5.** English and Jewish: variant spelling of MANN. **6.** Dutch: from Middle Dutch *man* 'man', 'husband', 'vassal', 'arbiter'. **7.** French: from the Germanic personal name *Manno* (see MANN 2). **8.** Jewish (Ashkenazic): from the personal name *Man*, derived from Yiddish 'man'.
GIVEN NAMES Chinese 18%. *Wai* (4), *Chan* (2), *Cheuk* (2), *Kin* (2), *Kwok* (2), *Sai* (2), *Shek* (2), *Tong* (2), *Chi, Choong, Chung Yee, Hin.*

Manago (145) **1.** Southern Italian and Greek (**Managos**): from the Greek personal name *Managos*, a dialect variant of PANAGOS. **2.** Altered form of French MANIGAULT.
GIVEN NAMES Italian 14%; Spanish 9%. *Carmello, Domenico, Saverio; Alonzo, Angel, Basilio, Jose, Manuel, Pablo, Rosemaria.*

Manahan (731) Irish: shortened Anglicized form of Gaelic **Ó Mainchín** (see MONAHAN).
GIVEN NAMES Irish 4%. *Delma* (3), *Donal.*

Manak (132) Czech (**Maňák**): from the name for a man who was the son or husband of a woman called *Marie*, from a pet form of the female personal name *Máňa*, itself a pet form of *Marie* (see MARIA).

Manalo (374) **1.** Filipino: unexplained. **2.** alternatively, perhaps Catalan (**Manaló**), variant spelling of *Maneló*, pet form of the personal name *Manel*, short form of EMANUEL.
GIVEN NAMES Spanish 42%. *Josefina* (4), *Ramon* (4), *Edgardo* (3), *Felipe* (3), *Mariano* (3), *Alberto* (2), *Arsenio* (2), *Arturo* (2), *Carlito* (2), *Luz* (2), *Nilo* (2), *Virgilio* (2); *Antonio* (2), *Dante* (2), *Angelo, Ceasar, Federico, Gilda, Gildo, Ireneo, Lorenzo, Luciano, Romeo, Sal.*

Manansala (128) Filipino: unexplained.
GIVEN NAMES Spanish 48%; Italian 7%. *Artemio* (2), *Felino* (2), *Miguel* (2), *Renato* (2), *Wilfredo* (2), *Abelardo, Agapito,*

Arsenio, Augusto, Bienvenido, Dulce, Eduardo; Leonardo (2), Dante, Romeo.

Manard (142) Dutch: from the Germanic personal name *Manhard*, composed of the Germanic elements *man* 'man', 'human' + *hard* 'hardy', 'brave', 'strong'.

Manary (133) Irish: variant of **Menary**, an Anglicized form of Gaelic **Mac Náradhaigh**, described by Woulfe as 'a rare Ulster surname'.

Manas (160) Spanish (**Mañas**): nickname for a devious person or alternatively for an astute or skillful person, from the plural of Spanish *maña* 'trick', 'strategem' (Late Latin *mania*, a derivative of *manus* 'hand').
GIVEN NAMES Spanish 11%. *Arturo* (2), *Francisco* (2), *Angelito, Diego, Hermenegildo, Joaquin, Juan, Mauricio, Reynaldo, Roberto; Angelo* (2), *Carmel* (2), *Bruna, Cira.*

Manasco (476) Origin unidentified. According to one family tradition, it is of northern Spanish or southern French origin. The etymology is unknown. It seems to have reached North America via England. FOREBEARS The name was well established in colonial North America. A Manasco family was recorded in Amherst Co., VA, in 1749. James and Jeremiah Minasco are recorded as land holders in Anson Co., NC, in 1763.

Manasse (142) French: from the Biblical Hebrew personal name *Manasseh*, from *nashah* 'make to forget'. This was the name of Joseph's elder son, brother of Ephraim, so named in the hope that Joseph's father Jacob might begin to forget the sorrows of the past.
GIVEN NAMES French 9%; German 6%. *Henri* (2), *Armand, Lucienne, Pierre; Claus.*

Manatt (112) Irish or Scottish: probably a variant of McNatt.
FOREBEARS Robert Manatt (1792–1864) emigrated fron Co. Down, Ireland, to Poweshiek Co., IA.

Manbeck (262) German: unexplained.
FOREBEARS Rudolph Manbeck was born in 1743 in Germany and died in January 1794 in Tulpehocken, Berks Co., PA.

Manca (114) Italian (Sardinian): nickname for a left-handed person, from Sardinian *(manu) manka* 'left hand', hence by extension a nickname for a left-handed person (see Manco).
GIVEN NAMES Italian 13%. *Alessandra, Angelo, Enzo, Giuseppe, Lorenzo, Luigi, Piero.*

Mance (633) **1.** English (Devon): unexplained. **2.** Croatian: unexplained.

Mancebo (183) Spanish: occupational or status name for a serf or servant, also 'youth', 'single man', Old Spanish *mancebo* (Late Latin *mancipus*, from classical Latin *mancipium* 'slave').
GIVEN NAMES Spanish 28%; Portuguese 9%. *Manuel* (6), *Jose* (4), *Lino* (3), *Roberto* (3), *Adalberto, Arnaldo, Carlos, Cesar,*

Eugenio, Francisca, Joaquin, Josefina; Joao.

Mancera (123) Italian, Spanish, or Portuguese: unexplained.
GIVEN NAMES Spanish 66%. *Carlos* (3), *Jose* (3), *Juan* (3), *Luis* (3), *Arturo* (2), *Elena* (2), *Enrique* (2), *Javier* (2), *Jose Luis* (2), *Miguel* (2), *Rafael* (2), *Roberto* (2).

Mancha (362) **1.** Spanish: regional name from La Mancha, which extends through the provinces of Ciudad Real, Toledo, Cuenca, and Albacete. The place name is a derivative of Arabic *ma-nya* 'high plain'. **2.** Spanish and Portuguese: possibly from *mancha* 'stain' (Latin *macula*).
GIVEN NAMES Spanish 46%. *Jose* (10), *Manuel* (9), *Jesus* (6), *Juan* (5), *Javier* (4), *Ramon* (4), *Guadalupe* (3), *Jorge* (3), *Pedro* (3), *Raul* (3), *Ricardo* (3), *Roberto* (3).

Manchester (2078) English: habitational name from the city in northwestern England, formerly part of Lancashire. This is so called from *Mamucio* (an ancient British name containing the element *mammā* 'breast', and meaning 'breast-shaped hill') + Old English *ceaster* 'Roman fort or walled city' (Latin *castra* 'legionary camp').

Mancia (239) Italian, Spanish, or Portuguese: unexplained.
GIVEN NAMES Spanish 48%; Portuguese 13%. *Jose* (13), *Ana* (7), *Guillermo* (4), *Julio* (4), *Carlos* (3), *Dinora* (3), *Gilberto* (3), *Berta* (2), *Miguel* (2), *Nestor* (2), *Ricardo* (2), *Salvador* (2); *Ligia; Angelo* (2), *Amerigo, Antonio, Giovanna, Guido, Lucio.*

Mancil (280) **1.** Variant spelling of English MANSELL. **2.** Possibly also an Americanized form of Spanish MANCILLA.

Mancill (102) **1.** Variant spelling of English MANSELL. **2.** Possibly also an Americanized form of Spanish MANCILLA.

Mancilla (440) **1.** Spanish: from *mancilla* 'mole', 'birthmark' or 'blot', 'stain' (Latin *manucella*), hence a nickname for someone with a blemish on their skin or their character. **2.** Asturian-Leonese: habitational name from *Mancilla*, a village in Lleón province, northern Spain.
GIVEN NAMES Spanish 55%. *Jose* (15), *Juan* (8), *Luis* (8), *Miguel* (7), *Carlos* (5), *Alejandro* (4), *Eduardo* (4), *Ricardo* (4), *Salvador* (4), *Arturo* (3), *Javier* (3), *Manuel* (3).

Mancillas (247) Spanish: variant (plural) of MANCILLA.
GIVEN NAMES Spanish 47%. *Jose* (4), *Pedro* (4), *Francisco* (3), *Luis* (3), *Manuel* (3), *Angel* (2), *Francisca* (2), *Javier* (2), *Jorge* (2), *Juan* (2), *Lauro* (2), *Mateo* (2); *Antonio* (2), *Amadeo, Eliseo, Leonardo, Sal.*

Mancinelli (403) Italian: from a diminutive of MANCINI.
GIVEN NAMES Italian 13%. *Enrico* (3), *Aldo* (2), *Amerigo, Angelo, Carlo, Ceasar,*

Dante, Dino, Giampiero, Gildo, Leno, Rocco.

Mancini (3934) Italian: patronymic or plural form of the nickname MANCINO.
GIVEN NAMES Italian 19%. *Angelo* (19), *Antonio* (18), *Rocco* (17), *Dante* (11), *Domenic* (11), *Luigi* (9), *Carmine* (8), *Salvatore* (7), *Guido* (6), *Pasquale* (6), *Sal* (6), *Aldo* (5).

Mancino (513) Italian: nickname for a left-handed person, *mancino* (from Latin *mancinus*).
GIVEN NAMES Italian 25%. *Salvatore* (6), *Angelo* (3), *Sal* (3), *Alfonso, Alfonzo, Alicia, Annalisa, Antonio, Cataldo, Ciro, Cosimo, Domenic, Domenico, Genaro, Giuseppe, Mario, Placido.*

Mancl (168) Czech form of German **Manzel**, a pet form of the German personal name MANZ.

Manco (183) Southern Italian, Spanish, and Portuguese: nickname from *manco*, originally meaning 'one-armed', 'maimed' (Latin *mancus* 'one-armed', 'defective', 'maimed'). In Italian this is a descriptive epithet for a left-handed person.
GIVEN NAMES Italian 9%; Spanish 7%. *Angelo, Ottavio, Santo; Carlos, Estela, Fernando, Jesus.*

Mancusi (199) Southern Italian: patronymic or plural form of MANCUSO.
GIVEN NAMES Italian 17%. *Mario* (3), *Carmine* (2), *Alberto, Aldo, Angelo, Evaristo, Guido, Italo, Pasquale.*

Mancuso (3546) Italian (Sicilian and Calabrian): nickname for a left-handed or maladroit person, Sicilian *mancusu* (from Latin *mancosus*, a derivative of *mancus* 'one-armed', 'defective', 'maimed').
GIVEN NAMES Italian 14%. *Salvatore* (21), *Angelo* (18), *Sal* (12), *Antonio* (7), *Carlo* (7), *Carmine* (6), *Santo* (5), *Domenic* (4), *Rocco* (4), *Carmela* (3), *Ciro* (3), *Ettore* (2).

Mand (178) **1.** Indian (Panjab): Sikh name, probably from Panjabi *mən* 'skill'. It is based on the name of a Jat clan. **2.** Dutch: from a short form of the personal name *Amand(us)*.
GIVEN NAMES Indian 7%; German 5%. *Jasvir* (2), *Dalbir, Jagdish; Alois, Ewald, Gerda.*

Manda (174) **1.** Indian (Andhra Pradesh): Hindu (Brahman) name based on the name of a subgroup of Brahmans. **2.** Czech and Slovak: from a derivative of the female personal name *Magdalena* (see MAUDLIN).
GIVEN NAMES Indian 17%. *Srinivas* (3), *Asha, Ashok, Bhaskar, Bose, Shanti, Sivaram, Vasantha, Vijay.*

Mandal (103) Indian (northern states): Hindu name found in several communities, from Sanskrit *maṇala*, which has several meanings, including 'sphere' and 'halo'.
GIVEN NAMES Indian 71%. *Chandi* (2), *Sanjay* (2), *Sankar* (2), *Somnath* (2), *Aditi, Aditya, Ajit, Amala, Amitabha, Anil, Anirudh, Aparna.*

Mandala (142) Italian (Sicily; **Mandalà**): **1.** occupational name for a seller of scarves, from Greek *mandilas*. **2.** altered form of *Mannalà*, a name of Arabic origin, derived from *mann Allāh* 'grace of Allāh'. The surname is characteristic of the Palermo region and eastern Sicily.
GIVEN NAMES Italian 24%. *Salvatore* (2), *Carmela, Filippo, Gaspare, Girolamo, Mario, Marta.*

Mandarino (222) Italian: possibly from *mandarino* 'mandarin orange'.
GIVEN NAMES Italian 18%. *Carmello* (2), *Carmine* (2), *Angelo, Guido, Luigina, Mario, Sal.*

Mandato (158) Southern Italian: from the old Tuscan personal name *Mandatus*, probably an omen name derived from *mandato (da Dio)* 'gift (of God)'.
GIVEN NAMES Italian 14%. *Vito* (2), *Graziano, Oreste, Sal.*

Mandel (3174) **1.** German, Dutch, and Jewish (Ashkenazic): from Middle High German *mandel*, Middle Dutch *mandel*, or Yiddish *mandl* 'almond'. This could have been a topographic name for someone who lived by an almond tree or a metonymic occupational name for a seller of almonds. In the case of the Jewish name, it is one of the many ornamental surnames referring to different types of trees and their fruit. This is also found as a Slovenian name in the form **Mandelj**. **2.** German: possibly a habitational name from any of various places named Mandel, for example near Bingen, or Mandeln. **3.** South German and Austrian: variant of MANDL. **4.** Dutch: from Middle Dutch *mandel(e)*, a term denoting a certain number of sheaves of harvested wheat (12–15). **5.** Jewish (Ashkenazic): variant of MENDEL.
GIVEN NAMES Jewish 7%. *Hyman* (5), *Chaim* (4), *Emanuel* (3), *Moshe* (3), *Zelig* (3), *Aron* (2), *Devorah* (2), *Ilya* (2), *Isidor* (2), *Pincus* (2), *Shlomo* (2), *Yaakov* (2).

Mandelbaum (629) Jewish (Ashkenazic): ornamental name from German *Mandelbaum* 'almond tree'.
GIVEN NAMES Jewish 18%. *Chaim* (4), *Aron* (3), *Uri* (3), *Yehuda* (3), *Benzion* (2), *Hyman* (2), *Leib* (2), *Mordechai* (2), *Morry* (2), *Moshe* (2), *Yehudah* (2), *Arek.*

Mandell (1656) Variant spelling of German or Dutch MANDEL.

Mandella (200) Origin uncertain. Possibly a variant of Italian MANDALA.
GIVEN NAME Italian 5%. *Sal.*

Mander (205) **1.** English: of uncertain origin. It may be a nickname for a beggar, from an agent derivative of *maund* 'beg' (probably from Old French *mendier*, Late Latin *mendicare*); this word is not attested before the 16th century, but may well have been in use earlier. Alternatively it may be an occupational name for a maker of baskets, from an agent derivative of Middle English *maund* 'basket' (Old French

mande, of Germanic origin); or perhaps for someone in some position of authority, from a shortened form of Middle English *coma(u)nder* (from *coma(u)nden* 'to command'). **2.** German: habitational name from places called Mandern, in Hesse and the Rhineland. **3.** Belgian (**van der Mander**): habitational name from a place called Ter Mandere or Mandel, in West Flanders, derived from the river name Mandel. **4.** Indian (Panjab): Sikh (Dogar, Jat) name of unknown meaning, based on the names of clans in these communities.
GIVEN NAMES Indian 8%. *Balwinder, Bikram.*

Manderfeld (136) Dutch: habitational name from a place so called near Liège, Belgium.

Manderfield (125) Americanized form of Dutch MANDERFELD.

Manders (660) **1.** English: patronymic from MANDER 1. **2.** Dutch: variant of MANDEL.

Manderscheid (186) German: habitational name from a place so named in the Eifel region.

Manderson (212) Scottish: patronymic from MANDER 1.
FOREBEARS A branch of the family established themselves in French-speaking Canada in the mid 19th century. Others went to South Africa.
GIVEN NAMES French 8%. *Easton* (2), *Paulet* (2), *Alphonse, Monique.*

Mandery (103) **1.** English: variant of **Mandry** (a local pronunciation of *Mainwaring*). **2.** Dutch and German: from *Mand(e)rick*, a derivative of a Germanic personal name *Manric*. **3.** Possibly an Americanized form of Polish **Mądry** (see MONDRY).

Mandes (117) Spanish: unexplained.
GIVEN NAMES Spanish 5%. *Pedro* (2), *Armando, Joaquin, Jose Inez, Tomasa.*

Mandeville (1045) English and Irish (of Norman origin), and French: habitational name from any of various places in France called Mann(e)ville (from the Germanic personal name *Manno* (see MANN 2) + Old French *ville* 'settlement') or *Magneville* (from Old French *magne* 'great' + *ville* 'settlement').
GIVEN NAMES French 9%. *Marcel* (4), *Andre* (2), *Armand* (2), *Gabrielle* (2), *Camille, Emile, Fernand, Fernande, Gaston, Jean-Paul, Lucien, Michel.*

Mandia (120) Southern Italian (Campania): unexplained.
GIVEN NAMES Italian 8%. *Carmel, Carmela, Carmine, Salustiano.*

Mandich (234) Croatian and Serbian (**Mandić**): metronymic from *Manda*, a pet form of the personal name *Magdalena* (see MAUDLIN).
GIVEN NAMES South Slavic 4%. *Nenad, Sinisa, Zarko.*

Mandigo (325) Origin unidentified.

Mandile (150) Southern Italian: from medieval Greek *mandilin* 'headscarf', pre-

sumably a metonymic occupational name for someone who sold scarves or a nickname for someone who habitually wore a scarf. **Mandilas** is also found as a Greek family name, with derivatives such as **Mandilakis**.
GIVEN NAMES Italian 17%. *Francesco, Gaetano, Vito.*

Mandl (210) **1.** South German: nickname for a small man, from Middle High German *man* 'man' + the diminutive suffix *-l*. **2.** Jewish (Ashkenazic): variant of MANDEL 1, 4.
GIVEN NAMES German 7%; Hungarian 4%. *Hans* (3), *Alois, Klaus, Otto*; *Bela* (2), *Zoltan.*

Mandle (102) Jewish: American variant spelling of MANDEL.
GIVEN NAME Jewish 8%. *Aron.*

Mandler (199) **1.** South German and Dutch: occupational name from an agent derivative of Middle High German *mandeln* 'to push through a mangle'. **2.** South German: patronymic from MANDL. **3.** Jewish (Ashkenazic): from an agent derivative of MANDEL.
GIVEN NAMES Jewish 5%. *Meyer* (2), *Avner.*

Mandley (142) Probably an Americanized form of a German, Slavic, or Jewish form of MANDEL.

Mandracchia (112) Italian (Sicily): habitational name from a place called Mandracchia, named with medieval Greek *mandrakia*, plural of *mandrakion* 'yard', a diminutive of *mandra* 'enclosure'. It may also be a topographic name for someone living by an enclosure. *Mandraki* is a common place name in Greece, and **Mandrakis** is also found as a Greek family name.
GIVEN NAMES Italian 20%. *Mario* (2), *Pietro* (2), *Salvatore, Vito, Zulma.*

Mandrell (356) Americanized spelling of Polish **Mądrala**, nickname derived from the vocabulary word *mądry* 'wise' (see MONDRY).

Mandry (130) **1.** Americanized spelling of Polish **Mądry**, nickname from *mądry* 'wise' (see also MONDRY). **2.** perhaps a variant spelling of Catalan *Mandri*, unexplained.
GIVEN NAMES Spanish 9%. *Ramon* (2), *Alejandro, Jose, Luis, Manuel, Orlando, Salvadore.*

Mandt (245) Dutch: **1.** variant spelling of MAND. **2.** (**de Mandt**): metonymic occupational name for a basketweaver, from *mand* 'basket'.

Mandujano (332) Spanish (from Basque): possibly a variant spelling of the habitational name *Mandojano*, from Basque *Mandoiana*, a town in Araba province, Basque Country.
GIVEN NAMES Spanish 59%. *Jose* (11), *Pedro* (6), *Juan* (5), *Francisco* (4), *Jesus* (4), *Luis* (4), *Manuel* (4), *Roberto* (4), *Alberto* (3), *Alvaro* (3), *Carlos* (3), *Enrique* (3); *Antonio* (5), *Leonardo, Lucio, Silvano.*

Mandy (189) Hungarian (**Mándy**): old spelling of **Mándi**, a habitational name for someone from a place called Mánd in Szatmár county.

GIVEN NAMES Hungarian 4%. *Szabolcs, Zoltan.*

Mane (87) Indian (Maharashtra); pronounced as two syllables: Hindu (Maratha) name, probably from Sanskrit *māna* 'respect' or *mānya* 'respectable'.

Manecke (135) North German: variant of MAHNKE.

GIVEN NAMES German 9%. *Kurt, Siegmund.*

Maneely (105) Irish: variant of MCNEELY.

Manella (111) Southern Italian and Greek (**Manellas**): nickname or occupational name from the Greek vocabulary word *manela* 'lever', 'crank', Italian *maniglia*.

Maner (624) German: **1.** (**Mäner**) occupational name from Middle High German *mener* 'cattle driver'. **2.** (**Mahner**) nickname or perhaps an occupational name for a summons server or bill collector.

Manera (129) Italian (mainly northwestern): **1.** (**Manèra**): according to Felice, from a Frankish name composed of the elements *magin* 'strength', 'might' + *hari* 'army', which became *Mainero* in Italy. **2.** possibly a habitational name from either of two places named Manera, in Cuneo and Como provinces.

GIVEN NAMES Italian 27%. *Angelo* (3), *Domenico* (2), *Mariano* (2), *Agapito, Alfredo, Antonio, Armando, Bonifacio, Claudio, Domenic, Genaro, Mario, Salvatore.*

Maneri (153) Southern Italian: patronymic or plural form of *Ma(i)nero*, a Germanic personal name composed of the elements *magin* 'strength', 'might' + *hari* 'army'. Compare MAINER.

GIVEN NAMES Italian 15%. *Angelo, Carmine, Ciro, Gaspare, Remo, Sal, Salvatore, Vincenzo.*

Maners (233) Variant spelling of English MANNERS.

Manes (1168) **1.** Dutch: variant of MAGNUS. **2.** Dutch: from a short form of the personal name *Germanus, Germanes*. **3.** Dutch: variant of MENNEN. **4.** Czech (**Mánes**): from *Mánek*, a pet form of the personal name *Emanuel*.

Maness (2921) Probably a variant of Dutch MANES.

Manetta (179) Italian: **1.** according to de Felice, from the female personal name, feminine form of **Manetto**, a pet form of MAINO, or from Old French *Mainet*, a pet form of *(Charle)magne*, which was introduced into Italy during the Carolingian period, but possibly from a feminine derivative of *mano* 'hand'. **2.** It may also be from a shortened pet form of the personal name *Emanuele* (see EMANUEL). **Manettas** is also found as a Greek family name.

GIVEN NAMES Italian 16%. *Salvatore* (2), *Benedetto, Camillo, Carmelo, Cesare, Igino, Luciano, Rosaria, Sal.*

Maneval (244) French: habitational name from a locality in Eure named Menneval (recorded in early documents as *Manneval, Maneval*).

Maney (1194) Irish: Anglicized form of Gaelic **Ó Maine** 'descendant of *Maine*', a popular early personal name of unexplained origin.

FOREBEARS Martin Maney was born in about 1749 in Ireland, married in 1781 in Jonesborough, TN, and died on April 15, 1830 in Paint Fork, Yancey Co., NC.

Manford (116) English: possibly a habitational name from a lost or unidentified place.

Manfra (119) Southern Italian (Naples): reduced form of **Manfrida**, a variant of MANFREDO.

GIVEN NAMES Italian 7%. *Angelo, Dario.*

Manfre (296) Italian (Sicily): from a short form of MANFREDO.

GIVEN NAMES Italian 22%. *Salvatore* (8), *Agostino* (2), *Angelo* (2), *Gaspare* (2), *Antonio, Biagio, Carmine, Enzo, Franco, Ignazio, Marco, Sal.*

Manfred (190) German and Dutch: evidently from the Germanic personal name *Manfred*, composed of the elements *man* 'man' + *frid* 'peace'. The surname is rare in Germany, however, while the personal name was common in Lombardy, and Italian sources derive the first element from *magin* 'strength'. Compare MANFREDO.

Manfredi (913) Italian: patronymic or plural form of MANFREDO.

GIVEN NAMES Italian 13%. *Angelo* (4), *Rocco* (3), *Alfonse* (2), *Antonio* (2), *Cesare* (2), *Cosmo* (2), *Dante* (2), *Gino* (2), *Amerigo, Carlo, Carmine, Corrado.*

Manfredo (203) Italian: from the Germanic personal name *Mag(in)frid*, composed of the elements *mag(in)* 'strength', 'might' + *frid* 'peace' (common in Lombardic records in the mid- and late 8th century). Compare MANFRED. The name was most famously borne by Manfredo (*c.*1232–66), king of Sicily 1258–66, son of the Holy Roman emperor Frederick II.

GIVEN NAMES Italian 11%. *Aldo, Geno, Nunzio, Salvatore.*

Manfredonia (152) Italian: habitational name from the region of Manfredonia in Apulia, named for Manfredo, king of Sicily (see MANFREDO).

GIVEN NAMES Italian 9%. *Antonio* (2), *Filomena, Giulio, Luciano, Sal.*

Manfull (128) English (Midlands): probably a variant of MANDEVILLE. Compare MANVILLE.

Mang (575) **1.** German (Baden–Württemberg): from *Mangnus*, a dialect form of MAGNUS. **2.** Southeast Asian: unexplained.

Mangal (107) **1.** Indian (northern states): Hindu (Bania) and Jain name from Sanskrit *mangala* 'auspicious'. The Agarwal Banias have a clan called Mangal. **2.** Name found among people of Indian origin in Guyana and Trinidad: from the Indian personal name *Mangal*, also from Sanskrit *mangala* 'auspicious'.

GIVEN NAMES Indian 51%; Muslim 7%. *Ram* (3), *Ajay* (2), *Keshav* (2), *Mamta* (2), *Indira, Jaikaran, Kishore, Krishna, Latchman, Madan, Manish, Nirmal; Abdul, Abdul Hamid, Ahmad, Hussein, Kamal, Sameer, Wali.*

Mangan (2232) **1.** Irish: Anglicized form of Gaelic **Ó Mongáin** 'descendant of *Mongán*', originally a byname for someone with a luxuriant head of hair (from *mong* 'hair', 'mane'), borne by families from Connacht, County Limerick, and Tyrone. It is also a Huguenot name, traced back to immigrants from Metz. **2.** Irish: see MANNING. **3.** English (of Norman origin): nickname for a glutton, from Old French *manger* 'to eat'. **4.** English: occupational name from old Spanish *mangón* 'small trader'.

GIVEN NAMES Irish 5%. *Brendan* (2), *Ciaran, Declan.*

Manganaro (315) Southern Italian: occupational name from *manganaro*, agent noun from MANGANO in any of its various senses. **Manganaris** and **Manganaras** are also found as Greek family names.

GIVEN NAMES Italian 14%. *Salvatore* (4), *Angelo* (3), *Sal* (2), *Antonio, Gennaro, Giuseppe, Vito.*

Manganelli (141) Southern Italian: patronymic or plural form of MANGANELLO.

GIVEN NAMES Italian 15%. *Carmine* (2), *Amato, Aniello, Gelsomina, Oresto, Sal.*

Manganello (266) Southern Italian: from a diminutive of MANGANO.

GIVEN NAMES Italian 13%. *Angelo* (3), *Salvatore* (2), *Cosmo, Luigi, Marino, Pasquale, Sal, Santo, Vito.*

Manganiello (273) Italian: variant of MANGANELLO.

GIVEN NAMES Italian 13%. *Carmine* (3), *Angelo, Antonio, Biagio, Concetta, Gaetano, Giuseppe, Nicola, Rocco, Romeo, Sal, Veto.*

Mangano (932) Italian: **1.** occupational name from *mangano* 'mangle' (a device consisting of a pair of rollers used to press textiles and clothes) or 'calender' (a similar device used in making paper). The term *mangano* also denoted a bucket elevator (used for raising water from a well) and any of various other devices, including a catapult. **2.** habitational name from Mangano, a place in Catania province, Sicily.

GIVEN NAMES Italian 18%. *Angelo* (5), *Salvatore* (5), *Antonio* (4), *Carmine* (3), *Gaetano* (3), *Leonardo* (3), *Santo* (3), *Biaggio* (2), *Cosimo* (2), *Dino* (2), *Rocco* (2), *Carmello.*

Mangas (221) **1.** Spanish and Portuguese: probably from a byname from *manga* 'sleeve'. **2.** Spanish: habitational name from Mangas in Zaragoza province. **3.** Greek: nickname from *mangas* 'smart', 'clever', 'cunning'.

Mangat (107) Indian (Panjab): Sikh name based on the name of a Jat tribe.
GIVEN NAMES Indian 88%. *Harcharn* (2), *Hardev* (2), *Prem* (2), *Ameet, Amrit, Bahadur, Bhajan, Brij, Lachman, Nahar, Raghubir.*

Mange (125) French: from a shortened form of the personal name *Demange*, in Lorraine a dialect form of *Dominique* (see DOMINGO).
GIVEN NAMES Spanish 6%. *Angel, Francisco, Jesus, Joaquin, Leobardo, Leticia, Luis.*

Mangel (239) **1.** German: from a reduced form of the Germanic personal name *Managwald* (see MANGOLD). This name is also established in Greece. **2.** Jewish (Ashkenazic): from German *Mangel* 'privation', 'need', a nickname or one of surnames selected at random from vocabulary words by government officials when surnames were made compulsory.
GIVEN NAMES Jewish 4%. *Emanuel* (2), *Mendel, Nochum, Yisroel, Zvi.*

Mangels (554) North German: patronymic from MANGEL.
GIVEN NAMES German 5%. *Egmont, Frieda, Gerd, Hans, Hermann, Kurt, Otto.*

Mangelsdorf (164) German (Hamburg): habitational name from Mangelsdorf in Brandenburg.
GIVEN NAMES German 7%. *Horst, Lorenz, Udo.*

Mangen (193) Dutch: patronymic from a variant of MAGNUS.

Manger (508) **1.** English, Dutch, and German: occupational name for a retail trader, Middle English *manger, monger*, Middle Dutch *manger, menger*, Middle High German *mangære, mengære* (from Late Latin *mango* 'salesman', with the addition of the Germanic agent suffix). **2.** Norwegian: habitational name from a farmstead in southwestern Norway named as *Mángr* in Old Norse, perhaps from *már* 'sea gull' + *angr* 'fjord'.
GIVEN NAMES German 5%. *Kurt* (2), *Wendelin* (2), *Ingeborg.*

Manges (623) **1.** Variant of German MENGES. **2.** This name is also recorded in Britain in the late 19th century. It may be a variant of Scottish MENZIES, of which the traditional pronunciation is *Mingies.*

Mangham (476) English (South Yorkshire): habitational name from Manningham near Bradford, recorded in the 13th century as *Maingham.*

Mangiafico (162) Southern Italian: from *mangia* 'eat' (from *mangiare* 'to eat') + *fico* 'fig', probably an allusion to a bird (the fig eater) and thence to a man associated with

or thought to resemble the bird, rather than to a man who ate figs.
GIVEN NAMES Italian 32%. *Emanuele* (3), *Salvatore* (3), *Enrico* (2), *Rosario* (2), *Santo* (2), *Aldo, Carmelo, Corrado, Dino, Ernesto, Lorenzo, Luciano, Marco, Paolino.*

Mangiapane (161) Southern Italian: nickname from *mangia* 'eat' (from *mangiare* 'to eat') + *pane* 'bread'.
GIVEN NAMES Italian 24%. *Cesare* (2), *Sal* (2), *Vito* (2), *Antonio, Carmella, Giuseppe, Lorenzo, Niccolo, Nicolo, Rosario, Salvatore.*

Mangiaracina (252) Sicilian and southern Italian: nickname from Italian *mangia* 'eat' (from *mangiare* 'to eat') + Sicilian *racina* 'grapes'.
GIVEN NAMES Italian 16%. *Salvatore* (2), *Vito* (2), *Angelo, Antonio, Dominico, Francesco, Gasper, Leonardo, Pietro, Sal.*

Mangieri (201) Italian: according to Caracausi, from the personal name *Mangiero*, (Latin forms *Mangerius* or *Mangiarinus*), from a nickname derived from *mangiare* 'to eat', or alternatively a variant of the Germanic personal name *Malgerius*, composed of the elements *Amal* + *gār, gēr* 'spear'.
GIVEN NAMES Italian 19%. *Gaspar* (2), *Mario* (2), *Angelo, Arsenio, Mafalda, Orazio, Rocco, Silvio.*

Mangin (406) **1.** French: derivative of MANGE. **2.** English and Irish: variant of MANGAN, perhaps, in the case of the Irish name, of MANNING.
GIVEN NAMES French 4%. *Berthe, Christophe, Jeanne Marie, Monique, Octave.*

Mangine (183) Possibly Italian, a variant of MANCINI?
GIVEN NAMES Italian 7%. *Angelo, Carmine, Vito.*

Manginelli (121) Italian: variant of MANCINELLI.
GIVEN NAMES Italian 28%. *Rocco* (5), *Angelo* (2), *Vito* (2), *Domenico, Nunzia, Pasquale.*

Mangini (676) Southern Italian: patronymic or plural form of MANGINO.
GIVEN NAMES Italian 9%. *Angelo* (3), *Carmine* (3), *Rocco* (3), *Salvatore* (2), *Dante, Emedio, Flavio, Luigi, Marino, Nicola, Sal.*

Mangino (531) Southern Italian: variant of MANCINO.
GIVEN NAMES Italian 14%. *Angelo* (4), *Rocco* (4), *Cosmo* (2), *Domenic* (2), *Saverio* (2), *Amerigo, Antonio, Camillo, Carmine, Concetta, Guido, Salvatore.*

Mangione (559) Italian: nickname for a glutton, *mangione*.
GIVEN NAMES Italian 18%. *Salvatore* (7), *Angelo* (2), *Cataldo* (2), *Gaetano* (2), *Pasquale* (2), *Sal* (2), *Agostino, Alessandro, Benedetta, Ciro, Dante, Dino.*

Mangis (113) See MANGES.

Mangle (113) Americanized spelling of German and Jewish MANGEL.

Mango (531) **1.** Italian: possibly a southern variant of MANCO, but more likely a variant

of MAGNO 2. **2.** Italian: in some cases possibly a habitational name from Mango, a place in Cuneo province. **3.** Hungarian: metronymic from the old secular female personal name *Manga.*
GIVEN NAMES Italian 12%. *Angelo* (4), *Rocco* (4), *Carmine* (2), *Alessandro, Gianni, Raffaela.*

Mangold (1459) **1.** English: of uncertain origin. Reaney gives it as a variant of **Mangnall**, which he derives from Old French *mangonelle*, a war engine for throwing stones. It may alternatively be identical in origin with the German name in 2 below, but there is no evidence of its introduction to Britain as a personal name by the Normans, which is normally the case for English surnames derived from Continental Germanic personal names. **2.** German and French: from a Germanic personal name *Managwald*, composed of the elements *manag* 'much' + *wald* 'rule'.

Mangone (295) Italian: **1.** habitational name from Magone, a place in Cosenza province. **2.** occupational name for a merchant from Latin *mango* (genitive *mangonis*) 'dealer', 'slave trader'. **3.** possibly from a Germanic personal name (see MANGOLD 2, MANIGAULT).
GIVEN NAMES Italian 17%. *Antonio* (2), *Pasquale* (2), *Salvatore* (2), *Carmela, Elio, Leonardo, Marco.*

Mangrum (1306) English: said to be a variant of MANGUM, though the insertion of *-r-* is hard to account for.

Mangual (167) Portuguese: from a byname from *mangual* 'threshing flail' (from Latin *manualis*). In the spelling **Mengual**, this name is also common in southern Spain.
GIVEN NAMES Spanish 49%. *Angel* (4), *Jose* (4), *Juan* (4), *Jorge* (3), *Amado* (2), *Ricardo* (2), *Aida, Alfredo, Amaro, Americo, Armando, Aurelio.*

Mangum (3343) English: unexplained. Probably an Americanized form of English MANGHAM.

Mangus (947) Perhaps a German variant of MAGNUS (cf. MANG).

Manhardt (116) German: from the Germanic personal name *Manhard*, composed of the Germanic elements *man* 'man', 'human' + *hard* 'hardy', 'brave', 'strong'.

Manhart (419) Americanized spelling of Dutch MANARD or German MANHARDT.

Manheim (260) Jewish (Ashkenazic), French (of German origin), and Dutch: habitational name from the city of Mannheim in southwestern Germany (formerly the residence of the electors Palatine), so named from the Germanic personal name *Manno* (see MANN 2) + Old High German *heim* 'homestead'. Mannheim was not fortified or chartered until the beginning of the 17th century, until which time it was just a small fishing village.
GIVEN NAMES Jewish 5%. *Avraham, Moshe, Surie, Zalman.*

Manheimer (153) Jewish (Ashkenazic), French (of German origin), and Dutch: habitational name for someone from the city of Mannheim (see MANHEIM).
GIVEN NAMES Jewish 4%. *Chaim, Sol.*

Mani (385) **1.** Indian (southern states): reduced form of SUBRAMANIAN. **2.** Indian (Kerala): among Christians from Kerala, a pet form of EMMANUEL. It is only a given name in Kerala, but in the U.S. used as a family name among people from Kerala.
GIVEN NAMES Indian 46%. *Lalitha* (4), *Mani* (4), *Rajesh* (4), *Siva* (3), *Arun* (2), *Chitra* (2), *Jayashree* (2), *Raghu* (2), *Suresh* (2), *Varughese* (2), *Balu, Bhavani.*

Mania (110) Polish: unexplained.

Maniaci (428) Southern Italian: habitational name from Maniace in Catania province, Sicily.
GIVEN NAMES Italian 29%. *Vito* (9), *Nunzio* (4), *Salvatore* (4), *Antonio* (3), *Marco* (2), *Matteo* (2), *Rocco* (2), *Rosario* (2), *Alfonse, Alfonso, Alphonso, Angelo, Ciro, Dino, Emanuele, Rosalia, Teo, Teodoro.*

Maniatis (171) Greek: habitational name for someone from the Mani peninsula in the southwest Peloponnese. This is also found as a composite name with personal names, e.g. *Maniatogiannis* 'John from Mani'.
GIVEN NAMES Greek 14%. *Sotirios* (2), *Stavros* (2), *Marinos, Paraskevas, Sarantos, Vassilios.*

Manier (295) French: **1.** derivative of the Germanic personal name *Maginhari*, composed of the elements *magin* 'strength', 'might' + *hari* 'army'. **2.** nickname from Old French *manier* 'manual', also 'skillful', 'adroit'. **3.** occupational name for a miller, Old French *mounier, mannier.*

Manieri (135) Italian: patronymic or plural form of MAINIERO.
GIVEN NAMES Italian 17%. *Biagio, Leonardo, Pasquale, Rocco, Vincenzo.*

Manifold (267) English: unexplained. It may be a variant of MINNIFIELD, which is likewise unexplained.

Manigault (355) French: from the Germanic personal name *Managwald*, composed of *manag* 'much' + *wald* 'rule'. Compare MANGOLD.

Manigo (124) Altered form of French MANIGAULT.

Manikas (104) Greek: occupational name for a maker of handles (e.g. of knives), from medieval Greek *manikion* 'sleeve', 'handle', from Latin *manicae* 'sleeve, manacle'.

Manikowski (124) Polish: variant of MANKOWSKI.

Manilow (135) Jewish (from Ukraine): patronymic from the male personal name *Manele*, a pet form of EMANUEL.

Manion (2087) Variant spelling of Irish MANNION.

Manire (124) Origin unidentified. According to family tradition, the name is of French Huguenot origin.

Manis (1518) **1.** Greek: from the personal name *Manis*, a pet form of *Emmanouel* (see EMANUEL). **2.** Czech (**Maniš**): from German *Mann*, or from a Germanic personal name such as MANFRED. **3.** French: unexplained. **4.** Jewish (eastern Ashkenazic): from the Yiddish personal name *Mane* + the Yiddish possessive suffix -*s*. As a male name, this represents a variant of MAN 8. As a female name, it is derived from a form of *Mary* borrowed from Slavic Christians.

Maniscalco (972) Southern Italian: occupational name from *maniscalco* 'marshall', altered from *marescalco* by folk etymology, probably influenced by *mano* 'hand', from medieval Latin *mariscalcus, marescalcus*. Compare MARSHALL.
GIVEN NAMES Italian 16%. *Salvatore* (6), *Vito* (6), *Sal* (4), *Antonio* (3), *Ignazio* (3), *Carmelo* (2), *Francesco* (2), *Gaspare* (2), *Saverio* (2), *Antonino, Carlo, Damiano.*

Manix (114) Irish: variant spelling of MANNIX.

Manjarrez (192) Spanish: habitational name from Manjarrés, a village in La Rioja province.
GIVEN NAMES Spanish 48%. *Jesus* (5), *Carlos* (4), *Ignacio* (3), *Jose* (3), *Raymundo* (3), *Cesar* (2), *Jaime* (2), *Juan* (2), *Luis* (2), *Miguel* (2), *Abelardo, Alfredo; Antonio* (3), *Ciro, Clemente, Leonardo.*

Mank (321) Dutch: nickname from *mank*, 'lame', 'crippled'.

Manka (353) Polish (**Mańka**): **1.** nickname for a left-handed person, from *mańka* 'left-hander'. **2.** from a pet form of the personal name *Emanuel* (see EMANUEL).

Manke (832) North German: **1.** variant of MAHNKE. **2.** Germanized form of Polish **Mańka** (see MANKA).
GIVEN NAMES German 5%. *Kurt* (4), *Christoph, Erwin, Gerhart, Siegfried.*

Manker (317) Jewish (eastern Ashkenazic): habitational name for someone from Manki, a village in Belarus.

Mankey (181) **1.** English (Cornwall): habitational name from Mankea in Cornwall, named with Corinsh *men* 'stone' + *kee* 'bank', 'hedge'. **2.** Americanized form of German MANKE.

Mankin (711) English: from a pet form of the personal name *Man(n)* (see MANN 2), or a nickname from a diminutive of the noun *man*, with the sense of 'little man'.

Mankins (333) English: patronymic from MANKIN.

Manko (302) **1.** Polish (**Mańko**) and Ukrininan: from a pet form of the personal name EMANUEL. **2.** Americanized spelling of Slovak *Mańko*, from the personal name *Máňa*. **3.** Hungarian (**Mankó**): from *mankó* 'crutch', hence a nickname for a lame person.
GIVEN NAMES Polish 4%. *Ignacy, Krzysztof.*

Mankowski (429) Polish (**Mańkowski**) and Jewish (from Poland): habitational name for someone from a place called Mańkowice or Mańkowo.
GIVEN NAMES Polish 7%. *Bogdan* (2), *Andrzej, Dariusz, Jolanta, Jozef, Kazimierz, Teofil, Zbigniew.*

Mankus (131) Lithuanian: unexplained.

Manley (8811) **1.** English: habitational name from places in Devon and Cheshire, named in Old English as 'common wood or clearing', from *(ge)mæne* 'common', 'shared' + *lēah* 'woodland clearing'. The surname is still chiefly found in the regions around these villages. **2.** English: nickname from Middle English *mannly* 'manly', 'virile', 'brave' (Old English *mannlīc*, originally 'man-like'). **3.** Irish (County Cork): Anglicized form of **Ó Máinle** (and often pronounced *Mauly*), of unexplained origin. Compare MALLEY. **4.** Irish (Connacht and Donegal): shortened Anglicized form of Gaelic **Ó Maonghaile** 'descendant of *Maonghal*', a personal name derived from words meaning 'wealth' and 'valor'.

Manlove (399) English: unexplained.

Manly (607) English: variant spelling of MANLEY.
GIVEN NAME French 4%. *Andre.*

Mann (31430) **1.** English, German, Dutch (**De Mann**), and Jewish (Ashkenazic): nickname for a fierce or strong man, or for a man contrasted with a boy, from Middle English, Middle High German, Middle Dutch *man*. In some cases it may have arisen as an occupational name for a servant, from the medieval use of the term to describe a person of inferior social status. The Jewish surname can be ornamental. **2.** English and German: from a Germanic personal name, found in Old English as *Manna*. This originated either as a byname or else as a short form of a compound name containing this element, such as HERMANN. **3.** Jewish (Ashkenazic): from the Yiddish male personal name *Man* (cognate with 1). **4.** Indian (Panjab): Hindu (Jat) and Sikh name of unknown meaning.

Manna (834) **1.** Southern Italian: topographic name from Sicilian *manna* 'ash tree'. **2.** Southern Italian: from a feminine form of MANNO. **3.** Southern Italian: possibly from **La Manna**, with loss of the definite article, from Old Italian *Alamanna* 'Germania'. **4.** Dutch: from a personal name derived from the Germanic personal name *Man(n)hard*, composed of the elements *mann* 'man', 'human' + *hard* 'hardy', 'brave', 'strong'.
GIVEN NAMES Italian 15%. *Antonio* (3), *Angelo* (2), *Domenic* (2), *Gennaro* (2), *Luigi* (2), *Otello* (2), *Pasquale* (2), *Sal* (2), *Salvatore* (2), *Tullio* (2), *Aldo, Arduino.*

Mannan (124) **1.** Muslim: from a personal name based on Arabic *mannān* 'benevolent', 'bountiful'. *Al-Mannān* 'the Bountiful' is an attribute of Allah, and this name is found in combinations such as *'Abd-ul Mannān* 'servant of the Bountiful'.

This is a common name in Bangladesh, Pakistan, and India. **2.** Indian (Tamil Nadu): Hindu name meaning 'king' in Tamil. It is found as a personal name in India, but is also used as a family name in the U.S. among families from Tamil Nadu.
GIVEN NAMES Muslim 67%; Indian 8%. *Abdul* (24), *Mohammed* (7), *Mohammad* (3), *Chowdhury, Ghalib, Ghazi, Golam, Kazi, Muhammad, Nadim, Sayeeda, Sheikh; Ashok, Bindu, Dev, Jugal, Ramasamy, Sapna, Sarwan, Satish.*

Mannarino (323) Italian: in Calabria this word denotes a horse born and raised in a stall, elsewhere a gelding; in Sicily it can be derived from *mannara* 'axe'; it can also mean a sheepfold and may even be derived from *lupo mannarino* 'werewolf'. These meanings mostly suggest nicknames, though in the case of the sheepfold, an indirect occupational name for a shepherd is more likely.
GIVEN NAMES Italian 28%. *Mario* (4), *Angelo* (2), *Antonio* (2), *Enrico* (2), *Franco* (2), *Giuseppe* (2), *Romeo* (2), *Armando, Aurelio, Domenico, Emanuele, Franca, Francesco, Giovanna, Natale.*

Manne (180) **1.** Indian (Andhra Pradesh); pronounced as two syllables: Hindu name, of unexplained etymology. **2.** Dutch (**De Manne**): variant of MANN. **3.** French (Picardy): metonymic occupational name for a maker of a kind of basket with two handles, called *manne* in Old French. **4.** Jewish (Ashkenazic): from the Yiddish male personal name *Mane*, a variant of MAN 8.
GIVEN NAMES Indian 8%; Jewish 7%. *Anuradha* (2), *Kiran, Kishore, Murthy, Prabhakar, Prasad, Rao; Akiva, Shmuel, Yaakov.*

Mannel (125) German (**Männel**): from a pet form of MANN 2.

Mannella (251) Italian: from a diminutive of MANNA.
GIVEN NAMES Italian 20%. *Antonio* (2), *Guido* (2), *Mario* (2), *Angelo, Eugenio, Francesco, Marco, Orlando, Sal.*

Mannen (166) Possibly Dutch, a patronymic from a Germanic personal name formed with -*man* 'man'.

Manner (327) **1.** German: variant of **Männer** (see MANER). **2.** English: unexplained. Perhaps a variant of MANNERS. **3.** Finnish: ornamental name from *manner* 'continent'. This name occurs throughout Finland, but chiefly in the southwestern part.
GIVEN NAMES Finnish 4%; German 4%. *Aarne, Aimo, Esa, Mikko, Reijo, Vaino; Heimo.*

Mannering (168) **1.** English (Kent): variant of MANWARING. **2.** Irish: name used as an Anglicized form of Gaelic **Ó Manaráin**, which Woulfe believes to be a dissimilated form of **Ó Manannáin** (see MURNAN).

Manners (666) English (of Norman origin): habitational name from Mesnières in Seine-Maritime, recorded in the 13th century as *Maneria*, a derivative of Latin *manere* 'to remain, abide, reside'. See also MENZIES.

Mannes (275) **1.** German: patronymic from MANN 1 and 2. **2.** Dutch: variant of MAGNUS, MANNEN, or MANES 1. **3.** Norwegian: habitational name from a farm name in Rogaland, composed of an uncertain first element (possibly Old Norse *man* 'thrall', 'slave') + *nes* 'promontory'.
GIVEN NAMES Scandinavian 6%; German 5%. *Aase, Erik, Lars; Klaus* (2), *Kurt.*

Manney (321) Irish: variant of MANEY.

Mannheimer (124) Jewish (Ashkenazic), French (of German origin), and Dutch: variant of MANHEIM with agent suffix -*er*.
GIVEN NAMES German 9%; Scandinavian 7%. *Egon, Kurt, Manfred; Sig* (2), *Jorgen.*

Manni (244) **1.** Italian: patronymic or plural form of MANNO. **2.** Finnish: ornamental name from *manni* 'man' (see MANNINEN).
GIVEN NAMES Italian 9%. *Angelo* (3), *Domenic, Giacomo, Luigi, Primo.*

Mannie (138) Scottish spelling of Irish MANEY.

Mannina (136) Italian: from the feminine form of MANNINO.
GIVEN NAMES Italian 21%. *Angelo, Antonino, Carmelo, Gaspare, Gasper, Giuseppe, Pietro, Salvatore, Vito.*

Manninen (192) Finnish: **1.** ornamental name from *manni* 'man' + the common surname suffix -*nen*. **2.** also from Swedish *man* or German *Mann*, either as an element of a soldier's name or as a short form of a personal name such as HERMANN or EMANUEL.
GIVEN NAMES Finnish 8%; Scandinavian 4%. *Arto, Arvo, Jarmo, Reino, Tenho, Wilho; Erik, Nils.*

Manning (25725) **1.** English: patronymic from MANN 1 and 2. **2.** Irish: adopted as an English equivalent of Gaelic **Ó Mainnín** 'descendant of *Mainnín*', probably an assimilated form of *Mainchín*, a diminutive of *manach* 'monk'. This is the name of a chieftain family in Connacht. It is sometimes pronounced *Ó Maingín* and Anglicized as MANGAN.
FOREBEARS Anstice Manning, widow of Richard Manning of Dartmouth, England, came to MA with her children in 1679. Her great-great-grandson Robert, born at Salem, MA, in 1784, was the uncle and protector of author Nathaniel Hawthorne. Another early bearer of the relatively common British name was Jeffrey Manning, one of the earliest settlers in Piscataway township, Middlesex Co., NJ. His great-grandson James Manning (1738–91) was a founder and the first president of Rhode Island College (Brown University).

Mannings (126) Irish: variant of MANNING 2, with the addition of English patronymic -*s*.
GIVEN NAMES Irish 5%. *Donovan, Eamonn, Ronan.*

Mannino (1099) Italian: from a pet form of MANNO.
GIVEN NAMES Italian 26%. *Salvatore* (18), *Vito* (17), *Sal* (7), *Angelo* (6), *Francesco* (5), *Gaspare* (3), *Salvator* (3), *Antonio* (2), *Filippo* (2), *Lorenzo* (2), *Marcello* (2), *Matteo* (2).

Mannion (1230) **1.** Irish: Anglicized form of Gaelic **Ó Mainnín** (see MANNING). **2.** English and Irish: variant of MANGAN.
GIVEN NAMES Irish 7%. *Malachy* (4), *Brendan* (2), *Aislinn, Brigid, Ciaran, Declan, Dermot, Kieran, Liam, Maeve, Siobhan.*

Mannis (221) **1.** Irish: shortened variant of McMANUS. **2.** Jewish: variant of MANIS.

Mannix (910) Irish: Anglicized form of the Gaelic (Munster) name **Ó Mainchín**, a variant of **Manahan** (see MONAHAN).
GIVEN NAME Irish 5%. *Kieran.*

Manno (948) Italian: from a personal name *Manno*, medieval Latin *Mannus*, a short form of names ending in -*manno*, such as *Ermanno, Riccomanno,* or directly from the Germanic personal name *Manni*.
GIVEN NAMES Italian 18%. *Salvatore* (13), *Vito* (6), *Angelo* (4), *Pietro* (2), *Romano* (2), *Vincenzo* (2), *Cosimo, Cosmo, Dino, Federico, Filomena, Francesca.*

Mannon (555) French: from a Germanic personal name (see MANN 2), with the Old French oblique case ending.

Mannor (104) Possibly English: see MANOR.

Manns (1631) German: patronymic from MANN 1 and 2.

Manny (293) Irish: variant of MANEY.

Mano (157) **1.** Japanese: meaning 'true field'. The name is not common in Japan. **2.** Spanish: from **De la Mano**, from *mano* 'hand'.
GIVEN NAMES Japanese 21%; Spanish 6%. *Akira* (2), *Yuichi* (2), *Kiyoshi, Michi, Minoru, Mitsunori, Seiji, Shinya, Takako, Tetsuro, Toru, Tosh; Manuel* (2), *Arnaldo, Elena, Jose, Patrocinio, Renato, Roberto.*

Manocchio (173) Southern Italian: of uncertain derivation; perhaps originally a nickname, from *mal(o)* + *occhio*, i.e. 'evil eye', later changed to obscure its meaning (compare **Manacorda**, from *mal(o)* + *cor(d)* 'bad heart', and similar). Caracausi's Greek etymology is not plausible.
GIVEN NAMES Italian 34%. *Angelo* (4), *Antonio* (4), *Mario* (3), *Domenic* (2), *Alberto, Carmine, Damiano, Dario, Gino, Giovanni, Giulio, Marco, Michael Angelo, Nunzia, Orlando, Pasquale, Renato, Tino.*

Manolis (185) Greek: from the personal name *Manolis*, the usual pet form of *Emmanouël* (see EMANUEL).

GIVEN NAMES Greek 21%. *Demetrios* (3), *Costas, Demos, Evangelos, Konstantinos, Koula, Pericles, Sotirios, Spiro, Spiros, Stylianos, Vasilios.*

Manon (168) French: variant spelling of MANNON.

GIVEN NAMES Spanish 24%. *Luis* (4), *Marcos* (2), *Adolfo, Alejandro, Ana, Ana Maria, Angel, Bienvenido, Cristobal, Eduardo, Ernesto, Fernando.*

Manoogian (291) Western Armenian: variant of MANOUKIAN.

GIVEN NAMES Armenian 13%. *Manoog* (4), *Haig* (3), *Ara* (2), *Dickran* (2), *Sarkis* (2), *Anahid, Aram, Armen, Azniv, Berj, Hagop, Kevork.*

Manor (1136) **1.** Jewish (Israeli): modern Hebrew name meaning 'loom'. **2.** English: unexplained.

Manos (1189) **1.** Greek: from the personal name *Manos*, pet form of MANOLIS, itself a pet form of *Emmanouēl* (see EMANUEL). **2.** Spanish: from the plural of *mano* 'hand'.

Manoukian (190) Armenian: patronymic from classical Armenian *manuk* 'child'.

GIVEN NAMES Armenian 54%; French 5%. *Avedis* (3), *Aram* (2), *Avetis* (2), *Berj* (2), *Sarkis* (2), *Vahe* (2), *Anahid, Anahit, Anoush, Araxi, Armen, Arpenik; Edouard, Michel, Pierre, Serge.*

Manous (138) Probably a shortened and altered form of Irish McMANUS.

Manring (330) English and Irish: reduced form of MANNERING.

Manrique (391) Spanish: possibly from the Occitan personal name *Aimeric* (in southern France), composed of the Germanic elements *haim* 'homeland', 'village' + *rīc* 'power'.

GIVEN NAMES Spanish 52%. *Carlos* (8), *Luis* (8), *Juan* (6), *Jose* (5), *Fernando* (4), *Manuel* (4), *Jesus* (3), *Jorge* (3), *Mario* (3), *Raul* (3), *Roberto* (3), *Ruben* (3).

Manriquez (689) Spanish (**Manríquez**): patronymic from MANRIQUE.

GIVEN NAMES Spanish 46%. *Jose* (15), *Roberto* (8), *Ruben* (7), *Jesus* (6), *Carlos* (5), *Rafael* (5), *Sergio* (5), *Armando* (4), *Felipe* (4), *Juan* (4), *Manuel* (4), *Alberto* (3); *Antonio* (5), *Lorenzo* (3), *Aldo, Clementina, Flaminio, Heriberto, Luciano.*

Manross (159) Origin unidentified.

Manry (302) Irish: variant of **Menary**; see MANERY.

FOREBEARS This name, in the form **Manery**, was brought to New York from Ireland by Pat Manery some time between 1845 and 1865.

Mans (418) Dutch: variant of MANN.

Mansbach (114) German: habitational name from a place so called near Hersfeld.

GIVEN NAMES German 5%. *Gerda, Kurt.*

Mansberger (136) German or Jewish: habitational name from a place called Mansberg.

Manseau (240) French: habitational or regional name for someone from Le Mans or

the surrounding area of *Maine*. Compare English MANSELL 1.

GIVEN NAMES French 8%. *Adelard* (2), *Francois, Jean Pierre, Normand.*

Mansel (173) English: variant spelling of MANSELL.

Mansell (1294) English (chiefly West Midlands): **1.** (of Norman origin): habitational or regional name from Old French *mansel* 'inhabitant of Le Mans or the surrounding area of *Maine*'. The place was originally named in Latin *(ad) Ceroman-nos*, from the name of the Gaulish tribe living there, the *Ceromanni*. The name was reduced to *Celmans* and then became *Le Mans* as a result of the mistaken identification of the first syllable with the Old French demonstrative adjective. **2.** status name for a particular type of feudal tenant, Anglo-Norman French *mansel*, one who occupied a *manse* (Late Latin *mansa* 'dwelling'), a measure of land sufficient to support one family. **3.** some early examples, such as Thomas *filius Manselli* (Northumbria 1256), point to derivation from a personal name, perhaps the Germanic derivative of MANN 2 Latinized as *Manzellinus*.

Manser (426) English: **1.** from the male personal name *Manasseh*, Hebrew *Menashe* 'one who causes to forget' (see MANASSE), borne in the Middle Ages by Christians as well as by Jews. Hebrew *Menashe* and its reflexes in other Jewish languages have always been popular among Jews. **2.** occupational name for someone who made handles for agricultural and domestic implements, from an agent derivative of Anglo-Norman French *mance* 'handle' (Old French *manche*, Late Latin *manicus*, a derivative of *manus* 'hand').

Mansfield (7104) **1.** English: habitational name from a place in Nottinghamshire. The early forms, from Domesday Book to the early 13th century, show the first element uniformly as *Mam-*, and it is therefore likely that this was a British hill-name meaning 'breast' (compare MANCHESTER), with the later addition of Old English *feld* 'pasture', 'open country' (see FIELD) as the second element. The surname is now widespread throughout Midland and southern England and is also common in Ireland. **2.** Irish: when not an importation of 1, this is an altered form of the Norman name **Manville** (see MANDEVILLE). **3.** Americanized form of German and Jewish (Ashkenazic) **Mansfeld**, a habitational name for someone from a place so called in Saxony.

Manship (353) English: habitational name from Minskip in West Yorkshire, Manships Shaw in Surrey, or Manchips Field in Bishop's Stortford, Hertfordshire, all named with the same Old English word, *gemǣnscipe* 'community', 'fellowship', also 'land held in common'.

Mansi (119) Italian: patronymic or plural form of MANSO.

GIVEN NAMES Italian 9%. *Cosmo, Flavio, Pasquale.*

Mansilla (121) Spanish: habitational name from *Mansilla*, a place in La Rioja province.

GIVEN NAMES Spanish 61%. *Gustavo* (3), *Aura* (2), *Jose* (2), *Luis* (2), *Manuel* (2), *Mario* (2), *Osvaldo* (2), *Rafael* (2), *Rosendo* (2), *Aida, Avelina, Carlos.*

Mansir (127) Probably a variant of Muslim MANSUR.

Manske (825) German: **1.** spelling variant of Eastern German **Manzke**, probably of Slavic origin. **2.** reduced form of **Schi-mansky**, derivative of a Slavic form of the personal name SIMON.

GIVEN NAMES German 4%. *Kurt* (3), *Eldred.*

Mansker (327) Americanized form of German **Mainzger**, a habitational name for someone from the city of Mainz in Germany. Compare MAINZER.

FOREBEARS Ludwig Maintzger (1726–76) came from near Karlsruhe in Germany to Philadelphia in 1749, and settled in Lancaster Co., PA. In North America he spelled his name *Lodowick Minsker*. His descendants are associated with Dauphin Co., PA, and Sumner Co., TN.

Manso (216) Spanish, Portuguese, and Italian: nickname for a mild, inoffensive person, from *manso* 'tame', 'docile' (Late Latin *mansus*, classical Latin *mansuetus* 'tamed', literally 'accustomed to the hand').

GIVEN NAMES Spanish 38%. *Jesus* (4), *Jose* (4), *Jorge* (3), *Luis* (3), *Concepcion* (2), *Evelio* (2), *Gilberto* (2), *Juan* (2), *Justo* (2), *Mireya* (2), *Roberto* (2), *Adriana.*

Manson (2378) **1.** Scottish (common in the Northern Isles): patronymic from the personal name MAGNUS. **2.** English: patronymic from the Middle English nickname or byname MANN. **3.** Jewish (Ashkenazic): patronymic from MAN 8.

Mansoor (132) Muslim: variant of MANSUR.

GIVEN NAMES Muslim 65%. *Salim* (3), *Tariq* (3), *Abdul* (2), *Ahmad* (2), *Arshad* (2), *Aslam* (2), *Mahmood* (2), *Mansoor* (2), *Mohamed* (2), *Shahid* (2), *Syed* (2), *Tahir* (2).

Mansour (1124) **1.** Muslim: variant spelling of MANSUR. **2.** Egyptian Arabic: habitational name from the city of Mansoura, in in the Nile Delta. It was named for a battle in 1250 in which the Saracens destroyed a Crusader force, capturing King Louis IX of France and holding him and many of his knights to ransom. **Mansouras** is also found as a Greek family name; there was a large Greek community in Mansoura until comparatively recently.

GIVEN NAMES Arabic 39%. *Mansour* (10), *Mohamed* (9), *Samir* (8), *Ahmed* (7), *Nabil* (6), *Ali* (5), *Mahmoud* (5), *Hassan* (4), *Kamal* (4), *Nasser* (4), *Amal* (3), *Farid* (3).

Mansouri (107) Muslim: from an adjectival derivative of MANSOUR in either sense.
GIVEN NAMES Muslim 87%. *Ali* (4), *Bijan* (3), *Hadi* (3), *Behzad* (2), *Hamid* (2), *Hossein* (2), *Mehdi* (2), *Mehran* (2), *Safa* (2), *Abbas, Aghdas, Alireza.*

Manspeaker (143) Americanized form of German MANSBERGER.

Mansueto (106) Southern Italian: from the medieval personal name *Mansueto*, from Latin *Mansuetus*, meaning 'docile', 'gentle'.
GIVEN NAMES Italian 29%. *Mario* (3), *Donato* (2), *Angelo, Biagio, Carlo, Franco, Gaetano, Rocco, Savino.*

Mansur (533) Muslim: from a personal name based on Arabic *manṣūr* 'victorious', 'triumphant'. This word is found in compound names such as *Manṣūr-ud-Dīn* 'victorious in religion'. The second of the Abbasid khalifs was Al-Manṣūr Abu-Ja'far (*c.* 712–75), who built the city of Baghdad in 762 and is considered the real founder of the Abbasid khalifate.
GIVEN NAMES Muslim 4%. *Aamer, Ahsan, Aly, Amera, Arzu, Ashfaque, Baber, Faruq, Hala, Hamed, Haris, Hossein.*

Mantei (197) German: variant of MANTHEI.
GIVEN NAMES German 9%; French 4%. *Inge* (2), *Erwin, Otto; Marcel* (2), *Auguste.*

Mantel (485) **1.** English, German, French, and Dutch: metonymic occupational name for a cloak maker or a nickname for someone who wore a cloak of a particularly conspicuous design, from Anglo-Norman, Middle High German, Old French, and Middle Dutch *mantel* 'cloak', 'coat' (Late Latin *mantellus*). **2.** Jewish (Ashkenazic): probably from German *Mantel* or Yiddish *mantl* 'coat', which are related to 1 above. **3.** German: topographic name from Middle High German *mantel* 'Scots pine'.
GIVEN NAMES Jewish 4%. *Menachem, Shlomo, Sol.*

Mantell (420) English and Jewish (Ashkenazic): variant spelling of MANTEL.
GIVEN NAMES Jewish 4%. *Asher, Elihu, Sol, Yetta.*

Manter (268) English: probably a variant of MANDER.
FOREBEARS Belcher Manter is recorded in Plymouth, MA, in 1657. John Manter (1658–1744), possibly a son of Belcher, was the founder of a family associated with Martha's Vineyard.

Manternach (183) Habitational name from a place so called in Luxembourg.
GIVEN NAME French 4%. *Elodie.*

Manteufel (163) German: from Low German *Mandüvel*, a nickname composed of the elements *Man* 'man' + *Düvel* 'devil', 'devil's fellow'. This was the name of a Pomeranian noble family.

Manteuffel (104) Variant spelling of German MANTEUFEL.
GIVEN NAMES German 9%. *Erwin, Gerhard.*

Mantey (243) German: **1.** variant of the habitational name MANTHEI. **2.** Perhaps a variant of the personal name MANTHE.

Manthe (285) German (Westphalia): from a short form of a personal name formed with Germanic *magin* 'strength', 'might' as the first element.

Manthei (523) German: habitational name for someone from a place called Manthei in Schwerin province. This name is also established in Poland.
GIVEN NAMES German 7%. *Uwe* (5), *Lothar* (2), *Otto* (2), *Gebhard.*

Manthey (868) German: variant of MANTHEI.

Mantia (369) **1.** Southern Italian: shortened form of **Amantia**, a habitational name from Amantea in Cosenza province. **2.** Dutch: variant of MANTEL 1.
GIVEN NAMES Italian 9%. *Cosmo* (2), *Salvatore* (2), *Agostino.*

Mantilla (211) Spanish: from *mantilla* 'mantilla', 'scarf worn over the head and shoulders', presumably an occupational name for a maker of mantillas or a descriptive name for someone who habitually wore such a garment.
GIVEN NAMES Spanish 59%. *Jorge* (7), *Javier* (6), *Jose* (6), *Carlos* (4), *Jaime* (4), *Luz* (4), *Manuel* (4), *Armando* (3), *Luis* (3), *Mauricio* (3), *Noelio* (3), *Ramon* (3).

Mantini (106) Italian: from the personal name *Mantino*, a pet form of *Mantio* (see MANTIONE).
GIVEN NAMES Italian 17%. *Angelo* (2), *Carlo* (2), *Gaetano, Secondo, Vito.*

Mantione (184) Italian (Sicily): augmentative of the personal name *Mantio*, from a Germanic personal name based on the element *Mand.*
GIVEN NAMES Italian 26%. *Angelo* (9), *Salvatore* (5), *Piero.*

Mantle (482) **1.** English: variant spelling of MANTEL 1. **2.** Americanized spelling of German MANTEL.

Manton (345) **1.** English: habitational name from any of the various places so called, for example in Leicestershire, Lincolnshire, Nottinghamshire, and Wiltshire. For the most part the first element is either Old English *(ge)mǣne* 'common', 'shared' (see MANLEY, MANSHIP), or the Old English byname *Mann(a)* (see MANN). However, in the case of Manton in Lincolnshire the early forms show clearly that it was Old English *m(e)alm* 'sand', 'chalk', with reference to the poor soil of the region. The second element is in each case Old English *tūn* 'enclosure', 'settlement'. **2.** Irish (Cork): Anglicized form of Gaelic **Ó Manntáin** 'descendant of *Manntán*', a personal name derived from a diminutive of *manntach* 'toothless'.

Mantooth (727) Probably an altered form of Scottish MONTEITH or **Mantach**, a nickname from Gaelic *manntach* 'stammering'

(also 'toothless' in Irish), of which one early Welsh recorded form is *Mantath.*

Mantor (124) Variant of English MANTER.

Mantovani (126) Italian: patronymic or plural form of **Mantovano**, a habitational name for someone from the city of Mantua.
GIVEN NAMES Italian 14%. *Ugo* (2), *Aldo, Alessia, Carlo, Cosmo, Guerino, Guido, Pierluigi.*

Mantyla (112) Finnish (**Mäntylä**): topographic and ornamental name from *mänty* 'pine' + the local suffix *-la.* Common as a habitational name in western Finland in the 19th century.
GIVEN NAMES Finnish 18%. *Pasi* (2), *Aune, Ilmari, Jarmo, Jouni, Martti, Reino.*

Mantz (797) South German: variant spelling of MANZ.

Manuel (6378) **1.** Spanish, Portuguese, French, and German: from the personal name *Manuel*, a short form of EMANUEL. **2.** Catalan and Spanish: possibly also a habitational name from Manuel in Valencia province. **3.** Americanized form of any of various other European family names derived from EMANUEL, for example the Greek patronymic **Manouilidis.**

Manuele (177) Italian: from a short form of the personal name EMANUELE.
GIVEN NAMES Italian 33%. *Salvatore* (5), *Ernesto* (2), *Mario* (2), *Rocco* (2), *Vito* (2), *Angelo, Carmel, Carmelo, Enrico, Marcello, Santo.*

Manus (833) Irish: shortened form of MCMANUS.

Manville (469) **1.** English: variant of MANDEVILLE. **2.** French: habitational name from Menville in the Haute-Garonne.

Manwaring (530) English (of Norman origin): see MAINWARING.

Manwarren (192) Perhaps an altered form of English MANWARING.

Manweiler (111) German (**Mannweiler**): habitational name from Mannweiler in the Palatinate.
GIVEN NAMES German 9%; Scandinavian 5%. *Erna, Kurt, Orlo.*

Manwell (163) **1.** Variant of English MANDEVILLE. **2.** Americanized form of German **Mannweiler** (see MANWEILER).

Manwill (105) Origin unidentified. **1.** Perhaps a variant of English MANDEVILLE. **2.** Perhaps an Americanized form of German **Mannweiler** (see MANWEILER).

Manwiller (187) Americanized spelling of German **Mannweiler** (see MANWEILER).
GIVEN NAME German 4%. *Kurt.*

Many (256) **1.** French: habitational name from Masny in Nord or Many in Moselle. **2.** Variant of Irish MANEY.
GIVEN NAMES French 5%. *Cecile* (3), *Micheline* (2).

Manz (845) Southern German: **1.** (Alemannic, Swabian) from a short form or pet form of the personal name MANGOLD. **2.** (Bavarian, Austrian) from a short form of the personal name *Mannhart* (see MAN-HART). **3.** (eastern) from a derivative of the Slavic male personal name *Manslaw*.

GIVEN NAMES German 4%. *Albrecht, Erhardt, Hilde, Johannes, Kurt, Matthias, Monika, Reinhard.*

Manza (117) Italian: variant of MANZO.

GIVEN NAMES Italian 9%. *Carmine, Rocco, Salvatore.*

Manzanares (808) Spanish: habitational name from the city of Manzanares in Ciudad Real province.

GIVEN NAMES Spanish 29%; Portuguese 6%. *Jose* (12), *Manuel* (9), *Ruben* (8), *Carlos* (7), *Juan* (6), *Luis* (4), *Arturo* (3), *Javier* (3), *Jorge* (3), *Adolfo* (2), *Jesus* (2), *Juanita* (2); *Godofredo.*

Manzano (888) Spanish: habitational name from any of various minor places named Manzano, or a topographic name for someone who lived by an apple tree or orchard, from Spanish *manzano* 'apple tree', Old Spanish *maçano*, from *maçana* 'apple', Late Latin *(mala) Mattiana*, a type of apple named in honor of the 1st century BC horticultural writer Gaius Matius.

GIVEN NAMES Spanish 49%. *Jose* (23), *Luis* (12), *Manuel* (12), *Juan* (11), *Pedro* (8), *Jorge* (7), *Jaime* (6), *Carlos* (5), *Ana* (4), *Francisco* (4), *Ricardo* (4), *Roberto* (4).

Manzella (713) Italian (Sicily): from a feminine diminitive of *manso* 'docile'.

GIVEN NAMES Italian 19%. *Vito* (8), *Salvatore* (7), *Antonino* (2), *Bartolo* (2), *Benedetto* (2), *Pasquale* (2), *Sal* (2), *Antonio, Carlo, Carmine, Concetta, Domenico.*

Manzer (495) German: habitational name for someone from Manze in Silesia or Manzen in Bavaria.

Manzi (986) Italian: patronymic or plural form of MANZO.

GIVEN NAMES Italian 11%. *Salvatore* (8), *Orest* (3), *Antonio* (2), *Ciro* (2), *Pasquale* (2), *Rocco* (2), *Aldo, Alesio, Carmela, Carmine, Domenic, Franco.*

Manzione (161) Italian (Sicily): augmentative of **Manzio**, from the Latin personal name *Amantius*.

GIVEN NAMES Italian 14%. *Pasquale* (2), *Cono, Vito.*

Manzo (1806) Italian: **1.** nickname for someone supposedly resembling an ox, *manzo* (from Late Latin *mansus* 'tame' (see MANSO), with a particular sense of an ox tamed to the plow), or metonymic occupational name for someone who worked with oxen. **2.** nickname from *manso* 'gentle', 'mild' (from the same Late Latin word as 1). **3.** possibly from a Germanic personal name formed with *magin* 'strength', 'might'. Compare MAIN.

GIVEN NAMES Spanish 20%; Italian 14%. *Jose* (20), *Juan* (13), *Jesus* (11), *Luis* (11), *Raul* (7), *Enrique* (6), *Francisco* (6), *Manuel* (6), *Ricardo* (6), *Carlos* (5), *Miguel* (5), *Roberto* (5); *Salvatore* (9), *Angelo* (8), *Antonio* (7), *Rocco* (6), *Guido*

(5), *Marco* (5), *Sal* (4), *Carmine* (3), *Gino* (3), *Giuseppe* (3), *Carmela* (2), *Enrico* (2).

Manzolillo (110) Italian: from a pet form of MANZO.

GIVEN NAMES Italian 27%. *Carmine* (3), *Cono* (3), *Domenico, Giovanni, Rocco.*

Mao (737) **1.** Chinese 毛: from the name of an area called Mao, in present-day Henan province, during the Zhou dynasty (1122–221 BC. Bo Dan, the ninth son of Wen Wang, was granted this following the establishment of the Zhou dynasty in 1122 BC). In due course his descendants adopted the place name Mao as their surname. This character also means 'hair' or 'feather'. This was the family name of Mao Zedong (1893–1976), the Chinese Communist Party chairman. **2.** Chinese 茅: another son of Wen Wang—the third, Mao Shu—was granted a different state, whose name is also pronounced *Mao*. Descendants adopted the name of this state as their surname. This character also means 'thatched' or 'type of grass used in thatching'. **3.** Cambodian: unexplained.

GIVEN NAMES Chinese 38%; Cambodian 4%. *Chea* (4), *Hong* (3), *Chan* (2), *Chi* (2), *Guoliang* (2), *Hua* (2), *Hui* (2), *Ming* (2), *Ping* (2), *Shun* (2), *Chung, Pai, Sinh, Tam; Chhay* (2), *Sarin* (2), *Ba, Binh, Dang, Ky, Lan, Long, Ly, Quoi, Saroeun, Sophea, Tan.*

Mapel (259) English: variant spelling of MAPLE.

Mapes (2208) Possibly a plural form of French *Mape* 'piece of fabric', 'napkin'; if so a metonymic occupational name.

Maphis (118) Variant of German MAVES.

Maple (1548) **1.** English: topographic name for someone who lived by a maple tree, Middle English *mapel* (Old English *mapul*). **2.** French: from Latin *mapula*, a diminutive of *mappa* 'piece of cloth', 'napkin', presumably a metonymic occupational name for a cloth merchant or a weaver.

Maples (3940) English: variant of MAPLE.

Mapp (1102) English: **1.** from a variant of the medieval female personal name *Mab(be)*, a short form of Middle English, Old French *Amabel* (from Latin *amabilis* 'loveable'). This has survived into the 20th century in the short form *Mabel*. **2.** possibly from an unattested Old English male personal name, *Mappa*. **3.** Welsh: from Old Welsh *map, mab* 'son', which was used as a distinguishing epithet.

Mapson (106) English: metronymic from the medieval female personal name *Mab(be)* (see MAPP).

GIVEN NAME Ethiopian 5%. *Yared.*

Mapstone (121) English (Somerset and Gloucester): unexplained. Perhaps a habitational name from a lost or unidentified place.

Mar (939) **1.** Spanish, Portuguese, Galician, Asturian-Leonese, and Catalan: topographic name for someone living by the sea, from

mar 'sea' (Latin *mare*). **2.** German: nickname from Middle High German *mar(w)* 'tender', 'delicate'. **3.** Hungarian (**Már**): from a short form of the personal name *Márkus* or *Márk*, Hungarian forms of *Marcus* and *Mark*; or possibly from the personal name *Márton*, Hungarian form of MARTIN. **4.** Chinese: variant of MA.

GIVEN NAMES Chinese 5%. *Gim* (3), *Wai* (3), *Fong* (2), *Hong* (2), *Man Chung* (2), *Moo* (2), *Mun* (2), *Quon* (2), *Wing* (2), *Yat* (2), *Bok, Chun.*

Mara (873) **1.** Irish: shortened form of O'MARA. **2.** Hungarian: from a pet form of the personal names *Márkus* (Hungarian form of *Marcus*) or *Márton* (Hungarian form of MARTIN), or from a short form of the old ecclesiastical name *Marcel* (see MARCEL). **3.** Czech (**Mára**): from a pet form of the personal name MAREK or MARTIN.

Marabella (150) Italian (Sicily): variant of MIRABELLA.

GIVEN NAMES Italian 21%. *Angelo* (3), *Salvatore* (2), *Santo* (2), *Carmelo, Nuncio, Nunzio, Paolo.*

Marable (965) English: from the feminine personal name *Mirabel*, equated in medieval records with Latin *mirabilis* 'marvellous', 'wonderful' (in the sense 'extraordinary').

Maracle (116) Altered spelling of French or Dutch **Marical** or **Marécal** variants of MARICLE.

Maradiaga (111) Spanish (chiefly Central America): unexplained.

GIVEN NAMES Spanish 50%; Portuguese 13%; Jewish 4%; Italian 4%. *Juan* (3), *Luis* (2), *Mario* (2), *Pedro* (2), *Santos* (2), *Adan, Alicia, Alma Rosa, Ana, Angel, Argentina, Armando; Ligia; Miriam* (2); *Antonio.*

Maragos (123) Greek: occupational name meaning 'carpenter', from Italian (Venetian) *marangon*.

GIVEN NAMES Greek 13%. *Demetrios* (2), *Iraklis, Nikos, Spiro, Stathis.*

Maraj (106) Name found among people of Indian origin in Guyana and Trinidad: altered form of Indian MAHARAJ.

GIVEN NAMES Indian 36%. *Bal, Indira, Indrani, Khemraj, Mahadeo, Mukesh, Nisha, Raj, Ramesh, Ramsaran, Sattie.*

Marak (287) Czech (**Marák**): **1.** from a pet form of the personal names MARTIN or MAREK. **2.** (**Mařák**): name for a man who was the son or husband of a woman called *Mářî*, a pet form of *Marie* (see MARIA).

Maraldo (103) Italian: from a Lombard personal name of Germanic origin.

GIVEN NAMES Italian 27%. *Renzo* (2), *Angelo, Dante, Dino, Domenico, Ennio, Giuseppi, Quinto, Romano, Salvatore, Secondo.*

Maran (149) French and Romanian (**Măran**): topographic name from an adjective derived from Latin *marinus* 'marine', 'maritime'. Alternatively, it is said by some authorities to be an altered form of the element *maren(c)*, which occurs in the word *cormoran* 'cormorant', from Latin *corvus marinus* 'sea raven'.

Maranda (159) Romanian (**Măranda**): from the female personal name *Maranda*, a shortened form of *Smarand*, from the name *Smaragd*, meaning 'emerald'.
GIVEN NAMES French 12%. *Alexandre, Armand, Jacques, Luc, Marcel, Serge.*

Marando (196) Southern Italian: from a reduced form of the Greek personal name *Amarantos* 'unfading' (see AMARANTE).
GIVEN NAMES Italian 29%. *Rocco* (4), *Salvatore* (3), *Giuseppe* (2), *Amerigo, Angelo, Carlo, Domenico.*

Marandola (125) Italian (Milan): possibly from a Lombard personal name of Germanic origin.
GIVEN NAMES Italian 19%. *Italo* (2), *Pasco* (2), *Antonio, Carlo, Guido, Luigi, Olindo.*

Marano (1067) Italian: habitational name from any of various places named with the Latin personal name *Marius* + the suffix *-anu*, notably Marano di Napoli (Campania), Marano Marchesato (Cosenza, Calabria), and Marano dei Marsi (L'Aquila, Abruzzo).
GIVEN NAMES Italian 19%. *Salvatore* (9), *Angelo* (6), *Carlo* (5), *Rocco* (5), *Carmine* (3), *Antonio* (2), *Nunzio* (2), *Pasquale* (2), *Aldo, Alessandro, Annamarie, Attilio.*

Maranto (310) Italian (Sicily): probably a variant of MARANDO.
GIVEN NAMES Italian 8%. *Salvatore* (2), *Antonino, Antonio, Immaculata, Vincent Joseph.*

Marantz (148) Jewish (eastern Ashkenazic): ornamental name from Yiddish *marants* 'orange' (compare POMERANTZ).
GIVEN NAMES Jewish 7%. *Hirsh, Yakov, Zev.*

Maranville (166) French: habitational name from Maranville in Haute-Marne.

Maras (324) **1.** Polish (also **Marasz**), Czech, and Slovak: from a derivative of the personal names MAREK or MARTIN. **2.** Czech (**Máras**): from the name for a man who was the son or husband of a woman called *Mári*, Czech form of MARIA. **3.** Croatian: from a pet form of any of several personal name beginning with *Mar-*, e.g. *Marijan, Marin, Marko.* **4.** Polish: topographic name from Polish dialect *maras* 'marsh'. **5.** Greek: nickname from Albanian *marrë* 'crazy', 'wild', 'strong'. This element is also found as part of composite names such as **Maragiannis** 'crazy John'.

Marasco (839) Southern Italian: topographic name from the Salentine dialect word *marascu* 'mullein' (Latin *verbascum*).
GIVEN NAMES Italian 9%. *Angelo* (6), *Nicola* (2), *Canio, Dante, Dario, Domenic, Giacinto, Gino, Guido, Italo, Marcello, Romolo.*

Marasigan (124) Filipino: unexplained.
GIVEN NAMES Spanish 38%; Italian 7%. *Alberto, Alicia, Armando, Benito, Caridad,*

Carmelita, Cesar, Conchita, Conrado, Domingo, Eduardo, Emelita; Antonio (3), *Eliseo.*

Maratea (123) Southern Italian: habitational name from Maratea, a place in Potenza province, named with Greek *maratho* 'fennel'. *Marathia* is also a common place name element in Greece.
GIVEN NAMES Italian 20%. *Gennaro* (3), *Carlo, Gaetano, Liberato, Nicoletta.*

Maravilla (343) Spanish: nickname from Latin *mirabilia* 'extraordinary thing', 'marvel'.
GIVEN NAMES Spanish 54%. *Jose* (8), *Juan* (7), *Luis* (6), *Jesus* (5), *Jose Luis* (5), *Manuel* (4), *Ricardo* (4), *Roberto* (4), *Ignacio* (3), *Alfonso* (2), *Felipe* (2), *Francisco* (2).

Marbach (308) German: habitational name from Marbach on the Neckar river, named with Old High German *marca* 'boundary' + *bah* 'stream', 'creek'.
GIVEN NAMES German 4%. *Udo* (2), *Erwin, Frieda, Ralf.*

Marberry (231) Altered spelling of English MARBURY.

Marble (1941) Southern French (**Marblé**): probably from a form of the adjective *marbré* '(of) marble' (from *marbre* 'marble'), hence an occupational name for a quarrier or worker in marble.

Marbry (127) Variant of English MARBURY.

Marburger (703) German: habitational name from Marburg in Hesse + the agent suffix *-er*. The place name is composed of Old High German *marca* 'boundary' + *burg* 'fortified town', 'stronghold'.

Marbury (568) English: habitational name from Marbury in Cheshire, named in Old English as 'stronghold by the lake', from *mere* 'pool', 'lake' + *burh* 'fortified place' (dative *byrig*).

Marbut (294) Origin unidentified.

Marc (246) French and Catalan: from the personal name *Marc* (see MARK 1).
GIVEN NAMES French 23%. *Andre* (4), *Aurele* (3), *Alexandre, Edeline, Lucien, Lucner, Mireille, Pierrot, Renald, Rochenel.*

Marcano (435) Spanish: of uncertain origin. Possibly a habitational name from *Marcano*, a region of Margarita Island in the Caribbean, northeast of the mainland of Venezuela.
GIVEN NAMES Spanish 41%. *Jose* (15), *Juan* (9), *Luis* (7), *Carlos* (5), *Andres* (4), *Pedro* (4), *Jesus* (3), *Julio* (3), *Alfredo* (2), *Ana* (2), *Angel* (2), *Enrique* (2).

Marcantel (491) French (southeastern): from a diminutive of MARCHAND.

Marcantonio (463) Italian: from a composite personal name formed with MARCO + ANTONIO.
GIVEN NAMES Italian 17%. *Rocco* (5), *Vito* (4), *Angelo* (2), *Antonio* (2), *Donato* (2), *Canio, Carlo, Emedio, Ezio, Gianfranco, Giulio, Igino.*

Marceau (663) French: variant of MARCEL.

GIVEN NAMES French 9%. *Andre* (3), *Normand* (3), *Fernand* (2), *Aime, Alphonse, Francois, Ghislain, Gilles, Henri, Jacques, Marcelle, Napoleon.*

Marceaux (273) French: variant of MARCEL.
GIVEN NAMES French 6%. *Arsene, Curley, Eraste, Thierry.*

Marcel (500) French, also Hungarian: from the personal name *Marcel* (Latin *Marcellus*, a diminutive of *Marcus* (see MARK 1), which was borne by a 3rd-century missionary to Gaul who was martyred at Bourges with his companion Anastasius).
GIVEN NAMES French 8%. *Benoit* (2), *Pierre* (2), *Alphonse, Andre, Angelle, Antoine, Gislaine, Henri, Raymonde, Yanick, Yvanne.*

Marcelin (191) **1.** French: from the personal name *Marcel(l)in*, from the Latin name *Marcellinus*, a double derivative of *Marcus* (see MARK) borne by several early saints, including a pope who died in the persecutions instigated by Diocletian. **2.** Galician (**Marcelín**): habitational name from *Marcelín*, a village in Galicia, northern Spain.
GIVEN NAMES French 39%; Spanish 5%; German 4%. *Andre* (3), *Pierre* (3), *Mireille* (2), *Anselme, Calixte, Constant, Dominique, Elysee, Francois, Georges, Jean Claude, Jean- Claude; Luis* (4), *Carlos, Enrique, Marcial, Mario, Raul, Rolando; Ernst, Fritz.*

Marcelino (197) Portuguese and Spanish: from the personal name *Marcelino*, Latin *Marcellinus*, a derivative of *Marcellus* (see MARCELLO), borne by several early saints, including the friend of St. Augustine to whom *De Civitate Dei* was dedicated.
GIVEN NAMES Spanish 36%; Portuguese 13%. *Jose* (4), *Manuel* (3), *Atilano* (2), *Eduardo* (2), *Felipe* (2), *Hector Luis* (2), *Luis* (2), *Pedro* (2), *Rosalina* (2), *Adriano, Alfredo, Alicia; Albano, Joaquim; Antonio* (3), *Francesco, Martino, Rizalino.*

Marcell (359) Catalan and southern French (Occitan): possibly a variant of the personal name *Marcel* (see MARCELLO).

Marcella (363) Southern Italian: from the personal name, feminine form of MARCELLO.
GIVEN NAMES Italian 9%. *Antonio* (4), *Angelo* (2), *Italia, Luigi, Pasquale, Vito.*

Marcelle (232) French: from a feminine form of MARCEL. From the 8th century the personal name was popularized in Provence in particular by the cult of St. Marcelle, who, according to a popular myth, was the servant of Martha of Bethany and traveled with her to Gaul.
GIVEN NAMES French 4%. *Andre, Christophe, Normand.*

Marcelli (218) Italian: patronymic or plural form of MARCELLO.
GIVEN NAMES Italian 26%. *Dario* (2), *Luigi* (2), *Mario* (2), *Orlando* (2), *Angelo, Attilio,*

Elpidio, Fernando, Franco, Gino, Marcello, Marco, Rocco, Vittoria.

Marcellino (350) Italian: from a pet form of the personal name MARCELLO or from Latin *Marcellinus*, a double diminutive of *Marcus* (see MARK).

GIVEN NAMES Italian 15%. *Domenic* (3), *Salvatore* (2), *Carmelina, Carmine, Enrico, Gennaro, Giuseppe, Luigi, Petrina, Rocco, Santina, Vito.*

Marcello (814) Italian and Spanish: from the personal name *Marcello*, Latin *Marcellus*, a diminutive of *Marcus* (see MARK 1). This was borne by a large number of minor early saints, and consequently became popular as a personal name during the Middle Ages.

GIVEN NAMES Italian 15%. *Angelo* (4), *Vito* (4), *Rocco* (3), *Sal* (3), *Antonio, Berardino, Carmine, Carmino, Domenico, Francesco, Gino, Giovanna.*

Marcellus (550) Latinized form of MARCELLO or MARCEL.

GIVEN NAMES French 8%. *Pierre* (2), *Alphonse, Andre, Camille, Clermont, Ghislaine, Micheline, Octa, Pascal, Renaud.*

Marcelo (230) Portuguese and Spanish: from the personal name *Marcelo* (see MARCELLO).

GIVEN NAMES Spanish 53%. *Jose* (4), *Bernardino* (2), *Domingo* (2), *Jesus* (2), *Juan* (2), *Luis* (2), *Pedro* (2), *Vicente* (2), *Wilfredo* (2), *Adriana, Angelina, Angelito.*

Marcey (148) Possibly an altered spelling of French **Marcé**, a habitational name from places in Indre-et-Loire, Maine-et-Loire, Loir-et-Cher, and Sarthe, all named with the Gallo-Roman demesne name *Marciacum*. Alternatively, it may be a variant spelling of English MARCY.

March (3860) **1.** English: topographic name for someone who lived on the border between two territories, especially in the Marches between England and Wales or England and Scotland, from Anglo-Norman French *marche* 'boundary' (of Germanic origin; compare MARK 2). In some cases, the surname may be a habitational name from March in Cambridgeshire, which was probably named from the locative case of Old English *mearc* 'boundary'. **2.** English: from a nickname or personal name for someone who was born or baptized in the month of March (Middle English, Old French *march(e)*, Latin *Martius (mensis)*, from the name of the god *Mars*) or who had some other special connection with the month, such as owing a feudal obligation then. **3.** Catalan: from the personal name *March*, Catalan equivalent of MARK 1.

Marchak (147) Ukrainian or Americanized form of Polish MARCZAK.

GIVEN NAME Polish 4%. *Casimir.*

Marchal (272) French: status name or occupational name from Old French *maresc(h)al* 'marshal'. The term is of Ger-

manic origin (from *marah* 'horse', 'mare' + *scalc* 'servant') and was originally applied to a man who looked after horses. In the Middle Ages it also came to be used on the one hand as an occupational name for a farrier, and on the other as a status name for an officer of state, in particular a member of a royal household with military responsibilities. Compare MARSHALL.

GIVEN NAMES French 10%. *Gilles, Jacques, Maryse, Philippe, Pierre, Veronique.*

Marchan (142) **1.** French: unexplained. **2.** Filipino: unexplained.

GIVEN NAMES Spanish 49%. *Jose* (4), *Juan* (3), *Andres* (2), *Evaristo* (2), *Francisco* (2), *Jesus* (2), *Nonito* (2), *Ramon* (2), *Alejandra, Arturo, Atanacio, Audilia.*

Marchand (2458) French and English: occupational name for a buyer and seller of goods, from Old French, Middle English *march(e)ant*, Late Latin *mercatans*, from Latin *mercari* 'to trade', from *merx* 'commerce', 'exchange', 'merchandise'. In the Middle Ages the term was used mainly to denote a wholesale dealer.

GIVEN NAMES French 12%. *Marcel* (7), *Andre* (4), *Armand* (4), *Pierre* (4), *Emile* (3), *Jacques* (3), *Lucien* (3), *Normand* (3), *Alphonse* (2), *Camille* (2), *Cecile* (2), *Colette* (2).

Marchant (2151) English and French: variant of MARCHAND.

FOREBEARS John Marchant (*c.*1600–*c.*1668) was in Newport, RI, before 1638. In that year he moved to Braintree, MA, then to Watertown, MA (1642), and finally to Yarmouth, MA (1648). His descendants included many sea captains and other prominent people.

Marchbank (116) Scottish: variant of MARCHBANKS.

GIVEN NAME French 4%. *Camille.*

Marchbanks (557) Scottish: variant of the surname **Marjoribanks**, which according to Black was adopted by a family previously known as JOHNSTON, when, in the early 16th century, they acquired the lands of Ratho-Marjoribankis in Renfrewshire. This estate was so called from having been bestowed on Robert the Bruce's daughter *Marjorie* (see MARGESON) on her marriage in 1316 to Walter the High Steward.

Marchel (132) **1.** Anglicized spelling of Polish **Marczel**, a derivative of the personal name MAREK. **2.** Variant of French MARCHAL.

GIVEN NAMES Polish 5%; German 4%. *Jacek, Ryszard; Ernst.*

Marchello (121) Italian (mainly northern and central Italy): from a pet form of the personal name MARCO.

GIVEN NAMES Italian 16%. *Ettore, Ezio, Guido, Mario, Sal.*

Marchesani (211) Northern Italian: patronymic or plural form of MARCHESANO.

GIVEN NAMES Italian 16%. *Angelo* (3), *Cesare* (2), *Domenic, Rocco.*

Marchesano (129) Northern Italian: regional name for an inhabitant of Marche province.

GIVEN NAMES Italian 31%. *Santo* (3), *Cono* (2), *Concetta, Sal, Tito.*

Marcheschi (132) Italian: from an adjectival form of MARCHESE.

GIVEN NAMES Italian 13%. *Angelo* (2), *Agostino, Eligio, Fiore, Gino, Matteo, Renzo.*

Marchese (2179) Italian: from the title of rank *marchése* 'marquis' (in Italy the rank immediately below that of duke), probably applied as a nickname for someone who behaved like a marquis, or an occupational name for a servant in the household of a marquis. However, 13th- and 14th-century documents show that the term was also used as a personal name at that time.

GIVEN NAMES Italian 16%. *Salvatore* (22), *Vito* (9), *Angelo* (7), *Rocco* (6), *Sal* (6), *Antonio* (3), *Carlo* (3), *Giuseppe* (3), *Santo* (3), *Donato* (2), *Franco* (2), *Gaetano* (2).

Marchesi (253) Italian: patronymic or plural form of MARCHESE.

GIVEN NAMES Italian 23%. *Giancarlo* (2), *Gino* (2), *Mario* (2), *Aldo, Angelo, Annamarie, Carlo, Ennio, Franco, Giuseppe, Guido, Lorenzo, Luigi, Renato, Sergio.*

Marchessault (155) French: perhaps a variant of **Marcheseuil**, habitational name from a place in Liernais, Côte d'Or, named with the dialect word *marchais* 'marsh'.

GIVEN NAMES French 8%. *Berthe, Gaetan, Jacques, Lucien.*

Marchetta (165) Southern Italian: **1.** from a feminine form of **Marchetto** (see MARCHETTI). **2.** from a diminutive of *marca* 'boundary', 'territory', 'district', hence a status name denoting someone owning or associated with a piece of land.

GIVEN NAMES Italian 22%. *Rocco* (3), *Angelo* (2), *Gino* (2), *Aldo, Attilio, Enzo, Leonardo.*

Marchetti (1590) Italian: patronymic or plural form of **Marchetto**, from a pet form of the personal name MARCO.

GIVEN NAMES Italian 15%. *Gino* (13), *Angelo* (10), *Aldo* (7), *Marco* (5), *Carlo* (4), *Dario* (4), *Carmine* (3), *Silvio* (3), *Vito* (3), *Antonio* (2), *Elio* (2), *Guido* (2).

Marchewka (188) Polish and Jewish (from Poland): from a diminutive of *marchew* 'carrot', as a Polish name a nickname for a person with carrot-colored hair. The Jewish surname is usually ornamental.

GIVEN NAMES Polish 9%. *Danuta, Dorota, Kazimierz, Mieczyslaw, Stanislaw, Wojciech, Zofia.*

Marchi (477) Italian: patronymic or plural form of MARCO.

GIVEN NAMES Italian 13%. *Angelo* (4), *Guido* (3), *Aldo* (2), *Carlo* (2), *Domenic* (2), *Gino* (2), *Marco* (2), *Vito* (2), *Alfio, Antonio, Bruna, Egidio.*

Marchiano (139) Southern Italian: variant of MARCIANO.

GIVEN NAMES Italian 22%. *Sal* (2), *Angelo, Pietro, Salvatore, Vito.*

Marchini (198) Italian: patronymic or plural form of a pet form of the personal name MARCO.

GIVEN NAMES Italian 18%. *Angelo* (2), *Aldo, Alfonso, Claudio, Francisco, Gino, Giorgio, Italia, Juliano, Mario, Remo.*

Marchio (194) Southern Italian: probably from a variant of the Latin personal name *Marcius* influenced by Greek.

GIVEN NAMES Italian 18%. *Riccardo* (2), *Angelo, Carlo, Carmine, Franco, Nicola.*

Marchionda (121) Italian: unexplained.

GIVEN NAMES Italian 21%. *Carmine* (2), *Gaetano* (2), *Nino* (2), *Attilio, Ennio, Salvatore, Sandro, Tonino.*

Marchione (427) Southern Italian: nickname from *marchione* 'marquis', from medieval Latin *marchio*, genitive *marchionis*, from Germanic *marka* 'borderland'. See also MARCHESE.

GIVEN NAMES Italian 15%. *Mario* (4), *Rocco* (4), *Angelo* (2), *Vito* (2), *Adriana, Aldo, Armando, Evo, Pasquale, Rodolfo, Romolo, Salvatore.*

Marchioni (138) Southern Italian: patronymic or plural form of MARCHIONE.

GIVEN NAMES Italian 14%. *Dante* (2), *Aldo, Angelo, Carlo, Dario, Dino, Fedele, Filippo, Tullio.*

Marchitelli (104) Italian: from a pet form of MARCHITTO, itself a pet form of MARCO.

GIVEN NAMES Italian 33%. *Americo* (2), *Dante* (2), *Guido* (2), *Angelo, Donato, Gaetano, Pietro, Romeo, Sal, Vittorio.*

Marchitto (157) Southern Italian: variant of **Marchetto**, from a pet form of the personal name MARCO.

GIVEN NAMES Italian 16%. *Angelo* (2), *Pasquale* (2), *Carmine, Rocco.*

Marchman (445) English: topographic name for someone who lived by a border or boundary, from Anglo-Norman French *marche* 'boundary'.

Marchuk (144) Ukrainian and Jewish (Ashkenazic): patronymic from the personal name *Marko*, a variant of MARCUS.

GIVEN NAMES Russian 14%. *Igor* (2), *Vladimir* (2), *Dmitriy, Mikhail, Misha, Valeriy, Vasiliy, Vasily.*

Marcia (120) Italian and Spanish: presumably from the female personal name *Marcia*, Latin feminine form of *Marcius*, derivative of *Marcus* (see MARK). Marcia was the name of several early saints and martyrs.

GIVEN NAMES Spanish 26%. *Emilia* (3), *Jose* (3), *Berta, Consuelo, Eduardo, Francisco, Jose Tomas, Leopoldo, Margarita, Mario, Miguel Angel, Raul.*

Marcial (283) Spanish, Portuguese, and Galician: from the personal name *Marcial*, Latin *Martialis* 'martial', literally 'of or pertaining to Mars' (the god of war).

GIVEN NAMES Spanish 46%; Portuguese 10%. *Jose* (7), *Manuel* (4), *Rogelio* (4), *Fran-*

cisco (3), *Jesus* (3), *Juan* (3), *Luis* (3), *Armando* (2), *Carlos* (2), *Gustavo* (2), *Juana* (2), *Margarita* (2); *Ligia*; *Antonio* (2), *Michelangelo* (2), *Eliseo, Julieta, Silvano.*

Marciano (847) Southern Italian: 1. habitational name from any of various places named Marciano. 2. from the personal name, from Latin *Marcianus*, a derivative of *Marcius*, derived in turn from *Marcus* (see MARK), or, with the stress on the last syllable (**Marcianò**), from the Greek form of this name, *Markianos.*

GIVEN NAMES Italian 14%. *Rocco* (5), *Salvatore* (3), *Carmine* (2), *Giovanni* (2), *Santo* (2), *Angelo, Antonio, Benedetto, Domenic, Francesco, Gaetano, Giacomo.*

Marciante (154) Southern Italian: probably an occupational name for a merchant, *mercante*, in a form altered under the influence of French *marchand* (from Late Latin *mercatans*, from Latin *mercari* 'to trade').

GIVEN NAMES Italian 33%. *Pellegrino* (3), *Sal* (2), *Salvatore* (2), *Vito* (2), *Alfonso, Alphonso, Angelo, Antonio, Augusto, Carmelo, Luigi, Mario, Stefano.*

Marciel (135) Spanish: presumably a variant of MARCIAL.

Marcil (296) French: from the personal name, a vernacular form of Latin *Marcilius.*

GIVEN NAMES French 13%. *Yvon* (2), *Alain, Alphonse, Amie, Andre, Hilaire, Jacques, Jean Charles, Jean Jacques, Jean-Jacques, Leandre, Normand.*

Marcille (115) French: variant of MARCIL.

Marcin (373) 1. French: from the personal name (a popular form of *Marcian*), derived from the Latin family name *Marcianus*, popularized through the cult of a local saint. 2. Polish: from the personal name *Marcin* (see MARTIN).

Marcinek (286) Polish: from a pet form of the personal name *Marcin* (see MARTIN).

GIVEN NAMES Polish 4%. *Jerzy, Piotr, Zofia.*

Marciniak (1006) Polish: patronymic from the personal name *Marcin* (see MARTIN).

GIVEN NAMES Polish 6%. *Eugeniusz* (2), *Ewa* (2), *Agnieszka, Bartosz, Boleslaw, Ignatius, Jaroslaw, Jerzy, Krystyna, Ryszard, Slawomir, Stanislawa.*

Marcinkiewicz (147) Polish: patronymic from the personal name *Marcinek*, a pet form of *Marcin* (see MARTIN).

GIVEN NAMES Polish 7%. *Henryk* (2), *Beata, Elzbieta, Janina.*

Marcinko (409) Slovak: from a pet form of a personal name equivalent to MARTIN.

Marcinkowski (283) Polish: habitational name for someone from a place called Marcinkowo or Marcinkowice.

GIVEN NAMES Polish 9%. *Beata* (2), *Casimir* (2), *Jozef* (2), *Jacek, Janusz, Jerzy, Tadeusz, Wladyslaw.*

Marcinowski (112) Polish: habitational name for someone from any of the places called Marcinów, Marcinowa, Marcino-

wice, or any of numerous other places in Poland named with the personal name *Marcin* (see MARTIN).

GIVEN NAMES Polish 9%. *Aleksander, Bogdan, Jerzy, Zbigniew, Zigmund.*

Marciszewski (57) Polish: habitational name for someone from a place called Marcisze or Marciszów.

GIVEN NAMES Polish 12%. *Henryk, Ryszard.*

Marck (119) 1. Dutch: from the personal name, Dutch form of MARK 1. 2. Dutch (**van Marck**): habitational name from places called Marke, Maarke, Langemark, Kortemark, Marck, or Marcq. 3. Dutch (**van der Marck**): topographic name for someone who lived by a border or boundary, from Middle Dutch *marke, merke* 'borderland'. 4. French: habitational name from Marck in the Pas-de-Calais, of the same etymological origin as MARK 2.

GIVEN NAME French 6%. *Brunel.*

Marcks (329) German and Dutch: patronymic from MARK 1.

GIVEN NAMES German 4%. *Hans, Heinz, Kurt, Merwin.*

Marco (994) 1. Spanish and Italian: from the personal name *Marco*, from Latin *Marcus* (see MARK 1). 2. Catalan (**Marcó**): from the personal name *Marc*, Latin *Marcus* (see MARC).

GIVEN NAMES Italian 4%. *Angelo* (2), *Aldo, Antonio, Carmela, Gino, Julieta, Paolo, Rocco, Salvatore.*

Marcoe (164) Variant of French MARCOUX.

Marcolini (123) Italian: from the personal name *Marcolino*, a pet form of MARCO.

GIVEN NAMES Italian 7%. *Angelo, Enrico.*

Marcom (246) Altered spelling of English MARKHAM.

Marcon (184) 1. French and English: from the old oblique case of the Germanic personal name *Marco*, a short form of compound names formed with *mark* 'borderland' as the first element. 2. Italian: from an augmentative of MARCO.

GIVEN NAMES Italian 16%; French 6%. *Mario* (3), *Arturo* (2), *Guido* (2), *Alberto, Giacinto, Guilio, Leno, Luigi, Nilo, Rino, Romeo*; *Francois, Renold.*

Marcone (157) Italian: from an augmentative of the personal name MARCO.

GIVEN NAMES Italian 26%. *Mario* (3), *Guido* (2), *Angelo, Eliseo, Ferdinando, Luigi, Sal.*

Marconi (995) Italian: patronymic or plural form of MARCONE.

GIVEN NAMES Italian 23%. *Gino* (4), *Guido* (4), *Angelo* (3), *Primo* (3), *Aldo* (2), *Attilio* (2), *Dante* (2), *Geno* (2), *Libero* (2), *Marco* (2), *Nazzareno* (2), *Antonio.*

Marcos (510) Spanish and Portuguese: from the personal name *Marcos* (see MARK 1).

GIVEN NAMES Spanish 37%; Portuguese 12%. *Jose* (15), *Juan* (7), *Ricardo* (7), *Jorge* (5), *Emilio* (4), *Jesus* (4), *Manuel* (4), *Pedro* (4), *Andres* (3), *Eduardo* (3), *Mario* (3), *Miguel* (3); *Marcio*; *Antonio* (2), *Clemente,*

Eligio, Federico, Flavio, Leonardo, Mauro, Romeo, Sal.

Marcott (349) French: variant of MAR-COTTE.

Marcotte (2381) French (Picardy): **1.** from a pet form of the personal name *Marc*, French form of MARK 1. **2.** metonymic occupational name for a vine-grower, from Old French *marcotte* 'vineshoot forming a layer'.

GIVEN NAMES French 10%. *Armand* (7), *Andre* (6), *Lucien* (5), *Marcel* (4), *Normand* (4), *Alphonse* (3), *Fernand* (3), *Henri* (3), *Michel* (3), *Pierre* (3), *Rosaire* (3), *Adrien* (2).

Marcou (166) French: variant of MARCOUX.
GIVEN NAME French 4%. *Jean Claude.*

Marcoux (1058) French: from a personal name derived from the Germanic personal name *Markwulf*, *Markolf*, composed of the elements *mark* 'borderland' + *wulf* 'wolf'. The name was borne by a 6th-century abbot of Cotentin, who is commemorated in various place names in Normandy: for example Saint-Marcouf in Calvados and Manche.

GIVEN NAMES French 15%. *Andre* (5), *Lucien* (5), *Gaston* (3), *Normand* (3), *Alphonse* (2), *Cecile* (2), *Michel* (2), *Roch* (2), *Yvan* (2), *Yves* (2), *Adrien, Alcide.*

Marcrum (151) Origin unidentified.

Marcucci (535) Italian: patronymic or plural form of a pet form of the personal name MARCO.

GIVEN NAMES Italian 28%. *Guido* (3), *Mario* (3), *Romolo* (3), *Dante* (2), *Lido* (2), *Lilio* (2), *Pasquale* (2), *Rocco* (2), *Aldo, Alvaro, Americo, Angelo, Assunta, Carmello, Corrado, Italo, Liberato; Ines, Jose, Miguel, Nelida, Reina, Santos.*

Marcum (5205) Americanized form of English MARKHAM.

Marcus (7747) German, Dutch, French, Swedish, Danish, and Jewish (Ashkenazic): from the Latin personal name *Marcus* (see MARK 1).

Marcussen (231) North German, Dutch, Danish, and Norwegian: patronymic from MARCUS.

GIVEN NAMES Scandinavian 15%; German 4%. *Erik* (2), *Alf, Britt; Hans, Kurt, Otto.*

Marcy (1083) English (of Norman origin) and French: habitational name from places so called in Aisne, Nièvre, and Rhône, all named with the Gallo-Roman demesne name *Marciacum*.

Marczak (274) Polish: patronymic from the personal name *Marek* (see MAREK).
GIVEN NAMES Polish 13%; German 5%. *Bogdan, Feliks, Ignatius, Janina, Jerzy, Krzysztof, Tadeusz, Wieslaw, Witold, Wojciech, Zbigniew; Alfons* (2), *Hedwig.*

Marden (874) English: habitational name from any of various places so called. One in Wiltshire was named in Old English 'valley at a boundary', from *mearc* 'boundary' + *denu* 'valley'; one in Sussex was named as 'boundary hill' (Old English *(ge)mǣre*

'boundary' + *dūn* 'hill'); one in Kent was named 'mares' pasture' (Old English *m(i)ere* 'mares' + *denn* 'pasture'); while the one in Herefordshire was named with British *magno-* 'plain' + Old English *worðign* 'enclosure'.

Marder (630) **1.** Jewish (Ashkenazic): ornamental name from German *Marder*, Yiddish *marder* 'pine marten' (see 2). **2.** German: nickname from Middle High German *marder* 'pine marten'. This was sometimes used as a nickname for a thief.

GIVEN NAMES Jewish 10%. *Chaim* (3), *Avrum* (2), *Hyman* (2), *Isadore* (2), *Miriam* (2), *Bluma, Gerson, Meyer, Moshe, Moysey, Shoshana, Sol.*

Mardesich (117) Croatian (**Mardešić**): patronymic from the old personal name *Mrdeša*. This surname comes from the Dalmatian island of Vis and the city of Split.

Mardirosian (142) Armenian: patronymic from the personal name *Mardiros* 'martyr', from Greek *martyros*.

GIVEN NAMES Armenian 21%. *Aram* (4), *Garabet* (2), *Anahid, Aris, Ashot, Deran, Haig, Horen, Hovik, Kevork, Sebouh, Vartan.*

Mardirossian (109) Armenian: variant of MARDIROSIAN.
GIVEN NAMES Armenian 62%; French 4%. *Garo* (5), *Kevork* (4), *Aris* (3), *Markar* (3), *Armen* (2), *Gagik* (2), *Raffi* (2), *Vahe* (2), *Vartkes* (2), *Viken* (2), *Adik, Agop; Antoine, Armand, Marcelle.*

Mardis (972) Origin unidentified. Probably a variant of MARTIS.

Mardock (120) Scottish: variant of MURDOCH.

Mare (108) **1.** French and English: topographic name from *mare* 'pond', 'pool', or a habitational name from one of the places in Normandy called La Mare (see DELAMAR). **2.** Italian and Spanish: topographic name for someone living by the sea, from Latin *mare* 'sea'. **3.** Dutch (**de Mare**): nickname from the Germanic word *mari*, *meri* 'famous', 'renowned'.

GIVEN NAMES Spanish 9%; Portuguese 8%; Italian 8%; Dutch 5%. *Americo, Cesareo, Fernando, Ines, Javier, Jose, Marcos; Henrique; Antonio, Gino, Olindo, Silvio, Vito; Andries.*

Maready (183) Irish and Scottish: variant of MCCREADY.

Marean (183) Scottish: probably a variant spelling of MARION.

Marecek (118) Czech (**Mareček**): from a pet form of MAREK.
GIVEN NAMES Czech and Slovak 6%. *Lubor, Ludmila, Milan.*

Marecki (105) Polish: habitational name for someone from any of various places in Poland called Marki, named from the personal name MAREK.
GIVEN NAMES Polish 11%. *Tadeusz* (2), *Casimir, Jerzy.*

Maree (123) Irish: Anglicized form of Gaelic **Ó Mearadhaigh** (see MERRY).

Marek (2957) **1.** Polish, Czech, and Slovak: from the West Slavic personal name *Marek*, a vernacular form of Latin *Marcus* (see MARK). **2.** Czech: from a pet form of the personal name MARTIN.

Marella (199) Italian: from a feminine form of *Marello* (see MARELLI).
GIVEN NAMES Italian 11%. *Nicola* (2), *Aldo, Rocco, Silvio, Vito.*

Marelli (128) Italian: **1.** from a pet form of MARE. **2.** from a pet form of the Greek personal name *Mavros* 'black'.
GIVEN NAMES Italian 14%. *Rocco* (3), *Giuseppe* (2), *Angelo, Dante.*

Maren (102) **1.** Dutch (**Van (der) Maren**): topographic name for someone who lived by a watercourse, Middle Dutch *mare*, or a habitational name from a place named Maren or Maar, from this word. **2.** German: unexplained. **3.** Possibly an altered spelling of Irish MARRON.
GIVEN NAME German 4%. *Ilse.*

Marenco (151) Italian: variant of MARENGO. This name is also found in El Salvador.
GIVEN NAMES ; Italian 28%; Spanish 14%. *Alvaro* (4), *Carlo* (3), *Marcela* (2), *Mario* (2), *Ricardo* (2), *Rolando* (2), *Dario, Flavio, Marco, Romeo, Silvio; Jose* (5), *Adelaida, Alejandro, Amparo, Ana, Blanca, Carlos.*

Marengo (269) Italian: **1.** habitational name from Marengo in Alessandria province or Marengo-Talloria in Cuneo. **2.** from *maréngo*, *marénco* 'of the sea', 'maritime' (medieval Latin *marincus*, from *mare* 'sea'), which were often used as personal names or nicknames in the Middle Ages.

GIVEN NAMES Italian 5%. *Guido* (3), *Domenic, Domenico, Gaetano, Gasper, Nunzio, Pasquale, Salvatore.*

Mareno (163) **1.** Spanish: possibly a variant of MORENO. **2.** Italian: habitational name from Mareno di Piave in Treviso province.

GIVEN NAMES Spanish 12%; Italian 5%. *Mario* (3), *Pablo* (2), *Angel, Azucena, Claudio, Fernando, Idolina, Jose, Ramona, Ricardo, Rodolso; Marco* (2), *Antonio, Carmelo.*

Marentette (130) Canadian French: unexplained.

Mares (1888) **1.** Catalan (**Marès**, also **Marés**): topographic name from Catalan *marès* 'by the sea'. **2.** English (of Norman origin): topographic name from Old French *marais* 'marsh' (Norman and Picard *marese*), or a habitational name from (Le) Marais in Calvados, Normandy. **3.** Dutch: metronymic from the personal name MARIE. **4.** Czech and Slovak (**Mareš**): from a derivative of the personal names MAREK or MARTIN.

GIVEN NAMES Spanish 29%. *Jose* (43), *Juan* (14), *Manuel* (10), *Francisco* (7), *Jesus* (7),

Luis (7), *Mario* (7), *Ruben* (7), *Arturo* (6), *Guadalupe* (6), *Rafael* (6), *Ramon* (6).

Maresca (696) Southern Italian: see MARESCO.

GIVEN NAMES Italian 17%. *Salvatore* (6), *Angelo* (4), *Luigi* (4), *Giuseppe* (3), *Pasquale* (3), *Rocco* (3), *Carmine* (2), *Aniello, Carlo, Ciro, Constantino, Sal.*

Maresco (176) Italian (Sicily): probably from a place so called, named with *marisco*, denoting a species of reed (from Latin *mariscus*), or a topographic name for someone who lived by a reed bed. However, there is some evidence that *Marisco* is also an old personal name, with MARESCA as a feminine form and a patronymic form **Maresci**.

GIVEN NAMES Italian 12%. *Carmine* (3), *Antonio, Gasper, Pasquale.*

Maresh (495) Americanized form of Czech and Slovak **Mareš** (see MARES 4).

Maret (214) French: from a pet form of the female personal name *Mar(ie)* (MARIE).

GIVEN NAME German 4%. *Wolfgang.*

Marett (271) Probably an altered spelling of MARET.

Marez (422) **1.** probably a Castilianization of Catalan **Marès** or **Marés** (see MARES). **2.** French: variant of MARET.

GIVEN NAMES Spanish 30%. *Jose* (6), *Lupe* (4), *Jesus* (3), *Armando* (2), *Juan* (2), *Juanita* (2), *Leandro* (2), *Ruben* (2), *Adelfa, Alfredo, Amalia, Ana.*

Margerum (259) Altered spelling of English **Marjoram**, a Norfolk name, apparently from the name of the herb, Middle English *majorane, mageram* (via Old French from medieval Latin *majorana*, of obscure derivation). However, it is more probably a derivative of the female personal name *Margery* (see MARGESON).

Margeson (403) English: metronymic from a short form of the personal name *Margery* or *Margaret* (of which *Margery* was the usual Middle English form), derived via Old French *Marguerite* and Latin *Marguerite*, from Greek *margarītēs* 'pearl' (see MARGETTS).

Margetts (128) English: metronymic from a form of the female personal name *Margaret*, via Late Latin *Margarita* from Greek *margarītēs* 'pearl'. This was borne by several early Christian saints, and became a popular female personal name throughout Europe. The vocabulary word was borrowed into Latin and Greek from a Semitic source, and is probably ultimately from Persian *morvarid* 'pearl'.

Margheim (127) German: habitational name from an unidentified place.

Margiotta (415) Southern Italian: unexplained.

GIVEN NAMES Italian 23%. *Antonio* (2), *Emanuele* (2), *Gino* (2), *Ignazio* (2), *Salvatore* (2), *Silvio* (2), *Adelmo, Angelo, Anselmo, Antonino, Attilio, Carmine, Elio, Emidio, Mario.*

Margis (106) English: metronymic from a short form of the personal name *Margery* (see MARGETTS).

Margison (101) English: variant spelling of MARGESON.

Margo (236) **1.** Italian (Sicily): probably from a personal name, *Margo*, variant of MARCO. **2.** Possibly an altered spelling of French **Margot**, from a pet form of the female personal name *Marguerite* (see MARGESON).

Margolies (418) Jewish (Ashkenazic): variant of MARGOLIS.

GIVEN NAMES Jewish 4%. *Chaim, Emanuel, Yaakov.*

Margolin (813) Jewish (from Belarus): **1.** metronymic from the Yiddish female personal name *Margole* + the Slavic suffix *-in* (see MARGOLIS). **2.** Slavicized form of MARGOLIS.

GIVEN NAMES Jewish 10%; Russian 6%. *Aron* (2), *Chaim* (2), *Ephraim* (2), *Ilya* (2), *Sol* (2), *Yakov* (2), *Avi, Devorah, Iren, Jakov, Mendel, Miriam; Mikhail* (5), *Vladimir* (4), *Boris* (2), *Leonid* (2), *Lev* (2), *Semyon* (2), *Aleksandr, Alexei, Evgeny, Grigory, Igor, Maks.*

Margolis (2195) Jewish (from Belarus, Lithuania, and northeastern Poland): from the female personal name *Margolis*, meaning 'pearls' in Hebrew. The Hebrew word is ultimately of Greek origin, as in Greek *margaron, margarītēs* 'pearl' (see MARGETTS).

GIVEN NAMES Jewish 5%. *Hyman* (3), *Isadore* (3), *Moises* (3), *Meyer* (2), *Avi, Avrohom, Chaim, Ilya, Itzhak, Izak, Khanna, Maier.*

Margosian (135) Armenian: patronymic from the personal name *Margos*, Armenian form of MARK.

GIVEN NAMES Armenian 12%. *Zaven* (2), *Araxie, Aris, Ashken, Diran, Mesrop, Papken.*

Margotta (108) Italian: perhaps from the French female personal name *Margot*, a pet form of *Marguerite* (see MARGESON).

GIVEN NAMES Italian 20%. *Angelo* (2), *Canio* (2), *Gaetano, Vita, Vito.*

Margraf (212) German and Dutch: variant of MARKGRAF.

GIVEN NAMES German 4%. *Kurt* (2), *Mathias.*

Margrave (169) Possibly an altered spelling of MARKGRAF.

Margulies (643) Jewish (from Ukraine and Poland): variant of MARGOLIS.

GIVEN NAMES Jewish 6%. *Sol* (3), *Mendel* (2), *Mayer, Rochel, Shaul, Simche, Yetta.*

Margulis (363) Jewish (from Ukraine and Poland): variant of MARGOLIS.

GIVEN NAMES Russian 12%; Jewish 8%. *Boris* (2), *Efim* (2), *Igor* (2), *Yury* (2), *Aleksandr, Arkadiy, Eugeny, Iliya, Inessa, Iosif, Konstantin, Leonid; Emanuel* (2), *Yakov* (2), *Isaak, Marat, Naum, Rozalia.*

Marhefka (230) Altered spelling of Slovak *Marhevská*: **1.** from a derivative of the German personal name *Marhold* (see MAROLT). **2.** from a derivative of the personal name *Mareš* (see MARES).

Mari (406) **1.** Italian: patronymic from a short form of the medieval personal name *Ademaro, Adimaro*, derived from a Germanic personal name composed of the elements *adal* 'noble' + *mari, meri* 'famous'. In southern Italy, it is more often from a short form of AMARI, or a nickname from *amaro, amaru*, also *maru* 'unlucky'. **2.** Italian: patronymic from the personal name MARIO. **3.** Catalan (**Marí**): occupational name from *marí* 'mariner' or nickname for someone who lived by the sea. **4.** Hungarian: from the personal name *Mári*, a pet form of *Márton* (see MARTIN) or *Márkus* (see MARK), or of the female name *Mária* (see MARIA).

GIVEN NAMES Spanish 11%; Italian 10%. *Manuel* (3), *Jorge* (2), *Jose* (2), *Justo* (2), *Luis* (2), *Miguel* (2), *Andres, Elena, Evelio, Fernando, Francisco, Horacio; Angelo* (3), *Antonio* (3), *Caesar, Francesco, Giancarlo, Giuseppe, Guido, Loredana, Luigi, Olindo, Salvatore, Vincenzo.*

Maria (490) Spanish (**María**), Italian, Portuguese, and Hungarian (**Mária**): from the female personal name, Latin *Maria*, which arose as a back-formation from the early Christian female name *Mariam*. This was mistaken for an accusative case, with the usual Latin feminine accusative ending *-am*, but in fact it is an Aramaic form of the Hebrew name *Miryam* (see MARIE).

GIVEN NAMES Spanish 28%; Portuguese 7%; Italian 6%. *Jose* (6), *Ana* (4), *Elena* (3), *Manuel* (3), *Pedro* (3), *Juan* (2), *Miguel* (2), *Rafael* (2), *Santa* (2), *Alejandro, Amado, Amandio; Joaquim; Antonio* (4), *Angelo* (2), *Salvatore* (2), *Albertina, Antonino, Cataldo, Filiberto, Ignazio, Plinio, Sal.*

Marian (247) **1.** Romanian: from the personal name *Marian*, from Latin *Marianus* (see MARIANO). **2.** English and French: from a pet form of MARIE.

GIVEN NAMES Romanian 7%. *Radu* (2), *Laurentiu, Mihaela, Tiberiu, Vasile, Viorica.*

Mariani (1585) Italian: **1.** patronymic or plural form of MARIANO. **2.** in some cases, a habitational name from Mariano in Bergamo, or Mariano Comense in Como, although as a Lombardic surname it is unlikely to have contributed greatly to the American surname.

GIVEN NAMES Italian 16%. *Angelo* (8), *Gino* (5), *Enrico* (4), *Luigi* (4), *Vito* (4), *Antonio* (3), *Domenic* (3), *Marco* (3), *Rocco* (3), *Vincenzo* (3), *Carlo* (2), *Elio* (2).

Mariano (1606) Italian and Spanish: from the personal name *Mariano*, from the Latin family name *Marianus* (a derivative of the ancient personal name *Marius*, of Etruscan origin). In the early Christian era it came to be taken as an adjective derived from *Maria*, and was associated with the cult of the Virgin Mary. It was borne by various early saints, including a 3rd-century martyr in Numibia and a 5th-century hermit of Berry, France.

GIVEN NAMES Spanish 15%; Italian 12%. *Jose* (7), *Carlos* (4), *Pablo* (4), *Alfonso* (3), *Ernesto* (3), *Fernando* (3), *Gregorio* (3), *Jesus* (3), *Luz* (3), *Manuel* (3), *Marcelo* (3), *Rolando* (3); *Antonio* (8), *Angelo* (6), *Rocco* (5), *Vito* (5), *Nicola* (3), *Fausto* (2), *Federico* (2), *Mabini* (2), *Romeo* (2), *Alessandra, Arcangelo, Caesar*.

Marich (289) Serbian and Croatian (**Marić**); Slovenian (**Marič**, from Prekmurje): metronymic from the female personal name *Marija* (see MARIA), or its pet form *Mara*.

GIVEN NAMES South Slavic 4%. *Milan* (4), *Mirko* (2).

Marick (121) Germanized or Americanized spelling of Czech **Mařík** (see MARIK).

Maricle (449) Altered spelling of French or Dutch **Marical** or **Marécal**, Norman, Picard, and Flemish forms of MARCHAL.

Mariconda (111) Italian: perhaps from a personal name of Germanic origin.

GIVEN NAMES Italian 24%. *Sal* (2), *Salvatore* (2), *Mario* (2), *Antonio, Dante, Geremia, Giuseppe*.

Marie (1004) **1.** French and English: from the popular medieval female personal name, Latin *Maria*. This was the name of the mother of Christ in the New Testament, as well as several other New Testament figures. It derives from Aramaic *Maryam* (Biblical Hebrew *Miryam*), but the vernacular forms have been influenced by the Roman family name *Marius* (which is of uncertain origin). The Hebrew name is likewise of uncertain etymology, but perhaps means 'wished-for child', from an Egyptian root *mrj* with the addition of the Hebrew feminine diminutive suffix *-am*. St. Jerome understood it as a compound of *mar* 'drop' + *yam* 'sea', which he rendered as Latin *stilla maris*, later altered to *stella maris* 'star of the sea', whence the medieval Christian liturgical phrase. **2.** French (**Marié**): nickname for a man newly married, from the past participle of *marier* 'to marry'.

GIVEN NAMES French 10%. *Jacques* (3), *Oneil* (3), *Cecile* (2), *Alain, Benoit, Camille, Edouard, Francoise, Jean Jacques, Jean-Philippe, Stephane*.

Marien (311) **1.** Dutch and German: metronymic from the personal name *Maria* (see MARIE). **2.** German: topographic name for someone who lived by a church named for one of the Marys of the New Testament: Mary the Mother of Jesus, Mary Magdalene, or Mary sister of Martha. **3.** French and Picard: from the Old French oblique case of MARIE 1. **4.** French: from the masculine personal name *Marien* (popularized by the 6th-century St. Marien of Auxerre), derived from Latin *Marianus* (see MARIANO).

GIVEN NAME French 4%. *Armand*.

Marier (281) French: cult name for a devotee of the virgin Mary (see MARIE).

GIVEN NAMES French 16%. *Adelard* (2), *Jacques* (2), *Marcel* (2), *Edouard, Florent, Gilles, Origene, Pierre, Veronique*.

Marietta (407) Italian: from a pet form of the female personal name MARIA.

Marietti (104) Italian: from the personal name *Marietto*, a pet form of MARIO.

GIVEN NAMES Italian 18%. *Luigi* (2), *Renzo* (2), *Domenic, Leno*.

Marik (220) Czech (**Mařík**) and German (of Slavic origin): from a pet form of the personal names MAREK, MARTIN, or *Máří* (see MARIA).

Marin (4214) **1.** Spanish (**Marín**), French, English, Slovenian, Croatian, and Romanian: from the Latin personal name *Marinus*, borne by several minor early saints. Originally this was a Roman family name derived from *Marius* (compare MARIE), but was often taken to mean 'of the sea'. **2.** Italian (Venetia): variant of MARINO. **3.** Serbian, Croatian, and Slovenian: from the personal name *Marija* or its short form *Mara* (see MARIA). **4.** Galician and Spanish: habitational name from a place called Marín, in particular the one in Pontevedra, Galicia. **5.** French: occupational name for a sailor, Old French *marin* (Late Latin *marinus*, a derivative of *mare* 'sea'). **6.** Asturian-Leonese (**Marín**): occupational name for a sailor in Asturies.

GIVEN NAMES Spanish 42%; Portuguese 10%. *Jose* (99), *Carlos* (51), *Luis* (45), *Juan* (44), *Manuel* (37), *Jesus* (24), *Mario* (20), *Miguel* (18), *Rafael* (18), *Jorge* (17), *Pedro* (17), *Francisco* (15); *Ligia* (3), *Sebastiao*.

Marina (181) Spanish and Catalan: **1.** topographic name meaning 'coast', 'coastal area', or a habitational name from a place called Marina. **2.** in some cases, perhaps from the female personal name *Marina*.

GIVEN NAMES Spanish 23%. *Jose* (7), *Alfonso* (2), *Carlos* (2), *Luis* (2), *Miguel* (2), *Beatriz, Blanca, Dorita, Eduardo, Elena, Gonzalez, Jaime; Salvatore*.

Marinacci (130) Italian: patronymic or plural form of MARINACCIO.

GIVEN NAMES Italian 5%. *Nicola, Pietro*.

Marinaccio (366) Italian: from a derivative of MARINO 2.

GIVEN NAMES Italian 19%. *Vito* (6), *Carmine* (4), *Antonio* (2), *Rocco* (2), *Angelo, Luigi, Marco, Nicola, Philomena*.

Marinari (123) Italian: from a patronymic or plural form of MARINARO.

GIVEN NAMES Italian 21%. *Salvatore* (3), *Dante* (2), *Alfonse, Angelo, Pasquale, Rocco*.

Marinaro (458) Italian: occupational name for a sailor, *marinaro* (from Late Latin *marinus*, a derivative of *mare* 'sea'). In the form **Marinaros** this is also found as a Greek family name.

GIVEN NAMES Italian 22%. *Domenic* (2), *Rocco* (2), *Sal* (2), *Amato, Angelo, Antonio, Cosmo, Dino, Ettore, Francesco, Franco, Giuseppe*.

Marine (965) **1.** French: variant of MARIN. **2.** Catalan (**Mariné**): variant spelling of **Mariner**, an occupational name for a sailor, *mariner* (from Late Latin *marinus*, a derivative of *mare* 'sea').

Marineau (181) French: from a pet form of MARIN 1.

GIVEN NAMES French 8%. *Armand, Jacques, Marcel, Yves*.

Marinelli (1660) Italian: patronymic or plural form of MARINELLO.

GIVEN NAMES Italian 15%. *Vito* (11), *Angelo* (9), *Carmine* (4), *Domenic* (4), *Dante* (3), *Dino* (3), *Giuseppe* (2), *Lorenzo* (2), *Marcello* (2), *Marco* (2), *Nicola* (2), *Salvatore* (2).

Marinello (537) Italian: from a pet form of the personal name MARINO.

GIVEN NAMES Italian 21%. *Sal* (5), *Salvatore* (5), *Angelo* (3), *Rocco* (3), *Vito* (3), *Antonio* (2), *Mario* (2), *Santo* (2), *Alessandro, Alfonso, Camillo, Carlo, Carmine, Elio*.

Mariner (555) **1.** English: occupational name for a sailor, Anglo-Norman French *mariner* (Old French *marinier, marnier, merinier*). Compare MARIN 2. **2.** Catalan: occupational name for a sailor, Catalan *mariner* (Latin *marinarius*).

Marines (171) Catalan and Asturian-Leonese: habitational name from any of several towns called Marines, in Valencia and Asturies.

GIVEN NAMES Spanish 44%. *Jose* (5), *Juan* (3), *Erasmo* (2), *Ignacio* (2), *Luis* (2), *Ricardo* (2), *Roberto* (2), *Rosendo* (2), *Alejandro, Alicia, Amador, Ambrosio*.

Marinez (195) Spanish (**Marínez**) and Galician (**Maríñez**): patronymic from MARIN 1.

GIVEN NAMES Spanish 46%. *Jose* (4), *Carlos* (3), *Fernando* (2), *Jorge* (2), *Juan* (2), *Luis* (2), *Pedro* (2), *Rodolfo* (2), *Alfonso, Alfredo, Altagracia, Ana*.

Maring (459) North German: habitational name from any of several places so named in the Rhineland.

Marini (1235) Italian: patronymic or plural form of MARINO.

GIVEN NAMES Italian 24%. *Mario* (11), *Angelo* (7), *Gino* (6), *Enrico* (5), *Dante* (4), *Antonio* (3), *Lino* (3), *Natale* (3), *Sal* (3), *Attilio* (2), *Armando* (2), *Francesco* (2), *Franco* (2), *Geno* (2), *Gerardo* (2), *Giovanni* (2).

Marinich (104) Croatian (**Marinić**) and Slovenian (**Marinič**): patronymic from the medieval personal name *Marin* (Latin *Marinus*; see MARIN 1), or metronymic from the female personal name *Marina*, which is both a feminine form of *Marin* and a derivative of *Marija*.

GIVEN NAMES Slavic 8%. *Andrei* (2), *Vladimir*.

Marinko (127) Slovenian (central Slovenia), Croatian (Dalmatia), and Slovak: derivative of the personal name MARIN, formed with the diminutive suffix *-ko*.

Marinkovich (162) Serbian and Croatian (**Marinković**): patronymic from MARINKO.
GIVEN NAMES South Slavic 16%. *Milan* (5), *Dragomir*, *Marko*, *Mile*, *Obrad*, *Zorica*, *Zorka*.

Marino (10403) **1.** Italian: from the personal name *Marino*, from Latin *Marinus* (see MARIN 1). **2.** Italian: habitational name from any of various places named Marino. **3.** Spanish and Galician (**Mariño**): occupational name for a sailor, *marino* (from Latin *marinus* 'of the sea').
GIVEN NAMES Italian 18%; Spanish 9%. *Salvatore* (48), *Angelo* (37), *Sal* (32), *Antonio* (31), *Rocco* (16), *Carlo* (13), *Carmine* (12), *Pasquale* (12), *Carmela* (11), *Vito* (10), *Domenic* (9); *Mario* (20), *Jose* (12), *Rosario* (12), *Alfonso* (9), *Jorge* (9), *Manuel* (8), *Carlos* (5), *Ricardo* (5), *Alfredo* (4), *Angel* (4), *Claudio* (4), *Emilio* (4).

Marinoff (156) **1.** Bulgarian: alternative spelling of **Marinov**, a patronymic from the personal name MARIN. **2.** Jewish (from Belarus): unexplained.
GIVEN NAME Jewish 6%. *Hyman* (2).

Marinos (254) Greek: from the personal name *Marinos*, from Latin *Marinus* (see MARIN 1), or a shortened form of a patronymic derivative such as **Marinopoulos**.
GIVEN NAMES Greek 12%. *Evangelos* (3), *Constantinos* (2), *Tasos* (2), *Anastasios*, *Angelos*, *Christos*, *Demetrios*, *Despina*, *Dimitris*, *Efstratios*, *Pantelis*, *Spiro*.

Marinovich (121) **1.** Croatian and Serbian (**Marinović**): patronymic from MARIN. **2.** Variant spelling of Ukrainian **Marynovych**, patronymic from MARIN.

Marinucci (293) Italian: from a pet form of MARIN.
GIVEN NAMES Italian 16%. *Antonio* (2), *Gino* (2), *Luigi* (2), *Aldo*, *Angelo*, *Carlo*, *Carmela*, *Concetta*, *Enrico*, *Nicoletta*, *Pio*, *Rocco*.

Mario (196) Italian, Spanish, and Portuguese: from the personal name *Mario*, from the Latin personal name *Marius*, which is probably of Etruscan origin, but was widely adopted from an early date in the Christian era as a male equivalent of the female Christian name MARIA.
GIVEN NAMES Italian 12%; Spanish 10%. *Carlo* (2), *Angelo*, *Carmine*, *Giovanna*, *Natale*, *Sal*, *Vito*; *Jose* (3), *Alfonso*, *Fernandez*, *Garcia*, *Jesus*, *Jorge*, *Mario*, *Martinez*, *Ortiz*, *Paz*, *Rodriguez*, *Rosalina*.

Marion (4839) French and English: from a pet form of MARIE 1.
FOREBEARS Benjamin Marion, a Huguenot and a native of Poitou, France, came to SC in about 1690. His descendants established themselves in St. John's Parish, Berkeley Co., SC, and in 1773 they acquired Pond Bluff on the Santee River.
GIVEN NAMES French 4%. *Armand* (6), *Andre* (5), *Jacques* (3), *Adelard* (2), *Antoine* (2), *Julien* (2), *Pierre* (2), *Alain*, *Camille*, *Cecile*, *Emile*, *Fernand*.

Mariotti (443) Italian: patronymic or plural form of the personal name *Mariotto*, a pet form of MARIO.
GIVEN NAMES Italian 14%. *Aldo* (2), *Angelo* (2), *Rocco* (2), *Benedetta*, *Camillo*, *Dario*, *Domenic*, *Ennio*, *Enrico*, *Francesco*, *Franco*, *Gabriella*.

Maris (614) **1.** English: variant spelling of MARES 2. **2.** Dutch: variant of MARES 3. **3.** Dutch and Belgian (**van Maris**): habitational name for someone from Merris in French Flanders or possibly from Maris in Dutch Limburg. **4.** Greek: probably a metronymic from the female personal name MARIA.

Mariscal (708) Spanish: status name or occupational name from *mariscal* 'marshal'.
GIVEN NAMES Spanish 56%. *Jose* (22), *Juan* (18), *Manuel* (12), *Jesus* (11), *Carlos* (9), *Francisco* (8), *Jorge* (7), *Pedro* (7), *Guadalupe* (6), *Luis* (6), *Javier* (5), *Lupe* (5).

Maritato (101) Southern Italian: nickname meaning 'married (man)', Italian *maritato*, Sicilian *maritatu*.
GIVEN NAMES Italian 31%. *Mario* (3), *Carmela*, *Carmine*, *Concetta*, *Eugenio*, *Gennaro*, *Oreste*, *Sal*, *Vito*.

Mark (5051) **1.** English and Dutch: from Latin *Marcus*, the personal name of St. Mark the Evangelist, author of the second Gospel. The name was borne also by a number of other early Christian saints. *Marcus* was an old Roman name, of uncertain (possibly non-Italic) etymology; it may have some connection with the name of the war god *Mars*. Compare MARTIN. The personal name was not as popular in England in the Middle Ages as it was on the Continent, especially in Italy, where the evangelist became the patron of Venice and the Venetian Republic, and was allegedly buried at Aquileia. As an American family name, this has absorbed cognate and similar names from other European languages, including Greek MARKOS and Slavic MAREK. **2.** English, German, and Dutch (**van der Mark**): topographic name for someone who lived on a boundary between two districts, from Middle English *merke*, Middle High German *marc*, Middle Dutch *marke*, *merke*, all meaning 'borderland'. The German term also denotes an area of fenced-off land (see MARKER 5) and, like the English word, is embodied in various place names which have given rise to habitational names. **3.** English (of Norman origin): habitational name from Marck, Pas-de-Calais. **4.** German: from *Marko*, a short form of any of the Germanic compound personal names formed with *mark* 'borderland' as the first element, for example MARKWARDT. **5.** Americanization or shortened form of any of several like-sounding Jewish or Slavic surnames (see for example MARKOW, MARKOWITZ, MARKOVICH). **6.** Irish (northeastern Ulster): probably a short form of MARKEY (when not of English origin).

Markarian (541) Armenian: patronymic, probably from classical Armenian *margarē* 'prophet'.
GIVEN NAMES Armenian 33%. *Markar* (5), *Aram* (4), *Armen* (4), *Ara* (3), *Garabed* (3), *Hagop* (3), *Mihran* (3), *Noubar* (3), *Sarkis* (3), *Vartan* (3), *Arsen* (2), *Avedis* (2).

Markee (397) **1.** Variant spelling of Irish MARKEY. **2.** Americanized spelling of German **Marke**, a variant of MARK.

Markel (1488) **1.** Dutch and German: from a pet form of the Germanic personal name *Markolf*, composed of the elements *marc*, *merc* 'boundary' + *wolf* 'wolf'. **2.** Americanized form of Slovenian **Markelj**, a derivative of the personal name *Marko*, Latin *Marcus*, + the suffix *-elj*.

Markell (453) Altered spelling of MARKEL.

Marken (316) **1.** Norwegian: habitational name from any of several farmsteads so named from Old Norse *mǫrk* 'forest pasture' or *mark* 'field', 'land'. **2.** Swedish (**Markén**): probably an ornamental name from *mark* 'land' + the adjectival suffix *-én*, from Latin *-enius*.

Marker (2141) **1.** English: topographic name for someone who lived by a boundary (see MARK 2). It is notable that early examples of the surname tend to occur near borders, for example on the Kent-Sussex boundary. **2.** English: possibly an occupational name from an agent derivative of Middle English *mark(en)* 'to put a mark on', although it is not clear what the exact nature of the work of such a 'marker' would be. **3.** English: relatively late development of MERCER. There is one family in Clitheroe, Lancashire, who spelled their name **Mercer** or **Marcer** in the 16th century, but **Marker** in the 17th. **4.** Jewish (Ashkenazic): occupational name from Yiddish *marker* 'servant'. **5.** German: status name for someone who lived on an area of land that was marked off from the village land or woodland, Middle High German *merkære*. **6.** Danish: from a short form of the Germanic personal name *Markward*.

Markert (837) German and Dutch: from a reduced form of a Germanic personal name composed of the elements *mark* 'borderland' + *hard* 'hardy', 'brave' or *ward(e)* 'guardian'.
GIVEN NAMES German 4%. *Bernhard*, *Caspar*, *Frieda*, *Fritz*, *Heinz*, *Otto*.

Markes (140) English: variant spelling of MARKS.

Market (233) English: topographic name for someone who lived by a market, Middle English *market*.

Markey (2123) Irish (Monaghan): Anglicized form of Gaelic **Ó Marcaigh** 'descendant of *Marcach*', a byname meaning 'horseman', 'knight', from *marc* 'horse'.

GIVEN NAMES Irish 6%. *Brendan* (2), *Donal, Donovan, Fergal.*

Markgraf (375) German and Dutch: status name from Middle High German *marc-grāve* 'margrave' (from *marc* 'boundary' + *grāve* 'royal judge'). In some cases the title may have been applied as a nickname for someone with overbearing behavior or as an metonymic occupational name for a servant in the household of a margrave.

GIVEN NAMES German 5%. *Kurt* (3), *Gerhard, Wolf.*

Markham (5050) **1.** English: habitational name from a place in Nottinghamshire, named in Old English as 'homestead at a (district) boundary', from *mearc* 'boundary' + *hām* 'homestead'. **2.** Irish: English surname used as an equivalent of Gaelic **Ó Marcacháin** 'descendant of *Marcachán*', a diminutive of *Marcach* (see MARKEY). This is a Galway surname, which is sometimes 'translated' as RYDER.

Markie (128) **1.** Variant spelling of Irish MARKEY. **2.** Shortened form of Polish MARKIEWICZ.

Markiewicz (933) Polish: patronymic from the personal name MAREK.

GIVEN NAMES Polish 4%. *Aleksander, Andrzej, Beata, Grazyna, Ignatius, Janina, Jozef, Leszek, Mariusz, Miroslaw, Wieslaw, Zigmund.*

Markin (451) **1.** English: from a pet form of the personal name *Mary* (MARIE) or possibly sometimes from a pet form of the much less common male personal name MARK 1. **2.** Jewish (eastern Ashkenazic): patronymic from the Yiddish personal name *Marke*, a variant of MARK.

Marking (210) English: variant of MARKIN.

Markins (141) English: metronymic or patronymic from MARKIN.

GIVEN NAME German 4%. *Otto.*

Markland (777) English (Lancashire): **1.** habitational name from a place in the parish of Wigan (now in Greater Manchester), so called from Old English *mearc* 'boundary' + *lanu* 'lane'. **2.** topographic name for someone who lived by a stretch of border or boundary land (see MARK 2) or a status name for someone who held land with an annual value of one mark.

Markle (2132) **1.** Americanized spelling of German and Dutch MARKEL. **2.** Scottish and English: habitational name from Markle in Lothian, Scotland, or from Much Marcle or Little Marcle in Herefordshire, England, named in Old English with *mearc* 'boundary' + *lēah* 'woodland clearing'.

Markley (2819) English: habitational name from Markly in Heathfield, Sussex.

Marklin (106) South German (also **Märklin**) and French (Alsatian): from a pet form of a personal name such as MARKWARDT, *Markhart,* or *Markolf.*

Markman (590) **1.** Jewish (eastern Ashkenazic): occupational name for a market trader, from Yiddish *mark* 'marketplace' +

man 'man'. **2.** German (**Markmann**): status name for someone who lived on an area of land that was marked off from village land or woodland, from Middle High German *mark* 'marked land' or 'border land' (see MARKER) + *man* 'man'.

GIVEN NAMES Jewish 7%; Russian 4%. *Emanuel* (2), *Fayvel* (2), *Irina* (2), *Faina, Ilya, Meyer, Naum, Semen, Sol, Yetta; Leonid* (3), *Boris* (2), *Gennady* (2), *Arkady, Lef, Lev, Mikhail, Raisa, Yefim.*

Marko (1046) **1.** Polish and Slovak: from a derivative of the personal name *Marek* (see MARK). **2.** Ukrainian and Slovenian: from the personal name *Marko* (see MARK) **3.** Hungarian (**Markó**): from a pet form of the personal name *Márkus,* Hungarian form of MARK.

Markoe (105) Origin uncertain; possibly an altered spelling of Slavic MARKO.

FOREBEARS Abraham Markoe (1727–1806) was born at St. Croix in the Virgin Islands. About 1770 he moved to Philadelphia, where he organized the Philadelphia Light Horse in 1774. His son (*c.* 1752–1792) was the poet and playwright Peter Markoe, listed in 1775 in the Pennsylvania Archives as captain of Light Horse, 3d Battalion, Philadelphia City Militia.

Markoff (324) Russian or Bulgarian: alternative spelling of MARKOV.

Markos (348) **1.** Greek: from the personal name *Markos* (see MARK) or a shortened form of patronymic derivatives of this, for example **Markopoulos, Markakis,** or composite names such as **Markantonakis** 'son of Mark Anthony'. **2.** Hungarian: variant of **Márkus,** a Latinized Hungarian form of MARK. **3.** Hungarian: possibly a nickname from *markos* 'strong' (from *marok* 'palm of the hand', *markol* 'to grip').

GIVEN NAMES Greek 8%. *Vasilios* (3), *Euripedes* (2), *Christos, Constantions, Evangelos, Theofanis.*

Markoski (101) Polish and Ukrainian: variant of MARKOWSKI.

Markov (149) Russian, Bulgarian, and Jewish (eastern Ashkenazic): patronymic from the personal name *Marko* (see MARK).

GIVEN NAMES Russian 23%; Jewish 10%; South Slavic 14%. *Igor* (2), *Oleg* (2), *Sergey* (2), *Vladimir* (2), *Yefim* (2), *Arkady, Dmitry, Dmytro, Galina, Grigoriy, Iosif, Lev; Etya; Milan* (3), *Marko, Sreten, Zivan.*

Markovic (293) Serbian and Croatian (**Marković**); Slovenian (**Markovič**): patronymic from the personal name *Marko,* a vernacular form of the personal name *Marcus* (see MARK).

GIVEN NAMES South Slavic 33%. *Milan* (6), *Petar* (3), *Dejan* (2), *Milenko* (2), *Branko, Dragan, Dragica, Gojko, Goran, Lazar, Marko, Milija, Miloje, Radmila, Zdenek.*

Markovich (965) **1.** Serbian and Croatian (**Marković**) or Slovenian (**Markovič**): see

MARKOVIC. **2.** Ukrainian, Belorussian, and Jewish (eastern Ashkenazic): patronymic from the personal name *Marko* or *Mark* (see MARK 1).

GIVEN NAMES Jewish 4%; Russian 4%. *Aizik, Dror, Hagit, Irina, Khaim, Lenoid, Naum, Yakov; Mikhail* (3), *Michail* (2), *Boris, Josip, Mayya, Mikhial, Milutin, Nadezda, Nadezhda, Nikolai, Svetlana, Valeriy.*

Markovits (110) **1.** Jewish (eastern Ashkenazic): patronymic from the personal name *Marko* (see MARKOVICH). **2.** Hungarian spelling of the Slavic name MARKOVICH.

GIVEN NAMES Hungarian 8%. *Miklos* (2), *Gabor, Istvan, Tamas.*

Markovitz (326) Variant spelling of Slavic and Jewish MARKOVICH, MARKOVIC, or MARKOWICZ.

GIVEN NAMES Jewish 7%. *Shoshana* (2), *Meir, Meyer, Morry, Moshe.*

Markow (222) **1.** Russian (**Markov**) and Jewish (eastern Ashkenazic): patronymic from a Slavic form of MARK. **2.** Shortened form of Jewish MARKOWITZ.

Markowicz (183) Polish and Jewish (from Poland): patronymic from MAREK.

GIVEN NAMES Jewish 6%; Polish 5%. *Moty* (2), *Mandel, Nuta; Aleksander, Janina, Jolanta, Zbigniew.*

Markowitz (2165) Jewish (Ashkenazic): see MARKOVICH.

GIVEN NAMES Jewish 9%. *Sol* (8), *Aron* (4), *Hyman* (4), *Arie* (3), *Emanuel* (3), *Miriam* (3), *Benzion* (2), *Isadore* (2), *Mayer* (2), *Meyer* (2), *Shimshon* (2), *Zalman* (2).

Markowski (1277) **1.** Polish, Ukrainian, Belorussian, and Jewish (eastern Ashkenazic): habitational name for someone from any of various places called Markowa, Markowice, Markowo, Marków, etc., named with the personal name MAREK. **2.** Jewish (Ashkenazic): patronymic from the personal name MAREK.

GIVEN NAMES Polish 5%. *Jacek* (3), *Andrzej* (2), *Leszek* (2), *Zbigniew* (2), *Aleksander, Czeslaw, Eugeniusz, Henryk, Ignatius, Janina, Janusz, Jerzy.*

Marks (19072) **1.** English and Dutch: patronymic from MARK 1. **2.** English: variant of MARK 2. **3.** German and Jewish (western Ashkenazic): reduced form of *Markus,* German spelling of *Marcus* (see MARK 1).

Marksberry (286) Variant spelling of English MARKSBURY.

Marksbury (155) English: habitational name from Marksbury in Somerset (now Avon), which was named in Old English either as '*Mǣrec*'s or *Mearc*'s stronghold' (from an Old English male personal name + *burh* 'stronghold', 'fortified place', dative *byrig*), or as 'stronghold on a boundary' (from *mearc* 'boundary', possibly a reference to the Wansdyke, + *burh, byrig*).

Markson (250) English and Jewish (Ashkenazic): patronymic from the personal name MARK.

Markstrom (119) Swedish (**Markström**): ornamental name composed of the elements *mark* '(border)land' + *ström* 'river'. GIVEN NAMES French 4%; Scandinavian 4%; German 4%. *Nels*; *Jochen*.

Markt (106) German (also **Märkt**): topographic name for someone who lived by a market.

Markum (328) Americanized form of English MARKHAM.

Markunas (174) Lithuanian (**Markūnas**): patronymic from the personal name *Markus*, a pet form of MARK.

Markus (1525) **1.** German, Dutch, and Hungarian (**Márkus**): from the personal name, from Latin *Marcus* (see MARK 1). **2.** Swedish: variant spelling of MARCUS.

Markuson (221) Swedish (**Markusson**): patronymic from MARKUS.

Markussen (115) Danish and Norwegian: patronymic from the personal name *Markus* (see MARK). GIVEN NAMES Scandinavian 15%. *Erik* (2), *Bjorg*.

Markward (158) North German: variant of MARKWARDT.

Markwardt (347) North German: occupational name for a frontier guard or the guardian of a fenced-off area (such as a woodland), Middle Low German *markward*, from *mark* 'borderland' + *ward(e)* 'guardian'. In medieval folk stories *Markwart* occurs as a nickname for a jay; it is possible that this use may have influenced the acquisition of the surname in some cases. GIVEN NAMES German 4%. *Kurt* (2), *Otto* (2), *Gerhardt*.

Markwell (506) English: habitational name from a place of this name in Cornwall.

Markwith (106) Americanized form of German MARKWARDT.

Markwood (284) part-translation of German **Markwald**, from a Germanic personal name (**Marcowald**) composed of *marc* 'boundary' + *waltan* 'to rule', or from a topographic name meaning 'boundary woods'.

Markworth (122) **1.** variant of German MARKWARDT. **2.** It may also be an English habitational name, but no place of this name is known in the British Isles.

Marland (210) **1.** English (southern Lancashire): habitational name from a minor place in the parish of Rochdale, named from Old English *mere* 'lake', 'pool' + *land* 'tract of land', 'estate', 'cultivated land'. There may also have been some confusion with MARKLAND. **2.** Dutch: habitational name from Maarland in Eijsden, Dutch Limburg. **3.** possibly a variant of Dutch **Merlan**, from French *merlan* 'whiting', a metonymic occupational name for a fisherman or seller of these fish.

Marlar (593) English (Essex): probably a variant spelling of MARLER.

Marlatt (893) Of French origin: variant of MARLETT.

Marler (2411) English: occupational name for someone who hewed or quarried marl, or a topographic name for someone who lived on a patch of clay soil, from a derivative of Middle English *marl* (Old French *marle*, Late Latin *margila*, from earlier *marga*, probably of Gaulish origin, with the ending added under the influence of the synonymous *argilla*).

Marlett (420) Americanized spelling of French **Marlet** or **Merlet**, a nickname from a diminutive of *merle* 'blackbird'. FOREBEARS Gideon Merlet from Roussy in Champagne, France, married Marguerite Martijn on 21 August 1644 at Leiden in the Netherlands. In 1662 they emigrated to the Dutch colony of New Amsterdam.

Marlette (347) French: variant of **Marlet** (see MARLETT).

Marley (2188) English: habitational name from any of the various places so called, for example in Devon, Kent, and West Yorkshire. According to Ekwall, the first element of these place names is respectively Old English *(ge)mǣre* 'boundary', *myrig* 'pleasant', and *mearð* '(pine) marten'. The second element in each case is Old English *lēah* 'woodland clearing'. This surname was taken to Ireland by a Northumbrian family who settled there in the 17th century.

Marlin (1923) English and French: variant of MERLIN.

Marling (326) English: variant of MERLIN. GIVEN NAME French 5%. *Patrice*.

Marlo (143) Variant spelling of English MARLOW.

Marlow (4462) English: **1.** habitational name from the place in Buckinghamshire on the Thames, named in Old English with *mere* 'lake', 'pool' + *lāfe* 'remnants', 'leavings', i.e. a boggy area remaining after a lake had been drained. **2.** possibly also a variant of MARLEY.

Marlowe (2561) English: variant of MARLOW.

Marmer (162) Jewish (eastern Ashkenazic): ornamental name from Yiddish *marmer* 'marble' (see MARMOR). GIVEN NAMES Jewish 5%; Russian 4%. *Herschel*, *Ilya*; *Grigoriy*, *Igor*, *Oleg*.

Marmion (203) **1.** English (of Norman origin) and French: nickname from Old French *marmion* 'monkey', 'brat'. **2.** Irish: as well as being a Norman English name as in 1, this has been used in recent times for MERRIMAN.

Marmo (311) Italian: from *marmo* 'marble'; perhaps a topographic name for someone who lived in an area of marble, a metonymic occupational name for a stonemason or quarryman, or a nickname for a cold, unresponsive person. GIVEN NAMES Italian 22%. *Angelo* (4), *Antonio* (2), *Carmine* (2), *Salvatore* (2),

Caesar, *Dante*, *Fermin*, *Generoso*, *Giovanni*, *Luigi*, *Mario*, *Rosario*.

Marmol (210) **1.** Spanish (**Mármol**): from *mármol* 'marble'; perhaps a topographic name for someone who lived in an area of marble, a habitational name from either of two places called El Mármol (in Cádiz and Jaén provinces), a metonymic occupational name for a stonemason or quarryman, or a nickname for a cold, unresponsive person. **2.** Polish: nickname from Polish dialect *marmolić* 'to dawdle'; also meaning 'to get dirty'. GIVEN NAMES Spanish 48%. *Jose* (5), *Manuel* (3), *Ricardo* (3), *Carlos* (2), *Eduardo* (2), *Fermin* (2), *Francisco* (2), *Guillermo* (2), *Julio* (2), *Nestor* (2), *Rafael* (2), *Ramon* (2); *Antonio* (2), *Donato* (2), *Fausto* (2), *Anastasio*.

Marmolejo (429) Spanish: habitational name from a place called Marmolejo in Jaén province. GIVEN NAMES Spanish 45%. *Jose* (17), *Manuel* (8), *Juan* (6), *Luis* (6), *Francisco* (4), *Miguel* (4), *Reyes* (3), *Ricardo* (3), *Alfonso* (2), *Alfredo* (2), *Alicia* (2), *Arturo* (2).

Marmon (418) Possibly an altered spelling of French **Marmont**, a habitational name from Marmont-Pachas (Lot-et-Garonne) or Marmont (Ain), orignially meaning 'bad or evil hill'.

Marmor (182) Jewish (Ashkenazic): ornamental name from German *Marmor* 'marble'. GIVEN NAME Jewish 4%. *Tali*.

Marn (120) **1.** Irish, Scottish, or English: unexplained. **2.** Slovenian: unexplained.

Marnell (362) Irish: altered form of English WARNELL, associated with Kilkenny since the mid 16th century.

Marner (205) English (of Norman origin) and German: occupational name for a sailor (see MARINER), from Anglo-Norman French *mariner*, Middle High German *marnære* 'seaman'.

Marney (372) English (of Norman origin): habitational name from Marigni in La Manche, so called from the Gallo-Roman personal name *Marinius* + the locative suffix *-acum*.

Maro (178) **1.** Italian: from a short form of the medieval personal name *Ademaro*, *Adimaro*, derived from a Germanic personal name composed of the elements *adal* 'noble' + *mari*, *meri* 'famous'. **2.** Hungarian (**Maró**): from a pet form of the personal names *Márk* (see MARK) or *Márton* (see MARTIN). GIVEN NAMES Italian 11%. *Angelo*, *Remo*, *Salvator*, *Salvatore*.

Marocco (132) Italian: **1.** variant spelling of MARROCCO. **2.** perhaps from *Marocco* 'Morocco', an ethnic name for someone from Morocco or a nickname for someone who had dealings with that country.

GIVEN NAMES Italian 17%. *Angelo* (2), *Eligio, Emilio, Luigi, Orlando, Pio, Sal, Vania.*

Marohl (209) Probably a derivative of the Germanic personal name *Marhold* (see MAROLT).

Marohn (238) Eastern German: from an Old Prussian personal name.

GIVEN NAMES German 4%. *Gerd, Ingeborg, Klaus, Kurt.*

Marois (233) French (Normandy and Picardy): topographic name from Old French *mareis, marois* 'marshy ground'.

GIVEN NAMES French 18%. *Armand* (3), *Normand* (3), *Andre* (2), *Germain* (2), *Monique* (2), *Alphonse, Gaston, Rejean, Rosaire, Serge.*

Marold (170) Dutch and Slovenian: variant of MAROLT.

GIVEN NAMES German 4%. *Erwin, Hubertus.*

Marolda (107) Italian: from a feminine form of the Lombard personal name *Maroldo*, a variant of *Maraldo*, of Germanic origin. Compare MAROLT.

GIVEN NAMES Italian 10%. *Carmela, Pasquale.*

Marolf (220) German: from the Germanic personal name *Marwolf*, composed of the elements *mari, meri* 'famous' + *wolf* 'wolf'.

Marolt (186) **1.** Dutch and Slovenian: from the Germanic personal name *Marholt*, composed of the elements *mari, meri* 'famous' + *wald* 'rule'. **2.** Slovenian: possibly also a nickname for an educated or studious person, from the obsolete Slovenian word *marovt* 'student'.

Maron (608) **1.** French: from the Old French oblique case of the Germanic personal name *Maro*, a short form of compound names with the initial element *mari, meri* 'famous'. **2.** French: habitational name from either of the places so called Indre and Meurthe-et-Moselle. **3.** Polish (**Maroń**): from a derivative of the personal name MAREK, or alternatively from a Slavic form of the personal name MARTIN.

GIVEN NAMES German 6%. *Erwin* (2), *Kurt* (2), *Manfred* (2), *Udo* (2), *Ernst, Gerhard, Hans, Lothar, Otto, Rudi.*

Maronde (102) Of French origin (**Marande**, a habitational name from Marande in Nièvre, or perhaps, as Morlet suggests, from Latin *merenda* 'afternoon luncheon', denoting in Old French 'collation to eat outdoors'); probably a Huguenot name brought to the U.S. via Germany.

Marone (453) Italian: **1.** from an augmentative of *Mare*, perhaps from the Germanic personal name *Adimar* (see MARI). **2.** from the personal name *Maronius*.

GIVEN NAMES Italian 8%. *Angelo* (2), *Rocco* (2), *Concetta, Salvatore, Severino.*

Maroney (1646) Irish: variant spelling of MORONEY.

GIVEN NAMES Irish 4%. *Eoin, Thomas Patrick* (2).

Maroni (213) **1.** Italian: patronymic or plural form of MARONE. **2.** possibly also a habitational name from Marone in Lombardy.

GIVEN NAMES French 5%. *Jacques* (2), *Yves.*

Maroon (345) Origin uncertain. Possibly a variant of Arabic MAROUN 'Maronite Christian'.

Marose (104) Origin unidentified. Possibly a derivative of the Latin personal name *Ambrosius* (see AMBROSE), but the language of origin has not been identified.

Marotta (1471) Southern Italian: from a reduced form of *Mariotta*, a female pet form of MARIO, probably via French MAROTTE.

GIVEN NAMES Italian 16%. *Carmine* (9), *Angelo* (8), *Salvatore* (6), *Rocco* (4), *Gaetano* (3), *Gino* (3), *Sal* (3), *Antonio* (2), *Carmelo* (2), *Domenic* (2), *Enrico* (2), *Santo* (2).

Marotte (154) **1.** French: from a pet form of the female personal name MARIE. **2.** Belgian (**De Marotte**): habitational name from 't Marot in Wormhout, Marote in Lichtervelde, or Marottes in Klabbeek, Brabant.

GIVEN NAMES French 14%. *Alphonse* (2), *Marcel* (2), *Emile, Normand.*

Marotti (172) Southern Italian: patronymic or plural form of MAROTTO.

GIVEN NAMES Italian 16%. *Levio* (2), *Amedeo, Antonio, Carmine, Domenic, Maurizio, Reno, Silvio.*

Marotto (214) Italian: from a pet form of the personal name *Adimaro* (see MARI) or, alternatively, possibly from French *Marot*, a pet form of *Maraud*.

GIVEN NAMES Italian 21%. *Angelo* (2), *Francisco* (2), *Marco* (2), *Carlo, Dante, Gino, Piera, Primo, Salvatore, Valentino.*

Marotz (176) German (Sorbian): from a Slavic personal name such as *Maroslaw.*

Maroun (166) **1.** Muslim: variant, under French influence, of a personal name based on Arabic *marwan* 'granite'. It was the name of two Abbasid khalifs, Marwan I ben al-Hakam (ruled 684–5) and Marwan II al-Himar (ruled 744–750). **2.** Arabic (**Mārūn**): identifying name for a Maronite Christian.

GIVEN NAMES French 13%; Arabic 10%. *Emile* (3), *Michel* (2), *Camil, Camille, Pascal; Maroun* (2), *Said* (2), *Charbel, Majeed, Nabih, Nabil, Nader, Naji, Nasif, Salem, Samir.*

Marousek (104) Czech (**Maroušek**): pet form of the personal names *Maruše* (a derivative of *Mářĭ* (see MARIA), MAREK, or MARTIN).

Marovich (179) Serbian (**Marović**): patronymic from the personal name *Maro*, a pet form of *Marko*, Serbian form of MARK.

Marple (1029) English: habitational name from a place in Cheshire, named in Old English as 'boundary *((ge)mǣre)* stream *(pyll)*'.

Marquand (123) French (Normandy and Picardy): variant of MARCHAND.

Marquard (366) Altered spelling of MARKWARDT.

Marquardt (3774) German: variant spelling of MARKWARDT.

GIVEN NAMES German 5%. *Otto* (12), *Kurt* (10), *Hans* (4), *Erwin* (3), *Wolfgang* (3), *Franz* (2), *Markus* (2), *Arno, Ekkehard, Ernst, Fritz, Gerhard.*

Marquart (1107) German: variant spelling of MARKWARDT.

GIVEN NAMES German 4%. *Kurt* (6), *Baerbel, Ernst, Erwin, Otto.*

Marques (1554) **1.** Portuguese: patronymic from the personal name MARCOS. **2.** Southern French (Occitan), Catalan (**Marquès**), and Spanish (**Marqués**): from *marqués* 'marquis', from the French word, either a nickname for someone who behaved like a marquis or an occupational nickname for a servant in the household of a marquis.

GIVEN NAMES Spanish 31%; Portuguese 17%. *Manuel* (46), *Jose* (42), *Carlos* (22), *Mario* (14), *Luis* (10), *Fernando* (9), *Jorge* (6), *Armando* (5), *Ana* (4), *Joaquin* (4), *Julio* (4), *Marcos* (4); *Joao* (13), *Joaquim* (4), *Paulo* (4), *Henrique* (2), *Lourenco, Seraphine, Vanderlei, Vasco; Antonio* (35), *Federico* (2), *Leonardo* (2), *Silvio* (2), *Augustino, Elio, Francesco, Lorenzo, Romeo, Sal, Salvatore.*

Marquess (317) English: variant of MARQUIS.

Marquette (967) French (Picardy): habitational name from Marquette-lès-Lille or Marquette-en-Ostrevant in Picardy.

GIVEN NAMES French 4%. *Numa* (3), *Andre* (2), *Marcel* (2), *Jacques, Ludger.*

Marquez (9676) Spanish (**Márquez**): patronymic from the personal name MARCOS.

GIVEN NAMES Spanish 46%; Portuguese 11%. *Jose* (265), *Manuel* (131), *Jesus* (95), *Juan* (88), *Carlos* (86), *Luis* (66), *Francisco* (58), *Miguel* (48), *Raul* (47), *Ruben* (44), *Pedro* (42), *Rafael* (41); *Ligia* (2), *Godofredo.*

Marquina (120) Spanish (from Basque): Spanish form of a habitational name from any of several Basque towns called Markina, in Araba and Biscay provinces.

GIVEN NAMES Spanish 58%. *Jose* (6), *Juan* (3), *Ruben* (3), *Fernando* (2), *Gilberto* (2), *Graciela* (2), *Guillermo* (2), *Javier* (2), *Reynaldo* (2), *Ricardo* (2), *Adelina, Agustina.*

Marquis (3470) **1.** French (of Norman origin) and English: nickname for someone who behaved like a marquis or an occupational name for a servant in the household of a marquis, from Old Northern French *marquis*. The title originally referred to the governor of a border territory (from a Germanic word; compare MARCH 1 and MARK 2). Marquises did not form part of the original French feudal structure of nobility; the title was first adopted by the Counts of Toulouse because of their possessions in the border region beyond the Rhône. **2.** Scottish: shortened form of **McMarquis** (Gaelic **Mac Marcuis**), a patronymic from the personal name *Marcus* (see MARK).

GIVEN NAMES French 10%. *Emile* (7), *Normand* (7), *Marcel* (6), *Fernand* (5), *Lucien* (5), *Rosaire* (5), *Andre* (4), *Armand* (4), *Camille* (4), *Cecile* (4), *Jacques* (4), *Francois* (3).

Marquiss (182) English: variant spelling of MARQUIS.

Marr (4226) **1.** Scottish: habitational name from Mar in Aberdeenshire, the etymology of which is uncertain, possibly Old Norse *marr*, a rare word generally denoting the sea, but perhaps also a marsh or fen, as reflected in modern dialect forms. **2.** English: habitational name from Marr in West Yorkshire, whose name is likewise of uncertain origin; possibly the same as 1. **3.** German: from the Germanic personal name *Marro*.

Marra (2026) **1.** Southern Italian: habitational name from places so called in central and southern Italy, from *marra* 'heap of stones'. **2.** Italian: from *marra* 'hoe' (from Latin *marra*), presumably a metonymic occupational name for a maker of such implements or a metonymic occupational name for an agricultural laborer. The surname is also found in Spain and Portugal in this sense.

GIVEN NAMES Italian 13%. *Angelo* (10), *Antonio* (9), *Rocco* (7), *Carmine* (6), *Salvatore* (5), *Enrico* (3), *Pasquale* (3), *Sal* (3), *Vincenzo* (3), *Alessandro* (2), *Gaetano* (2), *Marino* (2).

Marraccini (138) Southern Italian: from a diminutive of MARRA.

GIVEN NAMES Italian 9%. *Angelo*, *Dante*, *Egisto*, *Enrico*, *Guido*, *Ofelio*, *Orlando*, *Silvio*.

Marrano (140) Italian: nickname for a ruffian or villain, or for a convert to Christianity from Judaism or Mohammedanism, *mar(r)ano*, Sicilian *marranu*.

GIVEN NAMES Italian 13%. *Angelo*, *Saverio*, *Vito*.

Marrazzo (221) Italian: **1.** probably from a pejorative form of MARRA. **2.** from the Calabrian dialect word *marrazzu* 'butcher's knife', presumably a metonymic name for a butcher.

GIVEN NAMES Italian 19%. *Salvatore* (3), *Tobia* (2), *Carmine*, *Caterina*, *Cesare*, *Ciro*, *Dante*, *Domenic*, *Natale*, *Salvator*, *Saverio*.

Marre (103) **1.** French: nickname for a stubborn or narrow-minded man, from Old French *marre* 'ram'. **2.** English: variant spelling of MARR. **3.** Italian: from the plural of *marra* (see MARRA).

GIVEN NAME French 5%; Italian 5%. *Jacques*.

Marren (315) English: variant spelling of MARRIN.

Marrero (2433) Spanish: occupational name for a stone breaker, *marrero*, a derivative of *marra* 'hammer'.

GIVEN NAMES Spanish 44%. *Jose* (84), *Luis* (33), *Pedro* (30), *Carlos* (27), *Juan* (27), *Angel* (25), *Miguel* (25), *Manuel* (24), *Rafael* (20), *Ana* (17), *Francisco* (13), *Jorge* (12).

Marrese (108) Italian: habitational name for someone from any of various places called Marra, named with *marra* 'heap of stones'.

GIVEN NAMES Italian 25%. *Rocco* (2), *Angelo*, *Dante*, *Erminio*, *Luigi*, *Nino*, *Oreste*, *Pasco*.

Marrin (204) English: from a relatively rare medieval personal name derived from the Latin saint's name *Marinus* (or possibly from its feminine equivalent, *Marina*).

Marrinan (165) Irish: Anglicized form of Gaelic **Ó Maranáin** 'descendant of *Maranán*', a dissimilated form of *Manannán* (see MURNAN).

Marriner (336) English: variant spelling of MARINER 1.

Marriott (1891) English: from the medieval female personal name *Mariot*, a pet form of *Mary* (see MARIE).

Marris (158) **1.** English: variant of MARES 2. **2.** Dutch: variant of MARES 3.

GIVEN NAME French 4%. *Berard*.

Marrison (114) English (chiefly Norfolk): metronymic from MARIE 1, or perhaps from a misdivision of a name such as *Tom Harrison*.

Marro (496) **1.** Southern Italian: probably a masculine form of MARRA. **2.** Spanish: nickname from *marro* 'ram'.

GIVEN NAMES Italian 13%. *Angelo* (2), *Carmine* (2), *Pasco* (2), *Carlo*, *Pasquale*, *Philomena*, *Pietro*, *Rinaldo*, *Sal*, *Salvatore*, *Savino*.

Marrocco (266) Italian: probably a topographic name from a derivative of *marro* 'pile of stones'.

GIVEN NAMES Italian 16%. *Aldo* (2), *Luigi* (2), *Salvatore* (2), *Benedetto*, *Constantino*, *Dante*, *Gaetano*, *Giuseppe*, *Guido*, *Salvator*, *Umberto*.

Marron (1082) **1.** Irish: Anglicized form of Gaelic **Ó Mearáin** 'descendant of *Mearán*', a personal name from a diminutive of *mear* 'lively'. This is a Monaghan name. Compare MERRY. **2.** Spanish (**Marrón**): derivative of French *marron* 'chestnut', which now means 'brown'. **3.** French: diminutive of **Marre**, a nickname from Old French *marre* 'ram' (Occitan MARRO).

GIVEN NAMES Spanish 6%; Irish 4%. *Jose* (9), *Jesus* (5), *Armando* (4), *Juan* (4), *Mario* (4), *Carlos* (3), *Enrique* (3), *Joaquin* (3), *Rafael* (3), *Alfonso* (2), *Alfredo* (2), *Alvaro* (2); *Ciaran*, *Parnell*.

Marrone (1276) Southern Italian: from *marrone* 'chestnut', probably applied as a topographic name, or possibly as a nickname for someone with chestnut colored hair.

GIVEN NAMES Italian 13%. *Angelo* (8), *Salvatore* (5), *Vito* (5), *Carmine* (3), *Antonio* (2), *Carmela* (2), *Gino* (2), *Lorenzo* (2), *Pasquale* (2), *Aldo*, *Augustino*, *Benedetto*.

Marroquin (1449) Portuguese and Spanish (**Marroquín**): ethnic name for someone from Morocco.

GIVEN NAMES Spanish 52%; Portuguese 14%. *Jose* (47), *Juan* (24), *Carlos* (20), *Manuel* (19), *Mario* (14), *Jorge* (13), *Luis* (13), *Francisco* (11), *Miguel* (10), *Jesus* (9), *Ricardo* (9), *Pedro* (8); *Ligia*, *Wenseslao*.

Marrow (889) English: nickname from Middle English *marwe* 'companion', 'mate', 'lover'.

Marrs (2165) English and Scottish: variant of MARR.

Marrufo (290) Spanish: of uncertain derivation; possibly from *marrufo* literally, 'lay brother'; figuratively, 'cunning', 'sly'.

GIVEN NAMES Spanish 55%. *Jose* (10), *Manuel* (8), *Jesus* (6), *Jaime* (4), *Javier* (4), *Juan* (3), *Ramon* (3), *Alfredo* (2), *Blanca* (2), *Carlos* (2), *Felipe* (2), *Francisco* (2).

Marrujo (176) Hispanic: unexplained.

GIVEN NAMES Spanish 31%. *Manuel* (3), *Fernando* (2), *Jose* (2), *Jose Luis* (2), *Ramon* (2), *Alfredo*, *Andres*, *Azucena*, *Carlos*, *Claudio*, *Concepcion*, *Crescencio*.

Marry (116) Irish: variant of MAREE.

Mars (1402) **1.** English: variant of MARSH. **2.** French: habitational name from places so named in Ardèche, Ardennes, Gard, Loire, Nièvre, and Meurthe-et-Moselle, from the Latin personal name *Marcius*, used adjectivally. **3.** French: from the personal name *Meard*, *Mard*, *Mart*, vernacular forms of the saint's name *Médard*. Morlet notes that there are a number of places called Saint-Mars, formerly recorded in Latin as *Sanctus Medardus*. **4.** French: from the name of the month, *mars* 'March', denoting seed sown in March, and hence a metonymic name for an arable grower. **5.** French (**De Mars**): habitational name from Mars in the Ardennes. **6.** Dutch: from a short form of the personal name *Marsilius*.

GIVEN NAMES French 4%. *Cecile*, *Fernand*, *Jean Claude*, *Julien*, *Marceau*, *Pierre*, *Serge*, *Simonne*, *Yvon*.

Marsala (454) Sicilian and southern Italian: habitational name from Marsala on the west coast of Sicily, in Trapani province, so named from Arabic *marsā* '*Alī* 'port of Ali'.

GIVEN NAMES Italian 16%. *Salvatore* (6), *Angelo* (3), *Carmelo* (2), *Gaspare* (2), *Nicolo* (2), *Antonino*, *Carmine*, *Domenico*, *Franco*, *Gasper*, *Giovanni*, *Leonardo*.

Marsalis (202) Dutch: probably a variant of MARCHAL.

FOREBEARS The name **Marselis** is recorded in Beverwijck in New Netherland (Albany, NY) in the mid 17th century.

Marsan (192) French: habitational name from a place so named in Gers.
GIVEN NAMES French 14%. *Jean-Claude* (2), *Lucien* (2), *Adelard*, *Andre*, *Gaetan*, *Philippe*, *Pierre*, *Raoul*.

Marsch (295) North German: topographic name for someone who lived by a marsh or fen, Middle Low German *marsch*.
GIVEN NAMES German 4%. *Kurt* (2), *Erwin*.

Marschall (469) German: occupational name for a man in the service of a member of the nobility, originally one who looked after the horses, Middle High German *marschalc* (from *mar(c)* 'noble horse' + *schalk* 'servant'). In time the term came to be used for a military rank or a certain court official. Compare MARSHALL.
GIVEN NAMES German 7%. *Kurt* (3), *Erwin*, *Hedwig*, *Juergen*, *Reinhard*, *Theresia*, *Wilfried*.

Marschel (116) German: **1.** variant of MARSCHALL. **2.** from a pet form of a Slavic personal name such as *Maresch* (see MARES 4).
GIVEN NAME German 6%. *Klaus*.

Marschke (226) German (Silesia, Saxony, and Bohemia): patronymic from a Slavic personal name such as *Maresch* (see MARES 4).
GIVEN NAMES German 5%. *Kurt* (3), *Erwin*, *Otto*.

Marschner (198) German **1.** (Silesia, Saxony, and Bohemia): patronymic from the Czech personal name MAREK, or a metronymic from *Marusch*, a pet form of the female personal name *Margaret* (see MARGESON). **2.** topographic name for someone who lived by a marsh or fen, a derivative of Middle Low German *marsch* 'marsh'.
GIVEN NAMES German 9%. *Ernst* (2), *Kurt*.

Marsden (1836) English: habitational name from places in Lancashire and West Yorkshire, so named from Old English *mearc* 'boundary' (see MARK 2) + *denu* 'valley' (see DEAN 1), i.e. a valley forming a natural boundary.

Marse (122) Northern French (**Marsé**): topographic name from a dialect variant of French *marché* 'market'.
GIVEN NAMES French 7%. *Gaston*, *Julien*.

Marsee (334) Variant of Northern French MARSE.

Marsella (362) Italian: variant of MARZELLA.
GIVEN NAMES Italian 14%. *Angelo* (3), *Antonio* (3), *Romolo* (2), *Bruna*, *Dante*, *Dino*, *Filippo*, *Gaetano*, *Gianna*, *Gino*, *Luigi*, *Nichola*.

Marsh (23280) English: topographic name for someone who lived by or in a marsh or fen, Middle English *mershe* (Old English *mersc*), or a habitational name from any of various minor places named with this word, for example in Shropshire and Sussex.

Marshak (198) Jewish (eastern Ashkenazic): acronymic name from the Hebrew expression *Morenu Harav Rabbi Shmuel Koidanover* 'our teacher Rabbi Samuel Koidanover', the name of a talmudic scholar and preacher from eastern Europe who lived in the 17th century.

Marshal (186) Variant spelling of English and Scottish MARSHALL or German MARSCHALL.

Marshalek (145) Americanized spelling of Czech **Maršálek** or Polish **Marszałek** (see MARSZALEK).

Marshall (61191) English and Scottish: status name or occupational name from Middle English, Old French *maresc(h)al* 'marshal'. The term is of Germanic origin (compare Old High German *marah* 'horse', 'mare' + *scalc* 'servant'). Originally it denoted a man who looked after horses, but by the heyday of medieval surname formation it denoted on the one hand one of the most important servants in a great household (in the royal household a high official of state, one with military responsibilities), and on the other a humble shoeing smith or farrier. It was also an occupational name for a medieval court officer responsible for the custody of prisoners. An even wider range of meanings is found in some other languages: compare for example Polish **Marszałek** (see MARSZALEK). The surname is also borne by Jews, presumably as an Americanized form of one or more like-sounding Jewish surnames.
FOREBEARS As the fourth chief justice of the U.S., John Marshall (1755–1835) was the principal architect in consolidating and defining the powers of the Supreme Court. He was a descendant of John Marshall of Ireland, who settled in Culpeper Co., VA, sometime before 1655.

Marshburn (704) English or Scottish, probably a habitational name from an unidentified place named as 'marsh stream'.

Marshman (319) English: topographic name for someone who lived in a marsh (see MARSH).

Marsicano (215) Italian: habitational name for someone from MARSICO, or from the Marsica, an area in Abruzzo, with the agent suffix *-ano*.
GIVEN NAMES Italian 13%. *Angelo*, *Benedetto*, *Gabriele*, *Gennaro*, *Serafino*.

Marsico (492) Southern Italian: habitational name from Marsico Nuovo and Marsico Vetere in the region of Potenza, Basilicata province, so named from the Latin personal name *Marsicus*.
GIVEN NAMES Italian 21%. *Alfonso* (2), *Rocco* (2), *Sal* (2), *Salvatore* (2), *Vito* (2), *Agostino*, *Aldo*, *Annamarie*, *Carmela*, *Carmine*, *Clodomiro*, *Elena*, *Eugenio*, *Federico*, *Franco*, *Gaetano*, *Mario*, *Roberto*.

Marsiglia (196) Italian: habitational name from Marseilles in southern France (Italian *Marsiglia*).

GIVEN NAMES Italian 6%. *Salvatore* (3), *Flavio*.

Marsili (146) Italian: from the personal name MARSILIO.
GIVEN NAMES Italian 18%. *Gino* (2), *Alfio*, *Angelo*, *Caesar*, *Dario*, *Dino*, *Enio*, *Enrico*, *Ercole*, *Guido*, *Pietro*, *Silvio*.

Marsilio (136) Italian: from the personal name *Marsilio* (from Latin *Marsilius*).
GIVEN NAMES Italian 18%. *Liberato* (2), *Mario* (2), *Emilio*, *Salvadore*.

Marske (123) English: from either of two places so called in North Yorkshire, name with Old English *mersc* 'marsh', the *-sk* being the result of Scandinavian influence.

Marsland (218) English (chiefly southern Lancashire): habitational name, probably from some place named as being a boggy place, from Old English *mersc* 'marsh' + *land* 'land'. Alternatively, it may be a variant of MARKLAND.

Marsman (111) Dutch: **1.** topographic name for a dweller in marshland, from Middle Dutch *marsch*, *mersch* 'marsh' + *man* 'man'. **2.** occupational name for a traveling salesman, from Middle Dutch *me(e)rseman*, *maers(e)man*.
GIVEN NAME Dutch 4%. *Berend* (2).

Marso (191) Probably an Americanized spelling of French MARCEAU.

Marsocci (100) Italian: unexplained; perhaps from a suffixed form of the personal name *Marso* (see MARSI).
GIVEN NAMES Italian 7%. *Angelo*, *Antonio*, *Lorenzo*, *Velio*.

Marsolek (268) Polish: variant spelling of **Marszołek** (see MARSZALEK).

Marson (554) **1.** English: variant of the habitational name MARSTON. The two forms seem to have been used interchangeably. **2.** French: habitational name from places so called in Marne and Meuse, or from Marçon in Sarthe.

Marsteller (402) German: occupational name for a stable boy in or for the supervisor of the stables on a noble estate, from Middle High German *mar(c)* 'noble horse' *stall* 'stable' + the agent suffix *-er*.

Marsters (241) English: variant spelling of MASTERS.

Marston (2646) English: habitational name from any of the numerous places so called, of which there are examples in at least sixteen counties. All get their names from Old English *mersc* 'marsh' + *tūn* 'enclosure', 'settlement'.

Marszalek (358) Polish (**Marszałek**): occupational name or status name from the vocabulary word *marszałek* 'marshal', denoting anything from a high court official, a field marshal, or the chairman of the Polish parliament, to the senior servant in a great household. Compare English MARSHALL.
GIVEN NAMES Polish 10%. *Piotr* (2), *Alicja*, *Andrzej*, *Eugeniusz*, *Henryk*, *Jerzy*, *Kazimierz*, *Mieczyslaw*, *Wieslaw*, *Zbigniew*, *Zofia*, *Zygmunt*.

Mart (437) **1.** English: from an early Middle English personal name, *Mert* or *Mart*, or perhaps a nickname from Old English *mearð* '(pine) marten'. **2.** German (Alsace-Lorraine): from a short form of MARTIN.

Marta (272) **1.** Spanish, Portuguese, and Catalan: from *marta* 'marten'. **2.** Slavic and Hungarian (**Márta**): from the female personal name which appears in the New Testament as *Martha* (Aramaic *Marta* 'lady'), borne by the sister of Lazarus and Mary (of Bethany).
GIVEN NAMES Spanish 14%. *Manuela* (2), *Alfaro, Angel, Arturo, Cuca, Fernando, Isidro, Jose, Jose Alfredo, Juan, Manuel, Margarito; Carlo, Carmela, Fausto, Marino, Romano.*

Marte (666) **1.** Portuguese and Galician: variant of MARTA. **2.** Italian: probably from medieval Greek *Martios* 'March' or the Calabrian dialect word *marti* 'Tuesday', in either case probably denoting someone with some particular association with the month or the day. **3.** English: variant spelling of MART 1. **4.** German: from a short form of MARTIN.
GIVEN NAMES Spanish 48%. *Jose* (23), *Ana* (8), *Rafael* (8), *Juan* (7), *Luis* (6), *Pedro* (6), *Francisco* (5), *Margarita* (5), *Mercedes* (5), *Jorge* (4), *Luz* (4), *Ramon* (4).

Martel (3056) **1.** English and German: from a medieval personal name, a pet form of MARTIN or MARTA. **2.** English and French: metonymic occupational name for a smith or a nickname for a forceful person, from Old French *martel* 'hammer' (Late Latin *martellus*). Charles Martel, the grandfather of Charlemagne, gained his byname from the force with which he struck down his enemies in battle. **3.** Spanish and Portuguese: from Portuguese *martelo*, Old Spanish *martel* 'hammer' (Late Latin *martellus*), or an Iberianized form of the Italian cognate MARTELLO.
GIVEN NAMES French 13%. *Lucien* (12), *Andre* (10), *Armand* (10), *Normand* (8), *Marcel* (7), *Adrien* (4), *Aime* (4), *Benoit* (4), *Laurent* (4), *Yvan* (4), *Jacques* (3), *Michel* (3).

Martell (3048) **1.** English, French, and German: variant spelling of MARTEL. **2.** Catalan: metonymic occupational name for a smith, or nickname for a forceful person, from *martell* 'hammer' (Late Latin *martellus*).

Martella (398) Southern Italian: from a feminine form of MARTELLO.
GIVEN NAMES Italian 7%. *Angelo* (3), *Bruna, Rocco, Romeo.*

Martelle (176) French: from a feminine form of MARTEL 2.

Martelli (505) Italian: patronymic or plural form of MARTELLO.
GIVEN NAMES Italian 23%. *Antonio* (3), *Mario* (3), *Angelo* (2), *Carmine* (2), *Francesco* (2), *Gino* (2), *Goffredo* (2),

Luigi (2), *Rafael* (2), *Vito* (2), *Camillo, Domenic, Emanuele, Emilio, Fabio, Fabrizio, Jacinto, Manuel, Ricardo.*

Martello (777) Southern Italian: nickname for someone with a forceful personality, from Italian *martèllo* 'hammer' (Late Latin *martellus*), or a metonymic occupational name for someone who used a hammer in their work.
GIVEN NAMES Italian 15%. *Angelo* (8), *Rocco* (4), *Sal* (3), *Salvatore* (3), *Carlo* (2), *Pasquale* (2), *Romeo* (2), *Saverio* (2), *Tommaso* (2), *Aldo, Antonio, Bartolomeo.*

Marten (1125) Dutch and German form of MARTIN.
GIVEN NAMES German 4%. *Hans* (2), *Klaus* (2), *Otto* (2), *Eugen, Fritz, Gerhardt, Johannes, Lorenz.*

Marteney (191) Perhaps an altered form of a French surname such as **Martigny** (a habitational name from places in Aisne, Manche, Calvados, Seine-Maritime, Vosges, and Saône-et-Loire, named in Latin as 'estate of *Martinius*', from the Latin personal name + the suffix *-acum*), or **Martinet, Martenet** (pet forms of MARTIN).
GIVEN NAME French 4%. *Pierre.*

Martens (4384) **1.** North German and Dutch: patronymic from MARTEN. **2.** English: variant of MARTINS.
GIVEN NAMES German 4%. *Hans* (6), *Otto* (5), *Ernst* (3), *Kurt* (3), *Armin* (2), *Claus* (2), *Erwin* (2), *Heinz* (2), *Horst* (2), *Rainer* (2), *Sibert* (2), *Wilhelm* (2).

Martensen (370) North German, Dutch, and Danish (**Mårtensen**): patronymic from the personal name MARTEN.
GIVEN NAMES Scandinavian 5%; German 5%. *Carsten, Erik; Armin, Ernst, Hans, Jurgen, Otto.*

Martenson (335) Respelling of Swedish **Mårten(s)son** or any of various Scandinavian or North German patronymic forms cognate with MARTENSEN.
GIVEN NAMES Scandinavian 11%. *Anders* (2), *Elof, Nels, Sven.*

Marter (303) **1.** English: nickname from Middle English *martre, marter* 'marten' (Old French *martre*). **2.** Dutch: possibly from *marter* 'marten'.

Martes (123) Hispanic or southern Italian: unexplained.
GIVEN NAMES Spanish 35%. *Juan* (2), *Angel, Augustina, Dionisio, Eduardo, Germania, Grecia, Hilario, Jorge, Jose, Juliano, Luz; Antonio, Luciano.*

Marth (626) German: **1.** from a short form of MARTIN. **2.** habitational name from any of several places named Marth.

Martha (120) Portuguese, Spanish, Catalan, Dutch, Greek (**Marthas**), etc.: metronymic from the female personal name, which appears in the New Testament as *Martha* (Aramaic *Marta* 'lady') (see MARTA).

GIVEN NAMES Spanish 9%. *Alejandro, Garcia, Juan, Lozano, Maribel, Roberto, Rogelio, Sergio.*

Marthaler (397) **1.** Swiss German: habitational name for someone from Marthalen near Schaffhausen. **2.** German and Dutch: habitational name for someone from Martental near Laubach.

Marthaller (100) German and Dutch: variant spelling of MARTHALER.

Marti (1298) **1.** Swiss German: from a pet form of MARTIN 1. **2.** Italian: probably from medieval Greek *Martios* 'March', a nickname for someone who was born or baptized in March or had some other association with the month. **3.** Catalan (**Martí**) and southern French (Occitan): from the personal name *Martí* (see MARTIN). **4.** Hungarian: topographic name from *mart* 'small hill', 'waterfront'. **5.** Hungarian: from *Marti*, a pet form of the personal name *Márton*, Hungarian form of MARTIN.
GIVEN NAMES Spanish 15%. *Jose* (16), *Luis* (8), *Ramon* (6), *Juan* (5), *Enrique* (4), *Marta* (4), *Sergio* (4), *Alfredo* (3), *Jorge* (3), *Ricardo* (3), *Alberto* (2), *Andres* (2).

Martian (118) Origin unidentified.

Martie (106) **1.** Scottish: from the personal name *Martie*, a pet form of MARTIN. **2.** French and Swiss German: variant of MARTY.

Martignetti (127) Italian: from a patronymic of plural form of *Martignetto*, a pet form of MARTINO.
GIVEN NAMES Italian 22%; Spanish 10%. *Erminio* (2), *Alessandro, Angelo, Antonio, Carmine, Gaetano, Pasquale, Sal, Silvio; Adriano.*

Martin (238747) **1.** English, Scottish, Irish, French, Dutch, German, Czech, Slovak, Spanish (**Martín**), Italian (Venice), etc.: from a personal name (Latin *Martinus*, a derivative of *Mars*, genitive *Martis*, the Roman god of fertility and war, whose name may derive ultimately from a root *mar* 'gleam'). This was borne by a famous 4th-century saint, Martin of Tours, and consequently became extremely popular throughout Europe in the Middle Ages. As a North American surname, this form has absorbed many cognates from other European forms. **2.** English: habitational name from any of several places so called, principally in Hampshire, Lincolnshire, and Worcestershire, named in Old English as 'settlement by a lake' (from *mere* or *mær* 'pool', 'lake' + *tūn* 'settlement') or as 'settlement by a boundary' (from *(ge)mære* 'boundary' + *tūn* 'settlement'). The place name has been charged from *Marton* under the influence of the personal name *Martin*.

Martina (375) **1.** Italian: from the feminine form of the personal name MARTINO. **2.** Czech: from a derivative of the personal name MARTIN.

GIVEN NAMES Italian 6%. *Elio* (2), *Amerigo*, *Antonio*, *Carlo*, *Guido*, *Leno*, *Maurizio*, *Vittorino*.

Martinak (101) Polish, Slovak (**Martinák**), and Czech: patronymic derivative of the personal name MARTIN.

GIVEN NAMES German 4%. *Florian*, *Rainer*.

Martincic (130) Slovenian (**Martinčič**); Croatian and Serbian (**Martinčić**): patronymic from the personal name MARTIN. The name is also found in Italy, in Venezia Giulia.

GIVEN NAME Italian 4%. *Silvio*.

Martindale (2595) English: habitational name from a place in Cumbria, first recorded in 1220 in its present form. There is a chapel of St. Martin here, and the valley (see DALE) may be named from this. Alternatively, there may have been a landowner here called *Martin*, and the church dedication may be due to popular association of his name with that of the saint.

Martindell (112) English: variant of MARTINDALE.

Martine (538) French: from the feminine form of MARTIN 1.

Martineau (1766) **1.** French (western): from a pet form of MARTIN 1. **2.** English: habitational name from Martineau in France. The name was also taken to England by Huguenot refugees in the 17th century (see below).

FOREBEARS Harriet Martineau (1802–76), the English writer, was the daughter of a Norwich manufacturer. She was descended from a family of French Huguenots who owned land around Poitou and Touraine in the 15th century. They included a number of surgeons in the 17th century. In the 19th century a branch of the family was firmly established in Birmingham, England; others went to North America.

GIVEN NAMES French 14%. *Emile* (7), *Marcel* (6), *Pierre* (6), *Andre* (4), *Jacques* (4), *Lucien* (4), *Armand* (3), *Michel* (3), *Raoul* (3), *Antoine* (2), *Camille* (2), *Huguette* (2).

Martinec (167) **1.** Czech and Slovak: derivative of the personal name MARTIN. **2.** Slovenian and Croatian (northern and eastern Croatia): diminutive or patronymic from the personal name MARTIN.

GIVEN NAME German 4%. *Otto* (2).

Martinek (666) Czech (**Martínek**), Slovak, Croatian (northern and western Croatia), and Slovenian: from a pet form of the personal name MARTIN.

Martinell (112) Italian (Venice): shortened form of MARTINELLI.

Martinelli (1797) Italian: from a pet form of the personal name MARTINO.

GIVEN NAMES Italian 13%. *Guido* (8), *Angelo* (6), *Gino* (5), *Dante* (3), *Luigi* (3), *Nicola* (3), *Rocco* (3), *Domenic* (2), *Donato* (2), *Evo* (2), *Giulio* (2), *Italo* (2).

Martines (487) Portuguese and Spanish: variant of MARTINEZ.

GIVEN NAMES Spanish 26%; Portuguese 7%; Italian 6%. *Francisco* (4), *Jose* (4), *Manuel* (4), *Jesus* (3), *Carlos* (2), *Juan* (2), *Luis* (2), *Mario* (2), *Miguel* (2), *Pablo* (2), *Ramon* (2), *Ricardo* (2); *Joao*; *Salvatore* (2), *Antonio*, *Maurizio*, *Ottavio*.

Martinet (130) French: from a pet form of the personal name MARTIN.

GIVEN NAMES French 23%. *Colette* (2), *Jacques* (2), *Pierre* (2), *Dominique*, *Jean Pierre*, *Micheline*.

Martinetti (115) Italian: from a pet form of MARTINO.

GIVEN NAMES Italian 11%; Spanish 10%. *Aldo*, *Domenic*, *Gino*; *Victorio* (3), *Julio* (2), *Levia*.

Martinez (94105) Spanish (**Martínez**): patronymic from the personal name MARTIN.

GIVEN NAMES Spanish 45%; Portuguese 10%. *Manuel* (916), *Carlos* (712), *Luis* (703), *Jesus* (688), *Francisco* (495), *Pedro* (486), *Miguel* (474), *Raul* (444), *Mario* (429), *Jorge* (424), *Roberto* (379), *Ruben* (353); *Ligia* (5), *Paulo* (4), *Armanda* (3), *Catarina* (3), *Gonsalo* (3), *Marcio* (3), *Wenceslao* (3), *Anatolio* (2), *Godofredo* (2), *Lidio* (2), *Sil*, *Zulmira*.

Marting (212) Dutch: variant of MARTIN 1.

Martinho (105) Portuguese: derivative of MARTIN or of any of its Portuguese variants, MARTINS and *Martim*.

GIVEN NAMES Spanish 26%; Portuguese 20%. *Jose* (4), *Luis* (2), *Manuel* (2), *Zeferino* (2), *Adelino*, *Basilio*, *Carlos*, *Francisco*, *Jose Luis*, *Mario*, *Rogerio*; *Joao*, *Joaquim*; *Antonio* (4).

Martini (2668) **1.** Italian: patronymic form of MARTINO. **2.** German: Latinized patronymic from MARTIN 1.

GIVEN NAMES Italian 7%. *Angelo* (6), *Luigi* (6), *Guido* (5), *Antonio* (4), *Elio* (4), *Rinaldo* (4), *Rocco* (4), *Silvio* (4), *Dino* (3), *Gino* (3), *Cesidio* (2), *Enrico* (2).

Martinie (107) Derivative of MARTIN; language unidentified.

Martinka (181) Czech, Slovak, and Ukrainian: from a derivative of the personal name MARTIN.

Martinko (131) Altered spelling of Polish **Marcinko** or **Martynko**, Slovak MARCINKO or **Martinčko**, or some other Slavic form of the personal name MARTIN.

Martinkus (88) Lithuanian: patronymic from a derivative of the personal name MARTIN.

Martino (4508) Italian: from the personal name *Martino* (see MARTIN).

GIVEN NAMES Italian 14%. *Angelo* (26), *Vito* (14), *Carmine* (13), *Rocco* (12), *Domenic* (11), *Sal* (11), *Antonio* (8), *Carlo* (6), *Pasquale* (6), *Concetta* (4), *Dino* (4), *Donato* (4).

Martinovich (180) Ukrainian; Serbian and Croatian (**Martinović**): patronymic from the personal name MARTIN.

Martins (2202) **1.** Portuguese: patronymic from the personal name *Martim*, vernacular

form of Latin *Martinus* (see MARTIN). **2.** English and Dutch: patronymic from the personal name MARTIN.

GIVEN NAMES Spanish 30%; Portuguese 20%. *Manuel* (89), *Jose* (80), *Carlos* (36), *Fernando* (23), *Francisco* (22), *Mario* (14), *Luis* (12), *Armando* (8), *Alvaro* (7), *Ana* (7), *Marcelo* (6), *Sergio* (6); *Joaquim* (15), *Joao* (10), *Paulo* (7), *Agostinho* (3), *Henrique* (3), *Afonso* (2), *Batista* (2), *Ademir*, *Amadeu*, *Anabela*, *Caetano*, *Heitor*; *Antonio* (75), *Luciano* (4), *Marco* (3), *Angelo* (2), *Lucio* (2), *Aldino*, *Ciro*, *Clementina*, *Egidio*, *Emidio*, *Enio*, *Fausto*.

Martinsen (710) Dutch, North German, Danish, and Norwegian: patronymic from MARTIN 1.

GIVEN NAMES Scandinavian 8%. *Knut* (2), *Lars* (2), *Alf*, *Helmer*, *Hilmar*, *Ove*.

Martinson (3429) English, Swedish (**Martinsson**), Norwegian and Danish (**Martinsen**): patronymic from the personal name MARTIN.

Martiny (158) French (southeastern) and German: variant of MARTIN 1.

Martir (123) Spanish or Portuguese: from *mártir* 'martyr', probably a nickname for someone devoted to the religious cult of a martyr, or perhaps one who had played the part of a martyr in a religious play. Compare Italian MARTIRE.

GIVEN NAMES Spanish 38%. *Jose* (4), *Luis* (3), *Manuel* (3), *Miguel* (3), *Julio* (2), *Angel*, *Benito*, *Carlos*, *Cresencio*, *Hermino*, *Honorio*, *Joaquin*.

Martire (206) Italian: from *martire* 'martyr', probably a nickname for someone who had played the part of a martyr in a religious play. However, there was a St. Martire and so the surname may be derived from a personal name.

GIVEN NAMES Italian 20%. *Antonio* (3), *Angelo* (2), *Dante* (2), *Agostino*, *Carlo*, *Enrico*, *Luigi*, *Matteo*, *Ottavio*, *Pietro*, *Salvatore*.

Martis (283) **1.** German: patronymic from MARTI 1. **2.** Galician: patronymic from a vernacular form of Latin *Martinus* (see MARTIN). **3.** Greek: from the month of March, Greek *Marti(o)s*, used as a nickname for a capricious or tempestuous person because of the associations of the vocabulary word with unpredictable stormy weather. **4.** Hungarian: from a pet form of the ecclesiastical name *Márton* (see MARTIN).

GIVEN NAMES Spanish 5%. *Jose* (3), *Armando*, *Carolina*, *Catalina*, *Emilia*, *Jorge*, *Lisandra*, *Manuel*, *Odalis*, *Onesimo*.

Marto (114) Spanish: **1.** habitational name from a place called Marto in Andalusia. **2.** probably also a masculine variant from MARTA.

GIVEN NAMES Spanish 4%. *Alicia*, *Augusto*, *Julio*, *Manual*.

Martocci (173) Italian: **1.** from a derivative of MARTA or MARTE. **2.** otherwise possibly from a derivative of the root *Mart-* of *Martinus*. Compare MARTONE 2.

GIVEN NAMES Italian 8%. *Gino, Rocchina, Rocco, Sal.*

Marton (600) **1.** English: habitational name from any of several places so called, principally in Lincolnshire, Warwickshire, and North Yorkshire, named in Old English as 'settlement by a lake' (from *mere* or *mær* 'pool', 'lake' + *tūn* 'settlement') or as 'settlement by a boundary' (from *(ge)mære* 'boundary' + *tūn* 'settlement'). Compare MARTIN 2. **2.** Hungarian (**Márton**): from the Hungarian personal name *Márton* (see MARTIN 1).

GIVEN NAMES Hungarian 8%. *Laszlo* (3), *Antal* (2), *Arpad* (2), *Geza* (2), *Andras, Bela, Denes, Endre, Gaza, Imre, Istvan, Janos.*

Martone (984) Southern Italian: **1.** from an augmentative of the Old Tuscan personal name *Marte*, from Latin *Mars*, genitive *Martis* (the Roman god of war). **2.** from MARTINO, with a change of suffix.

GIVEN NAMES Italian 11%. *Angelo* (2), *Carmine* (2), *Dino* (2), *Giacomo* (2), *Lorenzo* (2), *Rocco* (2), *Salvatore* (2), *Agostino, Aldo, Carmel, Ciro, Clemente.*

Martorana (469) Southern Italian (Sicily): variant of MARTORANO.

GIVEN NAMES Italian 26%. *Salvatore* (5), *Franco* (3), *Vito* (3), *Angelo* (2), *Antonio* (2), *Giovanni* (2), *Aldo, Calogero, Carmelo, Domenico, Filippo, Francesco, Mario, Teodora.*

Martorano (402) Italian: habitational name from either of two places in Emilia-Romagna named Martorano, but more probably, in an American context, a habitational name from Martirano (see MARTURANO).

GIVEN NAMES Italian 21%. *Sal* (6), *Salvatore* (4), *Angelo, Dino, Gustavo, Marco, Mario, Vito.*

Martorella (130) Italian (Sicily): from a feminine diminutive of the personal name *Martoro* (see MARTORELLI).

GIVEN NAMES Italian 17%. *Dante* (2), *Mario* (2), *Aldo, Alfredo, Francesco.*

Martorelli (175) Italian: patronymic form of a diminutive of **Martoro**, probably a variant of MARTIRE.

GIVEN NAMES Italian 21%. *Sal* (2), *Angelo, Mario, Pasquale, Quido, Ricco, Rosario, Salvatore.*

Martos (116) Spanish or Portuguese: unexplained.

GIVEN NAMES Spanish 35%. *Humberto* (3), *Jorge* (3), *Jose* (3), *Alfredo* (2), *Francisco* (2), *Jesus* (2), *Joaquin* (2), *Armando, Carlos, Cesar, Dionisio, Eduardo; Antonio* (2), *Francesca, Leonardo.*

Marts (504) German: probably a variant of **März** (see MARTZ).

Martsolf (115) French (Alsatian): from a derivative of the Latin personal name *Marcellus* (see MARCELLO).

FOREBEARS The surname Martzolf is associated with Memmelshoffen and Betschdorf in Alsace, France. In 1833, Johann Heinrich and Diebold Martzolf came to America and settled around Hanover and Abottstown, PA.

Marttila (153) Finnish: habitational name from a farm so named, from the personal name *Martti*, Finnish form of *Martin* + the local suffix *-la*, i.e. 'Martti's place'. The name can be traced back to the 15th century.

GIVEN NAMES Finnish 6%. *Annikki, Eino, Paavo, Risto.*

Martucci (835) Southern Italian: **1.** from a plural derivative of MARTA or MARTE. **2.** otherwise possibly from a derivative of the root *Mart-* of *Martinus*. Compare MARTONE 2.

GIVEN NAMES Italian 12%. *Angelo* (4), *Vito* (3), *Pasquale* (2), *Antonio, Augustino, Carmela, Carmine, Dino, Domenic, Elio, Rocco.*

Marturano (143) Southern Italian: probably a habitational name from either of two places in Catanzaro province: Martirano or Marturano Lombardo.

GIVEN NAMES Italian 21%. *Angelo, Antonio, Caesar, Carmela, Carmine, Salvatore, Sofio.*

Martus (164) German: humanistic name, probably a variant spelling of **Martius**, Latinized form of MERZ.

Marty (1703) South German, Swiss German, southern French, and English: from the personal name *Marty*, a pet form of MARTIN.

Martyn (655) **1.** English and Dutch: variant spelling of MARTIN 1. **2.** Ukrainian: from the personal name *Martyn* (see MARTIN).

Martz (3147) German: **1.** (also **Märtz**): from a nickname or personal name for someone who was born or baptized in the month of March, Middle High German *merz* (see MARCH 2), or who had some other special connection with the month, such as owing a feudal obligation then. **2.** (**Märtz**): from a short form of a personal name such as MARTIN 1 or MARK 1. **3.** from a Germanic personal name, *Marizo* (which became *Mar(t)zo*), a pet form of compound names formed with *mari* 'famous' as the first element.

Martzall (127) Altered form of Alsatian **Martzolf** (see MARTSOLF).

Maruca (302) Southern Italian: nickname from Calabrian dialect *maruca* 'snail' (Latin *maruca*).

GIVEN NAMES Italian 13%. *Umberto* (3), *Angelo, Caesar, Federico, Ippolito, Natale, Santo.*

Marucci (351) Italian: from a patronymic form of **Maruccio**, a derivative of MARE or MARI, or a reduced form of *Mariuccio*, a derivative of MARIO.

GIVEN NAMES Italian 14%. *Rocco* (3), *Antonio* (2), *Silvio* (2), *Angelo, Carmela,*

Domenic, Donato, Egidio, Guido, Licinio, Lorenzo, Luciano.

Marullo (217) Italian: **1.** from a pet form of MARI. **2.** from the medieval Greek surname **Maroulles, Maroullos**. This is either a metronymic from *Maroulla*, a pet form of MARIA, or an occupational name for someone who grew and sold lettuces, modern Greek *marouli* 'lettuce', medieval Greek *maroulion*.

FOREBEARS The Byzantine humanist scholar Michael Maroullos (d. 1499) fled to Venice after the fall of Constantinople (1453) and ultimately settled in Florence, where he was an influential figure in the Italian Renaissance.

GIVEN NAMES Italian 15%. *Salvatore* (3), *Carlo* (2), *Biagio, Gaetano, Gennaro, Nunzio, Paolo, Vittoria.*

Marum (119) Norwegian: habitational name from either of two farmsteads named *Marheimar* in Old Norse, most likely from *marr* 'horse' + *heimr* 'homestead', 'farmstead'.

GIVEN NAMES German 4%. *Hans, Helmut.*

Maruna (101) Czech: from a derivative of the personal names MAREK or MARTIN.

Marusak (130) **1.** Czech and Slovak (**Marušák**), Polish (**Maruszak**), and Ukrainian (**Marushak**): metronymic from Czech *Maruše*, or some other Slavic pet form of the female personal name *Maria* (see MARIE). **2.** In Polish and Ukrainian it is possibly also a nickname, from a derivative of the dialect word *marucha* 'bear'.

Maruschak (125) Germanized spelling of Slavic MARUSAK.

Marusich (117) Croatian (**Marušić**) and Slovenian (**Marušič**): metronymic from the personal name *Maruša*, derivative of *Marija* (see MARIA).

Maruska (253) Czech (**Maruška**) and Ukrainian (**Marushka**): from a pet form of the female personal name Czech *Maruše*, Ukrainian *Marush*, itself a pet form of MARIA (Czech *Máří*, Ukrainian *Marija*).

Marut (150) Polish: from a derivative of the personal names *Marcin, Marek*, or *Maria*.

GIVEN NAMES Polish 7%. *Krzysztof* (2), *Agnieszka, Tadeusz.*

Maruyama (291) Japanese (mainly central Japan): topographic name meaning 'round mountain'. It can be derived from an actual mountain name or from any of the the many large, round, man-made mounds from the tomb period (*c.* 250–710), found throughout Japan.

GIVEN NAMES Japanese 70%. *Hiroshi* (4), *Kazuo* (4), *Toru* (4), *Takashi* (3), *Akiko* (2), *Akira* (2), *Atsuko* (2), *Hideo* (2), *Hiroyuki* (2), *Kiyoshi* (2), *Koji* (2), *Mieko* (2).

Marvel (1419) English: **1.** nickname for a person considered prodigious in some way, from Middle English, Old French *merveille* 'miracle' (Latin *mirabilia*, originally neuter plural of the adjective *mirabilis* 'admirable', 'amazing'). The nickname was no doubt sometimes given with mocking intent. **2.** (of Norman origin): habitational name, from places called Merville. The one in Nord is named from Old French *mendre* 'smaller', 'lesser' (Latin *minor*) + *ville* 'settlement'; that in Calvados seems to have as its first element a Germanic personal name, probably a short form of a compound name with the first element *mari*, *meri* 'famous'.

Marvin (3997) English: **1.** from the Middle English personal name *Merewine* (Old English *Maerwin*, from *mær* 'fame' + *win* 'friend'). **2.** from the Old English personal name *Merefinn*, derived from Old Norse *Mora-Finnr*. **3.** from the Old English personal name *Mærwynn*, composed of the elements *mær* 'famous', 'renowned' + *wynn* 'joy'. **4.** from the Welsh personal name *Merfyn*, *Mervyn*, composed of the Old Welsh elements *mer*, which probably means 'marrow', + *myn* 'eminent'.
FOREBEARS Mathew Marvin was one of the founders of Hartford, CT, (coming from Cambridge, MA, with Thomas Hooker) in 1635.

Marwitz (107) German: habitational name from a place so named in Brandenburg, Pomerania, or East Prussia.
GIVEN NAMES German 7%. *Kurt, Otto*.

Marx (5279) Dutch, German, Czech, and Jewish (western Ashkenazic): variant spelling of MARKS 3.
GIVEN NAMES German 4%. *Otto* (8), *Hans* (6), *Heinz* (5), *Kurt* (4), *Gunther* (3), *Manfred* (3), *Franz* (2), *Guenther* (2), *Lothar* (2), *Ulrich* (2), *Benno, Bernhard*.

Marxen (200) North German: patronymic from MARK 1.
GIVEN NAMES German 4%. *Hans, Horst*.

Marxer (120) Dutch: patronymic from the personal name *Marx* (see MARK).

Mary (361) French: habitational name from places in Saône-et-Loire, Seine-et-Marne, and Nièvre, named in Latin as *Mariacum* 'estate of Marius'.
GIVEN NAMES French 6%. *Michel, Myrtha, Pierre*.

Maryanski (109) Polish: variant of **Marjański**: **1.** habitational name for someone from a place called Martjany in Toruń voivodeship. **2.** possibly also a derivative of the personal name *Marian* with the common surname suffix -*ski*.

Maryott (136) English: variant spelling of MARRIOTT.

Marz (402) German (**März**): variant spelling of MARTZ.

Marzan (184) Spanish (**Marzán**): habitational name from any of the many places in Galicia named Marzán, from Latin *villa Martiani*, a derivative of the personal name *Martius*.
GIVEN NAMES Spanish 46%. *Jose* (5), *Ana* (4), *Carlos* (2), *Miguel* (2), *Pedro* (2), *Adelaida, Agapita, Angel, Aniceto, Camilo, Carolina, Catalina; Antonio, Geronimo, Guido, Leonardo*.

Marzano (580) Southern Italian: habitational name from either of two places in Campania: Marzano Appio, in Caserta province, or Marzano di Nola, in Avellino province.
GIVEN NAMES Italian 11%. *Angelo* (5), *Vito* (3), *Ciro* (2), *Guido* (2), *Antonio, Gennaro, Giuseppe, Nunzio, Rocci, Rocco, Salvatore, Santo*.

Marzec (362) Polish: from Polish *marzec* (derived from Latin *Martius (mensis)*, from the name of the god *Mars*), a nickname or personal name for someone who was born or baptized in the month of March or who had some other special connection with the month, such as owing a feudal obligation then.
GIVEN NAMES Polish 10%. *Tadeusz* (4), *Boleslaw, Cecylia, Edyta, Halina, Marcin, Stanislaw, Wladyslaw, Zdzislaw, Zigmund, Zosia*.

Marzella (147) Italian: from a feminine pet form MARZO.
GIVEN NAMES Italian 19%. *Angelo* (2), *Antonio, Carlo, Pasquale, Remo, Reno, Ugo, Vincenzo*.

Marzen (113) North German: variant of **Märtz** (see MARTZ).

Marzette (123) Possibly an altered spelling of French **Marzet**, a habitational name from the Rhone region.
GIVEN NAME French 4%. *Monique*.

Marzilli (160) Italian: **1.** from the patronymic or plural form of a pet form of *Marzio*, from Latin *Martius*, a derivative of *Mars*, genitive *Martis*, the Roman god of war. **2.** possibly from a patronymic or plural form of MARZULLO, from a pet form of the personal name MARZO.
GIVEN NAMES Italian 22%. *Rocco* (5), *Luigi* (2), *Salvatore* (2), *Antonio, Franca, Gaetano, Santino, Tommaso, Vincenzo*.

Marzo (174) **1.** Spanish and Italian: from a nickname or personal name given to someone who was born or baptized in the month of March, Spanish and Italian *Marzo* (Latin *Martius (mensis)*, from the name of the war god *Mars*), or nickname for someone who had some other special connection with the month, such as owing a feudal obligation then. **2.** Italian: from a reduced form of the personal name *Marzio* (see MARZILLI).
GIVEN NAMES Italian 11%; Spanish 9%. *Salvatore* (2), *Cataldo, Egidio, Leonardo, Massimiliano; Mariano* (3), *Blanca, Javier, Juan, Lourdes, Orlando, Pastora, Rosita, Teresita*.

Marzolf (385) German and French (Alsace): from a germanicized form of the personal name *Marcellus*.
GIVEN NAMES German 4%. *Erna, Kurt, Reinhold*.

Marzullo (505) Southern Italian: from a pet form of MARZO.
GIVEN NAMES Italian 18%. *Angelo* (3), *Carmelo* (3), *Vito* (3), *Giovanni* (2), *Sal*

(2), *Aldo, Alfonse, Benedetto, Domenic, Donato, Francesco, Giuseppe*.

Mas (317) **1.** North German and Dutch: from a short form of THOMAS. Compare MAAS 1 and MASS. **2.** Catalan and southern French (Occitan): topographic name for someone who lived in an isolated dwelling in the country, rather than in a village, from Catalan and Occitan *mas* 'farmstead' (Late Latin *mansum, mansus*).
GIVEN NAMES Spanish 39%. *Ramon* (7), *Francisco* (6), *Jose* (6), *Juan* (5), *Pedro* (5), *Jaime* (4), *Luis* (4), *Carlos* (3), *Raul* (3), *Ana* (2), *Angel* (2), *Aquiles* (2).

Masaitis (110) Lithuanian: patronymic from the personal name *Masys*.
GIVEN NAMES Lithuanian 6%. *Aleksas, Antanas, Brone*.

Masaki (157) Japanese: variously written, mostly with the characters for 'correct' and 'tree'. It is not very common, and different families bearing this name are descended from the TAIRA, northern FUJIWARA, and MINAMOTO clans.
GIVEN NAMES Japanese 65%. *Koichi* (5), *Ichiro* (3), *Kenji* (2), *Ryo* (2), *Takahisa* (2), *Akira, Etsuro, Fumio, Hideki, Hiroshi, Hirotsugu, Hiroya*.

Masar (100) Origin unidentified.

Masarik (125) Czech (**Masařík**) and Slovak: occupational name from *masař* 'butcher'.
FOREBEARS Tomáš Masaryk (1850–1937) was the first president of the Czechoslovak Republic (1918–35). His son Jan Masaryk (1886–1948) was foreign minister (1941–48), who disappeared in mysterious circumstances at the time of the Communist takeover.
GIVEN NAME French 4%. *Ludger*.

Mascarenas (511) Spanish (**Mascareñas**; Philippines **Mascarenas**): variant of Portuguese MASCARENHAS.
GIVEN NAMES Spanish 20%. *Jose* (8), *Manuel* (7), *Alfonso* (3), *Carlos* (3), *Eloy* (3), *Cresencio* (2), *Ruben* (2), *Alicia, Amalia, Apolonio, Benedicto, Benito*.

Mascarenhas (159) Portuguese: habitational name from one of the towns called *Mascarenhas* in Portugal. This name is also found in India, where it was taken by Portuguese colonists.
GIVEN NAMES Portuguese 9%; Spanish 5%; German 4%; Indian 4%; Italian 4%. *Henrique, Joaquim; Luis* (2), *Amaro, Ana, Jose, Julio, Mario; Franz* (2), *Konrad; Dinesh, Snehlata, Vijay; Angelo, Giovanni, Sylvana*.

Mascari (423) Italian: **1.** patronymic or plural form of MASCARO. **2.** possibly a habitational name from Mascari in Colosimi, Cosenza province.
GIVEN NAMES Italian 15%. *Salvatore* (3), *Carlo, Gino, Luciano, Mario, Rocci, Sal*.

Mascaro (598) **1.** Italian and Catalan (**Mascaró**): from the Old Tuscan personal name *Mascaro*. **2.** Italian: possibly from Arabic *al-mu'askari* 'soldier'. **3.** Catalan from a medieval personal name of Germanic origin.

GIVEN NAMES Italian 22%; Spanish 9%. *Angelo* (8), *Pasquale* (3), *Alberto* (2), *Carmine* (2), *Emilio* (2), *Giuseppe* (2), *Guillermo* (2), *Mario* (2), *Aldo*, *Attilio*, *Gaspare*, *Gildo*, *Orlando*, *Rocco*, *Salvatore*; *Jorge* (3), *Juan* (2), *Carlos*, *Jose*, *Marisa*, *Pedro*.

Masch (136) **1.** North German: topographic name from Middle Low German *masch* 'marsh', 'fen', a variant of *marsch*. Compare English MARSH. **2.** German (Alemannic; **Mäsch**): nickname from Middle High German *mast* 'fat', 'stout'. Compare MAST 3. **3.** Jewish (Ashkenazic): variant of MASH.

GIVEN NAMES German 8%; Jewish 6%. *Fritz* (2), *Erwin*, *Horst*, *Ralf*; *Ber*, *Sima*.

Mascher (100) German: habitational name for someone from a place called Masch or Maschau in Westphalia and Bavaria.

Masching (106) Possibly German: unexplained.

Maschino (254) French (from Lorraine) or German: probably a pet form of THOMAS.

Maschke (154) German (of Slavic origin): from a pet form of the personal names THOMAS (compare MAAS), MAS, or MATTHIAS.

Masci (248) Southern Italian: **1.** variant of MASI. **2.** from a patronymic or plural form of MASCIO.

GIVEN NAMES Italian 32%. *Angelo* (4), *Antonio* (4), *Carlo* (2), *Armando*, *Berardino*, *Demetrio*, *Fernando*, *Gennaro*, *Gilda*, *Gino*, *Giosue*, *Justino*, *Margarita*, *Mario*, *Nicoletta*, *Pierina*, *Pietro*, *Roberto*, *Rocco*.

Mascia (404) Southern Italian: **1.** from a feminine form of MASCIO. **2.** occupational name from Sicilian *mascia* 'dressmaker'. **3.** from Salentine *mascia* 'mask'.

GIVEN NAMES Italian 18%. *Angelo* (7), *Carmine* (3), *Antonio*, *Cosmo*, *Domenic*, *Gino*, *Giorgio*, *Giovanni*, *Giuseppe*, *Salvatore*.

Masciantonio (137) Southern Italian: from a compound name, a title of respect, formed from *mascio*, dialect form of *mastro* 'master craftsman' (see MASCIO) + the personal name ANTONIO.

GIVEN NAMES Italian 25%. *Angelo* (5), *Attilio*, *Florio*, *Gino*, *Nicolo*, *Piera*.

Masciarelli (197) Southern Italian: from a diminutive of **Masciari**.

GIVEN NAMES Italian 24%. *Mario* (3), *Dante* (2), *Rocco* (2), *Alberico*, *Amalio*, *Antonio*, *Armando*, *Camillo*, *Domenic*, *Luca*, *Marco*.

Mascio (183) Southern Italian: **1.** variant of MASI (or the Albanian form *Mashi*). **2.** (Salento and Apulia): from a dialect form of MASTRO.

GIVEN NAMES Italian 9%. *Antonio*, *Carlo*, *Gino*, *Luigi*, *Paolo*, *Salvatore*.

Mascioli (177) Italian: from a diminutive of MASCIO.

GIVEN NAMES Italian 28%. *Rocco* (4), *Mario* (3), *Angelo* (2), *Antonio* (2), *Dino* (2), *Aldo*, *Bernardino*, *Claudio*, *Colombo*, *Domenic*, *Donato*, *Fernando*, *Giustino*, *Guido*, *Lelio*, *Nino*, *Nuncio*.

Mascola (194) Southern Italian: variant of MASCOLO.

GIVEN NAMES Italian 11%. *Sal* (4), *Carmel*, *Cosmo*, *Salvatore*.

Mascolo (258) Southern Italian: **1.** from southern Italian *màscolo*, *màsculo* 'male', used as personal name. **2.** from a short form of the medieval personal name *Dolcemascolo* 'sweet man'.

GIVEN NAMES Italian 14%. *Carlo* (2), *Salvatore* (2), *Angelo*, *Antonio*, *Carmine*, *Dino*, *Gennaro*, *Sal*.

Mascorro (261) Spanish (mainly Mexico): unexplained.

GIVEN NAMES Spanish 46%. *Jose* (10), *Jesus* (4), *Alfredo* (3), *Rafael* (3), *Ramon* (3), *Roberto* (3), *Angel* (2), *Ernesto* (2), *Luis* (2), *Neftali* (2), *Pedro* (2), *Salvador* (2); *Antonio* (4), *Camillo*, *Ceasar*, *Cesario*, *Luciano*.

Masden (259) English: probably a variant of MARSDEN.

Mase (380) **1.** Jewish (eastern Ashkenazic): from a Hebrew acronym meaning 'of the seed of Aharon the priest'. **2.** Japanese: written with characters meaning 'space' and 'strait'. This name is not common in Japan.

GIVEN NAMES Japanese 4%. *Eriko*, *Hiroyuki*, *Junji*, *Kazumi*, *Makoto*, *Shinji*, *Yukari*.

Masek (573) Czech (**Mašek**): from a short form of the personal name *Tomášek* (see TOMASEK) or possibly of a personal name beginning with *Ma-*, e.g. *Matěj* (see MATTHEW), MARTIN, or *Mauricius* (see MORRIS).

Masel (104) German: from a pet form of a short form of THOMAS.

GIVEN NAME German 6%. *Kurt*.

Masella (258) Italian: from a feminine pet form of the personal name *Maso* (see MASI).

GIVEN NAMES Italian 22%. *Mario* (4), *Rinaldo* (2), *Carmine*, *Dino*, *Domenico*, *Gaetano*, *Leandro*, *Nino*, *Orlando*, *Pasquale*, *Ugo*, *Virgilio*, *Vittorio*.

Maselli (508) Southern Italian: patronymic from a pet form of *Maso* (see MASI).

GIVEN NAMES Italian 26%. *Mario* (3), *Vito* (3), *Donato* (2), *Enrico* (2), *Aldo*, *Alfonso*, *Angelo*, *Augusto*, *Claudio*, *Dino*, *Domenic*, *Egidio*, *Firmino*, *Flavio*, *Gino*, *Giorgio*.

Masengale (121) English: variant of **Masongill** (see MASSENGILL).

GIVEN NAME French 4%. *Vernice*.

Maser (709) **1.** German: nickname for someone with boils or lumpy skin, or perhaps for a hunchback, from Middle High German *maser* 'lump', 'protuberance'. **2.** German and English: from Middle High

German *maser*, Middle English *maser* 'maple-wood bowl' (Old French *masere*, of Germanic origin), hence a metonymic occupational name for a wood-turner producing such ware. **3.** English: variant spelling of **Macer**, an occupational name for a mace-bearer, from Old French *maissier*, *massier*, a derivative of Old French *masse* 'mace'. **4.** German (**Maaser**): pet form of THOMAS.

Mash (602) **1.** English: variant of MARSH. **2.** Americanized spelling of German MASCH. **3.** Jewish (Ashkenazic): unexplained; possibly an acronymic name.

Mashak (125) Americanized form of a Slavic pet form of THOMAS.

Mashaw (151) Origin unidentified. It may be an Americanized form of French *Machaut*.

Mashburn (2517) English: probably a variant of MARSHBURN.

FOREBEARS Edward Mashburn came from London to Onslow Co., NC, in 1698.

Mashek (258) Americanized form of Czech MASEK.

Masi (1053) Italian: patronymic or plural form of *Maso*, a short form of the personal name *Tommaso* (see THOMAS).

GIVEN NAMES Italian 23%. *Angelo* (9), *Carmine* (5), *Mario* (5), *Vito* (5), *Carlo* (4), *Antonio* (3), *Alfonso* (2), *Armando* (2), *Filomena* (2), *Gerardo* (2), *Giovanni* (2), *Salvatore* (2), *Alfonse*, *Alfonsina*, *Amato*, *Anello*, *Canio*, *Emilio*.

Masias (117) **1.** Catalan: variant spelling of **Masies**, habitational name from any of numerous places called Masies, from the plural of *masia* 'farmstead' (from Late Latin *mansum*, *mansus*). **2.** Spanish: variant spelling of MACIAS.

GIVEN NAMES Spanish 27%. *Celestino* (2), *Julio* (2), *Miguel* (2), *Sergio* (2), *Armando*, *Balbino*, *Bonifacia*, *Eleno*, *Enedina*, *Humberto*, *Javier*, *Jose*.

Masiello (579) Southern Italian (chiefly Neapolitan): from a pet form of the personal name *Tommaso* (see THOMAS).

GIVEN NAMES Italian 19%. *Carlo* (3), *Rocco* (3), *Angelo* (2), *Carmine* (2), *Franco* (2), *Salvatore* (2), *Antonio*, *Carmino*, *Domenic*, *Domenica*, *Francesco*, *Mauro*.

Masih (104) Arabic and Muslim (found in the Indian subcontinent as well as in the Arab world): from a personal name based on Arabic *masīḥ* 'Messiah'. It is sometimes found in combinations such as *'Abd-ul Masīḥ* 'servant of the Messiah'. It is used by Christians as well as Muslims. 'Isa (Jesus) is mentioned as the Messiah and a Prophet in the Qur'an (4:171).

GIVEN NAMES Muslim 41%; Indian 23%. *Javed* (2), *Abu*, *Amir*, *Aqueel*, *Ashraf*, *Aslam*, *Bashir*, *Didar*, *Fazal*, *Inayat*, *Jamal*, *Maqbool*; *Ajay*, *Amrit*, *Anil*, *Arun*, *Ashish*, *Ashok*, *Lalit*, *Manjula*, *Meena*, *Neelesh*, *Nirmal*, *Ravi*.

Masin (173) **1.** Czech (**Mašín**): from the personal name *Mašín*, a pet form of any personal name beginning with *Ma-*, in particular *Matěj* (see MATTHEW), MARTIN, and *Mauritius* (see MORRIS). It may also be from a short form of *Tomáš* (see THOMAS). **2.** Dutch: from a pet form of THOMAS. **3.** Italian (Veneto): shortened form of MASINO.

Masini (192) Italian: patronymic or plural form of MASINO.

GIVEN NAMES Italian 26% French 4%. *Duilio* (2), *Mauro* (2), *Aldo, Antonio, Assunta, Dino, Domenic, Ermanno, Fabio, Giorgio, Lino, Marco, Mario, Massimo, Pasquale, Pio, Rico, Telmo*; *Camille, Stephane.*

Masino (297) Italian: from a short form of **Tommasino**, a pet form of the personal name *Tommaso* (see THOMAS).

GIVEN NAMES Italian 7%. *Angelo* (2), *Ciro, Larraine.*

Mask (1023) **1.** German and Dutch: from a pet form of the personal name THOMAS. **2.** English: unexplained.

Maska (107) Probably German or Dutch: variant of MASKE.

Maske (457) German and Dutch: from a pet form of the personal name *Tom(m)aso* (see THOMAS).

GIVEN NAMES Italian 10%. *Nunzio* (2), *Pio* (2), *Antonio, Fiore, Sal.*

Maskell (374) English and Scottish: variant of MARSHALL, derived from an Anglo-Norman French form of Old French *maresc(h)al* 'marshal'.

Masker (279) **1.** English or Scottish: unexplained. **2.** German and Dutch: probably a variant of MASKE.

Maslak (136) **1.** Polish (**Maślak**), Ukrainian, and Jewish (from Poland): **2.** from the vocabulary word *maślak*, name of a species of edible fungus. **3.** patronymic from a personal name or nickname derived from *masło* 'butter', perhaps a metonymic occupational name for maker or seller of dairy produce, or a nickname for someone who was 'as soft as butter'.

GIVEN NAME Polish 4%. *Kazimierz.*

Maslanka (341) Polish (**Maślanka**) and Jewish (from Poland): Polish nickname or metonymic occupational name, or Jewish ornamental name, from Polish *maślanka* 'buttermilk'.

GIVEN NAMES Polish 7%. *Bartosz* (2), *Beata, Boguslawa, Janina, Krystyna, Piotr, Stanislaw, Stanislawa, Zygmunt.*

Maslar (124) Serbian: occupational name for a producer of dairy products, from *maslo* 'butter'.

Maslen (141) English: variant spelling of MASLIN.

Masley (175) Perhaps an Americanized spelling of Ukrainian **Maslij** or Polish **Maślej**, from *masło* 'butter', hence probably a metonymic occupational name for a dairyman or perhaps a nickname for a fat person.

Maslin (233) English and French: **1.** from the medieval personal name *Masselin*. This originated as an Old French pet form of Germanic names with the first element *mathal* 'speech', 'counsel'. However, it was later used as a pet form of MATTHEW. Compare MACE. A feminine form, *Mazelina*, was probably originally a pet form of *Matilda*. **2.** possibly a metonymic occupational name for a maker of wooden bowls, from Middle English, Old French *maselin* 'bowl or goblet of maple wood' (a diminutive of Old French *masere* 'maple wood', of Germanic origin). In some cases it may derive from the homonymous dialect terms *maslin*, one of which means 'brass' (Old English *mæslen, mæstling*), the other 'mixed grain' (Old French *mesteillon*).

Masloski (114) Variant of Polish **Masłow-ski** (see MASLOWSKI).

Maslow (272) **1.** Russian (**Maslov**): patronymic from *maslo* 'butter', presumably applied as a metonymic occupational name for a dairyman or a seller of dairy products. **2.** Possibly a shortened form of Polish and Jewish MASLOWSKI.

GIVEN NAMES Jewish 4%; French 4%. *Eph, Yaakov*; *Emile, Luce.*

Maslowski (545) Polish (**Masłowski**) and Jewish (eastern Ashkenazic): habitational name for someone from places called Masłowo, Masłowice, or Masłów.

GIVEN NAMES Polish 8%. *Jerzy* (2), *Mikolaj* (2), *Bogdan, Grazyna, Henryka, Karol, Leszek, Mieczyslaw, Ryszard, Weislaw, Zdzislaw, Zigmund.*

Maslyn (112) English: variant spelling of MASLIN.

Mason (54197) **1.** English and Scottish: occupational name for a stonemason, Middle English, Old French *mas(s)on*. Compare MACHEN. Stonemasonry was a hugely important craft in the Middle Ages. **2.** Italian (Veneto): from a short form of MASONE. **3.** French: from a regional variant of *maison* 'house'.

FOREBEARS George Mason (1725–92), the American colonial statesman who framed the VA Bill of Rights and Constitution, which was used as a model by Thomas Jefferson when drafting the Declaration of Independence, was a VA planter, fourth in descent from George Mason (?1629–?86), a royalist soldier of the English Civil War who had received land grants in VA. As well as being prominent in the affairs of VA, the family also produced the first governor of MI. Two other families of this name were among the early English settlers in America. John Mason (1586–1635) was born in King's Lynn, Norfolk, became governor of Newfoundland in 1615, and was one of the founders of NH. His namesake, John Mason (?1600–72), emigrated before 1633 and was one of the founders of Norwich, CT.

Masone (284) Italian: from an augmentative of *Maso*, a short form of the personal name *Tom(m)aso* (see THOMAS).

GIVEN NAMES Italian 10%. *Nunzio* (2), *Pio* (2), *Antonio, Fiore, Sal.*

Masoner (261) German (Tyrol): probably from a Rhaeto-Romansh occupational term for a stonemason or bricklayer.

Masood (154) Muslim: from a personal name based on Arabic *mas'ūd* 'lucky', 'fortunate', 'happy'. 'Abdullah ibn Mas'ūd was one of the Companions of the Prophet Muhammad.

GIVEN NAMES Muslim 80%; Indian 5%. *Syed* (8), *Khalid* (4), *Tariq* (4), *Ahmed* (3), *Mohammad* (3), *Shahid* (3), *Adnan* (2), *Ahmad* (2), *Anwer* (2), *Arshad* (2), *Imran* (2), *Javed* (2); *Anju, Asim, Burhan, Nehal, Shaila.*

Masotti (136) Italian: from the personal name *Masotto*, a pet form of *Maso*, a short form of *Tom(m)aso* (see THOMAS).

GIVEN NAMES Italian 18%. *Vito* (3), *Dino, Luigi, Pasquale, Reno, Umberto, Vincenza.*

Masri (220) Muslim: ethnic name for an Egyptian, a variant of Arabic *Miṣrī* 'Egyptian'. Compare MITRI.

GIVEN NAMES Muslim 59%. *Nabil* (4), *Zahi* (3), *Adnan* (2), *Ahmad* (2), *Akram* (2), *Bashar* (2), *Bassam* (2), *Fouad* (2), *Ghassan* (2), *Hani* (2), *Hassan* (2), *Issam* (2).

Mass (848) **1.** North German and Dutch: from a short form of the personal name THOMAS. Compare MAAS, MAS. **2.** Jewish (Ashkenazic): metonymic occupational name from German *Mass* 'measure', 'measurement'.

Massa (1984) Southern Italian: habitational name from any of various places called Massa, for example Massa Lubrense or Massa di Somma, both in Naples province, or Masse d'Albe in Aquila, all named from medieval Latin *massa* 'holding', 'estate' (from Latin *massa* 'mass', 'lump', 'pile', Greek *maza*).

GIVEN NAMES Italian 7%. *Salvatore* (8), *Angelo* (6), *Sal* (5), *Antonio* (4), *Silvio* (2), *Annamarie, Biagio, Caesar, Carmela, Dante, Elisabetta, Ennio.*

Massad (220) Altered spelling of Dutch **Massaad**, a variant of MASSART.

Massar (190) French (found mainly in French-speaking Belgium): from a short form of *Thomassard*, a pet form of the personal name THOMAS.

Massara (154) Italian: feminine form of MASSARO or from the equivalent occupational or status name in medieval Greek, *massaras* 'peasant', 'share cropper', from *massaria* 'small farm'.

GIVEN NAMES Italian 15%. *Angelo* (2), *Camillo* (2), *Attilio, Marco, Nuncio.*

Massarelli (161) Italian: patronymic or plural form of *Massarello*, a diminutive of MASSARO.

GIVEN NAMES Italian 8%. *Angelo* (2), *Mauro* (2), *Dario*, *Massimo*.

Massari (327) Southern Italian: patronymic or plural form of MASSARO.

GIVEN NAMES Italian 18%; Spanish 7%. *Mario* (4), *Aldo* (2), *Alessandro*, *Angelo*, *Domenic*, *Florio*, *Mariano*, *Marina*, *Nicola*, *Reinaldo*, *Rocco*, *Salvatore*, *Silvano*, *Tito*; *Esteban*, *Jose*, *Wilfredo*.

Massaro (1621) Italian: occupational or status name from *massaro*, which in northern Italy denoted a tenant farmer or share cropper and in central and southern Italy could also denote an agent or steward of a rural estate, from medieval Latin *massarius*, a derivative of *massa* 'farm', 'estate'. Compare MASSA 1.

GIVEN NAMES Italian 16%. *Angelo* (16), *Salvatore* (8), *Carmine* (4), *Pasquale* (4), *Rocco* (4), *Antonio* (3), *Gennaro* (3), *Vito* (3), *Carlo* (2), *Gaetano* (2), *Nunzio* (2), *Antoninette*.

Massart (127) French: from a pet form of THOMAS.

GIVEN NAMES French 7%; German 4%. *Francois* (2), *Emile*; *Fritz*.

Masse (1223) **1.** English: variant of MACE 1. **2.** French (Picardy): metonymic occupational name from *masse* 'mace', 'hammer'. **3.** French: habitational name from places called Masse (Allier and Cô-d'Or), or La Masse (Eure, Lot, Puy-de-Dôme, Saône-et-Loire). **4.** French (**Massé**): habitational name from a place called Massé in Maine-et-Loire, so named from Gallo-Roman *Macciacum* (from the personal name *Maccius* + the locative suffix *-acum*). **5.** Dutch: from Middle Dutch *masse* 'clog'; 'cudgel', perhaps a metonymic occupational name for someone who wielded a club. **6.** Dutch: possibly a variant of MAAS 1, or a patronymic from MAS.

GIVEN NAMES French 15%. *Armand* (11), *Marcel* (8), *Normand* (8), *Pierre* (6), *Lucien* (2), *Michel* (2), *Serge* (2), *Alain*, *Alban*, *Alcide*, *Andre*, *Aurele*.

Massee (142) Possibly an altered spelling of **Massé** (see MASSE 4) or MASSEY.

GIVEN NAME French 4%. *Germain*.

Massena (103) Southern French: probably from a pet form of MASSON.

Massenburg (328) Origin unidentified. This name is recorded in VA in the early 18th century. It may be an altered form of English **Massingberd**, the etymology of which is likewise uncertain. Reaney suggests Old Norse *messing* 'brass', 'brazen' + *berd* 'beard', but the early citations are from Sussex and Surrey, which were not areas of Norse settlement.

Massengale (1192) English: variant of **Masongill** (see MASSENGILL).

Massengill (1256) English: habitational name from a place in North Yorkshire called Masongill. The surname has died out in England.

Masser (334) English (Midlands): possibly a variant of MESSER.

Massett (162) Probably a variant spelling of English and French **Masset**, from a feminine pet form of the personal name *Masse*, a variant of MATTHEW.

GIVEN NAMES Irish 7%. *Brendan*, *Eamon*.

Massetti (120) Italian: patronymic or plural form of *Massetto*, a pet form of the personal name *Tommaso* (see THOMAS).

GIVEN NAMES Italian 14%. *Amerigo*, *Angelo*, *Ennio*, *Pasquale*, *Reno*, *Secondo*.

Massey (18537) **1.** English and Scottish (of Norman origin) and French: habitational name from any of various places in northern France which get their names from the Gallo-Roman personal name *Maccius* + the locative suffix *-acum*. **2.** English (of Norman origin): habitational name from Marcy in La Manche. This surname is preserved in the English place name Stondon Massey. **3.** English: from a pet form of MATTHEW. **4.** Altered spelling of French **Massé** (see MASSE 4).

Massi (300) Italian: patronymic or plural form of MASSO.

GIVEN NAMES Italian 24%. *Guido* (3), *Dante* (2), *Geno* (2), *Pasquale* (2), *Carlo*, *Enrico*, *Galileo*, *Guilio*, *Mario*, *Nino*, *Norberto*, *Orlando*.

Massicotte (159) Altered spelling of French **Massicot**, from a pet form of THOMAS.

GIVEN NAMES French 11%. *Cecile*, *Fernand*, *Jean Louis*, *Marcel*, *Mathieu*, *Normand*, *Roch*.

Massie (3581) Scottish (Aberdeen): variant spelling of MASSEY.

Massimino (199) Italian: from a pet form of MASSIMO (Latin *Maximinus*).

GIVEN NAMES Italian 14%. *Mario* (3), *Sal* (2), *Concetta*, *Cosimo*, *Enrico*, *Italo*, *Lorenzo*, *Primo*, *Reno*, *Rinaldo*.

Massimo (149) Italian: from the personal name *Massimo*, (Latin *Maximus* 'greatest', superlative of *magnus* 'great'; compare MAGNUS), borne by a number of minor early Christian saints.

GIVEN NAMES Italian 15%. *Amerigo* (2), *Antonio* (2), *Aldo*, *Angelo*, *Gennaro*, *Nicolo*, *Salvatore*.

Massing (206) German: habitational name from a place so named in Bavaria.

Massingale (293) English: variant of **Masongill** (see MASSENGILL).

Massingill (707) English: variant of **Masongill** (see MASSENGILL).

Massman (358) Americanized spelling of North German MASSMANN.

Massmann (181) North German: pet form of MASS.

GIVEN NAMES German 8%. *Erwin* (2), *Johann* (2), *Fritz*, *Klaus*.

Masso (228) **1.** Italian: masculinized form of MASSA. **2.** Catalan (**Massó**): probably variant spelling of *maçó* 'pickaxe', nick-

name for someone who worked as stone-cutter, from the diminutive of *maça* 'mace'.

GIVEN NAMES Spanish 14%; Italian 9%. *Jose* (4), *Juan* (2), *Miguel* (2), *Alvaro*, *Angelina*, *Arturo*, *Enrique*, *Genoveva*, *Hernan*, *Jaime*, *Jesus*, *Libardo*; *Dante* (2), *Pasco* (2), *Antonio*, *Guido*, *Silvio*.

Masson (972) **1.** Scottish (Aberdeen): variant of MASON, or possibly an assimilated form of MANSON 1. **2.** French: from a pet form of THOMAS. **3.** French: occupational name for a stonemason, Old French *mas(s)on*.

GIVEN NAMES French 10%. *Emile* (3), *Lucien* (3), *Alain* (2), *Henri* (2), *Pierre* (2), *Yves* (2), *Agathe*, *Aime*, *Cecile*, *Clovis*, *Francois*, *Francoise*.

Massoni (184) Italian: from an augmentative of MASSO.

GIVEN NAMES Italian 14%. *Evo* (2), *Gino* (2), *Camillo*, *Cesare*, *Dante*, *Elio*, *Otello*, *Piero*, *Romano*.

Massoth (141) German (Hesse): unexplained.

Massoud (166) Muslim: variant of MASOOD. In this spelling the name is particularly common in North Africa.

GIVEN NAMES Muslim 36%; French 7%. *Hany* (2), *Hisham* (2), *Hossein* (2), *Nazy* (2), *Nidal* (2), *Said* (2), *Adly*, *Afifa*, *Aly*, *Assad*, *Bahram*, *Bassam*; *Pierre* (2), *Philippe*, *Piere*.

Massucci (143) Italian: variant spelling of MASUCCI.

GIVEN NAMES Italian 10%. *Romeo* (2), *Angelo*, *Fiore*.

Mast (3518) **1.** Dutch: nickname for a tall, lanky man, from Middle Dutch *mast* '(ship's) mast'. **2.** Dutch: metonymic occupational name for a swineherd, from Middle Dutch *mast* 'mast', 'swine fodder' (the same word as the English word for beechnuts). **3.** Dutch (**van de(r) Mast**): topographic name for someone from a place rich in animal fodder, for example acorns. **4.** German and Swiss German: nickname from Middle High German *mast* 'fat', 'stout'.

Mastalski (113) Polish (**Masztalski**): derivative of the occupational term *masztalerz* 'groom'.

Mastandrea (255) Southern Italian: variant of MASTRANDREA formed with *masto* 'master craftsman', Campanese form of *mastro*.

GIVEN NAMES Italian 16%. *Amadeo* (2), *Angelo* (2), *Vito* (2), *Carmel*, *Dario*, *Domenico*, *Pietro*, *Saverio*, *Tommaso*.

Mastel (225) **1.** Ukrainian: unexplained, probably of German origin. **2.** Of Italian origin: possibly a shortened form of **Mastellone** (unexplained).

Masteller (295) German: probably a variant of MOSTELLER.

Masten (1345) Dutch: from a pet form of a Germanic personal name, either the female name *Machthild* (see MOULD) or the male name *Machtolf*, composed of the elements *maht*, *meht* 'strength', 'might' + *wulf* 'wolf'.

Mastenbrook (122) Americanized form of the Dutch surname **Mastenbroek**, a habitational name from a place so named in Overijssel.

Master (898) **1.** English and Scottish: nickname for someone who behaved in a masterful manner, or an occupational name for someone who was master of his craft or a schoolmaster, from Middle English *maister* (Old French *maistre*, Latin *magister*). In early instances this surname was often borne by people who were franklins or other substantial freeholders, presumably because they had laborers under them to work their lands. In Scotland Master was the title given to administrators of medieval hospitals, as well as being born by the eldest sons of barons; thus, the surname may also have been acquired as a metonymic occupational name by someone in the service of such. See also MCMASTER. **2.** Either a dialect form or an Americanized form of German MEISTER. **3.** Indian (Gujarat and Bombay city): Parsi occupational name for someone who was a master of his craft, from the English word *master*.
GIVEN NAMES Indian 9%. *Amar* (2), *Dhimant* (2), *Pravin* (2), *Amit*, *Aruna*, *Bhanu*, *Gaurang*, *Gopal*, *Haren*, *Jagu*, *Jayesh*, *Kalpesh*.

Masterman (240) English: occupational name for the servant of a master craftsman, or a man known as MASTER.

Masters (8834) English: patronymic from MASTER. Reaney notes the medieval example *atte Maysters* (1327), and suggests this might have denoted someone who lived at a master's house, a master's servant or perhaps an apprentice.

Masterson (4454) English: patronymic from MASTER.

Masterton (109) Scottish: habitational name from the lands of Masterton in Fife, so named because they were once held by the master (*magister*) of the Abbey church of Dunfermline.

Mastin (1350) French: partly an occupational name for a household servant, from Old French *mastin* 'watchdog'; 'manservant' (from Latin *mansuetudinus* 'domestic'). The Old French word had the further sense of a bad-tempered dog, and was used as an adjective in the sense of 'bad', 'cruel'.

Maston (522) English: unexplained. Possibly a variant of MARSTON, reflecting a local pronunciation, or a habitational name from Mastin Moor in Derbyshire.

Mastrandrea (112) Italian: from a compound name, a title of respect formed with *mastro* 'master craftsman' + the personal name *Andrea* (see ANDREAS).
GIVEN NAMES Italian 31%. *Vito* (3), *Emilio* (2), *Mario* (2), *Carlo*, *Carmella*, *Giuseppe*, *Lorenzo*, *Sabatino*.

Mastrangelo (868) Southern Italian: from a compound name, a title of respect formed from *mastro* 'master craftsman' + the personal name ANGELO.
GIVEN NAMES Italian 17%. *Angelo* (12), *Rocco* (8), *Antonio* (4), *Domenic* (3), *Marco* (2), *Carmelo*, *Carmine*, *Dino*, *Domenico*, *Donato*, *Fiore*, *Francesca*.

Mastrianni (224) Italian: reduced form of MASTROIANNI.
GIVEN NAMES Italian 10%. *Carmine*, *Domenic*, *Federico*, *Sal*, *Salvatore*, *Silvio*, *Vincenzo*.

Mastriano (145) Italian: perhaps an altered form of MASTROIANNI.
GIVEN NAMES Italian 15%. *Domenic*, *Gennaro*, *Natale*, *Rocco*.

Mastro (669) Southern Italian: occupational name for a teacher, or for a master craftsman, from *maestro* 'master' (Latin *magister*). The Portuguese and Spanish surnames, from *mastro* 'mast', 'flagpole', appear not to have contributed significantly to the American surname.
GIVEN NAMES Italian 10%. *Vito* (3), *Aldo* (2), *Dante* (2), *Sal* (2), *Alfonse*, *Angelo*, *Gino*, *Giustino*, *Oreste*.

Mastrocola (226) Southern Italian: from a compound name, a title of respect formed from *mastro* 'master craftsman' + *Còla*, a short form of the personal name *Nicola* (see NICHOLAS).
GIVEN NAMES Italian 34%. *Antonio* (3), *Marcello* (3), *Vittorio* (3), *Carlo* (2), *Luigi* (2), *Nicola* (2), *Rocco* (2), *Aldo*, *Angelo*, *Armando*, *Assunta*, *Camillo*, *Domenico*, *Elio*, *Mario*.

Mastrogiacomo (116) Italian: from a compound name, a title of respect formed from *mastro* 'master craftsman' + the personal name GIACOMO, Italian equivalent of JAMES.
GIVEN NAMES Italian 27%. *Angelo* (5), *Carlo* (2), *Giovanni* (2), *Pasquale* (2), *Francesco*, *Remo*, *Vincenzo*.

Mastrogiovanni (161) Southern Italian: from a compound name, a title of respect ('Master John'), formed from *mastro* 'master craftsman' + the personal name GIOVANNI, Italian equivalent of JOHN.
GIVEN NAMES Italian 21%. *Marco* (2), *Carmine*, *Luciano*, *Pasquale*, *Sal*, *Salvatore*, *Vito*.

Mastroianni (727) Southern Italian: from a compound name, a title of respect formed from *mastro* 'master craftsman' + *Ianni*, a central and southern dialect form of the personal GIOVANNI, now preserved only in the surname.
GIVEN NAMES Italian 28%. *Antonio* (13), *Angelo* (10), *Mario* (7), *Gaetano* (4), *Luigi* (4), *Donato* (3), *Guido* (3), *Americo* (2), *Armando* (2), *Carmine* (2), *Cesare* (2), *Giulio* (2), *Raffaele* (2), *Remo* (2), *Vincenzo* (2), *Carmella*, *Emilio*, *Francisco*, *Leopoldo*, *Mariano*, *Placido*, *Rosario*.

Mastromarino (128) Italian: from a compound name, a title of respect formed from *mastro* 'master craftsman' + the personal name MARINO.
GIVEN NAMES Italian 13%. *Angelo*, *Carmine*, *Vito*.

Mastromatteo (108) Italian: from a compound name, a title of respect formed from *mastro* 'master craftsman' + the personal name MATTEO.
GIVEN NAMES Italian 11%. *Giovanni*, *Onofrio*.

Mastronardi (270) Southern Italian: patronymic or plural form of the compound name *Mastronardo*, a title of respect formed from *mastro* 'master craftsman' + the personal name *Nardo*, a short form of *Bernardo*, *Leonardo*, etc.
GIVEN NAMES Italian 23%. *Gerardo* (3), *Angelo* (2), *Filomena* (2), *Nicola* (2), *Olindo* (2), *Annamaria*, *Domenic*, *Emilio*, *Enrico*, *Ernesto*, *Giovanni*, *Guido*, *Pasquale*, *Saverio*, *Umberto*.

Mastropietro (206) Southern Italian: from a compound name, a title of respect formed from *mastro* 'master craftsman' + the personal name *Pietro*, an Italian equivalent of PETER.
GIVEN NAMES Italian 22%. *Carmine* (2), *Aldo*, *Aniello*, *Antonio*, *Cesare*, *Dino*, *Donato*, *Marcello*, *Nicola*, *Nino*, *Nunzio*.

Masucci (502) Italian: from a derivative of the personal name **Maso**.
GIVEN NAMES Italian 13%. *Rocco* (3), *Angelo* (2), *Antonio* (2), *Carmine* (2), *Sal* (2), *Dante*, *Domenic*, *Domenica*, *Gaetano*, *Gaspare*, *Gino*, *Italo*.

Masuda (513) Japanese: 'increasing rice paddy'; variously written, it is found throughout Japan and the Ryūkyū Islands.
GIVEN NAMES Japanese 66%. *Tokuo* (6), *Koji* (4), *Hiroshi* (3), *Kenji* (3), *Kiyoshi* (3), *Mitsuo* (3), *Satoshi* (3), *Shigeru* (3), *Akira* (2), *Chieko* (2), *Isao* (2), *Junji* (2).

Masullo (172) Italian: from a pet form of the personal name *Tommaso* (see THOMAS).
GIVEN NAMES Italian 26%. *Angelo* (7), *Carmine* (2), *Antonio*, *Dino*, *Fernando*, *Gerardo*, *Giulio*, *Mario*, *Pasquale*, *Pietro*, *Rosario*, *Sal*, *Salvatore*.

Masur (221) German: ethnic name for a member of the Masur people, who gave their name to the area known as Masuren in the former German province of East Prussia.
GIVEN NAMES German 5%. *Kurt* (2), *Helmut*, *Inge*, *Rainer*.

Mata (4023) **1.** Portuguese and Spanish: habitational name from any of numerous places in Portugal and Spain named Mata, from *mata* 'wood', 'forest'. **2.** Catalan: topographic name from *mata* 'scrub'. **3.** Hungarian: from a pet form of the personal name *Máté* (see MATTHEW).
GIVEN NAMES Spanish 51%; Portuguese 11%. *Jose* (111), *Juan* (67), *Manuel* (45), *Carlos*

(44), *Jesus* (42), *Francisco* (29), *Luis* (27), *Mario* (25), *Arturo* (22), *Pedro* (22), *Raul* (22), *Jose Luis* (21); *Joao*.

Matalon (166) Spanish (**Matalón**) and Jewish (Sephardic): nickname from *matalón* 'worn-out horse', a derivative of *matar* 'to flog (an animal)', 'flog to death'.
GIVEN NAMES Jewish 19%. *Ahron* (2), *Dror*, *Hyman*, *Itai*, *Moshe*, *Nissim*, *Sabi*, *Shabtay*, *Shaul*, *Yehuda*.

Matamoros (308) Spanish: from *Matamoros* meaning 'killer of Moors', a title given to Spain's patron saint, St. James, in the Middle Ages (from *matar* 'to kill' + *moros* 'Moors'). According to legend, the saint appeared to a 9th-century Spanish king during a battle, and enabled him to massacre 60,000 Saracens.
GIVEN NAMES Spanish 47%; Portuguese 12%. *Jose* (10), *Andres* (4), *Aurelio* (4), *Juan* (4), *Luis* (4), *Manuel* (4), *Mario* (4), *Carlos* (3), *Gustavo* (3), *Miguel* (3), *Rafael* (3), *Raul* (3); *Figueroa*; *Antonio*, *Filiberto*, *Franco*, *Marcellino*, *Marco Tulio*.

Matar (136) Muslim: variant of MATTAR.
GIVEN NAMES Muslim 47%. *Nabil* (4), *Fouad* (2), *Ghassan* (2), *Mounir* (2), *Said* (2), *Zeina* (2), *Abdallah*, *Ahmad*, *Ali*, *Aly*, *Bassam*, *Fadi*.

Matarazzo (558) Italian (Sicily): from Sicilian dialect *matarazzu* 'mattress', a derivative of Arabic *maṭraḥ* 'place to lie down'.
GIVEN NAMES Italian 18%. *Carmine* (8), *Angelo* (5), *Antonio* (3), *Ciro* (3), *Salvatore* (3), *Santo* (3), *Luciano* (2), *Sal* (2), *Aniello*, *Elio*, *Enrico*, *Giuseppe*.

Matarese (276) Italian: habitational name for someone from MATERA, from *materräisë*, a local adjectival form of the place name (in standard Italian *materano*).
GIVEN NAMES Italian 17%. *Antonio* (5), *Vito* (5), *Rocco* (2), *Salvatore* (2), *Carmine*, *Domenic*, *Gaetano*, *Giro*, *Pasquale*, *Vincenzo*.

Matarrese (110) Italian: variant of MATARESE.
GIVEN NAMES Italian 18%. *Vito* (3), *Giovanni*, *Giuseppe*.

Matas (212) **1.** Spanish: variant (plural) of MATA 1. **2.** Catalan: variant spelling of MATES. **3.** Czech (**Maťas**), Slovak (**Maťaš**), and Croatian: from the personal name *Mathias*, Croatian *Matija* or *Matej* (see MATTHEW). **4.** Lithuanian: from the personal name *Matas*, Lithuanian form of Latin *Matthaeus* (see MATTHEW).
GIVEN NAMES Spanish 12%. *Jose* (2), *Raul* (2), *Adriana*, *Alina*, *Armando*, *Arturo*, *Carlos*, *Carlos Antonio*, *Domitilo*, *Fransico*, *Guillermo*, *Humberto*.

Matassa (197) Italian (Sicily): metonymic occupational name for a producer of silk, from Sicilian *matassa* 'hank', 'skein', also the name of a type of silk.
GIVEN NAMES Italian 18%. *Angelo* (4), *Francesco* (2), *Franco*, *Nunzio*.

Matava (107) Origin unidentified.

Mataya (154) Americanized spelling of Polish MATEJA.

Matchett (797) Northern Irish: of uncertain origin, possibly a pet form of MATTHEW.

Matchette (122) Variant spelling of northern Irish MATCHETT.

Matczak (135) Polish: patronymic from a pet form of the personal name *Maciej* (see MATTHEW).
GIVEN NAMES Polish 5%. *Ewa* (2), *Jacek*.

Mate (386) **1.** Hungarian (**Máté**): from the ecclesiastical personal name *Máté*, Hungarian form of MATTHEW. **2.** Slovenian: from a pet form of the personal name *Matevž*, Latin *Matthaeus* (see MATTHEW). **3.** Spanish (**Maté**): variant of MATEO. **4.** Greek: see MATES. **5.** French (**Maté**): from a pet form of the personal name MATHIEU, French form of MATTHEW.
GIVEN NAMES Hungarian 4%. *Arpad*, *Bela*, *Elek*, *Imre*, *Laszlo*, *Tibor*.

Matecki (142) Polish: habitational name for someone from a place called Matcze in Zamość voivodeship.
GIVEN NAMES Polish 8%. *Feliks*, *Jaroslaw*.

Mateer (532) Scottish and Irish (Ulster): reduced form of MCATEER.

Mateja (188) Polish and Czech (**Matěja**): from a derivative of Polish *Mateusz*, Czech *Matěj*, or some other Slavic form of the Latin personal name *Matthaeus* or *Mathias* (see MATTHEW).
GIVEN NAMES Polish 8%. *Casimir*, *Cecylia*, *Jacek*, *Jerzy*, *Stanislaw*.

Matejcek (152) Czech (**Matějček**) and Slovak (**Matejček**, **Matejčík**): from a pet form of the personal name *Matěj*, Czech form of Latin *Matthaeus* or *Mathias* (see MATTHEW).

Matejek (104) Polish and Czech (**Matějek**) and Slovak (**Matejek**): from a pet form of the personal name *Mateusz* (Polish) or *Matěj* (Czech).
GIVEN NAMES Polish 16%. *Pawel* (2), *Walenty*, *Witold*, *Zofia*.

Matejka (465) Czech (**Matějka**): from a pet form of the personal name *Matěj* (see MATTHEW).

Matelski (178) Polish: from a derivative of the personal name *Mateusz* (see MATTHEW).

Mateo (947) Spanish: from the personal name *Mateo* (see MATTHEW).
GIVEN NAMES Spanish 50%; Portuguese 10%. *Jose* (17), *Juan* (13), *Pedro* (11), *Carlos* (9), *Luis* (9), *Francisco* (8), *Andres* (6), *Mario* (6), *Angel* (5), *Jesus* (5), *Jorge* (5), *Manuel* (5); *Catarina*.

Mateos (120) Spanish or Portuguese: from the personal name *Mateo* (see MATTHEW).
GIVEN NAMES Spanish 50%. *Alberto* (3), *Francisco* (3), *Arturo* (2), *Carlos* (2), *Claudio* (2), *Humberto* (2), *Jose* (2), *Rafael* (2), *Rodolfo* (2), *Agapito*, *Alfredo*, *Armando*; *Antonio*.

Mater (223) Belgian (**van Mater**): habitational name from Mater in East Flanders.

Matera (472) Italian: habitational name from Matera in Basilicata region.
GIVEN NAMES Italian 20%. *Angelo* (5), *Rocco* (5), *Pasquale* (3), *Domenic* (2), *Lia* (2), *Salvatore* (2), *Alessio*, *Amerigo*, *Biagio*, *Canio*, *Domenico*, *Enrico*.

Matern (226) German and Dutch: variant spelling of MATTERN.
GIVEN NAMES German 6%. *Erwin*, *Ingo*, *Kurt*, *Otto*, *Wilhelmina*.

Materna (154) Polish and Czech: nickname from Latin *materna*, feminine form of the adjective *maternus* 'maternal'. It may also be from a this word as a personal name (see MATTERN).

Mates (288) **1.** Hungarian: from a pet form of the personal name *Máté*, Hungarian form of MATTHEW. **2.** Catalan: from the plural of *mata* 'scrub' (see MATA). **3.** Greek (**Matis**): from a pet form of the personal name *Stamatios* (see STAMATIS). **4.** Jewish (Ashkenazic): from a personal name equivalent to MATTHEW.

Matesic (147) Croatian (**Matešić**): patronymic from the personal name *Mateša*, a pet form of *Matija* or *Matej* (see MATTHEW).
GIVEN NAMES Italian 11%; South Slavic 5%; Spanish 4%. *Grazia* (2), *Nino*; *Dinko*, *Sime*, *Zlatko*; *Adriana*, *Benito*, *Mario*.

Mateus (142) Portuguese: from the personal name *Mateus* (see MATTHEW).
GIVEN NAMES Spanish 36%; Portuguese 26%. *Manuel* (6), *Carlos* (5), *Jose* (4), *Luis* (3), *Cesar* (2), *Jorge* (2), *Miguel* (2), *Armando*, *Avelino*, *Blanca*, *Elidio*, *Enrique*; *Joaquim* (5), *Joao* (2), *Aderito*, *Fernandes*, *Serafim*.

Matey (242) **1.** Ukrainian: from the personal name *Matey* (see MATTHEW). **2.** Americanized spelling of Czech *Matěj* or Slovak *Matej*. **3.** French (eastern): from a regional variant of the personal name MATHIEU. **4.** Possibly also Galician: a habitational name from Matey, a minor place in Lugo province, Galicia.

Math (133) Jewish (American): unexplained. Possibly a shortened form of an unidentified Ashkenazic surname.
GIVEN NAME German 5%; Jewish 5%. *Yisrael*.

Mathai (332) **1.** Indian (Kerala): derivative of Greek *Matthaios* or its Hebrew original form, variant of MATTHEW, used as a given name among Christians in Kerala (southern India). In the U.S. it has come to be used as a surname among families from Kerala. **2.** Hungarian (**Máthay**): archaic spelling variant of **Mátai**, a habitational name for someone from a place called Máta in Szabolcs county.
GIVEN NAMES Indian 43%. *Mathai* (7), *Varughese* (3), *Amit* (2), *Babu* (2), *Ninan* (2), *Raju* (2), *Anil*, *Anish*, *Jaimini*, *Marykutty*, *Oommen*, *Prasad*.

Mathe (320) **1.** Hungarian: variant of MATE. **2.** French: from a pet form of the personal name *Mathieu*, French form of

MATTHEW. **3.** Spanish: possibly a variant of **Maté** (see MATE).

GIVEN NAMES Hungarian 9%. *Denes* (2), *Zoltan* (2), *Attila, Gyula, Istvan, Janos, Miklos.*

Matheis (377) German: from a variant of the personal name *Matthäus* or *Mathias* (see MATTHEW).

GIVEN NAMES German 6%. *Armin, Helmut, Nikolaus, Otto, Ulrich, Wolfgang.*

Mathena (473) Variant of MATHENY.

Matheney (496) Variant of MATHENY.

Mathenia (139) Variant of MATHENY.

Matheny (3231) English: of French (possibly Huguenot) origin. According to family tradition, this is a habitational name from a place called Mathenay in the French Alps. FOREBEARS Daniel Matheny came to MD from London in the latter half of the 17th century.

Mather (2750) English: **1.** occupational name for a mower or reaper of grass or hay, Old English *mǣðere*. Compare MEAD, MOWER. Hay was formerly of great importance, not only as feed for animals in winter but also for bedding. **2.** in southern Lancashire, where it has long been a common surname, it is probably a relatively late development of **Madder** (see MADER). FOREBEARS The prominent Mather family of New England were established in America by Richard Mather (1596–1669) in 1635. He was a Puritan clergyman from a well-established family of Lowton, Lancashire, England. After he emigrated, he was in great demand as a preacher, finally settling in Dorchester, MA. His son Increase Mather (1639–1723) was a diplomat and president of Harvard. He married his stepsister Maria Cotton, herself the daughter of an eminent Puritan divine, John Cotton. Their son Cotton Mather (1663–1728) bore both family names. The latter was a minister who is remembered for his part in witchcraft trials, but he was also a man of science and a fellow of the Royal Society in London.

Matherly (889) English: unexplained. It may be a habitational name from an unidentified place name, or possibly a variant of MADELEY.

Mathern (229) German: variant of MATTERN.

Matherne (1202) Probably a respelling of MATHERN.

GIVEN NAMES French 5%. *Armand* (2), *Emile* (2), *Landry* (2), *Mederic* (2), *Monique* (2), *Antoine, Autrey, Eusebe, Gillis, Jacques, Michel.*

Mathers (1561) English: patronymic from MATHER.

Matherson (153) English and Scottish: **1.** patronyic from MATHERS. **2.** Altered form of MATHESON.

Mathes (2367) **1.** English: patronymic from a pet form of MATTHEW. **2.** French (**Mathès**) and German: from the personal names *Mathias* or *Mattheus* (see MATTHEW).

Matheson (3050) Scottish: patronymic from a short form of MATTHEW.

Matheus (190) **1.** Dutch: from the personal name *Mattheus* (see MATTHEW). **2.** Portuguese: variant spelling of MATEUS.

GIVEN NAMES Spanish 15%. *Alfredo* (3), *Manuel* (3), *Gustavo* (2), *Rafael* (2), *Alejandro, Arnoldo, Eduardo, Elva, Ernesto, Genoveva, Gerardo, Germano.*

Mathew (1817) English, Scottish, and Indian (southern states): variant spelling of MATTHEW. It is found as a personal name among Christians in India, and in the U.S. is used as a family name among families from southern India.

GIVEN NAMES Indian 32%. *Mathai* (16), *Babu* (11), *Oommen* (9), *Saji* (9), *Varughese* (9), *Raju* (8), *Reji* (6), *Sunil* (5), *Prakash* (4), *Prasad* (4), *Shaji* (4), *Cheriyan* (3).

Mathews (18304) English: patronymic from MATHEW; a variant spelling of MATTHEWS. In the U.S., this form has absorbed some European cognates such as German **Matthäus**. FOREBEARS Among the earliest bearers of the name in North America was Samuel Mathews (*c.*1600–*c.*1657), who came to VA from London in about 1618. He established a plantation at the mouth of the Warwick River, which was at first called Mathews Manor; later its name was changed to Denbigh. He was one of the most powerful and influential men in the early affairs of the colony. He (or possibly his son, who bore the same name) was governor of the colony from 1657 until his death in 1660.

Mathewson (1406) English: patronymic from MATTHEW.

Mathey (328) **1.** French (eastern): from a regional variant of the personal name MATHIEU. **2.** Dutch: from a variant of the personal name *Mattheus* (see MATTHEW).

Mathia (151) **1.** German (**Mathiä**) and Dutch: from a variant of the personal name *Mathias* (see MATTHEW). **2.** French: from an old regional form of MATHIAS 1.

Mathias (3290) **1.** French, Dutch: from the personal name *Mathias* (see MATTHEW). **2.** Spanish and Portuguese: variant spelling of MATIAS. **3.** Welsh: a late surname formation from the Biblical personal name *Mathias* (see MATTHEW).

Mathiasen (188) Danish and Norwegian: patronymic from the personal name *Mat(t)hias* (see MATTHEW).

GIVEN NAMES German 7%; Scandinavian 6%. *Mathias* (2), *Math*; *Erik, Niels.*

Mathiason (236) **1.** Swedish: patronymic from the personal name *Mathias*, Swedish form of MATTHEW. **2.** Respelling of MATHIASEN.

Mathie (234) **1.** French: from a variant of the personal name MATHIEU. **2.** Scottish: habitational name from the former parish of M(e)athie, next to Inverarity. **3.** Scottish: possibly from a pet form of MATTHEW.

Mathies (376) **1.** English: patronymic from a pet form of MATTHEW. **2.** Dutch: from a variant of the personal name *Mathias* (see MATTHEW).

Mathiesen (445) Danish, Norwegian, and Dutch: patronymic from the personal name *Mathias* (see MATTHEW).

GIVEN NAMES Scandinavian 8%. *Erik* (2), *Alf, Johan, Kristjan, Per.*

Mathieson (656) **1.** Scottish: patronymic from a pet form of MATTHEW. **2.** Scandinavian: patronymic from the personal name *Mathies* (see MATTHEW).

Mathieu (1850) French: from the personal name *Mathieu*, vernacular derivative of Latin *Mathias* or *Matthaeus* (see MATTHEW).

GIVEN NAMES French 16%. *Marcel* (8), *Normand* (6), *Andre* (5), *Lucien* (5), *Pierre* (5), *Yvon* (5), *Armand* (3), *Rosaire* (3), *Alphonse* (2), *Dominique* (2), *Emile* (2), *Fernand* (2).

Mathiowetz (156) Germanized form of Polish MACKIEWICZ.

GIVEN NAMES German 5%. *Aloysius, Othmar, Reinhold.*

Mathis (16186) **1.** Dutch and French: from a variant of the personal name *Mathias* (see MATTHEW). **2.** English: patronymic from a pet form of MATTHEW.

Mathisen (644) Dutch, Danish, and Norwegian: patronymic from the personal name *Mathi(a)s* (see MATTHEW).

GIVEN NAMES Scandinavian 11%. *Erik, Johan, Mauritz, Oivind, Oystein, Sig, Steinar, Tor.*

Mathison (1724) **1.** Scottish: variant spelling of MATHESON. **2.** Scandinavian: patronymic from a pet form of the personal name *Mathi(a)s* (see MATTHEW).

Mathre (126) Norwegian: habitational name from either of two farmsteads in Hordaland named with *Matr*, originally a fjord name of disputed etymology, possibly related to Old Norse *matr* 'food (fish)' or to an unidentified word meaning 'wet place'.

GIVEN NAMES Scandinavian 5%. *Erik, Lars.*

Mathson (159) Reduced form of Scottish MATHISON.

Mathur (525) Indian (north central): Hindu (Kayasth) name, based on the name of a subgroup of the Kayasth community, from Sanskrit *māthura* 'of Mathura', a city to the south of Delhi. Some Brahmans and Banias are also reported to bear this family name.

GIVEN NAMES Indian 93%. *Anil* (11), *Sanjay* (11), *Raj* (9), *Vijay* (7), *Ravi* (6), *Alok* (5), *Ashok* (5), *Mukesh* (5), *Rajiv* (5), *Sharad* (5), *Sunil* (5), *Amit* (4).

Mathurin (172) French: from a personal name, Latin *Maturinus* (a derivative of *Maturus* 'timely'), borne by a 3rd-century saint who was responsible for spreading the gospel in the district of Sens.

GIVEN NAMES French 43%. *Andre* (3), *Emile* (3), *Pierre* (2), *Serge* (2), *Alain*, *Andree*, *Armand*, *Carmelle*, *Donat*, *Etienne*, *Germain*, *Jean-Paul*.

Mathus (116) Dutch: from a variant of the personal name *Matheus* (see MATTHEW).

Mathwig (201) German: irregular derivative of the personal name *Mathias* or *Matthäus* (see MATTHEW), influenced by names such as *Ludwig*.

GIVEN NAMES German 7%. *Erwin*, *Ewald*, *Horst*, *Reinhardt*.

Mathy (168) French: from a variant of the personal names *Mathias* or *Mathieu* (see MATTHEW).

Mathys (276) Dutch: variant spelling of MATHIS.

Matias (897) **1.** Spanish (**Matías**), Portuguese, and Dutch: from the personal name (see MATTHEW). **2.** Americanized form of Czech **Mat'áš** (from Czech *Matěj*), or of some other Slavic form of the personal name *Mathias* (see MATTHEW).

GIVEN NAMES Spanish 42%; Portuguese 15%. *Jose* (36), *Manuel* (12), *Jorge* (7), *Ernesto* (6), *Luis* (6), *Alfredo* (5), *Carlos* (5), *Pedro* (5), *Enrique* (4), *Jesus* (4), *Juan* (4), *Julio* (4); *Agostinho* (2), *Joao* (2), *Wenceslao*.

Matic (134) Croatian and Serbian (**Matić**): patronymic from the personal name *Matija* or *Matej* (see MATTHEW), or from the pet forms *Mate* (Croatian) or *Mato*.

GIVEN NAMES South Slavic 40%. *Dusan* (3), *Miodrag* (2), *Bosko*, *Branko*, *Davor*, *Goran*, *Gordana*, *Jure*, *Ljubisa*, *Milan* (2), *Milos*, *Natasa*, *Nenad*, *Pero*, *Petar*.

Matich (200) Croatian and Serbian (**Matić**): see MATIC.

GIVEN NAMES South Slavic 7%. *Zika* (3), *Bozidar*, *Mladen*, *Momir*, *Nenad*.

Matin (152) Muslim: from a personal name based on Arabic *matīn* 'strong', 'powerful'. *Al-Matīn* 'the Almighty' is an attribute of Allah, and this name is found in combinations such as *'Abd-ul Matīn* 'servant of the Almighty'.

GIVEN NAMES Muslim 66%. *Abdul* (10), *Mohammed* (4), *Shaikh* (3), *Aliasghar* (2), *Amir* (2), *Hamid* (2), *Mohammed Abdul* (2), *Abdol*, *Abu*, *Afsaneh*, *Afshin*, *Akbar*.

Matis (446) **1.** French: from a variant or pet form of *Matthias* (see MATTHEW). **2.** English: patronymic from a pet form of MATTHEW. **3.** Greek: see MATES. **4.** Hungarian (**Mátis**): from *Mátis*, or *Matis*, pet forms of the personal name *Máté*, Hungarian form of MATTHEW. **5.** Czech and Slovak: variant of MATAS. **6.** Variant of Lithuanian **Matyĺfs**, from the personal name MATAS. **7.** Jewish (Ashkenazic): variant of MATES.

Matison (108) Variant spelling of Scottish and northern English MATTISON.

Matkin (286) English: from a pet form of MATTHEW.

Matkins (211) English: patronymic from a pet form of MATTHEW.

Matkovich (176) Croatian and Serbian (**Matković**) and Slovenian (**Matkovič**): patronymic from the personal name *Matko*, a pet form of *Matija* or *Matej* (see MATTHEW).

Matkowski (106) Polish: habitational name from Matków (now in Ukraine), named with the personal name *Matek*, pet form of *Mateusz* (see MATTHEW).

Matlack (529) Variant of English MATLOCK.
FOREBEARS William Hancock Matlack (b. 1648 in Cropwell Bishop, Northamptonshire, England) came to America in 1677 as an indentured servant aboard the *Kent*. He was one of the founders of Burlington, NJ.

Matley (140) English: habitational name from any of various minor places called Matley, in particular Matley in Greater Manchester, Matley Heath and Matley Wood in Hampshire, or Matley Moor in Derbyshire.

Matlick (185) Probably a variant of English MATLOCK.

GIVEN NAMES Jewish 5%. *Mort* (2), *Sol*.

Matlin (219) **1.** Jewish (eastern Ashkenazic): metronymic from the Yiddish personal name *Matle* (of Germanic origin) + the Slavic possessive suffix *-in*. **2.** Possibly also a variant of German **Mattlin**, a topographic name from a diminutive of Middle High German *matte* 'alpine meadow'.

GIVEN NAMES Russian 9%; Jewish 9%. *Vladimir* (4), *Yefim* (2), *Boris*, *Grigory*, *Igor*, *Iosif*, *Leonid*, *Lev*, *Mikhail*; *Nisan* (2), *Gershon*, *Isaak*.

Matlock (3955) English: habitational name from Matlock in Derbyshire, named in Old English as 'meeting-place oak', from *mæthel* 'meeting', 'gathering', 'council' + *āc* 'oak'.

Matney (1805) American variant of English MATTINGLY.
FOREBEARS Walter Mattingley (1747– c.1804), of Montgomery Co., VA, and subsequently Washington Co., VA, is also recorded as Walter Matney.

Mato (141) **1.** Galician and Portuguese: widespread habitational name from any of numerous places in Galicia and Portugal named Mato, from *mata* 'brushwood', 'scrub', 'thicket'. **2.** Spanish: topographic name from *mato* 'scrub'. **3.** Catalan (**Mató**): metonymic occupational name for a dairyman, from a word meaning 'cream'; 'curds', 'curd cheese'. **4.** Hungarian (**Mató**): from a pet form of the personal name *Maté*, Hungarian form of MATTHEW.

GIVEN NAMES Spanish 21%. *Jose* (3), *Mario* (3), *Juan* (2), *Manuel* (2), *Pablo* (2), *Ricardo* (2), *Aida*, *Argelio*, *Armando*, *Carlos*, *Galo*, *Jesus*.

Matocha (127) Czech and Slovak: from a derivative of the personal name *Matěj*, Czech form of Latin *Matthaeus* or *Mathias* (see MATTHEW).

Matos (2394) **1.** Portuguese: widespread habitational name from any of numerous places in Portugal named Matos, from *mata* 'brushwood', 'scrub', 'thicket'. **2.** Spanish: topographic name, from the plural of MATO. **3.** Hungarian: variant of MATUS.

GIVEN NAMES Spanish 43%; Portuguese 13%. *Jose* (76), *Luis* (32), *Manuel* (32), *Angel* (21), *Juan* (21), *Carlos* (19), *Rafael* (17), *Pedro* (15), *Ana* (14), *Francisco* (13), *Miguel* (13), *Jorge* (11); *Joao* (3), *Paulo* (2), *Albano*, *Henrique*, *Joaquim*, *Ligia*, *Serafim*, *Vasco*.

Matott (213) Altered spelling of French **Mat(th)ot**, from a pet form of the personal name *Mathieu* (see MATTHEW).

Matous (133) Czech (**Matouš**): from the personal name *Matouš* from *Matěj*, Czech form of Latin *Matthaeus* or *Mathias* (see MATTHEW).

Matousek (395) Czech (**Matoušek**): from a pet form of **Matouš** (see MATOUS).

Matovich (139) Serbian and Croatian (**Matović**): patronymic from *Mato*, a pet form of *Matija* or *Matej* (see MATTHEW).

GIVEN NAMES South Slavic 5%. *Velimir* (2), *Marko*.

Matranga (414) Southern Italian and Greek (**Matrangas**): of Albanian origin. There are numerous places in Greece called Matranga, centers of settlement by Arvanites, Greeks of Albanian origin.

GIVEN NAMES Italian 15%. *Angelo* (3), *Carlo* (2), *Giuseppe*, *Liborio*, *Marco*, *Sal*.

Matras (113) Polish: from the vocabulary word *matras* (derived from Italian *materazzo*), either a nickname or an occupational name for a maker of mattresses. Compare Italian MATARAZZO.

GIVEN NAMES Polish 9%. *Casimir*, *Danuta*, *Jozef*.

Matre (112) Possibly a French habitational name from a place in Seine Maritime called Le Matré.

Matrone (115) Italian: perhaps a masculinized form of **Matrona**, from the personal name *Matrona*, from Latin *matrona* 'married woman', 'wife'.

GIVEN NAMES Italian 14%; Spanish 9%. *Concetta*, *Sal*; *Santa* (2), *Silvana*.

Matsen (170) Scandinavian: patronymic from *Mats*, a short form of the personal name *Mathias* (see MATTHEW).

GIVEN NAMES Scandinavian 5%. *Erik*, *Thor*.

Matsko (250) Americanized spelling of MACKO.

Matson (4979) English, Dutch, and Swedish: patronymic from a short form of English MATTHEW or Dutch and Swedish *Mathias*.

Matsubara (157) Japanese (mainly western Japan and the Ryūkyū Islands): habitational name meaning 'pine tree plain', from any of the many places so named throughout Japan. Some families bearing this name are of MINAMOTO or FUJIWARA descent.

GIVEN NAMES Japanese 65%. *Atsushi* (2), *Hideki* (2), *Hiroshi* (2), *Katsumi* (2),

Kazunori (2), *Shigeru* (2), *Yo* (2), *Akiko, Eiji, Etsuko, Fujio, Haruhiko.*

Matsuda (679) Japanese (mainly western Japan and the Ryūkyū Islands): habitational name from any of the many places in Japan so named, meaning 'pine tree rice paddy'. The word *matsu* 'pine' also means 'wait', in this sense implying hope of a divine visitation to a sacred rice paddy. It is also related to the verb *matsuru* 'to perform religious ceremonies'; the name therefore has connections with priestly families of the Shintō religion. Other names with similar religious derivations include MATSUMOTO and MATSUOKA. Several families of noble (especially FUJIWARA) descent have taken the name.

GIVEN NAMES Japanese 58%. *Hiroshi* (6), *Kenji* (6), *Takeshi* (5), *Fujio* (3), *Hiroko* (3), *Hiroyuki* (3), *Kaoru* (3), *Kiyoshi* (3), *Sachiko* (3), *Seigo* (3), *Takashi* (3), *Yuji* (3).

Matsui (318) Japanese (mainly west-central Japan and the Ryūkyū Islands): ancient name meaning 'pine tree well'.

GIVEN NAMES Japanese 61%. *Kunio* (3), *Masato* (3), *Takashi* (3), *Akira* (2), *Hiroshi* (2), *Nobuo* (2), *Osamu* (2), *Takeshi* (2), *Tamotsu* (2), *Tetsuo* (2), *Toshiyuki* (2), *Yu* (2).

Matsumoto (1460) Japanese (common in western Japan and the Ryūkyū Islands): from a common place name; many bearers therefore may be unrelated. According to folklore, a habitation near a pine tree (*matsu*) from which a deity would issue to visit mortals would be named *Matsumoto*: 'place of the (divine) pine tree'. See also MATSUDA and MATSUOKA.

GIVEN NAMES Japanese 57%. *Hiroshi* (11), *Takashi* (7), *Yoshio* (7), *Masao* (6), *Shigeru* (6), *Tadashi* (6), *Teruo* (6), *Takayuki* (5), *Toshio* (5), *Hirotaka* (4), *Kazuo* (4), *Kenji* (4).

Matsumura (354) Japanese: habitational name meaning 'pine tree village', found throughout Japan and the Ryūkyū Islands. Several families of this name have samurai connections.

GIVEN NAMES Japanese 49%. *Akihiko* (3), *Akira* (3), *Fumio* (3), *Akemi* (2), *Hiroshi* (2), *Ichiro* (2), *Isao* (2), *Keiko* (2), *Kenichi* (2), *Makoto* (2), *Masaru* (2), *Nobuo* (2).

Matsunaga (259) Japanese (mostly found in the island of Kyūshū and Okinawa Island): habitational name from two villages in Fukui and Mie prefectures, written with characters meaning 'pine tree' and 'lengthy'.

GIVEN NAMES Japanese 51%. *Takeshi* (4), *Haruo* (2), *Katsuo* (2), *Shiro* (2), *Takashi* (2), *Takehisa* (2), *Yutaka* (2), *Aiko, Daisuke, Eiko, Harumi, Hideaki.*

Matsuno (134) Japanese (mostly west-central Japan and Okinawa Island): 'pine tree field'. One family, descended from the Utsunomiya family, took its name from a

village in Shimotsuke (now Tochigi prefecture).

GIVEN NAMES Japanese 57%. *Hiroshi* (2), *Minoru* (2), *Chiyoko, Fumihiko, Hanako, Hiromu, Hiroyuki, Hitoshi, Isao, Kaori, Kengi, Kenichi.*

Matsuo (272) Japanese (mostly found in the islands of Kyūshū and Okinawa): written with characters meaning 'pine tree' and 'lower slope (of a mountain)'. One family is of priestly (Shintō) origin; two others descend from branches of the TAIRA and MINAMOTO clans.

GIVEN NAMES Japanese 72%. *Kiyoshi* (4), *Hideo* (3), *Kenji* (3), *Hiroshi* (2), *Kazuyuki* (2), *Kenichi* (2), *Kyoko* (2), *Mami* (2), *Miyoko* (2), *Naoko* (2), *Takashi* (2), *Tomoyuki* (2).

Matsuoka (358) Japanese (found throughout Japan and the Ryūkyū Islands): 'pine tree hill', usually denoting a sacred hilltop grove. Small Shintō shrines, always surrounded by trees and usually on hilltops, are found all over the country. See also MATSUDA and MATSUMOTO.

GIVEN NAMES Japanese 51%. *Hiroshi* (4), *Masao* (2), *Miyoko* (2), *Seiki* (2), *Shiro* (2), *Takao* (2), *Yukio* (2), *Aiko, Akifumi, Akihiro, Akiko, Chiaki.*

Matsushima (166) Japanese (mainly eastern Japan and the Ryūkyū Islands): 'pine tree island'.

GIVEN NAMES Japanese 57%. *Aki* (3), *Masumi* (2), *Akio, Akira, Chiyo, Haruo, Hideko, Hideo, Hideto, Hiroshi, Junko, Kazuo.*

Matsushita (197) Japanese: 'beneath the pine tree'. Two families, one of Tōtōmi (now part of Shizuoka prefecture), the other of Mikawa (now part of Aichi prefecture), both descend from the SASAKI family. The name is also found in the Ryūkyū Islands.

GIVEN NAMES Japanese 75%. *Seiji* (4), *Hiroshi* (3), *Yoshiko* (3), *Hideo* (2), *Hiromi* (2), *Kanji* (2), *Masanobu* (2), *Midori* (2), *Nobuyuki* (2), *Shinya* (2), *Toshi* (2), *Toshio* (2).

Matsuura (312) Japanese (mostly found in the island of Kyūshū and the Ryūkyū Islands): 'pine tree bay'. It was originally taken from ancient Matsura province, in what is now Nagasaki prefecture, and is listed in the Shinsen shōjiroku. The alternate pronunciation **Matsura** is also found.

GIVEN NAMES Japanese 57%. *Hiroshi* (4), *Kazuo* (3), *Shigeru* (3), *Kenji* (2), *Machiko* (2), *Masami* (2), *Tadashi* (2), *Takeshi* (2), *Tetsuya* (2), *Akiyoshi, Hajime, Hiroaki.*

Matsuyama (142) Japanese (mainly western Japan and the Ryūkyū Islands): 'pine tree mountain'. One family is descended from the CHIBA branch of the TAIRA clan; another descends from the TAKEDA branch of the MINAMOTO clan.

GIVEN NAMES Japanese 64%. *Akito* (3), *Rumi* (3), *Atsuko* (2), *Hideo* (2), *Hiroshi* (2),

Kenji (2), *Yuji* (2), *Chiaki, Hajime, Hideki, Hiromi, Itaru.*

Matsuzaki (105) Japanese: 'pine tree cape'. This name is found mostly in both the Tōkyō area and on the island of Kyūshū, where it is pronounced *Matsusaki*.

GIVEN NAMES Japanese 72%. *Hiro* (2), *Yasuhiro* (2), *Chiyo, Daisuke, Etsuko, Hajime, Hide, Hidemi, Hiroshi, Hisao, Katsuyoshi, Kazuhiro.*

Matt (1327) **1.** English: from a short form of the personal name MATTHEW. **2.** German: from a short form of the personal name *Matthias* or *Matthäus* (see MATTHEW). **3.** German and Dutch: variant of MATTE 'meadow'.

Matta (1019) **1.** Southern Italian: from a feminine form of MATTO. **2.** Slovak: from the personal name *Matúš*, Slovak form of MATTHEW. **3.** Hindu and Sikh name of unknown meaning, found among people from Sind, Pakistan.

GIVEN NAMES Spanish 11%; Indian 6%. *Jose* (9), *Manuel* (7), *Carlos* (6), *Enrique* (4), *Alfonso* (3), *Juan* (3), *Luis* (3), *Alfredo* (2), *Angel* (2), *Gerardo* (2), *Jaime* (2), *Julio* (2); *Mahendra* (3), *Amit, Ananda, Anil, Ash, Ashwin, Balraj, Deepak, Gurmukh, Hari, Jyoti, Lalita.*

Mattaliano (133) Italian: possibly as Caracausi suggests, from the Biblical name *Magdala* (see MAUDLIN).

GIVEN NAMES Italian 8%. *Sal, Salvatore.*

Mattar (122) Muslim: **1.** variant of **Mu'attar**, a personal name based on Arabic *mu'attar* 'perfumed', 'scented'. **2.** possibly a derivative of *matar* 'rain'.

GIVEN NAMES Muslim 29%. *Afif* (2), *Nabil* (2), *Selim* (2), *Ahmed, Ali, Ameen, Bassam, Emad, Fady, Fouad, Ghassan, Joumana.*

Mattas (132) Greek: origin uncertain. **1.** possibly a reduced form of a surname containing the syllable *Mat-*, such as the patronymic *Mattheou*. **2.** Alternatively, perhaps from Aromanian *mata*, denoting an animal (mule or sheep) with red around the eyes.

GIVEN NAME Greek 4%. *Christos.*

Matte (804) **1.** South German: topographic name for someone who lived near a meadow, from Middle High German *matte* 'meadow'. **2.** Dutch (**van der Matt(e)**): topographic name for someone who lived by a meadow, or habitational name from any of various places named Made or Maete, from Middle Dutch *matte, matta* 'meadow'. **3.** Southern French: possibly a habitational name from the common demesne name La Matte, La Mathe, derived from Occitan *mata* 'bush', 'shrub', 'thicket', 'brush'. Compare MATA 1.

GIVEN NAMES French 6%. *Marcel* (3), *Andre* (2), *Armand* (2), *Cecile, Gervais, Jean Pierre, Jean-Claude, Leonce, Pierre.*

Mattei (675) Italian: patronymic or plural form of MATTEO.

GIVEN NAMES Italian 19%; Spanish 11%. *Angelo* (7), *Marino* (3), *Salvatore* (3), *Mario* (2), *Remo* (2), *Rocco* (2), *Aldo, Alessandra, Antonio, Arcangelo, Attilio, Augusto, Caesar, Clemente, Eduardo; Carlos* (2), *Carmelita, Cruz, Dominga, Javier, Jorge, Josue.*

Matteis (102) Italian: from a patronymic or plural form of DE MATTEIS.

GIVEN NAMES Italian 13%. *Dino, Fiore, Rocco, Sal.*

Matteo (690) Italian: from the personal name *Matteo*, derivative of Latin *Matthaeus* or *Matthias* (see MATTHEW).

GIVEN NAMES Italian 10%. *Rocco* (5), *Antonio* (3), *Amedeo, Augustino, Carmine, Domenic, Nicolino, Pasquale, Salvatore, Sante.*

Matter (1080) **1.** German: topographic name for someone who lived by a meadow, from MATTE 1 + *-er,* suffix denoting an inhabitant. **2.** English and Dutch: occupational name for a maker of mats, from an agent derivative of Middle English *matte,* Middle Dutch *mat* 'mat'.

Mattera (652) Italian (Naples): **1.** variant of MATERA. **2.** possibly from a local form *mat(t)era* 'wood', from Spanish *madera.*

GIVEN NAMES Italian 27%. *Salvatore* (7), *Elena* (3), *Mario* (3), *Sal* (3), *Gilio* (2), *Gino* (2), *Giovanni* (2), *Giuseppe* (2), *Pasquale* (2), *Vincenzo* (2), *Agostino, Angelo, Antonio, Arnaldo, Attilio, Emilio, Ernesto, Geremia, Julio, Orlando, Rafael, Tiberio, Tito.*

Mattern (1772) **1.** German (especially Silesia) and Dutch: from the medieval personal name *Matern,* a derivative of the Roman personal name *Maternus* (from Latin *mater* 'mother'), which was the name of a legendary saint. **2.** Dutch: from *materne* 'prioress', hence presumably a nickname.

Matters (204) **1.** English: variant of MATTER. **2.** English: probably a metonymic occupational name for a mattress maker or seller, from Middle English, Old French *materas,* or less likely for a maker of crossbow bolts, spears, and lances, from the Middle English homonym *materas.* **3.** Dutch: variant of MATTER 2.

Mattes (1111) **1.** English: patronymic from a pet form of MATTHEW. **2.** Hungarian and Jewish (Ashkenazic): variant of MATES.

GIVEN NAMES German 4%. *Reinhold* (4), *Hans* (3), *Erwin, Klaus, Konrad, Kurt, Manfred, Wolfgang.*

Matteson (2800) **1.** Scottish and northern English: variant spelling of MATTISON. **2.** Respelling of Swedish **Mattesson,** a patronymic from the personal name *Mattes* or *Mattis,* Swedish forms of MATTHEW.

Matteucci (310) Italian: from a pet form of the personal name MATTEO.

GIVEN NAMES Italian 18%. *Angelo* (3), *Gino* (2), *Remo* (2), *Alberico, Bruna, Camillo, Carlo, Dante, Domenic, Ermanno, Gianni, Guido.*

Mattey (130) Variant spelling of German MATTHEY.

Mattfeld (104) Americanized form of German **Mad(t)feld,** habitational name from Madfeld in Westphalia or Madtfeld in the Ruhr.

GIVEN NAME German 4%. *Johann.*

Matthai (116) **1.** German: from a variant of the personal name *Matthäus* (see MATTHEW). **2.** Indian: variant spelling of MATHAI.

GIVEN NAMES German 11%; Indian 4%. *Arno* (2), *Heinz, Sieglinde, Waltraud; Ashok.*

Mattheis (252) German: from a variant of the personal name *Matthäus* (see MATTHEW).

GIVEN NAMES German 5%. *Bernd, Erwin, Ewald, Friedrich.*

Matthes (737) **1.** German: from a variant of the personal name *Matthäus* (see MATTHEW). **2.** English: from a variant of the personal name MATTHEW.

GIVEN NAMES German 6%. *Kurt* (5), *Dieter* (3), *Klaus* (2), *Otto* (2), *Eldred, Gunter, Juergen, Monika, Ulrich.*

Matthew (1716) **1.** English and Scottish: from the Middle English personal name *Ma(t)thew,* vernacular form of the Greek New Testament name *Matthias, Matthaios,* which is ultimately from the Hebrew personal name *Matityahu* 'gift of God'. This was taken into Latin as *Mat(t)hias* and *Matthaeus* respectively, the former being used for the twelfth apostle (who replaced Judas Iscariot) and the latter for the author of the first Gospel. In many European languages this distinction is reflected in different surname forms. The commonest vernacular forms of the personal name, including English *Matthew,* Old French *Matheu,* Spanish *Mateo,* Italian *Matteo,* Portuguese *Mateus,* Catalan and Occitan *Mateu* are generally derived from the form *Matthaeus.* The American surname **Matthew** has also absorbed European cognates from other languages, including Greek MATHIAS and **Mattheos.** Compare MATHEW, MATHAI. **2.** It is found as a personal name among Christians in India, and in the U.S. is used as a family name among families from southern India.

Matthews (43160) **1.** English: patronymic from MATTHEW. In North America, this form has assimilated numerous vernacular derivatives in other languages of Latin *Mat(t)hias* and *Matthaeus.* **2.** Irish (Ulster and County Louth): used as an Americanized form of MCMAHON.

Matthewson (166) Northern English: patronymic from MATTHEW.

Matthey (122) **1.** English: from a pet form of MATTHEW. **2.** Dutch: from a derivative of *Mattheus* (see MATTHEW). **3.** German: from a shortened form of *Matthäus* (see MATTHEW).

GIVEN NAME German 4%. *Erwin* (2).

Matthias (926) **1.** German and Dutch: from the personal name *Matthias* (see MATTHEW). **2.** English (chiefly Wales): learned variant of MATTHEW. **3.** Greek: variant of MATHIAS.

Matthies (702) North German and Dutch: derivative of the personal name MATTHIAS.

GIVEN NAMES German 5%. *Ernst* (3), *Hans* (2), *Kurt* (2), *Detlef, Heinrich, Otto, Wilhelm.*

Matthiesen (462) North German, Dutch, Danish, and Norwegian: patronymic from the personal name *Matthias* (see MATTHEW).

GIVEN NAMES German 4%. *Hans* (3), *Heinz* (2), *Armin, Horst.*

Matthiessen (136) North German, Danish, and Norwegian: patronymic from the personal name *Matthias* (see MATTHEW).

GIVEN NAMES German 6%. *Hans, Joerg, Nikolaus.*

Matthieu (105) French: variant spelling of MATHIEU.

GIVEN NAMES French 9%. *Aldor, Renella, Ulysse.*

Matthis (376) Dutch, French, and English: variant of MATHIS.

Matthys (406) Dutch, French, and English: variant of MATHIS.

Matti (200) **1.** Swiss German: from a pet form of the personal name *Matthaeus* (see MATTHEW). **2.** Shortened form of Finnish MATTILA or some other surname based on the personal name *Matti,* a Finnish form of MATTHEW.

Mattia (548) Southern Italian: from the personal name *Mattia,* a variant of MATTEO, Italian equivalent of MATTHEW.

GIVEN NAMES Italian 15%. *Angelo* (3), *Alfonse* (2), *Marco* (2), *Aldo, Antonio, Cosimo, Domenic, Egidio, Gesualdo, Giacomo, Gino.*

Mattiace (109) Italian: unexplained; perhaps from a derivative of the personal name *Mattia* (see MATTHEW).

GIVEN NAMES Italian 19%. *Angelo, Donato, Isabele, Nicola.*

Mattice (906) Origin unidentified. Perhaps a variant of Italian MATTIACE.

Mattick (224) English (of Welsh origin): variant of MADDOCK.

Mattie (416) Scottish: from a pet form of the personal name MATTHEW.

Mattiello (106) Italian: from a pet form of the personal name MATTEO.

GIVEN NAMES Italian 19%. *Assunta, Carmine, Filomena, Gino, Giorgio, Marco, Mario, Paolo.*

Mattila (557) Finnish: from the personal name MATTI + the local suffix *-la,* originally a habitational name from a farm or village so named in western Finland.

GIVEN NAMES Finnish 6%. *Reino* (2), *Sulo* (2), *Toivo* (2), *Yalmer* (2), *Arvo, Esko, Heikki, Ilmari, Jaakko, Kaino, Martti, Pertti.*

Mattimore (132) Irish: unexplained. Perhaps a derivative of a pet form of MATTHEW, with the addition of Gaelic *mor* 'big'.
GIVEN NAMES Irish 4%. *Aileen, Donovan.*

Mattina (219) Italian: **1.** diminutive of MATTO. **2.** habitational name from a place in Caggiano, Salerno province, named Mattina, or from Matina, a place in San Marco Argentano, in Cosenza province.
GIVEN NAMES Italian 22%. *Salvatore* (5), *Angelo* (3), *Salvator* (2), *Luigi, Orazio.*

Mattingley (155) English: variant spelling of MATTINGLY.

Mattingly (5464) English: habitational name from Mattingley in Hampshire, named in Old English as *Mattinglēah* 'woodland clearing (*lēah*) associated with (-*inga*) a man called *Matta*'.

Mattinson (162) Northern English: patronymic from a pet form of MATTHEW.

Mattioli (437) Italian: from a pet form of a personal names MATTIA, MATTEO, or *Mattio*, Italian equivalents of MATTHEW.
GIVEN NAMES Italian 24%. *Gaetano* (3), *Salvatore* (3), *Angelo* (2), *Marco* (2), *Orlando* (2), *Albino, Aldo, Amadeo, Americo, Antonio, Caesar, Carmelo, Carmine, Dante, Elia, Elio, Ellio, Eraldo, Ernesto, Mario, Mauricio, Roberto.*

Mattis (831) **1.** Dutch and French: from a variant of the personal name *Mathias* (see MATTHEW). **2.** English: patronymic from a pet form of MATTHEW.

Mattison (2633) **1.** Scottish and northern English: patronymic from a pet form of MATTHEW. **2.** Respelling of Swedish **Mattisson**, a patronymic from the personal name *Mattis*, a Swedish form of MATTHEW.

Mattix (439) English (of Welsh origin): variant of MADDOX.

Mattke (234) German (of Slavic origin): from a pet form of the personal name *Matt*, a short form of *Matthäus* (see MATTHEW).
GIVEN NAMES German 4%. *Ernst, Guenter, Juergen.*

Matto (136) **1.** Italian: nickname from a dialect variant of *pazzo* 'mad', 'eccentric'. **2.** Italian: from the Germanic personal name *Matto*, from Germanic *Matha-*. **3.** Hungarian (**Mattó**): variant of *Mató*, from a pet form of the personal name *Máté*, Hungarian form of MATTHEW.

Mattocks (640) English (of Welsh origin): variant of MADDOX.

Matton (174) French: from a pet form of the personal name MATHIEU (see MATTHEW).
GIVEN NAMES French 13%. *Philias* (2), *Alphonse, Clermont, Emile, Jean-Luc.*

Mattoon (564) Variant of French MATTON.

Mattos (993) **1.** Portuguese and Spanish: spelling variant of MATOS. **2.** Hungarian: variant of MATUS.
GIVEN NAMES Spanish 10%; Portuguese 5%. *Manuel* (15), *Juan* (4), *Mario* (4), *Carlos* (3), *Alberto* (2), *Fernando* (2), *Gustavo* (2),

Adela, Albino, Alfonso, Ana, Armando; *Joaquim* (3), *Marcio, Sebastiao.*

Mattox (3456) English (of Welsh origin): variant of MADDOX.

Matts (228) English: patronymic from a pet form of MATTHEW.

Mattsen (102) Danish and Norwegian: patronymic from the personal name *Mats*, Scandinavian form of the personal name *Matthaeus* (see MATTHEW).
GIVEN NAMES Scandinavian 11%. *Lars* (2), *Erik, Rigmor, Thorvald.*

Mattson (6975) **1.** Americanized form of Swedish MATTSSON. **2.** Variant of English MATSON.

Mattsson (162) Swedish: patronymic from Swedish *Mat(t)s*, Swedish form of the personal name *Matthaeus* (see MATTHEW).
GIVEN NAMES Scandinavian 34%. *Anders* (2), *Erik* (2), *Matts* (2), *Nils* (2), *Bjorn, Gunvor, Per, Sten, Thor, Thorvald, Torvald.*

Mattucci (158) Italian: patronymic or plural from a pet form of the personal name MATTEO or MATTO.
GIVEN NAMES Italian 15%. *Alessio* (3), *Emelio* (2), *Alfonse, Evo, Gino, Rocco.*

Mattus (101) German: from a reduced form of **Matthäus** (see MATTHEW).

Matty (331) Swiss German: variant spelling of MATTI.

Matula (694) **1.** Czech, Slovak, and Polish: from a pet form of the personal name *Matěj* (see MATTHEW). **2.** Czech: nickname from the vocabulary word *matula* 'butterfly'. **3.** Polish and Ukrainian: nickname from *matula* 'little mother', 'mummy', a pet form of *matka* 'mother'.

Matulewicz (113) Polish: patronymic from the personal name MATULA.

Matulich (191) Croatian (**Matulić**): patronymic from the personal name *Matula*, a derivative of *Matija* or *Matej* (see MATTHEW).
GIVEN NAMES Italian 8%. *Aldo* (2), *Carlo, Marco.*

Matulis (175) Lithuanian: patronymic from the personal name *Matula*, a Lithuanian form of *Matthaeus* (see MATTHEW).
GIVEN NAMES Lithuanian 5%. *Vacys* (2), *Stasys.*

Matura (142) **1.** Croatian: probably a derivative of the personal name *Matija* or *Matej* (see MATTHEW), or alternatively from the Italian surname MATURO. This name comes from the Dalmatian city of Šibenik. **2.** Czech: from the personal name *Matěj*, Czech form of MATTHEW.
GIVEN NAMES South Slavic 7%. *Dragutin, Ivica.*

Maturin (109) French: variant spelling of MATHURIN.
GIVEN NAMES French 7%; Dutch 5%. *Sylvain*; *Derk.*

Maturo (343) Italian: nickname from *maturo* 'mature', 'middle aged', possibly denoting someone who was mature beyond his years.

GIVEN NAMES Italian 15%. *Rocco* (4), *Pasquale* (2), *Vito* (2), *Amedeo, Cosimo, Federico, Giovanni, Luco, Orazio.*

Matus (766) **1.** Czech (Moravian) and Slovak (**Matúš**); Polish; Croatian (Slavonia, **Matuš**); and Slovenian (eastern Slovenia, **Matuš**): from Slavic forms of the Latin personal name *Matthaeus* (see MATTHEW). **2.** Hungarian: from a pet form of *Máté*, Hungarian form of MATTHEW. **3.** Jewish (Ashkenazic): variant of MATES.
GIVEN NAMES Spanish 10%. *Jose* (5), *Carlos* (4), *Juan* (4), *Luis* (4), *Roberto* (4), *Alvaro* (3), *Francisco* (3), *Jorge* (3), *Armida* (2), *Julio* (2), *Manuel* (2), *Mario* (2).

Matusek (202) Czech (**Matušek**) and Slovak (**Matúšek**): from a dialect pet form of the personal name *Mat(o)uš* (see MATTHEW).

Matusiak (226) Polish: patronymic from the personal name *Matusz* (see MATTHEW).
GIVEN NAMES Polish 8%. *Feliks, Grzegorz, Jadwiga, Slawomir, Zbigniew, Zdzislaw.*

Matusik (200) Polish, Czech and Slovak (**Matušík**): from a pet form of the personal name *Matusz* (Polish), *Matouš* (Czech), or *Matúš* (Slovak) (see MATTHEW).
GIVEN NAMES Polish 4%. *Halina, Jerzy, Zbigniew.*

Matuska (295) Czech and Slovak (**Matuška**): from a pet form of the personal name **Mat(o)uš** (see MATTHEW).

Matuszak (525) Polish: patronymic from the personal name *Matusz* (see MATTHEW).

Matuszewski (465) Polish: derivative of the personal name *Matusz* (see MATTHEW), with the addition of -*ewski* by analogy with other surnames (mostly habitational) with this ending, or possibly a habitational name for someone from an unidentified place named with this personal name.
GIVEN NAMES Polish 9%; German 4%. *Bogdan* (2), *Ryszard* (2), *Zbigniew* (2), *Aleksander, Boleslaw, Casimir, Janusz, Jerzy, Kazimierz, Miroslaw, Piotr, Wiktor*; *Alfons* (2), *Hedwig.*

Matute (197) Spanish: habitational name from Matute, towns in La Rioja and Soria provinces.
GIVEN NAMES Spanish 57%. *Jose* (10), *Luis* (7), *Juan* (6), *Carlos* (4), *Miguel* (3), *Pedro* (3), *Santos* (3), *Jaime* (2), *Manuel* (2), *Reynaldo* (2), *Rodrigo* (2), *Salvador* (2); *Marco* (3), *Antonio* (2), *Dante, Fausto, Renzo.*

Matyas (457) Hungarian (**Mátyás**) and Czech (**Matyáš**): from vernacular forms of the personal name *Mathias* (see MATTHEW).
GIVEN NAMES Hungarian 5%. *Attila* (3), *Bela* (3), *Gyula, Lajos, Tibor, Zoltan.*

Matye (100) German form of Hungarian MATYI.
GIVEN NAME German 4%. *Reinhard.*

Matyi (96) Hungarian: from a pet form of the personal name *Mátyás* (see MATTHEW).

Matz (2139) South German: from a pet form of the personal names *Mattheus* or *Matthias* (see MATTHEW).

Matza (199) Jewish (eastern Ashkenazic): occupational name for a baker of Jewish unleavened bread, from Yiddish (of Hebrew origin) *matse* 'matzah' (unleavened bread).

GIVEN NAMES Jewish 8%. *Hyman, Nissim, Sol.*

Matzek (195) German (of Slavic origin): Germanized spelling of Czech and Slovak MACEK. See also MATZ.

Matzen (445) **1.** North German: patronymic from a pet form of the personal name *Matthäus* or *Matthias* (see MATTHEW). **2.** German and Dutch: habitational name from Matzen in the Eifel region.

GIVEN NAMES German 4%. *Hans, Heintz, Juergen, Kurt, Lorenz, Otto.*

Matzinger (194) South German: habitational name for someone from either of two places named Matzing, in Bavaria and in Austria (Salzburg), or from Matzingen (in Thurgau canton) in Switzerland.

Matzke (793) German (of Slavic origin): from a pet form of the personal name *Matthäus* or *Matthias* (see MATTHEW).

GIVEN NAMES German 5%. *Kurt* (2), *Otto* (2), *Bernhard, Ernst, Erwin, Gerhard, Heinz.*

Matzner (151) **1.** German and Dutch: habitational name for someone from Matzen (see MATZEN 2). **2.** Variant of German METZNER 1. **3.** Jewish (Ashkenazic): variant of MATZA, with the Yiddish agent suffix *-ner.*

GIVEN NAMES German 11%; Scandinavian 6%; Jewish 5%. *Oskar* (2), *Hans, Markus, Otto; Gitla, Hyman.*

Mau (1095) **1.** North German and Dutch: nickname for a dandy or an affluent person, from Middle Low German *mouwe*, Dutch *mouw*, 'sleeve', referring to a wide sleeve of expensive, ornamented fabric. **2.** Portuguese: nickname from *mau* 'bad', 'evil' (Latin *malus*). **3.** Breton: nickname or occupational name from *mao* 'young boy', 'servant'. **4.** Chinese: variant of MAO.

Mauceri (221) Italian (Sicily): variant of MAUGERI. The spelling with *-c-* reflects a local pronunciation.

GIVEN NAMES Italian 24%. *Sal* (3), *Salvatore* (3), *Giuseppe* (2), *Angelo, Palma, Pietrina.*

Mauch (929) German: nickname for a glutton, though possibly connected with *much* 'rotten(ness)' (Swiss German *mauch*) or Middle High German *müchen* 'to be secretive'.

Mauck (1079) **1.** German: unexplained. **2.** Americanized spelling of German MAUCH.

Maude (182) English: from a female personal name (see MOULD). MacLysaght notes that this name was taken to County Kilkenny in the 17th century, and also oc-

curs among Irish-speaking people in County Connemara, Ireland.

GIVEN NAME Irish 8%. *Brian Patrick.*

Maudlin (338) English: from the Middle English vernacular form, *Maudeleyn*, of the New Testament Greek personal name *Magdalēnē*. This is a byname, meaning 'woman from *Magdala*' (a village on the Sea of Galilee, deriving its name from Hebrew *migdal* 'tower'), denoting the woman cured of evil spirits by Jesus (Luke 8:2), who later became a faithful follower. In Christian folk belief she was generally identified with the repentant sinner who washed Christ's feet with her tears in Luke 7; hence the name came to be used as a byname for a prostitute, also a tearful woman. The popularity of the personal name increased with the supposed discovery of her relics in the 13th century.

Maudsley (104) English: variant of MAWDSLEY.

Maue (237) German (**Maue**): variant of MAU.

Mauel (122) German: habitational name from any of several places so named in the Rhineland.

Mauer (1311) **1.** German: variant of MAURER. **2.** German and Jewish (Ashkenazic): topographic name for someone who lived by a wall, Middle High German *mūre*, German *Mauer*. As a Jewish name it can be ornamental.

Mauerman (110) German (**Mauermann**): occupational name for a bricklayer, literally 'wall man'.

GIVEN NAMES German 4%. *Kurt, Otto.*

Maugans (117) German: probably an altered spelling of the Frisian personal name *Magens*, which is either a derivative of MAGNUS or a patronymic from the personal name *Magino*, a short form of any of various Germanic personal names formed with *magin* 'strength' as the first element.

Mauger (612) **1.** English: variant of MAJOR 1. **2.** French: from the same personal name as 1, or from a short form of the personal name *Amauger*, from a Germanic personal name composed of the elements *amal* 'strength', 'vigor' + *gār, gēr* 'spear'. **3.** South German: dialect variant of *Maunker*, nickname for a morose person.

Maugeri (183) Southern Italian: probably a habitational name from Maugeri in Catania, although Caracausi explains the name as a variant of **Malgeri**, which he associates with a Germanic personal name composed of the elements *amal* 'strength', 'energy' + *gār, gēr* 'spear', 'lance'.

GIVEN NAMES Italian 22%. *Carmine* (2), *Ignazio* (2), *Salvatore* (2), *Angelo, Camillo, Giuseppe, Orazio, Pietro.*

Maughan (1054) Irish: variant of MAHAN.

Maughon (115) Variant spelling of Irish MAHAN.

Mauk (1288) German (Swabian): from Middle High German *māc, māge* 'relative', 'kinsman' (see MAAG).

Maul (1116) **1.** German: nickname for someone with a deformed mouth, or for someone who made excessive use of the mouth in eating, drinking, or talking, from Middle High German *mūl* 'mouth'. **2.** German: possibly a nickname from Middle High German *mūl* 'mule'. **3.** English: from *Mall*, a medieval pet form of the female personal name *Mary* (see MARIE 1).

Maulden (236) English: variant spelling of MAULDIN.

Mauldin (3606) English: habitational name from Malden in Surrey (now in Greater London) or Maldon in Essex. Both places were named in Old English as 'hill with a cross or monument', from *mǣl* 'monument', 'cross' (crucifix) + *dūn* 'hill'.

Maulding (234) English: variant of MAULDIN or a metathesized spelling of **Maudling**, a variant of MAULDIN.

Maule (594) **1.** German (**Mäule**): variant of MAUL 1. **2.** English: variant of MAUL 2.

Mauler (135) Southern German: **1.** occupational name from a dialect form of MAHLER. **2.** nickname for a complainer, from Middle Low German *mūlen* 'to complain', 'to be angry'.

Maull (274) English: variant of MAUL 2.

GIVEN NAME French 4%. *Camille.*

Mauller (126) From a dialect variant of German MAHLER.

Maulsby (162) English: variant of MAULTSBY.

Mault (143) English: variant of MOULD.

Maultsby (396) English: habitational name from Mautby in Norfolk, named in Old Norse as 'the farmstead (*býr*) of a man called Malti' or 'the farmstead where malt is made'.

Maun (120) Irish: variant spelling of MAUNE.

Maund (183) English: **1.** variant of MANDER 1. **2.** habitational name from Maund Bryan or Rose Maund in Herefordshire, possibly named in Old English as '(place at) the hollows', from the dative plural of *maga* 'stomach' (used in a topographical sense). Mills suggests it may alternatively be a survival of an ancient Celtic term *magnis*, probably meaning 'the rocks'.

Maunder (121) English: variant of MANDER.

Maune (172) Irish: possibly from the Norman personal name *Mayon*, a pet form of MATTHEW. In County Mayo it is a variant of MAHAN.

GIVEN NAMES German 5%. *Dietrich, Kurt.*

Mauney (1134) Probably an altered spelling of French **Mauny**, a habitational name from several places so called Seine-Maritime.

Maung (124) Burmese or other Southeast Asian: unexplained.

GIVEN NAMES Southeast Asian 51%. *Maung* (3), *Sein* (3), *Zaw* (3), *Han* (2), *Kan* (2), *Chen, Khin, Ming Wai, Sang, Soe, Wai; Tun* (2), *Cho, Min; Tin* (6), *Than* (2), *Ba, Phan, Tha*.

Maunu (119) Finnish: habitational name from a place so named, found chiefly in western and northern Finland.

GIVEN NAMES Finnish 17%; Scandinavian 4%. *Jarmo, Markku, Olavi, Reino, Sulo, Toivo*.

Maupin (2390) French: topographic name from Old French *mal, mau* 'bad' + *pin* 'pine (tree)'.

Maura (121) **1.** Catalan and French: variant of **Maure**, from the Latin personal name *Maurus* (see MOORE 2). **2.** Southern Italian: from a feminine variant of the personal name MAURO.

GIVEN NAMES Spanish 18%; Italian 8%; French 6%. *Mario* (3), *Eduardo* (2), *Humberto* (2), *Amada, Amalia, Armando, Bernardo, Carlos, Jesus, Jose, Juan, Luis; Antonio, Giuseppe, Rino, Romolo, Vincenzo; Myrlande* (2).

Maurer (8613) German and Jewish (Ashkenazic): occupational name for a builder of walls of stone or brick, from an agent derivative of Middle High German *mûre*, German *Mauer* 'wall' (from Latin *murus* 'wall', especially a city wall). In the Middle Ages the majority of dwellings were built of wood (or lath and plaster), and this term would have specifically denoted someone employed in building defensive walls, castles, churches, and other public buildings.

Mauri (185) **1.** Italian (mainly southern): patronymic or plural form of MAURO. **2.** Catalan: patronymic name from the personal name *Mauri*, from Latin *Maurus* (see MAURO). **3.** Catalan and Southern French (Occitan) (**Maurí**): probably from the personal name *Malric* (Germanic *Almaricus*).

GIVEN NAMES Spanish 12%; Italian 8%. *Ernesto* (2), *Ramon* (2), *Adela, Carlos, Eladio, Emilia, Estrella, Horacio, Jorge, Jose, Juan, Mario; Alessandra, Angelo, Cecilio, Cosimo, Gianfranco, Lorenzo, Mauro*.

Maurice (1149) French, English, Welsh, Scottish, and Irish: from the Old French personal name *Maurice*, Latin *Mauritius* (see MORRIS).

GIVEN NAMES French 11%. *Andre* (4), *Pierre* (3), *Armand* (2), *Denys* (2), *Gabrielle* (2), *Antoine, Benoit, Camille, Cecile, Francois, Gaston, Germain*.

Mauricio (458) Portuguese (**Maurício**) and Spanish: from the personal name *Maurício* (Portuguese), *Mauricio* (Spanish), derived from the Latin personal name *Mauritius* (see MORRIS).

GIVEN NAMES Spanish 40%; Portuguese 15%. *Jose* (15), *Manuel* (10), *Juan* (8), *Carlos* (4), *Mario* (4), *Roberto* (4), *Lilia* (3), *Luis* (3), *Adela* (2), *Andres* (2), *Antero* (2),

Cipriano (2); *Manoel; Antonio* (10), *Augustino, Clemente, Liberato, Marino*.

Mauriello (466) Italian (mainly southern): from a pet form of MAURO.

GIVEN NAMES Italian 15%. *Angelo* (6), *Flavio* (2), *Salvatore* (2), *Alfonse, Attilio, Carmine, Gino, Nicola, Nunzio, Sal, Vicenzo*.

Maurin (255) Italian and French: from a medieval personal name derived from the Latin personal name *Maurinus*, a derivative of *Maurus* (see MAURO), which was the name of a 6th-century martyr.

Mauritz (195) German and Dutch: from the personal name *Mauritz*, from the Latin personal name *Mauritius* (see MORRIS).

GIVEN NAMES German 10%. *Fritz* (2), *Armin, Frieda, Helmut, Kurt, Reinhold, Wolfgang*.

Maurizio (124) Italian: from the personal name *Maurizio*, from Latin *Mauritius* (see MORRIS).

GIVEN NAMES Italian 21%. *Carlo* (2), *Marcello, Marco, Mario* (2), *Fernando, Matteo, Natale, Sal, Valentino, Vito*.

Mauro (2653) Italian (mainly southern): from the personal name *Mauro*, derived from the Latin personal and ethnic name *Maurus*, meaning 'Moor', 'North African'; or from the same word, *mauro*, applied as a nickname or ethnic name. Compare MOORE 2 and 3.

GIVEN NAMES Italian 14%. *Salvatore* (17), *Angelo* (8), *Sal* (7), *Domenic* (5), *Giuseppe* (5), *Antonio* (4), *Carmine* (4), *Carmelo* (3), *Domenico* (3), *Gaetano* (3), *Nino* (3), *Pasquale* (3).

Maury (453) **1.** French: from a short form of the personal name *Amaury* (see EMERY). **2.** Southern French (Occitan): habitational name from Maury, in Basses Pyrénées. **3.** English: probably a variant of MOREY 2.

GIVEN NAMES French 6%; Spanish 4%. *Cecile, Chantal, Christophe, Jean-Luc, Lucien, Marcel, Michel, Monique, Phillippe, Sylvanie; Jose* (3), *Ruben* (3), *Carlos* (2), *Manuel* (2), *Alvaro, Antolin, Luis, Miguel, Pedro, Ramon, Roberto, Salvador*.

Maus (1414) **1.** German: nickname for someone supposedly resembling a mouse, in appearance or timidity, from Middle High German *mûs* 'mouse'. **2.** Jewish (Ashkenazic): from German *Maus* 'mouse', one of the most common of the unflattering surnames imposed on Jews by non-Jewish government officials in 18th- and 19th-century central Europe.

Mauser (491) German: occupational name for a mouse-catcher, from Middle High German *mûs* 'mouse' + the agent suffix -*er*.

GIVEN NAMES German 4%. *Ulrich* (2), *Alfons, Ewald*.

Mauseth (100) Norwegian: habitational name from any of several farms, named with an uncertain first element, possibly *maur* 'ant' or *maure* 'bedstraw' (Galium).

The second element is *set* 'farmstead', 'dwelling'.

Mausolf (178) German: variant of MUSOLF.

GIVEN NAMES German 5%. *Ernst, Reinhard*.

Mauss (197) German: variant spelling of MAUS.

GIVEN NAME German 4%. *Wilhelm*.

Mausser (150) German: variant spelling of MAUSER.

GIVEN NAMES German 10%. *Alois, Bernhard, Franz, Frieda, Helmut, Konrad*.

Maust (664) Possibly an altered form of German MAST.

Maute (194) French (**Mauté**): variant of **Mauthé** (see MAUTHE).

GIVEN NAMES German 9%. *Kurt* (3), *Bernhard, Gerhard*.

Mauter (114) French (Alsatian): occupational name from German *Mauter*, Middle High German *mûtære* 'collector of tolls or customs duty'. Compare MAUTNER.

Mauthe (214) **1.** French (**Mauthé**): nickname from Old French *malté, mauté* 'malice' (derived from *mal, mau* 'bad'). **2.** German: metonymic occupational name for a toll collector, from Middle High German *mûte* 'customs', 'duty', 'toll'.

Mautino (116) Italian (Piedmont): unexplained; probably from a personal name.

Mautner (258) German (Bavaria, Austria): occupational name from Middle High German *mûtære* 'collector of tolls or customs'.

GIVEN NAMES German 8%. *Erwin* (2), *Hans* (2).

Mautz (332) South German: **1.** nickname for a grouse or complainer, from Swabian dialect *mau(n)zen* 'to complain'. **2.** variant of MUTZ and MUTH.

Mauzey (138) See MAUZY.

Mauzy (419) Possibly an altered form of the French surname **Mauzé**, a habitational name from a place in Deux-Sèvres, named in Latin as *Malisiacum* or *Maletiacum* 'estate of Maletius', from the personal name *Maletius* + the locative suffix -*acum*.

Maver (105) Scottish: occupational name for a steward, from Gaelic *maor*.

GIVEN NAME French 4%. *Gabrielle*.

Maves (442) Altered spelling of German **Mewes**, a pet form of the personal name *Bartholomäus* (see BARTHOLOMEW).

FOREBEARS Bearers of this name are descended from Johannes Meivus, who landed in Philadephia in 1737.

Mavis (445) German: variant of MAVES.

GIVEN NAMES German 4%. *Erwin* (2), *Kurt, Otto*.

Mavity (205) Irish: reduced form of **MacVitty**, an Anglicized form of Gaelic **Mac an Bhiadhtaigh** 'son of the food provider', a class of people, i.e. farmers, under Irish law.

Mavros (105) Greek: from the personal name *Mavros*, originally a descriptive nickname for a person with a dark or swarthy complexion, Greek *mavros* 'black',

'Moorish', later also meaning 'poor fellow'. This nickname may also be the source of the surname. This element is also commonly found in compound names such as *Mavrogiannis* 'black John'.

GIVEN NAMES Greek 21%. *Anastasios, Apostolos, Despina, Konstantinos, Kyriacos, Nikolaos, Theodoros, Vassilios.*

Maw (384) English: **1.** name for someone who was related to an important local personality, from Middle English *maugh, maw* 'relative', especially by marriage (from Old English *māge* 'female relative'). In the north of England this term was used more specifically to mean 'brother-in-law'. **2.** topographic name from Middle English *mawe* 'meadow'. Some early forms, such as Sibilla de la Mawe (Suffolk 1275), clearly indicate a topographic origin, by reason of the preposition and article. **3.** probably also from a Middle English personal name, *Mawe*, Old English *Mēawa*, perhaps originally a byname from Old English *mǣw* 'sea mew', 'seagull' (compare MEW).

Mawby (136) English: habitational name from Mautby in Norfolk. Compare MAULTSBY.

Mawdsley (114) English: habitational name from Mawdesley in Lancashire, named in Middle English with the Anglo-Norman French female personal name *Maud* + Middle English *ley* 'clearing'.

Mawhinney (469) **1.** Scottish (Galloway) and northern Irish: Anglicized form of Gaelic **Mac Choinnich** (Scottish), **Mac Choinnigh** (Irish), a patronymic from the byname *Coinneach* (see MCKENZIE and KENNETH). **2.** Northern Irish (Antrim): possibly an Anglicized form of Gaelic **Mac Shuibhne** (see MCSWEENEY).

Mawn (139) Irish: variant spelling of MAUNE.

Mawson (240) English: **1.** patronymic from MAW 1. **2.** metronymic from a form of MOULD 1.

Mawyer (306) **1.** Americanized spelling of German MAYER. **2.** Possibly a variant of English **Mawer**, an occupational name for a reaper or mower, Middle English *mawer(e), mower*.

Max (925) German and Dutch: from a short form of the personal name *Maximilian* (Latin *Maximillianus*, a derivative of *Maximillus*, diminutive of *Maximus* 'greatest'), borne by a 3rd-century saint venerated particularly in the region of Passau, where he founded a church. The personal name was comparatively rare at the most productive period of surname formation; it gained popularity from the Holy Roman Emperor Maximilian I (born 1459), who was named by his father, Frederick III of Austria, in honor of the Roman heroes Q. Fabius Maximus and Scipio Aemilianus, as if with a combination of their names. The name is also borne by Ashkenazic Jews, presum-

ably as an adoption of the German surname.

Maxa (137) Czech: from the personal name *Makarius*, from Greek *Makarios* 'fortunate', 'blessed'.

GIVEN NAME French 4%. *Michel.*

Maxam (254) Variant spelling of MAXIM.

Maxcy (292) English: variant spelling of MAXEY.

Maxedon (131) Origin uncertain; possibly an altered form of Scottish MAXTON.

FOREBEARS A Maxedon family are recorded in Orange Co., SC, from 1781 onward, also found as **Maxident**.

Maxey (3818) **1.** English: habitational name from a place in Northamptonshire, so named from the genitive case of the northern English personal name MACK + Old English *ēg* 'island', 'low-lying land'. **2.** Irish: variant of **Mackesy**, an Anglicized form of Gaelic **Ó Macasa** 'descendant of *Macus*', a personal name which is probably a form of MAGNUS.

Maxfield (2180) English (South Yorkshire): habitational name from Maxfield in Sussex, or Maxfield Plain in North Yorkshire.

Maxham (192) Variant spelling of MAXIM, altered by folk etymology to resemble an English habitational name.

Maxie (589) Variant spelling of English or Irish MAXEY.

Maxim (551) French and Dutch: from the personal name *Maxim* (from Latin *Maximus* 'greatest', superlative of *magnus* 'great'), borne by a number of early Christian saints.

Maximo (102) Spanish (**Máximo**): from the personal name *Máximo* (Latin *Maximus* 'greatest', superlative of *magnus* 'great'), borne by a number of early Christian saints.

GIVEN NAMES Spanish 50%; Italian 8%. *Arturo* (3), *Zosimo* (3), *Miguel* (2), *Roberto* (2), *Alfonso, Amador, Angel, Carlos, Corazon, Erasto, Fulgencio, Gonzalo; Flavio, Marino, Valentino.*

Maxin (108) Probably a variant of English MAXSON.

Maxon (937) English: variant of MAXSON.

Maxson (1851) Patronymic from the personal name *Maximilian* (see MAX).

FOREBEARS This surname is recorded as early as 1666 in Westerly, RI, with the birth of a John Maxson.

Maxted (146) English (Kent): habitational name from Maxted Street in Kent.

Maxton (186) Scottish: habitational name from a place so called in Roxburghshire (Borders), named as the 'settlement (*tūn*) of Maccus'. There is also a place of this name in Kent, England, but it does not seem to have given rise to a surname.

Maxwell (23548) **1.** Scottish: habitational name from a place near Melrose in Roxburghshire. The place name is first recorded in 1144 in the form *Mackeswell*

'Mack's spring or stream (Old English *well(a)*)'. **2.** Irish: this surname is common in Ulster, where it has sometimes been adopted as an alternative to MISKELL. **3.** Jewish: arbitrary adoption of the Scottish name, or Americanized form of one or more like-sounding Jewish surnames.

May (38472) **1.** English, French, Danish, Dutch, and German: from a short form of the personal name *Matthias* (see MATTHEW) or any of its many cognates, for example Norman French *Maheu*. **2.** English, French, Dutch, and German: from a nickname or personal name taken from the month of May (Middle English, Old French *mai*, Middle High German *meie*, from Latin *Maius (mensis)*, from *Maia*, a minor Roman goddess of fertility). This name was sometimes bestowed on someone born or baptized in the month of May; it was also used to refer to someone of a sunny disposition, or who had some anecdotal connection with the month of May, such as owing a feudal obligation then. **3.** English: nickname from Middle English *may* 'young man or woman'. **4.** Irish (Connacht and Midlands): when not of English origin (see 1–3 above), this is an Anglicized form of Gaelic **Ó Miadhaigh** 'descendant of *Miadhach*', a personal name or byname meaning 'honorable', 'proud'. **5.** French: habitational name from any of various places called May or Le May. **6.** Jewish (Ashkenazic): habitational name from Mayen, a place in western Germany. **7.** Americanized spelling of cognates of 1 in various European languages, for example Swedish **Ma(i)j**. **8.** Chinese 梅: possibly a variant of MEI 1, although this spelling occurs more often for the given name than for the surname.

FOREBEARS Cape May, at the mouth of Delaware Bay, is named after the Dutch explorer Cornelius Jacobsen May.

Maya (729) **1.** Spanish (from Basque): habitational name from Maya del Baztán in Navarre province, from Basque *Amaiur*. **2.** Catalan: variant spelling of *Maià*, habitational name from *Maià de Montcal* and other places (see MAIA)

GIVEN NAMES Spanish 45%. *Jose* (15), *Francisco* (11), *Carlos* (6), *Jaime* (6), *Juan* (6), *Luis* (6), *Miguel* (6), *Enrique* (5), *Jesus* (5), *Jorge* (5), *Manuel* (5), *Mario* (5).

Mayabb (112) Origin unidentified.

Mayall (186) English: variant spelling of MALE.

Maybee (396) Variant spelling of English MABEY.

Mayben (119) Northern Irish: variant spelling of MABEN.

Mayberry (4622) English and Irish: of uncertain origin; most probably an altered form of MOWBRAY. It is also found as **Maybury**, which has the form of an English habitational name. There is a place near Woking in Surrey so called; however, this is not recorded until 1885 and is probably derived from the surname. In England this surname is found mainly in the West Midlands; it has also spread into Wales. In Ireland this form is common in Ulster; MacLysaght records that it was taken there from England in the 17th century.

Maybin (208) Irish (Ulster): variant spelling of MABEN.

Maybury (296) English and Irish: see MAYBERRY. In Ireland this form is common in County Kerry.

Maycock (266) English: from a pet form of MAY 1.

Maycroft (100) English: unexplained.

Mayden (191) English: variant spelling of MAIDEN.

Maye (974) English: variant spelling of MAY.

Mayeaux (400) French: origin uncertain. Perhaps an altered spelling of **Mayaud**, a nickname from Occitan *maial, maiau* 'hog to be killed in May'.
GIVEN NAMES French 4%. *Andre, Clemile, Ferrel.*

Mayeda (303) Japanese: alternative spelling of MAEDA. The *-ye* spelling represents a sound lost from modern Japanese, now pronounced and spelled *-e*.
GIVEN NAMES Japanese 35%. *Minoru* (5), *Takashi* (3), *Hideo* (2), *Hiroshi* (2), *Kaz* (2), *Kenji* (2), *Masami* (2), *Sunao* (2), *Akie, Akiko, Akira, Fumio.*

Mayen (161) **1.** German: habitational name from a place so named in the Rhineland. The place name is related to *Maifeld*, the name of the area of which it is the main settlement, which is derived from the Celtic word *magos* 'field', 'plain'. **2.** French: from a diminutive of *mai*, which in the dialect of Savoy denoted pasture where cattle were allowed to graze in the spring and fall, and, by extension, a hut built for the cowherd nearby. This name is also established in Mexico.
GIVEN NAMES Spanish 42%. *Jose* (8), *Luis* (4), *Juan* (2), *Manuel* (2), *Mario* (2), *Rodolfo* (2), *Alda, Ana, Carlos, Carlos Humberto, Efrain, Enrique.*

Mayer (17136) **1.** English: status name for a mayor, Middle English, Old French *mair(e)* (from Latin *maior* 'greater', 'superior'; compare MAYOR). In France the title denoted various minor local officials, and the same is true of Scotland (see MAIR 1). In England, however, the term was normally restricted to the chief officer of a borough, and the surname may have been given not only to a citizen of some standing who had held this office, but also as a nickname to a pompous or officious person. **2.** German and Dutch: variant of MEYER 1. **3.** Jewish (Ashkenazic): variant of MEYER 2.
GIVEN NAMES German 4%. *Kurt* (26), *Otto* (18), *Hans* (10), *Franz* (7), *Helmut* (6), *Wilhelm* (6), *Erwin* (5), *Gerhard* (5), *Heinz* (5), *Ilse* (5), *Lorenz* (5), *Wolfgang* (5).

Mayerhofer (137) South German: habitational name for someone from Mayerhof in Bavaria, or from any of the numerous farms named Mayerhof, Maierhof, or Meyerhof.
GIVEN NAMES German 11%. *Helmut* (4), *Hans* (2), *Konrad* (2), *Bernhard, Ignatz.*

Mayernik (181) Czech and Slovak (**Majerník**): from a diminutive of German MEYER, a word which in Slavic-speaking regions often denoted a the steward of a farm, although farther west it usually denoted a tenant farmer.
GIVEN NAMES French 5%. *Simonne* (2), *Alphonse.*

Mayers (1716) **1.** English: patronymic from MAYER 1. **2.** German: patronymic from MAYER 2. **3.** Dutch: variant of MEYER 1 and 3.

Mayerson (167) Jewish (Ashkenazic): patronymic from MAYER.
GIVEN NAMES Jewish 8%. *Hyman, Meyer, Ronit, Sol.*

Mayes (7382) English: patronymic from the personal name *May* (see MAY).

Mayette (170) French: habitational name from places called Le Mayet in Allier and Puy-de-Dôme, or Mayet in Sarthe.

Mayeux (655) Northern French: from an old form of **Mayeur**, a variant of MAIRE.
GIVEN NAMES French 5%. *Landry* (2), *Alphonse, Andre, Armand, Colette, Monique, Theophile.*

Mayfield (9674) English: habitational name from places so named in Staffordshire and Sussex. The former was named in Old English as 'open country (*feld*) where madder (*mæddre*) grows', while the latter was named as 'open country where mayweed (*mægðe*) grows'. The surname is now most common in Nottinghamshire.

Mayhall (607) English: of uncertain origin. it may be a habitational name from an unidentified place (there is a Mayhall Farm in Buckinghamshire, but it is not clear whether the family name is derived from the farm name or vice versa). Alternatively it may be a variant of MAYALL, which is itself a variant of MALE.

Mayhan (215) Variant spelling of Irish MAHAN.

Mayher (148) Variant spelling of Irish MAHER.

Mayhew (3547) **1.** English: from the Norman French personal name *Mahieu*, a variant of *Mathieu* (see MATTHEW). **2.** Anglicized form of French MAILLOUX.
FOREBEARS Thomas Mayhew (1593–1682) came to Medford, MA, from Tisbury, Wiltshire, England, about 1632, and subsequently moved to Watertown, MA. In 1642 he established a settlement on Martha's Vineyard, with his son Thomas, who was the first English missionary to the Indians of New England.

Mayhorn (140) Probably English: unexplained.

Mayhue (308) Variant spelling of English MAYHEW.

Mayhugh (529) Variant spelling of English MAYHEW.

Mayland (159) English: habitational name from Mayland in Essex, possibly named in Old English as 'land or estate (*land*) where mayweed (*mægðe*) grows', or alternatively as '(place at) the island', from Old English *ēg-land*, with the initial *M-* derived from a preceding *ðǣm*, dative case of the definite article.

Mayle (1185) English: variant spelling of MALE.

Maynard (12924) English (of Norman origin) and French: from the Continental Germanic personal name *Mainard*, composed of the elements *magin* 'strength' + *hard* 'hardy', 'brave', 'strong'.

Mayne (1540) **1.** Scottish and English: variant spelling of MAIN. **2.** Irish: mainly of Norman English origin (see MAIN 3–6) but in County Fermanagh used sometimes to represent McMANUS. **3.** French: variant of MAINE.

Mayner (130) **1.** English: variant spelling of MAYNOR. **2.** Catalan: variant of MAINER.

Maynes (520) Irish: shortened Anglicized form of Gaelic **Mac Maghnuis** (see McMANUS).

Maynor (1369) English (of Norman origin): from a derivative of the Continental Germanic personal name *Maginhari*, composed of the elements *magin* 'strength', 'might' + *hari* 'army'.

Mayo (11294) **1.** English and Irish: variant of MAYHEW. **2.** Variant of French MAILHOT.
FOREBEARS A William Mayo born in Wiltshire, England, *c.* 1684 was a surveyor who settled in VA about 1623 and helped survey the VA-NC boundary and found Richmond and Petersburg, VA.

The Mayo Clinic in Rochester, MN, was founded by William Worrall Mayo (1819–1911), who immigrated to the U.S. from England, in 1845, and his sons, all gifted and innovative physicians and surgeons.

Mayol (102) Catalan: from a variant spelling of from *mallol* 'young vineyard', either a topographic name or a metonymic occupational name for a young winegrower.
GIVEN NAMES Spanish 26%. *Jose* (4), *Carlos, Cornelio, Efrain, Fernando, Jorge, Juan, Juan Carlos, Manuel, Miguel, Nilda, Orlando.*

Mayon (152) French: from a pet form of the female personal name *Marie* (see MARIE 1).
GIVEN NAME French 4%. *Alcee.*

Mayor (567) **1.** English (Lancashire): variant spelling of MAYER 1. **2.** Spanish and Jewish (Sephardic): nickname for an older man or a distinguishing epithet for the elder of two bearers of the same personal name, from Spanish *mayor* 'older' (Latin *maior* (*natus*), literally 'greater (by birth)'). **3.** Spanish and Jewish (Sephardic): occupational or status name, from *major* 'governor', 'chief'. **4.** Catalan: variant spelling of MAJOR. **5.** Jewish (Ashkenazic): variant of MEYER 2.

GIVEN NAMES Spanish 14%. *Carlos* (3), *Pedro* (3), *Agapito* (2), *Alberto* (2), *Cesar* (2), *Cosme* (2), *Javier* (2), *Jorge* (2), *Jose* (2), *Juan* (2), *Manuel* (2), *Orlando* (2).

Mayoral (155) Spanish and Catalan (variant spelling of *Majoral*): occupational name for the foreman of a gang of agricultural workers or the leader of a group of herdsmen, *mayoral* (Late Latin *maioralis*, originally an adjective derivative of *maior* 'greater').

GIVEN NAMES Spanish 57%. *Carlos* (4), *Jose* (4), *Luis* (4), *Jesus* (3), *Aida* (2), *Alberto* (2), *Gustavo* (2), *Jaime* (2), *Joaquin* (2), *Juan* (2), *Miguel* (2), *Osvaldo* (2).

Mayorga (774) Spanish: habitational name from Mayorga in Valladolid province (Latin *Maiorica*).

GIVEN NAMES Spanish 47%; Portuguese 11%. *Jose* (20), *Luis* (12), *Carlos* (8), *Jorge* (6), *Juan* (6), *Manuel* (6), *Alberto* (5), *Cesar* (5), *Guillermo* (5), *Miguel* (5), *Armando* (4), *Francisco* (4); *Marcio*.

Mayotte (352) Altered spelling of French **Mayot**, a habitational name from a place so named in Aisne.

GIVEN NAMES French 6%. *Armand* (3), *Mireille*.

Mayou (111) English (West Midlands): possibly a variant of MAYHEW.

Mayr (397) **1.** German, Czech (**Maýr**), and Slovak (**Majer**): variant of MEYER 1. **2.** Jewish (eastern Ashkenazic): variant of MEYER 2.

GIVEN NAMES German 24%. *Franz* (5), *Otto* (4), *Siegfried* (4), *Ernst* (2), *Hans* (2), *Helmut* (2), *Konrad* (2), *Kurt* (2), *Armin*, *Bernd*, *Dieter*, *Fritz*.

Mayrand (137) Possibly an altered spelling of French **Mayran**, a habitational name from a place so named in Aveyron.

GIVEN NAMES French 9%. *Andre*, *Fernand*, *Germaine*, *Remi*, *Stephane*.

Mays (11651) English: patronymic from the personal name *May* (see MAY).

Mayse (527) English: patronymic from the personal name *May* (see MAY).

Mayson (170) Northern English: **1.** patronymic from the personal name *May* (see MAY). **2.** variant spelling of MASON.

Maysonet (124) Spanish or Portuguese: unexplained.

GIVEN NAMES Spanish 42%. *Angel* (4), *Jose* (4), *Rafael* (3), *Eugenio* (2), *Manuel* (2), *Abimael*, *Agustin*, *Antonio*, *Efrain*, *Eusebio*, *Francisco*, *Gilberto*, *Juan*.

Mayton (511) Probably of English origin, a habitational name from an unidentified place, perhaps Mayton Hall in Norfolk.

Maytum (117) English (Kent): unexplained.

Mayville (412) French?

Maywald (118) Partly Americanized spelling of German **Maiwald**, a habitational

name from Maiwaldau in Silesia, or a topographic name from a wood named as 'May wood'.

GIVEN NAME German 12%. *Christoph* (3).

Mayweather (236) Probably an altered form of English MERRIWEATHER.

Maza (299) **1.** Spanish: metonymic occupational name for someone who had a mace as a symbol of office or who carried one in ceremonial possessions, from Spanish *maza* 'mace' (Late Latin *mattea*, probably of Germanic origin). In some cases it may have been used as a metonymic occupational name for a soldier who used a mace in its original function as a weapon. **2.** Polish: nickname derived from *mazać* 'to smear', 'sully', 'rub out'. The exact meaning of the nickname is unclear. Compare MAZIARZ.

GIVEN NAMES Spanish 34%. *Luis* (8), *Jose* (6), *Angel* (4), *Carlos* (4), *Manuel* (4), *Ana* (3), *Cesar* (2), *Juan* (2), *Mario* (2), *Pedro* (2), *Refugio* (2), *Ricardo* (2).

Mazak (123) Slovak (**Mazák**): nickname from *mazáč* 'smear'.

Mazanec (223) Czech and Slovak: from *mazanec* 'Easter cake', 'big round cake', hence a nickname for someone with a big round face.

Mazar (144) Jewish (eastern Ashkenazic): possibly, occupational name for a dealer in tar, wheel grease, or cart grease, from Ukrainian *mazyar*. Compare Polish MAZIARZ.

GIVEN NAMES Jewish 8%. *Moshe*, *Polina*, *Rivka*, *Shimon*.

Mazariegos (250) Spanish: habitational name from Mazariegos, a town in Palencia province.

GIVEN NAMES Spanish 52%. *Jorge* (9), *Carlos* (4), *Blanca* (3), *Cesar* (3), *Juan* (3), *Julio* (3), *Luis* (3), *Manuel* (3), *Silvia* (3), *Armando* (2), *Arturo* (2), *Augusto* (2); *Manfredo* (2), *Antonio*, *Flavio*, *Leonardo*.

Maze (1541) **1.** French (**Mazé**): habitational name from a place in Maine-et-Loire, named in Latin as *Masiacum* 'estate of Masius', from the personal name *Masius* + the locative suffix *-acum*. **2.** French (Forez): topographic name from a feminine form of *mas* 'farmhouse', 'house in the country' (see MAS 2), or a habitational name from a place called La Maze (Ardèche) or Les Maze (Hérault), named with the same word. **3.** French (**Mazé**): from a pet form of THOMAS. **4.** Northern Irish: of uncertain origin; possibly a variant of MAY. **5.** Slovenian: possibly from a short form of the personal name *Tomaž* or its pet form *Tomaže(j)* (see THOMAS).

Mazeika (199) Lithuanian (**Mažeika**): nickname for a short person, from *mažas* 'short'.

GIVEN NAMES Lithuanian 5%. *Aldona*, *Alfonsas*, *Antanas*, *Juozas*, *Mykolas*, *Nida*, *Vytautas*.

Mazer (712) Jewish (eastern Ashkenazic): variant of MAZUR.

GIVEN NAMES Jewish 4%. *Emanuel* (2), *Herschel* (2), *Hedva*, *Isadore*, *Mendel*, *Meyer*, *Sol*.

Mazerolle (100) Respelling of French **Mazerolles**, a habitational name from any of several places named Mazerolles, in Aude, Charente, Landes, Vienne, and elsewhere.

GIVEN NAMES French 23%. *Alcide* (3), *Antoine*, *Armand*, *Chantel*, *Mathieu*, *Yvon*.

Mazey (102) **1.** Jewish (from Ukraine): Americanized spelling of *maziej*, an occupational name from Ukrainian *mazij* 'worker with tar, wheel grease, or cart grease'. **2.** Americanized spelling of Slovenian **Mazej**, variant of MAZE.

Maziarz (359) Polish: metonymic occupational name from *maziarz* 'dealer in tar, wheel grease, or cart grease', an agent noun derivative of *mazać* 'to smear'.

GIVEN NAMES Polish 10%. *Wladyslaw* (3), *Casimir* (2), *Bogdan*, *Genowefa*, *Jerzy*, *Jozef*, *Kazimierz*, *Malgorzata*, *Slawomir*, *Stanislawa*, *Witold*.

Mazie (104) Jewish (from Belarus): acronymic name from the Hebrew expression *mi zera Israel Isserlin* 'descendant of Israel Isserlin', famous rabbinical scholar from Central Europe (1390–1460). .

Mazin (101) Jewish (eastern Ashkenazic): metronymic from the Yiddish female personal name *Maze*, a pet form of Mariam (see MARIE).

GIVEN NAMES Jewish 25%; Russian 13%. *Ilya*, *Isaak*, *Naum*, *Zalmon*; *Boris* (3), *Mikhail* (2), *Vladimir* (2), *Igor*, *Leonid*, *Oleg*.

Mazingo (105) Variant of MOZINGO.

Mazmanian (106) Armenian: patronymic of unexplained origin, probably from a Persian personal name.

GIVEN NAMES Armenian 17%. *Anahit*, *Aram*, *Araxie*, *Arshag*, *Asdghig*, *Haig*, *Krekor*, *Mardiros*, *Sarkis*, *Vartan*.

Mazo (220) **1.** Spanish: nickname for a forceful person or metonymic occupational name for someone who used a mallet, Spanish *mazo* (a byform of MAZA 1). **2.** Spanish (from Galician and Asturian-Leonese): habitational name from any of a number of places so named in Galicia, Asturies, and Lleón. **3.** Jewish (eastern Ashkenazic): variant of MASE.

GIVEN NAMES Spanish 21%; Russian 8%; Jewish 8%. *Manuel* (3), *Lourdes* (2), *Maria Teresa* (2), *Nieves* (2), *Alejandro*, *Cruz*, *Domingo*, *Eloy*, *Fabiola*, *Jairo*, *Jesus*, *Jose*; *Galina* (2), *Mikhail* (2), *Anatoly*, *Dmitry*, *Gennady*, *Grigoriy*, *Vladimir*, *Yevgeniy*; *Aron*, *Hyman*, *Leyb*, *Miriam*, *Yakov*.

Mazon (298) **1.** Spanish (**Mazón**): from an augmentative of MAZA 1. **2.** Galician (**Mazón**): habitational name from Mazón, a town in Lugo province, Galicia. **3.** French: variant of MAISON.

GIVEN NAMES Spanish 23%. *Jose* (3), *Luis* (3), *Enriqueta* (2), *Guillermo* (2), *Gustavo* (2), *Manuel* (2), *Sergio* (2), *Adolfo*, *Alejandra*, *Alejandrina*, *Alfredo*, *Angelina*.

Mazor (224) Jewish (eastern Ashkenazic): variant of MAZUR.

GIVEN NAMES Jewish 18%; Russian 5%. *Baruch* (2), *Haim* (2), *Miriam* (2), *Arie*, *Avi*, *Limor*, *Mort*, *Moshe*, *Naum*, *Nir*, *Ravit*, *Shmuel*; *Boris* (2), *Galina*, *Igor*, *Leonid*, *Liya*, *Mikhail*, *Svetislav*.

Mazur (3347) Polish, Ukrainian, and Jewish (eastern Ashkenazic): **1.** regional name for someone from the medieval province of Masovia (Polish *Mazowsze*), which includes modern Masuria. **2.** Polish: nickname from Polish *mazur* 'rustic'.

GIVEN NAMES Polish 6%. *Zbigniew* (5), *Andrzej* (3), *Beata* (3), *Jacek* (3), *Stanislaw* (3), *Wladyslaw* (3), *Wojciech* (3), *Zygmunt* (3), *Henryk* (2), *Lech* (2), *Piotr* (2), *Wieslaw* (2).

Mazure (149) French: topographic name from Old French *masure* 'country house', 'house with land', 'estate' (from Latin *mansura*), or a habitational name from any of several places named with this word, for example Le Masure in Audresselles (Pas-de-Calais), Le Mazure in Savoy, and Les Mazures in Ardennes.

GIVEN NAME French 4%. *Philippe* (2).

Mazurek (1078) Polish and Ukrainian: diminutive of MAZUR.

GIVEN NAMES Polish 8%. *Jerzy* (3), *Jozef* (3), *Dorota* (2), *Krystyna* (2), *Stanislaw* (2), *Witold* (2), *Alicja*, *Andrzej*, *Casimir*, *Edyta*, *Elzbieta*, *Ewa*.

Mazurkiewicz (396) Polish: patronymic from MAZUREK.

GIVEN NAMES Polish 9%. *Andrzej* (2), *Bogdan*, *Jacek*, *Jozef*, *Lech*, *Marcin*, *Przemyslaw*, *Ryszard*, *Stanislawa*, *Tadeusz*, *Urszula*, *Zbigniew*.

Mazurowski (191) Polish: habitational name for someone from places called Mazurowice or Mazurowiec, or even Mazury.

Mazyck (284) Americanized spelling of Polish **Mazik**, a derivative of *mazać* 'to smear', 'sully', or 'rub out', probably a nickname for a messy person.

Mazza (2898) Italian: **1.** nickname or metonymic occupational name from *mazza* 'club', 'mace', 'sledge hammer'. **2.** nickname for a destructive individual, from a derivative of Italian *(am)mazzare* 'to kill or destroy' (Latin *mactare*).

GIVEN NAMES Italian 13%. *Angelo* (14), *Salvatore* (8), *Domenic* (7), *Sal* (6), *Carmine* (4), *Vito* (4), *Antonio* (3), *Carmelo* (3), *Enrico* (3), *Gaetano* (3), *Italo* (3), *Biagio* (2).

Mazzaferro (219) Italian: probably a nickname for a particularly strong or invincible man, from the verb *(am)mazzare* 'to kill' + *ferro* 'iron'.

GIVEN NAMES Italian 24%. *Aldo* (2), *Domenic* (2), *Rocco* (2), *Amedeo*, *Carmela*, *Carmello*, *Gino*, *Giorgio*, *Guiseppe*, *Luigi*, *Natale*.

Mazzanti (243) Italian: from a derivative of MAZZA, possibly denoting a butcher or slaughterer.

GIVEN NAMES Italian 11%. *Stefano* (4), *Agostino*, *Aldo*, *Angelo*, *Emidio*, *Geno*, *Italo*, *Pasquale*, *Reno*.

Mazzara (248) Italian (Sicily): habitational name from the port of Mazzara del Vallo on the west coast of Sicily, which takes its name from the Mazzaro river.

GIVEN NAMES Italian 27%. *Vito* (5), *Salvatore* (4), *Sal* (3), *Carmelo* (2), *Antonio*, *Claudio*, *Filomena*, *Isidoro*, *Leonarda*, *Mario*, *Rosario*.

Mazzarella (669) Italian: from a diminutive of MAZZA.

GIVEN NAMES Italian 13%. *Angelo* (7), *Antonio* (3), *Alfonse*, *Antonietta*, *Carmelo*, *Carmine*, *Gaetano*, *Giosue*, *Luigi*, *Raffaele*, *Rocco*, *Rosaria*.

Mazzarelli (157) Italian: patronymic or plural form of **Mazzarello**, a diminutive of MAZZA.

GIVEN NAMES Italian 19%. *Angelo* (3), *Carmine* (2), *Antonio*, *Claudio*, *Corrado*, *Fernando*, *Fiorenzo*, *Giulio*, *Mauro*, *Nicola*, *Ovidio*, *Santo*.

Mazzarese (108) Italian: habitational name for someone from Mazara del Vallo, from an adjectival form of the first element.

GIVEN NAMES Italian 20%. *Angelo* (5), *Aldo* (3), *Antonio*, *Ignazio*, *Sal*.

Mazzariello (100) Italian: perhaps from a diminutive of MAZZARO.

GIVEN NAMES Italian 18%. *Vito* (3), *Antonio* (2), *Luigi* (2).

Mazzaro (123) Italian: occupational name for a maker or seller of clubs or maces, from an agent derivative of *mazza* 'club', 'mace'. This surname may also have denoted the mace-bearer of a magistrat or bishop, who would walk at the head of a procession, holding the symbolic mace.

GIVEN NAMES Italian 26%. *Vito* (3), *Carmine* (2), *Salvatore* (2), *Angelo*, *Biaggio*, *Domenic*, *Nicola*, *Sal*.

Mazzei (670) Southern Italian: patronymic or plural form of MAZZEO.

GIVEN NAMES Italian 20%. *Angelo* (5), *Carmine* (4), *Antonio* (2), *Gaetano* (2), *Livio* (2), *Luigi* (2), *Marino* (2), *Mario* (2), *Moreno* (2), *Aldo*, *Arnaldo*, *Carmino*, *Dante*, *Dino*, *Elvio*.

Mazzella (761) Southern Italian: from a diminutive of MAZZA or alternatively of *Mazzeo*, a variant of MATTEO.

GIVEN NAMES Italian 32%. *Silvio* (8), *Silverio* (7), *Mario* (6), *Carmine* (5), *Angelo* (4), *Antonio* (3), *Nicola* (3), *Salvatore* (3), *Aldo* (2), *Attilio* (2), *Elio* (2), *Guido* (2), *Sal* (2), *Camillo*, *Luciana*, *Luisa*, *Paola*, *Roberto*.

Mazzeo (866) Southern Italian: from the personal name *Mazzeo*, a variant of *Matteo*, Italian equivalent of MATTHEW.

GIVEN NAMES Italian 22%. *Angelo* (4), *Rocco* (4), *Mario* (3), *Santo* (3), *Constantino* (2), *Guido* (2), *Vito* (2), *Antonio*, *Biagio*, *Biago*, *Caesar*, *Camillo*, *Roberto*, *Rodolfo*, *Rosario*.

Mazzetti (176) Italian: **1.** from a plural diminutive of MAZZA. **2.** from a patronymic or plural form of a derivative of MAZZO or MAZZEO.

GIVEN NAMES Italian 16%; French 6%. *Remo* (3), *Flavio* (2), *Gianluca* (2), *Renzo* (2), *Aldo*, *Angelo*, *Dino*, *Franco*; *Armand* (2), *Camille*, *Sylvie*.

Mazzie (242) Americanized spelling of Italian MAZZEI.

GIVEN NAMES Italian 8%. *Antonio*, *Cosimo*, *Remo*, *Salvatore*.

Mazzilli (155) Italian: from the patronymic or plural form of a derivative of MAZZO or MAZZEO.

GIVEN NAMES Italian 13%. *Vito* (3), *Aldo*, *Carmela*, *Francesco*, *Libero*, *Matteo*, *Mauro*.

Mazzio (102) Italian: from the personal name *Mazzio*, a variant of *Matteo*, Italian equivalent of MATTHEW.

GIVEN NAMES Italian 14%. *Rocco*, *Vito*.

Mazziotta (102) Italian: derivative of MAZZIO.

GIVEN NAME Italian 10%. *Salvatore*.

Mazziotti (135) Italian: from the patronymic or plural form of *Mazziotto*, a pet form of the personal name MAZZIO.

GIVEN NAMES Italian 18%. *Alfonso*, *Americo*, *Mario*, *Massimo*, *Salvatore*.

Mazzo (146) Italian: **1.** from the Old Tuscan personal name *Mazzus*, from the Germanic personal name *Maz(z)o*. **2.** possibly from a short form of *Giacomazzo*, a pejorative derivative of the personal name *Giacomo* (see JAMES).

GIVEN NAMES Italian 14%. *Angelo*, *Antonio*, *Carmine*, *Cosmo*, *Domenic*, *Massimo*, *Rocco*.

Mazzocchi (157) Italian: patronymic or plural form of MAZZOCCO.

GIVEN NAMES Italian 16%. *Salvatore* (2), *Antonio*, *Carlo*, *Elio*, *Pierina*.

Mazzocco (211) Italian: **1.** from a plural or patronymic form of **Mazzocca**, from a derivative of MAZZA. **2.** possibly a habitational name from Mazzocco, a locality in Mogliano Veneto, Treviso province.

GIVEN NAMES Italian 19%. *Dante* (3), *Angelo* (2), *Carmel* (2), *Adelmo*, *Domenic*, *Ennio*, *Giulio*, *Leandro*, *Marco*, *Nino*, *Ricci*, *Rinaldo*, *Ulises*.

Mazzola (1357) Southern Italian: from a diminutive of MAZZA.

GIVEN NAMES Italian 14%. *Salvatore* (6), *Vito* (5), *Antonio* (4), *Angelo* (3), *Ciro* (3), *Donato* (3), *Carmine* (2), *Gaetano* (2), *Nazzareno* (2), *Pasquale* (2), *Sal* (2), *Santo* (2).

Mazzoli (155) Italian: patronymic or plural form of *Mazzolo*, a pet form of MAZZO.
GIVEN NAMES Italian 10%. *Angelo* (2), *Vito* (2), *Enrico, Luigi, Pasquale, Romano*.

Mazzone (808) Italian: **1.** from an augmentative of MAZZA or MAZZO. **2.** possibly from a shortened augmentative of *Giacomazzo*, a pejorative derivative of the personal name *Giacomo* (see JAMES).
GIVEN NAMES Italian 16%. *Angelo* (6), *Salvatore* (4), *Vito* (3), *Antonio* (2), *Gaetano* (2), *Giuseppe* (2), *Marco* (2), *Pasquale* (2), *Rocco* (2), *Aldo, Carmelo, Clemente*.

Mazzoni (454) Italian: patronymic from MAZZONE.
GIVEN NAMES Italian 13%. *Aldo* (6), *Carlo* (2), *Marco* (2), *Renzo* (2), *Alessio, Dante, Elio, Giampiero, Gino, Giuseppe, Neno, Pietro*.

Mazzotta (337) Italian: from a pet form of the personal names MAZZO or MAZZEO.
GIVEN NAMES Italian 25%; Spanish 9%. *Carmelo* (5), *Salvatore* (5), *Giuseppe* (3), *Domenic* (2), *Sal* (2), *Santo* (2), *Antonio, Carmine, Clementina, Dante, Francesco, Gaetano; Mario* (3), *Orlando* (2), *Roberto* (2), *Rosario* (2), *Alejandro, Alfonso, Casimiro, Celestino, Cesar, Julio, Marina, Renato*.

Mazzotti (108) Italian: from a pet form of the personal names *Mazzo* or MAZZEO.
GIVEN NAMES Spanish 10%; Italian 9%. *Carlos, Ernesto, Guillermo, Rolando; Aldo, Luca, Marco*.

Mazzuca (263) Italian (Sicily): from Greek *matsouka* 'club', 'mace', itself from medieval Latin *maxuca*. Compare MAZZA.
GIVEN NAMES Italian 16%. *Silvio* (2), *Carlo, Corinda, Giovanni, Maurizio, Ornella, Rocco, Santo*.

Mazzucco (191) Italian: from a derivative of the personal names MAZZO or MAZZEO.
GIVEN NAMES Italian 18%. *Angelo* (4), *Carmine* (2), *Massimo* (2), *Biagio, Cesare, Gennaro, Giulio, Salvatore*.

Mazzullo (107) Italian: from a pet form of the personal names MAZZO or MAZZEO.
GIVEN NAMES Italian 8%. *Antonio, Mario, Salvatore*.

McAbee (1385) Irish: Anglicization of Gaelic **Mac an B(h)eatha** 'son of life', i.e. 'man of religion', originally a term denoting a monk, but later used as a personal name.

McAda (112) Scottish and northern Irish: Anglicization of Gaelic **Mac Ádaidh** 'son of *Ádadh*', Gaelic form of ADAM.

McAdam (916) Scottish and Irish: Anglicized form of Gaelic **Mac Adaim** 'son of ADAM'. In Ireland, it has also been adopted as a surname by bearers of the names MCCADDEN (in County Armagh) and MCCAW (in County Cavan), as well as by bearers of a number of unrelated names including BARRY (a Norman family in County Cork).
GIVEN NAME Irish 4%. *Brendan*.

McAdams (4381) Northern Irish: variant of MCADAM with the redundant addition of the English patronymic ending *-s*.

McAden (139) Scottish: variant of MCADAM or MCCADDEN.

McAdoo (1203) Northern Irish (Connacht): Anglicized form of Gaelic **Mac Conduibh** 'son of *Cú Dhubh*', a personal name or byname meaning 'black hound', from *cú* 'hound' (genitive *con*) + *dubh* 'black'. It is also Anglicized as CUNNIFF and MCNIFF.

McAdory (265) Northern Irish (County Antrim): rare Anglicized form of Gaelic **Mac an Deoraidh** 'son of the stranger'.

McAdow (149) Northern Irish: variant of MCADOO.

McAfee (4260) Scottish and northern Irish: Anglicized form of Gaelic **Mac Dhuibhshíthe** 'son of *Duibhshíth*', a personal name composed of the elements *dubh* 'black' + *síth* 'peace'. Compare DUFFY.

McAffee (180) Scottish and northern Irish: variant spelling of MCAFEE.

McAlear (123) Northern Irish: variant spelling of MCALEER.
GIVEN NAME Irish 5%. *Egan*.

McAleer (916) Northern Irish (Armagh) and Scottish: Anglicized form of Gaelic **Mac Giolla Uidhir** (see MCCLURE).
GIVEN NAME Irish 4%. *Siobhan*.

McAleese (213) Scottish and northern Irish: Anglicized form of Gaelic **Mac Gille Íosa** (Scottish), **Mac Giolla Íosa** (Irish) (see MCLEISH).

McAlexander (605) Scottish: Anglicized form of Gaelic **Mac Alasdair** (see MCALLISTER), *Alexander* being regarded as the English equivalent of the Gaelic personal name *Alasdair*.

McAlhany (124) Irish: Anglicized form of Gaelic **Mac Giolla Choinnigh** (see MCELHINNEY).

McAlister (4225) Scottish and northern Irish: variant of MCALLISTER.

McAllaster (120) Scottish: variant spelling of MCALLISTER.

McAllen (206) **1.** Scottish: Anglicized form of Gaelic **Mac Ailín** or **Mac Aileáin** 'son of Allen' (see ALLEN). **2.** Irish: when not Scottish, it can be a variant of MCCALLION, in counties Donegal and Kerry.

McAllister (10625) Scottish and northern Irish: Anglicized form of Gaelic **Mac Alasdair** 'son of *Alasdair*', the Gaelic form of the personal name ALEXANDER.

McAloon (331) Northern Irish: Anglicized form of Gaelic **Mac Giolla Eóin** 'son of the servant of (Saint) John'. Compare MCLEAN.
GIVEN NAME Irish 5%. *Brendan* (2).

McAlpin (1127) Scottish and northern Irish: variant of MCALPINE.

McAlpine (1359) Scottish and northern Irish: Anglicized form of Gaelic **Mac Ailpein** (Scottish), **Mac Ailpín** (Irish) 'son of *Ailpean*', a personal name of uncertain etymology, possibly derived from *alp* 'lump'. The personal name was borne by Pictish kings, one of whom, Kenneth, son of Ailpín, Ailpean, became the ruler of the united Picts and Scots and is regarded as the founder of the somewhat disparate clan of this name.

McAmis (376) Irish: Anglicized form of Scottish Gaelic **Mac Sheumais** 'son of *Seumus*', Gaelic form of JAMES. Compare MCCAMISH.

McAnallen (145) Irish or Scottish: Anglicized form of Gaelic **Mac an Ailín**, of unexplained origin.

McAnally (1497) Northern Irish: Anglicized form of Gaelic **Mac an Fhailghigh** (see MCNALLY).

McAnany (198) Irish: variant of MCENANEY.

McAndrew (1588) Scottish and Irish (County Mayo): Anglicized form of Gaelic **Mac Aindreis** (Scottish), **Mac Aindriú** (Irish) 'son of Andrew'.

McAndrews (990) Scottish and Irish: variant of MCANDREW with the redundant addition of English patronymic *-s*.

McAnelly (266) Irish: variant of MCANALLY (see MCNALLY).

McAneny (121) Irish: variant of MCENANEY.

McAninch (753) Northern Irish: Anglicized form of Gaelic **Mag Aonghuis** (see MCINNIS).

McAnnally (181) Irish: Anglicized form of Gaelic **Mac an Fhailghigh** (see MCNALLY).

McAnulty (538) Irish: Anglicized form of Gaelic **Mac an Ultaigh**; MCNULTY.

McArdle (2303) Irish (Ulster) and Scottish: Anglicized form of Gaelic **Mac Árdghail** 'son of *Árdghal*', a personal name composed of the elements *ard* 'height' + *gal* 'valor'.
GIVEN NAMES Irish 6%. *Bridie, Colm, Dermot, Kieran, Sean Patrick*.

McAree (127) Scottish: Anglicized form of Gaelic **Mac Ara** 'son of the charioteer'.

McArthur (4541) Scottish: Anglicized form of Gaelic **Mac Artair**, a patronymic from the Gaelic form of the personal name ARTHUR.

McArtor (268) Scottish: variant of MCARTHUR.

McAskill (122) Scottish: variant of MCCASKILL.

McAtee (1686) Northern Irish: Anglicized form of Gaelic **Mac an tSaoi** 'son of the scholar or wise man'.

McAteer (848) Northern Irish: Anglicized form of Gaelic **Mac an tSaoir** 'son of the craftsman'. Compare Scottish MCINTYRE.
GIVEN NAMES Irish 4%. *Eoin, Nuala, Sean Patrick*.

McAulay (296) Northern Irish: Anglicized form of Gaelic **Mac Amhalghaidh** (see MCCAULEY).

McAuley (1605) Northern Irish: Anglicized form of Gaelic **Mac Amhalghaidh** (see McCauley).

GIVEN NAMES Irish 4%. *Brendan, Declan.*

McAuliff (200) Irish: variant spelling of McAuliffe.

GIVEN NAME Irish 5%. *Clancy.*

McAuliffe (2398) Irish (Cork): Anglicized form of Gaelic **Mac Amhlaoibh** 'son of *Amhlaoibh*', Gaelic form of the Old Norse personal name Olaf (see McCauley).

GIVEN NAMES Irish 5%. *Paddy* (2), *Liam.*

McAvoy (1928) Northern Irish: variant of McEvoy.

McBain (579) Scottish: 1. Anglicized form of Gaelic **Mac a' Ghille Bhàin** 'son of the pale or white-haired lad', in some cases a descriptive nickname for an albino. 2. variant of McBean.

McBane (232) Scottish: variant of McBain.

McBath (113) Variant of Scottish McBeth.

McBay (245) Scottish: variant of McBeth.

McBean (295) Scottish and northern Irish: Anglicized form of Gaelic **Mac Bheathain** 'son of *Beathan*' (see Bean).

GIVEN NAME French 4%. *Leonie.*

McBeath (386) Scottish: variant of McBeth.

McBee (2491) Scottish or Irish: variant of McBay, itself a shortened form of McBeth. In Gaelic, *-th-* is silent.

McBeth (1002) Scottish: Anglicization of Gaelic **Mac Beatha** 'son of life', i.e. 'man of religion', used as a personal name. Compare McAbee.

McBratney (115) Irish: Anglicized form of Gaelic **Mac an Bhreitheamhnaigh** 'son of the judge'.

McBrayer (1388) Variant of Scottish and northern Irish **MacBrair** or **MacBriar**, Anglicized forms of Gaelic **Mac Bràthar** 'son of the friar'.

McBreairty (117) Variant spelling of McBrearty.

McBrearty (242) Irish (mainly County Donegal): Anglicized form of Gaelic **Mac Mhuircheartaigh** 'son of *Muircheartach*', a personal name meaning 'navigator'. Compare Moriarty.

McBreen (224) Irish (County Kilkenny): Anglicized form of Gaelic **Mac Braoin** 'son of *Braon*', a personal name meaning 'drop'.

GIVEN NAME Irish 6%. *Brendan* (2).

McBride (21267) Irish (mainly County Donegal) and Scottish: Anglicized form of Gaelic **Mac Brighde**, from earlier **Mac Giolla Bhrighde** (Irish), **Mac Gille Brighde** (Scottish) 'son of the servant of (Saint) Brighid'. Compare Kilbride.

McBridge (111) Irish: variant of McBride, representing the original Gaelic pronunciation.

McBrien (415) Irish: Anglicized form of Gaelic **Mac Briain** 'son of Brian' (see

Bryan) or of **Mac Broin, Mac Brain** 'son of *Bran*', a personal name meaning 'raven'.

GIVEN NAMES Irish 5%. *Brendan, Seamus.*

McBroom (1624) Scottish: probably a variant of **MacBrayne**, an Anglicized form of Gaelic **Mac an Bhreitheamhan** 'son of the judge', from *breitheamh* 'judge' (see Brain). In Ireland the same name was Anglicized as **(Mc)Abraham**.

McBryar (167) Variant spelling of Scottish and northern Irish **McBriar** (see McBrayer).

McBryde (692) Scottish: variant of McBride.

McBurnett (289) Scottish: patronymic formation (with Gaelic *mac* 'son'), apparently from the Anglo-Norman surname Burnett 'little brown-haired one'. More probably, it may be an altered form of McBurney.

McBurney (899) Scottish and northern Irish: Anglicized form of Gaelic **Mac Biorna** 'son of *Biorna*', Gaelic form of the Old Norse personal name *Bjarni* 'bear'.

McBurnie (121) Scottish and northern Irish: variant spelling of McBurney.

GIVEN NAME French 5%. *Andre* (2).

McCaa (303) Scottish (Galloway): variant of McCaw.

McCabe (12048) Scottish and Irish (Cavan): Anglicized form of Gaelic **Mac Cába** 'son of *Cába*', a nickname or personal name of uncertain origin.

GIVEN NAMES Irish 8%. *Conall* (2), *Donovan* (2), *Aileen, Aisling, Brendan, Ciaran, Declan, Dermot, Eamon, Fintan, Kieran, Liam.*

McCadden (259) Irish and Scottish: Anglicized form of Gaelic **Mac Cadáin** 'son of *Cadán*', a rare surname from County Armagh; or of **Mac Adáin** or **Mac Aidín**, both based on a diminutive of the personal name Adam.

McCafferty (1901) Irish: Anglicized form of Gaelic **Mac Eachmharcaigh**, 'son of *Eachmharcach*', a personal name composed of the elements *each* 'horse' + *marcach* 'rider', 'knight'. The sound change *ch* to *f* also occurs in a number of other names. Compare Murphy. The surname is found in Donegal, probably a branch of the O'Dohertys.

GIVEN NAME Irish 4%. *Brendan.*

McCaffery (917) Northern Irish: variant of McCaffrey.

GIVEN NAMES Irish 5%. *Brendan* (2), *Patrick Do.*

McCaffrey (3431) Northern Irish: Anglicized form of Gaelic **Mac Gafraidh** or **Mac Gofraidh** 'son of *Gafradh*', a Gaelic form of the Old Norse personal name *Guðfróðr*, composed of the elements *guð* 'god' + *fróðr* 'wise', and equivalent to English Godfrey. An alternative Gaelic form of the personal name is *Gothraidh*, which gave rise to McGorry. In Ireland this is a branch of the Maguires of Fermanagh.

GIVEN NAMES Irish 6%. *Aidan, Caitlin, Donal, Eamon, Kaitlin, Maeve, Murphy.*

McCaghren (120) Irish: Anglicized form of Gaelic **Mac Eachráin** (see McEachern).

McCague (135) Irish (County Monaghan): variant of McCaig.

McCahan (173) Irish: Anglicized form of Gaelic **Mac Eacháin** (see McCaughan).

McCahill (281) Irish: Anglicized form of Gaelic **Mac Cathail** or of **Mac Cathmhaoil**, an Ulster name (see McCall).

GIVEN NAMES Irish 8%. *Brendan, Liam, Padraic.*

McCahon (105) Irish: Anglicized form of Gaelic **Mac Eacháin** (see McCaughan, McGahan).

McCaig (515) Irish (Galway) and Scottish (Ayr, Galloway): Anglicized form of Gaelic **Mac Thaidhg** (Scottish Gaelic **Mac Thaoig**) 'son of *Tadhg*', a name meaning 'poet', 'philosopher'.

McCain (5966) Irish: variant of Scottish McKean.

McCaleb (1072) Scottish or Irish: variant of McKillip. The spelling has been influenced by the Old Testament personal name Caleb.

McCalip (166) Variant of Scottish or Irish McKillip.

McCalister (368) Scottish: variant of McAllister.

McCall (14185) Irish and Scottish: 1. Anglicized form of Gaelic **Mac Cathmhaoil** 'son of *Cathmhaol*', a personal name composed of the elements *cath* 'battle' + *maol* 'chief'. 2. Anglicized form of **Mac Cathail** 'son of *Cathal*' (see Cahill).

McCalla (948) 1. Scottish and Irish (Donegal): variant of McCauley. 2. Irish (Armagh): variant of McCall 1.

McCallen (180) 1. Scottish: variant of McAllen. 2. Irish (County Fermanagh): variant of McCallion.

McCalley (240) Scottish and Irish: variant of McCauley.

GIVEN NAME Irish 5%. *Murphy* (2).

McCallie (352) Scottish variant of McCauley.

McCallion (304) Irish (Donegal and Derry) and Scottish (Argyllshire): Anglicized form of Gaelic **Mac Cailín** 'son of *Cailín* or *Caileán*', a personal name that is either a variant of Colin or a derivative of *coileán* 'puppy'.

GIVEN NAME Irish 5%. *Eamon.*

McCallister (2651) Scottish and northern Irish: variant of McAllister.

McCallon (129) Irish: variant of McCallion.

GIVEN NAME Irish 4%. *Joe Pat.*

McCallum (3738) Scottish: Anglicized form of Gaelic **Mac Coluim** 'son of *Colum*', a personal name derived from Latin *columba* 'dove' (now often found as *Calum*). This was the name of the 6th-century missionary known in English as St.

Columba (521–97), who converted the Picts to Christianity and founded an influential monastery on the island of Iona.

McCally (102) Irish: variant of MCCALLEY.

McCalman (129) Scottish and northern Irish: variant of MCCALMONT.

McCalmon (123) Scottish and northern Irish: variant of MCCALMONT.

McCalmont (162) Scottish and northern Irish: Anglicized form of Gaelic **Mac Colmáin** 'son of *Colmán*' (earlier *Columbán*), a diminutive of the personal name *Colum*. See also COLEMAN, MCCALLUM. The addition of *-t* is due to English speakers' perception of the devoicing of Gaelic final *-n*.

McCambridge (360) Northern Irish and Scottish: Anglicized form of Gaelic **Mac Ambróis** 'son of AMBROSE'.
GIVEN NAME Irish 5%. *Kieran*.

McCamey (338) Scottish: variant of **MacCamie** 'son of Jamie', a pet form of JAMES. See also MCCAMISH.

McCamish (247) Scottish or Irish: Anglicized form of **Mac Sheumais** 'son of *Seumas*', Gaelic form of JAMES.

McCammack (123) Of Scottish or Irish origin: possibly an Anglicized form of Scottish Gaelic **Mac Thamaig** 'son of Tommie'.

McCammon (1248) Scottish and northern Irish (County Down): Anglicized form of Gaelic **Mac Ámoinn** 'son of *Ámoinn*', a Gaelic form of the Norse personal name *Amundr*, which is composed of the elements *ag* 'awe', 'fear', or 'edge', 'point' + *mundr* 'protection'.

McCampbell (551) Patronymic formation from Scottish CAMPBELL.

McCamy (184) Scottish: see MCCAMEY.

McCan (143) Irish: variant spelling of MCCANN.

McCance (320) Scottish and Irish: Anglicized form of Gaelic **Mac Aonghuis** 'son of *Aonghus*' (see ANGUS). Compare MCINNIS, MCGINNIS.

McCandless (2068) Northern Irish: Anglicized form of Gaelic **Mac Cuindlis** 'son of *Cuindleas*', an early personal name of uncertain origin.

McCandlish (209) Northern Irish: Anglicized form of Gaelic **Mac Cuindlis** (see MCCANDLESS).

McCane (343) Irish: variant of MCKEAN or MCCAHAN.

McCanless (288) Variant of northern Irish MCCANDLESS.

McCann (13754) Irish (northern Armagh): Anglicized form of Gaelic **Mac Cana** 'son of *Cana*', a personal name or byname meaning 'wolf cub'.
GIVEN NAMES Irish 4%. *Brendan* (11), *Malachy* (3), *Donovan* (2), *Liam* (2), *Aidan*, *Aileen*, *Brigid*, *Colum*, *Conan*, *Donal*, *Kiernan*, *Ronan*.

McCanna (332) Irish: variant of MCCANN.

McCannon (315) Irish: Anglicized form of Gaelic **Mac Canann** (see CANNON).

McCants (1410) Scottish and Irish: variant of MCCANCE.

McCard (153) Scottish or Irish: variant of MCCART.

McCardell (394) Scottish and Irish: variant of MCARDLE.

McCardle (749) Scottish and Irish: variant of MCARDLE.

McCarey (184) Irish: variant spelling of MCCARY.
GIVEN NAME Irish 6%. *Bridie*.

McCargar (165) Irish or Scottish: Anglicized form of Gaelic **Mac Ardghair** 'son of *Ardghar*', a variant of the personal name *Ardghal* (see MCARDLE).

McCargo (176) Scottish (Galloway): of uncertain origin; perhaps an altered form of MCHARG.

McCarl (310) Irish: probably an Americanized form of MCCARROLL.

McCarley (1496) Irish: Anglicized form of Gaelic **Mac Fhearghaile** 'son of *Fearghal*', a personal name meaning 'valiant man'.

McCarn (294) Irish (County Monaghan): reduced form of MCCARRON.

McCarney (278) Northern Irish: Anglicized form of Gaelic **Mac Cearnaigh** 'son of *Cearnach*', a personal name meaning 'victorious'. Much commoner in Ireland is the shortened form CARNEY.

McCarrell (323) Variant spelling of Irish MCCARROLL (see CARROLL).

McCarren (279) Variant of Irish MCCARRON.

McCarrick (392) Irish: **1.** Anglicized form of Gaelic **Mac Con Charraige** 'son of *Cú Charraige*', a personal name meaning 'hound of the rock'. **2.** Anglicized form of **Mac Con Chathrach** 'son of *Cú Chathrach*', a personal name meaning 'hound of the fort'.

McCarroll (1098) Irish: Anglicized form of Gaelic **Mac Cearbhaill** (see CARROLL).

McCarron (1370) Irish: **1.** Anglicized form of Gaelic **Mac Cearáin**, a form of **Mac Ciaráin** 'son of *Ciarán*', a personal name meaning 'little dark one', often Anglicized as *Kieran*. **2.** Anglicized form of Gaelic **Mac Carrghamhna** 'son of *Corrghamhain*', a personal name composed of the elements *corr* 'sharp' + *gamhain* 'calf' (young bull).
GIVEN NAMES Irish 5%. *Aidan*, *Fidelma*, *Liam*, *Sean Patrick*, *Siobhan*.

McCarry (154) Irish: variant of MCCARY.

McCarson (304) Northern Irish: perhaps an elaborated form of CARSON.

McCart (902) Northern Irish: Anglicized form of Gaelic **Mac Airt**, 'son of *Art*', a personal name meaning 'bear'.

McCartan (295) Northern Irish: Anglicized form of Gaelic **Mac Artáin** 'son of *Artán*', a diminutive of the personal name *Art* 'bear'. This is a chieftain family in County Down.

GIVEN NAMES Irish 8%. *Aileen*, *Brendan*, *Conn*.

McCarten (182) Northern Irish: variant spelling of MCCARTAN.
GIVEN NAME Irish 6%. *Briana*.

McCarter (3288) Scottish and northern Irish: Anglicized form of Gaelic **Mac Artair** 'son of ARTHUR'.

McCartha (170) Variant of Scottish MCARTHUR.

McCarther (92) Variant of Scottish MCARTHUR.

McCarthy (33792) Irish: Anglicized form of Gaelic **Mac Cárthaigh** 'son of *Cárthach*', a personal name meaning 'loving'. This is the name of an important Munster family.
GIVEN NAMES Irish 6%. *Brendan* (39), *Donal* (7), *Liam* (5), *Cormac* (4), *Niall* (4), *Aileen* (3), *Brigid* (3), *Conor* (3), *Declan* (2), *Dermod* (2), *Dermot* (2), *Finbar* (2).

McCartin (350) Irish: variant spelling of MCCARTAN.

McCartney (4947) Scottish (Galloway) and northern Irish: Anglicized form of Scottish Gaelic **Mac Artaine**, 'son of *Artan*' a diminutive of the personal name *Art* 'bear' or 'hero'. Compare Irish **Mac Artáin** (see MCCARTAN), of which this is a variant.

McCartt (174) Scottish and Irish: variant spelling of MCCART.

McCarty (13410) Irish: variant of MCCARTHY, reflecting the common southern Irish pronunciation of *th*.

McCarver (781) Irish: variant of MCCARVILLE (see CARROLL).

McCarville (430) Irish: Anglicized form of Gaelic **Mac Cearbhaill** 'son of *Cearbhall*' (see CARROLL).
GIVEN NAME Irish 6%. *Seamus*.

McCary (819) Irish: variant of MCGARRY or, in counties Galway and Westmeath, an Anglicized form of Gaelic **Mac Fhiachra** 'son of *Fiachra*', a personal name possibly meaning 'battle king'.

McCaskey (525) Scottish and Irish: Anglicized form of Gaelic **Mac Ascaidh** 'son of *Ascadh*', a Gaelic pet form of the Old Norse personal name *Ásketill* (see MCCASKILL).

McCaskill (1715) Scottish: Anglicized form of Gaelic **Mac Asgaill** 'son of *Asgall*', a reduced Gaelic form of the Old Norse personal name *Ásketill*, composed of the elements *óss*, *áss* 'god' + *ketill* 'kettle'.

McCasland (788) Irish: variant of MCCASLIN. The addition of *-d* is due to English speakers' perception of the devoicing of Gaelic final *-n*.

McCaslin (1806) Irish: Anglicized form of Gaelic **Mac Ausaláin** 'son of *Ausalán*' (see MCCAUSLAND).

McCathern (144) Irish or Scottish: probably an altered form of **McCahern** or **McGahern**, Anglicized forms of Gaelic **Mac Eachráin** (see MCEACHERN).

McCaughan (298) Northern Irish: Anglicized form of Gaelic **Mac Eacháin** 'son of *Eachán*', a personal name derived from a diminutive of *each* 'horse'.

McCaughey (683) Irish: variant of McGAUGHEY.
GIVEN NAMES Irish 4%. *Brendan, Eamon, Sheelagh.*

McCaul (384) Irish: variant spelling of McCALL.
GIVEN NAMES Irish 7%. *Cormac* (2), *Colm, Conor.*

McCauley (9034) **1.** Scottish (Dumbartonshire) and Irish (Westmeath): Anglicized form of Gaelic **Mac Amhalghaidh** 'son of *Amhalghadh*', a personal name of uncertain origin. **2.** Scottish (Hebrides) and Irish (Fermanagh): Anglicized form of Gaelic **Mac Amhlaoibh** or **Mac Amhlaidh** 'son of Olaf', from Gaelic forms of the Old Norse personal name *Áleifr, Óláfr*. Compare McAULIFFE.

McCaulley (521) Scottish and Irish: variant of McCAULEY.

McCausland (741) Scottish and northern Irish: probably a variant of **MacAuslan**, which according to Black is an Anglicization of **Mac Ausaláin** 'son of Absolom', from the name of an early 13th-century cleric. However, there may rather be an underlying Gaelic personal name, possibly *Caisealán*, meaning 'little one of the castle'.

McCauslin (215) Probably a variant of Irish McCASLIN or Scottish **McAuslan** (see McCAUSLAND).

McCaw (903) Northern Irish and Scottish: Anglicized form of Gaelic **Mac Ádhaimh** 'son of *Ádhamh*', Gaelic form of the personal name ADAM.

McCawley (466) Irish: variant spelling of McCAULEY.

McCay (971) Northern Irish and Scottish: Anglicized form of Gaelic **Mac Aodha** (see McCOY).

McChesney (1517) Scottish (Galloway) and northern Irish: probably an Anglicized form of Gaelic **Mac an tSasanaigh** 'son of the Saxon (i.e. the Englishman)'. Another Anglicized version of this name is **McAtasney**.

McChristian (245) Northern Irish: patronymic from the personal name CHRISTIAN.

McClafferty (294) Scottish and northern Irish: Anglicized form of Gaelic **Mac Fhlaithbheartaigh** 'son of *Flaithbheartach*' (see McLAFFERTY).
GIVEN NAMES Irish 9%. *Eamon* (2), *Liam.*

McClaflin (192) Variant of Irish McLAUGHLIN.
GIVEN NAMES French 4%. *Camille, Nolton.*

McClain (14317) Variant of Scottish or Irish McLEAN.

McClaine (279) Variant of Scottish or Irish McLEAN.

McClam (246) Irish: Anglicized form of Gaelic **Mac Fhlaithimh** (see McCLAVE). Compare McLAMB.

McClammy (130) Scottish: patronymic from a pet form of LAMONT.

McClamrock (105) Of Scottish or Irish origin: unexplained.

McClanahan (3616) Scottish and Irish: Anglicized form of Gaelic **Mac Gille Onchon** 'son of the servant of (Saint) *Onchú*', an Old Irish personal name perhaps meaning 'mighty hound'. St. Onchú was a 6th-century Irish pilgrim and collector of holy relics. See also McCLENAHAN.

McClane (393) Scottish or Irish: variant of McLEAN.

McClaran (301) Variant of Scottish McLAREN.

McClard (328) Irish or Scottish: variant of **McLardy**, a mainly Scottish variant of McLAFFERTY.

McClaren (415) Scottish: variant of McLAREN.

McClarin (139) Variant of Scottish McLAREN.

McClarnon (166) Irish and Scottish: Anglicized form of Gaelic **Mac Giolla Earnáin** (Irish), **Mac Gille Earnain** (Scottish) 'son of the devotee of (Saint) *Earnan*', a personal name possibly derived from *iarn* 'iron'.
GIVEN NAME Irish 6%. *Brendan.*

McClarren (165) Variant of Scottish McLAREN.

McClarty (162) Scottish and Irish: variant of McLAFFERTY.

McClary (1786) Irish: variant of McCLEARY.

McClaskey (571) Irish: variant of McCLOSKEY.

McClatchey (317) Northern Irish and Scottish (Ayr, Galloway): Anglicized form of Gaelic **Mac Gille Eidich**, possibly 'son of the ugly lad', from *éidigh* 'ugly'.

McClatchy (204) Northern Irish and Scottish: variant of McCLATCHEY.

McClaugherty (150) Irish: variant of McLAFFERTY.
GIVEN NAME Scottish 4%. *Maire.*

McClaughry (136) Irish: possibly of Scottish origin, an Anglicized form of Gaelic **Mac Clochaire** 'son of the stone worker'.

McClave (172) **1.** Irish: Anglicized form of Gaelic **Mac Fhlaithimh** 'son of *Flaitheamh*', a personal name meaning 'prince'. See also CLAFFEY. **2.** Scottish: Anglicized form of Gaelic **Mac Clochaire** 'son of the stone worker'.

McClay (733) Scottish and northern Irish: probably an Anglicized form of Scottish Gaelic **Mac an Léigh** 'son of the physician', Irish **Mac an Leagha** (Antrim).

McCleaf (159) Irish: variant of McCLAVE.

McClean (936) Scottish and Irish: variant of McLEAN.

McClearn (130) Irish (East Galway and County Down): possibly a rare variant of McLAREN.

McCleary (2390) Northern Irish and Scottish: **1.** Anglicized form of Gaelic **Mac Cléirich** 'son of the cleric' (see CLEARY). **2.** Anglicized form of **Mac Giolla Arraith** 'son of the servant of *Arraith*', or Woulfe suggests of **Mac Giolla an Raith** 'son of the prosperous youth'.

McCleave (178) Irish: variant of McCLAVE.

McCleery (725) Northern Irish: variant spelling of McCLEARY.

McClees (177) Scottish and Irish: variant of McLEISH.

McCleese (224) Scottish and Irish: variant of McLEISH.

McClellan (9164) Scottish and Irish: Anglicized form of Gaelic **Mac Gille Fhaolain** (Scottish) and **Mac Giolla Fhaoláin** (Irish) 'son of the servant of (Saint) Faolán' (see WHELAN).

McClelland (5350) Northern Irish: variant of McCLELLAN, with excrescent -d due to the devoicing of palatalized -n in Gaelic.

McClellen (156) Northern Irish: variant of McCLELLAN.

McClement (107) Scottish and northern Irish: variant of McCLYMONT, assimilated to the English personal name *Clement*.

McClements (142) Scottish and northern Irish: variant of McCLYMONT, assimilated to the English personal name *Clement*, with English patronymic -s.

McClenaghan (142) Irish: variant spelling of McCLENAHAN.
GIVEN NAME Irish 5%. *Fergal.*

McClenahan (471) **1.** Irish (mainly Counties Derry and Antrim): Anglicized form of Gaelic **Mac Leanacháin** 'son of *Leanachán*', a personal name derived from *leanach*, which MacLysaght translates as 'possessing mantles' (from *leann* 'mantle', 'cloak'). **2.** Scottish: variant of McCLANAHAN.

McClenathan (159) Scottish or Irish: variant of McCLENAHAN.

McClendon (4956) Irish: variant of McCLINTON.

McClennen (135) Scottish: variant of McLENNAN.

McClenney (115) Scottish or Irish: probably a variant of McELHINNEY.

McClenny (400) Scottish or Irish: probably a variant of McELHINNEY.

McClenton (112) Irish: variant of McCLINTON.

McCleod (159) Scottish and Irish: variant of McLEOD.

McClernon (112) Irish: variant of McLARNON.

McCleskey (671) Irish: variant of McCLOSKEY.

McClimans (265) Scottish and northern Irish: variant of McCLYMONT, with English patronymic -s.

McClimon (105) Scottish and northern Irish: variant of McCLYMONT.

McClintic (562) Altered spelling of McCLINTOCK.

McClintick (345) Scottish: variant of McCLINTOCK.

McClintock (3633) Scottish and northern Irish: Anglicized form of Gaelic **Mac Gille Fhionndaig** (Scottish), **Mac Giolla Fhionntóg** (Irish) 'son of the servant of (Saint) *Finndag*', a personal name derived from a pet form of *fionn* 'white'. According to Woulfe, the Scottish family settled in Donegal in the late 16th century.

McClinton (1198) Northern Irish: Anglicization of Gaelic **Mac Gille Fhionntain** (Scottish), **Mac Giolla Fhionntáin** (Irish) 'son of the servant of (Saint) *Fintán*', a personal name derived from a pet form of *fionn* 'white', or *Fintan*, an older name composed of the elements *find* 'white' + *senos* 'old'.

McClish (422) Variant of Scottish McLEISH.

McClone (103) Irish: variant of McCLUNE.

McClory (271) Northern Irish (Counties Down and Armagh) and Scottish (Galloway): Anglicized form of Gaelic **Mac Labhradha** 'son of *Labhraidh*', a personal name meaning 'speaker', 'spokesman'.
GIVEN NAMES Irish 5%. *Brendan, Eamon.*

McCloskey (4290) Irish: Anglicized form of Gaelic **Mac Bhloscaidh** 'son of *Bloscadh*' a personal name probably derived from *blosc* 'resounding noise', 'blast'. This surname is the name of a family from County Derry descended from the O'Kanes; it is also found in Scotland, mainly in Glasgow.
GIVEN NAMES Irish 4%. *Aileen, Brendan, Bridie, Dermot, Seamus.*

McClosky (178) Irish: variant spelling of McCLOSKEY.

McCloud (3920) Scottish: variant of McLEOD.

McCloughan (105) Irish: possibly, as proposed by Sean de Bhulbh, an Anglicized form of Gaelic **Mac Lugháin**.

McCloy (638) Scottish and northern Irish: Anglicized form of Gaelic **Mac Lughaidh** 'son of *Lugaidh*' (see LEWIS).

McCluer (181) Variant spelling of Scottish McCLURE.

McClune (238) Northern Irish: Anglicized form of Gaelic **Mac Giolla Eoin** 'son of the servant of (Saint) John'.

McCluney (294) Scottish: variant of McCLUNG.

McClung (3786) Scottish: Anglicized form of Gaelic **Mac Luinge** 'son of *Lunge*', a personal name probably meaning 'seafarer', although the literal meaning is 'ship', from Latin *navis longa*.

McClure (17914) Scottish and northern Irish: **1.** Anglicized form of Gaelic **Mac Gille Uidhir** (Scottish), **Mac Giolla Uidhir** (Irish), probably 'son of the sallow lad'. **2.** Anglicized form of Scottish Gaelic **Mac Gille Dheòradha**, Irish **Mac Giolla Dheóradha** 'son of the servant of the pilgrim'.

McClurg (1359) Scottish: Anglicized form of Gaelic **Mac Luirg** 'son of *Lorg*', a personal name meaning 'footman' (literally 'track'). Alternatively, it may be a reduced Anglicized form of Gaelic **Mac Cléirich** 'son of the scribe or cleric' (Gaelic *cléireach*). Compare CLEARY.

McClurkin (288) Irish: Anglicized form of Gaelic **Mac Cléireacháin** 'son of the little priest', from a diminutive of *cléireach* 'priest', 'cleric'.

McCluskey (2463) Irish: variant of McCLOSKEY.
GIVEN NAMES Irish 4%. *Aidan* (3), *Donovan* (2), *Brendan, Eamon, Seamus.*

McClusky (470) Irish: variant of McCLOSKEY.

McClymonds (135) Scottish and northern Irish: variant of McCLYMONT, with English patronymic *-s*.

McClymont (149) Scottish and northern Irish: Anglicized form of Gaelic **Mac Laomuinn** 'son of *Laomann*', a personal name meaning 'law giver' (see LAMONT).

McCoach (129) Scottish or Irish: of uncertain origin, perhaps a variant of Scottish **McCosh**, which is an Anglicized form of Gaelic **Mac Mhic Coise** 'son of the messenger'.

McCoid (117) Irish: variant of McQUAID.

McCoig (131) Scottish: of uncertain origin; probably a variant of McCAIG.

McCoin (249) Northern Irish: Anglicized form of Gaelic **Mac Eoghain** 'son of Eoghan' (see McEWEN) or 'son of *Eoin*', a personal name from Latin *Johannes* (see JOHN).

McCole (283) Irish: variant of McCOOL 2.
GIVEN NAME Irish 5%. *Ernan.*

McColgan (467) Irish and Scottish: Anglicized form of Gaelic **Mac Colgan** 'son of *Colga*', a personal name based on Irish *colg* 'thorn', 'sword'.
GIVEN NAMES Irish 6%. *Eamon* (2), *Kaitlin.*

McColl (574) Scottish and Irish: Anglicized form of Gaelic **Mac Colla** (earlier *Conla(e)*).

McCollam (298) Northern Irish: variant of McCOLLUM.

McColley (434) Irish: probably a variant of McCULLOUGH, or an Anglicized form of Gaelic **Mac Duinnshléibhe** (see DUNLEAVY). Seán de Bhulbh notes that there was an Ulster family called **Mac Colla**, though this was usually Anglicized as COLL.

McCollister (496) Scottish and northern Irish: variant of McALLISTER.

McColloch (235) Scottish: variant of McCULLOUGH.

McCollom (575) Northern Irish: variant of McCOLLUM.

McCollough (1581) Irish: variant of McCULLOUGH.

McCollum (7242) Northern Irish: Anglicized form of Gaelic **Mac Coluim** 'son of *Colum*'. See McCALLUM, which is the usual spelling of this name in Scotland.

McColly (108) Irish: variant of McCOLLEY.

McColm (209) Scottish: variant of McCOLLUM.

McComas (1724) Northern Irish: Anglicized form of Gaelic **Mac Thómais** 'son of THOMAS'.

McComb (2064) Scottish and northern Irish: Anglicized form of Gaelic **Mac Thóm** 'son of *Thóm*', a Gaelic short form of the personal name THOMAS.

McCombe (140) Scottish and northern Irish: variant of McCOMB.

McComber (202) Irish: Anglicized form of a Gaelic name, probably **Mac Ciaragáin** 'descendant of *Ciaragán*', a personal name based on a diminutive of *ciar* 'black', 'dark' (see KERRIGAN), but erroneously identified with *cíor* 'comb'. However, the Irish evidence is for **Ó Ciaragáin**, not **Mac Ciaragáin**, so the *Mac* prefix is surprising.

McCombie (177) Scottish: Anglicized form of Gaelic **Mac Thomaidh** 'son of *Thomaidh*', a Gaelic pet form of the personal name THOMAS.

McCombs (3163) Northern Irish: variant of McCOMB, formed with the redundant addition of the English patronymic ending *-s*.

McComiskey (117) Irish: Anglicized form of Gaelic **Mac Cumascaigh** 'son of *Cumascach*', a byname from *cumascach* 'mixer', 'confuser'. See also COMERFORD.

McCommon (241) Irish: Anglicized form of Gaelic **Mac Comáin** 'son of *Comán*', a personal name of uncertain origin.

McCommons (171) Altered form of Irish McCOMMON, formed with the redundant addition of English patronymic ending *-s*.

McComsey (195) Irish: variant of McCOMISKEY or possibly McCOMAS.

McConachie (144) Scottish: Anglicized form of Gaelic **Mac Dhonnchaidh** 'son of *Donnchadh*', equivalent to Irish McCONAGHY.

McConaghy (358) Northern Irish: Anglicized form of Gaelic **Mac Dhonnchaidh** 'son of *Donnchadh*', a widely used personal name meaning 'brown one or chief of battle', from *donn* 'brown-haired' or 'chief' + *cath* 'battle', which is Anglicized as *Donagh* or *Duncan*. Derivatives in which the personal name is unlenited include DONAHUE and McDONOUGH; these derive from the early genitive form, *Donnchadha*. Forms ending in *-y* derive from the later genitive, *Donnchaidh*.

McConaha (155) Northern Irish: variant of McCONAGHY.

McConahay (174) Northern Irish: variant of MCCONAGHY.

McConahy (182) Northern Irish: variant of MCCONAGHY.

McConathy (272) Northern Irish: variant of MCCONAGHY.

McConaughey (197) Northern Irish: variant of MCCONAGHY.

McConaughy (192) Northern Irish: variant of MCCONAGHY.

McConchie (147) Scottish: variant of MCCONACHIE.

McCone (224) Irish: Anglicized form of Gaelic **Mac Comhdhain** 'son of *Comhdhan*', a personal name of uncertain origin. This is the name of an ecclesiastical family in County Armagh.

McConico (163) Altered form of Scottish MCCONACHIE or Irish MCCONAGHY.

McConkey (1034) Northern Irish: variant of Scottish MCCONACHIE or Irish MCCONAGHY.

McConkie (135) Scottish: variant of MCCONACHIE.

McConn (156) Irish: **1.** Anglicized form of Gaelic **Mac Cuinn** 'son of *Conn*', a personal name meaning 'chieftain' (literally 'head' or 'sense'). **2.** variant of the Ulster surname MacIlchon, an Anglicized form of Gaelic **Mac Mhíolchon** 'son of *Míolcha*', a personal name meaning 'hare-hound', from *míol* 'hare' + *cú* 'hound', genitive *con*.

McConnaughey (394) Altered form of Irish MCCONAGHY.

McConnaughy (99) Altered form of Irish MCCONAGHY.

GIVEN NAME Irish 6%. *Caitlin*.

McConnel (235) Scottish and Irish: variant spelling of MCCONNELL.

McConnell (15660) **1.** Scottish and Irish: Anglicized form of Gaelic **Mac Dhomhnuill** 'son of *Domhnall*' (see MCDONALD). **2.** Irish: Anglicized form of Gaelic **Mac Conaill** 'son of *Conall*', a personal name probably composed of the elements *con*, an inflected form of *cú* 'hound' or 'wolf', + *gal* 'valor'. This was borne by many early chieftains and warriors of Ireland, including the Ulster hero Conall Cearnach, and one of the two sons of Niall of the Nine Hostages, who gave his name to *Tir Conaill* 'Conall's land', otherwise known as County Donegal. It was further popularized by the fame of a 7th-century Irish saint, abbot of Inis Caoil.

McConnon (201) Irish: Anglicized form of Gaelic **Mac Canann**, **Mac Canáin** or **Mac Canannáin**, all patronymics from *cano*, an element meaning 'wolf cub', or its diminutives. See CANNON.

GIVEN NAMES Irish 8%. *Aine, Brendan*.

McConville (999) Northern Irish: Anglicized form of Gaelic **Mac Conmhaoil** 'son of *Cú Mhaol*', a personal name apparently composed of the elements *cú* 'hound' + *maol* 'bald'. (This was the original form of the nominative, which was later replaced by the inflected form *Conmhaol*.)

GIVEN NAMES Irish 6%. *Brendan, Donal, Donovan, Maeve, Niall, Sean Michael*.

McCooey (158) Irish: Anglicized form of Gaelic **Mac Cumhaighe** 'son of *Cú Mhaighe*', a personal name meaning 'hound of the plain'. This was the original form from the nominative, which replaced the genitive form **Mac Con Mhaighe**.

McCook (595) Scottish and northern Irish: **1.** Anglicized form of Gaelic **Mac Cúg** 'son of *Húg* (Hugo)', a personal name that was used as an Anglicized form of Gaelic *Aodh* (see MCCOY). **2.** Anglicized form of Irish Gaelic **Mac Dhabhóg** 'son of David'.

McCool (2578) **1.** Scottish and northern Irish: Anglicized form of Gaelic **Mac Dhubhghaill** (see MCDOWELL). **2.** Scottish and northern Irish: Anglicized form of Gaelic **Mac Gille Chomhghaill** (Scottish), **Mac Giolla Comhghaill** 'son of the servant of (Saint) *Comhghall*', a personal name, possibly an intensive of *gall* 'stranger', borne by an early Irish saint. **3.** Irish: possibly an Anglicized form of Gaelic **Mac Cumhaill** 'son of *Cumhall*', a byname meaning 'champion'. Fionn Mac Cumhaill is the name of a famous hero in traditional Irish literature.

McCoppin (127) Probably an altered form of Scottish and northern Irish **McCappin**, which is a variant of MCALPINE.

McCord (6365) Northern Irish and Scottish: Anglicized form of Gaelic **Mac Cuairt** or **Mac Cuarta**, apparently meaning 'son of a journey', which Woulfe suggests may be a reduced form of **Mac Muircheartaigh** (see MCMURTRY).

McCorkel (161) Scottish and Irish: variant spelling of MCCORKLE.

McCorkell (172) Scottish and Irish: variant spelling of MCCORKLE.

McCorkle (3176) Scottish and Irish: Anglicized form of Gaelic **Mac Thorcaill** 'son of *Thorkell*', a personal name of Old Norse origin, meaning 'Thor's kettle'.

McCormac (265) Variant spelling of Scottish and Irish MCCORMICK.

GIVEN NAME Irish 4%. *Fintan*.

McCormack (7151) Scottish and Irish: variant of MCCORMICK.

GIVEN NAMES Irish 4%. *Brendan* (7), *Aidan* (3), *Dermot* (2), *Eamon* (2), *Niall* (2), *Aine, Caitlin, Colm, Declan, Donovan, Fitz, Liam*.

McCormic (143) Variant spelling of Scottish and Irish MCCORMICK.

McCormick (24370) Scottish and Irish: Anglicized form of Gaelic **Mac Cormaic** 'son of *Cormac*', a personal name composed of the elements *corb* 'raven' + *mac* 'son'.

McCornack (135) Scottish: variant of MCCORMACK (see MCCORMICK).

McCorquodale (210) Scottish: Anglicization of Gaelic **Mac Thorcadail**, 'son of *Torcadal*', a personal name of Old Norse origin meaning 'Thor's kettle'.

McCorry (258) Northern Irish: Anglicized form of Gaelic **Mac Gothraidh** 'son of *Gothradh*', Gaelic form of the personal name GODFREY.

McCort (252) Irish and Scottish: variant of MCCORD.

GIVEN NAME Irish 4%. *Brendan*.

McCorvey (317) Scottish (Kintyre): Anglicized form of Gaelic **Mac Fhearghaidh** 'son of *Fearghaidh*', a pet form of the personal name FERGUS.

McCory (154) Irish: probably a variant of MCCORRY.

McCosh (254) Scottish and northern Irish: Anglicized form of Gaelic **Mac Coise** 'son of *Cos*', a byname meaning 'messenger' or 'foot soldier' (from *cos* 'foot', 'leg').

McCoskey (283) Possibly an altered form of Irish **McAskie**, an Anglicized form of Gaelic **Mac Ascaidh**, a patronymic from a diminutive of an Old Norse name, possibly Ascall, Asketil; or an Anglicized form of **Mac Coscraich** 'son of *Coscrach*' (see COSGROVE).

McCotter (285) Scottish and northern Irish: Anglicized form of Gaelic **Mac Oitir** 'son of *Oitir*', Gaelic form of the Old Norse personal name *Óttarr*, composed of the elements *ótti* 'fear', 'dread' + *herr* 'army'.

GIVEN NAME Irish 5%. *Seamus*.

McCoubrey (110) Scottish and Irish: Anglicized form of Gaelic **Mac Cúithbreith** 'son of Cuthbert'.

McCoun (150) Irish or Scottish: probably a reduced form of MCCOWAN or MCKEOWN.

McCourt (1366) Irish and Scottish: variant of MCCORD.

GIVEN NAMES Irish 4%. *Brendan, Eamon*.

McCourtney (103) Irish: variant of MCCARTNEY.

McCoury (118) Irish: probably a variant of MCCORRY.

McCowan (1305) Scottish: **1.** Anglicized form of Gaelic **Mac Eoghain** (see MCEWEN). **2.** Anglicized form of Gaelic **Mac Gille Comhghain** 'son of the servant of (Saint) *Comhghan*' (see MCELHONE).

McCowen (362) Scottish: variant spelling of MCCOWAN.

McCowin (166) Variant spelling of Scottish MCCOWAN.

McCown (1893) Scottish and Irish: variant of MCCOWAN, MCCUNE, etc.

McCoy (34738) Irish (Limerick): Anglicized form of Gaelic **Mac Aodha** 'son of *Aodh*', an ancient personal name meaning 'fire', originally the name of a pagan god. Thus it has the same origin as MCGEE, MCKAY and MCKEE.

FOREBEARS The McCoy clan of KY, led by Randolph McCoy, was involved in one of the bitterest mountain feuds, with the Hatfield clan of WV, from the Civil War to the end of the 19th century. The expression 'the real McCoy' probably originated with an American boxer, Norman Selby (1873–1940), who adopted the name "Kid McCoy" distinguish himself from another fighter of the same name.

McCracken (7463) Northern Irish and Scottish (Galloway): Anglicized form of Gaelic **Mac Reachtain**, Ulster variant of **Mac Neachtain** (see MCNAUGHTON), with the replacement of *n* by *r* in the cluster *cn* that is characteristic of Ulster Irish.

McCrackin (362) Northern Irish and Scottish (Galloway): variant spelling of MCCRACKEN.

McCrady (536) Irish and Scottish: variant of MCCREADY.

McCrae (680) Scottish: variant of MCRAE.

McCraney (523) Variant of Irish **Mac Cranny**, an Anglicized form of a Gaelic patronymic, possibly **Mac Bhranaigh** 'son of *Branach*', a personal name derived from *bran* 'raven'.

McCranie (570) Irish: see MCCRANEY.

McCrann (121) Irish: Anglicized form of Gaelic **Mac Bhroin**, a patronymic from a name derived from *bran* 'raven'. GIVEN NAME Irish 8%. *Brendan*.

McCrary (4156) Scottish and northern Irish: variant of MCCREARY.

McCraven (110) Irish (Louth, Monaghan): Anglicized form of Gaelic **Mac Crabháin** 'son of *Crabhán*', possibly meaning 'religious'.

McCravy (193) Northern Irish: variant of MCGREEVY.

McCraw (2027) Irish: variant of MCGRATH, which is based on the personal name **Mac Raith**, of which this is a phonetic development; the *-th*, having been pronounced in the early period, became silent in later Gaelic. Compare MCRAE.

McCray (6229) Scottish and northern Irish: variant spelling of MCRAE.

McCrea (2121) Scottish and northern Irish: variant of MCRAE.

McCreadie (161) Scottish: variant spelling of MCCREADY.

McCready (1722) Irish and Scottish: Anglicized form of Gaelic **Mac Riada** 'son of *Riada*', a personal name meaning 'trained', 'expert'.

McCreary (3025) Scottish and northern Irish: Anglicized form of Gaelic **Mac Ruidhrí**, a variant of **Mac Ruaidhrí**, which has been connected to Irish *ruadh* 'red' (see MCCRORY) and to the Old Norse personal name *Hrothrekr*, whence RODERICK.

McCredie (147) Scottish: variant spelling of MCCREADY.

McCree (649) Scottish: variant of MCRAE.

McCreedy (287) Irish: variant spelling of MCCREADY.

McCreery (935) Irish: variant spelling of MCCREARY.

McCreight (590) Scottish (Galloway) and northern Irish: reduced Anglicized form

of Gaelic **Mac Neachtain** (see MCNAUGHTON).

McCreless (161) Irish or Scottish: perhaps a variant of MCNELIS. Compare MCCRILLIS.

McCrery (121) Scottish and northern Irish: variant of MCCREARY.

McCrickard (145) Irish: patronymic from the personal name *Ricard* (see RICHARD).

McCright (289) Variant of Scottish and northern Irish MCCREIGHT.

McCrillis (207) Of Irish or Scottish origin; perhaps a variant of MCNELIS.

McCrimmon (485) Scottish: Anglicized form of Gaelic **Mac Ruimein** 'son of *Ruimen*', Gaelic form of the Old Norse personal name *Hroðmundr*, composed of the elements *hród* 'fame' + *mundr* 'protection'. This was the name of a famous family of pipers.

McCrobie (107) Scottish: patronymic from a Gaelic form of the personal name *Robbie*, a pet form of ROBERT.

McCrocklin (137) Variant of Irish MCLAUGHLIN.

McCrohan (127) Irish (Kerry): Anglicized form of Gaelic **Mac Criomhthainn** 'son of *Criomhthann*', an ancient personal name meaning 'fox'. Criomhthann was the name of one of the warriors associated with Finn mac Cumhaill. It was also the name of an early saint and is said to have been St. Columba's original first name.

McCrone (281) Scottish and Irish: Anglicized form of Gaelic **Mac Cróin** 'son of the swarthy one', from *crón* 'swarthy'.

McCrorey (232) Northern Irish and Scottish: variant spelling of MCCRORY.

McCrory (2083) Northern Irish: Anglicized form of Gaelic **Mac Ruaidhrí** 'son of *Ruaidhrí*' (see RORIE).

McCroskey (909) Scottish: metathesized Anglicized form of Gaelic **Mac Cosgraich** 'son of *Coscrach*', a byname meaning 'victorious', 'triumphant'. Compare Irish COSGROVE.

McCrossen (153) Irish and Scottish: Anglicized form of Gaelic **Mac an Chrosáin** 'son of the satirist', a patronymic from *crosán* 'reciter of satirical verse', 'satirist' (originally a cross bearer in a religious procession).

McCrossin (141) Irish and Scottish: variant spelling of MCCROSSEN.

McCroy (109) Irish: variant of MCROY.

McCrudden (194) Northern Irish: Anglicized form of Gaelic **Mac Rodáin**, 'son of *Rodán*', a personal name derivative from *rod* 'spirited'.

McCrum (337) Scottish and northern Irish (County Down): Anglicized form of Scottish Gaelic **Mac Cruim** or **Mac a' Chruim** 'son of the cripple', from *crom* 'bent', 'twisted'.

McCrumb (191) Altered spelling of Scottish and northern Irish: variant of MCCRUM.

McCrystal (206) Northern Irish (Counties Armagh and Tyrone): Anglicized form of **Mac Criostal**, a variant of *Criostar*, Gaelic form of CHRISTOPHER.

McCuaig (129) Scottish: Anglicized form of Gaelic **Mac Dhubhaig**, a patronymic from a nickname derived from *dubh* 'black'.

McCuan (166) Scottish: variant of MCEWEN.

McCubbin (882) Scottish: Anglicized form of Gaelic **Mac Giobúin**, a patronymic from the pet form of a Gaelic form of the personal name GILBERT.

McCubbins (394) Scottish: Anglicized form of Gaelic **Mac Giobúin**, a patronymic from the pet form of a Gaelic form of the personal name GILBERT.

McCue (3266) Northern Irish: variant of MCHUGH (see MCCOY). GIVEN NAMES Irish 4%. *Clancy*, *Niall*.

McCuen (664) Scottish: variant of MCEWEN.

McCuin (240) Irish: variant of MCQUINN.

McCuistion (397) Altered spelling of MCCUTCHEON.

McCuiston (468) Altered spelling of MCCUTCHEON.

McCulla (155) Probably a variant of MCCULLAGH, though perhaps alternatively a form of **McColla**, a Scottish patronymic from the Gaelic personal name *Colla*, or from Irish *coll* 'hazel', as in QUILL.

McCullagh (260) Irish (especially Ulster): variant of MCCULLOUGH. GIVEN NAME Irish 5%. *Connor*.

McCullah (319) Variant of Irish MCCULLOUGH or Scottish MCCULLOCH or MCKELLAR.

McCullar (721) Variant of Scottish MCKELLAR.

McCullars (162) Variant of Scottish MCKELLAR, with redundant English patronymic *-s*.

McCullen (715) Irish: Anglicized form of Gaelic **Mac Cuilinn**, a patronymic from a personal name derived from *cuileann* 'holly'.

McCuller (199) Scottish and Irish: variant of Scottish MCKELLAR.

McCullers (515) Scottish and Irish: variant of Scottish MCKELLAR, with redundant English patronymic *-s*.

McCulley (2008) Scottish: variant of MCCULLOCH.

McCullick (132) Northern Irish: variant of MCCULLOUGH.

McCulloch (3438) Scottish form of Irish MCCULLOUGH, long established as a family name in southwestern Scotland.

McCullock (112) Northern Irish: variant of MCCULLOUGH.

McCulloh (261) Variant of Irish MCCULLOUGH or Scottish MCCULLOCH.

McCullom (123) Scottish and northern Irish: variant of MCCOLLUM.

McCullough (16158) Irish (especially Ulster): Anglicized form of the Gaelic surname **Mac Cú Uladh**, a patronymic from *Cú Uladh* 'hound of Ulster'. Compare MCNALLY, which is from **Mac Con Uladh**, genitive form of the same name. It has sometimes been erroneously associated with Gaelic *cullach* 'wild boar', and some families in County Sligo have translated it into English as **Boar**.

McCullum (615) Scottish and northern Irish: variant of MCCOLLUM.

McCully (1184) **1.** Scottish: variant of MCCULLOCH. **2.** Irish: see CULLY.

McCumber (837) Variant of Irish MCCOMBER.

McCumbers (121) Variant of Irish MCCOMBER, with the addition of English patronymic *-s*.

McCune (3569) Scottish and Irish: Anglicized form of Gaelic **Mac Eoghain** (see MCEWEN).

McCurdy (4566) Scottish and Irish (County Antrim): Anglicized form of Gaelic **Mac Mhuircheartaigh**, a patronymic from *Muircheartach*, a personal name composed of the elements *muir* 'sea' + *ceartach* 'ruler', hence 'skilled seaman'. Compare MORIARTY.

McCurley (1017) Irish (mainly Counties Galway and Roscommon): Anglicized form of Gaelic **Mac Thoirdhealbhaigh**, a patronymic from the personal name *Toirdhealbhach* 'Thor-shaped'. Compare TURLEY, from the unlenited form.

McCurry (2638) **1.** Northern Irish and Scottish: variant of MCMURRAY. **2.** Irish: variant of MCCORRY.

McCurtain (114) Irish: Anglicized form of Gaelic **Mac Curtáin**, a variant of **Mac Cruitín** 'son of the hunchback' (see CURTIN).

McCusker (1320) Northern Irish and Scottish: Anglicized form of Gaelic **Mac Oscair**, a patronymic from the Gaelic personal name *Oscar* 'deer-lover' or from a Gaelic form of the Old Norse personal name *Ásgeirr*, composed of the elements *ans* 'god' + *geirr* 'spear'.
GIVEN NAMES Irish 5%. *Eamon, Niall.*

McCuskey (141) Irish: variant of MCCASKEY.

McCutchan (490) Variant of Scottish and northern Irish MCCUTCHEON.

McCutchen (1366) Variant of Scottish and northern Irish MCCUTCHEON.

McCutcheon (3425) Scottish and northern Irish (of Scottish origin): Anglicized form of Gaelic **Mac Uisdein**, a patronymic from the personal name *Uisdean*, a Gaelicized form of Old French *Huchon*, a pet form of *Hu(gh)e* (see HUGH).

McCutchin (113) Variant of Scottish and northern Irish MCCUTCHEON.

McDade (2244) Irish: Anglicized form of Gaelic **Mac Daibhéid** (see MCDEVITT).

McDaid (276) Irish: variant spelling of MCDADE.
GIVEN NAMES Irish 10%. *Brendan, Colm, Eamon.*

McDanel (292) Variant of Irish MCDONNELL (see MCDANIEL).

McDaniel (29848) Altered form of Irish MCDONNELL 'son of Donal', from an incorrect association of the Gaelic patronymic with the personal name DANIEL.

McDaniels (1971) Irish: variant of MCDANIEL, with redundant addition of English patronymic *-s*.

McDannald (135) Variant of Irish MCDONNELL. Compare MCDANIEL.

McDannel (150) Variant of Irish MCDONNELL.

McDannell (137) Variant of Irish MCDONNELL.

McDannold (106) Variant of Irish MCDONNELL. Compare MCDANIEL.

McDaris (266) Anglicized form of Gaelic **Mac Dubhruis** 'son of *Dubhros*', a personal name composed of the elements *dubh* 'black' + *ros* 'wood'. See DORIS.

McDavid (1012) Scottish and Irish: quasi-Gaelic patronymic from DAVID. Compare MCDADE, MCDEVITT.

McDavitt (232) Irish: variant of MCDEVITT.

McDearmon (138) Scottish: variant of MCDIARMID with excrescent *-n-*.

McDermed (135) Scottish: variant of MCDIARMID.

McDermid (315) Scottish: variant of MCDIARMID.

McDermitt (266) Irish: Anglicized form of Gaelic **Mac Diarmada** 'son of *Diarmaid*', a personal name possibly composed of the separative prefix *di-* + *farmat* 'envy', hence meaning 'free from envy'. This name was borne in Celtic legend by the lover of Gráinne, and, in historical times, by Diarmaid Mac Murchadha, the 12th-century king of Leinster whose appeal to the English for support led directly to the Anglo-Norman presence in Ireland. Mac Diarmada was an important name in Connacht.

McDermott (12113) Irish: Anglicized form of Gaelic **Mac Diarmada** 'son of *Diarmaid*', a personal name possibly composed of the separative prefix *di-* + *farmat* 'envy', hence meaning 'free from envy'. This name was borne in Celtic legend by the lover of Gráinne, and, in historical times, by Diarmaid Mac Murchadha, the 12th-century king of Leinster whose appeal to the English for support led directly to the Anglo-Norman presence in Ireland. Mac Diarmada was an important name in Connacht.
GIVEN NAMES Irish 5%. *Brendan* (7), *Fergus* (6), *Dermod* (3), *Dermot* (2), *Aidan, Bridie, Clancy, Colm, Fitzgerald, Kieran, Kiernan, Liam.*

McDevitt (2838) Irish: Anglicized form of Gaelic **Mac Daibhéid**, a patronymic from

the Gaelic equivalent of DAVID. Compare MCDADE.
GIVEN NAMES Irish 5%. *Brendan, Clancy, Donal, Seamus.*

McDiarmid (297) Scottish: Anglicized form of Gaelic **Mac Diarmaid** 'son of *Diarmaid*', a personal name said to mean 'free of envy' (from *di* 'without' + *airmait* 'envy'). Etymologically, therefore, it is the same name as Irish MCDERMOTT.
GIVEN NAME Scottish 5%. *Murdo.*

McDiffett (107) Variant of Scottish and Irish MCDEVITT.

McDill (451) Scottish: variant of MCDOWELL.

McDivitt (355) Scottish and Irish: variant of Irish MCDEVITT.

McDole (564) Irish: variant of MCDOWELL.

McDonagh (745) Irish: variant of MCDONOUGH.
GIVEN NAMES Irish 9%. *Brendan* (2), *Bridie* (2), *Aisling, Declan, Dympna, Malachy, Siobhan.*

McDonald (64356) Scottish: Anglicized form of Gaelic **Mac Dhomhnuill**, a patronymic from the personal name *Domhnall*, which is composed of the ancient Celtic elements *domno-* 'world' + *val-* 'might', 'rule'.
FOREBEARS This was the clan name of the Lords of the Isles in medieval Scotland. There was considerable interaction between Gaelic speakers and Norse speakers in the Hebrides, and the name of the founder of the clan, Gaelic *Somhairle*, English *Sorley*, is itself of Scandinavian origin, from Old Norse *Sumarliðr* "summer traveler" or "summer warrior". The Macdonalds are the largest of the Scottish clans.

McDonel (114) Variant spelling of Irish MCDONNELL.

McDonell (728) Variant spelling of Irish MCDONNELL.
GIVEN NAME Irish 4%. *Brendan* (2).

McDoniel (138) Irish: variant of MCDONNELL. The spelling is influenced by the personal name DANIEL. Compare MCDANIEL.

McDonnel (117) Irish: variant spelling of MCDONNELL.
GIVEN NAME Irish 5%. *Brendan.*

McDonnell (5971) Irish: Anglicized form of Gaelic **Mac Dhomhnuill**, a patronymic from the personal name *Domhnall* (see MCDONALD).
GIVEN NAMES Irish 6%. *Brigid* (3), *Dermot* (3), *Colm* (2), *Donal* (2), *Eamonn* (2), *Aidan, Brendan, Brian Patrick, Bridgid, Caitlin, Ciaran, Conor.*

McDonough (9189) Irish: Anglicized form of Gaelic **Mac Donnchadha**, patronymic from the personal name *Donnchadh*, a personal name composed of the elements *donn* 'brown', possibly 'chieftain' + *cath* 'battle'.
GIVEN NAMES Irish 5%. *Brendan* (6), *Callahan* (2), *Aileen, Brennan, Brigid, Caitlin,*

Dermot, Donal, Donovan, Eamon, Kieran, Seamus.

McDorman (362) Irish: perhaps an Anglicized form of Gaelic **Mac Dornáin** 'descendant of *Doirnín*', a byname from a diminutive of *dorn* 'fist'. Compare DORNAN. However, this may alternatively be an irregularly formed patronymic from the English surname DORMAN, which is well established in Ireland.

McDougal (2476) Scottish: variant spelling of McDOUGALL.

McDougald (921) Scottish: variant of MCDOUGALL.

McDougall (2633) Scottish: Anglicized form of Gaelic **Mac Dubhghaill**, 'son of *Dubhghall*', a personal name composed of the elements *dubh* 'black' + *gall* 'stranger'. This was originally a byname used to distinguish the darker-haired Danes from the fair-haired Norwegians. Compare DOYLE.

McDougle (554) Variant spelling of Scottish McDOUGALL.

McDow (496) Scottish and Irish: patronymic from the Gaelic personal name *Dubh* meaning 'black'; thus, it is of the same origin as McDUFF.

McDowall (316) Scottish variant of McDOWELL.

GIVEN NAME Scottish 4%. *Alasdair.*

McDowell (16616) Scottish and Irish: Anglicized form of Gaelic **Mac Dubhghaill** 'son of *Dubhghall*', a byname meaning 'dark stranger', used among the Gaels to distinguish the darker-haired Danes from fair-haired Norwegians. According to MacLysaght, this is the Irish form of the name of the Scottish clan McDOUGALL, borne by a branch which went to Ireland from the Hebrides as mercenaries. However, Black shows that both forms were current in Scotland.

McDuff (554) Scottish and northern Irish: Anglicized form of Gaelic **Mac Duibh**, a patronymic from the personal name *Dubh* 'black', 'dark'.

GIVEN NAMES French 6%. *Armand* (2), *Gaston, Jean Marie, Laurent, Lucien, Marie-Jeanne, Numa, Pierre.*

McDuffee (494) Variant spelling of Irish and Scottish McDUFFIE.

McDuffey (126) Variant spelling of Irish and Scottish McDUFFIE.

McDuffie (2690) Scottish and Irish: Anglicized form of Gaelic **Mac Duibhshíthe** 'son of *Duibhshíth*', a personal name composed of the elements *dubh* 'black' + *síth* 'peace'. Compare DUFFY 2.

McDuffy (225) Irish and Scottish: variant spelling of McDUFFIE.

McDunn (112) Irish: Anglicized form of Gaelic **Mac Duinn** 'son of *Donn*', a byname meaning 'brown-haired', 'dark', 'swarthy'.

McEachen (108) Scottish: variant of McEACHIN.

McEachern (1616) Irish and Scottish: Anglicized form of Gaelic **Mac Eichthigheirn** 'son of *Eichthighearn*', a personal name composed of the elements *each* 'horse' + *tighearna* 'lord'.

McEachin (359) Scottish: Anglicized form of Gaelic **Mac Eachainn** 'son of *Eachann*', a personal name composed of Celtic *each* 'horse' + *donn* 'lord' and Anglicized as HECTOR.

McEachran (133) Scottish: variant of McEACHERN.

McEachron (155) Scottish: variant of McEACHERN.

McElderry (265) Irish (mainly northern): Anglicized form of Gaelic **Mac Giolla Dhorcha** 'son of the dark-haired lad'.

McEldowney (434) Northern Irish: Anglicized form of Gaelic **Mac Giolla Dhomhnaigh** 'son of the servant of the Church'.

McElduff (104) Northern Irish: Anglicized form of Gaelic **Mac Giolla Duibh** 'son of the servant of *Dubh*', a by-name meaning 'dark', 'black'.

McEleney (126) Irish: variant of McELHINNEY.

McElfish (134) Variant of Scottish McELFRESH.

McElfresh (812) Scottish (Western Isles): Anglicized form of Gaelic **Mac Gille Bhris**, patronymic from a personal name meaning 'servant of (Saint) Bricius'. This was the name of a 5th-century Gaulish saint whose cult was popular in Scotland in the 12th–14th centuries.

McElhaney (1360) Irish: variant of McELHINNEY.

McElhannon (298) Irish: Anglicized form of Gaelic **Mac Giolla Chonáin** 'son of the servant of (Saint) Conán'.

McElhany (169) Variant of Irish McELHINNEY.

McElheney (158) Variant of Irish McELHINNEY.

McElhenney (141) Variant of Irish McELHINNEY.

McElhenny (117) Irish: variant of McELHINNEY.

McElheny (282) Irish: variant of McELHINNEY.

McElhiney (335) Irish: variant of McELHINNEY.

McElhinney (452) Irish (mainly Ulster): Anglicized form of Gaelic **Mac Giolla Choinnigh** 'son of the servant of (Saint) *Coinneach*' (see KENNY).

GIVEN NAME Irish 4%. *Liam.*

McElhinny (208) Irish: variant spelling of McELHINNEY.

McElhone (178) Irish (mainly County Tyrone): Anglicized form of Gaelic **Mac Giolla Chomhghain** 'son of the servant of (Saint) *Comhghan*', a personal name composed of the elements *comh* 'together' + *gan-, gen-* 'born', hence a byname for a

twin. This name was borne by an 8th-century Irish prince who lived as a monk in Scotland.

GIVEN NAME Irish 5%. *Liam.*

McElligott (684) Irish: Anglicized form of Gaelic **Mac Uileagóid**, a patronymic from a pet form of the Gaelic form of WILLIAM.

GIVEN NAMES Irish 5%. *Brigid* (2), *Brendan, Seamus.*

McElmurray (153) Irish: Anglicized form of Gaelic **Mac Giolla Muire** 'son of the servant of Mary', the surname of a chieftain family in County Down. It is more commonly Anglicized as GILMORE.

GIVEN NAMES French 5%. *Ancil, Clovis.*

McElmurry (295) Variant of Irish McELMURRAY.

McElrath (1003) Irish: Anglicized form of Gaelic **Mac Giolla Riabhaigh** 'son of the brindled lad'.

McElravy (176) Variant of northern Irish McIlravy, an Anglicized form of Gaelic **Mac Giolla Riabhaigh** (see McELRATH).

McElreath (378) Variant of northern Irish McELRATH.

McElroy (9084) Irish: Anglicized form of Gaelic **Mac Giolla Ruaidh** 'son of the red-haired lad' (from *ruadh* 'red'). Compare GILROY.

McElvain (384) Scottish: variant of McELWAIN.

McElveen (1223) Irish (County Down): Anglicized form of Gaelic **Mac Giolla Mhín** 'son of the gentle lad'.

McElwain (1315) **1.** Scottish: Anglicized form of Gaelic **Mac Gille Bheathain** 'son of the servant of (Saint) *Beathan*', a personal name representing a diminutive of *beatha* 'life'. **2.** Irish: Anglicized form of Gaelic **Mac Giolla Bháin** 'son of the white-haired (i.e. 'ash blond') lad'. In Ulster this surname can be the Scottish name as in 1.

McElwee (1412) Irish: Anglicized form of Gaelic **Mac Giolla Bhuidhe** 'son of the yellow-haired lad'. Compare McEVOY 1.

GIVEN NAMES Irish 4%. *Gearold, John Patrick, Liam, Maeve.*

McElyea (690) Irish: perhaps an altered spelling of McELWEE.

McEnaney (347) Irish: Anglicized form of Gaelic **Mac an Déaghanaigh** 'son of the dean'. This surname is sometimes Anglicized as BIRD, part of the name being taken erroneously for Irish *éan* 'bird'.

McEnany (180) Irish: variant spelling of McENANEY.

McEndree (188) Irish: variant of McHENRY.

McEneaney (132) Irish: variant spelling of McENANEY.

McEnerney (178) Irish: variant of McINERNEY.

McEnery (286) Irish (Limerick): Anglicized form of Gaelic **Mac Innéirghe** 'son of

Innéirghe', a personal name, apparently a derivative of *éirghe* 'to arise', 'to ascend'. GIVEN NAME Irish 7%. *Cormac* (2).

McEniry (119) Irish: variant spelling of MCENERY.

McEnroe (446) Irish: **1.** (Munster) Anglicized form of Gaelic **Mac Conchradha** 'son of *Conchradh*', a personal name composed of the elements *cú* 'hound' + *crádh* 'torment', genitive *crádha*. **2.** (southern Ulster) Anglicized form of Gaelic **Mac Con Rubha** 'son of *Cú Rubha*', meaning 'hound of the promontory'.

McEntee (1064) Irish: variant of MCATEE. GIVEN NAMES Irish 4%. *Brendan, Jarlath*.

McEntire (1444) Respelling of Scottish MCINTYRE.

McEntyre (436) Scottish: variant spelling of MCINTYRE.

McErlean (174) Scottish: Anglicized form of Gaelic **Mac an Fhirléighinn** 'son of the lector', from *fear léighinn* 'man of reading'. This was the title held by the head of a monastic school. GIVEN NAMES Irish 11%. *Brendan, Declan, Donal, Eamon*.

McEuen (397) Scottish: variant spelling of MCEWEN.

McEver (239) Scottish: variant of MCIVER.

McEvers (247) Scottish: variant of MCIVER.

McEvilly (202) Irish: Anglicized form of Gaelic **Mac an Mhílidh** 'son of the knight' (from Gaelic *míleadh* 'warrior', 'knight'). In County Mayo a family of English origin changed their name from STAUNTON to McEvilly. GIVEN NAME Irish 8%. *Eamonn*.

McEvoy (2365) **1.** Irish (Ulster) and Scottish: Anglicized form of Gaelic **Mac Giolla Bhuidhe** 'son of the yellow-haired lad'. **2.** Irish: Anglicized form of Gaelic **Mac Fhíodhbhuidhe**, a patronymic, originally (the genitive has been altered) from *fíodhbhadhach* 'woodman'. In east Ulster this surname has sometimes been used in place of MCVEIGH. GIVEN NAMES Irish 6%. *Kieran* (3), *Aileen, Colm, Cormac, Finbar, Seamus*.

McEwan (962) Scottish: variant spelling of MCEWEN.

McEwen (2961) Scottish and Irish: **1.** Anglicized form of Gaelic **Mac Eoghain** 'son of *Eoghan*', a widespread and ancient personal name, possibly derived from *eo* 'yew', meaning 'born of yew'. It was Latinized as *Eugenius* (see EUGENE), and was also regarded as a Gaelic form of JOHN. This was the name of one of the two sons of Niall of the Nine Hostages; the other was Conall. **2.** Anglicized form of **Mac Eathain** 'son of *Eathan*', a Scottish Gaelic form of Latin *Johannes* (see JOHN). *John* was taken into Irish as *Eoin* at first; *Seán* is a later form. In later Irish, as in the surnames, the personal names *Eoghan* and *Eoin* were often confused.

McFadden (9677) Scottish and Irish: Anglicized form of Gaelic **Mac Phaid(e)in** (Scottish) and **Mac Pháidín** (Irish), patronymics from Gaelic pet forms of the personal name PATRICK.

McFaddin (324) Scottish and Irish: variant spelling of MCFADDEN.

McFaden (138) Scottish and Irish: variant spelling of MCFADDEN.

McFadin (221) Scottish and Irish: variant spelling of MCFADDEN.

McFadyen (404) Scottish and Irish: variant spelling of MCFADDEN.

McFall (2721) Scottish and Irish: Anglicized form of Gaelic **Mac Phàil** (Scottish) and **Mac Phóil** (Irish), patronymics from Gaelic forms of the personal name PAUL.

McFalls (783) Northern Irish: variant of MCFALL, formed with redundant addition of the English patronymic -*s*.

McFann (279) Variant of Irish **McVann**, itself a variant of MCBEAN.

McFarlain (117) Scottish and northern Irish: variant spelling of MCFARLANE.

McFarlan (208) Scottish: variant of MCFARLANE. GIVEN NAME French 5%. *Andre*.

McFarland (14696) Northern Irish: variant of MCFARLANE.

McFarlane (2635) Scottish and northern Irish: Anglicized form of Gaelic **Mac Pharthaláin**, a patronymic from the personal name *Parthalán*, which is most probably from Latin *Bartholomaeus* (see BARTHOLOMEW). FOREBEARS McFarlane is one of the most important Scottish clans, originally associated with Arrochar on Loch Long. Robert McFarlane came to NY in 1835 and was editor of *Scientific American* magazine (1848–65.

McFarlen (117) Scottish and northern Irish: variant spelling of MCFARLANE.

McFarlin (1534) Scottish and northern Irish: variant spelling of MCFARLANE.

McFarling (322) Altered form of Scottish MCFARLANE.

McFarren (337) Irish: variant of MCFERRIN. Compare FARREN.

McFate (226) Scottish: Anglicized form of Gaelic **Mac Phaid**, a patronymic from a pet form of the Gaelic form of the personal name PATRICK.

McFatridge (212) Irish and Scottish: variant of MCFETRIDGE.

McFatter (172) Scottish: variant of MCPHEETTERS.

McFaul (449) Variant of Scottish and Irish MCPHAIL.

McFayden (147) Scottish: variant of MCFADDEN. GIVEN NAME French 4%. *Andre* (2).

McFeaters (129) Scottish: variant spelling of MCPHEETERS.

McFee (741) Scottish and Irish: variant spelling of MCPHEE.

McFeeley (143) Irish: variant spelling of MCFEELY.

McFeely (299) Irish (Counties Donegal and Derry): Anglicized form of Gaelic **Mac Fithcheallaigh**, a patronymic from *Fithcheallach* 'chess player'.

McFeeters (176) Scottish: variant of MCPHEETERS.

McFerran (274) Northern Irish: variant spelling of MCFERRIN.

McFerren (344) Northern Irish: variant spelling of MCFERRIN.

McFerrin (554) Northern Irish: **1.** Anglicized form of Gaelic **Mac Fearáin** 'son of *Fearán*', a personal name from a diminutive of *fear* 'man'. **2.** Anglicized form of Gaelic **Mac Mhearáin** 'son of *Mearán*', a personal name derived from *mear* 'swift'.

McFerron (181) Northern Irish: variant spelling of MCFERRIN.

McFetridge (255) Scottish and Irish (County Antrim): Anglicized form of Scottish Gaelic **Mac Pheadruis**, patronymic from a Gaelic form of the personal name PETER.

McField (109) Scottish or Irish: Anglicized form of Gaelic **Mac Phàil** (see MCPHAIL).

McGaffey (149) Irish: **1.** Anglicized form of Gaelic **Mac Eochadha** or **Mac Eachaidh** 'son of *Eachaidh*', a byname meaning 'horseman' (a derivative of *each* 'horse'). **2.** Anglicized form of Gaelic **Mac Gáibhthigh**, patronymic from a personal name based on *gáibhtheach* 'fierce', 'eager' (earlier *gáibhthech*). Compare GAFFEY and CAUGHEY.

McGaffin (119) Northern Irish: Anglicized form of Gaelic **Mac Eacháin** 'son of *Eachán*' (see MCGAHAN).

McGaha (1311) Irish: Anglicized form of Gaelic **Mac Eachaidh** (see MCGAFFEY).

McGahan (583) Northern Irish: Anglicized form of Gaelic **Mac Eacháin**, 'son of *Eachán*' a diminutive of *Eachaidh*, a personal name based on *each* 'horse'. Compare KEOGH.

McGahee (539) Irish: variant of MCGAUGHEY.

McGahey (511) Irish: variant of MCGAUGHEY.

McGalliard (317) Irish: possibly an Anglicized form of Irish **Mac Giolla Aird** 'son of the tall lad'.

McGann (1543) Irish: **1.** Connacht form of MCCANN. **2.** possibly a reduced form of MCGAHAN.

McGannon (273) Irish: Anglicized form of Gaelic **Mag Fhionnáin** 'son of *Fionnán*' (see MCLENNAN). This name, from a diminutive of *fionn* 'white', 'fair', was borne by several early Irish saints. GIVEN NAME Irish 7%. *Connor*.

McGarey (123) Scottish: variant of MCGARRY.

McGarity (714) Irish: Anglicized form of Gaelic **Mag Oireachtaigh** 'son of *Oireach-*

tach', a byname meaning 'member of the assembly' or 'frequenting assemblies'. Compare GERAGHTY.

McGarr (397) Irish or Scottish: probably a variant of McGIRR.

McGarrah (321) Irish: shortened form of **McGarraher**, an Anglicized form of Gaelic **Mag Fhearchair** 'son of *Fearchar*', a personal name composed of the elements *fear* 'man' + *car* 'dear', 'loving'.

McGarrigle (203) Irish: Anglicized form of Gaelic **Mag Fhearghail** 'son of *Fearghal*', a personal name composed of the elements *fear* 'man' + *gal* 'valor'.

McGarrity (446) Irish: variant spelling of McGARITY.

McGarry (2794) Irish and Scottish: Anglicized form of Gaelic **Mac Fhearadhaigh** 'son of *Fhearadhach*', a personal name meaning 'manly', 'brave' (from *fear* 'man').
GIVEN NAMES Irish 5%. *Kieran* (5), *Brendan* (2), *Eamon, James Patrick, Mairead, Sean Patrick*.

McGarty (129) Irish: reduced form of McGARITY.

McGarvey (1535) Irish (County Donegal) and Scottish (Galloway): Anglicized form of Gaelic **Mac Gairbhshíth** 'son of *Gairbhshíth*', a personal name derived from *garbh* 'rough', 'cruel' + *síth* 'peace'.
GIVEN NAMES Irish 4%. *Cormac, Declan*.

McGary (995) Irish: variant of McCARY.

McGath (170) Scottish (Ayrshire): perhaps an Anglicized spelling of Gaelic **Mag Eathach**, a variant of **Mac Eachach**.

McGaugh (453) Irish: perhaps a variant of McGOUGH or McGAW.

McGaughey (1336) Irish: Anglicized form of Gaelic **Mac Eachaidh** 'son of *Eochaidh* or *Eachaidh*', meaning 'horseman' (a derivative of *each* 'horse').

McGaughy (434) Irish: variant spelling of McGAUGHEY.

McGauley (283) Irish: variant of McCAULEY.

McGavin (223) Scottish (Elgin and Galloway): possibly variant of McGOWAN.

McGavock (176) Irish or Scottish: Anglicized form of Gaelic **Mac Dhabhóig** 'son of *Dabhóg*', a Gaelic pet form of the personal name DAVID.

McGaw (451) Northern Irish and Scottish: Anglicized form of Gaelic **Mag Ádhaimh** 'son of Adam'. Compare McCAW.

McGeachy (172) Scottish: variant of Irish McGAUGHEY.

McGeady (117) Irish (Donegal): Anglicized form of Gaelic **Mag Céadaigh**, from *céadach* 'hundredfold' used as personal name.
GIVEN NAMES Irish 12%. *Eamonn* (2), *Kieran*.

McGeary (548) Irish (Counties Tyrone and Armagh): variant of McGARRY.

McGee (23438) Irish and Scottish: Anglicized form of Gaelic **Mac Aodha** 'son of *Aodh*' (see McCOY).

McGeehan (620) Irish (Ulster): Anglicized form of Gaelic **Mac Gaoithín** 'son of *Gaoithín*', a personal name derived from the diminutive of *gaoth* 'clever', 'wise'.
GIVEN NAMES Irish 5%. *Brendan, Brigid*.

McGeeney (104) Respelling of Irish (Ulster) **McGeaney**, an Anglicized form of Gaelic **Mac Géibheannaigh**, a patronymic from a personal name formed from *géibheannach* 'fettered'.

McGeever (179) Irish (Donegal): variant of McIVER.
GIVEN NAME Irish 10%. *Brendan*.

McGehee (2494) Irish: probably a variant of McGAUGHEY.

McGeorge (668) Scottish: Anglicized form of Gaelic **Mac Deoraidh** 'son of the pilgrim or relic keeper' (see DEWAR 1).

McGeough (208) Irish and Scottish (Galloway): Anglicized form of Gaelic **Mag Eochadha**, **Mac Eochadha**, variant genitive forms of *Eochaidh* (see McGAUGHEY).
GIVEN NAME Irish 7%. *Liam*.

McGettigan (417) Northern Irish (Donegal): Anglicized form of Gaelic **Mag Eiteagáin**, patronymic from the personal name *Eiteagán*, a diminutive of *eite* 'wing' (perhaps originally a byname for a swift runner).
GIVEN NAMES Irish 8%. *Brendan, Declan*.

McGettrick (103) Scottish and northern Irish: variant of McKITTRICK.
GIVEN NAMES Irish 8%. *Brendan, Malachy*.

McGhan (164) Irish: probably a variant of McGANN or McCANN.
GIVEN NAME Irish 4%. *Pegeen*.

McGhee (6439) Scottish and Irish: variant of McGEE.

McGhie (288) Scottish: variant of McGEE.

McGibbon (348) Scottish and Irish: Anglicized form of Gaelic **Mac Giobúin**, a patronymic from a pet form of the personal name GILBERT, found in Connacht and Limerick in Ireland, and also in Scotland, where it is sometimes Anglicized as McKIBBEN.

McGibney (105) Irish: Anglicized form of Gaelic **Mac Gibne** 'son of *Gibne*', a byname meaning 'hound'.

McGiboney (127) Irish: variant of McGIBNEY.

McGiffin (140) Irish: Anglicized form of Gaelic **Mag Dhuibhfinn**, a patronymic from the personal name *Duibhfionn*, composed of the elements *dubh* 'black' + *fionn* 'fair'.

McGilberry (132) Irish: Anglicized form of Gaelic **Mac Giolla Bhearaigh** 'son of the servant of (Saint) Bearach'.

McGill (9318) **1.** Scottish (Galloway) and Irish: Anglicized form of Gaelic **Mac an Ghoill** 'son of the stranger' (see GALL 1). **2.** Irish: short form of Gaelic names beginning with *Mac Giolla* 'son of the servant (or devotee) of' (see for example McELROY). **3.** Scottish: Anglicized form of **Mac Ghille Mhaoil**, otherwise Anglicized as McMILLAN.

McGillen (137) Irish: probably an Anglicized form of Gaelic **Mag Giolláin**, a patronymic from *giollán* 'little lad'; Woulfe, on the other hand, proposes an Anglicized form of **Ó Gealáin** meaning 'bright'.

McGillicuddy (476) Irish: Anglicized form of Gaelic **Mac Giolla Chuda**, 'son of the servant of (Saint) *Chuda*', a personal name of unexplained origin. This was the name of a 7th-century abbot-bishop of Rathin in County Westmeath.
GIVEN NAMES Irish 7%. *Ciaran, Dermot, Siobhan*.

McGillis (265) Scottish: Anglicized form of Gaelic **Mac Gille Iosa** 'son of the servant of Jesus'. Compare McLEISH.

McGillivary (112) Scottish: variant of McGILLIVRAY.
GIVEN NAME Irish 5%. *Aisling*.

McGillivray (546) Scottish: Anglicized form of Gaelic **Mac Gille Bhràtha**, a patronymic from a personal name meaning 'servant of judgment'.
FOREBEARS The leading negotiator between the Creek nation and the U.S. government in the years after the American Revolution was a Creek chief who bore the unlikely name Alexander McGillivray (b. *c.*1759). He was in fact of mixed descent; his father was Lachlan McGillivray, a Scottish trader, but he owed his position in the Creek nation to matrilineal descent through his mother, who was half Creek and half French.

McGilton (156) Northern Irish: reduced form of **McGiltenan**, an Anglicized form of Gaelic **Mac Giolla tSeanáin**, a patronymic from a personal name meaning 'servant of (Saint) Senan'.

McGilvary (140) Scottish: variant of McGILLIVRAY.

McGilvery (187) Scottish: variant of McGILLIVRAY.

McGilvray (484) Scottish: variant of McGILLIVRAY.

McGimsey (116) Irish: Anglicized form of Gaelic **Mac Díomasaigh** 'son of *Díomasach*', a byname meaning 'proud', 'haughty', from *díomas* 'pride'. Compare DEMPSEY.

McGinity (146) Irish: variant of McGINTY.
GIVEN NAME Irish 8%. *Brigid*.

McGinley (2741) Irish (Donegal): Anglicized form of Gaelic **Mag Fhionnghaile**, a patronymic from the personal name *Fionnghal*, composed of the elements *fionn* 'fair' + *gal* 'valor'.
GIVEN NAMES Irish 6%. *Liam* (2), *Brendan, Brigid, Caitlin, Conal, Declan, Michael Patrick*.

McGinn (2414) Irish: Anglicized form of Gaelic **Mag Finn**, a patronymic from the personal name *Fionn* (see FINN). This is the name of an ecclesiastical family in County Down.

GIVEN NAMES Irish 5%. *Brendan* (2), *Malachy*.

McGinnes (218) Irish and Scottish: variant spelling of MCGINNIS.

McGinness (696) Irish and Scottish: variant spelling of MCGINNIS.

McGinnis (10305) Irish (also Galloway in western Scotland): Anglicized form of Gaelic **Mag Aonghuis** 'son of *Aonghus*' (see ANGUS). Compare Scottish MCINNIS. This is the surname of a chieftain family in western County Down.

McGinniss (183) Irish and Scottish: variant spelling of MCGINNIS.

McGinnity (225) Irish: variant of MCGINTY.

McGinty (2355) Irish: Anglicized form of Gaelic **Mag Fhionnachtaigh**, a patronymic from the personal name *Fionnshneachtach*, composed of the elements *fionn* 'white' + *sneachtach* 'snowy'.

GIVEN NAMES Irish 5%. *Brendan, Patrick Sean, Seamus.*

McGirr (417) Scottish and northern Irish: Anglicized form of Gaelic **Mac an Gheairr** 'son of the short man', sometimes translated into English as SHORT.

GIVEN NAME Irish 4%. *Eamon.*

McGirt (297) Northern Irish: variant of MCCORD.

McGivern (579) Northern Irish: Anglicized form of Gaelic **Mac Uidhrín**, a patronymic from a personal name which is from a diminutive of *odhar* 'dun'. This surname is also found in Galloway in Scotland, where it is of Irish origin.

McGivney (356) Irish (especially County Cavan): Anglicized form of Gaelic **Mac Dhuibhne**, a patronymic from *Duibhne*, a personal name from *duibhne* 'disagreeable', 'ill-going'.

GIVEN NAME Irish 7%. *Brendan.*

McGlade (303) Northern Irish: Anglicized form of Gaelic **Mag Léid**, which may be a variant of MCLEOD.

McGlamery (327) Of Scottish or Irish origin: unexplained; probably related to MCCLAMROCK.

McGlashan (181) Scottish and Irish (western Ulster): Anglicized form of Gaelic **Mac Glasáin** (see MCGLASSON). In Ireland, in many cases, this surname has been translated as GREEN.

McGlasson (482) Scottish: Anglicized form of Gaelic **Mac Glasain**, a patronymic from the personal name *Glasan*, from a diminutive of *glas* 'gray', 'green', 'blue'.

McGlathery (120) Irish: variant of **McGladdery**, an Anglicized form of Gaelic **Mac Gleadra**.

McGlauflin (104) Northern Irish: variant of MCLAUGHLIN, from Gaelic **Mag Lochlainn**.

McGlaughlin (388) Northern Irish: variant of MCLAUGHLIN, from Gaelic **Mag Lochlainn**.

McGlaun (207) Irish: variant of MCGLONE.

McGlinchey (387) Irish (Donegal): Anglicized form of Gaelic **Mag Loingsigh**, a patronymic from the personal name *Loingseach* meaning 'mariner' (from *long* 'ship'). Compare LYNCH.

GIVEN NAMES Irish 7%. *Dermot* (2), *James Patrick, Parnell.*

McGlinn (199) Irish: variant of MCGLYNN.

McGlocklin (208) Irish or Scottish: variant of MCLAUGHLIN.

McGloin (327) Irish: variant of MCGLONE.

GIVEN NAMES Irish 7%. *Eamonn, Eoin, Padraig.*

McGlone (1281) Irish: Anglicized form of Gaelic **Mac Giolla Eóin** 'son of the devotee of St. John (Irish *Eóin*)'. Compare MONDAY, MCLEAN.

McGlory (153) Irish (Ulster): variant of MCCLORY, from Gaelic **Mag Labhradha**.

McGlothen (129) Of Scottish or Irish origin: unexplained. Perhaps a variant of MCLAUGHLIN.

McGlothin (407) Of Scottish or Irish origin: unexplained. Perhaps a variant of MCLAUGHLIN.

McGlothlen (123) Variant of Irish and Scottish MCLAUGHLIN.

McGlothlin (1356) Variant of Irish and Scottish MCLAUGHLIN.

McGlumphy (137) Probably a respelling of Scottish **McClumpha**, an Anglicized form of Gaelic **Mac Gille Iomchadha** 'son of the servant of (St) Iomchadh'.

McGlynn (1632) Irish: Anglicized form of Gaelic **Mag Fhloinn**, patronymic from the personal name *Flann* 'red', 'crimson'.

GIVEN NAMES Irish 6%. *Brendan, Bridie, Colm, Declan, Donovan, Sean Patrick, Thomas Patrick.*

McGoey (175) Irish (Counties Leitrim and Longford): variant of MCGAUGHEY.

McGoff (243) Irish: variant of MCGOUGH.

McGoldrick (1188) Irish (Ulster and Connacht): Anglicized form of Gaelic **Mag Ualghairg**, patronymic from the personal name *Ualgharg*, composed of Celtic elements meaning 'proud' + 'fierce'. It is sometimes Anglicized as GOLDEN.

GIVEN NAMES Irish 7%. *Aileen* (3), *Fergal.*

McGonagill (103) Variant spelling of Irish and Scottish MCGONIGLE.

McGonagle (671) Irish (Donegal): variant spelling of MCGONIGLE.

GIVEN NAMES Irish 5%. *Colm, Liam, Seamus.*

McGonegal (109) Irish (Donegal): variant spelling of MCGONIGLE.

GIVEN NAME Irish 7%. *Donal.*

McGonigal (564) Irish (Donegal): variant spelling of MCGONIGLE.

McGonigle (826) Irish (Donegal) and Scottish (Glasgow): Anglicized form of Gaelic **Mac Conghail**, a patronymic from

the personal name *Conghal*, composed of Celtic elements meaning 'hound' + 'valor'.

McGoogan (115) Irish: variant of MCGUIGAN.

GIVEN NAMES German 4%. *Otto, Wilhelmina.*

McGorry (141) Irish (County Cavan) and Scottish: Anglicized form of Gaelic **Mac Gothraidh** 'son of *Gothradh*', a Gaelic equivalent of English *Godfrey*. Compare MCCAFFREY.

McGorty (104) Irish: variant spelling of MCGOURTY.

GIVEN NAME Irish 7%. *Aileen.*

McGory (102) Irish: variant of MCGORRY.

McGougan (100) Irish: variant of MCGUIGAN.

McGough (1968) Irish: Anglicized form of Gaelic **Mag Eochadha**, a patronymic from the personal name *Eochaidh*, variant *Eachaidh*, 'horseman', a derivative of *each* 'horse'.

McGourty (251) Irish: probably an altered form of **McGourkey**, Anglicized form of Gaelic **Mac Dhorchaidh**, a patronymic from the personal name *Dorchadh*, a derivative of *dorcha* 'dark'.

McGovern (6695) Irish and Scottish: Anglicized form of Gaelic **Mag Shamhr(adh)áin**, a patronymic from the personal name *Samhradháin*, a diminutive of *samhradh* 'summer'.

GIVEN NAMES Irish 5%. *Brendan* (3), *Eamon* (2), *Ciaran, Dermot, Dierdra, Kevin Patrick, Liam, Niall, Padraic.*

McGowan (11667) Scottish and Irish: Anglicized form of Gaelic **Mac Gobhann** (Scottish) and **Mac Gabhann** (Irish) 'son of the smith'.

GIVEN NAMES Irish 4%. *Brendan* (5), *Siobhan* (3), *Cormac* (2), *Seamus* (2), *Aileen, Colm, Eithne, Kieran, Niall, Paddy.*

McGowen (1376) Scottish and Irish: variant spelling of MCGOWAN.

McGowin (260) Scottish and Irish: variant spelling of MCGOWAN.

McGown (480) Scottish and Irish: variant spelling of MCGOWAN.

McGrade (108) Irish: variant of MCGRADY.

McGrady (1388) Irish (County Down): Anglicized form of Gaelic **Mag Bhrádaigh**, a patronymic from the personal name *Brádach*, probably from a word meaning 'proud'.

GIVEN NAMES Irish 4%. *Seamus* (2), *Liam.*

McGrail (891) Irish: Anglicized form of Gaelic **Mac Réill** (earlier **Mac Néill**), a patronymic from the personal name *Niall* (see NEILL). The substitution of *-r-* for *-n-* occurs in a number of Irish *Mac-* names.

GIVEN NAME Irish 5%. *Dympna.*

McGrain (178) Scottish and Irish: variant of MCGRANE.

McGranaghan (117) Irish: variant spelling of MCGRANAHAN.

McGranahan (371) Irish and Scottish (Galloway): Anglicized form of Irish

Gaelic **Mac (Mag) Reannacháin**, a patronymic from the personal name *Reannachán*, probably derived from *reannach* 'sharp', 'pointed'.

McGrane (688) Irish: Anglicized form of Gaelic **Mac Ráighne**, a patronymic from a pet form of a Gaelic form of REYNOLD (see RAINEY).

McGrann (161) Irish: variant of McGRANE.

McGrath (14369) Irish: Anglicized form of Gaelic **Mac Craith**, a patronymic from a personal name, possibly **Mac Raith** 'son of grace', from *rath* 'grace', 'prosperity'.
GIVEN NAMES Irish 5%. *Brendan* (4), *Briana* (2), *Finbarr* (2), *Kieran* (2), *Malachy* (2), *Aileen, Brennan, Ciaran, Connor, Conor, Declan, Dermot.*

McGraw (7641) Northern Irish: variant of McGRATH.

McGray (167) Variant of Irish McGRATH or Scottish McRAE.

McGreal (310) Irish: variant of McGRAIL.
GIVEN NAME Irish 6%. *Cathal.*

McGreevey (141) Northern Irish: variant spelling of McGREEVY.

McGreevy (986) Northern Irish: Anglicized form of Gaelic **Mac Riabhaigh** (Irish), **Mac Riabhaich** (Scottish), a patronymic from the byname *Riabhach* 'brindled', 'grizzled'.
GIVEN NAMES Irish 5%. *Seamus* (2), *Brendan.*

McGregor (5803) Scottish: Anglicized form of Gaelic **Mac Griogair** 'son of *Griogar*', Gaelic form of the personal name GREGORY.

McGregory (148) Scottish: variant of Mc-GREGOR.

McGrew (3400) Irish: altered form of MUL-GREW.

McGriff (1468) Irish: of uncertain origin. Perhaps an altered form of McNIFF.

McGroarty (393) Irish and Scottish: Anglicized form of Gaelic **Mac Robhartaigh**, patronymic from the personal name *Robhartach*, meaning 'flood tide', hence 'abundance', 'prosperity'.

McGrogan (224) Northern Irish: Anglicized form of Gaelic **Mac Gruagáin** 'son of *Gruagán*', possibly from *gruag* 'hair' or *grug* 'fierceness'.

McGrory (441) Scottish and Irish: variant of McCRORY.
GIVEN NAMES Irish 7%. *Brendan, Liam.*

McGruder (798) Scottish: Anglicized form of Gaelic **Mac Grudaire**, a patronymic from the occupational byname *grudaire* 'brewer'.

McGuane (155) Irish: Anglicized form of Gaelic **Mac Dhubháin**, a patronymic from the personal name *Dubhán*, a derivative of *dubh* 'dark', 'black'.
GIVEN NAME Irish 7%. *Brennan.*

McGuckin (535) Irish: variant of McGUI-GAN.

McGue (155) Northern Irish: variant of McCOY. Compare McHUGH.

McGuff (126) Irish: Anglicized form of Gaelic **Mac Dhuibh**, a patronymic from the personal name or byname *Dubh* 'black'.

McGuffee (237) Variant spelling of Scottish and Irish McGUFFEY.

McGuffey (527) Scottish and Irish: **1.** Anglicized form of the Gaelic patronymic **Mac Dhubhthaigh** or **Mac Dhuibhshíthe** (see DUFFY). **2.** Scottish: according to Black this may be a variant of **McGuffog**, which may represent Gaelic **Mac Dhabhoig**, a patronymic from *Davuc*, a pet form of DAVID.

McGuffie (191) Scottish variant spelling of McGUFFEY.
GIVEN NAME French 4%. *Pierre.*

McGuffin (716) Irish: older Anglicized form of Gaelic **Mag Dhuibhfinn** (see McGIFFIN).

McGugan (139) Irish: variant of McGUI-GAN.

McGuigan (1396) Northern Irish and Scottish: Anglicized form of Gaelic **Mag Uiginn** 'son of the viking' (see HIGGINS) or **Mac Guagáin**, an altered version of **Mag Eochagáin** (see GEOGHEGAN).
GIVEN NAMES Irish 5%. *Brendan, Liam, Mairead.*

McGuiggan (102) Irish: variant of McGUIGAN.

McGuiness (443) Irish: variant spelling of McGINNIS.
GIVEN NAME Irish 5%. *Ciaran.*

McGuinn (445) Irish: variant of McQUINN.
GIVEN NAMES Irish 6%. *Brendan, Briann, John Patrick.*

McGuinness (1652) Irish: variant spelling of McGINNIS.
GIVEN NAMES Irish 7%. *Brendan* (5), *Ciaran, Ethna, Fergus, Kieran, Malachy, Niall, Niamh, Seamus.*

McGuire (23838) Irish and Scottish: Anglicized form of Gaelic **Mag Uidhir** 'son of *Odhar*', a byname meaning 'sallow'. This was the name of the ruling family of Fermanagh from the 13th–17th centuries.
GIVEN NAMES Irish 4%. *Brendan* (9), *Brigid* (2), *Caitlin* (2), *Kieran* (2), *Aidan, Aislinn, Clancy, Conley, Connor, Cormac, Donal, Fionnuala.*

McGuirk (913) **1.** Scottish and Irish: Anglicized form of Gaelic **Mag Cuirc**, patronymic from the personal name *Corc* 'heart'. **2.** Irish (Ulster): Anglicized form of Gaelic **Mag Oirc**, patronymic from the personal name *Orc*, from *orc* 'pig'.
GIVEN NAMES Irish 5%. *Brendan, Eithne, Kieran, Liam.*

McGuirl (109) Irish: possibly a variant of **McGirl**, an Anglicized form of **Mag Fhearghail**.

McGuirt (285) Irish: variant of McCORD.

McGurk (681) Scottish and Irish: variant of McGUIRK.
GIVEN NAMES Irish 6%. *Aileen, Brendan, Brigid, Malachy, Siobhan.*

McGurl (121) Irish: Anglicized form of Gaelic **Mag Fhearghail** 'son of *Fearghal*' (see FARRELL).

McGurn (309) Irish: variant of McGURRIN.

McGurrin (139) Irish (Connacht): Anglicized form of Gaelic **Mag Corraidhín**, a patronymic from a personal name derived from *corradh* 'spear'.

McGuyer (157) Irish: variant of McGUIRE.

McHaffie (214) Scottish and Irish: Anglicized form of the Gaelic patronymic **Mac Dhuibhshíthe** (see DUFFY 2).

McHale (2581) Irish: **1.** Anglicized form of Gaelic **Mac Céile**, a patronymic from the byname *Céile* 'companion'. This was the surname of a Mayo family, tenants of church lands. **2.** from **Mac Haol** 'son of *Haol*', a Gaelicized form of HOWELL which was adopted by a Welsh family of this name who settled in County Mayo.
GIVEN NAMES Irish 5%. *Brendan* (2), *Brigid, Kieran, Liam, Padraic.*

McHam (156) Scottish: Anglicized form of Gaelic **Mac Tham**, a patronymic from a Gaelic pet form of the personal name THOMAS.

McHan (274) Irish: probably a variant of McCANN or McGANN.

McHaney (353) Scottish or Irish: unexplained. Perhaps an unusual Anglicized form of Gaelic **Mac Giolla Choinnigh** 'son of the servant of (St.) Canice'.

McHardy (113) Scottish: Anglicized form of Gaelic **Mac Chardaidh** 'son of the sloe'.

McHarg (138) Irish and Scottish: Anglicized form of Gaelic **Mac Conchairge**, patronymic from *Cú Chairge* 'hound of the rock' or *Giolla Chairge* 'lad of the rock'.

McHargue (630) Scottish or Irish: variant spelling of McHARG.

McHatton (189) Scottish and northern Irish: Anglicized form of Scottish Gaelic **Mac Gille Chatain** (Irish Gaelic **Mac Giolla Chatáin**), a patronymic from a personal name meaning 'servant of (Saint) *Catan*', a little-known saint who was revered on the Scottish west coast and islands.

McHenry (4212) Irish: Anglicized form of Gaelic **Mac Éinrí**, a patronymic from a Gaelic form of the personal name HENRY. Compare McKENDRICK.

McHone (612) Irish: of uncertain origin; possibly a variant of McCUNE or McCONE.

McHugh (7594) Irish and Scottish: variant of McCOY.
GIVEN NAMES Irish 6%. *Brendan* (9), *Conal* (2), *Sinead* (2), *Brigid, Conall, Cormac, Eamon, Eamonn, Fintan, Kieran, Malachy, Patrick Sean.*

McIlhenny (218) Irish (western Ulster): variant of McELHINNEY.

McIllwain (104) Scottish: variant of McEL-WAIN 1.

McIlrath (317) Scottish and Irish: variant of McELRATH.

McIlroy (541) Northern Irish and Scottish: variant of MCELROY.

McIlvain (535) Scottish: variant of MCELWAIN 1.

McIlvaine (457) Scottish: variant of MCELWAIN 1.

McIlveen (136) **1.** Scottish: variant of MCELWAIN 1. **2.** Irish (County Down): Anglicized form of Gaelic **Mac Giolla Mhín** 'son of the smooth or gentle lad'.

McIlvoy (102) Scottish: variant of MCEVOY.

McIlwain (1065) Scottish: variant of MCELWAIN 1.

McIlwaine (122) Scottish: variant of MCELWAIN 1.

McIlwee (133) Irish and Scottish: variant of MCELWEE.

McInally (112) Irish: Anglicized form of Gaelic **Mac an Fhailghigh** (see MCNALLY).

McIndoe (131) Scottish: of uncertain origin; perhaps an Anglicized form of Gaelic **Mac Iain Duibh** 'son of black(-haired) Ian' (see JOHN).

McInerney (1856) Irish: Anglicized form of Gaelic **Mac an Airchinnigh** 'son of the overseer (of church lands)', Gaelic *airchinneach*, often Anglicized as *erenagh*. The surname arose in different places, notably Munster and Roscommon.
GIVEN NAMES Irish 6%. *Brendan, Bridie, Liam, Maeve.*

McInerny (216) Irish: variant spelling of MCINERNEY.

McInnes (678) Scottish: variant spelling of MCINNIS.

McInnis (2874) Scottish: Anglicized form of Gaelic **Mac Aonghuis**, a patronymic from the personal name *Aonghus* (see ANGUS). Compare Irish MCGINNIS.

McInroy (183) Scottish: Anglicized form of Gaelic **Mac Ian ruaidh** 'son of red *Ian*', a Gaelic form of JOHN.

McIntee (259) Irish: variant of MCATEE.

McInteer (105) Scottish: variant of MCINTYRE.

McIntire (4053) Scottish: variant of MCINTYRE.

McIntosh (13815) Scottish: Anglicized form of Gaelic **Mac an Toisich** 'son of the chief'.

McInturf (146) Irish or Scottish: variant of MCINTURFF.

McInturff (587) Irish or Scottish: probably an Anglicized form of Gaelic **Mac an Tairbh** 'son of the bull'.

McIntyre (16072) Scottish: Anglicized form of Gaelic **Mac an tSaoir** 'son of the craftsman'. Compare Irish MCATEER.

McInvale (163) Scottish or Irish: unexplained. Possibly and Anglicized form of Gaelic **Mac Giolla M(h)aoil** 'son of the bald lad'.

McIrvin (117) Irish: Anglicized form of Gaelic **Mac hEireamhóin** 'son of *Eireamhón*' (see IRVIN). See also IRWIN.

McIsaac (496) Scottish: patronymic from ISAAC.

McIver (1833) Scottish and northern Irish: Anglicized form of Gaelic **Mac Íomhair** 'son of *Íomhar*', Gaelic form of the Old Norse personal name *Ivarr*.

McIvor (365) Scottish: variant spelling of MCIVER.

McJunkin (610) Irish: Anglicized form of Gaelic **Mac Seancín** 'son of *Seancín*', Gaelic form of the Middle English personal name JENKIN.

McJunkins (211) Irish: variant of MCJUNKIN, with the addition of English patronymic -*s*.

McKague (123) Irish: variant of MCCAIG.

McKahan (103) Irish: variant spelling of MCCAHAN.

McKaig (422) Scottish and Irish: variant of MCCAIG.

McKain (702) Scottish and Irish: variant of MCKEAN.

McKamey (424) Variant spelling of Scottish MCCAMEY.
GIVEN NAMES Irish 4%. *Aileen, Teague.*

McKamie (148) Variant spelling of Scottish MCCAMEY.

McKane (368) Northern Irish and Scottish: variant of MCKEAN, possibly also of MCCAHAN.
GIVEN NAME Irish 4%. *Brendan.*

McKanna (158) Irish and Scottish: variant of MCKENNA.

McKaskle (140) Variant spelling of Scottish MCCASKILL.

McKaughan (135) Irish: variant of MCCAUGHAN.

McKay (14107) Scottish and northern Irish: Anglicized form of Gaelic **Mac Aodha** 'son of *Aodh*', an ancient personal name meaning 'fire'. Etymologically, this is the same name as MCCOY.

McKeag (216) Scottish and northern Irish: variant of MCCAIG.

McKeage (113) Scottish and northern Irish: variant of MCCAIG.

McKeague (180) Scottish and northern Irish: variant of MCCAIG.

McKean (1976) Scottish: Anglicized form of Gaelic **Mac Iain** 'son of *Ian*', a Gaelic form of JOHN.

McKeand (165) Scottish: variant of MCKEAN.

McKearney (112) Northern Irish (Ulster): Anglicized form of Gaelic **Mac Cearnaigh**.

McKechnie (598) Scottish: Anglicized form of Gaelic **Mac Eacharna**, a patronymic from the personal name *Eacharn*, a derivative of *each* 'horse' + *tighearna* 'lord', which in Scotland is usually Anglicized as MCEACHERN.

McKee (17288) Northern Irish and Scottish: variant of MCKAY.

McKeegan (190) Northern Irish: Anglicized form of Gaelic **Mac Aodhagáin** 'son of *Aodhagán*', a pet form of the ancient Irish personal name *Aodh* 'fire' (see MCKAY).

McKeehan (876) Irish: Anglicized form of Gaelic **Mac Caocháin**, a patronymic from a personal name or byname derived from *caoch* 'blind', 'purblind'.

McKeel (639) Irish: of uncertain origin; perhaps an Anglicized form of Gaelic **Mac Cathmhaoil** (see MCCALL).

McKeeman (178) Northern Irish: **1.** Anglicized form of **Mac Shíomóin** 'son of Simon'; i.e. a Gaelicized variant of FITZSIMMONS. **2.** alternatively, perhaps an Anglicized form of Gaelic **Mac Eamoinn** 'son of *Eamonn*', a patronymic from the Gaelic form of the English personal name EDMOND.

McKeen (853) Northern Irish: variant spelling of MCKEAN.

McKeever (2722) Scottish and Irish: Anglicized form of Gaelic **Mac Íomhair** 'son of *Iomhar*' (see MCIVER).

McKeighan (126) Irish: variant of MCKEEHAN.

McKeithan (451) Variant of Irish MCKEEHAN.

McKeithen (333) Variant of Irish MCKEEHAN.

McKell (215) Northern Irish and Scottish: shortened Anglicized form of a Gaelic name beginning with *Mac Giolla* 'son of the lad' (see for example MCELROY).

McKellar (1037) Scottish: Anglicized form of Gaelic **Mac Ealair**, a patronymic from the personal name *Ealair*, Gaelic equivalent of HILLARY.

McKeller (188) Scottish: variant spelling of MCKELLAR.

McKellips (219) Scottish or Irish: variant of MCKILLIP, formed with the addition of redundant English patronymic -*s*.

McKelvey (2667) **1.** Scottish: Anglicized form of Gaelic **Mac Shealbhaigh**, 'son of *Sealbhach*', a personal name from the adjective *sealbhach* 'rich in herds', 'rich'. **2.** Irish: Anglicized form of Gaelic **Mac Giolla Bhuidhe** (see MCEVOY).

McKelvie (276) Scottish: variant spelling of MCKELVEY.

McKelvin (109) Scottish: unexplained. Possibly a variant of Irish MCILVEEN 2.

McKelvy (557) Scottish: variant spelling of MCKELVEY.

McKemie (137) Scottish or Irish: variant of MCKIMMY.

McKendree (361) Northern Irish: variant spelling of MCHENRY.

McKendrick (392) Irish and Scottish: Anglicized form of Gaelic **Mac Eanruig** (Scottish) and **Mac Éanraic** (Irish), patronymics from a Gaelic form of the personal name HENRY.

McKendry (401) Irish (northeastern Ulster): variant of MCHENRY.

McKenna (10669) Irish and Scottish: Anglicized form of Gaelic **Mac Cionaodha** or

Mac Cionaoith 'son of *Cionaodh*' (see McKINNEY 1).

GIVEN NAMES Irish 6%. *Brendan* (7), *Kieran* (3), *Aidan* (2), *Caitlin* (2), *Eamon* (2), *Eamonn* (2), *Seamus* (2), *Siobhan* (2), *Aileen*, *Colum*, *Donal*, *John Patrick*.

McKenney (2767) Scottish: variant of McKINNEY 1.

McKennon (293) Irish and Scottish: Anglicized form of Gaelic **Mac Fhionnáin**, a patronymic from the personal name *Fionnán*, a personal name representng a diminutive of *fionn* 'white'.

McKenny (347) Scottish: variant of McKINNEY 1.

McKenrick (168) Irish and Scottish: variant of McKENDRICK.

McKenzie (18667) Scottish: Anglicized form of Gaelic **Mac Coinnich**, patronymic from the personal name *Coinneach* meaning 'comely'. Compare MENZIES.

McKeon (3022) Northern Irish: variant of McEWEN.

GIVEN NAMES Irish 5%. *Brendan* (4), *Fergal* (2), *Kieran*, *Liam*, *Murph*.

McKeone (212) Northern Irish: variant of McEWEN.

McKeough (228) Irish: Anglicized form of Gaelic **Mac Eochaidh** 'son of *Eochaidh*', a personal name based on *each* 'horse'.

GIVEN NAME Irish 6%. *Brendan*.

McKeown (3007) Northern Irish and Scottish: variant of McEWEN.

GIVEN NAMES Irish 4%. *Brendan* (2), *Liam* (2), *Declan*, *Donovan*, *Niall*.

McKercher (172) Scottish: Anglicized form of Gaelic **Mac Fhearchair**, a patronymic from the personal name *Fearchar* (see FARQUHAR).

McKern (219) Irish: variant of McCARRON.

McKernan (1058) Northern Irish: variant of McKIERNAN.

GIVEN NAME Irish 5%. *Brendan*.

McKerrow (121) Scottish: of uncertain derivation. Some sources believe it to be an Anglicized form of Gaelic **Mac Cearrach**, **Mac Cearrbhaich** 'son of the gambler', while Woulfe derives it from **Mac Ciothruadha** 'son of *Ciothruaidh*', a personal name of Norse origin.

McKesson (167) Scottish: Anglicized form of Gaelic **Mac Cessáin** 'son of *Cessán*', a personal name derived from *cess* 'wickerwork', probably applied in the sense 'thick or matted hair'.

McKethan (165) Irish: Anglicized form of Gaelic **Mac Eacháin** (see McCAUGHAN).

McKevitt (273) Irish: Anglicized form of Gaelic **Mac Daibhéid**, with lenited personal name (see McDEVITT).

GIVEN NAME Irish 8%. *Fergal*.

McKewen (105) Scottish and northern Irish: variant of McEWEN.

McKey (532) Scottish and northern Irish: variant of McCOY.

McKibben (1756) **1.** Irish: Anglicized form of Gaelic **Mac Fhibín**, a patronymic from *Fibín*, a pet form of PHILIP. **2.** Scottish: Anglicized form of Gaelic **Mac Giobúin** (see McGIBBON).

McKibbin (622) Irish and Scottish: variant spelling of McKIBBEN.

McKibbon (142) Irish and Scottish: variant spelling of McKIBBEN.

McKiddy (149) Scottish: Anglicized form of Gaelic **Mac Ádaidh**, a patronymic from a Gaelic pet form of ADAM.

McKie (892) Scottish: variant of McCOY.

McKiernan (873) Northern Irish: Anglicized form of Gaelic **Mac Thighearnáin**, a patronymic from a lenited diminutive of the personal name *Tighearna* 'lord', 'master' (Old Irish *tigern*). Compare TIERNAN.

GIVEN NAMES Irish 7%. *Brendan* (3), *Fergus* (2), *Bridie*, *Eamonn*, *Ethna*, *Kieran*.

McKillip (680) Scottish and northern Irish (County Antrim): Anglicized form of Gaelic **Mac Fhilib** 'son of Philip' (see PHILIP).

McKillop (590) Scottish: variant of McKILLIP.

McKim (1523) Scottish: Anglicized form of Gaelic **Mac Shim**, a patronymic from a Gaelic pet form of the personal name SIMON.

McKimmey (130) Scottish: variant spelling of McKIMMY.

McKimmy (188) Scottish: Anglicized form of Gaelic **Mac Shimidh**, a patronymic from a Gaelic pet form of SIMON.

McKinlay (351) Scottish: variant spelling of McKINLEY.

GIVEN NAME Scottish 5%. *Alastair*.

McKinley (8466) Scottish: Anglicized form of Gaelic **Mac Fionnlaigh**, a patronymic from the early personal name *Fionnlaoch* (see FINLEY).

FOREBEARS William McKinley (1843–1901), 25th U.S. president, was born at Niles, OH, a descendant of David McKinley, known as 'David the Weaver', of Scotch–Irish stock, who settled in York Co., PA, about 1743. William McKinley's family were iron founders who tracked the ore from the Susquehanna Valley in PA to Columbiana Co., OH.

McKinnell (119) Scottish: unexplained. Perhaps an Anglicized form of the Gaelic patronymic **Mac Fhionnghail** ('fair valour').

McKinney (27133) **1.** Scottish: Anglicized form of Gaelic **Mac Cionaodha** or **Mac Cionaoith** 'son of *Cionaodh*', a personal name which is probably composed of the elements *cion* 'respect', 'affection' + *Aodh*, a Gaelic personal name, originally the name of the Celtic god of fire. The personal name thus probably means 'beloved of Aodh'. **2.** Northern Irish: Anglicized form of Gaelic **Mac Coinnigh** 'son of *Coinneach*', an Old Irish personal name

equivalent to Scottish KENNETH. Compare KENNY. Also the Scottish name as in 1.

McKinnie (723) Variant spelling of Scottish or northern Irish McKINNEY.

McKinnis (658) Scottish: variant of McINNIS.

McKinniss (102) Variant of Scottish McINNIS.

McKinnon (5243) Scottish: Anglicized form of Gaelic **Mac Fhionghuin**, a patronymic from a Gaelic personal name meaning 'fair born' or 'fair son'. It is also translated as LOVE, and has been taken as being from Gaelic **Mac Ionmhuinn** 'son of the beloved one'.

McKinny (114) Scottish: variant spelling of McKINNEY 1.

McKinsey (549) Perhaps a respelling of **McKinzie**, a variant of McKENZIE.

McKinstry (1046) Northern Irish: Anglicized form of Gaelic **Mac an Aistrigh**, a simplified version of **Mac an Aistrighthigh** 'son of the traveler'. The name is now largely confined to Ulster, but seems to have originated in Galloway (southwestern Scotland).

McKinzey (115) Variant of Scottish McKENZIE.

McKinzie (1268) Scottish: variant of McKENZIE.

McKissack (464) Scottish and Irish (of Scottish origin): variant of McISAAC.

McKissic (120) Scottish: variant of McISAAC.

McKissick (930) Scottish: variant of McISAAC.

McKissock (101) Scottish: variant of McISAAC.

GIVEN NAME Scottish 4%. *Ewan*.

McKitrick (412) Scottish and northern Irish: variant spelling of McKITTRICK.

McKittrick (770) Scottish and northern Irish: Anglicized form of Gaelic **Mac Shitrig**, a patronymic from a Gaelic form of the Old Norse personal name *Sigtryggr*, which is composed of the elements *sigr* 'victory' + *tryggr* 'true'.

McKiver (123) Scottish: variant of McIVER.

McKneely (132) Variant of Scottish and northern Irish McNEELY.

McKnelly (109) Variant of Scottish McNELLY.

McKnight (10374) Irish: **1.** (Ulster) Anglicized form of Scottish **Mac Neachtain**, which is usually Anglicized as McNAUGHTON. **2.** part translation of Gaelic **Mac an Ridire** 'son of the horseman (Gaelic *ridire*)'.

McKone (308) Irish (County Louth): variant of McCUNE.

McKowen (195) Irish and Scottish: variant of McEWEN.

McKown (1485) Irish and Scottish: variant of McEWEN.

McKoy (1548) Scottish and Irish: variant spelling of McCOY.

McKune (213) Scottish: variant spelling of McCUNE.

McKusick (156) Variant of Scottish or Irish McISAAC.

McLachlan (723) Scottish: variant spelling of McLAUGHLIN.

McLafferty (186) Scottish and northern Irish: Anglicized form of Gaelic **Mac Fhlaithbheartaigh** 'son of *Flaithbheartach*' (see LAFFERTY).

McLagan (146) Scottish: Anglicized form of Gaelic **Mac Gille Adhagain** 'servant of *Adocan*', a pet form of *Adamnan*.

McLain (6525) Scottish and Irish: variant of McLEAN.

McLaine (144) Scottish and Irish: variant of McLEAN.

McLallen (123) Scottish: variant of McLEL-LAN.

McLamb (1182) Irish: Anglicized form of Gaelic **Mac Fhlaithimh** (see McCLAVE). Compare McCLAM.

McLamore (107) Irish: variant of Mc-LEMORE.

McLanahan (173) Scottish: variant of Mc-CLANAHAN.

McLane (2186) Scottish and Irish: variant of McLEAN.

McLaney (119) Irish: probably a variant of McELHINNEY.

McLaren (2250) Scottish and northern Irish: Anglicized form of Gaelic **Mac Labhrainn** 'son of *Labhrann*', Gaelic form of the personal name LAWRENCE.

McLarney (173) Irish: Anglicized form of Gaelic **Mac Giolla Earna** 'son of *Giolla Earna*', a personal name meaning 'servant of (Saint) Earna'. This is an old, rare Monaghan name.

McLarnon (110) Irish and Scottish: Anglicized form of Gaelic **Mac Giolla Earnáin** 'son of the servant or devotee of St. *Earnan*'.

McLarty (722) Scottish: variant of McLAF-FERTY.

McLauchlan (167) Scottish: variant of Mc-LAUGHLIN.

McLauchlin (280) Scottish: variant of Mc-LAUGHLIN.

McLaughlan (134) Irish: variant of Mc-LAUGHLIN.

McLaughlin (29719) Irish and Scottish: Anglicized form of Gaelic **Mac Lochlainn** 'son of the Scandinavian', a patronymic from the personal name *Lochlann* (see LAUGHLIN).
GIVEN NAMES Irish 8%. *Brendan* (12), *Donal* (5), *Siobhan* (3), *Aileen* (2), *Caitlin* (2), *Keane* (2), *Liam* (2), *Padric* (2), *Aine*, *Ciaran*, *Conan*, *Conley*.

McLaurin (2025) Scottish: variant of McLAREN.

McLaury (181) Scottish and northern Irish: patronymic from LAURIE.

McLawhorn (476) Northern Irish: probably an Americanized form of Gaelic **Mac Labhrainn** 'son of *Labhrann*' (see Mc-LAREN).

McLaws (111) Perhaps a Americanized form of Scottish or Irish McLEISH.

McLay (279) Scottish: variant of McCLAY.

McLean (14920) **1.** Scottish: Anglicized form of Gaelic **Mac Gille Eathain**, a patronymic from a personal name meaning 'servant of (Saint) John'. The family bearing this name were chieftains in several islands of the Inner Hebrides. **2.** Irish: Anglicized form of Gaelic **Mac Giolla Eóin**, cognate with 1, from a different Gaelic form of *Johannes* (*John*). Compare McGLONE.

McLear (175) Irish: Anglicized form of Gaelic **Mac Giolla Uidhir** 'son of the swarthy lad' or 'son of the servant of *Odhar*', a byname from *odhar* (genitive *uidhir*) 'dun-colored', 'weatherbeaten'. Compare McALEER. See also McCLURE.

McLeary (157) Irish: variant of McCLEARY.

McLees (324) Scottish and Irish: variant of McLEISH.

McLeese (112) Scottish and Irish: variant of McLEISH.

McLeish (317) Northern Irish (Ulster) and Scottish: Anglicized form of Gaelic **Mac Gille Íosa**, patronymic from a personal name meaning 'servant of Jesus'.

McLeland (210) Scottish: variant of Mc-CLELLAN.

McLellan (2607) Scottish: variant of Mc-CLELLAN.

McLelland (666) Scottish and northern Irish: variant of McCLELLAN.

McLemore (3383) Irish: probably an Anglicization of Gaelic **Mac Giolla Mhuire** 'son of the servant of (the Virgin) Mary' (see GILMORE).

McLendon (2866) Altered form of Mc-CLENDON.

McLennan (951) Scottish: Anglicized form of Gaelic **Mac Gille Fhinneain**, a patronymic from a personal name meaning 'servant of (Saint) *Fionnán*', a personal name representng a diminutive of *fionn* 'white'. There were several early Irish saints of this name, most notably a 7th-century bishop who governed the Church established in Northumbria and evangelized parts of southern England.

McLeod (11118) Scottish: Anglicized form of Gaelic **Mac Leòid**, a patronymic from a Gaelic form of the Old Norse personal name *Ljótr* 'ugly'.
FOREBEARS One prominent bearer of this prominent Scottish name, Alexander McLeod (1774–1833), a Reformed Presbyterian clergyman, author, and editor, emigrated to the U.S. in 1792 from the island of Mull in the Hebrides. He taught Greek at Schenectady, NY, and was a pastor in New York City after 1800.

McLernon (113) Irish: variant of McLAR-NON.
GIVEN NAMES Irish 14%. *Aidan* (3), *Aine*.

McLeroy (593) Irish: reduced Anglicized form of Gaelic **Mac Giolla Ruaidh** (see GILROY).

McLerran (209) Northern Irish: variant of McLAREN.

McLeskey (121) Irish: variant of McCLOS-KEY.

McLester (184) Irish: variant of McAL-LISTER.

McLin (784) Variant of Scottish and Irish McLEAN. See also MACKLIN.

McLinden (187) Irish and Scottish: Anglicized form of Gaelic **Mac Gille Fhionntain** (Scottish), **Mac Giolla Fhionntáin** (Irish) (see McCLINTON).

McLinn (143) Northern Irish: variant of McLEAN.

McLoone (128) Irish: Anglicized form of Gaelic **Mac Giolla Eóin** (see McGLONE).

McLoud (339) Scottish: variant of McLEOD.

McLoughlin (1878) Irish: variant of McLAUGHLIN.
GIVEN NAMES Irish 7%. *Brendan* (4), *Niall* (2), *Aileen*, *Brigid*, *Eamon*, *Eithne*, *Peadar*.

McLouth (185) Of Scottish or Irish origin: unexplained. Possibly an Americanized form of McLEOD.

McLucas (282) Scottish: Anglicized form of Gaelic **Mac Lùcais**, patronymic from the personal name LUCAS.

McLuckie (167) Scottish: patronymic from a pet form of LUCAS.

McLure (208) Scottish and northern Irish: variant of McCLURE.

McMackin (486) Irish: Anglicized form of Gaelic **Mac Maicín** 'son of the young man', from a pet form of *mac* 'son', 'youth'.

McMahan (5477) Irish: variant spelling of McMAHON.

McMahen (171) Irish: variant spelling of McMAHON.

McMahill (156) Of Scottish or Irish origin: unexplained; possibly an Anglicized form of Gaelic **Mac Micheáil**, usually Anglicized as McMICHAEL, or of a patronymic from a personal name found in **Ó Machail** (which is Anglicized as **Mackle**).

McMahon (15896) Irish: Anglicized form of Gaelic **Mac Mathghamhna**, a patronymic from the byname *Mathghamhain* meaning 'good calf'. This was the name of two (unrelated) chieftain families in counties Clare and Monaghan. In northern Ireland it is sometimes Anglicized as MATTHEWS, since *Matha* was the Irish form of the Biblical name.
GIVEN NAMES Irish 5%. *Brendan* (7), *Liam* (6), *Kieran* (3), *Maeve* (2), *Seamus* (2), *Brigid*, *Connor*, *Dermot*, *Eamon*, *Fergus*, *Grainne*, *James Patrick*.

McMain (141) Irish: variant of McMAHON.

McMains (464) Northern Irish: variant of McMANUS.

McMaken (142) Variant spelling of Irish McMACKIN.

McMakin (342) Variant spelling of Irish McMackin.

McManama (159) Irish: variant of McMenamy.

McManaman (247) Irish: variant of McMenamin.

McManamon (240) Irish: variant of McMenamin.
GIVEN NAME Irish 9%. *Aileen.*

McManamy (152) Irish: variant of McMenamy. Black records this (in the form **McManamny**) as a name of Irish origin occurring in the Scottish county of Galloway.

McManaway (272) Irish (Roscommon): variant of McMenamy. This surname is also recorded in Scotland, in Galloway.

McManigal (265) Variant of Irish McMonagle.

McManigle (97) Variant of Irish McMonagle.

McManis (436) Irish and Scottish: variant of McManus.

McMann (950) Irish: variant of McMahon.

McMannis (209) Irish and Scottish: variant of McManus.

McManus (9437) Irish: Anglicized form of Gaelic **Mac Maghnuis**, patronymic from a Gaelic form of the Scandinavian personal name Magnus. As an Irish name this is found chiefly in Roscommon and Fermanagh and is connected with the O'Connors or the Maguires; in Scotland it is connected with the Colquhouns.
GIVEN NAMES Irish 8%. *Brendan* (7), *Connor* (2), *Donovan* (2), *Dympna* (2), *Murphy* (2), *Siobhan* (2), *Aidan, Aileen, Declan, Kieran, Kiernan, Michael Patrick.*

McMartin (390) Scottish: Anglicized form of Gaelic **Mac Mhàrtainn** or **Mac Mhàrtuinn**, formerly **Mac Gille Mhartainn**, a patronymic from a personal name meaning 'servant of (Saint) Martin'.

McMaster (2582) Scottish: Anglicized form of Gaelic **Mac Maighstir** or **Mac A'Mhaighstir** 'son of (the) master', from Gaelic *maighstir*, a title for a clergyman.

McMasters (1042) Scottish: variant of McMaster.

McMath (737) Scottish and northern Irish: Anglicized form of Gaelic **Mac Matha**, a patronymic from a Scottish Gaelic form of Matthew.

McMeans (570) Variant of Irish McMahon, with the addition of English patronymic *-s*.

McMeekin (391) Northern Irish and Scottish (Galloway): Anglicized form of Gaelic **Mac Miadhacháin**, a patronymic from the personal name *Miadhachán*, a diminutive of *miadhach* 'honorable'.

McMeen (231) Irish: variant of McMahon.

McMellon (155) Irish: **1.** probably an Anglicized form of Gaelic **Mac Mealláin** 'son of *Meallán*', a personal name formed as a diminutive of *meall* 'pleasant'. **2.** alternatively perhaps an Anglicized form of

the Gaelic patronymic **Mac Maoláin**, which is more commonly Anglicized as McMillan.

McMenamin (828) Irish: Anglicized form of Gaelic **Mac Meanman**, a patronymic from the personal name *Meanma* meaning 'spirited'. *Meanman* is an older form of the genitive than *Meanm(n)a*, which lies behind McMenamy.
GIVEN NAMES Irish 6%. *Brigid, Donal, Eamonn, Liam.*

McMenamy (294) Irish: Anglicized form of Gaelic **Mac Meanm(n)a**, a patronymic from a personal name meaning 'spirited'.

McMenemy (149) Irish: variant of McMenamy.

McMichael (2796) Scottish: Anglicized form of Gaelic **Mac Mìcheil** (probably earlier **Mac Gille Mhìcheil**), a patronymic from a Gaelic form of the personal name Michael.

McMichen (187) Scottish and northern Irish: variant of McMeekin.

McMicken (122) Irish and Scottish (Galloway): variant of McMeekin.

McMickle (265) Scottish or Irish: variant of McMichael.

McMillan (13879) Scottish: Anglicized form of Gaelic **Mac Maoláin**, a patronymic from the byname *Maolán*, a diminutive of *maol* 'bald', 'tonsured'. In Scotland the usual spelling is Macmillan. Compare Mullen.

McMillen (3995) Northern Irish: variant spelling of McMillin or McMillan.

McMiller (323) Scottish: patronymic from the occupational byname Miller.

McMillian (2764) Scottish: variant of McMillan.

McMillin (2122) Irish: reduced Anglicized form of Gaelic **Mac Maoilfhinn** 'son of *Maoilfhinn*', a personal name meaning 'fair(-haired) chief'.

McMillion (1093) Altered spelling of McMillan.

McMillon (860) Scottish: variant spelling of McMillan.

McMinn (1901) Scottish and northern Irish: Anglicized form of Gaelic **Mac Méinn**, a patronymic from the Gaelic form of the surname Menzies.

McMonagle (443) Irish and Scottish: Anglicized form of Gaelic **Mac Maonghail**, a patronymic from the personal name *Maonghal*, composed of the elements *maoin* 'wealth' + *gal* 'valor'. In this form the consonant cluster *-ngh-* has been 'delenited'. Compare Manley, which is based on an earlier form of the genitive.
GIVEN NAME Irish 6%. *Cahal.*

McMonigal (135) Irish: variant spelling of McMonagle.

McMonigle (278) Irish: variant spelling of McMonagle.

McMorran (155) Irish (originally Connacht) and Scottish (Argyllshire): Angli-

cized form of Gaelic **Mac Mo(gh)ráin**, a patronymic from a personal name, originally *Mughròn*, from *mug* 'slave' + *rón* (Scottish *ròn*) 'seal'.

McMorris (879) Scottish and Irish: Anglicized form of Gaelic **Mac M(h)uiris**, a patronymic from a Gaelicized form of Morris.

McMorrow (718) Irish: **1.** Anglicized form of Gaelic **Mac Murchadha**, a patronymic from the personal name *Murchadh* 'sea warrior', from *muir* 'sea' + *cath* 'battle'. In Leinster this name is usually Anglicized as **McMurrough** and in Ulster as Murphy. **2.** usual Anglicized form of Gaelic **Mac Muireadhaigh** (see McMurray).
GIVEN NAME Irish 6%. *Colm.*

McMullan (1125) Irish form of McMillan.
GIVEN NAME Irish 4%. *Brendan.*

McMullen (7570) Irish form of McMillan.

McMullin (2009) Irish form of McMillan.

McMunn (367) Scottish (also found in Donegal): Anglicized form of Gaelic **Mac Gille Mhunna** 'son of the servant of (Saint) *Munnu*'. This name, which is also found in the form *Mundu*, from earlier *Mo-Fhindu*, is a hypocoristic form of *Fionntan* with the affective prefix *mo-* 'my'.

McMurdo (162) Scottish: Anglicized form of Gaelic **Mac Murchaidh** or **Mac Murchadha**, a patronymic from the personal name *Murchadh*, composed of the elements *muir* 'sea' + *cath* 'battle'. Compare Irish McMurphy.

McMurphy (373) Irish: Anglicized form of Gaelic **Mac Murchadha**, a patronymic from the personal name *Murchadh* 'sea warrior', from *muir* 'sea' + *cath* 'battle'. Compare McMorrow, McMurdo.

McMurray (3525) Northern Irish: Anglicized form of Gaelic **Mac Muireadhaigh**, a patronymic from the personal name *Muireadhach* 'seafarer' (see Murdock).

McMurrey (172) Northern Irish: variant spelling of McMurray.

McMurrin (121) Irish: variant of McMorran.

McMurry (1478) Northern Irish: variant spelling of McMurray.

McMurtrey (507) Northern Irish and Scottish: variant spelling of McMurtry.

McMurtrie (446) Northern Irish and Scottish: variant spelling of McMurtry.

McMurtry (973) Northern Irish and Scottish: Anglicized form of Gaelic **Mac Muircheartaigh** 'son of *Muircheartach*', a personal name meaning 'navigator', from *muir* 'sea' + *ceartach* 'ruler'.

McNab (638) Scottish and northern Irish: variant spelling of McNabb.

McNabb (3701) Scottish and northern Irish: Anglicized form of Scottish Gaelic **Mac an Aba(dh)** 'son of the abbot'. In Scotland, monasteries often had hereditary lay abbots, who were not bound by rules of celibacy. The McNabs seem to have originated at the monastery of St. Faolan in Strathfillan.

McNair (4512) Scottish: **1.** Anglicized form of Gaelic **Mac Iain Uidhir** 'son of sallow John'. This form is associated mainly with Ross-shire. **2.** Anglicized form of Gaelic **Mac an Oighre** 'son of the heir'. This form is associated mainly with Perthshire. **3.** Anglicized form of Gaelic **Mac an Mhaoir** 'son of the steward or keeper'. The same name in Ireland was commonly Anglicized as WEIR.

McNairy (232) Variant of Irish MCNEARY.

McNall (359) Scottish or Irish: probably a shortened form of MCNALLY, but no longer found in Scotland or Ireland.

McNalley (134) Irish: variant spelling of MCNALLY.

McNally (6261) Irish: **1.** Anglicized form of Gaelic **Mac an Fhailghigh** 'son of the poor man'. **2.** in Ulster more probably an Anglicized form of Gaelic **Mac Con Uladh** 'son of the hound of Ulster'.
GIVEN NAMES Irish 5%. *Brendan* (3), *Kieran* (3), *Aidan, Brennan, Cathal, Cormac, Donal, Grainne, Seamus, Ulick.*

McNamar (134) Irish: variant of MC-NAMARA.

McNamara (11006) Irish: Anglicized form of Gaelic **Mac Conmara**, a patronymic from *Cú Mhara*, a personal name composed of the elements *cú* 'hound' + *muir* 'sea'.
GIVEN NAMES Irish 6%. *Brendan* (5), *Parnell* (3), *Aidan* (2), *Conor* (2), *Dermot* (2), *Brigid, Conan, James Patrick, Liam, Michael Patrick, Nuala, Ronan.*

McNamee (2303) Irish: Anglicized form of Gaelic **Mac Conmidhe**, a patronymic from the personal name *Cú Mhidhe*, meaning 'hound of Meath'. This family were hereditary poets in Ulster.
GIVEN NAMES Irish 5%. *Brendan* (4), *Donovan* (2), *Aileen, Declan.*

McNamer (179) Irish: probably a variant of MCNAMARA.

McNaney (175) Irish: variant of MC-ENANEY or of the less common surname **McNanany**. The latter is an Anglicization of Gaelic **Mac Conaonaigh**, a patronymic from *Cú Aonaigh* 'hound of the fair'.

McNary (888) Irish: Anglicized form of Gaelic **Mac Náraigh** 'son of *Nárach*', a byname meaning 'modest', more commonly Anglicized as NEARY.

McNatt (986) Evidently of Irish or Scottish origin: probably a variant of MCNUTT.

McNaught (421) **1.** Scottish and Irish: shortened form of MCNAUGHTON. **2.** Irish: in Donegal, a variant of MCKNIGHT.

McNaughton (1657) Scottish and Irish: Anglicized form of Gaelic **Mac Neachtain**, a patronymic from the personal name *Neachtan*, a name of the god of water in Irish mythology. This is cognate with Latin *Neptunus* 'Neptune', the Roman sea-god.

McNay (307) Scottish and Irish: Anglicized form of Gaelic **Mac Niadh**, a patronymic from the byname *Nia* 'champion'.

McNeal (5346) Scottish and Irish: variant spelling of MCNEIL.

McNealy (466) Scottish and northern Irish: variant spelling of MCNEELY.

McNear (463) Scottish or Irish: variant spelling of MCNAIR.

McNearney (103) Irish: variant of MCINER-NEY.

McNeary (152) Irish: Anglicized form of Gaelic **Mac Naradhaigh**, a patronymic from the personal name *Naradhach*, probably a derivative of *nárach* 'modest'.

McNease (177) Variant of Irish MCNEESE.

McNee (229) Scottish and Irish: Anglicized form of Gaelic **Mac Niadh** 'son of *Nia*', a byname meaning 'champion'.

McNeece (287) Variant spelling of Mc-NEESE.

McNeel (528) Scottish: variant spelling of MCNEIL.

McNeeley (518) Scottish and northern Irish: variant spelling of MCNEELY.

McNeely (4118) **1.** Scottish (Galloway) and northern Irish: Anglicized form of Gaelic **Mac an Fhilidh** 'son of the poet'. **2.** Irish: Anglicized form of the Connacht name **Mac Conghaile** 'son of *Conghal*' (see CONNOLLY).

McNeer (262) Probably a variant spelling of Scottish MCNAIR.

McNees (503) Irish: variant spelling of MCNEESE.

McNeese (1074) Irish: Anglicized form of Gaelic **Mac Naois**, a patronymic from a shortened form of the personal name *Aonghus* (see ANGUS).

McNeff (267) Irish and Scottish: variant of MCNIFF.

McNeice (233) Irish: variant spelling of MCNEESE.

McNeil (10448) Irish and Scottish: Anglicized form of Gaelic **Mac Néill**, a patronymic from the personal name *Niall* (genitive *Néill*), thought to mean 'champion' (see NEILL). In Scotland MacNeills are associated with Barra and Gigha in the Hebrides; some of them went to Antrim and Derry in Ireland.

McNeill (6725) Irish and Scottish: variant spelling of MCNEIL.

McNeilly (690) Scottish and northern Irish: variant of MCNEELY.

McNeish (188) Irish: variant of MCNEESE.
GIVEN NAMES Irish 4%. *Brigid, Murphy.*

McNelis (541) Irish (western Ulster): Anglicized form of Gaelic **Mac Niallghuis** 'son of *Niallghus*', a personal name (probably originally a compliment) composed of the personal name *Niall* 'champion' + *gus* 'choice' or 'vigor'.
GIVEN NAMES Irish 8%. *Dermot* (2), *Brendan.*

McNelley (129) Scottish (Galloway) and northern Irish: variant of MCNEELY.

McNellis (394) Irish: variant spelling of MCNELIS.

McNelly (587) Scottish (Galloway) and northern Irish: variant of MCNEELY.

McNemar (349) Probably a variant of Irish MCNAMARA.

McNerney (1008) Irish: variant of MCINER-NEY.

McNett (609) Possibly an altered form of Irish MCNUTT.

McNevin (188) Scottish and Irish: Anglicized form of Gaelic **Mac Naoimhín** or **Mac Cnáimhín** (see NEVIN).

McNew (1585) Apparently an altered spelling of an unidentified Scottish or Irish surname. This form is not found in Britain or Ireland.

McNichol (524) Scottish and Irish: Anglicized form of Gaelic **Mac Niocaill**, patronymic from the Gaelic form of NICHOLAS.

McNicholas (758) Irish: patronymic from NICHOLAS. Compare MCNICHOL. In Ireland this was the surname of a Gaelicized Norman family.

McNichols (764) Scottish and Irish: variant of MCNICHOL with the addition of English patronymic *-s*.

McNickle (211) Northern Irish: variant spelling of MCNICHOL.

McNicol (247) Scottish and Irish: patronymic from the personal name *Nicol*, Scottish form of NICHOLAS.

McNiece (139) Variant spelling of MCNEESE.

McNiel (639) Scottish and Irish: variant spelling of MCNEIL.

McNiff (558) Irish and Scottish: Anglicized form of Irish Gaelic **Mac Conduibh**, a patronymic from the personal name *Cú Dhubh*, composed of the elements *cú* 'hound' (genitive *con*) + *dubh* 'black'. It is also Anglicized as CUNNIFF and MCADOO.
GIVEN NAMES Irish 6%. *Brigid, Donovan.*

McNinch (420) Irish: reduced form of MCANINCH.

McNish (394) Scottish and Irish: variant of MCNEESE.

McNitt (537) Variant of Scottish MCNUTT or MCNAUGHTON.

McNiven (118) Scottish: Anglicized form of Gaelic **Mac Naoimhín** (see NEVIN).

McNorton (148) Scottish and Irish: Anglicized spelling of Gaelic **Mac Neachtain** (see MCNAUGHTON).

McNulty (5359) Irish: Anglicized form of Gaelic **Mac an Ultaigh** 'son of the Ulsterman'. This is the name of a Donegal family originally from County Down.
GIVEN NAMES Irish 5%. *Brendan* (2), *Aidan, Brennan, Brigid, Dermot, Dympna, Kieran, Michael Patrick, Niall.*

McNutt (3514) Irish (especially Ulster): **1.** Anglicized form of a rare Gaelic name, **Mac Nuadhat**, a patronymic from the personal name *Nuadha*, the name of an ancient

Celtic god. **2.** (originally Scottish) reduced form of McNAUGHTON.

McOmber (219) Irish: variant of Mc-COMBER.

McOsker (149) Scottish and Irish: variant of McCOSKEY.

McOwen (138) Irish: Anglicized form of Gaelic **Mac Eoghain** (see McEWEN).

McPadden (143) Irish: Anglicized form of Gaelic **Mac Páidín**, a patronymic from *Páidín*, a Gaelic pet form of PATRICK. This is the same name as McFADDEN, without lenition.
GIVEN NAMES Irish 4%. *Brighid, Donal.*

McParland (295) Northern Irish: variant of McPARTLAND.

McPartlan (100) Northern Irish: variant of McPARTLAND.

McPartland (645) Northern Irish: local equivalent of McFARLANE, without lenition.

McPartlin (214) Northern Irish: northern Irish: variant of McPARTLAND.
GIVEN NAME Irish 8%. *Conor* (2).

McPeak (1290) Northern Irish: Anglicized form of Gaelic **Mac Péice**, a patronymic from the personal name *Péic*, which Woulfe links to Old English *Pic* (see PIKE 5), although MacLysaght derives it from Old English *peac* 'thickset man'.

McPeake (231) Northern Irish: variant spelling of McPEAK.

McPeck (148) Probably a variant of Irish McPEAK.

McPeek (858) Variant spelling of Irish McPEAK.

McPeters (366) Scottish: variant of Mc-PHEETERS.

McPhail (1993) Scottish and Irish: Anglicized form of Gaelic **Mac Phàil** (Scottish) and **Mac Phóil** (Irish), patronymics from Gaelic forms of the personal name PAUL.

McPhatter (204) Scottish: variant of Mc-PHEETERS.

McPhaul (300) Scottish and Irish: variant spelling of McPHAIL.

McPhearson (267) Scottish: variant of McPHERSON.
GIVEN NAMES French 4%. *Andre, Collette.*

McPhee (1591) Scottish and Irish: Anglicized form of Gaelic **Mac Dhuibhshíthe** 'son of *Duibhshíth*' (see DUFFY).

McPheeters (511) Scottish: Anglicized form of Gaelic **Mac Gille Pheadair**, a patronymic from a Gaelic personal name meaning 'servant of (Saint) PETER'.

McPheron (316) Scottish: possibly a variant of Irish McFERRIN.

McPherson (12380) Scottish: Anglicized form of Gaelic **Mac an Phearsain** 'son of the parson' (see PARSONS). This is the surname of various ecclesiastical families in Aberdeenshire and Argyll; it is also established in northern Ireland.

McPheters (121) Scottish: variant of Mc-PHEETERS.

McPhetridge (148) Scottish and Irish: variant spelling of McFETRIDGE.

McPhie (175) Scottish: variant spelling of McPHEE.

McPhillips (743) Scottish and Irish: Anglicized form of Gaelic **Mac Philib**, a patronymic from a Gaelic form of the personal name PHILLIP. See also McKILLIP.
GIVEN NAMES Irish 6%. *Brendan, Fitzgerald.*

McPike (360) Variant of McPEAK, now unknown in Scotland and Ireland.

McQuade (1706) Irish: variant spelling of McQUAID.
GIVEN NAMES Irish 5%. *Brendan, Kieran, Murphy, Patrick Joseph.*

McQuaid (998) Irish: Anglicized form of Gaelic **Mac Uaid** 'son of *Uad*', Gaelic form of the personal name *Wat* (see WALTER).
GIVEN NAMES Irish 4%. *Brendan, Colum, Nuala.*

McQuaide (274) Irish: variant spelling of McQUAID.

McQuaig (330) Irish: Anglicized form of Gaelic **Mac Cuaig** (unexplained). Compare QUIGG.

McQuain (315) Irish: Anglicized form of Gaelic **Mac Cuáin** 'son of *Cuán*', a personal name or byname formed from a diminutive of *cú* 'hound'. Compare COYNE.

McQuarrie (373) Scottish: Anglicized form of Gaelic **Mac Guaire**, a patronymic from a Gaelic personal name meaning 'proud', 'noble'.

McQuary (222) Scottish: variant of Mc-QUARRIE.

McQuate (125) Irish: variant spelling of McQUAID.

McQuay (557) Scottish (Galloway) and Irish: variant of McCOY.

McQueary (629) Variant of Scottish McQUARRIE.

McQueen (5732) Scottish: Anglicized form of Gaelic **Mac Shuibhne** 'son of *Suibhne*' a byname meaning 'pleasant'. Compare McSWEENEY. This name was also used as a Gaelic equivalent of the Old Norse byname *Sveinn* (see SWAIN).

McQueeney (380) Irish: variant of McSWEENEY, from the lenited Gaelic form **Mac Shuibhne**. Compare MAWHINNEY 2.
GIVEN NAME Irish 6%. *Cait.*

McQuerry (196) Irish or Scottish: variant of McQUARRIE.

McQuigg (133) Irish: variant of McQUAIG.
GIVEN NAME Irish 4%. *Clancy.*

McQuiggan (116) Irish: variant of McGUIGAN.

McQuilkin (305) Irish and Scottish: Anglicized form of Gaelic **Mac Uilcín** (Irish), **Mac Cuilcein** (Scottish), patronymics from the personal name *Uilcín*, a Gaeliced form of English WILKIN.

McQuillan (1013) **1.** Irish: Anglicized form of Gaelic **Mac Uighilín** 'son of *Huguelin*', a double diminutive of the Norman personal name HUGH. This is the name of an

important family in County Antrim. **2.** Irish: Anglicized form of Gaelic **Mac Cuilinn** (see McCULLEN). **3.** Scottish (of Irish origin): Anglicized form of Gaelic **Mac Coilín** (Irish), **Mac Cailein** (Scottish), a patronymic from the personal name *Coilín* or *Cailean*. See COLLINS.
GIVEN NAMES Irish 7%. *Brendan* (2), *Donal, Niamh, Seamus, Siobhan.*

McQuillen (759) Irish: variant spelling of McQUILLAN.

McQuillin (185) Irish and Scottish: variant spelling of McQUILLAN.

McQuinn (547) Irish: Anglicized form of Gaelic **Mac Cuinn** 'son of *Conn*' (see CONN).

McQuire (166) Scottish and Irish: variant of McGUIRE.

McQuirter (103) Scottish: possibly a variant of McWHIRTER.

McQuistion (126) Scottish and Irish: variant of McQUISTON.

McQuiston (895) Scottish and Irish: Anglicized form of Gaelic **Mac Uisdein** (see McCUTCHEON).

McQuitty (249) Northern Irish: Anglicized form of Gaelic **Mac Fhaoitigh** (see McWHITE).

McQuoid (123) Irish: variant of McQUAID.

McQuown (382) Variant spelling of Scottish McEWEN.

McRae (5963) Scottish: Anglicized form of a patronymic from the Gaelic personal name *Macraith*, meaning 'son of grace'.

McRaney (210) Scottish or Irish: variant of McCRANEY.

McRay (244) Scottish: variant spelling of McRAE.

McRea (105) Probably a metathesized form of Scottish McRAE.

McRee (735) Variant of Scottish McRAE.

McReynolds (2925) Northern Irish: Anglicized form of Gaelic **Mac Raghnaill**, a patronymic from the personal name *Raghnall*, derived from a Norse personal name of the same origin as REYNOLDS.

McRight (143) **1.** Irish: variant spelling of McWRIGHT. **2.** Respelling of Scottish and northern Irish McCREIGHT.

McRill (119) Probably a Gaelicized spelling of English **Mackrill**, a variant of MACK-RELL.

McRobbie (102) Scottish (Highlands): patronymic from the personal name *Robbie*, a pet form of ROBERT.
GIVEN NAME Scottish 5%; Scandinavian 4%. *Alastair.*

McRoberts (1403) Scottish: Anglicized form (with English genitive *-s*) of Gaelic **Mac Roibeirt**, a patronymic from a Gaelic form of the personal name ROBERT.

McRobie (109) Scottish: variant of McROBBIE.

McRorie (221) Scottish: variant spelling of McCRORY.

McRoy (484) Irish: Anglicized form of Gaelic **Mac Rúaidh**, a patronymic from the personal name or byname *Rúadh* 'red'.

McShan (370) Variant of northern Irish and Scottish MCSHANE.

McShane (1901) Northern Irish and Scottish: Anglicized form of Gaelic **Mac Seáin** 'son of *Seán*' (Irish form of JOHN). GIVEN NAMES Irish 6%. *Brendan* (2), *Conal, Declan, John Patrick, Kieran, Liam, Seamus.*

McSharry (136) Irish: Anglicized form of Gaelic **Mac Searraigh** (see MCSHERRY).

McShea (342) Irish: Anglicized form of Gaelic **Mac Séaghdha** 'son of *Séaghdha*', a byname meaning 'fine' or 'fortunate'. This is a rare Fermanagh name. GIVEN NAME Irish 6%. *Aileen.*

McSherry (825) **1.** Irish (southern Ulster): Anglicized form of Gaelic **Mac Searraigh** 'son of *Searrach*', a personal name based on *searrach* 'foal'. It is sometimes further Anglicized as FOLEY. **2.** Irish: Anglicized form of Gaelic **Mac Séartha** 'son of *Séartha*', a personal name equivalent to English GEOFFREY. This was the patronymic surname adopted by a County Cork family of Welsh origin, formerly named HODNETT. **3.** Scottish: Anglicized form of Gaelic **Mac Siridh** 'son of *Siridh*', a personal name of Old Norse origin, either from the male name *Sigfrid* or *Sigurðr* or from the female *Sigfríðr*. The first element in each is *sigr* 'victory', while the final elements are, respectively, *frid* 'peace', *vörðr* 'guardian', and *fríðr* 'fair', 'beautiful'. GIVEN NAMES Irish 5%. *Aidan, Eamon, Kieran, Padraic.*

McSorley (690) Scottish: Anglicized form of Gaelic **Mac Somhairle** 'son of *Somhairle*', a Gaelicized form of an Old Norse personal name composed of the elements *sumar* 'summer' + *liðr* 'seafarer'. GIVEN NAMES Irish 5%. *Brendan, Brigid.*

McSpadden (990) Scottish and Irish: Anglicized form of Gaelic **Mac Spáidín**, a patronymic from *spádán* or *spáidín*, diminutives of *spád* 'spade'.

McStay (138) Northern Irish (County Down): altered form of Irish **Mustey**, which is an Anglicized form of Gaelic **Ó Maoilstéighe** 'descendant of *Maoilstéighe*', a personal name of unknown origin.

McSwain (2041) Scottish and Irish: probably an Anglicized form of Gaelic **Mac Suibhne** (see MCSWEENEY) or of a Gaelic patronymic based on Old Norse *sveinn* 'boy', 'servant', which was also used as a personal name.

McSween (232) Scottish: variant of MCSWAIN.

McSweeney (1534) Irish: Anglicized form of Gaelic **Mac Suibhne** 'son of *Suibhne*', a byname meaning 'pleasant'. Compare MCQUEENEY, which is from the lenited form.

GIVEN NAMES Irish 5%. *Eamonn* (2), *Brendan, Fergus.*

McSweeny (139) Irish: variant of MC-SWEENEY. GIVEN NAME Irish 6%. *Conor.*

McTaggart (802) Scottish and northern Irish: Anglicized form of Gaelic **Mac an t-Sagairt** 'son of the priest' (see TAGGART).

McTague (414) Irish: variant of MCTIGUE.

McTavish (213) Scottish: Anglicized form of Gaelic **Mac Tamhais**, patronymic from a Lowland Scots form of the personal name THOMAS.

McTeague (166) Irish: variant of MCTIGUE. GIVEN NAMES Irish 11%. *Conor, Liam.*

McTee (123) Northern Irish: reduced form of MCATEE.

McTeer (233) Irish: reduced form of MC-ATEER.

McTernan (227) Irish: variant of MCTIER-NAN. GIVEN NAME Irish 6%. *Brennan.*

McTier (178) Scottish and Irish: variant of MCINTYRE and MCATEER.

McTiernan (256) Irish: Anglicized form of Gaelic **Mac Tighearnáin** (see MCKIER-NAN).

McTighe (342) Irish: Anglicized form of Gaelic **Mac Taidhg**, a patronymic from the byname *Tadhg* 'poet', 'philosopher'. Compare MCCAIG. GIVEN NAME Irish 5%. *Aidan.*

McTigue (532) Irish: Anglicized form of Gaelic **Mac Taidhg**, a patronymic from the byname *Tadhg* 'poet', 'philosopher'. Compare MCCAIG. GIVEN NAME Irish 6%. *Brendan* (2).

McTyre (124) Scottish and Irish: probably an Anglicized form of Gaelic **Mac Tír** 'son of the land' (a euphemism for the wolf). It could also be a variant of MCINTYRE.

McVaugh (144) Probably a variant of Scottish and Irish MCVEIGH.

McVay (2888) Scottish: variant spelling of MCVEY.

McVea (172) Northern Irish: probably a variant of MCVEY.

McVean (118) Scottish: Anglicized form of Gaelic **Mac Bheathain** 'son of *Beathan*'. Compare MCELWAIN. GIVEN NAMES Scottish 7%; Irish 4%. *Ewan; Brigid.*

McVeigh (1150) Variant spelling of Scottish MCVEY. GIVEN NAMES Irish 5%. *Brendan* (2), *Grainne, Seamus.*

McVey (3472) Scottish: variant of MCBETH, from the aspirated Gaelic form **Mac Bheatha**.

McVicar (319) Scottish and Irish (Ulster, of Scottish origin): Anglicized forms of Gaelic **Mac áBhiocair** (Scottish) or **Mac an Bhiocaire** (Irish) 'son of the vicar', from Latin *vicarius*.

McVicker (1448) Scottish and Irish: variant spelling of MCVICAR.

McVittie (71) Scottish and northern Irish: Anglicized form of Gaelic **Mac Bhiadhtaigh** 'son of the victualer' (see BEATTY).

McVoy (146) Irish or Scottish: Anglicized form of Gaelic **Mac Bhuidhe** 'son of the yellow-haired man' (from *buidhe* 'yellow'), or **Mac Fhíodhbhuidhe** 'son of the woodcutter' (see MCEVOY).

McWade (129) Irish: variant spelling of MCQUAID. GIVEN NAME Irish 5%. *Brendan.*

McWain (156) Irish: variant of MCQUAIN.

McWaters (489) Scottish: Anglicized form (with English genitive *-s*) of **Mac Bhàtair**, a patronymic from a Gaelicized form of the personal name WALTER.

McWatters (230) Scottish (Caithness) and northern Irish: Anglicized form (with English genitive *-s*) of Gaelic **Mac Uaitéir**, a patronymic from a Gaelicized form of the personal name WALTER.

McWeeney (183) **1.** Irish: Anglicized form of Gaelic **Mac Mhaonaigh** 'son of *Maonach*', a personal name meaning either 'dumb'. **2.** variant of Scottish MCWHIN-NEY.

McWethy (198) Irish or Scottish: unexplained.

McWherter (364) Variant spelling of MCWHIRTER.

McWhinney (161) Scottish and northern Irish: Anglicized form of Gaelic **Mac Choinnigh**, a patronymic from the byname *Coinneach* (see MCKENZIE and KENNETH).

McWhinnie (112) Scottish and northern Irish: variant spelling of MCWHINNEY.

McWhirt (208) Irish: variant of MCCORD.

McWhirter (1087) Scottish (Ayrshire) and northern Irish: Anglicized form of Gaelic **Mac an Chruiteir** 'son of the harpist or fiddler', from Gaelic *cruitear* 'harpist', 'fiddler'.

McWhite (292) Irish: partly translated Anglicized form of Gaelic **Mac Faoitigh**, a patronymic from a Gaelic form of English WHITE.

McWhorter (3510) Variant of Scottish and northern Irish MCWHIRTER.

McWilliam (289) **1.** Scottish and northern Irish: Anglicized form of Gaelic **Mac Uilleim**, a patronymic from a Gaelicized form of WILLIAM, frequently Anglicized as WILLIAMSON. **2.** Northern Irish: variant of MCQUILLAN. GIVEN NAMES Scottish 5%. *Iain, Morag.*

McWilliams (7512) Irish: Anglicized form of Gaelic **Mac Uilleim**, a patronymic from a Gaelicized form of WILLIAM, with the redundant addition of English patronymic *-s*. In many cases it represents a partial Gaelicization of Welsh WILLIAMS.

McWright (115) Irish: probably a part translation of MCINTYRE 'son of the wright'.

McZeal (126) Scottish: of uncertain origin. The letter *z* was used in Older Scots to represent the obsolete letter {yogh} (yogh), pronounced variously as 'y', 'g', or a gutteral fricative, so this may be a Scottish variant of McGill.

Meacham (2495) English: variant of Machen. This is a late (17th-century) form.

Meachem (124) English: see Machen.

Meachum (306) English: see Machen.

Mead (9083) English: **1.** topographic name for someone who lived by a meadow, from Middle English *mede* 'meadow' (Old English *mǣd*). **2.** metonymic occupational name for a brewer or seller of mead (Old English *meodu*), an alcoholic beverage made by fermenting honey.

Meade (7818) Irish: variant of English Mead.

Meader (872) English: **1.** topographic name for someone who lived by a meadow, from Mead 1 + the suffix *-er*, denoting an inhabitant. **2.** occupational name for a brewer or seller of mead, Middle English *med(i)er* (see Mead 2).

Meaders (375) English: variant of or patronymic from Meader.

Meador (4081) English: variant of Meader.

Meadors (1346) English: variant of or patronymic from Meader.

Meadow (376) English: topographic name for someone who lived by a meadow. Compare Mead. The form *meadow* derives from *mǣdwe*, the dative case of Old English *mǣd*.

Meadowcroft (215) English: habitational name from Meadowcroft in Middleton, Lancashire.

Meadows (14676) English: variant of Meadow.

Meads (813) English: variant of Mead 1.

Meager (136) English and Irish (of Norman origin): nickname for a thin person, from Old French *maigre* 'thin', 'slender' (Latin *macer* 'delicate').

Meagher (2558) **1.** Irish (midlands): Anglicized form of Gaelic **Ó Meachair** (see Maher). **2.** English and Irish (of Norman origin): variant spelling of Meager.
GIVEN NAMES Irish 6%. *Brendan* (3), *Niall* (3), *Cormac* (2), *Kieran* (2), *Padric* (2), *Declan, Dermot, Seamus, Siobhan*.

Meahl (109) Origin unidentified.

Meaker (181) English (Somerset): possibly a variant of Meager.

Meakin (147) English (chiefly Nottinghamshire): variant of Makin 1.
GIVEN NAME Irish 5%. *Brennan*.

Mealer (442) English: probably a variant of Mellor. Compare Mealor, Meeler.

Mealey (680) Irish: variant of Malley.

Mealing (141) English (Avon): unexplained; possibly a variant of Melling.

Mealor (178) English (Cheshire): probably a variant of Mellor. Compare Mealer, Meeler.

Meals (437) English: metonymic occupational name for a grinder or seller of flour, Middle English *mele*.

Mealy (502) Irish: variant spelling of Mealey.

Meaney (821) Irish: Anglicized form of Gaelic **Ó Maonaigh** (see Mooney).
GIVEN NAMES Irish 5%. *Colm, Declan*.

Meanor (175) Irish?

Means (5484) **1.** Irish: shortened form of McMeans. **2.** English: habitational name from East and West Meon in Hampshire, which take their names from the Meon river. The word is Celtic but of uncertain meaning, possibly 'swift one'. **3.** nickname from Middle English *mene* 'inferior in rank', 'of low degree' (from Old English *gemǣne*), or from Middle English *mene* 'moderate in behaviour' (from Old French *mëen, mean*).

Meany (470) Irish: variant spelling of Meaney.

Meara (236) Irish: shortened form of **O'Meara**, a variant of O'Mara.
GIVEN NAME Irish 4%. *Brendan*.

Meares (596) English: variant spelling of Mears.

Mearns (293) Scottish: habitational name from a place so named in Renfrewshire or from a region called The Mearns, more or less co-extensive with Kincardineshire, named in Gaelic as *an Mhaoirne*, a derivative of *maor* 'beadle' (see Mair).

Mears (3698) English: **1.** topographic name for someone who lived by a pond, Old English *mere*. **2.** topographic name for someone who lived near a boundary, Old English *(ge)mǣre*.

Meas (227) **1.** English: variant of Mease or Meece. **2.** Norwegian (Sør Trøndelag): habitational name from a farmstead named Meås, from *me* 'middle' + *ås* 'hill', 'ridge'. **3.** French (**Méas**): habitational name from a locality so named in Nièvre. **4.** Cambodian: unexplained.
GIVEN NAMES Cambodian 44%. *Sarin* (4), *Chan* (3), *Rin* (3), *Sok* (2), *Chea, Heng, Hok, Kan, Lim, Man, Pich, Sambath; Samnang* (2), *Saroeun* (2), *Be, Dam, Hum, Ky, Ly, Nhan, Sophal, Sophan, Sophea, Yen; Vuthy* (2), *Chhath, Chhin, Chhon, Oeun, Savath, Sophath, Sovann, Thoeun; Pheng*.

Mease (806) English: **1.** probably a patronymic from May 1. **2.** variant of Meece.

Measel (179) Origin unidentified.

Meason (109) English: perhaps a variant of Meacham.

Meath (235) Irish: part-translation of Gaelic **Mac Conmidhe** 'son of the hound of Meath' (see McNamee).
GIVEN NAME Irish 5%. *William Kevin*.

Meaux (837) French: habitational name from a place in Seine-et-Marne, so named from the Gaulish tribal name *Meldi*, or from Meaux-la-Montagne in Rhône.

GIVEN NAMES French 5%. *Andrus* (2), *Amede, Camille, Eves, Maudry, Michel, Pierre, Raywood, Theogene*.

Mebane (522) Probably a variant of Scottish McBain.

Mecca (702) Italian: from a pet form of a feminine form of the personal name *Domenico* (see Domingo).
GIVEN NAMES Italian 18%. *Angelo* (9), *Salvatore* (9), *Donato* (5), *Vito* (3), *Mauro* (2), *Rocco* (2), *Dante, Dino, Domenic, Gabriele, Gilda*.

Meccia (112) Italian (Sicilian): feminine form **Meccio**, which may is probably a nickname from Sicilian *mecciu* 'curl', 'ringlet'.
GIVEN NAMES Italian 10%. *Alessandro, Arcangelo, Vito*.

Mech (291) **1.** German: from a short form of any of various Germanic personal names beginning with *Mag-*, for example *Magwart*. **2.** Polish, Czech, and Sorbian: topographic name from Western Slavic *mech* 'moss'. **3.** Czech (**Měch**) and Polish (**Miech**): possibly a derivative of Czech *měch* 'skin' or Polish *miech* 'bag'. **4.** Americanized spelling of Hungarian **Mécs**, probably an occupational name for a candle maker, from *mécs* 'wick'.

Mecham (1112) Variant of English Meacham.

Mechanic (144) Jewish (eastern Ashkenazic): occupational name for a craftsman, from Polish *mechanik* or Russian *mekhanik*.
GIVEN NAME Jewish 10%. *Mayer* (2).

Meche (634) French (**Mèche**): nickname from *mèche* 'lock (of hair)', 'forelock'.
GIVEN NAMES French 6%. *Clovis* (2), *Curley* (2), *Anatole, Emile, Etienne, Landry, Placide, Remi, Theophile*.

Mechem (170) Variant of English Meacham.

Mechler (260) **1.** German: occupational name for a broker or middleman, Middle High German *mecheler*, ultimately from Middle Low German (see Meckler). **2.** Belgian: habitational name for someone from Mechelen in Antwerp province.
GIVEN NAMES German 7%. *Otto* (3), *Kurt*.

Mechling (440) German: diminutive of Mech or spelling variant of *Michling*, a derivative of Michael.

Meck (610) German and Dutch: from a short form of the Germanic personal name *Macco* (see Mack 2).

Mecke (134) German and Dutch: variant of Meck.
GIVEN NAMES German 9%. *Bernhard, Horst, Jurgen*.

Meckel (215) German: **1.** from a pet form of Meck. **2.** (Hesse): from a short or pet form of the female personal name *Mechthild* (see Metz). **3.** habitational name from Meckel in the Eifel region, south of Bitburg.

Meckes (295) German: patronymic from MECK.

Meckfessel (102) Southern German: altered form of **Methfessel**, from Middle High German *met* 'mead' + a diminutive of *faz* 'vat', 'barrel', a metonymic occupational name for a brewer of mead, or perhaps a habitational name from a tavern so called.

Mecklenburg (283) German and Jewish (Ashkenazic): regional name for someone from the province of this name in northern Germany, so called from Old Saxon *mikil* 'big', 'great' + *burg* 'castle'.

Meckler (260) North German and Jewish: occupational name for a broker or middleman, Middle Low German *mekeler* (from Middle Low German *maken* 'to make') and Yiddish *mekler*.

GIVEN NAMES Jewish 5%; German 4%. *Chani, Yakov; Otto.*

Meckley (621) **1.** Variant of English MACKLEY. **2.** Probably also an altered form of German MECKLER.

Meckstroth (150) German (Westphalia): topographic name for someone living near an area of swampy underbrush or in a hollow, from *Meck* (probably from the personal name, see MECK) + Low German *Strut(h), Stroth* 'underbrush', 'hollow'.

GIVEN NAME German 4%. *Kurt* (2).

Mecum (303) English or Irish: unexplained. Perhaps an Anglicized form of Gaelic **Mac Thom** 'son of Tom'.

Meda (113) **1.** Galician: habitational name from Meda, a village in Galicia. **2.** Indian (Andhra Pradesh): Hindu name from Telugu *mēa* 'mansion'.

GIVEN NAMES Spanish 15%; Indian 14%. *Jose* (3), *Alfonso, Alfredo, Angel, Consuelo, Esperanza, Francisco, Imelda, Javier, Jesus, Jose Maria, Manuel; Amar, Gautam, Gowri, Ravindranath, Sridhar, Uma, Vijay.*

Medaglia (149) Southern Italian: according to Caracausi, a hypercorrected spelling of **Meraglia**, a variant of MIRAGLIA, but possibly a metonymic occupational name for a medal maker, from Italian *medaglia* 'medal'.

GIVEN NAMES Italian 24%. *Rocco* (4), *Emelio, Mario, Salvatore.*

Medal (108) Galician: possibly a derivative of MEDA.

GIVEN NAMES Spanish 26%. *Mireya* (2), *Pablo* (2), *Adolfo, Carlos, Eduardo, Fernando, Francisco, Humberto, Jesus, Jose, Maria Del Socorro, Mario.*

Medaris (201) Probably an altered form of Portuguese and Galician MEDEIROS.

Medbery (126) Variant spelling of English **Medbury**, a habitational name from Medbury Farm in Bedfordshire.

Medcalf (467) English: variant of METCALF.

Medd (152) English: variant of MEAD 1.

Meddaugh (290) Of uncertain origin; perhaps Irish, related to **Midheach** (see MEAD).

Medders (669) English: unexplained; possibly a variant of MEADOWS (see MEADOW), reflecting a local pronunciation.

Meddings (151) English: derivative of MEAD.

Meddock (106) English: variant of MADDOCK.

Medearis (333) Altered form of Portuguese and Galician MEDEIROS.

Medeiros (5457) Portuguese and Galician: habitational name from any of various places named Medeiros, from Portuguese and Galician *medeiro* 'place where shocks of maize are gathered' (a derivative of *meda* 'shock', 'stack', Latin *meta* '(pyramid-shaped) post').

GIVEN NAMES Spanish 14%; Portuguese 9%. *Manuel* (187), *Jose* (63), *Carlos* (34), *Mario* (15), *Luis* (14), *Alvaro* (5), *Ana* (5), *Augusto* (5), *Eduardo* (5), *Francisco* (5), *Jaime* (5), *Armando* (4); *Joao* (15), *Joaquim* (5), *Paulo* (5), *Duarte* (3), *Guilherme* (2), *Valentim* (2), *Zulmira* (2), *Agostinho, Anabela, Caetano, Fernandes, Vasco.*

Medel (318) Spanish: **1.** from the personal name *Medel*, possibly a derivative of the Latin name *Emetherius*. **2.** habitational name from San Medel, a town in Salamanca province.

GIVEN NAMES Spanish 44%; Portuguese 8%. *Juan* (5), *Mario* (4), *Ruben* (4), *Enrique* (3), *Jorge* (3), *Manuel* (3), *Angel* (2), *Ernesto* (2), *Leticia* (2), *Magda* (2), *Rafael* (2), *Ramon* (2); *Paulo.*

Medellin (596) Spanish (**Medellín**): habitational name from a place so named in Badajoz province, Latin *(Caecilia) Metellina*, derived from the name of a 1st-century Roman proconsul in Spain, Cecilio Metello Pio.

GIVEN NAMES Spanish 43%. *Jose* (10), *Juan* (7), *Pedro* (7), *Jesus* (6), *Carlos* (5), *Javier* (5), *Sergio* (4), *Alfredo* (3), *Ernesto* (3), *Guadalupe* (3), *Luis* (3), *Manuel* (3); *Antonio* (6), *Lorenzo* (2), *Carmelo, Cecilio, Donato, Eliseo, Federico, Heriberto, Marco.*

Medema (293) Frisian: patronymic from the personal name *Mede*, short form of *Médard* (see MARS).

Medendorp (162) Dutch: topographic name for someone who lived 'in the middle of a village' or in a place known as 'the middle village'.

Meder (534) German: variant of MADER 2.

GIVEN NAMES German 6%. *Ewald* (2), *Gunther* (2), *Manfred, Siegfried.*

Medero (102) Spanish: Castilianized form of Portuguese and Galician MEDEIROS.

GIVEN NAMES Spanish 46%. *Jose* (4), *Jesus* (3), *Juan* (3), *Angel* (2), *Adela, Alejandro, Ana Elizabeth, Dulce, Enrique, Felicita, Francisco, Guillermo.*

Mederos (337) Spanish: Castilianized form of MEDEIROS.

GIVEN NAMES Spanish 52%. *Juan* (11), *Jose* (9), *Francisco* (5), *Jesus* (4), *Luis* (4), *Alberto* (3), *Armando* (3), *Fernando* (3), *Gerardo* (3), *Humberto* (3), *Manuel* (3), *Mario* (3).

Medford (1476) Apparently an English habitational name from an unidentified place. Possibly it originated in North America, from Medford, MA, which is named as 'the ford by the meadow'.

Mediate (109) **1.** English: unexplained. **2.** Southern Italian: unexplained.

GIVEN NAMES Italian 28%. *Rocco* (6), *Giovanni.*

Medich (133) Serbian and Croatian (**Medić**): patronymic from *Medo*, a nickname derived from a diminutive of *medved* 'bear'.

GIVEN NAMES South Slavic 4%. *Dragoljub, Marko.*

Medici (328) Italian: patronymic or plural form of MEDICO.

GIVEN NAMES Italian 24%. *Angelo* (4), *Mario* (4), *Antonio* (3), *Domenic* (2), *Palma* (2), *Amedeo, Americo, Caesar, Carlo, Dante, Dario, Demetrio, Giovanni, Guido, Lorenzo, Osvaldo, Renato.*

Medick (106) English: from a nickname for a physician.

Medico (178) Italian (mainly southeastern): occupational name for a physician, Italian *medico* (Latin *medicus*, from *medere* 'to heal').

GIVEN NAMES Italian 9%. *Angelo* (2), *Aldo, Cataldo, Cosmo, Gilda, Lorenzo.*

Medin (181) Galician (**Medín**): habitational name from Medín, a place in A Coruña province.

Medina (16607) Spanish: habitational name from any of the several places, as for example Medina-Sidonia in Cádiz province and Medina del Campo in Valladolid, so called from Arabic *medīna* 'city'. The surname is also borne by Sephardic Jews.

GIVEN NAMES Spanish 46%; Portuguese 11%. *Jose* (444), *Juan* (222), *Manuel* (176), *Luis* (156), *Carlos* (139), *Jesus* (108), *Francisco* (97), *Pedro* (86), *Miguel* (83), *Ramon* (82), *Mario* (79), *Rafael* (77); *Lidio* (2), *Ligia* (2), *Anatolio, Duarte, Joao.*

Medine (122) French: unexplained. This is a Louisiana name.

GIVEN NAME French 5%. *Cecile.*

Medinger (229) German: habitational name for someone from any of several places called Medingen.

Meditz (158) Germanized spelling of Slavic MEDICH.

GIVEN NAMES German 9%. *Alois, Friedrich, Gerhard, Helmuth.*

Medland (100) English (Devon and Cornwall): topographic name for someone who lived by the 'meadow (Old English *mǣd*) land (Old English *land*)'.

Medlar (130) Possibly English, a variant spelling of MEDLER, or perhaps from a habitational name from place in Lancashire called Medlar, meaning 'middle shieling'.

Medlen (281) English (Cornwall): variant spelling of MEDLIN.

Medler (354) English (Norfolk): habitational name from Madehurst in Sussex, which gets its name from Old English *mǣd* 'meadow' (see MEAD 1) + *hyrst* 'wooded hill'. This place name appears in 12th-century records in the Normanized form *Medl(i)ers*. The surname is found in Norfolk as early as the 13th century in the form *de Medlers*; the landowning family that bore it was in vassalage to the Earl of Surrey, who had large estates in both Sussex and Norfolk.

Medley (4271) English: **1.** habitational name, either a variant of Madeley (a name common to several places, including one in Shropshire and two in Staffordshire), named in Old English as 'Māda's clearing', from an unattested byname, *Māda* (probably a derivative of *mād* 'foolish') + *lēah* 'woodland clearing'; or from Medley on the Thames in Oxfordshire, named in Old English with *middel* 'middle' + *ēg* 'island'. **2.** nickname for an aggressive person, from Middle English, Old French *medlee* 'combat', 'conflict' (Late Latin *misculata*).

Medlin (3798) **1.** English (Cornwall): unexplained. **2.** Czech (**Medlín**): derivative of **Medla**, a name of uncertain origin; perhaps a nickname from *mdlý* 'faint', or an occupational name for a brewer or seller of mead from *med* 'honey', 'mead'.

Medlock (1988) English: variant of MATLOCK.

Mednick (334) Jewish (eastern Ashkenazic): occupational name from Russian *mednik* 'coppersmith'.

GIVEN NAMES Jewish 4%. *Sol* (2), *Emanuel, Miriam.*

Medoff (197) **1.** Alternative spelling of Bulgarian **Medov**, a patronymic from *Medo*, a short form of the personal name *Metodij* (from Greek *Methodios*). **2.** Shortened form of Jewish (eastern Ashkenazic) **Medovoj**, meaning 'of honey' in Russian, hence an occupational name for a mead maker.

GIVEN NAMES Jewish 4%. *Sol* (2), *Ari.*

Medow (101) Jewish: variant of MEDOFF.

GIVEN NAMES Jewish 7%; German 6%. *Rivkah, Sol; Gerhard.*

Medrano (3207) Spanish: habitational name from a place in Soria province.

GIVEN NAMES Spanish 52%; Portuguese 12%. *Jose* (98), *Juan* (50), *Jesus* (37), *Carlos* (29), *Francisco* (27), *Manuel* (24), *Mario* (22), *Raul* (21), *Ruben* (21), *Rafael* (20), *Jorge* (19), *Miguel* (19); *Ligia, Wenseslao.*

Medsker (267) Perhaps an altered spelling of METZGER.

Meduna (126) Czech: affectionate nickname from *medunný* 'as sweet as honey', from *med* 'mead', 'honey'.

Medve (119) Variant of Slavic MEDVED.

Medvec (128) Slovak: nickname from a derivative of *medved'* 'bear' (see MEDVED).

Medved (489) Ukrainian, Belorussian, Slovak (**Medved'**), Czech (**Medvěd**), Slovenian, Croatian, and Jewish (eastern Ashkenazic): from the nickname *Medved* 'bear', applied to a large, strong, or clumsy person. In some cases this name may be a reduced form of Ukrainian or Belorussian **Medvedev**, a patronymic name of the same origin.

GIVEN NAMES Russian 4%. *Leonid* (3), *Galina, Oleg, Vasiliy, Vladimir.*

Medwid (124) Polish form of Ukrainian and Belorussian MEDVED 'bear'.

GIVEN NAMES Polish 7%. *Andrzej, Wasyl.*

Mee (880) **1.** Irish: reduced form of McNAMEE or MEEHAN. **2.** Irish: Anglicized form of Gaelic **Ó Miadhaigh** 'descendant of *Miadhach*', a byname meaning 'honorable'. **3.** French (**Mée**): habitational name from places called (Le) Mée in Mayenne, Eure-et-Loir, and Seine-et-Marne, derived from Old French *me(i)s* 'farmstead' (Latin *mansus*).

Meece (1063) **1.** English: habitational name from Meece in Staffordshire, named in Old English with *mēos* 'moss'. **2.** Possibly a variant of Dutch MEESE.

Meech (279) English: nickname from Old English *mecca* 'companion', 'friend'.

Meeder (277) Variant of English MEADER.

Meeds (162) Variant spelling of MEADS.

Meegan (391) Irish: variant of MEEHAN.

GIVEN NAME Irish 5%. *Brendan.*

Meehan (6138) Irish: **1.** Anglicized form of Gaelic **Ó Miadhacháin** 'descendant of *Miadhachán*', a diminutive of *Miadhach*, a byname meaning 'honorable'. **2.** Anglicized form of Gaelic **Ó Maotháin** 'descendant of *Maothán*', a personal name representing a diminutive of *maoth* 'moist', 'soft', 'tearful'. **3.** in some instances, an assimilated form of MEHEGAN.

GIVEN NAMES Irish 5%. *Brendan* (3), *Eamon* (2), *Aileen, Caitlin, Conan, Cormac, Donal, Donovan, Patrick Michael.*

Meehl (167) Possibly a variant of Norwegian MEHL.

Meek (5763) English and Scottish: nickname for a self-effacing person or a gentle and compassionate one, from Middle English *meke* 'humble', 'submissive', 'merciful' (Old Norse *mjúkr*).

Meeker (3385) Dutch and Belgian: **1.** occupational name from Middle Dutch *maker*, Brabant-Limburg dialect *meker* 'maker', 'craftsman'. **2.** from the Germanic personal name *Magherus*.

Meekhof (129) Dutch: habitational name of unexplained origin.

GIVEN NAMES Dutch 4%; German 4%. *Gerrit* (3); *Kurt.*

Meekins (1045) English: patronymic from MAKIN 1.

Meeks (9131) English: variant of MEEK.

Meeler (237) English: probably a variant of MELLOR. Compare MEALOR, MEALER.

Meenach (120) **1.** Perhaps Irish: variant of MINNICK. **2.** Alternatively, perhaps German: variant of MINNICH.

Meenan (350) Irish (mainly County Donegal): Anglicized form of Gaelic **Ó Mianáin** 'descendant of *Mianán*', a personal name derived from *mian* 'goodwill'.

Meents (157) Frisian: patronymic from a Frisian form of the personal name MEINERT.

Meer (308) **1.** Dutch: topographic name for someone who lived by a body of water, Middle Dutch *mere* 'lake'. **2.** Jewish: variant of MEYER 2. **3.** Muslim: from a Persian title, a shortened form of Arabic *amīr* 'prince', 'commander' (see AMIR). This name is found throughout the Indian subcontinent.

GIVEN NAMES Muslim 4%. *Shahid* (2), *Zaheer* (2), *Bashir, Faisal, Naima, Sayed, Syed, Wahab, Waqar.*

Meerdink (123) Altered form of Dutch **van Meerdonk**, a habitational name for someone from Meerdonk in East Flanders in Belgium.

Meers (505) **1.** English: variant of MEARS. **2.** Dutch: topographic name from *meers(ch)* denoting lush, alluvial land by a watercourse.

Mees (438) Dutch: **1.** from a short form of the personal name *Bartholomeus* (see BARTHOLOMEW 1). **2.** variant of MAAS or MEESE 2.

Meese (796) **1.** English: variant spelling of MEECE. **2.** German and Dutch: nickname from the bird name *mees* 'titmouse', or a metonymic occupational name for a bird-catcher. **3.** Dutch: possibly a metonymic occupational name for a basketweaver, from Middle Dutch *mese* '(fish) basket'. **4.** Dutch: patronymic from a short form of the personal name *Bartolomeus*.

Meester (283) North German and Dutch: nickname for someone who behaved in a masterful manner, or an occupational name for a teacher or lecturer, or someone who was master of his craft, from Latin *magister*.

Meetze (272) German: possibly a habitational name from a place called Meetzen.

Meeuwsen (203) Dutch: patronymic from a short form of the personal name *Bartholomeus* (see BARTHOLOMEW).

Mefferd (221) Variant of MEFFERT.

Meffert (221) German and Dutch: from a Germanic personal name composed of the elements *mahti* 'strength', 'might' + *frithu* 'peace'.

GIVEN NAMES German 4%. *Jurgen, Manfred.*

Mefford (1309) Probably an Americanized spelling of German and Dutch MEFFERT.

Mega (137) **1.** Greek (**Megas**): nickname from Greek *megas* 'big', often used in combination with a personal name, for example **Megagiannis** 'big John', **Megapanos** 'big Panos' (see PANOS). **2.** Eastern German: nickname from German dialect *mege* 'goat'.

Megahan (111) Irish: **1.** with the stress on the first syllable, this is an Anglicized form of Gaelic **Ó Maothagáin** 'descendant of *Maothagán*', a derivative of *maoth* 'soft'. **2.** with the stress on the second syllable, it is a variant of McGAHAN.

Megan (121) Irish: **1.** with the stress on the first syllable, this is an Anglicized form of Gaelic **Meighan**, which, according to MacLysaght, is usually a variant of MEEHAN or occasionally of MEGAHAN. **2.** with the stress on the second syllable, a variant of McGAHAN.

Megee (234) Variant of Irish MAGEE.

Meger (166) German: nickname from Middle High German *mager, meger* 'lean', 'thin'. This surname is also found in Poland.

Meggers (129) North German: patronymic from the Low German *Megger*, a variant of MEYER 'tenant farmer', 'steward', or 'headman'.

Meggett (110) **1.** English: from a pet form of the female personal name *Magg, Megg* (see MAGGS). **2.** Scottish: habitational name from Megget in the parish of Yarrow, Selkirkshire.
GIVEN NAME French 4%. *Cecile.*

Megginson (325) English: variant of MEGGISON, with intrusive -*n*-.

Meggison (177) English: metronymic from *Meggot*, a pet form of the personal name *Margaret*.

Meggitt (108) English: variant of MEGGETT.

Meggs (401) English: metronymic from *Megg*, a reduced form of the personal name *Margaret* (see MARGESON).
FOREBEARS Vincent Meggs (*c.*1583–1658) came to Weymouth, MA, from East Devon, England, in or before 1639.

Megill (287) Variant spelling of Irish MAGILL.

Meglio (128) Italian: from a personal name derived from Latin *melior* 'better', or from a shortened form of AMELIO.
GIVEN NAMES Italian 22%; French 7%; Spanish 4%. *Angelo* (3), *Antonio* (2), *Franco, Nicola, Sal, Vito; Jean-Paul, Jeanpaul; Angelina* (2), *Mario, Olivio, Raimundo.*

Megna (328) Italian: habitational name from a shortened form of Omegna in Novara province.
GIVEN NAMES Italian 10%. *Salvatore* (2), *Guiseppe, Vito.*

Mehaffey (685) Irish: Anglicized form of Gaelic **Mac Dhuibhshíthe** 'son of *Duibhshíth*', a personal name composed of the elements *dubh* 'black' + *síth* 'peace'. According to Woulfe, this was originally a

Scottish name (usually Anglicized there as McPHEE), which was taken to Antrim in the 16th century.

Mehaffie (108) Variant of Scottish and Irish MAHAFFEY.

Mehaffy (126) Variant of Irish MAHAFFEY.

Mehalic (149) Altered form of Slovenian **Mihelič** or **Mihalič**, or of Croatian **Mihalić**, patronymics from the personal *Mihal*, or from some other, similar Slavic derivative of the Biblical name MICHAEL.

Mehalick (114) Americanized form of Ukrainian **Myhalik**, Slovak **Mihálik**, or a similar name in another Slavic language. Compare MEHALIC.

Mehalko (138) **1.** Variant transcription of Ukrainian **Myhalko**, from a pet form of the personal name *Myhajlo*, Ukrainian form of MICHAEL. **2.** Americanized spelling of Slovak **Mi(c)halko** or some other similar surname derived from a Slavic pet form of the personal name MICHAEL.

Mehall (177) Americanized spelling of Hungarian **Mihály**, Slovak **Mihál**, Ukrainian **Myhal**, or some other form of the personal name MICHAEL.

Mehan (319) **1.** Variant spelling of Irish MEEHAN. **2.** Indian (Panjab): Hindu (Khatri) name of unknown meaning.
GIVEN NAMES Indian 6%. *Arun* (2), *Ashok* (2), *Vijay* (2), *Dharam, Geeta, Naveen, Ramesh.*

Meharg (239) Irish: variant of McHARG.

Mehegan (128) Irish: Anglicized form of Gaelic **Ó Maothagáin** 'descendant of *Maothagán*', a personal name derived from a diminutive of *maoth* 'soft'.

Mehl (1172) **1.** German: metonymic occupational name for a miller or flour merchant, from Middle High German *mel* 'flour'. This surname is also established in Denmark and Sweden. **2.** Norwegian: habitational name from any of several farmsteads in southwestern Norway, originally named with Old Norse *melr* 'sandbank', 'gravel bank'.
GIVEN NAMES German 4%. *Kurt* (6), *Bernhard, Ernst, Gerd, Gerhard, Gottfried, Otto.*

Mehlberg (200) **1.** North German: habitational name from any of several places named Mehlberg or Me(h)hlbergen. **2.** Jewish (Ashkenazic): ornamental name composed of German *Mehl* 'flour' + *Berg* 'mountain', 'hill'.
GIVEN NAME German 5%. *Wolfgang.*

Mehle (154) **1.** Dutch and German: possibly from a short form of the personal name *Amelis, Amilius*, a Latinization of a Germanic compound name with initial *Amal*- 'bravery', 'vigor'; or of the Roman family name *Aemilius*. **2.** German: habitational name from a place called Mehle near Elze in Lower Saxony. **3.** Slovenian: unexplained; possibly an adoption of the German name. In Slovenia this name is found mainly in the capital, Ljubljana. **4.** Norwe-

gian (**Mæ(h)le**): habitational name from any of numerous farmsteads in western Norway named Mele, from *meli*, the dative case of Old Norse *melr* 'sandbank', 'gravel bank'. (Compare MAHLE 2.)

Mehlenbacher (162) German: habitational name for someone from a place called Mehlenbach.

Mehler (485) **1.** Jewish (Ashkenazic): occupational name for a miller or flour merchant, from an agent derivative of German *Mehl* 'flour'. **2.** German (Rhineland, Hesse): variant of MAHLER.

Mehlhaff (214) Variant of German MEHLHOFF.
GIVEN NAME German 4%. *Helmut.*

Mehlhoff (196) North German (Westphalia): topographic name for someone who lived on (or owned) a farm in marshy ground, from Middle Low German *mel* 'mud' (Bahlow) + *hoff* 'farmstead', 'manor farm'.
GIVEN NAMES German 5%. *Milbert* (2), *Kurt.*

Mehlhorn (173) North German: topographic name from Middle Low German *mel* 'mud', 'dirt' (Bahlow) + *horn* 'corner'.
GIVEN NAMES German 11%. *Klaus* (4), *Hans, Otto, Rainer, Uwe.*

Mehling (434) German: patronymic from a short form of a compound name formed with *mahal* 'gathering place', 'court' (medieval *thing*) as the first element.
GIVEN NAMES German 4%. *Alois, Benno, Fritz, Othmar, Otto.*

Mehlman (320) German (**Mehlmann**) and Jewish (Ashkenazic): occupational name for a miller or flour merchant. The German name is from Middle High German *mel* 'flour' + *man* 'man'. The Yiddish name is from modern German *Mehl* 'flour'+ *Mann* 'man'.
GIVEN NAMES Jewish 6%. *Gerson* (2), *Mordechai* (2), *Chaya, Hyman, Meyer, Moshe.*

Mehner (155) **1.** North German: variant of MEINERT. **2.** South German: variant of **Mäner** (see MANER).
GIVEN NAMES German 16%; Dutch 4%. *Hans* (2), *Fritz, Gerhart, Gunter, Gunther, Heinz, Otto; Dierk.*

Mehnert (162) North German: variant of MEINERT.
GIVEN NAME German 4%. *Ralf.*

Mehok (138) Origin unidentified.

Mehr (453) German: habitational name from any of several places so named.

Mehra (278) Indian (Panjab): from Panjabi *mehrā* 'chief', 'master'. Compare MALHOTRA.
GIVEN NAMES Indian 93%. *Anil* (6), *Sanjay* (6), *Vijay* (6), *Arun* (4), *Prem* (4), *Rajiv* (4), *Ravi* (4), *Ajay* (3), *Dev* (3), *Pradeep* (3), *Sanjeev* (3), *Ashok* (2).

Mehrens (138) North German: patronymic from a short form of a compound name with the first element *mar* 'horse', or from a homonym meaning 'magnificent', 'famous'.

GIVEN NAMES German 4%. *Arno, Monika.*

Mehrer (259) German: nickname for an industrious person, from an agent derivative of Middle High German *meren* 'to increase'.

GIVEN NAMES German 4%. *Fritz, Kurt, Otto.*

Mehrhoff (136) German: probably a variant of MEYERHOFER.

Mehring (474) German: habitational name from any of several places named Mehring or Mehringen.

GIVEN NAMES German 6%. *Wilfried* (3), *Horst, Kurt.*

Mehringer (342) German: habitational name for someone from any of several places named Mehring or Mehringen.

Mehrotra (137) Indian: variant of MALHOTRA.

GIVEN NAMES Indian 94%. *Sushil* (8), *Deepak* (7), *Sharad* (4), *Prem* (3), *Rakesh* (3), *Rohit* (3), *Sanjay* (3), *Vivek* (3), *Ajay* (2), *Anshuman* (2), *Ashok* (2), *Manish* (2).

Mehrtens (243) North German: variant of MERTENS.

GIVEN NAMES German 4%. *Armin, Erwin, Otto.*

Mehta (2513) Indian (Gujarat, Rajasthan, Panjab, and Bombay city): Hindu (Bania, Vania, Brahman, Khatri), Jain, Parsi, and Sikh name meaning 'chief' in several modern Indian languages, from Sanskrit *mahita* 'praised', 'great' (from *mah-* 'to praise or magnify'). In Gujarati it has come to mean 'teacher', 'accountant', probably because teachers and accountants were respectfully so addressed in Gujarat. The Oswal and Porwal Banias and the Panjabi Khatris also have clans called Mehta.

GIVEN NAMES Indian 91%. *Ashok* (26), *Dilip* (24), *Anil* (21), *Rajesh* (20), *Ramesh* (20), *Bharat* (19), *Deepak* (18), *Sanjay* (18), *Pankaj* (17), *Sunil* (17), *Prakash* (15), *Vinod* (15).

Mehus (143) Norwegian: habitational name from any of about fifteen farmsteads named from *me* 'middle' + *hus* 'house', referring to a farm in the middle of something.

Mei (975) **1.** Chinese 梅: from the name of an area called Mein during the Shang dynasty. Under the reign of the corrupt and cruel last king of the Shang dynasty, Zhou Xin (1154–1123 BC), a high counselor's position was occupied by the prince of the area of Mei. The prince of Mei was loyal but outspoken, and many times criticized his ruler's extravagant and dissolute behavior. This enraged the king, who executed the prince. The deceased's descendants subsequently adopted the place name Mei as their surname. **2.** Dutch: variant of MAY. **3.** Italian: from a patronymic or plural form of a short form of the personal names BARTOLOMEO, ROMEO, or TOLOMEO. **4.** Italian: see MEO.

GIVEN NAMES Chinese 44%. *Hui* (7), *Jing* (5), *Wei* (5), *Hong* (4), *Feng* (3), *Guo Quan* (3), *Jianping* (3), *Liang* (3), *Mei* (3), *Qiao* (3), *Wen* (3), *Xiao* (3), *Min* (2), *Chang, Cho, Shen.*

Meidinger (479) German: habitational name for someone from Meitingen in Württemberg.

GIVEN NAMES German 4%. *Otto* (2), *Gerhardt, Gottfried, Milbert.*

Meidl (177) German: possibly a nickname from Middle High German *meidel* 'young woman', 'female servant'.

Meier (10953) **1.** German, Dutch, Czech, Slovak (**Majer**), and Polish: status name for a tenant farmer, steward, overseer, or village headman, a variant spelling of German MEYER 1. **2.** Jewish (Ashkenazic): variant spelling of the personal name *Meyer* (see MEYER 2). **3.** Danish: occupational name from *meiere* 'reaper', 'harvester'.

GIVEN NAMES German 5%. *Kurt* (28), *Otto* (20), *Hans* (19), *Erwin* (9), *Manfred* (8), *Heinz* (6), *Armin* (5), *Bernhard* (5), *Lorenz* (4), *Franz* (3), *Gerhard* (3), *Helmut* (3).

Meierotto (135) Despite its Italianate appearance, this unusual name is probably German, most likely a variant of MEIER, with the personal name *Otto* tacked on.

Meiers (511) Dutch and North German: patronymic from MEYER.

Meiggs (106) English: variant of MEGGS.

Meighan (339) Irish: variant of MEEHAN, or sometimes of **Meekin**, an Anglicized form of Gaelic **Mac Miadhacháin** 'son of *Miadhachán*', a personal name representing a diminutive of *miadhach* 'honorable'.

Meighen (162) Irish: variant of MEIGHAN.

GIVEN NAME German 4%. *Kurt.*

Meigs (607) English: variant of MEGGS.

Meijer (144) Dutch: variant of MEYER.

GIVEN NAMES Dutch 18%; German 13%; Scandinavian 11%. *Harm* (2), *Adriaan, Cornelis, Derk, Henk, Pieter, Willem; Hans* (3), *Ernst, Inge, Johannes, Otto; Berent, Johan.*

Meikle (616) Scottish: variant of MICKLE.

Meiklejohn (163) Scottish: distinguishing name for the largest or eldest (see MICKLE) of two or more bearers of the personal name JOHN.

Meile (122) Dutch and German: from a short form of any of several Germanic personal names formed with *mag-* 'might' or *māg* 'kinsman' as the first element.

Meili (129) Dutch and German: variant of MEILE.

GIVEN NAMES German 13%. *Kurt* (2), *Otto* (2), *Fritz.*

Meilinger (103) German: habitational name for someone from any of several places named Meiling or Meilingen in Bavaria.

GIVEN NAME Dutch 4%. *Dirk.*

Meiller (119) Americanized form of French MEILLEUR.

Meilleur (131) French: nickname from French *meilleur* 'better', 'best'.

GIVEN NAMES French 17%. *Marcel* (2), *Emile, Euclide, Gilles, Laurent, Marcelle, Muguette, Philippe, Sylvie.*

Mein (237) **1.** German and Dutch: from the Germanic personal name *Maino, Meino*, a short form of the various compound names with a first element *magin* 'strength', 'might', for example MEINHARDT. **2.** German: from a byname from Middle High German *mein* 'mean', 'nasty'. **3.** Scottish: variant of MAIN.

Meinberg (113) German: habitational name from Meinberg in Westphalia.

GIVEN NAMES German 11%. *Erwin* (2), *Juergen, Klaus, Kurt.*

Meincke (159) North German: from a pet form of MEIN.

GIVEN NAMES German 6%. *Arno, Heinz, Otto.*

Meinders (284) North German: patronymic from the personal name *Meinhard* (see MEINERT).

GIVEN NAMES German 5%. *Kuno, Kurt.*

Meindl (187) South German: from a pet form of MEIN.

GIVEN NAMES German 4%. *Aloysius, Johann.*

Meine (181) North German: **1.** variant of MEIN. **2.** habitational name from Meine near Brunswick.

GIVEN NAMES German 5%. *Heinz, Klaus, Kurt.*

Meinecke (399) North German: from a pet form of MEIN.

GIVEN NAMES German 6%. *Gerd* (2), *Gerhard* (2), *Inge* (2), *Kurt* (2), *Eberhard.*

Meineke (165) North German: variant spelling of MEINECKE.

Meinel (102) South German: from a pet form of MEIN 1 or MEINE + the diminutive ending *-el.*

GIVEN NAMES German 12%. *Kurt* (2), *Helmut.*

Meinen (361) **1.** North German: patronymic from MEIN. **2.** German: variant of MEINE 2. **3.** Dutch: metronymic from a feminine form of MEIN.

GIVEN NAMES German 6%. *Kurt* (3), *Dieter, Ernst.*

Meiner (161) German: variant of MEINERT.

Meiners (804) Northern German and Dutch: patronymic from MEINERT.

Meinert (758) Dutch and North German: from the personal name *Meinert* (see MEINHARDT).

Meinhardt (650) German: from the Germanic personal name *Meinhard(t)*, composed of the elements *magin* 'might', 'strength' + *hard* 'hardy', 'brave', 'strong'.

GIVEN NAMES German 4%. *Erwin, Fritz, Hans, Kurt, Otto, Rudi, Wolf.*

Meinhart (218) Variant of German MEINHARDT.

Meinhold (159) German and Dutch: from the Germanic personal name *Meinold*, composed of the elements *magin* 'might', 'strength' + *wald* 'rule'.

GIVEN NAMES German 4%. *Otto, Wilfried.*

Meinholz (182) German: variant of MEINHOLD.

Meininger (435) German: habitational name from Meiningen on the Werra river. The place name is derived from a personal name with *magin* 'might', 'strength' as the first element.

Meinke (662) North German and Dutch: from a pet form of MEIN.

GIVEN NAMES German 5%. *Kurt* (3), *Dieter* (2), *Erwin, Fritz, Hertha, Otto.*

Meinking (106) North German: patronymic from the personal name *Meinke*, pet form of MEIN 1.

GIVEN NAME German 4%. *Ewald.*

Meins (147) German: variant of MEINTS.

GIVEN NAMES German 4%. *Erna, Kurt.*

Meints (373) North German: **1.** patronymic from MEIN. **2.** habitational name from any of several places named Meins or Meinsen.

Meinzer (254) **1.** German: habitational name for someone from any of several places named Meins or Meinsen. **2.** Jewish (Ashkenazic): variant spelling of MAINZER.

GIVEN NAMES German 4%. *Gerhard, Konrad, Otto.*

Meir (166) Jewish (Ashkenazic): variant of MEYER 2.

GIVEN NAMES Jewish 23%. *Itzchak* (2), *Yoav* (2), *Amikam, Aryeh, Asher, Avi, Avner, Avraham, Dror, Eran, Gadi, Itshak.*

Meiring (180) German: habitational name from any of several places called Maiering (Bavaria, Upper Palatinate) or Mairing (Bavaria, Austria).

Meis (551) **1.** German: variant of MEISE. **2.** German: variant of MEISS. **3.** Dutch: from a short form of the personal name *Remeis*, from the Latin personal name *Remigius* (see REMY), which was born by two early medieval bishops in Normandy. **4.** Dutch: from a reduced form of the personal name *Meinso*, a variant of MEIN. **5.** Dutch: possibly a late variant of **Mys** (see MIS), or a metronymic from the personal name *Clemeinse, Clementia*, from the Latin female personal name *Clementia* (meaning 'mercy') or from a derivative of *clemens* 'merciful'.

Meisch (191) Dutch: variant of MAAS.

Meise (217) **1.** German: nickname, probably for someone who was agile, from Middle High German *meise* 'titmouse'; or perhaps in some cases a metonymic occupational name for a fowler (a bird catcher). **2.** German: habitational name from any of several places called Meise or Meisa. **3.** German: occupational name for someone who made panniers or used one in his work, Middle High German *meise*. **4.** Dutch: variant of MEIS 4.

GIVEN NAMES German 6%. *Albrecht, Helmut, Kurt.*

Meisel (853) **1.** German: occupational name from Middle High German *meizel* 'lumberjack', 'wood cutter'. **2.** German: nickname for someone thought to resemble a mouse, from a diminutive of Middle High German *mūs*, German MAUS. **3.** Jewish (Ashkenazic): from the Yiddish personal name *Mayzl*, of uncertain origin.

Meiselman (142) Jewish: elaborated form of MEISEL.

GIVEN NAME Jewish 5%. *Meyer.*

Meisels (228) Jewish: patronymic from MEISEL.

GIVEN NAMES Jewish 36%; German 4%. *Moshe* (6), *Asher* (3), *Zalmen* (3), *Zev* (3), *Bernat* (2), *Chaim* (2), *Hirsch* (2), *Hirsh* (2), *Mendl* (2), *Ruchel* (2), *Sol* (2), *Aryeh*; *Kurt, Manfred.*

Meisenbach (112) German: habitational name from any of several places so named.

GIVEN NAMES German 9%. *Kurt* (2), *Ernst.*

Meisenheimer (455) German: habitational name for someone from Meisenheim in the Palatinate.

Meisenhelder (101) German: habitational name for someone from a place named Maisenhälden, near Neckarsulm.

Meisenzahl (115) German: jocular nickname seemingly meaning 'titmouse tail', from Middle High German *meise* + *zagel*, but it may originally have derived from central German *Meis, Meise* 'cow' when *Meis* also meant 'vulva'.

Meiser (530) German: **1.** occupational name for a fowler, from an agent derivative of MEISE 1. **2.** topographic name for someone who lived in an area where timber had been felled (see MEISS). **3.** habitational name for someone from a place called Mais in Bavaria.

GIVEN NAMES German 4%. *Kurt* (2), *Alois, Manfred.*

Meisinger (492) South German: habitational name for someone from any of several places called Meising in Bavaria.

GIVEN NAMES German 5%. *Alois* (2), *Kurt* (2), *Otto* (2), *Erwin, Jurgen.*

Meisler (183) **1.** Variant of German **Meissler**, an occupational nickname for someone who used a chisel in his work, from Middle High German *meizel* 'chisel' + the agent suffix *-er*, or a nickname for a philanderer, from the same word in the sense 'penis'. **2.** Jewish (Ashkenazic): variant of MEISEL.

GIVEN NAMES Jewish 5%. *Isadore, Miriam.*

Meisner (1432) German and Jewish (Ashkenazic): variant of MEISSNER.

Meiss (136) German: topographic name from Middle High German *meiss* 'felling area', 'felled timber'.

GIVEN NAME German 4%. *Heinz* (2).

Meissner (1698) German and Jewish (Ashkenazic): habitational name from Meissen in Germany, earlier (968 AD) recorded as *Misna, Misina*, named for the small river Misna (today Meisabach), whose name is

very ancient, probably pre-Slavic. The place was famous in the Middle Ages for the fine linen cloth produced there, and the German surname may also be an occupational name for a manufacturer or seller of such wares.

GIVEN NAMES German 6%. *Kurt* (7), *Gerhard* (4), *Erwin* (3), *Hans* (3), *Claus* (2), *Fritz* (2), *Heinz* (2), *Siegfried* (2), *Eldred, Ewald, Hanns, Helmuth.*

Meister (3167) German and Jewish (Ashkenazic): status name for someone who was master of his craft, from Middle High German *meister* 'master' (from Latin *magister*). The surname **Meister** is established throughout central Europe; in Poland it is also spelled **Majster**. As an Ashkenazic Jewish surname it denoted a rabbi as a leading figure in a Jewish community.

GIVEN NAMES German 4%. *Kurt* (13), *Konrad* (3), *Otto* (3), *Fritz* (2), *Hans* (2), *Klaus* (2), *Alois, Bernhard, Dieter, Ewald, Hellmut, Helmut.*

Meitner (114) German: unexplained.

Meitz (134) German: habitational name from any of several places called Meitz or Meitze.

GIVEN NAMES German 6%. *Erwin, Guenter, Siegfried.*

Meitzler (201) German: possibly a variant of **Meissler** (see MEISLER).

Meixell (116) Americanized form of German **Meixl**, a pet form of any of various Germanic personal names formed with *mag-* 'strength' or *Māg* 'kinsman' as the first element.

Meixner (545) German: variant of MEISSNER. This form is frequent also in central and eastern Europe, especially in Bohemia.

GIVEN NAMES German 4%. *Alois, Gerhard, Helmut, Joerg, Kurt.*

Meixsell (108) Probably of German origin: unexplained. Compare MEIXELL.

Mejia (6474) Spanish (**Mejía**): probably from a religious byname (possibly under Jewish influence), from a vernacular form of Latin, Greek *Messias* 'Messiah', from Hebrew *māšīaḥ* 'anointed'.

GIVEN NAMES Spanish 55%; Portuguese 13%. *Jose* (233), *Juan* (118), *Carlos* (82), *Luis* (80), *Manuel* (63), *Francisco* (62), *Miguel* (44), *Mario* (40), *Jesus* (39), *Jorge* (39), *Pedro* (35), *Rafael* (32); *Adauto, Anabela, Batista, Catarina, Lidio, Marcio, Wenceslao.*

Mejias (454) Spanish (**Mejías**): variant of **Mejía** (see MEJIA).

GIVEN NAMES Spanish 47%. *Jose* (10), *Juan* (8), *Angel* (7), *Rafael* (7), *Luis* (6), *Manuel* (5), *Fernando* (4), *Francisco* (3), *Mario* (3), *Pedro* (3), *Roberto* (3), *Aida* (2); *Antonio* (3), *Carmelo* (2), *Aldo, Angelo, Dario.*

Meka (111) Indian (Andhra Pradesh): Hindu name from Telugu *mēka* 'goat'.

GIVEN NAMES Indian 21%. *Hari* (2), *Seshagiri* (2), *Chandra, Jayasree, Mallika, Prasad, Rama, Rukmini.*

Mekeel (152) Origin unidentified. Possibly a much altered form of Irish MCHALE.

Mekelburg (153) German: altered form of **Meckelburg**, variant of MECKLENBURG.
GIVEN NAMES German 4%. *Gerhard, Helmut.*

Mekonnen (121) Ethiopian: unexplained.
GIVEN NAMES Ethiopian 72%. *Mesfin* (4), *Getachew* (3), *Teferi* (3), *Amare* (2), *Mehari* (2), *Melaku* (2), *Tesfaye* (2), *Admasu, Alem, Alemayehu, Ashenafi, Ayele.*

Melamed (497) Jewish (Ashkenazic and Sephardic): Hebrew occupational name for a primary school teacher.
GIVEN NAMES Jewish 25%; Russian 11%. *Chaim* (3), *Aron* (2), *Hyman* (2), *Ilya* (2), *Moisey* (2), *Asher, Avraham, Doron, Hedva, Ilan, Isadore, Isidor; Boris* (6), *Igor* (3), *Semyon* (3), *Yefim* (3), *Leonid* (2), *Vladimir* (2), *Aleksandr, Dmitry, Efim, Gennady, Grigoriy, Lev; Mordecai.*

Melancon (2317) French: nickname from a dialect word meaning 'melancholic'.
GIVEN NAMES French 7%. *Antoine* (6), *Andre* (4), *Gilles* (4), *Monique* (4), *Clovis* (2), *Elrick* (2), *Gillis* (2), *Yves* (2), *Alcee, Alphe, Camille, Cecile.*

Meland (356) Norwegian: habitational name from any of numerous farmsteads in southwestern Norway so named from Old Norse *Meðalland* 'the mid land'.
GIVEN NAMES Scandinavian 6%. *Nils* (2), *Erik, Nels, Selmer, Thor.*

Melander (424) **1.** German: from a humanist translation of *Schwarzmann* 'black man' into a Greek compound derived from *melas* 'black' + *anēr* 'man', 'male', genitive *andros*. **2.** Swedish: either the same as 1, or an ornamental name composed of the elements *Mel-*, an unexplained element of Swedish place names, + *-ander*, a popular learned surname suffix, taken from Greek *andr-* 'man'.
GIVEN NAME German 5%. *Kurt* (5).

Melanson (1797) Possibly of English origin; unexplained.
GIVEN NAMES French 6%. *Armand* (7), *Alcide* (2), *Andre* (2), *Normand* (2), *Alphee, Alphonse, Amedee, Antoine, Arsene, Benoit, Eloi, Euclide.*

Melara (248) Italian: unexplained.
GIVEN NAMES Spanish 51%; Portuguese 17%. *Jose* (13), *Carlos* (9), *Jorge* (8), *Ricardo* (4), *Julio* (3), *Leticia* (3), *Manuel* (3), *Corina* (2), *Humberto* (2), *Jorge Alberto* (2), *Luis* (2), *Marta* (2); *Ligia.*

Melaragno (139) Italian: unexplained.
GIVEN NAMES Italian 24%. *Antonio* (3), *Mario* (3), *Aldo* (2), *Angelo, Benigno, Biagio, Dino, Edoardo, Emidio, Enrico, Luca, Pasquale, Renzo, Sabatino.*

Melber (119) **1.** South German: occupational name for a miller or flour merchant, from an agent derivative of Middle High German *mel* (genitive *melwes*) 'flour'. **2.** Jewish: unexplained.
GIVEN NAMES Jewish 7%. *Shmuel, Yaakov.*

Melberg (192) **1.** Norwegian: habitational name from a farm name in southwestern Norway, originally *Meðalberg* in Old Norse, from *meðal* 'middle' + *berg* 'rock', 'hill', 'cliff'. **2.** Swedish: possibly an ornamental name with the same etymology as 1, or from an unexplained first element (perhaps a place name element) + *berg* 'mountain', 'hill'.
GIVEN NAMES Scandinavian 7%; German 4%. *Carsten, Nils; Fritz, Guenter.*

Melbourne (229) English (mainly East Midlands): habitational name from any of various places. Melbourne in former East Yorkshire is recorded in Domesday Book as *Middelburne*, from Old English *middel* 'middle' + *burna* 'stream'; the first element was later replaced by the cognate Old Norse *meðal*. Melbourne in Derbyshire has as its first element Old English *mylen* 'mill', and Melbourn in Cambridgeshire probably Old English *melde* 'milds', a type of plant.

Melby (1109) Norwegian: habitational name from any of about 25 farmsteads in eastern Norway, originally named *Meðalbýr* in Old Norse, from *meðal* 'middle' + *býr* 'farmstead'.
GIVEN NAMES Scandinavian 4%. *Alf, Erik, Lars, Nils, Thor, Thoralf.*

Melbye (145) Variant of Norwegian MELBY.
GIVEN NAME Scandinavian 5%. *Hartvig.*

Melcer (110) **1.** Jewish (from Poland and Lithuania); also Polish and Czech: Slavic spelling of German MELTZER 'maltster'. **2.** Catalan: variant of the occupational name MERCER.
GIVEN NAMES Jewish 8%; Spanish 4%. *Chaim, Rivky; Enrique* (2), *Carlos, Jacobo, Miguel.*

Melcher (1990) German and Dutch: variant of MELCHIOR. This name also occurs frequently in central Europe, especially Bohemia.

Melchert (405) German and Dutch: variant of MELCHIOR.
GIVEN NAMES German 5%. *Bernhard, Elke, Otto, Reinhardt, Udo, Willi.*

Melchi (105) Hispanic (Mexican and Central America): unexplained. Possibly from a short form of MELCHIOR.

Melching (178) South German: habitational name from Melchingen in Württemberg.
GIVEN NAME German 6%. *Kurt.*

Melchior (584) German, Danish, Dutch, Spanish, Portuguese, and French: from the personal name *Melchior* (a derivative of Hebrew *melech* 'king' + *or* 'light', 'splendor'). This was in use as a slightly unusual personal name throughout the Middle Ages, having been ascribed in popular Christian tradition to one of the Magi. The surname is also borne by Ashkenazic Jews, in which case it is an adoption of the German surname.

Melchiori (117) Italian: from a patronymic or plural form of MELCHIORRE.

GIVEN NAMES Italian 8%. *Dario* (2), *Remo* (2), *Aldo, Enrico, Ugo.*

Melchiorre (309) Italian: from the personal name *Melchiorre*, Italian equivalent of MELCHIOR.
GIVEN NAMES Italian 13%. *Domenico* (2), *Angelo, Antonio, Camillo, Carlo, Carmine, Cosmo, Deno, Donato, Giovanna, Rocco.*

Melchor (620) Spanish and Dutch: from a variant of the personal name MELCHIOR.
GIVEN NAMES Spanish 45%. *Jose* (16), *Juan* (8), *Pedro* (7), *Carlos* (6), *Francisco* (5), *Luis* (5), *Miguel* (5), *Ignacio* (4), *Manuel* (4), *Raul* (4), *Alfredo* (3), *Fidel* (3).

Meldahl (119) Swedish: ornamental name composed of possibly a place name element, as in Mellby, which could be from Old Norse *meðal* 'mid(dle)' + *dahl*, an ornamental spelling of *dal* 'valley'.
GIVEN NAME Jewish 4%. *Meyer.*

Melde (135) South German: occupational name from a derivative of Middle High German *melden* 'to announce or proclaim'.
GIVEN NAME German 9%. *Gerhard.*

Melder (294) German: occupational name from Middle High German *mëldære* 'town crier', 'carrier of news', also applied as a nickname for a gossip or a traitor.
GIVEN NAMES German 4%. *Hans* (2), *Fritz, Johannes.*

Meldrum (815) Scottish: habitational name from a place in Aberdeenshire, first recorded in 1291 as *Melgedrom*, from an obscure first element + Gaelic *druim* 'ridge'.

Mele (1476) **1.** Southern Italian: affectionate nickname from *mele* 'honey', a dialect form of *miele*. **2.** Italian: possibly a habitational name from Mele in Genoa province. **3.** French (southeastern): topographic name for someone who lived by a medlar, Old French *mesle*. **4.** Norwegian (**Mæle**): variant of **Mæhle** (see MEHLE).
GIVEN NAMES Italian 17%. *Angelo* (11), *Rocco* (8), *Salvatore* (7), *Dante* (5), *Sal* (5), *Carmine* (4), *Nicola* (3), *Vito* (3), *Antonio* (2), *Carmela* (2), *Domenic* (2), *Mauro* (2).

Melear (145) Origin unidentified.

Melena (125) Spanish and Portuguese: probably a nickname from *melena*, a term denoting a piece of leather placed on the horns of an ox so that the yoke would not harm them, possibly applied to someone in charge of an ox as a draft animal. By extension, *melena* came to mean 'mane' and 'long hair', probably applied to someone with long or untidy hair.
GIVEN NAMES Spanish 31%. *Jose* (3), *Efrain* (2), *Adan, Alvaro, Ana, Angel, Angelina, Aurelio, Blanca, Caridad, Carolina, Consuelo.*

Melendez (4926) Spanish (**Meléndez**): variant of **Menéndez** (see MENENDEZ).
GIVEN NAMES Spanish 47%; Portuguese 12%. *Jose* (163), *Carlos* (72), *Juan* (69), *Luis* (53), *Manuel* (47), *Angel* (41), *Jorge* (36), *Miguel* (36), *Pedro* (29), *Francisco* (27),

Roberto (27), *Mario* (26); *Anabela, Ligia, Wenceslao.*

Melendrez (402) Galician: variant of **Menéndez** (see MENENDEZ).
GIVEN NAMES Spanish 38%. *Manuel* (11), *Jesus* (6), *Jose* (4), *Juan* (4), *Alfredo* (3), *Arturo* (3), *Pedro* (3), *Adolfo* (2), *Angel* (2), *Florentino* (2), *Joaquin* (2), *Juanita* (2).

Melendy (345) Of Scottish, Welsh, or English origin, but uncertain etymology. It is recorded in the 17th century in Scotland and subsequently in Boldre, Hampshire. Most probably it is a habitational name from Welsh *melin* 'mill' + *dy*, lenited form of *ty* 'house'. Place names of Welsh origin are found not only in Wales and western England, but also in southern Scotland, where Welsh was spoken in earlier centuries.

Melerine (131) Probably of French origin: unexplained. This is a Louisiana name.
GIVEN NAME French 4%. *Emile.*

Melero (166) Spanish: occupational name for a collector or seller of honey, *melero* (Late Latin *mellarius*, an agent derivative of *mel*, genitive *mellis*, 'honey').
GIVEN NAMES Spanish 53%. *Jose* (5), *Francisco* (4), *Alicia* (2), *Jaime* (2), *Javier* (2), *Juan* (2), *Manuel* (2), *Mario* (2), *Salvador* (2), *Alfredo, Alvarado, Anastacio.*

Meleski (200) Polish: unexplained; possibly a variant of MALESKI.
GIVEN NAMES Polish 5%. *Casimir, Zygmunt.*

Melfi (373) Southern Italian: habitational name from a place so named in Potenza province.
GIVEN NAMES Italian 14%. *Vito* (4), *Pasquale* (2), *Antonio, Carmela, Dino, Riccardo, Romeo, Sabatino.*

Melgaard (172) **1.** Norwegian: habitational name from any of several farmsteads in eastern Norway named Melgård, from Old Norse *Meðalgarðr*, a compound of *meðal* 'mid(dle)' + *garðr* 'farmstead', 'dwelling', 'enclosure'. **2.** Danish: habitational name from a farmstead named with the same elements as 1.
GIVEN NAMES Scandinavian 17%. *Bjorn* (2), *Erik, Juel, Nels.*

Melgar (530) **1.** Spanish: topographic name for someone who lived by a field of lucerne, Spanish *melgar* (a collective derivative of *mielga* 'lucerne', Late Latin *melica*, for classical Latin *Medica (herba)* 'plant' from Media). There are several places in Spain named with this word, and the surname may be a habitational name from any one of them. **2.** Dutch: variant of MELCHIOR.
GIVEN NAMES Spanish 56%; Portuguese 14%. *Jose* (24), *Carlos* (13), *Juan* (10), *Roberto* (6), *Ana* (4), *Blanca* (4), *Cesar* (4), *Francisco* (4), *Julio* (4), *Luis* (4), *Miguel* (4), *Pedro* (4); *Godofredo* (2).

Melgarejo (119) Spanish: unexplained.
GIVEN NAMES Spanish 54%. *Jose* (5), *Enrique* (2), *Francisca* (2), *Gerardo* (2), *Mario* (2),

Pablo (2), *Rafael* (2), *Rodolfo* (2), *Adolfo, Alfredo, Ana, Ana Paula; Federico.*

Melgoza (380) Spanish: **1.** probably an altered spelling of *Melgosa*, which Tibón treats as a derivative of MELGAR. **2.** habitational name from *Melgosa*, in Cuenca province.
GIVEN NAMES Spanish 53%. *Jose* (10), *Rafael* (9), *Arturo* (6), *Manuel* (6), *Jesus* (5), *Ruben* (5), *Gerardo* (4), *Jaime* (4), *Luis* (4), *Salvador* (4), *Alberto* (3), *Alfonso* (3); *Antonio* (2), *Federico* (2), *Carmel, Dino, Gabriella, Heriberto, Leonardo, Mario Antonio, Rosaria.*

Melhorn (397) German: variant of MEHL-HORN.
GIVEN NAMES German 5%. *Otto* (2), *Dieter, Erwin, Helmut.*

Melhus (106) Norwegian: **1.** habitational name from the name of several farmsteads in Trøndelag, named with *mel* 'middle' + *hus* 'house', i.e. 'the house (or farm) in the middle'. **2.** spelling variant of **Mjølhus**, a habitational name from any of seven places (in Rogaland, for instance), named with Old Norse *mjøl* 'flour' + *hus* 'house'

Meli (455) Italian: **1.** patronymic or plural form of the personal name *Melo*, a short form of *Carmelo* or some other personal name ending in *-melo*. **2.** from a medieval Greek personal name, MELIS, or an affectionate nickname from Sicilian *meli* 'honey'.
GIVEN NAMES Italian 24%. *Salvatore* (8), *Angelo* (3), *Carmelo* (3), *Ernesto* (3), *Sal* (2), *Antonio, Cosmo, Domenica, Francesco, Giuseppe, Ignazio, Mariano, Mario, Pietro, Renaldo, Rosario, Santo.*

Melia (615) **1.** Southern Italian: habitational name from any of various places in Sicily and southern Italy named Melia, as for example in the provinces of Messina or Reggio Calabria. **2.** Italian: possibly from a short form of the female personal name *Amelia.* **3.** Irish: variant of MALLEY. **4.** Dutch: from a derivative of the Latin personal name *Amelius, Amilius* (see MEHLE). **5.** Catalan (**Melià**): from the Latin personal name *Aemilianus.* **6.** Georgian: from a Georgian local name.

Melichar (296) Czech: from a vernacular form of the personal name MELCHIOR.

Melick (549) Dutch (**(van) Melick**): habitational name from Melick in Dutch Limburg.

Melikian (195) Armenian: patronymic from Turkish *melik* 'ruler', from Arabic *malik* 'king'.
GIVEN NAMES Armenian 15%; French 4%. *Armen* (4), *Ashod* (2), *Karnig* (2), *Aram, Arax, Ardemis, Garbis, Garen, Garnik, Haig, Takvor, Zaven; Andre, Odette.*

Melillo (896) Southern Italian: **1.** from a pet form of MELI. **2.** from the Neapolitan dialect word *melillo* 'crab apple', hence a nickname, possibly for someone with a sour disposition, a topographic name, or a

metonymic occupational name for a grower or seller of apples. **3.** possibly a regularized form of Melilli, a habitational name from a place so named in Siracusa, Sicily.
GIVEN NAMES Italian 14%. *Angelo* (6), *Carmine* (3), *Rocco* (3), *Domenic* (2), *Lorenzo* (2), *Pasquale* (2), *Salvatore* (2), *Antonello, Antonio, Bartolomeo, Carmela, Elio.*

Melin (823) **1.** Swedish: probably an ornamental name composed of the place name element *mel* from Old Norse *meðal* 'mid(dle)' + the common surname suffix *-(l)in*, from Latin *-(l)inius.* **2.** French: from a short form of the personal name *Amelin.* **3.** French: habitational name from places in Haute-Saône and Côte d'Or, all named with the dialect word *melin* 'mill', from Latin *molinum.* **4.** Breton: topographic name for someone who lived at a mill or an occupational nickname for a miller, from *milin, melin* 'mill'. **5.** Czech (**Melín**): derivative of the personal name *Melichar* (see MELCHIOR). **6.** Slovenian (eastern Slovenia): unexplained.
GIVEN NAMES Scandinavian 4%. *Alvar* (2), *Anders* (2), *Hilmer* (2), *Hiltrud, Sven.*

Meline (231) French: from a shortened feminine form of the personal name *Amelin.*

Meling (114) Norwegian: habitational name from any of six farmsteads so named in southwestern Norway, probably from the unattested Old Norse place name *Miðlingr* 'the farm in the middle'.
GIVEN NAME Scandinavian 9%. *Per* (2).

Melino (105) Italian: from the personal name *Melino*, probably a short form of *Carmelino* or *Amelinus.*
GIVEN NAMES Italian 8%. *Angelo, Dino.*

Melis (134) **1.** English: variant spelling of MELLIS 1. **2.** German: variant of MELIUS. **3.** Dutch (**(van) Melis**): variant of MILLIS 2. **4.** Czech and Slovak (**Meliš**), and Hungarian: from a short form of the Biblical personal name *Melichar* (see MELCHIOR). **5.** Greek: from the personal name *Melis*, a pet form of *Meletios* or *Meliton* (names of various early saints and martyrs). The personal names are derived from either *meli* 'honey' or *meletan* 'care for', 'study'. **6.** Italian (Sardinia and southern Italy): habitational name from a place so named in Sardinia. **7.** Lithuanian: nickname from *melis* 'blue'. **8.** Latvian: unflattering nickname from *melis* 'liar'. **9.** Latvian: variant of MELLIS.

Melita (140) Italian: from *Melita*, the Latin name for Malta, hence an ethnic name for someone from Malta or someone with trade or other connections with the island. This has beena family name since Byzantine times.
GIVEN NAMES Italian 19%. *Salvatore* (3), *Alfio, Carmela, Orazio, Rosaria, Santo.*

Melito (266) Southern Italian: habitational name from Melito di Napoli in Naples province, Melito Irpino in Avellino, or

Melito Porto Salvo in Reggio Calabria, which takes its name from the Melito river, from Greek *potamos tou melitos* 'river of honey'.
GIVEN NAMES Italian 21%. *Angelo* (3), *Calogero, Carmelo, Carmine, Giacomo, Mario, Orlando, Salvatore, Vito.*

Melius (457) German: from the personal name *Amelius* (see MEHLE 2).

Melka (150) Polish and Czech: from *melka* 'half-ground grain', hence an metonymic occupational name for a miller or a nickname from the same word in Polish dialect denoting a flour soup.
GIVEN NAMES French 5%. *Gabrielle, Philippe.*

Melko (142) Slovak: from a pet form of the personal name MELCHIOR.

Melkonian (292) Armenian: patronymic from the personal name *Mel'kon*, Armenian form of MELCHIOR.
GIVEN NAMES Armenian 34%. *Ara* (4), *Armen* (4), *Avedis* (2), *Garo* (2), *Haik* (2), *Nejdeh* (2), *Nerses* (2), *Zareh* (2), *Zaven* (2), *Agob, Anahid, Anahit.*

Mell (750) **1.** English: variant of MILL. **2.** German: variant of MELLE.

Mella (206) Galician and Basque: habitational name from Mella or La Mella in La Coruña province, Galicia, or from La Mella in Biscay, Basque Country.
GIVEN NAMES Spanish 25%; Italian 9%. *Jose* (5), *Salvador* (3), *Americo* (2), *Ana* (2), *Enrique* (2), *Luis* (2), *Asuncion, Bartolome, Carlos, Eduvigis, Evangelina, Francisco; Dante* (3), *Carmine* (2), *Carlo, Raffaele, Romeo.*

Mellado (117) Spanish: nickname from *mellado* 'nicked', for someone who missed one or more teeth, from *mellar* 'to nick'.
GIVEN NAMES Spanish 49%. *Jose* (4), *Luis* (4), *Manuel* (3), *Carlos* (2), *Gustavo* (2), *Rafael* (2), *Alicia, Ana, Bernando, Cesar, Claudio, Edmundo.*

Melland (220) Norwegian: variant of MELAND.

Mellard (123) English: variant of MILLWARD.

Mellas (106) **1.** English and Scottish: unexplained. Perhaps a variant spelling of MALLIS. **2.** Greek: occupational name for a seller of honey, from *meli* 'honey' + the agent noun suffix *-as*.

Mellberg (136) Swedish: see MELBERG.
GIVEN NAME Scandinavian 4%. *Alf.*

Melle (187) **1.** North German: habitational name from Melle near Osnabrück, earlier *Menele*, probably from Old Saxon *gimēni* 'public' + *lō* 'woods'. **2.** Dutch and Belgian (**van Melle**): habitational name from places in East Flanders and North Brabant. **3.** Galician: habitational name from a village so named in Lugo province, Galicia. **4.** French: metonymic occupational name from Old French *melle* 'buckle', 'ring'. **5.** French: habitation from Melle-sur-Béronne in Deux-Sèvres.

GIVEN NAMES German 5%. *Heinz, Horst, Kurt, Otto.*

Mellem (161) Norwegian: habitational name from any of several farmsteads in eastern Norway, so named from *mellom* 'between', i.e. a farmstead situated between two others.

Mellema (255) Frisian: unexplained.
GIVEN NAMES Dutch 4%. *Dirk* (2), *Gerrit, Gerritt.*

Mellen (1099) Dutch: variant of MELIN.

Mellencamp (110) Belgian and northern French: Dutch-influenced variant of **Millecamp**, a habitational name for someone who lived in a house 'amid the fields' (northern French dialect *mi les camps*).

Mellenthin (121) German: habitational name from places so called near Berlin and on the island of Usedom.
GIVEN NAMES German 7%. *Eldor, Frieda.*

Meller (539) **1.** Americanized form of German **Möller** (see MOELLER). **2.** German: habitational name for someone from MELLE. **3.** German, Jewish (Ashkenazic), and Polish: occupational name for a miller or flour merchant, from an agent derivative of German *Mehl* 'flour'. **4.** English: variant of MILLER.
GIVEN NAMES German 5%; Jewish 4%. *Uwe* (2), *Alois, Armin, Bernd, Dieter, Erwin, Hartmann, Manfred, Nikolaus, Ute; Arie, Baruch, Emanuel, Gershon, Ilya, Moisey, Moshe, Sol.*

Mellert (132) German: probably a variant of MELLER 3.
GIVEN NAMES German 4%. *Konrad* (2), *Erwin.*

Mellett (233) Irish: variant of MILLETT.
GIVEN NAME Irish 6%. *Jarlath.*

Mellette (123) French: **1.** variant of MILLET. **2.** altered spelling of Irish MELLETT.
GIVEN NAMES French 4%. *Monique, Patrice.*

Melley (157) Variant spelling of Irish **Melly**, an Anglicized form of Gaelic **Ó Meallaigh**, from *meall* 'pleasant'.
GIVEN NAME Irish 6%. *Brendan.*

Mellgren (147) Swedish: ornamental name composed of the elements *Mel-* (probably a place name element meaning 'middle') + *gren* 'branch'.
GIVEN NAME Scandinavian 12%. *Erik.*

Mellick (222) Variant spelling of Dutch MELICK.

Mellies (121) German: variant of MELIUS.
GIVEN NAME German 5%. *Wolfgang.*

Mellin (440) **1.** English: variant of MELVILLE. **2.** German: from any of various places so called.

Melling (366) **1.** English (Lancashire): habitational name from places near Lancaster and near Liverpool. Both are probably so called from the Old English tribal name *Me(a)llingas* 'people of *Mealla*'. **2.** English: variant of MELVILLE. **3.** German: habitational name from a place called Mellingen (see MELLINGER).

Mellinger (1349) German: habitational name for someone from Mellingen in Thuringia and Aargau or Möllingen in Hesse-Nassau.

Mellis (196) **1.** English: habitational name from a place in Suffolk, named in Old English with *mylenas*, plural of *mylen* 'mill'. **2.** Scottish and northern Irish (of Scottish origin): from an Anglicized form of the Gaelic personal name *Maol Íosa* 'devotee of Jesus'. **3.** Greek: variant of MELIS. **4.** Dutch: unexplained. **5.** Latvian: nickname from *mells* 'black'.
GIVEN NAMES Greek 5%. *Spiro* (2), *Christos, Spero.*

Mellish (211) **1.** English: habitational name from Melhuish in Devon, so called from Old English *mǣl(e)* 'brightly colored', 'flowery' + *hīwisc* 'hide' (a measurement of land). **2.** Scottish: variant of MELLIS 2.

Mellman (159) **1.** German (**Mellmann**): variant of MELLE 2, with the addition of Middle High German *man* 'man'. **2.** Swedish: probably of German origin or an ornamental compound of *Mel-* (probably a place name element meaning 'middle') + *man* 'man'. **3.** Jewish (Ashkenazic): variant of MELLER 2.
GIVEN NAMES Jewish 7%. *Miriam, Myer.*

Mello (3860) **1.** Italian: probably from a short form of a personal name ending with the hypocoristic suffix *-ello*, such as *Giacomello*. **2.** Portuguese: variant spelling of MELO. **3.** Dutch and Belgian (**van Mello**): habitational name from Mellelo, a place named for a wood near Melle in East Flanders (see MELLE 3) + *lo* 'grove'.
GIVEN NAMES Spanish 8%; Portuguese 5%. *Manuel* (95), *Jose* (12), *Carlos* (7), *Adelino* (5), *Ana* (4), *Joaquin* (4), *Acacio* (3), *Claudio* (3), *Cristina* (3), *Fernando* (3), *Americo* (2), *Enrique* (2); *Duarte* (2), *Joaquim* (2), *Armanda, Joao, Paulo, Serafim.*

Mellon (1700) **1.** Northern Irish: shortened Anglicized form of Gaelic **Ó Mealláin** 'descendant of *Meallán*', a personal name that is a diminutive of *meall* 'pleasant'. **2.** English (of Norman origin): habitational name from Meulan in Seine-et-Oise. **3.** Dutch (**van Mellon**): habitational name from Millun bij Keulen.
FOREBEARS Thomas and Sarah Jane Mellon came to Pittsburgh, PA, from Lower Castletown, Tyrone, Ireland, in 1818. Their grandson, the industrialist and financier Andrew William Mellon (1855–1937) is remembered not only as a businessman but also as an art collector. He served as secretary of the Treasury from 1921 to 1932.

Mellone (126) Italian: from an augmentative of MELLO.
GIVEN NAMES Italian 13%. *Antonio, Emidio, Luigi, Pasquale.*

Mellor (1475) English: habitational name from places in Lancashire, West Yorkshire, and Derbyshire, earlier recorded as *Melver*, and named from ancient British words that are ancestors of Welsh *moel* 'bare' + *bre* 'hill'.

Mellott (1585) Irish: variant of MILLETT.

Mellow (289) English (Cornwall): perhaps a variant of MELLOR.

Melloy (166) **1.** Variant spelling of Irish MALLOY. **2.** Variant spelling of Norwegian **Meløy** (see MELOY).

Mells (108) English: topographic name for someone who lived in a place where there was more than one mill, Middle English *melles* 'mills', or habitational name for someone from Mells in Somerset, named with this word.

Mellum (141) Norwegian: variant of MELLEM.

Melman (208) **1.** Jewish (Ashkenazic): variant of MELLER 2. **2.** Dutch: variant of MELLE 2. **3.** Altered spelling of German **Mellmann** (see MELLMAN).
GIVEN NAMES Jewish 13%; Russian 4%. *Avi, Itta, Jakov, Meyer, Yakov, Zelig*; *Arkady, Gennadiy, Mikhail, Yefim.*

Melms (124) North German: probably a topographic name, from Low German *melm* 'dust', 'sand'.

Melnick (1354) Americanized or Germanized spelling of MELNIK.

Melnik (417) **1.** Jewish (eastern Ashkenazic): occupational name from Russian *melnik* 'miller' (from *melit* 'to grind'). **2.** Polish: habitational name for someone from a place called Mielnik. **3.** Polish: occupational name from *mielnik* 'miller'.
GIVEN NAMES Russian 16%; Jewish 8%. *Vladimir* (7), *Nikolay* (3), *Anatoliy* (2), *Anatoly* (2), *Dmitry* (2), *Galina* (2), *Leonid* (2), *Mikhail* (2), *Oleg* (2), *Raisa* (2), *Vladmir* (2), *Dmitri*; *Semen* (2), *Moshe, Yosef, Zalman, Zvi.*

Melnikoff (105) Russian and Jewish (from Ukraine and Belarus): alternative spelling of **Melnikov**, a patronymic from MELNIK.
GIVEN NAMES Jewish 12%. *Meyer* (2), *Sol.*

Melnyk (500) Jewish (eastern Ashkenazic): variant spelling of MELNIK.

Melo (1138) Portuguese: habitational name from any of numerous places named with Portuguese *merlo* 'blackbird' (Latin *merulus*).
GIVEN NAMES Spanish 40%; Portuguese 19%. *Manuel* (46), *Jose* (42), *Luis* (21), *Francisco* (12), *Carlos* (11), *Juan* (9), *Jorge* (8), *Mario* (7), *Fernando* (5), *Julio* (5), *Luiz* (5), *Raul* (5); *Joao* (9), *Paulo* (5), *Agostinho* (2), *Albano, Goncalo, Guilherme, Joaquim, Vasco*; *Antonio* (37), *Angelo* (3), *Constantino* (2), *Federico* (2), *Vitorino* (2), *Caio, Egidio, Eliseo, Luciano, Rocco, Salvatore, Silvio.*

Meloche (301) Respelling of French **Maloche**, probably a habitational name from Les Malochets in Allier or alternatively a variant of **Malosse**, also a habitational name, from a place so named in Chaudey-

rolles in Haute-Loire or from La Malosse in Seine-et-Marne.
GIVEN NAMES French 8%. *Gilles, Jacques, Lucien, Michel, Yvon.*

Melody (347) Irish: Anglicized form of Gaelic **Ó Maoiléidigh** 'descendant of *Maoléidigh*', a byname composed of the elements *maol* 'chief' + *éidigh* 'ugly'.

Melone (622) Southern Italian: **1.** from an augmentative of MELI or of the personal name *Melo* (see MELI). **2.** metonymic occupational name for a grower or seller of melons, from Calabrese *melune* or Sicilian *miluni* 'melon'.
GIVEN NAMES Italian 8%. *Antonio* (2), *Gino* (2), *Angelo, Benedetta, Carlo, Domenic, Domenico, Guido, Marco, Pasco, Remo, Rocco.*

Meloni (263) Italian: patronymic from MELONE.
GIVEN NAMES Italian 15%. *Salvatore* (2), *Antonio, Domenic, Edoardo, Francesca, Francesco, Giorgio, Luigi, Maurizio, Piero, Umberto, Vito.*

Melott (152) **1.** Of French origin: variant of MARLETT. **2.** Irish: variant of MILLETT.

Meloy (640) **1.** Norwegian (**Meløy**): habitational name from any of several farmsteads on islands so named, from Old Norse *meðal* 'middle' (or *melr* 'sandbank', 'gravel bank') + *øy* 'island'. **2.** Norwegian (**Mjøløy**): habitational name from a farmstead named with *mjøl* 'flour', 'sand' + *øy* 'island'. **3.** Irish: variant of MALLOY.

Melquist (154) Swedish: ornamental name composed of either *mell-* (from the place name element meaning 'middle') or *mäl-* (also a place name element, an altered form of *mal* 'gravel') + *quist*, an old or ornamental spelling of *kvist* 'twig'.

Melrose (518) Scottish: habitational name from a place near Galashiels in the Scottish Borders, so named from British words that were ancestors of Welsh *moel* 'bare', 'barren' + *rhos* 'moor', 'heath'. The Breton and Irish equivalents of the second element mean 'promontory', and this may also have been the sense here.

Melroy (147) Variant of Irish MULROY.
GIVEN NAME French 5%. *Philippe.*

Melsheimer (112) French (Alsatian): habitational name from a place called Melsheim in Alsace.

Melson (1439) English: **1.** patronymic from the personal name *Miles* (of Norman origin but uncertain derivation; possibly related to *Michael* or Latin *miles* 'soldier', or even the Slavic name element *mil* 'grace', 'favor'), or a metronymic from the female personal name *Milla*. **2.** metronymic from the old female personal name *Milde, Milda*, from Old English *milde* 'mild', 'gentle'.

Melton (16660) Northern English: habitational name from any of various places, for example in Leicestershire, Lincolnshire, Norfolk, and Yorkshire, all of which have the same origin as MIDDLETON, with Old

English *middel* replaced by its Old Norse equivalent *meðal* after the Scandinavian settlement of northern and eastern England.

Meltz (207) Eastern German: habitational name from Melz in Mecklenburg.

Meltzer (1866) German and Jewish (Ashkenazic): occupational name for a maltster, a brewer who used malt, from German *Meltzer* (an agent derivative of Middle High German *malt* 'malt', 'germinated barley'), Yiddish *meltser* 'maltster'. This surname is also established in Poland.
GIVEN NAMES Jewish 6%. *Hyman* (4), *Meyer* (3), *Sol* (2), *Yaakov* (2), *Ari, Benzion, Gilat, Hillel, Isadore, Mayer, Oded, Rimma.*

Melucci (161) Italian: from a derivative of the personal name *Melo* (see MELI).
GIVEN NAMES Italian 18%; German 4%. *Remo* (3), *Antonio* (2), *Evo* (2), *Antonietta, Cosmo, Elio, Francesco, Pasquale, Salvatore*; *Otto, Rainer.*

Melugin (180) Origin unidentified.

Melville (1586) **1.** Scottish (of Norman origin): habitational name from any of the various places in Normandy called Malleville, from Latin *mala* 'bad' + *ville* 'settlement'. **2.** Irish (mainly Ulster): English surname adopted by bearers of Gaelic **Ó Maoilmhichíl** 'descendant of *Maoilmhichíl*', a personal name meaning 'devotee of (Saint) Michael'.
FOREBEARS The American novelist Herman Melville (1819–91) was a descendant of the Scottish Melvilles. His maternal grandfather was the revolutionary war general Peter Gansevoort (b. 1749 in Albany, NY). His paternal grandfather was Maj. Thomas Melville of Boston. Irish bearers of the name claim descent from Maol Mhichíl, a chief of Síol Muireadhaigh (Co. Roscommon) in the 9th century.

Melvin (6510) **1.** Scottish: Anglicized form of Gaelic **Mac Gille Bheathain** (see MCILWAINE). **2.** Scottish: variant of MELVILLE 1. **3.** Irish: Anglicized form of Gaelic **Ó Maoil Mhín** 'descendant of the devotee of *Maoilmhín*', a personal name meaning 'gentle chieftain'.

Melzer (721) German and Jewish (Ashkenazic): variant of MELTZER 'maltster'.
GIVEN NAMES German 5%. *Kurt* (3), *Otto* (2), *Berthold, Erhardt, Frieda, Helmut, Klaus, Manfred, Walburga.*

Membreno (156) Hispanic: unexplained.
GIVEN NAMES Spanish 54%. *Jose* (11), *Luis* (3), *Mario* (3), *Carlos* (2), *Francisco* (2), *Juan* (2), *Manuel* (2), *Mauricio* (2), *Miguel* (2), *Adela, Agustin, Alberto.*

Memmer (268) German: **1.** Frisian habitational name for someone from the island of Memmert, between Borkum and Juist (in the North Sea). **2.** reduced form of the personal name *Meinhart* (see MEINHARDT).

Memmott (285) English (Sheffield): of uncertain origin; perhaps a variant of MINETTE.

Memoli (166) Italian: **1.** patronymic or plural form of a pet form of the personal name **Guglielmo**, Italian form of WILLIAM. **2.** possibly a habitational name for someone from Nemoli in Potenza province.

GIVEN NAMES Italian 14%. *Ciro, Francesco, Luciano, Natale, Nino.*

Memon (165) Indian (Gujarat): Muslim name, from Arabic *momin* 'believer'. The Memons are a well-known business community of Gujarat.

GIVEN NAMES Muslim 88%. *Abdul* (14), *Mohammed* (12), *Mohammad* (6), *Altaf* (3), *Haji* (3), *Iqbal* (3), *Ahmed* (2), *Ali* (2), *Ghulam* (2), *Haroon* (2), *Liaquat* (2), *Muhammad* (2).

Memory (162) Altered form of English MOWBRAY, altered by folk etymology to resemble the English vocabulary word *memory*.

Men (127) **1.** English: unexplained. **2.** Jewish (from Ukraine): from the Yiddish male personal name *Men*, a pet form of either MENDEL or Biblical *Menachem*. **3.** Cambodian: unexplained.

GIVEN NAMES Southeast Asian 23%; Russian 8%; Jewish 8%. *Bunthoeun, Chamroeun, Chhath, Chhoeun, Moeun, Noeun, Oeurn, Sophat, Yoeun; Chin, Feng, Hongbin, Lei, Man, Sarin, Shu-Wen, Soeun, Yin; Anatoli, Boris, Igor, Svetlana, Veniamin, Vladimir; Borukh, Khana.*

Mena (1781) **1.** Spanish and Jewish (Sephardic): habitational name from Mena, in Castile and León provinces. **2.** Greek (**Menas**): see MINAS.

GIVEN NAMES Spanish 50%; Portuguese 12%. *Carlos* (41), *Jose* (37), *Juan* (21), *Manuel* (20), *Luis* (16), *Pedro* (14), *Ricardo* (14), *Alberto* (12), *Javier* (11), *Jorge* (11), *Rafael* (11), *Jesus* (10); *Marcio, Paulo; Antonio* (11), *Marco* (6), *Angelo* (2), *Ceasar* (2), *Didio* (2), *Luciano* (2), *Annalisa, Bartolo, Cecilio, Clemente, Clementina, Dario.*

Menaker (210) Jewish (Ashkenazic): occupational name from a Hebrew word for a butcher who removed veins for koshering meat.

GIVEN NAMES Jewish 6%; Russian 4%. *Hyman, Khana, Miriam; Enya, Galina, Yefim, Yelizaveta.*

Menapace (218) Italian: probably from a personal name, *Menapace*, meaning 'bring peace', from *menare* 'to take or lead' + *pace* 'peace'.

Menard (4055) French (**Ménard**): variant of MAYNARD.

GIVEN NAMES French 11%. *Pierre* (12), *Andre* (10), *Armand* (6), *Laurent* (5), *Marcel* (5), *Michel* (5), *Normand* (5), *Antoine* (4), *Gilles* (4), *Lucien* (4), *Luc* (3), *Raoul* (3).

Menasco (151) Variant of MANASCO.

Menashe (128) Jewish: from the Biblical male personal name *Menashe* (Hebrew form; see MANASSE).

GIVEN NAMES Jewish 11%. *Dror* (2), *Nissim* (2), *Nissin, Sima, Sol, Yaacov.*

Mencer (214) **1.** Variant spelling of German **Mentzer**, a habitational name for someone from a place called Mentz (possibly Mainz) or Menz. **2.** English: probably a variant of MANSER. Compare MENSER.

Mench (190) Variant of MENSCH.

Menchaca (975) Spanish (of Basque origin): habitational name from Basque *Mentxaka* in Biscay province.

GIVEN NAMES Spanish 43%. *Jose* (17), *Juan* (17), *Manuel* (15), *Mario* (9), *Armando* (8), *Arturo* (8), *Ruben* (8), *Rafael* (7), *Guadalupe* (5), *Sergio* (5), *Enrique* (4), *Jesus* (4).

Mencher (109) Jewish: **1.** occupational name for a flour dealer (Polish *maczarz*). **2.** habitational name for someone from Menchi, a village in the Shavli district of the former Russian empire.

GIVEN NAMES Jewish 7%. *Dvora, Meyer.*

Menck (103) German: variant of MENK.

GIVEN NAMES German 10%. *Dietmar* (2), *Hans.*

Mencke (106) North German and Dutch: from a pet form of a Germanic compound name with the initial element *man(n)*, 'man' or *magin* 'strength', 'might'. See MEIN.

GIVEN NAMES German 8%. *Kurt* (2), *Erhard.*

Menconi (164) Italian: patronymic from an augmentative of a reduced form of the personal name *Domenico*, Latin *Dominicus* (see DOMINGO).

GIVEN NAMES Italian 6%. *Annamaria, Fiore, Gino, Marco, Primo.*

Mende (297) German: **1.** topographic name for someone who lived on the outskirts of a village or settlement, from Middle High German *am ende* 'at the end' (see ENDE). **2.** habitational name from any of various places so called in the Rhineland and Westphalia. **3.** from a short form of the personal name *Menath.*

GIVEN NAMES German 12%. *Hans* (4), *Elfriede, Gunter, Heinz, Hellmut, Helmut, Horst, Karl-Heinz, Markus.*

Mendel (1172) **1.** Jewish (Ashkenazic): from the Yiddish personal name *Mendl*, a diminutive of *Man* (see MANN 3). **2.** South German: variant of MEINDL.

GIVEN NAMES German 4%. *Otto* (5), *Erwin* (3), *Florian* (2), *Kurt* (2), *Alois, Monika, Taube.*

Mendell (499) Respelling of Jewish and German MENDEL.

GIVEN NAMES French 4%. *Andre* (2), *Emile.*

Mendelsohn (1169) Jewish: variant of MENDELSON.

GIVEN NAMES Jewish 4%. *Avner, Eliezer, Hyman, Irit, Isadore, Labe, Menachem, Pola, Rifka, Shmuel, Sol, Syma.*

Mendelson (1375) Jewish (Ashkenazic): patronymic from the Yiddish personal name MENDEL.

GIVEN NAMES Jewish 6%. *Haim* (4), *Ari* (2), *Emanuel* (2), *Hyman* (2), *Miriam* (2), *Myer*

(2), *Boruch, Leib, Mayer, Menachem, Naum, Nisson.*

Menden (171) German: habitational name from any of several places so named in the Rhineland.

Mendenhall (3763) English: habitational name for someone from either of two places called Mildenhall, in Suffolk and Wiltshire. The place in Suffolk may have been named in Old English as 'middle nook of land', from *middel* + *halh*, or it may be of the same origin as the Wiltshire place name, 'Milda's nook of land', from an unattested Old English personal name + *halh*. The spelling Mendenhall does not appear in English sources, and this may be a U.S. variant.

Mendes (1915) Portuguese: patronymic from the personal name *Mendo*, a reduced form of *Menendo* (see MENENDEZ).

GIVEN NAMES Spanish 19%; Portuguese 12%. *Manuel* (42), *Jose* (34), *Carlos* (15), *Mario* (6), *Pedro* (5), *Alberto* (4), *Sergio* (4), *Armando* (3), *Cesar* (3), *Domingos* (3), *Francisco* (3), *Luis* (3); *Joao* (11), *Joaquim* (4), *Paulo* (4), *Agostinho, Amadeu, Armanda, Guilherme, Henrique, Sebastiao, Valentim; Antonio* (36), *Leonardo* (2), *Agnelo, Aldo, Anastasio, Enrico, Luciano, Marino, Mauro, Mirella, Paolo, Romeo.*

Mendez (12500) Galician (**Méndez**): patronymic from the personal name *Mendo* (see MENDES, of which this is the Galician equivalent).

GIVEN NAMES Spanish 49%; Portuguese 11%. *Jose* (367), *Juan* (170), *Manuel* (133), *Carlos* (112), *Luis* (108), *Jesus* (92), *Francisco* (82), *Pedro* (79), *Miguel* (76), *Raul* (68), *Jorge* (66), *Rafael* (57); *Ligia* (3), *Godofredo, Ilidio, Paulo, Serafim.*

Mendicino (248) Southern Italian: habitational name from Mendicino, a place in Cosenza province.

GIVEN NAMES Italian 13%. *Carmine* (2), *Angelo, Antonio, Gasper, Guido, Guiseppe, Pasquale, Salvatore, Santo.*

Mendieta (313) Basque: habitational name from any of the numerous places named Mendieta, from *mendi* 'mountain' + the plural suffix *-eta*.

GIVEN NAMES Spanish 56%. *Carlos* (9), *Jose* (6), *Juan* (6), *Manuel* (6), *Luis* (5), *Armando* (4), *Francisco* (4), *Jorge* (4), *Roberto* (4), *Alejandro* (3), *Ana* (3), *Cesar* (3); *Amadeo, Antonio, Constantino, Duilio, Marco, Mirella.*

Mendillo (164) Southern Italian (Campania): from a pet form of a personal name, possibly a reduced form of *Menico*, from *Domenico.*

GIVEN NAMES Italian 18%. *Angelo* (5), *Alfonse, Elio, Pasquale, Rocco.*

Mendiola (1052) Basque: habitational name from any of several places named Mendiola, in Araba, Gipuzkoa, and Biscay provinces, so named from Basque *mendi* + the topographic suffix *-ola.*

GIVEN NAMES Spanish 45%. *Jose* (21), *Juan* (21), *Carlos* (13), *Manuel* (10), *Luis* (9), *Raul* (9), *Pedro* (6), *Armando* (5), *Ricardo* (5), *Rolando* (5), *Guadalupe* (4), *Ignacio* (4).

Menditto (101) Italian: probably from a short form of the Spanish personal name *Mendo*, a reduced form of *Melendo*, of Germanic origin.
GIVEN NAMES Italian 9%. *Salvatore* (2), *Arturo, Ricardo*.

Mendivil (224) Spanish (of Basque origin): habitational name from Basque Mendibil, towns in Navarre and Biscay provinces; the place name is formed with Basque *mendi* 'mountain'.
GIVEN NAMES Spanish 38%. *Manuel* (7), *Jorge* (3), *Jose* (3), *Alfonso* (2), *Carlos* (2), *Enrique* (2), *Francisco* (2), *Juan* (2), *Mario* (2), *Alberto, Alejandro, Armando*.

Mendizabal (126) Basque: topographic name from Basque *mendi* 'mountain' + *-zabal* 'wide', 'spacious'.
GIVEN NAMES Spanish 48%. *Jorge* (5), *Jose* (3), *Manuel* (3), *Rodolfo* (3), *Carlos* (2), *Graciela* (2), *Julio* (2), *Octavio* (2), *Abelardo, Alejandro, Crus, Diego*.

Mendler (119) German: occupational name for a maker of coats, from an agent derivative of Middle High German *mantel, mandel, mendel* 'coat'.

Mendlowitz (107) Jewish (eastern Ashkenazic): Germanized form of a Slavic patronymic from MENDEL.
GIVEN NAMES Jewish 42%. *Mendel* (2), *Shimon* (2), *Shmuel* (2), *Sholem* (2), *Chaim, Eliezer, Feivel, Hershy, Mendy, Moshe, Shraga*.

Mendola (428) Italian: nickname or more often a habitational name from places named with the dialect term *(a)mendola, mendula* 'almond' (also 'almond tree'). Related names include AMENDOLA, LAMENDOLA.
GIVEN NAMES Italian 20%. *Angelo* (7), *Salvatore* (6), *Giovanni* (2), *Sal* (2), *Agostino, Antonino, Carmine, Ignazio, Nicolo, Vincenzo*.

Mendolia (172) Italian: from Greek *amygdalia* 'almond', influenced by Sicilian *mennula*. Compare MENDOLA.
GIVEN NAMES Italian 20%. *Sal* (3), *Carmine* (2), *Antonino, Biagio, Franca, Gaspare, Justo, Mario, Rosario, Salvatore*.

Mendonca (932) Portuguese (**Mendonça**): habitational name from Mendonça, in Portugal.
GIVEN NAMES Spanish 22%; Portuguese 13%. *Manuel* (32), *Jose* (20), *Carlos* (7), *Luis* (5), *Fernando* (4), *Jorge* (3), *Luiz* (3), *Manuela* (3), *Ana* (2), *Antero* (2), *Armando* (2), *Eduardo* (2); *Guilherme* (2), *Joao* (2), *Agostinho, Duarte, Marcio; Antonio* (12), *Angelo* (3), *Dino, Flavio, Franco, Leno, Palma*.

Mendonsa (161) Variant spelling of Portuguese MENDONCA.

Mendosa (123) Spanish and Portuguese (of Basque origin): variant spelling of MENDOZA.
GIVEN NAMES Spanish 41%. *Carlos* (4), *Jose* (4), *Fernando* (2), *Pedro* (2), *Ramon* (2), *Adolfo, Alberto, Anselmo, Benito, Bernadino, Consuelo, Domitila; Antonio* (3), *Bartolo*.

Mendoza (17593) Basque: habitational name from several places in the provinces of Arava and Biscay called Mendoza, named with Basque *mendi* 'mountain' + *otz* 'cold' + the definite article *-a*.
GIVEN NAMES Spanish 50%; Portuguese 11%. *Jose* (466), *Juan* (244), *Manuel* (175), *Jesus* (167), *Carlos* (156), *Luis* (141), *Francisco* (111), *Miguel* (102), *Ramon* (90), *Pedro* (87), *Roberto* (86), *Jorge* (82); *Anatolio* (2), *Godofredo* (2), *Anabela, Catarina, Ligia, Marcio, Paulo, Sil*.

Mendyk (122) Polish and eastern German: status name for a mendicant (a beggar, impoverished person, or perhaps a member of a mendicant order of minor friars), from Polish *mendyk* 'beggar' (Latin *mendicus*).
GIVEN NAME German 4%. *Klaus* (2).

Menear (257) English (Devon; of Cornish origin): topographic name for someone who lived by a menhir, i.e. a tall standing stone erected in prehistoric times (Cornish *men* 'stone' + *hir* 'long').

Meneely (254) Northern Irish: variant of McNEELY.

Menees (224) Variant of **Mannice**, an Ulster form of McNEECE and McNISH.

Menefee (1400) Probably Irish, but of unexplained origin.

Meneley (137) Probably northern Irish, a variant of McNEELY.

Menendez (2034) Spanish (**Menéndez**): patronymic from the medieval personal name *Mendendo*, a hypercorrected form of the Visigothic personal name *Hermenegild*, composed of the elements *ermen, irmen* 'whole', 'entire' + *gild* 'tribute'. This personal name was borne by a 6th-century member of the Visigothic royal house, who was converted from Arianism to the Catholic faith and became an enormously popular saint, as a result of which the personal name was very common in Spain in the Middle Ages.
GIVEN NAMES Spanish 45%; Portuguese 14%. *Jose* (81), *Manuel* (45), *Carlos* (30), *Luis* (28), *Juan* (20), *Ramon* (20), *Angel* (14), *Jorge* (14), *Fernando* (12), *Francisco* (12), *Rafael* (12), *Mario* (11); *Marcio; Antonio* (10), *Marco* (3), *Lorenzo* (2), *Luciano* (2), *Silvio* (2), *Angelo, Bruna, Carmela, Carmin, Ceasar, Clementino, Constantino*.

Meneses (733) **1.** Spanish: habitational name from Meneses de Campos (Palencia, Castile), or for an ethnic name for someone from the Mena valley in Burgos. **2.** Portuguese: habitational name from any of the several places named Meneses in Portugal.

GIVEN NAMES Spanish 48%; Portuguese 16%. *Jose* (17), *Carlos* (13), *Luis* (10), *Manuel* (9), *Jorge* (8), *Francisco* (6), *Mario* (6), *Juan* (5), *Orlando* (5), *Alejandro* (4), *Arturo* (4), *Benigno* (4); *Joao* (2), *Mateus* (2), *Henrique, Joaquim, Ligia; Antonio* (8), *Luciano* (3), *Marco* (2), *Marco Antonio* (2), *Alfonse, Carmela, Elio, Geronimo, Heriberto, Liberato, Mauro, Silvano*.

Menezes (469) Portuguese: variant of MENESES. This name is common in India, where it was taken by Portuguese colonists.
GIVEN NAMES Spanish 14%; Portuguese 10%; Indian 4%. *Jose* (5), *Manuel* (5), *Luiz* (3), *Marcos* (3), *Sergio* (3), *Alberto* (2), *Antero* (2), *Eduardo* (2), *Adelino, Alda, Ana, Ana Maria; Ademir* (2), *Almir, Guilherme, Marcio, Paulo; Geetha, Jeevan, Naresh, Rahul, Rohit, Shalini, Vinod, Vivek*.

Meng (1095) **1.** Chinese 孟: during the Spring and Autumn period (722–481 BC), there were two sources of the name Meng. A son of a prince in the state of Lu was called Meng Sun, while a duke of the state of Wei had a 'style name' of Meng Zhi. Descendants of both adopted the Meng portion of their names as their surname. This was the family name of Meng Zi, known to the West as Mencius, the Confucian philosopher. **2.** Chinese 蒙: two sources of this surname are a General Men of the Qin Dynasty (221–206 BC) and a place named Mengshuang in Hebei province. Additionally, the Yuan Dynasty (1271–1368 AD) was under the rule of Mongolia, known in Chinese as *Menggu*. *Menggu* became a surname, which in later times was generally shortened to *Meng*. **3.** German: from a form of the personal name MAGNUS. **4.** German: variant of MENGER. **5.** Danish: habitational name from a place so named. **6.** Danish: variant of MANG.
GIVEN NAMES Chinese 11%. *Yuan* (4), *Bin* (3), *Ching* (3), *Hsien-Ming* (3), *Jin* (3), *Li* (3), *Heng* (2), *Hong* (2), *Jin Hong* (2), *Ming* (2), *Ping* (2), *Qiang* (2).

Menge (522) German: variant of MENG.
GIVEN NAMES German 5%. *Franz* (2), *Helmut* (2), *Berthel, Ruediger*.

Mengel (861) **1.** German: occupational name for a market trader or stallholder, from Middle High German *menglære*, a variant of *mengære* (see MENGER). This surname is also established in Poland. **2.** Dutch: from a pet form of the personal name *Meinger*, derived from a Germanic personal name composed of the elements *magin* 'strength' + *gār, gēr* 'spear'; or a pet form of the personal name MANGOLD. **3.** Dutch: possibly an occupational nickname, from Middle Dutch *mengel, mingel*, a liquid measure equal to 2 pints.

Menger (264) German: **1.** occupational name for a market trader, Middle High German *mengære, mangære* (from Late Latin *mango* 'salesman', with the addition of the Germanic agent suffix). **2.** from the

Germanic personal name *Meginger*, composed of *magin* 'might', 'force' + *gār, gēr* 'spear'.

GIVEN NAMES German 7%. *Kurt* (2), *Fritz*, *Heinz*.

Menges (703) **1.** German: from an altered form of the personal name MAGNUS. **2.** German: from the personal name *Me(i)ngoss*, from Germanic *magin* 'strength', 'might' + *gōt* 'Goth'. **3.** Hungarian (**Mengesz**): Magyarized spelling of the German family name.

Menghini (159) Italian: from a pet form of the personal name *Doménico* (see DOMINGO).

GIVEN NAMES Italian 4%. *Enzo, Leno*.

Mengle (114) Variant spelling of German MENGEL.

Menicucci (105) Italian: from *Menicucco*, a pet form of *Menico*, a short form of DOMENICO.

GIVEN NAMES Italian 16%. *Angelo* (3), *Dante, Giulio, Guido*.

Menifee (105) Origin unidentified. Compare MENEFEE.

Menius (111) German: humanistic surname of unexplained etymology.

Menjivar (453) Basque: unexplained.

GIVEN NAMES Spanish 59%. *Jose* (32), *Carlos* (9), *Miguel* (6), *Juan* (5), *Ana* (4), *Efrain* (4), *Luis* (4), *Manuel* (4), *Mario* (4), *Pedro* (4), *Edgardo* (3), *Francisco* (3).

Menk (309) North German and Dutch: from a pet form of any of several Germanic personal names formed with *magin* 'might', 'force' as the first element (see, for example, MEINHARDT).

Menke (1813) North German and Dutch: variant of MENK.

GIVEN NAMES German 4%. *Kurt* (6), *Fritz* (5), *Wilhelm* (3), *Alfons, Alois, Aloys, Aloysius, Bernhard, Detlef, Dietrich, Elfriede, Ewald*.

Menken (280) North German: from a pet form of MEIN.

GIVEN NAMES German 4%. *Klaus, Kurt*.

Menkes (144) Dutch: patronymic from MENCKE.

GIVEN NAMES Russian 5%. *Evgueni, Gennadiy, Sheyva*.

Menking (115) German: variant of MEINKING.

GIVEN NAMES German 9%. *Manfred* (2), *Helmut, Kurt*.

Menn (229) **1.** German: variant of MEIN. **2.** Breton: nickname from *menn* 'kid', 'young goat', perhaps denoting an agile person.

GIVEN NAMES Russian 4%; German 4%. *Anatoly, Boris, Dmitry, Svetlana; Kurt* (2), *Otto*.

Menna (357) Italian: **1.** from the personal name *Menna*, from Greek *Mēnas* (see MENA). In Italian it came to be treated as a feminine name; so, for example, the place name Santamenna in Salerno, is recorded in the masculine form Santomenna until the end of the 8th century. **2.** variant of *Menno*, a reduced form of the personal name *Domenico* (see DOMINGO).

GIVEN NAMES Italian 25%. *Alfonso, Angelo* (4), *Silvio* (3), *Carmine* (2), *Marco* (2), *Pasquale* (2), *Aniello, Concetta, Elio, Ennio, Gaetano, Gilda, Giovanni, Isidoro*.

Menne (453) German: **1.** variant of MENN. **2.** habitational name from Menne in Westphalia.

Mennella (290) Southern Italian: from a pet form of MENNA.

GIVEN NAMES Italian 16%. *Salvatore* (2), *Carlo, Carmela, Concetta, Federico, Giuseppa, Giuseppe, Luigi, Nicolina, Raffaele, Sabastian, Vincenza*.

Mennen (190) Dutch: patronymic from a Germanic name formed with the initial element *man* 'man' or *magin* 'strength', 'might'.

Mennenga (259) North German and Frisian: patronymic from a form of the personal name MEIN.

GIVEN NAME Jewish 4%. *Hyram* (3).

Menner (118) **1.** German and Hungarian: occupational name from Middle High German *mener* 'cattle drover'. **2.** German: habitational name for someone from MENNE.

GIVEN NAME Hungarian 4%. *Lorant*.

Mennig (101) German: variant of MENNING.

Menning (383) German: **1.** patronymic from MEIN. **2.** habitational name from a place named Menning in southern Germany.

Menninger (194) German: habitational name from places named Menningen, Menning, or Meiningen, all in southern Germany.

GIVEN NAMES German 8%. *Florian* (2), *Manfred* (2), *Erwin, Konrad*.

Meno (196) Spanish or Italian: unexplained.

GIVEN NAMES Spanish 6%. *Jose* (3), *Ramon* (2), *Braulio, Francisco, Gregorio, Jesus, Luis, Serafin*.

Menold (111) German: from the personal name *Mainold*, composed of the Germanic elements *magin* 'might', 'strength' + *walt* 'rule'.

Menon (425) Indian (Kerala): Hindu (Nayar) name, from Malayalam *mēnōn*, usually used to mean 'accountant', but literally 'exalted one' (earlier *mēnavan, mēlavan*, from *mēl* 'high' + the third person singular masculine pronoun, *avan* 'he'). Originally, this was a hereditary title conferred by the rulers of various kingdoms in Kerala.

GIVEN NAMES Indian 93%. *Anil* (6), *Sanjay* (6), *Vijay* (6), *Anand* (5), *Hari* (5), *Krishna* (5), *Satish* (5), *Suresh* (5), *Prem* (4), *Arvind* (3), *Bal* (3), *Bhaskar* (3).

Menor (179) Spanish, Portuguese and Catalan: distinguishing name for the younger of two bearers of the same first name, from *menor* 'smaller', 'lesser'; 'younger' (Latin *minor*).

GIVEN NAMES Spanish 24%. *Candido* (2), *Rodolfo* (2), *Rosita* (2), *Alejandro, Benedicto, Camilo, Catalino, Constancia, Damaso, Ernesto, Eugenio, Evelio*.

Menotti (119) Italian: from *Menotto*, a pet form of *Menico*, a short form of DOMENICO.

GIVEN NAMES French 6%; Italian 4%. *Gaston; Renzo*.

Mensah (343) African: unexplained.

GIVEN NAMES African 14%. *Kofi* (5), *Kwabena* (3), *Kwaku* (3), *Tetteh* (3), *Afia, Akwasi, Kwame, Kwasi, Kweku, Kwesi, Moi, Nii*.

Mensch (634) **1.** South German: status name for a serf or feudal vassal, Middle High German *mensch*. **2.** North German and Dutch: from *Menseke*, a pet form of a Germanic compound personal name formed with the initial element *magin* 'strength', 'might' or *man*.

Mensching (132) North German: patronymic from MENSCH 2.

Mense (143) North German: patronymic from a short form of any of the group of personal names identified at MEIN.

Mensen (125) Norwegian: patronymic from **Mens**, a pet form of the German personal names **Meinhard** or **Meinrich**.

Menser (355) English: probably a variant of MANSER.

Mensik (163) Czech (**Menšik**): from *menšík* 'smaller', comparative of *malý* 'small', typically used as a byname for a younger brother or for the smaller of two bearers of the same personal name.

Mensing (424) North German: patronymic from a short form of any of the group of personal names identified at MEIN.

GIVEN NAME French 4%. *Philomene*.

Mensinger (240) South German: habitational name from for someone from Mansingen (today called Mansie), near Wederstede in Lower Saxony.

Menta (132) Southern Italian: topographic name from *menta* '(pepper)mint' (Latin *menta*), or a habitational name from any of various places named with this word.

GIVEN NAMES Italian 22%. *Guido* (2), *Enrico, Filomena, Luciano, Luigi, Michael Angelo, Rodelio, Rocco, Salvatore, Vincenzo*.

Mentch (109) Americanized spelling of German MENSCH.

Mente (145) **1.** North German: from a short form of a Germanic compound name formed with *magin* 'strength', 'might' as the first element, for example MEINHARDT. **2.** Dutch: topographic name from Middle Dutch *mente* '(pepper)mint'. **3.** Dutch: from the female personal name *Mente*, a short form of *Clemente*, feminine form of CLEMENS. **4.** Hungarian: metonymic occupational name from *mente* 'short coat'.

Mentel (172) German: **1.** from a pet form of a short form of a personal name formed with Germanic *magin* 'strength', 'might' (see MENTE 1). **2.** metonymic occupational name for a rag-and-bone collector, from *Mäntel* 'overcoat'.

Menter (316) English: **1.** (of Norman origin): nickname from Old French *mentur* 'liar'. **2.** variant spelling of MINTER.

Menth (148) Dutch and North German: variant of MENTE 1 and MANTHE.

Menting (154) Dutch: variant of MENTINK.

Mentink (200) Dutch: **1.** patronymic derivative of a short form of the personal name CLEMENT. **2.** from a derivative of MEINERT.

Mento (268) Italian: from a short form of any of various medieval personal name ending with *-mento*, as for example *Agromento, Comento, Fundamento, Palmento*, or *Saramento*, all of which have now fallen into disuse.
GIVEN NAMES Italian 11%. *Antonio, Carmel, Carmine, Dante.*

Menton (252) Irish: perhaps a variant of MANTON.

Mentor (119) **1.** French: unexplained. **2.** English: unexplained. **3.** Possibly a respelling of **Menter**, an unexplained name of German origin.
GIVEN NAMES French 16%; Spanish 6%; Scandinavian 4%. *Cecile, Philippe, Pierre; Felipe, Ramon, Ricardo.*

Mentz (325) Variant spelling of German MENZ.

Mentzel (220) Variant spelling of German MENZEL.
GIVEN NAME German 5%. *Kurt* (2).

Mentzer (1353) German: habitational name with the agent suffix *-er*, either from Mainz, earlier *Mentz*, derived from the medieval Latin name *Mogontia* (Latin *Mogontiacum*, probably from the Celtic personal name *Mogontios*), or from Menz in Brandenburg and Saxony.

Meny (125) French: topographic name from a spelling variant of *ménil* 'house', 'dwelling'. Compare DUMESNIL.
GIVEN NAME French 8%. *Normand* (2).

Menz (571) **1.** North German: from a short form of a Germanic compound name with the same initial element *magin* 'strength', 'might'. **2.** North German: habitational name from Menz in Mecklenburg or Mainz (see MENTZER). **3.** South German: variant of *Manz*, a derivative of a compound name with the initial element *man* (see, for example, MANHART).

Menza (139) Italian: from a feminine form of **Menzo**, from Sicilian *menzo* 'middle', possibly in the sense 'middle son', presumably applied to the older of twin boys who have an older brother, or possibly a nickname for someone of small stature, from the same word in the sense 'half'.
GIVEN NAMES Italian 7%. *Angelo, Rocco.*

Menze (196) German: variant of MENZ.

Menzel (1059) **1.** German: from a pet form of MENZ. **2.** German (Silesia, Saxony,

Bohemia): from a pet form of the personal name HERMANN or CLEMENS, under the influence of Czech pet forms such as *Hermannec*, leading to medieval name forms recorded as, for example, *Hermenczel*, and later *Menczel*.
GIVEN NAMES German 7%. *Horst* (3), *Gunther* (2), *Hans* (2), *Klaus* (2), *Kurt* (2), *Rainer* (2), *Ute* (2), *Claus, Erhard, Erwin, Ewald, Fritz.*

Menzer (284) German: variant spelling of MENTZER.

Menzie (340) Variant of Scottish MENZIES.

Menzies (796) Scottish: variant of MANNERS, in which the *z* originally represented Middle English letter *Ê'* (yogh), representing a sound similar to modern English *y*. The surname is still pronounced *mingiz* in Scotland. It has been Gaelicized as **Méinn**, from which come the English forms **Mein** and **Mien**. The patronymic forms **McMenzies, McMon(n)ies, McMin(n)**, and **McMyn** represent adapations of the name to the predominant pattern of Highland surnames.

Meo (302) Italian: from a short form of the personal names BARTOLOMEO, ROMEO, or TOLOMEO, or possibly from a reduced form of *Matteo, Mazzeo* (Italian equivalents of MATTHEW).
GIVEN NAMES Italian 25%. *Sal* (3), *Alphonso* (2), *Antonio* (2), *Mario* (2), *Ciro, Gasper, Iolanda, Nicola, Onofrio, Rocco, Santi, Santo, Vito.*

Meola (574) Italian (**Meòla**): from a pet form of a feminine form of MEO.
GIVEN NAMES Italian 13%. *Angelo* (4), *Carmine* (3), *Vito* (2), *Benedetto, Donato, Flavio, Giuseppe, Nicola, Sal, Salvatore, Tosca, Umberto.*

Meoli (106) Italian: from *Meolo*, a pet form of MEO.
GIVEN NAMES Italian 27%. *Luco* (4), *Angelo* (2), *Enrico* (2), *Giuseppe, Rocco, Sal, Saverio.*

Mepham (100) English: habitational name from a place in Kent named Meopham, from an Old English personal name *Mēapa* + Old English *hām* 'homestead', 'settlement'.

Mera (226) **1.** Galician: habitational name from any of the several placed named Mera in Galicia. **2.** Romanian: habitational name for someone from the village of Mera (Hungarian *Méra*) in Transylvania.
GIVEN NAMES Spanish 48%. *Jose* (9), *Luis* (6), *Carlos* (5), *Fernando* (4), *Andres* (3), *Alberto* (2), *Francisco* (2), *Galo* (2), *Glicerio* (2), *Jaime* (2), *Jorge* (2), *Juan* (2).

Meranda (196) Italian: probably a variant of MIRANDA.

Merante (113) Italian: variant of MIRANTE.
GIVEN NAMES Italian 22%. *Antonio* (2), *Italo, Nicola, Pasquale, Rocco, Valentino.*

Meraz (568) Spanish: variant of Asturian-Leonese **Merás**, a habitational name from Merás in Asturies.

GIVEN NAMES Spanish 58%. *Jose* (21), *Jesus* (14), *Juan* (13), *Manuel* (13), *Carlos* (10), *Miguel* (6), *Ruben* (6), *Raul* (5), *Adan* (4), *Francisco* (4), *Guadalupe* (4), *Guillermo* (4); *Antonio* (5), *Marco Antonio* (4), *Lorenzo* (3), *Carmelo, Eligio, Eliseo, Filiberto, Julieta, Marco.*

Mercadante (405) Southern Italian: occupational name for a merchant, Old Italian *mercadante, mercatante.*
GIVEN NAMES Italian 20%. *Pasquale* (2), *Sal* (2), *Alfonso, Angelo, Aracely, Deno, Dino, Dominico, Emilio, Filomena, Mario, Rino, Rocco, Salvatore.*

Mercado (5519) Spanish: from *mercado* 'market', topographic name for someone living by a market or metonymic occupational name for a market trader.
GIVEN NAMES Spanish 46%; Portuguese 11%. *Jose* (152), *Juan* (67), *Luis* (62), *Manuel* (54), *Carlos* (47), *Angel* (40), *Jesus* (38), *Francisco* (37), *Pedro* (32), *Raul* (27), *Miguel* (26), *Jorge* (25); *Godofredo, Goncalo, Ligia.*

Mercaldo (113) Italian (Campania): unexplained; perhaps from a much altered form of some Germanic personal name.
GIVEN NAMES Italian 9%. *Angelo, Aniello, Antonio, Marco.*

Merced (349) Spanish: from a short form of the Marian name *Nuestra Señora de la Merced* 'Our Lady of Grace', from *merced* 'grace', 'mercy'.
GIVEN NAMES Spanish 43%. *Jose* (9), *Jorge* (6), *Carlos* (5), *Angel* (4), *Alberto* (3), *Francisco* (3), *Aurelio* (2), *Juan* (2), *Julio* (2), *Luis* (2), *Margarita* (2), *Noemi* (2); *Angelo, Antonio, Caesar, Dino, Heriberto, Saturnina.*

Mercedes (281) Spanish: from the Marian name *Nuestra Señora(or María) de las Mercedes*, from the plural of *merced* 'grace', 'mercy'.
GIVEN NAMES Spanish 58%; Portuguese 12%. *Jose* (12), *Manuel* (6), *Ramon* (6), *Rafael* (5), *Francisca* (3), *Juan* (3), *Luis* (3), *Miguel* (3), *Ana* (2), *Angel* (2), *Beatriz* (2), *Carolina* (2); *Duarte.*

Mercer (12532) English and Catalan: occupational name for a trader, from Old French *mercier*, Late Latin *mercarius* (an agent derivative of *merx*, genitive *mercis*, 'merchandise'). In Middle English the term was applied particularly to someone who dealt in textiles, especially the more costly and luxurious fabrics such as silks, satin, and velvet.

Merchant (4617) **1.** English: occupational name for a buyer and seller of goods, from Old French, Middle English *march(e)ant*, Late Latin *mercatans* (see MARCHAND). **2.** Indian (Gujarat and Bombay city): Muslim and Parsi occupational name for a trader, from the English vocabulary word *merchant.*

Merchen (147) Possibly a variant of English MERCHANT.

Mercier (3126) English and French: occupational name for a trader, from Old French *mercier* (see MERCER).

GIVEN NAMES French 11%. *Armand* (10), *Marcel* (8), *Andre* (7), *Pierre* (6), *Gaston* (5), *Lucien* (5), *Aurele* (4), *Jacques* (4), *Normand* (4), *Laurent* (3), *Michel* (3), *Valmont* (3).

Mercil (139) Origin uncertain. This name was in Quebec, Canada, from the 19th century or earlier; it may be of Czech origin.

Merck (608) **1.** Dutch: from the personal name, a form of MARK 1. **2.** German and French: from a short form of a Germanic compound personal name with initial element *mark* 'boundary', 'border area', for example, MARKWARDT.

Mercure (389) French: from a personal name popularized by the fame of St. Mercurius of Cappadocia (see Italian MERCURIO).

GIVEN NAMES French 11%. *Lucien* (2), *Michel* (2), *Ovide* (2), *Treffle* (2), *Adrien*, *Francois*, *Gabrielle*, *Monique*, *Normand*, *Ovila*.

Mercuri (277) Southern Italian: patronymic from the personal name MERCURIO.

GIVEN NAMES Italian 19%. *Domenic* (3), *Carmela* (2), *Domenico* (2), *Angelo*, *Antonio*, *Francesco*, *Franco*, *Giuseppe*, *Nicola*, *Pasquale*, *Romeo*, *Sal*.

Mercurio (1741) Southern Italian: from a medieval personal name popularized by the cults of various saints of this name, including St. Mercurius of Cappadocia, martyred by order of the 4th-century Emperor Julian the Apostate. The name is derived from the Latin personal name *Mercurius*, which was originally the name of the Roman god of commerce.

GIVEN NAMES Italian 14%. *Salvatore* (9), *Sal* (7), *Angelo* (5), *Antonio* (5), *Rocco* (5), *Pasquale* (4), *Vito* (4), *Domenic* (3), *Luigi* (3), *Cosmo* (2), *Donato* (2), *Marco* (2).

Mercy (198) **1.** French: habitational name from places so named in Allier, Meuthe-et-Moselle, and Yonne, derived from the Latin personal name *Marcius*, *Martius*, or *Mercius* + the locative suffix *-acum*. **2.** French: from a Picard or Walloon form of MERCIER.

GIVEN NAME French 4%. *Jean Robert*.

Meredith (9054) Welsh: from the personal name *Maredudd*. In Welsh the stress is on the second syllable. The Old Welsh form is *Morgetiud*, of which the first element may mean 'pomp, splendor' and the second is *iudd* 'lord'.

Merenda (314) **1.** Italian: from *merenda*, from Late Latin *merenda* 'evening meal'; however, it may have retained the meaning of Latin *merere* 'to merit' in the sense 'worthy cause', 'thing of merit'. **2.** Portuguese: from *merenda* 'light meal', cognate with 1.

GIVEN NAMES Italian 21%. *Antonio* (3), *Carmelo* (2), *Giuseppe* (2), *Mario* (2),

Rosario (2), *Angelo*, *Domenic*, *Domenico*, *Giulio*, *Nicola*, *Oreste*, *Silvestro*, *Umberto*.

Merendino (217) Italian: from a diminutive of MERENDA.

GIVEN NAMES Italian 24%. *Angelo* (2), *Rosario* (2), *Salvatore* (2), *Aldo*, *Gaetano*, *Gaspare*, *Giovanni*, *Giusto*.

Mereness (136) Scandinavian?

Merfeld (273) German: habitational name from a place so named near Dülmen in Lower Saxony.

Mergel (111) **1.** German and Dutch: topographic name from Middle High German *mergel* 'marl'. **2.** German: metronymic from *Mergel*, an old pet name from the personal name *Maria* (see MARIE 1). **3.** German: variant of MERKEL. **4.** German (Hesse): from a West Middle German nickname for a lean or gaunt man. **5.** Dutch (**van de(n) Mergel**): habitational name from Le Merghele in Rinxent in the Pas-de-Calais (France), Mergele in Ronse, or Mergelput ('marl pit') in Anzegem, Oostkamp, and St-Pieters-Kapelle, all named with this word.

Mergen (337) Dutch: of uncertain origin and meaning, possibly from the older family name **Amargant**, thought to be an occupational name for a maker of fastenings, from Middle Dutch *margant* 'hook', 'clasp'.

Mergens (128) German: unexplained; perhaps a respelling of **Mehrkens**, a patronymic from a pet form of a personal name formed with *Mer-*, for example, *Merolf*, *Merbod*.

Mergenthaler (212) German: habitational name for someone from a place called Mergenthal, probably named with a pet form of the personal name *Maria* (see MARIE 1) + Middle High German *tal* 'valley'.

FOREBEARS Ottmar Mergenthaler, the inventor of the Linotype print-composing machine, was born into a poor family in Hachtel, Germany. He emigrated to America in 1872, his fare paid for by a family friend. At the time of his death in 1899, Mergenthaler held over 50 patents.

GIVEN NAME German 5%. *Otto*.

Merges (101) German: unexplained.

Mergler (131) South German: topographic name for someone who lived by a marl pit, or occupational name for someone who sold marl for fertilizer or brick making, from German *Mergel* 'marl' (see MERGEL 1) + the agent suffix *-er*.

Merhar (109) Slovenian (central Slovenia): from *mrhar*, an agent derivative of *mrha* 'carrion', hence an unflattering nickname for someone regarded as a vulture or carrion crow (in a figurative sense), or a nickname meaning 'bear', or possibly an occupational name for someone who flayed animal hides.

GIVEN NAME South Slavic 5%. *Milan* (2).

Merica (258) Romanian: either from a pet form of the personal name *Mera*, from *Miron*, of Greek origin (see MYRON), or a habitational name.

Merical (135) Altered form of French **Marécal** (see MARICLE, MARCHAL).

Mericle (498) Altered form of French **Marécal** (see MARICLE, MARCHAL).

Merida (418) Spanish (**Mérida**): habitational name from the city of Mérida in Badajoz province. One of the most important Roman cities of the Iberian peninsula, it was named *Augusta Emerita*, and established as a *colonia* of retired soldiers. Latin *emerita* is the past participle of *emerere* 'earn out', 'merit', i.e. 'complete one's term of military service' (from *e*, *ex* 'out of' + *merere* 'to deserve').

GIVEN NAMES Spanish 34%. *Luis* (7), *Juan* (6), *Cesar* (5), *Jose* (5), *Angel* (3), *Jorge* (3), *Rafael* (3), *Arturo* (2), *Manuel* (2), *Mario* (2), *Octavio* (2), *Pedro* (2).

Merideth (616) Variant of Welsh MEREDITH.

Meridith (248) Variant of Welsh MEREDITH.

Merillat (212) French (**Mérillat**): nickname from a reduced diminutive of *esmeril* 'merlin' (a small falcon).

Merin (125) **1.** Spanish (**Merín**): possibly a variant of **Marín** (see MARIN), or in some cases perhaps a habitational name from one of the places in Galicia named Merín (A Coruña and Pontevedra provinces). **2.** Jewish (from Belarus): metronymic from the Yiddish female personal name *Mere*, a pet form of the personal name of *Miryam* (see MIRKIN).

Merino (1023) Spanish: occupational or status name from Spanish *merino*, the title of a royal or seigneurial functionary who had wide legal and military jurisdiction over a district. The word is from Late Latin *maiorinus*, a derivative of *maior*. Compare MAYER and MAYORAL.

GIVEN NAMES Spanish 46%. *Jose* (21), *Juan* (12), *Carlos* (10), *Pedro* (10), *Mario* (9), *Miguel* (9), *Luis* (8), *Ricardo* (8), *Jesus* (7), *Angel* (6), *Ramon* (6), *Armando* (5).

Merithew (128) English and Irish: variant of MERRIHEW.

Meritt (282) English: variant spelling of MERRITT.

Meriweather (209) English: variant spelling of MERRIWEATHER.

Meriwether (723) English: variant spelling of MERRIWEATHER.

Merk (490) **1.** Dutch: variant of MARK 1. **2.** Dutch: (**van de Merk**): variant of MARK 4. **3.** German: from a short form of the personal name MARKWARDT.

GIVEN NAMES German 5%. *Erhard*, *Gerhart*, *Guenther*, *Inge*, *Nikolaus*, *Otto*.

Merkel (2829) **1.** South German and Swiss German: from a pet form of a short form of a personal name such as MARKWARDT. **2.** German: from a pet form of the personal name *Mark* (see MARK 4).

Merker (405) **1.** German: variant of MAR-KER. **2.** South German and Jewish (Ashkenazic): occupational name from Middle High German *merker*, German *Merker* 'watchman', 'lookout'.

GIVEN NAME Jewish 4%. *Reuven* (2).

Merkes (118) Jewish (eastern Ashkenazic): metronymic from the Yiddish female personal name *Merke, Mirke* (see MIRKIN).

Merkey (160) Probably a variant of Irish MARKEY.

GIVEN NAME French 4%. *Marcel.*

Merkin (216) Jewish (eastern Ashkenazic): variant of MIRKIN.

GIVEN NAMES Russian 8%; German 6%; French 5%. *Vyacheslav* (2), *Galina, Leonid, Lev, Osip; Hermann* (3); *Serge* (3).

Merkl (150) **1.** German: variant of MER-KEL. **2.** Czech: from the personal name *Markus* (see MARK), or possibly in some cases from the personal name MARTIN.

GIVEN NAMES German 9%. *Eldred, Hermann, Manfred, Mathias, Theodor, Wolfgang.*

Merkle (1553) Variant spelling of German MERKEL.

GIVEN NAMES German 4%. *Kurt* (4), *Alfons* (3), *Armin* (2), *Gerhard* (2), *Klaus* (2), *Aloysius, Dieter, Ernst, Gotthilf, Guenter, Hellmut, Inge.*

Merklein (117) German: from a pet form of MERKEL.

GIVEN NAMES German 14%. *Hans* (2), *Friedrich, Guenter, Helmut, Konrad, Wolf.*

Merkley (601) Probably an Americanized form of German MERKEL.

Merklin (183) German: from a pet form of MERKEL.

Merkling (127) German: habitational name from either of two places called Merklingen, near Stuttgart and Ulm.

Merklinger (114) German: habitational name for someone from either of two places called Merklingen (see MERKLING).

Merkt (174) German: topographic name from Middle High German *merket* 'market(place)'.

GIVEN NAMES German 8%. *Erwin, Hedwing, Hermann, Manfred, Wilfried.*

Merl (110) Jewish (Ashkenazic): metronymic from the Yiddish female personal name *Merl*, a pet form of Hebrew *Miryam* (see MIRKIN).

GIVEN NAME Jewish 4%. *Baruch.*

Merle (469) **1.** German and French: nickname, possibly for a good or habitual singer or whistler, from Middle High German, Old French *merle* 'blackbird' (Latin *merula*). See MERLO. **2.** German: from a pet form of a short form of a personal name formed with German *mar, mer* 'famous' as the first element.

GIVEN NAMES French 6%. *Pierre* (3), *Etienne, Henri, Jean-Paul.*

Merli (127) Italian: from a patronymic or plural form of MERLO.

GIVEN NAMES Italian 7%. *Carlo, Gino, Luigi.*

Merlin (381) **1.** English, French, and Spanish (**Merlín**): from the Old French personal name *Merlin*, Latin *Merlinus* was derived from the Welsh personal name *Myrddin*. *Merlinus* was a Latinized form of *Myrddin* devised by Geoffrey of Monmouth and popularized in the Arthurian romances. **2.** Jewish (eastern Ashkenazic): metronymic from the Yiddish female personal name *Merle*, a pet form of *Miryam* (see MIRKIN).

GIVEN NAMES Jewish 4%. *Aron, Arye, Sura.*

Merlini (110) Italian: patronymic or plural form of MERLINO.

GIVEN NAMES Italian 14%. *Angelo, Cosmo, Livio, Luigi, Neri, Rocco, Silvio.*

Merlino (902) Italian: **1.** from the Arthurian personal name *Merlino*, borrowed from French MERLIN. **2.** from a diminutive of MERLO. **3.** possibly in some cases, a Lombardic habitational name from Merlino in Milan province.

GIVEN NAMES Italian 14%. *Angelo* (7), *Salvatore* (5), *Antonio* (4), *Rocco* (3), *Aldo, Attilio, Biagio, Carlo, Carmela, Carmelo, Carmine, Ciro.*

Merlo (880) Italian and Spanish: nickname from Italian and medieval Spanish *merlo* 'blackbird' (Latin *merula*). In the Middle Ages this bird seems to have been regarded at times as foolish and gullible, and at other times as cunning and wily. In some cases the surname may have arisen as a metonymic occupational name for a bird catcher.

GIVEN NAMES Spanish 9%; Italian 8%. *Jose* (4), *Mario* (4), *Arturo* (2), *Jesus* (2), *Luis* (2), *Raul* (2), *Adan, Adela, Agustin, Azucena, Baldemar, Dalila; Aldo* (3), *Angelo* (3), *Carlo* (2), *Santo* (2), *Vito* (2), *Antonio, Carmela, Elvio, Enrico, Franco, Grazia, Mauro.*

Merlos (112) Spanish and Portuguese: from the personal name *Merlos* (see MERLO).

GIVEN NAMES Spanish 57%. *Fidel* (2), *Francisco* (2), *Jorge* (2), *Juan* (2), *Lazaro* (2), *Manuel* (2), *Miguel* (2), *Adelso, Alonso, Ana, Angel, Cesar.*

Merman (108) Americanized spelling of North German **Meermann**, a topographic name for someone living by a large lake.

GIVEN NAME German 8%. *Elfriede* (2).

Mermelstein (435) Jewish (Ashkenazic): ornamental name from Yiddish *mermlshteyn* 'marble'.

GIVEN NAMES Jewish 11%; German 6%. *Bluma* (2), *Yehuda* (2), *Aharon, Ahuva, Aron, Berka, Isidor, Mendy, Naum, Raizy, Sol, Tovia; Armin, Egon, Erwin, Eugen, Frederika, Lothar, Otto.*

Mero (431) **1.** Galician: topographic name from Mero, a river in Galicia. **2.** Spanish and Catalan: probably a nickname from *mero* 'grouper' (the fish). **3.** Italian: possibly from *mero* 'pure', 'sheer' (Latin *merus*). Theoretically, this could also be a source of the Spanish name, but in any case

it is difficult to explain its application. **4.** Hungarian (**Mérő**): occupational name for someone who worked with scales, from *mérő* 'measure', 'measurer', a noun derivative of *mérni* 'to measure'.

GIVEN NAMES Spanish 5%. *Carlos* (3), *Jose* (3), *Amparo, Ana, Beatriz, Carols, Cesar, Digna, Emilia, Gonzalo, Narcisa, Ninfa.*

Merola (748) Southern Italian: nickname from Neapolitan *merula* 'female blackbird', from Latin *merula* (see MERLO).

GIVEN NAMES Italian 14%. *Angelo* (4), *Carmine* (3), *Marco* (3), *Sal* (3), *Alfonse* (2), *Guido* (2), *Lorenzo* (2), *Pasquale* (2), *Salvatore* (2), *Antonio, Carlo, Fiore.*

Merolla (195) Southern Italian: **1.** possibly from Neapolitan *merolla* '(bone) marrow'. **2.** possibly a diminutive of MERO.

GIVEN NAMES Italian 21%. *Amedeo* (3), *Antonio* (2), *Rocco* (2), *Sal* (2), *Carmine, Carmino, Dante, Domenic, Gennaro, Gino, Giuseppe, Salvatore.*

Meroney (204) Probably a variant spelling of Irish MORONEY.

Merrell (3051) English: variant spelling of MERRILL.

Merren (102) English: variant of MERRIN.

Merrett (131) English: variant spelling of MERRITT.

Merriam (1226) English: habitational name from Merriams in Leeds, Kent.

Merrick (3306) **1.** Welsh: from the Welsh personal name *Meurig*, a form of *Maurice*, Latin *Mauritius* (see MORRIS). **2.** English: from an Old French personal name introduced to Britain by the Normans, composed of the Germanic elements *meri, mari* 'fame' + *rīc* 'power'. **3.** Scottish: habitational name from a place near Minigaff in the county of Dumfries and Galloway, so called from Gaelic *meurach* 'branch or fork of a road or river'. **4.** Irish: when not Welsh or English in origin, probably an Anglicized form of Gaelic **Ó Mearadhaigh** (see MERRY).

Merricks (211) Variant or patronymic form of MERRICK.

Merrifield (1382) English: habitational name from any of various places, such as Merryfield in Devon and Cornwall or Mirfield in West Yorkshire, all named with the Old English elements *myrige* 'pleasant' + *feld* 'pasture', 'open country' (see FIELD).

Merrigan (487) Irish: Anglicized form of Gaelic **Ó Muireagáin** 'descendant of *Muireagán*' a personal name representing a name beginning with *muir* 'sea'. Earlier found in the Irish midlands and southern Ulster, this surname is now found throughout Ireland.

GIVEN NAME Irish 5%. *Eamon.*

Merrihew (234) English and Irish: most probably an altered form of Welsh MEREDITH (which is found as **Meriday** in 16th and 17th century English sources), or possibly of English MAYHEW.

Merrill (12951) English: habitational name from any of several minor places named with the Old English elements *myrige* 'pleasant' + *hyll* 'hill'.

Merriman (3304) **1.** English: nickname, an elaborated form of MERRY 1. **2.** Irish: Anglicized form of an unidentified Gaelic name.

Merrin (131) English (East Midlands): unexplained; possibly a variant of MARRIN.

Merring (100) English: variant of MERRIN.

Merriott (223) English: variant of MERRITT.

Merris (104) English: possibly a variant of MARES.

Merrithew (132) English and Irish: variant of MERRIHEW.

Merritt (16161) English: **1.** habitational name from Merriott in Somerset, named in Old English as 'boundary gate' or 'mare gate', from *(ge)mǣre* 'boundary' or *miere* 'mare' + *geat* 'gate'. **2.** variant (as a result of hypercorrection) of MARRIOTT, or of **Marryat**, which is from a Middle English personal name, *Meryet*, Old English *Mǣrgēat*, composed of the element *mǣr* 'boundary' + the tribal name *Gēat* (see JOSLIN).

Merritts (169) English: variant of or patronymic from MERRITT 2.

Merriweather (935) English: nickname for someone of a sunny disposition, from Middle English *merry* (see MERRY) + *wether* 'weather' (Old English *weder*).

Merriwether (187) English: variant spelling of MERRIWEATHER.

Merrow (538) English: habitational name from Merrow in Surrey, possibly so named from Old English *mearg* 'marrow' used figuratively to mean 'fertile ground'.

Merry (1490) **1.** English: nickname for someone with a blithe or happy disposition, from Middle English *merry* 'lively', 'cheerful' (Old English *myr(i)ge* 'pleasant', 'agreeable'). **2.** Irish: Anglicized form of Gaelic **Ó Mearadhaigh**, **Ó Meardha** 'descendant of *Mearadhach*', 'descendant of *Meardha*', personal names derived from an adjective meaning 'lively', 'wild', 'wanton'. **3.** French: from a vernacular form of the personal name *Médéric*, derived from a Germanic personal name conposed of *mecht* 'strength', 'might' + *rīc* 'power'; 'ruler'. **4.** French: habitational name from Merry in Yonne or Merri in Orne, derived from the Latin personal name *Matrius* + the suffix *-acum*.

Merryfield (243) English: variant spelling of MERRIFIELD.

Merryman (1492) English: variant spelling of MERRIMAN.

Merryweather (127) English: variant spelling of MERRIWEATHER.

Mers (122) Dutch: variant of MEERS 2, or of MARS 5.

GIVEN NAMES German 5%. *Alois, Kurt.*

Mersch (300) German: topographic name from Middle High German, Middle Low German *mersch* 'marsh'.

Mersereau (281) Altered spelling of French **Mercereau**, an occupational name from a diminutive of Old French *mercier* 'merchant' (from vulgar Latin *merciarius*, a derivative of *merx*, genitive *mercis* 'merchandise').

Mershon (750) Americanized spelling of French MARCHAND.

Mersinger (126) German: habitational name for someone from Merzingen in Bavaria.

GIVEN NAME French 4%. *Amie* (2).

Mersky (115) Origin unidentified.

Mersman (161) **1.** German: variant of MERSCH with the addition of Middle Low German *man* 'man'. **2.** Dutch: variant of MEERS 2. **3.** Dutch: occupational name from Middle Dutch *me(e)rseman*, *maers(e)man* 'peddler', 'traveling merchant'.

Merson (495) **1.** Jewish (Ashkenazic): patronymic from a reduced form of MEYER 2, + German *Sohn* 'son'. **2.** French: metonymic occupational name for a trader, from Old French *mers* (Latin *merx*) 'wares', 'merchandise'. **3.** Scottish: probably a metronymic from a short form of the female personal name *Mary* (see MARIE).

Merta (176) Polish: from the female personal name *Merta* (see MARTA).

GIVEN NAMES Polish 4%. *Ewa, Zdzislawa.*

Mertel (122) **1.** South German: variant of MARTEL 1. **2.** French: variant of MARTEL 2.

GIVEN NAMES German 8%. *Wolf, Wolfgang.*

Merten (785) North German and Dutch: from a variant of the personal name MARTIN.

Mertens (1729) North German and Dutch: patronymic from a variant of the personal name MARTIN.

Mertes (670) North German and Dutch: variant of MERTENS.

Mertins (210) German and Dutch: patronymic from a variant of MARTIN.

GIVEN NAMES German 8%. *Erwin, Gerhard, Hans, Kurt, Otto, Siegfried, Ulrich.*

Merton (176) English: habitational name from places called Merton in London, Devon, Norfolk, and Oxfordshire, named in Old English with *mere* 'lake', 'pool' + *tūn* 'enclosure', 'settlement'. Compare MARTON, MARTIN 2.

Mertz (3233) German: **1.** (northern): patronymic from a form of the personal name MARTIN. **2.** variant of MARTZ. This surname is also established in Poland, where it is now usually spelled *Merc*.

Merullo (118) Southern Italian: **1.** from a feminine diminutive of MERO. **2.** either from Calabrian *merullu* 'marrow', 'brains' or directly from Latin *merula*.

GIVEN NAMES Italian 11%. *Carmine* (2), *Pasquale* (2), *Domenic, Santo.*

Mervin (154) English: variant of MARVIN.

Mervine (271) Variant of English MARVIN.

Mervis (199) **1.** Dutch: patronymic from an altered form of **Mevis**, a reduced short form of the personal name *Bartholomeus* (see BARTHOLOMEW). **2.** Jewish (eastern Ashkenazic): unexplained.

GIVEN NAMES Jewish 4%. *Hyman, Isadore.*

Merwin (1038) English: variant of MARVIN.

Mery (108) French: **1.** variant of MERRY 3, or from a short form of the personal name *Aimery* (see EMERY). **2.** habitational name from places in Ardennes, Aube, Calvados, Marne, and Val-d'Oise, all derived from the same Gallo-Roman name as MERRY 4.

GIVEN NAMES Spanish 12%; French 9%. *Sergio* (2), *Alicia, Carolina, Enrique, Felipe, Javier, Jorge, Manuel, Mario, Miguel; Michel* (2), *Camille.*

Merz (1867) German: variant spelling of MERTZ.

GIVEN NAMES German 5%. *Otto* (6), *Hans* (3), *Otmar* (2), *Alois, Bernhard, Egon, Eldor, Ernst, Erwin, Fritz, Gerhard, Helmut.*

Mesa (1908) Spanish: probably a habitational name from any of various places, mainly in southern Spain, named La Mesa, from Latin *mensa* 'table', with reference to a topographic feature.

GIVEN NAMES Spanish 49%; Portuguese 11%. *Jose* (52), *Juan* (26), *Manuel* (19), *Carlos* (18), *Luis* (17), *Jorge* (15), *Francisco* (14), *Rafael* (13), *Ruben* (13), *Orlando* (12), *Ramon* (11), *Angel* (10); *Armanda.*

Mesaros (250) **1.** Serbian and Croatian (Slavonia) (**Mesaroš**): Slavicized form of Hungarian *Mészáros*, an occupational name for a butcher, itself derived from South Slavic *mesar* 'butcher'. **2.** Americanized spelling of Hungarian **Mészáros** 'butcher' (see MESZAROS).

Mescall (122) English and Scottish: from a medieval variant of MARSHALL.

Mesch (225) **1.** German and Jewish (eastern Ashkenazic): metonymic occupational name for a brazier, from Middle High German *mess(e)*, Yiddish *mesh* 'brass'. **2.** German: variant of MERSCH.

GIVEN NAMES Jewish 8%. *Dov* (2), *Avi, Meyer.*

Mescher (376) German: possibly an occupational name for a brazier, from an agent derivative of Middle High German *mess(e)* 'brass'.

Meschke (241) Eastern German (of Slavic origin): variant of *Metschke*, a pet form of the personal name *Matthias* (see MATTHEW).

GIVEN NAMES German 6%. *Bernhardt, Fritz, Guenter, Manfried.*

Mesecher (137) German: probably from a Sorbian personal name, *Mesech.*

Meseck (116) German: probably from a Sorbian personal name, *Mesech.*

Meseke (124) German: probably from a Sorbian personal name, *Mesech.*

Mesenbrink (186) North German: topographic name from Middle Low German *mēse* 'titmouse' + *brink* 'edge', 'slope', 'grazing land'.

Meserole (191) Origin unidentified.

Meserve (663) French (Channel Islands; **Meservé**): unexplained.

FOREBEARS Clement Meserve (born 1645 in Gorey Grouville, Jersey, in the Channel Islands) came to Portsmouth, NH, in about 1670. His grandson Nathaniel, who had 11 children, was one of the 12 leading men who purchased claims to NH territory in 1746.

Meservey (260) French (Channel Islands): variant of MESERVE.

Mesh (137) Americanized spelling of Jewish and German MESCH.

GIVEN NAMES Russian 10%; Jewish 9%. *Mikhail* (2), *Anatoly, Arkagy, Gennadiy, Gennady, Leonid*; *Yakov* (2).

Meshell (227) Probably an Americanized spelling of French MICHEL.

Mesich (118) Probably Bosnian, Serbian, or Croatian (**Mesić**): patronymic from the personal name *Meso*, pet form of the Muslim name *Mehmed*, Turkish form of MUHAMMAD.

Mesick (312) Americanized form of Bosnian, Serbian, and Croatian MESICH.

Meske (247) **1.** North German: from Middle Low German *mēseke* 'titmouse', possibly a nickname for someone who was agile or a metonymic occupational name for a bird catcher. **2.** Swedish: possibly of the same origin as 1.

GIVEN NAMES German 5%. *Erhardt, Gerhard, Kurt.*

Mesker (218) Americanized form of German METZGER 'butcher'.

Meskill (183) Irish: variant spelling of MISKELL.

Meskimen (158) Variant of Irish MISKIMEN.

Meskin (120) **1.** Jewish (from Belarus and Lithuania): metronymic from the Yiddish female personal name *Meske*, a pet form of Hebrew *Miryam* (see MIRKIN). **2.** Muslim: from Arabic *meskīn* 'poor', 'humble'.

GIVEN NAMES Jewish 8%; Russian 6%; Muslim 5%. *Isaak*; *Leonid* (2), *Yefim*; *Farid, Khalil, Shahram.*

Mesko (225) **1.** Slovak (**Meško**): from a pet form of the personal name *Mečislav*. **2.** Slovenian (**Meško**): probably from a derivative of the personal name *Mihael* (see MICHAEL).

Mesler (299) **1.** German: variant spelling of MESSLER. **2.** Americanized form of German METZLER.

Mesman (114) **1.** Dutch: occupational name for a hawker or travelling salesman, Middle Dutch *me(e)rseman*. **2.** Dutch: habitational name for someone from any of numerous places named ter or de Meers(ch). **3.** German: unexplained; possibly a variant of MASSMANN. **4.** English: unexplained.

Mesmer (280) Altered spelling of German MESSMER.

Mesnard (130) French: variant of MAYNARD; a hypercorrected spelling of MENARD.

Mesner (154) Variant spelling of German MESSNER.

Mesquita (173) **1.** Portuguese: probably a topographical name from *mesquita* 'mosque'. **2.** Spanish: topographic name from a variant spelling of *mezquita* 'mosque'.

GIVEN NAMES Spanish 23%; Portuguese 21%; Italian 9%. *Manuel* (3), *Jose* (2), *Pedro* (2), *Roberto* (2), *Adriana, Alfredo, Alvaro, Armando, Camila, Fernando, Filipe, Francisco*; *Joao* (3), *Henrique*; *Antonio* (4), *Angelo, Caio.*

Mesrobian (103) Armenian: patronymic from the personal name *Mesrop*, of unknown origin. St. Mesrop (*c.* 350–439) was a scholar and evangelist who devised the Armenian alphabet and promoted Christianity in Armenia.

GIVEN NAMES Armenian 36%; French 9%. *Sarkis* (3), *Ara* (2), *Harout* (2), *Kegham* (2), *Armen, Grigor, Haig, Hratch, Krikor, Mesrob, Minas, Ovanes*; *Gilles* (2).

Mess (282) South German: possibly a metonymic occupational name for a brazier, from Middle High German *mess(e)* 'brass'.

Messa (205) Southern Italian and Spanish: unexplained.

GIVEN NAMES Italian 17%; Spanish 5%. *Carlo* (2), *Vito* (2), *Angelo, Mario, Onofrio, Orlando, Vita*; *Carlos, Manuel, Marcos.*

Messamore (144) Origin unidentified. Probably a variant of MESSIMER.

Messana (232) Southern Italian: unexplained.

GIVEN NAMES Italian 32%. *Rocco* (4), *Sal* (3), *Salvatore* (3), *Angelo* (2), *Mariano* (2), *Gioacchino, Giuseppe, Luigi, Mario, Nicolo, Paolo, Pasquale, Rosario, Silvio.*

Messano (111) Italian (Campania): habitational name for someone from the Sicilian city of Messina, the former name of which was *Messana*.

GIVEN NAMES Italian 19%. *Angelo, Carmine.*

Messenger (2191) English: occupational name, from Middle English, Old French *messag(i)er* 'carrier of messages' (an agent derivative of *message*, Late Latin *missaticum*, from *missus* 'sent').

Messer (6970) **1.** German and Jewish (Ashkenazic): metonymic occupational name for a cutler, from Middle High German *mezzer* 'knife', from Old High German *mezzirahs, mezzisahs*, a compound of *maz* 'food', 'meat' + *sahs* 'knife', 'sword'. The Jewish name is from German *Messer* 'knife' or Yiddish *meser* 'knife'. **2.** German: occupational name for an official in charge of measuring the dues paid in kind by tenants, from an agent derivative of Middle High German *mezzen* 'to measure'. **3.** English and Scottish: occupational name for someone who kept watch over harvested crops, Middle English, Older Scots *mess(i)er*, from Old French *messier* (see MESSIER).

Messerli (203) Swiss German: from a diminutive of MESSER 'knife (maker)'.

GIVEN NAMES German 7%. *Franz* (2), *Fritz, Kurt.*

Messerly (342) Swiss German: variant spelling of MESSERLI.

Messerschmidt (492) German: occupational name for a cutler, from Middle High German *mezzer* 'knife' + *smit* 'smith'. See also MESSER 1.

GIVEN NAMES German 5%. *Ewald, Franz, Frieda, Hans, Kurt, Rudi.*

Messersmith (880) Part-translation of German MESSERSCHMIDT.

Messex (106) Probably a variant of French **Messac** (see MESSICK).

Messick (2500) Probably an altered form of French **Messac**, a habitational name from any of several places with this name, named in Gallo-Roman times as the estate of someone called *Mettius*.

FOREBEARS Julian Messick or Mezeck was a French Huguenot who came to MD in 1664.

Messier (1621) French: occupational name for someone who kept watch over harvested crops, Old French *messier* 'harvest master' (Late Latin *messicarius*, agent derivative of *messis* 'harvest').

GIVEN NAMES French 12%. *Andre* (9), *Armand* (8), *Marcel* (8), *Normand* (6), *Rosaire* (3), *Clovis* (2), *Emile* (2), *Gilles* (2), *Adelard, Adrien, Aldor, Edouard.*

Messimer (204) German: occupational name for a sexton, churchwarden, or verger (see MESSMER, MESSNER).

Messina (4564) Southern Italian: habitational name from the Sicilian city of this name. It was named *Messana* in the 5th century BC when it was captured by Anaxilaos of Rhegium; previously it had been known as *Zancle*. This is a very common surname in Sicily, especially in Palermo and Catania.

GIVEN NAMES Italian 16%. *Salvatore* (47), *Angelo* (26), *Sal* (14), *Santo* (9), *Vito* (9), *Domenic* (6), *Antonio* (4), *Carlo* (4), *Concetta* (4), *Gaetano* (4), *Gasper* (4), *Stefano* (4).

Messineo (376) Southern Italian: habitational name from an Italianized form of *Messineos*, the Greek adjective form of Messina (standard Italian **Messinese**).

GIVEN NAMES Italian 13%. *Dino* (2), *Alessandra, Annamaria, Antonino, Antonio, Concetta, Corrado, Leonardo, Luigi, Nino, Rocco, Sal.*

Messing (818) German: metonymic occupational name for a brazier, from Middle High German *messinc* 'brass' (see MESSINGER 2).

Messinger (1757) **1.** English: variant spelling of MESSENGER. **2.** German and Jewish (Ashkenazic): occupational name for a brazier, from an agent derivative of Middle High German *messinc* 'brass', German *Messing*, from Greek *mossynoikos (khalkos)* 'Mossynoecan bronze', named after the people of northeastern Asia Minor who first produced the alloy. **3.** German: habitational name from Mössingen in Baden-Württemberg (Messingen in the local dialect), which is recorded as *Masginga* in 789, probably from the personal name *Masco* + *ingen*, suffix of relationship.

Messler (272) German: habitational name for someone from Messel near Darmstadt.

Messman (362) **1.** German (**Messmann**): habitational name for someone from Messa (see MESSA). **2.** occupational name or nickname for someone who transported or sold dung, variant of **Mistmann**, from Middle High German *mist*, Middle Low German, Dutch *mest* 'dung', 'cesspool'.

Messmer (1130) German (Alemannic and Swabian): variant of MESSNER, the alteration being by analogy with surnames in *-mer* from place names in *-heim* 'homestead'.

Messmore (269) Possibly an altered form of MESSMER. (cf. Messamore)

Messner (1929) South German: occupational name for a sexton, churchwarden, or verger, Middle High German *mesnære* (Old High German *mesināri*, from Late Latin *ma(n)sionarius*, a derivative of *mansio*, genitive *mansionis*, 'house (of God)', 'church'). The double *-s-* is the result of association with *Messe* 'Mass'.

Messore (112) Italian: occupational name from Old Italian *messore* 'reaper', 'harvester'.

GIVEN NAMES Italian 15%. *Alessandro, Angelo, Duilio, Giacomo, Guido, Immacolata, Rocco, Salvatore.*

Mest (177) French (Breton): occupational name, from a variant of MAITRE.

Mestas (432) Spanish: habitational name from Las Mestas in Cáceres province, or Castilianized form of Asturian-Leonese *Les Mestes*, name of a town and several villages in Asturies, all named with the plural of *mesta* 'common (sheep) pasture' (from Latin *mixtas*, past participle (plural) of *miscere* 'to mix', 'to mingle').

GIVEN NAMES Spanish 16%. *Conrado* (3), *Manuel* (3), *Eduardo* (2), *Juan* (2), *Roberto* (2), *Abelardo, Alfonso, Alfonzo, Alonzo, Aniceto, Armondo, Carlos.*

Mestayer (127) French: from a medieval form of **Métayer** (see METAYER).

GIVEN NAMES French 8%. *Gaston, Monique, Raoul.*

Mester (449) **1.** North German form of MEISTER or Dutch variant of MEESTER. **2.** Hungarian: occupational name for a teacher, or master craftsman, from the vocabulary word *mester* 'master', 'craftsman', or alternatively a status name for a learned person. Compare MEISTER.

Meston (103) Scottish (Aberdeenshire): unexplained.

Mestre (230) **1.** Catalan, southern French (Occitan), and Portuguese: from *mestre* 'master (craftsman)', denoting the head of a craft or trade guild. Compare French MAITRE. **2.** Jewish (Sephardic, especially in Italy): status name for a rabbi, translation of Aramaic *Rabbī* 'teacher'. **3.** Italian: habitational name from Mestre, now one of the most densely populated areas of Venice.

GIVEN NAMES Spanish 49%; Portuguese 16%. *Jorge* (9), *Jose* (8), *Rolando* (6), *Carlos* (4), *Juan* (4), *Octavio* (4), *Alberto* (3), *Francisco* (3), *Alvaro* (2), *Ana* (2), *Arsenio* (2), *Cesar* (2); *Amadeu.*

Meszaros (671) Hungarian (**Mészáros**): occupational name for a butcher, from the Slavic loanword *mészár*, from *męso* 'meat'. Compare Czech MASARIK.

GIVEN NAMES Hungarian 11%. *Laszlo* (7), *Tibor* (4), *Imre* (3), *Attila* (2), *Ferenc* (2), *Gabor* (2), *Janos* (2), *Karoly* (2), *Zoltan* (2), *Arpad, Bela, Denes.*

Metallo (170) Southern Italian: from the Greek vocabulary word *metallo* 'metal', used as a nickname for a miner or for someone with a clear or metallic tone of voice.

GIVEN NAMES Italian 11%. *Canio, Nicola, Rocco, Vincenzo.*

Metaxas (119) Greek: occupational name for a silkworm breeder, silk merchant, or silk manufacturer, from *metaxi* 'silk' + *-as*, suffix of occupational names. See also MATASSA.

GIVEN NAMES Greek 21%. *Andreas, Angelos, Constantine, Euripides, Gerasimos, Marios, Panagiotis, Spiros, Takis, Tassos.*

Metayer (157) French (**Métayer**): status name for a tenant farmer who held land on condition of sharing its produce equally with the landlord, Old French *meitier* (an agent derivative of *meitié* 'half', Late Latin *medietas*, from *medius* 'middle').

GIVEN NAMES French 23%. *Marcel* (3), *Lucien* (2), *Michel* (2), *Andre, Armand, Charlemagne, Edline, Francklin, Guerda, Jacques, Jean-Michel, Marcelle.*

Metcalf (8906) English (Yorkshire): of uncertain origin, probably from Middle English *metecalf* 'food calf', i.e. a calf being fattened up for eating at the end of the summer. It is thus either an occupational name for a herdsman or slaughterer, or a nickname for a sleek and plump individual, from the same word in a transferred sense. The variants in *med-* appear early, and suggest that the first element was associated by folk etymology with Middle English *mead* 'meadow', 'pasture'.

Metcalfe (1936) English: variant spelling of METCALF.

Metellus (115) French: unexplained.

GIVEN NAMES French 45%; German 4%. *Antoine* (2), *Dominique* (2), *Philomene* (2), *Andree, Brunel, Fabienne, Franck, Georges, Luc, Lucien, Lucner, Marise; Ernst, Fritz.*

Meter (168) Dutch: occupational name, literally 'measurer', denoting an official responsible for dispensing grain from a central warehouse, from an agent derivative of Middle Dutch *meten* 'measure out'.

Meth (213) German and Jewish (Ashkenazic): metonymic occupational name for a brewer or seller of mead, from Middle High German *met(e)*, German *Met* 'mead'.

GIVEN NAMES Jewish 5%; German 4%. *Bina, Emanuel, Meyer, Miriam, Reuven, Shaya; Eugen, Ute.*

Methe (157) German: **1.** habitational name from Methau in Saxony. **2.** (eastern): probably from a derivative of the Sorbian personal name *Mjeto* (see MARTIN).

GIVEN NAMES French 11%. *Laurent* (2), *Normand, Philippe.*

Metheney (184) Variant of MATHENY.

Metheny (787) Variant of MATHENY.

Methner (133) German: variant of METHE 2.

GIVEN NAMES German 8%. *Fritz, Lothar, Otto.*

Method (117) Origin unidentified. Compare French METHOT.

Methot (201) French Canadian: probably a respelling of **Matthot**, from a pet form of the personal name *Mathieu* (see MATTHEW).

GIVEN NAMES French 13%. *Michel* (3), *Armand, Christien, Germain, Normand.*

Methven (162) Scottish: habitational name from Methven near Perth, recorded in 1150 in the form *Matefen*, at the end of the same century as *Mafen*, and at the beginning of the 13th century as *Methfen*. The place name is probably cognate with Welsh *medd* 'mead' + *maen* (mutated to *faen*) 'stone'.

Methvin (447) Scottish: variant of METHVEN.

Metivier (516) French (**Métivier**): occupational name for a harvester, or rather a feudal tenant who owed a particular duty of service at the time of the harvest, from an agent derivative of Old French *métive* 'harvest' (Latin *messis aestiva* 'summer harvest').

GIVEN NAMES French 11%. *Armand* (3), *Cecile* (2), *Alcide, Aldor, Andre, Benoit, Emile, Luc, Lucien, Nazaire, Normand, Oliva.*

Metler (126) Eastern German: variant of METTLER.

GIVEN NAME German 4%. *Alois.*

Metoyer (532) French (**Métoyer**): variant of METAYER.

GIVEN NAMES French 7%. *Numa* (2), *Silton* (2), *Cecile, Emile, Michel, Patrice.*

Metrick (215) Jewish (eastern Ashkenazic): unexplained.

Metro (465) **1.** Greek (**Metros**): variant of **Mitros** (see MITRO). **2.** Slovak: variant of MITRO. **3.** Perhaps an altered spelling of French **Métreau**, a diminutive of MAITRE. **4.** Spanish: from *metro* 'metre', 'measure', 'rule'.

Metsch (116) German (of Slavic origin): from a short form of a personal name related to Slovak and Slovenian *meč*, Polish *miecz* 'sword' or to Polish *miedza* 'boundary' (of a field, for example).
GIVEN NAMES German 9%. *Fritz, Guenter.*

Metscher (105) German: unexplained.
GIVEN NAMES German 5%. *Hermann, Johann.*

Metsker (189) Americanized form of German METZGER.

Mette (277) **1.** North German and Dutch: from a pet form of the female personal name *Mechthild* (see METZ). **2.** French: topographic name from Old French *mete* 'boundary stone', 'boundary' (from Latin *meta* 'bounded estate').

Mettee (107) Possibly a respelling of French **Metté**, a derivative of METTE.

Metteer (107) Origin unidentified. Possibly an altered form of French **Métier**, from *métier*, Old French *mestier* 'official responsibility', 'duty', 'calling', hence a metonymic occupational name for an official of some kind.

Metten (111) German: habitational name from a place called Metten in Westphalia.
GIVEN NAMES German 5%. *August, Hans.*

Metter (193) German: **1.** variant of METH. **2.** from a Germanic personal name based on *mahal* 'gathering place', 'court'.
GIVEN NAME German 4%. *Horst.*

Metters (107) English (Devon): unexplained; perhaps a variant of MATTERS, itself a variant of MATTER.

Mettert (107) German: unexplained.

Mettille (103) Possibly a variant of French **Metteil**, from *méteil* 'mixed crop of wheat and rye', hence possibly a metonymic occupational name for a grain farmer or a topographic name.

Metting (109) North German and Dutch: unexplained; perhaps a variant of **Meding**, a habitational name from any of various places named Medingen.
GIVEN NAME German 5%. *Ewald.*

Mettler (1197) **1.** Eastern German: probably a patronymic from *Metel*, a pet form of the personal name *Matthias* (see MATTHEW). **2.** Swiss German: habitational name for someone from any of the many places in Switzerland called Mettlen.

Metts (1328) Americanized spelling of German METZ.

Metty (110) German: unexplained.
GIVEN NAMES German 5%. *Aloys, Eldred.*

Metz (8170) **1.** German: from a short form of the female personal name *Mechthild*, composed of Germanic *maht* 'might', 'strength' + *hild* 'strife', 'battle'. **2.** German and Jewish (Ashkenazic): habitational name from Metz in Lorraine, which took its name from a Gaulish tribe, the *Mediomatrici*; in the name of the place this became abbreviated to *Mettis*, hence the modern name. **3.** German: from *Mätz*, a short form of the personal name *Matthias* (see MATTHEW). **4.** North German: metonymic occupational name for a cutler, from Middle Low German *messet*, *metset* 'knife', 'dagger' or Middle High German *metz(e)* 'knife'. Compare MESSER 1. This name is also established in Poland.
FOREBEARS Christian Metz, the founder of the Amana colonies in IA, was born in Neuwied, Prussia, in 1794. His group arrived in NY in 1842 and proceeded to the Midwest in 1855, where they were able to establish an experimental life style that was more successful than most other Utopian communal religious settlements of the time.

Metze (136) German: **1.** metronymic from a short form of the personal name *Mechthild* (see METZ 1). **2.** habitational name from Metze near Kassel.
GIVEN NAMES German 6%. *Armin, Gerhard, Gernot.*

Metzel (127) **1.** German: from a pet form of any of various personal names, for example *Matz* (from MATTHIAS), *Metz* (see METZ 1), or a Germanic personal name such as *Matzo*. **2.** German (Rhineland): variant of METZLER. This name is also established in Poland.

Metzen (131) German: metronymic from METZE or METZ 4.
GIVEN NAME German 4%. *Mathias.*

Metzer (213) **1.** German and Jewish (Ashkenazic): habitational name for someone from METZ. **2.** Dutch: occupational name for a bricklayer, Middle Dutch *metsere*.

Metzgar (540) Variant, under Slavic influence, of German METZGER.

Metzger (8559) South German and Jewish (Ashkenazic): occupational name for a butcher, Middle High German *metziger*, *metzjer*, German *Metzger* (probably a loan word from Latin, but of uncertain lineage).

Metzinger (355) German: habitational name from places called Metzingen, in Württemberg, Lorraine, and near Lüneburg, in northern Germany.

Metzker (191) Variant of German METZGER.

Metzler (2756) German (Middle Rhineland): occupational name for a butcher, Middle High German *metzeler*, from Latin *macellarius* 'dealer in meat', from *macellum* 'stall (at a market)', 'meat market'.

Metzner (543) **1.** German (Silesia, Saxony, Bavaria, and Austria): from Middle High German *metze*, a small dry-measure for grain or flour, hence a metonymic occupational name for a maker of measures or for a miller's assistant (who measured the quantity of flour due to the miller as pay-ment in kind). **2.** South German: occupational name for a butcher, from an agent derivative of Middle High German *metzjen*, *metzigen* 'to butcher'. **3.** German: habitational name for someone from Metzen in Lower Bavaria.

Meucci (157) Italian: patronymic from the personal name *Meuccio*, a pet form of MEO.
GIVEN NAMES Italian 13%. *Gino* (2), *Otello* (2), *Aldo, Angelo, Dario, Enrico, Enza, Guilio.*

Meuer (107) German: habitational name for someone from Meura near Saalfeld (Thuringia) or Meuro near Wittenberg.
GIVEN NAMES German 8%. *Frieda, Gerd, Ingeburg.*

Meulemans (194) Dutch: patronymic from **Meuleman**, an occupational name for a miller, from *molen*, *meulen* 'mill' (Latin *molina*) + *man* 'man'.
GIVEN NAME French 4%. *Elzear.*

Meunier (1126) French: occupational name for a miller, *meunier* (Old French *mounier*, from an agent derivative of Latin *molina* 'mill').
GIVEN NAMES French 12%. *Jacques* (4), *Marcel* (4), *Andre* (3), *Armand* (3), *Cecile* (2), *Emile* (2), *Fernand* (2), *Michel* (2), *Pierre* (2), *Yvon* (2), *Aldor, Alyre.*

Meurer (724) German and Jewish (Ashkenazic): variant of MAURER.

Meuret (104) French: from a diminutive of Old French *meure* 'mulberry', probably applied as a nickname for someone with a dark complexion, or perhaps as an occupational name for someone who grew or sold mulberries.

Meuse (397) Dutch (**van der Meuse**): topographic name from Middle Dutch *mose* 'mud', 'mire'.

Meusel (116) Dutch and North German: occupational name for a bagpipe player.
GIVEN NAMES German 15%. *Juergen* (2), *Fritz, Kurt.*

Meuser (266) **1.** German: occupational name for a mouse catcher, from Middle High German *mūs* 'mouse' + the agent suffix *-er*. **2.** Dutch: occupational name from *musen* 'to play the bagpipes'.
GIVEN NAMES German 5%. *Ernst, Horst, Otto.*

Meuth (182) German: unexplained.

Meuwissen (117) Dutch (**Mewissen**, **Meeuwesen**, etc.): patronymic from the personal name *Meus, Mewis*, short forms of *Bartholomeus* (see BARTHOLOMEW).
GIVEN NAMES German 4%; French 4%. *Franz, Matthias; Etienne, Hilaire.*

Meverden (141) Origin unidentified.

Mew (169) English: **1.** from an Old English nickname *mǣw*, *mēaw* 'seagull', or the same word used as a personal name, *Mēawa*. Compare MAW. **2.** metonymic occupational name for someone in charge of a mew, a cage for hawks and falcons, especially while moulting, from Old French *mue*, a derivative of *muer* 'to moult' (from Latin *mutare* 'to change').

Mewborn (380) English: unexplained. Perhaps a variant of NEWBORN. This name occurs frequently in NC.

Mewbourn (104) Variant of English MEWBORN.

Mewes (219) **1.** North German: from a short form of the personal name *Bartholomäus* (see BARTHOLOMEW). **2.** English: habitational name from Meaux (pronounced 'Myoos') in Humberside, formerly in East Yorkshire. This was named in Old Norse as 'sandbank pool', from *melr* 'sandbank', 'sandhill' + *sær* 'sea', 'lake', and subsequently assimilated by folk etymology to a French place name.
GIVEN NAMES German 10%. *Hans* (2), *Alfons, Horst, Klaus, Manfred, Otto, Uwe, Wilhelm.*

Mewhinney (101) Variant of Scottish and northern Irish MAWHINNEY.

Mewhorter (100) Variant of Scottish and northern Irish MCWHORTER.

Mews (164) German and English: variant spelling of MEWES.
GIVEN NAMES German 10%. *Detlef, Kurt, Otto, Siegfried, Willi, Wolfgang.*

Mey (258) English, Dutch, and German: variant spelling of MAY or MEI.
GIVEN NAMES German 4%. *Helmuth, Horst, Udo, Ulli, Wilhelmina.*

Meyer (65510) **1.** German and Dutch: from Middle High German *meier*, a status name for a steward, bailiff, or overseer, which later came to be used also to denote a tenant farmer, which is normally the sense in the many compound surnames formed with this term as a second element. Originally it denoted a village headman (ultimately from Latin *māior* 'greater', 'superior'). **2.** Jewish (Ashkenazic): from the Yiddish personal name *Meyer* (from Hebrew *Meir* 'enlightener', a derivative of Hebrew *or* 'light'). **3.** Irish: Anglicized form of Gaelic **Ó Meidhir**, from *meidhir* 'mirth'. **4.** Danish: variant spelling of MEIER 3.

Meyerhofer (162) South German: habitational name for someone who lived at a farm named Meyerhof (from Middle High German *meier* 'steward', 'bailiff', 'tenant farmer' + *hof* 'manor farm').
GIVEN NAME German 6%. *Dietrich* (2).

Meyerhoff (454) German (Westphalia): habitational name for someone who lived at a farm named Meyerhof (see MEYERHOFER).
GIVEN NAMES German 4%. *Erwin, Ilse, Otto.*

Meyering (223) North German: patronymic from the status name MEYER 1, meaning 'descendant of the tenant farmer (or steward or bailiff)'.

Meyerowitz (197) Jewish (Ashkenazic): Germanized spelling of a Slavic patronymic from MEYER 2.
GIVEN NAMES Jewish 8%. *Meyer, Shula.*

Meyers (22803) **1.** English: patronymic meaning 'son of the mayor' (see MAYER 1). **2.** Jewish (Ashkenazic): patronymic from the personal *Meyer* (see MEYER 2). **3.** American form of German MEYER, with excrescent -*s*. **4.** Irish: variant of MEYER 3.

Meyerson (782) Jewish (Ashkenazic): patronymic from the personal name MEYER 2.
GIVEN NAMES Jewish 5%. *Meyer* (2), *Emanuel, Irina, Isadore, Mort.*

Meyette (101) French: **1.** Possibly a respelling of **Myet** (see MYETTE). **2.** In some cases, it may be a respelling of English MYATT.
GIVEN NAMES French 7%. *Andre, Armand.*

Meylor (100) **1.** English: occupational name for an enameler, from Middle English *ameillur*, Old French *esmailleur* (see MAILER). **2.** English and Welsh: from the Welsh personal name *Meilyr*. **3.** Scottish: habitational name from Mailer in Forteviot, Perthshire.

Meyn (294) North German: variant spelling of MEIN.
GIVEN NAMES German 7%. *Klaus* (2), *Elke, Frieda, Gunter, Kurt, Otto, Reiner.*

Meza (3526) possibly Basque: unexplained.
GIVEN NAMES Spanish 53%; Portuguese 12%. *Jose* (119), *Juan* (53), *Jesus* (50), *Carlos* (45), *Manuel* (34), *Luis* (32), *Francisco* (26), *Jorge* (23), *Miguel* (21), *Roberto* (21), *Javier* (19), *Mario* (18); *Ligia* (2), *Godofredo, Zaragoza.*

Mezera (226) Origin unidentified.

Mezey (149) Hungarian: topographic name for someone who lived near a field or a meadow, or an occupational name for a farmer (see MEZO).
GIVEN NAMES Hungarian 8%; Jewish 4%; German 4%. *Kalman* (2), *Bela, Ildiko, Laszlo; Isadore; Siegmund.*

Mezger (248) German and Jewish (Ashkenazic): variant spelling of METZGER.
GIVEN NAMES German 8%. *Fritz* (4), *Erwin, Hermann, Ilse, Kurt.*

Mezick (116) Probably a variant of French **Messac** (see MESSICK).

Mezo (192) **1.** Hungarian (**Mező**): from *mező* 'field', 'meadow', hence probably a metonymic occupational name for a farmer or farmworker. **2.** Spanish (of Basque origin): unexplained.

Mezzacappa (107) Variant spelling of Italian **Mezzacapa**, an unflattering nickname for someone of limited intelligence, from *mezza* 'half' + *capa* 'head'. Compare MEZZATESTA.
GIVEN NAMES Italian 37%. *Enrico* (2), *Angelo, Antonio, Carmine, Ciro, Giovanni, Nicola, Pietro.*

Mezzanotte (131) Italian: from *mezzanotte* 'midnight', probably an anecdotal nickname, although Caracausi suggests it may have been a personal name alluding to the time of birth of the bearer.
GIVEN NAMES Italian 10%. *Antonio, Arcangelo, Domenic, Donato, Romolo.*

Mezzatesta (103) Italian: unflattering nickname for someone of limited intelligence, from *mezza* 'half' + *testa* 'head'. Compare MEZZACAPPA.
GIVEN NAMES Italian 23%; Spanish 10%. *Angelo* (2), *Sal* (2); *Alberto, Orlando.*

Mhoon (129) Southeast Asian: variant of MOON.

Miah (256) Muslim: variant of MIAN. In Panjab and Rajasthan it is also found as a Hindu name among a class of Hill Rajputs.
GIVEN NAMES Muslim 75%; Indian 7%. *Mohammed* (22), *Abdul* (5), *Mohammad* (4), *Muhammed* (3), *Nurul* (3), *Siraj* (3), *Syed* (3), *Abdus* (2), *Ahmed* (2), *Harun* (2), *Malek* (2), *Malik* (2); *Lal* (2), *Manik* (2), *Bachu, Bakul, Dulal, Suruj.*

Mian (251) Muslim: from a title of respect, Urdu *mian* 'sir' (from Persian *miyān* 'between'), used to address an older man. In Bangladesh this is common as a suffix added to the name of a respected person, especially a senior member of a village community.
GIVEN NAMES Muslim 85%. *Mohammad* (11), *Muhammad* (6), *Abdul* (5), *Tahir* (5), *Humayun* (4), *Javed* (4), *Khalid* (4), *Mohammed* (4), *Zahid* (4), *Nisar* (3), *Riaz* (3), *Shahid* (3).

Miano (594) Southern Italian: **1.** from a short form of the personal name DAMIANO or *Emiliano*, Latin *Aemilianus* (see EMILE). **2.** habitational name from Miano in Naples, Parma, and Teramo; Miane in Treviso; or Mian in Belluno.
GIVEN NAMES Italian 16%. *Salvatore* (7), *Rocco* (3), *Angelo* (2), *Gaetano* (2), *Sal* (2), *Alfio, Carmela, Carmelo, Carmine, Dino, Domenic, Gino.*

Miao (258) **1.** Chinese 苗: from the name of an area called Miao. During the Spring and Autumn period (722–481 BC) this area was granted to the son of a senior adviser of the state of Chu. The character for *Miao* also denotes the Miao ethnic group in China, but the surname does not have a Miao origin. **2.** Chinese 缪: from a title posthumously bestowed upon the duke of Miao from the state of Qin during the Spring and Autumn period (722–481 BC).
GIVEN NAMES Chinese 43%. *Wei* (3), *Lan* (2), *Li* (2), *Ping* (2), *Tao* (2), *Xue* (2), *Chang, Chun Mei, Dong Sheng, Feng Ying, Gang, Guo Jun, Hai, Haiping, Han Yong, Min, Xuan, Yen, You.*

Miars (105) Probably a variant spelling of English and Irish MYERS.

Miazga (167) Polish: nickname from *miazga* 'pulp', 'crush', probably a nickname for someone who had been crushed by something.
GIVEN NAMES Polish 8%. *Danuta, Edyta, Genowefa, Irena, Izydor, Mariola, Tadeusz.*

Mical (122) Polish (**Micał**, also **Miczał**): from the personal name *Michał* (see MICHAEL) or *Mikołaj* (see NICHOLAS).

GIVEN NAMES Polish 10%. *Janina, Jerzy, Mieczyslaw, Zygmund.*

Micale (317) Southern Italian: from the Greek personal name *Mikhalis*, vernacular form of *Mikhaēl* (see MICHAEL).

GIVEN NAMES Italian 25%. *Angelo* (4), *Carlo* (4), *Domenic* (2), *Salvatore* (2), *Antonio, Ferdinando, Filippo, Natale, Nicola, Orlando, Remo, Rocco, Rosario, Santo.*

Micalizzi (142) Italian: patronymic from a pet form of the personal name MICALE. In the form **Mihalitsis** this is also found as a Greek family name.

GIVEN NAMES Italian 22%. *Salvatore* (3), *Angelo* (2), *Gaetano* (2), *Carmelo, Guiseppe, Rocco.*

Micallef (300) Probably an altered spelling of Bulgarian *Mihalev*, patronymic from the personal name *Mihal* (see MICHAEL).

GIVEN NAMES French 6%; Italian 4%. *Francois, Susette; Carmelina, Romeo, Santo.*

Micciche (315) Italian (**Micciché**): habitational name from a place (recorded in Greek as *Mitzēkenion*), which stood on the site of present-day Villalba or Alimena.

GIVEN NAMES Italian 10%. *Salvatore* (4), *Angelo* (3), *Romano* (2), *Antonio, Lorenzo, Sal.*

Miccio (153) Italian: **1.** probably from Southern Italian Greek *miććo* 'small'. **2.** Alternatively, from an Old Tuscan nickname, *Miccio*, from the vocabulary word *miccio* 'ass', 'donkey'. **3.** from Sicilian *micciu* 'wick', applied as a nickname for a tall thin man.

GIVEN NAMES Italian 15%. *Salvatore* (4), *Nunziato, Sal.*

Micco (159) Italian: from a short form of the personal name *Domenico*, Latin *Dominicus* (see DOMINGO).

GIVEN NAMES Italian 11%. *Pasquale* (2), *Angelo, Giovanni.*

Micek (493) Czech (**Miček**) and Polish: from a pet form of a personal name such as *Michal, Michał* (see MICHAEL), or *Mikuláš, Mikołaj* (see NICHOLAS).

Miceli (1635) Sicilian and southern Italian: from a southern variant of the personal name *Michele* (see MICHAEL), influenced by the Greek form *Mikhailis*.

GIVEN NAMES Italian 23%. *Salvatore* (15), *Angelo* (6), *Sal* (6), *Vito* (6), *Mario* (5), *Giuseppe* (4), *Luciano* (4), *Rosario* (3), *Santo* (3), *Arturo* (2), *Carlo* (2), *Giuseppi* (2), *Luca* (2), *Paolo* (2), *Pasquale* (2), *Salvador* (2), *Aida, Alfredo, Augusto, Ildo, Lino, Marta.*

Mich (199) **1.** English: from a pet form of the medieval personal name *Michel* (see MITCHELL). **2.** Polish: from a short form of any of various personal names such as *Michał* (Polish equivalent of MICHAEL) or *Mikołaj* (Polish equivalent of NICHOLAS).

Michael (13800) English, German, Dutch, and Jewish: from the personal name *Michael*, ultimately from Hebrew *Micha-el*

'Who is like God?'. This was borne by various minor Biblical characters and by one of the archangels, the protector of Israel (Daniel 10:13, 12:1; Rev. 12:7). In Christian tradition, Michael was regarded as the warrior archangel, conqueror of Satan, and the personal name was correspondingly popular throughout Europe, especially in knightly and military families. In English-speaking countries, this surname is also found as an Anglicized form of several Greek surnames having *Michael* as their root, for example **Papamichaelis** 'Michael the priest' and patronymics such as **Michaelopoulos**.

Michaelides (121) Greek: patronymic from the personal name *Mikhaēl* (see MICHAEL). The *-ides* patronymic is classical; it was revived in the 19th century, mainly by Greeks from the Black Sea.

GIVEN NAMES Greek 38%. *Costas* (4), *Demetrios* (3), *Alkis, Christos, Demetris, Efstathios, Evangelos, Ioannis, Manos, Michalakis, Paraskevas, Pavlos.*

Michaelis (1351) German, Dutch, and Jewish: Latinized patronymic from the personal name MICHAEL.

GIVEN NAMES German 6%. *Kurt* (4), *Gunther* (2), *Arno, Bernhard, Elke, Erwin, Frieda, Gerd, Gerda, Guenther, Gunter, Horst.*

Michaels (6903) English, German, and Dutch: patronymic from the personal name MICHAEL. This form has also absorbed cognates from other European languages.

Michaelsen (416) Danish and Norwegian, Dutch, and North German: patronymic from the personal name MICHAEL.

GIVEN NAMES Scandinavian 4%; German 4%. *Helle, Kerstin, Knud, Niels; Dieter, Eldred, Erwin, Fritz, Hans.*

Michaelson (1679) **1.** English: patronymic from the personal name MICHAEL. **2.** Americanized spelling of MICHAELSEN.

Michal (359) Polish (**Michał**), Czech, Slovak, and Ukrainian: from the personal name *Michal*, Polish *Michał* (see MICHAEL).

Michalak (1415) Polish: patronymic from the personal name *Michał* (see MICHAEL).

GIVEN NAMES Polish 4%. *Casimir* (3), *Miroslaw* (2), *Agnieszka, Andrzej, Boleslaw, Iwona, Jacek, Janina, Jaromir, Krzysztof, Piotr, Zbigniew.*

Michalczyk (128) Polish: from a pet form of the personal name *Michał* (see MICHAEL).

GIVEN NAMES Polish 11%. *Janina, Jozef, Piotr, Ryszard, Zbigniew.*

Michalec (371) Czech, Slovak, and Polish: from a derivative of the personal name *Michal* (Czech), *Michał* (Polish) (see MICHAEL).

Michalek (890) Czech and Slovak (**Michálek**) and Polish (**Michałek**): from a pet form of the personal name *Michal* (Czech) or *Michał* (Polish) (see MICHAEL).

Michalik (613) Polish: from a pet form of the personal name *Michał* (see MICHAEL).

GIVEN NAMES Polish 7%. *Andrzej* (3), *Jaroslaw* (2), *Stanislaw* (2), *Boleslaw, Dariusz, Henryk, Irena, Janusz, Krystyna, Wojciech.*

Michalk (120) German (Saxony): variant of MICHALKE.

Michalke (111) Germanized form of a Slavic pet form of the personal name MICHAL.

GIVEN NAMES German 14%. *Gernot* (2), *Otto* (2), *Erwin, Fritz, Klaus.*

Michalko (125) Ukrainian: from a derivative of the personal name MICHAL.

GIVEN NAME German 4%. *Helmut.*

Michalowski (514) Polish (**Michałowski**): habitational name from a place called Michałowice.

GIVEN NAMES Polish 12%. *Jerzy* (3), *Franciszek* (2), *Ryszard* (2), *Slawomir* (2), *Alicja, Bogdan, Bronislaw, Jaroslaw, Krzysztof, Mariusz, Matylda, Miroslaw.*

Michals (258) Variant of MICHAELS in Slavic languages.

Michalski (2647) **1.** Polish and Jewish (from Poland): habitational name for someone from a place called Michale in Bydgoszcz voivodeship, or Michały in Płock voivodeship. **2.** Jewish (from Poland): patronymic from personal name *Michal* (see MICHAEL).

GIVEN NAMES Polish 4%. *Janusz* (3), *Casimir* (2), *Ewa* (2), *Grzegorz* (2), *Izydor* (2), *Wladyslaw* (2), *Zbigniew* (2), *Andrzej, Bartosz, Bronislaw, Darek, Jacek.*

Michalsky (144) Variant (mainly Ukrainian) of MICHALSKI.

Michaud (5769) French: from a variant of the personal name *Michel* (see MICHAEL).

GIVEN NAMES French 14%. *Armand* (25), *Lucien* (18), *Andre* (11), *Benoit* (8), *Fernand* (8), *Normand* (8), *Ludger* (7), *Adrien* (6), *Philippe* (6), *Pierre* (6), *Camille* (5), *Henri* (5).

Michaux (266) French: variant of MICHAUD.

Micheal (131) Variant of MICHAEL.

Micheals (108) Variant of MICHAELS.

GIVEN NAME French 4%. *Damien.*

Micheau (125) French: variant of MICHAUD.

Michel (6608) **1.** French, German, and Dutch: from the personal name *Michel* (see MICHAEL). **2.** Basque: variant from the personal name *Mitxel*, equivalent of MICHAEL. **3.** Polish: from a variant of the personal name *Michał* (see MICHAEL). **4.** Greek: shortened form of any of various patronymic derivatives of MICHAEL, for example **Michelakis, Michelakakis,** or **Michelakos**.

GIVEN NAMES French 7%. *Pierre* (8), *Andre* (6), *Jacques* (5), *Micheline* (4), *Patrice* (4), *Dominique* (3), *Emile* (3), *Gisele* (3), *Laurent* (3), *Lucien* (3), *Philippe* (3), *Raymonde* (3).

Michela (105) Italian: variant of MICHELE.

GIVEN NAME Italian 6%. *Domenic.*

Michele (175) Italian: from the personal name *Michele*, Italian equivalent of MICHAEL.
GIVEN NAMES Italian 10%. *Angelo, Antonio, Gioia, Guiseppe.*

Micheletti (317) Italian: form a patronymic or plural form of a pet form of the personal name MICHELE.
GIVEN NAMES Italian 8%. *Angelo* (2), *Aldo, Gildo, Gino, Guido, Libero, Marco, Umberto.*

Micheli (405) Italian: from a patronymic form of the personal name MICHELE.
GIVEN NAMES Italian 18%. *Sergio* (5), *Silvano* (3), *Aldo* (2), *Amelio* (2), *Angelo* (2), *Carlo* (2), *Elio* (2), *Annibale, Antonio, Domenico, Edo, Francesco, Gino, Mario, Orlando.*

Michelin (163) French: from a pet form of *Michel*, French form of MICHAEL.
GIVEN NAMES French 6%. *Andre, Jacques.*

Michelini (187) Italian: patronymic or plural form of a pet form of MICHELE.
GIVEN NAMES Italian 10%. *Guido* (4), *Franco* (2), *Aldo, Angelo, Carmelo, Gennaro, Massimo, Pasquale.*

Michell (507) English (mainly Devon and Cornwall): variant spelling of MITCHELL.
GIVEN NAMES French 4%. *Jacques* (2), *Etienne, Yvrose.*

Michelle (192) French: from the female personal name *Michelle*, feminine form of *Michel*, French form of MICHAEL.
GIVEN NAMES Italian 5%; French 4%. *Angelo, Carlo, Gennaro; Colette, Odile.*

Michelli (171) Variant spelling of Italian MICHELI.
GIVEN NAMES Italian 8%. *Angelo, Gasper, Nicolo, Silvio.*

Michelman (150) **1.** German (**Michelmann**): patronymic or pet form of the personal name *Michel*, a variant of MICHAEL. **2.** English: occupational name for the servant (Middle English *man*) of a man called *Michel* (see MITCHELL).
GIVEN NAME German 6%. *Kurt.*

Michelotti (167) Italian: patronymic or plural form of a pet form of the personal name MICHELE.
GIVEN NAMES Italian 16%. *Aldo* (2), *Carlo* (2), *Remo* (2), *Romano* (2), *Gioia, Italo, Pietro, Renzo.*

Michels (2928) German and Dutch: patronymic from the personal name *Michel* (see MICHAEL).

Michelsen (543) North German, Dutch, Danish, and Norwegian: patronymic from the personal name *Michel* (see MICHAEL).
GIVEN NAMES Scandinavian 8%. *Erik* (3), *Johan* (2), *Niels* (2), *Per, Sofus, Sophus, Thor.*

Michelson (1580) **1.** Jewish (Ashkenazic): patronymic from the Yiddish personal name *Mikhl* (see MICHAEL). **2.** English: patronymic from the medieval personal name *Michel* (see MITCHELL). **3.** Dutch: patronymic from the personal name

Michel, a Dutch variant of MICHAEL. **4.** Americanized spelling of MICHELSEN.
GIVEN NAMES Jewish 4%. *Ilya* (3), *Kerith* (2), *Zev* (2), *Ari, Dorit, Elihu, Ilanit, Isadore, Meyer, Miriam, Pnina, Yaacov.*

Michener (796) Variant spelling of English MITCHENER.

Michetti (165) Italian: patronymic or plural form of a pet form of the personal name *Mico*, a short form of MICHELE.
GIVEN NAMES Italian 19%; French 4%; Spanish 4%. *Angelo* (2), *Antonio, Dante, Domenica, Gennaro, Giustino, Liberato, Marco, Marino; Armand* (2), *Alphonse; Mario, Tito.*

Michie (523) Scottish: from the old Scottish personal name *Michie*, a pet form of MICHAEL.

Michiels (246) Dutch: patronymic from a variant form of the personal name MICHAEL.
GIVEN NAMES French 9%. *Pierre* (2), *Andre, Jean Pierre, Luc, Marcel, Michel.*

Michl (214) German (Bavaria) and Jewish (Ashkenazic): from a variant form of the personal name MICHAEL.
GIVEN NAMES French 4%; German 4%. *Andre, Girard; Ernst, Kurt.*

Michler (149) South German: **1.** patronymic from the personal name *Michel* (see MICHAEL). **2.** habitational name for someone from any of several places called Michelau.
GIVEN NAMES German 9%. *Kurt, Markus, Otto.*

Michlig (123) Swiss German: unexplained.
GIVEN NAME French 4%. *Celestine.*

Michna (257) Czech and Slovak: from a pet form of the personal name *Michal.*

Michniewicz (112) Polish: patronymic from the personal name MICHNO.
GIVEN NAME Polish 7%. *Irena.*

Michno (102) Polish: from a pet form of the personal name *Michał* (see MICHAEL).
GIVEN NAMES Polish 7%; German 4%. *Jadwiga, Tomasz; Florian.*

Michon (362) French and Dutch: from a pet form of *Miche*, a short form of the personal name *Michel* (see MICHAEL).
GIVEN NAMES French 7%. *Emile* (2), *Normand* (2), *Andre, Eugenie, Michel.*

Michonski (100) Polish: from a derivative of the personal name MICHNO.

Mick (1912) **1.** North German and Dutch: metonymic occupational name from Middle Low German and Middle Dutch *micke* '(wheat or rye) bread'. **2.** German (Saxon): from a short form of the Slavic personal name *Mikolaj*, a form of NICHOLAS. **3.** German (northern and central): from a byname related to Middle Low German *micke* 'forked stick'. **4.** Irish: reputedly a surname taken to County Limerick from the Rhine Palatinate in the 18th century.

Micka (233) **1.** Czech and Slovak (also **Mička**): from a pet form of the personal

names *Mikuláš* (see NICHOLAS) or *Michal* (see MICHAEL). **2.** Polish (also **Mićka, Miczka**): from a pet form of the personal names *Mikołaj* (see NICHOLAS) or *Dymitr* (Latin *Demetrius*; see DEMETRIOU).

Micke (236) Dutch and German: variant of MICK.

Mickel (755) **1.** German: from the personal name, a variant of MICHAEL. **2.** Altered spelling of German and Dutch MICHEL. **3.** Scottish: variant spelling of MICKLE.

Mickels (164) Possibly an altered spelling of MICHELS, or of Dutch **Mikels** or **Mickils**, patronymics from a variant of MICHAEL.

Mickelsen (598) Danish and Norwegian: patronymic from the personal name *Michel* (see MICHAEL).
GIVEN NAMES Scandinavian 7%. *Erik* (5), *Einer, Ludvig.*

Mickelson (3080) Respelling of Swedish **Mickelsson**, a patronymic from the personal name *Mickel* (see MICHAEL).

Mickens (999) Origin uncertain. Evidently a patronymic from a form of the personal name MICHAEL, perhaps in English, though the surname is not found in England.

Mickey (1349) Americanized spelling of Dutch and German MICKE or MUECKE.

Mickiewicz (205) Polish: patronymic from *Micko*, a pet form of the personal names *Mikołaj* (see NICHOLAS) or *Dymitr* (Latin *Demetrius*; see DEMETRIOU).
GIVEN NAMES Polish 10%. *Jacek* (2), *Andrzej, Henryk, Krzysztof, Tadeusz.*

Mickle (1257) **1.** Shortened form of Scottish or Irish McMICKLE. **2.** Scottish and northern English: nickname for a big man, from Older Scots and northern Middle English *meikle, mekill* 'great', 'large' (Old Norse *mikill*). **3.** Altered spelling of German MICKEL.

Mickler (462) Americanized spelling of MICHLER.

Mickles (285) Variant of Dutch MICHIELS or some other derivative of the personal name MICHAEL.

Mickley (425) Americanized form of German MICKEL.

Micklos (129) Americanized spelling of Hungarian **Miklós** (see MIKLOS).

Mickus (162) Lithuanian: from a reduced pet form of the personal name *Dimitriju*, from Greek *Dēmētrios* (Latin *Demetrius*; see DEMETRIOU).
GIVEN NAMES Lithuanian 8%. *Albinas* (2), *Antanina, Juozas, Nida, Vytautas.*

Micucci (200) Italian: patronymic or plural form of a pet form of the personal name *Mico*, a short form of MICHELE.
GIVEN NAMES Italian 13%. *Angelo* (3), *Lorenzo, Rocco, Tonino, Vito.*

Midcap (134) Origin unidentified.

Middaugh (857) Americanized spelling of German MITTAG.

Middendorf (812) German: topographic name from the residence of an inhabitant 'in the middle of the village', from Middle Low German *midde*, Middle High German *mitte* 'midst' (adjective) + Middle Low German *dorp*, Middle High German *dorf* 'village'.

Middlebrook (910) English: from Middle English *middel* 'middle' + *broke* 'brook', 'stream', hence denoting someone who lived by a stream so called.

Middlebrooks (1237) Variant form of English MIDDLEBROOK.

Middlecamp (101) Dutch (**Middelkamp**): topographic name for someone who lived in the middle of a field or by the 'middle field'.

Middlekauff (186) Partly Americanized form of German **Mittelkauff**, an occupational name for a broker or middleman, from Middle High German *mittel* 'middle' + *kauf* 'purchase'.

Middleman (149) literal translation of German **Mittelmann**, a status name for an arbitrator.
GIVEN NAME French 7%. *Raoul* (3).

Middlemas (104) Scottish: regional name from Middlemass, a district near Kelso in the Borders region, so named from northern Middle English *midelmast* 'middlemost'.

Middlemiss (168) Scottish and northern English: variant of MIDDLEMAS.

Middlesworth (180) Possibly of English origin, a habitational name from a lost or unidentified place, possibly so named from Old English *midel* 'middle' + *worð* 'enclosure', 'settlement'.

Middleton (13995) English and Scottish: habitational name from any of the places so called. In over thirty instances from many different areas, the name is from Old English *midel* 'middle' + *tūn* 'enclosure', 'settlement'. However, Middleton on the Hill near Leominster in Herefordshire appears in Domesday Book as *Miceltune*, the first element clearly being Old English *micel* 'large', 'great'. Middleton Baggot and Middleton Priors in Shropshire have early spellings that suggest *gemȳðhyll* (from *gemȳð* 'confluence' + *hyll* 'hill') + *tūn* as the origin.
FOREBEARS A Scottish family of this name derives it from lands at Middleto(u)n near Kincardine. The Scottish physician Peter Middleton practiced in New York City after 1752 and was one of the founders of the medical school at King's College (now Columbia University) in 1767. One of the earliest of the Charleston, SC, Middleton family of prominent legislators was Arthur Middleton, born in Charleston in 1681.

Midgett (977) Perhaps altered spelling of French **Miget**, from a pet form of the personal name *Migel*, a southern personal name, Occitan form of MICHAEL.

Midgette (404) French: see MIDGETT.

Midgley (530) English: habitational name from any of several places in West Yorkshire, or minor places in Cheshire, named in Old English as 'midge glade', from *micg(e)* 'midge' + *lēah* 'wood'; 'clearing', 'glade'.

Midkiff (1759) Americanized form of German **Mittelkauff**, an occupational name for a broker or middleman, from Middle High German *mittel* 'middle' + *kauf* 'purchase'. Compare MIDDLEKAUFF.

Midthun (191) Norwegian: habitational name from any of about ten farmsteads in western Norway named Midtun, from Old Norse *mið* 'middle' + *tún* 'enclosure', 'farmstead'.

Midura (225) Polish: unexplained. Perhaps an unflattering nickname from Old Polish *midera* 'ruin', 'baseness'.
GIVEN NAMES Polish 8%. *Andrzej, Mieczyslaw, Stanislaw.*

Midyett (185) English: unexplained.

Midyette (167) Variant (under French influence) of English MIDYETT.

Miears (159) Respelling of MEARS or MIERS.

Mieczkowski (241) Polish: habitational name from places called Mieczkowo, Mieczków, and Mieczk, named with a derivative of *mieci-* 'to throw', or from the personal name *Miecisław*.
GIVEN NAMES Polish 18%. *Krzysztof* (2), *Andrzej, Aniela, Bogdan, Boguslaw, Casimir, Czeslaw, Danuta, Genowefa, Jaroslaw, Jerzy, Jozef.*

Miedema (480) Frisian: unexplained.

Mielcarek (195) Polish: from a diminutive of *mielcarz* 'maltster'. Compare German MELTZER.

Miele (1331) **1.** Southern Italian: from a personal name or affectionate nickname from *miele* 'honey'. **2.** French: metonymic occupational name for a producer of honey, from a feminine form of *miel* 'honey'. **3.** Dutch: from a personal name, perhaps of Germanic origin, or from a reduced form of the personal names *Amilius, Amelis,* or *Emilia.*
GIVEN NAMES Italian 16%. *Angelo* (16), *Pasquale* (6), *Agostino* (4), *Salvatore* (4), *Franco* (3), *Rocco* (3), *Sal* (3), *Vito* (3), *Aniello* (2), *Benedetto* (2), *Carmel* (2), *Carmine* (2).

Mielke (2390) **1.** Eastern German (of Slavic origin): from a pet form of a Slavic compound personal name with the first element *Milo-,* from *mil* 'favor', 'grace'. **2.** Dutch: from a pet form of MIELE 3.
GIVEN NAMES German 4%. *Otto* (5), *Erwin* (3), *Erna* (2), *Kurt* (2), *Reinhard* (2), *Arno, Eldred, Erhardt, Ernst, Ewald, Frieda, Fritz.*

Mier (829) **1.** English: variant spelling of MYER. **2.** Spanish: habitational name from a village in Santander province, so named from *mies* 'ripe grain', 'harvest time' (Latin *messis aestiva* 'summer har-

vest'). **3.** Dutch: nickname from *mier* 'ant'; perhaps denoting an industrious person. **4.** Dutch and Belgian (**van de Mier**): topographic name from a Brabantine form of *moere* 'bog', 'marsh' (modern *moeras*), or a habitational name from Moere in West Flanders.
GIVEN NAMES Spanish 19%. *Carlos* (11), *Manuel* (6), *Jesus* (5), *Jose* (4), *Luis* (4), *Miguel* (4), *Joaquin* (3), *Juan* (3), *Pedro* (3), *Salvador* (3), *Faustino* (2), *Gonzalo* (2).

Miera (269) Spanish: habitational name from Miera, a place in Santander province.
GIVEN NAMES Spanish 20%. *Alberto* (3), *Carlos* (3), *Manuel* (3), *Raul* (3), *Bernardo* (2), *Eloy* (2), *Jose* (2), *Luis* (2), *Orlando* (2), *Asencion, Emilia, Medardo.*

Mieras (176) Spanish (of Catalan and Asturian-Leonese origin): Castilianized form of **Mieres**, a habitational name from Catalan and Asturian-Leonese Mieres, towns in Catalonia and Asturies.

Mierau (124) German: habitational name from a place named Mierau (West Prussia), Mirau (East Prussia, Posen), or Mirow (several examples in Mecklenberg). This was one of the German names established in Ukraine in the 19th century.

Miers (744) **1.** English: patronymic from a variant spelling of MAYER 1. **2.** English: variant of MYERS. **3.** Spanish: variant of MIER 2. **4.** Dutch: variant of MIER 3. **5.** Dutch (**van der Miers**): variant of MEERS 2.

Mierzejewski (273) Polish: habitational name for someone from a place called Mierzejewo, named with *mierzeja* 'spit', 'sandbar'.
GIVEN NAMES Polish 12%. *Piotr* (3), *Ignacy* (2), *Bogdan, Dariusz, Justyna, Slawomir, Stanislaw, Stanislawa, Wieslaw, Wladyslaw.*

Mierzwa (238) Polish: unflattering nickname from *mierzwa* 'manure', 'muck'.
GIVEN NAMES Polish 11%. *Andrzej, Jaroslaw, Jozef, Malgorzata, Ryszard, Stanislaw, Wieslawa, Witold.*

Mies (294) **1.** South German: topographic name for someone who lived by a peat-bog, Middle High German *mies*; or a habitational name from Mies, named with the same word. **2.** Dutch: from a short form of the personal name *Bartholomeus* (see BARTHOLOMEW). **3.** Dutch (**van der Mies**): variant of MEERS 2.

Miesch (126) Swiss German: variant of MIES.
GIVEN NAME French 4%. *Jean Marie.*

Miesen (123) Dutch: variant of MIES 2.
GIVEN NAMES German 6%. *Fritz, Konrad.*

Miesner (294) Variant of German and Jewish MEISSNER.

Miesse (136) Dutch: variant of MIES 2.

Mietus (112) Polish (**Miętus**): from *miętus* 'burbot', either a nickname or a metonymic occupational name for a fisherman.

GIVEN NAMES Polish 21%. *Casimir* (2), *Bogdan, Bronislaw, Ewa, Stanislaw, Tadeusz, Wieslaw, Wladyslaw, Zdzislaw, Zophia*.

Mietz (100) German: from a Slavic personal name based on *meč* 'sword'.

GIVEN NAMES German 7%. *Gerhard, Otto*.

Mifflin (385) English: unexplained.

FOREBEARS John Mifflin (born 1640) came to Delaware from Warminster, Wiltshire, England, in the 1670s. He is probably the same person as the John Mifflin, a Quaker, who built his home, 'Fountain Green', in Fairmont Park, Philadelphia, in 1679. His fourth-generation descendant Thomas Mifflin (1744–1800) was a member of the Continental Congress, a revolutionary soldier, and governor of PA.

Mifsud (216) Arabic: from a personal name based on either *mifṣad* 'lancet' or *mafṣūd* 'lanced'.

GIVEN NAMES Italian 5%. *Carmelo, Guido, Martino, Reno*.

Miga (152) Polish: nickname from a derivative *migać* 'to twinkle or wink'.

GIVEN NAMES Polish 7%. *Zdzislaw* (2), *Alojzy, Tadeusz*.

Migdal (259) Polish (**Migdał**) and Jewish (eastern Ashkenazic): from *migdał* 'almond' (from Greek *amygdalia*), probably a metonymic occupational name for an almond seller. As a Jewish name it is mainly ornamental name.

GIVEN NAME Jewish 4%. *Meyer*.

Miggins (141) English and Irish: variant of HIGGINS, resulting from a misdivision of a name such as *Tom Higgins*.

GIVEN NAME Irish 5%. *Brendan*.

Might (126) English: presumably a nickname for a strong man.

Migl (112) German: unexplained. Perhaps a pet form of **Mieg**, which is from a short form of the personal name *Remigius* (see REMY).

GIVEN NAMES German 6%. *Kurt, Otto*.

Migliaccio (534) Italian: **1.** derogatory derivative of MIGLIO. **2.** (Sicily): topographic name from Sicilian *migghiazzu* 'burdock' or 'millet'.

GIVEN NAMES Italian 17%. *Vito* (4), *Angelo* (3), *Giovanni* (3), *Clemente* (2), *Concetta* (2), *Sal* (2), *Alessandra, Carlo, Carmine, Dino, Dominico, Fausto*.

Miglio (117) Italian: **1.** from a short form of the personal name EMILIO. **2.** possibly a nickname or occupational name from Italian *miglio* 'millet'.

GIVEN NAMES Italian 16%; Spanish 10%. *Salvatore* (2), *Carmela, Concetta, Domenico, Giulio; Mario* (3), *Carlos* (2), *Juanita, Miguel, Teresita, Tito*.

Migliore (799) Southern Italian (**Miglióre**): from the personal (omen) name *Migliore*, from Latin *melior* 'better'.

GIVEN NAMES Italian 13%. *Sal* (7), *Angelo* (4), *Salvatore* (4), *Carmelo* (3), *Carmine*

(2), *Ciro* (2), *Gasper* (2), *Nunzio* (2), *Rocco* (2), *Santo* (2), *Amelio, Calogero*.

Migliori (159) Southern Italian: patronymic from the personal name MIGLIORE.

GIVEN NAMES Italian 19%. *Mario* (3), *Rocco* (2), *Alberto, Angelo, Fabio, Guido, Renato*.

Migliorini (104) Italian: from a pet form of the personal name MIGLIORE.

GIVEN NAMES Italian 16%. *Angelo* (2), *Aldo, Carlo, Deno*.

Migliozzi (130) Italian: from a pet form of the personal name MIGLIORE.

GIVEN NAMES Italian 15%. *Antonio* (2), *Armando, Mario, Pasquale, Stefano*.

Mignano (172) Southern Italian: habitational name from Mignano Monte Lungo, in Caserta province.

GIVEN NAMES Italian 19%. *Antonio, Benedetto, Bino, Fernando, Gino, Giovanni, Salvatore*.

Migneault (153) Variant of French **Mignaud** or **Migneau(x)**, variants of the Old French nickname *Mignel*, a diminutive of *mignon, mignot*, 'pleasing', 'charming', 'attractive'.

GIVEN NAMES French 9%. *Alphonse, Armand, Chantal, Gaston, Normand*.

Mignogna (263) Southern Italian: in part, a habitational name from Mignogna, a minor place in Foggia province.

GIVEN NAMES Italian 6%. *Elio* (2), *Salvatore*.

Mignon (100) French: nickname from *mignon, mignot*, 'pleasing', 'charming', 'attractive'.

GIVEN NAMES French 10%. *Dominique, Francois, Michel*.

Mignone (338) **1.** Italian: possibly from an augmentative of an unattested personal name *Migno*, or alternatively from French *Mignon* 'pleasing'. **2.** French: nickname from French *mignon(ne)* (see MIGNEAULT), meaning 'sweetheart' or 'lover'. This may also be a descriptive name from Old French *mignon* 'beggar'.

GIVEN NAMES Italian 19%. *Pasquale* (4), *Marino* (2), *Aldo, Biagio, Carmine, Constantino, Dino, Domenico, Enzo, Federico, Gaetano, Gilda*.

Miguel (1040) Spanish and Portuguese: from the personal name *Miguel*, equivalent to MICHAEL.

GIVEN NAMES Spanish 35%; Portuguese 9%. *Manuel* (21), *Jose* (12), *Luis* (8), *Ana* (7), *Miguel* (7), *Carlos* (5), *Jorge* (5), *Juan* (5), *Alicia* (4), *Raul* (4), *Adolfo* (3), *Alberto* (3); *Catarina, Joao, Joaquim; Antonio* (14), *Angelo* (4), *Leonardo* (2), *Antonino, Cecilio, Constantino, Donato, Gabino, Geronimo, Lorenzo, Marco Antonio*.

Migues (283) Portuguese (and Galician **Migués**): variant of MIGUEZ.

Miguez (251) Portuguese and Galician (**Míguez**): patronymic from MIGUEL, a reduced form of *Miguelez*.

GIVEN NAMES Spanish 17%; French 4%. *Jose* (6), *Francisco* (2), *Margarita* (2), *Adolfo, Albino, Andres, Arturo, Beatriz, Domingo,*

Elba, Elena, Gerardo; Colette, Minos, Ovide, Vernice.

Mihal (195) **1.** Greek: variant spelling of MICHAEL, or short form of a patronymic derivative such as **Mihalidis**. **2.** Slovak (**Mihál**): from the Slovak personal name *Mihál* (see MICHAEL). **3.** Ukrainian: from the personal name *Mychajlo*, Ukrainian form of MICHAEL. **4.** Variant of Hungarian **Mihály** (see MICHAEL).

Mihalek (238) Slovak (**Mihálek**) and Croatian (Slavonia): from a pet form of the personal name *Mihál*, variant of *Michal* (Slovak) or *Mihajlo* (Croatian) (see MICHAEL).

Mihalic (196) Croatian and Serbian (**Mihalić**); Slovak and Slovenian (**Mihalič**): patronymic from the personal name *Mihal*, variant of *Michal* (Slovak), *Mihovil* (Croatian), *Mihajlo* (Serbian), and the old Slovenian dialect form *Mihal* (Slovenian) (see MICHAEL).

Mihalick (116) Germanized or Americanized spelling of Slovak **Mihalík** (see MIHALIK).

Mihalik (578) Slovak (**Mihalík**) and Ukrainian: from a pet form of the personal name *Michal*.

Mihalko (381) Ukrainian: from a pet form of the personal name *Mychajlo*, Ukrainian form of MICHAEL.

Mihalovich (127) Croatian and Serbian (**Mihajlović, Mihalović**); Ukrainian (**Mychajlovich**); or Belorussian (**Michajlovich**): patronymic from a local Slavic form of MICHAEL.

Mihaly (214) Hungarian (**Mihály**): from the personal name *Mihály*, Hungarian form of MICHAEL.

GIVEN NAMES Hungarian 6%. *Laszlo* (2), *Balint, Tamas, Zoltan*.

Mihara (108) Japanese: 'three plains'. This name is found mostly in western Japan.

GIVEN NAMES Japanese 62%. *Kenichiro* (3), *Kenji* (3), *Kazuo* (2), *Yoko* (2), *Akio, Ayako, Azusa, Chie, Haruo, Hiroki, Hiroshi, Kenichi*.

Mihelcic (61) Slovenian (**Mihelčič**): patronymic from the personal name *Mihel*, an old spelling of *Mihael* (see MICHAEL).

Mihelic (138) Slovenian (**Mihelič**): patronymic from the personal name *Mihel*, an old spelling of *Mihael* (see MICHAEL).

Mihelich (382) Slovenian (**Mihelič**): see MIHELIC.

Mihm (425) German: unexplained.

Mihok (202) Hungarian (**Mihók**): from a pet form of *Mihály*, Hungarian form of MICHAEL.

Mijares (319) Spanish: habitational name from a place named Mijares, in particular the one in Ávila province, named from the plural of *mijar* 'millet field', from *mijo* 'millet'.

GIVEN NAMES Spanish 48%. *Jose* (12), *Manuel* (8), *Carlos* (5), *Francisco* (5), *Juan* (5), *Enrique* (3), *Ignacio* (3), *Tomas* (3),

Agustin (2), *Alberto* (2), *Alicia* (2), *Amalia* (2).

Mika (817) Hungarian, Polish, Czech (**Míka**), and Slovak: from a pet form of a central and eastern European personal name equivalent to NICHOLAS: Hungarian *Miklós*, Czech and Slovak *Mikuláš*, Polish *Mikołaj*.
GIVEN NAMES Polish 4%. *Bronislawa, Grazyna, Jacek, Jaroslaw, Jozef, Justyna, Maciej, Pawel, Waclaw, Zofia.*

Mikaelian (161) Armenian: patronymic from the personal name *Mikael*, Armenian form of MICHAEL.
GIVEN NAMES Armenian 37%. *Ovanes* (2), *Sarkis* (2), *Anahid, Anait, Antranig, Ara, Arakel, Armenouhi, Arsen, Artine, Avanes, Berj.*

Mikami (146) Japanese (mostly northeastern Japan): variously written, usually with characters meaning 'three' and 'above', and meaning 'something bestowed from above' (from one's superior or a deity).
GIVEN NAMES Japanese 49%. *Kuni* (2), *Naoko* (2), *Seiko* (2), *Takayuki* (2), *Akira, Eiichiro, Emiko, Haruo, Hiromu, Isao, Kazunori, Kei.*

Mikan (114) Origin unidentified.

Mike (760) Hungarian: from a pet form of the personal name *Miklós*, Hungarian form of NICHOLAS, or possibly from a short form of *Mihály*, Hungarian form of MICHAEL.

Mikeal (139) Origin uncertain. Presumably it is a variant of one of the forms of the personal name MICHAEL.

Mikel (765) Polish (also **Mikiel**): from a pet form of the personal name *Mikołaj* (see NICHOLAS).

Mikell (851) Variant spelling of MIKEL.

Mikels (414) Dutch: patronymic from the personal name *Mikel* (see MICHAEL).

Mikelson (261) Partly Americanized spelling of Danish and Norwegian MIKKELSEN.

Mikes (335) Hungarian; also Czech (**Mikeš**): from a pet form of a personal name equivalent to NICHOLAS (Hungarian *Miklós*, Czech *Mikuláš*).

Mikesell (1325) Americanized spelling of German MEIXELL.
FOREBEARS Andreas Meixel or Meissel came to Lancaster Co., PA, about 1715 from Leimen, Germany.

Mikesh (169) Americanized spelling of Hungarian or Czech MIKES.

Mikeska (376) Polish and Czech (**Mikeška**): from a derivative of the personal name *Mikołaj* (see NICHOLAS).

Mikhail (311) **1.** Arabic: from the personal name *Mīkā'īl* (see MICHAEL). **2.** variant transcription of Greek MICHAEL.
GIVEN NAMES Muslim 59%. *Samir* (5), *Labib* (4), *Nabil* (4), *Bishoy* (3), *Emad* (3), *Makram* (3), *Ezzat* (2), *Fouad* (2), *Hany* (2), *Ibrahim* (2), *Karim* (2), *Maher* (2).

Miki (104) Japanese: 'three trees'. This name is found mostly in western Honshū,

where there is a castle town by that name.
GIVEN NAMES Japanese 70%. *Masaharu* (2), *Masato* (2), *Shojiro* (2), *Yasuhiro* (2), *Akira, Asako, Eiji, Gaku, Hiroko, Hisato, Ikuyo, Katsumi.*

Mikita (242) Ukrainian (**Mykyta**), Slovak, and Polish: from the personal name *Mykyta* or *Mikita*, Greek *Nikētas* (see NIKITAS). The Polish and Slovak surnames may be of Ukrainian origin or alternatively derivatives of the personal names *Mikołaj* (Polish) or *Mikuláš* (Slovak) (see NICHOLAS).

Mikkelsen (916) Danish, Norwegian, and Dutch: patronymic from the personal name *Mikkel* (see MICHAEL).
GIVEN NAMES Scandinavian 11%. *Erik* (3), *Niels* (3), *Gorm* (2), *Knut* (2), *Nels* (2), *Nils* (2), *Aksel, Bente, Carsten, Egil, Kjeld, Lars.*

Mikkelson (990) Altered spelling of MIKKELSEN.
GIVEN NAMES Scandinavian 4%. *Nels* (2), *Erik, Estrid, Hjalmer, Thoralf.*

Mikkola (200) Finnish: from the personal name *Mikko* (a Finnish pet form of MICHAEL) + the local suffix *-la*, i.e. 'Mikko's place'. The surname occurs mainly in western Finland.
GIVEN NAMES Finnish 18%; German 4%. *Hannu* (2), *Kaisa* (2), *Toivo* (2), *Jussi, Kauko, Niilo, Pentti, Raimo, Tauno, Waino, Wilho*; *Kurt, Otto.*

Miklas (204) Czech and Slovak (**Mikláš**), Polish (also **Miklasz**), and Sorbian: from a pet form of the personal name *Mikołaj* (see NICHOLAS).

Mikle (129) Hungarian and Slovak: from a pet form of Hungarian *Miklós* or Slovak *Mikuláš* (see NICHOLAS).
GIVEN NAMES Hungarian 6%. *Laszlo* (2), *Mihaly.*

Mikles (193) German: from a Slavic or Hungarian form of NICHOLAS.

Miklos (530) Hungarian (**Miklós**): from the personal name *Miklós*, Hungarian form of NICHOLAS.

Miko (239) Hungarian (**Mikó**): from a pet form of the personal names *Miklós* (Hungarian form of NICHOLAS) or *Mihály* (Hungarian form of MICHAEL).
GIVEN NAMES Hungarian 4%. *Bela* (2), *Arpad, Zoltan.*

Mikol (118) Frenchified form of Hungarian **Mikó** (see MIKO).
GIVEN NAMES French 10%; German 4%. *Yves* (3); *Erwin.*

Mikolajczak (232) Polish: patronymic from the personal name *Mikołaj* (see NICHOLAS).
GIVEN NAMES Polish 8%. *Alojzy, Andrzej, Casimir, Ignatius, Iwona, Jacek, Janina, Jerzy.*

Mikolajczyk (425) Polish (**Mikołajczyk**): from a pet form of the personal name *Mikołaj* (see NICHOLAS).

FOREBEARS Stanisław Mikołajczyk (1901–66) was prime minister of the Polish government in exile in London during the World War II. From 1944 he was deputy prime minister of the Government of National Unity in Poland, and subsequently the chief organizer of the Polish.
GIVEN NAMES Polish 10%. *Andrzej, Bernadeta, Bogdan, Czeslaw, Halina, Ireneusz, Jolanta, Krzysztof, Mariola, Ryszard, Szymon, Waclaw.*

Mikolajewski (100) Polish (**Mikołajewski**): habitational name for someone from any of various places called Mikołajew or Mikołajewo, named with the personal name *Mikołaj* (see NICHOLAS).
GIVEN NAME Polish 5%. *Maciej.*

Mikolay (108) Americanized spelling of Polish **Mikołaj**, from the Polish personal name so spelled. See NICHOLAS.

Mikols (101) Origin unidentified.

Mikos (371) **1.** Polish (**Mikosz, Mikoś**), Slovenian (**Mikoš**), and Hungarian: from a derivative of a personal name equivalent to NICHOLAS: Polish *Mikołaj*, Slovenian *Miklavž*, or Hungarian *Miklós*. **2.** Greek: from the Greek personal name *Mikos*, which is of uncertain origin. It may be a reduced and altered pet form of *Dēmētrios* (Latin *Demetrius*; see DEMETRIOU).
GIVEN NAMES Polish 5%. *Kazimierz, Krzysztof, Stanislaw, Tadeusz, Zdzislaw.*

Mikowski (142) Polish: habitational name for someone from any of various places called Mikowa or Mików, named with the personal name MIKA, a derivative of *Mikołaj* (see NICHOLAS).

Mikrut (228) Polish: of uncertain origin; perhaps a derivative of the personal name *Mikołaj* (see NICHOLAS).
GIVEN NAMES Polish 9%. *Casimir* (2), *Janusz, Jerzy, Ryszard, Stanislaw.*

Miksch (223) Eastern German (Silesia, Lausitz, and Saxony): from a pet form of the Slavic personal name *Mikolaj* (see NICHOLAS).

Mikula (892) Polish (**Mikuła**), Ukrainian (**Mykula**), Czech and Slovak (**Mikula**): from Slavic forms of the Greek personal name *Nikolaos* (see NICHOLAS).

Mikulak (184) Czech, Slovak, and Ukrainian (**Mykulak**): patronymic from the personal name *Mikula* or *Mykula*, Slavic forms of Greek *Nikolaos* (see NICHOLAS).

Mikulas (103) Czech and Slovak (**Mikuláš**): from a pet form of the personal name *Mikuláš* (see NICHOLAS).

Mikulec (140) Czech, Slovak, and Polish: from a pet form of a Slavic personal name, Czech *Mikula*, Polish *Mikuła* (see NICHOLAS).
GIVEN NAMES Polish 5%. *Krystyna, Zbigniew.*

Mikulecky (129) Czech and Slovak (**Mikulecký**): from a pet form of the personal name *Mikula* (see NICHOLAS).

Mikulich (168) Ukrainian and Belorussian: patronymic from *Mikula*, Ukrainian and Belorussian form of NICHOLAS.

Mikulka (134) Czech and Slovak: from a pet form of the personal name *Mikuláš*, Czech and Slovak form of NICHOLAS.
GIVEN NAME German 4%. *Heinz.*

Mikulski (442) Polish: habitational name for someone from a place called Mikuły or Mikulice, named with the personal name **Mikuła** (see MIKULA).
GIVEN NAMES Polish 5%. *Piotr* (2), *Jozef*, *Stanislaw.*

Mikus (425) Czech, Slovak, Croatian (northern and northwestern Croatia), and Slovenian (**Mikuš**); Polish (**Mikuś**, **Mikusz**); Ukrainian; and Hungarian: derivative of a personal name equivalent to NICHOLAS: Czech and Slovak *Mikuláš*, Slovenian *Miklavž*, Polish *Mikołaj*, Ukrainian *Mykola*, Hungarian *Miklós.*

Milam (4349) English: variant spelling of MILHAM.

Milan (1341) **1.** Italian, Spanish (**Milán**), and French: habitational name from the Italian city of Milan (see MILANO). **2.** Spanish (**Milán**): nickname from *milán* 'kite' (the bird of prey). **3.** Czech, Slovak, and Ukrainian: from the Slavic personal name *Milan*, a derivative of names such as *Bohumil* and *Miloslav*, containing the element *mil* 'grace', 'favor'.
GIVEN NAMES Spanish 10%. *Francisco* (4), *Jose* (4), *Carlos* (3), *Juan* (3), *Modesto* (3), *Nestor* (3), *Alfonso* (2), *Angel* (2), *Jesus* (2), *Joaquin* (2), *Jorge* (2), *Miguel* (2).

Miland (125) **1.** French: variant of MILAN 2. **2.** altered spelling of German **Mieland**, a derivative of any of several German or Slavic personal names, for example *Miloslav.*

Milanes (113) Spanish (**Milanés**): habitational name for someone from Milan in Italy (*Milano*), from *milanés*, an adjectival form of the place name.
GIVEN NAMES Spanish 52%. *Jose* (7), *Dulce* (3), *Jorge* (3), *Arturo* (2), *Carlos* (2), *Jesus* (2), *Miguel* (2), *Adela*, *Alberto*, *Ana*, *Angel*, *Carolina.*

Milanese (197) Northern Italian (**Milanése**) and Jewish (from Italy): habitational name for someone from the city of Milan in Lombardy (Italian *Milano*), with the ethnic suffix *-ése.*
GIVEN NAMES Italian 24%. *Aldo* (2), *Carlo* (2), *Sandro* (2), *Alfonso*, *Antonio*, *Gino*, *Giovanni*, *Girolamo*, *Marco*, *Nino*, *Pasquale*, *Roberto*, *Sal*, *Santino.*

Milani (574) Italian: variant of MILANO. This is a typical Lombardic surname; there almost all surnames derived from place names have a pluralized form.
GIVEN NAMES Italian 13%. *Angelo* (3), *Carlo* (3), *Renzo* (3), *Umberto* (3), *Aldo* (2), *Dino* (2), *Italo* (2), *Silvio* (2), *Caterina*, *Cesare*, *Dante*, *Domenico.*

Milano (1805) **1.** Italian and Jewish (from Italy): habitational name from Milan, Italian *Milano* (from Latin *Mediolan(i)um*, composed of Celtic elements meaning 'middle' + 'plain'). **2.** In some instances the surname may be Spanish, of the same origin as 1 or a habitational name from Milano in Salamanca province.
GIVEN NAMES Italian 12%. *Salvatore* (8), *Angelo* (7), *Vito* (5), *Antonio* (4), *Carmelo* (4), *Ciro* (2), *Domenic* (2), *Francesca* (2), *Luigi* (2), *Matteo* (2), *Pasquale* (2), *Rocco* (2).

Milanovich (141) Serbian and Croatian (**Milanović**): patronymic from the personal name *Milan* (see MILAN 3).

Milanowski (243) Polish: habitational name for someone from a place called Milanowo, Milanów, or Milanówek, all named with the personal name *Milan* (see MILAN 3) or with a derivative of the adjective *miły* 'pleasant', 'favorable'.
GIVEN NAMES Polish 8%. *Jerzy* (2), *Ryszard* (2), *Wencel* (2), *Krystyna*, *Marzanna*, *Stanislaw.*

Milardo (168) Italian: probably from a Germanic personal name composed of the elements *mil* 'gracious', 'good' + *hard* 'hardy', 'brave', 'strong'.
GIVEN NAMES Italian 14%. *Angelo* (2), *Carmelo* (2), *Sebastiano.*

Milas (240) **1.** Greek: probably an occupational name for an apple seller, from *mēlon* 'apple' + the occupational suffix *-as*, or a reduced form of some other surname containing the syllable *-mil-*, for example **Koromilas** 'plum'. **2.** Czech and Slovak: derivative of a short form of an old Slavic name such as *Miloslav* or *Bohumil* (see MILAN 3).
GIVEN NAMES Greek 5%. *Eleni*, *Gerasimos*, *Nicolaos*, *Pavlos*, *Spiro.*

Milavec (104) Slovenian: **1.** nickname from an unexplained obsolete dialect word. The surname comes mainly from the city of Postojna in the Notranjska region of southwestern Slovenia. **2.** habitational name for someone from the village of Milava in the southwestern Slovenia.

Milazzo (1034) Italian (Sicily): habitational name from Milazzo in Messina.
GIVEN NAMES Italian 18%. *Salvatore* (12), *Angelo* (11), *Sal* (6), *Antonio* (3), *Carmelo* (3), *Gasper* (3), *Pasquale* (3), *Ciro* (2), *Gaetano* (2), *Concetto*, *Damiano*, *Dino.*

Milbauer (182) Partly Americanized form of German and Jewish MUEHLBAUER.
GIVEN NAMES Jewish 5%. *Peretz*, *Yaakov.*

Milberg (161) **1.** Partly Americanized form of German **Mühlberg**, a habitational name from any of several places named with German *Mühl* 'mill' + *Berg* 'mountain', 'hill'. It is also found as a Swedish name, where it may be of ornamental origin. **2.** Jewish (Ashkenazic): ornamental name from German *Mühl* 'mill' + *Berg* 'hill' (see 1).
GIVEN NAME Jewish 4%. *Alter.*

Milberger (205) Partly Americanized form of German **Mühlberger**, a habitational name for someone from a place called Mühlberg (see MILBERG).

Milbert (128) French: from a Germanic personal name composed of the elements *mil* 'gracious', 'good' + *berht* 'bright', 'famous'.

Milbourn (300) English: variant spelling of MILBOURNE.

Milbourne (302) English: habitational name from places in Northumbria and Wiltshire, named in Old English as 'mill stream' (see MILBURN).
GIVEN NAMES French 4%; German 4%. *Monique*; *Erwin* (2), *Otto.*

Milbrandt (386) German: variant of MILBRATH.

Milbrath (299) German (of Slavic origin): from the Slavic personal name *Milobrat*, composed of the elements *mil* 'grace', 'favor' + *brat* 'brother'.

Milburn (2751) English (Northumbria and Cumbria): habitational name from a place in Cumbria, named in Old English as 'mill-stream', from *mylen* 'mill' + *burna* 'stream'.

Milbury (108) English (Hampshire): perhaps a habitational name from a lost or unidentified place.

Milby (818) English: habitational name from Milby in North Yorkshire, named in Old Norse as 'Mildi's homestead', from the personal name *Mildi* + *býr* 'homestead', 'village' (Old Danish *by*).

Milch (165) German: **1.** metonymic occupational name for a seller of milk, from Middle High German *mil(i)ch* 'milk'. **2.** reduced form of MILICH.

Milde (125) **1.** German and Dutch: nickname from Middle High German *milde*, Middle Dutch *mild(e)* 'kind', 'gentle', 'compassionate', 'generous'. **2.** German: habitational name from Milda in Thuringia.
GIVEN NAMES German 8%. *Helmut* (2), *Hans.*

Mildenberger (149) German: variant of MILTENBERGER.

Milder (280) Perhaps an altered spelling of the Dutch occupational name **Mulder** 'miller' or of **van Milders**, a habitational name from Te Mulders in Mollem, meaning 'at the miller's (house)'.

Mildner (106) North German: occupational name for a trough maker, Middle Low German *muldener.*
GIVEN NAMES German 8%. *Horst*, *Otto.*

Mildren (101) English (Cornwall): unexplained.

Mileham (159) English: habitational name from Mileham in Norfolk, so named from Old English *myln* 'mill' + *hām* 'homestead'.

Milek (119) Polish: nickname from a derivative of *miły* 'pleasant', 'nice', or from a pet form of a Polish compound name with this as a first element.

GIVEN NAMES Polish 9%. *Andrzej* (2), *Dariusz, Jacek.*

Milem (125) English: variant spelling of MILEHAM.

Miler (271) Polish, Croatian (eastern Croatia), Slovenian, and Jewish (Ashkenazic): Slavicized and Yiddishized form of German **Müller**, an occupational name for a miller (see MUELLER).

Miles (26447) **1.** English (of Norman origin): via Old French from the Germanic personal name *Milo*, of unknown etymology. The name was introduced to England by the Normans in the form *Miles* (oblique case *Milon*). In English documents of the Middle Ages the name sometimes appears in the Latinized form *Milo* (genitive *Milonis*), although the normal Middle English form was *Mile*, so the final *-s* must usually represent the possessive ending, i.e. 'son or servant of Mile'. **2.** English: patronymic from the medieval personal name *Mihel*, an Old French contracted form of MICHAEL. **3.** English: occupational name for a servant or retainer, from Latin *miles* 'soldier', sometimes used as a technical term in this sense in medieval documents. **4.** Irish (County Mayo): when not the same as 1 or 3, an Anglicized form of Gaelic **Ó Maolmhuire**, *Myles* being used as the English equivalent of the Gaelic personal name *Maol Muire* (see MULLERY). **5.** Jewish (eastern Ashkenazic): unexplained. **6.** Dutch: variant of **Miels**, a variant of MIELE 3.

FOREBEARS John Miles or Myles (*c.*1621–83), born probably in Herefordshire, England, was a pioneer American Baptist minister who emigrated to New England in 1662 and had a pastorate in Swansea, MA. Many of his descendants spell their name Myles.

Mileski (318) Polish: variant of MILEWSKI.
GIVEN NAME Polish 4%. *Zigmund* (2).

Miletich (149) Croatian and Serbian (**Miletić**): patronymic from the male personal name *Mileta*, a derivative of *Mile*, from the Old Slavic adjective *mil* 'gentle', 'dear'.

Mileto (101) Southern Italian: habitational name from Mileto in Catanzaro province.
GIVEN NAMES Italian 23%. *Angelo* (3), *Rocco, Salvatore.*

Milette (107) Probably a respelling of French **Milet**, from a pet form of the personal name *Émile.*
GIVEN NAMES French 24%. *Andre* (2), *Francois* (2), *Emilien, Laurent, Marcel, Yvon.*

Milewski (945) Polish: habitational name for someone from a place called Milew or Milewo, named with *miły* 'nice', 'pleasant'.
GIVEN NAMES Polish 9%. *Janusz* (3), *Jozef* (3), *Dariusz* (2), *Jerzy* (2), *Kazimierz* (2), *Aleksander, Alicja, Andrzej, Bogdan, Boleslaw, Jaroslaw, Karol.*

Miley (2466) Irish: Anglicized form of a Gaelic name, probably **Ó Maol Aodha** 'descendant of *Maol Aodha*', a personal name meaning 'devotee of (Saint) *Aodh*' (see McCOY).

Milford (1168) **1.** English (Devon): habitational name from any of numerous places, for example in Derbyshire, Devon, Hampshire, Norfolk, Staffordshire, and Surrey, named in Old English as 'mill ford', from *mylen* 'mill' (see MILL) + *ford* 'ford'. **2.** Irish: Anglicized form of Gaelic **Ó Maolfhoghmhair** 'descendant of *Maolgfhoghmhair*', a personal name meaning 'chief of harvest'. The Gaelic name was first Anglicized as **Mullover**, which was later assimilated to Milford.

Milgram (176) Jewish (Ashkenazic): ornamental name from Yiddish *milgrim, milgroym* 'pomegranate' (ultimately from Late Latin *mille granata* 'thousand seeds').
GIVEN NAMES Russian 6%; Jewish 5%; French 4%. *Aleksandr, Arkady, Mikail, Mikhail, Raissa; Inna, Miriam; Andre, Thierry.*

Milgrim (143) Jewish (Ashkenazic): variant of MILGRAM.

Milgrom (128) Jewish (Ashkenazic): variant of MILGRAM.
GIVEN NAMES Jewish 9%; German 4%. *Hyman, Isadore, Jakob, Miriam.*

Milham (198) English: possibly a habitational name from Mill Ham, Devon, or Millham Farm in Cornwall and Hereford, or perhaps a variant of MILEHAM.

Milhoan (253) Probably an American variant of Irish MULQUEEN.

Milholland (342) Variant of Irish MULHOLLAND.

Milhorn (193) Variant of Irish **Mulhorn**, which is unexplained.

Milhous (119) Variant spelling of English MILLHOUSE.

Milhouse (194) English: variant spelling of MILLHOUSE.

Milia (102) Southern Italian: habitational name from any of various minor places so named, or in some cases from a short form of the personal name EMILIO.
GIVEN NAMES Italian 20%; Spanish 9%. *Carmelo* (3), *Angelo* (2), *Gaetano, Gaeton, Rocco, Sal; Beatriz, Ernesto, Francisco, Liborio, Marina, Nestor.*

Milian (401) Spanish (**Milián**) and Polish: from a reduced form of the Latin personal name *Aemilianus* (a derivative of *Aemilius*, a Roman family name probably derived from *aemulus* 'rival'). This was borne by various early saints and hence was widely used throughout Europe as a personal name in the Middle Ages.
GIVEN NAMES Spanish 50%. *Jose* (13), *Juan* (8), *Alberto* (5), *Francisco* (5), *Luis* (5), *Raul* (5), *Carlos* (4), *Mario* (4), *Pedro* (4), *Ramon* (4), *Alfredo* (3), *Ana* (3); *Antonio* (2), *Elio* (2), *Aldo, Leonardo.*

Milich (265) **1.** German: variant of **Mühlich** (via the form **Miehlich**), an unflattering nickname from Middle High German *müelich* 'troublesome', 'difficult to get on with'. **2.** Eastern German (of Slavic origin): from a pet form of a Polish compound name with the first element *miły* 'nice', 'pleasant', or possibly an Americanized spelling of the Polish name **Milicz**, which has the same origin. **3.** Serbian and Croatian (**Milić**): patronymic or metronymic from the personal names *Mile, Milo* (male), or *Mila, Milica* (female), derivatives of the Old Slavic adjective *mil* 'gentle', 'dear'.
GIVEN NAMES South Slavic 7%. *Marko* (3), *Dragisa, Novak, Predrag, Zarko.*

Milici (197) Southern Italian: habitational name from any of various places named with this word, as for example Rodi Milici in Messina province, Sicily.
GIVEN NAMES Italian 14%. *Carmelo* (3), *Antonio, Giuseppe, Sal.*

Milillo (153) Italian: variant of MELILLO.
GIVEN NAMES Italian 27%. *Carlo* (2), *Angelo, Antonio, Carmello, Domenic, Nicola, Pasquale, Silvio, Vito.*

Militello (716) Sicily and southern Italian: habitational name from a place called Militello in Val di Catania, in Catania, or Militello Rosmarino in Messina, named from the diminutive of Latin *meletum*, formed from *melus* 'apple tree' + the suffix *-etum* indicating abundance.
GIVEN NAMES Italian 16%. *Santo* (7), *Salvatore* (6), *Angelo* (5), *Antonio* (3), *Sal* (3), *Giuseppe* (2), *Antonino, Carmello, Carmelo, Cosimo, Cosmo, Gaetano.*

Milito (172) Italian: probably a variant of MELITO.
GIVEN NAMES Italian 18%. *Salvatore* (3), *Carlo, Francesco, Giuseppe, Mario, Ottavio, Rodolfo, Vincenzo.*

Milius (193) Dutch: from a short form of the personal name *Aemilius* (see MILIAN).

Milk (115) **1.** English (Norfolk): probably from Middle English *milk* 'milk', applied as a metonymic occupational name for a producer or seller of milk. **2.** In some instances, probably a translation of German MILCH, a variant of Slavic MILICH, or Dutch **Mielke** (a pet form of MIELE), or a shortening of Slavic MILKOVICH.

Milke (243) Variant of Dutch **Mielke**, a pet form of MIELE.

Milkey (135) Americanized form of Dutch **Mielke**, a pet form of MIELE 3.

Milkie (119) Americanized form of Dutch **Mielke**, a pet form of MIELE 3.

Milko (161) **1.** Polish (**Miłko**): from a short form of a Polish compound personal name such as *Miłosław*, with a first element *Mił-* (Old Slavic *mil* 'nice', 'pleasant', or 'favor'). **2.** nickname from a derivative of the adjective *miły* 'nice', 'pleasant'. **3.** Shortened form of MILKOVICH or a similar name.
GIVEN NAME French 5%. *Jeanmarie.*

Milkovich (186) Serbian and Croatian (**Milković**); Slovak (**Milkovič**); Ukrainian: patronymic from the personal name *Milko*, a pet form of *Miloslav*, a derivative of Old Slavic *mil* 'grace', or some other Slavic personal name composed with this element.

Milkowski (186) Polish (**Miłkowski**): habitational name for someone from any of various places called Miłków, Miłkowa, or Miłkowo, named with the personal name *Miłek* (see MILKO).

GIVEN NAMES Polish 11%; German 4%. *Zbigniew* (2), *Andrzej, Henryk, Kazimierz, Sławomir, Zdzisław; Kurt* (2), *Hedwig.*

Milks (527) Variant of MILK. Middle English *milk* 'milk', presumably applied as a metonymic occupational name for a seller of milk. Alternatively, it may be a translation (again, with an excrescent *-s*) of German MILCH, or a variant of Slavic MILICH.

Mill (615) **1.** Scottish and English: topographic name for someone who lived near a mill, Middle English *mille, milne* (Old English *myl(e)n*, from Latin *molina*, a derivative of *molere* 'to grind'). It was usually in effect an occupational name for a worker at a mill or for the miller himself. The mill, whether powered by water, wind, or (occasionally) animals, was an important center in every medieval settlement; it was normally operated by an agent of the local landowner, and individual peasants were compelled to come to him to have their grain ground into flour, a proportion of the ground grain being kept by the miller by way of payment. **2.** English: from a short form of a personal name, probably female, as for example *Millicent.*

Milla (148) Catalan (**Millà**): from a reduced form of a personal name from Latin *Aemilianus* (see MILIAN).

GIVEN NAMES Spanish 36%. *Carlos* (3), *Jose* (3), *Luis* (3), *Aura* (2), *Julio* (2), *Miguel* (2), *Domingo, Esteban, Jesus, Jorge, Jorge Alberto, Juan.*

Millage (260) English: variant spelling of MILLEDGE.

Millam (128) English: variant spelling of MILHAM.

Millan (1159) **1.** Spanish (**Millán**): variant of **Milián** (see MILIAN). **2.** Galician: patronymical name from *Millán*, from a reduced form of a personal name from Latin *Aemilianus* (see MILIAN). **3.** Galician: in some cases, possibly a habitational name from any of the places in Galicia called Millán, from Latin *villa Aemiliani* 'villa of Aemilianus'. **4.** Scottish: shortened form of MCMILLAN.

GIVEN NAMES Spanish 40%; Portuguese 8%. *Jose* (17), *Carlos* (11), *Juan* (9), *Manuel* (9), *Miguel* (9), *Pedro* (7), *Luis* (6), *Mario* (6), *Cesar* (5), *Fernando* (5), *Ramon* (5), *Ruben* (5), *Vasco* (2).

Millar (2625) Scottish and northern Irish: variant spelling of MILLER.

Millard (4942) **1.** English (chiefly Gloucestershire and Worcestershire): variant of MILLWARD. **2.** French (northern): from a Germanic personal name composed of the elements *mil* 'good', 'gracious' + *hard* 'hardy', 'brave', 'strong'. **3.** Southern French: from a variant spelling of Occitan *milhar* 'millet field' (from *mil* 'millet').

Millay (388) Perhaps a respelling of **Millais**, an English habitational name of Norman origin, from Miliez in Nord, or French MILLET.

Mille (129) **1.** French: from the Germanic personal name *Milo* (see MILES 1). **2.** English: variant spelling of MILL. **3.** Dutch: variant of MIELE.

GIVEN NAMES French 8%. *Herve, Lucien, Michel.*

Millea (174) Irish: variant of MILEY.

Milledge (261) English: habitational name from Milwich in Staffordshire, so named from Old English *myln* 'mill' + *wīc* 'dairy farm'; '(trading) settlement'.

Millen (1082) **1.** Irish: variant of MULLEN. **2.** English: from Old French *Milon*, an inflected form of the personal name *Miles* (see MILES 1). **3.** English: from Middle English *milne*, adjectival form of *mille* 'mill', or perhaps a topographic name for someone living in a lane leading to a mill, from Middle English *mille, milne* 'mill' + *lane, lone* 'lane'. **4.** Dutch: patronymic from MIELE 3.

Millender (382) Probably an altered form of German MELANDER.

GIVEN NAMES French 5%. *Chantel* (2), *Andre, Micheline.*

Miller (421078) **1.** English and Scottish: occupational name for a miller. The standard modern vocabulary word represents the northern Middle English term, an agent derivative of *mille* 'mill', reinforced by Old Norse *mylnari* (see MILNER). In southern, western, and central England MILLWARD (literally, 'mill keeper') was the usual term. The American surname has absorbed many cognate surnames from other European languages, for example French MEUNIER, DUMOULIN, **Demoulins**, and MOULIN; German MUELLER; Dutch MOLENAAR; Italian MOLINARO; Spanish **Molinero**; Hungarian **Molnár**; Slavic MLINAR, etc. **2.** Southwestern and Swiss German and Jewish (Ashkenazic): variant of **Müller** (see MUELLER).

Millerick (159) Irish: Anglicized form of Gaelic **Ó Maoilgheiric** 'descendant of *Maoilgheiric*', a personal name meaning 'devotee of (Saint) Geiric', probably to be identified with St. Cyriacus.

Milles (139) English: variant spelling of MILLS.

Milleson (196) Scottish: metronymic from the female personal name *Mille*, a derivative of Old English *milde* 'mild', 'gentle'. Compare MELSON.

FOREBEARS Sander (Alexander) Milleson

was one of 150 Scottish prisoners captured in the English Civil War and brought to Boston as an indentured servant in 1652 aboard the *John and Sara.*

Millet (1036) **1.** French: metonymic occupational name for a grower or seller of millet or panic grass, from a diminutive form of Old French *mil* (Latin *milium*). In some cases it may have been a nickname for someone suffering from a skin disease, with blisters resembling grains of millet. Compare the English term *miliary fever.* **2.** French and English: from a pet form of the personal name MILES. **3.** Catalan: topographic name for someone who lived by a field of millet, Catalan *millet* (Latin *milietum*, a derivative of *milium* 'millet').

GIVEN NAMES French 5%. *Leonce* (2), *Aime, Aubert, Celine, Herve, Julien, Leandre, Marcel, Monique, Patrice, Raymonde, Roussel.*

Millett (1520) **1.** English: variant spelling of MILLET. **2.** Irish (mainly County Mayo): Anglicized form of Gaelic **Ó Mealóid**, from an occupational or status name derived from Latin *miles* 'soldier'.

Millette (864) Altered spelling of French MILLET; the spelling reflects the Canadian practice of sounding the final *-t*.

GIVEN NAMES French 10%. *Armand* (6), *Emile* (2), *Jacques* (2), *Adelard, Andre, Aurore, Camille, Gilles, Jean Noel, Lucien, Monique, Normand.*

Milley (237) **1.** Americanized spelling of French MILLET. **2.** Hungarian: archaic variant of **Mil(l)ei**, a habitational name for someone from a place called Milej in Zala county or Mile in Torna county.

Millham (131) English: variant spelling of MILHAM.

Millholland (104) Irish: variant of MULHOLLAND.

Millhollin (129) Variant of Irish MULHOLLAND.

Millhouse (533) English: topographic name for a miller, who lived 'at the mill house' (Middle English *mille* + *hus*; compare MULLIS), or possibly a habitational name from any of various places so named.

Millian (106) Spanish or Galician: possibly a variant of **Millán** (see MILLAN).

GIVEN NAMES Spanish 10%. *Beatriz, Jaime, Jose, Juan, Mateo, Roberto.*

Milliard (122) Possibly a variant of French MILLARD.

GIVEN NAMES French 13%. *Gaston, Guillaume, Treffle.*

Millican (1413) Variant of Irish MILLIGAN.

Millien (125) French: from a short form of the personal name *Émilien* (Latin *Aemilianus*).

GIVEN NAMES French 19%; German 7%. *Jacques, Jean Pierre, Michel, Mireille, Serge, Yves; Ernst* (2), *Fritz.*

Milligan (7943) Irish: **1.** Anglicized form of Gaelic **Ó Maolagáin** 'descendant of *Maolagán*', a personal name from a double diminutive of *maol* 'bald', 'tonsured'. **2.** in some instances, a variant of MOLLOHAN.

Millikan (722) Irish: variant of MILLIGAN.

Milliken (2366) Irish: variant of MILLIGAN.

Millikin (510) Irish: variant of MILLIGAN.

Milliman (618) English (Devon): perhaps a variant of MILLMAN.

Millin (247) Irish: Anglicized form of Gaelic **Ó Maoilfhinn** 'descendant of *Maoilfhinn*', a personal name meaning 'fair(-haired) chief'.

Milliner (591) Scottish and English: unexplained; probably a variant of MILNER. The vocabulary word *milliner* 'seller of women's hats' (originally meaning 'native of Milan', hence 'maker of fancy goods', hence 'hat maker') is first recorded in the 16th century, probably too late to have given rise to a surname.

Milling (453) Irish: variant of MULLEN.

Millington (874) English: habitational name from places in Cheshire and East Yorkshire, so named from Old English *mylen* 'mill' + *tūn* 'enclosure', 'settlement'.

Million (1105) **1.** French (mainly southern): from *miloun* 'million'. **2.** Americanized form of Spanish or Polish MILIAN. **3.** Shortened form of Irish MCMILLION.

Milliren (159) Origin unidentified.

Milliron (781) Americanized form of German MUEHLEISEN.

Millirons (167) Of German origin: variant of MILLIRON.

Millis (823) **1.** English: variant of MILLS. **2.** Dutch: habitational name from Milheeze in the province of North Brabant. **3.** Dutch: from a short form of the personal name *Amilius* or *Amelis* (Latinized forms of a Germanic name with the initial element *amal* 'strength', 'vigor') or of the Latin personal name *Aemilius* (see MILIAN).

Millison (155) English: probably a variant of MELSON.

Millman (1270) English and Jewish (Ashkenazic): occupational name for a worker at a mill, from Middle English *mille* 'mill' + *man* 'man', Yiddish *mil* + *man*.
GIVEN NAMES Jewish 4%. *Meyer* (3), *Isadore* (2), *Golda, Iren, Miriam, Sol.*

Millner (992) English (northern and eastern): variant spelling of MILNER.

Millon (170) French: variant of MILON.
GIVEN NAMES Spanish 11%; French 7%. *Juan* (5), *Domingo* (2), *Carlos, Ernesto, Esperanza, Fernando; Alain, Antoine, Jean-Pierre, Monique, Vernice.*

Milloy (185) Scottish (Argyllshire and Isle of Bute): Anglicized form of Gaelic **Mac Lughaidh** 'son of *Lugaidh*' (see LEWIS).

Mills (52726) **1.** English and Scottish: variant of MILL 1. **2.** English: either a metronymic form of MILL 2, or a variant of MILES. **3.** Irish: in Ulster this is the English name, but elsewhere in Ireland it may be a translation of a Gaelic topographic byname, **an Mhuilinn** 'of the mill'.

Millsap (1512) English: nickname for a spiritless man, from Middle English *milksop* 'piece of bread soaked in milk'.

Millsaps (1124) Variant of English MILLSAP.

Millson (135) English: variant of MELSON.

Millspaugh (540) Altered spelling of German **Mühlsbach**, a habitational name from a place so named in Baden-Württemberg.

Millstein (308) **1.** Jewish (Ashkenazic): variant spelling of MILSTEIN. **2.** Partly Americanized form of German **Mühlstein**, a nickname for a heavy person, from Middle High German *mülstein* 'millstone', or a habitational name from Mühlstein in Baden-Württemberg.
GIVEN NAMES Jewish 8%. *Hyman, Isador, Isadore, Meyer.*

Millward (525) English (chiefly West Midlands): occupational name for someone in charge of a mill, from Old English *mylen* 'mill' + *weard* 'guardian'. In southern England and the West Midlands this was a standard medieval term for a miller. Compare MILLER.

Millwee (121) Scottish (Galloway): altered form of **McIlwee**, an Anglicized form of Gaelic **Mac Giolla Bhuidhe** (see MCEVOY).

Millwood (710) English: **1.** habitational name for someone from a place named as 'the wood with a mill in it'. **2.** variant of MILLWARD.

Milman (289) Jewish (eastern Ashkenazic) and English: variant spelling of MILLMAN.
GIVEN NAMES Russian 16%; Jewish 12%. *Boris* (4), *Mikhail* (4), *Lev* (3), *Aleksandr* (2), *Grigory* (2), *Iosif* (2), *Dmitry, Grigoriy, Konstantin, Leonid, Lyubov, Lyudmila; Ilya* (2), *Isaak* (2), *Aron, Chana, Mariya, Naum, Polina, Sarra, Yakov, Yehiel.*

Milne (2736) Scottish (common in Aberdeenshire): occupational name for a miller or someone who lived at a mill, Old English *mylen* 'mill' (see MILL, MILNER). The Scottish name found its way to Ireland; MacLysaght records that it has been in Dublin since the early 18th century. In some cases it has absorbed Irish MOYLE.

Milner (4591) Northern English (mainly Yorkshire) and Scottish: variant of MILLER, retaining the *-n-* of the Middle English word, which was a result of Scandinavian linguistic influence, as in Old Norse *mylnari*.

Milnes (449) English: variant of MILLS. Compare MILNER.

Milnor (143) English: variant spelling of MILNER.
GIVEN NAME French 5%. *Susette.*

Milo (681) **1.** Czech and Slovak: from a short form of the personal name *Miloslav*. **2.** Southern Italian: habitational name from Milo in Catania province, Sicily. **3.** Southern Italian: from a short form of the personal name *Emilio*, or the Germanic personal name *Milo*.
GIVEN NAMES Italian 5%. *Antonio* (2), *Ciro* (2), *Gabriella* (2), *Carmela, Carmine, Carmino, Fausto, Gennaro, Matteo, Pasquale, Rocco, Salvatore.*

Milon (123) French: variant of MILES 1 (from the Old French inflected form *Milon*).
GIVEN NAMES French 8%. *Jacques, Pascal, Stephane.*

Milonas (170) Greek: occupational name for a miller, from Greek *mylos* 'mill' + the suffix of occupational nouns *-as*. **Milonas** has been known as a Greek family name since Byzantine times.
GIVEN NAMES Greek 27%. *Spiros* (3), *Vasilios* (3), *Constantine* (2), *Andreas, Antonios, Argyrios, Constantinos, Demos, Dimitrios, Ioannis, Konstantinos, Panagiotis.*

Milone (623) Southern Italian: from the personal name MILO, either the oblique case of the Germanic name or an augmentative of the Italian.
GIVEN NAMES Italian 15%. *Salvatore* (7), *Angelo* (3), *Pasquale* (3), *Aniello* (2), *Antonio* (2), *Carmelo, Cono, Filippo, Francesca, Gino, Luigi, Margherita.*

Milord (102) French: nickname for an important or rich man, a borrowing of English *my lord*.
GIVEN NAMES French 18%; Spanish 5%. *Francois, Herve, Marie Carmel, Veronique; Berta, Lorenza, Narciso, Tulia.*

Milos (273) **1.** Polish: variant of **Miłosz**, a derivative of the personal name *Miłosław*, composed with the Old Slavic adjective *mil* 'gentle', 'nice', or some other personal name with this as a first element. **2.** Czech, Slovak, Croatian, and Serbian (**Miloš**): from the personal name *Miloš*, a derivative of *Miloslav* (see 1) or some other Old Slavic name with the Old Slavic adjective *mil* as its first element.
GIVEN NAMES Polish 9%. *Teofil* (3), *Zigmund* (3), *Boguslaw, Zbigniew.*

Milosevich (150) Serbian and Croatian (**Milošević**): patronymic from the personal name *Miloš*, a derivative of *Milosav* or *Miloslav*, composed with the Old Slavic adjective *mil* 'gentle', 'dear'.
GIVEN NAMES South Slavic 12%. *Lazo, Marko, Milorad, Rade, Velko, Vladan, Vojo.*

Milot (265) French: from a pet form of MILES 1.
GIVEN NAMES French 16%. *Andre, Armand, Camille, Cecile, Donat, Emilien, Fernand, Gaston, Jean Claude, Joffre, Lucien, Michel.*

Milota (133) **1.** Czech and Slovak: from a short form of *Miloslav, Bohumil* or some other personal name formed with Old Slavic *mil* 'grace', 'mercy'. **2.** Possibly an Americanized spelling of Hungarian **Milotai** or **Milotay**, a habitational name for someone from a village called Milota in Szatmár county in northeastern Hungary. The place name is of Slavic origin.

Milovich (144) Serbian and Croatian (**Milović**): patronymic from the personal name *Milo*, from the Old Slavic adjective *mil* 'gentle', 'dear', or from a short form of *Milosav* or *Miloslav* (see MILOSEVICH).
GIVEN NAMES South Slavic 5%. *Milos* (2), *Milan*.

Milroy (452) **1.** Scottish: variant of **McIlroy** (see GILROY). **2.** Irish: variant of MULROY.

Milsap (240) English: variant of MILLSAP.

Milson (148) English: variant of MELSON.
GIVEN NAME Jewish 5%. *Hyman*.

Milstead (1185) English: habitational name from Milstead in Kent, perhaps so named from Middle English *middel* 'middle' + *stede* 'place'.

Milstein (571) Jewish (Ashkenazic): metonymic occupational name for a miller, or ornamental name, from Yiddish *milshteyn* 'millstone'.
GIVEN NAMES Jewish 10%. *Isadore* (2), *Meyer* (2), *Sol* (2), *Asher*, *Bracha*, *Chaim*, *Doron*, *Eitan*, *Lazer*, *Pinchas*, *Pinkus*, *Pnina*.

Miltenberger (467) German: habitational name from Mildenberg in Brandenburg or Miltenberg on the Main river, which is recorded as *Miltinberg* in 1226, from Middle High German *milte* 'friendly', 'charming' + *berg* 'mountain'; this was originally the name of the castle, now known as the Mildenburg.

Miltner (201) German: possibly a habitational name for someone from Miltern near Stendal.

Milton (5847) English and Scottish: habitational name from any of the numerous and widespread places so called. The majority of these are named with Old English *middel* 'middle' + *tūn* 'enclosure', 'settlement'; a smaller group, with examples in Cumbria, Kent, Northamptonshire, Northumbria, Nottinghamshire, and Staffordshire, have as their first element Old English *mylen* 'mill'.

Miltz (109) German: variant spelling of MILZ.

Milum (178) English: variant spelling of MILHAM.

Milward (181) English: variant spelling of MILLWARD.

Milz (171) **1.** German: nickname for a cantankerous individual, from Middle High German *milz(e)* 'spleen'. According to medieval theory of humors, an excess of bile from the spleen was responsible for ill temper. **2.** German: habitational name from a place so named in Thuringia. **3.** German and Dutch: from a personal name of uncertain etymology.
GIVEN NAMES German 10%. *Otto* (2), *Alois*, *Dieter*, *Fritz*, *Wolfram*.

Mimbs (221) English: variant of MIMS.

Mimms (486) English: variant spelling of MIMS.

Mimnaugh (167) Irish: Anglicized form of Gaelic **Muimhneach**, a regional name for someone from the province of Munster.

Mims (5313) English: habitational name from Mimms (North and South Mimms) in Hertfordshire, most probably derived from an ancient British tribal name, *Mimmas*.

Min (1118) **1.** Korean: there is only one Chinese character used for the Min surname. There is a legend that the Min clan's founding ancestor, Ch'ing-do, was a descendant of Ch'a kŏn, one of the ten disciples of Confucius. Ch'ing-do, an emissary from China to the Koryŏ kingdom, decided to stay and settled in the Yŏhŭng area. The surname Min can be found throughout Korea, but it is particularly concentrated in Chŏlla and Kyŏngsang provinces. **2.** Chinese 闵: the source of this name was the character's former meaning, 'sympathy for those who die young'. The descendants of various people who died young adopted Min as their surname. **3.** Dutch: nickname from Middle Dutch *minne* 'beloved', 'sweetheart'. **4.** Dutch: from a reduced form of the personal name *Dominicus* (see DOMINICK).
GIVEN NAMES Chinese/Korean 60%. *Kyung* (15), *Young* (13), *Kyong* (10), *Byong* (9), *Sung* (9), *Sun* (6), *Byoung* (5), *Eun* (5), *Hong* (5), *Yong* (5), *Choong* (4), *Joon* (4); *Byung* (28), *Chang* (4), *Chung* (4), *Pyong* (4), *Kyong Su* (3), *Myong* (3), *Sik* (3), *Eun-Young* (2), *Hyun Sook* (2), *Jeong* (2), *Kyung Soo* (2), *Kyung Won* (2).

Mina (481) **1.** Portuguese: ethnic name for someone from or who had been to the (Costa da) Mina in Africa. **2.** Spanish: habitational name from any of the numerous places named Mina, La Mina, from Spanish and Portuguese *mina* 'mine'. **3.** Greek: variant of MINAS. **4.** Muslim: from a personal name based on Arabic *minaḥ* 'gifts', 'favors'.
GIVEN NAMES Spanish 18%; Muslim 12%; Portuguese 4%; Italian 4%. *Carlos* (3), *Jose* (3), *Rolando* (3), *Azael* (2), *Domingo* (2), *Felicitas* (2), *Jorge* (2), *Miguel* (2), *Roberto* (2), *Salvador* (2), *Alejandro*, *Alfredo*; *Gamil* (4), *Sami* (3), *Mazin* (2), *Refaat* (2), *Adil*, *Amir*, *Ansar*, *Assaf*, *Ehab*, *Essam*, *Ezzat*, *Fayek*; *Joao*; *Aldo*, *Antonio*, *Elio*, *Emiliana*, *Gioia*, *Vitaliano*, *Vito*.

Minadeo (130) Italian (Molise): unexplained.

Minahan (394) Irish: variant of MOYNIHAN.
GIVEN NAME Irish 5%. *Brendan*.

Minami (216) Japanese: topographic name meaning 'south', taken from places all over Japan and the Ryūkyū Islands, meaning someone who lived to the south of everyone else in the village. Some families have samurai connections.
GIVEN NAMES Japanese 49%. *Koji* (2), *Masaru* (2), *Yasuo* (2), *Akie*, *Akira*, *Atsushi*, *Eiji*, *Fumi*, *Haru*, *Hiro*, *Hiroaki*, *Hirokazu*.

Minamoto (40) Japanese: meaning 'source', 'origin'. With the FUJIWARA and TAIRA, this is one of the three most prominent clans in Japanese history. It is listed in the Shinsen shōjiroku. The name itself is not common today, as most of the descendant families have taken other surnames, usually from their places of residence. In 814, the Emperor Saga created the surname for those of his children who were to become commoners. Later emperors did likewise, so the various branches of the clan were distinguished by the names of their parent-emperors. The Minamoto are also commonly called *Genji*, from the Sino-Japanese pronunciation of *minamoto* plus the word for clan.
GIVEN NAMES Japanese 66%. *Shigeo* (2), *Eizo*, *Etsuko*, *Hiroshi*, *Junichi*, *Kazuko*, *Keiko*, *Masaji*, *Masatake*, *Noboru*, *Noriaki*, *Tadashi*.

Minar (211) Czech (**Minář**): occupational name from a variant of *mlynář* 'miller'.

Minard (1106) French: variant of MAYNARD.

Minardi (407) Italian: patronymic from a personal name, *Minardo*, equivalent to MAYNARD.
GIVEN NAMES Italian 12%. *Angelo* (3), *Antonio* (2), *Carmine* (2), *Sal* (2), *Salvatore* (2), *Silvio* (2), *Corrado*, *Emanuele*, *Gino*, *Giorgio*, *Luciano*, *Natale*.

Minarik (343) Czech (**Minařík**) and Slovak (**Minárík**): from a diminutive of **Minář** (see MINAR).

Minas (126) **1.** Greek: from the personal name *Mēnas*. This was a popular name among early Christians and is celebrated in the Greek Orthodox Church as the name of seven martyrs and a patriarch. The story goes that St. Menas was named by his mother for the word *Amen*, which she heard on conceiving him; more prosaically, it is derived from the pre-Christian Egyptian name *Mena*, borne by the Pharaoh Mena (or Menes) who unified Upper and Lower Egypt in 3100 BC. **2.** Spanish: from the plural of MINA.
GIVEN NAMES Spanish 5%; French 4%. *Salvador* (2), *Frederico*, *Lupe*, *Matias*; *Andre*, *Michel*.

Minasian (343) Armenian: patronymic from the personal name MINAS, of Greek origin.
GIVEN NAMES Armenian 33%. *Armen* (5), *Minas* (4), *Raffi* (3), *Ara* (2), *Garabed* (2), *Haig* (2), *Karnig* (2), *Norik* (2), *Sarkis* (2), *Agop*, *Antranig*, *Arakel*.

Minassian (309) Armenian: variant of MINASIAN.
GIVEN NAMES Armenian 57%; French 6%. *Armen* (6), *Sarkis* (6), *Hagop* (5), *Minas* (4), *Raffi* (4), *Aram* (3), *Ashot* (3), *Antranik* (2), *Ara* (2), *Ghazar* (2), *Karnik* (2), *Vazgen* (2); *Serge* (3), *Edouard* (2), *Andre*, *Gregoire*.

Minaya (189) Spanish: habitational name from Minaya, a town in Albacete province.

GIVEN NAMES Spanish 46%. *Jose* (8), *Altagracia* (3), *Jorge* (3), *Luis* (3), *Luz* (3), *Ana* (2), *Maximo* (2), *Miguel* (2), *Rafael* (2), *Ramon* (2), *Adelso*, *Alba*.

Mince (199) **1.** English (Gloucester): probably a variant spelling of MINNS. **2.** French (**Mincé**): from a diminutive of *mince* 'slender', 'thin'.

Mincer (227) **1.** Jewish (from Poland): Polish spelling of the occupational surname MINTZER 'moneyer'. **2.** English: unexplained. Perhaps a metonymic occupational name for a butcher, a cook, or a warrior, from a derivative of Middle English *mince(n)* 'to mince', 'to cut into small pieces'.

Mincey (1308) Possibly of English or Irish origin: unexplained. Compare MINCHEY, MINCY.

Minch (780) Irish: **1.** reduced form of **Minnish**, a variant of MCNEESE. **2.** shortened form of the English surname MINCHIN.

Mincher (228) English (West Midlands): unexplained.

Minchew (546) Altered spelling of Bulgarian **Minchev**, a patronymic from *Mincho*, a pet form of the personal name *Mihail*, Bulgarian form of MICHAEL

Minchey (134) Origin uncertain; probably a variant of English MINCEY.

Minchin (121) **1.** English: nickname from Old English *mynecen* 'nun' (a derivative of *munuc* 'monk'). **2.** French: from a diminutive of Picard *minche*, a dialect form of French *mince* 'slender', 'thin'. **3.** Bulgarian: from a pet form of the female personal name *Dimitra*, from Greek *Dēmētrios* (see DEMETRIOU).

Minck (138) **1.** North German: variant of MINK 2. **2.** German: nickname from Middle High German *mün(i)ch* 'monk'. See also MINNICH. **3.** German: variant of MINKE 2 or MENCKE.

Minckler (172) German: probably a nickname for a servant of a monk (see MINCK).

Mincks (245) German: variant of MINCK.

Mincy (275) Of Irish or English origin: unexplained. Compare MINCEY, MINCHEY.

Mindel (215) Jewish (Ashkenazic): from the Yiddish female personal name *Mindl*, a pet form of *Mine*, a name of similar origin to *Minna*.
GIVEN NAMES Jewish 9%. *Nissan* (2), *Pinkas* (2), *Gilah*, *Herschel*.

Mindell (115) Jewish (Ashkenazic): variant spelling of MINDEL.

Minden (230) German: habitational name from any of various places so named, for example in Westphalia.
GIVEN NAMES German 4%. *Erwin*, *Matthias*.

Minder (524) North German and Dutch: **1.** variant of MEINDERS. **2.** distinguishing nickname from Middle High German, Middle Dutch *minder* 'smaller', 'younger'.

Mindlin (216) Jewish (eastern Ashkenazic): metronymic from the Yiddish personal name *Mindle*, a pet form of *Mine* (see MINDEL).
GIVEN NAMES Jewish 7%; Russian 6%. *Sol* (2), *Ilya*, *Zelik*; *Mikhail* (2), *Boris*, *Efim*, *Genady*, *Leonid*, *Vladimir*.

Mindrup (115) North German and Danish: presumably a habitational name from an unidentified place name formed with *-rup* 'farmstead', 'hamlet'.

Mindt (125) German: from a reduced form of the personal name MEINHARDT.

Minear (514) Americanized form of Dutch MYNHIER.

Mineau (199) French: diminutive of *mine*, a measurement of capacity equal to about 12 ounces (a short form of *hémine*), hence possibly a nickname for a small person or a metonymic occupational name for an official who checked weights.

Mineer (156) Americanized form of Dutch MYNHIER.

Minehan (106) Irish: variant of MOYNIHAN.

Minehart (235) Americanized spelling of German MEINHARDT.

Minella (218) Southern Italian: from a pet form of the female personal name *Mina*, a short form of *Guglielmina*, *Giacomina*, etc.
GIVEN NAMES Italian 19%. *Gaeton* (2), *Rocco* (2), *Vito* (2), *Angelo*, *Concetta*, *Domenic*, *Giacomo*, *Giulio*, *Ricci*, *Sal*.

Minelli (203) Italian: patronymic or plural form of *Minello*, a pet form of the personal name *Mino*, which is a short form of a personal name formed with the hypocoristic suffix *-mino*, such as *Adimino*, *Giacomino*, *Guglielmino*, etc.
GIVEN NAMES Italian 11%. *Biagio* (2), *Lorenzo* (2), *Angelo*, *Livio*, *Matteo*, *Tiziano*.

Mineo (518) Italian (Sicily): habitational name from Mineo, a place in Catania province.
GIVEN NAMES Italian 15%. *Sal* (4), *Angelo* (2), *Gino* (2), *Giovanni* (2), *Salvatore* (2), *Santo* (2), *Sebastiano* (2), *Stefano* (2), *Agostino*, *Antonino*, *Antonio*, *Carmine*.

Miner (7951) English: occupational name for someone who built mines, either for the excavation of coal and other minerals, or as a technique in the medieval art of siege warfare. The word represents an agent derivative of Middle English, Old French *mine* 'mine' (a word of Celtic origin, cognate with Gaelic *mein* 'ore', 'mine').

Minerd (147) Perhaps an altered spelling of MEINERT.

Minerich (111) Croatian: unexplained.

Minerva (242) Italian: from the female personal name *Minerva*, from the name of the Roman goddess of wisdom, corresponding to Greek *Athena*.
GIVEN NAMES Italian 14%. *Vito* (5), *Domenic* (2), *Angelo*, *Giuseppe*, *Italia*, *Salvatore*.

Minervini (257) Italian: patronymic or plural form of MINERVINO.

GIVEN NAMES Italian 24%. *Mario* (3), *Mauro* (3), *Vito* (3), *Anello* (2), *Corrado* (2), *Gaetano* (2), *Rocco* (2), *Saverio* (2), *Carmelo*, *Fabio*, *Pina*, *Rinaldo*, *Vincenzo*.

Minervino (106) Italian: probably a habitational name from either of two places, Minervino di Lecce and Minervino Murge, in the provinces of Lecce and Bari, which take their names from ancient temples dedicated to the Roman goddess Minerva.
GIVEN NAMES Italian 12%. *Rocco* (2), *Enrico*, *Salvatore*, *Tommaso*.

Mines (778) **1.** Of German origin: probably an Americanized spelling of MEINS. **2.** Jewish (eastern Ashkenazic): metronymic from the Yiddish female personal name *Mine* (see MINDEL) + the Yiddish possessive suffix *-s*.

Minett (131) English and French: **1.** nickname from Old French *mignot* 'dainty', 'pleasing'. **2.** from *Minnota*, a pet form of the female personal name *Minna*. This was originally a Germanic personal name from Old High German *minna* 'love', but later it was also used as a short form of *Willemina*, a feminine version of WILLIAM.

Minette (163) French: from *Minet*, a pet form of a personal name such as *Dominique*, *Jacquemine* or *Guillemine*. Also a pet nickname from Old French *minet* 'very small'. The *-ette* ending is a standard variation in North American French of *-et*; it does not necessarily indicate derivation from a feminine personal name.
GIVEN NAME French 5%. *Henri* (2).

Minetti (182) Italian: patronymic or plural form of **Minetto**, a pet form of the personal name *Mino* (see MINELLI).
GIVEN NAMES Italian 17%. *Rocco* (4), *Angelo* (3), *Antonio* (2), *Dario* (2), *Guido*, *Rino*.

Ming (831) **1.** English: of uncertain origin; possibly from a reduced form of the personal name DOMINICK. **2.** Chinese 明: from the name of Meng Mingshi, a senior minister of the state of Qin in the Spring and Autumn period (722–481 BC). His descendants adopted the first character of his given name, which means 'bright', as their surname.
GIVEN NAMES Chinese 16%. *Chen* (2), *Fung* (2), *Hing* (2), *Ming* (2), *Tzu* (2), *Wing* (2), *Xing* (2), *Chi*, *Choo*, *Fan*, *Guang*, *Guo Wei*.

Minga (147) **1.** Eastern German: from a Slavic pet form of the Germanic personal name MEINHARDT. **2.** Greek (**Mingas**): nickname among Greeks of Aromanian origin, from Aromanian *mincu*, *mingu* 'small child'.

Minge (202) **1.** English: variant of **Mingy** (see MINGEE). **2.** German: from a pet form of the personal name MEINHARDT. **3.** German: altered form of French MUNIER 'miller'. **4.** Norwegian: habitational name from a farm name in Østfold, of obscure etymology.

GIVEN NAME Scandinavian 4%; German 4%. *Erik*.

Mingee (135) English (Suffolk): of uncertain derivation; **1.** perhaps from a reduced form of the personal name *Dominicus* (see DOMINICK). **2.** alternatively, as Reaney proposes, it may be from the Breton personal name *Menguy*, a compound of *men* 'stone' + *ki* 'dog'.

Minger (347) Dutch: **1.** from a Germanic personal name composed of the elements *magin* 'strength', 'might' + *gār, gēr* 'spear'. **2.** variant of MANGER 1.

Minges (305) **1.** Altered spelling of Scottish MENZIES, reflecting the traditional Scottish pronunciation of that name. **2.** German: variant of MENGES 1 or 2.

GIVEN NAMES German 6%. *Gunter* (2), *Kurt* (2).

Mingione (156) Italian (Campania): perhaps a variant of MANGIONE.

GIVEN NAMES Italian 24%; French 6%. *Rocco* (4), *Attilio, Carmela, Dino, Domenic, Pasquale, Santo*; *Armand, Thierry*.

Mingle (410) Perhaps an altered spelling of German MENGEL.

Mingledorff (116) German: presumably a habitational name from an unidentified village called Mingeldorf.

GIVEN NAME German 10%. *Kurt* (3).

Mingo (1006) Spanish and Italian: from a short form of the personal name DOMINGO, Italian *Domenico*.

Mings (366) Scottish: variant of MINGUS.

Mingus (638) Scottish: variant of MENZIES, which is traditionally pronounced 'mingiz'.

Minh (73) **1.** Vietnamese: unexplained. **2.** Cambodian: unexplained.

GIVEN NAMES Vietnamese 56%; Other Southeast Asian 25%. *Tran* (8), *Hien* (2), *Lam* (2), *Phu* (2), *Da, Dang Van, Dao, Doan, Dung, Duong, Ha, Huynh*; *Chu, Kyoung*.

Minhas (110) **1.** Indian (Panjab): Hindu (Rajput) and Sikh name based on the name of Rajput and Jat tribes. **2.** Muslim: possibly an altered form of **Minhāj**, a personal name based on Arabic *minhāj* 'method', 'order', 'way'. Minhāj al-Siraj was the author of a well-known 13th-century history of India.

GIVEN NAMES Muslim 47%; Indian 40%. *Ashfaq* (3), *Rashid* (2), *Raza* (2), *Tasleem* (2), *Ahmad, Babar, Faqir, Farooq, Haji, Hameed, Hamid, Iftakhar*; *Amit, Harcharn, Jit, Joga, Pritam, Rajpal, Sohan*.

Mini (192) Italian: short form of any of the many diminutive name forms ending in -*mini*, for example GIACOMINI.

GIVEN NAMES Italian 20%. *Salvatore* (3), *Aida, Angelo, Augusto, Enrico, Gabriela, Mario, Pietro, Salvatore*.

Miniard (229) Possibly English: unexplained. Compare MINYARD.

Minich (694) Czech: nickname from the vocabulary word *mnich* 'monk'.

Minichiello (233) Italian: from a pet form of *Minico*, a short form of the personal name *Domenico* (see DOMINGO).

GIVEN NAMES Italian 15%. *Angelo* (6), *Antonio, Luigi, Modestino, Orazio, Rocco, Salvatore, Vittorio*.

Minick (904) Perhaps an Americanized spelling of Ukrainian **Mynik**, Polish **Minik**, of uncertain origin, possibly a short form of the personal name *Dominik* (see DOMINGO).

Minicozzi (111) Italian: from a derivative of the personal name *Minico*, a short form of DOMENICO.

GIVEN NAMES Italian 14%. *Angelo* (2), *Salvatore*.

Minicucci (175) Italian: from a patronymic form of *Minicuccio*, a pet form of *Minico*, which is a short form of the personal name *Domenico* (see DOMINGO).

GIVEN NAMES Italian 18%. *Rocco* (2), *Amerigo, Angelo, Carmine, Cosmo, Fulvio, Rinaldo, Sal, Salvatore, Saverio*.

Minier (429) **1.** Perhaps a variant of Dutch MYNHIER. **2.** Spanish: possibly a Castilianized form of French MEUNIER.

GIVEN NAMES Spanish 6%. *Mario* (3), *Carlos* (2), *Altagracia, Ana, Baudilia, Bernardo, Carolina, Dulce, Jose, Juan, Juana, Luis*.

Minieri (113) Italian: possibly a reduced form of MAINIERO.

GIVEN NAMES Italian 18%. *Americo, Carmine, Domenica, Salvatore*.

Minihan (191) Irish: **1.** Anglicized form of Gaelic **Ó Mionacháin**, a variant of **Ó Manacháin** (see MONAHAN). **2.** variant of MOYNIHAN.

GIVEN NAME Irish 8%. *Brendan*.

Mininger (188) German: variant of MEININGER.

Minion (171) French: occupational name for a miner, from a diminutive of *minier* 'miner' (see MINER).

Minish (253) Irish: variant of MCNEESE.

Minium (160) Origin unidentified.

Minix (544) Perhaps a variant of Irish MANNIX.

Minjares (177) Spanish: variant of MINJAREZ.

GIVEN NAMES Spanish 46%. *Jose* (6), *Raul* (4), *Alfredo* (2), *Eloy* (2), *Gerardo* (2), *Juanita* (2), *Agustina, Alfonso, Alonzo, Amador, Amalia, Andres*.

Minjarez (219) Spanish (**Minjárez**): patronymic from an unidentified personal name.

GIVEN NAMES Spanish 39%. *Luis* (4), *Jose* (3), *Manuel* (3), *Francisco* (2), *Jesus* (2), *Raul* (2), *Ruben* (2), *Agapito, Alfonso, Alfredo, Angel, Arturo*.

Mink (2123) **1.** Czech: from a reduced form of the personal name *Dominik* (see DOMINGO). **2.** North German and Dutch: from a pet form of the personal name MEIN. **3.** Dutch: nickname from Middle Dutch *menke, minke* 'physical defect', 'infirmity', 'mutilation'. **4.** German: variant of MINKE 2.

Minke (192) **1.** Dutch: variant of MINK 2 and 3. **2.** German: habitational name from any of several places called Minken in Brandenburg and Silesia.

Minkel (243) Jewish (Ashkenazic): from the female personal name *Minkl*, a pet form of *Mine* (see MINDEL).

Minker (113) Jewish (from Lithuania): habitational name for someone from a place called Minkiai in Lithuania.

Minkin (317) Jewish (from Belarus): from the Yiddish personal name *Minke*, a pet form of *Mine* (see MINDEL).

GIVEN NAMES Jewish 8%; Russian 4%. *Hyman* (2), *Ilya, Isaak, Meyer, Miriam, Semen, Sol*; *Leonid* (2), *Yury* (2), *Boris*.

Minkler (415) German: from Middle High German *menkeler*, a variant of *mengaere* 'trader', 'peddler' (see MENGER).

Minkley (102) **1.** English (Midlands): unexplained. **2.** possibly an Americanized spelling of German MINKLER.

GIVEN NAME German 7%. *Arno* (2).

Minko (107) Polish and Ukrainian: probably a derivative of a reduced form of the personal name *Dominik* (Latin *Domenicus*).

GIVEN NAMES Polish 8%. *Czeslaw, Jacek, Malgorzata*.

Minkoff (323) Alternative spelling of **Minkov**: **1.** Bulgarian: patronymic from the personal name *Mino*. **2.** Jewish (from Belarus): metronymic from the female personal name *Minke* (see MINKIN).

GIVEN NAMES Jewish 4%. *Faige, Miriam, Sol*.

Minks (543) Altered form of Polish and Jewish MINKUS.

Minkus (141) **1.** Polish: perhaps from a reduced form of the personal name *Dominik* (Latin *Domenicus*). **2.** Polish: alternatively perhaps a nickname from Polish *minka* 'person who used to pull faces'. **3.** Jewish (Ashkenazic): metronymic from the personal name *Minke* (see MINKIN).

Minnear (102) Americanized form of Dutch MYNHIER.

Minneci (111) Italian: perhaps an altered form of *mendico* 'beggar', 'mendicant'.

GIVEN NAMES Italian 19%. *Santo* (2), *Antonio, Francesco, Giuseppe, Pietro, Sal, Salvatore, Vito*.

Minnehan (156) Variant spelling of Irish MINIHAN.

Minnella (102) Southern Italian: from a derivative of the Calabrian and Sicilian dialect word *minna* 'breast'.

GIVEN NAMES Italian 19%. *Salvatore* (2), *Carmelo, Ciro, Corrado, Pietro, Rocco*.

Minneman (133) German (**Minnemann**): nickname for an attractive or amorous man, from Middle High German *minne* 'love' + *man* 'man'.

Minner (637) **1.** German: nickname from Middle High German *minnære* 'lover'. **2.** Dutch: variant of MEINERT.

Minnerly (111) Probably an Americanized form of South German **Minnerle**, pet form of MINNER 'lover'.

Minney (355) English: unexplained. Compare MINNIE.

Minnich (1725) **1.** German: from Middle High German *münich* 'monk' (see MONK), probably denoting someone who worked for the monks in a local monastery. **2.** North German: from a pet form of a local form of the personal name MEIN.

Minnick (2690) Irish: probably an Anglicized form of Gaelic **Ó Muineóg**, perhaps derived from a diminutive *manach* 'monk'.

Minnie (166) Scottish and English: unexplained. Compare MINNEY.

GIVEN NAME French 5%. *Armand* (2).

Minniear (247) Perhaps a variant of Dutch MYNHIER.

Minniefield (140) Origin unidentified.

Minnifield (141) Variant of MINNIEFIELD.

Minnig (154) German: variant of MINNICH.

GIVEN NAMES German 5%. *Hansi, Merwin.*

Minning (112) German: variant of MINNICH.

Minnis (914) Irish (eastern Ulster): variant of MCNEESE.

Minniti (201) Southern Italian: from a derivative of the personal name MENNA, of Greek origin.

GIVEN NAMES Italian 22%. *Angelo* (2), *Caterina* (2), *Salvatore* (2), *Eugenio, Lorenzo, Orlando, Ronaldo, Santo, Tito.*

Minnix (430) Perhaps a variant of Irish MANNIX.

Minns (239) English (chiefly Norfolk): metronymic from a medieval female personal name, *Minna* (see MINETT).

Mino (319) **1.** Galiciam, Asturian-Leonese and Spanish (**Miño**): habitational name from any of several places in Galicia, Asturies, and Soria called Miño, which take their name from the Miño river on which they stand. **2.** Japanese (rare): variously written, usually with characters meaning 'three fields', though the actual meaning is 'straw raincoat'.

GIVEN NAMES Spanish 11%; Japanese 5%. *Jorge* (3), *Mario* (3), *Carlos* (2), *Andres, Armondo, Cesar, Claudio, Cristobal, Efrain, Fidelia, Humberto, Jaime; Yoshiaki* (2), *Hiroshi, Kaoru, Takeshi, Toshiyuki, Yutaka.*

Minogue (517) Irish: Anglicized form of Gaelic **Ó Muineog** 'descendant of *Muineog*', a variant of *Manóg*, a personal name representing a diminutive of *manach* 'monk'.

GIVEN NAMES Irish 6%. *Brendan* (3), *Aine.*

Minor (9308) **1.** English: variant spelling of MINER. **2.** German: nickname, meaning 'small(er)', from Latin *minor* 'less', 'smaller'. **3.** French: nickname meaning 'younger', from the same word as in 2.

Minot (196) French: **1.** variant of MINEAU. **2.** from a pet form of a masculine personal name ending in *-min*, such as *Jacquemin* or *Guillemin.*

Minott (293) **1.** Altered spelling of French MINOT, written thus to preserve the final *-t*, which is pronounced in Canadian French. **2.** English: variant of MINETT.

GIVEN NAMES French 4%. *Andre, Eugenie, Remy.*

Minotti (211) Italian: from a pet form of the personal name *Mino* (see MINELLI).

GIVEN NAMES Italian 13%. *Angelo* (2), *Carlo* (2), *Aldo, Marcello, Salvatore.*

Minser (105) Jewish (Ashkenazic): variant spelling of the occupational surname MINTZER 'moneyer'.

Minshall (402) English: habitational name from a pair of villages in Cheshire, on either side of the Weaver river, recorded in Domesday Book as *Maneshale*, from the genitive case of the Old English personal name *Mann* + Old English *scylf* 'shelf', 'ledge'.

Minshew (501) English: variant of MINSHALL.

Minsky (394) **1.** Russian, Belorussian, and Jewish (eastern Ashkenazic): habitational name for someone from Minsk, now the capital of Belarus. **2.** Jewish (from Poland): habitational name for someone from Mińsk Mazowiecki, in Poland.

GIVEN NAMES Jewish 11%. *Hyman* (3), *Naftaly* (2), *Sol* (2), *Hershel, Meir, Menachem, Meyer, Schneur, Yair, Yaron.*

Minson (385) **1.** English: unexplained. **2.** Dutch (**Minsen**) patronymic from the Germanic personal name *Me(g)inzo.*

Minster (337) Altered spelling of German **Münster** (see MUNSTER).

Minteer (231) Irish: variant of MCATEER, in which Gaelic *Mac an* ('son of the') has become *Min-* in the Anglicized form.

Minten (166) Dutch: patronymic from a variant of MENTE 3.

GIVEN NAMES German 4%. *Johann, Kurt.*

Minter (3249) English: occupational name for a moneyer, Old English *myntere*, an agent derivative of *mynet* 'coin', from Late Latin *moneta* 'money', originally an epithet of the goddess Juno (meaning 'counselor', from *monere* 'advise'), at whose temple in Rome the coins were struck. The English term was used at an early date to denote a workman who stamped the coins; later it came to denote the supervisors of the mint, who were wealthy and socially elevated members of the merchant class, and who were made responsible for the quality of the coinage by having their names placed on the coins.

Minto (401) Scottish: habitational name from a place near Denholm in the Borders, originally named with British *minit* (cognate with Welsh *mynydd* 'hill'), with the later addition of Middle English *ho(e)* 'ridge', 'hill' after the original meaning of the first element had been forgotten.

Minton (4918) English: habitational name from a place in Shropshire, so named from Welsh *mynydd* 'hill' + Old English *tūn* 'enclosure', 'settlement'.

Mintun (108) Variant of English MINTON.

Minturn (198) Probably an altered form of the English habitational name **Mintern(e)**, from Minterne in Dorsetshire, named in Old English as the 'mint house', from *minte* 'mint' (the herb) + *ærn* 'building', 'dwelling'.

Mintz (2654) German and Jewish (Ashkenazic): habitational name from the city of Mainz in Germany.

GIVEN NAMES Jewish 6%. *Sol* (5), *Ari* (3), *Chaim* (3), *Avrohom* (2), *Avrom* (2), *Eliyohu* (2), *Emanuel* (2), *Hyman* (2), *Meyer* (2), *Rebeckah* (2), *Zalman* (2), *Zelik* (2).

Mintzer (460) Jewish (Ashkenazic): occupational name for a moneyer, Yiddish *mintser.*

Minucci (121) Italian: from a pet form of the personal name *Mino* (see MINELLI).

GIVEN NAMES Italian 27%. *Salvatore* (2), *Saverio* (2), *Vito* (2), *Attilio, Biagio, Carmela, Ignazio, Nunzio, Rocco.*

Minus (169) **1.** English: unexplained. **2.** German unexplained.

Minx (100) Probably an altered form of German MINTZ: unexplained.

Minyard (837) Possibly English: unexplained. Compare MINIARD.

Mioduszewski (103) Polish: derivative of the nickname *Miodusz* (a pet form of *Miód*, from *miód* 'honey') + the common surname ending *-ewski.*

GIVEN NAMES Polish 14%. *Czeslaw, Katarzyna, Miroslaw, Tadeusz, Wojciech.*

Mion (160) **1.** Italian: variant of MIONE. **2.** French: nickname from Old French *mion* 'small', 'insignificant'.

GIVEN NAMES Italian 14%; Spanish 9%. *Mario* (3), *Antonio* (2), *Carlo, Corrado, Enrico, Lino* (2), *Lorenzo, Primo, Romano; Luis* (2), *Alejandro, Carlos.*

Mione (150) Italian: (**Mióne**): from an augmentative form of the personal name MEO.

GIVEN NAMES Italian 19%. *Salvatore* (3), *Angelo, Carlo, Flavio, Giuseppe, Pietro, Vito.*

Miotke (166) Germanized form of Polish **Miotka**, a nickname derived from *miotać* 'to throw or toss'.

Mir (291) **1.** Muslim (common in Pakistan, Bangladesh, and India): from a title of Persian origin, a short form of Arabic AMIR 'prince', 'commander'. **2.** Polish: from a short form of any of various Old Polish personal names containing the element *mir* 'peace', 'quiet', 'esteem', for example *Mirosław* or *Jaromir*. **3.** Catalan: patronymic from *Mir*, a medieval personal name of Germanic origin (see MIRO). **4.** French: variant of MIRE 1.

GIVEN NAMES Muslim 43%; Spanish 13%; Portuguese 5%. *Mohammad* (5), *Ali* (4), *Rizwan* (3), *Tariq* (3), *Javed* (2), *Jawed* (2),

Mahmood (2), *Majid* (2), *Muhammad* (2), *Naeem* (2), *Rasul* (2), *Saghir* (2); *Jose* (6), *Carlos* (3), *Florentino* (3), *Juan* (3), *Rafael* (3), *Amado* (2), *Julio* (2), *Nestor* (2), *Araceli*, *Arnaldo*, *Eduardo*, *Francia*; *Armanda*.

Mira (291) **1.** Galician and Portuguese: probably a habitational name from any of the places in Galicia and Portugal named Mira. **2.** Catalan: of uncertain origin; possibly from the Arabic personal name *Amira*, or a derivative of MIR. **3.** Italian: apparently from the personal name *Mira*, feminine form of *Miro*, from Late Latin *Mirus* and *Mira*, respectively, from Latin *mirus* 'wonderful', 'marvellous'. **4.** Czech and Polish: from a pet form of any of various personal names formed with the element *mir* 'peace', 'quiet', 'esteem' (see MIR).
GIVEN NAMES Spanish 26%; Italian 8%. *Manuel* (3), *Mario* (3), *Roberto* (3), *Alfredo* (2), *Herminio* (2), *Jose* (2), *Ramon* (2), *Alfonso*, *Ana Maria*, *Blanca*, *Carlos*, *Eloy*; *Antonio* (3), *Angelo* (2), *Sal* (2), *Alessandra*, *Antonietta*, *Francesco*, *Lorenzo*.

Mirabal (453) Aragonese: probably a variant of **Miraval**, a habitational name from Miraval, in Aragon, formed with *mirar* 'to look', 'survey', 'admire' + *vall* 'valley'.
GIVEN NAMES Spanish 37%. *Jose* (8), *Manuel* (7), *Pedro* (6), *Fernando* (5), *Pablo* (5), *Miguel* (4), *Carlos* (3), *Luis* (3), *Elena* (2), *Gerardo* (2), *Guillermo* (2), *Hortensia* (2).

Mirabella (565) Italian (Campania and Sicily): habitational name from Mirabella Eclano in Avellino or Mirabella Imbaccari in Catania, or from various places with the name Mirabello, all named from medieval Latin *mira* 'viewpoint' + *bella* 'beautiful'.
GIVEN NAMES Italian 12%. *Angelo* (3), *Gino* (3), *Salvatore* (2), *Alfonse*, *Carmello*, *Enrico*, *Natale*, *Rachele*, *Rocco*, *Sal*, *Santo*.

Mirabelli (220) Italian (**Mirabèlli**): **1.** patronymic from the personal name *Mirabello*, from medieval Latin *mirus (et) bellus* 'amazing and handsome'. **2.** habitational name from a plural form of the common place name Mirabello, as for example Mirabello Monferrato in Alessandria province or Mirabello Sannitico in Campobasso.
GIVEN NAMES Italian 16% French 4%. *Oreste* (3), *Carlo*, *Cesare*, *Dante*, *Francesca*, *Gildo*, *Marcello*, *Raffaele*; *Mario* (9), *Jorge*, *Sergio*; *Andre* (2), *Manon*.

Mirabile (377) Italian: nickname from *mirabile* 'admirable' (Latin *Mirabilis*).
GIVEN NAMES Italian 20%. *Santo* (6), *Salvatore* (4), *Alfonso* (2), *Angelo* (2), *Carmelo* (2), *Giuseppe* (2), *Rocco* (2), *Antonio*, *Benito*, *Cosmo*, *Domenic*, *Filippa*, *Gasper*.

Mirabito (227) Southern Italian (especially eastern Sicily and Calabria): variant of MORABITO.

GIVEN NAMES Italian 10%. *Angelo* (4), *Salvatore* (2), *Fiorella*.

Miracle (1870) **1.** Southern French (Occitan) and Catalan: from the Marian name *Mare de Déu del Miracle*, or nickname from *miracle* 'miracle', 'wonder' (Latin *miraculum*), applied perhaps to someone who had had a miraculous escape from death or disaster. **2.** Variant of MARACLE.

Miraglia (514) Southern Italian: from the Old Sicilian title *miraglia di mari* 'admiral'.
GIVEN NAMES Italian 13%. *Sal* (2), *Salvatore* (2), *Vittorio* (2), *Angelo*, *Attillo*, *Carmela*, *Cirino*, *Domenic*, *Gianni*, *Giuseppe*, *Guilio*, *Nichola*.

Miramontes (681) Galician: habitational name from Miramontes in A Coruña province, so named from *mirar* 'to look' + *montes* 'mountains'.
GIVEN NAMES Spanish 56%. *Jose* (28), *Carlos* (10), *Guadalupe* (8), *Juan* (8), *Jesus* (7), *Ramon* (7), *Javier* (6), *Raul* (6), *Salvador* (6), *Arturo* (5), *Leticia* (5), *Luis* (5).

Miranda (9057) Spanish, Portuguese, and Jewish (Sephardic): habitational name from any of numerous places in Spain and Portugal called Miranda. The derivation of the place name is uncertain; it may be of pre-Roman origin, or from Latin *miranda* 'view', 'outlook'. This name is also found in western India, where it was taken by Portuguese colonists.
GIVEN NAMES Spanish 41%; Portuguese 10%. *Jose* (195), *Manuel* (94), *Carlos* (90), *Luis* (86), *Juan* (83), *Jorge* (56), *Miguel* (51), *Jesus* (46), *Pedro* (46), *Francisco* (43), *Mario* (39), *Rafael* (34); *Paulo* (5), *Joaquim* (4), *Godofredo* (3), *Joao* (3), *Albano*, *Amadeu*, *Anatolio*, *Lidio*, *Marcio*, *Zaragoza*; *Antonio* (59), *Angelo* (16), *Lorenzo* (8), *Marco* (7), *Salvatore* (7), *Luciano* (5), *Carmelo* (4), *Dario* (4), *Fausto* (4), *Federico* (4), *Sal* (4), *Gilda* (3).

Mirando (214) Italian and Spanish: from the personal name *Mirando*, Latin *Mirandus*, from Latin *mirandus* 'wondrous', 'lovely'.
GIVEN NAMES Italian 11%; Spanish 8%. *Salvatore* (3), *Cosmo*, *Modesto*, *Silvio*; *Ana*, *Carlos*, *Gonzalo*, *Isidro*, *Julio*, *Olimpia*, *Rodrigo*.

Mirante (160) **1.** Southern Italian: from a short form of **Almirante**, an occupational or honorific name (or possibly a nickname for someone with a self-important manner), from Spanish *almirante* 'admiral', which is from Arabic *al amīr* 'commander'. **2.** Portuguese: possibly a habitational name from any of the places so named, from *mirante* 'watch tower', 'look out', or from the same word in the sense 'watch', 'vigilance', 'sentry duty'.
GIVEN NAMES Italian 15%. *Antonio* (2), *Carlo*, *Domenico*, *Filippo*, *Gaetano*, *Marcello*, *Salvatore*.

Mirarchi (155) Southern Italian: status name from medieval Greek *moirarchos* 'captain', from *moira* 'squadron', 'company' + *archos* 'chief', 'head'.
GIVEN NAMES Italian 29%. *Saverio* (4), *Dante* (2), *Vincenzo* (2), *Domenico*, *Mario*, *Marisa*, *Orlando*, *Romano*, *Salvatore*, *Ugo*.

Mirchandani (167) Hindu name found among people from Sind, Pakistan, meaning 'of (or descended from) Mirchand'. *Mirchand* must be an ancestral name; it is a compound of Arabic *mīr* 'head', 'chief', + Indic *chand* (from Sanskrit *čandra* 'shining', 'pleasant'), a common final element in compound names.
GIVEN NAMES Indian 84%. *Kishore* (5), *Prakash* (4), *Chandru* (3), *Sunder* (3), *Anjali* (2), *Dilip* (2), *Dinesh* (2), *Gagan* (2), *Haresh* (2), *Kapil* (2), *Karuna* (2), *Lal* (2).

Mire (926) French: occupational name from Old French *mire* 'physician'.
GIVEN NAMES French 8%. *Laurent* (3), *Lucien* (3), *Emile* (2), *Michel* (2), *Alcide*, *Andrus*, *Angelle*, *Clovis*, *Curley*, *Fernest*, *Germaine*, *Jacques*.

Mirecki (73) Polish: habitational name for someone from a place called Mircze in Zamość voivodeship.
GIVEN NAMES Polish 18%. *Casimir*, *Irena*, *Kazimierz*, *Leszek*, *Zygmunt*.

Mireles (1468) Spanish (Canary Islands): probably a variant of Portuguese **Meireles**, which is of uncertain derivation.
GIVEN NAMES Spanish 49%; Portuguese 10%. *Jose* (59), *Juan* (29), *Carlos* (15), *Jesus* (15), *Manuel* (11), *Ricardo* (11), *Francisco* (10), *Ramon* (10), *Pedro* (10), *Raul* (9), *Ruben* (8), *Armando* (7); *Ligia*, *Paulo*.

Mirelez (154) Spanish: variant of MIRELES.
GIVEN NAMES Spanish 33%. *Jorge* (3), *Ramon* (3), *Cayetano* (2), *Enrique* (2), *Fortino* (2), *Jose* (2), *Manuel* (2), *Alfonso*, *Alfredo*, *Armando*, *Blasa*, *Carlos*.

Mirenda (149) Southern Italian (Sicily): possibly a variant of MERENDA.
GIVEN NAMES Italian 11%. *Cirino*, *Pasquale*.

Mires (365) **1.** English (Kent): perhaps a variant spelling of MYERS. **2.** Greek (pronounced as two syllables): nickname from Albanian *mirë* 'good', 'honest'.

Mirick (152) Americanized form of Polish or Czech **Mirek** or **Mirík**, pet forms of several personal names formed with the element *mir* 'peace'.

Mirkin (242) Jewish (eastern Ashkenazic): metronymic from the Yiddish female personal name *Mirke*, a pet form of the Biblical Hebrew name *Miryam*, a very ancient name of uncertain etymology, perhaps meaning 'wished-for child', from an Egyptian root *mrj* with the addition of the Hebrew feminine diminutive suffix *-am*.
GIVEN NAMES Russian 12%; Jewish 9%. *Boris* (6), *Leonid* (2), *Mirk* (2), *Ekaterina*, *Emiliya*, *Georgy*, *Mikhail*, *Mikhial*, *Raisa*, *Semion*, *Sergei*, *Vladimir*; *Isadore*, *Zehava*.

Mirkovich (101) Croatian and Serbian (**Mirković**): patronymic from the personal name *Mirko*, a pet form of *Miroslav* or any of various other male names composed with *mir* 'peace'.
GIVEN NAMES South Slavic 11%; German 4%. *Andrija, Nikolina, Rajko, Zvonko; Reinhard.*

Mirman (162) Jewish (eastern Ashkenazic): from Yiddish female personal name *Mire*, a pet form of *Miryam* (see MIRKIN) + Yiddish *man* 'man', in the sense 'husband of'.
GIVEN NAME Jewish 5%. *Avi.*

Miro (301) Catalan (**Miró**): from the medieval personal name *Mir, Mirone,* of Germanic origin.
GIVEN NAMES Spanish 29%; Portuguese 7%; Italian 5%. *Carlos* (5), *Jose* (4), *Julio* (3), *Rafael* (3), *Jose Mario* (2), *Juan* (2), *Lourdes* (2), *Luis* (2), *Manuel* (2), *Pedro* (2), *Ramon* (2), *Aida; Serafim; Antonio* (6), *Tommaso* (2), *Gasper, Julieta, Marco, Sal.*

Miron (647) **1.** Spanish (**Mirón**): Castilianized spelling of Catalan **Miró** (see MIRO). **2.** Spanish (**Mirón**): from *mirón,* a derivative of *mirar* 'to look' (Latin *mirare*), possibly a nickname in the sense 'nosy', 'inquisitive'. **3.** French: from a diminutive of MIRE. **4.** Greek: variant of MYRON.
GIVEN NAMES Spanish 5%; French 4%. *Jose* (4), *Carlos* (2), *Elia* (2), *Francisco* (2), *Raul* (2), *Ricardo* (2), *Alberto, Ana, Angel, Ayala, Baldomero, Cesar; Marcel* (2), *Andre, Emile, Gilles, Jean Louis, Yves.*

Mirowski (91) Polish: habitational name for someone from any of various places called Mirów or Mirowo.
GIVEN NAMES Polish 10%. *Casimir, Jacek, Pawel.*

Mirra (274) Southern Italian: from *mirra* 'myrrh', either an occupational name for someone who sold myrrh or perhaps from a medieval Greek female personal name dervied from this word.
GIVEN NAMES Italian 16%. *Emilio* (2), *Mario* (2), *Angelo, Antonio, Aurelio, Carmine, Cosmo, Dino, Domenica, Domenico, Gennaro, Leonardo, Nicola, Salvatore, Saverio.*

Mirro (141) Italian: possibly from a short form of a personal named formed with *-miro,* with a doubling of the *r.*
GIVEN NAMES Italian 7%. *Antonio* (2), *Carmela, Rocco.*

Mirski (32) Polish: habitational name from any of various places named with the element *mir* 'peace', 'quiet', or with MIR as a personal name.

Mirsky (401) Jewish (eastern Ashkenazic): habitational name for someone from Mir, a place in Belarus.
GIVEN NAMES Jewish 5%. *Isaak, Miriam, Moshe, Rebekah, Sol, Yehudah.*

Mirto (157) **1.** Italian: habitational name from Mirto in Messina province, Sicily, or from Mirto, a district of Crosia, which is in Cosenza province, or a topographic name from *mirto* 'myrtle' (from Greek *myrtis*). **2.** Possibly also Greek, a shortened form of *Mirtoglou,* a metronymic from the female personal name *Myrto* 'Myrtle' (classical Greek *Myrtis*).
GIVEN NAMES Italian 16%. *Armando, Basilio, Domenic, Erminio, Gilda, Sal, Salvatore.*

Mirza (641) Muslim (Bangladesh, India, and Pakistan): from a personal name based on the Persian honorific title *Mīrzā,* a shortened form of *mir-zadeh* 'child of a prince'.
GIVEN NAMES Muslim 76%. *Mohammad* (20), *Imran* (8), *Mohammed* (7), *Khalid* (6), *Muhammad* (5), *Ahmed* (4), *Ali* (4), *Asif* (4), *Javed* (4), *Masood* (4), *Nadeem* (4), *Abdul* (3).

Mis (183) **1.** Polish (**Miś**): from a pet form of the personal name *Michał* (see MICHAEL). **2.** Polish (**Miś**): perhaps also a nickname from *miś* 'bear'. **3.** Slovenian (**Miš**): nickname from the vocabulary word *miš* 'mouse'. **4.** Dutch: from a reduced form of the personal name *Amijs,* a derivative of Latin *amicus* 'friend'.
GIVEN NAMES Polish 6%. *Ryszard, Stanislaw, Wojciech.*

Misak (114) Czech (**Mišák**) and Slovenian (**Mišak**): nickname from the vocabulary word *mišak* 'he-mouse'.

Misch (395) German **1.** (Silesia and Lausitz): from a Slavic pet form of a personal name equivalent to MICHAEL. Compare Polish **Miś** (see MIS). **2.** habitational name from any of several places in the Rhineland called Müsch.
GIVEN NAMES German 5%. *Franz* (2), *Dieter, Hans, Horst, Manfred, Rainer.*

Mische (116) German: variant of MISCH 1.
GIVEN NAME German 4%. *Franziska.*

Mischel (252) German: pet form of MISCH.

Mischke (400) German (Silesia and Lausitz): **1.** from a Slavic pet form (*Miszka*) of any of various personal names, such as Polish *Michał* (see MICHAEL), *Mikołaj* (see NICHOLAS), or a compound name such as *Miłosław* or *Mirosław,* the latter formed with *mir* 'peace'. **2.** habitational name from any of several places so named in eastern Germany.
GIVEN NAMES German 7%. *Erwin* (2), *Christoph, Egon, Fritz, Hermann, Irmgard, Juergen, Kurt, Otto.*

Mischler (378) Swiss German: occupational name for a baker, from Middle High German *mutschel,* diminutive of *mutze* 'bread roll'.
GIVEN NAMES German 4%. *Heinz, Otmar.*

Mischo (104) German (of Slavic origin): from the Serbian and Croatian personal name *Mišo,* a pet form of *Miroslav* or MICHAEL.

Misek (152) Czech (**Míšek**): nickname from a diminutive of the vocabulary word *měch* 'leather purse', 'bag'.

Misencik (121) Probably Belorussian, a variant Americanized form of **Mishenchyk.**

Misener (344) Americanized form of German MEISSNER.

Misenheimer (471) Variant of German MEISENHEIMER.

Misenhimer (119) Variant of German MEISENHEIMER.

Miser (400) **1.** Catalan: probably variant of **misser,** from Vulgar Latin *mi senior,* which was used as a title for men of letters. **2.** Possibly a variant of German **Misser,** a topographic name for someone who lived by a bog.

Miserendino (135) Southern Italian (Sicily): ethnic name from Arabic *manzil sindī* 'native of Sind', a province of southern Pakistan, which is traversed by the Indus river.
GIVEN NAMES Italian 14%. *Calogero, Gino, Giovanni, Giuseppe, Luciano, Santo.*

Misfeldt (162) North German: topographic name for someone who lived by a swampy area of open country, from a Middle Low German word for 'swamp' + *velt* 'open country'.

Mish (337) Americanized spelling of German MISCH or Slovenian **Miš** (see MIS).

Mishkin (370) **1.** Russian: patronymic from the personal name *Mishka,* a pet form of *Mikhail,* Russian form of MICHAEL. **2.** Jewish (eastern Ashkenazic): patronymic from *Mishke,* a pet form of the Yiddish personal names *Mikhl* (MICHAEL) and *Moyshe* (MOSES).
GIVEN NAMES Jewish 4%. *Arnon, Eliezer, Meyer, Sol.*

Mishler (1330) Americanized spelling of Swiss German MISCHLER.

Mishoe (366) Perhaps an Americanized spelling of the French surname **Michau,** a vocalized form of *Michel,* French form of MICHAEL.

Mishra (330) Indian: variant of MISRA.
GIVEN NAMES Indian 88%. *Sanjay* (11), *Ashok* (6), *Ajay* (4), *Asha* (4), *Rakesh* (4), *Manoj* (3), *Pradeep* (3), *Prateek* (3), *Rajesh* (3), *Sanjeev* (3), *Usha* (3), *Vinod* (3).

Misiak (281) Polish: patronymic from the personal name *Miś* (see MIS).
GIVEN NAMES Polish 7%. *Casimir* (2), *Jolanta* (2), *Andrzej, Miroslaw, Wladyslaw.*

Misiaszek (229) Polish: from a pet form of the personal name *Miś* (itself a pet form of *Michał*) or from *Miś* as a nickname meaning 'bear'. See MIS.
GIVEN NAMES Polish 7%. *Czeslaw, Jacek, Witold.*

Misiewicz (233) Polish: patronymic from **Miś** (see MIS).
GIVEN NAMES Polish 9%. *Stanislaw* (2), *Casimir, Halina, Jozef, Wojciech, Zigmond.*

Miska (287) **1.** Hungarian: from a pet form of the personal name *Mihály,* Hungarian form of MICHAEL. **2.** Czech (**Miška**): from a pet form of the personal name *Mikuláš,* Czech form of NICHOLAS, or *Michal,* Czech form of MICHAEL. **3.** Slovenian (**Miška**): nickname from *miška* 'little mouse'.

GIVEN NAMES German 5%. *Kurt* (2), *Jutta*, *Wolfgang*.

Miske (250) Hungarian: from a pet form of the personal name *Mihály*, Hungarian form of MICHAEL, or *Miklós*, Hungarian form of NICHOLAS.

GIVEN NAMES German 6%. *Kurt* (2), *Erwin*, *Frederich*.

Miskell (411) Irish: Anglicized form of Gaelic **Ó Meisceall** 'descendant of *Meiscill*', a personal name of unexplained etymology. See also MAXWELL.

Miskelly (118) Irish: variant of **MacScally**, an Anglicized form of Gaelic **Mac Scalaidhe**, a patronymic, probably from a variant of *scolaidhe* 'scholar' (see SCULLY).

Miskiewicz (114) Polish (**Miśkiewicz**): patronymic from the personal name *Misiek*, a pet form of *Miś* (see MIS).

GIVEN NAME Polish 7%; German 4%. *Krystyna*.

Miskimen (115) Northen Irish: from the Galloway (Scotland) name **Mac Skimming**, a patronymic from an unidentified personal name.

Miskin (133) Jewish (from Belarus): patronymic from the male personal name *Miske*, a pet form of MICHAEL.

GIVEN NAMES Russian 4%. *Leonid* (2), *Vladimir*.

Miskinis (113) Lithuanian (**Miškinis**): topographic name from *miškinis* 'forest', 'forest spirit'. This name is also established in Poland.

GIVEN NAMES Lithuanian 5%; Polish 4%. *Algirdas*, *Kestutis*, *Vytenis*; *Danute* (2).

Misko (334) **1.** Ukrainian; Slovak and Slovenian (**Miško**): from a pet form of a Slavic name derived from the Biblical name *Michael*: Ukrainian *Mychajlo*, Slovak *Michal*, Slovenian *Mihael*. **2.** Ukrainian; Slovak (**Miško**): from a pet form of a Ukrainian *Mykola*, Slovak *Mikuláš*, or some other Slavic equivalent of the personal name NICHOLAS. **3.** Greek: shortened form of *Miskopoulos*, patronymic from the Albanian nickname MISKA 'turkey'.

Misner (1162) Variant of German MEISSNER.

Misra (319) Indian (north central and northeast): Hindu (Brahman) name, from Sanskrit *miśra*, originally meaning 'mixed', 'manifold', but later applied after a name as an honorific epithet meaning 'honorable'.

GIVEN NAMES Indian 87%. *Ram* (4), *Ramesh* (4), *Ajay* (3), *Amaresh* (3), *Arun* (3), *Brijesh* (3), *Chandra* (3), *Sudarsan* (3), *Suresh* (3), *Alok* (2), *Amit* (2), *Anand* (2).

Missel (169) German: variant of **Müssel**, from a pet form of a short form of the personal name *Hieronymus* (see JEROME).

GIVEN NAMES German 8%. *Fritz* (2), *Frieda*, *Hans*, *Kurt*.

Missey (180) Perhaps an altered spelling of MUSSEY.

Missildine (209) Probably of English origin, a habitational name from a lost or unidentified place.

Missimer (165) German: variant of MESSIMER.

Missler (174) German: variant spelling of MISTLER.

GIVEN NAME German 5%. *Othmar*.

Mister (302) Probably an Americanized form of the southern French surname *Mistre*, a variant of MAITRE.

Mistler (206) German: nickname for someone thought to resemble a mistle thrush in some way, Middle High German *misteler*.

Mistretta (940) Italian (Sicily): habitational name from Mistretta in Messina province, Sicily, so named from Latin *Amestratus*.

GIVEN NAMES Italian 21%. *Sal* (6), *Salvatore* (6), *Gaetano* (5), *Gaspare* (3), *Antonino* (2), *Caesar* (2), *Cosmo* (2), *Franco* (2), *Giacomo* (2), *Mario* (3), *Onofrio* (2), *Rosario* (2), *Angelo*, *Carlo*, *Orlando*.

Mistry (459) Indian (Gujarat and Bombay city): Hindu and Parsi name meaning 'skilled artisan' in Gujarati, from Portuguese *mestre* 'master', 'expert'. This word has come to mean 'carpenter', 'cook', 'mason', 'tailor', 'teacher' in the various Indian languages into which it has been borrowed from Portuguese.

GIVEN NAMES Indian 82%. *Kiran* (6), *Kishor* (5), *Anil* (4), *Arvind* (4), *Bharat* (4), *Dilip* (4), *Hasmukh* (4), *Jayesh* (4), *Jehangir* (4), *Kirit* (4), *Nilesh* (4), *Pravin* (4).

Misuraca (333) Southern Italy: habitational name from a place named Mesoraca, in Catanzaro province.

GIVEN NAMES Italian 19%. *Salvatore* (5), *Sal* (4), *Antonino* (2), *Agostino*, *Angelo*, *Cesare*, *Gaspare*, *Natale*, *Paolo*, *Vincenzo*, *Vito*.

Mita (116) **1.** Japanese: meaning 'three rice paddies', the name is more common in eastern Japan. It is also pronounced *Santa* or *Sanda* in western Japan. **2.** Polish: from a pet form of the personal name *Dymitr* (Latin *Demetrius*; see DEMETRIOU).

GIVEN NAMES Japanese 30%; Polish 5%. *Sachiko* (2), *Yoshio* (2), *Fukiko*, *Fumi*, *Hiroko*, *Hiroto*, *Katsumi*, *Katsunori*, *Kazuo*, *Keisuke*, *Kenji*, *Kunihiko*; *Grzegorz*, *Zygmont*.

Mital (139) Indian: variant of MITTAL.

GIVEN NAMES Indian 46%. *Paresh* (3), *Chetna* (2), *Harish* (2), *Mohan* (2), *Ajay*, *Alka*, *Amit*, *Bhanu*, *Chandra*, *Deepak*, *Indira*, *Mayank*.

Mitch (303) Origin uncertain. **1.** Probably an Americanized spelling of Czech **Mič**, a derivative of the personal name *Michal* (see MICHAEL). **2.** Possibly a short form of English or Irish MITCHELL. **3.** Alternatively, an Americanized spelling of *Mitsch*, a German surname of Slavic origin (see MISCHKE).

Mitcham (773) English: habitational name from Mitcham in Surrey, so named from Old English *micel* 'big' + *hām* 'homestead', 'settlement'.

Mitchel (868) English: variant spelling of MITCHELL.

Mitchell (122922) Scottish, English, and Irish: **1.** from the Middle English, Old French personal name *Michel*, vernacular form of MICHAEL. **2.** nickname for a big man, from Middle English *michel*, *mechel*, *muchel* 'big'. **3.** Irish (County Connacht): surname adopted as equivalent of MULVIHILL.

Mitchelson (128) English: patronymic from MITCHELL.

Mitcheltree (223) Northern Irish (Tyrone): unexplained. It is probably a topographic name of Scottish origin, meaning 'big tree'.

Mitchem (1412) English: variant spelling of MITCHAM.

Mitchener (351) English (Hampshire and Dorset): habitational name, possibly from Michen Hall in Godalming, Surrey.

Mitchiner (110) English: variant spelling of MITCHENER.

Mitchner (181) English: variant of MITCHENER.

Mitchum (1161) English: variant spelling of MITCHAM.

Mitchusson (117) Respelling of English **Mitcheson**, a patronymic from the personal names *Mich* or *Michie*.

Mitman (157) Americanized spelling of German **Mittmann** (see MITTMAN).

Mitnick (293) Ukrainian and Jewish (eastern Ashkenazic): occupational name from Ukrainian *mytnyk*, Polish *mytnik* 'toll collector'.

GIVEN NAMES Jewish 11%. *Mordecai* (2), *Yitzchok* (2), *Yosef* (2), *Itzik*, *Meyer*, *Mordechai*, *Shaindy*, *Shimon*, *Simcha*, *Yaakov*.

Mitra (368) Indian (Bengal) and Bangladeshi: Hindu (Kayasth) name, from Sanskrit *mitra* 'friend', 'ally'. Mitra is the name of an important deity in the Vedas; the name also refers to the sun as a deity.

GIVEN NAMES Indian 71%. *Raj* (5), *Sumanta* (5), *Amit* (4), *Pradip* (4), *Indrani* (3), *Shyamal* (3), *Amitava* (2), *Anirban* (2), *Anjan* (2), *Arun* (2), *Atanu* (2), *Bhaskar* (2).

Mitrani (124) Jewish (Sephardic, from Italy): habitational name from Hebrew *mi Trani* 'from Trani' (a town in Italy where there was a substantial Jewish community).

GIVEN NAMES Spanish 19%; Jewish 5%. *Alberto* (3), *Jaime* (2), *Jose* (2), *Julio* (2), *Roberto* (2), *Jacobo*, *Raul*, *Salomon*, *Salvador*, *Susana*; *Moises* (2), *Hyman*, *Nissim*.

Mitrano (177) Jewish (from Italy): variant of MITRANI, altered by folk etymology as if it were an Italian family name.

GIVEN NAMES Italian 24%. *Salvatore* (3), *Nicola* (2), *Biagio*, *Cesare*, *Ciro*, *Cosmo*, *Domenic*, *Donato*, *Gaetano*, *Giro*, *Vito*.

Mitri (112) **1.** Muslim: probably an ethnic name for an Egyptian, a variant of Arabic *Miṣrī* 'Egyptian', a derivative of *Miṣr* 'Egypt'. Compare MASRI. **2.** Italian: from a patronymic or plural form of MITRO.

GIVEN NAMES Muslim 19%; French 7%; Italian 4%. *Habib* (2), *Anis, Dima, Imad, Mitri, Moufid, Omar, Rami, Ramzi, Samir, Talaat, Zahi*; *Emile, Pierre*; *Antonio, Francesco, Romeo*.

Mitro (153) **1.** Southern Italian and Greek (**Mitros**): from the personal name *Mitros* (Italian *Mitro*), a pet form of Greek *Dēmētrios*, Italian *Demetrio, Dimitri* (Latin *Demetrius*; see DEMETRIOU). In Greek this element is also found as a patronymic in composite names such as **Mitrogiannis** 'John son of Mitros', **Mitrogiorgos** 'George son of Mitros', and **Mitrothanassis** 'Athanasios son of Mitros', and in patronymics such as **Mitropoulos**. **2.** Czech and Slovak: from *Mít*, a short form of the personal names *Metoděj* or *Dmitrij*.

Mitrovich (134) Serbian and Croatian (**Mitrović**): patronymic from the personal name *Mitar*, a pet form of *Dimitrije*, a vernacular form of Greek *Dēmētrios* (Latin *Demetrius*; see DEMETRIOU).

GIVEN NAMES South Slavic 11%; Russian 4%. *Milenko* (2), *Drago, Gordana, Milorad, Predrag, Uros*; *Ksenija, Milutin, Vladimir*.

Mitsch (263) Eastern German: from a pet form of a Slavic form of NICHOLAS.

Mitschke (177) German (Silesia, Lausitz): from a pet form of a Slavic form of NICHOLAS, Slavic forms of this personal name generally begin with *M-*.

GIVEN NAMES German 7%. *Otto* (2), *Kurt, Lothar*.

Mittag (206) German: **1.** from Middle High German *mittag* 'midday', 'south', hence a nickname for someone who lived or held property which lay to the south of a main settlement. **2.** (eastern: Saxony and Lausitz): from *Mittak*, a Sorbian pet form of the personal name *Matthias* (see MATTHEW).

GIVEN NAMES German 9%. *Otto* (2), *Gerhardt, Heinz, Juergen, Rudi*.

Mittal (217) Indian (north-central and Panjab): Hindu (Bania) and Jain name based on the name of a clan in the Agarwal Bania community, probably derived from Sanskrit *mitra* 'friend', 'ally' (see MITRA).

GIVEN NAMES Indian 87%. *Ashok* (3), *Anand* (3), *Anurag* (3), *Raj* (3), *Rakesh* (3), *Ram* (3), *Saurabh* (3), *Vijay* (3), *Alok* (2), *Amrit* (2), *Anil* (2), *Arun* (2).

Mittan (149) Probably a variant of English MITTON.

Mittel (118) German: literally 'middle', probably a topographic name from a farm occupying a middle position in a settlement. Compare MITTER.

Mittelman (307) **1.** Jewish (Ashkenazic): nickname from Yiddish *mitlman* 'man of moderate means'. **2.** German (**Mittel-**

mann): from a byname from Middle High German *mittelman* 'mediator', 'arbitrator'.

GIVEN NAMES Jewish 10%. *Moshe* (2), *Devorah, Emanuel, Hershy, Hyman, Mendel, Meyer, Mordechai, Myer, Nachman*.

Mittelstadt (411) German (**Mittelstädt**): see MITTELSTAEDT.

GIVEN NAMES German 4%. *Lorenz* (2), *Gunther*.

Mittelstaedt (372) German (**Mittelstädt**): habitational name from any of several places in Bavaria and Baden-Württemberg called Mittelstedt or Mittelstadt, from Middle High German *mitte* 'middle' + **stat** 'place', 'town'.

GIVEN NAMES German 4%. *Hans* (2), *Eldor, Erwin, Gerhard, Guenther*.

Mittelsteadt (189) Variant of German **Mittelstädt** (see MITTELSTAEDT).

GIVEN NAMES German 5%. *Kurt, Otto*.

Mitten (464) English: variant spelling of MITTON.

Mittendorf (217) German: habitational name from a place in Baden-Württemberg, so named from Middle High German *mitte* 'mid', 'middle' + *dorf* 'village'.

Mitter (141) **1.** German (Bavaria): topographic name for someone who lived on or owned a property that was in the middle between two or more others, especially if the others were both held by men with the same personal name (for example, *Mitter Hans*), from the strong form of Middle High German *mitte* 'mid', 'middle'. **2.** Indian (Panjab): Hindu (Arora) and Sikh name from Sanskrit *mitra* 'friend'.

GIVEN NAMES Indian 8%; German 4%. *Jagdish* (2), *Navnit*; *Kurt, Markus*.

Mittleider (144) German and Jewish (Ashkenazic): nickname for a compassionate person, from a derivative of German *Mitleid* 'compassion'.

GIVEN NAMES German 4%. *Bernhardt, Herta*.

Mittleman (355) Jewish: Americanized spelling of MITTELMAN.

GIVEN NAMES Jewish 6%. *Isadore, Meyer, Moshe*.

Mittler (293) German: **1.** topographic name from Middle High German *mittel* 'middle' (see MITTER). **2.** byname from Middle High German *mitteler* 'mediator', 'arbitrator'.

Mittman (231) **1.** German (**Mittmann**): status name for a tenant farmer who paid rent, or an occupational name for a day laborer or journeyman, from a dialect pronunciation with short vowel of Middle High German *miete* 'rent' + *man* 'man'. **2.** Jewish (Ashkenazic): probably a variant of MITTELMAN.

GIVEN NAMES Jewish 4%. *Emanuel* (2), *Hyman* (2), *Mazal*.

Mitton (610) English: **1.** topographic name for someone who lived in the center of a village, from Middle English *midde* 'mid' + *toun* 'village', 'town'. **2.** habitational

name from places in Lancashire, Worcestershire, and West Yorkshire, so named in Old English as 'farmstead at a river confluence', from *(ge)mȳðe* 'river confluence' + *tūn* 'farmstead', 'settlement'.

Mitts (624) **1.** Probably an American form of Dutch **De Mits**, an occupational name from Middle Dutch *mets(e)* 'bricklayer'. The name is recorded in England in the 19th century. **2.** Alternatively, perhaps, it may be an Americanized spelling of Jewish MITZ.

Mitz (155) Jewish (eastern Ashkenazic): metonymic occupational name for a maker of caps, from Yiddish *mits* 'cap'.

GIVEN NAMES Jewish 9%. *Morry* (3), *Meyer*.

Mitzel (747) Perhaps an altered form of METZEL.

Mitzner (255) Jewish (Ashkenazic): occupational name for a cap maker, from Yiddish *mits* 'cap' + the agent suffix *-ner*.

GIVEN NAMES Jewish 4%. *Avi, Isador*.

Miu (117) **1.** Chinese: variant of MIAO. **2.** Romanian: unexplained.

GIVEN NAMES Chinese 11%; Romanian 5%. *Chi Wing* (2), *Ming* (2), *Kin, Ping, Siu Wah, Sung, Wai Lin, Yim, Yung*; *Bung, Hung, Tu*; *Nicolae* (2).

Miura (414) Japanese (mostly northeastern): 'three bays', although the original meaning was probably 'august bay'. One prominent family, descended from the TAIRA clan, settled in a place called Miura, in Sagami (now Kanagawa prefecture), taking the name of the place as the surname.

GIVEN NAMES Japanese 62%. *Akio* (3), *Akira* (3), *Takahiro* (3), *Tsutomu* (3), *Hajime* (2), *Hideyuki* (2), *Isamu* (2), *Kazuto* (2), *Mamoru* (2), *Shinjiro* (2), *Tsuneo* (2), *Yasuhiko* (2).

Miville (104) Variant spelling of French **Mivelle**, a topographic name for someone who lived in the middle of the town: *(en) mi ville*.

GIVEN NAMES French 22%. *Armand, Cecile, Fernand, Laurent, Marcel, Normand, Roch, Yvon*.

Mix (1898) **1.** Of German origin: perhaps a respelling of **Micksch**, from *Mikusch*, a pet form of *Mikolaj*, a Slavic form of NICHOLAS. **2.** Probably English: unexplained.

Mixell (124) Variant of Scottish and English MITCHELL.

Mixer (295) English (East Anglia): unexplained.

Mixon (4047) English: **1.** habitational name from Mixon in Staffordshire, named from Old English *mixen* 'dungheap', or a topographic name for someone who lived by a dungheap. **2.** patronymic from a pet form of MICHAEL.

Mixson (533) English: variant of MIXON 2.

Mixter (168) Perhpas an Anglicized form of the southern French surname *Mistre*, a variant of MAITRE.

Miya (124) Japanese: the name could mean 'three arrows', 'three valleys' or 'shrine', the latter being the most common. Some occurrences in America are the result of shortening longer names.
GIVEN NAMES Japanese 35%. *Hideo* (3), *Akira, Chizuru, Hisa, Hitoshi, Ikuko, Katsu, Kaz, Kazuhiro, Mako, Masami, Naoko.*

Miyagawa (106) Japanese: meaning 'shrine river', the name is found mostly in the Ryūkyū Islands.
GIVEN NAMES Japanese 53%. *Ichiro* (2), *Mieko* (2), *Osamu* (2), *Emiko, Hajime, Haruyo, Hiro, Katsuki, Kazuhisa, Kazunori, Kiyoshi, Koichi.*

Miyahara (128) Japanese (mostly eastern): from a term meaning 'plain of the shrine'. Families of Kii (now Wakayama prefecture) and Kazusa (now part of Chiba prefecture) are of MINAMOTO descent; while a family of Hyūga (now Miyazaki prefecture) descends from the Taira clan. The name is listed in the Shinsen shōjiroku.
GIVEN NAMES Japanese 48%; German 5%. *Koji* (2), *Ayumi, Fumitaka, Gengo, Harumi, Hideo, Hiro, Hiroji, Hiromi, Hisashi, Ikuko, Kanichi; Helmut* (3).

Miyahira (135) Japanese (rare in Japan proper, but more common in the Ryūkyū Islands): written with characters meaning 'shrine' and 'level', probably a topographic name denoting a shrine on a flat place rather than, as is more usual, on a hill.
GIVEN NAMES Japanese 35%. *Yasunobu* (2), *Eiichi, Fujiko, Ichiro, Kiyoshi, Koichi, Mitsuru, Miyoshi, Nanae, Nobuo, Tetsuo, Toshio.*

Miyake (310) Japanese: variously written, usually with characters meaning 'three houses'. In the 5th and 6th centuries, Japanese rulers based in the Yamato region (present-day Nara prefecture) established royal rice-growing estates (*miyake*) throughout their realm in order to increase their income and consolidate their power. Many unrelated stewards and residents of these estates, or their descendants, adopted the term as a surname, which is listed in the Shinsen shōjiroku. Bearers of this surname, now found mostly in west-central Japan, spread throughout Japan, but many of their descendants later took local surnames.
GIVEN NAMES Japanese 55%. *Hiroshi* (4), *Takashi* (3), *Yoshiko* (3), *Akira* (2), *Daisuke* (2), *Maki* (2), *Masaki* (2), *Masao* (2), *Rie* (2), *Shinichi* (2), *Tetsuo* (2), *Toshio* (2).

Miyamoto (729) Japanese: habitational name meaning '(one who lives) at the shrine', found mostly in western Japan and the island of Okinawa. Several noted samurai families bear this name, but the widespread existence of Shintō shrines in Japan indicates that most bearers are unrelated and are not of samurai rank.
GIVEN NAMES Japanese 50%. *Eiji* (5), *Yoshiaki* (4), *Akira* (3), *Asami* (3), *Hiroshi* (3), *Kazuko* (3), *Keiko* (3), *Kenji* (3),

Masami (3), *Masao* (3), *Mitsuru* (3), *Osamu* (3).

Miyasaki (161) Japanese: alternate pronunciation of MIYAZAKI.
GIVEN NAMES Japanese 23%. *Fumiko, Hidemi, Kats, Kazuko, Kenzo, Kiyoshi, Koshi, Masanobu, Minoru, Rikio, Saburo, Tadami.*

Miyasato (195) Japanese: meaning 'shrine village', the name is rare in Japan proper, but more common in the island of Okinawa.
GIVEN NAMES Japanese 26%. *Shigeru* (2), *Chiyoko, Eishi, Emiko, Isamu, Kanako, Kotaro, Naoto, Noriko, Satoru, Seichi, Seiichi.*

Miyashiro (474) Japanese: meaning 'shrine castle', the surname is found mostly in the Ryūkyū Islands. The same characters are also pronounced **Miyagi, Miyagushiku,** and **Miyagusuku.**
GIVEN NAMES Japanese 33%. *Masao* (3), *Mitsuo* (3), *Yoshio* (3), *Hideo* (2), *Kiyoshi* (2), *Shigeo* (2), *Susumu* (2), *Tomiko* (2), *Tsuneo* (2), *Akira, Chiyo, Fumiko.*

Miyashita (111) Japanese: meaning '(one who lives) below the shrine', the name is found mostly in eastern Japan.
GIVEN NAMES Japanese 75%. *Kei* (3), *Masashi* (2), *Norio* (2), *Sumio* (2), *Toshio* (2), *Akihiko, Chiaki, Fujie, Fumio, Fusako, Hideo, Hiroaki.*

Miyata (181) Japanese: meaning 'rice paddy of the shrine', the surname is found throughout Japan and the Ryūkyū Islands.
GIVEN NAMES Japanese 63%. *Masaaki* (2), *Noboru* (2), *Noriyuki* (2), *Yuko* (2), *Aiko, Chiyo, Fumiko, Haruo, Hidefumi, Hirofumi, Hiroki, Hisako.*

Miyazaki (198) Japanese: meaning 'shrine cape', the surname is found throughout Japan. Some residents of Miyazaki prefecture may have adopted the name as their surname.
GIVEN NAMES Japanese 80%. *Takashi* (4), *Hiroshi* (3), *Kenji* (3), *Yoshio* (3), *Yukiko* (3), *Akira* (2), *Hideyuki* (2), *Masaaki* (2), *Mayumi* (2), *Yasuo* (2), *Aiko, Akiko.*

Miyoshi (171) Japanese: variously written, usually with characters meaning 'three' and 'good'. The name is also found in the Ryūkyū Islands. Different families descend variously from the MINAMOTO and FUJIWARA clans, and from a family of the ancient Korean kingdom of Paekche.
GIVEN NAMES Japanese 56%. *Hiroshi* (3), *Mitsuru* (3), *Hiroko* (2), *Takashi* (2), *Toru* (2), *Yasuyo* (2), *Akihito, Akito, Ayumu, Chiemi, Emiko, Hideaki.*

Mizak (121) Polish and Slovak (**Mizák**): derivative of the dialect word *mizać* 'to string beads or thread pearls'.

Mize (4370) Origin unidentified. Possibly an Americanized form of Dutch MEIS or German MEISE.

Mizell (1885) Respelling of German MEISEL.

Mizelle (581) Respelling of German MEISEL.

Mizener (103) Americanized spelling of German MEISSNER.

Mizer (600) Respelling of German MEISER.

Mizerak (147) Polish: unflattering descriptive nickname from *mizerak* 'starveling', 'weakling', 'miserable creature' (a derivative of Latin *miserus* 'wretch').

Mizner (244) Americanized spelling of German MEISSNER.

Mizrachi (174) Jewish (Ashkenazic and Sephardic): variant of MIZRAHI.
GIVEN NAMES Jewish 31%. *Moshe* (2), *Nissim* (2), *Shlomo* (2), *Aharon, Amnon, Amram, Aron, Avi, Aviva, Ayal, Bracha, Chana.*

Mizrahi (662) Jewish (Ashkenazic and Sephardic): from Hebrew *mizrachi* 'easterner', 'man from the East'.
GIVEN NAMES Jewish 21%. *Moshe* (10), *Avi* (4), *Aviv* (3), *Sol* (3), *Haim* (2), *Meir* (2), *Menahem* (2), *Rebekah* (2), *Shalom* (2), *Shaul* (2), *Shimon* (2), *Avraham.*

Mizuno (248) Japanese: habitational name meaning 'water field', from a village so named in Owari (now part of Aichi prefecture). The surname is found mostly along the eastern seaboard and on the island of Okinawa.
GIVEN NAMES Japanese 64%. *Makoto* (3), *Ayako* (2), *Jiro* (2), *Katsumi* (2), *Kazuo* (2), *Kiyoshi* (2), *Masaaki* (2), *Masao* (2), *Riko* (2), *Shigeru* (2), *Takashi* (2), *Tetsuo* (2).

Mizzell (249) Origin unidentified. Compare MIZELL.

Mizzi (144) **1.** Italian: from the plural of **Mizio,** probably from a pet form of the personal name *Domizio,* from Latin *Domitius.* **2.** Italian: nickname from Southern Italian Greek *miććo* 'small'.
GIVEN NAMES Italian 6%. *Carmel, Romeo, Salvatore.*

Mjelde (101) Norwegian: habitational name from any of several farms, probably named from Old Norse *mjǫl* 'flour', referring to the fine sandy soil of the place.

Mlakar (131) Slovenian: topographic name for a person who lived near a pool, from *mlaka* 'pool', or a habitational name for someone from a place called Mlaka or Mlake, named with the same word in the singular and plural form respectively.
GIVEN NAME South Slavic 4%. *Jasna.*

Mleczko (120) Polish: from *mleczko,* diminutive of *mleko* 'milk', a nickname for someone who liked milk or an occupational name for a milkman.
GIVEN NAMES Polish 13%. *Andrzej, Bronislaw, Casimir, Lucyna, Marzena, Urszula.*

Mlinar (163) Slovenian, Croatian and Serbian: occupational name from *mlinar* 'miller', from *mlin* 'mill' + *-ar* suffix of agent nouns. Compare MALNAR.
GIVEN NAMES German 4%. *Angelika, Ignatz.*

Mlodzik (112) Polish (**Młodzik**): nickname from *młodzik* 'young person'.

Mlynarczyk (124) Polish (**Młynarczyk**): occupational name from a pet form of *młynarz* 'miller' (see MLYNARSKI), or a patronymic from the family name or byname *Młynarz*.

GIVEN NAMES Polish 18%. *Stanislaw* (2), *Arkadiusz, Kazimierz, Krzysztof, Malgorzata, Pawel, Piotr, Tomasz, Walenty*.

Mlynarski (138) Polish (**Młynarski**) and Jewish (eastern Ashkenazic): occupational name for a miller, Polish *młynarz* (from Latin *molinarius* 'miller'), or habitational name from a place named with this word.

GIVEN NAMES Polish 17%. *Tadeusz* (2), *Zbigniew* (2), *Andrzej, Bogdan, Grzegorz, Jozef, Tytus*.

Mlynek (101) Polish (**Młynek**): occupational name from a pet form of *młynarz* 'miller' (see MLYNARSKI).

GIVEN NAME Polish 4%. *Tadeusz*.

Mo (455) **1.** Chinese 莫: from the name of a place called Mo City (莫), said to have been founded by Zhuan Xu, legendary emperor who lived in the 26th century BC. The current Chinese character for *Mo* replaces another, rare or obsolete character. Another source of this name was a government post called Mo'ao, which existed during the Spring and Autumn period (722–481 BC) in the state of Chu. Descendants of a holder of the post adopted the first character of the title as their surname. **2.** Chinese 巫: variant of WU 5. **3.** Chinese 毛: variant of MAO 1. **4.** Chinese 武: variant of WU 3. **5.** Norwegian: variant of MOE.

GIVEN NAMES Chinese/Korean 47%. *Wei* (4), *Siu* (3), *Wai* (3), *Mei Juan* (2), *Shu* (2), *Sung* (2), *Wenzhong* (2), *Zhong* (2), *Bin, Cheong, Ching, Chun Keung*; *Chung* (2), *Chang, Cheol, Chong Soon, Jung Soon, Sangki, Yeon, Yiming*.

Moad (233) Scottish and English: unexplained. It may be a topographic name from the English word *moat*. See also MODE.

Moak (947) English: variant spelling of MOCK.

Moake (102) Variant spelling of English MOCK.

Moan (247) **1.** Irish: reduced form of MOHAN. **2.** Variant (the definite plural form) of Norwegian MOE.

GIVEN NAME Irish 6%. *Connor* (2).

Moat (190) Scottish (Borders): habitational name from either of two places in Dumfriesshire called Moat, named from Middle English *mote* 'moat', 'ditch', originally referring to the whole system of fortifications (see MOTTE). In some cases it may have been a topographic name for someone who lived in or near a moated dwelling.

Moates (489) English (Norwich): variant of MOAT.

Moats (1838) English: variant of MOAT.

Mobbs (395) English (Norfolk): metronymic from the medieval female personal name *Mab(be)* (see MAPP 1).

Moberg (1278) Swedish: ornamental or topographic name composed of the elements *mo* 'sandy heath' + *berg* 'mountain', 'hill'.

GIVEN NAMES Scandinavian 5%. *Iver* (2), *Nils* (2), *Anders, Erik, Eskil, Gunhild, Lars, Per, Sven*.

Moberley (112) English: habitational name from Mobberley in Cheshire, named in Old English as 'clearing with a fortified site where assemblies are held', from *(ge)mōt* 'meeting', 'assembly' + *burh* 'enclosure', 'fortification' + *lēah* 'wood', 'clearing'.

Moberly (894) English: variant spelling of MOBERLEY.

Mobilia (135) Italian: altered form of **Mabilia**, from the old female personal name *Mabile*, from Latin *Amabilis*.

GIVEN NAMES Italian 21%. *Angelo* (2), *Carmine, Carmino, Domenic, Luciano, Nicola*.

Mobley (8638) English: reduced form of MOBERLEY.

Mocarski (183) Polish: **1.** habitational name for someone from either of two places called Mocarze in Bielsko-Biała, Łomża, and Nowy Sącz voivodeships. **2.** Possibly also a nickname from *mocarz* 'strongman' or 'warlord' (from *moc* 'strength').

GIVEN NAMES Polish 9%. *Andrzej, Czeslaw, Krystyna, Miroslaw, Zdzislaw*.

Moccia (403) Italian: from a feminine pet form of a personal name ending with *-moccio* (see MOCCIO).

GIVEN NAMES Italian 21%. *Angelo* (4), *Mario* (4), *Salvatore* (4), *Carmine* (3), *Elvira* (2), *Rocco* (2), *Vito* (2), *Alberto, Aldo, Amedeo, Benedetto, Carlo, Elena, Enrico, Ernesto, Filippo, Fulvio, Genesio, Ninfa, Teodoro*.

Moccio (188) Italian: from a short pet form of a personal name formed with the ending *-moccio*, such as *Giacomoccio* from *Giacomo* (Italian equivalent of JAMES).

GIVEN NAMES Italian 18%. *Salvatore* (6), *Carmine, Gaetano, Guido, Pasquale, Vito*.

Moceri (267) Italian: variant of MAUCERI, itself a variant of MAUGERI.

GIVEN NAMES Italian 21%. *Salvatore* (4), *Vito* (3), *Carlo* (2), *Dino* (2), *Angelo, Carmelo, Carmine, Gaetano, Rocco, Sal*.

Moch (242) **1.** German (also **Möch**): variant of MOCK 2. **2.** Eastern German (of Slavic origin): topographic name for someone who lived in a marshy place. **3.** Polish: unflattering nickname from *moch* in either of its senses, 'insect' and 'wheedler'.

GIVEN NAMES German 4%. *Franz, Matthias, Otto*.

Mochel (162) German: Swabian nickname from a diminutive of MOCH.

Mochizuki (208) Japanese (mostly central Japan): habitational name meaning 'full moon', from a village in Shinano (now Nagano prefecture).

GIVEN NAMES Japanese 66%. *Masao* (3), *Ayako* (2), *Ichiro* (2), *Itaru* (2), *Kaoru* (2), *Keiko* (2), *Kiyo* (2), *Makoto* (2), *Megumi* (2), *Minoru* (2), *Shinobu* (2), *Shintaro* (2).

Mock (5955) **1.** English (Devon): from the rare Old English masculine personal name *Mocca*, which may be related to a Germanic stem *mokk-* 'to accumulate', 'to be heaped up', and hence may originally have been a nickname for a heavy, thickset person. Alternatively, it could be from Middle English *mokke* 'trick', 'joke', 'jest', 'act of jeering', a derivative of *mokke(n)* 'to mock', from Old French *moquer*. **2.** German: variant of MAAG. **3.** German: nickname for a short, thickset man, Middle High German *mocke*. **4.** Dutch: nickname from Middle Dutch *mocke* 'dirty or wanton woman', 'slut', or from West Flemish *mokke* 'fat child'.

Mockabee (108) Americanized form of Irish MCABEE or MCEVOY.

Mockbee (127) Americanized form of Irish MCABEE or MCEVOY.

Mockler (388) English and Irish (of Norman origin): nickname from Old French *mau* 'bad' + *clerc* 'cleric'.

Mockus (164) Lithuanian: from a derivative of the personal name *Motiejus*, from Latin *Matthaeus* (see MATTHEW).

GIVEN NAMES Lithuanian 9%. *Audris* (2), *Laima, Vladas, Vytautas*.

Moctezuma (169) Nahuatl: American Indian name adopted in honor of *Moctezuma*, the name of the last ruler of the Aztec empire, who was killed by the Spanish in 1520.

GIVEN NAMES Spanish 57%. *Jose* (4), *Juan* (4), *Alfredo* (2), *Alvaro* (2), *Angel* (2), *Cruz* (2), *Demetrio* (2), *Javier* (2), *Jesus* (2), *Julio* (2), *Manuel* (2), *Pedro* (2).

Moczygemba (270) Polish (**Moczygęba**): nickname for a heavy drinker, from *moczyć* 'to soak' + *gęba* 'mouth', 'gob'.

GIVEN NAME French 4%. *Alphonse*.

Modafferi (108) Southern Italian: probably a variant of **Modaffari**, a nickname from Arabic *muẓaffar* 'victorious'.

GIVEN NAME Italian 12%. *Cosimo*.

Mode (429) English (Surrey): unexplained. Compare MOAD.

Model (159) **1.** South German: from Middle High German *model* 'measure', 'size', hence a metonymic occupational name for a maker of weights and measures. **2.** German: possibly a habitational name from the Slavic place name Modlau. **3.** Polish: from *model* 'model', 'fashion'. **4.** Jewish (eastern Ashkenazic): from the Yiddish personal name *Modl*, a pet form of MORDECAI.

Modell (208) Variant spelling of German MODEL.

Moden (142) Swedish (**Modén**): ornamental name, probably from *mo* 'sandy heath' + the adjectival suffix *-én*, a derivative of Latin *-enius*.

Modena (161) Italian and Jewish (from Italy): habitational name from the city of Modena in Emilia-Romagna.
GIVEN NAMES Italian 9%. *Silvio* (2), *Angelo*, *Pasquale*, *Peppino*, *Salvatore*.

Moder (281) **1.** Dutch: from a Germanic personal name composed of the elements *mōda* 'courage' + *heri*, *hari* 'army'. **2.** Slovak and Polish: from Middle High German *māder* 'reaper'. **3.** Polish: from Middle Low German *moder* 'mother', 'womb', or 'mare'. **4.** Slovenian: nickname for a wise man, from the adjective *moder* 'wise', 'prudent'. **5.** Swedish (**Modér**): ornamental name, probably from *mo* 'sandy heath' + the surname suffix *-(d)ér*, derived from Latin *-(d)erius*.

Modesitt (279) Probably of French origin. Compare MODISETTE. There are clusters of this name in IN and WV; the name is recorded in WV in the 18th century.

Modeste (126) French: from the personal name *Modeste*, a vernacular form of Latin *Modestus*, from the adjective *modestus* 'reserved', 'gentle', 'virtuous'. Compare Italian MODESTO.
GIVEN NAMES French 9%; German 5%. *Andre*, *Pierre*; *Kurt*.

Modesto (215) Spanish, Portuguese, and Italian: either a nickname from *modesto* 'modest', 'unassuming' or from the personal name *Modesto*, from Late Latin *Modestus* (meaning 'moderate', 'gentle', 'temperate'). The name was borne by several early saints, including a child martyred at Alexandria, Egypt, and an 8th-century evangelist of Carinthia.
GIVEN NAMES Spanish 37%; Italian 7%. *Miguel* (3), *Narciso* (3), *Jose* (2), *Mario* (2), *Octavio* (2), *Rafael* (2), *Albaro*, *Alfredo*, *Ambrosio*, *Ana*, *Angel*, *Arturo*; *Salvatore* (3), *Aldo*, *Carmelo*, *Selvino*.

Modglin (259) Origin unidentified.

Modi (413) Indian (Gujarat, Rajasthan, and Bombay city): Hindu (Bania, Vania), Jain, and Parsi name, from *modi* meaning 'grocer', 'grain merchant' in the various languages of this region. There is a clan called Modi among the Oswal Banias.
GIVEN NAMES Indian 88%. *Hemant* (7), *Ramesh* (7), *Jitendra* (6), *Manoj* (6), *Sunil* (6), *Jayesh* (5), *Pravin* (5), *Bhupendra* (4), *Hasmukh* (4), *Rajendra* (4), *Vinod* (4), *Anil* (3).

Modic (132) Slovenian: unexplained.

Modica (863) Italian (Sicily): habitational name from a place named Modica, in Ragusa province.
GIVEN NAMES Italian 10%. *Salvatore* (4), *Antonino* (2), *Natale* (2), *Agostino*, *Angelo*, *Benedetto*, *Carlo*, *Corrado*, *Domenic*, *Edmondo*, *Francesco*, *Gino*.

Modin (116) **1.** Jewish (from Belarus): patronymic from the Yiddish male personal name *Modye*, a pet form of MORDECAI. **2.** Swedish: variant of **Modén** (see MODEN).

GIVEN NAMES German 6%; Jewish 4%. *Kurt* (2); *Mosey*.

Modine (118) Swedish: variant of **Modén** (see MODEN).
GIVEN NAMES Scandinavian 8%; German 4%. *Nels* (2), *Erik*; *Kurt*.

Modisette (298) French: unexplained. Compare MODESITT.

Modjeski (154) Germanized or Americanized spelling of Polish MODRZEJEWSKI, MODRZEWSKI, or some other derivative of *modrzew* 'larch' or possibly *modry* 'dark blue'.

Modlin (919) **1.** Jewish (from Belarus): patronymic from a Yiddish personal name, *Modle*, a pet form of MORDECAI. **2.** Northern English: unexplained.

Modrak (141) **1.** Polish: patronymic from a nickname based on *modry* 'deep blue'. **2.** Eastern German: nickname for a clever person, from Sorbian *mudrack*, *mudrach*.

Modrall (105) English: see MODRELL.

Modrell (125) English (Northumberland and Durham): unexplained.

Modrow (123) Polish and Sorbian: nickname from the possessive case of *modry* 'dark blue'. This name is well established in eastern Germany.

Modrzejewski (59) Polish: habitational name for someone from any of several places called Modrzewie, e.g. in Kielce voivodeship, all named with *modrzew* 'larch'.
FOREBEARS Helena Modrzejewska (1840–1909) was a Polish American actress famous for her performances in Shakespearian roles; she came to the U.S. in 1876 and settled in CA.
GIVEN NAMES Polish 8%; Slavic 5%; German 4%. *Ryszard*; *Casmir*.

Modrzewski (11) Polish: habitational name for someone from Modrze in Poznań voivodeship or Modrzewie in Piła voivodeship, both named with *modrzew* 'larch'.

Modugno (224) Southern Italian: habitational name from Modugno in Bari province, recorded in medieval Latin as *Medunium*.
GIVEN NAMES Italian 16%. *Antonio* (5), *Rocco* (2), *Alberico*, *Angelo*, *Carmello*, *Gennaro*, *Giuseppe*, *Nicola*, *Salvatore*.

Mody (317) Indian: variant spelling of MODI.
GIVEN NAMES Indian 80%. *Harshad* (4), *Hasmukh* (4), *Ashish* (3), *Kalpana* (3), *Naresh* (3), *Panna* (3), *Pravin* (3), *Sanjay* (3), *Suresh* (3), *Ajay* (2), *Ajit* (2), *Amit* (2).

Modzelewski (313) Polish and Jewish (from Poland): habitational name for someone from places in Poland called Modzel or Modzele, from *modzel* 'hard place', 'callus'.
GIVEN NAMES Polish 15%. *Tadeusz* (3), *Zygmunt* (3), *Casimir* (2), *Krzysztof* (2), *Wieslaw* (2), *Jozef*, *Kazimierz*, *Slawomir*.

Moe (4680) **1.** Norwegian: habitational name from any of numerous farmsteads named Moe or (modernized) Mo, from Old Norse *mór* 'plain', 'moor', 'heath'. **2.** Swedish: ornamental or topographic name from *mo* 'sandy heathland'.
GIVEN NAMES Scandinavian 5%. *Erik* (8), *Knute* (3), *Carsten* (2), *Helmer* (2), *Aagot*, *Alf*, *Ardeen*, *Bergit*, *Bernt*, *Gunhild*, *Gunner*, *Iver*.

Moebius (181) German (**Möbius**): from a reduced form of the personal name *Bartholomäus* (see BARTHOLOMEW).
GIVEN NAMES German 13%; Scandinavian 4%. *Kurt* (3), *Bernd*, *Eberhard*, *Helmuth*, *Otto*, *Wolfgang*; *Alf*, *Erik*.

Moeck (102) German (**Möck**): variant of MOCK 2.
GIVEN NAMES German 10%. *Frieda*, *Johannes*, *Kurt*, *Otto*.

Moeckel (261) German (**Möckel**): from a diminutive of MOCK 2.
GIVEN NAMES German 5%. *Egon*, *Fritz*, *Klaus*, *Kurt*.

Moede (291) **1.** German (**Möde**): habitational name from a place called Moide in Lower Saxony. **2.** from an Old Prussian personal name.
GIVEN NAMES German 4%. *Ewald*, *Hans*, *Kurt*, *Otto*.

Moeder (137) German (**Möder**): habitational name for someone from MOEDE.
GIVEN NAME German 4%. *Kurt*.

Moehle (289) North German (**Möhle**): topographic name for someone living near a mill, or a metonymic occupational name for a miller or worker in a mill, from Middle Low German *mole* 'mill'
GIVEN NAMES German 7%. *Kurt* (4), *Grete*, *Heinz*, *Orlo*, *Otto*.

Moehling (115) German: unexplained; perhaps a hypercorrected spelling of **Möhlin**, a habitational name from a place so named in Aargau, Switzerland.

Moehlman (153) North German (**Möhlmann**): occupational or topographic name for someone who worked in or lived at a mill, from Middle Low German *mole* 'mill' + *man* 'man'.

Moehn (115) German (**Möhn**): habitational name for someone from a place called Möhn near Trier.
GIVEN NAMES Irish 6%; German 5%. *Tague*; *Franz*, *Math*.

Moehring (406) North German (**Möhring**): variant of MORING 2, 3.
GIVEN NAMES German 6%. *Kurt* (2), *Erwin*, *Florian*, *Fritz*, *Manfred*, *Ute*, *Wilhelm*, *Wilhelmina*.

Moeller (5864) North German (**Möller**): occupational name for a miller, from Middle Low German *möller*.
GIVEN NAMES German 5%. *Hans* (16), *Kurt* (10), *Otto* (5), *Heinz* (4), *Helmut* (4), *Armin* (3), *Dieter* (3), *Erwin* (3), *Fritz* (3), *Gerhard* (3), *Uwe* (3), *Arno* (2).

Moellering (229) German (Westphalia; **Möllering**): patronymic from MOELLER.
GIVEN NAMES German 4%. *Heinz* (2), *Otto*.

Moen (3550) **1.** Dutch: from a short form of the personal name *Simo(e)n* (see SIMON). **2.** Belgian (**van Moen**): habitational name for someone from Moen in West Flanders. **3.** Norwegian: habitational name from any of numerous farmsteads all over Norway, so named from the definite singular form of *mo*, from Old Norse *mór* 'plain', 'moor', 'heath'.
GIVEN NAMES Scandinavian 5%. *Erik* (6), *Selmer* (5), *Egil* (3), *Alf* (2), *Anders* (2), *Ardeen, Hilmer, Juel, Knut, Nels, Obert, Orvald.*

Moench (353) German (**Mönch**): nickname for someone of monkish habits or appearance, or an occupational name for a servant employed at a monastery, from Middle High German *münich* 'monk' (Latin *monachus*).

Moening (225) German (**Möning**): habitational name from places called Möning, in the Palatinate and near Nuremberg.

Moerbe (175) North German (**Mörbe**): nickname for a weak person, from Middle Low German *morwe* 'crumbly', 'soft'.

Moerke (149) German (**Mörke**): from a diminutive of **Mohr** (see MOHR 2).

Moerman (145) Dutch and Belgian: **1.** topographic name for someone who lived in the vicinity of marshy ground, *moere* (related to modern Dutch *moeras* 'marsh'), or a habitational name for someone from Moere in West Flanders, named with this word. **2.** occupational name for someone who dug and sold peat. **3.** variant of MOERS.

Moers (151) **1.** German (**Mörs**): habitational name from Moers in the Rhineland or from any of several places called Mörse or Mörsen. **2.** German (**Mörse**): from a variant of the personal name MORITZ. **3.** Dutch: variant of MOORS 2 and 3.

Moes (334) Dutch: **1.** Limburg variant of MAAS. **2.** (**de Moes**): nickname, or metonymic occupational name for a cook, from Middle Dutch *moes* 'food', 'porridge', 'stewed vegetables'. **3.** (**van Moes**): possibly a habitational name from Moerzeke in East Flanders, or a topographic name for someone who lived by the Maas river.
GIVEN NAMES German 4%. *Heinz* (2), *Gerda.*

Moesch (180) German (**Mösch**): topographic name for someone who lived in the vicinity of a marsh.
GIVEN NAMES German 6%. *Elfriede, Helmut, Ralf.*

Moeser (217) German (**Möser**): see MOSER 1 and 2.
GIVEN NAMES German 6%. *Otto* (2), *Hans, Ulrich.*

Moessner (123) German (**Mössner**): variant of MESSNER.
GIVEN NAMES German 14%. *Erwin, Hedwig, Heinz, Helmut, Kurt, Otto.*

Moffa (376) Italian (mainly southern): unexplained.

GIVEN NAMES Italian 10%. *Salvatore* (3), *Aldo, Antonio, Carmine, Pasquale, Remo, Sisto.*

Moffat (1321) Scottish and northern Irish: variant spelling of MOFFATT.

Moffatt (1743) Scottish and northern Irish: habitational name from Moffat in Dumfriesshire, named in Gaelic as 'the long plain', from *magh* 'plain' + *fada* 'long'.

Moffet (394) **1.** Scottish and northern Irish: variant of MOFFATT. **2.** French: variant form of **Maufait**, a nickname composed of the elements *mal, mau* 'badly' + *fait*, past participle of *faire* 'to do or make'.

Moffett (4091) Scottish and northern Irish: variant of MOFFATT.

Moffit (382) Scottish and northern Irish: variant of MOFFATT.

Moffitt (3715) Scottish and northern Irish: variant of MOFFATT.

Mofield (190) Origin uncertain. Perhaps a variant of Scottish and northern Irish MOFFATT.

Moga (172) Romanian (Transylvania and Moldavia): nickname from Hungarian *mogos, mogus, magos* 'big', 'tall' (Romanian *mogo*).
GIVEN NAMES Romanian 8%. *Aurel* (3), *Vasile* (2), *Mihai, Mircea, Niculae, Viorel.*

Mogan (328) Irish (Connacht): of uncertain etymology; possibly either a variant of MOHAN (via the form **Moughan**), or from Gaelic **Ó Mógáin** 'descendant of *Mógán*'.

Mogavero (339) Italian: variant of MUGA-VERO.
GIVEN NAMES Italian 16%. *Angelo* (3), *Salvatore* (3), *Maurizio* (2), *Dante, Domi-nico, Franco, Gilda, Matteo, Nunzio, Sal, Vincenza.*

Mogck (133) German: variant of MOOG or MAAG. This is one of the German names that became established in Ukraine and Moldova in the 19th century.

Mogel (199) **1.** German: probably from a diminutive of MOOG. **2.** Jewish (Ashkenazic): perhaps an altered spelling of **Mohel** (see MOHL).
GIVEN NAMES German 4%; Jewish 4%. *Otto; Mort* (2).

Mogen (132) **1.** Norwegian: habitational name from any of several farmsteads, especially in Telemark, named from a dialect form of MOEN. **2.** Danish: from a truncated form of the personal name *Mogens*, Danish form of MAGNUS.
GIVEN NAMES Scandinavian 6%. *Hilma, Sigvard.*

Mogensen (443) Danish and Norwegian: patronymic from the personal name *Mogens*, Danish form of MAGNUS.
GIVEN NAMES Scandinavian 8%; German 4%. *Erik, Niels, Palle; Erwin, Kurt.*

Moger (213) **1.** Dutch: from a Germanic personal name composed of the elements *madal* 'council' + *gār, gēr* 'spear'. **2.** Southern English: unexplained.

Mogg (279) English: from the medieval female personal name *Mag(ge)*, a reduced form of *Margaret* (see MARGESON).

Moghadam (116) Arabic: from *muqaddam* 'administrator', also denoting a military rank (major or lieutenant colonel).
GIVEN NAMES Arabic 74%. *Ali* (3), *Hamid* (3), *Nasrin* (3), *Bijan* (2), *Fariba* (2), *Fatima* (2), *Hassan* (2), *Ahmad, Amir, Fatemeh, Ghassem, Hossein.*

Moghaddam (106) Muslim: variant of MOGHADAM.
GIVEN NAMES Muslim 82%. *Ali* (4), *Bahram* (3), *Amir* (2), *Azita* (2), *Mehran* (2), *Mohammed* (2), *Nader* (2), *Ahmad, Akram, Arash, Bejan, Farideh.*

Mogle (236) Probably an altered spelling of Jewish MOGEL.

Moglia (204) Italian: probably a topographic name for someone in a swampy area, from Sicilian *moghia* 'mud', 'mire', or Italian *moia* 'marshy', 'boggy'.
GIVEN NAMES Italian 15%. *Ettore* (3), *Aldo, Carlo, Emidio, Giovanni, Giuseppe, Luigi, Pietro, Romano, Savino, Silvio.*

Mogren (137) Swedish: ornamental name composed of the elements *mo* 'sandy heath' + *gren* 'branch'.

Mogul (155) **1.** Turkish (**Mügül**), Iranian, Pakistani, or Indian: from Persian *Moghol*, literally 'Mongol'. This was the name of the dynasty, of Mongolian origin, which ruled most of northern India from the 16th to the 19th centuries, noted for their military prowess, efficient administration, and religious tolerance. **2.** As an English word, this term became extended to denote any powerful ruler or businessman; it may be an English nickname for a powerful person of an autocratic disposition.

Mohabir (132) Name found among people of Indian origin in Guyana and Trinidad: variant of MAHABIR.
GIVEN NAMES Indian 51%. *Angad, Anil, Ganesh, Gangaram, Indranie, Jagat, Kawall, Latchman, Mohan, Naresh, Parmanand, Rajendra.*

Mohamad (159) Muslim: variant of MU-HAMMAD.
GIVEN NAMES Muslim 76%. *Ali* (4), *Mohamad* (4), *Ahmad* (3), *Abdalla* (2), *Abdul* (2), *Ahmed* (2), *Ibrahim* (2), *Khalid* (2), *Abdelhamid, Abdu, Abdulkarim, Adib.*

Mohamed (1582) Muslim: variant of MU-HAMMAD. See also MOHAMMED.
GIVEN NAMES Muslim 76%. *Mohamed* (49), *Ahmed* (45), *Ali* (25), *Hassan* (16), *Bibi* (14), *Ibrahim* (11), *Abdul* (10), *Saleh* (9), *Hesham* (8), *Abdi* (7), *Mohamud* (7), *Salah* (7).

Mohammad (643) Muslim: variant of MU-HAMMAD.
GIVEN NAMES Muslim 86%. *Mohammad* (15), *Amin* (12), *Ahmad* (6), *Ali* (6), *Iqbal* (6), *Khan* (6), *Noor* (6), *Wali* (6), *Hamid* (5), *Syed* (5), *Tariq* (5), *Abdul* (4).

Mohammadi (166) Muslim: adjectival derivative of MUHAMMAD.

GIVEN NAMES Muslim 82%. *Hamid* (7), *Mohammad* (7), *Ali* (6), *Aghajan* (2), *Hassan* (2), *Hossein* (2), *Jahan* (2), *Khalil* (2), *Mohsen* (2), *Rafiq* (2), *Abbas*, *Ahmad*.

Mohammed (1452) Muslim: variant of MUHAMMAD. This is the traditional English-language spelling. It is also common as a name adopted by Black Americans on conversion to Islam.

GIVEN NAMES Muslim 70%. *Ali* (19), *Ahmed* (16), *Abdul* (11), *Ibrahim* (10), *Mohammed* (10), *Noor* (7), *Rasheed* (7), *Abbas* (6), *Nazim* (6), *Shaheed* (6), *Amin* (5), *Amir* (5).

Mohan (1335) **1.** Irish: Anglicized form of Gaelic **Ó Mocháin** 'descendant of *Mochán*', a personal name from a diminutive of *moch* 'early', 'timely'. In Connacht this name was changed to MAHON; it is also found translated into English as EARLY. It has been used to represent the Norman habitational surname **de Mohun**. **2.** Indian (Panjab and southern states): Hindu name from Sanskrit *mohana* 'fascinating', 'infatuating', an epithet of the god Krishna. In the Panjab, it is a Brahman name based on the name of a clan in the Mohyal subgroup of Saraswat Brahmans; it probably evolved from an ancestral personal name. In the southern states this is only found as a male given name; it has also come to be used as a family name in the U.S. among familes from South India.

GIVEN NAMES Indian 34%. *Ram* (11), *Krishna* (9), *Madan* (8), *Chandra* (7), *Brij* (5), *Rakesh* (5), *Vivek* (4), *Anil* (3), *Chander* (3), *Leela* (3), *Raj* (3), *Sanjay* (3).

Mohanty (109) Indian (Orissa): Hindu (Brahman, Kayasth) name, from Sanskrit *mahant-* 'great'.

GIVEN NAMES Indian 87%. *Gopal* (2), *Prasanna* (2), *Arun*, *Atanu*, *Bani*, *Bidyut*, *Bikash*, *Bikram*, *Chandra*, *Ganesh*, *Himansu*, *Jagannath*.

Mohar (249) Irish: variant of MOHER.

Moher (183) Irish (western County Waterford and eastern County Cork): Anglicized form of Gaelic **Ó Mochair** 'descendant of *Mochar*', from *mochar* 'place overgrown with brushwood'.

GIVEN NAME Irish 4%. *Siobhan*.

Mohiuddin (145) Muslim (common in Bangladesh, Pakistan, and India): from Arabic *muḥyī-ud-dīn* 'reviver of religion'. This title was bestowed on the religious scholar and saint Sheikh 'Abdul Qadīr Jīlānī (1077–1166).

GIVEN NAMES Muslim 86%. *Syed* (20), *Mohammed* (19), *Ahmed* (7), *Mohammad* (5), *Anwar* (3), *Khaja* (3), *Asif* (2), *Hamid* (2), *Muhammad* (2), *Abdul*, *Abid*, *Ahmad*, *Alam*.

Mohl (389) **1.** North German (**Möhl**): variant of MOEHLE. **2.** Jewish (Ashkenazic): possibly from Hebrew *mohel*, an occupational name meaning 'circumciser'.

GIVEN NAMES German 5%. *Erhardt*, *Ewald*, *Juergen*, *Otto*, *Reinhard*.

Mohler (2542) German (**Möhler**): dialect variant of MAHLER, found chiefly in Bavaria.

Mohlman (201) North German (**Möhlmann**): see MOEHLMAN.

Mohn (1283) German: **1.** metonymic occupational name for a grower of poppies, from Middle High German *mān* 'poppy'. **2.** from a short form of the Germanic personal name *Monrad*, composed of the elements *mun* 'spirit', 'thought' + *rat* 'counsel'. **3.** variant of German **Möhn** (see MOEHN).

Mohney (652) Possibly a variant of Irish MAHONEY.

Mohon (290) Altered spelling of Irish MOHAN or MAHON.

Mohr (7295) **1.** North German: topographic name for someone who lived in a fen, Middle Low German *mōr*. **2.** German and Dutch: nickname for a man of swarthy complexion, from Middle High German *mōr*, Middle Dutch *mo(e)r* 'Moor'. **3.** German: from a short form of an old personal name, *Morhart* (see MORATH).

Mohrbacher (131) German: habitational name for someone from any of various places called Morbach, in the Palatinate, the Rhineland, and elsewhere, so named from Middle High German *muor* 'swamp' + *bach* 'stream', 'brook'.

Mohring (163) North German (**Möhring**): variant of **Möring** (see MORING 2, 3).

GIVEN NAMES German 12%. *Ewald*, *Gunter*, *Gunther*, *Klaus*, *Kurt*, *Manfred*, *Otto*.

Mohrman (348) Variant of German and Dutch MOHRMANN.

Mohrmann (295) North German and Dutch: **1.** topographic name for someone who lived in a fen, Middle Low German *mōr*, + *man* 'man'. **2.** nickname for a man of swarthy complexion, from Middle High German *mōr*, Middle Dutch *mo(e)r* 'Moor', + *man* 'man'.

GIVEN NAMES German 4%. *Otto*, *Rinehart*.

Mohs (445) German: variant of MOOS.

Mohundro (101) Variant of OMOHUNDRO.

Moilanen (298) Finnish: from the Karelian personal name *Moila* (a form of SAMUEL) + the common surname suffix *-nen*. This is an eastern Finnish surname dating back to the 16th century.

GIVEN NAMES Finnish 8%. *Eino* (2), *Oiva* (2), *Jaana*, *Rauha*, *Reino*, *Toivo*, *Tyyne*, *Waino*, *Wiljo*, *Yalmer*.

Moir (916) Scottish: variant of MUIR.

Moisan (239) Breton and western French: from the old oblique case of the personal name *Moïse*, a French form of MOSES.

GIVEN NAMES French 12%. *Armand* (3), *Andre* (2), *Jean Louis*, *Ludger*, *Maxime*, *Pierre*, *Rolande*.

Moise (663) **1.** French (**Moïse**) and Jewish: from the personal name *Moise* (see MOSES). **2.** Italian (also **Moisé**): from a variant of the personal name *Mosè*, Italian equivalent of MOSES.

GIVEN NAMES French 22%; German 4%. *Serge* (3), *Gessy* (2), *Jacques* (2), *Monique* (2), *Odette* (2), *Pierre* (2), *Roch* (2), *Agathe*, *Benoit*, *Bonard*, *Colette*, *Collette*; *Fritz* (4).

Moises (120) Spanish (**Moisés**), Jewish (Sephardic), and Portuguese: from the personal name *Moisés*, Spanish equivalent of MOSES. **Moissis** is also found as a family name in Greece.

GIVEN NAMES Spanish 38%; French 4%. *Ernesto* (2), *Raymundo* (2), *Adela*, *Adolfo*, *Adriana*, *Alfonso*, *Alvarez*, *Ana*, *Aurelio*, *Carlos*, *Clarita*, *Domingo*; *Michel*, *Pierre*.

Moist (188) English: unexplained. This name occurs chiefly in PA.

Moix (129) Swiss: unexplained.

Mojica (1180) Spanish (of Basque origin): variant of **Mújica** (see MUJICA).

GIVEN NAMES Spanish 48%; Portuguese 9%. *Jose* (29), *Carlos* (18), *Juan* (16), *Jesus* (11), *Luis* (11), *Alberto* (10), *Francisco* (9), *Rafael* (9), *Julio* (8), *Manuel* (7), *Jorge* (6), *Miguel* (6); *Paulo*; *Antonio* (8), *Marco* (3), *Angelo* (2), *Heriberto* (2), *Aldo*, *Carlo*, *Carmelo*, *Clemente*, *Dante*, *Dario*, *Dino*, *Eliseo*.

Mok (557) **1.** Korean: there is only one Chinese character for the Mok surname, which was much more common in the past than it is today. Many members of the Sach'ŏn Mok clan held prominent government positions in the Koryŏ period (AD 918–1392) and the subsequent Chosŏn period. The clan's founding ancestor, Mok Hyo-gi, was a Koryŏ general. **2.** Chinese 莫: variant of Mo 1. **3.** Dutch: variant of MOCK 3. **4.** Hungarian (**Mók**): from the secular personal name *Mók*, probably a pet form of *Mózes*, Hungarian form of MOISES.

GIVEN NAMES Chinese/Korean 25%. *Wai* (6), *Wing* (4), *Chiu* (3), *Jung* (2), *Kam* (2), *Kwok* (2), *Man* (2), *Pui* (2), *Yin* (2), *Yuen* (2), *Chak*, *Chee*; *Hung*, *Mai*, *Pha*, *Phat*, *Sau*.

Moke (113) English and Dutch: variant of MOCK.

GIVEN NAMES German 6%. *Kurt*, *Otto*.

Mokry (201) Polish, Czech, and Slovak (**Mokrý**): nickname from Slavic *mokry* 'wet'.

Mol (220) Dutch: **1.** nickname from Middle Dutch *mol* 'mole', perhaps for a very short-sighted or blind person, or someone with dark hair. **2.** (**van Mol**): habitational name for someone from Mol in Antwerp province.

GIVEN NAMES Dutch 5%. *Adrianus*, *Cornelis*, *Hendrick*, *Pieter*.

Mola (244) **1.** Italian: habitational name from any of numerous minor places named with Latin *mola* 'mill', 'millstone'. **2.** Catalan and Aragonese: habitational name from any of various places named Mola in Catalonia and Aragon, in particular the one in Teruel province (Aragon), from Latin *mola* 'mill', 'millstone'. **3.** Greek (**Molas**): see MULA.

GIVEN NAMES Italian 14%; Spanish 13%. *Pasquale* (2), *Salvatore* (2), *Angelo*, *Antonio*, *Gennaro*, *Giulio*, *Primo*, *Sal*, *Secondo*, *Stefano*; *Jose* (3), *Luis* (3), *Efrain* (2), *Emilio* (2), *Mario* (2), *Ana*, *Berta*, *Blanca*, *Digna*, *Edilberto*, *Elena*, *Estrella*.

Molaison (160) French: unexplained. This is a Louisiana name.

GIVEN NAMES French 9%. *Antoine*, *Gillis*, *Jacques*, *Ulysse*.

Moland (195) Norwegian: habitational name from any of several farmsteads named from Old Norse *mór* 'plain', 'moor', 'heath' + *land* 'land'.

GIVEN NAME Scandinavian 5%. *Hilmar*.

Molander (259) Swedish: ornamental name composed of the elements *Mol-* (probably taken from a place name such as Molanda) + *-ander*, a common surname suffix derived from Greek *andr-* 'man'.

GIVEN NAMES Scandinavian 6%. *Alfhild*, *Jarl*, *Lars*.

Molano (215) Hispanic: unexplained. Perhaps a habitational name for someone from Mola.

GIVEN NAMES Spanish 49%. *Jose* (4), *Rodolfo* (4), *Orlando* (3), *Rafael* (3), *Raul* (3), *Alberto* (2), *Alvaro* (2), *Carlos* (2), *Erlinda* (2), *Francisco* (2), *Jorge* (2), *Julio* (2).

Molchan (224) Ukrainian: nickname for a taciturn individual, from *molchat* 'to be silent'.

Molde (111) English: variant spelling of MOULD.

Molden (446) English: unexplained; possibly a variant spelling of MALDEN.

Moldenhauer (921) North German: occupational name for a maker of wooden bowls, Middle Low German *moldenhauer*, from *molde* 'bowl', 'trough', 'tub' (from Latin *mulctra* 'milking tub') + an agent derivative of *hauen* 'hew'; 'carve'.

GIVEN NAMES German 5%. *Erwin* (3), *Kurt* (3), *Egon*, *Eldor*, *Fritz*, *Hans*, *Hertha*, *Juergen*, *Lorenz*, *Otto*.

Molder (303) **1.** German (Lorraine): occupational name from an agent derivative of Middle High German *mulde* 'trough', 'tub' (see MOLDENHAUER). **2.** Dutch and North German (also **Mölder**): occupational name for a miller, Middle Dutch *molder(e)*.

Moldovan (366) Romanian, Ukrainian, and Jewish (eastern Ashkenazic): ethnic name for a Moldavian or regional name for someone from Moldavia, the area lying between the eastern range of the Carpathians and the Prut river.

GIVEN NAMES Romanian 10%. *Petru* (3), *Gheorghe* (2), *Alexandru*, *Costel*, *Dorel*, *Dumitru*, *Floare*, *Iacob*, *Mihai*, *Nicolae*, *Sorin*, *Vasile*.

Mole (483) **1.** English: nickname for someone supposedly resembling a mole (the burrowing mammal), Middle English *mol(le)* (from Dutch or Low German *mol*), for example in having poor eyesight. **2.** English: nickname for someone with a prominent mole or blemish on the face, from Middle English *mole* (Old English *māl*). **3.** English: from an Old English masculine personal name, *Moll*. **4.** English: from Old Norse *moli* 'crumb', 'grain', possibly a nickname for a small man. **5.** French: metonymic occupational name for a knife grinder or a maker of whetstones, from a variant of *meule* 'whetstone', 'grindstone', 'millstone'. **6.** Italian: variant of MULE. **7.** Slovenian: probably a nickname for a extremely religious man, from *mole* 'zealot', a derivative of *moliti* 'to pray'.

Molek (109) **1.** Polish: nickname from a diminutive of *mol* 'moth'; also meaning 'bookworm'. **2.** Slovenian: probably a nickname for a religious man, from *molek* 'rosary', a derivative of *moliti* 'to pray'.

GIVEN NAMES Polish 9%. *Czeslaw*, *Krysztof*, *Wladyslaw*, *Wojciech*.

Molen (250) **1.** Swedish (**Molén**): ornamental surname from *mo* 'sandy heath' + the adjectival suffix *-én*, a derivative of Latin *-enius*. **2.** Dutch: topographic name from *molen* 'mill'. **3.** Dutch (**van der Molen**): habitational name from any of numerous places named Ter Molen or Ter Meulen (from *molen* 'mill').

Molenaar (254) Dutch: occupational name from *molenaar* 'miller'.

GIVEN NAMES Dutch 7%; German 4%. *Jacobus* (2), *Pieter* (2), *Cornelis*, *Diederik*, *Gerrit*; *Hans*, *Johannes*.

Molenda (309) Polish (also **Molęda**): occupational name for a miller, from a derivative of Latin *molendinator*.

GIVEN NAMES Polish 5%. *Janina* (2), *Grzegorz*, *Tadeusz*.

Moler (683) German and Danish: probably a variant of **Möller** (see MOLLER).

Moles (970) **1.** English: patronymic from MOLE 3 and 4. **2.** Catalan: habitation name from any of various minor places named Moles, from the plural of *mola* (see MOLA).

Moleski (219) Polish: probably a variant of MOLSKI.

Molesky (178) Polish: probably a variant of MOLSKI.

Molesworth (190) English: habitational name from a place in Cambridgeshire, named in Old English as 'Mūl's enclosure', from *Mūl*, a personal name or byname meaning 'mule' + *worð* 'enclosure'. It may also be derived from Mouldsworth in Cheshire, so called from Old English *molda* 'crown of the head', 'top of a hill' + *worð* 'enclosure'.

Molette (105) Variant spelling of French MOLLET.

Moley (122) Variant of Irish MOLLOY.

Molin (354) **1.** English (of Norman origin) and French: topographic name from Old French *molin* 'mill'. **2.** English (of Norman origin): habitational name from a place in

France called Moline(s). **3.** Swedish: ornamental name from *mo* 'sandy heath' + the common ornamental suffix *-lin*. **4.** In some cases, possibly Italian, a variant of MOLINO.

GIVEN NAMES Scandinavian 7%; French 4%. *Lars* (2), *Gunard*, *Jarl*, *Nils*; *Moliere*, *Pascale*, *Victoire*.

Molina (8603) Spanish and Catalan: habitational name from any of numerous places named Molina, in particular the one in Guadalajara province.

GIVEN NAMES Spanish 48%; Portuguese 10%. *Jose* (225), *Juan* (122), *Carlos* (110), *Luis* (75), *Manuel* (71), *Jesus* (65), *Francisco* (55), *Jorge* (54), *Mario* (51), *Miguel* (49), *Ana* (43), *Roberto* (43); *Joao*, *Margarida*.

Molinar (483) Spanish (of Basque origin): habitational name from any of the numerous minor places named Molinar, in particular the one in Biscay province, so named from a derivative of *molina* 'mill'.

GIVEN NAMES Spanish 41%. *Manuel* (12), *Jose* (9), *Carlos* (7), *Luis* (7), *Alberto* (4), *Alfonso* (4), *Francisco* (4), *Ricardo* (4), *Ruben* (4), *Alfredo* (3), *Alicia* (3), *Jaime* (3).

Molinari (1083) Italian: patronymic or plural form of MOLINARO.

GIVEN NAMES Italian 24%. *Mario* (11), *Rocco* (4), *Angelo* (3), *Dante* (2), *Elio* (2), *Fabiola* (2), *Gennaro* (2), *Raffaele* (2), *Roberto* (2), *Aldo*, *Antonio*, *Attilio*, *Dino*, *Eduardo*, *Enrico*, *Fabio*, *Gaetano*.

Molinaro (1026) Italian: occupational name from *molinaro* 'miller', an agent derivative of *molino* 'mill'.

GIVEN NAMES Italian 15%. *Angelo* (6), *Salvatore* (3), *Carmine* (2), *Dante* (2), *Franco* (2), *Giuseppe* (2), *Pietro* (2), *Silvio* (2), *Umberto* (2), *Amedeo*, *Antonio*.

Moline (1269) **1.** French: variant of MOLINA 2. **2.** French (**Moliné**): occupational name for a miller, a variant of *molinier*, an agent derivative of Old French *molin* 'mill'. **3.** Catalan (**Moliné**): variant of the occupational name *molinier* 'miller'.

Molineaux (116) Variant spelling of English, Irish, and French MOLYNEUX.

GIVEN NAMES French 11%. *Alban*, *Emile*, *Jean-Paul*.

Molinelli (180) Italian (**Molinèlli**): from a plural diminutive of MOLINO, possibly from a minor place so called.

GIVEN NAMES Italian 8%. *Angelo* (2), *Attilio*, *Italo*, *Pietro*.

Molini (105) Italian: patronymic or plural form of MOLINO.

GIVEN NAMES Italian 7%. *Alberto*, *Benito*, *Josefa*.

Molino (354) Italian and Spanish: habitational name from any of numerous places named Molino, from *molino* 'mill', or a topographic name for someone who lived at a mill. **Molinos** is also found as a Greek name.

GIVEN NAMES Italian 14%; Spanish 9%. *Angelo* (2), *Gino* (2), *Remo* (2), *Cosmo*,

Dante, Marco, Nino; *Alfredo* (2), *Amando* (2), *Alberto, Alfonso, Armando, Dagoberto, Dominga, Edmundo, Elena, Emilio, Eusebia, Fidencio.*

Molis (130) **1.** German: unexplained. **2.** Possibly a variant of Belgian French **Malis**, **Molisse**, a nickname from French *malice* 'mischief'. **3.** Lithuanian: from *molius* 'brickmaker' or *molis* 'clay', also used in a transferred senses as a nickname for a dirty person.

Molitor (1455) From Latin *molitor* 'miller', a humanistic name adopted as a Classicized equivalent of German MUELLER, Dutch MOLENAAR, Polish **Młynarz**, etc.

Molitoris (158) Patronymic from the genitive case of Latin MOLITOR.

Moll (2917) **1.** English (Norfolk): from the medieval female personal name *Moll(e)*, a pet form of *Mary* (see MARIE 1). **2.** German: nickname from a dialect term for a plump, stout person. This surname is widely established throughout central Europe, from Alsace-Lorraine to Poland. **3.** Catalan: nickname for a weak or ineffectual person, from Catalan *moll* 'soft', 'weak' (Latin *mollis*). **4.** Dutch: variant of MOL 1. **5.** (**van Moll**): variant of MOL 2.

Molla (129) **1.** Muslim: status name for someone with a qualification in Islamic religious learning, from Persian *mulla*, a derivative of Arabic *maulā, maulwī* 'scholar' (usually transcribed in English as *mullah*). **2.** Ethiopian: unexplained. **3.** Catalan: from a feminine form of MOLL. **4.** Catalan (**Mollà**): variant spelling of the habitational name from any of the several places called *Mollar* in Catalonia and Valencia.

GIVEN NAMES Muslim 16%; Ethiopian 14%; Spanish 4%. *Mahbub* (2), *Abul, Ahamed, Farid, Mohammad, Nazrul, Rafiqul, Saiful, Selim, Shamsul; Adane, Alemnesh, Belayneh, Belete, Berhanu, Getachew, Mesfin, Sisay, Worku; Juan* (2), *Marcelino* (2), *Jose, Osvaldo.*

Mollard (124) French: habitational name from any of numerous minor places named Molard, from a regional term denoting a rise in elevation, a small hill, or a large pile of stones.

GIVEN NAMES French 11%. *Francois* (2), *Camille, Philippe.*

Molle (325) **1.** German: variant of MOLL. **2.** North German: metonymic occupational name for a maker of wooden bowls, from Middle Low German *molde* 'bowl', 'trough', 'tub' (from Latin *mulctra* 'milking tub'). **3.** Dutch: variant of MOL 1. **4.** Dutch (**van Molle**): variant of MOL 2. **5.** French: topographic name from a diminutive of *mol, mou* 'soft', denoting boggy ground. **6.** Southern French: variant of MOLE 'knife grinder'.

GIVEN NAMES French 5%. *Andre, Cecile, Emile, Jacques, Sylvain.*

Mollen (123) Irish: variant of MULLEN.

Mollenhauer (231) North German: variant of MOLDENHAUER.

GIVEN NAMES German 7%. *Claus, Gerhard, Hans, Juergen, Kurt.*

Mollenkopf (241) South German: nickname for an obstinate person, related to the Swabian dialect word *Molle* 'ox' + *Kopf* 'head'.

Moller (1737) Dutch, North German (also **Möller**), and Danish (**Møller**): occupational name for a miller. See also MOELLER. In the form **Moller**, this name is established from the Netherlands to Poland. It is also found in Sweden (**Möller**), where it is of either German or Danish origin, and in Norway, where it is of Danish origin.

GIVEN NAMES Scandinavian 10%; German 6%. *Erik* (9), *Jorgen* (5), *Borge* (3), *Nels* (3), *Sven* (3), *Anders, Bent, Bernt, Dagny, Gudrun, Hakon, Holger; Kurt* (6), *Hans* (4), *Claus* (3), *Erwin* (3), *Horst* (2), *Wilhelm* (2), *Wolfgang* (2), *Elke, Ernst, Gerda, Gerhard, Gottfried.*

Mollere (115) French: variant of **Molière**, a habitational name from any of several places so named as being on soft or damp ground, from Latin *mollis* 'soft' + the locative suffix *-aria*.

Mollet (299) **1.** French, Channel Islands, and English: from a pet form of the personal name *Moll*, a pet form of *Mary* (see MARIA). **2.** French: topographic name for someone who lived in a muddy or boggy place, from a diminutive of *mol* 'marsh', 'bog' (see MOLLE). **3.** Catalan: habitational name from any of various places named Mollet, especially in the provinces of Barcelona and Girona.

GIVEN NAMES French 4%. *Andre, Jacques, Jean Claude.*

Mollett (430) French: variant of MOLLET.

Mollette (152) French: variant of MOLLET.

Molleur (133) French: unexplained; perhaps an altered spelling of **Malheux**, an old variant of *malheur* 'misfortune', 'adversity', or of MOLLER, which is found in Alsace.

GIVEN NAMES French 12%. *Marcel* (2), *Armand, Gilles, Jacques, Raoul.*

Mollica (624) Southern Italian: from *mollica* 'crumb', 'soft part (of bread)', perhaps a nickname for a small person or a soft-hearted one.

GIVEN NAMES Italian 21%. *Salvatore* (6), *Rosario* (4), *Antonio* (2), *Sal* (2), *Angelo, Bartolo, Benito, Carlo, Fernando, Francesco, Gaetano, Gino, Marco, Mario, Mauro, Virgilio.*

Mollick (128) English: unexplained.

Mollison (201) Scottish (Aberdeen): metronymic from the personal name *Molly* (see MOLL 1).

Mollman (142) German (**Möllmann**): variant of **Möhlmann** (see MOHLMAN).

Mollner (143) North German (also **Möllner**): occupational name from Middle Low German *molner* 'miller', an agent derivative of *malen* 'to mill'.

Mollo (314) **1.** Southern Italian: possibly a nickname from Sicilian *moddu* 'soft', 'delicate'. **2.** Catalan: habitational name from *Molló* in Girona province, or from Prats de Molló in northern Catalonia, east Pyrenees. **3.** Southern French (Occitan): topographic name from a diminutive of Old French *mol* 'soft', 'muddy'.

GIVEN NAMES Italian 13%; French 4%. *Guido* (2), *Luciano* (2), *Vincenzo* (2), *Aldo, Alessandro, Angelo, Antonio, Constantino, Cosimo, Domenico, Pasquale, Salvatore; Camille, Donat.*

Mollohan (447) Irish: **1.** Anglicized form of Gaelic **Ó Mothlacháin** 'descendant of *Mothlachán*', a byname or personal name from a diminutive form of *mothlach* 'shaggy'. **2.** Anglicized form of Gaelic **Ó Maolacháin** 'descendant of *Maolachán*', a personal name.

Molloy (3025) Irish: **1.** shortened Anglicized form of Gaelic **Ó Maolmhuaidh** 'descendant of *Maolmhuadh*', a personal name composed of the elements *maol* 'chieftain' + *muadh* 'noble', 'grand', 'big'. **2.** shortened Anglicized form of Gaelic **Ó Maol Aodha** 'descendant of the devotee of *Aodh*' (see McCOY). **3.** reduced Anglicized form of Gaelic **Ó Maol Mhaodhóg** 'descendant of the devotee of (Saint) *Maodhóg*'. Compare LOGUE. **4.** variant of MULVIHILL and SLOWEY.

GIVEN NAMES Irish 6%. *Brendan* (5), *Brigid* (2), *Eamon* (2), *Fintan* (2), *Brid, Caitlin, Colm, Cormac, Dermot, Ethna, Kevin Patrick, Kieran.*

Molnar (3290) **1.** Hungarian (**Molnár**) and Jewish (from Hungary): occupational name from *molnár* 'miller', probably a Magyarized form of the Slavic word for a miller, *mlinar*. *Molnar* is also found as a Slovenian surname. **2.** Dutch: variant of MOLENAAR 'miller'.

GIVEN NAMES Hungarian 7%. *Bela* (15), *Laszlo* (10), *Ferenc* (6), *Zoltan* (6), *Imre* (5), *Arpad* (4), *Geza* (4), *Gyula* (4), *Istvan* (4), *Gabor* (3), *Janos* (3), *Miklos* (3).

Molner (177) Variant spelling of German MOLLNER.

Molock (138) Origin unidentified. This is a MD name.

Moloney (1216) Irish: variant spelling of MALONEY.

GIVEN NAMES Irish 8%. *Brendan* (2), *Kieran* (2), *Brigid, Dermot, Fergal, Liam, Niall, Siobhan.*

Molony (302) Irish: variant spelling of MALONEY.

Molpus (100) Scottish and English: variant of MALPASS.

Molski (120) Polish: habitational name for someone from any of several places in Poland called Mole, named with Polish *mol* 'moth' (see MOLEK).

GIVEN NAME Polish 5%. *Casimir* (2).

Molstad (218) Norwegian: habitational name from any of several farmsteads in

southeastern Norway named either Mold-stad (in Old Norse *Moldastaðir*, from the personal name *Moldi* + *staðr* 'farmstead', 'dwelling') or Molstad, from an unexplained element, *Mol-* + *staðr*.
GIVEN NAMES Scandinavian 5%. *Egil* (2), *Erik*.

Molt (196) **1.** German: topographic name from Middle High German *molte* 'fine, dry soil'. **2.** North German: metonymic occupational name for a maltster, from Middle Low German *molt* 'malt'.

Molter (669) North German: occupational name for a maltster, from an agent derivative of Middle Low German *molten* 'to produce malt'.

Molton (204) English: variant spelling of MOULTON.

Moltz (230) German: habitational or topographic name of unexplained etymology, from any of several places and fields so named.

Molyneaux (381) English and Irish: variant spelling of MOLYNEUX.

Molyneux (402) **1.** English and Irish (of Norman origin): habitational name from Moulineaux in Seine-Maritime, so named from the plural of Old French *moulineau*, a diminutive of *moulin* 'mill'. In some cases this may have been an occupational name as in 2. **2.** French: occupational name for a miller, from *molineux*, a variant of Old French *molineur* 'miller'. **3.** Irish: Anglicized form of MULLIGAN. **4.** Irish (Co. Kerry): Anglicized form of Gaelic **Ó Maol an Mhuaidh** 'descendant of *Maol an Mhuaidh* (follower of the noble)'.

Molz (149) German: variant spelling of MOLTZ.
GIVEN NAME German 5%. *Otto* (2).

Molzahn (205) German: habitational name from Moltzahn in Pomerania or Molzahn in Mecklenburg.

Moman (263) Swedish: ornamental name from *mo* 'sandy heath' + *man* 'man'.

Momberg (101) Dutch and German: habitational name from a place so named.

Momberger (104) German: variant of MOMBERG.
GIVEN NAME German 6%. *Kurt* (2).

Moment (103) English (Lincolnshire and Yorkshire): unexplained.

Momin (288) Muslim: from a personal name based on Arabic *mu'min* 'believer (in Islam)', 'pious person'. Al-Mu'min 'the Believer' is one of the names of Allah (Qur'an 59:23). It is also the title of the 40th sura of the Qur'an.
GIVEN NAMES Muslim 91%. *Karim* (13), *Akbar* (6), *Zulfiqar* (6), *Amirali* (5), *Sadruddin* (5), *Nasir* (4), *Salim* (4), *Sultan* (4), *Ahmed* (3), *Amir* (3), *Inayat* (3), *Nizar* (3).

Mommaerts (112) Dutch: from a derivative of the Middle Dutch verb *mommen* 'to dress up', 'to disguise', 'to put on a mask'.

Mommsen (106) North German: variant of MOMSEN.
GIVEN NAMES German 8%. *Gerhard*, *Hans*, *Katharina*.

Momon (124) Origin unidentified.

Momsen (149) North German (**Mommsen**): patronymic from the personal name *Mumm(o)* (see MUMM 1).

Mon (184) **1.** English: variant of MUNN, MANN, or possibly MOON. **2.** German: probably a variant of MANN. **3.** Catalan: from the Marian name *Mare de Déu del Món*, from Girona province. This name is very common in northern Catalonia. **4.** Asturian-Leonese or Aragonese: habitational name from Mon in Asturies, or from El Mon in Uesca, Aragón. **5.** Chinese 万: variant of WAN 1.
GIVEN NAMES Spanish 18%; Chinese 5%. *Jorge* (2), *Jose* (2), *Armando*, *Dulce*, *Eduardo*, *Emilio*, *Enedina*, *Francisca*, *Gregorio*, *Guillermina*, *Jose Luis*, *Josefa*; *Chin*, *Hon*, *Hyeon*, *Jin*, *Kam Shing*, *Khin*, *Kin*, *Maung*, *Mei*, *Seng*, *Sing*, *Zhi Ming*.

Mona (171) **1.** Italian and Greek: from a feminine form of **Moni**, a short form of the personal name *Simone* (Italian equivalent of SIMON). **2.** Muslim: from a personal name based on Arabic *munā* 'wishes', 'desires', plural of *munya* 'wish'.
GIVEN NAMES Muslim 6%. *Mohammed* (2), *Wedad* (2), *Ghalib*, *Jamal*, *Khadijah*, *Muna*, *Showkat*.

Monacelli (256) Italian (**Monacèlli**): patronymic or plural form of *monacello*, a diminutive of MONACO.
GIVEN NAMES Italian 12%. *Guido* (2), *Cesare*, *Egidio*, *Elio*, *Enrico*, *Fausto*, *Gianfranco*, *Naldo*, *Pasquale*, *Querino*, *Tommaso*.

Monachino (130) Italian: from a diminutive of MONACO.
GIVEN NAMES Italian 12%. *Alfonso*, *Francesca*, *Mario*.

Monaco (3020) Italian (**Mònaco**): nickname for someone of monkish habits or appearance, or an occupational name for a servant employed at a monastery, from Italian *monaco* 'monk' (from Greek *monakhos* 'monk', 'solitary'). **Monachos** is also found as a Greek family name. Compare English MONK.
GIVEN NAMES Italian 15%. *Angelo* (25), *Salvatore* (10), *Luigi* (7), *Antonio* (5), *Domenic* (5), *Pasquale* (5), *Rocco* (5), *Carmine* (4), *Donato* (4), *Aldo* (3), *Francesco* (3), *Gino* (3).

Monaghan (3091) Irish: variant spelling of MONAHAN.
GIVEN NAMES Irish 6%. *Brendan* (6), *Aidan* (2), *Brigid*, *Colm*, *Liam*, *Patrick James*, *Siobhan*.

Monagle (151) Irish: shortened Anglicized form of Gaelic **Mac Maonghail** (see McMONAGLE).
GIVEN NAME Irish 8%. *Ronan*.

Monahan (6111) Irish: Anglicized form of Gaelic **Ó Manacháin** 'descendant of

Manachán', a personal name representing a diminutive of *manach* 'monk'. See also MONK. The Gaelic name is sometimes interpreted as if it were *Ó Muineacháin* 'descendant of the little shrubbery', and is sometimes translated as THORNTON. Compare the place name *Monaghan*.
GIVEN NAMES Irish 5%. *Brendan* (4), *Fergus* (4), *Murphy* (2), *John Patrick*, *Kevin Patrick*, *Paddy*.

Monarch (217) Origin unidentified. Perhaps a translation of French **Monarque**, **Monarc**, a nickname for a high-handed or haughty person, from Old French *monarque* 'monarch'.

Monarrez (204) Spanish **Monárrez**: variant of *Munárriz*, a Castilianized form of Basque Munarritz, name of a town in Navarre province, Basque Country.
GIVEN NAMES Spanish 51%. *Jose* (8), *Francisco* (4), *Javier* (3), *Rafael* (3), *Alberto* (2), *Alejandro* (2), *Dionicio* (2), *Jesus* (2), *Juan* (2), *Manuel* (2), *Miguel* (2), *Ruben* (2); *Lorenzo* (3), *Federico*, *Flavio*, *Mauro*.

Monasmith (101) Americanized form of German **Mahnenschmidt**, an unexplained compound of SCHMIDT 'smith'.

Monast (136) French (Acadian): unexplained.
GIVEN NAMES French 6%; Spanish 4%. *Pierre*; *Ramon* (4).

Monastero (126) Italian: topographic name for someone living at or near a monastery or who worked in one as a servant of the monks.
GIVEN NAMES Italian 28%. *Sal* (4), *Salvatore* (3), *Alfonso*, *Antonino*, *Carlo*, *Domenico*, *Giacomo*, *Mario*, *Salvy*.

Monastra (108) Southern Italian: habitational name from a place called *Monastra*, named with Greek *monastria* 'nun'.
GIVEN NAMES Italian 24%. *Cesare* (3), *Salvatore* (3), *Antonio*, *Aurello*, *Dante*, *Dino*.

Monat (120) **1.** French: unexplained. Perhaps a respelling of **Monatte**, a habitational name from either of two localities named La Monatte: in Craponne-sur-Arzon in Haute-Loire, or Saint-Bonnet-le Coureau in Loire. **2.** Jewish (Ashkenazic): ornamental name from German *Monat* 'month'.
GIVEN NAME French 6%. *Colette*.

Moncada (789) Catalan: variant of *Montcada*, a habitational name from any of the places so named in Valencia and Catalonia.
GIVEN NAMES Spanish 49%. *Jose* (17), *Carlos* (13), *Luis* (13), *Manuel* (10), *Juan* (9), *Pedro* (9), *Javier* (8), *Armando* (6), *Jesus* (6), *Mario* (6), *Jaime* (5), *Raul* (5).

Moncayo (187) Spanish or Aragonese: habitational name, probably from either of two places in Andalusia named Moncayo (in Granada and Córdoba provinces), or for someone who lived in the area of Montcayo, a remarkable mountain in the Aragonese Pyrenees.

GIVEN NAMES Spanish 43%. *Jose* (4), *Manuel* (4), *Francisco* (3), *Julio* (3), *Cesar* (2), *Jorge* (2), *Juan* (2), *Luis* (2), *Ruben* (2), *Soledad* (2), *Abelardo, Adalberto.*

Monce (109) Scottish (Angus): unexplained. Perhaps related to the Irish (Galway) name **Mons**, also unexplained.

Monceaux (278) French: habitational name from any of numerous places in northern France named Monceau (plural *Monceaux*), from Old French *moncel* 'little mountain', Late Latin *monticellum*, a diminutive of *mons* 'mountain', genitive *montis*.
GIVEN NAMES French 5%. *Colette, Easton, Francois, Noemie.*

Moncivais (153) Variant spelling of Mexican Spanish MONSIVAIS.
GIVEN NAMES Spanish 46%. *Jose* (5), *Guadalupe* (4), *Eugenio* (2), *Jesus* (2), *Jorge* (2), *Jose Trinidad* (2), *Ricardo* (2), *Agapito, Alejandro, Alfredo, Alma Rosa, Andres*; *Lorenzo* (3), *Leonardo* (2), *Antonio, Ciro.*

Monck (121) English: variant spelling of MONK.

Monckton (116) English: habitational name from any of various places named Monkton, from Old English *munuc* 'monk' + *tūn* 'farmstead', 'settlement', in particular those in Devon and Kent, although there are other, less important, examples (often with distinguishing affixes).

Moncrief (1549) Scottish: habitational name from Moncreiff Hill near Perth, so called from Gaelic *monadh* 'hill' + *craoibhe*, genitive of *craobh* 'tree'.

Moncrieff (158) Scottish: variant spelling of MONCRIEF. This is the more common spelling in Scotland.
GIVEN NAME French 5%. *Patrice* (2).

Moncur (175) Scottish: habitational name from a place on Tayside, or possibly of Norman origin from an unidentified place in Normandy. The first known bearer of the name is Michael de Muncur, who witnessed a charter in the first half of the 13th century.

Moncure (211) Variant spelling of Scottish MONCUR.

Moncus (222) Origin unidentified. Possibly an altered form of English **Monkhouse**, a topographic name for someone who lived and worked at a monastery, a house of monks.

Monda (255) Italian: possibly a nickname from *monda* 'clean', 'pure', feminine form of *mondo* (from Latin *mundus*); otherwise it could be from a short form of a female form of a personal name ending with -*mondo* (see MONDO), although such names were found almost exclusively in the masculine form in the medieval period.
GIVEN NAMES Italian 8%. *Antonio* (2), *Bartolomeo, Giuseppe, Luigi, Sal.*

Mondale (51) Americanized form of Norwegian MUNDAHL.

Monday (1567) **1.** English: from the Old Norse personal name *Mundi*, a short form of the various compound names containing the element *mundr* 'protection'. **2.** English: nickname for someone who had a particular association with this day of the week (Old English *mōnandæg* 'day of the moon'), normally because he owed feudal service then. It was considered lucky to be born on a Monday. **3.** Irish (Ulster): quasi-translation of **Mac Giolla Eoin** 'son of the servant of *Eoin*', by confusion of the last part of the name with Irish *Luain* 'Monday'.

Mondelli (181) Italian: patronymic or plural form of MONDELLO.
GIVEN NAMES Italian 21%. *Vito* (4), *Carlo* (2), *Luigi* (2), *Franco, Leonardo, Lorenzo, Pasquale, Rocco, Trifone.*

Mondello (460) Italian: from a pet form of the personal name MONDO.
GIVEN NAMES Italian 20%. *Sal* (3), *Salvatore* (3), *Rocco* (2), *Antonino, Basilio, Benedetto, Carmella, Carmine, Francesca, Guido, Mario, Natale, Nunzio, Placido, Tino.*

Mondesir (158) French: nickname from a phrase meaning literally 'my desire'.
GIVEN NAMES French 48%; German 5%. *Andre* (2), *Micheline* (2), *Yvon* (2), *Anatole, Elcie, Francoise, Gabrielle, Jean Baptiste, Jean Claude, Jean Robert, Laure, Lucien*; *Hermann, Liesl.*

Mondi (143) Italian: patronymic or plural form of MONDO.
GIVEN NAMES Italian 16%. *Angelo, Massimo, Santo.*

Mondloch (123) German: unexplained; perhaps a habitational name from either of two places in Bavaria called Muntlach.
GIVEN NAMES German 5%. *Alois* (2), *Kurt.*

Mondo (191) Italian: from a short form of a personal name ending with -*mondo*, as for example *Belmondo, Boemondo, Raimondo.*
GIVEN NAMES Italian 9%; French 4%. *Rocco* (2), *Caesar, Franco, Giuseppe*; *Laure, Odette.*

Mondor (231) French (Massif Central): possibly a habitational name from Mont-Dore in Puy-de-Dôme (named with Old French *mont* 'hill', 'mountain' (Latin *mons*, genitive *montis*) + a pre-Celtic element, *dur*), or from Saint-Didier au Mont-d'Or in Rhône (named with *or* 'gold').
GIVEN NAMES French 7%. *Andree, Henri, Jacques, Normand.*

Mondragon (1429) **1.** Spanish (**Mondragón**): habitational name from Basque Mondragoe ('dragon mountain'), a place in Gipuzkoa province. **2.** French: habitational name from Montdragon in Tarn.
GIVEN NAMES Spanish 42%. *Jose* (28), *Juan* (17), *Manuel* (12), *Francisco* (10), *Miguel* (9), *Jesus* (8), *Alejandro* (7), *Carlos* (7), *Jorge* (6), *Marcos* (6), *Mario* (6), *Gustavo* (5).

Mondry (183) **1.** French: from a Germanic personal name composed of the elements *mund* 'protection' + *rīc* 'power'. **2.** Polish: nickname from *mądry* 'wise'.

Monds (229) Irish (County Roscommon): unexplained. According to MacLysaght, this is equivalent to the Galway name **Mons**, also unexplained.

Mondschein (144) **1.** German: habitational name from a house name meaning 'moonshine', or a nickname for someone who was bald, from the same word, Middle High German *mōne, mān(d)e* + *schein*. **2.** Jewish (Ashkenazic): ornamental name from the German word *Mondschein* 'moonshine' (see 1).
GIVEN NAMES Jewish 6%; German 5%. *Sol*; *Alois, Franz.*

Mondt (102) Dutch: variant of MONT.
GIVEN NAME German 4%. *Manfred.*

Mondy (295) English: variant of MONDAY.

Mone (300) Irish: variant of MOHAN.

Monell (286) Probably an altered spelling of French **Monel**, from a shortened pet form of the personal name SIMON.

Mones (181) **1.** Catalan (**Monés**): probably a variant spelling of the plural of Old Catalan *moner* 'mill', a topographical name for someone who lived by or worked in a mill (Latin *molinarius*), or habitational name from any of the so-called places in Catalonia. **2.** Galician or Asturian-Leonese: habitational name place in Ourense (Galicia) or Asturies called Mones.
GIVEN NAMES Spanish 23%. *Jose* (4), *Manuel* (3), *Rodrigo* (2), *Tino* (2), *Ulises* (2), *Alberto, Alfonso, Alfredo, Augusto, Carolina, Cipriano, Crisanto.*

Monet (115) **1.** French: from a shortened pet form of SIMON or another personal name ending in -*mon*, such as *Aymon* (from the Germanic personal name *Haimo*, a derivative of *haim* 'home'). **2.** Italian: unexplained.
GIVEN NAMES French 10%; Spanish 9%. *Philippe, Pierre*; *Domingo* (2), *Carlos, Cesar.*

Moneta (110) Italian: from *moneta* 'money', probably applied as a nickname for a rich man or as a metonymic occupational name for a moneyer or money lender.
GIVEN NAMES Italian 6%. *Angelo, Luigi.*

Monett (108) Variant of French MONET.

Monette (1020) **1.** French: from a pet form of the female personal name *Simone* (see SIMON). **2.** North American spelling of French MONET.
GIVEN NAMES French 4%. *Jacques* (2), *Pierre* (2), *Germain, Germaine, Philippe.*

Monetti (147) Italian: patronymic or plural form of *Monetto*, a shortened pet form of the personal name *Simone* (see SIMON).
GIVEN NAMES Italian 16%. *Alessandro* (2), *Luciano* (2), *Domenico, Gabriele, Gino, Giuliano, Raffaele, Sal, Salvatore.*

Money (2115) **1.** English: from Middle English *money(e)* 'money' (Old French *moneie*, Latin *moneta*), hence a nickname for a rich man or a metonymic occupational name for a moneyer. Compare MINTER. **2.** Irish: Anglicized form of Gaelic **Ó Maonaigh** (see MEANEY).

Moneyhun (111) Most probably an American respelling of Irish MONAHAN.

Moneymaker (287) Translated form of German **Geldmacher** or **Geldschläger**, occupational names for a coiner.

Moneypenny (279) English and Scottish: probably a nickname for a rich man or a miser, from Middle English *many* 'many' (Old English *manig*, *monig*) + *peny* 'penny' (see PENNY).

Monfils (175) French: nickname which Morlet ascribes to the over-use of the phrase *mon fils* 'my son' in conversation, whereas Debrabandere believes it more likely to be *mau fils* 'bad son'.
GIVEN NAMES French 11%. *Armand* (2), *Georges* (2), *Emile*, *Marcel*, *Pierre*.

Monfort (344) French and English: variant of MONTFORT.
GIVEN NAMES French 4%. *Jacques*, *Marcel*, *Monique*, *Wilner*.

Monforte (168) **1.** Italian and Spanish: habitational name from any of numerous places named Monforte, from Latin *mons* 'mountain' (genitive *montis*) + *fortis* 'strong', was probably a reference to the strategic position of these locations. This name is common in Mexico. **2.** Possibly a variant of English MONTFORT.
GIVEN NAMES Italian 19%; Spanish 5%. *Angelo* (3), *Salvatore* (2), *Carmela*, *Carmine*, *Rocco*, *Rosaria*, *Sal*; *Carlos*, *Francisco*, *Luis*, *Medardo*.

Mong (592) **1.** Norwegian: habitational name from a farmstead in Rogaland, probably originally named in Old Norse as *Mángr*, from *már* 'gull' + *angr* 'small fjord'. **2.** Korean: unexplained.

Mongan (326) Irish: Anglicized form of Gaelic **Ó Mongáin** (see MANGAN).

Mongar (110) English: variant spelling of MONGER.

Monge (822) **1.** Portuguese and Spanish: from Portuguese *monge*, Spanish *monje* 'monk' (a loanword from Old Occitan, from Latin *monachus*). **2.** French: from a short form of **Demonge**, a pet form of the personal name *Dominique* (see DOMINGO). **3.** Norwegian: habitational name from a farmstead in Romsdal named Monge.
GIVEN NAMES Spanish 38%. *Jose* (15), *Julio* (11), *Carlos* (10), *Luis* (10), *Juan* (8), *Manuel* (7), *Mario* (6), *Francisco* (5), *Jesus* (5), *Rafael* (5), *Sergio* (5), *Alberto* (4).

Mongeau (389) French: from a pet form of MONGE 1.
GIVEN NAMES French 6%. *Laurent* (2), *Colette*, *Dominique*, *Gilles*, *Jacques*.

Mongelli (293) Italian (Milan): of uncertain derivation; possibly a shortened form of

Amoncelli, an unexplained family name, or alternatively from a derivative of the personal name *Moncio* (as preserved in the surnames *Monci*, *Moncino*, etc.), or from a reduced form of *Monicello* 'little monk'.
GIVEN NAMES Italian 18%. *Rocco* (5), *Sal* (2), *Aldo*, *Alfredo*, *Amelio*, *Antonio*, *Caesar*, *Carmela*, *Cesare*, *Concetta*, *Cosmo*, *Emanuele*, *Franco*, *Mario*.

Mongelluzzo (132) Italian: from a derivative of **Mongello** (see MONGELLI).
GIVEN NAMES Italian 20%. *Angelo* (4), *Antonio* (2), *Amato*, *Carmela*, *Carmine*, *Pasquale*, *Romeo*.

Mongeon (416) French: probably a derivative of MONGE 2.
GIVEN NAMES French 10%. *Adrien* (2), *Armand* (2), *Alain*, *Camil*, *Francois*, *Ghislaine*, *Herve*, *Julien*, *Laurent*, *Marcel*, *Normand*, *Roch*.

Monger (764) English: occupational name for a retail trader or a stallholder in a market, Middle English *monger*, *manger* (see MANGER).

Mongiello (208) Italian: variant of **Mongello** (see MONGELLI).
GIVEN NAMES Italian 19%. *Angelo* (3), *Carmine* (2), *Americo*, *Cosmo*, *Enrico*, *Gerardo*, *Primo*, *Romeo*, *Roberto*.

Mongillo (372) Italian: variant of **Mongello** (see MONGELLI).
GIVEN NAMES Italian 9%. *Antonio*, *Enrico*, *Evo*, *Italo*, *Nicola*, *Pasquale*.

Mongold (575) Altered form of English or German MANGOLD.

Mongrain (100) French: unexplained.
GIVEN NAMES French 16%. *Marcel* (2), *Andre*, *Leonce*.

Monheit (100) German: unexplained.

Monhollen (212) Irish, Scottish, or English: unexplained. Possibly an altered form of Irish MULHOLLAND.

Monica (373) **1.** Italian: from a feminine form of MONICO. **2.** Spanish **Mónica**: from the female personal name *Monica*, the name of the mother of St. Augustine. She was a Carthaginian, so the name may well be of Phoenician origin. However, in the early Middle Ages, it was taken to be a derivative of Latin *monere* 'to warn or advise', and was associated with the spiritual guidance that she gave to her famous son.

Monical (206) Origin unidentified.

Monico (319) Italian, Spanish and Portuguese (**Mónico**): from the personal name *Mónico*, a masculinized form of MONICA.
GIVEN NAMES Spanish 13%; Italian 9%. *Juan* (3), *Jose* (2), *Candido*, *Carlos*, *Cristina*, *Emilio*, *Enrique*, *Esperanza*, *Jesus*, *Jose Antonio*, *Jose De Jesus*, *Luis Ernesto*; *Angelo* (2), *Domenic*, *Gino*, *Nunzio*, *Prisco*, *Salvatore*.

Monie (139) French (**Monié**): variant of MONNIER.

Monier (279) French: variant of MONNIER.
GIVEN NAMES French 4%. *Huguette*, *Jacques*, *Lisanne*.

Monigold (161) Americanized form of French MANIGAULT.

Monin (143) French: from a pet form of the personal name SIMON.

Moninger (163) German: possibly a habitational name (**Möning**) for someone from Möning in Bavaria.

Moniot (102) French: from a diminutive of Old French *mon(n)ier* 'moneyer'.

Moniz (1613) Portuguese: from a patronymic form of the medieval personal name *Munho*.
GIVEN NAMES Spanish 12%; Portuguese 9%. *Manuel* (56), *Jose* (22), *Carlos* (5), *Mario* (3), *Fernando* (2), *Hilario* (2), *Jorge* (2), *Rogerio* (2), *Adelino*, *Adriano*, *Alberto*, *Alfredo*; *Joao* (6), *Agostinho*, *Duarte*, *Guilherme*, *Henrique*.

Monjaras (102) Hispanic (Mexico, El Salvador): unexplained.
GIVEN NAMES Spanish 50%. *Jose* (4), *Guadalupe* (2), *Leticia* (2), *Luis* (2), *Madaleno* (2), *Ana*, *Angeles*, *Armando*, *Arturo*, *Bernabe*, *Carlos*, *Cirilo*.

Monje (293) Spanish: from *monje* 'monk' (a loanword from Old Occitan, from Latin *monachus*). Compare MONGE.
GIVEN NAMES Spanish 34%. *Jose* (5), *Marta* (4), *Carlos* (3), *Arturo* (2), *Gonzalo* (2), *Manuel* (2), *Ramon* (2), *Ricardo* (2), *Ysidro* (2), *Angelita*, *Armando*, *Beatriz*.

Monk (3962) **1.** English: nickname for someone of monkish habits or appearance, or an occupational name for a servant employed at a monastery, from Middle English *munk*, *monk* 'monk' (Old English *munuc*, *munec*, from Late Latin *monachus*, Greek *monakhos* 'solitary', a derivative of *monos* 'alone'). **2.** North German (**Mönk**) and Dutch: equivalent of 1, from Middle Low German *monik*, Middle Dutch *moni(n)c*, *mun(i)c*. **3.** Irish: translation of Gaelic **Ó Muineaog** (see MINOGUE) or **Ó Manacháin** (see MONAHAN). **4.** Jewish (eastern Ashkenazic): occupational name for a miller or flour merchant, from Polish *mąka* 'flour', 'meal'.

Monkman (147) English: occupational name for a servant in a monastery, from Middle English *munk*, *monk* (see MONK 1) + *man* 'serving man'.

Monks (997) English and Dutch: patronymic from MONK 1 and 2, or an occupational name for a servant in a monastery or a monk's servant.

Monn (324) **1.** German: variant of MOHN 2. **2.** Altered form of MANN.

Monnett (261) North American French spelling of MONET (see MONETT).

Monnier (379) French: **1.** occupational name from Old French *mon(n)ier* 'minter', 'money-changer'. **2.** from a dialect variant of MEUNIER.
GIVEN NAMES French 5%. *Octave* (2), *Solange* (2), *Henri*, *Jean-Baptiste*, *Yves*.

Monnig (272) German (**Mönnig**): from Middle Low German *monik* 'monk', hence a nickname for someone of monkish habits or appearance, or an occupational name for a servant employed at a monastery. See also MONK 2.

GIVEN NAMES German 4%; French 4%. *Franz, Kurt, Otto; Roch* (2).

Monnin (468) **1.** Dutch: from a shortened pet form of the personal name SIMON. **2.** French: from a shortened pet form of the personal name *Simon*. Compare MONNOT.

Monninger (131) German: see MONINGER.

Monnot (150) French: from a shortened pet form of the personal name *Simon*.

GIVEN NAMES French 5%. *Herve, Michel*.

Monohan (119) Irish: variant spelling of MONAHAN.

Monopoli (101) Italian: habitational name from a place called Monopoli, from Greek *monē polis* 'single town'.

GIVEN NAMES Italian 19%. *Angelo, Carmela, Domenico, Gaetano, Mauro, Salvatore, Sante, Vito*.

Monreal (501) Spanish and Aragonese: habitational name from any of the places called Monreal, for example in Cuenca, Teruel, and Zaragoza provinces.

GIVEN NAMES Spanish 45%. *Jose* (9), *Juan* (6), *Manuel* (6), *Carlos* (5), *Francisco* (5), *Jesus* (5), *Ricardo* (5), *Jaime* (4), *Luis* (4), *Pedro* (4), *Amador* (3), *Guadalupe* (3).

Monro (144) Scottish: variant spelling of MONROE.

Monroe (17345) Scottish: according to tradition, this is a rare example of a Gaelic surname of topographic origin, the first element of which is probably Gaelic *mun*, a mutated form of *bun* 'foot', or British *minit* 'hill'. In Ireland this name has sometimes been used as an equivalent of **O'Mellan** (see MELLON) and MILROY 2.

FOREBEARS Scottish bearers of this name are descended from Donald O'Kane, who in the 11th century migrated from the mouth of the Roe to Ferrindonald in Cromarty, Scotland. There his descendants, as barons of Foulis and vassals of the earls of Ross, held lands along the Firth of Cromarty. James Monroe (1758–1831), 5th president of the U.S. (1817–25), came from a cadet branch of this family.

Monroy (919) Spanish: habitational name from Monroy ('red mountain'), a place in Cáceres province.

GIVEN NAMES Spanish 50%. *Jose* (17), *Juan* (14), *Manuel* (9), *Enrique* (8), *Francisco* (8), *Jorge* (8), *Armando* (7), *Carlos* (7), *Miguel* (7), *Cesar* (6), *Jaime* (6), *Juana* (6); *Antonio* (9), *Marco* (5), *Ceasar* (2), *Clementina* (2), *Camillo, Cecilio, Costantino, Elio, Filiberto, Gilda, Leonardo, Lorenzo*.

Mons (111) **1.** French: habitational name from any of numerous places named Mons. **2.** Catalan: topographic name from the plural of *mont* 'mountain'.

GIVEN NAMES French 6%; Spanish 4%. *Alain; Consuelo, Juan, Orestes, Valeria*.

Monsalve (155) Spanish (also **Monsalvé**): unexplained.

GIVEN NAMES Spanish 57%; Italian 7%. *Carlos* (5), *Jorge* (4), *Jose* (4), *Luz* (4), *Sergio* (4), *Alba* (3), *Jaime* (3), *Juan* (3), *Luis* (3), *Adolfo* (2), *Fidelino* (2), *Margarita* (2); *Dario* (3), *Marcello, Marco*.

Monsanto (138) Spanish and Portuguese: habitational name from Monsanto ('sacred mountain') in Beira or one of the other places so named.

GIVEN NAMES Spanish 25%. *Enrique* (3), *Adolfo* (2), *Carlos* (2), *Jose* (2), *Ruben* (2), *Ana, Anastacio, Angel, Esperanza, Ines, Juana, Nereida*.

Monsees (295) Origin unidentified.

Monsen (467) Norwegian and Danish: patronymic from the personal name *Mons*, from MAGNUS.

GIVEN NAMES Scandinavian 10%. *Monrad* (3), *Erik* (2), *Nels* (2), *Anders, Maren*.

Monserrate (115) **1.** Portuguese: habitational name from any of various places in Portugal named Monserrate. **2.** Spanish: Castilianized form of the Catalan habitational name *Montserrat*, after the famous monastery of *Mare de Déu de Montserrat*, in Barcelona. Christopher Columbus christened the Caribbean Island of Montserrat with reference to this name of the Virgin.

GIVEN NAMES Spanish 45%. *Luis* (3), *Carlos* (2), *Jorge* (2), *Jose* (2), *Adriana, Alberto, Amparo, Angel, Cesar, Cruz, Felicita, Hernandez; Angelo, Filomena*.

Monsivais (158) Spanish (**Monsiváis**): Mexican variant of a topographic name derived from Latin *mons silvaticus* 'wooded mountain'.

GIVEN NAMES Spanish 53%. *Jose* (7), *Santos* (4), *Francisco* (3), *Juan* (3), *Luis* (3), *Eduardo* (2), *Javier* (2), *Juanita* (2), *Mario* (2), *Roberto* (2), *Adriana, Agustina; Antonio* (2), *Marco* (2), *Donato, Lorenzo*.

Monsma (123) Frisian: unexplained.

Monson (4156) American respelling of Swedish **Månsson**, a patronymic from an assimilated form of the personal name MAGNUS (compare Danish MONSEN).

Monsour (397) French: ironical nickname from *monsor*, a dialect form of *Monsieur* 'my Lord'.

GIVEN NAMES French 4%. *Andre, Edmound, Emile*.

Mont (205) **1.** Catalan and French: topographic name for someone who lived on or near a hill, from Catalan and Old French *mont* 'mountain', 'hill' (Latin *mons*, genitive *montis*). **2.** Dutch: nickname from Middle Dutch *monde* 'mouth', perhaps denoting someone with a large or loud one. **3.** Dutch: from a short form of a Germanic personal name ending in *-mond* (from *mund* 'protection'; compare RAYMOND.) **4.** Dutch (**de Mont**): kinship name from Middle Dutch *mond* 'guardian'.

GIVEN NAMES Spanish 11%. *Carlos* (2), *Jose* (2), *Juan* (2), *Cristina, Domingo, Fran-*

cisco, Jorge, Luis, Mariano, Ramon, Trinidad.

Montag (721) German and Jewish (Ashkenazic): from Middle High German *māntac*, German *Montag* 'Monday'. As a German name, this was a nickname for someone who had a particular association with this day of the week, probably because he owed feudal service then. As a Jewish name, it is either ornamental or it may have been adopted or given with reference to the day of registration of the surname.

Montagna (453) Italian: topographic name for someone who lived on or near a mountain or mountains, Italian *montagna*, from Late Latin *montanea*, originally the neuter plural of an adjective derivative of *mons* (see MONTE 1), or a habitational name from one of the many places named with this word.

GIVEN NAMES Italian 16%. *Angelo* (3), *Sal* (3), *Gaetano* (2), *Alessandro, Antonino, Attilio, Carlo, Carmelo, Cosmo, Dino, Enrico, Oreste*.

Montagne (292) French: topographic name for someone who lived on or near a hill, from Old French *montaine* 'hill', '(small) mountain' (see MONTAGNA); or a habitational name from any of the many places in France so called.

GIVEN NAMES French 7%. *Andre* (2), *Francoise, Herve, Marcel, Philippe, Pierre*.

Montagnino (144) Italian: from a diminutive of MONTAGNA or **Montagno**, possibly denoting a mountain dweller (compare MONTANARO), but also found as a medieval personal name in the form *Montaninus*.

GIVEN NAMES Italian 20%. *Salvatore* (3), *Antonino, Antonio, Franca, Nino, Pietro*.

Montague (3934) **1.** English (of Norman origin): habitational name from a place La Manche in France, so named from Old French *mont* 'hill' (see MONT 1) + *agu* 'pointed' (Latin *acutus*, from *acus* 'needle', 'point'). **2.** Irish: English surname adopted as equivalent of Gaelic **Mac Taidhg**, a patronymic from the byname *Tadhg* (see McTIGUE).

Montalbano (1175) Southern Italian: habitational name from Montalbano di Elicona in northeastern Sicily (earlier simply Montalbano), Montalbano Jonico (Matera province), or the district of Montalbano in Fasano, Brindisi.

GIVEN NAMES Italian 13%. *Salvatore* (6), *Vito* (6), *Angelo* (3), *Calogero* (2), *Gaetano* (2), *Luigi* (2), *Sal* (2), *Antonino, Carlo, Carmelo, Carmine*.

Montalbo (173) **1.** Spanish: habitational name from any of the places called Montalbo, in the provinces of Cuenca, Jaen, and Logroño, named in Latin as 'white mountain', from *mons* 'mountain' (genitive *montis*) + *albus* 'white'. **2.** Italian: habitational name from a place named Montalbo ('white mountain').

GIVEN NAMES Spanish 39%; Italian 6%. *Juan* (3), *Salomon* (3), *Prudencio* (2), *Adalberto, Agusto, Alba, Alfredo, Ana, Anastacio, Arturo, Candido, Cayetano*; *Raffaele* (2), *Dante, Heriberto, Tillio*.

Montalto (495) **1.** Italian: habitational name from any of various places called Montalto or Montaldo, especially Montalto Uffugo in Cosenza province. **2.** Portuguese: habitational name from a place named Montalto, from *monte* 'hill' + *alto* 'high' (Latin *altus*).
GIVEN NAMES Italian 21%. *Salvatore* (5), *Vito* (5), *Angelo* (4), *Carmine* (3), *Domenico* (2), *Giovanni* (2), *Sal* (2), *Agostino, Alessandra, Alessia, Antonio, Emilio, Franco*.

Montalvan (110) Spanish (**Montalván**): habitational name from Montalbán in Lugo province, from an old spelling of the place name, or from various other places in Spain called Montalbán, in particular in Teruel.
GIVEN NAMES Spanish 56%. *Carlos* (5), *Ricardo* (3), *Joaquin* (2), *Juan* (2), *Luis* (2), *Ruben* (2), *Alberto, Alicia, Alonso, Alvaro, Ana Lydia, Andres*.

Montalvo (2470) Portuguese and Spanish: habitational name from places named Montalvo. See MONTALBO.
GIVEN NAMES Spanish 44%; Portuguese 10%. *Jose* (62), *Juan* (37), *Luis* (28), *Jesus* (18), *Rafael* (18), *Manuel* (17), *Mario* (15), *Angel* (14), *Carlos* (14), *Pedro* (14), *Francisco* (13), *Miguel* (12); *Duarte, Marcio*.

Montana (1165) **1.** Spanish (**Montaña**): topographic name from *montaña* 'mountain'. **2.** Italian: from a feminine form of MONTANO.
GIVEN NAMES Spanish 9%; Italian 6%. *Jose* (9), *Eduardo* (4), *Juan* (4), *Armando* (3), *Jorge* (3), *Mario* (3), *Andres* (2), *Carlos* (2), *Enrique* (2), *Francisco* (2), *Gustavo* (2), *Lupe* (2); *Angelo* (5), *Rocco* (3), *Salvatore* (3), *Antonio* (2), *Carmine* (2), *Aldo, Camillo, Carmello, Cesario, Francesco, Ignazio, Lucio*.

Montanari (278) Italian: patronymic or plural form of MONTANARO.
GIVEN NAMES Italian 7%. *Romano* (2), *Antonio, Dino, Fulvio, Luigi, Olindo*.

Montanaro (452) Italian (especially Emilia): topographic name from medieval Latin *montanarius* 'mountain dweller', or a habitational name from places called Montanara (for example, in Cremona and Mantua) or Montanaro (for example in Turin and Milan).
GIVEN NAMES Italian 15%; Spanish 7%. *Carmella* (3), *Alfredo* (2), *Angelo* (2), *Cosimo* (2), *Vito* (2), *Antonio, Carmine, Ciro, Concetta, Dino, Donato, Emilio, Gino, Guido, Italo*; *Carlos* (2), *Domingo* (2), *Alejandra, Alicia, Juan Luis, Lisandro*.

Montandon (124) Swiss French: habitational name from Montandon in Doubs, France.
GIVEN NAMES French 6%. *Henri, Michel*.

Montanez (1366) Spanish (**Montáñez**): of uncertain derivation; either a habitational name from Montáñez, a minor place in Granada or an altered spelling of *montañées* 'from the mountains', an adjectival derivative of *montaña* 'mountain'.
GIVEN NAMES Spanish 47%. *Jose* (35), *Luis* (20), *Juan* (16), *Jesus* (15), *Ramon* (13), *Carlos* (10), *Miguel* (10), *Pedro* (10), *Angel* (9), *Manuel* (9), *Francisco* (8), *Ricardo* (8).

Montani (149) Italian (especially Liguria): patronymic or plural form of MONTANO.
GIVEN NAMES Italian 15%. *Nino* (2), *Angelo, Gino, Luigi, Pietro, Rocco, Santo*.

Montanino (117) Italian: from the personal name *Montanino*, a pet form of MONTANO.
GIVEN NAMES Italian 23%. *Aniello, Carmela, Enrico, Gennaro, Rocco, Sal, Salvatore, Saverio*.

Montano (3247) **1.** Spanish and Portuguese: nickname or topographic name from the adjective *montano* 'from the mountains'. **2.** Italian: topographic name from Italian *montano* 'mountain', or a habitational name from a place called Montano, in particular Montano Antilia in Salerno province, or the district of Caianello in Caserta so named. **3.** Italian: from the personal name *Montano*, from Latin *montanus* 'mountain dweller'.
GIVEN NAMES Spanish 34%. *Jose* (56), *Juan* (31), *Manuel* (30), *Carlos* (24), *Jesus* (18), *Francisco* (16), *Luis* (14), *Pedro* (12), *Ruben* (12), *Mario* (11), *Alfonso* (9), *Jorge* (9).

Montante (208) Italian: from French **Montant**, from the personal name *Montant*, from Latin *Montanus*; alternatively it may be from a nickname from Old French *montant* 'brave', or a habitational name from Le Montant in Aube or other, minor places so named.
GIVEN NAMES Italian 16%; Spanish 10%. *Angelo* (3), *Gaetano* (3), *Luigi* (2), *Salvatore* (2), *Antonio, Carmelina, Carmelo, Domenic, Marco, Philomena, Sal*; *Jose* (4), *Lourdes* (2), *Armando, Avelino, Carlota, Francisco, Guillermo, Luisa, Luzviminda, Manual, Mario*.

Montanye (290) Probably an altered spelling of French **Montane**, **Montaigne**, variants of MONTAGNE.
GIVEN NAMES German 4%. *Fritz, Kurt, Philo*.

Montavon (181) Swiss French: habitational name from Montavon in Jura canton.

Monte (1462) **1.** Italian (Lombardy and Emilia-Romagna), Spanish, Portuguese, and Jewish (from Italy): topographic name for someone who lived on or near a mountain, Italian, Spanish, Portuguese *monte* (Latin *mons*, genitive *montis*). **2.** Italian and Jewish (from Italy): habitational name from any of the places named with Monte or Monti.
GIVEN NAMES Italian 10%; Spanish 7%. *Carlo* (10), *Mario* (4), *Domenic* (3), *Salvatore* (3), *Aldo* (2), *Angelo* (2), *Antonio*

(2), *Arturo* (2), *Carmelo* (2), *Gaspare* (2), *Carmela, Ciro, Gasper, Philomena*; *Jose* (7), *Manuel* (3), *Carlos* (2), *Edgardo* (2), *Emilia* (2).

Monteagudo (178) Spanish: habitational name from any of numerous places called Monteagudo ('pointed mountain'), from *monte* 'mountain' + *agudo* 'sharp', 'pointed' (Latin *acutus*, from *acus* 'needle'), for example in the provinces of Murcia, Teruel, A Coruña, and Navarre.
GIVEN NAMES Spanish 48%. *Jorge* (6), *Jose* (5), *Francisco* (4), *Jesus* (3), *Blanca* (2), *Eduardo* (2), *Luis* (2), *Manuel* (2), *Pilar* (2), *Ramon* (2), *Roberto* (2), *Sergio* (2); *Aldo* (2), *Antonio* (2), *Marco*.

Montealegre (118) Spanish: habitational name from Montealegre in Vallodolid province or Montealegre del Castilo in Albacete, so named from *monte* 'mountain' + *alegre* 'happy', 'joyful'.
GIVEN NAMES Spanish 50%. *Alvaro* (3), *Carlos* (3), *Jaime* (3), *Julio* (3), *Mario* (3), *Enrique* (2), *Juan* (2), *Marcelo* (2), *Miguel* (2), *Ramiro* (2), *Alberto, Alfonso*.

Montecalvo (283) **1.** Italian: habitational name from any of various places called Montecalvo ('bald mountain'), especially Montecalvo Irpino in Avellino province. **2.** Galician: habitational name from either of two places in Galicia called Montecalvo, from *monte* 'mountain' + *calvo* 'bald'. However, the American surname appears to be predominantly of Italian origin.
GIVEN NAMES Italian 13%. *Antonio* (3), *Angelo* (2), *Carlo* (2), *Vito* (2), *Saverio*.

Montee (177) Possibly an altered spelling of MONTE, written thus to preserve the second syllable.

Monteforte (217) Italian: habitational name from Monteforete Cilento in Salerno province or Montefore Irpino in Avellino.
GIVEN NAMES Italian 24%. *Carmine* (10), *Angelo* (3), *Antonio, Gaetano, Pietro, Rino, Salvatore*.

Montefusco (240) Southern Italian: habitational name from, Montefusco, a place in Avellino province, recorded in medieval Latin as *Mons Fusculus*, from Latin *mons*, genitive *montis* 'mountain' + *fusculus*, either a derivative of *fuscus* 'dark', 'obscure' or from the personal name *Fusculus*.
GIVEN NAMES Italian 16%. *Antonietta* (2), *Antonio* (2), *Angelo, Carmino, Cesare, Domenic, Enrico, Franco, Luigina, Mattia, Nichola, Renzo*.

Monteiro (1228) Portuguese and Galician: occupational name for a hunter, *moneiro*. This name is also found in western India, where it was taken by Portuguese colonists.
GIVEN NAMES Spanish 24%; Portuguese 16%. *Jose* (32), *Manuel* (28), *Pedro* (10), *Carlos* (8), *Mario* (7), *Luis* (6), *Fernando* (5), *Alberto* (3), *Alfredo* (3), *Ana* (3), *Armando* (3), *Ernesto* (3); *Joao* (8), *Guilherme* (3), *Marcio* (3), *Paulo* (3), *Joaquim* (2), *Aderito, Afonso, Duarte, Margarida,*

Messias, Sebastiao, Vasco; Antonio (25), Albertina (2), Carmela (2), Marcello (2), Alessandra, Clementino, Filomena, Gino, Lorenzo, Marco, Sal.

Monteith (1254) Scottish: habitational name from a place in Perthshire, named in Gaelic as 'hill pasture (above) the Teith', from *monadh* 'hill pasture' + *Teith*, a river name of obscure origin. This name was introduced to Ulster, where it is now quite numerous in certain areas, particularly County Tyrone.

Montejano (257) Spanish: habitational name for someone from a place called MONTEJO, from an adjectival form of the place name.

GIVEN NAMES Spanish 49%; Portuguese 11%. *Jose (7), Carlos (5), Manuel (5), Angel (3), Francisco (3), Javier (3), Raul (3), Ruben (3), Elvira (2), Emilio (2), Juan (2), Mario (2); Adauto; Eliseo (2), Marco (2), Antonio, Dario, Romeo.*

Montejo (158) Spanish: **1.** topographic name from a diminutive of MONTE 1. **2.** habitational name from any of places called Montejo ('little mountain'), in particular those in the provinces of Salamanca, Segovia, and Soria.

GIVEN NAMES Spanish 52%. *Raul (4), Carlos (3), Eduardo (3), Abelardo (2), Alberto (2), Julio (2), Mario (2), Mauricio (2), Miguel (2), Miguel Angel (2), Alejandro, Alfonso.*

Montel (120) Southern French: topographic name from Occitan *montell* 'little mountain'.

Monteleone (1186) Italian: habitational name from any of numerous places called Monteleone, notably Monteleone di Puglia in Foggia province, Monteleone Sabino in Rieti, or Monteleone di Calabria (formerly in Catanzaro), which was renamed in 1928 as Vibo Valentia. The place name is composed of the elements *monte* 'mountain' + the personal name *Leone*.

GIVEN NAMES Italian 16%. *Vito (6), Salvatore (5), Angelo (4), Antonio (4), Cosmo (4), Carmine (3), Sal (3), Domenico (2), Cosimo, Domenica, Elio, Ettore.*

Montella (255) **1.** Italian: habitational name from Montella, a place in Avellino province. **2.** Catalan (**Montella** and **Montellà**): habitational name from any of various places named Montellà or Montella, in Lleida and Girona provinces.

GIVEN NAMES Italian 18%. *Angelo (3), Salvatore (3), Pasquale (2), Aniello, Antonio, Carmine, Emidio, Gaetano, Lucio, Oreste, Saverio, Sebastiano.*

Montellano (124) Spanish: **1.** habitational name from Montellano in Seville province, derived from *monte* 'mountain' + *llano* 'plain' or 'flat'. **2.** Castilianized form of Basque **Mendizelai**, habitational name from a town in Biscay province, derived from *mendi* 'mountain' + *zelai* 'field', 'plain'.

GIVEN NAMES Spanish 40%; Italian 7%. *Jose (3), Ernesto (2), Guadalupe (2), Juventino (2), Manuel (2), Pedro (2), Adolfo, Andres, Angel, Eduardo, Efrain, Enrique; Antonio, Dino, Eliseo.*

Montello (227) Italian: from a diminutive of MONTE.

GIVEN NAMES Italian 6%. *Biagio, Carmela, Marco.*

Montelongo (684) **1.** Galician: habitational name from places so named in Ourense and A Coruña in Galicia. **2.** Italian: habitational name from Montelongo in Campobasso province, so named from *monte* 'mountain' + *longo* 'long'.

GIVEN NAMES Spanish 50%. *Jose (21), Juan (13), Manuel (9), Arturo (8), Francisco (6), Guadalupe (6), Ruben (6), Mario (5), Roberto (5), Angel (4), Carlos (4), Domingo (4).*

Montemarano (213) Italian: habitational name from Montemarano in Avellino province.

GIVEN NAMES Italian 29%. *Carmine (5), Angelo (3), Antonio (3), Mauro (2), Romeo (2), Vito (2), Antonietta, Enrico, Filomena, Gennaro, Gino, Giuseppe.*

Montemayor (1127) Spanish: habitational name from any of several places called Montemayor, from *monte* 'mountain' + *mayor* 'main', 'larger', 'greater', in particular in the provinces of Cordova, Salamanca, and Valladolid.

GIVEN NAMES Spanish 48%. *Jose (23), Juan (19), Carlos (12), Ruben (12), Jesus (10), Raul (10), Manuel (8), Miguel (7), Ramon (7), Arturo (6), Cesar (6), Enrique (6).*

Montemurro (203) Southern Italian: habitational name from a place Montemurro in Potenza province, so named from *monte* 'mountain' + *murro*, a variant of Lucanese *morro*, a pre-Roman term relating to rock spikes, heights, and strongholds.

GIVEN NAMES Italian 22%. *Antonio (2), Carmine (2), Leonardo (2), Rocco (2), Angelo, Domenic, Emilio, Francesco, Gerardo, Giuseppe, Raffaele, Salvatore, Santo.*

Montenegro (996) Spanish, Portuguese, and Italian: habitational name from any of various places in Spain, Portugal, and Italy called Montenegro ('black mountain').

GIVEN NAMES Spanish 47%; Portuguese 13%; Italian 5%. *Jose (30), Jorge (11), Juan (10), Miguel (10), Carlos (9), Enrique (9), Mario (9), Francisco (7), Manuel (7), Raul (7), Fernando (6), Luis (6); Paulo; Antonio (8), Elio (3), Lucio (3), Caesar (2), Leonardo (2), Marco (2), Romeo (2), Albertina, Aldo, Dario, Enio, Flavio.*

Monter (161) Catalan: variant spelling of the occupational name *munter*, denoting a person in charge of the dogs at a hunt (see MONTERO).

GIVEN NAMES Spanish 8%. *Angel (2), Arturo, Enrique, Ernesto, Francisca, Gerardo,*

Guillermo, Juan, Juan Luis, Maria De La Paz.

Montera (106) Spanish: probably from *montera* 'cap', 'hat', in particular the type of hat worn by bullfighters, so either an occupational name for someone who made such hats or a nickname for someone who habitually wore one.

GIVEN NAMES Spanish 10%. *Constancio, Jose, Mario, Rojelio.*

Montero (1761) Spanish: occupational name for a beater or other assistant at a hunt, from an agent derivative of *monte*, which, as well as meaning 'mountain', 'hill', could be used in the transferred sense of a game forest on wooded upland. The occupational term was itself also used as a title for any of various palace functionaries, and some cases of the surname may derive from this.

GIVEN NAMES Spanish 45%; Portuguese 10%. *Jose (47), Carlos (29), Juan (25), Luis (23), Manuel (15), Pedro (15), Jesus (12), Miguel (12), Jorge (10), Roberto (10), Angel (9), Rafael (9); Ligia.*

Monterosso (144) Southern Italian (Sicily): habitational name from any of numerous places called Monterosso, as for example Monterosso Calabro in Vibo Valentia, or Monterosso Almo in Ragusa, which takes its name from *monte* 'mountain' + the personal name *Russo, Rosso*.

GIVEN NAMES Italian 20%. *Angelo, Damiano, Domenic, Francesco, Gino, Natale, Raffaele, Rocco, Sal, Vita.*

Monterrosa (104) Spanish: variant of MONTERROSO. This name is mainly found in Mexico and Central America.

GIVEN NAMES Spanish 55%. *Ricardo (6), Jose (5), Juan (4), Ana (2), Guillermo (2), Jorge (2), Adelio, Carlos, Eduardo, Elena, Ernesto, Fernando.*

Monterroso (163) **1.** Spanish and Galician: habitational name from Monterroso in Galicia, or possibly from Monterroso in Málaga. **2.** Portuguese: habitational name from any of several places named Monterroso.

GIVEN NAMES Spanish 46%; Italian 9%. *Carlos (3), Aura (2), Jorge (2), Luis (2), Marta (2), Miguel (2), Roberto (2), Sergio (2), Adela, Adilio, Armando, Arnulfo; Egidio (2), Marco (2), Romeo (2), Antonio, Carlo, Eliseo, Giovanni, Lucio.*

Montes (3846) **1.** Spanish and Portuguese: topographic name, a plural form of MONTE. **2.** Dutch: patronymic from a short form of a Germanic compound personal name formed with *-mund* 'protection' as the final element. Compare RAYMOND.

GIVEN NAMES Spanish 51%; Portuguese 10%. *Jose (121), Juan (50), Jesus (41), Manuel (40), Jorge (32), Luis (32), Francisco (30), Miguel (28), Carlos (27), Alfredo (25), Ramon (25), Raul (25); Joaquim, Vanderlei.*

Montesano (443) **1.** Southern Italian: habitational name from Montesano Salentino in Lecce province or Montesano sulla Marcellana in Salerno province, so named from *monte* 'mountain' + *sano* 'healthy'. **2.** Possibly also Spanish: habitational name for someone from Montesa in Valencia province, from an adjectival form of the place name. However, the American surname appears to be predominantly of Italian origin.
GIVEN NAMES Italian 12%. *Amedeo* (2), *Carmelo* (2), *Rocco* (2), *Vito* (2), *Angelo*, *Giovanni*, *Luigi*, *Salvatore*, *Santo*.

Montes de Oca (404) Spanish: topographic name from a range of mountains forming the watershed between the rivers Ebro and Duero in northern Spain, named with the plural of *monte* 'mountain' + *oca* 'goose'.
GIVEN NAMES Spanish 56%. *Jose* (17), *Juan* (10), *Luis* (9), *Carlos* (8), *Jorge* (8), *Francisco* (7), *Fernando* (5), *Pedro* (5), *Jesus* (4), *Julio* (4), *Mario* (4), *Raul* (4).

Montesi (184) Southern Italian: **1.** habitational name for someone from a place called MONTE, from an adjectival form of the place name. **2.** from the plural of **Montese**, a habitational name from Montese in Modena province. **3.** from a patronymic form of the medieval personal name *Montese* (from *monte* 'mountain'). **4.** from a short form of the 13th-century Florentine name **Chiermontese**, a habitational name for someone name from the French city of Clermont, from an adjectival form of the place name. Late Latin *monte-nis* 'of or belonging to mountains', or various other habitational names such as **Chiaromontese**, denoting someone from Chiaromonte, etc.

Montesino (157) Spanish and Jewish (Sephardic): topographic name for someone who lived on a mountain, from a derivative of *monte* 'mountain' (Latin *mons*, gentive *montis*).
GIVEN NAMES Spanish 55%. *Jose* (6), *Luis* (4), *Juan* (3), *Ramon* (3), *Roberto* (3), *Blanca* (2), *Candido* (2), *Jorge* (2), *Julio* (2), *Luisa* (2), *Manuel* (2), *Reynaldo* (2); *Antonio*, *Marino*, *Mauro*.

Montesinos (155) Spanish: probably a habitational name from Montesinos in Murcia province or Los Montesinos in Badajoz or Alacant.
GIVEN NAMES Spanish 55%. *Luis* (7), *Jose* (5), *Miguel* (4), *Arturo* (3), *Carlos* (3), *Manuel* (3), *Adolfo* (2), *Cesar* (2), *Felipe* (2), *Javier* (2), *Pablo* (2), *Roberto* (2); *Antonio*, *Clementina*, *Lia*, *Marco*.

Montet (117) French: topographic name, from a diminutive of *mont* 'mountain' (Latin *mons*, gentive *montis*), or a habitational name from any of various places so named.
GIVEN NAMES French 7%. *Curley*, *Michel*.

Monteverde (230) **1.** Galician: habitational name from Monteverde in Ourense

province, Galicia. **2.** Italian: habitational name from any of various places called Monteverde, for example in Avellino province, from *monte* 'mountain' (Latin *mons*, gentive *montis*) + *verde* 'green' (Latin *viridis*).
GIVEN NAMES Spanish 20%. *Carlos* (3), *Eduardo* (2), *Enrique* (2), *Francisco* (2), *Aurelio*, *Gustavo*, *Ines*, *Jaime*, *Jorge*, *Jose*, *Juan*, *Leticia*.

Montez (1304) **1.** Portuguese (**Montez**, also **Montês**): topographic name for a mountain dweller, from *montês* 'of the mountain'. **2.** Spanish: from a variant of the adjective *montés*, having the same meaning as 1.
GIVEN NAMES Spanish 32%; Portuguese 6%. *Manuel* (16), *Juan* (14), *Jose* (13), *Carlos* (7), *Guadalupe* (7), *Francisco* (6), *Miguel* (6), *Raul* (6), *Jesus* (5), *Lupe* (5), *Ruben* (5), *Domingo* (4); *Sil*, *Vasco*.

Montford (338) English: **1.** variant of MONTFORT. **2.** habitational name from Montford in Shropshire, named in Old English as *Maneford*, from *(ge)mǣne* or *mann* (genitive plural *-a*) 'communal', 'of the community' + *ford* 'ford'; or from Mundford in Norfolk, named in Old English as 'Munda's ford', from *Munda*, an unattested Old English personal name, + *ford* 'ford'.

Montfort (272) French and English (of Norman origin): habitational name from any of the numerous places called Montfort, from Old French *mont* 'hill' (see MONT 1) + *fort* 'strong', 'impregnable' (Latin *fortis*). A Norman bearer of this name, from Montfort-sur-Risle in Eure, near Brionne, accompanied William the Conqueror in his invasion of England in 1066.

Montgomery (39082) English, Scottish, and northern Irish (of Norman origin): habitational name from a place in Calvados, France, so named from Old French *mont* 'hill' + a Germanic personal name composed of the elements *guma* 'man' + *rīc* 'power'. In Ireland this surname has been Gaelicized as **Mac Iomaire** and in Scotland as **Mac Gumaraid**.

Monti (1096) Italian: variant of MONTE, from the plural.
GIVEN NAMES Italian 13%. *Angelo* (5), *Salvatore* (4), *Aniello* (3), *Pasquale* (3), *Aldo* (2), *Carmel* (2), *Elio* (2), *Enrico* (2), *Gaetano* (2), *Marco* (2), *Marino* (2), *Philomena* (2).

Monticello (171) Italian: habitational name from any of numerous places, especially in northern Italy, called Monticello, from Late Latin *monticellus* 'mount', 'small mountain'.
GIVEN NAMES Italian 8%. *Angelo* (2), *Rocco*, *Salvatore*.

Montie (229) Perhaps a variant spelling of English MONTY.

Montiel (811) Spanish: habitational name from Montiel, a place in Ciudad Real province.
GIVEN NAMES Spanish 50%; Portuguese 9%. *Jose* (17), *Francisco* (12), *Juan* (11), *Manuel* (11), *Carlos* (10), *Luis* (7), *Armando* (6), *Roberto* (6), *Alejandro* (5), *Cesar* (5), *Leticia* (5), *Miguel* (5); *Godofredo*.

Montieth (141) Variant spelling of Scottish MONTEITH.

Montigny (117) French: habitational name from a place named Montigny, from a Romano-Gallic estate name, *Montiniacum*.
GIVEN NAMES French 11%. *Armand*, *Henri*, *Jacques*, *Normand*, *Remi*.

Montijo (353) Spanish and Portuguese: habitational name from any of several places called Montijo, in particular one in Badajoz province.
GIVEN NAMES Spanish 33%. *Juan* (4), *Luis* (4), *Ramon* (4), *Blanca* (3), *Jesus* (3), *Jose* (3), *Miguel* (3), *Ruben* (3), *Armando* (2), *Carlos* (2), *Horacio* (2), *Javier* (2).

Montilla (179) Spanish: habitational name from Montilla, a place in Córdoba province.
GIVEN NAMES Spanish 48%. *Fernando* (3), *Jesus* (3), *Manuel* (3), *Alfredo* (2), *Alicia* (2), *Ana* (2), *Juan* (2), *Julio* (2), *Lino* (2), *Ramon* (2), *Rosita* (2), *Alejandro*; *Carmine*.

Montini (185) Italian (Milan): **1.** from a diminutive plural of MONTE. **2.** patronymic from the medieval personal name *Montino* (a derivative of *monte* 'mountain').
GIVEN NAMES Italian 21%. *Enio* (2), *Pietro* (2), *Arsenio*, *Concetta*, *Dante*, *Dino*, *Domenic*, *Eliseo*, *Lorenzo*, *Marco*, *Mauro*, *Quirino*, *Ricco*, *Tulio*.

Montjoy (131) Either an altered form of MOUNTJOY or, more likely, an Americanized spelling of French **Montjoie**, a habitational name from a place so named, for example in Pas-de-Calais. This name occurs chiefly in SC.
GIVEN NAME French 5%. *Gaston*.

Montminy (226) French: perhaps a habitational name from Montmin in Haute Savoie, so named from Latin *medianus*, Old French *main* 'middle', 'central'.
GIVEN NAMES French 21%. *Lucien* (4), *Armand* (2), *Aime*, *Alcide*, *Alphonse*, *Emile*, *Fernand*, *Gilles*, *Jean-Francois*, *Laurier*, *Normand*, *Pierre*.

Montney (128) Americanized form of French **Montenay**, a habitational name from places in Mayenne and Indre, so named from Latin *Montanus*.

Monto (122) Catalan (**Montó**): variant of **Muntó**, a topographic name from a diminutive of *mont* 'mountain'.

Montone (179) Italian: **1.** nickname from *montone* 'ram' (from medieval Latin *multo*, genitive *multonis*). **2.** habitational name from any of numerous localities called Montone ('big mountain').
GIVEN NAMES Italian 13%. *Angelo*, *Bruna*, *Natale*, *Pasco*, *Vito*.

Montooth (141) Probably an altered form of Scottish MONTEITH.

Montoro (148) **1.** Spanish: habitational name from any of the places named Montoro, in particular those in Córdoba or Teruel provinces. **2.** Italian: habitational name from any of the places called Montoro, in particular Montoro Inferiore and Montoro Superiore in Avellino province.
GIVEN NAMES Spanish 16%; Italian 10%. *Julio* (2), *Carlos, Celso, Enrique, Jose, Juan, Lazaro, Luiz, Manuel, Miguel, Rafael, Raul; Angelo, Dante, Giuseppe, Marco.*

Montour (231) Possibly a respelling of French **Montoir**, a habitational name from a place called Montoir-de-Bretagne.
GIVEN NAMES French 9%. *Alain* (2), *Andre* (2), *Julienne, Mirlene, Myrtha, Renold.*

Montoya (9024) Spanish: unexplained. This is a frequent name in Spain.
GIVEN NAMES Spanish 33%; Portuguese 6%. *Jose* (121), *Juan* (88), *Manuel* (64), *Carlos* (62), *Luis* (53), *Mario* (35), *Ruben* (32), *Jesus* (31), *Jorge* (27), *Ramon* (24), *Francisco* (22), *Miguel* (21); *Godofredo, Marcio, Zaragoza.*

Montpetit (132) French: nickname possibly representing *maupetit* 'bad child', from Old French *mal, mau* 'bad' + *petit* 'small (one)'. Compare MONFILS.
GIVEN NAMES French 11%. *Andre, Lucien, Marcel, Romain, Yvon.*

Montplaisir (107) French: habitational name from any of various places called Montplaisir, in Allier, Aude, Hérault, and Nord.
GIVEN NAMES French 11%; Irish 5%. *Jacques, Philippe, Raoul.*

Montreuil (150) French: habitational name from any of a number of places in northern France, so named from Latin *monasteriolum*, a diminutive of *monasterium* 'monastery'.
GIVEN NAMES French 12%. *Armand, Carolle, Edouard, Jean-Pierre, Marcel, Veronique.*

Montrose (372) Scottish: habitational name from the place so named in the county of Angus.

Montross (319) Perhaps an older form of MONTROSE.

Montroy (346) French: habitational name from either of the places so called, in Charente-Maritime and Puy-de-Dôme.

Monts (372) Catalan: topographic name for someone who lived in the mountains, from Catalan *monts* (Latin *montes*), plural of *mont* 'mountain' (see MONT).

Montuori (236) Italian: from the plural form of **Montuoro**, a variant of MONTORO.
GIVEN NAMES Italian 16%. *Antonio* (3), *Salvatore* (2), *Alfonse, Amerigo, Angelo, Carmine, Dante, Gennaro, Giuseppe.*

Montville (247) Variant of French MON-VILLE.
GIVEN NAMES French 4%. *Emile, Vernice.*

Monty (592) **1.** English (County Durham): unexplained. **2.** French: topographic name for a mountain dweller, from Old French *mont* 'mountain' (Latin *mons, montis*). **3.** Walloon (Belgian French): habitational name from either of two places called Monty, from Late Latin *montile* 'hill': in Carneux, Liège province or in Corroy-le-Château, Namur province.
GIVEN NAMES French 6%. *Emile* (3), *Amedee, Chantelle, Francoise, Henri, Michel, Micheline, Ovila.*

Montz (491) **1.** Variant spelling of German MANTZ. **2.** from a Germanic personal name formed with *mun* 'thought'.

Monville (110) French: habitational name from Monville in Calvados or Montville in Seine-Maritime, both named with Old French *mont* 'mountain', 'hill' (see MONT 1) + *ville* 'demesne', 'estate' (later 'village', 'town'). In some instances the name may be from Monville in Fronville in Namur province, Belgium.

Monzingo (186) Variant of MOZINGO.

Monzo (221) **1.** Catalan (**Monzó**): variant of **Montsó**, habitational name from a place in Aragon (see MONZON). **2.** Italian: possibly a variant of **Monsu**, which may be an occupational name for a cook, Calabrian *munsu*, or a nickname or title from Milanese *monsu* 'sir', 'lord', 'gentleman'.
GIVEN NAMES Spanish 11%; Italian 5%. *Adela* (3), *Francisco* (2), *Juan* (2), *Rafael* (2), *Guadalupe, Jose Antonio, Mario, Pablo; Angelo* (2), *Concetta.*

Monzon (556) Spanish (**Monzón**): habitational name from Monzón, a place in Uesca province, which is probably named from Latin *montione* 'big mountain'.
GIVEN NAMES Spanish 50%. *Jose* (21), *Luis* (12), *Carlos* (10), *Jorge* (9), *Juan* (9), *Alberto* (6), *Julio* (6), *Ricardo* (6), *Ramon* (5), *Alvaro* (4), *Armando* (4), *Manuel* (4).

Mooberry (152) Origin unidentified.

Moock (119) Dutch: variant of **van Mook** (see MOOK).

Mood (295) English (Northumberland and Durham): unexplained. Compare MOAD, MODE.

Moodie (484) Scottish spelling of MOODY.

Moody (21888) English and Irish: nickname for a courageous, arrogant, or foolhardy person, or one quickly moved to anger, from Middle English *modie* 'impetuous', 'haughty', 'angry' (Old English *mōdig* 'brave', 'proud', from *mōd* 'spirit', 'mind', 'courage'). This English name has been established in Ireland since the late 13th century.

Mooers (484) Dutch: **1.** patronymic from a short form of the Latin personal name *Mauritius* (see MORRIS). **2.** possibly a variant of MOOR 2.

Moog (274) **1.** German: nickname for someone who was related to an important local personality, from Middle High German *māc, māge* 'relative'. Compare

MAAG. **2.** Dutch: variant of **van Mook** (see MOOK).

Mook (543) Shortened of Dutch **van Mook**, a habitational name from a place called Mook, in Dutch Limburg.

Moomaw (398) Origin unidentified. Compare MUMAU, MUMAW. This surname is found mainly in VA and OH.

Moomey (323) Origin unidentified. Compare MUMMEY.

Moon (14672) **1.** Irish: Anglicized form of Gaelic **Ó Mocháin** (see MOHAN). **2.** English (of Norman origin): habitational name from Moyon in La Manche, named from the Gallo-Roman personal name *Modius* (from Latin *modus* 'measure') + the locative suffix *-o* (genitive *-onis*). **3.** English: nickname from Anglo-Norman French *moun* 'monk' (see MONK). **4.** Cornish: nickname for a slender person, from Cornish *mon* 'thin'. **5.** Korean: variant of MUN.

Moonan (146) Irish: Anglicized form of Gaelic **Ó Muanáin**, a northern form of **Ó Maonáin**, from the diminutive of *maon* 'dumb'.

Moone (193) Irish and English: variant spelling of MOON.

Moonen (134) Dutch: from a shortened pet form of the personal name SIMON.
GIVEN NAMES Dutch 5%. *Henk* (2), *Dirk.*

Mooney (12814) Irish: Anglicized form of Gaelic **Ó Maonaigh**, 'descendant of *Maonach*', a personal name derived from *maoineach* 'rich'.

Mooneyham (996) Altered form of Irish MOYNIHAN.

Mooneyhan (289) Irish: variant of MOYNIHAN.

Moor (799) English, Irish, Scottish, and Welsh: variant spelling of MOORE.

Mooradian (346) Armenian: patronymic from the personal name *Moorad*, from the Turkish personal name *Murad* 'wish', 'desire', from Arabic *murād* (see MURAD).
GIVEN NAMES Armenian 17%. *Aram* (3), *Hagop* (3), *Arsen* (2), *Arshag* (2), *Sarkis* (2), *Ararat, Avak, Berge, Boghos, Gayane, Hrach, Nubar.*

Moore (239230) **1.** English: from Middle English *more* 'moor', 'marsh', 'fen', 'area of uncultivated land' (Old English *mōr*), hence a topographic name for someone who lived in such a place or a habitational name from any of the various places named with this word, as for example Moore in Cheshire or More in Shropshire. **2.** English: from Old French *more* 'Moor' (Latin *maurus*). The Latin term denoted a native of northwestern Africa, but in medieval England the word came to be used informally as a nickname for any swarthy or dark-skinned person. **3.** English: from a personal name (Latin *Maurus* 'Moor'). This name was borne by various early Christian saints. The personal name was introduced to England by the Normans, but it was never as popular in England as it was on the Continent. **4.** Irish: Anglicized form of Gaelic **Ó Mórdha** 'descendant of *Mórdha*', a byname meaning 'great', 'proud', or 'stately'. **5.** Scottish: see MUIR. **6.** Welsh: from Welsh *mawr* 'big', applied as a nickname or distinguishing epithet.

Moorefield (748) English (Lancashire): probably an altered form of the Norman baronial name **de Morville**, borne by a family who held land in Yorkshire and northern Lancashire in the 12th and 13th centuries.

Moorehead (1561) Northern Irish (eastern Ulster): variant of MUIRHEAD.

Moorehouse (243) English (chiefly Yorkshire): variant spelling of MOREHOUSE.

Moorer (1139) Perhaps an altered spelling of MAURER.

Moores (934) English: **1.** topographic name for someone who lived on the moors (see MOORE 1). **2.** patronymic from *Moore* as a personal name (see MOORE 3).

Moorhead (1902) Northern Irish: variant of MUIRHEAD.

Moorhouse (590) English (chiefly Yorkshire): variant spelling of MOREHOUSE.

Mooring (581) English: from a diminutive of MOORE 2 or 3.

Moorman (2773) **1.** English and Scottish: topographic name for someone who lived and worked on a moor (see MOORE 1). In Scotland the term denoted an official responsible for a moor, whose duties included overseeing the branding of the cattle which roamed on the moor. **2.** Dutch and North German: variant of MOHRMANN.

Moormann (115) Dutch and North German: variant of MOHRMANN.
GIVEN NAMES German 7%. *Helmuth* (2), *Kurt*.

Moors (314) **1.** English: variant spelling of MOORES. **2.** Dutch: nickname for a man of swarthy complexion or ethnic name for a North African, from *moor* 'Moor' (see MOORE 2). **3.** Dutch: patronymic from a short form of the Latin personal name *Mauritius* (see MORRIS 1).

Moos (786) **1.** German: topographic name for someone who lived by a peat bog, Middle High German *mos*. **2.** Dutch: variant of MAAS.

Moosbrugger (109) South German: variant of MOSBRUCKER.
GIVEN NAME German 4%. *Kurt*.

Moose (1317) Perhaps an altered spelling of MOOS; it occurs chiefly in NC.

Moosman (157) Americanized form of the German topographic surname **Moosmann**, a variant of MOOS 1 with the addition of Middle High German *man* 'man'.
GIVEN NAME French 4%. *Ferrel*.

Moot (133) Dutch: topographic name from *mot(t)e* 'mott' (Old French *mote*), a mound or small hill on which a castle keep was built. This occurs in a number of place

names, for example La Motte in Lessen, Hainault province.

Moothart (175) Variant spelling of German **Muthard**, from a personal name composed of the Germanic elements *mut* 'spirit' + *hard* 'hardy', 'brave', 'strong'.

Moots (291) Altered spelling of German MUTZ.

Mooty (209) **1.** Apparently of Irish or Scottish origin, but unexplained. It may be a variant of MOODY. **2.** Possibly an Americanized form of German **Mutig**, a nickname meaning 'cheerful'.

Mootz (339) Altered spelling of German MUTZ.

Moppin (119) Origin unidentified. Perhaps an Americanized form of French MAUPIN.

Moquin (528) French: nickname for someone given to irony, mocking, or derision, from a diminutive noun derivative of *moquer* 'to mock'.
GIVEN NAMES French 7%. *Armand* (2), *Henri* (2), *Adelard*, *Emile*, *Marcel*, *Raoul*.

Mor (159) Jewish: unexplained.
GIVEN NAMES Jewish 22%. *Ari*, *Arie*, *Avi*, *Eliezer*, *Erez*, *Etty*, *Haim*, *Hedva*, *Ilan*, *Itai*, *Moshe*, *Noam*.

Mora (5131) **1.** Portuguese, Spanish, and Catalan (**Móra**): habitational name from any of the places named Mora, in some cases from *mora* 'mulberry' (Late Latin *mora*, originally the plural of classical Latin *morum*). **2.** Occitan and Catalan (**Morà**): from *Morandus*, an old personal name of uncertain derivation and meaning. **3.** Italian: topographic name from Old Italian *mora* 'pile of stones'. **4.** Hungarian (**Móra**): from a pet form of the personal name *Móricz*, Hungarian form of MORRIS. **5.** Czech and Polish: from a short form of a personal name, e.g. Czech *Mauric*, Polish *Maurycy*, derived from Latin *Mauritius* (see MORRIS). **6.** Polish: possibly a nickname from *mora* 'sickness', 'plague'. **7.** Czech: possibly a nickname from *mora* 'vampire'.
GIVEN NAMES Spanish 45%; Portuguese 10%. *Jose* (138), *Juan* (65), *Luis* (51), *Manuel* (44), *Carlos* (41), *Jorge* (34), *Miguel* (32), *Jesus* (31), *Francisco* (29), *Roberto* (26), *Mario* (24), *Pedro* (23); *Ligia* (2), *Lidio*.

Morabito (846) Italian (Sicily): nickname for a teetotaler, Sicilian *murabbitu*, from Arabic *murābiṭ* 'hermit', 'ascetic'.
GIVEN NAMES Italian 16%. *Rocco* (8), *Angelo* (4), *Antonio* (3), *Domenic* (3), *Carmelo* (2), *Salvatore* (2), *Cosmo*, *Enzo*, *Filomena*, *Francesco*, *Gaetano*, *Giovanna*.

Morace (220) **1.** French: variant of MAURICE. **2.** Italian (Sicily): possibly from the Greek personal name *Morakēs* (see MORRIS).
GIVEN NAMES French 6%. *Andre*, *Silton*.

Morad (187) Muslim and Jewish (Israeli): variant of Arabic MURAD.
GIVEN NAMES Muslim 23%; Jewish 9%. *Ammar* (2), *Saeed* (2), *Said* (2), *Salim* (2),

Ahmad, *Ali*, *Ayman*, *Faraj*, *Habib*, *Hamid*, *Jamal*, *Laila*; *Yosef* (2), *Arieh*, *Ilan*, *Sholomo*, *Yacov*, *Yael*.

Moradi (143) Muslim: from a derivative of MURAD.
GIVEN NAMES Muslim 70%. *Ali* (10), *Hamid* (4), *Mohammad* (3), *Saeed* (3), *Alireza* (2), *Amir* (2), *Saied* (2), *Ahmad*, *Atour*, *Ezat*, *Farid*, *Fattah*.

Morado (175) Spanish and Portuguese: from Spanish and Portuguese *morado* 'deep violet', presumably a nickname.
GIVEN NAMES Spanish 45%. *Jose* (8), *Ramon* (3), *Rodrigo* (3), *Alfredo* (2), *Estanislado* (2), *Guadalupe* (2), *Jorge* (2), *Juan* (2), *Manuel* (2), *Miguel* (2), *Modesto* (2), *Ricardo* (2); *Antonio* (4), *Heriberto*, *Lucio*.

Moraes (156) Portuguese: topographic name for someone living among mulberry trees, from the plural of *moral* 'mulberry'. Compare Spanish MORALES.
GIVEN NAMES Spanish 23%; Portuguese 16%. *Fernando* (3), *Manuel* (3), *Francisco* (2), *Marcelo* (2), *Pedro* (2), *Roberto* (2), *Adriano*, *Agnaldo*, *Ana*, *Anselmo*, *Carlos*, *Claudio*; *Joao*, *Manoel*, *Paulo*; *Alessandra*, *Alessandro*, *Antonio*, *Sandro*.

Moraga (250) Spanish: from *moraga* 'barbecue', from Arabic.
GIVEN NAMES Spanish 25%; Italian 10%; French 5%. *Blanca* (2), *Francisco* (2), *Guillermo* (2), *Jose* (2), *Juan Francisco* (2), *Luis* (2), *Alvaro*, *Andres*, *Angel*, *Elfego*; *Antonio* (2), *Arturo* (2), *Gino* (2), *Mario* (2), *Giovanni*, *Severino*; *Gaston* (2), *Michel*.

Moragne (152) Possibly of French origin: unexplained; it could be a metathesized form of **Morange**, a habitational name from a place named Moranges, for example in Puy-de-Dôme, Haute-Loire, and Cantal.

Morahan (177) Irish: Anglicized form of Gaelic **Ó Murcháin** 'descendant of *Murchán*', a personal name, a pet form of *Murchadh* 'sea-warrior'.

Morain (203) French: variant of MORIN.

Morais (477) Portuguese: variant of MORAES, a topographic name meaning 'mulberry trees'.
GIVEN NAMES Spanish 27%; Portuguese 21%; French 4%. *Jose* (25), *Manuel* (16), *Fernando* (6), *Carlos* (4), *Francisco* (3), *Amaro* (2), *Armando* (2), *Domingos* (2), *Elia* (2), *Geraldo* (2), *Mario* (2), *Norberto* (2); *Joao* (7), *Albano* (3), *Joaquim* (3), *Vasco* (3), *Paulo* (2), *Aderito*, *Ilidio*, *Ligia*, *Marcio*; *Adrien* (2), *Aime*, *Chanel*, *Donat*, *Elodie*, *Fernande*, *Jean-Louis*, *Marcel*, *Sylvie*, *Valmond*.

Moraitis (155) Greek: regional name for someone from the Peloponnese, a derivative of *Mórea* 'Peloponnese', named as the land of mulberry trees, from *mōrea* 'mulberry'.
GIVEN NAMES Greek 20%. *Dimitrios* (3), *Evangelos* (2), *Isidoros* (2), *Constantine*,

Costas, Gerasimos, Markos, Stavros, Vasilios, Zaharias.

Morales (24584) Spanish: topographic name from the plural of *moral* 'mulberry tree'.

GIVEN NAMES Spanish 48%; Portuguese 10%. *Jose* (654), *Juan* (353), *Carlos* (263), *Luis* (248), *Manuel* (197), *Jesus* (188), *Jorge* (166), *Miguel* (161), *Francisco* (156), *Pedro* (154), *Raul* (131), *Roberto* (126); *Ligia* (6), *Paulo* (4), *Catarina* (2), *Anabela, Armanda, Godofredo, Henrique, Omero, Wenceslao.*

Moralez (429) Spanish (**Morález**): variant of MORALES.

GIVEN NAMES Spanish 34%; Portuguese 9%. *Manuel* (8), *Miguel* (6), *Jose* (5), *Ignacio* (3), *Armando* (2), *Carlos* (2), *Catarino* (2), *Ernesto* (2), *Fidel* (2), *Francisco* (2), *Jaime* (2), *Jesus* (2); *Gonsalo*; *Antonio* (4), *Carmel* (2), *Elio, Eliseo, Geronimo, Lorenzo.*

Moran (25911) **1.** Irish: Anglicized form of Gaelic **Ó Móráin** 'descendant of *Mórán*', a personal name meaning 'great', 'large'; the stress is normally on the first syllable. **2.** English: variant of MORANT, normally pronounced with the stress on the second syllable. **3.** Spanish (**Morán**): habitational name from places called Morán in Asturies, Galicia (Pontevedra) and Aragon (Zaragoza).

GIVEN NAMES Irish 4%. *Brendan* (13), *Liam* (6), *Kieran* (5), *John Patrick* (4), *Aileen* (3), *Eamon* (3), *Dermot* (2), *Seamus* (2), *Aidan, Cathal, Colm, Colum.*

Morand (304) French and Swiss French: **1.** variant of MORANT. **2.** habitational name from places so called in Indre-et-Loire, Allier, Loire, and Haute-Saône.

GIVEN NAMES French 6%. *Jacques, Lucien, Margaux, Remi, Solange, Yolene.*

Morandi (181) Italian: patronymic or plural form of the personal name MORANDO.

GIVEN NAMES Italian 14%; Spanish 4%. *Mario* (2), *Reno* (2), *Aldo, Angelo, Carlo, Geno, Giovanni, Italo, Leno, Remo*; *Angel, Carlos, Enrique.*

Morando (186) Italian and Spanish: from the medieval personal name *Morando* (medieval Latin *Morandus*), of uncertain derivation.

GIVEN NAMES Italian 17%; Spanish 12%. *Rocco* (3), *Salvatore* (3), *Angelo* (2), *Carlo* (2), *Sal*; *Jesus* (2), *Augusto, Eusebio, Javier, Jose Manuel, Luz Maria, Mariano, Marta, Ramon, Raul, Roberto, Vicente.*

Morang (253) Probably an Americanized spelling of MORAIN or of **Morange**, a habitational name from places called Moranges in Puy-de-Dôme, Haute-Loire, and Cantal. This name occurs chiefly in ME and MI.

Morano (994) **1.** Italian: habitational name from a place called Morano Calabro, in Cosenza province. **2.** Italian and Spanish: from the personal name *Morano*, a derivative of *Maurus* (see MORO).

GIVEN NAMES Italian 10%. *Angelo* (4), *Antonio* (3), *Rocco* (3), *Silvio* (3), *Carmelo* (2), *Carmine* (2), *Domenic* (2), *Domenico, Enrico, Francesco, Franco.*

Morant (281) **1.** English, French, and German: from an Old French personal name of uncertain etymology. It appears to be a byname meaning 'steadfast', 'enduring', from the present participle of Old French *(de)morer* 'to remain or stay', but this may be no more than the reworking under the influence of folk etymology of a Germanic personal name. The later may be from the elements *mōd* 'courage' + *hramn* 'raven'. Another possibility is derivation from Latin *Maurus* + suffix *-andus* (following the pattern of names formed from a verbal noun, such as *Amandus*). **2.** French: habitational name, a variant of MORAND.

Morante (149) Spanish and Italian: from a personal name, probably a variant of MORANDO under French influence.

GIVEN NAMES Spanish 32%; Italian 5%. *Jose* (4), *Angel* (2), *Carlos* (2), *Francisco* (2), *Juan* (2), *Manuel* (2), *Alberto, Alfredo, Andres, Arturo, Enrrique, Felipe*; *Giovanni, Paolo.*

Moranville (134) French: habitational name from Moranville in Meuse, probably so named from the personal name MORAND + Latin *villa* 'demesne', 'estate'.

Morar (107) **1.** Indian (Gujarat): Hindu name of unknown origin. **2.** Romanian: unexplained.

GIVEN NAMES Indian 18%; Romanian 8%. *Piyush* (2), *Ashok, Govind, Kishor, Nilesh, Pranav, Satish*; *Dumitru, Florin, Ionel, Vasile.*

Moras (116) Spanish: habitational name from any of the places named Moras, plural form of MORA.

GIVEN NAMES Spanish 5%. *Angel, Guadalupe, Manuel, Marina, Rafael, Santiago.*

Morasch (162) German (of Slavic origin): probably from a place called Moratz (in Pomerania), or from a Slavic topographic name meaning 'cloudberry' (Polish *morosz*).

Morasco (116) Italian: ethnic name for a Moor, someone from North Africa, a derivative of MORO, a variant of Italian *moresco* 'Moorish'.

GIVEN NAME Italian 5%. *Francesco.*

Morash (163) Americanized spelling of MORASCH.

Moraski (159) Polish: **1.** habitational name for someone from a place in Sieradz voivodeship called Morasy, possibly named with Polish dialect *morasić* 'to destroy'. **2.** variant of MORAWSKI.

GIVEN NAME Polish 5%. *Zigmund* (2).

Morast (100) Probably a variant of German MORASCH.

Morataya (109) Spanish: variant of **Moratalla**, habitational name from a village in Murcia province.

GIVEN NAMES Spanish 56%. *Jose* (12), *Juan* (3), *Julio* (3), *Luis* (3), *Cesar* (2), *Mario* (2), *Vicente* (2), *Alicia, Armando, Bertila, Edgardo, Felipe.*

Morath (195) South German: from the Germanic personal name **Morhart** (see MOREHART).

GIVEN NAMES French 4%; German 4%. *Camille, Gaston; Erhardt, Kurt.*

Moravec (741) Czech and Slovak: regional name for someone from Moravia (Czech *Morava*), a region in the eastern part of what is now the Czech Republic, named for the river which flows through it. From the 11th century onwards it was a crownland of the kingdom of Bohemia.

Moravek (200) Czech (**Morávek**): regional name for someone from Moravia.

Morawski (348) Polish: habitational name for someone from Morawy in Ciechanów or Włocławek voivodeships, or places called Morawa, Morawce, Morawczewice, or Morawka, all named with *morawa* 'wet grassy area', or a topographic name from this word.

GIVEN NAMES Polish 12%. *Lech* (2), *Zygmunt* (2), *Aleksander, Jaroslaw, Jerzy, Kazimierz, Leszek, Mieczyslaw, Ryszard, Szymon, Walerian, Wlodek.*

Morby (133) English: habitational name from Moreby in Yorkshire or Moorby in Lincolnshire, both named in Old Scandinavian as 'farmstead (*býr*) in the moor or marshland (*mór*)'.

Morck (129) **1.** Danish (**Mørck**): nickname for someone with dark hair or a swarthy complexion, from Old Norse *myrkr* 'dark'. **2.** Norwegian (**Mørck**): variant of MORK 2.

GIVEN NAMES Scandinavian 8%; German 5%. *Erik, Niels, Sven; Theos.*

Morcom (229) English (Devon): habitational name, probably from Morecombelake in Dorset (recorded as *Mortecumbe* in 1240). The second element of this is Old English *cumb* 'short valley', 'combe' (see COOMBE); the first is probably either an Old English personal name, *Morta* (see MORT) or *mort* 'young salmon or similar fish'. The surname is not from Morecambe in Lancashire, which is an 18th-century coinage, based on identification of Morecambe Bay with *Morikambē* 'great gulf' in the work of the ancient Greek geographer Ptolemy.

Morcos (138) Arabic: from *Morqūs*, Arabic form of the name of the apostle MARK.

GIVEN NAMES Arabic 55%; French 5%. *Samir* (4), *Samy* (4), *Laila* (3), *Nabil* (3), *Emad* (2), *Hany* (2), *Mounir* (2), *Raed* (2), *Tarek* (2), *Amal, Atef, Ehsan; Antoine, Lucienne, Marcelle, Piere.*

Mordan (122) English: variant spelling of MORDEN.

GIVEN NAME French 4%. *Nadege.*

Mordecai (321) **1.** Jewish: from a Hebrew Biblical personal name, etymologically related to that of the Babylonian god *Marduk*.

Mordecai was the name of a captive Jew in the palace of the Persian king Ahasuerus; he was guardian to his orphaned cousin Esther, who became Ahasuerus's queen and saved the Jews in his kingdom from threatened destruction (as recorded in the Old Testament Book of Esther). **2.** Welsh: from the Biblical personal name (see 1).

Morden (438) English: habitational name from Morden in Dorset or Surrey, Guilden or Steeple Morden in Cheshire, or Moredon in Wiltshire, all of which were named in Old English as 'hill (dūn) in marshland (mōr)'.

Mordhorst (147) North German: topographic name, probably from Middle Low German mōr 'fenland', 'swamp' + horst 'scrubland', 'wild place'.
GIVEN NAMES German 6%. Helmut (2), Johann.

More (1176) **1.** Scottish: variant spelling of MUIR. **2.** Welsh: from mawr 'big' (see MOORE). **3.** French: nickname for a dark-skinned person, from Old French more 'Moor' (Latin maurus) (see MOORE 2). **4.** French (also Moré): nickname from Old French of more 'Moor' or from moré, moret 'dark brown' (diminutive forms). The term was also used to refer to dark-colored cloth. **5.** French (Moré): from a short pet form of a Germanic personal name beginning with Maur-, Mor- 'Moor', for example, Morbold (+ bold 'bold', 'brave') or Morbert (+ berht 'bright', 'famous'). **6.** Indian (Maharashtra); pronounced as two syllables: Hindu (Maratha) name, probably from Marathi mor 'peacock' (Sanskrit mayūra). It is based on the name of a Maratha clan.
FOREBEARS Richard More (1614–c.1695), the illegitimate son of Jacob Blakeley and Katherine More, wife of Samuel More, was shipped to America aboard the Mayflower to be raised with the Pilgrims and avoid the social stigma of being bastardized. He became a mariner and sea captain with polygamous families on both sides of the ocean. Nicholas More, born in England, emigrated to PA in 1682 and became chief justice of PA and the lower counties.
GIVEN NAMES Indian 4%. Dilip (2), Pratap (2), Sanjiv (2), Vineet (2), Anand, Anil, Anjali, Harish, Hemant, Lata, Manjula, Maruti.

Morea (312) **1.** Italian (Apulia): unexplained. **2.** Spanish and Catalan: habitational name from any of the places named Morea in Navarre, Lleida, or Badajoz provinces.
GIVEN NAMES Italian 13%; Spanish 8%. Angelo (2), Saverio (2), Domenic, Ferdinando, Rocco; Manuel (2), Carlos, Cesar, Elvira, Jesus, Mauricio.

Moreau (3359) French: from a derivative of MORE 4 or 5.
GIVEN NAMES French 12%. Andre (12), Pierre (9), Jacques (7), Armand (6), Lucien (6), Marcel (6), Normand (5), Gaston (4),

Laurent (3), Michel (3), Ovide (3), Philippe (3).

Morecraft (111) English: topographic name for someone who lived at a moorland croft.

Moredock (116) Variant of Scottish MURDOCH.

Moree (539) French (Morée): habitational name from a place so named in Loir-et-Cher.

Morefield (658) English: see MOOREFIELD.

Morehart (303) Altered spelling of German Morhar(d)t, from the Germanic personal name Morhart, composed of an unidentified first element + hart 'hardy', 'brave', 'strong'.

Morehead (2857) Northern Irish and Scottish: variant of MUIRHEAD.

Morehouse (2462) English (chiefly Yorkshire): habitational name from any of various places, for example Moorhouse in West Yorkshire, named from Old English mōr 'marsh', 'fen' + hūs 'house'.

Morein (136) **1.** Irish: an Anglicized form of Gaelic Ó Móráin (see MORAN). **2.** Russian: unexplained.
GIVEN NAMES Irish 8%; Russian 5%. Donovan (2), Brigid; Vitaly (2), Gleb.

Moreira (1099) Portuguese and Galician: habitational name from any of the numerous places in Portugal and Galicia called Moreira, from moreira 'mulberry tree'.
GIVEN NAMES Spanish 38%; Portuguese 15%. Jose (33), Manuel (23), Carlos (20), Jorge (9), Ana (7), Luis (7), Roberto (7), Julio (6), Miguel (6), Fernando (5), Francisco (5), Mario (5); Joao (5), Joaquim (5), Paulo (5), Ademir, Albano, Almir, Amadeu, Conceicao, Heitor, Manoel, Marcio.

Morejon (328) Spanish (Morejón): probably from a derivative moro 'Moor' (Latin Maurus).
GIVEN NAMES Spanish 59%. Jose (11), Luis (9), Carlos (8), Juan (8), Raul (8), Jesus (5), Jorge (5), Pedro (5), Eduardo (4), Julio (4), Alberto (3), Francisco (3); Antonio (6), Lorenzo (2), Elio, Guido, Leonardo, Rosaria, Sal, Silvio.

Morel (1474) **1.** French, Occitan, Catalan, and English: from the medieval personal name Morel, a diminutive vernacular form of Latin Maurus (see MOORE 3), with the hypocoristic suffix -el. Compare MORRELL. **2.** German: from the personal name and saint's name Maurelius.
GIVEN NAMES Spanish 12%; French 9%. Jose (8), Ana (7), Luis (5), Francisco (4), Juana (4), Rafael (4), Ramon (4), Jorge (3), Juan (3), Julio (3), Miguel (3), Pedro (3); Armand (4), Andre (2), Franck (2), Francois (2), Francoise (2), Marcel (2), Normand (2), Pierre (2), Alphonse, Benoit, Camille, Cecile.

Morelan (118) Variant of Scottish and English MORELAND.

Moreland (6082) Scottish and northern English: habitational name from any of various places, notably in the Borders region

and in Kinross, named Moreland, from Old English mōr 'marsh', 'fen', 'moor' + land 'land'.

Morell (1180) **1.** English: variant spelling of MORRELL or MOREL. **2.** Catalan: habitational name from any of several places called Morell in Tarragona and Girona provinces or Majorca and Minorca Islands, from a vernacular form of Latin Maurellus 'dark-skinned', diminutive of Maurus 'Moor'.
GIVEN NAMES Spanish 9%. Jose (7), Jorge (5), Armando (3), Gerardo (3), Angel (2), Carolina (2), Elba (2), Francisco (2), Justo (2), Manuel (2), Miguel (2), Modesto (2).

Morella (212) Italian: **1.** from a feminine form of the personal name MORELLO. **2.** topographic name for someone who lived where brambles grew, from Old Sicilian morella, Sicilian mureddha 'blackberry'. **Morellas** is also found as a Greek family name.
GIVEN NAMES Italian 12%. Giovanni (2), Prisco (2), Cono, Raffaele, Reno, Salvatore, Silvano, Vito.

Morelli (2321) Italian: patronymic or plural form of MORELLO.
GIVEN NAMES Italian 14%. Angelo (11), Antonio (10), Aldo (6), Luigi (5), Remo (5), Carmine (4), Rocco (4), Salvatore (4), Domenic (3), Gino (3), Dino (2), Domenico (2).

Morello (1129) Southern Italian: **1.** from a pet form or diminutive of MORO. **2.** from a short form of **Amorello**, from a pet form of the personal name Amore (from a term of endearment meaning 'love').
GIVEN NAMES Italian 15%. Salvatore (10), Angelo (6), Antonio (3), Gaetano (3), Rocco (3), Carmela (2), Carmine (2), Cesare (2), Filippo (2), Luciano (2), Silvio (2), Aldo.

Morelock (880) Americanized spelling of German MORLOCK.

Morelos (190) Spanish: habitational name from any of various places called Morelos, including one in Mexico that gave its name to a state of Mexico.
GIVEN NAMES Spanish 45%. Jose (8), Alfredo (2), Luis (2), Rafael (2), Ramon (2), Ricardo (2), Adelina, Alejandro, Amalia, Anel, Angel, Carlos.

Moreman (155) **1.** Scottish and English: variant of MOORMAN. **2.** Dutch: variant of MOERMAN 1 and 2.

Moren (479) **1.** Dutch: from a pet form of a Germanic compound personal name formed with Maur-, Mor-, meaning 'Moor' as the first element. **2.** Swedish (Morén): probably an ornamental name composed of the place name element mor 'copse', 'marshy wood' + the adjectival suffix -én, a derivative of Latin -enius.

Morena (201) **1.** Spanish: shortened form of **De la Morena**, which either refers to the Sierra Morena, or is a matronymic from a feminine form of a nickname from moreno

'brown'. Compare MORENO. **2.** Southern Italian: from a feminine form of MORENO.
GIVEN NAMES Spanish 16%; Italian 11%. *Jose* (2), *Alejandro, Buenaventura, Carmella, Cesar, Diego, Gerardo, Guadalupe, Juan, Leticia, Lucila, Manuel*; *Gino* (2), *Alfonse, Angelo, Carmelo, Clementina, Donato, Giovanna, Rocco, Salvatore.*

Morency (580) French: perhaps a shortened form of **Montmorency**, a habitational name from a place so named in Val-d'Oise; or an altered spelling of **Morancé**, a habitational name from Morencé in Rhône, named in Latin as *Maurentiacum*, from the personal name *Maurentius* + suffix *-acum*.
GIVEN NAMES French 16%. *Fernand* (3), *Gisele* (2), *Jacques* (2), *Laurent* (2), *Normand* (2), *Adrien, Amedee, Armand, Auguste, Carmelle, Cecile, Chantale.*

Moreno (17556) Spanish, Portuguese, and Jewish (Sephardic): nickname for someone with dark hair and a swarthy complexion, from Spanish and Portuguese *moreno* 'dark-haired', a word of uncertain origin, probably from Late Latin *maurinus*, a derivative of classical Latin *Maurus* 'Moor'. Compare MOORE 2.
GIVEN NAMES Spanish 46%; Portuguese 10%. *Jose* (425), *Juan* (220), *Manuel* (178), *Luis* (156), *Carlos* (152), *Jesus* (141), *Mario* (138), *Jorge* (102), *Miguel* (100), *Francisco* (99), *Ruben* (96), *Raul* (83); *Gonsalo* (2), *Ligia* (2), *Omero, Vasco.*

Morenz (133) Of German origin: unexplained.

Morera (183) Spanish and Catalan: habitational name from a place called Morera or La Morera, especially Morera in Badajoz province, or La Morera de Montsant in Catalonia, named with Spanish and Catalan *morera* 'mulberry tree'.
GIVEN NAMES Spanish 52%. *Angel* (5), *Jose* (5), *Luis* (5), *Juan* (4), *Carlos* (3), *Jorge* (3), *Julio* (3), *Justo* (3), *Manuel* (3), *Miguel* (2), *Alberto, Alfredo*; *Antonio, Carlo, Elio.*

Mores (140) **1.** English: variant of MOORES. **2.** Dutch: from the personal name *Maurits* (see MORRIS).

Moreschi (122) Italian: from the plural of *moresco* 'Moorish'.
GIVEN NAMES Italian 9%. *Ettore, Pasquale.*

Moresco (158) Italian **1.** (**Morésco**) from a medieval personal name or a nickname for someone from North Africa or a swarthy or dark-haired person, from medieval Latin *Mauriscus* 'Moor' (see MOORE 2). **2.** habitational name from Moresco in Ascoli Piceno province.
GIVEN NAMES Italian 11%. *Primo* (2), *Gino, Luciano, Riccardo.*

Moresi (141) Italian (**Morési**): possibly patronymic or plural form of *morese*, an ethnic name for a Moor.
GIVEN NAMES Italian 6%. *Angelo* (3), *Dante, Ezio.*

Moret (336) French: nickname from a diminutive of MORE 4 or 5.

GIVEN NAMES French 6%. *Lucien* (2), *Andre, Marcel, Pascal, Remy.*

Moreton (286) **1.** English: variant spelling of MORTON 1. **2.** French: nickname from a double diminutive of MORE 2. **3.** Spanish (**Moretón**): from *moretón* 'brown', 'tanned' (of skin).

Moretti (1376) Italian: patronymic or plural form of MORETTO.
GIVEN NAMES Italian 12%. *Angelo* (7), *Aldo* (3), *Dante* (3), *Dino* (3), *Enrico* (3), *Guido* (3), *Marco* (3), *Antonio* (2), *Carmela* (2), *Marino* (2), *Massimo* (2), *Natale* (2).

Moretto (246) Italian: from a pet form or diminutive of the medieval personal name and nickname MORO.
GIVEN NAMES Italian 11%. *Angelo* (2), *Julio* (2), *Alberto, Albino, Antonio, Enzo, Fiore, Gino, Gustavo, Luciano, Mario, Martino, Rocco.*

Moretz (687) German and Dutch: variant of MORITZ.

Morey (4058) **1.** Irish: Anglicized form of Gaelic **Ó Mórdha** (see MOORE). **2.** English (of Norman origin): from the Old French personal name *Mory*, a short form of *Amaury* (see EMERY).

Morfin (269) English and French: unexplained; possibly a variant of **Morfey**, an unflattering nickname meaning 'cursed', 'ill-omened', 'ill-fated', Medieval Latin *malefatus*. This surname is also established in Mexico.
GIVEN NAMES Spanish 51%. *Jose* (5), *Francisco* (4), *Angel* (3), *Elena* (3), *Jaime* (3), *Javier* (3), *Jesus* (3), *Juan* (3), *Manuel* (3), *Rafael* (3), *Ramon* (3), *Ruben* (3).

Morfitt (106) English: variant of **Moorfoot**, a topographic name for someone who lived 'at the foot of the moor'.

Morford (1156) English (Kent): apparently a habitational name from a lost or unidentified place, but possibly a variant of **Moorfoot** (see MORFITT).

Morga (137) **1.** Spanish: habitational name from Morga in Biscay province. **2.** Italian: from the Salento dialect word *morga* 'marc (of olives)', 'dregs', possibly applied as a derogatory nickname. **3.** Polish: from *morga*, a term denoting a unit of land measuring 5,600 square meters, hence a nickname for a wealthy landowner.
GIVEN NAMES Spanish 35%; Italian 10%. *Alfredo* (3), *Angel* (2), *Francisco* (2), *Jesus* (2), *Jose* (2), *Aida, Ana, Andres, Anselmo, Araceli, Benito, Carlos*; *Antonio* (3), *Carmine* (2), *Pasquale.*

Morgado (308) Portuguese and Spanish: distinguishing name for the eldest son of a family, from Portuguese *morgado* 'first-born', 'heir', Late Latin *maioricatus*, a derivative of *maior* (see MAYOR 2).
GIVEN NAMES Spanish 37%; Portuguese 13%. *Manuel* (12), *Jose* (7), *Carlos* (5), *Abilio* (3), *Acacio* (3), *Armando* (3), *Mario* (3), *Edmundo* (2), *Eduardo* (2), *Miguel* (2), *Adolfo, Alejandra*; *Henrique.*

Morgan (97713) **1.** Welsh: from the Old Welsh personal name *Morcant*, which is of uncertain but ancient etymology. **2.** Irish: importation of the Welsh surname, to which has been assimilated more than one Gaelic surname, notably **Ó Muireagáin** (see MERRIGAN). **3.** Scottish: of uncertain origin; probably from a Gaelic personal name cognate with Welsh *Morcant*.
FOREBEARS Morgan is one of the oldest and commonest of Welsh surnames, but there is also a Scottish family called Morgan, established from medieval times in Aberdeenshire, with connections with the McKays. The Scottish name is probably not the result of Welsh migration, but was established independently. Abel Morgan (1673–1722), a baptist clergyman, was born in Cardiganshire, South Wales, and emigrated to Philadelphia in 1712, establishing churches in PA, DE, and NJ.

Morganelli (121) Italian: unexplained; possibly from a derivative of the personal name *Morgana*.

Morgano (151) Italian: **1.** masculinized form of **Morgana**, from a female personal name of Celtic origin, which was widespread throughout the medieval world as a result of the Arthurian romances. **2.** habitational name from a place so named in Treviso province.
GIVEN NAMES Italian 23%. *Salvatore* (3), *Biagio* (2), *Vito* (2), *Amedio, Angelo, Carlo, Carmelo, Carmine, Dante.*

Morgans (200) Welsh: variant of MORGAN, with the addition of English patronymic *-s*.

Morganstein (134) Jewish (Ashkenazic): **1.** altered form of MORGENSTERN. **2.** ornamental name compound from German *Morgen* 'morning' + *Stein* 'stone'.
GIVEN NAME Jewish 4%. *Morry.*

Morganstern (178) Jewish: variant of MORGENSTERN.
GIVEN NAME Jewish 4%. *Moshe.*

Morgante (180) Italian: from Old Italian *Morgante*, Old French *Morgant* (in medieval French an adjective meaning 'proud', 'scornful'), the name of a giant in a poem by Pulci.
GIVEN NAMES Italian 16%; French 5%. *Alessandro, Angelo, Calogero, Chiara, Donato, Elio, Enzo, Gino, Guiseppe, Mino, Nazzareno, Nino*; *Armand, Prosper.*

Morganti (371) Italian: patronymic form of MORGANTE.
GIVEN NAMES Italian 12%. *Angelo* (6), *Sal* (2), *Alessandra, Cesare, Dino, Egidio, Marco, Rocco, Romeo, Sandro.*

Morgart (163) Origin unidentified. It occurs chiefly in PA.

Morgen (284) German, Dutch, and Danish: **1.** topographic name from Middle High German, Middle Dutch *morgen* (literally 'morning'), a measurement of land representing an area that could be plowed in one morning (approximately one acre). **2.** from a German personal name of uncertain origin. It is not known as a personal name in Scandinavia, but it could possibly be a Germanization or Americanization of Danish *Mogens* (see MAGNUS).

Morgenroth (257) **1.** German: nickname for an early riser, from Middle High German *morgenrōt* 'sunrise', 'dawn' (literally 'morning red'). **2.** Jewish (Ashkenazic): from German *Morgenrot* 'dawn', one of the ornamental names taken from words referring to natural phenomena.

Morgensen (122) Danish, Norwegian, and North German: of uncertain derivation; apparently from a personal name *Morgen*, although no such personal name exists in Scandinavia. Compare MORGEN.

Morgenstein (142) Jewish (Ashkenazic): **1.** altered form of MORGENSTERN. **2.** ornamental name compound from German *Morgen* 'morning' + *Stein* 'stone'.
GIVEN NAMES Jewish 5%. *Fishel, Zinaida.*

Morgenstern (1131) **1.** Jewish (Ashkenazic): from German *Morgenstern* 'morning star', Yiddish *morgn-shtern*, one of the Jewish ornamental names taken from natural phenomena. **2.** German: habitational name for someone living at a house distinguished by a sign depicting the morning star, Middle High German *morgensterne*.
GIVEN NAMES Jewish 8%. *Hyman* (4), *Amrom* (2), *Dvora* (2), *Mendel* (2), *Miriam* (2), *Moshe* (2), *Pincus* (2), *Shlomo* (2), *Shmuel* (2), *Sol* (2), *Basya, Dov.*

Morgenthaler (294) German: variant of MERGENTHALER, the first element having been transformed by folk etymology to *Morgen* 'morning'.
GIVEN NAMES German 4%. *Erwin* (2), *Hans, Inge, Willi.*

Morgese (108) Italian (Bari): habitational name of uncertain origin, possibly a variant of **Murghese**, denoting someone from Murga.
GIVEN NAMES Italian 19%. *Vito* (5), *Domenico.*

Morgeson (106) English: unexplained.

Morgillo (102) Italian: diminutive of **Morgia**, a variant of MURGIA.
GIVEN NAMES Italian 23%. *Angelo* (2), *Carmela, Pietro, Salvatore, Vincenza.*

Morgret (115) Origin uncertain. Perhaps an altered form of French **Maigret**, a nickname from a diminutive of *maigre* 'thin'.

Mori (1262) **1.** Japanese: variously written, but most often with a character meaning 'forest', and denoting the sacred grove around a Shintō shrine. The character used to list the name in the Shinsen shōjiroku means 'guard' or 'keeper'. The name is mostly found in west-central Japan, the island of Shikoku, and in the Ryūkyū Islands. Another name, properly Romanized as **Mōri**, is written phonetically with the characters for 'hair' and 'advantage', but bearers of this name are also of the original Mori family. There were several daimyō families named Mōri, the greatest originating in Aki (now part of Hiroshima prefec-

ture). From their base in Chōshū (Nagato: now part of Yamaguchi prefecture), they ruled much of western Honshū in the 16th century, until restricted by Shōgun Tokugawa Ieyasu to Chōshū. **2.** Italian: patronymic form of MORO. **3.** German (**Möri**): from a pet form of the personal name *Morhart* (see MORATH). **4.** Hungarian (**Móri**): habitational name for someone from a place called Mór in Fejér county of Hungary. **5.** Hungarian: patronymic from the personal name *Mór*, from Latin *Maurus*.
GIVEN NAMES Japanese 41%. *Yoshiko* (7), *Takashi* (6), *Yasuo* (6), *Kiyoshi* (5), *Akira* (4), *Hiroshi* (4), *Nobuo* (4), *Akiko* (3), *Junko* (3), *Kazuo* (3), *Kenji* (3), *Masako* (3).

Moriarity (512) Irish: altered form of MORIARTY.
GIVEN NAME Irish 6%. *Brendan.*

Moriarty (4262) Irish (Kerry): shortened Anglicized form of Gaelic **Ó Muircheartaigh** 'descendant of *Muircheartach*', a personal name composed of the elements *muir* 'sea' + *ceardach* 'skilled', i.e. 'skilled navigator'. A Meath and Monaghan name of the same form is Anglicized as MURTAGH.
GIVEN NAMES Irish 7%. *Brendan* (5), *Liam* (2), *Seamus* (2), *Aidan, Bridie, Caitlin, Dermot, Fergus, Paddy.*

Morice (187) French and English: from the Old French personal name *Maurice* (see MORRIS).
GIVEN NAMES Italian 5%; Spanish 4%. *Salvatore* (4), *Mario, Rodolfo*; *Raul* (2), *Carlos, Jorge, Leticia, Rafael.*

Morici (233) **1.** Italian: patronymic form of the personal name *Maurice* (see MORRIS). **2.** Hungarian: patronymic form of the personal name *Móric*, Hungarian form of MORRIS. **3.** Hungarian: possibly a habitational name for someone from a place called Móric in Somogy county or in the Nagykunság.
GIVEN NAMES Italian 17%. *Salvatore* (4), *Antonio* (2), *Gasper* (2), *Aldo, Angelo, Annamarie, Elvio, Giuseppe, Sal, Santo, Vito.*

Moriconi (131) Italian: habitational name from Moricone, a place in Rome province.
GIVEN NAMES Italian 10%. *Rino* (2), *Alfio, Gianfranco, Luca, Marco, Silvio.*

Morie (105) **1.** Scottish spelling of Irish MOREY 1. **2.** English and French: from the personal name *Amaury* (see MOREY 2).

Morikawa (232) Japanese: 'forest river'; mostly found in western Japan and the island of Okinawa. One daimyō family of Owari (now part of Aichi prefecture) descended from the MINAMOTO clan through the SASAKI.
GIVEN NAMES Japanese 51%. *Hideo* (3), *Hiroshi* (3), *Eiji* (2), *Minoru* (2), *Sumiko* (2), *Yoshito* (2), *Akemi, Akihiro, Akiko, Akira, Chie, Chiyo.*

Morillo (292) Spanish: habitational name from Morillo de Monclús in Uesca province, from a diminutive of *moro* 'Moor'.
GIVEN NAMES Spanish 48%. *Jose* (11), *Carlos* (5), *Juan* (5), *Manuel* (5), *Ana* (4), *Cesar* (4), *Arturo* (3), *Ademar* (2), *Belkys* (2), *Camilo* (2), *Estela* (2), *Juana* (2).

Morimoto (487) Japanese: '(one who lives) near the forest', or '(one who is) from the forest'; mostly found in western Japan and the island of Okinawa. A family of Settsu (now part of Hyōgo prefecture) descended from the Ono family, while another of Kai (now Yamanashi prefecture) descended from the MINAMOTO clan through the TAKEDA.
GIVEN NAMES Japanese 50%. *Hiroshi* (6), *Akira* (3), *Isamu* (3), *Hitoshi* (2), *Kaz* (2), *Kiyoshi* (2), *Kunio* (2), *Masaharu* (2), *Masao* (2), *Naoki* (2), *Nobuyuki* (2), *Satoshi* (2).

Morin (9659) **1.** English and French: from a diminutive of the medieval nickname and personal name *More* (see MOORE). **2.** Italian: Venetian variant of MORINI. **3.** Spanish (**Morín**): possibly a derivative of MORO. **4.** Dutch: from a short pet form of a Germanic compound personal name beginning with *Maur-, Mor-* (see MORE 4).
GIVEN NAMES French 11%. *Armand* (29), *Marcel* (20), *Lucien* (19), *Emile* (18), *Pierre* (15), *Andre* (14), *Normand* (14), *Gilles* (13), *Jacques* (11), *Fernand* (10), *Adrien* (9), *Gaetan* (6).

Morine (196) Japanese: 'forest root' or 'prosperous root'; from the island of Okinawa.

Moring (539) **1.** English: from a diminutive of MOORE 2, 3. **2.** North German (**Möring**): patronymic from the nickname *Mohr* (see MOHR 2). **3.** North German (**Möring**): habitational name from Möringen or Möhringen near Stendal and Stettin. **4.** Dutch: variant of MORIN.

Morini (196) Italian: patronymic or plural form of MORINO.
GIVEN NAMES Italian 25%. *Mario* (5), *Amedeo* (2), *Claudio* (2), *Modesto* (2), *Aldo, Angelo, Elio, Enrico, Ermando, Lino, Marta, Reno, Sal, Silvio, Tonino.*

Morino (128) **1.** Italian: from a pet form of the medieval personal name and nickname *Moro*, meaning 'Moor' (see MOORE 2). **2.** Spanish: probably from the Latin personal name *Maurinus*. **3.** Japanese: meaning 'forest field'; the name is not common in Japan.
GIVEN NAMES Japanese 21%; Spanish 7%; Italian 6%. *Kimiko* (2), *Akihito, Fumio, Kasumi, Koki, Makoto, Masanobu, Takashi, Toyoko, Yasuhiro, Yoko, Yoshio*; *Alfonso, Alphonso, Juan, Luis, Mariano, Mario, Miguel, Pedro*; *Alessandro, Angelo, Lucio.*

Morioka (162) Japanese: 'forest hill'; mostly found in western Japan and the island of

Okinawa. One family of Satsuma (now Kagoshima prefecture) was samurai. A few bearers may have taken the name of the city of Morioka, in Iwate prefecture in the far north, which is written with characters meaning 'prosperous hill'.

GIVEN NAMES Japanese 35%. *Makoto* (2), *Takashi* (2), *Asako, Haruko, Hideo, Hiroshi, Ichio, Isao, Katsuto, Kazuko, Keiko, Koji.*

Moris (233) **1.** English, Welsh, and Scottish: variant of MORRIS. **2.** Dutch and North German: variant of MORITZ. **3.** French: variant of MAURICE. **4.** Latvian: nickname for a dark person, from *Moris* 'Moor', 'Negro'. Compare Moore 2. **5.** Lithuanian: possibly a nickname from *morylfs* 'lazy person'.

Morisette (152) French: variant spelling of MORISSETTE.

GIVEN NAMES French 5%. *Adelore, Emile.*

Morishige (101) Japanese: written with characters meaning 'forest' and 'heavy'. This name is not common in Japan.

GIVEN NAMES Japanese 39%. *Noboru* (2), *Eiko, Fumiko, Haruo, Iwao, Juichi, Kaoru, Katsumi, Kazuaki, Nobuo, Sachi, Shinsuke.*

Morishita (139) Japanese: '(one who lives) below the forest'; mostly found in the Kyōto–Ōsaka region and the island of Okinawa.

GIVEN NAMES Japanese 62%. *Takao* (4), *Shigeo* (3), *Hisano* (2), *Kenichi* (2), *Koji* (2), *Akira, Ayumu, Hiroyuki, Hisashi, Joji, Kana, Katsumi.*

Morison (381) English and Scottish: patronymic from MORRIS.

Morisset (102) Variant spelling of French **Maurisset**, from a pet form of the personal name *Maurice* (see MORRIS).

GIVEN NAMES French 26%. *Jacques* (2), *Pierre* (2), *Camille, Edouard, Jean-Guy, Ulysse, Yvon.*

Morissette (379) North American French spelling of MORISSET.

GIVEN NAMES French 21%. *Armand* (3), *Fernand* (2), *Marcel* (2), *Alain, Andre, Cecile, Damien, Emile, Francois, Gaston, Henri, Herve.*

Morita (620) Japanese: rice paddy near the forest, a common place name, variously written. The surname is mostly found in western Japan and the Ryūkyū Islands.

GIVEN NAMES Japanese 57%. *Takeshi* (5), *Akio* (4), *Satoshi* (4), *Aki* (3), *Kazuo* (3), *Koichi* (3), *Masao* (3), *Shigeru* (3), *Tomoyo* (3), *Toshio* (3), *Hiroko* (2), *Hiroshi* (2).

Moritz (2585) German, Dutch, Danish and Jewish (Ashkenazic): from the personal name *Moritz*, a variant of *Mauritz* (see MORRIS). Among Jews it was sometimes assumed as a surname by bearers of the personal name MOSES, as the two names have some phonetic similarity.

GIVEN NAMES German 4%. *Hans* (5), *Erwin* (3), *Gerhard* (2), *Kurt* (2), *Berthold, Ewald,*

Friedrich, Fritz, Gunter, Juergen, Klaus, Manfred.

Moriyama (131) Japanese: usually written with characters meaning 'forest mountain' or 'protecting mountain'. The latter version could be taken from any of three widely scattered place names in Owari (now part of Aichi prefecture), Iwaki (now part of Fukushima prefecture), or Etchū (now Toyama prefecture). The 'forest mountain' version could be taken from even more numerous place names. Neither version is common as a surname in Japan; they are found mainly in the Ryūkyū Islands.

GIVEN NAMES Japanese 41%. *Takeshi* (2), *Hatsue, Hideki, Hidemi, Hiroko, Hisako, Katsu, Katsutoshi, Kazuo, Keiichiro, Masahiro, Masako.*

Mork (992) **1.** Danish (**Mørk**) and Swedish (**Mörk**): nickname for someone with dark hair or a swarthy complexion, from Danish *mørk*, Swedish *mörk* 'dark' (Old Norse *myrkr*, whence also the English word *murk(y)*). **2.** Norwegian: habitational name from any of about 20 farmsteads so named, from Old Norse *mǫrk* 'wood'.

GIVEN NAMES Scandinavian 6%. *Lars* (2), *Bent, Erik, Gudrun, Hjalmer, Jarl, Jorgen, Nils, Viggo.*

Morken (353) **1.** Norwegian: habitational name from any of numerous farmsteads so named, from the definite form of Old Norse *mǫrk* 'wood'. **2.** Irish: Anglicized form of Gaelic **Ó Murcháin** 'descendant of *Murchán*', a diminutive of the personal name *Murchadh* (see MURPHY).

GIVEN NAME Scandinavian 5%. *Knut* (2).

Morlan (875) Spanish (**Morlán**): habitational name from Santa María Morlán in the province of A Coruña.

Morland (309) **1.** Northern English and Scottish: variant spelling of MORELAND. **2.** Dutch: topographic name for someone living in an area of peat. **3.** Norwegian: habitational name from any of numerous farmsteads so called. The name has different origins according to its location; in all cases, the second element is from Old Norse *land* 'land'.

Morley (4254) **1.** English: habitational name from any of the various places called Morley (for example in Cheshire, Derbyshire, County Durham, Norfolk, and West Yorkshire), or Moreleigh in Devon, all of which are named from Old English *mōr* 'marsh', 'fen' + *lēah* 'woodland clearing'. **2.** Possibly an altered spelling of French **Morlet**, a nickname from a diminutive of Old French *mor* 'brown', 'dark' (from Latin *Maurus* 'Moor').

Morlock (897) German (Baden and Württemberg): nickname for someone with black hair, from Middle High German *mōr* 'Moor' + Early New High German *locke* 'lock (of hair)'.

GIVEN NAMES German 4%. *Dieter* (2), *Armin, Baerbel, Gerhardt, Hans, Kurt, Reinhold, Ute, Volker.*

Morman (893) **1.** Scottish and English: variant of MOORMAN. **2.** Variant of German MOHRMANN.

Mormann (132) German: variant of MOHRMANN.

Mormile (156) Southern Italian (Naples): possibly related to *Mormilis*, which is recorded as the name of an archbishop's palace.

GIVEN NAMES Italian 7%. *Angelo, Antonio, Carmine, Ettore.*

Mormino (154) Italian (Sicily): probably from a shortened pet form of *Gilormu*, a variant of the personal name *Girolamo* (see JEROME).

GIVEN NAMES Italian 11%. *Angelo, Carlo, Giacinto, Salvatore.*

Morneau (393) French: contracted form of *Morineau*, a double diminutive of MORE 2.

GIVEN NAMES French 17%. *Andre* (3), *Armand* (3), *Lucien* (3), *Adrien, Emile, Gaston, Gilles, Henri, Herve, Hilaire, Laurent, Napoleon.*

Morneault (274) French: variant spelling of MORNEAU.

GIVEN NAMES French 17%. *Adrien* (2), *Camille* (2), *Gaston* (2), *Rosaire* (2), *Armand, Cecile, Emile, Normand, Octave, Odile, Oneil, Remi.*

Morning (273) Translation of German MORGEN.

Morningstar (934) Jewish (American): English translation of MORGENSTERN.

Moro (701) **1.** Spanish: ethnic name from *moro* 'Moor'. **2.** Italian: variant of MAURO.

GIVEN NAMES Spanish 10%; Italian 8%. *Jose* (4), *Carlos* (3), *Mario* (3), *Alberto* (2), *Jorge* (2), *Lino* (2), *Luis* (2), *Luiz* (2), *Manuel* (2), *Ramiro* (2), *Adolfo, Aida; Angelo* (2), *Pino* (2), *Pio* (2), *Remo* (2), *Antonio, Ciro, Cosmo, Elio, Enrico, Geno, Giancarlo, Gino.*

Morocco (225) Italian: ethnic name for someone from Morocco, or a nickname for someone with some connection with Morocco. This name is common in Peru.

GIVEN NAME Italian 4%. *Salvatore.*

Moron (109) **1.** Spanish (**Morón**): habitational name from Morón de Almazán in Soria province or Morón de la Frontera in Seville. The former, and possibly the latter also, is probably named from Arabic *maurūr* 'hidden', from the past participle of *wárrà* 'to hide or bury'. **2.** Spanish (**Morón**): in some cases, from a derivative of *moro* 'Moor'. **3.** French: possibly from the old personal name *Maurone*. **4.** French: possibly in some cases a nickname from Old French *moron* 'dreamer'.

GIVEN NAMES Spanish 50%; French 5%. *Juan* (4), *Armando* (2), *Eduardo* (2), *Guadalupe* (2), *Miguel* (2), *Orlando* (2), *Adelaida, Adelfa, Blanca, Bonifacio, Carlos, Cesar; Jacques, Marcel.*

Morone (149) Italian: **1.** from an augmentative form of MORO. **2.** possibly a variant of MORRONE.

GIVEN NAMES Italian 5%. *Angelo, Pasquale.*

Morones (309) Spanish: possibly a habitational name from Los Morones in Granada province.

GIVEN NAMES Spanish 37%. *Jose* (8), *Mario* (5), *Juan* (4), *Manuel* (4), *Ricardo* (4), *Francisco* (3), *Gerardo* (3), *Javier* (3), *Jesus* (3), *Ruben* (3), *Trinidad* (3), *Luis* (2).

Moroney (935) Irish: Anglicized form of Gaelic **Ó Maolruanaidh** 'descendant of *Maolruanaidh*', a personal name meaning 'devotee of (Saint) *Ruanadh*' (see ROONEY).

GIVEN NAME Irish 7%. *Brendan* (2).

Morong (156) Americanized spelling of French MORON.

Moroni (245) Italian: patronymic from an augmentative of the personal name or nickname MORO.

GIVEN NAMES Italian 21%. *Aldo* (2), *Angelo* (2), *Armando* (2), *Graciela* (2), *Remo* (2), *Antonio, Carlo, Demetrio, Deno, Edgardo, Elio, Enrico, Enzo, Giulio, Luca, Osvaldo.*

Moros (140) **1.** Spanish: habitational name from Moros in Zaragoza province, so named from the plural of *moro* 'Moor', i.e. 'the place where the Moors live'. **2.** Greek: ethnic name for a Moor, from Greek *Moros* 'Moor'.

GIVEN NAMES Spanish 17%; Greek 5%. *Carlos* (4), *Alberto* (2), *Julio* (2), *Aida, Alejandro, Francisco, Jorge, Maria Elisa, Mercedes, Pedro, Rafael; Gerasimos, Stelios, Theodoros.*

Morosky (114) Germanized form of an eastern Slavic name based on the word *moroš* 'cloudberry' or possibly *m(o)roz* 'frost'.

Moroz (456) **1.** Ukrainian, Belorussian, Slovak, Polish, and Jewish (eastern Ashkenazic): nickname from the eastern Slavic word *m(o)roz* 'frost'. **2.** Romanian: from Russian *moroz* 'frost' or Bulgarian *moruza* 'grain'.

GIVEN NAMES Russian 8%; Jewish 5%; Polish 4%. *Galina* (2), *Lev* (2), *Mikhail* (2), *Vladimir* (2), *Aleksandr, Anatoliy, Asya, Boris, Dmitriy, Grigory, Iyla, Leonid; Inna, Khaim, Mariya, Rakhil, Yakov, Yuly; Danuta, Henryk, Krzysztof, Miroslawa, Piotr, Wasil.*

Morphew (537) English: **1.** descriptive nickname from Middle English *morphew* 'blemish', 'birthmark', from Italian *morfea*. **2.** According to Reaney, an Anglo-Norman French nickname from Old French *malfé, malfeü*, from Latin *malefatus, malefatutus* 'ill-fated', a derogatory term for a Saracen or the devil.

Morphis (458) Variant of Irish MURPHY.

Morphy (117) Irish: variant of MURPHY.

GIVEN NAMES Spanish 5%; Irish 4%. *Augusto, Jaime, Javier, Luis, Patricio; Donovan.*

Morquecho (104) Galician or Basque: unexplained.

GIVEN NAMES Spanish 50%. *Juan* (4), *Ruben* (3), *Francisco* (2), *Nieves* (2), *Adan, Alberto, Alejandro, Alfredo, Carlos, Cesar, Eduardo, Elicia.*

Morr (381) Perhaps an altered spelling of German MARR 3. It occurs chiefly in OH.

Morra (486) Italian (Campania): habitational name from any of numerous places called Morra, as for example Morra De Sanctis, formerly Morra Irpino.

GIVEN NAMES Italian 15%. *Antonio* (4), *Gino* (3), *Luciano* (3), *Pasquale* (3), *Rocco* (3), *Dino* (2), *Vincenzo* (2), *Angelo, Annamarie, Lorenzo, Lucio, Luigi.*

Morrall (158) English: **1.** variant spelling of MORRELL. **2.** topographic name for someone living at a hall or large house on a moor, from Middle English *more* 'moor', 'marsh', 'fen' + *halle* 'hall'.

GIVEN NAMES French 4%. *Andre, Vernice.*

Morreale (829) Italian (Sicily): variant of **Monreale**, a habitational name from Monreale near Palermo, Sicily, so named from *monte regale* 'regal mountain'.

GIVEN NAMES Italian 12%. *Salvatore* (11), *Antonio* (6), *Angelo* (3), *Sal* (2), *Antonino, Carmel, Carmine, Franco, Gaetano, Gilda, Giuseppe, Santo.*

Morrell (4099) English: from the medieval personal name *Morel*, a diminutive vernacular form of Latin *Maurus* (see MOORE 3), with the hypocoristic suffix *-el*.

Morren (226) **1.** English: from a diminutive of MOORE 2 or 3. **2.** English: from an unattested Old English personal name, *Mōrwine*. **3.** Dutch: nickname for a grumbler, from Middle Dutch *murren, morren* 'to grumble or growl'.

Morrey (109) English: variant of MOREY 2.

Morrical (232) Probably a respelling of French *Marical* or **Marécal** (see MARICLE). It occurs chiefly in IL and IN.

Morrice (113) Mainly Scottish: variant spelling of MORRIS.

Morrill (3304) English: variant spelling of MORRELL.

Morrin (316) English: from a diminutive of MOORE 2 or 3.

GIVEN NAME Irish 5%. *Dermot.*

Morris (110158) **1.** English and Scottish: from *Maurice*, an Old French personal name introduced to Britain by the Normans, Latin *Mauritius*, a derivative of *Maurus* (see MOORE). This was the name of several early Christian saints. In some cases it may be a nickname of the same derivation for someone with a swarthy complexion. **2.** Irish: Anglicized form of Gaelic **Ó Muirghis**, a variant of **Ó Muirgheasa** (see MORRISSEY). **3.** Welsh: Anglicized form of the Welsh personal name *Meurig* (from Latin *Mauritius*), which was gradually superseded in Wales by *Morus, Morys*, a derivative of the Anglo-Norman French form of the name (see 1). **4.** German: variant of

MORITZ. **5.** Americanized form of any of various like-sounding Jewish surnames (see MORSE).

FOREBEARS Morris was the name of an extensive and powerful family in colonial North America, whose members played a leading part in the emergence of the nation. They were descended from Richard Morris (d. 1672), who fought in Oliver Cromwell's army and then became a merchant in Barbados. His son Lewis (1671–1746) established the "manor" of Morrisania in NY. His grandson, Lewis (1726–98), third owner of that manor, was a signer of the Declaration of Independence. Two other grandsons, Richard and Gouverneur, were also key figures in the Revolution. Their half-brother Staats Morris (1728–1800) was a general in the British army who was appointed governor of Quebec. Another signer of the Declaration, Robert Morris (1734–1806), had emigrated to America from Liverpool at the age of 13. He became known as the "Financier of the Revolution" and was the founder of the Bank of North America. Despite his reputation, he was personally ruined by unwise (or unfortunate) speculation.

Morrisett (122) Variant spelling of French MORISSET.

Morrisette (386) Variant spelling of French MORISSET.

GIVEN NAMES French 4%. *Gaetan, Laurette, Lucien, Yvon.*

Morrisey (630) Irish: variant spelling of MORRISSEY.

Morrish (209) English (Devon): variant of MORRIS 1.

Morrison (44572) Scottish: patronymic from the personal name MORRIS.

Morrisroe (170) Irish (County Roscommon): Anglicized form of Gaelic **Mac Muiris Rua** 'son of red Morris' (see MORRIS 2).

Morriss (633) English: variant spelling of MORRIS 1.

Morrissette (1167) Canadian spelling of French MORISSET, from a pet form of the personal name *Morisse* (see MORRIS 1).

GIVEN NAMES French 10%. *Normand* (6), *Lucien* (3), *Jacques* (2), *Pierre* (2), *Alain, Andre, Anselme, Armand, Donat, Fernand, Germaine, Gilles.*

Morrissey (5764) Irish: Americanized form of **Ó Muirgheasa** 'descendant of *Muirgheas*', a personal name apparently derived from *muir* 'sea' + *geas* 'taboo', 'prohibition'. However, according to MacLysaght, this surname is also derived from the Norman name *de Marisco*.

GIVEN NAMES Irish 5%. *Donal* (3), *Aileen, Clodagh, Cormac, Declan, Fergus, James Patrick, John Patrick, Liam, Malachy, Paddy.*

Morrisson (129) English: variant spelling of MORRISON.

GIVEN NAME French 6%. *Clovis* (2).

Morro (186) **1.** Spanish: nickname for someone with a prominent nose or lips, from *morro* 'snout'. **2.** Spanish and Italian: topographic name from *morro* in the sense 'hill'.
GIVEN NAMES Italian 8%. *Angelo* (2), *Rocco* (2), *Carmela*.

Morrone (870) Southern Italian: habitational name from Morrone del Sannio in Campobasso, named with a pre-Latin term *murro* 'stone', 'rock'.
GIVEN NAMES Italian 22%. *Mario* (7), *Amedeo* (4), *Emilio* (4), *Sal* (3), *Carmelo* (2), *Amerigo, Angelo, Annamarie, Antonio, Augusto, Aurelio, Caesar, Carlo, Carmine, Claudio, Cristino, Domenic, Egidio, Roberto, Rosario.*

Morrow (20634) Irish: shortened Anglicized form of Gaelic **Mac Murchadha** (see McMorrow).

Morsch (239) German: **1.** (also **Mörsch**) topographic name for someone living near a bog, from an adjectival derivative of German *Moor* (Middle Low German *mōr*) 'swamp', or a habitational name from places called Mörsch in Baden and the Palatinate. **2.** variant of MARSCH. **3.** variant of MURSCH.

Morse (17258) **1.** Welsh and English: variant of MORRIS. **2.** Americanized form of any of various like-sounding Jewish surnames, especially MOSES. Compare MORRIS.
FOREBEARS Samuel Morse (1791–1872), inventor of the electric telegraph and of Morse code, was a direct descendant of Anthony Morse of Wiltshire, England, who had emigrated to MA in 1635.

Morsey (105) Irish: probably a reduced form of MORRISSEY.
GIVEN NAME French 6%. *Marcelle*.

Morson (166) English: patronymic from MORSE?

Morss (229) English: variant of MORRIS 1.

Morstad (129) Norwegian: habitational name from farmsteads in eastern Norway named Morstad, from an unexplained first element (possibly a personal name) + *staðir*, plural of *staðr* 'farmstead', 'dwelling', or Mørstad, probably from Old Norse *maurr* 'ant' + *staðir*.
GIVEN NAME Scandinavian 5%. *Erik*.

Mort (922) **1.** English (Lancashire): of uncertain origin. The most plausible suggestion is that it is a Norman nickname from Old French *mort* 'dead' (Latin *mortuus*), presumably referring to a person of deathly pallor or unnaturally still countenance, or possibly to someone who played the part of death in a pageant. However, it could also be the result of survival into the Middle English period of an Old English personal name, *Morta*, or an Old English vocabulary word *mort* 'young salmon or trout', both postulated by Ekwall to explain various place names (see for example MORCOM). **2.** French: either a nickname from Old

French *mort* 'dead' (see above), or an alteration, by folk etymology, of the personal name *Mor(e)* (see MOORE 3).

Mortara (101) Italian: habitational name from Mortara in Pavia province (Lombardy).

Mortell (295) Irish (of Norman origin): from the Latin nickname *Martellus* or its Old French derivative *Martel* 'hammer'. In Ireland, this surname is found in counties Tipperary, Limerick, and Cork.

Mortellaro (179) Italian: occupational name for a seller of myrtle berries, which in the medieval period were used in tanning.
GIVEN NAMES Italian 17%. *Angelo* (2), *Carlo* (2), *Antonino, Gasper, Gerlando, Ignazio, Santo.*

Morten (201) English (of Norman origin): habitational name from Mortagne in La Manche, France. This surname may have been sometimes confused with MORTON.

Mortensen (3882) Danish and Norwegian, Dutch, and North German: patronymic from the personal name *Morten* (see MARTIN 1).
GIVEN NAMES Scandinavian 6%. *Erik* (10), *Niels* (7), *Lars* (3), *Morten* (3), *Einer* (2), *Jorgen* (2), *Bent, Britt, Carsten, Egil, Gunner, Hartvig.*

Mortenson (1741) Americanized spelling of Swedish **Mårtensson** or Danish and Norwegian MORTENSEN, patronymics from Scandinavian forms of the personal name MARTIN.

Morter (211) Catalan: topographic name for someone who lived by a gully, or perhaps an occupational name for an alchemist or seller of spices (from *morter* 'mortar', from Latin *mortarium* 'mortar').

Morthland (114) Scottish: habitational name of uncertain origin. Black tentatively derives it from a place called Merchland, near Eglinton, now lost.

Mortier (165) French: **1.** from Old French *mortier* 'mortar', perhaps an occupational name for an alchemist or spicer, or perhaps derived from a house sign. **2.** habitational name from various places in France and Belgium, called Mortiers, for example, in Aisne and Charente-Maritime in France, or Mortier, for example, in the Belgian province of Liège.
GIVEN NAME French 4%. *Emile*.

Mortillaro (107) Italian: possibly a variant of MORTELLARO or a habitational name from a place called Mortillaro.
GIVEN NAMES Italian 21%. *Gino* (2), *Santo* (2), *Enzo, Sal, Vito.*

Mortimer (2122) English, Welsh, Scottish, and Irish (of Norman origin): habitational name from Mortemer in Seine-Maritime, France, so called from Old French *mort(e)* 'dead' + *mer* 'sea' (Latin *mare*). The place name probably referred to a stagnant pond or partly drained swamp; there may also have been an allusion to the Biblical Dead Sea seen by crusaders. The Norman sur-

name was taken to Ireland from England in the medieval period, where it has also been adopted by bearers of the Gaelic surnames **Mac Muircheartaigh** and **ÓMuircheartaigh**, commonly Anglicized as **McMurty** and **Mortagh**. Compare McMurdo.

Mortimore (336) English (Devon): variant of MORTIMER.

Mortland (185) Scottish: variant of MORTHLAND.

Morton (22291) **1.** English and Scottish: habitational name from any of the many places called Mor(e)ton, named in Old English as 'settlement (*tūn*) by or on a marsh or moor (*mōr*)'. **2.** Swedish: variant of MARTIN. **3.** French: contracted form of MORETON 2. **4.** Americanized form of one or more like-sounding Jewish surnames or of various other non-English names bearing some kind of similarity to it.
FOREBEARS The name Morton was established early in North America. George Morton (1585–1624), one of the Pilgrims, was probably born in Scrooby, Nottinghamshire, England. He and his son Nathaniel (b. 1613 in Leiden, the Netherlands) settled in Plymouth in 1623. John Morton (c.1724–77), one of the signers of the Declaration of Independence, was born in PA, of Swedish descent. His grandfather, Morten Mortenson, had emigrated from Gothenburg in 1654.

Morua (110) Spanish (of Basque origin): Castilinanized form of the Basque topographic name *Murua*, from *muru* 'crag' + the definite article *-a*
GIVEN NAMES Spanish 42%. *Domingo* (3), *Alfredo* (2), *Armando* (2), *Esteban* (2), *Juan* (2), *Lupe* (2), *Manuel* (2), *Ramon* (2), *Alejandra, Artemio, Carlos, Ernesto; Antonio, Cecilio, Lorenzo.*

Morvan (111) French: **1.** regional name for someone from Morvan in Burgundy. **2.** from the old Breton personal name *Morvan*.
GIVEN NAMES French 19%. *Yves* (2), *Arnaud, Christophe, Guillaume, Jacques, Jean Claude, Lucienne.*

Morvant (514) Breton: from an old personal name, known from the 10th century on, which Morlet suggests may be an altered form of the Old Breton personal name *Morman* (also known from 10th-century records). *Morman* is probably composed of Breton *mor* 'sea', or 'great', + *man* 'thought'.
GIVEN NAMES French 8%. *Antoine* (2), *Irby* (2), *Numa* (2), *Ulysse* (2), *Camille, Felicie, Raoul.*

Morvay (131) Hungarian: regional name for someone from Moravia, or a habitational name for someone from a village called Morva in Zemplén county.
GIVEN NAMES Hungarian 8%. *Gabor, Geza, Tibor, Zoltan.*

Morway (138) Variant of Hungarian MORVAY.

Mory (170) **1.** English: variant spelling of MOREY 2. **2.** French: topographic name from French *mûrier* 'mulberry tree', or a habitational name from Mouriez in Pas-de-Calais, or from Mourier in Villers-St-Paul, Oise. **3.** French: possibly a short form of AMORY, from the Germanic personal name *Amalric*.

GIVEN NAMES German 4%. *Claus, Fritz, Inge.*

Mosakowski (104) Polish: habitational name for someone from a place called Mosaki in Ciechanów voivodeship, named with the personal name *Mosak*, a pet form of various names beginning with *Mo-*, for example *Mojsław*.

GIVEN NAMES Polish 9%. *Henryk, Janusz, Witold.*

Mosbacher (140) German and Jewish (Ashkenazic): habitational name for someone from any of numerous places called Mo(o)sbach, named with Old High German *mos* 'peat bog' + *bach* 'stream'.

GIVEN NAMES Jewish 7%. *Moshe* (2), *Aryeh, Chaim, Gerson.*

Mosbrucker (198) South German: topographic name for someone who lived by a bridge over a swamp, from Middle High German *mos* 'bog', 'swamp' + *brucke* 'bridge'.

Mosby (1944) **1.** English (Yorkshire): habitational name, probably from Mosbrough in South Yorkshire, recorded in Domesday Book as *Moresburh*, from Old English *mōres*, genitive singular of *mōr* 'marsh', 'fen', 'moor' + *burh* 'fortress'. **2.** Norwegian: habitational name from any of several farmsteads in southern Norway, so named from Old Norse *mós* (genitive case of *mór* 'sandy plain') + *býr* 'farm'.

Mosca (843) Italian, Portuguese, and Spanish: nickname from Italian, Portuguese, and Spanish *mosca* 'fly' (from Latin *musca*), possibly denoting an annoying, importunate person.

GIVEN NAMES Italian 15%. *Antonio* (7), *Salvatore* (6), *Angelo* (5), *Domenic* (2), *Guido* (2), *Luca* (2), *Oreste* (2), *Rocco* (2), *Alfonse, Berardino, Carlo.*

Moscaritolo (100) Italian: unexplained.

GIVEN NAMES Italian 19%. *Rico* (3), *Angelo* (2), *Antonio, Grazio, Mario, Silvio.*

Moscatelli (136) Italian: patronymic or plural form of MUSCATELLO.

GIVEN NAMES Italian 14%. *Eligio, Ezio, Guiseppe, Oreste, Pasquale, Remo, Salvatore.*

Moscatello (118) Italian: variant of MUSCATELLO.

GIVEN NAMES Italian 16%. *Carmela, Carmine, Guido, Italo, Oresto, Salvatore.*

Moscato (435) **1.** Italian: variant of the personal name MUSCATO. **2.** Americanized spelling of Greek **Moskatos**, a metonymic occupational name for a grower of muscat grapes, a derivative of Greek *moskhos*, denoting fragrant, sweet-smelling grapes, or

wine made from such grapes, from *moskos* 'musk', from Persian *moshk* 'musk'.

GIVEN NAMES Italian 18%. *Angelo* (6), *Salvatore* (6), *Antonio* (3), *Sal* (2), *Vito* (2), *Amedeo, Aniello, Filomena, Gianni, Pasquale, Prisco, Vincenza.*

Mosch (102) German (also **Mösch**): **1.** variant of MESCH 1. **2.** (Westphalian) nickname from dialect *Mosch* 'sparrow'. **3.** variant of MARSCH.

GIVEN NAMES German 9%. *Hans* (2), *Klaus, Otto.*

Moschel (103) Jewish (Ashkenazic): from the Yiddish male personal name *Moshl*, a pet form of MOSES.

GIVEN NAME French 5%; Jewish 4%. *Sol.*

Moschella (386) Italian: nickname from a diminutive of MOSCA.

GIVEN NAMES Italian 14%. *Carmine* (5), *Sal* (3), *Angelo* (2), *Salvatore* (2), *Soccorso* (2), *Gilda, Rocco.*

Moschetti (257) Italian: patronymic or plural form of MOSCHETTO.

GIVEN NAMES Italian 10%. *Vito* (3), *Angelo* (2), *Rocco* (2), *Antonio, Dino, Gilda.*

Moschetto (126) Italian: nickname from a diminutive of MOSCA.

GIVEN NAMES Italian 7%. *Carmela, Salvatore.*

Moscinski (107) Polish: habitational name for someone from any of various places called Mosty, nmed with *most* 'bridge'.

GIVEN NAMES Polish 8%. *Casimir, Iwona, Kazimierz.*

Mosco (227) **1.** Italian and Spanish: from *mosco* 'mosquito', 'gnat', hence a nickname for a small, annoying, or persistent person. **2.** Americanized form of Greek **Moschos, Moskos**, from the personal name *Moskhos, Moskos* 'sweet-smelling', 'fragrant', from *moskhos* 'musk', from Persian *moshk* 'musk'. This name is also found in compounds such as *Moskogiannis* 'musky John', *Moskopoulos* 'musky Paul', *Moskolias* 'musky Elias'.

GIVEN NAMES Italian 6%. *Angelo* (2), *Marino, Sal, Salvatore, Sisto.*

Moscone (137) Italian: from an augmentative form of MOSCA.

GIVEN NAMES Italian 9%. *Antonio, Dante, Emidio, Giacomo, Marcello, Serafino.*

Mosconi (135) Italian: patronymic or plural form of MOSCONE.

GIVEN NAMES Italian 9%. *Aldo, Dario, Dino, Enrico.*

Moscoso (291) Spanish and Galician: habitational name from any of the places, mainly in Galicia, called Moscoso, named with an adjectival derivative of *mosca* 'fly', denoting a place where there were many flies.

GIVEN NAMES Spanish 45%; Portuguese 9%. *Manuel* (6), *Jose* (5), *Carlos* (4), *Ana* (3), *Cesar* (3), *Luis* (3), *Mario* (3), *Pedro* (3), *Eloy* (2), *Guillermo* (2), *Hernan* (2), *Jaime* (2); *Paulo.*

Moscowitz (122) Jewish (eastern Ashkenazic): variant spelling of MOSKOWITZ.

GIVEN NAMES Jewish 9%. *Hyman, Menachem.*

Mose (453) **1.** Italian (pronounced as two syllables): from the Biblical name *Mose*, Italian equivalent of MOSES. This surname is widespread in northern Italy, and is especially common Trieste and Venetia. **2.** Catalan (**Mosé**): from *Mossé*, Catalan and Occitan (southern France) form of the Biblical name MOSES. **3.** Danish: topographic name from *mose* 'swamp', 'bog'.

Moseby (103) **1.** English (Midlands): unexplained; perhaps a habitational name from a lost or unidentified place. **2.** Norwegian: habitational name from a farmstead in eastern Norway, named from *mos* '(bog) moss' + *by* 'farm'.

GIVEN NAMES Scandinavian 6%. *Erik, Morten.*

Mosel (210) German: **1.** habitational name from any of several places so named, of unexplained etymology. **2.** topographic name from the Mosel river in western Germany, a tributary of the Rhine that rises in the Vosges and flows through Lorraine and then a deep, winding valley from Trier to Koblenz.

Moseley (6760) English: variants MOSLEY. The form *Moseley* occurs mainly in the West Midlands.

Mosely (889) English: variants MOSLEY. The form *Moseley* occurs mainly in the West Midlands.

Moseman (377) German (**Mosemann**): variant of **Moosmann** (see MOOSMAN).

Moseng (113) Norwegian: habitational name from any of several farms named from *mos* 'moss' + *eng* 'meadow', 'pasture'.

GIVEN NAMES Scandinavian 8%. *Selmer* (2), *Helmer.*

Moser (11991) **1.** South German: topographic name for someone who lived near a peat bog, Middle High German *mos*, or a habitational name from a place named with this word. **2.** North German (**Möser**): metonymic occupational name for a vegetable grower or seller, from an agent noun based on Middle Low German *mōs* 'vegetable'.

Moses (11775) Jewish; also Welsh and English: from the Biblical name borne by the Israelite leader who led the Israelites out of Egypt, as related in the Book of Exodus. The Hebrew form of the name, *Moshe*, is probably of Egyptian origin, from a short form of any of various ancient Egyptian personal names, such as *Rameses* and *Tutmosis*, meaning 'conceived by (a certain god)'. However, very early in its history it acquired a folk etymology, being taken as a derivative of the Hebrew root verb *mšh* 'draw (something from the water)', and was associated with a story of the infant Moses being discovered among the bullrushes by Pharaoh's daughter (Exodus 2: 1–10). *Moses* is the usual English spelling. As a Welsh family name, it was adopted among Dissenter families in the 18th and 19th centuries. As a North American family name, it has absorbed forms of the name from other languages, for example MOISE and **Moshe**.

Mosey (271) English: from a vernacular form of the personal name MOSES.

Mosgrove (103) English: variant of MUS-GROVE.

Mosher (6191) **1.** English: unexplained. **2.** South German and Swiss German: unexplained.
FOREBEARS This name is said to be a variant of English **Moger** (the origin of which is likewise unexplained), and to have been brought from Somerset, England, to RI and ME in the mid 17th century.

Moshier (688) Variant of MOSHER.

Mosholder (104) Variant of German MOSS-HOLDER.

Mosier (3048) English: unexplained. Compare MOSHIER and MOSHER.

Mosiman (164) Swiss German (**Mosimann**): variant of MOSSMAN.

Moskal (757) Polish and Jewish (from Poland): ethnic name for a Muscovite, also used to refer to Russians in general (often with a slightly pejorative sense).
GIVEN NAMES Polish 6%. *Jozef* (3), *Arkadiusz* (2), *Wieslaw* (2), *Andrzej, Czeslawa, Jacek, Janina, Jozefa, Ludwika, Piotr, Stanislaw, Zofia.*

Mosko (247) Polish (**Mośko**), Ukrainian, Slovak (**Moško**), and Jewish (eastern Ashkenazic): from the personal name *Mosko*, a Slavic pet form of MOSES.

Moskovitz (306) Jewish (eastern Ashkenazic): variant of MOSKOWITZ.
GIVEN NAMES Jewish 9%. *Avi* (2), *Alter, Arie, Isadore, Myer, Reuven.*

Moskow (174) Shortened form of Jewish MOSKOWITZ.

Moskowitz (2500) Jewish (eastern Ashkenazic): Germanized form of a Slavic patronymic from the Yiddish personal name *Moshke*, a pet form of *Moshe* (see MOSES).
GIVEN NAMES Jewish 9%. *Hyman* (5), *Sol* (5), *Aron* (4), *Emanuel* (4), *Miriam* (4), *Ari* (3), *Moshe* (3), *Chana* (2), *Mendel* (2), *Mendy* (2), *Sholem* (2), *Aviva.*

Moskwa (123) Polish: habitational name from Moscow, Polish *Moskwa*; also used, with a slightly pejorative sense, as an ethnic name or a nickname for a Russian. Compare MOSKAL.
GIVEN NAMES Polish 6%. *Danuta, Zbigniew.*

Mosler (148) German: topographic name for someone who lived by the Mosel river (see MOSEL).
GIVEN NAMES German 8%. *Alois, Dieter, Gerhard, Heinz, Ingeborg.*

Mosley (11628) English (chiefly southern Yorkshire and Lancashire): habitational name from any of several places called Mos(e)ley in central, western, and northwestern England. The obvious derivation is from Old English *mos* 'peat bog' + *lēah*

'woodland clearing', but the one in southern Birmingham (*Museleie* in Domesday Book) had as its first element Old English *mūs* 'mouse', while one in Staffordshire (*Molesleie* in Domesday Book) had the genitive case of the Old English byname *Moll.*

Mosman (333) **1.** Scottish: variant of MOSSMAN. **2.** Swiss German (**Mosmann**): see MOSSMAN.

Mosner (115) German (**Mösner**): variant of MESSNER.

Mosqueda (688) Spanish: probably a nickname from a derivative of *mosca* 'fly' (see MOSCA).
GIVEN NAMES Spanish 48%; Portuguese 11%. *Jose* (27), *Manuel* (12), *Juan* (10), *Arturo* (8), *Francisco* (6), *Jesus* (6), *Alberto* (5), *Alicia* (5), *Raul* (5), *Ruben* (5), *Carlos* (4), *Eduardo* (4); *Gonsalo.*

Mosquera (374) **1.** Spanish: topographic name for someone who lived in a place that was infested with flies or mosquitos, from a derivative of *mosca* 'fly' (see MOSCA). **2.** Catalan: habitational name from any of the numerous places named *Mosquera* in Catalonia, Valencia and Andorra.
GIVEN NAMES Spanish 54%. *Carlos* (8), *Jose* (6), *Eduardo* (5), *Jorge* (5), *Juan* (5), *Luis* (5), *Manuel* (5), *Guillermo* (4), *Hernan* (4), *Jaime* (4), *Claudio* (3), *Hernando* (3).

Moss (26430) **1.** English and Welsh: from the personal name *Moss*, a Middle English vernacular form of the Biblical name MOSES. **2.** English and Scottish: topographic name for someone who lived by a peat bog, Middle English, Old English *mos*, or a habitational name from a place named with this word. (It was not until later that the vocabulary word came to denote the class of plants characteristic of a peat-bog habitat, under the influence of the related Old Norse word *mosi*.) **3.** Americanized form of MOSES or some other like-sounding Jewish surname. **4.** Irish (Ulster): part translation of Gaelic **Ó Maolmhóna** 'descendant of *Maolmhóna*', a personal name composed of the elements *maol* 'servant', 'tonsured one', 'devotee' + a second element which was assumed to be *móin* (genitive *móna*) 'moorland', 'peat bog'.

Mossa (137) Italian: perhaps a habitational name from Mossa in Gorizia province.
GIVEN NAMES Italian 17%. *Vito* (4), *Domenica* (2), *Francesco, Pasquale, Silvio; Manuel* (2), *Angelina, Josefina, Paola, Ramon.*

Mossbarger (196) Altered spelling of German **Mossberger**, a topographic name for someone who lived near a hill in a swampy area, from Middle High German *mos* 'swamp' + *berg* 'hill', 'mountain'.

Mossberg (221) **1.** Swedish: ornamental name composed of the elements *mosse* 'peat bog' + *berg* 'mountain', 'hill'. **2.** Jewish (Ashkenazic): ornamental exten-

sion of MOSES, with German *Berg* 'mountain', 'hill'.
GIVEN NAMES Scandinavian 10%; German 4%; Jewish 4%. *Sven* (2), *Bjorn, Ludvig; Bernhard* (2), *Kurt; Chaya, Herschel, Hyman.*

Mossburg (246) Possibly an altered spelling of MOSSBERG.

Mosser (967) German (also **Mösser**): occupational name for a producer or seller of must, i.e. unfermented grape juice, from an agent noun based on a dialect variant of German *Most* (see MOST).

Mossey (263) Possibly an altered form of the southeastern French surname **Mossé**, a form of MOSES.

Mossholder (126) German: altered spelling of **Massholder**, a topographic name meaning 'maple tree', from Middle High German *mazalter.*

Mossing (121) **1.** Norwegian: habitational name from a farm name in Trøndelag, probably named with *mose* 'moss' + *vin* 'meadow'. **2.** German and Dutch: habitational name, **Mössing**, from Mössingen in Baden-Württemberg.

Mossman (1004) **1.** Scottish and northern English: topographic name for a man who lived by a peat bog. **2.** German (**Mossmann**): occupational name for a producer or seller of must, i.e. unfermented grape juice, from an agent noun based on a dialect variant of German *Most* (see MOST). **3.** probably also a spelling variant of MASSMAN. **4.** Jewish (Ashkenazic): elaborated form of MOSES.

Mosso (189) **1.** Italian: of uncertain derivation; possibly from a shortened pet form of a personal name ending in *-mo*, such as ANSELMO, GIACOMO, or GUGLIELMO, or alternatively a habitational name from Mosso Santa Maria in Biella province. **2.** Catalan: occupational name from *mosso* 'young man', 'apprentice'. **3.** Spanish and Portuguese: variant from Spanish *mozo*, Portuguese *mọo* 'youth', 'young man', 'apprentice'.
GIVEN NAMES Italian 13%; Spanish 11%. *Pasquale* (4), *Nino* (2), *Vito* (2), *Bartolo, Nichola; Carlos* (2), *Francisa, Hipolito, Ignacio, Nestor, Rafael, Ramiro, Rey, Rosendo.*

Mossop (102) English (Cumbria): probably a habitational name from a lost or unidentified place.

Mossor (160) Variant of German MOSSER.

Most (735) **1.** German: metonymic occupational name for a producer or seller of must, i.e. unfermented grape juice, Middle High German *most* (Latin *mustum vinum* 'young (i.e. fresh) wine'). The same term was also used to denote perry and cider, since these do not keep well and need to be drunk while still fresh. **2.** Dutch: topographic name for someone who lived in a place where moss grew. Compare MOSS. **3.** Polish and Jewish (eastern Ashkenazic):

topographic name from Slavic *most* 'bridge', or habitational name from any of several places named with this word.

Mostad (123) Norwegian: habitational name from any of several farmsteads named with a personal name or Old Norse *mór* 'moor', 'sandy plain' + Old Norse *staðir*, plural of *staðr* 'farmstead', 'settlement'.

GIVEN NAMES Scandinavian 6%; German 4%. *Fredrik*; *Manfred*, *Orlo*.

Mostafa (154) Muslim: variant of MU-STAFA.

GIVEN NAMES Muslim 84%. *Mohammed* (7), *Mohamed* (5), *Ahmed* (4), *Ali* (4), *Mohammad* (4), *Hassan* (3), *Kamal* (3), *Mostafa* (3), *Samir* (3), *Amr* (2), *Ashraf* (2), *Begum* (2).

Mostek (181) Polish: topographic name from *mostek* 'little bridge'.

Mosteller (922) German: unexplained.
FOREBEARS Peter Masteller (born 1706) is recorded as an immigrant at the Port of Philadelphia, PA, in 1736.

Moster (157) Catalan: either a habitational name from Almoster in Tarragona, or an occupational name derived from *most* 'unfermented grape juice'.

Mostert (105) Dutch: occupational name for a grower or seller of mustard, from Middle Dutch *mostaert* (Old French *mo(u)starde*).

GIVEN NAMES Dutch 12%. *Pieter* (2), *Willem* (2), *Hendrik*.

Mostoller (196) Origin unidentified. Compare MOSTELLER.

Mostrom (163) **1.** Norwegian: habitational name from any of several farmsteads named Mostrøm, from Old Norse *mór* 'moor', 'sandy plain' + *strøm* 'current'. **2.** Probably Swedish (**Moström**): ornamental name with the same etymology as 1.
GIVEN NAME German 4%. *Kurt*.

Mostyn (142) Welsh: habitational name from Mostyn in North Wales. This surname was adopted by a 16th-century Lord of Mostyn, Thomas ap Richard ap Hywel, and his brother Piers.

Mota (1040) **1.** Spanish and Portuguese: topographic name for someone who lived by a fortified stronghold, from *mot(t)a*, a borrowing from Old French *motte* (see MOTTE 1). **2.** Spanish: habitational name from places in the provinces of Cuenca and Valladolid named Mota. **3.** Catalan: topographic name from *mota* 'hillock', denoting someone who lived by a hillock. **4.** Catalan: habitational name from places in Girona and Valencia.

GIVEN NAMES Spanish 52%; Portuguese 14%. *Jose* (49), *Luis* (21), *Carlos* (13), *Manuel* (13), *Juan* (9), *Rafael* (9), *Fernando* (8), *Pedro* (8), *Armando* (6), *Guillermo* (6), *Jesus* (6), *Agustin* (5); *Joao* (3), *Duarte* (2), *Agostinho*, *Guilherme*.

Mote (1530) French and English: variant of MOTTE 1.

Motel (102) French: topographic name from a derivative of Old French *motte* 'fortified stronghold' (see MOTTE).

Moten (819) Dutch: topographic name for someone who lived by a fortified stronghold, Middle Dutch *mote* (see MOTTE 1).

Motes (1136) Catalan: from the plural of *mota* 'hillock' (see MOTA). The name occurs chiefly in Valencia.

Mothersbaugh (106) Origin unidentified.

Mothershead (220) English: variant of **Mottershead** or **Mottishead**, a habitational name from a lost place in the parish of Mottram, Cheshire, recorded in the 13th century as *Mottresheved*, from the genitive case of the Old English byname *Mōtere* 'speaker' + Middle English *heved* 'head(land)', 'hill'.

Mothershed (260) English: variant of MOTHERSHEAD.

Motil (121) **1.** Variant of German MOTL. **2.** Possibly a variant of Czech or Slovak **Motýl**, a nickname from *Modýl* 'butterfly'.

Motl (300) South German: from a short pet form of the personal name *Matthäus* (see MATTHEW).

Motley (3175) English: probably a nickname for someone who wore parti-colored clothes, from Middle English *motteley* 'motley'.

Motola (156) **1.** Italian: habitational name from Mottola in Taranto province (Puglia). **2.** Jewish (Sephardic): unexplained.
GIVEN NAMES Spanish 10%; Italian 7%; Jewish 4%. *Alberto*, *Blanca*, *Enrique*, *Estrella*, *Jaime*, *Mario*, *Pepe*, *Violeta*; *Rocco* (2), *Angelo*; *Asher*, *Eliezer*, *Emanuel*, *Rina*, *Sol*.

Moton (702) Probably a variant of English MORTON.

Motschenbacher (114) German: variant of **Mutschenbäcker** or **Mutzenbäcker**, an occupational name for a baker, from Middle High German *mutze*, *mutsche(l)* 'bread roll', 'loaf of white bread' + *bäcker* (agent noun from *backen* 'to bake').

Motsenbocker (115) Americanized spelling of German MOTSCHENBACHER.

Motsinger (640) Altered spelling of German MATZINGER.

Mott (6493) **1.** English: variant spelling of MOTTE 1. **2.** English: from *Motte*, a medieval pet form of the personal name *Matilda* (see MOULD). **3.** German: topographic name for someone who lived by or owned property in a marshy area, from Middle High German *mot* 'mud', 'swamp'.

Motta (1021) **1.** Italian (mainly northern): topographic name from *motta* 'fortified stronghold', or a habitational name from any of the numerous places named with this word, as for example Motta Camastra and Motta d'Affermo in Messina, Sicily, Mottafollone in Cosenza province, Motta Montecorvino in Foggia; Motta Baluffi in Cremona, Motta di Livenza in Treviso, and Motta Visconti in Milan, etc. **2.** Portuguese: variant of MOTA.

GIVEN NAMES Spanish 12%; Italian 8%; Portuguese 5%. *Manuel* (16), *Mario* (5), *Carlos* (3), *Jose* (3), *Luis* (3), *Alberto* (2), *Alvaro* (2), *Armando* (2), *Cesar* (2), *Felipe* (2), *Jaime* (2), *Jorge* (2); *Angelo* (3), *Salvatore* (3), *Santo* (3), *Amedeo*, *Antonino*, *Antonio*, *Carlo*, *Carmelo*, *Dino*, *Domenic*, *Flavio*, *Giuseppe*; *Paulo* (3), *Joao*, *Joaquim*.

Motte (250) **1.** French and English: topographic name for someone who lived by a fortified stronghold, Old French, Middle English *motte*. The surname may also be a habitational name from any of the places in France named with this word. **2.** English: variant spelling of MOTT 2. **3.** German: habitational name from Motte in the Saarland or Motten in Bavaria.
FOREBEARS The settlement that became the city of Detroit was founded in 1701 by Antoine de la Mothe, Sieur de Cadillac (1658–1730), governor of LA. He was born into the minor nobility in Gascony, France, where his father owned the seigneury of Cadillac. Marie Joseph Paul Yves Roch Gilbert du Motier, Marquis de Lafayette (1757–1834), the French aristocrat who played a leading part in both the French and the American Revolutions, came of a family who had owned the estate of Lafayette in the Auvergne since the 13th century.

GIVEN NAMES French 7%; German 4%. *Edouard*, *Etienne*, *Monique*, *Yves*; *Klaus*, *Reinhard*.

Motter (1015) German: topographic name from Middle High German *mot* 'mud', 'mire' + the suffix *-er* denoting an inhabitant.

Mottern (283) German: variant of MOTTER.

Mottl (177) South German: variant of MOTL.

Mottley (240) English: variant spelling of MOTLEY.

Motto (534) **1.** Italian: when not a masculinized form of MOTTA, from a shortened pet form of a personal name ending in *-mo*. **2.** Scottish: perhaps a habitational name from a lost place named with Middle English *motte* 'fortified stronghold' + *ho(e)* 'ridge', 'hill'.

GIVEN NAMES Italian 7%. *Rocco* (4), *Salvatore* (2), *Carmela*, *Carmelo*, *Carmine*, *Primo*, *Vita*.

Mottola (476) Southern Italian: habitational name from Mottola, a place in Taranto province.

GIVEN NAMES Italian 13%. *Angelo* (3), *Elia* (2), *Adolfo*, *Antonio*, *Carmine*, *Enrico*, *Ernesto*, *Fiore*, *Gustavo*, *Horacio*, *Luigi*, *Rocco*, *Romeo*, *Sabato*, *Sal*, *Salvatore*, *Vincenzo*.

Motton (101) English: variant of MUTTON.

Mottram (181) English: habitational name from either of two places in Cheshire. It is possible that the name originally denoted a building where village assemblies were held, named in Old English as 'meeting-house', from *(ge)mōt* 'meeting' + *ærn* 'house', 'hall'. Other possibilities are that the name derives from Old English *(ge)mōt-rūm* 'meeting space', or *(ge)mōt-treum* 'assembly trees'.

Motts (169) English: metronymic from MOTT 2.

Motycka (128) Polish (**Motyczka**): from a derivative of MOTYKA.

Motyka (460) Polish, Ukrainian, Slovak: from *motyka* 'hoe', a nickname for someone given to going off on a wild goose chase.

GIVEN NAMES Polish 9%. *Jozef* (2), *Alicja, Dariusz, Franciszek, Ignatius, Jadwiga, Janina, Jozefa, Krzysztof, Leszek, Miroslawa.*

Motyl (139) Polish: nickname from *motyl* 'butterfly'.

GIVEN NAMES Polish 6%. *Alicja, Krystyna, Mariusz.*

Motz (926) South German: **1.** (also **Mötz**) nickname for a grubby, unkempt individual, or an obstinate one, from Swabian dialect *motz* 'dirt'. **2.** variant of MAUTZ. **3.** short form of the personal name *Matthäus* (see MATTHEW).

Motzer (154) South German: variant of MOTZ 1 and 2.

GIVEN NAMES German 6%. *Hans, Otto.*

Motzko (162) **1.** Germanized spelling of Ukrainian **Mochko**, a pet form of any of various male personal names beginning with *Mo-*. **2.** Germanized spelling of Polish **Moczko**, a derivative of *moczyć się* 'to soak or bathe'.

Mou (102) **1.** Chinese 牟: from the name of a state of Mou that existed during the Zhou dynasty (1122–221 BC). Descendants of the ruling class of this state adopted its name as their surname. **2.** Chinese 莫: variant of MO 1. **3.** Laotian: unexplained.

GIVEN NAMES Chinese 25%. *Cheng, Chia, Chih Chung, Ching, Kai Chung, Kuen, Mei, Wah, Xue, Yiwen, Yung.*

Moua (897) Laotian: unexplained.

GIVEN NAMES Southeast Asian 65%. *Chao* (16), *Ying* (12), *Mee* (10), *Tou* (10), *Yia* (9), *Chue* (8), *Kou* (8), *Nhia* (8), *Tong* (8), *Yang* (8), *Yee* (8), *Chia* (6); *Pao* (17), *Vang* (16), *Neng* (15), *Blia* (11), *Chong* (11), *Koua* (11), *Yer* (10), *Houa* (7), *Shoua* (6), *Thai* (6), *Blong* (5), *Soua* (5); *Mai* (13), *Long* (6), *Thao* (6), *Dang* (4), *Thong* (3), *Bao* (2), *Pha* (2), *Be, Hue, Ly, Mang, Nang.*

Moubray (138) English and French: variant of MOWBRAY.

GIVEN NAME French 4%. *Michel.*

Mouch (109) Nickname meaning 'fly', from French *mouche* or Czech *moucha*.

Moudry (160) Czech (**Moudrý**): nickname for a wise man, from *moudrý* 'wise'.

Moudy (396) English or Irish: variant of MOODY.

Moul (438) Variant spelling of English MOULE.

Mould (331) English: from the Middle English female personal name *Mau(l)d*, a

reduced form of the Norman name *Mathilde, Matilda*, composed of the Germanic elements *maht* 'might', 'strength' + *hild* 'strife', 'battle'. The learned form *Matilda* was much less common in the Middle Ages than the vernacular forms *Mahalt, Maud* and the reduced pet form TILL. The name was borne by the daughter of Henry I of England, who disputed the throne of England with her cousin Stephen for a number of years (1137–48). In Germany the popularity of the name in the Middle Ages was augmented by its being borne by a 10th-century saint, wife of Henry the Fowler and mother of Otto the Great.

Moulden (307) English: unexplained; possibly a variant of MOULTON.

Moulder (858) English: occupational name for a maker of measures or a measurer, derived from Old French *moule* 'measure'.

Moulds (367) English: metronymic from MOULD.

Moule (113) English: variant of MULE.

Moulin (277) French: topographic name from Old French *molin* 'mill', Latin *molina* (see MILL). This was normally a metonymic occupational name for a miller or mill worker.

GIVEN NAMES French 13%. *Gaston* (2), *Michel* (2), *Pierre* (2), *Andre, Cecile, Chantal, Gabrielle, Herve, Jacques.*

Moulis (118) French: habitational name from places called Moulis in Ariège, Gironde, and Haute-Loire, or from Moulis-en-Médoc.

GIVEN NAME French 4%. *Alain.*

Moulthrop (162) Possibly of English origin, a habitational name from a lost or unidentified place.

Moulton (5033) English: habitational name from any of the various places with this name, as for example in Cheshire, Lincolnshire, Norfolk, Northamptonshire, Suffolk, and North Yorkshire. For the most part these were named in Old English as 'Mū-la's settlement', from the Old English personal name or byname *Mūla* 'mule' + *tūn* 'enclosure', 'settlement', but in some cases they may have been originally farms where mules were reared or kept. In the case of the Norfolk place name the first element was probably a personal name *Mōda*, a short form of the various compound names with a first element *mōd* 'spirit', 'mind', 'courage'.

Moultrie (842) Scottish: unexplained. According to Black the first known bearer of the name in Scotland was Adam de Multreve; the *de* suggests it may have been a Norman habitational name.

Moultry (112) Variant spelling of Scottish MOULTRIE.

Mounce (966) **1.** English (Devon): unexplained. **2.** Possibly an Americanized form of German MANZ.

Mound (126) English: presumably a variant of MOUNT.

Mounger (242) Perhaps an altered spelling of MANGER; it is found chiefly in TX, MA, and TN.

Mounsey (197) English (of Norman origin): habitational name from Monceaux in Calvados and Orne, or their name from the plural form of Old French *moncel* 'hillock' (Late Latin *monticellum*, a diminutive of *mons*).

Mount (3294) **1.** English: topographic name for someone who lived on or near a hill, Middle English *mount* (from Old English *munt*, reinforced by Old French *mont*). **2.** Scottish: probably a habitational name from places so called in Peeblesshire, Fife, and Lanarkshire.

Mountain (1214) **1.** English: topographic name from Old French *montagne* 'mountain' (see MONTAGNE). **2.** Irish: either of Norman origin, as 1, or an Anglicized form of Gaelic **Ó Manntáin** (see MANTON 2).

Mountcastle (254) **1.** Irish: in part at least, probably a further Anglicization of the Irish surname **Mountcashell**, itself an Anglicized form of Gaelic **Ó Maolchaisil** (see CASHEL 2), which was associated with Ballymulcashell in County Clare. Woulfe says that a registrar in Munster changed the name to Mountcashel *c.* 1840. **2.** English: in England, this name is common in Lincolnshire. While this may well be the result of migration from Ireland, the possibility of a habitational name from an unidentified place should not be ruled out.

Mountford (331) English (chiefly West Midlands): **1.** variant of MONTFORT. **2.** possibly a habitational name from Mundford in Norfolk (see MUNFORD).

Mountjoy (378) English (of Norman origin): habitational name from Montjoie in La Manche, France, named with Old French *mont* 'hill', 'mountain' (see MONT) + *joie* 'joy'.

Mounts (1297) Probably an altered form of English MOUNT or German MANTZ.

Mountz (310) Probably an altered spelling of German MANTZ; it is concentrated in PA.

Moura (442) **1.** Portuguese and Galician: habitational name from Moura in Beja, Portugal, or from any of the like named places in Galicia. **2.** Southern French: dialect variant of MORE 3.

GIVEN NAMES Spanish 26%; Portuguese 16%; Italian 5%. *Manuel* (15), *Jose* (12), *Fernando* (4), *Ana* (3), *Carlos* (3), *Silvino* (3), *Domingos* (2), *Geraldo* (2), *Luis* (2), *Luiz* (2), *Mario* (2), *Pedro* (2), *Heitor* (2), *Joao* (2), *Henrique, Joaquim, Marcio, Paulo; Antonio* (15), *Arcilio, Flavio, Marco, Sylvio.*

Mourad (174) Muslim: variant of MURAD.

GIVEN NAMES Muslim 50%; French 7%. *Bassam* (4), *Ahmad* (2), *Ghassan* (2), *Habib* (2), *Jamal* (2), *Maher* (2), *Nazih* (2), *Samiha* (2), *Sana* (2), *Tamin* (2), *Walid* (2),

Zaki (2); *Pierre* (2), *Antoine, Flore, Jean-Paul.*

Mouradian (221) Armenian: variant of MOORADIAN.

GIVEN NAMES Armenian 37%; French 5%. *Sarkis* (3), *Andranik* (2), *Hagop* (2), *Hratch* (2), *Krikor* (2), *Vahram* (2), *Anahid, Arakel, Araxie, Aroutioun, Artin, Avedis*; *Pierre* (2), *Edouard.*

Mourer (225) Southern French (Gascon): topographic name from a dialect equivalent of French *mûrier* 'mulberry tree'.

Mourey (146) French: **1.** from Old French *moré* 'brown', 'black', also 'dark colored material', hence a metonymic occupational name for someone who made or sold such fabrics. **2.** habitational name from a place in Indre-et-Loire called Moré.

Mourning (259) Of German origin, through translation and misspelling. See MORNING.

Mousa (141) Muslim: variant of MUSA (Moses).

GIVEN NAMES Muslim 60%. *Mohamed* (3), *Abdel* (2), *Amir* (2), *Hayat* (2), *Mahmoud* (2), *Mousa* (2), *Nabil* (2), *Sana* (2), *Abdelsalam, Ahmad, Ahmed, Awad.*

Mouse (121) Americanized form of German MAUS.

Mousel (229) Americanized form of the German **Mäusl**, from a diminutive of MAUS.

Mouser (1055) Possibly an Americanized form of German MAUSER.

Mousley (155) English: variant spelling of MOSLEY.

Moussa (292) Muslim: variant of MUSA (Moses).

GIVEN NAMES Muslim 63%. *Mohamed* (7), *Moussa* (6), *Ayman* (3), *Fadi* (3), *Hassan* (3), *Sameh* (3), *Samir* (3), *Afif* (2), *Ahmed* (2), *Amr* (2), *Antoun* (2), *Aziz* (2).

Mousseau (481) French: habitational name from any of various places named with Mousseaux, for example Mousseaux-Neuville in Eure, Seine-et-Oise, or Mousseaux-lès-Bray in Seine-et-Marne.

GIVEN NAMES French 7%. *Adelard, Aime, Gaetan, Jacques, Marcel, Michel, Ovila.*

Moustafa (112) Muslim: variant of MUSTAFA.

GIVEN NAMES Muslim 81%. *Mohamed* (8), *Moustafa* (6), *Ahmed* (4), *Amr* (3), *Emad* (3), *Abdalla* (2), *Azem* (2), *Samir* (2), *Samy* (2), *Tarek* (2), *Yasser* (2), *Abbas.*

Mouton (1795) French: nickname from Old French *mouton* 'sheep', doubtless used to denote a docile and unintelligent person, perhaps someone easily led.

GIVEN NAMES French 8%. *Andre* (5), *Antoine* (4), *Curley* (4), *Camille* (2), *Elphege* (2), *Emile* (2), *Michel* (2), *Ravis* (2), *Adhemar, Adrien, Alcee, Alcide.*

Moutray (175) Scottish: variant of MOULTRIE.

Mouw (375) Possibly an altered form of Dutch **Mouws**, from Dutch *mouw* 'sleeve'

(see MAU 3); or a nickname from Middle Dutch *mouwe* 'thick or protruding lip'.

GIVEN NAMES Dutch 4%. *Gerrit* (2), *Gerritt* (2), *Dirk, Hendrik, Marinus.*

Mouzon (303) French: habitational name from either of the places so called in Ardennes and Charente, probably originally named with a Gaulish personal name (unattested), *Mausos, Mosos.*

Mow (217) **1.** Scottish: habitational name from Mow (formerly Molle) in the parish of Morebattle, Roxburghshire. **2.** Variant spelling of English **Mowe**, a variant of MAW.

Mowad (123) Muslim: from a personal name based on Arabic *mu'ādh* 'protected'. Mu'ādh bin Jabal was a judge in Yemen appointed by the Prophet Muhammad.

GIVEN NAMES Muslim 5%. *Samir* (3), *Ghassan* (2), *Haifa.*

Mowat (222) Scottish and northern English: variant of MOWATT.

Mowatt (360) Scottish and northern English: **1.** from a medieval female personal name, *Mohaut*, a variant of *Mau(l)d* (see MOULD). **2.** occupational name for an official in charge of communal pasture land, Middle English *moward, maward*, from Old English *māwe* 'meadow' + *weard* 'guardian' (see WARD 1). **3.** habitational name from any of various places in northern France called Mon(t)haut, from Old French *mont* 'hill' (see MONT 1) + *haut* 'high' (Latin *altus*).

Mowbray (777) English (of Norman origin): habitational name from Montbrai in La Manche, France, named in Old French as 'mud hill', from Old French *mont* 'hill' (see MONT 1) + *brai* 'mud', 'slime' (of Gaulish origin).

Mowder (141) Possibly an Americanized form of a South German surname, **Mauder**, originally a nickname for a grumbling, peevish person.

GIVEN NAMES German 4%. *Merwin* (2), *Erwin.*

Mowdy (287) English or Irish: variant of MOODY.

Mowell (243) English: from Middle English *moul*, an older form of *mule* 'mule', which was altered under Norman French influence (see MULE). This would have been a nickname for a stubborn person or a metonymic occupational name for a driver of pack animals.

Mowen (472) Irish: Anglicized form of Gaelic **Ó Mocháin** (see MOHAN).

Mower (1197) **1.** English (East Anglia, chiefly Norfolk): occupational name for someone who mowed pasture lands to provide hay, from an agent derivative of Middle English *mow(en)* 'mow' (Old English *māwen*). **2.** Welsh: nickname from *mawr* 'big' (see MOORE 6). **3.** German (**Möwer**): nickname from an agent derivative of Middle High German *mōven* 'to torment, trouble, or burden'.

Mowers (501) English: variant of MOWER.

Mowery (2953) English: variant of MOWRY.

Mowles (158) English: **1.** metronymic from MULE 3. **2.** patronymic from MULE 1 or 2 (the Middle English word being *moul* until replaced by Old French *mule*), or a metronymic from MOULD.

Mowrer (560) Americanized spelling of German MAURER.

Mowrey (1023) English: variant of MOWRY.

Mowry (2033) English: probably a variant of the Anglo-Norman French personal name *Mory*, a short form of *Amaury* (see EMERY, MOREY).

FOREBEARS Roger Mowry (*c.* 1612–66) emigrated from England to MA before 1634, when he married Mary Johnson in Roxbury, Suffolk Co., MA.

Mox (137) **1.** Dutch: metronymic or patronymic from MOCK 3; **2.** Walloon: nickname from Walloon *moxhe* 'fly' (Old French *mosche*, Latin *musca*), denoting an annoying, importunate person; **3.** habitational name from Moxhe in the province of Liège.

GIVEN NAME German 4%. *Eldred.*

Moxey (150) English: unexplained.

Moxham (126) English: habitational name from a lost placed called Moxhams, in Atworth, Wiltshire.

Moxley (1675) English: habitational name from a minor place in the West Midlands called Moxley.

Moxon (223) English (Yorkshire): metronymic from the medieval personal name *Mag(ge)*, a reduced form of *Margaret* (see MARGESON); but in some cases a patronymic from the Old English personal name *Mocca.*

Moy (2434) **1.** Irish (County Donegal): Anglicized form of Gaelic **Ó Muighe** 'descendant of *Muighe*', of unexplained etymology. The English surname (see 2) has also become established in Ulster. **2.** English (Norfolk): unexplained. Compare MOY 1. **3.** French: habitational name from places so called in Aisne and Saône-et-Loire, named in Latin as *Modiacum* '(estate) of Modius' (see MOYA 2). **4.** Norwegian: habitational name from any of several farmsteads in southwestern Norway named Moi, from Old Norse *mói*, the dative case of *mór* 'sandy plain'. **5.** Chinese: possibly a variant spelling of MEI 1.

GIVEN NAMES Chinese 9%. *Wah* (8), *Ming* (7), *Wai* (7), *Wing* (7), *Hing* (6), *Kin* (5), *Sun* (4), *Hong* (3), *Kee* (3), *Kwong* (3), *Lai* (3), *Siu* (3).

Moya (1861) **1.** Spanish: habitational name from Moya, in Cuenca, or from places so named Valencia, Lugo, and the Canaries. **2.** Catalan (**Moyà**): variant spelling of the habitational name from Moià in Barcelona province, named in Late Latin as *Modianus* '(estate) of *Modius*' (a personal name derived from Latin *modus* 'measure').

GIVEN NAMES Spanish 39%. *Jose* (43), *Juan* (21), *Manuel* (16), *Luis* (12), *Carlos* (11), *Miguel* (11), *Ruben* (11), *Jesus* (10), *Mario* (10), *Pedro* (8), *Roberto* (8), *Alejandro* (7).

Moyano (103) Spanish: habitational name for someone from MOYA, from an adjectival form of the place name.

GIVEN NAMES Spanish 48%. *Carlos* (3), *Luis* (3), *Ricardo* (3), *Alberto* (2), *Cesar* (2), *Javier* (2), *Jose* (2), *Juan Carlos* (2), *Manuel* (2), *Diego, Emilio, Gustavo; Carlo, Fausto, Marcello, Marco.*

Moye (2303) **1.** English (Suffolk, Essex): unexplained. **2.** French: habitation name from Moye in Haute-Savoie. **3.** Dutch (**de Moye**): nickname from Middle Dutch *moy, moeie*, 'fine', 'handsome', denoting a well-dressed person or a dandy. **4.** Spanish: see MOYA.

Moyer (14444) **1.** Irish: possibly a shortened form of **MacMoyer**, Anglicized form of Gaelic **Mac an Mhaoir** 'son of the steward', from *maor* 'steward'. **2.** Americanized form of German MEYER 1. **3.** Dutch: occupational name for a mower or reaper.

Moyers (1872) **1.** Americanized form of German MAYER with an excrescent -*s*. **2.** Dutch: variant of MOYER 3, or of **Moyaers**, a nickname for a dandy, from a derivative of Middle Dutch *moy, moeie* 'fine', 'handsome'. **3.** Shortened form of Irish **MacMoyers** (see MOYER).

Moyes (444) Scottish and English: from the Middle English personal name *Moise* (see MOSES).

Moylan (1055) **1.** Irish: Anglicized form of Gaelic **Ó Maoláin** (see MULLEN). **2.** Perhaps Welsh, an Anglicized form of the nickname *moelyn*, a diminutive of *moel* 'bald' (see MOYLE).

GIVEN NAMES Irish 7%. *Brendan* (2), *Patrick Do* (2), *Declan, Dermot, Eamon, John Patrick, Kiernan, Liam.*

Moyle (857) Cornish and Welsh: descriptive nickname meaning 'bald', from Cornish *moyl*, Welsh *moel*.

Moyles (146) Irish (now mainly County Mayo): Anglicized form of Gaelic **Ó Maolmhuire** (see MULLERY).

Moynahan (312) Irish: variant of MOYNIHAN.

GIVEN NAMES Irish 4%. *Brendan, Brigid.*

Moynihan (1859) Irish: Anglicized form of Gaelic **Ó Muimhneacháin** 'descendant of *Muimhneachán*', a diminutive of the byname *Muimhneach* 'Munsterman', i.e. someone belonging to the province of Munster. (In County Mayo this surname has sometimes been changed to **Munster**.)

GIVEN NAMES Irish 7%. *Brendan* (2), *Patrick James* (2), *Donal, Eamon, Finbarr, Kieran, Niall.*

Moyse (174) **1.** Jewish: variant of MOSES. **2.** English (Devon and Norfolk) and French: from a medieval variant of the personal name MOSES (Middle English *Moise*, Old French *Moïse*).

GIVEN NAMES German 8%; Jewish 4%. *Hermann* (3), *Viktor* (2); *Faina, Josif, Shlema.*

Mozee (139) Americanized spelling of French **Mozé**, a habitational name from Mouzé-le-Louet or Mozé in Maine-et-Loire, originally named as *Mausiacum*, '(estate) of *Maletius* or *Mausos*' (the former a Latin personal name, the latter Gaulish).

Mozena (157) Americanized form of French **Mo(u)ginet**, a pet form derived from MONGE.

FOREBEARS John Mozena or Mozeney (Jean Mo(u)ginet; 1747–1830) came to North America from Mont-le-Vignoble, near Strasbourg, with Lafayette to fight in the American Revolution. He settled in Monroe Co., OH.

Mozer (224) Altered spelling of German MOSER.

GIVEN NAMES German 9%. *Kurt* (2), *Albrecht, Erwin, Gottlob, Manfred, Reinhold.*

Mozes (145) Variant of MOSES, in this spelling typically a Jewish Hungarian name.

GIVEN NAMES Jewish 19%; Hungarian 7%. *Eyal* (2), *Ari, Asher, Chaim, Efrom, Icek, Miriam, Mordche, Shalom, Shmuel, Tzvi; Kalman* (3), *Laszlo* (2), *Miklos.*

Mozingo (1174) Origin uncertain. Most probably an Americanized form of an unidentified French Huguenot name. There are several references in family lore to origin in the South of France or the Pyrenees. It has also been suggested that this is an Italian name, which seems less likely.

Mozley (197) English: variant spelling of MOSLEY.

Mrachek (107) Americanized spelling of Czech **Mráček** or Slovak **Mráčik**, a diminutive of **Mrak**, from *mrak* 'cloud', an unflattering nickname for a disgruntled person who was always complaining.

Mraz (854) Slovenian; Czech and Slovak (**Mráz**): nickname from Slovenian *mraz*, Czech and Slovak *mráz* 'frost', a nickname for someone with white hair or possibly for someone of an icy disposition.

Mrazek (232) Czech (**Mrázek**) and Slovak (**Mrázik**): pet form of **Mráz** (see MRAZ).

Mrazik (137) Czech and Slovak (**Mrázik**): pet form of **Mráz** (see MRAZ).

Mroczek (217) Polish: nickname for a person of a gloomy disposition, from Polish *mroczek* 'small dark cloud' (a diminutive of *mrok* 'cloud', also used in the sense 'gloom', 'darkness'). This word also means 'bat', which could also lie behind the nickname.

GIVEN NAMES Polish 12%. *Pawel* (2), *Tadeusz* (2), *Boguslaw, Krzysztof, Stanislawa, Wieslaw, Wieslawa.*

Mroczka (185) Polish: variant of MROCZEK.

GIVEN NAMES Polish 9%. *Agnieszka, Beata, Casimir, Leszek, Wladyslaw, Zbigniew.*

Mroczkowski (239) Polish: habitational name for someone from any of various

places called Mroczkowa, Mroczków, or Mroczkowice, named with *mroczek* 'bat'.

GIVEN NAMES Polish 16%. *Stanislaw* (2), *Tomasz* (2), *Andrej, Andrzej, Ireneusz, Jacek, Ludmilla, Ludwik, Miroslaw, Stanislaus, Szczepan, Tadeusz.*

Mross (115) Germanized form of Polish **Mróz** (see MROZ) or Czech **Mráz** (see MRAZ).

GIVEN NAME German 6%. *Juergen* (2).

Mrotek (169) Polish: reduced form of **Mamrotek**, a nickname for someone who mumbled or talked incomprehensibly, from a derivative of *mamrotać* 'to mumble or gibber'.

Mrowka (113) Polish (**Mrówka**): nickname from Polish *mrówka* 'ant', denoting a busily active small person.

GIVEN NAME French 4%. *Lucien.*

Mroz (961) Polish (**Mróz**): **1.** nickname for a white-haired man or alternatively for one of an icy and unsociable disposition, from Polish *mróz* 'frost'. **2.** from a reduced form of the personal name *Ambroży* (see AMBROSE).

GIVEN NAMES Polish 11%. *Zbigniew* (4), *Wojciech* (3), *Bogdan* (2), *Casimir* (2), *Eugeniusz* (2), *Janina* (2), *Jaroslaw* (2), *Jerzy* (2), *Jozef* (2), *Ryszard* (2), *Stanislaw* (2), *Tomasz* (2).

Mrozek (576) Polish: pet form of MROZ.

GIVEN NAMES Polish 7%. *Janusz* (3), *Alojzy, Casimir, Dorota, Jadwiga, Krystyna, Krzysztof, Malgorzata, Marcin, Pawel, Zdzislaw.*

Mrozinski (400) Polish (**Mroziński**): habitational name for someone from any of several places called Mrozy.

GIVEN NAMES Polish 4%. *Casimir, Dariusz, Ignacy, Stanislaw.*

Mrozowski (101) Polish: habitational name for someone from Mrozowo in Bydgoszcz voivodeship, or from any of several places called Mrozy.

GIVEN NAMES Polish 14%. *Jadwiga, Jarek, Krzysztof, Witold, Wojciech.*

Mruk (162) Polish: nickname from *mruk*, denoting a taciturn individual, a man who said little.

GIVEN NAMES Polish 8%. *Jacek, Lech, Wieslaw, Wlodzimierz.*

Mu (187) **1.** Chinese 穆: in the state of Song during the Spring and Autumn period (722–481 BC) there existed a leader who was posthumously given the name of the duke of Mu. His descendants adopted Mu as their surname. **2.** Chinese 牟: variant of MOU 1. **3.** Hawaiian: unexplained.

GIVEN NAMES Chinese 50%. *Chung* (3), *Chang* (2), *Jian* (2), *Li* (2), *Tong* (2), *Bin, Chao, Cheng, Chin, Chuan, Der, Feng, Fung, Hua.*

Mucci (828) Italian: patronymic or plural form of MUCCIO.

GIVEN NAMES Italian 12%. *Gennaro* (3), *Gino* (3), *Angelo* (2), *Domenic* (2), *Geno* (2),

Pasquale (2), *Antonio, Carlo, Dante, Dario, Donato, Emidio.*

Mucciarone (109) Italian: from an augmentative form of the personal name MUCCIO.
GIVEN NAMES Italian 11%. *Antonio, Armando, Carmine, Mario, Orlando.*

Muccino (123) Italian: from a pet form of the personal name MUCCIO.
GIVEN NAMES Italian 11%. *Silvio* (2), *Angelo, Savino.*

Muccio (199) Italian: from the personal name *Muccio*, a short form of the pet names *Anselmuccio, Giacomuccio*, or a pet form of any other name ending with *-mo*.
GIVEN NAMES Italian 13%. *Angelo* (2), *Salvatore* (2), *Carmel, Marco.*

Much (260) **1.** German: habitational name from a place near Cologne named Much. **2.** Scottish and English: variant of MUTCH.
FOREBEARS Johann G. and Ernestine Sontag Much migrated with their four children to WI in 1862, probably from Cologne (Köln), Germany.
GIVEN NAMES German 6%. *Otto* (3), *Fritz.*

Mucha (1003) Polish, Ukrainian, Czech dialect, and Slovak: nickname from *mucha* 'fly', denoting an irritating person or someone considered of no importance.
GIVEN NAMES Polish 6%. *Alojzy, Andrzej, Boleslaw, Eugeniusz, Grazyna, Iwan, Janina, Jerzy, Jozef, Mariusz, Miroslaw.*

Muchmore (280) English (Cornwall): unexplained.

Muchnick (181) Jewish (from Ukraine): occupational name from Russian and Yiddish *muchnik* 'dealer in flour'.
GIVEN NAMES Jewish 12%. *Hyman* (2), *Meyer* (2), *Herschel, Miriam, Mordecai.*

Muchow (422) **1.** German: habitational name from a place so named near Ludwigslust in Mecklenburg. **2.** Polish: from the possessive form of MUCHA.
GIVEN NAMES German 5%. *Kurt* (2), *Ewald, Fritz, Gerhart, Ralf.*

Muck (605) German (also **Mück(e)**): nickname from Middle High German *mucke* 'midge', 'gnat', denoting a small person, an irritating person, or someone considered to be of no importance.

Muckelroy (91) Variant of Scottish **McIlroy** (see GILROY), the first two syllables having being altered by folk-etymological association with Scots *muckle* 'big'.

Muckenfuss (153) German: nickname for someone with bony or weak legs, from Middle High German *mucke* 'midge', 'gnat' + *fuos* 'foot'.

Mucker (105) German: nickname from an agent derivative of *mucken* 'to bridle or bristle', 'to rebel', denoting a person of prickly or rebellious character.

Muckerheide (115) German: topographic name of uncertain origin; perhaps from someone who lived on a heath where gnats or mosquitos bred, from German *Mücke* 'gnat', 'mosquito' + *Heide* 'heath'.

Muckey (253) Americanized form of German **Mücke** (see MUECKE).

Muckle (213) **1.** English (Northumberland): nickname for a big man, from Middle English *muchel* 'big' (Old English *mycel*). Compare MICKLE. **2.** German (**Mückle**; South German **Muckle**): from a diminutive of MUCK 'gnat'.

Muckler (106) Origin uncertain. **1.** Possibly Irish or Manx: unexplained. **2.** Alternatively, perhaps, a respelling of Alemannic **Möckle**, a nickname from a diminutive of Middle High German *mocke* 'lump', 'awkward or inept person', or of German **Mückle**, a nickname from a diminutive of Middle High German *mugke* 'restless person'.

Muckleroy (201) Irish: variant of McELROY.

Mucklow (108) English: habitational name from Mucklows Hill in Worcestershire or Muckley Corner, near Lichfield, Staffordshire. Both are named with Old English *micel* 'large' + *hlāw* 'hill'.

Mudd (2374) English: **1.** from a medieval personal name, a variant of *Maud* (see MOULD). **2.** from the Old English personal name *Mōd(a)*, a short form of the various compound names containing the element *mōd* 'spirit', 'mind', 'courage'. **3.** topographic name for someone who lived in a particularly muddy area, from Middle English *mud(de)* 'mud', perhaps also a metonymic occupational name for a dauber (one who constructed buildings of wattle and daub).

Muddiman (103) English: nickname from Middle English *modie* 'impetuous', 'haughty', 'angry' (see MOODY) + *man* 'man'.

Mudge (964) English (Devon): from an unattested Old English personal name, *Mugga.*

Mudgett (462) English: from a pet form of MUDGE.

Mudie (108) Mainly Scottish: variant spelling of English MOODY.
GIVEN NAME Scottish 4%. *Iain.*

Mudra (124) Czech: variant of MOUDRY.

Mudrak (123) Czech and Slovak (**Mudrák**) and Ukrainian: from a derivative of Slavic *mudry* (Czech *moudrý*, Ukrainian *mudryj*) 'wise'.

Mudrick (213) Americanized spelling of Czech **Mudřík**, Slovak **Mudrík**, or Ukrainian and Jewish (from Ukraine) **Mudryk**, all derivatives of an adjective meaning 'wise'. Compare Czech MOUDRY.

Mudry (219) Ukrainian; Slovak (**Múdry**); Serbian and Croatian (**Mudri**): nickname for a wise man, from the adjective *mudryj* (Ukrainian), *múdry* (Slovak), *mudar* (Serbian and Croatian), all meaning 'wise'.

Mueck (112) German (**Mück**): see MUCK.
GIVEN NAME German 6%. *Horst.*

Muecke (245) German (**Mücke**): **1.** from Middle High German *mucke* 'midge', 'gnat', nickname for an irritating person or someone considered to be of no importance. Compare MUCK. **2.** In Silesia this can also be from the Slavic personal name *Micka*, a pet form of MICHAEL, or a habitational name from Mücka (Upper Lausitz).
GIVEN NAMES German 8%. *Hans* (4), *Otto* (2), *Georg, Manfred.*

Muegge (195) North German (**Mügge**): nickname meaning 'midge', 'gnat' and used to denote an irritating person, or someone considered of no importance. Compare MUCK.

Muehl (237) German (**Mühl**): variant of **Mühle** (see MUHLE).
GIVEN NAMES German 5%. *Aloysius, Kurt, Mathias.*

Muehlbauer (316) German (**Mühlbauer**) and Jewish (Ashkenazic): occupational name from German **Mühlbauer** 'millwright', 'mill builder', Middle High German *mül(e)* 'mill' + *būwære* 'builder'.
GIVEN NAMES German 7%. *Kurt* (3), *Alois, Erhart, Otto.*

Muehlberger (119) German (**Mühlberg**): habitational name for someone from a place called Mühlberg.

Muehleisen (108) German (**Mühleisen**): metonymic occupational name for a miller, from Middle High German *mülīsen*, literally 'mill-iron', meaning the shaft of the mill-wheel.
GIVEN NAMES German 11%. *Otto* (2), *Otmar, Theodor.*

Muehlhausen (101) German: topographic name for someone who lived 'at the mill houses', or a habitational name from a place named with these elements.

Muehling (129) German (**Mühling**): **1.** nickname for a troublesome, awkward person, derived from Middle High German *müelich* 'difficult (to get on with)', 'troublesome', 'tiresome'. **2.** habitational name from Mühlingen in Baden.

Mueller (27888) German (**Müller**) and Jewish (Ashkenazic): occupational name for a miller, Middle High German *müller*, German *Müller*. In Germany Müller, Mueller is the most frequent of all surnames; in the U.S. it is often changed to Miller.
GIVEN NAMES German 8%. *Kurt* (84), *Otto* (59), *Hans* (56), *Erwin* (38), *Fritz* (24), *Gerhard* (24), *Klaus* (20), *Heinz* (19), *Helmut* (18), *Wolfgang* (17), *Manfred* (15), *Horst* (13).

Muellner (229) German (**Müllner**): variant of **Müller** (see MUELLER), from Middle High German *mülner*.
GIVEN NAMES German 5%. *Benno, Math, Mathias.*

Muench (1174) German (**Münch**) and French (Alsace): see MUNCH.
FOREBEARS Friedrich Münch (Muench), pastor and humanist, was born in Niedergründen, Hesse, in 1799. In 1833, after being involved in the failed revolution of 1832, he fled Germany for America, where

he became one of the founders of MO. Largely as a result of his personal popularity and rhetorical skills, MO did not intervene in the Civil War on the side of the South.
GIVEN NAMES German 7%. *Kurt* (4), *Arno* (2), *Ernst* (2), *Hans* (2), *Konrad* (2), *Lothar* (2), *Bernd, Christoph, Ewald, Fritz, Gerhardt, Guenter.*

Muenchow (207) German (**Münchow**): habitational name from a place so named in Upper Franconia.
GIVEN NAMES German 5%. *Karlheinz, Kurt, Otto.*

Muenks (106) German (**Münks**): from **Münk**, variant of **Mönch** (see MOENCH) + excrescent -*s*.

Muenster (191) German (**Münster**): see MUNSTER.
GIVEN NAMES German 9%. *Ernst, Juergen, Ralf, Reinhard.*

Muenz (100) German: variant spelling of **Münz** (see MUNZ).
GIVEN NAMES German 19%. *Manfred* (4), *Kurt* (3), *Hans, Oskar.*

Muenzer (125) German (**Münzer**) and Jewish: see MUNZER.
GIVEN NAMES German 9%. *Gerhard, Hans, Horst, Mathias.*

Mues (126) Dutch: variant of MAAS.

Muessig (131) German (**Müssig**): nickname for an idle person from Middle High German *müessic* 'leisured'.
GIVEN NAMES German 7%. *Hans, Siegfried.*

Mueth (144) German: see MUTH.
GIVEN NAMES German 5%. *Aloys, Erwin.*

Mueting (101) German: unexplained.

Muetzel (125) South German and Swiss German: from a diminutive of MUTZ.
GIVEN NAME German 4%. *Manfred.*

Muff (291) **1.** English: variant of MAW 2. **2.** South German: nickname for a sulky or surly person, from Middle High German *muff, mupf* 'pout', 'drooping mouth'.
GIVEN NAMES German 4%. *Erwin, Leonhard.*

Muffett (107) Scottish and northern Irish: variant of MOFFATT.

Muffley (204) Americanized form of South German **Muffele**, nickname for a surly person, from a diminutive of MUFF.

Muffoletto (138) Italian (Sicily): from Sicilian *muffulettu* 'soft spongy bread', applied as a nickname for a flabby person or possibly as a metonymic occupational name for a baker.
GIVEN NAMES Italian 11%. *Antonio, Concetta, Giuseppe, Salvatore.*

Mugavero (195) Southern Italian (Sicilian): nickname from Arabic *maghāwīr* (plural) 'aggressive', 'bold'. The nickname was bestowed originally on a troop of Aragonese soldiers sent as a garrison from Aragon following the Sicilian Vespers uprising in 1282, which expunged Angevin rule and paved the way for Aragonese rule.
GIVEN NAMES Italian 12%. *Salvatore* (3), *Antonio* (2), *Angelo, Franca, Nunzio.*

Mugford (242) English (Devon): evidently a habitational name, but of unknown origin. It may be a variant of **Mudford**, from a place so named in Somerset, from Old English *muddig* 'muddy' + *ford* 'ford'.

Mugg (135) English: variant of MUDGE.

Mugge (118) **1.** English: variant of MUDGE. **2.** German: German (**Mügge**):

Muggli (134) Swiss German (**Müggli**, also **Mügeli**): derisive nickname meaning 'little gnat', from a diminutive of MUECKE.
GIVEN NAMES German 6%. *Ewald, Gerhard, Ruedi.*

Mugler (121) South German: nickname for a portly individual, from a reduced form of *mugeler* 'plump man'.

Muglia (124) Italian: habitational name from a minor place named Muglia or Moglia.
GIVEN NAMES Italian 28%. *Aldo* (2), *Silvio* (2), *Alfonse, Alfonso, Domenico, Gaetano, Luigi, Mario, Oreste, Pasquale, Vincenzo.*

Muha (336) **1.** Slovenian: nickname for an annoying, restless, or difficult person, especially someone who kept changing his mind, from *muha* 'fly'. Compare MUCHA. **2.** Variant of Ukrainian MUCHA.

Muhammad (1337) Muslim: from a personal name based on Arabic *muḥammad* 'praiseworthy' (derived from the verb *ḥamida* 'praise'). This is the name of the founder of Islam, the Prophet Muhammad (570–632). He began to receive spiritual revelations at the age of 40. The Qur'an, the holy book of Islam, was revealed to him by the Angel Jibril (Gabriel). As a personal name, this name is extremely common throughout the Muslim world.
GIVEN NAMES Muslim 67%. *Abdul* (18), *Abdullah* (18), *Ali* (12), *Bilal* (8), *Hassan* (8), *Ibrahim* (7), *Omar* (7), *Wali* (7), *Ahmad* (6), *Yahya* (6), *Yusuf* (6), *Akbar* (5).

Muhammed (115) Muslim: variant of MUHAMMAD.
GIVEN NAMES Muslim 71%. *Abdul* (4), *Wali* (2), *Abdul Hakim, Abdulai, Abdullah, Ajmal, Akram, Alhaji, Ali, Aly, Anwar, Anwer.*

Muhl (256) **1.** North German form of MAUL 1. **2.** German (**Mühl**) and Jewish (Ashkenazic): topographic name from *Mühl(e)* 'mill' (see MUHLE).
GIVEN NAMES German 4%. *Guenter* (2), *Franz.*

Muhlbach (101) German (**Mühlbach**): topographic name meaning 'mill stream'.

Muhlbauer (163) German (**Mühlbauer**): see MUEHLBAUER.
GIVEN NAMES German 8%. *Claus, Erwin, Gunter, Kurt.*

Muhle (130) **1.** German (**Mühle**) and Jewish (Ashkenazic): from Middle High German *mül(e)*, German *Mühle* 'mill'. This was normally a metonymic occupational name for a miller or mill worker, though it may sometimes have been no more than a topographic name for someone living near

a mill. See also MILL. **2.** North German form of MAUL 1, from Middle Low German *mule*.
GIVEN NAMES German 4%. *Aloys, Kurt.*

Muhleman (124) Swiss German (**Mühlemann**): occupational name for a miller or worker at a mill, from Middle High German *mül(e)* 'mill' + *man* 'man'.

Muhlenkamp (232) German (**Mühlenkamp**): topographic name for someone who lived near a mill. *Kamp* is a dialect word meaning 'enclosure', 'field', or 'domain'.

Muhlestein (126) German (**Mühl(e)stein**): from a German word meaning 'millstone'.

Muhlhauser (100) German (**Mühlhauser**): topographic name for someone who lived at a mill house.
GIVEN NAMES German 11%. *Eckhard, Fritz, Hans, Lorenz.*

Muhr (286) **1.** German (Bavaria): topographic name from Middle High German *muor* 'marsh', 'bog', or 'moor'. **2.** North German and Swiss: variant of MAUER 2.
GIVEN NAMES German 5%. *Karlheinz, Otto, Ulrich, Willibald.*

Muhs (390) German: unexplained.

Mui (788) **1.** Chinese: variant of MEI. **2.** Tongan and Samoan: unexplained.
GIVEN NAMES Chinese 36%. *Wing* (12), *Kwok* (6), *Chun* (5), *Chung* (4), *Kin* (3), *Kwong* (3), *Mei* (3), *Ming* (3), *Ting* (3), *Wai* (3), *Yim* (3), *Yuk* (3), *Chi* (2); *Diep* (2), *Coong, Dat, Hung, Huynh, Lap, Lieu, Ngai, Ngo, Sau; Yuet* (3), *Woon* (2), *Chong Man, Poy, Toi, Yit.*

Muilenburg (316) Dutch: habitational name from a place named as 'mill castle'.

Muir (4436) Scottish: topographic name for someone who lived on a moor, from a Scots form of Middle English *more* 'moor', 'fen'.

Muirhead (925) Scottish: habitational name from any of the places in southern Scotland so called, from northern Middle English *muir* 'moor' + *heid* 'head', 'end'.

Muise (578) Probably an altered spelling of MOISE 1.

Mujica (253) Spanish (of Basque origin; **Mújica**): habitational name from Basque *Muxika*, in Biscay province, Basque Country.
GIVEN NAMES Spanish 50%. *Jose* (7), *Juan* (5), *Pedro* (5), *Alfredo* (3), *Gonzalo* (3), *Jorge* (3), *Ramon* (3), *Raul* (3), *Rodrigo* (3), *Agustin* (2), *Eduardo* (2), *Jesus* (2).

Mukai (303) Japanese: 'the well on the other side'; mostly found in western Japan and the Ryūkyū Islands.
GIVEN NAMES Japanese 37%. *Shigeto* (2), *Toshimitsu* (2), *Yoichi* (2), *Yoshio* (2), *Aiko, Chiyoko, Fujie, Futoshi, Hajime, Hanayo, Hatsuko, Hidenori.*

Mukherjee (384) Indian (Bengal) and Bangladeshi: Hindu (Brahman) name, of which the Sanskrit version, *Mukhyopadhyaya*, is ostensibly composed of *mukhya* 'principal', 'chief' + *upadhyaya* 'teacher'.

However, in fact the first element relates to a Bengali place name, probably *Mukhati*. The Sanskrit version, with its rather grander meaning, is a later coinage based on this name, which actually means 'teacher from a place called Mukhati (or similar)'. Compare CHATTERJEE.

GIVEN NAMES Indian 85%. *Partha* (5), *Amit* (4), *Arun* (4), *Mita* (4), *Sunil* (4), *Arup* (3), *Ashish* (3), *Dilip* (3), *Kalyan* (3), *Sankar* (3), *Sonali* (3), *Amitabha* (2).

Mukhopadhyay (100) Indian (Bengal) and Bangladeshi: Altered form of MUKHERJEE, to its supposed original Sanskrit form meaning 'principal teacher'.

GIVEN NAMES Indian 92%. *Sunil* (3), *Amitabha* (2), *Bhaskar* (2), *Dipankar* (2), *Satya* (2), *Somnath* (2), *Tapas* (2), *Ajay*, *Alpana*, *Amarnath*, *Amit*, *Anup*.

Mula (182) **1.** Spanish: habitational name from Mula, a city in the Murcia province. **2.** Possibly also Catalan (**Mulà**): topographic name from a variant of *molar* 'millstone', or habitational name from any of several places named with this word. **3.** Southern Italian (**Mulà**) and Greek (**Moulas**): occupational name for a muleteer, from medieval Greek *moula* 'mule' + the occupational suffix *-as*. **4.** Greek (**Moulas**): status name from Turkish *molla* 'chief judge', 'learned man', 'one who has studied (Islamic) theology' (from Persian *mullah*).

GIVEN NAMES Italian 16%; Spanish 9%. *Salvatore* (3), *Angelo* (2), *Antonio*, *Giuseppe*, *Luigi*, *Pasquale*; *Americo* (2), *Rosario* (2), *Felisa*, *Fransico*, *Silvana*.

Mulac (112) Origin unidentified.

GIVEN NAME German 5%. *Otto* (2).

Mulanax (171) Irish and English: variant of MULLINAX.

Mularz (90) Polish: occupational name for a builder, from *mularz*, a dissimilated variant of *mumarz* 'builder', 'mason'.

Mulberry (180) **1.** English: variant of MOWBRAY, altered by folk etymology. **2.** Irish: Anglicized form of Gaelic **Ó Maoilbhearaigh** 'descendant of the devotee of (Saint) *Bearach*'.

Mulcahey (407) Irish: variant spelling of MULCAHY.

Mulcahy (2833) Irish: Anglicized form of Gaelic **Ó Maolchathaigh** 'descendant of the devotee of (Saint) *Cathach*', a personal name meaning 'warlike'.

GIVEN NAMES Irish 5%. *Brendan* (2), *Clodagh*, *Colm*, *Declan*, *Sean Patrick*.

Mulcare (151) Irish: Anglicized form of Gaelic **Ó Maoilchéire** 'descendant of *Maolchiar*', a personal name meaning 'dark chieftain'.

Mulder (2669) **1.** Dutch: occupational name from *mulder* 'miller'. **2.** German: occupational name for a maker of wooden bowls, from Middle High German *mulde* 'bowl', 'trough', 'tub' + the agent suffix *-er*. **3.** variant of **Müller** (see MUELLER).

Mulderig (111) Respelling of Irish **Mulderrig**, a shortened Anglicized form of Gaelic **Ó Maoildeirg**.

Muldoon (1688) Irish: Anglicized form of Gaelic **Ó Maoldúin** 'descendant of *Maoldúin*', a personal name composed of the elements *maol* 'chieftain' + *dún* 'fortress'. This is a name associated with Fermanagh, Sligo, and Munster.

GIVEN NAMES Irish 5%. *Brendan* (2), *Delma*, *Fintan*.

Muldowney (460) Irish: Anglicization of Gaelic **Ó Maol Dhomhnaigh** (see MALONEY).

GIVEN NAMES Irish 7%. *Eamon*, *Kieran*.

Muldrew (203) Irish (Ulster): **1.** Anglicized form of Gaelic **Ó Maoldoraidh**, 'descendant of *Maoldoraidh*' meaning 'contentious chief'. **2.** possibly a variant of MULGREW.

Muldrow (585) Variant of Irish MULDREW.

Mule (460) **1.** English: from a medieval personal name, perhaps Old English *Mūl* (from Old English *mūl* 'mule', 'halfbreed'). This was the name of a brother of Ceadwalla, King of Wessex (died 675), and is also found as a place name element. However, it may not have survived to the Conquest, and Domesday Book *Mule*, *Mulo* may instead represent Old Norse *Mūli*, which is probably from Old Norse *mūli* 'muzzle', 'snout'. **2.** English: nickname for a stubborn person or metonymic occupational name for a driver of pack animals, from Middle English *mule* 'mule' (Old English *mūl*, reinforced by Old French *mule*, both from Latin *mula* 'she-mule'). **3.** English: from the medieval female personal name *Mulle*, variant of *Molle*, a pet form of *Mary* (see MARIE). **4.** French: nickname from *mule* 'mule' (see 2). **5.** Dutch: nickname for a gossip or someone with a large mouth, from Middle Dutch *mule* 'mouth', 'snout'. **6.** Dutch: metonymic occupational name for a maker of slippers, from Middle Dutch *mule* 'slipper'. **7.** Italian (also **Mulé**): from the medieval nickname *Mulé*, *Molé*, from Arabic *mawlā* 'gentleman', 'lord', 'master', *m(a)uley* 'my lord'. **8.** Sicilian and southern Italian: status name, from Arabic *mawlā* 'master', 'owner'.

GIVEN NAMES Italian 20%. *Salvatore* (7), *Vito* (5), *Angelo* (2), *Antonio* (2), *Matteo* (2), *Sal* (2), *Carmelo*, *Concetta*, *Francesco*, *Gaetano*, *Gaspare*, *Gino*, *Rosario*.

Mulford (1151) English: habitational name from Milford in Wiltshire, so named from Old English *myln* 'mill' + *ford* 'ford'.

Mulgrew (271) Irish (Ulster): Anglicized form of Gaelic **Ó Maolchraoibhe** 'descendant of *Maolchraoibhe*', a personal name meaning 'chief of Craobh', a place on the Bann river.

GIVEN NAME Irish 5%. *Kieran*.

Mulhall (730) Irish (Leinster): Anglicized form of Gaelic **Ó Maolchathail** 'descendant of *Maolchathail*', a personal name

meaning 'devotee of (Saint) *Cathal*' (see CAHILL).

Mulhearn (277) Irish: variant spelling of MULHERN.

GIVEN NAME Irish 8%. *John Patrick*.

Mulherin (468) Irish and Scottish: variant of MULHERN.

Mulhern (1239) Irish (midland and Ulster): Anglicized form of Gaelic **Ó Maoilchiaráin** 'descendant of *Maoilchiaráin*', a personal name meaning 'devotee of (Saint) *Ciarán*' (a personal name from a diminutive of *ciar* 'black').

GIVEN NAMES Irish 6%. *Meave*, *Pegeen*, *Sinead*.

Mulheron (111) Irish: variant of MULHERN.

GIVEN NAME Irish 4%. *Francis Pat*.

Mulhollan (124) Irish: variant of MULHOLLAND.

Mulholland (2438) Irish (Ulster): Anglicized form of Gaelic **Ó Maolchalann** 'descendant of *Maolchalann*', a personal name meaning 'chief of the calends'.

GIVEN NAMES Irish 4%. *Brendan* (5), *Liam*, *Seamus*.

Mulhollen (153) Irish: variant of MULHOLLAND.

Mulick (106) Irish: Anglicized form of Gaelic **Mac Míoluic**, a patronymic from a diminutive of *Milo*.

Mulka (153) Polish and Sorbian: nickname from the dialect term *mulka* 'little kiss' or 'whey'.

GIVEN NAMES Polish 7%. *Casimir* (2), *Andrzej*, *Zygmunt*.

Mulkern (334) Irish: variant of MULHERN.

GIVEN NAME Irish 8%. *Brendan* (2).

Mulkey (2002) Irish: variant of MULCAHY.

Mulkins (135) Irish: shortened Anglicized form of Gaelic **Mac Maolchaoin** 'son of the pleasant chief'.

Mull (3308) Scottish, Irish, or English: unexplained.

Mullady (150) Irish or English: variant of MELODY.

Mullahy (120) Irish: shortened Americanized of **Ó Maolaithche** 'descendant of the servant or devotee of *Aithche*', a personal name which, according to Woulfe, means 'votary of regeneration'.

GIVEN NAMES Irish 13%. *Aileen*, *Brendan*.

Mullally (473) Irish: Anglicized form of Gaelic **Ó Maolalaidh** 'descendant of *Maolaladh*', a personal name composed of the elements *maol* 'chieftain' + *aladh* 'speckled', 'piebald'. This was originally a Galway name.

GIVEN NAMES Irish 7%. *Brendan*, *Conn*.

Mullaly (353) Irish: variant spelling of MULLALLY.

GIVEN NAME Irish 6%. *Brendan*.

Mullan (736) Irish: variant spelling of MULLEN.

GIVEN NAMES Irish 5%. *Brendan* (3), *Caitlin*.

Mullane (813) Irish: variant of MULLEN.

GIVEN NAME Irish 5%. *Brendan*.

Mullaney (1727) Irish (Connacht): Anglicized form of Gaelic **Ó Maoil Sheanaigh** 'descendant of *Maoilsheanaigh*', a personal name meaning 'devotee of (Saint) *Seanach*', a personal name based on *sean* 'ancient', 'old'. Because most Connacht spellings omit the *Sh* (pronounced as *h*), it has been suggested that the original name might have been **Ó Maoileanaigh** 'descendant of *Maoileanach*', a personal name meaning 'chief of the marsh'. There was a different Ulster family of this name, now extinct in Ireland.
GIVEN NAMES Irish 6%. *Brendan* (2), *Brennan*.

Mullany (189) Irish: variant spelling of MULLANEY.
GIVEN NAME Irish 7%. *Fergus*.

Mullarkey (483) Irish: shortened Anglicized form of Gaelic **Ó Maoilearca** 'descendant of *Maoilearca*', a personal name meaning 'devotee of (Saint) *Earc*', (a personal name with two possible meanings: 'speckled', 'dark red', or 'salmon').
GIVEN NAME Irish 7%. *Brendan*.

Mullee (112) Irish: variant of MILEY.

Mullen (14371) **1.** Irish: Anglicized form of the common and widespread Gaelic name **Ó Maoláin** 'descendant of *Maolán*', a byname meaning 'tonsured one', 'devotee' (from a diminutive of *maol* 'bald'). **2.** English: topographic name for someone who lived by a mill, or a metonymic occupational name for a miller, from Anglo-Norman French *mo(u)lin*, *mulin* 'mill' (see MILL). In some instances it may be a variant of MILLEN, from Middle English *mullelane*. **3.** Dutch and Belgian (**van Mullen**): habitational name from Mullem in East Flanders, Mullem in West Flanders, or possibly Mollen in Brabant. **4.** Dutch (**van (der) Mullen**): variant of **van der Molen** (see MOLEN 4).

Mullenax (454) Irish and English: variant of MULLINAX.

Mullenbach (178) German: variant spelling of **Mühlenbach**, a topographic name for someone living by a mill stream, from Middle High German *mül(e)* 'mill' + *bach* 'stream'.
GIVEN NAMES German 4%. *Gebhard*, *Otto*.

Mullendore (324) altered spelling of German **Mühlentor**, topographic name for someone who lived at a place named as the 'mill gate'.

Mullenix (806) Irish and English: variant of MULLINAX.

Mullennix (129) Irish and English: variant of MULLINAX.

Mullens (1387) English and Irish: variant of MULLINS.

Muller (11107) **1.** German (**Müller**) and Jewish (Ashkenazic): see MUELLER. **2.** Dutch: variant of MULDER.
GIVEN NAMES German 6%. *Kurt* (26), *Hans* (17), *Otto* (16), *Erwin* (8), *Ernst* (6), *Fritz*

(6), *Franz* (5), *Gerhard* (5), *Uwe* (5), *Dieter* (4), *Heinz* (4), *Jurgen* (4).

Mullery (159) Irish: Anglicized form of Gaelic **Ó Maolmhuire** 'descendant of *Maolmhuire*', a personal name meaning 'servant of (the Virgin) Mary'. This is an Ulster name, now rare.
GIVEN NAME Irish 7%. *Brendan*.

Mullet (540) **1.** English and French: from Middle English *molet*, *mulet* 'mullet', a metonymic occupational name for a fisherman or seller of these fish. **2.** nickname from a diminutive of MULE 2.

Mullett (766) **1.** English: variant spelling of MULLET. **2.** Irish (County Wexford): possibly a variant of MILLETT.

Mulley (131) **1.** English (Suffolk): unexplained. **2.** Irish: variant of MILEY.

Mullican (691) Irish: Anglicized form of Gaelic **Ó Maolagáin** (see MILLIGAN).

Mulligan (5777) Irish: Anglicized form of Gaelic **Ó Maolagáin** (see MILLIGAN).
GIVEN NAMES Irish 6%. *Brendan* (5), *Brigid* (3), *Malachy* (3), *Siobhan* (2), *Brennan*, *Colm*, *Connor*, *Donal*, *Fintan*, *Kieran*, *Seamus*.

Mulliken (159) Irish: Anglicized form of Gaelic **Ó Maolagáin** (see MILLIGAN).

Mullikin (1113) Irish: Anglicized form of Gaelic **Ó Maolagáin** (see MILLIGAN).

Mullin (4675) Irish: variant of MULLEN.
GIVEN NAMES Irish 4%. *Brennan* (2), *Assumpta*, *Brendan*, *Bridie*, *Caitlin*, *Declan*, *Jarlath*, *Padraic*.

Mullinax (1720) Irish and English: altered form of the Anglo-Norman French surname MOLYNEUX, via the intermediate form **Mullineaux**, in which the final -*x* was pronounced.

Mullineaux (207) Irish and English: variant of MULLINAX.

Mulliner (113) English: occupational name for a miller, from an agent derivative of Anglo-Norman French *mo(u)lin*, *mulin* 'mill'.

Mullings (489) English: variant of MULLINS.

Mullinix (637) Irish and English: variant of MULLINAX.

Mullinnix (102) Irish and English: variant of MULLINAX.
GIVEN NAME German 6%. *Eldred* (2).

Mullins (23100) English and Irish: occupational name from Old French *molineux* 'miller' (see MOLYNEUX).
FOREBEARS William Mullins (d. 1621) was one of the Pilgrims who sailed on the *Mayflower* in 1620. He, his wife, and his son died during the first winter at Plymouth Colony, leaving behind his daughter Priscilla, who married John Alden, by whom she had eleven children.

Mullis (3209) English (West Midlands): topographic name for someone who lived at a millhouse (from Middle English *mulle* + *hus*; compare MILLHOUSE), or a meto-

nymic occupational name for someone who worked in one.

Mullner (100) Germanized variant of Hungarian MOLNAR.
GIVEN NAMES Hungarian 5%. *Csaba*, *Nandor*.

Mullowney (139) Irish (Connacht): Anglicized form of Gaelic **Ó Maol Dhomhnaigh** (see MALONEY).

Mulloy (693) Irish: variant spelling of MOLLOY.
GIVEN NAMES Irish 6%. *Brigid*, *Padraic*, *Seamus*.

Mulnix (183) Irish and English: variant of MULLINAX.

Mulqueen (331) Irish: Anglicized form of Gaelic **Ó Maolchaoine** 'descendant of *Maolchaoine*', a personal name meaning 'devotee of (Saint) Caoine'.

Mulready (128) Irish: Anglicized form of Gaelic **Ó Maoilbhrighde**, 'descendant of *Maoilbhrighde*', a personal name meaning 'devotee of (Saint) Brigid'. The modern Irish spelling of this name is **Ó Maoilbhríde**.

Mulroney (137) Irish: Anglicized form of Gaelic **Ó Maol Ruanaidh** (see MORONEY).
GIVEN NAME Irish 5%. *Conor*.

Mulrooney (485) Irish: Anglicized form of Gaelic **Ó Maol Ruanaidh** (see MORONEY).
GIVEN NAME Irish 6%. *Brennan*.

Mulroy (591) Irish (Mayo): Anglicized form of Gaelic **Ó Maolruaidh** 'descendant of *Maolruadh*', a personal name composed of the elements *maol* 'chief' + *ruadh* 'red', i.e. 'red-haired chieftain'. This surname has sometimes been changed to MUNROE.

Mulry (203) Irish: variant of MULROY or MULLERY.

Multer (157) **1.** North German: variant of MOLTER. **2.** South German: topographic name denoting a bowl-shaped hollow, Middle High German *multer*. Compare MULDER 2.

Mulvaney (1278) Irish: Anglicized form of Gaelic **Ó Maoilmheana** 'descendant of *Maoilmheana*', a personal name meaning 'chieftain of the Main (river)'. In Donegal it may be an Anglicized form of **Ó Maolmhaghna**.
GIVEN NAMES Irish 5%. *Kieran* (2), *Brendan*, *Brigid*, *Donovan*, *Liam*.

Mulvany (218) Irish: variant of MULVANEY.
GIVEN NAME Irish 6%. *Sean Patrick*.

Mulvehill (192) Irish: variant spelling of MULVIHILL.

Mulvenna (108) Irish: shortened Anglicized form of Gaelic **Ó Maoilmheana** (see MULVANEY).
GIVEN NAME Irish 8%. *Brendan*.

Mulvey (1644) Irish: Anglicized form of Gaelic **Ó Maoilmhiadhaigh** 'descendant of *Maoilmhiadhach*', a personal name meaning 'honorable chief'.
GIVEN NAME Irish 5%. *Ronan*.

Mulvihill (1329) Irish: reduced Anglicized form of Gaelic **Ó Maoil Mhichíl** 'descen-

dant of the devotee of St. Michael' (see MELVILLE). In Counties Clare and Galway Mulvihill has been changed to **Mulville** and MELVILLE, and in Ulster MITCHELL has been adopted as an equivalent.
GIVEN NAME Irish 4%. *Paddy.*

Mulville (106) Irish: reduced form of MULVIHILL.

Muma (263) Romanian: from *mumă*, an old variant of *mamă* 'mother'.

Mumau (134) Origin unidentified. Compare MOOMAW, MUMAW.

Mumaw (529) Origin unidentified. Compare MOOMAW, MUMAU.

Mumby (223) English: habitational name from a place in Lincolnshire, so named from the Old Norse personal name *Mundi* (see MONDAY 1) + Old Norse *býr* 'farm', 'settlement'.

Mumford (2278) English: **1.** variant of MONTFORD. **2.** variant of MUNFORD.

Mumm (801) North German: **1.** from the medieval personal name *Mummo*. This is probably a short form of a Germanic personal name composed of the elements *mund* 'protection' + a second element beginning with *m-*, such as *man* 'man' or *muot* 'courage'. **2.** (Swabian): nickname for a grumpy individual, from *mummen* 'to mumble'.

Mumma (939) Origin unidentified. Possibly a respelling of German MUMME.

Mumme (232) North German: variant of MUMM 1.

Mummert (981) German: from a byname from Middle High German *muntbor* 'protector', 'guardian'.

Mummey (187) Possibly an Americanized spelling of German MUMME.

Mumper (318) **1.** German: from a byname from Middle High German *muntbor* 'protector', 'guardian'. **2.** Possibly also an altered spelling of German **Mümpfer**, a habitational name for someone from Mumpf, near Säckingen, Switzerland.

Mumphrey (203) Variant of Welsh and English HUMPHREY, by misdivision of a forename-surname pair such as *Tom Humphrey.*

Mumpower (283) Probably an Americanized spelling of German MUMPER, or of **Mummenbrauer**, an occupational name in Braunschweig (Brunswick) for a brewer of a local beer called Mumme. A heavily hopped barley beer with low alcohol content, it was first brewed in 1492 by a man named Mumme.

Mun (352) **1.** Scottish and English: unexplained; possibly a respelling of **Munn**, from Old Norse *Munni, Munnr*, a byname meaning 'mouth'. **2.** Korean: there are two Chinese characters for the surname Mun. Although some records indicate that there are as many as 131 Mun clans, only three can be traced. The founding ancestor of the oldest of these, the Namp'yŏng Mun clan, was named Mun Ta-sŏng and was born in 472. According to legend, he was found by

Shilla King Chabi Maripkan in a stone box at the end of a rainbow by a lotus pond. The Chinese character Mun was inscribed in the box, so the king gave that as a surname to the child. The founders of the other two Mun clans were originally named CHA and KIM, but after studying in China they changed their names to Mun (the Chinese character *Mun* means 'writing' or 'literature').
GIVEN NAMES Korean 63%. *Young* (8), *Yong* (4), *Chong* (3), *Hyung* (3), *In* (3), *Song* (3), *Bok* (2), *Dae* (2), *Hui* (2), *Jae* (2), *Kwang* (2), *Kyong* (2), *Kyong Tae* (2), *Kyung* (2), *Myung* (2), *Ae, Cheol, Chul, Chul Ho, Chung, Hak, Hong Suk, Hyung Chul, In Ho.*

Munafo (176) Italian (**Munafò**): variant of MONACO.
GIVEN NAMES Italian 22%. *Alfio, Alfredo, Angelo, Mario, Maurizio, Placido, Rosario, Salvatore, Santi, Santo.*

Munce (183) Possibly an Americanized form of German MUN(T)Z or MAN(T)Z.

Muncey (294) English (Cambridgeshire): variant spelling of MUNSEY.

Munch (907) German (**Münch**) and French (Alsace): variant of **Mönch** (see MOENCH). This name is also established in Scandinavia, especially Denmark.
GIVEN NAMES German 4%. *Erwin* (2), *Otto* (2), *Achim, Egon, Gerhard, Gunther, Helmut, Kurt.*

Muncie (333) Scottish: variant spelling of MUNSEY.

Munck (140) Dutch and Scandinavian: from Middle Dutch *munc* 'monk', Danish, Norwegian, and Swedish *munk* (Old Norse *munkr*), a nickname for someone thought to resemble a monk or a metonymic occupational name for someone in the service of a monastery.
GIVEN NAMES Scandinavian 9%; German 4%. *Jorgen, Peer, Thora; Hans.*

Muncrief (114) Variant spelling of Scottish MONCRIEF.

Muncy (1709) English: variant spelling of MUNSEY.

Mund (478) **1.** English: from an unattested Old English personal name, *Munda*, a short form of some compound name formed with *mund* 'protection'. **2.** German: variant of MUNDT.
GIVEN NAMES German 4%. *Klaus* (2), *Otto, Wilhelm.*

Munda (108) **1.** Slovenian: from a short form of the personal name *Rajmund* (see RAYMOND), formed with the suffix *-a*. **2.** Slovenian: nickname from the dialect word *munda* (of uncertain origin), used as a name for a bull. **3.** Hispanic (Mexico): unexplained.
GIVEN NAMES Italian 9%. *Rino* (2), *Arturo, Guillermo, Leonardo, Orlando, Romolo.*

Mundahl (123) Norwegian: habitational name from places in Sogn and Hordaland named Mundal, from a first element proba-

bly derived from a river name + Old Norse *dalr* 'valley'.
GIVEN NAME Scandinavian 5%. *Erik* (2).

Munday (1202) English and Irish: variant spelling of MONDAY.

Mundell (957) Scottish (of Norman origin): habitational name from Magneville in Normandy. Medieval forms of the name were often spelled with a *-d-* (e.g. *Mandeville*), hence this form.

Munden (688) English: habitational name from a place in Hertfordshire, so named from the Old English personal name *Munda* (a short form of any of the various compound names formed with *mund* 'protection') + *denu* 'valley'.

Mundhenk (109) German: nickname meaning 'Henk with the mouth' (see MUNDT, HENK).
GIVEN NAMES German 4%. *Heinrich, Kurt.*

Mundie (232) Scottish: variant spelling of MUNDY 2.

Mundine (112) English: probably a variant of MUNDEN.

Mundinger (196) German: habitational name for someone from places called Mundingen, in Württemberg and Baden.
GIVEN NAMES German 9%. *Gerhard* (3), *Kurt* (3).

Mundis (190) **1.** Greek: nickname from Greek *moundis*, in Byzantine Greek meaning 'dark reddish brown' but later acquiring the transferred sense 'sulky', 'gloomy', 'dismal'. Either of these senses could have given rise to the surname. **2.** Also of German origin: unexplained.

Mundo (216) **1.** Catalan (**Mundó**): probably a variant of **Montdony**, a habitational name from a place of this name in Vallespir, northern Catalonia. The name is found mainly in Girona province. **2.** Italian: unexplained.
GIVEN NAMES Spanish 31%. *Jose* (5), *Francisco* (2), *Luis* (2), *Manuel* (2), *Marcial* (2), *Nazario* (2), *Rafael* (2), *Sergio* (2), *Alejandra, Alejandro, Alfonso, Andres; Domenico* (2), *Nicolo* (2), *Vito.*

Mundorf (182) German: habitational name from various places called Mondorf, notably in Saarland.

Mundorff (152) German: variant spelling of MUNDORF.
GIVEN NAMES German 9%. *Fritz* (2), *Guenther, Liesl.*

Mundt (1361) German: **1.** nickname for someone with a big mouth or whose mouth was in some other way remarkable, from Middle High German *munt* 'mouth'. **2.** nickname for a guardian or trustworthy person, from Middle High German *munt* 'guardian', 'protector'.

Mundy (3452) **1.** English: variant of MONDAY. **2.** Scottish: probably a habitational name from Munday (formerly Mundy) in Perthshire.

Munford (652) English (Norfolk): habitational name from Mundford in Norfolk, so named from the Old English personal name *Munda* (from *mund* 'protection') + *ford* 'ford'.

Munger (2234) English: variant of MONGER.

Mungia (199) Basque: habitational name from Mungia in Biscay province.
GIVEN NAMES Spanish 48%. *Jose* (6), *Pedro* (3), *Juan* (2), *Lupe* (2), *Manuel* (2), *Sergio* (2), *Adan*, *Adelina*, *Adolfo*, *Alejandro*, *Alfonso*, *Amalia*; *Antonio*, *Geronimo*.

Mungin (228) Probably an Americanized form of French MONGEON.
GIVEN NAME French 4%. *Andre* (2).

Mungle (157) Scottish: habitational name from Mungall in Stirlingshire.

Mungo (327) Scottish: from the personal name *Mungo*, of uncertain derivation. It was an alternative name for St. Kentigern, the patron saint of Glasgow, who was a 6th-century apostle of southwestern Scotland and northwestern English.

Mungovan (123) Irish (Connacht): rare, shortened Anglicized form of Gaelic **Ó Mongabháin** 'descendant of *Mongabhán*', a byname from *mongbhán* 'white hair'.
GIVEN NAMES Irish 6%. *Brendan*, *Liam*.

Munguia (817) Spanish (of Basque origin; **Munguía**): Castilianized form of the Basque habitational name MUNGIA, from a place in Biscay province.
GIVEN NAMES Spanish 53%. *Jose* (30), *Juan* (14), *Ruben* (12), *Carlos* (11), *Francisco* (8), *Jorge* (6), *Luis* (6), *Fernando* (5), *Manuel* (5), *Salvador* (5), *Alfonso* (4), *Gerardo* (4).

Munhall (115) Scottish: unexplained. Black records the surname **Mungall**, a habitational name from Mungall in Stirlingshire; Munhall may be a variant of this.

Muni (100) 1. Indian (Gujarat): Hindu (Vania) name derived from Sanskrit *muni* 'sage', 'hermit, in particular one who has taken a vow of silence'. 2. Southern Italian (Sicilian): from a short form of the personal name *Simuni*, Sicilian form of SIMON. 3. Southern Italian (**Monì**): possibly from modern Greek *Monias*, which may be from *mónos* 'alone' and hence a nickname for a solitary person.
GIVEN NAMES Indian 27%; Italian 7%. *Haresh* (2), *Ashok*, *Bharti*, *Chandra*, *Indu*, *Ketan*, *Kirit*, *Muralidhar*, *Narendra*, *Raj*; *Orlando* (2), *Antonio*, *Carmine*, *Domenic*.

Munier (149) French: occupational name for a miller, from a regional variant of *meunier* 'miller'.
GIVEN NAMES French 11%. *Emile* (3), *Jacques*, *Thibaut*.

Munir (138) Muslim: from a personal name based on Arabic *munīr* 'bright', 'brilliant', 'radiant'.
GIVEN NAMES Muslim 77%; Indian 5%. *Mohammad* (10), *Muhammad* (10), *Nasir* (3), *Choudhry* (2), *Isam* (2), *Khan* (2), *Mohamad* (2), *Shahid* (2), *Yusuf* (2), *Adnan*, *Ahmed*, *Aminah*; *Asim* (2), *Asis*.

Muniz (3291) 1. Galician, Asturian-Leonese, and Spanish (**Muñiz**): patronymic from the old personal name *Muño* (see MUNOZ). 2. Portuguese: variant of MONIZ.
GIVEN NAMES Spanish 45%. *Jose* (90), *Juan* (55), *Luis* (43), *Carlos* (39), *Manuel* (28), *Francisco* (27), *Jorge* (20), *Jesus* (19), *Raul* (18), *Miguel* (16), *Angel* (15), *Ramon* (14).

Munk (691) 1. English: variant spelling of MONK. 2. German (**Münk**), Scandinavian, and Dutch: from Middle High German *münich*, Middle Dutch *munc*, Scandinavian *munk* 'monk', a nickname for someone thought to resemble a monk, or a metonymic occupational name for someone in the service of a monastery. 3. Jewish (Ashkenazic): from the male personal name *M(o)unka*, a Czech pet form of SOLOMON.
GIVEN NAMES Jewish 5%. *Ezriel* (4), *Pinchos*, *Rivka*, *Shimon*, *Shmuel*, *Zev*.

Munkres (143) Origin unidentified.

Munley (408) Irish (Connacht and Donegal): Anglicized form of Gaelic **Ó Maonghaile** (see MANLEY).

Munn (3393) 1. Scottish: Anglicized form of Gaelic **Mac Gille Mhunna** (see McMUNN). 2. English: nickname from Anglo-Norman French *moun* 'monk' (see MONK).

Munnell (128) Possibly an altered form of MUNDELL.

Munnelly (124) Irish: shortened Anglicized form of Gaelic **Ó Maonghaile** (see MANLEY).

Munnerlyn (236) Origin unknown.

Munno (108) Italian: assimilated form of MUNDO.
GIVEN NAMES Italian 21%. *Salvatore* (2), *Antonio*, *Ennio*, *Lorenzo*, *Matteo*, *Oreste*, *Pasquale*, *Rocco*.

Munns (589) English: patronymic from MUNN.

Muno (106) Spanish (**Muño**): from the old personal name *Muño*. The name in this form is common in Mexico and the Dominican Republic.

Munos (201) Spanish: probably a variant spelling of **Muñoz** (see MUNOZ).
GIVEN NAMES Spanish 41%. *Jose* (9), *Juan* (3), *Luis* (3), *Jaime* (2), *Pablo* (2), *Rafael* (2), *Raul* (2), *Adolfo*, *Alfonso*, *Balentin*, *Beatriz*, *Carlos*.

Munoz (14273) Spanish (**Muñoz**): patronymic from the old personal name *Muño*.
GIVEN NAMES Spanish 49%; Portuguese 10%. *Jose* (449), *Juan* (209), *Manuel* (148), *Carlos* (144), *Luis* (133), *Jesus* (124), *Miguel* (96), *Francisco* (94), *Mario* (77), *Ruben* (77), *Pedro* (72), *Jorge* (71); *Wenceslao* (3), *Catarina* (2), *Paulo* (2), *Anatolio*.

Munro (2895) 1. Scottish: variant of MONROE. 2. In Ireland, Munroe has come to replace the surname MULROY in some cases.

Munroe (2349) 1. Scottish: variant of MONROE. 2. In Ireland, Munroe has come to replace the surname MULROY in some cases.

Muns (259) 1. Catalan: variant spelling of *Munts*, plural of MUNT. 2. French: from a Germanic personal name, *Munzo* or *Munso*, pet forms of *Muno* or *Mundo*, from either *mun* (related to Gothic *munan* 'to think') or *mund* 'protection'. 3. Dutch: patronymic from a short form of the personal name *Simon*, *Simoen* (see SIMON).

Munsch (447) Alsatian variant of French MONGE.

Munsell (745) 1. English: variant of MANSELL. 2. in some cases perhaps an Americanized spelling of German **Munzel**, a habitational name from a place so named near Hannover or from Monzel near Trier.

Munsen (127) 1. Norwegian and Danish: variant of MONSEN. 2. Swedish (**Munsén**): probably an ornamental variant of **Månsson** (see MONSON), with the ending altered by analogy with the many Swedish surnames ending in *-én*.
GIVEN NAMES Scandinavian 5%. *Bernt*, *Johan*.

Munsey (981) English (of Norman origin): habitational name from places called Monceaux, in Calvados and Orne, or Monchaux, in Nord and Seine-Maritime. These get their name from the plural form of Old French *moncel* 'hillock', Late Latin *monticellum*, a diminutive of *mons*. Compare MONT.

Munshi (122) Indian (northern states): Hindu and Muslim name meaning 'clerk', 'writer', from Arabic *munshi'*. It is widely used as an honorific title for an educated man.
GIVEN NAMES Indian 51%; Muslim 36%. *Kersi* (3), *Rajiv* (2), *Snehal* (2), *Sushil* (2), *Abhay*, *Ajit*, *Amit*, *Anil*, *Anuradha*, *Aparna*, *Bhargav*, *Gaurang*; *Anwar* (4), *Imtiaz* (2), *Abdul*, *Abdulla*, *Aisha*, *Ashraf*, *Ebrahim*, *Habib*, *Hafizur*, *Ilyas*, *Imran*, *Mahmood*.

Munshower (122) Americanized spelling of German **Monschauer**, habitational name for someone from Monschau (near Aachen), which supposedly derives from French *Montjoie*.

Munsinger (156) German: 1. (**Münsinger**) habitational name for someone from a place called Münsingen. 2. altered form of **Munzinger**, from any of several places call Munzingen.

Munson (7175) English: patronymic from MUNN.

Munster (303) 1. German and Dutch (**Munster**, **Münster**): habitational name from places called Munster or Münster, derived from Latin *monasterium* 'monastery', or a topographic name for someone who lived near a monastery. 2. Irish: see MOYNIHAN.
GIVEN NAMES German 5%. *Gerhard* (2), *Egon*, *Jurgen*.

Munsterman (313) German (**Munster-mann, Münstermann**) and Dutch: variant of MUNSTER.

Munt (104) **1.** Catalan: variant of MONT, topographic name from *munt* 'hill', denoting someone who lived on or near a hill, Latin *mons*. **2.** English: variant of MOUNT.

Muntean (250) Romanian: **1.** ethnic name for someone from Wallachia (Romanian *Muntania* 'the mountain region'). **2.** topographic name from *muntean* 'mountain dweller'.

GIVEN NAMES Romanian 16%. *Vasile* (4), *Petru* (3), *Nicolae* (2), *Sorin* (2), *Aurelian*, *Filon*, *Georgeta*, *Mircea*, *Radu*.

Munter (373) **1.** North German (**Münter**), Dutch, and Scandinavian: occupational name for a moneyer (see MINTER). **2.** Catalan: occupational name from *munter*, applied to a person in charge of the dogs at a hunt

Muntz (561) German (**Müntz**): habitational name from Müntz near Jülich.

Munyan (212) Irish: Anglicized form of Gaelic **Ó Mainnín** (see MANNION, MANNING).

Munyon (452) Irish: Anglicized form of Gaelic **Ó Mainnín** (see MANNION, MANNING).

Munz (627) **1.** German and Jewish (Ashkenazic): metonymic occupational name for a moneyer, from German *Münze* 'mint'. Compare MINTER. **2.** German (also **Münz**): from a pet form of a Germanic personal name, *Muno* or *Mundo* (see MUNS 2).

GIVEN NAMES German 7%. *Otto* (3), *Willi* (2), *Armin*, *Fritz*, *Heinz*, *Katharina*, *Lothar*, *Manfred*, *Rudi*.

Munzer (163) German (**Münzer**) and Jewish (Ashkenazic): occupational name for a moneyer, Middle High German *münzære*, German *Münzer*.

GIVEN NAMES Jewish 6%; German 4%. *Emanuel* (2), *Doron*, *Hyman*, *Miriam*; *Alois*, *Benno*, *Otto*.

Muoio (199) Italian: most likely a habitational name from Muoio, a district of Agropoli in Salerno province.

GIVEN NAMES Italian 18%. *Gennaro* (3), *Salvatore* (2), *Luigi*, *Pasquale*, *Piero*, *Vittorio*.

Mura (265) **1.** Japanese: ornamental name, now rare in Japan, from *mura* 'village'; listed in the Shinsen *shōjiroku*. Occurrences in America probably originated in the Ryūkyū Islands, or may be shortened forms of other names containing this word. **2.** French: according to Morlet, a topographic name from a dialect variant of *mure* 'ruined wall(s)', from *mur* 'wall', Latin *murus*, or a habitational name from places called La Mure in Alpes-de-Haute-Provence, Isère, Rhône, and Puy-de-Dôme. **3.** Italian (southern Sardinia): topographic name or nickname from Sardinian *mura* 'mulberry' or 'blackberry'. **4.** Catalan: habitational name from Mura in Barcelona. **5.** Czech

and Slovak: from *Muric*, a personal name equivalent to *Maurice* (see MORRIS).

GIVEN NAMES Japanese 6%; French 5%. *Akio*, *Hideo*, *Masao*, *Nanako*, *Tsutomu*, *Yoshi*; *Alphonse*, *Amie*, *Henri*.

Murabito (126) Southern Italian: nickname from Sicilian *murabbitu* 'teetotaler', from Arabic *murābit* 'hermit'.

GIVEN NAMES Italian 17%. *Angelo* (2), *Salvatore* (2), *Santo* (2), *Alfio*.

Muraca (125) Italian: variant of MORACE.

GIVEN NAMES Italian 28%. *Angelo* (2), *Antonio*, *Cesare*, *Marcello*, *Mario*, *Ottavio*, *Pasquale*, *Pietro*, *Valentino*.

Murach (117) German: habitational name from any of several places such as Murach in Bavaria or Maurach in Tyrol, Austria.

Muraco (110) Italian: variant of MORACE.

GIVEN NAMES Italian 15%. *Angelo*, *Carlo*, *Carmine*, *Gasper*.

Murad (445) Muslim: from a personal name based on Arabic *murād* 'will', 'purpose', 'wish'. This was the name of a son of the 16th-century Mughal emperor Akbar.

GIVEN NAMES Muslim 26%; French 6%. *Ahmed* (4), *Ali* (4), *Mohammed* (4), *Ferid* (2), *Fuad* (2), *Hani* (2), *Husain* (2), *Nabil* (2), *Nidal* (2), *Raed* (2), *Abdullah*, *Aly*; *Marcel* (3), *Antoine*, *Camille*, *Carolle*, *Franck*, *Pierre*, *Thierry*.

Murai (156) **1.** Japanese: 'village well'; mostly found in the Kyōto-Ōsaka region. **2.** Hungarian: habitational name for someone who lived by the river Mura.

GIVEN NAMES Japanese 60%. *Shigeo* (3), *Atsushi* (2), *Mamiko* (2), *Norio* (2), *Osamu* (2), *Akio*, *Hajime*, *Haruka*, *Hirofumi*, *Hiroyuki*, *Hisayuki*, *Ichiro*.

Murakami (908) Japanese: 'above the village'; found mostly in west-central Japan and the island of Okinawa. It is also the patronymic of the Murakami Genji, a branch of the MINAMOTO clan descended from several sons of the Emperor Murakami (926–967).

GIVEN NAMES Japanese 52%. *Takashi* (10), *Katsumi* (5), *Koji* (4), *Mitsuo* (4), *Tadashi* (4), *Akiko* (3), *Akira* (3), *Hiroshi* (3), *Kazuo* (3), *Kiyoshi* (3), *Koichi* (3), *Masayuki* (3).

Muramoto (168) Japanese: '(one who lives) below the village'; found throughout Japan, but not in large numbers.

GIVEN NAMES Japanese 41%. *Toshio* (3), *Hideto* (2), *Takeo* (2), *Hideko*, *Hideo*, *Hiroko*, *Hisato*, *Itsuo*, *Jiro*, *Kameko*, *Kazumasa*, *Masaji*.

Muranaka (130) Japanese: '(one who lives) in the center of the village'; found throughout Japan, but not in large numbers.

GIVEN NAMES Japanese 49%. *Hideo* (2), *Nobuo* (2), *Shigemi* (2), *Tamotsu* (2), *Tomio* (2), *Akio*, *Haruko*, *Kaoru*, *Koji*, *Masashi*, *Momoyo*, *Sadamu*.

Murano (266) **1.** Italian: habitational name for someone from Murano. **2.** Japanese: 'village field'; found throughout Japan, but not in large numbers.

GIVEN NAMES Italian 11%; Japanese 8%. *Carmine* (2), *Salvatore* (2), *Aniello*, *Carlo*, *Donato*, *Rocco*, *Sal*, *Serafino*; *Atsuko*, *Chikara*, *Eiichi*, *Isao*, *Keni*, *Kiyo*, *Kohei*, *Masaaki*, *Taro*, *Tomoko*.

Muraoka (250) Japanese: 'village hill'; found throughout Japan, but not in large numbers.

GIVEN NAMES Japanese 41%. *Hiroshi* (4), *Atsushi* (2), *Mamoru* (2), *Masao* (2), *Mitsugi* (2), *Takashi* (2), *Aiko*, *Akane*, *Aki*, *Akio*, *Fumi*, *Haruko*.

Muraski (212) Polish: variant of MURAWSKI.

Murat (119) French: habitational name from any of various places named Murat, in Allier, Cantal, Corrèze, Puy-de-Dôme, and Tarn.

GIVEN NAMES French 18%. *Andre*, *Armand*, *Chantelle*, *Emile*, *Marie Anne*, *Raynald*, *Solange*.

Murata (414) Japanese: 'village rice paddy'; a name that is found throughout Japan, but not in large numbers.

GIVEN NAMES Japanese 55%. *Hiroshi* (7), *Hideyuki* (3), *Kiyoshi* (3), *Koji* (3), *Akira* (2), *Kazu* (2), *Kazuo* (2), *Kenji* (2), *Makoto* (2), *Minoru* (2), *Naoki* (2), *Osamu* (2).

Muratore (354) Southern Italy and Sicily: from *muratore*, a derivative of Late Latin *murare* 'to make walls', hence an occupational name for a builder or mason.

GIVEN NAMES Italian 13%. *Angelo* (4), *Rocco* (2), *Antonio*, *Carmine*, *Caterina*, *Gaetano*, *Gasper*, *Guido*, *Paolo*, *Raffaele*, *Salvatore*.

Muratori (105) Italian: from a patronymic or plural form of MURATORE.

GIVEN NAMES Italian 15%. *Attilio*, *Dante*, *Filippo*, *Francesca*, *Giorgio*, *Silvio*.

Murawski (1094) Polish: habitational name for someone from placed called Murawa or Murawy, named with *murawa* 'lawn', 'green'.

Murayama (147) Japanese: meaning 'the mountain near the village'. The name is more common in eastern Japan and the Ryūkyū Islands. Listed in the Shinsen *shōjiroku*.

GIVEN NAMES Japanese 62%. *Atsuko* (3), *Takashi* (3), *Kaoru* (2), *Kei* (2), *Kohei* (2), *Masaaki* (2), *Masao* (2), *Noritaka* (2), *Akihiko*, *Akiko*, *Atsuhiko*, *Chikako*.

Murbach (126) German: habitational name from any of several places so called in Baden and Bavaria.

Murch (742) **1.** English (Devon): nickname for a dwarf, Middle English *much(e)*. **2.** French (Lorraine): nickname for a lethargic, feeble man, from a Middle High German loanword, *mursch*, *murz*.

Murchie (220) Scottish: shortened Anglicized form of Gaelic **Mac Mhurchaidh** (see MURCHISON).

Murchison (1260) Scottish and northern Irish: Anglicized form (in which the Gaelic patronymic prefix *Mac* has been translated into the English patronymic suffix *-son*), of

Gaelic **Mac Mhurchaidh**, a patronymic from the personal name *Murchadh*, composed of the elements *muir* 'sea' + *cath* 'battle', hence 'sea warrior'.

Murcia (166) Spanish: habitational name from the city so named.
GIVEN NAMES Spanish 54%; Portuguese 15%. *Jose* (7), *Carlos* (5), *Jaime* (3), *Jorge* (3), *Luis* (3), *Manuel* (3), *Roberto* (3), *Alfonso* (2), *Alvaro* (2), *Consuelo* (2), *Fernando* (2), *Juan* (2); *Ligia*.

Murcko (136) Slovak: from a pet form of the personal name *Muric*, Slovak form of *Maurice* (see MORRIS).

Murdaugh (402) Altered spelling of MUR-DOCH.

Murden (345) English (Nottingham): variant of MORDEN.

Murdick (181) Variant of northern Irish MURDOCK.

Murdoch (1518) **1.** Scottish: from an Anglicized form of the Gaelic personal names *Muire(adh)ach*, a derivative of *muir* 'sea' (hence the usual translation as 'mariner') and *Murchadh* 'sea battler'. These may originally have been patronymics, the prefix *Mac* having been dropped at a later stage. **2.** Irish (Ulster): when not of Scottish origin, a variant of MURTAGH.

Murdock (7051) Northern Irish: variant of Scottish MURDOCH.

Murdough (128) Variant of Scottish MURDOCH.

Murdy (198) Scottish: probably a variant of MURDOCH.

Muren (110) Slovenian: nickname from *muren* 'cricket' (the insect), probably denoting a cheerful person.

Murer (103) Norwegian and Danish (**Mürer**): occupational name from *Mur* 'brick wall', originally German.
GIVEN NAMES Scandinavian 8%; German 6%. *Erik* (2); *Kaspar, Klaus, Otto*.

Murff (405) Possibly an altered spelling of Swiss German **Morff**, which may be a contracted form of the personal name *Morolf*.

Murfin (232) English (chiefly Nottinghamshire, Derbyshire, and Yorkshire): from an Old English personal name, *Merewine, Merefinn*, or *Mǣrwynn* (see MARVIN).
FOREBEARS The first Murfins in North America were Nottinghamshire Quakers. Robert and Ann Murfin and their daughter Mary sailed from Hull, England, in 1678 on the ship *Shield of Stockton* and settled at Chesterfield, near Burlington, NJ.

Murga (163) **1.** Spanish: habitational name from Murga in Navarre province. **2.** Romanian (**Murgă**) and Greek (**Mourgas**): nickname meaning 'dark-skinned', from Romanian *murg* 'black'. The Greek name was also used to denote a Greek of Aromanian origin. It is sometimes found in combinations such as *Mourgagiannis* 'dark-skinned John' or 'Aromanian John'.
GIVEN NAMES Spanish 42%. *Armando* (5), *Jose* (5), *Jorge* (3), *Victoriano* (3), *Alberto*

(2), *Estela* (2), *Francisco* (2), *Jesus* (2), *Manuel* (2), *Aida, Aleida, Alfredo*.

Murgatroyd (114) English (West Yorkshire): habitational name from a lost place near Halifax, apparently named with the medieval personal name *Marg(ar)et* (see MARGESON) + northern Middle English *royd* 'clearing' (Old English *rod*).

Murgia (123) **1.** Italian: topographic name from *murgia* 'rock'. **2.** Italian (Sardinian): nickname from Sardinian *murgia* 'brine' or *murcia* 'marc (of olives)', 'dregs' (compare MORGA). **3.** Basque: habitational name from either of the two towns called Murgia, in Araba and Gipuzkoa provinces, Basque Country.
GIVEN NAMES Italian 19%; Spanish 10%. *Antonio* (2), *Cecilio, Chiara, Marco, Silvano; Cruz* (2), *Jose* (2), *Beatriz, Guadalupe, Paola, Ramon*.

Murgo (114) Italian: habitational name from places called Morco or Murga. This name is also common in Mexico.
GIVEN NAMES Italian 18%. *Salvatore* (3), *Angelo* (2), *Antonio, Gaetano, Sal*.

Murguia (368) Spanish (of Basque origin): Castilianized form of Basque MURGIA, habitational name from either of two places called Murgia, in Araba and Gipuzkoa provinces.
GIVEN NAMES Spanish 49%. *Jose* (10), *Jesus* (6), *Eduardo* (5), *Francisco* (5), *Salvador* (5), *Carlos* (4), *Manuel* (4), *Jose Luis* (3), *Juana* (3), *Luis* (3), *Raul* (3), *Alberto* (2).

Muri (158) **1.** Norwegian: habitational name from a farmstead in Sunnmøre called Muri, probably originally *Mærvin*, from Old Norse *mærr* 'illustrious', 'glorious' + *vin* 'meadow'. **2.** Swiss German: unexplained; perhaps a variant of **Möri** (see MORI 3).
GIVEN NAMES French 4%; German 4%. *Pierre; Heinz* (2).

Murie (138) **1.** Scottish: habitational name from Murie in Perthshire. **2.** possibly a variant spelling of Norwegian MURI.
GIVEN NAME French 4%. *Michel*.

Muriel (158) **1.** Spanish: habitational name from any of the places called Muriel, in Soria, Gaudalajara, or Valladolid. **2.** English (East Anglia): from the female personal name *Muriel*, of Breton origin. This was common in East Anglia during the Middle Ages, where it was introduced by Breton settlers following the Norman invasion.
GIVEN NAMES Spanish 46%. *Jose* (4), *Carlos* (3), *Fernando* (3), *Alfredo* (2), *Angel* (2), *Francisco* (2), *Javier* (2), *Juan* (2), *Alejo, Amador, Candido, Diego*.

Murillo (3383) Spanish: habitational name from any of several places called Murillo, notably in Navarre, Logroño, and Zaragoza provinces, so named from a diminutive of *muro* 'wall'.
GIVEN NAMES Spanish 51%; Portuguese 11%. *Jose* (110), *Manuel* (46), *Juan* (43), *Jesus* (38), *Carlos* (36), *Jorge* (29), *Miguel* (25),

Francisco (23), *Luis* (22), *Javier* (20), *Pedro* (18), *Ruben* (17); *Marcio, Paulo, Wenceslao*.

Murin (205) **1.** Jewish (eastern Ashkenazic) and Ukrainian: nickname for someone with a dark complexion, from Belorussian and Yiddish *murin*, Ukrainian *muryn* 'moor'. **2.** Jewish (eastern Ashkenazic): habitational name from Muriny in Belarus.

Murk (163) Americanized or Germanized spelling of Swedish **Mörk** or Norwegian and Danish **Mørk, Mørck, Mørch** (see MORK).
GIVEN NAMES German 6%. *Alfons, Ewald*.

Murley (608) **1.** Irish (County Cork): Anglicized form of Gaelic **Ó Murthuile**, 'descendant of *Murthuile*', a personal name from *murthuile* 'sea tide' (*muir* 'sea' + *tuile* 'tide', 'flood'). **2.** Irish (Donegal and Mayo): Anglicized form of Gaelic **Ó Murghaile** 'descendant of *Murghal*', a personal name from *muir* 'sea' + *gal* 'valor'. **3.** English: possibly of Irish origin, but it occurs chiefly in southwestern counties, suggesting that it may be a variant of the habitational name MORLEY, from Moreleigh in Devon.

Murman (116) German (**Mürmann**): variant of **Mauermann** (see MAUERMAN).
GIVEN NAME German 7%. *Wessel*.

Murnahan (108) Irish (Ulster): shortened Anglicized form of Gaelic **Ó Muirneacháin** 'descendant of *Muirneachán*', a byname from *muirneach* 'lovable'.

Murnan (148) Irish: variant of MURNANE.
GIVEN NAME French 4%. *Emile*.

Murnane (634) Irish (County Cork): Anglicized form of Gaelic **Ó Murnáin**, a reduced and dissimilated form of **Ó Manannáin** 'descendant of *Manannán*', name borne in Celtic mythology by a sea god associated with the Isle of Man.

Murner (139) South German and Swiss German: habitational name for someone from a place called Murn or Murnau.

Muro (963) **1.** Spanish: habitational name from any of numerous places named Muro, from *muro* 'wall'. **2.** Southern Italian: habitational name from a place named Muro. **3.** Southern Italian (**Murò**): nickname from medieval Greek *mouros* 'stupid', 'foolish' (classical Greek *mōros*).
GIVEN NAMES Spanish 39%; Portuguese 7%; Italian 6%. *Manuel* (16), *Jose* (14), *Jesus* (13), *Juan* (9), *Miguel* (7), *Alejandro* (6), *Arturo* (5), *Francisco* (5), *Luis* (5), *Ruben* (5), *Margarita* (4), *Alfonso* (3); *Armanda; Antonio* (5), *Angelo* (3), *Pasquale* (2), *Rocco* (2), *Salvatore* (2), *Carmelo, Carmine, Cira, Filomena, Heriberto, Luigi, Mirella*.

Murph (450) See MURFF.

Murphey (1548) Irish: variant of MURPHY.

Murphree (1806) Probably a variant of Irish MURPHY.

Murphrey (151) Probably a variant of Irish MURPHY.

Murphy (115601) Irish: Anglicized form of Gaelic **Ó Murchadha** 'descendant of *Murchadh*', a personal name composed of the elements *muir* 'sea' + *cath* 'battle', i.e. 'sea-warrior'. This was an important family in Tyrone.

GIVEN NAMES Irish 4%. *Brendan* (64), *Liam* (12), *Aileen* (9), *Kieran* (9), *Brigid* (8), *Donal* (8), *Siobhan* (8), *Eamon* (7), *Aidan* (6), *Dermot* (6), *John Patrick* (6), *Declan* (5).

Murr (906) German (common in Munich): nickname for a morose person, from Middle High German, Middle Low German *murren* 'to grumble'.

Murra (127) **1.** Probably an Americanized form of Scottish MURRAY. **2.** Italian (Sicily): topographic name from Sicilian *murra* 'large rock', 'mass of rocks' or a habitational name from a place named with this word.

Murrah (483) Probably an Americanized form of Scottish MURRAY.

Murray (66484) **1.** Scottish: regional name from Moray in northeastern Scotland, which is probably named with Old Celtic elements meaning 'sea' + 'settlement'. **2.** Irish (southern Ulster): reduced Anglicized form of Gaelic **Ó Muireadhaigh** 'descendant of *Muireadhach*' (the name of several different families in various parts of Ireland), or a shortened form of McMURRAY. **3.** Irish: reduced form of MacIlmurray, Anglicized form of Gaelic **Mac Giolla Mhuire** (see GILMORE).

Murrell (3522) English: variant of MERRILL.

Murren (234) Irish: variant of MURRIN.

Murrey (382) English, Scottish, and Irish: variant of MURRAY.

Murri (139) Probably a variant spelling of Scottish MURRAY.

Murrie (132) Scottish: variant spelling of MURRAY.

Murrieta (199) Basque: habitational name from Murrieta in Biscay province.

GIVEN NAMES Spanish 47%. *Jesus* (8), *Manuel* (7), *Joaquin* (4), *Blanca* (2), *Francisco* (2), *Adalberto, Agustin, Alberto, Alfonso, Alfonzo, Amado, Armando.*

Murrill (353) English: variant of MERRILL or MORRELL.

Murrillo (120) Spanish: variant of MURILLO.

GIVEN NAMES Spanish 55%. *Jose* (5), *Juan* (3), *Guadalupe* (2), *Jesus* (2), *Pedro* (2), *Ricardo* (2), *Roberto* (2), *Ruben* (2), *Beatriz, Blanca, Evangelina, Everardo.*

Murrin (476) **1.** Irish: Anglicized form of Gaelic **Ó Muireáin** 'descendant of *Muireán*', most probably a diminutive of a personal name beginning with *muir* 'sea'. **2.** English (Devon): unexplained; possibly a variant of MORRIN.

Murrow (473) Irish and Scottish: variant of MORROW.

Murry (2440) Variant spelling of MURRAY 1–4.

Mursch (104) German: nickname for a frail person, from Middle High German *mursch* 'brittle'.

GIVEN NAMES German 7%. *Horst, Jurgen.*

Murtagh (736) Irish: **1.** (Meath and Monaghan) Anglicized form of Gaelic **Ó Muircheartaigh** 'descendant of *Muircheartach*', a personal name from *muir* 'sea' + *ceardach* 'skilled', i.e. 'skilled navigator'. A Kerry surname of the same form is Anglicized as MORIARTY. **2.** (County Roscommon) Anglicized form of *Mac Muircheartaigh* (originally Anglicized as MacMoriarty) (see McMURTRY). **3.** (Ulster): sometimes of Scottish origin, an alternative to MURDOCK.

GIVEN NAMES Irish 9%. *Brendan, Ciaran, Declan, Eamon, Eamonn, Fintan, Maeve.*

Murtaugh (644) Irish: variant of MURTAGH.

Murtha (1277) Irish (mainly County Meath): variant of MURTAGH.

GIVEN NAME Irish 4%. *Brendan* (2).

Murthy (416) Indian (Karnataka): Hindu name from Sanskrit *mūrti* 'manifestation', 'image'. As a personal name, this appears to have evolved from the final element of compound names such as **Ramamurthy** 'manifestation of Rama' and KRISHNAMURTHY 'manifestation of Krishna'. It is only a given name in India, but has come to be used as a surname among South Indians in the U.S.

GIVEN NAMES Indian 93%. *Krishna* (21), *Keshava* (9), *Ravi* (5), *Arun* (4), *Narasimha* (4), *Vasudeva* (4), *Ananda* (3), *Ganesh* (3), *Harsha* (3), *Nagesh* (3), *Naresh* (3), *Prahlad* (3).

Murto (103) Finnish: topographic name from *murto* 'forest clearing'. This was also adopted as an ornamental name during the name conversion movement at the beginning of the 20th century. It is found mostly in western Finland.

GIVEN NAMES Finnish 5%. *Tauno, Wilho.*

Murton (171) Northern English: habitational name from any of various places, in Cumbria, County Durham, North Yorkshire, and elsewhere, all named in Old English as 'settlement or enclosure at the marsh or moor', from *mōr* 'marsh', 'fen', 'moor' + *tūn* 'enclosure', 'settlement'.

Murty (187) **1.** Indian: variant of MURTHY. **2.** Irish: shortened Anglicized form of Gaelic **Mac Muircheartaigh** (see McMURTRY).

GIVEN NAMES Indian 18%. *Ramana* (3), *Sudarshan* (2), *Hari, Hema, Krishna, Lakshmi, Radhika, Ram, Sanjay, Uma, Veni.*

Murzyn (191) Polish: nickname for a dark-skinned person, from *murzyn* 'Moor'. Compare MOORE 2.

Musa (447) **1.** Muslim: from the Arabic personal name *Musa* (the Biblical MOSES). The Qur'an says (19:51): 'He was specially chosen, and he was a Messenger and a Prophet.' **2.** Southern Italian: habitational name from a place called Musa, particularly the one in Melito di Porto Salvo in Reggio Calabria, and the one in Nissorìa in Enna province, Sicily.

GIVEN NAMES Muslim 33%; Spanish 4%. *Mohammad* (7), *Ibrahim* (3), *Mohammed* (3), *Mustafa* (3), *Sami* (3), *Abdal* (2), *Bassam* (2), *Hussein* (2), *Jamal* (2), *Mazen* (2), *Muhammad* (2), *Musa* (2); *Jorge* (2), *Jose* (2), *Mario* (2), *Narciso* (2), *Carmelita, Cleofas, Eduardo, Esperanza, Jesus, Juan, Luis, Luz.*

Musacchia (132) Italian (Sicily): Italianized form of the Albanian family name **Muzaqi**. The Muzaqi were an Albanian princely family, prominent in the 13th century.

GIVEN NAMES Italian 18%. *Carmela* (2), *Antonino, Carmine, Giovanni, Nicolo, Salvatore, Salvatrice.*

Musacchio (225) Southern Italian: variant of MUSACCHIA.

GIVEN NAMES Italian 11%. *Angelo, Carlo, Lelio, Pasquale.*

Musante (400) Italian (Genoa): unexplained.

GIVEN NAMES Italian 6%. *Angelo* (3), *Attilio* (2), *Aldo, Carlo, Guido, Renzo, Tiziana, Vito.*

Musarra (169) Italian (Sicilian): probably from a personal name based on Arabic *masarruh* 'happiness'.

GIVEN NAMES Italian 26%. *Angelo* (3), *Salvatore* (3), *Sal* (2), *Antonio, Francesco, Giuseppina, Rosario, Stefano.*

Muscarella (542) Sicilian and southern Italian: nickname from a diminutive of *musca* 'fly' (see MOSCA).

GIVEN NAMES Italian 18%. *Angelo* (4), *Sal* (4), *Salvatore* (4), *Antonio* (2), *Armelio, Concetta, Mariano, Natale, Rocco, Rosario, Silvestre.*

Muscarello (139) Italian: masculinized form of MUSCARELLA.

GIVEN NAMES Italian 14%. *Angelo* (2), *Sal, Santo.*

Muscari (114) Variant spelling of Italian MASCARI.

Muscat (267) **1.** Maltese and Italian: variant of MUSCATO. **2.** German and Jewish (Ashkenazic): variant spelling of MUSKAT. **3.** English: probably a variant spelling of MUSCOTT.

GIVEN NAMES Italian 8%; Spanish 5%. *Angelo* (2), *Alessio, Carmela, Egidio, Mario, Orlando; Carlos, Erlinda, Manuel.*

Muscatello (146) Italian: **1.** from a pet form of the personal name MUSCATO. **2.** metonymic occupational name for a producer or seller of a sweet, musk-scented wine, Italian *muscatello*. Compare MOSCATO.

GIVEN NAMES Italian 9%. *Carlo, Pierina.*

Muscato (283) Italian: **1.** from the personal name *Muscato*, ultimately a derivative of Latin *muscus* 'moss'. **2.** variant of MOSCATO.

GIVEN NAMES Italian 7%. *Antonio, Natale, Rocco, Salvatore.*

Musch (305) **1.** North German (**Müsch**): topographic name meaning 'bog', or habitational name from a place called Müsch in the Eifel. **2.** Dutch and German: nickname meaning 'house sparrow', perhaps given to a busy person or a small, weak man.

Musco (258) Italian: **1.** topographic name from *musco* 'moss' (Latin *muscus*). **2.** nickname from Sicilian *muscu* 'miser' 'untrustworthy or lawless person'.

GIVEN NAMES Italian 19%. *Salvatore* (5), *Angelo* (3), *Lucio* (2), *Sal* (2), *Carlo, Enrico, Nunzio, Santo.*

Muscott (87) English: habitational name from Muscott, a minor place in Northamptonshire, or Muscoates in North Yorkshire, both named from Old English *mūs* 'mouse' + *cot* 'hut', 'small dwelling', 'shelter'.

Muse (3658) French: nickname for a dissolute person, from Old French *muse* 'amusement', 'dissipation'.

Musel (112) French: diminutive of MUSE.

Musella (134) Italian: probably from a diminutive plural of MUSA or MOSE.

GIVEN NAMES Italian 12%. *Salvatore* (3), *Domenica, Giacomo, Sal.*

Muser (115) South German (**Müser**): variant of MOSER 1.

GIVEN NAMES German 8%. *Christoph, Kurt, Wolf.*

Musgrave (1999) English (Cumbria): variant of MUSGROVE.

Musgraves (117) Northern English: variant of MUSGROVE.

Musgrove (2375) English (Cumbria): habitational name from either of two villages in Cumbria, named in Old English with *mūs* 'mouse' (perhaps a byname) + *grāf* 'grove' (see GROVE 1). The Norman surname *de Mucegros*, established in Herefordshire and elsewhere in the 12th and 13th centuries, is unrelated and has died out.

Mushinski (153) **1.** Jewish (eastern Ashkenazic): habitational name for someone from Moshny, in Ukraine. **2.** Altered spelling of Slovak **Mušinský**, Polish **Muszyński** (see MUSZYNSKI), or Ukrainian **Mushensky**, all habitational names.

Mushrush (178) Possibly an altered form of German **Moscherosch**, Germanized form of Spanish **(de) Museros**, a habitational name for someone from the city of Museros in Valencia province.

Musial (663) Polish (**Musiał, Musieł**): nickname meaning 'he had to do it', from the masculine singular past tense of *musieć* 'must', 'be required to do something'. Compare MUSIL.

GIVEN NAMES Polish 10%. *Boguslaw* (2), *Casimir* (2), *Eugeniusz* (2), *Alicja, Andrzej, Bogdan, Bronislaw, Elzbieta, Jacek, Jacenty, Janina, Jaroslaw.*

Music (1101) **1.** Serbian and Croatian (**Mušić**): patronymic from the personal name *Musa*, a pet form of the Biblical name *Mojsije* (see MOSES). **2.** Slovenian (**Mušič**): patronymic from the nickname MUHA, or possibly a topographic name from *mušič*, a dialect word for foxtail grass (genus Setaria).

Musich (212) Serbian and Croatian (**Mušič**) or Slovenian (**Mušič**): see MUSIC.

Musick (2396) Dutch: **1.** metonymic occupational name for a musician, from Middle Dutch *musike* 'music'. **2.** Altered form of **Muschick** (an eastern German name of Slavic origin), or Czech MUZIK.

Musielak (104) Polish: patronymic from **Musiał** (see MUSIAL).

GIVEN NAMES German 7%; Polish 6%. *Fritz, Lutz; Casimir, Zdzislaw.*

Musil (617) Czech; also Polish (**Musił**): anecdotal nickname from a lost anecdote, meaning something like 'he had to', from the past tense of Czech *musit*, Polish *musieć* 'to have to', 'to be required to do something'.

Musilli (115) Italian: of uncertain origin; perhaps a variant of Italian **Muselli** (see MUSELLA).

GIVEN NAMES Italian 17%. *Antonio* (3), *Cesare* (2), *Caterina, Corrado, Filomena, Gaetano, Gennaro, Silvestro.*

Muska (214) **1.** Czech and Slovak (**Muška**): nickname from *muška*, diminutive of *moucha* 'fly'. **2.** Hungarian: Americanized spelling of *Muszka*, an old ethnic name for a Russian.

Muskat (158) German and Jewish (Ashkenazic): metonymic occupational name for a spice merchant, from Middle High German *muscāt*, German *Muskat* 'nutmeg', 'mace'. As a Jewish name it is mainly of ornamental origin.

GIVEN NAMES Jewish 8%. *Chaim, Shalom.*

Muske (158) North German: nickname from a diminutive of Middle Low German *mūs* 'mouse' (see MAUS 1).

Muskin (106) English: unexplained.

Muskopf (153) German: nickname for a stupid person, from Middle High German *muos* 'pulp' + *kopf* 'head'.

Musolf (264) German: from *Mutwolf*, a Germanic personal name composed with *mut* 'spirit', 'intent' + *wolf* 'wolf'.

Musolino (169) Italian: **1.** metonymic occupational name for a seller of muslin, Old Italian *musolino* (from Arabic *mauṣilī*, from the name of Mosul in Mesopotamia (now Iraq), the place where muslin was first manufactured). **2.** from a pet form of MUSSO.

GIVEN NAMES Italian 16%. *Angelo* (2), *Bruna, Enzo, Lorenzo, Salvatore; Alicia, Elena, Mario.*

Mussa (123) Muslim: variant of MUSA (Moses).

GIVEN NAMES Muslim 41%. *Ahmed* (6), *Fuad* (3), *Ibrahim* (2), *Abdallah, Ashraf, Dawud, Fatima, Fatuma, Fozia, Haitham, Hani, Huda.*

Mussell (176) English (Southampton): metonymic occupational name for a seller of shellfish, from Middle English *mussel* 'mussel', 'shellfish' (Old English *muscelle*).

Musselman (2389) Swiss German (**Müsselmann**): probably an occupational name for a woodman, from Middle High German *müsel* 'log' + *man* 'man'.

FOREBEARS Christian Musselmann (1665–1734) was a Mennonite who came to PA from Lauperswil, Berne, Switzerland, at the beginning of the 18th century.

Musselwhite (617) Southern English (Wiltshire): unexplained.

Mussen (133) **1.** Dutch: from a shortened pet form of a personal name ending with the syllable *-mus* (for example, Hieronymus). **2.** Possibly a variant spelling of English MUSSON.

Musser (3607) German: probably a variant of MOSER.

FOREBEARS Jost (Joseph) Musser (*c.*1692–1761) came on the ship *Molly*, which arrived at Philadelphia, PA, on 30 September, 1727. He settled in Lampeter Township, PA.

Mussett (99) English (eastern counties): unexplained. Possibly a variant of **Masset** (see MASSETT).

Mussey (123) **1.** English: nickname from Middle English *mūs* 'mouse' + *ēage* 'eye'. **2.** Possibly an altered spelling of French **Musset** (see MUSSETT 1).

Musslewhite (123) English: variant spelling MUSSELWHITE.

Mussman (334) German (**Mussmann**): from Middle Low German *mūs* 'mouse' + *man* 'man', either a nickname for someone thought to resemble a mouse, or an occupational name for a mouse catcher.

Musso (922) **1.** Italian (Sicily): nickname for someone with some peculiarity of the mouth, Sicilian *mussu*, Italian *muso* (from Late Latin *musum*). **2.** Northern Italian: from the personal name *Musso*, a northern form of *Giacomo* (see JAMES).

GIVEN NAMES Italian 21%; Spanish 10%. *Salvatore* (5), *Angelo* (3), *Mario* (3), *Vito* (3), *Biagio* (2), *Giuseppe* (2), *Santo* (2), *Alessandro, Ambrogio, Antonino, Antonio, Carlo, Dino, Lino, Mariano, Osvaldo, Rosario; Carlos* (3), *Juan* (2), *Calisto, Gaspar, Salvador.*

Musson (457) **1.** English (East Midlands): of uncertain origin, ostensibly a patronymic, though Reaney believes it to be a nickname from Anglo-Norman French *muisson* 'sparrow'. **2.** French: variant of *Musset* (see MUSSETT 1). **3.** French: nickname from Old French *moisson, mousson,* 'sparrow'. **4.** French: habitational name from Mousson in Meuse-et-Moselle, named with the Latin personal name *Montius* + the suffix *-onem*, or alternatively, with Latin *mons* 'mountain' + the suffix *-ionem*.

Mustafa (570) **1.** Muslim: from a personal name based on Arabic *muṣṭafā* 'chosen', from Arabic *ṣafā* 'to be pure', 'to be select'.

For Muslims, *Al-Muṣṭafā* is an epithet referring to the Prophet Muhammad, while among Arabic-speaking Christians it is applied to St. Paul. Muṣṭafa is among the most popular personal names in the Islamic world. In Turkey, it is often chosen in honor of Mustafa Kamal Atatürk (1881–1938), founder of modern Turkey. **2.** Spanish (of Arabic origin): from the Arabic personal name (see 1 above). **3.** Italian: from the Arabic personal name (see 1 above), or from a nickname from Calabrian *mustafà* 'strong man with a walrus moustache'.
GIVEN NAMES Muslim 74%. *Ghulam* (16), *Ahmad* (8), *Kamal* (8), *Ibrahim* (7), *Jamal* (7), *Mohammad* (7), *Mustafa* (7), *Syed* (7), *Ali* (6), *Ahmed* (5), *Omar* (5), *Abdul* (4).

Mustain (498) English: unexplained; perhaps a variant spelling of Welsh MOSTYN. Compare MUSTIAN.

Mustard (563) Northern English and Scottish: metonymic occupational name for a dealer in spices, or a nickname for someone with a hot temper or a vicious tongue, from Middle English, Old French *mo(u)starde* 'mustard' (a derivative of *mo(u)st* 'unfermented wine' (see MOST 1), in which the mustard seeds were originally prepared). Black draws attention to an early Scottish form (*van Mouster*, 1414), which appears to be a Dutch habitational name.

Muster (207) **1.** Dutch: variant of MUNSTER 1. **2.** English: variant of **Musters**, a habitational name of Norman origin, from Les Moutiers-Hubert in Calvados, France. **3.** Slovenian (eastern Slovenia): old form of MOSTAR 'bridge keeper', an agent derivative of *must*, an archaic spelling of *most* 'bridge'. This name is also found in German-speaking countries.
GIVEN NAMES German 8%. *Franz* (2), *Hans* (2), *Bernhard*, *Heinz*.

Mustian (121) English: unexplained; see MUSTAIN.

Mustin (294) English (West Midlands): origin uncertain; possibly a variant of MUSTON or perhaps of MUSTO.

Musto (838) **1.** English: topographic name for someone who lived near a piece of open ground used as a meeting place, from Middle English *motestow* 'meeting', 'assembly' (Old English *(ge)mōt* + *stōw* 'place', 'site' (see STOW). The surname Musto is now found mainly in South Wales. **2.** Italian and Greek (**Moustos**): probably from Greek *moustos*, Latin *mustus* 'must' (fermenting wine), hence perhaps a nickname for someone who made wine. Combinations such as **Moustogiannis** 'musty John' are also found.
GIVEN NAMES Italian 15%. *Angelo* (6), *Antonio* (4), *Carmine* (4), *Pasquale* (4), *Alessandro* (3), *Carlo* (2), *Luigi* (2), *Mauro* (2), *Rocco* (2), *Amerigo*, *Annamarie*, *Beniamino*.

Mustoe (179) English: variant spelling of MUSTO.

Muston (141) English: habitational name from either of the places in Leicestershire and North Yorkshire so named, from Old English *mūs* 'mouse' + *tūn* 'enclosure', 'settlement'. The Yorkshire Muston may alternatively have been called 'Músi's farmstead', from an Old Scandinavian personal name + *tūn*.

Musumeci (313) Southern Italian: unexplained.
GIVEN NAMES Italian 32%. *Salvatore* (12), *Angelo* (5), *Alfio* (4), *Sal* (4), *Antonino* (2), *Antonio*, *Camillo*, *Carlo*, *Carmela*, *Carmelo*, *Carmine*, *Concetta*; *Rosario* (3), *Andres*, *Armando*, *Arturo*, *Isidoro*, *Mariano*, *Rosairo*.

Muszynski (555) Polish (**Muszyński**): habitational name for someone from places called Muszyna in Nowy Sącz voivodeship and elsewhere, named with *mucha* 'fly' (see MUCHA 1).
GIVEN NAMES Polish 5%. *Jozefa*, *Kazimierz*, *Krystyna*, *Stanislaw*, *Wojtek*, *Zbigniew*, *Zigmund*, *Zofia*.

Mutch (474) Scottish and English: nickname for a large (tall or fat) person, from Middle English *muche* 'great', a shortened form (probably a back-formation, as if from a diminutive with the Anglo-Norman French suffix *-el*) of *muchel*, Old English *mycel* 'great', 'large'.

Mutchler (733) Americanized spelling of German MUTSCHLER.

Muter (122) English: nickname for a spokesman, from Middle English *mutere*, *motere* 'one who speaks at public meetings', Old English *mōtere*, an agent derivative of *(ge)mōt* 'gathering', 'meeting'. See also MUSTO.

Muth (2072) German (also **Müth**): **1.** from the Germanic personal name *Muoto*, a short form of compound names with the first element *mut* 'spirit'. **2.** nickname for a brave, determined individual, from Middle High German *muot* 'high spirit'.

Muthig (107) German: nickname for a high-spirited or courageous man, German *mutig*.

Muto (518) **1.** Italian (mainly central-southern Italy) and Greek (**Moutos**): nickname from *muto* 'mute', 'unable to speak'. The Greek name is also found in combinations such as *Mutogiorgios* 'mute George'. **2.** Japanese (**Mutō**): 'warrior wisteria', meaning 'Fujiwara of Musashi' (*Musashi no Fujiwara*). These Mutō claim descent from Fujiwara no Hidesato (10th century), of the northern branch of the clan. Other bearers, descended from the MINAMOTO through the TAKEDA, sometimes pronounce the name **Takefuji**. All are found mainly in eastern Japan.
GIVEN NAMES Japanese 18%; Italian 8%. *Koji* (3), *Hiroshi* (2), *Takao* (2), *Takeshi* (2), *Asuka*, *Fumihiko*, *Fumio*, *Futoshi*, *Hidehito*, *Hideo*, *Hiko*, *Hiroyuki*; *Antonio* (2), *Enrico* (2), *Alfonse*, *Angelo*, *Caterina*, *Cesare*, *Enzio*, *Ercole*, *Francesco*, *Nichola*, *Nunzio*, *Rocco*.

Mutschler (434) German: occupational name for a baker who specialized in making white bread, Middle High German *mutsche*, *mutschel*, *mutze* + the agent suffix *-er*.

Mutter (756) **1.** South German (also **Mütter**): occupational name for an official employed to measure grain, from Middle High German *mutte*, *mütte* 'bushel', 'grain measure' (Latin *modius*) + the agent suffix *-er*. **2.** English: variant spelling of MUTER.

Mutti (110) **1.** Indian (Panjab): Hindu and Sikh name based on the name of a clan in the Kamboh community. **2.** Italian: of uncertain derivation; perhaps a nickname from *muto* 'dumb', 'mute'. **3.** German: unexplained.
GIVEN NAMES Indian 7%; Italian 6%; German 5%. *Giovanni* (2), *Massimo*, *Umberto*; *Fritz*, *Schmidt*.

Mutton (125) English (chiefly Devon): nickname for someone thought to resemble a sheep (e.g. a gentle but unimaginative person), or metonymic occupational name for a shepherd, from Anglo-Norman French *muto(u)n* 'sheep' (Old French *mouton*, probably of Gaulish origin; compare Breton *maout* 'sheep').

Mutz (539) South German: **1.** probably a metonymic occupational name for a baker, from Middle High German *mutze* 'white bread', 'roll' (see MUTSCHLER). **2.** nickname either for a short person, from Middle High German *mutzen* 'to cut or shorten', or for a fop or dandy, from the same word in the sense 'to decorate or adorn'.

Muzik (187) Czech and Slovak (**Mužík**): affectionate nickname for a man of short stature, from a derivative from *muž* 'man'.

Muzio (234) Northern Italian: from a medieval personal name derived from the Latin personal name *Mucius* or *Mutius*.
GIVEN NAMES Italian 12%; French 4%. *Salvatore* (2), *Aldo*, *Angelo*, *Domenic*, *Gaetano*, *Nino*; *Achille*, *Monique*.

Muzny (115) Czech and Slovak (**Mužný**): nickname for a virile, bold, or manly individual, from an adjective meaning 'male'.

Muzquiz (130) possibly Spanish (of Basque origin; **Múzquiz**): from **Muzqui**, Castilianized form of Basque Muzki, habitational name from name of a town in Navarre.
GIVEN NAMES Spanish 37%. *Enrique* (3), *Alberto* (2), *Armando* (2), *Felipe* (2), *Guadalupe* (2), *Javier* (2), *Jorge* (2), *Jose* (2), *Jose Luis* (2), *Julio* (2), *Luis* (2), *Marcelo* (2).

Muzyka (213) Polish and Czech: nickname for a musical person, from Polish and Czech (old spelling) *muzyka* 'music'.
GIVEN NAMES Polish 4%. *Wasyl* (2), *Ferdynand*.

Muzzarelli (112) Italian: diminutive of MUZZI.
GIVEN NAMES Italian 9%. *Carlo*, *Dante*, *Giovanni*, *Riccardo*.

Muzzey (177) Possibly a variant spelling of English MUSSEY. Compare MUZZY. As a

British name, this is found mainly in South Wales.

Muzzi (124) Italian: **1.** from a Latin name *Mucius* or *Mutius*, which continued into the medieval period. **2.** in some cases, possibly from a short form of the personal name *Giacomuzzo*, a pet form of GIACOMO (see JAMES).

GIVEN NAMES Italian 27%. *Domenic* (2), *Nazareno* (2), *Elodia, Orlando, Pasquale, Primo, Salvatore.*

Muzzy (503) Variant spelling of English MUSSEY. Compare MUZZEY.

Myatt (1194) English (chiefly West Midlands): from the Middle English personal name *Myat*, formed from *My*, a truncated version of *Mihel* (an Old French form of MICHAEL) + the diminutive suffix *-at* (from Old French *-et*, crossed with the originally pejorative Old French *-ard*).

Myer (2479) English: **1.** occupational name from Old French *mire* 'physician'. **2.** topographic name from Middle English *mire* 'marsh' (Old Norse *mýrr*) . **3.** variant of MAYER 1.

Myers (84848) **1.** English (mainly Yorkshire): patronymic from MAYER 1, i.e. 'son of the mayor'. **2.** English: patronymic from *mire* 'physician' (see MYER 1). **3.** Irish: Anglicized form of Gaelic **Ó Midhir**, probably a variant of **Ó Meidhir** 'mayor' (see MAYER 1).

Myerson (346) English: patronymic from MAYER or MYER.

Myette (213) Possibly a Canadian spelling of French **Myet**, from a short form of the personal name *Amiet*, a pet form of *Ami*.

GIVEN NAMES French 10%. *Alphonse, Andre, Emilien, Jacques, Napoleon, Ovide, Pierre.*

Mygatt (103) English: unexplained.

Myhand (156) Origin unidentified; possibly an altered form of Irish **Myhan**, a variant of MEEHAN.

Myhr (122) Norwegian: habitational name from any of several farmsteads named Myr, from *myr* 'bog', 'swamp' (Old Norse *mýrr*).

GIVEN NAMES Scandinavian 15%. *Anders* (2), *Niklas.*

Myhre (1293) Norwegian: habitational name from any of numerous farmsteads named Myre, most from the dative case of *myr* 'bog', 'swamp' (Old Norse *mýrr*). Compare MYHR.

GIVEN NAMES Scandinavian 8%. *Thor* (3), *Erik* (2), *Helmer* (2), *Petter* (2), *Erlend, Knut, Lars, Lief, Nels, Nils, Sig, Steinar.*

Myint (108) Southeast Asian: unexplained.

GIVEN NAMES Southeast Asian 34%. *Maung* (4), *Kyaw* (3), *Khin* (2), *Kan, Sein, Soe, Zaw; Tun* (2), *Min, Shwe, Thein, Than, Tin.*

Myklebust (159) Norwegian: habitational name from any of several farmsteads in western Norway, so named from Old Norse *Myklibólstaðr* from *mikill* 'large' + *bólstaðr* 'farm'. This is a very frequent name in Norway.

GIVEN NAMES Scandinavian 27%. *Ludvig* (3), *Aslaug, Erik, Helmer, Nels, Paal, Per, Toralf, Truls.*

Myler (410) Irish: variant of **Meyler**, which was taken to Wexford, Ireland by a Welsh family so named. The surname is from the Welsh personal name *Meilyr* (Brythonic *Maglorix*, of which the second element is *rhi* 'king'), and was Gaelicized as **Mac Maoilir**.

Myles (2983) English and Irish: variant of MILES.

FOREBEARS This spelling of the name is used by many descendants of the 17th-century MA Baptist minister John Miles or Myles (see MILES).

Mylin (104) **1.** Swiss German: possibly a respelling of **Meilen**, a habitational name from Meilen in Zürich, or a variant of **Meilan**, from the personal name *Megelanus*. **2.** English or Scottish: unexplained.

Mylott (143) Irish: variant spelling of MILLETT.

Mynatt (692) English: variant of **Mynott** (see MINETT).

Mynes (148) **1.** English: possibly a variant of MINNS. **2.** Perhaps an Americanized spelling of Dutch **Mijnes**, which can be a nickname or occupational name from Middle Dutch *minne* 'beloved', 'sweetheart', or a metronymic from a short form of a female personal name such as *Jacqueminne* or *Willeminne*. Compare MIN 2. **3.** Possibly a variant spelling of MINES.

Mynhier (167) Dutch: variant of Dutch **Mijnheer, Menheer**, a nickname taken from the title of address used for a monarch, nobleman, or other personage of high status, meaning 'my Lord'. As a surname, it probably originated as an ironic nickname.

Myott (120) English: variant of MYATT.

Myracle (145) Most probably an altered spelling of French **Marical** or **Marécal** (see MARICLE).

Myran (122) Variant (definite plural form) of Norwegian MYREN.

GIVEN NAMES Scandinavian 6%. *Lars, Nels.*

Myre (260) Norwegian: variant of MYHRE.

Myren (220) Norwegian: habitational name from numerous farmsteads all over Norway named Myra, from the definite singular form of *myr* 'bog', 'swamp' (Old Norse *mýrr*).

GIVEN NAMES Scandinavian 5%. *Nels, Selmer, Sven.*

Myres (341) Scottish: habitational name from Myres in the parish of Auchtermuchty, Fife.

Myrick (4293) Altered spelling of Welsh **Meyrick** (see MERRICK).

Myricks (120) Welsh: variant of MYRICK.

Myrie (128) Origin unidentified.

GIVEN NAMES Spanish 5%. *Jorge* (2), *Adolfo, Alphonso, Ernesto, Nereida.*

Myron (380) **1.** Greek: from the personal name *Myron* (from *myron* 'myrrh') or possibly a shortened form of a patronymic de-

rivative such as **Myronakis** or **Myronidis**. **2.** Scottish: unexplained.

Myrtle (151) **1.** English: topographic name for someone who lived where the shrub myrtle grew. **2.** Americanized form of Greek **Myrtoglou** or a metronymic of similar derivation, from the Greek female personal name *Myrto* (see MIRTO).

Myslinski (250) Polish (**Myśliński**): **1.** habitational name for someone from Myślin in Ciechanów voivodeship or Myślina in Częstochowa voivodeship. **2.** Possibly also a nickname for a deep thinker, from a derivative of *myśleć* 'to think'.

GIVEN NAMES Polish 6%; French 4%. *Jolanta* (2), *Kazimierz, Zigmont, Zosia; Andre, Jeanmarie.*

Mysliwiec (231) Polish (**Myśliwiec**): occupational name for a hunter or gamekeeper, from a derivative of *myśliwy* 'hunter'.

GIVEN NAMES Polish 10%. *Jozef* (2), *Aleksander, Andrzej, Boguslaw, Grazyna, Jadwiga, Jaroslaw, Waclaw, Wieslawa, Zygmunt.*

Myszka (236) Polish: nickname for a man of small stature, from *myszka* 'mouse'.

Myszkowski (113) Polish and Jewish (from Poland): habitational name for someone from a place called Myszkowo, Myszków, or Myszkowice, all named with *myszka* 'mouse'.

FOREBEARS This name was borne by many nobles who played a significant role in Polish history, amongst them Piotr Myszkowski (1505–91), bishop of Kraków, and Zygmunt Myszkowski (1562–1615), grand marshal of Poland.

GIVEN NAMES Polish 15%. *Zbigniew* (3), *Andrzej, Jacek, Krzysztof.*

Myung (127) Korean: variant of **Myŏng**. In 1363, Myŏn Ok-jin established the Ha (Summer) Kingdom between Korea's Koryŏ Kingdom and China's Yuan Kingdom and declared himself emperor. This was a time of shifting political alliances between Korea and China, and several such small kingdoms appeared on the borderlands between the two nations. Myŏng Ok-jin died in 1366 and his son, Myŏng Sŏng, ascended the throne of the Ha Kingdom. At this time, however, China's Yuan nation was falling and the new Ming Dynasty seized the Ha kingdom's territory. Myŏng Sŏng returned to Koryŏ and was given the right by the Koryŏ king to live in Songdo, Korea. Later, when the Koryŏ kingdom fell to the Chosŏn kingdom, Myŏng Sŭng associated with the Yi Dynasty's founding king, Yi Sŏng-gye. Most members of the present-day Myŏng family live in North Korea's P'yŏnan North Province.

GIVEN NAMES Korean 70%. *Kwang* (3), *Duk* (2), *Hong* (2), *Hyeong* (2), *Sang* (2), *Young* (2), *Yung* (2), *Chan Ho, Choon Ho, Chung, Duk Young, Eunha, Hae, Hwa Young, Hyo, Jaeyong, Jung Hee, Nam, Seoung, Sun Hee, Sung Jun, Youn.*

N

Na (406) **1.** Korean: there is only one Chinese character for the Na surname. Some sources indicate that there are 46 different Na clans, but only two of them can be documented, and it is believed that these two sprang from a common founding ancestor. The Na clan's founding ancestor, Na Pu, migrated from China sometime during the mid-seventh century and settled in the Naju area. **2.** Chinese 那: there are two sources of this surname. One is the state of Na that existed during the Zhou dynasty (1122–221 BC). The other source is the Hu ethnic group, some of whom adopted Na as their surname.

GIVEN NAMES Korean/Chinese 69%. *Sung* (7), *Kwang* (6), *Sang* (5), *Seung* (5), *Byung* (4), *Chong* (4), *Jae Eun* (3), *Jin* (3), *Song* (3), *Chang* (2), *Chul* (2), *Hong* (2), *Hyo* (2), *Seong* (2), *Yong* (2), *Yoon* (2), *Young* (2), *Young Man* (2), *Chong Ho, Chong Sik, Dong In, Doyoung, Hae.*

Naab (328) German: habitational name from Naab in Bavaria or from the Naab river, a tributary of the Danube. The word is of pre-Germanic origin meaning 'damp', 'moist' and is related to German *Nebel* 'fog', 'mist'.

Naar (107) Dutch and North German: from a short form of the personal name *Bernaert*, a variant of BERNHARD.

GIVEN NAMES French 11%; Jewish 4%; Scandinavian 4%. *Antoine, Gisele, Jacques, Yves; Hyman; Anders.*

Naas (446) **1.** German: variant of NASE. **2.** Norwegian: habitational name from farmsteads in Møre og Romsdal and Telemark, named with Old Norse *n{o,}s* 'nose', used with reference to a nose-like formation in the landscape, for example, a precipitous crag or mountain peak. **3.** Dutch: from a short form of the personal name *Donaas*, a derivative of the Latin personal name *Donatius*, which was known as a saint's name in medieval times.

FOREBEARS Johannes Naas (1669–1741), a Brethren elder, was a native of Nordheim (near Worms) in the Palatinate, Germany, and a minister in the Marienborn area around 1714. When the Brethren were expelled in 1715, the Naas family, which included five children, moved to Krefeld. Naas was married twice; his first wife died in Krefeld in 1725, and he married again in 1727. With his second wife and a daughter, he emigrated to PA in the autumn of 1733. The family settled in Amwell, NJ, where

Naas developed a flourishing congregation. He also helped start congregations in PA, especially at Northkill and Great Swamp. Naas was one of the great preachers and church leaders of the Brethren, both in Europe and in colonial America. He died on 12 May 1741 and was buried near Amwell.

Naasz (144) **1.** German: variant of NAAS. **2.** German: from a short form of the medieval personal name *Ignaz*, a vernacular form of *Ignatius* (see IGNACIO).

GIVEN NAMES German 6%; Scandinavian 4%. *Kurt, Milbert, Otto; Sig.*

Naatz (126) German: variant of NAASZ 2.

Nabb (180) Scottish, northern English, and northern Irish: reduced form of MCNABB.

Naber (919) **1.** North German: nickname from Low German *Naber* 'neighbor'. Compare NEIGHBOR. **2.** Southwestern German: from a personal name given in honor of St. Nabor; or a habitational name from a place in Alsace. In Württemberg there is a place name Nabern, derived from the river name Naber, which might have contributed to the surname. **3.** German: occupational name for a maker of wheel hubs, Middle High German *nabegēr*, from *nabe* 'hub'.

Nabers (183) German: variant of NABER.

Nabholz (103) German: metonymic occupational name for a wheelwright or cartwright, from Middle High German *nabeholz* 'hub wood'.

Nabor (110) Spanish and Catalan: from the personal name *Nabor*, which was borne by a saint believed to have been martyred in Milan in the 4th century, about whom nothing else is known. The personal name is probably a derivative of Hebrew *barar* 'to choose', 'to purify', which evolved into *nabar* 'honest', 'ernest', 'clean'.

GIVEN NAMES Spanish 18%. *Jose* (2), *Pedro* (2), *Aurelio, Belen, Eusebio, Fidel, Francisco, Gaudencio, Marciano, Maximo.*

Nabors (1938) Variant of English NEIGHBOR.

Nabours (111) Variant of English NEIGHBOR.

Nabozny (214) Polish (**Nabożny**): nickname from *nabożny* 'pious' 'devout'.

Naccarato (596) Southern Italian (Sicily): **1.** nickname from Sicilian *nnaccaratu* 'graceful', 'charming', 'dear'. **2.** possibly from the old Ligurian term *macharatus* 'drums'.

GIVEN NAMES Italian 13%. *Angelo* (4), *Carmine* (3), *Filippo* (2), *Antonio, Concetta, Dante, Domenico, Ercole, Geno, Guiseppe, Italo, Luigi.*

Nace (1205) **1.** Irish: reduced Anglicized form of Gaelic **Mac Naois** (see MCNEESE). **2.** Americanized spelling of Dutch and German NEES, NEESE, or NIES.

Nacey (104) Americanized spelling of German and Dutch NEESE 2.

Nachazel (109) Origin unidentified.

Nachbar (168) **1.** German: nickname from Middle High German *nāchbūre* 'neighbor'. **2.** Jewish (Ashkenazic): from German *Nachbar* 'neighbor', the reasons for its adoption being unknown.

Nachman (477) Jewish: from the Hebrew post-Biblical male personal name *Nachman* 'consoler'.

GIVEN NAMES Jewish 4%; German 4%. *Hyman* (2), *Miriam, Mordecai; Erwin* (2), *Lothar* (2), *Inge, Wolf.*

Nachreiner (241) South German: from German *Nachreiner*, an expression meaning 'neighboring farmer' or 'farmer living on the outskirts of a village', from Middle High German *nāch* 'near' + *rein* 'edge', 'margin' + *-er* suffix denoting an inhabitant. Compare NACHBAR.

GIVEN NAME French 4%. *Camille.*

Nacht (149) **1.** German: possibly, as Brechenmacher suggests, an occupational nickname for a night watchman, from Middle High German *naht* 'night'. **2.** Jewish (Ashkenazic): ornamental name from German *Nacht* 'night'.

GIVEN NAMES German 5%. *Otto, Siegfried.*

Nachtigal (188) German and Jewish (Ashkenazic): variant spelling of NACHTIGALL.

Nachtigall (132) **1.** German: nickname from Middle High German *nachtegal* 'nightingale' (from Old High German *galan* 'to sing'), probably denoting a good singer, or possibly for a birdcatcher, birdseller, or birdlover. **2.** Jewish (Ashkenazic): ornamental name from German *Nachtigall* 'nightingale'.

GIVEN NAMES German 9%. *Arno, Fritz, Guenter, Hedwig, Konrad.*

Nachtman (119) **1.** Jewish (Ashkenazic): variant of NACHMAN. **2.** Jewish (Ashkenazic): ornamental name from German *Nacht* 'night' + *Mann* 'man'. **3.** German (**Nachtmann**): occupational name for a night watchman.

Nachtwey (115) North German: a topographic name, a reduced form of *Nachtweide* 'night pasture', for someone who owned land for grazing cattle or sheep at night.

Nack (394) **1.** German and Dutch: variant of NACKE 1. **2.** German (**Näck**): from a variant of *Neck*, the name of a water sprite. **3.** Americanized spelling of German KNACK. **4.** English: variant spelling of NACKE.

FOREBEARS This name is recorded in Beverwijck in New Netherland (Albany, NY) in the mid 17th century.

GIVEN NAMES German 4%. *Achim, Hermann, Kurt, Madel.*

Nacke (159) **1.** German and Dutch: nickname from Middle High German *nac, nacke*, Middle Dutch *necke* 'neck', perhaps denoting someone with a stiff neck, in either the literal or figurative sense. **2.** English: from the Old Norse personal name *Hnaki.*

Naclerio (187) Italian: occupational name from Latin *nauclerus* 'shipowner', 'ship's captain', which was also used as a personal name.

GIVEN NAMES Italian 13%. *Matteo* (2), *Salvatore* (2), *Saverio* (2).

Nadal (293) Catalan and southern French (Occitan): from the personal name *Nadal*, from *nadal* 'Christmas' (from Latin *natalis* 'birthday'). Compare NOEL.

GIVEN NAMES Spanish 32%. *Carlos* (7), *Miguel* (4), *Francisco* (3), *Jose* (3), *Luis* (3), *Caridad* (2), *Digna* (2), *Jaime* (2), *Juan* (2), *Juan Carlos* (2), *Manuel* (2), *Otilio* (2).

Nadeau (4988) French: according to Morlet, from a variant of NADAL.

GIVEN NAMES French 14%. *Armand* (20), *Andre* (16), *Marcel* (14), *Lucien* (13), *Fernand* (10), *Normand* (9), *Aime* (8), *Cecile* (6), *Benoit* (4), *Emile* (4), *Jacques* (4), *Yves* (4).

Nadel (728) German and Jewish (Ashkenazic): metonymic occupational name for a maker of needles, or in some cases for a tailor, from Middle High German *nādel(e)*, German *Nadel* 'needle'.

GIVEN NAMES Jewish 5%. *Emanuel* (2), *Abbe, Dov, Moishe, Ofer, Sol.*

Nadell (191) Jewish (Ashkenazic): variant spelling of NADEL.

GIVEN NAMES Jewish 6%; German 5%. *Avrom, Gerson, Mayer, Sol; Bernhardt, Johannes, Theodor.*

Nadelman (111) Jewish (Ashkenazic): variant of NADEL.

GIVEN NAMES Jewish 8%; German 5%. *Ari, Emanuel.*

Naden (156) Possibly an altered form of German **Nöthen**, from an old personal name from Old High German *nōt* 'distress', 'compulsion', 'force', or a habitational name from a place so named near Aachen.

Nader (812) **1.** Arabic: from a personal name based on Arabic *nādir* 'extraordi-

nary', 'rare', 'exceptional'. **2.** German (also **Näder**): occupational name for an embroiderer, later a tailor, from an agent derivative of Middle High German *næjen* 'to embroider or sew'.

GIVEN NAMES Muslim 9%; French 4%. *Nader* (4), *Walid* (3), *Adib* (2), *Bahjat* (2), *Jamal* (2), *Nabil* (2), *Raheem* (2), *Abed, Ali Reza, Alireza, Amir, Azar; Marcel* (3), *Colette* (2), *Alexandre, Andre, Emile, Eugenie.*

Naderi (115) Muslim: from an Arabic name based on an adjectival derivative of NADER.

GIVEN NAMES Muslim 82%. *Hamid* (6), *Nader* (5), *Masood* (3), *Mohammad* (3), *Abdul* (2), *Ali* (2), *Amir* (2), *Sassan* (2), *Afsaneh, Akbar, Basir, Faird.*

Nadig (104) **1.** German: nickname for a kind, benevolent person, from Old High German *(gi-)nādig* 'kind'. **2.** Indian (Karnataka): Hindu name meaning 'village superintendent', derived from an official title based on Kannada *nāu* 'district' + the agentive suffix *-iga*.

GIVEN NAMES Indian 8%. *Balu, Mahesh, Vinay.*

Nading (270) Variant of German and Swiss NADIG.

Nadkarni (100) Indian (Goa, Karnataka): Hindu (usually Brahman) name meaning 'district accountant', from Kannada *nāu* 'province', 'district' + Sanskrit *karana* 'writer' or *karnī* 'helmsman'. It used to be the title of a hereditary official, equivalent to DESHPANDE in other areas.

GIVEN NAMES Indian 92%. *Shyam* (4), *Ashok* (3), *Prakash* (3), *Vinay* (3), *Arun* (2), *Girish* (2), *Govind* (2), *Shirish* (2), *Sunil* (2), *Uday* (2), *Anil, Anupama.*

Nadler (1472) German, Jewish (Ashkenazic), and English: occupational name for a maker of needles, from an agent derivative of Middle High German *nādel(e)*, German *Nadel* 'needle', Middle English *nedle, nadle*. Needles in the Middle Ages were comparatively coarse articles made from bone. In some cases, especially as a Jewish name, it may also be an occupational name for a tailor.

GIVEN NAMES Jewish 4%. *Emanuel* (4), *Zev* (2), *Batia, Isadore, Miriam, Moshe, Pinchus, Rivka, Sol, Yudi, Zvi.*

Nadolny (476) Polish, Jewish (from Poland), and Sorbian: topographic name from Polish *nadół*, Sorbian *nadol* 'downwards', denoting someone who lived lower down in a village on a slope, or on relatively low-lying ground.

Nadolski (352) Polish: topographic name for someone who lived *na dole* 'lower down', or *na dołach* 'by the pits or caves'.

Nadon (147) French: from a pet form of a personal name ending in *-nard* (assimilated to *-nad*), for example BERNARD; or possibly from one such as GERARD, with medial *-r-* mutated to *-n-*.

GIVEN NAMES French 15%. *Andre* (2), *Etienne, Guylaine, Marcel, Remi, Sylvie, Yves.*

Naef (202) **1.** Dutch: metonymic occupational name for a wheelwright, from Middle Dutch *nave, naef* 'hub'. **2.** Variant of Swiss German **Näf** (see NEFF).

GIVEN NAMES German 6%. *Fritz, Markus.*

Naegele (510) South German (**Nägele**): see NAGEL.

GIVEN NAMES German 6%. *Otto* (2), *Alois, Bernhard, Erwin, Heinz, Hilde, Manfred, Matthias, Wolfgang.*

Naegeli (204) South German (**Nägeli**): variant of NAGEL.

GIVEN NAMES German 7%. *Markus, Otto, Wolfgang.*

Naeger (243) German (**Näger**): see NAGER.

GIVEN NAMES German 6%. *Kurt* (2), *Alois, Florian, Reinhard.*

Naegle (190) Reduced form of South German **Nägele** (see NAGEL).

Naeve (206) German (**Näve**): see NEVE 1.

Nafe (107) **1.** Probably an Americanized form of German NEFF or **Näve** (see NEVE). **2.** Tongan: unexplained.

Naff (405) **1.** South German and Swiss German (also **Näff**): variant of NEFF. **2.** Altered spelling of **Knaf**, from the Low German form of *Knabe* 'boy', 'journeyman'.

FOREBEARS By 1776, more than twenty families named Näff, Naff, or Neff had come to PA from Germany. Progenitors of Brethren Naff or Neff families comprise four groups. Brothers Francis and Johann Heinrich Neiff (Neff) were Swiss Mennonites who fled first to Alsace and then to Lancaster Co., PA, prior to 1715. Both had prominent descendants. Dr. John Henry Neff, a physician, probably a descendant of one of these two, settled in Shenandoah Co., VA, about 1750. Henry Neff and his wife joined the Conestoga congregation in PA on 24 April 1748. He was minister of Codorus in 1770. Brothers Jacob and Rudolph Naff arrived in Philadelphia on 11 September 1749, on the *Priscilla* and settled at Germantown, PA. Sebastian Naff came from the Swiss-German border. He was followed by his brother, Jacob, who arrived in Philadelphia on the *Dragon* on 26 September 1749. In 1782 Jacob settled in Franklin Co., VA, and was joined there in 1793 by Sebastian. Descendants who moved to the Midwest before the Civil War changed their name to Neff; those who remained in VA or moved to TN retained the form Naff.

Naffziger (204) Variant spelling of German **Nafzger**, a nickname meaning 'sleepyhead', from a noun derivative of Middle High German *nafzen* 'to take a nap'.

Naftzger (126) Variant of German **Nafzger**, a nickname for a sleepyhead, from a noun derivative of Middle High German *nafzen* 'to take a nap'.

Nafus (111) Origin unidentified.

Nafziger (474) Variant of German **Nafzger** (see NEFZGER).

FOREBEARS Matheias and Peter Nafsker and

Rudolf Nafzger sailed to North America on the *Phoenix*, arriving in Philadelphia on 15 September 1749. Rudolph settled in Washington Co., PA. His son John moved to Montgomery Co., OH, about 1800 with several of his married children. Others in the 1750s, Amish Mennonites, originated in Thun, Bern Canton, Switzerland.

Nagai (338) Japanese: written in either of two ways, both with characters meaning 'long' and 'well'. Bearers of either version of the name appear to be descended from either the SAITO or MIURA families. This name is now also established in Hawaii.
GIVEN NAMES Japanese 69%. *Takao* (3), *Takashi* (3), *Akira* (2), *Hideaki* (2), *Hideo* (2), *Hideyuki* (2), *Hirokazu* (2), *Isami* (2), *Masao* (2), *Nobuyuki* (2), *Reiko* (2), *Shigeru* (2).

Nagamine (149) Japanese: variously written with characters meaning 'long' and 'peak'; from a place name. Two versions of the name are more common in eastern Japan and the Ryūkyū islands, and a third is found in western Japan. This name is also established in Hawaii.
GIVEN NAMES Japanese 37%. *Hiroshi* (2), *Yasumasa* (2), *Yasuo* (2), *Eiko*, *Hiroko*, *Hiroyuki*, *Kazuo*, *Kiku*, *Kosei*, *Kyoko*, *Masaya*, *Michie*.

Nagano (162) Japanese: 'long field'; from a very common place name. The name, which is listed in the Shinsen shōjiroku, is written in two ways, in roughly equal numbers, one being found mostly in eastern Japan and the other in western Japan; both are also found in Okinawa Island. Many bearers are unrelated; some are of Sakanoue, Gotō, or Kikuchi descent.
GIVEN NAMES Japanese 64%. *Hiroaki* (2), *Isao* (2), *Koichi* (2), *Masakazu* (2), *Masato* (2), *Akira*, *Emiko*, *Etsuko*, *Fumiko*, *Hideki*, *Hiro*, *Hironobu*.

Nagao (173) Japanese: 'long tail'; from a common place name, the 'tail' therefore being topographic, denoting the lower slope of a mountain, not an animal's tail. The surname is found mostly on the islands of Shikoku and Okinawa. Many bearers have samurai connections.
GIVEN NAMES Japanese 45%. *Toru* (3), *Koji* (2), *Takashi* (2), *Daisuke*, *Hideki*, *Hikaru*, *Hiro*, *Hiroki*, *Hiromi*, *Hiroshi*, *Hiroyuki*, *Junichi*.

Nagar (110) **1.** Indian (northern states): Hindu (Kayasth) name, from Sanskrit *nāgara* 'urban' (from Sanskrit *nagara* 'city'). **2.** Jewish (Sephardic and Israeli): occupational name from Hebrew *nagar* 'carpenter'. As an Israeli name, it sometimes represents a translation into Hebrew of Ashkenazic names with the same meaning, for example ZIMMERMANN and TESLER.
GIVEN NAMES Indian 43%; Jewish 18%. *Anil* (3), *Devesh* (2), *Lakshmi* (2), *Prashant* (2), *Priya* (2), *Rajeev* (2), *Sat* (2), *Arathi*, *Arvind*, *Bhupesh*, *Deepa*, *Dev*; *Avi* (4),

Amnon, *Avner*, *Azriel*, *Mazal*, *Menachem*, *Nissim*, *Ronit*, *Yaakov*, *Yoav*.

Nagarajan (114) Indian (Kerala, Tamil Nadu): Hindu name from Sanskrit *nāgarāja* 'serpent king' (from *nāga* 'serpent' + *rāja* 'king'), an epithet of the serpent king Shesha + the Tamil-Malayalam third-person masculine singular suffix *-n*. This is only a given name in India, but has come to be used as a family name in the U.S.
GIVEN NAMES Indian 98%. *Raj* (3), *Gopalan* (2), *Krishna* (2), *Sivakumar* (2), *Sundar* (2), *Ashok*, *Bala*, *Ganesh*, *Gopal*, *Kasturi*, *Krishnaswamy*, *Kumar*.

Nagasawa (138) Japanese: 'long swamp'; though written with different characters today, it is of the same origin as NAKAZAWA, both being common place names. The surname is found mostly in central Japan. One family of MINAMOTO origin came from *Nagasawa-zato* in Etchū (now Toyama prefecture).
GIVEN NAMES Japanese 53%. *Takashi* (3), *Isamu* (2), *Noriko* (2), *Sumi* (2), *Fumio*, *Hatsumi*, *Hiro*, *Kaname*, *Kazuhiko*, *Kazuyo*, *Kimio*, *Masao*.

Nagata (413) Japanese: 'long rice paddy'; from a common place name. The majority of bearers today are descended from the SASAKI branch of the MINAMOTO clan, and took the name from a village in Ōmi (now Shiga prefecture). Listed in the Shinsen shōjiroku, the characters are pronounced OSADA or *Chōda* by some families. All three versions are found in eastern Japan. The name is also found in the Ryūkyū Islands.
GIVEN NAMES Japanese 48%. *Hiroshi* (4), *Makoto* (4), *Takashi* (4), *Toshio* (3), *Akihiro* (2), *Ayako* (2), *Hideki* (2), *Hideo* (2), *Kaoru* (2), *Masaaki* (2), *Ryuzo* (2), *Shigeo* (2).

Nagel (6199) German, Dutch, Scandinavian, and Jewish (Ashkenazic): from Middle High German, Middle Dutch *nagel*, German *Nagel* 'nail', hence a metonymic occupational name for a maker of nails. Compare English NAIL.
GIVEN NAMES German 4%. *Erwin* (8), *Heinz* (7), *Hans* (6), *Otto* (6), *Kurt* (4), *Armin* (3), *Franz* (3), *Fritz* (3), *Udo* (2), *Wilhelm* (2), *Aloys*, *Eldred*.

Nagele (201) South German (**Nägele**): variant of NAGEL.
GIVEN NAMES German 6%. *Jutta* (2), *Erwin*, *Rainer*, *Siegfried*.

Nagengast (230) German: nickname for a grasping innkeeper from Middle High German *nagen* 'to gnaw', 'to be stingy' + *gast* 'guest', literally 'be stingy with the guest'.

Nageotte (104) French: **1.** from the female personal name. **2.** habitational name from Nageot in Haute-Marne or other minor places so named.

Nager (255) **1.** German (**Näger**): occupational name for a tailor or embroiderer, from an agent derivative of Middle High

German *næjen* 'to sew', 'to embroider'. **2.** Jewish (Ashkenazic): variant of NAGAR (showing alteration of the final vowel under Yiddish influence).
GIVEN NAMES German 4%. *Urs* (2), *Wolfgang*.

Nagi (143) **1.** Muslim: variant of Arabic **Naji**, from an Arabic word meaning 'close friend'. *Najiullah* 'friend of Allah' is an epithet of the Prophet Muhammad. **2.** Indian (Panjab): Hindu and Sikh name based on the name of a subgroup of the Tank goldsmiths of the Panjab, from Sanskrit *nāgī* 'one with serpents', which is an epithet of the god Shiva.
GIVEN NAMES Muslim 36%; Indian 14%. *Abdo* (4), *Ali* (3), *Mohamed* (3), *Abdulkarim*, *Ahmed*, *Akram*, *Fathia*, *Hesham*, *Kamal*, *Mansor*, *Mansour*, *Mohamad*; *Vinod* (2), *Amar*, *Rachna*, *Rakesh*, *Ravi*, *Sukhbir*.

Nagle (4476) **1.** Irish (County Cork): variant of NANGLE or, according to Woulfe, possibly an Anglicized form of Gaelic **Mac an Óglaigh** 'son of the soldier' (a County Sligo name formerly Anglicized as **MacNogly**). **2.** German and Dutch: Americanized spelling of NAGEL or dialect **Nägle**.

Nagler (468) German and Dutch: occupational name for a nail maker, from Middle High German, Middle Dutch *nagel* 'nail' + the agent suffix *-er*.
GIVEN NAMES German 4%. *Hans*, *Hedwig*, *Kurt*, *Otto*.

Nagley (109) Variant of Dutch or German NAGLE.

Nagode (102) Slovenian: nickname for a troublesome person or for a prematurely born child. It is a respelling of the noun *negode*, a derivative of the obsolete noun *negod* 'wrong time'.

Nagorski (168) Polish and Jewish (from Poland and Ukraine): habitational name from any of several places called Nagórze in Poland, or from a village in Ukraine called Nagortsy.
GIVEN NAMES Polish 7%. *Zygmunt* (2), *Henryk*, *Zigmund*.

Nagy (5861) **1.** Hungarian and Jewish (from Hungary): nickname for a large or powerful person, from Hungarian *nagy* 'big'. The family name is contrasted with KISS and was sometimes used to describe the older of two bearers of the same personal name. **2.** Indian: variant of NAGI.
GIVEN NAMES Hungarian 9%. *Sandor* (26), *Laszlo* (23), *Tibor* (17), *Bela* (15), *Zoltan* (15), *Ferenc* (9), *Karoly* (8), *Attila* (7), *Kalman* (7), *Gabor* (6), *Geza* (6), *Imre* (6).

Nahabedian (117) Armenian: patronymic from classical Armenian *nahapet* 'leader'.
GIVEN NAMES Armenian 35%; Scandinavian 4%. *Sarkis* (4), *Yervant* (3), *Aram* (2), *Ardashes* (2), *Bedros*, *Hagop*, *Hovanes*, *Hrair*, *Kerop*, *Kevork*, *Raffi*, *Roupen*.

Nahas (342) Arabic and Jewish (Sephardic): occupational name from Arabic *naḥḥās* 'coppersmith'.
GIVEN NAMES Arabic 9%; French 6%. *Nabil* (3), *Abbas, Ali, Amin, Bassam, Cherif, Fadi, Issam, Karim, Majeed, Marwan, Nabeel; Michel* (4), *Dominique* (2).

Nahigian (123) Armenian: patronymic from a personal name of unexplained origin.
GIVEN NAMES Armenian 4%. *Araxi, Diran, Zaven.*

Nahm (167) **1.** German: possibly a nickname for a robber or thief, from Middle High German, Middle Low German *name* 'loot'. **2.** Korean: variant of NAM.

Nahmias (153) Jewish (Sephardic; **Nahmías**): from the Hebrew name *Nechemia* 'the Lord consoles', 'the Lord will console' (English *Nehemiah*). According to Tibón this surname originated in Toledo. The distinctively French forenames are borne by Jewish migrants from former French colonies in North Africa.
GIVEN NAMES Jewish 9%; French 4%. *Avi, Meyer, Shlomo; Andre, Michel.*

Nahrwold (112) German: from a Germanic personal name composed of *nerjan* (older stem *nar*) 'to save', 'keep alive', 'heal' + *walt* 'rule'.

Naidu (183) Indian (Andhra Pradesh): Hindu name that occurs in several communities of Andhra Pradesh. It is *nāyu* in Telugu, composed of a stem from Sanskrit *nāya* 'leader', 'chief' + the Telugu third personal masculine suffix *-u*.
GIVEN NAMES Indian 82%. *Vijay* (3), *Ajit* (2), *Bhaskar* (2), *Dharma* (2), *Narain* (2), *Rajesh* (2), *Subra* (2), *Anand, Anil, Arun, Asha, Hari.*

Naifeh (165) Arabic: from a personal name based on Arabic *nāfi* 'beneficial', 'profitable'.

Naik (455) Indian: Hindu name found in several communities meaning 'chief', 'leader', from Sanskrit *nāyaka*.
GIVEN NAMES Indian 92%. *Dilip* (6), *Bharat* (5), *Ramesh* (5), *Vijay* (5), *Jayant* (4), *Jayesh* (4), *Prakash* (4), *Rajendra* (4), *Rajesh* (4), *Rupal* (4), *Sumant* (4), *Suresh* (4).

Nail (2094) **1.** English: from Middle English *naile, nayle* 'nail' (from Old English *nægel*), applied as a metonymic occupational name for a maker of nails, or as a nickname for a tall thin person. **2.** Americanized form of German NAGEL.

Naill (188) Variant of English NAIL or Irish NEILL.

Naillon (102) French: from an inflected form of *Nail* a Germanic personal name formed with *nah* 'sufficient', 'adequate'.

Nailor (310) English: variant spelling of NAYLOR.

Nails (274) Origin unidentified; possibly an altered form of NAIL.

Naim (157) Muslim and Jewish (Sephardic): from a personal name based on Arabic *na'īm* 'bliss', 'happiness'.
GIVEN NAMES Muslim 46%; Jewish 11%; French 4%. *Mohammad* (3), *Naji* (2), *Syed* (2), *Zafar* (2), *Abdul, Ahmad, Ali, Alia, Amir, Bassam, Essam, Faiza; Ari* (3), *Ofer* (2), *Uri* (2), *Avital, Moises, Shaul, Yehuda; Antoine, Philippe.*

Naiman (310) Jewish (Ashkenazic): Yiddish equivalent of German NEUMANN 'newcomer'.
GIVEN NAMES Jewish 11%. *Yosef* (2), *Ari, Chaya, Elimelech, Emanuel, Hyman, Isadore, Mayer, Polina, Shlomo, Sol, Yitzchok.*

Nair (875) **1.** Indian (Kerala): Hindu (Nayar) name denoting membership of the Nayar community, which is from Malayalam *nāyar* 'leader', 'lord', 'soldier' (from Sanskrit *nāya(ka)* 'leader' + the honorific plural ending *-r*). The Nayars were regarded as protectors of the land. **2.** Northern Irish: reduced form of McNAIR.
GIVEN NAMES Indian 74%. *Hari* (9), *Suresh* (9), *Radhakrishnan* (8), *Vinod* (8), *Rajesh* (7), *Mohan* (6), *Satish* (6), *Chandra* (5), *Usha* (5), *Balachandran* (4), *Gopal* (4), *Krishna* (4).

Nairn (415) Scottish: habitational name from the place of this name, east of Inverness, named for the river at whose mouth it stands. The river name is of pre-Celtic origin.
FOREBEARS First mentioned in the Carolina plantation records in 1698, the name appears with Thomas Nairne, a landowner on St. Helena Island. He went on to be a SC assemblyman and an Indian agent.

Naiser (114) **1.** German: nickname from Middle High German *neiser* 'pursuer', 'persecutor'. **2.** German: possibly a short form of *Dionysos* (see DENIS).

Naish (142) English (chiefly Wiltshire and Somerset): variant spelling of NASH 1.

Naismith (138) Scottish and English: variant of NESMITH. In the British Isles, this is the commonest form of the surname.

Naito (245) Japanese (**Naitō**): 'inner wisteria'; a name taken by two branches of the northern FUJIWARA clan. One is descended from the famous warrior Hidesato (10th century), the other from Michinaga (966–1027), the statesman who took his family to its greatest heights of power, and on whom the main character of the classic novel *Genji monogatari* ('The tale of Genji') is based.
GIVEN NAMES Japanese 58%. *Hideo* (3), *Hiroshi* (2), *Hisayuki* (2), *Jiro* (2), *Kiyomi* (2), *Kiyoshi* (2), *Megumi* (2), *Minako* (2), *Ryo* (2), *Shinobu* (2), *Yukio* (2), *Akemi.*

Najar (363) Spanish: **1.** most probably a habitational name from Najar, Alacant. **2.** alternatively, it may be an occupational name derived from Arabic *najjār* 'carpenter'.
GIVEN NAMES Spanish 28%. *Jose* (6), *Manuel* (4), *Juan* (3), *Rodolfo* (3), *Alfonso* (2), *Alicia* (2), *Armando* (2), *Camilo* (2), *Candido* (2), *Guillermo* (2), *Ramon* (2), *Refugio* (2).

Najarian (455) Armenian: patronymic from Turkish dialect *nacar* 'carpenter', from Arabic *najjār*.
GIVEN NAMES Armenian 26%. *Berj* (4), *Haig* (4), *Sarkis* (4), *Aram* (3), *Berge* (3), *Antranik* (2), *Armen* (2), *Arsen* (2), *Hasmik* (2), *Nubar* (2), *Vahe* (2), *Varant* (2).

Najarro (132) Spanish: habitational name from Najarro in Cáceres province.
GIVEN NAMES Spanish 56%. *Jose* (6), *Carlos* (4), *Ana* (3), *Blanca* (3), *Arturo* (2), *Francisco* (2), *Marina* (2), *Miguel* (2), *Pedro* (2), *Reyes* (2), *Ricardo* (2), *Adolfo* (2).

Najera (1271) Spanish (**Nájera**): habitational name from Najera, a city in Logroño province.
GIVEN NAMES Spanish 51%. *Jose* (29), *Juan* (21), *Jesus* (15), *Miguel* (14), *Manuel* (12), *Francisco* (11), *Guadalupe* (10), *Carlos* (9), *Mario* (8), *Pedro* (8), *Raul* (8), *Roberto* (7).

Najjar (388) Arabic and Jewish (Sephardic): occupational name from Arabic *najjār* 'carpenter'.
GIVEN NAMES Muslim 36%; French 4%. *Samir* (4), *Abdallah* (3), *Maher* (3), *Nabil* (3), *Samer* (3), *Ali* (2), *Amjad* (2), *Bassam* (2), *Hisham* (2), *Mohammed* (2), *Namir* (2), *Omar* (2); *Dominique, Eugenie, Marcel, Michel.*

Nakada (121) Japanese: variant of NAKATA.
GIVEN NAMES Japanese 53%. *Tetsuo* (2), *Yutaka* (2), *Akihiro, Eiichi, Genichi, Haruto, Hisano, Junko, Kazumi, Kazuyoshi, Koichi, Kuni.*

Nakagawa (797) Japanese: 'middle river'; from a common place name. A few bearers are of FUJIWARA or MINAMOTO origin.
GIVEN NAMES Japanese 53%. *Hiroshi* (6), *Makoto* (5), *Hiroyuki* (4), *Keiko* (4), *Osamu* (4), *Akiko* (3), *Akira* (3), *Fujio* (3), *Kenji* (3), *Kiyoshi* (3), *Koji* (3), *Minoru* (3).

Nakahara (253) Japanese: 'central plain'; mostly found in the island of Kyūshū. Borne by descendants of the Mononobe clan, the name is listed in the Shinsen shōjiroku. It is pronounced **Nakabaru** on Okinawa island.
GIVEN NAMES Japanese 52%. *Shoichi* (3), *Toshio* (3), *Akito* (2), *Asuka* (2), *Hiroyasu* (2), *Masato* (2), *Akio, Bunji, Chika, Daisuke, Eiji, Fujio.*

Nakai (210) **1.** Japanese: 'central well'; it originated in Mikawa (now part of Aichi prefecture), and is also found in the island of Okinawa. **2.** Navajo name for someone from Mexico.
GIVEN NAMES Japanese 46%. *Katsumasa* (2), *Kazuo* (2), *Tomoko* (2), *Fumio, Harue,*

Haruo, Hideaki, Hideo, Junichi, Junko, Kaoru, Keiko.

Nakajima (281) Japanese: 'middle island'; a more common pronunciation is NAKASHIMA.

GIVEN NAMES Japanese 90%. *Takashi* (6), *Hiroshi* (4), *Shigeru* (4), *Hideo* (3), *Kazuo* (3), *Kunio* (3), *Masayuki* (3), *Mihoko* (3), *Nobuyuki* (3), *Shigeki* (3), *Shinya* (3), *Akemi* (2).

Nakama (196) Japanese: variously written; the meaning could be 'midway', 'companions', among others. Found mostly in western Japan and the Ryūkyū islands.

GIVEN NAMES Japanese 38%. *Akira* (2), *Sueo* (2), *Takeo* (2), *Tsuneo* (2), *Yuki* (2), *Chikako, Haruko, Hiroshi, Kameko, Kaoru, Keiko, Kiyoko.*

Nakamoto (488) Japanese: 'central origin' or '(one who lives) in the middle'; found mostly in the Ryūkyū islands.

GIVEN NAMES Japanese 36%. *Kenji* (3), *Kazuo* (2), *Minoru* (2), *Naoko* (2), *Ryoko* (2), *Shigeru* (2), *Tetsuo* (2), *Asako, Atsushi, Chiyo, Eiji, Goro.*

Nakamura (2552) Japanese: variously written, usually with characters meaning 'village in the middle'. One of the ten most common surnames, it is very ancient and also a very common place name. Listed in the Shinsen shōjiroku.

GIVEN NAMES Japanese 53%. *Kenji* (13), *Hiroshi* (9), *Masao* (9), *Noboru* (9), *Takeshi* (9), *Toru* (9), *Koichi* (8), *Takashi* (8), *Toshio* (8), *Akira* (7), *Katsumi* (7), *Akihiro* (6).

Nakanishi (310) Japanese: 'center of the west'; a habitational name taken from villages in Yamato (now Nara prefecture), Bizen (now part of Okayama prefecture), and others. Mostly found in western Japan and Okinawa island.

GIVEN NAMES Japanese 57%. *Hiroshi* (3), *Toru* (3), *Toshio* (3), *Atsuko* (2), *Hideyuki* (2), *Isao* (2), *Kazuhiko* (2), *Koji* (2), *Makoto* (2), *Masanobu* (2), *Shinichi* (2), *Tetsuo* (2).

Nakano (710) Japanese: 'central field'; from a common place name. It is a frequent surname, found mostly in western Japan. As it is listed in the Shinsen shōjiroku, some bearers can be assumed to be of ancient, noble origin.

GIVEN NAMES Japanese 55%. *Takashi* (8), *Hiroshi* (5), *Hiroko* (4), *Koji* (4), *Hideo* (3), *Hiroyuki* (3), *Kenji* (3), *Shigeru* (3), *Yoshiko* (3), *Yukio* (3), *Yutaka* (3), *Akiko* (2).

Nakao (258) Japanese: 'middle tail', 'tail' being topographic and denoting the lower slope of a mountain, not an animal's tail. Three separate families descend from the southern FUJIWARA through the Kudō family, from the Akamatsu family, and from the TAIRA clan. The name is also found on the island of Okinawa.

GIVEN NAMES Japanese 54%. *Hiroshi* (4), *Koji* (2), *Mayumi* (2), *Takashi* (2), *Tamotsu* (2), *Tetsuya* (2), *Toshio* (2), *Yoko* (2), *Yoshihiro* (2), *Yoshiko* (2), *Aki, Akinori.*

Nakashima (547) Japanese: 'middle island'; also pronounced NAKAJIMA. The sense of 'island' is not necessarily land surrounded by water, but can denote a property surrounded by other holdings. Compare NAKAMURA.

GIVEN NAMES Japanese 39%. *Masao* (5), *Takeshi* (5), *Takeo* (3), *Hiro* (2), *Ichiro* (2), *Kaneo* (2), *Keisuke* (2), *Kiyoshi* (2), *Masaru* (2), *Morio* (2), *Satoshi* (2), *Shigeru* (2).

Nakasone (313) Japanese: found in the Ryūkyū Islands, usually written with characters for 'center', 'monk', and 'root'.

GIVEN NAMES Japanese 31%. *Aiko* (2), *Seiko* (2), *Akira, Asayo, Ayano, Chiyo, Fumio, Hajime, Hideko, Hideo, Hiromitsu, Hiroshi.*

Nakata (455) Japanese: 'central rice paddy'; from a common place name found throughout Japan. The surname occurs mostly in western Japan and the Ryūkyū Islands. A common alternate pronunciation is **Nakada**. Some bearers have southern FUJIWARA or MINAMOTO connections.

GIVEN NAMES Japanese 39%. *Hideo* (3), *Kenichi* (3), *Yoshio* (3), *Hiroshi* (2), *Masahiro* (2), *Masaichi* (2), *Masaru* (2), *Osamu* (2), *Shigeo* (2), *Shigeru* (2), *Takeo* (2), *Akemi.*

Nakatani (178) Japanese: 'central valley'; found mostly in western Japan and the island of Okinawa. An alternate reading in eastern Japan is **Nakaya**.

GIVEN NAMES Japanese 59%. *Etsuko* (3), *Yoshio* (3), *Akira* (2), *Iwao* (2), *Rumiko* (2), *Aiko, Ayako, Chie, Fumihiko, Isamu, Isao, Katsutoshi.*

Nakatomi (7) Japanese (no longer common); an important priestly, noble clan in ancient Japan, and the ancestral name of the greatest clan of classical times, the FUJIWARA. Listed in the Shinsen shōjiroku, the name originally was *Naka-tsu-omi*: 'minister of the center', denoting an ancient, hereditary office as intermediary between men and deities. The clan claimed descent from Ame no Koyane, a son of the deity Takamimusubi and a companion of the mythical hero Ninigi. Nakatomi no Kamako (mid 6th century) was a leader of the faction opposing the importation of the Buddhist religion, which was sponsored by the Soga clan. Kamako's great-grandson, Kamatari, was a key figure in the downfall of the Soga and, as founder of the FUJIWARA clan, the principal architect of his family's greatness.

Nakayama (485) Japanese: 'central mountain'; a common place name, the surname is mostly found in western Japan and on the island of Okinawa. A few bearers descend from the northern FUJIWARA clan.

GIVEN NAMES Japanese 65%. *Takashi* (5), *Hideo* (3), *Isamu* (3), *Noboru* (3), *Shigeru* (3), *Takao* (3), *Yoshiko* (3), *Yoshinari* (3), *Hiroshi* (2), *Kazuo* (2), *Keiko* (2), *Kenichi* (2).

Nakazawa (122) Japanese: 'central swamp'; mostly found in central Japan and on the island of Okinawa. Though written with different characters today, it is of the same origin as NAGASAWA; both are common place names. Several bearers are of MINAMOTO origin, through various lines.

GIVEN NAMES Japanese 75%. *Hiroshi* (8), *Akio* (2), *Takao* (2), *Chiyoko, Fumiko, Goichi, Hajime, Hideo, Hideyuki, Hikari, Hiroki, Ichiro.*

Nalbandian (242) Armenian: patronymic from Turkish *nalbant* 'farrier', a word of Persian origin.

GIVEN NAMES Armenian 49%. *Anahit* (3), *Haig* (3), *Aram* (2), *Garbis* (2), *Hagop* (2), *Jirair* (2), *Mihran* (2), *Rouben* (2), *Sarkis* (2), *Vartan* (2), *Andranik, Antranig.*

Nalbone (158) Italian: of uncertain derivation; possibly a topographic or habitational name from an unidentified place, perhaps Narbonne in France.

GIVEN NAMES Italian 10%. *Angelo* (3), *Santo.*

Nalder (130) Probably a metathesized variant of German NADLER.

GIVEN NAME French 4%. *Michel.*

Nale (539) Altered spelling of German **Nähle**, from a pet form of the personal name CORNELIUS.

Nalepa (283) Polish: nickname from *nalepa* 'fireside corner', 'ingle nook'.

GIVEN NAMES Polish 6%. *Janusz* (3), *Ewa, Krystyna.*

Nall (2364) **1.** reduced form of Scottish or Irish MCNALL. **2.** Possibly an altered spelling of German **Nahl**, a reduced form of NAGEL.

FOREBEARS Martin Nall (1677–1728) emigrated from England to Tappahonnock, VA, in 1699.

Nalle (145) Variant of NALL 1.

Nalley (1585) Variant spelling of Irish NALLY (see MCNALLY).

Nalls (630) Probably an American derivative of NALL, or a variant of NILES. This name is borne mainly by African Americans.

GIVEN NAMES *Amaziah, Caloosa, Iretha, Lubirta, Radious, Redious, Terrika, Ulyeses.*

Nally (1041) Irish: reduced form of MCNALLY.

GIVEN NAMES Irish 4%. *Brendan* (2), *Siobhan.*

Nam (968) Korean: there is only one Chinese character for the surname *Nam*, meaning 'south'. As many as fifty-seven Nam clans are mentioned in the records, but of these only four can be positively documented. The founding ancestor of the Nam clans was a man named Kim Ch'ung. He was an emissary from Tang, China, on his way to

Japan when a southerly storm blew his ship northward and forced it aground in Shilla, Korea. The Shilla king Kyŏngdŏk (742–765), noting that he had come from the south, renamed the emissary *Nam* in 755.
GIVEN NAMES Korean 59%; Vietnamese 4%. *Sang* (23), *Young* (13), *Seung* (7), *Chong* (6), *Jung* (6), *Kyung* (6), *Yong* (6), *Chang* (5), *Kwang* (5), *Song* (5), *Sung* (5), *Myong* (4), *Yong Woo* (4), *Young Sook* (4), *Chung* (3), *Dae Woo* (3), *Hak* (3), *Ji Young* (3), *Seong* (3), *Seung Woo* (3), *Sook* (3), *Young Woo* (3), *Byung* (2); *Nguyen* (3), *Du, Ho Van, Nguyen Van, Pham, Pu, To, Truong.*

Naman (123) Respelling of French **Namon** or **Namin**, respectively an inflected and a pet form of the Germanic personal name *Namo*.
GIVEN NAMES French 5%. *Emile, Marcelle.*

Namanny (112) Origin unidentified.

Namba (145) Japanese: written with the characters for 'difficult' and 'wave' used phonetically, the original meaning is unclear. The name is mostly found in the island of Shikoku, and is also Romanized as **Nanba**.
GIVEN NAMES Japanese 59%. *Nobuaki* (2), *Shizuo* (2), *Chihiro, Chizuko, Hiroki, Hiroshi, Ikuo, Isamu, Iwao, Katsuhiro, Kazuo, Kazushi.*

Nameth (126) Variant of Hungarian **Németh** 'German' (see NEMETH).

Namey (108) Perhaps an Americanized form of Hungarian **Németh** 'German' (see NEMETH).

Nancarrow (205) Cornish: habitational name from places in the parishes of St. Allen and St. Michael Penkivel, so named from Cornish *nans* 'valley' + *carow* 'deer', 'stag' or *garow* 'rough'.

Nance (7815) Americanized spelling of German NANTZ.

Nanda (169) Indian (Panjab): Hindu (Khatri) and Sikh name based on the name of a Khatri clan.
GIVEN NAMES Indian 88%. *Ashok* (3), *Ashwini* (3), *Amitabh* (2), *Anil* (2), *Arun* (2), *Kavita* (2), *Madhu* (2), *Meenu* (2), *Mohit* (2), *Nikhil* (2), *Rajesh* (2), *Rajiv* (2).

Nanez (265) Spanish (**Náñez**): unexplained; possibly a reduced form of some patronymic.
GIVEN NAMES Spanish 43%. *Jose* (5), *Manuel* (4), *Luis* (3), *Sergio* (3), *Angel* (2), *Armando* (2), *Benito* (2), *Esperanza* (2), *Jaime* (2), *Juan* (2), *Juanita* (2), *Lupe* (2).

Nangle (440) Irish (brought to Ireland by Normans from Pembrokeshire): habitational name from a place in Pembrokeshire named with Middle English *atten angle* 'at the angle', i.e. 'dweller in the nook'.
FOREBEARS Gilbert de Angulo was a Norman baron, a follower of Strongbow, who came to Ireland in the 12th century. Many of his linear male descendants bear the surnames Nagle or Neagle, and members of the family held estates in County

Cork and in Connacht. In Connacht they adopted the Gaelic surname **Mac Oisdealbhaigh** (see COSTELLO).
GIVEN NAME Irish 4%. *Brendan.*

Nania (135) Southern Italian: from a reduced form of the personal name ANANIA.
GIVEN NAMES Italian 29%. *Salvatore* (3), *Antonino* (2), *Orlando* (2), *Americo, Emilio, Lorenzo, Pasquale, Rosalino.*

Nankervis (140) Cornish: habitational name from a place in St. Enoder parish, so called from Cornish *nans* 'valley' + an uncertain second element, possibly *cerwys*, an unattested plural of *carow* 'stag'.

Nann (105) **1.** Probably a shortened form of German **Nanne**, from an old nursery name. **2.** North German and Frisian: from a short form of a Germanic personal name based on *nanthjan* 'to dare'.
GIVEN NAME German 7%; Scandinavian 4%. *Hermann.*

Nanna (197) Italian: either from a feminine form of the personal name *Nanno* (see NANNI), or from an pet form of the female personal name *Marianna*.
GIVEN NAMES Italian 7%. *Angelo, Carmela, Dino, Domenic, Vito.*

Nannen (112) North German and Frisian: patronymic form from a short form of a personal name ending with -*nand*, such as *Gernand, Signand,* or *Wignand*. Compare NANN).

Nanney (857) **1.** Welsh: habitational name from a place called Nannau in Meirioneth. **2.** Possibly also a reduced and altered form of Irish MCNANEY.

Nanni (389) Italian (mainly central and northeastern): from a reduced pet form of *Giovanni* (Italian equivalent of JOHN), or from *Nanno*, a reduced form of BONANNO. In the form **Nannis** this is also found as a Greek family name.
GIVEN NAMES Italian 30%. *Leopoldo* (4), *Enrico* (3), *Mario* (3), *Giulio* (2), *Liborio* (2), *Tito* (2), *Aldo, Alesio, Alfredo, Amerigo, Antonio, Bernardino, Dario, Edmondo, Elio, Enzo, Giovanni, Luciano.*

Nanninga (179) North German and Dutch (Frisian): patronymic from a Frisian personal name, in origin probably a nursery term, but in the Middle Ages also taken as a short form of various Germanic compound names containing the element *nand* 'daring', 'brave' (see, for example, FERDINAND). Compare NANN.

Nannini (193) Italian: from a pet form of NANNI.
GIVEN NAMES Italian 12%. *Enzo* (3), *Guido* (2), *Mauro* (2), *Orazio* (2), *Elio, Evo, Geno, Luigi, Reno.*

Nanny (148) Variant spelling of NANNEY.

Nanos (136) Greek: **1.** from the personal name *Nanos*, a pet form of *Giovanos*, from Italian *Giovanni* (see JOHN). **2.** descriptive nickname from the vocabulary word *nanos* 'dwarf'.
GIVEN NAMES Greek 5%. *Kosmas, Stelios.*

Nansel (105) German: probably a variant spelling of **Nensel**, a variant of NANN.
GIVEN NAMES German 4%. *Conrad, Kurt.*

Nantz (635) South German: from a pet form of a Germanic compound name formed with *Nant-* (for example, *Nantwig, Nantger*); its meaning is reflected in Middle High German *nenden* 'to dare'.

Napier (5783) **1.** Scottish: occupational name for a producer or seller of table linen or for a naperer, the servant in charge of the linen in use in a great house, Middle English, Old French *nap(p)ier*, an agent derivative of Old French *nappe* 'table cloth' (Latin *mappa*). Compare NAPPER. **2.** Shortened form of Polish NAPIERALA or a similar name.
FOREBEARS An extensive Scottish family called Napier, who once held the earldom of Lennox, are descended from the hereditary naperers to the Kings of Scotland in the 12th century.

Napierala (217) Polish (**Napierała**): nickname for an insistent person, from a derivative of *napierać* 'advance', 'press', 'urge'.

Napieralski (114) Polish: derivative of **Napierała** (see NAPIERALA).
GIVEN NAME Polish 4%. *Tadeusz.*

Napierkowski (134) Polish: habitational name for someone from a place called Napierki in Olsztyn voivodeship.
GIVEN NAME Polish 6%. *Zigmont.*

Naples (887) Americanized form of Italian NAPOLI or Spanish and Portuguese NAPOLES.
GIVEN NAMES Italian 7%. *Angelo* (3), *Rocco* (3), *Caesar, Carlo, Carmine, Dante, Domenic, Romeo.*

Napoleon (526) French (**Napoléon**) and Spanish (**Napoleón**): from a Corsican personal name (see NAPOLEONE). It was made famous by the French Emperor Napoleon (1769–1821), and in some cases may have been adopted as a surname in his honor.
GIVEN NAMES French 7%; Italian 4%. *Armand, Berthony, Dominique, Germaine, Jacques, Jean Francois, Maryse, Mireille, Monique, Serge; Angelo, Rocco, Rosaria.*

Napoleone (117) Italian: from the Corsican personal name *Napoleone*, of uncertain origin.
GIVEN NAMES Italian 33%. *Giuseppe* (2), *Luigi* (2), *Nunzio* (2), *Umberto* (2), *Angelo, Antonio, Dante, Filiberto, Gino, Maddalena, Pietro, Rocco.*

Napoles (237) Spanish and Portuguese (**Nápoles**): habitational name from the Italian city of Naples (see NAPOLI).
GIVEN NAMES Spanish 57%. *Juan* (7), *Jose* (6), *Francisco* (5), *Jesus* (5), *Pedro* (5), *Ernesto* (4), *Luis* (4), *Manuel* (4), *Ignacio* (3), *Miguel* (3), *Ramon* (3), *Rolando* (3).

Napoletano (153) Southern Italian: habitational name for someone from Naples, from an adjectival derivative of NAPOLI.
GIVEN NAMES Italian 25%. *Mario* (2), *Mauro* (2), *Aldo, Antonio, Assunta, Cataldo, Emo,*

Guido, Guiseppe, Luigi, Marco, Sal, Sergio, Vito.

Napoli (1772) Southern Italian: habitational name from the Campanian city of Naples, now the third largest city in Italy. The place name, Italian *Napoli*, Latin *Neapolis*, is from Greek *nea* 'new' + *polis* 'city'. It was an ancient Greek colony taken over by the Romans in the 4th century BC.
GIVEN NAMES Italian 18%. *Salvatore* (14), *Angelo* (7), *Rocco* (7), *Antonio* (6), *Carmine* (6), *Santo* (4), *Carmela* (3), *Sal* (3), *Vito* (3), *Bartolo* (2), *Carmelo* (2), *Domenic* (2).

Napolitan (210) Reduced form of Italian NAPOLITANO.
GIVEN NAMES Italian 7%. *Angelo, Carlo, Carmela, Sal.*

Napolitano (2380) Southern Italian: habitational name for someone from Naples, perhaps from Neapolitan dialect *Napulitanë*, an adjectival derivative of NAPOLI. Compare standard Italian NAPOLETANO.
GIVEN NAMES Italian 18%. *Carmine* (24), *Sal* (12), *Angelo* (10), *Salvatore* (10), *Carmela* (5), *Pasquale* (5), *Aniello* (4), *Domenic* (3), *Fiore* (3), *Vincenzo* (3), *Antonio* (2), *Clemente* (2).

Napora (151) Polish: nickname for an interfering person, Polish *napora*, derivative of *napierać* 'to insist on somebody doing something'.
GIVEN NAMES Polish 4%. *Jaroslaw, Krystyna.*

Napp (269) **1.** English: metonymic occupational name for a producer or seller of table linen, from Old French *nappe* 'table cloth'. **2.** English: either a variant spelling of KNAPP or a reduced variant of Scottish MCNABB. **3.** Altered spelling of German KNAPP. **4.** German: metonymic occupational name for a bowl and cup maker, from Middle Low German *nap* 'bowl', 'mug', or alternatively, from an old personal name formed with an element cognate with Old High German *(gi-)nāda* 'grace', 'benevolence'.

Nappa (142) Southern Italian: nickname with various possible derivations. **1.** from *nappa* 'gib', 'large nose'; **2.** from Calabrian *nappa* 'clay dish', or the same word in Sicilian meaning 'dish', 'protruding chin (for want of teeth)'; **3.** from *(n)nappa* 'ingenue'.
GIVEN NAMES Italian 17%. *Carmine* (3), *Angelo, Pasquale, Pellegrino.*

Napper (809) **1.** English: occupational name for a naperer, the servant in charge of the linen in use in a great house, Middle English, Old French *nap(p)ier*. Compare Scottish NAPIER. **2.** Dutch: nickname from an agent derivative of Middle Dutch *nappen* 'prick', 'sting', 'bite'. **3.** Dutch: occupational name from an agent derivative of *nap* 'cup', denoting a turner who made cups, dishes, and bowls. **4.** Altered spelling of German KNAPPER.

Nappi (891) Italian: plural form of NAPPA.

GIVEN NAMES Italian 13%. *Angelo* (4), *Antonio* (4), *Benedetto* (2), *Natale* (2), *Salvatore* (2), *Severino* (2), *Alfonse, Amato, Aniello, Carmine, Chiara, Dino.*

Nappier (301) Scottish: variant spelling of NAPIER.

Nappo (209) Southern Italian: **1.** perhaps a metonymic occupational name for a potter, from Calabrian *nappo* denoting a type of cup. **2.** variant of NAPPA.
GIVEN NAMES Italian 16%. *Angelo* (3), *Antonio* (3), *Gino, Sal, Salvatore, Veto, Vincenzo.*

Naquin (1384) French: occupational name for a young lad or serving man, Old French *naquin* (apparently a diminutive of *naque* 'mucus', 'snot', a word of uncertain origin).
GIVEN NAMES French 6%. *Camille* (3), *Chantel* (2), *Emile* (2), *Eves* (2), *Oneil* (2), *Alphonse, Andre, Anicet, Antoine, Chanel, Etienne, Evest.*

Naqvi (199) Muslim: adjectival derivative of Arabic *naqī* 'pure', 'clean'. It is a family name denoting a descendant or follower of 'Ali ibn Muhammad Naqī, tenth imam of the Shiites.
GIVEN NAMES Muslim 90%. *Syed* (40), *Ali* (9), *Haider* (2), *Irfan* (2), *Mohsin* (2), *Nasim* (2), *Nazar* (2), *Raza* (2), *Saiyid* (2), *Shams* (2), *Abbas, Adnan.*

Naragon (111) Spanish (**Naragón**): regional name for someone from the province of Aragon (see ARAGON).

Narain (144) **1.** Indian: variant of NARAYAN. **2.** variant of NARINE in Guyana and Trinidad.
GIVEN NAMES Indian 69%. *Arvind* (2), *Vijay* (2), *Ajay, Amar, Amitabh, Ashok, Bindu, Brahm, Chandra, Deonarine, Hardat, Harish.*

Naramore (354) English (Devon): variant spelling of NARRAMORE.

Narang (163) Indian (Panjab): Hindu (Arora) and Sikh name based on the name of a clan in the Arora community, from Sanskrit *nāranga* 'orange'.
GIVEN NAMES Indian 90%. *Ramesh* (6), *Anil* (3), *Ashok* (3), *Lalit* (3), *Prem* (3), *Rajeev* (3), *Arun* (2), *Ashish* (2), *Kamini* (2), *Mukesh* (2), *Rakesh* (2), *Ram* (2).

Naranjo (1564) Spanish: topographic name for someone who lived by an orange grove, from Spanish *naranjo* 'orange tree' (from *naranja* 'orange', Arabic *nāránjya*), or a habitational name from a place named Naranjo in A Coruña and Códoba provinces. (The word *orange* reached English from Spanish via Old French and Old Provençal, in which languages the initial *n-* had already been sporadically lost.)
GIVEN NAMES Spanish 46%. *Jose* (32), *Carlos* (18), *Juan* (15), *Luis* (15), *Roberto* (15), *Javier* (11), *Manuel* (11), *Pedro* (10), *Francisco* (8), *Miguel* (8), *Raul* (8), *Jaime* (7).

Narasimhan (131) Indian (Kerala, Tamil Nadu): Hindu name from Sanskrit *narasimha* 'man lion' (from *nara* 'man' + *simha* 'lion', name of the fourth incarnation of Vishnu, in which he was half man and half lion) + the Tamil-Malayalam third-person masculine singular suffix -*n*. This is only a given name in India, but has come to be used as a family name in the U.S.
GIVEN NAMES Indian 96%. *Ravi* (5), *Lakshmi* (4), *Srinivasan* (3), *Chitra* (2), *Ramesh* (2), *Sridhar* (2), *Akila, Anand, Arun, Bhanu, Bharati, Charu.*

Narayan (338) Indian (northern and southern states): Hindu name from Sanskrit *nārāyaṇa*, an epithet of the god Vishnu. In the northern states, it appears to have evolved into a family name from the final element of compound personal names such as *Ramnarayan* (from *Ram*, name of an incarnation of Vishnu, + *Narayan*). In South India, it is used only as a male given name, but has become a family name among South Indians in the U.S. It is a variant of NARAYANAN among Tamil and Malayalam speakers who have migrated from their home state.
GIVEN NAMES Indian 85%. *Ram* (10), *Shankar* (6), *Hari* (5), *Prakash* (4), *Ravi* (4), *Anand* (3), *Geetha* (3), *Satya* (3), *Sriram* (3), *Suresh* (3), *Uma* (3), *Anil* (2).

Narayanan (290) Indian (Kerala, Tamil Nadu): Hindu name from Sanskrit *nārāyaṇa* (an epithet of Vishnu; see NARAYAN) + the Tamil-Malayalam third-person masculine singular suffix -*n*. This is only a given name in India, but has come to be used as a family name in the U.S.
GIVEN NAMES Indian 94%. *Ram* (5), *Ramesh* (5), *Ravi* (5), *Suresh* (5), *Manoj* (4), *Hari* (3), *Lakshmi* (3), *Mahesh* (3), *Murali* (3), *Suriya* (3), *Vijay* (3), *Anand* (2).

Narciso (273) Portuguese and Spanish: from a medieval personal name (Latin *Narcissus*, from Greek *Narkissos*, the name of a flower). This name was borne, according to classical myth, by a vain youth who was so transfixed by his own beauty that he ignored the blandishments of the nymph Echo and stared at his own reflection in water until he faded away and turned into the pale but lovely flower that bears his name. It was also borne by several early Christian saints, in particular by a bishop who was said to have been put to death, together with his deacon Felix, in Catalonia AD *c.* 307. The personal name owes its popularity to this saint rather than to the mythological youth.
GIVEN NAMES Spanish 21%; Italian 11%. *Alfredo* (4), *Jose* (3), *Carlos* (2), *Sergio* (2), *Adolfo, Arturo, Benito, Carmelita, Eduardo, Emiliano, Emilio, Enrique*; *Antonio* (4), *Angelo* (2), *Luca, Nicola, Romeo, Sabatino, Salvatore, Saturnina, Vito.*

Narcisse (427) French: from the personal name *Narcisse*, French form of *Naricissus* (see NARCISO).

GIVEN NAMES French 13%. *Andre, Andree, Antoine, Cecile, Celine, Dieudonne, Francois, Maudry, Michel, Micheline, Myrtha, Odette.*

Nard (130) French: from a short form of the personal name *Bernard.*

Nardella (344) Italian: from a pet form of NARDO.

GIVEN NAMES Italian 14%. *Angelo* (4), *Amato, Benedetto, Carlo, Cosmo, Gaetano, Giuseppe, Luigi, Matteo, Pasquale, Salvatore, Silvio.*

Nardelli (284) Italian: patronymic or plural form of **Nardello**, a pet form of NARDO.

GIVEN NAMES Italian 16%. *Antonio* (5), *Camillo* (2), *Vito* (2), *Carlo, Carmela, Ettore, Flavio, Marco, Nicolina, Orazio, Primo.*

Nardi (1057) Italian: patronymic or plural form of NARDO.

GIVEN NAMES Italian 11%. *Angelo* (3), *Gino* (3), *Primo* (3), *Dario* (2), *Remo* (2), *Santo* (2), *Vito* (2), *Aldo, Attilio, Carlo, Carmela, Domenic.*

Nardiello (169) Italian: from a Neapolitan pet form of the personal name NARDO.

GIVEN NAMES Italian 17%. *Aldo* (2), *Silvio* (2), *Gennaro, Gesualdo, Rocco, Vincenzo.*

Nardin (120) French and Italian (Venetian): from a reduced pet form of the personal name BERNARD (French), BERNARDO (Italian). Compare NARDO.

GIVEN NAMES French 8%; Italian 6%. *Pierre* (2); *Concetta, Dante, Raffaele.*

Nardini (333) Italian: from *Nardino*, a pet form of the personal name NARDO.

GIVEN NAMES Italian 23%. *Mario* (5), *Dino* (2), *Domenic* (2), *Gino* (2), *Lilio* (2), *Alfio, Alfredo, Alida, Alvaro, Amadio, Angelo, Carlo, Dante, Enrico, Levia, Lino, Matteo, Piero, Reno, Silvio.*

Nardo (300) Italian: from the personal name *Nardo*, originally a short form of any of the various personal names (of Germanic origin) ending with *-nardo*, for example, *Bernardo, Leonardo.*

GIVEN NAMES Italian 14%; Spanish 10%; French 4%. *Salvatore* (2), *Angelo, Antonio, Dino, Italo, Nicola, Rino, Romeo, Silvio, Vito; Carlos* (3), *Rafael* (2), *Concepcion, Ernesto, Felipe, Ildefonso, Jose, Juan, Luis, Mario, Miguel; Damien, Marcel.*

Nardolillo (100) Italian: from a pet form of the personal name NARDO.

GIVEN NAMES Italian 19%. *Angelo* (3), *Domenic* (2), *Giacinto, Nichola.*

Nardone (1138) Italian: from an augmentative of the personal name NARDO.

GIVEN NAMES Italian 14%. *Angelo* (10), *Enrico* (3), *Salvatore* (3), *Ugo* (3), *Carlo* (2), *Luciano* (2), *Oreste* (2), *Amedeo, Carmela, Concetta, Cosimo, Cosmo.*

Nardozzi (191) Italian: from the personal name *Nardozzo*, a pet form of NARDO.

GIVEN NAMES Italian 16%. *Sal* (2), *Salvatore* (2), *Carmine, Donato, Mauro, Pasquale, Rocco.*

Narducci (311) Italian: from a pet form of the personal name NARDO.

GIVEN NAMES Italian 11%. *Domenic* (5), *Lorenzo* (2), *Angelo, Antonio, Donato, Filomena, Nicola, Saverio, Vito.*

Narehood (106) Origin unidentified.

Narez (114) Spanish (**Nárez**): unexplained.

GIVEN NAMES Spanish 50%. *Francisco* (4), *Bulmaro* (3), *Armando* (2), *Jesus* (2), *Jorge* (2), *Jose* (2), *Rafael* (2), *Alfrado, Alfredo, Ana, Candelario, Carmella; Antonio, Erminio, Sal.*

Nargi (143) Italian (Campania): unexplained.

GIVEN NAMES Italian 13%. *Carmine* (2), *Angelo, Antonio, Marco, Salvatore, Vincenzo.*

Narine (145) Name found among people of Indian origin in Guyana and Trinidad: altered form of Indian NARAYAN.

GIVEN NAMES Indian 45%. *Deo* (2), *Jasodra* (2), *Leela* (2), *Suraj* (2), *Suruj* (2), *Adesh, Dhanraj, Drupatie, Geeta, Ghanshyam, Gopal, Gopaul.*

Narkiewicz (115) Polish: patronymic from the Lithuanian personal name *Narkus*, *Norkus*.

Narlock (144) Probably an altered spelling of German **Narloch** or **Norloch**, a topographic name composed of Middle High German *nord* 'north' (frequently shortened to *nor-*) + *lōch* 'wood', 'copse'.

GIVEN NAME French 5%. *Cecile.*

Naro (206) Southern Italian: habitational name from Naro in Agrigento province, Sicily.

GIVEN NAMES Italian 8%. *Angelo* (3), *Salvatore* (2).

Naron (323) Galician (**Narón**): habitational name from Narón in A Coruña province, Galicia.

Narr (132) German: nickname for a foolish or silly person, from Middle High German *narr* 'fool', 'jester'.

GIVEN NAMES German 5%. *Erwin, Heinz.*

Narramore (292) English: habitational name for someone living in a place known as the 'north moor', as for example Narramore in Devon.

GIVEN NAME French 4%. *Gillis.*

Narron (448) Americanized spelling of Scottish NAIRN.

Narrow (121) Jewish: Americanized form of some like-sounding Ashkenazic name.

GIVEN NAMES German 4%; Jewish 4%. *Erwin; Mayer.*

Nartker (133) German (**Närtker**): perhaps a topographic name for someone who lived in a basin, from Middle High German *narte* 'trough'.

Narula (110) Indian (Panjab): Hindu (Arora) and Sikh name based on the name of an Arora clan.

GIVEN NAMES Indian 88%. *Vijay* (4), *Arun* (2), *Deepak* (2), *Prem* (2), *Raj* (2), *Sita* (2), *Alok, Amit, Anju, Anupam, Anuradha, Anurag.*

Narum (209) Norwegian: **1.** habitational name from farmsteads in eastern Norway, named in Old Norse as *Nórheimar*, from *nór* 'narrows', 'narrow passage (in a river, fjord, or lake)' + *heimr* 'homestead', 'home'. **2.** Americanized form of **Nærum**, a habitational name from a farmstead so named from Old Norse *Njarðarheimr*, which is a compound of *Njǫrð* (the name of a heathen god) + *heimr*.

Narvaez (1028) Spanish (**Narváez**): habitational name from a place so called near Almagro, in Ciudad Real province.

GIVEN NAMES Spanish 45%. *Jose* (21), *Juan* (16), *Luis* (14), *Carlos* (9), *Jorge* (9), *Pedro* (7), *Julio* (6), *Rafael* (6), *Francisco* (5), *Ana* (4), *Eduardo* (4), *Jaime* (4).

Narveson (195) Americanized spelling of Norwegian **Narvesen**, a patronymic from the personal name *Narve*, Old Norse *Narfi*, ultimately from a word meaning 'narrow' (compare NARUM).

GIVEN NAME German 5%. *Kurt* (2).

Nary (181) Irish: variant of NEARY. Compare MCNARY.

Nasby (170) English: habitational name from Naseby in Northamptonshire, named with the genitive of the Old English personal name *Hnæf* + Old English *byrig*, dative case of *burh* 'fortified place'.

Nasca (310) Southern Italian (Sicily): from Sicilian *nasca* 'nose', hence a nickname for someone with a snub, flat, or turned-up nose.

GIVEN NAMES Italian 13%. *Angelo* (6), *Salvatore* (3), *Carlo, Dominico.*

Nascimento (413) Portuguese: religious byname from Portuguese *nascimento* 'birth', 'nativity' (Late Latin *nascimentum*, from *nasci* 'to be born'). This was one of the epithets of the Virgin Mary (*Maria do Nascimento*), and was also used as a given name for children born at Christmas.

GIVEN NAMES Spanish 27%; Portuguese 17%. *Jose* (13), *Manuel* (7), *Carlos* (5), *Fernando* (3), *Raimundo* (3), *Cesar* (2), *Francisco* (2), *Luiz* (2), *Marcelo* (2), *Osmar* (2), *Sergio* (2), *Adelmo; Joao* (4), *Paulo* (3), *Ademir, Damiao, Goncalo, Guilherme, Joaquim, Sebastiao, Vasco; Antonio* (13), *Marcello* (2), *Marco* (2), *Elio, Flavio, Paolo, Rosangela, Silvio, Umberto.*

Nase (274) German: nickname from Middle High German *nase* 'nose', denoting someone with an unusually big or otherwise remarkable nose.

GIVEN NAMES German 6%. *Erwin* (2), *Kurt* (2), *Aloysius.*

Naser (293) **1.** Arabic: variant of NASSER. **2.** German (**Näser**): nickname for a gourmand, from Middle High German *nēser* 'shoulder bag for food'. **3.** German: topographic name from German *Nase* 'nose', i.e. a projecting piece of land.

GIVEN NAMES Arabic 33%. *Abdel* (3), *Mohamed* (3), *Mohammad* (3), *Salameh* (3), *Ibrahim* (2), *Mohammed* (2), *Nidal* (2), *Zaki* (2), *Abdalla, Abdul, Adbul, Ahmad.*

Nash (19889) **1.** English: topographic name for someone who lived by an ash tree, a variant of ASH by misdivision of Middle English *atten ash* 'at the ash', or a habitational name from any of the many places in England and Wales named Nash, from this phrase, as for example Nash in Buckinghamshire, Herefordshire, or Shropshire. The name was established from an early date in Wales and Ireland. **2.** Jewish: of unknown origin, possibly an Americanized form of one or more like-sounding Jewish surnames.

FOREBEARS The surname Nash was taken to Ireland from England or Wales by a family who established themselves in Co. Kerry in the 13th century, during the second wave of Anglo-Norman settlement. Abner Nash (?1740–86), governor of NC, was of Welsh origin, his parents having emigrated to VA from Wales in 1730. His brother Francis (?1742–77) was a general in the Continental army; the city of Nashville, TN, was named in his honor.

Nasi (114) Italian: patronymic or plural form of NASO.

GIVEN NAMES Italian 11%. *Enrico* (2), *Angelo, Antonio, Carlo, Duilio, Franco, Giovanni.*

Nasir (195) Muslim: **1.** from a personal name based on *naṣīr* 'supporter', 'helper' (Qur'an 9:116). **2.** from a personal name based on *nāṣir* 'protector'. It is found in compounds such as **Nasruddin** (Arabic *Nāṣir ud-Dīn*) 'protector of religion', i.e. 'defender of the faith (Islam)'. Compare NASSER.

GIVEN NAMES Muslim 77%. *Mohammad* (7), *Mohammed* (5), *Syed* (4), *Mokhtar* (3), *Nabih* (3), *Abdul* (2), *Ahmad* (2), *Bassem* (2), *Ghulam* (2), *Iqbal* (2), *Ismail* (2), *Jamal* (2).

Naslund (296) Swedish (**Näslund**): ornamental or topographic name composed of the elements *näs* 'narrow neck of land', 'headland' + *lund* 'grove'.

GIVEN NAMES Scandinavian 8%. *Helmer, Lennart, Nels, Petter.*

Naso (252) Italian: **1.** possibly a nickname from *naso* 'nose' (Latin *nasus*), denoting someone with a prominent, snub, or otherwise remarkable nose. **2.** habitational name from Naso in Messina province, Sicily.

GIVEN NAMES Italian 11%. *Angelo* (2), *Salvatore* (2), *Benedetta, Giovanna, Serafino, Vito.*

Nason (2179) French: nickname from a diminutive of Old French *nes* 'nose'. Compare NASO.

Nasr (275) Muslim: from a personal name based on Arabic *naṣr* 'victory'. *Al-Nasr* 'the Victory' is the title of the 110th sura of the Qur'an.

GIVEN NAMES Muslim 62%. *Mohamed* (8), *Mostafa* (4), *Munir* (4), *Ahmed* (3), *Aziz* (3), *Ghassan* (3), *Walid* (3), *Abdulla* (2), *Ali* (2), *Farid* (2), *Karim* (2), *Khaled* (2).

Nasrallah (117) Muslim: from a personal name based on Arabic *naṣr-ullah* 'victory through Allah'. See the Qur'an (sura 110): 'With Allah's help victory comes'.

GIVEN NAMES Muslim 49%. *Abdo* (2), *Amal* (2), *Nadim* (2), *Salah* (2), *Walid* (2), *Amer, Antoun, Anwar, Bahjat, Fadi, Faisal, Farid.*

Nass (892) **1.** English: variant of NESS. **2.** German: from Middle High German *naz* 'wet', a nickname for a heavy drinker or a topographic name for someone living on wet land.

GIVEN NAMES German 5%. *Kurt* (4), *Gerhard* (3), *Alois, Fritz, Gerhart, Hans, Otto, Volker.*

Nassar (679) Arabic: from a personal name based on Arabic *naṣṣār* 'granter of victory'.

GIVEN NAMES Arabic 32%; French 5%. *Nassar* (6), *Ramzi* (4), *Hani* (3), *Jamil* (3), *Nadim* (3), *Said* (3), *Wadih* (3), *Abdel* (2), *Ahmed* (2), *Ali* (2), *Emad* (2), *Essam* (2); *Antoine* (4), *Emile* (3), *Michel* (2), *Amie, Autrey, Clemence, Georges, Monique.*

Nassau (156) German, Dutch, and Jewish (western Ashkenazic): habitational name from the town of Nassau, formerly the seat of an independent duchy. The place name derives from Old High German *naz* 'damp', 'wet' + *ouwa* 'water meadow'.

FOREBEARS The royal house of Nassau traces its descent from Dudo, Count of Lauenberg, who flourished between 1093 and 1117. His family acquired the county of Nassau in the 12th century. The Dutch king Willem van Oranje-Nassau, otherwise known as William the Silent, was the leader of the Dutch revolt against Spain in the 17th century.

GIVEN NAME French 4%; Jewish 4%. *Ehud.*

Nasser (761) **1.** Muslim: from an Arabic personal name based on *nāṣir* 'granter of victory'. Compare NASIR, NASSAR. **2.** German: habitational name for someone from any of the places called Nassen, in Rhineland-Palatinate, Hesse, and Bavaria. **3.** German (**Näßer**): variant of NASER 2.

GIVEN NAMES Muslim 33%. *Ali* (8), *Mohamed* (7), *Ahmed* (5), *Ibrahim* (4), *Bassam* (3), *Mohamad* (3), *Saleh* (3), *Wafa* (3), *Ahmad* (2), *Arwa* (2), *Chafic* (2), *Ezzat* (2).

Nassif (403) Muslim: from a personal name based on Arabic *nāṣif* 'just', 'fair'.

GIVEN NAMES Muslim 14%. *Farid* (3), *Walid* (3), *Amir* (2), *Amine, Amr, Bassam, Fadia, Fady, Faten, Fouad, Fuad, Ghassan.*

Nasso (135) **1.** Italian: widespread throughout Italy, this name has various possible sources: as a habitational name from a place called Nasso (Latin *Naxus*) or from a

reduced form of various personal names or nicknames formed with this suffix, as for example *Satanasso*, the name of the Devil, or Venetian *Canasso*. **2.** Greek: from the personal name *Nassos*, a pet form of *Athanassios* (see ATHANAS).

GIVEN NAMES Italian 22%. *Domenic* (2), *Angelo, Antonio, Rocco, Santo, Serafino, Vito.*

Nast (422) German: topographic name for someone who lived in a thickly wooded area, or a metonymic occupational name for a woodcutter, from Middle High German *nast* 'branch', a regional variant of *ast*, resulting from the misdivision of forms such as *ein ast* 'a branch'.

Nasta (174) **1.** Southern Italian: from a reduced form of the personal names ANASTASIO (Italian), Greek *Anastasios* (see ANASTAS). **2.** Hindu name of unknown meaning found among people from Sind, Pakistan.

GIVEN NAMES Italian 14%; Indian 8%. *Vito* (3), *Angelo, Antonio, Cosmo, Massimo, Pasqualino; Deep, Hansa, Mahesh, Manish, Naresh, Sucheta.*

Nastase (103) Romanian: from a reduced form of the personal name ANASTAS.

GIVEN NAMES Romanian 15%. *Doina, Dragos, Gheorghe, Ilie, Liviu, Radu, Sorin, Viorel; Orazio.*

Nastasi (458) Southern Italian: patronymic from a reduced form of the personal name ANASTASIO.

GIVEN NAMES Italian 28%. *Antonio* (4), *Salvatore* (4), *Vito* (3), *Angelo* (2), *Agostino, Aldo, Basilio, Carmel, Carmella, Ernesto, Gaspar, Giuseppe, Lorenzo, Mariano, Marino, Mario, Matteo, Natale.*

Nastri (165) Italian: possibly a nickname from the plural of *nastro* 'ribbon'.

GIVEN NAMES Italian 9%. *Carmine* (2), *Horacio* (2), *Angelina, Carmela, Mariano, Orlando, Pasquale.*

Nasuti (152) Italian: nickname from *nasuto* 'person with a big nose'.

Nasworthy (149) English (Devon): variant of NORSWORTHY.

Natal (341) Portuguese and Spanish: from the personal name *Natal* (from Latin *Natalis*), bestowed on someone born at Christmas or with reference to the Marian epithet *María del Natal*.

GIVEN NAMES Spanish 36%. *Jose* (12), *Angel* (7), *Luis* (4), *Manuel* (4), *Ana* (2), *Arcangel* (2), *Eduardo* (2), *Pedro* (2), *Rafael* (2), *Adalberto, Armando, Arturo.*

Natale (1992) Italian: nickname from the personal name *Natale* 'Christmas' (see NOEL). As a personal name this referred originally to the day of a martyr's or saint's death, i.e. birth to eternal life; later it was given in honor of the Christmas festival.

GIVEN NAMES Italian 16%. *Pasquale* (12), *Angelo* (10), *Antonio* (8), *Rocco* (7), *Salvatore* (5), *Dante* (4), *Domenic* (4),

Gennaro (3), *Sal* (3), *Carmine* (2), *Ciro* (2), *Domenico* (2).

Natali (265) Italian: patronymic or plural form of NATALE.

GIVEN NAMES Italian 13%. *Angelo* (3), *Cosimo, Enrico, Enzo, Franco, Luigi, Marco, Tonino, Vito.*

Natalie (222) French: from the female personal name Natalie, Latin *Natalia*, derived from *natalis* (see NOEL). This was the name of a saint and martyr, which gave it popularity in the Middle Ages.

GIVEN NAMES Italian 12%. *Nunzio* (3), *Angelo, Dino, Rocco.*

Natarajan (277) Indian (Kerala, Tamil Nadu): Hindu name from Sanskrit *naṭarāja* 'king of dancers' (from *naṭa* 'dancer' + *rāja* 'king', an epithet of the god Shiva) + the Tamil-Malayalam third-person masculine singular suffix -*n*. This is only a given name in India, but has come to be used as a family name in the U.S.

GIVEN NAMES Indian 91%. *Murali* (6), *Raj* (5), *Ganesh* (4), *Senthil* (4), *Siva* (4), *Raju* (3), *Shiva* (3), *Subramanian* (3), *Sundar* (3), *Swaminathan* (3), *Balu* (2), *Chandra* (2).

Nate (150) French: from a short form of the personal name *Donat* (Latin *Donatus* 'given').

Nath (611) Indian: Hindu name from Sanskrit *nātha* 'lord'. This commonly occurs as the final element of compound personal names, from which it appears to have evolved into a surname.

GIVEN NAMES Indian 45%. *Prem* (5), *Vijay* (5), *Amar* (3), *Anil* (3), *Aditya* (2), *Aloke* (2), *Amita* (2), *Jagan* (2), *Kailash* (2), *Manju* (2), *Nakul* (2), *Narendra* (2).

Nathan (2864) Jewish, English, and German: from the Biblical Hebrew personal name *Natan* 'given' (i.e. by God). Sometimes this is also a Jewish short form of *Jonathan* or *Nathaniel*. The personal name was comparatively rare among non-Jews in the Middle Ages (although always common among Jews); as a modern surname it is most frequently Jewish.

Nathaniel (309) From the Biblical Hebrew personal name meaning 'given by God'. This was borne by a minor prophet in the Bible (2 Samuel 7:2). It is found as both a Jewish and Gentile surname in Europe. In South India it is used as a given name among Christians, and in the U.S. it has come to be used as a family name among South Indian Christians.

GIVEN NAMES Indian 4%. *Satya* (2), *Ashish, Sashi.*

Nathans (118) Jewish: patronymic from NATHAN.

GIVEN NAME Jewish 4%. *Meyer.*

Nathanson (1093) Jewish: patronymic from NATHAN.

GIVEN NAMES Jewish 5%. *Sol* (3), *Hyman* (2), *Miriam* (2), *Morry* (2), *Avram, Reuven, Shai, Zelig.*

Nathe (254) German: from a short form of a Germanic personal name formed with an element cognate with Old High German (*gi-)nāda* 'grace', 'benevolence'.

Nation (2404) English (West Midlands): most probably a variant of NATHAN, altered by folk etymology under the influence of the English vocabulary word *nation*.

Nations (1353) English: variant of NATION.

Natividad (484) Spanish: from the personal name *Natividad* 'nativity', 'Christmas', from Latin *nativitas* 'birth', genitive *nativitatis*, usually bestowed with reference to the Marian epithet *María de la Natividad*. Compare NATAL.

GIVEN NAMES Spanish 43%. *Juan* (8), *Jose* (7), *Manuel* (6), *Ramon* (6), *Jesus* (5), *Ernesto* (4), *Jaime* (4), *Guadalupe* (3), *Luis* (3), *Miguel* (3), *Rafael* (3), *Raul* (3); *Antonio* (3), *Romeo* (2), *Annalisa, Donato, Emiliana, Enrico, Franco, Julieta, Leonardo, Lorenzo.*

Natoli (774) Italian: from a reduced form of the personal name *Anatoli*, Late Latin *Anatolius*, a derivative of Greek *anatolē* 'sunrise', 'dawn'.

GIVEN NAMES Italian 22%. *Angelo* (10), *Carmelo* (8), *Salvatore* (6), *Bartolo* (5), *Rocco* (4), *Domenico* (2), *Orlando* (2), *Rosario* (2), *Sal* (2), *Santo* (2), *Aldo, Gaetano, Gianfranco, Marino.*

Natt (136) **1.** Indian (Panjab): Sikh name based on the name of a Jat clan. **2.** Evidently also a reduced form of Irish or Scottish McNATT. **3.** Jewish (American): shortened form of NATHAN.

GIVEN NAMES Indian 11%. *Anit, Gagan, Jagbir, Malkit, Nasib.*

Natter (209) German: **1.** from a Germanic personal name based on an element cognate with Old High German (*gi-)nāda* or Old Saxon *nadha* 'favor', 'grace'. **2.** occupational nickname for a snake catcher, from Middle High German *nāter* 'snake'.

GIVEN NAMES German 10%. *Hans* (2), *Wolfgang* (2), *Franz, Kurt, Uwe.*

Nattress (123) Northern English: habitational name from a place called Nattrass in Alston, Cumbria.

Natvig (143) Norwegian: habitational name from any of several places so named. One example, in Sogn, is named with Old Norse *naddr* 'stud', 'nail' (relating to the shape of a headland) + *vik* 'bay', 'inlet'; another, in Agder, is from Old Norse *knǫttr* 'hummock' + *vik*; and a third, in Sunnmøre is from *not* 'nut' + *vik*.

GIVEN NAME Scandinavian 5%. *Juel.*

Natwick (115) Americanized spelling of Norwegian **Natvig.**

Natzke (237) German: from a pet form of the personal name *Ignatz*, from Latin *Ignatius* (see IGNACIO). This was the name borne by a bishop of Antioch *c.*100 AD, the object of a widespread cult in the Middle Ages.

Nau (1111) **1.** German: variant of NEU. **2.** French: metonymic occupational name for a boatman, from Occitan *nau* 'ship', 'boat' (Latin *navis*). **3.** French: from a reduced form of a personal name such as *Arnaud* (see ARNOLD) or *Renaud* (see REYNOLD).

GIVEN NAMES French 5%. *Alain* (2), *Altagrace, Andre, Fernande, Germaine, Joselle, Michel, Serge, Wesner, Wilner, Yvan.*

Naud (100) French: variant of NAULT.

GIVEN NAME French 7%. *Jacques.*

Nauer (148) **1.** German: occupational name for a ferryman, Middle High German *næware.* **2.** Altered spelling of German KNAUER.

Nauert (232) German: **1.** variant of NAUER with the addition of an excrescent -*t*, which is common in west-central German dialects. **2.** in the north, perhaps a nickname from a reduced form of Middle Low German *nouwe-rāt* 'good advice'.

Naugher (124) Irish (Ulster): reduced Anglicized form of Gaelic **Mac Conchobhair** 'son of *Conchobhar*' (see O'CONNOR). This form seems to have arisen from a common pronunciation of the personal name as *Cnochúr*, with loss of the initial *k*- in the process of Anglicization.

Naughton (2076) **1.** Irish: reduced form of McNAUGHTON. **2.** English: habitational name from a place in Suffolk, named in Old English with *nafola* 'navel' + *tūn* 'enclosure', 'settlement', i.e. 'settlement in the navel or depression'.

GIVEN NAMES Irish 6%. *Brendan, Brigid, Ciaran, Eamonn, John Patrick.*

Naugle (1299) Americanized form of German NAGEL.

Nault (1073) French: from a short form of various medieval personal names derived from Germanic personal names formed with *wald* 'rule' as the final element, in particular ARNOLD.

GIVEN NAMES French 10%. *Armand* (6), *Alphonse* (5), *Andre* (4), *Normand* (3), *Adelard* (2), *Emile* (2), *Marcel* (2), *Adlore* (2), *Alexandre, Aurele, Aurelien, Aurore.*

Naulty (107) Irish: reduced form of **Mc Naulty**, a variant of McNULTY.

GIVEN NAME Irish 7%. *Brendan* (2).

Naum (123) Romanian: unexplained.

GIVEN NAMES Romanian 4%. *Dumitru, Vasile.*

Nauman (1402) German (**Naumann**) and Jewish (Ashkenazic): see NEUMANN.

Naumann (1394) German: variant of NEUMANN.

GIVEN NAMES German 7%. *Hans* (6), *Otto* (5), *Kurt* (4), *Erwin* (3), *Fritz* (3), *Horst* (2), *Joerg* (2), *Arno, Bernd, Bernhardt, Berthold, Egon.*

Naus (245) **1.** Dutch: patronymic from a reduced form of the Middle Dutch personal name *Arnoud* (see ARNOLD). **2.** German: habitational name from places called

Nausen (Lower Saxony) or Naus (near Trier).

Nauss (203) German: variant of Naus.

Nauta (279) Italian: possibly an occupational name for a sailor, from *nauta* 'helmsman' (from Latin *nauta* 'sailor').
GIVEN NAMES Dutch 4%. *Antje, Douwe, Frans, Gerrit, Pieter, Wiebe.*

Nava (2641) Spanish, Catalan, and Asturian-Leonese: habitational name from any of numerous places named Nava, from *nava* 'treeless plateau', a word of pre-Roman origin, most probably from Basque *naba* 'plain next to mountains'. The name is also borne by Sephardic Jews.
GIVEN NAMES Spanish 54%. *Jose* (74), *Juan* (35), *Jesus* (33), *Carlos* (21), *Luis* (20), *Pedro* (20), *Manuel* (19), *Alfredo* (15), *Francisco* (15), *Ruben* (15), *Javier* (14), *Enrique* (13).

Navar (167) Spanish: probably a topographic name from a collective form of *nava* 'treeless plateau' (see Nava).
GIVEN NAMES Spanish 48%. *Jesus* (3), *Joaquin* (3), *Jose* (3), *Raul* (3), *Alfredo* (2), *Arturo* (2), *Erasmo* (2), *Ezequiel* (2), *Gilberto* (2), *Juan* (2), *Manuel* (2), *Miguel* (2); *Flavio, Lucio, Vito.*

Navarette (293) Variant of Spanish Navarrete.
GIVEN NAMES Spanish 43%. *Jose* (6), *Manuel* (4), *Armando* (3), *Mario* (3), *Adon* (2), *Agustina* (2), *Andres* (2), *Carlos* (2), *Fernando* (2), *Francisco* (2), *Jesus* (2), *Jorge* (2).

Navarra (532) Spanish and Portuguese, Italian, and Jewish (Sephardic) (from Basque): regional name from Navarre (Basque *Nafarroa*), a region now divided between Spain and France, but in the Middle Ages an independent Basque kingdom. The place name derives from Basque *naba* 'plain next to mountains'.
GIVEN NAMES Italian 16%; Spanish 5%. *Sal* (3), *Edgardo* (2), *Guido* (2), *Santo* (2), *Vito* (2), *Angelo, Annamarie, Antonio, Benedicto, Camillo, Dante, Emilio, Fausto, Gaetano, Giuseppe, Mario, Romulo, Sergio; Agustin, Herlinda, Manuel, Solita.*

Navarre (994) French: regional name for someone from Navarra.
GIVEN NAMES French 5%. *Emile* (3), *Jacques* (2), *Anatole, Angelle, Camille, Marcelle, Oneil.*

Navarrete (1414) Spanish and Aragonese (of Basque origin): habitational name from any of the places in La Rioja, Aragon, and Basque Country named Navarrete, from Basque (spoken in all those areas in pre-Roman times) *Nafarrete* 'plateau between two small valleys', a derivative of *naba* (see Nava, Navarra).
GIVEN NAMES Spanish 56%. *Jose* (51), *Juan* (23), *Manuel* (19), *Carlos* (17), *Jesus* (16), *Pedro* (13), *Raul* (11), *Luis* (10), *Miguel* (9), *Roberto* (9), *Salvador* (9), *Francisco* (8).

Navarrette (544) Respelling of Spanish Navarrete.
GIVEN NAMES Spanish 37%. *Manuel* (10), *Jose* (5), *Ruben* (5), *Felipe* (4), *Ricardo* (4), *Adan* (3), *Angel* (3), *Eduardo* (3), *Fernando* (3), *Jaime* (3), *Raul* (3), *Alfredo* (2).

Navarro (9119) Spanish, Italian, and Jewish (Sephardic) (of Basque origin): regional name denoting someone from Navarre (see Navarra).
GIVEN NAMES Spanish 47%. *Jose* (251), *Juan* (127), *Manuel* (100), *Carlos* (90), *Jesus* (85), *Luis* (75), *Ramon* (71), *Francisco* (59), *Miguel* (55), *Rafael* (48), *Jorge* (47), *Pedro* (47).

Navas (497) **1.** Asturian-Leonese and Spanish: plural form of Spanish and Asturian-Leonese Nava (see also Naves). **2.** In some cases possibly Catalan (**Navàs**): variant spelling of **Navars**, habitational name from a place so called in Barcelona province, from a regional name denoting someone from Navarre (see Navarra) **3.** In some cases possibly French: variant (old form) of Naves.
GIVEN NAMES Spanish 40%. *Luis* (13), *Jose* (10), *Jorge* (5), *Julio* (5), *Manuel* (5), *Roberto* (5), *Armando* (4), *Arturo* (4), *Alejandro* (3), *Carlos* (3), *Enrique* (3), *Francisco* (3); *Antonio* (4), *Aldo* (2), *Biagio* (2), *Marco Tulio, Sandro.*

Nave (1715) **1.** English: occupational name for a servant, from Middle English *knave* 'boy', 'youth', 'servant'. **2.** English: possibly a metonymic occupational name for a maker of wheel-hubs, Middle English *nave* (from Old English *nafa, nafu*). **3.** German (also **Näve**): variant of **Neff** (see Neve). **4.** Dutch (**de Nave**): variant of Naef 1. **5.** In some cases possibly Portuguese: topographic name from *nave* 'plain' (a variant of *nava*), or a habitational name from a place named with this word. Compare Nava.

Naves (167) **1.** Portuguese: habitational name from a place named Naves, examples of which are found in Guarda and Castelo Branco. **2.** Asturian-Leonese and Galician: habitational name from any of the towns called Naves in Asturies and Galicia. **3.** French: habitational name from a place named Naves, notably in Allier and Corrèze, from the pre-Celtic word *nava* 'plain'. Compare Nava.
GIVEN NAMES Spanish 10%. *Manuel* (2), *Angel, Carlos, Carols, Cesar, Eugenio, Fernando, Jose, Mario, Rigoverto.*

Navia (117) Galician and Asturian-Leonese: habitational name from either of two places named Navia, in Galicia and Asturies.
GIVEN NAMES Spanish 53%. *Carlos* (9), *Jose* (4), *Adriana* (3), *Alfonso* (2), *Jaime* (2), *Juan* (2), *Manuel* (2), *Pedro* (2), *Adolfo, Alvaro, Andres, Arturo.*

Navickas (139) Lithuanian form of Polish Nowicki.

GIVEN NAMES Lithuanian 8%. *Arunas, Vytautas.*

Navin (489) Scottish and Irish: variant of Nevin.

Navis (219) Dutch: unexplained.

Navone (100) Italian: probably a habitational name from a place so named.
GIVEN NAMES Italian 8%. *Aldo, Remo.*

Navratil (465) Czech (**Navrátil**): from the masculine singular past tense of *navrátit* 'to return', a nickname for someone who had returned to his native community after a prolonged absence.
GIVEN NAMES Czech and Slovak 4%. *Blanka, Stanislav, Vaclav, Zdenek.*

Nawaz (127) Muslim (frequent in Pakistan): from a personal name based on Persian *nawāz* 'one who caresses, cherishes, or soothes'. Thus, *'Alī Nawāz* means 'cherished by Ali'.
GIVEN NAMES Muslim 87%. *Mohammad* (22), *Muhammad* (5), *Shahid* (3), *Ahmad* (2), *Ahmed* (2), *Mian* (2), *Mohamed* (2), *Mohammed* (2), *Nadeem* (2), *Zafar* (2), *Abdul, Ahamed.*

Nawrocki (935) Polish: **1.** from *nawrócić* 'to be converted', hence a name for a religious convert, in particular a Jew who had converted to Christianity. **2.** possibly also a habitational name for someone from Nawrotów in Kalisz voivodeship. The name is well established in Germany.
GIVEN NAMES Polish 4%. *Casimir* (5), *Andrzej, Dariusz, Janina, Jerzy, Karol, Mariusz, Wieslaw.*

Nawrot (148) Polish: derivative of Polish *nawrócić* 'to be converted' (see Nawrocki).
GIVEN NAMES Polish 10%. *Franciszek, Grzegorz, Irena, Jadwiga, Jerzy, Kazimierz, Leszek.*

Nay (1092) **1.** Scottish and Irish: reduced form of McNay. **2.** English: variant of Nye. **3.** French: habitational name from places so called in Manche and Pyrénées Atlantiques, possibly named with Latin *Nadium*, from a Gaulish personal name, *Nadius*. **4.** Dutch: metonymic occupational name for a tailor or embroiderer, from a derivative of *naaien* 'to sew'. **5.** Jewish (Ashkenazic): Yiddish equivalent of German Neu.

Nayak (221) Indian: variant of Naik.
GIVEN NAMES Indian 92%. *Satish* (5), *Suresh* (5), *Ashok* (4), *Sunil* (4), *Naresh* (3), *Pradeep* (3), *Ramesh* (3), *Shankar* (3), *Vasudev* (3), *Hari* (2), *Ramachandra* (2), *Ramnath* (2).

Nayar (115) Indian: variant of Nair.
GIVEN NAMES Indian 91%. *Arun* (4), *Ravi* (3), *Bala* (2), *Deepak* (2), *Gopal* (2), *Krishan* (2), *Lalit* (2), *Rajiv* (2), *Ramesh* (2), *Sanjay* (2), *Ajith, Ambika.*

Naylon (128) English: habitational name from Nayland in Suffolk, or a topographic name, from misdivision of Middle English *atten eylond, eiland* 'at the island' (Old English *æt ðǣm ēgland*).

Naylor (6185) **1.** English (mainly northern): occupational name for a maker of nails, from an agent derivative of Middle English *nayle* 'nail' (see NAIL). **2.** Americanized form of German **Nahler**, a variant of NAGLER.

Nayman (118) Jewish (eastern Ashkenazic): from Yiddish *nayman* 'new man' (see NEUMANN).
GIVEN NAMES Jewish 10%; Russian 4%. *Esfir, Shmuel, Yakov; Lev, Mikhail, Oleg, Yelena.*

Nazar (206) **1.** Muslim: from a personal name based on Arabic *naẓẓār* 'esteem', 'regard'. **2.** Basque: habitational name from Nazar in Navarre.
GIVEN NAMES Muslim 11%. *Abdol, Ahamed, Ali, Behzad, Bijan, Davoud, Massoud, Muhammad, Naved, Nuri, Saeid, Sheikh.*

Nazarenus (100) German: surname adopted with reference to Latin *Nazarenus* 'of or pertaining to Nazareth', the birthplace of Christ. The surname was adopted in particular among a group of German speakers who settled in the Volga basin in Russia in the 19th century.

Nazareth (126) Indian, Dutch, and French: from a personal name adopted with reference to Jesus of Nazareth. In India, it is found among Christians in Goa, Mangalore, and elsewhere.
GIVEN NAMES Indian 13%; French 4%. *Anand* (2), *Aruna* (2), *Vasanthi, Vijay, Vivek; Andre.*

Nazari (151) **1.** Arabic: adjectival variant of NAZAR. **2.** Reduced form of Armenian NAZARIAN.
GIVEN NAMES Muslim 56%; Armenian 13%. *Ali* (3), *Hamid* (3), *Mahmood* (3), *Mohammad* (2), *Mohammed* (2), *Shahram* (2), *Abbas, Abed, Afagh, Ahmad, Ahmed, Amin; Norik* (2), *Asatour, Edik, Ghazar, Hovik, Hrand, Khachik, Razmik, Serop, Vazgen.*

Nazarian (463) Armenian and Iranian: patronymic from the personal name *Nazar*, from Arabic *naẓẓār* 'esteem', 'regard'.
GIVEN NAMES Armenian 29%; Muslim 16%. *Vartan* (4), *Edik* (3), *Hagop* (3), *Razmik* (3), *Sarkis* (3), *Armen* (2), *Artin* (2), *Ashot* (2), *Berge* (2), *Hasmik* (2), *Narbeh* (2), *Nerses* (2); *Nazar* (5), *Hamid* (2), *Rahim* (2), *Zakaria* (2), *Abrahim, Aziz, Bahram, Davoud, Ebrahim, Eliahou, Ezatollah, Habib.*

Nazario (706) Portuguese (**Nazário**) and Spanish: from the personal name *Nazario*, from the Late Latin personal name *Nazarius* 'of Nazareth'.
GIVEN NAMES Spanish 45%. *Jose* (25), *Luis* (13), *Carlos* (10), *Rafael* (8), *Angel* (5), *Emilio* (5), *Enrique* (5), *Jorge* (5), *Manuel* (5), *Ruben* (5), *Francisco* (4), *Juan* (4).

Naze (123) Respelling of German NASE.

Nazelrod (130) Americanized form of German **Nesselroth**, a variant spelling of NESSELRODT.
FOREBEARS Bearers of this name are descended from Friedrich Wilhelm Nesselroth, a Hessian mercenary who was brought to North America to fight for the British during the Revolutionary War.

Nazir (105) Muslim: from a variant of Arabic *nadhīr* 'warner'. *Al-Nadhīr* 'the Warner' is an epithet of the Prophet Muhammad, in the sense 'one sent by Allah to warn mankind' (Qur'an 7:188).
GIVEN NAMES Muslim 86%. *Mohammed* (7), *Javed* (5), *Mohammad* (5), *Shahid* (5), *Khalid* (4), *Muhammad* (4), *Tariq* (4), *Asif* (2), *Faisal* (2), *Husain* (2), *Mohamed* (2), *Abdul.*

Nazworth (103) English: variant of NORSWORTHY.

Nazzaro (481) Italian: from a personal name representing a vernacular form of Latin *Nazareus* or Greek *Nazarios*, a derivative of *Nazareth* (Hebrew *Natserat*, perhaps from a root meaning 'to guard or protect'), applied to early Christians as followers of Jesus of Nazareth and accepted by them as an honorable personal name.
GIVEN NAMES Italian 11%. *Salvatore* (3), *Carmine* (2), *Rocco* (2), *Angelo, Camillo, Dante, Enrico, Guido, Pellegrino, Romeo, Vittorio.*

Ndiaye (186) African: unexplained. Possibly from Arabic *nadīy* 'generous', 'open-handed'.
GIVEN NAMES African 47%; Muslim 25%; French 4%. *Amadou* (6), *Mamadou* (6), *Boubacar* (3), *Modou* (3), *Aliou* (2), *Fatou* (2), *Momar* (2), *Ousmane* (2), *Aminata, Awa, Cheikh, Demba; Moussa* (5), *Abdoulaye* (3), *Mohamed* (3), *Abdou* (2), *Cherif, Daouda, Habib, Ibraham, Ibrahima, Karim, Khadim, Lamine; Adrien, Dieudonne.*

Neace (684) **1.** Americanized spelling of German or Dutch NIES or NEESE **2.** Reduced and altered form of Irish McNEESE.

Nead (282) **1.** English: possibly a metonymic nickname for a needy person, from Middle English *ne(e)d* 'need'. **2.** Respelling of German NIED.

Neagle (442) English and Irish (of Norman origin): variant of NANGLE.

Neal (28379) **1.** English, Scottish, and Irish: from an Anglo-Scandinavian form of the Gaelic name *Niall* (see NEILL). This was adopted by the Scandinavians in the form *Njal* and was introduced into northern England and East Anglia by them, rather than being taken directly from Gaelic. It was reinforced after the Norman Conquest by the Anglo-Norman French and Middle English forms *Neel, Nihel,* and *Nigel,* which were brought to England by the Normans. **2.** Scottish and Irish: reduced form of McNEAL (see McNEIL).

Neale (1568) English, Scottish, and Irish: variant of NEAL.

Nealey (433) Irish: reduced variant of McNEELY.

Nealis (334) Irish: variant of NELLIS.

Neall (108) English and Irish: variant spelling of NEAL.
GIVEN NAME French 4%. *Gabrielle.*

Neally (116) Irish: reduced variant of McNEELY.

Nealon (800) Irish: Anglicized form of Gaelic **Ó Nialláin** 'descendant of *Niallán*', a personal name formed from a diminutive of *Niall* (see NEILL).
GIVEN NAME Irish 4%. *Declan.*

Neals (100) **1.** Variant spelling of Dutch and North German **Niels** or NEELS. **2.** Perhaps also a variant of Irish NEILL, with the addition of English patronymic *-s.*

Nealy (1114) Irish: reduced and altered form of McNEELY.

Near (609) Probably of Scottish or Irish origin, a reduced and altered form of McNAIR.

Nearhood (157) Americanized spelling of German **Nierhuth**, a reduced form of **Niederhuth** (North German **Nedderhod**), a nickname referring to a particular style of headgear, from *nieder* 'low' + *hut* 'hat', or, in the south, a topographic name from Middle High German *nider* 'low' + *huott(e)* '(field) range', 'pasture'.

Nearhoof (130) Americanized spelling of North German **Nierhof(f)**, a reduced form of **Niederhof**, a topographic name composed of the elements *nieder* 'low(er)' + *hof* 'farmstead', 'manor farm'.

Nearing (324) Americanized spelling of German **Niering**, a habitational name from a place so named in Westphalia, or possibly an altered spelling of NEHRING.
GIVEN NAME French 4%. *Alouis* (2).

Neary (1951) Irish: Anglicized form of Gaelic **Ó Náradhaigh** 'descendant of *Náradhach*', a byname meaning 'modest'.
GIVEN NAMES Irish 5%. *Seamus, Siobhan.*

Neas (383) **1.** Americanized form of German or Dutch NIES or NEESE **2.** **2.** Irish: reduced and altered form of McNEESE.

Nease (849) **1.** Irish: reduced form of McNEESE. **2.** Americanized form of German or Dutch NIES or NEESE **2.**

Neason (127) **1.** Irish: variant spelling of NEESON. **2.** Probably an altered spelling of Dutch or German NIESEN.

Neat (205) English: metonymic occupational name for a herdsman in charge of cattle or a nickname for someone thought to resemble an ox or a cow, from Middle English *neat* 'ox', 'cow' (Old English *nēat*). The modern English adjective *neat* (via French from Latin *nitidus* 'clean', 'shining') does not occur before the 16th century, after the main period of surname formation.

Neatherlin (108) Americanized form of NETHERLAND.

Neathery (408) Scottish and northern Irish: variant of NETHERY.

Neaton (102) English: possibly a habitational name from Neaton in Norfolk. However, the modern surname occurs chiefly in the English Midlands suggesting a different source may be involved.

Neault (217) French: habitational name from Neau in Mayenne, derived from the Latin personal name *Nigellus* 'black'.
GIVEN NAMES French 10%. *Armand, Donat, Leontine, Marcel, Renald.*

Neave (153) **1.** English (Norfolk): variant spelling of NEVE 'nephew'. **2.** Scottish: from a place called Nevay in Angus.
GIVEN NAMES Spanish 14%. *Manuel* (2), *Alfonso, Amador, Bulmaro, Florentina, Javier, Jesus, Jose, Juanita, Luis, Marcos, Maria Elena.*

Neaves (317) **1.** English (Kent): patronymic from NEVE, i.e. 'son of the nephew'. **2.** Scottish: probably a habitational name from a reduced form of Balneaves, a minor place in the parish of Kinkell, Angus.
GIVEN NAMES Spanish 4%. *Jose* (3), *Pedro* (2), *Alvino, Cruz, Francisco, Humberto, Jose Angel, Juan, Manuel, Ricardo, Santiago, Sergio.*

Nebeker (407) Variant of North German **Niebecker**, an occupational name for a baker who was new in town, or a habitational name from Niebeck (near Uelzen).

Nebel (866) **1.** German and Jewish (Ashkenazic): from German *Nebel* 'fog', 'mist', Middle High German *nēbel*. This could be a nickname, or alternatively a habitational name from any of several places so named in Schleswig-Holstein and Bavaria. In some cases it may be a shortened form of the Germanic personal name *Nibelunc, Nebelung.* **2.** Altered spelling of German KNEBEL.
GIVEN NAMES German 7%. *Kurt* (5), *Gerhard* (2), *Hans* (2), *Otto* (2), *Annice, Armin, Dieter, Erwin, Ewald, Ingeborg, Raimund.*

Nebergall (150) German: variant of NIEBERGALL.

Nebgen (102) German: from a diminutive of **Nebe** (see NEFF 1) (*-gen* is the central German variant of standard German *-chen*).

Neblett (549) English: apparently a variant of NIBLETT.

Necaise (498) Altered spelling of French **Nicaise**, which is from a personal name of Greek origin, *Nikasios* 'victorious', based on Greek *nikē* 'victory'. This name was borne by three saints, and may have been considered to refer to spiritual victory over sin and death.

Necessary (331) Probably a variant, by folk etymology, of ESSARY, an English surname of unexplained origin.

Necker (135) **1.** South German: habitational name from a place on the Neckar river, or a topographic name for someone living on or by a prominence, from an agent derivative of *Nock* 'hill(top)', 'rock'. **2.** Dutch

(**de Nekker**) and North German: from Middle Dutch, Middle Low German *necker* 'watersprite', 'goblin', 'devil', hence a nickname for someone thought to resemble a goblin in some way.
GIVEN NAMES German 7%. *Heinz, Helmut.*

Ned (191) Origin unidentified.

Nedd (258) Origin unidentified.
GIVEN NAMES French 4%. *Dominique, Orelia.*

Neddo (207) Perhaps an altered spelling of French NADEAU.

Nedeau (175) Southern French: variant of NADEAU.

Neder (115) **1.** German: variant of NADER. **2.** Dutch (**van Neder**): variant of **van Neer** (see NEER).
GIVEN NAMES Spanish 8%; German 4%. *Alberto* (2), *Luis* (2), *Aida, Carlos, Glicerio, Julio, Lourdes; Willi.*

Nederveld (103) Reduced form of Dutch **van Nedervelde**, a habitational name for someone from any of various minor places named Ne(d)erveld.

Nedley (106) English and Scottish: unexplained; possibly a habitational name from a lost or unidentified place.

Nedrow (332) Americanized form of German **Niederauer**, topographic name for someone who lived 'at the lower meadow', from *nieder* 'lower' + *Au* 'water meadow'.
FOREBEARS Michael Niederauer emigrated from Germany to Germantown, PA, in 1747.

Nedved (278) Czech (**Nedvěd**): nickname meaning 'bear', from a dialect form of the vocabulary word *medvěd* 'bear'.

Nedza (113) Polish (**Nędza**): nickname from *nędza* 'misery'.
GIVEN NAMES Polish 5%. *Casimir, Grazyna.*

Nee (989) Irish or Scottish: reduced Anglicized form of Gaelic **Ó Niadh** 'descendant of *Nia*' or **Ó Niadh** 'son of *Nia*'. Compare MCNEE.
GIVEN NAMES Irish 4%. *Dermot* (2), *John Patrick.*

Neeb (388) German: from an unexplained old personal name.

Neece (666) **1.** Irish: reduced Anglicized form of Gaelic **Mac Naois** (see MCNEESE). **2.** Americanized form of German or Dutch NEESE 2 or NIES.

Need (106) Variant spelling of NEAD.

Needels (100) Variant spelling of NEEDLES.

Needham (4278) **1.** English: habitational name from places in Derbyshire, Norfolk, and Suffolk, so named from Old English *nēd* 'need', 'hardship' + *hām* 'homestead', i.e. a place that provided a poor living. **2.** Irish (County Mayo): English surname adopted as an equivalent of Irish **Ó Niadh** (see NEE).
FOREBEARS English explorer James Needham carried the name to the southern Carolina settlement, arriving from Barbados in 1670 as a young man.

Needle (407) **1.** English: from Middle English *nedle, nadle* 'needle' (Old English *nǣdle*), hence a metonymic occupational name for a maker of needles, or in some cases perhaps for a tailor. See also NADLER. **2.** Jewish (American): translation of NADEL.
GIVEN NAMES Jewish 6%. *Emanuel* (2), *Sol* (2).

Needleman (377) Jewish (American): English translation of NADELMAN or NUDELMAN.
GIVEN NAMES Jewish 4%. *Hyman, Meyer.*

Needler (173) **1.** English: occupational name for a maker of needles (see NADLER). **2.** Jewish: Americanized form of NADLER.

Needles (413) Apparently an altered form of NEEDLE.

Needs (193) English (mainly South Wales and southwestern England): variant of NEAD.

Needy (167) English: unexplained.

Neef (168) **1.** Dutch: variant of NEVE, from *neef* 'nephew', 'cousin'. **2.** German (southwestern): variant of NEFF.

Neel (2904) Irish and Scottish: variant of NEILL.

Neeland (124) Probably a respelling of Dutch **Nieland**, a habitational name from any of numerous places named Nieland or Niewland, denoting newly reclaimed land.

Neeld (236) Irish and Scottish: variant of NEILL. The excrescent *-d* results from an English mishearing of the devoicing of final *-l* in Gaelic.

Neeley (3133) Irish: reduced form of MCNEELY.

Neels (168) Dutch and North German: patronymic from the personal name *Neel*, a reduced form of either CORNELIUS or *Daneel* (see DANIEL).

Neely (8219) Irish: reduced form of MCNEELY.

Neeman (150) Jewish: occupational name from a Hebrew term meaning 'treasurer of the community'. In some cases this may represent a Hebraized (Israeli) form of NEUMANN.
GIVEN NAMES Jewish 12%. *Aron* (2), *Giora* (2), *Menashe* (2), *Amnon, Limor, Moshe, Shaul.*

Neenan (268) Irish: Anglicized form of Gaelic **Ó Naoidheannáin** 'descendant of *Naoidheanán*', from *naoidheán* 'infant', often now assimilated to NOONAN.

Neeper (182) Probably an altered spelling of German **Nieper**, from the Germanic personal name *Nidperht*, based on an element cognate with Old High German *nīt* 'hostility', 'hatred'.

Neer (860) **1.** Dutch (also **van Neer**): habitational name from a place called Neer in the Netherlands. **2.** German: variant of NEHER. **3.** Jewish: (Ashkenazic): variant of NEIER.

Neering (99) **1.** Dutch: from a derivative of any of various Germanic personal names containing the element *nar-*, *ner-* 'food'. **2.** Altered spelling of German **Niering** (see NEARING) or **Nehring** (see NEHRING).

Nees (596) **1.** Irish: reduced Anglicized form of Gaelic **Mac Naois** (see MCNEESE). **2.** Americanized form of German or Dutch NIES or NEESE 2.

FOREBEARS Henry Nees (1833–1904) emigrated from Germany to Fort Wayne, IN, in 1850, but the name was already established in North America before that date. Earlier bearers are probably of Irish origin.

Neese (1895) **1.** Irish: reduced Anglicized form of Gaelic **Mac Naois** (see MCNEESE). **2.** North German and Dutch: from a short form of the female personal name *Agnes* (see ANNIS). **3.** Americanized form of German NIES or possibly KNIESS (see KNEZ).

Neeser (128) **1.** Swiss German: unexplained; possibly a habitational name for someone from either of two places in North Rhine-Westphalia: Neesen or Niesen. **2.** Swiss German: metronymic from the personal name *Agnes* (see NEESE 2).

Neeson (204) **1.** Irish: reduced Anglicized form of Gaelic **Mac Naois** 'son of Naois', usually Anglicized as MCNEESE. **2.** Altered form of Dutch or German NIESEN.

Neet (161) Possibly a respelling of German **Nieth**, a habitational name from Nied on the Nidda river in Hesse, or of **Niet**, which is possibly a nickname from Middle High German *niet* 'eager'.

Neff (9151) **1.** German and Swiss German: from Middle High German *neve* 'nephew' (later rather broader in application, rather like *cousin* in English), hence probably a distinguishing name for a close relation or familiar of a prominent personage. **2.** Dutch: variant of NEVE, cognate with 1. **3.** Jewish (Ashkenazic): from German *Neffe* 'nephew'. **4.** Reduced form of Irish MCNEFF (see MCNIFF).

Nefzger (117) German: variant of **Nafzger**, a nickname for a sleepyhead, from a noun derivative of Middle High German *nafzen* 'to take a nap'.

Negaard (146) Norwegian: habitational name from any of several farmsteads named *ne* 'lower' + *gård*.
GIVEN NAMES Scandinavian 5%; German 4%. *Selmer*; *Hans*, *Kurt*.

Negley (502) Altered spelling of Swiss German **Nägele**, **Naegeli**, or **Nägeli**, variants of NAGEL.

Neglia (188) Italian (mainly Sicily): from Sicilian and southern Italian *neglia*, *neghia* 'fog', 'mist', possibly a nickname for someone with poor eyesight.
GIVEN NAMES Italian 25%. *Vito* (4), *Angelo* (2), *Quirico* (2), *Ciro*, *Claudio*, *Matteo*, *Mauro*, *Sal*, *Salvatore*.

Negrete (1177) Spanish: possibly from *negrete*, denoting a member of a 15th-century

faction based in the mountainous area of Santander.
GIVEN NAMES Spanish 45%. *Jose* (29), *Juan* (20), *Jorge* (18), *Jesus* (16), *Manuel* (10), *Luis* (9), *Miguel* (9), *Carlos* (8), *Fernando* (8), *Francisco* (8), *Pedro* (8), *Ruben* (8).

Negri (626) Italian and Jewish (from Italy): patronymic or plural form of NEGRO.
GIVEN NAMES Italian 8%. *Salvatore* (2), *Amerigo*, *Bartolo*, *Carmine*, *Franco*, *Gilda*, *Giovanna*, *Luigi*, *Nino*, *Rinaldo*, *Silvano*, *Vito*.

Negrin (266) **1.** Spanish (**Negrín**) and Italian (Venetian): from a diminutive of NEGRO. **2.** Jewish (Sephardic): unexplained; probably an adoption of the Spanish or Italian name.
GIVEN NAMES Spanish 20%; Jewish 7%. *Jose* (4), *Pedro* (4), *Manuel* (3), *Fernando* (2), *Jesus* (2), *Orlando* (2), *Sergio* (2), *Alberto*, *Alejandro*, *Alfredo*, *Ana*, *Antolina*; *Sol* (3), *Haim*, *Hyman*, *Meyer*, *Moises*.

Negro (198) Italian, Spanish, Portuguese, and Jewish: **1.** nickname or ethnic name from *negro* 'black' (Latin *niger*), denoting someone with dark hair or a dark complexion. **2.** from a medieval continuation of the Latin personal name *Niger*.
GIVEN NAMES Italian 23%; Spanish 5%. *Armando* (2), *Mario* (2), *Sergio* (2), *Alberto*, *Carlo*, *Dante*, *Giovanna*, *Salvatore*, *Saverio*, *Secondo*; *Juan*, *Marcela*.

Negron (1882) Spanish (**Negrón**) and French: variant of NEGRO.
GIVEN NAMES Spanish 43%. *Jose* (63), *Luis* (36), *Angel* (27), *Miguel* (26), *Carlos* (25), *Juan* (17), *Ana* (14), *Jorge* (13), *Rafael* (12), *Pedro* (10), *Wilfredo* (10), *Jaime* (9).

Negus (383) **1.** English: unexplained. **2.** Romanian: occupational name for a merchant (Late Latin *negotiator*, from *negotiari* 'to trade, deal', a derivative of *negotium* 'business', 'affair').

Neher (835) German: occupational name for a tailor or embroiderer, from an agent derivative of Middle Low German *nehen* 'to sew', 'to embroider'. Compare NAGER 1.
FOREBEARS Johann Martin Neher (1713–97) and his family came to North America from Durwangen, Württemberg, Germany, arriving in Philadelphia aboard the *Osgood* on September 29, 1750.

Nehl (162) North German and Dutch: from a reduced form of the personal name CORNELIUS or *Daneel* (see NEELS).

Nehls (604) North German and Dutch: patronymic from NEHL.

Nehmer (153) Jewish (Ashkenazic): from German *Nehmer* 'taker', 'recipient'; perhaps selected as a surname because of its phonetic similarity to the Jewish male personal name *Nehemia* (see NAHMIAS).

Nehrbass (100) German: nickname for a gourmand or a greedy person, literally '(I) feed (my)self better', from Middle High German *ner(e)n* 'to feed', 'support'.
GIVEN NAMES German 6%. *Eldred*, *Kurt*.

Nehring (923) German: **1.** nickname for a miser or someone who guarded his possessions jealously, from Middle High German *nerung*, *narung*, Middle Low German *neringe* 'food', 'livelihood'. **2.** habitational name from Nehringen in Pomerania, or a topographic name from *nehrung*, *nehring* 'long narrow spit of land'.
GIVEN NAMES German 5%. *Otto* (3), *Ewald* (2), *Klaus*, *Siegfried*, *Ulrich*, *Uwe*, *Viktor*, *Wolfgang*.

Neibauer (204) Variant of German NEUBAUER.

Neibaur (104) Variant of German NEUBAUER.

Neibert (191) German: variant of **Neubert**, a reduced form of NEUBAUER with the addition of an excrescent *-t*, or a variant of *Nieper* (see NEEPER).

Neice (204) Reduced form of Irish **McNeice** (see MCNEESE).

Neider (356) German: **1.** habitational name for someone from Neida near Coburg or Neiden near Torgau. **2.** variant of NIEDER.

Neiderer (147) German: probably a variant of NIEDERER.

Neiderhiser (126) Possibly a respelling of Swiss German **Niederhäuser**, a topographic name for someone living at the 'lower houses', or a habitational name from a place named Niederhausen in the Palatinate.

Neidert (310) German: reduced form of NEIDHARDT.
GIVEN NAMES German 4%. *Fritz* (2), *Konrad*.

Neidhardt (292) German: from the medieval personal name *Nīthart*, composed of the Germanic elements *nīt* 'ambition', 'hatred' + *hard* 'hardy', 'brave', 'strong'.
GIVEN NAMES German 6%. *Kurt* (2), *Berthold*, *Jurgen*.

Neidhart (171) German and Swiss German: variant of NEIDHARDT.

Neidich (119) Jewish (also **Naydich**, from Belarus and Ukraine): **1.** habitational name from a village called Nayda, now in Belarus. **2.** patronymic form of Ukrainian *nayda* 'foundling'.
GIVEN NAMES Jewish 5%. *Dov*, *Hyman*.

Neidig (473) German: nickname for a hostile, envious person, from Middle High German *nīt* 'hatred', 'ambition'.

Neidigh (222) Americanized spelling of German NEIDIG.

Neidlinger (376) German: habitational name for someone from Neidlingen in Württemberg.
GIVEN NAMES German 6%. *Kurt* (2), *Dieter*, *Helmuth*, *Hermann*, *Otto*.

Neier (160) German and Jewish (Ashkenazic): occupational name for a tailor, from an agent derivative of Middle High German *næjen*, German *nähen* 'to sew'.
GIVEN NAMES Jewish 6%; German 5%. *Aryeh*; *Erwin* (4).

Neifert (250) German: from a Germanic personal name composed with an element cognate with Old High German *niuwi* 'new'.

Neiger (263) German and Swiss German: variant of NEIER.

GIVEN NAMES German 4%. *Heinz* (2), *Merwin*.

Neighbor (233) **1.** English: from Middle English *neghebour*, a compound of Old English *nēah* 'near' + *gebūr* 'dweller'. Compare BAUER. This may have been used as a nickname for someone who was a 'good neighbor', or more probably it derives from the common use of the word as a term of address. **2.** Translation of German NACHBAR.

Neighbors (1778) English: variant of NEIGHBOR.

Neighbours (144) English: variant of NEIGHBOR.

Neihart (140) Probably a respelling of German **Niehardt**, a variant of **Neuhardt** (see NEUHART).

Neiheisel (146) Altered spelling of South German **Neuhäus(e)l** ('new little house'), a topographic name or a habitational name from any of three places so named in the Palatinate, Rhineland, and Austria.

Neikirk (300) Dutch: habitational name from Nykerk, a city in Gelderland whose name is itself a dialect variant of Nieuwekerk, or a topographic name for someone living by a new church.

Neil (3470) Irish and Scottish: reduced form of MCNEIL or variant of NEILL.

Neilan (267) Irish (Munster and Connacht): Anglicized form of Gaelic **Ó Nialláin** 'descendant of *Niallán*', a diminutive of the personal name *Niall* (see NEILL).

Neild (200) Irish and Scottish: variant of NEILL. The excrescent *-d* results from an English mishearing of the devoicing of final *-l* in Gaelic.

Neill (3841) Irish and Scottish: reduced form of Irish Gaelic **Ó Néill** or Scottish Gaelic **Mac Néill** 'descendant (or son) of *Niall*', a personal name of Irish origin, thought to mean 'champion'. The personal name was adopted by Norsemen in the form *Njáll*, and was brought to England both directly from Ireland by Scandinavian settlers and indirectly (via France) by the Normans. Among the latter it had taken the form *Ni(h)el*, which was altered by folk etymology to the Latin name *Nigellus*.

Neils (278) **1.** German: from a reduced form of the personal name CORNELIUS. **2.** Irish: variant of NEILL, with English patronymic *-s*.

GIVEN NAMES German 7%. *Gerhard* (3), *Eldor* (2), *Kurt*.

Neilsen (784) Altered spelling of NIELSEN or NILSEN.

GIVEN NAMES Scandinavian 6%. *Erik* (2), *Ejnar, Gurli, Jorgen, Nels, Niels*.

Neilson (2485) **1.** Scottish: patronymic from NEILL. **2.** Americanized form of Swedish NILSSON.

Neily (111) Irish and Scottish: reduced variant of MCNEELY.

Neiman (1455) Nickname meaning 'newcomer' in various languages: **1.** Jewish (Ashkenazic) and German (**Neimann**): variant of NEUMANN. **2.** Dutch: variant of NIEMAN. **3.** Swedish: variant of NYMAN.

GIVEN NAMES Jewish 7%. *Moshe* (4), *Pincus* (3), *Chaim* (2), *Hershel* (2), *Sender* (2), *Avrohom, Baruch, Bronia, Elchonon, Eliyohu, Gershon, Hyman*.

Neimeyer (153) Variant of German NIEMEYER.

Nein (195) German: unexplained. Perhaps from a short form of a Germanic personal name formed with an element cognate with Old High German *niuwi* 'new'.

GIVEN NAMES German 5%. *Hans, Reinhold*.

Neinast (101) South German: probably from a topographic name meaning 'new pasture', or from a habitational name with dialect *Ast(en)* 'pasture'.

Neira (292) Galician: habitational name from any of several places in Lugo province named Neira.

GIVEN NAMES Spanish 49%. *Carlos* (8), *Jorge* (4), *Jose* (4), *Juan* (4), *Manuel* (4), *Julio* (3), *Mercedes* (3), *Rogelio* (3), *Amado* (2), *Eduardo* (2), *Fernando* (2), *Guillermo* (2).

Neis (528) **1.** German (Rhineland): from a short form of the medieval personal name *Dionysius* (see DENNIS). **2.** Dutch: from a short form of the personal name *Denijs* (see DENNIS).

Neisen (268) **1.** German and Dutch: patronymic from NEIS 2. **2.** Respelling of German and Dutch NIESEN. **3.** German: habitational name from a place called Neisen in Hesse.

GIVEN NAME French 4%. *Romain*.

Neiser (117) German: variant of German **Neisser**, a habitational name for someone from Neisse in Silesia.

Neises (289) German: nickname for a new settler or neighbor, from Middle High German *niuwe* 'new' + *sez* 'dwelling'.

Neish (136) Scottish: reduced Anglicized form of Gaelic **Mac Naois** 'son of *Naos*'. Compare Irish MCNEESE.

Neisius (117) Dutch or German humanistic name: a Latinized form of NIES or a similar name.

Neisler (296) **1.** German: nickname for someone who was finicky with food, inept in his work, or tentative in speech, from Middle High German *niusen* 'to probe', 'try out'. **2.** Altered spelling of **Kneisler**, a nickname from Middle High German *knūz* 'cheeky', 'irritable'.

Neiss (287) German: nickname for a distrustful, suspicious person, from Middle High German *niusen* 'to probe'.

Neiswander (113) Respelling of German **Neuschwender**, a variant of NEUSCHWANDER.

Neiswender (242) Respelling of German **Neuschwender**, a variant of NEUSCHWANDER.

Neiswonger (136) German: see NISWONGER.

Neitz (239) German: perhaps from a Slavic pet form of the personal name *Nikolaus* (see NICHOLAS). Compare NITZ.

Neitzel (943) German: **1.** from a Slavic pet form of the personal name *Nikolaus* (see NICHOLAS), or from a Germanic personal name formed with *nīt* 'hostility'. **2.** nickname for an obnoxious person, from Middle High German *nīt* 'hostility'.

GIVEN NAMES German 4%. *Ewald* (3), *Ernst* (2), *Erwin, Florian, Hans, Hertha, Hilde, Klaus, Kurt*.

Neitzke (346) German: variant of NEITZ, a pet form of the personal name *Nikolaus* (see NICHOLAS).

GIVEN NAMES German 4%. *Dieter* (2), *Kurt*.

Nejman (110) Polish and Jewish (eastern Ashkenazic): Polish form of German NEUMANN.

GIVEN NAMES Polish 10%. *Jadwiga, Jerzy, Zygmunt*.

Nekola (136) Czech: nickname for a stubborn person, from Czech *ne* 'not' + *kola* 'instability'.

Nelan (104) Variant of Irish NEALON.

GIVEN NAME Irish 4%. *Conor*.

Neldon (107) Possibly an English habitational name from a lost or unidentified place.

Nelis (161) **1.** Irish: reduced form of MCNELIS. **2.** Dutch: reduced form of CORNELIUS or DANIELS.

Nelkin (123) Jewish (eastern Ashkenazic): Slavicized form of ornamental name from German *Nelken* 'cloves', 'carnation'.

GIVEN NAMES Jewish 10%. *Meyer* (2), *Dov*.

Nell (760) **1.** Dutch and German: from the personal name *Nel*, a reduced form of CORNELIUS. **2.** South German: nickname from Middle High German *nelle* 'crown of the head', perhaps denoting an obstinate person. **3.** English: from the Middle English personal name *Nel(le)*, a variant of NEILL.

Nelle (126) **1.** Dutch and North German: from the personal name *Nelle*, a pet form of CORNELIUS. **2.** South German: variant of NELL 2. **3.** Altered spelling of German KNELL.

Neller (163) German: **1.** contracted form of NADLER or NAGLER. **2.** topographic name for someone living on top of a hill or on a pass, from Middle High German *nel(le)* 'point', 'vertex'. **3.** Altered spelling of German KNELLER.

Nelles (222) Dutch: patronymic from the personal name *Nelis*, a short form of **Cornelis** (see CORNELIUS).

Nellessen (114) Dutch: patronymic from the personal name *Nelis*, a short form of **Cornelis** (see CORNELIUS).

Nelli (121) Italian (mainly Tuscany): patronymic from the personal name *Nello*, a short form of a personal name formed with the hypocoristic suffix *-ello* following the final consonant *-n*, for example *Antonello*, *Brunello*, *Giovannello*.
GIVEN NAMES Italian 13%. *Guido* (2), *Aldo*, *Carmello*, *Nicola*, *Sylvio*, *Vincenzo*.

Nelligan (469) Irish (Munster): Anglicized form of Gaelic **Ó Niallagáin** 'descendant of *Niallagán*', a double diminutive of the personal name *Niall* (see NEILL).
GIVEN NAME Irish 5%. *Brendan* (2).

Nellis (1053) **1.** Dutch: variant spelling of NELIS. **2.** Possibly also Irish: reduced form of McNELIS.

Nellums (112) English: variant of NELMS.

Nelms (2528) English: topographic name for someone who lived near or amid a grove of elm trees, from misdivision of Middle English *atten elmes* 'at the elms' (see ELM).

Neloms (130) Variant of English NELMS.

Nelon (154) Perhaps an altered spelling of French **Nellon**, from a pet form of a personal name, *Isnel*.

Nelsen (2768) **1.** Danish and Norwegian: variant of NIELSEN. **2.** Dutch: patronymic from NELIS.
GIVEN NAMES Scandinavian 4%. *Nels* (8), *Erik* (4), *Einer* (2), *Berger*, *Folmer*, *Holger*, *Iver*, *Juel*, *Morten*, *Thor*, *Uffe*.

Nelson (160009) **1.** English and Scottish: patronymic from the medieval personal name *Nel* or *Neal*, Anglo-Scandinavian forms of the Gaelic name *Niall* (see NEILL). This was adopted by the Scandinavians in the form *Njal* and was introduced into northern England and East Anglia by them, rather than being taken directly from Gaelic. **2.** Americanized spelling of the like-sounding Scandinavian names NILSEN, NIELSEN, and NILSSON.
FOREBEARS The Nelson name was an important one in 18th-century VA, starting with Thomas 'Scotch Tom' Nelson, who emigrated to VA at the close of the 17th century from Penrith, Cumbria, where the Nelsons were numerous. Scotch Tom settled about 1700 at Yorktown, VA, where he became a successful merchant and landholder. His son was sheriff and a member of the VA Council, and his grandson, Thomas Nelson (1738–89), a signer of the Declaration of Independence, was governor of VA.

Neltner (110) German: variant of NADLER.

Neman (112) **1.** Jewish (Sephardic and Ashkenazic): variant of NEEMAN, a status name meaning 'treasurer'. **2.** Dutch and North German (**Nemann**): variant of NIEMAN 'newcomer'. **3.** Muslim: perhaps from a personal name based on Arabic *nu'mān* 'blood'. *Nu'mān* was the name borne by the kings of Hirah in Arabia. It was the name of one of the Companions of the Prophet Muhammad, also the surname of Abu Hanifa, founder of the Hanafi school of law.
GIVEN NAMES Muslim 21%; Jewish 6%; German 5%. *Ebrahim*, *Farnaz*, *Malek*, *Maryam*, *Moussa*, *Nahid*, *Nazila*, *Nourollah*, *Said*, *Soliman*, *Youness*; *Itshak*, *Rimma*, *Yoel*, *Yosi*; *Kurt*, *Walther*.

Nembhard (143) German: **1.** from the Germanic personal name *Nan(d)hart*, composed with *nand* 'daring' + *hard* 'hard', 'strong'. **2.** nickname for a greedy or grasping person, from Middle High German *nemen* 'to take' + *hard* 'hard'.

Nemcek (110) Czech (**Němček**): variant of **Němeček** (see NEMECEK).

Nemec (1332) **1.** Czech and Slovak (**Němec**): ethnic name for a German or German-speaker, from *němec* 'German'. In Old Czech this word was used to denote any foreigner, being derived from *němý* 'mute', referring to an inability to speak Czech. This name is also found in Germany. **2.** Slovenian: ethnic name from *Nemec* 'German', a derivative of the adjective *nem* 'mute' (see 1). Germans (mainly Bavarians) were brought in large numbers by feudal overlords to the territory of present-day Slovenia and of the early medieval Slovenian state Carantania (present-day Carinthia and Styria, now divided between Austria and Slovenia).

Nemecek (511) Czech (**Němeček**): from a diminutive of NEMEC 'German'.

Nemechek (140) Americanized spelling of Czech **Němeček** (see NEMECEK).

Nemer (237) Jewish (American): shortened form of **Nemerovski** or **Nemirovski** (see NEMEROFF).
GIVEN NAMES Jewish 7%. *Meyer* (2), *Batia*, *Myer*.

Nemeroff (165) Jewish (Ashkenazic): alternative spelling of **Nemirov**, habitational name from Nemirov in Ukraine or Niemirów in eastern Poland. In some cases it could also be a form shortened in America from **Nemerovski** or **Nemirovski**, a surname derived from these place names.

Nemes (362) Hungarian and Jewish (from Hungary): from *nemes* 'possessing noble rights and privileges', hence a status name, sometimes denoting a servant of a nobleman, or possibly a nickname for an honorable or distinguished-looking person. As a Jewish name it is mainly of ornamental origin.
GIVEN NAMES Hungarian 6%; Romanian 4%. *Jeno* (2), *Aladar*, *Arpad*, *Dezso*, *Janos*, *Katalin*, *Miklos*, *Tibor*; *Vasile* (2), *Dorel*, *Ilie*, *Petru*, *Rodica*.

Nemet (102) Hungarian (**Német**) and Jewish (from Hungary): variant of NEMETH.
GIVEN NAME Jewish 8%. *Shlomo* (2).

Nemeth (3098) Hungarian (**Németh**): ethnic name from Hungarian *német* 'German'. Compare NEMEC. The name is also found in Germany and Austria.
GIVEN NAMES Hungarian 8%. *Laszlo* (15), *Zoltan* (11), *Geza* (5), *Imre* (5), *Sandor* (5), *Andras* (4), *Attila* (4), *Bela* (4), *Kalman* (4), *Miklos* (4), *Vilmos* (4), *Dezso* (3).

Nemetz (476) German (of Slavic origin): originally from an adjective which meant 'mute', referring to an inability to speak the (Slavic) language, and then became an ethnic name denoting a German. Compare NEMEC.

Nemiroff (129) Jewish: variant of NEMEROFF.
GIVEN NAME Jewish 6%. *Elihu*.

Nemirovsky (112) Jewish (eastern Ashkenazic): habitational name from Nemirov in Ukraine or Niemirów in eastern Poland.
GIVEN NAMES Jewish 30%; Russian 27%. *Gady* (2), *Ofer* (2), *Yakov* (2), *Aron*, *Bension*, *Borukh*, *Ilya*, *Irina*, *Isaak*, *Naum*, *Sima*, *Sunya*; *Igor* (2), *Leonid* (2), *Maksim* (2), *Mikhail* (2), *Sergey* (2), *Anatoly*, *Boris*, *Dmitry*, *Efim*, *Fanya*, *Iosif*, *Lyudmila*.

Nemitz (530) Slavic and German (of Slavic origin): habitational name, for example from Nemitz in Wendland, of the same origin as NEMETZ.
GIVEN NAMES German 5%. *Otto* (2), *Edeltraud*, *Gerhard*, *Kurt*, *Reinhard*, *Udo*.

Nemmers (272) German: variant of **Nemmert**, itself a variant of NEMBHARD.

Nemo (106) English: variant of NIMMO.

Nenni (129) Italian: patronymic or plural form of NENNO.
GIVEN NAMES Italian 6%. *Fulvio* (2), *Silvio* (2), *Oresto*.

Nennig (148) German: habitational name from a place in the Saar area called Nennig.

Nenninger (270) German: habitational name for someone from Nenningen in Württemberg.
GIVEN NAMES German 4%. *Fritz*, *Jutta*.

Nenno (100) Italian: unexplained; possibly from a short form of a personal name formed with the hypocoristic suffix *-enno*.

Nentwig (105) German: from the medieval personal name *Nantwig*, *Nentwig*, composed of the elements *nand* 'bold', 'brave' + *wīg* 'battle'.
GIVEN NAMES German 7%. *Gerhard* (2), *Klaus*.

Nephew (418) English: kinship name from Old French *neveu* 'nephew'.

Nepomuceno (146) Spanish: from the byname of the 14th-century saint Johannes Nepomucenus, patron saint of Bohemia.
GIVEN NAMES Spanish 38%. *Ricardo* (3), *Cesar* (2), *Alberto*, *Alfonso*, *Angelito*, *Arsenia*, *Caridad*, *Catalina*, *Clarita*, *Conrado*, *Edilberta*, *Eugenio*.

Nepper (141) **1.** German: metonymic occupational name for a wheelwright, from Middle High German *nebegēr* 'pointed iron tool' (for drilling a wheel hub). **2.** Altered spelling of German KNEPPER. **3.** Dutch: variant of NAPPER.

Neppl (195) South German: possibly from a pet form of *Nepomuk*, the name of the 14th century patron saint of Bohemia, Johann von Nepomuk, which became a personal name in Bavaria in the 18th century.

Neptune (471) Possibly of French origin: unexplained.

GIVEN NAMES French 6%. *Andre* (2), *Armand*, *Elmire*, *Gisele*, *Jean-Luc*, *Luce*, *Magalie*.

Nerad (155) **1.** Czech and Sorbian: unflattering nickname for a fussy, picky person, from *nerad* 'dislike'. **2.** Slovenian: perhaps a nickname from the adverb *nerad* 'unwillingly', 'reluctantly'.

GIVEN NAMES German 8%. *Otto* (4), *Kurt*.

Nerby (117) Norwegian: habitational name from any of several farmsteads in southeastern Norway, named in Old Norse as *Neðribýr* 'the lowest (*neðri*) farm (*býr*)'.

Nerenberg (199) Jewish (Ashkenazic): variant of NIERENBERG.

GIVEN NAME Jewish 5%. *Hyman*.

Neri (1238) **1.** Spanish: from a personal name, from the name of a 16th-century Italian saint, Filippo Neri (see 2). **2.** Italian (Tuscany): from a short form of the personal name *Raineri*, *Ran(i)eri*, or *Rin(i)eri*, or in some cases from later personal names such as *Guarniero*, *Falconiere*, *Soldaniero*.

GIVEN NAMES Spanish 20%; Italian 14%. *Jose* (8), *Juan* (8), *Mario* (5), *Francisco* (4), *Jorge* (4), *Alfonso* (3), *Esteban* (3), *Florencio* (3), *Guadalupe* (3), *Lino* (3), *Manuel* (3), *Raul* (3); *Salvatore* (8), *Angelo* (4), *Geno* (4), *Dino* (2), *Gildo* (2), *Giovanni* (2), *Luca* (2), *Pasquale* (2), *Pietro* (2), *Rocco* (2), *Sal* (2), *Umberto* (2).

Nerio (130) Hispanic (mainly Mexico, EL Salvador, and Peru): unexplained.

GIVEN NAMES Spanish 35%. *Jose* (4), *Mario* (4), *Elvira* (2), *Jesus* (2), *Jorge* (2), *Juan* (2), *Aleyda*, *Alfredo*, *Ana*, *Blanca*, *Carlos*, *Dionicia*.

Nerison (158) Probably Norwegian: patronymic from *Neri*, a comparatively rare personal name, from Old Norse *Neriðr*, a compound or *ner-* 'strong', 'healthy' + a second element meaning either 'isthmus' or 'brilliance', 'beauty'.

GIVEN NAMES Scandinavian 7%. *Erik*, *Nels*, *Nils*, *Ove*.

Nerney (175) Irish: reduced form of MCINERNEY.

Nero (1154) Italian: nickname from *nero* 'black' (Latin *niger*).

Nerone (186) Italian: from an augmentative of NERO.

GIVEN NAMES Italian 5%. *Amerigo*, *Marco*.

Nerren (166) Origin unidentified.

Nersesian (111) Armenian: patronymic from the classical Armenian personal name

Nersēs (from Middle Iranian *Nerseh*), a name borne by patriarchs of the Armenian Church from the 4th century onward.

GIVEN NAMES Armenian 29%. *Serop* (3), *Nerses* (2), *Varouj* (2), *Agop*, *Ara*, *Aram*, *Armen*, *Carnig*, *Hagop*, *Hakop*, *Raffi*, *Stepan*.

Nerud (107) Czech: unexplained.

Nervig (102) Origin unidentified.

Nery (129) Spanish and Portuguese: variant of NERI.

GIVEN NAMES Spanish 35%; Portuguese 9%. *Jose* (5), *Jose Roberto* (2), *Adelfa*, *Alfonso*, *Alfredo*, *Andres*, *Benedicto*, *Carlos*, *Constancio*, *Cristina*, *Edmundo*, *Efren*; *Paulo* (2).

Nesbit (1748) Scottish (Borders) and northern English: variant spelling of NESBITT.

Nesbitt (4494) Scottish (Borders), northern English, and northern Irish: habitational name from any of several places in the Border region of Scotland called Nesbit(t) or Nisbit, named in northern Middle English with *nese* 'nose' + *bit* 'mouthful', 'piece of ground' (Old English *bita*) or *bit* 'bend' (Old English *byht*, modern *bight*). The place names refer either to a piece of raised land sticking up like a nose, or to a bend in a river shaped like a nose.

Nesby (169) Norwegian: habitational name from a farm name from Old Norse *nesbýr* 'the farm on the headland'. Compare NESHEIM.

Nesci (170) Southern Italian: unexplained; possibly of Arabic origin.

GIVEN NAMES Italian 26%. *Salvatore* (4), *Carmela* (2), *Rocco* (2), *Antonio*, *Carmine*, *Domenic*, *Francesco*, *Saverio*.

Nese (106) **1.** Norwegian: variant of NESS. **2.** Italian: possibly from a short form of a habitational name formed with the suffix *-ese*, such as Bolognese.

GIVEN NAMES Italian 5%; French 4%. *Angelo*, *Lucio*; *Patrice*.

Nesheim (371) Norwegian: habitational name from any of about ten farmsteads so named, mainly in Rogaland and Hordaland, from Old Norse *Nesheimr*, a compound of *nes* 'headland', 'promontory' + *heim* 'homestead', 'home'.

GIVEN NAMES Scandinavian 6%. *Britt*, *Erik*, *Lars*, *Nils*.

Neske (113) German: from a pet form of the female medieval personal name *Nes*, a short form of *Agnes* (see NESS 4).

GIVEN NAME German 4%. *Horst*.

Nesler (304) South German: variant spelling of NESSLER.

Nesmith (1940) Scottish and English: occupational name for a maker of knives or of nails, from Middle English *knyf* 'knife' or *nayl* 'nail' + *smith* (see SMITH).

Nespoli (102) Italian and Sicilian: topographic name from Italian *nespolo*, Sicilian *nespulu* 'medlar tree' (from Latin *mespilus*).

GIVEN NAMES Italian 15%. *Leonardo*, *Livio*, *Sal*, *Salvatore*.

Ness (4669) **1.** Scandinavian (especially Norwegian), Scottish, and northern English: topographic name for someone who lived on a headland or promontory, Old Norse *nes*, or a habitational name from any of the numerous places named with this word; there are over a hundred farms in Norway and many settlements in Scotland and northern England so named **2.** English: according to Reaney and Wilson, a variant of NASH. **3.** German: habitational name from places called Nesse in Oldenburg and Friesland. **4.** German: from a short form of the female personal name *Agnes* (see AGNES 1).

GIVEN NAMES Scandinavian 4%. *Erik* (6), *Hilma* (3), *Lars* (2), *Monrad* (2), *Alf*, *Anders*, *Helmer*, *Hilmer*, *Juel*, *Nels*, *Nils*.

Nessel (191) **1.** German: nickname for a waspish person, from Middle High German *nezzel* 'nettle'. **2.** Dutch: variant of NESTEL.

Nesselrodt (134) German: from a topographic name denoting a clearing (from Middle High German *riuten*, *roten* 'to clear land [for cultivation or settlement])'.

Nessen (151) **1.** German and Danish: metronymic from the personal name *Agnes* (see AGNES 1). **2.** German: habitational name from any of several places in Lower Saxony called Nesse.

GIVEN NAMES Scandinavian 4%. *Anders*, *Nils*.

Nesser (216) **1.** German: possibly a habitational name, a variant of NESS. **2.** Altered spelling of German **Nösser**, an occupational name for a trader in livestock, from an agent derivative of Middle High German *nōz* 'domestic animals', 'cattle'.

Nesset (117) Norwegian: variant of NESSETH.

GIVEN NAME Scandinavian 4%; German 4%. *Kurt*.

Nesseth (186) Norwegian: habitational name from a farmstead named Nesset, in one case possibly from Old Norse *neyti* 'herd of cattle' + *set* 'farm', but most from the more common farm name *Neset*, meaning 'the headland' (from the definite singular form of Old Norse *nes*).

GIVEN NAME Scandinavian 4%. *Hjalmer*.

Nessler (246) South German: **1.** variant of NESTLER. **2.** topographic name from *in den Nesseln* 'in the nettles' (see NESSEL). **3.** occupational name for a weaver of cotton fabric, from an agent derivative of *Nessel* 'cotton'.

GIVEN NAMES German 6%. *Otto* (3), *Konrad*.

Nessmith (138) Scottish and English: variant of NAISMITH.

Nesson (117) Irish: probably a reduced Anglicized form of Gaelic **Mac Naois** (see McNEESE).

Nest (102) Welsh: from the medieval female personal name *Nest*, possibly a diminutive form of *Agnes*.

Nesta (156) Italian: from a reduced form of the medieval female personal name *Onesta*, from *onesto* 'man of dignity and integrity'. This name is also well established in Mexico.

GIVEN NAMES Italian 20%; Spanish 6%. *Angelo* (2), *Nicola* (2), *Rocco* (2), *Salvatore* (2), *Alessandro, Giovanni*; *Amador, Cruz, Garcia Manuel, Jesus, Maria Elena*.

Nestel (135) German, Dutch, and Jewish (Ashkenazic): metonymic occupational name for a ribbon and cord maker, from Middle High German, Middle Dutch *nestel* '(shoe)lace', 'drawstring', 'cord'.

GIVEN NAMES German 8%; Jewish 4%. *Kurt* (3), *Wolfram*; *Aron, Hyman*.

Nester (2000) **1.** German: presumably a topographic name from Middle High German *nest* 'nest', 'hideout', 'home', or possibly a nickname for a surly person, from a derivative of Middle High German *nast* 'knot' (see NAST). **2.** German: habitational name for someone from Nest, a place near Köslin in eastern Germany. **3.** Possibly an altered spelling of NESTOR.

Nestico (111) Italian: variant of **Nistico**, a nickname from medieval Greek *nēstikos* 'hungry', 'fasting'.

GIVEN NAMES Italian 20%. *Pasquale* (2), *Salvatore* (2), *Aurelio, Elena, Vincenzo, Vito*.

Nestle (243) Swiss German: **1.** from a diminutive of NAST. **2.** variant spelling of NESTEL.

Nestler (382) German and Dutch: occupational name for a maker of strings and laces, from Middle High German, Middle Dutch *nestel* '(shoe)lace', 'drawstring' + the agent suffix *-er*.

GIVEN NAMES German 7%; Scandinavian 4%. *Gunter* (2), *Hans* (2), *Heinz* (2), *Helmut, Kurt*.

Nestlerode (113) German: Americanized form of **Nesselrode** (see NESSELRODT).

GIVEN NAME German 6%. *Franz* (2).

Nestor (1935) **1.** Irish (Munster): reduced Anglicized form of Gaelic **Mac an Adhastair**, formerly **Mac Girr an Adhastair**, a patronymic from a byname meaning 'short man of the halter'. **2.** Humanistic Dutch and German name from a classical Greek personal name, borne by a king of Pylos who was one of the Greek leaders in the Trojan war, noted for his age and wisdom. In Homer's Odyssey, the aged Nestor gives wise advice to Odysseus' son Telemachos. According to Debrabandere, in Dutch this was a nickname sometimes given to the oldest person in a group.

Neth (371) German: **1.** probably a habitational name from Nethen in Oldenburg, or from the Nethe river near Höxter, or the Nethen, a tributary of the Dijle. **2.** from a

reduced form of the female personal name *Agnethe*, variant of *Agnes*.

Nethercott (118) English: a topographic name for someone who lived in a cottage at the lower end of a settlement, from Middle English *nether(e)* 'lower' (Old English *neoðera*) + *cot* 'cottage', or a habitational name from any of various places named with these elements, as for example Nethercote or Nethercott in Oxfordshire, Nethercote in Warwickshire, or Nethercott in Devon.

Nethercutt (179) Variant of English NETHERCOTT.

GIVEN NAME German 4%. *Kurt* (2).

Netherland (430) Anglicized form of German **Niederland**, a topographic name for someone who lived in a low-lying area or an ethnic name for a Dutchman.

Nethers (163) German: variant of **Näther**, an occupational name for a tailor, from an agent derivative of Middle High German *næjen* 'to embroider', 'to sew'. Compare NADER.

Netherton (648) English: habitational name from a place named with Old English *neoðera* 'lower' + *tūn* 'enclosure', 'settlement'. This could be the one in Worcestershire or the one in Northamptonshire, but is more likely to be from one of the eight places so called in Devon, where the surname is most common.

Nethery (516) Scottish and northern Irish (Tyrone): unexplained; probably a habitational name from a lost or unidentified place in the British Isles.

Netland (129) Norwegian: habitational name from any of seven farmsteads in Agder and Rogaland, named in Old Norse as *Nesland* 'the farm (*land*) on the headland (*nes*)'.

GIVEN NAMES Scandinavian 11%. *Anders* (2), *Arlys, Bernt, Bjorn*.

Neto (296) Portuguese and Galician: from *neto* 'grandson'. Compare NIETO.

GIVEN NAMES Spanish 38%; Portuguese 23%. *Jose* (19), *Manuel* (11), *Carlos* (8), *Francisco* (4), *Joaquin* (3), *Mario* (3), *Adelino* (2), *Aires* (2), *Jorge* (2), *Luiz* (2), *Pedro* (2), *Abilio*; *Joao* (3), *Joaquim* (3), *Paulo* (2), *Agostinho, Mateus*.

Nett (579) **1.** German: from a Slavic personal name, perhaps composed with Old Slavic *netu* 'burning', 'fire'. **2.** Respelling of the German habitational name **Nette**, from any of several places so named and a river near Osnabrück. **3.** Irish: variant of McNETT.

Netter (343) **1.** English: occupational name for a net-maker, from an agent derivative of Middle English *net* 'net'. **2.** English: variant of **Nettard**, an occupational name for a cattle herd, from Middle English *neat* 'cattle' + *hi(e)rde* 'herdsman'. **3.** German: variant of NADER. **4.** German: habitational name for someone from any of various places called Nette, for example in Lower

Saxony and Westphalia. **5.** Jewish (Ashkenazic): unexplained.

Netterville (220) Irish (now rare in Ireland): of Anglo-Norman origin, probably a habitational name from an unidentified place in France.

GIVEN NAME French 4%. *Andre* (2).

Nettesheim (215) German: habitational name from a place so named in the Rhineland.

GIVEN NAMES German 5%. *Hans, Kurt, Reiner, Ulrich*.

Netti (121) Italian: patronymic or plural form of NETTO.

GIVEN NAMES Italian 20%. *Antonio, Carmel, Domenic, Lorenzo, Mauro, Nicola, Paolo, Salvatore, Stefano*.

Nettle (234) **1.** English (Cornwall): probably a topographic name for someone who lived at a place overgrown with nettles, Middle English *net(t)el*. **2.** Respelling of North German **Nettel**, a nickname for an obnoxious person, from Middle Low German *nettel* 'nettle'.

Nettles (3344) English: variant of NETTLE.

Nettleton (878) English (Yorkshire): habitational name from a place so named, probably the one in Lincolnshire, although there is also one in Wiltshire. The place name is derived from Old English *netele* 'nettle' + *tūn* 'enclosure', 'settlement'.

Netto (305) **1.** Portuguese and Galician: variant spelling of NETO. **2.** Italian: from a short pet form of a personal name ending in *-ne*, as for example *Baronetto* (from BARONE), *Leonetto* (from LEONE), or *Simonetto* (from SIMONE).

GIVEN NAMES Spanish 6%; Portuguese 5%; Italian 5%. *Manuel* (4), *Carlos, Christiano, Jorge, Julio, Luis, Pedro*; *Guilherme, Paulo*; *Amalia, Renato, Roberto, Theodoro*.

Netz (269) **1.** German: habitational name from any of various places called Neetze or Netze, from the Netze river, or from certain other localities such as Netzkamp in northern Germany. **2.** German: metonymic occupational name for a maker of nets, from Middle High German *netz* 'net'. **3.** Jewish (Ashkenazic): ornamental name from German *Netz* or Yiddish *nets* 'net'.

Netzel (363) German: **1.** (also **Nötzel**) nickname for a person in need or distress, from Middle High German *nōt* 'hardship', 'distress', 'suffering'. **2.** possibly from a pet form of *Notz*, a short form of the personal name *Norbert*. **3.** southern metonymic occupational name for a maker of nets, from Middle High German *netzel(īn)*, a diminutive of *netz* 'net' (see NETZ).

GIVEN NAMES German 4%. *Aloysius, Egon, Erwin, Kurt, Willibald*.

Netzer (371) **1.** South German and Jewish (Ashkenazic): occupational name for a fisherman who used nets, from Middle High German *netz* 'net' + the agent suffix *-er*. **2.** Eastern and northern German: habitational name for someone from Netz, Netze, or Netzen in northern Germany.

GIVEN NAMES German 5%; Jewish 4%. *Siegfried* (3), *Erwin, Heinz, Helmut, Kurt; Aharon* (2), *Emanuel, Giora, Malca, Miriam, Shula.*

Netzley (183) Americanized spelling of South German **Netzle**, from a pet form of the personal name *Ignaz* (see IGNACIO), or a Swabian variant of NETZ.

Neu (1701) German and Jewish (Ashkenazic): nickname for a newcomer to an area, from Middle High German *niu(we)*, German *neu* 'new'.

GIVEN NAMES German 4%. *Gebhard* (2), *Hans* (2), *Kurt* (2), *Otto* (2), *Alois, Eldred, Horst, Manfred, Nikolaus, Ralf, Wilhelm, Wolfgang.*

Neubarth (104) German: variant of NEUBAUER (with excrescent -*t*).

Neubauer (2548) **1.** German: epithet for a settler who was new to an area, from Middle High German *niu(we)* 'new' + *(ge)būre* 'settler', 'resident', 'peasant' (see BAUER). **2.** Jewish: either an adoption of the German surname (Jews were not usually agricultural workers at the time when surnames were acquired) or an artificial creation of a name from the German vocabulary word without any relationship to the actual occupation of the first Jewish bearer.

GIVEN NAMES German 5%. *Kurt* (8), *Fritz* (7), *Hans* (3), *Erwin* (2), *Math* (2), *Otto* (2), *Willi* (2), *Beate, Dieter, Eldred, Erna, Ernst.*

Neubaum (107) German: topographic name meaning 'new tree', or a habitational name from a place so named.

Neubeck (142) Dutch: distinguishing name for a 'new baker', either one new to the place where he was working, or perhaps one who had newly finished his apprenticeship.

Neubecker (197) German: **1.** nickname for a baker who was new in a village or town, from *neu* 'new' + *becker* 'baker'. **2.** in northern Germany it may sometimes be a habitational name for someone from a place called Niebe(c)k, meaning 'new stream', or a topographic name for someone who lived by a stream so named.

Neuber (146) German: reduced form of NEUBAUER.

GIVEN NAMES German 8%; Scandinavian 4%. *Dietmar, Fritz, Karl Heinz; Kerstin.*

Neuberger (696) **1.** German and Jewish (Ashkenazic): habitational name from any of several places called Neuberg (Hesse) or Neuburg (Bavaria, Palatinate, Mecklenburg). **2.** Jewish (Ashkenazic): ornamental name from a derivative of German *Neuberg* 'new mountain'.

GIVEN NAMES German 6%; Jewish 4%. *Hans* (3), *Kurt* (2), *Egon, Eldor, Ernst, Hilde, Lothar, Mathias, Maximilian, Reinhold; Ari* (3), *Miriam* (2), *Shraga* (2), *Yaakov* (2),

Boruch, Joachim, Meyer, Tsvi, Yosef, Zipporah.

Neubert (905) German (mainly Saxony): reduced form of NEUBAUER with excrescent -*t*. Compare NEUBER.

GIVEN NAMES German 8%. *Hans* (5), *Kurt* (3), *Ulrich* (3), *Armin, Dieter, Egon, Erhard, Ernst, Erwin, Franz, Frieda, Fritz.*

Neuburger (226) German and Jewish (Ashkenazic): habitational name for someone from any of several places named Neuburg ('new town') in Swabia, Bavaria, and the Upper Palatinate.

GIVEN NAMES German 8%. *Kurt* (2), *Elke, Helmut.*

Neudecker (163) German: habitational name from any of several places called Neudeck, in Saxony, Thuringia, Silesia, Bavaria, former East Prussia, and Württemberg. See also NYDEGGER.

GIVEN NAMES German 7%. *Bernd* (2), *Bernhard, Hans.*

Neuendorf (281) German: habitational name from any of the numerous places so named throughout Germany (three of which are now in Poland).

GIVEN NAMES German 8%. *Erwin* (2), *Guenter, Klaus, Kurt, Ralf, Willi, Wolfgang.*

Neuenfeldt (228) German: habitational name for someone from places so named in Brandenburg and Pomerania, or from places in Lower Saxony or Westphalia called Neuenfelde.

GIVEN NAME German 5%. *Ernst* (2).

Neuens (152) **1.** Dutch and Luxembourgeois: patronymic from the medieval personal name *Noudin*, a derivative of *Arnoud*, of Germanic origin (see ARNOLD). **2.** German and Luxembourgeois: possibly from a French name.

Neuenschwander (669) German: nickname for someone farming or occupying newly cleared land, from Middle High German *niuwe* 'new' + *swant* 'land cleared of forest', or a habitational name for someone from Neuenschwand in Bavaria.

FOREBEARS This is an old Bernese name, found in Signau district and in the villages of Niederstocken, Höfen, and Lützelflüh, which had long associations with the Mennonites. Jacob Neiswanger, his wife, and Ann Neiswanger were members of the Codorus, PA, congregation in 1770. A Joseph Niswanger was with a Brethren group that settled in Cape Girardeau Co., MO, about 1790. A Michael Neuenschwander, grandson of Peter Neuenschwander, who had moved with his family to Cortébert in the Jura in 1729, arrived in Wayne Co., OH, in 1823.

Neuer (141) German: inflected (masculine) form of NEU (as in *neuer Mann* 'new man').

GIVEN NAMES German 9%. *Otto* (3), *Frederich.*

Neufeld (1282) **1.** German: habitational name from any of several places called Neufeld, also the German name for Konielspol near Łódź in Poland. **2.** Jewish (Ashkenazic): ornamental name from German *Neufeld* 'new field'.

GIVEN NAMES German 5%. *Gerhard* (3), *Hans* (3), *Heinrich* (2), *Erna, Ernst, Frieda, Helmut, Irmgard, Katharina, Kurt, Otto.*

Neufeldt (100) German: variant of NEUFELD.

Neufer (105) Variant spelling of German NEUFFER.

Neuffer (123) German: habitational name for someone from Neuffen in Württemberg. Compare NEIFERT.

GIVEN NAME German 5%. *Kurt.*

Neugebauer (695) German and Jewish (Ashkenazic): variant of NEUBAUER.

GIVEN NAMES German 7%. *Hans* (3), *Kurt* (3), *Otto* (2), *Christoph, Erwin, Heinz, Helmut, Helmuth, Juergen, Leonhard, Lorenz, Manfred.*

Neugent (238) Variant spelling of English NUGENT.

Neuhalfen (128) North German: from *neu* 'new' + Low German *half* 'half', a nickname for a new owner or tenant farmer of half an estate or of a holding of half a land unit, or for a newcomer whose tax obligation amounted to half his harvest.

Neuhardt (108) German: variant of NEUHART.

GIVEN NAME German 6%. *Otto.*

Neuhart (164) German: variant of NEIDHARDT, from *nīt*, wrongly reduced to *nī* and standardized to *neu*.

Neuharth (279) Variant of German NEUHART.

GIVEN NAMES German 5%. *Erwin* (3), *Helmuth, Reinhold.*

Neuhaus (999) German and Jewish (Ashkenazic): topographic name for someone who lived in a new house, Middle High German *niuwe hūs*, modern German *neu Haus*, or a habitational name for someone from any of several places named Neuhaus ('new house') in various parts of Germany and Austria, also in Bohemia.

GIVEN NAMES German 7%. *Armin* (3), *Fritz* (3), *Kurt* (2), *Alois, Arno, Bernhard, Eberhard, Eldor, Elfriede, Gerhard, Heinz, Helmut.*

Neuhauser (368) German (**Neuhäuser**) and Jewish (Ashkenazic): variant of NEUHAUS, with the suffix -*er* denoting an inhabitant.

GIVEN NAMES German 7%. *Hans* (4), *Lenz* (2), *Dietrich, Fritz, Heinz, Otto.*

Neuhoff (217) **1.** German: distinguishing epithet for the owner or tenant of a new farm or manor, standardized from Middle Low German *nie* 'new' + *hof* 'farmstead', 'manor farm' or a habitational name from any of several places so named, for example in Saxony and Thuringia. Compare

NIEHOFF. **2.** Jewish (Ashkenazic): ornamental name from German *Neuhof* 'new yard'.
GIVEN NAMES German 6%; Jewish 4%. *Lorenz* (3), *Kurt*; *Mayer* (2), *Chaim*, *Chanie*.

Neujahr (155) German: from Middle High German *niuwe* 'new' + *jār* 'year', a nickname for someone who owed feudal dues at the New Year, or sometimes a name given to someone born on that day.
GIVEN NAMES German 4%. *Ewald, Wolfgang*.

Neukam (189) Altered spelling of German **Neukamm** or **Neukomm**, a nickname for a newcomer, from Middle High German *niuwe* 'new' + a derivative of Middle High German *komen* 'to come'.

Neukirch (103) German: topographic name for someone who lived by the new church, Middle High German *niuwe* 'new' + *kirche* 'church', or a habitational name from any of several places so named.

Neumaier (153) South German: variant spelling of NEUMEYER.
GIVEN NAMES German 7%. *Gerhard, Hans, Lothar*.

Neuman (3703) Jewish (Ashkenazic): variant of NEUMANN.

Neumann (7091) German, Danish, and Jewish (Ashkenazic): nickname for a newcomer to a place, from Middle High German *niuwe*, German *neu* 'new' + Middle High German *man*, German *Mann* 'man'.
GIVEN NAMES German 9%. *Kurt* (29), *Hans* (14), *Otto* (12), *Gunter* (9), *Helmut* (9), *Erwin* (8), *Heinz* (7), *Dieter* (5), *Guenter* (5), *Bernd* (4), *Ernst* (4), *Fritz* (4).

Neumayer (238) South German: variant spelling of NEUMEYER.
GIVEN NAMES German 6%. *Alois, Kurt, Maximilian, Otto*.

Neumeier (278) German: variant spelling of NEUMEYER.
GIVEN NAMES German 7%. *Gunter, Heinz, Hermann, Wolfgang*.

Neumeister (359) German: distinguishing name for a master craftsman who had newly settled in a particular community, from Middle High German *niuwe* 'new' + *meister* 'master'.

Neumeyer (481) German: distinguishing name for a newly appointed steward or tenant farmer, or one who was a newcomer to an area, from Middle High German *niuwe* 'new' + *meier* 'steward', 'tenant farmer' (see MEYER 1). In compound names *-meyer* and *-man(n)* were often treated as near synonyms and were used interchangeably, as for example **Neumann, -meyer**, **Nettemann, -meyer**, **Schmittmann, -meyer**.

Neumiller (295) Americanized form of German **Neumüller**, a nickname for a newly arrived miller, from Middle High German *niuwe* 'new' + *mülnære* 'miller'.

Neuner (446) South German: occupational nickname for a member of a council made up of nine (literally, a 'niner'), from Middle High German *niun* 'nine' + the agent suffix *-er*.

Neupert (152) German: variant of NEUBERT (see NEUBAUER).
GIVEN NAMES German 10%. *Elke, Frieda, Hermann, Kurt*.

Neurohr (168) South German: topographic name for someone who lived near a reed bed, from Middle High German *niuwe* 'new' + *rōr* 'reed(s)'.
GIVEN NAMES German 4%. *Helmut, Nikolaus*.

Neuroth (259) German: habitational name from any of various places called Neurode, originally a field name meaning 'new clearing', or topographic name for someone living in a new clearing in woodland.
GIVEN NAMES German 4%. *Kurt* (2), *Florian*.

Neuschwander (156) South German: variant of NEUENSCHWANDER.

Neuse (102) German: of uncertain origin. Possibly a nickname from dialect *neusen* 'to eat on the sly'.
GIVEN NAMES German 10%. *Erhard, Herta*.

Neuser (187) German: **1.** habitational name for someone from Neuss near Düsseldorf. **2.** nickname for a suspicious or distrustful person, from an agent derivative of Middle High German *niusen* 'to test or probe'.

Neustadt (228) German and Jewish (Ashkenazic): habitational name from any of many places in Germany and Austria called Neustadt ('new town'), or from a German translation of various Slavic place names with similar meaning.
GIVEN NAMES Jewish 7%. *Anshel, Chaim, Miriam, Mordechai*.

Neustadter (123) German (**Neustädter**) and Jewish: habitational name for someone from any of many places in Germany and Austria called NEUSTADT.
GIVEN NAMES German 9%. *Gerhard, Kurt*.

Neuville (181) French: habitational name from any of the many places, mainly in northern France, so named from Latin *nova villa* 'new villa, estate' (later, 'town'). The surname is also established in French Switzerland and may have been brought to the U.S. from there.

Neuwirth (441) German and Jewish (Ashkenazic): nickname for a new innkeeper, from Middle High German *niuwe* 'new' + *wirt* and German *neu* + *Wirt* 'master of a house', 'innkeeper'.
GIVEN NAMES Jewish 4%. *Arieh, Chana, Channa, Emanuel, Ilan, Miriam, Sol, Zeev*.

Neuzil (214) Czech (**Neužil**): nickname for a miser, from Czech *ne* 'not' + *užilý* 'generous'.

Neva (128) Finnish: topographic name from *neva* 'marsh' (in Karelian 'waterway'), or habitational name from a farm named with this word.

Nevala (199) Finnish: variant of NEVA with the local suffix *-la*.

GIVEN NAMES Finnish 4%. *Eino* (2), *Tarja, Weikko*.

Nevares (123) Asturian-Leonese: habitational name from Nevares, a locality in the town of Parres in Asturies, named with the plural of *nevar* 'snow-covered', a derivative of *nieve* 'snow'.
GIVEN NAMES Spanish 44%. *Jesus* (3), *Luis* (2), *Adela, Agueda, Alberto, Alfredo, Amalio, Andres, Anselma, Camilo, Dulce, Engracia*.

Nevarez (1450) Spanish (from Asturian-Leonese): Castilianized variant of Asturian-Leonese NEVARES.
GIVEN NAMES Spanish 50%. *Jose* (33), *Manuel* (20), *Jesus* (17), *Juan* (14), *Francisco* (13), *Miguel* (13), *Carlos* (12), *Rafael* (11), *Pedro* (10), *Armando* (8), *Luis* (8), *Alfredo* (7).

Neve (459) **1.** English, Dutch, Danish, and Swedish: from Middle English, Old Norse, Middle Dutch *neve* 'nephew', presumably denoting the nephew of some great personage. **2.** French (**Nève**): Lyonnais habitational name from the Rhône place name En Nève, which derives from misdivision of *En ève* 'in water' (modern standard French *en eau*). **3.** Italian: from the personal name *Neve*, which may be from *neve* 'snow' (Latin *nix*, genitive *nivis*, possibly denoting a white-haired or very pale-complexioned person, or, according to Caracausi, may be a variant of the personal name *Neves*, from the Marian epithet *Madonna della Neve* or *Maria Santissima ad nives* 'Mary of the Snows'. **4.** Portuguese and Galician: from *neve* 'snow'. Compare 3.
FOREBEARS A family by the name Neve traces its descent from Robert le Neve, living in Tivetshall, Norfolk, in the 14th century.

Neveau (148) Variant spelling of French NEVEU.

Nevel (294) **1.** German: variant of NEBEL. **2.** Jewish (Israeli): new Hebrew name meaning 'harp'.

Nevells (106) Irish: variant of NEVILLE.

Nevels (828) **1.** Scottish: variant of Irish NEVILLE. **2.** Dutch: probably an altered form of **Nevens**, a patronymic from NEVE 1.

Nevens (112) Dutch: patronymic from NEVE.

Nevers (442) French and English: habitational name from the city of Nevers in France. The 1881 British census records a William Nevers, born in Norfolk, and eight bearers of the name Albrecht de Nevers, the eldest of whom, Edward, was born in Germany.

Neves (1206) Portuguese and Galician: **1.** religious byname, from the Marian title *Maria das Neves* 'Mary of the Snows' (see NIEVES). **2.** Galician and Asturian-Leonese: habitational name from any of the places named Neves in the provinces of

Pontevedra, Lugo, and A Coruña (Galicia), and Asturies.

GIVEN NAMES Spanish 15%; Portuguese 11%. *Manuel* (27), *Jose* (14), *Carlos* (7), *Jorge* (6), *Luis* (6), *Fernando* (5), *Gilberto* (5), *Mario* (4), *Ricardo* (3), *Augusto* (2), *Horacio* (2), *Joaquin* (2); *Joao* (7), *Joaquim* (3), *Agostinho, Catarina, Manoel, Paulo*.

Neveu (335) French: from Old French *neveu* 'nephew' (Latin *nepos*, genitive *nepotis*), presumably denoting the nephew of some great personage.

GIVEN NAMES French 10%. *Armand* (3), *Lucien* (2), *Normand* (2), *Aliette, Andre, Marcel*.

Nevil (256) Irish and English: variant spelling of NEVILLE.

Nevill (385) Irish and English: variant spelling of NEVILLE.

Neville (4368) **1.** Irish and English (of Norman origin): habitational name from Neuville in Calvados or Néville in Seine-Maritime, both so called from Old French *neu(f)* 'new' (Latin *novus*) + *ville* 'settlement' (see VILLA). **2.** Irish (Munster): assimilation of the Gaelic name **Ó Niadh** (see NEE) and sometimes of **Ó Cnaimhín** (see NEVIN).

FOREBEARS George Neville came to VA in or about 1700 and settled on the headwaters of the Occoquan River, acquiring a large estate. His descendants, bearing the surnames Neville and Craig, were of considerable importance in Pittsburgh, PA, and Cincinnati, OH.

Nevills (214) English: variant of NEVILLE.

Nevils (254) English: variant of NEVILLE.

Nevin (1214) **1.** Scottish and Irish (Leinster): reduced Anglicized form of Gaelic **Mac Naoimhín**, a patronymic from a personal name representing a diminutive of *naomh* 'saint'. **2.** Irish: reduced Anglicized form of Gaelic **Mac Cnáimhín** 'son of *Cnámhín*', a Galway name, or **Ó Cnáimhín**, a Munster name meaning 'descendant of *Cnámhín*', a byname meaning 'little bone', used to refer to a thin man.

Nevins (2015) Scottish and Irish: variant of NEVIN, with English patronymic *-s*.

Nevis (161) English: unexplained. Perhaps a variant of Scottish NEVINS.

Nevitt (628) Welsh (Merioneth): Anglicized form of the personal name *Ednyfed*, of unexplained etymology.

Nevius (488) German: humanistic name, a Latinized form of NEFF.

New (4325) **1.** English: nickname for a newcomer to an area, from Middle English *newe* 'new'. **2.** English: topographic name for someone who lived by a yew tree, from a misdivision of the Middle English phrase *atten ewe* 'at the yew' (Old English *æt ðæm ēowe*). **3.** German and Jewish (American): Translation of German NEU.

Newark (126) English: habitational name from Newark in Cambridgeshire or Newark

on Trent in Nottinghamshire, both named from Old English *nīwe* 'new' + *weorc* 'fortification', 'building'.

Newbanks (137) Possibly an Americanized spelling of North German **Niebank**, a nickname for a new market trader, from Low German *nie* 'new' + *bank* 'bench', 'vendor's booth or stand', or alternatively an altered form of English EUBANKS.

Newbauer (248) Altered form of German **Neubauer**, with the initial element Americanized.

Newberg (779) Jewish (American): Americanized form of **Neuberg** (see NEUBERGER).

Newberger (239) Altered form of NEUBERGER, with the first syllable Americanized.

GIVEN NAME Jewish 4%. *Sol*.

Newbern (582) Possibly an altered form of NEWBURN, NEWBORN, or **Neuborn** (see NEWBORN).

Newberry (4608) English: habitational name from any of the many places called Newbury, named with the Old English elements *nēowe* 'new' + *burh* 'fortress', 'fortified town' (see BERRY 1 and BURY).

FOREBEARS Thomas Newberry emigrated from Devon, England, to Dorchester, MA, in 1634. Among his descendants were a number of very successful manufacturers and entrepreneurs, including the brothers Oliver (1789–1860) and Walter (1804–68) Newberry, whose prosperity was linked with the growth and development of Chicago.

Newbert (106) Americanized spelling of German NEUBERT.

Newbery (132) English: variant spelling of NEWBERRY.

GIVEN NAMES Spanish 6%. *Jorge* (2), *Ernesto, Facundo, Ricardo, Santiago, Tomas*.

Newbill (562) Probably an Americanized spelling of German **Nübel**, a habitational name from any of several places in Schleswig-Holstein named Nübel, or possibly of NIEBEL.

Newbold (1196) English: topographic name for someone who lived in a newly constructed dwelling, from Middle English *newe* 'new' + *bold* 'building'. There are several places (in Cheshire, Derbyshire, Lancashire, Leicestershire, Northamptonshire, Nottinghamshire, Warwickshire, and Worcestershire) named with the same elements in Old English (*nēowe* + *bold*), and the surname may also be derived from any or all of them.

Newborn (371) **1.** English: habitational name from Newbourn in Suffolk or Newburn in Tyne and Wear (formerly part of Northumberland), both named with Old English *nīwe* 'new' + *burna* 'stream', perhaps denoting a stream that had changed its course. **2.** Possibly an Americanized form of German **Neugebo(h)ren**, **Neugeborn** (a nickname meaning 'newborn').

Newbrough (311) English: **1.** habitational name from Newbrough in Northumberland, named from Old English *nīwe* 'new' + *burh* 'fortification'. **2.** In some instances, possibly a variant of NEWBERRY.

Newburg (207) Part Americanized form of German **Neuburg**, a habitational name from any of numerous places in Germany and Austria called Neuburg.

Newburger (117) Americanized form of German **Neuburger**, a habitational name for someone from any of the many places in Germany and Austria called Neuburg.

Newburn (465) Scottish: habitational name from places so called in Fife and near Stirling.

Newbury (809) English: variant spelling of NEWBERRY.

Newby (3876) English: habitational name from any of the various places in northern England named with the Middle English elements *newe* 'new' + *by* 'farm', 'settlement' (of Old Norse origin).

Newcom (292) **1.** Americanized form of Swiss German **Neukomm** (see NEUKAM). **2.** Possibly an altered spelling of English NEWCOMB.

Newcomb (5623) **1.** English: nickname for a new arrival in a place, from Middle English *newe-come(n)* 'recently come', 'just arrived'. The intrusive *-b-* is the result of the influence of place names ending in *-combe* (see COOMBE). **2.** Americanized form of German **Neukamm**, possibly arising from a misinterpretation of its etymology as *neu* 'new' + *Kamm* 'comb' (see NEUKAM).

FOREBEARS According to family tradition, Capt. Andrew Newcomb was born in England in 1618 and died in Boston, MA, in 1686, leaving family who settled both in MA and in Kittery, ME. Among his descendants was the internationally renowned astronomer Simon Newcomb (1835–1909).

Newcombe (663) **1.** English: variant spelling of NEWCOMB. **2.** Possibly an Americanized form of German **Neukamm** (see NEWCOMB 2).

Newcome (275) **1.** English: variant spelling of NEWCOMB. **2.** Probably an Americanized form of German **Neukomm** or NEUKAM.

Newcomer (2129) Jewish (American): Americanized name of any of various European originals with this meaning.

Newell (12001) **1.** English and Irish: variant of NEVILLE. **2.** English: variant of NOEL. **3.** Irish (north County Kildare): Anglicized form of Gaelic **Ó Tnúthghail** 'descendant of *Tnúthgal*', a personal name composed of the elements *tnúth* 'desire', 'envy' + *gal* 'valor'.

Newey (187) English (West Midlands): topographic name for someone who lived at a 'new enclosure' (from Middle English *newe* + *hawe* or *heye*), or a habitational name from some minor place named with these elements (in Old English, *nēowe* + *haga*). Newhay and Newhey occur several times as place names in Cheshire and Yorkshire.

Newfield (277) **1.** Jewish (American): English translation of Ashkenazic NEUFELD. **2.** English: habitational name from any of many places named Newfield, especially in northern England and Scotland.
GIVEN NAMES Jewish 6%. *Aron* (2), *Shlomo* (2), *Meyer*, *Sol*.

Newgard (226) Americanized form of Scandinavian **Nygard**, **Nygaard**, or **Nygård** (see NYGAARD) or of German **Neugart**, a habitational name from places in Mecklenburg and Brandenburg named Neugarten or from Naugard in Pomerania.

Newgent (145) Variant spelling of English NUGENT.
GIVEN NAMES German 5%. *Kurt*, *Wendelin*.

Newhall (623) English: topographic name from Middle English *newe* 'new' + *hall* 'hall', denoting someone who lived by or worked in a newly built hall or manor house, or possibly a habitational name from any of various minor places so named (from Old English *nīwe* + *hall*), for example in Cheshire and Derbyshire.

Newham (149) English: habitational name from any of the various places, for example in Northumbria and North Yorkshire, so named from Old English *nēowe* 'new' + *hām* 'homestead'.

Newhard (343) Americanized form of German NEUHART.

Newhart (521) Americanized form of German NEUHART.

Newhouse (2449) **1.** English: topographic name for someone who lived in a 'new house', from Middle English *newe* + *hous*, or a habitational name from any of various minor places named with these elements, for example in Cheshire and West Yorkshire. Newsham in Lincolnshire was often *Neuhouse* in the medieval period, the modern form in *-ham* representing an alternative from Old English dative plural *-um*. **2.** Translation of Scandinavian NYHUS, German and Ashkenazic Jewish NEUHAUS (topographic or habitational names), or Hungarian **Újházi**, a habitational name for someone from any of various places named with *új* 'new' + *ház* 'house'.

Newill (157) English and Irish: variant of NEVILLE.

Newingham (167) English: variant of **Newenham**, itself a variant of NEWHAM, with the adjective (Old English *nēowe* 'new') retaining the weak dative *-an* inflection, originally used after a preposition and article. The English surname is also established in Ireland (County Cork), having been taken there by an English family in the mid 17th century.

Newitt (123) English: unexplained.

Newkirk (3547) Americanized form of the Dutch topographic name **Nieuwekerk** 'new church' (see NEIKIRK).

Newlan (117) Americanized form of Scandinavian NYLAND.
GIVEN NAME French 5%. *Napoleon*.

Newland (2672) **1.** English: topographic name, from Middle English *newe* 'new' + *land* 'land', for someone who lived by a patch of land recently brought into cultivation or recently added to the village, or a habitational name from any of a number of settlements called Newland for this reason. **2.** Translation of Scandinavian NYLAND or of German **Neuland** and North German **Nieland**, from any of several habitational names from places named Neuland or Nieland(e) in Westphalia and Schleswig-Holstein.

Newlander (107) Americanized form of Swedish NYLANDER.

Newlands (115) Scottish: habitational name from either of two places so called, a barony in Kincardine and a parish in Peebles. Compare English NEWLAND.

Newlin (1686) **1.** English: from the Old French personal name *Nevelon*, continental Germanic *Neveling*, *Nivelung* (see NIEBLING). **2.** English: possibly a habitational name from East Newlyn, Cornwall, which takes its name from the patron saint of the church there, *Niwelina*. **3.** Probably an Americanized form of German **Neuling**, a nickname for a newcomer or inexperienced person, from Middle Low German *nilinge* 'newly', 'recent'. **4.** Americanized form of Norwegian and Swedish NYLUND.

Newlon (686) **1.** English: unexplained. **2.** Americanized form of Norwegian and Swedish NYLUND.

Newlove (115) English: perhaps a nickname with reference to some anecdote or episode now irrecoverably lost. Compare BREEDLOVE.

Newlun (187) Americanized form of Norwegian and Swedish NYLUND.

Newman (39339) English: nickname for a newcomer to a place, from Middle English *newe* 'new' + *man* 'man'. This form has also absorbed several European cognates with the same meaning, for example NEUMANN. (For other forms, see Hanks and Hodges 1988.)

Newmann (212) Americanized form of German NEUMANN.
GIVEN NAMES German 4%. *Heinz*, *Markus*.

Newmark (587) Americanized form of Scandinavian **Nymark**, a common habitational name from farms named with *ny* 'new' + *mark* 'field', or of German and Ashkenazic Jewish **Neumark**, a habitational name from any of several places so named in all eastern German provinces and in Bavaria and Bohemia. The German surname may also derive from Neumark, a region in Brandenburg.

GIVEN NAMES Jewish 5%. *Emanuel* (3), *Sol* (3), *Chayim*, *Meyer*, *Shlomo*, *Vigdor*.

Newmeyer (193) Americanized form of German NEUMEYER.

Newmyer (149) Americanized form of German NEUMEYER.

Newnam (361) English: variant of NEWNHAM.

Newnham (140) English: habitational name of the same etymology as NEWHAM. The middle *-n-* comes from the weak dative form, *nēowan* of Old English *nēowe*, originally used after a preposition. There are places named Newnham in Bedfordshire, Cambridgeshire, Gloucestershire, Hampshire, Hertfordshire, Kent, Northamptonshire, Oxfordshire, Warwickshire, and Worcestershire.

Newnum (125) Variant of English NEWNHAM.

Newport (1504) Southern English: habitational name from any of several places so called, from Old English *nēowe* 'new' + *port* 'market town' (see PORT 2).
FOREBEARS The earliest known bearer of this name in North America was Christopher Newport (died 1617), an English mariner who served with Sir Francis Drake's Cadiz expedition of 1587. In 1592 he commanded a successful privateering expedition to the West Indies, taking 19 Spanish vessels. He married three times and had two daughters and two sons, one of whom, John, lived to acquire land in VA.

Newquist (376) Partly Americanized form of Swedish NYQUIST.
GIVEN NAMES Scandinavian 4%. *Erik*, *Ole*.

Newsham (286) English (chiefly Lancashire): variant of NEWSOME.

Newsom (3983) English: variant spelling of NEWSOME.

Newsome (6332) English (chiefly Yorkshire): habitational name from a place named with the Old English phrase *(æt ðǣm) nēowan hūsum* '(at the) new houses'. This and some of the variants listed below are common as place names in northern England. In the form Newsom, the surname is also established in Ireland, being the name of a Quaker family in County Cork.

Newson (951) English (East Anglia): **1.** variant of NEWSOME. **2.** patronymic from NEW 1.

Newstead (104) English: habitational name from any of various places called Newstead, in particular the one in Nottinghamshire, which is named from Old English *nīwe* 'new' + *stede* 'monastic site'.

Newstrom (194) Partly Americanized form of NYSTROM.

Newsum (131) English: variant spelling of NEWSOME.

Newswanger (271) Americanized form of Dutch **Nijswanger** 'newcomer', or German **Neuschwanger** (see NISWONGER and NEUENSCHWANDER).
GIVEN NAMES German 6%. *Phares* (5), *Erwin*.

Newth (119) English (Gloucestershire): unexplained.

Newton (25953) English: habitational name from any of the many places so named, from Old English *nēowe* 'new' + *tūn* 'enclosure', 'settlement'. According to Ekwall, this is the commonest English place name. For this reason, the surname has a highly fragmented origin.

Newtown (102) **1.** English: variant of NEWTON. **2.** Probably a translation of equivalents in other European languages, such as French NEUVILLE or German NEUSTADT.
GIVEN NAME French 5%. *Albon.*

Newville (258) **1.** Americanized form of French NEUVILLE. **2.** Possibly also a variant of Irish and English NEVILLE.

Ney (1286) **1.** English: variant of NYE. **2.** Irish: reduced form of O'NEY. **3.** North German and Jewish (Ashkenazic): variant of NEU. The Jewish surname may sometimes be a shortened form of a name such as NEUBURGER. **4.** German: habitational name from a place near Boppard. **5.** North German: nickname from Middle Low German *ni(g)e*, *ney(g)e* '(the) new one'. **6.** Dutch: from a short form of the personal name *Aarnoud* (see ARNOLD). **7.** Dutch (**de Ney**): variant of NAY 3.

Neyens (178) Dutch: patronymic from NEY 4.

Neyer (271) German, Swiss, and Jewish (Ashkenazic): occupational name for a tailor, from an agent derivative of Middle High German *næjen* 'to embroider', 'to sew', or Yiddish *neyen*, 'to sew'.

Neyhart (210) Probably an altered spelling of German NEUHART.

Neyland (337) Irish: variant of NEALON.

Neylon (275) Irish: variant of NEALON.
GIVEN NAME Irish 4%. *Marypat.*

Neyman (467) **1.** Jewish (eastern Ashkenazic): variant of NEUMANN. **2.** Dutch: variant of NIEMAN.
GIVEN NAMES Russian 9%; Jewish 8%. *Boris* (5), *Lev* (3), *Vladimir* (3), *Aleksandr* (2), *Igor* (2), *Leonid* (2), *Vladmir* (2), *Anatoliy, Anatoly, Brukha, Dmitry, Gennadiy; Izya, Moisey, Mordukh, Polina, Shaya, Sima, Yakov, Yuly.*

Nez (171) French: from *nez* 'nose', applied as a nickname for someone with a big or otherwise remarkable nose.

Nezat (102) French: unexplained.
GIVEN NAME French 6%. *Clothilde.*

Ng (6924) **1.** Chinese 吳: variant of WU 1. **2.** Chinese 伍: variant of WU 4.
FOREBEARS Born in South China in 1866, Ng Poon Chew followed relatives to CA and rose to prominence as a promoter of Chinese culture among Americans and of American ingenuity among the Chinese. He was a 32d-degree Mason, the first Chinese in CA to become a Shriner, and the most prominent bearer of the name Ng

Poon, which began appearing on the west coast in the 19th century.
GIVEN NAMES Chinese 27%; Other Southeast Asian 5%. *Wing* (35), *Kin* (34), *Wai* (31), *Kam* (26), *Kwok* (25), *Ming* (14), *Ping* (13), *Chun* (11), *Pui* (11), *Siu* (11), *Chi* (10), *Ching* (10); *Chung* (16), *Pak* (16), *Kok* (7), *Cho* (6), *Chong* (5), *Woon* (5), *Yiu* (5), *Yuet* (5), *Shiu* (4), *Moon* (3), *Siew* (3), *Yook* (3).

Ngai (332) **1.** Chinese 倪: variant of NI. **2.** Chinese 魏: variant of WEI 1.
GIVEN NAMES Chinese 22%; Vietnamese 6%. *Kwok* (3), *Kwong* (3), *Ming* (3), *Kwok Kwan* (2), *Wai* (2), *Yuet Ming* (2), *Cheung, Chi, Chi Kin, Chin, Chun, Fong; Hung* (2), *Chau, Dai, Tuan, Tung.*

Ngan (156) Chinese 顏: variant of YAN 3.
GIVEN NAMES Chinese 28%; Vietnamese 11%. *Fung* (3), *Hon* (2), *Kong* (2), *Hang, Heng, Hok, Kai Ming, Kan, Kwun, Ming, Mu, Sang, Weng; Dinh, Huynh, Mui, Nguyen, Soi, Tri.*

Nghiem (176) Vietnamese: unexplained.
GIVEN NAMES Vietnamese 71%. *Thanh* (5), *Dung* (3), *Hung* (3), *Nguyen* (3), *Diep* (2), *Loi* (2), *Tuan* (2), *Anh, Ba, Bao, Bich, Binh.*

Ngo (3709) **1.** Vietnamese (**Ngô**): unexplained. **2.** Chinese 敖: variant of AO.
GIVEN NAMES Vietnamese 66%; Chinese 14%. *Thanh* (53), *Hung* (46), *Minh* (45), *Dung* (39), *Hoa* (31), *Tuan* (26), *Quang* (25), *Son* (25), *Thu* (25), *Binh* (24), *Duc* (23), *Hoang* (23), *Tam* (15), *Phong* (14), *Nam* (13), *Tuong* (7), *Thai* (6), *Sinh* (5), *Tuoi* (5), *Tinh* (4), *Manh* (3), *Thach* (3), *Tham* (3); *Chi* (14), *Dong* (13), *Hong* (13), *Man* (9), *Sang* (9), *Chung* (5), *Han* (5), *Tong* (5), *Hang* (3), *Ho* (3), *Meng* (3), *Ming* (3), *Chan* (2).

Ngu (109) **1.** Vietnamese: unexplained. **2.** Filipino: unexplained.
GIVEN NAMES Vietnamese 53%; Other Southeast Asian 22%. *Hung* (3), *Tuan* (3), *Ha To* (2), *Long* (2), *Minh* (2), *Nguyet* (2), *Chau, Cuong, Dat, Du, Hoa, Khanh; Phong* (2), *Chung, Ming, Tso, Ung; Nam, Siew, Thai.*

Nguy (173) Vietnamese: unexplained.
GIVEN NAMES Vietnamese 67%. *Hung* (5), *Hoa* (4), *Minh* (4), *Quang* (3), *Thanh* (3), *Hao* (2), *Hue* (2), *Phat* (2), *Theng, Thuy* (2), *Tinh* (2), *Vinh* (2), *Anh, Au, Thai, Thay, Tuong.*

Nguyen (43992) Vietnamese (**Nguyễn**): unexplained. This was the family name of a major Vietnamese royal dynasty.
GIVEN NAMES Vietnamese 75%. *Thanh* (715), *Hung* (682), *Dung* (443), *Tuan* (442), *Minh* (423), *Hoa* (402), *Hai* (337), *Son* (310), *Tam* (305), *Hoang* (304), *Thuy* (293), *Long* (283), *Anh* (267), *Hong* (208), *Nam* (204), *Thai* (145), *Phong* (139), *Chi* (107), *Sang* (107), *Dong* (101), *Hang* (81), *Tuong* (78), *Tinh* (63), *Tong* (55), *Thach* (51), *Chien* (50), *Manh* (49), *Man* (47), *Chung* (44), *Han* (43), *Sinh* (42), *Lai* (43), *Chan* (41), *Ho* (40), *Uyen* (33), *Tuoi* (27).

Nhan (160) Vietnamese: unexplained.
GIVEN NAMES Vietnamese 62%; Chinese 11%. *Kiet* (3), *Nguyen* (3), *Thuong* (3), *Tran* (3), *Binh* (2), *Hoa* (2), *Huy* (2), *Kien* (2), *Minh* (2), *Quang* (2), *Tai Tan* (2), *Tan* (2); *Hong, Song, Sun.*

Ni (455) Chinese 倪: from the place name Ni. During the Zhou dynasty (1122–221 BC) there existed a fief of Ni (你). After the state of Chu conquered Ni, descendants of the Ni aristocracy adopted Ni as their surname. The character for this Ni was not the same as that of the present-day surname however; later descendants, in order to evade their enemies, changed the form of the character, allowing the pronunciation to stay the same.
GIVEN NAMES Chinese 66%. *Jian* (7), *Pei-Lin* (4), *Kong* (3), *Min* (3), *Ming* (3), *Yung* (3), *Bin* (2), *Cao* (2), *Huang* (2), *Jing* (2), *Wen* (2), *Zhen* (2), *Biao, Chang, Chi, Quan, Yaping.*

Niazi (107) Muslim (prevalent in India and Pakistan): from a personal name based on Persian *niyāzi* 'friend'.
GIVEN NAMES Muslim 83%. *Mohammad* (6), *Abdul* (3), *Imran* (3), *Tariq* (3), *Assadullah* (2), *Khalid* (2), *Mohammed* (2), *Suad* (2), *Syed* (2), *Ali, Amanullah, Amir.*

Nibarger (109) Altered form of German and Jewish NEUBERGER.

Nibbe (157) North German: nickname meaning 'beak', or from a short form of a Germanic personal name *Nippo*, composed of Old High German *nīt* 'hostility', 'eagerness' + *boto* 'messenger'.
GIVEN NAMES German 4%. *Ewald, Frederick Fritz, Hans.*

Nibbelink (109) Possibly a variant of German **Nibelung**, from a personal name recorded since the 8th century.

Nibert (314) German: variant spelling of **Nibbeling**, a variant of NEBEL.

Niblack (262) Variant of Scottish and northern Irish NIBLOCK.

Niblett (462) English: unexplained; possibly a nickname from a double diminutive of Middle English *nibbe*, a dialect form of *neb* 'beak', referring to someone with a prominent or beaklike nose.

Niblick (103) Variant of Scottish and northern Irish NIBLOCK.

Niblock (247) Scottish and northern Irish: unexplained. The surname has been established in county Antrim since the 17th century, believed to be of English origin.

Nicastro (675) Southern Italian: habitational name from Nicastro, a place in Catanzaro province named from Latin *Neocastro* 'new camp', from medieval Greek *neokastron*.
GIVEN NAMES Italian 16%. *Salvatore* (5), *Carmine* (4), *Sal* (3), *Carmelo* (2), *Gennaro* (2), *Orazio* (2), *Vito* (2), *Antonio, Carlo, Ciriaco, Cosmo, Dino.*

Niccolai (107) Variant spelling of Italian NICOLAI.

GIVEN NAMES Italian 12%. *Aldo, Attilio, Carlo, Lido, Marino, Remo.*

Niccoli (158) Italian: from a Tuscan variant of the personal name *Nicola*, Italian form of NICHOLAS.

GIVEN NAMES Italian 7%; French 5%. *Santo, Serafino, Silvio; Colette, Dominique.*

Niccum (535) respelling of German **Nickum** (see NEUKAM).

Nice (1227) **1.** English (Essex) and French: nickname from Middle English, Old French *nice* 'foolish', 'simple' (Latin *nescius* 'ignorant'). In the 14th century the English word also acquired the sense 'wanton' and in the 15th century 'coy', 'shy', both of which meanings may be reflected in the surname. The sense 'fastidious', 'precise', 'minute' developed only in the 16th century, probably too late to have given rise to any surnames, and the present-day sense of general approbation is not clearly attested until the late 19th century. **2.** Americanized spelling of German NEIS.

Niceley (114) Americanized spelling of German **Neißl** or **Nissle** (see NISSLEY).

Nicely (1672) Americanized spelling of German **Neißl** or **Nissle** (see NISSLEY).

Nicewander (145) Americanized form of German NEUSCHWANDER.

GIVEN NAME German 6%. *Kurt* (3).

Nicewarner (125) Americanized form of German NEUSCHWANDER.

Nichelson (329) Dutch: patronymic from a short form of the personal name *Nikolaus* (see NICHOLAS).

Nichol (1319) **1.** English and Scottish: from the northern Middle English personal name *Nicol* or its Gaelic equivalent (see NICHOLAS and MCNICHOL). **2.** Dutch: from a short form of the personal name *Nikolaus* (see NICHOLAS).

Nicholas (8918) English and Dutch: from the personal name (Greek *Nikolaos*, from *nikān* 'to conquer' + *laos* 'people'). Forms with -*ch*- are due to hypercorrection (compare ANTHONY). The name in various vernacular forms was popular among Christians throughout Europe in the Middle Ages, largely as a result of the fame of a 4th-century Lycian bishop, about whom a large number of legends grew up, and who was venerated in the Orthodox Church as well as the Catholic. In English-speaking countries, this surname is also found as an Americanized form of various Greek surnames such as **Papanikolaou** '(son of) Nicholas the priest' and patronymics such as **Nikolopoulos**.

FOREBEARS The colonial official and revolutionary patriot Robert Carter Nicholas was from a prominent VA family on both sides. His father was a British navy surgeon who emigrated in about 1700 from Lancashire, England, to Williamsburg, VA.

Nicholes (419) English and Dutch: patronymic from the personal name NICHOL.

Nicholl (502) Northern Irish: variant spelling of NICHOL.

Nicholls (2246) English and Dutch: patronymic from the personal name NICHOL.

Nichols (53183) **1.** English and Dutch: patronymic from NICHOL. **2.** Jewish (American): Americanized form of any of various like-sounding Jewish names.

Nicholson (20489) Northern English and Scottish: patronymic from NICHOL.

Nichter (296) German: nickname from Middle High German *nüchter(n)* 'sober'.

Nick (977) **1.** English: from a pet form of NICHOLAS. **2.** South German and Dutch: from a pet form of the personal name *Nikolaus* (see NICHOLAS). **3.** Jewish (American): Americanized form of any of various like-sounding Jewish names.

Nickel (3368) **1.** Dutch and German: from a pet form of *Nick*, a short form of the personal name *Nikolaus* (see NICHOLAS). **2.** English: variant spelling of NICHOL.

GIVEN NAMES German 4%. *Kurt* (7), *Dieter* (3), *Armin* (2), *Bernd* (2), *Gerhard* (2), *Hans* (2), *Helmut* (2), *Adelheid, Dietrich, Erhard, Ewald, Franz.*

Nickell (2221) Dutch, German, and English: variant spelling of NICKEL.

Nickels (1728) Dutch, German, and English: patronymic from NICKEL.

Nickelsen (130) Danish, North German, and Dutch: patronymic from the personal name *Nikolaus* (see NICHOLAS).

GIVEN NAMES German 10%; Scandinavian 6%. *Ralf* (2), *Kurt; Nelle.*

Nickelson (994) **1.** Americanized spelling of NICKELSEN. **2.** English: variant spelling of Scottish and northern English NICHOLSON.

Nickens (846) Apparently a patronymic from a pet form of NICK; the language of origin could be Dutch or English.

Nickerson (5957) English (Norfolk): patronymic from a pet form of NICHOLAS.

Nickeson (155) English: patronymic from a pet form of NICHOLAS.

Nickey (236) Americanized spelling of German **Nicke** or **Nickig**, from pet forms of the personal name *Nikolaus* (see NICHOLAS).

Nicklas (726) German: variant of NICKOLAUS.

Nicklaus (369) German: variant of NICKOLAUS.

GIVEN NAMES German 4%. *Reinhold* (2), *Gerhard, Heinz.*

Nickle (732) **1.** English: variant of NICHOL. **2.** Variant of German NICKEL.

Nickles (1283) **1.** German: variant of NICKLAS. **2.** Possibly an altered spelling of German **Nickels** (see NICKEL) or English NICHOL(L)S.

Nickless (285) English (West Midlands): variant spelling of NICHOLAS.

Nicklin (209) English (West Midlands): from a pet form of NICHOLAS.

Nicklow (212) Origin uncertain; presumably a variant of NICHOLAS.

Nickol (239) **1.** English: variant spelling of NICHOL. **2.** German: from a variant of the personal name *Nikolaus* (see NICHOLAS).

Nickolas (151) Variant spelling of German *Nikolaus* or English NICHOLAS.

Nickolaus (122) German: from the personal name *Nikolaus*, a German form of NICHOLAS.

Nickoloff (150) Bulgarian: alternative spelling of **Nikolov**, patronymic from the personal name *Nikol*, Bulgarian form of NICHOLAS.

Nickols (412) English: variant of NICHOLS.

Nickolson (165) English: variant of NICHOLSON.

Nicks (1183) German: patronymic from a short form of *Nikolaus*, a German form of NICHOLAS.

Nickson (422) **1.** English (Lancashire) and Scottish: variant spelling of NIXON. **2.** Dutch: patronymic from a short form of NICHOLAS.

GIVEN NAME French 4%. *Andre* (2).

Nickum (173) Americanized form of German **Niekum**, itself a variant of NEUKAM.

Nicley (152) Variant of German NICKLE.

Nicodemus (795) Spanish: from a personal name of Greek origin, composed of the elements *nikē* 'victory' + *dēmos* 'people'. This is the name borne in the New Testament by a Greek Jew who defended Jesus before the religious leaders (John 7:50) and was present at his burial (John 19:39).

Nicol (1894) Scottish: from a Scottish vernacular form of NICHOLAS.

Nicola (611) Italian: from the male personal name *Nicola*, from Greek *Nikolaos* (see NICHOLAS). This was a very common Italian name in the Middle Ages.

Nicolai (781) **1.** Italian: patronymic from the personal name *Nicolao*, a variant of NICOLA. **2.** North German, Dutch, and French (**Nicolaï**): Latinate (humanistic) patronymic from NICHOLAS.

GIVEN NAMES German 4%. *Ralf* (2), *Dietmar, Erwin, Frieda, Heino, Leonhard, Lothar, Otto.*

Nicolaides (160) Greek: patronymic from the personal name *Nikolaos* (see NICHOLAS). The -*ides* patronymic is classical, and was revived in the 19th century, in particular by Greeks from the Black Sea area.

GIVEN NAMES Greek 15%. *Nicos* (2), *Aristotle, Costas, Demetris, Despina, Panos, Stelios, Stratos, Yiannis.*

Nicolaisen (196) Danish, Norwegian, Dutch, and North German: patronymic from *Nicolai* (otherwise *Nikolai*), the genitive of *Nikolaus* (see NICHOLAS).

GIVEN NAMES Scandinavian 9%; German 4%. *Knut* (2), *Johan, Thor; Hans* (4).

Nicolaou (124) Greek (Cyprus): patronymic from the personal name *Nikolaos* (see NICHOLAS).

GIVEN NAMES Greek 37%; German 4%. *Andreas* (6), *Nicos* (4), *Christakis* (3), *Marios* (3), *Charalambos*, *Christos*, *Constantinos*, *Demetris*, *Panayiota*, *Panos*, *Vasiliki*.

Nicolas (909) **1.** Spanish (**Nicolás**), French, Dutch, Greek, etc: from the personal name *Nicolas*, the usual spelling of Greek *Nikolaos* in many languages (see NICHOLAS). **2.** English (common in Wales): variant spelling of NICHOLAS.

GIVEN NAMES Spanish 20%; French 13%. *Alberto* (4), *Angelito* (3), *Emilio* (3), *Fernando* (3), *Francisco* (3), *Manuel* (3), *Mario* (3), *Ricardo* (3), *Rodolfo* (3), *Ruben* (3), *Alfredo* (2), *Angel* (2); *Luc* (3), *Pierre* (3), *Andre* (2), *Georges* (2), *Jacques* (2), *Marcellin* (2), *Yves* (2), *Adrien*, *Alain*, *Camille*, *Celina*, *Dominique*.

Nicolau (125) **1.** Portuguese, Galician, Catalan, and southern French (Occitan): from the personal name *Nicolau* (see NICHOLAS). **2.** Romanian: patronymic from the personal name *Nicolai* (see NICHOLAS).

GIVEN NAMES Spanish 15%; Romanian 9%; German 6%. *Gabriela* (2), *Manuel* (2), *Alberto*, *Alfredo*, *Emilia*, *Francisca*, *Jaime*, *Jose*, *Juan Angel*, *Mariela*, *Miguel*, *Sergio*; *Anca* (2), *Constantin*, *Nicolae*, *Serban*; *Erwin* (2), *Theodor* (2).

Nicolaus (206) Dutch and German: variant of NICHOLAS.

GIVEN NAMES German 6%. *Dieter*, *Otto*.

Nicolay (349) **1.** Variant of NICOLAI 2. **2.** English: variant of NICHOLAS.

GIVEN NAMES German 4%. *Dieter*, *Franz*, *Helmuth*, *Ilse*, *Ingo*.

Nicolaysen (100) Danish, Norwegian, and North German: variant spelling of NICOLAISEN.

GIVEN NAMES Scandinavian 17%; German 6%. *Thor* (2), *Erik*; *Erwin*, *Frieda*.

Nicolazzo (101) Italian: from a pejorative form of the personal name NICOLA.

GIVEN NAMES Italian 15%; Spanish 10%. *Antonio* (2), *Marco* (2), *Francesco*, *Michelangelo*, *Salvatore*; *Domingo*, *Jose*, *Pascual*.

Nicole (157) French: from the personal name *Nicole*, feminine form of NICOLAS.

GIVEN NAMES French 9%. *Andre*, *Elzear*.

Nicolella (122) Italian: from a pet form (feminine) of the male personal name NICOLA.

GIVEN NAMES Italian 14%. *Angelo* (2), *Amadeo*, *Domenic*, *Mario*.

Nicolet (205) French: from a pet form of the personal name *Nicolas* (see NICHOLAS).

GIVEN NAMES French 5%. *Andre*, *Laure*, *Pascale*.

Nicoletta (151) Italian: from a female pet form of NICOLA.

GIVEN NAMES Italian 23%. *Angelo* (2), *Rocco* (2), *Antonietta*, *Antonio*, *Carmelo*, *Carmine*, *Enrico*, *Nunziata*, *Pasquale*, *Raffaele*, *Sal*, *Salvatore*.

Nicolette (175) French: from a pet form of NICOLAS. The ending is not feminine, but represents the full pronunciation of the final *t* that is characteristic of North American French names.

GIVEN NAMES Italian 6%. *Rocco*, *Sal*, *Vito*.

Nicoletti (896) Italian: from a pet form of the male personal name NICOLA.

GIVEN NAMES Italian 13%. *Rocco* (7), *Angelo* (4), *Antonio* (4), *Carmine* (2), *Dino* (2), *Dante*, *Domenica*, *Ezio*, *Federico*, *Fiore*, *Francesca*, *Francesco*.

Nicoli (213) **1.** Italian: variant spelling of NICCOLI. **2.** Greek (**Nikolis**): from the personal name *Nikolis*, pet form of *Nikolaos* (see NICHOLAS).

GIVEN NAMES Italian 7%. *Gino* (2), *Reno* (2), *Dario*, *Guido*, *Luciano*.

Nicolini (276) Italian: patronymic from *Nicolino*, a pet form of NICOLA.

GIVEN NAMES Italian 14%. *Enrico* (2), *Reno* (2), *Antonio*, *Carmela*, *Francesca*, *Giancarlo*, *Luciano*, *Premo*, *Riccardo*, *Rocco*, *Sal*, *Salvatore*.

Nicoll (948) Scottish: variant spelling of NICOL.

Nicolls (183) English, Scottish, and Irish: patronymic from NICOL.

GIVEN NAME Irish 4%. *Aileen* (2).

Nicolo (199) **1.** Southern Italian (mainly Sicily; **Nicolò**): from the personal name *Nicolo*, a reduced form of *Nicolao*, from Greek *Nikolaos* (see NICHOLAS). **2.** Greek: use of the Italian surname as a reduced form of Greek patronymic surnames such as **Nikolopoulos** or **Nikologlou**, or of compound names used as patronymics, such as **Nikolodimos** 'Dimitrios son of Nicholas', **Nikolothanassis** 'Athanasios son of Nicholas', or **Nikologiannis** 'John son of Nicholas'.

GIVEN NAMES Italian 22%; Spanish 5%. *Angelo* (2), *Rocco* (2), *Antonio*, *Carmine*, *Decio*, *Donato*, *Enrico*, *Mauro*, *Pasquale*, *Salvatore*, *Vincenzo*; *Diego* (2), *Demetrio*, *Fernando*, *Palmira*.

Nicoloff (142) Bulgarian: variant of NICKOLOFF.

Nicolosi (687) Italian (Sicily): habitational name from a place so called in Catania, which takes its name from a monastery dedicated to St. Nicholas.

GIVEN NAMES Italian 18%. *Angelo* (5), *Sal* (3), *Salvatore* (3), *Carmelo* (2), *Filippo* (2), *Nunzio* (2), *Santo* (2), *Vincenzo* (2), *Alessandra*, *Alfio*, *Antonella*, *Carmela*.

Nicols (170) English and Dutch: variant spelling of NICHOLS.

Nicolson (269) Scottish: patronymic from the personal name *Nicol* (see NICHOLAS).

GIVEN NAMES Scottish 8%. *Iain* (2), *Murdo* (2).

Nicosia (1028) Italian (Sicily): habitational name from a place so called in Enna.

GIVEN NAMES Italian 15%. *Salvatore* (14), *Angelo* (5), *Rocco* (3), *Sal* (3), *Santo* (3), *Antonio* (2), *Attilio* (2), *Giuseppe* (2), *Nunzio* (2), *Antonino*, *Benedetto*, *Carmelo*.

Nicoson (187) Variant of Scottish NICOLSON.

Nicotera (184) Southern Italian: habitational name from Nicotera in Calabria, which is named with the Greek personal name *Nikoteras* meaning 'miracle of victory'.

GIVEN NAMES Italian 22%. *Angelo* (4), *Vito* (3), *Antonino*, *Antonio*, *Raffaele*, *Rocco*, *Salvatore*, *Santo*.

Nicotra (265) Southern Italian (Sicily): from a reduced form of NICOTERA. This is one of the most common surnames in Catania province.

GIVEN NAMES Italian 20%. *Rosario* (5), *Salvatore* (5), *Alfio* (3), *Angelo* (2), *Antonio*, *Gerardo*, *Luigi*, *Marco*, *Sal*, *Santo*.

Nicpon (101) Origin unidentified.

Nida (478) German: habitational name from Nidda, a town (also a river) in Hesse. In some cases the surname was run together with the preposition *von* 'from', 'of', giving rise to the form **Vonada**, which is common in PA, and **Vonnieda** in Germany.

Niday (325) Probably an altered form of German NIDA.

Nidiffer (245) Americanized form of German **Neudorfer**, a habitational name for someone from any of numerous places called Neudorf, meaning 'new village'.

Nie (250) **1.** English: variant spelling of NYE. **2.** Chinese 聂: from the name of Nie City, which existed during the Spring and Autumn period (722–481 BC). It was granted to a son of a duke of the state of Qi; his descendants adopted the name of the city as their surname.

GIVEN NAMES Chinese 15%. *Xiaosong* (2), *Cui*, *Dawei*, *Fei*, *Fen*, *Feng*, *Geng*, *Hui*, *Hui Ling*, *Huiming*, *Jin*, *Jing*.

Niebauer (227) German: partly standardized form of Low German **Niebuhr** (see NEUBAUER).

Niebel (127) German: **1.** variant of NEBEL. **2.** habitational name from Niebel near Treuenbrietzen, or possibly a topographic name from the medieval river name *Nibel*.

Nieberding (111) German: Westphalian patronymic from *Nieber*, from the Germanic personal name *Nīdperht*, composed of *nīt* 'eagerness', 'hatred' + *berht* 'bright', 'famous'.

Niebergall (134) South German: nickname for someone who habitually failed to repay his debts, from Middle High German *nie* 'never' + a derivative of *vergelten* 'to repay'.

Nieblas (127) Spanish: apparently a topographic name for someone living in a place that was prone to fog, *niebla*, or possibly a habitational name. Niebla in Aragon is named with this word.

GIVEN NAMES Spanish 29%. *Jose* (4), *Jorge* (3), *Jose Luis* (2), *Abelardo*, *Alejandro*, *Arely*, *Arturo*, *Bernardo*, *Francisco*, *Idalia*, *Jesus*, *Miguel*.

Niebling (157) German: from a medieval personal name, representing the Germanic clan name *Nibelung* 'descendant of mist (or fog)' (from a name cognate with German *Nebel* 'mist', 'fog'). In Germanic mythology the Nibelungs were the doomed possessors of an immense hoard of treasure.
GIVEN NAME French 6%. *Andre* (2).

Nieboer (125) Dutch: epithet for a farmer who was new to an area, from Middle Low German *nie* 'new' + *boer* 'farmer'. Compare German NEUBAUER.

Niebrugge (138) Dutch and North German (**Niebrügge**): topographic name for someone living by a 'new bridge'.
GIVEN NAME German 4%. *Otto*.

Niebuhr (516) North German and Danish equivalent of NEUBAUER, or, as Søndergaard proposes, from a dialect form of German *Nachbar* 'neighbour'.
GIVEN NAMES German 8%. *Guenter* (2), *Hermann* (2), *Kurt* (2), *Frieda*, *Gerhard*, *Hans*, *Hertha*, *Horst*, *Otto*, *Ralf*, *Reinhold*.

Niebur (159) North German and Danish: variant of NIEBUHR.

Niec (110) Polish: origin uncertain. Possibilities include: **1.** diminutive from a variant of the given name *Mikołaj*, Latin *Nicolaus* (see NICHOLAS). **2.** from Old Polish *nieć* 'nephew or niece'.

Niece (344) Scottish and Irish: reduced form of MCNIECE, a variant spelling of MCNEESE.

Nied (236) South German: habitational name from Nied in Hesse.

Niedbala (141) Polish (**Niedbała**): nickname from *niedbały* 'negligent', 'careless', 'untidy'.
GIVEN NAMES Polish 5%. *Bronislaw*, *Kazimierz*.

Niedbalski (175) Polish: **1.** derivative of **Niedbała** (see NIEDBALA). **2.** possibly also a habitational name for someone from a place called Niedbałki.

Nieder (246) German and Jewish (Ashkenazic): topographic name for someone who lived at the lower end of a settlement, from Middle High German *nider*, German *nieder* 'lower', or a habitational name from any of many places called Nied (in Hesse), Niede, or Nidda.
GIVEN NAMES German 6%. *Klaus* (2), *Manfred* (2), *Otto*.

Niederberger (108) German and Swiss German: habitational name from any of various places named Niederberg, for example in North Rhine-Westphalia and the Rhineland Palatinate.
GIVEN NAMES German 11%. *Franz* (2), *Hans* (2), *Otto*.

Niederer (224) German: variant of NIEDER, from the inflected (masculine) form.

GIVEN NAMES German 8%. *Otto* (2), *Hans*, *Heino*, *Helmut*, *Wilhelm*.

Niederhauser (226) Swiss and German (also **Niederhäuser**): habitational name from any of numerous places named Niederhaus or Niederhausen, denoting the lower of two dwellings or settlements or one in a low-lying position.

Niederkorn (136) German: from Middle High German *nider* 'lower' + *korn* 'grain', possibly a nickname of anecdotal origin.

Niederman (162) Jewish (Ashkenazic) and German (**Niedermann**): elaborated form of NIEDER.
GIVEN NAMES Jewish 6%. *Asher*, *Gitty*.

Niedermayer (105) German: variant spelling of German NIEDERMEYER.

Niedermeier (181) German: variant spelling of NIEDERMEYER.
GIVEN NAMES German 9%. *Otto* (2), *Friedrich*, *Hans*, *Johann*.

Niedermeyer (281) German and Dutch: distinguishing name for a farmer (see MEYER) who had a farm lower (Middle High German *nider(e)*) than the neighboring one(s).
GIVEN NAMES German 5%. *Ernst*, *Franz*, *Otto*.

Niedert (146) German: **1.** contracted form of **Nithart** (see NEIDHART). **2.** variant of NIEDER with the addition of an excrescent *-t*.

Niedfeldt (153) German: topographic name for someone who lived 'by the lower area of open land', from Middle Low German *nider* 'lower' + *feld* 'open country'.

Niedringhaus (125) German: apparently a habitational name from a place called Niedringhausen, near Lübbeke, Westphalia; the place name, however, may be derived from the family name, which may have arisen as a topographic name, from Middle Low German *neddering(e)* 'depression', 'low lying (marsh) land' + *hüsen* '(at the) houses'.
GIVEN NAMES German 4%. *Kurt*, *Otto*.

Niedzielski (233) Polish: habitational name for someone from a place called Niedzieliska in the voivodeships of Płock, Tarnów, or Zamość, or Niedzielsko in Sieradz voivodeship. All of these places were probably named with *niedziela* 'Sunday' or with *Niedziel*, a nickname from *nie dzielić* 'don't divide'.
GIVEN NAMES Polish 7%. *Andrzej*, *Jacek*, *Jerzy*, *Tadeusz*, *Wasyl*.

Niedzwiecki (451) Polish (**Niedźwiecki**, **Niedźwiedski**): habitational name for someone from a place called Niedźwiedź, named with Polish *niedźwiedź* 'bear' (Old Polish *miedźwiedź*; compare MEDVED).
GIVEN NAMES Polish 9%. *Boguslawa*, *Czeslaw*, *Henryk*, *Ignatius*, *Jacek*, *Janusz*, *Jerzy*, *Kazimierz*, *Krzysztof*, *Malgorzata*, *Ryszard*, *Stanislaw*.

Niehaus (1415) North German: topographic name from Middle Low German *nie*

'new' + *hūs* 'house'; or a habitational name from a common North German and Westphalian farm name with the same meaning.

Niehoff (441) North German: topographic name from Middle Low German *nie* 'new' + *hof* 'farmstead', 'manor farm', or a habitational name from a common farm name with the same meaning.

Niehues (120) Dutch and North German: variant of NIEHUS.
GIVEN NAMES German 7%. *Fritz*, *Matthias*.

Niehus (157) North German: variant of NIEHAUS, with Low German *hus* as the second element.

Niekamp (263) North German and Dutch: topographic name from Middle Low German *nie* 'new' + *kamp* 'field', 'domain'.

Niel (105) Irish: variant spelling of NEILL.
GIVEN NAME Irish 4%. *Conley*.

Nieland (395) **1.** Dutch and North German: topographic name from Low German *nie* 'new' + *land* 'land', denoting newly reclaimed marshland, or a habitational name from places so named in Schleswig-Holstein and Westphalia. **2.** Irish: variant of NEALON.

Nield (325) Irish and Scottish: variant of NEILL. The excrescent *-d* results from an English mishearing of the devoicing of final *-l* in Gaelic.

Nielsen (16859) Danish, Norwegian, and North German (especially Schleswig-Holstein): patronymic from the personal name *Niels*, a reduced form of *Nikolaus* (see NICHOLAS).
GIVEN NAMES Scandinavian 9%. *Erik* (67), *Niels* (44), *Jorgen* (12), *Knud* (11), *Lars* (11), *Nels* (10), *Bent* (7), *Borge* (6), *Holger* (6), *Ove* (6), *Einer* (5), *Oluf* (5).

Nielsen (16859) Danish, Norwegian, and North German (especially Schleswig-Holstein): patronymic from the personal name *Niels*, a reduced form of *Nikolaus* (see NICHOLAS) or CORNELIUS.
GIVEN NAMES Scandinavian 9%. *Erik* (67), *Niels* (44), *Jorgen* (12), *Knud* (11), *Lars* (11), *Nels* (10), *Bent* (7), *Borge* (6), *Holger* (6), *Ove* (6), *Einer* (5), *Oluf* (5).

Nieman (1945) Dutch, North German (**Niemann**), and Danish: **1.** nickname for a newcomer to a place, from *nie* 'new' (variant of German *neu* or Dutch *nieuw*) + *man* 'man'. **2.** Perhaps also from *niemand* 'nobody', hence a nickname for an orphan or a person of no account.

Niemann (1760) North German form of NEUMANN, from Middle Low German *nie* + *man*.
GIVEN NAMES German 4%. *Kurt* (4), *Hans* (3), *Claus* (2), *Ernst* (2), *Erwin* (2), *Eldred*, *Erna*, *Gerhard*, *Hasso*, *Irmgard*, *Jochen*, *Juergen*.

Niemczyk (390) Polish and Jewish (from Poland): ethnic or regional name from a diminutive or patronymic from Polish NIEMIEC 'German'.

GIVEN NAMES Polish 5%. *Andrzej, Casimir, Jacek, Miroslaw*.

Niemeier (506) German: variant spelling of NIEMEYER.

Niemela (307) Finnish (**Niemelä**): from *niemi* 'peninsula', 'headland' + the local suffix -*la*, either ornamental or a habitational name from a farm name. This surname occurs predominantly in western Finland.

GIVEN NAMES Finnish 9%; Scandinavian 4%. *Eino* (2), *Reino* (2), *Waino* (2), *Armas, Arto, Esko, Helvi, Raino, Veikko*; *Jarl, Lars, Nels*.

Niemeyer (1797) North German: nickname for a newly arrived steward or tenant farmer, from Middle Low German *nie* 'new' + MEYER.

GIVEN NAMES German 4%. *Kurt* (3), *Elke* (2), *Lorenz* (2), *Otto* (2), *Claus, Eldred, Erna, Frieda, Gerhart, Guenter, Ulrich*.

Niemi (1999) Finnish: from *niemi* 'peninsula', 'headland', originally a habitational name from a farm so named for its situation. In the late 19th century it was a popular ornamental adoption, so much so that people then began to change it for a less common name. It occurs chiefly in western Finland. In America, it is also found as an abbreviation of other surnames containing this element, such as **Rajaniemi, Sotaniemi**, and **Syrj(a:)niemi**.

GIVEN NAMES Finnish 7%. *Eino* (10), *Reino* (7), *Arvo* (4), *Waino* (4), *Eero* (3), *Niilo* (3), *Urho* (3), *Armi* (2), *Lempi* (2), *Onni* (2), *Sulo* (2), *Vieno* (2).

Niemiec (808) Polish and Jewish (from Poland): ethnic or regional name from the vocabulary word *niemiec* 'German'. Compare NEMEC.

GIVEN NAMES Polish 7%. *Stanislaw* (2), *Casimier, Casimir, Henryk, Ignatius, Ireneusz, Jadwiga, Janusz, Jerzy, Krystyna, Ludwik, Mieczyslaw*.

Niemuth (246) German: probably a nickname, either for a cheerful person, from Middle Low German *nie, nige mōt* 'new spirit'; or, in the south, for a belligerent or aggressive person, from Middle High German *nīt* 'hostile attitude' + *muot* 'attitude', 'sense'.

Nienaber (396) North German: nickname from Low German *nie* 'new' + *nabur* 'neighbor'.

Nienhaus (193) North German: partly standardized form of **Nienhus**, a North German equivalent of NEUHAUS, in which the first element is inflected (i.e. 'at the new house').

GIVEN NAMES German 5%. *Aloys, Juergen, Uli, Ulrike*.

Nienhuis (269) Dutch: topographic name for someone living at a 'new house' (a reduced form of *nieuwenhuis*).

GIVEN NAMES German 4%. *Erwin* (2), *Eldred*.

Nienow (241) German: unexplained. It is probably a variant of German **Nienau**, which is also unexplained.

Nienstedt (117) **1.** German and Dutch: topographic name for someone living in 'the new town'. **2.** German: habitational name from any of several places named Nienstedt in northern Germany, Saxony, and former East Prussia.

Nier (183) **1.** South German: contracted form of NIEDER. **2.** German: from the personal name *Nithart* (see NEIDHART). **3.** German: variant of NEER (see NEHER). **4.** Southern French (Occitan) and Catalan: nickname from Occitan *nier* 'black' (from Latin *niger*).

GIVEN NAME French 5%. *Henri* (2).

Nierenberg (232) Jewish (Ashkenazic): habitational name from the city of Nuremberg in northern Bavaria, Yiddish name *Nirnberg*, German name *Nürnberg*, or from another place similarly named.

Nierman (317) **1.** Jewish (Ashkenazic): of uncertain origin, perhaps from Yiddish *nir* or German *Niere* 'kidney' + German *Mann* 'man'. This surname is now well established in Mexico. **2.** Respelling of German NIERMANN.

GIVEN NAMES Jewish 4%. *Dov* (2), *Gittel, Yaffa*.

Niermann (144) **1.** North German: variant of **Nee(h)rmann**, a nickname from *nee(h)r*, a reduced form of Low German *neder* 'low' + *man* 'man'. **2.** German: enlarged form of NIEMANN with inflected (masculine) form as the first part, *neuer Mann* 'new man'.

GIVEN NAMES German 10%. *Gerhard, Guenter, Hans, Klaus, Volker*.

Nies (875) North German and Dutch: **1.** from a reduced form of the personal name *Dionys* (see DENNIS), which was stressed on the last syllable; this was a popular personal name as a result of the influence of the French Saint Denis. **2.** possibly in some cases from the female personal name *Agnes*, also a saint's name, in the form of *Agnise*.

Niese (353) North German and Dutch: **1.** variant of NIES. **2.** habitational name from a place so named near Detmold.

Niesen (636) **1.** Dutch: patronymic from the personal name *Nijs*, a reduced form of *Denijs* (see DENNIS). **2.** German (frequent in the Rhineland): metronymic from a reduced form of the personal name *Agnes*. **3.** German: variant of NIES.

Niess (170) German: variant of NIES 1.

GIVEN NAMES German 5%. *Berthold, Irmgard*.

Niessen (127) German (Rhineland): patronymic from the personal name NIES.

GIVEN NAMES German 11%. *Wolfgang* (2), *Guenter, Hans, Manfred, Wolfram*.

Nieters (145) German: patronymic from the Germanic personal name *Nither*, composed of *nīt* 'ambition', 'hatred' + *heri* 'army'.

Nietfeld (102) North German: variant of NIEDFELDT.

Nieto (2504) Spanish: nickname for someone descended from a prominent elder in a community or one whose memory was respected, from Spanish *nieto* 'grandson' (Latin *nepos*, genitive *nep(o)tis*, 'grandson', 'nephew').

GIVEN NAMES Spanish 45%. *Jose* (77), *Juan* (33), *Manuel* (22), *Jesus* (20), *Carlos* (19), *Francisco* (17), *Luis* (15), *Mario* (12), *Pedro* (12), *Armando* (11), *Guadalupe* (11), *Miguel* (11).

Nietupski (102) Polish: habitational name for someone from Nietupa in Białystok voivodeship.

GIVEN NAMES Polish 5%. *Kasmier, Wladyslawa*.

Nietz (107) German: variant of NITZ.

Nieuwenhuis (150) Dutch: topographic name for someone living in a new house, from Middle Dutch *n(i)uwe* 'new' + *huus* 'house', or a habitational name from a place so named.

GIVEN NAMES German 5%; Dutch 4%. *Kurt; Dirk, Gerrit*.

Nieves (3260) Spanish: **1.** religious byname, from the title *María de las Nieves* 'Mary of the Snows', given particularly to children born on 5 August, on which date the Virgin allegedly once caused it to snow in Rome. It is possible that the surname derives in part from a nickname for someone with snow-white hair. **2.** Castilianized form of the Galician and Asturian-Leonese habitational name NEVES.

GIVEN NAMES Spanish 45%. *Jose* (91), *Luis* (57), *Miguel* (33), *Carlos* (31), *Juan* (28), *Angel* (26), *Rafael* (24), *Francisco* (19), *Jesus* (19), *Luz* (18), *Manuel* (17), *Ramon* (16).

Niewald (115) North German: from a Low German variant of German **Neuwald** 'new forest'.

Niewiadomski (117) Polish: habitational name for someone from Niewiadom in Katowice voivodeship or Niewiadoma in Siedlce voivodeship, probably both places so named from *niewiadomy* 'unknown'.

GIVEN NAMES Polish 11%. *Andrzej, Jaroslaw, Leszek, Mariusz, Zdzislaw*.

Niewiarowski (41) Polish: habitational name for someone from Niewiarów in Kraków voivodeship, or places called Niewiarowa in Białystok and Łomża voivodeships, probably so named from *niewiara* 'disbelief'.

Niewinski (104) Polish: habitational name for someone from Niewino in Białystok voivodeship.

GIVEN NAMES Polish 19%. *Ewa, Henryk, Ireneusz, Jacek, Jerzy, Krzysztof, Mikolaj, Walerian*.

Niewoehner (136) North German (**Niewöhner**): nickname for a new neighbor or settler, from Low German *nie* 'new' +

wöhner 'dweller', 'settler' (an agent derivative of *wohnen* 'to dwell').

Niezgoda (189) Polish: nickname for a quarrelsome person, from *niezgoda* 'discord'.

GIVEN NAME Polish 4%. *Grazyna*.

Niffenegger (100) Swiss German: probably a topographic name of the same origin as **Niffern**, a habitational name from Nufringen in Swabia, formerly Nüfferen, Niffern + *egger*, from Middle High German *ecke* 'corner'.

Nifong (293) Probably an altered spelling of German **Neufang**, a nickname for a new settler or a topographic name for someone who lived on newly cleared land, from Middle High German *niuvanc*.

Nigam (110) Indian (northern states): Hindu (Kayasth) name, based on the name of a subgroup of the Kayasth community. In Hindi, the word *nigəm* (from Sanskrit *nigama*) has several meanings, including 'path', 'market', and 'determination'.

GIVEN NAMES Indian 93%. *Anil* (3), *Ashok* (3), *Madhu* (3), *Ravi* (3), *Alok* (2), *Archna* (2), *Chander* (2), *Himanshu* (2), *Pratap* (2), *Rishi* (2), *Vivek* (2), *Ajay*.

Nigg (215) South German and Swiss German: from a short form of the personal name *Niklaus*, a German form of NICHOLAS.

Nigh (679) Probably an altered spelling of English NYE, or possibly an Americanized spelling of German NEU or NEY.

Nighswander (122) Americanized spelling of NEUSCHWANDER.

Nighswonger (169) Americanized spelling of NEUSCHWANDER.

Nightengale (354) English: variant of NIGHTINGALE.

Nightingale (1514) **1.** English: nickname for someone with a good voice, from Middle English *nighti(n)gale* (Old English *nihtegal*, from *niht* 'night' + *galan* 'sing'). **2.** Probably a translation of German and Jewish NACHTIGALL, or cognates in other languages.

Nigl (104) Respelling of South German and Austrian **Niggl**: from a pet form of the personal name NIKOLAUS.

GIVEN NAME German 9%. *Otto* (2).

Nigrelli (177) Southern Italian: patronymic from a diminutive of NIGRO.

GIVEN NAMES Italian 20%. *Antonino* (2), *Santo* (2), *Aldo*, *Cosimo*, *Cosmo*, *Domenic*, *Domenico*, *Francesco*, *Lucio*, *Sal*, *Sebastiano*, *Vito*.

Nigro (1807) Southern Italian: nickname from *nigro* 'black' (Latin *niger*).

GIVEN NAMES Italian 13%. *Angelo* (10), *Rocco* (9), *Salvatore* (7), *Antonio* (5), *Carmine* (5), *Vito* (5), *Dante* (3), *Dino* (3), *Vincenzo* (2), *Alfonse*, *Amato*, *Aniello*.

Nihart (201) German: variant of NEUHART.

Nihill (132) Irish (County Clare): variant of O'NEILL.

GIVEN NAME Irish 6%. *Brendan*.

Nihiser (129) Altered spelling of German **Neuhäuser** (see NEUHAUSER).

Nii (112) Japanese: variously written, sometimes with characters used phonetically, the most probable meanings are 'two wells' or 'new well'. The name is not common in Japan.

GIVEN NAMES Japanese 41%. *Yuko* (3), *Aiko*, *Hideaki*, *Hiroki*, *Hiroyuki*, *Isamu*, *Kaoru*, *Katsumi*, *Keiichiro*, *Kenji*, *Masako*, *Masayuki*.

Nikas (113) Greek: from the personal name *Nikas*, a pet form of *Nikolaos* (see NICHOLAS) or NIKITAS.

GIVEN NAMES Greek 22%. *Demetrios* (2), *Dimitrios* (2), *Dimitris* (2), *Andreas*, *Despina*, *Kalliope*, *Vasilis*.

Nikirk (138) Americanized spelling of Dutch NEIKIRK.

Nikitas (111) Greek: from the personal name *Nikētas*, a derivative of *nikān* 'conquer'. This name was popular among early Christians as an allusion to Christ's victory over death, and was borne by several saints, including a 4th-century converted Ostrogoth and a 5th-century missionary to Dacia. Both have a more active cult in the Orthodox Church than the Roman Catholic.

GIVEN NAMES Greek 6%. *Dimitrios*, *Rigas*, *Stavroula*.

Nikkel (387) Possibly an altered spelling of Dutch **Nikel**, from the personal name, a Dutch form of NICHOLAS.

Niklas (112) German: variant of NIKOLAUS.

GIVEN NAME German 4%. *Otto*.

Nikodem (107) German and central European: from a personal name of Greek origin, composed of the elements *nikē* 'victory' + *dēmos* 'people'. This is the name borne in the New Testament by a Greek Jew who defended Jesus before the religious leaders (John 7:50) and was present at his burial (John 19:39).

Nikolai (282) North German and Dutch: from the Latin genitive case (patronymic) of the personal name *Nikolaus* (see NICHOLAS).

GIVEN NAMES German 6%. *Erhard* (2), *Hans*, *Kurt*, *Willi*, *Wolfram*.

Nikolas (119) **1.** German: variant of NIKOLAUS. **2.** Greek: from the personal name *Nikolaos* (see NICHOLAS), or a reduced form of derivative surnames such as **Papanikolaou** '(son of) Nicholas the Priest' and **Hatzinikolaou** '(son of) Nicholas the Pilgrim'.

Nikolaus (180) German: from the personal name, a German form of the Greek personal name *Nikolaos* (see NICHOLAS). After *Johann* and *Peter*, *Nikolaus* was the third most popular personal name in medieval Germany.

Nikolic (165) Serbian and Croatian (**Nikolić**): patronymic from the personal name *Nikola*, Serbian and Croatian form of NICHOLAS.

GIVEN NAMES South Slavic 58%; Russian 6%. *Dragan* (3), *Miodrag* (3), *Budimir* (2), *Radovan* (2), *Aleksandar*, *Blagoje*, *Bogoljub*, *Bosko*, *Branimir*, *Branislav*, *Branka*, *Branko*, *Djordje*, *Dragica*, *Dusan*, *Milan*, *Zlata*; *Igor*, *Jelena*, *Josip*, *Milutin*, *Pavle*, *Sava*.

Nikolich (128) Serbian and Croatian (**Nikolić**): see NIKOLIC.

GIVEN NAMES South Slavic 20%; Russian 4%; Czech and Slovak 4%. *Branko*, *Dragi*, *Drago*, *Gordana*, *Jonce*, *Milovan*, *Petar*, *Sanja*, *Slavko*, *Srdjan*, *Srecko*; *Aleks*, *Boris*, *Luka*; *Milan* (2), *Radmila*, *Zdenka*.

Nikula (105) Finnish: from the personal name *Niku*, Finnish form of NICHOLAS + the local suffix *-la*. Common nowadays in western Finland.

GIVEN NAMES Scandinavian 6%; Finnish 6%. *Erik*; *Eino*, *Heimo*, *Orvo*.

Nilan (219) Irish: variant of NEALON.

Niland (452) **1.** Variant spelling of Scandinavian NYLAND. **2.** Irish: variant of NEALON. **3.** Probably an altered spelling of German or Dutch NIELAND.

Nile (158) English: perhaps a variant of NEIL.

Niles (3513) **1.** English: perhaps a patronymic from the medieval personal name *Nel* or *Neal* (see NELSON). **2.** Possibly a variant of German NEILS, a derivative of the personal name CORNELIUS.

FOREBEARS John Niles from England was known to have been in Dorchester, MA, as early as 1634 before putting down roots in Braintree, MA, where his grandson Samuel was a Congregational clergyman for many years.

Nilges (226) North German: from a reduced and altered pet form of the personal name CORNELIUS.

GIVEN NAME French 4%. *Jean-Marie*.

Nill (315) **1.** North German: from a personal name, a reduced form of CORNELIUS. **2.** South German: nickname for a big, crude or unmannered person, related to Middle High German *nel* 'peak' or *nol* 'rounded elevation'.

GIVEN NAMES German 4%. *Eldred*, *Hans*, *Ulrich*.

Nilles (503) North German: patronymic from NILL 1.

Nilsen (1649) Norwegian: patronymic from the personal name *Nils*, a reduced form of *Nikolaus* (see NICHOLAS).

GIVEN NAMES Scandinavian 18%; German 4%. *Erik* (14), *Nils* (9), *Alf* (5), *Bjorn* (5), *Lars* (5), *Per* (4), *Nels* (3), *Anders* (2), *Bente* (2), *Tor* (2), *Arnfinn*, *Astrid*; *Hans* (5), *Kurt* (5), *Ralf* (2), *Arnulf*, *Otto*.

Nilson (1124) Americanized spelling of Swedish NILSSON or Norwegian NILSEN.

GIVEN NAMES Scandinavian 7%. *Nils* (5), *Erik* (2), *Alvar*, *Holger*, *Kristoffer*, *Mats*, *Sven*.

Nilsson (1327) Swedish: patronymic from the personal name *Nils*, a reduced form of *Nikolaus* (see NICHOLAS).

GIVEN NAMES Scandinavian 27%; German 5%. *Erik* (12), *Lars* (12), *Nils* (11), *Per* (9), *Anders* (5), *Egil* (3), *Lennart* (3), *Sven* (3), *Birgit* (2), *Fredrik* (2), *Sten* (2), *Algot; Kurt* (5), *Hans* (3), *Otto* (2), *Gerhard, Gotthard, Karl-Heinz*.

Niman (147) **1.** English: variant of NEWMAN. **2.** Americanized form of various European cognates with the same meaning, for example NEUMANN. (For other forms, see Hanks and Hodges 1988.)

Nimmer (309) **1.** German: habitational name from Nimmer, Westphalia, derived from a prehistoric word *nim, nam*, with a probable meaning of 'marsh'. **2.** South German: from the personal name *Nidmar*, composed of Old High German *nīt* 'hostility' + *mar* 'famous'.

GIVEN NAMES German 4%. *Armin, Kurt, Otto*.

Nimmo (1051) Scottish: unexplained. According to Black, the earliest forms of this name are *Newmoch* (1459), *Nemoch* (1490), and *Nemok* (1587). Forms with *-i-* are not found before the 17th century.

Nimmons (297) Northern Irish: probably a variant of Scottish NIMMO.

Nimon (135) Probably a variant of Scottish NIMMO.

GIVEN NAMES Jewish 5%. *Aron, Fira, Yael*.

Nims (711) Origin uncertain. **1.** It is most probably an altered from of German NIMTZ (see NEMETZ). **2.** It has also been suggested that it may be an Anglicized form of French **Nîmes**, and so a habitational name from the city of this name. However, the evidence in support of this hypothesis seems to depend largely on the similarity in spelling.

Nimtz (240) German (of Slavic origin): see NEMETZ.

Nimz (178) German: variant of NIMTZ.

Nine (373) Americanized spelling of German NEIN or **Neun**, from Middle High German *niun* 'nine' (see NEUNER).

Niner (192) Altered spelling of German NEUNER.

Ning (155) Chinese 宁: from the name of a place called Ning, which existed in the state of Wei during the Spring and Autumn period (722–481 BC).

GIVEN NAMES Chinese 58%. *Kuan* (2), *Ping* (2), *Aihua, Chi, Chin, Ching, Chong, Chun, Fong, Gang, Guang, Hongjun, Hsiao, Hu, Nu, Quan, Xuan, Yen*.

Nini (128) **1.** Italian: patronymic or plural form of NINO. **2.** Greek (**Ninis**): probably from the Italian personal name NINO.

GIVEN NAMES Italian 21%. *Antonio, Dante, Eduardo, Eufronio, Gumersindo, Liliana, Marco, Primo, Remo, Roberto, Sebastiano*.

Ninneman (266) Variant of North German NINNEMANN.

Ninnemann (116) North German: unexplained. Probably a variant of **Nünemann**,

an occupational name or a status name for someone on a council of nine men, from Middle Low German *niun* 'nine' + *man* 'man'.

Nino (933) **1.** Spanish (**Niño**): nickname from Spanish *niño* 'child', 'boy'. This was often given to a first-born son as a familiar name. **2.** Italian: from the personal name *Nino*, a short form of *Antonino* or *Giovannino*, pet forms of ANTONIO and GIOVANNI respectively. **3.** Greek (**Ninos**): from the personal name *Ninos*, a pet form of *Konstantinos* (see CONSTANTINE).

GIVEN NAMES Spanish 47%. *Jose* (29), *Juan* (15), *Carlos* (13), *Manuel* (13), *Jesus* (10), *Luis* (7), *Raul* (7), *Ruben* (6), *Alfredo* (5), *Andres* (5), *Arturo* (5), *Jaime* (5).

Nipp (282) German: probably a nickname for an alert, sharp person, from Middle Low German *nip* 'of keen eyesight and hearing' (in Altmark dialect now meaning 'well mannered', 'cute').

Nipper (1340) German: **1.** habitational name for someone from Nippe in Hesse. **2.** nickname for an alert, astute person, from Middle Low German *nip* 'exact', 'sharp'' (of sight and hearing)', the *-er* reflecting the full (masculine) ending.

Nippert (170) German: from a Germanic personal name composed of the elements *nīt* 'hatred', 'hostility' + *berht* 'bright', 'illustrious', or a habitational name derived from Nippern in Silesia.

GIVEN NAME French 4%. *Clovis*.

Nipple (117) Americanized spelling of German **Nippel**, which is probably from a Germanic personal name composed of the elements *nīt* 'hostility' + *bald* 'brave'.

Nipps (112) English: unexplained; perhaps a variant of **Nopps**, itself a variant of NOBBS. Compare KNIBBS.

Niquette (203) Probably an altered spelling of French **Niquet**, a nickname from Old French *niquet* 'nod', or from a pet form of *Nique*, a short form of NICOLAS. The spelling reflects the Canadian practice of sounding the final *-t*, which is not the practice in France.

GIVEN NAMES French 12%. *Armand* (4), *Clemence* (2), *Aristide, Emile, Flore, Lucien, Manon*.

Nirenberg (176) Jewish (eastern Ashkenazic): variant spelling of NIERENBERG.

GIVEN NAMES Jewish 12%; Russian 9%. *Bentsion, Hyman, Isaak, Meyer, Rimma, Shalom; Mikhail* (5), *Boris, Gennady, Raisa, Serafima, Vladimir*.

Niro (186) Italian: southern variant of NERO, from *niro, niru* 'black' (Latin *niger*).

GIVEN NAMES Italian 22%. *Antonio* (3), *Pietro* (3), *Donato* (2), *Enrico* (2), *Alfonse, Arsenio, Benito, Berardino, Corrado, Cosimo, Domenic, Gennaro, Luciano, Marco*.

Nirschl (107) South German: unexplained.

Nisbet (905) Scottish: variant of NESBITT.

Nisbett (227) Scottish: variant of NESBITT.

Nish (150) **1.** Scottish and Irish: reduced variant of MCNEESE. **2.** Altered spelling of German **Nisch**, from a pet form of the personal name *Nikolaus* (see NICHOLAS).

Nishi (282) Japanese: 'west'; mostly found in the islands of Kyūshū, where two samurai families were based, and Okinawa. In some cases, the name may be a shortened form of other names beginning with *Nishi-*.

GIVEN NAMES Japanese 56%. *Tomohiko* (12), *Masao* (3), *Yoshio* (3), *Kazuo* (2), *Masahiko* (2), *Nobuo* (2), *Noriko* (2), *Akihiko, Akihiro, Akira, Akiyo, Etsuko*.

Nishida (372) Japanese: 'western rice paddy'; mostly found in western Japan and the island of Okinawa.

GIVEN NAMES Japanese 57%. *Kazuo* (3), *Hiroshi* (2), *Katsumi* (2), *Katsunori* (2), *Kosaku* (2), *Masa* (2), *Masao* (2), *Norimasa* (2), *Shigeru* (2), *Takaaki* (2), *Takeshi* (2), *Tomoko* (2).

Nishihara (121) Japanese: 'western plain'; mostly found in western Japan and the island of Okinawa, where it is also pronounced **Nishibaru**. Some bearers have MINAMOTO or FUJIWARA origins.

GIVEN NAMES Japanese 44%. *Hide* (2), *Masa* (2), *Atsuo, Hidehiro, Kazuaki, Kenji, Kimie, Koichi, Mikio, Mitsugi, Noboru, Ryuzo*.

Nishikawa (294) Japanese: 'western river'; mostly found in western Japan and the Ryūkyū Islands. A less common, alternative pronunciation, **Saikawa**, is from eastern Japan. A few bearers are of samurai origin.

GIVEN NAMES Japanese 64%. *Keizo* (4), *Hiroshi* (3), *Kazuo* (3), *Koji* (3), *Masao* (3), *Takashi* (3), *Akihiro* (2), *Hiro* (2), *Kenji* (2), *Kimiko* (2), *Kiyo* (2), *Kiyoshi* (2).

Nishimoto (434) Japanese: '(one who lives) to the west'; mostly found in western Japan and the Ryūkyū Islands.

GIVEN NAMES Japanese 36%. *Masao* (4), *Hideo* (2), *Kazuo* (2), *Masami* (2), *Shig* (2), *Torao* (2), *Yoko* (2), *Yoshiji* (2), *Akira, Atsushi, Emiko, Fumio*.

Nishimura (889) Japanese: 'western village', a common place name and surname; the surname is found mostly in northeastern Japan and the island of Okinawa. Some bearers are of samurai descent.

GIVEN NAMES Japanese 46%. *Akira* (4), *Hiroshi* (4), *Koichiro* (4), *Makoto* (4), *Fumiko* (3), *Hiro* (3), *Hiroyuki* (3), *Ichiro* (3), *Keiji* (3), *Shigeru* (3), *Takashi* (3), *Akio* (2).

Nishioka (203) Japanese: 'western hill', a common place name and surname; the surname is found mostly in western Japan and the island of Okinawa. Some bearers are of samurai descent.

GIVEN NAMES Japanese 49%. *Kenji* (3), *Toshio* (3), *Masao* (2), *Rikio* (2), *Takeshi* (2), *Tsutomu* (2), *Akira, Arata, Atsumi, Atsuo, Chie, Chiyoko*.

Nishiyama (173) Japanese: 'western mountain', a common place name and surname;

the surname is found mostly in western Japan and the island of Okinawa. Some bearers are descended from the FUJIWARA clan.

GIVEN NAMES Japanese 62%. *Kaoru* (4), *Hitoshi* (3), *Fumie* (2), *Hiroshi* (2), *Masanori* (2), *Shigeru* (2), *Yasuo* (2), *Yosuke* (2), *Akira, Emiko, Fumio, Ikuko.*

Niska (116) Finnish: topographic name from a place named with *niska* 'neck', i.e. an isthmus.

GIVEN NAMES German 5%. *Kurt* (2), *Hans.*

Niskanen (169) Finnish: from *niska* 'neck' + the common surname suffix *-nen,* applied either as a topographic name referring to some geographical feature such as a mountain ridge, rapids, or an isthmus, or as a nickname for a stubborn person. It is found chiefly in central Finland and can be traced back to the 16th century.

GIVEN NAMES Finnish 8%; Scandinavian 4%. *Armas, Eino, Heikki, Olavi, Sulo, Veijo; Erland.*

Nisley (203) Of German origin: see NISS-LEY.

Nisly (157) Of German origin: see NISSLEY.

Niss (128) **1.** German and Danish: assimilated form of *Nils,* a contraction of *Nikolaus* (see NICHOLAS). **2.** Americanized spelling of German **Nüss** 'nut' (see NUSS 2). **3.** Jewish (from Ukraine and Poland): ornamental name from Yiddish dialect *nis* 'nut' (cognate with German *Nüss;* see 1).

GIVEN NAME Jewish 4%. *Batya.*

Nissan (139) Jewish (Israeli): ornamental name from the name of the Jewish month during which Passover takes place.

GIVEN NAMES Jewish 21%; Muslim 20%. *Amnon* (2), *Avraham, Doron, Ilan, Limor, Ofer, Reuven, Ronen, Uzi, Zahava; Sami* (3), *Samir* (2), *Akram, Batoul, Farid, Hani, Imad, Khalid, Muhannad, Nabeel, Nawal, Nazar.*

Nissen (2180) **1.** Jewish (Ashkenazic): from the Yiddish male personal name *Nisn,* from Hebrew *nisan,* the Jewish month during which Passover takes place, originally given to boys born in that month. Compare ODER and NISSAN. **2.** German and Danish: patronymic from the Scandinavian personal name *Nis,* variant of *Nils* (see NICHOLAS).

GIVEN NAMES German 4%. *Hans* (4), *Inge* (3), *Lorenz* (3), *Kurt* (2), *Bernhardt, Egon, Helmut, Helmuth, Horst, Lieschen, Mathias, Otto.*

Nissenbaum (195) Jewish (Ashkenazic): ornamental name from German *Nüsse* 'nuts' + *Baum* 'tree'. The transformation of *ü* into *i* (unrounding) is due to Yiddish influence.

GIVEN NAMES Jewish 8%. *Hillel, Meyer, Miriam, Moshe.*

Nissim (118) Jewish (Sephardic): from the Hebrew male personal name *Nissim,* meaning 'miracles'.

GIVEN NAMES Jewish 22%; French 7%. *Itzhak* (2), *Igal, Meir, Moshe, Nissim, Pinhas, Sasson, Yosi; Marcel* (2), *Alphonse.*

Nissley (481) **1.** Americanized spelling of German **Nissle,** a pet form of the personal names *Dionys* (DENIS) or *Nikolaus* (see NICHOLAS). **2.** Americanized spelling of German **Nüssli, Nüssle, Nüsslein,** topographic names for someone who lived near a place where nut trees grew, from Middle High German *nuz* 'nut' + the diminutive suffix *-le, -lein.* **3.** Altered spelling of North German **Nissler** or **Nüssler,** a nickname for a slow worker, from Low German *nusse* 'slow, weak person'.

Nisson (132) Jewish: variant of NISSEN.

GIVEN NAME French 5%. *Andre.*

Nist (252) Welsh: variant of NEST.

Nistler (314) German: variant of NESTLER.

GIVEN NAMES German 4%. *Erwin* (2), *Florian, Kurt, Reinhart.*

Niswander (318) Altered spelling of German NEUSCHWANDER (see NEUEN-SCHWANDER) or of the Dutch cognate **Nijswander.**

Niswonger (507) Altered spelling of German NEUSCHWANGER, variant of **Neuschwander** (see NEUENSCHWANDER) or of the Dutch cognate, **Nijswander.**

Nitchman (114) Probably an Americanized form of German **Nitschmann,** a derivative of NITSCH.

Nitka (181) Polish and Jewish (from Poland): nickname from Polish *nitka,* 'thread'; either a nickname for a thin man or (as a Jewish name) also a metonymic occupational name for a tailor. This name is also established in Germany.

GIVEN NAMES French 4%. *Gaston, Laurette.*

Nitsch (316) Eastern German (Silesian; under Slavic influence): from a pet form of the personal name *Nikolaus* (see NICHOLAS).

GIVEN NAMES German 9%. *Guenther* (2), *Erhard, Gunter, Helmuth, Kurt, Otto, Wolfgang.*

Nitsche (254) German: variant of NITSCH.

GIVEN NAMES German 7%. *Gerhard, Johannes, Manfred, Otto, Rainer.*

Nitschke (604) Eastern German (Silesia; under Slavic influence): from a pet form of the personal name *Nikolaus* (see NICHOLAS).

GIVEN NAMES German 8%. *Kurt* (3), *Klaus* (2), *Arno, Dieter, Erwin, Georg, Horst, Lorenz, Otto.*

Nitta (289) Japanese: 'new rice paddy'; mostly found in western Japan. The most famous Nitta family took the name from their residence in Kōzuke (now Gunma prefecture). They descended from Minamoto no Yoshishige (died 1202), who was also the ancestor of the Tokugawa. One descendant, Nitta Yoshisada (1301–38) was the major opponent of Ashikaga Takauji in the latter's bid for the Shogunate, in which Takauji was confirmed the year of Yoshi-

sada's death in battle. At this time there was a schism in the imperial family, with rival emperors ruling from separate courts. Takauji supported each side in turn, as it suited him politically, but Yoshisada is to this day revered as the champion of the southern (considered 'legitimate') court. Alternative readings of the surname are **Arata** (mostly found in the Ryūkyū Islands) and **Shinden.**

GIVEN NAMES Japanese 41%. *Isao* (2), *Junichi* (2), *Masako* (2), *Naoki* (2), *Yoshiko* (2), *Akihiko, Atsuko, Fujio, Goro, Hiroshi, Hisako, Isamu.*

Nitti (276) Italian: patronymic from the personal name *Nitto,* a pet form of *Benedetto,* or more likely of the Latin form, *Benedictus* (see BENEDICT), or of GIOVANNI.

GIVEN NAMES Italian 12%. *Gino* (2), *Vito* (2), *Carmel, Giuseppe, Luigi.*

Nitz (941) German (under Slavic influence): from a pet form of the personal name *Nikolaus* (see NICHOLAS).

GIVEN NAMES German 5%. *Benno* (2), *Kurt* (2), *Erwin, Gerhardt, Guenter, Gunter, Hans, Hertha, Klaus, Lothar, Manfred, Wendelin.*

Nitzberg (137) Jewish (from Belarus): of unknown origin.

GIVEN NAMES Jewish 8%. *Hyman, Meyer.*

Nitzel (171) Eastern German (under Slavic influence): from a pet form of the personal name *Nikolaus* (see NICHOLAS).

Nitzsche (192) German: from a pet form of the personal name *Nikolaus* (see NICHOLAS).

GIVEN NAMES German 9%. *Horst* (2), *Heinz, Helmut, Jurgen, Monika.*

Niu (174) **1.** Chinese 牛: this name probably arose during the Zhou dynasty (1122–221 BC) in the area of Gansu province; the details are unclear. It was borne by a person named Niu Wen, who was a descendant of the eldest brother of the last king of the Shang dynasty, Zhou Xin (1154–1123BC). **2.** Chinese 钮: a second character pronounced **Niu** came into use as a surname during the Eastern Jin dynasty (317–420 AD) in Jiangsu province south of the Yangtze river. **3.** Tongan: unexplained.

GIVEN NAMES Chinese 37%. *Ming* (2), *Baohua, Cheng, Chi-Sheng, Chien, Chuan, Feng, Gang, Jiayi, Kejian, Li, Li Min.*

Niva (100) Finnish: topographic name from *niva* 'small rapids', 'river shallows', or 'ford'. This name is found chiefly in northern Finland.

GIVEN NAMES Finnish 4%. *Eino, Ilkka.*

Niven (602) Scottish: variant of NEVIN.

Nivens (593) Scottish: variant of NEVIN.

Niver (345) Americanized spelling of Dutch **Knijver,** borne by a family that is recorded in the 17th-century Dutch colony of New Amsterdam.

Nivison (157) Scottish: patronymic from NEVIN.

Niwa (104) Japanese: variously written, sometimes with characters used phonetically, the most probable meanings are 'two wings' or 'garden'. Two noble families, one descended from the MINAMOTO and the other from the FUJIWARA, both originated in Owari (now part of Aichi prefecture). The name is not common in Japan and is found mostly along the southeastern seaboard.

GIVEN NAMES Japanese 62%. *Yuko* (3), *Hiromi* (2), *Junichiro* (2), *Rie* (2), *Akio, Atsuhiko, Hiroo, Hiroshi, Hisao, Kensuke, Kiyohiko, Kunihiko.*

Nix (8784) **1.** English, German, and Dutch: patronymic from a pet form of NICHOLAS (German *Nikolaus*). **2.** Irish (County Limerick): Anglicized form of Gaelic **Mac Nioceais** 'son of Nicholas', which was taken by some Limerick families named WOULFE. **3.** German (southern and Upper Rhine): from a nickname from Middle High German *nickes(e), nixe* 'water sprite'.

Nixdorf (180) Eastern German: habitational name from a place east of Sebnitz, formerly named Niklasdorf.

GIVEN NAMES German 8%. *Frieda, Gerhard, Gunther, Klaus.*

Nixon (12503) **1.** Northern English, Scottish, and northern Irish: patronymic from the Middle English personal name *Nik(k)e*, a short form of NICHOLAS. **2.** French: variant of a contracted form of *Nickesson*, a pet form of *Nick*, from NICOLAS.

Niziolek (155) Polish (**Niziołek**): nickname for a short person or literal descriptive name for a dwarf, from Polish dialect *niziołek* 'dwarf'.

GIVEN NAMES Polish 5%. *Andrzej, Jadwiga.*

Niznik (257) Jewish (Ashkenazic): nickname from Ukrainian *nizhnyj* 'affectionate', 'tender', or from an agent noun, *kniznik*, based on Russian *knigi* 'books'.

No (286) **1.** Korean: there are three Chinese characters for the No surname, one of which is extremely rare. Between the three characters, there are a total of sixteen clans. All of the clans are descended from founding ancestors from China. One of the founding ancestors, No Su, migrated from China in 755 and brought with him his nine sons. Each of his sons went on to found another clan. **2.** Japanese (**Nō**): written with the character for 'ability'; found in the Ryūkyūan island of Amami.

FOREBEARS No is a very common surname in Korea, and is found throughout the peninsula. Roh Tae Wu, a former president of the Republic of Korea, belongs to one of the No clans.

GIVEN NAMES Korean 73%. *Sung* (4), *Chae* (3), *Jong* (3), *Song* (3), *Yong* (3), *Hong* (2), *Hyo* (2), *Hyo Sun* (2), *Jae* (2), *Kun* (2), *Kyong* (2), *Kyoung* (2); *Chong* (3), *Chang* (2), *Dae* (2), *Chong Kun, Chong Sik, Inho,*

Insoo, Jae In, Jae Yoon, Jeong, Jin Sung, Jong Hwan.

Noa (184) **1.** Spanish: from the Biblical personal name NOAH. **2.** German (**Noä**) and Jewish: variant spelling of NOAH.

GIVEN NAMES Spanish 32%. *Carlos* (3), *Pedro* (3), *Arnoldo* (2), *Asterio* (2), *Mario* (2), *Orestes* (2), *Roberto* (2), *Angel, Argelio, Armando, Arnaldo, Dagoberto; Antonio* (3), *Angelo, Geronimo.*

Noack (1036) German and eastern European: **1.** variant of NOAH. **2.** variant of NOWAK.

GIVEN NAMES German 7%. *Hans* (4), *Klaus* (3), *Arno* (2), *Otto* (2), *Achim, Ernst, Erwin, Gerhard, Gerhardt, Heinrich, Katharina, Kurt.*

Noah (1681) **1.** English, German, and Jewish (Sephardic and Israeli): from the Biblical personal name *Noah* (see NOE). **2.** English: probably a variant spelling of **Noar**, a topographic name derived from misdivision of the Middle English phrase *atten ore* 'at the bank or steep slope' (Old English *ōra*).

Noakes (583) English (southeastern and central): topographic name for someone who lived by some oak trees, from misdivision of Middle English *atten okes* 'at the oaks' (see NOCK).

Nobbe (285) **1.** Variant spelling of English **Nobb**, from the medieval personal name *Hob*, a pet form of ROBERT. **2.** North German: from a short form of a Germanic personal name formed with *nōt* 'distress', 'forse'.

GIVEN NAMES German 5%. *Aloys, Ernst, Erwin, Mathias.*

Nobbs (128) English (Norfolk): patronymic from the personal name *Nobb* (see NOBBE).

Nobel (312) **1.** Swedish: shortened form of **Nobelius**, a Latinized habitational name from a place called Nöbbelöv. This is one of the rare genuine habitational names in Swedish, as distinct from ornamental coinages, which sometimes look like place names. **2.** German (also **Nöbel**): from a short form of a Germanic personal name composed with *nōt* 'distress', 'force'. **3.** German (also **Nöbel**): in some cases a habitational name from a place so named near Danzig (Polish Gdańsk) and (**Nöbel**) from Nöbeln in Saxony. **4.** Jewish (Ashkenazic): ornamental name from German *nobel* 'noble'.

GIVEN NAMES Jewish 4%. *Arie* (2), *Aviva, Barak.*

Nobert (113) French: from the Germanic personal name *Norbert*, composed of the elements *nord* 'north' + *berht* 'bright', 'shining'.

GIVEN NAMES French 16%. *Normand* (2), *Gaston, Henri, Huguette, Marcel.*

Nobile (587) Italian: nickname from *nobile* 'noble' (see NOBLE).

GIVEN NAMES Italian 13%; French 4%. *Salvatore* (7), *Rocco* (6), *Angelo* (2),

Agostino, Antonio, Carmine, Ciro, Gaetano, Giovani, Giovanni, Lucio, Onofrio; Camille, Michelene, Philippe.

Nobis (220) German: nickname of disputed origin: *Nobis* was a euphemism for the devil; alternatively, the name may be taken from *Nobiskrüge* ('Nobis taverns'), a term denoting an outlying tavern, on the edge of civilization.

GIVEN NAMES German 7%. *Otto* (2), *Fritz, Gunter, Siegried.*

Noble (14980) **1.** English, Scottish, and Irish (of Norman origin); also French: nickname from Middle English, Old French *noble* 'high-born', 'distinguished', 'illustrious' (Latin *nobilis*), denoting someone of lofty birth or character, or perhaps also ironically someone of low station. The surname has been established in Ireland since the 13th century, but was re-introduced in the 17th century and is now found mainly in Ulster. **2.** Jewish (Ashkenazic): Americanized form of **Knöbel**, a surname derived from an archaic German word for a servant. This was the name of a famous rabbinical family which moved from Wiener Neustadt to Sanok in Galicia in the 17th century; several members subsequently emigrated to the U.S. **3.** Jewish: Americanized form of NOBEL. **4.** German: probably a Huguenot name (see 1). **5.** Possibly an altered form of German KNOBEL or NOBEL.

Nobles (3942) English: patronymic from NOBLE 1.

Noblet (160) English, Irish, and French: from a diminutive of NOBLE. The Irish name is of Huguenot origin.

Noblett (363) English (Lancashire): **1.** variant spelling of NOBLET. **2.** from a pet form of the medieval personal name *Nobb* (see NOBBE).

Noblin (362) **1.** Possibly a respelling of German **Nobiling**, a derivative of NOBEL.

Noblit (147) Variant spelling of English NOBLETT.

Noblitt (616) Variant spelling of English NOBLETT.

Noboa (122) Galician: variant from the Galician habitational name Nóvoa (see NOVOA).

GIVEN NAMES Spanish 41%. *Luis* (6), *Carlos* (5), *Julio* (4), *Jose* (3), *Alvaro* (2), *Fernando* (2), *Juan* (2), *Ana, Bolivar, Francisco, Gonzalo, Jacinto.*

Nobrega (228) Portuguese (**Nóbrega**): habitational name from the former juridical district Terra da Nóbrega.

GIVEN NAMES Spanish 18%; Portuguese 11%. *Jose* (5), *Manuel* (5), *Jorge* (3), *Americo* (2), *Luis* (2), *Alberto, Christiano, Fernando, Filipe, Gilberto, Julio, Lino; Agostinho; Antonio, Caesar, Cesario.*

Nobriga (191) Portuguese (**Nóbriga**): variant of NOBREGA.

GIVEN NAMES Spanish 5%. *Manuel* (3), *Carlos, Joaquin.*

Noce (350) Italian: topographic name for someone who lived where nut trees grew, from *noce* 'nut' (Latin *nux*, genitive *nucis*).
GIVEN NAMES Italian 15%. *Angelo* (4), *Franco* (3), *Carlo* (2), *Salvatore* (2), *Amerigo, Carmelo, Domenic, Fausto, Gennaro, Gino, Marco, Natale.*

Nocella (290) Italian: from a diminutive of NOCE.
GIVEN NAMES Italian 12%. *Angelo* (4), *Pasquale* (2), *Rocco* (2), *Luciano, Olindo, Sal.*

Nocera (539) Southern Italian: habitational name from Nocera Inferiore and Superiore in Salerno province, or Nocera Terinese in Catanzaro province, all named with Latin *Nuceria*.
GIVEN NAMES Italian 20%. *Angelo* (3), *Salvatore* (3), *Cosmo* (2), *Dante* (2), *Domenic* (2), *Erminio* (2), *Gaetano* (2), *Michelangelo* (2), *Rocco* (2), *Annunziato, Antonio, Arduino.*

Nocerino (120) Italian (Campania): habitational name for someone from Nocera Inferiore or Nocera Superiore (see NOCERA), from an adjectival derivative of the place name. (The term for a native of Nocera Terinese, on the other hand, is *nocerese.*)
GIVEN NAMES Italian 22%. *Assunta, Ciro, Dante, Gennaro, Giovanni, Giro, Silvio.*

Nocito (158) **1.** Italian: topographic name from Latin *nucetum* 'walnut orchard'. **2.** Spanish: Castilianized form of *Nozito*, habitational name from a town so called in Uesca province, Aragon.
GIVEN NAMES Italian 12%. *Carlo, Genoveffa, Vincenzo.*

Nock (646) **1.** English: topographic name for someone who lived by an oak tree, from misdivision of Middle English *atten oke* 'at the oak'. **2.** South German (also **Nöck**): from Tyrolean *nock, nog* 'rounded hill', 'rock', hence a topographic name for someone who lived by such a feature, or a nickname from the same word used in the sense 'short and fat'.

Noda (333) **1.** Japanese: 'rice paddy in the field', a common place name and surname throughout Japan. **2.** Spanish (Canary Islands): unexplained.
GIVEN NAMES Japanese 45%; Spanish 12%. *Masao* (4), *Akira* (2), *Koichi* (2), *Koji* (2), *Makoto* (2), *Masaaki* (2), *Mikiko* (2), *Minoru* (2), *Shinichiro* (2), *Takeshi* (2), *Yuji* (2), *Yukio* (2); *Blanca* (2), *Carlos* (2), *Felipe* (2), *Isidra* (2), *Jose* (2), *Lazara* (2), *Pedro* (2), *Ricardo* (2), *Adelfa, Andres, Atilio, Aurea.*

Nodal (91) Hispanic (mainly Mexico): unexplained.
GIVEN NAMES Spanish 59%. *Jose* (6), *Rafael* (3), *Armando* (2), *Blanca* (2), *Eduardo* (2), *Luis* (2), *Pedro* (2), *Raul* (2), *Ronaldo* (2), *Adelaida, Adolfo, Aleida; Leonardo* (2), *Guido, Mirella.*

Nodarse (114) Hispanic: unexplained.

GIVEN NAMES Spanish 51%. *Jose* (4), *Carlos* (3), *Ernesto* (3), *Alberto* (2), *Caridad* (2), *Ovidio* (2), *Raul* (2), *Tomas* (2), *Alfredo, Alicia, Amado, Cristobal.*

Nodine (435) French: probably from a pet form personal name of Germanic origin, *Nodo*, a short form of *Nodolf* (see NOLF).

Nodland (134) Norwegian: habitational name from a farm name in southwestern Norway, probably composed of Old Norse *nata* 'small nettle' + *land* 'land', 'farmstead'.
GIVEN NAMES Scandinavian 15%. *Borge* (2), *Gudmund, Karsten.*

Noe (4149) English, German, Dutch, French (**Noé, Noë**), Spanish (**Noé**), Catalan (**Noè**): from the Biblical personal name *Noach* 'Noah', which means 'comfort' in Hebrew. According to the Book of Genesis, Noah, having been forewarned by God, built an ark into which he took his family and representatives of every species of animal, and so was saved from the flood that God sent to destroy the world because of human wickedness. The personal name was not common among non-Jews in the Middle Ages, but the Biblical story was an extremely popular subject for miracle plays. In many cases, therefore, the surname probably derives from a nickname referring to someone who had played the part of Noah in a miracle play or pageant, rather than from a personal name.

Noecker (374) **1.** South German and Dutch: from the Germanic personal name *Notker* (*Notger*), composed of the elements *not* 'battle throng' + *gār, gēr* 'spear'. **2.** North German: nickname for a complainer, from Low German *nöckern* 'to moan or grumble'. **3.** South German (**Nöcker**): topographic name from Tyrolean *nock, nogg* '(rounded) hill', 'rock'.

Noel (9087) English and French: nickname for someone who had some special connection with the Christmas season, such as owing the particular feudal duty of providing a yule-log to the lord of the manor, or having given a memorable performance as the Lord of Misrule. The name is from Middle English, Old French *no(u)el* 'Christmas' (Latin *natalis (dies)* 'birthday'). It was also used as a given name for someone born during the Christmas period.
GIVEN NAMES French 6%. *Andre* (12), *Pierre* (12), *Normand* (6), *Antoine* (4), *Jacques* (4), *Alphonse* (3), *Leonce* (3), *Lucien* (3), *Marcel* (3), *Damien* (2), *Emile* (2), *Francois* (2).

Noelke (125) German (**Nölke**): from a reduced pet form of the personal name *Arnold*.

Noell (631) **1.** German (**Nöll**): habitational name from any of several places in Rhineland and Westphalia named Nöll. **2.** Catalan: nickname from NOVELL 'young', 'new' (Latin *novellus* 'new'). Compare NEW.

Noelle (104) **1.** German: respelling of NOELL. **2.** Respelling of French NOEL.

Noeske (124) German (**Nöske**): nickname for someone with a remarkable nose, from Sorbian *nósk*, a diminutive of *nos, nós* 'nose'. Compare NOSKO.
GIVEN NAMES German 11%. *Erwin, Hans, Heinz, Helmuth, Herta, Ottmar.*

Noeth (169) South German (**Nöth**): from a Germanic personal name composed with an element cognate with Old High German *nōt* 'distress', 'travail', 'force'.
GIVEN NAMES German 4%. *Hans* (2), *Guenther, Klaus.*

Noetzel (158) German (**Nötzel**): **1.** from a pet form of NOETH. **2.** diminutive of NOTZ, from Middle High German *næzel* 'domestic animals', 'cattle', hence a metonymic occupational name for someone who tended animals.
GIVEN NAMES German 6%. *Ewald, Georg, Hans, Manfred.*

Noffke (289) Eastern German (Sorbian): nickname for a newcomer to a district, from a diminutive of *novy* 'new'. Compare Polish NOWAK, Czech NOVAK.

Noffsinger (689) German: Americanized form of **Nafziger** (see NEFZGER).

Nofsinger (262) German: Americanized form of **Nafziger** (see NEFZGER).

Noftz (113) German: nickname for a sleepyhead, from a noun derivative of Middle High German *nafzen* 'to take a nap'. Compare NEFZGER.

Nofziger (326) German: variant of NAFZIGER.

Noga (576) Polish: from Polish *noga* 'leg', used as a derogatory nickname for a totally incompetent person.
GIVEN NAMES Polish 6%. *Krzysztof* (2), *Leszek* (2), *Casimir, Cecylia, Dorota, Grazyna, Krystyna, Mieczyslaw, Piotr, Stanislaw.*

Nogales (106) Spanish: habitational name from either of two places named Nogales: in Badajoz and Málaga provinces.
GIVEN NAMES Spanish 47%. *Jose* (3), *Javier* (2), *Jorge* (2), *Juan* (2), *Manuel* (2), *Roberto* (2), *Alejandra, Alfredo, Alicia, Belia, Carlos, Delfina; Antonio.*

Noggle (546) Possibly a respelling of German **Nöggel**, a variant of **Nöckel**, a South German topographic name from *Nock* 'hill', 'peak', 'rock', or of NAGEL 1.

Nogle (272) Possibly an altered spelling of German NAGEL 1.

Noguchi (239) Japanese: 'entrance to the field', found mostly along the southeastern coast of Japan and in the Ryūkyū Islands. Some families have samurai connections.
GIVEN NAMES Japanese 68%. *Hiroshi* (4), *Fumio* (3), *Hideo* (3), *Maki* (3), *Hideki* (2), *Jiro* (2), *Makiko* (2), *Seiji* (2), *Sumiko* (2), *Yoshiaki* (2), *Yoshio* (2), *Yuji* (2).

Nogueira (350) Portuguese and Galician: habitational name from any of numerous places in Portugal and Galicia so named from *nogueira* 'walnut tree' (Late Latin *nucarius*, from *nux*, genitive *nucis*, 'nut').

GIVEN NAMES Spanish 34%; Portuguese 17%. *Jose* (12), *Manuel* (8), *Carlos* (7), *Fernando* (4), *Alicia* (3), *Alvaro* (3), *Eduardo* (3), *Jorge* (3), *Claudio* (2), *Geraldo* (2), *Juan* (2), *Mario* (2); *Joaquim* (2), *Paulo* (2), *Afonso*, *Joao*, *Manoel*; *Antonio* (5), *Alessandra*, *Enrico*, *Marco*.

Noguera (235) **1.** Spanish: habitational name from Noguera, a town in Teruel, probably from Catalan *noguera* 'walnut tree' (Latin *nucarius*). **2.** Catalan: topographic name for someone who lived by any of the rivers called Noguera, in northern Catalonia.

GIVEN NAMES Spanish 54%. *Jose* (7), *Carlos* (4), *Juan* (4), *Eduardo* (3), *Enrique* (3), *Cesar* (2), *Elia* (2), *Geraldo* (2), *Javier* (2), *Jesus* (2), *Jorge* (2), *Luis* (2).

Noh (319) **1.** Korean: variant of NO. **2.** Mexican (Mayan): nickname or ornamental name from a word meaning 'big', 'big or chief thing', 'right hand', or 'irregularly shaped gourd'.

GIVEN NAMES Korean 54%. *Jae* (7), *Jung* (5), *Young* (5), *Sang* (4), *Jin* (3), *Sung* (3), *Zung* (3), *Dong* (2), *Heung* (2), *Hwan* (2), *Chae*, *Eui*; *Chang* (2), *Boksoon*, *Byung*, *Chong*, *Chul*, *Chul Soo*, *Doyoung*, *Hae*, *Hak*, *Hee Sook*, *Hyung Sik*, *Hyunsik*.

Nohe (114) German: variant of NOAH.

Nohl (144) **1.** German: probably a variant of NOLL 2, in Switzerland and Tyrol denoting a naive or inept person. **2.** Dutch: from a reduced form of the personal name ARNOLD.

GIVEN NAME French 4%. *Andre*.

Nohr (211) **1.** Norwegian: habitational name from a farmstead named Nor, from Old Norse *nór* 'narrows', denoting either a narrow passage in a fjord or lake, or a short stream leading from a lake into a river. **2.** German: probably a habitational name from Nohra in Thuringia, originally named with elements meaning 'marshy stream'; or, in Holstein, a topographic name from *Nohr* 'stagnant water', 'lake'. **3.** German (**Nöhr**): from a reduced form of medieval personal name *Apollinaris* (a derivative of Greek *Apollo*). This name was borne by a Christian martyr whose cult was centered on Remagen (Rhineland), where it is found in old forms such as *Pollenoris*, *Bolinoris*.

Noia (115) **1.** Galician: habitational name from the town of Noia, in Galicia. **2.** Catalan: variant of the topographic name *Anoia*, for someone living by the Anoia river in Catalonia.

GIVEN NAMES Spanish 10%. *Jose* (4), *Juan*.

Noice (115) English: variant spelling of NOYCE.

Nokes (668) English: variant of spelling NOAKES.

Nola (209) Southern Italian: habitational name from Nola in Naples province.

GIVEN NAMES Italian 5%. *Angelo* (2), *Francesca*.

Nolan (16929) Irish (Leinster and Munster): Anglicized form of Gaelic **Ó Nualláin** 'descendant of *Nuallán*', a personal name representing a diminutive of *nuall* 'famous', 'noble'.

GIVEN NAMES Irish 8%. *Brendan* (12), *John Patrick* (3), *Liam* (3), *Cathal* (2), *Clancy* (2), *Conor* (2), *Fergus* (2), *Kieran* (2), *Seamus* (2), *Siobhan* (2), *Aileen*, *Brigid*.

Noland (3472) **1.** Irish: variant of NOLAN. **2.** French: from a Germanic personal name composed of the elements *not* 'need' + *land* 'land'.

Nolasco (628) Portuguese and Spanish: from the personal name *Nolasco*, derived from the name of *Petrus Nolascus* (Saint Peter of Nolasco), who was born in Carcassone in 1189 and died in Barcelona in 1256, where he was co-founder and leader of the order of S. Maria della Mercede 'Our Lady of Ransom', known in English as the Mercedarians.

GIVEN NAMES Spanish 52%; Italian 6%. *Jose* (15), *Manuel* (8), *Carlos* (7), *Juan* (7), *Mario* (6), *Pedro* (6), *Fernando* (5), *Jesus* (5), *Julio* (5), *Ramon* (5), *Miguel* (4), *Alfredo* (3); *Antonio* (6), *Romeo* (2), *Filiberto*, *Gino*, *Giovanni*, *Lorenzo*, *Marco*, *Quirino*, *Sal*.

Nold (598) **1.** North German: from the short form of the personal name ARNOLD. **2.** Probably an altered form of NOLDE (which is much more frequent in Germany).

Nolde (218) **1.** German and Dutch: from a short form of the personal name ARNOLD. **2.** German: in some cases a metonymic occupational name for a needlemaker, from Middle High German *nālde* 'needle' (variant of *nādel*). Compare NADLER. **3.** German: habitational name from a place so named in Schleswig-Holstein.

Nolden (299) Dutch and German: patronymic from NOLDE 1.

GIVEN NAMES German 4%. *Kurt* (3), *Aloys*.

Nolder (279) German: probably an altered form of **Noeld(n)er**, an occupational name for a needlemaker, from an agent derivative of Middle High German *nālde* 'needle', metathesized form of *nādele* (see NADLER).

Nole (237) Italian (Potenza; **Nolè**): unexplained.

GIVEN NAMES Italian 13%; French 4%. *Angelo* (4), *Vito* (4), *Salvatore* (2), *Alfonse*, *Canio*, *Donato*; *Girard*, *Jean-Louis*, *Monique*.

Nolen (3672) **1.** Dutch and North German: from a Germanic personal name formed with an element cognate with Middle Low German *nōt* 'distress', 'power'. **2.** Swedish: probably an ornamental or habitational name formed with *Nol-*, from *Nord-* 'north', plus the adjectival suffix *-én*, from Latin *-en(i)us*. However, it may also be a variant of **Nolin**, which in at least one

case is derived from a place called *Skällsäter*, by Latinization of *Skäll-*, erroneously thought to be derived from Swedish *skälla* 'little bell', Latin *nola*. The place name is in fact derived either from Swedish dialect *skäll* 'barren', 'infertile', or from Swedish *sköld* 'shield'. **3.** Irish: variant spelling of NOLAN. **4.** Jewish: unexplained.

Noles (1198) Possibly an altered spelling of KNOWLES.

Nolet (243) French: from a reduced pet form of a personal name such as *Arnaud*, *Bernaud*, *Renaud*.

GIVEN NAMES French 6%. *Andre*, *Philippe*, *Rodrigue*.

Nolette (230) French: variant of NOLET.

GIVEN NAMES French 12%. *Alderic*, *Armand*, *Aurore*, *Lucienne*, *Normand*, *Philippe*, *Raoul*.

Nolf (250) **1.** German and Dutch: from a short form of the personal name *Arnolf*, composed of the Germanic elements *arn* 'eagle' + *wulf* 'wolf'. **2.** Dutch: from a reduced form of *Nodolf*, derived from the personal name *Odolf* by transfer of the final *-n* in a preceding personal name such as *Jan*, *Simoen*. *Odolf* is composed of the Germanic elements *aud* 'wealth' + *wulf* 'wolf'.

Nolfi (141) Italian: patronymic from a reduced pet form of the personal names *Arnolfo* (see NOLF) or *Dinolfo*.

GIVEN NAMES Italian 10%. *Angelo*, *Marco*, *Salvatore*, *Salvo*.

Nolin (948) French: from a pet form of the personal name BERNARD.

GIVEN NAMES French 7%. *Armand* (4), *Alphe*, *Andre*, *Benoit*, *Cecile*, *Colette*, *Emile*, *Gervais*, *Gisele*, *Jean-Charles*, *Lucien*, *Marthe*.

Noll (4241) **1.** German: from a short form of any of various medieval personal names derived from Germanic personal names ending in *-n* + *wald* 'rule', for example ARNOLD and REINWALD. **2.** South German: nickname for a rotund or naive person, from Middle High German *nol* 'hillock', 'knoll'. **3.** Jewish (Ashkenazic): of uncertain origin; perhaps an occupational name from Yiddish *nol* 'awl'.

Nolle (125) **1.** German: variant of NOLL. **2.** North German: habitational name from the Nolle district in Westphalia. **3.** North German (**Nölle**): topographic name from Middle High German *nol*, *nel(le)* 'peak', 'summit', also the name from several streams so named in Westphalia. **4.** German (**Nölle**): variant of NOLL 1. **5.** French (**Nollé**): variant of NOLET.

GIVEN NAMES German 7%; French 4%. *Horst*, *Klaus*, *Kurt*; *Jacques*, *Rolande*.

Nollen (111) German: variant of NOLEN.

Noller (436) German (also **Nöller**) and Dutch: occupational name for a needle maker (see NADLER).

GIVEN NAMES German 4%. *Dieter* (2), *Hans* (2), *Gerhard*, *Kurt*.

Nollette (107) Respelling of French **Nolet**, **Nollett**, from a reduced form of the personal name *Bernolet* or *Renolet*.

Nolley (441) **1.** Probably a reduced form of Irish **Nohilly**, an Anglicized form of Gaelic **Ó Neothallaigh** or **Ó Neothaille**. **2.** Alternatively, it may be a respelling of German NOLLE.

Nolt (750) Altered spelling of German NOLTE.
GIVEN NAME German 4%. *Phares.*

Nolta (101) Respelling of German NOLTE.

Nolte (2645) German (also **Nölte**): from a short form of any of various medieval personal names derived from Germanic personal names ending with *-n* + *wald* 'rule', for example ARNOLD and REINWALD. Compare NOLL 1.
GIVEN NAMES German 5%. *Kurt* (6), *Erwin* (3), *Heinz* (3), *Erna* (2), *Frieda* (2), *Hans* (2), *Horst* (2), *Johann* (2), *Juergen* (2), *Ewald, Guenter, Heinrich.*

Nolting (604) North German (also **Nölting**): patronymic from the personal name *Nolte*, a variant of NOLL.
GIVEN NAMES German 4%. *Arno, Erwin, Kurt, Otto, Ralf.*

Nolton (112) **1.** French: from a diminutive of **Nolet** (see NOLLETTE). **2.** Possibly an Americanized form of German **Nolten**, patronymic from NOLT.
GIVEN NAME German 4%. *Hilde* (2).

Nomura (486) Japanese: 'village in the field', a common place name. The surname is mostly found in western Japan and the island of Okinawa.
GIVEN NAMES Japanese 45%. *Kazuo* (7), *Kiyoshi* (3), *Koji* (3), *Satoru* (3), *Akihiro* (2), *Akira* (2), *Hiroshi* (2), *Katsumi* (2), *Kazuhiro* (2), *Kenji* (2), *Mitsuhiro* (2), *Shigeo* (2).

Nonaka (126) Japanese: '(one who lives) in the middle of the field'; the name is found mostly in eastern Japan. Listed in the Shinsen shōjiroku; when that record was compiled the name was pronounced *Nunaka.*
GIVEN NAMES Japanese 52%. *Hiroshi* (2), *Manabu* (2), *Taro* (2), *Akihiko, Atsuko, Chieko, Goro, Hatsuko, Hideko, Hideo, Iwao, Junichi.*

Nondorf (106) **1.** German (Austria): habitational name from either of two places so named in Lower Austria. **2.** German: probably from a habitational or topographic name with an unexplained *Non-* as the first part, as in the family name **Noneder**.

Nonemaker (124) Americanized form of German **Nonnemacher** (see NONNEN-MACHER).

Nonn (100) **1.** North German: from a Frisian personal name recorded in the 15th century as *Nonno* and in the 16th as *Nonne.* **2.** South German: short form of NONNENMACHER, an occupational name for someone who castrated hogs, from Middle High German *nonne, nunne* 'cas-

trated pig' + *macher*, an agent derivative of *machen* 'to make'.

Nonnemacher (199) German: variant of NONNENMACHER.

Nonnenmacher (142) German: occupational name for a gelder of hogs, from Middle High German *nunne, nonne* 'nun', and by transfer 'castrated hog' + an agent derivative of *machen* 'to make'.
GIVEN NAMES German 10%. *Heinz, Helmut, Hermann.*

Noojin (108) Origin unidentified.

Noon (1055) **1.** Irish: variant spelling of NOONE. **2.** English, Scottish, and Dutch: from Middle English *none*, Middle Dutch *noene* 'noon', the time of brightest sunshine, hence perhaps nickname for a bright and cheerful person or for someone born at that time of day. The word is derived from Latin *nona (hora)* 'ninth (hour)', i.e. about three o'clock. The change in meaning of the vocabulary word from mid-afternoon to midday, probably occurred as a result of monastic meal times being brought forward.
GIVEN NAME Irish 4%. *Brendan.*

Noonan (5425) Irish (Munster): Anglicized form of Gaelic **Ó hlonmhaineáin** 'descendant of *Ionmhaineán*', a personal name derived from the diminutive of *Ionmhain* 'beloved', 'dear'.
GIVEN NAMES Irish 6%. *Brendan* (3), *Brigid, Declan, Dermot, Donal, Eamonn, Egan, Paddy, Seamus, Sinead.*

Noone (972) Irish (Connacht): Anglicized form of Gaelic **Ó Nuadháin** 'descendant of *Nuadhán*', a personal name derived from *Nuadha*, the name of an ancient Celtic gods.
GIVEN NAMES Irish 5%. *Brendan* (2), *Malachy* (2), *Kieran, Peadar.*

Nooner (164) Americanized spelling of German **Nunner**, an occupational name for someone who castrated animals, from Middle High German *nunnen* 'to castrate'.

Nooney (236) Irish: variant of NOONE.

Noonkester (158) Americanized spelling of German NUNGESSER.
GIVEN NAME Jewish 6%. *Hershel* (3).

Noor (209) **1.** Muslim: from a personal name based on Arabic *nūr* 'light', 'illumination'. *Al-Nūr* 'the Light', is an attribute of Allah. It is also found in compound names such as *Nūr Allah* (*Nurullah*) 'Light of Allah' and *Nūr ud-Dīn* (*Nuruddin*) 'Light of Religion'. **2.** Dutch: ethnic name for a Norwegian.
GIVEN NAMES Muslim 53%. *Ahmed* (3), *Mohammad* (3), *Mohammed* (3), *Abdirahman* (2), *Mustafa* (2), *Aban, Abdi, Abdul, Abdul Hakim, Afzal, Ahmad, Alam, Anjum, Jehangir, Lavanya, Mehar, Shamsher, Suman.*

Noorani (119) Muslim: from a personal name based on Persian *nūrānī* 'luminous', 'bright', a derivative of Arabic *nūr* 'light'.

GIVEN NAMES Muslim 82%. *Salim* (5), *Abdul* (3), *Ali* (3), *Mohammed* (3), *Sultan* (3), *Amin* (2), *Anis* (2), *Aziz* (2), *Hamid* (2), *Rahim* (2), *Saleem* (2), *Ahmed.*

Noorda (102) Origin unidentified.

Noori (123) Muslim: from a personal name based on Arabic *nūrī* 'bright', 'shining', 'full of light'.
GIVEN NAMES Muslim 83%. *Ahmad* (5), *Mohammad* (5), *Majid* (3), *Mostafa* (3), *Afsaneh* (2), *Assadullah* (2), *Bibi* (2), *Jalal* (2), *Rahim* (2), *Sadiq* (2), *Amir, Arif.*

Nooyen (111) Origin unidentified.

Nopper (128) German: occupational name for someone whose job was to remove burls from newly made cloth, from an agent derivative of Middle High German *nop(pe)* 'tuft of wool'. Compare English NAPPER.

Nora (223) **1.** Italian and German: from a short form of the feminine personal name *(E)leonora*. **2.** Southern Italian: perhaps a habitational name from localities named Nora in Modica and Scicli. **3.** Portuguese: habitational name from any of the numerous places called Nora, from *nora* 'draw well'.

Norbeck (202) Belgian (**van Norbeck, van Oorbeek**): habitational name from Oorbeek (meaning 'across the creek'), in Brabant, or from Orbais in Brabant (from an earlier form, *Orbec*).
GIVEN NAME French 4%. *Colette.*

Norberg (1125) **1.** Swedish: ornamental name composed of the elements *norr, nord* 'north' + *berg* 'mountain', 'hill'. **2.** Norwegian: variant of NORDBERG.
GIVEN NAMES Scandinavian 6%. *Erik* (2), *Alvar, Britt, Lennart, Sven.*

Norbury (229) English: habitational name from any of various places, for example in Cheshire, Derbyshire, Shropshire, Staffordshire, and Surrey, so called from Old English *norð* 'north' + *burh* 'fortress', 'fortified town'.

Norbut (111) Lithuanian: nickname from a derivative of *noreti* 'to want' + *būti* 'to be'.

Norby (971) **1.** English: habitational name from Norby in Thirsk, North Yorkshire. **2.** Swedish (**Norrby**): habitational name from a farmstead named with *norr* 'north' + *by* 'farm', or an ornamental name formed with the same elements.
GIVEN NAMES Scandinavian 4%. *Bendt, Borge, Erik, Kresten, Niels.*

Norcia (208) Italian and Jewish (from Italy): habitational name from Norcia in Perugia province.
GIVEN NAMES Italian 10%. *Carmine* (2), *Antonio, Concetta, Matteo, Rocci, Salvatore.*

Norcott (134) English: variant of NORTH-CUTT.

Norcross (1200) English (Lancashire): habitational name from a minor place near Blackpool, so named from Old English *norð* 'north' + *cros* 'cross'.

Norcutt (150) English: variant of NORTH-CUTT.

Nord (1923) **1.** Scandinavian and Dutch: topographic or ornamental name from Scandinavian *nord*, Dutch *noord* 'north'. As a topographic name it would have denoted someone who lived in the northern part of a village or to the north of a main settlement or someone who had migrated from the north. **2.** Jewish (Ashkenazic): from German *Nord* 'north'. **3.** Dutch, German, and French: from a short form of a Germanic personal name with the first element *nord* 'north', for example *Norbert*.
GIVEN NAMES Scandinavian 5%. *Erik* (5), *Helmer* (2), *Alvar, Knute, Nels, Per*.

Nordahl (301) **1.** Swedish: ornamental name formed with *norr, nord* 'north' + *dahl*, an ornamental spelling of *dal* 'valley'. **2.** Norwegian: habitational name from any of various farmsteads named with *nord* 'north' + *dal* 'valley'.
GIVEN NAMES Scandinavian 11%. *Erik* (3), *Jorgen, Ove*.

Nordan (244) English: variant spelling of NORDEN.

Nordberg (568) **1.** Norwegian: habitational name from any of several farmsteads named from *nord* 'north' + *berg* 'mountain'. **2.** Swedish: variant of NORBERG.
GIVEN NAMES Scandinavian 9%; German 4%. *Nils* (3), *Erik, Helmer, Ingman, Svein; Kurt* (2), *Erwin, Inge*.

Nordby (728) **1.** Norwegian: habitational name from any of fifty or more farmsteads named in Old Norse as *Norðbýr* 'the north farm'. **2.** Swedish: ornamental name formed with the same elements as 1. Compare NORBY 2.
GIVEN NAMES Scandinavian 6%. *Erik* (2), *Knut* (2), *Gudrun, Hilmer, Sigvald*.

Nordeen (395) Swedish: variant of NORDEN.

Nordell (229) Swedish: ornamental name composed of the elements *nord* 'north' + the common surname element *-ell*, a derivative of the Latin adjectival ending *-elius*.
GIVEN NAMES Scandinavian 6%. *Joakim, Lars, Nils*.

Norden (740) **1.** Swedish (**Nordén**): ornamental name formed with *norr, nord* 'north' + the common surname suffix *-én*, from Latin *-enius*. **2.** North German and Jewish (Ashkenazic): habitational name from any of several places so called in East Friesland, Schleswig-Holstein, and former East Prussia. The German surname may have arisen as a topographic name from a field so named because of its northerly aspect. **3.** Dutch: patronymic from NORD 3. **4.** English: habitational name from a minor place name, probably Norden in West Alvington, Devon, or possibly Norton Green in Stockbury, Kent.

Norder (171) **1.** German: habitational name for someone from a place called NORDEN. **2.** German: regional name for a northerner, a derivative of Middle High German *norden* 'north'. **3.** Swedish: probably an ornamental name formed with *nord* 'north' + the suffix *-ér*, derived from Latin *-erus* 'descendant of'.

Nordgren (402) Swedish: ornamental name composed of the elements *nord* 'north' + *gren* 'branch'.
GIVEN NAMES Scandinavian 9%. *Erik* (5), *Berger, Ludvig, Nels, Sigfrid*.

Nordhagen (110) German: habitational name from either of two places called Nordhagen: in Schleswig-Holstein and North Rhine-Westphalia.

Nordhaus (119) German: topographic name for someone who lived at the 'north house', or a habitational name from a place so named.

Nordhausen (115) German: habitational name from any of several places called Nordhausen, in Thuringia, Lower Saxony, and Baden-Württemberg, or a topographic name for someone who lived at the 'north houses'.
GIVEN NAMES German 15%. *Juergen* (2), *Arno, Bernd, Erwin, Otto*.

Nordheim (106) Norwegian: habitational name from any of several farmsteads named from *nord* 'north' + *heim* 'home', 'farmstead'.
GIVEN NAME Scandinavian 13%. *Erik* (2).

Nordhoff (173) North German: habitational name from any of the numerous farms so named, from Middle Low German *nord* 'north' + *hof* 'farmstead', 'manor farm' (see HOFF). This is a common farm name in northern Germany, especially Westphalia.

Nordholm (110) **1.** Norwegian: habitational name from a farm name composed of *nord* 'north' + *holm* 'islet'. **2.** Swedish: ornamental name formed with the same elements as 1.
GIVEN NAME Scandinavian 7%. *Erik* (2).

Nordick (129) **1.** Probably an altered form of German **Nordeck**, a habitational name from a place so named in Hesse. **2.** German: habitational name from a place so named near Bocholt, in the Lower Rhine area.

Nordin (1066) **1.** Swedish: ornamental name formed with *norr, nord* 'north' + the common surname suffix *-in*, derived from Latin *-inius* 'descendant of'. **2.** Dutch: patronymic from NORD 3.
GIVEN NAMES Scandinavian 8%. *Erik* (4), *Lars* (3), *Sven* (2), *Alvar, Anders, Einer, Kerstin, Nels, Nils, Obert*.

Nordine (239) Respelling of Swedish NORDIN.

Nordland (134) Norwegian: habitational name from any of several farms, named with *nord* 'north' + *land* 'land', 'farmstead'.
GIVEN NAMES German 5%. *Gerhard, Kurt*.

Nordling (292) Swedish: ornamental name formed with *norr, nord* 'north' + the suffix *-ling*, denoting a person.

GIVEN NAMES Scandinavian 6%. *Nels* (2), *Swen*.

Nordlund (450) Swedish: ornamental compound name composed of the elements *nord* 'north' + *lund* 'grove'.

Nordman (593) **1.** German and Jewish (Ashkenazic): variant of NORDMANN. 1 **2.** Dutch: ethnic name for a Norseman, from *nord* 'north' + *man* 'man'.
GIVEN NAMES German 4%. *Kurt* (3), *Angelika, Wilhelm*.

Nordmann (197) German and Jewish (Ashkenazic): topographic name from German *Nord* 'north' + *man* 'man' (see NORTH 1).
GIVEN NAMES German 5%. *Hans* (2), *Gunther*.

Nordmark (154) **1.** Swedish: ornamental name composed of the elements *nord* 'north' + *mark* 'land'. **2.** Norwegian: habitational name from a farmstead named with the elements *nord* 'north' + *mark* 'wood', 'forest'.
GIVEN NAMES Scandinavian 12%; German 4%. *Erik* (2), *Helmer, Hjalmer, Nils, Tor; Hans, Meggan*.

Nordmeyer (299) German: distinguishing name for a tenant farmer whose farm was to the north of a settlement, from Middle High German, Middle Low German *nord* 'north' + MEYER.

Nordness (150) Norwegian: habitational name from the common farm name *Nordnes* 'northern headland'.
GIVEN NAMES Scandinavian 7%; German 6%. *Hjalmer, Knut, Ordell; Gerhard, Kurt*.

Nordquist (981) Swedish: ornamental name composed of the elements *nord* 'north' + *quist*, an old or ornamental spelling of *kvist* 'twig'.
GIVEN NAMES Scandinavian 5%; German 4%. *Erik* (2), *Bjorn, Lars, Nels, Ove, Sigfrid; Kurt* (4), *Otto, Siegfried*.

Nordrum (140) Norwegian: habitational name from any of five farms in eastern Norway, named in Old Norse as *Norðrheimr* (see NORDHEIM).

Nordstrand (101) Swedish: ornamental name composed of the elements *nord* 'north' + *strand* 'shore'.
GIVEN NAME Scandinavian 5%. *Nils*.

Nordstrom (2443) Swedish (**Nordström**): ornamental name composed of the elements *nord* 'north' + *ström* 'river'.
GIVEN NAMES Scandinavian 6%. *Lars* (4), *Nils* (4), *Erik* (3), *Elof, Evald, Lennart, Mauritz, Nels, Sven*.

Nordwall (143) Swedish: ornamental name composed of the elements *nord* 'north' + *vall* 'bank'.

Nordyke (499) Americanized spelling of Dutch **Noorddijk**, a topographic name for someone living at 'the north dike'.

Nore (136) **1.** Norwegian: habitational name from a farmstead named from Old Norse *nór* 'narrows' (see NOHR 1), or, in Nordfjord, a compound of *nór* + *á* 'small river'. **2.** English: probably a habitational name from Nore in Surrey.

GIVEN NAMES Scandinavian 13%. *Iver* (2), *Alf, Per.*

Nored (177) Norwegian: probably an Americanized form of **Nordeid**, a habitational name from any of several farms, a compound of *nord* 'north' + *eid* 'isthmus'.

Noreen (390) Swedish: ornamental name formed with *norr* 'north' + the adjectival suffix *-een*, variant of *-én*, a derivative of Latin *-enius*.

GIVEN NAME Scandinavian 5%. *Sten.*

Noreika (111) Possibly of Lithuanian origin.

Norell (250) Swedish: ornamental name formed with *norr* 'north' + the suffix *-ell*, taken from the Latin adjectival ending *-elius*.

GIVEN NAMES Scandinavian 4%. *Per* (2), *Sven.*

Norelli (123) Italian: from a diminutive of NORA.

GIVEN NAMES Italian 25%. *Angelo* (4), *Aracely* (3), *Gianfranco* (2), *Fiore, Guido, Lucio, Mario, Tino.*

Norem (260) English: variant of **Norham** (see NORTHAM).

Noren (675) Swedish (**Norén**): ornamental compound of *nor* 'north' + the adjectival suffix *-én*, from Latin *-enius*.

GIVEN NAMES Scandinavian 7%. *Helmer* (2), *Juel* (2), *Lennart, Nels, Nils.*

Norenberg (197) **1.** German (**Nörenberg**): habitational name from a Pomeranian place name. **2.** Swedish: probably an ornamental compound of *nor(d)* 'north' + *berg* 'mountain'.

GIVEN NAMES German 4%. *Frederich, Otto.*

Norfleet (1199) English: habitational name from a place called Northfleet in Kent, from *north* + Old English *flēot* 'stream' or 'estuary'.

FOREBEARS Thomas Norfleet, from Kent, England, was in VA by 1666.

Norfolk (292) English: regional name from the county of Norfolk in East Anglia, so called from an Old English tribal name composed of the elements *norð* 'north' + *folc* 'people' (in contrast to the *sūðfolc* of Suffolk).

Norford (112) English (Suffolk): probably a variant of NORFOLK.

Norgaard (523) **1.** Norwegian: habitational name from any of numerous farmsteads named Nordgård, from *nord* 'north' + *gård* 'farm'. **2.** Swedish: ornamental name or habitational name based on a farm name with the same etymology as 1.

GIVEN NAMES Scandinavian 8%. *Lars* (2), *Asger, Carsten, Erik, Orvald.*

Norgard (298) Norwegian: variant of NORGAARD 1.

GIVEN NAMES Scandinavian 4%. *Iver, Selmer.*

Norgren (324) Swedish: variant of NORDGREN.

GIVEN NAMES Scandinavian 4%. *Lars* (2), *Elof.*

Norheim (112) Norwegian: either a variant of NORDHEIM or from a farm name composed of Old Norse *nór* 'narrows' (see NOHR 1) + *heimr* 'homestead', 'home'.

GIVEN NAMES Scandinavian 13%. *Nels, Oddvar.*

Nori (108) **1.** Indian (Andhra Pradesh): Hindu (Brahman) name of unknown meaning. **2.** Italian: from the personal name *Noro* or *Norio*, a short form of *Onorio* ('honor').

GIVEN NAMES Indian 28%; Italian 13%. *Srinivas* (3), *Anil* (2), *Mani* (2), *Bala, Madhav, Meera, Murthy, Ram, Sekhar, Vasu, Vijay; Angelo* (2), *Carlo, Franco, Pasquale, Pietro, Rocco, Valentino.*

Noriega (1454) Asturian-Leonese: habitational name from Noriega in Asturies.

GIVEN NAMES Spanish 45%. *Jose* (36), *Juan* (22), *Jesus* (16), *Manuel* (15), *Carlos* (11), *Fernando* (10), *Ramon* (9), *Guadalupe* (8), *Ana* (6), *Luis* (6), *Pedro* (6), *Ruben* (6).

Norin (109) Swedish: ornamental name composed of the elements *nor* 'north' + the common surname suffix *-in*, derived from Latin *-inius* 'descendant of'.

GIVEN NAMES Scandinavian 5%. *Alf, Lasse.*

Nork (159) **1.** German: possibly from an unexplained Old Prussian personal name or from a Slavic word for a diving bird (for example, a duck). **2.** Swedish: unexplained.

Norkus (289) Lithuanian: **1.** nickname from a derivative of *noras* 'wish', 'desire', 'will' or *noréti* 'to want'. **2.** derivative of the personal name *Norkantas*.

GIVEN NAMES Lithuanian 4%. *Kazys, Petras, Pranas, Vytautas.*

Norland (282) **1.** English: topographic name from Middle English *north* 'north' + *land* 'land', or a habitational name from Norland in West Yorkshire, named with Old English *norð* 'north' + *land* 'land', 'estate', 'district', 'part of a settlement'. **2.** Norwegian: habitational name from a farmstead so named, from Old Norse *nord* 'north' + *land* 'land', 'farmstead'.

GIVEN NAMES Scandinavian 8%. *Nils* (3), *Erik* (2), *Thor* (2), *Selmer.*

Norlander (235) Swedish: ornamental name composed of the elements *norr* 'north' + *land* 'land' + the habitational suffix *-er*.

Norlin (301) Swedish: topographic name for someone who lived to the north of a settlement, from *norr* 'north' + the surname suffix *-(l)in*, derived from Latin *-(l)inius*.

GIVEN NAMES Scandinavian 8%; German 4%. *Anders, Erik, Per, Sven; Kurt, Otto.*

Norling (504) Swedish: ornamental name formed with *norr* 'north' + the suffix *-ling* denoting a person.

GIVEN NAMES Scandinavian 5%. *Hilmer, Lars.*

Norman (22685) **1.** English, Irish (Ulster), Scottish, and Dutch: name applied either to a Scandinavian or to someone from Normandy in northern France. The Scandinavian adventurers of the Dark Ages called themselves *norðmenn* 'men from the North'. Before 1066, Scandinavian settlers in England were already fairly readily absorbed, and *Northman* and *Normann* came to be used as bynames and later as personal names, even among the Saxon inhabitants. The term gained a new use from 1066 onwards, when England was settled by invaders from Normandy, who were likewise of Scandinavian origin but by now largely integrated with the native population and speaking a Romance language, retaining only their original Germanic name. **2.** French: regional name for someone from Normandy. **3.** Dutch: ethnic name for a Norwegian. **4.** Jewish (Ashkenazic): variant of NORDMAN. **5.** Jewish: Americanized form of some like-sounding Ashkenazic name. In at least one case it is an Americanized form of **Novominsky**, the name of a family from Uman in Ukraine. On coming to the United States around 1900, a member of this family changed his name to *Norman*, after which some relatives in Russia adopted this name in place of *Novominsky*. **6.** Swedish: from *norr* 'north' + *man* 'man'.

FOREBEARS Albert Andriessen Bradt, a settler in Rensselaerswijck on the upper Hudson River in NY, was originally from Norway and was known as *de Norrman* ('the Norwegian'). The waterway south of Albany which powered his mills became known as the *Normanskill* ('the Norman's Waterway'), by which name it is still known today.

Normand (1249) French (also Scottish): regional name for someone from Normandy (see NORMAN).

GIVEN NAMES French 8%. *Gaston* (3), *Andre* (2), *Laurent* (2), *Marcel* (2), *Pierre* (2), *Amie, Donat, Emile, Herve, Jacques, Jean Noel, Jean-Michel.*

Normandeau (160) French: from a diminutive of NORMAND.

GIVEN NAMES French 6%. *Lucien, Marcel.*

Normandin (745) French: from a diminutive of NORMAND.

GIVEN NAMES French 10%. *Armand* (3), *Alain* (2), *Serge* (2), *Adrien, Andre, Aurore, Celine, Clovis, Emile, Gaetan, Gilles, Laurier.*

Normandy (101) English: regional name for someone from Normandy in northern France.

Normann (147) German and Scandinavian: variant of NORDMANN.

GIVEN NAMES Scandinavian 21%; German 7%. *Erik* (2); *Gerd* (2).

Norment (288) Northern French (**Le Norment**): variant of NORMAND.

Normile (296) Irish: Anglicized form of Gaelic **Mac Confhormaoile**, a patronymic from *Cú Fhormaoile*, a personal name meaning 'hound of Formoyle', a place in County Clare. This and the variant **Normoyle** are found in Counties Clare and Limerick.

Normington (215) English (West Yorkshire): apparently a habitational name, probably from any of various places called Normanton, notably the one in West Yorkshire, which are named with Old English *Northman* 'Norseman', 'Viking' + *tūn* 'settlement'.

Normoyle (170) Irish: variant of NORMILE.
GIVEN NAME Irish 6%. *Kieran*.

Noronha (129) Portuguese: originally from Asturian-Leonese **Noroña**, variant of the habitational name Noreña, a town in Asturies. This name is common in the former Portuguese colony of Goa and elsewhere in western India, where it was taken by Portuguese colonists.
GIVEN NAMES Spanish 17%; Portuguese 11%; Indian 7%. *Carlos* (3), *Augusto* (2), *Jose* (2), *Adelio, Alda, Alfredo, Fernando, Frederico, Luis, Manuel, Mauricio, Santana; Guilherme, Joaquim; Anil, Arun, Priya, Roshni, Sunita*.

Norquist (388) Swedish: ornamental name composed of the elements *norr, nord* 'north' + *quist*, an old or ornamental spelling of *kvist* 'twig'.

Norr (174) **1.** Swedish: probably an ornamental name from *norr* 'north'. **2.** German (**Nörr**): variant of NOHR 3. **3.** Perhaps a respelling of German KNORR.

Norred (444) **1.** English: variant of NORROD. **2.** Norwegian: variant of NORED.

Norrell (658) Swedish: ornamental name composed of the elements *norr* 'north' + the common surname element *-ell*, a derivative of the Latin adjectival ending *-elius*.

Norrick (122) English: unexplained. Probably a variant of **Northwick**, a habitational name from Old English *north* 'north' + *wīc* 'outlying (dairy) farm'. There is a place of this name in Gloucestershire.

Norrid (156) English: variant of NORROD.

Norrie (198) **1.** Scottish: variant of NORRIS. Black offers evidence that this name was interchangeable with **Norn**, an old Orkney surname derived from Old Norse *Norrœna*, the name of the Norse language; alternatively, it may be from Old Norse *Noregr* 'Norway'. **2.** English: variant of NORTHEY.

Norrington (154) English: **1.** topographic name for someone living to the north of a main settlement, Middle English *north in toun*, or a habitational name from any of the places named with this phrase (Old English *norð in tūne*), as for example Norrington in Wiltshire. **2.** variant of **Northampton**, a habitational name from the city of this name, which was named with Old English

norð 'north' + *hām* + *tūn* 'homestead', 'home farm'.

Norris (31450) English, Scottish, and Irish: **1.** regional name for someone who had migrated from the North (i.e. further north in England, or from Scotland or Scandinavia), from Old French *nor(r)eis* 'northerner'. **2.** topographic name for someone who lived in a house on the north side of a settlement or estate, from Middle English *north* 'north' + *hous* 'house'. **3.** occupational name for a wet-nurse or foster mother, from Old French *nurice, norrice* (Latin *nutrix*, genitive *nutricis*).

Norrod (239) **1.** English: variant of NORWOOD. **2.** Possibly an altered spelling of German **Naurod**, a habitational name from Naurod near Wiesbaden, or **Nauroth**, a habitational name from Nauroth in the Westerwald, both denoting settlements on newly cleared land. Compare NEUROTH.
FOREBEARS Benjamin Isaac Norrod (1735–1816) came from Buckinghamshire, England, to MD in 1735, and moved on to Stewart Co., TN.

Norstrom (148) Swedish (**Norström**): ornamental name composed of the elements *norr, nord* 'north' + *ström* 'river'.

Norsworthy (869) English: habitational name from Norseworthy in Walkhampton, Devon.

North (7504) **1.** English: topographic name, from Middle English *north* 'north', for someone who lived in the northern part of a village or to the north of a main settlement (compare NORRINGTON 1), or a regional name for someone who had migrated from the north. Compare NORRIS 1. **2.** Irish: regional name for someone from Ulster, the northern area of Ireland, in part as an Anglicized form of Gaelic **Mac an Ultaigh** (see MCNULTY) or (in Westmeath) of **Ultach**. **3.** German: from a short form of a Germanic personal name composed with a cognate of Old High German *nord* 'north'.

Northam (567) English (Devon): habitational name from Northam in Devon, named in Old English with *norþ* 'north' + *hamm* 'enclosure hemmed in by water' or 'promontory'.

Northcott (401) English: variant of NORTHCUTT.

Northcraft (217) English: topographic name for someone who lived on a croft to the north of the main settlement, from Middle English *north* 'north' + *croft* 'enclosure', 'small enclosed field', or a habitational name from a place named with these elements, as for example Northcroft in Cheshire. The dialect spelling *craft* seems to belong to southern and western counties.

Northcutt (2395) English: habitational name from any of many minor places, notably in Devon, called Northcott or Northcote, named in Old English with *norð* 'north' + *cot* 'cottage', 'shelter'.

Northen (144) English: variant of NORTHERN.

Northern (989) English: topographic name, from an adjectival form of NORTH.

Northey (419) English (Devon): habitational name, probably from Northay in Hawkchurch, Devon, named with Old English *norð* 'north' + *(ge)hæg* 'enclosure', or from various other places called Northey.

Northington (690) English: variant of NORRINGTON.

Northrip (116) Variant of English NORTHRUP.

Northrop (1648) English: variant of NORTHRUP. This is the most frequent form of the surname in the British Isles.

Northrup (2155) English: habitational name from Northorpe in the former East Riding of Yorkshire, named with Old Norse *norðr* or Old English *norþ* 'north' + *þorp* or *þrop* 'dependent outlying farmstead', 'hamlet'.

Northup (1071) English: habitational name from Northop in Flintshire, named with Old English *norð* 'north' + *hop* 'enclosure (in marsh or moor)', 'enclosed valley'.

Northway (419) English: topographic name for someone living on the north side of a road, from Middle English *north* 'north' + *weye* 'way', 'path', 'road', or a habitational name from a minor place name of the same origin.

Nortman (156) German (**Nortmann**): variant of NORDMANN.
GIVEN NAMES French 5%. *Henri, Monique*.

Norton (24449) **1.** English: habitational name from any of the many places so called, from Old English *norð* 'north' + *tūn* 'enclosure', 'settlement'. In some cases, it is a variant of NORRINGTON. **2.** Irish: altered form of NAUGHTON, assimilated to the English name. **3.** Jewish (American): adoption of the English name in place of some like-sounding Ashkenazic name.
FOREBEARS Nicholas Norton (1610–90) came from Broadway, Somerset, England, to Weymouth, MA, in 1635–37. In about 1657 he moved to Edgartown on Martha's Vineyard. He had ten children and many prominent descendants.

Nortz (118) **1.** North German: from a short form of a Germanic personal name (see NORTH 3). **2.** South German: perhaps a metonymic occupational name for someone who trapped otters or for someone who dealt in otter skins, from Middle High German *norz, nörz* 'otter'.

Norum (168) **1.** Norwegian: habitational name from any of four farmsteads named in Old Norse as *Nórheimr*, from *nór* 'narrow passage in a river', 'strait' + *heimr* 'homestead', 'farmstead'. **2.** Swedish: ornamental name formed with the same elements as 1.

Norvell (1405) Scottish: reduced form of the Norman habitational name Normanville, derived from either of two places so called in Normandy.

Norville (520) English: see NORVELL.

Norwich (114) English: habitational name from the city of Norwich in East Anglia, named from Old English *north* 'north' + *wīc* 'trading center', 'harbor', or a topographic name with the same meaning.

Norwick (116) **1.** Scottish (Orkney): habitational name from Norwick in Shetland. **2.** Possibly an altered spelling of NORWICH.

Norwood (7002) English: habitational name from any of the many places so called, from Old English *norð* 'north' + *wudu* 'wood'.

Nosal (436) Polish, Czech (**Nosál**), and Slovak (**Nosál'**): nickname for someone with a big nose.

GIVEN NAMES Polish 4%. *Piotr, Ryszard, Tadeusz.*

Nosbisch (155) Altered form of German **Nosbüsch** or **Nussbusch**, a topographic name for someone who lived by a nut tree, typically a hazel.

Nosek (331) Czech and Polish: nickname for someone with a snub nose, from Czech, Polish *nosek* 'little nose'.

GIVEN NAMES Polish 5%. *Andrzej, Bogumil, Jacek, Pawel.*

Noser (138) **1.** Swiss German: perhaps an altered form of **Nösser**, an occupational name from an agent derivative of Middle High German *nōss* 'working stock (cattle)'; or alternatively perhaps a habitational name from Nossen in Saxony, the *-er* suffix denoting an inhabitant. **2.** German and Swiss German (**Nöser**): occupational name for a cattle dealer or someone who raised cattle or other domestic animals, an agent noun from Middle High German *nōz* 'domestic animals' (see NOTZ and NOSS).

Noseworthy (190) English: variant of NORSWORTHY.

Noska (188) Polish: nickname for someone with a snub nose, from a derivative of *nosek* 'little nose' (see NOSEK).

Nosko (122) German (of Slavic origin): nickname for someone with a snub nose.

GIVEN NAME German 4%. *Otto.*

Noss (496) **1.** Norwegian: habitational name from any of various farmsteads named Noss, from Old Norse *nǫs* 'nose', in reference to any natural feature, such as a crag or mountain peak, that is shaped like a nose. **2.** German (of Slavic origin): see NOSEK. **3.** German: variant of NOTZ. **4.** English: variant of NESS 1.

Nossaman (125) Origin unidentified.

Nostrand (161) Dutch: see VAN NOSTRAND.

Nostrant (105) Dutch: see VAN NOSTRAND.

Nosworthy (99) English: variant of NORSWORTHY.

Notarangelo (127) Italian: distinguishing name for a clerk (see NOTARO) called ANGELO.

GIVEN NAMES Italian 10%. *Antonio, Lorenzo, Lucio, Mario, Pietro.*

Notarianni (153) Italian: distinguishing name for a clerk (see NOTARO) named *Ianni*, a variant of *Giovanni* (see JOHN).

GIVEN NAMES Italian 24%. *Antonio* (2), *Pasco* (2), *Aldo, Emilio, Fernando, Giovanni, Giuseppe, Luigi, Pasquale, Renato, Romeo.*

Notaro (593) Italian: occupational name for a scribe or clerk, medieval Italian *notaro*, from Latin *notarius*, an agent derivative of *nota* 'mark', 'sign'. *Notaro* is widespread in southern Italy.

GIVEN NAMES Italian 15%. *Salvatore* (4), *Angelo* (3), *Antonio, Carmelo, Carmine, Dante, Giacomo, Giovanni, Giuseppe, Mauro, Natale, Nicola.*

Notch (186) Perhaps an Americanized spelling of German NOTZ.

Noteboom (331) Dutch: topographic name for someone who lived by a walnut tree, Dutch *note(n)boom*.

Notestine (270) Altered form of German NOTHSTEIN.

Noth (145) German (also **Nöth**): nickname from Middle High German *nōt* 'distress', 'need', 'travail', or from a short form of a Germanic personal name formed with a cognate of this word, as for example *Notger, Gernot*.

GIVEN NAMES German 6%. *Egon, Kurt, Orlo, Theodor.*

Nothdurft (140) German: nickname for a poverty-stricken person, from Middle High German *nōtdurft* 'need'.

GIVEN NAMES German 5%. *Franz, Wilhelm.*

Nothnagel (152) South German: metonymic occupational name for a farrier, from Early New High German *nöte* (from Middle High German *nötstal*) denoting a special stall for horses used for shoeing and other operations + *Nagel* 'nail'.

GIVEN NAME German 5%. *Kurt.*

Nothstein (142) German: from a Germanic personal name composed of Old High German *nōt* 'distress', 'force' + *stein* 'stone', 'rock', 'castle'.

GIVEN NAMES German 5%. *Erwin, Fritz.*

Notley (142) English: probably a habitational name from Black and White Notley in Essex, named from Old English *hntu* 'nut tree' + *lēah* 'clearing'.

Notman (125) **1.** Scottish and northern English: probably an occupational name for a dealer in nuts, from Middle English *not(e)*, nut + *man*, although Black expresses reservations about this derivation, and it may perhaps be an occupational name for the 'servant (Middle English *man*) of someone called NOTT'. **2.** Jewish (Ashkenazic): nickname for a poor man, from German *Not* 'need', 'want' + *Mann* 'man'. **3.** Respelling of German **Nothmann**, from a short form of a Germanic personal name formed with a cognate of Old High German *nōt* 'distress', 'force' + *man* 'man'.

4. North German: from Middle Low German *note* 'companion' + *man* 'man'.

Noto (1179) Italian (Sicily): habitational name from Noto in Siracusa province.

GIVEN NAMES Italian 16%. *Salvatore* (18), *Sal* (4), *Angelo* (3), *Antonio* (3), *Aldo* (2), *Dino* (2), *Giovanni* (2), *Pasquale* (2), *Saverio* (2), *Vito* (2), *Alfonse, Baldassare.*

Nott (843) **1.** English: nickname for a bald man or one who kept his hair extremely close-cropped, from Middle English *not(te)* 'bald' (Old English *hnott*). **2.** English: variant spelling of KNOTT. **3.** German: of uncertain origin; perhaps either a nickname for an inconspicuous person, from Middle Low German *not(e)* 'nut', or a derivative of Middle Low German *note* 'companion'.

Nottage (212) English: nickname from Middle English *notehache* 'nuthatch' (a bird name, apparently from Old English *hnutu* 'nut' + *haccian* 'to break, crack').

Notte (172) **1.** Italian: from a short form of the personal name **Bonanotte**, from *buona* 'good' + *notte* 'night', given with reference to the time of birth. **2.** French: occupational name for a choral singer, from *not(t)er* 'to sing'. **3.** Dutch: from a reduced form of a personal name ending in *-n* (for example, *Johann, Jan*) with the diminutive suffix *-otte*. **4.** Dutch and Belgian (**van der Notte**): habitational name from any of various places called Ter Noot, for example in Borre, French Flanders. **5.** German (also **Nötte**): variant of NOTT.

GIVEN NAMES Italian 15%. *Dante* (2), *Angelo, Benedetto, Luigi, Nicola, Quido, Rocco, Serafino.*

Notter (219) **1.** German and Swiss German: variant of a Germanic personal name formed with Old High German *nōt* 'distress', 'force' + *hart* 'strong'. **2.** South German: nickname for someone versed in the art of writing, from Middle High German *noter* 'notarius', 'literate (lay) person'.

GIVEN NAMES German 4%. *Erwin, Ewald.*

Nottingham (1479) English: habitational name from the city of Nottingham in the East Midlands, named in Old English as 'homestead (*hām*) of Snot's people'. The initial *S-* was lost in the 12th century, due to the influence of Anglo-Norman French (the combination *sn-* is alien to French).

Notz (198) German and Swiss German: **1.** probably from Middle High German *nōz* 'domestic animals', 'cattle', hence a byname for a dealer in livestock. Compare NOETZEL. **2.** from a short form of a Germanic personal name formed with *nōt* 'distress', 'force'.

GIVEN NAMES German 5%; French 5%. *Otto* (2); *Thierry* (2), *Gregoire.*

Nour (104) Muslim: variant of NOOR.

GIVEN NAMES Muslim 62%; French 6%; Romanian 4%. *Ramez* (3), *Ashraf* (2), *Bakr* (2), *Mohamed* (2), *Mostafa* (2), *Nabil* (2), *Samir* (2), *Abdalla, Adib, Ali, Amir,*

Ebrahim; *Emile* (2), *Antoine*; *Sorin* (2), *Dragos*.

Nouri (166) Muslim: variant of NOORI.
GIVEN NAMES Muslim 70%. *Ahmad* (3), *Hossein* (3), *Keyvan* (3), *Mohammad* (3), *Abderrahmane* (2), *Adiba* (2), *Ali* (2), *Fatima* (2), *Karim* (2), *Mohamad* (2), *Mohamed* (2), *Nader* (2).

Nourie (137) Origin unidentified.

Nourse (638) English, Scottish, and Irish: variant of NORRIS 3.

Noury (144) French: **1.** from a Germanic personal name composed of the elements *nod*, *not* 'need' + *rīc* 'power', 'rule'. **2.** habitational name from Nourry in Nièvre, derived from a Gallo-Roman estate name, *Nutriacum*. **3.** according to Debrabandere, from Old French *norri* 'fed', hence a nickname for a lodger.
GIVEN NAMES French 9%. *Armand*, *Lucien*, *Normand*, *Serge*.

Nova (287) **1.** Asturian-Leonese and Spanish: habitational name from any of the towns called Nova in Albacete or Asturies. **2.** Galician: literally 'new', probably a habitational name from a place named Vila Nova. **3.** Italian: unexplained.
GIVEN NAMES Spanish 40%. *Carlos* (6), *Rafael* (4), *Juan* (3), *Manuel* (3), *Mercedes* (3), *Alfredo* (2), *Dominga* (2), *Francisco* (2), *Gonzalo* (2), *Luz* (2), *Maribel* (2), *Aida*.

Novacek (362) Czech (**Nováček**): from a diminutive of NOVAK.

Novack (1079) Germanized or Americanized spelling of NOVAK.

Novak (14184) **1.** Czech and Slovak, Croatian and Serbian, Slovenian, Hungarian (**Novák**), and Jewish (eastern Ashkenazic): from Slavic *novy* 'new', denoting a newcomer to a place. Compare English NEWMAN. **2.** Slovenian: also a topographic name for a peasant who settled on newly cleared land.

Novakovich (168) Serbian and Croatian (**Novaković**): patronymic from NOVAK.
GIVEN NAMES South Slavic 5%. *Stanko*, *Zarko*, *Zeljko*.

Novakowski (143) Altered spelling of Polish NOWAKOWSKI.

Novara (119) Italian (Sicily): habitational name from Novara di Sicilia in Messina province, Sicily, possibly so named from Sicilian *nuara* 'vegetable plot', 'place where vegetables are grown'.
GIVEN NAMES Italian 8%. *Caesar*, *Domenic*, *Gasper*, *Romano*.

Novell (155) Catalan: nickname from *novell* 'young', 'new' (Latin *novellus* 'new'). Compare NEW.

Novella (137) **1.** Catalan: probably a nickname from the feminine form of NOVELL 'young' or from *novella* 'news'. **2.** Italian: variant (feminine form) of NOVELLO.
GIVEN NAMES Spanish 13%; Italian 8%. *Felipe*, *Francisco*, *Jesus*, *Juan*, *Julio*, *Luis*,

Mario, *Milagros*, *Rolando*, *Rosario*; *Giuseppe*, *Sal*, *Salvatore*.

Novelli (437) Italian: patronymic or plural form of NOVELLO.
GIVEN NAMES Italian 17%. *Angelo* (6), *Enrico* (2), *Salvatore* (2), *Dante*, *Domenic*, *Ercole*, *Francesca*, *Gaetano*, *Luciano*, *Lucio*, *Marco*, *Nicola*.

Novello (511) **1.** Italian: from the nickname and personal name *Novello* 'new', 'young'. As a nickname it may have denoted a newcomer to an area, from a diminutive of *nuovo* 'new', or been used to distinguish the younger of two bearers of the same personal name in the same family; as a personal name it may have been bestowed on the youngest child. **2.** Catalan (**Novelló**): from a diminutive of NOVELL.
GIVEN NAMES Italian 21%; Spanish 6%. *Salvatore* (3), *Angelo* (2), *Gaetano* (2), *Guido* (2), *Mario* (2), *Mauro* (2), *Rocco* (2), *Rodolfo* (2), *Aldo*, *Antonino*, *Antonio*, *Carmine*, *Fausto*, *Francesco*, *Rudolfo*; *Elvira*, *Jesus*, *Jose*, *Ruben*, *Santos*.

November (156) **1.** Dutch: nickname from the name of the month, probably denoting someone born or baptized in November. **2.** Jewish (Ashkenazic): probably an ornamental adoption of the name of the month, from German.
GIVEN NAME Jewish 6%. *Mort*.

Novey (161) Possibly an altered spelling of NOVY.

Novich (116) Serbian and Croatian (**Nović**): patronymic from *Novica* or *Novo*, pet forms of NOVAK.

Novick (1324) **1.** Americanized form of a Slavic name such as NOVAK, denoting a newcomer to a place. **2.** Jewish (from Belarus): habitational name from a village in Belarus called Noviki.
GIVEN NAMES Jewish 4%. *Sol* (2), *Aron*, *Ber*, *Dov*, *Elihu*, *Emanuel*, *Hyman*, *Meyer*, *Miriam*.

Novicki (199) Altered spelling of Polish NOWICKI.
GIVEN NAME French 4%. *Alphonse*.

Noviello (160) Italian: Neapolitan variant of NOVELLO.
GIVEN NAMES Italian 18%. *Alfonso*, *Antonio*, *Giacomo*, *Luigi*, *Orlando*, *Vito*.

Novik (133) Jewish (from Belarus): habitational name from a village in Belarus called Noviki.
GIVEN NAMES Russian 24%; Jewish 14%. *Boris* (3), *Anatoly* (2), *Gariy* (2), *Anatoliy*, *Dmitry*, *Fima*, *Fyodor*, *Grigoriy*, *Igor*, *Iosif*, *Pesya*, *Raisa*; *Aron*, *Esfir*, *Faina*, *Genya*, *Sol*, *Yakov*.

Novikoff (111) **1.** Russian (**Novikov**): patronymic from *novik* 'newcomer'. **2.** Jewish (from Belarus): habitational name from the Belorussian village of Noviki.

Novinger (224) Possibly an altered form of German **Nofsinger** (see NOFFSINGER).

Novitski (190) Jewish (eastern Ashkenazic) and Polish: altered form of NOWICKI.

Novitsky (224) Jewish (eastern Ashkenazic) and Polish: altered form of NOWICKI.
GIVEN NAMES Russian 5%. *Vladimir* (2), *Anatoly*, *Oksana*, *Sergei*.

Novo (222) Portuguese and Galician: nickname from Portuguese and Galician *novo* 'new', 'young' (Latin *novus*). The word was also occasionally used in the Middle Ages as a personal name, particularly for a child born after the death of a sibling, and this may also be a source of the surname.
GIVEN NAMES Spanish 41%; Portuguese 11%. *Jose* (5), *Manuel* (4), *Roberto* (4), *Jesus* (3), *Miguel* (3), *Cristina* (2), *Eduardo* (2), *Elena* (2), *Ignacio* (2), *Juan* (2), *Lazaro* (2), *Ramon* (2); *Joaquim*; *Antonio* (4), *Angelo*, *Claudina*.

Novoa (431) Galician (**Nóvoa**): habitational name from the former Galician juridical district Terra de Nóvoa, in Ourense province.
GIVEN NAMES Spanish 51%. *Jose* (19), *Luis* (8), *Jorge* (7), *Mario* (7), *Carlos* (6), *Jesus* (6), *Joaquin* (6), *Angel* (5), *Manuel* (5), *Ricardo* (5), *Roberto* (5), *Ana* (4).

Novosad (317) Jewish (eastern Ashkenazic) and Belorussian: habitational name from places named Novosady, of which there are several in Belarus and one in Poland. In some cases it could be a shortened form of **Novosadski**.

Novosel (421) Ukrainian and Jewish (eastern Ashkenazic): nickname for a newcomer to a place, Ukrainian *novosel*.

Novotney (214) Americanized spelling of Czech NOVOTNY.

Novotny (2895) Czech (**Novotný**) and Jewish (Ashkenazic): nickname denoting a newcomer to a place. This is the third most common Czech surname.

Novy (661) **1.** Czech (**Nový**) and Jewish (Ashkenazic): variant of NOVAK. **2.** Southern French: from old Occitan *novi* 'newlywed husband', derived from Latin *novius*.

Nowack (485) German (of Slavic origin): Germanized spelling of Czech and Slovak NOVAK or Polish NOWAK.
GIVEN NAMES German 5%. *Gerhard* (3), *Lorenz* (2).

Nowacki (649) Polish: habitational name for someone from places called Nowaki in the voivodeships of Nowy Sącz, Opole, Siedlce, and elsewhere, named with *nowy* 'new'.
GIVEN NAMES Polish 7%. *Stanislaw* (3), *Jacek* (2), *Tadeusz* (2), *Bogdan*, *Casimir*, *Izabela*, *Janina*, *Kazimierz*, *Pawel*, *Walenty*, *Zbigniew*.

Nowaczyk (267) Polish: nickname for a newcomer to a district, from a diminutive of NOWAK.
GIVEN NAMES Polish 4%. *Jerzy*, *Jozef*, *Sylwester*.

Nowak (7201) Polish and Jewish (eastern Ashkenazic): nickname for a newcomer to a district or someone new to a profession or occupation, from a derivative of Polish *nowy* 'new'. This is an extremely common Polish surname.

GIVEN NAMES Polish 6%. *Andrzej* (11), *Janusz* (9), *Jozef* (7), *Stanislaw* (7), *Zbigniew* (7), *Janina* (5), *Jerzy* (5), *Boguslaw* (4), *Casimir* (4), *Lech* (4), *Piotr* (4), *Tadeusz* (4).

Nowakowski (1430) Polish: habitational name for someone from Nowakowa in Nowy Sącz voivodeship, or Nowakowo in Poznań voivodeship.

GIVEN NAMES Polish 8%. *Jerzy* (4), *Boleslaw* (2), *Grzegorz* (2), *Zbigniew* (2), *Zdzislaw* (2), *Andrzej*, *Bogdan*, *Boguslaw*, *Casimir*, *Dariusz*, *Izabela*, *Jacek*.

Nowell (2143) English: variant spelling of NOEL.

Nowels (106) Altered form of NOWELL or NOEL.

Nowicki (2320) **1.** Polish and Jewish (from Poland): variant of NOWAK 'newcomer'. **2.** Polish: habitational name for someone from a place called Nowica or Nowice, named with *nowý* 'new'.

GIVEN NAMES Polish 5%. *Jerzy* (3), *Stanislaw* (3), *Bogdan* (2), *Jadwiga* (2), *Ryszard* (2), *Witold* (2), *Zdzislaw* (2), *Zigmund* (2), *Alojzy*, *Arkadiusz*, *Ewa*, *Franciszek*.

Nowik (124) Polish and Jewish (eastern Ashkenazic): nickname for a newcomer, from a derivative of *nowy* 'new' (see NOWAK).

GIVEN NAMES Polish 19%. *Ryszard* (2), *Teofil* (2), *Henryka*, *Izydor*, *Mariusz*, *Waclaw*.

Nowinski (220) Polish (**Nowiński**) and Jewish (eastern Ashkenazic): habitational name for someone from any of many places in Poland, Ukraine, and Belarus called (in Polish) Nowina, Nowiny, Nowinka, Nowinki, etc., all named with *nowina* 'fallow land'.

GIVEN NAMES Polish 7%. *Leszek* (2), *Bogdan*, *Jozef*, *Kazimierz*, *Lucjan*, *Piotr*.

Nowlan (367) Irish: variant spelling of NOLAN.

GIVEN NAMES French 4%. *Adelard*, *Germaine*, *Patrice*, *Raoul*.

Nowland (448) **1.** English: possibly a variant of NEWLAND or Irish NOLAN. **2.** Possibly a respelling of German **Nauland** (see NEWLAND).

Nowlen (140) Probably a variant spelling of Irish NOLAN.

Nowlin (2273) Probably a variant spelling of Irish NOLAN.

Nowling (371) Possibly a hypercorrected spelling of Irish NOLAN (see NOWLIN).

Nowotny (232) Polish: nickname from *nowotny* 'newcomer'.

GIVEN NAMES German 6%. *Alois*, *Erwin*, *Franz*, *Kurt*, *Volker*.

Noxon (203) English: probably a habitational name from a place so called in Gloucestershire.

Noy (145) **1.** English: variant of NOE. **2.** Jewish (Israeli): ornamental name from Hebrew *noy* 'decoration', 'adornment', in

part adopted as a Hebraicized form of various Ashkenazic surnames containing the unrelated German element *neu*, e.g. **Neumann** (see NEWMAN). **3.** Catalan: variant of **Noi**, nickname from *noi* 'boy', 'lad'.

GIVEN NAMES Jewish 14%; Spanish 9%. *Moshe* (2), *Eliezer*, *Ilan*, *Yacov*, *Yael*, *Yigal*, *Zahava*; *Jose* (2), *Juan* (2), *Alfredo*, *Ana*, *Eugenio*, *Jesus*, *Luis*, *Mario*, *Miguel*, *Ruberto*.

Noya (119) **1.** Galician: variant of the habitational name NOIA. **2.** Catalan: variant spelling of NOIA, truncated form of the habitational name **Anoia**. **3.** Japanese: written with characters meaning 'field' and 'arrow'. This name is not common in Japan.

GIVEN NAMES Spanish 32%; Japanese 5%. *Jose* (5), *Brunilda* (2), *Domingos* (2), *Ernesto* (2), *Juan* (2), *Ramon* (2), *Alicia*, *Ana*, *Angel*, *Aurelio*, *Cesar*, *Edmundo*; *Fumiaki*, *Takahiro*, *Yasuko*, *Yoshiko*.

Noyce (230) English: patronymic from the medieval personal name *Noye*, vernacular form of *Noah* (see NOE).

Noyd (135) English: unexplained.

Noye (108) English, French (**Noyé**), and Dutch: variant of NOE, from a vernacular form of NOAH.

GIVEN NAME French 4%. *Andre*.

Noyer (116) **1.** French: topographic name from *noyer* 'walnut tree'. **2.** German: probably a Huguenot name of the same origin and meaning as 1.

GIVEN NAMES German 4%. *Erwin*, *Phares*.

Noyes (4165) English (South Wales): patronymic from NOE.

Noyola (288) Spanish (from Basque): probably a variant of LOYOLA.

GIVEN NAMES Spanish 53%. *Jose* (12), *Juan* (10), *Carlos* (4), *Francisco* (4), *Benito* (3), *Javier* (3), *Raul* (3), *Angel* (2), *Armando* (2), *Arturo* (2), *Catalina* (2), *Guadalupe* (2).

Nuber (163) **1.** South German: variant of NUFER. **2.** Reduced form of German NEUBAUER.

Nucci (309) Italian (Tuscany and central–southern Italy): from a patronymic or plural form of NUCCIO.

GIVEN NAMES Italian 16%. *Dino* (4), *Angelo* (3), *Annamaria* (2), *Domenic* (2), *Marcello* (2), *Aniello*, *Antonio*, *Domenico*, *Valentino*, *Vincenza*.

Nuccio (506) Italian: from a short form of a personal name formed with the suffix *-uccio* following a final consonant *-n-*, for example *Antonuccio*, *Benuccio*, *Giovannuccio*, *Rinuccio*, *Stefanuccio*.

GIVEN NAMES Italian 16%; Spanish 5%. *Sal* (4), *Carlo* (3), *Mario* (3), *Salvatore* (3), *Vito* (3), *Pietro* (2), *Antonino*, *Antonio*, *Attilio*, *Carmin*, *Dino*, *Domenic*, *Ettore*, *Juan*, *Ramon*, *Salvador*.

Nuce (113) English: unexplained; perhaps a variant of NOYCE.

Nuchols (117) Variant of NICHOLS.

Nuckels (108) **1.** North German **Nückels**: pet form of *Nikolaus* (see NICHOLAS). Compare NUCKOLS. **2.** German: habitational name from a place called Nückel in Lower Saxony near Geestemünde. **3.** Altered spelling of *Nuckel*, an Old Prussian personal name.

Nuckles (414) Americanized form of North German **Nückels** (see NUCKELS).

Nuckolls (620) Of North German origin: variant spelling of NUCKOLS.

Nuckols (1054) Americanized form of North German **Nückel** (see NUCKELS), a pet form of *Nikolaus* (see NICHOLAS).

Nudd (192) English (Norfolk): unexplained. It may be a result of misdivision of some personal name ending in *-n* + the surname *Hudd* (see HUTT).

Nudell (101) Jewish (from Ukraine and Poland): metonymic occupational name for a tailor or a needle maker, from Yiddish dialect *nudl* 'needle'.

GIVEN NAMES Jewish 12%. *Avi*, *Chaim*, *Mayer*, *Moishe*, *Shira*.

Nudelman (389) Jewish (from Ukraine and Poland): occupational name for a tailor or a maker of needles, from Yiddish dialect 'needle' + *man* 'man'. Compare NADLER.

GIVEN NAMES Jewish 16%; Russian 10%. *Yakov* (4), *Haim* (2), *Mendel* (2), *Aron*, *Bronya*, *Gersh*, *Ilya*, *Irina*, *Miriam*, *Rachmil*, *Semen*, *Sima*; *Mikhail* (5), *Boris* (3), *Lev* (2), *Yefim* (2), *Aleksandr*, *Aleksey*, *Alik*, *Arkady*, *Iosif*, *Khava*, *Pesya*, *Polya*.

Nuding (125) German: patronymic from a Germanic personal name formed with an element cognate with Old High German *nōt* 'distress', 'need', 'force'.

Nudo (178) Italian: from *nudo* 'naked', perhaps a nickname for a destitute man, or a topographic name for someone who lived in a barren area.

GIVEN NAMES Italian 17%. *Angelo* (2), *Santo* (2), *Domenico*, *Raffaele*, *Rocco*, *Silvio*, *Tommaso*.

Nuechterlein (105) German (**Nüchterlein**): nickname from Middle High German *nüchtern* 'sober'. Compare NICHTER.

Nuehring (133) German (**Nühring**): of uncertain origin.

GIVEN NAMES German 9%. *Otto* (2), *Eldred*, *Erwin*, *Kurt*.

Nuelle (101) **1.** North German (**Nülle**): topographic name from *nul* 'bog', 'mire', or a habitational name from a place named with this word. **2.** South German: nickname for a big, awkward person.

Nuernberg (112) German: variant spelling of **Nürnberg** (see NURNBERG).

GIVEN NAMES German 6%; Scandinavian 4%. *Guenther*, *Hans*.

Nuernberger (137) German: variant spelling of **Nürnberger** (see NURNBERGER).

GIVEN NAMES German 7%. *Franz*, *Guenther*, *Wolfgang*.

Nuessle (104) Swiss German (**Nüssle**): **1.** from a field name, *Nüssle* 'hazel bush'. **2.** from the personal name *Nissle*, a pet form of *Dionysius* (see DENNIS).

Nufer (136) Swiss German (also **Nüfer**): nickname from Swiss German *nuefer* 'cheerful', 'lively', 'active'.
GIVEN NAMES German 5%. *Bernd, Kurt.*

Nuffer (188) **1.** Swiss German: see NUFER. **2.** German: from a personal name derived from *Onuphrius*, name of a local saint.
GIVEN NAMES German 4%. *Fritz, Gerhard.*

Nugen (160) Probably a variant of English and Irish NUGENT.

Nugent (6133) English and Irish (of Norman origin), and northern French: habitational name from any of several places in northern France, such as Nogent-sur-Oise, named with Latin *Novientum*, apparently an altered form of a Gaulish name meaning 'new settlement'.
FOREBEARS The Anglo-Norman family of this name is descended from Fulke de Bellesme, lord of Nogent in Normandy, who was granted large estates around Winchester after the Conquest. His great-grandson was Hugh de Nugent (died 1213), who went to Ireland with Hugh de Lacy, and was granted lands in Bracklyn, County Westmeath. The family formed itself into a clan on the Irish model, of which the chief bore the hereditary title of *Uinsheadun* (Irish *Uinnseadún*), from their original seat at Winchester. They have been Earls of Westmeath since 1621. The name is now a common one in Ireland, and has been adopted there by some who have no connection with the clan.

Nuhfer (166) Variant of German NUFFER or NUFER.

Nuhn (164) German: unexplained. Perhaps from *Nunno*, an Old High German personal name and ultimately a nursery word.
GIVEN NAMES German 7%. *Manfred* (3), *Heinrich.*

Nulf (143) Variant of Dutch and German NOLF.

Null (2574) **1.** Jewish (Ashkenazic): variant of NOLL 3. **2.** German (also **Null**): a variant of NOLL and NUELLE 2.

Nulph (261) Classicized spelling of Dutch and German NULF (see NOLF).

Nulton (138) Probably a spelling variant of German **Nolten**, a patronymic of NOLTE.

Nulty (283) Irish: reduced form of McNULTY.
GIVEN NAME Irish 4%. *Eamonn.*

Nunamaker (281) Americanized form of German NONNENMACHER.

Nunan (286) Irish: variant spelling of NOONAN.
GIVEN NAME Irish 5%. *Seamus* (2).

Nuncio (117) Spanish and Portuguese: of uncertain derivation. Possibly from *nuncio* 'messenger', 'envoy' or a personal name from the same word (possibly alluding to the Angel Gabriel).

GIVEN NAMES Spanish 32%. *Juan* (3), *Jose* (2), *Ricardo* (2), *Anacleto, Domingo, Ernesto, Jesus, Juanita, Lino, Manuel, Mario, Mateo.*

Nunemaker (372) Americanized spelling of German NONNENMACHER.

Nunes (3061) Portuguese or Galician: patronymic from the personal name NUNO.
GIVEN NAMES Spanish 14%; Portuguese 9%. *Manuel* (76), *Jose* (29), *Carlos* (15), *Francisco* (12), *Luis* (12), *Mario* (9), *Alberto* (4), *Domingos* (4), *Ricardo* (4), *Americo* (3), *Ana* (3), *Armando* (3); *Joao* (10), *Joaquim* (5), *Paulo* (4), *Guilherme* (2), *Aderito, Fernandes, Ilidio, Vasco, Zulmira.*

Nunez (10562) Spanish (**Núñez**): patronymic from the personal name *Nuño* (see NUNO).
GIVEN NAMES Spanish 49%; Portuguese 10%. *Jose* (346), *Juan* (176), *Luis* (111), *Manuel* (101), *Carlos* (83), *Jesus* (78), *Francisco* (75), *Miguel* (70), *Rafael* (65), *Pedro* (62), *Jorge* (61), *Ramon* (60); *Guilherme, Joaquim, Vasco, Wenceslao.*

Nungesser (233) German: **1.** apparently a variant spelling of **Nonnengasse**, from a street name meaning 'nuns' lane'. **2.** Possibly a variant of **Gnugesser**, a nickname for a big eater, from *g(e)nug* 'enough' + *esser* 'eater' (from *essen* 'to eat'). **3.** Alternatively, it may be a habitational name for someone from Nunkas, a place in the Upper Palatinate.

Nungester (119) Variant of German NUNGESSER.

Nunley (2662) English: habitational name from Nunley Farm in Wroxhall, Warwickshire.

Nunn (5334) **1.** English (mainly East Anglia): nickname for a pious and demure man, or an occupational name for someone who worked at a convent, from Middle English *nunn* 'nun' (Old English *nunne*, from Latin *nonna*, originally a respectful term of address for an elderly woman. The Latin word probably originated as a nursery term). **2.** German: from an Old High German personal name *Nunno*, said to be a nursery word.

Nunnally (1432) Irish: probably a variant of MUNNELLY.

Nunnelee (165) Variant of Irish NUNNALLY.

Nunnelley (250) Variant of Irish NUNNALLY.

Nunnelly (175) Variant of Irish NUNNALLY.

Nunnery (842) English: perhaps from Middle English *nonnerie* 'nunnery', applied as a topographic name for someone who lived by a nunnery or a metonymic occupational name for someone who worked at one.

Nunno (107) Italian (Sicily): nickname from Sicilian *nunnu* 'charming', 'agreeable'.
GIVEN NAMES Italian 18%. *Gino* (3), *Angelo, Biagio, Rocco, Umberto.*

Nuno (543) Spanish (**Nuño**), Portuguese, and Galician: from a medieval personal name, first attested in the Latin form *Nunnus*, of uncertain derivation.
GIVEN NAMES Spanish 54%; Portuguese 12%. *Jose* (19), *Juan* (13), *Jesus* (9), *Salvador* (8), *Alfredo* (6), *Carlos* (6), *Francisco* (6), *Jose Luis* (6), *Miguel* (6), *Luis* (5), *Manuel* (5), *Alfonso* (4); *Joao, Joaquim, Paulo*; *Antonio* (7), *Aldo, Dante, Flavio, Gabino, Sal.*

Nunziata (187) Italian: from a reduced form of the Marian personal name ANNUNZIATA.
GIVEN NAMES Italian 12%. *Sal* (2), *Salvatore* (2), *Alfonse, Antonio, Gennaro.*

Nunziato (223) Italian: from a reduced form of the personal name ANNUNZIATO.
GIVEN NAMES Italian 14%; French 5%. *Gennaro* (2), *Angelo, Carmela, Concetta, Sal, Salvatore*; *Andre* (2), *Armand.*

Nupp (111) Estonian: unexplained.

Nurenberg (133) Jewish (Ashkenazic): variant of NIERENBERG.

Nurmi (292) Finnish: ornamental name from Finnish *nurmi* 'lawn' or 'pasture'. The surname dates from the 16th century, becoming popular in the late 19th century, when it was taken by people who hitherto had no surname, and during the name conversion movement of the 19th and early 20th centuries, when it was frequently adopted as a replacement for a Swedish or other foreign family name. It occurs chiefly in southwestern Finland.
GIVEN NAMES Finnish 20%; Scandinavian 6%. *Paavo* (3), *Arvo* (2), *Eino* (2), *Oiva* (2), *Reino* (2), *Tauno* (2), *Waino* (2), *Ahti, Annikki, Arvi, Eero, Jorma*; *Fredrik, Johan, Nels.*

Nurnberg (145) **1.** German (**Nürnberg**): habitational name from the city of Nürnberg in Bavaria. **2.** Jewish (Ashkenazic): variant of NIERENBERG.
GIVEN NAME German 6%. *Kurt* (2).

Nurnberger (151) German (**Nürnberger**) and Jewish (western Ashkenazic): habitational name for someone from the city of Nürnberg in Bavaria.
GIVEN NAMES German 9%. *Otto* (2), *Hans, Rudi.*

Nurre (199) Origin unidentified.
GIVEN NAMES French 4%. *Gabrielle* (2), *Camille.*

Nurse (619) English, Scottish, and Irish: variant of NORRIS 3.

Nusbaum (1220) Variant spelling of German and Jewish NUSSBAUM.

Nuse (159) German (**Nüse**): variant of NIES 1.

Nuss (1604) **1.** German: from Middle High German *nuz* 'nut', hence a metonymic occupational name for a gatherer and seller of nuts, or a (sometimes derogatory) nickname for a man thought to resemble a nut in some way (for example in having a round head and a brown complexion). **2.** (**Nüss**): variant of NIES.

Nussbaum (1936) **1.** German: topographic name from Middle High German *nuz* 'nut' + *boum* 'tree'. **2.** Jewish (Ashkenazic): ornamental name from German *Nussbaum* 'nut tree'.

GIVEN NAMES Jewish 5%; German 4%. *Yehudah* (3), *Aron* (2), *Dovid* (2), *Ephraim* (2), *Moshe* (2), *Chain*, *Hyman*, *Menachem*, *Yecheskel*; *Kurt* (4), *Hans* (3), *Fritz* (2), *Erwin*, *Hellmuth*, *Inge*, *Manfred*, *Monika*, *Otto*, *Rudi*, *Siegfried*.

Nussbaumer (220) German: topographic name for someone who lived by a nut tree (see NUSSBAUM).

GIVEN NAMES German 7%. *Christoph*, *Ernst*, *Gerhard*, *Inge*, *Klaus*.

Nusser (335) South German (also **Nüsser**): probably an occupational name for a collector or seller of nuts, from an agent derivative of Middle High German *nuzzen* 'to pick nuts'.

Nusz (227) German: old spelling of **Nuss** (see NUSS).

Nute (331) English (Devon): probably a variant of NUTT.

Nuth (106) **1.** English: origin uncertain; perhaps a variant of NUTT. **2.** German: variant of **Nöth** (see NOTH), or a habitational name from Nutha in Saxony. **3.** Cambodian: unexplained.

GIVEN NAMES Cambodian 15%. *Hoeun*, *Oeurn*, *Ly*, *Phal*, *Sanh*, *Saroeun*, *Son*.

Nuti (111) Italian: patronymic from a reduced form of the personal name BENVE-NUTO.

GIVEN NAMES Italian 14%. *Aldo* (2), *Bruna*, *Gino*, *Manlio*, *Pasquale*, *Pietro*, *Romano*, *Silvano*.

Nutile (149) Italian (mainly Campania): of uncertain derivation; perhaps an aphetic form of the rare surname **Inutile**, a nickname meaning 'useless'.

GIVEN NAME Italian 4%. *Attilio*.

Nutley (152) English: habitational name from places in Hampshire and Sussex called Nutley, from Old English *hnutu* 'nut tree' + *lēah* '(forest) clearing'. The surname has also been established in Ireland since the 17th century.

Nutsch (106) German: of uncertain origin.

GIVEN NAME German 4%. *Frieda*.

Nutt (2755) **1.** English: from Middle English *not(e)*, *nut* 'nut'; either a metonymic occupational name for a gatherer and seller of nuts, or a nickname for a man supposedly resembling a nut (for example in having a rounded head and brown complexion). **2.** Irish: reduced form of MCNUTT 1. **3.** North German: nickname for an industrious person, from Middle High German *nutte* 'useful', 'efficient'.

Nuttall (1114) English: habitational name from some place named with Old English *hnutu* 'nut' + *h(e)alh* 'nook', 'recess'. In some cases this may be Nuthall in Nottinghamshire, but the surname is common mainly in Lancashire, and a Lanca-shire origin is therefore more likely. Nuttall in Bury, Lancashire, was earlier *Notehogh*, from Old English *hnutu* + *hōh* 'hill-spur'.

Nutter (3134) English (Lancashire and Yorkshire): **1.** occupational name for a keeper of oxen, from an agent derivative of Middle English *nowt* 'beast', 'ox' (from Old Norse *naut*, a cognate of Old English *nēat*; compare NEAT). **2.** occupational name for a scribe or clerk, from Middle English *notere* (Old English *nōtere*, from Latin *notarius*, an agent derivative of *nota* 'mark', 'sign').

Nutting (1052) English: patronymic from NUTT.

Nuttle (194) Possibly an altered spelling of NUTTALL.

Nutty (111) **1.** Reduced form of **McNutty**, an unexplained Irish or Scottish name. **2.** English: unexplained.

Nuxoll (193) German: probably an irregular variant of NUCKOLS.

Nuzum (576) Irish (Dublin): variant of NEWSOME. This is now a rare name in Ireland.

Nuzzi (293) Southern Italian: patronymic or plural form of NUZZO.

GIVEN NAMES Italian 22%. *Angelo* (4), *Pasquale* (3), *Vito* (3), *Domenico* (2), *Carmine*, *Chiara*, *Dino*, *Guiseppe*, *Philomena*, *Raffaele*.

Nuzzo (686) Southern Italian: from a short form of a personal name formed with the suffix *-uzzo* following a final consonant *-n-*, for example *Antonuzzo*, *Benuzzo*, *Gio-vannuzzo*, *Rinuzzo*, *Stefanuzzo*.

GIVEN NAMES Italian 12%. *Salvatore* (5), *Sal* (3), *Angelo* (2), *Pasquale* (2), *Rocco* (2), *Antonio*, *Chiara*, *Concetta*, *Domenic*, *Donato*, *Michelina*, *Raffaele*.

Nwosu (108) African: unexplained.

GIVEN NAMES African 10%. *Emeka* (2), *Ngozi*; *Aloysius*, *Uli*.

Nyberg (1728) Scandinavian: habitational name from a farmstead so named, or an ornamental name formed with *ny* 'new' + *berg* 'hill'.

GIVEN NAMES Scandinavian 7%. *Anders* (5), *Erik* (2), *Alvar*, *Astrid*, *Fredrik*, *Holger*, *Mats*, *Niels*, *Sten*.

Nybo (172) Scandinavian: habitational name from any of various farmsteads named with *ny* 'new' + *bo* 'home', or an ornamental name with the same origin.

GIVEN NAME Scandinavian 9%. *Erik*.

Nyborg (206) Scandinavian: habitational name from a common farmstead name and place name, or an ornamental name. In either case, the name is formed with *ny* 'new' + *borg* 'fortress', 'castle', 'town'; this second element is commonly applied to natural formations which resemble fortifications.

GIVEN NAMES Scandinavian 7%. *Erik*, *Hasse*, *Nels*.

Nyce (342) Variant spelling of English or French NICE or German **Neiss**.

Nycum (135) Respelling of German **Niekum** (see NEUKAM).

Nycz (187) Polish: from a pet form of the personal name *Nikolaus* (Polish form *Mikołaj*), or possibly a Polonized form of German NITZ.

GIVEN NAME Polish 4%. *Tadeusz*.

Nydam (218) Dutch (**Nijdam**) and Danish: topographic name for someone living at 'the new (*ny*) dam or pond (*dam*)'.

Nydegger (181) **1.** Probably a respelling of German **Niederegger**, from NIEDER + ECKER, a topographic name for someone who lived at the 'lower corner'. **2.** Dutch: altered form of **Nieuwegger** 'new harrow-er', with epenthetic *-d-*.

GIVEN NAMES German 6%. *Hans* (2), *Fritz*, *Juerg*.

Nye (4807) English (southeastern): topo-graphic name arising from a misdivision of Middle English *atten (e)ye* which means ei-ther 'at the river' or 'at the island', from Old English *ēa* 'river' and *ēg* 'island' re-spectively. Both these words were feminine in Old English, and so should have been preceded only by Middle English *atter* (see RYE), but distinctions of gender ceased to be carefully maintained in the Middle Eng-lish period.

Nyenhuis (233) Dutch: habitational name from a place name meaning 'new house'.

Nygaard (1243) Scandinavian: habitational name from any of numerous farmsteads so named, from *ny* 'new' + *gård* 'farm'.

GIVEN NAMES Scandinavian 7%; German 4%. *Erik* (3), *Oddvar* (2), *Asmund*, *Bernt*, *Helmer*, *Lars*, *Niels*, *Obert*, *Thor*, *Viggo*; *Kurt* (7), *Egon*, *Gerhard*, *Grete*, *Hans*, *Johannes*, *Klaus*, *Konrad*, *Otto*.

Nygard (570) Scandinavian (**Nygård**): vari-ant of NYGAARD.

GIVEN NAMES Scandinavian 9%. *Lars* (2), *Sven* (2), *Bjorn*, *Holger*, *Iver*, *Ludvig*, *Nels*, *Nils*, *Sig*, *Sigfred*, *Viljo*.

Nygren (819) Swedish: ornamental name formed with *ny* 'new' + *gren* 'branch'.

GIVEN NAMES Scandinavian 8%. *Anders* (2), *Lars* (2), *Sten* (2), *Evald*, *Lennart*, *Mats*, *Per*, *Thor*, *Vidar*.

Nyhan (137) Irish: Anglicized form of Gaelic **Ó Niatháin** 'descendant of *Niathán*', a diminutive of *Niath* 'warrior' (a later spelling of *Nia(dh)*; compare NEE).

GIVEN NAME Irish 4%. *Donal*.

Nyholm (166) Swedish: ornamental name formed with *ny* 'new' + *holm* 'island'.

GIVEN NAMES Scandinavian 14%. *Per* (2), *Erik*, *Holger*, *Iver*.

Nyhuis (126) Possibly a respelling of Dutch **Nijhuis**, a habitational name from any of various places named with *ny* 'new' + *huijs* 'house'.

Nyhus (348) Scandinavian (mainly Norwe-gian): habitational name from any of nu-merous farmsteads and places named with *ny* 'new' + *hus* 'house', 'farm'.

GIVEN NAMES Scandinavian 8%; German 4%. *Hjalmer, Ordell, Sigfred; Eldred, Gerhard, Hans.*

Nykamp (166) Variant of Dutch **Nijkamp** (see NIEKAMP).
GIVEN NAME German 4%. *Hans* (3).

Nykiel (138) Polish: from the personal name *Nicolaus*, the Latin form of NICOLAS (Polish *Mikołaj*), or a Polonized form of German NICKEL.
GIVEN NAME Polish 8%. *Zbigniew* (2), *Stanislaw.*

Nyland (594) **1.** Scandinavian, especially Norwegian: habitational name from any of several farmsteads or places named with *ny* 'new' + *land* 'land', 'farm'. **2.** Americanized form of a common Dutch habitational name (**Nieland, Nilant, Nijland(e)**), denoting newly reclaimed land.

Nylander (411) **1.** Swedish: topographic or ornamental name meaning 'dweller on new land', from *ny* 'new' + *land* 'land' + -*er*. suffix denoting an inhabitant. **2.** Dutch: variant of NYLAND, the suffix -*er* denoting an inhabitant.
GIVEN NAMES Scandinavian 8%. *Erik* (2), *Anders, Kristoffer, Lars, Tor.*

Nylen (244) Swedish (also **Nylén**): ornamental name, probably formed with *ny* 'new' + the common surname suffix -*en*,

from Latin -*enius*, with intrusive -*l*- for euphony. Alternatively the first element may have been part of a place name such as *Nyland.*
GIVEN NAMES Scandinavian 13%. *Anders* (3), *Per* (2), *Arlis, Erik, Sven.*

Nylin (136) Swedish: variant of NYLEN.

Nylund (439) Scandinavian, especially Norwegian: habitational name from a farm named with *ny* 'new' + *lund* 'grove'. In Swedish it also occurs as an ornamental name.
GIVEN NAMES Scandinavian 6%. *Sven* (3), *Erik, Lars, Mats, Sig.*

Nyman (1279) **1.** Danish and Swedish: nickname for a newcomer to a place, from Scandinavian *ny* 'new' + *man* 'man'. The Swedish name may also be of ornamental origin. **2.** Jewish: American spelling variant of NAIMAN 'newcomer'.
GIVEN NAMES Scandinavian 7%. *Lars* (3), *Johan* (2), *Anders, Hilmer, Joakim, Knute, Lennart, Nels, Nils, Ove, Sven, Thor.*

Nyquist (825) Swedish: ornamental name composed of the elements *ny* 'new' + *quist*, an old or ornamental spelling of *kvist* 'twig'.
GIVEN NAMES Scandinavian 4%. *Erik* (2), *Alvar, Anders, Hjalmer, Walfrid.*

Nyren (119) Swedish (**Nyrén**): ornamental or habitational name from Swedish *ny* 'new' + the adjectival suffix -*én*, from Latin -*enius*, with the consonant -*r*- introduced for euphony.

Nys (117) French: from a reduced form of the personal name *Denys*, a variant spelling of *Denis* (see DENNIS).
GIVEN NAMES French 8%. *Andre* (2), *Yves.*

Nystrom (1826) Swedish (**Nyström**): ornamental name composed of the elements *ny* 'new' + *ström* 'river'.
GIVEN NAMES Scandinavian 7%; German 4%. *Erik* (7), *Lars* (2), *Per* (2), *Britt, Iver, Lennart; Brunhilde* (2), *Fritz* (2), *Kurt* (2), *Claus, Erwin, Johannes, Otto, Walther.*

Nystuen (103) Norwegian: habitational name from any of several farmsteads named from *ny* 'new' + *stue* 'cottage', denoting a small farm.

Nytes (100) Possibly an altered spelling of English **Knights**, a variant of KNIGHT.

Nzuyen (121) Vietnamese: variant of NGUYEN.
GIVEN NAMES Vietnamese 80%. *Minh* (3), *Duc* (2), *Hai* (2), *Lan* (2), *Loc* (2), *Loi* (2), *Ngan* (2), *Thanh* (2), *Anh, Ba Van, Bach, Bao.*